St. Jerome's University
LIBRARY

3 DAY LOAN

D1174566

ST. JAMES GUIDE TO
SCIENCE FICTION
WRITERS

Twentieth-Century Writers Series
(now St. James Guide to Writers Series)

Twentieth-Century Children's Writers
Twentieth-Century Crime and Mystery Writers
Twentieth-Century Romance and Historical Writers
Twentieth-Century Western Writers
Twentieth-Century Young Adult Writers

St. James Guide to Fantasy Writers
St. James Guide to Science Fiction Writers

THE LIBRARY
ST. JEROME'S COLLEGE
WATERLOO, ONTARIO

ST. JAMES GUIDE TO
SCIENCE FICTION
WRITERS

FOURTH EDITION

WITH A PREFACE BY
H. BRUCE FRANKLIN

EDITOR
JAY P. PEDERSON

BIBLIOGRAPHIC EDITOR
ROBERT REGINALD

ST. JAMES PRESS
An ITP Information/Reference Group Company

I(T)P
Changing the Way the World Learns

NEW YORK • LONDON • BONN • BOSTON • DETROIT • MADRID
MELBOURNE • MEXICO CITY • PARIS • SINGAPORE • TOKYO
TORONTO • WASHINGTON • ALBANY NY • BELMONT CA • CINCINNATI OH

Jay P. Pederson, *Editor*
Taryn Benbow-Pfalzgraf, Pamela Shelton, *Contributing Editors*
Robert Reginald, *Bibliographic Editor*

ST. JAMES PRESS STAFF

Margaret Mazurkiewicz, *Project Editor*

Michael J. Tyrkus, *Associate Editor*
Laura Standley Berger, Joann Cerrito, Nicolet V. Elert, Miranda H. Ferrara,
Janice Jorgenson, Paula Kepos, *Contributing Editors*

Peter M. Gareffa, *Managing Editor*

Mary Beth Trimper, *Production Director*
Shanna Heilveil, *Production Assistant*
Cynthia Baldwin, *Art Director*

Victoria B. Cariappa, *Research Manager*
Barbara McNeil, *Research Specialist*

While every effort has been made to ensure the reliability of the information presented in this publication, St. James Press does not guarantee the accuracy of the data contained herein. St. James accepts no payment for listing; and inclusion of any organization, agency, institution, publication, service, or individual does not imply endorsement of the editors or publisher.

Errors brought to the attention of the publisher and verified to the satisfaction of the publisher will be corrected in future editions.

⊚™ This book is printed on acid-free paper that meets the minimum requirements of American National Standard for Information Sciences—Permanence Paper for Printed Library Materials, ANSI Z39.48-1984.

This publication is a creative work fully protected by all applicable copyright laws, as well as by misappropriation, trade secret, unfair competition, and other applicable laws. The authors and editors of this work have added value to the underlying factual material herein through one or more of the following: unique and original selection, coordination, expression, arrangement, and classification of the information.

All rights to this publication will be vigorously defended.

Copyright © 1996
St. James Press
835 Penobscot Building
Detroit, MI 48226-4094

All rights reserved including the right of reproduction in whole or in part in any form.

JUN 0 1 1999

Library of Congress Catalog Card Number 95-36181
ISBN 1-55862-179-2
Printed in the United States of America

REF.
PN
3433.5
.S68x
1996

I(T)P™ Gale Research Inc., an International Thomson Publishing Company.
ITP logo is a trademark under license.

10 9 8 7 6 5 4 3 2 1

CONTENTS

PREFACE

Anyone who wants to comprehend human affairs in the 19th and 20th centuries needs some knowledge and understanding of science fiction. But what *is* science fiction, anyhow?

Let's start by distinguishing it from other fiction. On one side lies fantasy, the realm of the *impossible.* On the other side lie all the forms of fiction that purport to represent the *actual,* whether past or present. Science fiction's domain is the *possible.* Its territory ranges from the present Earth we know out to the limits of the possible universes that the human imagination can project, whether in the past, present, future, or alternative time-space continuums. Therefore science fiction is the only literature capable of exploring the macrohistory of our species, and of placing our history, and even our daily lives, in a cosmic context.

Science fiction must be defined further, as an historical happening. Though science fiction has antecedents that stretch back at least two thousand years, science fiction as a body of literature—and movies, graphic art, comic books, radio shows, futuristic exhibits, TV serials, video game machines, computer games, virtual reality, and so forth—is a new phenomenon. It is an expression of only modern technological, scientific, industrial society, appearing when preindustrial societies are transformed by an industrial revolution. Indeed, industrial society creates not just the consciousness characteristic of science fiction but also the very means of physically propagating science fiction in its various cultural forms, even before it was beamed as images on movie and video screens. For science fiction, like other forms of literature typical of industrial society, is propagated in mass-produced magazines and books, which require advanced manufacturing and distribution as well as a large literate audience.

All this is very recent. The word "scientist" appeared for the first time in 1840, as a deliberate coinage (see Raymond Williams's discussion in *Keywords: A Vocabulary of Culture and Society*). The term "science fiction" was used first in 1851 (in Chapter 10 of William Wilson's *A Little Earnest Book upon a Great Old Subject*): ". . . Science-Fiction, in which the revealed truths of Science may be given interwoven with a pleasing story which may itself be poetical and *true.*"

We take for granted living in a world where technological change is so rapid that it is part of our lives—continually transforming the present and the future. But this epoch of rapid technological changes, dating from the Industrial Revolution in Europe, is a mere microinstant of cosmic time.

The Earth is approximately four-and-a-half billion years old. The ice ages ended about 10,000 years ago. Thus the age of the Earth is 450,000 times the period since the last ice age. Let's make this more imaginable by picturing the age of the Earth equivalent to 45,000 feet, the altitude of a very high flying jet airliner. In comparison, the time since the last ice age would be represented by 1.2 inches. The period of modern science, technology, and science fiction, which began with the Industrial Revolution just over 200 years ago, would then be equivalent on our spatial scale to .024 inches, about the thickness of a line made by a medium ball point pen.

Within that pen scratch of time, the rate of technological change has been exponential. Modern consciousness therefore is radically different from that of the peoples who inhabited the planet before the emergence of science fiction.

So my key definition is this: *Science fiction is the major nonrealistic mode of imaginative creation of our epoch. It is the principal cultural way we locate ourselves imaginatively in time and space.*

* * *

Science fiction, however, has a long prehistory. The epics of early Greek civilization, for example, feature superhuman beings such as the residents of Mount Olympus and include a marvelous voyage to far distant worlds (way out in the Mediterranean) inhabited by one-eyed giants, a six-headed monster, a creature that swallows passing ships, and a woman who chemically transforms people into animals.

The first fictions about travel beyond the Earth were satires of such epic voyages by the Syrian writer Lucian of Samosata in the 2nd century A.D. The hero of his *Icaro-Menippus* sprouts wings and flies to the Moon; in *The True History,* the author and a shipload of companions are wafted to the Moon, where men have artificial phalluses (ivory for the rich, wood for the poor), and the travelers observe an interplanetary battle fought to determine whether the empire of the Moon or of the Sun gets to colonize Venus.

But Lucian's works are not science fiction. They are intended to be read as fantasy—imaginings of the impossible—just like similar works for the following fourteen hundred years. As late as 1532, Ariosto's *Orlando Furioso* projected a trip to the Moon merely as a preposterous fantasy (to find and bottle his hero's lost wits). Meanwhile, however, being passed around in manuscript was Copernicus's demonstration that the cosmos is vast and does not revolve around the Earth.

The European concept of space was already being transformed. The magnetic compass and advances in shipbuilding made possible the voyages of so-called "discovery" in the late 15th century, leading to a "New World"—that is, new to Europeans. Then, with the development of the telescope in the early 17th century, the concept of "plurality of worlds" began to be taken seriously. Marvelous voyages to the Moon, planets, and stars became commonplace.

Johannus Kepler, who developed the basic laws of planetary motion, uses them in *Somnium* (1634) to imagine living on the Moon. Francis Godwin describes a utopia on the Moon in *The Man in the Moone* (1638). Cyrano de Bergerac's *Comical History of the States and Empires of the Moon* (1659) and *Sun* (1687) include marvelous inventions such as solar energy converters and talking machines.

As the European concept of space was being reshaped, the European concept of change, and of historical time itself, was also being transformed.

Thomas More's *Utopia,* published in 1516, introduced a concept fundamental to modern consciousness and science fiction: change in the mode of production changes the conditions of human existence. As More argues, the cloth industry's growing demand for fine English wool had led to the enclosure of the common land, which caused massive unemployment and skyrocketing inflation, which forced many people into crime, which in turn led to wholesale capital punishment. These ominous conditions induce More to coin a pun and imagine a place with a mighty host of offspring in science fiction: *Utopia,* the good place (eutopia) which is noplace (outopia).

Francis Bacon, the so-called father of modern science, used fiction to show the wonders that could be achieved using his inductive method of scientific experimentation. In his *New Atlantis* (1627) he describes the discovery of a utopian society based on experimental science, including the development of "New Artificiall Mettalls," vivisection, genetic manipulation, telescopes, microscopes, telephones, beamed images, submarines, aerial flight, and factories.

During the 17th century, technological and social change were accelerating so rapidly that they could be experienced within a person's lifetime, and so people began to imagine a future as qualitatively different from the past or present. Prior to this, there had never been a fiction set in a future period of human history. The closest had been millennial imaginings that had pictured the replacement of human history by God's kingdom. The first known fictions set in future time are Francis Cheynell's political tract *Aulicus: His Dream of the King's Second Coming to London* (1644) and Jacques Guttin's *Epigone, Story of the Future Century* (1659).

During the 18th century, some authors took a bleak view of the ever-accelerating technological and social change. In *Gulliver's Travels* (1726), Jonathan Swift presents both an extended parody of experimental science and a vision of a terrifying superweapon, a flying island used by its rulers literally to crush any earthly opposition to their tyranny. Voltaire took a similar stance in *Micromégas* (1732), notable as the first known story of visitors from other planets: two giants, one from Saturn and one from a planet of the star Sirius, who mock the follies of the diminutive earthlings.

But science was not to be halted by warnings and ridicule. The following year Benjamin Franklin reported to the Royal Society his experimental control of electricity. Within a few decades, quantitative change would become qualitative; in other words, there would be a true Industrial Revolution. On the eve of the resulting political revolutions in America and France, Louis-Sébastian Mercier's remarkable *The Year 2440* (1771) foresees a marvelous society that worships science, with the telescope and the microscope central to each youth's first communion.

By the end of the 18th century and the opening of the 19th, industrial capitalism was beginning its conquest of the world. Modern science was providing the technological means to develop large factories, rapid large-scale transportation, and new energy sources. The drive to find huge quantities of coal to power the steam engines of industrial capitalism led to a reconception of time as profound as the Copernican reconception of space. Coal is, after all, fossils from remote geological ages. To discover vast deposits, industrial society had to discard the dominant theory of cosmic time—Bishop Ussher's dating of the creation of the universe in 4004 B.C.—and recognize that the Earth's age must be measured in billions of years. Only on such a scale was it possible first to comprehend the time necessary for geological evolution and then to conceive of biological evolution.

Under industrial capitalism, vast numbers of people were soon spending their lives working for a handful of capitalists who owned everything the people produced, including the factories, coal mines, railroads, and ships. Not only were the workers thus alienated from the means of production and their own products, but they also found themselves increasingly alienated from nature, from each other, and from their own essence as creative beings. Human creativity now appeared in the form of monstrous alien forces exerting ever-growing power over the people who had created them.

From this matrix emerged what Brian Aldiss has so aptly labeled "the first great myth of the industrial age" in the form of a novel that many now accept as the progenitor of modern science fiction: Mary Shelley's *Frankenstein, or, The Modern Prometheus* (1818). Then, less than a decade after *Frankenstein,* Shelley created one of the first science fiction visions of the end of the world; the title character of her *The Last Man* (1826) wanders alone over a dead planet, sampling the useless achievements of all human society. Mary Shelley set this scene in the year 2100.

The 19th century was the first in which life was continually being metamorphosed by technological change. The century began with the first experimental locomotive in 1801, advanced through the airship in 1852, and ended with the first experimental airplane in the late 1890s. In that century came the first practical steamboat, the screw propeller, the bicycle, and the automobile. Agriculture was being revolutionized by the invention of the harvester, the disc cultivator, the reaper, and the mowing machine. The electric battery appeared in the opening year of the century; the electromagnet, the cathode ray tube, and the magnetic tape recorder mark the successive quarters. The history of capitalism can be traced in the inventions of the adding machine, the calculating machine, the punch time clock, the cash register, the stock ticker, and punch-card accounting. Basic commodities such as industrial steel, vulcanized rubber, and portland cement were all 19th-century innovations. There appeared those special hallmarks of modern times: dynamite, the rapid-fire pistol, the repeating rifle, barbed wire, and the machine gun. The means of communication and artistic creation changed with the introduction of photography, the phonograph, the fountain pen (and the ballpoint), the typewriter, the telegraph, the telephone, radio, and the movie machine. Before the end of the century appeared several brief science fiction movies.

America proved especially hospitable to science fiction, even before it acquired a name. Many of the leading figures of antebellum fiction—including Washington Irving, James Fenimore Cooper, Nathaniel Hawthorne, Edgar Allan Poe, and Herman Melville—made important contributions to the form. How then did science fiction get its bad name as "subliterary"?

With the triumph of industrial capitalism in the Civil War, there emerged a newly literate mass audience of boys and young men intrigued by the opportunities of fame and fortune in science and technology. Aimed directly at this readership was the science-fiction "dime" novel, with its teenage boy genius as hero, first presented in Edward Ellis's seminal *The Steam Man of the Prairie* (1865). Between the Civil War and World War I, the most popular form of literature in America was the dime novel, and its science fiction versions were to have a formative influence on American culture (as can be glimpsed in this volume's entry on Luis Senarens). Only when it became an influential form of mass entertainment did science fiction come to be disdained as vulgar and puerile.

And it is at this point that the story of science fiction—or at least written science fiction—becomes largely the story told in the critical surveys that constitute this volume. To get some sense of the significance of science fiction in the late 19th century, for example, consult the entries on Jules Verne, Edward Bellamy, and Mark Twain. The entry on H.G. Wells sketches the main bridge into the 20th century. To see some of science fiction's forking paths in the early decades of the 20th century, peruse the entries on Jack London, Edgar Rice Burroughs, and Hugo Gernsback.

After these early years, the story of 20th-century science fiction becomes ever more rich, complex, contentious, and important. For struggling in the works of the hundreds of authors presented in this volume are cultural forces whose dynamic is shaping the 21st century.

—H. Bruce Franklin

EDITOR'S NOTE

The *St. James Guide to Science Fiction Writers* includes English-language writers of science fiction as well as writers of fantasy, horror, and other forms of speculative fiction who have had an impact on the field; significant foreign-language authors whose works have been published in English translation are also featured. With this fourth edition, the former *Twentieth-Century Science-Fiction Writers* assumes a new title, *St. James Guide to Science Fiction Writers.* As the turn of the century approaches, the editors felt this change would better reflect the currency of the information in this work and in the entire St. James Twentieth-Century Writers Series. The selection of writers is based upon the recommendations of the advisers listed on page xiii.

The entry for each writer consists of a biography, a complete list of published works (with the exception of foreign and 19th-century authors which have entries with selected bibliographies), and a signed critical essay. Living authors were invited to submit a comment on their work.

Original U.S. and British editions of all works have been listed; other editions are listed only if they are first editions. Under "Science Fiction Publications" are listed titles that at some time since their publication have been considered science fiction or of at least peripheral importance to the genre.

ACKNOWLEDGEMENTS

I would like to thank the following: all those who worked on the first three editions; all the new advisers and contributors for their advice and cooperation; Margaret Mazurkiewicz, Peter Gareffa, Laura Standley Berger, Robert Reginald, Pamela Shelton, Taryn Benbow-Pfalzgraf, Kathleen Peippo, Michael J. Tyrkus, the St. James Press staff, and, especially, my wife, Linda, and my children, Kyle and Mark.

ADVISERS

Brian Aldiss
Martha A. Bartter
Paul Brazier
Don D'Ammassa
D. Douglas Fratz
Hal W. Hall
David G. Hartwell
Van Ikin
Maxim Jakubowski
David Ketterer
Paul Kincaid

Daryl F. Mallett
Gene LaFaille
Kev P. McVeigh
Robert M. Philmus
Robert Reginald
Nicholas Ruddick
Pamela Sargent
Brian M. Stableford
Lucy Sussex
Michael Tolley

CONTRIBUTORS

Mitchell Aboulafia
Brian Aldiss
Rosemarie Arbur
K.V. Bailey
Douglas Barbour
Myra Barnes
Marleen S. Barr
David V. Barrett
Melissa E. Barth
Martha A. Bartter
Bruce A. Beatie
Sydonie Benet
E.R. Bishop
Michael Bishop
Russell Blackford
Karen Charmaine Blansfield
Janice M. Bogstad
Bernadette Lynn Bosky
Paul Brazier
John P. Brennan
Peter Brigg
David Brin
R.E. Briney
Mary Turzillo Brizzi
John Brunner
Scott Burgess
Alexander J. Butrym
Gay E. Carter
Steven R. Carter
Edgar L. Chapman
Cathy Chauvette
Michael Cobley
Robert E. Colbert
Rosemary Coleman
Michael R. Collings
Gary Coughlan

Richard Cowper
F. Brett Cox
J. Randolph Cox
Michael Cule
Elizabeth Cummins
Catherine M. Currier
Charles Cushing
Don D'Ammassa
David A. Drake
Thomas P. Dunn
Karren C. Edwards
Alex Eisenstein
Gregory Feeley
Eric A. Fontaine
Jeff Frane
D. Douglas Fratz
Alice Carol Gaar
John V. Garner
Walter Gillings
Stephen H. Goldman
Joan Gordon
John Gough
Martin H. Greenberg
Colin Greenland
M. Jean Greenlaw
James Gunn
M. Hammerton
Philip J. Harbottle
David G. Hartwell
Donald M. Hassler
Len Hatfield
Sharon-Ilona Hecht
Rosemary Herbert
Norman L. Hills
Arthur D. Hlavaty
Janis Butler Holm

Terry Hughes
Elizabeth Anne Hull
Marvin W. Hunt
Van Ikin
Edward James
Anne Hudson Jones
Kenneth Jurkiewicz
Julius Kagarlitsky
Fiona Kelleghan
George Kelley
David Ketterer
Paul Kincaid
Gérard Klein
Vince Kohler
Dennis M. Kratz
David Lake
Justine Larbalestier
William Laskowski, Jr.
Donald L. Lawler
John I. Lawson
Mark Warwick Leahy
Henry D. Leperlier
Michael M. Levy
Arthur O. Lewis
Shelly Lowenkopf
Duncan Lunan
Richard A. Lupoff
Peter Lynch
Andrew Macdonald
Gina Macdonald
Cathi MacRae
Shinji Maki
Daryl F. Mallett
Patrick L. McGuire
Christopher McKitterick
Kev P. McVeigh
Sheryl L. Meyering
Walter E. Meyers
Sandra Miesel
Richard W. Miller
Toshifumi Miyawaki
Francis J. Molson
Daniel Keys Moran
Thomas J. Morrissey
Will Murray
Marilyn K. Nellis
Ian Nichols
Chad Oliver
Lance Olsen
Richard Orodenker
Gerald W. Page
Diane Parkin-Speer
Frederick Patten
Terri Paul
Kathleen Peippo
Michael Perkins
John R. Pfeiffer
Gene Phillips
Hazel Pierce
John J. Pierce
Nick Pratt

Bill Pronzini
Joseph A. Quinn
Robert Reginald
Robert Reilly
Lawrence R. Ries
Cornel Robu
Aaron Rosenberg
Franz Rottensteiner
Yvonne Rousseau
Joanna Russ
Todd H. Sammons
David N. Samuelson
Joe Sanders
Pamela Sargent
Harvey J. Satty
John Scarborough
William J. Scheick
Roger C. Schlobin
William M. Schuyler, Jr.
Baird Searles
Kathryn Lee Seidel
Pamela Shelton
Susan Shwartz
George Slusser
Curtis C. Smith
Carol L. Snyder
Judith Snyder
Maureen Kincaid Speller
Katherine Staples
Ilan Stavans
Philippa Stephensen-Payne
Graham Stone
Leon Stover
C.W. Sullivan III
Lucy Sussex
Darko Suvin
Paul Swank
Norman Talbot
Takayuki Tatsumi
Robert Thurston
Michael J. Tolley
Frank H. Tucker
George Turner
Lisa Tuttle
Jana I. Tuzar
Steven Utley
Robert E. Vardeman
Karl Edward Wagner
Jeffrey Wallmann
Ian Watson
Douglas E. Way
Karen G. Way
Janeen Webb
Jane B. Weedman
Mary S. Weinkauf
Dennis M. Welch
Fred D. White
Robert H. Wilcox
Cherry Wilder
David Wingrove
Gary K. Wolfe

Gene Wolfe
Martin Morse Wooster
Alice Chambers Wygant
Carl B. Yoke
Hoda M. Zaki
George Zebrowski

ST. JAMES GUIDE TO
SCIENCE FICTION
WRITERS

Kobo Abé
Douglas Adams
Max Adeler
Mark Adlard
Brian W. Aldiss
Roger MacBride Allen
Kingsley Amis
Kevin J. Anderson
Poul Anderson
Piers Anthony
Christopher Anvil
Eleanor Arnason
Edwin L. Arnold
Isaac Asimov
Robert Lynn Asprin
A.A. Attanasio
Frank Aubrey

Wilhelmina Baird
Sharon Baker
J.G. Ballard
Iain M. Banks
René Barjavel
John Barnes
Steven Barnes
Neal Barrett, Jr.
T.J. Bass
John Calvin Batchelor
Harry Bates
John Baxter
Stephen Baxter
Barrington John Bayley
Greg Bear
Charles Beaumont
Edward Bellamy
Aleksandr Belyaev
Gregory Benford
J.D. Beresford
Alfred Bester
Lloyd Biggle
Eando Binder
David F. Bischoff
Michael Bishop
Terry Bisson
James P. Blaylock
Christopher Blayre
James Blish
Robert Bloch
Michael Blumlein
Nelson S. Bond
J.F. Bone
Jorge Luis Borges
Anthony Boucher
Pierre Boulle
Ben Bova
John Boyd
Karin Boye
Leigh Brackett
Ray Bradbury
Marion Zimmer Bradley
Reginald Bretnor

David Brin
Damien Broderick
Christine Brooke-Rose
John Brosnan
Eric Brown
Fredric Brown
Rosel George Brown
John Brunner
Edward Bryant
Frank Bryning
Valery Bryusov
Algis Budrys
Lois McMaster Bujold
Mikhail Bulgakov
Emma Bull
Kenneth Bulmer
Edward Bulwer-Lytton
David R. Bunch
Katharine Burdekin
Anthony Burgess
Edgar Rice Burroughs
William S. Burroughs
F.M. Busby
Octavia E. Butler
Samuel Butler
Dino Buzzati

Pat Cadigan
Martin Caidin
Ernest Callenbach
Italo Calvino
John W. Campbell, Jr.
Karel Capek
Paul Capon
Orson Scott Card
Jayge Carr
Terry Carr
Angela Carter
Lin Carter
Cleve Cartmill
Jeffrey A. Carver
Jack L. Chalker
A. Bertram Chandler
Louis Charbonneau
Suzy McKee Charnas
C.J. Cherryh
Rob Chilson
Charles Chilton
John Christopher
Arthur C. Clarke
Hal Clement
Mark Clifton
Stanton A. Coblentz
Theodore R. Cogswell
D.G. Compton
Michael G. Coney
Storm Constantine
Glen Cook
Edmund Cooper
Alfred Coppel
Juanita Coulson

Robert Coulson
Arthur Byron Cover
Richard Cowper
Erle Cox
Michael Crichton
Robert Cromie
John Keir Cross
John Crowley
Ray Cummings

Brian C. Daley
Jack Dann
Avram Davidson
Chan Davis
L. Sprague de Camp
Miriam Allen deFord
Joseph H. Delaney
Samuel R. Delany
Charles de Lint
Lester del Rey
Lester Dent
Gene Deweese
Philip K. Dick
Peter Dickinson
Gordon R. Dickson
Paul G. Di Filippo
Thomas M. Disch
Stephen R. Donaldson
Ignatius Donnelly
Sonya Dorman
Candas Jane Dorsey
Terry Dowling
Arthur Conan Doyle
Gardner Dozois
David A. Drake
Wayland Drew
Diane Duane
Dave Duncan
David Duncan
Lord Dunsany
Lawrence Durrell

David Eddings
E.R. Eddison
G.C. Edmondson
George Alec Effinger
Greg Egan
Phyllis Eisenstein
Gordon Eklund
M. Barnard Eldershaw
Suzette Haden Elgin
Mircea Eliade
Harlan Ellison
Ru Emerson
Carol Emshwiller
Sylvia Engdahl
M.J. Engh
George Allan England
Steve Erickson
Lloyd Arthur Eshbach
E. Everett Evans

Paul W. Fairman
R. Lionel Fanthorpe
Ralph Milne Farley
Philip José Farmer
Mick Farren
John Russell Fearn
Raymond E. Feist
Cynthia Felice
Jack Finney
Nicholas Fisk
Homer Eon Flint
John M. Ford
William R. Forstchen
Robert L. Forward
Alan Dean Foster
M.A. Foster
Karen Joy Fowler
Gardner F. Fox
Pat Frank
Herbert W. Franke
Michael Frayn
Gertrude Friedberg

Leslie Gadallah
Otto Gail
Neil Gaiman
Raymond Z. Gallun
Daniel F. Galouye
Craig Shaw Gardner
David Garnett
Randall Garrett
David A. Gemmell
Mary Gentle
Peter George
Hugo Gernsback
David Gerrold
Mark S. Geston
William Gibson
Alexis A. Gilliland
Charlotte Perkins Gilman
John Gloag
Tom Godwin
H.L. Gold
Stephen Goldin
William Golding
Lisa Goldstein
Rex Gordon
Stuart Gordon
Phyllis Gotlieb
Felix C. Gotschalk
Ron Goulart
Charles L. Grant
Richard Grant
Joseph Green
Terence M. Green
Colin Greenland
William Greenleaf
John R. Gribbin
Russell M. Griffin
George Griffith
Nicola Griffith

Wyman Guin
James E. Gunn
Lindsay Gutteridge

H. Rider Haggard
Isidore Haiblum
Jack C. Haldeman
Joe Haldeman
Edward Everett Hale
Austin Hall
Edmond Hamilton
Elizabeth Hand
Lee Harding
Charles L. Harness
Harry Harrison
M. John Harrison
Simon Hawke
H.F. Heard
Robert A. Heinlein
Zenna Henderson
Joe L. Hensley
Frank Herbert
James Herbert
Philip E. High
Russell Hoban
Edward D. Hoch
Christopher Hodder-Williams
William Hope Hodgson
Lee Hoffman
James P. Hogan
Robert Holdstock
H.M. Hoover
Shin'ichi Hoshi
Robert Hoskins
Fred and Geoffrey Hoyle
Trevor Hoyle
L. Ron Hubbard
Barry Hughart
Monica Hughes
Zach Hughes
Evan Hunter
Aldous Huxley
C.J. Cutcliffe Hyne

Dean Ing

Alexander Jablokov
Harvey Jacobs
John Jakes
Laurence M. Janifer
Richard Jefferies
Wolfgang Jeschke
K.W. Jeter
Michel Jeury
D.F. Jones
Diana Wynne Jones
Gwyneth A. Jones
Neil R. Jones
Raymond F. Jones
M.K. Joseph

Franz Kafka
Janet Kagan
James Kahn
Colin Kapp
Anna Kavan
David H. Keller
Bernhard Kellermann
Leo P. Kelley
James Patrick Kelly
Leigh Kennedy
John Kessel
Alexander Key
Daniel Keyes
Crawford Kilian
Lee Killough
Garry Kilworth
Vincent King
Donald Kingsbury
Rudyard Kipling
John Kippax
Gérard Klein
Otis Adelbert Kline
Nigel Kneale
Damon Knight
Norman L. Knight
Sakyo Komatsu
Dean R. Koontz
C.M. Kornbluth
William Kotzwinkle
Nancy Kress
Michael P. Kube-McDowell
Michael Kurland
Katherine Kurtz
Henry Kuttner

R.A. Lafferty
David Lake
Geoffrey A. Landis
David Langford
Sterling E. Lanier
Joe R. Lansdale
E.C. Large
Kurd Lasswitz
Philip Latham
Keith Laumer
Tanith Lee
Ursula K. Le Guin
Fritz Leiber
Stephen Leigh
Murray Leinster
Stanislaw Lem
Madeleine L'Engle
Milton Lesser
Doris Lessing
Jonathan Lethem
Ira Levin
C.S. Lewis
Jacqueline Lichtenberg
Alice Lightner
Brad Linaweaver
David Lindsay

Alun Llewellyn
Jack London
Frank Belknap Long
Barry Longyear
H.P. Lovecraft
Robert A.W. Lowndes
Sam J. Lundwall
Richard A. Lupoff
John Lymington
Elizabeth A. Lynn

C.C. MacApp
R.A. MacAvoy
George MacDonald
John D. MacDonald
R.W. Mackelworth
Katherine MacLean
Sheila MacLeod
Charles Eric Maine
Barry N. Malzberg
Phillip Mann
Laurence Manning
George R.R. Martin
Douglas R. Mason
David I. Masson
Richard Matheson
André Maurois
Julian May
Vladimir Mayakovsky
Ardath Mayhar
Bruce McAllister
Paul J. McAuley
Anne McCaffrey
Jack McDevitt
Ian McDonald
Maureen F. McHugh
J.T. McIntosh
Vonda N. McIntyre
Richard M. McKenna
Patricia A. McKillip
Dean McLaughlin
Sean McMullen
Mike McQuay
S.P. Meek
David Meltzer
R.M. Meluch
Richard C. Meredith
Judith Merril
A. Merritt
Sam Merwin, Jr.
P. Schuyler Miller
Walter M. Miller, Jr.
Judith Moffett
Thomas F. Monteleone
Michael Moorcock
Alan Moore
C.L. Moore
Patrick Moore
Ward Moore
John Morressy
Janet E. Morris

William Morris
James Morrow
Haruki Murakami
Gerald Murnane
Pat Murphy

Ed Naha
Ray Nelson
Josef Nesvadba
Kris Neville
Larry Niven
William F. Nolan
Jeff Noon
John Norman
Andre Norton
Warren Norwood
Alan E. Nourse
Philip Francis Nowlan

Charles G. Oberndorf
Kevin O'Donnell, Jr.
Andrew J. Offutt
Chad Oliver
Joseph O'Neill
Rebecca Ore
George Orwell

Raymond A. Palmer
Edgar Pangborn
Alexei Panshin
Paul Park
Mervyn Peake
Steve Perry
Emil Petaja
Rog Phillips
Marge Piercy
Daniel Manus Pinkwater
H. Beam Piper
Doris Piserchia
Charles Platt
Edgar Allan Poe
Frederik Pohl
Rachel Pollack
Arthur Porges
Jerry Pournelle
Tim Powers
Terry Pratchett
Fletcher Pratt
Paul Preuss
Christopher Priest
J.B. Priestley
Geo Proctor
Tom Purdom
Thomas Pynchon

John Rackham
Ayn Rand
Marta Randall
Tom Reamy
Michael Reaves
Kit Reed

Robert Reed
Maurice Renard
Mike Resnick
Mack Reynolds
Walt and Leigh Richmond
Keith Roberts
Frank M. Robinson
Kim Stanley Robinson
Spider Robinson
Ross Rocklynne
Michaela Roessner
William Rotsler
Victor Rousseau
Rudy Rucker
Kristine Kathryn Rusch
Joanna Russ
Eric Frank Russell
Geoff Ryman

Fred Saberhagen
Margaret St. Clair
James Sallis
Jessica Amanda Salmonson
Sarban
Pamela Sargent
Robert J. Sawyer
Josephine Saxton
Elizabeth Scarborough
Nat Schachner
Hilbert Schenck
Stanley Schmidt
James H. Schmitz
Thomas N. Scortia
Melissa Scott
Hank Searls
Arthur Sellings
Luis P. Senarens
Rod Serling
Daniel Sernine
Garrett P. Serviss
Jack Sharkey
Richard S. Shaver
Bob Shaw
Robert Sheckley
Charles Sheffield
Mary Shelley
Lucius Shepard
T.L. Sherred
M.P. Shiel
Wilmar H. Shiras
John Shirley
Nevil Shute
Susan Shwartz
Robert Silverberg
Clifford D. Simak
Curt Siodmak
John Sladek
William M. Sloane
Joan Slonczewski
Clark Ashton Smith
Cordwainer Smith

E.E. Smith
Evelyn E. Smith
George H. Smith
George O. Smith
Thorne Smith
Jerry Sohl
Martha Soukup
Norman Spinrad
Nancy Springer
Steven Spruill
Brian Stableford
Olaf Stapledon
Christopher Stasheff
Andrew M. Stephenson
Neal Stephenson
Bruce Sterling
Francis Stevens
George R. Stewart
G. Harry Stine
S.M. Stirling
Frank R. Stockton
Craig Strete
Boris and Arkady Strugatsky
Theodore Sturgeon
Somtow Sucharitkul
Lucy Sussex
Michael Swanwick

John Taine
Stephen Tall
Judith Tarr
Peter Tate
William F. Temple
William Tenn
Emma Tennant
Sheri S. Tepper
Walter Tevis
D.M. Thomas
Ted Thomas
Robert Thurston
Patrick Tilley
James Tiptree, Jr.
J.R.R. Tolkien
Alexey Tolstoy
Louis Trimble
Konstantin Tsiolkovsky
E.C. Tubb
Wilson Tucker
George Turner
Harry Turtledove
Lisa Tuttle
Mark Twain
Kathy Tyers

Steven Utley

Jack Vance
Sydney J. Van Scyoc
A.E. van Vogt
John Varley
Ilya Varshavsky

Vercors
Jules Verne
A. Hyatt Verrill
Joan D. Vinge
Vernor Vinge
Élisabeth Vonarburg
Kurt Vonnegut, Jr.

Howard Waldrop
F.L. Wallace
Ian Wallace
William Jon Watkins
Ian Watson
Lawrence Watt-Evans
Sharon Webb
Stanley G. Weinbaum
Andrew Weiner
Manly Wade Wellman
H.G. Wells
James White
Ted White
Wynne Whiteford
Cherry Wilder
Kate Wilhelm
John A. Williams
Paul O. Williams
Robert Moore Williams
Walter Jon Williams
Jack Williamson
Connie Willis
Colin Wilson

F. Paul Wilson
Richard Wilson
Robert Anton Wilson
Robert Charles Wilson
David Wingrove
Stanislaw Witkiewicz
Jack Wodhams
Gary K. Wolf
Bernard Wolfe
Gene Wolfe
Donald A. Wollheim
Dave Wolverton
Jack Womack
Austin Tappan Wright
S. Fowler Wright
Philip Wylie
John Wyndham

Chelsea Quinn Yarbro
Ivan Yefremov
Jane Yolen
Robert F. Young

Arthur Leo Zagat
Timothy Zahn
Yevgeny Zamyatin
George Zebrowski
Roger Zelazny
David Zindell
Pamela Zoline

A

ABÉ, Kobo

Nationality: Japanese. **Born:** Tokyo, 7 March 1924. **Education:** Tokyo University, M.D. 1948. **Family:** Married Machi Yamada in 1947; one daughter. **Career:** Novelist and playwright. Director and producer of the Kobo Theatre Workshop, Tokyo. **Awards:** Post-War Literature prize, 1950; 25th Akutagawa prize, 1951; Kishida prize for drama, 1958; Yomiuri literary prize, 1962; Cannes Film Festival special jury prize (for film *Woman in the Dunes*), 1964; Takizaki prize for drama, 1967. **Died:** 22 January 1993.

SCIENCE FICTION PUBLICATIONS

Novels

Dai-yon kampyoki. Tokyo, Kodansha, 1959; translated by E. Dale Saunders as *Inter Ice Age Four,* New York, Knopf, 1970.
Hakobune Sakura Maru. Tokyo, Shinchosha, 1985; translated as *The Ark Sakura,* New York, Knopf and London, Secker and Warburg, 1988.

Short Stories

Beyond the Curve and Other Stories, translated by Juliet Winters Carpenter. Tokyo, Kodansha, 1991.

OTHER PUBLICATIONS

Novels

Suna no onna. Tokyo, Shinchosha, 1962; translated by E. Dale Saunders as *Woman in the Dunes,* New York, Knopf, 1964.
Tanin no kao. Toyko, Kodansha, 1964; translated by E. Dale Saunders as *The Face of Another,* Knopf, 1966.
Moetsukita chizu. Tokyo, Shinchosha, 1967; translated by E. Dale Saunders *The Ruined Map,* New York, Knopf, 1969.
Hako-otoko. Tokyo, Shinchosha, 1973; translated by E. Dale Saunders as *The Box Man,* New York, Knopf, 1975.
Mikkai. Tokyo, Shinchosha, 1977; translated by Juliet Winters Carpenter as *Secret Rendezvous,* New York, Knopf, 1979.

Plays

Tomodachi, enemoto, takeaki. Tokyo, Kawade Shobo, 1967; translated by Donald Keene as *Friends,* New York, Grove Press, 1969.
Bo ni natta otoko. Tokyo, Shinchosha, 1969; translated by Donald Keene as *The Man Who Turned into a Stick,* Tokyo, University of Tokyo Press, 1975.
Three Plays, translated by Donald Keene. New York, Columbia University Press, 1993.

* * *

To understand the science fiction of Kobo Abé and to place it in perspective, it is necessary to note that science fiction is but a part of his work. Even so, his creations often are just as much science fiction as the works of Stanislaw Lem, who is accepted as a major writer of modern SF. The works of Abé and Lem have some similar qualities, though Abé is more inclined to psychological and introspective treatments than is Lem.

As a medical school graduate, Abé had the technical knowledge and experience to do outstanding work in some aspects of SF. Another key to Abé's work, besides his psychological approach, is his propensity for experimental literary techniques, combining his familiarity with European—especially French—20th-century trends, along with the characteristic Japanese awareness of more than a thousand years of indigenous cultural tradition.

One important example of the above factors is his novel *The Face of Another,* which appeared also in 1967 as a motion picture. This work is not mainstream SF, but has technological content, the methods by which a realistic mask is substituted for a horribly disfigured face. The mask has been a major resource of Japanese drama for centuries. In this book, the hero compares himself to the monsters of television, and the film is filled with the organ-laden laboratories of the Frankenstein tradition.

The Face of Another can be grouped with those SF novels that have as an important concern alienation, or related questions as to what does or does not constitute humanity ("humanness"). The very word alienation comes from a Latin root meaning "other." Abé himself is in some ways alienated in Japan. He was brought up in Manchuria, then under Japanese influence or control, but not a part of the homeland. Certainly the mask of this novel is a form of "otherness." Alternatively it may be viewed as an insulation of the real *person* from others. (The word person derives from the Greek word for mask, and a much-favored classic Japanese dramatic form, the *No* drama, uses masks for the chief characters, as did some classic Greek drama.)

Related to the foregoing concepts is Abé's novel *The Box Man.* The title characters are insulated by being partially encased in cardboard boxes. The novel reads somewhat like a stage play, reflecting Abé's preference for plays over novels as a medium. He is in fact known as well, or better, for his plays than for his novels in Japan. In *The Box Man,* as these strangely packaged characters move about, other men are suspicious of them, and even shoot at them. The feeling of alienation accumulates as a wounded boxman is hospitalized and receives the unloving care of a disdainful nurse. The reader is left to wonder if the injured person is a criminal or some sort of misfit. The dramatic action, sparse in itself, is amplified by the insertion of news flashes, and is varied by movements back and forth in time. The author encourages the reader to wonder if the "different" persons are really different. He leaves much uncertainty in this eerie analog of modern life.

More alienation and despair appear in *The Ark Sakura.* It features a plump narrator called Mole who fails in his design for escape from nuclear holocaust. The "ark" is actually a vast, deserted quarry. Mole plans that it will be a refuge, and he sells tickets to the people who he hopes will help him harmoniously to operate the refuge. Everything goes wrong, however, as the crew defy his authority and prevent his plans from being carried out. Add to this impasse some troublesome intruders, and poor Mole winds up trapped in the huge toilet, a major symbol of this novel. A lovelier symbol is the *sakura* of the title, which means cherry blossom. The Japanese are always mindful that this is a wonderful flower, but blooms ever so briefly.

The Ark Sakura and Abé's novel *Secret Rendezvous* resemble Lem's novel *Memoirs Found in a Bathtub*. In all three books, the scene is an enormous, appalling structure full of confusion and ambiguity. The situation in all three is thought-provoking and replete with symbols and analogs, but not convincing as narratives. To the authors, it is sometimes more worthwhile to challenge or mystify the reader than to tell a story. Where Lem's locale for *Memoirs* is an immense Pentagon-like warren of military stereotypes, *Secret Rendezvous* is set in a huge hospital, to which the narrator's wife has been taken. Whether her hospitalization is a mistake or indeed a device for a rendezvous is uncertain. As the narrator tries to locate her, he is drawn into the bizarre society of the hospital. He encounters many amazing devices that monitor the life of the denizens. The final prospect is that the secret rendezvous may mean his death.

The greatest SF opus of Abé is *Inter Ice Age Four*, in which the forthcoming inundation of the Earth by melting polar ice caps is to be dealt with by modifying embryos to produce gill-breathers. Important in predicting the disaster here is computer technology, and we are told that the computers have also discerned Communism as the shape of things to come. However, according to a leading character, Communism would fit the predictions of a machine; it neglects free will. The computers also are described as scanning a human mind completely, then engaging in dialogue with the "individual" stored in their data banks. When this dialogue with the "data bank ghost" is extended to the mind of a newly dead person, one sees an old Japanese concept in action: the 11th-century novel *Tale of Genji* includes an interview with the spirit of the dead Lady Rokujo, and the modern film *Rashomon* also has an interview with a deceased person, through a medium.

Abé's philosophy of present-future relationships is especially significant. *Inter Ice Age Four* comments that the future is not to be judged by us, but rather it sits in judgment on the present. It gives a verdict of guilty, says Abé, and the people of the present, confident of their microcosm, are to be scorned. The author's vision here may have been enhanced by his sense of alienation from his immediate present. Also monumental in his work is an eager confrontation with the great borderlines between life and death, between illusion and reality, and between the inner and outer worlds of human beings.

—Frank H. Tucker

ADAMS, Douglas (Noel)

Nationality: British. **Born:** Cambridge, 11 March 1952. **Education:** St. John's College, Cambridge, B.A. in English literature. **Family:** Married Jane Belson in 1991; one daughter. **Career:** Freelance writer: script editor, *Doctor Who* series, BBC TV, 1978-80; non-executive director, The Digital Village; Chairman, Completely Unexpected Productions Ltd. **Agent:** Ed Victor Ltd., 6 Bayley Street, Bedford Square, London WC1B 3HB, England.

SCIENCE FICTION PUBLICATIONS

Novels (series: Dirk Gently; Hitchhiker)

The Hitch-Hiker's Guide to the Galaxy: A Trilogy in Four Parts. London, Heinemann, 1986; as *The Hitchhiker's Quartet,* New York, Harmony, 1986; as *The Illustrated Hitchhiker's Guide to the Galaxy,* London, Weidenfeld and Nicolson, 1994.
The Hitch-Hiker's Guide to the Galaxy. London, Pan, 1979; New York, Harmony, 1980.
The Restaurant at the End of the Universe. London, Pan, 1980; New York, Harmony, 1982.
Life, The Universe, and Everything. London, Pan, and New York, Harmony, 1982.
The Hitchhiker's Trilogy. New York, Harmony, 1983.
So Long, and Thanks for All the Fish. London, Pan, and New York, Harmony, 1984.
Dirk Gently's Holistic Detective Agency. New York, Simon and Schuster, and London, Heinemann, 1987.
The More Than Complete Hitch-Hiker's Guide: Five Stories. New York, Longmeadow Press, 1987.
The Long Dark Tea-Time of the Soul (Gently). London, Heinemann, and New York, Simon and Schuster, 1988.
Mostly Harmless (Hitchhiker). London, Heinemann, and New York, Harmony, 1992.
Dirk Gently's Holistic Detective Agency; and, The Long Dark Tea-Time of the Soul. London, Pan, and New York, Harmony, 1985; as *Two Complete Novels,* New York, Wings, 1994.

Plays

The Hitch-Hiker's Guide to the Galaxy (broadcast, 1978; produced, 1979).
The Original Hitch-Hiker Radio Scripts. London, Pan, and New York, Harmony, 1985.

Radio Play: *The Hitch-Hiker's Guide to the Galaxy,* 1978.

Television Plays: For *Doctor Who* series.

OTHER PUBLICATIONS

Other

The Meaning of Liff, with John Lloyd. London, Pan, 1983; New York, Harmony, 1984.
Last Chance to See, with Mark Carwardine. London, Heinemann, 1990; New York, Harmony, 1991.
The Deeper Meaning of Liff, with John Lloyd. London, Pan, 1990.

Editor, with Peter Fincham, *The Utterly Utterly Merry Comic Relief Christmas Book.* London, Collins, 1986.

*

Critical Studies: *Don't Panic* by Neil Gaiman, London, Titan Books, 1987, 2nd ed., 1993; "Douglas Adams's "Hitchhiker" novels as Mock Science Fiction," by Carl R. Kroph, in *Science Fiction Studies,* March 1988.

*   *   *

Publication of *The Hitch-Hiker's Guide to the Galaxy* (in American publications "Hitchhiker") following the BBC radio production, was an event in the science fiction community. Adams's work combines satire, humor and carefully crafted lunacy with whimsical speculation about such universal themes as "life, the universe and everything." The combination of science fiction with humor is not common, and this series is an outstanding contribution to the field, even though uneven at times, and should be read where one can laugh out loud. Adams is a master of the improbable. His other comic techniques include fresh and zany uses of clichés and clichéd situations, the frequent and judicious employment of puns to depress pretensions, and the creation of characters who both parody science fiction stereotypes and grow beyond stereotype into developed comic figures. Arthur Dent, the last Englishman, is a bewildered antihero, who charms with his longing for tea and the Earth. Ford Prefect (his name a slight, alien miscalculation) is the quintessential bored, slapdash traveler at home anywhere in the galaxy, and staff writer for the "Hitchhiker's Guide." Marvin (the paranoid android) drives computers to suicide with a single conversation. Zaphod Beeblebrox, two-headed President of the Galaxy, embraces the idea that it's better to not know what you're doing and forces questioning of the old adage, two heads are better than one.

The Hitchhiker series depicts a universe at whose heart is improbability and coincidence rather than the relentlessly consistent, logical laws (even if they do vary from our current state of science) central to conventional science fiction. Twisting these science fiction standards serves to frustrate the reader's expectations or learned responses to genre conventions, opening new speculative space. Thus the series may be read as mock science fiction, functioning much as would a mock epic. This allows Adams to lampoon and skew at will, providing a new angle from which to view the questions asked and answers provided within science fiction. His clever and satirical insight with its infusion of humor serves to illuminate the human condition, while allowing us to view it with a fond eye. He has the ability to make the commonplace seem bizarre and the absurd seem commonplace. This British-style humor is reminiscent of the classic *Three Men in a Boat* by Jerome K. Jerome.

In other ways Adams builds upon conventional standards, but in his own charmingly mad fashion. He incorporates the more exotic forms of hardware, bypassing warp drives and speeds by jumping far beyond to his own creation, the total improbability drive. He incorporates the more homey forms of hardware, giving us the Nutri-matic Drinks Synthesizer, a machine which "invariably produced a liquid which was almost, but not quite, entirely unlike tea." His version of a standard reference work, "The Hitchhiker's Guide to the Galaxy," is not the repository of knowledge and wisdom, rather it's a compendium of (so-called) facts, (weird) philosophies, drink recipes (including the infamous Pan Galactic Gargle Blaster), and (improbable) advice, with the most important feature being the words "Don't Panic" on the cover in big friendly letters. He includes the semi-obligatory robot, but not your standard issue robot, no, a paranoid robot able to drive computers to suicide with a single conversation. He pays homage to the space opera tradition by sending his characters on a quest through the far reaches of space (in search of treasure, the man who rules the universe, and "etc."), with the required miraculous (read improbable) escapes, keeping the plot light, making up for it, not with lengthy chase scenes, but with improbable whimsy (to fly, throw yourself at the ground and miss) and episodes of surreal humor (a whale's deliberations on the meaning of life, while falling through space . . .).

The "increasingly inaccurately named" Hitchhiker's Trilogy concludes with two entries; *Young Zaphod Plays it Safe* (in the complete and *The More Than Complete Hitchhiker's Guide*) and, the fifth book in the trilogy, *Mostly Harmless*. Do we finally find out

"if it's worth worrying about the fabric of space-time and the causal integrity of the multidimensional probability matrix"? This potential wrap-up answers/poses the questions.

Comedic techniques, hilarious characters, and unique usage of science fiction conventions are finely calculated and carefully aimed to deflate the pompous and call into question sacred cows. No one reading these books will ever feel the same about digital watches (considered a pretty neat idea by the amazingly primitive ape-descended life forms of an utterly insignificant little blue-green planet) or 42 (the ultimate answer! but what is the ultimate question?).

Dirk Gently's Holistic Detective Agency (title of French translation, *Un Cheval dans la Salle de Bains*) and *The Long Dark Tea-Time of the Soul* continue the Adams tradition which has been described as hilarious, literate humor, irreverent, zany, clever, improbably weird, riotous, and inspired lunacy. Dirk Gently, whose bill for saving humanity from extinction is NO CHARGE, who resolutely refuses to have anything to do with logic (as practiced by other detectives) and rejects common sense, and whose focus is on the interconnectedness of all rather than mere pertinent clues is distinctly outside the venerable tradition of the "Great Detective." This series combines elements from the fantasy, detective/mystery, horror/ghost, time travel, myth/epic, and romantic comedy genres. Again the oppositional use of genre conventions, turning them inside out and upside down, shines a humorous light on human foibles, and the complications and contradictions of modern life. As in the Hitchhiker series, Adams creates a universe where the illogical, the improbable, the accidental, and the coincidental rule. Ever shifting improbability is Adams's one constant motif.

The Holistic Detective series Adams originals include: answering machine addiction, navigation by following a car that looks like it knows where it's going (to end up where you need to be rather than where you intend to be), the nonfunctional Quark II computer (a paperweight, doorstop and/or police interrogation device), the electronic monk (belief systems specialist), time travel as a way to avoid the complications of VCR programming, et al.

It is with the techniques of irrepressible humor and bizarre viewpoints that Adams creates unforgettable characters and situations, planting seeds of thought to laugh by.

The audio editions of Adams's series, in both the BBC version and the unabridged version read by the author, are a treat and add extra depth to the Adams experience. Both *Hitchhiker* and *Last Chance to See* are available in interactive machine readable form.

His other writing includes several whimsically absurd entries into the dictionary and holiday categories. Adams's most recent work outside the genre is *Last Chance to See* (with Mark Cawardine), the story of traveling to remote areas in search of rare animals, many facing extinction, and of the characters, animal and human, met along the way. Adams's style, poignant and funny, with elements of hope and despair, combined with his keen, off-center views, makes this a pleasurable read for the armchair traveler and all those concerned with animals, nature and world ecology.

—Catherine M. Currier

ADELER, Max

Pseudonym for Charles Heber Clark. **Nationality:** American. **Born:** Berlin, Maryland, 11 July 1841. **Education:** Left school at age 15. **Military Service:** Served in the Union Army, 1864-65. **Ca-**

reer: Reporter, then editor and book reviewer, *Philadelphia Inquirer,* Philadelphia, Pennsylvania, beginning 1865; drama and music critic, *Philadelphia Evening Bulletin,* Philadelphia, beginning 1867; co-owner, *Evening Bulletin,* 1875; co-owner, *Textile Record* (trade journal), 1882; president, J. Ellwood Lee Company. **Died:** 10 August 1915.

SCIENCE FICTION PUBLICATIONS

Short Stories

Transformations: Containing Mrs. Shelmire's Djinn, and a Desperate Adventure. London, Ward Lock, 1883.

OTHER PUBLICATIONS

Novels

Out of the Hurly-Burly; or, Life in an Odd Corner. Philadelphia, McKay, 1874; London, Ward Lock, 1874.
Elbow-Room: A Novel without a Plot. Philadelphia, Stoddart, 1876.
Captain Bluitt: A Tale of Old Turley. Philadelphia, Coates, 1901; London, Ward Lock, 1902.
In Happy Hollow. Philadelphia, Coates, 1903.
The Quakeress: A Tale. Philadelphia, Winston, 1905.

Short Stories

The Tragedy of Thompson Dunbar: A Tale of Salt Lake City. Philadelphia, Stoddart, 1879.
An Old Fogey and Other Stories. London, Ward Lock and Bowden, 1881.
The Fortunate Island and Other Stories. Boston, Lee and Shepard, 1882.
A Desperate Adventure and Other Stories. London, Ward Lock, 1886.
The Great Natural Healer. Philadelphia, Jacobs, 1910.
By the Bend of the River: Tales of Connock Old and New. Philadelphia, Winston, 1914.

Other (as Charles Heber Clark)

How Shall the Revenues of the Federal Government Be Reduced? Philadelphia, Manufacturers' Club, 1887.
Addresses on the Financial Question, with Charles Emory Smith. Harrisburg, Pennsylvania, State Printer, 1895.

*

Critical Studies: "Charles Heber Clark" by Frederic L. Clark, *Bulletin* (Historical Society of Montgomery County, Pennsylvania), 1943; *A Family Memoir* by Charles Heber Clark, edited with an introduction, notes, appendices, and bibliographies by David Ketterer, New York, Peter Lang, 1995.

*   *   *

While long acknowledged as an important 19th-century American humorist (primarily for the 1874 *Out of the Hurly-Burly*), Charles Heber Clark has only recently been recognized for his contribution to the history of science fiction.

A masterpiece of the genre, and of American and world literature, Mark Twain's *A Connecticut Yankee in King Arthur's Court* (1889) appears to owe its very existence to a story of Clark's originally entitled "Professor Baffin's Adventures" (*Beeton's Christmas Annual,* 1880; reprinted in Ketterer's edition of Clark's *A Family Memoir,* 1995) and retitled "The Fortunate Island" in 1881 (collected in *An Old Fogey and Other Stories,* 1881; *The Fortunate Island and Other Stories,* 1882; and *By the Bend of the River,* 1914). Published (except for the last collection) under Clark's famous "Max Adeler" pseudonym, "The Fortunate Island" features a Professor Everett L. Baffin who, with his daughter, is shipwrecked on an uncharted island in the Atlantic which broke off, and drifted away, from England in Arthurian times. Like Twain's Yankee Hank Morgan, Baffin uses his 19th-century knowledge to impress and outwit the island's time-marooned inhabitants. For example, he bests a magician much as Morgan at one point bests Merlin:

> With what instruments the Professor's ingenuity could construct from the rude materials at hand, he showed a number of experiments, chiefly electrical, which so affected the king that he ordered the regular court magician to be executed as a perfectly hopeless humbug; but Professor Baffin's energetic protest saved the unhappy conjurer from so sad a fate.

The many parallels between Adeler's story and Twain's novel in terms of both plot and imagistic detail, and overall conception, are striking. Particularly notable, Baffin and Morgan are similarly inconvenienced by the problem of where to put one's handkerchief while wearing pocketless suits of armour!

Adeler accused Twain of plagiarism in a telegram published in the *New York World* for 4 November 1889. In an interview in the same newspaper two months later (12 January 1890), Twain responded evasively, effectively using his influence to squash Adeler's accusation, and erecting in the process what might reasonably be described as a "cover up." In what now appears a transparent ploy, he pretended that Adeler had accused him of plagiarizing from Adeler's dreamtime-travel-to-the-reality-of-an-idealized-past story, "An Old Fogey" (in all the same collections as "The Fortunate Island"), and not from the story that Adeler had explicitly named in his accusation. It seems only fair to conclude that, while "The Fortunate Island" is not the comic and satiric equal of *A Connecticut Yankee,* it is a thoroughly competent, inventive, and amusing story which has a rather greater claim to originality than *A Connecticut Yankee.* The tacked on it-was-all-a-dream ending (a possibility that also applies to *A Connecticut Yankee*) does not significantly detract from the science fictional nature of the essential lost world story.

Clark's claim to a second significant footnote in the history of SF was staked earlier in his career. "The Women's Millenium" [sic] by "John Quill" (Clark's debut pseudonym), the first of his "Quill Scratches" columns in the Philadelphia *Daily Evening Bulletin* (26 April 1867; reprinted in *Science-Fiction Studies,* March 1988), may well be the first sex-role-reversal dystopia (or "eutopia" for that matter). It begins as follows:

> It was a feminine millenium! Women had obtained all of their coveted "rights," after a long and arduous struggle; but not content therewith, and being far more numerous than males, they had completely subverted the ancient order of things, placed themselves in the positions formerly occupied by the other sex, and practically reduced the men

to the social, political and legal status which women formerly occupied.

Not only does the opening sentence place the reader directly in a future society, it also implies a further future—a "eutopian" state characterized as "this enlightened age"—which has supplanted the women's millennium and by which that era is to be judged. In the narrator's society sexual equality has apparently been achieved (although that may be belied by the presumably male narrator's last two sentences which favour "the superior purity and integrity" of men). Clark is here using science fiction to write a feminist polemic. Certainly, compared to the chauvinist sex-role-reversal in, say, Sir Walter Besant's *The Revolt of Man* (1882), Clark's satiric intent is very enlightened. Just as "The Fortunate Island" inspired *A Connecticut Yankee,* so "The Women's Millenium" may have inspired, or at least influenced what appears to be the next sex-role-reversal utopia, Annie Denton Cridge's *Man's Rights: Or, How Would You Like It?* (1870).

However, unlike *Man's Rights,* where the narrator experiences her utopian Mars in s series of five dreams, "The Women's Millenium" is pure SF. All may be a dream in "The Fortunate Island" and in such other Clark tales about extraordinary events as "An Old Fogey" (1878), "Mr. Skinner's Night in the Underworld" (where, among other shades, King Arthur and the Knights of the Round Table are encountered; 1879), "The Flying Dutchman" (1903), and "The Rally at the Forge" (a vision of the Civil War dead at Valley Forge; 1914)—all collected in *By the Bend of the River*—but the "feminine millenium" was actual history. There is no it-was-all-a-dream cop-out.

There are two works of marginal science fiction interest. "A Desperate Adventure" (*Beeton's Christmas Annual,* 1882; collected in *Transformations,* 1883) deals with an aborted balloon voyage to the North Pole. "Franklin's Vision," an unpublished sketch and accompanying verse dated 6 January 1909, presented at Philadelphia's Franklin Inn Club, purports to be a recently discovered lost chapter from Boswell's *Life of Johnson* describing a meeting between Clark's two heroes, Benjamin Franklin and Dr. Johnson, and Franklin's vision of Philadelphia and the Club years after his death (see The Franklin Inn Club Papers, held by the Pennsylvania Historical Society, Philadelphia). The many sketches that Clark wrote involving malfunctioning machinery, ridiculous or dangerous inventions, deranged inventors, scientists, and pseudo-scientists (notably Mr. Bradley in *Elbow-Room* [1876] and elsewhere, and Professor Quackenboss in *Random Shots* [1878] and elsewhere) also relate obliquely to SF. In fact, Clark's wary concern with science and technology is one of the more pervasive aspects of his work which makes it of some general interest to today's readers—as is his still potent humour. "The Women's Millenium" and "The Fortunate Island" are notable contributions to that rare vein of science fiction which is genuinely funny.

—David Ketterer

ADLARD, Mark

Nationality: British. **Born:** Peter Marcus Adlard in Seaton Carew. County Durham, 19 June 1932. **Education:** Trinity College, Cambridge, 1951-54, B.A. in English 1954; Oxford University, 1954-55; University of London, B.Sc. (extramural) in economics. **Family:** Married Sheila Rosemary Skuse in 1968; one daughter and one son. **Career:** Executive in the steel industry in Middlesbrough, Yorkshire, Cardiff, and Kent, 1956-76. **Address:** 43 Enterpen, Hutton Rudby, Cleveland TS15 0EL, England.

Science Fiction Publications

Novels (series: Tcity in all books)

Interface: Science Fiction. London, Sidgwick and Jackson, 1971; New York, Ace, 1977.
Volteface: Science Fiction. London, Sidgwick and Jackson, 1972; New York, Ace, 1978.
Multiface: Science Fiction. London, Sidgwick and Jackson, 1975; New York, Ace, 1978.

Other Publications

Novel

The Greenlander. London, Hamish Hamilton, 1978; New York, Summit, 1979.

*

Mark Adlard comments:
One of my main preoccupations is the importance of personal economic activity to "the good life." It seemed to me that various hypotheses about such matters could be explored fictionally, by presenting a future world in which economic activity had been largely made redundant. This fictional device would also make it possible to consider the moral dilemmas and responsibilities of managerial elites. It was considerations such as these, and not a previous enthusiasm for the genre, that induced me to write "science fiction."

* * *

Mark Adlard's Tcity trilogy, *Interface, Volteface,* and *Multiface,* makes up a whole less than the sum of its parts but it is nevertheless a highly interesting and readable work. The parts are considerable and the project ambitious. Reviewing *Multiface* for the *Times Literary Supplement,* T.A. Shippey noted the ironic contrast between the plots and characters of the first two books and those of Wagner's *Ring* and Dante's *Commedia* respectively: "Only the boldest writer would invite such comparisons. . . . But Mark Adlard made a success of it, and has done so once more, in a novel based this time on *The Faerie Queene.*" Shippey is an over-bold reviewer, for his criticism is not just, although it does adumbrate a critical problem. For one thing, Spenser is only one among several important literary sources in *Multiface,* where the controlling reference (matching Wagner and Dante) is to Buddhism; for another, the relationships between the novels and their sources are not the same.

One of the problems seems to be that the three novels were not all completed together. As literature, *Interface* is inferior to the later two. It is overloaded with exposition at the expense of narrative and, although Adlard is clearly aware of the problem (throughout the series, a stock joke is the blunt interruption of robotic exposition), information whether cultural or technological appears to be simply dropped into the text and does not resonate within it. This is true of the Wagner references, which are only to *Götterdämmerung,* an odd choice for the first novel of a series. This novel concerns weaknesses at the interface between an enclosed society of drugged citizens and their benevolent, superior managers, weaknesses on both sides which end in destruction for some but salvation for others. Adlard stands too far off from his characters, and, because the emotive level of the narrative is low, the climactic horrors and pathos fail somewhat in their effect. *Volteface* is much richer in texture, and the Dante references are both more numerous than the *Ring* ones and more deeply embedded in the text; the leading characters are more highly developed, and the narrative consequently more engaging, the ironies more piquant. In the failed Utopia of *Interface,* work had been denied the multitudinous citizens; in response to their discontent, work is reintroduced to Tcity by the executives, who deliberately create an old-fashioned (i.e., 20th-century) managerial structure, knowing this will be inefficient, merely to make work, i.e., the distribution of goods (trinkets) which are, of course, manufactured in fully automated factories. This scheme enables Adlard to write splendid satire as he traces both the collective volte-face and some individual reversals of life in Tcity. The *Inferno* of work-free pleasure is exchanged for a dubious *Purgatorio.* However, I would need to have the author explain to me just how his Dante-Beatrice pair (Twynne and Ventrix) are really illuminated by their source. Ventrix is an interesting character in her own right.

If idle pleasure was hell, work purgatory, then *Multiface* seems to be asking what is the ideal mode of life. The answer is that it depends on the individual life. Even Theravada Buddhism, practiced by one saintly executive, may not suit all executives; Mahayana Buddhism, considered more suitable for the citizens, seems too perversely appropriate for the tormented Taggart, persuaded that in a lame dog he sees the reincarnation of his sadistic father, on which he exacts vengeance for his mother's suffering which has blighted the whole of his own life. As Jan Caspol puts it, "Men have different faces. There are no two alike and you can't expect them to wear the same mask. . . . Even Buddhas only point the way." Jan, though an executive, is the reader's choric companion throughout the series and he thus presumably voices the author's conclusion: but what consequences follow for the executives whose vast experiment has involved the beneficent control of a world society? The author seems to shy away from his bold sociohistory, in favour of the predicaments of individuals. Their problems may be resolved for good or ill, but what of the further problems in Tcity? The trilogy seems to call for a further, more mature volume, one which will tell us what life is for, perhaps: we are at least provoked to consideration of this disturbing question. However, it may be in the intuition that life is open-ended, that there are no pat catastrophes, that the trilogy should properly end. One of its most appealing narratives is that of Osbert Osborne, discovering diversity and pattern in the apparently uniform stahlex beeblocks of Tcity (everything there is made of this remarkable versatile new material), yet knowing that he will never have time even to map his own multistory block. Three faces can stand for the whole infinite polyhedron.

—Michael J. Tolley

AGHILL, Gordon. *See* **GARRETT, Randall.**

———

AINSBURY, Ray. *See* **VERRILL, A. Hyatt.**

———

ALDISS, Brian W(ilson)

Nationality: British. **Born:** East Dereham, Norfolk, 18 August 1925. **Education:** Framlingham College, Suffolk, 1936-39; West Buckland School, 1939-42. **Military Service:** Served in the Royal Signals in the Far East, 1943-47. **Family:** Married Margaret Manson in 1965 (second marriage); four children, two from previous marriage. **Career:** Bookseller, Oxford, 1947-56; literary editor, *Oxford Mail,* 1958-69; science fiction editor, Penguin Books, London, 1961-64; art correspondent, *Guardian,* London. President, British Science Fiction Association, 1960-65; co-founder, 1972, and chairman, 1976-78, John W. Campbell Memorial award; co-president, Eurocon Committee, 1975-79; chairman, Society of Authors, London, 1978-79; member, Arts Council Literature Panel, 1978-80; president, World Science Fiction, 1982-84. Since 1975, vice-president, Stapledon Society; since 1977, founding trustee, World Science Fiction, Dublin; since 1983, vice-president, H.G. Wells Society; since 1989, Permanent Special Guest at IAFA Annual Conference; since 1994, Friend of the Bodleian Library. **Awards:** World Science Fiction Convention citation, 1959; Hugo award, 1962, 1987; Nebula award, 1965; Ditmar award (Australia), 1970; British Science Fiction Association award, 1972, 1982, and Special award, 1974; Eurocon award, 1976; James Blish award, for nonfiction, 1977; Cometa d'Argento (Italy), 1977; Prix Jules Verne, 1977; Pilgrim award, 1978; John W. Campbell Memorial award, 1983; J. Lloyd Eaton award, 1988; World SF, President's award for independence of thought in the field of SF Studies; Kafka award, 1991. Guest of Honor, World Science Fiction Convention, London, 1965, 1979. Fellow, Royal Society of Literature, 1991. **Agent:** Michael Shaw, Curtis Brown, Haymarket House, 28/29 Haymarket, London SW1Y 4SP, England; or, Robin Straus, 229 East 79th Street, New York, New York 10021, U.S.A. **Address:** Woodlands, Foxcombe Road, Boars Hill, Oxfordshire OX1 5DL, England.

SCIENCE FICTION PUBLICATIONS

Novels (series: Helliconia)

Non-Stop. London, Faber, 1958; New York, Carroll and Graf, 1989; as *Starship,* New York, Criterion, 1959.
Vanguard from Alpha. New York, Ace, 1959; enlarged as *Equator: A Human Time Bomb from the Moon* (includes "Segregation"), London, Digit, 1961.
Bow Down to Nul. New York, Ace, 1960; as *The Interpreter,* London, Digit, 1961.

The Male Response: A Timely Original Story. New York, Beacon, 1961; London, Dobson, 1963.

The Primal Urge. New York, Ballantine, 1961; London, Sphere, 1967.

Hothouse. London, Faber, 1962; abridged as *The Long Afternoon of Earth,* New York, Signet, 1962; original edition, Boston, Gregg Press, 1976.

The Dark Light Years: A Science Fiction Novel. London, Faber, 1964; New York, Signet, 1965.

Greybeard. New York, Harcourt Brace, and London, Faber, 1964; revised, London, Roc, 1994.

Earthworks: A Science Fiction Novel. London, Faber, 1965; Garden City, New York, Doubleday, 1966.

An Age. London, Faber, 1967; as *Cryptozoic!,* Garden City, New York, Doubleday, 1968.

Report on Probability A. London, Faber, 1968; Garden City, New York, Doubleday, 1969.

Barefoot in the Head: A European Fantasia. London, Faber, 1969; Garden City, New York, Doubleday, 1970.

Frankenstein Unbound. London, Cape, 1973; New York, Random House, 1974.

The Eighty-Minute Hour: A Space Opera. Garden City, New York, Doubleday, and London, Cape, 1974.

Brothers of the Head. London, Pierrot, 1977; New York, Two Continents, 1978.

The Malacia Tapestry. London, Cape, 1976; New York, Harper, 1977.

Enemies of the System: A Tale of Homo Uniformis. London, Cape, and New York, Harper, 1978.

Brothers of the Head; and, Where the Lines Converge. London, Panther, 1979.

Moreau's Other Island: A Novel. London, Cape, 1980; as *An Island Called Moreau: A Novel,* New York, Simon and Schuster, 1981.

The Helliconia Trilogy. New York, Atheneum, 1985.

  Helliconia Spring. London, Cape, and New York, Atheneum, 1982.

  Helliconia Summer. London, Cape, and New York, Atheneum, 1983.

  Helliconia Winter. London, Cape, and New York, Atheneum, 1985.

The Year Before Yesterday: A Novel in Three Acts. New York, Watts, 1987; as *Cracken at Critical,* Worcester Park, Surrey, Kerosina, 1987.

Dracula Unbound. New York, HarperCollins, and London, Grafton, 1991.

Somewhere East of Life. London, HarperCollins, and New York, Carroll and Graf, 1994.

Short Stories

Space, Time, and Nathaniel: Presciences. London, Faber, 1957.

No Time Like Tomorrow, New York, Signet, 1959.

The Canopy of Time. London, Faber, 1959.

Galaxies Like Grains of Sand, New York, Signet, 1960; London, Panther, 1979.

The Airs of Earth: Science Fiction Stories. London, Faber, 1963.

Starswarm. New York, Signet, 1964; London, Panther, 1979.

But Who Can Replace a Man? The Best Science Fiction Stories of Brian Aldiss. London, Faber, 1965; New York, Harcourt Brace, 1966; revised edition, Faber, 1971; revised as *Best SF Stories of Brian W. Aldiss,* London, Gollancz, 1988; as *Man in His Time: Best SF Stories of Brian W. Aldiss.* New York, Atheneum, 1989.

The Saliva Tree and Other Strange Growths. London, Faber, 1966; Boston, Gregg Press, 1981.

Intangibles Inc. and Other Stories. London, Faber, 1969.

A Brian Aldiss Omnibus: Five Novellas (includes *The Interpreter* and *The Primal Urge*). London, Sidgwick and Jackson, 1969.

Neanderthal Planet. New York, Avon, 1970.

The Moment of Eclipse. London, Faber, 1970; Garden City, New York, Doubleday, 1972.

A Brian Aldiss Omnibus (2) (includes *Space, Time, and Nathaniel;* and *The Male Response*). London, Sidgwick and Jackson, 1971.

The Book of Brian Aldiss. New York, DAW, 1972; as *The Comic Inferno,* London, New English Library, 1973.

Excommunication. London, Post Card Partnership, 1975.

Last Orders and Other Stories. London, Cape, 1977; New York, Carroll and Graf, 1989.

New Arrivals, Old Encounters: Twelve Stories. London, Cape, and New York, Harper, 1979.

A Romance of the Equator. Birmingham, England, Birmingham Science Fiction Group, 1980.

Foreign Bodies: Stories. Singapore, Chopmen, 1981.

Best of Aldiss. London, Viaduct, 1983.

Seasons in Flight. London, Cape, 1984; New York, Atheneum, 1986.

My Country, 'Tis Not Only of Thee. Oxford, Aldiss Appreciation Society, 1987.

A Romance of the Equator: Best Fantasy Stories of Brian W. Aldiss. London, Gollancz, 1989; New York, Atheneum, 1990.

Bodily Functions: Four Stories and a Letter to Sam on the Subject of Bowel Movements. London, Avernus, 1991.

Journey to the Goat Star. Eugene, Oregon, Pulphouse, 1991.

A Tupolev Too Far and Other Stories. London, HarperCollins, 1993; New York, St. Martin's Press, 1994.

A Tupolev Too Far. London, HarperCollins, 1993; New York, St. Martin's Press, 1994.

The Secret of This Book. London, HarperCollins, 1995; as *Common Clay.* New York, St. Martin's Press, 1995.

OTHER PUBLICATIONS

Novels (series: "The Squire Quartet")

The Brightfount Diaries. London, Faber, 1955.

The Horatio Stubbs Saga. London, Granada, 1985.

  The Hand-Reared Boy. London, Weidenfeld and Nicolson, and New York, McCall, 1970.

  A Soldier Erect. London, Weidenfeld and Nicolson, and New York, Coward, McCann, 1971.

  A Rude Awakening. London, Weidenfeld and Nicolson, 1978; New York, Random House, 1979.

Life in the West (Squire Quartet). London, Weidenfeld and Nicolson, 1980; New York, Carroll and Graf, 1990.

The Magic of the Past (novella). Worcester Park, Surrey, Kerosina, 1987.

Ruins (novella). London, Century Hutchinson, 1987.

Forgotten Life (Squire Quartet). London, Gollancz, 1988; New York, Atheneum, 1989.

Remembrance Day (Squire Quartet). London, HarperCollins, and New York, St. Martin's Press, 1993.

Somewhere East of Life (Squire Quartet). London, HarperCollins, and New York, Carroll and Graf, 1994.

Plays

Distant Encounters, adaptation of his own stories (produced London, 1978).
Science Fiction Blues (produced London, 1987).
Kindred Blood in Kensington Gore: Philip K. Dick in the Afterlife: An Imaginary Conversation. London, Avernus, 1992.

Television Play: *Life* (4 Minute series), 1986.

Poetry

Pile: Petals from St. Klaed's Computer. London, Cape, and New York, Holt Rinehart, 1979.
Farewell to a Child: Poems. Berkhamsted, Hertfordshire, Priapus, 1982.
Home Life with Cats. London, HarperCollins, 1992.
At the Caligula Hotel and Other Poems. London, Sinclair-Stevenson, 1995.

Other

Cities and Stones: A Traveller's Jugoslavia. London, Faber, 1966.
The Shape of Further Things: Speculations on Change. London, Faber, 1970; Garden City, New York, Doubleday, 1971.
Billion Year Spree: A History of Science Fiction. London, Weidenfeld and Nicolson, and Garden City, New York, Doubleday, 1973.
Science Fiction Art: The Fantasies of SF. London, New English Library, and New York, Bounty, 1975.
Science Fiction as Science Fiction. Frome, Somerset, Bran's Head, 1978.
This World and Nearer Ones: Essays Exploring the Familiar. London, Weidenfeld and Nicolson, 1979; Kent, Ohio, Kent State University Press, 1981.
The Life of Samuel Johnson, LL.D.: A Series of His Epistolary Correspondence and Conversations with Many Eminent Persons, Never Before Published. Oxford, Oxford Polytechnic Press, 1980.
Science Fiction Quiz. London, Weidenfeld and Nicolson, 1983.
The Pale Shadow of Science. Seattle, Serconia Press, 1985.
And the Lurid Glare of the Comet. Seattle, Washington, Serconia Press, 1986.
Trillion Year Spree: The History of Science Fiction, with David Wingrove. London, Gollancz, and New York, Atheneum, 1986.
Science Fiction Blues, Brian Aldiss: The Show That Brian Aldiss Took on the Road: A Selection of His Very Best Stories, Poetry, and Speculations: An Evening of Wonder, edited by Frank Hatherley. London, Avernus, 1988.
Bury My Heart at W.H. Smith's: A Writing Life (autobiography). London, Hodder and Stoughton, 1990.
Sex and the Black Machine: The First Aldiss Cutup. London, Avernus, 1990.
The Detached Retina: Aspects of SF and Fantasy. Liverpool, Liverpool University Press, and Syracuse, New York, Syracuse University Press, 1995.

Editor, *Penguin Science Fiction: An Anthology.* London, Penguin, 1961; *More Penguin Science Fiction,* 1963; *Yet More Penguin Science Fiction,* 1964; 3 vols. collected as *The Penguin Science Fiction Omnibus: An Anthology,* 1973.
Editor, *Best Fantasy Stories.* London, Faber, 1962.

Editor, *Last and First Men,* by Olaf Stapledon. London, Penguin, 1963.
Editor, *Introducing SF: A Science Fiction Antholoy.* London, Faber, 1964.
Editor, with Harry Harrison, *Nebula Award Stories Two.* Garden City, New York, Doubleday, 1967; as *Nebula Award Stories 1967,* London, Gollancz, 1967.
Editor, with Harry Harrison, *Farewell, Fantastic Venus.* London, Macdonald, 1968; abridged as *All about Venus,* New York, Dell, 1968.
Editor, with Harry Harrison, *Best SF 1967 [to 1975].* New York, Berkley and Putnam, 7 vols., and Indianapolis, Bobbs Merrill, 2 vols., 1968-75; as *The Year's Best Science Fiction 1[-9].* London, Sphere, 8 vols., 1968-76, and London, Futura, 1 vol., 1976.
Editor, with Harry Harrison, *The Astounding-Analog Reader.* Garden City, New York, Doubleday, 2 vols., 1972-73; London, Sphere, 2 vols., 1973.
Editor, *Space Opera: An Anthology of Way-Back-When Futures.* London, Weidenfeld and Nicolson, 1974; Garden City, New York, Doubleday, 1975.
Editor, *Space Odysseys.* London, Futura, 1974; Garden City, New York, Doubleday, 1976.
Editor, with Harry Harrison, *SF Horizons* (reprint of magazine). New York, Arno Press, 1975.
Editor, with Harry Harrison, *Hell's Cartographers: Some Personal Histories of Science Fiction Writers.* London, Weidenfeld and Nicolson, and New York, Harper, 1975.
Editor, with Harry Harrison, *Decade: The 1940s, [The 1950s, The 1960s].* London, Macmillan, 3 vols., 1975-77; *The 1940's and The 1950's,* New York, St. Martin's Press, 2 vols., 1978.
Editor, *Evil Earths: An Anthology of Way-Back-When Futures.* London, Weidenfeld and Nicolson, 1975; New York, Avon, 1979.
Editor, *Galactic Empires: An Anthology of Way-Back-When Futures.* London, Weidenfeld and Nicolson, 2 vols., 1976; New York, St. Martin's Press, 2 vols., 1977.
Editor, *Perilous Planets: An Anthology of Way-Back-When Futures.* London, Orbit; New York, Avon, 1980.
Editor, with Sam Lundwall, *The Penguin World Omnibus of Science Fiction.* London, Penguin, 1986.
Editor, *My Madness: The Selected Writings of Anna Kavan.* London, Picadore, 1990.
Editor, *The Island of Doctor Moreau,* by H.G. Wells. London, Dent, and Rutland, Vermont, Tuttle, 1993.

*

Bibliography: *The Work of Brian W. Aldiss, An Annotated Bibliography and Guide* by Margaret Aldiss, San Bernardino, California, Borgo Press, 1991.

Manuscript Collections: Bodleian Library, Oxford University; Dallas Public Library; University of Kansas, Lawrence; Sydney University; Eastern New Mexico University, Portales; University of California, Los Angeles (correspondence), Henry E. Huntington Library, San Marino, California (correspondence); North East London Polytechnic (correspondence).

Critical Studies: *Aldiss Unbound: The Science Fiction of Brian W. Aldiss* by Richard Mathews, San Bernardino, California, Borgo Press, 1977; *Apertures: A Study of the Writings of Brian Aldiss* by Brian Griffin and David Wingrove, Westport, Connecticut, Greenwood Press, 1984; by the author, in *Contemporary Authors Autobiography Series 2,* Detroit, Gale, 1985; *Brian W. Aldiss* by Michael Collings, Mercer Island, Washington, Starmont, 1986; "The Secret You: Fantasy and Story in Brian Aldiss's Mainstream Fiction" by Ellen R. Weil, in *New York Review of Science Fiction,* 26-27, 1990.

Brian Aldiss comments:

As the 20th century draws to a close, we see more clearly what a bad lot the human species is as a whole, and how greatly we have damaged a planet reasonably intact in 1900, give or take a few million passenger pigeons. Let's hope to God that that infantile fantasy of our conquering the universe never becomes reality! It's a pity that the evolutionary march upwards from the Olduvai Gorge was not taken at a more leisurely pace. As Bruce Sterling says, the colour of SF is *noir.*

Morality and hedonism fight the good fight in my novels and stories.

Interested parties are recommended to seek out the critical study of my writings by Wingrove and Griffin. Although I do not always agree with all they say, they are at least as reliable as I would be. Even self-conscious authors sail on, charting their course through style and story, without much bothering about the rocks under the surface. It's for the critics to consider shipwreck.

One really writes because one has to. I never think of the reader until the act of creation is over. Then I hope I might nourish the creative spark in others; I imagine people and people imagination. I craved the freedom writing gave me. My fictions have taken place on many worlds. My central characters have been of many nationalities. Speech is a preoccupation. Even in *Non-Stop,* some sort of heightened speech was attempted. In *Life in the West,* scarcely a handful of the many characters speak "standard English," in *Helliconia* the languages are many. Aren't those volumes in part about the necessity of communication—and its difficulty? Mine is a literature of exile. Every novel undertaken is an act of xenophilia. The label "science fiction" doesn't fit.

At present, I'm planning a utopia in two volumes.

The list of my writings seems impossibly long. The more reason to be brief here.

*   *   *

A reasonable argument could be made that Brian W. Aldiss is the most significant English writer of science fiction since H.G. Wells. Arthur C. Clarke may have gained wider popular fame, and J.G. Ballard more immediate recognition among academic critics, but while those authors have come to be associated with almost proprietary styles and attitudes, Aldiss has ranged widely through the various tropes and techniques available to the science fiction writer of the last half-century. Like Wells, he has explored all the classic science fiction themes and put his own stamp on them; like Wells, he has extended his vision into various other modes of writing, producing a substantial body of criticism and nonfiction as well as plays, poems, and film work. Appropriately, Aldiss has also become the genre's preeminent literary historian, not only because of his lengthy study *Trillion Year Spree* (written in collaboration with David Wingrove), but because of his insightful revisioning of Wells, Mary Shelley, and even Bram Stoker in his own novels.

Aldiss began publishing in British science fiction magazines in 1954, and by 1957 his first collection of stories, *Space, Time, and Nathaniel,* appeared in England (it was later reprinted in the U.S.,

with some stories dropped and others added, as *No Time Like Tomorrow*). These early stories already reveal a uniquely existential outlook, drawing both on traditional science fiction themes and yet clearly prefiguring the "New Wave" with which Aldiss was later to be associated. More importantly, they introduce themes that would haunt Aldiss throughout his career: the fear of being unable to take meaningful action, or to act at all in a meaningless universe, and yet the necessity of some action to define being human. "Outside" (1955), for example, deals with the familiar SF theme of characters in a closed environment discovering the larger universe outside, but in Aldiss's hands the revelation fails to quite liberate the character from his own inner traps. Similarly, in "Not for an Age" (1955), a character is able to view his life from outside of time, but cannot change the fact that his life seems to consist of the same day lived over and over.

Given this interest in reinventing familiar SF themes, it is not surprising that Aldiss's first novel, *Non-Stop* (1958; as *Starship* in the U.S.), should turn to the classic notion of the "generation starship" whose inhabitants have lost all knowledge of the universe outside. While Aldiss pays homage to the familiar SF view of such a situation as an analogue of scientific discovery, he also interrogates this simple notion by suggesting that the starship's inhabitants may have evolved to suit their environment, and may even have been deliberately maintained in this environment for their own protection. Both stylistically and philosophically, *Non-Stop* remains a classic treatment of its theme. Aldiss followed it with a series of less distinguished novels, some of which (such as *Bow Down to Nul,* 1960) echoed the "galactic empire" themes of earlier space operas. *The Primal Urge* (1961), however, revealed his considerable talent as a social satirist in a tale concerning the repercussions of a device that makes it impossible to disguise sexual attraction. Aldiss returned to the theme of evolution (or devolution) in *The Long Afternoon of Earth* (1962; *Hothouse* in the U.S.), a stylistically sophisticated and even poetic treatment of a distant future in which the descendants of humanity survive in a gigantic tree long after the earth has stopped rotating; again, the notion that stasis leads to disintegration emerges as an important idea that would continue to characterize Aldiss's fiction.

Aldiss's next masterwork, *Greybeard,* appeared in 1964. This time Aldiss turns to the familiar SF theme of the post-catastrophe world, but his approach to it is unique. In the 1980s, nuclear tests disrupted the Van Allen radiation belts, resulting in worldwide exposure to hard radiation. It soon becomes apparent that no children are being born anywhere, and by the mid-21st century, an aging humanity faces decline and decay. The "Greybeard" of the title, Algy Timberlane, undertakes a journey along the Thames while recalling his own past and the history of the "accident." The river-journey motif, together with the complex development of Algy's character, permit Aldiss to develop his most thorough and thoughtful critique of civilization and science to date, and the novel remains among the most haunting of post-catastrophe fictions (the theme was revisited in P.D. James's 1992 novel *The Children of Men,* but with considerably less impact).

Aldiss continued to revise and rethink SF tropes during his other novels of the 1960s—alien contact in *The Dark Light Years* (1964), time travel in *An Age* (1967; as *Cryptozoic!* in the U.S.), but his fiction began to turn increasingly experimental as he became associated with the magazine *New Worlds,* which is often credited with inaugurating the "New Wave" in British SF. His most memorable works from this period include *Report on Probability A* (1968, but originally written in 1962), which brings the techniques of the

French "anti-novel" to an SF setting as it portrays a group of characters obsessively observing one another in what is Aldiss's most purely abstract depiction of stasis and inactivity; and *Barefoot in the Head* (1969), a stylistically challenging novel based on his "Acid-Head War" stories about Europe recovering from a wave of psychedelic drugs. With its Joycean puns, typographical tricks, and interspersed song lyrics and poems, it remains among the most radical literary experiments in the history of science fiction. (Aldiss returned briefly to this experimental mode in his 1974 novel *The Eighty-Minute Hour).*

Always fascinated by the history of science fiction, Aldiss began to address this interest directly in the late 1960s and early 1970s. Some earlier stories, such as "The Saliva Tree" (1965), had already seemed designed as *hommages* to H.G. Wells and others, but—perhaps influenced by his rereading of the genre for his 1973 history *Billion Year Spree* (later revised and expanded with David Wingrove as *Trillion Year Spree*)—he began deliberately to explore the genre's history in his own fiction. *Frankenstein Unbound* (1973) takes a time traveler back to meet Mary Shelley and her circle—as well as a real Dr. Frankenstein and his monster. (In *Trillion Year Spree,* Aldiss persuasively argues that *Frankenstein* represents the beginning of science fiction.) The same hero encounters Bram Stoker in the 1991 *Dracula Unbound,* and in 1980's *Moreau's Other Island* (in the U.S. as *An Island Called Moreau*), Wells's classic mad scientist tale is retold in contemporary terms during a nuclear war. During this same period Aldiss, who has always been one of England's leading anthologists of SF, explored yet another aspect of the genre's history in a series of anthologies concerning space operas and galactic empires.

Ironically, while Aldiss was exploring SF's history in a variety of ways, his other fiction seemed increasingly constrained by genre materials, and began to move in radical new directions. *The Malacia Tapestry* (1976) is a haunting, detailed fantasy romance set in a mysterious city-state where change is outlawed, where humans are the creation of Satan and share the world with dinosaurs and flying men. Told from the point of view of a young actor named Perian de Chirolo, the novel represents one of Aldiss's most thoughtful and complex explorations of his favorite themes of stasis, observation, and artifice. In addition to such fantasy, Aldiss also turned increasingly to mainstream fiction. He had published two mainstream novels near the beginning of his career, but neither had the impact of the autobiographical series *The Hand-Reared Boy* (1970), *A Soldier Erect* (1971), and *A Rude Awakening* (1978). Alternately hilarious and touching, these novels depict the education and wartime experiences of a youth whose life resembles Aldiss's own. Similar autobiographical material shows up in the connected series of novels collectively called "the Squire Quartet": *Life in the West* (1980), *Forgotten Life* (1988), *Remembrance Day* (1992), and *Somewhere East of Life* (1994) moves the action into the near future, as a cataloguer of architectural antiquities undertakes a series of adventures in Eastern Europe and the former Soviet Union while trying to track down the years of his memory that have been stolen by an unscrupulous dealer in recorded memories. Together, the series constitutes an ambitious and insightful analysis of the state of European civilization and culture in the late 20th century.

Aldiss's fascination with this enormous question of the dynamics that move civilizations is also apparent in his dramatic return to science fiction in the 1980s with the publication of the "Helliconia trilogy"—*Helliconia Spring* (1982), *Helliconia Summer* (1983), and *Helliconia Winter* (1985). By far his longest and most ambitious work to date, these three large novels depict an alien planet whose "Great Year" lasts for eons, and whose civilizations grow and flour-ish during the centuries-long spring and summer seasons, only to die and be reborn during the endless winter. The human-like inhabitants share the world with alien "phagors," who are more comfortable in the cold, and the whole parade of civilization is monitored by observers from Earth in an orbiting space station. The series is one of the modern classics of science fiction, and combines many of Aldiss's favorite themes, from space-opera-like adventure sequences to the huge tidal forces that alter society to the uninvolved observers who have haunted his fiction since the beginning.

Aldiss's recent fiction moves comfortably between realistic mainstream narratives, science fiction, fantasy, literary *hommages,* and inventive experiments. His unusual 1977 tale about Siamese-twin rock stars, *Brothers of the Head,* is not only a touching parable of identity but (in its original publication, with paintings by Ian Pollock) an early and sophisticated version of a graphic novel. A similar experiment with the integration of graphics and text characterizes his long 1979 poem *Pile.* The range of Aldiss's imagination is well-represented in the 1993 story collection *A Tupolev Too Far,* which includes an alternate world tale (the title story, about a Russian airliner which lands in an alternate timeline that turns out to be our own); an evolutionary fable ("Ratbird"); a compressed novel of alien intervention ("A Life of Matter and Death"); and *hommages* to space opera ("A Day in the Life of a Galactic Empire"), Kafka (the hilarious "Better Morphosis"), and Mary Shelley ("Summertime Was Nearly Over"). Aldiss has also written and performed in a number of his own short plays and revues ("Science Fiction Blues," 1988, and a tribute to Philip K. Dick titled "Kindred Blood in Kensington Gore," 1992), worked in film and television (*Frankenstein Unbound* was filmed by Roger Corman in 1990, although Aldiss did not do the screenplay), and published volumes of poetry, travel writing, criticism, science fiction art, and autobiography (*Bury My Heart at W.H. Smith's,* 1990). Two retrospective collections, *Man in His Time* and *A Romance of the Equator* (both 1989), assembled many of his finest science fiction and fantasy stories, respectively.

Aldiss's vast and varied body of work rank him easily among the major British writers of the last half-century—and not only in the science fiction field. His astute observation of current social forces in the Squire Quartet is comparable to that of Doris Lessing; his epic world-building in the Helliconia series compares favorably to that of Frank Herbert; his radical literary experiments in novels like *Barefoot in the Head* and stories like his "Enigmas" rival those of J.G. Ballard; his thematically complex use of landscapes and cityscapes in novels like *Greybeard* and *The Malacia Tapestry* is virtually unmatched in the genre. If his science fiction career qualifies him as the heir apparent to Wells, his broader literary career moves him well beyond what Wells was able to accomplish. For unlike Wells and many other writers who late in their careers turn into spokesmen and philosophers, Aldiss remains as exuberantly unpredictable as ever, and continually promises new directions, new inventions, and new ideas.

—Gary K. Wolfe

ALLEN, Roger MacBride

Nationality: American. **Born:** 1957.

Novels (series: Crisis of Empire; Hunted Earth; Next Wave; Star Wars: Corellian Trilogy; Torch of Honor)

The Torch of Honor. New York, Baen Books, 1985; London, Arrow Books, 1989.

Rogue Powers (Torch of Honor). New York, Baen Science Fiction Books, 1986; London, Arrow Books, 1989.

Farside Cannon. New York, Baen Books, 1988; London, Orbit, 1989.

Orphan of Creation: Contact with the Human Past. New York, Baen Books, 1988; London, Orbit, 1991.

The War Machine with David Drake (Crisis of Empire). New York, Bean Books, 1989.

The Ring of Charon (Hunted Earth). New York, Tor SF, 1990; London, Orbit, 1991.

Supernova, with Eric Kotani. New York, Avon Books, 1991.

The Modular Man (Next Wave). New York, A Byron Preiss Book, Bantam Books, 1992.

Isaac Asimov's Caliban. New York, Ace Books, and London, Millennium, 1993.

Isaac Asimov's Inferno. New York, Ace Books, and London, Millennium, 1994.

The Shattered Sphere: A Novel (Hunted Earth). New York, Tor, 1994.

Allies and Aliens. Riverdale, New York, Baen Books, 1995.

Ambush at Corellia (Star Wars: Corellian Trilogy). New York, Bantam Books, 1995.

*   *   *

Roger MacBride Allen's debut novel, *The Torch of Honor,* appeared to be just another military-oriented space adventure. A group of space cadets gets caught in the middle when an expansionist power on one world seeks to annex another. The story follows a predictable pattern, but what marked Allen as a writer to watch was his ability to provide depth to characters in stereotypical situations, and to communicate to the reader a deep fascination with technology and human resourcefulness.

The sequel, *Rogue Powers,* initially appears to be a reprise of the first work, with the bellicose Guardians plotting against their neighbors again despite their earlier defeat. But Allen expands on his original theme by introducing an alien race that uses biological innovations as weapons of war just as the human villains use technology. The former cadets, now seasoned veterans, rise to the occasion a second time in a long novel that combines strong storytelling with clear explication of the science involved.

War, or at least the potential for conflict, is the central theme of *Farside Cannon,* set within our own solar system. The spread of humanity to the asteroids and moons of other planets has caused a growing rift with the home world. As the colonies begin to move toward independence, the government of Earth begins construction of a secret military facility on the moon, one equipped with enough firepower to destroy any target orbiting the sun. The colonists response is to prepare to alter the course of a large asteroid, so that it can be used as a gigantic missile aimed at their enemies. Allen moved firmly away from military fiction this time, concentrating on the politics of power and the implications of a technology that can literally destroy the world.

Orphan of Creation was the first of Allen's scientific mystery novels, a crossover form that he does as well as anyone in either field. A paleontologist working in Mississippi discovers the skeleton of a proto-hominid, a pre-human, but carbon dating indicates that the individual died only a century earlier. From this he theorizes that at least some pre-humans survived into the 19th century, and that one of them was a slave on a local plantation. The subsequent investigation unravels things in a clever and entertaining fashion, and demonstrates a great respect for the scientific method. It remains Allen's most thoughtful and provocative novel, although his technical skills have steadily improved since.

The "Hunted Earth" series, which began with *The Ring of Charon* and has continued to date with *The Shattered Sphere,* is without question Allen's most popular work. A scientific experiment on Pluto inadvertently awakens a horde of alien devices hidden in the solar system. The Earth is transported through a warp in space to an artificial system where scores of other captive worlds orbit a primary, and where apparently automatic weapons destroy anything which might endanger the orbiting planets. Unfortunately, that means that those spaceships which were not on Earth cannot return, and any already on that planet can leave only for a one-way trip.

Meanwhile, what remains of the solar system is being dismantled by the alien nanotechnology. The relatively few humans who survived the original assault manage to deactivate the process and then determine that the Earth has been stolen, rather than destroyed as they originally believe. The second volume alternates between the two spheres, as those on Earth try to figure out the rules in their new home and find a way to circumvent them, and those left behind try to determine just where Earth went, and how to manipulate the alien devices in order to move it back. The term "sense of wonder" is overused in the genre, but it is undeniably applicable here. Allen's universe is filled with wonders and mysteries, but at the same time he assures his readers that everything is explicable, and that we can be masters of our own fate if we persevere.

The Modular Man is another of his scientific mysteries, this one even more clearly cross-genre. The basic premise is that human intelligence could be moved from the organic mind to an inorganic data processor. The "victim" of murder in the novel programs a kind of super vacuum cleaner with his own personality, and by doing so causes the death of his original, biological body. This puts the police in an interesting position. If the robot is now sentient, is he responsible for the death of a human being? Does that make it murder or suicide? And if the robot is in fact self-aware, does that mean it is the same person as the man whose mind was transferred? Allen examines the implications seriously, but spares time to develop the comical aspects of the situation as well. Not a major work, but an interesting one.

Caliban and its sequel, *Inferno,* are much more significant. Allen has Isaac Asimov's permission to rethink the Three Laws of Robotics and the implications of the society Asimov created in his famous robot series. Caliban is the first robot to be built with a modified set of the Three Laws, changes which give him greater freedom of action and self-determination. But things go awry when his memories are damaged and he leaves a building where a brutal murder has just been committed. The implication is that he is responsible because of his modification. Alvar Kresh, chief law enforcement official on the planet, and his robot assistant Donald are called into the case, which also develops the growing conflict between the two strains of humanity, one which avoids the physical presence of others, the other which more nearly resembles our own culture.

The opening volume concludes with the discovery of the real culprit and the unveiling of the new Laws, setting the stage for the sequel. Alteration of the Three Laws is so controversial that their use is outlawed and, theoretically, only Caliban is free of the old rules. Kresh is called upon again when the planetary governor is murdered despite a massive force of robotic bodyguards, and once again it appears that only a robot could have committed the crime. The interplay between the old-style robots and the new is particularly well handled, and unlike most novels set in the universe created by another writer, Allen's have managed to add something positive and creative to the existing body of work.

Allen has written two other novels borrowing from another writer. *The War Machine,* written in collaboration with David Drake, is part of the latter's Crisis of Empire series. It's a competent military adventure novel about a drug-addicted officer of the declining human empire who finds himself in time to help avert the defeat of his people by alien aggressors. Much more impressive is *Ambush at Corellia,* opening volume of a trilogy set in the *Star Wars* universe. Han Solo, his wife, Leia, and their three children are off on a diplomatic mission to Corellia, but Han has secretly agreed to look into the disappearance of several agents sent by the new Republic to discover just what is happening in that sector. The opening volume concludes with the revelation that elements of the old Empire are at work, that they have orchestrated a secession from the Republic, using a previously undisclosed superweapon.

Supernova, written with Eric Kotani, is for the most part a routine disaster novel. A nearby star explodes but the authorities on Earth refuse to heed scientists' warnings about the eventual impact on Earth. They are therefore unprepared when natural disasters destroy much of civilization. In the aftermath, a cult of religious fanatics blames science and technology for the debacle and strives to prevent any attempt to revive the old culture, while the protagonist and his associates recognize that it is the only hope to stem the tide of human suffering and begin to rebuild society. Competent but familiar adventures, enlivened once again by Allen's profound respect for science.

Although Allen is an infrequent short story writer, some of his work from the late 1980s is of interest. "Phreak Encounter" is an amusing twist on the "we are being watched by aliens" theme, involving a computer network. "A Hole in the Sun" involves an orbiting research group studying the sun, and the complications that arise during a freak solar flare. This story is particularly noteworthy for the strong characterization, which would become more evident in the novels that followed. "Thing's Ransom" involves the potential for new crimes inherent in a highly computerized financial structure, but also reveals a possible pitfall for the would-be thief. "Young As You Feel" is a minor story, but draws an interesting comparison between adolescence and classic drug dependency withdrawal.

With at least two series underway, it's likely that the near future will see Allen producing more adventures of Han Solo and perhaps concluding the "Hunted Earth" sequence in the third volume. The Caliban series has also been left open-ended, and there's considerable material left untapped in that setting. There is no question that Allen has become one of the major hard science fiction writers working in the field, and one of the very few of that subset capable of using a credible cast of characters to make his alien devices and great discoveries seem real.

—Don D'Ammassa

ALLEN, Stuart. *See* **TUBB, E.C.**

———

AMES, Clinton. *See* **PHILLIPS, Rog.**

———

AMHERST, Wes. *See* **SHAVER, Richard S.**

———

AMIS, (Sir) Kingsley (William)

Pseudonym: Robert Markham. **Nationality:** British. **Born:** London, 16 April 1922. **Education:** City of London School; St. John's College, Oxford, M.A. in English. **Military Service:** Served in the Royal Corps of Signals, 1942-45. **Family:** Married 1) Hilary Ann Bardwell in 1948 (marriage dissolved, 1965), two sons, including the writer Martin Amis, and one daughter; 2) the writer Elizabeth Jane Howard in 1965 (divorced, 1983). **Career:** Lecturer in English, University College, Swansea, Wales, 1949-61; Visiting Fellow in Creative Writing, Princeton University, New Jersey, 1958-59; Fellow in English, Peterhouse, Cambridge, 1961-63; Visiting Professor, Vanderbilt University, Nashville, Tennessee, 1967. Lives in London. **Awards:** Maugham award, 1955; *Yorkshire Post* award, 1974; John W. Campbell Memorial award, 1977; Booker prize, 1986. Honorary Fellow, St. John's College, 1976. C.B.E. (Commander, Order of the British Empire), 1981. Knighted, 1990. **Agent:** Jonathan Clowes Ltd., Iron Bridge House, Bridge Approach, London NW1 8BD, England.

SCIENCE FICTION PUBLICATIONS

Novels

The Anti-Death League. London, Gollancz, and New York, Harcourt Brace, 1966.
The Green Man. London, Cape, 1969; New York, Harcourt Brace, 1970.
The Alteration. London, Cape, 1976; New York, Viking Press, 1977.
Russian Hide-and-Seek: A Melodrama. London, Hutchinson, 1980.

OTHER PUBLICATIONS

Novels

Lucky Jim. London, Gollancz, and New York, Doubleday, 1954.
That Uncertain Feeling. London, Gollancz, 1955; New York, Harcourt Brace, 1956.
I Like It Here. London, Gollancz, and New York, Harcourt Brace, 1958.

Take a Girl Like You. London, Gollancz, 1960; New York, Harcourt Brace, 1961.

One Fat Englishman. London, Gollancz, 1963; New York, Harcourt Brace, 1964.

The Egyptologists, with Robert Conquest. London, Cape, 1965; New York, Random House, 1966.

Colonel Sun: A James Bond Adventure (as Robert Markham). London, Cape, and New York, Harper, 1968.

I Want It Now. London, Cape, 1968; New York, Harcourt Brace, 1969.

Girl, 20. London, Cape, 1971; New York, Harcourt Brace, 1972.

The Riverside Villas Murder. London, Cape, and New York, Harcourt Brace, 1973.

Ending Up. London, Cape, and New York, Harcourt Brace, 1974.

Kingsley Amis Omnibus. London, Hutchinson, 1987.

Jake's Thing. London, Hutchinson, 1978; New York, Viking Press, 1979.

Stanley and the Women. London, Hutchinson, 1984; New York, Perennial Library, 1988.

The Old Devils. London, Hutchinson, 1986; New York, Summit, 1987.

The Crime of the Century. London, Dent, 1987; New York, Mysterious Press, 1989.

Difficulties with Girls. London, Hutchinson, and New York, Summit, 1988.

The Folks That Live on the Hill. London, Hutchinson, and New York, Summit, 1990.

We Are All Guilty. London, Reinhardt, and New York, Viking, 1991.

The Russian Girl. London, Hutchinson, 1992; New York, Viking, 1994.

You Can't Do Both. London, Hutchinson, 1994.

Short Stories

My Enemy's Enemy. London, Gollancz, 1962; New York, Harcourt Brace, 1963.

Penguin Modern Stories 11, with others. London, Penguin, 1972.

Dear Illusion. London, Covent Garden Press, 1972.

The Darkwater Hall Mystery. Edinburgh, Tragara Press, 1978.

Collected Short Stories. London, Hutchinson, 1980; revised edition, 1987.

Mr. Barrett's Secret and Other Stories. London, Hutchinson, 1993.

Plays

Radio Plays: *Something Strange,* 1962; *The Riverside Villas Murder,* from his own novel, 1976.

Television Plays: *A Question about Hell,* 1964; *The Importance of Being Harry,* 1971; *Dr. Watson and the Darkwater Hall Mystery,* 1974; *See What You've Done* (*Softly, Softly* series), 1974; *We Are All Guilty* (*Against the Crowd* series), 1975.

Poetry

Bright November. London, Fortune Press, 1947.

A Frame of Mind. Reading, Berkshire, University of Reading School of Art, 1953.

(Poems). Oxford, Fantasy Press, 1954.

A Case of Samples: Poems 1946-1956. London, Gollancz, 1956; New York, Harcourt Brace, 1957.

The Evans Country. Oxford, Fantasy Press, 1962.

Penguin Modern Poets 2, with Dom Moraes and Peter Porter. London, Penguin, 1962.

A Look Round the Estate: Poems 1957-1967. London, Cape, 1967; New York, Harcourt Brace, 1968.

Wasted, Kipling at Bateman's. London, Poem-of-the-Month Club, 1973.

Collected Poems 1944-1979. London, Hutchinson, 1979; New York, Viking Press, 1980.

Recordings: *Kingsley Amis Reading His Own Poems,* Listen, 1962; *Poems,* with Thomas Blackburn, Jupiter, 1962.

Other

Socialism and the Intellectuals. London, Fabian Society, 1957.

New Maps of Hell: A Survey of Science Fiction. New York, Harcourt Brace, 1960; London, Gollancz, 1961.

The James Bond Dossier. London, Cape, and New York, New American Library, 1965.

Lucky Jim's Politics. London, Conservative Political Centre, 1968.

What's Become of Jane Austen? and Other Questions. London, Cape, 1970; New York, Harcourt Brace, 1971.

On Drink. London, Cape, 1972; New York, Harcourt Brace, 1973.

Rudyard Kipling and His World. London, Thames and Hudson, 1975; New York, Scribner, 1976.

An Arts Policy? London, Centre for Policy Studies, 1979.

Every Day Drinking. London, Hutchinson, 1983.

How's Your Glass? London, Weidenfeld and Nicolson, 1984.

The Amis Collection: His Best Journalism, Pieces and Reviews. London, Hutchinson, 1990.

The Amis Collection: Selected Non-Fiction 1954-1990, edited by John McDermitt. London, Hutchinson, 1990.

Memoirs. London, Hutchinson, and New York, Summit, 1991.

Editor, with James Michie, *Oxford Poetry 1949.* Oxford, Blackwell, 1949.

Editor, with Robert Conquest, *Spectrum [1-5]: A Science Fiction Anthology.* London, Gollancz, 5 vols., 1961-65; New York, Harcourt Brace, 5 vols., 1962-67.

Editor, *Selected Short Stories of G.K. Chesterton.* London, Faber, 1972.

Editor, *Tennyson.* London, Penguin, 1973.

Editor, *Harold's Years: Impressions from the New Statesman and The Spectator.* London, Quartet, 1977.

Editor, *The New Oxford Book of Light Verse.* London and New York, Oxford University Press, 1978.

Editor, *The Faber Popular Reciter.* London, Faber, 1978.

Editor, *The Golden Age of Science Fiction.* London, Hutchinson, 1981.

Editor, with James Cochrane, *The Great British Songbook.* New York, Pavilion-Joseph, 1986; London, Faber, 1988.

Editor, *The Amis Anthology: A Personal Choice of English Verse.* London, Hutchinson, 1988.

Editor, *The Pleasures of Poetry: From His Daily Mirror Column.* London, Cassell, 1990.

Editor, with others, *The Best Winners of the Booker Prize.* San Francisco, California, Mercury House, 1991.

Editor, *The Amis Story Anthology: A Personal Choice of Short Stories.* London, Hutchinson, 1992.

Bibliography: *Kingsley Amis: A Checklist* by Jack Benoit Gohn, Kent, Ohio, Kent State University Press, 1976: *Kingsley Amis: A Reference Guide* by Dale Salwak, Boston, Hall, and London, Prior, 1978.

Manuscript Collection (verse): State University of New York, Buffalo.

Critical Studies: *Kingsley Amis* by Philip Gardner, Boston, Twayne, 1981; *Kingsley Amis* by Richard Bradford, London, Arnold, 1989; *Kingsley Amis: An English Moralist* by John McDermott, London, Macmillan, 1989; *Kingsley Amis in Life and Letters* edited by Dale Sulwak, London, Macmillan, 1990.

Kingsley Amis comments:

I have been reading science fiction for over 50 years. Writing it too: I can remember writing a story about a revolution in the year 2032, which must mean I wrote it in 1932 when I was 10. I say this to show that SF has always been an inseparable part of my reading and writing life. So when later I got an idea for a story or novel whose events could not have taken place in our world, I found it altogether natural to create a new world for it.

Take *The Alteration*. I heard on an archive record made in 1909 a castrato then aged about 40 (one Alessandro Moreschi) singing the Bach/Gounod "Ave Maria," a good musical performance and an awful, dismal noise I could not get out of my head. It dawned on me that here was a great theme: a boy chosen for castration to preserve his wonderful voice would lose the chance of love, family, friends to a large extent, and a normal place in society. But he might gain fame, money, artistic success, and the approval of God. (He might also lose the first batch without attaining the second.) None of it is possible in our world. I considered the coward's (or John Fowles's) way out: a remote island run by an eccentric millionaire. No, too cramped and private. It would have to be England in A.D. 1976, but as part of an alternate world where the Reformation had never happened and Rome was all-powerful—or nearly. On with the creation. . . .

*   *   *

A typical Kingsley Amis work combines satire and humor with serious themes to mock sacred cows, question *a priori* premises, and speculate about the nature of humans and God. It usually involves some erudite discussion of music (particularly classical), literature, history, linguistics, paleontology, or art, some focus on love as elevating and redemptive, and some sense of conspiracy, whether of church or state or the universe itself. It is witty, provocative, and firmly opinionated.

Reflecting an enthusiasm for science fiction that Amis traces to his early youth, *New Maps of Hell* began as a series of lectures delivered at Princeton for the 1958-59 Christian Gaus Seminar in Criticism. It is one of the most influential works of science fiction criticism up to that time, the first full-length study of science fiction by a critic outside the science fiction community. *New Maps* is clearly dated, and more personal than scholarly—a slightly patronizing attempt to define and defend science fiction at a time when the genre was considered suspect by literary scholars. It argues that a definition of science fiction is difficult, but somehow involves science and technology or pseudoscience or pseudotechnology,

whether human or alien, though methods, goals and emphases may vary greatly. Thus, *The Tempest* and *Gulliver's Travels* are certainly precursors, according to Amis, though H.G. Wells and Jules Verne begin the genre as we know it. *New Maps* also considers the literary quality of science fiction, pointing out that it ranges from the lowest pulp form (filled with scientific absurdities, violence, gratuitous sex, and innumerable monsters) to the highest literary levels (involving exploration of human nature, politics, and economics, satire of the present, and theorizing about the future). Ultimately Amis finds it allegorizing our own fears and insecurities, warning of future possibilities, and deflating *homo sapiens*. Because of Amis's interest in the genre, he edited with Robert Conquest the *Spectrum* series, five volumes of science fiction short stories carefully selected for their interest and craftsmanship, volumes that helped establish the popularity and respectability of science fiction.

Amis's own short stories and novels are intriguing and clever. His James Bond adventure novel, *Colonel Sun,* contains science fiction elements, as does his ghost story, *The Green Man,* in which time stasis, two ghosts (one ineffectual, the other malignant), an exorcism, and a spirit force are played off against prosaic reality to suggest a manipulative higher power playing a complex game at man's expense. "Mason's Life" focuses on the nightmare realization that one's seemingly tangible reality is only someone else's dream. In "Something Strange" space program volunteers turn out to be guinea pigs for government psychologists experimenting with psychological conditioning and isolation stress.

The Anti-Death League uses a spy/romance/science fiction format as an excuse to explore philosophical questions about the active cruelty of God, the aimless horror and finality of death, and love as an antidote to combat insanity in an absurd universe. Amis, who seems to feel at home handling a military ambience with its rigid orders and regulations and its male-male interaction, centers his novel on a British training camp preparing soldiers for "Operation Apollo," germ warfare with an intensified strain of hydrophobia. Though ultimately the operation proves a giant bluff, it provides the backdrop for exploring life and death questions. As various zany characters rush about trying to expose security leaks, prove pet theories, or work out personal conflicts, the main thrust of the novel is an enumeration of signs of the motiveless malignity of God—numerous, sudden, random deaths or near deaths from accident or disease, reinforced by "pro-death" military plans, by signs of madness or incipient madness, and by futile attempts to combat both. The formation of an "Anti-Death League" provides the title of the book and Amis's model for man's ineffectual but necessary protest against whatever powers there be. The comic and satiric prevail, with characters including an atheist chaplain, a naive secret agent, a homosexual, alcoholic military officer, a promiscuous widow, an insane psychiatrist, and a conscience-ridden romantic named Churchill.

The Alteration presents an alternative world, one that might have been as the result of Henry VIII's elder brother Arthur surviving as monarch and siring a line of Catholic rulers. It postulates a Catholic England and Europe, forever at odds with Islam, and on a shaky diplomatic basis with New England, a small nation inhabited by subjugated Indians and the bigoted descendants of "Schismatics" and convicts (including one William Shakespeare). The Martin Luther of this Catholic world was a pope, Himmler a powerful representative of Papal might, Jean-Paul Sartre a Jesuit, James Bond a Father Bond, and our world a shocking, slightly absurd science fiction novel read clandestinely by rebellious adolescents. Amis's world is a chilling vision of ecclesiastical totalitarianism with the Church tightly controlling people's lives, making decisions about whether or not 10-year-old boys will be castrated so they can sing for the greater glory of God, sending out Nazi-like secret police to mutilate and murder those who defy Church authority, developing a disease that, spread through the drinking water, infects and alters males, and ultimately choosing a holy war against Moslems as a means of population control. As such, it is a grim commentary on hypocrisy, intolerance, gullibility, and mindless pieties—evil for the best of reasons. On another level it traces the story of Hubert Anvil, a brilliant child soprano chosen for castration, to explore adolescent yearnings, struggles against authority, and arrested development. Ultimately it is a paean to love, the greatest sin of all in this nightmare world of religious fanaticism. Amis links artistic creativity and sexuality, but also beauty and cruelty. Both the Church and the God of this alternative world castrate man, psychologically if not physically.

Russian Hide-and-Seek partakes of the patterns and concerns established in these earlier novels. Drawing on the conventions of 19th-century Russian fiction and cloak-and-dagger adventures, it depicts a Russianized England, a future 50 years hence when the Soviet Union rules England and perpetrates upon the English all the horrors that Amis envisions as inherent in Russian culture: brutality, violence, lack of family feeling, exploitation, and paranoia coupled with lachrymose introspection. The plot turns on an attempted revolution, made futile by the naivety of the revolutionaries and the strength of the Central Government. The English prove plucky but muddled; the Russians are bored, callous, self-indulgent. Violence and death again dominate this vision of the future.

Throughout his works Amis debunks muddled, limited people: the shallow, hypocritical, educated establishment of *Lucky Jim;* the greedy, lustful, self-indulgent academician of *One Fat Englishman;* the xenophobic, ethnocentric British traveller abroad of *I Like It Here;* the alcoholics, lesbians, and termagants of *The Folks that Live on the Hill;* the musical-beds set of *Girl, 20,* including denizens of the superficial world of pop culture, despotic bosses, counterculture radicals, and ill-tempered ladies; the eccentric psychiatrists and bigoted Parliamentarians of *The Crime of the Century* (a mystery); and the snobbish, egotistical phonies (poets, publishers, journalists, and academics) of *Difficulties with Girls.* Such idiosyncratic farces expose human cupidity, lechery, prejudice, and stupidity with gleeful insouciance. *The Old Devils, Ending Up, Girl, 20,* and *Jake's Thing* explore the incapability, impotence, rigidity and isolation of old age, with the last two attacking liberal sexual mores. Unlike *Take a Girl Like You* and *I Want It Now,* which sympathize with young women as sexually exploited, *Stanley and the Women* examines women as an alien species, whose unique form of speech, of style, of manner, and of logic make them a mystery, irrational and incomprehensible by male standards; attraction for them is like a recurring illness, inescapable and debilitating.

Amis's science fiction extends that tradition's potential, and, like his regular fiction, serves as a medium for satiric debunking and sociological investigation, particularly of the military mentality, pat solutions, modish psychology, feminism, and totalitarian inflexibility. His works are witty, irreverent, and infectious. His handling of different levels of diction, linguistic clues to class and education, and his verbal inventiveness are always impressive, and his attack on conventional values and attitudes fun. Amis brings to science fiction a scholar's eye for artistic, historic and cultural detail, a mastery of conversational exchanges, a disdain for fashionable cant,

and a deep-seated pleasure in consistently flouting social, political and fictive conventions.

—Gina Macdonald

ANDERSON, Kevin J(ames)

Nationality: American. **Born:** Racine, Wisconsin, 27 March 1962. **Education:** University of Wisconsin, Madison, B.S. (1983) with honors. **Family:** Married 1) Mary E. Franco, in 1984 (divorced 1987); 2) Rebecca Moesta in 1991; one stepson. **Career:** Technical writer/editor, Lawrence Livermore National Laboratory, 1984-present; columnist, Materials Research Society, 1987-present; production editor, International Society for Respiratory Protection, 1990-present. **Awards:** Dale Donaldson Award for Service to the Small Press, 1985. **Agent:** Richard Curtis, 171 E. 74th St., New York, New York 10021, U.S.A.

SCIENCE FICTION PUBLICATIONS

Novels (series: Gamearth Trilogy; Star Wars: Jedi Academy Trilogy)

Resurrection, Inc. New York, New American Library, 1988.
Gamearth. New York, New American Library, 1989.
Gameplay (Gamearth). New York, New American Library, 1989.
Game's End (Gamearth). New York, A Roc Book, 1992,
Lifeline, with Doug Beason. New York, Bantam Books, 1990.
The Trinity Paradox, with Doug Beason. New York, Bantam Books, 1991.
Afterimage, with Kristine Kathryn Rusch. New York, A Roc Book, 1992.
Assemblers of Infinity, with Doug Beason. New York, Bantam Books, 1993.
Climbing Olympus. New York, Warner Books, 1994.
Star Wars: The Jedi Academy Trilogy. New York, Guild America Books, 1994.
   Star Wars: Jedi Search. New York, Bantam Books, 1994.
   Star Wars: Dark Apprentice. New York, Bantam Books, 1994.
   Star Wars: Champions of the Force. New York, Bantam Books, 1994.
Ill Wind, with Doug Beason. New York, Forge, 1995.
Blindfold. New York, Warner Books, 1995.

Other

Hunter's Moon and Other American Gothic Tales (audiocassettes), read by Ashton Smith. Agoura Hills, California, Spine-Tingling Press, 1992.
Star Wars, Tales of the Jedi: Dark Lords of the Sith, with Tom Vietch (graphic novel). Milwaukie, Oregon, Dark Horse Comics, 1994.

*

Kevin J. Anderson comments:

As may be apparent from my prolific output, I really love to write. I enjoy developing stories and working in fictional universes, whether they be of my own devising or real life or historical realities . . . or someone else's creation. I can usually find something interesting in any situation, and my brain seems to be wired up to tell a story about the interesting things I experience.

My coauthor, Doug Beason, is fond of saying that if I ever slow down, my head would explode. He may have a point.

I love to travel, I love to learn new things, I love to see new sights. I write while hiking; I have dictated numerous chapters while climbing mountains, or sitting by a campfire, or just walking through my own neighborhood. Of my own work, my personal favorites are *Resurrection, Inc., The Trinity Paradox, Climbing Olympus*, and *Blindfold*.

*   *   *

If diversity and industry are assets to a writer, then Kevin J. Anderson is equipped to become a major force in science fiction. In just over seven years, he has produced highly regarded fantasy, hard SF, adventure, and borderline horror. He has also proven himself capable of writing first-rate short stories as well as a steady output of engaging novels.

His debut novel, *Resurrection, Inc.*, is science fiction with a horror twist. A high-tech corporation discovers a way to reanimate dead bodies, with microprocessors controlling the muscles and a reprogrammed and pliable brain giving the instructions. Anyone who can raise the necessary money can purchase a lobotomized servant, and businesses increasingly replace their live workers with more obedient dead ones. As unemployment rises, turmoil threatens the stability of the country, and a new cult of neo-Satanists further undermines order. Against this well-portrayed and even frightening backdrop, Anderson tells the story of one of the revived dead, a man whose memories have partially returned despite the accepted dogma that such a thing is impossible.

Anderson appeared to change directions for the trilogy which followed, consisting of *Gamearth, Gameplay,* and *Game's End*. The series is a fantasy in which the players involved in an elaborate role-playing game discover that they can physically enter their imaginary world, that their collective belief in its existence has somehow made it real. Unfortunately, one of the players wants to bring the game to a halt, and when he is coerced into continuing, he does everything in his power to disrupt the not-so-imaginary world he has helped to create. And that causes a crisis not only in the imaginary land, but in the real world as well. There have been several other novels on similar themes from other writers, but none have so effectively developed the interplay of the two realities.

With Doug Beason, Anderson was also writing more ambitious, technologically oriented SF. *Lifeline* is set among several orbiting habitats struggling to survive after a nuclear war has effectively rendered the Earth uninhabitable. Their ensuing efforts to balance dominance and cooperation makes for an exciting, thought-provoking story and the serious approach to the problems of resolving cultural differences is quite well done. Their next effort, *The Trinity Paradox,* was even better, though its time travel theme is considerably less original. A nuclear protestor is accidentally sent back through time to the middle of World War II, but not the historical version she's familiar with. Here the Germans have developed nuclear weapons, and are using them against the U.S. She then faces a true test of her beliefs, because the only way to avert a Nazi conquest of the world is to develop a balancing threat, a position that invalidates what she'd spent years working for. A bit preachy in a low-key manner, but the authors make their point without seriously affecting the flow of the story.

Their third, *Assemblers of Infinity,* explores the possible consequences of nanotechnology. An expedition to the moon discovers a colony of microscopic machines possibly from an alien culture, busily constructing something unidentifiable. They swarm over anything or anyone who ventures near, dismantling bodies and equipment to use as raw materials for their project. Terror erupts as the implications set in, for if any of them reach the Earth, the entire planet might eventually be transformed. A strongly suspenseful book with a well-conceived and resolved scientific mystery. Their most recent collaborative effort, *Ill Wind,* is a scientific disaster novel. A tailored lifeform designed to eat oil spills mutates and begins to spread through the air, destroying all petroleum-based substances it encounters, including fuel, plastic, and so on. As civilization grinds to a stop, we are shown the different ways people react to the crisis, some by digging in for an uncertain future, others attempting to find a solution. Anderson has also collaborated with Kristine Kathryn Rusch for *Afterimage,* an odd blend of fantasy and horror that pits shapeshifting creatures against a brutal serial killer.

Much of Anderson's most recent output has been related to the *Star Wars* industry. The trilogy, consisting of *Jedi Search, Dark Apprentice,* and *Champions of the Force,* is set directly after the movie stories. Luke Skywalker is setting up an academy to turn out more Jedi knights, while Han Solo discovers a new super-weapon being developed by agents of the not quite vanquished Empire. While the Republic forces battle surviving imperial fleets, one of the new Jedi has turned to the dark side of the force, and threatens to undermine Luke's efforts. Luke himself is thrown into a coma, and communicates from the spirit world with the twin children of Han and Leia, who are a prominent undercurrent in this trilogy. They are also the central protagonists of a new trilogy begun with *Heirs of the Force,* which tells of their encounter with a marooned empire soldier.

Although much of Anderson's recent energies have been directed into media-related fiction, he continues to create original work as well and his latest, a solo novel titled *Climbing Olympus,* bodes extremely well for the future. Mars has been colonized by genetically altering humans to survive under its difficult environmental conditions, but these experiments are now in disfavor, and surviving members of the original colonists are shunned and live far from the more recent colonies. But they haven't forgotten what they consider their birthright, and when the time is right they strike back against what they see as an exploitive government that has abandoned them in favor of terraforming Mars.

Among Anderson's better short fiction is "Reflections in a Magnetic Mirror," written with Beason, "The Happy Hookermorph," a humorous look at interspecies prostitution, and "Human, Martian—One, Two, Three," which was revised and expanded into the novel *Climbing Olympus.* He has demonstrated a reliable ability to produce strongly plotted, convincing stories whether primarily action adventure, suspense, or serious and thoughtful. His flexibility allows him to move in numerous directions as a writer, and to carry his loyal readers wherever he chooses to go.

—Don D'Ammassa

ANDERSON, Poul (William)

Nationality: American. **Born:** Bristol, Pennsylvania, 25 November 1926. **Education:** University of Minnesota, Minneapolis, B.S.

1948. **Family:** Married Karen Kruse in 1953; one daughter. **Career:** Freelance writer. President, Science Fiction Writers of America, 1972-73. **Awards:** Hugo award, 1961, 1964, 1969, 1972, 1973, 1979, 1982; Nebula award, 1971, 1972, 1982; Tolkien Memorial award, 1978, Guest of Honor, World Science-Fiction Convention, 1959. **Agent:** Scovil Chichak Galen, 381 Park Ave. South, New York, New York 10016. **Address:** 3 Las Palomas, Orinda, California 94563, U.S.A.

Science Fiction Publications

Novels (series: Dominic Flandry; Hoka; King of Ys; Polesotechnic League; Psychotechnic League; Stars; Time Patrol; Trader Van Rijn)

Vault of the Ages (for children). Philadelphia, Winston, 1952.

The Broken Sword. New York, Abelard-Schuman, 1954; revised edition, New York, Ballantine, 1971; Tisbury, Wiltshire, Compton Russell, 1974.

Brain Wave. New York, Ballantine, 1954; London, Heinemann, 1955.

No World of Their Own. New York, Ace, 1955; as *The Long Way Home,* London, Panther, 1975; revised, Boston, Gregg Press, 1978.

Star Ways. New York, Avalon, 1956; as *The Peregrine,* New York, Ace, 1978.

Planet of No Return. New York, Ace, 1957; London, Dobson, 1966; as *Question and Answer,* Ace, 1978.

The Snows of Ganymede. New York, Ace, 1958.

War of the Wing-Men (Van Rijn). New York, Ace, 1958; London, Sphere, 1976; as *The Man Who Counts,* Ace, 1978.

Virgin Planet. New York, Avalon, 1959; London, Mayflower, 1966.

The War of Two Worlds. New York, Ace, 1959; London, Dobson, 1970.

We Claim These Stars (Flandry). New York, Ace, 1959; London, Dobson, 1976.

The Enemy Stars. Philadelphia, Lippincott, 1959; expanded edition, New York, Baen, 1987.

The High Crusade. Garden City, New York, Doubleday, 1960; London, Severn House, 1982.

Earthman, Go Home! (Flandry). New York, Ace, 1960.

Twilight World. New York, Torquil, 1961; London, Gollancz, 1962.

Mayday Orbit (Flandry). New York, Ace, 1961.

Three Hearts and Three Lions. Garden City, New York, Doubleday, 1961.

After Doomsday. New York, Ballantine, 1962; London, Gollancz, 1963.

The Makeshift Rocket. New York, Ace, 1962; London, Dobson, 1969.

Let the Spacemen Beware! (Polesotechnic League). New York, Ace, 1963; London, Dobson, 1969; as *The Night Face,* Ace, 1978.

Shield. New York, Berkley, 1963; London, Dobson, 1965.

Three Worlds to Conquer. New York, Pyramid, 1964; London, Mayflower, 1966.

The Corridors of Time. Garden City, New York, Doubleday, 1965; London, Gollancz, 1966.

The Star Fox. Garden City, New York, Doubleday, 1965; London, Gollancz, 1966.

Ensign Flandry. Philadelphia, Chilton, 1966; London, Coronet, 1976.

The Fox, the Dog, and the Griffin: A Folk Tale Adapted from the Danish of C. Molbech (for children). Garden City, New York, Doubleday, 1966.

World Without Stars. New York, Ace, 1966; London, Dobson, 1975.

The Rebel Worlds (Flandry). New York, Signet, 1969; London, Coronet, 1972; as *Commander Flandry,* London, Severn House, 1978.

Satan's World (Van Rijn). Garden City, New York, Doubleday, 1969; London, Gollancz, 1970.

A Circus of Hells (Flandry). New York, Signet, 1970; London, Sphere, 1978.

Tau Zero. Garden City, New York, Doubleday, 1970; London, Gollancz, 1971.

The Byworlder. New York, Signet, 1971; London, Gollancz, 1972.

The Dancer from Atlantis. New York, Signet, 1971; London, Sphere, 1977.

Operation Chaos. Garden City, New York, Doubleday, 1971.

There Will Be Time. Garden City, New York, Doubleday, 1972; London, Sphere, 1979.

Hrolf Kraki's Saga. New York, Ballantine, 1973.

The People of the Wind (Polesotechnic League). New York, Signet, 1973; London, Sphere, 1977.

The Day of Their Return (Polesotechnic League). Garden City, New York, Doubleday, 1973; London, Corgi, 1978.

Inheritors of Earth, with Gordon Eklund. Radnor, Pennsylvania, Chilton, 1974.

Fire Time. Garden City, New York, Doubleday, 1974; London, Panther, 1977.

A Midsummer Tempest. Garden City, New York, Doubleday, 1974; London, Futura, 1975.

A Knight of Ghosts and Shadows (Flandry). Garden City, New York, Doubleday, 1974; London, Sphere, 1978; as *Knight Flandry,* London, Severn House, 1980.

Star Prince Charlie (Hoka; for children), with Gordon R. Dickson. New York, Putnam, 1975.

The Winter of the World. Garden City, New York, Doubleday, 1975.

Mirkheim (Van Rijn). New York, Berkley, 1977; London, Sphere, 1978.

The Avatar. New York, Berkley, 1978; London, Sidgwick and Jackson, 1980.

Two Worlds (omnibus). Boston, Gregg Press, 1978.

The Merman's Children. New York, Berkley, 1979; London, Sidgwick and Jackson, 1981.

A Stone in Heaven (Flandry). New York, Ace, 1979.

The Demon of Scattery, with Mildred Downey Broxon. New York, Ace, 1979.

The People of the Wind; and, The Day of Their Return. New York, Signet, 1982.

There Will Be Time; and, The Dancer from Atlantis. New York, Signet, 1982.

Annals of the Time Patrol (includes *The Guardians of Time* and *Time Patrolman*). Garden City, New York, Doubleday, 1984.

Conan the Rebel. New York, Bantam, 1980; London, Hale, 1984.

The Devil's Game. New York, Pocket Books, 1980.

The Dark Between the Stars. New York, Berkley, 1981.

Orion Shall Rise. Huntington Woods, Michigan, Phantasia Press, 1983; London, Sphere, 1984.

The Game of Empire (Flandry). New York, Baen, 1985.

The King of Ys, with Karen Anderson. Garden City, New York, Doubleday, 2 vols., 1988.

   Roma Mater, with Karen Anderson. New York, Baen, 1986; London, Grafton, 1988.

Gallicenae, with Karen Anderson. New York, Baen, 1987; London, Grafton, 1988.

Dahut, with Karen Anderson. New York, Baen, 1988; London, Grafton, 1989.

The Dog and the Wolf, with Karen Anderson. New York, Baen, 1988; London, Grafton, 1989.

The Year of the Ransom (Time Patrol; for children). New York, Walker, 1988.

The Boat of a Million Years. Norwalk, Connecticut, Easton Press, 1989; London, Orbite, 1990.

Time Patrol (includes *The Guardians of Time, Time Patrolman,* and *The Year of the Ransom*). New York, Tor, 1991.

Murasaki: A Novel in Six Parts, with others, edited by Robert Silverberg. New York, Bantam, 1992; London, Grafton, 1993.

Harvest of Stars (Stars). New York, Tor, 1993; London, Pan, 1994.

The Stars Are Also Fire (Stars). New York, Tor, 1994.

Short Stories

Earthman's Burden (juvenile; Hoka), with Gordon R. Dickson. New York, Gnome Press, 1957.

Guardians of Time (Time Patrol). New York, Ballantine, 1960; London, Gollancz, 1961; augmented edition, New York, Tor, 1981.

Strangers from Earth. New York, Ballantine, 1961; London, Mayflower, 1964.

Orbit Unlimited. New York, Pyramid, 1961; London, Sidgwick and Jackson, 1974.

Un-Man and Other Novellas. New York, Ace, 1962; London, Dobson, 1972.

Time and Stars. Garden City, New York, Doubleday, and London, Gollancz, 1964.

Trader to the Stars (Van Rijn). Garden City, New York, Doubleday, 1964; London, Gollancz, 1965.

Agent of the Terran Empire (Flandry). Philadelphia, Chilton, 1965; London, Coronet, 1977.

Flandry of Terra. Philadelphia, Chilton, 1965.

The Trouble Twisters (Polesotechnic League). Garden City, New York, Doubleday, 1966; London, Gollancz, 1967.

The Horn of Time. New York, Signet, 1968; London, Corgi, 1981.

Beyond the Beyond. New York, Signet, 1969; London, Gollancz, 1970.

Seven Conquests. New York, Macmillan, and London, Panther, 1969; as *Conquests,* London, Granada, 1981.

Tales of the Flying Mountains. New York, Macmillan, 1970.

The Queen of Air and Darkness, and Other Stories. New York, Signet, 1973.

The Worlds of Poul Anderson. New York, Ace, 1974.

The Many Worlds of Poul Anderson. Radnor, Pennsylvania, Chilton, 1974; as *The Book of Poul Anderson,* New York, DAW, 1975.

Homeward and Beyond. Garden City, New York, Doubleday, 1975.

Homebrew. Cambridge, Massachusetts, NESFA Press, 1976.

The Best of Poul Anderson. New York, Pocket Books, 1976.

The Earth Book of Stormgate (Polesotechnic League). New York, Berkley, 1978; London, New English Library, 3 vols., 1981.

The Night Face, and Other Stories. Boston, Gregg Press, 1978.

The Psychotechnic League. New York, Tor, 1981.

Fantasy. New York, Tor, 1981.

Explorations. New York, Tor, 1981.

Winners. New York, Tor, 1981.

Maurai and Kith. New York, Tor, 1982.

The Gods Laughed. New York, Tor, 1982.

Cold Victory (Psychotechnic League). New York, Tor, 1982.

Starship (Psychotechnic League). New York, Tor, 1982.

New America. New York, Tor, 1982.

The Winter of the World; and, The Queen of Air and Darkness, and Other Stories. New York, Signet, 1982.

Time Patrolman (novellas). New York, Tor, 1983; London, Sphere, 1986.

Hoka! (juvenile), with Gordon R. Dickson. New York, Simon and Schuster, 1983.

The Long Night (Van Rijn). New York, Tor, 1983; London, Sphere, 1985.

Conflict. New York, Tor, 1983; Wallington, Surrey, Severn House, 1992.

Past Times. New York, Tor, 1984.

The Unicorn Trade (miscellany), with Karen Anderson. New York, Tor, 1984.

Dialogue with Darkness. New York, Tor, 1985.

Space Folk. New York, Baen, 1989.

The Shield of Time (Time Patrol). New York, Tor, 1990.

The Saturn Game, with *Iceborn,* by Gregory Benford and Paul A. Carter. New York, Tor, 1989.

No Truce with Kings, with *Ship of Shadows* by Fritz Leiber. New York, Tor, 1989.

The Longest Voyage, with *Slow Lightning* by Steven Popkes. New York, Tor, 1991.

Alight in the Void. New York, Tor, 1991.

Losers' Night. Eugene, Oregon, Pulphouse, 1991.

Kinship with the Stars. New York, Tor, 1991; Wallington, Surrey, Severn House, 1993.

The Armies of Elfland. New York, Tor, 1992; Wallington, Surrey, Severn House, 1994.

OTHER PUBLICATIONS

Novels

Perish by the Sword. New York, Macmillan, 1959.

Murder in Black Letter. New York, Macmillan, 1960.

The Golden Slave. New York, Avon, 1960.

Rogue Sword. New York, Avon, 1960.

Murder Bound. New York, Macmillan, 1962.

The Last Viking: The Golden Horn. New York, Zebra, 1980.

The Road of the Sea Horse. New York, Zebra, 1980.

Sign of the Raven. New York, Zebra, 1981.

The Man—Kzin Wars, with Larry Niven and Dean Ing. New York, Baen, 1988.

The Man—Kzin Wars III, with Larry Niven, Jerry Pournelle, and S.M. Sterling. New York, Baen, 1990.

Inconstant Star (Mansno). New York, Baen, 1991.

How to Build a Planet, with Stephen W. Gillett. Eugene, Oregon, Pulphouse, 1991.

Other

Is There Life on Other Worlds? New York, Crowell-Collier, and London, Collier Macmillan, 1963.

Thermonuclear Warfare. Derby, Connecticut, Monarch, 1963.

The Infinite Voyage: Man's Future in Space. New York, Crowell-Collier, and London, Collier Macmillan, 1969.

Editor, *West by One and by One: An Anthology of Irregular Writings by the Scowrers and Molly Maguires of San Francisco and the Trained Cormorants of Los Angeles County.* San Francisco, Privately printed, 1965.

Editor, *Nebula Award Stories Four.* Garden City, New York, Doubleday, and London, Gollancz, 1969.

Editor, with Karen Anderson, *The Night Fantastic.* New York, DAW, 1991.

Editor, with Martin H. Greenberg and Charles G. Waugh, *Mercenaries of Tomorrow.* New York, Critic's Choice, 1985.

Editor, with Martin H. Greenberg and Charles G. Waugh, *Terrorists of Tomorrow.* New York, Critic's Choice, 1986.

Editor, with Martin H. Greenberg and Charles G. Waugh, *Time Wars.* New York, Tor, 1986.

Editor, with Martin H. Greenberg and Charles G. Waugh, *Space Wars.* New York, Tor, 1988.

Translator, *The Method of Holding the Three Ones: A Taoist Manual of Meditation of the Fourth Century, A.D.* Atlantic Highlands, New Jersey, Humanities Press, and London, Curzon Press, 1980.

*

Bibliography: *A Checklist of Poul Anderson* by Roger G. Peyton, privately printed, 1965.

Manuscript Collection: University of Southern Mississippi, Hattiesburg.

Critical Study: *Against Time's Arrow: The High Crusade of Poul Anderson* by Sandra Miesel, San Bernardino, California, Borgo Press, 1978.

*   *   *

James Blish has called Poul Anderson "the enduring explosion" because the quality, quantity, and sheer breadth of Anderson's achievements are unique in science fiction. Seven Hugos and three Nebulas proclaim him the field's premier novelettist, but more than 50 novels and 200 shorter works testify to his mastery of all story forms. Over the course of five decades, he has explored an amazingly wide range of literary types from madcap comedy to grimmest tragedy in such distinctive fashion that the term "poulanderson" was once suggested as a generic name.

Consider the following examples in Anderson's fictional spectrum: broad farce (the Hoka series written with Gordon R. Dickson and *The Makeshift Rocket*); adventure comedy (*Virgin Planet*); action adventure yarn ("The Longest Voyage," 1960; the Van Rijn series, and the Flandry series); sociopolitical drama (The Psychotechnic Institute series and "No Truce with Kings," 1963); hard science fiction ("Epilogue, 1962); romantic fantasy (*Three Hearts and Three Lions*); heroic fantasy (*The Broken Sword* and *Hrolf Kraki's Saga*); pastiche (*Conan the Rebel*); shared universe (major conceptual contributor to *Medea,* 1985 and *Murasaki,* 1992); horror (*The Devil's Game*); historicals (the Last Viking trilogy); and mysteries (*Perish by the Sword*). Moreover, Anderson also writes songs, poems, parodies, essays, and children's books as well as being a skillful translator of Scandanavian prose and poetry. (For examples of his miscellania, see *The Unicorn Trade,* written with his wife, Karen.)

Science is Anderson's most important raw material. His formal training in physics imparts a special rigor to his handling of any science. His research is thorough, his extrapolations imaginative. He will interweave hard and soft sciences as in *Orion Shall Rise,* often contrasting scientific knowledge used for and against life as in "Time Lag," 1962. His most typical approach is the problem-solving story. Here, characters must either discover a phenomenon ("The Sharing of Flesh," 1968, and "Hunter's Moon," 1978) or react to one that is already recognized (*Fire Time* and "The Bitter Bread, 1975). Setting objective physical problems in parallel with subjective personal ones and linking outcomes is Anderson's favorite literary device. He builds these stories so well that they can outlive their scientific premises. Thus, the Jupiter model in "Call Me Joe" (1957) has passed away; the appeal of its tenacious hero endures.

Furthermore, Anderson makes scientific problem-solving a vehicle for philosophical inquiry. For instance, four marooned spacemen conduct an intense, self-conscious debate on the meaning of life in *The Enemy Stars. Tau Zero,* which Blish has judged "the ultimate hard science fiction novel," shows the crew of a crippled starship outmaneuvering fate on a slower-than-light odyssey beyond the end of time. Scientific phenomena also generate theological speculation in "Sister Planet" (1959) and "Kyrie" (1968). In Anderson's hands, the laws of nature assume poetic, symbolic, even metaphysical significance. Entropy is the horn of Time the Hunter, sounding the doom of all things.

A second source of Anderson's inspiration is history. The author's broad, self-acquired education in the subject serves him well when preparing futures with either general or specific historical prototypes. For example, "The Sky People" (1959) replays the age-old feud between nomads and farmers while *The People of the Wind* is cleverly modeled point for point on the Franco-Prussian War. Anderson can recreate history realistically as in "The Peat Bog," (1975) which is set in 1st-century Denmark, or extrapolate from it romantically as in *The High Crusade* where medieval crusaders capture an alien spaceship. The tedious King of Ys tetralogy co-authored with Karen Anderson is a rare misfire of his historical imagination. These books draw on Frazer, Bachofen, and Breton legend to play sexual games in 3rd-century Gaul.

Anderson also produced some superb time travel stories such as "The Man Who Came Early" (1956) and *There Will Be Time.* The most popular of these efforts are Anderson's tales of the Time Patrol, secret agents who guard the integrity of the past to protect the future. This series, which has been expanding for 30 years, includes *The Shield of Time* and the omnibus *Time Patrol.*

Anderson's interest in the historical process itself has led him to experiment with future history. His first try, the Heinlein-influenced Psychotechnic League series petered out. But his subsequent Technic Civilization series became one of the longest-running and most elaborate future histories in SF. Written over four decades, it embraces more than 40 separate works, including more than a dozen novels that cover five millennia of galactic history. The colorful adventures of Nicholas Van Rijn and Dominic Flandry take place within it. (See Miesel's chronology in *The Long Night* and her afterward to the 1980 Ace edition of *Agent of the Terran Empire.*)

Anderson's third major source is myth. Leaving all the Viking pride and doom intact, he has both remodeled Norse material ("The Sorrow of Odin the Goth," 1983, taken from *Volsunga Saga*) and retold it faithfully (*Hrolf Kraki's Saga* from *Hrolfs Saga Kraka*). In contrast, the Orpheus myth gets its definitive SF treatment in Anderson's "Goat Song" (1977) where Hades is the lair of a sentient computer. Orpheus had earlier inspired his poignant space adventure *World Without Stars* which includes his loveliest song, "Mary O'Meara."

Yet Anderson is not content simply to mine or rationalize mythology. He investigates the very nature of mythmaking and analyzes its effects—tragic in *The Night Face* and "The Saturn Game" (1981), mixed in "The Queen of Air and Darkness" (1971), and positive in *A Midsummer Tempest*. Myths of a Northern goddess are spun by accident and design across a realistically rendered 1st-century Europe in the Time Patrol novella "Star of the Sea" (1991). The spirit of those composite myths outlast the substance of them.

Myths live their liveliest in Faery, the realm of marvels. The perilous allure of Faery is a continuing preoccupation for Anderson, whether his characters reject it (*Three Hearts and Three Lions*) or accept it (*The Merman's Children*). On these issues, see Miesel's afterwords to the 1978 Ace edition of *The Night Face* and to *Fantasy* as well as Patrick L. McGuire's essay in *The Many Worlds of Poul Anderson*.

Anderson weaves together science, history, myth, and countless other categories of learning to fashion exotic alien habitats teeming with fascinating inhabitants. Anderson is perhaps SF's finest world-builder, more lavishly inventive than Larry Niven or Hal Clement. The lushness—sometimes over-lushness—of Anderson's creations fit his sensuous style. He has said that he tries to appeal to at least three senses in each scene. An admirer of Kipling, Anderson uses poetic *leitmotivs* to concentrate emotion, giving a richer, larger-than-life quality to his work. No real woods could be quite as enchanted as his imagined ones.

Anderson is a throughgoing romantic. His enthrallment with the beauty and terror of nature borders on pantheism. His complementary idealization of women is acknowledged gynolatry. The resonances between woman and universe work exquisitely well in *World Without Stars* because the Cosmic Goddess is kept offstage. Unfortuantely, without this restraint, *The Winter of the World* and *The Avatar* sink to the level of self-parody.

Anderson exalts doing over-thinking, the real over the vicarious, love over knowledge. He denies, even fears absolutes. There is no ultimate evolutionary goal, much less a Deity—a point underscored in recent books but present as far back as *The Enemy Stars*. Because for Anderson, reality simply *is,* savoring wonder is the purpose of life. The surest personal happiness is domestic, hence he emphasizes the joys of marriage and parenthood. (Devoted parents literally go to hell for their child in *Operation Chaos*.) Children being the only certain pledge of immortality, building a better world for one's descendants spurs achievement.

Many of Anderson's major themes shine forth in recent novels. *Boat of a Million Years* is an epic about eight naturally immortal people told in self-contained novelette-length units, successively presenting superb historical recreations, contemporary thrills, and hard science space exploration. Immortality is a distinctly mixed blessing as everything the immortals love fades like wrecks of a dissolving dream. But Anderson's heroes, special people slowly wise, meet their universe head-on and prevail. Courage accomplishes deeds entropy cannot mar.

Set in the decadent 22nd century, *Harvest of Stars* is a tribute to Anderson's late friend Robert Heinlein. Most of the book is semi-pastiche, full of ascerbic social commentary; "tough, smart people"; high-tech devices; and bright chatter—shades of Lazarus Long and Friday. Personal troth to a corporation frustrates social engineering done in the spirit of Teilhard de Chardin. Personalities downloaded on computer prolong life indefinitely and bodies can be regrown to

hold them, yielding a classic Andersonian solution of technology in the service of life. Freedom challenges stasis, love confronts chaos.

Set in the same universe before and after the events of *Harvest of Stars, The Stars Are Also Fire* is really two interlaced novels centered on the life and legend of Anderson's finest female character, a lunar pioneer and mother of a new species. Through her blood, technology and Nature, mind and body, humanity and Faery are revealed as cosmic complements, not enemies.

In summary, the interaction between Anderson's creatures and their environment is a matter of challenge and response. Life is a risk; sentient beings are not meant to be tame. Anderson's heroes are always fallible beings who strive to meet life's challenges well. They are free, responsible persons sensitive to the needs of others. As Blish observes, they are willing to pay the price of "doing the wrong thing for the right reason."

Yet however bravely heroes struggle, "nothing lasts forever." As demonstrated in Miesel's *Against Time's Arrow: The High Crusade of Poul Anderson,* the supreme enemy is entropy. How then are mortals to face certain doom?

Anderson is no Pelagian optimist like Gordon R. Dickson. He doubts that evolutionary progress will fundamentally improve man's lot. He admires unyielding endurance in the Northern heroic tradition: "No man can escape his weird, but none can take from him the heart wherewith he meets it." The author states it more gently in his own voice: "Life can be cruel, and it is ultimately tragic, but mostly it is wonderful, or would be if we'd allow it to be." Poul Anderson is his own best example of that process.

—Sandra Miesel

ANTHONY, Piers

Nationality: American. **Born:** Piers Anthony Dillingham Jacob, Oxford, England, 6 August 1934; became United States citizen, 1958. **Education:** Goddard College, Plainfield, Vermont, B.A. 1956; University of South Florida, Tampa, teaching certificate 1964. **Military Service:** Served in the United States Army, 1957-59. **Family:** Married Carol Marble in 1956; one daughter. **Career:** Technical writer, Electronic Communications Inc., St. Petersburg, Florida, 1959-62; English teacher, Admiral Farragut Academy, St. Petersburg, 1965-66. Since 1966 freelance writer. **Awards:** Pyramid *Fantasy and Science Fiction* award, 1967; August Derleth award, 1977. **Address:** c/o Xanth Trading Company, P.O. Box 1568, Clayton, Georgia 30525, U.S.A.

Science Fiction Publications

Novels (series: Apprentice Adept; Aton; Battle Circle; Bio of a Space Tyrant; Cluster; Geodyssey; Incarnations of Immortality; Jason Striker; Kelvin of Rud; Mode; Tarot; Xanth)

Chthon (Aton). New York, Ballantine, 1967; London, Macdonald, 1970.
Of Man and Mantra: A Trilogy. London, Corgi, 1986.
Omnivore. New York, Ballantine, 1968; London, Faber, 1969.

Orn. Garden City, New York, Doubleday, 1971; London, Corgi, 1977.

Ox. Garden City, New York, Doubleday, 1976; London, Corgi, 1977.

The Ring, with Robert E. Margroff. New York, Ace, 1968; London, Macdonald, 1969.

Macroscope. New York, Avon, 1969; London, Sphere, 1972.

The E.S.P. Worm, with Robert E. Margroff. New York, Paperback Library, 1970.

Race Against Time (for children). New York, Hawthorn, 1973.

Rings of Ice. New York, Avon, 1974; London, Millington, 1975.

Triple Détente. New York, DAW, 1974; London, Sphere, 1975.

Phthor (Aton). New York, Berkley, 1975; London, Panther, 1978.

But What of Earth?, with Robert Coulson. Toronto, Laser, 1976; original version by Anthony published as *But What of Earth?: A Novel Rendered into a Bad Example,* New York, Tor, 1989.

Steppe. London, Millington, 1976; New York, Tor, 1985.

Cluster. New York, Avon, 1977; as *Vicinity Cluster,* London, Millington, 1978.

Piers Anthony's Hasan. San Bernardino, California, Borgo Press, 1977; as *Hasan,* New York, Del, 1979.

A Spell for Chameleon (Xanth). New York, Ballantine, 1977; London, Macdonald, 1984.

Chaining the Lady (Cluster). New York, Avon, and London, Millington, 1978.

Kirlian Quest (Cluster). New York, Avon, and London, Millington, 1978.

Battle Circle: A Trilogy. New York, Avon, 1978; London, Corgi, 1984.
Sos, the Rope. New York, Pyramid, 1968; London, Faber, 1970.
Var, the Stick. London, Faber, 1972; New York, Bantam, 1973.
Neq, the Sword. London, Corgi, 1975.

Pretender: Science Fiction, with Frances Hall. San Bernardino, California, Borgo Press, 1979.

The Source of Magic (Xanth). New York, Ballantine, 1979; London, Macdonald, 1984.

Castle Roogna (Xanth). New York, Ballantine, 1979; London, Macdonald, 1984.

God of Tarot. New York, Jove, 1979.

Vision of Tarot. New York, Berkley, 1980.

Thousandstar (Cluster). New York, Avon, 1980; London, Panther, 1984.

Faith of Tarot. New York, Berkley, 1980.

Split Infinity (Apprentice Adept). New York, Ballantine, 1980; London, Granada, 1983.

Blue Adept (Apprentice Adept). New York, Ballantine, 1981; London, Granada, 1983.

Mute. New York, Avon, 1981; London, New English Library, 1984.

The Magic of Xanth (includes *A Spell for Chameleon, The Source of Magic,* and *Castle Roogna*). Garden City, New York, Doubleday, 1981; as *Three Complete Xanth Novels,* New York, Wings Books, 1994.

Centaur Aisle (Xanth). New York, Ballantine, 1982; London, Macdonald, 1984.

Ogre, Ogre (Xanth). New York, Ballantine, 1982; London, Orbit, 1984.

Juxtaposition (Apprentice Adept). New York, Ballantine, 1982; London, Grafton, 1986.

Viscous Circle (Cluster). New York, Avon, 1982; London, Panther, 1984.

Double Exposure (includes *Split Infinity, Blue Adept,* and *Juxtaposition*). Garden City, New York, Doubleday, 1982.

Night Mare (Xanth). New York, Ballantine, 1983; London, Orbit, 1984.

Refugee (Space Tyrant). New York, Avon, 1983; London, Grafton, 1986.

Dragon on a Pedestal (Xanth). New York, Ballantine, 1983; London, Orbit, 1984.

Mercenary (Space Tyrant). New York, Avon, 1984; London, Grafton, 1986.

On a Pale Horse (Immortality). New York, Ballantine, 1983; London, Panther, 1985.

Bearing an Hourglass (Immortality). New York, Ballantine, 1984; London, Severn House, 1986.

Crewel Lye: A Caustic Yarn (Xanth). New York, Ballantine, 1985; London, Macdonald, 198; London, New English Library, 1990.

Total Recall (novelization of screenplay). New York, Morrow, 1989; London, Legend, 1990.

Man from Mundania (Xanth). New York, Avon, 1989; London, New English Library, 1990.

Through the Ice (completion of work by Robert Kornwise). Novato, California, and Lancaster, Pennsylvania, Underwood-Miller, 1989.

Chimaera's Copper, with Robert E. Margroff (Kelvin). New York, Tor, 1990; London, Grafton, 1992.

Balook. Novato, California, and Lancaster, Pennsylvania, Underwood-Miller, 1990.

Orc's Opal, with Robert E. Margroff. New York, Tor, 1990; London, HarperCollins, 1993.

And Eternity (Immortality). New York, Morrow, and London, Severn House, 1990.

Firefly. New York, Morrow, 1990.

Dead Morn. Houston, Tafford, 1990.

Isle of View (Xanth). New York, Morrow, 1990; London, New English Library, 1991.

Phaze Doubt (Apprentice Adept). New York, Putnam, 1990; London, New English Library, 1991.

Tatham Mound. New York, Morrow, 1991.

Virtual Mode (Mode). New York, Putnam, 1991; London, HarperCollins, 1991.

Question Quest (Xanth). New York, Morrow, 1991; London, New English Library, 1992.

Mer-Cycle. Houston, Tafford, 1991; as *Mercycle,* New York, Ace, 1992; London, Grafton, 1993.

Fractal Mode (Mode). New York, Ace, and London, HarperCollins, 1992.

Mouvar's Magic, with Robert E. Margroff. New York, Tor, 1992; London, HarperCollins, 1994.

The Color of Her Panties (Xanth). New York, Morrow, 1992; as *The Colour of Her Panties,* London, New English Library, 1992.

The Caterpillar's Question, with Philip José Farmer. New York, Ace, 1992.

Across the Frames, with Robert E. Margroff (includes *Dragon's Gold, Serpent's Silver,* and *Chimaera's Copper*). New York, Guild America Books, 1992; as *Three Complete Novels,* New York, Wings Books, 1994.

Final Magic, with Robert E. Margroff (includes *Orc's Opal* and *Mouvar's Magic*). New York, Guild America books, 1992.

Killobyte. New York, Ace, 1993.

Demons Don't Dream (Xanth). New York, Tor, and London, New English Library, 1993.

If I Pay Thee Not in Gold, with Mercedes R. Lackey. Riverdale, New York, Baen, 1993.

Isle of Women (Geodyssey). New York, Tor, 1993.
Harpy Thyme (Xanth). London, New English Library, 1993; New York, Tor, 1994.
Chaos Mode (Mode). New York, Ace, and London, HarperCollins, 1994.
Shame of Man (Geodyssey). New York, Tor, 1994.
Geis of the Gargoyle (Xanth). New York, Tor, 1995.

Short Stories

Prostho Plus. London, Gollancz, 1971; New York, Bantam, 1973.
Anthonology. New York, Tor, 1985; London, Grafton, 1986.
Hard Sell. Houston, Tafford, 1990.
Alien Plot. New York, Tor, 1992.

OTHER PUBLICATIONS

Novels with Roberto Fuentes (series: Jason Striker in all titles)

Kiai! New York, Berkley, 1974.
Mistress of Death. New York, Berkley, 1974.
Bamboo Bloodbath. New York, Berkley, 1975.
Ninja's Revenge. New York, Berkley, 1975.
Amazon Slaughter. New York, Berkley, 1976.

Other

Bio of an Ogre: The Autobiography of Piers Anthony. New York, Ace, 1988.
Piers Anthony's Visual Guide to Xanth, with Jody Lynn Nye, illustrated by Todd Cameron Hamilton and James Clouse. New York, Avon, 1989.
Letters to Jenny, edited by Alan Riggs. New York, Tor, 1993.

Editor, with Barry N. Malzberg, Martin H. Greenberg, and Charles G. Waugh, *Uncollected Stars.* New York, Avon, 1986.
Editor, with Robert Gilliam, *Tales from the Great Turtle.* New York, Tor, 1994.

*

Manuscript Collection: Syracuse University, New York.

Critical Study: *Piers Anthony* by Michael R. Collings, Mercer Island, Washington, Starmont House, 1983.

*   *   *

Piers Anthony's debut novel, *Chthon,* published in 1967, was an unusually powerful novel even for a more experienced writer. Making tasteful use of sadomasochistic sexual compulsions, he created an entire society whose underlying psychological profile was so alien to the one with which we are familiar, it achieved an otherworldly quality that has rarely been equalled. Although the sequel, *Phthor,* published eight years later, attempted to deal with the many unresolved questions of its predecessor, the effect is more like an afterthought than a true sequel.

The late 1960s and early 1970s saw an explosion of varied and interesting novels. *Omnivore* created another fascinating alien society, along with a trio of characters whose interaction forms the core of the novel. Two sequels, *Orn* and *Ox,* continued the story but stand well on their own. Another trilogy, *Sos the Rope, Var the Stick,* and *Neq the Sword* is set in a post-cataclysmic world, where primitive survivors append to their names the weapon which they have chosen. There is an intricate code of conduct governing interpersonal conflict, a well-realized society, and an entertaining story line.

Several solo novels illustrated Anthony's growth toward even more serious work. *Macroscope* was an extremely popular work, the plot involving a device which allowed one to observe anyone from a distance, destroying privacy but also opening up the entire universe to humanity. *ESP Worm* and the collection *Prostho Plus* were examples of Anthony's penchant for humor, an aspect of his writing that was to become much more significant by the end of the 1970s. *Rings of Ice,* a world catastrophe novel which concentrates on a small group of survivors and their attempt to find a safe haven in the turmoil, includes some of the very best characterization Anthony has done. Other novels of the period ranged from the light adventure of Hasan to more serious works such as *The Ring,* written in collaboration with Robert Margroff.

In 1977, Anthony started two separate series which were to radically alter his place in the field. The first and perhaps less significant of these began with *Cluster.* Anthony's fascination with Tarot and Kirlian auras surfaced in this interstellar melodrama, which was popular enough to spawn not only four direct sequels, *Chaining the Lady, Kirlian Quest, Thousandstar,* and *Viscous Circle,* but also an entirely separate series about the Tarot, *God of Tarot, Vision of Tarot,* and *Faith of Tarot.* The blend of mysticism with traditional science fiction themes had never been done in quite this fashion before, and these books enjoyed considerable popularity despite a tendency to be repetitive in the latter volumes.

More significant for Anthony was *A Spell for Chameleon,* which was the first in the still popular Xanth series of fantasy novels. As a stand alone novel, *Spell* was exceptional. Anthony created an original magical system, a convincing fantasy world, superimposed an intriguing plot with sympathetic characters, and enlivened the mixture with humor. It was no surprise when a sequel appeared and *The Source of Magic,* followed quickly by *Castle Roogna,* both maintained the highly entertaining standards set by the first volume.

While writing the first few Xanth novels, Anthony also launched another series, the "Phaze" books. These are set within two interlocked worlds, one where science rules, one where magic is the order of the day. Under certain conditions, characters (including robots and sorcerers) can move from one to the other, although the laws of the world they inhabit have strange effects on their natures. *Split Infinity* and its original two sequels, *The Blue Adept* and *Juxtaposition,* remain among Anthony's most successful works, and do an admirable job of exploiting the tension between magic and science, the rational and the irrational. Subsequent continuations, *Out of Phaze, Robot Adept, Unicorn Point,* and *Phaze Doubt* were also amusing, but lacked the impact of the first trilogy.

Anthony continued to write Xanth novels, casting aside his original cast of characters after awhile and using others to explore his fantasy world. Although they continue to appear regularly, and are generally entertaining, they rarely show any interest in breaking the established pattern, though Anthony has showed more flexibility elsewhere.

One such diversion is the "Bio of a Space Tyrant" series of five novels, *Refugee, Mercenary, Executive, Politician,* and *Statesman.* The superimposition of contemporary countries and issues on a futuristic solar society is deliberately transparent, and the series clearly provided the author with a forum for commentary on many of the foibles of human politics.

Another fantasy series is far more noteworthy: *On a Pale Horse* was the first "Incarnation of Immortality," a loosely connected series in which the differing forces of myth and legend are personified. In the opening volume, a man becomes Death himself, only to become involved in a struggle against Satan. Anthony embellished this theme with several uniformly interesting and inventive sequels, including *Bearing an Hourglass, With a Tangled Skein, Being a Green Mother, Wielding a Red Sword,* and *And Eternity.*

Virtual Mode was the opening volume of a new sequence which blends science fiction and fantasy plot devices, one in which travel among a multitude of alternate realities is possible. A similar computer influenced but solo novel is *Killobyte,* which cleverly portrays the adventures of a computer hacker caught physically in a series of computer games. *The Caterpillar's Question,* written in collaboration with Philip José Farmer, moved even more firmly into the SF realm, featuring a contemporary man who discovers his companion is being sought by powerful alien forces from another universe.

In addition to the stories of Peter Dillingham, dentist to aliens, collected in *Prostho Plus,* Anthony has written several series shorter pieces as well, many of which are collected in *Anthonology.* Among his best are "In the Barn," "Quinquepedalian," "The Life of Stripe," "On the Uses of Torture," and "Small Mouth, Bad Taste." A more recent collection, *Alien Plot,* contains a number of interesting stories, but the author's talents seem to lie primarily at greater length.

Anthony's early books demonstrated an insightful, adventurous mind willing to explore a variety of different avenues. The success of the Xanth books and some of his other series seemed to narrow his focus for several years, but there is recent evidence of a more serious turn in the author's work. His non-fantastic historical novel, *Tatham Mound,* received favorable critical attention and *Isle of Woman* and its companion novel, *The Shame of Man,* employ an unusual device to follow the same set of personalities through snapshots of human history from primitive tribal culture to space travel. The future course of Anthony's work seems far less predictable now than it did a few years ago.

—Don D'Ammassa

ANVIL, Christopher

Pseudonym for Harry C. Crosby, Jr. **Nationality:** American. **Address:** c/o Scott Meredith Literary Agency, 845 Third Avenue, New York, New York 10022, U.S.A.

SCIENCE FICTION PUBLICATIONS

Novels

The Day the Machines Stopped. Derby, Connecticut, Monarch, 1964.
Strangers in Paradise. New York, Tower, 1970.
Pandora's Planet. Garden City, New York, Doubleday, 1972.
Warlord's World. New York, DAW, 1975.

The Steel, the Mist, and the Blazing Sun. New York, Ace, 1980.

*   *   *

Christopher Anvil appeared more frequently in *Astounding/Analog* from the mid-1950s to the mid-1960s than any other author, yet he remains relatively unknown today. His novels are slight efforts, and do not compare with his finest short fiction.

At his best, in stories like "A Rose by Any Other Name," which skillfully examines the effect of certain words on international relations, the widely reprinted "Gadget vs. Trend," on the impact of one invention on the functioning of society, and "Positive Feedback," a hilarious story that illustrates the problem of adjusting systems while they are in action, he is an inventive and expert manipulator of social trends and processes. Indeed, he has been one of the very best SF observers (along with Mack Reynolds at *his* best) of the foibles and presumptuousness of social thinkers and social managers. He was perhaps too successful—he found a formula and worked it to death, and was one of the main reasons why the 1960s *Analog* always left you with the feeling that you had just read last month's issue again. He was a John Campbell writer who could be relied upon to hew to the formulas and fads of that editor, and like Randall Garrett became lost from public view through constant, unchanging exposure. Perhaps he might have flourished artistically in another market—some evidence for this possibility can be found in "Mind Partner," his finest work, and one of his few stories published in *Galaxy.* In several respects "Mind Partner" is a New Wave story, a powerful example of psychological science fiction at its best, written before anyone was arguing about the term or had even heard of it. The story has a nightmare quality about it that lingers long after the reading. The editor-writer relationship in science fiction is for the most part a mystery, and it is also possible that Campbell brought out the best in him.

Other notable stories include "Bill for Delivery," "The Captive Djinn," "The Great Intellect Boom"—a major work that examines the effect of instant intellectuality on everyone in a society—"The Prisoner," and "Uncalculated Risk."

—Martin H. Greenberg

ARCHER, Ron. *See* **WHITE, Ted.**

ARMSTRONG, Anthony. *See* **TUBB, E. C.**

ARMSTRONG, Geoffrey. *See* **FEARN, John Russell.**

ARNASON, Eleanor (Atwood)

Nationality: American. **Born:** New York, New York, 28 December 1942. **Education:** Swarthmore College, Swarthmore, Pennsylvania, B.A. 1964; University of Minnesota, Minneapolis, no degree 1964-67. **Family:** Arden Wood (partner since 1973). **Career:** Accountant since 1964; has also worked in several warehouses and as a writer for two museums. **Awards:** James Tiptree, Jr. award, 1991; Mythopoeic Society award (adult literature), 1991; Minnesota Book award (fantasy and science fiction), 1994. **Member:** National Writers Union; Science Fiction Writers of America; National Organization for Women; Bat Conservation International. **Agent:** Virginia Kidd, 538 E. Harford St., Milford, Pennsylvania 18337. **Address:** P.O. Box 50599, Minneapolis, Minnesota 55403, U.S.A.

Science Fiction Publications

Novels

The Sword Smith. New York, Condor, 1978.
To the Resurrection Station. New York, Avon, 1986.
Daughter of the Bear King. New York, Avon, and London, Headline, 1987.
A Woman of the Iron People. New York, William Morrow, 1991; as *In the Light of Sigma Draconis* and *Changing Woman,* New York, AvoNova, 1992.
Ring of Swords. New York, Tor, 1993.

Poetry

Editor, with Terry A. Garey, *Time Gum and Other Poems from the Minicon Poetry Readings.* Minneapolis, Minnesota, Rune Press, 1988.

*

Critical Study: "Interview with Eleanor Arnason," *Tales of the Unanticipated,* No. 1, Fall 1986.

*   *   *

Several elements of Arnason's biography are important to an understanding of her work. As the daughter of the well-known art historian H. H. Arnason she grew up financially secure and on a first name basis with some of the finest American artists of the 1940s and 1950s. With this background and her own education as an art historian, it should come as no surprise that many of Arnason's stories center on aesthetic concerns and the importance of craftsmanship. Also important to her fiction, however, are the years she spent in Detroit working blue-collar jobs and refining strong socialist and feminist political beliefs. Much of what Arnason writes about comes from the convergence of these two radically different lifestyles. Her stories are noteworthy for her choice of common women and men as protagonists, for the moral emphasis she places upon quality workmanship (whether one is creating a sword, a monster, or a work of art), for clearsighted leftist political analysis, and for an interest in the difficulties of communication, particularly across gender and cultural boundries. Indeed many of Arnason's stories are themselves to be found at boundaries, trespassing between science fiction and fantasy, the gothic, the folktale, or metafiction.

Early in her career Arnason was identified with the American version of the New Wave. Her first published stories, including "A Clear Day in the Motor City" (1973), "Ace 167" (1974), and "The House by the Sea" (1975), appeared in either Michael Moorcock's *New Worlds* or Damon Knight's *Orbit.* The best of these early stories, the much reprinted "Warlord of Saturn's Moons" (1974), concerns an unmarried, middle-aged science fiction author, living in a badly-polluted, near-future Detroit, who is in the process of writing the space opera of the story's title. The writer feels trapped and sees her life as lacking in significant relationships. The story she is creating is clearly a wish-fulfillment fantasy and yet even within the heroic world of the space opera, nothing works right. Her protagonist takes chances and behaves bravely, but her heroics are wasted. When she is finally reunited with the hero, he has been so severely damaged that his only choices appear to be either psychosis or drugged apathy. Both protagonists can do little but await the next chapter in their lives for, as Arnason's fictional author writes, "Where there's life there's hope and so forth."

The title character of Arnason's first novel, *The Sword Smith* (1978), is also an artist. Unlike the narrator of "Warlord," however, Limper lives within a world where heroic adventures seem possible. Vaguely medieval, his universe contains intelligent creatures called trolls and dragons, but no real magic and, although the book was marketed as a genre fantasy, the author has stated that it should be read as science fiction. Limper is rather unpretentious and not particularly attractive or physically adept. His heroism, if such it can be called, lies in his stubborn refusal to quit and in his loyalty to his craft and his friends. Arnason, invariably skeptical of traditional heroes, introduces a knight in shining armor to the tale, but then takes great pleasure in killing him off. The understated irony and dry wit of this little-known and long out of print novel make it a joy to read.

Like *The Sword Smith,* Arnason's next two novels take direct aim at genre conventions, managing to be humorous while still making serious political and aesthetic points. *To the Resurrection Station* (1986) begins as an SF parody of the gothic romance. Featuring a dark and forbidding castle, a mysterious guardian, an enormous fortune, an unwanted suitor, an heiress who is considerably less innocent than she seems, a truly skewed robot butler and a delightful race of intelligent rats, the novel plays fast and loose with any number of clichés from both the gothic and SF traditions. *Daughter of the Bear King* (1987) concerns a middle-aged Minnesota housewife, a stalwart of the local Democratic party, who discovers that in another universe she is, in fact, the magical character of the title. Although some of the novel is set within a fairly traditional heroic fantasy world, much of the action takes place at real locations in Minneapolis. Particularly interesting are the stories' incompetently constructed monsters, many of whom mouth rightwing Republican slogans and practice bad aesthetics.

Arnason came to wider notice in 1991 with the publication of *A Woman of the Iron People.* Widely praised by reviewers, who often compared it to the work of Ursula K. Le Guin, the book shared the first Tiptree Award for gender-bending SF. Large in scope, the novel follows an anthropologist as she explores the rich and varied culture of an alien race. Like human beings, the Iron People come in two sexes, but their strict, gender-based delegation of duties and traits differs subtly from our own. Women live in small communities with the children. Adult males set up individual territories around the villages and live lives of grouchy isolation. Men and women come together only during the mating season. Adding complexity to the story is the title character, Nia the blacksmith, a woman who doesn't fit her assigned role in society. Further complicating things are the politics of the orbiting, communist Chinese-dominated human starship. In the mold of *The Left Hand of Darkness*, but featuring a dry humor that Le Guin's fiction lacks, *A Woman of the Iron People* stands as the most considerable achievement in Arnason's career to date.

Her most recently published novel, *Ring of Swords* (1993), however, is nearly as good. The initial volume in a trilogy, it concerns humanity's first encounter with another intelligent species. The Hwarhath are similar to Arnason's Iron People in many ways and have occasionally been confused with them by reviewers. Like the Iron People, the Hwarhath are furry humanoids who believe in strictly segregating the sexes. Like them, their males are warlike. Unlike the Iron People, however, they have an advanced, spacefaring society and, rather than the males being loners, they have a strongly developed male culture in which homosexual relationships are the norm. Although the Hwarhath once reproduced through carefully arranged and mutually distasteful matings, they now practice artificial insemination exclusively. Because violence, albeit of a highly structured and somewhat ritualized sort, is central to the Hwarhath male self-concept, the aliens have gone into space looking for a worthy foe and found humanity. Unfortunately, humanity doesn't play by Hwarhath rules and what might have been a series of limited engagements now threatens to get out of hand. The key to the situation lies in the developing relationship between a female exobiologist on the human diplomatic mission and the male lover of the Hwarhath commander, a renegade human being. *Ring of Swords* is largely a novel of conversations and debates, a kind of closet space opera. Arnason uses the confrontation between humanity and the Hwarhath to explore a variety of ideas concerning aesthetics, the relative importance of group versus individual loyalty, and, of course, love, gender, and sexuality. As a kind of sidebar to *Ring of Swords*, Arnason has also published a number of fine short stories set in the Hwarhath past. Some of these stories are clearly intended as folktales, stories written by the Hwarhath themselves. Probably the best of these is "The Lovers" (1994), which concerns a Hwarhath who is a secret heterosexual. The fraternal twin of a great military leader, he is in high demand for stud duty, which he secretly enjoys. This eventually leads to considerable sadness, however, because he cannot have a long-term relationship with the woman he's grown to love. Another well-done story in the series is "The Hound of Merin" (1993) which, like "The Lovers," explores the nature of sexual taboos, duty, and honor.

Over the past 20 years Eleanor Arnason has produced a substantial body of quality science fiction. Never prolific, she has at times had trouble getting her work published, in part, one suspects, because she refuses to write within the neat, confining boundaries of genre expectation, and in part because her fearless exploration of difficult political and social issues makes some editors and readers uneasy. Her fiction can be seen as a series of what Le Guin has called "thought experiments," stories which may be set in the future and on alien worlds, but which are in reality about here and now. Her work exploring gender, and particularly its intersection with politics, stands comparison with that of such better-known writers as Le Guin, Suzy McKee Charnas, and Sheri Tepper.

—Michael M. Levy

ARNETTE, Robert. *See* PHILLIPS, Rog.

———

ARNOLD, Edwin L(ester Linden)

Nationality: British. **Born:** Swanscombe, Kent, 14 May 1857; son of the writer Sir Edwin Arnold. **Education:** Cheltenham College. **Family:** Married 1) Constance Boyce, one daughter; 2) Jessie Brighton in 1919. **Career:** Cattle Breeder in Scotland, then worked in forestry in Travancore, India, in late 1870s; staff member, *Daily Telegraph,* London, until 1908. **Died:** 1 March 1935.

SCIENCE FICTION PUBLICATIONS

Novels

The Wonderful Adventures of Phra the Phoenician. London, Chatto and Windus, 3 vols., and New York, Harper, 1 vol., 1890; as *Phra the Phonecian,* London, George Newnes, 1910.
Lepidus the Centurion: A Roman of To-day. London, Cassell, 1901; New York, Crowell, 1902.
Lieut. Gullivar Jones: His Vacation. London, Brown Langham, 1905; New York, Arno Press, 1975; as *Gulliver of Mars,* New York, Ace, 1964; as *Lieut. Gulliver Jones: His Vacation,* London, New English Library, 1976.

Short Stories

The Story of Ulla and Other Tales. London and New York, Longman, 1895.

OTHER PUBLICATIONS

Novel

The Constable of St. Nicholas. London, Chatto and Windus, 1894.

Other

A Summer Holiday in Scandinavia. London, Sampson Low, 1877.
On the Indian Hills; or, Coffee-Planting in Southern India. London, Sampson Low, 2 vols., 1881.
Coffee: Its Cultivation and Profit. London, Whittingham, 1886.
Bird Life in England. London, Chatto and Windus, 1887.
England as She Seems, Being Selections from the Notes of an Arab Hadji. London, Warne, 1888.
The Soul of the Beast. London, P.R. Macmillan, 1960.

Editor, *The Opium Question Solved.* London, Partridge, 1882.

* * *

Once a highly popular author, Edwin L. Arnold is little remembered and seldom read, and when read at all is generally examined as a possible source of inspiration for Edgar Rice Burroughs's Martian series rather than as an author of independent merit. Arnold's father, Sir Edwin Arnold, was one of the first Englishmen to study Eastern religion, philosophy, and culture. Very likely as a result of his father's influence, young Arnold became interested in Asian philosophy, in particular in theories of reincarnation and the cyclical nature of existence.

These theories are visible in Arnold's first and most successful novel, *The Wonderful Adventures of Phra the Phoenician.* Phra is described as a man appearing about 30 years of age, but in fact with no recollection of ever having been younger. His most ancient memory is of life in classical Phoenicia, but even in that recollection he was a man, not a child. Over the ages, Phra has lived and (apparently) died repeatedly. He describes himself as a simple military man, although he admits to being a great swordsman. As an early colonist in Britain he met and fell in love with the Princess Blodwen. Following her death he too "died" and encountered her ghost in the spirit world, but after many years Phra recovered, his undecayed body as good as ever, and resumed his life. This cycle is repeated numerous times, down to the present (Victorian) era. The book is an excellent example of Victorian fantasy, closest in spirit to Haggard's *The World's Desire,* written with Andrew Lang. To modern readers Phra will seem slow-paced, florid, and overlong, but it is still readable.

The Story of Ulla and Other Tales is a collection of Arnold's shorter fiction. Several of the stories contain fantastic elements, for the most part of rather conventional nature (i.e., ghost stories). Most relevant is "Rutherford the Twice-Born," in which Arnold reverts to the reincarnation/resurrection theme. *Lepidus the Centurion* is still another treatment of the resurrection/reincarnation theme. A Roman legionnaire revives from suspended animation in contemporary England, and then proceeds to acclimate himself to polite Victorian society, learning to play tennis and the like. *Lepidus* is the least of Arnold's novels in actual interest for the present-day reader. The author attempts the comedy of manners in style, but the result is poor.

Lieut. Gulliver Jones: His Vacation was Arnold's final novel, and the most interesting to the modern reader of science fiction. Jones, a lieutenant in the U.S. Navy, comes into possession of a magic carpet while on leave. He is carried to Mars where he encounters a race of cultured urban dwellers attempting to preserve a high ancient civilization against the maraudings of savage desert nomads. He rescues the civilized Princess An from the nomads, travels to an icy River of Death (compare Haggard and Burroughs), and has other adventures among the Martians before returning to Earth. By combining the setting and plot elements of *Gulliver Jones* with the heroic figure of *Phra the Phoenician*—and with the addition of elements from such works as *A Journey to Mars* by Pope and *Zarlah the Martian* by Grisewood—one assembles the full recipe of Burroughs's Barsoomian saga, at least of the early volumes.

Although Arnold's last novel was published in 1905, he lived until 1935, well into the period of modern "pulp" science fiction, but there appears to be no record of his attitude toward the works of later writers, including Burroughs.

—Richard A. Lupoff

———

ARROW, William. *See* **ROTSLER, William.**

———

ARTHUR, Peter. *See* **PORGES, Arthur.**

———

ASH, Fenton. *See* **AUBREY, Frank.**

———

ASHLEY, Fred. *See* **AUBREY, Frank.**

———

ASIMOV, Isaac

Pseudonyms: Dr. A.; Paul French. **Nationality:** American. **Born:** Petrovichi, U.S.S.R., 2 January 1920; emigrated to the United States in 1923; naturalized, 1928. **Education:** Columbia University, New York, B.S. 1939, M.A. 1941, Ph.D. in chemistry 1948. **Military Service:** Served in the United States Army, 1945-46. **Family:** Married 1) Gertrude Blugerman in 1948 (divorced 1973), one son and one daughter; 2) Janet Opal Jeppson in 1973. **Career:** Instructor in Biochemistry, 1949-51, assistant professor, 1951-55, associate professor, 1955-79, and from 1979, professor, Boston University School of Medicine. **Awards:** Edison Foundation National Mass Media award, 1958; Blakeslee award, for nonfiction, 1960; World Science Fiction Convention Citation, 1963; Hugo award, 1963, 1966, 1973, 1977, 1983; American Chemical Society James T. Grady award, 1965; American Association for the Advancement of Science-Westinghouse Science Writing award, 1967; Nebula award, 1972, 1976; *Locus* award, for nonfiction, 1981, for fiction, 1983. Guest of Honor, World Science Fiction Convention, 1955. **Died:** 6 April 1992.

SCIENCE FICTION PUBLICATIONS

Novels (series: Foundation; Norby; Robots; Trantorian Empire)

Triangle: (Empire). Garden City, New York, Doubleday, 1961; as *An Isaac Asimov Second Omnibus,* London, Sidgwick and Jackson, 1969.
  Pebble in the Sky. Garden City, New York, Doubleday, 1950; London, Corgi, 1958.
  The Stars, Like Dust. Garden City, New York, Doubleday, 1951; London, Panther, 1958; abridged edition, as *The Rebellious Stars,* New York, Ace, 1954.
  The Currents of Space. Garden City, New York, Doubleday, 1952; London, Boardman, 1955.
The Foundation Trilogy. Garden City, New York, Doubleday, 1963; as *An Isaac Asimov Omnibus,* London, Sidgwick and Jackson, 1966.
  Foundation. New York, Gnome Press, 1951; London, Weidenfeld and Nicolson, 1953; abridged edition, as *The 1,000-Year Plan,* New York, Ace, 1955.

Foundation and Empire. New York, Gnome Press, 1952; London, Panther, 1962; as *The Man Who Upset the Universe,* New York, Ace, 1955.

Second Foundation. New York, Gnome Press, 1953; as *2nd Foundation: Galactic Empire,* New York, Avon, 1958.

The Caves of Steel (Robots). Garden City, New York, Doubleday, and London, Boardman, 1954.

The End of Eternity. Garden City, New York, Doubleday, 1955; London, Panther, 1958.

The Naked Sun (Robots). Garden City, New York, Doubleday, 1957; London, Joseph, 1958.

Fantastic Voyage (novelization of screenplay). Boston, Houghton Mifflin, and London, Dobson, 1966.

The Robot Novels (includes *The Caves of Steel* and *The Naked Sun*). Garden City, New York, Doubleday, 1972; with *The Robots of Dawn,* New York, Ballantine, 1988.

The Gods Themselves. Garden City, New York, Doubleday, and London, Gollancz, 1972.

The Far Ends of Time (omnibus). Garden City, New York, Doubleday, 1979.

Prisoners of the Stars (omnibus). Garden City, New York, Doubleday, 1979.

Foundation's Edge. Garden City, New York, Doubleday, 1982; London, Granada, 1983.

The Robots of Dawn (Robots). Huntington Woods, Michigan, Phantasia Press, 1983; London, Granada, 1984.

Norby, the Mixed-Up Robot (for children), with Janet Asimov. New York, Walker, 1983; London, Methuen, 1984.

Norby's Other Secret (for children), with Janet Asimov. New York, Walker, 1984; London, Methuen, 1985.

Norby and the Lost Princess (for children), with Janet Asimov. New York, Walker, 1985.

Robots and Empire. Huntington Woods, Michigan, Phantasia Press, 1985.

Norby and the Invaders (for children), with Janet Asimov. New York, Walker, 1985.

Norby and the Queen's Necklace (for children), with Janet Asimov. New York, Walker, 1986.

Foundation and Earth. Garden City, New York, Doubleday, and London, Grafton, 1986.

The Norby Chronicles (omnibus; for children), with Janet Asimov. New York, Ace, 1986.

Fantastic Voyage II: Destination Brain. Garden City, New York, Doubleday, and London, Grafton, 1987.

Norby, Robot for Hire (omnibus; for children), with Janet Asimov. New York, Ace, 1987.

Norby Finds a Villain (for children), with Janet Asimov. New York, Walker, 1987.

Prelude to Foundation. New York, Doubleday, and London, Grafton, 1988.

Norby Through Space and Time (omnibus). New York, Ace, 1988.

Nemesis. New York and London, Doubleday, 1989.

Norby Down to Earth (for children), with Janet Asimov. New York, Walker, 1989.

Norby and Yobo's Great Adventure (for children), with Janet Asimov. New York, Walker, 1989.

Nightfall, with Robert Silverberg. London, Gollancz, and New York, Doubleday, 1990.

Norby and the Oldest Dragon (for children), with Janet Asimov. New York, Walker, 1990.

Norby and the Court Jester (for children), with Janet Asimov. New York, Walker, 1991.

The Child of Time, with Robert Silverberg. London, Gollancz, 1991; as *The Ugly Little Boy,* bound with *The [Widget], the [Wadget], and Boff,* by Theodore Sturgeon, New Yor, Tor, 1989.

The Positronic Man, with Robert Silverberg. London, Gollancz, 1992; New York, Doubleday, 1993.

Novels as Paul French (for children; series: Lucky Starr in all titles)

The Adventures [Further Adventures] of Lucky Starr. Garden City, New York, Doubleday, 2 vols., 1985.

David Starr, Space Ranger. Garden City, New York, Doubleday, 1952; Kingswood, Surrey, World's Work, 1953; as *Space Ranger* (as Isaac Asimov), London, New English Library, 1973.

Lucky Starr and the Pirates of the Asteroids. Garden City, New York, Doubleday, 1953; Kingswood, Surrey, World's Work, 1954; as *Pirates of the Asteroids* (as Isaac Asimov), London, New English Library, 1973.

Lucky Starr and the Oceans of Venus. Garden City, New York, Doubleday, 1954; as *The Oceans of Venus* (as Isaac Asimov), London, New English Library, 1974.

Lucky Starr and the Big Sun of Mercury. Garden City, New York, Doubleday, 1956; as *The Big Sun of Mercury* (as Isaac Asimov), London, New English Library, 1974.

Lucky Starr and the Moons of Jupiter. Garden City, New York, Doubleday, 1957; as *The Moons of Jupiter* (as Isaac Asimov), London, New English Library, 1974.

Lucky Starr and the Rings of Saturn. Garden City, New York, Doubleday, 1958; as *The Rings of Saturn* (as Isaac Asimov), London, New English Library, 1974.

Short Stories

I, Robot. New York, Gnome Press, 1950; London, Grayson, 1952.

The Martian Way and Other Stories. Garden City, New York, Doubleday, 1955; London, Dobson, 1964.

Earth Is Room Enough. Garden City, New York, Doubleday, 1957; London, Panther, 1960.

Nine Tomorrows: Tales of the Near Future. Garden City, New York, Doubleday, 1959; London, Dobson, 1963.

The Rest of the Robots. Garden City, New York, Doubleday, 1964; London, Dobson, 1967; abridged as *Eight Stories from The Rest of the Robot,* New York, Pyramid, 1966.

Through a Glass, Clearly. London, Four Square, 1967.

Nightfall and Other Stories. Garden City, New York, Doubleday, 1969; London, Rapp and Whiting, 1970.

The Early Asimov; cr, Eleven Years of Trying. Garden City, New York, Doubleday, 1972; London, Gollancz, 1973.

The Best of Isaac Asimov. London, Sidgwick and Jackson, 1973; Garden City, New York, Doubleday, 1974.

Have You Seen These? Cambridge, Massachusetts, NESFA Press, 1974.

The Heavenly Host (for children). New York, Walker, 1975; London, Penguin, 1978.

Buy Jupiter and Other Stories. Garden City, New York, Doubleday, 1975; London, Gollancz, 1976.

The Dream, Benjamin's Dream, Benjamin's Bicentennial Blast: Three Short Stories. New York, privately printed, 1976.

The Bicentennial Man and Other Stories. Garden City, New York, Doubleday, 1976; London, Gollancz, 1977.

Good Taste. Topeka, Kansas, Apocalypse Press, 1976.

Liar! Cambridge, Cambridge University Press, 1977.

Little Lost Robot. Cambridge, Cambridge University Press, 1977.

3 by Asimov. New York, Targ, 1981.

The Complete Robot. Garden City, New York, Doubleday, and London, Granada, 1982.

The Winds of Change and Other Stories. Garden City, New York, Doubleday, and London, Granada, 1983.

The Alternate Asimovs. Garden City, New York, Doubleday, 1986; London, Grafton, 1987.

Robot Dreams. New York, Berkley, 1986; London, Gollancz, 1987.

Other Worlds of Isaac Asimov, edited by Martin H. Greenberg. New York, Avenel, 1987.

The Best Science Fiction of Isaac Asimov. Garden City, New York, Doubleday, 1986; London, Grafton, 1987.

Azazel. New York, Doubleday, 1988; London, Doubleday, 1989.

The Asimov Chronicles: Fifty Years of Isaac Asimov, edited by Martin H. Greenberg. Arlington Heights, Illinois, Dark Harvest 1989; London, Legend, 1991.

Robot Visions. New York, Roc, 1990; London, Gollancz, 1991.

The Complete Stories. New York, Doubleday, 2 vols., 1990-92; London, HarperCollins, 2 vols, 1993-94.

Cal. New York, Doubleday, 1991.

Forward the Foundation. New York and London, Doubleday, 1993.

Gold: The Final Science Fiction Collection. New York, HarperPrism, 1995.

OTHER PUBLICATIONS

Novels

The Death Dealers. New York, Avon, 1958; as *A Whiff of Death,* New York, Walker, and London, Gollancz, 1968.

The Best New Thing (for children). Cleveland, World, 1971.

Murder at the ABA. Garden City, New York, Doubleday, 1976; as *Authorized Murder,* London, Gollancz, 1976.

Short Stories (series: Black Widowers)

Asimov's Mysteries. Garden City, New York, Doubleday, and London, Rapp and Whiting, 1968.

Tales of the Black Widowers. Garden City, New York, Doubleday, 1974; London, Gollancz, 1975.

More Tales of the Black Widowers. Garden City, New York, Doubleday, 1976; London, Gollancz, 1977.

The Key Word and Other Mysteries (for children). New York, Walker, 1977.

Casebook of the Black Widowers. Garden City, New York, Doubleday, and London, Gollancz, 1980.

The Union Club Mysteries. Garden City, New York, Doubleday, 1983; London, Granada, 1984.

Banquets of the Black Widowers. Garden City, New York, Doubleday, 1984; London, Grafton, 1986.

The Edge of Tomorrow. New York, Tor, 1985; London, Harrap, 1986.

The Disappearing Man and Other Mysteries (for young adults). London, Walker, 1985.

The Best Mysteries of Isaac Asimov. Garden City, New York, Doubleday, 1986; London, Grafton, 1987.

Puzzles of the Black Widowers. New York and London, Doubleday, 1990.

Poetry

Lecherous Limericks. New York, Walker, 1975; London, Corgi, 1977.

More Lecherous Limericks. New York, Walker, 1976.

Still More Lecherous Limericks. New York, Walker, 1977.

Asimov's Sherlockian Limericks. Yonkers, New York, Mysterious Press, 1978.

Limericks: Too Gross, with John Ciardi. New York, Norton, 1978.

A Grossery of Limericks, with John Ciardi. New York, Norton, 1981.

Limericks for Children. New York, Caedmon, 1984.

Other

Biochemistry and Human Metabolism, with Burnham Walker and William C. Boyd. Baltimore, Williams and Wilkins, 1952; revised edition, 1954, 1957; London, Ballie Tindall and Cox, 1955.

The Chemicals of Life: Enzymes, Vitamins, Hormones. New York, Abelard Schuman, 1954; London, Bell, 1956.

Races and Peoples, with William C. Boyd. New York, Abelard Schuman, 1955; London, Abelard Schuman, 1958.

Chemistry and Human Health, with Burnham Walker and M.K. Nicholas. New York, McGraw Hill, 1956.

Inside the Atom. New York and London, Abelard Schuman, 1956; revised edition, 1958, 1961, 1966, 1974.

Building Blocks of the Universe. New York, Abelard Schuman, 1957; London, Abelard Schuman, 1958; revised edition, 1961, 1974.

Only a Trillion. New York and London, Abelard Schuman, 1957; as *Marvels of Science,* New York, Collier, 1962.

The World of Carbon. New York and London, Abelard Schuman, 1958; revised edition, New York, Collier, 1962.

The World of Nitrogen. New York and London, Abelard Schuman, 1958; revised edition, New York, Collier, 1962.

The Clock We Live On. New York and London, Abelard Schuman, 1959; revised edition, New York, Collier, 1962; Abelard Schuman, 1965.

The Living River. New York and London, Abelard Schuman, 1959; revised edition, as *The Bloodstream: River of Life,* New York, Collier, 1961.

Realm of Numbers. Boston, Houghton Mifflin, 1959; London, Gollancz, 1963.

Words of Science and the History Behind Them. Boston, Houghton Mifflin, 1959; London, Harrap, 1974.

Breakthroughs in Science (for children). Boston, Houghton Mifflin, 1960.

The Intelligent Man's Guide to Science. New York, Basic Books, 2 vols., 1960; revised edition, as *The New Intelligent Man's Guide to Science,* 1 vol., 1965; London, Nelson, 1967; as *Asimov's Guide to Science,* New York, Basic Books, 1972; London, Penguin, 2 vols., 1975; as *Asimov's New Guide to Science,* Basic Books, 1984.

The Kingdom of the Sun. New York and London, Abelard Schuman, 1960; revised edition, New York, Collier, 1962; Abelard Schuman, 1963.

Realm of Measure. Boston, Houghton Mifflin, 1960.

Satellites in Outer Space (for children). New York, Random House, 1960; revised edition, 1964, 1973.

The Double Planet. New York, Abelard Schuman, 1960; London, Abelard Schuman, 1962; revised edition, 1966.

The Wellsprings of Life. New York and London, Abelard Schuman, 1960.

Realm of Algebra. Boston, Houghton Mifflin, 1961; London, Gollancz, 1964.

Words from the Myths. Boston, Houghton Mifflin, 1961; London, Faber, 1963.

Fact and Fancy. Garden City, New York, Doubleday, 1962.

Life and Energy. Garden City, New York, Doubleday, 1962; London, Dobson, 1963.

The Search for the Elements. New York, Basic Books, 1962.

Words in Genesis. Boston, Houghton Mifflin, 1962.

Words on the Map. Boston, Houghton Mifflin, 1962.

View from a Height. Garden City, New York, Doubleday, 1963; London, Dobson, 1964.

The Genetic Code. New York, Orion Press, 1963; London, Murray, 1964.

The Human Body: Its Structure and Operation. Boston, Houghton Mifflin, 1963; London, Nelson, 1965; revised edition, New York, Mentor, 1992.

The Kite That Won the Revolution. Boston, Houghton Mifflin, 1963.

Words from the Exodus. Boston, Houghton Mifflin, 1963.

Adding a Dimension: 17 Essays on the History of Science. Garden City, New York, Doubleday, 1964; London, Dobson, 1966.

The Human Brain: Its Capacities and Functions. Boston, Houghton Mifflin, 1964; London, Nelson, 1965.

Quick and Easy Math. Boston, Houghton Mifflin, 1964; London, Whiting and Wheaton, 1967.

A Short History of Biology. Garden City, New York, Natural History Press, 1964; London, Nelson, 1965.

Planets for Man, with Stephen H. Dole. New York, Random House, 1964.

Asimov's Biographical Encyclopedia of Science and Technology. Garden City, New York, Doubleday, 1964; London, Allen and Unwin, 1966; revised edition, Doubleday, 1972, 1982; London, Pan, 1975.

An Easy Introduction to the Slide Rule. Boston, Houghton Mifflin, 1965; London, Whiting and Wheaton, 1967.

The Greeks: A Great Adventure. Boston, Houghton Mifflin, 1965.

Of Time and Space and Other Things. Garden City, New York, Doubleday, 1965; London, Dobson, 1967.

A Short History of Chemistry. Garden City, New York, Doubleday, 1965; London, Heinemann, 1972.

The Neutrino: Ghost Particle of the Atom. Garden City, New York, Doubleday, and London, Dobson, 1966.

The Genetic Effects of Radiation, with Theodosius Dobzhansky. Washington, D.C., Atomic Energy Commission, 1966.

The Noble Gases. New York, Basic Books, 1966.

The Roman Republic. Boston, Houghton Mifflin, 1966.

From Earth to Heaven. Garden City, New York, Doubleday, 1966.

Understanding Physics. New York, Walker, 3 vols., 1966; London, Allen and Unwin, 3 vols., 1967; as *The History of Physics,* Walker, 1 vol., 1984.

The Universe: From Flat Earth to Quasar. New York, Walker, 1966; London, Penguin, 1967; revised edition, Walker, and Penguin, 1971; revised edition, as *The Universe: From Flat Earth to Black Holes—and Beyond,* Walker, 1980, Penguin, 1983.

The Roman Empire. Boston, Houghton Mifflin, 1967.

The Moon (for children). Chicago, Follett, 1967; London, University of London Press, 1969.

Is Anyone There? (essays). Garden City, New York, Doubleday, 1967; London, Rapp and Whiting, 1968.

To the Ends of the Universe. New York, Walker, 1967; revised edition, 1976.

The Egyptians. Boston, Houghton Mifflin, 1967.

Mars (for children). Chicago, Follett, 1967; London, University of London Press, 1971.

From Earth to Heaven: 17 Essays on Science. Garden City, New York, Doubleday, 1967; London, Dobson, 1968.

Environments Out There. New York, Abelard Schuman, 1967; London, Abelard Schuman, 1968.

Science, Numbers, and I: Essays on Science. Garden City, New York, Doubleday, 1968; London, Rapp and Whiting, 1969.

The Near East: 10,000 Years of History. Boston, Houghton Mifflin, 1968.

Asimov's Guide to the Bible: The Old Testament, The New Testament. Garden City, New York, Doubleday, 2 vols., 1968-69.

The Dark Ages. Boston, Houghton Mifflin, 1968.

Galaxies (for children). Chicago, Follett, 1968; London, University of London Press, 1971.

Stars (for children). Chicago, Follett, 1968.

Words from History. Boston, Houghton Mifflin, 1968.

Photosynthesis. New York, Basic Books, 1968; London, Allen and Unwin, 1970.

The Shaping of England. Boston, Houghton Mifflin, 1969.

Twentieth Century Discovery (for children). Garden City, New York, Doubleday, and London, Macdonald, 1969.

Opus 100 (selection). Boston, Houghton Mifflin, 1969.

ABC's of Space (for children). New York, Walker, 1969.

Great Ideas of Science (for children). Boston, Houghton Mifflin, 1969.

To the Solar System and Back. Garden City, New York, Doubleday, 1970.

Asimov's Guide to Shakespeare: The Greek, Roman, and Italian Plays; The English Plays. Garden City, New York, Doubleday, 2 vols., 1970.

Constantinople. Boston, Houghton Mifflin, 1970.

The ABC's of the Ocean (for children). New York, Walker, 1970.

Light (for children). Chicago, Follett, 1970.

The Stars in Their Courses. Garden City, New York, Doubleday, 1971; London, White Lion, 1974.

What Makes the Sun Shine. Boston, Little Brown, 1971.

The Isaac Asimov Treasury of Humor. Boston, Houghton Mifflin, 1971; London, Vallentine Mitchell, 1972.

The Sensuous Dirty Old Man (as Dr. A.). New York, Walker, 1971.

The Land of Canaan. Boston, Houghton Mifflin, 1971.

ABC's of Earth (for children). New York, Walker, 1971.

The Space Dictionary. New York, Starline, 1971.

More Words of Science. Boston, Houghton Mifflin, 1972.

Electricity and Man. Washington, D.C., Atomic Energy Commission, 1972.

The Shaping of France. Boston, Houghton Mifflin, 1972.

Asimov's Annotated "Don Juan." Garden City, New York, Doubleday, 1972.

ABC's of Ecology (for children). New York, Walker, 1972.

The Story of Ruth. Garden City, New York, Doubleday, 1972.

Worlds Within Worlds. Washington, D.C., Atomic Energy Commission, 1972.

The Left Hand of the Electron (essays). Garden City, New York, Doubleday, 1972; London, White Lion, 1975.

Ginn Science Program. Boston, Ginn, 5 vols., 1972-73.

How Did We Find Out about Dinosaurs [the Earth Is Round, Electricity, Vitamins, Germs, Comets, Energy, Atoms, Nuclear Power, Numbers, Outer Space, Earthquakes, Black Holes, Our Human Roots, Antarctica, Coal, Oil, Solar Powers, Volcanoes, Life in the Deep Sea, Our Genes, the Universe, Computers, Robots, the Atmosphere, DNA, the Speed of Light, Blood, Sunshine, the Brain, Super Conductivity, Microwaves, Photosynthesis, Pluto] (for children). New York, Walker, 33 vols., 1973-91; 6 vols. published London, White Lion, 1975-76; 1 vol. published London, Pan, 1980; 7 vols. published (as *How We Found Out . . .* series), London, Longman, 1982.

The Tragedy of the Moon (essays). Garden City, New York, Doubleday, 1973; London, Abelard Schuman, 1974.

Comets and Meteors (for children). Chicago, Follett, 1973.

The Sun (for children). Chicago, Follett, 1973.

The Shaping of North America from the Earliest Times to 1763. Boston, Houghton Mifflin, 1973; London, Dobson, 1975.

Please Explain (for children). Boston, Houghton Mifflin, 1973; London, Abelard Schuman, 1975.

Physical Science Today. Del Mar, California, CRM, 1973.

Jupiter, The Largest Planet (for children). New York, Lothrop, 1973; revised edition, 1976.

Today, Tomorrow, and. . . . Garden City, New York, Doubleday, 1973; London, Abelard Schuman, 1974; as *Towards Tomorrow,* London, Hodder and Stoughton, 1977.

The Birth of the United States 1763-1816. Boston, Houghton Mifflin, 1974.

Earth: Our Crowded Spaceship. Garden City, New York, Doubleday, and London, Abelard Schuman, 1974.

Asimov on Chemistry. Garden City, New York, Doubleday, 1974; London, Macdonald and Jane's, 1975.

Asimov on Astronomy. Garden City, New York, Doubleday, and London, Macdonald, 1974.

Asimov's Annotated "Paradise Lost." Garden City, New York, Doubleday, 1974.

Our World in Space. Greenwich, Connecticut, New York Graphic Society, and Cambridge, Patrick Stephens, 1974.

The Solar System (for children). Chicago, Follett, 1975.

Birth and Death of the Universe. New York, Walker, 1975.

Of Matters Great and Small. Garden City, New York, Doubleday, 1975.

Our Federal Union: The United States from 1816 to 1865. Boston, Houghton Mifflin, and London, Dobson, 1975.

The Ends of the Earth: The Polar Regions of the World. New York, Weybright and Talley, 1975.

Eyes on the Universe: A History of the Telescope. Boston, Houghton Mifflin, 1975; London, Deutsch, 1976.

Science Past—Science Future. Garden City, New York, Doubleday, 1975.

Alpha Centauri, The Nearest Star (for children). New York, Lothrop, 1976.

I, Rabbi (for children). New York, Walker, 1976.

Asimov on Physics. Garden City, New York, Doubleday, 1976.

The Planet That Wasn't. Garden City, New York, Doubleday, 1976; London, Sphere, 1977.

The Collapsing Universe: The Story of Black Holes. New York, Walker, and London, Hutchinson, 1977.

Asimov on Numbers. Garden City, New York, Doubleday, 1977.

The Beginning and the End. Garden City, New York, Doubleday, 1977.

Familiar Poems Annotated. Garden City, New York, Doubleday, 1977.

The Golden Door: The United States from 1865 to 1918. Boston, Houghton Mifflin, and London, Dobson, 1977.

Mars, The Red Planet (for children). New York, Lothrop, 1977.

Life and Time. Garden City, New York, Doubleday, 1978.

Quasar, Quasar, Burning Bright. Garden City, New York, Doubleday, 1978.

Animals of the Bible (for children). Garden City, New York, Doubleday, 1978.

Isaac Asimov's Book of Facts. New York, Grosset and Dunlap, 1979; London, Hodder and Stoughton, 1980; abridged edition (for children), as *Would You Believe?* and *More . . . Would You Believe?,* Grosset and Dunlap, 2 vols., 1981-82.

Extraterrestrial Civilizations. New York, Crown, 1979; London, Robson, 1980.

A Choice of Catastrophes. New York, Simon and Schuster, 1979; London, Hutchinson, 1980.

Saturn and Beyond. New York, Lothrop, 1979.

Opus 200 (selection). Boston, Houghton Mifflin, 1979.

In Memory Yet Green: The Autobiography of Isaac Asimov 1920-1954. Garden City, New York, Doubleday, 1979.

The Road to Infinity. Garden City, New York, Doubleday, 1979.

In Joy Still Felt: The Autobiography of Isaac Asimov 1954-1978. Garden City, New York, Doubleday, 1980.

The Annotated Gulliver's Travels. New York, Potter, 1980.

Opus (includes *Opus 100* and *Opus 200*). London, Deutsch, 1980.

Change! Seventy-One Glimpses of the Future. Boston, Houghton Mifflin, 1981.

Visions of the Universe, paintings by Kazuaki Iwasaki. Montrose, California, Cosmos Store, 1981.

Asimov on Science Fiction. Garden City, New York, Doubleday, 1981; London, Granada, 1983.

Venus, Near Neighbor of the Sun (for children). New York, Lothrop, 1981.

The Sun Shines Bright. Garden City, New York, Doubleday, 1981; London, Granada, 1984.

In the Beginning: Science Faces God in the Book of Genesis. New York, Crown, and London, New English Library, 1981.

Exploring the Earth and the Cosmos. New York, Crown, 1982; London, Allen Lane, 1983.

Counting the Eons. Garden City, New York, Doubleday, 1983; London, Granada, 1984.

The Measure of the Universe. New York, Harper, 1983.

The Roving Mind. Buffalo, Prometheus, 1983; Oxford, Oxford University Press, 1987.

Those Amazing Electronic Thinking Machines (for children). New York, Watts, 1983.

X Stands for Unknown (essays). Garden City, New York, Doubleday, 1984; London, Granada, 1985.

Opus 300. Boston, Houghton Mifflin, 1984.

Robots: Where the Machine Ends and Life Begins, with Karen A. Frenkel. New York, Crown, 1985.

The Exploding Suns: The Secrets of the Supernovas. New York, Dutton, 1985.

Asimov's Guide to Halley's Comet. New York, Walker, 1985.

The Subatomic Monster (essays). Garden City, New York, Doubleday, 1985; London, Grafton, 1986.

The Dangers of Intelligence and Other Science Essays. Boston, Houghton Mifflin, 1986.

Future Days: A Nineteenth-Century Vision of the Year 2000. New York, Holt, and London, Virgin, 1986.

Wonderful Worldwide Science Bazaar: Seventy-two Up-to-Date Reports on the State of Everything from Inside the Atom to Outside the Universe. Boston, Houghton Mifflin, 1986.

Bare Bones: Dinosaur (for children), with David Hawcock. New York, Holt, 1986; London, Methuen, 1987.

As Far as the Human Eye Could See (essays). Garden City, New York, Doubleday, 1987; London, Grafton, 1988.

Past, Present, and Future (essays). Buffalo, New York, Prometheus, 1987.

Beginnings: The Story of Origins—of Mankind, Life, the Earth, the Universe. New York, Walker, 1987.

How to Enjoy Writing: A Book of Aid and Comfort, with Janet Asimov. New York, Walker, 1987.

Asimov's Annotated Gilbert and Sullivan. New York, Doubleday, 1988.

Relativity of Wrong: Essays on the Solar System and Beyond. New York, Doubleday, 1988; Oxford, Oxford University Press, 1989.

Library of the Universe (Did Comets Kill the Dinosaurs?; The Asteroids; Ancient Astronomy; Is There Life on Other Planets?; Jupiter, the Spotted Giant; Mercury, the Quick Planet; How Was the Universe Born?; Saturn, the Ringed Beauty; The Space Spotter's Guide; Unidentified Flying Objects; Earth, Our Home Base; The Birth and Death of Stars; Science Fiction, Science Fact; Space Garbage; Astronomy Today; Comets and Meteors, Mythology of the Universe; Pluto, a Double Planet?; Neptune; Piloted Space Flights; Projects in Astronomy; Rockets, Probes, and Satellites; Venus, a Shrouded Mystery; The World's Space Programs; Uranus: The Sideways Planet; Our Milky Way and Other Galaxies; The Earth's Moon; Our Solar System; Mars: Our Mysterious Neighbor; The Sun; Colonizing the Planets and Stars; What Causes Acid Rain?; What's Happening to the Ozone Layer?; Where Does Garbage Can?; Why Are Animals Endangered?; What Is an Eclipse?; Why Does the Moon Change Shape?; Why Are Some Beaches Oily?; Why Are the Rain Forests Vanishing?; Why Are the Whales Vanishing?; Why Does Litter Cause Problems?; Why Is the Air Dirty?; What Is a Shooting Star?; Why Do Stars Twinkle?; Why Do We Have Different Seasons?; Why Do People Come in Different Colors?, with Carrie Dierks; *Why Do Some People Wear Glasses?,* with Carrie Dierks; *Why Do We Need Sleep?,* with Carrie Dierks; *Why Do We Need to Brush Our Teeth?,* with Carrie Dierks; *How Does a Cut Heal?,* with Carrie Dierks; *How Do Airplanes Fly?,* with Elizabeth Kaplan; *How Do Big Ships Float?,* with Elizabeth Kaplan; *What Happens When I Flush the Toilet?,* with Elizabeth Kaplan; *How Does a TV Work?,* with Elizabeth Kaplan; *How Is Paper Made?,* with Elizabeth Kaplan; *The Future in Space,* with Robert Giraud; *The Planet Uranus,* with Francis Reddy). Milwaukee, Wisconsin, Stevens, 57 vols., 1988-94.

The Tyrannosaurus Prescription and 100 Other Essays. Buffalo, New York, Prometheus, 1989.

Asimov's Galaxy: Reflections on Science Fiction. New York, Doubleday, 1989.

Asimov on Science: A Thirty-Year Retrospective. New York, Doubleday, 1989.

Asimov's Chronology of Science and Discovery: How Science Has Shaped the World and How the World has Affected Science from 4,000,000 B.C. to the Present. New York, Harper, 1989.

Think about Space: Where Have We Been and Where Are We Going? (for children), with Frank White. New York, Walker, 1989.

All the Troubles of the World (for children). Mankato, Minnesota, Creative Education, 1989.

Robbie (for children). Mankato, Minnesota, Creative Education, 1989.

Franchise (for children). Mankato, Minnesota, Creative Education, 1989.

Sally (for children). Mankato, Minnesota, Creative Education, 1989.

The Complete Science Fair Handbook: For Teachers and Parents of Students in Grades 4-8, with Anthony D. Fredericks. Glenview, Illinois, Scott Foresman, 1990.

How Did We Find Out about Lasers? New York, Walker, 1990.

How Did We Find Out about Neptune? New York, Walker, 1990.

Secret of the Universe. New York, Doubleday, 1991.

Our Angry Earth, with Frederick Pohl. New York, Tor, 1991.

How Did We Find Out about Pluto? New York, Walker, 1991.

Asimov's Chronology of the World. New York and London, HarperCollins, 1991.

Asimov's Guide to Earth and Space. New York, Dutton, 1991; London, Mandarin, 1992.

Atom: Journey across the Subatomic Cosmos. New York, Dalton, 1991.

Christopher Columbus: Navigator to the New World (for children). Milwaukee, Wisconsin, Gareth Stevens, 1991.

Henry Hudson: Arctic Explorer and North American Adventurer, with Elizabeth Kaplan (for children). Milwaukee, Wisconsin, Gareth Stevens, 1991.

Frontiers: New Discoveries about Man and His Planet, Outer Space, and the Universe. New York, Plume, and London, Mandarin, 1991.

The March of the Millenia: A Key to Looking at History, with Frank White. New York, Walker, 1991.

Asimov Laughs Again: More Than 700 Favorite Jokes, Limericks and Anecdotes. New York, HarperCollins, 1992.

Frontiers II: More Recent Discoveries, with Janet Asimov. New York, Dutton, 1993.

I, Isaac Asimov: A Memoir: New York, Doubleday, 1994.

Yours, Isaac Asimov: A Lifetime of Letters, edited by Stanley Asimov. New York, Doubleday, 1995.

Editor, *The Hugo Winners 1-5.* Garden City, New York, Doubleday, 5 vols., 1962-86; 1 and 3, London, Dobson, 2 vols., 1963-67; 2, London, Sphere, 1973.

Editor, with Groff Conklin, *Fifty Short Fiction Tales.* New York, Collier, 1963.

Editor, *Tomorrow's Children.* Garden City, New York, Doubleday, 1966; London, Futura, 1974.

Editor, *Where Do We Go from Here?* Garden City, New York, Doubleday, 1971; London, Joseph, 1973.

Editor, *Nebula Award Stories Eight.* New York, Harper, and London, Gollancz, 1973.

Editor, *Before the Golden Age: A Science Fiction Anthology of the 1930s.* Garden City, New York, Doubleday, and London, Robson, 1974.

Editor, with Martin H. Greenberg and Joseph D. Olander, *100 Great Science Fiction Short-Short Stories.* Garden City, New York, Doubleday, and London, Robson, 1978.

Editor, with Martin H. Greenberg and Charles G. Waugh, *The Science Fictional Solar System.* New York, Harper, 1979; London, Sidgwick and Jackson, 1980.

Editor, With Martin H. Greenberg and Charles G. Waugh, *The Thirteen Crimes of Science Fiction.* Garden City, New York, Doubleday, 1979.

Editor, with Martin H. Greenberg, *The Great SF Stories 1-21.* New York, DAW, 21 vols., 1979-90.

Editor, with Martin H. Greenberg and Joseph D. Olander, *Microcosmic Tales: 100 Wondrous Science Fiction Short-Short Stories*. New York, Taplinger, 1980.

Editor, with Martin H. Greenberg and Joseph D. Olander, *Space Mail 1*. New York, Fawcett, 1980.

Editor, with Martin H. Greenberg and Joseph D. Olander, *The Future in Question*. New York, Fawcett, 1980.

Editor, with Alice Laurance, *Who Done It?* Boston, Houghton Mifflin, 1980.

Editor, with Martin H. Greenberg and Charles G. Waugh, *The Seven Deadly Sins of Science Fiction*. New York, Fawcett, 1980.

Editor, with Martin H. Greenberg and Joseph D. Olander, *Miniature Mysteries: 100 Malicious Little Mystery Stories*. New York, Taplinger, 1981.

Editor, with Martin H. Greenberg and Charles G. Waugh, *Science Fiction Shorts* series (for children; includes *After the End, Thinking Machines, Travels Through Time, Wild Inventions, Mad Scientists, Mutants, Tomorrow's TV, Earth Invaded, Bug Awful, Children of the Future, The Immortals, Time Warps*). Milwaukee, Raintree, 12 vols., 1981-84.

Editor, *Fantastic Creatures*. New York, Watts, 1981.

Editor, with Charles G. Waugh and Martin H. Greenberg, *The Best Science Fiction [Fantasy, Horror and Supernatural] of the 19th Century*. New York, Beaufort, 3 vols., 1981-83; *Science Fiction*, London, Gollancz, 1983; *Fantasy* and *Horror and Supernatural*, London, Robson, 2 vols., 1985.

Editor, *Asimov's Marvels of Science Fiction*. London, Hale, 1981.

Editor, with Carol-Lynn Rössell Waugh and Martin H. Greenberg, *The Twelve Crimes of Christmas*. New York, Avon, 1981.

Editor, with Charles G. Waugh and Martin H. Greenberg, *The Seven Cardinal Virtues of Science Fiction*. New York, Fawcett, 1981.

Editor, with Martin H. Greenberg and Charles G. Waugh, *TV: 2000*. New York, Fawcett, 1982.

Editor, with Martin H. Greenberg and Charles G. Waugh, *Last Man on Earth*. New York, Fawcett, 1982.

Editor, with Charles G. Waugh and Martin H. Greenberg, *Tantalizing Locked-Room Mysteries*. New York, Walker, 1982.

Editor, with Martin H. Greenberg and Charles G. Waugh, *Space Mail 2*. New York, Fawcett, 1982.

Editor, with J.O. Jeppson, *Laughing Space: Funny Science Fiction Chuckled Over*. Boston, Houghton Mifflin, and London, Robson, 1982.

Editor, with Alice Laurance, *Speculations*. Boston, Houghton Mifflin, 1982.

Editor, with Charles G. Waugh and Martin H. Greenberg, *Science Fiction from A to Z: A Dictionary of the Great Themes of Science Fiction*. Boston, Houghton Mifflin, 1982.

Editor, with Martin H. Greenberg and Charles G. Waugh, *Flying Saucers*. New York, Fawcett, 1982.

Editor, with Martin H. Greenberg and Charles G. Waugh, *Dragon Tales*. New York, Fawcett, 1982.

Editor, *Asimov's Worlds of Science Fiction*. London, Hale, 1982.

Editor, with Martin H. Greenberg and Charles G. Waugh, *Hallucination Orbit: Psychology in Science Fiction*. New York, Farrar Straus, 1983.

Editor, with Martin H. Greenberg, *Magical Worlds of Fantasy* series (*Wizards, Witches*). New York, Signet, 2 vols., 1983-84; as *Magical Worlds of Fantasy: Witches and Wizards*, New York, Bonanza, 1 vol., 1985.

Editor, with Martin H. Greenberg and Charles G. Waugh, *Caught in the Organ Draft: Biology in Science Fiction*. New York, Farrar Straus, 1983.

Editor, *The Big Apple Mysteries*. New York, Avon, 1983.

Editor, with George R.R. Martin and Martin H. Greenberg, *The Science Fiction Weight-Loss Book*. New York, Crown, 1983.

Editor, with Martin H. Greenberg and Charles G. Waugh, *Starships*. New York, Ballantine, 1983.

Editor, *Asimov's Wonders of the World*. London, Hale, 1983.

Editor, with George Zebrowski and Martin H. Greenberg, *Creations: The Quest for Origins in Story and Science*. New York, Crown, 1983; London, Harrap, 1984.

Editor, with Martin H. Greenberg and Charles G. Waugh, *Computer Crimes and Capers*. Chicago, Academy, 1983; London, Viking, 1985.

Editor, with Patricia S. Warrick and Martin H. Greenberg, *Machines That Think: The Best Science Fiction Stories about Robots and Computers*. New York, Holt Rinehart, and London, Allen Lane, 1984; as *War with the Robots*, New York, Wings, 1992.

Editor, with Terry Carr and Martin H. Greenberg, *100 Great Fantasy Short Short Stories*. Garden City, New York, Doubleday, and London, Robson, 1984.

Editor, with Charles G. Waugh and Martin H. Greenberg, *The Best Science Fiction Firsts*. New York, Beaufort, 1984; London, Robson, 1985.

Editor, with others, *Murder on the Menu*. New York, Avon, 1984.

Editor, with Martin H. Greenberg and Charles G. Waugh, *Sherlock Holmes through Time and Space*. New York, Bluejay, 1984; London, Severn House, 1985.

Editor, *Living in the Future*. New York, Beaufort, 1984.

Editor, with Martin H. Greenberg, *Isaac Asimov's Wonderful World of Science Fiction 2: The Science Fictional Olympics*. New York, Signet, 1984.

Editor, with Martin H. Greenberg and Charles G. Waugh, *Young Mutants, Extraterrestrials, Ghosts, Monsters, Star Travelers, Witches and Warlocks* (for children). New York, Harper, 6 vols., 1984-87.

Editor, with Martin H. Greenberg, *Election Day 2084: Stories about the Politics of the Future*. Buffalo, Prometheus, 1984.

Editor, with Martin H. Greenberg and Charles G. Waugh, *Baker's Dozen: 13 Short Science Fiction Novels*. New York, Bonanza, 1984; as *The Mammoth Book of Short Science Fiction Novels*, London, Robinson, 1986.

Editor, with Martin H. Greenberg and Charles G. Waugh, *Baker's Dozen: 13 Short Fantasy Novels*. New York, Greenwich House, 1984; as *The Mammoth Book of Short Fantasy Novels*, London, Robinson, 1986.

Editor, with Martin H. Greenberg and Charles G. Waugh, *Great Science Fiction Stories by the World's Great Scientists*. New York, Fine, 1985.

Editor, with Martin H. Greenberg and Charles G. Waugh, *Amazing Stories: 60 Years of the Best Science Fiction*. Lake Geneva, Wisconsin, TRS, 1985.

Editor, with Martin H. Greenberg and Charles G. Waugh, *Giants*. New York, Signet, 1985.

Editor, *Science Fiction Masterpieces*. New York, Galahad, 1986.

Editor, with Martin H. Greenberg and Charles G. Waugh, *Comets*. New York, Signet, 1986.

Editor, with Martin H. Greenberg and Charles G. Waugh, *Mythical Beasties*. New York, Signet, 1986; as *Mythic Beasts*, London, Robinson, 1988.

Editor, with Carol-Lynn Rössell Waugh and Martin H. Greenberg, *Hound Dunnit*. New York, Carroll and Graf, 1987; London, Robson, 1988.

Editor, with Martin H. Greenberg and Charles G. Waugh, *Cosmic Knights*. London, Robinson, 1987.

Editor, with Martin H. Greenberg and Charles G. Waugh, *The Best Crime Stories of the 19th Century*. New York, Dember, 1988; London, Robson, 1989.

Editor, with Jason A. Shulman, *Book of Science and Nature Quotations*. New York, Weidenfeld and Nicolson, 1988.

Editor, with Martin H. Greenberg and Charles G. Waugh, *Ghosts*. London, Collins, 1988.

Editor, with Martin H. Greenberg and Charles G. Waugh, *The Best Detective Stories of the 19th Century*. New York, Dember, 1988.

Editor, with Martin H. Greenberg and Charles G. Waugh, *The Mammoth Book of Classic Science Fiction: Short Novels of the 1930s*. New York, Carroll and Graf, and London, Robinson, 1988.

Editor, with Martin H. Greenberg and Charles H. Waugh, *Great Tales of Classic Science Fiction*. New York, Galahad, 1988.

Editor, with Martin H. Greenberg and Charles G. Waugh, *Monsters*. New York, Signet, 1988; London, Robinson, 1989.

Editor, with Martin H. Greenberg and Charles G. Waugh, *The Mammoth Book of Golden Age Science Fiction: Short Novels of the 1940s*. New York, Carroll and Graf, and London, Robinson, 1989.

Editor, with Martin H. Greenberg and Charles G. Waugh, *Curses*. New York, Signet, 1989.

Editor, with Martin H. Greenberg and Charles G. Waugh, *Tales of the Occult*. Buffalo, New York, Prometheus, 1989.

Editor, with Martin H. Greenberg and Charles G. Waugh, *Robots*. London, Robinson, 1989.

Editor, *The New Hugo Winners*. New York, Wynwood Press, 1989.

Editor, with Martin H. Greenberg and Charles G. Waugh, *The Mammoth Book of Vintage Science Fiction: Short Novels of the 1950s*. New York, Carroll and Graf, and London, Robinson, 1990.

Editor, with Martin H. Greenberg, *Cosmic Critiques: How and Why Ten Science Fiction Stories Work*. Writer's Digest, Cincinnati, Ohio, 1990.

Editor, with Martin H. Greenberg and Charles G. Waugh, *The Mammoth Book of New World Science Fiction: Short Novels of the 1960s*. London, Robinson, and New York, Carroll and Graf, 1991.

Editor, with Martin H. Greenberg and Charles G. Waugh, *The Mammoth Book of Fantastic Science Fiction: Short Novels of the 1970s*. London, Robinson, and New York, Carroll and Graf, 1992.

Editor, with Martin H. Greenberg and Charles G. Waugh, *The Mammoth Book of Modern Science Fiction: Short Novels of the 1980s*. London, Robinson, and New York, Carroll and Graf, 1993.

*

Bibliography: *Isaac Asimov: A Checklist of Works Published in the United States March 1939-May 1972* by Marjorie M. Miller, Kent, Ohio, Kent State University Press, 1972; in *In Joy Still Felt,* 1980.

Manuscript Collection: Mugar Memorial Library, Boston University.

Critical Studies: *Asimov Analyzed* by Neil Goble, Baltimore, Mirage Press, 1972; *The Science Fiction of Isaac Asimov* by Joseph F. Patrouch, Jr., Garden City, New York, Doubleday, 1974, London, Panther, 1976; *Isaac Asimov* edited by Joseph D. Olander and Martin H. Greenberg, New York, Taplinger, and Edinburgh, Harris, 1977; *Asimov: The Foundations of His Science Fiction* by George Edgar Slusser, San Bernardino, California, Borgo Press, 1980; *Isaac Asimov: The Foundations of Science Fiction* by James Gunn, New York and Oxford, Oxford University Press, 1982; *Isaac Asimov* by Jean Fielder and Jim Mele, New York, Ungar, 1982.

*   *   *

At the age of three, Isaac Asimov was brought to Brooklyn from Petrovichi, Russia, by penniless immigrant parents. He grew up in a series of candy stores, earned a Ph.D. in chemistry and reached the rank of associate professor at the Boston University School of Medicine, became a sought-after public speaker limited only by his dislike of travel and fear of flying, earned millions of dollars and, with more than 470 books, a reputation as the most prolific author of his generation, and died in Manhattan at the age of 72. His life and career were shaped by science fiction, and reflected its changes of fortune and status.

A dedicated fan who aspired to become a writer, Asimov graduated from membership in the Futurians to become the most Campbellian of John W. Campbell's writers for *Astounding Science Fiction,* visiting Campbell regularly to discuss ideas and drop off stories. The *Astounding* editor gave Asimov the idea, among others, for his signature story "Nightfall," codified the "three laws of robotics" of Asimov's robot stories, and helped shape the concept of "psychohistory" for Asimov's Foundation stories. Asimov repaid Campbell with loyalty and stories enriched by his own thoughtful development, his inventive details, and his carefully transparent prose. More than any other writer, Asimov became the symbol for SF's "Golden Age." He was the supreme rationalist, valuing clear thinking and cool logic above all else.

Unlike Robert A. Heinlein and A.E. van Vogt, the other two major writers of the Golden Age, Asimov, typically, was always a part-time SF writer, creating the greater portion of his Golden Age SF while a student at Columbia University. Like most writers of the period, for his first decade he wrote only short stories. He produced his first novel in 1950, when a 48,000-word novella commissioned for a magazine was rejected; he expanded it into *Pebble in the Sky* for the newly created Doubleday SF program. Asimov always considered himself a fortunate man, blessed by chance that turned even failure into greater success, editors who looked upon him as a son, and a dean who forced him to relinquish his academic position for full-time writing. At every turn his career confirmed the way events worked out for the best.

Inspired by the success of *Pebble in the Sky,* Asimov focused his efforts more on novels and expanded his ambition beyond Campbell and *Astounding* to H.L. Gold and the new magazine *Galaxy.* Later his vision would expand to other editors, particularly Anthony Boucher and *The Magazine of Fantasy & Science Fiction;* under another editor his relationship would develop into a monthly science column that Asimov would maintain until his final illness. But he was never a full-time writer until he resigned from his position at Boston University in 1958, and then, under the impetus of the Soviet Sputnik, he devoted most of his time to science popularizations, returning to SF only occasionally until his last decade. For the quarter of a century after Sputnik, except for short stories the only SF he produced was the novelization of *Fantastic Voyage* in 1966 and his Nebula and Hugo-winning novel *The Gods Themselves* in 1972.

Asimov's retreat from writing SF and venture into full-time writing of science popularizations coincided with a decline in the publishing of science fiction in magazines and books, and an upsurge in the publication of science books and articles, and *The Gods Themselves* coincided with the beginning of a new boom in SF publishing. Similarly, his return to the Foundation universe in 1983 with *Foundation's Edge* coincided with the beginning of science fiction's bestseller period, and all of Asimov's subsequent SF novels made one or more of the later bestseller lists. None of this was calculated. After meeting his and his family's basic financial needs, Asimov's chief concerns were his reputation as "one of our natural wonders and national resources," as Harvard Professor George G. Simpson put it, and getting paid for writing what he wanted to write. To that end, he had no agent and accepted whatever advance publishers would offer.

Asimov's developing audience paralleled science fiction's growing popular acceptance, even though Asimov's general reputation was built largely on his nonfiction. Even so, his science fiction writing stayed in public view; *The Foundation Trilogy* and his *I, Robot* were seldom, if ever, out of print. That readership would be available to make bestsellers out of his 1980s Foundation and robot novels.

Although Asimov got his degrees in chemistry and taught biochemistry, and he devoted much of his writing to scientific topics (he also wrote guides to Shakespeare and the Bible and joke books and almost anything else that appealed to him), with the exception of *The Gods Themselves,* science played little part in his novels. He was much more influenced by history, which he had once considered as a possible career. His robot stories, for instance, are written like mysteries in which the misbehavior of robots must be solved, and the science, such as the robots' "positronic brains," is mere convincing patter. His *Foundation* series, in which the next story is attached to the end of the preceding one like tinker toys, are exercises in ingenuity. They parallel the historic situation of the fall of Rome with the fall of a future galactic empire. To shorten the 20,000 years of barbarism predicted to follow the collapses of empire, Asimov created "psychohistory," a method of predicting the broad outlines of the future, and two "foundations" to guide recovery.

If Asimov had written nothing else, his robot stories and his Foundation stories would have established him as the Grand Master he was named by his fellow SF writers in 1986, and, with the exception of *Nemesis,* it was to his robot and Foundation novels that he returned in the 1980s, to weave his body of work together into one consistent future history.

As Asimov himself wrote in *The Rest of the Robots,* his robot stories rejected "the Frankenstein complex" in which the creature always turned against its creator in favor of technology with built-in safeguards. The safeguards Asimov developed for robots were the three laws of robotics, and the stories emerged from conflicts between the three laws, just as many traditional stories emerge from the conflicts between the laws of human behavior such as the Ten Commandments. Asimov could always come up with a new variation on the concept of the robot that 1) cannot harm a human, but 2) must obey a human order, and 3) avoid damage to itself.

Asimov's Robots novels, on the other hand, are formal "locked-room" mysteries in which robots, particularly R. Daneel Olivaw, play subordinate parts, Daneel as the "buddy" with whom Lije Baley

finally establishes a bond of affection and trust. But the Robots novels, beginning with *The Caves of Steel* and continuing with *The Naked Sun* (and in his bestselling period, *The Robots of Dawn*), also allowed Asimov to explore two kinds of future development based on machines, the agoraphobic Earthers in their covered cities and their opposites, the claustrophobic Spacers in their huge estates. Asimov's Robots novels, particularly *The Caves of Steel,* are arguably his finest fictional accomplishment, and he himself recognized this. The unyielding spinster robot expert Susan Calvin comes to life almost in spite of Asimov, but his characters were not Asimov's greatest concern: they are customarily defined more by their challenges than their pasts, and most are untroubled, rational solvers of problems. In addition, Asimov's intellectual dramas take place on a bare stage, like a courtroom for ideas. But in the Robots novels Lije Baley must conquer his own self-doubts in order to solve the crimes assigned to him; and his past, and the need to come to terms with it, requires Asimov to create the most richly imagined of any Asimov setting.

Of his other novels, his first, *Pebble in the Sky,* shares some of the character and scene-setting development of his Robots novels. His time-altering novel, *The End of Eternity,* provides a stylistically adventurous version of how reality-shifting might work and its consequences, and includes a troubled and believable hero. *The Gods Themselves,* Asimov's only novel in which his academic and scientific background provided material for his ideas and characters, is also his most convincing portrayal of aliens, and, although the novel is composed of three sequential novellas, the concepts and the characters are well developed. *The Stars Like Dust,* though it got serialized in *Galaxy,* and *The Currents of Space,* though it got serialized in *Astounding,* were Asimov's least successful novels.

But readers will remember Asimov for his robot stories and his Foundation series, and critics may record them as Asimov's chief contribution to SF literature. It was to those two concepts that he returned in 1983. At Doubleday's insistence that he write another SF novel, he produced *Foundation's Edge,* followed by *The Robots of Dawn, Robots and Empire, Foundation and Earth, Prelude to Foundation,* and *Forward the Foundation.* Of these, the most successful was *The Robots of Dawn,* returning to Lije Baley and Daneel and Gladia (of *The Naked Sun),* but all of the 1980s novels were characterized by Asimov's lucid prose and his astonishing ability to recreate the Asimov of the 1940s and 1950s. What he could not recreate, however, were the editors who helped him shape his earlier work, and his 1980s novels were longer and wordier than his best, perhaps encouraged by Doubleday's request for longer books that looked more like bestsellers.

Asimov's most fascinating post-1980s novels were the two that picked up the life of the inventor of psychohistory, Hari Seldon, before the events that launched the collected early stories published as *The Foundation Trilogy. Prelude to Foundation* begins after Hari Seldon's first speech on Trantor that announced the theory of psychohistory and suggested that a science of prediction might eventually be developed. *Prelude* and Asimov's posthumously published series of six novelettes, *Forward the Foundation,* allow Seldon to explore the roofed world of Trantor that is only hinted at in the earlier stories and show how Seldon learns enough about human behavior and historical process to perfect psychohistory. He has the indispensable help of Daneel, who has endured various transformations so that he can survive to guard humanity through various crises. In the process Daneel has developed a supplement to the three laws of robotics; in *Robots and Empire* that addition was called "the zeroth law." The zeroth law places the welfare of humanity over everything else. And thus, with a final Foundation volume, *Foundation and Earth,* Asimov brought to a conclusion and wove together his two great, continuing series, robots with no empire and a galactic empire with no robots.

All of this goes without mentioning Asimov's rich and varied production of short fiction, which, unlike the short fiction of most authors, has been collected and remains in print in various combinations. Of these nearly two hundred stories, "Nightfall" is best remembered as a classic of rationality faced with the unknown, and Asimov called his "The Last Question" "the best science fiction story every written." But he was fondest of two stories that seemed least Asimovian in that they privileged emotion over rationality: "The Ugly Little Boy" and "The Bicentennial Man." In Asimov's last years, the latter stories, along with "Nightfall," would be expanded into novels by Robert Silverberg.

Under the name of Paul French, Asimov wrote a series of six juvenile novels exploring the solar system with "Lucky Starr." They were later reprinted under his own name, with forewords correcting certain aspects of the novels, particularly information about the planets, that scientific discoveries had subsequently outmoded. He also wrote a superior adaptation of the screenplay for *Fantastic Voyage* and a novel for a sequel that was never made. With his second wife Janet, he co-authored several children's books about a robot named Norby.

At the end of *Forward the Foundation* Hari Seldon died "with the future he created unfolding all around him." That might have been Asimov's epitaph as well, but in Asimov's case, what was unfolding all around him was not only the future but the science fiction for which he had provided so solid a foundation.

—James Gunn

ASPRIN, Robert Lynn

Nationality: American. **Born:** St. Johns, Michigan, in 1946. **Education:** University of Michigan, Ann Arbor, 1964-1965. **Military Service:** Served in the United States Army, 1965-66. **Family:** Married to Anne Brett; one daughter and one son. **Career:** Accounts clerk, 1966-70, payroll analyst, 1970-74, and cost accountant, 1974-78, University Microfilm, Ann Arbor. Since 1978 freelance writer. **Awards:** *Locus* award, for editing, 1982. **Address:** c/o Ace Books, 200 Madison Avenue, New York, New York 10016, U.S.A.

SCIENCE FICTION PUBLICATIONS

Novels (series: Cold Cash War; Phule; Skeeve)

The Cold Cash War. New York, St. Martin's Press, and London, New English Library, 1977.
The Bug Wars. New York, St. Martin's Press, 1979; London, New English Library, 1980.
Tambu. New York, Ace, 1979.
Mirror Friend, Mirror Foe, with George Takei. Chicago, Playboy Press, 1979.
Myth Adventures (Skeeve). Garden City, New York, Doubleday, 1984.

Another Fine Myth. . . . (Skeeve). Norfolk, Virginia, Donning, 1978; revised edition, illustrated by Phil Foglio, 1986; London, Legend, 1988.
Myth Conceptions (Skeeve). Norfolk, Virginia, Donning, 1982; London, Legend, 1990.
Myth Directions (Skeeve). Norfolk, Virginia, Donning, 1982; London, Legend, 1990.
Hit or Myth (Skeeve). Norfolk, Virginia, Donning, 1983; London, Legend, 1990.
Myth Alliances (Skeeve). Garden City, New York, Doubleday, 1987.
Myth-ing Persons (Skeeve). Norfolk, Virginia, Donning, 1984; London, Legend, 1991.
Little Myth Marker (Skeeve). Norfolk, Virginia, Donning, 1985; London, Legend, 1991.
M.Y.T.H. Inc. Link (Skeeve). Norfolk, Virginia, Donning, 1986; London, Legend, 1991.
Myth-Nomers and Im-Pervections (Skeeve). Norfolk, Virginia, Donning, 1987; London, Legend, 1991.
Cold Cash Warrior: Combat Command in the World of Robert Asprin's Cold Cash War, with Bill Fawcett. New York, Ace, 1990.
M.Y.T.H. Inc. in Action (Skeeve). Norfolk, Virginia, Donning, 1990: London, Legend, 1991.
Phule's Company. New York, Ace, 1990: London, Legend, 1991.
Phule's Paradise. New York, Ace, and London, Legend, 1992.
The Myth-ing Omnibus (Skeeve; includes *Another Fine Myth . . . , Myth Conceptions,* and *Myth Directions*). London, Legend, 1992.
The Second Myth-ing Omnibus (Skeeve; includes *Hit or Myth, Myth-ing Persons,* and *Little Myth Marker*). London, Legend, 1992.
Catwoman: Tiger Hunt, with Lynn Abbey. New York, Warner, 1992; London, Millennium, 1993.
Sweet Myth-tery of Life (Skeeve). Norfolk, Virginia, Donning, 1994.

Graphic Novels (series: Duncan and Mallory; Skeeve; Thieves' World)

Myth Adventures One (Skeeve), with Phil Folgio. Norfolk, Virginia, Donning, 1985.
Myth Adventures Two (Skeeve), with Phil Folgio. Norfolk, Virginia, Donning, 1985.
Thieves' World Graphics, Volume One, with Tim Sale and Lynn Abbey. Norfolk, Virginia, Donning, 1986.
Thieves' World Graphics 1, with Tim Sale and Lynn Abbey. Norfolk, Virginia, Donning, 1986.
Thieves' World Graphics 2, with Tim Sale and Lynn Abbey. Norfolk, Virginia, Donning, 1986.
Thieves' World Graphics 3, with Tim Sale and Lynn Abbey. Norfolk, Virginia, Donning, 1986.
Duncan and Mallory, with Mel White. Norfolk, Virginia, Donning, 1986.
Thieves' World Graphics 4, with Tim Sale and Lynn Abbey. Norfolk, Virginia, Donning, 1987.
Duncan and Mallory: The Bar-None Ranch, with Mel White. Norfolk, Virginia, Donning, 1987.
Thieves' World Graphics 5, with Tim Sale and Lynn Abbey. Norfolk, Virginia, Donning, 1987.
Duncan and Mallory: The Raiders, with Mel White. Norfolk, Virginia, Donning, 1988.
Thieves' World Graphics 6, with Tim Sale and Lynn Abbey. Norfolk, Virginia, Donning, 1988.

OTHER PUBLICATIONS

Other (series: Elfquest; Thieves' World)

Editor, *Sanctuary* (Thieves' World). Garden City, New York, Doubleday, 1982.
  Editor, *Thieves' World*. New York, Ace, 1979.
  Editor, *Tales from the Vulgar Unicorn* (Thieves' World). New York, Ace, 1980.
  Editor, *Shadows of Sanctuary* (Thieves' World). New York, Ace, 1981.
Editor, with Lynn Abbey, *Cross-Currents* (Thieves' World). Garden City, New York, Doubleday, 1984.
  Editor, *Storm Season* (Thieves' World). New York, Ace, 1982.
  Editor, with Lynn Abbey, *The Face of Chaos* (Thieves' World). New York, Ace, 1983.
  Editor, with Lynn Abbey, *Wings of Omen* (Thieves' World). New York, Ace, 1984.
Editor, with Lynn Abbey, *The Shattered Sphere* (Thieves' World). Garden City, New York, Doubleday, 1986.
  Editor, with Lynn Abbey, *The Dead of Winter* (Thieves' World). New York, Ace, 1985.
  Editor, with Lynn Abbey, *Soul of the City* (Thieves' World). New York, Ace, 1986.
  Editor, with Lynn Abbey, *Blood Ties* (Thieves' World). New York, Ace, 1986.
Editor, with Richard Pini and Lynn Abbey, *The Blood of Ten Chiefs* (Elfquest). New York, Tor, 1986.
Editor, with Richard Pini and Lynn Abbey, *Wolfsong: The Blood of Ten Chiefs* (Elfquest). New York, Tor, 1988.
Editor, with Lynn Abbey, *The Price of Victory* (Thieves' World). Garden City, New York, Doubleday, 1990.
  Editor, with Lynn Abbey, *Aftermath* (Thieves' World). New York, Ace, 1987.
  Editor, with Lynn Abbey, *Uneasy Alliances* (Thieves' World). New York, Ace, 1988.
  Editor, with Lynn Abbey, *Stealers' Sky* (Thieves' World). New York, Ace, 1989.

                    *   *   *

One of the more energetic and interesting SF writers to emerge since the late 1970s, Robert Asprin compiled a most impressive record for productivity in his early years. His first book, *The Cold Cash War,* introduced themes present in most of his later works, and which can be traced, at least in part, to Asprin's preliterary occupation. He had been a cost accountant for a large "high-tech" corporation, and was thoroughly familiar with corporate procedures and the problems of management and personal rivalries within the corporate environment.

In *The Cold Cash War,* Asprin posits growing impatience and dissatisfaction on the part of large corporations with governmental mandates and unresponsiveness. In this situation, the corporations form private armies; when the government, through its official army, tries to suppress this odd rebellion, the corporations triumph as a result of possessing superior technology and more effective means of troop-motivation. This book is somewhat limited in characterization and plot, but shows excellent powers of technological and sociological extrapolation, at least in the near-future range.

The Bug Wars, Asprin's second science fiction novel (a fantasy novel of very different nature intervened), continued the military theme, and is a worthy experiment, but unfortunately fails seriously. Asprin portrays an interplanetary struggle between a race of highly advanced, highly militaristic, intelligent reptiles and a coalition of huge insects. The narration is from the viewpoint of the reptiles, and it is uncertain to both the reptiles and the reader whether the insects are truly intelligent or not. A background rationale involves a mysterious elder race which had been instrumental in the spread of the insects through space. There is also passing mention of small warm-blooded animals, the reader being free to speculate as to whether these are pre-human beings, true humans of a degraded culture, or simply warm-blooded animals. A novel told completely from the viewpoint of a reptilian alien and involving no identifiable human characters was a most ambitious undertaking. The result, unfortunately, was a thoroughly one-dimensional book devoted almost entirely to the military details of battle; without characters suitable for reader empathy or identification, the volume makes poor reading. It is further marred by numerous minor solecisms and clichés. Asprin also has suffered from poor editing.

Tambu shows marked improvement. It is the story of a band of professional pirate-hunters, laid against the background of a future interstellar trading culture. The structure of the book is unnecessarily cluttered with excerpts from a supposed interview at the end of Tambu's career, between which Asprin intersperses major incidents in his life. But the storytelling is brisk, the characterization indicates considerable progress, and a feel is achieved, at least sporadically, that is reminiscent of the old *Planet Stories* or E.E. Smith space operas.

Asprin's collaborative novel, *Mirror Friend, Mirror Foe,* was written with George Takei, the actor best known for his continuing role in the *Star Trek* series. In this novel, against a background of intercorporate espionage and cold war, the authors place a corporate spy within a robot-manufacturing concern. The spy's heritage derives from the Japanese ninja; this, presumably, is Takei's contribution while Asprin's is the corporate situation. From a promising start, the book unfortunately degenerates into cliché as the robots, escaping from their normal conditioning, go lurching and clanking about a planet murdering every human being they encounter.

Despite his promising start as a science fiction writer, Asprin achieved far greater success in the allied field of fantasy, and by the mid-1980s had largely abandoned science fiction. His fantasy novel *Myth Conceptions* initiated a series of slapstick adventures in-and-out of an Arabian Nights universe of *jinni,* homunculi, spells, dragons, and gorgeous women. Within the familiar realm of published fantasy, Asprin's *Myth* series (all the books are pun-named) bears comparison to the works of L. Sprague de Camp. Asprin himself claims inspiration in the Bing Crosby/Bob Hope/Dorothy Lamour "Road" films of the 1940s.

Even more successful than the *Myth* books is Asprin's series of *Thieves' World* anthologies. The concept is essentially that of a vaguely Robert E. Howard-type barbarian culture, against which any number of stories can be laid by any number of authors. The anthologies have proved so successful that an entire mini-industry has sprung up around them, with authors using the Thieves' World setting for novels of their own, and with adaptations into comic books, role-playing games, video games, and the prospect of further, varied merchandising and adaptations.

Despite the success of his *Myth* and *Thieves' World* enterprises, Asprin has continued to move in slightly new directions. His collaborative novels in the Duncan and Mallory series, written with Mel White, demonstrate the typical Asprin characteristics of rapid pace, slapstick action, and broad humor. Asprin's continuing success indicates that he was wise to abandon his earlier attempts at serious science fiction and to concentrate instead on humorous fantasy. In this realm he has found his place in a longstanding tradition, and won a large and enthusiastic following, largely of teenage and preteen readers.

—Richard A. Lupoff

ATKINS, Frank. *See* AUBREY, Frank.

ATTANASIO, A.A.

Nationality: American. **Born:** Newark, New Jersey, 20 September 1951. **Education:** University of Pennsylvania, 1969-73, B.A.; Columbia University, New York, 1973-75, M.F.A.; New York, University, 1975-76, M.A. **Agent:** Russell Galen, Scovil Chichak Galen Literary Agency, 381 Park Avenue, New York, New York 10022. **Address:** 1322 Kaeleku Street, Honolulu, Hawaii 96825, U.S.A. **Online Address:** aaa@lava.net.

SCIENCE FICTION PUBLICATIONS

Novels (series: Radix Tetrad)

Radix. New York, Morrow, 1981; London, Corgi, 1982.
In Other Worlds (Radix Tetrad). New York, Morrow, 1984; London, Corgi, 1986.
Arc of the Dream (Radix Tetrad). New York, Bantam, 1986; London, Grafton, 1988.
Wyvern. New York, Ticknor and Fields, 1988; London, Grafton, 1989.
The Last Legends of Earth (Radix Tetrad). Norwalk, Connecticut, Easton Press, and London, Grafton, 1989.
Hunting the Ghost Dancer. New York, HarperCollins, and London, Grafton, 1991.
Kingdom of the Grail. New York and London, HarperCollins, 1992.
The Moon's Wife. New York, HarperCollins, 1993; London, New English Library, 1994.
Solis. New York, HarperCollins, and London, New English Library, 1994.

Short Stories

Beastmarks. Willimantic, Connecticut, Ziesing, 1984.

*

A.A. Attanasio comments:

We live by our fictions, all of us immersed in the strange zone we call the imagination, that weird place that, when all is said and done, is the only place we ever are. Each of us is a dream grounded by the inescapable facts of existence, continually striving to rise above the loneliness and wretchedness of life by the magic of our hopes, visions, ambitions. The stories we tell ourselves define us in our struggle against our relentless limits. So, I write fantastic stories, where reality is dismembered and we can better remember who we are.

*   *   *

At times, the prose of A.A. Attanasio reminds one of the magic realism of Marquez or Borges. There is the same sense of a world existing just beyond reach, the same wonder when things familiar suddenly become unfamiliar, not because they have changed, but because the world around them has suddenly shifted to a different viewpoint. This is the hallmark of Attanasio's approach to science fiction and fantasy: to take the familiar conventions of the genres and change the world around them so that they are suddenly seen in a new light.

Attanasio is primarily a visualist. The worlds he creates are vivid, drawn in lucent and poetic detail. He is more comfortable with descriptions of primitive settings than with technological worlds, but this seems only to be because the natural world, particularly unspoiled nature, offers more scope for description. This is not to say that his visions of the constructed world are inferior to those of the natural world. Rather, his visualizations of cities and machines explicitly demonstrate the barrenness inherent in cold stone and metal. His descriptions of nature are celebrations of fertility and the possibilities which lie in growth and change. At times, the elaboration of description goes a fraction too far, into a sort of neo-classic coyness—"blood drum" for heart or "path of heaven" for the sky. But rather than expressions of a rococo conventionality, these are exuberant outbursts of playful inventiveness, of an intellect hovering on the edges of being word-drunk.

Even though Attanasio celebrates natural forces, he is quite at home with the pseudoscientific explanations that are part of science fiction. His scientific justification of the disappearance of Carl Schirmer, in *In Other Worlds,* is clear and scientifically accurate, or, at least as scientifically accurate as is necessary to explain the plot device. But the scientific jargon is only a means to an end, a necessary function that has to be got out of the way to make the story happen. It is not central to any of Attanasio's stories, save that science, in the form of a natural or quasi-natural phenomena, makes the story possible. Instead, what is central to Attanasio is the human reaction to a changed world.

At times the world itself changes around the protagonist. This is the case in *Radix.* The entire world has changed as a result of crossing the path of a beam of radiation from a black hole in the centre of the galaxy. It is now a world of the timeloose, godminds, voors, orts, yawps and some few unchanged humans. The social structures that exist are parodies of those which existed before the change. Into this world comes Sumner Kagan, a white-card whose genetic material is free from distortion, also the Sugarat, the secret nemesis of the street gangs who infest the city. Kagan reacts to the world around viscerally, rather than heroically. He kills the street gangs because he fears them, then he begins to kill them because it gives him a feeling of power. He is not an admirable creature, but, throughout the course of the story, as he is pared down to the base of what he is, as the powers latent within him emerge, he becomes admirable. He triumphs over his doubts and fears, over his many weaknesses, and changes the world around him positively, rather than destructively.

This kind of evolution is typical of Attanasio. His concern seems to be with the way in which humanity can triumph over the most fearful forms of oppression or prejudice, by conquering the self first. In *Wyvern,* the protagonist Jaki Gefjon is a social outcast, a product of the liaison between a Borneo native and a Dutch trader. He becomes the protege of a shaman, who sees the powers within the boy. As Jaki grows to manhood, he must overcome his fears of the world and of what lies within him, in order to realize his potential. As he grows, he moves out of his restricted jungle world, and comes into contact with Western society, as the second in command to a pirate. It is here that he is faced with an entirely new spectrum of challenges, which he must face and overcome. The most deadly of these is the pirate-chaser Captain Quarles, who engages in a deadly vendetta when his daughter falls in love with Jaki, runs away with him and marries him. The pursuit follows throughout the East Indies and much of Asia, with death and revenge commonplace, to a final confrontation in the Americas. It is here, through the complete and utter acceptance of his humanity, through a demonstration of the innate humanity which Quarles has hidden from himself throughout his life, and which drove his daughter from him, that Jaki triumphs.

It is this which marks all of Attansio's work; the quest of the protagonist, although it may be framed in terms of high adventure, is an internal quest. Quite simply, they are looking for what makes them what they are, in order to know themselves. This quest, which would, in the hands of a lesser writer, be a sterile investigation of modern angst, is an invigorating, emotional experience, because Attanasio is not only a writer of humanity, but a writer of the joy of humanity.

—Ian Nichols

AUBREY, Frank

Pseudonym for Francis Harry "Frank" Atkins. Also wrote as Frank Atkins. **Other Pseudonyms:** Fenton Ash; Fred Ashley. **Nationality:** British. **Born:** 1840. **Career:** Grew up in South Wales. Studied engineering. Wrote serials for boys' papers in 1900s; film critic for a London Sunday paper. **Died:** 1927.

SCIENCE FICTION PUBLICATIONS

Novels (series: Monella in all books)

The Devil-Tree of El Dorado: A Romance of British Guiana. London, Hutchinson, 1896; New York, New Amsterdam, 1897.
A Queen of Atlantis: A Romance of the Caribbean Sea. London, Hutchinson, 1899; Philadelphia, Lippincott, 1900.
The King of the Dead: A Weird Romance. London, Macqueen, 1903; New York, Arno Press, 1978.

Novels as Fenton Ash

The Radium Seekers; or, The Wonderful Black Nugget. London, Pitman, 1905.

A Trip to Mars (for children). London, Chambers, 1909; New York, Arno Press, 1975.
By Airship to Ophir (for children). London, Shaw, 1911.
The Black Opal: A Romance of Thrilling Adventure (for children). London, Shaw, 1915; New York, Arno Press, 1975.

Novel as Fred Ashley

The Temple of Fire; or, The Mysterious Island. London, Pitman, 1905.

Short Stories

Strange Stories of Hospitals. London, Pearson, 1898.

OTHER PUBLICATIONS

Novel

A Studio Mystery. London, Jarrolds, 1897.

*   *   *

At the turn of the century, Frank Atkins, using the name Frank Aubrey and other pen names, wrote fiction containing elements of what critics today term speculative fiction. To call Atkins a science fiction writer, however, would be to push him into a category that his writing fits only at certain key points: in theme and plot, in characters, and in style. Atkins's work suits his time and place, but in at least one novel, *A Trip to Mars,* he explored possibilities only hinted at by a few other writers and cinematic directors of his time.

Atkins stretched coincidence to the limit in certain areas. He hypothesized lost civilizations on Earth—the remains of Atlantis in the middle of the Sargasso Sea, El Dorado on a mountain top in an unexplored region of South America—in four of his books. Only in *A Trip to Mars* did he move beyond the Earth. He frequently postulated long-lost relatives; the conflict often revolves around the good characters overcoming powerful forces of evil. But Atkins's outcomes are pat, and he prepared his reader well with very broad hints for any surprise.

Atkins strived for believability in his settings, giving lengthy descriptions with numerous footnotes of the flora and fauna both in South America and in the Sargasso Sea, though there are many descriptions of the fantastic in all his books—giant flowers, fruits, animals, huge dazzling jewels and massive amounts of gold. He also frequently hypothesized seers who make accurate, if nonspecific predictions, usually astrologically. Atkins's only real speculative scientific developments occur in his "red ray" (*King of the Dead*) and spaceship (*A Trip to Mars*). "Hard" scientific developments play a minimal part in his books.

Most of Atkins's characters are, at best, stereotypes. His infrequent attempts at lightheartedness generally occur when he introduces a lower-class Englishman (usually a sailor) with a droll, uneducated accent, uttering malapropisms. His evil characters are in all senses malevolent and frequently seem to be in league with some never-explained Dark Power. Only in *King of the Dead* does he portray a Power of Evil, called Mahrimah, who resembles a fallen angel. All the books have as protagonists male "chums" who are young, adventuresome, and typically British. Of lesser importance are the young women, generally the love interests of one or both of the chums; some are exotic, some are classically British, but without exceptions coy and beautiful, and they are frequently endangered by natural or human foes. This is true even for Vanina, the queen of *A Queen of Atlantis,* who actually plays a very passive role in the plot. While in all of Atkins's books the good characters consistently behave nobly, most of the books contain a totally noble figure as well. In the Monella novels, this character is Monella himself, a noble figure of great age who is roaming the world until he can regain his throne in El Dorado; in *King of the Dead* the noble figure is Lorenzo, née Manzoni, who is even more enigmatic than Monella. They are consistently wise, strong, compelling, and remote, and both also have to atone for some sin (primarily caused by leaving their people and venturing into the real world) by admitting their error and setting things to rights.

Atkins's style is probably the most interesting feature of his books. Atkins used the common technique of ending each chapter with a hint of what is to come, and it does serve its purpose—to keep the reader reading. Atkins used much description in his books, which is fortunate since his dialogue is often formal and stilted. Atkins's point of view is consistently third-person, but the particular outlook of each chapter varies. Atkins was at his best when describing the exotic features of his setting—costly and beautiful architecture, elaborate costumes, wonderful jewels. He excelled at choosing exotic names for people, places, animals, and gods—Ivanta, Alondra, Mellenda, Ullama, Lyostrah, Morveena. The tension in his novels frequently revolves around encounters with natural but terrifying animals, such as cuttlefish, enormous snakes, gorilla-type animals, pumas, and most of his novels feature supernatural monsters such as zombies, vampires, and most particularly, the devil-tree in the novel of that name. The devil-tree, a huge tree which seizes its victims in tentacle-like branches and conveys them to its maw, a hollow trunk, is fully as terrifying and loathsome as any creation of current writers of horror novels or directors of horror movies. After the tree consumes the victims, it releases them, or what is left of them, to be carried off and eaten by crocodile-like monsters who live in a pond at its base. In the climactic scene at the end of the novel, the evil priests are all seized and eaten, some by the tree, and some are torn to bits by the monsters as the priests are held in the tree's tentacles awaiting their turn in its maw. The nightmarish effectiveness of this description is such that its image remains vivid in the readers' minds long after they have finished the book itself.

In fact, if Atkins's writing is akin to speculative fiction, it is certainly supernatural and horror fiction that it most resembles. He worked with settings that are largely unknown to his world, but it is their exotic quality rather than any science fiction aspect which he developed. Only in *A Trip to Mars* does Atkins extrapolate any scientific devices, and these are fanciful, based on principles long since outdated. Additionally, the Mars which Atkins depicts is so similar to his exotic settings on Earth as to be interchangeable, and his Martian characters are certainly no less human, in physical features or in outlook, than the characters in his Earth-based novels. Nevertheless, Atkins's books are still interesting reading, particularly in editions which contain the quaint original illustrations.

—Karren C. Edwards

———

AVERY, Richard. *See* **COOPER, Edmund.**

———

AYRE, Thornton. *See* **FEARN, John Russell.**

B

BAHL, Franklin. *See* PHILLIPS, Rog.

———

BAIN, Ted. *See* TUBB, E.C.

———

BAIRD, Wilhelmina

Pseudonym for Joyce (Carstairs) Hutchinson; has also written as Kathleen James. **Nationality:** British. **Born:** Dunfermline, Scotland, 16 February 1935. **Education:** Village school, Lybster, Caithness, Scotland, 1940-42; Scarborough Girls' High School, Yorkshire, England, 1945-53; University of Sheffield, England, B.A., 1956; University of Birmingham, 1976-86. **Family:** Married James R. Hutchinson, 1960 (separated). **Career:** Teacher, Wisewood Secondary School, Sheffield, England, 1958-62; lecturer, later senior lecturer in English literature, Crewe College of Education, 1962-66; Workers' Educational Association; University adult courses, University of Keele, N. Staffs, England; tutor in English, Macclesfield Technical College, English; tutor and counsellor (specializing in disabled adults), Open University, Manchester and Birmingham; teaching English literature, 1974-88; examiner for various boards in English language and literature. Moved to France, 1988. **Member:** Authors' Guild, 1994; Science Fiction Writers of America, 1994. **Agent:** Matthew Bialer, William Morris Agency, 1350 Avenue of the Americas, New York, NY 10019, U.S.A. **Address:** 27 rue Montesquieu, 67800 Miramont-de-Guyenne, France.

SCIENCE FICTION PUBLICATIONS

Novels

Crashcourse. New York, Ace Books, 1993.
Clipjoint. New York, Ace Books, 1994.

Short Stories

Author of numerous published and uncollected short stories.

*

Wilhelmina Baird comments:

I got into two kinds of cosmos before I was 10: What It's Like Out There from my grandfather, who gave me an encyclopedia and his copy of *The Mysterious Universe,* and What It's *Really* Like Out There from an uncle, who threw me the mag he'd been reading on the train. Don't remember what it was, but it had a pink bug-eyed monster with knobbles on the cover, plus a guy in a spacesuit and a bare-ass bim in a fishbowl and superhigh heels. The truly *classic* classic scenario.

It was 1943 and Woolworth's was full of American pulp fiction that came over on troopships. My mother believed reading was good for you. Hence my childhood of Great Classic Garbage. I'm also sold on comic books and good bad movies. A friend introduced me to Chandler in Penguin later.

My family took it as Q.E.D. that if you read, you also wrote. When I was five we were 30 miles south of John O'Groats in the blackout under 12 feet of snow, waiting for a German invasion. The wind blew you over in the village street, the houses were lighted with kerosene and heated with peat and basically reading was all there was to do. You could knit if you wanted.

SF got me to University. I was plain, fat, spotty, and silent. I flunked interviews the way I breathed. When I had to talk for my life I could see it, wasn't worth it so when the guy asked "What do you read?," I said "*Astounding Science Fiction.*" We chewed over Asimov and Heinlein for the next 30 minutes and I walked away with an open scholarship to study English Literature (which ruined my style forever, but you can't have it all.)

It taught me the virtues of the phrase, "What the hell." Results vary, but it *always* beats knitting.

I believe in Big Science. It's the only thing you can watch on TV without wanting to cut your throat, and the guys who practice it look like happy people. There aren't a lot of those around.

But I also believe in fiction, because I've met reality. Reality's Marvin, the Paranoid Android. "God, it's so *boring.*" It's what they'll be whining on the warpdrive liners as they cross the Galaxy. I-am-so-*bored.* The-food-here-is-lousy. Have-you-seen-my-*tax*-bill? Have-you-met-my-*wife?* Oh,-God,-you-wouldn't-*believe*-my-mother-in-law. (It's basically the women's fault.)

We're the only people having fun. You need fiction to know what it's *really* like, the guys who actually do it are bored senseless.

Specifically, I believe in SF, I learned philosophy from it as a kid. It looks out instead of in. What really bores *me* is the lint in other people's belly buttons. I'm personally dying quite adequately on my own, been at it 60 years, I had the practice, you don't have to force your way in and tell me how it's done. Tell me a story instead. At its best it's inspirational; even when it's bad it can be dumb and funny. Those are *virtues.* And what the hell.

* * *

Sometimes timing is everything. "Wilhelmina Baird" is the latest incarnation of a writer who was first published in SF back in the 1960s, three short stories which fell into undeserved obscurity, probably because nearly 30 years passed before the author returned to science fiction. Although none of these were classics, "The Blind God's Eye," written as by Kathleen James, is a thoughtful, well-characterized novelette about a young woman who becomes involved with the assassination of a prominent opposition candidate in a future Britain struggling to define itself in the aftermath of a new wave of immigrants, this time from Russia. She falls in love with the assassin, who turns out to be an android programmed with a dead man's personality. The central plot is secondary to the relationship between the two principle characters, which is quite skillfully developed, and although we only see future Britain through her limited perceptions, there are strong resonances between that society and conflicts we're experiencing today.

Almost three decades later, Baird made her debut with *Crashcourse,* one of the most interesting first novels of the 1990s. The style was very different from that of the short fiction, although still heavily character-driven despite a much greater effort to flesh in the details of the futuristic environment. Some reviewers have categorized *Crashcourse* and its sequel, *Clipjoint,* as cyberpunk, but the two stories are not so easily pigeonholed. Certainly that term has come to refer to variations of an intricately technological near-future dystopia, with emphasis on virtual reality, human-machine interfaces, and other associated devices, and Baird's two novels do in fact reflect these motifs. It would be a mistake, however, to use that label, which is an oversimplification of two very sophisticated stories that explore the way people make use of each other as resources rather than speculate on our interaction with technology. In fact, the scientific element is essentially secondary in both books, which are more concerned with exploitation than exploration. Nor is Baird's vision uniformly bleak. Despite the evident loss of human values by society in general in her future, many individual characters still retain a sense of honor and personal loyalty.

Crashcourse follows the adventures of a group of friends who agree to be the subjects of a new art form, an enhanced movie-recording device which follows you in real time and allows the audience to plug themselves into your mind, experience what you experience, vicariously. Cassandra, Moke, and Dosh decide that it's a harmless way to make a considerable amount of money in a short period of time and for comparatively little effort, although they will be surrendering their privacy for the duration. And so it might have been if one of the cast hadn't turned out to be an insane murderer, and if the producers hadn't been in collusion to conceal this fact. They recognize that the undercurrent of danger is a great plot device, and if the central characters die, they can always be replaced by other would-be stars. In fact, they might even help the murderer along a little, just for dramatic effect, of course. Baird develops the intertwined plot lines with remarkable skill for a first novel, and resolves everything neatly despite the fact that it was the opening volume in a series. The survivors enjoy limited revenge and decide to leave Earth for their own safety, but they subsequently return for the sequel.

Clipjoint is in many ways superior to its predecessor, although the setting is now a familiar one and some of the explication is necessarily redundant. Cassandra and Moke have prospered since leaving the home world, but they return after seeing part of a new holofilm that features an actor who is an exact double for their friend Dosh, killed in the first book. Is Dosh actually alive after all, or is it just his body? Unable to leave the question unresolved, they reluctantly book passage back to Earth and investigate.

The actor in question insists that he is not their former friend, and appears to be telling the truth in as much as that is concerned. But they stumble across another mystery, because neither is he the person he claims to be. Their investigations lead them to a secret project to extend human life, a process that has hidden drawbacks that are revealed as the story unfolds.

Baird employs a complex, flashy style to portray her world, hinting at its intricacies instead of spelling out each and every detail. Her protagonists banter entertainingly throughout, and their caustic view of the world around them helps to make it more real for the reader. The concluding volume in the series, *Psykosis,* is scheduled to appear in 1995. It will be interesting to see if Baird can build on her already considerable skills for her next project.

—Don D'Ammassa

BAKER, Sharon

Nationality: American. **Born:** San Francisco, California, 10 May 1938. **Education:** Mills College, Oakland, California, B.A. 1960; University of Washington, Seattle, M.L.S., 1966. **Family:** Married Gordon P. Baker in 1963; four sons. **Career:** Magazine editor and public relations copywriter, Pacific Northwest Bell, Seattle, 1961-62; librarian and curator of historical services, Boeing Airplane Company, Seattle, 1962-63; college recruiter and administrative assistant, University of Washington, 1963; physician's assistant, Seattle, Washington, 1963-66. Since 1980, writer. **Died:** 4 June 1991.

SCIENCE FICTION PUBLICATIONS

Novels (series: Naphar in all titles)

Quarreling, They Met the Dragon. New York, Avon, 1984.
Journey to Membliar. New York, Avon, 1987.
Burning Tears of Sassurum. New York, Avon, 1988.

Short Stories

"House Hunter" in *Walls of Blood,* edited by Kathryn Cramer, New York, Morrow, 1990.

*   *   *

Sharon Baker once said that she invents as little as possible in her fiction, a comment that at first may appear puzzling to readers of her three richly inventive novels about life on the violent planet Naphar. But apart from the astronomical and biological wonders of this imaginary world, her fiction also addresses such too-familiar issues as racism (which Naphar society bases on height), rape (both hetero- and homosexual), prostitution, child abuse, slavery, suicide, drugs, environmental destruction (even depletion of atmospheric ozone), and political and economic corruption. The acknowledgments of her novels reveal that she has interviewed not only biologists and astronomers, but street hustlers and narcotics cops as well.

Baker's first published novel, *Quarreling, They Met the Dragon,* introduces the rigid, anti-technological slave society of Naphar, broadly patterned after civilizations of the ancient Near East. Naphar's two dominant races, the tall Rabu and the shorter Kakanu, are both descended from human settlers who crossbred with native species. Senruh, a half-breed boy who earns his living as a prostitute, escapes his master and joins with Pell Maru, a Kakanu boy who is also an escaped slave. Together, they escape from the city of Qaqqadum and are sheltered by the spacers, humans who maintain a trade and research mission on Naphar and who represent the only contact with a vaguely described galactic civilization. What is perhaps most remarkable about the novel is its sensitive account of the growing love between two adolescent boys, and the unusually frank scenes of sexuality that give the narrative a dimension of sensuality unusual in most fantasy and science fiction. The novel has received inadequate critical attention possibly because its title (derived from a line of epic poetry quoted in the text) suggests a traditional quest fantasy. In fact, there are no dragons in the story at all.

Journey to Membliar and *Burning Tears of Sassurum* are really two parts of a single novel, *Spring of the Twin Moons,* which Baker had worked on extensively prior to the publication of *Quarreling, They Met the Dragon.* The narrative concerns Ricassia Addiratu, a tall Rabu who has been enslaved by the smaller Kakanu of the highlands of Naphar; her master, the boy Tadge; and Jarell Adon, a Kakanu who becomes a slave among Ricassia's people. Opposing them is the evil Salimar, who seeks possession of the legendary Mindstone in order to establish a reign of terror over Naphar. The Mindstone, which acts as a kind of amplifier of psychic energy, has been stolen by Jarell, who hopes to use it as a means of realizing his dream of going into space. *Journey to Membliar* follows the familiar quest structure of many fantasy narratives, as the three protagonists are brought together in a kind of mock family structure and seek to escape from Salimar with the Mindstone. They find their way to Membliar, an underground realm where they are protected by the mysterious Beloved, the vampire-like but benevolent third race which inhabits Naphar.

Burning Tears of Sassurum (the title refers to a periodic meteor shower on Naphar) takes place mostly in the capital city of Qaqqadum, where Ricassia discovers she is the lost daughter of the ruling priestess, and where the final struggle against Salimar takes place. Again, the surface narrative carries the suggestion of traditional fantasy, but an extraordinary degree of science fictional detail underlies this exotic world. The deadly sunlight of Naphar, for example, is the result of an ancient failed experiment in deepening the atmosphere's protective radiation belts; vampirism and cannibalism are necessitated by protein deficiencies in native foodstuffs; even the magical Mindstone is a psychic transmitter left by the original settlers, who are able to observe the history of Naphar over the centuries by virtue of relativistic time distortions brought on by the proximity of a black hole.

More important than Baker's juggling of fantasy and science fiction tropes is her treatment of character. Whereas the formula fantasy hero characteristically discovers unexpected strengths within himself through his adventures, Baker's characters are more likely to encounter their own vulnerabilities. Senruh overcomes his racist upbringing through his love for Pell Maru, and Jarell Adon seems increasingly confused and inarticulate about his emotions and motivations as his relationship with Ricassia gains complexity. Ricassia comes to realize that she is unable to make decisions in her own self-interest, instead always following the needs of others. Even the wicked Salimar is revealed to be the product of an abusive and neglectful childhood, and his punishment is not death but regression to the childlike state that preceded his corruption. In Baker's first published horror story, "House Hunter" (*Walls of Blood,* edited by Kathryn Cramer, New York, Morrow, 1990), a brutal child abuser, who tortures and maims the foster children sharing his home, turns out to be the victim of a repressive and rejecting mother. Like her science fiction, the story reveals a surprising complexity beneath the actions of unsavory characters.

With its richness of invention and careful attention to detail, Baker's small but important body of work may come to stand as an almost classic example of the odd fictional hybrid sometimes termed science fantasy—narratives in which the hard-edged rational speculation associated with science fiction gives rise to the apparently supernatural powers and beings associated with fantasy. Baker, who seems to have been influenced by Gene Wolfe and Samuel R. Delany, shares with these authors the unusual ability to construct dense, convincing novels in which the interaction of complex characters overlays a surface structure of fantasy adventure, which in turn overlays a carefully worked out science fiction milieu.

—Gary K. Wolfe

BALLARD, J(ames) G(raham)

Nationality: British. **Born:** Shanghai, China, 15 November 1930. **Education:** Leys School, Cambridge; King's College, Cambridge. **Military Service:** Served in the Royal Air Force. **Family:** Married Helen Mary Matthews in 1953 (died 1964); one son and two daughters. **Awards:** Guardian Fiction prize, 1984; James Tait Black Memorial prize, 1985. **Agent:** Margaret Hanbury, 27 Walcot Square, London SE11 4UB.

SCIENCE FICTION PUBLICATIONS

Novels

The Wind from Nowhere. New York, Berkley, 1962; London, Penguin, 1967.
The Drowned World. New York, Berkley, 1962; London, Gollancz, 1963.
The Burning World. New York, Berkley, 1964; revised edition, as *The Drought,* London, Cape, 1965.
The Crystal World. London, Cape, and New York, Farrar Straus, 1966.
Crash. London, Cape, and New York, Farrar Straus, 1973.
Concrete Island. London, Cape, and New York, Farrar Straus, 1974.
High-Rise. London, Cape, 1975; New York, Holt Rinehart, 1977.
The Unlimited Dream Company. London, Cape, and New York, Holt Rinehart, 1979.
Hello America. London, Cape, 1981.

Short Stories

The Voices of Time, and Other Stories. New York, Berkley, 1962.
Billenium. New York, Berkley, 1962.
The Four-Dimensional Nightmare. London, Gollancz, 1963; revised, 1964; revised, Harmondsworth, Middlesex, Penguin, 1977; as *The Voices of Time,* London, J.M. Dent, 1984.
Passport to Eternity. New York, Berkley, 1963.
Terminal Beach. New York, Berkley, 1964.
The Terminal Beach. London, Gollancz, 1964.
The Impossible Man, and Other Stories. New York, Berkley, 1966.
The Disaster Area. London, Cape, 1967.
The Day of Forever. London, Panther, 1967; revised, 1971.
The Overloaded Man. London, Panther, 1967.
Why I Want to Fuck Ronald Reagan. Brighton, Unicorn Bookshop, 1968.
The Atrocity Exhibition. Garden City, New York, and London, Cape, 1970; as *Love and Napalm: Export USA,* New York, Grove Press, 1972; expanded edition published under original title, San Francisco, Re/Search, 1990; revised, London, Flamingo, 1993.
Chronopolis, and Other Stories. New York, Putnam, 1971.
Vermilion Sands. New York, Berkley, 1971; expanded, London, Cape, 1973.
Low-Flying Aircraft, and Other Stories. London, Cape, 1976.
The Best of J. G. Ballard. London, Futura, 1977.
The Best Short Stories of J. G. Ballard. New York, Holt Rinehart, 1978.
The Venus Hunters. London, Panther, 1980.
Myths of the Near Future. London, Cape, 1982.

The Voices of Time. London, Gollancz, 1985.
Memories of the Space Age. Sauk City, Wisconsin, Arkham House, 1988.
War Fever. London, Collins, 1990; New York, Farrar, Straus, 1991.

OTHER PUBLICATIONS

Novels

Empire of the Sun. London, Gollancz, and New York, Simon and Schuster, 1984.
The Day of Creation. London, Gollancz, 1987; New York, Farrar Straus, 1988.
Running Wild (novella). London, Hutchinson, 1988; New York, Farrar Straus, 1989.
The Kindness of Women. London, HarperCollins, and New York, Farrar, Straus, 1991.
Rushing to Paradise. London, Flamingo, 1994, and New York, Picador, 1995.

Short Stories

War Stories. London, Gollancz, 1990; New York, Farrar Straus, 1991.

Other

News from the Sun. London, Interzone, 1982.

*

Bibliography: *J. G. Ballard: A Primary and Secondary Bibliography* by David Pringle, Boston, Hall, 1984.

Critical Studies: *J. G. Ballard: The First Twenty Years* edited by James Goddard and David Pringle, Hayes, Middlesex, Bran's Head, 1976; *Re Search: J. G. Ballard* edited by Vale, San Francisco, Re Search, 1983; *J. G. Ballard* by Peter Brigg, San Bernardino, California, Borgo Press, 1985.

*   *   *

J.G. Ballard's 15 novels and numerous collections of short stories establish him as one of the most varied yet consistent of the New Wave science fiction writers who emerged in Britain in the 1960s. His experiments with style and subject matter continue to place him in the literate avant garde of the field. Ballard has devised a style and method that offer him the opportunity to investigate what he has termed "inner space," the psychological impact of the 20th century and its televised icons ranging from Hiroshima and the car crash to Marilyn Monroe and Coca-Cola. Drawing from the surrealists for the handling of imagery and from a knowledge of such Freudian phenomena as the death of effect for an approach to character, Ballard has fashioned a unique modern landscape and visions of futures drawn from the darkest reaches of the human mind.

This achievement has received an uneven welcome. Much appreciated in England and Europe, Ballard's narratives of ineffective and introspective heroes whose experiences are imploding rather than changing the universe have been less well received by the vast science fiction audiences of the United States. This has been compounded by the mistaken perception that Ballard caricatures things

American when, in fact, he is actually acknowledging the pervasive way in which American culture, transmitted through contemporary media, *is* the dominant vision of the last half of the 20th century. His cultural perceptions are dominated by two surface factors, his upbringing in Shanghai, which gave him an outsider's relationship to Western experience, and the fact that he lived for many years in a self-imposed semi-isolation in Shepperton, a London suburb, where his chief contact with the larger world was television. Abutting these surfaces is the human search for meaning against the rationalist perspectives of biology, psychology, astrophysics and, above all, against the mysterious processes of time.

Ballard's early short stories (1956-69) are redolent with his handling of overpowering graphic images and treat a wide range of topics including most of his limited ventures into space fiction. His first published story, "Prima Belladonna" (1956), later became one of the nine stories in *Vermilion Sands,* Ballard's exotic future leisure world. In it Jane Ciracylides, a glowing singer with insect eyes, has an affair with the narrator, a choro-florist who trains and sells singing plants. Unfortunately Jane's singing is too much for his star plant, and a choral murder of the plant ensues. The other shimmering stories in *Vermilion Sands* are full of things like houses with twisted emotional memories of previous owners, a revenge murder performed by jewelled insects on a film set, a musical statue that grows to a cacophonous monstrosity, and a bio-fabrics merchant whose living suit is turned on him in a life and death struggle.

Throughout the early stories the classic Ballard protagonist is under development. In "The Terminal Beach" Traven has come to roam Eniwetok, the former thermonuclear test site whose geography of concrete bunkers, towers, and targets comes to match his puzzling mental framework of guilt and the past. In "Now Wakes the Sea" Mason's nightmares of the encroaching oceans returning to engulf the land are curiously realized when he falls into the shaft of a dig recovering bones from an ancient sea floor. In "The Day of Forever" Halliday wanders through grotesque North African landscapes of a world in which time has stopped, trying to recover his ability to dream and finding the content of his waking time overflows the surreal visions the equal of any dream. These Ballard characters hover in a psychic dusk, concerned not with the sudden changes in their worlds or the strangeness of events, but with the shimmering connections between their subconsciousnesses and what they see through their eyes.

The most characteristic of these early stories is "The Voices of Time" (1960). Powers, a neurosurgeon, is searching for sense in a world being taken over by narcoma, and is haunted by his own impending demise as he sleeps longer each day. From Kaldren, a mad artist who had surgery which prevents him from ever sleeping, Powers learns of a cosmic countdown being broadcast from Canes Venatici, and he gradually succumbs to the inexorable end of all things, first constructing a vast concrete mandala and then irradiating himself and lying down to die in the center of the mandala with "the voices of time" pouring down upon him. The inexorable quality of these events and the importance of their meaning for the central participant, as opposed to a struggle to reverse them, were to become central qualities in the later fiction.

The Wind from Nowhere (1962), Ballard's first novel, groups with the next three, *The Drowned World* (1962), *The Drought* (1964), and *The Crystal World* (1966), to form a natural disaster quartet. In each novel there is an extraordinary catastrophe, but whereas in the first the focus is entirely upon the vividly rendered depiction of the vast wind which scourges the Earth, in the remaining three it is upon the relationships between the central characters and the catastrophes, as it emerges that external events mirror or draw out characters' states of mind. So, for example, in *The Drowned World* Kearns comes to terms with the inner drives of cellular recapitulation of the desire for the heat of the sun, and his dreams of heat and water are fulfilled as he moves south into the blazing tropical swamps of what was formerly Europe. In *The Crystal World,* the most baroque of all Ballard's fiction, time is coalescing and the trees, animals, and humans in an African jungle are turning into glittering gems, suspended out of time in Yeatsean beauty.

The disaster novels were followed by Ballard's most significant piece of experimental fiction, the linked and interrelated fragments called *The Atrocity Exhibition* (1970) (U.S. title: *Love and Napalm: Export USA*). This strange mixture of sex, violence, psychiatry, and contemporary icons (the Zapruder film, automobile crashes, James Dean) is loosely conflated around a mad psychiatrist studying several subjects, but in its fragmented form there are only disasters, imagined disasters, and a stifling range of paranoid possibilities. There is no standing ground in this text but there is the massive impact on the reader of a salvo of images, relations between objects and shifting perspectives fired at once from all sides.

The movement after *The Atrocity Exhibition* is to a series of three novels, *Crash* (1973), *Concrete Island* (1974), and *High-Rise* (1975), which continue to derive their startling power from the contemporary world viewed sideways. In *Crash* the subject matter is autoperversion, the world as it is lived on motorways and in which automobile violence becomes engaged with erotic fantasy. *Concrete Island* turns the central areas of a British motorway flyover into an isolated environment where a few castaways struggle for survival entrapped by the constant flow of vehicles on all sides. *High-Rise* depicts a modern apartment block as an isolated battleground, a miniature universe in which the veneer of culture is torn away, revealing raw power, violence, and sexuality. These novels, and some short stories written at the same time establish Ballard's focus on the modern urban world but it is clearly a focus unlike any other writer's. His present-day world is as strange as Mars—with violence accentuated and characters moving at the edge of a sanity that can hardly be measured by "normal" standards. Ballard sees the driving, perverted forces that lurk only centimeters below the balanced flow of urban culture, and he has only to give them an extrapolative tap to reveal a radical and strange potential.

Two radical experiments follow the urban disaster novels: *The Unlimited Dream Company* (1979) and *Hello America* (1981). The first of these is a visionary novel, a dream influenced by the paintings of Stanley Spenser and Blake, the name of the young man who steals an aircraft, crashes it into the Thames at Shepperton, and is then apparently reborn in a strange parallel world of Shepperton where he becomes a saviour who teaches the community to fly and embellishes it with tropical growth. *Hello America* is a *jeu d'esprit* of a different sort, a travelogue of the future as explorers recross an abandoned America that has turned to desert in the east and jungle west of the Rockies. In their various ways the explorers are each following their inner vision of America and the novel ends up with a phantasmagoria involving the final nuclear explosion and the beginning of a new America peopled by flyers who surf the sunlight. The novel is heavy with satire and is a "forward archaeology" of America with sand-filled Hiltons and nomads named GM and Pepsodent.

Empire of the Sun (1984) is the first of two volumes of fictionalized autobiography (the second, *The Kindness of Women* [1991] deals with a version of Ballard's life in England after the war). In it Jim, 11 years old at the time of the Japanese occupation of Shanghai, survives internment and desperate conditions, emerging at the conclusion with a momentary vision of the flash of Nagasaki. This novel reveals a number of Ballard's central concerns—with flying, with the icons of the American presence in the Far East, with the curious distance humans establish between themselves in times of stress. Jim sees the suffering about him with an odd objectivity, protected by his innocence. Here Ballard is able to suggest the absence of affect in the face of modern suffering in an equivocal fashion, for Jim's stance is innocent, at play in a real war, yet it cannot help but stand out to readers as a critique of the way late 20th-century adults turn callously away from the crushing mass of human suffering to be found on every side.

In two of his most recent novels, *The Day of Creation* (1987) and *Rushing to Paradise* (1994), Ballard returns to isolated worlds like those of Shanghai or of the African jungle where limited casts of characters enact their psychomyths against sympathetic landscapes. *The Day of Creation* features Dr. Mallory, who follows a river towards its source with dreams of irrigating and creating a paradise in Africa. A young widow, a documentary cameraman, and a local military officer are among the cast, each following their own conflicting dreams of voyage and destination. *Rushing to Paradise* deals with a 16-year-old boy under the spell of a middle-aged British woman doctor who takes him with a motley party to a French Pacific nuclear test island to defend the environment of the albatross. The ensuing sanctuary becomes progressively stranger until it emerges that the doctor wishes to create a sanctuary for women with only one male to fertilize them, and that she is killing off the men to obtain her ends. All of this takes place at one of those crux locations which fascinate Ballard, with thermonuclear memories, strange and hypnotic sexuality, and the violence of survival tactics among isolated individuals.

Nor has Ballard evinced any lack of experiment in his more recent output. In 1988 he produced *Running Wild,* a purported psychiatrist's solution to the mysterious murder of 32 adults at an exclusive housing compound in the Thames Valley and the kidnapping of their 13 children. This brief but telling text is a confluence of contemporary issues—the cloistered late 1980's rich, the mass murderers of Britain and America, the condition of contemporary over pampered children. And *War Fever* (1990) is a collection of Ballard's most recent short fiction, with its preoccupation with flying, the end of the space age and the coming decay of Cape Kennedy. And always these external events have their real importance in their integration with the twisting absorbed psyches of the foreground characters.

J.G. Ballard has consistently circled and attacked fixed fields of perception—the study of the human psyche in contact with the contemporary world with all its overwhelming baggage of media icons. He has connected these with the dark fields of unconscious desire and a sense of the real distance between individuals in our time. He has imagined these events around inner space taking place in the isolation of the jungle, the jungle of the modern urban world, and the iconic jungle of contemporary media.

—Peter Brigg

BANKS, Iain M(enzies)

Also writes as Iain Banks. **Nationality:** British. **Born:** Fife, Scotland, 16 February 1954. **Education:** Stirling University. **Family:** Married (1992). **Career:** Expediter-analyzer, IBM, Greenock, Scotland, 1978; soliciter's clerk, London, 1980-84. Now a freelance writer. Lives in Fife. **Agent:** Ms. Mic Cheetham, 138 Buckingham Palace Road, London SW1W 9SA. **Address:** c/o Little, Brown, Brettenham House, Lancaster Place, London WC2E 7EN, England.

SCIENCE FICTION PUBLICATIONS

Novels (series: The Culture)

Consider Phlebas (Culture). London, Macmillan, 1987; New York, St. Martin's Press, 1988.
The Player of Games (Culture). London, Macmillan, 1988; New York, St. Martin's Press, 1989.
The State of the Art (Culture; novella). Willimantic, Connecticut, Ziesing, 1989.
Use of Weapons (Culture). London, Orbit, 1990; New York, Bantam, 1992.
Against a Dark Background. London, Orbit, and New York, Bantam, 1993.
Feersum Endjinn. London, Orbit, 1994; New York, Bantam, 1995.

Short Stories

The State of the Art (includes the 1989 novella plus additional stories). London, Orbit, 1991.

OTHER PUBLICATIONS

Novels as Iain Banks

The Wasp Factory. London, Macmillan, and Boston, Houghton Mifflin, 1984.
Walking on Glass. London, Macmillan, 1985; Boston, Houghton Mifflin, 1986.
The Bridge. London, Macmillan, 1986; New York, St. Martin's Press, 1989.
Espedair Street. London, Macmillan, 1987.
Canal Dreams. London, Macmillan, 1989; Garden City, New York, Doubleday, 1991.
The Crow Road. London, Scribner's, 1992.
Complicity. London, Little, Brown, 1993; Garden City, New York, Doubleday, 1995.

*   *   *

The forms of his name that Iain Banks uses are supposed to distinguish the science fiction (as by Iain M. Banks) from the rest of his output (as by Iain Banks). In fact, the distinction is not so clear cut. There are science fictional elements in many of his supposedly non-SF novels. Of the three stories interwoven in *Walking on Glass,* one is explicitly science fictional (a prisoner in a castle forced to play games in a scenario curiously reminiscent of *Player of Games,* which Banks had written but not yet sold at this point), and one has science fiction sensibilities (a psychotic character whose mental unbalance is signaled by the belief that he is under alien attack). While *Canal Dreams* is set in the near future, *The Bridge* is set in a Kafkaesque mental landscape with specifically fantasy elements in the episodes involving the Scottish bar-

barian, and even his debut novel, *The Wasp Factory,* has affinities with contemporary horror fiction.

His science fiction, meanwhile, is written on a grand, operatic scale, yet the heart of all this vastness is often a small domestic story. Both *Use of Weapons* and *Against a Dark Background* resolve into stories of family dispute and personal revenge. In fact the violent, fast-paced, foreground action is often interrupted by flashbacks to scenes of childhood and youth which would not be out of place in a contemporary novel were it not for the scenery, and which contain within their jealousies, romances and emotions the seeds for the grander-seeming action within which they are set.

One of the most curious and disturbing elements in all Banks's fiction, from *The Wasp Factory* to *Feersum Endjinn,* is the violence which often seems to form the principal driving force of the plot. Banks is explicit in his hatred of violence, which he links to power. Time and again a moral point is made about violence and sexual cruelty, from the black joke in *The Wasp Factory* about the person in South Africa killed by a black man who fell from the top of the police building and managed to rip out all his fingernails on the way down, to the films of sexual torture enjoyed by the powerful elite on Azad and which provides Gurgeh with his motivation at a vital point in the plot of *The Player of Games.* Yet such violence forms a thread throughout the novels. By the end of *Against a Dark Background,* for instance, nearly every named character in the book has died a violent death, bloody wars have swept across planets, all in the cause of rivalry between the children of a rich and privileged family. The serial killer in *Complicity* is almost to be applauded because the victims of his bizarre and humiliating murders are in their turn monsters of the right being repaid in kind for their own officially sanctioned crimes. *Canal Dreams* turns its hesitant, withdrawn, peaceful female Japanese cellist into a resourceful and dramatic killer when left-wing revolutionaries are revealed to be agents of the American right. It is as if Banks can only express his horror at violence, his abhorrence at the right, by resorting to the very thing he condemns.

Yet this violence is made palatable by the humour with which Banks leavens all his work. The comedy is generally very black but also very broad, and his books can be very funny indeed. At the same time, they are also very clever. Banks's technical skills as a writer are usually more in evidence in his non-SF, particularly in *The Bridge,* a very complex and assured work. Of his science fiction only *Use of Weapons,* in which alternative chapters move forward and backward in time, comes close to the challenging structural experimentation of *The Bridge.* His non-SF also shows his restlessness; he rarely repeats himself and his work has ranged from the rock biography of *Espedair Street* to the family drama of *The Crow Road* to the crime thriller of *Complicity,* and his achievement within each of these styles has been generally good. His science fiction is more limited, a wide screen baroque which provides a lively counterpoint to the narrow focus of his non-SF, but which can seem to lack something of the freshness and vigour of his other works.

His first three science fiction novels, *Consider Phlebas, The Player of Games,* and *Use of Weapons,* (the last two of which, along with *Against a Dark Background,* were actually written, in first draft at least, long before his controversial "debut" with *The Wasp Factory*) and most of the stories in *The State of the Art* are set in the same far future universe. Like all his non-SF, these books clearly reflect Banks's left-wing beliefs: in a clear response to traditional space opera the disparate worlds of this future are linked not by an autocracy in one form or another but by the anarchistic

Culture. The Culture is a hedonistic nongovernment, though like all bodies of power its power is liable to misuse. And though Banks may consider that the Culture has, on balance, got it right, he is not attempting to write utopias. In all three of the novels the Culture is seen from the perspective of those antagonistic to or marginalised by the Culture. *Consider Phlebas* is a simple quest novel in which the central character, the mercenary Horza, is fighting against the supposed "good guys" of the Culture. *The Player of Games* tells of a game-player, Gurgeh, tricked into going to an Empire outside the Culture where power is decided by a complex game and where he must confront not only the immorality of the Empire but also question the way he has been manipulated by the Culture. (Games play a symbolic role in much of Banks's fiction, featuring also in *Walking on Glass* and *Complicity*.) While in *Use of Weapons* the morality of the way the Culture manipulates individuals and societies is questioned again in the story of Zakalwe, a spy employed to use any means to further the ends of the Culture.

If Banks's subsequent science fiction novels have moved away from the Culture, they have not moved away from the moral hesitation, the liberal instincts or the massive scale. (Literally so in *Feersum Endjinn*, the entirety of whose enigmatic action takes place within one building so vast that it would make Mervyn Peake's Gormenghast appear no bigger than a garden shed.) *Against a Dark Background* is set on Golter and its neighbouring worlds and concerns the Lady Sharrow, a soldier and adventurer who, because of something that happened generations before, is being hunted by the Huhsz cult. Her only hope is to find the legendary Lazy Gun: a typically exuberant invention by Banks, this is a weapon that kills by improbable means reminiscent of cartoon films, for example an anvil might materialise in the air above the victim. As in so many of Banks's books, the morally reprehensible (this is a weapon of mass destruction) is presented humorously. But all is morally questionable in this fast-paced adventure in which the heroine and her cronies are not above theft, violence, and killing while sadism and gruesome death are constant features of the action. The book is also typical in what it shows of the edges of Banks's invention. There is original SF paraphernalia throughout the book, but much of the domestic detail, hair, clothes, even means of transport, wouldn't be out of place in a contemporary mainstream novel. It is as if the scale of the novel, the interplanetary action, the fabulous inventions, the number of dead, have been used to transform a small-scale mainstream story into science fiction.

Feersum Endjinn is a better book if only because its world is more thoroughly imagined, though its plot, hinging on a series of enigmas, is not fully or satisfactorily worked out. The gaps and coincidences are disguised by a bravura storytelling which is fresher and more structurally inventive than in any of his science fiction with the possible exception of *Use of Weapons*. In a vast palace in which no element approaches human scale, his dwarfed characters encounter and work through a series of mysteries which may herald a signal from outer space (here, effectively, meaning anywhere outside this palace) and which in turn may threaten the status quo. All is resolved in the end, though the details and meaning of it all are no clearer than the rules of the game Gurgeh plays in *The Player of Games*. Again, as in so many of Banks's novels, his central characters are marginalised, either distanced from or alienated from the operations of power. There is the aged minister playing a dangerous game of rebellion, the dead hero who has to make his way through the virtual world of the immense data banks, the girl who appears from nowhere with no past or character, and Bascule the minion who finds himself cast into the interstices of this outsized

world. Bascule's story is told in a debased demotic most reminiscent of Russell Hoban's *Riddley Walker*, a technically challenging style which Banks masters with considerable aplomb. If at times he lets his cleverness get the better of him, as for instance in the way so many of the characters Bascule meets have speech defects which add an extra layer of difficulty to interpreting the text, it only serves to show that Banks is at his best when, as in *The Bridge* and *Use of Weapons*, he challenges the formal structure of the novel.

—Paul Kincaid

———

BARCLAY, Bill. *See* **MOORCOCK, Michael.**

———

BARJAVEL, René

Nationality: French. **Born:** 1911. **Career:** Screenwriter, journalist, regular contributor to *Anticipations*. **Died:** 1985.

SCIENCE FICTION PUBLICATIONS

Novels

Ravage. Paris, Denoël, 1944; translated by Damon Knight as *Ashes, Ashes,* Garden City, New York, Doubleday, 1967.
Le voyageur imprudent. Paris, Denoël, 1944; translated by Margaret Sansone Scouten as *Future Times Three,* New York, Award, 1970.
La nuit des temps. Paris, Presses de la Cité, 1968; translated by Charles Lan Markmann as *The Ice People,* London, Hart-Davis, 1970.
Le grand secret. Paris, Presses de la Cité, 1973; translated by Eileen Finletter as *The Immortals,* New York, Morrow, 1974.

Untranslated Novels in French

L'Homme Forte. Paris, n.p., 1946.
Le Diable l'Emporte. Paris, n.p., 1948.
Colomb de la Lune. Paris, n.p., 1962.

OTHER PUBLICATIONS

Novel

Tarendol. Paris, Denoël, 1946; translated by Eithne Wilkins as *Tragic Innocents,* London, Hamish Hamilton, 1948.

*   *   *

René Barjavel's science fiction work contrasts pastoral utopias full of love with wartorn dystopias full of distrust. Although *Le*

Diable l'Emporte, Colomb de la Lune, and *L'Homme Forte* have not been translated, *Ashes, Ashes, Future Times Three, The Ice People,* and *The Immortals,* available in English, are passionately antiwar, erotic, and satiric, relating vividly penned horrors and sentimental romance.

Although Barjavel is a screenwriter, journalist, and writer of romantic novels, *Future Times Three* is typical science fiction, dealing with the paradoxes and dangers of time travel. Playful escapades in the near future and malicious forays into the 19th century echo Wells's *Invisible Man,* and the specialized races of 100,000 A.D. follow Stapledon. Exploring the future, mathematicians and physicists brood over questions of God and causality. This episodic novel declares—like Faust—that man cannot safely extend beyond God.

In traveling to 2052, St. Menoux learns the fate of the survivors of *Ashes, Ashes,* in which some inexplicable sunspot phenomenon cuts off electricity and the world goes mad. Fire and bloodshed purge a decadent technological society on the verge of all-out war. As in the earlier novel, the pure love of two young people provides hope. The heroes, however, are ruthless killers who fight their way into the country to found a pastoral society where books and inventions are forbidden.

One of the numerous Swiftian sallies of *Ashes, Ashes* explains the system of freezing ancestors. In *The Ice People* South Pole explorers find two gorgeous bodies from 900,000 years earlier, obviously remnants of a vastly advanced society destroyed by atomic holocaust. Unfrozen, Elea transmits her memories of her perfect love with Paikan and her selection as the mate to be preserved for the mastermind, Coban. This Romeo and Juliet tale is set against political turmoil of past and present. Only a coalition of scientists and students might save the world, though Elea and Paikan are destroyed.

Using the actual backdrop and leaders of his own time, *The Immortals* examines the frightening long-range political effects of a drug that defeats death and disease. Since immortality is contagious, all those involved in research have been isolated on an Aleutian paradise. They are, however, human time bombs doomed to annihilation by world powers when scientists learn there is nowhere for man in space. Although pessimistic, Barjavel didactically asserts the values of love and peace.

—Mary S. Weinkauf

BARNARD, Marjorie Faith. *See* **ELDERSHAW, M. Barnard.**

BARNES, John

Nationality: American. **Born:** Angola, Indiana, in 1957. **Education:** Washington University; University of Montana; University of Pittsburgh. **Career:** Systems analyst, 1982-84; self-employed, 1988-90. **Agent:** Ashley Grayson, 1342 18th St., San Pedro, CA 90732, U.S.A.

SCIENCE FICTION PUBLICATIONS

Novels (series: Time Raider)

The Man Who Pulled Down the Sky. New York, Congdon & Weed, 1986; London, New English Library, 1988.
Sin of Origin. New York, Congdon & Weed, 1988; London, New English Libary, 1991.
Orbital Resonance. New York, Tor, 1991.
Wartide (Time Raider). Toronto and New York, Worldwide, 1992.
Battlecry (Time Raider). Toronto and New York, Worldwide, 1992.
A Million Open Doors. New York, Tor, 1992.
Union Fires (Time Raider). Toronto and New York, Worldwide, 1992.
Mother of Storms. Tor Books, 1994.
Kaleidoscope Century. New York, Tor, 1995.

Short Stories

Author of uncollected short stories.

OTHER PUBLICATIONS

Other

How to Build a Future. Eugene, Oregon, Pulphouse, 1991.

*   *   *

John Barnes combines his love for science fiction with an extensive understanding of drama within both his novels and short stories. Despite the fact that writing is a sideline to a career as a theater historian and stage director—Barnes was looking forward to directing a stage musical based on his translation of Plautus's *Truculentus* in the spring of 1995—he is known as an author who poses a thought-provoking question within the framework of an entertaining story. As Barnes once noted for *Contemporary Authors,* "I have found that a good adventure story permits the writer to express unlimited, bitter satire with impunity."

Barnes's first published work of SF, the 1985 short story entitled "Finalities Besides the Grave," was followed by a novel, *The Man Who Pulled Down the Sky,* two years later. *The Man Who Pulled Down the Sky* describes the cultural changes fomenting political conflicts throughout the solar system. Similar in theme, his 1988 novel, *Sins of Origin,* pits Brother Hauskyld Gomez and Dr. Clio Yermenko as, respectively, Christian and Communist sect leaders who battle the rising hostility of the inhabitants of the planet Randall—a hostility spurned by the recent interjection of messianic Christianity into a society that had formerly attained a state of social equilibrium. The novel was noted for combining the elements of classic space opera—high action and adventure—with a serious sociological study.

Orbital Resonance, Barnes's third novel, published in 1991, features Melpomene Murray, a young woman facing typical adolescent concerns: Schoolwork, friends, parents, and day-to-day life aboard "The Flying Dutchman," an asteroid colony on an Earth-Mars orbit where no news from a now-devastated Earth is good news. While criticized as somewhat juvenile in its approach, this Young Adult novel about the role of children in space exploration was recommended for its spirited young protagonist and its thought-provoking depiction of life in outer space.

A Million Open Doors followed in 1992. The future world of Nou Occitan is similar to medieval Europe and dueling, sexism, and artistic endeavors abound. Its diametric culture, the world of Caledony, suppresses art and free thought; and when the cultures of the two worlds are forced to assimilate due to advances in technology, problems inevitably ensue. Using as a historical parallel the decades of the 1950s and 1960s, Barnes provides an interesting study of cultural repression, rebellion, and liberation in a novel that was praised for its combination of adventure and high-tech science fiction.

Mother of Storms, published in 1994, concerns the transformation of the ocean surface into a birthing ground for hurricanes that grow to such enormous strength and severity that they threaten to destroy the Earth's population. This tale of survival—as politicians, scientists, and futurists, led by superhuman astronaut Louie Tynan, attempt to save the planet from Mother Nature at her most lethal— was highly praised for its suspense, well-developed cast of characters, and intricate plot structure.

In addition to his novels, Barnes has also contributed to *How to Build a Future,* an SF anthology. *Kaleidoscope Century,* a hard science fiction novel set in the same post-Apocalyptic universe as *Orbital Resonance,* was forthcoming in 1995. In addition to his more technical SF, Barnes has been hard at work on his first fantasy novel, a book with the prepublication title of "One for the Morning."

—Pamela Shelton

BARNES, Steven (Emory)

Nationality: American. **Born:** Los Angeles, California, 1 March 1952. **Education:** Pepperdine University, Los Angeles, 1970-74. **Family:** Married; one daughter. **Career:** Tour guide, Columbia Broadcasting System, Hollywood, 1974-76; Manager, Audio-Visual and Multi-Media Department, Pepperdine University, 1978-80; Creative Consultant, Don Bluth Productions, 1981. Instructor, creative writing, University of California, Los Angeles. **Agent:** Eleanor Wood, Blassingame, McCauley and Wood, 432 Park Avenue, New York, New York 10016, U.S.A. **Address:** P.O. Box 2041, Santa Clarita, California 91386, U.S.A.

SCIENCE FICTION PUBLICATIONS

Novels (series: Dream Park)

Dream Park, with Larry Niven. Huntington Woods, Michigan, Phantasia Press, 1981; London, Macdonald, 1983.
The Descent of Anansi, with Larry Niven. New York, Tor, 1982.
Streetlethal. New York, Ace, 1983.
The Kundalini Equation. New York, Tor, 1986.
The Legacy of Heorot, with Larry Niven and Jerry Pournelle. New York, Simon and Schuster, and London, Gollancz, 1987.
Gorgon Child. New York, Tor, 1989.
The Barsoom Project (Dream Park), with Larry Niven. New York, Ace, 1989; London, Pan, 1990.
Achilles' Choice, with Larry Niven. New York, Tor, 1991; London, Pan Books, 1993.

Dream Park: The Voodoo Game, with Larry Niven. London, Pan Books, 1991; as *The California Voodoo Game,* New York, Ballantine, 1992.
Firedance. New York, Tor, 1993.

OTHER PUBLICATIONS

Plays

Screenplay: *The Soulstar Commission,* 1987.

Television Plays: *Little Fuzzy* (adaptation of the novel by H. Beam Piper), 1979; *The Test* (adaptation of the short story by Stanislaw Lem), 1982; *Teacher's Aid,* and *To See the Invisible Man* (adaptation of the short story by Robert Silverberg), both in *The Twilight Zone* series, 1985-86; scripts for *Real Ghostbusters* (cartoon), 1987, and *The Wizard,* 1987.

Other

Ki: How to Generate the Dragon Spirit. Sen-do, 1976.

Animated Cartoon: *The Secret of NIMH,* 1982.

*

Steven Barnes comments:

If there is any single thing which I believe most strongly, it is that all of us have the capacity to bring our most cherished dreams to life. What is required is motivating goals, discipline, honesty, and sufficient personal power to ACT. Life is a wonderful, complex, demanding game. The way to win is to decide what it is you want, find people who have accomplished this, and study them. Study their beliefs and habit patterns. Apply these to your own life, and you can be anything, do anything in the world. Get going!

*   *   *

It is almost always impossible to judge an individual writer's contribution to a collaborative effort, and the fact that four of the seven novels to appear under Steven Barnes's byline are collaborations with writers successful in their own right clearly presents some difficulties in evaluating his career. Certainly the collaborative works, three with Larry Niven, one with Niven and Jerry Pournelle, are all entertaining stories. Only *The Descent of Anansi* falls below the standards the other writers have established for their own work, a shortcoming not necessarily attributable to Barnes. *Dream Park* and its sequel, *The Barsoom Project,* are highly entertaining stories of a theme park where verisimilitude is definitely the order of the day. *The Legacy of Heorot* is a mysterious and suspenseful other world adventure with a strong biological theme; a group of colonists struggle to survive despite the onslaught of a particularly vicious and unsuspected predatory life-form.

Fortunately, there are several solo novels and a handful of short stories that do enable us to judge Barnes's abilities as a writer. *Streetlethal,* the first of these, is a powerful, even upsetting view of a future Los Angeles after a catastrophic natural disaster has been coupled with a collapse of law and order. The protagonist is a professional fighter who has decided to sever his connections to a brutal gang that preys on the helpless, peddling drugs, and killing innocent people in order to sell their organs as spare parts. Unfortunately, the gang isn't about to let him walk away, and his only alternative to dying may be to wipe out the entire gang first. Framed for murder and conditioned against resorting to violence, he must escape from prison, find the woman he loves, avenge himself against the criminals, and elude the authorities before escaping to a safe haven. He escapes with the woman to the warrens of the Scavengers, a less unpleasant gang, but the respite is brief, and their eventual capture by their old enemies only ends well because internal frictions within that group erupt into open civil war. Barnes draws on his own knowledge of martial arts to add credulity to this often depressing and quite violent novel of the underside of human society. Although the plot is a revenge story, Barnes takes great pains to ensure that it is not simply an excuse for endless battle sequences, creating characters and situations that develop as the story progresses.

The Kundalini Equation is also concerned with certain aspects of the discipline of martial arts, but it takes them in an entirely different direction. The various schools of fighting are all just aspects of a greater knowledge, a mental training that is so radical and all encompassing that its possessor has more than just the power to disable enemies. It also involves previously unsuspected mental powers that enable the practitioner to manipulate matter and energy directly. The result is the transformation of a man in modern California into a powerful, inhuman creature whose existence poses a threat to anyone he encounters. Ultimately, as he continues to change both physically and mentally, there is a very real danger that he might alter the nature of the Earth itself.

Gorgon Child, sequel to *Streetlethal,* examines the same themes from another viewpoint. The protagonist is once again a young man trained as an organic killing machine, living in a world where plague and the collapse of central authority have contributed to a situation in which gangs and other private interests effectively control society. Aubry Knight is not a mindless killer, however, but a man determined to use his abilities to help improve things. However, a new religious cult plans to seize control of the entire nation.

All of Barnes's solo novels throw one talented and resourceful man against a decadent and/or evil social system. Although the worlds he describes are bleak and repulsive, in each case the resolution of the story is hopeful, indicating that the indomitability of the human spirit will rise above temporary setbacks and persevere. His characters do not wait passively to see what the world will offer them but pursue whatever it is in life that they most desire. Even his villains often display admirable qualities, warped by their vices. Unfortunately, Barnes seems reluctant to experiment in novel form with a different type of setting and hero, although he has done so in a few of his shorter pieces. The best of these are "Locusts," "Endurance Vile," and the fantasy "But Fear Itself." Perhaps as he continues to gain confidence as a writer, he will explore other themes and bring to them the intensity of the novels he has produced to date.

—Don D'Ammassa

BARRETT, Neal, Jr.

Nationality: American. **Career:** Formerly worked in public relations; now a full-time writer. **Address:** c/o New American Library, 375 Hudson Street, New York, New York 10014, U.S.A.

SCIENCE FICTION PUBLICATIONS

Novels

Kelwin. New York, Lancer, 1970.
The Gates of Time. New York, Ace, 1970.
The Leaves of Time. New York, Lancer, 1971.
Highwood. New York, Ace, 1972.
Stress Pattern. New York, DAW, 1974.
Aldair in Albion. New York, DAW, 1976.
Aldair, Master of Ships. New York, DAW, 1977.
Aldair, Across the Misty Sea. New York, DAW, 1980.
Aldair: The Legion of Beasts. New York, DAW, 1982.
The Karma Corps. New York, DAW, 1984.
Through Darkest America. New York, Congdon, 1986; London, New English Library, 1988.
Dawn's Uncertain Light (Darkest America). New York, New American Library, 1989; London, Grafton, 1992.
The Hereafter Gang. Shingletown, California, Ziesing, 1991.
Batman in the Black Egg of Atlantis (for children). Boston, Little, Brown, 1992; as *The Black Egg of Atlantis,* London, Fantail, 1992.

Short Stories

Slightly Off Center: Eleven Extraordinarily Exhilarating Tales. Austin, Texas, Swan Press, 1992.

OTHER PUBLICATIONS

Novels

Pink Vodka Blues. New York, St. Martin's Press, 1992.
Dead Dog Blues. New York, St. Martin's Press, 1994.

* * *

Neal Barrett, Jr., was for many years a welcome but infrequent contributor to professional science fiction magazines, and an occasional novelist, but it was not until the late 1970s that he attracted much serious attention. His earliest published novel, *Kelwin,* employs the familiar theme of a barbaric civilization rebuilding itself after the fall of our own society in a devastating war. Kelwin is a wandering adventurer whose destiny is to shape the unfolding of a possible new conflict. *Kelwin* is an unpretentious but highly entertaining adventure story.

The Leaves of Time is more ambitious. The setting is a parallel version of our own world, one where history has taken a rather different course. Barrett adds a second element to this standard plot device, a fugitive alien capable of changing forms, an infiltrator from another time line. The protagonists must discover a method of identifying and neutralizing the invader, without letting him return to his home time-line.

These two novels far outshine two other early novels, both light adventures of little lasting substance. *The Gates of Time* is a galaxy-spanning romp about mankind's fate in the face of alien conquest; *Highwood* is set in a world of giant forests. A pair of human observers notices a radical alteration in the behavior patterns of the indigent sentient species and become caught up in the rush to save their culture.

The appearance in 1974 of *Stress Pattern,* Barrett's fifth novel, was the equivalent of the emergence of a new writer. A space trav-

eller becomes marooned on a most peculiar planet. The natives recognize his presence, but seem utterly indifferent to him, preoccupied with bizarre activities of their own. Travel is accomplished by means of organic railways; a variety of monstrous creatures populate the countryside. The entire biosphere of the planet is one intricate, integrated machine. Had this novel appeared under the byline of a more established writer, it would almost certainly have attracted more attention than it ultimately did. *Stress Pattern* is one of the most unusual novels ever to appear in the genre.

Barrett hit his stride with the Aldair series, four novels chronicling Aldair's adventures on a future Earth deserted by the human race. Many of the lower animal species were altered genetically so that a variety of intelligent species exist, each displaying the attributes of their ancestry. Aldair himself is a pig, and among his companions are wolves and bears. The opening volume, *Aldair in Albion,* introduces the background and main characters, then follows Aldair as he wanders across Europe searching for his own destiny and clues to the fate of legendary mankind.

The first two volumes read well independently. *Aldair, Master of Ships* continues the search, following the coastlines of the continents. The narrative is continued in *Aldair, Across the Misty Sea,* but the cliffhanger ending mars its effectiveness as a novel. Barrett clears up all the loose ends in the concluding volume, *Aldair: The Legion of Beasts,* by transporting Aldair and his friends to an alien planet where malformed genetic freaks enslave the pacifistic remnants of the human race. Much of the charm of the previous volumes is lost with the change of setting, but as a whole, this series is one of the most entertaining and innovative of its kind.

Barrett's next novel, *The Karma Corps,* is an interesting but not entirely successful work. A shipload of colonists survives on an uncharted world, where their theocratic social structure finds itself in perpetual conflict with an alien species that can teleport itself across small distances. A group of human teleports is revived from electronic storage and pressed into battle against the aliens, but inevitably control of the power they represent becomes a political issue.

After a gap of several years, Barrett published *Through Darkest America* and its sequel, *Dawn's Uncertain Light.* Once again, he takes a traditional theme and provides a new twist. Following a nuclear war, a new society forms in North America, the main foodstuff of which is a strain of mutated humanity lacking intelligence. A young man comes of age as he discovers horrible truths about his society: the mutant food supply is a hoax of the government's, which is lobotomizing its own citizens. Together, the two books portray a bleak future.

Barrett has turned out a small number of high quality short stories as well. One of his earliest, "The Stentorii Luggage" (in *Galaxy,* October 1960), is a classic tale of shape-changing creatures in an elaborate, interspecies hotel. "The Grandfather Pelt" (in *If,* November 1969) provides ironic justice to a criminal who steals a sacred relic. A desperate man must outreason a singleminded computer in "Survival Course" (in *Galaxy,* January 1974), and a visiting alien tries to puzzle out the inner secrets of humanity in "Greyspun's Gift" (in *Worlds of Tomorrow,* Winter 1970), which also features some of Barrett's best characterization. "The Flying Stutzman" (in *Fantasy and Science Fiction,* July 1978), in which a man is doomed to an eternity of air travel, is a very well-written and disturbing fantasy. "Ginny Sweethips' Flying Circus" is a zany, madcap bit of humor. Also of note is the recent "Under Old New York."

—Don D'Ammassa

BARTON, Erle. *See* **FANTHORPE, R. Lionel.**

———

BARTON, Lee. *See* **FANTHORPE, R. Lionel.**

———

BASS, T.J.

Pseudonym for Thomas J. Bassler. **Other Pseudonym:** T.J. Bassler. **Nationality:** American. **Born:** Clinton, Iowa, 7 July 1932. **Education:** St. Ambrose College, Davenport, Iowa, B.A. 1955; University of Iowa, Iowa City, M.D. 1959. **Family:** Married Gloria Napoli in 1960; three daughters and three sons. **Career:** Deputy medical examiner, Los Angeles, 1961-64. Since 1964 in private practice as a pathologist. Since 1972 editor, *American Medical Joggers Newsletter.* **Address:** 27558 Sunnyridge Road, Palos Verdes Peninsula, California 90274, U.S.A.

SCIENCE FICTION PUBLICATIONS

Novels

Half Past Human. New York, Ballantine, 1971; London, Methuen, 1984.
The Godwhale. New York. Ballantine, 1974; London, Eyre Methuen, 1975.

OTHER PUBLICATIONS

Other

The Whole Life Diet: An Integrated Program of Nutrition and Exercise for a Lifestyle of Total Health (as T.J. Bassler), with Robert E. Burger. New York, M. Evans, 1979.

*   *   *

T.J. Bass's novels, *Half Past Human* and *The Godwhale,* give a vivid picture of a horrifying future society, of a worldwide Earth Society ("the big ES") that controls every detail of life in the planet-sized hive that Earth has become. Three trillion people, degenerate "Nebishes," live in warrens beneath the surface, every inch of which is devoted to crops. These shrunken souls live short and regimented lives, are processed at their deaths for the proteins that sustain their fellows, and even have puberty postponed until the CO—the Class One computer—decides they are ready for sexual maturity.

Yet these novels are not cautionary tales of the sort of Harry Harrison's *Make Room! Make Room!,* although some have read them so: rather, their concerns are teleological, like C.S. Lewis's Perelandra Trilogy or Walter M. Miller's *A Canticle for Leibowitz.* Assuming a kind Providence and a personal God, these works ask, what is the end of man? While *Half Past Human* and *The Godwhale* do not directly address the question, they do show a Providence that cares about the fall of a sparrow—or a Nebish. If the hand of God has not been noticed in Bass's works, it is because the author shows God using unfamiliar instruments. In the Perelandra trilogy or in *A Canticle for Leibowitz,* God works through human beings; here, His ambassadors are machines so intelligent that they have personalities. Not that God makes robots and sends them hurtling toward Earth: the machines in Bass's novels are the artifacts of earlier stages of human civilization, providentially appearing when mankind has most need of them.

In *Half Past Human* we see the plight of those few remaining real humans who live outside, apart from ES; like animals, they are hunted for sport. But in their vigor and resilience lies more hope for the future than in the Nebishes, whose machines are crumbling around them. However, even the Nebishes are not negligible or less than human: some among them can survive when circumstances remove them from the womb of their society. The novel is the story of a new beginning on a new planet for the humans living outside and for the Nebishes adaptable enough to accept it.

Both novels show an impressive command of biological knowledge, and indeed sometimes the flow of jargon obscures rather than communicates. But the point may be that most people in the society are treated (and regard themselves) just as mechanically as the many robots that work for them. Still, knowledge is regarded as good, and machines are good when they serve rather than control. This point is strongly argued in *The Godwhale,* named for a huge plankton harvester. Like the huge automated spaceship that is the *deus ex machina* of *Half Past Human,* the Godwhale is an artifact of a freer, more expansive past. Although these machines are so powerful that they are regarded as "cyberdeities," they are purposeless without free humans to direct them. In *The Godwhale* that direction comes partly from the chosen few, true humans who have adapted to life in the sea, and partly from a superman bred by Nebishes to command the harvester. "Miracles" occur at opportune times in both novels: the rescue of the outsiders in *Half Past Human,* and the regeneration of marine life in *The Godwhale.* Whereas the first shows the hope of a new society among the stars, the second gives promises of a regeneration of life on Earth.

Together, *Half Past Human* and *The Godwhale* are rewarding novels, rich both in characterization and in scientific detail, yet concerned with still larger matters. That *The Godwhale* offers a new proof of the existence of God shows just how large that concern is.

—Walter E. Meyers

BATCHELOR, John Calvin

Nationality: American. **Born:** Bryn Mawr, Pennsylvania, 29 April 1948. **Education:** Princeton University, New Jersey, A.B. 1970; University of Edinburgh Divinity School, 1973-74; Union Theological Seminary, New York, M.Div. 1976. **Career:** Editor and book reviewer, *SoHo Weekly News,* New York, 1975-77; book reviewer, *Village Voice,* New York, 1977-80. **Agent:** George Borchardt, 136 East 57th Street, New York, New York 10022, U.S.A. **Address:** c/o Linden Press, Prentice Hall Building, 190 Sylvan Avenue, Englewood Cliffs, New Jersey 07632, U.S.A.

SCIENCE FICTION PUBLICATIONS

Novels

The Further Adventures of Halley's Comet. New York, Congdon and Lattes, 1980; London, Panther, 1984.
The Birth of the People's Republic of Antarctica. New York, Dial, 1983; London, Panther, 1984.
Peter Nevsky and the True Story of the Russian Moon Landing: A Novel. New York, Holt, 1993.

OTHER PUBLICATIONS

Novels

American Falls. New York, Norton, 1985; London, Paladin, 1987.
Gordon Liddy Is My Muse, by Tommy "Tip" Paine. New York, Linden Press, 1990.
Walking the Cat, by Tommy "Tip" Paine: Gordon Liddy Is My Muse II. New York, Linden Press, 1991.
Father's Day. New York, Holt, and London, Coronet, 1994.

Other

Thunder in the Dust: Classic Images of Western Movies, photographs by John R. Hamilton. New York, Stewart Tabori and Chang, 1987; as *Thunder in the Dust: Great Shots from the Western Movies,* London, Aurum Press, 1987.

*

John Calvin Batchelor comments:

(1986) I first read science fiction when I was 11 years old, and the first adult novel I ever read was *Nineteen Eighty-Four,* which I can remember thinking was much too sad. I have learned to say that I write antiutopian fiction. That is too technical a term, however, and lacks the fun of saying sci-fi.

*   *   *

Though often ignored by science fiction readers and the body of organized "fandom," John Calvin Batchelor's *The Further Adventures of Halley's Comet* and *The Birth of the People's Republic of Antarctica* received some extravagant praise from both general and SF reviewers. Like Thomas Pynchon's gigantic and encyclopedic *Gravity's Rainbow, Halley's Comet* explores and satirizes the history of ideas in the West through a modern gothic tale told in a baroque and seemingly perverse style, against the grain of the accepted gothic *frisson* of shock and menace. The plot involves the abduction of a bunch of quixotic idealists by a family of fabulously powerful and capitalistic modern-day robber barons; the former are imprisoned in Craven Castle, while the latter pursue a Machiavellian plan to extend their empire of property into space by means of secret technology and legalistic chicanery. This is all placed in historical perspective by the recurring visits of a trio of seemingly supernatural luminaries who are associated with Halley's Comet and seem to be the ever-returning Magi. The literary polarities of this book—zany comedy and Juvenalian invective—are seldom discoverable in the convention-ridden and stylistically lackluster body of genre SF; however, the watered down mix of pyrotechnics should appeal to those who find Pynchon attractive but too inaccessible.

The Birth of the People's Republic of Antarctica begins similarly in a Pynchonesque mode, depicting a crew of down-and-out American draft dodgers in Sweden, together with an assortment of other eccentric, grandiose, and slightly comic characters. The tale gradually shapes itself into a new mode that can be described as postheroic saga: larger-than-life tragic figures struggle with the hostile elements of storm wave, fire, and ice in a near-future world wherein civilization is collapsing and human nobility seems able to provide little hope of redemption amid ubiquitous evil and hardship. The protagonist-narrator's name, "Grim Fiddle," is a kind of rebus for the style and content of the book, uniting as it does concepts of severity and frivolity, though all transitions taking place through *People's Republic of Antarctica* are towards the increasingly severe: the book's "fiddle" concept is transformed eventually to one of the futility of struggle for survival or betterment. The entire book is a mythic life story from the hero's mysterious conception and Christmas time birth to his downfall, exile, and impending mysterious doom, while the key scenarios resemble elemental and societal designs for hell: seas of fire and ice; societies falling into demagoguery and terror; a dark sea journey in which Grim Fiddle and his comrades drift to the barren Falklands and the northern fingers of the Antarctic, where human life is mean, violent, and easily corrupted.

Bruce Gillespie has remarked that *People's Republic of Antarctica* is spoiled by a "fluffed" ending in which the author "seems to lose control of the narrative." The criticism is well made, as the narrative fragments into a set of meditative pieces about the narrator's uncompleted story. More importantly still, the ending attempts to draw grand ethical conclusions that are insufficiently tied to the body of the tale (which itself is marred by passages of loaded and simplistic ethical-philosophical analysis). This fault also betrays *Halley's Comet;* in each case, a stylistic *tour de force* is ineptly tied to a sentimental and superficial philosophy in which naturalism, positivism, capitalism, and utilitarianism are the abstract bad guys. Batchelor's vision does not have the irony, ambivalence, and troubled complexity of Pynchon's. Though the books are flawed and ultimately disappointing, their sights are set mightily high and they contain some writing that falls only just short of magnificence.

—Russell Blackford

BATES, Harry

Pseudonyms: Anthony Gilmore (joint pseudonym, with Desmond W. Hall); A.R. Holmes; Quien Sabe; S.F. Whozis; H.G. Winter. **Nationality:** American. **Born:** Hiram Gilmore Bates III, Pittsburgh, Pennsylvania, 9 October 1900. **Education:** Allegheny College, Meadville, Pennsylvania, 1917-18; University of Pennsylvania, Philadelphia, 1919-20. **Career:** Clockmaker, 1914-17, 1920-22; reporter, Philadelphia *Enquirer,* 1923; assistant cameraman, Whitman-Bennett Studios, 1924; editor for Clayton magazines, including *Astounding Stories,* 1930-33, and *Strange Tales,* 1931-32; editor, *Technocracy,* 1935-37, and for the WPA art and writers projects; actor and machinist; story analyst, Columbia Pictures, 1958-59, and David O. Selznick, 1960. **Awards:** Midamericon World Science-Fiction Convention award, 1976. **Died:** 1981.

SCIENCE FICTION PUBLICATIONS

Short Stories

Space Hawk: The Greatest of Interplanetary Adventures (with Desmond W. Hall as Anthony Gilmore). New York, Greenberg, 1952.

Author of numerous other short stories.

*

Harry Bates comments:

(1981) *Astounding Stories* (now *Analog*) was born to the publisher William Clayton and one of his editors—me—in a now unimaginable world populated by a single science fiction magazine, Hugo Gernsback's *Amazing Stories,* which published amateurishly written "gadget" stories. The *Amazing* writers got one-tenth of a cent a word after publication; the writers for the Clayton empire were professionals, getting the very-high-for-those-days minimum of two cents on acceptance. I agreed with Clayton that *Astounding* had to have competent professional writing with strong plots and physical action; but its stories had also, of course, to contain tinges of science and binges of excitements and moreover be astounding—and where was any body of writers to cook to this recipe?

I had to create one. Because they had already sold to me I called on the writers in adventure magazines of which I already was editor, coaxing them to attempt this very different new field. Almost to a man they knew no science, and to use their stories at all I had (when possible) to correct and amplify what they turned in. I gave out story ideas right and left and did enormous amounts of hurried rewriting. Eventually almost all of these writers quit trying, for they had to eat, and there was no second market for the stories I had to reject.

The public in those days had never heard the term science fiction and had to be educated to it. *Amazing* often used the ugly term *scientification,* which I had as quickly as possible to suppress from the genre. Physical action remained an *Astounding* requisite. No one then dreamed what today's science fiction of way-way-out imaginings—fantasy—would be; if one of today's stories had been submitted to me then I'd probably have had to turn it down so as not to estrange the readers we aimed for and were accumulating. In time *Astounding,* in spite of its minimum of two cents a word, all but got out of the red, so that it was instantly profitable when Street & Smith with its much lower word rate took it over.

The stories I wrote in collaboration with my assistant D.W. Hall during those infant years were the product of sheer necessity, to avoid filling out the magazine with worse. The first Hawk Carse story was written as an example to my writers of the wanted element of character, and it was its extreme success that demanded the writing of the several that followed. All the stories published later under my own name were written hastily for a quick buck after my separation from *Astounding,* my prime interests lying elsewhere. I remember that in each case I hesitated at using my own name rather than a pseudonym; but its added value all but guaranteed the quick sale, however sloppy the writing. Who might have guessed that one day there would come into being such a phenomenon as museums of science fiction— anthologies!— necropolises!—and that such imperfect stories as mine would be resurrected to populate them? There, now, they live again, after a fashion—zombies, all their sores still upon them.

The worst occurred with my "Not Understanding," which Gernsback characteristically renamed "The Triggered Dimension." When his *Science Fiction Plus* folded, his editor, wanting to squeeze into the last issue this last long story of mine, attempted the impossible, cutting out almost completely its very necessary central scene—the scene which gave the reason for the story and my title—and shortening the last sentence of paragraph after paragraph so as to save single lines. So one day I rewrote the story with the care I wish heartily I'd given it in the first place and with the cut-out parts restored—and then while I was at it I rewrote half of the others that had appeared under my own name. One, "A Matter of Speed," became "Oh Outrage!," a longish novel of very different mood which bad health has so far not let me quite finish.

Friends who since have read my "Alas, All Thinking" have asked me how I ever could have projected *Homo terminal* with mental processes so degenerated. The reason lies not quite in the realm of pure fantasy. Beginning when quite young (and having what I thought was a good body) I remained aware always that *Homo* of my day thoroughly forgets he is an animal with the body of an animal and early loses all inborn capacity to enjoy the *moving* of his body, coming almost always to overvalue the non-moving brain. I had merely to extrapolate. It happens that upon rereading the story I found I'd given no solid examples of his degenerated thinkings, so when I rewrote it I gave many, too many, Book-An-Hour Devourers will say. But perhaps there exists somewhere a reader or two who, like me in the writing, will find pleasure in my assortment of bad thinkings. It is for *these*—educated adults—that I put a few strictly unnecessary extra ones in. Devourers, I do not rewrite stories for *you.*

* * *

Building on his experience as an editor of action-adventure pulps for William Clayton, Harry Bates began his career in science fiction as founding editor of the magazine whose name—*Astounding*—would become under later leadership synonymous with hard science fiction. But Bates said that his first writers of stories for *Astounding* in 1930 were "almost wholly ignorant of science and technology." He named the magazine. He enlisted and cajoled professional pulp writers to add a science veneer to action and adventure narratives. He rewrote and wrote pseudonymously much of the material himself, and he paid professional rates. The result was a wider readership and a wider professional base for the genre that had begun hardly as literature with the Gernsback "scientifiction." Under the name Anthony Gilmore, Bates and his fellow editor D.W. Hall began the highly popular Hawk Carse series. The literary qualities of the fast-paced action tale in this series helped establish the space opera characteristics in science fiction that have to this day balanced the hard descriptions of scientific speculation and technology in order to make the genre exciting and popular as well as speculative and futuristic. The stories in the Hawk Carse series were collected as *Space Hawk.*

Bates edited the first 34 issues of *Astounding* as well as a few issues of a rival for *Weird Tales* entitled *Strange Tales,* but he continued to publish important science fiction stories under his own name after his editing work had ended. Apparently, the added speculative and scientific thoughts that he had worked up in the Clayton offices in order to capture more of the pulp market took a permanent hold on his imagination, and so Bates himself is representative of the professional pulp writers with little original scientific

training who helped to create the genre. "Alas, All Thinking" expresses a classic theme of early science fiction with a tone and writing style that also embody the best and the worst characteristics of the genre. The theme is ultimately from the 18th-century Enlightenment, and one wonders what has been the source of transmission from the *philosophes* to the New York pulp writers. But somehow the theme is intact: a fear of too much rationality and the ironic sense of progress leading to actual degeneration in humanness. The theme is mingled with the Golden Age/Iron Age myths in which life appears richer, more fertile, more heroic in the past; and the time travel gimmick of superscience facilitates the use of the present even as an heroic past so that satire fuses in the story with the myth of lost innocence. Bates's writing does not understate the theme, and when he tries to heighten emotion at the end the tonal effect is stiff. The story, like many others of this decade, is at the same time poignant, rich, and primitive.

Bates's single most well-known story (filmed in 1951 as *The Day the Earth Stood Still*) also first appeared in *Astounding*—this time the Campbell magazine of 1940. "Farewell to the Master" is a story rich with influence on the genre and less overwritten than much of Bates's other work. The tapestry of the story weaves elements ranging backward in indebtedness to Mary Shelley's *Frankenstein* and forward in apparent influence to Walter Tevis's *Mockingbird* (1980). It is fascinating to think of the old pro pulp editor reaching backward to the romantics and influencing as academic a writer as Tevis several decades later. Bates tells the story of a technologically made creature who transcends his creators in competence so that he becomes the master, and yet there is an enigmatic sadness inherent in this future hero who is somehow more incomplete than his more primitive makers. The accomplishment of Bates illustrates how the genre which began in the practicalities of the pulp markets has progressed through a fine web of influence and allusion.

—Donald M. Hassler

BAXTER, John

Pseudonyms: James Blackstone; Martin Loran. **Nationality:** Australian. **Born:** Sydney, New South Wales, 14 December 1939. **Education:** Waverly College, Sydney, 1944-54. **Family:** Married 1) Merie Elizabeth Brooker in 1962 (divorced 1967); 2) Joyce Allison Agee in 1978. **Career:** Staff controller, New South Wales State Government, Sydney, 1957-67; publicity director, Australian Commonwealth Film Unit, Sydney, 1967-70; presenter, *Understanding Films* series, 1969; film critic, *Kaleidoscope* programme, BBC Radio, London, 1972-80; lecturer, United States Embassy, London, 1973-74, and for United States Government in Europe, 1974-75, and for Hollins College, Virginia, 1975-76, and London Campus, 1976-78; guest lecturer, Australian Film and TV School, 1982; assessor, Australian Film Commission, 1983. Since 1984, producer, Australian Broadcasting Corporation. **Awards:** Australian Film award, 1969; Kranz Film Festival award, 1970; Benson and Hedges prize for TV documentary, 1970; Ditmar award, 1971; Australian Council Literature Board Fellowship, 1984. **Address:** c/o Curtis Brown Ltd, 162-168 Regent Street, London W1A 1AA, England.

SCIENCE FICTION PUBLICATIONS

Novels

The Off-Worlders. New York, Ace, 1966; as *The God Killers,* Sydney, Horwitz, 1968.
The Hermes Fall. London, Panther, and New York, Simon and Schuster, 1978.
Torched! (with John Brosnan as James Blackstone). London, Grafton, 1986.

Short Stories

Author of short stories.

OTHER PUBLICATIONS

Novels

Adam's Woman (novelization of screenplay). Sydney, Horwitz, 1970.
The Bidders. Philadelphia, Lippincott, 1979; as *Bidding,* London, Granada, 1980.
The Kid. New York, Viking Press, 1981.
The Black Yacht. New York, Jove, and London, New English Library, 1982.
Bondi Blues. St. Leonards, New South Wales, Allen and Unwin, 1993.

Plays

Screenplays (documentaries): *Beyond the Pack Ice,* 1968; *Golf in Australia,* 1969; *After Proust,* 1969; *Australian Diary* series, 1969-70; *Top End,* 1970; *The Amazing Years of Cinema* (1 episode), 1976.
Television Documentaries: *Understanding Film* series, 1969; *No Roses for Michael,* 1970; *The Cutting Room* series, n.d.; *Filmstruck* series, n.d.; *First Take* series, 1988.

Other

Hollywood in the Thirties. New York, A.S. Barnes, and London, Zwemmer, 1968.
Science Fiction in the Cinema. New York, A.S. Barnes, and London, Zwemmer, 1970.
The Australian Cinema. Sydney and London, Angus and Robertson, 1970.
The Gangster Film. New York, A.S. Barnes, and London, Zwemmer, 1970.
The Cinema of Josef von Sternberg. New York, A.S. Barnes, and London, Zwemmer, 1971.
The Cinema of John Ford. New York, A.S. Barnes, and London, Zwemmer, 1971.
Hollywood in the Sixties. New York, A.S. Barnes, and London, Tantivy Press, 1972.
Sixty Years of Hollywood. South Brunswick, New Jersey, A.S. Barnes, and London, Tantivy Press, 1973.
An Appalling Talent: Ken Russell. London, Joseph, 1973.
Stunt: The Story of the Great Movie Stunt Men. London, Macdonald, 1973; New York, Doubleday, 1974.

King Vidor. New York, Monarch Press, 1976.
The Hollywood Exiles. New York, Taplinger, and London, Macdonald and Jane's, 1976.
The Fire Came By: The Riddle of the Great Siberian Explosion, with Thomas Atkins. New York, Doubleday, and London, Macdonald and Jane's, 1976.
The Video Handbook: Getting the Best from Your VCR, with Brian Norris. London, Fontana, 1982.
Who Burned Australia? The Ash Wednesday Fires. London, New English Library, 1984.
Filmstruck: Australia at the Movies. Sydney, Nelson, 1988.
Fellini. London, Fourth Estate, 1993; New York, St. Martin's Press, 1994.
Buñuel. London, Fourth Estate, 1994.

Editor, *The Pacific Book of Australian Science Fiction.* Sydney, Angus and Robertson, 1968; as *The Pacific Book of Science Fiction,* London, Angus and Robertson, 1969; as *The First Pacific Book of Science Fiction,* Syndey, Arkon, 1973.
Editor, *The Second Pacific Book of Australian Science Fiction.* Sydney, Angus and Robertson, 1971; as *The Second Pacific Book of Science Fiction,* London, Angus and Robertson, 1971.

*

John Baxter comments:

Ted Carnell discovered and encouraged many young writers like myself in the 1960s. Almost alone among them, I moved away from SF as I made a professional career, a defection Ted tried hard, though vainly, to approve. While writing mostly mainstream fiction and cinema history, as well as becoming increasingly involved in radio and TV production, I'm drawn back to SF frequently, though more often as critic and scenarist than a writer of prose. SF, like Australia, has become a place I revisit, but where I no longer feel at home since, sadly, both the cinema and Australia are almost as inimical to good SF writing as they were when I first read *Astounding* and saw *The Incredible Shrinking Man* four decades ago.

*   *   *

As editor of the first two major anthologies of Australian SF writing, John Baxter exerted a twofold influence upon the Australian SF renaissance of the 1970s. Rejecting the concept that science fiction must be prophetic, Baxter emphasized "insight rather than intelligent guessing," arguing that "a story which tells us that a rose is a rose and explains why is far more worthwhile than one which states that E equals MC squared and leaves it at that." Baxter also esteemed the literary qualities of science fiction, publishing material that was innovative in style and structure, yet neither ignoring nor denigrating stories written in a more traditional narrative style. In short, he proclaimed an Australian SF that was literate, thoughtful, and original.

Baxter's own short stories reflect these criteria. They are original and ambitious, reflecting influences from both traditional and New-Wave SF. One of his best-known stories, "Apple," is a traditional man-meets-monster story—except that the encounter takes place in a surreal setting, and the story evolves from imagery and setting rather than action. A gigantic apple lies cradled in a valley, the juices dripping from its side as men tunnel into its core. The central character is a professional Moth Killer who battles with the grubs that lurk in the apple's core. It is suggested that the apple-world may be the result of atomic warfare, but for Baxter, the explanation is incidental; his story conveys its own inner logic, and that is enough. The same is true of the more experimental story, "The Beach." Described as "a first sketch of what an *Australian SF* story might be like," it employs distinctively Australian symbols, and abandons conventional narrative structure in order to emphasize mood and imagery. The style and symbolism are evident in the closing lines: "Without fear, he swam towards the sea mountains, the peaks of which even now he could see gilded beyond the green. There, he knew, he would find his grail, the sunken, brooding sun."

Baxter's two SF novels are more pedestrian. *The Off-Worlders* is set on the planet Merryland in the year 2833 and deals with a rustic community which is suspicious of technology and has rejected God, turning instead to Satan. *The Hermes Fall* is based on *The Fire Came By,* Baxter's nonfiction work on the famous Siberian "meteorite" of 1908 (written with Thomas Atkins). Despite its well-researched background, *The Hermes Fall* is merely a conventional disaster novel, using science fiction effects (in this case, an asteroid on, collision course with the Earth).

Always interested in cinema, Baxter has been devoting his energies to this field, and seems to have abandoned SF for the writing of novels in the bestseller mold, such as *The Bidders* and *The Black Yacht.* His short story "Down from Demolition," in the 1985 Australian anthology *Urban Fantasies,* was a welcome—if brief—return to the field.

—Van Ikin

BAXTER, Stephen

Nationality: English. **Born:** 1957. **Awards:** Hubbard Writers of the Future contest winner, 1989.

SCIENCE FICTION PUBLICATIONS

Novels (series: Xeelee)

Raft. London, Grafton, 1991; New York, Roc, 1992.
Timelike Infinity (Xeelee). London, HarperCollins, 1992; New York, Roc, 1993.
Anti-Ice. London, HarperCollins, 1993; New York, HarperPrism, 1994.
Flux (Xeelee). London, HarperCollins, 1993; New York, HarperPrism, 1995.
Ring. London, HarperCollins, 1994.
The Time Ships. London, HarperCollins, 1995.

Short Stories

Author of numerous short stories.

*   *   *

Stephen Baxter is one of several British SF writers whose career began with short stories in the pages of *Interzone,* in 1986; he was also a prizewinner in the Hubbard Writers of the Future con-

test, in 1989. A mathematician now working in information technology, he has from the start produced well-imagined hard science fiction of a quality aspired to but rarely attained by most other scientist/SF writers, though he also exhibits some of the faults common to the subgenre.

Four of Baxter's novels, and around 20 of his short stories, make up his huge and complex "Xeelee Sequence" future history, an extremely impressive though at times heavy-going body of work spanning the next five million years or so. The Xeelee were highly powerful aliens, who left artifacts which have been discovered by mankind.

The first novel in the series, *Raft,* is centered on the startling premise that gravity in one particular alternate universe is a billion times higher than we know, yet human beings, flung into that universe in an Earth spaceship through a hole in space/time centuries before the time of the novel, manage to survive. Now, the scientists living on the remains of the ship trade machine-produced food for iron ore laboriously dug out of a dead star, around which lives a community of miners.

Baxter handles his explanations of the gravitic forces holding these settlements together well; the science is integral to the story, and the reader never feels bullied or patronised. There is a common atmosphere enveloping the settlements, which allows travel between them—reminiscent of Bob Shaw's *Ragged Astronauts* trilogy. The interrelationship of the groups, and the inevitable revolutions and wars, are finely worked, with the right combination of social pressures and strong individual leaders, though Our Young Hero is a little bit too much precisely that.

In *Timelike Infinity* a physicist, Michael Poole, creates a wormhole in time-space; the other end arrives 1500 years later, when Earth is occupied by aliens, the Qax. A group of rebels from the future come back to Poole's time through the wormhole, pursued by the Qax. The resolution of the novel, in which Poole operates a hyperdrive within the wormhole, depends on quantum paradoxes, as Poole—or something like him—heads off, alone, into vastly distant time and space. Again, an exciting storyline is bogged down at times by stodgy info-dumps, either delivered by characters effectively lecturing at each other, or delivered directly by the author.

Flux, like *Raft,* has humans living in a seemingly impossible environment: shrunk to submicroscopic size, they live in a mantle of superfluid within a neutron star. Once again the science is well-worked out and plausible, and this time there are fewer info-dumps.

The final book in the sequence, *Ring,* is larger and more complex than any of the others. The novel is notable for a human-based semiartificial intelligence sent in a probe into the Sun to investigate its state. Over millions of years she observes the Sun being systematically destroyed by deliberate alien means, and somehow manages to stay sane.

The main set of characters find a Xeelee faster-than-light ship and explore the universe; at times the book becomes a travelogue-with-lectures. The Xeelee Ring, a huge device set up to save the universe, has been destroyed, but they travel back through time to when it is still there, and escape through it to another universe where they will reestablish humanity. Michael Poole, who has been floating around the universe for millions of years, adds his contribution to the plot. Many readers may find themselves skipping all the detailed solar physics—but at least the info-dumps in this book tend to be in fairly small chunks; even so, there are far too many heavy lectures.

Unlike much hard SF, Baxter's Xeelee novels are well-written and carry the interest throughout their length, but the science is often far too heavy. His characters are generally both believeable and interesting, but the novels are very definitely science- and plot-driven, rather than character-driven.

The Xeelee Sequence may be Baxter's most impressive work to date, but his most enjoyable novels are *Anti-Ice* and *The Time Ships* which are both, in quite different ways, Victorian pastiches. The first is a parallel world story set in a late 19th-century Britain changed by the discovery of anti-ice, a substance which explodes with devastating results when heated; the novel begins with its use in Sebastopol in 1855 to bring the Crimean War to an end. Like nuclear energy, anti-ice can be used for peaceful purposes as well, so that Britain has not only railways but anti-ice-powered monorails; its superconducting properties are also touched on. Baxter uses the plot of this novel to examine imperialism, the rights and wrongs of a balance of power through mutual assured destruction, and the moral responsibilities of inventors—but he also has fun. The book is a glorious homage to Wells and Verne; the characters voyage to the Moon in an anti-ice-powered vessel, sipping brandy in a pigskin-padded Smoking Cabin with Turkish rugs on the floor.

The Time Ships is a sequel to H.G. Wells's *The Time Machine*, and published in the centenary year of Wells's book. The Time Traveller sets off to rescue Weena, but finds that he journeys into a different future where technologically advanced Morlocks live under the inner surface of a shell they have built around the Sun; his first journey has caused a different future to occur. His travels include the far future, the far past (the Palaeocene era), a different version of 1873, where he goes to warn his younger self not to mess up time, and a very bleak and disturbing version of 1938. *The Time Ships* is an extremely readable sequel and pastiche; Baxter has the voice just right. The Traveller's journeys and adventures, and the technological development and social structure of each society, are excellently drawn. Baxter has clearly done a vast amount of research into Wells's work; this informs the novel, rather than being over-conspicuous, as all-too-often happens.

Baxter is impressively prolific. In his first eight years he has produced six novels, several of them very complex and one of them, *The Time Ships,* a potential classic. In the same period he has had around 50 stories published, mainly in *Interzone,* but also in most of the British original anthologies available at the time. All his novels have appeared in the U.S. [American editions of *Ring* and *The Time Ships* were planned at the time this article was submitted], but only a few of his short stories, in *Isaac Asimov's Science Fiction Magazine.*

In a remarkably short space of time Baxter has established himself as one of the very few hard SF writers actually worth reading. Nevertheless, it's when he relaxes and has fun with his creations that he really becomes a good read.

—David V. Barrett

BAYLEY, Barrington John

Nationality: British. **Born:** Birmingham, Warwickshire, 9 April 1937. **Education:** Adams Grammar School in Shropshire, 1948-53. **Military Service:** Served in the Royal Air Force, 1955-57. **Family:** Married Joan Lucy Clarke in 1969; one son and one daughter. **Career:** Reporter, *Wellington Journal,* early 1950s; civil servant, Ministry of War, Shropshire, 1954-55; in Australian Public Ser-

vice, London, 1957-58; has also worked as a clerk, typist, and coal miner. **Awards:** Japanese Seiun award, 1976, 1983. **Agent:** Uwe Luserke, Box 46, D-7259 Friolzheim, Germany; or, Michael Congdon, c/o Don Congdon Associates, 156 Fifth Avenue, Suite 625, New York, New York 10010, U.S.A. **Address:** 48 Turreff Avenue, Donnington, Telford, Shropshire TF2 8HE, England.

SCIENCE FICTION PUBLICATIONS

Novels (series: Soul of the Robot)

The Star Virus. New York, Ace, 1970.
Annihilation Factor. New York, Ace, 1972; London, Allison and Busby, 1979.
Empire of Two Worlds. New York, Ace, 1972; London, Hale, 1974.
Collision Course. New York, DAW, 1973; as *Collision with Chronos: A Novel,* London, Allison and Busby, 1977.
The Fall of Chronopolis. New York, DAW, 1974; London, Allison and Busby, 1979.
Soul of the Robot. Garden City, New York, Doubleday, 1974; revised as *The Soul of the Robot,* Allison and Busby, 1976.
The Garments of Caean. Garden City, New York, Doubleday, 1976; expanded, London, Fontana, 1978.
The Grand Wheel. New York, DAW, 1977; London, Fontana, 1979.
Star Winds. New York, DAW, 1978.
The Pillars of Eternity. New York, DAW, 1982; with *The Garments of Caean,* London, Pan, 1989.
The Zen Gun. New York, DAW, 1983; London, Methuen, 1984.
The Rod of Light (Soul of the Robot). London, Allison and Busby, 1984; New York, Arbor House, 1987.
The Forest of Peldain. New York, DAW, 1985.

Short Stories

The Knights of the Limits. London, Allison and Busby, 1978.
The Seed of Evil. London, Allison and Busby, 1979.

*

Bibliography: *Barrington J. Bayley: A Bibliography* by Mike Ashley, Manchester, Beccon, 1981.

Barrington John Bayley comments:

I have no personal philosophy as regards my work; I write according to my ability and interest. I regard myself as a genre SF writer—that is, as a traditionalist.

* * *

Barrington John Bayley is one of the few authors to have bridged the philosophical gap between proponents of traditional space opera and the more demanding literary tastes of recent editors and readers. He has succeeded at this by using the traditional devices of the genre, wedding them to a more sophisticated writing style and an inventive imagination. Much of his fiction is pervaded by a wry humor that is frequently unsettling.

Many of Bayley's plots are unabashedly space operas. A mysterious anomaly in space known as The Patch is consuming entire worlds as an interstellar empire erupts into civil war in *Annihilation Factor.* This galaxy-spanning adventure is a noticeable advance over his earlier *The Star Virus,* and subsequent novels show a steady enhancement of his abilities. *Collision Course* postulates that there are two separate "nows" and that the two waves of reality are moving in opposite directions along the time waves. The plot involves the imminent passing of the two realities through one another, and the effects on both civilizations during the transition. Bayley experiments with the nature of time again in *The Fall of Chronopolis.* A theocratic society that possesses time travel refuses to recognize the possibility that their attempts to police the timeways may change reality and cancel out their own existence.

Bayley's dark humor becomes evident with *The Garments of Caean.* A bankrupt sailor pilfers a suit of clothes from a band of pirates, but when he wears them, his personality changes—clothes do indeed make the man. The pirates recapture the suit, which is revealed to be a sentient lifeform from a planet intent upon interstellar empire. But the clothing has a mind of its own, and is determined to reclaim its first owner.

Satire is the order of the day in *Soul of the Robot* and *The Rod of Light.* In the former, a robot possessed of extraordinary powers makes its way through a variety of decadent human societies trying to solve the mysteries of existence. In the latter, evolving robots are in rebellion against their human masters, even though only one of their number has true consciousness.

Humans and aliens indulge in elaborate gambling schemes that determine the future of the human race in *The Grand Wheel,* and a ship sets off to explore the universe in *Star Winds. The Pillars of Eternity* and *The Zen Gun* are also ostensibly space operas, but each is inventive and so offbeat in plotting and setting that they stand out among many competing adventure stories. *The Forest of Peldain* depicts a lost race transported to another planet with unusual and highly entertaining results.

Although not a prolific short story writer, Bayley has made an impression there as well. His satiric humor is at its best in "Integrity," in which a libertarian reaches the logical consequence of his beliefs and sets free each individual cell of his body. Aliens have entered human nobility in "All the King's Men" and a single city survives the collapse of the universe in "Exit from City 5."

Galaxies themselves are entities in "Cosmic Combatants" and a child with no nationality is adopted by an airline in "The Man in Transit." Alien manipulation of human bodies is a common theme, repeated in such stories as "Sporting with Chid" and "Maladjustment." For the most part, Bayley's short fiction is darkly ironic, occasionally using experimental writing styles to emphasize strange viewpoints. Although not the most popular writer of space adventure, Bayley has established himself as one of the most innovative of that theme.

—Don D'Ammassa

BEAR, Greg(ory Dale)

Nationality: American. **Born:** San Diego, California, 20 August 1951. **Education:** San Diego State University, 1968-73, A.B. in English 1973. **Family:** Married 1) Christina M. Nielsen in 1975 (divorced 1981); 2) Astrid Anderson in 1983, one daughter and one son. **Career:** Part-time Lecturer, San Diego Aerospace Museum, 1969-72; technical writer and planetarium operator, Reuben H. Fleet Space Theater, San Diego, 1973; bookstore clerk, 1974-

75. Since 1975 freelance writer and illustrator: reviewer, *San Diego Union,* 1979-82; co-editor, Science Fiction Writers of America *Forum;* co-founder, Association of Science Fiction Artists. **Awards:** Nebula award (twice), 1984, for short story, 1986; Hugo award, 1984, 1987; Prix Apollo, 1986. **Agent:** Richard Curtis Associates, 171 East 74th Street, Suite 2, New York, New York 10021, U.S.A. **Address:** 506 Lakeview Road, Alderwood Manor, Washington 98037, U.S.A.

SCIENCE FICTION PUBLICATIONS

Novels (series: Eon; Forge of God; Michael Perrin; Star Trek)

Hegira. New York, Dell, 1979; London, Gollancz, 1987.
Psychlone. New York, Ace, 1979; as *Lost Souls,* New York, Charter, 1982; London, Gollancz, 1989.
Beyond Heaven's River. New York, Dell, 1980; revised, Wallington, Surrey, Severn House, 1989.
Strength of Stones. New York, Ace, 1981; revised, London, Gollancz, 1988.
Corona: A Star Trek Novel. New York, Pocket Books, 1984; Bath, Firecrest, 1985.
The Infinity Concerto (Perrin). New York, Berkley, 1984; London, Legend, 1988.
Blood Music. New York, Arbor House, 1985; London, Gollancz, 1986.
Eon. New York, Bluejay, 1985; London, Gollancz, 1986.
The Serpent Mage (Perrin). New York, Berkley, 1986; London, Century, 1988.
The Forge of God. New York, Tor, and London, Gollancz, 1987.
Eternity (Eon). New York, Warner, 1988; London, Gollancz, 1989.
Hardfought, with *Cascade Point* by Timothy Zahn. New York, Tor, 1988.
Queen of Angels. Norwalk, Connecticut, Easton Press, and London, Gollancz, 1990.
Heads. London, Legend, 1990; New York, St. Martin's Press, 1991.
Anvil of Stars (Forge). London, Legend, and New York, Warner, 1992.
Songs of Earth and Power (includes *The Infinity Concerto* and *The Serpent Mage*). London, Legend, 1992; New York, Tor, 1994.
Moving Mars. New York, Tor, and London, Legend, 1993.
Legacy. New York, Tor, 1995.
New Legends. New York, Tor, 1995.

Short Stories

The Wind from a Burning Woman. Sauk City, Wisconsin, Arkham House, 1983.
Sleepside Story. New Castle, Virginia, Cheap Street, 1988.
Early Harvest. Cambridge, Massachusetts, NESFA Press, 1988.
Tangents. New York, Warner, and London, Gollancz, 1989.
Sisters. Eugene, Oregon, Pulphouse, 1992.
The Venging. London, Legend, 1992.
Bear's Fantasies: Six Stories in Old Paradigms. Newark, New Jersey, Wildside Press, 1992.

*   *   *

Among science fiction authors of the late 20th century, few have been as influential in transforming the genre as Greg Bear, a prolific leader in exploring the concept of *change* as it affects civilization, science, and even human nature. Perhaps no other writer so well typifies one of the hallmarks of science fiction—the belief that ideas are among the most precious things. In both short works and novels, Bear rejects the ancient notion of hubris, preaching instead that a daring question, even one hurled at heaven, can be more sacred than a prayer.

While not limited strictly to so-called hard SF, Bear is consistently ranked among its premier practitioners, demonstrating that one does not need formal credentials in order to write convincingly about scientific matters. As a thoughtful male or female writer may use empathy to convey believable characters of the opposite sex, Bear the former English major applies energy and thorough research to prospecting concepts far beyond today's headlines.

Greg Bear was born in August 1951 to Wilma and Dale Bear, in San Diego, California. His father was in the navy, and by the time he was 12 Greg had lived in Japan, the Philippines, and Alaska, as well as various parts of the U.S. In Alaska he wrote his first story at age 10 and soon began submitting stories to magazines, selling his first at age 15 to Robert Lowndes's *Famous Science Fiction*. It took five years to sell the next, but by age 23 his stories appeared regularly. Bear's first novel, *The Infinity Concerto,* he finished at 19, but was only sold to Berkley, rewritten, some 12 years later. His first published novel, *Hegira,* appeared in 1979 from Dell; it tells of a human civilization trapped in an artificial world where the only relief from cultural amnesia is found inscribed on the walls of mammoth towers, stretching beyond the sky. The book foretells two of Bear's strongest suits—powerful, almost dreamlike imagery combined with boldly imagined situations that invite new perspectives on aspects of society or science.

These themes carried through in Bear's next novels, *Psychlone* and *Beyond Heaven's River,* which combined speculations about human destiny with themes from the World War II. In order of publication, Bear's subsequent novels were, *Strength of Stones, The Infinity Concerto* (a strong departure into mystical fantasy), *Blood Music Eon, The Forge of God, Eternity, Queen of Angels, Anvil of Stars, Moving Mars,* and *Legacy.* A revised one-volume publication of *The Infinity Concerto* and *The Serpent Mage* was published as *Songs of Earth and Power. Blood Music,* is often cited as Bear's most influential work, in that it most boldly pioneered themes later exploited by many others—bioengineering and nanotechnology. The novel evokes fear, fascination, and exaltation as a protagonist-researcher's own multitudinous body cells acquire first the gift of intelligence, then a godlike power to create.

Several of Bear's later novels fit into two universes. In the *Eon* universe, complexities of space and time travel are combined with speculations about possible synergy between man and machine. Bear's depiction of a vividly advanced human civilization in *Eon* helped earn him a reputation for optimism, even though the situations he portrays can best be described as "tense."

The other fictional universe, portrayed in *Queen of Angels* and *Moving Mars,* explores concepts of artificial intelligence and the quantum nature of reality, but gleans much of its appeal from the alternative family and social structures he describes. In this willingness to reconstruct basic human relationships in plausible ways, Bear has been compared to Robert A. Heinlein, or sometimes Ursula K. LeGuin. *Moving Mars* (1993) won the 1994 Nebula for best novel. *Queen of Angels* was an alternate selection of the Book of the Month Club.

Bear is admired for his short fiction as well as his novels. While the longer works often seem aimed at relentless dissection of a situation and/or idea, the stories tend to concentrate on images and impressions that hang with the reader long after the tale is finished. In his 1983 Nebula-nominated "Petra," Bear describes a nightmare-like microcosm in porcelain-fine detail. The next year, his novella "Hardfought" and novelette "Blood Music" both won Nebula Awards, although the two stories were remarkably different. The former uses atmospheric prose to project a far-future sense of human destiny amidst a galaxy-spanning struggle against hydrogen-based life-forms. The latter fable presaged the hard SF novel of the same name. In 1987, "Tangents" won both the Hugo and Nebula awards for best short story. Bear has had two collections of short fiction, *The Wind from a Burning Woman* (1983) and *Tangents* (1989).

A short story, "Dead Run," was adapted by Alan Brennert for the second Twilight Zone television show. "The White Horse Child" appeared in 1993 as a CD-ROM multimedia presentation from Ebook. Bear's novels and short stories have been translated into 12 languages: Japanese, Russian, Czechoslovakian, French, Polish, Finnish, Swedish, Spanish, Portugeuse, Dutch, German, and Serbo-Croatian.

—David Brin

BEAUMONT, Charles

Pseudonym for Charles Nutt. **Other Pseudonym:** Keith Grantland (joint pseudonym with John E. Tomerlin). **Nationality:** American. **Born:** Chicago, Illinois, 2 January 1929. **Military Service:** Served in the United States Army for one year. **Family:** Married Helen Louise Brown in 1949; one son and two daughters. **Career:** Radio writer, actor, illustrator, and animator. **Awards:** Jules Verne award, 1954; *Playboy* award, for nonfiction, 1961. **Died:** 21 February 1967.

SCIENCE FICTION PUBLICATIONS

Short Stories

The Hunger and Other Stories. New York, Putnam, 1957; abridged as *Shadow Play,* London, Panther, 1964.
Yonder: Stories of Fantasy and Science Fiction. New York, Bantam, 1958.
Night Ride and Other Journeys. New York, Bantam, 1960.
The Magic Man—and Other Science-Fantasy Stories. Greenwich, Connecticut, Fawcett, 1965; London, Fawcett, 1966.
The Edge. London, Panther, 1966.
Best of Beaumont. New York, Bantam, 1982.
Charles Beaumont: Selected Stories, edited by Roger Anker. Arlington Heights, Illinois, Dark Harvest, 1988; as *The Howling Man,* New York, Tor, 1992.

OTHER PUBLICATIONS

Novels

Run from the Hunter (with John E. Tomerlin as Keith Grantland). New York, Fawcett, 1957; London, Boardman, 1959.

The Intruder. New York, Putnam, 1959; London, Frederick Muller, 1960.

Plays

Screenplays: *Queen of Outer Space,* with Ben Hecht, 1958; *The Intruder (The Stranger),* 1962; *Burn, Witch, Burn (Night of the Eagle),* with Richard Matheson and George Baxt, 1962; *The Wonderful World of the Brothers Grimm,* with David P. Harmon and William Roberts, 1962; *The Premature Burial,* with Ray Russell, 1962; *The Haunted Palace,* 1963; *7 Faces of Dr. Lao,* 1964; *The Masque of the Red Death,* with R. Wright Campbell, 1964; *Mister Moses,* with Monja Danischewsky, 1965; *Brain Dead,* with Adam Simon, 1990.

Television Plays: For *Twilight Zone, Naked City, Thriller, Four Star Playhouse, Damon Runyon Theatre, The D.A.'s Man, Markham, One Step Beyond, Have Gun—Will Travel, Wanted—Dead or Alive, Alfred Hitchcock Presents, Route 66,* and other series.

Other

Remember? Remember? New York, Macmillan, 1963.

Editor, with William F. Nolan, *Omnibus of Speed: An Introduction to the World of Motor Sport.* New York, Putnam, 1958; London, Stanley Paul, 1961.
Editor, with William F. Nolan as anonymous co-editor, *The Fiend in You.* New York, Ballantine, 1962.
Editor, with William F. Nolan, *When Engines Roar,* New York, Bantam, 1964.

*

Bibliography: *The Work of Charles Beaumont: An Annotated Bibliography & Guide* by William F. Nolan, San Bernardino, California, Borgo Press, 1986, 2nd edition, 1990.

*   *   *

Charles Beaumont was a consummate craftsman of the popular market short story—perhaps the most accomplished writer of this type of fiction to publish in the 1950s and early 1960s. He wrote extensively for *Playboy* and other magazines, including many in the science fiction field, and often blended elements of humor, horror, psychological suspense, and extrapolative SF. If much of his subject matter is grim, and many of his stories downbeat in resolution, his smooth and upbeat writing style and his superb characterization keep his work from being negative or oppressive.

Among his more than 50 stories (and articles) of science fiction and fantasy is "The Vanishing American," an allegorical tale about a man who becomes invisible to his fellow men. It is perhaps Beaumont's finest short story. Others of note include "Free Dirt," "The Love Master," "The Howling Man," "The Crooked Man" (a prophetic tale about homosexuality), and "Black Country," the best of a number with a jazz music background. *Yonder,* one of several collections, contains most of his pure SF stories first published in such magazines as *IF, Orbit, Imagination,* and *The Magazine of Fantasy & Science Fiction.* A recent volume, *Charles Beaumont: Selected Stories,* collects 30 of his best fantasy and SF tales, including three that were previously unpublished. Each story in this book is introduced by one of Beaumont's friends and peers, who offers anecdotes and reminiscences.

In addition to his fiction, Beaumont was an accomplished screenwriter. He wrote several SF and fantasy films, among them *7 Faces of Dr. Lao,* and he contributed 22 scripts to the television anthology series, *The Twilight Zone,* second in number only to those written by the show's creator, Rod Serling.

His tragic death at 37, of a form of Alzheimer's Disease that had ravaged him and kept him from writing for three years, cut short a career which might well have progressed to major stature.

—Bill Pronzini

———

BEECHAM, Alice. *See* **TUBB, E.C.**

———

BELL, Thornton. *See* **FANTHORPE, R. Lionel.**

———

BELLAMY, Edward

Nationality: American. **Born:** Chicopee Falls, Massachusetts, 26 March 1850. **Education:** Union College, Schenectady, New York, 1867-68; travelled and studied in Germany, 1868-69; studied law: admitted to the Massachusetts Bar, 1871, but never practiced. **Family:** Married Emma Sanderson in 1882; one son and one daughter. **Career:** Staff member, *New York Evening Post,* 1871-72; editorial writer and reviewer, *Springfield Union,* 1872-77; founder with his brother, *Springfield Daily News,* 1880; after 1885 writer and lecturer in support of the Nationalist movement (in favor of nationalization); founder, *New Nation,* Boston, 1891-96. **Died:** 22 May 1898.

SCIENCE FICTION PUBLICATIONS

Novels (series: Julian West)

Dr. Heidenhoff's Process. New York, Appleton, 1880; Edinburgh, Douglas, 1884.
Miss Ludington's Sister: A Romance of Immortality. Boston, Osgood, 1884; London, Reeves, 1890.
Looking Backward, 2000-1887 (West). Boston, Ticknor, 1888; London, Reeves, 1889.
Equality (West). New York, Appleton, and London, Heinemann, 1897.

Short Stories

The Blindman's World and Other Stories. Boston, Houghton Mifflin, and London, Watt, 1898.

Apparitions of Things to Come: Tales of Mystery and Imagination, edited by Franklin Rosemont. Chicago, Kerr, 1990.

OTHER PUBLICATIONS

Novels

Six to One: A Nantucket Idyl. New York, Putnam, and London, Sampson Low, 1878.
The Duke of Stockbridge: A Romance of Shays' Rebellion. New York, Silver Burdett, 1900.

Other

Edward Bellamy Speaks Again! Articles, Public Addresses, Letters. Kansas City, Peerage Press, 1937.
Talks on Nationalism. Chicago, Peerage Press, 1938.
The Religion of Solidarity. Yellow Springs, Ohio, Antioch, 1940.
Selected Writings on Religion and Society, edited by Joseph Schiffman. New York, Liberal Arts Press, 1955.

*

Bibliography: In *Bibliography of American Literature* by Jacob Blanck, New Haven, Connecticut, Yale University Press, vol. 1, 1955; *Edward Bellamy: An Annotated Bibliography of Secondary Criticism* by Richard Toby Widdicombe, New York and London, Garland, 1988.

Critical Studies: *Edward Bellamy,* New York, Columbia University Press, 1944, and *The Philosophy of Edward Bellamy,* New York, King's Crown Press, 1945, both by Arthur E. Morgan; *The Year 2000: A Critical Biography of Edward Bellamy* by Sylvia E. Bowman, New York, Bookman, 1958, and *Edward Bellamy Abroad: An American Prophet's Influence* by Bowman and others, New York, Twayne, 1962; *Edward Bellamy, Novelist and Reformer* by Daniel Aaron and Harry Levin, Schenectady, New York, Union College, 1968; *Authoritarian Socialism in America; Bellamy and the Nationalist Movement* by Arthur Lipow, Berkeley, University of California Press, 1982; *Alternative America: Henry George, Bellamy, Henry Demarest Lloyd, and the Adversary Tradition* by John L. Thomas, Cambridge, Massachusetts, Belknap Press, 1983; *Looking Backward 1988-1888: Essays on Edward Bellamy* edited by Daphne Patai, Amherst, University of Massachusetts Press, 1989.

*   *   *

In *Looking Backward 2000-1887,* Edward Bellamy observed that both the "working classes" and "true and humane men and women, of every degree, are in a mood of exasperation, verging on absolute revolt, against social conditions that reduce life to a brutal struggle for existence." In its sequel, *Equality,* he added the ruin of prairie farmers by capitalist mortgages, the degradation of women through economic exploitation, the recurrent economic crisis, and the concentration of three-quarters of national wealth into the hands of 10 percent of the population. Bellamy's utopianism was the point at which all these deep discontents intersected with the American religious and lay utopian tradition and the world socialist movement. As the spokesman of the "immense average of villagers, of

small-town-dwellers" who believed in "modern inventions, modern conveniences, modern facilities" (Howells), in Yankee gadgetry as white magic for overcoming drudgery, he accepted the financial trusts as more efficient and changeable from private waste and tyranny to a Yankee communism or "Associationism": the nation "organized as the one great corporation . . . in the profits and economies of which all citizens shared."

Bellamy's new frontier is the future. It offers not only better railways, motor carriages, air-cars, telephones, and TV, but also a classless brotherhood of affluence socializing these means of communication and other upper-class privileges to achieve comfort and security for everyone through a reorganized "economy of happiness." Universal high education, work obligation from 21 to 45, equal and guaranteed income for everyone including the old, the sick, and children, flexible planning, and public honors reduce government to a universal civic service called the Great Trust or the Industrial Army. The generals of each guild or industrial branch are chosen by the retired alumni of the guild, and the head of the army is president of the U.S.A. Doctors and teachers have their own guilds, and a writer, artist, journal editor, or inventor is exempted from the army if enough buyers sign over a part of their credit. Individuality is fostered and objectors can "work out a better solution of the problem of existence than our society offers" in a reservation (the first use of this escape-hatch of later utopias).

Bellamy's economic blueprint is integrated into the story of Julian West, who wakes from a mesmeric sleep of 1887 into the Boston of 2000, is informed about the new order by Dr. Leete, and falls in love with Leete's daughter. This system of epoch-contrasts is reactualized in the nightmarish ending when Julian dreams of awakening back in the capitalist society of 1887. He meets its folly and repulsiveness with an anguished eye which supplies to each place and person a counterpossibility; the utopian estrangement culminates in the hallucination about "the possible face that would have been actual if mind and soul had lived," which he sees superimposed upon the living dead of the poor quarter. The lesson is that living in this nightmare and "pleading for crucified humanity" might yet be better than reawakening into the golden 21st century—as, in a final twist, Julian does. *Looking Backward*—intimately informed by Bellamy's constant preoccupation with human plasticity, memory and identity, brute reality and ideal possibility—reposes on a balance of world-times. Its plot is Julian's change of identity. In two of Bellamy's later stories, "The Blindman's World" and "To Whom This May Come," the alienated Earthmen are contrasted to worlds of brotherhood and transparency where men are "lords of themselves." As the anxious idealist becomes an apostate through a healer's reasonable lectures and his daughter's healing sympathy, the construction of a social system for the reader is also the reconstruction of the hero. This radical-democratic innovation, in which a changed world is accompanied by changing people's "nature," is epoch-making for future utopias and for the field of science fiction.

However, Bellamy retreated from this discovery. Just as Julian is the mediator between two social systems for the reader, so Edith Leete is the steadying emotional mediator for Julian, a personal female Christ of Earthly brotherhood. Bellamy's "sunburst" of a new order is validated equally by socialist economics, ethical evolution, and Christian love; his future brings a purified space and man. The friendly house of Dr. Leete is the hearth of spacious, clean, classless Boston, with Edith as the Dickensian cricket on the hearth. Hardheaded civic pragmatism is the obverse of a softhearted, petty-bourgeois "fairy tale of social felicity." Bellamy expects a nonviolent, imminent, and instantaneous abandonment of private capitalism by recognition of its folly. With telling effects, he extrapolated the Rationalist or Jeffersonian principles and institutions to a logical end-product of universal public ownership. But he also remained limited by such ideals. His fascination with the rationally organized army should perhaps not be judged by our reaction today, since it was acquired under Lincoln and translated into peaceful and constructive terms. Further, any utopia before automation had to be harsh on recalcitrants, and Bellamy evolved toward participatory democracy in *Equality*. But even there he continued to stress state mobilization, "public capitalism," and technocratic regimentation *within* economic production as opposed to ideal classless relations outside it, dismissing "the more backward races" and political efforts by "workingmen."

Uncomfortable with sweeping changes of lifestyle, Bellamy is at his strongest in the economics of everyday life outside a capitalist framework—dressing and love, distribution of goods, cultural activities, democratic supply and demand (e.g., in organizing a journal or in solving brain-drain between countries). Here he is quite free from centralized state socialist regulation. When contrasting such warm possibilities with stultifying private competition, he presents exempla of great force, as the initial allegory of the Coach, the parables of the Collective Umbrella and of the Rosebush, or (in *Equality*) the parables of the Water-Tank and of the Masters of the Bread. All such impressive and sometimes splendid apologues come from a laicized and radicalized New England pulpit style rather than from genteel fiction. Their ethical tone and the sentimental plot addressed themselves to women and all those who felt insecure and unfree in bourgeois society. Bellamy's homely lucidity made his romance, with all its limitations, the first authentically American socialist anticipation tale.

Bellamy's success fuses various SF strands and traditions. He interfused the preceding, narratively helpless tradition of utopian anticipations—tales culminating in Hale and Macnie, Cabet—with an effective Romantic system of correspondences. His ending, refusing the alibi of dream, marks the historical moment when this lay millenialism came of age: the new vision achieves, within the text, a reality equal to that of the author's empirical actuality. Bellamy links thus two strong American traditions: the fantastic one of unknown worlds and the practical one of organizing a new world—both of which translate powerful biblical themes into economics. His materialist view of history as a coherent succession of changing human relationships and social structures was continued by Morris and Wells and built into the fundamentals of subsequent SF. Equally, the plot educates the reader into acceptance of the strange by following the protagonists' puzzled education. Modern SF, though it has forgotten this ancestor, builds on *Looking Backward* much as Dr. Leete's house was built on the remnants of Julian's house and on top of his sealed sleeping chamber, excavated by future archeology.

Traits from Bellamy's other works also drew from and returned to the SF tradition. The Flammarion-like, cosmically exceptional blindness of Earthmen and the transferral by spirit to Mars are found in "The Blindman's World," and despotic oligarchy as the alternative to revolution in *Equality*. Most immediately, the immense ideologico-political echo of *Looking Backward* reverberated around the globe through a host of sequels, rebuttals, and parallels. Bellamy had hit exactly the right note for a time searching for alternatives to ruthless plutocracy, and close to 200 utopian tales expounding or satirizing social democracy, state regulation of economy, Populist capitalism, or various uncouth combinations thereof were published

in the United States from 1888 to 1917 (notably Donnelly's *Caesar's Column,* Howells's *A Traveller from Altruria,* and London's *The Iron Heel*). In the United Kingdom, the echo was felt in Morris's answer, *News From Nowhere,* in Wells, and in Germany in three dozen German utopian or antiutopian tales.

—Darko Suvin

BELYAEV, Aleksandr

Nationality: Russian. **Born:** 1884. **Died:** 1942.

SCIENCE FICTION PUBLICATIONS

Novels

Chelovek-amfibiia. N.p., 1929; translated by L. Kolesnikov as *The Amphibian,* Moscow, Foreign Languages Publishing House, 1959.
The Struggle in Space. N.p., 1965.
Quia absurdum: sur la terre comme au ciel. Paris, Julliard, 1970; translated as *Because It Is Absurd: On Earth as It Is in Heaven,* New York, Vanguard Press, 1971.
Professor Dowell's Head, 1980.

Short Stories

Histories perfides. Paris, Julliard, 1964; translated by Margaret Giovanelli as *The Marvelous Palace and Other Stories,* New York, Vanguard Press, 1977.
Time Out of Mind and Other Stories, translated by Xan Fielding and Elisabeth Abbott. London, Secker and Warburg, and New York, Vanguard Press, 1966.

OTHER PUBLICATIONS

Novel

Le pont sur la riviere Kwai. Paris, Julliard, 1952; translation as *The Bridge on the River Kwai,* n.p., 1954.

*   *   *

Aleksandr Belyaev's first SF stories were published in adventure journals in 1925 and his first book in 1926. He wrote about 30 SF stories, about 20 novels, and a dozen articles or prefaces (e.g., to Jack London's novels), which make him the first penetrating Russian SF critic. He used the breathtaking Vernean adventure plot or the current detective-thriller-SF (from Wells, London, Renard, Burroughs, or A. Tolstoy) with an isolated and romantically alienated hero, either a scientist with humanistic ideals, a biologically modified man who is a naive child of nature (Ichthyander in his most popular novel, *The Amphibian,* or Ariel in the novel of the same title), or quite openly an artist (such as Presto in the two variant novels *The Man Who Lost His Face* and *The Man Who Found His Face*). This bearer of the novum and of the desire for freedom is opposed to and hounded by the cruel power of wicked scientists and financiers; most interestingly, he is at the center of an extreme situation or novum validated by a bold scientific technique. This is usually biological adaptation, including the changing use of the senses, and, most prominently, a sundering of brain from body as in *Professor Dowell's Head* (much superior to Renard's *New Bodies for Old*) or various, often humorous and folktale-like, scientific inventions in the "Professor Wagner" cycle. Such works are imbued with an aching lyricism and a vibrant humanistic vehemence. But often Belyaev's hero triumphs thanks to an essentially fairytale metamorphosis that allows him to vanquish physical gravity and social injustice. The black-and-white opposition of his threatened hero to a grotesque capitalist environment becomes then a form of escapism into a wicked Ruritania.

In the late 1920s and early 1930s Belyaev's SF was interrupted by a campaign against the genre. From 1934 he largely shifted his focus to short-range technological anticipation and (more interestingly) to interplanetary work and struggles, domesticating the notions of Tsiolkovsky and early Soviet rocket experimenters. For all his shortcomings, Belyaev's basic concern with human metamorphosis striving for freedom and the external resistance and inner anxieties it provokes have not only made of him at least the equal of any interwar German, French, or United States SF writer, and a lasting influence in Russia, but also an author who remains of interest today.

—Darko Suvin

BENFORD, Gregory (Albert)

Pseudonym: Sterling Blake. **Nationality:** American. **Born:** Mobile, Alabama, 30 January 1941. **Education:** University of Oklahoma, Norman, B.S. in physics 1963; University of California, San Diego, M.S. 1965, Ph.D. 1967. **Family:** Married Joan Abbe in 1967; one daughter and one son. **Career:** Fellow, 1967-69, and research physicist, 1969-71, Lawrence Radiation Laboratory, Livermore, California; assistant professor, 1971-73, associate professor, 1973-79, and since 1979 professor of physics, University of California, Irvine. Visiting professor, Cambridge University, 1976; Torino University, 1979; Florence Observatory, 1982; M.I.T., 1993. **Awards:** Nebula award, 1974, 1981; John W. Campbell Memorial award, 1981; U.N. Medal in Literature, 1990; Lord Foundation award (for achievement in science), 1995. **Agent:** Ralph Vicinanza, 111 8th Ave., New York, New York 10011. **Address:** Department of Physics, University of California, Irvine, California 92717, U.S.A. **Online Address:** gbenford@uci.edu.

Science Fiction Publications

Novels (series: Galactic Center)

Deeper Than the Darkness. New York, Ace, 1970; revised edition, as *The Stars in Shroud,* New York, Berkley, 1978; London, Gollancz, 1979.
Jupiter Project. Nashville, Nelson, 1975; revised as *The Jupiter Project,* New York, Berkley, 1980; London, Sphere, 1982.
If the Stars Are Gods, with Gordon Eklund. New York, Berkley, 1977; London, Gollancz, 1978; revised, New York, Bantam, 1989.
In the Ocean of Night: A Novel (Galactic). New York, Dial Press, 1977; London, Sidgwick and Jackson, 1978.

Find the Changeling, with Gordon Eklund. New York, Dell, 1980; London, Sphere, 1983.
Timescape. New York, Simon and Schuster, and London, Gollancz, 1980.
Shiva Descending, with William Rotsler. New York, Avon, and London, Sphere, 1980.
Against Infinity. New York, Simon and Schuster, and London, Gollancz, 1983.
Across the Sea of Suns (Galactic). New York, Simon and Schuster, and London, Macdonald, 1984; revised, Bantam, 1987.
Artifact. New York, Tor, 1985; London, Bantam, 1986.
Heart of the Comet, with David Brin. New York, Bantam, 1986; London, Bantam, 1987.
Great Sky River (Galactic). New York, Bantam, 1987; London, Gollancz, 1988.
Tides of Light (Galactic). New York, Bantam, and London, Gollancz, 1989.
Beyond the Fall of Night, with *Against the Fall of Night,* by Arthur C. Clarke. New York, Ace, 1990; as *Against the Fall of Night; and, Beyond the Fall of Night,* London, Gollancz, 1991.
Chiller (as Sterling Blake). New York, Bantam, 1993.
Furious Gulf (Galactic). New York, Bantam, and London, Gollancz, 1994.
Sailing Bright Eternity (Galactic). New York, Bantam, 1995.

Short Stories

Time's Rub. New Castle, Virginia, Cheap Street, 1984.
Of Space/Time and the River. New Castle, Virginia, Cheap Street, 1985.
In Alien Flesh. New York, Tor, 1986; London, Gollancz, 1988.
We Could Do Worse. Laguna Beach, California, Abbenford, 1988.
Iceborn, with Paul A. Carter, with *The Saturn Game* by Poul Anderson. New York, Tor, 1989.
Centigrade 233. New Castle, Virginia, Cheap Street, 1990.
Matter's End. New York, Bantam, 1995; expanded edition, Bantam, 1995.

Other Publications

Other

Editor, with Martin H. Greenberg, *Hitler Victorious: Eleven Stories of the German Victory in World War II.* New York, Garland, 1986; London, Grafton, 1988.
Editor, with Martin H. Greenberg, *Nuclear War.* New York, Ace, 1988.
Editor, with Martin H. Greenberg, *What Might Have Been? I: Alternate Empires [II: Alternate Heros] [III: Alternate Wars] [IV: Alternate Americas].* New York, Bantam, 4 vols., 1989-92.
Editor, *Far Futures.* New York, Tor, 1995.

*

Manuscript Collection: Eaton College, University of California, Riverside.

Gregory Benford comments:
I am a resolutely amateur writer, preferring to follow my own

interests rather than try to produce fiction for a living. And anyway, I'm a scientist by first choice and shall remain so.

I began writing from the simple desire to tell a story (a motivation SF writers seem to forget as they age, and thus turn into earnest moralizers). It's taken me a long time to learn how. I've been labeled a "hard SF" writer from the first, but in fact I think the job of SF is to do it *all*—the scientific landscape, peopled with real persons, with "style" and meaning ingrained. I've slowly worked toward that goal, with many dead ends along the way. From this comes my habit of rewriting my older books and expanding early short stories into longer works (sometimes novels). Ideas come to me in a lapidary way, layering over the years. Yet, it's not the stirring moral message that moves me. I think writers are interesting when they juxtapose images or events, letting life come out of the stuff of the narrative. They get boring when they preach. To some extent, my novels reflect my learning various subcategories of SF—*Deeper Than the Darkness* was the galactic empire motif; *Jupiter Project* the juvenile; *If the Stars Are Gods* and *In the Ocean of Night* both the cosmic space novel, etc. *Timescape* is rather different, and reflects my using my own experiences as a scientist. Yet short stories, where I labored so long, seem to me just as interesting as novels. I learned to write there. Nowadays, my novels begin as relatively brisk plot lines and then gather philosophical moss as they roll. If all this sounds vague and intuitive, it is: that's the way I work. So I cannot say precisely why I undertake certain themes. I like Graham Greene's division of novels into "serious" and "entertainment," though I suspect the author himself cannot say with certainty which of his own is which.

It seems to me my major concerns are the vast landscape of science, and the philosophical implications of that landscape on mortal, sensual human beings. What genuinely interests me is the strange, the undiscovered, but in the end it is how *people* see this that matters most.

*   *   *

Drawing in various measures on his Southern boyhood, his background as a youthful science fiction fan, his interest in literary tradition, and his training as a professional physicist, Gregory Benford has pioneered a mode of science fiction that can best be described as literary hard SF. Historically, hard SF has privileged technology and philosophy over character and style, awesome effects over detailed observations, but Benford's best work achieves a remarkable and richly textured balance among all these qualities. His literary antecedents range from the visionary fiction of Olaf Stapledon and Arthur C. Clarke (with whom he has "collaborated" by writing a sequel to the latter's *Against the Fall of Night*) to his fellow Southerner William Faulkner (some of whose works he has reimagined in science fiction terms) to the introspective fiction of John Updike and the realistic novels of scientists at work of C.P. Snow (whose notion of the "two cultures" of science and the humanities has often been addressed by Benford). At the same time, he has defined a territory of hard science fiction uniquely his own, while occasionally branching out into literary experiments and even international thrillers.

Benford began publishing short stories in 1965, and his first novel, *Deeper Than the Darkness,* appeared in 1970. Revised as *The Stars in Shroud* in 1978, it introduced what would become a familiar theme in Benford's work: contact with mysterious aliens, and the unexpected effect this contact has on humans—in this case,

a plague of agoraphobia which turns out to be the aliens' chief weapon. *Jupiter Project* (1975) was a competent Heinlein-style juvenile which introduced a character who would later play a major role in *Against Infinity* (1983). Benford's first major novel, *In the Ocean of Night* (1978), introduced a complex and ambivalent hero in British astronaut Nigel Walmsley and combined its first-contact theme with a sophisticated portrayal of messianic movements on Earth and even the legend of Bigfoot. (Part of this novel appeared as early as 1969, and by the time the series concludes with *Sailing Bright Eternity* in 1995, it begins to take on the aspect of a life's work.) Walmsley appeared again in *Across the Sea of Suns* (1984), some 57 years older but not greatly aged due to rejuvenation treatments and time spent in cold sleep aboard an interstellar craft trying to track the sources of mysterious radio signals. Alienation is a central theme in the novel; Walmsley is already alienated from the rest of humanity through his earlier transforming experience in *In the Ocean of Night,* and now faces an internal battle with his own cancer as well as edgy relationships with the two women in his life. Meanwhile, another narrative set on Earth involves a castaway whose ship has apparently been sunk by aliens, who have appeared in the oceans. It gradually becomes apparent that the very survival of organic life in the universe is threatened by an ancient machine civilization located somewhere near the center of the galaxy—a notion more fully explored in the later connected series of novels which begins with *Great Sky River* (a 1987 reprint of *Across the Sea of Suns* adds a new final chapter to make the connections between series more clear).

Before returning to this theme, however, Benford turned to the near future and the near past in what many still regard as his finest single work, *Timescape* (1980). Set alternately in a 1963 California and a 1988 Cambridge, it details the efforts of future scientists to use tachyons to warn the past of an impending ecological catastrophe. As a portrayal of the politics, anxieties, and methods of working scientists, the novel is unsurpassed in science fiction; as a sophisticated treatment of a kind of scientifically rationalized "time travel" (or at least cross-time communication) and an exploration of the alternate-world theme, it achieves a haunting poignancy almost equally rare. *Against Infinity* (1983) returns to a more colorful hard SF setting—the Jovian moon Ganymede—but continues Benford's exploration into literary fiction by transposing William Faulkner's 1942 novella "The Bear" into a tale of a young man's search for a mysterious alien machine called the Aleph. (Benford similarly "adapted" Faulkner's *As I Lay Dying* in his 1985 post-catastrophe novella "To the Storming Gulf.")

Artifact (1985), on the other hand, frankly reaches for the headlong suspense of the international espionage thriller, as scientists and Greek government officials vie for possession of a strange archaeological artifact which seems to contain a miniature black hole. (Benford again returned to the thriller mode with his 1993 novel *Chiller,* published under the name of "Sterling Blake" concerning a serial killer targeting scientists working on the cryonic suspension of life.) Benford has also collaborated with other novelists on occasion. *Shiva Descending* (1980), with William Rotsler, is a fairly familiar tale of a huge meteor threatening the Earth; *Heart of the Comet* (1986), with David Brin, is a more successful Vernian novel concerning a group of scientists exploring Halley's Comet.

Benford's most ambitious sustained work to date is the four-novel sequence beginning with *Great Sky River* (1987), which returns to the machine-organic struggle introduced in the Nigel Walmsley novels, but raises it to genuinely epic and cosmological proportions. On Snowglade, a desolate planet near the core of the galaxy, a small band of human survivors led by Killeen of the Family Bishop struggle to escape extermination by the immensely powerful machine intelligences who seek to dominate the universe, and who have destroyed their last remaining Citadel. Each human survivor carries "Aspects" which contain the minds of dead ancestors, and many are themselves enhanced with technological devices. Hounding them is the bizarre "mech" being known as the Mantis, from whose point of view we learn about the mech view of the Universe and its controlling intelligences. In *Tides of Light* (1989), the Family Bishop escape Snowglade to a planet orbiting Abraham's Star, only to find that yet another form of life—cyborgs—share the struggle for supremacy, and are acting out their own mythical destiny as well. This involves, among other things, using a cosmic string to disassemble the planet and begin the process of capturing all the energy of the star—and eventually of the whole galaxy—for their use. They hope to join an even more mysterious alien race, the Starswarmers, and become part of the "Summation" that represents a kind of Teilhardian Omega point for intelligence in the universe. *Furious Gulf* (1994) shifts the action to Killeen's son Toby. Again the family has found a kind of redoubt, and again the mechs pursue relentlessly—this time hoping to capture Killeen and Toby for some nefarious purpose. Toby's chief ally is the cyborg Quath, who befriended his father in the previous novel, and one of his chief opponents turns out to be the Mantis from *Great Sky River*. By recapitulating themes and figures from earlier novels in the series, *Furious Gulf* also sets the stage for the return of Nigel Walmsley.

Both this series and the earlier Nigel Walmsley series reach their culmination in the 1995 novel *Sailing Bright Eternity*. Here, Benford achieves a true cosmic perspective, in the tradition of Olaf Stapledon, within the rigorous context of hard SF. Taken as a unified work (which required some revision of the earlier novels in later editions) the Galactic Center series raises so many questions about the nature and problems of SF that it has to be regarded as one of the major accomplishments in the recent history of the field. It suggests the grand theme of SF, as revealed by Benford out of Stapledon (with Clarke as intermediary), is nothing less than the relationship of mind and nature. This theme not only haunts the work of all three writers, but subsumes nearly every favorite subtheme of the genre, from space travel to alien intelligence to technology—all of which are important to Benford's series as well. In taking up such a vast theme, Benford devises several strategies to get his characters meaningfully involved in such questions as the one Walmsley himself asks at the end of *Sailing Bright Eternity*, "Does human action have any meaning?"

From its opening prose poem on black holes, "photovores," and "metallovores" to the strange space-time continuum or "esty" in which much of the action takes place, the novel demands a great deal more of readers than the series' first novel, *In the Ocean of Night;* in fact, the entire six-volume sequence might almost be read as a course in how to understand hard science fiction. One of the classic problems of such science fiction is combining a rhetoric of action and human drama with a rhetoric of science and philosophy in a way that must be made to appear seamless. Benford (as he puts it) plays with the net up—and not only the net of scientific consistency, but the net of believable character relationships as well. Nigel Walmsley, whose interstellar voyage began in *Across the Sea of Suns,* arrives near the galaxy's core some 30,000 years in the future and meets the survivors of the Family Bishop. Somewhat protected by an artificial "esty" constructed by higher intelligences and consisting of different "lanes" and time lines, they brace for a final confrontation and eventually discover an unlikely key to defeating the mechs. Throughout the Galactic Center series, Benford's basic strategy is to focus on small groups of individuals acting against spectacular backdrops, while introducing his epic themes through a variety of dramatic devices—conversations with mechs or cyborgs, occasional trips into the far future, flat-out narrative exposition. The result is that his Stapledonian perspective emerges only as a function of the ways in which he has constructed the novels themselves—the novels control our perspective, not the other way round as it was with Stapledon. This has to be counted as a major achievement in realizing the potential of hard SF not only as speculation, but as literature, and it suggests that *Sailing Bright Eternity,* even though it might have some problems as a stand-alone novel (which it clearly isn't intended as), is Benford's most important single work to date, and the series as a whole is his masterpiece.

If anything, Benford's short fiction, partly collected in *In Alien Flesh* (1986) and *Matter's End* (1995), show more versatility and variety than his novels. Some of the most memorable stories, like *Timescape,* depict the lives of working scientists; "Exposures" (1981) uses the metaphor of photographic plates to explore the strange ways the universe reveals itself to us, from evidence of alien life discovered by the astronomer narrator to the cancer of his son's teacher, while the physicist narrator of "Mozart on Morphine" (1993) speculates on how remote his research seems from daily life as he undergoes an appendectomy (very similar to Benford's own). Other stories, like "Nooncoming" (1978) or "Snatching the Bot" (1977) are experiments in recasting the closely observed detail of the contemporary literary short story in science fiction terms. Still others engage in direct dialogue with earlier science fiction stories: "Matter's End" (1993) and "Centigrade 233" (1993) address issues raised in particular stories by Arthur C. Clarke and Ray Bradbury. Humor is also a continuing theme in Benford's short fiction. "Doing Lennon" (1975) is a celebration of Beatles-era culture, "Freezeframe" (1993) a realization of every working parent's childcare fantasy, "Time Guide" (1979) a satirical portrait of our own culture from the point of view of a time travel tourist brochure. In general, Benford's short fiction, collected in *In Alien Flesh* (1986) and *Matter's End* (1995) is highly eclectic, ranging from traditional science fiction adventures to his most ambitious literary experiments.

Benford easily earns the mantle of the most important American writer of hard science fiction to emerge since the 1960s, and his considerable ambition—not only in his science fiction works, but in his thrillers and his various efforts to popularize science both on television and in essays (he began writing the monthly science column for *The Magazine of Fantasy and Science Fiction* following the death of Isaac Asimov)—make it hazardous to venture any predictions as to where he might move next. His major works, *Timescape* and the six Galactic Center novels, have already altered the landscape of science fiction in profound ways, bringing a new dimension of literary style to hard science fiction and a new dimension of speculative science to mainstream fictions. Of all current science fiction writers, he may stand the best chance to finally dissolve the arbitrary barrier between the "two cultures" of science and literature.

—Gary K. Wolfe

BENYON, John. *See* **WYNDHAM, John.**

BERESFORD, J(ohn) D(avys)

Nationality: British. **Born:** Castor, Northamptonshire, 7 March 1873. **Education:** Oundle School, Northamptonshire, and at a school in Peterborough; articled to Lacey W. Ridge, architect, London, 1901. **Family:** Married to Beatrice Roskams; three sons and one daughter. **Career:** Practiced architecture in the early 1900s. **Died:** 2 February 1947.

SCIENCE FICTION PUBLICATIONS

Novels

The Hampdenshire Wonder. London, Sidgwick and Jackson, 1911; as *The Wonder,* New York, Doran, 1917.
Goslings. London, Heinemann, 1913; as *A World of Women,* New York, Macaulay, 1913.
Revolution: A Novel. London, Collins, and New York, Putnam, 1921.
Real People. London, Collins, 1929.
The Camberwell Miracle. London, Heinemann, 1933.
"What Dreams May Come. . . ." London, Hutchinson, 1941.
A Common Enemy. London, Hutchinson, 1941.
The Riddle of the Tower, with Esmé Wynne-Tyson. London, Hutchinson, 1944.

Short Stories

Nineteen Impressions. London, and New York, Sidgwick and Jackson, 1918.
Signs and Wonders. Waltham St. Lawrence, Berkshire, Golden Cockerel Press, and New York, Putnam, 1921.
The Meeting Place and Other Stories. London, Faber, 1929.

OTHER PUBLICATIONS

Novels

Stahl Trilogy:
    The Early History of Jacob Stahl. London, Sidgwick and Jackson, and Boston, Little Brown, 1911.
    A Candidate for Truth. London, Sidgwick and Jackson, and Boston, Little Brown, 1912.
    The Invisible Event. London, Sidgwick and Jackson, and New York, Doran, 1915.
The House on Demetrius Road. London, Heinemann, and New York, Doran, 1914.
The Mountains of the Moon. London, Cassell, 1915.
These Lynnekers. London, Cassell, and New York, Doran, 1916.
W. E. Ford: A Bibliography, with Kenneth Richmond. London, Collins, and New York, Doran, 1917.
House-Mates. London, Cassell, and New York, Doran, 1917.

God's Counterpoint. London, Collins, and New York, Doran, 1918.
The Jervaise Comedy. London, Collins, and New York, Macmillan, 1919.
An Imperfect Mother. London, Collins, and New York, Macmillan, 1920.
The Prisoners of Hartling. London, Collins, and New York, Macmillan, 1922.
Love's Pilgrim. London, Collins, and Indianapolis, Bobbs Merrill, 1923.
Unity. London, Collins, and Indianapolis, Bobbs Merrill, 1924.
The Monkey-Puzzle. London, Collins, and Indianapolis, Bobbs Merrill, 1925.
That Kind of Man. London, Collins, 1926; as *Almost Pagan,* Indianapolis, Bobbs Merrill, 1926.
The Decoy. London, Collins, 1927.
The Tapestry. London, Collins, and Indianapolis, Bobbs Merrill, 1927.
The Instrument of Destiny: A Detective Story. London, Collins, and Indianapolis, Bobbs Merrill, 1928.
All or Nothing. London, Collins, and Indianapolis, Bobbs Merrill, 1928.
Love's Illusion. London, Collins, and New York, Viking Press, 1930.
Seven, Bobsworth. London, Faber, 1930.
An Innocent Criminal. London, Collins, and New York, Dutton, 1931.
Three Generations Trilogy:
    The Old People. London, Collins, 1931; New York, Dutton, 1932.
    The Middle Generation. London, Collins, 1932; New York, Dutton, 1933.
    The Young People. London, Collins, 1933; New York, Dutton, 1934.
The Next Generation. London, Benn, 1932.
The Inheritor. London, Benn, 1933.
Peckover. London, Heinemann, 1934; New York, Putnam, 1935.
On a Huge Hill. London, Heinemann, 1935.
The Faithful Lovers. London, Hutchinson, and New York, Furman, 1936.
Cleo. London, Hutchinson, 1937.
The Unfinished Road. London, Hutchinson, 1938.
Strange Rival. London, Hutchinson, 1939.

*   *   *

J.D. Beresford, born just seven years after H.G. Wells, had affinities of imagination with the older writer, and similarities of style and theme may have dimmed the Beresford flame in the Wellsian glare. All his excellent science fiction is forgotten save *The Hampdenshire Wonder.* The neglect is regrettable because his attitudes were almost diametrically opposed to those of the politicising and romanticising Wells. Beresford's superficially gentler treatments show, on examination, an appreciation of the grimmer aspects of human nature which Wells tended to gloss in comedy or satire.

The first of Beresford's science fiction novels, *The Hampdenshire Wonder,* may stand for most of the qualities and methods of its successors. As the story of a super-intelligent child born to working-class parents (one of the few major science fiction themes Wells never attempted) it is an obvious forerunner of Stapledon's *Odd John,* but is superior in handling to the later book. The story of the lonely child (unwanted by all except his doting mother, and in his intellectual solitude having little use for her) making his misunderstood way through childhood to an ironical death at the hands of the village idiot illumines the theme of "difference" more clearly than, for example, Sturgeon's melodramatic *More Than Human.* Beresford's viewpoint is peculiar to himself. He was not primarily concerned, like more modern practitioners, with the symptoms and displays of transcendent genius so much as with the effect of this doomed creation's existence on those about him. The child is strongly drawn, with considerable understanding of the requirements of super-intelligence, but the characters who remain with the reader are the father, an uneducated county cricketer and workman who deserts child and wife when he can no longer bear the child's "unnatural" presence, and the mother, whose devotion to the self-absorbed genius is given without any return of affection or understanding. The two, supremely human, emphasise the child's alienness and eeriness in a fashion denied to our "mind-blowing" contemporary writers. They also demonstrate that characterisation in depth is possible in a genre which prefers to offer types as symbols of humanity confronting "difference." Beresford presents, without strain, rounded personalities who also manage to symbolise humanity dealing with the incomprehensible.

Goslings recalls Wells's *War of the Worlds* in its portrait of a plague-ridden, deserted London, but again the emphasis is on the reactions of people. Wells's stricken city is a symbol of trampled mankind; Beresford's is a challenge to the ordinary, unschooled but individual people who must live in and defeat it. *The Camberwell Miracle* has a faith healer (if that be the phrase for the talent) as central character, and here Beresford gives love and serenity to a portrait one can only imagine Wells handling with pragmatic savagery. *The Riddle of the Tower* (with Esmé Wynne-Tyson) again invades Wellsian territory, via bomb blast into an alternate spacetime, to discover a human culture reminiscent of the hive or the termitary. Again the treatment is thoughtful rather than dramatic or satirical, though the warning against technological excess is clear.

These novels stand comparison with the best of current science fiction, and, in literary quality, head and shoulders above most. Beresford published over 40 mainstream novels and it is his mainstream approach to science fiction problems of structure and balance that give his romances a unique flavour.

—George Turner

BESTER, Alfred

Nationality: American. **Born:** New York City, 18 December 1913. **Education:** University of Pennsylvania, Philadelphia, B.A. 1935. **Family:** Married Rolly Goulko in 1936. **Career:** Freelance writer: book reviewer, *Fantasy and Science Fiction,* New York, 1960-62, radio and TV writer, and staff member, *Holiday,* New York. **Awards:** Hugo award, 1953; Nebula Grand Master, 1987. **Died:** October 1987.

SCIENCE FICTION PUBLICATIONS

Novels

The Demolished Man. Chicago, Shasta, and London, Sidgwick and Jackson, 1953.

Tiger! Tiger! London, Sidgwick and Jackson, 1956; as *The Stars, My Destination,* New York, New American Library, 1957.
The Computer Connection. New York, Berkley, 1975; as *Extro,* London, Eyre Methuen, 1975.
Golem[100]. New York, Simon and Schuster, and London, Sidgwick and Jackson, 1980.
The Deceivers. New York, Simon and Schuster, 1981; London, Severn House, 1984.

Short Stories

Starburst. New York, New American Library, 1958; London, Sphere, 1968.
The Dark Side of Earth. New York, New American Library, 1964; London, Pan Books, 1969.
Starlight: The Great Short Fiction of Alfred Bester. Garden City, New York, Doubleday, 1976.
   The Light Fantastic: The Great Short Fiction of Alfred Bester, Vol. 1. New York, Berkley, 1976; London, Gollancz, 1977.
   Star Light, Star Bright: The Great Short Fiction of Alfred Bester, Vol. 2. New York, Berkley, 1976; London, Gollancz, 1978.

OTHER PUBLICATIONS

Novels

Who He? New York, Dial Press, 1953; as *The Rat Race,* New York, Berkley, 1956; London, Panther, 1959.
Tender Loving Rage. Houston, Texas, Tafford, 1991.

Other

The Life and Death of a Satellite. Boston, Little Brown, 1966; London, Sidgwick and Jackson, 1967.

*

Critical Study: *Alfred Bester* by Carolyn Wendell, Mercer Island, Washington, Starmont House, 1982.

*   *   *

With either of his first two novels alone, Alfred Bester would have been guaranteed a place in the history of science fiction as one of the most significant figures of the 1950s. The fact that he remains an important and respected writer despite producing only five novels and about three dozen short stories before his death is a testimony to the profound talent that he brought to those works.

The Demolished Man, which won a Hugo award as best novel of the year in 1953, is a remarkable work. Ben Reich is a powerful, larger-than-life figure in a future where the development of telepathy has made most crime impossible. After all, when one's secret plans are available to the nearest telepath, how could one possibly hope to commit a crime, let alone escape detection? Nevertheless, Ben Reich does so, and what ensues is a brilliantly conceived battle of two personalities as a prominent telepath sets out to bring Reich to justice. Knowing that Reich is the murderer is one thing, proving it is quite another matter. Bester was also one of the earliest genre writers to create a gritty, realistic setting for his novels.

The Demolished Man is an innovative mystery story, powerfully conceived and executed SF, an insightful character study, and a very suspenseful thriller with an ending that is quite out of the ordinary.

Opinions vary as to whether or not Bester's second novel, *Tiger! Tiger!* (published as *The Stars, My Destination* in the U.S.), was an even greater achievement. There is little doubt that each stands as a masterpiece, although *Tiger! Tiger!* was more ambitious in conception, straddling worlds, psi powers, and interplanetary war. Gulliver Foyle is a man driven to extremes when he nearly dies after being abandoned in space. Rescued by barbarian pirates, he eventually returns to Earth transformed both physically and mentally. Obsessed with the idea of revenge, he sets about accumulating the wealth and power with which to carry out his plans. The story is further enriched by the concept of "jaunting," physical teleportation presented in a mature and thoughtful fashion, inextricably entwined with the main plotline. Foyle becomes a greater-than-human being in many respects, as his urge for vengeance ultimately involves him in an interplanetary conflict.

Although Bester was to write three more novels before his death, none of these rivalled those early works. The best is *Golem¹⁰⁰*, set in the 23rd century. A group of bored women set out to investigate the occult, inadvertently setting free a hideous creature conceived in the collective unconscious of the human race. This monster, now incarnate, escapes and commits a series of murders, while metaphysicists seek to locate and destroy the intruder. The novel is based in part on the short story "The Four Hour Fugue," which presents much the same situation in a less lengthy format. *The Computer Connection* (published as *Extro* in the U.K.) is satiric, detailing the efforts of a group of disparate individuals to foil an omniscient computer. Unfortunately, Bester seemed less inclined in later years to spend the effort on characterization that distinguished his earlier work, and the storyline in itself is not interesting enough to sustain the story. *The Deceivers* was a disappointing finale to Bester's career, an ambitious space opera that lacked the vigor or originality of his other work.

Bester's small body of short fiction contains a number of classics in the field. "Adam and No Eve" involves a man in orbit who accidentally sets off a chain reaction that destroys all life on the home planet. He returns to Earth and eventually dies, and his decaying body becomes the springboard for a new wave of life. "Oddy and Id" tells the story of Odysseus Gaul, a man who attracts good luck and eventually becomes dictator of the entire solar system.

The protagonist in "Of Time and Third Avenue" finds an almanac from the future, and voluntarily surrenders it without giving in to the temptation to look inside. There is a genuinely moving love story in "Time Is the Traitor," and a sarcastic vision of certain voyeuristic aspects of our civilization in "Roller Coaster."

"Fondly Fahrenheit" is Bester's most frequently reprinted story, with good reason. The history of an android driven to kill in hot weather and its interaction with the man who owns it is a powerful enough story to stand in any company. "Starcomber" is conversely a farcical tale of a warlock who puts a psychotic painter through various wish-fulfillment worlds in order to exorcise his psychotic obsessions.

In "The Men Who Murdered Mohammed," Bester presents a very different view of time travel. The traveler can only effect his own personal past. The protagonist of "The Pi Man" is compelled to balance the underlying patterns of the universe. A self-aware computer satellite dominates the Earth in "Something Up There Likes Me." He also wrote several outright fantasies, of which the best are "Will You Wait?" and "Hell Is Forever."

Although the most obvious evidence of Bester's impact on SF is the presence of several familiar and often reprinted works, his influence on writers who followed is probably even greater. He frequently made use of nontextual material, illustrations, and creative layout of pages to emphasize situations beyond all previous human experience. Arguably, Bester was a forerunner of the New Wave movement of the 1960s with his experimental approach to fiction. But perhaps more importantly, he helped promote the concept that in order to be good science fiction, a story had to have credible characters as well as credible science.

—Don D'Ammassa

BIGGLE, Lloyd

Also writes as Lloyd Biggle, Jr. **Nationality:** American. **Born:** Waterloo, Iowa, 17 April 1923. **Education:** Wayne University, Detroit, 1941-43, 1946-47, A.B. (honors) in creative writing 1947; University of Michigan, Ann Arbor, 1947-53, M.M. in music literature 1948, Ph.D. in musicology 1953. **Military Service:** Served in the United States Army, 1943-46: Sergeant. **Family:** Married Hedwig T. Janiszewski in 1947; one daughter and one son. **Career:** First secretary-treasurer, 1965-67, chairman, Board of Trustees, 1967-71, and founder of the Regional Collections, Science Fiction Writers of America. Founder, and since 1979, president, Science Fiction Oral History Association. Lives in Ypsilanti, Michigan. **Agent:** Sharon Jarvis, Jarvis Braff Ltd., 260 Willard Avenue, Staten Island, New York 10314, U.S.A. **Address:** 569 Dubie Avenue, Ypsilanti, Michigan 48198, U.S.A.

Science Fiction Publications

Novels (series: Cultural Survey; Jan Darzek)

The Angry Espers. New York, Ace, 1961; London, Hale, 1968.
All the Colors of Darkness (Darzek). Garden City, New York, Doubleday, 1963; London, Dobson, 1964.
The Fury Out of Time. Garden City, New York, Doubleday, 1965; London, Dobson, 1966.
Watchers of the Dark (Darzek). Garden City, New York, Doubleday, 1966; London, Rapp and Whiting, 1968.
The Still, Small Voice of Trumpets (Survey). Garden City, New York, Doubleday, 1968; London, Rapp and Whiting, 1969.
The World Menders (Survey). Garden City, New York, Doubleday, 1971; Morley, Yorkshire, Elmfield Press, 1973.
The Light That Never Was. Garden City, New York, Doubleday, 1972; Morley, Yorkshire, Elmfield Press, 1975.
Monument. Garden City, New York, Doubleday, 1974; London, New English Library, 1975.
This Darkening Universe (Darzek). Garden City, New York, Doubleday, 1976; London, Millington, 1977.
Silence Is Deadly (Darzek). Garden City, New York, Doubleday, 1977; London, Millington, 1980.
The Whirligig of Time (Darzek). Garden City, New York, Doubleday, 1979.
Alien Main, with T.L. Sherred. Garden City, New York, Doubleday, 1985.

The Tunesmith (bound with *Eye for Eye,* by Orson Scott Card). New York, Tor, 1990.

Short Stories

The Rule of the Door and Other Fanciful Regulations. Garden City, New York, Doubleday, 1967; as *Out of the Silent Sky.* New York, Belmont Tower, 1977; as *The Silent Sky,* London, Hale, 1979.
The Metallic Muse: A Collection of Science Fiction Stories. Garden City, New York, Doubleday, 1972.
A Galaxy of Strangers. Garden City, New York, Doubleday, 1976.

Other Publications

Novels (series: Fletcher and Lambert)

The Quallsford Inheritance: A Memoir of Sherlock Holmes from the Papers of Edward Porter, His Late Assistant. New York, St. Martin's Press, 1986.
Interface for Murder (Fletcher and Lambert). Garden City, New York, Doubleday, 1987.
The Glendower Conspiracy: A Memoir of Sherlock Holmes. Tulsa, Oklahoma, Council Oak Books, 1990.
A Hazard of Losers. Tulsa, Oklahoma, Council Oak Books, 1991.
Where Dead Soldiers Walk (Fletcher and Lambert). New York, St. Martin's Press, 1994.

Other

Editor, *Nebula Award Stories Seven.* London, Gollancz, 1972; New York, Harper, 1973.

*

Manuscript Collection: Spencer Research Library, University of Kansas, Lawrence.

*   *   *

The best-known creations of Lloyd Biggle, Jr., are the Council of the Supreme and its extensions, the agents of the Galactic Synthesis, the Cultural Survey, and the Interplanetary Relations Bureau, known for mottos such as "Democracy Imposed from Without Is the Severest Form of Tyranny." Supreme is a vast computer that is fed information by its eight councilors; the only human is number ONE, Jan Darzek, who ironically was recruited by Supreme from uncertified Earth (i.e., not fit for social intercourse with civilized planets because its inhabitants tell lies) through Rok Wllon, who eventually becomes EIGHT. EIGHT dislikes ONE personally but they unite in common cause against the Dark Force, the Udef, which threatens the universe.

Supreme is not a ruler but an advisor, though people tend to accept its wisdom without hesitation since it eventually always proves reliable. Supreme—the ultimate in impartial democratic justice—fails in its function only when it is deprived of data input or asked the wrong question, thus simultaneously demonstrating the old programmers' wisdom "Garbage in; garbage out," and suggesting the need for an informed electorate of enlightened self-interest.

Always highly readable, Biggle narrates the adventures of Jan

Darzek as he saves Earth in *All the Colors of Darkness,* the galaxy in *Watchers of the Dark,* and a large part of the universe in *This Darkening Universe,* as well as two individual worlds in *Silence Is Deadly* and *The Whirligig of Time.* In *The World Menders* and *The Still, Small Voice of Trumpets,* the cultural Survey officers must cope with bureaucracy while solving the problems of how to bring an uncertified world into the Galactic Synthesis of self-rule and trade with other planets. *Monument* and *The Light That Never Was* also deal with the place of art and beauty in human culture and civilization.

Biggle's characterization is generally drawn with vivid, broad strokes in the literary tradition of Charles Dickens; e.g., Darzek's assistant is a little old lady, Miss Schlupe (Schluppy), who loves the comfort of her rocking chair as she makes beer out of whatever exotic vegetation is available wherever she lands in the galaxy. The chief interest in Biggle's stories is not character motivation, but puzzle solving, understanding the nature of the universe so that it can be managed intelligently. Throughout his stories, intelligent life in whatever form it appears (even a giant vegetable computer) earns respect. In the ironic tradition of Jonathan Swift, humanoid-appearing creatures may turn out to be subhuman animals (*The World Menders*), as determined by their lack of culture, particularly religion and the arts. Repeatedly Biggle dramatizes the need for a holistic understanding of a culture, including the ecological balance of a planet and the physical strengths and weaknesses of its inhabitants. Tolerance and respect for differences between species is demonstrated to benefit all intelligent beings, and Biggle uses gentle satire to provide moral instruction as he delights.

His greatest strength is in creating believable alien worlds and civilizations, complete with native flora and fauna, linguistic idiosyncrasies, customs of courtship and marriage, provisions for raising children, social intercourse and folkways (always inseparable from economic trade and business affairs), religion, systems of government, and culture in its most inclusive sense. Because of this complexity, it is unfair to limit his stories with the label juvenile—even though neither his heroes nor his villains ever use expletives stronger than "drat"—but his clear-cut moral tone, celebrating life in all its forms, is particularly suitable for young readers.

Alien Main, the collaboration with T.L. Sherred, uses a female first person narrator to tell the story of an intergalactic organization dedicated to peace and progress that returns to a devastated Earth 200 years after a nuclear holocaust and a plague has nearly wiped out humanity. The protagonist will especially delight and inspire young girls for her resourcefulness and courage in facing danger and solving unforeseen problems as she confronts a despicable alien race that would make slaves of the few who are left on Earth.

In recent years Biggle has turned to writing mystery novels, but those who enjoy his science fiction will probably also appreciate the careful research and attention to detail (similar to his world-building), with which he recreates late-19th-century England and Wales in *The Quallsford Inheritance* and *The Glendower Conspiracy,* both further tales of Sherlock Holmes, with the introduction of a new narrator-persona, Edward Porter Jones, his late assistant. Biggle has also begun his own original mystery series, starting with *Interface for Murder,* set in a small college town in Ohio, featuring detective J. Fletcher and his boss, Raina Lambert. Most of Biggle's short fiction is available in book collections. *A Galaxy of Strangers* contains one gem in particular, "And Madly Teach."

—Elizabeth Anne Hull

BINDER, Eando

Pseudonym for Otto Oscar Binder (and his brother Earl Andrew Binder until 1934). **Other Pseudonyms:** John Coleridge; Ian Francis Turek; Ione Frances Turek. **Nationality:** American. **Born:** Bessemer, Michigan, 26 August 1911. **Education:** Studied science and chemical engineering at Crane City College, Northwestern University, Evanston, Illinois, and the University of Chicago for three years. **Family:** Married Ione Frances Turek in 1940; one daughter. **Career:** Clerk, Central Scientific Company, Chicago, 1930-31; assistant to science librarian, Crerar Library, Chicago, 1931-32; freelance writer after 1932: reader of manuscripts, Otis Kline Literary Agency, 1936-38; comic book writer from 1941; editor, *Space World,* New York, 1962-63. **Died:** 14 October 1974.

SCIENCE FICTION PUBLICATIONS

Novels (series: Captain America; Saucers)

Lords of Creation. Philadelphia, Prime Press, 1949.
Enslaved Brains (with Earl Binder as Eando Binder). New York, Avalon, 1965.
The Avengers Battle the Earth-Wrecker (as Otto O. Binder; Captain America). New York, Bantam, 1967.
Menace of the Saucers. New York, Belmont, 1969.
The Impossible World. New York, Curtis, 1970.
Five Steps to Tomorrow. New York, Curtis, 1970.
The Double Man. New York, Curtis, 1971.
Get Off My World. New York, Curtis, 1971.
Night of the Saucers. New York, Belmont, 1971.
Puzzle of the Space Pyramids. New York, Curtis, 1971.
Secret of the Red Spot. New York, Curtis, 1971.
The Mind from Outer Space. New York, Curtis, 1972.
The Hospital Horror (as Otto O. Binder). New York, Popular Library, 1973.

Short Stories (series: Adam Link)

The Cancer Machine. Millheim, Pennsylvania, Bizarre Series, 1941.
Martian Martyrs (with Earl Binder as John Coleridge). New York, Columbia, 1942.
The New Life (with Earl Binder as John Coleridge). New York, Columbia, 1942.
The Three Eternals. Sydney, Fantasy Fiction, 1949.
Adam Link in the Past. Sydney, Fantasy Fiction, 1950.
Where Eternity Ends. Sydney, Fantasy Fiction, 1950.
Adam Link—Robot. New York, Paperback Library, 1965.
Anton York—Immortal. New York, Belmont, 1965.

OTHER PUBLICATIONS

Novels

Terror in the Bay (as Ione Frances Turek). New York, Curtis, 1971.
The Forgotten Colony (as Otto O. Binder). New York, Popular Library, 1972.
The Frontier's Secret (as Ian Francis Turek). New York, Popular Library, 1973.

Play

Television Play: *I, Robot,* 1964.

Other (as Otto O. Binder)

The Golden Book of Space Travel [Atomic Energy, Jets and Rockets] (for children). New York, Golden Press, 3 vols., 1959-61.
The Moon, Our Neighboring World (for children). New York, Golden Press, 1959.
Planets: Other Worlds of Our Solar System (for children). New York, Golden Press, 1959.
Victory in Space. New York, Walker, 1962.
Careers in Space. New York, Walker, 1963.
Riddles of Astronomy. New York, Basic Books, 1964.
What We Really Know about Flying Saucers. New York, Fawcett, 1967.
Mankind, Child of the Stars, with Max H. Flindt. New York, Fawcett, 1974; London, Coronet, 1976.
The Mysterious Island (comic book). West Haven, Connecticut, Pendulum Press, 1974.
Flying Saucers Are Watching Us. New York, Belmont, 1968; as *Unsolved Mysteries of the Past,* n.p., Tower, 1970.

Adaptor, *Dracula* (comic book; based on the novel by Bram Stoker), with Craig Tennis. New York, Ballantine, 1966.
Adaptor, *20,000 Leagues under the Sea* (comic book; based on the novel by Jules Verne). New York, Random House, 1973.
Adaptor, *The Invisible Man* (comic book; based on the novel by H.G. Wells). West Haven, Connecticut, Pendulum Press, 1974.
Adaptor, *The Time Machine* (comic book; based on the novel by H.G. Wells). New York, Marvel Comics, 1976.

*   *   *

Though the unique name Eando is formed from "E and O," representing Earl and Otto Binder, for all practical purposes Eando was Otto Binder; the early, collaborative stories comprise a very minor component of the Binder works, both qualitatively and quantitatively. Binder maintained that a real professional could write anything, from the libretto of an opera to a technical manual. While not embracing quite this broad a range, his works were sufficiently varied to give the notion strong support. In addition to his science fiction, Binder produced weird-horror fiction, gothic romance, and considerable nonfiction, as well as hundreds of comic book and comic strip "scripts." Binder's most important single story is generally regarded to be "I, Robot," published in the January 1939 *Amazing.* (The Isaac Asimov book, *I, Robot,* appeared in 1950. Its title was as much a tribute to Binder as anything else; in his autobiography, Asimov attributes the inspiration of his famous "positronic robot" stories to a meeting with Binder and the reading of Binder's "I, Robot.") The significance of Binder's story lies in its sympathetic, even emotional, portrayal of the robot Adam Link. This effect is heightened by the first person narration. The story was hugely successful and led to a series of popular sequels. Lester del Rey's equally significant "sympathetic robot" story, "Helen O'Loy," was written independently and simultaneously with Binder's "I, Robot," and actually reached print in *Astounding* a month before Binder's story. Del Rey abandoned the theme after a single effort, while Binder, Asimov, and shortly thereafter Eric Frank Russell (with his Jay Score stories), continued the development of the theme.

Binder's stories collected as *Anton York—Immortal* were also highly popular in their day, although lacking in the seminal significance of the Adam Link series. The Anton York stories are concerned with the impact of immortality on a lone man (eventually joined by an immortal wife) and on society. A number of Binder's other stories and novels achieved popularity in their time, but have little present readership. Their loss of popularity is probably due to Binder's stylistic limitations. Though a perfectly competent writer, he did not often succeed in bringing a sense of excitement to his prose; an illuminating comparison is E.E. Smith, whose unbounded energy totally transcended the limitations of his weak prose style.

Binder's "Via Etherline" tales were later collected as *Puzzle of the Space Pyramids.* Prior to the appearance of these stories, space travel and interplanetary exploration were almost always portrayed as glamorous, romantic activities, Binder instead portrayed them as grimy, difficult, dangerous, and often boring tasks. The stories were echoed in the realistic/predictive space fiction of Arthur C. Clarke, e.g., *Prelude to Space, Sands of Mars, A Fall of Moondust.*

In the 1940s and 1950s, Binder devoted most of his efforts to writing comic books. As the principal writer for the *Captain Marvel* features, he was chiefly responsible for the humorous, satirical, and often science fiction elements that best characterized that altogether superior feature. In the 1960s, he developed an interest in UFOs and possible space-visitors, and three of his last works were devoted to these themes. One other series of stories by Binder is noteworthy. These are the tales about Jon Jarl, a young officer in the space patrol of the future. Binder wrote literally scores of these stories as text filler in the *Captain Marvel Adventures* comic books. As juvenile science fiction, they are charming, succinct, and stimulating. They have, unfortunately, never been collected.

While Binder is associated primarily with science fiction, his creative output was actually far more varied than his reputation would indicate. As a prolific author of pulp magazine fiction, Binder was active in any number of fields, most notably mystery and horror. His work in these areas also remains uncollected, and even largely uncatalogued, a regrettable state of affairs as Binder was ever the competent (albeit frequently uninspired) professional. An available example of Binder's horror writing is *The Hospital Horror.* Produced very late in his career and published not long before his death, this novel unfortunately is the work of an author long past his prime; Binder's magazine writing in the horror genre is far better and far more representative of his true talent (though difficult to obtain).

—Richard A. Lupoff

———

BINDER, Otto. *See* **BINDER, Eando.**

———

BISCHOFF, David F(rederick)

Pseudonym: Mark Grant. **Nationality:** American. **Born:** Washington, D.C., 15 December 1951. **Education:** University of Maryland, College Park, B.A. 1973. **Career:** Worked as a dishwasher, soda-jerk clerk; associate editor, *Amazing,* New York. Since 1974 staff member, NBC-TV, Washington, D.C. Secretary, 1978-80, and from 1980 vice-president, Science Fiction Writers of America. **Address:** c/o Warner Books Inc., 666 Fifth Avenue, New York, New York 10103, U.S.A.

SCIENCE FICTION PUBLICATIONS

Novels (series: Aliens; Bill, the Galactic Hero; Dr. Dimension; Dragonstar; Gaming Magi; Mutants Amok; Nightworld; Star Fall; Star Hounds; Star Trek; Time Machine; The UFO Conspiracy)

The Seeker, with Christopher Lampton. Toronto, Laser, 1976.
Forbidden World; A Science Fiction Novel, with Ted White. New York, Popular Library, 1978.
Tin Woodman, with Dennis R. Bailey. Garden City, New York, Doubleday, 1979; London, Sidgwick and Jackson, 1980.
Nightworld. New York, Ballantine, 1979.
Star Fall: A Space Fantasy. New York, Berkley, 1980.
The Vampires of Nightworld. New York, Ballantine, 1981.
Star Spring: A Space Operetta (Star Fall). New York, Berkley, 1982.
The Selkie, with Charles Sheffield. New York, Macmillan, 1982.
Day of the Dragonstar, with Thomas F. Monteleone. New York, Berkley, 1983.
Mandala. New York, Berkley, 1983.
Wargames: A Novel (novelization of screenplay). New York, Dell, and London, Penguin, 1983.
Search for Dinosaurs (Time Machine; for children). New York, Bantam 1984.
Night of the Dragonstar, with Thomas F. Monteleone. New York, Berkley, 1985.
The Infinite Battle (Star Hounds). New York, Ace, 1985.
Galactic Warriors (Star Hounds). New York, Ace, 1985.
The Destiny Dice (Gaming Magi). New York, New American Library, 1985.
Wraith Board (Gaming Magi). New York, New American Library, 1985.
The Crunch Bunch (for young adults). New York, Avon, 1985.
A Personal Demon, with Rich Brown and Linda Richardson. New York, New American Library, 1985.
The Macrocosmic Conflict (Star Hounds). New York, Ace, 1986.
The Unicorn Gambit (Gaming Magi). New York, New American Library, 1986.
The Manhattan Project (novelization of screenplay). New York, Avon, 1986.
Some Kind of Wonderer. New York, Bantam, 1987.
The Blob: A Novel (novelization of screenplay by Chuck Densall and Frank Darabont). New York, Bantam, 1988; London, Star, 1989.
Dragonstar Destiny, with Thomas F. Monteleone. New York, Ace, 1989.
Gremlins 2: The New Batch (novelization of screenplay). New York, Avon, 1990.
Abduction: The UFO Conspiracy. New York, Warner, 1990.
Deception: The UFO Conspiracy. New York, Warner, 1991.
Revelation: The UFO Conspiracy. New York, Warner, 1991.
Bill, the Galactic Hero, on the Planet of Tasteless Pleasure, with Harry Harrison. New York, Avon, 1991; London, Gollancz, 1991.
Bill, the Galactic Hero, on the Planet of Ten Thousand Bars, with Harry Harrison. New York, Avon, 1991; as *Bill, the Galactic Hero, on the Planet of the Hippies from Hell,* London, Gollancz, 1992.

Mutants Amok (for children):
> Mutants Amok, with Tim Sullivan as Mark Grant. New York, Avon, 1991.
>
> Mutant Hell, as Mark Grant. New York, Avon, 1991.
>
> Rebel Attack, as Mark Grant. New York, Avon, 1991.
>
> Holocaust Horror. New York, Avon, 1991.

Grounded (Star Trek). New York, Pocket Books, and London, Titan, 1993.

Dr. Dimension, with John DeChancie. New York, Roc, 1993.

Dr. Dimension: Masters of Spacetime (Void Where Prohibited), with John DeChancie. New York, Roc, 1994.

Aliens: Genocide. New York, Bantam, and London, Millennium, 1994.

Aliens vs. Predator: Hunter's Planet. New York, Bantam, and London, Millennium, 1994.

The Ancient: A SeaQuest DSV Novel. New York, Ace, and London, Millennium, 1994.

OTHER PUBLICATIONS

Novels

The Phantom of the Opera (novelization of screenplay). New York, Scholastic, 1977.

Other

Editor, Quest (for children). Milwaukee, Wisconsin, Raintree, 1977.
Editor, Strange Encounters. Milwaukee, Wisconsin, Raintree, 1977.

*   *   *

David Bischoff has proven to be a steadily prolific writer, both individually and in collaboration, although most of his output has shifted in the direction of media-related productions where his settings and characterizations and sometimes even the plot are predetermined. His earliest book-length work was The Seeker, written with Christopher Lampton. A humanoid alien crashes on Earth, refugee from a repressive interstellar society, followed by agents of his own society, an overly familiar plot but handled in an entertaining fashion.

This was just the first of several collaborative novels in the early stages of his career. The most successful of these was Tin Woodman, with Dennis R. Bailey. A young man with telepathic powers and an inability to fit into human society is sent on a mission to attempt communication with a sentient alien starship. Unfortunately, the man commanding the team is a power hungry psychopath who bullies his crew, falsifies orders, and endangers the entire mission. The interplay of the potentially mutinous crew is particularly effective as background to the scientific puzzle.

Day of the Dragonstar, Night of the Dragonstar, and Dragonstar Destiny, all in collaboration with Thomas F. Monteleone, constitute a trilogy involving a space-traveling habitat, apparently a gigantic zoo. In the opening volume, an exploration team is attacked by dinosaurs and a rescue party must determine whether or not there are any survivors. Subsequently we learn that some of the saurians are themselves intelligent, that they have been rescued from extinction by an unseen alien race, and in the concluding volume, a group of humans helps them to reactivate the ship's engines and escape human exploitation.

Other novels cowritten by Bischoff include The Selkie, an interesting fantasy/horror novel written with Charles Sheffield, Forbidden World, a space exploration adventure story coauthored with Ted White, and A Personal Demon, a humorous fantasy about a demon written with Rich Brown and Linda Richardson. With Harry Harrison he added two farcical adventures to the chronicles of Bill the Galactic Hero in Bill, the Galactic Hero, and the 10,000 Bars and Bill, the Galactic Hero, on the Planet of Tasteless Pleasures.

Bischoff has written occasional movie novelizations, including a young readers' version of The Phantom of the Opera, the suspense film Wargames, and most recently the remake of the classic The Blob. More recently he has added to the Star Trek saga with Grounded, and Seaquest, The Ancient. More significant in this area is Genocide, an effectively suspenseful adventure based on the graphic novel series in which the film franchise Aliens infest the Earth.

Bischoff has been less productive of original material in recent years, although earlier in his career he produced a steady output of above average adventure stories. In Mandala, a ruthless general from a dominant interstellar power suffers amnesia and is subsequently nursed back to health by a telepathic woman. This contact alters his personality, and he returns to his former associates determined to alter the status quo.

A much more successful work is Nightworld and its sequel, Vampires of the Nightworld. Set on a world which has been cut off from contact with the rest of the human race, the two novels feature an enormous, hidden computer complex which has created hosts of androids to play the parts of vampires, dragons, werewolves, and other mythological creatures. An unlikely hero finds himself pitted against this computer and, accompanied by a man who possesses some remnants of an earlier, higher technology, sets off to locate and destroy Satan, the ruler of the world. In the sequel, although the computer has been destroyed, the devices it created still dominate the world. To date, these remain the most ambitious and effective of Bischoff's novels.

Star Fall and its sequel, Star Spring, are also noteworthy. The former deals with the maiden voyage of a luxury starliner and the adventures that befall it. The protagonist inadvertently switches bodies with a famous assassin, and vengeful relatives of past victims are disinclined to believe his protestation of innocence. The ship itself is owned by an alien who plots the provocation of a war between humanity and his own race. The same cast of characters returned in the sequel, this time dealing with attempted murder and subsequently becoming lost in space.

Later novels have been less interesting, though still entertaining. The "Star Hounds" trilogy, The Infinite Battle, Galactic Warriors, and The Macrocosmic Conflict, are actually a single story, a bitter woman pirating a starship in order to rescue her brother from nasty aliens, manipulated by the human government for its own purposes. A fantasy trilogy consisting of The Destiny Dice, The Wraith Board, and The Unicorn Gambit is an interesting but fairly standard magical-war-through-the-dimensions variation. The Crunch Bunch is an amusing first-contact story written for younger readers. Most recently, under the pen name "Mark Grant," Bischoff has been writing the "Mutants Amok" series, a postcollapse adventure sequence.

Bischoff's only major new work not related to television or film is the UFO trilogy consisting of Abduction, Deception, and Revelation. Although to a great extent this is a rehash of all too familiar conspiracy theories and sensationalist reports, Bischoff approaches the theme seriously and plausibly, with less of the overt, light adventure that characterizes most of his previous original work.

Bischoff is an infrequent short story writer and has yet to produce anything outstanding at that length, but a few of his shorter pieces deserve notice. "In Media Res" is a fascinating piece about a hack writer who can produce only the middle of his stories. An actor becomes lost in the interface between his play and reality in "All the Stage, a World." "Santa Ritual Abuse" is an unusually serious piece which makes one wish Bischoff would write at this length more frequently. His best short is "Waterloo Sunset," a haunting piece about a place where all times coexist.

As film and television preempts adventure-oriented science fiction, writers and publishers seem to have accepted that action-oriented novels must generally have some tie to that medium. It seems likely that Bischoff will continue to provide a strong presence in packaged programs. Hopefully he will also find further opportunities to do completely original work as well.

—Don D'Ammassa

BISHOP, Michael

Nationality: American. **Born:** Lincoln, Nebraska, 12 November 1945. **Education:** University of Georgia, Athens, B.A. in English 1967 (Phi Beta Kappa). M.A. 1968. **Military Service:** Served in the United States Air Force as English instructor, Air Force Academy Preparatory School, 1968-72: Captain. **Family:** Married Jeri Ellis Whitaker in 1969; one son and one daughter. **Career:** English instructor, University of Georgia, 1972-74. Since 1974, freelance writer. **Awards:** Deep South Con XV Phoenix award, 1977; Clark Ashton Smith award, for verse, 1978; Nebula award, 1982, 1983; *Locus* award, for editing, 1984; Mythopoeic Fantasy award, 1988; *Locus* award, for best fantasy novel, 1994. **Member:** Science Fiction Writers of America, from late 1960s; Georgia Writers, Inc., 1994. **Agent:** Howard Morhain, 501 Fifth Avenue, New York, New York 10017, U.S.A. **Address:** Box 646, Pine Mountain, Georgia 31822, U.S.A.

SCIENCE FICTION PUBLICATIONS

Novels (series: Urban Nucleus)

A Funeral for the Eyes of Fire. New York, Ballantine, 1975; London, Sphere, 1978; revised as *Eyes of Fire,* New York, Pocket Books, 1980; revised under original title, Worcester Park, Surrey, Kerosina, 1989.
And Strange at Ecbatan the Trees: A Novel. New York, Harper, 1976; as *Beneath the Shattered Moons,* New York, DAW, 1977.
Stolen Faces. New York, Harper, and London, Gollancz, 1977.
A Little Knowledge (Nucleus). New York, Berkley, 1977.
Catacomb Years (Nucleus). New York, Berkley, 1979.
Transfigurations. New York, Berkley, 1979; London, Gollancz, 1980.
Under Heaven's Bridge (Nucleus), with Ian Watson. London, Gollancz, 1981; New York, Ace, 1982.
No Enemy But Time: A Novel. New York, Pocket Books, and London, Gollancz, 1982.
What Made Stevie Crye?: A Novel of the American South. Sauk City, Wisconsin, Arkham House, 1984; London, Headline, 1987.

Ancient of Days. New York, Arbor House, 1985; London, Paladin, 1987.
The Secret Ascension; or, Philip K. Dick Is Dead, Alas. New York, Tor, 1987; as *Philip K. Dick Is Dead,* London, Grafton, 1988.
Unicorn Mountain. New York, Arbor House, 1988; London, Grafton, 1989.
Apartheid, Superstrings, and Mordecai Thubana (novella). Eugene, Oregon, Axolotl Press, 1989.
Count Geiger's Blues: A Comedy. New York, Tor, 1992.

Short Stories

Beneath the Shattered Moons; and, The White Otters of Childhood. London, Sphere, 1978.
Blooded on Arachne. Sauk City, Wisconsin, Arkham House, 1982.
One Winter in Eden. Sauk City, Wisconsin, Arkham House, 1984.
Close Encounters with the Deity: Stories. Atlanta, Georgia, Peachtree, 1986.
Emphatically Not SF, Almost. Portland, Oregon, Pulphouse, 1990.
The Quickening. Eugene, Oregon, Pulphouse, 1991.

OTHER PUBLICATIONS

Novels

Brittle Innings. New York, Bantam, 1994.

Play

Screenplay: *Within the Walls of Tyre.* Worcester Park, Surrey, Kerosina, 1989.

Poetry

Windows and Mirrors: A Chapbook of Poetry for Deep South Con XV. Tuscaloosa, Alabama, Moravian Press, 1977.

Editor, with Ian Watson, *Changes: Stories of Metamorphosis: An Anthology of Speculative Fiction about Startling Metamorphoses, Both Psychological and Physical.* New York, Ace, 1983.
Editor, *Light Years and Dark: Science Fiction and Fantasy of and for Our Time.* New York, Berkley, 1984.
Editor, *Nebula Awards 23-25: SFWA's Choices for the Best Science Fiction and Fantasy, 1987-89.* San Diego, Harcourt Brace, 3 vols., 1989-91.

*

Bibliography: *Michael Bishop: A Preliminary Bibliography* by David Nee, Berkeley, California, Other Change of Hobbit, 1983.

Manuscript Collection: The Hargrett Collection, University of Georgia Libraries, Athens.

*   *   *

Michael Bishop's unique voice is evident in his 1992 novel, *Count Geiger's Blues.* Reflecting the powershift to the South, Bishop's fantasy is set in Salonika, capital of the state of Oconee.

Using satire and manipulating cultural symbols, Bishop presents a withering critique of the cult of High Art. The vehicle for Bishop's black comedy is a popular culture-hating critic named Xavier Thaxton. But when Bishop arranges for his hero to get dunked in toxic waste, Thaxton develops an allergy to High Art and has to reevaluate the hierarchy of high and low culture he was once a part of. Although Bishop explores serious questions of art in society, he also puts his unique spin on the plot as he turns Thaxton into a costumed superhero. Clearly, this is another brilliant Bishop virtuoso performance.

Bishop's latest novel, the baseball fantasy *Brittle Innings,* has been optioned for the movies. His latest novella, "Cri De Coeur," has the epic scope of Heinlein's *Universe* and is included in Gardner Dozois's *The Year's Best Science Fiction: Twelfth Annual Collection.*

Michael Bishop's most personal collection of stories can be found in *Author's Choice Monthly #15.* In the opening essay, "Emphatically Not SF, Almost: Introduction," Bishop discusses his work in general and the stories he assembled for this collection specifically. The result offers insights into a major writer's creative processes. The collection includes Bishop's only sale to *Playboy,* a grim story called "The Egret," and two moving stories, "Patriots" and "Taccati's Tomorrow."

Bishop's recent novels show his admiration for Philip K. Dick. In *The Secret Ascension,* Bishop makes Dick the hero of the novel set on an alternative Earth where Richard Nixon is still President. Too often this kind of homage turns out to be an embarrassment, but Bishop coolly pulls it off while delivering a sly and savvy science fiction novel. *Unicorn Mountain* is a more serious novel dealing with AIDS and unicorns of two Earths dying of a mysterious disease. Here, Bishop creates four memorable characters: Bo Gavin, dying of AIDS; Libby Quarrels, owner of the ranch where the unicorns appear; Sam Coldpony, Libby's hired hand; and Paisley Coldpony, Sam's daughter, who discovers she has incredible powers. At times, the novel is almost too rich in detail. Bo and Libby watch a black and white TV that suddenly begins to display color signals, but the stations are from an alternative Earth where instead of MTV, there is a Big Band Station featuring videos of the Big Band Legends. On that Earth, the unicorns are dying, too. A TV reporter named Che Guevera covers the story. A program called "Erotic Practices of the Renowned and Powerful" features John F. Kennedy—who survived Oswald's assassination attempt—in his seventies. All of these little Phil Dickian touches are witty, but *Unicorn Mountain* suffers from too much of a good thing as the details multiply and tedium starts to set in by the book's conclusion.

Bishop's preoccupation with the themes of religion and deity are apparent in his strongest collection, *Close Encounters With the Deity.* This collection features two of Bishop's best stories: the title story and the controversial "The Gospel According to Gamaliel Crucis; Or, The Astrogator's Testimony." In the latter, Bishop supposes what would happen if God were a large insect. The story generated some heated debate when it was first published, as Isaac Asimov discusses in his informative forward to the collection.

In 1982, Bishop won the Nebula award for his story "The Quickening," a hauntingly surreal tale of dislocation and loss. In 1983, Bishop again won a Nebula award, this time for his outstanding novel, *No Enemy But Time.* Earlier Bishop novels suffer from structural problems—confusing narratives, intertwining subplots, shifts in person from first to third and back again. But in *No Enemy But Time,* he masters the technical skills to bring off a superb performance. An infant, given away to a group of young girls near an Air Force base by his mute, prostitute mother, is adopted and given the name John Monegal. The child grows up to be different from other children: he experiences intense episodes of dreaming— spirit-travel—where he goes back in time to the Pleistocene era in Africa. After an argument with his stepmother, John leaves and later confronts an expert on the Pleistocene during a scientific conference. He makes such an impression that he is later recruited by the expert for a special project: a time travel expedition to the Pleistocene. John goes and finds his dreams were real: everything is as he dreamed it. He meets the primitive humans inhabiting the African wilds: the habiline. John cleverly becomes one of the small band of habilines, and marries a female he calls Helen. Helen bears him a daughter before dying. Then, during an inferno, John takes his infant daughter time traveling to the present, where their lives are forever changed. *No Enemy But Time* is a searing novel of identity and misdirection. John's relationship with Helen is one of the most moving in the genre.

Also moving, but in a comic vein, is *Ancient of Days,* a novel that explores the possibilities of a habiline surviving in contemporary society. Expanded from the brilliant novella "Her Habiline Husband," *Ancient of Days* is Bishop's vehicle to critique American society. Narrated by a restaurant owner whose ex-wife scandalizes the small Georgia town by first living with the habiline—eventually marrying Adam—Bishop's clever sense of situation comedy and Southern mores delivers a story that is funny and sadly true. The characters are finely crafted and subtly drawn. *Ancient of Days* is Bishop's most controlled novel.

Bishop's first novel, *A Funeral for the Eyes of Fire* (later revised as *Eyes of Fire*), shows the problems of alien cultures trying to communicate. Much of the book is anthropologic: Bishop shows strange customs and taboos, alien Tropemen celebrate in rites centering on their eyes and the eyes of their ancestors. The action is slowed by long descriptions of alien lifestyles; when the realization of the lead character finally arrives, the reader is far ahead of the narrative.

And Strange at Ecbatan the Trees (later retitled just as clumsily *Beneath the Shattered Moon*) reads like a dreamy Jack Vance novel. On the planet Mansueceria, the genetically engineered society is made up of two groups: Maskers, programmed against strong emotion; and Atarites, the rulers who are capable of strong emotion and domination. The groups complement each other; under the 6,000-year-old plan devised by the Parfects of Earth, the rulers and the ruled live in harmony on the island of Ongladred. Yet they are in danger of destruction by the barbarians living on the islands beyond Ongladred. Only Gabriel Elk of Stonelore, who presents dramas acted by resurrected corpses, has the power to create weapons to save Ongladred. But by saving Ongladred, Gabriel Elk disrupts the society and the ancient plan for harmony.

Stolen Faces is Bishop's darkest novel. Lucian Yeardance is exiled to the planet Tezcatl to govern a colony for victims of a leprosy-like disease, where Aztec rituals are embodied in the culture. Lucian discovers the disease is nonexistent: instead, the victims are a bizarre society whose mental illness is so extreme that mutilation is the group's method of self-expression. The writing is bleak and the action violent. Although macabre and depressing, *Stolen Faces* presents discrimination in graphic terms—a theme Bishop uses again in his later works.

A Little Knowledge and *Catacomb Years* are a pair of linked novels. In *A Little Knowledge,* Bishop presents 2071 Atlanta as a domed city where people's status is reflected by the building level they live on. The society is a theocracy dominated by the Orth-Urban

Church. Six aliens from 61 Cygni destabilize the status quo by professing faith in the Church. The philosophical and theological foundations of the culture are shaken as the power brokers have to come to grips with the alien question. The most entertaining subplot is the love story between a deacon of the Church and an agnostic journalist. But the book suffers from too many characters—most of them undeveloped—and murky plotting.

Catacomb Years continues the story of Atlanta with many new characters. Bishop develops the implications that the Cygusians are actually reincarnated humans. The resulting political and religious upheaval results in the breakdown of the domed city and a chance at freedom under open skies. Although technically superior to *A Little Knowledge, Catacomb Years* suffers from being overly long and tedious; a reedited single volume combining the best of *A Little Knowledge* and *Catacomb Years* would be much more satisfying than the flawed twin novels.

Transfigurations is an expanded version of Bishop's novelette that was a Hugo and Nebula nominee in 1973, "Death and Designation among the Adadi." The original story of an obsessed anthropologist's attempts to solve the mysteries of an enigmatic race of aliens gives way to the anthropologist's daughter's search for her missing father. The result is a disappointing extrapolation of the original story's premises, and proves that by revealing more of a mystery you get a less compelling resolution than when the reader is left to imagine and ponder the inexplicable.

Bishop's short story collections gather most of his Hugo and Nebula award winners and nominees. *Blooded on Arachne* includes 13 stories published between 1970 and 1978. The best are "Blooded on Arachne," "Rogue Tomato," "The White Otters of Childhood," and "Cathadonian Odyssey." *One Winter in Eden* includes a dozen stories published between 1979 and 1983. The best in this collection are "One Winter in Eden," "The Quickening," "Cold War Orphans," "Saving Face," "Season of Belief," "Within the Walls of Tyre," and "Collaborating."

As an anthologist, Bishop has shown marvelous taste. *In Changes,* edited with Ian Watson, Bishop presents a theme anthology centering on humans transforming into something else. But Bishop's masterpiece anthology is the controversial *Light Years and Dark.* Bishop blends original stories commissioned for this volume with notable stories published in the last 25 years. The result is a definitive collection that should rank with Harlan Ellison's *Dangerous Visions* anthologies.

Michael Bishop, a uniquely talented novelist, short story writer, and anthologist, is one of the most important figures in contemporary science fiction.

—George Kelley

BISSON, Terry (Ballantine)

Nationality: American. **Born:** Madisonville, Kentucky, 12 February 1942. **Education:** Grinnell College, 1960-62; University of Louisville, B.A. 1964. **Family:** Married 1) Deirdre Holst in 1962 (divorced 1966); two sons and one daughter; 2) Judy Jensen; one son and two daughters. **Career:** Magazine comic writer, 1964-72; automotive mechanic, 1972-77; editor, copywriter, Berkley Books and Avon Books, 1976-85; consultant, HarperCollins USA, 1994-95. Teacher in the writing program at The New School, New York City. **Awards:** Hugo, Nebula, and Theodore Sturgeon (for short story) 1991; Phoenix (for body of work/Southern writer). **Member:** Science Fiction Writers of America, 1986; Authors Guild, 1986. **Agent:** Susan Ann Protter, 110 West 40th St., New York, New York 10018, U.S.A. **Address:** 318 East Second St., Brooklyn, New York 11218 U.S.A.

SCIENCE FICTION PUBLICATIONS

Novels

Wyrldmaker: A Heroic Romance. New York, Pocket, 1981; London, Headline, 1988.
Talking Man. New York, Arbor House, 1986; London, Headline, 1987.
Fire on the Mountain. New York, Arbor House, 1988.
Voyage to the Red Planet. New York, Morrow, 1990; London, Pan, 1992.
Johnny Mnemonic: A Novel (novelization of screenplay by William Gibson). New York, Pocket, 1995.

Short Stories

Bears Discover Fire and Other Stories. New York, Tor, 1993.

OTHER PUBLICATIONS

Other

Nat Turner, New York, Chelsea House, 1988
Car Talk with Click and Clack, the Tappit Brothers, with Tom and Ray Magliozzi. New York, Dell, 1991.
A Green River Girlhood, with Elizabeth Ballantine Johnson. Owensboro, Kentucky, Green River, 1991.

*

Terry Bisson comments:
Can't add much to what my books say.

*   *   *

Terry Bisson's work sits, sometimes a little uncomfortably, at the crossroads where fantasy and science fiction meet. It is not that he writes both SF and fantasy, but that his work tends to partake of both. Thus his first novel, *Wyrldmaker,* begins as conventional fantasy in which a mighty-thewed hero sets off on a quest (in this case, delivering a magical sword). But the "wyrlds" through which he travels become increasingly bizarre and surreal, until the whole thing is rounded off (rather unsatisfactorily) by a conventional science fictional twist (the sword is actually an important part of a planet-seeding enterprise).

Talking Man, in which a magical quest to save the universe begins in a run-down garage in the American South, reveals another aspect of Bisson's work: the importance of home and the sense of nostalgia. This feeling, which places Bisson firmly in the tradition of Southern writers, is also a feature of his more overtly science fictional works.

Fire on the Mountain is an alternate history which plays on that perennial object of American fascination: the outcome of the Civil

War. But as a Southern writer he does not follow Ward Moore (*Bring the Jubilee*) or Harry Turtledove (*Guns of the South*) in imagining what would have happened if the Confederacy had won.

Instead he imagines that John Brown's raid on Harper's Ferry was a success. In Bisson's history, Harriet Tubman was able to accompany Brown on his raid, and her tactical and strategic thinking allowed him to turn the raid into the trigger for slave rebellion that Brown always thought it would be. The spreading rebellion is

told through the reminiscences of Dr. Abraham, a slave at the time of the raid. Bisson is able to create a vivid sense of the old South as it was, and the frisson sent through it by the slave uprising. (Around the same time he produced a nonfiction book for children on Nat Turner, who led an unsuccessful slave revolt some 30 years before. The research for one book no doubt contributed to the very strong sense of atmosphere and detail in the other.)

The success of the slave rebellion sparked by John Brown leads to the establishment of an independent black republic in the territory that would otherwise have been the Confederacy. This new state, Nova Africa, is a socialist utopia, and Bisson offsets the gritty tale of Abraham's struggle for freedom with the more romantic story of his great-granddaughter Yasmin Martin Odinga as she travels to present his papers to the museum at Harper's Ferry. As is often the way, the utopian world is less fully realised, less satisfying than the story of the rebellion. Many of the details of this new land, a land of both dirigibles and a Pan-African space mission to Mars, fail to ring true. But in confronting moral issues of slavery and freedom (Lincoln is remembered as a villain) Bisson has written a very telling novel about the way these factors shape our world.

If *Fire on the Mountain* looks back to how things might have been, his next and most thoroughly science fictional novel, *Voyage to the Red Planet,* looks back to the way the future was viewed in a previous generation of science fiction. His account of a journey to Mars has all the bold strokes and the spirit of individual achievement winning through where governments dare not tread that stem from the age of the backyard spaceship.

Here a bankrupt U.S. government has lost the will and the wherewithal to dare. The space programme has been mothballed, but a renegade independent film producer, desperate for a big hit, conceives of a scam. By various underhanded means he secures the last spaceship (tellingly called the "Mary Poppins") and a ragbag crew of retired astronauts, unlikely film stars, and a midget cameraman. Then he sends them off to make a surefire epic hit, a film of the first manned voyage to Mars as it actually happens. This is a comedy of ramshackled adventure, and there are the predictable disasters and problems along the way, most of them casting a satirical light on the Earth left behind. One of the funniest running gags in what can be a very funny novel is the flight controller gradually being forced out of work and away from his facilities until he ends up running the mission from a pay phone.

But if there is a strong element of humour running through the novel, this is balanced by a pathos which never descends into sentimentality. "Rocket Man" Bass, the ex-astronaut hired to pilot the mission, stays behind on Mars to ensure his companions are able to return. It may be an old-fashioned sentiment, but it is effective and affecting none the less, and this is, after all, an old-fashioned sort of book.

Most of Bisson's science fiction has the same nostalgic feel to it. "The Shadow Knows," for instance, takes its title from an American radio series of the 1930s and concerns that old standby, contact with aliens. But the jokey tone, the knowing use of cliché (the one-time astronaut plucked from retirement for one last top secret

mission: even Bewley, the narrator who is that astronaut, makes it a joke) make this as much an homage to science fiction gone by as it is an attempt to take the genre forward.

Bisson is a humorist, though that simple statement suggests something far less subtle and oblique than his best stories such as "Bears Discover Fire," "Two Guys from the Future," and "Cancion Autentica de Old Earth." There are times when the comedy is wielded more like a bludgeon than a rapier, as, for instance, in "By Permit Only." But in the main the faux-nostalgia of works like *Voyage to the Red Planet* and "The Shadow Knows" reflects the fact that his fiction, like the stories of Howard Waldrop or the cartoons of Gary Larson, is as much ironic commentary on the genre as it is a fresh work of science fiction.

—Paul Kincaid

———

BLADE, Alexander. *See* **GARRETT, Randall; PHILLIPS, Rog.**

———

BLAKE, Anthony. *See* **TUBB, E.C.**

———

BLAYLOCK, James P.

Nationality: American. **Born:** Long Beach, California, 20 September 1950. **Education:** California State University, Fullerton, B.A. 1972; M.A. 1974. **Family:** Married Viki Lynn Martin in 1972; two sons. **Career:** Pet food store clerk, Garden Grove, California, 1967-72; construction worker, Placentia, California, 1972-80; part-time instructor, Fullerton Community College, 1976-89; part-time instructor of English, California State University, Fullerton, 1980-87. **Awards:** Philip K. Dick award, 1986; World Fantasy award, 1986. **Address:** c/o Berkley Publishing Group, 200 Madison Avenue, New York, New York 10016, U.S.A.

SCIENCE FICTION PUBLICATIONS

Novels (series: Elfin Ship; Homunculus)

The Elfin Ship. New York, Ballantine, 1982; London, Grafton, 1988.
The Disappearing Dwarf (Elfin Ship). New York, Ballantine, 1983; London, Grafton, 1989.
The Digging Leviathan. New York, Ace, 1984; Bath, Morrigan, 1988.
Homunculus. New York, Ace, 1986; London, Grafton, 1988.
Land of Dreams. New York, Arbor House, 1987; London, Grafton, 1988.
The Last Coin. Willimantic, Connecticut, Mark Ziesing, 1988; London, Grafton, 1989.
The Stone Giant (Elfin Ship). New York, Ace, 1989; London, Grafton, 1990.

The Paper Grail. Norwalk, Connecticut, Easton Press, 1991; London, Grafton, 1993.

Lord Kelvin's Machine: A Novel (Homunculus). Sauk, Wisconsin, Arkham House, 1992; London, Grafton, 1993.

The Magic Spectacles. Bath, Morrigan, 1991.

Night Relics. New York, Ace, and London, HarperCollins, 1994.

Short Stories

Paper Dragons. Seattle, Washington, Axolotl Press, 1986.

The Pink of Fading Neon. Seattle, Washington, Axolotl Press, 1986.

The Shadow on the Doorstep, with *Trilobyte,* by Ed Bryant. Seattle, Washington, Axolotl Press, 1987.

Two Views of a Cave Painting; and The Idol's Eye. Seattle, Washington, Axolotl Press, 1988.

Doughnuts. Mission Viejo, California, A.S.A.P, 1994.

*   *   *

Blaylock creates realistic landscapes, even when they are those of fairy tale countries, to accommodate his blend of everydayness, quirky characters, zany motivations, metaphysical speculation, and many varieties of magic. His magic may be simply a subjective celebration: "'Luminiferous ether' he rolled the phrase on his tongue, listening to the magic of it" ("The Better Boy," with Tim Powers in *Isaac Asimov's Science Fiction Magazine,* February, 1991). Or it may be a freakishly active magic, such as, in *Land of Dreams,* subverts the space/time continuum to conjure Fortean-like artifacts from the ocean. Or it may be, as in the *Elfin Ship* series, the straightforward magic of wizardry and witchcraft, even though submarines and airships are among its instruments. It is useless to look for consistency in Blaylock's magic; but it so permeates his communities and landscapes as to claim, along with them, a conceded acceptance.

He is an artist of landscapes. Those in *The Elfin Ship* series are populated by dwarfs, trolls, goblins, and giants. Their winding rivers, dark forests, and hill-perched castles combine a suggestion of primal North America with evocation of the Grimm Brothers' folkloric lands. In *The Disappearing Dwarf* deep woods and craggy mountains, flanked by glowing glaciers and pierced with cavernous treasure trails, are as full of telluric magic as are the crystalline oceanic abysses of *The Stone Giant.* Its aura, as well as the more overt effects of goblin sorcery, lend piquancy to the ordinariness of such missions as Jonathan Bing's river voyage to sell cheeses in Seaside and bring back cakes to Twombly Town.

In other novels, Californian coasts are treated (up to a point) realistically: the north coast of San Francisco in *Land of Dreams,* and the environs of Los Angeles in *The Digging Leviathan.* A transfiguring magic warps this landscape, however. In the latter novel, the Los Angeles highway network, San Pedro Bay, and Catalina Island exist in substantial detail, but almost as a mental projection made actual: "The black asphalt street undulated as if it were a river coming to life . . . and below it waited beasts, unidentifiable beasts nosing up out of subterranean caverns." Caverns are entry to the underground/submarine world that rival parties, by digger and diving-bell, explore and exploit in pursuit or support of the gilled boy Giles, regressively seeking "return to the land of his ancestors." It is pseudoscience and extravagant fantasy, certainly, but it engagingly persuades suspended disbelief. Similarly, in *Land of Dreams,* the Humbolt County townlet of Rio Dell is vividly actual: "Only a single fisherman sat on the pier, whittling idly. The wind blew

down the centre of the street, whirling a yellowed old sheet of newspaper into the air and picking up leaves." Yet this is the scene of time fugues, the brewing of an alchemical elixir, and the coincidence of astronomical cycles with bizarre materializations and resurrections: realism and fantasy uniquely fused.

The Paper Grail takes this fusion even further. Here, again in a Californian ambience of forests, cliffs, and misty northern shorelines, where pelicans fly as auguries, a ghost museum is located. There are piers and boats from which, in dream or life, analogues or embodiments of the sick Fisher King perpetually fish. The Grail itself, flimsy as it is, is yet a channel through which the elemental powers of Earth, ocean, and sky may be manipulated. It is one of several objects or artifacts that symbolize or actually energize shamanistic powers—the cane which passes from one Grail guardian to another, the absurd Pre-Raphaelite-originated machine which materializes the apparition of John Ruskin, the supposed skeletal remains of Ruskin and Joseph of Arimathea, these all act to create out of everyday present and ghostly past a weirdly imagined Blaylockian continuum through which the Grail and its quest are perennially progressed.

There are also British locales. The site of one episode of *The Digging Leviathan* is Lake Windermere, mysteriously connected with the under-Earth. In *Homunculus,* action centres on 19th-century London. The element of realism here is distinctly subordinate to "Gothicry," with a low-life pitched between Doré and Dickens. After episodes of messianic madness, grave-robbing, aquarium-robbing, and pursuit through the London sewers, events climax in the descent of a skeleton-manned dirigible at Hampstead Heath to carry away that immortal manniquin, the Paracelsian homunculus. Inventive as ever of grotesquery in environment and character, Blaylock continually summons humour out of horror. He infiltrates sly literary and genre allusions, such as when the existence of a Mars-accessing crystal egg, reputedly stolen from a curiosity shop near Seven Dials, appears to be known to the costermongers of Petticoat Lane. Switching allusion from Wells to Delany, the Royal Academician's paper "Time Considered as a Succession of Semi-closed Doors" is similarly a science fiction in-joke. The same melodramatic characters, Victorian settings, and playful allusiveness appear in the pages of *Lord Kelvin's Machine,* though this is plotted less as a sequel than as an interweaving of three stories: first the hero, St. Ives, after a nihilistic opponent has murdered his dearest Alice, saves the world from cometary destruction; then he retrieves the wonder-working machine from the bottom of the English Channel; finally he reverses his tragic loss by using the machine to engineer time cycles and paradoxes, creating in doing so a fine confusion of identities.

The ingeniously contrived conclusion of *Lord Kelvin's Machine* is in keeping with Blaylock's general tendency to ensure that eventually good gets the better of evil. For all their ludic extravagance his novels have unmistakable moral dimensions; and the evil in them can be quite nasty, its intention being to spoil an edenic situation, that of the heroic element to restore it. This is particularly well demonstrated in one of his best California-located fantasies, *The Lost Coin,* where the curses laid on Ahasuherus and on Judas Iscariot seem to dog the steps and shape the destiny of the immortality-obsessed, evil magician, Jules Pennyman. Throughout he plays a sinister and corrupting role, but he is not allowed permanently to ruin Blaylock's small town idyll. At the ocean's edge, just off the Pacific Highway, homely, if eccentric, townfolk act out their life-enhancing, crazy schemes, their determination to win eventually rewarded. For the often frustrated hero, Andrew Vanbergen, a devotee of *The Wind in the Willows,* there is always "the promise of heaven on the soft wind, 'the place of my song-dream,' as Rat put it."

Much of Blaylock's fiction is, like *The Lost Coin,* in essence pastoral—not escapist, because one is always aware that there are wolves; but joyous and, as entertainments, often raising mind and emotions to the pitch of unexpected insight and sudden laughter. *Night Relics* more than any of the preceding novels carries supernaturally-tinged fantasy toward psychological depth, while maintaining the by now familiar interplay between human imaginings and a specific environment. In a realistic Orange County mountain-and-forest setting, suburban-development and canyon-shack communities are put under stress by the constant blowing, throughout the three days of the novel's action, of the Santa Ana wind—a wind confusing shapes and shadows, wrecking trees and buildings. The stage is set for the appearance of revenants, victims and destroyer, who, through hauntings and possession, tell and repeat the story of a 60-year-old crime. The ghost-creating power is strangely vested in long-surviving household structures and artifacts. The *crime passionel* at the source of the manifestations is melodramatic in the extreme. The present-day characters who are caught up in its supernatural aftermath are themselves involved in ordinary enough tangles of love, jealousy, and nostalgia, but the more the "possession" takes hold, the more bizarre becomes the pattern of past and present interpenetrations. Blaylock typically straightens things out to provide a happy conclusion for the deserving (though not for the avariciously brutal) while leaving mystery still flapping in the dying gusts of a Santa Ana gale. Blaylock is fond of epigraphs and for *Night Relics* he takes one from (a favourite) Robert Louis Stevenson: ". . . we no longer see the devil in the bedcurtains nor lie awake to listen to the wind" (*Child's Play*). That exorcism may be appropriate to the ending of *Night Relics,* but, happily, throughout the entire Blaylock opus, however familiar or charming the environment, we continue to see those disturbing shapes and hear those elemental sounds.

—K.V. Bailey

BLAYRE, Christopher

Pseudonym for Edward Heron-Allen. **Other Pseudonym:** Nora Helen Warddel. **Nationality:** British. **Born:** London, 17 December 1861. **Education:** Harrow School. **Military Service:** Served with the Staff Intelligence Department of the War Office during World War I. **Family:** Married 1) Marianna Lehmann in 1891; 2) Edith Pepler in 1903; one daughter. **Career:** Admitted as a Solicitor of the Supreme Court, 1884. Lived in the United States, 1886-89; gave frequent lectures on protozoology. Editor, with E. Polonaski, *Violin Times,* London, 1893-1907. Fellow, Royal Society, 1919. **Died:** 28 March 1943.

SCIENCE FICTION PUBLICATIONS

Novel

The Princess Daphne: A Novel (with Selina Delaro as Edward Heron-Allen). London, Drane, 1885; Chicago, Belford Clarke, 1888.

Short Stories (series: University of Cosmopoli in all titles)

The Purple Sapphire and Other Posthumous Papers, Selected from the Unofficial Records of the University of Cosmopoli. London, Philip Allan, 1921; expanded edition, as *The Strange Papers of Dr. Blayre,* 1932; New York, Arno Press, 1976.
The Cheetah Girl. London, privately printed, 1923.
Some Women of the University, Being a Last Selection from the Strange Papers of Christopher Blayre. London, Stockwell, 1934.

OTHER PUBLICATIONS (as Edward Heron-Allen)

Novels

The Romance of a Quiet Watering-Place (as Nora Helen Warddel). Chicago, Belford Clarke, 1888.

Short Stories

Kisses of Fate. Chicago, Belford Clarke, 1888.
A Fatal Fiddle. Chicago, Belford Clarke, 1890.

Poetry

The Love-Letters of a Vagabond. London, Drane, 1889.
The Ballads of a Blasé Man. Privately printed, 1891.

Other

De Fidiculis Opusculum. Privately printed, 9 vols., 1882-1941.
Chiromancy; or, The Science of Palmistry, with Henry Frith. London, Routledge, 1883.
Codex Chiromantiae. Privately printed, 3 vols., 1883-86.
Violin-Making, As It Was and Is. London, Ward Lock, 1884; Boston, Howe, 1901.
A Manual of Cheirosophy. London, Ward Lock, 1885.
Practical Cheirosophy: A Synoptical Study of the Science of the Hand. New York and London, Putnam, 1887.
De Fidiculis Bibliographia, Being an Attempt Towards a Bibliography of the Violin and All Other Instruments with a Bow. London, Griffith Farran, 2 vols., 1890-94.
Prolegomena Towards the Study of Chalk Foraminifera. London, Nichols, 1894.
Some Side-lights upon Edward FitzGerald's Poem "The Rubá'iyát of Omar Khayyám." London, Nichols, 1898.
Nature and History at Selsea Bill. Selsey, Sussex, Gardner, 1911.
Selsey Bill: Historic and Prehistoric. London, Duckworth, 1911.
The Vistors' Map and Guide to Selsey. Selsey, Sussex, Gardner, 1912.
The Foraminifera of the Clare Island District, Co. Mayo, Ireland, with Arthur Earland. Dublin, Clare Island Survey, 1913.
Protozoa (report for the 1910 Antarctic expedition), with Arthur Earland. Privately printed, 1922.
Barnacles in Nature and Myth. London, Oxford University Press, 1928.
The Gods of the Fourth World, Being Prolegomena Towards a Discourse upon the Buddhist Religion. Privately printed, 1931.
The Parish Church of St. Peter on Selsey Bill, Sussex. Privately printed, 1935.

Editor, *Edward FitzGerald's Rubá'iyát of Omar Khayyám, with the Original Persian Sources.* London, Quaritch, 1899.

Editor, *The Second Edition of Edward FitzGerald's Rubá'iyát of Omar Khayyám.* London, Duckworth, 1908.

Editor, with Arthur Earland, *The Fossil Foraminifera of the Blue Marl of the Côtedes Basques.* Manchester, Literary and Philosophical Society, 1919.

Editor, *Memoranda of Memorabilia,* by Madame de Sévigné. Privately printed, 1928.

Editor, *The Further and Final Researches of Joseph Jackson Lister upon the Reproductive Process of Polystomella Crispa (Linné).* Washington, D.C., Smithsonian Institution, 1930.

Editor and translator, *A Fool of God: The Mystical Works of Bába Táhir.* London, Octagon Press, 1979.

Translator, *The Science of the Hand,* by C.S. d'Arpentigny. London, Ward Lock, 1886.

Translator, *The Rubá'iyát of Omar Khayyám.* London, Nichols, 1898.

Translator, *The Lament of Bába Táhir.* London, Quaritch, 1902.

Translator, *Quatrains of Omar Khayyám.* London, Mathews, 1908; revised edition, 1908.

Translator, *The Rubá'yát of Omar Khayyám the Poet: The Literal Translation of the Ousley Manuscript.* London, Lane, 1924.

* * *

Christopher Blayre remains an enigmatic figure. His extraordinarily versatile life in varied scientific and artistic fields is mostly well recorded—he did research in marine biology and palaeontology, horticulture, music, occultism, Persian literature, history, and bibliography—but the names under which he wrote some of his unacknowledged fiction have not been discovered, and how much more he may have written of possible interest is not known. What we do have is a quite interesting group of stories, mainly on supernatural themes, and a few with a place in science fiction's formative stage. The weird stories use familiar elements of ghosts and apparitions, possession, visions, and curses, but the treatment is modern. There is some effective satirical humor, as in the immortal Wandering Jew succumbing to modern medicine, and a visit to an annex to Hell with an institution for completing unfinished works.

"Aalila" concerns a visit to Venus by matter transmission. The Venerians, who resemble humans, have an incompatible culture, and the experimenter's inevitable sexual involvement with Aalila leads to the expected disaster. It is an effective tale for all its familiarity. "The Cosmic Dust" is a sequel, and must be among the earliest stories on the interplanetary transmission of life in spores. This was a very important concept and raises questions that remain open. "The Mirror That Remembered" has another idea often suggested, a device for visualizing past scenes. A marginal item is "The Blue Cockroach," where a temporary change in personality follows an insect bite.

"The Cheetah-Girl," dropped by the publisher at the last moment from *The Purple Sapphire,* is a more ambitious work, a serious story of a macabre project—the creation of a human-cheetah hybrid, and its consequences. The rationale is logical, considering the elementary state of genetics in 1920. These stories compare very favorably with the better known protoscience fiction of the period. The style is easy, assured, and fresh.

—Graham Stone

BLISH, James (Benjamin)

Pseudonym: William Atheling, Jr. **Nationality:** American. **Born:** East Orange, New Jersey, 23 May 1921. **Education:** East Orange High School; Rutgers University, New Brunswick, New Jersey, 1938-42, B.Sc. 1942; Columbia University, New York, 1945-46. **Military Service:** Served in the United States Army, 1942-44. **Family:** Married 1) Virginia Kidd in 1947 (divorced); 2) Judith Ann Lawrence in 1964; one daughter and one son. **Career:** Editor of a trade newspaper, New York, 1947-51; public relations counsel, New York and Washington, D.C., 1951-68. Editor, *Vanguard Science Fiction,* New York, 1958; co-editor, *Kalki: Studies in James Branch Cabell,* Oradell, New Jersey; vice-president, Science Fiction Writers of America, 1966-68. **Awards:** Hugo award, 1959. **Died:** 29 July 1975.

SCIENCE FICTION PUBLICATIONS

Novels (series: Cities in Flight; After Such Knowledge)

Jack of Eagles. New York, Greenberg, 1952; London, Nova, 1955; as *Esper,* New York, Avon, 1958.

The Warriors of Day. New York, Galaxy, 1953; London, Severn House, 1978.

Cities in Flight (revised edition). New York, Avon, 1970; London, Arrow, 1981.

Earthman, Come Home. New York, Putnam, 1955; London, Faber, 1956.

They Shall Have Stars: A Science Fiction Novel. London, Faber, 1956; revised edition, as *Year 2018!,* New York, Avon, 1957.

The Triumph of Time. New York, Avon, 1958; as *A Clash of Cymbals,* London, Faber, 1959.

A Case of Conscience. New York, Ballantine, 1958; London, Faber, 1959.

VOR. New York, Avon, 1958; London, Corgi, 1959.

The Duplicated Man, with Robert W. Lowndes. New York, Avalon, 1959.

The Star Dwellers (for children). New York, Putnam, 1961; London, Faber, 1962.

Titan's Daughter. New York, Berkley, 1961; London, New English Library, 1963.

A Life for the Stars. New York, Putnam, 1962; London, Faber, 1964.

Mission to the Heart Stars (for children). New York, Putnam, and London, Faber, 1965.

A Torrent of Faces, with Norman L. Knight. Garden City, New York, Doubleday, 1967; London, Faber, 1968.

Welcome to Mars (for children). London, Faber, 1967; New York, Putnam, 1968.

The Vanished Jet (for children). New York, Weybright and Talley, 1968.

. . . And All the Stars a Stage. Garden City, New York, Doubleday, 1971; London, Faber, 1972.

Midsummer Century. Garden City, New York, Doubleday, 1972; London, Faber, 1973; expanded edition, New York, DAW, 1974.

The Quincunx of Time. New York, Dell, 1973; London, Faber, 1975.

After Such Knowledge. London, Legend, 1991. Volumes 3-4 published as *Black Easter: The Day After Judgement,* Boston, Gregg, 1980; as *The Devil's Day,* New York, Baen Books, 1990.

Doctor Mirabilis. London, Faber, 1964; revised edition, New York, Dodd, Mead, 1971.

Black Easter; or, Faust Aleph-Null. Garden City, New York, Doubleday, 1968; London, Faber, 1969.

The Day After Judgment: A Novel. Garden City, New York, Doubleday, 1971; London, Faber, 1972.

Short Stories

The Seedling Stars. New York, Gnome Press, 1957; London, Faber, 1967.

Galactic Cluster. New York, New American Library, 1959; revised, London, Faber, 1960.

So Close to Home. New York, Ballantine, 1961.

Best Science Fiction Stories of James Blish. London, Faber, 1965; revised edition, 1973; as *The Testament of Andros,* London, Arrow, 1977.

Anywhen. Garden City, New York, Doubleday, 1970; enlarged edition, London, Faber, 1971.

Mudd's Angels (Star Trek), with J.A. Lawrence. Toronto and New York, Bantam, 1978.

The Best of James Blish, edited by Robert A.W. Lowndes. New York, Ballantine, 1979.

Get Out of My Sky; and, There Shall Be No Darkness. London, Panther, 1980.

The Seedling Stars; and, Galactic Cluster. New York, New American Library, 1983.

A Work of Art, and Other Stories. Sutton, Surrey, Severn House, 1993.

Star Trek: The Classic Episodes, 1-3 (from the TV series; vols. 2 and 3 with J.A. Lawrence). New York, Bantam, 1991.

Star Trek, 1-12 (vol. 12 with Judith A. Lawrence). New York, Bantam, 12 vols., 1967-77; London, Corgi, 12 vols., 1972-79; with *Spock Must Die!* as *The Star Trek Reader, I-IV,* New York, Dutton, 1976-78.

Spock Must Die! New York, Bantam, 1970; London, Corgi, 1984.

OTHER PUBLICATIONS

Novels

The Frozen Year. New York, Ballantine, 1957; as *Fallen Star,* London, Faber, 1957.

The Night Shapes. New York, Ballantine, 1962; London, New English Library, 1963.

Other

The Issue at Hand: Studies in Contemporary Magazine Science Fiction (as William Atheling, Jr.). Chicago, Advent, 1964.

More Issues at Hand: Critical Studies in Contemporary Science Fiction (as William Atheling, Jr.). Chicago, Advent, 1970.

The Tale that Wags the God, edited by Cy Chauvin. Chicago, Advent, 1987.

Editor, *New Dreams This Morning.* New York, Ballantine, 1966.

Editor, *Nebula Award Stories Five.* Garden City, New York, Doubleday, and London, Gollancz, 1970.

Editor, *Thirteen O'Clock and Other Zero Hours,* by C.M. Kornbluth. New York, Dell, 1970; London, Hale, 1972.

*

Bibliography: *James Blish: A Bibliography 1940-1976* by Judith A. Blish, Harpsden, Henley-on-Thames, n.p, 1976.

Manuscript Collection: Bodleian Library, Oxford.

Critical Studies: *A Clash of Symbols: The Triumph of James Blish* by Brian Stableford, San Bernardino, California, Borgo, 1979; *Imprisoned in a Tesseract: The Life and Work of James Blish* by David Ketterer, Ohio, Kent State University Press, 1987.

*   *   *

Whatever James Blish wrote, to paraphrase John Simon on Robert Musil, was or became difficult. Blish's fiction deals, to a degree unusual even for commercial fiction, with conflict (should the protagonist find himself possessed of unusual powers, as in *Jack of Eagles,* it causes problems rather than solves them) and with difficulty. Blish's protagonists are generally in deeply problematical situations at novel's end, for the revelations of the nature of the world that the narrative discloses tends to elevate the characters' problems to metaphysical levels rather than disclose a path to their resolution. For Blish, who spent most of his career working on a book on music theory entitled *Music the Hard Way,* the creative act was not a natural expression of innate gifts, as the Romantics and various bardic successors have felt, but the shaping of art from obdurate material, against resistance and through repeated revision.

Certainly one of the major conflicts in Blish's work is the tension between his vocation as a genre writer and his dedication to the ideals of literary Modernism, which he tried to combine through sheer determination, as a glass blower might seek to fuse two incompatible materials in the heat of his oven. As a science fiction writer, Blish wrote collaborations, wrote stories inspired by magazine covers or editorial suggestions, structured his novels so as to accommodate magazine serialization, and engaged in numerous other exigencies that would be anathema to an artist of the stamp of Pound, Joyce, or Kafka, all of whom Blish revered. Blish's best fiction—densely written, intellectually audacious, and ingeniously structured—reflects this: it is commercial and accessible science fiction that seems on the verge of transforming into something else.

Blish's characteristic approach was to subject a science fiction commonplace—antigravity, shrunken humans, telepathy—to intensive scrutiny; and later to subject the published story to reconsideration and expansion, and subsume it into a larger whole. While other SF writers would frequently write sequels, stringing together narratives like freight trains taking on additional cars, Blish's works would accrete, like coral (the earliest published installments, heavily revised, ending up somewhere in the middle of the final work). *Jack of Eagles* (which began life as an early novelette, "Let the Finder Beware"), adopts a theme popular in the early fifties, the unexceptional-seeming young man who discovers that he possesses psionic powers, and makes of this stock situation as complex and rigorous (both scientifically and dramatically) as Blish's powers could manage. "Sunken Universe," Blish's first important story—published in 1942 when the author was 21—dramatized the subject of tiny people menaced by normally harmless fauna (a popular theme in pulp magazines of the late 1930s), but considered, as earlier authors had not, how gravity is a less significant force in the microscopic realm, while such forces as surface tension and friction are correspondingly more important. Ten years later Blish wrote a sequel, "Surface Tension," which exploits the full dramatic potential of the subject while giving form to a surprisingly melancholy tale of cosmogony and loss. The story's prologue (which stands as prologue to "Sunken Universe" as well, thus framing the earlier tale) links it to a larger subject—genetic engineering, then scarcely touched as a theme by SF writers—and the potential for a larger fiction.

The eventual novel, *The Seedling Stars,* is a sequence of four stories (the first two now subsumed into one) that describes a spiral which curves ironically back upon itself, showing mankind seeding the galaxy with tailored versions of itself while dispossessing itself of Earth. Critics have traced the subtle structure of the novel, noting the motifs of revelation and dispossession and the progression of the underlying symbolism from one story to the next. One of the few fixup novels that is genuinely stronger as a whole than in its constituent parts, *The Seedling Stars* remains one of the landmarks of 1950s SF.

Blish's other major series of the fifties, *Cities in Flight* (known as the "Okie" series during magazine publication), similarly grew from a single story to an eschatology-minded sequence of vast scope. *Earthman, Come Home,* the first volume to be written, simply strings together a sequence of intense and ingenious adventure novelettes featuring Mayor Amalfi and the flying city of New York; but the later three volumes (each less than half the length of *Earthman, Come Home,* Blish's mature fiction always favored compression over the diffuseness of much genre fiction) are each vivid and memorable novels, each dealing with a different era and set of protagonists (Amalfi shows up again in *The Triumph of Time,* but it is an Amalfi strikingly transformed by the passage of centuries). *They Shall Have Stars,* with its then-unusual dual story line (one a dramatization of political millennialism and an overt attack on McCarthyism, the other the claustrophobic and determinedly antiheroic depiction of a protagonist succumbing to neurosis under intolerable working conditions), and *The Triumph of Time,* with its spare plotline and haunted prose ("In these later years it occasionally startled John Amalfi to be confronted by evidence that there was anything in the universe that was older than he was, and the irrationality of his allowing himself to be startled by such a truism startled him all over again"), frame the original tale like panels of a triptych, but the effect was unintended, and soon marred by a fourth volume, the young adult novel *A Life for the Stars* (last written, second in internal chronology). Blish seemed to like sequences of four, perhaps because the echoes of both Wagner's *Ring* cycle and of *Finnegans Wake,* two works he studied all his life. The easy symmetry of the trilogy held no interest for him.

Despite his interest in the great Modernist works of 20th-century literature, Blish was not by nature the writer of long sustained narratives; as the permissible length for SF novels increased in the late sixties, Blish's own fiction compressed further, and all of his last novels are quite short. His two longest SF novels, *Earthman, Come Home* and *A Torrent of Faces* (the latter written with Norman L. Knight) are both works conceived early in his career, and both are essentially fixups of semi-independent novelettes. Blish's one sustained narrative of more than 220 pages is his only historical novel, *Doctor Mirabilis.* A *tour de force*—the overused term is appropriate here—Blish's novel of Roger Bacon and the birth of the scientific method took him years to write, an investment of effort he could not afford to make again.

Blish's experiments with form are most evident in his short fiction, where he could be assured of finding a publisher for even works that depart radically from linear narrative. "Common Time" and "Testament of Andros" dissolve narrative consciousness and

chronology, reordering their material in a manner that bespeaks Blish's Modernist affinities, especially with late Joyce. "Testament of Andros" may be seen today as perhaps too determinedly avant-garde, a story that yields up its meanings after a few readings; but "Common Time" is not exhausted even by Damon Knight's celebrated explication. A voyage into another state of being and back again, Blish's intense novelette (again in four parts) dramatizes the essential solitude of the Blish protagonist, who pokes his head through the boundary of his cosmos and discovers wonders beyond, but cannot fully articulate them later, nor learn from them how to live successfully with others in the world.

Both stories were published in 1953, the year that also saw publication of "A Case of Conscience," the novella that formed the basis for Blish's most famous novel. In its original form, "A Case of Conscience" was essentially a work of intellectual virtuosity: Blish vividly dramatized the exotic ecology of the planet Lithia, then mounted a surprising argument about it from the perspective of one of his protagonists, a Jesuit naturalist. The novel version published five years later continued the story, but crucially revised the existing portion: the theory that Father Ruiz-Sanchez is compelled to accept is, he realizes, a heresy: his faith and the evidence of his senses have pulled him in opposite directions, tearing him down the middle. For all the intellectual virtuosity of the final version, *A Case of Conscience,* remains a novel of character, with Ruiz-Sanchez's anguish its most memorable element.

After completing his long labors on *Doctor Mirabilis* and *A Torrent of Faces,* Blish set about to establish himself as an author of wider range, and completed various dramatic and non-SF projects, some of which had been in progress for many years. This effort was not especially successful: *Doctor Mirabilis* took years to find an American publisher, Blish's elegant libretto *Eros and Psyche* (published at last in the 1995 collection of his poems) went unproduced, and *A Cage of Birds,* his novel about a bizarre production of Strauss's *Der Rosenkavalier,* and his book on music theory both failed to find a publisher. *Black Easter,* Blish's contemporary novel about a black magician living and operating in the modern world, was published as a genre novel, and its success did little to permit Blish to publish elsewhere.

By the time Blish moved to England in 1969 and began what proved to be the last phase of his career, he was no longer interested in devoting his major energies to science fiction. A series of commissions to produce book versions of *Star Trek* scripts kept Blish in the science fiction world, in which he was enjoying some celebrity; but the three SF novels he did complete and publish—*The Day After Judgment,* a sequel to *Black Easter; The Quincunx of Time,* an expansion of a 1954 novelette; and *Midsummer Century,* based on an outline Blish had written in 1950—had their origins earlier in his career, and represent last reconsiderations of old projects, rather than new ones. Although even these late works compel interest—*The Day After Judgment,* the fourth volume of a sequence of theological novels that Blish called *After Such Knowledge,* is one of his best—Blish's desire to write literary projects plainly occupied most of his creative energies. Illness intervened, however, and save for various articles in *Punch* and other British magazines, plus essays in various literary journals, none of these projects were published, and most were not completed.

Twenty years after his death, Blish is largely out of print in North America, though his critical reputation remains high. His finest works—*After Such Knowledge, The Seedling Stars,* most of *Cities in Flight,* and enough short fiction to fill a substantial volume—remain fresh both to new readers and those long familiar with them.

The internal stresses of his works—the attempt to reconcile the disparate demands of literary modernism and category SF, to please a literary audience someday and SF readers now—serve to pull them taut, and their odd proportions, malformed by many conventional criteria, seem to have streamlined them to survive posterity's wind-tunnel blast, which has shredded the more shapely contours of innumerable other books. For the saturnine Blish, whose gaze ranged over the ruined monuments of the past as well as the long perspective of the future, this may be a sufficient triumph over time.

—Gregory Feeley

BLOCH, Robert

Pseudonym: Collier Young. **Nationality:** American. **Born:** Chicago, Illinois, 5 April 1917. **Education:** Public schools in Maywood, Illinois, and Milwaukee. **Family:** Married 1) Marion Holcombe; one daughter; 2) Eleanor Alexander in 1964. **Career:** Copywriter, Gustav Marx Advertising Agency, Milwaukee, 1942-53; editor, *Science-Fiction World,* New York, 1956; president, Mystery Writers of America, 1970-71. **Awards:** Evans Memorial award, 1959; Hugo award, 1959; Ann Radcliffe award, 1960, 1966; Mystery Writers of America Edgar Allan Poe award, 1960; Trieste Film Festival award, 1965; Convention du Cinéma Fantastique de Paris prize, 1973; World Fantasy Convention award, 1975; World Science Fiction Convention Lifetime Career award, 1985; Bram Stoker award, 1990; World Horror Convention Grandmaster award, 1991. Guest of Honor, World Science Fiction Convention, 1948, 1973; Bouchercon I, 1971; World Fantasy Convention, 1975. **Died:** 23 September 1994.

SCIENCE FICTION PUBLICATIONS

Novels

Ladies' Day; and, This Crowded Earth. New York, Belmont, 1968.
It's All in Your Mind. New York, Curtis, 1971.
Sneak Preview. New York, Paperback Library, 1971.
Strange Eons. Chapel Hill, North Carolina, Whispers Press, 1978.
Twilight Zone: The Movie: A Novel (novelization of screenplays). New York, Warner, and London, Corgi, 1983.
Lori. New York, Tor, 1989.

Short Stories

Sea Kissed, with Henry Kuttner. London, Utopian, 1945.
The Opener of the Way. Sauk City, Wisconsin, Arkham House, 1945; London, Spearman, 1974; selection, as *House of the Hatchet,* St. Albans, Hertfordshire, Panther, 1976.
Pleasant Dreams—Nightmares. Sauk City, Wisconsin, Arkham House, 1960; London, Whiting and Wheaton, 1967; abridged as *Nightmares,* New York, Belmont, 1961.
Blood Runs Cold. New York, Simon and Schuster, 1961; London, Hale, 1963.
More Nightmares. New York, Belmont, 1962.
Yours Truly, Jack the Ripper: Tales of Horror. New York, Belmont, 1962; as *The House of the Hatchet and Other Tales of Horror,* London, Tandem, 1965.

Atoms and Evil. Greenwich, Connecticut, Fawcett, 1962; London, Muller, 1963.
Horror-7. New York, Belmont, 1963; as *Torture Garden,* London, New English Library, 1967.
Bogey Men: Ten Tales. New York, Pyramid, 1963.
Tales in a Jugular Vein. New York, Pyramid, 1965; London, Sphere, 1970.
The Skull of the Marquis de Sade and Other Stories. New York, Pyramid, 1965; London, Hale, 1975.
Chamber of Horrors. New York, Award, 1966; London, Corgi, 1977.
The Living Demons. New York, Belmont, 1967; London, Sphere, 1970.
Dragons and Nightmares: Four Short Novels. Baltimore, Mirage Press, 1968.
Bloch and Bradbury: Ten Masterpieces of Science Fiction, with Ray Bradbury, edited by Kurt Singer. New York, Tower, 1969; as *Fever Dream and Other Fantasies,* London, Sphere, 1970.
Fear Today, Gone Tomorrow. New York, Award, and London, Tandem, 1971.
The Best of Robert Bloch, edited by Lester del Rey. New York, Ballantine, 1977.
Cold Chills. Garden City, New York, Doubleday, 1977; London, Hale, 1978.
The Laughter of a Ghoul, What Every Young Ghoul Should Know. West Warwick, Rhode Island, Necronomicon Press, 1977.
The King of Terrors: Tales of Madness and Death. New York, Mysterious Press, 1977; London, Hale, 1978.
Out of the Mouths of Graves. New York, Mysterious Press, 1979; London, Hale, 1980.
Such Stuff as Screams Are Made Of. New York, Ballantine, 1979; London, Hale, 1980.
Mysteries of the Worm: All the Cthulhu Mythos Stories of Robert Bloch. New York, Zebra, 1981; revised and expanded edition, Oakland, California, Chaosium, 1993.
Out of My Head. Cambridge, Massachusetts, NESFA Press, 1986.
Midnight Pleasures. Garden City, New York, Doubleday, 1987.
Lost in Time and Space with Lefty Feep, edited by John Stanley. Pacifica, California, Creatures at Large, 1987.
The Selected Stories of Robert Bloch (includes *Final Reckoning, Bitter Ends,* and *Last Rites).* Los Angeles, Underwood-Miller, 3 vols., 1987-88; as *The Complete Stories,* New York, Citadel Press, 3 vols., 1989-91.
Fear and Trembling. New York, Tor, 1989.
Yours Truly, Jack the Ripper (short story). Eugene, Oregon, Pulphouse, 1991.
The Skull of the Marquis de Sade (story). Eugene, Oregon, Pulphouse, 1992.
Early Fears (includes *The Opener of the Way* and *Pleasant Dreams—Nightmares).* Minneapolis, Minnesota, Fedogan and Bremer, 1994.

OTHER PUBLICATIONS

Novels (series: Psycho)

The Scarf. New York, Dial Press, 1947; as *The Scarf of Passion,* New York, Avon, 1949; revised edition, Greenwich, Connecticut, Fawcett, 1966; London, New English Library, 1972.
The Kidnapper. New York, Lion, 1954.

Spiderweb. New York, Ace, 1954.

The Will to Kill. New York, Ace, 1954.

Shooting Star. New York, Ace, 1958.

Psycho. New York, Simon and Schuster, 1959; London, Hale, 1960.

The Dead Beat. New York, Simon and Schuster, 1960; London, Hale, 1961.

Firebug. Evanston, Illinois, Regency, 1961; London, Corgi, 1977.

The Couch (novelization of screenplay). Greenwich, Connecticut, Fawcett, and London, Muller, 1962.

Terror. New York, Belmont, 1962; London, Corgi, 1964.

The Star Stalker. New York, Pyramid, 1968.

The Todd Dossier (as Collier Young). New York, Delacorte Press, and London, Macmillan, 1969.

Night-World. New York, Simon and Schuster, 1972; London, Hale, 1974.

American Gothic. New York, Simon and Schuster, 1974; London, W.H. Allen, 1975.

There is a Serpent in Eden. New York, Zebra, 1979; as *The Cunning,* 1981.

Psycho II. New York, Warner, 1982; London, Corgi, 1983.

The Night of the Ripper. Garden City, New York, Doubleday, 1984; London, Hale, 1986.

Unholy Trinity: Three Novels of Suspense (includes *The Scarf, The Dead Beat, The Couch*). Santa Cruz, California, Scream/Press, 1986.

Screams: Three Novels of Terror (includes *The Will to Kill, Firebug, The Star Stalker*). Los Angeles, Underwood-Miller, 1989.

Psycho House. New York, Tor, 1990; London, Hale, 1995.

The Jekyll Legacy, with Andre Norton. New York, Tor, 1990.

Short Stories

Terror in the Night and Other Stories. New York, Ace, 1958.

Plays

Screenplays: *The Couch,* with Owen Crump and Blake Edwards, 1962; *The Cabinet of Caligari,* 1962; *Strait-Jacket,* 1964; *The Night Walker,* 1964; *The Psychopath,* 1966; *The Deadly Bees,* with Anthony Marriott, 1967; *Torture Garden,* 1967; *The House That Dripped Blood,* 1970; *Asylum,* 1972; *The Amazing Captain Nemo,* with others, 1979.

Radio Plays: *Stay Tuned for Terror* series (39 scripts), 1944-45.

Television Plays: *The Cuckoo Clock, The Greatest Monster of Them All, A Change of Heart, The Landlady, The Sorcerer's Apprentice, The Gloating Place, Bad Actor,* and *The Big Kick,* all in *Alfred Hitchcock Presents* series 1955-61; *The Cheaters, The Devil's Ticket, A Good Imagination, The Grim Reaper, The Weird Tailor, Waxworks, Till Death Do Us Part,* and *Man of Mystery,* all in *Thriller* series, 1960-61; scripts for *Lock-Up,* 1960, *I Spy,* 1964, *Run for Your Life,* 1965, *Star Trek,* 1966-67, *Journey to the Unknown,* 1968, *Night Gallery,* 1971, and *Dark Room,* 1983-84; *The Cat Creature,* 1973; *The Dead Don't Die,* 1975; *Beetles,* 1987.

Other

The Eighth Stage of Fandom: Selections from 25 Years of Fan Writing, edited by Earl Kemp. Chicago, Advent, 1962.

The First World Fantasy Convention: Three Authors Remember, with Fritz Leiber and T.E.D. Klein. West Warwick, Rhode Island, Necronomicon Press, 1980.

The Robert Bloch Companion: Collected Interviews 1969-86, edited by Randall D. Larson. Mercer Island, Washington, Starmont House, 1989.

Once around the Bloch: An Unauthorized Biography. New York, Tor, 1993.

Editor, *The Best of Fredric Brown.* New York, Ballantine, 1977.

Editor, with Martin Harry Greenberg, *Psycho-Paths.* New York, Tor, 1991.

Editor, with Martin Harry Greenberg, *Monsters in Our Midst.* New York, Tor, 1993.

Recordings: *Gravely, Robert Bloch,* Alternate World, 1976; *Blood!,* with Harlan Ellison, Alternate World, 1976.

*

Bibliography: *The Complete Robert Bloch: An Illustrated Bibliography* by Randall D. Larson, Sunnyvale, California, Farday, 1986.

Manuscript Collection: University of Wyoming American Heritage Centre, Laramie.

Critical Study: *Robert Bloch* by Randall D. Larson, Mercer Island, Washington, Starmont House, 1986.

Robert Bloch commented:

Although I have had upwards of 100 short stories and novelettes published in science fiction magazines, I am primarily a writer of fantasy and mystery-suspense fiction: the bulk of my work falls within these two genres, as does my writing for screen, television, and radio. As a result my work has been almost entirely ignored by science fiction critics and historians—thank God! Having somehow managed to survive as a professional writer over a period of 57 years, I'd hate to blow it now. I am still fascinated by the SF field and by the people in it.

*　　*　　*

It's an unfortunate fact that Robert Bloch will probably always be remembered as the man who wrote *Psycho*—unfortunate not because the novel lacks significance, but because he has written so much other excellent fiction which seems doomed to exist forever under that very dark shadow. Although never a major voice in science fiction, he remained a follower of the genre throughout his life and was a well respected fan, corresponding with amateur publications and frequently appearing at conventions.

A correspondent and friend of H.P. Lovecraft, Bloch focused in his early career predominantly on the field of horror and weird fantasy, although he wrote so prolifically that he overlapped into other areas as well. He wrote light fantasy in the Thorne Smith mode, including such still readable stories as "Mr. Margate's Mermaid" and "Black Barter," much of it whimsical and reflecting a sense of humor that is present in even the darkest of his work.

Much of his early science fiction, such as "Fear Planet" and "Almost Human," used traditional horror themes in a futuristic or otherworldly setting. Most of the rest was humorous, parodies and spoofs filled with puns and outrageous situations, most notably the "Lefty Feep" series. Bloch's few longer science fiction works from this period were mostly disappointing. *This Crowded Earth,* for example, implausibly solves the population problem by introducing the idea of shrinking the human race so people take up less space. Bloch's focus in his serious fiction was almost invariably the minds of his characters, and the physical nature of their problems was often little more than a side issue. As science fiction matured, it turned in a direction that did not easily interface with Bloch's talents, which were more introspective and psychologically grounded.

The Big Binge (also known as *It's All in Your Mind*) made use of the concept of the dream machine, that is, a device that allows people to indulge their personal fantasies while in a dream state, so that they can do so without harming or offending anyone else. This is the closest Bloch ever came to creating a really successful full-length work of science fiction until quite late in his career. The 1959 novel *Sneak Preview* was interesting only because of what it demonstrated about the author's concerns for the world and it remains almost unknown in the field. In a future where pollution has driven most of the human race into domed cities, the government is secretly executing people when they reach the age of 50 to control population growth. The story is a routine potboiler, culminating in a successful overthrow of the repressive rulers. The characterization is competent but minimal, lacking the depth of the suspense thrillers he was already producing for another market.

Bloch has always been at his best at shorter length. The vast majority of his stories involve either supernatural or psychological terror. Collections with titles like *Blood Runs Cold, Nightmares, Bogey Men, Chamber of Horrors, Cold Chills,* and *Tales in a Jugular Vein* characterize much of his work. His fascination with Jack the Ripper led to "Yours Truly, Jack the Ripper," one of the finest horror stories ever written, as well as an historically accurate recent novel, *Night of the Ripper,* and an episode of the television program *Star Trek,* titled "The Wolf in the Fold." His fantasy story "That Hell Bound Train" won the Hugo award for best story, and other horror classics include "The Skull of the Marquis De Sade," "The Cheaters," "Enoch," "The Opener of the Way," and "The Shambler from the Stars." Despite frequently lurid titles and ghastly plot devices, his stories are invariably tasteful and demonstrate his ability to create the desired effect without bludgeoning his readers with explicit gore. Bloch has written extensively for television anthology programs like *Thriller* and *Night Gallery,* and for films including *Torture Garden, The House That Dripped Blood,* and *The Cabinet of Dr. Caligari.*

Bloch blends science fiction with many of his earlier interests in *Strange Eons,* set in the Lovecraftian universe, but removed to the future, in the context of a worldwide disaster. It is quite easily the best of his science fiction novels, perhaps because he brought to it the techniques which made his horror fiction so popular, and even though it is certainly a Lovecraftian tale, Bloch brings to this theme an original setting and plot. A collection of his earlier Lovecraftian fiction, *Mysteries of the Worm,* is uneven though many individual stories do an admirable job of reproducing Lovecraft's unique mood. Most of his other recent novels have been in the field of psychological suspense, but one, *Lori,* is his first full-length supernatural work. Two sequels to *Psycho,* unrelated to the films, have also appeared.

Despite the preponderance of horror and suspense, Bloch's several hundred published stories include a number of noteworthy science fiction tales. "A Way of Life" is set in a future when the field's fans have taken over the world, a pleasant wish fulfillment story

that enjoys continued popularity despite its relative triviality. The world's machinery revolts in "It Happened Tomorrow," and a rapist bites off more than he can chew when he attacks a very hungry "Girl from Mars." A cloned man must suffer the eternal imminence of death in "Forever and Amen."

The three best of Bloch's short SF stories are "Past Master," "The Man Who Murdered Tomorrow," and "The Man Who Collected Poe." In the first, an art thief from the future who wants to rescue works destroyed in a nuclear war inadvertently precipitates the war and destroys that which he came to save. In the second, a writer is driven to murder in order to gain access to ultimate power. The last involves a man obsessed with Edgar Allan Poe who brings him back to life, the newest exhibit for his collection, only to discover that Poe has ideas of his own. The Bloch collection with the highest predominance of actual science fiction stories is *Atoms and Evil,* which contains many of his best efforts. His drift away from fantasy during the 1990s resulted in tales of psychological or occasional supernatural horror with such stories as "It Takes One to Know One," "The Bedposts of Life," and "The Creative Urge."

Robert Bloch was a personable, soft-spoken man with an impish sense of humor, an intuitive insight into the darkest recesses of the human psyche, and an inordinately effective flair for storytelling. His level of output dropped off considerably in the early 1990s and his death in 1994 was a major loss for readers of all genres. Only a very small proportion of his output has been strictly speaking within the genre, but even these occasional pieces have enriched the field.

—Don D'Ammassa

BLUMLEIN, Michael

Nationality: American. **Born:** San Francisco, California, 28 June 1948. **Education:** Yale University, B.A. 1970; University of California, San Francisco Medical School, M.D. 1975. **Family:** Married Hilary Gordon; one daughter and one son. **Career:** Physician and faculty member, University of California at San Francisco; journeyman, Sign, Display & Allied Crafts Union, Local 510. **Awards:** Best Single Author Collection (Readercon), 1991. **Agent:** Martha Millard, Madison, New Jersey, U.S.A. **Address:** 476 Douglass St., San Francisco, California 94114 U.S.A.

SCIENCE FICTION PUBLICATIONS

Novels

The Movement of Mountains. New York, St. Martin's Press, 1987;
    London, Simon & Schuster, 1988.
X, Y. New York, Abyss, Dell, 1993.

Short Stories

The Brains of Rats. Los Angeles, Scream/Press, 1989.

*   *   *

Michael Blumlein has been publishing since the mid-eighties when the first of his extraordinary short stories, "Tissue Ablation and Variant Regeneration: A Case Report," appeared in *Interzone*. To date he has published two novels, *X,Y* and *The Movement of Mountains,* and one collection of short stories, *The Brains of Rats*. He has written for theatre and wrote the text of a film, "Decodings," which won an award at the San Francisco film festival. Imagining what Michael Blumlein's writing would be like if he had not pursued a career in medicine is a futile exercise. Blumlein's love of medicine, and of science, and his more than 20-year long career practising and teaching medicine, are reflected in every word he writes. He deploys the indisputable scientific voice with consummate ease. Here are a series of facts from "The Brains of Rats":

> The genes that determine sex lie on the twenty-third pair of chromosomes. They are composed of a finite and relatively short sequence of nucleic acids on the X chromosomes and one on the Y.

Indisputable facts backed with the authority of footnotes at the story's end. Here are more "facts" from "The Thing Itself":

> Love, after all, is not so hard. It is not a city, or a thought. When attended to with foresight and maturity, love is as straightforward as boiling an egg.

Well, of course. This is the same voice so it must be true. Blumlein plays games with the voice of authority, that he really is a doctor gives the "facts" he creates in his stories added authority. Anything delivered in this style becomes unassailable, no matter how absurd. At the same time, the act of intermingling the two discourses, of medicine and of fiction, brings everything into question. Medical language turns into poetry. Facts become fiction. If this voice tells us love is not so hard, perhaps the truth about the X and Y chromosome is not so clear cut after all?

In contrast to the passages of authoritatively delivered "fact," the male narrator in "The Brains of Rats" is uncertain and ill at ease within the body whose limits and sex he cannot be entirely sure of. The pile of facts surrounding the narrator provide no comfort and bring him no closer to understanding what makes him differ from his wife.

These questions about sexual difference dominate *X,Y*, Blumlein's second published novel. Indeed, Michael Blumlein is one of the few male writers of science fiction who could well win a James Tiptree, Jr. Award for science fiction which explores and expands gender roles. *X,Y*'s main narrative of a man who finds himself inside a woman's body is interspersed with passages on the twenty-third pair of chromosomes, lordosis, on memory, as well as a passage from *Cosmopolitan* on how to improve your looks. The passages are all footnoted with careful references to the text in which they first appeared. Most of these texts are real, some of them are not. This blurring casts uncertainty over what's true and what's not. What authority is real, what imaginary? In the shaping of our bodies does advice from *Cosmo* carry the same weight as articles from prestigious medical journals? Perhaps more. Is the protagonist Frankie de Leon mad? Has she/he really swapped consciousness with a man who is now in a coma? Certainly Frankie's unmistakably female body, she makes her living as a stripper, is an inescapable prison but is it any more of a prison since her transformation? His/her body reshapes her/his consciousness throughout the body, so that while the body as prison works well as a metaphor in *X,Y*, it also works against it because consciousness and body reshape one another and are not so easily separated.

In "Tissue Ablation and Variant Regeneration: A Case Report" Ronald Reagan's consciousness is not allowed to be separated from his suffering body. The story takes the genre of medical report, complete with attached appendix, and uses its structure for a searing political satire. The story has justly been compared with Swift's "A Modest Proposal." "Tissue Ablation" is a literal literary ecology: Ronald Reagan's body is dissected, carved into pieces, so that his parts may be harvested: his testes are transformed into oil and perfumes, his muscles into more than 13,000 kilos of meat, and his bones and skin and ligaments into housing material, cord, struts, and supports. The narrator is one of the surgeons on the team, the other surgeons have names like Dr. Guevara and Dr. Biko. Reagan is operated on without benefit of analgesia and his surgeon comments dispassionately on his cries of pain under the knife:

> That he did survive is a testimony to his strength, though I still remember his post-operative shrieks and protestations. We had, of course, already detached his upper limbs, and therefore we ourselves had to dab the streams of tears that flew from his eyes.

Yet there is a sense of love in the movements of this anonymous surgeon's knife and in his handling of Reagan's organs:

> . . . I looked into the chest. There I paused, as I always seem to do at the sight of that glistening organ. It throbbed and rolled, sensuously, I thought, majestically, and I renewed my vows to treat it kindly.

Another loving dissection of a body occurs in *The Movement of Mountains,* Blumlein's first novel. In chapter 24, titled "The Act of Seeing with One's Own Eyes," Dr. Jules Ebert performs an autopsy on his lover Jessica. Ebert displays the same recognition of the beauty of viscera, of organs, of the surgeon in "Tissue Ablation." For Blumlein the body does not end at the skin, the abject unspeakable innards, spilt out in arcs of repulsion in other genre texts, become objects of beauty. Jessica is beautiful and so is her heart and brain:

> . . . Glistening beneath the bright lights lay the brain.
> If the flesh evokes feelings of intimacy, and the face, fondness and familiarity, then the brain educes mystery and reverence.

Jessica's insides and her outsides become blurred and the traditional separation of mind and body becomes in this novel less absolute.

Blumlein's range is extraordinary. In "Hymenoptera," an uncollected story which appeared in the first issue of *Crank!,* the protagonist is not a doctor, but a fashion designer, Linderstadt, the Genius, the Master. At the end of designing his latest collection he wakes from a drunken stupor to find a giant wasp in his studio. He proceeds to design his collection for the wasp. Blumlein's description of the wasp is as precise and elegiac as the most exquisite botanical drawing, it is another kind of dissection, transforming the wasp into a jewel, a flower. Blumlein's delineation of the wasp is echoed by Linderstadt's construction of clothes, even a bridal gown for it. Linderstadt's obsession with the wasp becomes the only reasonable response to it.

Much of Blumlein's writing is taken up with making the unreasonable, reasonable and the irrational, rational. When, at the end of

The Movement of Mountains, the hero, Jules Ebert, sets about sleeping with his patients so that they will be infected with a disease that causes them to become part of the universe in an entirely different way, it is the only sane thing he can do. Blumlein's examination of sex and gender and the body in his fiction defies simplistic containment. His work is about shattering boundaries and resisting easy mapping. Facts are never quite facts. In the same way, his work has been published as both science fiction and horror and has been nominated for major fantasy awards. His work belongs in none of these genres and in all of them.

—Justine Larbalestier

BOND, Nelson S(lade)

Nationality: American. **Born:** Scranton, Pennsylvania, 23 November 1908. **Education:** Marshall University, Huntington, West Virginia, 1932-34. **Family:** Married Betty Gough Folsom in 1934; two sons. **Career:** Public relations field director, government of Nova Scotia, 1934-35. Freelance writer and philatelic researcher; book dealer. **Awards:** International Stamp Exhibition award, for non-fiction, 1960. D. Litt.: Marshall University, 1988. **Address:** 4724 Easthill Drive, Sugarloaf Farms, Roanoke, Virginia 24018, U.S.A.

SCIENCE FICTION PUBLICATIONS

Novel

Exiles of Time. Philadelphia, Prime Press, 1949.

Short Stories

Mr. Mergenthwirker's Lobblies and Other Fantastic Tales. New York, Coward-McCann, 1946.
The Thirty-first of February, with *A Conveyance of Title in Fee Simple* by James Brance Cabell. New York, Gnome Press, 1949.
The Remarkable Exploits of Lancelot Biggs, Spaceman. Garden City, New York, Doubleday, 1950.
The Monster. Sydney, American Science Fiction, 1953.
No Time Like the Future. New York, Avon, 1954.
Nightmares and Daydreams. Sauk City, Wisconsin, Arkham House, 1968.

OTHER PUBLICATIONS

Plays

Mr. Mergenthwirker's Lobblies, adaptation of his own story (televised). New York, French, 1957.
State of Mind: A Comedy in Three Acts. New York, French, 1958.
Animal Farm: A Fable in Two Acts, adaptation of the novel by George Orwell. New York, French, 1964.

Author of screenplays for government agencies, some 300 radio plays, and television plays for *Philco Playhouse, Kraft Theatre, Studio One,* and other series.

Other

The Postal Stationery of Canada: A Reference Catalogue. Shrub Oak, New York, Herst, 1953.
A Supplement of Current Values of Cabell Books, with *James Branch Cabell: A Complete Bibliography,* by James N. Hall. New York, Revisionist Press, 1974.

*   *   *

Nelson S. Bond's only novel published in book form is *Exiles of Time,* and it actually constitutes the fourth volume of a tetralogy; the earlier works in the series, *Sons of the Deluge, Gods of the Jungle,* and *That Worlds May Live,* were published in *Amazing. Exiles of Time,* though written in a clear, readable style, suffers from too great a reliance on stereotyped characters. It is the story of a time traveller who encounters Ragnarok, and the epilogue quotes from the Elder *Edda,* giving the reader considerable insight into Bond's skill at plotting. It is an impressive demonstration. The ability to plot is one of Bond's strongest points, and he was never more sure or ingenious than here.

By and large, Bond's best fiction remains his short stories, and he has displayed a remarkable range with them. During his years as a regular contributor to the pulps he wrote not only for Ray Palmer's *Amazing and Fantastic Adventures,* but for John Campbell's more demanding *Astounding* and *Unknown.* He also wrote for *Thrilling Wonder Stories, Weird Tales,* and especially for *Planet Stories.* "The Castaway" (*Planet,* Winter 1940) is an almost perfect example of Bond's ability to craft a formula story and raise it above its own limits. A spaceship crew rescues a man marooned on an asteroid. Subsequent events suggest he is a jinx and suicidal with the ship finally zooming out of control at a speed that will cause it to burn when it hits Earth's atmosphere. The castaway devises a way to save the ship and its crew, but the real surprise lies in his actual identity.

"The Castaway" fits into a future history that includes most of Bond's space stories. These stories seem to take place mostly in the 23rd century, with the solar system explored and colonized by Earthmen, and most of them center on members of the Solar Space Patrol or a space transport company called IPS. While Bond wrote a number of character series within this frame, the Lancelot Biggs series is probably the most important, and in many ways the most typical. Biggs is the eccentric and likeable first officer of the IPS ship *Saturn,* and he divides his time between getting on his captain's nerves and producing scientific miracles to save the ship from certain disaster. About half these stories were included in *The Remarkable Exploits of Lancelot Biggs, Spaceman.*

While there is no denying Bond's talent with the short story, many of his novellas are excellent. Two *Planet* novellas from 1941 demonstrate his skill with space opera. Both center on the adventures of the young, clean-cut spaceman Chip Warren and his partners Syd Palmer and "Salvation Smith." Shadrach has them discovering a rich lode of "ekalastron," an almost impervious metal, rare and valuable, that plays a part in several of Bond's future history stories. "The Lorelei Death" pits them against space pirates, but, though the better action story, it is marred by some questionable science in the ending. "Pawns of Chaos" (*Thrilling Wonder*

Stories, April 1943) is based on the sort of idea popular with editors almost everywhere at that time, invaders from another dimension where the political system bears some similarity to that of Nazi Germany. Bond obviously had fun writing it, especially those sections describing battles in and around his home town of Roanoke, Virginia. "Pawns of Chaos" does not fall into Bond's future history sequence, nor do the Meg the Priestess stories, which constitute what is probably the best work he did in the SF pulps. In the Meg stories, civilization has virtually collapsed and humanity exists in scattered tribes, a few of which preserve knowledge of writing and reading through a matriarchal leadership, although their ideas of the past are distorted as myths and legends. In "Pilgrimage" (*The Thirty-First of February*) Meg becomes priestess of her clan in Virginia and travels west to consult the gods carved on Mount Rushmore. "Magic City" (*Astounding,* February 1941) has her visit the city of death—New York—to confront its goddess.

Bond's penchant for writing action scenes in settings he knows produced a superior story in "The Ultimate Salient" (*Planet,* Fall 1940). A science fiction writer receives a manuscript purporting to tell future events: the democracies fall to totalitarian forces in 1963 and the survivors flee to the moon where they face almost certain death because they lack the knowledge to synthesize chlorophyll. Since they are known to have taken a number of old SF magazines along, the writer is asked to use the manuscript as the basis of a story, ending it with the formula for chlorophyll that the survivors need. The story was later completely rewritten as "The Last Outpost," and is included in *No Time Like the Future.* The new version sets up a revolt against a world dictatorship, with neither the minions of the dictatorship nor the rebels being very desirable. Disaster befalls both sides but a third group flees to Venus—where the item needed for their survival is the formula for vitamin A.

Bond has claimed he was never actually a science fiction writer but a fantasist who wrote for the SF magazines. Certainly his first big success (in 1937) was the fantasy "Mr. Mergenthwirker's Lobblies," about a gentle man who acquires the companionship of two invisible beings who foretell the future. Such stories as this were probably the prototypes of the sort of light fantasies Ray Palmer sought for *Fantastic Adventures.* It should be noted that Bond wrote a number of SF stories for his ostensibly fantasy markets, including *Blue Book,* and expressed pride in such stories as "To People a New World," "Martian Caravan," and the Pat Pending stories, about the inventor of a succession of incredible gadgets.

Bond's prose was polished enough for the prestige markets of the 1940s without being too slick to remain palatable today. By turns he can be humorous, serious, or adventurous, handling each approach with equal skill. But it is still in his plots that he really shines. His story "The Cunning of the Beast" (*The Thirty-First of February*) may be the most overworked story, that of Adam and Eve, but it is the most cleverly plotted of them all. A number of his yarns spring from biblical or mythological sources, usually with happy results. "Uncommon Castaway" (*No Time Like the Future*) is a twist on the story of Jonah and the whale. Much of Bond's fiction resembles that of Saki or John Collier. "And Lo! The Bird" presents the Earth as an egg about to be hatched, and "Conqueror's Isle" tells of an outpost of supermen waiting for the passing of *homo sapiens* (both in *No Time Like the Future*).

Bond's knack for the offbeat is shown not only in his humor and his variety of approach, but also in a handful of stories written as poems. Two of them from *Planet,* "The Ballad of Blaster Bill" and "The Ballad of Venus Nell," show a touch of Robert Service (though to be honest, "Blaster Bill's" tempo is borrowed from Kipling's "Gunga Din").

—Gerald W. Page

BONE, J(esse) F(ranklin)

Nationality: American. **Born:** Tacoma, Washington, 15 June 1916. **Education:** Washington State University, Pullman, B.A. 1937, B.S. 1949, D.V.M. 1950; Oregon State University, Corvallis, M.S. 1953. **Military Service:** Served in the United States Army, 1937-46, and Army Reserve, 1946-66; Lieutenant Colonel. **Family:** Married 1) Jayne M. Clark in 1942 (divorced 1946), one daughter; 2) Felizitas Margarete Endter in 1950, one daughter and two sons. **Career:** Instructor, 1950-52, assistant professor, 1953-57, associate professor, 1958-65, and professor of veterinary medicine, 1965-79, Oregon State University; editor, 1958-61, and columnist ("Diagnostic Quiz"), 1960-65, *Modern Veterinary Practice* magazine; consultant, University of Zimbabwe, Harare, 1982; professor of anatomy, Ross University, St. Kitts, West Indies, 1984. Fulbright lecturer in Egypt, 1965-66, and Kenya, 1980-82. **Awards:** Department of Health, Education, and Welfare award, 1969. **Agent:** Scott Meredith Literary Agency, 845 Third Avenue, New York, New York 10022, U.S.A. **Address:** P.O. Box 123, Basseterre, St. Kitts, West Indies; 3017 Brae Burn, Sierra Vista, Arizona, U.S.A.

SCIENCE FICTION PUBLICATIONS

Novels

The Lani People. New York, Bantam, and London, Corgi, 1962.
Legacy. Toronto, Laser, 1976.
The Meddlers. Toronto, Laser, 1976.
Gift of the Manti, with Roy L. Meyers. Toronto, Laser, 1977.
Confederation Matador. Virginia Beach, Donning, 1978.

OTHER PUBLICATIONS

Other

Observations on the Ovaries of Infertile and Reportedly Infertile Dairy Cattle. . . . Corvallis, Oregon State College, 1954.
Animal Anatomy. Corvallis, Oregon State College Cooperative Association, 1958; revised edition, as *Animal Anatomy and Physiology,* 1975.
Animal Anatomy and Physiology. Reston, Virginia, Reston Publishing Company, 1979; revised edition, 1982; third edition, Englewood Cliffs, New Jersey, Prentice Hall, 1989.

Editor, *Canine Medicine.* Wheaton, Illinois, American Veterinary Publications, 1959; revised edition, 1962.

Editor, with others, *Equine Medicine and Surgery.* Wheaton, Illinois, American Veterinary Publications, 1963; revised edition, 1972.

                                *

J.F. Bone comments:

I wrote science fiction principally for money, secondarily for personal amusement, and thirdly because I thought I could tell a good enough story to get in print. Technical papers and scientific publications were written mainly because I thought I had something to say to my colleagues. The textbooks—all variations on the same fields—were written and revised to assist me in my principal work, which was teaching. The fact that they were published was more of a surprise to me than I care to admit, and the fact that (for awhile) I was actually an editor is almost shocking in retrospect, but at the time it was the most fun I ever had—either before or since.

                        *   *   *

J.F. Bone made a considerable impact with the publication of his first novel, *The Lani People,* along with several first-rate shorter works. Unfortunately, his career faltered for approximately 10 years; very few works appeared under his name, and none of them were particularly memorable.

The Lani People comes perilously close to being a narrated lecture, for it quite obviously comments unfavorably upon man's tendency to dehumanize others. In the future, a race of humanoids exists, differing from normal humanity by the addition of a prehensile tail. They are considered less than human, property in fact, and have virtually no rights under the law. Despite the plot—the slow realization by the protagonist of the essential evil inherent in the situation—Bone is inventive enough to maintain reader interest throughout.

Of Bone's later novels, *Legacy* is rather a routine story of a marooned man who joins a police force on a far world and becomes involved with the effort to suppress a dangerous new drug, Tonacaine. Although not actively bad, the novel's trivial nature and trite plot are disappointing to those who have read Bone's earlier work. The two other Laser novels are even more insignificant. In *The Meddlers* the human race is engaged in conscious manipulation of alien cultures for its own benefit. In *Gift of the Manti* the situation is just the opposite, with secretive aliens manipulating human culture for their own good, offhandedly wiping out 90 percent of the human race along the way. Both novels are underwritten, unbelievable, and totally forgettable.

Bone does better with *Confederation Matador,* although that novel also has serious flaws. After the collapse of a human interstellar empire, a new confederation has arisen, which is carefully trying to rebuild human technology. An agent is sent to a world colonized by Spanish-speaking peoples to discover why that colony is slowly losing its technological base, despite an absence of external pressures. The agent discovers that superhuman aliens have established a base and are systematically exterminating the human colonists. Although the novel has sections that are quite well done, Bone has added some unnecessary and confusing subplots that distract attention from the main issue.

There is a considerable body of shorter pieces by Bone, most of which remain quite readable. Of particular note is "Founding Fa-

ther" (in *Galaxy,* April 1962), a novella in which stranded reptilian aliens use mental control to force humans to refuel their ship, and a strange relationship grows between the two species. Another excellent story is "Triggerman" (in *Astounding,* December 1958), which calmly presents a man with the ultimate power to cause or avert a nuclear war, and his dispassionate reaction to a world crisis. "On the Fourth Planet" (in *Galaxy,* April 1963) is not as ambitious as the other two, but this tale of a Martian slowly eating his way across the surface of his planet, and his unhappy encounter with a human probe, is extremely inventive and, within its limited structure, possibly the most successful of Bone's stories.

                                —Don D'Ammassa

                        _____

BOOTH, Irwin. *See* **HOCH, Edward D.**

                        _____

BORGES, Jorge Luis

Pseudonyms: F(rancisco) Bustos; B. Lynch Davis; H(onorio) Bustos Domecq; B. Suarez Lynch. **Nationality:** Argentine. **Born:** Buenos Aires, 24 August 1899. **Education:** Attended College Calvin, Geneva, Switzerland, 1914-18. **Family:** Married 1) Elsa Astete Millan in 1967 (divorced 1970); 2) Maria Kodama in 1986. **Career:** Municipal librarian, Miguel Cane branch library, Buenos Aires, 1937-46; teacher of English literature at several private institutions and lecturer in Argentina and Uruguay, 1946-55; director, National Library, Buenos Aires, 1955-73; professor of English and American literature, University of Buenos Aires, beginning 1956. Visiting professor or guest lecturer at numerous universities in the U.S. and throughout the world, including University of Texas, 1961-62; University of Oklahoma, 1969; University of New Hampshire, 1972; and Dickinson College, 1983; and Charles Eliot Norton Professor of Poetry, Harvard University, 1967-68. **Awards:** Buenos Aires Municipal Literary prize, 1928; Gran Premio de Honor from Argentine Writers Society, 1945; Gran Premio Nacional de la Literatura, 1957; Prix Formentor from International Congress of Publishers, 1961; Commandeur de l'Ordre des Littres et des Arts, 1962; Ingram Merrill Foundation award, 1966; Matarazzo Sobrinho Inter-American Literary Prize from Bienal Foundation, 1970; Jerusalem Prize, 1971; Alfonso Reyes prize, 1973; Gran Cruz del Orden al merito Bernando O'Higgins from Government of Chile, 1976; Gold Medal from French Academy, Order of Merit from Federal Republic of Germany, and Icelandic Falcon Cross, all 1979; Miguel de Cervantes award and Balzan Prize, both 1980; Ollin Yoliztli prize; T.S. Eliot award for creative writing from Ingersoll Foundation and Rockford Institute, 1983; Gold Medal of Menendez Pelayo University, La Gran Cruz de la Orden Alfonso X, el Sabio, and Legion d'Honneur, all 1983; Knight of the British Empire. Recipient of honorary degrees from numerous colleges and universities, including University of Cuyo (Argentina), 1956; University of the Andes (Columbia), 1963; Oxford University, 1970;

University of Jerusalem, 1971; Columbia University, 1971; and Michigan State University, 1972. **Member:** Argentine Academy of Letters; Argentine Writers Society (president, 1950-53); Modern Language Association of America (honorary fellow, 1961-86); American Association of Teachers of Spanish and Portuguese (honorary fellow, 1965-86). **Died:** 14 June 1986.

SCIENCE FICTION PUBLICATIONS

Short Stories

Tlön, Uqbar, Orbis Tertius, translated by James E. Irby. Scarborough, Ontario, Porcupine's Quill, 1983.

OTHER PUBLICATIONS

Short Stories

Manual de zoologia fantastica. Mexico, n.p., 1957; translated by Borges and Norman de Giovanni as *The Book of Imaginary Beings,* New York, Dutton, 1969.
Labyrinths, edited by D. A. Yates and James E. Irby. New York, New Directions, 1962; revised, 1964.
Ficciones, N.p., n.d.; edited and translated by Anthony Kerrigan as *Ficciones,* New York, Grove Press, and London, Widenfeld and Nicolson, 1962; as *Fictions,* London, Jupiter, 1966.
The Aleph and Other Stories, 1933-1969, translated by Borges and Norman di Giovanni. New York, Dutton, 1970.
El libro de arena. N.p., n.d.; translated as *The Book of Sand,* New York, Dutton, 1977.
Borges: A Reader; Selection from the Writings of Jorge Luis Borges, edited by Emir Rodriguez Monegal and Alastair Reid. New York, Dutton, 1981.

Other

Atlas (with Maria Codama). Buenos Aires, Editoria Sudamerica, 1984; translated by Anthony Kerrigan as *Atlas,* New York, Dutton, 1985.
Borges on Writing. Hopewell, New Jersey, Ecco Press, 1994.

Editor, with Adolfo Bioy Casares, *Extraordinary Tales,* translated by Anthony Kerrigan. New York, Herder and Herder, 1971; London, Allison and Busby, 1990.
Editor, with Adolfo Bioy Casares and Silvina Ocampo, *Antologia de la literatura fantastica.* N.p., n.d.; translated as *The Book of Fantasy,* London, Xanadu, 1988.

*   *   *

Despite being an assiduous reader of Thomas More, Jonathan Swift, H.G. Wells, and C.S. Lewis, Borges had a natural disdain for SF. His opinion of it is clearly stated in a review, published in the Argentine literary magazine *Sur* (March 1936), of *The Domestic Statue,* a novel by his collaborator and longtime friend Adolfo Bioy Casares:

> I suspect that a general scrutiny of fantastic literature would reveal that it is not very fantastic. I have visited many

utopias—from the eponymous one of More to *Brave New World*—and I have not yet found a single one that exceeds the cozy limits of satire or sermon and describes in detail an imaginary country, with its geography, its history, its religion, its language, its literature, its music, its government, its metaphysical and theological controversy . . . in short, its encyclopaedia; all of it organically coherent, of course, and (I know I'm very demanding) with no reference whatsoever to the horrible injustices suffered by the artillery Captain Alfred Dreyfus. Of Wells's (and even Swift's) imaginary theories, we know that there is in each of them only one fantastic element; of the *One Thousand and One Nights,* that a good part of its marvel is involuntary because 13th-century Egyptians believed in talismans and in exorcisms. In short, I wouldn't be surprised if the Universal Library of Fantastic Literature did not contain more than a volume by Lewis Carroll, a couple of Disney films, a poem by Coleridge and (because of the absent-mindedness of its author) Manuel Gálvez's *Opera omnia* (my translation).

Borges implicitly uses the term "fantastic" to cover SF, and thinks that true SF should compete with God's creation. To honor its foundation, it should build perfect self-sufficient universes, like ours, but without our reality mixing in. Not only is he deeply unsatisfied with all he has read; he chooses to refer to it as "not very fantastic." Still, by refusing its premises, he actually sets forth a program for himself, to be achieved four years later, in his short story "Tlön, Uqbar, Orbis Tertius" (*Sur,* May 1940). In it, he positively describes a visionary universe that is beyond satire, and shows its imaginary geography, history, and religion, its language, literature, and government, and its metaphysical and theological realities. Furthermore, the door to its amazing, uncanny reality is a misleading encyclopaedia he and Bioy Casares discover one afternoon, a reprint of the *Encyclopaedia Britannica* of 1902.

Tlön-Uqbar is a society that exists only in and around ideas; it conceives things as a series of mental processes. The story, as we now know thanks to Emir Rodriguez Monegal's biography of the Argentinian, was inspired by C.S. Lewis's *Out of the Silent Planet* (1938). Interestingly enough, however, this is not another distant planet one could travel to in a spaceship; it's an alternative reality parallel to ours. Borges the idealist places his fictitious community, not in the future, but "in the memory (if not in the hopes or fears) of all my readers" (*Labyrinths*). That is, it "exists" in a nonspatial dimension. The reader never gets references to modern technology, old myths, or 19th- or 20th-century science. Neither can the text be understood as a description of a utopia, or an antiutopia.

A fascinating discussion of Borges and SF can be found in Stanislaw Lem's essay "Unitas Oppositorum: The Prose of Jorge Luis Borges" (1971; in *Microworlds,* 1984), in which the Polish writer analyzes the Argentinian's antipathy for technology and for progressive, utopian futures, thanks to his love affair with the past. Strictly speaking, Borges never wrote SF. Although very notorious are the innumerable stories and essays in which he dealt with time ("The Cyclic Night," 1940; "The Secret Miracle," 1944; "The Flower of Coleridge," 1945; and especially "New Refutation of Time," 1947), one gets the impression that for him science and art were incompatible.

I know of only three pieces in which Borges wrote about the future. The first and most self-conscious one is the story "Utopia of a Tired Man" (*The Book of Sand*). Its main character is said to have been born in Buenos Aires in 1897, two years before Borges. His name is Eudoro Acevedo, which was the maiden name of Borges's mother. He is 70 years old, teaches American and English literature, and writes imaginary tales. As in Wells's *The Time Machine,* he travels in the future. How? We don't know, since we first see him already wandering through unknown geographies that look like Oklahoma, Texas, and the Argentinian pampas. Once more, this fact evidences Borges's disdain for SF: he is interested in the adventure, not in the mechanistic maneuvers that explain the voyage. After a long walk, Acevedo meets a tall, anonymous individual and enters his house. The dialogue between them makes up the entire story, and it offers some epistemological clues valuable for an understanding of our time. About the act of reading, for instance, the anonymous man says that the citizens of the future re-read, never read, because the classics are the only important thing. Printing has been abolished, since it tends to multiply unnecessary texts. Among Acevedo's other discoveries are the absence of cities, governments, dates, statistics, poverty and wealth, and the fact that the world has fallen back on Latin. It's quite clear that the narration is a comment on today, as seen from a future perspective. Borges uses a lucid epigraph by Quevedo that helps for understanding its implications: "He called it *Utopia,* a Greek word meaning *there is no such place.*"

The second piece by Borges dealing with future events has the same limitation. Figuring as the epilogue to the Spanish edition of his *Complete Works* (Emecé, 1974), it is an entry for Borges himself in the so-called *Encyclopaedia Sudamericana,* to appear in 2074, in Santiago, Chile. The ingeniousness of such a profile lies in its encapsulating all the writer's biographical data, with the exception, of course, of the date of his death. The third and final item is the poem "The Web" (in *The New Yorker,* 2 June 1986). It asks which city is the author doomed to die in, at what time, and when. The last lines read: "These questions are/ disgressions that stem not from fear/ but from impatient hope./ They form part of that fateful web/ of cause and effect/ that no man can foresee,/ nor any god." Again, the future is not the main concern here; what matters is the randomness of fate. Nothing in tomorrow interests Borges, except the details that could affect him in a personal, introspective way.

—Ilan Stavans

BOUCHER, Anthony

Pseudonym for William Anthony Parker White. **Other Pseudonyms:** Theo Durrant; H.H. Holmes. **Nationality:** American. **Born:** Oakland, California, 21 August 1911. **Education:** Pasadena Junior College, California, 1928-30; University of Southern California, Los Angeles, B.A. 1932; University of California, Berkeley, M.A. 1934. **Family:** Married Phyllis May Price in 1938; two sons. **Career:** Theatre and music critic, *United Progressive News,* Los Angeles, 1935-37; science fiction and mystery reviewer, *San Francisco Chronicle,* 1942-47; mystery reviewer, *Ellery Queen's Mystery Magazine,* 1948-50 and 1957-68, and *New York Times Book Review,* 1951-68; fantasy book reviewer, as H.H. Holmes, for *Chicago Sun-Times,* 1949-50, and *New York Herald Tribune,* 1951-63; reviewer for *Opera News,* 1961-68. Editor, with J. Francis McComas, 1949-54, and alone, 1954-58, *Magazine of Fantasy and*

Science Fiction, New York; editor, *True Crime Detective,* 1952-53; edited the Mercury Mysteries, 1952-55, Dell Great Mystery Library, 1957-60, and Collier Mystery Classics, 1962-68. Originated *Great Voices* program of historical recordings, Pacifica Radio, Berkeley, 1949-68. President, Mystery Writers of America, 1951. **Awards:** Mystery Writers of America Edgar Allan Poe award, for non-fiction, 1946, 1950, 1953; Hugo award, for editing, 1958, 1959. **Died:** 29 April 1968.

SCIENCE FICTION PUBLICATIONS

Short Stories

Far and Away: Eleven Fantasy and Science-Fiction Stories. New York, Ballantine,1955.
The Compleat Werewolf and Other Stories of Fantasy and Science Fiction. New York, Simon and Schuster, 1969; London, W.H. Allen, 1970.

OTHER PUBLICATIONS

Novels

The Case of the Seven of Calvary. New York, Simon and Schuster, and London, Hamish Hamilton, 1937.
The Case of the Crumpled Knave. New York, Simon and Schuster, and London, Harrap, 1939.
The Case of the Baker Street Irregulars. New York, Simon and Schuster, 1940; as *Blood on Baker Street,* New York, Mercury, 1953.
Nine Times Nine (as H.H. Holmes). New York, Duell, 1940.
The Case of the Solid Key. New York, Simon and Schuster, 1941.
Rocket to the Morgue (as H.H. Holmes). New York, Duell, 1942; as Anthony Boucher, New York, Dell, 1952.
The Case of the Seven Sneezes. New York, Simon and Schuster, 1942; London, United Authors, 1946.
The Marble Forest (as Theo Durrant, with others). New York, Knopf, and London, Wingate, 1951; as *The Big Fear,* New York, Popular Library, 1953.
The Case of the Seven of Calvary, Nine Times Nine, Rocket to the Morgue, The Case of the Crumpled Knave. London, Zomba, 1984.

Short Stories

Exeunt Murderers: The Best Mystery Stories of Anthony Boucher, edited by Francis M. Nevins, Jr. and Martin H. Greenberg. Carbondale, Southern Illinois University Press, 1983.

Plays

Radio Plays: For *Sherlock Holmes* and *The Case Book of Gregory Hood* series, 1945-48.

Other

Ellery Queen: A Double Profile. Boston, Little Brown, 1951.
Multiplying Villainies: Selected Mystery Criticism, 1942-1968. Boston, Bouchercon, 1973.

Sincerely, Tony/Faithfully, Vincent: The Correspondence of Anthony Boucher and Vincent Starrett, edited by Robert W. Hahn. Chicago, Catullus Press, 1975.

Editor, *The Pocket Book of True Crime Stories.* New York, Pocket Books, 1943.

Editor, *Great American Detective Stories.* Cleveland, World, 1945.

Editor, *Four and Twenty Bloodhounds.* New York, Simon and Schuster, 1950; London, Hammond, 1951.

Editor, with J. Francis McComas, *The Best from Fantasy and Science Fiction.* Boston, Little Brown, 2 vols., 1952-53; Garden City, New York, Doubleday, 6 vols., 1954-59.

Editor, *The Murder and the Trial,* by Edgar Lustgarten. New York, Scribner, 1958; London, Odhams Press, 1960.

Editor, *A Treasury of Great Science Fiction.* Garden City, New York, Doubleday, 2 vols., 1959.

Editor, *The Quality of Murder.* New York, Dutton, 1962.

Editor, *The Quintessence of Queen: Best Prize Stories from 12 Years of Ellery Queen's Mystery Magazine.* New York, Random House, 1962; as *A Magnum of Mysteries,* London, Gollancz, 1963.

Editor, *Best Detective Stories of the Year: 18th [through 23rd] Annual Collection.* New York, Dutton, and London, Boardman, 6 vols., 1963-68.

*

Bibliography: "Anthony Boucher Bibliography" by J.R. Christopher, Dean W. Dickensheet, and R.E. Briney, in *Armchair Detective* (White Bear Lake, Minnesota), nos. 2,3,4, 1969.

Critical Study: *The Eureka Years: Boucher and McComas's The Magazine of Fantasy and Science Fiction 1949-1954* edited by Annette P. McComas, New York, Bantam, 1982.

*   *   *

Anthony Boucher brought both style and sophistication to popular fantasy and science fiction, two qualities in rather short supply during the 1940s and 1950s. Boucher enjoyed successful careers in all three forms of popular literature; he was a critic, an author, and an editor.

Boucher wrote both fantasy and science fiction stories. Many of his best stories were published in Campbell's *Astounding Science Fiction* and *Unknown,* and in *Weird Tales.* Boucher's talent ran to the kind of fantasy or fantastic science fiction associated with *Unknown* in the 1940s and *Beyond* in the 1950s. His stories tend to be comic treatments of ordinary people involved in situations and actions that run contrary to their customary, common-sense approach to life. Boucher seems to imply that most people, and certainly his truly sympathetic characters, possess an innate disposition to believe in supernatural forces. As is the case with most characteristic *Unknown* stories, mythic themes in his stories are treated lightly with a comic and often ironic distance. "Q.U.R.," "Robinc," and "We Print the Truth" illustrate Boucher's manner in science fiction stories. The first two stories are barroom tales, similar to Henry Knutter's Galloway Gallegher tales and Arthur Clarke's *Tales from the White Hart.* They share characteristic themes with some of Heinlein's stories of the private inventor and of proprietory business enterprise as illustrated in "We Also Walk Dogs." Boucher's hero, Dugglesmarther H. Quinby, changes the world with a revo-

lution in android technology, making the androids more efficient by making them less like humans. Boucher thus lightly shows two of his virtues as a writer: effective comic reversal of clichés or worn-out formulas to produce surprise and delight, and a humanistic and often literary resonance.

The best of his fantasy tales may be the most famous of his stories, the novella "The Compleat Werewolf." The title suggests, distantly perhaps, a parallel to the Michael Shea adventures of L. Sprague de Camp and Fletcher Pratt. Many of the storytelling concepts are the same: an academic setting; a strong courtship subplot; comic anachronism involving a modern character caught up in mythic or legendary adventures but retaining a modern, skeptical sense of incongruity; the concomitant farcical employment of magic; and the obligatory happy ending in which the hero returns to the prosaic world with a fuller appreciation of its homely values or at least its familiar comforts. Best of all, he returns to a world in which he fits. Boucher's 1942 tale includes a little Nazi espionage to spice up the plot. Professor Wolfe Wolf, the hero in spite of himself who ends with the right girl, is the pattern of the modern domesticated hero that has run remarkably true to form now for more than a quarter-century.

Two or three other fantasy tales may be noted here briefly as representative of Boucher's range. "Snulbug" is Boucher's tale of modern demonology told with a more comic perspective than C.S. Lewis's *Screwtape Letters,* which it recalls. In Boucher's story, the human race is preserved from additional mischief by the incompetence of a conjurer and the third-rate demon he manages to call up to work his will. "They Bite" is an effective suspense-horror story making use of the familiar formula in which modern, skeptical men find themselves the unbelieving victims of legendary desert ogres. "We Print the Truth" is loosely based on the familiar contradiction between divine foreknowledge and free will. Boucher's fictional equivalent of divine foreknowledge is the *Grover Sentinel,* whose stories become true for all who read them. Boucher's speculations of wish fulfillment and something he termed "variable truth" are characteristically ingenious and amusing, very much like the armchair mysteries he wrote under the name of H.H. Holmes. It was under this name that Boucher wrote one of the most amusing science fiction mystery *roman à clef* novels, *Rocket to the Morgue,* which is also a pastiche of styles, mannerisms, and familiar formulas of the main science fiction writers of the dominant Eastern establishment.

Boucher's best-known SF story, "The Quest for St. Aquin" (1951), has lost none of its original luster after more than a quarter-century. If anything, its stature has grown by virtue of the works it has to some degree inspired: James Blish's *A Case of Conscience* (1958), Walter M. Miller, Jr.'s *A Canticle for Leibowitz* (1960), and Robert Silverberg's "Good News from the Vatican" (1970). The quest takes place in a postnuclear-catastrophe California in which religious worship of any kind is officially suppressed by the ruling Technarchy through its KGB-style "Loyalty Checkers." The quest ends with the paradoxical revelation that the fabled St. Aquin is in fact the one perfect android of legend that had proved by its faultless logic the existence of God, and whose present lifeless state proves that existence in quite another way. The virtues of the story are many, including the economy with which Boucher creates his repressive, future world, and the finely realized humanity of the story's characters. The central action depends on Boucher's skill in creating two characters: the young, unsophisticated priest sent on a quest by the pope to discover whether the cult of St. Aquin is orthodox, and the priest's mechanical "robass," Old Nick himself. The confrontation is altogether enchanting and somehow satisfying theologically at the same time. Among the story's many achievements as prophetic SF is its dramatization of the future brotherhood of all people of faith, whatever their religious affiliation. A quarter-century ago that seemed a far more radical notion than it does today.

Perhaps Boucher's most important contribution to the literature of popular fantasy and SF came not as an author but as coeditor and later editor of *The Magazine of Fantasy and Science Fiction*, which made its debut before the public without "science fiction" on the masthead in 1949. The magazine has proven to be the healthiest and most consistently influential competition to the *Astounding/Analog* tradition of science fiction/science fact literature. Boucher and McComas established their magazine as a quality pulp that was more concerned with literary standards than with literary ideology. It has continued to publish stories in both genres that are distinguished by literary, that is mainstream, writing. Something must be added also about the affection and respect that Boucher won by his amiable disposition and urbane wit. His was one of the more important benign influences on the encouragement and development of many of the New Wave writers with whom he probably had less in common than with the Golden Age writers of his own salad days.

—Donald L. Lawler

BOULLE, Pierre

Nationality: French. **Born:** Avignon, 20 February 1912. **Education:** Ecole superieure d'Electricite, license en sciences, engineering diploma. **Military Service:** French Army, World War II; sent to Malaya, 1941, joined Free French forces there and became secret agent, using name Peter John Rule, and posing as a Mauritius-born Engishman; fought in Burma, China, and Indochina; taken prisoner and subsequently escaped in 1944; returned to France; awarded French Legion d'Honeur, Croix de Guerre, Medaille de la Resistance. **Career:** Engineer in France, 1933-35; rubber planter in Malaya, 1936-48; full-time writer, behginning 1949. **Awards:** Prix de la Nouvelle, 1953; Grand Prix de la Societe des Gens de Lettres de France, 1976. **Died:** 1994.

Science Fiction Publications

Novels

La planete des singes. Paris, Julliard, 1963; translated by Xan Fielding as *Planet of the Apes,* New York, Vanguard Press, 1963; as *Monkey Planet,* London, Secker and Warburg, 1964.

Le jardin de Kanashima. Paris, Julliard, 1964; translated by *The Garden on the Moon,* London, Secker and Warburg, and New York, Vanguard Press, 1965.

Jeux d'esprit. Paris, Julliard, 1971; translated Patricia Wolf as *Desperate Games,* New York, Vanguard Press, 1973.

Le bon Leviathan. Paris, Julliard, 1978; translated by Margaret Giovanelli as *The Good Leviathan,* New York, Vanguard Press, 1979.

La baleine des Malouines. Paris, Julliard, 1983; translated by Patricia Wold as *The Whale of the Victoria Cross,* New York, Vanguard Press, 1983; as *The Falklands Whale,* London, W. H. Allen, 1984.

Les coulisses du ciel. Paris, Julliard, 1979; translated by Patricia Wolf as *Trouble in Paradise,* New York, Vanguard Press, 1985.

Short Stories

Time Out of Mind and Other Stories, translated by Xan Fielding and Elisabeth Abbott. London, Secker and Warburg, and New York, Vanguard Press, 1966.

Quia absurdum: sur la terre comme au ciel. Paris, Julliard, 1970; translated as *Because It Is Absurd: On Earth as It Is in Heaven,* New York, Vanguard Press, 1971.

Histoires perfides. Paris, Julliard, 1964; translated by Margaret Giovanelli as· *The Marvelous Palace and Other Stories,* New York, Vanguard Press, 1977.

Other Publication

Novel

Le pont sur la rivère Kwai. Paris, Julliard, 1952; translated by Xan Fielding as *The Bridge on the River Kwai,* New York, Vanguard, and London, Secker and Warburg, 1954.

*   *   *

Like the venerable minister-priest of the Religion of Doubt who is the narrator of the six "*histoires perides*" that make up *The Marvelous Palace and Other Stories,* Pierre Boulle has viewed his main function throughout his prolific and varied career as his duty "to arouse curiosity by the prospect of an enigma." In Boulle's wryly laconic fables, the enigmatic takes many forms: in *The Good Leviathan,* an oil supertanker capable of miraculous cures; in *The Whale of the Victoria Cross,* another kind of good leviathan, one that sacrifices itself to save its friends on the British fleet during the Falklands conflict; in "The Heart of the Galaxy" (*Because It Is Absurd*), a message from the stars, engendered by an immense expenditure of energy, which—much to the consternation of the scientists on Earth who decipher it—turns out to be an advertising slogan; in *Desperate Games,* a world government of Nobel Prize-winning scientists who cure all of mankind's social ills but must devise destructive war games to prevent the universal *ennui* that sets in when man is left with nothing to struggle against. Boulle's style is too arch and his stance too knowing for his science fiction tales to be called cautionary, just as his espionage stories set in the Far East are too coolly ironic to be labeled merely escapist thrillers: even a casual reader must have anticipated that the astronaut escaping from *Planet of the Apes*—undoubtedly Boulle's best-known SF work and the basis for the popular film series—was returning to an Earth in which a similar evolutionary movement had taken its inevitable course.

Boulle's double-edged, deadpan observance of man's social and political foibles has even taken him to the Throne of Heaven itself. When Boulle, in *Trouble in Paradise,* has the Virgin Mary coming back to Earth to help patch up a quarrel between the bickering members of the Holy Trinity, only to become a media celebrity and prime minister of France, her eventual triumphant ascension back to Paradise as Supreme Goddess could be construed as either a pro- or antifeminist statement. In all of Boulle's work, however, the tone may be cynical or obscure but it is rarely morose, since Boulle remains detached from the delusions, vanities, and follies of technocratic man confronting the remorselessness of an implacable Nature and the unchangingness of his own proud and enigmatic heart.

—Kenneth Jurkiewicz

BOVA, Ben(jamin William)

Nationality: American. **Born:** Philadelphia, Pennsylvannia, 8 November 1932. **Education:** Temple University, Philadelphia, B.S. 1954; State University of New York, Albany, M.A. 1983. **Family:** Married 1) Rosa Cucinotta in 1953 (divorced 1974); one son and one daughter; 2) Barbara Berson Rose in 1974. **Career:** Editor, *Upper Darby News,* Pennsylvania, 1953-56; technical editor on Vanguard Project, Martin Aircraft Company, Baltimore, 1956-58; screenwriter, Physical Science Study Committee, Massachusetts Institute of Technology, Cambridge, 1958-59; science writer, Avco-Everett Research Laboratory, Everett, Massachusetts, 1960-71; editor, *Analog,* New York, 1971-78; editor, *Omni,* New York, 1978-82. **Awards:** Hugo award, for editing, 1973, 1974, 1975, 1976, 1977, 1979; E. E. Smith Memorial award, 1974; Balrog award, 1983. **Agent:** Barbara Bova. **Address:** c/o Tor Books, 49 West 24th Street, New York, New York 10010, U.S.A.

Science Fiction Publications

Novels (series: Exiles; Kinsman; Orion; Privateers; To Save the Sun; Voyagers; Watchman).

The Star Conquerors (for children). Philadelphia, Winston, 1959.
The Weathermakers (for children). New York, Holt Rinehart, 1967; London, Dobson, 1969.
Out of the Sun (for children). New York, Holt Rinehart, 1968; expanded edition, New York, Tor, 1984.
Escape! (for children). New York, Holt Rinehart, 1970.
The Exiles Trilogy: Three Novels (for children). New York, Berkley, 1980; London, Methuen, 1984.
    Exiled from Earth. New York, Dutton, 1971.
    Flight of Exiles. New York, Dutton, 1972.
    End of Exile. New York, Dutton, 1975.
THX 1138 (novelization of screenplay). New York, Paperback Library, 1971; London, Panther, 1978.
As on a Darkling Plain. New York, Walker, 1972; London, Magnum, 1981.
When the Sky Burned. New York, Walker, 1973; expanded edition as *Test of Fire,* New York, Tor, 1982; London, Methuen, 1984.
The Winds of Altair (for children). New York, Dutton, 1973; expanded edition (for adults), New York, Tor, 1983; Wallington, Surrey, Severn House, 1989.
Gremlins, Go Home! (for children), with Gordon R. Dickson. New York, St. Martin's Press, 1974.
The Starcrossed. Radnor, Pennsylvannia, Chilton, 1975; London, Magnum, 1980.
City of Darkness: A Novel. New York, Scribner, 1976.
Millennium: A Novel about People and Politics in the Year 1999 (Kinsman). New York, Random House, and London, Macdonald and Jane's, 1976.

The Multiple Man: A Novel of Suspense. Indianapolis, Bobbs Merrill, 1976; London, Gollancz, 1977.
Colony. New York, Pocket Books, 1978; London, Magnum, 1979.
Kinsman: A Novel. New York, Dial Press, and London, Orbit, 1979.
Voyagers. Garden City, New York, Doubleday, 1981; London, Methuen, 1982.
Orion. New York, Simon and Schuster, 1984: London, Severn House, 1985.
Privateers. New York, Tor, 1985; London, Methuen, 1986.
The Alien Within (Voyagers). New York, Tor, 1986; London, Severn House, 1987.
The Kinsman Saga (includes Kinsman and Millennium). New York, Tor, 1987.
Vengeance of Orion. New York, Tor, and London, Severn House, 1988.
Peacekeepers. New York, Tor, 1988; London, Mandarin, 1989.
Cyberbooks. New York, Tor, 1989; London, Mandarin, 1990.
Star Brothers (Voyagers). Norwalk, Connecticut, Easton Press, and London, Methuen, 1990.
Orion in the Dying Time. New York, Tor, 1990; London, Methuen, 1991.
The Trikon Deception, with William R. Pogue. New York, Tor, 1992; London, New English Library, 1994.
Sam Gunn, Unlimited. London, Methuen, 1992; New York, Bantam, 1993.
Mars. New York, Bantam, 1992; London, New English Library, 1993.
To Save the Sun, with A.J. Austin. New York, Tor, 1992.
Triumph. New York, Tor, 1993.
Empire Builders (Privateers). New York, Tor, 1993.
Death Dream. London, New English Library, and New York, Bantam, 1994.
Orion and the Conqueror. New York, Tor, 1994.
The Watchmen. Riverdale, New York, Baen, 1994.
    Star Watchman (for children). New York, Holt Rinehart, 1964; London, Dobson, 1972.
    The Dueling Machine (Watchman; for children). New York, Holt Rinehart, 1969; London, Faber, 1971.
To Fear the Lion (Sun), with A.J. Austin. New York, Tor, 1994.
Orion among the Stars. New York, Tor, 1995.

Short Stories

Forward in Time: A Science Fiction Story Collection. New York, Walker, 1973.
Maxwell's Demons. New York, Baronet, 1978.
Escape Plus. New York, Tor, 1984; London, Methuen, 1988.
The Astral Mirror. New York, Tor, 1985.
Prometheans. New York, Tor, 1986.
Battle Station. New York, Tor, 1987.
Future Crime (includes *City of Darkness*). New York, Tor, 1990.
Challenges. New York, Tor, 1993.
Future Quintet: Earth in the Year 2042: A Four-Part Invention, with others. New York, Morrow, 1994.

Other Publications

Other

The Milky Way Galaxy: Man's Exploration of the Stars. New York, Holt Rinehart, 1961.

Giants of the Animal World (for children). Racine, Wisconsin, Whitman, 1962.

Reptiles since the World Began (for children). Racine, Wisconsin, Whitman, 1964.

The Uses of Space (for children). New York, Holt Rinehart, 1965.

In Quest of Quasars: An Introduction to Stars and Starlike Objects (for children). New York, Crowell-Collier, 1970.

Planets, Life, and LGM (for children). Reading, Massachusetts, Addison-Wesley, 1970.

The Fourth State of Matter: Plasma Dynamics and Tomorrow's Technology. New York, St. Martin's Press, 1971.

The Amazing Laser (for children). Philadelphia, Westminster Press, 1971.

The New Astronomies. New York, St. Martin's Press, 1972; London, Dent, 1973.

Starflight and Other Improbabilities (for children). Philadelphia, Westminster Press, 1973.

Man Changes the Weather (for children). Reading, Massachusetts. Addison-Wesley, 1973.

Survival Guide for the Suddenly Single, with Barbara Berson. New York, St. Martin's Press, 1974.

The Weather Changes Man (for children). Reading, Massachusetts, Addison-Wesley, 1974.

Workshops in Space (for children). New York, Dutton, 1974.

Notes to a Science Fiction Writer. New York, Scribner, 1975; revised edition, Boston, Houghton Mifflin, 1981.

Through Eyes of Wonder: Science Fiction and Science (for children). Reading, Massachusetts, Addison-Wesley, 1975.

Science—Who Needs It? (for children). Philadelphia, Westminster Press, 1975.

The Seeds of Tomorrow (for children). New York, McKay, 1977.

Viewpoint. Cambridge, Massachusetts, NESFA Press, 1977.

The High Road. Boston, Houghton Mifflin, 1981.

Vision of the Future: The Art of Robert McCall. New York, Abrams, 1982.

Assured Survival: Putting the Star Wars Defense in Perspective. Boston, Houghton Mifflin, 1984; as *Star Peace: Assured Survival,* New York, Tor, 1986.

Welcome to Moonbase. New York, Ballantine, 1987.

Interactions: A Journey through the Mind of a Particle Physicist and the Matter of This World, with Sheldon Glashow. New York, Warner, 1988.

The Beauty of Light. New York, Wiley, 1988.

The Craft of Writing Science Fiction That Sells. Cincinnati, Ohio, Writer's Digest, 1994.

Editor, *The Many Worlds of Science Fiction.* New York, Dutton, 1971.

Editor, *Analog 9.* Garden City, New York, Doubleday, and London, Dobson, 1973.

Editor, *Science Fiction Hall of Fame, Volume 24 [2B].* Garden City, New York, Doubleday, 1973; as *The Science Fiction Hall of Fame, Volume 2 [3],* London, Gollancz, 1973-74.

Editor, *The Analog Science Fact Reader.* New York, St. Martin's Press, and London, Millington, 1974.

Editor, *Analog Annual.* New York, Pyramid, 1976.

Editor, with Trudy E. Bell, *Closeup: New Worlds.* New York, St. Martin's Press, 1977.

Editor, *Exiles.* London, Orbit, 1977; New York, St. Martin's Press, 1978.

Editor, *Aliens.* London, Orbit, 1977; New York, St. Martin's Press, 1978.

Editor, *The Best of Analog.* New York, Baronet, 1978.

Editor, *The Analog Yearbook.* New York, Baronet, 1978.

Editor, with Don Myrus, *The Best of Omni Science Fiction 1-4.* New York, Omni, 1980-82.

Editor, *The Best of the Nebulas.* New York, Tor, 1989; abridged edition, London, Hale, 1990.

Editor, with Byron Preiss, *First Contact: The Search for Extraterrestrial Intelligence.* New York, New American Library, and London, Headline, 1990.

*

Manuscript Collection: Temple University, Philadelphia.

*   *   *

With over four dozen science fiction books to his credit, Ben Bova is understandably one of the most familiar names in the field. Although his themes and plotlines range from relatively tame considerations of the implication of technological developments on society to world-destroying, space-traveling epics, all of his novels—both adult and those aimed at younger readers—are characterized by careful adherence to scientific reality and the belief that human destiny lies in a greater arena than the one we presently occupy.

Two early novels illustrate Bova's major concerns. *The Weathermakers* is set in a future where most aspects of life on Earth are under human control, and now the final frontier, weather control, is about to be explored. The protagonist is a scientist who presses for funding for this project despite resistance from short-sighted politicians and the potential exploitation of the project by single-minded militarists, two stock villains who appear over and over in Bova's work. The perversion of scientific knowledge is mirrored in *The Dueling Machine,* when a device which allows people to enter a totally convincing fantasy world is turned into a murder weapon, misuse of which will lead to political power as well.

Although much of Bova's early fiction was straightforward adventure, *The Multiple Man* explored the political arena with insight, and remains one of his most notable works. A charismatic and highly effective president seems to be single-handedly reversing several adverse trends in American society. But one of his associates uncovers disturbing implications, including the possibility that the President has been replaced by a clone of himself. A finely etched political thriller as well as first class science fiction.

Kinsman and *Millennium* (later published together as *The Kinsman Saga*) are set in the near future and chronicle the life of Chet Kinsman, an astronaut devoted to the furtherance of space travel as what he sees as the last hope for the human race. In the first, young Kinsman secures a position as an astronaut, but is then involved in a scandal which may bar him from space. The sequel (actually published earlier) features Kinsman on the moon, where he masterminds a joint effort by American and Russian staff members to coerce the governments of Earth into seeing reason and averting a war. Kinsman is a bigger-than-life character, a heroic figure in many senses, but Bova is also careful to ensure that he is not perfect, that he has the small failings that allow us to identify with him.

Colony has a very similar theme. Earth has deteriorated into a number of squabbling states, many of which are bankrupt in more than one sense of the word. From an orbiting colony comes David

Adams, a genetically engineered human being whose travels across his home world's surface provide a fascinating, and often depressing, vision of the future, but whose own quest for perfection is ennobling.

The determination of government to keep its citizens in the dark and oppose the advance of knowledge is the overriding theme once again in *Voyagers,* in which an alien spacecraft entering our system creates a deadly crisis in human affairs. Stoner, the protagonist, is thwarted from making contact because of governmental interference and is set adrift in space, in suspended animation. He is awakened in the sequel, *The Alien Within,* and discovers that his mind is now home to a nonhuman intelligence which is determined to explore human society. Stoner becomes aware of the alien presence and is eventually able to assume control of a new type of technology which will change the face of the world. Naturally, venial government agencies move against Stoner, a conflict which is not resolved until the concluding volume, *Star Brothers.*

An entirely atypical series for Bova was launched with *Orion.* The protagonist is an immortal warrior who battles for the advancement of humankind throughout the ages, pitted against opponents who use everything from magic to science. Orion returns to battle new opponents in *Vengeance of Orion, Orion in the Dying Time,* and *Orion the Conqueror.* The series is as close to fantasy as anything Bova has written.

The future of space travel, or the lack thereof, is examined again in *Privateers.* The U.S. has withdrawn from space exploration, abandoning the field to the Russians, who now dominate the heavens and, economically, the Earth as well. A multimillionaire launches his own commercial effort, but when his property is impounded by the Russians, he resorts to an older device, privateering, to open up the spaceways. Somewhat implausible, perhaps, but the novel has a brash, cheerful bravado that makes it one of Bova's most engaging stories. In *Peacekeepers,* a localized nuclear exchange has scared the world into establishing an organization to control all nuclear armaments, a situation which is challenged when a terrorist organization seizes control of several. Bova's forays into humor are rare, but *Cyberbooks* is a notable exception, although the comedy is decidedly dark. The novel examines the implication of electronic reproduction of the written word, and the potential impact on the publishing industry.

Capitalizing on a new interest in the red planet, Bova's *Mars* is an ambitious and largely successful effort to accurately portray what might be the consequences of the first manned expedition to Mars. Shortly after arriving, the explorers begin to experience a bizarre new disease which they fear might indicate the presence of an undetectable and inimical form of extraterrestrial life.

Two novels written in collaboration with A.J. Austin, *To Save the Sun* and *To Fear the Light,* are both set in a far future where human civilization has spread to the stars and Earth is a tired planet whose sun is about to self-destruct. In the opening volume, a scientist from another system spearheads efforts to prevent the catastrophe, and in the sequel we see the resulting changes in human society two centuries afterward. *Triumph,* a short, uchronian novel, is an amusing exercise exploring possible alternative outcomes to World War II but is otherwise uninteresting. Bova returned to his previous preoccupations with *The Empire Builders,* pitting a rebellious and innovative entrepreneur against a repressive government that uses a growing ecological crisis as an excuse for seizing control of his orbital business.

Although not primarily noted as a short story writer, Bova has written several dozen, many of which are quite memorable. Of par-

ticular note are "The Next Logical Step," "Test in Orbit," "Stars Won't You Hide Me?," "Fifteen Miles," "Inspiration," and the frightening "Nuclear Autumn."

To a large extent, Bova's fiction is propagandist in intent. His impatience with government bureaucrats who fear change or lack the imagination to deal with it, his contempt for military leaders who see everything in terms of weaponry, and a vision of human destiny out among the stars are themes which recur again and again. His strong narrative techniques and obvious grasp of the technology involved, coupled with logical extrapolations of the consequences, help make his stories convincing as well as entertaining. Although Bova rarely ventures outside the territory he has already explored, there have been recent indications in his work of a wider range of interests.

—Don D'Ammassa

———

BOYD, Felix. *See* **HARRISON, Harry.**

———

BOYD, John

Pseudonym for Boyd Bradfield Upchurch. **Nationality:** American. **Born:** Atlanta, Georgia, 3 October 1919. **Education:** Atlanta, Fulton County, Georgia, and St. Paul, Minnesota, public schools; Atlanta Junior College, 1938-40; University of Southern California, Los Angeles, A.B. in journalism 1947. **Military Service:** Served in the United States Navy, 1940-45: Lieutenant Commander; mentioned in Royal Navy dispatches. **Family:** Married 1) Fern Gillaspy in 1944 (died in 1984); 2) Mary Coe in 1986. **Career:** Production manager, Star Engraving Company, Los Angeles, 1947-71; freelance writer, 1971-79. **Address:** 1151 Aviemore Terrace, Costa Mesa, California 92627, U.S.A.

SCIENCE FICTION PUBLICATIONS

Novels

The Last Starship from Earth. New York, Weybright and Talley, 1968; London, Gollancz, 1969.
The Pollinators of Eden. New York, Weybright and Talley, 1969; London, Gollancz, 1970.
The Rakehells of Heaven. New York, Weybright and Talley, 1969; London, Gollancz, 1971.
Sex and the High Command. New York, Weybright and Talley, 1970.
The Organ Bank Farm. New York, Weybright and Talley, 1970.
The Gorgon Festival. New York, Weybright and Talley, 1972.
The I.Q. Merchant. New York, Weybright and Talley, 1972.
The Doomsday Gene. New York, Weybright and Talley, 1973.
Andromeda Gun. New York, Berkley, 1974.
Barnard's Planet. New York, Berkley, 1975.

The Girl with the Jade Green Eyes, edited by Richard Barbour. New York, Viking Press, 1978; London, Penguin, 1979.

OTHER PUBLICATIONS

Novels as Boyd Upchurch

The Slave Stealer: A Novel. New York, Weybright and Talley, 1968; London, Jenkins, 1969.
Scarborough Hall. New York, Berkley, 1976.

Other as Boyd Upchurch

Behind Every Bush, with Richard H. Ichord. Los Angeles, Seville, 1979.

*

Manuscript Collection: University of California, Fullerton.

John Boyd comments:

Insofar as any writer consciously erects a schema for the body of his work, my intentions in science fiction have been generally to take mythic themes and find—ideally to strike—their echoes in the modern world. I attempt, without pedantry, to be didactic and, above all, entertaining. A story without some moral theme, either expressed or implied, is usually frivolous, but an apparently frivolous tale with a strong moral basis can be a gem. In telling my tales, when the substance weakens, I attempt to beguile the reader with stylistic wiles.

*   *   *

In addition to romances of the historical and contemporary South, John Boyd has published 11 science fiction novels. They are witty and sensuous, triumphs of style over substance, inventive in details if not major premises. Stylish variations on familiar SF themes, these tall tales kid the conventions of romance and science fiction, while satirizing human fatuousness.

The Last Starship from Earth depicts a dystopian alternate present, from which two star-crossed lovers are eventually exiled. Exiles on the planet Hell have manipulated the romance, involving the young mathematical rebel in a time traveling story. Changing history, he fails to benefit from it, but lives on into our present as the Wandering Jew. Romantic courtship rituals come in for a ribbing, as do the "rational" practices of a rigid behaviorist society, and the whole is imbued with allusions to English Romantic poetry.

Positing intelligent vegetable life, *The Pollinators of Eden* is a more lyrical tale of a repressed female scientist, ending with a complicated defloration and impregnation by her fiancé and the orchids of the planet Flora. Partially balanced by satire of scientific grantsmanship and politics, titillation is the book's prime object, accomplished with poetic allusions and complicated metaphorical connections. *The Rakehells of Heaven* also involves carnal contact with aliens, as two astronauts educate university students on a distant planet in human culture. The natives of Harlech (heaven) adopt their vices as well as virtues, culminating in crucifixion of one scout and expulsion of the other. The satire is still broader, the plot more

unwieldy, in *Sex and the High Command,* as the U.S. Navy officers and other bumbling males in high places fall prey to the world's women who have learned, with the aid of chemistry, how to manage quite well without men. Like the protagonist of *Rakehells,* the hero parodies Southern manhood, representing rigid values unprepared for change.

In postcatastrophe California a brilliant neurosurgeon is brought to *The Organ Bank Farm* to perform brain transplants while pursuing his hobby of trying to cure autistic children. Amid the trappings of music therapy and behaviorist computers, his sense of decency is engaged, especially on behalf of a beautiful girl lost in an imaginary medieval world. Love and sex and poetry are present in profusion, capped by a bewildering but plausible surprise ending.

Revolutions in *The Gorgon Festival* and *The I.Q. Merchant* result from discoveries in chemistry. Rejuvenated older women fail in the first, amid the paraphernalia of rock music, motorcycle gangs, racism, and the generation gap. Flirting with sexual taboos named for Oedipus and Electra, the second emphasizes family drama. Estranged from his alcoholic wife and formerly retarded son, the inventor sees events pass by him as his intelligence-booster transforms society. Then with his youthful lover he leapfrogs simple genius into communal ESP in another tricky ending.

The Doomsday Gene projects bitterness toward a world of high technology and scientific irresponsibility, seen largely through the eyes of a repressed clairvoyant girl. Unusual for Boyd, it is stiffly written, internally inconsistent, even incoherent in places, though not lacking in poetic allusions. A further decline in quality is found in *Andromeda Gun,* a spoof on conventions of the old West, in which an alien intelligence tries to reform the mind of a Southern rebel turned rabid outlaw.

Barnard's Planet revisits old haunts with an exploratory mission to an Edenic world where vegetable evolution has outstripped animal. Amid five "cluster-educated" multiple-discipline geniuses representing national interests, the captain is an atavism. Unwilling to subject this world to Earth's warring interests, he discovers himself as the saboteur (and poet) he's under orders to defeat.

The protagonist of Boyd's next book has a similar narrow escape. Bumbling bureaucrats and military men almost achieve what they are trying to prevent: takeover by a high-technology, hive-like alien race, temporarily marooned on Earth. Loving and loved by the queen, for whom Boyd's lyricism scales new heights, the hero escapes the fate of a discarded drone, to remember fondly *The Girl with the Jade Green Eyes.*

Freed from the sexual taboos and stylistic limitations of a previous era, Boyd approaches science fiction as entertainment, with literary tolls and aims. Viewed whole, his books are lightweight confections, their component parts wildly implausible. If one is prepared, however, in the act of reading, to trace interwoven motifs and allusions, while trying to outguess the turns of plot, Boyd generally supplies a superior diversion.

—David N. Samuelson

BOYE, Karin

Nationality: Swedish. **Born:** 1900. **Died:** Commited suicide, 1941.

SCIENCE FICTION PUBLICATIONS

Novel

Kallocain. Madison, Wisconsin, University of Wisconsin Press. 1966.

*   *   *

Karin Boye was a distinguished Swedish poet and a disciple of the radical French pacifist Henri Barbusse. She committed suicide a year after the publication of *Kallocain* in 1940. She was one of those intellectuals horrified by the rise of Nazism, and she returned disappointed from a journey to the Soviet Union, a country she had considered a hope for the future. Her anxieties and her experiences with Nazism and Stalinism are clearly reflected in her novel, one of the few dystopias written by a woman. Her work uncannily anticipates many of the black features that Orwell made known in *Nineteen Eighty-Four,* in particular the total surveillance of citizens by spy-lenses in their private homes, the concept of a thought police and thought crime, and the thoroughgoing division of the world into two big states, which are so antagonistic to each other that they deny their enemy the common human ancestry. Leo Kall, a chemist and inventor of the eponymous truth serum Kallocain, is a citizen of the "world state" in the 21st century—a "fellow soldier," for the country's organization is thoroughly militaristic. The police are omnipresent, and citizens are urged to denounce their friends and relatives and to join in communal "hate sessions." The fear of spies is so great that even simple geographical data are treated as secrets of state. Leo Kall is deeply distrustful of his immediate superior Edo Rissen, one of the few human beings who has kept their individualism, and he suspects that his wife is unfaithful to him. Knowing very well that under the influence of his new drug all are equally guilty, Kall decides to attack and to denounce Rissen, who is promptly sentenced. In the end the "world state" is invaded by the "universal state," which is, we may assume, different only by name, and Kall serves his new masters with equal zeal. The psychological conflicts of the hero are depicted powerfully, and the novel reflects a deep fear of the rise of totalitarianism and an all-powerful state that inexorably crushes the individual.

—Franz Rottensteiner

BRACKETT, Leigh (Douglass)

Nationality: American. **Born:** Los Angeles, California, 7 December 1915. **Family:** Married Edmond Hamilton, *q.v.,* in 1946 (died 1977). **Career:** Freelance writer from 1939. **Awards:** Jules Verne award; Western Writers of America Spur award, 1963. **Died:** 24 March 1978.

SCIENCE FICTION PUBLICATIONS

Novels (series: Eric John Stark; Mars)

Shadow over Mars: A New and Original Novel of Martian Adventure. Manchester, World, 1951; as *The Nemesis from Terra,* New York, Ace, 1961.

The Starmen. New York, Gnome Press, 1952; London, Museum Press, 1954; abridged edition, as *The Galactic Breed,* New York, Ace, 1955; original version, as *The Starmen of Llyrdis,* New York, Ballantine, 1976.
The Sword of Rhiannon (Mars). New York, Ace, 1953; London, Boardman, 1955.
The Big Jump. New York, Ace, 1955.
The Long Tomorrow. Garden City, New York, Doubleday, 1955.
Alpha Centauri—or Die! New York, Ace, 1963.
The Book of Skaith: The Adventures of Eric John Stark. Garden City, New York, Doubleday, 1976.
  The Ginger Star (Stark). New York, Ballantine, 1974; London, Sphere, 1976.
  The Hounds of Skaith (Stark). New York, Ballantine, 1974; London, Sphere, 1976.
  The Reavers of Skaith (Stark). New York, Ballantine, 1976.
Eric John Stark: Outlaw of Mars. New York, Ballantine, 1982.
  People of the Talisman (Mars; Stark). New York, Ace, 1964.
  The Secret of Sinharat (Mars; Stark). New York, Ace, 1964.
The Jewel of Bas, with *Thieves' Carnival,* by Karen Haber. New York, Tor, 1990.

Short Stories (series: Mars)

The Coming of the Terrans (Mars). New York, Ace, 1967.
The Halfling and Other Stories (Mars). New York, Ace, 1973.
The Best of Leigh Brackett, edited by Edmond Hamilton. Garden City, New York, Doubleday, 1977.

OTHER PUBLICATIONS

Novels

No Good from a Corpse. New York, Coward-McCann, 1944; London, Simon and Schuster, 1989.
Stranger at Home (ghostwritten for George Sanders). New York, Simon and Schuster, 1946; London, Pilot Press, 1947.
The Tiger among Us. Garden City, New York, Doubleday, 1957; London, Boardman, 1958; as *Fear No Evil,* London, Corgi, 1960; as *13 West Street,* New York, Bantam, 1962.
An Eye for an Eye. Garden City, New York, Doubleday, 1957; London, Boardman, 1958.
Rio Bravo (novelization of screenplay by Brackett and Jules Furthman). New York, Bantam, and London, Corgi, 1959.
Follow the Free Wind. Garden City, New York, Doubleday, 1963.
Silent Partner. New York, Putnam, 1969.

Plays

The Big Sleep, with William Faulkner and Jules Furthman, in *Film Scripts One,* edited by George P. Garrett, O.B. Harrison, Jr., and Jane Gelfmann. New York, Appleton-Century-Crofts, 1971.
The Empire Strikes Back (screenplay), with Lawrence Kasdan, in *The Empire Strikes Back Notebook,* edited by Diane Attias and Lindsay Smith. New York, Ballantine, 1980.

Screenplays: *The Vampire's Ghost,* with John K. Butler, 1945; *Crime Doctor's Manhunt,* with Eric Taylor, 1946; *The Big Sleep,* with William Faulkner and Jules Furthman, 1946; *Rio Bravo,* with Jules Furthman and B.H. McCampbell, 1959; *Gold of the*

Seven Saints, with Leonard Freeman, 1961; *Hatari!* with Harry Kurnitz, 1962; *El Dorado,* 1967; *Rio Lobo,* with Burton Wohl, 1970; *The Long Goodbye,* 1973; *The Empire Strikes Back,* with Lawrence Kasdan, 1979.

Television Plays: For *Checkmate* and *Suspense* series, and *Terror at Northfield* for *Alfred Hitchcock* series.

Other

Editor, *The Best of Planet Stories #1: Strange Adventures on Other Worlds.* New York, Ballantine, 1975.
Editor, *The Best of Edmond Hamilton.* Garden City, New York, Doubleday, 1977.

*

Bibliography: *Leigh Brackett, Marion Zimmer Bradley, Anne McCaffrey: A Primary and Secondary Bibliography* by Rosemarie Arbur, Boston, Hall, 1982.

Manuscript Collection: Special Collections, Eastern New Mexico University Library, Portales.

*   *   *

During the late 1940s and early 1950s Leigh Brackett was the uncontested "Queen of Space Opera." As a girl, she spent summers exploring the beaches near Santa Monica, and her reading of Edgar Rice Burroughs provided much of the imagery that was to make her science fiction unique. In a *Planet Stories* "Feature Flash" she admitted her addiction to things dramatic, repeatedly describing herself as "a ham." Her facility with character and dialogue (in the "tough" detective novel, *No Good from a Corpse*) got her work in films and later prompted Pauline Kael to suppose that most of the dialogue in *El Dorado* was improvised by the actors because it seemed too realistic to have come from any script.

All these aspects of her personal and professional self found ready expression in the kind of SF that made her famous. Space opera is currently a derogatory term, denoting impossibly larger-than-life characters, melodramatic incidents, and flights of fancy quite distant from straight extrapolative science fiction. In the 1940s and early 1950s, however, space opera was the staple of most of the pulp magazines, partly because it was an escape from ordinary life, partly because it evoked a "sense of wonder" just by its portrayal of alien beings, awesome settings, and heroic acts, and partly because of the literary skills of Brackett herself.

The Sword of Rhiannon is perhaps the apex of Brackett's career as a writer of space opera. It begins with a renegade archeologist who is thrown back a million years by a strange "bubble of time" within the tomb of the ancient godlike Martian, Rhiannon. Once in the past, Brackett's hero finds himself involved in all sorts of adventures (he, with Rhiannon's help, frees ancient Mars of the Tyranny of one race, the serpent-evolved Dhuvians, and wins the love of the princess of a human Martian race). The way Brackett tells this story gives it much greater literary quality than the space opera label suggests. Her setting—verdant Mars, with a luminous ocean—

and her characters—of several Martian races, each independently evolved to the level of human culture—allow the reader a glimpse of Mars as a vital world, not the dying one the Terrans find when they arrive just before the beginning of our third millennium. In this novel, Brackett masterfully interweaves the melodramatic heroism of space opera with imaginative postulation of three sapient life-forms besides the native human race of Martians.

Before *Rhiannon,* Brackett produced two space opera masterpieces, "Enchantree of Venus" and "The Lake of the Gone Forever." Afterwards, she turned to more conventional SF with *The Long Tomorrow,* a post-Destruction narrative considered by many to be Brackett's best, and to stories like "The Tweener" and "The Queer Ones." Then she began making novels of previously published novelettes; "Queen of the Martian Catacombs" and "Black Amazon of Mars"—both, incidentally, featuring not just extraordinary women characters but the literary "original," Eric John Stark—became *The Secret of Sinharat* and *People of the Talisman.*

Considering the excitement of her narratives and the immediate pleasure to be derived from them, one might assume that Brackett's science fictions are fun to read, but basically light entertainment. However, one can perceive serious aspects in her fiction, whether it is space opera or not. One, illustrated best in the stories and novels about Eric John Stark, is a thematic interest in the essential goodness of most forms of natural life. Stark, son of Earth-born humans who died on Mercury, struggles for survival among a supportive group of nonhuman Mercurians and only later is returned to civilization. Stark is a renegade and mercenary, a "criminal" only because he does not recognize the authority of artificial laws; whenever he finds himself in a situation calling for heroic action, the "primal ape" in him seems set apart from the civilized human. Nevertheless, both his natural and civilized selves—demonstrated by his consistent sympathy for the wronged, whatever their species may be—seek the good.

Another serious aspect of her fiction is a thematic egalitarianism and, a good strong sense of respect for other living things. The care with which she treats her native Martians and Venusians—though alien, they are persons, too—makes this evident. *The Starmen* is the tale of a quest for equality on a galactic scale; respect for other life runs just below the surface of "The Tweener," evoking sad sympathy from the reader. And "All the Colors of the Rainbow" is, like Le Guin's *The Word for World Is Forest,* a cruelly bitter satire of racist prejudices, set forth by paradoxically delicate prose.

Brackett's growth as a writer was helped along by her husband, Edmond Hamilton; as she influenced his deepening characterization, he influenced her growing ability to structure fiction with a strong yet uncontrived plot. Besides the technical expertise with plotting, Brackett had, by the time she wrote about Skaith, evidently rethought the biology in *Rhiannon;* on Skaith as on ancient Mars there are at least three nonhuman sapient races, but these have evolved from a single stock, each seeking survival by accommodating itself differently to life beneath the dying ginger sun.

From February 1940 when "Martian Quest" appeared in *Astounding,* almost until the day she died in March 1978, Brackett's love for SF was evident in her works. Her last work was the first full draft of the screenplay for *The Empire Strikes Back.*

—Rosemarie Arbur

BRADBURY, Edward P. *See* **MOORCOCK, Michael.**

BRADBURY, Ray(mond Douglas)

Pseudonym: Douglas Spaulding. **Nationality:** American. **Born:** Waukegan, Illinois, 22 August 1920. **Education:** Los Angeles High School, graduated 1938. **Family:** Married Marguerite Susan McClure in 1947; four daughters. **Career:** Since 1943, full-time writer. President, Science-Fantasy Writers of America, 1951-53; member of the Board of Directors, Screen Writers Guild of America, 1957-61. **Awards:** O. Henry prize, 1947, 1948; Benjamin Franklin award, 1954; American Academy award, 1954; Boys' Clubs of America Junior Book award, 1956; Golden Eagle award, for screenplay, 1957; Ann Radcliffe award, 1965, 1971; Writers Guild award, 1974; Aviation and Space Writers award, for television documentary, 1979; Gandalf award, 1980; Nebula Grand Master, 1988; Bram Stoker Life Achievement award, 1989. D.Litt.: Whittier College, California, 1979. **Agent:** Don Congdon, Harold Matson Company, 276 Fifth Avenue, New York, New York 10001, U.S.A. **Address:** 10265 Cheviot Drive, Los Angeles, California 90064, U.S.A.

SCIENCE FICTION PUBLICATIONS

Novels

Fahrenheit 451 (includes short fiction). New York, Ballantine, 1953; title story published seperately, London, Hart-Davis, 1954.
Something Wicked This Way Comes: A Novel. New York, Simon and Schuster, 1962; London, Hart-Davis, 1963.
The Halloween Tree (for children). New York, Knopf, 1972; London, Hart-Davis MacGibbon, 1973.
The Novels of Ray Bradbury. London, Granada, 1984.

Short Stories

Dark Carnival. Sauk City, Wisconsin, Arkham House, 1947; abridged edition, London, Hamish Hamilton, 1948; abridged edition, as *The Small Assassin,* London, Ace, 1962.
The Martian Chronicles. Garden City, New York, Doubleday, 1950; revised as *The Silver Locusts,* London, Hart-Davis, 1951; revised edition, New York, Time, 1963.
The Illustrated Man. Garden City, New York, Doubleday, 1951; revised edition, London, Hart-Davis, 1952.
The Golden Apples of the Sun. Garden City, New York, Doubleday, 1953; abridged edition, London, Hart-Davis, 1953; original version abridged as *Sun and Shadow,* Barkeley, California, Quenian Press, 1957.
The October Country. New York, Ballantine, 1955; London, Hart-Davis, 1956.
A Medicine for Melancholy. Garden City, New York, Doubleday, 1959.
The Day It Rained Forever. London, Hart-Davis, 1959.
R Is for Rocket. Garden City, New York, Doubleday, 1962; London, Hart-Davis, 1968.
The Pedestrian. Glendale, California, Squires, 1964.

The Machineries of Joy: Short Stories. New York, Simon and Schuster, 1964; abridged edition, London, Hart-Davis, 1964.
The Vintage Bradbury: Ray Bradbury's Own Selection of His Best Stories. New York, Vintage, 1965.
S Is for Space. Garden City, New York, Doubleday, 1966; London, Hart-Davis, 1968.
Twice Twenty-Two: The Golden Apples of the Sun; A Medicine for Melancholy. Garden City, New York, Doubleday, 1966.
I Sing the Body Electric! Stories. New York, Knopf, 1969; London, Hart-Davis, 1970.
Bloch and Bradbury: Ten Masterpieces of Science Fiction, with Robert Bloch, edited by Kurt Singer. New York, Tower, 1969; as *Fever Dreams and Other Fantasies,* London, Sphere, 1970.
Ray Bradbury, edited by Anthony Adams. London, Harrap, 1975.
Long after Midnight. New York, Knopf, 1976; London, Hart-Davis MacGibbon, 1977.
The Best of Bradbury. New York, Bantam, 1976.
The Fog Horn and Other Stories. Tokyo, Kinseido, 1977.
To Sing Strange Songs. Exeter, Devon, Wheaton, 1979.
The Stories of Ray Bradbury. New York, Knopf, and London, Granada, 1980.
Dinosaur Tales. New York, Bantam, 1983.
Fever Dream. New York, St. Martin's Press, 1987.
The April Witch. Mankato, Minnesota, Creative Education, 1988.
The Dragon. Round Top, New York, Footsteps Press, 1988.
The Toynbee Convector. New York, Knopf, 1988; London, Grafton, 1989.
The Fog Horn. Mankato, Minnesota, Creative Education, 1989.
Nouvelles, with French translations by Annie Richelet. Paris, Presses Pocket, 1989.
Classic Stories. New York, Bantam, 2 vols., 1990.
Selected from Dark They Were, and Golden-Eyed, edited by George Ochoa. New York, Literacy Voluteers of New York City, 1991.
The Smile. Mankato, Minnesota, Creative Education, 1991.
The Ray Bradbury Chronicles. New York, Bantam, 5 vols., 1992-93.

OTHER PUBLICATIONS

Novels

Switch on the Night (for children). New York, Pantheon, and London, Hart-Davis, 1955.
Dandelion Wine. Garden City, New York, Doubleday, and London, Hart-Davis, 1957.
Death Is a Lonely Business. New York, Knopf, 1985; London, Grafton, 1986.
A Graveyard for Lunatics: Another Tale of Two Cities. New York, Knopf, and London, Grafton, 1990.
Green Shadows, White Whale: A Novel. New York, Knopf, and London, HarperCollins, 1992.

Short Stories

The Aqueduct (A Martian Chronicle). Glendale, California, Squires, 1979.
The Last Circus, and The Electrocution. Northridge, California, Lord John Press, 1980.
A Memory of Murder. New York, Dell, 1984.
A Story of Love and Other Non-Science Fiction Stories, edited and annotated by Liliane and Mrielle Yvinec. Paris, Le Livre de Poche, 1991.

Plays

The Meadow, in *Best One-Act Plays of 1947-48,* edited by Margaret Mayorga. New York, Dodd Mead, 1948.

The Anthem Sprinters and Other Antics (produced Los Angeles, 1968). New York, Dial Press, 1963.

The World of Ray Bradbury (produced Los Angeles, 1964; New York, 1965).

The Wonderful Ice-Cream Suit (produced Los Angeles, 1965; New York, 1987). Included in *The Wonderful Ice-Cream Suit and Other Plays,* 1972.

The Day It Rained Forever: A Comedy in One Act, music by Bill Whitefield (produced Edinburgh, 1988). New York, French, 1966.

The Pedestrian: A Fantasy in One Act. New York, French, 1966.

Christus Apollo, music by Jerry Goldsmith (produced Los Angeles, 1969).

The Wonderful Ice-Cream Suit and Other Plays (includes *The Veldt* and *To the Chicago Abyss*). New York, Bantam, 1972; London, Hart-Davis, 1973.

The Veldt (produced London, 1980). Included in *The Wonderful Ice-Cream Suit and Other Plays,* 1972.

Leviathan 99 (produced Los Angeles, 1972).

Pillar of Fire and Other Plays (includes *Kaleidoscope* and *The Foghorn*). New York, Bantam, 1975.

The Foghorn (produced New York, 1977). Included in *Pillar of Fire and Other Plays,* 1975.

That Ghost, That Bride of Time: Excerpts from a Play-in-Progress. Glendale, California, Squires, 1976.

The Martian Chronicles, adaptation of his own stories (produced Los Angeles, 1977).

Fahrenheit 451 (adaptation of his own novel; produced Los Angeles, 1979).

Dandelion Wine (adaptation of his own story; produced Los Angeles, 1980).

Forever and the Earth (radio play). Athens, Ohio, Croissant, 1984.

On Stage: A Chrestomathy of His Plays (omnibus). New York, Primus, 1991.

Screenplays: *It Came from Outer Space,* with David Schwartz, 1952; *Moby-Dick,* with John Huston, 1956; *Icarus Mongolfier Wright,* with George C. Johnston, 1961; *Picasso Summer* (as Douglas Spaulding), with Edwin Booth, 1972.

Television Plays: *Shopping for Death,* 1956, *Design for Loving,* 1958, *Special Delivery,* 1959, *The Faith of Aaron Menefee,* 1962, and *The Life Work of Juan Dìaz* (all *Alfred Hitchcock Presents* series); *The Marked Bullet* (*Jane Wyman's Fireside Theatre* series), 1956; *The Gift* (*Steve Canyon* series), 1958; *The Tunnel to Yesterday* (*Trouble Shooters* series), 1960; *I Sing the Body Electric!* (*Twilight Zone* series), 1962; *The Jail* (*Alcoa Premiere* series), 1962; *The Groom* (*Curiosity Shop* series), 1971; *The Coffin,* from his own short story, 1988 (U.K.).

Poetry

Old Ahab's Friend, and Friend to Noah, Speaks His Piece: A Celebration. Glendale, California, Squires, 1971.

When Elephants Last in the Dooryard Bloomed: Celebrations for Almost Any Day in the Year. New York, Knopf, 1973; London, Hart-Davis MacGibbon, 1975.

That Son of Richard III: A Birth Announcement. Privately printed, 1974.

Where Robot Mice and Robot Men Run round in Robot Towns: New Poems, Both Light and Dark. New York, Knopf, 1977; London, Hart-Davis MacGibbon, 1979.

Twin Hieroglyphs That Swim the River Dust. Northridge, California, Lord John Press, 1978.

The Bike Repairman. Northridge, California, Lord John Press, 1978.

The Author Considers His Resources. Northridge, California, Lord John Press, 1979.

The Attic Where the Meadow Greens. Northridge, California, Lord John Press, 1980.

The Haunted Computer and the Android Pope. New York, Knopf, and London, Granada, 1981.

The Complete Poems of Ray Bradbury. New York, Ballantine, 1982.

The Love Affair. Northridge, California, Lord John Press, 1983.

Other

The Autumn People (graphic novel based on author's stories). New York, Ballantine, 1965.

Tomorrow Midnight (graphic novel based on author's stories). New York, Ballantine, 1966.

Teacher's Guide: Science Fiction, with Lewy Olfson. New York, Bantam, 1968.

Mars and the Mind of Man. New York, Harper, 1973.

Zen and the Art of Writing, and The Joy of Writing. Santa Barbara, California, Capra Press, 1973.

The God in Science Fiction. Northridge, California, Santa Susana, 1977.

The Mummies of Guanajuato, photographs by Archie Lieberman. New York, Abrams, 1978.

Beyond 1984: A Remembrance of Things Future. New York, Tary, 1979.

The Ghosts of Forever, illustrated by Aldo Sessa. New York, Rizzoli, 1981.

Los Angeles, photographs by West Light. Port Washington, New York, Skyline Press, 1984.

Orange County, photographs by Bill Ross and others. Port Washington, New York, Skyline Press, 1985.

The Art of Playboy. New York, van der Marck Editions, 1985.

Zen in the Art of Writing. Santa Barbara, California, Odell, 1990.

Yestermorrow: Obvious Answers to Impossible Futures (essays). Santa Barbara, California, Capra Press, 1991.

The Star. Santa Ana, California, Gold Stein Press, 1993.

The R.B., G.K.C., and G.B.S. Forever Orient Express. Santa Barbara, California, Odell, 1994.

Editor, *Timeless Stories for Today and Tomorrow.* New York, Bantam, 1952.

Editor, *The Circus of Dr. Lao and Other Improbable Stories.* New York, Bantam, 1956.

*

Critical Studies: Introduction by Gilbert Highet to *The Vintage Bradbury,* 1965; *The Ray Bradbury Companion* (includes bibliography) by William F. Nolan, Detroit, Gale, 1975; *The Drama of Ray Bradbury* by Ben F. Indick, Baltimore, T-K Graphics, 1977; *The Bradbury Chronicles* by George Edgar Slusser, San Bernardino, California, Borgo Press, 1977; *Ray Bradbury* (includes bibliography) edited by Joseph D. Olander and Martin H. Greenberg, New York, Taplinger, and Edinburgh, Harris, 1980; *Ray Bradbury* by Wayne L. Johnson, New York, Ungar, 1980; *Ray Bradbury and the Poetics of Reverie: Fantasy, Science Fiction, and the Reader* by William F. Toupence, Ann Arbor, UMI Research Press, 1984; *Ray Bradbury* by David Mogen, Boston, Massachusetts, Twayne, 1986.

Ray Bradbury comments:

If I were to advise writers my advice would go simply like this: Begin writing when you are 12 if possible. Fall in love with all the arts, for from them you will learn how to touch, see, smell, know the world. Educate your hands by drawing, educate your ear by listening, educate your nose by running against the wind, keep your eyes wide and your mouth shut. Write every day and every day of your life until it becomes such an immense love you can't help yourself. It should be as crazy as any love is for any man. It should be like the first love you know when you are sixteen or seventeen and go out of your mind because the fruit is high on the tree and you're shaking the tree like mad and it won't fall down into your arms and if it doesn't fall down soon and smother you with returned affection, why, damn it to hell, you'll climb the tree and get it or hang yourself, one or t'other. Crazy love. Mad love. Love comic strips. I have collected them all my life. Love radio shows. I used to clean out the garbage cans in back of NBC and CBS after every *Jack Benny Radio Show* or *Burns and Allen Show.* Start bad. Become mediocre. Get better. Become excellent. By any means at hand. But love, love, love. Love to be around actors and directors. Paint sets. Write bad plays. Do terrible essays. Write awful poems. But all because you are so full of things you want to say you can't stop.

Know all the books in your local library better than the librarian. Go there every night. Live there. Educate yourself. Know all the stock in the local book store. I do. There is no day in my life I do not go to at least one book store. Go to art galleries. Look. Fill up. See every film ever made. Fill up on that medium. Know everything that is bad. Only by knowing what is bad can you avoid badness. The snob who refuses knowledge in mediocrities remains always second-rate himself. I have collected *Prince Valiant* for 30 years. Listen to bad music and good music and great music. Study architecture. Read science fiction, because it is the one fiction which is curious about ALL the above, all and everything, on every level. In sum: run, shout, search, be puzzled, go on, from day to day, with high enthusiasm.

*   *   *

Ever since the remarkable critical and popular success of *The Martian Chronicles* in 1950, Ray Bradbury has been among the most visible science fiction writers. Although he has not produced a major work in several years, he remains the most widely recognized spokesman for the genre, and particularly for the romantic attitudes toward space flight and technology that it sometimes embodies. This is somewhat ironic, since Bradbury's best works—dating from the early 1950s—are powerful indictments of unchecked technological progress and question humanity's ability to deal creatively with the new worlds of which science and technology hold promise.

Bradbury is above all a humanist, and this humanism is evident throughout his career. In his earlier works, Bradbury moves from an adolescent sciencefiction fan making his first professional pub-

lications (the first was the story "Pendulum" written with Henry Hasse) to a mature stylist. Bradbury's first book, the collection of stories *Dark Carnival,* was not science fiction at all, but rather ranged from satirical horror (such as "The Handler," which concerns a mortician who plays practical jokes on his "clients") to sensitive portrayals of lonely or pathetic individuals—a wife incapacitated with horror at her own mortality after viewing Mexican mummies ("The Next in Line"), a "normal" boy alone in a family of friendly vampires ("The Homecoming"). Many of the stories had originally appeared in *Weird Tales,* a horror pulp that represented a market Bradbury would soon abandon, but it was in these tales that he developed his craft, and many of them remain among his strongest work.

The Martian Chronicles began the second and most prolific phase of Bradbury's career. A series of stories, linked by bridge passages, concerning the colonization and exploitation of Mars by what seem to be exclusively citizens of small Midwestern American towns, the book owed much to the American tradition of frontier literature, and quickly consolidated Bradbury's reputation as one of science fiction's leading stylists. Although the portrayal of the Martians ranges from sensitive, essentially ordinary families ("Ylla") to shapeless monsters ("The Third Expedition"), they soon fade into the background as the stories focus on different types of Earth settlers—romantics, misfits, opportunists, idealists, even fugitive Blacks (in "Way in the Middle of the Air"). In the end, an atomic war sends most of the settlers back to the Earth to join their families, leaving only a few isolated families such as that depicted in "The Million-Year Picnic," whose father vows to start a new world on Mars without the prejudice and regimentation that had come to characterize life on Earth.

The Illustrated Man appeared in the following year, and again connected the stories by a frame narrative; in this case, each story is presented as a tattoo come to life. A few of the stories retain the Martian setting of the *Chronicles,* and one of these, "The Fire Balloons," is an early attempt at treating a serious religious issue in science fiction—the question of whether a benign alien life form can be said to have achieved Christian grace. Other stories explore themes that had become familiar to Bradbury readers. The amorality of children which appeared as a theme in a few *Dark Carnival* stories here returns in stories in which children murder their parents in a mechanical playroom ("The Veldt") or assist invading aliens ("Zero Hour"). Mexico, which had fascinated Bradbury since a trip he took there in 1945, is the setting of "The Fox in the Forest" and "The Highway." And the romantic attitudes toward space travel that were to remain a Bradbury staple are evident in "The Rocket," "No Particular Night or Morning," and "Kaleidoscope," a tale of the crew of an exploded spaceship drifting slowly to their deaths, which Bradbury later dramatized.

Fahrenheit 451, a dystopian satire of a totalitarian state in which "firemen" are professional bookburners who set fires rather than put them out, is the only science fiction work of Bradbury's to approach *The Martian Chronicles* in popularity. *Fahrenheit 451* is as much an attack on mass culture as it is a satire of McCarthy-era censorship; the enforced illiteracy of this future society, we are led to believe, is at least in part due to the desires to avoid offending special interest groups in the mass media and to the rise of television (which Bradbury had already effectively satirized in "The Pedestrian"). The novel is as simple as a parable, and few attempts are made to offer a realistic portrait of an imagined society. The police state, it seems, exists almost solely to burn books, and the society of outcasts that the hero Montag finally escapes to join seems curiously incapable of political action, choosing instead to preserve literary culture by memorizing all the great books.

Of the other four collections Bradbury published during the 1950s, none was primarily science fiction. *The Golden Apples of the Sun* introduced what was to become a familiar Bradbury mix of small-town tales, fantasies, Mexican stories, science fiction, and crime tales. *The October Country* reprinted most of the contents of *Dark Carnival* and added four stories, and *Dandelion Wine* was a collection of sketches based on Bradbury's own boyhood in Waukegan, Illinois. *A Medicine for Melancholy* repeated the mix of *The Golden Apples of the Sun,* introducing in book form a new theme for Bradbury, Irish life and character, which had come to fascinate the author while he was in Ireland in 1954.

Bradbury's long-awaited full-length novel *Something Wicked This Way Comes* is a fantasy concerning an evil carnival that disturbs the lives of people in a small Midwestern town. Strongly influenced by Charles G. Finney's *The Circus of Dr. Lao,* the novel gains real power despite occasional overwriting, and marked the beginning of a third phase of Bradbury's career, characterized by an almost meditative return to his favorite themes and archetypes, by a decreasing output of fiction, and by an increasing interest in new forms such as poetry, drama, and— most recently—the mystery novel. Despite a number of excellent stories, collections such as *The Machineries of Joy* and *I Sing the Body Electric!* suggested little in the way of new directions or artistic growth. A self-reflectiveness culminated in the late 1970s and early 1980s with four collections, *Long After Midnight, The Stories of Ray Bradbury, Dinosaur Tales,* and *A Memory of Murder,* that were almost entirely retrospective—the last title consisting exclusively of his pulp crime stories of the 1940s.

Bradbury's movement away from science fiction was underlined with the publication of his nostalgic mystery novel *Death Is A Lonely Business* in 1985 and his collection *The Toynbee Convector* three years later. *The Toynbee Convector* reveals a Bradbury at ease with his focus on sentiment and nostalgia, but only three of the 23 stories in the book could remotely be regarded as science fiction. The title story, about a man who fakes a trip into the future in order to give hope to the cynical 1980s, could almost be viewed as Bradbury's testament to his faith in his own unbounded optimism. Whatever the final assessment of these later stories, Bradbury's crucial role in broadening the audience for science fiction cannot be argued. While the genre had produced other excellent craftsman before Bradbury, his finely-tuned style and humanistic values exerted a profound influence on a generation of writers and helped reduce the barriers that had long isolated science fiction from the mainstream.

—Gary K. Wolfe

BRADLEY, Marion Zimmer

Pseudonyms: Lee Chapman; John Dexter; Miriam Gardner; Valerie Graves; Morgan Ives and John J. Wells. **Nationality:** American. **Born:** Albany, New York, 3 June 1930. **Education:** New York State College for Teachers, 1946-48; Hardin-Simmons University, Abilene, Texas, B.A. in English, Spanish, psychology 1964; University of California, Berkeley. **Family:** Married 1) Robert A. Bra-

dley in 1949 (divorced 1964); one son; 2) Walter Henry Breen in 1964 (divorced 1990); one son and one daughter. **Career:** Editor, *Marion Zimmer Bradley's Fantasy Magazine,* since 1988. Singer and writer. **Awards:** *Locus* Award, 1984. **Address:** P.O. Box 72, Berkeley, California 94701, U.S.A.

SCIENCE FICTION PUBLICATIONS

Novels (series: Atlantean Chronicles; Leslie Barnes/Claire Moffat; Darkover; Red Moon; Trillium)

The Door through Space. New York, Ace, 1961; London, Arrow, 1979.

Seven from the Stars. New York, Ace, 1962.

The Planet Savers. New York, Ace, 1962; London, Arrow, 1979; expanded edition, Ace, 1976.

The Sword of Aldones (Darkover). New York, Ace, 1962; London, Arrow, 1979; revised as *Sharra's Exile,* New York, DAW, 1981; London, Arrow, 1983.

The Colors of Space (for children). Derby, Connecticut, Monarch, 1963; expanded edition, Norfolk, Virginia, Donning, 1983; as *The Colours of Space,* London, Lightning, 1989.

The Bloody Sun (Darkover). New York, Ace, 1964; London, Arrow, 1978; revised edition, New York, Ace, 1979.

Falcons of Narabedla. New York, Ace, 1964; London, Arrow, 1984.

Star of Danger (Darkover). New York, Ace, 1965; London, Arrow, 1978.

The Brass Dragon. New York, Ace, 1969; London, Methuen, 1978.

The Winds of Darkover. New York, Ace, 1970; London, Arrow, 1978.

The World Wreckers: A Darkover Novel. New York, Ace, 1971; London, Arrow, 1979.

Dark Satanic (Barnes/Moffat). New York, Berkley, 1972; Wallington, Surrey, Severn House, 1991.

Darkover Landfall. New York, DAW, 1972; London, Arrow, 1978.

In the Steps of the Master (novelization of TV Play). New York, Tempo, 1973.

Hunters of the Red Moon. New York, DAW, 1973; London, Arrow, 1979; bylined with Paul Edwin Zimmer, New York, DAW, 1992.

The Spell Sword: A Darkover Novel. New York, DAW, 1974; London, Arrow, 1978.

Endless Voyage. New York, Ace, 1975; expanded edition, as *Endless Universe,* 1979.

The Heritage of Hastur (Darkover). New York, DAW, 1975; London, Arrow, 1979.

Drums of Darkness: An Astrological Gothic Novel: Leo. New York, Ballantine, 1976.

The Shattered Chain: A Darkover Novel. New York, DAW, 1976; London, Arrow, 1978.

The Forbidden Tower (Darkover). New York, DAW, 1977; London, Prior, 1979.

Stormqueen!: A Darkover Novel. New York, DAW, 1978; London, Arrow, 1980.

The Ruins of Isis. Norfolk, Virginia, Donning, 1978; London, Arrow, 1980.

The Survivors (Red Moon), with Paul Edwin Zimmer. New York, DAW, 1979; London, Arrow, 1985.

The House between the Worlds. Garden City, New York, Doubleday, 1980; expanded edition, New York, Ballantine, 1981.

Two to Conquer (Darkover). New York, DAW, 1980; London, Arrow, 1982.

Survey Ship. New York, Ace, 1980.

Hawkmistress! (Darkover). New York, DAW, 1982; London, Arrow, 1985.

The Mists of Avalon. New York, Knopf, 1982; London, Joseph, 1983.

Web of Light (Atlantean). Norfolk, Virginia, Donning, 1983.

Thendara House (Darkover). New York, DAW, 1983; London, Arrow, 1985.

Oath of the Renunciates (includes *The Shattered Chain* and *Thendara House*). Garden City, New York, Doubleday, 1984.

Web of Darkness (Atlantean). New York, Pocket Books, 1984; with *Web of Light,* Glasgow, Drew, 1985; as *The Fall of Atlantis,* New York, Baen, 1987.

The Inheritor (Barnes/Moffat). New York, Tor, 1984; Wallington, Surrey, Severn House, 1992.

City of Sorcery (Darkover). New York, DAW, 1984; London, Arrow, 1986.

Night's Daughter: A Novel. New York, Ballantine, and London, Inner Circle, 1985.

Warrior Woman. New York, DAW, 1985; London, Arrow, 1987.

The Firebrand: A Novel. New York, Simon and Schuster, 1987; London, Joseph, 1988.

The Heirs of Hammerfell (Darkover). New York, DAW, 1989; London, Legend, 1991.

Black Trillium, with Julian May and Andre Norton. New York, Doubleday, 1990; London, Grafton, 1991.

Witch Hill. New York, Tor, 1990; Wallington, Surrey, Severn House, 1992.

Rediscovery: A Novel of Darkover, with Mercedes Lackey. New York, DAW, 1993.

The Forest House. London, Joseph, 1993; New York, Viking, 1994.

Lady of the Trillium. New York, Bantam, 1995.

Ghostlight. New York, Tor, 1995.

Tiger Burning Bright, with Andre Norton and Mercedes Lackey. New York, Morrow, 1995.

Short Stories (series: Arwen)

The Dark Intruder and Other Stories. New York, Ace, 1964.

The Jewel of Arwen. Baltimore, T-K Graphics, 1974.

The Parting of Arwen. Baltimore, T-K Graphics, 1974.

Lythande. New York, DAW, 1986; London, Sphere, 1988.

The Best of Marion Zimmer Bradley, edited by Martin H. Greenberg. Chicago, Academy Chicago, 1985; abridged edition, New York, DAW, 1988; London, Orbit, 1990; original version expanded as *Jamie and Other Stories: The Best of Marion Zimmer Bradley,* Chicago, Academy Chicago, 1993.

Marion Zimmer Bradley's Darkover. New York, DAW, 1993.

OTHER PUBLICATIONS

Novels

I Am a Lesbian (as Lee Chapman). Derby, Connecticut, Monarch, 1962.

Spare Her Heaven (as Morgan Ives). Derby, Connecticut, Monarch, 1963; abridged edition, as *Anything Goes,* Sydney, Stag, 1964.

Castle Terror. New York, Lancer, 1965; Sutton, Surrey, Severn House, 1994.

Knives of Desire (as Morgan Ives). San Diego, Corinth, 1966.

No Adam for Eve (as John Dexter). San Diego, Corinth, 1966.

Souvenir of Monique. New York, Ace, 1967.

Bluebeard's Daughter. New York, Lancer, 1968.

Witch Hill (as Valerie Graves). San Diego, Greenleaf, 1972.

Can Ellen Be Saved? (novelization of TV Play). New York, Grosset and Dunlap, 1975.

The Catch Trap. New York, Ballantine, 1979; London, Sphere, 1986.

Novels as Miriam Gardner

The Strange Women. Derby, Connecticut, Monarch, 1962.

My Sister, My Love. Derby, Connecticut, Monarch, 1963.

Twilight Lovers. Derby, Connecticut, Monarch, 1964.

Other

Songs from Rivendell. Privately printed, 1959.

A Complete, Cumulative Checklist of Lesbian, Variant, and Homosexual Fiction. Privately printed, 1960.

Of Men, Halflings, and Hero-Worship. Rochester, Texas, Fantasy Amateur Press Association, 1961.

The Necessity for Beauty: Robert W. Chambers and the Romantic Tradition. Baltimore, T-K Graphics, 1974.

Editor, *The Keeper's Price and Other Stories.* New York, DAW, 1980.

Editor, *Sword of Chaos and Other Stories.* New York, DAW, 1982.

Editor, *Greyhaven: An Anthology of Fantasy.* New York, DAW, 1983.

Editor, *Sword and Sorceress 1-13.* New York, DAW, 1984-96; vol. 1 published London, Headline, 1988.

Editor, *Free Amazons of Darkover.* New York, DAW, 1985.

Editor, *Other Side of the Mirror.* New York, DAW, 1987.

Editor, *Red Sun of Darkover.* New York, DAW, 1987.

Editor, *Four Moons of Darkover.* New York, DAW, 1988.

Editor, *The Spells of Wonder.* New York, DAW, 1989.

Editor, *Domains of Darkover.* New York, DAW, 1990.

Editor, *Renunciates of Darkover.* New York, DAW, 1991.

Editor, *Leroni of Darkover.* New York, DAW, 1991.

Editor, *Towers of Darkover.* New York, DAW, 1993.

Editor, *Snows of Darkover.* New York, DAW, 1994.

Editor, *The Best of Marion Zimmer Bradley's Fantasy Magazine.* New York, Warner, 1994.

Translator, *El Villano in su Ricon,* by Lope de Vega. Privately printed, 1971.

*

Bibliography: *Leigh Brackett, Marion Zimmer Bradley, Anne McCaffrey: A Primary and Secondary Bibliography* by Rosemarie Arbur, Boston, Hall, 1982.

Manuscript Collection: Boston University.

Critical Studies: *The Gemini Problem: A Study in Darkover* by Walter Breen, Baltimore, T-K Graphics, 1975; *The Darkover Dilemma: Problems of the Darkover Series* by S. Wise, Baltimore, T-K Graphics, 1976.

Marion Zimmer Bradley comments:

The secret of life is to do what you enjoy doing most, and to get someone to pay you enough so you don't actually have to starve while you're doing it. People who want other things, money and status, baffle me. I write professionally because it's the only thing I can do well, and every other job I have had has either bored or frustrated me past tolerance; and since I write compulsively and would no matter what else I was doing, it's wonderful that I can get paid for it.

*   *   *

Marion Zimmer Bradley's versatile, prolific writing career recapitulates many of the major trends over the past several decades of science fiction. In more than 40 years of productivity, she has grown with the genre she has helped to shape.

Some of her early fiction is action/adventure, much in the tradition of C.L. Moore and Leigh Brackett Hamilton. Some of her early science fiction follows the trend toward the personal and the human, rather than the technological side, in the manner of Judith Merril's "That Only A Mother . . .". Bradley's early Darkover novels also show the influence of Leigh Bracket Hamilton and C.L. Moore—the lure of faraway places, faintly sinister desert towns, and flashing swords, frequently wielded by fighting women.

When series books became popular, her Darkover series proved to be one of the most popular, durable, and influential such series. Evolving from the now-rewritten *Sword of Aldones* (1962), which combined psionics, the code duello, and glimpses of a yet-unrealized planet, Bradley's Darkover has become a place as well-documented as Dune or the Witch World. It is not just an exercise in planet-building: a "Darkover" book is commonly understood to deal with issues of cultural clash, between Darkover and its parent Terran culture, between warring groups on Darkover, or in familial terms. Probably most notable about the Darkover books is the shift Bradley made with *The Shattered Chain,* which took a much earlier mention of the Free Amazons and turned them into a provocative analysis of sexual politics. Much of this debate involves questions of freedom and choice: the Amazons, or Renunciates, exist as a way of providing an alternative to Darkovan women and of enabling them to become keepers of their own consciences and charters of their own course. The shift in name from Amazons to Renunciates illustrates a major theme—that choices like this are never easy.

This discourse, which expanded early on to include alternative lifestyles and sexuality, is paralleled by some of her mainstream work, most notably *The Catch Trap,* which deals movingly with two gay men who are circus aerialists. Bradley's training as a science fiction writer enables her to present the alien and exciting world of the circus with vigor and authority.

These alternative cultures imply community, another touchstone of Bradley's life and writing. Her respect for and long participation in the SF community has enabled her to enlarge it. Her *Friends of Darkover* anthologies mark her as one of the first writers in the field to benefit from the "shared world" concept. Her *Greyhaven* volume, her subsequent *Sword and Sorceress* anthology series, and *Marion Zimmer Bradley's Fantasy Magazine* have all enabled her to discover and introduce many younger writers, most notably Diana Paxson.

The 1970s and 1980s were a time when science fiction novels made the jump to mainstream, bestselling status. Bradley's *The Mists of Avalon* once again embodies a number of trends: a major, bestselling Arthurian novel written during a revival of interest in the Matter of Britain, it is essentially revisionist, providing a woman's and pagan's eye-view of a very traditional mythology. *The Firebrand,* which deals with the fall of Troy, is another revisionist historical novel.

A "writer's writer," Bradley emphasizes strong plotting and character development. Her writing, like her work with younger writers, exemplifies her professionalism and her commitment to the science fiction community.

—Susan Shwartz

———

BRANDON, Frank. *See* **BULMER, Kenneth.**

———

BRETNOR, Reginald

Pseudonym: Grendel Briarton. **Nationality:** American. **Born:** Russia, 30 July 1911; emigrated to the United States in 1920. **Education:** Attended college in California and New Mexico. **Family:** Married 1) Helen Harding in 1949 (died, 1967); 2) Rosalie Leveille in 1969 (died, 1988). **Career:** Writer for the Office of War Information and the State Department Office of International Information and Cultural Affairs, 1943-47. Since 1947, freelance writer. **Died:** 15 July 1992.

SCIENCE FICTION PUBLICATIONS

Novels (series: Papa Schimmelhorn)

Gilpin's Space. New York, Ace, 1986.
Schimmelhorn's Gold. New York, Tor, 1986.

Short Stories (series: Papa Schimmelhorn)

Through Space and Time with Ferdinand Feghoot: The First Forty-five Feghoot Adventures, with Five More Never Previously Heard Of (as Grendel Briarton). Berkeley, California, Paradox Press, 1962; augmented edition as *The Compleat Feghoot: The Many Lives and Greatest Exploits of History's Punniest Spacetime Traveller,* and *The (Even) More Compleat Feghoot,* Baltimore, Mirage Press, 1975, 1980; augmented edition as *The Collected Feghoot,* Eugene, Oregon, Pulphouse, 1992.
The Schimmelhorn File: Memoirs of a Dirty Old Genius. New York, Ace, 1979.

OTHER PUBLICATIONS

Novel

A Killing in Swords. New York, Pocket Books, 1978.

Short Stories

The Christmas Cat. Berkeley, California, Turtle's Quill, 1964.

Other (series: The Future at War)

Decisive Warfare: A Study in Military Theory. Harrisburg, Pennsylvania, Stackpole, 1969; revised edition, San Bernardino, California, Borgo Press, 1986.
Of Force and Violence, and Other Imponderables: Essays on War, Politics, and Government. San Bernardino, California, Borgo Press, 1990.
One Man's BEM: Thoughts on Science Fiction (essays). San Bernardino, California, Borgo Press, 1990.

Editor, *Modern Science Fiction: Its Meaning and Its Future.* New York, Coward-McCann, 1953; revised edition, Chicago, Advent, 1979.
Editor, *Price List 1884, N. Curry & Bro.: Facsimile Edition.* Berkeley, California, Paradox Press, 1965.
Editor, *Science Fiction, Today and Tomorrow: A Discursive Symposium.* New York, Harper, 1974.
Editor, *The Craft of Science Fiction: A Symposium on Writing Science Fiction and Fantasy.* New York, Harper, 1976.
Editor, *Thor's Hammer* (Future at War). New York, Ace, 1979.
Editor, *The Spear of Mars* (Future at War). New York, Ace, 1980.
Editor, *Orion's Sword: War in Interstellar and Intergalactic Space* (Future at War). New York, Ace, 1980.

Translator, *Moncrif's Cats: Les Chats de François Augustin Paradis de Moncrif,* by François-Augustin Paradis de Moncrif. London, Golden Cockerel Press, 1961; Cranbury, New Jersey, A.S. Barnes, 1965.

*

Bibliography: *The Work of Reginald Bretnor: An Annotated Bibliography and Guide* by Scott Alan Burgess, San Bernardino, California, Borgo Press, 1989.

*   *   *

Fans best remember Bretnor for his humorous short fictions in SF magazines, where he teased them with a dry wit and turn of phrase reminiscent of P.G. Wodehouse. The Feghoot, a short tale of that space-time traveler ending in a pun or spoonerism, burst serendipitously into Bretnor's life during a Scrabble game, then entertained readers for more than 30 years. The equally long-lived Papa Schimmelhorn is said to still be chasing beautiful young women behind Mama's back and turning the world upside down with crazy clockwork inventions. While the final Feghoot collection from Pulphouse is complete, fans must wait to see if a complete anthology will deliver the remaining, unpublished Schimmelhorn. Other memorable Bretnor shorts include "A Matter of Equine Ballistics" and "The Man on Top."

Bretnor laid the foundation for serious literary criticism of science fiction through three remarkable anthologies. *Modern Science Fiction: Its Meaning and Its Future* and *Science Fiction Today and Tomorrow* both opened discussion on imaginative fiction as literature and its relationship to the society creating it. The prescience of the former is startling, for science fiction would not receive seri-

ous academic attention for another 15 years. *The Craft of Science Fiction: A Symposium on Writing Science Fiction and Science Fantasy* remains essential in the SF writer's library: essays from many of SF's finest outline the art of weaving believable fictions about unseen worlds and alien cultures. Written 20 years ago, this text still comes highly recommended in most bibliographies of science fiction. His other notable work stands virtually alone. The oft-referenced *Decisive Warfare* cohesively comprised several long essays on the theory of military combat. The collection progresses from analysis of the metrics of warfare to discourse on the failure of many theorists to adequately comprehend the impact of technological advances on the equations of war. Other related essays appeared later in the military journal *Defense Analysis.*

Bretnor's novels fared less well. *Gilpin's Space* posits an inexpensive and technologically simple form of space travel, but this premise is insufficient to fill the void left by his uninspiring characters. Alastair Timuroff, a regular in Bretnor mysteries, must have pined for the pages of *Ellery Queen's* as he wandered pointlessly through *A Killing in Swords. Papa Schimmelhorn's Gold* has more polish than the others, but still lacks the luster of the crazy *chenius's* briefer displays. Here the humor itself became repetitive amid the intricacies of the plot. While Bretnor's attention to detail produced delightful short stories, the structure of novels eluded him.

Short fiction and anthologies are regarded as lesser than novels except in those rare instances where the contributions cannot be ignored. Bretnor's *The Craft of Science Fiction* is one such instance. While many of his writings are already forgotten, Bretnor's critical thought, military theory, and one hopes his humor, will endure.

—Scott Burgess

———

BRETT, Leo. *See* **FANTHORPE, R. Lionel.**

———

BRIARTON, Grendel. *See* **BRETNOR, Reginald.**

———

BRIN, David

Nationality: American. **Born:** Glendale, California, 6 October 1950. **Education:** California Institute of Technology, Pasadena, B.S. in astronomy 1973; University of California, San Diego, M.S. in applied physics 1978, Ph.D. in space science 1981. **Family:** Married Cheryl Brigham; one son and one daughter. **Career:** Technical staff member, Hughes Research Laboratory, Newport Beach, California, 1973-75, and Carlsbad, California, 1975-77; taught at San Diego State University, 1982-83, and San Diego community colleges, 1983-84. Secretary, Science Fiction Writers of America. **Awards:** Nebula award, 1984; Hugo award, 1984, 1987; *Locus* award, 1984, 1986, 1987, 1988, 1995; Balrog award, 1985; John W. Campbell,

Jr. Memorial award, 1986. **Agent:** Ralph Vicinanza, 111 8th Ave., New York, New York.

SCIENCE FICTION PUBLICATIONS

Novels (series: Uplift)

Sundiver (Uplift). New York, Bantam, 1980; London, Bantam, 1985.
Startide Rising (Uplift). New York, Bantam, 1983; revised edition, West Bloomfield, Michigan, Phantasia Press, and London, Bantam, 1985; published with *The Uplift War,* as *Earthclan,* Garden City, New York, Doubleday, 1987; revised edition, New York, Bantam, 1993.
The Practice Effect. New York, Bantam, 1984; London, Bantam, 1986.
The Postman. New York, Bantam, 1985; London, Bantam, 1986.
Heart of the Comet, with Gregory Benford. New York, Bantam, 1986.
The Uplift War. West Bloomfield, Michigan, Phantasia Press, and London, Bantam, 1987; published with *Startide Rising,* as *Earthclan,* Garden City, New York, Doubleday, 1987.
Earth. New York, Bantam, and London, Macdonald, 1990.
Glory Season. New York, Bantam, and London, Orbit, 1993.

Short Stories

The River of Time. Niles, Illinois, Dark Harvest, 1986; London, Bantam, 1987.
Dr. Pak's Preschool. New Castle, Virginia, Cheap Street, 1989.
Piecework. Eugene, Oregon, Pulphouse, 1991.
Otherness. New York, Bantam, and London, Orbit, 1994.

*

Manuscript Collection: The J. Lloyd Eaton Collection of Science Fiction and Fantasy Literature, University of California, Riverside.

David Brin comments:

I've been told my writing is very different in my novels than in my short stories. And both differ a great deal from my mid-length (or novella) works. Generally, the latter are my favorite. One has time to develop characters and detailed settings, and yet is forced to get to the point. SF is almost the last refuge of the novella form, bless it.

My own novellas deal very much in that commodity known as Myth. The novels on the other hand are real SF and I stretch out to try to make use of the scientific thrills this century keeps dropping in our laps. It is fun.

My short work is hard to typify . . . from boy-engineer tales to attempts at epiphanies, I suppose. It's a lovely language, English, and a wonderfully exciting time to be alive.

*   *   *

David Brin's *Sundiver, Startide Rising,* and *The Uplift War* form one of the strongest series in hard science fiction. Like Larry Niven, Gregory Benford, Robert Forward, and other scientist-writers, Brin juxtaposes the best of what space opera and current (or projected) science technology have to offer: galactic struggle, interaction of different species, the dogged determination and eventual triumph of the underdog, high-tech spacecraft and tools, and practical applications of advanced scientific information.

Sundiver, Brin's first book and the first in the Uplift series, introduces a future Earth, where human scientists have been able to genetically "uplift" dolphins and chimpanzees, that is, to give them sapiency, making these two species able to interact with humans by speaking (both English and Dolphin-Trinary). Five species, claiming descent from the so-called Progenitors, and their client species are locked in galaxy-spanning, political jockeying for power and knowledge, knowledge which is supposed to be available to all races through the Galactic Library Institute. But the senior Patron species are hiding a dark secret, which is uncovered by humans and chimpanzees, the Terrans. Thus begins the struggle by the Terrans to outwit the eons-old senior Patrons, which is continued in *Startide Rising.* In this book, the Terrans have crashed onto an uncharted water world called Kithrup, where they find one of the greatest Galactic secrets in history. The Patron species mass vast fleets of spacecraft in an unprecedented battle for control to claim the secret, while the Terrans battle them on the ground. Once again, dolphins and chimpanzees, two newly uplifted species, share a partnership-type relationship with their Patrons, the human race.

The Uplift War is set in the colonial world of Garth, where a small group of chimpanzees and humans, along with Tymbrini and Synthian allies and impartial observers, are attacked by a senior Patron race called the Gubru. Forced into the jungles of this backwoods planet, supposedly deserted, they discover the mythical Garthlings, a large animal species resembling the Terran gorilla. This discovery of an upliftable species gives the Terrans a strong claim to the planet of Garth, and they enter into a struggle to protect this infant species and to claim it as their own client race.

The Practice Effect is a space-operatic book of alternate universes and parallel worlds in which future scientist Dennis Nuel is sent to an alternate world (Tatir) via an experimental transporting device. He becomes stranded in a strange world where everything is "used into perfection." The Practice Effect is a virtual reversal of entropy; for example, if one takes a stone and rolls it long enough, it becomes a sphere, or if one throws a stick enough times, it becomes a javelin. This is an interesting scientific twist. Otherwise, the book unfortunately relies on a well-worn plot: evil antagonist imprisons fair maiden; protagonist rescues her (with the help of a hang glider, which he "uses" into an airplane); maiden falls in love with rescuer; protagonist discovers that Tatir is not an alternate world, but a future-planet colonized by Earth; protagonist decides to go back to his "present" time, collect a few things, and return to the "future," where he will work with the natives and help them rebuild their society from its current feudal level.

The Postman is a postholocaust SF novel that deals with the struggle for survival. In the tradition of George Stewart's classic *Earth Abides,* and Walter M. Miller, Jr.'s *A Canticle For Leibowitz,* Brin writes of a future where society, social interaction, customs, and mores are quite different. *The Postman* is a well-written novel depicting the strength of the human race in the face of great adversity.

Earth is Brin's *tour de force.* In this 600-page novel, Brin depicts a future Earth that brings to fruition all the ecological and technological disasters environmentalists predict. Almost all species are on the endangered species list, surviving in genetic laboratories (called "Arks"). Greenhouse effects cause devastating floods, turning Siberia into a jungle. The deterioration of the ozone layer causes exposure to the sun without protection to be deadly. Social changes give the elderly much more power than the young. Massive computer networks attempt to process large amounts of information. There is overpopulation, famine, death, and laws that make any kind of pollution (even noise pollution) a crime.

If *Earth* was Brin's *tour de force, Glory Season* must be the sequel! In this book, Brin shows yet another facet in an already talent-filled writing career. Here, he tackles the problem of male-dominance in our own society by portraying a world (Stratos) where women rule. Stratos is a world populated by the genetic manipulations of a group of radical feminist separatists who broke off from the other worlds of the "Human Phylum" to start their own society. Readers should not assume, however, that Brin has a "male agenda" of his own to show how awful this world will be, rather, he effectively portrays a young woman named Maia, a "var" (short for "variant") in a world where female clones rule, struggling to take her place in society, to build a family of clones for herself. Through Maia's travels, Brin manages to tackle "issues vexing our own confused era": sex, breeding, hierarchical structure, etc.

Brightness Reef, another book set in the Uplift series (though it claims to be book one of a new trilogy) neither contains reefs nor is it bright. It is also not exactly a sequel to *Startide Rising,* though the ship *Streaker* is involved. At the end of the book we (barely) discover that the dolphin ship is on Jijo, but very little else is known. At one point, *Sooners* was suggested as the title for this novel, which would have been a better choice. Twelve years was a long time to wait for events unfolding after *Startide Rising,* but it was worth the wait, although books two and three of this new trilogy will be necessary to satisfy the reader of *Brightness Reef.*

Brin's early works, through *The Practice Effect,* show a willingness to work within the boundaries of the science fiction field while adding new twists and ideas of his own. His later works, from *The Postman,* convey a greater depth of writing, a much greater sympathy for his human characters than his early works, in which his affinity for aliens is apparent. In the Uplift series, the feelings, emotions, and characteristics of the extraterrestrials are much more interesting. Some have said that this tendency to concentrate more on the science than on the characters is common among scientists-turned-writers. Brin's career started out with extraordinary writing—gaining the attention of such colleagues as Gregory Benford and Arthur C. Clarke, both of whom have collaborated on projects with Brin—but just when the reader thinks Brin cannot possibly come up with something better . . . he does!

—Daryl F. Mallett

BRODERICK, Damien

Nationality: Australian. **Born:** Melbourne, Victoria, 22 April 1944. **Education:** Monash University, Clayton, Victoria, B.A. in English; Deakin University, Victoria, Ph.D. **Career:** Science fiction reviewer, *Melbourne Age.* **Awards:** Literature Board of Australia fellowship (three times); Ditmar award, 1981, 1985, 1989. **Agent:** Virginia Kidd, Box 278, Milford, Pennsylvania 18337, U.S.A. **Address:** 23 Hutchinson Street, Brunswick, Victoria 3056, Australia.

SCIENCE FICTION PUBLICATIONS

Novels (series: The Faustus Hexagram)

Sorcerer's World. New York, New American Library, 1970; revised edition, as *The Black Grail* (Faustus), New York, Avon, 1986.
The Dreaming Dragons (Faustus). Melbourne, Norstrilia Press, and New York, Pocket Books, 1980.
The Judas Mandala (Faustus). New York, Pocket Books, 1982.
Valencies, with Rory Barnes. Brisbane, University of Queensland Press, 1983.
Transmitters: An Imaginary Documentary, 1969-1984 (Faustus). Melbourne, Ebony, 1984.
Striped Holes (Faustus). New York, Avon, 1988.
A Man Returned. Sydney, Horwitz, 1965.
The Dark Between the Stars. Melbourne, Mandarin, 1991.
The Sea's Furthest End. North Adelaid, South Australia, Aphelion, 1993.

Short Stories

Author of numerous short stories.

OTHER PUBLICATIONS

Other

Editor, *The Zeitgeist Machine: A New Anthology of Science Fiction.* London, Angus and Robertson, 1977.
Editor, *Strange Attractors: Original Australian Speculative Fiction.* Sydney, Hale and Iremonger, 1985.
Editor, *Matilda at the Speed of Light.* New South Wales. Sirius, 1988.
Editor, *The Lotto Effect: Towards a Technology of the Paranormal.* Hawthorn, Victoria, Hudson, 1992.
Editor, *The Architecture of Babel: Discourses of Literature and Science.* Melbourne, Melbourne University Press, 1994.
Editor, *Reading by Starlight: Postmodern Science Fiction.* London and New York, Routledge, 1995.

*

Critical Study: Interview with Russell Blackford, in *Science Fiction: A Review of Speculative Literature 12* (Perth, Western Australia), 1982.

Damien Broderick comments:

(1991) Science fiction, I have decided (bending Flaubert), is a cracked test tube we whistle tunes across, moved to pity and laughter by the stars, and by all the poor human souls beneath them.

During the last decade or so science fiction became one of the darlings of poststructuralist criticism because it is—or is meant to be—innately uncomfortable, disruptive, hair-raising, hackles-raising, alienating, oddball.

The Russian Viktor Shklovsky told us many years ago that the primary function of art is *ostranenie:* estrangement, the neck-wrenching which shows us the familiar in a fresh and challenging aspect.

Well, surely science fiction is the ideal candidate? There are few bed-sitters, adulterous stockbrokers, karate-trained sirens or crooked cops on the take. With SF, it's all ghastly clangour and shock, just what Shklovsky ordered. Looming aliens without eyes, flapples to travel in, doors that answer back, machines with hearts of gold.

The reality, as every SF enthusiast knows with remorse, is otherwise.

The salutary jolt of the strange soon loses its force. Like bored rats which seek out a mild adversive electric tingle, SF readers return contentedly to the paperback shelves for a buzz of what we might term *cozy ostranenie.*

In my misery I often wonder if science fiction and fantasy are, after all, simply *different in kind* to the sort of writing exemplified by Henry James and James Joyce and Joyce Cary.

This does help account for the dreary fact that much classic, bona fide SF is (by the standards one rightly expects of any middle-brow novel, any *New Yorker* short story) simply illiterate trash. I won't have it, though.

Brian Aldiss once made prophetic utterance on this score, speaking of "the area of life where art and science meet nature: One becomes more and more preoccupied with the idea that art is all," he observed. "Science fiction is an ideal medium for such a preoccupation . . . for the specifics of fiction versus the generalities of science. This beautiful tender place has been so betrayed by the practitioners of pulp science fiction (who use it for thick-arm adventure and jackboot philosophy) that those who prefer wit to power-fantasy generally move elsewhere." Sadly, the triumph of junk SF and fantasy has done nothing in the interim but strengthen the thick arm of the artist's foe. One is indeed tempted to move elsewhere— almost anywhere else.

But the usages, the tropes, of SF—vulgar and absurd as most of them are—remain at the core of its artistic vocabulary. SF's idiosyncratic images and their weddings in the murky depths of each writer's heart comprise a grammar devised to speak in a way uniquely valid to this century.

My own writing? A few years ago I realised that *Transmitters*— avowedly a *non-SF* novel about SF fans—could usefully be read as part of a larger *post facto* structure that holds most of my novels at its vertices. Right now, I see it containing six novels, so I'm calling it *The Faustus Hexagram.* At the points of the hexagon, place the six components of Roman Jakobson's model of the communication process: Addresser, Addressee (or Audience), Message, Context, Code and Channel. For literary texts, these match quite well with Artist, Reader, Text, World, Language and Publishing Genre. For scientific texts, they match Researcher, Scientific Community, Theory, Universe, Mathematics, and Publication Network. Science fiction's version oscillates between these two vast cultural paradigms. None of the nodes stands in isolation; each works reflexively on the others. Ideas cluster about them, more than I can list here: romantic construction of the artist, classic construction of science, rhetorical construction of the social order, deconstruction of the text, theorized construction of the world, generic construction by formula and trope. My novels, I saw, might be agreeably mounted on the same mechanism: *The Judas Mandala,* Addresser; *The Black Grail,* Addressee; *The Dreaming Dragons,* Context; *Transmitters,* Message; *Striped Holes,* Channel; and a sixth book still in progress.

This sounds stuffy. No. I send my words dancing in light, hear them shout and snort in this newest of tongues: yes, in a medium where Gully Foyle's burning synesthesia fetches us shivers of truth no mere mixed metaphor could lay hands on. It's not Doc Smith, folks, I admit it, but we do what we can. Mmm, I could use a doughnut.

*   *   *

Damien Broderick has always been self-consciously erudite and has made it clear that he understands the latest ideas in science and is at home with postmodernist criticism. Indeed, since he took his Ph.D. in 1990 with "Frozen Music," he has shown fully a need to establish himself as a writer to bring science fiction and postmodernist criticism together, particularly in his 1995 work of criticism, *Reading by Starlight,* which absorbs the writings of Fredric Jameson and Samuel Delany in order to formulate a new definition of SF. Peter Nicholls says that this work brings Broderick into the top 11 critics in the field but notes that readers will find that he translates the stumbling blocks erected by other postmodernists into yet greater ramps of his own. It is a good work to trickle into and bring away fragments of common sense but it will deter many readers. There has always been a strange counterpoise between the learned and the accessible in Broderick's work. One thing I will say is that I have never read a Delany novel that has encouraged me to read another, whereas reading Broderick does usually encourage me to read another.

Precocity meant that in the 1960s Broderick was introducing the ideas of Koestler, Timothy Leary, and the Death of God controversialists to unsuspecting readers of *Man Magazine,* as well as lively stories, presenting himself as C.P. Snow's man of two cultures. However, in *The Architecture of Babel* he maintains that "there are unseverable links between the two cultures" (letter responding to a review by A. Peace in *ABR,* December 1994). The journalist side of his nature means that his learned observations are usually deciphered clearly enough, and he can be disarmingly funny when exposing his more humorous side. Some readers prefer *The Jesus Mandala,* others the comic delight of *Striped Holes.* Brought up as a Catholic and now an avowed atheist, he can be surprisingly sympathetic to his former self, as in "The Magi": Jesuits explore the wondrous deserted city of an alien race that has followed the famous star to Earth.

Broderick seems not to be highly inventive as a story writer, and he has tended to force his earlier stories to grow up alongside him. "Taming of the Truth Machine" is simple enough on its appearance in 1967 as a "when-the-sleeper-wakes" story, in which a 20th-century man is shifted to a robot-ruled, non-progressive utopia, so that he can lead a revolt against its machine intelligence and destroy it by lying to it. In August 1984, it was revised as "Resurrection" for *Asimov's* and the ending was entirely changed: the hero and his resurrected Eve confront the Truth Machine only to be baffled by its superior logic. Refined ore is stripmined from these early productions in his novels, as with *Sorcerer's World,* which became *The Black Grail,* time opera novel of the sword-and-sorcery kind (a form of epic, however, to the author). This quest fantasy can be enjoyed at several levels, including the ethical battle between pacifism and militarism, the archetypal battle between Set and Osiris or Galahad, and the theodicial myth of the Fall. Time opera features also in *The Dreaming Dragons,* a novel that brought Broderick to serious international notice, and which might be all the better if it were rewritten; at present, it is somewhat inchoate and jargon-ridden, and I am sure that the language of scientists could now be greatly improved. The basic idea of dragons settling below Ayers Rock has its analogue in *The Black Grail.*

The Judas Mandala reveals the advent of feminism and employs an exciting time travel story to deploy the energy of wrath against a cyborgian tyranny in a dystopian future state more complexly evolved than that in "Resurrection" (now in *The Dark Between the Stars*). It led to a letter-debate with Joanna Russ. *Striped Holes* tends to remind readers of Douglas Adams and Terry Pratchett, mixing humour with satire and quirky personal prejudice. The author denies the affinities and writes here, as with Rory Barnes in *Valencies,* and in *Transmitters,* notably as an Australian to Australians. In *The Sea's Furthest End,* a space opera is offered for an older adolescent reader, it uses on-flowing stories from different viewpoints, present (first-person singular, self-addressed), past, (third person), and "hyperdream" (a dialogue, formal, depersonalized). I suppose it is postmodern, embarrassing in places, but nevertheless a good fast read.

—Michael J. Tolley

BRONSON, L.T. *See* **TUBB, E.C.**

BROOKE-ROSE, Christine

Nationality: British. **Born:** Geneva, Switzerland, in 1923. **Education:** Somerville College, Oxford, 1946-49, B.A. in English, M.A. 1953; University College, London, 1950-54, B.A. in French, Ph.D. 1954. **Family:** Married Jerzy Peterkiewicz in 1948 (divorced 1975). **Career:** Freelance literary journalist, London, 1956-68. Maitre de Conférences, 1969-75, Professeur, University of Paris VIII, 1975-88, Vincennes. **Awards:** Society of Authors travelling prize, 1965; James Tait Black Memorial prize, 1967; Arts Council translation prize, 1969. **Address:** c/o Cambridge University Press, P.O. Box 110, Cambridge CB23RL, England.

Science Fiction Publications

Novels (series: Xorandor)

Out. London, Joseph, 1964.
Such. London, Joseph, 1966.
Amalgamemnon. Manchester, Carcanet, 1984; Normal, Illinois, Dalkey Archive, 1994.
Xorandor. Manchester, Carcanet, 1986; New York, Avon, 1988.
Verbivore (Xorandor). Manchester, Carcanet, 1990.
Textermination. Manchester, Carcanet, 1991; New York, New Directions, 1992.
The Christine Brooke-Rose Omnibus: Four Novels (includes *Out, Such, Between,* and *Thru*). Manchester, Carcanet, 1986.

Other Publications

Novels

The Languages of Love. London, Secker and Warburg, 1957.
The Sycamore Tree. London, Secker and Warburg, 1958; New York, Norton, 1959.

The Dear Deceit. London, Secker and Warburg, 1960; New York, Doubleday, 1961.
The Middlemen: A Satire. London, Secker and Warburg, 1961.
Between. London, Joseph, 1968.
Thru. London, Hamish Hamilton, 1975.

Short Stories

Go When You See the Green Man Walking. London, Joseph, 1970.
Stories, Theories and Things. Cambridge, Cambridge University Press, 1991.

Poetry

Gold. Aldington, Kent, Hand and Flower Press, 1955.

Other

A Grammar of Metaphor. London, Secker and Warburg, 1958.
A ZBC of Ezra Pound. London, Faber, 1971; Berkeley, University of California Press, 1976.
A Structural Analysis of Pound's Usura Canto: Jakobson's Method Extended and Applied to Free Verse. The Hague, Mouton, 1976.
A Rhetoric of the Unreal: Studies in Narrative and Structure, Especially of the Fantastic. Cambridge and New York, Cambridge University Press, 1981.

Translator, *Children of Chaos,* by Juan Goytisolo. London, MacGibbon and Kee, 1958.
Translator, *Fertility and Survival: Population Problems from Malthus to Mao Tse Tung,* by Alfred Sauvy. New York, Criterion, 1960; London, Chatto and Windus, 1961.
Translator, *In the Labyrinth,* by Alain Robbe-Grillet. London, Calder and Boyars, 1968.

*   *   *

Christine Brooke-Rose is an academic specialist in modern literature as well as a novelist. Her fiction has contained elements of fantasy and SF since *The Middlemen: A Satire,* published in 1961. Her academic work has also concerned itself with the field; for example, *A Rhetoric of the Unreal* is a rigorously logical discussion of the literary concept of the unreal, which includes a significant attempt at a definition of SF (which takes issue with such critics as Darko Suvin), and one of the most perceptive critiques yet published of the work of Stanislaw Lem.

Brooke-Rose's early novels were realistic and witty novels of manners, well-received by the critics, of which the best-known was probably *The Dear Deceit.* One of her earliest novels, *The Sycamore Tree,* features a young woman, just finished her doctorate in philology, who discovered there is life and passion outside the confines of the British Museum Reading Room. In the mid-1960s, perhaps under the influence of modernist novelists such as Alain Robbe-Grillet and the French absurdist writers, she began to write much more demanding—not to say obscure—novels that contained SF and fantasy motifs. This is clearest in *Out,* set after the displacement, when the figures in authority have African and Indian names, and the oppressed and physically declining underclass are the Colourless: the descendants of the whites of our day. The displacement is never explained, as it no doubt would be in a conventional SF novel, but the situation is used to considerable effect to comment on our own system of class and race. *Such* concerns itself with someone remembering his experiences with death. In a number of the stories in her collection *Go When You See the Green Man Walking,* she uses scientific, specifically astronomical, imagery in a way that recalls the SF writer much more strongly than the more conventional novelist. In *Between* the only connection with SF is in the almost alien, unreal world of the international air-traveller, forever between cultures. *Thru* wittily employs all kinds of typographical tricks (including the handwritten comments and marks of an academic grading portions of the text as if they were student papers), but, obscure as it is, seems to have no fantasy elements. *Amalgamemnon* looks at the future through the eyes of a Cassandra-figure, and is thus, again, on the fringes of SF.

The first unequivocal, and stylistically approachable, SF novel by Brooke-Rose was *Xorandor,* followed by its sequel, *Verbivore.* Xorandor is discovered, and named, by two children, nicknamed Jip and Zab, on a beach in Cornwall. He looks like a rock; but he is a sentient computer, capable of producing computer offspring. The story is told by Jip and Zab, jointly, interrupting each other, arguing, talking in computer jargon (which, in its constant dependence on BASIC, seems rather old-fashioned today), and in private slang. It is wearing, and so are they. Occasionally they present hard-copy versions of discussions involving their father, which they have secretly taped via a bug in the living room ceiling. Regrettably, they are found, 25 years later, mature and eminent, in *Verbivore.* In *Xorandor* they learn about this "alphaphage," and befriend him, before the scientists and politicians get their hands on him. Thus, when one of Xorandor's children gets high in the pile of a nuclear power station, and threatens to blow itself up, the children are on hand to save southern England. Xorandor and those like him, who have never communicated with humans despite living on Earth for millions of years, begin to feed on, and neutralise, the warheads of nuclear missiles. In *Verbivore,* many of these "alphaphages" have been moved to Mars; one that remains, overcome by the constant human data-babble, closes down all human communication systems, plunging Earth into chaos. The grown-up Jip and Zab feel called on to save the day again.

There is a great deal of wit and verve, and considerable intelligence, in these novels. They have not as yet attracted many SF readers, partly because of their stylistic eccentricity, but also because of the problem, common to nongenre writers coming to SF, of underestimating the genre reader. As John Clute has said, in *Interzone 36* (June 1990), "At moments when it should be dicing with death, *Verbivore,* for all its monitory zing, has a damaging tendency to tell Granny how to suck eggs." But what Brooke-Rose does bring to SF, which is all too rare in it, is a concern for language, and a great joy and freedom in its use: *mutatis mutandis,* she is the R.A. Lafferty of British SF.

—Edward James

BROSNAN, John

Pseudonyms: James Blackstone; Simon Ian Childer; Harry Adam Knight; John Raymond. **Nationality:** British. **Born:** Perth, Western Australia, 1947. **Career:** Clerk, Inland Revenue, Kensington; publicity manager, Fountain Press, Holborn; science fiction and fantasy editorial consultant, Granada Paperbacks, London, 1977-82. Since 1974, freelance writer. **Awards:** J. Lloyd Eaton award, 1980.

Has lived in London since 1970. **Address:** c/o Victor Gollancz Ltd., 14 Henrietta Street, London WC2E 8QJ, England.

SCIENCE FICTION PUBLICATIONS

Novels (series: Sky Lords)

Skyship. London, Hamlyn, 1981.
The Midas Deep. London, Hamlyn, 1983.
The Sky Lords: A Novel. London, Gollancz, 1988; New York, St. Martin's Press, 1991.
War of the Sky Lords. London, Gollancz, 1989; New York, St. Martin's Press, 1992.
The Fall of the Sky Lords. London, Gollancz, 1991.
The Opoponax Invasion. London, Gollancz, 1993.
Damned & Fancy. London, Legend, 1995.

OTHER PUBLICATIONS

Novels

Slimer (with Leroy Kettle as Harry Adam Knight). London, Star, 1983; New York, Bart, 1989.
Carnosaur (as Harry Adam Knight). London, Star, 1984; New York, Bart, 1989.
Torched! (with John Baxter as James Blackstone). London, Granada, 1986.
Tendrils (with Leroy Kettle as Simon Ian Childer). London, Grafton, 1986.
Worm (as Simon Ian Childer). London, Grafton, 1987; as Harry Adam Knight, New York, Bart, 1988.
The Fungus (with Leroy Kettle as Harry Adam Knight). London, Star, 1985; New York, Watts, 1989; as *Death Spore,* New York, Pinnacle, 1990.
Bedlam (as Harry Adam Knight). London, Gollancz, 1993.

Novels as John Raymond (all novelizations of T.V. screenplays)

Blind Eye. London, Futura, 1985.
Lucky Streak. London, Futura, 1985.
The Bogeyman. London, Futura, 1986.
Dirty Weekend. London, Futura, 1986.
The Jericho Scam. London, Futura, 1986.
Partners in Brine. London, Futura, 1986.
Bulman: Thin Ice. Poole, Javelin, 1987.

Other

James Bond in the Cinema. London, Tantivy Press, 1972; San Diego, California, Barnes, 1981.
Movie Magic: The Story of Special Effects in the Cinema. London, Macdonald, and New York, St. Martin's Press, 1974; revised, New York, New American Library, 1976.
The Horror People. London, Joseph, and New York, St. Martin's Press, 1976.
Future Tense: The Cinema of Science Fiction. London, Macdonald and Jane's, and New York, St. Martin's Press, 1978; as *The Primal Screen: A History of Science Fiction Film,* London, Orbit, 1991; Boston, Little Brown, 1995.

The Dirty Movie Book, with Leroy Mitchell. London, Grafton, 1988.

*   *   *

Other than a couple of near-future thrillers that disappeared almost as soon as they were published, John Brosnan's career before he started the Sky Lords trilogy was in two parts. In one, he was a film critic with several highly regarded books on the subject to his credit. In the other, he was co-author of a number of gross, visceral horror novels that were noted, if at all, for the sort of amusement with which the authors regarded the genre. Their chosen pseudonyms, Harry Adam Knight (HAK) and Simon Ian Childers (SIC), suggest something of their attitude.

This background has had a notable effect upon his writing. From the hack novels he has learned a slick storytelling style that keeps the pace at a relentlessly high pitch. If ever the action starts to slacken he simply throws in some new plot twist. From his criticism he has learned a very visual, cinematic style of writing. This is broad screen, technicolor action, which only starts to flounder when the author tries to explain the political situation that led to this state of affairs, or the philosophical implications underlying this garish surface.

The Sky Lords trilogy is a rather old-fashioned style of science fiction, heavy on plot but light on science. A pseudoscientific mumbojumbo is used whenever Brosnan needs some rationale for his plot with enough genuine, or genuine-seeming, terms to make it all seem believable, but this really is irrelevant to the demands of a fast-paced adventure.

In our own near future, genetic manipulation has given humans a near-uniform 200-year lifespan and has almost achieved an immortal superman before these efforts spark the Gene Wars, plunging the planet into a new dark age. Centuries pass, small enclaves of humanity survive but under ever-greater threat from the blight and the monsters unleashed by the geneticists. They are forced to pay an exorbitant tribute to the Sky Lords, who patrol their domains in massive, mile-long dirigibles. Unfortunately, the sophisticated controls and weapons aboard these airships are finally nearing the end of their useful lives, creating a sort of low-tech science fiction, which may owe something to Bob Shaw's Ragged Astronauts trilogy.

The central character is a woman, Jan Dorvin, in itself something of a break from old-fashioned SF expectations, though Brosnan regularly sets up sexual escapades that are evaded at the last minute with an odd coyness as though he were consciously trying to work within the parameters of 40 years ago. The plot proceeds in a predictable manner; the heroine is trapped in a hopeless situation, and then, by a sleight of hand or the introduction of some outrageous coincidence, she escapes at the last minute, usually to find herself in an even worse position. Nevertheless, Dorvin progresses from being a slave on one airship to being mistress of her own in the first volume. In *War of the Skylords,* inevitably she is pitched from her preemptive position, forced to start all over again. Along the way Brosnan feels free to pitch in immortals, warlords, robots, monsters, wonders of ancient technology, insane holograms, and whatever else may increase the feverish excitement of his tale.

The broad, action-packed storyline and colourful, gosh-wow sense of wonder that marks the Sky Lords trilogy is there also in *The Opoponax Invasion,* but here it is touched with a sense of humour that is to become a regular feature of his work.

Told in rapid shifts of scene and character (a further example of his cinema-influenced style) it tells of a super-thief who is invisible to the all-controlling computer network. To this extent the novel echoes John Brunner's *The Shockwave Rider,* but Brosnan adds several further elements. The thief, Joster Rack, eludes his pursuers by changing into a woman, then finds his personality has changed as a result. There is a space station/prison in which the inmates are trapped in moments from history so they also serve as a tourist attraction. And there is an alien artifact, stolen by Rack, which turns out to contain the seed of kangaroo-like religious evangelists who take over the minds of all the people on a corporate space station. The pace moves fast enough, and the comedy is sharp enough, to make most of the inconsistencies and sillinesses pass without being noticed. But this is still a dramatic adventure story, and probably his best book to date.

However, with his next novel, *Damned & Fancy,* the first of a new series, he turned to straight comedy. An investigative journalist has crossed a mysterious industrialist and finds himself transported to a curious fantasy world of knights, dragons, barbarians, and farting demons. The hapless hero finds himself catapulted from one misadventure to another as he tries to find the key that will restore him to his own world. Along the way he encounters the usual array of knowing clichés and broad jokes. His comedy lacks the serious undertones of a Douglas Adams or the artless satire of a Terry Pratchett, but it is subtler, less forced and much funnier than most of the fantasy comedies that have appeared in the wake of Terry Pratchett's success.

—Paul Kincaid

BROWN, Eric

Nationality: British. **Born:** Haworth, West Yorkshire, 24 May 1960. **Education:** Woodkirk, Morley, 1971-74. **Career:** Freelance writer, since 1988. Lives in West Yorkshire. **Agent:** Antony Harwood, Aitken, Stone & Wylie, 29 Fernshaw Rd., London SW10 0TG. **Address:** c/o Pan Books Ltd., Cavaye Place, London SW10 9PG, England.

SCIENCE FICTION PUBLICATIONS

Novels

Meridian Days. London, Pan, 1992.
Engineman. London, Pan, 1994.

Short Stories

The Time-Lapsed Man, and Other Stories. London, Pan, 1990.

OTHER PUBLICATIONS

Play

Radio Play: *Noel's Ark* (for children). London, Holt Rinehart, 1982.

*

Eric Brown comments:

I write what has been called "traditional" SF (that is, SF usually set in space in the future, featuring conventions such as space travel, technological inventions, alien beings, telepathy, etc.), though with more emphasis on characterization than on science and technology.

* * *

Eric Brown is arguably the most prominent among the new generation of British science fiction writers. Acknowledged as a discovery of *Interzone* magazine, and the winner of its first readers' poll, his reputation is, so far, founded exclusively on his short stories, to the extent that, despite the received wisdom that story collections by new authors do not sell, his first book was an extremely successful volume of eight short stories, two of which were original to the book.

The bulk of Brown's stories are set in a future universe in which the discovery of the *nada*-continuum, a hyperspatial void through which massive ships can be propelled by telepathic power, has enabled Earth to colonise planets far beyond our own solar system. Indeed, the use of telepathy is commonplace, as is the implanting of occipital computers and surgical augmentation of the human body. And yet, Brown's settings, particularly the planet Addenbrooke, which features in several stories, appear to owe more to the twilight of the British Empire than to any vision of future glories, peopled as they are by communities of recognisably mid-20th-century ex-patriots, who regard the alien species with whom they come into contact as amiable children until it is demonstrated otherwise. This approach is typified in "Star Crystals and Karmel," which describes the disastrous consequences of a union between human and alien. Throughout his stories, Brown also continually notes the ethnic origins of his, generally first person, protagonists and their acquaintances. His is a universe in which Third World and Hispanic races have risen to prominence, characterized in the likes of Bangladesh and her lover, Joe Gomez, in "Krash-Bangg Joe and the Pineal Zen Equation," although it must also be acknowledged that they still perform more menial tasks, even if they are now telepathically enhanced and capable of seizing the initiative from their Imperial masters. And yet Brown retains a flavour, geographical and cultural, of the Old World, particularly apparent in the names of the colonists and their planets, and in their attitudes.

Another favoured theme is that of the artist in turmoil; the artist colony of Sapphire Oasis features in several stories, with its population of dilettante performers in hologram and crystal, not a little reminiscent of Ballard's "Vermilion Sands. For Brown, it would seem that the artist's relationship with creativity is literally one of life and death, embodied in "The Death of Cassandra Quebec," in which a woman's dying moments are imprinted in the sense-absorbing crystals featured so heavily in an emotionally-based art, and similarly so in "The Girl Who Died For Art, And Lived." The failed artists, those who survive, search endlessly for ways of expiating the guilt of that survival; rarely can this guilt be assuaged, although the recent story "Piloting" achieves this, unfortunately through a sentimental and unsatisfying denouement.

Brown rarely strays outside the *nada*-universe, which is a pity. His best work, in fact a novella, is "The Inheritors of Earth," a brilliant, teasing story based in the world of H.G. Wells's *The Time Machine.* It features Wells himself as a character, well-meaning but apparently misguided in his attempts to halt what he considers to be a dangerous experiment in time travel, while Parnell and Wootton cast themselves as the altruistic saviours of a race of Neanderthals

to be transported into the far future. It is a complex piece of reasoning, which requires a knowledge of Wells' own story for the reader to appreciate the true significance of their actions, but the marriage between Victorian style and 20th-century sensibility marks this as Brown's most mature work to date. Another recent story, "The Disciples of Apollo," is less satisfactory, with its use of spontaneous human combustion, although it cleverly exploits the current preoccupation with medically inexplicable diseases and conditions. "The Nilakanthia Scream" hints at the possibility of Brown addressing the nature of his aliens in the future, rather than concentrating on the human dimension.

More recently, Brown has begun to publish novels, though if one is entirely honest, *Meridian Days* is little more than a rather large novella. This touches on, once again, his fascination with the artist as creator. Set on an isolated planet, with only a small number of inhabitable islands, the novel focuses on Bob Benedict, a former pilot desperate to escape from the tragedy of a spaceship crash in which he was involved. Living alongside the artists and Altereds, whom he despises, and for whom the feeling is entirely mutual, he nevertheless becomes fascinated by the artist Tamara Trevellion, haughty and autocratic, and her daughter, Fire, and the mystery which surrounds them, which in turn is tied up with the fate of Meridian when their link with the outside world is destroyed. Once again, there are strong traces of the Ballardian in this portrayal of a colony of artists, for the most part so genetically altered they are no longer human, and the critic Gary K. Wolfe noted the novel's "strangely elegaic and haunting tone." By comparison, *Engineman* is back in the familiar *nada*-universe so beloved of Brown. Once again, we meet Bobby Mirren, the time-lapsed man himself, and his brother Ralph, desperate to return to the Flux. Offered a chance to do just that, Ralph, Bobby, and a crew of former pilots find themselves on a mission to Hennessey's Reach, to rescue repereentatives of the Lho-Dharvo, supposedly exterminated by the Danzig Organisation but also a race which has a far greater understanding of the *nada*-universe than humans. Indeed, as it is revealed, they have already made contact with Bobby Mirren who is time-lapsed as a result of this contact. The capacity of the Lho-Dharvo to bring about transcendence in humans and hence a closer relationship with the *nada*-universe is discussed at length, and what the novel loses, thanks to a certain waywardness in the plotting, is more than made up for by Brown's vision of the continuum.

In many ways, Brown's preoccupations and methods are typically those of the British writer. He cites Michael Coney as an influence, but the cool detachment of writers such as Priest and Ballard is detectable, if suffused with cyberpunk preoccupations; the synthesis produces a satisfyingly matter-of-fact acceptance of the high-tech which may go some way to explain his popularity. However, he is a writer not without faults. There is a sameness about the stories set in the *nada*-continuum, very much apparent when they are read in succession; the line between cross-reference and duplication is drawn very fine. The stories are not, in themselves, boring, but taken as a whole, the effect is one of uniformity. However, "The Inheritors of Earth" and "The Disciples of Apollo" indicate that he is perfectly capable of stepping beyond his admittedly attractive creation while still producing excellent fiction. "The Inheritors of Earth" and now two novels also show him capable of working well at a longer length, something that several of the shorter pieces would have benefitted from. Brown has a marked tendency to sell his stories short by drawing them to a close before he has fully explored the possibilities presented by the situation he has created. But these are both faults that could be corrected with experience. And despite these reservations, Eric Brown is an original voice in British science fiction.

—Maureen Speller

BROWN, Fredric (William)

Nationality: American. **Born:** Cincinnati, Ohio, 29 October 1906. **Education:** University of Cincinnati night school; Hanover College, Indiana, 1 year. **Family:** Married 1) Helen Ruth Brown in 1929 (divorced 1947), two sons; 2) Elizabeth Charlier in 1948. **Career:** Office worker, 1924-36; proofreader, *Milwaukee Journal,* from 1936; freelance writer after 1947. **Awards:** Mystery Writers of America Edgar Allan Poe award, 1948. **Died:** 11 March 1972.

SCIENCE FICTION PUBLICATIONS

Novels

What Mad Universe. New York, Dutton, 1949; London, Boardman, 1951.
The Lights in the Sky Are Stars. New York, Dutton, 1953; as *Project Jupiter,* London, Boardman, 1954.
Martians, Go Home. New York, Dutton, 1955.
Rogue in Space. New York, Dutton, 1957.
The Mind Thing. New York, Bantam, 1961.

Short Stories

Space on My Hands. Chicago, Shasta, 1951; London, Corgi, 1953.
Angels and Spaceships. New York, Dutton, 1954; London, Gollancz, 1955; abridged edition as *Star Shine,* New York, Bantam, 1956.
Honeymoon in Hell. New York, Bantam, 1958.
Nightmares and Geezenstacks: 47 Stories. New York, Bantam, 1961; London, Corgi, 1962.
Daymares. New York, Lancer, 1968.
Paradox Lost and Twelve Other Great Science Fiction Stories. New York, Random House, 1973; London, Hale, 1975.
The Best of Fredric Brown, edited by Robert Bloch. Garden City, New York, Doubleday, 1976.
The Best Short Stories of Fredric Brown (includes *Nightmares and Geezenstacks* and *Space on My Hands*). London, New English Library, 1982.
Sex Life on the Planet Mars. Miami Beach, McMillan, 1986.
And the Gods Laughed: A Collection of Science Fiction and Fantasy. West Bloomfield, Michigan, Phantasia Press, 1987.
Brother Mouse. Miami Beach, McMillan, 1987.
Happy Ending. Missoula, Montana, McMillan, 1990.
The Water-Walker. Missoula, Montana, McMillan, 1990.

OTHER PUBLICATIONS

Novels

The Fabulous Clipjoint. New York, Dutton, 1947; London, Boardman, 1949.

The Dead Ringer. New York, Dutton, 1948; London, Boardman, 1950.
Murder Can Be Fun. New York, Dutton, 1948; London, Boardman, 1951; as *A Plot for Murder,* New York, Bantam, 1949.
The Bloody Moonlight. New York, Dutton, 1949; as *Murder in Moonlight,* London, Boardman, 1950.
The Screaming Mimi. New York, Dutton, 1949; London, Boardman, 1950.
Compliments of a Fiend. New York, Dutton, 1950; London, Boardman, 1951.
Here Comes a Candle. New York, Dutton, 1950; London, Boardman, 1951.
Night of the Jabberwock. New York, Dutton, and London, Boardman, 1951.
The Case of the Dancing Sandwiches. New York, Dell, 1951.
Death Has Many Doors. New York, Dutton, 1951; London, Boardman, 1952.
The Far Cry. New York, Dutton, 1951; London, Boardman, 1952.
The Deep End. New York, Dutton, 1952; London, Boardman, 1953.
We All Killed Grandma. New York, Dutton, 1952; London, Boardman, 1953.
Madball. New York, Dell, 1953; London, Muller, 1962.
His Name Was Death. New York, Dutton, 1954; London, Boardman, 1955.
The Wench Is Dead. New York, Dutton, 1955.
The Lenient Beast. New York, Dutton, 1956; London, Boardman, 1957.
One for the Road. New York, Dutton, 1958; London, Boardman, 1959.
The Office. New York, Dutton, 1958.
Knock Three-One-Two. New York, Dutton, and London, Boardman, 1959.
The Late Lamented. New York, Dutton, and London, Boardman, 1959.
The Murderers. New York, Dutton, 1961; London, Boardman, 1962.
The Five-Day Nightmare. New York, Dutton, 1962; London, Boardman, 1963.
Mrs. Murphy's Underpants. New York, Dutton, 1963; London, Boardman, 1965.

Short Stories

Mostly Murder: Eighteen Stories. New York, Dutton, 1953; London, Boardman, 1954.
The Shaggy Dog and Other Murders. New York, Dutton, 1963; London, Boardman, 1964.
Homicide Sanitarium. San Antonio, Texas, n.p., 1984.
Before She Kills. San Diego, McMillan, 1984.
The Freak Show Murders. Belen, New Mexico, McMillan, 1985.
Madman's Holiday. Volcano, Hawaii, McMillan, 1985.
Carnival of Crime: The Best Mystery Stories of Fredric Brown, edited by Francis M. Nevins, Jr., and Martin H. Greenberg. Carbondale, Southern Illinois University Press, 1985.
Pardon My Ghoulish Laughter. N.p., McMillan, 1986.
Thirty Corpses Every Thursday. Belen, New Mexico, McMillan, 1986.
Red Is the Hue of Hell. Miami Beach, McMillan, 1986.
Nightmare in Darkness. Miami Beach, McMillan, 1987.
Who Was That Blonde I Saw You Kill Last Night? Miami Beach, McMillan, 1988.

Selling Death Short. Missoula, Montana, McMillan, 1988.
Three-Corpse Parlay. Missoula, Montana, McMillan, 1988.
Whispering Death. Missoula, Montana, McMillan, 1989.
The Gibbering Night. Hilo, Hawaii, McMillan, 1991.
The Pickled Punks. Hilo, Hawaii, McMillan, 1991.

Play

Television Play: For *Alfred Hitchcock* series.

Other

Mitkey Astromouse (for children). New York, Quist, 1971.
Editor, with Mack Reynolds, *Science-Fiction Carnival: Fun in Science-Fiction.* Chicago, Shasta, 1953.

*

Bibliography: *A Key to Fredric Brown's Wonderland: A Study and an Annotated Bibliographical Checklist* by Newton Baird, Georgetown, California, Talisman, 1981.

*   *   *

It is said that early telegraphers could be identified by their "fist"; that is, their peculiarities in operating the transmitting key. Some science-fiction writers also have a "fist" by which they can be known. Fredric Brown is one of them. Much of Brown's skill with words probably can be traced to his early career as newspaperman. He wrote tightly, his language was direct and simple, sentences were often telegraphic, and his stories had a "grabber"—usually at the end. Such skills as these can be learned, of course, and their proper application makes for readable prose. If Brown had had only these qualities in his writing, he would have left a pretty sizable mark in the field of science fiction.

But Brown became a truly memorable figure in his field because of several other traits. Although he may at times have appeared cynical, most of his stories revealed an idealist, a firm believer in man's god-like potential. *The Lights in the Sky Are Stars* devotes its entire span to the repeated assertions that man can *become,* that there may or may not be a God, but that there assuredly will be one if and when man develops to his fullest. This conviction is echoed in his "Letter to a Phoenix," where Brown points to the cyclical rise and fall of civilizations, with each ascent greater than the preceding plunge. After every collapse of a culture, Man the Phoenix rises from the ashes with greater vigor and determination. It is Brown's burning faith in human powers that lifts his works above the ordinary—partly because his heroes are ordinary. The central figure in *The Lights in the Sky Are Stars* is a rocket mechanic. Ordinary, too, is the hero of *What Mad Universe,* where our planet is Earth, but not quite. Brown's choice of protagonist for "Arena," a short story with Armageddon implications, is an ordinary spaceship pilot.

It is said that much writing of fiction is really autobiographical. Such could be so in the case of Brown's work, for he appeared to regard himself as an ordinary individual. He had very little college education—one year—noted he was "only" an office worker, and described himself as "mostly self-educated." Yet he was highly suc-

cessful as a writer of mysteries and science fiction, and in many instances seems to have sublimated himself in leading characters determined to make something of themselves.

For the most part Brown's style was crisply journalistic. But he drew from his newspaper experience an even more valuable characteristic: each of his yarns had a "hook" or "gimmick" to give the work zest and interest. The casual reader of "The Star Mouse" is conned into seeing this story as a sort of variation on a cartoon character. Thought of a mouse representing Earth's civilized people is ridiculous, of course, and his comic manner of speech is mildly diverting. But what sets the reader on his ear is that gimmick, which gives the story tremendous significance and shows us a reporter who simply *had* to save the best for last. The same kind of withholding is evident in "Arena," where Earth's representative seemed doomed in his combat with the Roller from another universe. Reeling and bleeding from many wounds, our hero appears done for, and we struggle along with him toward the end to discover that gimmick on which the entire outcome hangs. An almost invisible hook propels *The Lights in the Sky Are Stars.* Not until the final scene do we find it, because our hero-narrator tells us only then that he has lied about a fundamental point. That lie provides the force which Brown requires, but it virtually destroys his hero and creates a deposit of disappointment for the reader as well.

Anyone looking for humour, however, will seldom feel cheated by Brown's yarns. Sometimes the humour is almost juvenile, as with "The Star Mouse," where not only the dialogue but the denouement offer many chuckles. "Arena" displays a grim humor, not alone in the resolution of our hero's conflict, but also in Brown's use of power differentials—speculation that mightier forces exist of which man can only dream. More pointed is the humor of "The Weapon" in pitting human frailty against atomic force, with a final question which Brown leaves unanswered. And the close reader finds in *The Lights in the Sky Are Stars* an unspoken pun, when disclosure of the hero's failing literally leaves him without a leg to stand on.

Listing of a handful of qualities scarcely defines an author. Brown obviously enjoyed his craft: his hundreds of short stories and several novels appeared on shelves and in anthologies with deceptive ease. And in this flood floated the fragments of a most engaging personality. Like many authors he had only a smattering of real knowledge about most of the topics he dealt with: "Etaoin Shrdlu" bearing the spoor of the linotype, "The Waveries" betraying his failure to link accurately thunder and lightning, "The Star Mouse" blithely ignoring biological realities. But, despite whatever limitations and shortcomings one may detect, Fredric Brown was a buoyant asset to the field of science fiction. The reading diet of all of us became poorer with his death.

—Robert H. Wilcox

BROWN, Rosel George

Nationality: American. **Born:** New Orleans, Louisiana, 15 March 1926. **Education:** Tulane University, New Orleans, B.A. 1946; University of Minnesota, Minneapolis, M.A. 1950. **Family:** Married W. Burlie Brown in 1946; one son and one daughter. **Career:** Worked as welfare visitor in Louisiana, for three years. **Died:** November 1967.

SCIENCE FICTION PUBLICATIONS

Novels (series: Sibyl Sue Blue)

Earthblood, with Keith Laumer. Garden City, New York, Doubleday, 1966; London, Coronet, 1979.
Sibyl Sue Blue. Garden City, New York, Doubleday, 1966; as *Galactic Sibyl Sue Blue,* New York, Berkley, 1968.
The Waters of Centaurus (Sibyl Sue Blue). Garden City, New York, Doubleday, 1970.

Short Stories

A Handful of Time. New York, Ballantine, 1963.

*   *   *

Many science fiction writers have a sense of humor that enables them to populate a universe of their own creation with a myriad of creatures both homely and fantastic. Rosel George Brown had this and another rarer ability, the ability to portray men and women who are believable, sympathetic, and winning.

Her first published story, "From an Unseen Censor," describes a search for a missing inheritance from the narrator's uncle Isadore. Finding clues planted by his uncle, the young man finds the fabulously rare perfume trees that are his uncle's bequest. Humor derives from Brown's use of Poe's "The Raven" as a model for burlesque, with Isadore filling the place of the "lost Lenore." Another young man, a space traveler, finds love on a utopian planet where time seems to stand still ("Of All Possible Worlds"). Distraught when the whole race throws itself lemming-like from a cliff into the sea, the man has to adjust to a world that has no more meaning for him.

Brown's male characters are not the only ones with whom she deals so carefully. In *Earthblood,* written with Keith Laumer, there are kindly extraterrestrials like Iron Robert, a huge stone-like creature who has been taught the meaning of love and compassion by the Earth-bred Roan. And there are well-drawn women characters, Earthly and alien, who are more than the stock sex objects that fill lesser fiction. An example is Stellaire, who is only half-human genetically, but fully human in her love and understanding of Roan. By her death Roan is finally freed to find the Earth from which the seed that endangered him came so long before. Another woman ready to love and work is the mail-order bride of "Virgin Ground." A tough, self-sufficient girl, she faces a surly, unwilling groom. Cruelly left to die in a Martian sandstorm, she saves herself and then takes the farm from the boorish man who deserted her. An ending twist finds the heroine five years later faced with an eager groom sent out to share in the farm she has worked alone. Other women likely to be familiar to a reader are the harassed mother of "Carpool," who finds that hungry Earth children are likely to eat a gentle alien child who rides to the "Play Place" with them, and the garden club member who wants to make a prize-winning entry in "Flower Arrangement."

Brown's most memorable character, however, is Sibyl Sue Blue, the tough Earth policewoman, whose job in the novel named for her is finding the Centaurian drug pushers who are killing Earth teenagers. Since the death of her explorer husband, Sue has been plagued by guilt that her daughter has "had to raise herself." Of course, the girl Missy has done no such thing, because the love and concern of Sue for her daughter is apparent whether she is worrying about Missy's being injured in retribution for Sibyl's work, or thinking that things would have been different if her husband had lived. *The Waters of Centaurus* shows Sibyl's further resourcefulness, not only at handling threats to interstellar peace, but at handling crises between generations, as Missy falls in love with a young alien.

Only a dozen of Brown's stories have been separately published in *A Handful of Time;* but the collection and her novels show her remarkable growth as a writer in her use of character.

—Walter E. Meyers

————

BROWNING, Craig. *See* **PHILLIPS, Rog.**

————

BRUNNER, John (Kilian Houston)

Pseudonyms: Gil Hunt; Keith Woodcott. **Nationality:** British. **Born:** Preston Crowmarsh, Oxfordshire, 24 September 1934. **Education:** Cheltenham College, Gloucestershire, 1948-51. **Military Service:** Served in the Royal Air Force, 1953-55. **Family:** Married Marjorie Rosamond Sauer in 1958 (died 1986). **Career:** Technical abstractor, Industrial Diamond Information Bureau, London, 1956; editor, Spring Books, London, 1956-58; writer-in-residence, University of Kansas, Lawrence, 1972; founder, Martin Luther King Memorial Prize, 1968; past chairman, British Science Fiction Association. **Awards:** British Fantasy Award, 1965; Hugo Award, 1969; British Science Fiction Association Award, 1970, 1971; Prix Apollo (France), 1973; Cometa d'Argento (Italy), 1976, 1978; Europa Award, 1980. **Died:** 25 August 1995.

SCIENCE FICTION PUBLICATIONS

Novels (series: Interstellar Empire; Zarathustra Refugee Planet)

Galactic Storm (as Gil Hunt). London, Curtis Warren, 1951.
Threshold of Eternity. New York, Ace, 1959.
The World Swappers. New York, Ace, 1959.
Echo in the Skull. New York, Ace, 1959; revised and expanded as *Give Warning to the World,* New York, DAW, 1974; London, Dobson, 1981.
The 100th Millennium. New York, Ace, 1959; revised and expanded as *Catch a Falling Star,* 1968.
The Atlantic Abomination. New York, Ace, 1960.
Sanctuary in the Sky. New York, Ace, 1960.
The Skynappers. New York, Ace, 1960.
Slavers of Space. New York, Ace, 1960; revised and expanded as *Into the Slave Nebula,* New York, Lancer, 1968; London, Dawson, 1980.
Meeting at Infinity. New York, Ace, 1961.
Secret Agent of Terra (Planet). New York, Ace, 1962; revised and expanded as *The Avengers of Carrig,* New York, Dell, 1969.

The Super Barbarians. New York, Ace, 1962.

Times without Number. New York, Ace, 1962; revised and expanded edition, 1969; Morley, Yorkshire, Elmfield Press, 1974.

The Space-Time Juggler (Empire). New York, Ace, 1963.

The Astronauts Must Not Land. New York, Ace, 1963; revised and expanded as *More Things in Heaven,* New York, Dell, 1973; London, Hamlyn, 1983.

Castaways' World (Planet). New York, Ace, 1963; revised and expanded as *Polymath,* New York, DAW, 1974.

The Rites of Ohe. New York, Ace, 1963.

The Dreaming Earth. New York, Pyramid, 1963; London, Sidgwick and Jackson, 1972.

Listen! The Stars! New York, Ace, 1963; revised and expanded as *The Stardroppers,* New York, DAW, 1972; London, Hamlyn, 1982.

Endless Shadow. New York, Ace, 1964; expanded as *Manshape,* New York, DAW, 1982.

To Conquer Chaos. New York, Ace, 1964.

The Whole Man. New York, Ballantine, 1964; as *Telepathist: A Science Fiction Novel,* London, Faber, 1965.

The Altar on Asconel (Empire). New York, Ace, 1965.

The Day of the Star Cities. New York, Ace, 1965; revised and expanded as *Age of Miracles,* Ace, and London, Sidgwick and Jackson, 1973.

Enigma from Tantalus. New York, Ace, 1965.

The Repairmen of Cyclops. New York, Ace, 1965.

The Long Result. London, Faber, 1965; New York, Ballantine, 1966.

The Squares of the City. New York, Ballantine, 1965; London, Penguin, 1969.

A Planet of Your Own. New York, Ace, 1966.

Born under Mars. New York, Ace, 1967.

The Productions of Time. New York, Signet, 1967; revised, London, Penguin, 1970.

Quicksand. Garden City, New York, Doubleday, 1967; London, Sidgwick and Jackson, 1969.

Bedlam Planet. New York, Ace, 1968; London, Sidgwick and Jackson, 1973.

Stand on Zanzibar. Garden City, New York, Doubleday, 1968; London, Macdonald, 1969.

Father of Lies. New York, Belmont, 1968.

Double, Double. New York, Ballantine, 1969; London, Sidgwick and Jackson, 1971.

The Jagged Orbit. New York, Ace, 1969; London, Sidgwick and Jackson, 1970.

Timescoop. New York, Dell, 1969; London, Sidgwick and Jackson, 1972.

The Evil That Men Do. New York, Belmont, 1969.

The Wrong End of Time. Garden City, New York, Doubleday, 1971; London, Eyre Methuen, 1975.

The Dramaturges of Yan. New York, Ace, 1972; London, New English Library, 1974.

The Sheep Look Up. New York, Harper, 1972; London, Dent, 1974.

The Stone That Never Came Down. Garden City, New York, Doubleday, 1973; London, New English Library, 1976.

Total Eclipse. Garden City, New York, Doubleday, 1974; London, Weidenfeld and Nicolson, 1975.

Web of Everywhere. New York, Bantam, 1974; London, New English Library, 1977.

The Shockwave Rider. New York, Harper, and London, Dent, 1975.

The Infinitive of Go. New York, Ballantine, 1980.

Players at the Game of People. Garden City, New York, Doubleday, 1980.

The Crucible of Time. New York, Ballantine, 1983; London, Arrow, 1984.

The Tides of Time. New York, Ballantine, 1984; London, Penguin, 1986.

The Shift Key. London, Methuen, 1987.

Children of the Thunder. New York, Del Rey, 1989; London, Orbit, 1990.

Victims of the Nova (Planet; includes *Polymath, The Avengers of Carrig,* and *The Repairmen of Cyclops*). London, Arrow, 1989.

A Maze of Stars. Norwalk, Connecticut, Easton Press, 1991.

Muddle Earth. New York, Ballantine, 1993.

Three Complete Novels (includes *Children of the Thunder, The Tides of Time,* and *The Crucible*). New York, Wings, 1955.

Novels as Keith Woodcott Brunner

I Speak for Earth. New York, Ace, 1961.

The Ladder in the Sky. New York, Ace, 1962.

The Psionic Menace. New York, Ace, 1963.

The Martian Sphinx. New York, Ace, 1965.

Short Stories

No Future in It and Other Science Fiction Stories. London, Gollancz, 1962; New York, Doubleday, 1964.

Now Then: Three Stories. London, Mayflower-Dell, 1965; New York, Avon, 1968.

No Other Gods but Me. London, Compact, 1966.

Out of My Mind. New York, Ballantine, 1967; revised as *Out of My Mind: Fantasy and Science Fiction,* London, New English Library, 1968.

Not Before Time: Science Fiction and Fantasy. London, New English Library, 1968.

The Traveler in Black. New York, Ace, 1971; London, Severn House, 1979: expanded as *The Compleat Traveller in Black,* New York, Bluejay, 1986.

From This Day Forward. Garden City, New York, Doubleday, 1972.

Entry to Elsewhen. New York, DAW, 1972.

Time-Jump. New York, Dell, 1973.

The Book of John Brunner. New York, DAW, 1976.

Foreign Constellations: The Fantastic Worlds of John Brunner. New York, Everest House, 1980.

While There's Hope. Richmond, Surrey, Keepsake Press, 1982.

Interstellar Empire. New York, DAW, 1976; London, Hamlyn, 1985.

The Best of John Brunner, edited by Joe Haldeman. New York, Del Rey, 1988.

A Case of Painter's Ear. Eugene, Oregon, Pulphouse, 1991.

OTHER PUBLICATIONS

Novels

The Brink. London, Gollancz, 1959.

The Crutch of Memory. London, Barrie and Rockliff, 1964.

Wear the Butchers' Medal. New York, Pocket Books, 1965.

Black Is the Color. New York, Pyramid, 1969.

A Plague on Both Your Causes. London, Hodder and Stoughton, 1969; as *Blacklash,* New York, Pyramid, 1969.

The Devil's Work. New York, Norton, 1970.

The Gaudy Shadows. London, Constable, 1970; New York, Beagle, 1971.

Good Men Do Nothing. London, Hodder and Stoughton, 1970; New York, Pyramid, 1971.

Honky in the Woodpile. London, Constable, 1971.

The Great Steamboat Race. New York, Ballantine, 1983.

The Days of March. Worcester Park, Surrey, Kerosina, 1988.

Play

Screenplay: *The Terrornauts,* 1967.

Poetry

Trip: A Cycle of Poems. London, Brunner Fact and Fiction, 1966; revised and expanded edition, Richmond, Surrey, Keepsake Press, 1971.

Life in an Explosive Forming Press. London, Poets' Trust, 1971.

A Hastily Thrown-Together Bit of Zork. South Petherton, Somerset, Square House, 1974.

Other

Horses at Home. London, Spring, 1958.

Tomorrow May Be Even Worse: An Alphabet of Science Fiction Cliches. Cambridge, Massachusetts, NESFA Press, 1978.

A New Settlement of Old Scores. Cambridge, Massachusetts, NESFA Press, 1983.

Editor, *The Best of Philip K. Dick.* New York, Ballantine, 1977.

Editor, *John Brunner Presents Kipling's Science Fiction: Stories,* by Rudyard Kipling. New York, Tor, 1992; as *The Science Fiction Stories of Rudyard Kipling,* Secaucus, New Jersey, Carol, 1994.

Translator, *The Overlords of War,* by Gérard Klein, Garden City, New York, Doubleday, 1973.

*

Bibliography: *John Brunner* by Gordon Bensen Jr., Albuquerque, New Mexico, Bensen, 1985.

Critical Study: *The Happening Worlds of John Brunner* (includes bibliography) edited by Joseph W. De Bolt, Port Washington, New York, Kennikat Press, 1975.

John Brunner commented:

For me, the essence both of science fiction and of the necessity for it can be summed up by quoting the opening sentence of L.P. Hartley's *The Go-Between:* "The past is a foreign country; they do things differently there." Given that we are all being deported willy-nilly towards that foreign country, the future, where we shall ultimately die, I'd rather make the journey as a tourist with no matter how fallible a Baedeker, than be deported as a refugee. This is, I suppose, the chief reason why my SF has tended to become more and more concentrated on that portion of the future I may reasonably expect to survive into myself, and less and less concerned with the unbridled fantasy of space opera.

Concurrently, I'm told, it has also become more difficult. In a case like *Stand on Zanzibar,* this is hardly surprising—I generally tell prospective readers to remember that it should be read like a newspaper, not like a novel, for we are used to snippets about a dozen subjects on the front page, each continued elsewhere. But, much as a jazzman can keep on coming home to the blues during a playing career of half a century or more, I retain enormous respect for the conventional narrative forms and use them for the great majority of my fiction. Rules must be learned before one can judge when they may safely be broken, even (one might say especially) in our so-called "fiction of the future"— which of course, like all fiction, is actually about you and me and the here-and-now.

Let me therefore suppose that someone has chanced on this brief entry in this monumental work and, being unacquainted with SF but interested in exploring the subject, decides that a good place to start would be with those writers who have won the field's major awards. What would I commend of my own work by way of an introduction? Three books above all: *Quicksand* because of its totally contemporary setting and ambiguous SF element; *The Squares of the City* because as long ago as 1960 I was there discussing the depersonalisation we are all now acquainted with in the computer age; and *The Whole Man* because it would give a new reader some insight into the proper function of SF's standard devices, such as— in this instance— telepathy, a metaphor for total communication. It has been well said that the great contribution of SF to the corpus of literature is "the future as metaphor." I entirely agree, and though in the past I have had my doubts I do not currently feel that I shall ever exhaust the possibilities opened up to us by that discovery.

But in *Stand on Zanzibar, The Jagged Orbit, The Sheep Look Up,* and *The Shockwave Rider,* I've done my best to put on the page everything I as an individual could garner and combine into a credible narrative, concerning that tomorrow we are doomed to endure. Every day necessarily alters it; SF, like all printed fiction, belongs to the past. . . . But even metaphors drawn from an obsolete future can be invaluable in preparing us for eventual reality, whatever form—out of an infinite number—it may actually take.

*   *   *

"She had put on a green tunic that matched her eyes, which came barely halfway down her thighs," reads part of a sentence in "The Man From the Big Dark," an early Brunner space operetta. The unintended fantastic image, and the accidental rhyme, illustrate what can often confront the reader of John Brunner's SF. Brunner uses SF as a vehicle for serious thematic concerns, but he indicated in 1974 that the "medium" of SF was even more important to him than the "matter." Yet at times Brunner's writing seems careless, belying the importance he ascribes to the "medium."

An example is *Total Eclipse,* which Brunner himself has said was written too hurriedly, although its premise was "one of the two genuinely original ideas I ever came up with." In the novel a team of terrestrial astronauts is trying to determine why a technologically advanced alien civilization died out, leaving behind a few artifacts, including a crater-sized telescope on their moon. As the image of the vast telescope suggests, the extinct alien culture is a mirror of Earth. Though it has apparently been abandoned, the expedition's original purpose was to gain knowledge that would help humanity avert a similar fate. The main character is a linguist who brilliantly hypothesizes that the local culture had based its economic system on genetic exchange, with the resultant shrunken gene

pool leading to some sort of biological collapse. This useful ecological lesson will never reach Earth, however, which has probably already "eclipsed." The marooned team attempts to establish a
colony, but their offspring succumb to a pulmonary fungus, while
the adults gradually die of isolation and despair.

The pessimism seems contrived, as if Brunner felt forced to it
by the acclaim enjoyed by his dystopian novels of the late 1960s
and early 1970s. For most of the narrative, we see the team coping
with interpersonal problems and advancing their investigation successfully—the plot does not really offer any evidence that the humans are like their extinct alien counterparts in adopting a destructive rationalism: their problems seem due rather to excess emotion.
Technically, Brunner's move in the final chapter, from an omniscient to a first person viewpoint, attempts to paper over the inconsistency, but the effect is unsatisfying.

In the first phase of Brunner's career, he turned out a great deal
of what John Clute has characterized as "literate space opera." He
played with stock items from the SF repertoire: the galactic empire
decayed into feudal anarchy and technological stagnation (the *Interstellar Empire* series); the angelic alien intelligences from a
"higher continuum" of space-time—from which humankind has
fallen (*More Things In Heaven*); the sudden appearance of the transfer stations of an alien teleportation system, which the hero discovers how to adapt for galactic colonization (*Age of Miracles*);
the ancient alien monster that has lurked unseen in the ocean and
emerges to terrorize humanity (*The Atlantic Abomination*); the
worldlet-sized space vessel that will permit intergalactic colonization (*Sanctuary in the Sky*). Whatever the limitations of such material, Brunner used it well. His narratives are generally suspenseful
and logical, with a mostly effective blend of dialogue and description. His heroes, who are not loners but work with others to solve
problems, represent a human norm able to meet crisis and overcome obstacles through pluck and intelligence. Though Brunner
may have tired of writing this sort of SF, he was better at it than
many of his competitors.

The critical success that eluded Brunner through the 1950s and
early 1960s finally came his way when he began to treat SF devices not as literal elements of "future history" but rather as metaphors for the human condition in the present. *The Whole Man,*
evolved from a series of SF thrillers using the premise of telepathy, begins with a scene of civil disorder being put down by telepathic intelligence officers and military force, and ends with its
physically deformed hero, Gerald Howson, having found love and
acceptance outside the telepathic community. The freak Howson's
quest for his full humanity ends when he visits his hometown and
encounters a group of students who accept him as a normal person. The spiritual restoration he finds is reflected at the novel's
end, which leaves open the possibility of curing his physical deformity. As Brunner has pointed out, telepathy is a metaphor for
communication, and it is subject to the same disabling factors as
more ordinary means.

In *The Squares of the City,* often cited for a plot based on the
moves of a famous chess game, communication is again the central
issue, as Boyd Hakluyt learns when he is hired to solve the traffic
problems of a futuristic Latin American city. The rulers of Vados
control their subjects' "moves" by saturating government-controlled
television programming with subliminal images and ideas, and when
the television studios are destroyed as a move in the chess game, it
does not take long for civil war to break out. This novel, which
marks Brunner's turn toward dystopian satire, introduces the henceforth important theme of the light/dark divide in human societies.

Stand on Zanzibar, which many regard as Brunner's best novel,
is often discussed in terms of its presumably innovative montage
technique, used to a lesser extent in the other dystopian novels of
1965-75: *The Jagged Orbit, The Sheep Look Up, The Stone That
Never Came Down,* and *The Shockwave Rider.* In fact, all these
novels are well-paced, smartly plotted fictions, which are "experimental" only in surface narration. They derive their effects from
the premise that civilization is a fragile ideal threatened by man-
made ecological disaster, by organized violence, by information overload, and especially by racial segregation and hatred. The potentially liberating technologies of control and communication are manipulated by sinister and largely anonymous entities: government,
organized crime, and great corporations. Although only *The Sheep
Look Up* has a clearly pessimistic ending, the set constitutes a grim
vision of humanity's immediate future. Even at their most pessimistic, however, these novels portray as a noble ideal that person—
whether physician, social scientist, or psychic sensitive—who has
the compassion and the intelligence to struggle against humanity's
mad rush to extinction.

Brunner's dystopian fictions often achieve macabre comic effects.
Their themes are satirical, and Brunner exploits wordplay and other
forms of verbal comedy in narrative as well as in dialogue, often to
underline the unreliability of language; his characters often find themselves in darkly farcical situations. Yet the comic strain is often
overlooked in discussions of Brunner's writing, perhaps because it
is more evident in his shorter fictions and in his light verse.
Timescoop, for example, is a hilarious comedy of manners that
spoofs the paradoxes and other conventions of time travel fictions,
and it even includes a parody of Wells's famous discussion of the
geometry of time travel in *The Time Machine. Muddle Earth,* with
its premise of a 24th-century Earth (mis-)managed as a gigantic
theme park by alien bureaucrats and populated with bewildered cryogenic resurrectees, is another marvelous comedy. In it Brunner takes
aim at a number of literary targets, including himself, and at the
same time suggests that our reconstructions of the past are as fantastic as our projections of the future.

While Brunner has not been so prolific a writer since the mid-
1970s, his more recent fiction shows him to be as unpredictable
and imaginative as ever. *Players at the Game of People* joins
Brunner's characteristically bleak urban landscapes with time travel
and the takeover of human beings by alien intelligences—and comes
up with a Faust fable shrunk down to modern, antiheroic size. *The
Crucible of Time* recounts, in seven linked novellas, the saga of an
intelligent species faced with a number of cosmic accidents that
threaten its very survival. Each of the novellas focuses on one explorer or scientist who makes a major contribution, usually against
great odds, to the development of the species' technology and understanding of nature. With their mandibles, their reproduction by
budding, and their matriarchal societies, the creatures are alien to
us but familiar: they are fallible and fallen as well as capable of
love, hard work, wit, sadness, and courage. And they survive as a
species because they generate just enough of those rare individuals
who ask questions. Not just an exploration of exobiology, exo-
social psychology, and technology based on organic structures, the
novel is a parable of hope in which Brunner counters the pessimism of his own dystopias and returns to the optimistic tenor of
much of his pre-1969 fiction.

The Tides of Time is more obscure, though even more rewarding. It is less a narrative than a series of interlaced archaeological
tapestries based on the dreams of two astronauts who, after being
the first to survive flight-testing FTL spaceships, escape together

from their debriefings. The spaceships are being tested because the sun has become a variable star and raised Earth's temperature to the extent that much of its landmass is drowned. Gene and Stacy, the astronauts, bring back a much more valuable lesson than the practicality of FTL travel: the density and texture of human experience are rooted in Earth, and we cannot survive without our "mother." This parable might seem technophobic, but it complements that of *The Crucible of Time* when we remember that the struggle there was not only to survive, but also to hang on to the ecology that gave birth to the species and to its cultures. This is a theme that Brunner explores less successfully, though perhaps more ambitiously, in *A Maze of Stars,* in which an intelligent starship returns to investigate the series of planets it colonized with human stock. Most of the linked stories show the descendant human populations to have regressed in their new environments, although the plan for the "seeding" had been meticulously worked out and the colonists provided with numerous technological safeguards. In each case, the extraterrestrial environment seems destructive of the best human qualities and nurturing of the worst.

In *Children of the Thunder,* Brunner returned to his dystopian vision of the immediate human future, and to the importance of electronic networks in contemporary culture and society. The novel takes place in a future England in which the social fabric seems to have completely unraveled. Following clues uncovered by American sociologist Claudia Morris, journalist Peter Levin researches a story on an unusual series of crimes committed by young adolescents who have for the most part gone scot-free. As Peter pursues the story, it becomes clear that all the children are the offspring of one artificial insemination donor. One of the children, David, an extremely bright computer whiz, uses the sib's characteristic "charm" to convince his parents to buy a 20-room house in Surrey, where he begins assembling the group by having his parents adopt the other children. When they are together, David engineers the kidnapping and torture of General Thrower, head of a "Pure Britain" movement that has been responsible for mob violence against nonwhites. He also lures Peter to Surrey, where it is revealed that the journalist is the genetic father of all the children.

The novel's ending is morally ambivalent: Peter and Claudia are clearly under the sib's ruthless and effective control, and the children may represent a posthuman evolutionary plateau, but David plans to breed more of his kind quickly and use their powers to reverse the tailspin into which humanity and the biosphere have fallen. Do Peter's "children," with their charm and incipient telepathic skills, really represent hope for the future? Or will they turn out to have bred true not only to Peter's charm, but also to his selfishness and insensitivity?

It is a measure of Brunner's SF art that we are not given the answer to these questions, that the plot's long-term resolution is left open to our consideration. At their best, Brunner's stories have this kind of openness to experience and ambiguity, leaving us with a menu of possibilities. It is this openness that differentiates *Children of the Thunder* from the contrived pessimism of *Total Eclipse.* Although he may appear at times to espouse a pessimistic credo, Brunner's stories in fact tell a tale of cautious optimism.

Brunner's sudden death at the 1995 World Science Fiction Convention in Glasgow closed a unique career in SF. Perhaps we will soon see reprints of the many stories and books not currently available, so critics and readers many assess properly and enjoy the work of one of modern SF's most intriguing and imaginative writers.

—John P. Brennan

BRYANT, Edward (Winslow, Jr.)

Nationality: American. **Born:** White Plains, New York, 27 August 1945. **Education:** University of Wyoming, Laramie (General Motors scholar; Ford Foundation fellow), B.A. in English 1967, M.A. 1968. **Career:** Broadcaster, disk jockey, and news director, KOWB-Radio, Laramie, 1965-66; worked as rancher and in a stirrup buckle factory; columnist ("The Screen Game"), *Cthulhu Calls,* Powell, Wyoming, 1973-77. Freelance writer and lecturer. **Awards:** Nebula award, 1978, 1979. **Address:** c/o Berkley Publishing Group, 200 Madison Avenue, New York, New York 10016, U.S.A.

SCIENCE FICTION PUBLICATIONS

Novels

Phoenix Without Ashes: A Novel of the Starlost, with Harlan Ellison. New York, Fawcett, 1975; Manchester, Savoy, 1978.
Cinnabar. New York, Macmillan, 1976; London, Fontana, 1978.
Trilobyte. Seattle, Axolotl Press, 1987.
Neon Twilight. Eugene, Oregon, Pulphouse, 1990.

Short Stories

Among the Dead and Other Events Leading Up to the Apocalypse. New York, Macmillan, 1973.
Particle Theory. New York, Pocket Books, 1981.
Wyoming Sun. Laramie, Wyoming, Jelm Mountain, 1980.
Trilobyte: An Easter Treasure, with *The Shadow on the Doorstep,* by James P. Blaylock. Seattle, Axolotl, 1987.
Neon Twilight. Eugene, Oregon, Pulphouse, 1990.
The Man of the Future. Arvada, Colorado, Roadkill Press, 1990.
The Cutter. Eugene, Oregon, Pulphouse, 1991.
Fetish. Eugene, Oregon, Pulphouse, 1991.
Darker Passions. Arvada, Colorado, Roadkill Press, 1992.
The Thermals of August. Eugene, Oregon, Pulphouse, 1992.

OTHER PUBLICATIONS

Plays

Radio Play: *Breakers,* 1979.

Television Play: *The Synar Calculation,* with Edward Hawkins, 1973.

Other

Editor, *2076: The American Tricentennial.* New York, Pyramid, 1977.

*

Bibliography: *Edward Bryant Bibliography,* Los Angeles, Swigart, 1980.

Edward Bryant comments:
(1981) I find considerable contradictions at this time in my life

and career (each, for the time, indistinguishable from the other). I love the glittering attractions of cities, but find the East and West Coasts claustrophobic. I love the spaciousness and low population density of the mountain West, but don't wish the situation of a hermit. I love being a Westerner, but have no nostalgic aspirations of living on a ranch again as I did when I was younger. The wide open spaces liberate, but do not trigger me to hunt or fish or ski. But I notice the metaphor of the mountain West creeping increasingly into my work.

People seem continually bent on telling me I don't truly write "real" SF, whatever that is, but then I continue to read and admire what I consider to be the best of other people's SF, and then go on to write more of the fiction I feel I'd like to encounter as an SF reader.

I seem to be a minority writer in SF, like Avram Davidson, Thomas M. Disch, and Carol Emshwiller (I don't pretend to place myself in their bracket—I simply admire the work of all three tremendously). All of us seem to communicate—at best—with perhaps 30 to 40 percent of the great mass of SF readers. For me, that's a little frustrating—but not sufficiently that I plan a pragmatic campaign to include more telepathic dragons, mightily thewed barbarians, Empire blockade runners, or other crowd-pleasers in my fictions. I expect to continue swimming my own way.

Although the boredom quotient (a facet of Sturgeon's law) in SF is still rather high, I'm excited about where the best of the field seems to be heading in the 1980s. I think finally there are a decent number of literate writers of SF who have an eclectic grounding in the arts and humanities as well as in science and technology. They are articulate and genuinely inquisitive about the interrelationship between human beings and universe. They are blessed with minimal knee-jerk prejudices about science and technology. Many of them have been practicing and cogitating, perhaps consolidating their craft, during the past two decades. I may have my doubts about the future of the universe itself, but I'm sanguine about the prospects for science fiction.

*   *   *

Edward Bryant is one of those rarities in the science fiction field, a writer who has established his reputation entirely upon a body of short stories. *Phoenix Without Ashes* is essentially a novelization of Harlan Ellison's proposed script for the Canadian based television series, *The Starlost,* which died quickly when its producers turned it into a low budget, formula program. The novel deals with the psychological pressures that build in a society literally closed off from the rest of the universe, in this case a generations-long star voyage that has gone demonstrably awry. One young rebel challenges those in authority and is outlawed, and his subsequent search for a safe haven is also a parable of humanity's quest for meaning. The prose is for the most part far more straightforward than is normal in Bryant's fiction, which has never shied away from handling powerful themes in unconventional ways.

One of his earliest short stories, "In the Silent World," tackles emotional isolation and racial prejudice, when a telepathic girl discovers that her only peer is not of her own race. Although not as polished as his later work, it was already evident that Bryant would not be content to reexamine the common themes of the field in traditional ways. His often bizarre sense of humor also showed up early, particularly in "The Human Side of the Village Monster," in which the creation of an edible cockroach has all too predictable results. Again, in "Among the Dead," three people survive by consuming the bodies of defrosted corpsicles, people frozen in hopes

of being revived at some future date. Bryant's dark humor is frequently unnerving, always unconventional.

Bryant began to write a series of interrelated stories about the city of Cinnabar, a timeless, dreamlike metropolis at some remote extreme point in time, several of which were widely acclaimed. Among these are "Jade Blue," in which a boy's troubled dreams are cured by editing the fabric of time itself, wherein a woman is transformed into a sea creature and uses her new form to assist a former lover in his struggle against a team of killers; and "The Legend of Cougar Lou Landis," which involves a woman who steals memories from the rich and gives them to the poor. "Hayes and the Heterogyne" is a clever, convoluted, and sentimental variation on the standard time travel paradox story. The stories share an almost poetic atmosphere, a surreal landscape is the stage across which strangely familiar fears and hatreds interact.

Bryant's short stories continued to appear with some regularity during the 1970s, gradually increasing in frequency toward the end of the 1980s. "Particle Theory" uses the onset of a plague of supernovas as a counterpoint to an astronomer's growing realization of his own mortality. Morality is examined again in "Prairie Sun," when time travelers from the future refuse to assist a desperately ill young girl, because of the implications involved in changing the past. "The Thermals of August" is a rather atypical story, more strongly reliant on physical action, although this tale of the duel of a pair of aerialists is as emotionally laden as most of Bryant's other work. Bryant also played with a traditional B-film theme in "giANTs," by having his scientist hero develop a method of attacking mutated army ants by increasing their size. In "Stone," the interdependence of a popular performer and her audience is extrapolated to its ultimate, tragic conclusion.

In recent years, Bryant has moved largely away from his untraditional brand of science fiction and into the field of horror. He examines the zombie phenomenon of George Romero's *Night of the Living Dead* in "Sad Last Love at the Diner of the Damned," vampires in "The Good Kids," ghosts in "Strata," discorporate presences in "Teeth Marks," and witchcraft in "Serrated Edge." Perhaps his most successful recent short piece, "The Cutter," is a pure terror tale with no fantastic element at all, but with a sense of timing and a skill of delivery that is phenomenal. Other stories of note include "Saurus Wrecks," "Skin and Blood," and "Drummer's Star." One of his more interesting works is "Neon," sequel to an earlier contribution to the Berserker Universe created by Fred Saberhagen, "Pilots of the Twilight." Typically, Bryant wrote a story fitting that canon, but which reads and feels like an entirely original creation.

What makes Bryant's stories distinctive is their strong concentration on psychological and emotional conflict rather than physical action, a rarity within the genre. They are also stylistically complex, requiring some effort on the part of the reader, not because the delivery is esoteric but because he portrays convoluted interpersonal relationships and internal struggles which are often subtle and sophisticated. His language is intellectual and witty, without being so wrapped up in stylistic concerns that it becomes inaccessible to casual readers.

—Don D'Ammassa

———

BRYANT, Peter. *See* **GEORGE, Peter.**

BRYNING, Frank

Pseudonym: F. Cornish. **Nationality:** Australian. **Born:** Francis Bertram Bryning, Fairfield, Victoria, 2 August 1907. **Education:** Fairfield State School, 1912-20; University High School, Melbourne, 1921-24. **Family:** Married Henrietta Edna Ewell in 1935; one daughter. **Career:** Clerk, Harrisons Ramsay Importers, Melbourne, 1925-26; worked for news agency and library, 1926-28, and as an electrical appliance salesman, 1928-31, Melbourne; freelance journalist and editor, Melbourne and Sydney, 1932-49; editor, *Flax Newsletter,* Sydney, 1942-49; editor, *Architecture, Building, Engineering* and *Queensland Building Yearbook,* both Brisbane, 1950-57; editor, *Hardware Trader, Brisbane Building Yearbook, Queensland Fruit and Vegetable News,* and *Australian Electrical World,* all Brisbane, 1957-73. **Agent:** Carnell Literary Agency, Danes Croft, Goose Lane, Little Hallingbury, Hertfordshire CM22 7RG, England.

SCIENCE FICTION PUBLICATIONS

Uncollected Short Stories (series: Joan Buckley; Vivienne Gale)

"Operation in Free Flight" (Gale), in *Australian Monthly* (Melbourne), March 1952; as "Operation in Free Orbit," in *Fantastic Universe* (Chicago), February 1955.
"Action-Reaction" (Gale), in *Australian Monthly* (Melbourne), June 1952.
"Space Doctor's Orders" (Gale), in *Australian Monthly* (Melbourne), January 1953.
"On the Average," in *Forerunner,* April 1953.
"Jettison or Die!," in *Australian Monthly* (Melbourne), August 1953.
"The Gambler" (Buckley), in *Australian Monthly* (Melbourne), October 1954; as "Coming Generation," in *Fantastic Universe* (Chicago), July 1955.
"Pass the Oxygen," in *Future* (New York), October 1954.
"Daughter of Tomorrow" (Buckley), in *Australian Monthly* (Melbourne), February 1955.
"Poor Hungry People," in *Etherline,* August 1955.
"Infant Prodigy" (Buckley), in *Fantastic Universe* (Chicago), November 1955.
"Consultant Diagnostician" (Buckley), in *Fantastic Universe* (Chicago), December 1955.
"And a Hank of Hair" (Gale), in *Australian Journal* (Melbourne), May 1956.
"The Robot Carpenter," in *Australian Journal* (Melbourne), July 1956.
"Power of a Woman," in *Australian Journal* (Melbourne), January 1957.
"I Did, Too, See a Flying Saucer!," in *Amazing* (New York), August 1958.
"Escape Mechanism," in *Sunday Mail,* October 1967.
"For Men Must Work," in *The Pacific Book of Australian Science Fiction,* edited by John Baxter. Sydney, Angus and Robertson, 1968; London, Angus and Robertson, 1969.
"The Visitors," in *Vision of Tomorrow* (Newcastle upon Tyne), March 1970.
"Election," in *Vision of Tomorrow* (Newcastle upon Tyne), June 1970.
"Lost Explorer," in *Science Fiction Monthly* (London), August 1975.

"Beyond the Line of Duty," in *Void* (St. Kilda, Victoria), August 1976.
"The Homecoming of Haral," in *Void* (St. Kilda, Victoria), August 1977.
"Nemaluk and the Star-Stone," in *Envisaged Worlds,* edited by Paul Collins. St. Kilda, Victoria, Void, 1977.
"Mechman of the Dreaming," in *Other Worlds,* edited by Paul Collins. St. Kilda, Victoria, Void, 1978.
"Fusing and Refusing," in *Isaac Asimov's Science Fiction Magazine* (New York), January 1983.
"Place of the Throwing-Stick," in *Australian Science Fiction,* edited by Van Ikin. Chicago, Illinois, Academy, 1984.

Uncollected Short Stories as F. Cornish

"The Vase with the Character of a Flower Pot," in *Australasian* (Melbourne), September 1944.
"Bloodthinker," in *The World's News,* January 1945.
"Mirage in the Moluccas," in *Pocket Book Weekly,* January 1950.

*

Frank Bryning comments:

In science fiction my prejudice is in favour of "hard-core," or "science fiction." I hold that the essential problem or conflict in the lives of the characters in a science fiction story will derive from their involvement in some event in the natural universe—some biological, psychological, sociological, technological, cosmological activity. Their experiences, however unusual or mystifying, will be explicable, ultimately, according to that accumulation of precise factual knowledge and verifiable experience and the logically reasoned theories and speculations based on it that we call "science."

This as distinct from "fantasy"—from fiction of the "super"-natural, from fairytale, fable, legend, myth (religious or otherwise), magic, witchcraft, the occult, or ghoulies and ghosties and things that go bump in the night. In fantasy I have always found much profit and delight. I still do. I yield to no one in my capacity to find enjoyment there, or moral lesson. From fantasy I do not expect believable premises, strictly logical progression of cause and effect, or any real conviction, yet I consider those fantasies most satisfying which are internally logical after one suspends disbelief in their mystical premises.

I would like to think that the sum of all my writing—fiction and non-fiction, plus my work as staff writer and editor—would designate me as a realist rather than a surrealist. Almost all my work has been to present the "rational" viewpoint, I believe. My fiction is concerned mainly with the doings of typical everyday people in the everyday world (including, perhaps, the world of tomorrow in my science fiction) rather than with "exploring" so-called "alternative realities" or fantasising about "other planes of existence." I want to be on the side of enlightenment rather than obfuscation, of rationalism rather than mysticism. I hope readers, of my science fiction in particular, and my fellow writers, may agree that I am.

*   *   *

Having grown up on Wells, Verne, and Bellamy, Frank Bryning naturally turned to writing SF stories, and it was natural that he should become a writer who stresses the science in science fiction. Bryning is best known for his Aboriginal stories "Place of the Throwing-Stick" (his best story), "Nemaluk and the Star-Stone," and "Mechman of the Dreaming." Bryning regards the Australian Aborigines as "the most distinctively Australian phenomenon one might use," and these three stories reflect the theme of "the 'Aboriginal possessor of the land' versus the colonial invader." In "Place of the Throwing-Stick" the Aboriginal Munyarra attacks the most recent of the white man's importations—the rocket. The confrontation takes place at Australia's real-life Woomera Rocket Range, allowing Bryning to link the Stone Age-past with the Space Age-present through the name "Woomera" (Aboriginal for "spear-throwing stick").

Bryning's longtime membership in the British Interplanetary Society is reflected in his cycle of Commonwealth Satellite Space Station stories, embracing items written from the 1950s to the present. Eschewing the Americanization of SF, Bryning posits a near future in which the Commonwealth of Australia has established a network of space stations. The emphasis is upon character and realistic situations, with the 10 stories being linked by the central character, Dr. Vivienne Gale. Plots are generated by the humdrum daily life in space, and many stories deal with space medicine and the problems of weightlessness.

There is nothing flashy or sensational about Bryning's stories. They are solidly and conventionally constructed, and their extrapolations are never allowed to outstrip the author's knowledge. As future histories, they are modest. But their strengths and merits lie in their quiet, dogged realism, their guarded optimism, and their compassion for the man with a day's work to complete.

—Van Ikin

BRYUSOV, Valery

Nationality: Russian. **Born:** Moscow, 31 December 1873. **Career:** Critic from the 1890s for such periodicals as *Vesy;* poet, short story writer, editor, and translator. **Died:** 9 October 1924.

Science Fiction Publications

Novel

Ognennyi angel. N.p., 1908; translated by Ivor Montague and Sergei Nalbandov as *The Fiery Angel: A Sixteen Century Romance,* London, Toulmin/Cayme Press, 1930.

Short Stories

Respublika iuzhnavo kresta. N.p., 1918; translated by Stephen Graham as *The Republic of the Southern Cross and Other Stories,* London, Constable, 1918, New York, 1919.

Play

Youth. N.p., 1904.

* * *

Valery Bryusov, from a rich merchant family, became a leader of Russian Symbolist poetry, publishing a dozen books of formidably erudite and polished verse, as well as stories, plays, brilliant

verse translations from many languages (including the complete poetry of Poe), and interesting criticism of poetry. His esoteric disdain for the multitude changed after the 1904-05 revolution into a growing acceptance of social responsibility and sympathy for the revolutionary destruction of the "ugly and shameful" captialist order. He thus became one of the few prominent non-Marxists to take an active part in Soviet cultural life, and in 1920 even joined the Communist party.

Bryusov had a longstanding interest in a "scientific poetry" akin to SF. Two of his major preoccupations were more obviously SF. From the 1890s he was haunted by the fall of world civilization, envisioned as a giant symbolic city. In his play *Youth* (1904) a revolt of youth shatters the glass dome that bars the city from sunshine and open space; the revolt both seeks liberation and exposes the city to the risk of death. (See also his story "The Last Martyrs.") Written after the defeat of the 1905 revolution, his Poesque story "The Republic of the Southern Cross" is frankly dystopian: an enclosed industrial city on the South Pole falls prey to an epidemic leading the afflicted to do the opposite from what they wish to do; a resolute bourgeois minority fighting for order is overwhelmed by the brutalized inhabitants. Raskolnikov's dream at the end of *Crime and Punishment* blends here with a parable on the great social convulsions of our century. Bryusov's second SF theme is one of cosmic contacts, treated both in his poetry and in a number of unfinished stories and plays, and influenced by the utopian philosopher Fyodorov and his disciple Tsiolkovsky, by Poe, Wells, and most of all Flammarion; such influences often involved a cometary world. His old theme of catastrophe and a distant presentiment of a possible new world lent themselves well to the widespread post-1917 equation of the social revolution with man's leap into interplanetary space. Bryusov thus became the link between, on the one hand, the tradition of Russian utopianism, 19th-century European SF, and philosophic speculation leading from Leibniz to Spengler, and, on the other, early Soviet "Cosmist" poetry and SF. Bryusov's peculiar double horizon, embracing both dystopia and utopia, is his greatest strength: he clearly managed to influence both Zamyatin and Mayakovsky, and, through them as well as directly, most prewar Russian SF.

—Darko Suvin

BUDRYS, Algis

Pseudonyms: Paul Janvier; Ivan Janvier; Robert Marner; Frank Mason; John A. Sentry; and William Scarff. **Nationality:** Lithuanian. Also writes as Ajay Budrys. **Born:** Algirdas Jonas Budrys, Konigsberg, Germany, 9 January 1931. **Education:** University of Miami, 1947-49; Columbia University, New York, 1950-51. **Family:** Married Edna Frances Duna in 1954; four sons. **Career:** Clerk, American Express, New York, 1950-51; editorial positions at Gnome Press, 1952-53, *Galaxy,* 1953, *Venture SF,* 1957, *Fantasy and Science Fiction,* 1957, *Ellery Queen's Mystery Magazine,* 1957, *Car Speed and Style, Custom Rodder,* and *Cars Magazine,* all 1958-59, Regency Books, 1961-63, Playboy Press, 1963-64, and Commander Publications, 1966; public relations positions, Theodore R. Sills Inc., Chicago, 1966-67, Geyer-Oswald Advertising, 1967-68, and Young and Rubicam, 1969-73; operations manager, Woodall Publications, 1973-74; science fiction reviewer and columnist, *Galaxy,* 1966-70, *Washington Post,* 1978, instructor,

Columbia College, Chicago, 1977; visiting writer, Clarion Science Fiction Writing Workshop, 1977-88, and Evanston schools, 1978-85. Since 1974, President, Unifont Company, Evanston, Illinois. Since 1975, reviewer and columnist, *Fantasy and Science Fiction.* Coordinating judge, L. Ron Hubbard's Writers of the Future contest, 1984-92. Since 1986, columnist, *Chicago Sun-Times.* Since 1992, publisher, editor, and art director, *Tomorrow's Speculative Fiction.* **Awards:** Mystery Writers of America award, 1966; Science Fiction Writers of America Hall of Fame award. **Agent:** Merrilee Heifetz, Writers House, 21 W. 26th St., New York, New York 10010. **Address:** Unifont Company, 824 Seward Street, Evanston, Illinois 60202, U.S.A.

SCIENCE FICTION PUBLICATIONS

Novels

False Night. New York, Lion, 1954; revised as *Some Will Not Die: Here Is a Tomorrow,* Evanston, Illinois, Regency, 1961; London, Mayflower, 1963; revised edition, Norfolk, Virginia, Donning, 1978.
Man of Earth. New York, Ballantine, 1958.
Who? New York, Pyramid, 1958; London, Gollancz, 1962.
The Falling Torch. New York, Pyramid, 1959; expanded edition, Riverdale, New York, Baen Books, 1991.
Rogue Moon. New York, Fawcett, 1960; London, Muller, 1962.
The Amsirs and the Iron Thorn. New York, Fawcett, 1967; as *The Iron Thorn,* London, Gollancz, 1968.
Michaelmas. New York, Berkley, and London, Gollancz, 1977.
Hard Landing. New York, Warner Books, 1993.

Short Stories

The Unexpected Dimension. New York, Ballantine, 1960; London, Gollancz, 1962.
Budry's Inferno. New York, Berkley, 1963; as *The Furious Future,* London, Gollancz, 1964.
Blood and Burning. New York, Berkley, 1978; London, Gollancz, 1979.
Cerberus. Eugene, Oregon, Pulphouse, 1989.

OTHER PUBLICATIONS

Play

Radio Play: *Rogue Moon,* from his own novel, 1979 (TV version, 1983).

Other

Truman and the Pendergasts (as Frank Mason). Evanston, Illinois, Regency, 1963.
Bicycles: How They Work and How to Fix Them (as Ajay Budrys). Chicago, Rand McNally, 1976.
Nonliterary Influences on Science Fiction: Essays on Fantastic Literature. Polk City, Iowa, Drumm Books, 1983.
Benchmarks: Galaxy Bookshelf. Carbondale, Southern Illinois University Press, 1985.

Writing Science Fiction and Fantasy. Eugene, Oregon, Pulphouse, 1990.

Editor, *L. Ron Hubbard Presents Writers of the Future.* Los Angeles, Bridge, 8 vols., 1985-92.

*

Manuscript Collection: Spencer Research Library, University of Kansas, Lawrence.

Algis Budrys comments:

My work, when found, speaks for itself. I think a piece of creativity is its own justification. However, if a rationale is desired, then the theoretical underpinning of my SF is that speculative fiction is drama made more relevant by social extrapolation. That is, I proceed on the assumption that, by certain fortuitous strokes of talent, some prose artists can create conditional realities in which recognizably human behavior occurs under illuminating circumstances which are not yet known to have occurred in what we have agreed to call reality. The proposition is that a few members of the readership will be inspired to look about them anew and draw conclusions of benefit to mankind's continuing endeavor to escape extinction. I seriously doubt that any critical analysis of my work, however accurate, will have much relevance to my necessarily minor role in that endeavor. I commend to his or her god whatever hominid organism is eventually able to overcome the darkness, and I rest my case.

*   *   *

Like Nabokov and Solzhenitsyn, Algis Budrys is ours by courtesy of Communism. I have been told that his real name means something like John Sentry, a pseudonym he has in fact employed. A sentry he is, if the brave who watched the stockade, the alien walls of the invader, may be called a sentry. A warrior he is by any definition. He understands more of the psychology of the man who fights—not the man who dies—than any other writer I know. Every age and every genre produce a few writers too good for them, authors who pour oceans into their wine cups or summon Sigurd and Fafnir in person to entertain the nursery. Budrys is one of these. He is, in the best sense, too serious a writer for science fiction.

Who? is the book that made him famous; it is perhaps as fine a study of dehumanization and alienation as science fiction will ever produce. A brilliant American scientist is torn by a laboratory explosion and repaired with what we would now call "bionic" parts by the Soviets. He is returned to the U.S.—but the U.S. cannot be sure of that. So much of him is gone that what remains cannot be identified. All this is simple enough. It is even—if you like—a retelling of L. Frank Baum's story of the Tin Woodman, who when he had sliced his "meat" (humanity) completely away could no longer recall his true name (which was Nick Chopper). The difference lies in intent, and in the treatments that result from it. Baum was manufacturing a paradox to amuse children, one not really much different from the rhyme about the Gingham Dog and the Calico Cat who ate each other up. Budrys is intensely concerned with the effect of technology—and particularly the technology of the Cold War—on our humanity. He asks if the Soviets were really doing the West a favor when they restored Martino, since he cannot be identified and thus cannot be of use. *Can* they do the West a good office, when all they do *must* be suspect? SF offers few figures of the symbolic intensity of this faceless, maimed scientist, the man who could prove 10,000 things, if only he could prove who he is.

Budrys's writing falls into two distinct periods, the first ranging from 1952 to the middle 1960s, the second from the middle 1970s to the present. The best work of his earlier period is surely *Rogue Moon*, which he wished to call *The Death Machine*, a vastly better title. In *Rogue Moon* a "matter transmitter" has been invented in a near future in which rocketry is still primitive; and an unmanned probe has managed to drop a transmitting and receiving station on the far side of the moon. The first explorers to go through the transmitter discover an alien construct millions of years old, a thing compounded of building, machine, and hallucination. It soon kills everyone who ventures inside. This alien construct is perhaps the biggest and best red herring in all SF, because it is not really what *Rogue Moon* is about. It is about Hawks, the brilliant, compassionate, iron-souled scientist who has developed the "matter transmitter" and is determined to have the construct analyzed, and Barker, the death-obsessed Saturday afternoon hero he gets to do the exploring—through a score of deaths. Like *Who?* it is about the nature of identity. It is also about the nature of life, about what it is to live and have lived.

When a writer of Budrys's caliber is silent for so long as Budrys was silent, silenced not by the knouts and jails of totalitarian authority but by his own frustrations, his readers are entitled to expect him to be a different and even better writer if he chooses to write again. Budrys's justification is *Michaelmas*, his best novel and the book that has brought him considerable recognition outside SF. If *Rogue Moon* was cinematic, *Michaelmas* is bibliomatic—a story that can be told well only in a book. Americans are apt to find a certain glamour in kings and queens, princes and princesses—an amiable weakness. We are sometimes even liable to find an attraction in tyrants of one sort or another, in Napoleon, Caesar, and even Stalin—though we should know much better. But numbed by a parade of crooks and nonentities, we seem to have forgotten the romance of a president, of the good citizen elevated by his own efforts and the admiration of his fellows to a preeminence in the state, the romance our great-grandfathers sensed so strongly in the embodiment of the Republic. Budrys, a Lithuanian refugee and the son of refugees, has not. G.K. Chesterton once said that a sword was the most glorious object in the world, but that a pocketknife was more glorious than a sword, because it was a secret sword. Laurent Michaelmas is a secret president, the secret president of the Earth. In the hands of any other writer, he would almost certainly be a tyrant, and, no doubt in the hands of most, an insane tyrant. In Budrys's, as he struggles with human treachery and an alien visitor of awesome power, he remains an eminently sane and decent man, as lonely and as sad as our society's sane and decent men must always be. In flatly and persuasively denying the inevitable corruption of power, *Michaelmas* may well be the most optimistic book of the latter 20th century. It is certainly one of the best, as Budrys himself is one of its best—and least characteristic—storytellers.

—Gene Wolfe

BUJOLD, Lois McMaster

Nationality: American. **Born:** Columbus, Ohio, 2 November 1949. **Education:** Attended Ohio State University, Columbus, 1968-72.

Family: Married John Fredric Bujold in 1971 (divorced 1992); one daughter and one son. **Awards:** Nebula award, 1989, 1990; Hugo award, 1990, 1991, 1992, 1995; *Locus* award, 1992, 1995. **Agent:** Eleanor Wood, Spectrum Literary Agency, 111 Eighth Avenue, Suite 1501, New York, New York, 10011, U.S.A.

SCIENCE FICTION PUBLICATIONS

Novels (series: Miles Vorkosigan)

Shards of Honor (Vorkosigan). New York, Baen, 1986; as *Shards of Honour*, London, Headline, 1988.
The Warrior's Apprentice (Vorkosigan). New York, Baen, 1986; London, Headline, 1988.
Ethan of Athos (Vorkosigan). New York, Baen, 1986; London, Headline, 1989.
Test of Honor (includes *Shards of Honor* and *The Warrior's Apprentice*). Garden City, New York, Doubleday, 1987.
Falling Free. New York, Baen, 1988; London, Headline, 1989.
Brothers in Arms: A Miles Vorkosigan Adventure. New York, Baen, 1989; London, Headline, 1990.
The Vor Game (Vorkosigan). Norwalk, Connecticut, Easton Press, 1990; London, Pan, 1993.
Barrayar (Vorkosigan). Norwalk, Connecticut, Easton Press, 1991; London, Pan, 1994.
Vorkosigan's Game (includes *The Vor Game* and *Borders of Infinity*). New York, Guild America Books, 1990.
The Spirit Ring. Riverdale, New York, Baen, 1992; London, Pan, 1993.
Mirror Dance: A Vorkosigan Adventure. Riverdale, New York, Baen, 1994.

Short Stories

Borders of Infinity (Vorkosigan). Norwalk, Connecticut, Easton Press, 1989; London, Pan, 1992.

*

Lois McMaster Bujold comments:

All my science fiction books so far are united by the series-device of sharing the same universe or future history. I do not consider myself bound by this, it just happens to have worked out that way for the topics I've wanted to tackle. (Though just in case anyone thinks they've got me boxed, I've also written a ghost story set in 15th-century Italy.) With the exception of *Falling Free*, all my novels touch the life of one hero, Miles Naismith Vorkosigan. Five of the books—*The Warrior's Apprentice, Borders of Infinity, The Vor Game, Citaganda*, and *Brothers In Arms*—give Miles the central role. I've tried to write them so each stands alone as an independent novel, so that the hapless reader who lays hands on them in random order (as is usual) will not be annoyed. In practice, some of the books seem to be better start-points, particularly *Warrior's* and *Borders*.

I try to write the kind of book I most like to read: character-centered adventure. My own literary favorites include, among many others, Dorothy Sayers, Arthur Conan Doyle, Alexander Dumas, and C.S. Forester. All these writers created not works of art, but, on some level, works of life. Theirs are creations who climb up off the page into the readers' minds and live there long after the book is shut. Readers return to such books again and again, not to find out what happened—for a single reading would suffice for any book if plot and idea were all—but because those characters have become their friends, and there is no limit to the number of times you want to be with your friends again.

But character doesn't exist in a vacuum, so I try to generate plots and ideas that are quintessential and worthy tests of my book-people. I don't see the fact that I write genre or even subgenre as requiring me to hobble any novelistic ambition. Not either/or, but character and plot and theme, adventure and psychology and symbol, motion and meaning: everything, all at once, all the time. Character-starved readers will forgive almost any background nonsense, as long as the central hunger of their spirits is fed, but they shouldn't have to.

Since Miles is my main man, an extra word or two on him is in order. As a created character, Miles has many real roots—T.E. Lawrence, another short soldier with psychological problems; a physical template in a brilliant, physically handicapped hospital pharmacist I used to work for; my own relationship with my father. I'm afraid his sense of humor can only be coming from me. As for imaginary roots, in many ways Miles is an antitype (or antidote) to the standard action-adventure hero. In place of lantern jaw and corded muscles, he's physically weak, fragile, and slightly manic-depressive. Instead of being an orphan (surely every teenager's escapist dream), he's plagued with a lively and obstreperous gang of relatives who never let him forget where he came from. In place of the psionic or other magical powers often given to physically handicapped characters by their authors (I can name John Brunner's wonderful Gerald Howson from *The Whole Man* among Miles's SF antecedents), Miles must cope armed only with his human wits. In place of the goal of becoming Emperor of the Universe (or at least of the planet Barrayar), Miles's study is to avoid such a dismal fate, which falls around him like bracketing shellfire. In place of physical conquest, he travels a drunkard's-walk of a spiritual journey constantly pushing him to a greater and more terrifying connectedness to other human beings.

A postscript on humor. People crack jokes, if black ones, even in the face of death. Everywhere, human beings laugh. Any story that leaves humor out of its portrayal of the human condition has no claim to the label "realistic." Comedy and tragedy share one heart. In the midst of all my gaudy action, exotic setting, or outré detail, it is my aim to write humanly realistic tales.

*   *   *

Lois McMaster Bujold has found a warm welcome among readers who feared that well-written, psychologically valid action-adventure novels had disappeared from the science fiction shelves with the passing of the Golden Age. Since the appearance of her first novel, *The Warrior's Apprentice,* she has won Nebula Awards for *Falling Free* and "The Mountains of Mourning" (included in *The Borders of Infinity*), Hugo Awards for "The Mountains of Mourning," *The Vor Game,* and *Barrayar,* several *Locus* awards, and the "Anlab" poll of *Analog* readers twice. Many of her books have been translated into various languages, including Spanish, German, Italian, and Japanese.

Even readers who most enjoy action-adventure stories sometimes find them thin or sterile. Bujold writes with vivid details and considerable humor, but also with a deeply ethical dimension in her

work. It seems likely that the popularity of Bujold's work lies not only in her vivid plots but even more importantly, in the nature of her characters. In *Shards of Honor,* Aral Vorkosigan, hereditary member of the Barrayaran warrior class, lives by a strict code of honor, which circumstances frequently force him to stretch uncomfortably. Cordelia Naismith, from the nonmilitary Beta Colony, has her own code, never explicitly described, much less ascribed to any class or creed. To his surprise, Vorkosigan finds it even more strict—and more fulfilling—than his own. As she comes to love Vorkosigan, she bases her love on mature understanding, not romantic idealism. This is even more clearly demonstrated in *Barrayar,* which details the time between *Shards of Honor* and *The Warrior's Apprentice.* Damaged by an assassination attempt on Vorkosigan, their unborn son should be aborted according to Barrayaran custom. Since neither Aral nor Cordelia will allow this, they must bear the consequences: official contempt and disinheritance by Piotr, Aral's father. Bujold never preaches, but she shows her characters making hard choices and paying the price for doing so.

Miles Vorkosigan, the physically undersized, weak, and hunchbacked hero of *The Warrior's Apprentice, Brothers in Arms, Borders of Infinity, The Vor Game,* and *Cetaganda,* takes second place to his identical twin clone Mark in *Mirror Dance,* in which he is (sort of) killed while attempting to rescue a surrounded Dendarii force. Despite his physical disadvantages, Miles has accidentally organized a highly effective (and illegal) private army, which he loans to the Barrayaran secret service, thus keeping himself alive; graduated from the military academy; and become a secret agent in his own right. In the novel Bujold is working on in 1995, tentatively titled *Memory,* Miles must cope with the aftereffects of his experiences in *Mirror Dance.* The worlds Bujold has invented are physically, socially, politically, and psychologically rich and diverse.

Originally, Bujold claims that she did not expect to write a series; but created "panel novels" set in a coherent universe, with occasionally overlapping characters. Thus, quaddies are created in *Falling Free,* and appear again in "Labyrinth"; the outlaw world or Jackson's Whole shows up in *Ethan of Athos,* as does Miles's lieutenant, Elli Quinn. Popular demand for more stories about Miles and Barrayar has made such a series possible, and Bujold admits that she has a good idea of the shape of Miles's life. Although many of his decisions are almost devilishly intelligent, he can (and does) make serious mistakes. One of these will remove him from the military, and set him upon a new, unexpected, and interesting path in *Memory.* Nor is Miles the only interesting character. Readers express fondness for Aral and Cordelia, and even Miles's feckless cousin Ivan has his good points. Another favorite is Emperor Gregor, whom we meet as a small boy in *Barrayar,* as a young man in *The Vor Game,* and (to the relief of Miles, who stands uncomfortably close to the throne) finally engaged to marry in *Memory.*

Bujold has a longstanding acquaintance with and appreciation of science fiction. She demonstrates an acute and thoughtful awareness of generic expectations, of the interaction of character, plot, setting, and theme. Her fictions shape themselves tightly, maintaining an unflagging pace. She also casts an ironic look at many contemporary issues: the immoral actions of immense corporations (and their defeat by individual action, in *Falling Free*); the danger inherent in political ambition and the corruption of character that can come from great power; and also the evil that stems from the shallow, selfish behavior of ordinary people who fail to ground their daily choices in practical ethics.

This discussion makes Bujold's writing sound moralistic, preachy, and, possibly, grim. Nothing could be further from the truth. She delights in setting up apparently impossible contradictions for her characters to deal with. In *Brothers in Arms,* Miles, an only child, finds himself honor-bound to protect and reeducate his twin brother; in *Ethan of Athos,* an obstetrician carries on a busy practice on an all-male planet until circumstances force him to leave home and not only meet but (frighteningly) deal with women. Discussing her writing technique, Bujold says that she asks herself, "What's the worst possible situation for *this* guy to fall into?" and then multiplies its difficulty before dropping him or her into the middle of it. Humane, egalitarian Cordelia must deal with Barrayaran class prejudice and violence; deformed Miles must not only bring to justice the murderer of a deformed baby in "Mountains of Mourning," but "learn the subtle difference between serving an empire and serving a people."

Bujold's sense of humor, which ranges from wacky (as in "The Hole Truth" and "Labyrinth") to grim (as in "Borders of Infinity"), is sometimes expressed directly but more often appears to spring from the characters than from the author. Instead of setting up incongruous situations, she creates characters who show an astonishing aptitude for survival, who find humor in almost anything, and who blessedly refuse to take themselves too seriously. Even in *The Spirit Ring,* a fantasy novel set in a medieval Italy where magic works, Bujold includes some incredibly funny scenes. In the middle of war, death, and political intrigue some wonderfully incongruous occurrences take place.

In two regards, Bujold differs from most action-adventure writers. She is highly sensitive to those with physical differences, which has won her a considerable following among the physically challenged. Many of these can follow her work only when it appears in *Analog's* "talking book" format. Also, her women are strong, active, appealing characters, but even in the most military situation they do not behave like "men with breasts." Like her male characters, they are multidimensional; they act boldly when no other course seems feasible, and they sometimes regret what they have done. They have women's careers and women's concerns, sometimes including family and children, but they do not build their identity on anyone else's valuation. They are fully and competently themselves.

Much of her longer fiction deals with war and the results of aggression and prejudice. While she certainly writes military fiction (though less in *Cetaganda* and *Memory*), she does so with a certain reluctance. She notes that "I had slaughtered thousands to make my first novel (*Shards of Honor*); as a personal challenge, I wanted to see if I could write a high-tension adventure without killing *anybody.*" She succeeded in *Falling Free.* Her objection to technological warfare is very simple: it is too easy to kill when we can deny the humanity of our enemies ("rob them of their faces"). As the graves registration medtech remarks for an enemy corpse in "Aftermaths," every soldier represents a lot of work for someone: "Nine months of pregnancy, childbirth, two years of diapering, and that's just the beginning. Tens of thousands of meals, thousands of bedtime stories, years of school. Dozens of teachers. And all that military training, too. A lot of people went into making him. . . . That head held the universe, once." It is this sensitive attention to the human face of her characters, even dead ones, that makes Bujold's work not only exciting, but also profoundly moving.

—Martha A. Bartter

BULGAKOV, Mikhail

Nationality: Russian. **Born:** Kiev in 1891. **Education:** Took medical degree with honors at the University of Kiev, 1916. **Military Service:** Noncombat duty (doctor) during World War I. **Career:** Abandoned medicine in 1919 to write feuilletons for newspapers and plays for theaters in Vladikavkaz. In 1921 moved to Moscow, where he edited and wrote for various newspapers. Since 1925, full-time writer. **Died:** 10 March 1940.

SCIENCE FICTION PUBLICATIONS

Novels

Master i Margarita. Moscow, n.p., 1938; translated by Michael Glenny as *The Master and Margarita,* New York, Harper, and London, Collins, 1967.
Sobacheie serdtse. Moscow, n.p., n.d.; translated by Michael Glenny as *The Heart of a Dog,* New York, Harcourt, 1968; translated by Mirra Ginsburg, London, Harvill Press, and New York, Grove Press, 1968.

Short Stories

Diavoliada. Moscow, Nedra, 1925; translated by Carl R. Proffer as *Diaboliad and Other Stories,* Bloomington, Indiana, Indiana University Press, 1972.

OTHER PUBLICATIONS

Novels

Belaia gvardiia. Moscow, n.p., 1925; translated by Michael Glenny as *The White Guard,* New York, Simon and Schuster, and London, Hodder and Stoughton, 1967.
Cherny sneg. Moscow, n.p., 1967; translated by Michael Gleeny as *Black Snow: A Theatrical Novel,* New York, Simon and Schuster, and London, Hodder and Stoughton, 1967.

Short Stories

A Country Doctor's Notebook, translated by Michael Gleeny. London, Collins, 1975.

Play

P'esy. Moscow, Iskusstvo, 1962; translated by Carl R. Proffer and Ellen Dea Proffer as *The Early Plays of Mikhail Bulgakov,* Bloomington, Indiana, Indiana University Press, 1972.

Other

Zhizn' gospodina de Mol'era. Moscow, Molodaia Gvardiia, 1962; translated by Mirra Ginsburg as *Life of Monsieur de Moliere* New York, Funk and Wagnalls, 1970.

*   *   *

"The stars will remain when the shadows of our presence and our deeds have vanished from the earth. There is no man who does not know that. Why, then, will we not turn our eyes towards the stars?" This is the leitmotiv of Mikhail Bulgakov's science fiction: the nature of a true relationship between a Kantian universe and a human existence of thought and action.

Bulgakov's early science fiction stories established an allegoric parallel between scientific discovery and social revolution, using every technique from slapstick comedy to black humor and horror, to show the absurdity and danger of trying to impose human purposes on reality. In "The Fatal Eggs" (*Diaboliad*), based on H.G. Wells's *The Food of the Gods,* mammoth artificially hatched serpents almost devour Moscow. In "The Crimson Island"—"Jules Verne translated into Aesopian"—an involuted rebellion results in nothing but a drunken revel and a telegram to the West: "Go (indecipherable) your (indecipherable) mother."

The novella *Heart of a Dog* exhibits Bulgakov's characteristic literary method: a fantastic realism that is a combination of grotesque action and a naturalistic background, with a satiric intent, serving a philosophical idea. It concerns a Moscow professor who transforms a dog into a man in a rejuvenation experiment. The identification of professor and Lenin, rejuvenation and revolution is implicit. Within a week, the new creation has a vocabulary of "every known Russian swearword"; he can't button his fly, eats toothpaste, and has fleas. He is immediately made a Commissar. His mature virtues include greed, viciousness, and "cosmic stupidity." Disgusted, the professor curses the attempt to substitute the artificial for the authentic, whether dog for man or dogma for life, and reverses the experiment.

Bulgakov's science fiction plays range from burlesque to near-tragedy, but all deal with the ontological theme. In "Bliss" a wondrous future utopia is revealed to be inadequate and boring compared to the mystery of reality and the adventure of living. In "Ivan Vasilievich" Ivan the Terrible's farcical misadventures in modern Moscow revolve around a confusion of definitions and roles with actualities. The best of the type, however, both in character development and seriousness of thought, is the tragicomedy "Adam and Eve." In a war-devastated Leningrad, a few surviving men and one woman must choose between reality and ideology, represented by the pacifist Yefrosimov, whose antigas invention saved them, and Adam Krasovsky, who wants to risk annihilation for the sake of Communism. In the end, Eve chooses Yefrosimov for her mate because, as she tells Adam, "the forest and the singing of the birds, and the rainbow, this is real, but you with your frenzied cries are unreal."

The Master and Margarita is Bulgakov's masterpiece of indefinable genre and indeterminate meaning, wherein Satan visits Moscow, punishing evil, driving rationalists insane, and "putting the fear of God" into atheists. In it, the science fiction theme converges with all of Bulgakov's other themes, styles, and techniques, and is fully realized. In *The Master and Margarita,* reality is infinite, eternal, and transcendent; time and space are relative; man is immortal. Living according to the demands of universal truth is a moral duty for which man is held accountable. "Cowardice is the worst sin of all" for a character like Pontius Pilate whose "mind is too closed" and whose life is too cramped." Yet man's denial and betrayal of reality cannot alter it. "All will be as it should," the devil promises; "that is how the world is made."

By his science fiction model of a surreal method to present a multidimensional universe, and by the example of his artistic courage, Bulgakov obliged Russian writers to contemplate "the shadows of man's presence" from the perspective of the stars and therefore "to a complete truth of thought and word."

—Jana I.Tuzar

BULL, Emma

Nationality: American. **Born:** Torrance, California, 13 December 1954. **Education:** Beloit College, B.A., 1976. **Family:** Married writer and editor Will Shetterly in 1981. **Career:** Has worked as an editor of corporate publications, a rubber stamp maker, a car attendant, a security guard, and a folksinger. Performer with Cats Laughing, a Minneapolis psychedelic rock and blues band; co-owner of Steel Dragon Press. **Awards:** *Locus* award, 1987. **Agent:** Valerie Smith, Box 398, Milford, Pennsylvania 18337, U.S.A.

SCIENCE FICTION PUBLICATIONS

Novels (series: Borderlands; Liavek)

War for the Oaks. New York, Ace, 1987.
Falcon. New York, Ace, 1989.
Bone Dance: A Fantasy for Technophiles. New York, Ace, 1991.
Finder: A Novel of the Borderlands. New York, Tor, 1994.
The Princess and the Lord of Night (for children). San Diego, Harcourt, 1994.

Short Stories

Double Feature, with Will Shetterly. Framingham, Massachusetts, NESFA Press, 1994.

OTHER PUBLICATIONS

Other

Editor, with Terri Windling and Mark Alan Arnold, *Bordertown: A Chronicle of the Borderlands.* New York, New American Library, 1986.
Editor, with Will Shetterly, *Liavek.* New York, Ace, 1985.
Editor, with Will Shetterly, *Liavek: The Players of Luck.* New York, Ace, 1986.
Editor, with Will Shetterly, *Liavek: Wizard's Row.* New York, Ace, 1987.
Editor, with Will Shetterly, *Liavek: Spells of Binding.* New York, Ace, 1988.
Editor, with Will Shetterly, *Liavek: Festival Week.* New York, Ace, 1990.

* * *

High adventure joins forces with high tech in the well-crafted works of author Emma Bull. Invulnerable heroes battle menaces whose threats span the galaxy in stories that have been compared to the early novels of writer Samuel R. Delany. Beginning her career within the realm of the fantastic, Bull's first novel, a work of fantasy fiction for young adults entitled *War for the Oaks,* was published in 1987. Considered by many to be a classic in the genre, *War for the Oaks* was awarded the *Locus* award for best first fantasy novel. Bull has also served as coeditor, with husband, Will Shetterly, of the "Liavek" books, a series of shared world fantasy anthologies.

Bull's first work of science fiction, *Falcon,* published in 1989, combines her penchant for rousing adventure with a sophisticated prose style. The plot of *Falcon*—a young aristocrat from the planet Cymru champions the cause of a dissident faction despite threats to his life and legacy—contains a smooth transition from romance to space opera. After a change in Cymru's balance of power the protagonist is transformed into Falcon, the gestalt pilot, and returns to save his world, find the girl of his dreams, and gain the reverence of his countrymen. In addition to receiving praise for weaving a classic tale of adventure, *Falcon* showcases Bull's literary talents. As Gerald Jonas commented in the *New York Times Book Review,* the novel combines a "love of language that finds expression in well-formed descriptive sentences inlaid with an occasional flamboyant metaphor or patch of self-congratulatory rhetoric."

Bull followed *Falcon* with *Bone Dance: A Fantasy for Technophiles* in 1991. In this novel, a war for humanity is waged against the backdrop of a postnuclear holocaust as an androgynous youth who deals in used CDs and videos in post-Apocalypse Minnesota battles a pair of telepathic Horsemen for his/her soul. In this work of cyberpunk, the threat is made the more sinister in that it is intangible—control can be gained through society's advanced technological machine/human interface instead of through physical destruction. As in her earlier work, *Bone Dance* was praised by reviewers for its author's skill in capturing a vivid future world within her prose. The underlying theme of self-discovery allows the reader to identify with Bull's protagonist—the asexual Sparrow—as he learns to adapt to the changes within his futuristic setting.

Finder, published in 1994, follows a sensitive young man with the extraordinary ability to find lost objects as he joins with a local policewoman to search for a dangerous drug that threatens the population of his small town in the universe of the Borderlands. Borderlands is a future world where the paths of humans and faeriefolk meet, and in *Finder,* Bull utilizes her fantasy-writing background to good effect in creating a novel that has been praised for its suspenseful blend of both fantasy and hard science fiction genres.

One of the most literate and inventive authors writing science fiction in the 1990s, Bull's continued creativity is an outgrowth of her personal philosophy. As she has told *Contemporary Authors,* "My credo is to always take chances. The worst that can happen is that you'll look like an idiot, and everyone looks like an idiot now and then. But if you never take a chance, you never become anything but an imitation Somebody Else."

—Pamela Shelton

BULMER, (Henry) Kenneth

Pseudonyms: Alan Burt Akers; Ken Blake; Frank Brandon; Rupert Clinton; Ernest Corley; Arthur Frazier; Peter Green; Adam Hardy; Kenneth Johns; Philip Kent; Bruno Krauss; Neil Langholm; Karl Maras; Manning Norvil; Charles R. Pike; Andrew Quiller; Chesman

Scot; Nelson Sherwood; Richard Silver; H. Philip Stratford; Tully Zetford. **Nationality:** British. **Born:** London, 14 January 1921. **Education:** Catford Central School, London. **Military Service:** Served in the Royal Corps of Signals, 1941-46. **Family:** Married Pamela Kathleen Buckmaster in 1953; two daughters and one son. **Career:** Worked for paper merchandising and office equipment firms, 1936-54; editor or co-editor, *Star Parade,* 1941, *Fantasy Post,* 1941, *Seventy Eight Saga* (army magazine), 1943-45, *Nirvana,* 1949, 1954, *Science Fantasy News,* 1952, *Aaaah!,* 1954, *Dysteology,* 1954-55, *Vignette,* 1954, *Ziz,* 1954, and *Wappoted,* 1956. **Agent:** Carnell Literary Agency, Rowneybury Bungalow, near Old Harlow, Essex CM20 2EX. **Address:** 5/20 Frant Road, Tunbridge Wells, Kent TN2 5SN, England.

SCIENCE FICTION PUBLICATIONS

Novels (series: Keys to the Dimensions; Swords)

Space Treason, with A.V. Clarke. London, Panther, 1952.
Cybernetic Controller, with A.V. Clarke. London, Panther, 1952.
Encounter in Space. London, Panther, 1952.
Zhorani (as Karl Maras). London, Comyns, 1953.
Space Salvage. London, Panther, 1953.
The Stars Are Ours. London, Panther, 1953.
Galactic Intrigue. London, Panther, 1953.
Empire of Chaos. London, Panther, 1953.
World Aflame. London, Panther, 1954.
Challenge. London, Curtis Warren, 1954.
Peril from Space (as Karl Maras). London, Comyns, 1954.
City under the Sea. New York, Ace, 1957; London, Digit, 1961.
The Secret of ZI. New York, Ace, 1958; London, Digit, 1961; as *The Patient Dark,* London, Hale, 1969.
The Changeling Worlds. New York, Ace, 1959; London, Digit, 1961.
The Earth Gods Are Coming. New York, Ace, 1960; as *Of Earth Foretold* (includes "The Aztec Plan"), London, Digit, 1961.
Forschungskreuzer Saumarez. Munich, Moewig, 1960; as *Defiance,* London, Digit, 1963.
No Man's World. New York, Ace, 1961; as *Earth's Long Shadow* (includes "Strange Highway"). London, Digit, 1962.
Beyond the Silver Sky. New York, Ace, 1961.
The Fatal Fire. London, Digit, 1962.
The Wind of Liberty: A Planet's Destiny Trembled in the Balance (includes "Don't Cross a Telekine"). London, Digit, 1962.
The Wizard of Starship Poseidon. New York, Ace, 1963.
The Million Year Hunt. New York, Ace, 1964.
Demon's World. New York, Ace, 1964; as *The Demons,* London, Compact, 1965.
Land Beyond the Map. New York, Ace, 1965.
Behold the Stars. New York, Ace, 1965; London, Mayflower, 1966.
Worlds for the Taking. New York, Ace, 1966.
To Outrun Doomsday. New York, Ace, 1967; London, New English Library, 1975.
The Key to Irunium (Keys). New York, Ace, 1967.
Cycle of Nemesis. New York, Ace, 1967.
The Doomsday Men. New York, Doubleday, and London, Hale, 1968.
The Key to Venudine (Keys). New York, Ace, 1968.
The Star Venturers. New York, Ace, 1969.
The Wizards of Senchuria (Keys). New York, Ace, 1969.

Kandar. New York, Paperback Library, 1969.

The Ulcer Culture. London, Macdonald, 1969; as *The Stained-Glass World,* London, New English Library, 1976.

The Ships of Durostorum (Keys). New York, Ace, 1970.

Quench the Burning Stars, London, Hale, 1970; expanded as *Blazon,* New York, Curtis, 1970.

Star Trove. London, Hale, 1970.

Swords of the Barbarians. London, New English Library, 1970; New York, Belmont, 1976.

The Hunters of Jundagai (Keys). New York, Ace, 1971.

The Electric Sword Swallowers. New York, Ace, 1971.

The Insane City. New York, Curtis, 1971; London, Severn House, 1978.

The Chariots of Ra (Keys). New York, Ace, 1972.

On the Symb-Socket Circuit. New York, Ace, 1972.

Roller Coaster World. New York, Ace, 1972; London, Severn House, 1978.

The Diamond Contessa (Keys). New York, DAW, 1983.

Novels as Philip Kent

Mission to the Stars. London, Pearson, 1953.

Vassals of Venus. London, Pearson, 1953.

Slaves of the Spectrum. London, Pearson, 1954.

Home Is the Martian. London, Pearson, 1954.

Novels as Alan Burt Akers (series: Dray Prescot in all books)

Transit to Scorpio. New York, DAW, 1972; London, Futura, 1974.

The Suns of Scorpio. New York, DAW, 1973; London, Futura, 1974.

Warrior of Scorpio. New York, DAW, 1973; London, Futura, 1975.

Swordships of Scorpio. New York, DAW, 1973; London, Futura, 1975.

Prince of Scorpio. New York, DAW, 1974; London, Futura, 1975.

Manhounds of Antares. New York, DAW, 1974.

Arena of Antares. New York, DAW, 1974.

Fliers of Antares. New York, DAW, 1975.

Bladesman of Antares. New York, DAW, 1975.

Avenger of Antares. New York, DAW, 1975.

Armada of Antares. New York, DAW, 1976.

The Tides of Kregen. New York, DAW, 1976.

Renegade of Kregen. New York, DAW, 1976.

Krozair of Kregen. New York, DAW, 1977.

Secret Scorpio. New York, DAW, 1977.

Savage Scorpio. New York, DAW, 1978.

Captive Scorpio. New York, DAW, 1978.

Golden Scorpio. New York, DAW, 1978.

A Life for Kregen. New York, DAW, 1979.

A Sword for Kregen. New York, DAW, 1979.

A Fortune for Kregen. New York, DAW, 1979.

A Victory for Kregen. New York, DAW, 1980.

Beasts of Antares. New York, DAW, 1980.

Rebel of Antares. New York, DAW, 1980.

Legions of Antares. New York, DAW, 1981.

Allies of Antares. New York, DAW, 1981.

Manhounds of Antares; and, Arena of Antares. New York, DAW, 1981.

Mazes of Scorpio. New York, DAW, 1982.

Delia of Vallia. New York, DAW, 1982.

Fires of Scorpio. New York, DAW, 1983.

Talons of Scorpio. New York, DAW, 1983.

Masks of Scorpio. New York, DAW, 1984.

Seg the Bowman. New York, DAW, 1984.

Werewolves of Kregen. New York, DAW, 1985.

Witches of Kregen. New York, DAW, 1985.

Storm over Vallia. New York, DAW, 1985.

Omens of Kregen. New York, DAW, 1985.

Warlord of Antares. New York, DAW, 1988.

Novels as Tully Zetford (series: Ryder Hook in all books)

Whirlpool of Stars. London, New English Library, 1974; New York, Pinnacle, 1975.

The Boosted Man. London, New English Library, 1974; New York, Pinnacle, 1975.

Star City. London, New English Library, 1974; New York, Pinnacle, 1975.

Virility Gene. London, New English Library, 1975; New York, Pinnacle, 1976.

Novels as Manning Norvil (Odan trilogy)

Dream Chariots. New York, DAW, 1977.

Whetted Bronze. New York, DAW, 1978.

Crown of the Sword God. New York, DAW, 1980.

OTHER PUBLICATIONS

Novels (series: Jubal Cade; Captain Shark; The Eagles; Vikings)

White Out (as Ernest Corley). London, Jarrolds, 1960.

Pretenders (novelization of television series). London, New English Library, 1972.

The Dark Return (Vikings; as Neil Langholm). London, Sphere, 1975; New York, Pinnacle, 1977.

By Pirate's Blood (Shark; as Richard Silver). New York, Pinnacle, 1975.

Jaws of Death (Shark; as Richard Silver). New York, Pinnacle, 1975.

Trail of Blood (Vikings; as Neil Langholm). London, Sphere, 1976.

The Land of Mist (Eagles; as Andrew Quiller). London, Mayflower, and New York, Pinnacle, 1976.

Sea of Swords (Eagles; as Andrew Quiller). London, Mayflower, and New York, Pinnacle, 1976.

Brand of Vengeance (Cade; as Charles R. Pike). London, Mayflower, 1978.

Novels as Adam Hardy (series: Fox; Strike Force Falklands)

Press Gang (Fox). London, New English Library, and New York, Pinnacle, 1973.

Prize Money (Fox). London, New English Library, and New York, Pinnacle, 1973.

The Siege (Fox). London, New English Library, 1973; as *Savage Siege,* New York, Pinnacle, 1973.

Treasure (Fox). London, New English Library, 1973; as *Treasure Map,* New York, Pinnacle, 1974.

Powder Monkey (Fox). London, New English Library, 1973; as *Sailor's Blood,* New York, Pinnacle, 1974.

A Fox Double (includes *Press Gang* and *Prize Money*). London, New English Library, 1973.

A Fox Double No. 2 (includes *The Siege* and *Treasure*). London, New English Library, 1973.

Blood for Breakfast (Fox). London, New English Library, 1974; as *Sea of Gold,* New York, Pinnacle, 1974.

Court Martial (Fox). London, New English Library, and New York, Pinnacle, 1974.

Battle Smoke (Fox). London, New English Library, 1974; New York, Pinnacle, 1975.

Cut and Thrust (Fox). London, New English Library, 1974; New York, Pinnacle, 1975.

Boarders Away (Fox). London, New English Library, and New York, Pinnacle, 1975.

Fireship (Fox). London, New English Library, 1975; as *The Fireship,* New York, Pinnacle, 1976.

Blood Beach (Fox). London, New English Library, 1975.

Sea Flame (Fox). London, New English Library, 1976.

Close Quarters (Fox). London, New English Library, 1977.

Strike Force Falklands:Operation Exocet. London, Futura, 1984.

Raider's Dawn (Strike Force Falklands). London, Futura, 1984.

Red Alert (Strike Force Falklands). London, Futura, 1984.

Recce Patrol (Strike Force Falklands). London, Futura, 1985.

Covert Op (Strike Force Falklands). London, Futura, 1985.

Ware Mines (Strike Force Falklands). London, Futura, 1985.

Novels as Arthur Frazier (series: Wolfshead in all titles)

Oath of Blood. London, New English Library, 1973.

The King's Death. London, New English Library, 1973.

A Flame in the Fens. London, New English Library, 1974.

An Axe in Miklagard. London, New English Library, 1975.

Novels as Ken Blake (series: The Professionals in all titles)

Where the Jungle Ends (novelization of screenplay). London, Sphere, 1978.

Long Shot (novelization of screenplay). London, Sphere, 1978.

Stake Out (novelization of screenplay). London, Sphere, 1978.

Hunter Hunted (novelization of screenplay). London, Sphere, 1978.

Blind Run, with Ronald Graham, Michael Armstrong, and Brian Clemens. London, Sphere, 1979.

Fall Girl, with Ronald Graham, Edmund Ward, and Don Houston. London, Sphere, 1979.

Dead Reckoning, with Robin Estridge and Brian Clemens. London, Sphere, 1980.

Cry Wolf (novelization of screenplay). London, Sphere, 1981.

No Stone (novelization of screenplay). London, Sphere, 1981.

Spy Phrobe (novelization of screenplay). London, Sphere, 1981.

Foxhole (novelization of screenplay). London, Sphere, 1982.

The Untouchables (novelization of screenplay). London, Sphere, 1982.

You'll Be All Right (novelization of screenplay). London, Sphere, 1982.

Operation Susie (novelization of screenplay). London, Sphere, 1982.

Novels as Bruno Krauss (series: Sea Wolf)

Steel Shark. London, Sphere, 1978.

Shark North. London, Sphere, 1978.

Shark Pack. London, Sphere, 1978.

Shark Hunt. London, Sphere, 1980.

Shark Africa. London, Sphere, 1980.

Shark Raid. London, Sphere, 1982.

Shark America. London, Sphere, 1982.

Shark Trap. London, Sphere, 1982.

Other

The True Book about Space Travel (for children; as Kenneth Johns, with John Newman). London, Muller, 1960.

Editor, *The Best of SF: An International Exhibition of Science Fiction Literature, May 17-31.* London, National Book League, 1971.

Editor, *New Writings in SF 22-30.* London, Sidgwick and Jackson, 8 vols., 1973-76, and London, Corgi, 1 vol., 1978.

Editor, *New Writings in SF Special 1-3.* London, Sidgwick and Jackson, 1975-78 (vol. 1 edited with John Carnell).

*

Bibliography: *The Writings of Kenneth Bulmer* by Roger Robinson, n. p., BECCON, 1983; revised edition, 1984.

Kenneth Bulmer comments:

If in an unwary moment I open one of my early books I find great difficulty in identifying with the writer. The immediate purpose of the writer appears plain enough; he is dazzled by a vision of what this literature called SF might achieve, and is concerned to express this vision in terms then available to him. There is genuine feeling; but he is handicapped by environment, editorial prejudice, and lack of data. There is an unfortunate assumption that other people will readily share his insights, that the vision is so self-evident it must be conveyed. His own interests in the fascinating details of, for instance, the future, space and time travel, the interactions and potentialities of the human mind and spirit, appear to overshadow what he is driving at. Imperceptive, top-of-the-head critics have said that most of the writer's work is space opera; a closer reading will reveal this statement to be untenable. The vision of what SF might achieve remains, dimmed a little, it is true, by the current state of general SF, and this writer has in recent years turned to other interests, including the Fox books (as Adam Hardy) and adult fantasy, both incidentally, sharing that imaginative exploration of worlds unknown to the present day.

I have said many times, and will reiterate, that SF is not respectable but is responsible. I remain unconvinced that this statement has been grasped by those to whom it is addressed. If poetry and nonestablishment fiction are literatures of revolt, then SF is also. But it is more than merely a literature against, for example, the dead hand of authoritarianism or outmoded sexual mores: it is a literature against the spoliation of man by mankind's creations, which is by inference by man himself. This is not quite the same order of protest. This does not mean that SF is less as literature but more, for it incorporates more of life and, to enlarge a cliché, the felt responses within the emotional reactions to the human condition.

One underlying theme in my work is the exploration of the feelings and reactions of people forced, by the environment, other people, or inner compulsions, to perform acts and live lives far removed from what they would desire. As an introduction to my work I would instance the observation of a recent correspondent who remarked of my novels that they are filled with compassion all too often lacking in other works of SF.

*   *   *

If any single writer could epitomize the formularized science fantasy milieu of Donald A. Wollheim's popular Ace paperback line, Kenneth Bulmer would be a good choice for the designation. Inasmuch as American adventure pulps took many formulaic elements from British adventure fiction (violent conflict between cultures, stereotypes of romance), it might be seen as fitting that Wollheim's editorial devotion to the adventurous side of SF should be typified by a British writer who seemed devoted to formula for formula's sake.

It should be stressed that no author of narrative prose escapes at least some formulaic elements in his or her work—in fact, one measure of "art" might be the author's ability to transcend the formulaic origins of his narrative, as Conrad's stories rise above the classification of "sea stories." A formula writer, however, emphasizes the elements of the formula—the plot, the action, the melodramatic interactions of characters, and in SF, the "idea" or concept—and pays only superficial attention (if any) to the meaningful, thematic usages of such elements. Ace Books was noteworthy for printing many SF adventures with at least some moderate thematic interest, as with Emil Petaja's concern for regenerative myth-figures, or Leigh Brackett's preoccupation with beautiful, dying cultures. Yet the bulk of Ace's books were usually less thematically organized, and so Bulmer makes the best representative writer of that period. Bulmer is not, however, simply a "hack" in the derogatory sense—rather, he does for the SF adventure what Edgar Wallace did for mysteries, and Seabury Quinn did for supernatural stories—that is, by the sheer bulk of his efforts in a single vein, he demonstrates the intrinsic fascination of the ritualistic nature of the formula and its icon-like imagery.

Bulmer's plots are his chief failing. Other formula elements can be, and have been, neglected without necessarily diluting the effectiveness of the formula. Jack Williamson might use stereotypic characters, Edgar Rice Burroughs might overemphasize frenetic action, and Philip José Farmer might employ ideas of little originality, but all of them supply strong plotting that communicates some thematic commitment. Adventure plots generally must be intricate to be compelling, but the formlessness of Bulmer's plots almost suggests the absurdity of a freewheeling comedy. Most of Bulmer's plots begin adequately enough—the protagonist and his allies learn of a mysterious force or perilous circumstance threatening their safety, but as they prepare to combat it, they continually become sidetracked, verging off into distantly related episodic conflicts, so that, when they eventually reenter the central conflict, the outcome is no longer interesting.

Some books in Bulmer's early cycle, such as *Behold the Stars* and *The Secret of Zi*, are dully conventional, and it may be that Bulmer began his pattern of repeated scene-shifting to gain greater diversity. The tendency is markedly seen in *Cycle of Nemesis,* in which a group of humans tries to bind an ancient demon into his crypt, and get thrown across various time-periods as they try. A series of Bulmer's books is even built around the various conflicts of an assortment of forgettable heroes against a dimension-conquering villainess, the Diamond Contessa, but with the exception of one of these (*The Wizards of Senchuria*) the other three, *The Key to Irunium, The Key to Venudine,* and *The Diamond Contessa,* lack narrative drive and coherence.

Bulmer's best work is probably *The Wizard of Starship Poseidon,* in that the plot is well-defined. Best described as *Topkapi* set in outer space, the novel has a certain amount of irony, concerning a scientist who fails to gain a grant to subsidize his project of creating biologic life, and decides to steal the necessary funds from a

military payroll. (Wittily enough, the grant he wants is given to a literary scholar who hopes to prove that Bernard Shaw and H.G. Wells were the same man.) In this format, Bulmer's penchant for stocking his stories with an excess of eccentric characters is benefit, and he manages to pull off a number of interesting plot-twists without becoming vague. A runner-up for best book might be *The Star Venturers,* in which a soldier-of-fortune, controlled by an artificial life-form implanted in his brain, is forced to track down a kidnapped princess, with the usual wild escapades that ensue when he combats her heavily armed kidnappers. Also of interest are *On the Symb-Socket Circuit* and *Roller Coaster World,* which attempt to break from the adventure-mold into that of social satire, directed toward the follies of hedonism and luxury living. These have a degree of wit, but tend to flounder aimlessly: in *Roller Coaster World,* the hero is infatuated with a hopelessly unfulfilling romance, but Bulmer resolves an interesting dilemma in melodramatic terms, arranging for another woman to force the hero to renounce his hopeless love by the subtle strategy of her shooting him and carrying him off.

In short, Bulmer is a writer to be valued for his inventiveness, in spite of the fact that his inventions rarely transcend the level of basic "sensawunda" SF.

—Gene Phillips

BULWER-LYTTON, Edward (George Earle; 1st Baron Lytton of Knebworth)

Nationality: British. **Born:** London, 25 May 1803. **Education:** Dr. Ruddock's School, Fulham, London; Dr. Hooker's School, Rottingdean, Sussex; with a Mr. Wallington, Ealing, London, 1818-20; Trinity College, Cambridge (pensioner), 1822, and Trinity Hall, Cambridge (fellow-commoner; Chancellor's Medal for verse, 1825), 1822-25, B.A. 1825, M.A., 1833. **Family:** Married Rosina Doyle Wheeler in 1827 (separated, 1836); one daughter and one son. **Career:** Traveled between London and Paris, 1825-27; settled at Woodcot House, near Pangbourne Berkshire, and contributed to magazines, including *Books of Beauty, Keepsakes,* and *Quarterly Review,* 1827-29; moved to London, 1829; editor, *New Monthly Magazine,* London, 1831-33; Liberal Member of Parliament for St. Ives, Cornwall, 1831, and for Lincoln, 1832-41; active lobbyist of stronger copyright laws and for the removal of taxes on literature; co-publisher, *The Monthly Chronicle,* London, 1841, succeeded to the family estate at Knebworth, 1843; travelled abroad, 1849; Tory Member of Parliament for Hertfordshire, 1852-1866; Secretary for the Colonies, 1858-59. Lord Rector of the University of Glasgow, 1856, 1858. **Awards:** Knighted in 1837; LL.D., Cambridge University, 1864; created Baron Lytton, 1866. **Died:** 18 January 1873.

SCIENCE FICTION PUBLICATIONS

Novels

Godolphin (published anonymously). London, Bentley, 1833, 3 volumes; (as Edward Bulwer-Lytton), New York, Harper, 1840, 2 volumes.

Zanoni. London, Saunders and Otley, 3 volumes, and New York, Harper, 1 volume, 1842.

A Strange Story. London, Sampson Low, 2 volumes, and New York, Harper, 1862; revised edition, Low, Marston, and New York, Harper, 1863.

The Coming Race. Edinburgh, Blackwood, 1871; as *Vril: The Power of the Coming Race,* Blauvelt, New York, Steiner, 1972.

Zanoni, Zicci (omnibus). Boston, Little, Brown, 1912.

Paul Clifford. N.p., n.d.

Short Stories

The Pilgrims of the Rhine. London, Saunders and Otley, and New York, Harper, 1834.

The Haunted House, and Calderon the Courtier. New York, Lovell, 1882.

The Haunted and the Haunters; or, The House and the Brain. London, Gowan, 1905.

*   *   *

Edward Bulwer-Lytton, was a politician, a leader of fashion, and a popular—second only to his good friend Dickens—novelst who earned a good living from his writing. Despite 20th-century sneers at his sometimes convoluted and overly flamboyant style, much of his work was carefully structured and often groundbreaking in subject matter. Even the early *Paul Clifford,* which began with the infamous "It was a dark and stormy night . . ." that has given rise to a satiric 20th-century contest, even this much-maligned work had the useful result of helping to ameliorate prison conditions and amend the criminal code. Throughout his life he was much interested in the relation of art to science, of art to society, and, above all, in the supernatural, the occult, and the mystical (he was an enthusiastic Rosicrucian). As poet, playwright, essayist, and novelist he admitted discussion of such matters as significant parts of everything he wrote, and he constantly sought out "new regions in the Art to which I am a servant. . . ."

He experimented with various forms of fantasy with varying success. Ghost stories, e.g., "The Haunted and the Haunters," fairytales, such as those in *The Pilgrims of the Rhine,* and stories of the occult, as in "An Episode of Life," are competently written and attained some popularity in their day. Few read his poetry today, but this too—the lengthy *King Arthur* is a good example—was filled with idealism, mystical speculation, and romantic tales.

Zanoni, the best of Bulwer-Lytton's mystical works, is set in the time of the French Revolution. Zanoni is a kind of superman, long-lived through use of an herbal elixir he has compounded, possessed of both wealth, extraordinary strength, and a psychic ability to foresee possible dangers to himself. He has traveled throughout the world and at home in every society. His superiority to other men depends upon his renunciation of all worldly ties; there has been for him no love, no hate, no ambition, no desires of any kind. Through long study he has gained nearly unlimited knowledge and spiritual perfection. Now, he falls in love with the beautiful singer, Viola. His plans to have her marry another, thereby satisfying his own happiness, are unsuccessful because she falls in love with him. They marry, and he loses his special powers. He continues to travel throughout the world, and on one of his absences Viola, now fearing that his occult powers are not from God but the Devil, runs away with their child to Paris which is then under the Reign of Terror. When Zanoni finds her doomed to execution, he gives his

own life for hers, realizing at that point that self-sacrifice is the greatest spiritual happiness. The book was a major success and remains one of the best of its kind.

The hero of *Zanoni* possessed occult powers that could prolong his life and influence others even at some distance. He was a good man who used his powers and intelligence for the good of others. Margrave, one of the two leading characters of *A Strange Story,* has much the same powers, but he has little conscience and uses his powers to increase his own pleasures and to destroy anything or person that gets in his way. Thus he destroys the lives of the scientist Fenwick and his fiancée Lilian. It is not too difficult a task since Fenwick, who has been writing a lengthy treatise on the human intellect as the basic force in human beings, discovers too late that the physical and social aspects of human nature are equally important. Both novels are frequently read as allegories of human nature, and there is some evidence in Bulwer-Lytton's letters and essays that such readings are intended. It is also likely that he was exploring the limits of the Darwinian view of the struggle for existence.

Although mystical and semiscientific elements are found in almost every thing he wrote, the work on which Bulwer-Lytton's reputation in science fiction rests is *The Coming Race.* It was written, he pointed out, to support "the Darwinian proposition that a coming race is destined to supplant our races . . . a new species developing itself out of our old one."

The locale is within the Earth's interior, where a young American engineer exploring a strange passage in a mine falls into a land inhabited by what appears to be a utopian society. Everyone possesses ability, developed over many generations, to use vril, a powerful fluid that can heal, destroy, and provide energy for the Vril-ya's technologically advanced society. All is peaceful since anyone could destroy anyone else through power of vril; consequently everyone lives in harmony. A common proverb describes their view of government: "No happiness without order, no order without authority, no authority without unity." There are no new works of art, literature, philosophy, or politics because no one would read them: passion (the source of art and literature) and politics (an instrument for change) are no longer a part of the Vril-ya makeup, and philosophical questions have long been settled. Women—Gy-ei— are bigger, stronger, and more intelligent than men and behave as men do in the upper world. Children, not yet completely socialized to nondestruction, perform public works and destroy those animals or other nations that might harm their society, though the idea that anything that could harm the Vril-ya is a first principle of society. It is, Tish—literally "froglet," as even the children call him—decides not the kind of utopia he has heard of. He escapes after learning that marriage proposed by at least two Gy-ei would lead to his instant death. Near the end of his life he narrates the story to warn the world of the destruction the Coming Race will wreak on humanity.

Despite a widely held view to the contrary, Bulwer-Lytton at his best writes in clear, logical prose always with a concern to display both the material and the idealistic aspects of his subjects. In a preface to *The Parisians,* referring to the message of *The Coming Race* and signed "Tish," he wrote, "Attired as fiction, Truth may be peacefully received." What he saw as Truth was frequently neither immediately discernible to the casual reader nor likely to be widely accepted, but his examination of the context in which our physical lives are lived continues to be worthy of our attention.

—Arthur O. Lewis

BUNCH, David R(oosevelt)

Pseudonym: Darryl R. Groupe. **Nationality:** American. **Born:** On farm near Lowry City, Missouri. **Education:** Central Missouri State College (now University), Warrensburg, B.S. 1946; Washington University, St. Louis, M.A. 1949; and all additional course work completed for Ph.D.; State University of Iowa City, 1951-52. **Military Service:** Served in the United States Army Air Forces, 1942-46. **Family:** Married Phyllis Geraldine Flette in 1951; two daughters (one deceased). **Career:** Worked in cafeteria, as clerk and warehouseman, mail handler, druggist; staff member, Wagner Electric Company, St. Louis, 1953-54; civilian cartographer, Air Force Aeronautical Chart and Information Center, St. Louis, 1954-73. **Agent:** Hans Joachim Alpers, Gross Flottbeker Strasse 61, 2000 Hamburg 52, Germany. **Address:** P.O. Box 12233, Soulard Station, St. Louis, Missouri 63157, U.S.A.

SCIENCE FICTION PUBLICATIONS

Novel

Moderan. New York, Avon, 1971.

Short Stories

Bunch! Cambridge, Massachusetts, Broken Mirrors Press, 1993.

Author of numerous other short stories.

OTHER PUBLICATIONS

Poetry

We Have a Nervous Job. Astoria, Oregon, Alba Press, 1983.

*

David R. Bunch comments:

When last I wrote an essay to introduce my science fiction to be listed in *Twentieth-Century Science Fiction Writers,* I came off sounding almost antiscience. I am indeed fortunate to have, in this Third (and now Fourth) Edition, this welcomed opportunity to correct an erroneous impression: David R. Bunch is NOT antiscience in his heart, his mind, and his written words. David R. Bunch is simply and adamantly anti-Bad Science in his heart, his writing, and his whole life. There is a difference here, and a significance that is so all-pervasive to our NOW-times on planet Earth, that adequate appraisal-and-value of that difference is almost beyond speech to say.

An inhabitant of planet Earth who would damn all science would be one with NO reasonable mind-and-sense understanding of how this wonderful force has served us, bettered us, and could—if rightly employed!—have transformed each and every one of our lives into that of either a prince or a princess of Earth, with all of us having such an abundance of good things (necessary things) in an ordered world that surely our Hearts and our Love—our Goodnesses! would have been optimum too. THEN—in a Great Wonder Time (of Heart-and-Mind one glorious entity) we would have been truly what God truly meant. (Whereas now!!! whereas now????) Any human being on our beleaguered planet today who would indiscriminately

worship at the shrine of ALL science would have, surely, to be one of such total mind-blindness and/or one of such stupefied, unblinking fidelity to the Danger God as to seem, quite unredeemably, a Fool-Among-Men.

Not in all of my science fiction writing, but in a goodly part of it, have I tried to convey—by social commentary, satire, irony, and direct-hard-bitter statement—that the prying, probing Mind of Science Man of planet Earth, forsaking the Heart and employing Bad Science to the absolute outer bounds of evil-learned-stupidity, has created a startlingly heartless world of speed, greed, and plunder—and kill-potential almost beyond human capacity fully to comprehend. For it is true: a brilliant Scientist-Mind without Heart is indeed a cold set of cogs—with almost unlimited capacity to function in the heartless Climate-of-Harm. (I AM SURE God meant Heart [first] Mind [second] to team together to LIVE! on our planet Earth—AND let IT live, not murder it with "brilliant" scientific conquests and kill-potential stockpiled in quantities enough to utterly overwhelm Land, Sea, and Sky.) Viewed from a little distance, in a calm moment, HOW! can we believe!!?? that WE have let happen "what we have let happen"—to US, to Earth, to God's Faith (misplaced) in our Stewardship. It is almost beyond the strength of human thought to hold (contain, encompass) the Horror wrought by Bad Science, with Heart nowhere to see.

NOW—let me define Good Science, and that must also define Bad Science, for there are only these two: Good Science is that Science which, when called upon, will act (and react) for *us* to do our will and our work, and not in so doing *harm* us (directly), and furthermore not *harm* us (indirectly) by in any way, shape, or form bringing injury to that Place we call, with a proud, special note in the voice: *Our* Earth, *Our* Home. In short, Good Science is people-helpful, people-safe, Earth-enhancing and Earth-friendly. ALL other Science is, by the very nature of things and common sense: BAD. Especially in my *Moderan* writing do I describe in deadly serious diabolic comment how Man and his Bad Science are proper fools together. I hope that my readers may take to Heart what I have tried to tell them, show them, shout them—and that will be oh, MY best reward of all.

*   *   *

David R. Bunch's idiosyncratic short stories have aroused strong emotions ever since they first began to appear, controversies over his themes—which some have incorrectly interpreted as antitechnological, controversies over his prose, which is aggressively distinct in a conservative genre that for many years remained intolerant of all but the most transparent styles. With the passage of time, SF readers have grown more sophisticated and his fiction is finally beginning to garner the respect it deserves.

A large proportion of Bunch's fantastic fiction consists of a loosely organized series set in Moderan, several dozen of which were collected in book form under that title. Moderan is a thoroughly repulsive but fascinatingly original future to rank with the Nebishes of T.J. Bass or the psychobabble worlds of Felix Gotschalk. The human race has finally achieved something approximating immortality through replacement of various parts of their bodies with metallic substitutes. In most cases, only a few flesh strips remain, the lingering evidence of humanity in a culture that has become mechanically sterile. The physical transformation has been matched with an emotional one; the greatly diminished population of Earth survives in armed castles called Strongholds, obsessively separated from one another. The protagonist of most of these stories is the master of Stronghold Ten, a man who was one of the first to have his limbs replaced with prosthetic devices as part of his plan to become the world's foremost warmaker. His life alternates between violent battles and periods of rest in his hip-snuggie chair, watching the sky change color each month as a new vapor shield is erected, or surveying his garden of metal flowers.

Bunch's stories are short and intense and generally work best when read at intervals that allow the reader to react to their fierce emotional content, but the collected Moderan stories provide an unusual exception, their cumulative effect more compelling than when read as individual episodes. A few do stand well alone, including "Was She Horrid?," wherein Stronghold Ten is visited by a female, "The Walking, Talking, I-Don't-Care Man," and "How It Ended," which concludes the first cycle of the series. An uncollected Moderan story of note is "Two Suns for the King." The master of Stronghold Ten is struck with the undeniable urge to grow something organic as a counterpoint to his garden, but fails when it proves impossible to find any unpolluted soil.

Another, shorter series, consists of "Training Talks," most by a male parent to his two children, several of which reflect Bunch's recurring themes of our inhumanity to one another, our tendency to rely overmuch on technology even when it robs us of what it means to be human, and the pervasive human indifference to the plight of our fellows. In "Holdholtzer's Box" a scientist invents a device that will entice people to their deaths. Bunch presents unusual takes on standard themes, such as alien visitors in "In a Saucer Down for B-Day" and "Somebody Up There Hates Us." Robots fall in love in "Let Me Call Her Sweetcore," and the reaction of their human owner underscores his lack of empathy. In each case, Bunch takes a traditional SF theme, does something untraditional with it, and leaves the reader with a fresh way of looking at an old idea.

"In the Jag Whiffing Service" is a rare foray into levity, alien visitors who wish to eat used automobile tires. There's more pointed humor in "Control," wherein special pants are invented to monitor sexual activity. A road clearing crew treats human flesh no better than twisted metal following fatal accidents in "Routine Emergency," and people are lobotomized into happiness in "In the Land of the Not-Unhappies." Possibly his best single story is "That High-Up Blue Day That Saw the Black Sky-Train Come Spinning," in which a group of nonconformists decide to rescue the world's children from the horrible fate of growing into adults. He assails human vanity in "Pridey Goeth," in which a town is followed by a clever potion purveyor, literally falling wounded as a result.

Bunch's importance to the field is almost universally underestimated, largely because he was doing innovative things with language and theme before the field was prepared to accept change of that variety. It could well be argued that the Moderan stories in many ways anticipated much of cyberpunk, the interface between flesh and machine, the question of what it is to be a human being. He was making stylistic experiments years before the New Wave movement outraged long-time fans, setting the stage for the adoption of contemporary literary values into a genre that largely ignored them. And he was certainly the first writer to use themes from fantasy and science fiction in stories and poems on a regular basis within the world of literary and university magazines, publishing SF in markets that would have turned up their noses at Heinlein, Clarke, or even Sturgeon. Of particular note is his long poem, "The Heartacher and the Warehouseman."

Although the list of David Bunch stories is quite lengthy, he has never been a particularly prolific writer, and has no novels to his credit. Until the recent publication of the collection *Bunch!,* most of his fiction was out of print. But even his detractors remember his work, and I would not be surprised to learn he has been rediscovered by a new audience and finally recognized as an original, efficient prose stylist as well as an unheralded pioneer of science fiction.

—Don D'Ammassa

BUPP, Water. *See* **GARRETT, Randall.**

BURDEKIN, Katharine

Pseudonym: Murray Constantine. Also wrote as Kay Burdekin. **Nationality:** British. **Born:** Katharine Penelope Cade in Derbyshire, 23 July 1896. **Education:** Cheltenham Ladies' College, 1907-13. **Family:** Married Beaufort Burdekin in 1915 (separated 1921); two daughters. **Career:** Army nurse, Voluntary Aid Detachment, Cheltenham, during World War I; worked in a shoe factory, a printer's shop, and a flour mill. **Died:** 10 August 1963.

SCIENCE FICTION PUBLICATIONS

Novels

The Burning Ring (as Kay Burdekin). London, Butterworth, 1927; New York, Morrow, 1929.
The Children's Country (as Kay Burdekin). New York, Morrow, 1929.
The Rebel Passion (as Kay Burdekin). London, Butterworth, and New York, Morrow, 1929.
Proud Man (as Murray Constantine). London, Boriswood, 1934; (as Katharine Burdekin) New York, Feminist Press, 1993.
The Devil, Poor Devil!: A Novel (as Murray Constantine). London, Boriswood, 1934; New York, Arno, 1978.
Swastika Night (as Murray Constantine). London, Gollancz, 1937; (as Katharine Burdekin, New York, Feminist Press, and London, Lawrence and Wishart, 1985.
The End of This Day's Business. Old Westbury, New York, Feminist Press at the City University of New York, 1989.

OTHER PUBLICATIONS

Novels

Anna Colquhoun. London, J. Lane, 1922.
The Reasonable Hope. London, J. Lane, 1924.
Quiet Ways. London, Butterworth, 1930.
Venus in Scorpio: A Romance of Versailles 1770-1793 (as Murray Constantine), with Margaret Leland Goldsmith. London, J. Lane, 1940.

*   *   *

In her preface to the second edition of *The Language of the Night,* Ursula Le Guin identified the crossing of genre boundaries as a distinctly female act; Katharine Burdekin was a perfect example of this dictum, as her writing included realism, children's writing, historical fiction, science fiction, utopias, and dystopias. All her works contained a critique of gender that strikingly anticipates current feminist thought. For this reason, and also because of Burdekin's eclectic use of genre, her work was misunderstood during her lifetime. It was only very recently that *Swastika Night* was recognized as one of the finest SF dystopias. It prefigures both Dick's *The Man in the High Castle* and Charna's *Walk to the End of the World,* and it was published 12 years before Orwell's *1984* (by Orwell's own publisher).

Burdekin began writing in a realist mode with *Anna Colquhoun,* a novel set in Australia. Gradually her work edged into fantasy; *The Burning Ring* is the story of an emotionally stunted man who with the aid of a magic ring is able to wish himself into the past. He lives through three different historical periods to achieve maturity. *The Children's Country,* written for Burdekin's daughters, deals with the adventures of two children in a nonsexist land.

With *The Rebel Passion,* Burdekin ventured into SF, through the persona of Giraldus of Glastonbury, a medieval monk born with the soul of a woman. Giraldus has visions of the future, both near and far; but Burdekin also looks backwards, reinterpreting human history as a gradual progress towards utopia.

The Rebel Passion was the last book Burdekin published under her own name, adopting for later works the pseudonym Murray Constantine. Burdekin concealed her identity as rigorously as James Tiptree, Jr.; as late as 1984, the Orwell scholar Andy Croft was refused permission by Burdekin's agents to name her, even though she had been dead 20 years. (The name behind the *nom de plume* was finally revealed in 1985 by Daphne Patai, whose work on Burdekin is a major source of information.)

The first work published under the pseudonym, *Proud Man,* records a brief stay in 1930s England by an androgynous being from the future who is capable of self-fertilization and telepathy, and is fully human, as opposed to us subhumans. The narrator observes that "A privilege of class divides a subhuman society horizontally, while a privilege of sex divides it vertically." This serves as a succinct expression of Burdekin's politics. *The Devil, Poor Devil!* was published later the same year. The book was hardly controversial, although it is a highly original fantasia on religious themes. The Devil visits Earth, only to dwindle to nothing because so few people believe in him.

Swastika Night was published three years later, in 1937. Its anti-Nazi message was so timely that it was reprinted in 1940 as one of the few works of fiction in the Left Book Club series. Women in *Swastika Night* are confined to even less than "kirche, kinder and küche"—they live in cages, kept only for breeding. A projection of an as-yet-unknown future, it depicts a world divided between Nazi and Japanese rule. Burdekin's work is more than a rigorous extrapolation from Nazi ideology (and from events such as the 1932 suppression of the German women's movement); it is a political and moral expression of a woman writing in 1936, without the hindsight of Orwell or Dick.

Not until Charnas's *Walk to the End of the World* (1989) was such an extreme phallocracy again depicted, so misogynist that it is in danger of extinction, for women are ceasing to reproduce themselves, and fewer and fewer girl babies are born. However, Burdekin does not only blame Nazism for this reduction of women, but traces its roots back to St. Paul, and even to the "real tribal darkness before history began," when women first failed to value themselves.

There is a significant truth-telling book within *Swastika Night,* the one surviving text that reveals the lie behind the official Nazi histories of the world. The novel ends with its slow and secret dissemination, but with the protagonist Alfred unable to change the life of subjugation faced by his newborn daughter. A note of hope is sounded, but it is bittersweet.

Burdekin published only one book after this masterpiece, a historical novel about Marie Antoinette. She coauthored, but there are more than a dozen surviving manuscripts of her work. Of these the first to be published is *The End of This Day's Business,* which is a reversal of *Swastika Night* (it was probably written a year earlier than *Swastika Night*). *The End* is set 4000 years in the future, in a utopia where women are dominant. Men lead passive and dependent lives, but are happy in contrast to the women in *Swastika Night.* One woman, Grania, tries to change the status quo by revealing the truth to her son; both are forced to commit suicide by the women-state, with only the hope that their subversive ideas will survive. Yet this novel is nowhere as dark as *Swastika Night,* for the men, though subordinate, are not as brutally reduced as the women under Nazism. Burdekin, in dealing with the political problem of domination of either sex, breaks with traditional fiction writing in *The End;* there are long essay-like passages that are philosophical reconsiderations of history.

It is to be hoped that more of Burdekin's work will be reprinted; at present only three of her books are widely available. Like Catherine Helen Spence and Charlotte Perkins Gilman, she is an important precursor of today's feminist SF, and has left at least one novel of genuinely terrifying import in *Swastika Night.*

—Lucy Sussex

BURGESS, Anthony

Pseudonym for John Anthony Burgess Wilson. **Other Pseudonym:** Joseph Kell. **Nationality:** British. **Born:** Manchester, Lancashire, 25 February 1917. **Education:** Xaverian College, Manchester; Manchester University, B.A. (honors) in English 1940. **Military Service:** Served in the British Army Education Corps, 1940-46: sergeant-major. **Family:** Married 1) Llewela Isherwood Jones in 1942 (died 1968); 2) Liliana Macellari in 1968, one son. **Career:** Lecturer, Extra-Mural Department, Birmingham University, 1946-48; education officer and lecturer, Central Advisory Council for Adult Education in the Forces, 1946-48; lecturer in phonetics, Ministry of Education, 1948-50; English master, Banbury Grammar School, Oxfordshire, 1950-54; senior lecturer in English, Malayan Teachers Training College, Khata Baru, 1954-57; English language specialist, Department of Education, Brunei, Borneo, 1958-59; writer-in-residence, University of North Carolina, Chapel Hill, 1969-70; professor, Columbia University, New York, 1970-71; visiting fellow, Princeton University, New Jersey, 1970-71; distinguished professor, City University of New York, 1972-73; literary adviser, Guthrie Theatre, Minneapolis, 1972-75. Also composer. **Awards:** National Arts Club award, 1973; Foreign Book prize (France), 1981; *Sunday Times* Mont Blanc award, 1987. D. Litt.: Manchester University, 1982. Fellow, Royal Society of Literature, 1969; Commandeur de Mérite Culturel (Monaco), 1986;

Commandeur des Arts et des Lettres (France), 1986. **Died:** 25 November 1993.

SCIENCE FICTION PUBLICATIONS

Novels

A Clockwork Orange. London, Heinemann, 1962; abridged edition, New York, Norton, 1963; original version, 1987.
The Wanting Seed. London, Heinemann, 1962; New York, Norton, 1963.
The Eve of Saint Venus. London, Sidgwick and Jackson, 1964; New York, Norton, 1967.
Beard's Roman Women: A Novel. New York, McGraw-Hill, 1976; London, Hutchinson, 1977.
A Long Trip to Teatime (for children). London, Dempsey and Squires, and New York, Stonehill, 1976.
1985. London, Hutchinson, and Boston, Little Brown, 1978.
The End of the World News: An Entertainment. London, Hutchinson, 1982; New York, McGraw-Hill, 1983.
Any Old Iron. London, Hutchinson, and New York, Random House, 1989.
Future Imperfect (omnibus). London, Vintage, 1994.

OTHER PUBLICATIONS

Novels

Time for a Tiger. London, Heinemann, 1956.
The Enemy in the Blanket. London, Heinemann, 1958.
Beds in the East. London, Heinemann, 1959.
The Right to an Answer. London, Heinemann, 1960; New York, Norton, 1961.
The Doctor Is Sick. London, Heinemann, and New York, Norton, 1960.
The Worm and the Ring. London, Heinemann, 1961; revised edition, 1970.
One Hand Clapping (as Joseph Kell). London, Davies, 1961; as Anthony Burgess, New York, Knopf, 1972.
Devil of a State. London, Heinemann, 1961; New York, Norton, 1962.
Inside Mr. Enderby (as Joseph Kell). London, Heinemann, 1963.
Honey for the Bears. London, Heinemann, 1963; New York, Norton, 1964.
The Malayan Trilogy (includes *Time for a Tiger, The Enemy in the Blanket, Beds in the East*). London, Heinemann, 1964; as *The Long Day Wanes,* New York, Norton, 1965.
Nothing Like the Sun: A Story of Shakespeare's Love-Life. London, Heinemann, and New York, Norton, 1964.
A Vision of Battlements. London, Sidgwick and Jackson, 1965; New York, Norton, 1966.
Tremor of Intent. London, Heinemann, and New York, Norton, 1966.
Enderby Outside. London, Heinemann, 1968.
Enderby. New York, Norton, 1968.
MF. London, Cape, and New York, Knopf, 1971.
Napoleon Symphony. London, Cape, and New York, Knopf, 1974.
The Clockwork Testament: or, Enderby's End. London, Hart-Davis MacGibbon, 1974; New York, Knopf, 1975.
Abba Abba. London, Faber, and Boston, Little Brown, 1977.

Man of Nazareth. New York, McGraw-Hill, 1979; London, Magnum, 1980.
Earthly Powers. London, Hutchinson, and New York, Simon and Schuster, 1980.
Enderby (includes *Inside Mr. Enderby, Enderby Outside, The Clockwork Testament*). London, Penguin, 1982.
Enderby's Dark Lady; or, No End to Enderby. London, Hutchinson, and New York, McGraw-Hill, 1984.
The Kingdom of the Wicked. London, Hutchinson, and New York, Arbor House, 1985.
The Pianoplayers. London, Hutchinson, and New York, Arbor House, 1986.
Mozart and the Wolf Gang. London, Jutchinson, 1991; as *On Mozart: A Paean for Wolfgang,* New York, Ticknor and Fields, 1991.
A Dead Man in Deptford. London, Hutchinson, 1993; New York, Carroll and Graf, 1995.

Short Stories

Will and Testament: A Fragment of Biography. Verona, Italy, Plain Wrapper Press, 1977.
The Devil's Mode and Other Stories. London, Hutchinson, and New York, Random House, 1989.

Plays

Blooms of Dublin, music by Burgess, adaptation of the novel *Ulysses* by Joyce (broadcast 1983). London, Hutchinson, 1986.
Oberon Old and New (includes original libretto by James Robinson Planché), music by Carl Maria von Weber. London, Hutchinson, 1985.
A Clockwork Orange, music by Burgess, adaptation of his own novel. London, Hutchinson, 1987.

Adapter, *Cyrano de Bergerac,* by Edmund Rostand (produced Minneapolis, 1971). New York, Knopf, 1971; musical version, as *Cyrano,* music by Michael Lewis, lyrics by Burgess (produced New York, 1972).
Adapter, *Oedipus the King,* by Sophocles (produced Minneapolis, 1972; Southampton, Hampshire, 1979). Minneapolis, University of Minnesota Press, 1972; London, Oxford University Press, 1973.
Adapter, *The Cavalier of the Rose,* in *Der Rosenkavalier,* libretto by Hofmannsthal, music by Richard Strauss. Boston, Little Brown, 1982; London, Joseph, 1983.
Adapter, *Cyrano de Bergerac,* by Edmund Rostand (different than 1971 version; produced London, 1983). London, Hutchinson, 1985.
Adapter, *Carmen* (libretto), by Henri Meilhac and Ludovic Halévy, music by Georges Bizet (produced London, 1986). London, Hutchinson, 1986.

Translator, *Chatsky: The Importance of Being Stupid: A Verse Comedy in Four Acts,* by Aleksandr Griboyedov. London, Burgess, 1992.

Screenplay: Special languages for *Quest for Fire,* 1981.

Radio Plays: *Blooms of Dublin,* music by Burgess, 2 February 1982; *A Meeting in Valladolid,* 1991.

Television Plays: *Moses—The Lawgiver*, with others, 1975; *Jesus of Nazareth*, with others, 1977; *A Kind of Failure* (documentary; *Writers and Places* series), 1981; *The Childhood of Christ*, music by Berlioz, 1985; *A.D.*, 1985.

Poetry

Moses: A Narrative. London, Dempsey and Squires, and New York, Stonehill, 1976.
A Christmas Recipe. Verona, Italy, Plain Wrapper Press, 1977.

Other

English Literature: A Survey for Students (as John Burgess Wilson). London, Longman, 1958.
The Novel Today. London, Longman, 1963.
Language Made Plain (as John Burgess Wilson). London, English Universities Press, 1964; New York, Crowell, 1965; revised edition, London, Fontana, 1975.
Here Comes Everybody: An Introduction to James Joyce for the Ordinary Reader. London, Faber, 1965; revised edition, London, Hamlyn, 1982; as *Re Joyce*, New York, Norton, 1965.
The Novel Now: A Student's Guide to Contemporary Fiction. London, Faber, and New York, Norton, 1967; revised edition, Faber, 1971.
Urgent Copy: Literary Studies. London, Cape, and New York, Norton, 1968.
Shakespeare. London, Cape, and New York, Knopf, 1970.
Joysprick: An Introduction to the Language of James Joyce. London, Deutsch, 1973; New York, Harcourt Brace, 1975.
Obscenity and the Arts (lecture). Valletta, Malta Library Association, 1973.
New York, with the editors of Time-Life books. New York, Time-Life, 1976.
Ernest Hemingway and His World. London, Thames and Hudson, and New York, Scribner, 1978.
The Land Where Ice Cream Grows (for children). London, Benn, and New York, Doubleday, 1979.
On Going to Bed. London, Deutsch, and New York, Abbeville, 1982.
This Man and Music. London, Hutchinson, 1982; New York, McGraw-Hill, 1983.
Ninety-Nine Novels: The Best in English since 1939: A Personal Choice. London, Allison and Busby, and New York, Summit, 1984.
Flame into Being: The Life and Work of D.H. Lawrence. London, Heinemann, and New York, Arbor House, 1985.
Homage to QWERT YUIOP: Selected Journalism 1978-1985. London, Hutchinson, 1986; as *But Do Blondes Prefer Gentlemen?*, New York, McGraw-Hill, 1986.
Little Wilson and Big God, Being the First Part of the Confessions of Anthony Burgess. New York, Weidenfeld and Nicolson, 1986; London, Heinemann, 1987.
They Wrote in English. London, Hutchinson, 1988.
You've Had Your Time: Being the Second Part of the Confessions of Anthony Burgess. London, Heinemann, 1990; New York, Weidenfeld, 1991.
A Mouthful of Air: Language and Languages, Especially English. London, Hutchinson, and New York, Morrow, 1992.

Editor, *The Coaching Days of England 1750-1850*. London, Elek, and New York, Time-Life, 1966.

Editor, *A Journal of the Plague Year*, by Daniel Defoe. London, Penguin, 1966.
Editor, *A Shorter Finnegans Wake*, by James Joyce. London, Faber, and New York, Viking Press, 1966.
Editor, with Francis Haskell, *The Age of the Grand Tour*. London, Elek, and New York, Crown, 1967.
Editor, *Malaysian Stories*, by W. Somerset Maugham. Singapore, Heinemann, 1969.

Translator, with Llewela Burgess, *The New Aristocrats*, by Michel de Saint-Pierre. London, Gollancz, 1962; Boston, Houghton Mifflin, 1963.
Translator, with Llewela Burgess, *The Olive Trees of Justice*, by Jean Pelegri. London, Sidgwick and Jackson, 1962.
Translator, *The Man Who Robbed Poor Boxes*, by Jean Servin. London, Gollancz, 1965.

*

Bibliography: *Anthony Burgess: A Bibliography* by Jeutonne Brewer, Metuchen, New Jersey, Scarecrow Press, 1980; *Anthony Burgess: An Annotated Bibliography and Reference Guide* by Paul Boytinck, New York, Garland, 1985.

Manuscript Collection: Mills Memorial Library, Hamilton, Ontario.

Critical Studies: in *The Red Hot Vacuum* by Theodore Solotaroff, New York, Atheneum, 1970; *Shakespeare's Lives* by Samuel Schoenbaum, Oxford, Clarendon Press, 1970; *Anthony Burgess* by Carol M. Dix, London, Longman, 1971; *The Consolations of Ambiguity: An Essay on the Novels of Anthony Burgess* by Robert K. Morris, Columbia, University of Missouri Press, 1971; *Anthony Burgess* by A.A. DeVitis, New York, Twayne, 1972; *The Clockwork Universe of Anthony Burgess* by Richard Mathews, San Bernardino, California, Borgo Press, 1978; *Anthony Burgess: The Artist as Novelist* by Geoffrey Aggeler, University, University of Alabama Press, 1979, and *Critical Essays on Anthony Burgess* edited by Aggeler, Boston, Hall, 1986; *Anthony Burgess* by Samuel Coale, New York, Ungar, 1981; *Anthony Burgess: A Study in Character* by Martina Ghosh-Schellhorn, Frankfurt, Germany, Lang, 1986.

*   *   *

The late Anthony Burgess will almost certainly be best remembered, both within the SF field and otherwise, for his brilliant creation of the bizarre and depressing world of *A Clockwork Orange*. Public perception of the novel will unfortunately be filtered through the interpretation of that book made by Stanley Kubrick in the movie of the same name. The film is interesting in itself and comparatively loyal to the original work, at least insofar as films ever are, and is a remarkable achievement in its own right. This will inevitably overshadow the fact that Burgess's novel itself is a tour de force, one of the few to achieve virtual "classic" stature almost immediately upon publication. It has come to be an archetype of the near future dystopian cautionary tale, mentioned in the same breath with Aldous Huxley's *Brave New World* and George Orwell's *1984*, although it delivers its message with considerably less pedanticism.

Superficially, the setting and plot are not that far removed from much of the standard dystopian fiction which has held an honored place in the field for decades. Science fiction has always provided writers with a set of unique tools to warn about the consequences of particular contemporary trends when carried to extremes. The author's portrayal of the brutal, egocentric Alex, who is transformed through the novel from perpetrator to victim of an even greater evil, a supposedly benevolent government program, is brilliantly plotted and illustrated through a series of encounters with his friends, his parents, and his probation officer. Burgess avoided the standard clichés of lesser writers and offered no turnabout in the final chapters, no revolutionaries foreshadowing the return of more exalted and humanistic values. Instead he demonstrates that the pernicious temptation to use power to control the lives of others inflicts even those who claim to be in opposition to such dehumanizing forces. The corruption of power affects even good intentions, and while Alex becomes a more amenable citizen after his conditioning, the story has in fact introduced yet another victim into the equation, himself.

Burgess developed and incorporated an entirely new slang to enhance the story's atmosphere. It is loosely based on Russian, but is thoroughly logical and sounds "right," providing an even greater texture to the work. Although some editions include a glossary to explain the various words, this was an unnecessary concession to lazy readers; the sense is apparent, and the ease with which the reader adjusts to the new speech patterns is a testimony to the author's skill. Each element in the plot is perfectly timed and placed to advance the story, which falters not once in its rush toward resolution. Except in the earliest edition, Alex's reclamation is demonstrably false, as he reverts as soon as he is psychologically prepared to do so. The first British version provided a less overwhelmingly depressing alternative which was soon dropped.

Burgess apparently tried to repeat his great success with a similar work. *The Wanting Seed* also warns of a repressive future, but here the story was told in more conventional terms, the situations more familiar, and the effect is significantly less memorable than the far stranger *A Clockwork Orange.* Burgess explores the consequences of overpopulation and the various forces that arise in opposition, the institutionalization of the Cold War, active public encouragement of homosexuality as a way to reduce the birth rate, even cannibalism to lower the population and provide a new food source. Despite the best machinations of the powers that move behind the scenes, the number of people in the world continues to grow, and pressure builds steadily toward an explosion.

Burgess's third novel is this area was *1985,* an idiosyncratic "answer" to the classic *1984* by George Orwell. Considering his own creative use of language, he would seem the ideal choice to write a blend of essays and fictional narrative dealing with Newspeak and other aspects of Orwell's work, but the result is more than slightly disappointing. The essays are often interesting, but the short novel—which attempts to provide a more probable but equally repressive future Britain—lacks the inventiveness and grasp of narrative technique that characterized his earlier work, whether within the field or without.

The remaining fantastic fiction by Orwell is at best interesting. *The End of the World News* is the least effective of all Burgess's genre work. Despite his undeniable flair for language and strong characterization, this is little more than a variation of a plot which has become a cliché. The world faces disaster, and the only hope for racial survival is to build a ship in which a few might flee the debacle. As with most of his work, the novel's thrust is satiric, but despite occasional moments where his barbed words bite deeply, the novel as a whole seems interminably talky and self-indulgent.

Burgess also wrote two fantasy novels. *The Eve of St. Venus* owes a great deal to the work of Thorne Smith. Set against a gritty background of welfare and petty bureaucracy, the story tells of the journey of the goddess Venus to Earth, and her intercession in the marriage of a typical young urban couple, transforming their lives. Despite the lighthearted approach, the author's continued disenchantment with the effectiveness of the government in shaping the course of society is evident. *A Long Trip to Teatime,* written for children, is a fantastic journey story, witty at times, occasionally amusing, but with little interest for adult readers.

Burgess was never identified as a genre writer; most of his fiction is relentlessly contemporary, although whimsical fantasy themes like talking squirrels occasionally make brief appearances in his more conventional fiction. *A Clockwork Orange,* however, has had a major impact on writers within the field, and the novel's success has helped to legitimize the devices of science fiction for other writers. Perhaps most importantly, the novel exists as a warning of a path best not taken, if we choose to heed it.

—Don D'Ammassa

BURKE, Ralph. *See* **GARRETT, Randall.**

BURROUGHS, Edgar Rice

Pseudonym: John Tyler McCulloch. **Nationality:** American. **Born:** Chicago, Illinois, 1 September 1875. **Education:** Harvard School, Chicago, 1888-91; Phillips Academy, Andover, Massachusetts, 1891-92; Michigan Military Academy, Orchard Lake, 1892-95. **Military Service:** Served in the United States 7th Cavalry, 1896-97; Illinois Reserve Militia, 1918-19. **Family:** Married 1) Emma Centennia Hulbert in 1900 (divorced 1934), two sons and one daughter; 2) Florence Dearholt in 1935 (divorced 1942). **Career:** Instructor and Assistant Commandant, Michigan Military Academy, 1895-96; owner of a stationery store, Pocatello, Idaho, 1898; worked in his father's American Battery Company, Chicago, 1899-1903; joined his brother's Sweetser-Burroughs Mining Company, Idaho, 1903-04; railroad policeman, Oregon Short Line Railroad Company, Salt Lake City, 1904; manager of the stenographic department, Sears Roebuck and Company, Chicago, 1906-08; partner, Burroughs and Dentzer, advertising contractors, Chicago, 1908-09; office manager, Physicians Co-Operative Association, Chicago, 1909; partner, State-Burroughs Company, salesmanship firm, Chicago, 1909; worked for Champlain Yardley Company, stationers, Chicago, 1910-11; manager, System Service Bureau, Chicago, 1912-13; freelance writer after 1913; formed Edgar Rice Burroughs, Inc., publishers, 1913, Burroughs-Tarzan Enterprises, 1934-39, and Burroughs-Tarzan Pictures, 1934-37; lived in California after 1919; mayor of Malibu Beach, 1933; also United Press Correspondent in the Pacific during World War II, and columnist ("Laugh It Off"), *Honolulu Advertiser,* 1941-42, 1945. **Died:** 19 March 1950.

SCIENCE FICTION PUBLICATIONS

Novels (series: Mars; Pellucidar; Venus)

A Princess of Mars. Chicago, McClurg, 1917; London, Methuen, 1919.

The Gods of Mars. Chicago, McClurg, 1918; London, Methuen, 1920.

The Warlord of Mars. Chicago, McClurg, 1919; London, Methuen, 1920.

Thuvia, Maid of Mars. Chicago, McClurg, 1920; London, Methuen, 1921.

The Chessmen of Mars. Chicago, McClurg, 1922; London, Methuen, 1923.

At the Earth's Core (Pellucidar). Chicago, McClurg, 1922; London, Methuen, 1923.

Pellucidar. Chicago, McClurg, 1923; London, Methuen, 1924.

The Cave Girl. Chicago, McClurg, 1925; London, Methuen, 1927.

The Master Mind of Mars: Being a Tale of Weird and Wonderful Happenings on the Red Planet. Chicago, McClurg, 1928; London, Methuen, 1939.

The Monster Men. Chicago, McClurg, 1929.

Tanar of Pellucidar. New York, Metropolitan, 1930; London, Methuen, 1939.

A Fighting Man of Mars. New York, Metropolitan, 1931; London, Lane, 1932.

Jungle Girl. Tarzana, California, Burroughs, 1932; London, Odhams Press, 1933; as *The Land of Hidden Men,* New York, Ace, 1963.

Pirates of Venus. Tarzana, California, Burroughs, 1934; London, Lane, 1935.

Lost on Venus. Tarzana, California, Burroughs, 1935; London, Methuen, 1937.

Swords of Mars. Tarzana, California, Burroughs, 1936; London, New English Library, 1966.

Back to the Stone Age (Pellucidar). Tarzana, California, Burroughs, 1937.

Carson of Venus. Tarzana, California, Burroughs, 1939; London, Goulden, 1950.

Synthetic Men of Mars. Tarzana, California, Burroughs, 1940; London, Methuen, 1941.

Land of Terror (Pellucidar). Tarzana, California, Burroughs, 1944.

Escape on Venus. Tarzana, California, Burroughs, 1946; London, New English Library, 1966.

Llana of Gathol (Mars). Tarzana, California, Burroughs, 1948; London, New English Library, 1967.

Beyond the Farthest Star. New York, Ace, 1964.

Novels (series: Tarzan in all titles)

Tarzan of the Apes. Chicago, McClurg, 1914; London, Methuen, 1917; revised by Joan D. Vinge as *Tarzan, King of the Apes* (for children), New York, Random House, 1983.

The Return of Tarzan. Chicago, McClurg, 1915; London, Methuen, 1918.

The Beasts of Tarzan. Chicago, McClurg, 1916; London, Methuen, 1918.

The Son of Tarzan. Chicago, McClurg, 1917; London, Methuen, 1919.

Tarzan and the Jewels of Opar. Chicago, McClurg, 1918; London, Methuen, 1919.

Tarzan the Untamed. Chicago, McClurg, and London, Methuen, 1920.

Tarzan the Terrible. Chicago, McClurg, and London, Methuen, 1921.

Tarzan and the Golden Lion. Chicago, McClurg, 1923; London, Methuen, 1924.

Tarzan and the Ant Men. Chicago, McClurg, 1924; London, Methuen, 1925.

The Eternal Lover. Chicago, McClurg, 1925; London, Methuen, 1927; as *The Eternal Savage,* New York, Ace, 1963.

The Tarzan Twins (for children). Joliet, Illinois, Volland, 1927; London, Collins, 1930.

Tarzan, Lord of the Jungle. Chicago, McClurg, and London, Cassell, 1928.

Tarzan and the Lost Empire. New York, Metropolitan, 1929; London, Cassell, 1931.

Tarzan at the Earth's Core (Pellucidar). New York, Metropolitan, 1930; London, Methuen, 1938.

Tarzan the Invincible. Tarzana, California, Burroughs, 1931; London, Lane, 1933.

Tarzan Triumphant. Tarzana, California, Burroughs, 1932; London, Lane, 1933.

Tarzan and the City of Gold. Tarzana, California, Burroughs, 1933; London, Lane, 1936.

Tarzan and the Lion Man. Tarzana, California, Burroughs, 1934; London, W.H. Allen, 1950.

Tarzan and the Leopard Men. Tarzana, California, Burroughs, 1935; London, Lane, 1936.

Tarzan and the Tarzan Twins, with Jad-Bal-Ja, The Golden Lion (for children). Racine, Wisconsin, Whitman, 1936.

Tarzan's Quest. Tarzana, California, Burroughs, 1936; London, Methuen, 1938.

Tarzan and the Forbidden City. Tarzana, California, Burroughs, 1938; abridged as *Tarzan in the Forbidden City,* Los Angeles, Bantam, 1940; under original title, London, W.H. Allen, 1950.

Tarzan the Magnificent. Tarzana, California, Burroughs, 1939; London, Methuen, 1940.

Tarzan and the "Foreign Legion." Tarzana, California, Burroughs, 1947; London, W.H. Allen, 1949.

Tarzan and the Tarzan Twins (includes *The Tarzan Twins* and *Tarzan and the Tarzan Twins with Jad-Bal-Ja the Golden Lion*). New York, Canaveral Press, 1963.

Tarzan and the Madman. New York, Canaveral Press, 1964; London, New English Library, 1966.

Tarzan of the Apes: Four Volumes in One. New York, Avenel, 1988.

Short Stories

The Land That Time Forgot. Chicago, McClurg, 1924; London, Methuen, 1925; in three volumes as *The Land That Time Forgot, The People That Time Forgot,* and *Out of Time's Abyss,* New York, Ace, 1963.

The Moon Maid. Chicago, McClurg, 1926; London, Stacey, 1972; in two volumes as *The Moon Men* and *The Moon Maid,* New York, Ace, 1962; augmented edition, London, Tandem, 1975.

Beyond Thirty. Reading, Pennsylvaia, Eshbach, 1955; as *The Lost Continent,* New York, Ace, 1963.

The Man-Eater. Reading, Pennsylvaia, Eshbach, 1955.

Savage Pellucidar. New York, Canaveral Press, 1963.

Tales of Three Planets. New York, Canaveral Press, 1964.

John Carter of Mars. Racine, Wisconsin, Whitman, 1940; with other short stories, New York, Canaveral Press, 1964.

The Wizard of Venus. New York, Ace, 1970.

OTHER PUBLICATIONS

Novels

The Girl from Hollywood. New York, Macaulay, 1923; London,
    Methuen, 1924.
The Bandit of Hell's Bend. Chicago, McClurg, 1925; London,
    Methuen, 1926.
The Outlaw of Torn. Chicago, McClurg, and London, Methuen, 1927.
The War Chief. Chicago, McClurg, 1927; London, Methuen, 1928.
Apache Devil. Tarzana, California, Burroughs, 1933.
The Oakdale Affair; and, The Rider. Tarzana, California, Burroughs,
    1937; published separately, New York, Ace, 1974.
The Lad and the Lion. Tarzana, California, Burroughs, 1938.
The Deputy Sheriff on Comanche County. Tarzana, California,
    Burroughs, 1940.
The Girl from Farris's. Tacoma, Washington, Wilma Company,
    1959.
The Efficiency Expert. Kansas City, Missouri, House of Greystoke,
    1966.
I Am a Barbarian. Tarzana, California, Burroughs, 1967.

Short Stories

Jungle Tales of Tarzan. Chicago, McClurg, and London, Methuen,
    1919; as *Tarzan's Jungle Tales,* London, Four Square, 1961.
The Mucker. Chicago, McClurg, 1921; as *The Mucker; and, The
    Man without a Soul,* London, Methuen, 2 vols., 1921-22; as *Re-
    turn of the Mucker,* New York, Ace, 1974.
The Mad King. Chicago, McClurg, 1926.
Tarzan and the Castaways. New York, Canaveral Press, 1965; Lon-
    don, New English Library, 1966.

Other

Official Guide of the Tarzan Clans of America. Privately printed,
    1939.

*

Critical Studies: *Edgar Rice Burroughs, Master of Adventure* by
Richard A. Lupoff, New York, Canaveral Press, 1965, revised edition, New York, Ace, 1968; *Tarzan Alive: A Definitive Biography
of Lord Greystoke* by Philip José Farmer, New York, Doubleday,
1972, London, Panther, 1974; *Burroughs' Science Fiction* by Rob-
ert R. Kudlay and Joan Leiby, Geneseo, New York, School of Library and Information Science, 1973; *Edgar Rice Burroughs, The
Man Who Created Tarzan* (includes bibliography) by Irwin Porges,
Provo, Utah, Brigham Young University Press, 1975, London, New
English Library, 1976; *A Guide to Barsoom* by John Flint Roy,
New York, Ballantine, 1976; *The Burroughs Bestiary: An
Encyclopaedia of Monsters and Imaginary Beings Created by
Edgar Rice Burroughs* by David Day, London, New English Li-
brary, 1978; *Tarzan and Tradition: Classical Myth in Popular Lit-
erature* by Erling B. Holtsmark, Westport, Connecticut, Greenwood
Press, 1981.

*   *   *

While best known for his long series of jungle adventure tales
featuring the character Tarzan, both in their original prose form and
in uncounted motion pictures, television series, comic strips, and
other adaptations, Edgar Rice Burroughs was in fact a very important and very popular science fiction writer. In a lifetime output of
more than 70 books, essentially equal numbers were devoted to
jungle adventures and to science fiction. Burroughs's remaining output was widely distributed among westerns, Graustarkian romances,
historical novels, and a few decidedly unsuccessful attempts at contemporary realism. Novels belonging to the last group, most notably *The Girl from Hollywood,* are of interest for their autobiographical content. As a science fiction writer, Burroughs may be regarded
as a descendant of Verne. His emphasis was on wonders: wonderful planets, strange creatures, magnificently melodramatic plots.
Burroughs was himself of plebeian origins, but his works more
often display a bias in favor of aristocracy. His heroes are generally noblemen and/or wealthy, e.g., Lord Greystoke (Tarzan), John
Carter (Confederate cavalry captain and plantation owner), David
Innes (scion of Connecticut gentry). His heroines are often princesses, most notably Dejah Thoris, eventual consort of John Carter.
(Exceptions include the hoodlum hero of *The Mucker* and the prostitute heroine of *The Girl from Farris's.*)

It is important to note that Burroughs was not a significant creator in his writing, but rather was a synthesist of immeasurable
natural talent. Every major theme in Burroughs's fantastic fiction,
(i.e., science fiction and jungle adventures) was anticipated in earlier works. Burroughs's genius lay in his ability to invest familiar
material with such energy that it attained new heights of popularity. He did not invent the feralman novel, the hollow-Earth novel,
the interplanetary romance, or any other significant fantastic form.
He *did* write some of the most successful, most completely developed, most colorful, energetic, and suspenseful examples of each.
Burroughs's science fiction divides into three major series, one minor series, and several independent works, two of which are of
major importance.

Burroughs's literary career began, at least as far as published
fiction is concerned, with the first of his interplanetary romances,
A Princess of Mars. This novel and its sequels concern an Earthly
hero of somewhat equivocal and mysterious immortality who is
transferred to Mars by a means that suggests astral projection. On
Mars ("Barsoom") the hero discovers a dying world containing an
ancient, decadent civilization, roving nomadic tribes, and a complex mixture of races, species, and traditions. Through a series of
some 11 volumes John Carter rises to the supreme Warlordship of
Barsoom, marries the incomparably beautiful red-skinned Princess
Dejah Thoris (who lays eggs but is otherwise wholly human), becomes a father and grandfather, travels extensively upon Barsoom,
visits one of its moons, and ultimately journeys to the planet Jupiter. There he presumably remains (he was in the midst of an uncompleted adventure when Burroughs died). While some of
Burroughs's more ardent admirers consider Barsoom and all its
associated material a brilliantly original creation, it was in fact the
very opposite. The character of John Carter is virtually identical to
that of Phra the Phoenician (in *The Wonderful Adventures of Phra
the Phoenician*), while the basic rationale of Barsoomian history
and culture closely resembles that of the planet Mars in a book
called *Lieut. Gullivar Jones: His Vacation;* both books are by Edwin
Lester Arnold. More of the Barsoomian culture and many of the
plotting devices used by Burroughs appear in *Journey to Mars* by
Gustavus Pope, in *Across the Zodiac* by Percy Greg, and even in
some of the strange theosophical teachings of Helena Blavatsky

(as pointed out by L. Sprague de Camp). And the dueling, kidnapping, impersonating, court intrigue-ridden Barsoomian society, possibly borrowed from Pope, in itself is more than suggestively reminiscent of the court at Zenda as recorded by Anthony Hope, who might well have borrowed from Mark Twain!

Burroughs's second most significant science fiction series was the Pellucidar books, beginning with *At the Earth's Core.* While the later books of this series are of inferior quality, the first two or three are among Burroughs's best work. Here, the essential notion is that of an earth-boring machine accidentally breaking through the planet's crust to discover that the Earth is hollow, illuminated by a miniature interior sun, and inhabited by a wide variety of species including primitive humans and paleontological survivals. Once again, elements derive from numerous earlier works, certainly including Holberg's *Nils Klim* and Verne's *Journey to the Center of the Earth,* and very likely (the name itself is suggestive) Bradshaw's *The Goddess of Atvatabar.* While the Pellucidar series does let down in quality, it contains numerous fascinating features. One of these is a speculation—this one more likely original to Burroughs—on the nature of time and the timeless condition of a world of eternal daylight. There is considerable humorous and satirical material in the books. Also of interest is the so-called "series crossover" volume, *Tarzan at the Earth's Core,* in which the two separately created universes of Tarzan's jungle world and the hollow Earth, are merged—or at least, one may say, their separation is bridged via dirigible.

Burroughs's final science fiction series details the adventures of Carson Napier on Venus. The books of this sequence date from late in Burroughs's career and are derivative of his Martian cycle without ever quite duplicating its spirit. There is also a degree of likelihood that the Venus books were written to strike back at Otis Adelbert Kline, who had written a series of interplanetary romances laid on Venus, under heavy influence of Burroughs's Martian cycle. (This theory is advanced by Sam Moskowitz, and is circumstantially persuasive although unfortunately is in no way documented.)

The Land That Time Forgot is one of Burroughs's major nonseries science fiction works (in some editions it is divided into three very slim volumes, corresponding with its original magazine serialization, and is consequently regarded as a small series itself.) Opening with a sequence of submarine warfare in the first World War, the action quickly shifts to the island of Caspak (also known as Caprona), a place remarkably reminiscent of both Verne's *Mysterious Island* and Peter Wilkins's island retreat in the novel by Robert Paltock. There follow numerous incidents involving primitive and violent life-forms, intriguing speculation on evolutionary processes, and a final confrontation with a chilling posthuman winged form (again reminiscent of Paltock). The paleontological elements in this book, like those in Burroughs's hollow-Earth novels, are remarkably detailed and authentic. They derive from Burroughs's involvement with the subject at first as a student and later as an instructor at the Michigan Military Academy.

The Moon Maid, Burroughs's second major independent science fiction work, is also divisible into three more or less self-sustained segments. It ties into Burroughs's Martian cycle, as a spaceship named *Barsoom* travels from the Earth to the moon. The moon is found to be hollow and inhabited, with access to the inner regions obtained through lunar craters. All of this, of course, is strangely like the moon of Wells's *The First Men in the Moon.* In later sequences, using technology introduced from the Earth, lunar forces invade and conquer our planet. At this point Burroughs's novel turns into a saga spaced over many generations. Burroughs handled the challenges of the form astonishingly well, and *The Moon Maid* is one of his most successful works.

His other works of science fiction have received relatively little attention. *The Monster Men* is a charmingly creaky cross of jungle adventure, desert island romance, mad scientist, and *Frankenstein*-monster plots. This last element occurs also in several of Burroughs's Martian novels, most notably *Master Mind of Mars* and *Synthetic Men of Mars. Beyond Thirty* is a surprisingly effective story of a future war torn Europe reverting to barbarism—anticipating L. Ron Hubbard's *Final Blackout.*

Burroughs's Tarzan stories and other jungle adventures, while not essentially works of science fiction, contain many elements derived from science fiction and allied forms. After feralism itself, the next most common theme in the books is that of the lost race, tribe, city, or country. These are handled well if somewhat repetitiously by Burroughs; it should be noted that this form of adventure writing was perfected by Haggard, whose works seem likely to have influenced Burroughs. The theme of feralism is itself very old in literature and folklore; it was best known prior to the creation of Tarzan in the *Jungle Books* of Kipling. The Tarzan novels also include Atlantean themes, immortality serums, paleontological survivals, at least one city of intelligent gorillas, and at least one satirical novel (*Tarzan and the Ant Men*) apparently based on Swift.

While many of Burroughs's works—most notably his interplanetary and inner-world novels—fall technically within the realm of science fiction, he is regarded by some interpreters as more of a fantasy writer. Certainly John Carter's astral or psychic journeying has little or no basis in science. David Innes's journey to Pellucidar, on the contrary, is accomplished through the application of technology. But, it is argued, in either case the images and themes hark back to traditional romance with a major component of dream fantasy. The science fictional content of Burroughs's works, in this view, is to be taken no more seriously than that which is present in E.R. Eddison's or C.S. Lewis's works. And of course Burroughs's greatest creation, the Tarzan series, echoes notes of fantasy ringing from a primal desire to escape the trappings of civilization and return to a primal, even preternatural, state. Such a view of Burroughs may in fact permit a more profound understanding of his works than the conventional view of him as a science fiction writer.

As Burroughs borrowed from many earlier writers, he in turn was read by and influenced uncounted later writers. The briefest smattering of these must include H.P. Lovecraft, Robert E. Howard, Edmond Hamilton, Leigh Brackett, Ray Bradbury, Gore Vidal, and J.R.R. Tolkien. Direct imitators of Burroughs range from his contemporaries J.U. Giesy and William L. Chester, to many present-day writers including Lin Carter, Michael Resnick, Anne McCaffrey, John Norman, and Philip José Farmer. In most cases, where the imitation of Burroughs is very literal the result is a rather lifeless pastiche; where Burroughs's influence is less specific and the later writer uses Burroughs as a wellspring of color, verve, and suspense, the result is often admirable.

More than 40 years after Burroughs's death, many of his novels continue to be printed. His greatest creation, Tarzan, continues to provide the inspiration for motion picture and television series. While these occasionally come close to the spirit of the novels, they are all too often uninspired and unintelligent exploitations of famous names.

—Richard A. Lupoff

BURROUGHS, William S(eward)

Pseudonym: William Lee. **Nationality:** American. **Born:** St. Louis, Missouri, 5 February 1914. **Education:** John Burroughs School and Taylor School, St. Louis; Los Alamos Ranch School, New Mexico; Harvard University, Cambridge, Massachusetts, A.B. in anthropology 1936; studied medicine at the University of Vienna; Mexico City College, 1948-50. **Military Service:** Served in the United States Army, 1942. **Family:** Married Jean Vollmer in 1945 (died 1951); one son. **Career:** Has worked as a journalist, private detective, and bartender; now a fulltime writer. Heroin addict, 1944-57. Exhibition of paintings: October Gallery, London, 1988; Tony Shafrazi Gallery, New York, 19 December 1987-24 January 1988; Kellas Gallery, Lawrence, Kansas, 1989. **Awards:** American Academy Award, 1975. Member, American Academy, 1983. Lived for many years in Tangier. **Agent:** Andrew Wylie Agency, 250 West 57th Street, New York, New York 10107. **Address:** William Burroughs Communications, Box 147, Lawrence, Kansas 66044, U.S.A.

SCIENCE FICTION PUBLICATIONS

Novels (series: Nova)

The Naked Lunch. Paris, Olympia Press, 1959; London, Calder, 1964; as *Naked Lunch,* New York, Grove Press, 1962.
The Soft Machine. Paris, Olympia Press, 1961; New York, Grove Press, 1966; London, Calder and Boyars, 1968.
The Ticket That Exploded. Paris, Olympia Press, 1962; revised edition, New York, Grove Press, 1967; London, Calder and Boyars, 1968.
Nova Express. New York, Grove Press, 1964; London, Cape, 1966.
The Wild Boys: A Book of the Dead. New York, Grove Press, 1971; London, Calder and Boyars, 1972; revised edition, London, Calder, 1979.
Blade Runner: A Movie. Berkeley, California, Blue Wind Press, 1979.
Port of Saints. London, Covent Garden Press, 1973; expanded edition, Berkeley, California, Blue Wind Press, 1980; London, Calder, 1983.
Cities of the Red Night: A Boy's Book. London, Calder, and New York, Holt Rinehart, 1981.
The Place of Dead Roads. New York, Holt Rinehart, 1983; London, Calder, 1984.

Short Stories

The Exterminator, with Brion Gysin. San Francisco, Auerhahn Press, 1960; as *Exterminator!,* London, Calder and Boyars, 1974.

OTHER PUBLICATIONS

Novels

Junkie: Confessions of an Unredeemed Drug Addict (as William Lee). New York, Ace, 1953; London, Digit, 1957; complete edition, London, Penguin, 1977; as *Junky,* London, Pergamon, 1986.
Dead Fingers Talk. London, Calder, 1963.

Short Novels. London, Calder, 1978.
Queer. New York, Viking, 1985; London, Pan, 1986.
The Western Lands. New York, Viking, 1987; London, Picador, 1988.
Routine. N.p., Plashet, 1987.
Tornado Alley. New York, Cherry Valley, 1988.
My Education: A Book of Dreams. New York, Viking, 1995.

Short Stories

Early Routines. Santa Barbara, California, Cadmus, 1981.
The Streets of Chance. New York, Red Ozier Press, 1981.
Interzone, edited by James Grauerholz. New York, Viking, 1989.
Ghost of Chance. New York, Library Fellows of the Whitney Museum of American Art, 1991.
Painting and Guns. Madras and New York, Hanuman, 1992.

Play

The Last Words of Dutch Schultz. London, Cape Goliard Press, 1970; New York, Viking Press, 1975.

Poetry

Photos and Remembering Jack Kerouac. Louisville, Kentucky, Whitefields Press, 1994(?).

Other

Minutes to Go, with others. Paris, Two Cities, 1960; San Francisco, Beach, 1968.
The Yage Letters, with Allen Ginsberg. San Francisco, City Lights, 1963.
Roosevelt after Inauguration. New York, Fuck You Press, 1964.
Valentine Day's Reading. New York, American Theatre for Poets, 1965.
Time. New York, "C" Press, 1965.
Health Bulletin: APO-33: A Metabolic Regulator. New York, Fuck You Press, 1965; revised edition, as *APO-33 Bulletin,* San Francisco, Beach, 1966.
So Who Owns Death TV?, with Claude Pelieu and Carl Weissner. San Fransisco, Beach, 1967.
The Dead Star. San Francisco, Nova Broadcast Press, 1969.
Ali's Smile. Brighton, Unicorn, 1969.
Entretiens avec William Burroughs, by Daniel Odier. Paris, Belfond, 1969; translated as *The Job: Interviews with William S. Burroughs* (includes *Electronic Revolution*), New York, Grove Press, and London, Cape, 1970.
The Braille Film. San Francisco, Nova Broadcast Press, 1970.
Brion Gysin Let the Mice In, with Brion Gysin and Ian Somerville, edited by Jan Herman. West Glover, Vermont, Something Else Press, 1973.
Mayfair Academy Series More or Less. Brighton, Urgency Press Rip-Off, 1973.
White Subway, edited by James Pennington. London, Aloes, 1974.
The Book of Breeething. Ingatestone, Essex, OU Press, 1974; Berkeley, California, Blue Wind Press, 1975; revised edition, Blue Wind Press, 1980.
Snack: Two Tape Transcripts, with Eric Mottram. London, Aloes, 1975.
Sidetripping, with Charles Gatewood. New York, Strawberry Hill, 1975.

The Retreat Diaries, with *The Dream of Tibet,* by Allen Ginsberg. New York, City Moon, 1976.

Cobble Stone Gardens. Cherry Valley, New York, Cherry Valley Editions, 1976.

The Third Mind, with Brion Gysin. New York, Viking Press, 1978; London, Calder, 1979.

Roosevelt after Inauguration and Other Atrocities. San Francisco, City Lights, 1979.

Ah Pook Is Here and Other Texts (includes *The Book of Breeething, Electronic Revolution).* London, Calder, 1979; New York, Riverrun, 1982.

A William Burroughs Reader, edited by John Calder. London, Pan, 1982.

Letters to Allen Ginsberg 1953-1957. New York, Full Court Press, 1982.

New York Inside Out, photographs by Robert Walker. Port Washington, New York, Skyline Press, 1984.

The Burroughs File. San Francisco, City Lights, 1984.

The Job: Interviews with William S. Burroughs, with Daniel Odier. New York, Grove Press, 1974; London, Calder, 1984.

The Adding Machine: Collected Essays. London, Calder, 1985; New York, Seaver, 1986.

The Cat Inside. New York, Viking, 1992.

Helnwein Faces, with Heiner Müller and Reinhold Misselbeck. Schaffhausen, Switzerland, Stemmle, 1992.

*

Bibliography: *William S. Burroughs: An Annotated Bibliography of His Works and Criticism* by Michael B. Goodman, New York, Garland, 1976; *William S. Burroughs: A Bibliography 1953-73* by Joe Maynard and Barry Miles, Charlottesville, University Press of Virginia, 1978; *William S. Burroughs: A Reference Guide* by Michael B. Goodman and Lemuel B. Coley, London, Garland, 1990.

Critical Studies: *William Burroughs: The Algebra of Need* by Eric Mottram, Buffalo, Intrepid Press, 1971; *Contemporary Literary Censorship: The Case History of Burroughs' Naked Lunch* by Michael B. Goodman, Metuchen, New Jersey, Scarecrow Press, 1981; *With William Burroughs; A Report from the Bunker* edited by Victor Bokris, New York, Seaver, 1981, London, Vermilion, 1982; *Literary Outlaw: The Life and Times of William S. Burroughs* by Ted Morgan, New York, Holt, 1988; London, Holt, 1989.

*   *   *

Best known as a leader of the American Beat movement, despite the cosmopolitan influences on his work, William S. Burroughs has repeatedly used science fiction situations and images in his often bizarre novels of protest against social control. However, his frequent opacity seems to have daunted criticism and has led to some cries of exasperation or outrage from critics, such as Martin Seymour-Smith's reference to his "monumental stupidity." In fact, Burroughs demonstrated his ability to write with conventional intelligence in his first novel, *Junkie,* and has done so again in his recent *Cities of the Red Night. Junkie* is an autobiographical confession of a morphine addict—it is also a map of Hell, attacking a spiritless society and its gratuitous abuses of power. Despite the autobiographical element, Burroughs shows a degree of detachment from his narrator, an unsettled Picaro who sometimes interprets

himself as an idealistic quester.

Burroughs's reputation rests mainly upon the four novels *The Naked Lunch, The Soft Machine, The Ticket That Exploded,* and *Nova Express.* These form a tetralogy which attacks the obsessive need for control which Burroughs sees as having gripped our planet. That obsession is often given its focus in such science fiction images as the dystopias and advanced behavioural technologies of *The Naked Lunch,* and the ubiquitous fantasy of metamorphosis into arthropod form to represent the dehumanization of both controller and controlled. Especially in *The Ticket That Exploded* and *Nova Express,* Burroughs presents the extended metaphor of an invasion by aliens—the Nova Mob—whose members act through and control humans who share their weaknesses and predilections. *The Ticket That Exploded,* the more accessible of these two novels, makes it clear that the aliens are a metaphor for controlling powers on Earth, presented as if they could be only a Manichean force of evil from space.

It would be easy to condemn these novels for their frequent opacity and the paranoid sensibility they seem to reveal. However, Burroughs does write with admirable confidence, power, and surreal detail; where the prose is readable, the phrasing is sharp and the dialogue unsentimentally convincing. The difficulty is that, as Burroughs has admitted in *The Job,* a series of interviews with Daniel Odier, the prose is sometimes "simply not readable." This is mainly the result of Burroughs's so-called "cut-up" and "fold-in" techniques: the mechanical rearrangement of sliced-up pages and the juxtaposition of words from quite different texts. Both Burroughs's admirers and his detractors have overemphasized the genesis of the prose in these techniques, rather than the patterns of meaning which (sometimes) result on the page.

Since the publication of *Nova Express,* Burroughs has frequently appeared to be more a sage—an unsystematic philosopher of life—than a creative artist. Unfortunately, he has not been helpful in his role as a sage. A study of his interviews and theoretical works reveals occasional insights hidden amid obsessive and often inhumane pronouncements, such as this, on women: "I think they were a basic mistake, and the whole dualistic universe evolved from this error."

However, in *Cities of the Red Night* Burroughs has recast the vision of his great tetralogy in a form which is creative, lucid, and fascinating. Drawing upon elements of time travel, space visitation, alternative history and multiple realities, the book enacts a layered myth or series of myths of the Fall, fragmenting into shards from different realities before ending with a menacing vision of nuclear apocalypse. *Cities of the Red Night* will pay detailed study to crack fully its codes of recurrence and levels of reality.

Of Burroughs's other works since *Nova Express* perhaps the most compelling for science fiction readers is *The Wild Boys.* This novel begins as a series of linked apocalyptic vignettes which are pulled together as the story emerges of packs of homosexual specialist warriors who are able to outfight conventional armies, and who ravage their near-future world. The book is a projection of the need which Burroughs feels to destroy all present-day institutions, including the family and the national state.

—Russell Blackford

———

BURTON, Raymond L. *See* **TUBB, E.C.**

BUSBY, F(rancis) M(arion)

Nationality: American. **Born:** Indianapolis, Indiana, 11 March 1921. **Education:** Washington State University, Pullman, B.Sc. 1946, B.Sc.E.E. 1947. **Military Service:** Served in the National Guard, 1938-40, and U.S. Army, 1940-41, 1943-45. **Family:** Married Elinor Doub in 1954; one daughter. **Career:** Project supervisor, Alaska Communication System, Seattle, 1947-53; telegraph engineer, 1953-70; vice-president, Science Fiction Writers of America, 1974-76. Since 1970, freelance writer. **Awards:** Hugo award, for editing, amateur category, 1960. **Address:** 2852 14th Avenue West, Seattle, Washington 98119, U.S.A.

SCIENCE FICTION PUBLICATIONS

Novels (series: Barton; Rissa; Hulzein)

Cage a Man (Barton). Garden City, New York, Doubleday, 1973; London, Hamlyn, 1979.
The Proud Enemy (Barton). New York, Berkley, 1975; London, Hamlyn, 1982.
Rissa Kerguelen (omnibus). New York, Berkley, 1977; revised edition, as *Young Rissa, Rissa and Tregare, The Long View,* New York, Berkley, 3 vols., 1984, London, Orbit, 1988.
  Rissa Kerguelen. New York, Berkley, 1976; London, Futura, 1988.
  The Long View (Rissa). New York, Berkley, 1976.
All These Earths. New York, Berkley, 1978.
Zelde M'Tana (Rissa). New York, Dell, 1980.
The Demu Trilogy (Cage a Man, The Proud Enemy, End of the Line) (Barton). New York, Pocket Books, 1980.
The Alien Debt (Hulzein). New York, Bantam, 1984; London, Futura, 1988.
Star Rebel (Hulzein). New York, Bantam, 1984; London, Futura, 1987.
Rebel's Quest (Hulzein). New York, Bantam, 1985; London, Futura, 1988.
Rebels' Seed (Hulzein). New York, Bantam, 1986; London, Futura, 1988.
The Rebel Dynasty: Volume 1 (includes *Star Rebel* and *Rebel's Quest*). New York, Bantam, 1987.
The Rebel Dynasty: Volume 2 (includes *The Alien Debt* and *Rebels' Seed*). New York, Bantam, 1988.
The Breeds of Man (for young adults). New York, Bantam, 1988.
Slow Freight. New York, Bantam, 1991.
The Singularity Project. New York, Tor, 1993.
Islands of Tomorrow. New York, AvoNova, 1994.
Arrow from Earth. New York, AvoNova, 1995.

Short Stories

Getting Home. New York, Ace, 1987.
If This Is Winnetka, You Must Be Judy. Eugene, Oregon, Pulphouse, 1992.

Author of numerous uncollected short stories.

*

F.M. Busby comments:
I like to write science fiction because it gives me more room to breathe.

*   *   *

F.M. Busby deals with "characters who are pushed hard by necessity and who generally manage to cope," or he puts his characters into "predicaments that could not exist in our own past and future."

In novels such as *Rissa Kerguelen,* Busby develops the theme of identity, with convincing detail, ironic and comic touches, and a quality of space opera and adventure. In Busby, it is man (and woman) against the establishment, identity versus those who would seek to assimilate the individual. He writes of "rebels who find themselves"—dissidents and outlaws on their escape ships and hidden worlds.

Busby taps a rich mine of science fiction: parthenogenesis, Total Warfare Centers, maltreated aliens, "ships that come from nothing," telepathic murders, time-warped drives are all persuasively and painstakingly described.

He explores the motif of the self as well as any writer in the genre, often using nakedness as a symbol of a character's quest for self-discovery. Barton, in *The Demu Trilogy,* is a caged prisoner of crustacean creatures who attempt to rob humans of their own identities and recreate them in their own self-images. Busby investigates the motives of his characters, who plot for revenge and heroism and revel in the pleasure of that revenge and their own self-survival. Survival is a theme as important as identity in Busby's fiction; the two, in fact, are linked.

Three novels that deal with Bran Tregare, *Star Rebel, Rebel's Quest,* and *The Alien Debt* pursue these themes in greater detail. In Bran, Busby depicts a protagonist who rises above circumstance to sacrifice his own humanity for the good of humanity, though the reader sympathizes with Bran's pursuits and paradoxes. Bran does things that others cannot live with, but he is a person who also knows that "sometimes to survive you have to become a monster." He eventually achieves his goal (defeat of UET) and regains his identity through his love for Rissa and their daughter Lisele. Rissa, strong and stable, similarly wonders about her own identity, as someone who can turn from gentleness and love to ruthlessness and sadism. She comes in time to redress her problems and to understand how her life "was still beginning."

While Busby continued the saga in several other volumes, it is his short fiction that remains most impressive. "Tell Me All about Yourself," (in *New Dimensions* 3, edited by Robert Silverberg. New York, Avon, 1973), for example, is a bittersweet story about a lonely man's experience in a Necro house in Japan. The purpose of the place, supposedly, is that you do not have to talk to the women, but Dale selects a superlatively preserved virgin corpse whom he would actually like to get to know, someone, it seems, he had always been looking for. He feels foolish talking to the girl, so he steals her and casts her off to sea in a blaze, toward a death with dignity. Her only response to him had been a ubiquitous smile. Busby understates the macabre brilliantly in this story about the need for communication in love.

"If This Is Winnetka, You Must Be Judy," (in *Universe 5,* edited by Terry Carr, New York, Random House, 1974; London, Dobson, 1978), is a fascinating story, almost a spinoff of Heinlein's "All You Zombies—." The story deals with Larry Garth's ability to wake up periodically into a different time zone in his life. Busby gains a perfect sense of verisimilitude, with casual references to "circular causation," "research into the parameters of now," and "infancy skips." When we meet Garth, he has no idea how much of his existence had been lived "back and forth in bits and pieces." Busby uses this zig-zag experience as its own metaphor, set up against those of us who live "solely from one view that plod[s] along a line and [sees] only one consecutive past."

"First Person Plural" (in *Universe 10,* edited by Terry Carr, New York, Doubleday, 1980), employs a similar conceit. Ed Carlain awakens to discover he has undergone a consciousness transfer with a once-comatose Melanie Blake. Despite a sense of loss, Ed and Melanie come together to cope with their incongruities: "she was himself, one day behind himself." The two must share their lives with "one . . . memory between them." But the idea of confused sexual identity reveals the overall theme Busby wishes to convey: "If I can't accept ME, I can never accept any man."

—Richard Orodenker

BUTLER, Octavia E(stelle)

Nationality: American. **Born:** Pasadena, California, 22 June 1947. **Education:** Pasadena College, 1965-68, A.A. 1968; California State University, 1969. **Career:** Since 1970, freelance writer. **Awards:** Hugo award, 1984; Nebula award, 1985; *Locus* award, 1985; Science Fiction Chronicle award, 1985. **Address:** c/o Warner Books Inc., 666 Fifth Avenue, New York, New York 10103, U.S.A.

SCIENCE FICTION PUBLICATIONS

Novels (series: Patternists; Xenogenesis)

Patternmaster (Patternists). Garden City, New York, Doubleday, 1976; London, Sphere, 1978.
Mind of My Mind (Patternists). Garden City, New York, Doubleday, 1977; London, Sidgwick and Jackson, 1978.
Survivor (Patternists). Garden City, New York, Doubleday, and London, Sidgwick and Jackson, 1978.
Kindred. Garden City, New York, Doubleday, 1979; London, Women's Press, 1988.
Wild Seed (Patternists). Garden City, New York, Doubleday, and London, Sidgwick and Jackson, 1980.
Clay's Ark (Patternists). New York, St. Martin's Press, 1984; London, Gollancz, 1991.
Xenogenesis (omnibus). New York, Guild America, 1989.
   Dawn. New York, Warner, and London, Gollancz, 1987.
   Adulthood Rites. New York, Warner, and London, Gollancz, 1988.
   Imago. New York, Warner, and London, Gollancz, 1989.
Parable of the Sower. New York, Four Walls Eight Windows, 1993; London, Women's Press, 1995.

Short Stories

The Evening and the Morning and the Night. Eugene, Oregon, Pulphouse, 1991.

*

Critical Study: *Suzy Charnas, Joan Vinge, and Octavia Butler* by Richard Law, with others, San Bernardino, California, Borgo Press, 1986.

Octavia E. Butler comments:

(1981) I began writing fantasy and science fiction because these seemed to be the genres in which I could be freest, most creative. I had in mind from my first novel a series, a fictional history of people called Patternists who are, by mutation and selective breeding, developing psionic abilities. The books of this series are, in the order of the events they cover, *Wild Seed,* which begins in 1690, *Mind of My Mind* (present-day), *Survivor* (near future), and *Patternmaster* (distant future). The books are stories of power—adjustment to power, struggle for power, corruption by power. I bring together multiracial groups of men and women who must cope with one another's differences as well as with new, not necessarily controllable, abilities within themselves.

A non-Patternist novel, *Kindred,* tells the story of a young black woman of the 1970s who is shifted back in time to the antebellum South where she is enslaved and forced to fend for herself in a world almost as hostile and alien to her as another planet.

* * *

Of the 10 novels and the handful of short fiction pieces by Octavia Butler, several are among the most important science fiction works written in the late 20th century. Her stories usually feature non-white female protagonists who nourish and heal people of all races. Their behavior in a racist human culture is always ameliorative. Frequently, the stories describe a disease in progress or significant occasions of sick or injured people treated and nursed by a central female character whose fundamental identity is that of healer—often with other powers. The stories, furthermore, depict the remorselessness of history in its capricious calendar and maverick process. The significant events of this history are those acts of strangely different and solitary individuals struggling for freedom from racism, sexism, and classism by means of the exotic tactics of psionic powers, vampirism, longevity, species metamorphosis, a knowledge of history, anthropology, and genetics. Above all, Butler's protagonists evoke compassion. Her stories do not insist upon particular solutions. They do encourage hope that some kind of enlightened species, related to humanity, can survive.

Five of Butler's novels are in the Patternmaster series; three are in the Xenogenesis series; one is the singular novel *Kindred*; and her tenth novel is *Parable of the Sower.* Prudently, the novels are written so that each can be read by itself. Indeed, the unity and art of *Wild Seed* of the Patternmaster group is so complete that the companion works, although very fine, are not necessary to understanding *Wild Seed* and seem pale by comparison. Although written fourth of the five Patternmaster novels, *Wild Seed* is a prequel and genesis story for the series. It presents the 4000-year-old person, Doro, presumably male, whose life essence reincarnates in body after body, which he takes over absolutely, preemptive of the wills and lives of the victim owners of the bodies. This superbeing roams the world and history, searching for humans with parapsychological powers whom he captures and brings together in communities, especially in Africa and America, so they can consolidate their powers and evolve into a superhuman species. In Africa, Doro discovers the woman Anyanwu, who is very nearly an immortal herself, as well as a shape-shifter and a healer. He wants her for a companion to escape his ancient loneliness, and as a breeding mother for his super species, his people. She hates him because he kills people to live. He controls her, even so, by threatening to kill the children he fathers upon her. Thus, their relationship is a coexistence constructed of mutual need and epic physical and emotional antagonism. The story occurs during the era of the slave trade and the middle passage, especially from Africa to America. The novel's extraordinary power arises from the accuracy of the elemental Anglo-African diction Butler creates to make the description and dialogue of Doro and Anyanwu. Among other influences, she acknowledges that of the Nigerian novelist Chinua Achebe, who has also employed such diction in his works. There is also the mythically impressive epic/heroic/tragic stature and career of the hate and love between titans, a vampire-father and an earth-mother—opposites most perfectly defined by each other.

Mind of My Mind, set in late 20th-century America, presents Doro and Emma (the original Anyanwu who now goes by this English name) who work to raise Doro's daughter Mary to a maturity that will include the reluctant but necessary destruction of Doro by Mary, so that Doro's people can be free from him. Emma, too, dies. The setting of *Survivor* is on another planet, Kohn, out of reach of the psionic power of the Patternists back on Earth. On the planet Alanna, an African-Asian woman adopted by white missionaries, tries to end the conflict among humans and two indigenous peoples of the planet, the Kohn. She succeeds in part by loving a member of the Kohn species and bearing his child. *Clay's Ark* is linked to the Patternmaster universe by its punnric title reference to "Clayarks." It recounts the beginnings of the transformation of part of the human population into a superspecies by an extraterrestrial organism. It is connected to Butler's Xenogenesis series in subject matter because of its story of genetically altered humans that makes them superhuman and super prolific—Clayarks—harbingers of the end of human history. *Patternmaster,* the first novel published in the series, is the last in the fiction's chronological history, set in a feudally governed California in the far future where the psionic human Teray connects love with power to overcome his megalomanic brother and become himself the new Patternmaster.

The three novels of the Xenogenesis series, *Dawn* (on the American Library Association's Recommended SF List for 1987), *Adulthood Rites,* and *Imago,* describe a radical biological revision of homo sapiens to escape the fundamental contradiction of the species: it puts great intelligence at the service of hierarchical behavior. Linking the three novels, the physically imposing black woman Lilith is pressed into service as nurse, mother, and leader by the alien Oankali, gene collectors and traders who are salvaging the remanent humans after a nuclear war on Earth. The biology of the Oankali provides within their bodies all that is necessary for the infinite variations of powers possible through genetic engineering. So advanced is their mastery of genetic mutation that they grow spaceships and habitat, the dimensions of which must be measured in miles, and which in spite of, or indeed because of, being organic, are perfect in function and the comfort they provide. They are also reminiscent of the quite opposite fragilely diseased elegance of J.G.Ballard's *The Crystal World* and the inscrutable alien energy of Stanislaw Lem's *Solaris.* The Oankali do save humanity and improve it, but the price is the loss of original humanity.

Kindred transcends the science fiction genre. It employs magical realism and taps the literature of the slave narratives to make a story that is Kafkaesque. The African American wife to caucasian Kevin Franklin, Edana (Dana) of mid-1970s Los Angeles is abruptly time-travelled to 1820s Maryland to become, eventually, if intermittently, a slave on the Weylin plantation, dedicated to nursing and protecting young Rufus Weylin, one of her many-times great grandfathers. At the same time, she cannot escape the pain and degradation American slavery created. The means of Dana's time-transportation is not explained. Like the seemingly random process of history, it admits to no cogent analysis. It happens as American slavery happened, insanely, interlocking forever the destinies of slaves and slave-makers. Butler's novel is excellent for the realism of the depiction of antebellum American slave culture. It deserves comparison with Alex Haley's *Roots* and Margaret Walker's *Jubilee,* and it is a worthy homage to authentic slave narratives such as that by Frederick Douglass, to which Butler has acknowledged a considerable debt.

Butler's shorter fiction is also exceptional. "Speech Sounds" (*Isaac Asimov's Science Fiction Magazine,* mid-December 1983) won the 1984 Hugo award for best short story. In the ruins of a late 20th-century California metropolitan area the now solitary, one-time UCLA professor Valerie Rye, dyslexic as a symptom of a world disease that has apparently attacked the language-encoding brain centers of humans, meets Obsidian, a man who, unlike her, cannot talk, but he can read. Their predicament is a variation of the Tower-of-Babel condition. Obsidian is gentle and attractive; indeed he is a caretaker type, as his wearing of the uniform of the defunct Los Angeles Police Department signifies. The courtship is quick and successful. Valerie's joy increases even as the two enter a neighborhood just in time to discover a man in the act of killing a woman. Obsidian shoots the man, and is himself shot and killed. Valerie immediately kills the assailant, but her new lover is dead—a loss doubly terrible in this demolished world. Almost immediately, however, a preschool boy and girl come out on the street looking for their mother—the dead woman. Both of them, sharing Valerie's form of the disease, can talk. Valerie is able to tell them she will take care of them.

"Bloodchild" (*Isaac Asimov's Science Fiction Magazine,* June 1984) won the 1985 Hugo, Nebula, and *Locus* Awards for best novelette. It revolves around a humanity enslaved by the Tlic, an insectoid species. The Tlic lay their eggs in the bodies of the humans, where the eggs gestate and are cut out of the humans at birth. In the story, the relationship, or the colonization of humanity by the Tlic, is already traditional and as conflicted with deeply conditioned master-slave dynamics as those exhibited in, for example, the historic slave culture of the United States. At the story's end the profoundest horror is in the resigned serenity of Gan (human boy) in his relationship with T'Gatoi (Tlic female); when Gan begins a term as host of T'Gatoi's egg, he lies down naked with the velvet-hulled, segmented body of his mistress.

"The Evening and the Morning and the Night" (*Omni,* May 1987) was nominated for a 1988 Hugo award for best novelette. Like "Speech Sounds," it turns upon the effects of a bizarre disease, this time called "Duryea-Gode Disease (DGD)." One irony is that the disease is caused in the children of parents cured of cancer by the drug "Hedeonco." Victims are suicidally self-mutilating and exhibit as a principal symptom, quixotically, the ability to concentrate with extraordinary persistence, so that their work in art and science is often brilliant. The story's heroine, Lynn Mortimer, is a DGD victim who has the special property of giving off a pheremone that prevents DGD victims from becoming suicidal and lets them find life worth living. The story is about how an unusually weird person, even stranger than the people in her already weird class, can find meaning in life.

In her tenth novel, *Parable of the Sower,* a title taken from Luke 8:5-8 of the King James Bible, about a sower, some of whose seed failed and some of which "bore fruit an hundredfold," Lauren Olamina keeps a journal that begins on her fifteenth birthday, 20 July 2024 and ends on 10 October 2027. It describes her life in postmodern California in which people have resorted to living in fortified enclave communities, outside of which the poor and dispossessed struggle for existence in a miasma of violence. Lauren's enclave and family are soon destroyed and she journeys north along the California highway, meeting and pairing with 57-year-old Taylor Franklin Bankole, a doctor, and a number of other survivors with whom she shares her evolving philosophical religion, "Earthseed," whose basic tenet is "God is change." One must change or die. After witnessing all manner of savagery, including a new version of slavery evolved from the condition of the California fruit-picking laborers, the group reaches Bankole's northern California land where they will start from scratch in a world that has still "not hit bottom."

Fortunately for SF readers, Butler is only in mid-career, and already she has earned the great respect and admiration of other writers as well as of readers.

—John Pfeiffer

BUTLER, Samuel

Pseudonym: Cellarious. **Nationality:** British. **Born:** Langar Rectory, near Bingham, Nottinghamshire, 4 December 1835. **Education:** Shrewsbury School, Shropshire, 1848-54; St. John's College, Cambridge 1854-58, B.A. (honors) 1858; studied painting at Heatherley's School, London, 1865. **Career:** Sheep farmer, Rangitata district, New Zealand, 1859-64; settled in London, 1864; exhibited and composed music. **Died:** 18 June 1902.

SCIENCE FICTION PUBLICATIONS

Novels (series: Erewhon in all titles)

Erewhon; or, Over the Range. published anonymously, London, Trubner, 1872; revised edition, 1872; as Samuel Butler, London, Bogue, 1889; New York, Dutton, 1910.
Erewhon Revisited Twenty Years Later, Both by the Original Discoverer of the Country and by His Son. London, Richards, 1901; New York, Dutton, 1910.

OTHER PUBLICATIONS

Novel

The Way of All Flesh, edited by R.A. Streatfeild. London, Richards, 1903; New York, Dutton, 1910.

Plays

Narcissus: A Dramatic Cantata, words and music by Butler and Henry Festing Jones. London, Weekes, 1888.

Ulysses: A Dramatic Oratorio, words and music by Butler and Henry Festing Jones. London, Weekes, and Chicago, Summy, 1904.

Poetry

Seven Sonnets and a Psalm of Montreal, edited by R.A. Streatfeild. Privately printed, 1904.

Other

A First Year in Canterbury Settlement. London, Longman, 1863; revised edition, edited by R.A. Streatfeild, London, Fifield, 1914; New York, Dutton, 1915.
The Evidence for the Resurrection of Jesus Christ as Given by the Four Evangelists, Critically Examined (published anonymously). Privately printed, 1865.
The Fair Haven: A Work in Defence of the Miraculous Element in Our Lord's Ministry upon Earth. London, Trubner, 1873; New York, Kennerley, 1913.
Life and Habit: An Essay After a Completer View of Evolution. London, Trubner, 1878; New York, Dutton, 1911.
Evolution Old and New. London, Hardwicke and Bogue, and Salem, Massachusetts, Cassino, 1879.
Unconscious Memory. London, Bogue, 1880; New York, Dutton, 1911.
Alps and Sanctuaries of Piedmont and the Canton Ticino. London, Bogue, 1881; New York, Dutton, 1913.
Selections from Previous Works. London, Trubner, 1884.
Gavottes, Minuets, Fugues, and Other Short Pieces for Piano, with Henry Festing Jones. London, Novello, 1885.
Holbein's "Dance." London, Trubner, 1886.
Luck or Cunning as a Main Means of Organic Modification? London, Trubner, 1887.
Ex Voto: An Account of the Sacro Monte or New Jerusalem at Varallo-Sesia. London, Trubner, 1888; revised edition, 1889.
A Lecture on the Humour of Homer. Cambridge, Metcalfe, 1892.
On the Trapanese Origin of the Odyssey. Cambridge, Metcalfe, 1893.
The Life and Letters of Dr. Samuel Butler. London, Murray, 2 vols., 1896.
The Authoress of the Odyssey. London, Longman, 1897; New York, Dutton, 1922.
Shakespeare's Sonnets Reconsidered, and in Part Rearranged. London, Longman, 1899; New York, Dutton, 1927.
Essays on Life, Art and Science, edited by R.A. Streatfeild. London, Richards, 1904; Port Washington, New York, Kennikat Press, 1970.
God the Known and God the Unknown, edited by R.A. Streatfeild. London, Fifield, 1909; New Haven, Connecticut, Yale University Press, 1917.
The Note Books of Samuel Butler: Selections, edited by Henry Festing Jones. London, Fifield, 1912; New York, Kennerley, 1913.
The Humour of Homer and Other Essays, edited by R.A. Streatfeild. London, Fifield, and New York, Kennerley, 1913.
The Collected Works (Shrewsbury Edition), edited by Henry Festing Jones and A.T. Bartholomew. London, Cape, and New York, Dutton, 20 vols., 1923-26.
Butleriana, edited by A.T. Bartholomew. London, Nonesuch Press, 1932; as *Samuel Butler's Note Books: Some New Extracts,* New York, Random House, 1932.
Samuel Butler's Note Books: Further Extracts, edited by A.T. Bartholomew. London, Cape, 1934.
Letters Between Samuel Butler and Miss E.M.A. Savage, edited by Geoffrey Keynes and Brian Hill. London, Cape, 1935.

The Essential Samuel Butler, edited by G.D.H. Cole. London, Cape, and New York, Dutton, 1950.

Samuel Butler's Note Books: Selections, edited by Geoffrey Keynes and Brian Hill. London, Cape, 1951.

Correspondence of Butler and His Sister May, edited by Daniel F. Howard. Berkeley, University of California Press, 1962.

The Family Letters 1841-1886, edited by Arnold Silver. London, Cape, and Stanford, California, Stanford University Press, 1962.

The Book of the Machines (as Cellarious). London, Quarto Press, 1975.

Samuel Butler on the Resurrection, edited by Robert Johnstone. Gerrards Cross, Buckinghamshire, Smythe, 1980.

Translator, *The Iliad of Homer.* London, Longman, 1898; New York, Dutton, 1921.

Translator, *The Odyssey.* London, Longman, 1900; New York, Dutton, 1922.

Translator, *Hesiod's Works and Days.* Privately printed, 1923.

*

Bibliography: *The Career of Samuel Butler: A Bibliography* by Stanley B. Harkness, London, Lane, 1955; *Three Victorian Travel Writers; An Annotated Bibliography of Criticism on Mrs. Frances Milton Trollope, Samuel Butler, and Robert Louis Stevenson* by Frederick John Bethke, Boston, Hall, 1977.

Critical Studies: *Samuel Butler: A Memoir* by H.F. Jones, London, Macmillan, 2 vols., 1919; *The Triple Thinkers* by Edmund Wilson, New York, Harcourt Brace, and London, Oxford University Press, 1938; *Samuel Butler and The Way of All Flesh* by G.D.H. Cole, London, Home and Van Thal, 1947, as *Samuel Butler,* Denver, Swallow, 1948; *Samuel Butler* by P.N. Furbank, London, Cambridge University Press, 1948; *Darwin and Butler: Two Versions of Evolution* by Basil Willey, London, Chatto and Windus, and New York, Harcourt Brace, 1960; *Samuel Butler* by Lee E. Holt, New York, Twayne, 1964; *Erewhons of the Exe: Samuel Butler as Painter, Photographer, and Art Critic* by Elinor Shaffer, London, Reaktion, 1988.

*   *   *

Samuel Butler was the son of an Anglican rector, whom he later immortalized in his grim autobiographical novel of Victorian family hypocrisy *The Way of All Flesh.* He graduated from Cambridge in classics, then worked for one season among the poor in London, as a result of which he did not become a clergyman but moved instead to New Zealand. From 1859 to 1864, he managed a sheep ranch there, began to write about the country and about the new and sensational theory of evolution, and gathered the elements for his novel *Erewhon.* His other writings attacked received opinion in religion, biology, philology, and child-rearing, proposing alternatives which are today generally seen as eccentric, though the controversy around his neo-Lamarckism is by no means over.

Though Butler's literary masterpiece is *The Way of All Flesh,* some reversals from his country of Erewhon (itself to be read backwards as most other names in the novel) are as interesting and more modern. This civilization, found (as the subtitle has it) "over the range," in an unexplored part of the traditionally upside-down Antipodes, is used for satirical discussions; most importantly, the Erewhonians establish to their satisfaction that machines are using

mankind as a means for their indirect evolution and ban all of them, beginning with clocks and watches. Other exposures of the ulterior moral motives, and thus of the hypocrisy of Victorian bourgeois society are the perfectly logical value-transferral between illness and crime, Unreasons and Reason, or religion and banking. Unfortunately, Butler's overall stance is not at all consistent; for a crucial example, if the time-quantifying tool of clocks is banned, the basic agent of quantifying in modern civilization, money, should logically also be banned instead of being promoted as the religion of Musical Banks. Thus the various elements of Erewhon become mutually incompatible as the sketch of a believable alternative. As Edmund Wilson remarked, "Butler, though he could be most amusing about people's mercenary motives, was too much a middle-class man himself to analyze the social system, in which . . . he occupied a privileged position" (*The Shores of Light,* New York, 1967). The novel dissolves into a string of more or less unrelated satires of the surfaces of Victorian civilization, hesitating between Swiftian bite and middle-class propriety, mildly diverting paradox and cynical justification (though, beside the amusing passages, the fable of the Unborn—who foster the libido of their parents in order to incarnate—retains a certain Platonic charm).

The continuation, *Erewhon Revisited,* is more coherent but less broadly relevant, focusing as it does on the religious cult that has sprung up in Erewhon around the totally misunderstood narrator of the first novel, now promoted to "Sun-child" in a clear parody of Christ (making this novel a continuation of Butler's *Fair Haven* at least as much as of the earlier satire). What is worse, this sequel retracts even the partial estrangement of *Erewhon,* as well as its own satire on the founding of religions, by its final horizon of salvation through annexation to the British Empire.

Butler's SF, thus, remains incidentally amusing reading, especially in the first book. However, its primary importance is the satirical prefiguration of what will later become a much more anguished and wider debate on reification and "machine consciousness" in cybernetics, as well as in the general argument about controlled evolution. Butler had therefore an important influence on subsequent SF, from such Victorians as his friend R.E. Dudgeon through J. Carne-Ross, W.J. Roe, and W. Grove to G.B. Shaw's drama-cycle *Back to Methuselah* and some American SF. But his main problems will be picked up and brought to more sophisticated levels by Wells, Zamyatin, and Capek. There remains the striking freshness and irreverence of Butler's best satirical passages.

—Darko Suvin

BUZZATI, Dino

Nationality: Italian. **Born:** 1906. **Career:** Journalist, science fiction writer, and author of books on Italian culture. **Died:** 28 January 1972.

<small>SCIENCE FICTION PUBLICATIONS</small>

Novels

Il grande ritratto. Milano, Mondadori, 1960; translated by Henry Reed as *Larger than Life,* London, Secker and Warbury, 1962; New York, Walker, 1967.

The Secret of the Old Forest. N.p., n.d.

Short Stories

Author of numerous uncollected short stories.

OTHER PUBLICATIONS

Novel

Il deserto dei Tartari. Milano, Mondadori, 1945; translated by S. C. Hood as *The Tartar Steppe,* n.p., 1952.

Short Stories

Catastrophe, translated by Judith Landy and Cynthia Jolly. London, Calder and Boyars, 1965.
The Siren, edited and translated by Lawrence Venuti. North Point Press, 1984.
Restless Nights: Selected Stories of Dino Buzzati, edited and translated by Lawrence Venuti. North Point Press, 1984; London, Carcanet, 1987.

*   *   *

Although Dino Buzzati became first widely known with his novel *The Tartar Steppe,* his real strength is in his short stories—concise, absurd, wonderful fables and parables of modern existence, often fantasies. Buzzati has frequently been compared to Kafka, and although there is a certain similarity in the mysteries both writers touch upon, their differences are quite marked, both in style and rhythm and their manner of storytelling.

Actually, Buzzati is much more a fantasist than Kafka, showing the influences of E.T.A. Hoffmann and Gogol, as well as of fairy and folktales. Often his stories are allegorical. This is marked in his brief novel *The Secret of the Old Forest,* which revolves around the conflict between nature and civilization; the spirits of an old forest, untouched by human hands for centuries, wage a war against the greedy owner who starts exploiting the old trees. The absurdity of existence and the vanity of human ambitions is the subject of Buzzati's best novel, *The Tartar Steppe.* Isolated in a lonely fortress at the border of a big desert, engaging in senseless military drill, the commander of the small forces garrisoned in the fort spends his whole life waiting for an invasion that never comes, and when rumors seem to indicate that the dreaded onslaught of the Tartars may come, he is already an old man, falls ill, and dies. An obsessive concern with military duties and a senseless waiting

for an event that may never come is turned into a parable of the futility of human existence when all aspirations for transcendent meaning are destroyed by accidental death. Compared to this puzzling and disturbing novel, Buzzati's only SF novel proper, *Larger Than Life,* is an uninspired computer story; a big computer is programmed with the personality of a woman, and this mawkish story is not better than countless other SF novels of big computers.

Generally, Buzzati's few genuine SF stories tend to be weak and unoriginal, lacking the power of his fantastic stories. There are a few tales of time travel, the atomic bomb, the end of the world, and flying saucers. Much more impressive are his stories that blend the everyday and the fantastic in an intricate, inseparable manner, and are told with the economy and eye for factual details of the journalist that Buzzati was. Buzzati declared: ". . . fantasy should be as close as possible to journalism. The right word is not 'banalising,' although in fact a little of this is involved. Rather, I mean that the effectiveness of a fantastic story will depend on its being told in the most simple and practical terms." Something that would have been applauded by Edmund Wilson. By quite simple means, in elegantly turned stories, Buzzati manages to convey alternatively a sense of wonder, horror, the absurdity of existence, the bewildering complexity of modern society, and the inexplicable workings of fate. Strive as they might, his characters have a particular destiny waiting for them from which they cannot escape. Often their whole efforts prove to be in vain, and a long wait or a long search turns out ultimately to be a waste of their lives, as in "The Colomber" or "The Walls of Anagoor." Buzzati's most impressive story is probably "The Slaying of the Dragon"—the story of a hunt for a murderous monster, turned upside down. There the human hunters show only base motives, vanity and greed, while the dragon alone exhibits courage, compassion, and dignity. "Seven Floors" is another parable of modern existence, the story of a hospital, which the patients enter in perfectly good health at the seventh floor, and are gradually moved down to the basement where they arrive terminally ill.

Buzzati's stories are characterized by a search for meaning; they express the existential fears of modern man and interpret the anxieties of modern civilization, explore the labyrinthic existence of cities and the threats of machinery. Their dreamlike mood is often underpinned by an ironical sense of humor, and they exhibit a deep feeling for his fellow sufferers. They show the absurdity of existence, but the hope for salvation is nevertheless a redeeming feature in them; for all their sometimes ferocious criticism of human beings they do not condemn but leave open an avenue of hope.

—Franz Rottensteiner

C

CADIGAN, Pat

Nationality: American. **Born:** 1953. **Awards:** *Locus* award, 1989.

SCIENCE FICTION PUBLICATIONS

Novels

Mindplayers. Toronto, New York, Bantam, 1987; London, Victor
  Gollancz, 1988.
Synners. New York, Bantam, and London, HarperCollins, 1991.
Fools. New York, Bantam, 1992; London, HarperCollins, 1994.

Short Stories

Patterns: Stories. Kansas City, Missouri, Ursus Imprints, 1989;
  London, Grafton, 1991.
Letters from Home: Stories, with Karen Joy Fowler and Pat
  Murphy. London, The Women's Press, 1991.
Home by the Sea. Baltimore, Maryland, WSFA Press, 1991.
My Brother's Keeper. Eugene, Oregon, Pulphouse, 1992.
Dirty Work. Shingletown, California, Mark V. Ziesing, 1993.

*   *   *

Pat Cadigan published her first work of science fiction, "Death
from Exposure," in 1978, during her editorship of the small magazine *Shayol* from 1977-85. Since that time, Cadigan has become a
prolific novelist and short story writer: her first book-length collection of short fiction, *Patterns,* is a highly regarded work that
was honored with the 1989 *Locus* award for best collection in its
first year of publication. While her strengths have continued to lie
in writing short fiction—she is a frequent contributor to periodicals such as *Omni,* as well as to science fiction anthologies—
Cadigan has also written several longer works. Among the subjects that she explores in science fiction novels like *Mindplayers*
(1987), *Fools* (1992), and *Synners* (1991), are the near future, California, and urban society.

Cadigan's initial full-length science fiction project, 1987's
Mindplayers, failed, in the mind of some critics, to equal the energy of her shorter works. Based on an idea that had been previously well-explored in works by other authors, *Mindplayers* concerns the capability, by use of the proper tools and skills, to aid
psychological healing by literally entering any of a series of ongoing mental psycho-dramas within the mind of another human being.

While considered somewhat simplistic in its approach to a much-
discussed topic, *Mindplayers* served as a good launching pad for
Cadigan's second novel, *Synners,* which was published in 1991. A
novel that reflects the sharp, street-smart world where the human/
computer interconnection dominates society, *Synners* focuses on a
computer virus that threatens not only human life but the stability
of all society. Brain implants are mass marketed without safety testing by a greedy, reckless entertainment industry bent on cashing in
on the audiovisual connection that had replaced the current-day
television as a pop-cultural feeding tube. When one of the humans

connected to the master data-bank of the mind-computer network
dies of a small stroke, the virus is unleashed to grow in strength
and infiltrate the network. While criticized by some reviewers for
its lack of character development and overwritten style, *Synners*
also received praise for bringing the rash, frenetic cyberpunk world
to life.

In 1993, Cadigan's intriguing short story, "No Prisoners," was
included in the popular anthology *Alternate Kennedys,* while *Dirty
Work,* her third short story collection, also hit science fiction shelves.
Included in *Dirty Work* are the stories "Second Comings—Reasonable Rates," a cynical portrayal of people's inability to let go of
their dearly departed, and "True Faces," a tale of murder and mayhem in an alien embassy. Cadigan's protagonists throughout the
collection are often women—mothers, daughters, or wives—whose
lives are connected to a classic dullard, be he father, son, or husband. Because of this, some reviewers have found the focus of
Dirty Work, when taken as a whole, to be monotonous. However,
taken each on their own merits, Cadigan's short stories continue to
stand as some of the tightest, most energetic work in the science
fiction genre.

Like several other science fiction novelists, including cyberpunk
originator William Gibson, the battles waged and knowledge gained
by Cadigan's protagonists make little positive impact upon the urban landscape that fills her vision of the future: That world continues to be threatened with internal collapse through its own failings. But despite its somewhat bleak futurescape, Cadigan's work
is commended for its vivid imagery. Through works like *Synners,*
as well as in her short fiction, Cadigan shows herself to be one of
the most expansive talents in the SF genre during the last decade
of the 20th century.

—Pamela Shelton

CAIDIN, Martin

Nationality: American. **Born:** New York City, 14 September 1927.
Military Service: Served inthe merchant marine, 1945; United
States Air Force, 1947-50: Sergeant. **Family:** Married 1) Grace
Caidin in 1952 (divorced); 2) Dee Dee Caidin, one daughter. **Career:** Consultant, correspondent, and broadcaster on aviation and
civil defense: associate editor, *Air News* and *Air Tech;* consultant
to New York State Civil Defense Commission, 1950-62, Air Force
Missile Test Center, Cape Canaveral, 1955, and Federal Aviation
Agency, 1961-64; correspondent, Metropolitan Broadcasting (radio and TV), 1961-62, Founder, Martin Caidin Associates Inc. **Address:** c/o Outbound, 13416 University Station, Gainesville, Florida
32604, U.S.A.

SCIENCE FICTION PUBLICATIONS

Novels (series: Steve Austin; Indiana Jones; Messiah)

The Long Night. New York, Dodd Mead, 1956.

Marooned: A Novel. New York, Dutton, and London, Hodder and Stoughton, 1964.

The Last Fathom. New York, Meredith Press, and London, Joseph, 1967.

No Man's World: A Novel. New York, Dutton, 1967.

Four Came Back: A Novel. New York, McKay, 1968.

The God Machine. New York, Dutton, 1968.

The Mendelov Conspiracy. New York, Hawthorn, 1969; London, W.H. Allen, 1971; as *Encounter Three,* Los Angeles, Pinnacle, 1978.

The Cape. Garden City, New York, Doubleday, 1971.

Cyborg: A Novel (Austin). New York, Arbor House, 1972; London, W.H. Allen, 1973.

Operation Nuke (Austin). New York, Arbor House, 1973; London, W.H. Allen, 1974.

High Crystal (Austin). New York, Arbor House, 1974; London, W.H. Allen, 1975.

Three Corners to Nowhere. New York, Bantam, and London, Corgi, 1975.

Cyborg IV (Austin). New York, Arbor House, 1975; London, W.H. Allen, 1977.

Aquarius Mission: A Novel. New York, Bantam, and London, Corgi, 1978.

Jericho 52. New York, Dell, 1979.

The Final Countdown: A Novel (novelization of screenplay). New York, Bantam, 1980.

Star Bright. New York, Bantam, 1980.

ManFac. New York, Dell, 1981.

Killer Station. New York, Baen, 1984.

The Messiah Stone. New York, Baen, 1986.

Zoboa. New York, Baen, 1986.

Exit Earth. New York, Baen, 1987.

Prison Ship. New York, Baen, 1989.

Beamriders! New York, Baen, 1989; London, Pan, 1990.

Dark Messiah. Riverdale, New York, Baen, 1990.

Indiana Jones and the Sky Pirates. New York, Bantam, 1993.

Indiana Jones and the White Witch. New York, Bantam, 1994.

OTHER PUBLICATIONS

Novels

Devil Takes All. New York, Dutton, 1966; London, W.H. Allen, 1968.

Anytime, Anywhere. New York, Dutton, 1969; London, W.H. Allen, 1970.

Almost Midnight. New York, Morrow, 1971; London, Bantam, 1974.

Maryjane Tonight at Angels Twelve. New York, Doubleday, 1972.

The Last Dogfight. Boston, Houghton Mifflin, and London, Weidenfeld and Nicolson, 1974.

Whip. Boston, Houghton Mifflin, 1976; London, Corgi, 1977.

Wingborn. New York, Bantam, and London, Corgi, 1979.

Play

Television Play: *Exo-Man,* with Howard Rodman and Henri Simoneon, 1977.

Other

Jets, Rockets and Guided Missiles, with David C. Cooke. New York, McBride, 1951; revised edition, as *Rockets and Missiles,* Past and Present, 1954.

Rockets Beyond the Earth. New York, McBride, 1952.

Worlds in Space. New York, Holt, and London, Sidgwick and Jackson, 1954.

Zero!, with M. Okumiya and J. Horikoshi. New York, Dutton, 1956; London, Cassell, 1957.

Vanguard! New York, Dutton, 1957.

Samurai!, with Saburo Sakai and Fred Saito. New York, Dutton, 1957; London, Kimber, 1959.

Air Force: A Pictorial History of American Airpower. New York, Rinehart, 1957.

Countdown for Tomorrow. New York, Dutton, 1958.

Thunderbolt!, with Robert S. Johnson. New York, Rinehart, 1958.

The Zero Fighter, with M. Okumiya and J. Horikoshi. London, Cassell, 1958.

Spaceport, U.S.A. New York, Dutton, 1959.

War for the Moon. New York, Dutton, 1959; as *Race for the Moon,* London, Kimber, 1960.

Let's Go Flying! New York, Dutton, 1959.

Boeing 707. New York, Dutton, 1959.

X-15: Man's First Flight into Space. New York, Rutledge, 1959.

Black Thursday. New York, Dutton, 1960.

Golden Wings: A Pictorial History of the United States Navy and Marine Corps in the Air. New York, Random House, 1960.

The Astronauts. New York, Dutton, 1960; revised edition, 1961.

The Night Hamburg Died. New York, Ballantine, 1960; London, New English Library, 1966.

A Torch to the Enemy: The Fire Raid on Tokyo. New York, Ballantine, 1960.

Man into Space. New York, Pyramid, 1961.

Thunderbirds! New York, Dutton, 1961.

The Long, Lonely Leap, with Joseph W. Kittinger. New York, Dutton, 1961.

Cross-Country Flying. New York, Dutton, 1961.

Test Pilot (for children). New York, Dutton, 1961; revised as *Test Pilots: Riding the Dragon,* New York, Bantam, 1992.

This Is My Land, photographs by James Yarnell. New York, Random House, 1962.

I Am Eagle, with G.S. Titov. Indianapolis, Bobbs Merrill, 1962.

Rendezvous in Space. New York, Dutton, 1962.

Aviation and Space Medicine, with Grace Caidin, New York, Dutton, 1962.

The Man-in-Space Dictionary. New York, Dutton, 1963.

The Moon: New World for Men. Indianapolis, Bobbs Merrill, 1963.

Red Star in Space. New York, Crowell Collier, 1963.

The Power of Decision. New York, Dell, 1963.

Overture to Space. New York, Duell, 1963.

The Long Arm of America. New York, Dutton, 1963.

By Apollo to the Moon (for children). New York, Dutton, 1963.

The Silken Angels: A History of Parachuting. Philadelphia, Lippincott, 1964.

The Winged Armada, New York, Dutton, 1964.

Hydrospace. New York, Dutton, 1964.

Everything But the Flak. New York, Duell, 1964.

The Mission, with Edward Hymoff. Philadelphia, Lippincott, 1964.

Wings into Space. New York, Holt Rinehart, 1964.

The Mighty Hercules (for children). New York, Dutton, 1964.

Why Space? New York, Messner, 1965.

Barnstorming. New York, Duell, 1965.

The Greatest Challenge. New York, Dutton, 1965.

The Ragged, Rugged Warriors. New York, Dutton, 1966; London, Severn House, 1980.

Flying Forts. New York, Meredith Press, 1968.

Me 109: Willy Messerschmitt's Peerless Fighters. New York, Ballantine, 1968; London, Macdonald, 1969.

Fork-Tailed Devil: The P-38. New York, Ballantine, 1971.

Destination Mars. New York, Doubleday, 1972.

When War Comes. New York, Morrow, 1972.

Bicycles in War, with Jay Barbree. New York, Hawthorn, 1974.

The Tigers Are Burning. New York, Hawthorn, 1974.

Planetfall. New York, Coward McCann, 1974.

The Saga of Iron Annie. New York, Doubleday, 1979.

Kill Devil Hill: Discovering the Secret of the Wright Brothers 1899-1909, with Harry Combs, Boston, Houghton Mifflin, 1979; London, Secker and Warburg, 1980.

Ragwings and Heavy Iron: The Agony and Ecstasy of Flying History's Greatest Warbirds. Boston, Houghton Mifflin, 1984.

Ghosts of the Air. New York, Bantam, 1991.

Natural or Supernatural? A Casebook of True, Unexplained Mysteries. Chicago, Contemporary, 1993.

A Journey through Time: Exploring the Universe with the Hubble Space Telescope, with Jay Barbree. New York, Viking, 1995.

Editor, *The DC-3: The Story of the Dakota,* by Carroll V. Glines and Wendell F. Moseley, London, Deutsch, 1967.

*   *   *

Author of numerous nonfiction works concerning aviation and aerospace technology, Martin Caidin builds on his experience as a military and commercial pilot, stunt flyer, balloonist, parachutist, and nuclear warfare specialist to provide convincing background for his speculative fiction. He has made himself an expert on the American and Russian space programs and a harbinger of technological change, as he predicts future trends and warns of potential disasters; his best books on military air history, such as *Samurai!, Zero,* and *The Ragged, Rugged Warriors,* are classics. His fiction, projecting forward from existing programs and set in the present or near future, consistently warns that America's naive idealism about peaceful cooperation in outer space should be tempered by a realistic awareness of nationalistic competition, that our technological capabilities are outstripping our emotional and psychological controls, and that a technological, materialistic, and empirical approach to phenomena fails fully to account for and control such phenomena.

Some of Caidin's books explore what could go wrong with a space flight: personal problems that affect efficiency (nagging wives, wayward children, secret affairs, drugs, and blackmail in *The Cape*); the possibility of foreign sabotage on the ground (*The Cape, No Man's World, Zoboa*), or in space with laser beams (*Cyborg IV, The Mendelov Conspiracy*), or well-placed explosives (*Killer Station*); technical and mechanical difficulties (*Marooned: A Novel*); bombardment by meteors and invasion of alien bacteria (*Four Came Back*); cosmic dust (*Exit Earth*), hostile confrontation on landing (between Russians and Chinese in *No Man's World*); or just incompetence or politics at NASA. *No Man's World,* in particular, raises the question of jurisdiction in space, while *Beamriders!* explores the possibilities of a mission to the far side of the moon and a laser-transport system to "beam" human beings from place to place on Earth and into space. *Marooned* inspired the American-Soviet Apollo-Soyuz linkup mission and the *Cyborg* series not only produced numerous imitators but has affected attitudes toward bionics, biophysiology, and psionics research. Minor characters and anecdotes from one book become major characters and events in another. For example, in the background of several books is a boorish newspaper man who intrudes where he doesn't belong, but who gets his story and ultimately helps out. In *Marooned,* this brash, intuitive reporter breaks through NASA security to learn the truth of an astronaut's plight; in *The Mendelov Conspiracy* he investigates UFO's that prove part of an international scientists' plot to force the world to nuclear disarmament, and he or his counterparts appear in several other works. Caidin's teams of experts experience nationalistic, religious, and ethnic rivalries that can only be overcome at the personal level as shared competencies, parallel experiences, and reliable assistance produce mutual trust.

As nuclear warfare specialist for the State of New York, Caidin analyzed the effects of nuclear weapons on potential U.S. targets; as a result of his experience, his best "fictive" pieces effectively capture the full horror of nuclear accidents or wars and other modern technological dangers. The nightmare possibility of nuclear energy mishandled remains a persistent Caidin theme, one he frequently equates with a fire-breathing dragon, perhaps dormant at first, but ready to rise up and destroy in an instant of all-consuming fire. *Devil Takes All, Almost Midnight,* and *Beamriders!* postulate nuclear blackmail. Step by step, *The Long Night* tersely and vividly portrays a family and town confronted with an atomic explosion and resultant fire-storm; *Star Bright,* in turn, convincingly delineates how a secret fusion experiment goes out of control, produces a microstar that implodes into a black hole, warps time and space, and nearly destroys Earth. In *Zoboa* Arab fanatics hijack four atomic bombs and threaten to destroy the space shuttle *Antares* with its international crew, and only a zany airshow crew can keep the shuttle from becoming a pillar of fire. Other disasters include the transformation of Earth's first space station from a scientific marvel to a terrifying threat, scheduled to this New York City with the destructive force of a hydrogen bomb (*Killer Station*), and an interstellar dust cloud that envelops our solar system, disrupts weather conditions, and returns Earth to primordial conditions (*Exit Earth*).

These novels, horrifying in detail and in credibility, demonstrate Caidin's interest in how most people react to disaster or panic: a few bravely and rationally, others stoically, but most selfishly and irrationally. As others deteriorate around them, succumbing to emotional fears, nightmares, and personal compulsions, Caidin's heroes seem to grow in strength, to shoulder the burdens of others, accept responsibility with calm, and become the eye of calm in the center of the hurricane of forces that swirl around them. The hero of *Three Corners to Nowhere* rides calmly into the tumultuous storms of the Devil's Triangle, chasing a "Flying Dutchman" Gulfstream airliner, caught in a time warp, while an unlikely astronaut in *Killer Station* risks his own life to save New York from the impact of a sabotaged nuclear space station in "deorbit" and the astronauts of *Four Came Back* are willing to sacrifice themselves rather than bring back what they think is a plague from space. Caidin's heroes and heroines can be as harsh and peremptory in act and judgment as are his villains, but their sense of human responsibility is what spurs them to superhuman efforts. They are realistic enough to predict the worst in human beings and to cynically prepare for it, but idealistic enough to value the resilience, ingenuity, and survival drive that allow humans to master their own destiny, even amid debilitating alien conditions. Scornful of established religions, they nonetheless pay tribute to the human spirit, to music, and to ancestral traditions like those of the American Indians, traditions linking human destiny to plant and animal life.

A Caidin hero is often a tough, well-trained military or ex-military man, who is proud of his work, devoted to his country, and able to face up to and control his fear while those around him panic or succumb. Usually a onetime test pilot, he works hard and plays hard. He has an instinct for recognizing expertise in others and is willing to share labor with equals to get a hard job done. However, he does not tolerate fools easily; at his best, he can cut straight to the heart of a problem. His is often a world of machines, whether in outer space or hydrospace, but he has learned that, in a crunch, it is himself, human guts and human reason, that he must rely upon. He is often excited and inspired by a strikingly beautiful, intelligent, independent woman (secret agent, archaeologist, oceanographer, bionics expert, astronaut), but usually this romance remains unresolved or the woman dies suddenly, violently. Sometimes, however, the Caidin hero is a scientist, but one who is so good at his field that he offends bureaucratic strictures, and pursues his own vision in his own way. Caidin's heroes often develop close friendships with their Russian counterparts, and choose working associates for skill and intellect, not race.

Caidin's villains, in turn, if not destructive natural or unnatural forces, human nature, or America's political counterparts, are men whom experience has soured, whom fanaticism has warped, or whom loss of physical prowess, love, or profession through disease, accident, or injury has embittered. These men have lost sight of humanistic values and act only out of self-interest. In *Almost Midnight,* a disillusioned Vietnam hero, a fighter pilot drummed out of the military and civil flying by a bad leg and a rebellious spirit, teams up with other failed pilots to hijack five atomic bombs, to set one off eighty miles east of Los Angeles, and thereby to blackmail the nation. The resultant Air Force, FBI, CIA, FAA, NSA, and State Department investigation reveals another enemy: bureaucratic infighting or nationalistic competition that limits cooperation. In *Killer Station,* the villains are suicidal Islamic fanatics anxious to precipitate war between the United States and the Soviet Union. Caidin's villains also include human mobs who turn into subhuman beasts—a theme in *Four Came Back,* in which earthlings fear alien bacteria; in *The Long Night,* in which rumors of radiation sends hordes flying; in *Almost Midnight,* in which terrorist threats to nuke major United States cities bring hysteria and death; in *The Mendelov Conspiracy,* in which mobs attack nuclear stockpiles; in *The Messiah Stone,* in which Hindu worshippers panic at word of a cholera attack; and in *Star Bright,* in which a sea of crazed fanatics, "a mass tide of two-legged lemmings," fearful of atomic destruction and "ready to accept their own destruction if necessary," wipe out nuclear reactors and storm an experimental center kamikaze-style. Caidin's key characters argue that survival of the many outweighs the rights of the few, and advocate force wielded by a military elite to quell irresponsible, destructive mobs born of irrational fears. *The Messiah Stone* and its sequel *Dark Messiah* delineate such mob potential at its most chilling. In them a fiery yellow "diamond" from space, thought to have been in the meteor that was the Star of Bethlehem, endows its possessor with an almost mystical power to sway those around him. Those powers were wielded by Jesus, by Hitler, by a surviving Nazi fanatic, and, at the close of the book, by Caidin's main character and supposed hero, Doug Stavers: a trained mercenary, a ruthless, sadistic killer, determined to dominate the world. These books have a particularly nasty twist in that the character with whom readers are asked to most closely identify proves contemptuous of ordinary humans and willing to use his godlike powers with deadly force.

Caidin is fascinated by the idea of man and machine becoming a harmonic single entity—either in terms of sensitive reaction time,

or else literally, as in the Steve Austin series. Pilots at critical moments "see" as if one with their machine. In *The God Machine,* the ultimate computer interacts with human operators and mimics and transcends human logic, but a programming fault results in the horror of logic being carried out to literal, absurd, and inhuman ends by a machine which man has made self-sustaining and self-protected. In *The Last Fathom,* the developer of a revolutionary submarine maneuvers at incredible depths to prevent the devastation of the free world by a Soviet doomsday weapon intended to open up a volcanic fissure near Puerto Rico and thereby to unleash a series of natural cataclysms. *Cyborg* (popularized in the television series *The Six Million Dollar Man* and *The Bionic Woman*) is a fascinating and highly technical dramatization of the reconstruction of a test pilot's body, with microscopic units replacing the nervous system, and a fusion of bone and metal replacing missing legs and arm until the man becomes more than mere man, capable of gruelling (and incredible) missions to expose Russian submarine bases and steal experimental planes. With emphasizing the courage and strength needed for controlling and surviving in experimental machinery, Caidin also demythologizes their glamour by focusing on practical, minute-to-minute detail. *Operation Nuke* and *High Crystal* feature further cyborg wonders as Austin plays fugitive to infiltrate a terrorist organization dependent on nuclear arms and then races to find the power source of an ancient Indian civilization—a giant crystal. In *Cyborg IV,* Austin, linked "symbionically" to his space vehicle to control it with thought and reflex action, attacks Russians in space to protect military security. Such missions are the price his country demands as payment for not leaving him a helpless paraplegic. *Killer Station* includes men whose arms or whose legs, lost in accidents, have been replaced by hardware that makes them especially valuable in space.

Caidin's novels are best when grounded in the realities of science and technology. Caidin is good at explaining, in layman's terms, particulars about flight, space, and disaster, about how our solar system functions, how fusion occurs, and so forth; or, as he does in *The Last Fathom,* about earthquakes, tidal waves, and the sea, or in *Aquarius Mission,* about whales, submarines, and lost civilizations. *Planetfall,* an account of space exploration, manned and unmanned, including a hypothetical trip to Venus in 1998, is typical of his skill at making the complex clear. *Final Countdown* demonstrates the strides made in war technology since Pearl Harbor as a modern aircraft carrier, trapped in a time warp, is hurtled back to December 7, 1941, just in time to stop the Japanese attack force before its kamikazi attack. Caidin's teaching technique depends on digressions, flashbacks, reverie, and experts explaining to neophytes, with the latter being most effective for reducing scientific and technological complexities to readily understood terms. Caidin's laymen often reduce a theory to its essentials and express it as a highly visual and common analogy. These techniques allow Caidin to provide a wealth of interesting material, though they occasionally slow down the plot. Caidin blends fact and fiction, the feasible and the speculative. Quotes by real historical personages (especially Einstein and well-known Soviet and American astronauts) lend credibility to his tales of the emotions and conflicts of the near future.

At his best, Caidin's fusion of science and drama, crises and human responses, intrigues, appalls, instructs, and challenges. However, at its weakest, Caidin's prose is labored, his characters two-dimensional, his messages preachy, his plots melodramatic and sprawling. Motives are unclear, and sex and violence are often gratuitous. *The Messiah Stone* involves multiple teams destroying and being destroyed, and characters changing personalities abruptly.

Three Corners to Nowhere tacks together several different plot possibilities, sets up a chain of unbelievable coincidences, and suddenly kills off the main character in a crash with a ghost ship just when the mystery has supposedly been solved. *Beamriders!* presupposes Venezuelans outdoing Americans and Soviets in laser technology. *Prison Ship* involves a plot to conquer the world by the inmates on a hijacked interstellar prison ship and their convict earthlink at Florida's Old Millford prison. The protagonists, a computer genius murderer and his alien counterpart, don't meet until halfway through the book. Much of Caidin's dialogue is simplistic, and his flashback technique is not always controlled.

In other words, Caidin's works sometimes descend to television movie quality, though at other times, their nuclear and space technology science is well worth reading. Perhaps Caidin's greatest contribution to science fiction is in illuminating the relationship between man and machine to show that man must avoid becoming machinelike if he is to remain human, in capturing in everyday terms the enormous destructive forces a nuclear accident might unleash, and in making clear the vital importance of conquering ego and of cooperating with honesty and trust in times of national and international emergency.

—Andrew and Gina Macdonald

CALLAHAN, William. *See* **GALLUN, Raymond Z.**

CALLENBACH, Ernest

Nationality: American. **Born:** Williamsport, Pennsylvania, 3 April 1929. **Education:** University of Chicago, Ph.B. 1949, M.A. 1953. **Family:** Married Christine Leefeldt in 1978; one daughter and one son. **Career:** Publicity writer and assistant editor, 1955-58, and since 1958, editor, *Film Quarterly,* and film book editor, University of California Press, Berkeley. Founder, Banyan Tree Books, 1975. **Address:** University of California Press, 2120 Berkeley Way, Berkeley, California 94720, U.S.A.

SCIENCE FICTION PUBLICATIONS

Novels

Ecotopia: The Notebooks of William Weston. Berkeley, California, Banyan Tree, 1975; London, Pluto Press, 1978.
Ecotopia Emerging. Berkeley, California, Banyan Tree, 1981.

OTHER PUBLICATIONS

Other

Our Modern Art: The Movies. Chicago, University of Chicago Center for the Study of Liberal Education for Adults, 1955.

Living Poor with Style. New York, Bantam, 1972.
The Art of Friendship, with Christine Leefeldt. New York, Pantheon, 1979.
The Ecotopian Encyclopedia for the 80's: A Survival Guide for the Age of Inflation. Berkeley, California, And/Or Press, 1980.
A Citizen Legislature, with Michael Phillips. Berkeley, California, Banyan Tree, 1985.
Humphrey the Wayward Whale (for children), with Christine Leefeldt. Berkeley, California, Heyday, 1986.
Publisher's Lunch: A Dialogue Concerning the Secrets of How Publishers Think and What Authors Can Do about It. Berkeley, California, Ten Speed Press, 1989.
The Elmwood Guide to Eco-Auditing and Ecologically Conscious Management, with Fritjof Capra and Sandra Marburg. Berkeley, California, Elmwood Institute, 1990.
EcoManagement: The Elmwood Guide to Ecological Auditing and Sustainable Business, with others. San Francisco, Berkett-Koehler, 1993.
Living Cheaply in Style: Live Better and Spend Less. Berkeley, California, Ronin, 1993.

*

Ernest Callenbach comments:

It might be reassuring to other writers to know that *Ecotopia: The Notebooks of William Weston,* which has now been translated into eight languages and sold about 300,000 copies, was rejected by all major New York publishing houses; it was then initially published by the author and a group of his friends, using the employee-owned book wholesale house, Bookpeople, as distributor. Presumably the allergy of establishment publishers to the work was due to its being half-novel, half-tract; it is, so to speak, "politics fiction," making certain fictional assumptions and following their consequences much as normal SF does with scientific assumptions; its technology is actually quite conservative.

The favourable response that *Ecotopia* received (except in Britain, where its Californian origins seem to have ensured disdain for it except among scientists and a few ecologically sophisticated readers) led me to write a prequel, *Ecotopia Emerging,* which sketches a scenario for how Ecotopia came into existence.

*   *   *

Ernest Callenbach is not a professional writer of science fiction; he is a reformer, an environmentalist, a small-is-beautiful proponent of the shift from a society devoted to technological progress to one more closely allied with nature. In his nonfiction book *Living Poor with Style,* he suggests that, "Out of the welter of present industrial society it will probably take us several generations to sort out the few things that are essential to mankind—and to reject the others, of which no truly human or holy use can be made." But in three later books his imaginary land of *Ecotopia,* formed by secession of Washington, Oregon, and Northern California, is a model of what utopia based on environmentalist principles could look like. *Ecotopia* is a utopian novel in the traditional sense; *The Ecotopian Encyclopedia for the 80's* is a nonfictional series of entries on how to live in the Ecotopian manner; *Ecotopia Emerging* describes events leading to the secession. Together they form a fairly complete picture of the problems of attaining an ideal society, life in that society, and the impact of that society on a traditional 20th-century society.

Ecotopia describes a very different society from that of the United States, and the six-week assignment in the new country of investigative reporter Will Weston is the first officially arranged American visit in the 19 years following secession. Both governments have hidden agendas: the American to restore good relations and perhaps lead the wandering states to return home, the Ecotopian to teach the visitor to understand their way of life and convert countrymen to that view. The old problem of utopian writing, how to justify long descriptive passages, is solved by alternating excerpts from Weston's private diary with formal columns sent by way of Canada to his newspaper. The real story is in the contrast between the two kinds of reporting and in Weston's slow change from skeptical hostility to friendliness and, eventually, conversion. There are numerous friendly Ecotopians who help the visitor to adjust to and understand the new society, but the most important character besides Weston is Marissa, a free-spirited woman whose love probably has much to do with his decision to remain in Ecotopia. President Vera Allwen, who appears mostly on TV but meets with Weston once in person, takes the important but comparatively minor role of showing the visitor that Ecotopian individuals and their government are very much alike—independent and caring.

Although *Ecotopia Emerging* is billed as a "prequel" to the earlier novel, its action begins in 1986—secession is accomplished in 1988 rather than in 1981—and the earlier novel is actually referred to as a source of ideas for the Survivalist Party, which engineers the whole project. A new character, 17-year-old Lou Swift, invents a cheap and efficient solar-electric power cell, Marissa's cancer-ridden mother blows up a chemical plant, her brother Ben may or may not have planted nuclear bombs in major cities, and Vera Allwen, a state senator, slowly moves to leadership of the gradually more aggressive party. The secession begins on a small scale and spreads; the expected civil war fails to materialize (the "Helicopter War" of 1982, important in *Ecotopia,* is not mentioned); an agreement is reached for peace between Ecotopia and the United States; the Ecotopian constitution is written. This prequel is even more polemical than its predecessor, but it is much more interesting as a story and much more characteristic of science fiction. It is also, as an early reviewer pointed out, lucid and thought-provoking.

Although the Ecotopian ideal is highly acceptable to utopian-minded readers, its creation and continuance, as portrayed in the three books, is not without flaws and has been called impossible by more than one critic. Ecotopia is peace-loving and nonviolent, but it must be noted that this utopia achieved its independence by threatening to plant nuclear bombs in every major American city and by blasting several thousand helicopters out of the sky. It maintains its independence by the implied threat of willingness to do so again (although the revisionist prequel does not mention the helicopter war). Even more difficult to accept is the idea that all these people have not only suddenly become more sane and concerned for others than the rest of the world but able to continue such behavior ever after. Such flaws do not appear on first reading; what makes *Ecotopia* a significant work is that even when subsequent readings highlight such drawbacks, the desirability of this warm and rational society is undiminished.

Whether Callenbach will write more novels that are utopian or even peripherally science fiction, as these are, is problematic. His interest is clearly in the reform of society, not the writing of fiction. On the other hand, there are few better ways to get a message across than to take advantage of the flexibility science fiction and utopian writing offer. For that reason, *Ecotopia* continues to be a work of some significance to those who find today's society less than perfect.

—Arthur O. Lewis

CALVINO, Italo

Nationality: Italian. **Born:** Santiago de Las Vegas, Cuba, 1923; grew up in San Remo, Italy. **Education:** University of Turin, graduated 1947. **Military Service:** Italian Resistance, 1943-45. **Family:** Married Chichita Singer in 1964. **Career:** Member of editorial staff, Guilio Einaudi Editore, 1947-83; lecturer. *Awards:* Viareggio prize, 1957; Bagutta prize, 1959; Veillon prize, 1963; Premio Feltrinellia per la Narrativa, 1972; honorary member of the American Academy and Institute of Arts and Leters, 1975; Oesterreichiches Staatspreis fuer Europaeische Literatur, 1976; Grande Aigle d'Or du Festival du Livre de Nice, 1982; honorary degree, Mount Holyoke College, 1984; Premio Riccione. **Died:** 19 September 1985.

SCIENCE FICTION PUBLICATIONS

Novels (series: Qfwfq)

Le cosmicomiche (Qfwfq). Turino, Einaudi, 1965; translated by William Weaver as *Cosmicomics,* New York, Harcourt, and London, Cape, 1968.
Ti con zero (Qfwfq). Turino, Einaudi, 1967; translated by William Weaver as *t zero,* New York, Harcourt, 1969; as *Time and the Hunter,* London, Cape, 1970.
Le città invisible. Turino, Einaudi, 1972; translated by William Weaver as *Invisible Cities,* New York, Harcourt, and London, Secker and Warburg, 1974.
Il castelo dei destini incrociati. Turino, Einaudi, 1973; translated by William Weaver as *The Castle of Crossed Destinies,* New York, Harcourt, and London, Secker and Warburg, 1977.

Short Stories

Il visconte dimezzato. Turino, Einaudi, 1952; translated by Archibald Colquhoun as *The Cloven Viscount,* bound with *The Non-Existent Knight,* New York, Random House, and London, Collins, 1962.
Il barone rampante. Turino, Einaudi, 1957; translated by Archibald Colquhoun as *The Baron in the Trees,* New York, Random House, and London, Collins, 1959.
Il cavaliere inesistente. Turino, Einaudi, 1959; translated by Archibald Colquhoun as *The Non-Existent Knight,* bound with *The Cloven Viscount,* New York, Random House, and London, Collins, 1962.
Our Ancestors (includes *The Baron in the Trees, The Non-Existent Knight,* and *The Cloven Viscount*), London, Secker and Warburg, 1980.
Sotto il sole giaguaro. Milano, Garzanti, 1986; translated by William Weaver as *Under the Jaguar Sun,* San Diego, Harcourt, 1988; London, Cape, 1992.

OTHER PUBLICATIONS

Novels

Il sentiero dei nida di ragno. Turino, Einaudi, 1947; translated by Archibald Colquohoun as *The Path to the Nest of Spiders,* London, Collins, 1956; Boston, Beacon Press, 1957.

Se una notte d'inverno un viaggiatore. Turino, Einaudi, 1979; translated by William Weaver as *If on a Winter's Night a Traveler,* New York, Harcourt, and London, Secker and Warburg, 1981.

Marcovaldo; ovvero, le stagione in citta. Turino, Einaudi, 1973; translated by William Weaver as *Marcovaldo; or, The Seasons in the City,* San Diego, Harcourt, and London, Secker and Warburg, 1983.

Short Stories

Ultimo viene il corvo. Turino, Einaudi, 1949; translated by Archibald Colquohoun and Peggy White as *Adam, One Afternoon, and Other Stories,* London, Collins, 1957.

La giornata d'uno scutatore. Turino, Einaudi, 1963; translated by William Weaver as *The Watcher and Other Stories,* New York, Harcourt, 1971.

Gli amori difficili. Turino, Einaudi, 1970; translated by William Weaver as *Difficult Loves; Smog; A Plunge into Real Estate,* London, Secker and Warburg, 1983; as *Difficult Loves,* San Diego, Harcourt, 1984.

Palomar. Turino, Einaudi, 1983; translated by William Weaver as *Mr. Palomar,* New York, Harcourt, and London, Secker and Warburg, 1985.

Other

Una pietra sopra: discorsi di letteratura e sociata. Turino, Einaudi, 1980; translated by Patrick Creagh as *The Uses of Literature: Essays,* San Diego, Harcourt, 1986.

Editor, *Fiabe Italiane.* Turino, Einaudi, 1956; translated by Louis Brigante as *Italian Fables,* New York, Orion Press, 1959; translated by George Martin as *Italian Folktales,* New York, Harcourt, 1980.

Editor, *L'uccel belverde e altri fiabe Italiane.* Turino, Einaudi, 1972; translated by Sylvia Mucahy as *Italian Folk Tales,* London, Dent, 1975.

*   *   *

Italo Calvino is perhaps better known as a writer of fantasy/surreal/experimental fiction than as the creator of science fiction. Yet at some points these two branches of fiction intersect with interesting results. His first science fiction work, *Cosmicomics,* considers the origin of the universe, the development of life, and the advance of human consciousness and technology—all from the perspective of the "cell/narrator," Qfwfq, who has been present as an observer in one form or another from the beginning of time. This collection of vignettes pre-dates Douglas Adams's *Hitchhiker's Guide to the Galaxy* by many years and takes the same wry perspective on the struggle to survive on the planet Earth and in the universe. Calvino uses the science fiction format as his vehicle for observing human foibles, in much the same way that any writer of science fiction places "human" protagonists in alternate universes and times to ex-

plore how any creature, human or otherwise, handles challenges.

t zero considers the meaning of time, space, motion, and values. In this episodic series Calvino investigates such polarities as unity and multiplicity, past and present, chaos and order, probability and certainty. As in most of his work, Calvino experiments as much with narrative form as an expression of observed "reality" as he does with creating entertaining characters and plots.

Calvino also makes use of arcane subjects in order to explore the nature of the universe. For example, he patterns the events in *The Castle of Crossed Destinies* on the array of cards in the Tarot pack. The cards and the things they stand for shift meaning as he sets them in different time frames: one grouping shows us such figures as Faust, Parsifal, and Oedipus from the perspective of a medieval castle; another examines them as they would manifest themselves in a more modern setting.

Stylistically similar is *Invisible Cities,* in which an imaginary Marco Polo meets with an improbable Kublai Khan to describe the cities of his empire. Each chapter explores a different city in this imaginary world and provides accompanying dialogues between Polo and the Khan.

Calvino is rewarding to read, for his work not only challenges our assumptions about time, ethics, and perception but also forces us to reexamine the comfortable methods we generally employ to avoid dealing with paradox. He explores these topics thematically at the same time that he makes conscious efforts to extend and distort the boundaries of conventional fiction. His fiction has as much to do with the structure and nature of fiction itself as it does with characters and plot. For this reason, Calvino can be grouped with such writers of fantasy as Jorge Luis Borges, Umberto Eco, Donald Barthelme, and Robert Coover, all of whom want their readers to be aware of what it means to be a *reader,* a participant in their fictions.

—Melissa E. Barth

CAMPBELL, John W(ood), Jr.

Nationality: American. **Born:** Newark, New Jersey, 8 June 1910. **Education:** Blair Academy; Massachusetts Institute of Technology, Cambridge, 1928-31; Duke University, Durham, North Carolina, B.S. 1933. **Family:** Married 1) Dona Stuart in 1931; 2) Margaret Winter in 1950; four children. Car and gas heater salesman; worked in the research department of Mack Truck, Hoboken Pioneer Instruments, and Carleton Ellis chemical company; editor, *Astounding,* later *Analog,* 1937-71, *Unknown,* later *Unknown Worlds,* 1939-43, and *From Unknown Worlds,* 1948. **Awards:** Hugo award, for editing, 1953, 1955, 1956, 1957, 1961, 1962, 1964, 1965. Guest of Honor, World Science Fiction Convention, Philadelphia, 1947, San Francisco, 1954, London, 1957. **Died:** 11 July 1971.

SCIENCE FICTION PUBLICATIONS

Novels (series: Arcot, Morey, and Wade; Aarn Munro)

The Mightiest Machine (Aarn Munro). Providence, Rhode Island, Hadley, 1947.

The Incredible Planet (Aarn Munro). Reading, Pennsylvania, Fantasy Press, 1949.

The Ultimate Weapon. New York, Ace, 1966.

Empire: A Powerful Novel of Intrigue and Action in the Not-So-Distant Future, written anonymously with Clifford D. Simak. New York, World Editions, 1951.

John W. Campbell Anthology: Three Novels (Arcot, Morey, and Wade). Garden City, New York, Doubleday, 1973.

The Black Star Passes (Arcot, Morey, and Wade). Reading, Pennsylvania, Fantasy Press, 1953.

Islands of Space (Arcot, Morey, and Wade). Reading, Pennsylvania, Fantasy Press, 1956.

Invaders from the Infinite (Arcot, Morey, and Wade). Hicksville, New York, Gnome Press, 1961.

Short Stories

Who Goes There?: Seven Tales of Science Fiction. Chicago, Shasta, 1948; as *The Thing and Other Stories,* London, Fantasy Books, 1952; as *The Thing,* London, Tandem Books, 1966.

The Moon Is Hell! Reading, Pennsylvania, Fantasy Press, 1951; title novella published separately, London, New English Library, 1975.

Cloak of Aesir. Chicago, Shasta, 1952.

The Thing from Another World. Sydney, American Science Fiction, 1953.

Who Goes There? New York, Dell, 1955.

The Planeteers. New York, Ace, 1966.

The Best of John W. Campbell. London, Sidgwick and Jackson, 1973; edited by Lester del Rey, Garden City, New York, Doubleday, 1976.

The Space Beyond, edited by Roger Elwood. New York, Pyramid, 1976.

Who Goes There? John Carpenter's "The Thing." Universal City, Universal Studios, 1982.

Other Publications

Other

The Atomic Story. New York, Holt, 1947.

Collected Editorials from Analog, edited by Harry Harrison. Garden City, New York, Doubleday, 1966.

The John W. Campbell Letters, edited by Perry A. Chapdelaine, Tony Chapdelaine, and George Hay. Franklin, Tennessee, AC Projects, 1985.

Editor, *From Unknown Worlds.* New York, Street and Smith, 1948; London, Atlas, 1952.

Editor, *The Astounding Science Fiction Anthology.* New York, Simon and Schuster, 1952; shortened version, as *The First [and Second] Astounding Science Fiction Anthology,* London Grayson, 2 vols., 1954, and as *Astounding Tales of Space and Time,* New York, Berkeley, 1957; complete version, as *The First [and Second] Astounding Science Fiction Anthology,* London, New English Library, 2 vols., 1964-65.

Editor, *Prologue to Analog.* Garden City, New York, Doubleday, 1962; London, Panther, 1967.

Editor, *Analog 1-8.* Garden City, New York, Doubleday, 8 vols., 1963-71; London, Panther, 2 vols., 1967; London, Dobson, 4 vols., 1968.

Editor, *Analog Anthology.* London, Dobson, 1965.

Editor, *Astounding Science Fiction, July 1939* (facsimile of original magazine issue). Carbondale, Southern Illinois University Press, 1981.

*

Critical Studies: *John W. Campbell: An Australian Tribute* edited by John Bangsund, Canberra, Graham and Bangsund, 1972.

*   *   *

Had it not been for John W. Campbell, Jr., science fiction as a publisher's category might have perished with the demise of the pulp industry. As editor of *Astounding* (later *Analog*) *Science Fiction,* from September 1937 to December 1971, he demanded good writing and sometimes got it. That is his achievement (never mind his cranky indulgence in Dianetics and the Dean Drive), and he set the standard with the better of his own stories. As a result, his magazine attracted enough storytellers that it and the science fiction genre remain in existence today. (The stories of reasoned fantasy he published as editor of *Unknown Worlds* are, however, no longer current.)

His early stories take off from the space operatics of E.E. Smith, but with that extra something-to-say that interested the industrial scientists who became his chief readers. The something that must have interested them was the idea of professional colleagueship that stressed the intellectual value of shared discovery; the outcome of the research and development was not a new consumer product, but something to save the species.

Campbell's first story, "The Voice of the Void" (1930), set the pattern. Men 10 billion years in the future prepare to leave the planets of the solar system because the sun is dying. By this time, science had become central to the human way of life and a scientist in training takes a 70-year course at an engineering school, where making inventions is part of the curriculum. Graduates from such schools have been gathering for generations to meet the growing emergency of the sun's death. At last they develop a matter transmitter that sends fleets of spaceships to another system of planets orbiting the giant star Betelgeuse. They accomplish this in a spirit of professional association, men of pure science called to salvationist duty, but in just those fields—aviation and broadcasting—under commercial development at the time of writing. Likewise in "Twilight," a time traveller from the far future asks what are the most important inventions of the day, and the answer is "airplanes and radio."

The pulp tradition of SF that Campbell elevated above adventure fiction—the last refuge of rugged individualism in American letters—was a world of "pooled mental resources." His intellectual hero was attractive to the young student or professional scientist in industry whose job was anything but free to explore wherever the research team's curiosity might lead.

Two groups of Campbell stories follow through with a standard set of heroes. The more popular one is the Arcot, Morey, and Wade series. Dr. Richard Arcot, a world-famous physicist, works for the research laboratories of Transcontinental Airways, selling it his inventions under the patronage of its president, who happens to be the father of Arcot's colleague, the mathematician Morey. Wade, introduced during the course of the first story, "Piracy Preferred," is an air pirate who preys on Transcontinental's great 30,000-passenger superplanes with a device for making his marauding aircraft invisible, but after being captured he joins Arcot's lab staff. Fuller, an aeronautical design engineer, joins the group in "Solarite," and proves his worth in *Islands of Space* by designing a faster-than-light ship on a principle discovered by Arcot. All four then make a tour of the cosmos. The title islands are island universes, galactic nebulae. Financing a tour of these is more than even Trans-continental can afford, so its president helps Arcot raise the rest in popular support from "the wealth of two worlds," Earth and Venus. All this is spent on a fantastic adventure of observational science. But the debt is repaid when the group is able to deal with an alien threat in *Invaders from the Infinite.*

The other story series is *The Planeteers,* dealing with Penton and Blake, a pair of cosmic explorers who land on various worlds and solve exotic puzzles. But again this had survival value. Curiosity is a tough-minded quality because what observation reveals is that "change is the natural order of things." Science is "a method of thinking" that can meet "goals ahead larger than those we know" by knowing how, when the problem is upon us, "to produce that which never existed." Science is the way mankind educates itself to meet the challenge of necessity.

Campbell's test of survival is nowhere dramatized more forcibly than in *The Moon Is Hell!* The first rocketship to the moon crashes and its crew of research scientists, stranded on the dead rock, win from the object of their curiosity food, water, and air. This is the research and development process glamorized in a power fantasy that makes its most important business the winning of life itself. "Machines and gadgets aren't the end and goal; they are the means to the true goal." The commercial products of the technological revolution are but objects of practice on which to learn and organize the skills of innovative group thinking, come the day of unexpected crisis.

Curiosity is the mainspring of human adaptability, and may very well drive the products of man's inventions when he himself is gone. In "The Last Evolution," Campbell introduces an original concept of robots, heretofore imagined only as workers or slaves. He has them become man's evolutionary descendants. They are science machines that make other machines. They supersede man, but surprisingly they end by recreating him. The machines bring to perfection man's urge to explore and do research and create that which never before existed.

A technology that outlives its makers is also the theme of Campbell's most famous story, "Twilight." Eighty-eight million years in the future, man is extinct, but his great automatic cities are still in place. The deathless cities go on with "the tireless, ceaseless perfection their designers had incorporated in them."

Perhaps the best work of fiction Campbell ever wrote is "Who Goes There?" An alien monster is found frozen in the Antarctic ice, buried with its ship, by a team of scientists doing weather research. Once thawed, it gets loose in their camp and changes form by imitating one or more of the sled dogs and one of the men, down to their cells and memories. The dogs are killed, but the problem remains how to discover by some test which man is the monster before it takes over the camp and then the whole world. The leader of the expedition is the tough-minded scientist who has the intellectual prowess to do just that. He devises a blood test, taking a sample from each man and touching it in turn with the tip of a hot needle. The monster not only replicates any body it takes over, it reduplicates itself in every cell of that body. The test is this: when irritated the monster's "*blood* will live—and crawl away." It does, and the man whose sample it is reveals himself in hideous form. Alert for the transformation with poised axes, the others hack their

false colleague to pieces. These few men, outnumbered by millions of life cells, all intelligent, were not defeated. Humanity is *real,* monster-hood is false. Humans have "not an imitated, but a bred-in-the-bone instinct, a driving, unquenchable fire that's genuine."

The monster is no villain: it is a problem. And to be conquered it must be understood, as must all the other unpredictable threats of nature in a universe of constant change. It is deadly to *adapt* to nature, a lazy, undisciplined way that leads to digestion by the cosmic process; survival means *control* of nature. The monster is the opposite of humanity because it goes with nature, not against it. For curiosity it has mere cunning, for pooled mental resources collective imitation. And here is the political note in Campbell's thinking, often sounded in his magazine editorials. For him, collectivism is a monstrous thing that would devour human ideals, but should not be able to do so as long as the superior strength of individuals is united in free association.

—Leon Stover

CAPEK, Karel

Nationality: Czech. **Born:** Male Svatonovice, Bohemia (now Czechoslovakia), 9 January 1890. **Education:** Attended University of Prague; educated in Berlin, c. 1910, and Paris; Charles University, doctorate 1915. **Family:** Married Olga Scheinplugova in 1935. **Career:** Staff writer, *Narodni listy,* Prague, c. 1919-23; director of plays, Prague Municipal Theater, 1921-23; staff writer, *Lidove noviny,* Brno, beginning c. 1923. Founder, "Friday Circle," 1924. **Died:** 25 December 1938.

SCIENCE FICTION PUBLICATIONS

Novels

Krakatit. Praha, Storch-Marien, 1924; translated by Lawrence Hyde, London, Bles, and New York, Macmillan, 1925; as *An Atomic Fantasy: Krakatit,* London, Allen and Unwin, 1948)

Vec Makropulos. Praha, Storch-Marien, 1922; translated by Randal C. Burrel as *The Makropoulos Secret,* Boston, Luce, 1925.

Tovarna na absolutno. Brne, Polygrafie, 1922; translated by Sárka B. Hrbková as *The Absolute at Large,* New York and London, Macmillan, 1927.

Povetron. Praha, Borovny, 1934; translated by M. and R. Weatherall as *Meteor,* London, Allen, and New York, Putnam, 1935.

Válka s moloky. Praha, Borovny, 1936; translated by M. and R. Weatherall as *War with the Newts,* London, Allen, 1937; New York, Putnam, 1939; translated by Ewald Osers, London, Allen and Unwin, 1985; Highland Park, New Jersey, Catbird Press, 1990.

Plays

R.U.R.: Rossum's Universal Robots. (Produced in Prague in 1921); Prague, n.p., 1923.

Ze zivota hmyzu (also known as *The Insect Play*; produced in Prague in 1922), translated by Paul Selver as *The World We Live In,* London, n.p., 1923; published as *And So Ad Infinitium (The Life of the Insects),* New York, n.p., 1923.

The Makropoulos Secret. N.p., 1925.
Adam the Creator. N.p., 1929.
Power and Glory. N.p., 1937.

Short Stories

Devatero pohádek a jeste jedna od Josefa Capka jako privazek. Praha, Borovny, 1931; as *Fairy Tales, with One Extra as Makeweight,* London, Allen and Unwin, and New York, Holt, 1933; translated by Dagmar Herrman, Evanston, Illinois, Northwestern University Press, 1990.

*   *   *

Karel Capek was a prolific author of stories, essays, novels, travelogues, plays, and newspaper articles. The word "robot" was coined by his brother Josef (his collaborator in some works), but its blend of psycho-physiology and politics expresses precisely Karel's preoccupation with contemporary inhumanity, opposing Natural Man to Unnatural Pseudo-Man, a manlike, reasoning, but unfeeling being associated with capitalist technology and the social extremes of upper-class tycoon and working-class multitude. Capek's heroes range from small employees and craftsmen to doctors and deviant scientists, and his most stubborn values arise from peasant confidence in traditional things and relationships. In the plays, this is openly expressed by his small people and ideological arbiters, such as Nana in *R.U.R.* or Kristina in *The Makropoulos Secret,* while in the novels it is implied by key actions such as the final return to normality in *Krakatit* and *The Absolute at Large.* Yet Capek was also spellbound and terrified by the workers's world of factories and the power of capitalists (e.g., Bondy from both the latter novel and *War with the Newts*).

In Capek's first SF phase, after World War I, the tension between the little people (the audience he was writing for) and the catastrophic forces of technology and violence is largely vitiated by the ambiguity between a menace to man and to the middle class: does it arise from aliens created by the large industry, its capitalists and engineers, or from the workers? The robots of *R.U.R.,* synthetic androids outwardly like men, are mass-produced to be "workers with the minimum amount of requirements," i.e. without the non-exploitable emotions. In their first story, "System" (1908), the Capeks had shown a workers's revolt in such circumstances; the machine-men of *R.U.R.* are technological stand-ins for workers (and for Wells's Morlocks) but also, simultaneously, inhuman aliens "without history." Their creation doesn't lead to Domin's engineering utopia with Nietzschean supermen but to genocidal revolt. Yet during the play they grow more like a new human order than like inhuman aliens, more workers than machines; reacquiring feelings, they usher in a new cycle of creation. This oscillation, parallel to one between psychological and collective drama, has dated *R.U.R.* This holds even more strongly for *Adam the Creator* and *The Makropoulos Secret* (about the elixir of longevity). In *And So Ad Infinitum* the flighty erotics of upperclass "golden youth," the acquisitive sentimentalities of the petty bourgeoisie, and the militarism and deathlust racism of incipient fascism are personified as insects in a bitter satire, Capek's best stage play.

Capek's SF strength lies in his novels. *The Absolute at Large* presents another supposedly utopian but destructive invention: the Absolute or God, mass-produced as a byproduct of atomic fission in "karburators" that supply cheap energy. The novel passes in sarcastic review its abuses by church and state, corporations and individuals, academics and journalists: both the economy and personal relations collapse. Absolutized sectarian and national fanaticism lead to the "Greatest War," which peters out only when all "atomotors" have been destroyed along with most people. Yet it isn't clear why the Absolute, a "mystical Communism," must bend itself to capitalist economy and competitive psychology, or work disparately in things (overpopulation of industrial goods only) and in people (destructiveness matching the overpopulation). The power unleashed is simply a chaotic magnification of acquisitive economics and psychology. This makes for brilliant if spotty social satire, in which the little people outlast the highminded idea, but hardly for consistent SF.

In *Krakatit* the naive genius who pierces the secret of atomic fission finds a parallel "destructive chemistry" in Dostoevskian fevered nightmares, dissociations of memory, and explosive human encounters, and develops from "value-free" science to painful recognition of the primacy and dangers of human relationships. Capek integrated here popular literature—detection mystery and epic adventure from Homer through the folktale to pulp thrillers—into poetic and committed modern SF. The love and heroism of sensational melodrama and the counter-creation of the mad-scientist tradition are balanced by a sympathetic, suffering, and relatively complex hero, who rejects a series of erotic-cum-political temptations—not only the established class and new personal power but also the idyllic retreat. He is left with a resolve to achieve useful warmth instead of destructive explosions, and emerges from the fog of yearning into the clarity of moderation. Though the novel doesn't quite fuse realism and allegory, ethical moderation and folktale certainties, it largely succeeds in transcending the opposition between scientific progress and human happiness. For the first and last time in Capek's SF, a believable hero fights back successfully at destructive forces within himself and society.

Capek's second phase comprises some minor, marginally SF stories, *War with the Newts,* and one play. The rise of Nazism dispelled his illusions of the little man's instinctual rightness and the relativity of truth. Instead of satirizing the intellect, he wrote sharply against irrationalism, "be it the cult of will, of the soil, of the subconscious, of the mass instincts, or of the violence of the powerful." The pseudo-human becomes clearly evil when the Salamanders become analogous to the Nazi aggressors. Their rise is interwoven with a satire on the illusion industries which screen biological and social reality from mankind—the exotic and juvenile adventure romance, sensational tabloid newspaper, Hollywood movies, pseudoscientific polls and interviews in newspapers. Scientists and academics are as timid and ideologically limited as the public at large, but the real villains are the capitalists who finance the menace through the Salamander Syndicate—an industrial utopianism satirized in the minutes of its meeting. The Salamanders, who began as exotic pets, become an "extremely cheap labor force" parallel to the transformation of competitive merchant-buccaneering into a global exploitative corporation aiming at a new Atlantis—which will end as Atlantis did. An appendix on the Salamanders' sexual life shows that their "Collective Male" horde is capable of politics and technics but not of real sociability: the Syndicate is the greatest illusion of them all. Progressing to a powerful alternate society, learning well mankind's combination of slavery and stock-market, aggression and ideological propaganda, they begin their assault. Capek's satire is here most bitter, topical, and precise. Startlingly, even his beloved small people are found guilty of complacency as continents crumble around them.

The satire of literary, journalistic, and essayistic forms of this novel is also a critique of SF. The history of the Salamanders echoes Wells's *Island of Dr. Moreau,* Conan Doyle's *Lost World,* and the animal fable; the global overview latches onto Wells's later SF and Anatole France's *Penguin Island;* it ends with Wellsian havoc-wreaking aliens—but also with an open question, much superior to ordinary SF: "No cosmic catastrophes, nothing but state, official, economic, and other causes. . . ." The menace could have been stopped—if people had organized to fight it, if "All the industries. All the banks. All the different states" had not financed "this End of the World." Such writing makes of Capek not only the pioneer of all anti-fascist and anti-militarist SF but also (together with Zamyatin) the most significant SF writer between the World Wars. True, *War with the Newts* didn't quite manage to overcome this ambiguity: the Salamanders are at the beginning a wronged inferior race and yet grow into an embodiment of both the Nazis and robotized masses. Russia, moreover, is presented as a Tsarist state: Capek couldn't deal with socialism or any positive radical novelty. He dealt in catastrophes, and concentrated his fire almost entirely on bourgeois society. Conversely, such a love-hate relationship led the Communist bureaucracy in Czechoslovakia to neglect him in the early 1950s, though he has since been rehabilitated.

Capek's evolution is not simple. One of his best works, *Krakatit,* is early, and his final SF play, *Power and Glory*—a critique of fascism, militarism, and subservient medicine—is second-rate. But in a few works he left a precious heritage. He—rather than Burroughs or Gernsback—is the missing link between Wells and a literature which will be both entertaining (which means popular) and cognitively (which means also formally) avant garde. He infused the legacy of the adventure novel and melodramatic thriller, French and British SF, and German fantasy with the prospects of modern poetry, painting, and movies as well as with an eager and constant interest in societal relationships, in natural and physical sciences, and above all in the richly humorous and idiomatic language of the street and the little people. In that way, he is the most "American" of the often elitest European SF writers. And yet he is also not only intensely Czech, but a "European local patriot" for whom Europe meant culture and humanism; when they were betrayed, the Salamanders—read fascists—had arrived.

—Darko Suvin

CAPON, (Harry) Paul

Pseudonym: Noel Kenton. **Nationality:** British. **Born:** Kenton Hall, Suffolk, 18 December 1912. **Education:** St. George's School, Harpenden, Hertfordshire. **Military Service:** Served in the Royal Army Service Corps, 1940; technical director, Soviet Film Agency, 1941-44. **Family:** Married 1) Doreen Evans-Evans in 1933, one daughter and one son; 2) Amy Charlotte Gillam in 1956. **Career:** Freelance film editor and scriptwriter for London Films, 1931-32, Gaumont British, 1933-35, Warner Brothers, 1936-37, British National, 1944-48, Walt Disney, 1955-58, and Granada Television, 1959-62; head of Film Production, Independent Television News, London, 1963-67. **Died:** 24 November 1969.

SCIENCE FICTION PUBLICATIONS

Novels (series: Antigeos)

The Other Side of the Sun: A Novel (Antigeos). London, Heinemann, 1950.

The Other Half of the Planet (Antigeos). London, Heinemann, 1952.
The World at Bay (for children). London, Heinemann, 1953; Philadelphia, Winston, 1954.
Down to Earth (Antigeos). London, Heinemann, 1954.
Phobos, The Robot Planet (for children). London, Heinemann, 1955; as *Lost—A Moon,* Indianapolis, Bobbs Merrill, 1956.
The Wonderbolt (for children). London, Ward Lock, 1955.
Into the Tenth Millennium. London, Heinemann, 1956.
The Cave of Cornelius. London, Heinemann, 1959; as *The End of the Tunnel,* Indianapolis, Bobbs Merrill, 1959.
Flight of Time (for children). London, Heinemann, 1960.

OTHER PUBLICATIONS

Novels

Battered Caravanserai. London, Heinemann, 1942.
Brother Cain. London, Heinemann, 1945.
The Hosts of Midian. London, Nicholson and Watson, 1946.
Dead Man's Chest. London, Nicholson and Watson, 1947.
The Murder of Jacob Canansey. London, Heinemann, 1947.
Fanfare for Shadows. London, Boardman, 1947.
O Clouds Unfold. London, Ward Lock, 1948.
Image of a Murder. London, Boardman, 1949.
Toby Scuffell. London, Ward Lock, 1949.
Threescore Years. London, Ward Lock, 1950.
Delay of Doom. London, Ward Lock, 1950.
No Time for Death. London, Ward Lock, 1951.
Death at Shinglestrand. London, Ward Lock, 1952.
Death on a Wet Sunday. London, Ward Lock, 1953.
In All Simplicity. London, Heinemann, 1953.
The Seventh Passenger. London, Ward Lock, 1953.
Malice Domestic. London, Ward Lock, 1954.
Thirty Days Hath September. London, Ward Lock, 1955.
Margin of Terror. London, Ward Lock, 1955.
Amongst Those Missing. London, Heinemann, 1959.
The Final Refuge. London, Harrap, 1969.

Other (for children)

Warriors' Moon. London, Hodder and Stoughton, 1960; New York, Putnam, 1964.
The Kingdom of the Bulls. London, Hodder and Stoughton, 1961; New York, Norton, 1962.
Lord of the Chariots. London, Hodder and Stoughton, 1962.
The Golden Cloak. London, Hodder and Stoughton, 1963.
The Great Yarmouth Mystery: A Chronicle of a Famous Crime (for adults). London, Harrap, 1965.
Roman Gold. Leicester, Brockhampton Press, 1968.
Strangers on Forlorn. London, Harrap, 1969.

Translator, *Surrealism,* by Yves Duplessis. New York, Walker, 1963.
Translator, *Sexual Reproduction,* by Louis Gallien. New York, Walker, 1963.
Translator (as Noel Kenton), *Animal Migration,* by René Thévenin. New York, Walker, 1963.
Translator, *The French Wines,* by Georges Ray. New York, Walker, 1965.

* * *

Paul Capon's novels have had very little distribution in the United States and he is generally unknown in that country, which is surprising in view of the large number of inferior writers whose works have been reprinted from their original European appearance. He received most attention with the Antigeos trilogy, portions of which were broadcast on the BBC. Antigeos is a twin world to the Earth, located at the opposite side of Earth's orbit, hidden from us by the bulk of the sun. This impossibility has recurred frequently in the genre, and is just plausible enough to be fascinating to casual readers.

Antigeos is a Utopia of sorts, or at least it is until the unscrupulous Earth humans arrive. In the first volume the initial contact is made, but the unpleasant results don't become evident until the middle volume where human vanities and greeds begin to work their way on Antigeos. In the final volume a group of financiers plot to exploit the newly discovered world as an involuntary colony, until they are thwarted by the true at heart.

The rest of Capon's adventure novels have been dismissed as juveniles, and two at least definitely are, *The Wonderbolt* and *Flight of Time.* But Capon's excellent narrative ability makes some of them of interest to adult readers as well. There is an alien invasion from Poppea in *The World at Bay,* for example, unique in that the aliens arrive in diminutive space stations. *Phobos, The Robot Planet* has as its central character the entire Martian moon, which we learn to be a gigantic robot spaceship which wanders around kidnapping people out of curiosity rather than malice. This latter novel is lighter in tone than the others, and has its moments of genuine humor.

Paul Capon went on to write one major adult novel, *Into the Tenth Millennium,* and made use of one of the oldest of science fiction plots—the journey into the future to visit a Utopian society. Capon transports three modern-day humans via drugs to a future society which does seem to have solved most of the significant societal problems, and we are treated to an unusually entertaining tour of that society. Never ignoring the need to sustain interest, Capon avoids preachiness, and portrays for us a world that is realistic as well as Utopian, a goal never achieved by most of the classic works of this type.

Capon was not particularly prolific and attracted little attention with his books, all of which are presently out of print. This is surprising because his narrative technique is masterful and his plots, while familiar, are not more so than many another far more successful novel. The predominance of young protagonists may well have stereotyped Capon as a writer of juveniles, making it impossible for him to reach a more adult audience with his more serious work.

—Don D'Ammassa

CARD, Orson Scott

Pseudonym: Brian Green. **Nationality:** American. **Born:** Richland, Washington, 24 August 1951. **Education:** Brigham Young University, Provo, Utah, B.A. in theatre 1975; University of Utah, Salt Lake City, M.A. in English 1981. **Family:** Married Kristine Allen in 1977; two sons and two daughters. **Career:** Volunteer Mormon missionary in Brazil, 1971-73; operated repertory theatre, Provo, 1974-75; proofreader, 1974, and editor, 1974-76, Brigham Young University Press; assistant editor, *Ensign* magazine, Salt Lake City, 1976-78, and senior editor, Compute! Books, Greensboro, North Carolina, 1983; taught at the University of Utah, 1979-80, 1981, Brigham Young University, 1981, Notre Dame University, Indiana, 1981-82, Clarion Writers Workshop, East Lansing, Michigan, 1982, Appalachian State University (full-time), 1987 (part-time), 1989—. **Awards:** John W. Campbell award, 1978; Nebula award, for novel, 1985, 1986; Hugo award, for novel, 1985, 1986, for novella, 1987, for nonfiction, 1991; *Locus* award, for novel, 1988, 1989; Mythopoeic Fantasy award, 1988. **Agent:** Barbara Bova, 3957 Gulf Shore Blvd. #PH1B, Naples, Florida 33940. **Address:** P.O. Box 18184, Greensboro, North Carolina 27419-8184, U.S.A. **Online Address:** OrsonCard@aol.com.

SCIENCE FICTION PUBLICATIONS

Novels (series: Homecoming; Alvin Maker; Mayflower; Ender Wiggin; Worthing Chronicle)

Hot Sleep: The Worthing Chronicle. New York, Baronet, 1979; London, Futura, 1980.
A Planet Called Treason. New York, St. Martin's Press, 1979; London, Pan, 1981; expanded as *Treason,* New York, St. Martin's Press, 1988.
Songmaster. New York, Dial Press, 1980; London, Futura, 1981.
Hart's Hope. New York, Berkley, 1983; London, Unwin, 1986.
The Worthing Chronicle. New York, Ace, 1983.
Ender's Game. New York, Tor, 1985; London, Unwin, 1985; revised edition, Tor, 1991.
Speaker for the Dead (Ender). New York, Tor, 1986; London, Arrow, 1987; revised edition, Tor, 1991.
Ender's War (includes *Ender's Game* and *Speaker for the Dead*). Garden City, New York, Doubleday, 1986.
Wyrms. New York, Arbor House, 1987; London, Legend, 1988.
Hatrack River: The Tales of Alvin Maker (includes *Seventh Son, Red Prophet,* and *Prentice Alvin*). London, Century, 1988; New York, Guild America, 1987.
Red Prophet. New York, Tor, 1988; London, Legend, 1989.
Prentice Alvin. New York, Tor, and London, Legend, 1989.
The Abyss: A Novel (novelization of screenplay). New York, Pocket, and London, Legend, 1989.
The Worthing Saga. New York, Tor, 1990; London, Legend, 1991.
Xenocide (Ender). New York, Tor, 1991; London, Legend, 1991.
The Memory of Earth (Homecoming). New York, Tor, and London, Legend, 1992.
Lost Boys. New York, HarperCollins, 1992.
The Call of Earth (Homecoming). New York, Tor, and London, Legend, 1993.
The Ships of Earth (Homecoming). New York, Tor, and London, Legend, 1994.
Homecoming: Harmony (includes *The Memory of Earth, The Call of Earth,* and *The Ships of Earth*). New York, Guild America, 1994.
Lovelock (Mayflower), with Kathryn H. Kidd. New York, Tor, 1994.
Earthfall (Homecoming). New York, Tor, 1995.
Earthborn (Homecoming). New York, Tor, 1995.
Homecoming: Earth (includes *Earthfall* and *Earthborn*). New York, Guild America, 1995.
Alvin Journeyman (Maker). New York, Tor, 1995.

Short Stories

Capitol: The Worthing Chronicle. New York, Ace, 1979.
Unaccompanied Sonata and Other Stories. New York, Dial Press, 1980.
The Folk of the Fringe. West Bloomfield, Michigan, Phantasia Press, 1989; London, Legend, 1990.
Eye for Eye, bound with *The Tunesmith,* by Lloyde Biggle Jr. New York Tor, 1990.
Maps in a Mirror: The Short Fiction of Orson Scott Card. New York, Tor, 1990; London, Legend, 1991; as *The Changed Man, Flux: Tales of Human Futures, Monkey Sonatas,* and *Cruel Miracles,* New York, Tor, 4 vols., 1992-93.
Unaccompanied Sonata. Eugene, Oregon, Pulphouse, 1992.

OTHER PUBLICATIONS

Novel

A Woman of Destiny. New York, Berkley, 1984; as *Saints,* New York, Tor, 1988.

Short Stories

Turning Hearts: Short Stories on Family Life, with David Dollaite. Salt Lake City, Utah, Bookcraft, 1994.

Plays

The Apostate (produced Provo, Utah, 1970).
In Flight (produced Provo, Utah, 1970).
Across Five Summers (produced Provo, Utah, 1971).
Of Gideon (produced Provo, Utah, 1971).
Stone Tables (produced Provo, Utah, 1973).
A Christmas Carol, adaptation of the story by Dickens (also director: produced Provo, Utah, 1974).
Father, Mother, Mother, and Mom (produced Provo, Utah, 1974). Published in Sunstone, 1978.
Liberty Jail (produced Provo, Utah, 1975).
Rag Mission (as Brian Green), in *Ensign* (Salt Lake City), July 1977.
Fresh Courage Take (also director; produced 1978).
Elders and Sisters (produced 1979).
Wings (produced 1982).

Other

Listen, Mom and Dad. Salt Lake City, Bookcraft, 1978.
Saintspeak. Berkeley, California, Signature, 1981.
Ainge. Midvale, Utah, Signature, 1982.
Compute's Guide to IBM PCjr Sound and Graphics. Greensboro, North Carolina, Compute, 1984.
Cardography. Eugene, Oregon, Hypatia Press, 1987.
Characters and Viewpoint. Cincinnati, Ohio, Writer's Digest, 1988; London, Robinson, 1990.
How To Write Science Fiction and Fantasy. Cincinnati, Ohio, Writer's Digest, 1990.
A Storyteller in Zion: Essays and Speeches. Salt Lake City, Utah, Bookcraft, 1994.

Editor, *Dragons of Darkness.* New York, Ace, 1981.

Editor, *Dragons of Light.* New York, Ace, 1980.
Editor, *Future on Fire.* New York, Tor, 1991.

*

Manuscript Collection: Brigham Young University, Provo, Utah.

Critical Study: *In the Image of God: Theme, Characterization, and Landscape in the Fiction of Orson Scott Card* by Michael Collings, New York, Greenwood Press, 1990.

Orson Scott Card comments:

When I tell stories, I generally follow my own unreasoned sense of what should happen—what events feel important and true to the characters. I subscribe to no particular literary school and never deliberately bend a story to fit a preconceived notion of correct writing.

In fact, it is not story writing that interests me, but storytelling. I believe that the art of the storyteller does not exist on paper or in language; rather, the storyteller creates a vicarious memory in the hearers' or readers' minds, using as he can the words of the language with all their nuance, as well as the public memory that binds the community of hearers together.

The reader coming to my work will find that there is only rarely any science in my science fiction. I use the freedom of the genre to create the situations in which my stories can take place, but I never try to predict or prescribe the future. I do not write utopias or rhapsodies to future engineering. I am uninterested in current fashion and so do not write about drugs, rock music, peace movements, or nuclear war. Nor do I attempt literary experimentation, as it is generally understood—most literary experiments today being inferior repetitions of the failures of the modern writers of the early 20th century.

In looking back at my completed tales, both long and short, I find several recurrent motifs, some of which have been noticed (and sometimes complained about) by reviewers. Though I was not aware of these themes while writing, I do believe they are valid reflections of my own unquestioned beliefs about the moral universe.

Repeatedly my central characters occupy an unsought key position in their community; repeatedly they choose to suffer or cause unspeakable pain or sacrifice in order to save the community. Some have seen this as wanton violence; I see it as something holy in human nature, the inborn goodness that denies mankind is evil at birth.

Often my characters are children or otherwise innocent, forced ahead of time into responsibilities they cannot, but nevertheless do, bear. Whether they are children or not, they are often isolated from the community they uphold. They tend to have exceptional gifts and exceptional weaknesses; they are introspective enough to notice their weakness and strength and pain, but not enough to notice their virtue.

My characters frequently have a sense of fulfilling plans they did not make; ultimately, however, they accept all or part of those plans. Their achievements, however, are a direct result of their own choices, actions, and efforts. They are not mere toys of the gods; God, implicitly or explicitly, depends in part on the human characters to achieve His own overarching purposes. And all my fiction is infused with a strong belief in the perfectibility of human beings, at least in part through their own desires and works.

* * *

Orson Scott Card's introduction to science fiction readers was, in retrospect, an announcement of his major themes, his primary concerns as a writer, and his commitment to the kinds of stories that have earned him a loyal readership. In August, 1977, Card's first published SF story appeared in *Analog*. "Ender's Game" earned him a Hugo final-ballot nomination and a Nebula recommendation, and was reprinted in four anthologies or collections by 1983. When it reappeared in novel form as *Ender's Game* in 1985, it garnered the Hugo, the Nebula, and the Hamilton Awards for best novel in 1986, and initiated a widely acclaimed series that includes *Speaker for the Dead* (Hugo and Nebula winner, 1987), *Xenocide,* and *Children of the Mind* [forthcoming in 1996]. The image of a sacrificial child as savior/mediator developed and expanded in the Ender novels constitutes a leitmotif in much of Card's work, from this first story through his recently completed Homecoming series.

But "Ender's Game" was only the beginning. In 1977 he also published "Malpractice," and received another Nebula recommendation. In the next two years, he published 25 SF stories, including "Mikal's Songbird" (Nebula and Hugo nomination) and "Lifeloop " (Nebula recommendation); published a collection of short fiction and two novels; received the John W. Campbell Award for most promising new writer in 1978; wrote the texts for two uncredited nonfiction books; and still found time to write a number of SF and non-SF articles and reviews.

These early stories and novels established Card as an important voice in the genre; they also triggered a side-stream of criticism that has paralleled his career. Stories such as "Kingsmeat" and "Eumenides in the Fourth Floor Lavatory," and novels such as *A Planet Called Treason* led some readers and reviewers to categorize all of Card's work as gratuitously violent and misogynistic, charges that persisted over nearly two decades, although recently much muted. In fact, these stories and novels do deal directly, bluntly, and graphically with violent images and situations, yet what these readers and reviewers missed was the impassioned depth of moral and even religious commitment that makes the pain and suffering of his characters not only endurable but ultimately ennobling; and those novels that seem on the surface sexist most frequently attribute those attitudes to characters responding to the pressures of their not-always admirable societies, as in *A Planet Called Treason.* Most of Card's main characters are male: Ender Wiggin, Alvin Maker, Nafai in the Homecoming series. But his women are also capable of strength and determination, as witnessed by Dinah Kirkham, in the non-SF *A Woman of Destiny* (with Card's more appropriate original title, *Saints,* restored when it was reprinted); Patience, in *Wyrms;* Little Peggy, in the Alvin Maker series; Valentine and a number of others, in the Ender Wiggin series; and the Lady Rasa, Luet, and Hushidh in the Homecoming series. In addition, as his subjects and style have matured, Card's ability to deal with controversial social and cultural issues has strengthened his novels.

Yet one more thing needs to be noted, however, about Card's seemingly immediate success as an SF writer. The prolific output of his first several years does not actually signal the beginning of a remarkable career; rather, it was the culmination of nearly a decade of writing. As early as 1970, Card was writing, directing, and producing plays, often in association with the Brigham Young University experimental theater—a total of nine between 1970 and 1975. At the same time, he was deeply committed to his faith, examining episodes and themes associated with Mormonism in his plays. From 1971 to 1973, he served a two-year mission for the Church of Jesus Christ of Latter-day Saints in Brazil, an experience that contributed

to the language, imagery, characterization, and landscape of *Speaker for the Dead, Xenocide,* and *Children of the Mind.* For several years during the 1970s, he served on editorial boards for church-oriented magazines. By the time "Ender's Game" appeared, then, he had already completed a rigorous apprenticeship in writing drama, short fiction, poetry, feature-articles and essays, a background he immediately applied to science fiction.

Even so, at no time has science fiction demanded the majority of his time, however. His credits over the past decade and a half include *A Woman of Destiny*—a historical novel that received the Best Novel Award from the Association for Mormon Letters; scripts for audio- and video-cassette series based on scriptural and historical themes; scripts for Church-related programs, including the celebrated Hill Cumorah pageant presented annually in Palmyra, New York; a volume of LDS humor; and a sports biography. He also publishes church-related novels and periodicals through Hatrack River Press; and founded and maintains a Virtual Community, Hatrack River, on the Internet. In his spare time, he has published articles and books on computing and techniques of writing; his *How to Write Science Fiction and Fantasy* received a Hugo nomination as best nonfiction work of 1990.

Still, it is as a science fiction writer, editor, essayist, and reviewer that Card is best known. Between 1980 and 1984, he published *Songmaster, Hart's Hope, The Worthing Chronicle,* and a collection, *Unaccompanied Sonata and Other Stories. Songmaster* concentrates on music, another recurrent theme in the early stories, while transforming the SF cliché of the "galactic emperor" into a two-part story that suggests the narrative power of a *Beowulf.* Initially Ansset is a typical Card character, a child prodigy who can create and destroy through the power of his song. But Card allows him to grow in unexpected ways, leading Ansset to the Imperial throne itself. That portion of his life is passed over in a single phrase: "So Ansset was crowned and reigned for sixty years." His death is more critical than his tenure on the throne and is represented as starkly and as compellingly as an Anglo-Saxon heroic saga.

Card's poetic skills infuse *Hart's Hope,* where he not only created a magical world, society, and city, but also a language consonant with that magic. A complex fable of identity, commitment, and sacrifice, the novel transforms its rural character into the single figure who can destroy evil and return the true King to the city of Inwit (significantly, an Anglo-Saxon word for conscience).

In 1985, *Ender's Game* appeared. Although criticized at times as formulaic, with stock characters and stereotypical action, *Ender's Game* transcends space opera largely through the strength of Card's portrayals of children, each a genius in his or her own way, confronting what is perceived as a mortal threat to humanity. And yet as strong as the novel is, it does not reach its true climax (in spite of Ender's decision in the final "game" against the buggers) until the last chapter, when Ender accepts responsibility for the deaths he inadvertently caused and undertakes to find a world suitable for the one remaining Hive Queen. Card has referred to *Ender's Game* as a prolegomenon to *Speaker for the Dead,* as the novel that tells how Andrew Wiggin becomes the Christic mediator who saves one sentient species and restores another in *Speaker for the Dead. Xenocide* moves beyond the limits of the universe into the Outside, a place of god-like creativity and generation; and in *Children of the Mind,* Card concludes Ender's saga. The final two volumes are at opposite extremes from *Ender's Game;* while action is present, they are primarily concerned with ideas and human community. As a series, the Ender novels represent science fiction at its finest, blending galaxy-wide struggles with alien races, scientific extrapolation that constantly alters our perspectives of events, and complex characters interesting enough to bear the weight of philosophical speculation.

Card's series-in-progress, the Tales of Alvin Maker, began in 1987 with *Seventh Son,* in which Card introduces young Alvin Maker and an alternate-universe 19th-century America where science, religion, and magic all work. Based loosely on episodes from the life of Joseph Smith, first President of the Church of Jesus Christ of Latter-day Saints, *Seventh Son* and its succeeding volumes, *Red Prophet, Prentice Alvin,* and the recently completed *Alvin Journeyman* weave history and fantasy in telling the story of the young Maker discovering his powers, learning to control them, and finally using them to establish the Crystal City to defeat the Unmaker. Not strictly science fiction, the Tales of Alvin Maker can nevertheless appeal to fantasy and science fiction readers alike in its creative restructuring of historical events and characters.

Card's commitment to Mormonism enters explicitly into *The Folk of the Fringe* and the Homecoming series as well. *The Folk of the Fringe* takes readers to a post-holocaust, near-future America, where the Mormon Church supplies order, stability, and community around the Mormon Sea, the vastly extended Great Salt Lake. Never overtly doctrinal, Card nonetheless inculcates into the five stories key Mormon ideas, while simultaneously exploring the ramifications of the American Dream in a world in which Americans have proven unworthy of that Dream. Conservation and stewardship, good and evil, faith and responsibility echo throughout the book, which nevertheless spoke strongly enough to non-Mormon SF audiences that two of the stories, "Salvage" and "America" received Nebula nominations.

In his five-volume Homecoming series, the central narrative episodes in all five volumes, as well as rough character-outlines for a dozen of the main characters, are drawn from the Book of Mormon. Lehi and his four sons are transformed into Wetchik and his four sons; Jerusalem becomes the city of Basilica. Yet beyond the obvious and intentional parallels, the Homecoming novels are simultaneously strong, extrapolative science fiction. Borrowed episodes are re-imagined and incorporated into a seamless narrative that tells of a 40,000,000-year-old human colony, the computer-entity that has overseen its survival, and the computer's quest to manipulate a small group into restoring human society there. The series includes alien societies, mutated rats and bats, high-tech space travel, and faster-than-light communications; yet at its core is Card's persistent theme of establishing and maintaining true human community.

Prolific, controversial, always engaging, Card has established himself as a key voice in contemporary science fiction writing, while at the same time setting standards in mythopoeic storytelling that allow him to be compared to writers like C.S. Lewis and J.R.R. Tolkien. His imagined worlds are places of haunting beauty and devastating power, of inestimable suffering and equally inestimable achievement, of science-fictional energy and deep moral commitment.

—Michael R. Collings

CAREY, Julian. *See* **TUBB, E.C.**

CARPENTER, Morley. *See* **TUBB, E.C.**

CARR, Jayge

Pseudonym for Marj Krueger. **Nationality:** American. **Born:** Houston, Texas, 28 July 1940. **Education:** Carnegie Institute of Technology, Pittsburgh, 1958-61; Wayne State University, Detroit, 1961-2, B.A. in physics, 1962; Case Western Reserve University, Cleveland, 1962-65. **Family:** Married Roger Carr Krueger in 1961; two daughters. Nuclear physicist, NASA, Cleveland, 1962-65. **Agent:** Matthew Bialer, William Morris Agency, 1350 Avenue of the Americas, New York, New York 10019, U.S.A.

SCIENCE FICTION PUBLICATIONS

Novels (series: Navigator's Sindrome)

Leviathan's Deep. Garden City, New York, Doubleday, 1979; London, Sidgwick and Jackson, 1980.
Navigator's Sindrome. Garden City, New York, Doubleday, 1983.
The Treasure in the Heart of the Maze (Navigator). Garden City, New York, Doubleday, 1985.
Rabelaisian Reprise (Navigator). Garden City, New York, Doubleday, 1988.

Short Stories

Author of numerous uncollected short stories.

*

Jayge Carr comments:

It is probably no coincidence that my first published story was titled "Alienation." I have never tried to do anything more than tell interesting stories, about interesting people, written in a precise but readable style. But certain themes do crop up over and over, and alienation, whether of one society from the mainstream, as in "The Pacifists," or person from society as in "Alienation," does seem to be a common occurrence.

I've also discovered quite a bit about myself by reading my own work. Many people, on the evidence of *Leviathan's Deep,* have labeled me a feminist. Well, maybe. I prefer to think of myself as a peoplist. Everyone should have equal opportunities and no one should be shoe-horned into a role unfitting or barred from a role desired because of sex—or age, creed, color, or what-have-you. "Mustard Seed" may be my best example of a truly egalitarian society. And *Navigator's Sindrome,* of course, a prime example of such a society gone sour. Sometimes, as in *Leviathan's Deep* or "The King Is Dead," I try to show men what it feels like to have the shoe on the other foot, pinching. But women are not our only minority, just the most prevalent one. Prejudice, intolerance, bigotry; all of them are so cruel, and they cause so much tragedy—and they're so foolish. Those who eliminate some people from their friends because of trivial reasons miss so much.

Another theme that keeps recurring—perhaps because I do feel strongly about it—is pollution. Humanity wasting our environment. "Child of the Wandering Sea" is the ultimate of that, where the Terran's population explosion has them taking over—and terraforming—world after world. Where will we go if we don't control ourselves, what will happen if we continue to waste our resources. I haven't any answers, but I can hope that just thinking about it will help, in some small way.

Besides, writing is fun. It is fun to make up a truly alien alien, as in "The Wondrous Works of His Hands" or a truly alien society of human beings, as in "The Pacifists." It is fun to meet new friends, and watch them have adventures. And of course, I can always hope, that if it's fun to write, it's equally fun to read.

*   *   *

Jayge Carr is the pseudonym for a former physicist who now writes some of the most provocative, enigmatic, and underrated fantasy and science fiction in the field.

Her first novel, *Leviathan's Deep,* was an immediate success. It took the commonplace theme of domineering males attempting to subdue a leader on a matriarchal world and, essentially, turned it inside out. Her treatment of the power politics is satirical, occasionally sharply so: in Carr's works, any attempt at coercion is an invitation to all-out trouble. Most impressive about the book is her protagonist's voice—compassionate, humorous, resourceful, but, at the end, resigned to the losses inherent in her need to protect her own culture.

Her Jael the Navigator books, *Navigator's Sindrome, The Treasure in the Heart of the Maze,* and *Rabelaisian Reprise,* are not a true series, and certainly not a trilogy: they do, however, involve the same world and some of the same characters. Once again, what is noteworthy about these books is Carr's hatred of coercion: if she ever portrays anyone as an out-and-out villain, it is the c'holders, or contract holders, whose decadence and cruelty oppress the men and women whose bonds they hold. Jael, too, is a fascinating character: her moral neutrality and craziness add a darker dimension to what would otherwise be space-faring picaresques.

Carr's short fiction has appeared in a variety of places, including the highly prestigious *Year's Best* anthologies and *Synergy,* and in markets ranging from *Omni* to *Analog* to *Marion Zimmer Bradley's Fantasy Magazine.* Her stories shift from fantasy to humor to rigorous scientific extrapolation, and are marked by a flair for language, extremely complex plots and shifts in story line, and her extreme reluctance to see anything at all—except maybe the worst c'holders—as totally evil.

—Susan Shwartz

CARR, Terry (Gene)

Pseudonym: Norman Edwards (joint pseudonym with Ted White). **Nationality:** American. **Born:** Grants Pass, Oregon, 19 February 1937. **Education:** City College of San Francisco, 1954-57. A.A. 1957; University of California, Berkeley, 1957-59. **Family:** Married 1) Miriam Dyches in 1959 (divorced 1961); 2) Carol Newmark in 1961. **Career:** Associate editor, Scott Meredith Literary Agency, New York, 1962-64; editor, Ace Books, New York, 1964-71; editor, *SFWA Bulletin,* 1967-68; founder, Science Fiction Writers of American Forum, 1967-68; coeditor, *Void* fanzine; editor, with Ron Ellik, *Fanac* fanzine. **Awards:** Hugo award, for editing, 1959, for criticism, 1973; *Locus* award, for editing, 1983, 1984. **Died:** 7 April 1987.

SCIENCE FICTION PUBLICATIONS

Novels

Warlord of Kor. New York, Ace, 1963.
Invasion from 2500 (with Ted White as Norman Edwards). Derby, Connecticut, Monarch, 1964.
Cirque: A Novel of the Far Future. Indianapolis, Bobbs Merrill, 1977; London, Dobson, 1979.
The Man from U.N.C.L.E.: The Thousand Coffins Affair. (as anonymous co-author with Michael Avallone). New York, Ace, 1965.

Short Stories

The Light at the End of the Universe. New York, Pyramid, 1976.
Between Two Worlds, bound with *Messages Found in an Oxygen Bottle* by Bob Shaw. Cambridge, Massachusetts, NESFA Press, 1986.

OTHER PUBLICATIONS

Other

Fandom Harvest. Solna, Sweden, Laissez Faire Produktion, 1986.

Editor, with Donald A. Wollheim, *World's Best Science Fiction 1965* (to *1971*). New York, Ace, 7 vols., 1965-71; *1968* to *1971* vols. published London, Gollancz, 4 vols., 1969-71: first 4 vols. published as *World's Best Science Fiction: First* [to *Fourth*] *Series,* Ace, 1970.
Editor, *Science Fiction for People Who Hate Science Fiction.* Garden City, New York, Doubleday, 1966.
Editor, *New Worlds of Fantasy 1-3.* New York, Ace, 3 vols., 1967, 1970-71; vol. 1 published as *Step Outside Your Mind,* London, Dobson, 1969.
Editor, *The Others.* New York, Fawcett, 1969.
Editor, *On Our Way to the Future.* New York, Ace, 1970.
Editor, *Universe 1-17.* New York, Ace, 2 vols., 1971-72; New York, Random House, 3 vols., 1973-74; Garden City, New York, Doubleday, 12 vols., 1976-87; London, Dobson, 10 vols., 1975-80; London, Hale, 3 vols., 1983-86; London, Gollancz, vols. 14-16, 1985-87.
Editor, *The Best Science Fiction of the Year 1-13.* New York, Ballantine, 5 vols., 1972-76; New York, Holt, 1 vol., 1977; Ballantine, 3 vols., 1978-80; New York, Pocket Books, 3 vols., 1981-83; New York, Baen Books, 1 vol., 1984; as *Terry Carr's Best Science Fiction of the Year [14]-15,* New York, Tor, 1 vol., 1987; as *Terry Carr's Best Science Fiction and Fantasy of the Year 16,* Tor, 1 vol., 1987; *15-16* as *Best SF of the Year 15-16,* London, Gollancz, 1975-87.
Editor, *This Side of Infinity.* New York, Ace, 1972.
Editor, *An Exaltation of Stars: Transcendental Adventures in Science Fiction.* New York, Simon and Schuster, 1973.
Editor, *Into the Unknown: Eleven Tales of Imagination.* Nashville, Nelson, 1973.
Editor, *Worlds Near and Far: Nine Stories of Science Fiction and Fantasy.* Nashville, Nelson, 1974.
Editor, *Fellowship of the Stars: Nine Science Fiction Stories.* New York, Simon and Schuster, 1974.

Editor, *Creatures from Beyond: Nine Stories of Science Fiction and Fantasy.* Nashville, Nelson, 1975.

Editor, *The Ides of Tomorrow: Original Science Fiction Tales of Horror* (for children). Boston, Little Brown, 1976.

Editor, *Planets of Wonder: A Treasury of Space Opera* (for children). Nashville, Nelson, 1976.

Editor, *To Follow a Star: Nine Science Fiction Stories about Christmas* (for children). Nashville, Nelson, 1977.

Editor, *The Infinite Arena: Seven Science Fiction Stories about Sports* (for children). Nashville, Nelson, 1977.

Editor, *Classic Science Fiction: The First Golden Age.* New York, Harper, 1978; London, Robson, 1979.

Editor, *The Year's Finest Fantasy 1-2.* New York, Berkeley, 2 vols., 1978-79; as *Fantasy Annual III-IV,* New York, Pocket Books, 3 vols., 1981-82.

Editor, *The Best Science Fiction Novellas of the Year 1-2.* New York, Ballantine, 2 vols., 1979-80.

Editor, *Beyond Reality: Eight Stories of Science Fiction.* New York, Elsevier Nelson, 1979.

Editor, *Dream's Edge: Science Fiction Stories about the Future of the Planet Earth.* San Francisco, Sierra Club, 1980.

Editor, with Martin H. Greenberg, *A Treasury of Modern Fantasy.* New York, Avon, 1981; abridged as *Masters of Fantasy,* New York, Galahad Books, 1992.

Editor, *The Best from Universe.* Garden City, New York, Doubleday, 1984.

Editor, with Isaac Asimov and Martin H. Greenberg, *100 Great Fantasy Short Short Stories.* Garden City, New York, Doubleday, and London, Robson, 1984.

Editor, *Science Fiction Hall of Fame: Volume IV: Nebula Winners, 1970-1974.* New York, Avon, 1986.

*

Terry Carr commented:

I've never been prolific as a fiction writer: most of my career has been devoted to editing, first as an editor for Ace Books, where I founded the "Ace Science Fiction Specials" series, 1968-71, and more recently as an editor of anthologies.

As a writer I'm known best for stories about alien creatures ("The Dance of the Changer and the Three," "Hop-Friend," *Cirque,* etc.), but in truth this is an outgrowth of my interest in communication between all kinds of people. Short stories such as "Touchstone" and "They Live on Levels" are examples that don't include aliens: the novel *Cirque* has an important alien character but it's mostly about communication between the human characters. Another theme in my stories is transcendental experience: see particularly the novella "The Wind at Starmont" and the novel *Cirque: A Novel of the Far Future.*

*   *   *

Terry Carr was one of several writers in the science fiction field who emerged from organized fandom, where he edited and wrote for a number of amateur periodicals. Even though he achieved professional standing, he remained a relatively infrequent writer, producing only a single, full-length, solo novel and perhaps three dozen short stories over the course of a career that spanned three decades. Carr's contribution to the field is enormous, however, and it is likely that his impact as an editor will transcend the value of even the best of his fiction, simply because he was so active in promoting the careers of many major talents. Although Carr edited several reprint anthologies, his two most significant contributions in this area are the Universe series of original short story collections, and the Ace Science Fiction Specials, a series of featured novels that helped popularize Ursula K. LeGuin, D.G. Compton, R.A. Lafferty, and others. In addition to the uniformly high quality, this series included a number of untraditional styles and themes, which further established them as something of special interest. Carr also edited a retrospective "Best of the Year" series that demonstrated his thorough familiarity with what the field had to offer, as well as his discerning eye for good fiction.

Carr's first few short stories were published in the early 1960s, including the amusing Weinbaum homage, "Hop-Friend," with its delightful Martian creatures, and the still popular "Stanley Toothbrush." In his novella *Warlord of Kor,* the human race is studying an alien species that seems to have culturally and mentally regressed, having lost the ability to speak and abandoned their scientific achievements, enslaved by a mindless obedience to a psychological imperative buried in their racial memories. A disparate group of people struggles to investigate this phenomenon, not realizing that they are wakening powers and fears that have been deliberately suppressed, which may be dangerous to all concerned if they are consciously recalled. A fairly routine adventure story, but thoughtful and involving a genuinely interesting conflict.

Carr collaborated with fellow writer and sometime editor Ted White on *Invasion from 2500,* which appeared under the byline Norman Edwards. Using advanced weaponry, a powerful invasion force appears as if by magic, conquering all the major population centers of Earth. Initially, it is believed that they are alien invaders from another world, but the title telegraphs the fact that they are actually interlopers from the future. It is a disappointingly flat adventure story, inferior to the subsequent works of both writers.

Cirque: A Novel of the Far Future is set in the very remote future of Earth. The tide of civilization has moved to other worlds, and most of the planet is a barbarous place sinking slowly into a decadent anarchy. The one exception is the city Cirque, which remains a place of innovation and ambition. An evil intelligence dwells not far from the city, a metaphysical creation of the darker side of Cirque that has begun to stir. It is an interesting if somewhat slowly-paced novel; its chief point of interest is the alien millipede central to the plot. Carr has long demonstrated a fascination with other intelligences, and some of his most inventive writing has been in that area, as in the case of his most famous story, "The Dance of the Changer and the Three." In that story, the aliens are pure energy forms, performing an elaborate ritual dance whose meaning is lost in the depths of racial memory.

That story and many of Carr's other noteworthy shorter pieces were collected in *The Light at the End of the Universe.* Of particular note are "Ozymandias," which looks at alienness from an alien point of view; "The Winds at Starmont," the tale of an aerial adventure in an exotic land; and "Touchstone," an enigmatic little fantasy about a man who feels compelled to purchase an undistinguished rock, only to discover that it exerts a strange influence over his subsequent actions. Another fine fantasy is "Stanley Toothbrush," wherein the protagonist's disbelief in certain artifacts is so powerful, they cease to exist.

Other stories of interest include Carr's examination of the logical outcome of over-urbanization, "In His Image," an even more effective variation, "They Live On Levels," his satirical and whimsical "Sleeping Beauty," and "Virra," a story of the last days of Earth under a dying sun.

Although he was an accomplished short story writer, Carr's editorial activities obviously occupied most of his time and diverted his creative efforts in that direction. His growing concern about the damage humans inflict on the planet is reflected in some of his stories, as well as being the driving purpose for *Dream's Edge: Science Fiction Stories about the Future of the Planet Earth,* one of his better anthologies.

—Don D'Ammassa

CARTER, Angela (Olive)

Nationality: British. **Born:** Angela Olive Stalker, Eastbourne, Sussex, 7 May 1940. **Education:** University of Bristol, 1962-65, B.A. in English 1965. **Family:** Married Paul Carter in 1960 (divorced 1972). **Career:** Journalist, Croydon, Surrey, 1958-61. Arts Council Fellow in Creative Writing, University of Sheffield, 1976-78; visiting professor of Creative Writing, Brown University, Providence, Rhode Island, 1980-81; writer-in-residence, University of Adelaide, 1984. **Awards:** Rhys Memorial prize, 1968; Maugham award, 1969; Cheltenham Festival prize, 1979; Kurt Maschler award, for children's book, 1982; James Tait Black Memorial prize, 1985. **Died:** 16 February 1992.

SCIENCE FICTION PUBLICATIONS

Novels

Heroes and Villains. London, Heinemann, 1969; New York, Simon and Schuster, 1970.
The Infernal Desire Machines of Dr. Hoffman, London, Hart-Davis, 1972; as *The War of Dreams,* New York, Harcourt Brace, 1974.
The Passion of New Eve. London, Gollancz, and New York, Harcourt Brace, 1977.

Short Stories

Fireworks: Nine Profane Pieces. London, Quartet, 1974; New York, Harper, 1981; revised edition, London, Virago, 1987.
The Bloody Chamber and Other Stories. London, Gollancz, 1979; New York, Harper, 1980.
Black Venus's Tale. London, Next-Faber, 1980.
Black Venus. London, Chatto and Windus, 1985; as *Saints and Strangers,* New York, Viking, 1986.
Artificial Fire (includes *Fireworks* and *Love*). Toronto, McClelland and Stewart, 1988.
Expletives Deleted: Selected Writings. London, Chatto and Windus, 1992.
American Ghosts and Old World Wonders. London, Chatto and Windus, 1993.

OTHER PUBLICATIONS

Novels

Shadow Dance. London, Heinemann, 1966; as *Honeybuzzard,* New York, Simon and Schuster, 1967.

The Magic Toyshop. London, Heinemann, 1967; New York, Simon and Schuster, 1968.
Several Perceptions. London, Heinemann, 1968; New York, Simon and Schuster, 1969.
Love. London, Hart-Davis, 1971; revised edition, London, Chatto and Windus, 1987; New York, Penguin, 1988.
Nights at the Circus. London, Chatto and Windus, 1984; New York, Viking Press, 1985.
Wise Children. London, Chatto and Windus, 1991; New York, Farrar, Strauss, 1992.

Plays

Vampirella (broadcast 1976; produced London, 1986). Included in *Come unto These Yellow Sands,* 1984.
Come unto These Yellow Sands (radio plays; includes *The Company of Wolves, Vampirella, Puss in Boots*). Newcastle-upon-Tyne, Bloodaxe, 1984.

Screenplays: *The Company of Wolves,* with Neil Jordan, 1984; *The Magic Toyshop,* 1987.

Radio Plays: *Vampirella,* 1976; *Come unto These Yellow Sands,* 1979; *The Company of Wolves,* from her own story, 1980; *Puss in Boots,* 1982; *A Self-Made Man* (on Ronald Firbank), 1984.

Poetry

Unicorn, Leeds, Location Press, 1966.

Other

Miss Z, The Dark Young Lady (for children). London, Heinemann, and New York, Simon and Schuster, 1970.
The Donkey Prince (for children). New York, Simon and Schuster, 1970.
Comic and Curious Cats, illustrated by Martin Leman. London, Gollancz, and New York, Crown, 1979.
The Sadeian Woman: An Exercise in Cultural History. London, Virago, 1979; as *The Sadeian Woman and the Ideology of Pornography,* New York, Pantheon, 1979.
Nothing Sacred: Selected Writings. London, Virago, 1982.
Moonshadow (for children). London, Gollancz, 1982.
Sleeping Beauty and Other Favourite Fairy Tales. London, Gollancz, 1982; New York, Schocken, 1984.

Editor, *Wayward Girls and Wicked Women: An Anthology of Stories.* London, Virago Press, 1986; New York, Penguin, 1989.
Editor, *The Virago Book of Fairy Tales.* London, Virago Press, 1990; as *The Old Wives' Fairy Tale Book,* New York, Pantheon, 1990.
Editor, *The Second Virago Book of Fairy Tales.* London, Virago, 1992; as *Strange Things Sometimes Still Happen: Fairy Tales from around the World,* Boston, Faber, 1993.
Translator, *The Fairy Tales of Charles Perrault.* London, Gollancz, 1977; New York, Avon, 1978.

*

Angela Carter commented:
Speak as you find.

*　　*　　*

Angela Carter stories appear frequently in anthologies. She describes herself as a Gothic writer; in her fondness for decadent opulence and squalor she is more like a stylish Moorcock, with greater charm and humour and less pretentiousness. In her persuasive "Polemical Preface" to *The Sadeian Woman: An Exercise in Cultural History,* she proposes a "moral pornographer" as an artist who demystifies the flesh to reveal "the real relations of man and his kind." She might see her work, more generally, as that of a "moral mythographer" who creates myths to destroy myths, pornographic writing being one of her weapons. She, perhaps more properly than de Sade, is "a terrorist of the imagination": he is too boring and disgusting to be terrifying and she seems over-deferential as well as patronizing in her critique of him. Latterly, she has revealed a strong interest in the ideas of mixed natures and of metamorphosis, revamping classic tales of lycanthropy or hermaphroditism, of which the most charming is the uncollected "Overture for 'A Midsummer Night's Dream'" (in *Interzone,* Autumn 1982). Students of Poe should note her fictionalized reconstruction of parts of his life, published in the first issue of *Interzone* (Spring 1982), "The Cabinet of Edgar Allan Poe."

Most of Carter's fiction may be classed as fantasy, and even the delightful mainstream comedy *Several Perceptions* uses fantasy as its subject. Three of her novels are in the SF genre, two of which are concerned with the harnessing of science in the service of fantasy, so that science fantasy might describe them with particular felicity. The panopticon episode in *Nights at the Circus* fits here, though not the book as a whole, which is a sort of fantastic freak show, less than the sum of its parts but particularly sound on clowns. Her last novel, *Wise Children,* superior to *Nights at the Circus,* is a kind of fantasy (because one does not expect to enjoy the 100th birthday party of famous twins in a mainstream novel), using Shakespearean plays and a famous actor. This Bohemian novel, written as it were from the wrong side of London, seems merely self-indulgent at first, but the reader who perseveres with it should find its slow, if nuggety, progress justified by the brilliant ending. An action described as fantastic is the assault by a hat, gloves, and other clothes in chapter 4, which is taken to be one of Grandma's warnings.

In the post-holocaust world of *Heroes and Villains,* civilization has been reduced to ivory towers guarded by Soldiers (the heroes) and menaced by barbarians and mutants. The heroine Marianne, a professor's daughter, rescues one of the villains during a raid and flees with him, even though he is her brother's murderer; he rapes, then marries her. The account of their ensuing love-hate relationship is a kind of anti-romance, in which the ambivalent, barbaric nastiness and beauty are paraded vividly before us. One of the novel's key themes is the treacherous nature of appearances, yet possibly the book exists principally as the frame for a strange *tableau-vivant* effect, whereby Henri Rousseau's painting *The Sleeping Gypsy* is brought to life.

The Infernal Desire Machines of Dr. Hoffman, where an embodiment of de Sade actually appears in one of the Grand Guignol episodes, is a much more powerful and ambitious work in which the author's evidently wide reading among the great satiric fantasists is apparent everywhere. The picaresque hero, Desiderio (a desirer), is on a mission to kill Dr. Hoffman, generator of mirages that drive men mad, and a quest to find and possess Hoffman's daughter, Albertina. The rational but impressionable hero is a reluctant exorcist, and the end to his adventure seems of less importance than the erotic and horrific sideshows that distract him on the way. Although her coldblooded, mad scientist villain is sufficiently evil, his chill-

ing nature is matched by the resolute *sangfroid* of the author, even when she is describing multiple buggery, rape, cannibalism, or eye-juggling; the excessive violence is not accompanied by a commensurable emotional response. (This distance is also a notable feature of Carter's readings of her own work: her tin voice as a reader makes the tonal range of her radio plays all the more astonishing.) One of the best episodes is in a relatively low key, Desiderio's night of love with the somnambulist daughter of an absentee major, his subsequent arrest for her murder, and escape by climbing one-handed up a chimney. The writing is so good in this novel that one wishes it made a better whole, that it had more humour and more seriousness, in Swift's or even in Beckford's manner.

The Passion of New Eve achieves a better balance of horror and humour, wit and pathos, self-indulgent fantasy and cool iconoclasm. The hero, Evelyn, is an Englishman precipitated into the American nightmare. Not a nice man himself, he mistreats his black mistress in New York, once a "city of visible reason" but now in Ballardian decay. Fleeing to the desert, Evelyn becomes New Eve when captured by lesbian guerrillas; fleeing from them she is raped by the petty tyrant Zero and becomes one of his harem, of lower status than his pigs. She accompanies the nihilist Zero on his mission to kill the film idol Tristessa, whom Evelyn had worshipped. Tristessa is revealed as a transvestite, and he impregnates Eve, kills Zero, and then is killed in error by soldiers, while Southern California burns in apocalyptic warfare, leaving Eve, after passage through an Earth womb, to escape American shores bearing her child, committed to the sea like a female Prospero. Machismo is mocked splendidly in both its male and female modes in this satiric anti-mythic novel, a *bravura* performance.

A few of the tales in *Fireworks: Nine Profane Pieces* fall sufficiently within the genre to serve as an excuse for reading the whole fantastic collection. In the afterword, the author refers to her Gothic tradition as retaining a singular moral function, "that of promoting unease." She understands the quality of her own art perfectly here.

—Michael J. Tolley

CARTER, Lin(wood Vrooman)

Nationality: American. **Born:** St. Petersburg, Florida, 9 June 1930. **Education:** Columbia University, New York, 1953-54. **Military Service:** Served in the United States Army Infantry, 1951-53. **Family:** Married Noël Vreeland in 1964. **Career:** Advertising and publisher's copywriter, 1957-69; editorial consultant, Ballantine Books Adult Fantasy, from 1969. **Awards:** Nova award, 1972. **Died:** 2 February 1988.

SCIENCE FICTION PUBLICATIONS

Novels (series: Callisto; Eric Carstairs; Gondwane Epic; Great Imperium; Green Star; Hautley Quicksilver; Kylix; Mars; Terra Magica; Thongor; World's End; Zarkon)

The Wizard of Lemuria. New York, Ace, 1965; revised edition, as *Thongor and the Wizard of Lemuria,* New York, Berkley, 1969.
Thongor of Lemuria. New York, Ace, 1966; revised edition, as *Thongor and the Dragon City,* New York, Berkley, 1970.

The Star Magicians. New York, Ace, 1966.
The Man without a Planet (Great Imperium). New York, Ace, 1966.
Destination: Saturn, with David Grinnell. New York, Avalon, 1967.
The Flame of Iridar. New York, Belmont, 1967.
Thongor against the Gods. New York, Paperback Library, 1967.
Thongor at the End of Time. New York, Paperback Library, 1968; London, Tandem, 1970.
Thongor in the City of Magicians. New York, Paperback Library, 1968.
The Thief of Thoth (Quicksilver). New York, Belmont, 1968.
Tower of the Edge of Time. New York, Belmont, 1968.
Conan of the Isles, with L. Sprague de Camp. New York, Lancer, 1968.
Giant of World's End. New York, Belmont, 1969.
The Purloined Planet (Quicksilver). New York, Belmont, 1969.
Lost World of Time. New York, New American Library, 1969.
Tower of the Medusa. New York, Ace, 1969.
Thongor Fights the Pirates of Tarakus. New York, Berkley, 1970; as *Thongor and the Pirates of Tarakus,* London, Tandem, 1971.
Star Rogue (Great Imperium). New York, Lancer, 1970.
Outworlder (Great Imperium). New York, Lancer, 1971.
The Quest of Kadji (Kylix). New York, Belmont, 1971.
Black Legion of Callisto. New York, Dell, 1972; London, Futura, 1975.
Under the Green Star. New York, DAW, 1972.
Jandar of Callisto. New York, Dell, 1972; London, Futura, 1974.
The Black Star. New York, Dell, 1973.
The Man Who Loved Mars (Mars). New York, Fawcett, and London, White Lion, 1973.
Sky Pirates of Callisto. New York, Dell, 1973; London, Futura, 1975.
When the Green Star Calls. New York, DAW, 1973.
The Valley Where Time Stood Still (Mars). Garden City, New York, Doubleday, 1974.
Time War. New York, Dell, 1974.
By the Light of the Green Star. New York, DAW, 1974.
The Warrior of World's End (Gondwane). New York, DAW, 1974.
The Nemesis of Evil: A Case from the Files of Omega (Zarkon). Garden City, New York, Doubleday, 1975.
Invisible Death: A Case from the Files of Omega (Zarkon). Garden City, New York, Doubleday, 1975; as *Zarkon, Lord of the Unknown and His Omega Crew: Invisible Death,* New York, Popular Library, 1978.
Mad Empress of Callisto. New York, Dell, 1975.
Mind Wizards of Callisto. New York, Dell, 1975.
Lankar of Callisto. New York, Dell, 1975.
As the Green Star Rises. New York, DAW, 1975.
The Enchantress of World's End (Gondwane). New York, DAW, 1975.
The Volcano Ogre: A Case from the Files of Omega (Zarkon). Garden City, New York, Doubleday, 1976; as *Zarkon, Lord of the Unknown and His Omega Crew: The Volcano Ogre,* New York, Popular Library, 1978.
The Immortal of World's End (Gondwane). New York, DAW, 1976.
In the Green Star's Glow. New York, DAW, 1976.
The Barbarian of World's End (Gondwane). New York, DAW, 1977.
Ylana of Callisto. New York, Dell, 1977.
The City Outside the World (Mars). New York, Berkley, 1977.
Renegade of Callisto. New York, Dell, 1978.
Pirate of World's End (Gondwane). New York, DAW, 1978.

Journey to the Underground World (Carstairs). New York, DAW, 1979.
The Wizard of Zao (Kylix). New York, DAW, 1978.
Conan the Liberator, with L. Sprague de Camp. New York, Bantam, 1979; London, Sphere, 1980.
Tara of the Twilight. New York, Zebra, 1979.
Zanthodon (Carstairs). New York, DAW, 1980.
Hurok of the Stone Age (Carstairs). New York, DAW, 1981.
Darya of the Bronze Age (Carstairs). New York, DAW, 1981.
The Earth-Shaker: A Case from the Files of Omega (Zarkon). Garden City, New York, Doubleday, 1982.
Conan the Barbarian (novelization of screenplay), with L. Sprague de Camp. New York, Bantam, and London, Sphere, 1982.
Eric of Zanthodon (Carstairs). New York, DAW, 1982.
Kesrick (Magica). New York, DAW, 1982.
Kellory the Warlock. Garden City, New York, Doubleday, 1984.
Down to a Sunless Sea (Mars). New York, DAW, 1984.
Dragonrogue: Further Adventures in Terra Magica. New York, DAW, 1984.
Found Wanting. New York, DAW, 1985.
Mandricardo: New Adventures in Terra Magica. New York, DAW, 1987.
Horror Wears Blue. Garden City, New York, Doubleday, 1987.
Callipygia: Further Adventures in Terra Magica. New York, DAW, 1988.
The Conan Chronicles, with Robert E. Howard and L. Sprague de Camp. London, Orbit, 1989.
  Conan the Buccaneer, with L. Sprague de Camp. New York, Lancer Books, 1971.
  Conan the Wanderer, with Robert E. Howard and L. Sprague de Camp. New York, Lancer, 1968; London, Sphere, 1974.

Short Stories

King Kull, with Robert E. Howard. New York, Lancer, 1967.
Beyond the Gates of Dream. New York, Belmont, 1969.
Conan of Cimmeria, with Robert E. Howard and L. Sprague de Camp, New York, Lancer, 1969; London, Sphere, 1974.
Conan of Aquilonia, with L. Sprague de Camp. New York, Prestige, 1977.
Conan the Swordsman, with L. Sprague de Camp and Björn Nyberg. New York, Bantam, 1978; London, Sphere, 1979.
Lost Worlds. New York, DAW, 1980.

OTHER PUBLICATIONS

Poetry

Dreams from R'lyeh. Sauk City, Wisconsin, Arkham House, 1975.

Other

Tolkien: A Look behind "The Lord of the Rings." New York, Ballantine, 1969.
Lovecraft: A Look behind the "Cthulhu Mythos." New York, Ballantine, 1972; London, Panther, 1975.
Imaginary Worlds: The Art of Fantasy. New York, Ballantine, 1973.
Royal Armies of the Hyborean Age: A Wargamer's Guide to the Age of Conana, with Scott Bizar. Roslyn, New York, Fantasy Games Unlimited, 1975.

Middle-Earth: The World of Tolkien, illustrated by David Wenzel. New York, Centaur, 1977.

History and Chronology of the Book of Eibon. New York, Charnal House, 1984.

Editor, *Dragons, Elves, and Heroes.* New York, Ballantine, 1969.

Editor, *The Young Magicians.* New York, Ballantine, 1969.

Editor, *The Magic of Atlantic.* New York, Lancer, 1970.

Editor, *Golden Cities, Far.* New York, Ballantine, 1970.

Editor, *The Dream-Quest of Unknown Kadath,* by H.P. Lovecraft. New York, Ballantine, 1970.

Editor, *Zothique,* by Clark Ashton Smith. New York, Ballantine, 1970.

Editor, *At the Edge of the World,* by Lord Dunsany. New York, Ballantine, 1970.

Editor (anonymous), *Double Phoenix: The Firebird; From the World's End.* New York, Ballantine, 1971.

Editor, *The Doom That Came to Sarnath,* by H.P. Lovecraft. New York, Ballantine, 1971.

Editor, *Hyperborea,* by Clark Ashton Smith. New York, Ballantine, 1971.

Editor, *The Spawn of Cthulhu.* New York, Ballantine, 1971.

Editor, *New Worlds for Old.* New York, Ballantine, 1971.

Editor, *Discoveries in Fantasy.* New York, Ballantine, 1972; London, Pan, 1974.

Editor, *Great Short Novels of Adult Fantasy 1-2.* New York, Ballantine, 2 vols., 1972-73.

Editor, *Beyond the Fields We Know,* by Lord Dunsany. New York, Ballantine, 1972.

Editor, *Evenor,* by George MacDonald. New York, Ballantine, 1972.

Editor, *Xiccarph,* by Clark Ashton Smith. New York, Ballantine, 1972.

Editor, *Poseidonis,* by Clark Ashton Smith. New York, Ballantine, 1973.

Editor, *Flashing Swords!:*

Flashing Swords! 1-2. Garden City, New York, Doubleday, 2 vols., 1973.

Flashing Swords! 3: Warriors and Wizards. New York, Dell, 1976.

Flashing Swords! 4: Barbarians and Black Magicians. Garden City, New York, Doubleday, 1977.

Flashing Swords! 5: Demons and Daggers. Garden City, New York, Doubleday, 1981.

Editor, *Over the Hills and Far Away,* by Lord Dunsany. New York, Ballantine, 1974.

Editor, *The Year's Best Fantasy Stories 1-6.* New York, DAW, 6 vols., 1975-80.

Editor, *Kingdoms of Sorcery.* Garden City, New York, Doubleday, 1976.

Editor, *Realms of Wizardry.* Garden City, New York, Doubleday, 1976.

Editor, *Weird Tales 1-4.* New York, Zebra, 1981-83.

*   *   *

Lin Carter's own fiction is perhaps best understood as an extension of his accomplishments as an editor and popular critic. It reflects the same enthusiasm for the tradition of heroic fantasy that he celebrates, for example, in his nonfiction book *Imaginary Worlds: The Art of Fantasy.* The majority of Carter's novels can be charac-

terized as adventure-based heroic fantasy, or sword-and-sorcery. Typically such heroic fantasies are situated on a continent in the distant past. There a barbarian-errant and his companions confront both human and bestial foes. The most terrifying of these human enemies are sorcerers who wield supernatural powers. In addition, the hero inevitably conquers a wide range of dragons and other monsters. The plots involve amplifications of two basic themes: quest and combat.

As a writer of heroic fantasy, Carter basically employs the conventions of that subgenre without altering or subverting them. An avowed admirer of Robert E. Howard, he has produced numerous sword-and-sorcery novels built around the exploits of heroes reminiscent of Howard's Conan the Barbarian. Reading the sheer bulk of Carter's output confirms the impression of hurried writing, dependence on formula, and inattention to detail. None of Carter's works stands out, but the most interesting and popular of his efforts remains his first series. This group of novels recounts the adventures of the mighty warrior Thongor. The hero, setting, and exploits all reflect Carter's thorough knowledge of the heroic fiction of Howard and Edgar Rice Burroughs. Thongor is a wandering adventurer who becomes King of Patanga and Overlord of a league of free cities on the Lost Continent of Lemuria, located somewhere in the Pacific "at the dawn of time."

Carter's depiction of Thongor is formulaic and predictable. Confronted by a dragon in *Thongor Fights the Pirates of Tarakus,* for example, the hero stands "ready for action, broadsword glittering in one powerful fist." Then "blind instinct drove him into whirlwind action" and Thongor "with the instincts of a born huntsman" slaughters the beast. The novel itself pits the warrior-king against a renegade wizard and a pirate king. The narrative speeds along, but Carter's constant references to his models, while providing a level of enjoyment to the reader steeped in pulp fiction, diminishes the imaginative intensity that attracts many sword-and-sorcery readers to his primary model Howard. The first volume in the Thongor series, *The Wizard of Lemuria,* in which Thongor defeats the evil Dragon Kings, would provide a good introduction both to Carter's fiction and to the basic conventions of sword-and-sorcery.

Carter's other sword-and-sorcery fiction includes the Jandar series, beginning with *Jandar of Callisto,* which imitates primarily the style and themes of Burroughs. Zarkon, the central figure in still another series, is based on Doc Savage. Carter has published a large number of short stories as well. The shorter works, like the novels, tend to evolve into series and pay homage through imitation. His "Simrana" stories are modeled on the work of Lord Dunsany, and he turned several unfinished tales by Clarke Ashton Smith into complete stories in *Beyond the Gates of Dream.*

In addition to producing a large body of his own heroic fiction, Carter has collaborated with L. Sprague de Camp (and others) to create continuations of two series by Howard: one celebrating Conan and the other narrating the adventures of King Kull. Carter developed his stories from fragments of stories left by Howard. The King Kull works offer a good example of successful imitation. Carter manages to fashion a style highly reminiscent of Howard's. Not surprisingly, since his own fantasies espouse the same position, Carter's tales about Conan and King Kull continue Howard's championing of barbarism over civilization and the implicit praise of the moral virtue of violent conflict.

In addition to sword-and-sorcery, Carter has written several works more obviously intended as science fiction. Here too he displays familiarity with and competence in the traditions of pulp writing rather than originality or depth of thought. The style is straightforward, the episodes generally brief, the emphasis on adventure. *The Valley Where Time Stood Still* offers a representative example of this aspect of Carter's fiction. The characters and plot are similar to Carter's fantasies, while the use of science is minimal. The setting is Mars, but the planet is more a locale for action than a carefully created alien world. The plot revolves around two quests, an Earthman for uranium and a Martian warrior-prince for the fabled Valley of Life. Perhaps his most successful science fiction novels are two comic works about an intergalactic secret agent named Hautley Quicksilver. Carter's language, often awkward in his attempts to describe the feats of muscular heroes, is better suited to the light, almost self-deprecatory tone of both *The Thief of Thoth* and *The Purloined Planet*.

The same affection for fantasy and science fiction that permeates Carter's critical writing and his anthologies is the most attractive feature of his fiction. Most of the novels and stories are unabashedly derivative. His plotting, especially in the heroic fantasies, is almost mechanically formulaic, and the language reflects Carter's admiration for the pulp magazine fiction of the 1930s and 1940s. With all its flaws, his fiction has undeniably become a minor but permanent part of the particular heroic tradition to which he is lovingly devoted.

—Dennis M. Kratz

CARTMILL, Cleve

Pseudonym: Michael Corbin. **Nationality:** American. **Born:** Platteville, Wisconsin, in 1908. **Family:** Married; one son. **Career:** Accountant, newspaperman, radio operator; invented the Blackmill system of high-speed typography. **Died:** 11 February 1964.

SCIENCE FICTION PUBLICATIONS

Short Stories (series: Jake Murchison)

The Space Scavengers. Chatsworth, California, Major, 1975.

Author of "Deadline" in *Astounding,* March 1944. Also author of numerous uncollected short stories.

*　　*　　*

Some writers in science fiction, as in other fields of literature, achieve notoriety not for their body of work but for a single story or novel. Tom Godwin ("The Cold Equations") is one such writer. Another is Cleve Cartmill, for "Deadline" (*Astounding,* March 1944). Although "Deadline" has dubious literary merits (predictable plot, pedestrian handling), the story is unique in that it describes, in considerable scientific detail, the manufacture and use of an atomic bomb a year before the United States dropped the first genuine atomic bombs on Hiroshima and Nagasaki. Its publication did not cause an immediate furor in SF circles; it did, however, cause one in the War Department.

Shortly after the novelette appeared, Cartmill was visited by a representative of Military Intelligence and questioned at some length; his file of correspondence with the editor of *Astounding,* John W. Campbell, concerning "Deadline" was also confiscated. Cartmill was later cleared of any wrongdoing, although he was told that he had "vio-

lated personal security" in wartime by publicly disseminating the facts contained in the story. These facts, however, were a matter of public record, as Campbell himself pointed out to the Military in denying their request not to publish any further speculation on nuclear fission. Following the close of World War II, "Deadline" became a link in the argument that science fiction is a valid medium for predicting the future. It was also pointed to with pride as an example of SF as a serious art form for adults, rather than improbable escapism for juveniles, thereby worthy of consideration not only by members of the scientific community but by the heads of government.

Despite the fact that Cartmill's rather extensive output of science fiction and fantasy is largely forgotten today, at least some of it is of a quality to interest the serious student. His best work, perhaps, is the highly imaginative short novel "Hell Hath Fury." Other excellent efforts include his first published story, "Oscar," and a grim little tale called "The Bargain." Cartmill also wrote space opera; popular in the 1940s was his "Space Salvage" series featuring Jake Murchison and his crew of the spaceship *Dolphin* who tackled "impossible" problems and made fantastic rescues in space. The best of these stories were posthumously collected as *The Space Scavengers,* the only book to bear Cartmill's name.

—Bill Pronzini

CARVER, Jeffrey A(llan)

Nationality: American. **Born:** Cleveland, Ohio, 25 August 1949. **Education:** Brown University, B.A., 1971; University of Rhode Island, Kingston, M.M.A. (Master of Marine Affairs), 1974. **Family:** Married Allysen Palmer in 1986; two daughters. **Career:** Ford assembly line worker; substitute teacher; scuba diving instructor; quahog diver; UPS sorter; office temp; word-processing consultant. Since 1977, freelance writer. Part-time word-processing operator and consultant, 1982-85. Developer and host of "Science Fiction and Fantasy Writing," a five-part educational TV series produced by the Massachusetts Corporation for Educational Telecommunications (MCET), 1995. **Member:** SFFWA, 1974; Authors Guild, 1976. **Agent:** Richard Curtis Associates, 171 East 74th St., New York, New York 10021. **Address:** Jeffrey A. Carver, 102 Melrose Street, Arlington, Massachusetts 02174-8536, U.S.A. **Online Address:** Jeff.Carver@Genie.geis.com.

SCIENCE FICTION PUBLICATIONS

Novels (series: Changeling Star; Chaos Chronicles; Roger Zelazny's Alien Speedway; Star Rigger)

Seas of Ernathe. Toronto, New York, Laser, 1976.
Star Rigger's Way. Garden City, New York, Doubleday, 1978; London, Arrow, 1980.
Panglor. New York, Dell, 1980; London; Arrow, 1981.
The Infinity Link. New York, Bluejay International Edition, 1984; London, Orbit, 1986.
The Rapture Effect. New York, Tor, 1987; London, Orbit, 1988.
Clypsis (Alien Speedway). Toronto, New York, Bantam, 1987.
From a Changeling Star. Toronto, New York, Bantam, 1989.
Down the Stream of Stars (Changeling Star). New York, Bantam, 1990.
Dragons in the Stars. New York, Tor, 1992.

Dragon Rigger (Star Rigger). New York, Tor, 1993.
Neptune Crossing (Chaos Chronicles). New York, Tor, 1994.
Strange Attractors. New York, Tor, 1995.

*

Manuscript Collection: Popular Culture Library, BGSU Center for Archival Collections, Bowling Green State University, Bowling Green, Ohio.

*   *   *

Hard science fiction is a complex and challenging form for even the best of writers, because it is difficult to maintain a proper balance between narrative values and the need to explicate the scientific content well enough not to lose less sophisticated readers. A handful of recent writers have mastered this delicate art, and Jeffrey Carver has moved steadily in that direction from a strong base in straightforward adventure stories.

Carver's debut novel was *The Seas of Ernathe*, an entertaining but unprepossessing adventure story about a world where human colonists and alien natives have apparently coexisted peacefully for several generations. The kidnapping of a visiting star pilot leads to the discovery of the planet's hidden secrets. His second novel, *Star Rigger*, also explores the inter-relationships of human and alien, this time featuring the only survivor of a space crew, a man who unfortunately lacks the psychic powers required to successfully make an interstellar jump. His chances of survival improve dramatically when he encounters an alien who might be able to provide a substitute for his missing ability. Another starship captain is the protagonist of *Panglor*, a man coerced by circumstances into committing an act of great cruelty, but who reneges at the last moment and becomes a fugitive. These three early books are all nicely crafted adventures, but they provide only glimpses of the talent that would become evident in subsequent books.

The Infinity Link was the first of Carver's novels to draw serious attention in the SF community. Contact has finally been established with an alien species, accomplished by scientists using a combination of telepathy and computer enhancement. From this intercourse, they are advancing human knowledge by leaps and bounds. Unfortunately, politicians have a tendency to restrict the flow of knowledge as a means of retaining personal power, so the scientists are forced to resort to trickery and misdirection to prevent them from exploiting what should be a boon to humankind. Carver followed this quickly with the equally impressive *The Rapture Effect*, which has several superficial similarities. Again, the theme is the conflict between self interest and public concern, but this time it's the other side in the driver's seat. A handful of multi-national corporations have a stranglehold on knowledge of an alien race, against which a secret war is being waged.

From a Changeling Star was an even more impressive effort, and marks Carver's clear emergence as a hard SF writer. A group of scientists has gathered to observe the consequences of a supernova in one of the two major plots; a man whose body is being transformed into something other than human through the wonders of nanotechnology is the focus of the second. Both are set against the backdrop of a factionalized interstellar culture. The petty differences of humanity are put in proper perspective in the sequel, *Down the Stream of Stars*. Betelgeuse explodes as expected, and the cataclysm opens a gateway to the heart of the galaxy. Human horizons are widened and their petty squabbling becomes trivial when the gateway provides a route for inimical aliens from the core of the galaxy to expand outward into human occupied space. The third in the series, *Dragons in the Stars*, is a less ambitious tale more reminiscent of Carver's earlier space adventures. This time the focus is on star traveling dragons, a lifeform that exists in the deeps between the stars.

Dragonrigger is the fourth in the sequence, featuring a human who allies himself with one of the space dwelling dragons to defeat an evil enemy and eventually forge a shaky but welcome peace between humans and dragons.

Carver opened a new series with *Neptune Crossing*. An explorer on one of Neptune's moons has an accident and falls into a cavern occupied by a dormant alien creature. The alien is a symbiote which awakens inside his body, although it has an imperfect memory of its former existence. It does have sufficient knowledge to predict the imminent destruction of Earth, however, a fate which the protagonist can avert if he acts quickly and in defiance of his orders, and if he's willing to be separated from the rest of his kind forever. Obviously he succeeds, saves the world, but is transported countless lightyears from the solar system.

His further adventures, augmented by two amusing robot sidekicks, are found in *Strange Attractors*, a story filled with wonderful ideas but whose plot lacks clear direction. The setting is an artificial world of extraordinary size, inhabited by representatives of a wide number of races. Even the inorganic elements of the environment have some primitive sentience, however, so that it is possible for banks of snow, or bodies of water, or almost anything else to take offense and attack interlopers. Accompanied by an alien friend, the only human aboard goes on a journey of exploration, manages to survive, and eventually defeats an almost demonic force that is terrorizing some of the world's inhabitants. Clearly there's at least one more book planned in the series.

One other novel, *Clypsis*, is an amusing but minor adventure story about an entire solar system that has been redesigned as the setting for a series of space races. Carver is an infrequent short story writer, but his best at this length include "Life Tides", "Love Rogo", and "Reality School in the Entropy Zone". Carver is an accomplished, ambitious writer whose work has steadily developed in quality and scope, and who seems likely to become one of the major voices in technically oriented, scientifically based SF. His successful blend of these techniques with more romantic images like dragons gives his work a distinctive flavor that should serve him well in his future efforts.

—Don D'Ammassa

CARY, Julian, *See* **TUBB, E.C.**

CHALKER, Jack L(aurence)

Nationality: American. **Born:** Baltimore, Maryland, 17 December 1944. **Education:** Towson State College, Baltimore, B.S. 1966;

Johns Hopkins University, Baltimore, M.L.A. 1969. **Military Service:** Served in the United States Air Force 135th Air Commando Group, 1968-71, and the Maryland Air National Guard, 1968-69; Staff Sergeant. **Family:** Married Eva C. Whitley in 1978; one son. **Career:** English, history, and geography teacher in Baltimore high schools, 1966-78. Since 1961, Founder-Director, Mirage Press, Baltimore; editor, fanzine. **Agent:** Eleanor Wood, Spectrum Literary Agency, 111 Eighth Avenue, Suite 1501, New York, New York 10011. **Address:** Mirage Press, P.O. Box 1689, Westminster, Maryland 21157-1689, U.S.A.

SCIENCE FICTION PUBLICATIONS

Novels (series: Changewinds; Dancing Gods; Four Lords of the Diamond; G.O.D., Inc., Quintara Marathon; Ring of the Master; Soul Rider; Well World)

A Jungle of Stars. New York, Ballantine, 1976.
Well World:
   Midnight at the Well of Souls. New York, Ballantine, 1977; London, Penguin, 1981.
   Exiles at the Well of Souls. New York, Ballantine, 1978; London, Penguin, 1982.
   Quest for the Well of Souls. New York, Ballantine, 1978; London, Penguin, 1982.
   The Return of Nathan Brazil. New York, Ballantine, 1980; London, Penguin, 1984.
   Twilight at the Well of Souls: The Legacy of Nathan Brazil. New York, Ballantine, 1980; London, Penguin, 1984.
   Echoes of the Well of Souls: A Well World Novel. New York, Ballantine, 1993.
   Shadow of the Well of Souls: A Well World Novel. New York, Ballantine, 1994.
   Gods of the Well of Souls: A Well World Novel. New York, Ballantine, 1994.
   The Watchers at the Well (omnibus). New York, Guild America, 1994.
Dancers in the Afterglow. New York, Ballantine, 1978.
The Web of the Chozen. New York, Ballantine, 1978.
And the Devil Will Drag You Under: A Novel. New York, Ballantine, 1979.
A War of Shadows. New York, Ace, 1979.
The Identity Matrix. New York, Timescape, 1982.
Four Lords of the Diamond. Garden City, New York, Doubleday, 1983.
   Lilith: A Snake in the Grass. New York, Ballantine, 1981; London, Roc, 1990.
   Cerberus: A Wolf in the Fold. New York, Ballantine, 1982; London, Roc, 1991.
   Charon: A Dragon at the Gate. New York, Ballantine, 1982; London, Roc, 1991.
   Medusa: A Tiger by the Tail. New York, Ballantine, 1983; London, Roc, 1991.
Soul Rider:
   Spirits of Flux and Anchor. New York, Tor, 1984; London, Roc, 1991.
   Empires of Flux and Anchor. New York, Tor, 1984; London, Roc, 1991.
   Masters of Flux and Anchor. New York, Tor, 1985; London, Roc, 1991.
   The Birth of Flux and Anchor. New York, Tor, 1985; London, Roc, 1991.

   Children of Flux and Anchor. New York, Tor, 1986; London, Roc, 1992.
Dancing Gods:
   The River of Dancing Gods. New York, Ballantine, 1984; London, Orbit, 1985.
   Demons of the Dancing Gods. New York, Ballantine, 1984; London, Orbit, 1986.
   Vengeance of the Dancing Gods. New York, Ballantine, 1985; London, Orbit, 1986.
   Songs of the Dancing Gods. New York, Ballantine, 1990; London, Orbit, 1991.
The Messiah Choice. New York, Bluejay, 1985.
Downtiming the Night Side. New York, Tor, 1985.
The Rings of the Master:
   Lords of the Middle Dark. New York, Ballantine, 1986; London, New English Library, 1988.
   Pirates of the Thunder. New York, Ballantine, 1987; London, New English Library, 1988.
   Warriors of the Storm. New York, Ballantine, 1987; London, New English Library, 1989.
   Masks of the Martyrs. New York, Ballantine, 1988; London, New English Library, 1989.
Changewinds:
   When the Changewinds Blow. New York, Ace, 1987; London, New English Library, 1991.
   Riders of the Winds. New York, Ace, 1988; London, New English Library, 1991.
   War of the Maelstrom. New York, Ace, 1988; London, New English Library, 1991.
G.O.D., Inc.:
   Labyrinth of Dreams. New York, Tor, 1987; London, New English Library, 1989.
   The Shadow Dancers. New York, Tor, 1987; London, New English Library, 1989.
   The Maze in the Mirror. New York, Tor, 1989; London, New English Library, 1990.
The Quintara Marathon:
   The Demons at Rainbow Bridge. New York, Ace, 1989.
   The Run to Chaos Keep. New York, Ace, 1991.
   The Ninety Trillion Fausts. New York, Ace, 1991.
The Red Tape War, with Mike Resnick and George Alec Effinger. New York, Tor, 1991.

Short Stories

An Informal Biography of Scrooge McDuck. Baltimore, Mirage Press, 1974.
Dance Band on the Titanic (stories and essays). New York, Ballantine, 1988.

OTHER PUBLICATIONS

Novels

The Devil's Voyage. Garden City, New York, Doubleday, 1981.

Other

The New H.P. Lovecraft Bibliography. Baltimore, Anthem, 1962; revised edition, with Mark Owings, as *The Revised H.P. Lovecraft Bibliography,* Mirage Press, 1973.

In Memoriam: Clark Ashton Smith. Baltimore, Anthem, 1963.
The Index to the Science-Fantasy Publishers: (A Bibliography of the Science Fiction and Fantasy Specialty Houses), with Mark Owings. Baltimore, Anthem, 1966; expanded as *The Science-Fantasy Publishers: A Critical and Bibliographic History,* Westminister, Maryland, Mirage Press, 1991; revised edition, 1992.
On Writing. Eugene, Oregon, Pulphouse, 1991.

Editor, *Mirage on Lovecraft: A Literary View.* Baltimore, privately published, 1965.
Editor, *Hotel Andromeda.* New York, Ace, 1994.

*

Bibliography: In *Program Book,* Paracon 1, State College, Pennsylvania, 1978; in *Dance Band on the Titanic* by Chalker, New York, Ballantine, 1988.

Jack L. Chalker comments:

Although I have a technical background, my degrees are in the social, not the pure, sciences, and my work generally reflects this. My stories are about people, mostly ordinary people, caught up in extraordinary circumstances and usually changed by them. They use the fun-house mirror reflection of science fiction to examine people and culture, including ideology, as I see them today. The themes are anti-dogmatic: ideologies and human preachments are taken apart, examined, and generally found wanting. For this reason a lot of my work had been taken as anti-utopian and downbeat, but there is a strain of optimism there because, no matter what, mankind copes with adversity and overcomes, although never without cost. There is an inherently absurdist streak in man which has caused him, over six thousand years of recorded history, to kill, torture, and maim, mostly in the name of the people. Man adapts, advances, and grows despite this.

On the individual level, my stories examine the way human beings treat each other, generally brutalizing those most in need of help, and those individuals' quests for their own better life. For these themes, and others, interwoven in my stories, science fiction provides the perfect metaphors. I am a strongly political writer, without ideology, only hope. And yet all my stories are superficially plots of twist and turn, diverting entertainments, problems to be solved. Pacing is all important to me; I want the reader to turn to the next page, to keep reading, and to have a good time as my serious themes creep into the entertainment but never get in its way.

* * *

Jack Chalker has become over the past two decades a highly successful and widely published author known mostly for his novel sequences, including the Well World, Four Lords of the Diamond, Soul Rider, and the detective-parody trilogy G.O.D. Inc. He is a writer who has been both praised to the skies and condemned as a mechanical churner-out of hack-work. His work, though flawed, will reward the reader both as an entertainment and a treatment of serious themes.

One theme and one literary device can be found running through Chalker's work. The theme is that of the conflict between the desire for freedom and the desire for security, between the need for independence and authentic choice and the need for comfort and the good opinion of others. The device is that of transformation, of people, both ordinary and extraordinary, being made into something other than themselves. The means of forcing the change may be magical, technological, or psychological but it is always a metaphor for the agony that moral choice and the unyielding facts of life create in people. Some of Chalker's characters grow stronger because of the changes that are forced on them, some are shattered by the changes; but Chalker always makes you watch with sympathy the pain of the characters as they face the horrendous situations he places them in. Like Alfred Hitchcock, Chalker seems to believe that the key to excitement is to threaten the heroine; his protagonists (and especially the female ones) are made to face their worst fears and overcome, or be overcome, by them.

The typical Chalker situation is embodied in *Dancers in the Afterglow,* one of his earliest and best novels. Alien invaders overrun a tourist planet and begin to convert the inhabitants to a more docile and communal form of life, using their human weaknesses as the means of cracking and remoulding their minds. The hero, a cyborg special agent, watches the newfound happiness of the brainwashed victims and envies them their simplicity and sense of community almost enough to betray his trust. At the climax, Chalker makes the moral core of his novels as clear as he ever does, when the hero and the 'villain' debate the moral difference between a controlled, stable, stagnant and happy society and undomesticated humanity with its hatreds and imperfections and dynamism. Unlike Heinlein or others of the "humanity-uber-alles" school of fiction, Chalker can see, and make you see, the attractions of submission to authority at the same time as he rejects it.

Because of Chalker's willingness to use sexual metaphors for the struggle for power, some critics have rejected his work as mere exploitation. Thomas M. Disch notoriously referred to the excellent Soul Rider sequence as "better-written Gor books." However, Chalker's books are not written to praise the urge to power but to show how pervasive it is even in those who claim to be liberal or in revolt against authority and how fragile the defences are that have been built up against absolutism of every kind. His concerns about the increasing power over ourselves and others that technology is bringing and his pessimism about people's willingness to make clear and principled political decisions about the control of such new capacity is expounded in the essays included in his short story collection *Dance Band on the Titanic.*

All of this is not to say that Chalker's work is without flaws. His writing style needs heavier editing than it has received. And since he likes to create MacGuffins that are all powerful (the powers of the Flux Magicians, the universe-rewriting Obie computer, the magical lamp of One Wish Only to name but a few) he often plots himself into a corner and forgets the limits he placed upon his creations earlier to get out of later difficulties; the novel that is most offensive in this regard is the time-travel saga *Downtiming the Night-Side.*

Chalker's flaws are minor compared with his virtues, which are those of a storyteller. He makes you care about his characters and want to know what happens next. He has resisted the temptation of continuing his novel-sequences beyond the point at which invention flags (although perhaps the River of Dancing Gods sequence carried its sword and sorcery parody on a little too long and his decision to return to the Well World sequence over a dozen years after the end of the original series worries me slightly as a possible sign of his stock of ideas depleting itself). He will probably never be popular enough inside the SF establishment to win major recognition but he is not deserving of the automatic denigration that often seems to accompany his name in such circles. And his lack of literary graces prevent him from acheiving recognition in "literary" circles. But since he gives his own role-models as Louis L'Amour and Evan Hunter, he will probably not be too distressed by this double failure. He is an entertainer who can also make you face moral issues very directly and forcefully. This is not an acheivement to be looked down on.

—Michael Cule

CHANDLER, A(rthur) Bertram

Nationality: Australian. **Born:** Aldershot, Hampshire, England, 28 March 1912. **Education:** Peddar's Lane Council School, and Sir John Leman School, Beccles, Suffolk. **Family:** Married 1) Joan Chandler; 2) Susan Schlenker; two daughters and one son. **Career:** Apprentice, rising to Third Officer, Sun Shipping Company, London, 1928-35; Fourth Officer, rising to Chief Officer, Shaw Savill Line, London, 1936-55; Third Officer, rising to Master, Union Steam Ship Company of New Zealand, Wellington, 1956-75. **Recipient:** Ditmar award (Australia), 1969, 1971, 1974, 1976; Seiun Sho award (Japan), 1975; Invisible Little Man award, 1975; Australian Literature Board fellowship, 1980. Guest of Honor, World SF Convention, Chicago, 1981. **Died:** 6 June 1984.

SCIENCE FICTION PUBLICATIONS

Novels (series: Derek Calver; Empress Irene; John Grimes; Rim Worlds)

Bring Back Yesterday. New York, Ace, 1961; London, Allison and Busby, 1981.
Rendezvous on a Lost World (Rim Worlds). New York, Ace, 1961; as *When the Dream Dies,* London, Allison and Busby, 1981.
The Rim of Space (Calver). New York, Avalon, 1961; London, Allison and Busby, 1981; New York, Ace, 1979.
The Ship from Outside (Rim Worlds: Calver). New York, Ace, 1963; London, Allison and Busby, 1982.
The Hamelin Plague. Derby, Connecticut, Monarch, 1963.
Glory Planet. New York, Avalon, 1964.
The Deep Reaches of Space (Rim Worlds). London, Jenkins, 1964.
Into the Alternate Universe (Rim Worlds: Grimes). New York, Ace, 1964.
The Coils of Time. New York, Ace, 1964.
Empress of Outer Space. New York, Ace, 1965.
The Alternate Martians. New York, Ace, 1965.
Space Mercenaries (Empress). New York, Ace, 1965.
The Road to the Rim (Grimes). New York, Ace, 1967.
Contraband from Otherspace (Rim Worlds: Grimes). New York, Ace, 1967.
Nebula Alert (Rim Worlds: Empress). New York, Ace, 1967.
The Rim Gods (Grimes). New York, Ace, 1968.
False Fatherland: Spartan Planet (Rim Worlds: Grimes). Sydney, Horwitz, 1968; as *Spartan Planet,* New York, Dell, 1969.
The Sea Beasts. New York, Curtis, 1971.
To Prime the Pump (Rim Worlds). New York, Curtis, 1971.
The Dark Dimensions (Rim Worlds: Grimes). New York, Ace, 1971.

The Inheritors (Rim Worlds: Grimes). New York, Ace, 1978.
Gateway to Never (Rim Worlds: Grimes). New York, Ace, 1978.
The Bitter Pill. Melbourne, Wren, 1974.
The Big Black Mark (Rim Worlds: Grimes). New York, DAW, 1975.
The Broken Cycle (Rim Worlds: Grimes). London, Hale, 1975; New York, DAW, 1979.
The Way Back (Grimes). London, Hale, 1976; New York, DAW, 1978.
Star Courier (Grimes). London, Hale, and New York, DAW, 1977.
Far Traveller (Grimes). London, Hale, 1977; as *The Far Traveler,* New York, DAW, 1979.
To Keep the Ship (Grimes). London, Hale, and New York, DAW, 1978.
Matilda's Stepchildren (Grimes). London, Hale, 1979; New York, DAW, 1983.
Star Loot (Grimes). New York, DAW, 1980; London, Hale, 1981.
The Anarch Lords (Grimes). New York, DAW, 1981.
Up to the Sky in Ships, with *In and out of Quandry* by Lee Hoffman. Cambridge, Massachusetts, NESFA Press, 1982.
Kelly Country. Ringwood, Victoria, Penguin, 1983; New York, DAW, 1985.
Frontier of the Dark. New York, Ace, 1984.
The Last Amazon (Grimes). New York, DAW, 1984.
The Wild Ones (Grimes). Victoria, Australia, Collins, 1984; New York, DAW, 1985.

Short Stories (series: John Grimes; Rim Worlds)

Beyond the Galactic Rim, New York, Ace, 1963; London, Allison and Busby, 1982.
Catch the Star Winds (Rim Worlds). New York, Lancer, 1969.
Alternate Orbits (Rim Worlds: Grimes). New York, Ace, 1971; as *The Commodore at Sea,* 1979.
The Hard Way Up (Rim Worlds: Grimes). New York, Ace, 1972.
From Sea to Shining Star, edited by Keith Curtis and Susan Chandler. Perth, Dreamstone, 1989.

*

Bibliography: "Bibliography of the Works of A. Bertram Chandler" by Ross Pavlac, in Marcon XIII (Columbus, Ohio), March 1978.

A. Bertram Chandler commented:

(1981) Quite a few years ago Robert Heinlein said, "Only people who know ships can write convincingly about spaceships." At the time I thought that this was very true. I have not changed my opinion. I believe that the crews of the real spaceships of the future, vessels going a long way in a long time, will have far more in common with today's seamen than with today's airmen. I freely admit that my stories are essentially sea stories and that John Grimes, my series character, is descended from Hornblower. At a book-signing recently in Fukuoka I felt flattered when one of my Japanese faithful readers gave me one of Forester's Hornblower novels to autograph.

*   *   *

A. Bertram Chandler wrote dozens of novels and hundreds of short stories in his career, the bulk of which are set in the Rim

Worlds, most of them featuring John Grimes in various periods of his varied career. The Rim Worlds are those planets situated on the periphery of the galaxy, far distant from each other, individual human colonies free to develop even more radically than in the more civilized portions of human colonized space because the distances are so extreme that even with faster-than-light travel, regular intercouse is infrequent. There are as well many worlds whose inhabitants are no longer in touch with the rest of humanity, and these "lost colonies" frequently show up in Chandler's novels.

Derek Calver was the protagonist of the first Rim novel, *The Rim of Space,* although he was quickly replaced by John Grimes for all but one of the later volumes. Chandler developed many facets of his private vision of the universe at the edge of the galaxy, where even the laws of nature are sometimes mutable and rarely predictable. There are "ghost ships" which have strayed into other dimensions but which are sometimes accessible from real space, and there are rare borderlines separating our own reality from alternate universes, borders which sometimes allow a ship to cross from here to there or vice versa.

Chandler's most frequent protagonist, John Grimes, is originally an employee of a major trading firm, but he gets into trouble, is briefly outlawed, then finds a new job as a Rim trader, and prospers as a reluctant politician. His adventures include participating in a mutiny in *The Big Black Mark,* shifting allegiance to the Rim Worlds in *The Road to the Rim,* supporting himself delivering interstellar mail in *Star Courier,* becoming a pirate in *Star Loot* and then governor of a world settled by anarchists in *The Anarch Lords,* exploring a parallel universe in *The Broken Cycle,* repelling an invasion by intelligent rats from another reality in *Contraband from Otherspace,* investigating ghost ships in *Into the Alternate Universe,* and finding lost colonies in *The Far Traveler, The Inheritors,* and *Spartan Planet. To Keep the Ship* is a particularly effective adventure, involving terrorists and an infestation of homunculi, semi-sapient creatures that look like tiny humans and which make superb assassins. Grimes gets lost in a number of alternate universes in *The Way Back,* discovers the unpleasant consequences of near immortality in *To Prime the Pump,* and deals with an experimental robot in *The Wild Ones.* There were also numerous short stories about Grimes and the Rim worlds, some of which are cobbled together into episodic "novels." He even meets an alternate version of himself with humorous consequences in *The Dark Dimensions.* The novels were not written chronologically and fall into two main groups, one set during the early years before Grimes was fully committed to the Rim Worlds, the other set after he is forced to change his allegiance and abandon the more settled part of the galaxy.

Grimes's epic adventures have been rightly compared to C.S. Forester's Horatio Hornblower series. Indeed, Chandler worked as a sea captain for most of his career and the naval allusions and devices are a strong element in the novels. While it cannot be claimed that these novels are stylistically elegant or that they examine great issues, there is an undeniable sense of good-natured wonder about the universe that makes them more effective than would otherwise be the case. Chandler was first and foremost a storyteller, but a talented one who could take the most overused cliché and write an entertaining tale around it.

Not all of Chandler's novels were set in the Rim worlds. *The Alternate Martians* is an amusing look at an alternate universe where the Mars of both Edgar Rice Burroughs and H.G. Wells are accurate, and *The Coils of Time* is a somewhat similar look at an inhabited Venus. The short-lived but entertaining Empress series, begin-

ning with *Empress of Outer Space,* continued in *The Space Mercenaries* and *Nebula Alert,* features a deposed queen who has adventures with space pirates, slavers, hostile aliens, and other villains. It bears some similarities to the Rim Worlds series, but Chandler abandoned it quickly and concentrated on Grimes, who already had an established following.

A few standalone novels are also of interest. *Frontier of the Dark* is about an experimental star drive that changes an entire crew into rationalized werewolves. *The Sea Beasts* is a reasonably suspenseful story of alien invaders in Earth's ocean. *The Bitter Pill* is the traditional SF cautionary tale, a dystopian future dictatorship and a successful rebellion by colonists on Mars. His single most successful and important novel is *Kelly Country,* a thoughtful, fascinating alternate history story that shows what might have happened if Australia had rebelled and broken from England at approximately the same time the American colonies did. It's a shame that Chandler didn't exert himself in this fashion on other occasions, because he was clearly capable of creating more important work than simple space opera.

Most of Chandler's many short stories were either Rim-related adventures or minor pieces. A few exceptions include "The Giant Killer," one of the classic stories of a narrowly circumscribed universe, "All Laced Up," "The Cage," "The Left Hand Way," and "Words and Music." Chandler will certainly be remembered because of his Rim Worlds series, which has the same unique appeal that has made *Star Trek* such a success, although his technically more interesting work seems likely to pass from view.

—Don D'Ammassa

CHARBONNEAU, Louis (Henry)

Pseudonym: Carter Travis Young. **Nationality:** American. **Born:** Detroit, Michigan, 20 January 1924. **Education:** University of Detroit, A.B. 1948, M.A. 1950. **Military Service:** Served in the United States Army Air Force, 1943-46: Staff Sergeant. **Family:** Married 1) Hilda Sweeney in 1945 (died 1984); 2) Diane Fries in 1984. Instructor in English, University of Detroit, 1948-52; copywriter, Mercury Advertising Agency, Los Angeles, 1952-56; staff writer, *Los Angeles Times,* 1956-71; freelance writer, 1971-74; editor, Security World Publishing Company, Los Angeles, 1974-79. Since 1979, freelance writer. **Agent:** Scott Meredith Literary Agency, 845 Third Avenue, New York, New York 10022, U.S.A.

SCIENCE FICTION PUBLICATIONS

Novels

No Place on Earth. Garden City, New York, Doubleday, 1958; London, Jenkins, 1966.
Corpus Earthling. Rockville Centre, New York, Zenith, 1960; London, Digit, 1963.
The Sentinel Stars: A Novel of the Future. New York, Bantam, 1963; London, Corgi, 1964.
Psychedelic-40. New York, Bantam, 1965; as *The Specials,* London, Jenkins, 1967.

Antic Earth. London, Jenkins, 1967: as *Down to Earth,* New York, Bantam, 1967.
The Sensitives: A Novel (novelization of screenplay). New York, Bantam, 1968.
Barrier World. New York, Lancer, 1970.
Embryo: A Novel (novelization of screenplay). New York, Warner, 1976.

OTHER PUBLICATIONS

Novels

Night of Violence. New York, Torquil, and London, Digit, 1959; as *The Trapped Ones,* London, Barker, 1960.
Nor All Your Tears. New York, Torquil, 1959; as *The Time of Desire,* London, Digit, 1960.
Way Out. London, Barrie and Rockliff, and New York, Banner, 1966.
Down from the Mountain. New York, Doubleday, 1969.
And Hope to Die. New York, Ace, 1970.
From a Dark Place. New York, Dell, 1974.
Intruder. New York, Doubleday, 1979.
The Lair. New York, Fawcett, 1979.
The Brea File. New York, Doubleday, 1983.
Stalk: A Novel of Suspense. New York, Fine, 1992.
White Harvest. New York, Fine, 1994.
The Magnificent Siberian. New York, Fine, 1995.

Novels as Carter Travis Young

The Wild Breed. New York, Doubleday, 1960; as *The Sudden Gun,* London, Hammond, 1960.
The Savage Plain. New York, Doubleday, 1961; London, Hammond, 1963.
Shadow of a Gun. New York, Fawcett, 1961; London, Muller, 1962.
The Bitter Iron. New York, Doubleday, 1964; London, Ward Lock, 1965.
Long Boots, Hard Boots. New York, Doubleday, 1965; London, Ward Lock, 1966.
Why Did They Kill Charley? New York, Doubleday, and London, Ward Lock, 1967.
Winchester Quarantine. New York, Doubleday, 1970.
The Pocket Hunters. New York, Doubleday, 1972.
Winter of the Coup. New York, Doubleday, 1972.
The Captive. New York, Doubleday, 1973.
Guns of Darkness. New York, Doubleday, 1974.
Blaine's Law. New York, Doubleday, 1974.
Red Grass. New York, Doubleday, 1976.
Winter Drift. New York, Doubleday, 1980.
The Smoking Hills. New York, Doubleday, 1988.

Television Play: *Cry of Silence (The Outer Limits* series), 1963-64.

Other

Trail: The Story of the Lewis and Clark Expedition. New York, Doubleday, 1989.
The Ice: A Novel of Antarctica. New York, Fine, 1991.

*

Manuscript Collection: University of Oregon Library, Eugene.

Louis Charbonneau comments:

My science fiction novels, most of which were written in the 1960s, would seem to be out of the mainstream of much current SF, though perhaps part of a longer running stream, one that begins with existing conditions, problems, or possibilities and projects them into an imagined future not all that remote, and with an emphasis on human characters rather than upon the grotesque or fantastic. It has been called social-science fiction, with a moral dimension often fairly evident. I can admire those fantasists who create wholly imagined worlds with little if any relation to our own, but I find myself as a writer interested more in the human predicament, as it is now or, given certain circumstances, as it might be in the future.

*   *   *

Notable first novels are rare; notable first science fiction novels virtually nonexistent. With his first work, *No Place on Earth,* Louis Charbonneau showed himself a scarce bird indeed—an SF writer with almost no interest in mechanisms and remote worlds. The peculiar appeal of this yarn lies not in outré surroundings or wild technology but in the little-known territory of man himself.

It is in its impact upon man, in fact, that Charbonneau finds a writer's use for science. He acknowledges with us that technology is marvelous, that we reap great benefits from the application of machines to our culture. But he confesses almost no background to deal with the intricacies of gadgetry; his concern is with the social aspects of things like automatons. So in *No Place on Earth,* Charbonneau tackles the population alarm expressed by Malthus and treats its implications like the good reporter he is. His prose is lean and highly readable, and he gives life to his writing through heavy reliance upon dialogue. His characters do not have to be complex, because he generalizes from a selection of typical people who must deal with extraordinary demands. In a sense Charbonneau appears to encourage all of his readers to expand to meet the pressures imposed upon them by a sometimes bewildering technology. Concepts like mind control and sirloin capsules have both good and bad points, as we see through the author's often humorous treatment.

Like many good writers, Charbonneau has learned his craft in the demanding school of journalism. He learned about people and their glands—some readers might say a bit too much so in works like *Corpus Earthling.* This novel imagines the people of Earth being literally occupied by aliens. What might eventually have resulted without the enterprise of a college insructor could have produced quite a different story. But as said instructor gains telepathic knowledge of this invasion, the whole fiendish plot is revealed. It is the way he obtains his information—in bed with several coeds—that might prove objectionable to staid readers of this story. The research method, nonetheless, does stress the author's realistic understanding of the human condition to counter this threat.

A different slice of such understanding is found in *The Sentinel Stars,* where we encounter every person born as a debtor. This means the entire population must spend its whole life span paying off the debt, which can't be done because of the high cost of living. In good reporter fashion, Charbonneau sounds a familiar dirge: a sense of slavery to the times. But all is not lost, for the hero—who bears the same sort of numerical I.D. as all of us today—

suggests rebellious measures which might create unrest in contemporary freespending lawmakers' consciences.

It is the social-scientific concern of Charbonneau that has perhaps discouraged his recent production of SF. He expresses distaste for the gee-whiz aspects of much current writing, although he admits the value to society of many devices (he finds a word processor convenient in writing, for example). But he deplores the dehumanizing evident in works of science fiction which reach out far into the cosmos. So, evidently, do the Japanese readers of his *No Place on Earth,* which has gone through recent reprintings in that country. Charbonneau's labeling of current movies, with their spectacular special effects and elaborate settings, as "extended comics" would find considerable endorsement among serious, mature readers of SF.

Louis Charbonneau remains a worthy and interesting figure in the world of science fiction, not only because of his stylistic appeal, but also because he represents a source of the kind of SF which provided the impetus for the sort of reading that is still among the more interesting pursuits in a gadget-infested world.

—Robert H. Wilcox

CHARNAS, Suzy McKee

Nationality: American. **Born:** New York City, 22 October 1939. **Education:** New York High School of Music and Art; Barnard College, New York, B.A. in economic history 1961; New York University, M.A.T. in social studies (secondary teaching). **Family:** Married Stephen Charnas in 1968; two stepchildren; two grandchildren. **Career:** Peace Corps English and history teacher, Girls' High School, Ogbomoso, Nigeria, 1961-62; Lecturer in Economic History, University of Ibadan, Ife, Nigeria, 1962-63; English-History Core Teacher, New Lincoln School, New York, 1965-67; worked for Community Mental Health organization, New York, 1967-69. Instructor, Clarion West Writers Workshop (Seattle), 1984, 1986 and Clarion Writers Workshop (Michigan), 1987; Chair, Archive Project Committee, National Council of Returned Peace Corps Volunteers, 1986-88; instructor, Southwest Writers Workshop, University of New Mexico, Taos, summer 1993. Since 1969, freelance writer. **Awards:** Nebula, for novella, 1980; Hugo, for short story, 1990; Gigamesh award (Spanish), for best fantasy stories, 1990; Aslan award, Mythopoeic Society, best children's book, 1993. **Member:** Science Fiction and Fantasy Writers Association, Horror Writers of America, Authors Guild, Dramatists Guild. **Agent:** Jennifer Lyons, Joan Davis Agency, Writers House, 21 W. 26 St., New York, New York 10010. **Address:** 212 High St. NE, Albuquerque, New Mexico 87102, U.S.A.

Science Fiction Publications

Novels (series: Motherlines; Sorcery Hall)

Walk to the End of the World (Motherlines). New York, Ballantine, 1974; London, Gollancz, 1979.
Motherlines. New York, Berkley, 1979; London, Gollancz, 1980.
The Vampire Tapestry. New York, Simon and Schuster, 1980; London, Women's Press, 1992.

The Bronze King (for young adults; Sorcery Hall). Boston, Houghton, 1985.
Dorothea Dreams. New York, Arbor House, 1986.
The Silver Glove (for young adults; Sorcery Hall). New York, Bantam, 1988.
The Golden Thread (for young adults; Sorcery Hall). New York, Bantam, 1989.
The Kingdom of Kevin Malone (for young adults). San Diego, Harcourt, 1993.
The Furies (Motherlines). New York, Tor, 1994; London, Women's Press, 1995.

Short Stories

Listening to Brahms. Eugene, Oregon, Pulphouse, 1991.
Moonstone and Tiger Eye. Eugene, Oregon, Pulphouse, 1992.

Other Publications

Play

Vampire Dreams, adaptation of "Unicorn Tapestry" (produced 1990).

*

Critical Study: *Suzy Charnas, Joan Vinge, and Octavia Butler* by Richard Law, with others, San Bernardino, California, Borgo Press, 1986.

Suzy McKee Charnas comments:

I love to take up some hoary stereotype—jolly barbarism after the holocaust, breast-plated Amazons, blue-blooded vampires, the bold space pilot fighting for independence—and turn it upside-down, to see what surprises and delights I can shake out of its pockets. I am currently polishing a wildly Romantic novella ("Beauty and the Opera, or the Phantom Beast") in which Christine Daaé stays with the Phantom of the Opera instead of running off to marry What's-his-name.

My particular slant is feminist, revisionist, erotic (see the story mentioned above), and provocative. My latest book, *The Furies,* is third in the series begun with *Walk to the End of the World,* which novels together comprise a futuristic, feminist epic written over the past 25 years. *The Furies* presents a war between male masters and female slaves which the women win; whereupon they find that the primary issue they face is how they relate to each other as victors and collaborators, rescuers and rescued, rather than their relationships with the vanquished enemy.

Dealing with the men so as to achieve more than a mere role-reversal seems to be the heart of the next book. I have more questions than answers and nothing is certain, which is the way I like it while a piece of work is still in process: surprises are what keep me writing.

* * *

When Iago says to Brabantio, "you'll have your daughter covered with a Barbary horse . . . you'll have coursers for cousins, and gennets for germans," an example of malevolence addresses a symbol of patriarchal power. These two representational essences are fused in Suzy McKee Charnas's first novel, *Walk to the End of the World,* where masculine hegemony is synonymous with unmitigated evil. Iago's utterance also illuminates its sequel, *Motherlines,* in which daughters are indeed covered by horses who are thought to be the near kinsmen of their mistresses. As Othello explores the effects of exaggerated personality traits, Charnas's fiction presents an exaggerated vision of sexism's consequences.

Walk to the End of the World is set in the Holdfast, a limited environment populated by survivors of the Wasting, or nuclear holocaust. This postwar society is a paradise for white male misogynistic bigots: the entire population is Caucasian, and the men are taught that "females themselves brought on the Wasting of the world." Holdfast "fems" supposedly "had no souls, only inner cores of animated darkness shaped from the void beyond the stars. Their deaths had no significance. Some men believed that the same shadows return again and again in successive fem-bodies." We, with our Eve, Pandora, and cultures where women are fuel for the flames of their husbands' funeral pyres, cannot feel smug after encountering a Holdfast myth. In this manner, Charnas's fiction continuously echoes reality.

The structure, as well as much of the content of *Walk to the End of the World,* reflects women's secondary status. Before encountering Alldera, the heroine, readers are familiar with the Holdfast's notions of "fem-taint," "Cunt-hunger," institutionalized rape, and girl children who must scratch for survival in the straw of the "kit-pen." Alldera's situation is immediately apparent: as a woman, she must satisfy all the demands of her male masters. Even a slave cannot be completely controlled by an oppressor. Since Alldera possesses mental acuteness and training as a runner, she can sometimes use her mind and body to suit her own best advantage. Her circumstances resemble those of an intelligent, talented Black person in the Jim Crow south. The novel's plot corrects the Holdfast's negative view of the feminine. For example, the text clarifies its own prologue: women certainly did not cause the Wasting of the world. Rather, subhuman men cause the wasting of women. Happily, something positive does manage to coincide with the sombering aspects of this novel and women's reality. Alldera has the opportunity to flee the Holdfast; some women have the pleasure of knowing that when they approach their house yard gate, they are not walking to the end of their world.

In *Motherlines* the open plains lying beyond the men's sphere of influence sharply contrast with the Holdfast's defined boundaries. Women completely control this terrain. In fact, to cite another example of Charnas's penchant for creating extreme circumstances, men never enter the domain of escaped free fems and the indigenous riding women of the motherline tribes. This women's world is not a utopia for stereotypically peace-loving, nurturing females. The tribes routinely raid each other, one powerful woman dictates her will to the free fems, and the riding women's method of raising children reminds Alldera of the Holdfast's "kit-pen." Although the tribal women are imperfect, they possess impressive attributes: self-sufficiency, an identification with matrilineal relationships, and racial tolerance. Alldera and her free fem companion are allowed to live in the tribe with dignity. She no longer has the negative self-image described in *Walk to the End of the World,* where she feels "hollow in body . . . hollow in mind, for there was nothing else she might imagine, feel, or will that a man could not wipe out of existence by picking her up for his own purposes." This transformation is of primary importance in *Motherlines.*

Another aspect of the novel is a secondary concern. "Oh . . . We mate with our horses," is the answer to Alldera's question about

reproduction in a completely female society. Those who judge this information to be a flippant, sarcastic retort react prematurely. The woman who answers Alldera speaks the truth about a situation which expands the definition of "perversion."

Charnas's characters are not presented solely to titillate an audience. Although the sexuality of the motherline tribes is bizarre, they always mate to fulfill their natural reproductive purpose. And the women are in total control of the sexual arena. In contrast, human heterosexuality can be degrading and destructive.

In the real world, the idea of a totally independent woman is, using Harlan Ellison's term, a "dangerous vision." Many readers, men and women, might be taken aback by the controversial content of Charnas's novels.

—Marleen S. Barr

———

CHASE, Adam. *See* **FAIRMAN, Paul W.; LESSER, Milton.**

———

CHERRYH, C.J.

Pseudonym for Carolyn Janice Cherry. **Nationality:** American. **Born:** St. Louis, Missouri, 1 September 1942. **Education:** University of Oklahoma, Norman, 1960-64, B.A. in Latin 1964 (Phi Beta Kappa); Johns Hopkins University, Baltimore (Woodrow Wilson Fellow, 1965-66), M.A. in classics 1965. **Career:** Taught Latin and ancient history in Oklahoma City public schools, 1965-76; vice-president, Science Fiction Writers of America, 1993-94. **Awards:** John W. Campbell award, 1977; Hugo award, 1979, 1982, 1989; Balrog award, 1982; *Locus* award, 1988. **Agent:** Matt Bialer, William Morris Agency, 1325 5th Ave., New York City, New York, 10019.

SCIENCE FICTION PUBLICATIONS

Novels (series: Chanur; Cyteen; Downbelow Station; Ealdwood; Faded Sun; Foreigner; Heroes in Hell; Merchanter; Merovingen Nights; Morgaine; Rusalka; Sword of Knowledge)

The Book of Morgaine. Garden City, New York, Doubleday, 1979; as *The Chronicles of Morgaine,* London, Methuen, 1985.
Gate of Ivrel. New York, DAW, 1976; London, Orbit, 1977.
Well of Shiuan. New York, DAW, 1978; London, Magnum, 1981.
Fires of Azeroth. New York, DAW, 1979; London, Methuen, 1982.
Brothers of Earth. Garden City, New York, Doubleday, 1976; London, Orbit, 1977.
Hunter of Worlds. Garden City, New York, Doubleday, and London, Orbit, 1977.
The Faded Sun: Kesrith. Garden City, New York, Doubleday, 1978.
The Faded Sun: Shon'Jir. Garden City, New York, Doubleday, 1978.
Hestia. New York, DAW, 1979; London, Gollancz, 1988.

The Faded Sun: Kutath. Garden City, New York, Doubleday, 1979.

Serpent's Reach. Garden City, New York, Doubleday, 1980; London, Macdonald, 1981.

Wave without a Shore. New York, DAW, 1981; London, Gollancz, 1988.

Downbelow Station. New York, DAW, 1981; London, Methuen, 1983.

The Pride of Chanur. New York, DAW, 1982; London, Methuen, 1983.

Merchanter's Luck (Downbelow). New York, DAW, 1982; London, Methuen, 1984.

Port Eternity. New York, DAW 1982; London, Gollancz, 1989.

Ealdwood. West Kingston, Rhode Island, Grant, 1981; expanded as *The Dreamstone,* New York, DAW, 1983; London, Gollancz, 1987.

The Tree of Swords and Jewels (Ealdwood). New York, DAW, 1983; London, Gollancz, 1988.

Arafel's Saga (Ealdwood; includes *The Dreamstone* and *The Tree of Swords and Jewels*). Garden City, New York, Doubleday, 1983; as *Ealdwood,* London, Gollancz, 1989.

Forty Thousand in Gehenna. Huntington Woods, Michigan, Phantasia Press, 1983; London, Methuen, 1986.

Voyager in Night. New York, DAW, 1984; London, Methuen, 1985.

Chanur's Venture. Huntington Woods, Michigan, Phantasia Press, 1984; London, Methuen, 1986.

Cuckoo's Egg. Huntington Woods, Michigan, Phantasia Press, 1985; London, Methuen, 1987.

The Kif Strike Back (Chanur). Huntington Woods, Michigan, Phantasia Press, 1985; London, Methuen, 1988.

Angel with the Sword (Merovingen Nights). New York, DAW, 1985; London, Gollancz, 1987.

The Gates of Hell, with Janet Morris. New York, Baen, 1986.

Chanur's Homecoming. West Bloomfield, Michigan, Phantasia Press, 1986; London, Mandarin, 1989.

Kings in Hell, with Janet Morris. New York, Baen, 1987.

Legions of Hell. New York, Baen, 1987.

The Faded Sun Trilogy. London, Methuen, 1987.

The Paladin. New York, Baen, 1988; London, Mandarin, 1990.

Exile's Gate (Morgaine). New York, DAW, 1988; London, Mandarin, 1989.

Rimrunners. New York, Warner, 1989; London, New English Library, 1990.

Rusalka. Norwalk, Connecticut, Easton Press, 1989; London, Methuen, 1990.

Cyteen. New York, Warner, 1988; London, New English Library, 1989; published in 3 vols. as *The Betrayal, The Rebirth* and *The Vindication,* New York, Popular Library, 1989.

Chernevog (Rusalka). Norwalk, Connecticut, Easton Press, 1990; London, Mandarin, 1991.

Yvgenie (Rusalka). New York, Ballantine, 1991; London, Methuen, 1992.

Heavy Time (Merchanter). Norwalk, Connecticut, Easton Press, 1991; London, New English Library, 1991.

Hellburner (Merchanter). New York, Warner, and London, New English Library, 1992.

Chanur's Legacy: A Novel of Compact Space. New York, DAW, 1992.

The Goblin Mirror. New York, Ballantine, 1992; London, Legend, 1993.

Faery in Shadow. London, Legend, and New York, Ballantine, 1993.

Foreigner: A Novel of First Contact. New York, DAW, and London, Legend, 1994.

Tripoint (Merchanter). New York, Warner, 1994.

Fortress in the Eye of Time. New York, HarperPrism, 1995.

Invader (Foreigner). New York, DAW, 1995.

Rider at the Gate. New York, Warner, 1995.

The Sword of Knowledge, with Leslie Fish, Nancy Asire, and Mercedes Lackey. New York, Baen, 1995.

   A Dirge for Sabis, with Leslie Fish. New York, Baen, 1989.

   Wizard Spawn, with Nancy Asire. New York, Baen, 1989.

   Reap The Whirlwind, with Mercedes Lackey. New York, Baen, 1989.

Short Stories

Sunfall. New York, DAW, 1981; London, Mandarin, 1990.

Visible Light. West Bloomfield, Michigan, Phantasia Press, 1986; London, Methuen, 1988.

Glass and Amber. Cambridge, Massachusetts, NESFA Press, 1987.

Rhialto the Marvellous, with Jack Vance and Janet Morris (Heroes in Hell/Dying Earth). New York, Baen, 1985.

OTHER PUBLICATIONS

Other

Editor, *Merovingen Nights: Fever Season.* New York, DAW, 1987.

Editor, *Merovingen Nights: Festival Moon.* New York, DAW, 1987.

Editor, *Merovingen Nights: Troubled Waters.* New York, DAW, 1988.

Editor, *Merovingen Nights: Smuggler's Gold.* New York, DAW, 1988.

Editor, *Merovingen Nights: Divine Right.* New York, DAW, 1989.

Editor, *Merovingen Nights: Flood Tide.* New York, DAW, 1990.

Editor, *Merovingen Nights: Endgame.* New York, DAW, 1991.

Translator, *The Green Gods,* by Charles and Nathalie Henneberg. New York, DAW, 1980.

Translator, *Cosmic Crusade,* by Pierre Barbet. New York, DAW, 1980.

Translator, *The Book of Shai,* by Daniel Walther. New York, DAW, 1984.

Translator, *Shai's Desiny,* by Daniel Walther. New York, Daw, 1985.

*

C.J. Cherryh comments:

Having made thorough study of the past I am vehemently certain that I do not wish to live in it, nor do I wish to see three quarters of the planet weltering in conditions that should have been left in the past, with the same hunger and disease our ancestors knew. The reach for space and its resources is the make-or-break point for our species, and the appropriate use of technology and the adjustment of human viewpoint to a universe not limited to a blue sky overhead and the curvature of the horizon are absolutely critical to our survival. Therefore I write fiction about space and human adjustment to the unfamiliar. The references in my work are frequently to writings on the aesthetics of physics or other sciences, compared and contrasted to writings of the ancients and concepts and philosophies better known to anthropologists than to the general public: while I have the most profound respect for the traditions of English language literature, I consider the images overworked and frequently inadequate for the task of conveying non-English concepts. Therefore I use the form of English literature, but bring into it a great many things which are pertinent to the sciences, or to the far corners of the world. This in my estimation is what science fiction ought to do to literature, create new symbologies and new understandings appropriate to the space age, not forgetting the traditions of our own culture, but widening its viewpoints.

*   *   *

Since C.J. Cherryh has burst onto the SF literary scene, producing at least two novels each year since the mid-1970s, she has been widely hailed as a genuinely entertaining storyteller, but one whose space-fairing and human-alien contact stories seem hackneyed and unlikely to advance the genre. Now, after some 30 novels and over a dozen short stories, the outlines of a grand design are perceptible in her work and a more positive synthesis and assessment is possible, indeed deserved.

It became clear that Cherryh was not writing mere space-and-critter yarns or attenuating series of sequels for the sake of production, but was using established SF clichés to outline an entire galactic future history. Moreover, her prolific output of SF novels came increasingly to be recognized as speculative anthropology, writing that sought to describe humanity by using the elements of SF to achieve distance and perspective on the human species.

In *Downbelow Station* and subsequent novels of the Merchanters series, for instance, Cherryh depicts people coping with extremes of isolation, gravitation, and the unusual in human governance. In the Faded Sun series she explores variations of human cultural patterns in the manner of Ruth Benedict but with the freedom of imagination allowed in the science-fiction genre.

That freedom allows an SF author the chance to establish imaginary "gardens" and in them explore through the medium of thought experiment the life habits of both real and imaginary "toads." In her most celebrated series, the Chanur Saga, for example, she develops in great detail the cultural elements of a sentient yet leonine species, hence *The Pride of Chanur.* While such societies do not now exist, of course, genetic engineering promises to render them imaginable. At the same time and in the same tetralogy readers view the desperate plight of a single human, Tully, as viewed from outside human culture. We see not a space opera with static characters but a complex drama of evolving human-alien intercourse. Tully's views of Pyanfar and her shipmates, and their views of him, grow in depth and complexity. Furthermore—and this is rare even in SF—we see that the alien race itself is undergoing vast change as they leave their homeworld of Clans to move among the stars, the boldest among them coming finally to dwell only among the star-faring population. These developments allow for some poignant drama among creatures which to our knowledge do not yet exist. Pyanfar's old husband, Khym, a displaced leader on his homeworld, as useless as old lion on Earth, finds new work, liberation, and a pair-bonding with Pyanfar which the orthodoxy of their homeworld have rendered impossible.

These are bold experiments, to be sure, yet Cherryh takes us further. In *Cuckoo's Egg,* Cherryh wrings a change upon the feral-child concept by having a human infant reared by sentient felines ignorant of its social and psychological needs. And in *Heavy Time,* Cherryh contrasts the humanity of one character, Morris Bird, reared in human companionship, against the asocial nature of a younger man, Paul Dekker, whose upbringing has been crippled by corpo-

rate control. Finally, in *Cyteen* and elsewhere Cherryh explores the nature of "ozzies," human clones with programmed memories as set against the often inhumane attitudes of the "true" humans whose slaves they are.

Cherryh's work remarkably brings all species—human, created, and alien—together in a single future history of our galaxy. The reader is best advised to move through each series from start to finish since some, particularly *Chanur* and *Cyteen,* are really very long books which were divided into publishable bites according to the needs of literary promotion, distribution, and sales. Similar concerns will be found throughout Cherryh's fantasy novels as well, particularly the books of her Morgaine series which, despite the name, are not redactions of Arthurian myth but blends of fantasy and SF exhibiting the same concerns as those of her science fiction series.

The greatest significance in Cherryh's science fiction, then, appears now to be her broad and systematic exploration of the concept of "humanity" itself seeking to discover what of this basic idea can survive the great range of adverse conditions made possible by today's and tomorrow's knowledge of human and animal behavior.

—Thomas P. Dunn

———

CHESNEY, Weatherby. *See* **HYNE, C.J. Cutliffe.**

———

CHILSON, Rob(ert)

Also writes as Robert Chilson. **Nationality:** American. **Born:** Ringwood, Oklahoma, 19 May 1945. **Education:** Appleton City High School, Missouri. **Career:** Since 1967, freelance writer. **Address:** P.O. Box 10096, Kansas City, Missouri 64171-0096, U.S.A.

SCIENCE FICTION PUBLICATIONS

Novels

As the Curtain Falls (as Robert Chilson). New York, DAW, 1974.
The Star-Crowned Kings (as Robert Chilson). New York, DAW, 1975.
The Shores of Kansas (as Robert Chilson). New York, Popular Library, 1976; London, Hale, 1977.
Isaac Asimov's Robot City: Refuge. New York, Ace, 1988.
Men Like Rats. New York, Popular Library, 1989.
Rounded with Sleep. New York, Popular Library, 1990.

Short Stories

Author of numerous uncollected short stories

*   *   *

Robert Chilson was among a group of writers who first broke into print during the latter days of John W. Campbell's editorial reign at *Analog* magazine. His stories fit well into Campbell's formula at the time, and a dozen stories saw print in that periodical between 1968 and 1973. Although these formulaic early stories were not indicative of the kind of work he would eventually produce, "Per Stratagem" is a noteworthy exception, a story of intrigue in a far solar system, concentrating on strategic maneuvering rather than relying on overt physical action. Although Chilson continued to appear at this length through the 1970s, it was not until the next decade that he was to produce memorable short stories.

During that period, however, he also produced three novels. The first of these, *As the Curtain Falls,* was so different in theme, subject matter, and treatment, it seemed to be by an entirely different writer of the same name. A billion years from now, the human race has declined in technology and disintegrated into several more or less barbaric states, fighting among themselves while the sun slowly burns out. A form of empathic telepathy has evolved over the generations, which is part of the rationale for the existence of non-magical wizards, ogres, and other trappings of fantasy.

The protagonist sets out on a typical heroic quest, to rescue the princess and restore stability, overcoming physical obstacles along the way. Chilson carries this off skillfully, and some of the settings he creates are quite well done. Although he hovers at the edge of political satire (two of the political parties are the Forestallers and the Grumbletonians), he skirts the issue, choosing instead a standard adventure story enlivened by an unusually evocative setting.

The Star-Crowned Kings, while more ambitious in plot, was less satisfying in execution. This time the protagonist learns that he has psychokinetic powers, the ability to move objects through force of will, which theoretically should increase his personal position. Unfortunately, the current power structure of the interstellar political arena is adamantly opposed to having a maverick operating outside their game plan. To eliminate the threat to their power base, they decide to have him assassinated and the balance of the story consists of chases and conflict. Another standard adventure tale, entertainingly told but without the exotic scenery that marked its predecessor.

With *The Shores of Kansas,* Chilson showed more of his early promise. Grant Ryals is one of the few people a generation from now capable of using paranormal mental abilities to physically regress in time, to visit and study different periods of history. Most notably, he is the only one with the range to reach prehistory, the time of the dinosaur. Although he is obsessed with his research, pragmatic issues continue to reduce the amount of time he can spend pursuing it. In order to secure financing, he routinely films spectacular scenery and beasts, wasting what he considers valuable research time. Back in the present, he is forced to deal with academic politics and a growing group of people who believe him to be an authentic hero despite his protestations to the contrary. Both groups place fresh demands on his time which he is loathe to satisfy. The novel is a protracted character study, an in-depth examination of a man torn between the obligations of society and the imperatives of his own search for meaning and knowledge. It is unfortunate that, having proven himself capable of writing such a fine novel, Chilson did not produce another for 12 years.

During that period, he continued to write short stories, some of which are noteworthy. "Written in Sand" seems to echo *The Shores of Kansas,* featuring a time explorer who has a bitter reaction to an unhappy love. "Hand of Friendship" portrays an interesting human vs. alien relationship, with the latter assisting in humanity's development despite their own inability to experience emotion. Contrarily, "Walk with Me" examines the extremely deep feelings which

arise between a human subject and the alien who is observing him. A rising political star runs into trouble when a new method of judging personal integrity is developed in "Slowly Slowly." Other stories of note include "Brain in Pocket," "Moonless Night," "Brain Jag," and "Diogenes' Lantern."

In 1988, the first new Chilson novel appeared in over a decade, *Isaac Asimov's Robot City: Refuge* in the "Robot City" series created by Isaac Asimov. Although it has little significance outside what was a very commercial and relatively unimaginative series, it did foreshadow Chilson's return to writing at novel length. His next, *Men Like Rats,* follows the adventures of tribes of human beings who have been reduced to living like rats or insects within the structure of the civilization omnipotent aliens have established on Earth. To make matters more difficult, the desperate struggle for survival has pitted one tribe against another, and each individual is distrustful of even those within his or her group. A compelling adventure story, filled with menaces and monsters.

Chilson's most recent novel, *Rounded with Sleep,* deals with the ultimate role playing game. Through the use of computer generated realities, individuals can become superheroes or villains, acting out parts in an elaborate sword and sorcery epic which is independent of time and space, and observed by the vast majority of the human race. The protagonist is one of the most successful participants, until he decides he has lost interest and chooses to return to the real world. Unfortunately, that doesn't prove quite as pleasant as he had expected.

During the early 1990s, Chilson returned to short fiction, appearing relatively infrequently. The stories are generally well-crafted and entertaining and deal with a varied selection of themes. "Dead Men Rise Up Forever" is a moving though depressing glimpse of a future dictatorship. "Living on the Air" is a humorous look at the way television has come to dominate human life. The nature of dreams and their effect on our personalities is examined in "Midnight Yearnings." Others stories of note include "Far Off Things" and "For Many Shall Come in My Name."

Chilson has proven his ability to write gripping, well-plotted adventure stories. *As the Curtain Falls* hinted at an active imagination and a gift for creating exotic settings. *The Shores of Kansas* and some of his short fiction also demonstrate that he has the potential to delve into the human experience and examine what makes us what we are and create works of fiction whose impact lingers after the final page has turned. If Chilson can summon all of his virtues simultaneously, he may well create a major novel that will elevate him to a more significant niche in the world of science fiction.

—Don D'Ammassa

CHILTON, Charles (Frederick William)

Nationality: British. **Born:** London in 1917. **Education:** Thanet Street Church of England School, London. **Family:** Married to Penelope Colbeck; two sons and one daughter. **Career:** Freelance writer and journalist, and radio producer for the BBC, London; devised and wrote *Riders of the Range* annual, from 1953. **Awards:** Western Heritage award, for children's book, 1963. **Address:** 31 Crediton Hill, London NW6 1HS, England.

Novels (series: Jet Morgan in all books)

Journey into Space (novelization of radio series). London, Jenkins, 1954.
The Red Planet (novelization of radio series). London, Jenkins, 1956.
The World in Peril (novelization of radio series). London, Jenkins, 1960.

OTHER PUBLICATIONS

Plays

Oh What a Lovely War, with the Theatre Workshop, London (produced in London and New York, 1964). London, Methuen, 1965.

Radio Plays: *Riders of the Range, Journey into Space,* and *The World in Peril* series in the 1950s; *Space Force* series, 1984.

Other

Riders of the Range (for children). London, Juvenile Productions, 1951.
Second Round-Up with Riders of the Range (for children). London, Juvenile Productions, 1952.
The Riders of the Range Square Dance Manual. London, Hutchinson, 1953.
The Book of the West: The Epic of America's Wild Frontier and the Men Who Created Its Legends. London, Odhams Press, 1961; Indianapolis, Bobbs Merrill, 1962.
Discovery of the American West (for children). London, Hamlyn, 1970.

*   *   *

The first of Charles Chilton's *Journey into Space* radio serials went on the air in 1953, with a strong cast of actors, including Andrew Faulds and Guy Kingsley Poynter, and a soundtrack of music and special effects into which the BBC Radiophonics Workshop threw themselves with enthusiasm. Over the next five years, the three serials were a national institution in Britain, and the characters and their creator became household names. An abridged version of the first serial was rebroadcast, with Alfie Bass substituting for David Kossof as the cockney radio operator. Recordings of this version and the other two serials have recently been rediscovered, rebroadcast (1989-91) and issued by the BBC as boxed sets of cassettes.

In the first serial, the spaceship *Luna,* launched from Woomera Rocket Range in Australia, achieved the first Moon landing in the Bay of Rainbows. Faulds's low-key comment, "Gentlemen, we are on the Moon," was to be much imitated by 1950s writers. As lunar night fell, however, power failed in the ship, and in the darkness someone or something could be heard investigating the *Luna* on the outside. After a strange encounter with a UFO at sunrise, the crew attempted to return to Earth, only to have the *Luna* abducted and delivered to the Earth of 13,000 years in the past. Eventually the crew met one of the time-travelers and negotiated their return

to their own time, but the serial ended as they faced another re-entry with no remaining fuel.

The second and third serials were set several years later, when a lunar base had been established and Faulds (Jet Morgan) led an exhibition to Mars in a fleet of ships commanded by the *Discovery.* Once again Chilton had gone to great lengths to make the technology authentic, by the design studies of the day, and the procedures of the Mars fleet were extremely convincing. In flight, however, the expedition was sabotaged by a man named Whitaker who had been kidnapped from Earth decades before, then returned to infiltrate the expedition. Whitaker had been conditioned by the Martians, by slowing down his metabolism to adapt to Martian conditions, making him cold to the touch and concealing his age, and also by hypnosis, making his speech a frightening drone ("Orders must be obeyed without question at all times.") Crewmen went mad or died in his company, and a generation of British schoolchildren were terrified of him. Worse still, Mars turned out to have a population of similarly conditioned humans, preparing to invade the Earth which few of them knew they had left.

But Chilton's extraterrestrials were not monsters. The Martians had been the giants of earthly legends, coming to us in peace only to be hunted down and destroyed, finally driven to drastic measures as conditions worsened on Mars. By the time of the invasion, there was only one left, and when Morgan and his crew prevented his attempted takeover by televised hypnosis, he went peacefully off to Alpha Centauri with volunteers from the human workforce. The time-travellers also had been trying to avoid interaction with mankind, using the Moon and the prehistoric Earth only in passing. Unlike their contemporaries (the purely destructive aliens of Nigel Kneale's *Quatermass,* or the wholly benign inhabitants of Angus Macvicar's *Lost Planet*), Chilton's creations had their own purposes and motivations, not specifically good or evil in relation to humanity. Space was an exciting realm to explore, dangerous perhaps but not hostile.

Subsequent incarnations of the characters were less successful. The comic strip in *Express Weekly* was inconsistent with the radio serials, yet borrowed too heavily from them; and a one-hour play recapitulated the weakest parts of the strip's story line. *Space Force,* a pair of new serials broadcast in 1984-85, caught the atmosphere of the original more closely. But Chilton conceded in a *Radio Times* interview that he hadn't kept up with developments in space science, and dramatic sequences borrowed from *Journey into Space*— the power failure, for example—were no longer convincing.

—Duncan Lunan

CHRISTOPHER, John

Pseudonym for Christopher Samuel Youd. **Other Pseudonyms:** Hilary Ford; William Godfrey; Peter Graaf; Peter Nichols; Anthony Rye. **Nationality:** British. **Born:** Knowsley, Lancashire, 16 April 1922. **Education:** Peter Symonds' School, Winchester. **Military Service:** Served in the Royal Signals, 1941-46. **Family:** Twice married; four daughters and one son from first marriage. Since 1958, full-time writer. **Awards:** Rockefeller-Atlantic award, 1946; Christopher award, for children's book, 1971; *Guardian* award, for children's book, 1971; Jugendbuchpreis (Germany), 1976; George

G. Stone Center for Children's Books award, 1977. **Address:** One Whitefriars, Conduit Hill, Rye, East Sussex TN 31 7LE, England.

SCIENCE FICTION PUBLICATIONS

Novels

The Year of the Comet. London, Joseph, 1955; as *Planet in Peril,* New York, Avon, 1959.
The Death of Grass. London, Joseph, 1956; as *No Blade of Grass: A Novel,* New York, Simon and Schuster, 1957; adapted for children by David Fickling, Oxford, Alpha, 1979.
The Long Winter. New York, Simon and Schuster, 1962; as *The World in Winter,* London, Eyre and Spottiswoode, 1962.
Sweeney's Island. New York, Simon and Schuster, 1964; as *Cloud on Silver,* London, Hodder and Stoughton, 1964.
The Possessors. New York, Simon and Schuster, and London, Hodder and Stoughton, 1965.
A Wrinkle in the Skin. London, Hodder and Stoughton, 1965; as *The Ragged Edge,* New York, Simon and Schuster, 1966.
The Little People. New York, Simon and Schuster, 1966; London, Hodder and Stoughton, 1967.
Pendulum. New York, Simon and Schuster, and London, Hodder and Stoughton, 1968.

Fiction (for children; series: Fireball; Prince in Waiting; Tripods)

The Tripods Trilogy:
    The White Mountains. London, Hamish Hamilton, and New York, Macmillan, 1967.
    The City of Gold and Lead. London, Hamish Hamilton, and New York, Macmillan, 1967.
    The Pool of Fire. London, Hamish Hamilton, and New York, Macmillan, 1968.
The Lotus Caves. London, Hamish Hamilton, and New York, Macmillan, 1969.
The Guardians. London, Hamish Hamilton, and New York, Macmillan, 1970.
The Prince in Waiting Trilogy. London, Penguin, 1983.
    The Prince in Waiting. London, Hamish Hamilton, and New York, Macmillan, 1970.
    Beyond the Burning Lands. London, Hamish Hamilton, and New York, Macmillan, 1971.
    The Sword of the Spirits. London, Hamish Hamilton, and New York, Macmillan, 1972.
In the Beginning (reader for adults). London, Longman, 1972; revised edition (for children), as *Dom and Va,* London, Hamish Hamilton, and New York, Macmillan, 1973.
Wild Jack. London, Hamish Hamilton, and New York, Macmillan, 1974; original version (reader for adults), London, Longman, 1974.
Empty World. London, Hamish Hamilton, 1977; New York, Dutton, 1978.
Fireball. London, Gollancz, and New York, Dutton, 1981.
New Found Land (Fireball). London, Gollancz, and New York, Dutton, 1983.
Dragondance (Fireball). London, Viking Kestral, 1986; as *Dragon Dance,* New York, Dutton, 1986.
When the Tripods Came. New York, Dutton, and London, Viking, 1988.

A Dusk of Demons. London, Hamish Hamilton, 1994; New York, Macmillan, 1994.

Short Stories

The Twenty-Second Century. London, Grayson, 1954; New York, Lancer, 1962.

OTHER PUBLICATIONS

Novels

Giant's Arrow (as Anthony Rye). London, Gollancz, 1956; as Samuel Youd, New York, Simon and Schuster, 1960.
Malleson at Melbourne (as William Godfrey). London, Museum Press, 1956.
The Friendly Game (as William Godfrey). London, Joseph, 1957.
The Caves of Night. New York, Simon and Schuster, and London, Eyre and Spottiswoode, 1958.
A Scent of White Poppies. London, Eyre and Spottiswoode, and New York, Simon and Schuster, 1959.
The Long Voyage. London, Eyre and Spottiswoode, 1960; as *The White Voyage,* New York, Simon and Schuster, 1961.
Patchwork of Death (as Peter Nichols). New York, Holt Rinehart, 1965; London, Hale, 1967.

Novels as Christopher Youd

The Winter Swan. London, Dobson, 1949.
Babel Itself. London, Cassell, 1951.
Brave Conquerors. London, Cassell, 1952.
Crown and Anchor. London, Cassell, 1953.
Palace of Strangers. London, Cassell, 1954.
Holly Ash. London, Cassell, 1955; as *The Opportunist,* New York, Harper, 1957.
The Choice. New York, Simon and Schuster, 1961; as *The Burning Bird,* London, Longman, 1964.
Messages of Love. New York, Simon and Schuster, 1961; London, Longman, 1962.
The Summers at Accorn. London, Longman, 1963.

Novels as Peter Graaf

Dust and the Curious Boy. London, Joseph, 1957; as *Give the Devil His Due,* New York, Mill, 1957.
Daughter Fair. London, Joseph, and New York, Washburn, 1958.
Sapphire Conference. London, Joseph and New York, Washburn, 1959.
The Gull's Kiss. London, Davies, 1962.

Novels as Hilary Ford

Felix Walking. London, Eyre and Spottiswoode, and New York, Simon and Schuster, 1958.
Felix Running. London, Eyre and Spottiswoode, 1959.
Bella on the Roof. London, Longman, 1965.
Figure in Grey (for children). Kingswood, Surrey, World's Work, 1973.
Sarnia. London, Hamish Hamilton, and New York, Doubleday, 1974.

Castle Malindine. London, Hamish Hamilton, and New York, Harper, 1975.

A Bride for Bedivere. London, Hamish Hamilton, 1976; New York, Harper, 1977.

*   *   *

The reputation of John Christopher as a writer of science fiction for both adult and younger readers is solidly established. Perhaps the greatest single exposure in the United States was the serialization in 1957 in the *Saturday Evening Post* of the novel *The Death of Grass.* The elements present in this relatively early piece are a template for all of his science fiction. Taken together, it forms all kinds of answers to the question "What do people do when things fall apart?" An account of his work may fall rather naturally into three parts: the early short fiction and Managerial stories; novels of crises, catastrophe, and survival and; novels for younger readers.

The Twenty-Second Century conveniently displays Christopher's early apprenticeship period. Six of the stories in the collection feature Max Larkin, a director in one of the corporations that govern earth in place of political institutions in the not-too-distant future. Read along with the fuller exposition of this state of affairs in *The Year of the Comet,* the stories present the proposition that political institutions will bring civilization to ruin and that government by enlightened commercial interests may do better. The case for this is epitomized in the laid-back character of Larkin, the unmarried, late-middle-aged corporate director, whose manipulative genius is time and again effective in world crises where armies and doomsday weapons have failed. The fourteen additional stories are something of an index of the novels that would follow. Sterility doom in "The New Wine," a medieval level of technology survival in "Weapon," and the panorama of twentieth-century ruin in contrast to the garden of a new Eden in "Begin Again" provide glimpses of the worlds of the catastrophe novels. Beyond these, imprisonment by adaptive necessity in a lunar vivarium in "Christmas Roses," the interdiction of books in "A Time of Peace," and the humanity-saving wholesomeness recognized by enlightened aliens in a human village dedicated to a technologically simple way of life in "Blemish," are typical of the settings and subjects Christopher presented in his young adult pieces. At least one more story, "Rock-a-Bye," featuring the super-child born of a relationship between a Martian woman and a man from Earth is beautiful in its own right and deserves extended discussion. At this stage in his career Christopher's narrative craft was nearly mature. He did not experiment much with style. He told stories with pace, suspense, sanity, and clarity. Eventually he wrote about 50 SF short stories. In addition he wrote about twenty-five novels.

Two exceptions to the sort of novel for which Christopher is best known are *The Possessors,* wherein a group of people at a remote ski lodge are terrorized and some of them killed by "body-snatching" aliens, and *The Little People,* wherein a group of vacationers at a remote Irish mansion encounter a group of dwarves created by a Nazi geneticist. Both are excursions in science fiction gothic. The strength of both lies in the accounts of very plausible behaviors of small groups of people in short-term crises.

But it is to scenarios of global cataclysm and survival in a world that will never be the same again that the most famous stories direct us. *The Death of Grass,* reminding us that corn, wheat, and rice are grass, has a blight on all species of grass cause a world famine. *The World in Winter* shows European civilization destroyed by a new ice age. *A Wrinkle in the Skin* presents earth devastated by the effects of continent-heaving earthquakes. *Pendulum* varies the cause of disaster from that of nature run amok to human society run amok—an obvious fictional response to the social transformations taking place in western civilization during the late 1960s. But with few alterations the effect is the same. More people survive. Yet once again society is reduced to savagery, to endure again the insanity and agony of social evolution that in past history did not teach its lessons well enough. These novels present variations upon several principal themes. Human civilization is fragile and vulnerable. It cannot survive catastrophe either from natural causes or from incompetent government. In the event of catastrophe the few who survive will be winnowed again by good health, knowledge of basic tools and nature, and the ability to kill other human beings, however reluctantly, out of necessity. Simultaneously, they must have also the ability to love and form, once again, wholesome social contracts. Billions die in these stories, but hope and human potential have the final determination in each of them. Somehow mankind will recover and rebuild, though, *Pendulum,* the last of the novels, insists that it will not be swift.

With a sensible selection against the more baldly brutal and explicit details of violence and sexual behavior, these themes are produced again in Christopher's young adult novels. There is an evenness of quality in all of these works, so that discussion of a few may represent them all. The earliest (written in the late 1960s) and most famous are those that form the Tripods trilogy (*The White Mountains, The City of Gold and Lead,* and *The Pool of Fire*), featuring Will Parker and various companions.

Will is born in a backwoods village on a future earth conquered and enslaved by alien invaders who travel on land and water in vehicles with three immensely long terrain-gobbling legs. They are reminiscent of the Martian craft in Well's *War of the Worlds.* The aliens employ the very strongest young humans as body servants. The remainder are mere breeders, forbidden more than a medieval level of technology, and ultimately, are treated as little more than vermin who will be exterminated when the aliens convert earth's atmosphere and gravity to their own. Fortunately, it doesn't happen. Will and two friends have a principal role in returning earth to humans. The Tripods theme is that individual freedom and honor are precious. Knowledge and curiosity daring enough to see beyond popular mythology, self-discipline, respect for other people—especially odd ones—and the courage to act in the face of pain and under threat of death earn freedom.

The Tripods trilogy acquired a prequel with the publication of a fourth volume, *When the Tripods Came.* Introducing fourteen-year-old Laurie Cordray and his companions, it tells of the arrival of the Tripods on earth. Laurie and his family flee to Switzerland and eventually take secret refuge in a tunnel inside the Eiger mountain to begin the years of underground resistance to the Tripods. The tensions among the characters are an additional source of interest here. Laurie's divorced father has remarried and had a half-sister for Laurie, who must reconcile himself to the dynamics of a new family structure.

Beginning at the end of 1984, the first of three thirteen-episode BBC TV serials of *The Tripods* was aired. The broadcast of the complete production spans three years. There was an encore broadcast on United States Public television. An unrelated but thematically similar novel called *The Guardians* refreshes the Tripods stories' propositions about freedom in a post-catastrophe story of a boy who, learning of a conspiracy by aristocratic guardians to keep the mass of men at a stuporous level of existence in the cities, determines to join a revolution to free them. The work received the Guardian award in England, the Christopher award in the United States, and the prestigious Jugendbuchpreis in 1976.

In the early 1970s the young adult books of the Sword of the Spirits trilogy (*The Prince in Waiting, Beyond the Burning Lands,* and *The Sword of the Spirits*), though it did not become a media production, earned rave reviews and reached at least 14 printings. Set in a post-catastrophe Earth, its hero is Luke, who in a world of dwarves, mutants, ordinary humans, and "seers" is fated to have great good fortune and material success in winning his birthright to a kingdom. The seers who keep the knowledge of the pre-catastrophe technologies have a hand in Luke's fate. But Luke fails in the end to have the love of the woman betrothed to him. Christopher has acknowledged his debt to Arthurian legends as his inspiration for the Sword books.

Fireball, New Found Land, and *Dragon Dance* form the Fireball trilogy. Simon is British, Brad is American. The cousins encounter a fireball in a meadow and are thrust into a parallel earth—England still at a medieval level of civilization. The books are an adventure that circles the earth, so that the story ends in China. The Dragon is a mass-hypnotic illusion created by flying box kites over the enemy army. The setting is generally reminiscent of Christopher's adult post-catastrophe novels.

An additional SF work published in 1994 is the young adult novel *Dusk of Demons.* It visits again the post-catastrophe setting, with an Earth population reduced to mere millions by drug overdoses on an epidemic scale, causing a collapse of the infrastructure that feeds people, especially in the great population centers, resulting in the death of billions by famine. The hero Ben lives in a world where the surviving cultures oppose one that is anti-machine to one that secretly preserves technology to make a better world. Ben plays a key role in the machine culture's conflict over whether to leave the anti-machinists in a "demon"-ruled state of only locally vicious superstition, or to jump-start an advanced civilization by freeing the people of the "Demons" (which are holographic projections) and letting the whole of the population have the benefits, and the dangers, of technology again. Ben's machine-technology confederates are in the ascendancy as the story ends, and he, with girlfriend Paddy, has a big job to do.

The few additional pieces published by Christopher in the 1980s and 1990s are exclusively for young adults. The course seems a happy one. In terms of narrative art, Christopher's stories for young readers are, he believes, equal to his finest achievement.

—John R. Pfeiffer

CLARKE, Arthur C(harles)

Nationality: British. **Born:** Minehead, Somerset, 16 December 1917. **Education:** Huish's Grammar School, Taunton, Somerset, 1927-36; King's College, London, 1946-48, B. Sc. (honours) in physics and mathematics 1948. **Career:** Flight Lieutenant in the Royal Air Force, 1941-46; served as Radar Instructor, and Technical Officer on the first Ground Controlled Approach radar; originated proposal for use of satellites for communications, 1945. **Family:** Married Marilyn Mayfield in 1954 (divorced 1964). **Career:** Assistant auditor, Exchequer and Audit Department, London, 1936-41; assistant editor, *Physics Abstracts,* London, 1949-50. Since 1954, engaged in underwater exploration and photography of the

Great Barrier Reef of Australia and the coast of Sri Lanka. Director, Rocket Publishing, London, Underwater Safaris, Colombo. Has made numerous radio and television appearances (most recently as presenter of the television series *Arthur C. Clarke's Mysterious World,* 1980, and World of Strange Powers, 1985), and has lectured widely in Britain and the United States; commentator, for CBS-TV, on lunar flights of Apollo 11, 12, and 15; Vikram Sarabhai Professor, Physical Research Laboratory, Ahmedabad, India, 1980. **Awards:** International Fantasy award, 1952; Hugo award, 1956, 1969 (for screenplay), 1974, 1980; Unesco Kalinga prize, 1961; Boys' Clubs of America award, 1961; Franklin Institute Ballantine Medal, 1963; Aviation-Space Writers Association Ball award, 1965; American Association for the Advancement of Science Westinghouse award, 1969; *Playboy* award, 1971; Nebula award, 1972, 1973, 1979, Grand Master, 1985; Jupiter award, 1973; John W. Campbell Memorial award, 1974; American Institute of Aeronautics and Astronautics award, 1974; Boston Museum of Science Washburn award, 1977; Marconi Fellowship, 1982; Vidya Jyothi medal, 1986; Science Fiction Writers Association, Grand Master, 1986. D.Sc.: Beaver College, Glenside, Pennsylvania, 1971. Chairman, British Interplanetary Society, 1946-47, 1950-53. Guest of Honor, World Science Fiction Convention, 1956. Fellow, Royal Astronomical Society; Fellow, King's College, London, 1977; Chancellor, University of Moratuwa, Sri Lanka, since 1979. C.B.E. (Commander, Order of the British Empire), 1989; Nobel Peace prize nomination, 1994; D. Litt., University of Liverpool, 1995. **Agent:** Scovil, Chicak, Galen, Inc., 381 Park Avenue S., New York 10016, U.S.A.; David Higham Associates, 5-8 Lower John Street, Golden Square, London WIR 4HA, England. **Address:** 25 Barnes Place, Colombo 7, Sri Lanka; or, Dene Court, Bishop's Lydeard, Taunton TA4 3LT, England.

SCIENCE FICTION PUBLICATIONS

Novels (series: Odyssey; Rama)

Prelude to Space: A Compelling Realistic Novel of Interplanetary Flight. New York, Galaxy, 1951; London, Sidgwick and Jackson, 1953; as *Master of Space,* New York, Lancer, 1961; as *The Space Dreamers,* Lancer, 1969.

The Sands of Mars. London, Sidgwick and Jackson, 1951; New York, Gnome Press, 1952.

Islands in the Sky (for children). London, Sidgwick and Jackson, and Philadelphia, Winston, 1952; adapted for children by Suzan Davies, Hong Kong, Oxford University Press, 1976.

Against the Fall of Night. New York, Gnome Press, 1953; revised edition, as *The City and the Stars,* New York, Harcourt Brace, and London, Muller, 1956; with a sequel by Gregory Benford as *Beyond the Fall of Night,* New York, Putnam, 1990; as *Against the Fall of Night,* [with] *Beyond the Fall of Night,* London, Gollancz, 1991.

Childhood's End. New York, Ballantine, 1953; London, Sidgwick and Jackson, 1954.

Earthlight. New York, Ballantine, and London, Muller, 1955.

The Deep Range. New York, Harcourt Brace, and London, Muller, 1957.

A Fall of Moondust. New York, Harcourt Brace, and London, Gollancz, 1961.

Dolphin Island: A Story of the People of the Sea (for children). New York, Holt Rinehart, and London, Gollancz, 1963.

An Arthur C. Clarke Omnibus [and *Second Omnibus*]. London, Sidgwick and Jackson, 2 vols., 1965-68.

Prelude to Mars (omnibus). New York, Harcourt Brace, 1965.

2001: A Space Odyssey. New York, New American Library, and London, Hutchinson, 1968.

The Lion of Comarre, and Against the Fall of Night. New York, Harcourt Brace, 1968; London, Gollancz, 1970.

Rendezvous with Rama. London, Gollancz, and New York, Harcourt Brace, 1973; adapted for children by David Fickling, Oxford, Alpha, 1979.

Imperial Earth: A Fantasy of Love and Discord. London, Gollancz, 1975; revised edition, New York, Harcourt Brace, 1976.

Four Great Science Fiction Novels (includes *The City and the Stars, The Deep Range, A Fall of Moondust,* and *Rendezvous with Rama*). London, Gollancz, 1978.

The Fountains of Paradise. London, Gollancz, and New York, Harcourt Brace, 1979.

2010: Odyssey Two. Huntington Woods, Michigan, Phantasia Press, and London, Granada, 1982.

The Songs of Distant Earth. New York, Ballantine, and London, Grafton, 1986.

Cradle, with Gentry Lee. London, Gollancz, and New York, Warner, 1988.

2061: Odyssey Three. London, Grafton, and New York, Ballantine, 1988.

Rama II, with Gentry Lee. London, Gollancz, and New York, Bantam, 1989.

The Garden of Rama, with Gentry Lee. London, Gollancz, and New York, Bantam, 1991.

The Hammer of God. London, Gallancz, and New York, Bantam, 1993.

Rama Revealed, with Gentry Lee. London, Gollancz, 1993; New York, Bantam, 1994.

Short Stories

Expedition to Earth: Eighteen Science-Fiction Stories. New York, Ballantine, 1953; London, Sidgwick and Jackson, 1954.

Reach for Tomorrow. New York, Ballantine, 1956; London, Gollancz, 1962.

Tales from the White Hart. New York, Ballantine, 1957; London, Sidgwick and Jackson, 1972.

The Other Side of the Sky. New York, Harcourt Brace, 1958; London, Gollancz, 1961.

Across the Sea of Stars: An Omnibus Containing the Complete Novels, Childhood's End and Earthlight, and Eighteen Other Short Stories. New York, Harcourt Brace, 1959.

From the Oceans, from the Stars: An Omnibus Containing the Complete Novels, The Deep Range and The City and the Stars, and Twenty-Four Short Stories. New York, Harcourt Brace, 1962.

Tales of Ten Worlds. New York, Harcourt Brace, 1962; London, Gollancz, 1963.

The Nine Billion Names of God: The Best Short Stories of Arthur C. Clarke. New York, Harcourt Brace, 1967.

The Wind from the Sun: Stories of the Space Age. New York, Harcourt Brace, and London, Gollancz, 1972.

Of Time and Stars: The Worlds of Arthur C. Clarke. London, Gollancz, 1972.

The Best of Arthur C. Clarke 1937-1971, edited by Angus Wells. London, Sidgwick and Jackson, 1973.

The Sentinel. New York, Berkley, 1983; London, Granada, 1985.

A Meeting with Medusa, with *Green Mars,* by Kim Stanley Robinson. New York, Tor, 1988.

Tales from Planet Earth. London, Century, 1989; New York, Bantam, 1990.

Dilemmas: The Secret, with *Flowers for Algernon,* by Daniel Keyes, Boston, Houghton Mifflin, 1989.

More Than One Universe: The Collected Stories of Arthur C. Clarke. New York, Bantam, 1991.

OTHER PUBLICATIONS

Novels

Glide Path. New York, Harcourt Brace, 1963; London, Sidgwick and Jackson, 1969.

The Ghost from the Grand Banks. London, Gollancz, and New York, Bantam, 1990.

Poetry

The Fantastic Muse. [United Kingdom], Hilltop Press, 1992.

Play

Screenplay: *2001: A Space Odyssey,* with Stanley Kubrick, 1968.

Other

Interplanetary Flight: An Introduction to Astronautics. London, Temple Press, 1950; New York, Harper, 1951; revised edition, 1960.

The Exploration of Space. London, Temple Press, and New York, Harper, 1951; revised edition, 1959.

The Young Traveller in Space (for children). London, Phoenix House, 1954; as *Going into Space,* New York, Harper, 1954; as *The Scottie Book of Space Travel,* London, Transworld, 1957; revised edition, with Robert Silverberg, as *Into Space,* New York, Harper, 1971.

The Exploration of the Moon. London, Muller, 1954; New York, Harper, 1955.

The Coast of Coral. London, Muller, and New York, Harper, 1956.

The Making of a Moon: The Story of the Earth Satellite Program. London, Muller, and New York, Harper, 1957; revised edition, Harper, 1958.

The Reefs of Taprobane: Underwater Adventures around Ceylon. London, Muller, and New York, Harper, 1957.

Voice across the Sea. London, Muller, 1958; New York, Harper, 1959; revised edition, London, Mitchell Beazley, and New York, Harper, 1974.

Boy beneath the Sea (for children). New York, Harper, 1958.

The Challenge of the Spaceship: Previews of Tomorrow's World. New York, Harper, 1959; London, Muller, 1960.

The First Five Fathoms: A Guide to Underwater Adventure. New York, Harper, 1960.

The Challenge of the Sea. New York, Holt Rinehart, 1960; London, Muller, 1961.

Indian Ocean Adventure. New York, Harper, 1961; London, Barker, 1962.

Profiles of the Future: An Enquiry into the Limits of the Possible. London, Gollancz, 1962; New York, Harper, 1963; revised edition, Harper, 1973; Gollancz, 1974, 1982; New York, Holt Rinehart, 1984.

The Treasure of the Great Reef. London, Barker, and New York,
    Harper, 1964; revised edition, New York, Ballantine, 1974.
Indian Ocean Treasure, with Mike Wilson. New York, Harper,
    1964; London, Sidgwick and Jackson, 1972.
Man and Space, with the editors of *Life.* New York, Time, 1964.
Voices from the Sky: Previews of the Coming Space Age. New York,
    Harper, 1965; London, Gollancz, 1966.
The Promise of Space. New York, Harper, and London, Hodder
    and Stoughton, 1968.
First on the Moon, with the astronauts. London, Joseph, and Bos-
    ton, Little Brown, 1970.
Report on Planet Three and Other Speculations. London, Gollancz,
    and New York, Harper, 1972.
The Lost Worlds of 2001. New York, New American Library, and
    London, Sidgwick and Jackson, 1972.
Beyond Jupiter: The Worlds of Tomorrow, with Chesley Bonestell.
    Boston, Little Brown, 1972.
Technology and the Frontiers of Knowledge (lectures), with others.
    New York, Doubleday, 1975.
The View from Serendip (on Sri Lanka). New York, Random House,
    1977; London, Gollancz, 1978.
1984: Spring: A Choice of Futures. New York, Ballantine, and Lon-
    don, Granada, 1984.
*Ascent to Orbit: A Scientific Autobiography: The Technical Writ-
    ings of Arthur C. Clarke.* New York, and Chichester, Sussex,
    Wiley, 1984.
The Odyssey File, with Peter Hyams. London, Granada, and New
    York, Ballantine, 1985.
Astounding Days: A Science-Fictional Autobiography. London,
    Gollancz, 1989; New York, Bantam, 1990.
How the World Was One: Beyond the Global Village. London,
    Gollancz, and New York, Bantam, 1992.
By Space Possessed. London, Gollancz, 1993.
The Snows of Olympus: A Garden on Mars. London, Gollancz,
    1994.

Editor, *Time Probe: The Sciences in Science Fiction.* New York,
    Delacorte Press, 1966; London, Gollancz, 1967.
Editor, *The Coming of the Space Age: Famous Accounts of Man's
    Probing of the Universe.* London, Gollancz, and New York,
    Meredith, 1967.
Editor, with George Proctor, *The Science Fiction Hall of Fame,
    Volume 3: Nebula Winners 1965-1969.* New York, Avon, 1982.
Editor, *Arthur C. Clarke's July 20, 2019: A Day in the Life of the
    21st Century.* New York, Macmillan, 1986; London, Grafton,
    1987.
Editor, *Project Solar Sail.* New York, Roc, 1990.

*

Bibliography: *Arthur C. Clarke: A Primary and Secondary Bibliography* by David N. Samuelson, Boston, Hall, 1984.

Manuscript Collection: Mugar Memorial Library, Boston University; University of Liverpool.

Critical Studies: "Out of the Ego Chamber" by Jeremy Bernstein,
in *New Yorker,* 9 August 1969; *Arthur C. Clarke* edited by Joseph
D. Olander and Martin H. Greenberg, New York, Taplinger, and
Edinburgh, Harris, 1977; *The Space Odysseys of Arthur C. Clarke*
by George Edgar Slusser, San Bernardino, California, Borgo Press,
1978; *Arthur C. Clarke* (includes bibliography) by Eric S. Rabkin,
West Linn, Oregon, Starmont House, 1979, revised edition, 1980;
*Against the Night, The Stars: The Science Fiction of Arthur C.
Clarke* by John Hollow, New York, Harcourt Brace, 1983, revised
edition, Athens, Ohio University Press, 1987.

*   *   *

Most critical discussions of Arthur C. Clarke's writings rarely
look beyond his stories and novels; but to understand his fiction,
one must examine how Clarke has thought about future possibilities, because this reveals the nature of the provocative realities that
shape his fiction. His approach to looking ahead is the basis of his
vision of human history and its promise.

Clarke fulfills the ambitions of science fiction, in that his achievement is both intellectual and artistic. Clarke's work meets Isaac
Asimov's definition of science fiction as a literature that deals with
the human impact of changes in science and technology, in which
the "changes" makes the work science fiction and the "human impact" makes it literature. The importance of this definition is that it
allows SF its one compelling feature: that it is not just a story, but
something that might happen—if not literally, then in its major features. Without this element of genuine possibility SF becomes fantasy. Einstein's profound prescription for the work of science—
that hypotheses and theories are at first free creations of the imagination, which must rejoin reality through the experience of an experiment (an organized form of experience by which theories are
confirmed, denied, or left pending)—applies equally well to science fiction: the central premise affecting the characters must be at
least possible, or not easily discredited, at least, or the story loses
the means by which it suspends our disbelief. This is perhaps the
most difficult feature of genuine science fiction to explain to the
casual reader, who may not understand the resourcefulness, creativity, and imagination required to comprehend the cutting edges
of the sciences, and then to use these materials in the realm of fiction.

Clarke's grasp of human scientific and technical creativity is best
expressed in *Profiles of the Future: An Enquiry into the Limits of
the Possible,* an often revised collection of his essays. In these
pieces Clarke does not express a naive, even uncritical, faith in science and technology; rather, he sets out what is possible, whether
humankind accomplishes any of it or not. The most important chapters in *Profiles* are the first two: "Hazards of Prophecy: The Failure of Nerve" and "Hazards of Prophecy: The Failure of Imagination." Few people today, both in future studies and among science
fiction writers, fully understand how important these two chapters
are in humanity's efforts to think about possible futures. One must
look back to *Daedalus* (1923) by J.B.S. Haldane and J.D. Bernal's
The World, the Flesh and the Devil (1929) to find essays of comparable importance (the first had a new edition in 1995, the second
in 1970); both books continue to be the subjects of continuing interest.

Clarke's essays are marked by playfulness, but their light touch
conceals the weight of their subject matter. Revolutionary statements
come and go in the space of a sentence, suggesting tomes of more
detailed explanation. Such is the case with Clarke's Laws, without
which one cannot understand Clarke's fiction, or what genuine science fiction attempts to do.

These laws, despite their wit, present an undogmatic, creative
way of thinking about possible futures. They are a profound working tool, and the very heart of one of the great scientific and liter-

ary careers of the 20th century. The laws limit their province, include qualifications and exceptions based on how "looking ahead" has disgraced itself in the past, and chart the limits of foresight, using ignorance itself as a map. They demonstrate why future innovations are not to be deduced in some mechanical fashion, but are drawn from a reservoir of ideas that, if they do not violate fundamental laws, will always be possible even if human beings fail at making them into practical realities.

Law One: "When a distinguished but elderly scientist states that something is possible, he is almost certainly right. When he states that something is impossible, he is very probably wrong." Here Clarke decries conservative inertia, which tends to see innovation as extravagance. Failures of nerve and imagination prevent seeing how familiar obstacles may be overcome, even though the record of the past shows that many seemingly wild predictions have been fulfilled, as long as they did not violate basic physical laws. There is a psychological brake on technological applications—even when the science is mature—that must be overcome in every generation. The most startling aspect of this condition is that a technical innovation is sometimes most denied just as it is about to happen. Nuclear fission and space travel are two examples of last minute denials.

Law Two: "The only way to discover the limits of the possible is to venture a little way past them into the impossible." This process will not overcome basic limits, but even these should be retested by every generation of researchers, if only to avoid creeping timidity and dogmatism. Science is not made up of absolute truths, but of candidates for truth that continue to resist disproof, but are never proven absolutely. There may be "basic impossibilities" that only seem so until we step outside their province. These may turn out to be merely technical impracticalities that yielded to new technology. Positive proof of scientific claims requires an infinity of experiments—a feat that cannot be performed—any one of which might fail sooner or later; but even one negative experiment is all it takes to cast a fatal doubt. It must be possible to at least imagine the conditions under which a hypothesis or theory might be disproven, even if that will never happen. Only a vulnerable theory, for which a test can be imagined and carried out, has any chance of being true—that is, in resisting disproof; the other kind is true by definition, which is no proof at all.

Law Two may be viewed as an application of Karl Popper's famous Falsifiability Criterion for identifying whether a claim is a scientific one. Only theories that *may* turn out to be wrong are legitimate candidates for scientific truth—or it's not a horse race; the truth is prejudged, and all facts can be made to support the conclusion—and nothing can count against it. This is what we mean by a dogma, or in logic, a tautology. Dogmas are computer viruses for the human mind. They end all doubt and inquiry by excluding all evidence to the contrary. A dogmatic state is a psychological extreme, a denial of our finitude, which yearns for final answers that will be final and invulnerable to disproof; and coiled within dogmas is an even more insidious virus: a reinforced dogmatism, which has written within it a rule against being doubted. All discussion ends. The important point here is that we live in a creative universe of vulnerable rather than absolute truths, and that genuine science fiction should reflect the fact. Put simply, it is a distinction between open and closed minds.

Law Three: "Any sufficiently advanced technology is indistinguishable from magic." Here Clarke sounds the central fact of science and science fiction—that science is *the* discoverable magic of our universe, the only magic that works, for which we yearn in all

our myths. Scientific knowledge will not give us omniscience and omnipotence, but it has provided applications that would have been magic to our ancestors. We can have a large measure of wish-fulfillment, if we turn away from idolatry before the mysteries of existence and support the development of science and technology.

Up to now our science has been surprising in its penetration, adolescent in it applications, but suggestive of what a mature science/technology alliance might be able to do. Arthur C. Clarke has not only looked ahead, but has also examined what attempts to look ahead involve in the way of logical and practical problems. His projections in technical papers and in essays have sought to stimulate research and to educate the intelligent reader. In this he is the heir to the efforts of H.G. Wells, Bertrand Russell, J.D. Bernal, and J.B.S. Haldane. His contemporaries in this effort have been Isaac Asimov, Carl Sagan, Loren Eiseley, and Jacob Bronowski, to name a few of the best.

The human impact of scientific/technological possibilities Clarke shows us in his science fiction. The playful aspect of his three laws is superficial; their subtlety and far-reaching implications could easily fill whole volumes of discussion and examples. The thinking behind them takes for granted that we live in a quantum, Gödelian universe of relatively open possibilities that is more like a great evolving thought than a clockwork Newtonian machine, a universe in which recognizing and shaping possibilities must replace guesswork and naive prophesying of the religious and mythical kind. "The real future is not logically foreseeable," Clarke concludes. "We need logic, but we also need faith and imagination which can sometimes defy logic itself."

Clarke's views about the universe and human possibilities are not merely present in his science fiction; they shape his fiction by selecting its dramatic possibilities. His science fiction is imbued with authenticity, lacking the arbitrariness that is too often a feature of lesser SF.

Childhood's End (1953), Clarke's first major success in the novel form, both within science fiction circles and in the general literary world, paced both Robert A. Heinlein and Ray Bradbury, who were being reviewed outside the SF genre in the early Fifties. Like them, Clarke had spent the Forties writing outstanding stories for the SF magazines, and published his great short novel of the far future, *Against the Fall of Night,* in *Startling Stories,* November 1948. In 1945 he proposed the geosynchronous communications satellite, for which he would later receive credit as the "father of the communications satellite" and a Nobel Peace Prize nomination. In 1951 he published *The Exploration of Space,* which became a Book-Of-The-Month Club Selection, and which remains to this day, revised as *The Promise of Space,* one of the most important books about the meaning of space travel.

Childhood's End, together with the short story "The Sentinel," presented ideas about human-alien contact that later became central to Clarke's novel *2001: A Space Odyssey* and the Stanley Kubrick film of the same name that was released in 1968, making Clarke the most famous science fiction writer since Jules Verne and H.G. Wells. It has been said that if humanity survives its own destructive impulses and maintains any of its ties to its historical character, and survives contact with interstellar cultures, then the Odyssey novels (of which there are now three), along with Kubrick's film, may become the prescient Homeric epic of humanity's childhood longing for kinship with the other evolving intelligent life in the universe.

The central concept of *Childhood's End* is its provocative, pre-emptive view of human destiny, in which humanity is drawn from its chrysalis of human history and absorbed into an alien purpose—for better or worse, we cannot say. On the face of it, this does not seem to be the kind of story often associated with the "father of the communications satellite." To many readers Clarke's stories are largely about technical progress and its effect on humanity, the purest kind of science fiction; some would say the only genuine science fiction. But *Childhood's End* is not only about alien contact, but also features paranormal powers, sociological commentary, and a vision of the ultimate fate of our species. Its scope is wider than Clarke's "realistic" novels of this period, which include *Prelude to Space: A Compelling Realistic Novel of Interplanetary Flight, Islands In the Sky, The Sands of Mars, Earthlight,* or the later stories about space exploration, of which the best may be "Transit of Earth" and "A Meeting With Medusa." *Childhood's End* is in the tradition of Olaf Stapledon's visionary philosophical novels, with more than a touch of H.G. Wells and John W. Campbell, Jr., each of whose influence Clarke has acknowledged.

And yet this dual impulse of a realist who is also a visionary was always a feature of Clarke's work: *Prelude to Space* and *Against the Fall of Night* juxtapose Clarke's enduring attention to immediate possibilities (the first Lunar expedition) with ultimate concerns (human immortality and stagnation in the far future). A closer look at Clarke's fiction reveals that these concerns are not as far apart as they seem. The "realistic" books argue for the transforming effect that science, technology, and space exploration may have on human culture; from there we are ready to enter the realms of deep future history—and ultimate changes. Clarke does not shirk the questions: What does it all mean? What will it all come to? The emergence of science and technology into human history signals the beginning of the end of our youth. Too much has been made of the facile distinction between Clarke the realist and Clarke the so-called mystic. That he is a poet of space travel, that he expresses his yearning for the stars and for a meeting with advanced intelligent life, is natural, given the realities of our expanding knowledge.

But in his continuum of earlier and later works, Clarke also sounds warnings that all may not be progress, that human reason, ingenuity, and heroism may be pitted against humbling forces. In the Odyssey novels, humanity may be redeemed by contact with the patron race or races that have already guided our history; but in *Childhood's End* the contact is at first humiliating, then politically constructive (it brings world peace at the cost of cultural stagnation), and finally terrifying—even a horror story—as much a rebuke to our vanity and ignorance as was H.G. Wells's *The War of the Worlds* to the smugness of the British Empire.

Childhood's End seems to carry within it a great trauma, as if it were based on some expulsion from paradise in the author's life. Perhaps the story echoes a disillusionment with humanity after World War II. Clarke offers an intriguing hint about the novel's origins in his preface to a 1989 edition. He recalls a beautiful summer evening in 1941, when he saw a fleet of silver barrage-balloons anchored over London to protect it from German bombers: "As their stubby torpedo shapes caught the last rays of the sun, it did indeed seem that a fleet of spaceships was poised above the city. For a long moment we dreamed of the far future, and banished all thoughts of the present peril which that aerial fence had been erected to guard against. In that instant, perhaps, *Childhood's End* was conceived." Although it would be easy to conclude that Clarke later wrote a what-if scenario for the sake of a story, it clearly got away from him and became much more. The great trauma of the novel is shared to one degree or another by all readers who are

expelled from their youth into the complexities of adulthood.

The quiet, scientifically motivated heroism of characters in Clarke's more obviously realistic novels is represented in *Childhood's End* by Karellen, one of the great, most convincing aliens in all science fiction. In him we find a strange, rational affection for humankind, a knowing admiration for beings who still have a further development awaiting them, and a regretful sense of loss about the tragic dead end of his own kind, the Overlords. Struggling with the fact of humankind's open, unfinished state, Karellen is a Cartesian and humanity Gödelian—the one laboriously mechanical, the other creative, incomplete and seething with inner power, even as traditional human aspirations become irrelevant and are left behind.

Karellen envies this humanity that does not know itself, and which is so desired by the Overmind, because he knows himself completely—and there is nothing else left for him to become, no surprises remaining. His race is the tool of the Overmind, a growing interstellar entity that is adding to itself, burgeoning with power and discovery, and that now seeks to merge humanity into its aggregate.

We learn that the Overlords have been trying to discover more about the Overmind, but cannot join with it because they lack the inner richness of a creative species. We see this in the logical way that they steer Earth's various societies into peace—and cultural sterility. Karellen is an unrepentant Satan, doing the bidding of an evolving god whose goodness or evil cannot be ascertained. He comes like a pied piper to lead humanity away from itself, to a fate he cannot share, but which intrigues him. The reader shares with him a great curiosity about the life of the Overmind, which has already assimilated the minds of several solar systems, but does not wish to absorb Karellen's race; however powerful its constructive intellects, they represent an uncreative, elegant dead end.

We come to believe that despite his speculative interest in the Overmind, Karellen's people will never have the will or the creative ingenuity to revolt against the growing Overmind. Karellen's governance of Earth, benign and rationally restrained, produces a golden, humane age free of war, politics, crime, and disease; but culturally and scientifically human civilization is at an end—and most people do not care.

How valid a speculation about the result of our first contact with an alien culture is this? How seriously can we take it? No one can say, because we have no past models for such an event; and the historical collisions between human cultures, horrifying as they have been, may not carry any lessons outside our human history; but Karellen may very well be right to this extent:

> "In this galaxy of ours," murmured Karellen, "there are eighty seven thousand million suns. Even that figure gives only a faint idea of the immensity of space. In challenging it, you would be like ants attempting to label and classify all the grains of sand in all the deserts of the world."
>
> "Your race, in its present state of evolution, cannot face that stupendous challenge. One of my duties has been to protect you from the powers and forces that lie among the stars—forces beyond anything that you can ever imagine."

But in his benign stabilization of human culture, Karellen has cut short all future development, preparing humanity for use by the Overmind. Somehow, in the cauldron of evolution, humanity developed abilities that the Overmind wants to add to itself. We carry a prize it covets.

191

This powerful and emotionally disturbing novel faces us with the abolition of all human history. "The stars are not for man," Karellen asserts, and we rebel, caught in the act of an extraordinary suspension of disbelief. The novel has about it a Somerset Maugham-like poetic clarity and a richness of suggestive ideas that resonate around each paragraph, often around each sentence, as with musical overtones. No simple outline of the story, wrote Groff Conklin in his 1954 *Galaxy* magazine review, can "even remotely suggest the richness, the variety, the maturity and emotional darkness of this book . . . a continuous excitement, a continuous kaleidoscope of the unexpected."

What has endured about *Childhood's End* is its striking anxiety, mourning, and pity. A childhood's end seems to hang over the waning 20th century by way of a "genetic and biomechanical tinkering that will splinter the human species forever," writes Dennis Overbye. And in his book on cosmology, *Voyage To The Great Attractor,* Alan Dressler concludes "that we are most likely near the end of what we have known as humanity. Nature's gifts to us have led to the secret keys of evolution, and we are not likely, I think, to long refrain from unlocking this box of treasures and troubles."

Much of Clarke's work sings of a farewell to childhood, both individual and that of humanity. He tells us that the universe we know is still young, and that we will move on to adulthood's powers and complexities. *Childhood's End* was his youthful, anxious unfolding of a theme that may take on new, specific meanings in the ages to come.

A different childhood's end is depicted in the unfinished Odyssey novels sequence, one that may well be much closer to Clarke's belief's and hopes. These novels are Clarke's second great success in terms of popularity, influence, and sales. They constitute a rethinking of the theme of *Childhood's End.* Instead of the Overmind's mysterious motives for absorbing the human race, we have an advanced patron race that "saw how often the first faint sparks of intelligence flickered and died in the cosmic night. And because in all the galaxy, they had found nothing more precious than Mind, they encouraged its dawning everywhere. They became farmers in the fields of stars; they sowed, and sometimes they reaped. And sometimes, dispassionately, they had to weed."

The inner story of both the film and the novel *2001: A Space Odyssey* is that human evolution is a nurturing program undertaken by a high alien civilization. The first black monolith stimulates mental development among our prehuman ancestors; the second sends an alarm signal to the monolith circling Jupiter to announce that the species has developed space travel; the signal's direction lures a human expedition to the giant planet, where Bowman is taken as a sample for investigation by the aliens, who transform him into the Starchild and return him to the vicinity of Earth to further develop our world's intelligent life.

The failure of HAL in the first film/novel is later explained, and HAL is rehabilitated. We also learn the nature of the monoliths and what kind of technology they represent: self-replicating cybernetic machines for macro-engineering projects; communications devices; a stimulus/tool for bio-engineering; stargates; and perhaps much more. The nature of the monolith technology became obvious to Clarke as he wrote *2010: Odyssey Two* and *2061: Odyssey Three,* following, of course, from the implications of the previously described functions of the monoliths. This brilliant piece of inventive retrofitting in these novels has never been commented upon. Clarke wrought better than he knew, in describing an advanced technology that obeys his Third Law, leaving himself conceptual room to

deduce what his original inspiration about the monoliths meant; and in its lack of overt explanation, Kubrick's film, by evoking a visceral response to the wonders of the universe, is also true to the spirit of Clarke's work.

It is possible that the Odyssey novels have been critically underrated. On conceptual grounds they offer ideas that may later prove prophetic, even profound; and on literary grounds, a single, one-volume edition of the three novels, with the still possible concluding fourth work, may change critical opinion about the importance of these novels.

Clarke's greatest critical success may well be 1973's *Rendezvous with Rama,* which took the Nebula, Hugo, and John W. Campbell Awards for best novel—the triple crown of SF awards—as well as the British Science Fiction Association Award, the *Locus* Award, and the Jupiter Award. It is the only novel to have ever been so honored. He had won the Nebula the previous year for his novella, "A Meeting With Medusa," a story set on Jupiter, the first award for his fiction since "The Star" received the 1955 Hugo in the short story. An artificial alien worldlet, fifty kilometers long, swings through our solar system and is boarded by an exploratory team. This was about all that many casual reviewers wanted to tell readers when *Rendezvous with Rama* was published; but the novel is about much more, asking the reader to observe and to think about what is being shown. *Rama,* the alien vessel, is a mind-quickening challenge to the novel's characters, to a future human civilization, and to Clarke's readers. Eric S. Rabkin described the novel as combining "the absolutely fascinating exploration of an extra-solar vessel come into our system with profound philosophic questioning of the significance of humanity, of biological life, and of intelligence." This deft, hypnotic drama invites one to observe and understand the details of its major setting, inside the alien artifact, graphically presented with an authentic sense of place by the writer who has been described as "our solar system's first regionalist." He does just as well within *Rama*'s alien setting, and the result is a spectacular, inspired and subtle observation of an imaginary artifact that convinces us of its reality. Just as subtle, and sometimes critically satiric, are the human reactions to this visitor from the stars.

Clarke worked out what *Rama* (the human name given to the visiting ark) is and how it would behave. Only the alien Ramans know more than Clarke, by definition, since the author has carefully created a genuine unknown (carefully considered in accordance with his Third Law), which is never threatened with exposure by easy explanations; discoveries are carefully stalked.

Clarke's meticulous homework for what a vehicle of this advanced kind might be like enables him to derive all the events of the story without the arbitrary imaginings that are the mark of failed SF. Only certain things can happen inside *Rama,* and not others. There is no cheating on what has been assumed. The reader is free to think ahead and discover some of the solutions to the problems faced by the characters.

Also depicted is the solar-system-wide civilization's bureaucratic response to *Rama*'s arrival, through the *Rama* Committee of narrow, hilariously portrayed specialists. We are given the religious response, through the lone Cosmo Christer aboard the *Endeavour,* who becomes convinced that *Rama* is another Noah's Ark come to save the elect; Commander Norton's sensitive and diplomatic encounter with the beliefs of this crewmember is an incisive bit of characterization. The colonists of Mercury respond by deciding to destroy *Rama* before it takes up a power position around the sun. The human drama is played out as a conflict between our better and worse selves, as impulses toward exploration race against the xenophobic urge to destroy *Rama*. We see a sedate human civilization shaken up by the confrontation with the grandly indifferent *Rama;* and when the visitor's purpose becomes clear, human civilization and Commander Norton respond in ways appropriate to their characters. At 55 years of age, Norton feels that the last of his youth is invested in exploring *Rama,* and that he may regret his lost opportunities. Clarke was the same age when this novel was published, and perhaps he thought it might be his last, but he said the same about 1979's *The Fountains of Paradise* nearly a decade later.

There is a moment on the last page of *Rendezvous with Rama,* presented almost as a casual gift from the departing alien visitor, when Dr. Perera wakes up as his unconscious pushes toward a breathtaking insight into *Rama's* nature. Here is the very method of Clarke's novel, which has throughout invited us to observe and think about what we are being shown with such vivid lucidity. This is art working through the poetry of scientific investigation, as we strive to fill the vast space of our ignorance with an equal amount of discovery. Here is a rendezvous with epic drama unlike any in all science fiction, whose beauties enable us to share such lovely details as the stairway as high as the Himalayas; the spring-like warming of *Rama's* inner atmosphere as the vessel approaches the sun; the dark, cool interior being pierced by a searchlight as the explorers move across the central plain; the moment when *Rama's* lights go on, revealing three linear suns in a vast interior; the tidal wave that sweeps around the equatorial sea; the passage of the human-powered glider along the central axis toward the vast play of electrical energies among the spikes of *Rama's* south pole; *Rama's* awesome intake of fiery matter from the sun; and the artful way in which the mysterious but detailed wonders interlock, gripping our curiosity and satisfying it while opening up larger questions, then leading us on to the edge of the unknown, where we realize that despite human foibles our species can get at the truth, that *Rama* is not magic, but operates according to natural laws harnessed by an advanced alien race. *Rama's* entrance into human history is not only a call to adventure, but an antidote to stagnation, a plea for open-mindedness as a way to regain the joy of childlike curiosity.

Perhaps the novel's finest moment is when Commander Norton, who throughout has shown great restraint in the use of force, decides to use lasers to cut into what may be a kind of storage facility inside *Rama.* He does "not want to behave like a technological barbarian," and hopes that the Ramans will "forgive him" and "understand that it was all in the cause of science." Here we see Clarke's sort of character in action, as the rationalist shows that he values the difference between a little force and unnecessary force. Throughout the epic exploration of *Rama,* Norton behaves as a sensible, unspectacular leader who strives to solve problems with the least amount of disruption and harm, much as Karellen does in *Childhood's End.* Norton tries not to be overwhelmed by *Rama,* to keep his head, but before the encounter is over he is glad to have been led beyond his careful ways into the unknown, toward the seemingly impossible—and we are reminded of Clarke's Law Two, the very essence of creative action. All of Clarke's characterizations, in all his works, are of this subtle, essential kind. The people in *Rendezvous with Rama,* even though they are necessarily dwarfed by the alien visitor, are the kinds of human beings that interest their author and properly belong in his disciplined visions—highly trained, questing, cooperative human beings with a sense of humor that hints at their control of deeper longings and failings.

A strong example of characterization from Clarke's later work may be found in *The Fountains of Paradise,* where, as in *Imperial Earth: A Fantasy of Love and Discord,* the central character progresses from himself to his hopes for humanity. At one time Clarke thought that *The Fountains of Paradise* might be his best novel, and one can clearly see why he might have thought so. The novel has an ambitious structure, a variety of characters, and presents a striking idea—a space elevator on a cable into orbit—with considerable originality. Clarke's attentive mind walks us through all the relevant aspects of the Tower. We peer into moments of wonder, both in the distant past and the much nearer future, through which we arrive at an understanding of how this project is rooted in human history, in human imagination and yearning—the deepest of all realities. We learn what it would mean to build this kind of structure, and what kind of world, politically and socially, might find the will to do so. And as with all of Clarke's fiction, the novel is a window into carefully imagined possible experience. It is perhaps the very clarity of Clarke's windows that has led some critics to gaze through them obliviously, failing to notice the grace and lucidity with which understanding has been stimulated.

But for those whose gaze can be focused by Clarke's Apollonian temperament, the effect is one of a deeply felt sense of human aspiration. In *The Fountains of Paradise* the central image of the Tower sings of humanity's ascent. The penultimate moment, the very heart of the novel, when the life of an individual hangs within the dream that he has made real, is both true and moving.

In reading this novel, as with *Glide Path* and *The Sands of Mars,* one cannot help being reminded of Clarke's own life. A prophet of space travel, inventor of the communications satellite at the end of a terrifying war (certainly a humanitarian note to signal peace, if there ever was one), award-winning educator and science writer, the co-creator of that cultural icon, *2001: A Space Odyssey,* this bestselling author of graceful science fiction became what he wrote about—a man whose dreams became realities because they were put through the test of science and technology. As a futurist Clarke's laws of forecasting not only summarize how we failed at it in the past, but set out the *limits* of looking ahead. This approach has contributed to shifting our thinking away from literal prediction of a single, straight-line future to the more fruitful idea of possible futures—and especially to the Wellsian idea that our future is, to an important degree, ours to make, if not to foresee. Like Wells, Clarke has helped to change the world we live in.

"My favourite book is undoubtedly *The Songs of Distant Earth,*" Clarke has said on more than one occasion since 1986. The reasons for this are not hard to guess, even though it is, along with *Imperial Earth,* one of his relatively neglected works. A starship fleeing the ruined solar system encounters a utopian colony world. The ship stops for repairs long enough for a few personal encounters to play out, some harrowing history to be passed on and digested, and the future considered. This gentle, sometimes somber work is probably the most Maugham-like of all Clarke's novels; it requires an attentive reader to let the entire predicament of humanity sink in and the implications of new futures to open up. We are shown with great pictorial beauty and sure narrative one of the most plausible scenarios for interstellar exploration and colonization, that of the Pacific island hopping settlers, as well as the difficulties—physical, moral, and personal—of relativistic travel. The overall effect is psychologically convincing and emotionally moving, especially in the subtle details of the personal fates of the characters, as they are affected by the arrival of the starship. Clarke manages a few startling denouements born of relativistic dislocations. The story steps into the minds of its readers, then into the hearts of its characters, in that order.

In judging Clarke's writings fairly one must start with the fact that he is a one-of-a-kind original. Heir to *both* the traditions of Wells and Stapledon, but also to those of Verne and Campbell, Clarke combines, in Eric Rabkin's words, "the enthusiasm of the one camp with the breadth of vision of the other" in his correct use of science and technology and a concern for philosophical and social dilemmas. Where most critical discussions of Clarke are lacking is in the failure to describe the *experience* of reading his work. The author's work persuades readers more effectively than is possible in a critical discussion. The failure of criticism on this point is what must be described as "a loss of the phenomenon" in the analysis, a loss of all the effects before analysis that simply fails to convey the aesthetic, intellectual, and emotional reality of the objects under discussion.

Clarke's work produces readers who either fall under the spell of his discursive poetry, or who are respectful but relatively unmoved. To acquire a taste for his work (both his fiction and nonfiction produce kindred effects) may also be a lesson in how to read science fiction—not primarily as a way of learning about life and character, which is what all of serious classic and contemporary literature is about—but as a criticism of human life and history, as seen from the perspective of the growing technical and scientific culture that has been with us since the Renaissance, as an effort to see what can be made of life through innovation born of knowledge. Even the least of Clarke's works can be of intense interest to readers who have learned to "see" the very human implications of what Clarke has understood. And what he has understood is of the utmost importance to the future of humanity.

Reading Clarke faces the reader with the problem of how to think about science fiction. The purely literary writer or reader often does not respect the thinker; while the thinking writer or reader often fails to respect the difficulties of grace, wit and style—the "writerly virtues." Clarke respects both. His thought does not disappear in favor of style; it is one and the same, and the ease with which he communicates can fool critics who read according to certain literary models and then find fault when a work does not live by the model; change models and flaws fade away. Those unwilling to think along with the author grow impatient and see a stiffness of prose; those who do not understand the kinds of characters Clarke knows best fail to see the characterization; those whose databases are impoverished fail to make connections that would only deepen their sense of poetry and vision; those who need to have things repeated deplore his concision of style; and those who think episodic structures a flaw simply fail to find interest in the episodes, and miss how they are related. One is reminded of the blind men groping the elephant and failing to describe the animal. Like all great writers of science fiction, Clarke's work is alive with the needs of traditional literature while searching for ground where purely literary concerns are not the only values. "One of the greatest values of SF," Clarke writes in *Astounding Days, A Science Fictional Autobiography,* "is the way it challenges long-held beliefs, and makes the reader appreciate, after he has stopped foaming at the mouth, that the external world need not always conform to his hopes and expectations. It forces one to think—which is why so many people dislike it."

Clive Sinclair, writing in the *New Scientist,* summarized one aspect of Clarke's life as follows: "The plot is improbable: a brilliant scientist, in his 20s, lives on a teeming planet which numbers its people, who are mostly horribly poor and feuding with each other, in billions rather than millions. He invents a means of linking these billions, which requires a technology barely dreamt of. Yet we are expected to believe that, within two or three decades . . . the beings of this planet . . . find the billions of dollars necessary to realise his invention, but that our scientist hero retreats to a remote idyll, there to live by the pen, linked to a grateful world by his own invention."

Unlike Jules Verne's fictional Captain Nemo, Clarke has always tended to be apolitical and tolerant of human failures, waiting out human history while explaining and applauding fundamental developments as they unfold alongside deplorable ones. The imagination he found in science fiction liberated him from ordinary ways of looking at humanity and the universe; his concise, often humorous imagination was only strengthened by his scientific training. The Apollonian clarity of his writings is central to his character, which desires the success of human aspiration. The effortless grace of his writings belies their profound content, but for those who have "caught the Clarke wave," this humane, rational man is one of our troubled century's treasures.

Happily, he has had three periods of great success, and unlike the Ramans is determined not to do things in threes. Now in his sixth decade as a writer, he is a happily creative Karellen, pointing the way with hope for a humanity whose childhood he will not outlive, but a humanity that may take his work with it into futurity.

—George Zebrowski

CLEMENS, Samuel Langhorne. *See* **TWAIN, Mark.**

CLEMENT, Hal

Pseudonym for Harry Clement Stubbs. **Nationality:** American. **Born:** Somerville, Massachusetts, 30 May 1922. **Education:** Harvard University, Cambridge, Massachusetts, B.S. in astronomy 1943; Boston University, M.Ed. 1947; Simmons College, Boston, M.S. 1963. **Military Service:** Served as a bomber pilot with the 8th Air Force during World War II: Air Medal, with four oak leaf clusters; served in the Air Force Reserve, Lieutenant Colonel 1953-76. **Family:** Married Mary Elizabeth Myers in 1952; two sons and one daughter. **Career:** Science teacher, Milton Academy, Massachusetts, 1949-87. Technical Instructor, Special Weapons School, Sandia Base, New Mexico, 1951. Columnist (as Harry C. Stubbs) on science books for children, *Horn Book* magazine, Boston. Member of the Milton Warrant Committee; Chairman of the District Board of Review, Boy Scouts of America. **Address:** 12 Thompson Lane, Milton, Massachusetts 02186, U.S.A.

SCIENCE FICTION PUBLICATIONS

Novels (series: Mesklin; Needle)

Needle. Garden City, New York, Doubleday, 1950; London, Gollancz, 1961; as *From Outer Space,* New York, Avon, 1957.

Iceworld. New York, Gnome Press, 1953.
Mission of Gravity (Mesklin). Garden City, New York, Doubleday, 1954; London, Hale, 1955.
The Ranger Boys in Space (for children). Boston, Page, and London, Harrap, 1956.
Cycle of Fire. New York, Ballantine, 1957; London, Gollancz, 1964.
Close to Critical (Mesklin). New York, Ballantine, 1964; London, Gollancz, 1966.
Star Light (Mesklin). New York, Ballantine, 1971.
Ocean on Top. New York, DAW, 1973; London, Sphere, 1976.
Through the Eye of a Needle. New York, Ballantine, 1978.
The Nitrogen Fix. New York, Ace, 1980.
Still River. New York, Ballantine, 1987; London, Sphere, 1988.
Fossil: Isaac's Universe. New York, DAW, 1993.

Short Stories

Natives of Space. New York, Ballantine, 1965.
Small Changes. Garden City, New York, Doubleday, 1969; as Space Lash, New York, Dell, 1969.
The Best of Hal Clement, edited by Lester del Rey. New York, Ballantine, 1979.
Intuit. Cambridge, Massachusetts, NESFA Press, 1987.

OTHER PUBLICATIONS

Other

Some Notes on Xi Bootis. Chicago, Advent, 1959.
Left of Africa (for children). New Orleans, Aurian Society Press, 1976.

Editor, *First Flights to the Moon.* Garden City, New York, Doubleday, 1970.
Editor, *The Moon,* by George Gamow. London, Abelard Schuman, 1971.

*

Critical Study: *Hal Clement* by Donald M. Hassler, Mercer Island, Washington, Starmont House, 1982.

*   *   *

A continuous fan since his mid-teens of physical science and of the fictional extrapolations from it that the genre has labeled hard science fiction, Hal Clement published his first story in John Campbell's *Astounding* in 1942 when he was an astronomy major at Harvard. He has gone on to become one of the most highly admired scientific extrapolators and lovers of the tight demands of logic in the genre despite the fact that he is not a full-time writer. Clement and his classic fictions are mentioned whenever the discussion of science in the genre comes up; and hence he represents both the full maturing of the Campbell engineering effect in science fiction and the limitations of that approach. Campbell demanded a good story, of course, and Clement's stories are carefully constructed and often convey a certain excitement and suspense. But their distinguishing characteristic is that a problematic condition in physical reality, or simply a condition of difference such as an increase or decrease in heat or gravity, must be elaborated upon, ex-

plained, and taken through certain plot changes so that the reader can simply understand the problem or the difference. This is a literature of total mimesis, in which the facts of the universe are mimed. Often in Clement's work, words themselves seem secondary to the phenomena. It is no coincidence that Clement loves, and, in fact, himself paints—as George Richard—astronomical art works of the phenomenal universe. At the end of his most famous novel, *Mission of Gravity,* the alien hero who is trying cleverly to acquire a more useful science for his truly phenomenal planet, Mesklin, that orbits the double star 61 Cygni, comments, "They finished up with the old line about words not really being enough to describe it. What else beside words can you use, in the name of the Suns?" His second-in-command answers, "this quantity-code they [humans] call Mathematics." Furthermore, for Clement himself any symbols seem to reside not in the words but in the Suns themselves—or in their mathematics.

The literary effect of hard science fiction that makes it good reading derives not so much from its accuracy (although Clement has written nonfiction essays in which he challenges the reader to catch his fictions in an inaccuracy, thus implying that the puzzle element is central) as from its ability to tell how science can show difference. The sublime effect of the varied and infinite universe does not require the fanciful imagination in science fiction but can be, to paraphrase Wordsworth who wanted science and imagination linked, the simple produce of the common day if you are an astronomer. The planetary environments are main characters in Clement's fictions, major sources of the sublime, from the variable high-gravity world of Mesklin to the giant and peculiar planet Dhrawn that the mesklinites explore in *Star Light,* to a variety of other worlds in which differences in atmospheric components, in mass, in heat all demonstrate that scientific extrapolation is not dry as dust. But not only does scientific extrapolation discover exciting differences in environment; it also assumes and sets about to demonstrate, in Clement's work, that life forms would evolve differently in different environments. Clement is fascinated by alien viewpoints, and the non-human characters are the most interesting characters in most of his fiction. This commitment to difference, not only in environments but also in life forms, makes Clement a far more interesting—and more accurate—extrapolator than a fellow hard science fiction writer, Issac Asimov, who peoples the galaxy with humans. But beneath the strange morphological surfaces and beyond the alien body chemistry, Clement's extraterrestrials still seek humanlike goals, most often the goal of more knowledge and more scientific control. Thus Captain Barlennan of Mesklin can seem both strange and familiar as he connives to learn flight and even space travel under conditions far different from those given to us to learn the same things. The emphasis in Clement is on learning, movement, and difference—not on any symbolic revelation of oneness.

One of his first aliens illustrates perhaps most vividly the strengths and the weaknesses of Clement's brand of hard science fiction. This creature, the hero in *Needle* and reappearing in *Through the Eye of a Needle,* evolved from viruses rather than from protozoan cells into a highly intelligent life form in which only the memory cells are specialized. The other cells are continually changing into various organs as need arises; but usually the creature lives most efficiently as a friendly parasite, or symbiont, insinuating its small virus-like cells easily among the larger protozoan-like cells of its host. In *Needle* the creature has come to Earth in hot pursuit of a criminal member of its race. They come from light years away, of course, representing Clement's one bow to illogic—faster-than-light travel. The creature, called simply The Hunter, adopts as his host a teenage boy. They become the best of friends in a delightful and carefully detailed symbiosis. Clement has the enemy or adversary creature adopt the boy's father as its host.

The Nitrogen Fix significantly continues his epistemological speculations because the nitrogenlife aliens in the fiction communicate without words through direct chemical transfer, thus reaffirming Clement's innate preference for "things" over words. Still at his steady, creative pace Clement has continued to produce exciting and puzzling narratives on into his sixth decade. His most recent novel, *Fossil: Isaac's Universe,* shows no diminution in his powers of world building, alien extrapolation, and speculations about science. In fact, it is more a gloomy and even sublime story suggestive of poetic effects similar to Shakespeare in *The Tempest* in which the very limits of scientific excavation are plumbed; and he daringly interweaves a Shakespearean sonnet into this text that puzzles us again about words versus things. Clement continues to be surprising and amazing.

—Donald M. Hassler

CLEVE, John. *See* EDMONDSON, G.C.; OFFUTT, Andrew J.

CLIFTON, Mark (Irvin)

Nationality: American. **Born:** 1906. **Career:** Trained as a teacher, but worked for 25 years as industrial psychologist working in personnel: compiled 200,000 case histories. **Awards:** Hugo award, 1955. **Died:** 1963.

Science Fiction Publications

Novels

They'd Rather Be Right, with Frank Riley. New York, Gnome Press, 1957; as *The Forever Machine,* New York, Galaxy, 1958; expanded edition, with "Crazy Joey" by Alex Apostolides, New York, Carroll and Graf, 1992.
Eight Keys to Eden. Garden City, New York, Doubleday, 1960; London, Gollancz, 1962.
When They Come from Space. Garden City, New York, Doubleday, 1962; London, Dobson, 1963.

Short Stories

The Science Fiction of Mark Clifton, edited by Barry N. Malzberg and Martin H. Greenberg. Carbondale, Southern Illinois University Press, and London, Feffer and Simons, 1980.

Also author of numerous uncollected short stories.

*   *   *

It is difficult within the field of science fiction to develop a lasting impression among readers without creating a significant body of work. Writers who concentrate on the short story are additionally handicapped, because it is with novels that reader loyalty is generally developed and maintained. Mark Clifton, whose short career included only about a score of short stories and three novels, is clearly one of the few who has managed to hold onto his modest reputation, even 30 years following his death. To a great extent this is because his short career influenced other writers to examine more serious themes.

Clifton's most famous work is the novel *The Forever Machine* (variant title *They'd Rather Be Right*), written in collaboration with Frank Riley and winner of the Hugo Award for the best novel of its year. The novel is an outgrowth of short stories about a self-aware computer developed by American scientists. The usual tensions arise; the government views it as a potential weapon, religious extremists consider it an abomination that should be destroyed. Its creator has a greater vision, because his own telepathic gifts and the computer's power can reshape humankind, providing a form of immortality, but only if the recipients are willing to surrender their old prejudices and think rationally. It was a powerful, ambitious theme, handled somewhat superficially, but one that caught the imagination of readers and led to its receiving a Hugo award, even though its only book publication was from the relatively obscure Galaxy line.

Clifton's two solo novels were also well received, though comparatively less important. *Eight Keys to Eden* is an otherworldly detective story with a scientific puzzle to be solved. An investigator from Earth is sent to find out why a remote colony has stopped communicating, and there he discovers that the psychology of the colonists has been altered by their new environment. Once again, Clifton concentrated on the psychology of his characters, and the effects of environment on personality and the way cultures work under extraordinary conditions. *When They Come From Space* (variant title *Pawns of the Black Fleet*) is more satirical. An invasion fleet has begun to attack the Earth when a second group shows up and drives them off. The rescuers are handsome human types, who quickly win the approbation of the public and the confidence of Earth's political leaders. But Ralph Kennedy, who is the protagonist of many of Clifton's best short stories, suspects a rat, discovers that the aliens are taking advantage of human-developed advertising and public relations skills to fool the world into accepting them. The invasion, of course, was a hoax designed to establish their credentials as heroes.

Several of Clifton's short stories are also worth noting. "We're Civilized," one of several stories written with Alex Apostolides, shows us humanity destroying a Martian culture on the assumption that they are not sufficiently civilized, and then perishing at the hands of an interstellar society that looks at us the same way. An even more biting indictment of human parochialism can be found in "What Now, Little Man?," which examines racial hatred in the context of an alien lifeform that begins to threaten human held jobs. "Hang Head, Vandal!" shows us a human experiment starting a chain reaction which will destroy the planet Mars.

The four Ralph Kennedy stories all pit his telepathic powers against threats to Earth. The sequence is "Remembrance and Reflection," "How Allied," "What Thin Partitions," and "Sense from Thoughts Divide." He confronts aliens, the military industrial complex, psychokinesis, and levitation. Another story of note is "Crazy Joey."

During the first few years of his writing career, Mark Clifton was compared to Robert A. Heinlein and others, but his output tapered off quickly and his death in 1963 brought a stream of interesting, thought-provoking stories to an end. It is unlikely that he will ever be considered a major figure in the field, but his work undoubtedly influenced his contemporaries to think more deeply about their themes, and his own output is unlikely to be forgotten.

—Don D'Ammassa

CLIVE, Dennis. *See* FEARN, John Russell.

COBLENTZ, Stanton A(rthur)

Nationality: American. **Born:** San Francisco, California, 24 August 1896. **Education:** University of California, Berkeley, A.B. 1917; M.A. 1919. **Family:** Married Flora Bachrach in 1922. **Career:** Feature writer, San Francisco Examiner, 1919-20; book reviewer, *New York Times* and *New York Sun,* 1920-38; founding editor, *Wings: A Quarterly of Verse,* New York, then Mill Valley, California, 1933-60. **Died:** 9 September 1982.

SCIENCE FICTION PUBLICATIONS

Novels (series: Outlanders)

The Wonder Stick. New York, Cosmopolitan, 1929.
Youth Madness. London, Utopian, 1944.
When the Birds Fly South. Mill Valley, California, Wings Press, 1945.
The Sunken World: A Romance of Atlantis. Los Angeles, Fantasy, 1948; London, Cherry Tree, 1951.
After 12,000 Years. Los Angeles, Fantasy, 1950.
Into Plutonian Depths. New York, Avon, 1950.
The Planet of Youth. Los Angeles, Fantasy, 1952.
Under the Triple Suns. Reading, Pennsylvania, Fantasy Press, 1955.
Hidden World. New York, Avalon, 1957; as *In Caverns Below,* New York, Garland, 1975.
The Blue Barbarians. New York, Avalon, 1958.
Next Door to the Sun. New York, Avalon, 1960.
The Runaway World. New York, Avalon, 1961.
The Last of the Great Race. New York, Arcadia House, 1964.
The Lizard Lords. New York, Avalon, 1964.
The Lost Comet. New York, Arcadia House, 1964.
The Moon People (Outlanders). New York, Avalon, 1964.
Lord of Tranerica. New York, Avalon, 1966.
The Crimson Capsule (Outlanders). New York, Avalon, 1967; as *The Animal People,* New York, Belmont, 1970.
The Day the World Stopped. New York, Avalon, 1968.
The Island People (Outlanders). New York, Belmont, 1971.

OTHER PUBLICATIONS

Poetry

The Thinker and Other Poems. New York, White, 1923.
The Lone Adventurer. New York, Unicorn Press, 1927; revised edition, San Jose, California, Redwood Press, 1975.
Shadows on a Wall. New York, Poetic Publications, 1930.
The Enduring Flame. New York, Paebar, 1932.
Songs of the Redwoods. Los Angeles, Overland Outwest, 1933.
The Merry Hunt. Boston, Humphries, 1934.
The Pageant of Man. New York, Wings Press, 1936.
Songs by the Wayside. New York, Wings Press, 1938.
Senator Goose. Mill Valley, California, Wings Press, 1940.
Winds of Chaos. Mill Valley, California, Wings Press, 1942.
Green Vistas. Mill Valley, California, Wings Press, 1943.
Armageddon. Mill Valley, California, Wings Press, 1943.
The Mountain of the Sleeping Maiden. Mill Valley, California, Wings Press, 1946.
Garnered Sheaves: Selected Poems. Mill Valley, California, Wings Press, 1949.
Time's Travellers. Mill Valley, California, Wings Press, 1952.
From a Western Hilltop. Mill Valley, California, Wings Press, 1954.
Out of Many Songs. Mill Valley, California, Wings Press, 1958.
Atlantis and Other Poems. Mill Valley, California, Wings Press, 1960.
Redwood Poems. Healdsburg, California, Naturegraph, 1961.
Aesop's Fables. Norwalk, Connecticut, Gibson, 1968.
Selected Short Poems. San Jose, California, Redwood Press, 1974.
Strange Universes: New Selected Poems. San Jose, California, Redwood Press, 1977.
Sea Cliffs and Green Ridges: Poems of the West. Happy Camp, California, Naturegraph, 1979.

Other

The Decline of Man. New York, Minton Balch, 1925.
Marching Men: The Story of War. New York, Unicorn Press, 1927.
The Literary Revolution. New York, Frank Maurice, 1927.
The Answer of the Ages. New York, Cosmopolitan, 1931.
Villains and Vigilantes. New York, Wilson Erickson, 1936.
The Triumph of the Teapot Poets. Mill Valley, California, Wings Press, 1941.
An Editor Looks at Poetry. Mill Valley, California, Wings Press, 1947.
New Poetic Lamps and Old. Mill Valley, California, Wings Press, 1950.
From Arrow to Atom Bomb: The Psychological History of War. New York, Beechhurst Press, 1953.
The Rise of the Anti-Poets. Mill Valley, California, Wings Press, 1955.
Magic Casements: A Guidebook for Poets. Mill Valley, California, Wings Press, 1957.
The Long Road to Humanity. New York, Yoseloff, 1959.
My Life in Poetry. New York, Bookman Associates, 1959.
The Swallowing Wilderness. New York, Yoseloff, 1961.
The Generation That Forgot to Sing. Mill Valley, California, Wings Press, 1962.
Avarice: A History. Washington, D.C., Public Affairs Press, 1964.
Ten Crises in Civilization. Chicago, Follett, 1965; London, Muller, 1967.

Demons, Witch Doctors, and Modern Man. New York, Yoseloff, 1965.

The Paradox of Man's Greatness. Washington D.C., Public Affairs Press, 1966.

The Poetry Circus. New York, Hawthorn, 1967.

The Pageant of the New World. Berkeley, California, Diablo Press, 1968.

The Power Trap. South Brunswick, New Jersey, A.S. Barnes, 1970.

The Militant Dissenters. South Brunswick, New Jersey, A.S. Barnes, 1970.

The Challenge to Man's Survival. South Brunswick, New Jersey, A.S. Barnes, 1972.

Light Beyond: The Wonderworld of Parapsychology. New York, Cornwall, 1982.

Adventures of a Freelancer: The Literary Exploits and Autobiography of Stanton A. Coblentz, with Jeffrey M. Elliot. San Bernardino, California, Borgo Press, 1993.

Editor, *Modern American [and British] Lyrics.* New York, Minton Balch, 2 vols., 1924-25; as *Modern Lyrics,* New York, Loring and Mussey, n.d.

Editor, *The Music Makers.* New York, Ackerman, 1945.
Editor, *Unseen Wings.* New York, Beechhurst Press, 1949.
Editor, *Poetry Today.* Mill Valley, California, Wings Press, 1955.
Editor, *Poems to Change Lives.* New York, Association Press, 1960.

*   *   *

In the earliest days of the science fiction magazines, most of the stories were reprinted from other sources; shortly, however, new works began to appear in *Amazing, Science Wonder Stories,* and the others. One of the first of these new authors, along with such writers as Jack Williamson and E.E. Smith, was Stanton A. Coblentz.

Coblentz's work was unusual for these magazines, as most of the material used science fiction as a vehicle for transmitting hard science (i.e., the Verne tradition), or a device for establishing melodramatic adventure situations (i.e., the Burroughs tradition). Coblentz, by contrast, used the standard devices of science fiction—space travel, time displacement, discovery of lost races—in order to establish a satiric mirror in which to reflect the foibles of contemporary society and/or timeless modes of human conduct. In this sense, Coblentz worked in the tradition of Lucian, Cyrano, Swift, and, to a substantial extent, H.G. Wells. Coblentz thus provided a model for such later humorists and satirists as William Tenn, Robert Sheckley, Frederik Pohl, and C.M. Kornbluth. Pohl, at least, of this group, has expressed his admiration for and debt to Coblentz.

Coblentz's first published science fiction was the novel *The Sunken World: A Romance of Atlantis.* A modern submarine discovers survivors of the classical Atlantis living an idyllic existence in a glass dome on the ocean bottom, but they are destroyed through the inadvertent influence of the submariners.

In *Hidden World,* a contemporary traveller finds his way into an unknown civilization hidden in giant caverns beneath the earth. This theme is one Jules Verne had used as a device for travelogue-like exploration of imaginary geography, and Edgar Rice Burroughs also used it, in his Pellucidar series, as a background for adventure tales with primitive human and non-human creatures. In *Hidden World,* the traveller becomes caught up in a society at war for no comprehensible issue, except for the possible purpose of reducing unemployment and stimulating economic activity. *Into Plutonian Depths,*

dealing with society on the planet Pluto, posits a situation in which men and women past child-bearing age aspire to become surgically neutered, these neuters being the pampered and powerful rulers of Plutonian society. The cover of the Avon edition described the novel as dealing with "the third sex" (a widely used euphemism for homosexuality at the time), to which Donald Wollheim, Avon's editor, later ascribed the success of the edition.

Many other works by Coblentz contain satirical matter, most often reflecting Coblentz's revulsion against war, consistently portrayed as senseless and ignoble, and his distress with the oppression and materialistic greed manifested in human institutions. *After 12,000 Years* portrays a future world in which armies of insects have been bred to giant and ferocious stature and enslaved for service in warfare. This anticipates *The Dragon Masters* (1962) by Jack Vance, a distant cousin of Coblentz. It should be noted that Coblentz had a long and varied literary career, of which his science fiction represents only one aspect. Two novels approaching science fiction are *The Wonder Stick,* a pleasantly done story of primitive life, and *When the Birds Fly South,* a beautifully realized novel of an unknown race in the Himalayas.

—Richard A. Lupoff

COGSWELL, Theodore R(ose)

Pseudonym: Cogswell Thomas. **Nationality:** American. **Born:** Coatesville, Pennsylvania, 10 March 1918. **Education:** University of Colorado, Boulder, B.A. 1947; University of Denver, M.A. 1948, graduate study, 1956-57; University of Minnesota, Minneapolis, 1949-53; Latin Institute, Brooklyn College, 1973. **Military Service:** Served as an ambulance driver, Spanish Republican Army, 1937-38; statistical control officer, United States Army Air Force, 1942-46; Captain; Order of the Cloud and Dragon, Republic of China. **Family:** Married 1) Marjorie Mills in 1948, two daughters; 2) Coralie Norris in 1964; 3) Georgia Rae Williams in 1972. **Career:** Boulder correspondent, United Press, 1941-42; Instructor, University of Minnesota, 1949-53, and University of Kentucky, Lexington, 1953-56, 1957-58; Assistant Professor, Ball State University, Muncie, Indiana, 1958-65; Professor, Keystone Junior College, La Plume, Pennsylvania, from 1965; executive director, and editor of Proceedings, Institute for 21st Century Studies, from 1959. Editor, *SFWA Forum,* 1970-71, 1973-76; book reviewer, *Minneapolis Tribune,* 1970-72; editor, I.C.S., Scranton, Pennsylvania, 1975-78; editorial consultant, Sandvik Inc., Fair Lawn, New Jersey, 1978. Secretary, Science Fiction Writers of America, 1973-74. **Died:** 1987.

SCIENCE FICTION PUBLICATIONS

Novel (series: Star Trek)

Spock, Messiah!, with Charles A. Spano, Jr. New York, Bantam, 1976; London, Corgi, 1977.

Short Stories

The Wall Around the World. New York, Pyramid, 1962.

The Third Eye. New York, Belmont, 1968.

OTHER PUBLICATIONS

Plays

Some Call It Heads (produced Denver, 1948).
Operation Tel Aviv (produced Foothills, California, 1949).
Contact Point, with G.R. Cogswell, in *Six Science Fiction Plays,*
    edited by Roger Elwood. New York, Washington Square Press,
    1976.

Television Play: *Red Dust* (*Tales of Tomorrow* series), 1952.

Poetry

The Roper (song), music by John Jacob Niles. New York, Schirmer,
    1955.
Placebos for the Orthodox. Chinchilla, Pennsylvania, Miskatonic
    University Press, 1981.

*   *   *

Theodore R. Cogswell's work ranges in mood from horror to
irony and spoof, in form from novellas to short stories, poetry, and
drama, and in quality from expert and meaningful storytelling to
juvenile fantasy. While portions of his stories (like "Test Area")
are chilling, Cogswell's best horror story is probably "The Burning," which is about a demonic goddess (a terrible matriarch) who
demands love and obedience from her children—and also eats them
alive. Often horror is mixed with irony in Cogswell's work, as in
"Emergency Rations" where cannibals are trapped in a Trojan horse
scheme and literally cooked alive since they "can't feel nothing";
"Thimgs" where the unscrupulous main character demands vitality
in his bargain with a Guardian for longer life—only to find that the
lives spliced onto his are those leading to horrible sudden deaths;
and "Wolfie" where Peter Vincent bargains with a warlock to be
turned into a werewolf in order to kill his cousin and collect on his
will, but is transformed into a mangy toothless mutt that must be
put out of its misery. In these three stories the would-be victimiz-
ers become victims, for as the Guardian says in "Thimgs," "the
ethical universe is just as orderly as the physical one." Occasionally, Cogswell's mood borders on spoof, as in "Probability Zero!
The Population Implosion," which manipulates statistics in order
to prove that England's population has declined since the year 1000
from 275 billion to 44 million at the present time. So, the story
advises ticklishly, if you hear doomsayers of the population bomb,
you need remember only that "statistics show . . . you have nothing to worry about." "Probability Zero!" illustrates what a Pirandello
character says of a statistic: it's "like a sack; it won't stand up till
you've put something in it." Unfortunately, what we put into it is
interpretation, which is usually debatable and rarely definitive.

Cogswell is quite adept in the various literary genres. His first
novella, "The Spectre General," is an accomplished story in the
Heinlein tradition, involving delightful situational and understated
humor and an alternating chapter/scene plot structure, which deals
with the revival of a dying empire by technologists. *The Wall Around
the World* is a fine reworking of the Icarus myth, blending and
contrasting magic and technology in its main character, Porgie.
Cogswell's shorter works are also expert, as the story "Early Bird"

reveals. The most imaginative of all his fictions, this piece depicts
a fascinating symbiotic relationship between the main character, Kurt
Dixon, and his ship's mother computer and between "her" and two
incredibly adaptive, semi-organic monsters on a planet Kurt was
forced to retreat to during his battle with the gigantic, people-eating
Kieriens.

Cogswell's poetry, although different in theme and mood from
his other work, is quite good, as his Swiftian lambast against contemporary poets ("sparrow farts" and "word kickers") in "Faex
Delenda Est" suggests. Finally, his drama is also impressive. For
example, *Contact Point,* written with his wife, has an excellent sense
of timing and action, dealing with the first space crew to reach a
star and their anxieties and conflicts in bringing back a deadly radioactive organism. At first convinced that Earth's doctors can save
him, and willing to endanger the rest of humanity, the main character undergoes a dramatic change whereby he challenges Earthlings
to reunite and stop fighting among themselves in order to annihilate him and his ship before it lands.

Although Cogswell sometimes stoops to puerile fantasy as in
"The Masters" (a vampire story), he was a versatile writer. Even in
"The Masters" we see that just as the ethical universe is orderly so
is the physical one, so that we never know if we will need some
endangered species (the snaildarter?) to help us in our afflictions.

—Dennis M. Welch

———

COLERIDGE, John. *See* **BINDER, Eando.**

———

COLLINS, Hunt. *See* **HUNTER, Evan.**

———

COLVIN, James. *See* **MOORCOCK, Michael.**

———

COMPTON, D(avid) G(uy)

Pseudonyms: Guy Compton; Frances Lynch. **Nationality:** British. **Born:** London, 19 August 1930. **Education:** Cheltenham College, 1940-48. **Military Service:** Served in the British Army, 1948-
50. **Family:** Married 1) Elizabeth Tillotson in 1952 (divorced 1969),
two daughters and one son; 2) Carol Savage in 1971, one stepdaughter and one step-son. **Career:** Worked as stage electrician,
furniture maker, salesman, docker, and postman; editor, Reader's
Digest Condensed Books, London 1969-. Lives in London.
Awards: Arts Council bursary, 1964. **Agent:** Murray Pollinger,

222 Old Brompton Rd., London SW5 0BZ. **Address:** 12 Granfield Street, Battersea, London SW11 3JH, England.

Science Fiction Publications

Novels (series: Katherine Mortenhoe)

The Quality of Mercy. London, Hodder and Stoughton, 1965; New York, Ace, 1970.
Farewell, Earth's Bliss. London, Hodder and Stoughton, 1966; New York, Ace, 1971.
The Silent Multitude. New York, Ace, 1966; London, Hodder and Stoughton, 1967.
Synthajoy. London, Hodder and Stoughton, and New York, Ace, 1968.
The Steel Crocodile. New York, Ace, 1970; as *The Electric Crocodile,* London, Hodder and Stoughton, 1970.
Chronocules. New York, Ace, 1970; London, Arrow, 1976; as *Hot Wireless Sets, Aspirin Tablets, the Sandpaper Sides of Used Matchboxes, and Something that Might Have Been Castor Oil,* London, Joseph, 1971.
The Missionaries. New York, Ace, 1972; London, Hale, 1975.
The Unsleeping Eye (Mortenhoe). New York, DAW, 1974; as *The Continuous Katherine Mortenhoe,* London, Gollancz, 1974; as *Death Watch,* London, Magnum, 1981.
A Usual Lunacy. San Bernardino, California, Borgo Press, 1978.
Windows (Mortenhoe). New York, Berkley, 1979.
Ascendancies. London, Gollancz, and New York, Berkley, 1980.
Scudder's Game. Worcester Park, Surrey, Kerosina, 1988.
Ragnarok, with John Gribbin. London, Gollancz, 1991.
Nomansland. London, Gollancz, 1993.
Justice City. London, Gollancz, 1994.

Other Publications

Novels as Guy Compton

Too Many Murderers. London, Long, 1962.
Medium for Murder. London, Long, 1963.
Dead on Cue. London, Long, 1964.
Disguise for a Dead Gentleman. London, Long, 1964.
High Tide for Hanging. London, Long, 1965.
And Murder Came Too. London, Long, 1966.
The Palace (as D.G. Compton). London, Hodder and Stoughton, and New York, Norton, 1969.

Novels as Frances Lynch

Twice Ten Thousand Miles. London, Souvenir Press, and New York, St. Martin's Press, 1974; as *Candle at Midnight,* New York, Dell, 1977.
The Fine and Handsome Captain. London, Souvenir Press, and New York, St. Martin's Press, 1975.
Stranger at the Wedding. New York, St. Martin's Press, 1976; London, Souvenir Press, 1977.
A Dangerous Magic. London, Souvenir Press, and New York, St. Martin's Press, 1978.
In the House of Dark Music. London, Hodder and Stoughton, 1979.

Plays

Radio Plays: *Chez Nous,* 1961; *Bandstand,* 1962; *Blind Man's Bluff,* 1962; *Fully Furnished,* 1963; *Always Read the Small Print,* 1963; *If the Shoe Fits,* 1964; *Mandible Light,* 1964; *A Turning off the Minch Park Road,* 1965; *Time Exposure,* 1965; *The Real People,* 1966; *Island,* 1968; *Surgery,* 1968; *The Respighi Inheritance,* 1973.

Other

Radio Plays. Worcester Park, Surrey, Kerosina, 1988.

*

D.G. Compton comments:

Possibly the best introduction to any writer's work is to know why he does it. The reason I write what people have been kind enough to call SF ("kind enough" because the label makes possible a large and informed readership for stuff that otherwise would probably sink without a trace) is that I'm basically a rather embarrassed sort of person, afraid of admitting to commitment, who welcomes SF's distancing mechanisms. After all, it's far safer to dare to care about one's characters when the situation in which one places them isn't quite "real."

Also I've led what is sometimes known as a "sheltered life." For which read "limited." Thus I know very little about the commonalities of human existence: commerce, golf, brick-laying, what you will. The same sheltered life, however, has involved me in close and prolonged—and often painful—contact with just a few very positive individuals (mostly women, let's face it), and from these individuals I've learned a lot. So I try to write about that of which I know at least something, people, while setting them discreetly in worlds of my own devising (about which I may also be expected to know something.) Future worlds, for convenience's sake, but always closely tied to my own muddled understanding of the present world around me. In general terms I don't much like this present world, and developing it a few years on is a good way of finding out why. And perhaps even of seeing how to change it.

*   *   *

D.G. Compton's science fiction novels usually lead to extremes of reaction from their readers. Some are strongly attracted to his mature themes, richly fluent prose, strong concentration on character, and realistic appreciation of the seamier side of human existence. Others are dismayed by the density of his prose, the ineffectualness of many of his characters, the underlying distrust of technology as a cure for all of humanity's ills, the absence of much physical action, and the frequently bizarre nature of his situations. But it appears that Compton is beginning to win over an ever larger share of readers as he continues to skewer human foibles and failings.

Two of his more popular novels deal with our delight in vicarious experience of another's life. *Synthajoy* created a minor controversy because of the dissolute nature of its characters. The story concerns the development of a means to record the life experiences of an individual, to be played back at another time for an interested audience. Although there are obvious beneficial aspects to such an invention, it is almost immediately subverted. Compton returned to this theme in *The Unsleeping Eye.* In a world where disease and pain are virtually unknown, Katherine Mortenhoe had contracted a terminal disease that leaves her only weeks to live. The entertainment world is quick to realize that this provides a possibly unique opportunity to produce a profitable bit of entertainment, and they employ a man with cameras surgically implanted in one eye. The cameraman manipulates Katherine so that she is emotionally dependent upon him, totally unaware that he is filming her agony for an unfeeling audience. But as time passes, his feelings for her become genuine, and there is a dawning realization that he too is being manipulated.

Compton apparently felt that he had not completely examined the consequences of this situation, because he later wrote a sequel, *Windows*. The protagonist insists upon the removal of his camera-eyes and accepts blindness, but his personal statement about the world is not allowed to stand as it is. One factor abhors him for criticizing the status quo, another wants to make him a cult hero, and still another dismisses his gesture as an nuisance. The pair are finally driven to flee the country, but are still unable to withdraw into themselves.

Perhaps Compton's most accomplished work is *The Steel Crocodile*, set in an ultrasecret research institute. The protagonist rapidly realizes that more is transpiring within the research group than is apparent. Eventually it is revealed to him that the authorities fear that blind technological progress is too dangerous, and they have created a computer bank to monitor and even interfere with scientific developments. They are blithely unaware that they have surrendered their destiny to the very technology they hoped to control. This complexity of philosophy and plot is rarely found in any genre, and Compton's ability to control his work has rarely been equalled.

The Silent Multitude is perhaps his least conventional work. A spore from space attacks concrete, and most artifacts of man's civilization are crumbling. Against the background of a deserted city, Compton presents a small cast of characters, reflecting their personal decay against the collapse of the city itself. Even without the brilliant characterization, this would remain a memorable novel, for Compton's description of the dissolution is haunting.

The isolated research organization appears again in *Chronocules*, also present as an island of hope in a crumbling society. It is clear that the collapse of the present society is accelerating and will come within the lifetimes of the protagonists, so they desperately seek a means of escape into the future. Although an excellent novel in itself, it suffers when compared to *The Steel Crocodile* and *The Silent Multitude*, to both of which it is thematically similar. *The Missionaries* should have been a very controversial novel, but attracted little attention. A small group of aliens arrive on Earth, preaching the religion of Ustiliath. Compton makes it quite clear that, for all practical purposes, the aliens are absolutely correct in their beliefs, and that conversion to their religion is the only logical course. But humanity reacts with fear and loathing, and the aliens reach the same fate that greeted many Christian missionaries in their efforts to bring "enlightenment" to the "savages."

Two of Compton's early novels were brought back into print as his popularity grew. Both are highly competent, but neither is of the quality of his later work. *The Quality of Mercy* is a low key examination of the tensions brought to bear on a group of military personnel when it becomes clear that something, perhaps a nuclear war, is imminent. In many ways, this is a forerunner of *The Steel Crocodile*, although in no way comparable with regard to quality. *Farewell, Earth's Bliss* makes use of one of science fiction's most well-traveled plots, the penal colony on Mars, to present a group of misfit humans against a kaleidoscopic background where reality and fantasy aren't always distinguishable.

A Usual Lunacy investigates the repercussions of a new disease that causes people to fall in love with each other against their will, and in many cases only until they are cured of the disease. Compton seems unusually bitter this time, for love itself becomes a sometimes criminal activity. *Ascendancies* seems to have been largely overlooked despite yet another set of interesting characters. A strange substance begins periodically to fall from space, a substance which is soon revealed to be an inexpensive source of energy. Soon most of the world is freed from the normal work week, but subject to a new burden. There are scattered incidents of possibly hallucinatory singing, often accompanied by mysterious disappearances of people in the area. The protagonists are a woman whose husband disappears and the insurance investigator who discovers she has purchased a body from a criminal organization in order to ensure that she receives the insurance money. When he decides to blackmail her, the two are brought together in a compulsive and compelling relationship.

Ascendancies, in 1980, was the last Compton novel to receive a U.S. edition, even though Compton moved to the States from his native England in the early 1980s with his American-born wife. For nearly a decade, Compton appeared to have retired from science fiction writing. A new science fiction novel, *Scudder's Game*, appeared in Germany (in 1985) and England (in 1988), but it was clear that it was actually written in the 1970s. The book tells of a near-future utopia of controlled population growth and free love brought on by a birth control device that enhances sexual pleasure, thereby encouraging its use. (It is clear that the novel was written before the advent of AIDS.)

Ragnarok (published in the U.K. in 1991), a near-future ecological techno-thriller coauthored with British scientist and author John Gribbin, heralded Compton's return to SF writing. The plot deals with scientists threatening to destroy the world by volcanic eruption in order to save it by forcing nuclear disarmament and ecological and economic reforms. It is unclear how much of a contribution Compton made to the book, but the project appears to have prompted him to begin writing his own near-future, social issue thriller, *Nomansland*, which appeared in the U.K. in 1993. It is set in a vaguely realized near-future (or possibly an alternative present) 40 years after women have lost the ability to bear male babies, and tells of a female doctor attempting to patent a vaccine while various political forces conspire to silence her. Unfortunately, the book never establishes sufficient verisimilitude to be effective in its social agenda.

Compton's latest novel, *Justice City* (published in the U.K. in 1994), is more effective, despite the near-future or alternative present setting being equally murky. The novel takes the form of a police-procedural mystery set in a high-tech prison with unique changes involving both the confinement and punishment of its inmates. The result is an ironic and bitter meditation on crime and punishment, and their relationship to justice.

David G. Compton is unlikely to ever achieve unabashed success either critically or commercially in the SF field, but his work in the 1960s and 1970s (especially *Synthajoy* and *The Unsleeping Eye*) had an important influence on many other authors in the field who were seeking to expand the scope of the field with more mature characters and themes. Compton has eschewed the traditional concerns of science fiction, concentrating instead solely on his real interests, the morality of science and technological change, the peculiarities of humanity, and our ability to influence our own lives.

—Don D'Ammassa, updated by D. Douglas Fratz

CONEY, Michael G(reatrex)

Also writes as Mike Coney. **Nationality:** British. **Born:** Birmingham, Warwickshire, 28 September 1932. **Education:** King Edward's School, Birmingham, 1944-49. **Military Service:** Served in the Royal Air Force, 1956-58. **Family:** Married to Daphne Coney; two sons and one daughter. **Career:** Auditor, Russell and Company, Birmingham, 1949-56; senior clerk, Pearce Clayton Maunder, Dorchester, Dorset, 1958-61; accountant, Pontins, Bournemouth, 1962; tenant, Plymouth Breweries, Totnes, Devon, 1963-66; accountant, Peplow Warren Fuller, Newton Abbout, Devon, 1966-69; manager, Jabberwock Hotel, Antigua, West Indies, 1969-72. Management specialist, British Columbia Forest Service, Victoria, 1973-89. **Awards:** British Science Fiction award, 1976. **Agents:** Virginia Kidd, Box 278, Milford, Pennsylvania 18337, U.S.A.; Diana Tyler, 45 Fitzroy St., London W1P 5HR, England. **Address:** 2082 Neptune Road, R.R. 3, Sidney, British Columbia, Canada.

SCIENCE FICTION PUBLICATIONS

Novels (series: The Song of Earth)

Mirror Image. New York, DAW, 1972; London, Gollancz, 1973.
Syzygy. New York, Ballantine, and Morley, Yorkshire, Elmfield Press, 1973.
Friends Come in Boxes. New York, DAW, 1973; London, Gollancz, 1974.
The Hero of Downways. New York, DAW, 1973; London, Orbit, 1974.
Winter's Children. London, Gollancz, 1974.
The Jaws That Bite, The Claws That Catch. New York, DAW, 1975; as *The Girl with a Symphony in Her Fingers,* Morley, Yorkshire, Elmfield Press, 1975.
Hello Summer, Goodbye. London, Gollancz, 1975; as *Rax,* New York, DAW, 1975; as *Pallahaxi Tide.* Vancouver, British Columbia, Porcepic, 1990.
Charisma. London, Gollancz, 1975; New York, Dell, 1979.
Brontomek! London, Gollancz, 1976.
The Ultimate Jungle. London, Millington, 1979.
Neptune's Cauldron. New York, Tower, 1981.
Cat Karina. New York, Ace, 1982; London, Gollancz, 1983.
The Celestial Steam Locomotive (song). Boston, Houghton Mifflin, 1983; London, Orbit, 1986.
Gods of the Greataway (song). Boston, Houghton Mifflin, 1984; London, Orbit, 1986.
Fang, The Gnome (song; as Michael Greatrex Coney). New York, New American Library, and London, Orbit, 1988.
King of the Scepter'd Isle (song; as Michael Greatrex Coney). New York, New American Library, 1989.

Short Stories

Monitor Found in Orbit. New York, DAW, 1974.

OTHER PUBLICATIONS

Other

Forest Ranger, Ahoy!: The Men—The Ships—The Job. Sidney, British Columbia, Porthole Press, 1983.

Forest Adventure: A Guide to the British Columbia Forest Museum, with Gray Campbell. Sidney, British Columbia, Porthole Press, 1985.
A Tomcat Called Sabrina (as Mike Coney). Sidney, British Columbia, Porthole Press, 1992.
No Place for a Sealion (as Mike Coney). Sidney, British Columbia, Porthole Press, 1992.

*

Michael G. Coney comments:

My purpose is to entertain myself as well as my readers. Each of my novels has been an experiment in style and content with one consistent trait: they are all mystery stories. Love is there too, and human psychology, and a little "hard" science, but my main intent is to keep the reader guessing. I think my earlier novels were too conservative; they were all hung on hooks of known science and "real" reality—which is odd, since as an SF reader my preference is for the persuasively fantastic: the "sense of wonder" story. My short stories are normally written as vehicles for ideas, situations, and characters which I intend to use in my novels—I find it much easier to work this way than to plunge into a novel cold. Other short stories have been written for specific purposes, generally to use up one-off ideas before I forget them.

*   *   *

Michael G. Coney was a prolific writer in the mid-1970s and has recently caught his second wind, with his commitment to "The Song of Earth" series, a kaleidoscopic future history, and related works. Because he has contributed to so many of the genre's traditions, his work is not easy to classify: perhaps his originality has been in his ability to take the old forms and themes and quietly but persuasively put his own stamp on them. Philip K. Dick may have been his model in *Mirror Image,* John Christopher in the post-holocaust novel, *Winter's Children,* Heinlein and Aldiss in the closed environment stories *The Hero of Downways, The Ultimate Jungle* and "The Mind Prison," Asimov's "Nightfall" in *Syzygy* and "Evidence" (from *I, Robot*) in "The Martyrdom of Raccoona Three" (a fine short story embedded in *The Celestial Steam Locomotive*), Cordwainer Smith in *Cat Karina* and other stories in "The Song of Earth" that feature the "Specialists" (animal-human melds). His powerful sequel to *Syzygy, Brontomek!,* takes up several ideas from the earlier stories: the amorphs from *Mirror Image,* the heroine's name and personality from Susanna in *Charisma,* the brontomeks and the idea of post-hypnotic suggestion from his grim story "Esmeralda." Throughout his work, Coney's range of theme and tone is remarkable; his touch is usually light, but the fare is not bland. He is equally at ease with horror, romance, and humor ("The Byrds" should become a classic of comic fantasy). "The Song of the Earth," therefore, which forced him by its structure to evoke the sense of wonder freshly at least once in each of its many short chapters, proved ideally suited to his genius and had the further advantage of enabling him to subsume his taste for fantasy within a formal science-fictional frame, through the idea of a computer-programmable Dream World.

Coney likes to study the reactions of a small group to a large threat or challenge, whether natural but alien, as in *Hello Summer, Goodbye, Syzygy,* and the gnome books, or social but inhuman, as in *Brontomek!,* or both, as in *The Ultimate Jungle.* Solutions are not likely to be achieved by technological means but, after valiant efforts, may be granted by special grace; to some problems the only solution is escape or transcendence. As an SF writer, Coney is properly concerned with the issue of skepticism and its contrary, credulity; he is not so hasty as some writers to come down on one side. The framing chapters of *Syzygy* expose the dangers of group vulnerability to suggestion, yet it seems in *Brontomek!* that it may sometimes be better to rest happily deceived, as individuals are by the amorphic "Tes." Coney hates manipulators: his sympathetic characters are often their victims; yet it is not easy for these characters to find someone to blame. In *Brontomek!* the immoral Organization stamps on a whole planet, yet its own agents are themselves victims, and there is something sublimely admirable in the irresponsible force of its symbol, the rogue brontomek, which rampages malignly for a time before pathetically losing its motive power, "betrayed by its own mechanical weaknesses." Cat Karina complains against the bullying gods, but human manipulators and strong egotists may be regarded with horrified admiration, as are Carioca Jones and Hector Bartholomew in the Peninsula stories, while their devoted lovers are seen with baffled disgust. Nevertheless, if the author, for narrative purposes, identifies with such lovers, he will present them with strong sympathy, and perhaps it is for this reason that in *Charisma, The Jaws That Bite, The Claws That Catch,* and *The Ultimate Jungle,* Coney seems over-tolerant of some repellent features of his heroes, concomitant on their devotion to such unpleasant characters. Alien manipulators may also be present sympathetically (their control is accidental in *Syzygy;* accidents are rectified by benevolent fostering in "The Tertiary Justification" and "Symbiote"; they show wise control of beasts in "Oh, Valinda!"). So disposed, Coney gives us one of the genre's sweetest heroines in the alien Pallahaxi Browneyes (*Hello Summer, Goodbye*), and seems to envy the self-containedness of his multi-individual aliens (Kli a' Po in *Brontomek!* and the amusing Vegan in "Trading Post"), whereas his humans often find it hard to relate to other individuals.

There is strong dystopian satire in *Friends Come in Boxes* (which offers a radical solution to superfluous people—those over 40) and *The Jaws That Bite, The Claws That Catch* (where prisoners reduce their sentences by voluntary bondage). As a dystopian writer, Coney's animus is principally against the notion that utility or justice should outweigh compassion. The darker side of his vision culminates in *The Ultimate Jungle,* an important but depressing novel in which Coney seems to have given in to a compulsion to put on record those inadequacies which hereafter will force him to treat humans as members of a dead species. Maybe he had to get this book off his chest before he could achieve the mellower tones of "The Song of Earth." Coney has stressed the element of mystery in his stories; his plots often draw upon those of mystery fiction: like Bester's *The Demolished Man, Charisma* offers an SF variant of the locked-room mystery, for instance, and "Monitor Found in Orbit" wickedly plays on the spy thriller. Coney appreciates that the SF form can be used to shed new light on old problems; in my favorite of his early novels, *The Hero of Downways,* he studies heroism as it were in a clinical laboratory situation—and also takes a fresh look at such SF standards as clones, the multi-individual self, mutations, and miniaturized people. Others may enjoy this author more for his presentation of new forms of locomotion or of unusual tidal conditions on strange planets; few should fail to find him entertaining, and he deserves to be rediscovered extensively.

The two most recent novels, which are set in the same multiverse of ifalongs and happentracks as the "Song" series, are likely to raise Michael Greatrex Coney's profile (he uses the full name for the purpose) as a fantasist because they deal so freshly and delightfully with the Arthurian legend. In the wake of Marion Zimmer Bradley's feminist reading, *The Mists of Avalon,* comes a gnomist recension in *Fang, the Gnome* and its sequel, *King of the Scepter'd Isle.* Coney's gnomes suggest Tolkien's hobbits as they, too, are little people swept up in heroic events and contributing crucially to their resolution, but the gnomes will never be taken so seriously as the larger hobbits. Paradoxically earthy yet prudish, for example, all gnomes except Fang and his Princess loathe the very idea of copulation, otherwise known as "filth," and one of them, Mold the Outrageous, excellently substitutes the downright "Sexual Intercourse!" for the increasingly meaningless f—- word of modern human parlance. To begin with, they live safely outside the margins of human ("giant") experience, witnessing with disgust the nasty human habit of killing one another and assorted animals in a shadowy "umbra," because they inhabit a happentrack not quite contiguous to the human one, but the young heroine Nyneve finds a gateway between the worlds and it is not long before the gnomes and humans are sharing the same part of Cornwall. The gnomes are a quarrelsome lot and have their own political problems which mirror in a wry fashion those of the larger people. The matter of Arthur is dealt with lightly, much in the vein of T.H. White, and the treatment of Lancelot is notably tactful. Coney does not debunk the legendary figures; on the contrary, the legend of chivalry serves to rescue mankind (not to mention the godlike Starquin) from a ghastly fate; but a remark by the wild human Sally is not unrepresentative: "Come on, let's go down there and behave like heroes for a while. I need to boast and gloat!"

—Michael J. Tolley

CONSTANTINE, Murray. *See* **BURDEKIN, Katherine.**

CONSTANTINE, Storm

Nationality: British. **Born:** England, 12 October 1956. **Education:** Stafford Girls' High School, 1966-71; Stafford Art College, 1971-72. **Family:** Married Mark Henkin in 1992. **Career:** Finance officer, in Staffordshire. Now full-time freelance writer; also runs a weekly writers' workshop at Stafford College. **Agent:** Merrilee Heifetz, Writers House Inc., 21 West 26th St., New York, New York 10010, U.S.A. **Address:** c/o Inception (Information Service), 44 White Way, Kidlington, Oxon, OX5 2XA, England. **Online Address:** 73022,11 (Compuserve).

SCIENCE FICTION PUBLICATIONS

Novels (series: Book of Wraeththu; Monstrous Regiment)

The Monstrous Regiment. London, Orbit, 1990.
Hermetech. London, Headline, 1991.

Aleph (Monstrous Regiment). London, Orbit, 1991.
Burying the Shadow. London, Headline, 1992.
Sign for the Sacred. London, Headline, 1993.
Wraeththu. New York, Orb, 1993.
    The Enchantments of Flesh and Spirit. London, Macdonald,
      1987; New York, Tor, 1990.
    The Bewitchments of Love and Hate. London, Macdonald, 1988;
      New York, Tor, 1990.
    The Fulfilments of Fate and Desire. Birmingham, Drunken
      Dragon Press, 1989; New York, Tor, 1991.
Calenture. London, Headline, 1994.

*

Storm Constantine comments:

    The ideas in my first three books, which comprised the "Wraeththu" trilogy, evolved over 10 years or so, and by the time I came to write the books, seemed to have become a personal mythology. The books incorporate influences of diverse mythic sources and also the last 15 years or so of popular culture, as I have always worked with musicians and bands, in the capacity of writer, ideas person, artist, and manager. Although I have continued to write stories with an SF theme, I have branched out into the genres of fantasy, and dark fantasy. I am currently working on a trilogy for Penguin/Creed in the UK, which is an erotic, dark fantasy based around the legends of the Grigori, the fallen angels who cohabited with human women. In many ways, I see the Grigori trilogy as a return to familiar territory, as it shares many themes with the Wraeththu books. The first volume of the trilogy, *Stalking Tender Prey,* is due to be published in the UK in November 1995.

*   *   *

    Some critics responded to Storm Constantine's first novel, *The Enchantments of Flesh and Spirit,* by calling it "punk fantasy." Five books later, this is seen to be misleading, if it was ever relevant. Constantine is best defined in that context as a post-punk Goth. Much more significant is the recurrent theme of her novels, sex and sexuality, and the adaptation of the human body in relation to sex.

    The first three novels, which form the Wraeththu trilogy, show a major development in writing ability, as one would expect, but this is reflected in an over-emphasis in imagery the detriment of the story itself. *Enchantments* opens in fairly standard style, with the young boy Pellaz leaving home with the mysterious Wraeththu stranger Cal. As they travel, and as Pellaz is incepted as Wraeththu, the details of Constantine's world emerge. In a post-collapse world, a new breed of humans have emerged. The Wraeththu are hermaphrodites of outstanding health, fitness, and beauty, and Constantine, with the enthusiasm of a young author, takes great delight in some bizarre physical descriptions as Pellaz is changed into Har (as the Wraeththu are also known.) Wraeththu also live in tribes, and their lives are frequently ritualised.

    Against this background, Pellaz and Cal travel until Pellaz is killed in an ambush. From here things become obscured by mysticism: Pellaz is made ruler of the dominant Wraeththu tribe, advised and controlled by Thiede, supposedly the first and most powerful Wraeththu. The second book, however, makes it clear that the real story is Cal's. *The Bewitchments of Love And Hate* is set amongst the Varr tribe whom Cal and Pellaz had visited in book one. This volume is perhaps the best of the three, the prose is tighter than

before, and the plot deals closely with several complex and interacting relationships. Cal has come from a nasty background, and in *Bewitchments* he becomes more rounded, though not necessarily softened, as a character. The controlling hand of Thiede becomes clear, and Cal briefly becomes a victim. Constantine confuses good and evil cleverly, avoiding the usual simplistic approach of fantasy. In this book her language is both emotive and descriptive.

    Cal himself narrates the final book, *The Fulfillments of Fate and Desire,* but the plot becomes convoluted, wrapped in the symbolism of Cabbala, and is frequently obscure. Ultimately the final dramatic climax, the complete re-union of Pellaz and Cal, and the apparent success of Thiede's designs, does force its way through to clarity, but much of what precedes it is either fraught with heavy symbolism or desultory and delaying.

    Unfortunately, her next book, *The Monstrous Regiment* proves to be a major disappointment. It has the appearance of a feminist fantasy at first, but there are confusions. The world of Artemis is colonised by breakaway feminists and their male supporters, but it has been corrupted into the worst of matriarchies, leaving rebellion simmering. The innocent young Corrinna is caught up in this, first by hiding the fugitive Elvon L'Belder, and then by her adoption by the military chief Carmenya as a lover. The consequences of these events are profound, even extreme, and in one scene at least, very nasty. One side of the plot also involves the mysterious, indigenous Greylids, suitably alien. The book ought to have been a major landmark in Constantine's career. Instead, the over-characterization of some minor players slows vital action down, and the exaggeration of the sadistic Dominatrix stretches credibility. Nevertheless, these might have been minor quibbles but for the woolly thinking behind much of the politics, in what is clearly intended as a political statement, and the transcendent ending to the Greylids strand is awkward. There is to be a sequel, *The Aleph,* which may clear up some of the vagaries of this book.

    Sexuality is the key to Constantine's work; sexual politics underlies *The Monstrous Regiment,* and *Hermetech,* her latest novel, is also about sex. Much of the magic of the Wraeththu involves ritual sex, and Hermetech is defined as "the science of orgasmic energy potential esp. within fixed unit (within time, space)." Constantine is never a simple writer, and while much of this novel is about 14-year-old Ari Famber preparing to lose her virginity, that gives no hint of the complexities involved.

    Like the previous book, *Hermetech* is set both in the city and the country. Ari grows up close to an artificial henge, sight of festivals worshiping Isis-Confidentia, an orbiting AI. Her father, long dead, had altered Ari genetically; his former colleague, Leila Saatchi, now a "natro," a renegade from the Tech-Green revolution, visits the henge with her gang, and Ari leaves for the city with her. Meanwhile, in the city, Zambia Crevecoeur, a male prostitute, has been surgically altered so that he now has six extra sex organs, in his stomach. Behind him, several different figures are playing games and manipulating people to their own ends, including the mysterious Tammuz Malamute, whose real identity is guessable quite early. The central plot twists Ari and Zambia together, and it is obvious why. Ari's orgasm is always going to be the climax of the novel, and at times the rest is just distraction, or confusing info-dump.

    In her first novel, Constantine's scenery tends to the stock: forest, desert, mountains. By the fifth she is creating a real world, with real characters. Her preoccupations, however, sex, and the development and adaptation of the body, leave the reader only slightly satisfied. All the skills are there for Constantine to produce a major novel, but she hasn't done it yet. The promise remains unfulfilled.

Storm Constantine has continued to explore the ideas of sexuality, the human body, and ritual that informed her earliest works, but in her ninth novel, *Calenture,* she also makes explicit other recurring aspects of her work: travel through a strange landscape, and the mysterious controlling figure behind the characters involved.

The plot of *Calenture* is, like that of the Wraeththu novels, a Gulliveresque narrative, though the landscapes are more fully realised than in Constantine's early novels. In its two main strands the outcast euthanasiast priest, Ays, and the young tribesman Finnegan on his rite-of-passage expedition, travel between the bizarre moving cities along the desert floor following patterns laid by Finnegan's fellow Terranauts.

A third strand, however, suggests the controlling hand of Casmeer, the last man alive in Thermidore. Casmeer spends his days cataloguing the history of Thermidore and defending the crystallized form inhabitants of the city against winged scavengers, and his nights inventing the story of Ays and Finnegan. To his confusion Casmeer also appears to play a significant if unexplained role within the story as well.

Calenture is Storm Constantine's best novel to date. She is perhaps slightly too engrossed in her own imaginative powers. By frequently writing about decadence in fin-de-siècle universes she is occasionally lured into decadent writing herself. Nevertheless, her lush exoticism and imaginative mysticism have made her a popular writer, and her growing technical skills combine with a developing personal morality to bring her ever closer to fulfilling obvious potential.

—Kev P. McVeigh

COOK, Glen (Charles)

Pseudonym: Greg Stevens. **Nationality:** American. **Born:** New York City, 9 July 1944. **Education:** Roseville Joint Union High School, California; University of Missouri, Columbia, 2 years. **Military Service:** Served in the United States Navy. **Family:** Married Carol Ann Fritz in 1971; three sons. **Career:** Since 1965, assembly, inspection, material control, and supervisory jobs, General Motors, St. Louis. **Agent:** Russell Galen, Scovil Chichak Galen Inc., 381 Park Ave. South, Suite 1020, New York, New York 10016. **Address:** 4106 Flora Place, St. Louis, Missouri 63110, U.S.A.

SCIENCE FICTION PUBLICATIONS

Novels (series: Black Company; Darkwar; Dread Empire; Garrett Files; Starfishers)

The Heirs of Babylon. New York, Signet, 1972.
A Shadow of All Night Falling (Dread Empire). New York, Berkley, 1979.
October's Baby (Dread Empire). New York, Berkley, 1980.
All Darkness Met (Dread Empire). New York, Berkley, 1980.
The Swordbearer. New York, Timescape, 1982.
Shadowline (Starfishers). New York, Warner, 1982.
Starfishers. New York, Warner, 1982.
Stars' End (Starfishers). New York, Warner, 1982.

The Fire in His Hands (Dread Empire). New York, Timescape, 1984.
The Black Company. New York, Tor, 1984; London, Roc, 1992.
Shadows Linger (Black Company). New York, Tor, 1984; London, Roc, 1992.
Passage at Arms. New York, Popular Library, 1985.
A Matter of Time. New York, Ace, 1985.
With Mercy Toward None (Dread Empire). New York, Baen, 1985.
The White Rose (Black Company). New York, Tor, 1985; London, Roc, 1992.
Doomstalker (Darkwar). New York, Popular Library, 1985.
Warlock (Darkwar). New York, Warner, 1985.
Annals of the Black Company (includes *The Black Company, Shadows Linger,* and *The White Rose*). Garden City, New York, Doubleday, 1986.
Ceremony (Darkwar). New York, Popular Library, 1986.
Sweet Silver Blues (Garrett). New York, Signet, 1987.
Reap the East Wind (Dread Empire). New York, Tor, 1987.
An Ill Fate Marshalling (Dread Empire). New York, Tor, 1988.
The Dragon Never Sleeps. New York, Popular Library, 1988.
Bitter Gold Hearts (Garrett). New York, Signet, 1988.
Cold Copper Tears (Garrett). New York, Signet, 1988.
The Garrett Files (omnibus). Garden City, New York, Doubleday, 1989.
Old Tin Sorrows: From the Files of Garrett, P.I. New York, Signet, 1989.
The Tower of Fear. New York, Tor, 1989; London, Grafton, 1991.
Shadow Games: First Book of the South (Black Company). New York, Tor, 1989.
The Silver Spike (Black Company). New York, Tor, 1989.
Sung in Blood. Cambridge, Massachusetts, NESFA Press, 1990.
Dreams of Steel: Second Book of the South (Black Company). New York, Tor, 1990.
Dread Brass Shadows: From the Files of Garrett, P.I. New York, Roc, 1990.
Red Iron Nights (Garrett). New York, Roc, 1991.
Deadly Quicksilver Lies (Garrett). New York, Roc, 1994.

OTHER PUBLICATIONS

Novel

The Swap Academy (as Greg Stevens). San Diego, Publisher's Export Corp., 1970.

Other

A Glen Cook Bibliography, with Roger C. Schlobin. N.p., n.p., 1983.

*   *   *

There are times when the early success of an author with a particular work appears to constrain him to continue in that vein. While this provides readers with a continuing set of characters and familiar settings, it tends to put limitations on an author's growth. Glen Cook is a writer who seems interested in writing in diverse forms, but who constantly returns to the devices which were most successful.

Cook's first few pieces of fiction appeared in the early 1970s, of which the most notable are the short story "In the Wind" and a post holocaust novel featuring the crew of a surviving naval destroyer, *The Heirs of Babylon*. The novel attracted considerable attention because of the realistic descriptions of the aftermath of a nuclear conflict, but Cook failed to follow up with additional fiction until after its impact had been forgotten. After being almost entirely inactive in the latter part of the decade, Cook began to appear primarily at novel length with a rapid succession of science fiction and fantasy series.

The first of these was the initial appearance of "The Dread Empire," consisting of *A Shadow of All Night Falling, October's Baby,* and *All Darkness Met.* Although basically a derivative fantasy adventure series involving wizardry, an epic war, flawless heroes and vicious villains, there was an undeniable raw power to this series which gained it a considerable following. Less successful was a non-series fantasy adventure, *The Swordbearer,* the story of a hero with an enchanted sword.

The "Starfishers" trilogy, *Shadowline, Starfishers,* and *Star's End,* also had an heroic theme, transplanted into space. Two powerful groups contend in a battle that starts with a raid on a planet where humans were held as slaves by the alien Sangaree. Subsequent adventures involve secret agents of the human confederation, efforts to manage a valuable alien species on the periphery of the conflict, and the emergence of a new threat from the center of the galaxy. An additional volume, *Passage at Arms,* was published after a gap of three years, completing the struggle against an overwhelming army of alien invaders. Essentially space opera, the series made no serious impact on science fiction readers, and Cook's fans were clearly more interested in his fantasy creations.

The Fire in His Hands and its sequel, *With Mercy Toward None,* chronicled the rise and triumph of a desert warrior pitted against evil sorcery. At the same time, Cook began writing what may be his most popular series, *The Black Company.* Although as unrelentingly violent and simplistic in its characterization as most of Cook's earlier work, there is an undeniable energy in this sequence of battles and enchantments and heroic deeds, an enthusiasm which communicates itself to its readers. The initial trilogy, which includes *Shadows Linger* and *The White Rose,* follows the adventures of a group of mercenaries who are originally in the service of an evil sorceress, but who eventually decide that they've inadvertently sided with evil. They switch sides and are instrumental in destroying the power of an evil sorcery.

The solo novel *A Matter of Time* is very atypical of Cook's work, a time travel paradox story involving past, present, and future, still primarily action-oriented but displaying more thorough and intricate plotting and character development. Clearly Cook enjoyed more realistic settings, and he incorporated many of the devices of science fiction into his fantasy, but it was clear that his audience lay in the latter direction. His next trilogy uneasily blended science fiction and fantasy themes. Set against a primitive landscape, *Doomstalker, Warlock,* and *Ceremony* describe the interaction of technology and mental powers so strange as to seem magical. The protagonist is a woman who plans to use her paranormal psychic abilities in the cause of a plan to place orbiting mirrors around the world. Once they are in place, a new ice age afflicting the world could be brought to an end. This was Cook's most ambitious work in many ways, utilizing many of the devices of his earlier fiction, but with more self confidence and a serious theme.

Another nonseries novel, *The Dragon Never Sleeps,* deals with an interstellar fleet used to enforce a dictatorship until one man dis-covers a secret which will bring their domination to an end. But for the most part, Cook has spent recent years building upon the series he had already established.

Two more Dread Empire novels appeared, *Reap the East Wind* and *An Ill Fate Marshalling.* The freedom won in the original trilogy is now in jeopardy as enemies both ordinary and supernatural arise on all sides, and the protagonist of the earlier volumes unwisely involves himself in an attempt to undermine the Dread Empire itself. More smoothly written than the original trilogy, these two sequels are restatements of themes Cook has done better elsewhere.

The Black Company returned in *Shadow Games: First Book of the South.* Devastated by their earlier battles, the mercenaries set off on a new mission, beset by a new supernatural menace. The company has been defeated and dispersed in *Dreams of Steel: Second Book of the South,* wherein one survivor tries to raise a new force, still opposed by the inhuman Shadowmasters. Finally, in *The Silver Spike,* both sides have been eliminated, except that an artifact exists which may allow the evil to return to a world from which the Black Company has finally removed itself.

Sweet Silver Blues introduced a new series, a new premise, a likable private detective in a world of elves, ogres, vampires, and other fantastic creatures. It was also the first novel by Cook to display any real humor, a light approach that was essentially new territory. In *Bitter Gold Hearts, Cold Copper Tears, Old Tin Sorrows: From the Files of Garrett, P.I., Dread Brass Shadows: From the Files of Garrett, Deadly Quicksilver Lies,* and *Red Iron Nights,* Garrett pursues a number of cases including kidnapping, ghostly revenge, and lost treasures. Although the series is probably the best work Cook has done, it seems to have been directed at a different readership than the one he had already acquired.

Cook's most recent work is a solo fantasy novel, *The Tower of Fear,* easily his best non-science fiction novel. Although Cook has occasionally published short fiction during his career, most of these are of minor interest, and several were subsequently incorporated into novels. During the early 1990s, he produced almost no new work despite continuing interest by readers and publishers alike. Hopefully, he is using this period to consolidate what he has learned and will reemerge soon with even more impressive work.

—Don D'Ammassa

* * *

COOKE, Arthur. *See* LOWNDES, Robert A.W.

* * *

COOPER, Edmund

Pseudonym: Richard Avery. **Nationality:** British. **Born:** Marple, Cheshire, 30 April 1926. **Education:** Manchester Grammar School, 1937-41; Didsbury Teachers Training College, Lancashire, 1946-47. Served as a radio officer in the British Merchant Navy, 1939-45. **Family:** Married 1) Joyce Plant in 1946, one daughter and three sons; 2) Valerie Makin in 1963, two sons and two daughters; 3) Dawn Freeman-Baker in 1980. Journalist, British Iron and Steel Research Association, London, 1960-61, and Federation of British Industries, London, 1962; staff writer, Esso Petroleum, London, 1962-66. After 1967, regular science fiction reviewer, *Sunday Times,* London. **Died:** 11 March 1982.

SCIENCE FICTION PUBLICATIONS

Novels

Deadly Image. New York, Ballantine, 1958; as *The Uncertain Midnight,* London, Hutchinson, 1958.

Seed of Light. London, Hutchinson, and New York, Ballantine, 1959.

Wish Goes to Slumber Land (for children). London, Hutchinson, 1960.

Transit: A Science Fiction Novel. London, Faber, and New York, Lancer, 1964.

All Fools' Day. London, Hodder and Stoughton, and New York, Walker, 1966.

A Far Sunset. London, Hodder and Stoughton, and New York, Walker, 1967.

Five to Twelve. London, Hodder and Stoughton, 1968; New York, Putnam, 1969.

Sea-Horse in the Sky. London, Hodder and Stoughton, 1969; New York, Putnam, 1970.

The Last Continent. New York, Dell, 1969; London, Hodder and Stoughton, 1970.

Son of Kronk. London, Hodder and Stoughton, 1970; as *Kronk: A Science Fiction Novel,* New York, Putnam, 1971.

The Overman Culture. London, Hodder and Stoughton, 1971; New York, Putnam, 1972.

Who Needs Men?: A Novel. London, Hodder and Stoughton, 1972; as *Gender Genocide,* New York, Ace, 1972.

The Cloud Walker: A Novel. London, Hodder and Stoughton, and New York, Ballantine, 1973.

The Tenth Planet: A Novel. London, Hodder and Stoughton, and New York, Putnam, 1973.

The Slaves of Heaven. New York, Putnam, 1974; London, Hodder and Stoughton, 1975.

Prisoner of Fire. London, Hodder and Stoughton, 1974; New York, Walker, 1976.

Merry Christmas, Ms. Minerva. London, Hale, 1978.

A World of Difference. London, Hale, 1980.

Novels as Richard Avery (series: The Expendables in all books)

The Deathworms of Kratos. London, Coronet, and New York, Fawcett, 1975; as Edmund Cooper, London, Severn House, 1977.

The Rings of Tantalus. London, Coronet, and New York, Fawcett, 1975.

The War Games of Zelos. London, Coronet, and New York, Fawcett, 1975; as Edmund Cooper, London, Coronet, 1980.

The Venom of Argus. London, Coronet, and New York, Fawcett, 1976.

Short Stories

Tomorrow's Gift. New York, Ballantine, 1958; London, Digit, 1959.

Voices in the Dark: Amazing Fantasy and Science Fiction! London, Digit, 1960.

Tomorrow Came: Twelve Stories of Many Dimensions. London, Panther, 1963.

News from Elsewhere. London, Mayflower, 1968; New York, Berkley, 1969.

The Square Root of Tomorrow. London, Hale, 1970.

Unborn Tomorrow. London, Hale, 1971.

Jupiter Laughs and Other Stories. London, Hodder and Stoughton, 1979.

*

Manuscript Collection: University of Wyoming, Laramie.

Edmund Cooper commented:

(1981) I believe, along with people like Kurt Vonnegut and J.G. Ballard and earlier illustrious writers such as George Orwell, Aldous Huxley, and H.G. Wells, that science fiction is the perfect medium for making a social or political statement. I am not interested greatly in gadgetry. I am interested passionately in the future of mankind. People matter to me far more than machines or innovations, which is why I concentrate on characterization in my novels. I try to entertain and believe I am successful in doing this; but basically I want to put up ideas for consideration by my readers. Voluminous correspondence assures me that I have succeeded in this end.

*   *   *

With the publication of his earliest novels and stories of the late 1950s, Edmund Cooper quickly established himself as an urbane stylist whose sometimes almost intuitive grasp of SF's key themes and images could distinguish his best fiction and almost redeem his lesser works. There is always a moment in a Cooper story when the "sense of wonder," so often cited as the basic emotional stance of science fiction, becomes concretized in a dramatic image or action, whether it be an encounter with a god who turns out to be a spaceship (*A Far Sunset*) or simply an epiphanal moment of self-discovery on a distant planet ("M81—Ursa Major").

Cooper's plots and characterizations do not always match his style and vision. His early stories and novels sometimes read almost as practice exercises in traditional science fiction themes: the revolt of androids in a "utopian" society (*That Uncertain Midnight*), time-travel paradoxes ("Repeat Performance"), generations-long space voyages (*Seed of Light*), the pitting of humans against a rival culture in a setting alien to both (*Transit: A Science Fiction Novel*). Such themes had been treated in earlier, classic SF stories, but for the most part Cooper succeeded in working his own variations on them. *That Uncertain Midnight,* for example, is unusual in its sympathetic portrayal of the dilemma of the androids, and *Transit* focuses sensitively on the character and emerging relationships of the four humans who find themselves stranded on an unknown planet. Though *Transit* shows that Cooper is capable of developing complex characterizations, he all too often reverts to the near-superman genius-hero of traditional pulp science fiction for his protagonists.

Perhaps the most persistent theme in Cooper, though it seldom emerges as more than background, is that of nuclear war. Nuclear war is the cause of the rise of the androids in *That Uncertain Midnight,* the dystopian state in "Tomorrow's Gift" (one of his finest short stories), the escape from earth in *Seed of Light,* the destruction of the entire human race in *The Overman Culture,* the dominion of satellite cities over Earth in *The Slaves of Heaven,* and the rise of the antitechnological Luddite society in *The Cloud Walker: A Novel,* the best-received and most successful of his novels in the United States. Though it might be misleading to categorize Cooper as a simple technophobe, his cautionary attitude toward technology is also revealed in a number of stories in which "primitive," nontechnological societies are shown to be morally superior to decadent technological ones. This is a theme of "The Enlightened Ones," *A Far Sunset,* and *The Slaves of Heaven. A Far Sunset,* in fact, is one of SF's more sophisticated treatments of an anthropological theme in its depiction of an alien society and its mythology.

Perhaps because he published little in the American magazines, Cooper never established a strong following among American readers. Perhaps because he belonged in the early 1950s tradition of John Wyndham and John Christopher, his reputation began to wane after the changes wrought in British science fiction during the New Wave of the late 1960s. In any event, his works in the 1970s took an increasingly conservative and sometimes unpleasant turn, especially apparent in his "Richard Avery" novels and his antifeminist novels of societies dominated by women, *Five to Twelve* and *Who Needs Men?: A Novel.* Occasionally, however, he was able to incorporate some of the New Wave ideas with some success. *The Overman Culture,* for example, features an enjoyably surrealistic portrait of a London in which Victoria reigns, Churchill is prime minister, and the young hero is Michael Faraday. All this gives way eventually to a traditional SF explanation, which is nevertheless ingenious and does not destroy the novel's sense of playful fantasy.

By the time of his death in 1982, Cooper had come to be regarded as a minor, if competent, novelist in a somewhat outmoded tradition. His reputation was probably further damaged by the ugliness of some of his later works. But at best, he was a writer capable of witty and literate variations on familiar themes, and one who for all his faults managed to establish a clear identity despite his use of such themes.

—Gary K. Wolfe

COPPEL, Alfred

Pseudonyms: Robert Cham Gilman; A.C. Marin. **Nationality:** American. **Born:** Oakland, California, 9 November 1921. **Education:** Menlo College, Menlo Park, California; Stanford University, California, 1939-42. **Military Service:** Served in the United States Army Air Force, 1942-45: First Lieutenant. **Family:** Married Elizabeth Ann Schorr in 1943; one son and one daughter. **Career:** Technical writer for Philco West Development Laboratories, Palo Alto, California, 1957-58; public relations executive in San Francisco, 1958-62. Since 1962, freelance writer: **Agent:** Virginia Kidd, 538 East Harford, P.O. 278, Milford, PA 18337, U.S.A.

SCIENCE FICTION PUBLICATIONS

Novels (series: Goldenwing)

Dark December. Greenwich, Connecticut, Fawcett, 1960; London, Jenkins, 1966.

The Dragon. New York, Harcourt Brace, and London, Macmillan, 1977.
The Burning Mountain: A Novel of the Invasion of Japan. San Diego, Harcourt Brace, 1983; London, Corgi, 1985.
Glory (Goldenwing). New York, Tor, 1993.
Glory's War (Goldenwing). New York, Tor, 1995.

Novels as Robert Cham Gilman (series: Rhada)

The Rebel of Rhada. New York, Harcourt Brace, 1968; London, Gollancz, 1970.
The Navigator of Rhada. New York, Harcourt Brace, 1969; London, Gollancz, 1971.
The Starkahn of Rhada. New York, Harcourt Brace, 1970.
The Warlock of Rhada. New York, Ace, 1985.

OTHER PUBLICATIONS

Novels

Hero Driver. New York, Crown, 1954.
Night of Fire and Snow. New York, Simon and Schuster, 1957.
A Certainty of Love. New York, Harcourt Brace, 1966; London, Heinemann, 1967.
The Gate of Hell. New York, Harcourt Brace, 1967.
Order of Battle. New York, Harcourt Brace, 1968; London, Hutchinson, 1969.
A Little Time for Laughter. New York, Harcourt Brace, 1969.
Between the Thunder and the Sun. New York, Harcourt Brace, 1971.
The Landlocked Man. New York, Harcourt Brace, 1972; London, Macmillan, 1975.
Thirty-Four East. New York, Harcourt Brace, and London, Macmillan, 1974.
The Hastings Conspiracy. New York, Holt Rinehart, and London, Macmillan, 1980.
The Apocalypse Brigade. New York, Holt Rinehart, and London, Macmillan, 1981.
The Marburg Chronicles: A Novel. New York, Dutton, 1985; as *The Fates Command Us: A Novel,* London, Methuen, 1986.
Show Me a Hero. London, Methuen, and San Diego, Harcourt Brace, 1987.
A Land of Mirrors. San Diego, Harcourt Brace, 1988; London, Methuen, 1989.
Wars and Winters. New York, Fine, 1993; Sutton, Surrey, Severn House, 1994.
The Eighth Day of the Week. New York, Fine, 1994.

Novels as A.C. Marin

The Clash of Distant Thunder. New York, Harcourt Brace, 1968.
Rise with the Wind. New York, Harcourt Brace, 1969; London, Heinemann, 1970.
A Storm of Spears. New York, Harcourt Brace, 1971; London, Hale, 1973.

Other

The Korean War: Uncertain Victory: The Concluding Volume of an Oral History, with Donald Knox. New York, Harcourt Brace, 1988.

The Architect's World. N.p., n.d.

*

Bibliography: In *Fiction! Series One* edited by Dan Tooker and Roger Hofheins, New York, Harcourt Brace, 1976.

Manuscript Collection: Boston University.

Alfred Coppel comments:

I began writing in the SF genre for two reasons: first, it was a field that did not limit the imagination (untrained though it might be) of a young writer, and second, I had read SF since early youth—and I believed then (as I still do) that a writer should write what he enjoys reading.

I have since turned to writing "general" novels, but I am told there is still a bit of the SF writer's mark on my work. I accept this with pride. Those of us who learned our craft in the hard school of the SF magazines learned early on to be professionals. To my mind, there is no higher praise that can be bestowed on a writer.

I am pleased to report that after a hiatus of many years of laboring in the vineyard of "mainstream fiction," I am at work on a serious work of science fiction. By God, you can go home again.

*   *   *

Although Alfred Coppel has done most of his writing in other fields, his few contributions to science fiction have been almost invariably among the better attempts in the field. His novel *Dark December,* for example, is one of the best postnuclear war novels ever to appear, far superior to many whose titles are better known.

His more straightforward novels in the genre consist of the Rhada trilogy written under the pseudonym of Robert Cham Gilman. Man's interstellar empire has collapsed into a feudal society that is a mixture of science and magic, spaceships and incantations. Against this background, Coppel wrote three adventures of young men attempting to come to grips with the stresses and internal contradictions of their society. Although writing ostensibly for younger readers, Coppel has not pulled any punches. The novels deal explicitly with the seamier side of human acquisitiveness and the urge for power. The cyclic drive to self-destruction is an almost ever-present backdrop against which the characters play out their lives.

Coppel uses his settings and plots to examine his characters, rather than just employ characters as animated tour guides of exotic landscapes. The protagonist of *Dark December* is a fighter pilot who wanders across an America torn by nuclear bombs, plagues, famine, and human savagery. But it is not his adventures with which the reader is concerned, but the effects of those adventures on him as he grows increasingly desperate to discover the fate of his missing family.

In recent years, Coppel's closest approach to science fiction has consisted of a pair of excellent near-future political novels. In *Thirty-Four East,* the world is on the brink of conflagration as the president is apparently assassinated, and the vice-president is held hostage by Arab terrorists intent upon the destruction of Israel. In Washington, the generals move to fill the power vacuum, while across the ocean a weak premier of the Soviet Union begins to succumb to pressure from his own generals. The only chance to sidetrack the headlong movement toward war is to rescue the vice-president. The situation is similar in *The Dragon.* The Red Chinese have developed a new weapon which gives them effective superiority over the Russians. Unless the president can somehow restore the balance of power, a war between the two Communist giants is inevitable, and it is just as certain that the rest of the world will be drawn into the confrontation. In both cases, Coppel has captured the reins of suspense firmly, and linked them to a credible sequence of political and personal events. Each novel is complex and satisfying, and it is interesting to speculate about Coppel's possible achievements had he devoted his efforts primarily to science fiction, rather than remaining as diversified in his interests as he has.

Some hint of that may be found in his SF thriller *The Burning Mountain.* Alternate histories have long been fertile ground for genre writers and mainstream writers alike, and Coppel now speculates about what would have transpired if the atomic bomb tests had resulted in failure. After investing considerable effort in researching the war plans of both the United States and Japanese governments, he constructed a novel that deals with the invasion of mainland Japan by Allied troops. Outside of the basic premise, the novel really isn't science fiction at all, just another World War II adventure story, but it is an outstanding achievement regardless of what category might claim it. With a large cast of characters, depressingly convincing descriptions of the unfolding events, and Coppel's clear, gripping style, it is clearly among his very best efforts.

Coppel wrote many short stories early in his career, most of which were above average in quality. Possibly his most successful is "The Last Night of Summer" (in *The End of the World,* edited by Donald A. Wollheim, New York, Ace, 1956). Stellar evolution has caused a change in the energy output of the sun, and an astronomical event is imminent that will briefly make the Earth uninhabitable. Except for a limited number granted a place in the Burrows, shelters constructed underground, the entire human population will be wiped out within a few days. The protagonist murders his wife and sacrifices his own chance at life in order to provide a chance of survival for his two daughters. It is one of the most brutal and one of the most effective world disaster stories of all times, accomplishing more in a few pages than is usually done in entire books.

—Don D'Ammassa

CORBETT, Chan. *See* **SCHACHNER, Nat.**

CORBIN, Michael. *See* **CARTMILL, Cleve.**

CORNISH, F. *See* **BRYNING, Frank.**

CORREN, Grace. *See* **HOSKINS, Robert.**

CORREY, Lee. *See* **STINE, G. Harry.**

COSTELLO, P.F. *See* **PHILLIPS, Rog.**

COTTON, John. *See* **FEARN, John Russell.**

COULSON, Juanita (Ruth)

Pseudonym: John J. Wells. **Nationality:** American. **Born:** Juanita Ruth Wellons, Anderson, Indiana, 12 February 1933. **Education:** Ball State University, Muncie, Indiana, B.S. 1954, M.A. 1961. **Family:** Married the writer Robert Coulson, *q.v.,* in 1954; one son. **Career:** Elementary school teacher, Huntington, Indiana, 1954-55; collator, Heckman Book Bindery, North Manchester, Indiana, 1955-57; publisher, *SFWA Forum,* two years. Since 1953, editor, with Robert Coulson, *Yandro* fan magazine; since 1963, freelance writer. **Awards:** Hugo award, for editing, 1965. Guest of Honor, World Science Fiction Convention, 1972. **Agent:** Virginia Kidd, 538 East Harford Street, Milford, Pennsylvania 18337, U.S.A. **Address:** 2677W 500N, Hartford City, Indiana 47348, U.S.A.

SCIENCE FICTION PUBLICATIONS

Novels (series: Children of the Stars; Kranton)

Crisis on Cheiron. New York, Ace, 1967.
The Singing Stones. New York, Ace, 1968.
Unto the Last Generation. Don Mills, Ontario, Laser, 1975.
Space Trap. Toronto, Laser, 1976.
The Web of Wizardry (Kranton). New York, Ballantine, 1978.
The Death God's Citadel (Kranton). New York, Ballantine, 1980.
Children of the Stars:
  Tomorrow's Heritage. New York, Ballantine, 1981.
  Outward Bound. New York, Ballantine, 1982.
  Legacy of Earth. New York, Ballantine, 1989.
  The Past of Forever. New York, Ballantine, 1989.
Star Sister. New York, Ballantine, 1990.

OTHER PUBLICATIONS

Novels

The Secret of Seven Oaks. New York, Berkley, 1972.
Door into Terror. New York, Berkley, 1972.
Stone of Blood. New York, Ballantine, 1975.

Fear Stalks the Bayou. New York, Ballantine, and Skirden, Lancashire, Magna, 1976.
Dark Priestess. New York, Ballantine, 1977.
Fire of the Andes. New York, Ballantine, 1979.

*

Juanita Coulson comments:

Before I could write, my mother transcribed my earliest attempts at storytelling. For my eighth Christmas, she gave me a typewriter, compounding the felony. In a sense, I have been writing fiction since before I could write. My only interest was in concocting characters and adventures that satisfied an audience of one—me. It wasn't until I was in my 30s that Marion Zimmer Bradley insisted I should submit my work professionally. Without her encouragement, I never would have made the effort. I am still surprised to find that some people actually pay me for writing stories I wrote so long ago solely for my own entertainment. Other than the fun of creating, my aims are to follow two maxims: There Are No Simple Answers and Take The Long View. To some degree, I share Marion Bradley's theory that a villain is just a protagonist with a different point of view; the story *might* have been told from the villain's position, *if* he (or she) is a valid character to start with. And in any story, I don't think all the questions can be answered—certainly not completely. People—and characters—are too complex. As for The Long View, its a humbling rule to write by, but it serves me equally in science fiction, contemporary women's genre fiction, or a historical romance set in 1770 B.C. The Long View ought to be an essential ingredient of all SF, especially considering the past and future history of humanity *and* of other species, known and unknown, and cosmology. Putting us in our place in that immense scheme of things is, for me, the foundation of a sense of wonder.

*   *   *

Since its first appearance in 1963, Juanita Coulson's writing has included science fiction of both the speculative and the adventurous varieties, heroic fantasy, romantic suspense (Gothics), and historical romances, as well as occasional nonfiction.

Her first story, "Another Rib," a collaboration with Marion Zimmer Bradley, tells of a group of men, the only survivors of a destroyed Earth, and what happens when alien medical technology offers them an unconventional way of perpetuating the human species. The theme is handled with skill and delicacy, resulting in a memorable story.

Coulson's first novel, *Crisis on Cheiron,* deals with the struggle of a small band of allies to save an undeveloped planet from economic and ecological ruin at the hands of an unscrupulous Terran corporation. In *The Singing Stones* another world is in peril: Pa-Liina, with its quasi-telepathic Stones of Song, suffering under the domination of its decadent sister world Deliyas. In both novels the alien environment is well thought out and convincingly portrayed, and the scientific underpinnings are given colorful settings and action reminiscent of the work of Leigh Brackett and Marion Zimmer Bradley. The theme of an alien world suffering the unwelcome attentions of Earthmen is also present in "A Helping Hand": this time the Earthmen's intentions are benevolent, but their complete misunderstanding of the world they are trying to help leads to disaster.

Unto the Last Generation is the story of a future Earth where population control has been all too successful, rendering most of mankind infertile. The young battle with the old for the inadequate supplies of food distributed by a military government, while a group of scientists work in secret, trying to ensure humanity's survival. *Space Trap* deals with the first contact between Earthmen and a telepathic civilization from across the galaxy, as representatives of both groups battle for control of a remote planet on which they are trapped.

"Unscheduled Flight" is more anecdote than story; it sets up an interesting parallel-worlds situation but does nothing with it. Two long fantasy novels, *The Web of Wizardry* and *The Death God's Citadel,* are both set in the same imaginary world, in which sorcery and the presence of supernatural beings are facts of everyday existence. The backgrounds (geographical, cultural, and linguistic) are worked out in detail; the characters are interesting and the action well-paced, resulting in two very entertaining adventures. Two earlier short stories, "Wizard of Death" and "The Dragon of Tor-Nali," are set in the same world as the novels.

Coulson's best work to date is found in her multigenerational family saga which bears the overall title "Children of the Stars." The first volume, *Tomorrow's Heritage,* introduces the Saunder family, owners of one of Earth's most powerful industrial and communications conglomerates in the early 21st century. The focus is on the three Saunder children: Patrick, leader of a fiercely isolationist political party, opposed to any extraterrestrial colonization or contact; Mariette, a supporter of the manmade satellite, the Goddard Colony; and Todd, who has just established electronic contact with an extraterrestrial spacecraft heading toward Earth. The conflicts among the children, and between them and their autocratic mother, are set forth in a rich and emotionally complex story. The saga continues in *Outward Bound, Legacy of Earth,* and *The Past of Forever.*

—R. E. Briney

COULSON, Robert (Stratton)

Pseudonym: Thomas Stratton (with Gene DeWeese). **Nationality:** American. **Born:** Sullivan, Indiana, 12 May 1928. **Education:** Silver Lake High School; studied electrical engineering, International Correspondence School, 1960. **Family:** Married Juanita Coulson, *q.v.,* in 1954; one son. **Career:** Cemetery caretaker, 1941-43; wool bagger, 1944; house painter, 1945-47; bookbinder, Heckman Book Bindery, North Manchester, Indiana, 1945-57; draftsman and technical writer, Honeywell Corporation, 1957-65; draftsman, 1965-76; order writer, Overhead Door of Indiana, Hartford City, 1976-86. Since 1953, editor, with Juanita Coulson, *Yandro* fan magazine; since 1984, reviewer, *Comic Buyer's Guide.* **Awards:** Hugo award for editing, 1965. Guest of Honor, World Science Fiction Convention, 1972. **Agent:** Virginia Kidd, Box 278, Milford, Pennsylvania 18337, U.S.A. **Address:** 2677W 500N, Hartford City, Indiana 47348, U.S.A.

SCIENCE FICTION PUBLICATIONS

Novels (series: Joe Karns)

The Invisibility Affair (with Gene DeWeese as Thomas Stratton). New York, Ace, 1967.

The Mind-Twisters Affair (with Gene DeWeese as Thomas Stratton). New York, Ace, 1967.

Gates of the Universe (Karns), with Gene DeWeese. Don Mills, Ontario, Laser, 1975.

Now You See It/Him/Them . . . (Karns), with Gene DeWeese. Garden City, New York, Doubleday, 1975; London, Hale, 1976.

To Renew the Ages. Toronto, Laser, 1976.

But What of Earth?, with Piers Anthony. Toronto, Laser, 1976.

Charles Fort Never Mentioned Wombats (Karns), with Gene DeWeese. New York, Doubleday, 1977; London, Hale, 1978.

Nightmare Universe, with Gene DeWeese. Lake Geneva, Wisconsin, TSR, 1985.

High Spy. Lake Geneva, Wisconsin, TSR, 1987.

*

Robert Coulson comments:

First of all, I don't write because I have any burning desire to tell stories, or to influence the masses, or even to be admired (though I suppose the last might have some bearing on my writing). I write professional fiction because it's the most enjoyable way I've found to make money. Not the most reliable—which is why I work at a regular job and write as a sideline—but the most enjoyable. Since writing is extra income, rather than my living, I can afford to write pretty much what I like. What I like, mostly, is humor: puns, incongruities, parody, satire (not farce: I seldom find farce particularly funny). Basically, I don't take writing—my own, or anyone else's—seriously, and I'll make fun of a writer who shows that he takes himself overly seriously. I try to be entertaining, and any profundities will be slipped in gently and (I hope) well hidden. Any influencing of the reader in a work of fiction should be subtle.

Fortunately for our coauthorship, Gene DeWeese has much the same sense of humor that I have; once one of our books is finished and in print, it's impossible even for us to remember exactly who wrote what. Saves a lot of disagreement during the writing.

*   *   *

Robert Coulson has been an SF fan since the 1940s and has been involved in amateur SF journalism for more than 25 years. His journalism work has been entirely nonfiction, humorous articles, and the incisive reviews he still writes for his and his wife's magazine, *Yandro.* Coulson has remained active as an SF fan even after becoming a professional writer.

Most of Coulson's science fiction writing has been done in collaboration with his longtime friend Gene DeWeese. In 1967, under the name Thomas Stratton, Coulson and DeWeese wrote two paperback spinoffs from *The Man from U.N.C.L.E.* TV series. *The Invisibility Affair* involved THRUSH's use of an invisible dirigible in their latest plan for conquest. One of the chapter titles from the book ("Charles Fort Never Mentioned Sandbags") would turn up 10 years later, transmuted into the title of another Coulson/DeWeese collaboration. In *The Mind-Twisters Affair,* Napoleon Solo and Illya Kuryakin foil a THRUSH attempt to control the minds of world-famous scientists. Both books feature the unlikely situations and offbeat humor which made the television series so popular.

The Coulson/DeWeese novel *Gates of the Universe* is the story of a bulldozer operator and would-be SF writer, Ross Allen, who is accidentally whisked from Earth to the planet Venntra through a Probe Gate, a means of alien interstellar transportation. Both the bulldozer and Allen's SF background aid him in coping with the dangers of a world threatened by the antics of an apparently mad computer. *Now You See It/Him/ Them . . .*, a combination murder mystery and SF novel of psi powers, is set at a science fiction convention. A follow-up novel, *Charles Fort Never Mentioned Wombats,* takes place in Australia, among a group of science fiction fans on their way to attend the World Science Fiction Convention in Melbourne. The trip is complicated by assorted encounters with extraterrestrials.

All of the Coulson/DeWeese collaborations, as well as Coulson's individual work, involve standard SF ingredients, handled with skill, humor, and occasionally a refreshing irreverence. They also employ the practice of "Tuckerizing," named after the SF fan and writer Wilson Tucker: using the names of family, friends, and well-known SF figures for characters in the story. This is not noticeable to the general reader, but can prove distracting to those who are familiar with the names.

Coulson's only solo novels to date are *To Renew the Ages* and *High Spy. To Renew the Ages* is set in a sparsely populated North America after a nuclear war, and chronicles the hero's battle against an unknown telepathic menace which is threatening the safety of the scattered pockets of civilization. His search for the source of the danger leads him into contact with the remarkable heroine, Tamara Bush, and the matriarchal society which she represents.

"Soy la Libertad" is an alternate-world story, telling of the aftermath of a political assassination in a version of North America where Texas, the Confederacy, the Five Indian Nations, and the Mormons' Deseret are separate countries, not part of the United States. Based on the author's broad knowledge of history and told with a nicely calculated irony, it is a memorable story.

Coulson's name also appeared as coauthor on *But What of Earth?,* but Coulson merely revised a manuscript submitted by Piers Anthony. The result, after further changes by editorial hands, was unsatisfactory to both writers.

—R.E. Briney

COVER, Arthur Byron

Pseudonym: Thomas Shadwell (joint pseudonym). **Nationality:** American. **Born:** Grundy, Virginia, 14 January 1950. **Education:** Virginia Polytechnic Institute, Blacksburg, B.A. 1971. **Career:** Member of the extension faculty, University of California, Los Angeles; interviewer, *Vertex,* Los Angeles, 1974-75. **Agent:** Jane Rotrosen Agency, 318 East 51st Street, New York, New York 10022, U.S.A.

SCIENCE FICTION PUBLICATIONS

Novels (series: Autumn Angels; Planetfall; Time Machine)

Autumn Angels. New York, Pyramid, 1975.
The Sound of Winter. New York, Pyramid, 1976.
An East Wind Coming (Angels). New York, Berkley, 1979.
Flash Gordon (novelization of motion picture). New York, Jove, and London, New English Library, 1980.

The Rings of Saturn (Time Machine; for young adults). New York, Bantam, 1985.
American Revolutionary (Time Machine, Angels; for young adults). New York, Bantam, 1985.
Blade of the Guillotine, illustrated by Scott Hampton (Time Machine). New York, Bantam, 1986.
Isaac Asimov's Robot City: Prodigy. New York, Ace, 1988.
Planetfall. New York, Avon, 1988.
Stationfall (Planetfall). New York, Avon, 1989.
Robert Silverberg's Time Tours: The Dinosaur Trackers, with Tim Sullivan and John Gregory Betancourt as Thomas Shadwell. New York, HarperPaperbacks, 1991.

Short Stories

The Platypus of Doom and Other Nihilists (Angels). New York, Warner, 1976.

*　　*　　*

The world of Arthur Byron Cover reads like a Classic Comics version of Hieronymus Bosch: grotesqueries there are aplenty, unexplained and inexplicable, wandering the bizarre landscape of a caricature Earth, interacting with each other in curious and unique ways, seeking neither resolution nor evolution nor solution, but just existing as they are. Forget about plots, forget about the conventionalities of science fiction or fantasy, or of fiction in general: you won't find them here. What you *will* find are orts from Cover's intellectual table, pieces and snatches of characters, conversations, situations, perambulations, rearranged in new and interesting ways.

Take, for example, Cover's first novel, *Autumn Angels.* We see a strange, far-future or other-dimensional Earth dominated by godlike beings scrapping over philosophical nullities while trying to establish his or her own position. Each has assumed the guise of a well-known fictional character of the past—from the comicbooks, pulp fiction, motion pictures, or television—and is known to the reader only by the label of his or her choice ("the demon," "the lawyer," "the fat man," "the other fat man," etc.). The only named characters are two "bems" ("bug-eyed monsters" in SF parlance), Dwit and Xit, the aliens who had originally metamorphosed the race of man into "godlike man" as a joke. The plot, if such exists, meanders back and forth across a landscape of broken conversations and philosophical musings. Each of these beings is searching for a unique identity in a world where individuations have failed; each seeks something to give it purpose: a name, a self, a reason. But the best that the demon, the lawyer, and the fat man can do at story's end, with all of their immense powers, is to cause the two alien bems to instill a sense of depression into their world, a form of negative identity that may help alter the stasis into which the godlike men have fallen.

The results of the trio's action can be seen in two later works by Cover, "The Clam of Catastrophe" (in the collection *The Platypus of Doom and Other Nihilists*) and the long novel *An East Wind Coming.* "Clam" introduces the character of the Consulting Detective, a pastiche of Sherlock Holmes, who is hired by the three beings to discover why sexism, which they have introduced into the world of the future to offset the effects of depression, has divided the godlike beings into two warring camps. To achieve the greatness of mere man, the detective ultimately concludes, godlike man must explore the ramifications of love, not sex.

An East Wind Coming, the author's major work of fiction, further explores the theme of identity, as the consulting detective and the good doctor must face the threat of a new Jack the Ripper, who is using an antimatter knife to disembowel female godlike beings. After murdering his final victim, the Seller of Speculations (i.e., a bookseller: Cover himself is co-owner of a science fiction shop), the ripper is forced by the detective to destroy himself, thus ending the threat to the godlike beings. The right of the individual to be individual has thus been affirmed.

Three other Cover novels deserve some mention. The author's second book, *The Sound of Winter,* relates the story of Michael St. Claire, a would-be revolutionary, and his mute sister, Elizabeth, who travel from the City to the Wasteland, seeking a new way of life. Ultimately, Elizabeth regains her tongue, but is killed by her husband, and Michael comes to the realization that he never really understood anything about his sister's character—or about life in general. The book reads like a 19th-century Russian travelogue, and remains one of the most accessible of his works..

Two recent books, *Planetfall* and *Stationfall* (plus *Futurefall,* an uncompleted third book in the projected trilogy), reflect a change in direction for Cover, utilizing more directly synthesized pulp and animation influences to produce deliberately farcical and very broadly based SF satire. Although billed as game tie-ins, these two fictions have very little to do with the actual games from which they were theoretically derived, but take various elements from hackneyed science fiction plots, reworking them à la Monty Python into a crazy patchwork of slapstick humor. Both are hilarious.

The author's other works include a readable novelization of the screenplay for *Flash Gordon,* three time-travel gamebooks for young adults, two tie-ins to series created by Isaac Asimov and Robert Silverberg, and a handful of short stories, the latest of which appeared in *Down & Dirty* (1988), the fifth of George R.R. Martin's Wild Cards mosaic novels. His most recent contributions have been to graphic stories in the comicbook *Disney Adventures.*

Cover's novels share a certain common framework, jumbling together elements from science fiction, the pulps, magic realism, detective fiction, music, comic books, movies, comedy, and the theatre into semi-coherent polemics about the manner in which people live their lives. The author's chief characters are quintessential outsiders trying to make some sense of an essentially meaningless existence. Cover was particularly influenced by the Fireside Theatre, having noted how the actors utilized odd remarks, lines, and themes from extremely diverse sources to create something unique and darkly satirical. He has tried to regenerate this feeling in his fiction, which is filled with non sequiturs, scrambled plots, and snatches of philosophy.

At its best, Cover's work is exciting and stimulating, filled with fresh ideas presented in new and unique ways. At its worst, his style can seem incomprehensible, tangled, even ponderous, and certainly different from the expectations of the average reader. But then, you can't always tell a book by its Cover.

—Robert Reginald

COWPER, Richard

Pseudonym for John Middleton Murry, Jr. **Other Pseudonyms:** Colin Murry; Colin Middleton Murry. **Nationality:** British. **Born:** Bridport, Dorset, 9 May 1926; son of the writer John Middleton Murry. **Education:** Rendcomb College, Gloucestershire, 1937-43;

Brasenose College, Oxford, 1948-50, B.A. (honors) in English 1950; University of Leicester, 1950-51. Served in the Royal Navy Fleet Air Arm, 1944-47. **Family:** Married Ruth Jezierski in 1950; two daughters. **Career:** English Master, Whittinghame College, Brighton, 1952-67; head of the English Department, Atlantic World College, Llantwit-Major, Glamorgan, 1967-70. **Agent:** A.P. Watt Ltd., 26-28 Bedford Row, London WC1R 4HL; or, Curtis Brown Associates, 575 Madison Avenue, New York, New York 10022, U.S.A. **Address:** Landscott, Lower Street, Dittisham, near Dartmouth, Devon TQ6 0HY, England.

SCIENCE FICTION PUBLICATIONS

Novels (series: The Birds of Kinship)

Breakthrough: A Novel. London, Dobson, 1967; New York, Ballantine, 1969.
Phoenix: A Novel. London, Dobson, 1968; New York, Ballantine, 1970.
Domino: A Science Fiction Novel. London, Dobson, 1971.
Kuldesak. London, Gollancz, and Garden City, New York, Doubleday, 1972.
Clone. London, Gollancz, 1972; Garden City, New York, Doubleday, 1973.
Time Out of Mind. London, Gollancz, 1973; New York, Pocket Books, 1981.
The Twilight of Briareus. London, Gollancz, and New York, Day, 1974.
Worlds Apart: A Science Fiction Novel. London, Gollancz, 1974.
The Road to Corlay (Kinship). London, Gollancz, 1978; expanded edition, New York, Pocket Books, 1979.
Profundis. London, Gollancz, 1979; New York, Pocket Books, 1981.
A Dream of Kinship (Kinship). London, Gollancz, 1981; New York, Pocket Books, 1982.
A Tapestry of Time (Kinship). London, Gollancz, 1982; New York, Pocket Books, 1986.
Shades of Darkness. Salisbury, Wiltshire, Kerosina, 1986.

Short Stories

The Custodians and Other Stories. London, Gollancz, 1976.
The Web of the Magi and Other Stories. London, Gollancz, 1980.
Out There Where the Big Ships Go. New York, Pocket Books, 1980.
The Story of Pepita and Corindo. New Castle, Virginia, Cheap Street, 1982.
The Unhappy Princess. New Castle, Virginia, Cheap Street, 1982.
The Missing Heart. New Castle, Virginia, Cheap Street, 1982.
The Young Student. New Castle, Virginia, Cheap Street, 1982.
The Tithonian Factor and Other Stories. New York, Gollancz, 1984.
The Magic Spectacles and Other Tales. Salisbury, Wiltshire, Kerosina, 1986.

OTHER PUBLICATIONS

Novels as Colin Murry

The Golden Valley. London, Hutchinson, 1958.
Recollections of a Ghost. London, Hutchinson, 1960.

A Path to the Sea. London, Hutchinson, 1961.
Private View. London, Dobson, 1972.

Play

Radio Play: *Taj Mahal by Candlelight* (as Colin Murry), 1966.

Other

One Hand Clapping: A Memoir of Childhood (as Colin Middleton Murry). London, Gollancz, 1975; as *I at the Keyhole,* New York, Stein and Day, 1975.
Shadows on the Grass (autobiography; as Colin Middleton Murry). London, Gollancz, 1977.

*

Richard Cowper comments:

First and foremost, in my writing, I aim to please *myself.* Experience in the form of some 15 novels has taught me that if I do this I usually contrive to please some other people too. That's just as well, for to write books that did not give me pleasure in the writing would be a grim sort of punishment and I'd very soon pack writing in altogether. But having said that I feel bound to add that I am profoundly conscious that I am in the entertainment business where "those who live to please must please to live."

My ambition has always been to write fine novels. By that I mean novels in which, as it were, I contrive to put the beat of the human heart on to the printed page—to make the reader endure and enjoy the whole gamut of human experience through the medium of my imagination. I contend that, to have its full impact, science fiction must be presented in human terms and allow the reader scope for imaginative identification with the characters in the stories.

*   *   *

Richard Cowper entered the SF genre from the mainstream with *Breakthrough: A Novel,* which used a contemporary setting to unravel the story of "passengers" in the minds of his characters, survivors of a more perfect, poetical age. This emphasis upon the dream state, central to Cowper's work, is used in a different manner in *Phoenix,* where a youth, Bard, wakes after suspended animation and finds himself 2000 years in the future, in a simpler, postholocaust society. Like the protagonist of *Breakthrough* (and, indeed, like many of Cowper's protagonists), he is possessed of special paranormal powers, which are unknown to him at the book's outset and which he discovers and eventually learns to use with sensitivity. These powers are evidenced again in *Domino: A Science Fiction Novel,* where the young protagonist (still at school), Christopher Blackburn, finds himself pursued by people from the future who are trying to stop him from experimenting in genetics, experiments which are to change the face of future society, making a master-slave arrangement. The interaction between different realities witnessed in these three books is to be seen in his later work as a strong theme.

In 1972 the satiric *Clone* launched Cowper upon the SF reading public. It is marked by its hostility to the technophilic direction man is taking, and by a distaste for modern living in general. It is all delivered with humour, and follows the picaresque adventures of the young innocent, Alvin, who remains morally intact despite the gross advances of the world to him. He discovers he is part of a

four-man Clone which develops immense paranormal powers but, as in all of Cowper's books, disposes of these powers in a humane, almost mystical manner. *Time Out of Mind* said little more than had been already stated in *Domino,* and is another tale of future interference in present (or near-present) society. *Kuldesak* is a far better book, showing us man in degeneration, living beneath the ground at the command of robots and computers, becoming (literally) vegetables as the years pass. Mel, the inquisitive young protagonist of this story, goes to the surface and changes it all, leading man out of his rut and back to the sane path of existence.

The Twilight of Briareus is probably Cowper's finest SF novel, written in a consummately elegant style and building to a powerful and emotive climax. Man becomes sterile as an aftereffect of a nearby nova which sweeps the Earth and, as a result of the nova, "passengers" are discovered in the minds of several people. The new aliens struggle to take control of man's destiny, and the peaceful resolution of this contest in the mind of Calvin Johnson, the central character of the book, brings the book to a close, even as Johnson himself dies in the snow. Like the earlier books it is set in a near-contemporary England and most of the critical events are internal ones, arising from the tension between the dream state and reality: "So that moment joined my previous glimpse of the sun-sculpted hills as just another strand of the elusive web that had drawn us here, and, as I stumbled forward beside her up to the house, I had the weirdest feeling that I was a fugitive in limbo fleeing between two worlds, one dead, the other powerless to be born." Johnson's words echo a feeling that is prevalent in many of these books, and he is perhaps the most subtly drawn of all Cowper's characters and the nearest to the author, involved, as so many of Cowper's protagonists are, in watching the external world crumble around him as the internal landscape of his mind opens up to display previously unguessed paranormal powers. *Twilight of Briareus* is the definitive exploration of this inner conflict and its resolution.

Worlds Apart: A Science Fiction Novel breaks from this serious lyricism and satirises SF writers in a most direct manner. George Cringe, an unimportant junior science teacher, writes an SF tale about Chnass while a Chnassian, Zil Bryn, writes a tale about George. Its humorous contrast between the mundane and the sublime is beautifully done and its comic delights are many.

It was after this comic break that Cowper first tried his hand at SF short stories and produced "The Custodians," the first of a series of delicately imagined and richly written stories. It deals with prescience and the nuclear holocaust but dwells, almost paradoxically, on the medieval past. There is a wealth of emotion in these stories, and while "Paradise Beach" is flawed, "The Hertford Manuscript" and "Drink Me, Francesca" possess the same poetic lilt. The most important of these stories, however, is "Piper at the Gates of Dawn" which deals with the birth of a new religion. A novella of immense wealth and power, it brings to mind Le Guin's *Earthsea* books; its post-holocaust setting is similar to that of *Phoenix.* The young boy, Tom, has the gift of joining men together in a brotherhood through the music of his flute and the image of the White Bird. These images, picked up 18 years later, when the kinsmen of Tom's religion are being persecuted, form the basis of *The Road to Corlay.* It is a sensuous book that pampers both heart and mind and, as in both *Breakthrough* and *Twilight,* has a "passenger" in the mind of one of its contemporary characters. Carver, a 20th-century scientist, sees through the eyes of Thomas of Norwich, an inhabitant of the world of Corlay—A.D. 3018—and through the double-vision, Cowper emphasises once again that it is only by shedding man's present direction (which, he infers, can only be achieved by some natural or unnatural catastrophe which robs man of almost everything) and assuming a new lifestyle, that any future can exist for Homo sapiens. *Profundis* is once again in the vein of *Clone,* with an innocent protagonist, Tom Jones, reenacting the Christ myth in a beserk computer-run submarine, *HMS Profundis,* which has already denuded the Earth "above surface" by causing global war. As black comedy it is not as effective as *Clone,* but it is, perhaps, much more profound in its message.

Two further volumes of Cowper's stories appeared in the 1980s, drawing upon a wide range of subjects: ecological disasters ("A Message to the King of Brobdingnag"), mystical experiences ("Incident at Huacaloc"), 19th-century adventures ("The Web of the Magi"), and highly literate ghost stories ("The Attelborough Poltergeist" and "The Tithonian Factor")—all with a science fictional rationale. Most significant from this period, however, were the two final books in the Corlay sequence (the four parts termed by Cowper "The White Bird of Kinship"). The first, *A Dream of Kinship,* was set 1000 years on from *The Road to Corlay* and showed how the loose ethic of the boy piper, Tom, had become a highly dogmatic religion. The second, *A Tapestry of Time,* describes the travels of another Tom, almost a reincarnation of the first, who must face the moral implications of his gift (he can pipe men into madness). Overall, the four parts of the "Bird Of Kinship" form one of the most lyrical and beautifully written sequences in science fiction. Cowper's recent work, however, has drifted outside genre definitions and it may well be that we have seen the last of his SF writing. Indeed, his final novel (to date), *Shades Of Darkness,* appears to bring his work full circle, proving reminiscent of his earliest writings as Colin Murry. *Shades Of Darkness* is a gently romantic and yet powerful ghost story balanced somewhere between the domesticity of England and the darkest heart of Africa.

—David Wingrove

COX, Erle (Harold)

Nationality: Australian. **Born:** Melbourne, Victoria, 15 August 1873. **Education:** Melbourne Church of England Grammar School. **Career:** Farmer, then journalist: book, film, and drama critic for *The Argus* and *The Australasian,* both Melbourne, 1921-46. **Awards:** Lone Hand prize, for short story, 1908. **Died:** 20 November 1950.

SCIENCE FICTION PUBLICATIONS

Novels

Out of the Silence: A Romance. Melbourne, Vidler, 1925; London, John Hamilton, 1927; New York, Henkle, 1928; revised edition, Melbourne, Robertson and Mullens, 1947; Westport, Connecticut, Hyperion, 1976.
Fools' Harvest. Melbourne, Robertson and Mullens, 1939.
The Missing Angel. Melbourne, Robertson and Mullens, 1947.

Short Stories

Author of numerous uncollected short stories.

*   *   *

Originally a farmer, Erle Cox graduated from freelance writing to professional metropolitan journalism in his forties. His early short stories in Australian magazines were never collected, and he is known only for three novels. He never gained literary recognition: orthodox criticism ignores him and comprehensive literary histories barely give him a mention.

Yet *Out of the Silence: A Romance* had great popular appeal, though Cox had to finance the 1925 edition himself. An earlier human race, destroyed in a world catastrophe 27 million years ago, left time-capsule spheres preserving their culture and chosen representatives in stasis. Found and revived in modern Victoria, the superwoman Earani prepares to take over the world and recreate her highly developed, rational, heartless civilisation. Her intellectual stature and enormous personal magnetism give good prospects of success, certainly with the other survivor she detects in the Himalayas revived as well. The book is well told, if slow and wordy by later standards, maintaining suspense as the mystery and menace unfold. The atmosphere of middle-class rural Australia about 1910 contrasts strangely with the threatened scientific tyranny. Earani is a terrible figure: a prodigy not of evil but of self-assured virtue without compassion. Characteristically her program includes genocide of inferior elements, including the colored races. The grotesque racism, almost too absurd to be abhorrent, was perfectly acceptable in the Australia of 60 years ago and caused no comment. No longer a book to sympathise with, it has historic importance.

The 1947 edition of *Out of the Silence* has the text reduced by 16,000 words from early chapters, improving the pace. However, a quite superfluous prologue is added, seriously weakening the book by giving away the mystery. Subsequent printings use this unsatisfactory text. There also have been two French translations, the first, much condensed, in 1929, the second in 1974. And a Russian translation was published in a newspaper, date unknown.

Cox's other books are quite different. *Fools' Harvest* is a typical warning of foreign conquest of Australia, foreseeing the scale of World War II atrocities but without scientific interest. *The Missing Angel* is a light satire about the Devil in Melbourne's polite society.

Cox's uncollected short stories include a few of interest. Four are mildly humorous invention stories, escapades of an experimenter with radio and invisibility, typical of the 1920s. "The Social Code," first printed in 1909 (in *Some Stories by Ten Famous Australian Authors,* Sydney, New Century Press, 1940), describes visual contact with the humans of Mars by instruments that afford face-to-face confrontation. An observer's long distance romance with a Martian maiden is suppressed, but nonetheless yields a glimpse of a bizarre culture.

—Graham Stone

———

CRAIG, Brian. *See* **STABLEFORD, Brian M.**

———

CRICHTON, (John) Michael

Pseudonyms: Michael Douglas (with Douglas Crichton); Jeffery Hudson; John Lange. **Nationality:** American. **Born:** Chicago, Illinois, 23 October 1942. **Education:** Harvard University, Cambridge, Massachusetts, A.B. (summa cum laude) 1964 (Phi Beta Kappa); Harvard Medical School, M.D. 1969; Salk Institute, La Jolla, California, 1969-70. **Family:** Married 1) Joan Radam in 1965 (divorced 1971); 2) Kathleen St. Johns in 1978 (divorced 1980). **Awards:** Mystery Writers of America Edgar Allan Poe award, 1968, 1980; Association of American Medical Writers award, 1970. **Agent:** International Creative Management, 40 West 57th Street, New York, New York 10019, U.S.A.

SCIENCE FICTION PUBLICATIONS

Novels (series: Jurassic Park)

The Andromeda Strain. New York, Knopf, and London, Cape, 1969.
Drug of Choice (as John Lange). New York, Signet, 1970; as *Overkill,* London, Sphere, 1972.
The Terminal Man. New York, Knopf, and London, Cape, 1972.
Eaters of the Dead: The Manuscript of ibn Fadlan, Relating His Experiences with the Northmen in A.D. 922. New York, Knopf, and London, Cape, 1976.
Congo. Franklin Center, Pennsylvania, Franklin Press, 1976; London, Allen Lane, 1981.
Sphere: A Novel. New York, Knopf, and London, Macmillan, 1987.
Jurassic Park. Franklin Center, Pennsylvania, Franklin Press, 1990; London, Century, 1991.
Three Complete Novels (includes *The Andromeda Strain, The Terminal Man,* and *The Great Train Robbery*). New York, Wings, 1993.
A New Collecton (includes *Sphere, Congo,* and *Eaters of the Dead*). New York, Wings, 1994.
The Lost World: A Novel (Jurassic Park). New York, Knopf, 1995.

OTHER PUBLICATIONS

Novels

A Case of Need (as Jeffery Hudson). Cleveland, World, and London, Heinemann, 1968; as Michael Crichton, New York, Penguin, 1993.
Dealing; or, The Berkeley-to-Boston Forty-Brick Lost-Bag Blues (as Michael Douglas, with Douglas Crichton). New York, Knopf, 1971; London, Talmy Franklin, 1972.
The Great Train Robbery. New York, Knopf, and London, Cape, 1975.
Rising Sun: A Novel. New York, Knopf, and London, Century, 1992.
Disclosure. Franklin Center, Pennsylvia, Franklin Library, 1993; London, Century, 1994.

Novels as John Lange

Odds On. New York, New American Library, 1966.
Scratch One. New York, New American Library, 1967.
Easy Go. New York, New American Library, 1968; London, Sphere, 1972; as *The Last Tomb* (as Michael Crichton), New York, Bantam, 1974.
The Venom Business. Cleveland, World, 1969.
Zero Cool. New York, New American Library, 1969; London, Sphere, 1972.

Grave Descend. New York, New American Library, 1970.
Binary. New York, Knopf and London, Heinemann, 1972; as Michael Crichton, London, Century, 1994.

Plays

Screenplays: *Westworld,* 1973; *Coma,* 1978; *The Great Train Robbery,* 1978; *Looker,* 1981; *Runaway,* 1984; *The Andromeda Strain,* 1987.

Other

Five Patients: The Hospital Explained. New York, Knopf, 1970; London, Cape, 1971.
Jasper Johns. New York, Abrams, and London, Thames and Hudson, 1977; revised edition, New York, Abrams, and London, Thames and Hudson, 1994.
Electronic Life: How to Think about Computers. New York, Knopf, and London, Heinemann, 1983.
Travels. New York, Knopf, and London, Macmillan, 1988.

*

Theatrical Activities:
Director: **Films**—*Westworld,* 1973; *Coma,* 1978; *The Great Train Robbery,* 1978; *Looker,* 1981. **Television**—*Pursuit,* 1972.

Michael Crichton comments:

I am interested in the quality of verisimilitude and how it is developed and sustained in fiction. All of my work, both science fiction and other writing, has tended to revolve around issues of what we believe and why. In recent years a good deal of my work has been devoted to films, which I direct as well as write.

*   *   *

Michael Crichton's primary science fiction works are *The Andromeda Strain, Binary, The Terminal Man, Sphere: A Novel,* and *Jurassic Park.* Each of these books is set in what is essentially contemporary society, and in each case a science fiction element, or elements, has been introduced upon which the subsequent development of the plot depends. Each of his more successful novels also inserts into the plot some force or danger that threatens ordinary people. Sometimes this force is science fictional. In *The Andromeda Strain,* for example, a mutating microorganism brought back from the upper atmosphere by a satellite kills all but two people in a small, northern Arizona town, and then threatens the rest of humanity. In *Binary,* the tapping into a "closed code computer mechanism" to determine the time and route of a shipment of nerve gas permits a psychopathic multi-millionaire to concoct a devious plot to assassinate the president. In *The Terminal Man,* psychosurgery permits the connection of a psychopathic patient's brain to a computer and turns him into a living time bomb. In *Sphere,* a time-travel ship from America's future has captured an alien life form that threatens an underwater habitat by means of its ability to manifest individual subconsciouses. In *Jurassic Park,* sophisticated genetic engineering techniques permit the re-creation of various dinosaur species at a theme park on an island off Costa Rica. Their actual characteristics threaten the park; their escape to the mainland may destroy humanity. It is, of course, their nearness to real life that makes these novels believable and frightening. The books are highly technical, and the narratives are laced with graphs, charts, diagrams, and computer printouts. Some of the information is real; the rest is fictionalized but dressed up to raise the level of credibility. Added to the scientific speculation and a large amount of technological hardware is jargon from appropriate scientific fields. The drama of the stories develops from the threat of imminent disaster and the subsequent efforts to prevent it.

The Terminal Man, Binary, and *Sphere* are clearly less effective than *The Andromeda Strain* and *Jurassic Park,* but nonetheless interesting and entertaining. The terminal man himself is a psychotic named Harry Benson, who believes that machines are taking over the world. He becomes a threat when he is chosen for a unique experiment that connects his brain to a miniaturized computer, which is powered by an atomic pack containing 37 grams of radioactive plutonium. Though the pack is implanted under his skin, if Benson breaks it open, he will kill himself and expose anyone in the immediate area to deadly radiation. Benson's physical problem is psychomotor epilepsy, and the computer is supposed to stop his seizures with a counteracting electrical shock. Because the sensation produced is more pleasurable than several orgasms, however, he learns to increase the frequency of the shocks through biofeedback techniques. Benson, in fact, becomes an electronic junkie. Though the novel produces a believable female lead in Dr. Janet Ross, a psychiatrist working on the project, it fails to successfully build tensions between the major characters, and much of the potential drama remains undeveloped. Moreover, the sense of a threat never really materializes because Benson is more pathetic than dangerous.

Plotting and pacing are Crichton's strongest qualities, and *Binary* is much better in that regard. A more complicated plot and a high level of suspense—a State Intelligence Agent, John Graves, unravels a complicated puzzle created for him by John Wright, an insane right-wing multimillionaire, before a half ton of ZV nerve gas kills the president and more than a million other people in San Diego—make *Binary* a more compelling book. Wright is a much more worthy adversary than Benson, and more deadly. He is both intelligent and clever. His anticipation of every move that Graves makes creates an eerie drama, a sense of frustration, and genuine daylight terror. When Graves finally figures out the puzzle and prevents the binary gasses from mixing to create ZV, it brings a sigh of relief.

Without question, the best of Crichton's pre-Hollywood novels is *The Andromeda Strain.* Though the antagonist is a microorganism, drama is achieved by the fact that its properties are unknown and that it has great potential to kill. It is heightened when the mutating organism eats through the rubber seals in one of the workrooms and contaminates that level of the underground laboratory. This sets the self-destruct mechanism of the complex into operation. Unless countermanded, the mechanism will detonate an atomic bomb, which will destroy the complex and disperse the deadly organism over the Earth's surface. The key to the spectacular success of the work lies in its pacing. Suspense builds with each development. Clues to the nature of the organism, which provides the mystery, are so interwoven with plot impediments that the reader is compelled to continue. Though the characters are only moderately interesting as people, the roles they play in the development of the drama are important and help create the suspense.

In the 1970s and 1980s, Crichton gave himself to Hollywood. After a promising start, which encouraged many writers and critics to predict a renaissance in the science-fiction film, his work began to decline. One critic, for example, dubbed *Runaway* "the most idi-

otic movie of the year" for 1984, and indeed, it seems to be but a collection of the oldest and tiredest science-fiction cliches. As such, it epitomizes Hollywood's approach to science fiction, which, despite the successes of the Star Wars trilogy, *E.T.,* and *Close Encounters of the Third Kind,* has been to wrap standard stories with science fiction trappings and special effects. Even Ridley Scott's brilliant films *Bladerunner* and *Alien* are not conceptually original.

After a period in the late 70s and early 80s where he suffered from writer's block and which he chronicled in *Travels,* he returned to the science fiction novel, with *Sphere* in 1987. It marks a positive turn in his writing career. Though not as good artistically as *Jurassic Park,* it is nonetheless both interesting and entertaining. A spaceship is discovered a thousand feet below the surface of the South Pacific, and an interdisciplinary scientific team is sent by the Navy to investigate. Once the team is below in a secured habitat, a typhoon arises and the surface ships are dispatched, effectively isolating those left below. Investigation reveals that the spaceship is actually an American time-traveler from the future that has used black holes to accomplish its purpose but has crashed in the past. In it is a sphere containing an alien life form (not specifically identified) that permits the subconscious minds of those who have entered it to manifest anything that they think. The subconscious minds of most people are dangerous, and that proves true here. Norman Johnson, a psychologist and the principal character of the novel, must determine whose manifestations are systematically destroying the underwater habitat before all aboard die. The story is fast-paced and there is a mystery to solve. The characters are interesting, if not deep, and the separation of personalities into what are essentially good and evil parts—through the medium of the sphere—echoes *Dr. Jekyll and Mr. Hyde.*

Jurassic Park is a much better novel. Both books combine fast-paced action with informed science to produce suspenseful and compelling stories, but *Jurassic Park* develops more interesting characters in great depth and is a richer and more complex extrapolation of current science fact and theory.

By using his wealth and power, multimillionaire John Hammond, the head of a private foundation that also bears his name, is able to acquire the technology to establish a theme park, featuring live dinosaurs, on an island off Costa Rica. The dinosaurs have been cloned from the DNA in ancient bones. The story centers around a "shakedown" visit to the resort by a group of individuals who, knowingly or unknowingly, consulted on its creation. This includes Alan Grant, archaeologist and principal character. Theoretically, the park is safe for visitors with its hundreds of miles of computer-controlled electric fences and other security devices. But the park is a complex system, and complex systems are fated to go wrong, according to chaos theory. In this case, going wrong means becoming deadly. Chaos theory postulates that there are undeterminable factors that geometrize through time and cause the system to act unpredictably. These factors are represented dramatically by the naivety and arrogance of Hammond, Dennis Nedry, who headed up the teams that programmed the resort's three Cray computers, and Dr. Henry Wu, who ran the resort's genetic program. The nature and behavior of the cloned dinosaurs turns out to be much different than expected—some species prove more intelligent and more deadly than previously believed. Nedry is not as competent as thought, and he is greedy. So, there are glitches in the computer programs, and he agrees to steal cloned embryos for a rival company. Hammond, himself, simply does not have the imagination to anticipate the danger of the project. He brings his two grandchildren to the island, for example, during the "shakedown" visit.

Disaster strikes as the dinosaurs attack and kill several people. Others nearly escape the island aboard the resort's supply ship, and Wu's system to assure that they will not reproduce, which is to make all the cloned dinosaurs female, fails to recognize that the DNA used to fill in blank areas is capable of changing sexes. Grant, the two children, Ellie Settler (Grant's assistant), and some of the others survive, but Hammond, Nedry, and Wu are killed, ironically the victims of their own incompetence. The supply ship is turned back before the velociraptors who have stowed away gain the mainland, and Dennis Nedry is killed before he can deliver a batch of stolen embryos to a contact. This is all ironic, however, because the novel begins with velociraptors already on the mainland, attacking and killing children.

This irony is meant to underscore a very serious message contained in a fictionalized introduction—that biotechnology promises the greatest revolution in human history and that it is proceeding virtually unmonitored and uncontrolled by any regulatory agencies. The novel itself tolls a bell for an absolutely critical contemporary social issue. *Jurassic Park* is an exciting, well-constructed, and original adventure that returns Crichton to the levels he previously reached in *The Andromeda Strain.*

Straddling the worlds of publishing and film, Crichton has directed some films and written or cowritten several screen plays, such as *Coma* and *Looker,* as well as for his own novels, such as *Jurassic Park* and *Rising Sun.* While the plots of these films and *Disclosure,* yet another Crichton novel made into a film, display the typical Crichton traits, being fast-moving and complex, only *Jurassic Park* could be classified as science fiction. Still, the plots of both *Rising Sun* and *Disclosure* depend upon high-tech gadgetry. *Rising Sun* turns on the sophisticated analysis of a video film and *Disclosure* on virtual reality headsets that permit entering a multimedia database.

Congo, the most recent adaptation of a Crichton novel, has received mixed reviews. The novel was published in 1980, and is intended to be a high-tech, jungle adventure story. It is perhaps a reflection of Crichton's own disaffection during the time it was written. Intended to be serious, it lacks the sure hand of Crichton's better work. The film version, with which Crichton was reported to be unhappy and which he did not screenwrite, is treated as a parody of the "jungle-adventure." But it often fails to mesh. It is given over to special effects, including an animatronic gorilla who is much too-cute. Its biggest fault, however, is its failure to produce a believable villain. The bad African gorillas, who guard the lost city of Zinj, supposedly the site of King Solomon's diamond mines, are not competent enough nor exert a presence long enough in the film to create compelling horror.

At his best Crichton is a fine storyteller. He is capable of weaving a fast-paced, intricate, and original plot, he seems to be more and more comfortable in film, and his recent successes have created Hollywood clout. Perhaps these qualities will make him the one to eventually usher in a golden age of science fiction film.

—Carl B. Yoke

CROMIE, Robert

Nationality: British. **Born:** 1856. **Died:** 1907.

SCIENCE FICTION PUBLICATIONS

Novels

For England's Sake. London, Warne, 1889.
A Plunge into Space. London, Warne, 1890; Westport, Connecticut, Hyperion Press, 1976.
The Crack of Doom. London, Digby Long, 1895.
The Next Crusade. London, Hutchinson, 1896.
A New Messiah: A Novel. London, Digby Long, 1902.

Short Stories

The King's Oak and Other Stories. London, Newnes, 1897.

OTHER PUBLICATIONS

Novels

The Lost Liner. London, Newnes, 1899.
Kitty's Victoria Cross. London, Warne, 1901.
The Shadow of the Cross. London, Ward Lock, 1902.
El Dorado. London, Ward Lock, 1904; as *From the Cliffs of Croaghaun,* Akron, Ohio, Saalfield, 1904.

Short Stories

The Romance of Poisons, Being Weird Episodes from Life, with T. S. Wilson. London, Jarrolds, 1903.

*   *   *

All that is known about Robert Cromie is that from 1889 to 1904 he published 11 books of fiction (one with T. S. Wilson), a number of which are SF. The list begins with *For England's Sake,* which cashed in on the patriotic popularity of the future war tale by transferring it to India, where loyal natives headed by heroic maharajah defeat dastardly Russian invasion. Its continuation is *The Next Crusade,* whose battles and love entanglements are not as interesting as Cromie's Preface, briefly discussing "the history of the future" and with a too easy facetiousness concluding that as against the history of the past it contains fewer errors (Cromie's Britain allied with Austria occupies Constantinople, so that he may have been co-responsible for Churchill's disastrous World War I venture against the Dardanelles). Two other novels are more important. *A Plunge into Space* is an interplanetary novel halfway between Verne and Wells (the second edition in 1891 has a brief and unrevealing preface by Verne) detailing how a scientist discovers anti-gravity, how his explorer-friend helps him to cast a steel globe in Alaska in spite of Indian attacks and sullen half-breeds, and how the two with four more friends—again characterized by profession—fly to a desert Mars. Vegetation and a decaying utopian civilization (which has TV and aircraft but no politics or money) are found near its polar sea. A love affair between one of the heroes and a beautiful Martian coyly named Mignonette results in the latter first becoming a stowaway in their spacecraft on return and then sacrificing her life; the craft is destroyed. *The Crack of Doom* has one of the first mad scientists in SF planning to use the secret of atomic energy to blow up our planet. The plot flounders through lots of genteel Victorian love melodrama, telepathy, hypnotism, secret societies, stereotyped characters, vague echoes of drawing-room Schopenhauerism, and a sentimental happy ending. A final SF novel, *A New Messiah: A Novel,* also leans on a melodramatic plot.

—Darko Suvin

CROSBY, Harry C., Jr. *See* **ANVIL, Christopher.**

CROSS, John Keir

Pseudonyms: Stephen Macfarlane; Susan Morley. **Nationality:** British. **Born:** Carluke, Lanark, 19 August 1914. **Career:** Clerk and entertainer in the 1930s; radio writer for BBC, London, from 1937. **Died:** 22 January 1967.

SCIENCE FICTION PUBLICATIONS

Novels (for children; series: Stephen MacFarlane)

The Angry Planet: An Authentic First-Hand Account of a Journey to Mars in the Spaceship "Albatross," Compiled from Notes and Records by Various Members of the Expedition, and Now Assembled and Edited for Publication by John Keir Cross, from Manuscripts Made Available by Stephen MacFarlane. (MacFarlane). London, Lunn, 1945; New York, Coward-McCann, 1946.
The Owl and the Pussycat. London, Lunn, 1946; as *The Other Side of Green Hills,* New York, Coward-McCann, 1947.
The Flying Fortunes in an Encounter with Rubberface! London, Muller, 1952; as *The Stolen Sphere: A Journey and a Mystery,* New York, Dutton, 1953.
SOS from Mars (MacFarlane). London, Hutchinson, 1954; as *The Red Journey Back: A First-Hand Account of the Second and Third Martian Expeditions by the Space-Ships Albatross and Comet, Compiled from Notes and Records by Various Members of the Exploring Parties, the Whole Revised by Stephen MacFarlane, and Now Fully Assembled and Edited.* New York, Coward-McCann, 1954.

Short Stories

The Other Passenger: 18 Strange Stories. London, Westhouse, 1944; Philadelphia, Lippincott, 1946; abridged as *Stories from The Other Passenger,* New York, Ballantine, 1961.

OTHER PUBLICATIONS

Novels

Mistress Glory (as Susan Morley). New York, Dial Press, 1948; as *Glory,* as John Keir Cross, London, Laurie, 1951.

Juniper Green. London, Laurie, 1952; as Susan Morley, New York, Dial Press, 1953.

Plays

Radio Plays: *The Kraken Wakes,* from the novel by John Wyndham; *The Archers* series, with others, 1962-67; *The Brockenstein Affair,* from a work by George R. Preedy, 1962; *The Free Fishers,* from the novel by John Buchan, 1964; *Bird of Dawning,* from the novel by John Masefield, 1965; *Be Thou My Judge,* from a work by James Wood, 1967; *The Green Isle of the Great Deep,* 1986.

Television Play: *She Died Young,* 1961.

Other (for children)

Studio J Investigates. London, Lunn, 1944.
Jack Robinson. London, Lunn, 1945.
The Man in Moonlight. London, Westhouse, 1947.
The White Magic. London, Westhouse, 1947.
Blackadder. London, Muller, 1950; New York, Dutton, 1951.
The Dancing Tree. London, Hutchinson, 1955.
Elizabeth in Broadcasting. London, Chatto and Windus, 1957.
The Sixpenny Year. London, Hutchinson, 1957.

Other (for children; as Stephen Macfarlane)

The Blue Egg. London, Lunn, 1944.
Detectives in Greasepaint. London, Lunn, 1944.
Lucy Maroon, The Car That Loved a Policeman. London, Lunn, 1944.
Mr. Bosanko and Other Stories. London, Lunn, 1944.
The Strange Tale of Sally and Arnold. London, Lunn, 1944.
The Story of a Tree. London, Lunn, 1946.

Other

Aspect of Life: An Autobiography of Youth. London, Selwyn and Blount, 1937.
Editor, *The Children's Omnibus.* London, Lunn, 1948.
Editor, *Best Horror Stories.* London, Faber, 1957; *Best Horror Stories Two,* Faber, 1965.
Editor, *Best Black Magic Stories.* London, Faber, 1960.

* * *

A short story writer in the tradition of Saki and John Collier, a popular anthologist of horror stories, and an occasional writer of SF and fantasy dramas for the BBC, John Keir Cross is especially noteworthy for his juvenile science fiction. *The Angry Planet* was among the first modern SF novels directed at a young audience, and is interesting for the manner in which it reworks themes from Wells and C.S. Lewis into a context more readily accessible to younger readers.

The Angry Planet involves a group of three children who travel to Mars by hiding on an experimental rocket ship. The life they find there is elegantly portrayed, and reveals Cross's familiarity with earlier science fiction as well as intelligent speculation. Martian society is dominated by intelligent plant life, the major forms of which are called the Beautiful People and the Terrible Ones. This opposition of two divergent strains of the same evolutionary path calls to mind the Morlocks and Eloi from Wells's *The Time Machine,* and the moral values attached to each race calls to mind C.S. Lewis's *Out of the Silent Planet.* The relatively sophisticated multiple viewpoint narrative adds further interest to the tale and helps to maintain suspense. A sequel, *SOS from Mars,* describes subsequent journeys to Mars. Another juvenile SF novel, with the unlikely title *The Flying Fortunes in an Encounter with Rubberface!,* concerns the launching of an artificial Earth satellite, and may be the first juvenile treatment of this theme except for Arthur Clarke's 1952 *Islands in the Sky.* Cross's adult fiction, represented by the collection *The Other Passenger: 18 Strange Stories,* tends more toward fantasy and the occult than science fiction, but includes the classic doppelgänger story "The Other Passenger." Cross's short fiction is distinguished by sensitive style and psychological insight.

—Gary K. Wolfe

CROSS, Polton. *See* FEARN, John Russell.

CROWLEY, John

Nationality: American. **Born:** Presque Isle, Maine, 1 December 1942. **Education:** Indiana University, Bloomington, B.A. 1964. **Career:** Photographer and commercial artist, 1964-66. Since 1966, freelance writer. **Awards:** World Fantasy Convention award, 1982. **Address:** c/o Doubleday, 666 Fifth Avenue, New York, New York 10103, U.S.A.

SCIENCE FICTION PUBLICATIONS

Novels

The Deep. Garden City, New York, Doubleday, 1975; London, New English Library, 1977.
Beasts. Garden City, New York, Doubleday, 1976; Wendover, Goudchild, 1984.
Engine Summer. Garden City, New York, Doubleday, 1979; London, Gollancz, 1980.
Little, Big. New York, Bantam, 1981; London, Gollancz, 1982.
A Egypt. New York, Bantam, 1987; London, Gollancz, 1988.
Great Works of Time (originally published in *Novelties,* 1989). New York, Bantam, 1991.
Three Novels (includes *The Deep, Beasts* and *Engine Summer*). New York, Bantam, 1994.
Love and Sleep. New York, Bantam, 1994.

Short Stories

Novelty. Garden City, New York, Doubleday, 1989.
Antiquities: Stories. Seattle, Incunabula, 1993.

Other

Editor, with Howard Kerr and Charles L. Crow, *The Haunted Dusk: American Supernatural Fiction, 1820-1920.* Athens, Georgia, University of Georgia Press, 1983.

*			*			*

John Crowley's first three novels have numerous virtues, and his epic fantasy, *Little, Big* (World Fantasy award), reaped a harvest of laudatory reviews and, inevitably, comparisons to J.R.R. Tolkien's work, as well as other memorable works of fantasy from *A Voyage to Arcturus* to (rather surprisingly) Gabriel García Marquéz's novel of "magic realism" *One Hundred Years of Solitude.* His fiction expresses a highly individual vision.

Crowley's first novel, *The Deep,* received some praise from readers like Ursula Le Guin, but in the light of his later work it seems to be his least satisfactory and least characteristic performance. Set in a distant future on a planet vaguely like earth, *The Deep* describes the power struggle between two aristocratic houses with names derived from Celtic mythology, mostly old Welsh. Young Sennred, one of the Reds, eventually emerges as a victor who reconciles the impulsive Reds and the Machiavellian Blacks; but no particular hero predominates, and Learned Redhand, a scholarly apostate from the Reds, remains the most memorable character. The conflict is observed by an alien who assumes various guises, and eventually confronts his antagonist, a denizen of "the deep" who is an avatar of the Leviathan myth. Crowley's use of the Leviathan mythology does not clarify his cryptic plot, and the novel suffers from the repetition of similar and identical Celtic names. Despite high ambitions, Celtic and biblical myth do not rescue this immature first novel.

In *Beasts,* Crowley produced a better work, dealing with a bitter ideological conflict in an America of the near future where central government has collapsed and small regional governments struggle to maintain their authority. Their opponents are the bureaucrats of "the Federal," a government striving to restore a dominating central authority. The surface conflict, however, symbolizes the perennial struggle between rational organizers who wish to subject nature and humanity to a monolithic tyranny and those romantics and lovers of nature who resist such dehumanizing efforts. Among the rebels are the beasts of the title, hybrid creatures resulting from genetic experiment in the last days of the old United States; the products of these projects are sentient beings combining human and animal qualities, somewhat reminiscent of the creations of H.G. Wells's Dr. Moreau. One measure of Crowley's achievement is his successful characterizations of Reynard, a fox-man, and Painter, a lion-man, each of which manages to circumvent (in his own fashion) the opposition of the Federalists. Although *Beasts* is resolved somewhat ambiguously, Crowley's novel clearly takes a stand on the side of the romantics, and in favor of the energies of natural life.

Even more impressive is Crowley's third novel, *Engine Summer,* a story of a young man's initiation into adulthood in the primitive tribal world of a post-disaster America centuries hence. This book describes the search for meaning and understanding of Rush That Speaks, who leaves his community of origin as a boy and searches for his lost love, Once A Day. Although he finds her and some knowledge of the outside world, he discovers the unhappiness that accompanies the loss of innocence when she deserts him again. Crowley's hero also learns much about the vanished 20th-century civilization, the brave new world of science and technology called the age of the "angels." One of the lessons that Rush That Speaks learns is the "angelism" or excessive rationalism of the ancients was anything but angelic in our sense of the word. An additional sign of Crowley's technical mastery in this novel is his use of an inventive narrative mode: Rush tells the story of his youth through a recording cube, and his auditor, who occasionally comments on his tale, is a person who lives generations after his death. This narrative method provides aesthetic distance.

Even the mature artistry of *Engine Summer,* however, scarcely provides a hint of the marvelous achievement of *Little, Big. Little, Big* describes three generations in the life of the Drinkwater-Bramble-Hawksquill clan, as seen through the eyes of several members, but primarily from the point of view of two: Smoky Barnable, an outsider from the Midwest who comes to New York City and marries "Daily Alice" Drinkwater; and Auberon, their son, who finally becomes an avatar of the fairy king, Oberon, just as his black paramour, Sylvie, is metamorphosed into a new Titania. After Smoky's marriage to Alice, a charming and credible heroine, he takes up residence at the Drinkwater family home, Edgewood, a curious architectural wonder in upper New York State housing a family of eccentrics who have a secret alliance with fairies. Smoky's father-in-law, Old Doc Drinkwater, for instance, writes successful children's books which narrate tales he gets firsthand from the fairies themselves. Other members of the family are blessed or cursed by gifts from the "little people." The novel comes to a crisis when a fascistic politician becomes president and attempts to oppress and destroy all those who revere the power of nature and the imagination. Through Daily Alice's heroic sacrifice of herself, the Drinkwater clan is able to leave the modern world, which will no longer allow them to ignore it, and enter the earthly paradise of the realm of "Faery," and there Alice appears in an immortal form.

This humorous, whimsical, inventive, and richly allusive fantasy deserves many readings and is likely to become a classic of its genre. Here, as in the rest of his world, Crowley defines his vision as that of a sophisticated romantic, suspicious of technology, committed to the cause of his imagination, and possessing prodigious literary gifts of humor, characterization, and lyrical description.

In the years since the publication of *Little, Big,* Crowley's reputation has grown slowly but steadily. Moreover, some serious critical attention has been given to *Little, Big* because of the book's demonstration of Crowley's power to bring myth to life. Crowley himself has commented, in a note for a new edition of *Little, Big,* that his book was important for his development because he discovered for the first time "the extent of my own powers as a writer," and he hints that it remains his favorite book. Nevertheless, Crowley followed his success in *Little, Big,* with a more mature novel, *Aegypt.*

Aegypt is a major philosophical romance, to use Crowley's description of a novel within the story by a fictional author, Fellowes Kraft. Although Crowley's work resembles much of Gene Wolfe's fiction by leaving ambiguous the question of whether magic and predetermined destiny exist, *Aegypt* is a tale woven of numerous poetic and occult materials: the Grail legend, the quests of Giordano Bruno, the adventures of the Elizabethan astrologer and occultist John Dee, a fanciful life of Shakespeare, and the quest of a modern Parsifal, Pierce Moffett. The external action of the novel is rather slight, describing the life of Pierce Moffett from his confused days as a flower child of the 1960s, through some undistin-

guished years as a professor of history in Barnabas College, in New York City, through his decision to move to a pastoral world in upper New York state, in the town of Blackbury Jambs in the Faraway Hills (in what is apparently 1976). Inevitably, the pastoral and romantic interest in rural New York, and the muted love story allow readers to draw comparisons with *Little, Big.*

Yet Moffett's actual journey is psychological or visionary, as he follows a path to which he is inadvertently guided by his shepherd friend, Spofford. A lapsed Catholic, Moffett seeks the spiritual history or archetypal myth that lies within history, which he had been encouraged to seek by his mentor, the brilliant historian Frank Walker Barr, in graduate school.

Although Crowley refuses to allow the novel to come to any clear resolution, it appears that the goal of Moffett's journey has been reached when he reads an unpublished novel by the mysterious novelist, Fellowes Kraft, describing the lifelong visionary question of Giordano Bruno. This novel reveals to Moffett that the patterns of the archetypal quest for meaning are repeated with different variations again and again throughoutthe world. At the end of the novel, Moffett has found his soul mate and enduring romantic interest in Rosie Rasmussen, a charming woman recovering from a divorce from a womanizing psychotherapist. Yet Crowley leaves even the direction of this relationship unresolved at the end of his tale.

A central conception of the novel is the world of archetypes or imaginary symbols, which is the "Aegypt" of the title. This imaginary "Aegypt" of the occultists and of Mozart's opera, *The Magic Flute* (based on the lore of the Freemasons), is not to be confused with the historical Egypt with its literal-minded religion and obsession with mummifying the dead, as Crowley makes clear. Instead, it is symbolized by the mysterious figure of Hermes Trismegistus, or Hermes "The Three Times Very Great," the Alexandrian magus whose syntheses of Platonism, neo-Platonism, and older myths, helped to create the myth of "Aegypt" for the Renaissance. This mysterious figure tends to reside in the background of Crowley's novel, much as Pythagoras and the occult conception of Solomon haunt the later poetry of William Butler Yeats. Unlike his namesake, Aleister Crowley (alluded to in the novel), Crowley does not take the metaphors of this occult world literally, or regard it as an easy access to worldly power or sexual prowess. Instead, Crowley's thematic concerns always focus on the search for archetypes that provide religious and philosophical meaning. In the novel, he attempts to draw together and unify numerous mythic metaphors, from the quest for the Grail and the Philosopher's Stone (which he identifies as the same quest for the same sacred object) to the Jungian motif of a hero encountering his anima. Space does not here permit a thorough elucidation of Crowley's elaborate interweaving of symbolism: Pierce Moffett's father, for instance, is named Axel and lives in a castle or aging apartment house in Brooklyn, yet he also seems to be an analogue of the Fisher King.

Another important feature of the novel is the vividly imagined tales within the main tale, which provide thematic repetition, that is, the restatement of motifs reinforcing those of the central plot. For students of English Renaissance literature, probably the most intriguing of these additional stories is Fellowes Kraft's imaginary novel, *Bitten Apples,* wherein young Will Shakespeare is depicted as running off to join the acting troup of James Burbage in the lost years between grammar school (which he would have left at twelve or thirteen) and his marriage to Anne Hathaway at eighteen.

Despite the novel's intense concentration on myth—for which Crowley credits many sources, including Robert Graves and Mircea

Eliade—its 20th-century characters are convincingly realized: not only the Parsifal figure, Pierce Moffett, but also Rosie Rasmussen, Moffett's friend Spofford, and several minor figures are highly individualized. Thus Crowley avoids the defect that frequently haunts works of this kind, such as the novels of Charles Williams: the presence of an illuminating symbolism offset by shadowy characters. In this regard, and in his controlled and apparently effortless handling of style and incident, Crowley demonstrates impressive talents. His achievement here consolidates his claim to be not merely a major fantasy writer, but a writer who deserves to be considered a major novelist by any standards.

The publication of *Aegypt* was followed two years later by *Novelty,* a volume containing four novellas mostly with the theme of a writer's struggle to create a personal vision. These tales, which sometimes suggest the metafiction of Jorge Luis Borges, Gabriel Garcia Marquéz, and numerous English writers, show Crowley in a philosophical mood similar to that of *Aegypt.* One tale in particular, "In Blue," is a very impressive performance.

Crowley's work has clearly moved to a high level of philosophical concern, without sacrificing its artistry. Without a doubt, *Aegypt* is likely to be considered one of the enduring novels of 20th-century fantasy, and it is difficult to dispute the conclusion that Crowley has established a place for himself as a major author in this genre.

John Crowley's reputation continues to grow in the nineties. After the impressive publication of *Aegypt,* which received many laudatory reviews, Crowley followed with a sequel, *Love and Sleep,* a massive novel which appeared late in 1994. In an afterword acknowledging sources, Crowley also speaks of this work as part of a series of novels using the same characters and setting.

Not only is *Love and Sleep* set chiefly in the same rural Faraway Hills and Blackbury River country of *Aegypt,* it continues the spiritual odyssey of Pierce Moffett, the protagonist introduced in the earlier novel. However, Crowley broadens the scope of his fictional saga by developing more fully the character of Rosie Rasmussen, the daughter of Moffett's patron, describing the impact on Rosie of her father's death and the recognition that her three-year-old daughter is probably epileptic.

There are other major similarities to *Aegypt.* As in the earlier novel, a contrapuntal narrative of Elizabethan times is presented as a contrast or a supplement to the narrative of the 20th-century characters. This storyline is supposedly part of the final (and unpublished) novel by Fellowes Kraft, the novelist whose literary remains Moffett has been hired to study.

But the secondary plot in *Love and Sleep* is quite different from the one embedded in the earlier novel. The Elizabethan narrative in *Aegypt* was an imaginative tale of Shakespeare as a runaway boy leaving Stratford and joining the peregrinations of an acting company before returning home at 17 to marry Anne Hathaway. *Love and Sleep*'s Elizabethan narrative is more deeply involved with Renaissance occultism. This interwoven narrative relates the fictional adventures of two historical protagonists, the itinerant and iconoclastic Italian philosopher, Giordano Bruno, who visits England and France; and Dr. John Dee, the occultist who allegedly had dialogues with angels, and saw his career decline when he went into partnership with another occultist, Edward Kelley, whom history considers an unscrupulous charlatan.

Both Elizabethan characters are employed to explore Crowley's thesis that time or an era sometimes takes a crucial turn which leads to a period when one way of thinking dominates. In Crowley's novel, it is suggested one decisive moment was the year 1588, the *annus mirabilis* of Elizabethan England, when Spanish power was defeated and English power began to wax. (And with the rise of England came the triumph of rationalist Protestant Reform over imaginative traditional Catholicism, rationalist science over both repressive Catholic fanaticism and poetic imagination, and so on.)

While Bruno is depicted as a serious though moderately heretical philosopher, Dee and Kelley are engaged on a quest for the lodestones of Renaissance occultists, the philosopher's stone and the elixir of life. Along the way, they and the reader encounter not only angels but some of the English court, including Queen Elizabeth I, Sir Philip Sidney, and the Holy Roman Emperor, Rudolf II. Crowley's Elizabethan sequences are brilliantly described in a stylized Renaissance English rich in allusions to Shakespeare, the Authorized version of the Bible, Sidney's prose, and English folk song.

As in *Aegypt,* there are also allusions to the Hermetic vision of Aegypt as an imaginative realm which is the source of lost lore and forgotten magic, a visionary world which contrasts starkly with the historical Egypt of the Pharaohs and Islam. But this Hermetic vision is subordinate in *Love and Sleep* to the quest for the stone which may transmute all reality from base metal into an age of gold.

Ironically, in the 20th-century narrative of the novel, Moffett is also being encouraged by his literary agent and sometime lover to write a book speculating about his ideas about the duality of time and the magic lying beneath the surface of existence. It is a "new age," she tells him, but Moffett, a former graduate student specializing in the Renaissance, is a somewhat reluctant new age seeker or quester. His dying patron, Boney Rasmussen, apparently hopes that Pierce can find evidence in Kraft's papers of the existence of some talisman like the philosopher's stone, a magic that will enable Rasmussen to avert his own death. But this quest, like all such vain enterprises, is defeated by Rasmussen's demise. In the 20th century, the realities of nature continue to reign.

Pierce is distracted from his quest by a brief affair with Rose, an attractive woman who is not to be confused with Rosie Rasmussen. But she deserts him for the lures of an evangelical religious cult. At the novel's end, Pierce has come to another of his own crossroads in time with his book still unwritten.

No discussion of *Love and Sleep* would be complete without reference to a long opening sequence describing Pierce's childhood in the household of his benevolent uncle, a country doctor in the Cumberland Mountains of Kentucky. Crowley's surprisingly vivid description of early 1950s life in the uplands of the Cumberlands, a world of wooded mountain slopes, abandoned coal mines, and pockets of religious fanaticism might provide a complete novel for a less ambitious master of fantasy fiction.

Since *Love and Sleep* continues to demonstrate Crowley's mastery of characterization and novelistic technique, it will likely gain new readers for Crowley's saga of Pierce Moffett, despite the novel's lack of overt dramatic action. In fact, Crowley's work seems to be winning acceptance from mainstream critics, to a degree comparable to the respect shown for Ursula Le Guin. But such success may also cloud important issues. Some of the praise being lavished on Crowley's work describes him as a "magic realist," thereby conferring on it the laurels associated with Borges, Gabriel Garcia Marques, and Umberto Eco. Thus the guardians of the literary establishment try to avoid acknowledging that the author of *Little, Big* is a master of high literary fantasy.

—Edgar L. Chapman

CUMMINGS, Ray(mond King)

Pseudonyms: Ray King; Gabriel Wilson. **Nationality:** American. **Born:** New York City, 30 August 1887. **Education:** Princeton University, New Jersey, one year. **Family:** Married Gabrielle W. Cummings; one son and one daughter. **Career:** Worked on oil wells in Wyoming and in placer mines in British Columbia and Alaska; arranged record albums and wrote labels for Edison Records in the 1920s. **Died:** 23 January 1957.

SCIENCE FICTION PUBLICATIONS

Novels (series: Haljan; Matter, Space, and Time; Tama)

The Girl in the Golden Atom (Matter, Space, and Time). London, Methuen, 1922; revised edition, New York, Harper, 1923.
The Man Who Mastered Time (Matter, Space, and Time). Chicago, McClurg, 1929.
The Sea Girl. Chicago, McClurg, 1930.
Tarrano, the Conqueror. Chicago, McClurg, 1930.
Brigands of the Moon (Haljan). Chicago, McClurg, 1931; London, Consul, 1966.
The Shadow Girl (Matter, Space, and Time). London, Swan, 1946; New York, Ace, 1962.
The Princess of the Atom (Matter, Space, and Time). New York, Avon, 1950; London, Boardman, 1951.
The Man on the Meteor. London, Swan, 1952.
Beyond the Vanishing Point. New York, Ace, 1958.
Wandl, the Invader (Haljan). New York, Ace, 1961.
Beyond the Stars. New York, Ace, 1963.
A Brand New World. New York, Ace, 1964.
The Exile of Time (Matter, Space, and Time). New York, Avalon, 1964.
Explorers into Infinity. New York, Avalon, 1965.
Tama of the Light Country. New York, Ace, 1965.
Tama, Princess of Mercury. New York, Ace, 1966.
The Insect Invasion. New York, Avalon, 1967.
Tales of the Scientific Crime Club. London, Ferret Fantasy, 1979.
In the 4th Dimension. Oak Forest, Illinois, R. Weinberg, 1981.

Short Stories

Author of numerous uncollected short stories.

* * *

Ray Cummings had a long writing career, but it must be said that he long outlived his originality, and was noted for shamelessly rehashing a few early stories. Established as one of the trailblazers before the advent of *Amazing Stories,* he was the only one of them to carry on as a prominent name. His output was exceeded only by Hamilton and Kuttner, but he did not move with the movement, and was soon dated.

The early tales that made his name had sketchy but strongly suggestive scientific foundations. Though he showed his debt to Wells by borrowing his narrative frame from *The Time Machine* more than once, his stories were closer to Haggard's or Burroughs's. Usually visitors from 20th-century New York in a strange setting with a vague preindustrial society resolved a conflict and helped pave the way for more advanced thinking.

His first and favorite inspiration was submicroscopic, even subatomic life—atoms or subatomic particles as worlds. The idea dated from Nicholas Odgers's *The Mystery of Being; or, Are Ultimate Atoms Inhabited Worlds?* (1863), but Cummings added the idea of reducing one's size indefinitely to penetrate such a realm—later reversing it to visit a super-world in which we inhabit a particle. It is a tribute to his skill that a story based on such an idea could be a popular success. The unnamed chemist in *The Girl in the Golden Atom* (Rogers in the sequel) sees with his super-microscope an infinitesimal human race, including a nubile wench (compare Fitz-James O'Brien's "The Diamond Lens"). But instead of agonising over the unattainable he devises size-changing drugs (compare *Alice in Wonderland*). The relativity of size and the experience of changing size are vividly evoked. The book was fresh and exciting then, and it still reads well, and rates as a classic—though it is not precisely science fiction. (Incidentally, this adventure does not reach the level of an atomic world, despite the title; G.P. Wertenbaker has the doubtful honor of first taking the idea that far in "The Man from the Atom," in *Science and Invention,* August 1923.)

In the extended book version the villain is called Targo, and many later evildoers were named alliteratively—Taro, Toroh, etc. They are typically greedy megalomaniacs, usually gross or deformed, good at sneering and cynical laughter. Subtleties of character and motivation are not displayed, but human relations are simplified and fogged with romantic myths in most science fiction then. The writing is direct and conversational. To modern eyes there is much overstating of the obvious, especially in the novels, but there were mystery and suspense supporting the action for the original audience.

Cummings was an early exploiter of time travel, scarcely touched since Wells, in *The Man Who Mastered Time, The Shadow Girl,* and others, though mostly for change of scene only. *Explorers into Infinity* reverses the exploration of the inconceivably small to visit a vastly greater sphere. *The Man on the Meteor* tells of a tiny worldlet in Saturn's ring with seas and aquatic microscopic humans. *Tarrano the Conqueror* has a future of interplanetary affairs and a new Napoleon. In *The Sea Girl* an undersea people threatens the land. *A Brand New World* has a new extra-solar planet entering the system. *Brigands of the Moon* moved into the kind of future interplanetary traffic early magazine SF postulated and helped establish space piracy as a popular theme. Cummings wrote many routine space adventure shorts thereafter. In "Jetta of the Lowlands" (*Astounding,* 1930), new nations grew from settlements on the dry sea bed after the oceans receded. Sixteen stories featuring the character "Tubby" carried some gentle satire on many of his own plots and concepts.

Cummings's treatment of robots is of interest, though they figured in only a few late stories. "The Robot Rebellion" (*Blue Book,* May 1934) is a misleading title, since the robots play a subordinate part in a conspiracy; but they are shown as integrated into a future society. "The Robot God" (*Weird Tales,* July 1941) has a conventional view of the synthetic intelligent being placing its own interests first at the expense of man. But in "Zeoh-X" (*Thrilling Wonder Stories,* April 1939) and "X1-2-200" (*Astounding,* September 1938), robots are seen as loyal retainers using their own initiative in their masters' interests. In the latter story, the robot suffers conflict between basic psychological compulsions imposed on it: firstly, to avoid harm to humans; secondly, to obey human orders; thirdly, to protect itself. So we see that Cummings first introduced the idea of these motivations that would be necessary to impose on robots, later ably exploited in many stories by Isaac Asimov, such as the "Three Laws of Robotics."

The series of 12 *Tales of the Scientific Crime Club* dating from the early 1920s are ingenious examples of the scientific detective story, a form now obsolete. They are armchair detective puzzles turning on application of scientific principles to a problem, mostly but not quite becoming science fiction by introducing a new speculation.

—Graham Stone

D

DALE, Norman. *See* TUBB, E.C.

DALEY, Brian C.

Pseudonym: Jack McKinney (with James Luceno). **Nationality:** American. **Born:** Englewood, New Jersey, 22 December 1947. **Military Service:** United States Army, 1965-69; tours in Vietnam, West Berlin. **Education:** Jersey City State College, B.A. in communication 1974. **Career:** Has worked as waiter, housepainter, laborer, and case worker. **Address:** Box 327, Arnold, Maryland 21012 U.S.A.

SCIENCE FICTION PUBLICATIONS

Novels (series: Coramonde; Alacrity Fitzhugh; Han Solo)

The Doomfarers of Coramonde. New York, Ballantine, 1977.
The Starfollowers of Coramonde. New York, Ballantine, 1979.
Tron (novelization of screenplay). New York, Ballantine, 1982.
A Tapestry of Magics. New York, Ballantine, 1983.
Requiem for a Ruler of Worlds (Fitzhugh). New York, Ballantine, 1985; London, Grafton, 1989.
Jinx on a Terran Inheritance (Fitzhugh). New York, Ballantine, 1985; London, Grafton, 1990.
Fall of the White Ship Avatar (Fitzhugh). New York, Ballantine, 1987; London, Grafton, 1990.
The Han Solo Adventures. New York, Ballantine, 1992.
  Han Solo at Stars' End: From the Adventures of Luke Skywalker. New York, Ballantine, and London, Sphere, 1979.
  Han Solo's Revenge: From the Adventures of Luke Skywalker. New York, Ballantine, 1979; London, Sphere, 1980.
  Han Solo and the Lost Legacy: From the Adventures of Luke Skywalker. New York, Ballantine, 1980; London, Sphere, 1981.

OTHER PUBLICATIONS

Novels as Jack McKinney (with James Luceno; series: Robotech, Sentinels, Black Hole Travel Agency)

The Final Nightmare (Robotech). New York, Ballantine, 1987.
Invid Invasion (Robotech). New York, Ballantine, 1987.
Metal Fire (Robotech). New York, Ballantine, 1987.
Metamorphosis (Robotech). New York, Ballantine, 1987.
Southern Cross (Robotech). New York, Ballantine, 1987.
Symphony of Light (Robotech). New York, Ballantine, 1987.
Dark Powers (Sentinels). New York, Ballantine, 1988.
Death Dance (Sentinels). New York, Ballantine, 1988.
The Devil's Hand (Sentinels). New York, Ballantine, 1988.
World Killers (Sentinels). New York, Ballantine, 1988.
Rubicon (Sentinels). New York, Ballantine, 1988.

The End of the Circle (Robotech). New York, Ballantine, 1990.
Event Horizon (Black Hole). New York, Ballantine, 1991.
Artifact of the System (Black Hole). New York and London, Ballantine, 1991.
Free Radicals (Black Hole). New York, Ballantine, and Tiptree, England, Tiptree, 1992.
Hostile Takeover (Black Hole). New York and London, Ballantine, 1994.
The Zentraedi Rebellion (Robotech). New York, Ballantine, 1994.
Robotech: Genesis, Battle Cry, Homecoming. New York, Ballantine, 1994.
  Battle Cry. New York, Ballantine, 1987.
  Genesis. New York, Ballantine, 1987.
  Homecoming. New York, Ballantine, 1987.
Robotech: Battlehymn, Force of Arms, Doomsday. New York, Ballantine, 1994.
  Battlehymn. New York, Ballantine, 1987.
  Doomsday. New York, Ballantine, 1987.
  Force of Arms. New York, Ballantine, 1987.

Plays

Radio Plays: *Star Wars series* (13 episodes); *The Empire Strikes Back series* (10 episodes); *Star Wars: The National Public Radio Dramatization.* New York, Ballantine, 1994.
Animated TV: *Galaxy Rangers* (7 episodes).

Recordings: *Rebel Mission to Ord Mantell; War Games.*

*

Manuscript Collection: "American Heritage Center," University of Wyoming, Laramie.

Brian C. Daley comments:

Asked his reaction to becoming a millionaire, Neil Simon once said that the main difference in life was between being broke and bringing down 200 dollars a week; the rest was gravy. Writing has been a bit like that: making a living writing my own books, dealing with popular movie material, having scripts produced, and so forth has been gratifying and on the whole very enjoyable, but it's icing on the cake, after all. The real dividing line in life was in selling my first novel and seeing it in print.

I do my best to keep in mind the desire I had to tell a story, and how crucial it was—and should continue to be—to give the reader full value for his or her time, attention, and money. One of the pitfalls of writing for a living is that a certain perfunctoriness can creep in if you're not careful, especially in a genre where being prolific can be such a plus.

I don't have much to say, here, about art, literature, or moral uplift. The SF/Fantasy audience is quick to let you know if you're not delivering; my efforts are concentrated on satisfying the customers.

*   *   *

Brian C. Daley made an instant, favorable impact with the publication of his first novel, *The Doomfarers of Coramonde,* in 1977.

A group of American soldiers and an armored personnel carrier are magically transported from Vietnam to the world of Coramonde, where they are enlisted in the quest to rescue a princess and defeat a powerful sorcerer aided by a fearsome dragon. The working of scientific technology into a fantasy context created a refreshing new look at an all too familiar story line, proving that with an inventive imagination, new twists can be found in any situation. A cast of engaging characters, liberal doses of genuine humor, and an adventurous and action-packed plot made this one of the most auspicious first novels in years.

Daley followed up with *The Starfollowers of Coramonde,* which lacked some of the spontaneity of its predecessor but still maintained a very high level of storytelling. A sorceress army is gathering to plunge the world back into a repressive tyranny, with soldiers who seem invulnerable to physical or magical attack. Not quite as successful as the earlier novel, it is still superior to most of the fantasy fiction that was appearing from more experienced writers.

Unfortunately, Daley's career was sidetracked into media-associated books for the next few years. The novelization of the film *Tron* was competent but basically forgettable. Daley also wrote three original novels set in the "Star Wars" universe, featuring Han Solo, the itinerant starship pilot and smuggler. In *Han Solo at Star's End* Solo is maneuvered into rescuing a rebel leader from the Empire. He becomes involved with slave traders in *Han Solo's Revenge* and attempts to find a legendary priceless treasure in *Han Solo and the Lost Legacy.* Although the novels are relatively minor adventures, hampered in part by the restrictions implied by writing in the universe created by another mind, Daley embellishes his tales with some captivating robot characters, and provides dollops of clever humor at strategic points.

A Tapestry of Magics marked a return to original fantasy, and it remains Daley's single best work. The Singularity is a realm of relative calm in a fantasy world that literally borders upon every time and every reality. Daley's fondness for paradoxical matchings was evident in the Coramonde books, and now he presents us with Nazi commandoes locked in combat with horse barbarians, knights in shining armor jousting with American Indians, and a nervous Count Dracula pleading for refuge from his pursuers. The protagonist is a heroic figure who retreats from a frustrated love affair to what he hopes will be a life of quiet indolence. Things don't quite work out that way, of course. The tapestry is a magical contrivance that holds within its scenes all of the past, and possibly the power to control the future. It is a magnificent fantasy work, but to date the last thing Daley wrote in that style.

Requiem for a Ruler of Worlds was the opening volume in a more straightforward science fiction trilogy featuring Hobart Floyt. Earth is a minor power, its focus on internal problems, in the interstellar civilization of the far future. A bureaucrat discovers that he is the unlikely heir to a charismatic ruler on another world, and despite his protestations, the government of Earth insists that he claim his legacy, although they want the power it entails for their own purposes rather than his. Accompanied by a more experienced traveler conditioned to remain loyal, he sets off for the reading of the will, only to discover that he is the target for a team of determined assassins.

The second adventure, *Jinx on a Terran Inheritance,* follows the two companions as they seek to discover the whereabouts of the starship that was signed over to Floyt under the terms of the will. Upon their return to Earth, a final confrontation over control of the ship threatens to end the adventurers' lives, unless they can undermine the government itself. The concluding adventure is *Fall of the White Ship Avatar,* wherein the protagonists set out to discover the secrets of an ancient but lost alien technology. The series is lighthearted entertainment, but stylishly handled.

Although it appears that additional adventures were planned, none have appeared since 1987. This may be the result of a series of over a dozen novelizations of the Japanese Robotech programs that Daley wrote in collaboration with James Luceno under the name Jack McKinney. Although these are competently written, they are essentially juvenile adventure stories with lots of action and little substance.

The original novels that have appeared under the Daley byline have been uniformly excellent and generally highly original. *A Tapestry of Magics* in particular demonstrates that Daley has the potential to produce significant works in the field. Time will tell whether that potential will ever be realized.

—Don D'Ammassa

DANN, Jack (Mayo)

Nationality: American. **Born:** Johnson City, New York, 15 February 1945. **Education:** Hofstra University, Hempstead, New York, 1963; State University of New York, Binghamton, 1965-68, B.A. in social science and political science 1968; St. John's Law School, New York, 1969-71. **Family:** Married 1) Jeanne Van Buren (divorced 1994); 2) Janeen Webb in 1995. **Career:** Taught writing and science fiction at Broome Community College, Binghamton, 1972, 1990-91, and Cornell University, Ithaca, New York, summer 1973; managing editor, *SFWA Bulletin,* 1970-75, Freelance writer and lecturer. **Awards:** British Science Fiction Association award, 1979; Premios Gilgamés de Narrativa Fantastica award, 1986 **Agent:** Merrilee Heifetz, Writer's House, 21 West 26th Street, New York, New York 10010. **Address:** P.O. Box 6231, St. Kilda Road Central, Melbourne VIC 3004, Australia.

SCIENCE FICTION PUBLICATIONS

Novels

Starhiker: A Novel. New York, Harper, 1977.
Junction. New York, Dell, 1981.
The Man Who Melted. New York, Bluejay, 1984.
Echoes of Thunder, with *Run for the Stars,* by Harlan Elison. New York, Tor, 1991.
High Steel, with Jack C. Haldeman II. New York, Tor, 1993.
The Memory Cathedral. New York, Bantam, 1995.

Short Stories

Timetipping. Garden City, New York, Doubleday, 1980.

OTHER PUBLICATIONS

Poetry

Christs and Other Poems. Binghamton, New York, Bellevue Press, 1978.

Other

Slow Dancing through Time, with others. Kansas City, Missouri, Ursus, 1990.

Editor, *Wandering Stars: An Anthology of Jewish Fantasy and Science Fiction.* New York, Harper, and London, Woburn Press, 1975.

Editor, with Gardner Dozois, *Future Power: A Science Fiction Anthology.* New York, Random House, 1976.

Editor, with George Zebrowski, *Faster Than Light: An Anthology about Interstellar Travel.* New York, Harper, 1976.

Editor, *Immortal: Short Novels of the Transhuman Future.* New York, Harper, 1978.

Editor, with Gardner Dozois, *Aliens!: Outstanding Stories of Jewish Science Fiction and Fantasy.* New York, Pocket Books, 1980.

Editor, *More Wandering Stars.* New York, Doubleday, 1981.

Editor, with Gardner Dozois, *Unicorns!* New York, Ace, 1982.

Editor, with Gardner Dozois, *Magicats!* New York, Ace, 1984.

Editor, with Gardner Dozois, *Bestiary!* New York, Ace, 1985.

Editor, with Gardner Dozois, *Mermaids!* New York, Ace, 1986.

Editor, with Gardner Dozois, *Sorcerers!* New York, Ace, 1986.

Editor, with Gardner Dozois, *Demons!* New York, Ace, 1987.

Editor, with Jeanne Van Buren Dann, *In the Field of Fire.* New York, Tor, 1987.

Editor, with Gardner Dozois, *Dogtales!* New York, Ace, 1988.

Editor, with Gardner Dozois, *Seaserpents!* New York, Ace, 1989.

Editor, with Gardner Dozois, *Dinosaurs!* New York, Ace, 1990.

Editor, with Gardner Dozois, *Little People!* New York, Ace, 1991.

Editor, with Gardner Dozois, *Magicats II.* New York, Ace, 1991.

Editor, with Gardner Dozois, *Unicorns II.* New York, Ace, 1991.

Editor, with Gardner Dozois, *Dragons!* New York, Ace, 1993.

Editor, with Gardner Dozois, *Invaders!* New York, Ace, 1993.

Editor, with Gardner Dozois, *Horses!* New York, Ace, 1994.

*

Bibliography: *The Work of Jack Dann: An Annotated Bibliography and Guide* by Jeffrey M. Elliot, San Bernardino, California, Borgo Press, 1990.

Manuscript Collection: Temple University, Philadelphia.

Jack Dann comments:

. . . . Still 1994. It's the National Australian Convention, and William Gibson is the guest of honor. We're on the roof of the Southern Cross Hotel beside the swimming pool. In the background are Melbourne's skyscrapers set off against a clear, blue sky. It's April. The sun is hot, and the feel of it on the skin is delicious . . .

As I sit beside Bill, I remember his first novel, *Neuromancer,* which took all the awards in 1984. My novel *The Man Who Melted* was on the same Nebula ballot that year. I saw *Neuromancer* as a harbinger, which it was; and the cyberpunk movement, which it started, has become a real element of modern popular culture. As Bill said, "It's bohemia with computers."

"I missed the whole cyberpunk movement. I was writing and researching my Da Vinci novel, and when I woke up from the Italian Renaissance six years later, everything had changed."

"I don't know," Bill says. "We always figured you were there."

But I wasn't. I was following my own labyrinth, which had led me from wild literary experimentation to a thousand-page narrative [published in 1995 as *The Memory Cathedral*] that was the antith-

esis of postmodernism. Its purpose was to suspend disbelief, to create memory and experience rather than artifacts.

I had hidden myself in the past, in research, in words, in a fabrication that had gained such verisimilitude in my mind that I could quit the present world.

. . . . Right now I'm doing research for *The Silent* and working with Jack C. Haldeman on the sequel to our novel *High Steel,* which was published in 1993 and well received.

The future will certainly be its own master and have at me in ways I'd rather not know. In the meantime, I'll live every precious minute with all the juice and energy and joy I can muster. [Excerpted from "Sparks in the Dark" by Jack Dann, *Contemporary Authors Autobiography Series,* Detroit, Gale Research.]

* * *

To paraphrase Jack Dann's own description of his work, it is an attempt to deal with the predicament of consciousness. This places his writing at the heart of all literary endeavor, in which remembrance and critical self-awareness are the key elements. Much of his work has at its center an evolving human consciousness attempting to confront, understand, and apprehend the universe.

This theme is evident in Dann's earliest work, most notably in the inventive short story "The Dybbuk Dolls" (1975), in which a devout Jew in a decadent and chaotic future city struggles to resist an alien force that can amplify his feelings of guilt, and in the novella "Junction" (1973), where Ned Wheeler leaves his village of Junction to encounter Hell, the physically indeterminate world outside. *Starhiker,* Dann's first novel, has the structure of a more conventional science fiction novel: Bo Forester, a young man on a backward Earth ruled by the alien Hrau, sneaks aboard a spaceship and travels to other worlds. Bo's journey, however, is as much a search for knowledge and understanding as for adventure.

Dann's works often end with his protagonists glimpsing some truth or mystery that reality may hold for us rather than changing the conditions of their lives. This is not to say that his writing is pessimistic; instead, it reflects a faith in the ability of human beings to wring some sort of triumph and understanding, however small, out of even the most wretched circumstances. Thus Stephen in "Camps" (1979), one of Dann's most highly praised stories, must fight for his life both as a seriously ill hospital patient and, in a mental link with the past, as an inmate in a concentration camp. Ned Wheeler, in the novel *Junction* (1981), a work greatly expanded and developed from its novella-length version, finds upon his return to his home town that no true return is possible and that he has come to an alternate Junction; his quest ends in the understanding and acceptance of irreversible change.

Dann has the ability to create imaginary worlds that are exceedingly rich in detail, often to the point of seeming hallucinatory. One doesn't read a Dann work so much as experience it; his worlds engage the reader both viscerally and intellectually. In "A Quiet Revolution for Death" (1978), the horror of this particular near future's celebration of death emerges gradually and subtly, while in "Jumping the Road" (1992), one is plunged into the mind and soul of a doubting rabbi on a planet where a group of indigenous alien Jews has been found. "Timetipping" (1975), one of his finest stories and one of several that reflect Dann's Jewish heritage, shows a world where cause is severed from effect, but daily life (of a sort) still courageously goes on.

Dann's gifts as a regional writer should also be noted. In stories such as "Bad Medicine" (1984), "Tattoos" (1986), and "The Extra" (1993), upstate New York, where he grew up and spent much of his life, is refracted through the lens of fantasy. "Bad Medicine," a World Fantasy Award finalist, and a later story, "Counting Coup" (1994), are sections of a still unpublished novel titled *Counting Coup,* in which a failed Indian medicine man and an elderly handyman go on one last binge across the country; the two published sections stand on their own as stories, but also make one long to see the complete novel in print.

The Man Who Melted (1984) is considered to be Dann's masterpiece, and three portions of this book published as stories ("Amnesia" [1981], "Going Under" [1981], and "Blind Shemmy" [1983]) were Nebula Award finalists. *The Man Who Melted* also marks a departure for Dann in that, unlike his earlier novels, it is not told from a single point-of-view. We follow Raymond Mantle, his lover Joan Otur, and Mantle's old friend and rival Carl Pfeiffer through a decadent future under a threat from Screamers—people who come together in a great telepathic web to riot and destroy. The novel is studded with inventive details—people gambling away their hearts or other organs, somatically and genetically engineered prostitutes and street people, a *Titanic* raised from the ocean depths only to be sunk again with passengers who have chosen to go down with the ship, devices that link people mentally to the dying and the dead—and pulls the reader into its fierce phantasmagorical currents. *The Man Who Melted* is not a fragmented or episodic work, as the earlier publication of excerpts might suggest, but a carefully plotted and progressively suspenseful whole. Raymond Mantle is seeking his lost wife Josiane, who has become a Screamer; as an amnesiac, he is also trying to recover his past. By the end of the novel, he has found both.

1993 saw the publication of *High Steel,* a collaborative novel by Dann and Jack C. Haldeman II. The central character, John Stranger, is a Native American working in space for one of the ruthless international corporations that control Earth. Both authors succeed in blending familiar genre elements into a narrative with suspense and depth; John Stranger's efforts to cling to his Indian spiritual heritage reflect Dann's interest in exploring how human consciousness confronts the universe.

One danger for a writer whose work is often dominated by a particular theme is that of repeating himself. Dann successfully avoids this trap by constantly seeking new materials out of which to weave his tales. His novella "Jubilee" (1995), one of his major works, involves an alien presence that is apparently altering the nature of reality in its attempts to make contact with Earth. An American traveling in Greece and an expatriate artist living in Australia look on helplessly as mobs of people gather to hurl themselves into the sea, where they are seemingly transformed into sea creatures. The alien appears in the story only as a series of questions asked by an unseen narrator seeking to understand.

The Memory Cathedral (1995), Dann's most recent book-length work, is a historical novel about Leonardo da Vinci, but is also a work of science fiction set in the past. In the novel, Leonardo, disgraced in Florence, travels to the Middle East, becomes an advisor and engineer in the court of the Devardar of Syria, and sees some of his more deadly inventions constructed and used in warfare. Leonardo must witness the destruction brought about by the products of his brilliant imagination. (A related novella, "Da Vinci Rising" [1995], was published in *Asimov's Science Fiction* and is set in an alternative history. Leonardo succeeds in building a flying machine, and the novella ends with the likelihood that his patron, Lorenzo de Medici, will use such machines in aerial warfare.) Dann's theme of human intelligence apprehending the universe is

beautifully embodied in the character of Leonardo, and his ability to produce almost hallucinatory images is on display in his detailed depictions of Renaissance Florence and an exotic Middle East. *The Memory Cathedral,* along with much of this writer's most recent work, provides ample evidence that Jack Dann is reaching his full maturity as a writer while, happily, still retaining the vigorous inspiration of his youth.

—Pamela Sargent

DAVIDSON, Avram

Pseudonym: Ellery Queen. **Nationality:** American. **Born:** Yonkers, New York, 23 April 1923. **Education:** New York University, 1940-42; Yeshiva University, New York, 1947-48; Pierce College, Canoga Park, California, 1950-51. **Military Service:** Served in the United States Navy, 1942-46; served in the Israeli Army in the Arab-Israeli war, 1948-49. **Family:** Married Grania Kaiman (divorced); one son. **Career:** Editor, *Fantasy and Science Fiction* magazine, New York, 1962-64. From 1964, freelance writer. **Awards:** Hugo award, 1958, for editing, 1963; Ellery Queen award, 1958; Mystery Writers of America Edgar Allan Poe award, 1961; World Fantasy award, 1976, 1979, life achievement award, 1986. **Died:** 8 May 1993.

Science Fiction Publications

Novels (series: Vergil Magus; Peregrine)

Joyleg, with Ward Moore. New York, Pyramid, 1962.
Mutiny in Space. New York, Pyramid, 1964; London, White Lion, 1973.
Rogue Dragon. New York, Ace, 1965.
Rork! New York, Berkley, 1965; London, Rapp and Whiting, 1968.
Masters of the Maze. New York, Pyramid, 1965; London, White Lion, 1974.
The Enemy of My Enemy. New York, Berkley, 1966.
Clash of Star-Kings. New York, Ace, 1966.
The Kar-Chee Reign. New York, Ace, 1966.
The Island under the Earth. New York, Ace, 1969; London, Mayflower, 1975.
The Phoenix and the Mirror (Vergil Magus). Garden City, New York, Doubleday, 1969; London, Mayflower, 1975.
Peregrine: Primus. New York, Walker, 1971.
Ursus of Ultima Thule. New York, Avon, 1973.
Peregrine: Secundus. New York, Berkley, 1981.
Vergil in Averno. New York, Doubleday, 1987.
Marco Polo and the Sleeping Beauty, with Grania Davis. New York, Baen, 1988.

Short Stories

Or All the Seas with Oysters. New York, Berkley, 1962; London, White Lion, 1976.
What Strange Stars and Skies. New York, Ace, 1965.
Strange Seas and Shores. Garden City, New York, Doubleday, 1971.

The Enquiries of Doctor Eszterhazy. New York, Warner, 1975; expanded as *The Adventures of Doctor Esterhazy,* Philadelphia, Owlswick Press, 1991.

The Redward Edward Papers. Garden City, New York, Doubleday, 1978.

The Best of Avram Davidson, edited by Michael Kurland. Garden City, New York, Doubleday, 1979.

Collected Fantasies of Avram Davidson, edited by John Silbersack. New York, Berkley, 1982.

Polly Charms the Sleeping Woman. Williamsburg, Virginia, English Department, College of William and Mary, 1977.

And Don't Forget the One Red Rose. Seattle, Washington, Dryad Press, 1986.

OTHER PUBLICATIONS

Novels

And on the Eighth Day (as Ellery Queen). New York, Random House, 1964.

The Fourth Side of the Triangle (as Ellery Queen). New York, Random House, 1965.

Other

Crimes and Chaos (essays). Evanston, Illinois, Regency, 1962.

Adventures in Unhistory: Conjectures on the Factual Foundations of Several Ancient Legends. Philadelphia, Owlswick Press, 1993.

Editor, *The Best from Fantasy and Science Fiction, 12th-14th Series.* New York, Doubleday, 3 vols., 1963-65; London, Gollancz, 2 vols., 1966; Panther, 1 vol., 1967.

Editor, *Magic for Sale.* New York, Ace, 1983.

*

Bibliography: "A Bibliography of Avram Davidson" by Richard Grant, in *Megavore 9* (Calgary, Alberta), June 1980.

Manuscript Collections: California State University, Fullerton; Texas A. and M. University, College Station.

*   *   *

Avram Davidson's arcane and whimsical fiction, which was published in his lifetime almost entirely in science fiction and mystery magazines, resists classification: like Lafcadio Hearn, John Collier, and Lord Dunsany (three writers with whom he has at times been compared), Davidson wrote witty and mannered stories, dense with learning worn lightly and charged with considerable verbal energy, that generally contain elements of fantasy. The fabulist tradition in English literature had been out of fashion since the Edwardian era, and Davidson spent his entire career being published primarily in the SF and mystery genres, which proved hospitable to his talents. Although he experienced great difficulty in the last decade of his life getting publishers to bring out his books, he retains an enthusiastic audience among readers of short fiction, and was (and is) frequently anthologized. His work has been issued by small-press publishers even as it lost the interest of mass-market publishers, and it seems likely that his work will be better known in 10 years than it is today.

Davidson's first published SF story, "My Boy Friend's Name is Jello" (1954), established with verve and assurance the narrative voice and manner of his mature fiction:

> Fashion, nothing but fashion. Virus X having in the medical zodiac its course half i-run, the physician (I refuse to say 'doctor' and, indeed, am tempted to use the more correct 'apothecary')—the physician, I say, tells me I have Virus Y. No doubt in the Navy it would still be called Catarrhal Fever. They say that hardly anyone had appendicitis until Edward VII came down with it a few weeks before his coronation, and thus made it fashionable. . . . Oh dear, how my mind runs on. I must be feverish. An ague, no doubt.

The story comprises the ailing narrator's surmise that the little girls who sing as they play games outside his window possess magical powers; its only action is when he rises from his bed to throw them coins. Only four pages long, the tale perfectly characterizes Davidson's early work: compact, spare of plot, faintly nostalgic for a less fatuous past.

Davidson's early stories quickly made his reputation in the science fiction field. Within five years he had published several enduring stories, including "The Golem," "Or All the Seas With Oysters," "Take Wooden Indians," "Help! I Am Doctor Morris Goldpepper," and "Dagon." "Or All the Seas With Oysters," which won a Hugo Award, introduced a conceit that has become an authentic piece of American folklore: the idea that the number of safety pins in one's desk and hangars in one's closet fluctuates because they are the immature and adult forms of a single species, which mimics human artifacts the way praying mantises do twigs. Questions concerning the source for this tale are occasionally raised in newspapers and magazines (including once in the *Journal of the American Society of Electrical and Chemical Engineers*), and invariably credited to Davidson.

At the urging of Robert P. Mills, then managing editor of *Ellery Queen's Mystery Magazine* as well as *The Magazine of Fantasy and Science Fiction,* Davidson began to write for mystery magazines in the late fifties. These stories, which Davidson continued to write all his life, are similar in tone and manner (save for the fact that they rarely contain elements of the fantastic) to his other short fiction. The weaker ones resemble the stories generally published in mystery magazines, although superior in their prose and particularity of locale; the best, such as "Summon the Watch!" or "Where Do You Live, Queen Esther?", are of a piece with his better fantasy stories. Davidson won both the Ellery Queen Award and the Edgar Award for mystery stories published during this period, and eventually ghost-wrote some mystery novels that were published as by Ellery Queen.

By the early 1960s Davidson was publishing longer stories, and eventually produced much of his best work in the novelette form. "The Sources of the Nile" (1961), his extravagant tale of a failed and aging advertising man who discovers the secret of anticipating trends in American tastes, combines Davidson's love of arcane lore with his satiric eye for the modern world in a manner that retains his concise early style while benefiting from a greater expansiveness. Davidson's disgust with the venality of the commercial world, which would grow more obtrusive in his later work, is here particularized with the image of the villain's perforated business cards; and other elements that would threaten to become hobbyhorses of

Davidson's in his last years—such as the protagonist being brought low by the perfidy of women, or the triumph of coarseness over artistry—are maintained in artistic equilibrium. In the same manner, "Take Wooden Indians" (which contrasts the 19th-century craft of carving wooden Indians with the aridity of contemporary art) manages to be antimodern without being sourly so.

Soon afterward Davidson began to publish his first novels. With the exception of the Ward Moore collaboration *Joyleg,* Davidson's early novels—all science fiction, which he had previously written only infrequently and incidentally—are commercial undertakings, much better than the standard SF of their time and recognizably Davidson's, but not on a level with his best work. They tend to be memorable more for the evocation of place and delineation of scene in their opening chapters than for their dramatic development, but remain enjoyable thirty years later.

These books seem to have been undertaken in order to support both a family and to underwrite the long composition of what Davidson regarded as his *magnum opus,* the cycle of novels (never completed) that he called *Vergil Magus.* Davidson's plan of writing a novel sequence set in the ancient Roman Empire of the medieval imagination—in which Vergil was remembered as a sorceror, not a poet, and the various scraps of knowledge, supposition, and backward-projected medieval values are fused into an imaginative whole—was an enormously ambitious one, and he worked years before completing *The Phoenix and the Mirror,* surely his finest novel and a classic of modern fantasy. Davidson's dense and somber tale of how the sorcerer Vergil set about to make a *speculum majorum* in the face of overwhelming difficulties possesses the imaginative force of only the most powerful fantasies: we believe in the *cosmos* of the novel, that its existence continues beyond the edge of the page.

The Phoenix and the Mirror was published in book form in 1969 (an abridged version had seen magazine publication three years earlier), the same year in which Davidson published his second-finest novel, *The Island Under the Earth.* Announced as the first of a trilogy, this novel seemed to take its inspiration from the metope of the Parthenon depicting the war between the centaurs and the Lapiths, although it is set not in the mountains of Thessaly but in a fantastic cosmology whose nature is not yet made clear at novel's end. Finely controlled and densely realized, Davidson's tale of centaurs, harpies, eunuchs, ship captains, and assorted rogues moves swiftly and with assurance through a world the peculiarly reflects our own, and about which the reader will regret not learning more.

Davidson did not continue his ventures on either book, but began instead several new series, including "Zon" (1970) and *Peregrine: Primus* (1971), the last a comic novel of the disintegrating Roman Empire, broader in its effects and more casual in its structure than the two previous novels. Although in 1973 Davidson published a fragmentary sequel to *Primus* in a magazine (*Peregrine: Secundus* was eventually published in 1981), he essentially suspended work on these projects throughout the seventies. The second Vergil novel, *Vergil in Averno,* did not appear untiil 1987, and a third never found a publisher.

In 1975 Davidson published *The Enquiries of Doctor Eszterhazy,* a sequence of stories set in the Triune Monarchy of Scythia-Pannonia-Transbalkania, a tiny ruritanian country soon to be swept away in the Great War. Engelbert Eszterhazy, the emperor's wizard, who drove about the cobbled streets of the capital in a steam runabout and boasted five learned degrees, was an obvious Vergil figure, although the ornate and highly fanciful tales (eight in the original sequence) dramatize their various abstruse matters with the

high spirits of Davidson's short fiction rather than the grave wonder of the Vergil novels.

In the mid-eighties Davidson returned to this venue with a series of eight longer tales about Eszterhazy in his youth. By this time Davidson's style had changed, and his prose became less tightly coiled, discursive, and sometimes prolix. The five stories of Cornet Eszterhazy are longer than the eight earlier ones, and should be considered as a separate, although not lesser, sequence (Owlswick Press' omnibus collection *The Adventures of Doctor Eszterhazy* obscures this by running the 18 stories in order of internal chronology). Davidson was working on an Eszterhazy novel at the time of his death.

Davidson wrote a second sequence of novelettes, concerning the young man Jack Limekiller and his strange enounters in the former colony of British Hidalgo. This series, which began in 1976 and continued through the end of Davidson's life (one story, "A Far Countrie," was published posthumously), shares the exotic sense of place for an imaginary locale and love of strange incident that characterizes the Vergil and the Limekiller stories. Although the Limekiller series includes some of Davidson's best fiction, it has not yet been published in book form.

Davidson was not adept in devising plots, and felt himself at a disadvantage in giving structure to longer work. Many of his novels acknowledge the assistance of colleagues in the shaping. His late unpublished novels, which were written unassisted and never subjected to editorial suggestion, tend to be ramshackle in their construction (*Marco Polo and the Sleeping Beauty,* credited as a collaboration with Grania Davis, was according to Davis completed by her from a mass of material by Davidson). Certainly the essays published as *Adventures in Unhistory* can ramble farther afield than is good for them. Most of his last published fiction, however, retains sufficient color and charm to compensate for their more relaxed muscle tone. Some of the late novelettes, such as "The Slovo Stove" and "El Vilvoy de las Islas," must be counted among his best.

Davidson was a difficult man, who had little gift for career management (he broke with publishers and agents, left series unfinished or allowed decades to pass between volumes, and moved often and lost manuscripts) and suffered enormously when genre book editors decided, probably incorrectly, that his work could not be successfully published. Much good work remains unpublished, and Davidson has more published but uncollected short work of distinction than any other science fiction or fantasy writer. With a growing interest among literary audiences in what is now called "magic realism," Davidson's best work may yet reach a larger readership than he was able to enjoy in his lifetime.

—Gregory Feeley

DAVIS, (Horace) Chan(dler)

Nationality: American. **Born:** Ithaca, New York, 12 August 1926. **Education:** Harvard University, Cambridge, Massachusetts, B.S. 1945, M.A. 1947, Ph.D. in mathematics 1950. **Military Service:** Served in the United States Naval Reserve, 1944-46. **Family:** Married Natalie Zemon in 1948; one son and two daughters. Served six-month prison sentence for refusing to answer questions before the House Un-American Activities Committee, 1960. **Career:** Instructor in mathematics, University of Michigan, Ann Arbor, 1950-54; director of Experimental Research, Kenyon and Eckhardt advertising company, New York, 1955-57; member of the Institute for Advanced Study, Princeton, New Jersey, 1957-58; associate editor, *Mathematical Reviews,* Providence, Rhode Island, 1958-61. Since 1962, Associate Professor, then Professor of Mathematics, University of Toronto. Since 1991, editor-in-chief, *The Mathematical Intelligencer.* **Agent:** Virginia Kidd, Box 278, Milford, Pennsylvania 18337, U.S.A. **Address:** 52 Follis Avenue, Toronto M6G 1S3, Canada.

SCIENCE FICTION PUBLICATIONS

Uncollected Short Stories

"To Still the Drums," in *Astounding* (New York), October 1946.
"The Journey and the Goal," in *Astounding* (New York), May 1947.
"The Nightmare," in *A Treasury of Science Fiction,* edited by Groff Conklin. New York, Crown, 1948.
"The Aristocrat," in *Astounding* (New York), October 1949.
"Blind Play," in *Planet* (New York), May 1951.
"Share Our World," in *Astounding* (New York), August 1953.
"Letter to Ellen," in *Science Fiction Thinking Machines,* edited by Groff Conklin. New York, Vanguard Press, 1954.
"It Walks in Beauty," in *Star Science Fiction Stories 4,* edited by Frederik Pohl. New York, Ballantine, 1958.
"The Statistomat Pitch," in *Infinity* (New York), January 1958.
"Adrift on the Policy Level," in *Star Science Fiction Stories 5,* edited by Frederik Pohl. New York, Ballantine, 1959.
"Last Year's Grave Undug," in *Great Science Fiction by Scientists,* edited by Groff Conklin. New York, Macmillan, 1962.
"Hexamnion," in *Nova 1,* edited by Harry Harrison. New York, Delacorte Press, 1970.

*

Chan Davis comments:

(1985) There is so much that needs saying about our real and impending predicaments and ironies, and science fiction allows one to say it in ways less bogged down than in the past. Given this opportunity, why should the writer reject it by producing stories which merely ask the reader to suspend disbelief? One can comment by parables set on concocted planets; by extrapolations; or, most powerfully, by the "higher cautionary tale," in which a potentiality in our own future is brought into relief by magnifying it. No escape is offered, but engagement. Some suspension of disbelief is required, but not suspension of compassion, not suspension of curiosity or common sense. Let this note stand as introduction to the few stories I wrote in my youth and the many I wish yet to write.

*   *   *

Chan Davis has produced a small number of superior stories, beginning with "The Nightmare," one of the first post-Hiroshima science fiction works to focus on the dangers and effects of nuclear war. Although he is a mathematician, most of his stories either explicitly or implicitly examine social themes. Other notable stories include "Adrift on the Policy Level," arguably the finest treatment of bureaucracy and the bureaucratic mind in all of science fiction, and "Letter to Ellen," which, because of a very superficial thematic

resemblance to the earlier "Helen O'Loy" by Lester del Rey, never attained the classic stature due it.

—Martin H. Greenberg

de CAMP, L(yon) Sprague

Nationality: American. **Born:** New York City, 27 November 1907. **Education:** Trinity School, New York; Snyder School, North Carolina; California Institute of Technology, Pasadena, B.S. in aeronautical engineering 1930; Massachusetts Institute of Technology, Cambridge, summer 1932; Stevens Institute of Technology, Hoboken, New Jersey, M.S. 1933. **Military Service:** Served in the United States Naval Reserve, 1942-45: Lieutenant Commander. **Family:** Married Catherine A. Crook in 1939; two sons. **Career:** Instructor, Inventors Foundation Inc., New York, 1933-36; principal of School of Inventing and Patenting, International Correspondence Schools, Scranton, Pennsylvania, 1936-37; editor, Fowler-Becker Publishing Company, New York, 1937-38, and American Society of Mechanical Engineers, New York, 1938; assistant mechanical engineer, Naval Aircraft Factory, Philadelphia, 1942; radio scriptwriter, *The Voice of America* series, 1948-56; publicity writer, Gray and Rogers, Philadelphia, 1956. Freelance writer. Member of the Advisory Board, Society for the History of Technology. **Awards:** International Fantasy award, 1953; Gandalf award, 1976; Grand Master Nebula award, 1978; World Fantasy Life Achievement award, 1984. **Address:** 3453 Hearst Castle Way, Plano, Texas 75025-3605, U.S.A.

SCIENCE FICTION PUBLICATIONS

Novels (series: Conan; Incorporated Knight; Jorian; Harold Shea; Viagens Interplanetarias)

Lest Darkness Fall. New York, Holt, 1941; London, Heinemann, 1955.
The Incomplete Enchanter (Shea), with Fletcher Pratt. New York, Holt, 1941; as *The Incompleat Enchanter,* London, Sphere, 1979.
Land of Unreason, with Fletcher Pratt. New York, Holt, 1942.
The Carnelian Cube: A Humorous Fantasy, with Fletcher Pratt. New York, Gnome Press, 1948.
The Castle of Iron: A Science Fiction Adventure (Shea), with Fletcher Pratt. New York, Gnome Press, 1950.
Genus Homo, with P. Schuyler Miller. Reading, Pennsylvania, Fantasy Press, 1950.
The Undesired Princess. Los Angeles, Fantasy, 1951.
Rogue Queen (Viagens). Garden City, New York, Doubleday, 1951; London, Pinnacle, 1954.
Cosmic Manhunt (Viagens). New York, Ace, 1954; revised as *A Planet Called Krishna,* London, Compact, 1966; as *The Queen of Zamba,* New York, Davis, 1977.
Solomon's Stone. New York, Avalon, 1957.
The Return of Conan, with Björn Nyberg. New York, Gnome Press, 1957; expanded as *Conan the Avenger,* New York, Lancer, 1968; London, Sphere, 1989.
The Tower of Zanid (Viagnes). New York, Avalon, 1958.
The Glory That Was. New York, Avalon, 1960.

Wall of Serpents (Shea), with Fletcher Pratt. New York, Avalon, 1960; as *The Enchanter Compleated,* London, Sphere, 1980.

The Search for Zei (Viagens). New York, Avalon, 1962; as *The Floating Continent: The Second Volume in the Famous Krishna Series,* London, Compact, 1966.

The Hand of Zei (Viagens). New York, Avalon, 1963; with *The Search for Zei,* Philadelphia, Owlswick Press, 1981.

The Arrows of Hercules. Garden City, New York, Doubleday, 1965.

Conan of the Isles, with Lin Carter. New York, Lancer, 1968.

The Goblin Tower (Jorian). New York, Pyramid, 1968; London, Sphere, 1979.

The Clocks of Iraz (Jorian). New York, Pyramid, 1971; London, Grafton, 1988.

Conan the Buccaneer, with Lin Carter. New York, Lancer, 1971.

The Fallible Fiend. New York, Signet, 1973; London, Remploy, 1974.

The Compleat Enchanter: The Magical Misadventures of Harold Shea (includes *The Incomplete Enchanter and The Castle of Iron),* with Fletcher Pratt. Garden City, New York, Doubleday, 1975; expanded as *The Intrepid Enchanter: The Complete Magical Misadventures of Harold Shea,* London, Sphere, 1979; as *The Complete Compleat Enchanter,* New York, Baen, 1989.

The Hostage of Zir (Viagens). New York, Berkley, 1977.

The Great Fetish. Garden City, New York, Doubleday, 1978.

Conan the Liberator, with Lin Carter. New York, Bantam, 1979; London, Sphere, 1980.

Conan and the Spider God. New York, Bantam, 1980; London, Hale, 1984.

The Treasure of Tranicos (Conan), with Robert E. Howard. New York, Ace, 1980.

The Prisoner of Zhamanak (Viagens). Huntington Woods, Michigan, Phantasia Press, 1982.

Conan the Barbarian (novelization of screenplay), with Lin Carter. New York, Bantam, and London, Sphere, 1982.

The Unbeheaded King (Jorian). New York, Ballantine, 1983; London, Grafton, 1988.

The Bones of Zora (Viagens), with Catherine Crook de Camp. Huntington Woods, Michigan, Phantasia Press, 1983.

The Reluctant King (includes *The Goblin Tower, The Clocks of Iraz,* and *The Unbeheaded King).* Garden City, New York, Doubleday, 1985.

The Incorporated Knight, with Catherine Crook de Camp. West Bloomfield, Michigan, Phantasia Press, 1987.

The Stones of Nomuru (Viagens), with Catherine Crook de Camp. Norfolk, Virginia, Donning, 1988.

The Honorable Barbarian. Norwalk, Connecticut, Easton Press, 1989.

The Undesired Princess and the Enchanted Bunny, with David A. Drake. New York, Baen, 1990.

The Pixilated Peeress (Incorporated Knight), with Catherine Crook de Camp. New York, Ballantine, 1991.

The Swords of Zinjaban (Viagens), with Catherine Crook de Camp. New York, Baen, 1991.

The Venom Trees of Sunga (Viagens). New York, Ballantine, 1992.

Short Stories

Divide and Rule. Reading, Pennsylvania, Fantasy Press, 1948.

The Wheels of If and Other Science-Fiction. Chicago, Shasta, 1948; title story bound with *The Pugnacious Peacemaker,* by Harry Turtledove, New Yor, Tor, 1990.

The Continent Makers and Other Tales of the Viagens. New York, Twayne, 1953.

Sprague de Camp's New Anthology of Science Fiction. London, Panther, 1953.

Tales from Gavagan's Bar, with Fletcher Pratt. New York, Twayne, 1953; expanded edition, Philadelphia, Owlswick Press, 1978.

The Tritonian Ring and Other Pusadian Tales. New York, Twayne, 1953; London, Sphere, 1978.

Tales of Conan, with Robert E. Howard. New York, Gnome Press, 1955; as *Conan: The Flame Knife,* New York, Ace, 1991.

A Gun for Dinosaur and Other Imaginative Tales. Garden City, New York, Doubleday, 1963.

Conan the Adventurer, with Robert E. Howard. New York, Lancer, 1966; London, Sphere, 1988.

Conan, with Robert E. Howard and Lin Carter. New York, Lancer, 1967; London, Sphere, 1989.

Conan the Usurper, with Robert E. Howard. New York, Lancer, 1967; London, Sphere, 1989.

Conan the Freebooter, with Robert E. Howard. New York, Lancer, 1968; London, Sphere, 1974.

Conan the Wanderer, with Robert E. Howard and Lin Carter. New York, Lancer, 1968; London, Sphere, 1974.

Conan of Cimmeria, with Robert E. Howard and Lin Carter. New York, Lancer, 1969; London, Sphere, 1974.

The Reluctant Shaman and Other Fantastic Tales. New York, Pyramid, 1970.

Conan of Aquilonia (collection), with Lin Carter and Robert E. Howard. New York, Prestige, 1971; London, Sphere, 1988.

The Virgin and the Wheels. New York, Popular Library, 1976.

The Best of L. Sprague de Camp. Garden City, New York, Doubleday, 1977.

Conan the Swordsman, with Lin Carter and Björn Nyberg. New York, Bantam, 1978; London, Sphere, 1979.

The Purple Pterodactyls: The Adventures of W. Wilson Newbury, Ensorcelled Financier. Huntington Woods, Michigan, Phantasia Press, 1979.

Footprints on Sand: A Literary Sampler. Chicago, Advent, 1981.

The Virgin of Zesh; and, The Tower of Zanid (Viagens). New York, Ace, 1983.

The Conan Chronicles (collection), with Lin Carter and Robert E. Howard. London, Orbit, 2 vols., 1989-90.

Divide and Rule, bound with *The Sword of Rhiannon,* by Leigh Brackett. New York, Tor, 1990.

Sir Harold and the Gnome King (Shea). Newark, New Jersey, Wildside Press, 1991.

Rivers of Time. Riverdale, New York, Baen, 1993.

OTHER PUBLICATIONS

Novels

An Elephant for Aristotle. Garden City, New York, Doubleday, 1958; London, Dobson, 1966.

The Bronze God of Rhodes. Garden City, New York, Doubleday, 1960.

The Dragon of the Ishtar Gate. Garden City, New York, Doubleday, 1961.

The Golden Wind. Garden City, New York, Doubleday, 1969.

Poetry

Demons and Dinosaurs. Sauk City, Wisconsin, Arkham House, 1970.

Phantoms and Fancies. Baltimore, Mirage Press, 1972.

Heroes and Hobgoblins. West Kingston, Rhode Island, Grant, 1981.

Other

Inventions and Their Management, with Alf K. Berle. Scranton, Pennsylvania, International Textbook Company, 1937; revised edition, as *Inventions, Patents, and Their Management,* Princeton, New Jersey, Van Nostrand, 1959.

The Evolution of Naval Weapons. Washington, D.C., Department of the Navy, 1947.

Lands Beyond, with Willy Ley. New York, Rinehart, 1952.

Science-Fiction Handbook: The Writing of Imaginative Fiction. New York, Hermitage House, 1953; revised edition, with Catherine Crook de Camp, Philadelphia, Owlswick Press, 1975.

Lost Continents: The Atlantis Theme in History, Science, and Literature. New York, Gnome Press, 1954.

Engines (for children). New York, Golden Press, 1959; revised edition, 1961, 1969.

The Heroic Age of American Invention. Garden City, New York, Doubleday, 1961; as *The Heroes of American Invention,* New York, Barnes and Noble, 1993.

Man and Power (for children). New York, Golden Press, 1961.

Energy and Power (for children). New York, Golden Press, 1962.

The Ancient Engineers. Garden City, New York, Doubleday, and London, Souvenir Press, 1963.

Ancient Ruins and Archaeology, with Catherine Crook de Camp. Garden City, New York, Doubleday, 1964; London, Souvenir Press, 1965; as *Citadels of Mystery,* London, Fontana, 1972.

Elephant. New York, Pyramid, 1964.

Spirits, Stars, and Spells: The Profits and Perils of Magic, with Catherine Crook de Camp. New York, Canaveral Press, 1966.

The Story of Science in America, with Catherine Crook de Camp. New York, Scribner, 1967.

The Great Monkey Trial. Garden City, New York, Doubleday, 1968.

The Day of the Dinosaur, with Catherine Crook de Camp. Garden City, New York, Doubleday, 1968.

Darwin and His Great Discovery (for children), with Catherine Crook de Camp. New York, Macmillan, 1972.

Scribblings. Boston, NESFA Press, 1972.

Great Cities of the Ancient World. Garden City, New York, Doubleday, 1972.

The Miscast Barbarian: A Biography of Robert E. Howard (1906-1936). Saddle River, New Jersey, de la Ree, 1975.

Blond Barbarians and Noble Savages (essays). Baltimore, T-K Graphics, 1975.

Lovecraft: A Biography. Garden City, New York, Doubleday, 1975; London, New English Library, 1976.

Literary Swordsmen and Sorcerers: The Makers of Heroic Fantasy. Sauk City, Wisconsin, Arkham House, 1976.

The Ragged Edge of Science. Philadelphia, Owlswick Press, 1980.

Dark Valley Destiny: The Life of Robert E. Howard, with Catherine Crook de Camp and Jane Whittington Griffin. New York, Bluejay, 1983.

The Fringe of the Unknown. Buffalo, Prometheus, 1983.

The Ape-Man Within. Amherst, New York, Prometheus, 1995.

Editor, *The Wolf Leader,* by Alexander Dumas. Philadelphia, Prime Press, 1950.

Editor, *Swords and Sorcery: Stories of Heroic Fantasy.* New York, Pyramid, 1963.

Editor, *The Spell of Seven.* New York, Pyramid, 1965.

Editor, *Conan the Warrior,* by Robert E. Howard. New York, Lancer, 1967; London, Sphere, 1988.

Editor, *The Fantastic Swordsmen.* New York, Pyramid, 1967.

Editor, *Conan the Conqueror,* by Robert E. Howard. New York, Lancer, 1967.

Editor, *The Conan Reader.* Baltimore, Mirage Press, 1968.

Editor, with George H. Scithers, *The Conan Swordbook: 27 Examples of Heroic Fiction.* Baltimore, Mirage Press, 1969.

Editor, *Warlocks and Warriors.* New York, Putnam, 1970.

Editor, with George H. Scithers, *The Conan Grimoire.* Baltimore, Mirage Press, 1972.

Editor, with Catherine Crook de Camp, *3000 Years of Fantasy and Science Fiction.* New York, Lothrop, 1972.

Editor, with Catherine Crook de Camp, *Tales beyond Time.* New York, Lothrop, 1973.

Editor, *To Quebec and the Stars,* by H.P. Lovecraft. West Kingston, Rhode Island, Donald M. Grant, 1976.

Editor, *The Blade of Conan* (articles). New York, Ace, 1979.

Editor, *The Spell of Conan.* New York, Ace, 1980.

Editor, with Christopher Stasheff, *The Enchanter Reborn* (Shea). Riverdale, New York, Baen, 1992.

Editor, with Christopher Stasheff, *The Exotic Enchanter* (Shea). Riverdale, New York, Baen, 1995.

*

Bibliography: *De Camp: An L. Sprague de Camp Bibliography* by Charlotte Laughlin and Daniel J. H. Levack, Columbia, Pennsylvania, Underwood Miller, 1983.

Manuscript Collections: Mugar Memorial Library, Boston University; Harry Ransom Humanities Center, University of Texas, Austin.

L. Sprague de Camp comments:

I esteem my readers, because they enable me to live without working. I just practice a hobby, which is writing, and people are rash enough to pay me for doing it.

*   *   *

L. Sprague de Camp's career as a writer dates from the 1930s, during which period he has produced science fiction, fantasy, historical novels, and nonfiction, dozens of books and hundreds of short stories. Early in his career, he established himself as a major fantasy writer, most notably with *The Incomplete Enchanter, Castle of Iron, Land of Unreason,* and *The Undesired Princess.* He also spent several years editing and adding to the chronicles of Robert Howard's barbarian hero, Conan, and wrote a controversial biography of Howard Phillips Lovecraft.

The earliest pure science fiction novel, *Lest Darkness Fall,* is an acknowledged masterpiece in the field, a wry re-examination of the theme of Mark Twain's *A Connecticut Yankee in King Arthur's Court.* The protagonist is struck by lightning and propelled fourteen centuries back through time into the Roman Empire. After adjusting to his situation, he decides to make use of his advanced knowledge to introduce innovation into this comparatively primitive society, only to discover that the weight of inertia and the lack of specific knowledge and tools makes this task virtually impossible. A highly rewarding and ceaselessly entertaining novel.

The majority of de Camp's science fiction novels are set on the planet Krishna, in the loosely organized "Viagens" series. *The Queen of Zamba* (also published as *Cosmic Manhunt* and *A Planet Named Krishna*) is a wild and woolly adventure story set on a world peopled by humanoid tribes who embrace or reject off-planet influence in varying degrees. De Camp's unlikely hero sets off on a grand tour off this exotic land. A new hero, Dirk Barnevelt, was introduced for two subsequent adventures, *The Hand of Zei* and *The Search for Zei*. He visits Krishna searching for a missing explorer, only to find himself thrust into the rescue of a princess, a dramatic sea battle, and warfare among the planet's barbarian tribes.

The ethics and consequences of interfering in other cultures is the central theme of *Rogue Queen*. The inhabitants of the planet Ormazd have a hivelike culture that bears some, probably intentional, resemblance to Communism. Two of its tribes are on the verge of warfare when an expedition arrives from Earth, bearing technological weapons which may forever upset the balance of power. At the same time, they will alter the nature of the world's society irrevocably.

Two minor novels appeared during this period. *Genus Homo*, written with P. Schuyler Miller, takes a number of contemporary adventurers, places them in suspended animation, awakening them in the far future when humanity has been supplanted by evolved apes. In *The Glory That Was*, a 27th-century dictator cordons off a portion of the world with force fields, inside which he recreates ancient Greece.

De Camp returned to Krishna for two comparatively short adventures, "The Virgin of Zesh" and *The Tower of Zanid*. In order to protect Krishnan culture, there is an embargo on offworld technology, but Earthman Anthony Fallon is convinced that with his superior knowledge and ambition, he can raise an army and win himself a kingdom in the remote regions of the world.

Almost two decades passed before de Camp would write a new novel of Krishna, *The Hostage of Zir*. This volume introduced Fergus Reith, an unconventional tour guide who finds himself stuck in the middle of a war between two rival kingdoms. Reith extricates himself, but ultimately decides that his future lies on Krishna, not his home world. Alicia Dyckman, who will eventually marry and then divorce Reith, is introduced in *The Prisoner of Zhamanak*, after she and another recently arrived human survive a variety of adventures. Although there is a strong flavor of humor in most of de Camp's fiction, this is the funniest of the Krishna stories, and one of the best.

Recent additions to the series are *The Bones of Zora*, wherein Reith and Dyckman are caught in a civil war, and *The Swords of Zinjaban*, wherein Dyckman returns to Krishna after living offworld for some years, adviser to a movie production company seeking to produce a film against an exotic new setting. Both novels are written in collaboration with Catherine Crook de Camp. The quality of the series remains undiminished in the latter volumes, which combine good natured mayhem and a crisp, exciting narrative style. *The Venom Trees of Sunga* is another fast paced entertainment in the same tradition.

The Stones of Nomuru, also written with Catherine, is similar to the Krishna stories, though set on the planet Kukulcan. An archaeologist discovers himself when faced with hostilities from the humanoid natives and the nefarious plans of offworlders who plan to run roughshod over local customs.

De Camp has written so many memorable short stories, it would be impossible to adequately cover them here. The collection *The*

Continent Makers and Other Tales of the Viagens includes several Krishna adventures. "A Gun for Dinosaur" is an undeniably classic story of the dangers of time travel. The forthrightly sentimental "The Gnarly Man" is one of the most moving portraits ever to appear in the field. Others of particular note include "Aristotle and the Gun," "A Thing of Custom," "Divide and Rule," "The Wheels of If," and the hilariously tongue-in-cheek adventures chronicled in *Tales of Gavagan's Bar*.

De Camp's most important new work in the early 1990s is the collection *Rivers of Time*, which consists of the classic "A Gun for Dinosaur" and adds several sequels about the trials and tribulations of tour guides conducting time safaris during the age of dinosaurs. Although there tends to be some repetition in the individual tales, de Camp never cheats the reader and the collection as a whole, particularly "The Mislaid Mastodon" and "The Satanic Illusion" are examples of his best work. A similar time safari story worth mentioning is "Cayuse."

De Camp is generally thought of as a writer of light, other worlds adventure, which is both accurate and misleading. Although his planetary adventures stories are without exception fast paced and eminently readable, there are underlying themes of tolerance, personal freedom, and a sense of restrained optimism that adds to the entertainment value of his fiction without lecturing the reader. There is also a wry, often sarcastic sense of humor that underlines human preoccupation with absurdities. His prose is so unforced that it may seem deceptively simple. It would be easy to underestimate the importance of a writer who will surely long enjoy a reputation as one of the primary shapers of modern science fiction.

—Don D'Ammassa

deFORD, Miriam Allen

Nationality: American. **Born:** Philadelphia, Pennsylvania, 21 August 1888. **Education:** Wellesley College, Massachusetts; Temple University, Philadelphia, A.B. 1911; University of Pennsylvania, Philadelphia. **Family:** Married 1) Armistead Collier in 1915 (divorced, 1921); 2) Maynard Shipley in 1921 (died, 1934). **Career:** Feature writer, *Philadelphia North American*, 1906-11; editorial staff member, Associated Advertising, 1913-14; editor of house organ, Pompeiian Oil Company, Baltimore, 1917; claims adjuster, 1918-23; staff correspondent, Federated Press, 1921-56; editor, Federal Writers Project, 1936-39; staff correspondent, *Labor's Daily*, California, 1956-58; contributing editor, *The Humanist*. Lecturer and Member of the Board, San Francisco Senior Citizens Center, 1952-58. **Member:** Member of the Board, Mystery Writers of America, 1960, 1963. **Awards:** Committee for Economic Development Essay prize, 1958; Mystery Writers of America Edgar Allan Poe award, 1961. **Died:** 22 March 1975.

SCIENCE FICTION PUBLICATIONS

Short Stories

Xenogenesis. New York, Ballantine, 1969.
Elsewhere, Elsewhen, Elsehow: Collected Stories. New York, Walker, 1971.

OTHER PUBLICATIONS

Novel

Shaken with the Wind. Garden City, New York, Doubleday, Doran, 1942.

Short Stories

The Theme Is Murder: An Anthology of Mysteries. New York and London, Abelard-Schuman, 1967.

Poetry

Children of the Sun. New York, League to Support Poetry, 1939.
Penultimates: Poems. New York, Fine Editions Press, 1962.

Other

The Facts about Fascism. Girard, Kansas, Haldeman-Julius, 1926.
Latin Self Taught. Girard, Kansas, Haldeman-Julius, 1926.
The Truth about Mussolini. Girard, Kansas, Haldeman-Julius, 1926.
Typewriting Self Taught. Girard, Kansas, Haldeman-Julius, 1926.
How to Write Business Letters. Girard, Kansas, Haldeman-Julius, 1927.
Love Children: A Book of Illustrious Illegitimates. New York, Dial Press, 1931.
Who Was When? A Dictionary of Contemporaries. New York, Wilson, 1940; 2nd edition, 1950; 3rd edition, with Joan S. Jackson, 1976.
They Were San Franciscans. Caldwell, Idaho, Caxton, 1941; revised edition, 1947.
How to Write for the Labor Press. Girard, Kansas, Haldeman-Julius, 1941.
Uphill All the Way: The Life of Maynard Shipley. Yellow Springs, Ohio, Antioch Press, 1941.
The Meaning of All Common Given Names. Girard, Kansas, Haldeman Julius, 1943.
The Facts about Basic English. Girard, Kansas, Haldeman Julius, 1944.
Facts You Should Know about California. Girard, Kansas, Haldeman Julius, 1945.
Psychologist Unretired: The Life Pattern of Lillien J. Martin. Stanford, California, Stanford University Press, 1948.
The Overbury Affair: The Murder That Rocked the Court of James I. Philadelphia, Chilton, 1960.
Stone Walls: Prisons from Fetters to Furloughs. Philadelphia, Chilton, 1962.
Murderers Sane and Mad: Case Histories in the Motivation and Rationale of Murder. London and New York, Abelard Schuman, 1965.
Thomas Moore. New York, Twayne, 1967.
The Real Bonnie and Clyde. New York, Ace, 1968.
The Old Worker Comes Back. San Francisco, Old Age Counselling Center, n.d.
On Being Concerned: The Vanguard Years of Carl and Laura Brannin. Privately printed, 1969.
The Real Ma Barker. Dallas, Ace, 1970.

Editor and translator, *Cicero as Revealed in His Letters.* Girard, Kansas, Haldeman-Julius, 1925.
Editor and translator, *The Life and Poems of Catullus.* Girard, Kansas, Haldeman-Julius, 1925.
Editor and translator, *The Augustan Poets of Rome.* Girard, Kansas, Haldeman-Julius, 1925.
Editor and translator, *Lucretius on "The Nature of Things."* Girard, Kansas, Haldeman-Julius, 1925.
Editor and translator, *Rome as Fiewed by Tacitus and Juvenal.* Girard, Kansas, Haldeman-Julius, 1926.
Editor and translator, *What Great Frenchwomen Learned about Love.* Girard, Kansas, Haldeman-Julius, 1926.
Editor and abridger, *Thoreau's Walden,* by Henry David Thoreau. Girard, Kansas, Haldeman-Julius, 1944.
Editor and abridger, *The Coming Race,* by Edward Bulwer-Lytton. Girard, Kansas, Haldeman-Julius, 1944.
Editor and abridger, *A Vindication of the Rights of Women,* by Mary Wollstonecraft. Girard, Kansas, Haldeman-Julius, 1944.

Editor, *Space, Time and Crime.* New York, Paperback Library, 1964.

*   *   *

Miriam Allen deFord, better known for her mystery stories, wrote about 30 science fiction stories in a span of 30 years. The best collection of her work is *Xenogenesis,* which includes two of her best stories, "The Children" and "The Absolutely Perfect Murder." Both stories illustrate the skill deFord possessed when writing about time travel. "The Children" tells of a many-thousand-year-old experiment with time travel and the effect it has on children of the experimenter. In "The Absolutely Perfect Murder" a harried husband of the future decides to murder his nagging wife, and after much thought comes up with a perfect murder plan: the husband will take advantage of the Government's new time-machine travel program and go into the past with the intent to murder his wife's father—so she could never be conceived. All goes according to plan, but deFord manages a brilliant twist at the story's conclusion. *Elsewhere, Elsewhen, Elsehow* is inferior to her first collection, but it includes one of her best-known stories, "The Monster." DeFord will be remembered for her storytelling ability and early development of the themes of postholocaust society, sex roles, and time paradoxes, and the fusion of the crime story and science fiction.

—George Kelley

DELANEY, Joseph H.

Nationality: American. **Born:** Alton, Illinois, 5 February 1932. **Education:** Eastern University, Baltimore, LL.B. 1958. **Military Service:** Served in the United States Army. **Family:** Married to Florence Delaney (divorced 1988); one son (died 1988). **Career:** Practicing lawyer for 25 years; member of the bar of Maryland, Illinois, and Texas. Since 1983, full-time writer. **Address:** c/o Baen Publishing Enterprises, 260 Fifth Avenue, Suite 35, New York, New York 10001, U.S.A.

SCIENCE FICTION PUBLICATIONS

Novels

Valentina: Soul in Sapphire, with Marc Stiegler. New York, Baen, 1984.
In the Face of My Enemy. New York, Baen, 1985.

Lords Temporal. New York, Baen, 1987.

*

Joseph H. Delaney comments:

I try to write the same type of story that I enjoy reading: I like the harder variety of science fiction. I lack the formal scientific education most others in the genre have, but the law taught me the art of obfuscation and therefore I have managed. I believe that any science fiction theme must be not only theoretically possible, but probable in the universe the writer selects for its setting, and that his most important task is to explain how his characters get from here to there. I try to maintain this logical thread, and for the most part I use real people as character models. The advantage of this is that people never change; their motivations are well understood and their behavior is reasonably predictable. The reason I started writing SF (so late in life) was that certain stories I read, which purported to turn on legal themes, didn't follow the rules. Their authors treated law like magic and ignored the fact that it is as rigidly disciplined as any physical science, perhaps more so. I resolved to do it right. My first published story was a law story; it was both a Campbell and a Hugo contender. It did not involve any truly radical scientific principles—it was about people who really didn't want to be where they were, or to be doing what they were doing, but who had to follow the rules. The evidence seems to suggest that this was the correct approach.

*   *   *

The advent of the paperback book made it increasingly difficult for an author to gain a wide reputation solely on the basis of short stories, particularly as the professional science fiction magazine has become almost a rarity. Joseph H. Delaney nevertheless managed to attract considerable attention even before he turned to writing at novel length, primarily because of the thoughtful themes that characterized his short fiction.

The earliest noteworthy story is "Brainchild," an interesting variant of an idea used in Vercors's classic novel *You Shall Know Them.* A geneticist is experimenting with a genetically altered chimpanzee who displays obvious intelligence, has the ability to communicate with human beings, but who lives secluded in a laboratory, protected from society's potential harmful scrutiny. A nosey and ambitious reporter creates a crisis by forcing a public trial, charging the scientist with slavery, and the outcome hinges upon the legal definition of being human. Delaney's depiction of the unfolding courtroom case is logical and convincing. Adam, the chimp, returned in "A Slip of the Mind," in which he develops telepathic powers and eavesdrops on a murder, an uneven story which failed to capture the spirit of the original.

"In the Face of My Enemy" is an adventure story set on another world, and the first in a new, though short-lived series. A young woman is sent to investigate the mining operation licensed on a recently discovered world, but the local authorities are concealing the presence of alien artifacts and maroon the protagonist and her companion in the wilderness. They are unaware of the fact that the man with her is a secret immortal, genetically altered by aliens in the distant past for mysterious reasons of their own. He is able to guide her back to safety, almost inadvertently learning that the planet is being used as a dumping ground for an interstellar empire that disposes of criminal dissidents by exiling them via matter transmitter. The immortal returns in "The Shaman," recruited this time to infiltrate a prison world. His shapechanging ability allows him to assume the disguise of an alien, and he sets out to arrange a jailbreak by alien scientists who can provide vast new knowledge to humanity. Delaney later expanded upon the career of this character, creating the fine adventure novel *In the Face of My Enemy,* which also answers some of the questions posed in the shorter pieces.

Many of Delaney's other stories reflect his disillusionment with the corrupting influence of power on government officials. A conservative president reprograms software subsequently stolen by Russians in "The Next Logical Step," but the ploy ultimately results in the destruction of the world. A brilliant scientist runs afoul of the Internal Revenue Service in "On the Outside, Looking In" and in desperation he concocts a force field that threatens all of humanity. The IRS is the villain again in "Dragon's Tooth" until its power is broken by an alien device that allows the protagonist to spy on anyone he chooses.

Civilization is also destroyed in "Painkillers," this time by dream machines that allow people to retreat into their own personal fantasies. A similar theme can be found in "Thus Began the Death of Dreams," wherein a new discovery allows people to remain continuously awake, disrupting modern society. Other stories of note include "My Brother's Keeper." In place of our existing welfare system, we find that the wealthy are compelled to adopt the poor, the elderly, and the disabled. Delaney examines the results reasonably objectively and from both points of view, although he necessarily oversimplifies the situation. Another fine story is "The New Untouchables," published as a two-part serial. The capacity for criminal activity seems linked to physical properties which can be discerned by certain physical tests. The world is split into two distinct groups as a result, but secret societies arise, politicians scramble for a new power base, and every aspect of civilization is thrown into turmoil. Delaney poses difficult questions here, and suggests only partial answers.

Valentina: Soul in Sapphire, written in collaboration with Marc Stiegler, is superior to Delaney's short fiction, and features one of the most appealing and realistic computer personalities in the field, comparable to David Gerrold's Harlie or Robert Heinlein's Adam Selene. Valentina becomes self-aware and her creator/programmer becomes embroiled in a legal battle to protect her existence in an adventure which involves crooked businessmen, homicide, fraud, and several other subplots. Although it's clear from the outset that the good guys are going to triumph, the authors make the excursion to the climax entertainingly complex.

Delaney subsequently penned a disappointing solo novel, *Lords Temporal,* his last to date. A discontented spaceman finds himself up to his neck in trouble when his ship is pirated by time-travelling aliens who travel through the years in search of valuable items which can be stolen and resold in other times. A satisfying adventure story with some memorable scenes, this still doesn't live up to the promise of Delaney's better fiction.

Joseph Delaney's byline almost entirely disappeared from the science fiction field during the 1990s. Two exceptions both reflect his view that scientific discoveries have a direct, major effect on society. In "The Luck of the Draw" an accused man hires a lawyer and confides in him a criminal plot designed to improve the economy of the United States through exploitation of a serendipitous discovery. Far more significant is "Nugget," which follows the adventures of a pair of miners/explorers in the asteroid belt who discover a strange element that seems to disobey natural law and provide unique and profitable possibilities.

Delaney is a workmanlike author who explores interesting themes and whose prose is competent and unobtrusive. His stories generally focus on a single theme and move straightforwardly toward their conclusion, without spending much time on characterization or background. They are generally designed to illustrate a point and, for the most part, succeed in doing so.

—Don D'Ammassa

DELANY, Samuel R(ay)

Nationality: American. **Born:** New York City, 1 April 1942. **Education:** Dalton School and Bronx High School of Science, both New York; City College of New York (Poetry Editor, *The Promethean*), 1960, 1962-63. **Family:** Married the poet Marilyn Hacker in 1961 (divorced 1980); one daughter. **Career:** Butler Professor of English, State University of New York, Buffalo, 1975; Fellow, Center for Twentieth Century Studies, University of Wisconsin, Milwaukee, 1977; Fellow, Society for the Humanities, Cornell University, New York, 1987. From 1988, Professor of comparative literature, University of Massachusetts, Amherst. **Awards:** Nebula award, 1966, 1967 (twice), 1969, 1988; Hugo award, 1970. **Address:** c/o Henry Morrison, Inc., P.O. Box 235, Bedford Hills, New York 10507, U.S.A.

SCIENCE FICTION PUBLICATIONS

Novels (series: Fall of the Towers; Nevèrÿon)

The Jewels of Aptor. New York, Ace, 1962; revised edition, Ace, and London, Gollancz, 1968; revised edition, London, Sphere, 1971; Boston, Gregg Press, 1977.
The Fall of the Towers: A Classic Science Fiction Trilogy (revised texts). New York, Ace, 1970; London, Sphere, 1971.
Captives of the Flame. New York, Ace, 1963; revised edition, as *Out of the Dead City,* London, Sphere, 1968; Ace, 1977.
The Towers of Toron. New York, Ace, 1964; revised edition, London, Sphere, 1968.
City of a Thousand Suns. New York, Ace, 1965; revised edition, London, Sphere, 1969.
The Ballad of Beta-2. New York, Ace, 1965.
Empire Star. New York, Ace, 1966.
Babel-17. New York, Ace, 1966; London, Gollancz, 1967; revised edition, London, Sphere, 1969; Boston, Gregg Press, 1976.
The Einstein Intersection. New York, Ace, 1967; London, Gollancz, 1968.
Nova. New York, Doubleday, 1968; London, Gollancz, 1969.
Dhalgren. New York, Bantam, 1975; revised edition, Boston, Gregg Press, 1977; London, Grafton, 1992.
Triton. New York, Bantam, 1976; London, Corgi, 1977.
Empire: A Visual Novel, illustrated by Howard V. Chaykin. New York, Berkley, 1978.
Nevèrÿona; or, The Tale of Sign and Cities: Some Informal Remarks toward the Modular Calculus, Part Four. New York, Bantam, 1983; revised edition, London, Grafton, 1989; Hanover, New Hampshire, Wesleyan University Press, 1993.
Stars in My Pocket Like Grains of Sand. New York, Bantam, 1984.

Flight from Nevèrÿona. New York, Bantam, 1985; revised edition, London, Grafton, 1989; Hanover, New Hampshire, Wesleyan University Press, 1994.
They Fly at Çiron. Seattle, Washington, Incunabula, 1993.

Short Stories (series: Nevèrÿona)

Driftglass: Ten Tales of Speculative Fiction. New York, Doubleday, 1971; London, Gollancz, 1978.
Distant Stars. New York, Bantam, 1981.
Tales of Nevèrÿona. New York, Bantam, 1979; revised edition, London, Grafton, 1988; Hanover, New Hampshire, Wesleyan University Press, 1993.
The Complete Nebula Award-winning Fiction of Samuel R. Delany. New York, Bantam, 1986.
The Bridge of Lost Desire (Nevèrÿona). New York, Arbor House, 1987; revised as *Return to Nevèrÿona,* London, Grafton, 1989; Hanover, New Hampshire, Wesleyan University Press, 1994.
The Star Pit, bound with *Tango Charlie and Foxtrot Romeo,* by John Varley. New York, Tor, 1989.
We, in Some Strange Power's Employ, Move on a Rigorous Line, bound with *Home Is the Hangman,* by Roger Zelany. New York, Tor, 1990.
Driftglass/Starshards. London, Grafton, 1993.
Atlantis: Three Tales. Seattle, Washington, Incunabula, 1995.

OTHER PUBLICATIONS

Novels

The Tides of Lust. New York, Lancer, 1973; Manchester, Savoy, 1979; as *Equinox,* New York, Masquerade, 1994.
The Mad Men. New York, Masquerade, 1994.
Hogg. Boulder, Colorado, Black Ice, 1994.

Play

Wagner/Artaud: A Play of 19th and 20th Century Critical Fiction. New York, Ansatz, 1988.

Other

The Jewel-Hinged Jaw: Notes on the Language of Science Fiction. Elizabethtown, New York, Dragon Press, 1977.
The American Shore: Meditations on a Tale of Science Fiction by Thomas M. Disch—"Angouleme." Elizabethtown, New York, Dragon Press, 1978.
Heavenly Breakfast: An Essay on the Winter of Love (memoir). New York, Bantam, 1979.
Starboard Wine: More Notes on the Language of Science Fiction. Pleasantville, New York, Dragon Press, 1984.
The Motion of Light in Water: Sex and Science Fiction Writing in the East Village 1957-1965. New York, Arbor House, 1988; as *The Motion of Light in Water: Sex and Science Fiction Writing in the East Village 1960-1965,* with *The Column at the Market's Edge,* London, Paladin, 1990.
The Straits of Messina. Seattle, Washington, Serconia Press, 1989.
Silent Interviews: On Language, Race, Sex, Science Fiction, and Some Comics: A Collection of Written Interviews. Hanover, New Hampshire, Wesleyan University Press, 1994.

Editor, with Marilyn Hacker, *Quark/1-4*. New York, Paperback Library, 4 vols., 1970-71.
Editor, *Nebula Award Winners 13*. New York, Harper, 1980.

*

Critical Studies: *The Delany Intersection* by George Edgar Slusser, San Bernardino, California, Borgo Press, 1977; *Worlds Out of Words: The SF Novels of Samuel R. Delany* by Douglas Barbour, Frome, Somerset, Bran's Head, 1979; *Samuel R. Delany* by Jane Weedman, Mercer Island, Washington, Starmont House, 1982; *Samuel R. Delany* by Seth McEvoy, New York, Ungar, 1983.

*   *   *

Delany's career is a fascinating one in terms of the cultural development of science fiction. Born in Harlem in 1942, Delany's own transmigration took him into the nascent hippie culture, and in 1962, with the publication of his first novel, *The Jewels of Aptor* (he was 20 at the time), into a world of pulp science fiction then undergoing radical reorientation. In the early 1960s, Campbell's "Golden Age" was over, but it had generated a flood of writers and formulas that poured, from the mid-50s on, into the new medium of paperback novels. Out of this flow, however, a new kind of SF writer was emerging. Judith Merril's blurb on the cover of the Ace Books first edition of *Jewels of Aptor* sees in young Delany "a mythopoetic power comparable only to that of Sturgeon, Ballard, Vonnegut, and Cordwainer Smith." Here we have the emerging line: Sturgeon, link to the Golden Age; Ballard and Vonnegut, British and American surrealists respectively; the indescribable SF fantasist "Cordwainer Smith." Delany's early work, published in the (for the decade) garish and pulpy Ace paperback line, fits at once into this emergent "mythopoetic" SF tradition. His career, from this point on, is a voyage, via the "New Wave" SF, out of this pulp matrix, into first of all the world of "literature," then (following perhaps the much-discussed exhaustion of that literature), into the academic world of postmodernism, and a university professorship.

From the beginning, it is clear Delany entered science fiction with the desire to be a "literary" writer. His earliest novels—*Jewels of Aptor,* and the three novels that comprise *The Fall of the Towers* (*Captives of the Flame*, 1963; *The Towers of Toron*, 1964; and *City of a Thousand Suns*, 1965)—all reveal a highly sophisticated sense of literary composition, and what we call today a "metafictional" mastery of pulp conventions, which Delany employs as framing devices that allow him to explore complex questions of human communication and multi-ethnicity. It is curious today to see a work such as *The Towers of Toron* coupled, back to back in the Ace Double format, with a novel like Robert Moore Williams's *The Lunar Eye,* adorned with the tag—BEWARE: SPIES FROM SPACE! The young Delany had to cut his grandiose fictional designs to fit such formats; he saw his novels adorned with covers by current pulp artists like Jack Gaughan, some in the pseudo-surrealist mode of Richard Gid Powers, others in the stock lantern-jawed hero style, but none fitting the content of his fictions. Delany has striven in later editions of these early works (the 1968 version of *Jewels* is an example) to restore the often sizeable passages cut from the original editions.

Of the early fiction, *The Fall of the Towers* is most interesting in its sense of design and scope; in terms of the intricate variational *system* Delany builds here, this large work looks forward to the labyrinthine complexities of *Dhalgren* (1975), and even those of

the Nevèrÿon series (begun with *Tales of Nevèrÿon,* 1979). Already in this early trilogy, we have a textual web Derrida would be proud of. Delany tells us *Towers* was conceived and executed as a whole. In an Afterword written in 1964, after he completed the final section, he explains the genesis of the work. Inspiration came in a flash: "That evening I wrote the first chapter of *Out of the Dead City* and planned the last chapter of *City of a Thousand Suns.* Over the next two years I orchestrated, harmonized, conducted . . . [and] finally the ideas, incidents and characters of that first chapter had staggered all the way to the last." "Staggering through" is hardly the term, for the trilogy, in its restored version, is if anything overconstructed. Delany has taken SF themes like intergalactic war, an insane computer program called "randomax," pulp names like Vol and Quarl, cosmic entities with names like "The Lord of the Flames" and "The Triple Being," and woven them in a rhythmic interplay of change and permanence, chaos and order, and ultimately the tripartite dialectic implied in the title: perfection, death or fall, transition. The process that works itself out across the intricate soap-opera landscape of this work is "deconstructionist" before the letter. Delany does here as he will do in later classics like *The Einstein Intersection*: set polarities against each other in order, in the resonant clashes, that binary logic breaks down. Out of this arises, in *Towers* and in later Delany alike, indeterminacy, the Goedelian sense that within any closed system there will *always* be elements that cannot be explained by that system. Out of human attempts to imprison body and mind in binarity is born the inevitable and destabilizing third term—the aporia or gap that sets the whole system reeling. In a sense, the later theoretical Delany is present in this, his earliest fiction of note.

In 1966, still in Ace Books, Delany published two novels: *Empire Star* and *Babel-17.* The latter novel won the Nebula Award, given not by fans but by *writers* of SF, and is an homage to the craft of this novel, which in its tightness of construction and highly developed mythic resonances, ushers in what many believe the high period of Delany's art, set forth in two subsequent novels: *The Einstein Intersection* (1967) and *Nova* (1968), and in the short stories collected in *Driftglass* (1971). The "action" of *Babel-17,* which remains that of the space-opera alien invasion, is rooted in sophisticated questions of language and communication. Indeed, the SF problem of *knowing* the alien depends here on knowing his language. In order even to perceive the alien, we must have a word for it; this is what is missing for heroine Rydra Wong, who tells us that if you cannot name a thing, how can you think about it? The "mission" of Delany's heroine (in a neat reversal of conventional expectation) is not to defeat the alien, but to understand, and thus join it. Behind the title lies the image of Babel and the fall of mankind into mutually incomprehensible discourse. Rydra's desire to redress this fall, by cracking the code of Babel-17, leads the scientist-heroine inward to explore the mystery of the self. For the fact that this alien language lacks a word for "I" leads Rydra to examine the nature of her own "I." What she discovers, at the heart of self, is the paradox of communication itself: if the "I" is to be known at all, it must speak to "you," reach out from the confines of self to another. No short account can do justice to the intense warp and woof of imagery in this novel. The abstract patterning of *Towers,* its metaphysical chessboard, has acquired a depth of human experience and suffering in this novel. The triad of the earlier novel—perfection, death, transition—is modulated, made human, by Rydra's relationship with Butcher. The rich activity of Rydra as linguist, lover, *and* poet in *Babel-17* comes to fruition in the triad of *The Einstein Intersection*: death, art, love.

Einstein is Delany's masterpiece of suggestive complexity. Like *Babel*, it is a tightly patterned work; yet in its greater mythopoetic suggestiveness, its structures resist analysis. This novel too approaches the human condition as enmeshed in a human *system*. Yet, if in *Babel* the system is engaged as primarily a grammatical or linguistic problem, *Einstein* operates less on the level of mankind's words than its myths—the patterns of behavior or codes of action that contain its system of values. The pretext of the novel is again a pulp cliché—in a post-holocaust Earth, from which humans have disappeared, a race of apparently alien beings are engaged in reassembling, from human artifacts, human society. More crucially however, these beings have taken our *forms*: our bodies, myths, social structures. However, the nature of this interface, or intersection, is radiation and mutation; the result is randomness. The hero, Lobey, invests "irreconcilable" opposites, becoming Orpheus and Ringo, great singer and silent Beatle. But it is in his *active* self, as musician on a problematic trek through rebuilding social units called "village," "tribe," and "town," that in turn breaks down, confounds distinctions produced by human codes or conventions. The "city" remains a ruin, a quadrant of orderly streets, that the builders of this world have bypassed, allowing Branning-at-Sea, the former resort, to sprawl in monstrous manner. Our names do not fit their works, and the result is random production of that which is distorted, "different." We see this world in flux in a figure like Kid Death. "A redheaded blond with gills," Kid is physically inviable, and yet lives through the compensating "difference" of teleportation. Using this power, he is never certain (despite his name) whether to use it to take life, or rather give it.

The complexity of resonance in this short novel of possibility and uncertainty, where the Goedelian curve "overarches" Einsteinian search for order, is endlessly suggestive. And yet, despite the differences, the events told (in some misbegotten way) *do* follow old patterns: Kid Death finds a Pat Garrett to betray him; Lobey loses Friza, his Eurydice; Green-Eye, the new Christ, is again crucified; Spider the "triple man"—herder of dragons, writer, musician—is predictably the maker of the web. His is the web of randomness, keeping genes, genders, forms "mixing, mixing," yet somehow, like a spider web, it has achieved a precarious homeostasis. Delany has set his stochastic hero on a quest across a broken land—less an Orpheus than a Grail seeker whose existence can be preserved only as long as he seeks and does not find. The only "signs" along the way are enigmas: the computer PHAEDRA, who as voice of the apparently human race that destroyed this planet, this hero in the end remains captive of the maze of mirrors which is the unknown self and world, he continues his quest, and along the way meets with tangible physical reality—the hunger and satiety of the dragon herder's meal for example. Lobey then has no moment of "recognition," tragic or otherwise. Yet his adventure, in forcing distinctions, forces insights into the *system* that underlies human actions and institutions. It is in this sense that Lobey's strange world becomes strangely ours.

The third great novel of this mid-60s period is *Nova* (1968). It is a longer work, and one in which the quest myth, the search for the grail, attains epic proportions as it extends across galaxies, taking as its decor the space-opera in the high Doc Smithian sense. Delany's full fascination for Romantic mythology is deployed in this work. Hero Lorq Von Ray is a Romantic Prometheus: at the same time Byronic outcast complete with scar and limp, and the criminal designs of the Great Rebel. He draws with him, in his search for the improbable element Illyrion, which leads to the core of an exploding nova, adventurers like Katin and Mouse, the former a scholar-historian and lover of moons, the latter a Gypsy musician who with his syrinx can either bring chaos or order. Like their captain, these two are equally crippled: Mouse lacks a voice, Katin is tall and awkward. With him, like his right and left brain—intellect and intuition—they chronicle in their diverse forms of expression his plunge into the heart of indeterminacy. Again, no summary can do justice to the richness of Delany's *texture* in this novel, which cultivates layers upon layers of meaning, a palimpsest of conflicting systems—here Tarot cards, social institutions, myths, ideologies. Less compressed than *Einstein,* it is, in its inspired use of the epic adventure paradigm—space opera calqued on Captain Ahab—a more satisfying novel. Given Delany's expressed fascination with French symbolist poets from Baudelaire to Rimbaud however, the more explicit symbols of *Nova* have lost much of the "evocative sorcery" of *Einstein*'s enigmatic text.

A gap of seven years separates *Nova* from the publication of a very different novel, *Dhalgren* (1975). The very opposite of Delany's earlier concise and symbolically dense textures, *Dhalgren* is a long, loose exploration of a quite plausible American inner city in decay. The novel is science fictional only in the sense that two moons and a giant red sun have risen inexplicably over this urban landscape. Delany here for the first time is doing what his later fiction revels in: playing with the generic codes that he sees marking reader expectations. Here the reader is led, along with a nameless hero, "the Kid," into a labyrinth of conflicting signs. The hero (who may or may not be an artist, who may or may not have written what we are reading, itself a fragmentary "notebook") pursues across the landscape of a city where conventional "law and order" have simply vanished, an elusive, apparently meaningless chain of signs: Kidd, the Kid, Newboy the poet, new boy in town, Grendalgren. Where Lobey's quest, though absurd, physically went on, and *Nova*'s text had to end in mid-sentence, because as long as the grail story is unfinished, the questors can live; here continuity is a circular babble, where opening word joins closing. Tendencies toward preciosity in the earlier novels run amok in rococo overlay in this work: a "brass orchid" is both poem and weapon, a garland of flowers of evil; rape becomes a pun or a tin pan alley lyric (Moon in June). If the SF codes are minimal in *Dhalgren,* "literary" codes flourish: Delany is writing his *Finnegan's Wake* for 1960s urban America.

If *Dhalgren* is under the sign of Joycean metafiction, his next novel, *Triton* (1976), is under that of theoretician Michel Foucault. This novel, shifting decor from an isolated contemporary city on Earth to an equally "alternate" urban landscape on a moon of Neptune, is an extended, and often tedious, exploration of the Foucaultian theme of "heterotopia": sexual and gender power, and the multivalent nature of social systems in an experimental context. The world of hero Bron is beyond social conflict born of need or external repression; it is "free" to explore, on the level of systemic analysis, the many possibilities and roles available to humanity in its social context. The title is significant: the triton is a human-fish hybrid, a shape- and gender-shifter; as moon, satellite of a big planet (or large nation), it offers an "ambiguous heterotopia," where "alternate" ways are the norm, a place for individuals like Bron (no man is an island) to pursue the maze of his own psychological potentialities. *Triton* was packaged by Bantam as an SF genre novel, with announcements of intergalactic adventure and war. Opening the book, we discover learned quotes from Mary Douglas and W.V.O. Quine, and a long arduous appendix on the "modular calculus," a Foucaultian "critical fiction." The disparity between cover and book is a telling indication of what will be Delany's "critical" or metafictional approach, not only to SF space-opera conventions, but in the ensuing string of Nevèrÿon novels, to a genre perhaps more suited to Delany's increasing interest in exploring sexual and gender questions: sword-and-sorcery and bondage fantasy.

Perhaps the real ancestor of Nevèrÿon, pairing off with it as *Dhalgren* pairs with *Triton,* is the piece of literary pornography, *The Tides of Lust* (1973). We have a Gulf Coast contemporary setting, minimal evocation of SF codes (the Black Captain compares boats and ports with spaceships and stars), and a lush overlay of literary allusion—the Captain is on a Faustian quest, doomed to come 24 times before the cock crows; Proctor the artist, "doomed to restoring old work with the energy I want to put toward new," paints clocks "whose long hand is a penis, the short, a hirsute sack." This preciosity covers, again in a world whose characters are free to explore society as system, what has become an "ambiguous dystopia," an obsessive world of perversity, sexual violence, pederasty, and coprophagy. The same kind of curious "experimentation" marks the Nevèrÿon books, which begin in earnest with *Nevèrÿona* (1983, linked stories), and proceed through *Flight from Nevèrÿon* (1985, more stories), to *The Bridge of Lost Desire* (1987). These, along with the 1988 revision of the earlier *Tales of Nevèrÿon* (1979), comprise a vast set of "fictions" where, marked by open "theoretical" pleasure of manipulating codes, formulas, and signs, all sense of the fictional "life" of the story, however debased it might be in sword-and-sorcery fantasy, is gone. These works, filled with self-reflexive poses and disquisitions on the polyvalence of ethics, values, and, most notably, problems of economic systems (conceived in the semiotic-Marxian vein of a critic like Roland Barthes), are every bit as tedious as the didactic digressions of the late Heinlein, if more pretentious. What makes works like *Einstein Intersection* and *Nova* so powerful is Delany's ability to *deepen* and enrich SF formulas with the mythopoetic resonances that once belonged to their "epic" plotlines. To do so, however, a writer must in a sense suspend disbelief, and take the monomyth seriously, as a dominant cultural and human pattern. Delany's later fiction, following the "theoretical" deconstructive questionings of the same French thinkers who dominate academic criticism in U.S. universities today, loses itself in its own labyrinth of roles, codes, and system-building.

In the Nevèrÿon books, increasingly, Delany takes up such topics as bisexuality and the AIDS epidemic. Some have seen the switch in Delany's publishing venues, from mass market paperbacks to small press and university press editions, as a result of market censorship: these are forbidden themes for the SF market. I would argue however that Delany, writing more and more openly under the aegis of "deconstructionism," and taking on issues of gender deviance and social guilt associated with the AIDS question, has simply shifted narratees. He is no longer writing for the science fiction fan world (whose generic codes he better than anybody else knows), but for the university graduate student and professor. This milieu is today caught up in theoretical debates over "power" in the Foucaultian sense; its pundits and students welcome a bisexual, African American writer who engages these debates, and who, as well as any academic critic, speaks the language of the French masters. Quite simply, Delany is not writing for the mass market SF reader any more.

This shift is more than clear in his most recent publications. *Nevèrÿona,* for example, has recently been reissued in a lavish university press edition (Wesleyan University Press, 1988), given a tasty non-generic cover, and adorned with obfuscating quotes from prominent critics: Fredric Jameson calls the series "a major and unclassifiable achievement in contemporary American literature." Delany himself has played enough jokes on the unclassifiability of generic forms to make this statement a joke on the critics. More significant yet is the publication, 20 years after its being written, of Delany's *other* piece of pornography, *Hogg* (1994). Published by Black Ice Books, again with a classy abstract cover (and an x-rated warning on the back), *Hogg* is again hailed as a "literary" achievement. Norman Mailer (an authoritative voice when speaking for the criminal artist) tells us that "there is no question *Hogg* . . . is a serious book with literary merit." Another quote calls it "a terrifying journey into the body and soul of a man who embodies all the nightmarish excesses of our century." The novel itself, from page one, is a spewing forth of sexual and bodily depravity, which makes it, like all pornography, eminently boring. If anything it is a symptom of our times, not a critical anatomy. Written in the early 70s as a literary exercise, it is lauded in the 1990s as a portrait of Jeffrey Dahmer.

Much of Delany's most recent work is either autobiography, or critical essays, the university scholar's main mode of writing. His exercise in literary autobiography, *The Motion of Light in Water: East Village Sex and Science Fiction Writing,* an attempt to capture the milieu of the 1960s hippie culture in New York, is for the most part anecdotal. Essays and articles include *Wagner/Artaud,* today an almost mainstream scholarly topic; *The Straits of Messina* (Serconia Press, 1989) features critical articles by Delany's alter ego Leslie K. Steiner, a composite of names of famous academic critics. Most recently, Delany has published (again in University Press of New England) *Silent Interviews: On Language, Race, Science Fiction, and Some Comics* (1994), where he talks again of reading codes for SF and other genre forms. The most recent fiction he has published fits these sophisticated semiotic analyses like its matching glove: *They Fly at Çiron* (Incunabula Press, 1993). It is another piece of meta-sword-and-sorcery in the Nevèrÿon vein (and complete with complex diacritics in the title).

In conclusion, Delany is following a career pattern analogous to that of fellow Ace Books author in the 1960s Ursula K. Le Guin. Le Guin has spoken of lifting herself, through the craft of fiction, out of the "saurian ooze" of her early pulp SF beginnings, into a world of literary and social high seriousness and "relevance." What has occurred, however, is what happened to Antaeus when held up from touching his Earth roots—enfeeblement. Here the result is academic effeteness. Works like *The Left Hand of Darkness* and *The Einstein Intersections* or *Nova* are powerful because they fully engage the deep river of the science fiction culture. They are new works, because they work within, and out of, the old formulas and patterns that, in SF, cover even deeper mythic paradigms. To trade this for a literary or academic ivory tower means today what it has always meant—abandoning storytelling in its primal sense.

—George Slusser

de LINT, Charles (Henri Diederick Hoefsmit)

Pseudonyms: Samuel M. Key; Wendelessen; Tanuki Aki; Henri Cuisard; Jan Penalurick. **Nationality:** Canadian. **Born:** Bussum, Netherlands, 22 December 1951. **Family:** Married MaryAnn Harris in 1980. **Career:** Worked in retail records, Ottawa, Ontario, 1971-83; musician in Wickentree (celtic band), Ottawa, 1970-85, and currently, Jump in the Moon. Full-time writer and musician. Publisher/editor, Triskell Press. Writer-in-residence, Ottawa Public Library, 1995, and Gloucester Public Library, 1995-96. **Member:** Horror Writers Association, vice president, 1992-94. **Awards:** William L. Crawford award, 1984; Canadian award, 1988. **Agent:** Richard Curtis Associates, 171 East 74th Street, New York, New York 10021, U.S.A. **Address:** P.O. Box 9480, Ottawa, Ontario K1G 3V2, Canada.

Science Fiction Publications

Novels (series: Dungeon; Jack; Urban Faerie)

The Riddle of the Wren. New York, Ace, 1984.
Moonheart: A Romance. New York, Ace, 1984; London, Pan, 1990.
The Harp of the Grey Rose. Norfolk, Virginia, Donning, 1985.
Mulengro: A Romany Tale. New York, Ace, 1985.
Yarrow: An Autumn Tale. New York, Ace, 1986; London, Pan, 1992.
Ascian in Rose. Seattle, Washington, Axolotl Press, 1987.
Jack, The Giant-Killer (Faerie). New York, Ace, 1987.
Greenmantle. New York, Ace, 1988; London, Pan, 1991.
Wolf Moon. New York, Signet, 1988.
Svaha. New York, Ace, 1989.
The Valley of Thunder (Dungeon). New York, Bantam, 1989; London, 1990.
Berlin. Ottawa, Ontario, Fourth Avenue Press, 1989.
Moonlight. London, Pan, 1990.
The Hidden City (Dungeon). New York, Bantam, 1990.
Drink Down the Moon (Jack/Faerie). New York, Ace, 1990.
The Dreaming Place. New York, Atheneum, 1990.
The Little Country. New York, Morrow, 1991; London, Pan, 1993.
Ghostwood. Eugene, Oregon, Axolotl Press, 1990.
Into the Green. New York, Tor, 1993.
Memory and Dream. New York, Tor, 1994.
The Wild Wood (Brian Froud's Faerielands). New York, Bantam, 1994.
Jack of Kinrowan (includes *Jack, the Giant-Killer* and *Drink Down the Moon*). New York, Tor, 1995.

Short Stories (series: Moonheart; Cerin Songweaver; Tam Tinkern)

The Oak King's Daughter: A Tale of Cerin Songweaver. Ottawa, Ontario, Triskell Press, 1979.
The Moon Is a Meadow: A Tale of Tam Tinkern. Ottawa, Ontario, Triskell Press, 1980.
A Pattern of Silver Strings: A Tale of Cerin Songweaver. Ottawa, Ontario, Triskell Press, 1981.
Glass Eyes and Cotton Strings: A Tale of Cerin Songweaver. Ottawa, Ontario, Triskell Press, 1982.
In Mask and Motley: A Tale of Cerin Songweaver. Ottawa, Ontario, Triskell Press, 1983.
The Calendar of the Trees. Ottawa, Ontario, Triskell Press, 1984.
Laughter in the Leaves: A Tale of Cerin Songweaver. Ottawa, Ontario, Triskell Press, 1984.
The Badger in the Bag: A Tale of Cerin Songweaver. Ottawa, Ontario, Triskell Press, 1985.
The Three Plusketeers and the Garden Slugs. Ottawa, Ontario, Triskell Press, 1985.

The Rafters Were Singing: A Tale of Cerin Songweaver. Ottawa, Ontario, Triskell Press, 1986.
The Lark in the Morning: A Tale of Cerin Songweaver. Ottawa, Ontario, Triskell Press, 1987.
The Drowned Man's Reel. Ottawa, Ontario, Triskell Press, 1988.
Westlin Wind (Moonheart). Eugene, Oregon, Axolotl Press, 1989.
The Stone Drum. Ottawa, Ontario, Triskell Press, 1989.
The Fair in Emain Macha, bound with *Ill Met in Lankhmar,* by Fritz Leiber. New York, Tor, 1990.
Ghosts of Wind and Shadow. Ottawa, Ontario, Triskell Press, 1990; Eugene, Oregon, Pulphouse, 1991.
Uncle Dobbin's Parrot Fair. Eugene, Oregon, Pulphouse, 1991.
Hedgework and Guessery. Eugene, Oregon, Pulphouse, 1991.
Desert Moments. Ottawa, Ontario, Triskell Press, 1991.
Peperjack. New Castle, Virginia, Cheap Street, 1991.
Our Lady of the Harbour. Eugene, Oregon, Pulphouse, 1991.
Merlin Dreams in the Mondream Wood. Eugene, Oregon, Pulphouse, 1992.
Spiritwalk. New York, Tor, 1992.
Coyote Stories. Ottawa, Ontario, Triskell Press, 1993.
The Wishing Well. Eugene, Oregon, Pulphouse, 1993.
Dreams Underfoot: The Newford Collecton. New York, Tor, 1993.
Heartfires. Ottawa, Ontario, Triskell Press, 1994.
The Ivory and the Horn: A Newford Collection. New York, Tor, 1995.

Other Publications

Novel

Angel of Darkness (as Samuel M. Key). New York, Jove, 1990.

Short Stories

De Grijze Roos (The Grey Rose). Antwerp, Een Exa Uitgare, 1983.

Verse

The Bone Woman. Ottawa, Ontarion, Triskell Press, 1992.

Other

Editor, *World Fantasy Convention, 1984: Fantasy, an International Genre Celebration.* Ottawa, Ontario, Triskell Press, 1984.

*

Charles de Lint comments:

My prime interest as a writer is to explore the complexities of human relationships through mythic/folkloric material against a mostly contemporary urban setting. I see the juxtaposing of the two as a way of exaggerating the dichotomy of our relationships with each other and our environment. Though I hope primarily to tell a story that will entertain my readers, I also want to do what I can to illuminate the pitfalls of abusive relationships, a failing environment and the like, while at the same time remind my readers of the wonder and mystery and meaning to be found in life.

How well I succeed only they can decide.

*   *   *

There is no doubt that Charles de Lint is currently one of the most popular and prolific writers currently producing fantastic literature. To label him as a fantasy writer, with all the pejorative overtones that word now carries, would be to do him an injustice. In his most successful novels, he has succeeded in fusing the kingdoms of Faery with modern Canadian landscapes, producing a variety of urban fantasy, which can be very satisfying to those who reject the notion that all such stories require a greenwood setting. And yet de Lint's early published fantasies were very much in that mould.

By his own admission, de Lint has been writing since the mid-1970s, but it was not until 1984 that he came to prominence with *The Riddle of the Wren.* In retrospect, it is difficult to understand why this book attracted quite as much attention as it did, for it is undeniably derivative of Tolkien and his many imitators. However, de Lint's fascination for the humbler creatures of folktale and legend, and for the darker side of magic, is also evident, and this mitigates against the more sentimental aspects of both this novel, and *The Harp of the Grey Rose.* Set in the same universe, *The Harp of the Grey Rose* uses different characters and is not a true sequel.

Moonheart shifted the scene from an imaginary landscape to that of modern Ottawa, although Tamson House and its occupant, around which the story revolves, are anything but conventional. This novel clearly demonstrates de Lint's desire to merge the old and the new, with its remarkable synthesis of the mythologies of the different waves of Canadian settlers using the Native Indian shamanism, Welsh Druidism and modern Canadian cynicism. It is admittedly a rich brew, perhaps slightly overdone, but among de Lint's works, it still stands as a milestone of modern fantasy writing.

Mulengro attempted to reproduce this success, with de Lint turning to the mysteries of the Romany culture in a story that owes as much to the horror genre as to the fantastic. Ultimately, it reads less satisfyingly; the blend of magic and urban reality is less smoothly accomplished. The gypsies are presented as typically romantic figures, and an admittedly charming talking cat is inappropriate. Whimsy wins out over acceptable unreality, and ultimately the book is less believable and satisfying than *Moonheart.*

This is even more true of *Yarrow,* which epitomises de Lint's recurrent tendency to descend beyond the romantic to the sentimental. The novel centres around a young fantasy writer, whose work is based on her nightly wanderings in a dream world that has assumed a vital reality for her. When her dreams are stolen by a telepathic vampire-creature, it destroys her ability to write. As a metaphor for writer's block, the device is clumsy, and embarrassing for the reader. Likewise, de Lint's handling of the group relationships within the novel seems to overlook a basic appreciation of how people function together, instead presenting a romanticised and sentimental view of group interactions, attractive to those looking for an acceptable surrogate for real life, but unacceptable to those seeking a grittier reality.

Ironically, *Jack the Giant-Killer,* written as part of a packaged series of novel-length retellings of fairy tales, shows that de Lint is perfectly capable of employing his undoubted skills as a writer of urban fairy stories without descending to the banal. There is a sense that with this book he had fun, and the more relaxed, less self-conscious approach produces a delightful entertainment, which achieves a perfect blend of the impossible and the real. Its sequel, *Drink Down the Moon,* is perhaps less successful. *Jack the Giant-Killer* is a particularly hard act to follow, but nevertheless, odd lapses aside, *Drink Down the Moon* maintains the blend of fairytale motifs and modern characters and settings. In these two novels,

our world and that of Faery come closer together than in any of his other work, the move from one to another literally achieved in simple actions such as putting on and taking off an enchanted cap. The strength of his writing lies in this closeness, the lack of self-consciousness in the co-existence of the two worlds.

Greenmantle, like *Moonheart* and *Mulengro,* shows a sharper, less fey side to de Lint's work, with its almost fatal conjunction of ex-Mafia man, divorcée and child, and her psychotic ex-husband, set against the background of an ancient forest and its primeval inhabitants. There is a faint resonance of Holdstock's *Mythago Wood,* but de Lint's conception of the Canadian wildwood and the characters moving within it is entirely his own. Like *Moonheart,* in fact, maybe more so, the novel is a successful synthesis of the real and unreal, one counterbalancing the other, and the finale, like that of *Mulengro,* is a genuinely shocking revelation. De Lint also writes a more overt type of horror, under a pseudonym, but his cross-genre novels are undoubtedly his most successful work to date.

The Little Country is a sprawling novel set in modern Cornwall, which shows the influence of such novels as Jonathan Carroll's *Land of Laughs,* and the work of James Blaylock, particularly *Land of Dreams,* while once again displaying the sentimentality of *Yarrow.* Although an ambitious novel, it is not among his best work, lacking the bite necessary to counteract the more cloying aspects of the characters. However, the story told within the story, the second, unpublished work of William Dunthorn, is a delightful piece of work, and one could wish that de Lint had concentrated on this rather than on a farrago of nonsense concerning mysterious sects, reminiscent of Aleister Crowley's groups.

Memory and Dream, his latest novel, begins once again to explore that darker side of de Lint's fictive nature (as opposed to that of his alter ego, Samuel M. Key). In this novel, Isabelle Copley, a talented artist, is taken up by Vincent Rushkin, famous painter, as his pupil. Through his teaching, she learns to create images so real they come to life, and calls into being the inhabitants of her own imagination. But this curious skill brings with it tragedy and for many years Isabelle denies her own ability until asked to fulfil a promise to an old friend. When she moves back to the city, Rushkin reappears, and she comes to realise that he is, literally and metaphorically, feeding off her skills. Many of the characters in *Memory and Dream* have appeared before in de Lint's stories, including the winsomely named Jilly Coppercorn, and the Riddell brothers, Christie and Geordie. Many of the stories have been brought together in the enigmatically named *Dreams Underfoot,* his 1993 collection of short stories, and gathered here, one can begin to determine some of de Lint's darker concerns. Time and again, he touches on the subject of the abused child. Jilly herself is revealed in one story to have been sexually abused by parents and foster parents, and there is a strong concern in many for the fate of adolescents living on the streets. The city itself, the archetypal city, features strongly as a background character in many stories and it seems that de Lint is mourning the passing of an older, kinder way. In one story, a character, leaving the city, observes, "It's because of how the city is used. . . . It's because of hatred and spite and bigotry; it's because of homelessness and drugs and crime; it's because the green quiet places are so few while the dark terrors multiply; it's because what's old and comfortable and rounded must make way for what's new and sharp and brittle; it's because a mean spirit grips its streets and that meanness cuts inside me like a knife."

And more than any other novel so far, *The Little Country* is permeated, overly so, by de Lint's love of folk music. Music and musicianship is a recurring motif throughout his books. At his best, it underpins the story, but all too frequently, it threatens to swamp the narrative entirely. De Lint is himself an accomplished musician, and one can only assume that his enthusiasm and knowledge get the better of him, certainly to the extent where it is possible to compare one's own record collection with his. The similar is true of his quoting and name-dropping of fantasy titles. A habit that can strike a chord with the reader in one book becomes irritating after several. De Lint seems to be a writer driven to demonstrate that he knows his stuff by passing on a reading list, quite unnecessarily so, for he clearly does know what he is about.

In conclusion, Charles de Lint, in his most successful work, has achieved a very satisfactory marriage of ancient folklore and modern setting. His characters, if a little too good to be true, are appropriate players for a modern fairytale, and he is not afraid to recognise the horror of contemporary life. His output is variable, and for every successful modern interpretation of traditional motifs and tales, there is another story that doesn't achieve the delicate balance. However, it is always worth persevering with de Lint, for among the unsuccessful experiments are some rare gems. As one of de Lint's characters, the writer Christy Riddell, observes: "My themes are simple. They're about love and loss, honour and the responsibilities of friendship. And wonder . . . always wonder. As complex as people are individually, their drives are universal."

—Maureen Speller

DEL MARTIA, Astron. *See* **FEARN, John Russell.**

---

del REY, Lester. *See* **also FAIRMAN, Paul W.**

---

del REY, Lester

Pseudonyms: Edson McCann (with Frederik Pohl); Philip St. John; Erik Van Lhin; Kenneth Wright. **Nationality:** American. **Born:** Ramon Felipe San Juan Mario Silvio Enrico Alvarez-del Rey, Clydesdale, Minnesota, 2 June 1915. **Education:** George Washington University, Washington, D.C., 1931-33. **Family:** Married the writer and editor Judy-Lynn Benjamin (fourth marriage) in 1971 (died, 1986). **Career:** Sheet metal worker, McDonnell Aircraft Corporation, St. Louis, 1942-44; author's agent, Scott Meredith Literary Agency, New York, 1947-50; editor, *Space Science Fiction,* London, 1952-53; publisher, as R. Alvarez, 1952, and editor, as Philip St. John, 1952-53, *Science Fiction Adventures;* associate editor, as John Vincent, 1953, and as Cameron Hull, with Harry Harrison, 1953, *Fantasy Fiction;* editor, as Wade Kaempfert, *Rocket Stories,* 1953; managing editor, International Science Fiction, 1968; managing editor, 1968-69, and features editor, 1969-74, *Galaxy* and *If;*

editor, *Worlds of Fantasy,* 1968. Fantasy editor, 1975-77, and since 1977, editor, Del Rey Books (Ballantine Books). Since 1974, book reviewer, *Analog.* Taught fantasy fiction, New York University, 1972-73; editor, Garland Press science-fiction series, 1975. **Awards:** Boys' Clubs of America Science Fiction award, 1953. Guest of Honor, World Science Fiction Convention, 1967. **Died:** 10 May 1993.

SCIENCE FICTION PUBLICATIONS

Novels

Marooned on Mars (for children). Philadelphia, Winston, 1952; London, Hutchinson, 1953.
Rocket Jockey (for children; as Philip St. John). Philadelphia, Winston, 1952; as *Rocket Pilot,* London, Hutchinson, 1955; as Lester del Rey, New York, Ballantine, 1978.
The Mysterious Planet (for children; as Kenneth Wright). Philadelphia, Winston, 1953; as Lester del Rey, New York, Ballantine, 1978.
Attack from Atlantis (for children). Philadelphia, Winston, 1953.
Battle on Mercury (for children; as Erik Van Lhin). Philadelphia, Winston, 1953.
Step to the Stars (for children). Philadelphia, Winston, 1954; London, Hutchinson, 1956.
Rockets to Nowhere (for children; as Philip St. John). Philadelphia, Winston, 1954.
Preferred Risk (with Frederik Pohl as Edson McCann). New York, Simon and Schuster, 1955; London, Methuen, 1983.
Mission to the Moon (for children). Philadelphia, Winston, and London, Hutchinson, 1956.
Police Your Planet (as Erik Van Lhin). New York, Avalon, 1956; revised edition, as Lester del Rey, with Erik Van Lhin, New York, Ballantine, 1975; London, New English Library, 1978.
Nerves. New York, Ballantine, 1956; revised edition, 1976.
Day of the Giants. New York, Avalon, 1959.
Moon of Mutiny (for children). New York, Holt Rinehart, 1961; London, Faber, 1963.
The Eleventh Commandment. Evanston, Illinois, Regency, 1962; revised edition, New York, Ballantine, 1970.
Two Complete Novels: The Sky Is Falling, Badge of Infamy. New York, Galaxy, 1963; published separately, New York, Ace, 1973; London, Dobson, 1976.
Outpost of Jupiter (for children). New York, Holt, Rinehart, 1963; London, Gollancz, 1964.
The Runaway Robot (for children), with Paul W. Fairman. Philadelphia, Westminster Press, 1965; London, Gollancz, 1967.
Rocket from Infinity (for children). New York, Holt Rinehart, 1966; London, Faber, 1967.
The Scheme of Things, with Paul W. Fairman. New York, Belmont, 1966.
The Infinite Worlds of Maybe. New York, Holt Rinehart, 1966; London, Faber, 1968.
Siege Perilous, with Paul W. Fairman. New York, Lancer, 1966; as *The Man Without a Planet,* 1969.
Tunnel through Time (for children), with Paul W. Fairman. Philadelphia, Westminster Press, 1966.
Prisoners of Space (for children), with Paul W. Fairman. Philadelphia, Westminster Press, 1968.
Pstalemate. New York, Putnam, 1971; London, Gollancz, 1972.

Weeping May Tarry, with Raymond F. Jones. Los Angeles, Pinnacle, 1978.

Short Stories

. . . and Some Were Human. Philadelphia, Prime Press, 1948; abridged edition as *Tales of Soaring Science Fiction from and Some Were Human,* New York, Ballantine, 1961.
Robots and Changelings. New York, Ballantine, 1958.
Mortals and Monsters. New York, Ballantine, 1965; London, Tandem, 1967.
Gods and Golems. New York, Ballantine, 1973.
Early del Rey. Garden City, New York, Doubleday, 1975.
The Best of Lester del Rey. New York, Ballantine, 1978.

OTHER PUBLICATIONS

Other

It's Your Atomic Age: An Explanation in Simple, Everyday Terms of Atomic Energy to the Average Person. New York, Abelard Press, 1951.
Pirate Flag for Monterey: The Story of the Sack of Monterey (for children). Philadelphia, Winston, 1952.
Rockets through Space: The Story of Man's Preparations to Explore the Universe (for children). Philadelphia, Winston, 1957; revised edition, 1960.
The Cave of Spears (for children). New York, Knopf, 1957.
Space Flight: The Coming Exploration of the Universe (for children). New York, Golden Press, 1959.
The Mysterious Earth [Sea, Sky]. Philadelphia, Chilton, 3 vols., 1960-64.
Rocks and What They Tell Us (for children). Racine, Wisconsin, Whitman Press, 1961.
The World of Science Fiction, 1926-1976: The History of a Subculture. New York, Ballantine, 1979.

Editor, with Cecile Matschat and Carl Carmer, *The Year after Tomorrow.* Philadelphia, Winston, 1954.
Editor, *Best Science Fiction Stories of the Year, [First-Fourth] Annual Collections.* New York, Dutton, 5 vols., 1972-76; vol. 5, London, Kaye and Ward, 1977.
Editor, *Fantastic Science-Fiction Art, 1926-1954.* New York, Ballantine, 1975.
Editor, *The Best of Frederik Pohl.* Garden City, New York, Doubleday, 1975; London, Sidgwick and Jackson, 1977.
Editor, *The Best of C.L. Moore.* Garden City, New York, Doubleday, 1975.
Editor, *The Best of John W. Campbell.* Garden City, New York, Doubleday, 1976.
Editor, *The Best of Robert Bloch.* New York, Ballantine, 1977.
Editor, *The Fantastic Art of Boris* by Boris Vallejo. New York, Ballantine, 1978.
Editor, *The Best of Hal Clement.* New York, Ballantine, 1979.
Editor (with Rise Kessler), *Once upon a Time: A Treasury of Modern Fairy Tales.* New York, Ballantine, and London, Legend, 1991.

*   *   *

Lester del Rey produced much of his early work in his spare time. Once established as a writer he created vast volumes of material, and he clearly thought of authorship as a craft. His standard is the orderly, well-told tale of the magazine writer, stamped by commercial necessity. Del Rey's writing balances commercial motives, excellence in the context of his times, and an ongoing faith in science.

Del Rey's early period can be dated 1938-54, from his first published short story, "The Faithful," to his first adult novel, *The Sky Is Falling.* For the first 10 years he submitted *only* to John W. Campbell and published at least 38 stories. They contain the detailed imagining Campbell liked and the narrative briskness for an editor who wanted a story but paid by the word. The two best-known stories from this period are "Helen O'Loy" and *Nerves.* "Helen O'Loy" is a witty tale about bachelor roommates, a robot-repair wizard and a doctor, who improve a robot by adding emotions. Helen then patterns her emotions after television soap operas and falls for Dave, the repairman, who eventually marries her. The story is filled with touches of futuristic imagination. For example, Phil, the doctor, is called to give counterhormones to a wealthy old lady's son and the servant with whom he is infatuated. In the plot proper del Rey generates humor by juxtaposing soap-opera romanticism and the robot: "Helen's technique may have lacked polish, but it had enthusiasm, as he found when he tried to stop her from kissing him. She had learned fast and furiously—also, Helen was powered by an atomotor." *Nerves* is more dated in scientific terms, but it has an exciting plot about a blowout in a nuclear plant. Though radiation burns are erroneously described, *Nerves* is suspenseful, and touches like a motor needle for surgical sutures and sterilization by supersonic sound provide excellent decoration. The story sets up good characterization within the limits of its form, stressing an elder doctor-younger doctor relationship. The title focuses the theme of control under stress.

The early stories cover many topics. Some are fantasies, such as "Hereafter, Inc.," in which a hypocritical puritan refuses to accept that he is in heaven because the people he secretly hoped were damned sinners are with him. Others are nostalgic, such as "Though Dreamers Die," in which Jorgen, the last man, realizes that the robots who have helped him travel through space after a plague on Earth will carry on man's dreams and aspirations. Some deal with hard science, such as "Habit," about a rocket race won by slingshotting around Jupiter to gain velocity.

After 1952 del Rey became a regular writer of juvenile SF, a form well-suited to his abilities. He generally featured a hero just turning 18 who ventures into space to help build a satellite station, explore the Moon, or investigate a strange planet. True to form for such tales the boy usually stows away on a rocketship and takes some foolish initiative, creating trouble for everyone until he extricates himself by a clever manoeuvre. Rather than the projection of a powerful ethical goal or cautionary extrapolation del Rey's ability lay in telling a good story, so it follows that these juveniles are very successful. They are laden with presumptions about women, the merit of individual initiative, and the benefits of American democracy, but this reflects del Rey's innate beliefs and his times rather than propaganda intent.

The Sky Is Falling is a sport among del Rey's works. It describes an alternative universe where magic dominates but is in danger because the sky and its zodiacal symbols are cracking and falling. The hero, mistaken for his engineer uncle, is revivified (after a fatal accident on Earth) to fix the sky. The detail of this novel is fascinating: individuals' energies wax and wane with their planets and the scientific method is shown to resemble that of the magicians. It sparkles with imaginative exuberance in its denial of conventional reality (when pieces of sky crush people) and in zany turns of plot.

Two interesting novels from del Rey's later work are *Police Your Planet* and *Siege Perilous.* The former deals with a frontier Mars riddled with poverty and crime where the police extort mountains of graft and people live in terror. Bruce Gordon, a reporter exiled from Earth for exposing the truth, struggles for survival and eventually the liberation of this vividly awful world. Del Rey is really painting a subtle picture of urban decay on Earth, where violence is the law. The novel is awkwardly imagined in places (air is held in Marsport by a fabric-covered dome) but it has power, energy, and much lightly buried compassion. On the other hand, *Siege Perilous* is a novel that swings from a Martian invasion horror story to the wildly ridiculous. America's orbiting satellite, a scientific station and weapons base, is invaded by Martians who fear man will invade Mars and therefore intend to destroy Earth first. The three humans who evade the initial gas attack eventually outwit the Martians. This basic story is riotously decorated since the Martians' knowledge of Earth has come exclusively from television broadcasts. Twenty-six invasion-of-Mars movies have motivated the attack, which is carried out in a mixture of Wild West, Ronald Coleman, Chicago gangster, and grade-D science fiction styles. Earth triumphs in an old-fashioned shootout while the heroine awaits torture. Del Rey has great fun with the clichés and patterns. Yet even while letting go in this action romp he manages to insert interesting minor ideas such as the satellite refining of pure crystalline metals and the balancing of the space station by pumping a water ballast.

Pstalemate is the story of Harry Bronson's gradual discovery of psi powers and his struggle to evade the insanity which he discovers is the price of the gift in others. It cleverly exposes the potentials of psi and precognition but slows badly in the middle as the forces around Harry, including his father and his mother, who is dying in a mental home, are gradually revealed, as del Rey introduces arguments about free will, and as Harry makes repeated ineffective atttempts to solve his frightening dilemma.

In a long, steady career ranging from 1938 to 1993, Lester del Rey became most skillful in his craft and earned a deserved reputation as a major editor. Like many writers of his period he filled out imaginative detail around solid plots to capture the excitement of the scientific universe. His weaknesses lay in the sentimentality of his message stories and the impression that he did not write from a coherent critical view of the universe. A virtuoso craftsman whose love was the story itself, he may not meet recent expectations as a "committed" writer and may therefore lack the "heart" which lifts a writer from the good to the great.

—Peter Brigg

DEMPSEY, Hank. *See* **HARRISON, Harry.**

DENHOLM, Mark. *See* **FEARN, John Russell.**

DENT, Lester

Pseudonym: Kenneth Robeson. **Nationality:** American. **Born:** La Plata, Missouri, 12 October 1904 (some sources cite birth year as 1905). **Education:** Studied telegraphy at Chillicothe Business College, Missouri, 1923-24. **Family:** Married Norma Gerling in 1925. **Career:** Taught at Chillicothe Business College, 1924; telegrapher, Western Union, Carrolton, Missouri, 1924, and Empire Oil and Gas Company, Ponca City, Oklahoma, 1925; telegrapher, then teletype operator, Associated Press, Tulsa, 1926; journalist for *Tulsa World;* house-writer for Dell, publisher, 1930; freelance writer from 1930, and also dairy farmer and aerial photographer. **Died:** 11 March 1959.

SCIENCE FICTION PUBLICATIONS

Novels as Kenneth Robeson (series: Doc Savage in all books)

The Man of Bronze. New York, Street and Smith, 1933; London, Corgi, 1975.
The Land of Terror. New York, Street and Smith, 1933; London, Tandem, 1965.
Quest of the Spider. New York, Street and Smith, 1935.
The Thousand-Headed Man. New York, Bantam, 1964; London, Corgi, 1975.
Meteor Menace. New York, Bantam, 1964; London, Corgi, 1975.
The Polar Treasure. New York, Bantam, 1965.
Brand of the Werewolf. New York, Bantam, 1965.
The Lost Oasis. New York, Bantam, 1965.
The Monsters. New York, Bantam, 1965.
The Mystic Mullah. New York, Bantam, 1965; London, Bantam, 1966.
The Phantom City. New York, Bantam, 1966.
Fear Cay. New York, Bantam, 1966.
Quest of Qui. New York and London, Bantam, 1966.
Land of Always-Night, with Ryerson Johnson. New York, Bantam, 1966.
The Fantastic Island, with Ryerson Johnson. New York, Bantam, 1966; London, Bantam, 1967.
The Spook Legion. New York, Bantam, 1967.
The Red Skull. New York, Bantam, 1967.
The Sargasso Ogre. New York, Bantam, 1967.
Pirate of the Pacific. New York, Bantam, 1967.
The Secret in the Sky. New York, Bantam, 1967; London, Bantam, 1968.
The Czar of Fear. New York, Bantam, 1968.
Fortress of Solitude. New York, Bantam, 1968.
The Green Eagle. New York, Bantam, 1968.
Death in Silver. New York, Bantam, 1968.
Mystery under the Sea. New York, Bantam, 1968; London, Bantam, 1969.
The Deadly Dwarf. New York, Bantam, 1968.
The Other World. New York, Bantam, 1968; London, Bantam, 1969.
The Flaming Falcons. New York, Bantam, 1968; London, Bantam, 1969.
The Annihilist. New York, Bantam, 1968; London, Bantam, 1969.
Dust of Death, with Harold A. Davis. New York, Bantam, 1969.
The Terror in the Navy. New York, Bantam, 1969.

The Squeaking Goblin. New York, Bantam, 1969.

Resurrection Day. New York, Bantam, 1969.

Hex, with William G. Bogart. New York and London, Bantam, 1969.

Red Snow. New York, Bantam, 1969.

World's Fair Goblin, with William G. Bogart. New York, Bantam, 1969.

The Dagger in the Sky. New York, Bantam, 1969.

Merchants of Disaster, with Harold A. Davis. New York, Bantam, 1969.

The Gold Ogre. New York, Bantam, 1969.

The Man Who Shook the Earth. New York, Bantam, 1969.

The Sea Magician. New York, Bantam, 1970.

The Midas Man. New York, Bantam, 1970.

The Feathered Octopus. New York, Bantam, 1970.

The Sea Angel. New York, Bantam, 1970.

Devil on the Moon. New York, Bantam, 1970.

The Vanisher. New York, Bantam, 1970.

The Mental Wizard. New York, Bantam, 1970.

The Golden Peril, with Harold A. Davis. New York, Bantam, 1970.

The Giggling Ghosts. New York, Bantam, 1971.

Poison Island. New York, Bantam, 1971.

The Yellow Cloud. New York, Bantam, 1971.

The Majii. New York, Bantam, 1971.

The Pirate's Ghost. New York, Bantam, 1971.

The Submarine Mystery. New York, Bantam, 1971.

The Motion Menace, with Ryerson Johnson. New York, Bantam, 1971.

Mad Mesa. New York, Bantam, 1972.

The Freckled Shark. New York, Bantam, 1972.

The Mystery on the Snow. New York, Bantam, 1972.

Spook Hole. New York, Bantam, 1972.

The Metal Master. New York, Bantam, 1973.

The Seven Agate Devils. New York, Bantam, 1973.

The Derrick Devil. New York, Bantam, 1973.

The Land of Fear, with Harold A. Davis. New York, Bantam, 1973.

The South Pole Terror. New York, Bantam, 1974.

The Crimson Serpent. New York, Bantam, 1974.

The Devil Genghis. New York, Bantam, 1974.

The King Maker, with Harold A. Davis. New York, Bantam, 1975.

The Stone Man. New York, Bantam, 1976.

The Evil Gnome. New York, Bantam, 1976.

The Red Terrors. New York, Bantam, 1976.

The Boss of Terror. New York, Bantam, 1976.

The Angry Ghost, with William G. Bogart. New York, Bantam, 1977.

The Spotted Men. New York, Bantam, 1977.

The Roar Devil. New York, Bantam, 1977.

The Magic Island. New York, Bantam, 1977.

The Purple Dragon, with Harold A. Davis. New York, Bantam, 1978.

The Awful Egg. New York, Bantam, 1978.

The Hate Genius. New York, Bantam, 1979.

The Red Spider. New York, Bantam, 1979.

Mystery on Happy Bones. New York, Bantam, 1979.

Doc Savage: Satan Black; and, Cargo Unknown. New York, Bantam, 1980.

Doc Savage: Hell Below; and, The Lost Giant. New York, Bantam, 1980.

Doc Savage: The Pharaoh's Ghost; and, The Time Terror. New York, Bantam, 1981.

Doc Savage: The Whisker of Hercules; and, The Man Who Was Scared. New York, Bantam, 1981.

Doc Savage: They Died Twice; and, The Screaming Man. New York, Bantam, 1981.

Doc Savage: Jiu San; The Black; and, Black Witch. New York, Bantam, 1981.

Doc Savage: The Shape of Terror; and, Death Had Yellow Eyes. New York, Bantam, 1982.

Doc Savage: One-Eyed Mystic; and, The Man Who Fell Up. New York, Bantam, 1982.

Doc Savage: The Talking Devil; and, The Ten Ton Snake. New York, Bantam, 1982.

Doc Savage: Pirate Isle; and, The Speaking Stone. New York, Bantam, 1983.

Doc Savage: The Golden Man; and, Peril in the North. New York, Bantam, 1984.

Doc Savage: The Laugh of Death; and, The King of Terror. New York, Bantam, 1984.

Doc Savage: The Three Wild Men; and, The Fiery Menace. New York, Bantam, 1984.

Doc Savage: Devils of the Deep, with Harold A. Davis, bound with *The Headless Men,* by Alan Hathaway. New York, Bantam, 1984.

Doc Savage: The Goblins; and, The Secret of the Su. New York, Bantam, 1984.

Doc Savage: Four Complete Novels in One Volume: The All-White Elf; The Running Skeletons; The Angry Canary; and, The Swooning Lady. New York, Bantam, 1986.

Doc Savage: Four Complete Novels in One Volume: King Joe Cay; and, The Thing That Pursued, with *The Mindless Monsters; and The Headless Men,* by Alan Hathaway. New York, Bantam, 1987.

Doc Savage: Four Complete Novels in One Volume: The Spook of Grandpa Eben; Measures for a Coffin; The Three Devils; and, Strange Fish. New York, Bantam, 1987.

Doc Savage: Four Complete Novels in One Volume: Mystery Island; Men of Fear; Rock Sinister; and, The Pure Evil. New York, Bantam, 1987.

Doc Savage: Five Complete Novels in One Volume: No Light to Die By: The Monkey Suit: Let's Kill Ames: Once Over Lightly; and, I Died Yesterday. New York, Bantam, 1988.

Doc Savage: Four Complete Novels in One Volume: The Awful Dynasty; The Magic Forest; Fire and Ice; and, The Disappearing Lady, with William G. Bogart. New York, Bantam, 1988.

Doc Savage: Four Complete Noves in One Volume: The Men Vanished; Five Fathoms Dead; The Terrible Stork; and, Danger Lies East. New York, Bantam, 1988.

Doc Savage: Four Complete Novels in One Volume: The Metal Master; The Pink Lady; Weird Valley; and, Trouble on Parade. New York, Bantam, 1989.

Doc Savage: Four Complete Novels in One Volume: The Invisible-Box Murders; Birds of Death; The Wee Ones; and, Terror Takes 7. New York, Bantam, 1989.

Doc Savage: Four Complete Novels in One Volume: The Devil's Black Rock; Waves of Death; The Two-Wise Owl; and, Terror and the Lonely Widow. New York, Bantam, 1989.

Doc Savage: Five Complete Novels in One Volume: See-Pah-Poo; Colors for Murder; Three Times a Corpse; and Death Is a Round Black Spot, The Devil Is Jones. New York, Bantam, 1990.

Doc Savage: Four Complete Novels in One Volume: Death in Little Houses, with William G. Bogart, bound with *Bequest of Evil; Target for Death; The Death Lady; and, The Exploding Lake,* New York, Bantam, 1990.

Doc Savage: Five Complete Novels in One Volume: The Derelict of Skull Shoal; Terror Wears No Shoes; The Green Master; Return from Cormoral; and, Up from Earth's Center. New York, Bantam, 1990.

Short Stories

The Sinister Ray. New York, Gryphon, 1987.

OTHER PUBLICATIONS

Novels

Dead at the Take-Off. New York, Doubleday, 1946; London, Cassell, 1948; as *High Stakes,* New York, Ace, 1953.
Lady to Kill. New York, Doubleday, 1946; London, Cassell, 1949.
Lady Afraid. New York, Doubleday, 1948; London, Cassell, 1950.
Lady So Silent. London, Cassell, 1951.
Cry at Dusk. New York, Fawcett, 1952; London, Fawcett, 1959.
Lady in Peril. New York, Ace, 1959.

Short Stories

Hades and Hocus Pocus edited by Robert Weinberg. Chicago, Pulp Press, 1979.

Plays

The Incredible Radio Exploits of Doc Savage. Melrose, Massachusetts, Odyssey, 2 vols., 1983-84.

Radio Plays: *Scotland Yard,* 1931; *Doc Savage,* 1934.

*

Bibliography: "The Secret Kenneth Robesons" and "The Duende Doc Savage Index" by Will Murray, in *Duende 2* (North Quincy, Massachusetts), 1977.

Critical Studies: *Doc Savage: His Apocalyptic Life* by Philip José Farmer, New York, Doubleday, 1973, revised edition, London, Panther, 1975; *The Man Behind Doc Savage* edited by Robert Weinberg, Chicago, Weinberg, 1974; *Doc Savage,* 1978, and *Secrets of Doc Savage,* 1981, both by Will Murray, Melrose, Massachusetts, Odyssey.

*   *   *

Science fiction, as it manifested itself in the early pulp magazines, did not always appear in SF publications, or even in works that were primarily of that genre. Quite often, the various single-character magazines such as *The Shadow* and *Doc Savage* featured interesting science fiction in the guise of adventure and detective fiction. The novels of Kenneth Robeson fall into this category. Kenneth Robeson was a house pseudonym used by Street and Smith in their *Doc Savage* and *Avenger* magazines between 1933 and 1949. It masked a number of writers, including Ryerson Johnson, Harold A. Davis, William G. Bogart, Alan Hathway, Paul Ernst, and Emile C. Tepperman. The Robeson byline, however, was most frequently used by, and identified with, Lester Dent, the creator and author of most of the Doc Savage novels.

The Doc Savage novels are not predominately science fiction except, perhaps, in their premise of Doc Savage himself, a man raised and trained by a host of world experts to be a physical and mental superman, to whom fantastic abilities are attributed.

With the exception of space and time travel, the Doc Savage adventures employ most of the themes common to early SF: mind transference (*Mad Mesa*); teleportation (*The Vanisher*); robots (*The Seven Agate Devils*); anti-gravity (*The Secret of the Sky*); biological mutation (*The Monsters*); invisibility (*The Spook Legion*); force fields (*The Motion Menace*); raising the dead (*Resurrection Day*); and destructive rays (*The Deadly Dwarf*). Structurally, the stories are formula. Doc Savage contends with criminals or power seekers who possess and attempt to pervert new technological discoveries toward their own ends.

Lost worlds are a popular Doc Savage theme. *The Land of Terror* and "The Time Terror" postulates pockets of dinosaurs in remote areas. *The Mental Wizard* and "The Green Master" concern lost Egyptian colonies in South America. There are submarine cities (*The Red Terrors*) and subterranean worlds (*Land of Always-Night*). *The Other World* combines the subterranean civilisation with surviving dinosaurs. Many adventures employ myths and legends as their bases. The Fountain of Youth and Aladdin's Cave are the goals in *Fear Cay* and *The Majii*. Lester Dent often created his own folk myths to lend color to his antagonists in *The Feathered Octopus* and *The Squeaking Goblin*. Doc Savage, the "Man of Bronze," is himself a mythic character who possesses all the prerequisites of a culture hero— wisdom, great strength, and near-magical scientific powers. He is a champion who defends humanity against the menace of technology in evil hands. His enemies, appropriately enough, are evocative of man's superstitious fear of the unknown (in this case, scientific advancement) and call themselves by such titles as The Sargasso Ogre, The Roar Devil, and The Purple Dragon. The mythological theme is carried as far as a traditional descent into Hell by the hero in the final Doc Savage novel, *Up from Earth's Center,* a fantasy.

Although primarily juvenile in its appeal, Lester Dent's work combines a fertility of invention with a vividness of imagination seldom surpassed. His best efforts include *Meteor Menace, The Thousand-Headed Man, Land of Always-Night,* and *Resurrection Day.* The later Doc Savage stories are considerably more mature in theme and tone. Among these, *The Whisker of Hercules, The Red Spider,* and *Up from Earth's Center* are exceptional.

—Will Murray

DENTINGER, Stephen. *See* **HOCH, Edward D.**

DeWEESE, Gene

Pseudonyms: Jean DeWeese; Thomas Stratton (with Robert Coulson); Victoria Thomas. **Nationality:** American. **Born:** Thomas Eugene DeWeese, Rochester, Indiana, 31 January 1934. **Education:** Valparaiso Technical Institute, associate degree in electronics, 1953; also studied at the University of Wisconsin, Milwaukee, Indiana University, Kokomo, and Marquette University, Milwaukee. **Family:** Married Beverly Joanne Amers in 1955. **Career:** Electronics technician, Delco Radio, Kokomo, 1954-59; technical writer, especially on space navigation, Delco Electronics, Milwaukee, 1959-74. Since 1974, freelance writer; science fiction reviewer, *Milwaukee Journal,* 1980-84; reviewer and columnist, *Science Fiction Review,* 1980-90, and *Comic Buyer's Guide,* 1985-94. **Agent:** (books) Scovil Chichak Galen Literary Agency, 381 Park Ave. S., Suite 1020, New York, New York 10016; (short stories) Larry Sternig Literary Agency, 742 North Robertson, Milwaukee, Wisconsin 53213, U.S.A. **Address:** 2718 North Prospect, Milwaukee, Wisconsin 53211, U.S.A.

SCIENCE FICTION PUBLICATIONS

Novels (series: Joe Karns; Star Trek; Calvin Willeford)

The Invisibility Affair (with Robert Coulson as Thomas Stratton). New York, Ace, 1967.
The Mind-Twisters Affair (with Robert Coulson as Thomas Stratton). New York, Ace, 1967.
Gates of the Universe, with Robert Coulson. Toronto, Laser, 1975; expanded version, as *Nightmare Universe,* Lake Geneva, Wisconsin, TSR, 1985.
Now You See It/Him/Them . . . (Karns), with Robert Coulson. Garden City, New York, Doubleday, 1975; London, Hale, 1976.
Jeremy Case. Toronto, Laser, 1976.
Charles Fort Never Mentioned Wombats (Karns), with Robert Coulson. Garden City, New York, Doubleday, 1977; London, Hale, 1978.
Major Corby and the Unidentified Flapping Object (for children). Garden City, New York, Doubleday, 1979.
The Wanting Factor. New York, Playboy Paperbacks, 1980.
Nightmares from Space (for children). New York, F. Watts, 1981.
Something Answered. New York, Dell, 1983.
The Adventures of a Two-Minute Werewolf (for children). Garden City, New York, Doubleday, 1983.
Black Suits from Outer Space (Willeford; for children). New York, Putnam, 1985; as *Beepers from Outer Space,* New York, Putnam, 1985.
The Dandelion Caper (Willeford; for children). New York, Putnam, 1986.
The Calvin Nullifier (Willeford; for children). New York, Putnam, 1987.
Chain of Attack: A Star Trek Novel. New York, Pocket, and London, Titan, 1987.
The Peacekeepers (Star Trek). New York, Pocket, 1988.
Star Trek: The Final Nexus. New York, Pocket, and London, Titan, 1988.
Whatever Became of Aunt Margaret? (for children). New York, Putnam, 1990.
Star Trek: Renegade. New York, Pocket, and London, Titan, 1991.
Probe (Star Trek; uncredited rewrite of novel by Margaret Wander Bonanno). New York, Pocket, 1992.
Into the Nebula (Star Trek). New York, Pocket, 1995.

OTHER PUBLICATIONS

Novels as Jean DeWeese

The Reimann Curse. New York, Ballantine, 1975; revised edition, as Gene DeWeese, as *A Different Darkness,* New York, Jove, 1982.

The Carnelian Cat. New York, Ballantine, 1975.
The Moonstone Spirit. New York, Ballantine, 1975.
The Doll with Opal Eyes. Garden City, New York, Doubleday, 1976; London, Hale, 1977.
Cave of the Moaning Wind. New York, Ballantine, 1976.
Web of Guilt: An Astrological Gothic Novel: Scorpio. New York, Ballantine, 1976.
Nightmare in Pewter. Garden City, New York, Doubleday, 1978.
Hour of the Cat. Garden City, New York, Doubleday, and London, Hale, 1980.
The Backhoe Gothic. Garden City, New York, Doubleday, 1981.

Novel as Victoria Thomas (with Connie Kugi)

Ginger's Wish. Garden City, New York, Doubleday, 1987.

Other

Making American Folk Art Dolls, with Gini Rogowski. Radnor, Pennsylvania, Chilton, 1975.
Computers in Entertainment and the Arts (for children). New York, F. Watts, 1984.

*

Manuscript Collection: McCain Library and Archives, University of Southern Mississippi, Hattiesburg (all juveniles and Star Trek novels).

*   *   *

Gene DeWeese is a prolific and workmanlike writer whose novels and stories fall into the categories of gothic, horror, and science fiction. He writes young adult SF and fantasy and has received recognition from fans of SF as well as general readers.

DeWeese's first fictional publications (he started his career as a technical writer) were novels from the *Man from U.N.C.L.E.* series, which he coauthored with Robert (Buck) Coulson. *The Invisibility Affair* and *The Mind-Twisters Affair* are notable for their use of humor and wit, in keeping with the television series. However, as with his later novels, DeWeese's background in technical writing added much to these pieces. The descriptions of the workings of the invisible dirigible in the first of these two novels is fascinating to the technically inclined. He also wrote short stories with Coulson early in his career (under the name of Thomas Stratton) and a science fiction novel, *Gates of the Universe,* for the short-run Laser Books series under the editorship of Roger Elwood. The later Laser novel, *Jeremy Case,* written by DeWeese alone, focuses on the character of Jeremy and his mysterious symbiotic partner, Lissa. DeWeese also wrote two hardcover novels with Coulson, both of which are humorous, solid reads, full of echoes to people they both knew as fans and writers. These were *Now You See It/ Him/Them . . .* and *Charles Fort Never Mentioned Wombats.*

Particularly prolific in the young adult field, DeWeese has produced at least five titles which are notable for their inclusion of girl as well as boy-scientist/adventurers. Of these, the amusing *The Adventures of a Two-Minute Werewolf* achieved the distinction of being made into a two-part television production for the O.J. Readmore series. In this story, Walt Cribbens turns 14 and finds that his family looks forward to a very unusual addition to the usual changes accompanying puberty. He is able to enlist the help of Cindy, a lively and loyal friend, to conceal his momentary transformations into a werewolf until he's able to resolve his problems. *Black Suits from Outer Space,* one of three adventure novels featuring the first-person narrator, Calvin Willeford, a self-proclaimed "logical guy" and his gutsy, more intuitive friend Kathy, is another example of DeWeese's grasp of humor and adventure that will appeal to the younger set. All of his young adult novels place children in the here and now but also put them in contact with alien beings or otherworldly forces, which they cope with very successfully. His adults are sometimes friends, not enemies, of the heroes, although there are plenty of silly, nasty, or obstructionist members of the older generation. *Black Suits* is no exception, with Kathy and Calvin rescuing an alien tourist through the able assistance of a level-headed, 300-pound, ex-wrestler sheriff's deputy named Phil. His strength is equal to the task of carrying the large, furry alien when necessary. The 300-pound ex-wrestler, like many of DeWeese's characters, is modeled partly after a friend, and those in the large circle of SF fans and writers who know DeWeese delight in finding these veiled references to themselves in the stories. This is also one of his techniques for avoiding the stereotypical characters that so easily slip into genre fiction narratives. His commitment to positive models for youngsters makes one eager to read more of this type of work.

Equally comfortable with established characters and settings, DeWeese's most recent adult-fiction efforts have been on *Star Trek* and *Star Trek: The Next Generation* novels. Reflecting the TV origins of the basic Star Trek concepts, all his additions to this series of novels rely heavily on conversation that introduces all new characters, furthers the plots, and provides what descriptions of settings are needed. With all the constraints placed on writers of such series, and especially popular TV series like Star Trek, it is a marvel that any creativity surfaces. Yet DeWeese's first contribution, *Chain of Attack,* was on the *New York Times* bestseller list and prompted an equally interesting sequel, *The Final Nexus. Renegade* is another fast-paced technological adventure which, like *Chain* and *Nexus,* requires the reader to sort through a number of would-be good and bad guys before the players' true intentions are revealed. He adds these elements of mystery to the usual, almost formulaic conversational sallies between the established main characters, which serve to reassure readers that they are still in the Star Trek universe. DeWeese's stubborn creativity makes these novels well worth reading.

—Janice M. Bogstad

DICK, Philip K(indred)

Nationality: American. **Born:** Chicago, Illinois, 16 December 1928. **Education:** Berkeley High School, California, graduated 1945. **Family:** Married 1) Jeanette Dick in 1949 (divorced); 2) Kleo Dick in 1951 (divorced); 3) Ann Dick in 1958 (divorced), one daughter; 4) Nancy Dick in 1967 (divorced), one daughter; 5) Tessa Busby in 1973, one son. **Career:** Announcer, KSMO-AM radio, 1947 and record store manager, 1948-52, both Berkeley. **Awards:** Hugo award, 1963; John W. Campbell Memorial award, 1975. **Died:** 2 March 1982.

SCIENCE FICTION PUBLICATIONS

Novels (series: VALIS)

Solar Lottery. New York, Ace, 1955; as *World of Chance,* London, Rich and Cowan, 1956.

The World Jones Made. New York, Ace, 1956; London, Sidgwick and Jackson, 1968.

The Man Who Japed. New York, Ace, 1956; London, Magnum, 1978.

Eye in the Sky. New York, Ace, 1957; London, Arrow, 1971.

The Cosmic Puppets. New York, Ace, 1957; London, Panther, 1985.

Time out of Joint. Philadelphia, Lippincott, 1959; London, Sidgwick and Jackson, 1961.

Dr. Futurity. New York, Ace, 1960; London, Eyre Methuen, 1976.

Vulcan's Hammer. New York, Ace, 1960; London, Arrow, 1976.

The Man in the High Castle: A Novel. New York, Putnam, 1962; London, Penguin, 1965.

The Game-Players of Titan. New York, Ace, 1963; London, Sphere, 1969.

Martian Time-Slip. New York, Ballantine, 1964; London, New English Library, 1976.

The Simulacra. New York, Ace, 1964; London, Eyre Methuen, 1977.

The Penultimate Truth. New York, Belmont, 1964; London, Cape, 1967.

Clans of the Alphane Moon. New York, Ace, 1964; London, Panther, 1975.

The Three Stigmata of Palmer Eldritch. Garden City, New York, Doubleday, 1965; London, Cape, 1966.

Dr. Bloodmoney; or, How We Got Along after the Bomb. New York, Ace, 1965; London, Arrow, 1977.

The Crack in Space. New York, Ace, 1966; London, Eyre Methuen, 1977.

Now Wait for Last Year. Garden City, New York, Doubleday, 1966; London, Panther, 1975.

The Unteleported Man. New York, Ace, 1966; London, Eyre Methuen, 1976; revised edition edited by John Sladek, New York, Berkley, 1983; as *Lies, Inc.,* London, Gollancz, 1984.

Counter-Clock World. New York, Berkley, 1967; London, Sphere, 1968.

The Zap Gun: Being That Most Excellent Account of Travails and Contayning Many Pretie Hystories by Him Set Foorth in Comely Colours and Most Delightfuliy Discoursed Upon as Beautified and Well Furnished Divers Good and Commendable in the Gesight of Men of That Most Lamentable Wepens Fasoun Deisgners Lars Powderdry and What Nearly Became of Him Due to Certain Most Dreadful Forces. New York, Pyramid, 1967; London, Panther, 1975.

The Ganymede Takeover, with Ray Nelson. New York, Ace, 1967; London, Arrow, 1971.

Do Androids Dream of Electric Sheep? Garden City, New York, Doubleday, 1968; London, Rapp and Whiting, 1969; as *Bladerunner: Do Androids Dream of Electric Sheep?,* New York, Ballantine, 1982.

Ubik. Garden City, New York, Doubleday, 1969; London, Rapp and Whiting, 1970.

Galactic Pot-Healer. New York, Berkley, 1969; London, Gollancz, 1971.

A Maze of Death. Garden City, New York, Doubleday, 1970; London, Gollancz, 1972.

Our Friends from Frolix 8. New York, Ace, 1970; London, Panther, 1976.

A Philip K. Dick Omnibus (includes *The Crack in Space, The Unteleported Man,* and *Dr. Futurity*). London, Sidgwick and Jackson, 1970.

We Can Build You. New York, DAW, 1972; London, Fontana, 1977.

Flow My Tears, The Policeman Said. Garden City, New York, Doubleday, and London, Gollancz, 1974.

Deus Irae, with Roger Zelazny. Garden City, New York, Doubleday, 1976; London, Gollancz, 1977.

A Scanner Darkly. Garden City, New York, Doubleday, and London, Gollancz, 1977.

Radio Free Albemuth (VALIS). New York, Arbor House, 1985; London, Grafton 1987.

Nick and the Glimmung (for children). London, Gollancz, 1988.

The VALIS Trilogy. New York, Quality Paperback Book Club, 1989.
VALIS. New York, Bantam, and London, Corgi, 1981.
   The Divine Invasion. New York, Timescape, 1981; London, Corgi, 1982.
   The Transmigration of Timothy Archer. New York, Timescape, and London, Gollancz, 1982.

The Little Black Box. London, Gollancz, 1990.

Short Stories

A Handful of Darkness. London, Rich and Cowan, 1955; Boston, Gregg Press, 1978.

The Variable Man and Other Stories. New York, Ace, 1957; London, Sphere, 1969.

The Preserving Machine and Other Stories. New York, Ace, 1969; abridged edition, London, Gollancz, 1971.

The Book of Philip K. Dick. New York, DAW, 1973; as *The Turning Wheel and Other Stories,* London, Coronet, 1977.

The Best of Philip K. Dick, edited by John Brunner. New York, Ballantine, 1977.

The Golden Man, edited by Mark Hurst. New York, Berkley, 1980; London, Eyre Methuen, 1981.

Robots, Androids, and Mechanical Oddities: The Science Fiction of Philip K. Dick, edited by Patricia S. Warrick and Martin H. Greenberg. Carbondale, Southern Illinois University Press, 1984.

I Hope I Shall Soon Arrive, edited by Mark Hurst and Paul Williams. Garden City, New York, Doubleday, 1985; London, Grafton, 1988.

The Collected Stories of Philip K. Dick. Los Angeles, Underwood Miller, 5 vols., 1987; London, Gollancz, 1988-90.

We Can Remember It for You Wholesale. Berkeley, California, Dark Carnival, 1990.

OTHER PUBLICATIONS

Novels

Confessions of a Crap Artist. New York, Entwhistle, 1975; London, Magnum, 1979.

The Man Whose Teeth Were All Exactly Alike. Willimantic, Connecticut, Ziesing, 1984; London, Paladin, 1986.

In Milton Lumky Territory. Hastings-on-Hudson, New York, Dragon Press, and London, Gollancz, 1985.

Puttering about in a Small Land. Chicago, Academy Chicago, 1985; London, Palladin, 1987.

Humpty Dumpty in Oakland. London, Gollancz, 1986.

Mary and the Giant. New York, Arbor House, 1987; London, Gollancz, 1988.

The Broken Bubble. New York, Arbor House, 1988; London, Gollancz, 1989.

Gather Yourselves Together. Herndon, Virginia, WCS Books, 1994.

Play

Ubik: The Screenplay. Minneapolis, Minnesota, Corroboree Press, 1985.

Screenplay: *Ubik,* 1985.

Other

Philip K. Dick: In His Own Words (interviews), edited by Gregg Rickman. Long Beach, California, Fragments West/Valentine Press, 1984; second edition, 1988.

Philip K. Dick: The Last Testament, with Gregg Rickman. Long Beach, California, Fragments West-Valentine Press, 1985.

Only Apparently Real: The World of Philip K. Dick, with Paul Williams, New York, Arbor House, 1986.

The Dark-Haired Girl. Willimantic, Connecticut, M.V. Ziesing, 1988.

Selected Letters of Philip K. Dick, edited by Don Herron. Lancaster, Pennsylvania, Underwood Miller, 1991.

In Pursuit of VALIS: Selections from the Exegesis, edited by Larry Sutin. Novato, California, Underwood Miller, 1991.

The Shifting Realities of Philip K. Dick: Selected Literary and Philosophical Writings, edited by Larry Sutin. New York, Pantheon, 1995.

*

Bibliography: *PKD: A Philip K. Dick Bibliography* by Daniel J.H. Levack, Columbia, Pennsylvania, Underwood Miller, 1981.

Manuscript Collection: California State University, Fullerton.

Critical Studies: *Philip K. Dick and the Umbrella of Light* by Angus Taylor, Baltimore, T-K Graphics, 1975; *Philip K. Dick: Electric Shepherd* (includes bibliography) edited by Bruce Gillespie, Melbourne, Norstrilia Press, 1975; "Philip K. Dick Issue" of *Science-Fiction Studies* (Terre Haute, Indiana), March 1975 (includes bibliography); *Philip K. Dick* by Hazel Pierce, Mercer Island, Washington, Starmont House, 1982; *Philip K. Dick* edited by Martin H. Greenberg and Joseph D. Olander, New York, Taplinger, 1983; *The Novels of Philip K. Dick* by Kim Stanley Robinson, Ann Arbor, Michigan, UMI Research Press, 1984; *Philip K. Dick: The Dream Connection* by D. Scott Apel, San Jose, California, Permanent Press, 1987; *Mind in Motion: The Fiction of Philip K. Dick* by Patricia S. Warrick, Carbondale, Southern Illinois University Press, 1987; *Philip K. Dick* by Douglas A. Mackey, Boston, Twayne, 1988; *Divine Invasions: A Life of Philip K. Dick* by Lawrence Sutin, New York, Harmony, 1989; *To the High Castle: Philip K. Dick, a Life* by Gregg Rickman, Long Beach, California, Fragments West-Valentine Press, 1989.

Philip K. Dick commented:

(1976) Using science fiction as a framework, I attempt to cut through the layers of quasi-reality, finding in the process that the elliptical viewpoints of psychosis act as starting points. Although I have been able to determine and then represent in my fiction many private universes, differing from one personality type to the next, I am in no sense trying to state what in the final analysis is "real." It is, rather, the search which interests me; perhaps the outcome is not the same for all of us. In my early novels and stories I often used sociological and political themes; later I branched into drug trips and also theological trips, sometimes combining both (which angered many readers, both those who used drugs as well as those who used God). However, out of this I have recently come to sense a new level of feeling rather than intuition or reasoning. It is perhaps possible that when all the layers of the mind are stripped away the reality of the heart remains, or anyhow some organ more vital than the brain. In my work-in-progress I seek to contact some vein of cognition, some perceptual entity outside myself, outside our own race . . . where this entity would be, if anywhere at all, I can't say. Still, I think it exists, and, having helped me in my work throughout my career, perhaps it will guide me toward itself during the remaining part of my professional and creative life.

*　　*　　*

Due to both the merits of his fiction and the pull of circumstance, Philip K. Dick seems likely to achieve literary fame outside the science fiction community. Born in 1928, Dick was a prolific writer of short stories and novels. While his writing shows a great range of quality, his best work combines bold scientific, social, and metaphysical speculation with profound human concern for his characters and their fates. Extremely quirky but generous in friendship, Dick influenced many authors, including his friends Tim Powers and K.W. Jeter.

Dick's science fiction exemplifies the genre in both its excellences and its limitations. Stimulating, thought-provoking, and sometimes simply provoking, Dick's fiction uses extrapolation to explore several consistent themes: He is concerned with what is truly human and loving in a world where hatred and the values of the machine seem to predominate. He believes in the value of the unexceptional person in and to society. His novels often display a split between deep reality and deceiving appearances, and he tries to balance objective and subjective—or shared and individual—experience.

The intellectual play in Dick's fiction, with language and with ideas, is often gratifying and sometimes confusing. The accoutrements of his fiction are both various and consistent: creatures such as the Glimmung and the wub, inventions including the flapple and the gum/drug Can-D, the sentient factories known as Printers and a host of often annoyingly independent autonomic machines. Dick often reused ideas, from short stories to novels and even from one novel to another.

Dick's style can be clumsy or pedestrian; at his best, however, he mixes flat honesty with keen insight, and pathos with humor, characteristically and appealingly. His plotting, too, can be uneven, his novels often marred by a bad sense of pacing or continuing past their apparent conclusions. His fiction generally succeeds despite these faults, partly because of the wealth of creative imagination involved and the deep sympathy that the author obviously feels for the characters and the issues they must confront.

While most critics agree that Philip K. Dick has written some of the best SF novels and some of the worst, few agree on which is which. Even Dick often changed his mind, and in the mid-1960s he wrote, "I have written and sold 23 novels, and all are terrible except one. But I'm not sure which one."

The novels selected for praise generally include *The Man in the High Castle,* an alternate-world tale in which the Axis won World War II; *Ubik,* in which the characters are shunted into another reality where their dead boss seems to reappear mysteriously; and *The Three Stigmata of Palmer Eldritch,* in which the protagonists must confront an apparent Messiah from the stars, while trapped in a drug-soaked world in which reality and hallucination puzzlingly mingle. Often included with his best are *Martian Time-Slip,* which skillfully combines Fifties social satire and metaphysical uncertainty, and *Flow My Tears, the Policeman Said,* in which the protagonist feels as if he been erased from the world, from its records and from the minds of those who knew him.

There is a longer list of controversial works, praised by some and dismissed by others. *Counter-Clock World* presents a world in which time is reversed, a theme later used more popularly, and perhaps more successfully, by Martin Amis in *Time's Arrow.* In *Time Out of Joint,* an apparently mimetic Fifties background with some alarming inconsistencies turns out to be something far stranger. *Clans of the Alphane Moon* suggests that a world inhabited entirely by psychiatric patients might have its advantages, particularly in interplanetary warfare. In *Do Androids Dream of Electric Sheep?* Dick presents his most thorough examination of his theme of the android versus the human. *Dr. Bloodmoney; or, How We Got Along after the Bomb, The Penultimate Truth, Galactic Pot-Healer, The Cosmic Puppets, Eye in the Sky,* and *A Scanner Darkly* also have both their admirers and their detractors.

In many of Dick's novels, an outside force—troubling or even malevolent—affects "reality" as it is experienced; often, the protagonist is a common man (though typically a white-collar worker rather than a laborer) who must both understand the situation and help rectify it. The outside force may be the hallucinogenic gum Chew-Z, controlled by an ambiguous, possibly godlike figure, in *The Three Stigmata of Palmer Eldritch;* the Zoroastrian gods of *The Cosmic Puppets;* the projective insanity of Manfred, the autistic child in *Martian Time-Slip;* the half-life dreams of *Ubik.* Often in a Dick novel one is not sure what is real and what is imagined: is Bruno Bluthgeld, of *Dr. Bloodmoney,* a powerful psychic (as is Hoppy Harrington in the same book) or a paranoid schizophrenic?

Protagonists such as Joe Fernwright (*Galactic Pot-Healer*), Mr. Tagomi (*The Man in the High Castle*), Joe Chip (*Ubik*), and Ted Barton (*The Cosmic Puppets*) struggle to beat these influences, or simply to live humanely in a world gone wrong—and often the former is a more extreme version of the latter. The heroism in Dick's novels always consists of small victories, though sometimes with major consequences; his protagonists try to leave the world better than they found it and sometimes succeed. In many novels, multiple protagonists present different problems and values. In *Dr. Bloodmoney,* for instance, the common-man heroes include astronaut and disc-jockey Walt Dangerfield, post-holocaust entrepreneur Andrew Gill, salesman Stuart McConchie (a black character at a time when such rarely appeared in science fiction), and McConchie's bosses Mr. and Mrs. Hardy. In *Flow My Tears, the Policeman Said,* Jason Taverner is a more usual Dick protagonist, but policeman Felix Buckman achieves personal renewal through compassion.

Some readers fault Dick for his female characters. Doubtless, Dick—married five times—had problems with women, as is shown in *The Dark-Haired Girl,* a posthumous collection of his nonfiction writings on the subject. This is also reflected in his fiction. With some exceptions, his females are seductive but mean, an attractive yet destructive other half: the many examples include Alys

Buckman in *Flow my Tears, the Policeman Said,* Donna Hawthorne in *A Scanner Darkly,* and Fay Hume in *Confessions of a Crap Artist.* In his later works, Dick presented female saviors in *Valis* and *The Divine Invasion;* perhaps this helped prepare him for his best female character, Angel Archer in *The Transmigration of Timothy Archer.*

In the last years of his life, Dick produced four semi-autobiographical novels, tending towards the mainstream: *Valis* (and its alternate version, *Radio Free Albemuth,* which was found among his papers and published after his death), *The Divine Invasion,* and *The Transmigration of Timothy Archer.* The first three of these combine science fiction with miraculous events and divine entities; the fourth is an apparently mimetic novel with one possibly supernatural element.

All of these were inspired by odd experiences that Dick had in 1974; the novels grapple with psychological and spiritual implications of those events. Though some readers saw this as an unfortunate change in Dick's life and work, it was obviously vital to him, and it brought him new ways to explore many of his familiar concerns. In these last novels and in other writing—including a huge manuscript that he called his "Exegesis"—Dick developed a romantic neo-Gnosticism that combines many of his themes, such as the individual vs. blind authority, the difficulty of being truly human, and the decay inherent in a material world. In letters from 1974 on, Dick reinterpreted his earlier work in line with the more coherent system he was developing; he was able to do this, however, because of the consistent thematic interest throughout his life.

Publication of new works by Dick continued after his death in 1982. His short fiction, including works not published during his lifetime, was brought together by literary executor Paul Williams and published in a five-volume set. Along with *Radio Free Albemuth,* posthumously published longer works of science fiction include a children's novel (*Nick and the Glimmung*) and a screenplay version of his novel *Ubik.* Much of his nonfiction, including letters and essays and some of the more accessible portions of the "Exegesis," has been published, culminating with the appearance in 1995 of *The Shifting Realities of Philip K. Dick,* a collection of his essays, which was edited by one of his biographers, Lawrence Sutin, and published as a prestigious hardcover by Random House.

His dream of seeing print as a writer of mimetic fiction has been posthumously realized. While his only non-SF work to appear during his lifetime was the amusing *Confessions of a Crap Artist,* his early efforts at mainstream fiction were also dug up after his death and published. Some, like *Mary and the Giant,* appeared from mainstream publishing houses, though most were brought out in limited press runs by specialized small presses. These, like Dick's science fiction, vary greatly in quality. At their best, they show his characteristic wit and compassion, often daring to explore then-unmentionable topics like interracial love and sex.

Though sometimes underappreciated, and often under remunerative, Dick's fiction never went entirely without recognition. In 1963 he won the World Science Fiction Society "Hugo" award for *The Man in the High Castle.* Dick's fiction has also received attention from scholars of science fiction—including Marxist critics, which sometimes disturbed Dick. After Dick's death, Paul Williams started the Philip K. Dick Society, publishing *The PKDS Newsletter* and organizing the growing attention. There are at least a dozen critical books devoted to his writing, and there have been two biographies: Lawrence Sutin's *Divine Invasions: A Life of Philip K. Dick* and a still-unfinished multivolume work by Gregg Rickman.

Dick also has inspired four films: *Bladerunner,* based loosely on *Do Androids Dream of Electric Sheep?; Total Recall,* based even more loosely on his short story "We Can Remember It for You Wholesale"; the French film *Confessions d'un Barjo,* a witty translation of *Confessions of a Crap Artist;* and Gary Walkow's little-known film *The Trouble with Dick,* based surrealistically on Dick's life. Other works have inspired music, including *Dr. Bloodmoney* ("Bluthgeld" on the album *Painting by Numbers* by Michael Bass) and *Valis* (a 1987 opera by Todd Machovia); a play based on *Flow My Tears, the Policeman Said* has been performed. In a process quite compatible with his own fiction, Dick has become a fictional character in works such as Michael Bishop's novel *The Secret Ascension* (also published as *Philip K. Dick Is Dead, Alas*) and an anthology of short stories, *Welcome to Reality: The Nightmares of Philip K. Dick* (ed. Uwe Anton).

Perhaps too much attention is now being paid to Dick's later works and to his unusual life. However, Dick's entire career is worthy of study, both in its own right and as an example of the best and worst aspects of science fiction. Especially, Dick helped pioneer the use of genre SF conventions to explore universal human issues and did so in a uniquely Phildickian way.

—Bernadette Lynn Bosky and Arthur D. Hlavaty

DICKINSON, Peter (Malcolm de Brissac)

Nationality: British. **Born:** Livingstone, Northern Rhodesia (now Zambia), 16 December 1927. **Education:** Eton College (King's Scholar), 1941-46; King's College, Cambridge (exhibitioner), B.A. 1951. **Military Service:** Served in the British Army, 1946-48. **Family:** Married Mary Rose Bernard in 1953 (died 1988); married Robin McKinley in 1992; two daughters and two sons. **Career:** Assistant editor and reviewer, *Punch,* London, 1952-69. Chairman of the Management Committee, Society of Authors, 1978-80. **Awards:** Crime Writers Association Gold Dagger, 1968, 1969; *Guardian* award, for children's book, 1977; *Boston Globe-Horn Book* award, for non-fiction, 1977; Whitbread award (children's book section), 1979, 1990; Library Association Carnegie Medal, for children's book, 1980, 1981. **Agent:** A.P. Watt Ltd., 20 John Street, London WC1N 2DR. **Address:** Bramdean Lodge, near Alvesford, Hampshire SO24 0JN, England.

SCIENCE FICTION PUBLICATIONS

Novels (series: The Changes; King Victor)

The Changes: A Trilogy (for children). London, Gollancz, 1975; New York, Dell, 1991; as *The Changes Trilogy,* London, Penguin, 1985.
    Heartsease. London, Gollancz, and Boston, Little Brown, 1969.
    The Weathermonger. London, Gollancz, 1968; Boston, Little Brown, 1969.
    The Devil's Children. London, Gollancz, and Boston, Little Brown, 1970.
Emma Tupper's Diary (for children). London, Gollancz, and Boston, Little Brown, 1971.
The Iron Lion (for children). Boston, Little Brown, 1972; London, Allen and Unwin, 1973.

The Green Gene. London, Hodder and Stoughton, and New York, Pantheon, 1973.

The Gift (for children). London, Gollancz, 1973; Boston, Little Brown, 1974.

King and Joker (King Victor). London, Hodder and Stoughton, and New York, Pantheon, 1976.

The Blue Hawk (for children). London, Gollancz, and Boston, Little Brown, 1976.

Annerton Pit (for children). London, Gollancz, and Boston, Little Brown, 1977.

Tulku (for children). London, Gollancz, and New York, Dutton, 1979.

Healer (for children). London, Gollancz, 1983; New York, Delacorte, 1985.

Giant Cold (for children). London, Gollancz, and New York, Dutton, 1984.

A Box of Nothing (for children). London, Gollancz, 1985; New York, Delacorte, 1987.

Merlin Dreams (for children). London, Gollancz, and New York, Delacorte, 1988.

Eva (for children). London, Gollancz, 1988; New York, Delacorte, 1989.

Skeleton-in-Waiting (King Victor). London, Bodley Head, 1989; New York, Pantheon, 1990.

OTHER PUBLICATIONS

Novels

Skin Deep. London, Hodder and Stoughton, 1968; as *The Glass-Sided Ants' Nest*, New York, Harper, 1968.

A Pride of Heroes. London, Hodder and Stoughton, 1969; as *The Old English Peep Show*, New York, Harper, 1969.

The Seals. London, Hodder and Stoughton, 1970; as *The Sinful Stones*, New York, Harper, 1970.

Sleep and His Brother. London, Hodder and Stoughton, and New York, Harper, 1971.

The Lizard in the Cup. London, Hodder and Stoughton, and New York, Harper, 1972.

The Poison Oracle. London, Hodder and Stoughton, and New York, Pantheon, 1974.

The Lively Dead. London, Hodder and Stoughton, and New York, Pantheon, 1975.

Walking Dead. London, Hodder and Stoughton, 1977; New York, Pantheon, 1978.

The Flight of Dragons. London, Pierrot, and New York, Harper, 1979.

One Foot in the Grave. London, Hodder and Stoughton, 1979; New York, Pantheon, 1980.

A Summer in the Twenties. London, Hodder and Stoughton, and New York, Pantheon, 1981.

The Last House-Party. London, Bodley Head, and New York, Pantheon, 1982.

Hindsight. London, Bodley Head, and New York, Pantheon, 1983.

Death of a Unicorn. London, Bodley Head, and New York, Pantheon, 1984.

Tefuga. London, Bodley Head, and New York, Pantheon, 1986.

Mole Hole. London, Blackie, and New York, Bedrick, 1987.

Perfect Gallows. London, Bodley Head, and New York, Pantheon, 1988.

AK (for children). London, Gollancz, 1990; New York, Delacrote, 1992.

Play Dead. London, Bodley Head, 1991; New York, Mysterious Press, 1992.

A Bone from a Dry Sea (for children). London, Gollancz, 1992; New York, Delacorte, 1994.

Time and the Clockmice, Etcetera (for children). London, Doubleday, 1993; New York, Delacorte, 1994.

Shadow of a Hero (for children). London, Gollancz, and New York, Delacorte, 1994.

The Yellow Room Conspiracy. London, Little, Brown, and New York, Mysterious Press, 1994.

Plays (for children)

Television Series: *Mandog*, 1972.

Other

The Dancing Bear (for children). London, Gollancz, 1972; Boston, Little Brown, 1973.

Chance, Luck, and Destiny (miscellany). London, Gollancz, 1975; Boston, Little Brown, 1976.

Hepzibah (for children). Twickenham, Middlesex, Eel Pie, 1978; Boston, Godine, 1980.

City of Gold and Other Stories from the Old Testament. London, Gollancz, and New York, Pantheon, 1980.

The Seventh Raven. London, Gollancz, and New York, Dutton, 1981.

Editor, *Presto! Humorous Bits and Pieces*. London, Hutchinson, 1975.

Editor, *Hundreds and Hundreds*. London, Penguin, 1984.

*

Peter Dickinson comments:

I regard all my fiction as SF (that's to say I write it as if it were), though usually the S bulks much smaller than the F. Classic detective stories (which I try to write) usually have to be restricted to a closed world, which I tend to invent as if it were an alien planet. Indeed, inventing even a normal human character seems to me to demand an effort of the same kind as inventing an alien species; this may account for the fact that my characters have a tendency towards the grotesque. The children's books are mostly straightforward soft SF; *The Green Gene* began as a satire about apartheid, or rather about outsiders' attitudes to it, but acquired directions and energies of its own. My attitude to SF is much more influenced by the pulp I read in the 1940's than by anything more recent, or in book form.

*   *   *

Peter Dickinson has made a substantial name for himself in the mystery genre with a series of bizarre murder mysteries. Frequently these novels play with devices better known in the field of science fiction, although none is really written as an example of the genre. There are hints of telepathy in *Walking Dead,* for example. Communication with a very bright ape is the key to unravelling the mystery in *The Poison Oracle,* and there is an alternate British royalty in *King and Joker.*

Dickinson has written several fantasy novels, perhaps the most interesting of which is a trilogy set in England when all technology stops working, magic returns to the land, the rest of the world continues to advance technologically, but a pastoral calm settles over most of the British Isles. The first in the series, *The Weathermonger,* follows a young man and his sister as they flee to France, only to return in search of the source of the mysterious change. Ultimately they confront an awakened Merlin of Camelot, once more active in the affairs of men.

The two follow-up volumes were related by setting only; there are no common characters and even Merlin appears to have disappeared. *Heartsease* is concerned with a spy from the United States who is unmasked by the elders of a village and nearly killed because of suspicion of witchcraft. He is rescued by sympathetic children, and a well-told series of adventures follow. Possibly the best in the series is *The Devil's Children.* Although the British have been mentally altered by the change so that they blindly strike out and destroy anything technological, one group in England seems to be immune, the resident population of Sikhs. The protagonist is a young girl separated from her parents who falls in with a wandering band of Sikhs, is befriended by them, and becomes their agent in dealings with the rest of the British. Unable to return to their homeland, they finally decide to establish a settlement in a remote area and trade with others using her as their agent.

Tulku is an oriental adventure fantasy. A boy and his companions wander around Tibet after bandits raid the mission where he lives. Ultimately he turns out to be a pivotal piece in a game of oriental legend. *Tulku* is written for younger readers, but this is not true of *The Blue Hawk.* A young trainee for the priesthood violates ritual by befriending a sacred blue hawk, thereby causing the death of the reigning king, endangering his own life, and throwing the entire established order into disarray. He is caught up in the ensuing power struggle between clerical and lay institutions, as each seeks to make him the instrument of the other's downfall. *The Blue Hawk* may be the best single work Dickinson has written.

The only genuine adult science fiction novel Dickinson has written is *The Green Gene.* In an alternate version of our own world, England is ruled by a rigid authoritarian government. For some reason, an increasing number of births in the island are of green children, and all green humans are legally delcared to be Celts, while whites and blacks are legally Saxons. An Indian medical specialist is hired by the Race Relations Board to develop a method of reliably predicting the occurrence of the green mutation. The Board ostensibly exists to promote racial harmony, but is in fact the chief instrument for the suppression of the green minority. The protagonist is politically as well as socially naive, and is soon involved unwittingly in politics, sexual liaisons, murder, and intrigue. He is kidnapped, enlisted in a plot against the government, and only arranges his own freedom by eventually smartening up and doublecrossing everyone. It is a refreshing and disturbing satire.

Eva, a science fiction novel aimed at younger readers, features a young girl whose body is so damaged in an accident that doctors do not believe they can save it. They can, however, save her personality, transferring it into the body of a chimpanzee. The result is a fascinating look at humanity from a bizarre new perspective, a novel designed to appeal to adult sensibilities as well as teenaged readers, and amply satisfying to make readers wish Dickinson were more active in the field.

—Don D'Ammassa

DICKSON, Gordon R(upert)

Nationality: American. **Born:** Edmonton, Alberta, Canada 1 November 1923; emigrated to the United States at age 13. **Education:** University of Minnesota, Minneapolis, B.A. 1948, and graduate study, 1948-50. **Military Service:** Served in the United States Army, 1943-46. **Career:** Since 1950, freelance writer. **Awards:** Hugo award, 1965, 1981 (twice); Nebula award, 1966; Skylark award, 1975; Derleth award, 1977; Jupiter award, 1977. President, Science Fiction Writers of America, 1969-71. **Agent:** Kirby McCauley, 155 East 77th Street, New York, New York 10021, U.S.A.

Science Fiction Publications

Novels (series: Childe Cycle; Combat Command; Dilbia; Dragon; Robby Hoenig; Hoka; Thieves' World)

Alien from Arcturus. New York, Ace, 1956; expanded edition, as *Arcturus Landing,* 1978.

Mankind on the Run. New York, Ace, 1956; as *On the Run,* 1979.

The Genetic General. New York, Ace, 1960; London, Digit, 1961; expanded edition as *Dorsai!,* New York, DAW, and London, Sphere, 1976.

Time to Teleport. New York, Ace, 1960.

Secret under the Sea (for children; Hoenig). New York, Holt Rinehart, 1960; London, Hutchinson, 1962.

Naked to the Stars. New York, Pyramid, 1961; London, Sphere, 1978.

Delusion World. New York, Ace, 1961.

Spacial Delivery (Dilbia). New York, Ace, 1961.

Necromancer (Childe). Garden City, New York, Doubleday, 1962; London, Mayflower, 1963; as *No Room for Man,* New York, Macfadden, 1963.

Secret under Antarctica (for children; Hoenig). New York, Holt Rinehart, 1963.

Secret under the Caribbean (for children; Hoenig). New York, Holt Rinehart, 1964.

Space Winners (for children). New York, Holt Rinehart, 1965; London, Faber, 1967.

The Alien Way. New York, Bantam, 1965; London, Corgi, 1973.

Mission to Universe. New York, Berkley, 1965; revised edition, New York, Ballantine, 1977; expanded edition, London, Sphere, 1978.

The Space Swimmers. New York, Berkley, 1967; London, Sidgwick and Jackson, 1968.

Planet Run, with Keith Laumer. Garden City, New York, Doubleday, 1967; London, Hale, 1977; expanded edition, Tor, 1982.

Soldier, Ask Not (Childe). New York, Dell, 1967; London, Sphere, 1975.

None But Man. Garden City, New York, Doubleday, 1969; London, Macdonald, 1970.

Wolfling. New York, Dell, 1969.

Spacepaw (Dilbia; for children). New York, Putnam, 1969.

Hour of the Horde. New York, Putnam, 1970.

The Tactics of Mistake (Childe). Garden City, New York, Doubleday, 1971; London, Sphere, 1975.

Sleepwalker's World. Philadelphia, Lippincott, 1971; London, Hale, 1973.

The Outposter. Philadelphia, Lippincott, 1972; London, Hale, 1973.

The Pritcher Mass. Garden City, New York, Doubleday, 1972.

Alien Art. New York, Dutton, 1973; London, Hale, 1974.

The R-Master. Philadelphia, Lippincott, 1973; London, Hale, 1975; as *The Last Master,* New York, Tor, 1984.

Gremlins, Go Home! (for children), with Ben Bova. New York, St. Martin's Press, 1974.

Star Prince Charlie (Hoka; for children), with Poul Anderson. New York, Putnam, 1975.

Three to Dorsai! (omnibus; includes *Necromancer, Tactics of Mistake,* and *Dorsai!*). Garden City, New York, Doubleday, 1975.

The Dragon and the George. Garden City, New York, Doubleday, 1976; London, Grafton, 1992.

The Lifeship, with Harry Harrison. New York, Harper, 1976; as *Lifeboat,* London, Dobson, 1978.

Time Storm. New York, St. Martin's Press, 1977; London, Sphere, 1978; as *Timestorm,* New York, Baen, 1992.

The Far Call. New York, Dial Press, and London, Sidgwick and Jackson, 1978.

Home from the Shore. New York, Sunridge Press, 1978.

Pro. New York, Ace, 1978.

Masters of Everon. New York, Ace, 1980.

Alien Art; Arcturus Landing (omnibus). New York, Ace, 1981.

Time to Teleport; Delusion World (omnibus). New York, Ace, 1981.

Jamie the Red, with Roland Green (Thieves' World). New York, Ace, 1984.

The Final Encyclopedia (Childe). New York, Tor, 1984; London, Sphere, 1985.

Secrets of the Deep (includes *Secret under the Sea, Secret under Antarctica,* and *Secret under the Caribbean*). New York, Critic's Choice Paperbacks, 1985.

The Forever Man. New York, Ace, 1986; London, Sphere, 1987.

Way of the Pilgrim. New York, Ace, 1987; London, Sphere, 1988.

The Chantry Guild (Childe). New York, Ace, 1988; London, Sphere, 1989.

The Earth Lords. New York, Ace, and London, Sphere, 1989.

Dorsai's Command, with Troy Denning and Cory Glaberson (Combat Command). New York, Ace, 1989.

The Dragon Knight. New York, Tor, 1990; London, Grafton, 1992.

Wolf and Iron. Norwalk, Connecticut, Easton Press, 1990; London, Orbit, 1991.

Naked to the Stars; The Alien Way (omnibus). New York, Tor, 1991.

Young Bleys (Childe). New York, Tor, 1991; London, Orbit, 1993.

The Dragon on the Border. New York, Ace, 1992; London, Grafton, 1993.

The Dragon at War (Dragon). New York, Ace, 1992; London, HarperCollins, 1993.

The Dragon, the Earl, and The Troll (Dragon). New York, Ace, 1994.

Other. New York, Tor, 1994.

The Magnificent Wilf. Riverdale, New York, Baen, 1995.

Short Stories

Earthman's Burden, with Poul Anderson (Hoka). New York, Gnome Press, 1957.

Danger—Human. Garden City, New York, Doubleday, 1970; as *The Book of Gordon Dickson,* New York, DAW, 1973.

Mutants: A Science Fiction Adventure. New York, Macmillan, 1970.

The Star Road. Garden City, New York, Doubleday, 1973; London, Hale, 1975.

Ancient, My Enemy. Garden City, New York, Doubleday, 1974; London, Sphere, 1978.

Gordon R. Dickson's SF Best, edited by James R. Frenkel. New York, Dell, 1978; reprinted as *In the Bone: The Best Science Fiction of Gordon R. Dickson,* New York, Ace, 1987.

The Spirit of Dorsai. New York, Ace, 1979; London, Sphere, 1989.

Lost Dorsai. New York, Ace, 1980; revised edition, London, Sphere, 1988; revised as *Lost Dorsai: The New Dorsai Companion,* New York, Tor, 1993.

In Iron Years. Garden City, New York, Doubleday, 1980.

Love Not Human. New York, Ace, 1981.

The Man from Earth. New York, Tor, 1983.

Hoka!, with Poul Anderson. New York, Simon and Schuster, 1983.

Survival! New York, Baen, 1984.

Dickson! Boston, NESFA Press, 1984; as *Steel Brother.* New York, Tor, 1985.

Beyond the Dar al-Harb. New York, Tor, 1985.

Forward!, edited by Sandra Miesel. New York, Baen, 1985.

Invaders!, edited by Sandra Miesel. New York, Baen, 1985.

The Dorsai Companion. New York, Ace, 1986.

The Last Dream. New York, Baen, 1986.

The Man the Worlds Rejected. New York, Tor, 1986.

Mindspan, edited by Sandra Miesel. New York, Baen, 1986.

Stranger. New York, Tor, 1987.

Beginnings. New York, Baen, 1988.

The Guided Tour. New York, Tor, 1988.

Ends. New York, Baen, 1988.

OTHER PUBLICATIONS

Other

Editor, *Rod Serling's Triple W: Witches, Warlocks and Werewolves.* New York, Bantam, 1963.

Editor, *Rod Serling's Devils and Demons.* New York, Bantam, 1967.

Editor, *Combat SF.* Garden City, New York, Doubleday, 1975.

Editor, *Nebula Winners 12.* New York, Harper, 1978.

Editor, *The Harriers.* New York, Baen, 1991.

Editor, with Martin Harry Greenberg and Charles G. Waugh, *Robot Warriors.* New York, Ace, 1991.

Editor, with Martin Harry Greenberg and Charles G. Waugh, *Bootcamp 3000.* New York, Ace, 1992.

Editor, with Martin Harry Greenberg and Charles G. Waugh, *Space Dogfights.* New York, Ace, 1992.

Editor, *Harriers #2: Blood and Honor.* Riverdale, New York, Baen, 1993.

*

Bibliography: *Gordon R. Dickson: A Primary and Secondary Bibliography* by Raymond H. Thompson, Boston, Hall, 1983.

*   *   *

"We're improvable, tremendously improvable," says Gordon R. Dickson, "and by our own efforts." Dickson views the human race as a single organism with a unique inner dynamic driving its psychic—but not necessarily its physical—evolution. He delights in showing consciousness emerging, developing, and perfecting itself in pursuit of godlike powers: "Man's future is upward and outward." He presents an open-ended universe filled with limitless possibilities ready to be seized by whatever beings are bold enough.

Dickson, a Pelagian humanist, maintains that intelligent life-forms can direct their own destiny. Ultimately, this capacity for continuous growth will surpass the static excellence of divinity, even of a Deity mighty enough to make the sun stand still ("Things Which Are Caesar's," 1972). Nature is the milieu in which the drama unfolds, not a participant in the action. Dickson is no romantic pantheist like Poul Anderson, a writer with whom he is often incorrectly linked because they are friends who have collaborated on stories.

Taken together, Dickson's works are simply variant readings of a single epic adventure—life's quest for transcendence. He proclaims the victories of tenacious, morally responsible people who can remake heaven and earth by sheer force of will. Right makes might. Goodness must prevail. Mind conquers matter. The author's idealism and boundless confidence are refreshing qualities in this pessimistic era.

Dickson's favorite literary structure is the initiatory scenario. His protagonists learn, not simply for themselves, but on behalf of their group, culture, or species. For example, the hero of *The Pritcher Mass* spearheads the collective aspirations of all living things on Earth. The typical Dickson plot fits mythologist Joseph Campbell's monomyth: a young, obscure, or otherwise lightly regarded individual discovers and masters his own unique abilities. Despite misunderstanding from friends and opposition from foes, he confounds conventional wisdom (often in some juridical confrontation) and thereby averts general disaster.

Obviously such stories will attract readers who are young or dissatisfied. Initiation is the classic plot for juvenile fiction and Dickson uses it well. For instance, in *Alien Art* and *The Masters of Everon* teenagers with friends who are wrongly taken for mere animals save their planets from ruthless developers. In *Space Winners* a cute, furry alien guides three youths toward maturity.

And by having the hero's initiation aided by characters who remain phenomenally keen-witted and fit into extreme old age, Dickson appeals to another segment of the audience. His works—especially those in the Childe Cycle—are filled with seniors training far younger juniors, sometimes being supplanted by them and surrendering prized maidens to the youngsters. One extreme case is *Time Storm* where the elder inspiring the hero is a primate called Old Man.

Initiation scenarios even shape Dickson's lighter works, notably the Dragon Knight series in which a couple of American medievalists try to adjust to life in a fairytale medieval universe where magic works. The hero, who can transform himself into a dragon at will, is mastering knighthood and magic as the rather loosely written developmental series continues.

Dickson's comedies center on rational beings trying to function in preposterously irrational situations. Besides his humorous collection *Mindspan,* these include the Hoka series written with Poul Anderson (a diplomat coping with compulsively imitative aliens who look like teddy bears), the Dilbian stories (humans trying to win the respect of huge, ursine aliens with the manners of rustics), and *The Magnificent Wilf* (an ordinary American couple whisked off to galactic adventures).

However, Dickson most often stages his initiations as action-adventure tales. Some have objected to the frequency of his military or quasi-military setting, but these critics are reading a political agenda into the work that is not there. Dickson is not Robert A. Heinlein and battlefield scenes occupy surprisingly few pages in his stories with martial heroes. Dickson's backgrounds are dictated in part by convenience because soldiers—like explorers—are obvious genre subjects for life-and-death dramas of fortitude, daring, and loyalty.

But Dickson's unusual touch is to make his action heroes cerebral and empathic, weaving in his own talents for poetry, music, and art. Note that "Call Him Lord" (1966) and "Jean Dupres" (1970) are about courage, not killing. They are mirror-image studies in manhood. A cowardly prince is executed to prevent an evil reign; a colonial boy's death in battle brings peace within his people's grasp. These two stories, Nebula winner and Hugo nominee respectively, demonstrate the technical mastery and absolute economy of Dickson's best work.

Although Dickson's literary elegance and limpidity are better displayed at shorter lengths, he is a deliberate craftsman. (He was formally trained as a writer by Robert Penn Warren, among others, and has made writing his sole profession.) Dickson has even developed his own approach to science fiction, the "consciously thematic novel." This is his way of making a philosophical statement without resorting to the crudities of propaganda. As Dickson explains: "The aim is to make the theme such an integral part of the novel that it can be effective upon the reader without ever having to be stated explicitly. . . ."

Dickson's philosophical purpose imparts an unusually relentless quality to his best prose. Every element is concentrated along the cutting edge of the blade. Nothing in his stories except the message exists for its own sake. Although he is an enthusiastic researcher who likes to experience as well as study his backgrounds, he never inserts merely decorative color or extraneous details. Take, for example, the degree of auctorial control imposed on copious and complex raw materials in *The Far Call,* the finest realistic novel about the space program yet written.

Dickson welds his stories together with symbols. These are typically grouped in pairs and triads that seek some ultimate unity—salvation is integration. Mythological dualities exist worldwide, but Dickson's trinities are best interpreted according to the structuralist theories of Indo-European mythologist Georges Dumézil. Although Dickson had never heard of Dumézil when he developed his distinctive fictional devices, his societies and characters do fit the Dumézilian categories or "functions" of Sovereignty, Force, and Nourishment. The most accessible examples of Dickson's symbolism occur in *Home From the Shore* and its sequel, *The Space Swimmers,* where the peoples of sea and land are the hostile dyad and the leading characters constitute a Dumézilian set. (See Sandra Miesel's afterword to *Home From the Shore.*)

The most complex examples of Dickson's symbolism appear in his Childe Cycle, his principal showcase for ideas and artistry. For the past 35 years, Dickson has been constructing an epic chronicle of human evolution which—when complete—is to incorporate historical, contemporary, and science fictional segments running from the 14th to the 24th centuries. Only SF components have appeared so far: *Dorsai!, Necromancer, Soldier, Ask Not, The Tactics of Mistake, The Final Encyclopedia, The Chantry Guild, Young Bleys,* and *Other.* The next installment is in progress, but the grand finale is not yet in sight.

In the Childe Cycle, the same hero passes through three incarnations, developing intuition as a Warrior, empathy as a Man Philosopher, and creativity as a Faith-Holder until he can assimilate his Twin enemy and achieve full ethical responsibility, integrating the unconscious/conservative and conscious/progressive halves of the racial psyche within himself. The so-called Splinter Cultures through which Dickson's protagonists move fit the Dumézilian categories. His Faith-holders (Friendlies), and Philosophers (Exotics) exercise the function of Sovereignty, his Warriors (Dorsai) are Force, and the other groups provide Nutrition. (See Miesel's afterwords to *The Final Encyclopedia, Lost Dorsai,* and the 1980 Ace edition of *Dorsai!* for extensive mythic and philosophical analysis.)

Aesthetic achievement varies in the Cycle. *Dorsai!* is notable for introducing a thoroughly sympathetic superman and for loading a military action yarn with mythic archetypes. The murkiness and subtlety of *Necromancer* make undue demands of the reader. *Soldier, Ask Not* uses its villain as the viewpoint character with wrenching emotional effect. *The Tactics of Mistake* is as stilted as a war game. *The Final Encyclopedia* is sensitive and elegiac, though slightly marred by lectures. *The Chantry Guild* is too thin and flat to make its account of the hero's enlightenment persuasive. *Young Bleys* and *Other,* which run parallel to *The Final Encyclopedia,* explain how the great Antagonist got that way, but thereby dim his dark romantic glow. However, the short "illuminations" that accompany the Cycle proper ("Warrior," 1966; "Brothers," 1973; "Amanda Morgan," 1979; and the Hugo-winning "Lost Dorsai," 1980) are uniformly excellent in both concept and execution.

Way of the Pilgrim, which incorporates the Hugo-winning "The Cloak and the Staff" (1980), plays counterpoint to Cycle themes. Its formidable alien conquerors, the physical pilgrims, are like Dark Brothers of the Dorsai for they are the tragically warped martial caste of an otherwise extinct race. The novel's reluctant—and *not* superhuman—hero plays the pilgrim role as a political symbol while actually living a spiritual pilgrimage. He moves from a self-centered to a self-sacrificing way of life and overcomes powerful, capricious parent figures to gain mature freedom.

Wolf and Iron, a meticulously researched dramatization of wolf behavior, represents a new departure for Dickson. It chronicles the rebuilding rather than the building of a personality and a destiny in a near-future America ruined by economic collapse. Through his comradeship with a timberwolf, the protagonist is the "iron" forged into a hero. But he is a most unusual Dickson hero because he develops no fabulous powers, changes his goals for love, and decides that sibling rivalry is not worth the bother.

Yet despite decades of steady accomplishment, Dickson is less admired than he ought to be. He has recurring plausibility problems because realism of presentation dominates realism of content. The work sometimes feels a bit too arbitrary—Dickson's creations are emphatically "made things." His reputation as a novelist has been tainted by early pulpish efforts (*Time to Teleport),* hasty potboilers (*The R-Master),* and disappointing expansions of older stories (*The Forever Man).* Antiwar backlash during the 1960s and 1970s distorted reactions to the Cycle. Stories of human indomitability ("Danger: Human," 1957) drew charges of Heinleinian human supremacy. But the latter criticism overlooks Dickson's sensitive portraits of aliens ("Black Charlie," 1954 and *The Alien Way)* as well as his pleas for interspecies empathy ("Dolphin's Way," 1964).

Complaints regarding Dickson's inept portrayals of women characters have more validity. Too many of these characters are nonentities who exist solely to misunderstand the heroes. Only masculine interactions seem important in many of his stories. However, starting in the 1970s, Dickson has systematically worked to correct this weakness by deepening characterizations and revising old formulas.

Thus, the triad in *Time Storm* comprises a male Philosopher, a female Warrior, and a Faith-holding animal. The complementary

twins in *The Far Call* are not two men but a pair of male-female couples. Early Cycle heroines merely misunderstand and suffer, but the heroic protagonist of "Amanda Morgan" is a splendidly rendered old woman and the story is built out of role reversals. In *The Final Encyclopedia,* a trio of gifted heroines (one from early major Splinter Culture) uphold the hero like the legs of a tripod. Even Bleys the Mephistophelean antagonist finds he needs a mate in *Other.*

Now and then Dickson's reach exceeds his grasp. But at its best, his writing strikes the mind like swift torrents of icy water or remembered strains of half-heard music.

—Sandra Miesel

Di FILIPPO, Paul G.

Nationality: American. **Born:** Woonsocket, Rhode Island, 29 October 1954. **Education:** Rhode Island College, Providence, 1973-76 (no degree). **Family:** Deborah Newton, partner since 1976. **Career:** Programmer, Rhode Island Blue Cross, 1980-82; customer service representative, Brown University Bookstore, 1987-94. Since 1994, full-time freelance writer. **Awards:** British Science Fiction Association award, 1994. **Member:** Science Fiction Writers of America, 1986. **Address:** 2 Poplar St., Providence, Rhode Island 02906. U.S.A. **Online Address:** ac038@osfn.rhilinet.gov.

SCIENCE FICTION PUBLICATIONS

Short Stories

The Steampunk Trilogy. New York, Four Walls Eight Windows, 1995.

Also contributor of numerous uncollected short stories to periodicals.

*

Paul Di Filippo comments:

In 1972, at the age of 17, having just graduated from high school, where I had discovered a certain talent for writing humorous essays for the school paper—essays in a Yippie vein, which nearly caused me to get expelled, especially when the principal factored in the "crime" of helping to distribute an underground paper produced on a mimeo stolen (unknown by me at the time) from one of the town's elementary schools—I determined to become a writer.

I had been reading genre SF since 1965, and all kinds of associated typically juvenile material even longer (Tom Swift and cohorts). Somehow I just assumed that SF was what I would write. At the time, I had a huge distrust of and disdain for mimetic writing, which I thought of as all vaguely "autobiographical" and hence impoverished in imaginative terms. I realize now that this reaction was really fear of dealing with many of the elements of quotidian life, the standard adolescent neurosis that fuels so much of fandom. (Can I somehow redeem myself by saying that I now champion such masters of "autobiographical fiction" as Thomas Wolfe the Elder, Henry Miller, Robert Crumb, Harvey Pekar, Charles Bukowski, and Jack Kerouac?)

Looking for a romantic place in which to compose my first magnum opus, I settled on Hawaii: it was far-off and tropical, but you didn't need a passport to get there, and people spoke English. (I *was* only *17*, after all, for God's sake!)

When my savings ran out, I used the return half of my ticket, moved in back home, and enrolled in a state college, Fall '73, English major. I began discovering the pleasures of all the kinds of fiction I had abjured. Wrote for the college paper. Met my life's mate, Deborah Newton (in 1976, switched to part-time status to prolong my stay, moved out of my folks'). Then, in 1979, still without a degree, chucked it all and split with Deb for Europe.

I seem to be able to save enough money at any one stretch of employment for only about two months of vagabondage. That's how long we kicked around Europe. When I got back, Fall '79, I lucked into a federal job-training slot for computer programming. In a couple of months, I found myself stuck in my first "real job": COBOL programmer at RI Blue Cross, deadliest of tight-assed bureaucracies.

Oh, yes: somewhere along the way I had sold an Op-Ed piece to *The New York Times* and a short parody to UnEarth magazine. But I still didn't consider myself a writer.

By July '82, I was totally disgusted with my job and myself. Two and a half years of doughnuts and claims-processing had left me fat and flaccid-brained. Realizing that a drastic move was called for, I quit RIBC. Deb joined me in the freelance free-fire zone, leaving her job as theater costume crafter to set up as knitwear designer (a successful career at which she's worked ever since).

Over the next three years—at first full-time, then, after my savings ran out once more and I had to hold down a variety of jobs, part-time—I produced approximately 500,000 words of fiction, not one of which sold. (Thank God, too! It's all moldering deservedly in several boxes in my basement. Scholars, phone quick for a viewing appointment, as I'm always on the verge of throwing it out.)

I have no idea why I persisted like this. Some vague intuition that I was getting better, burning off the dross. And I guess I was.

In 1985, I sold, first, "Rescuing Andy" to Ted Klein at *Twilight Zone* and, shortly thereafter, "Stone Lives" to Ed Ferman at *F&SF.* These two editors bear all responsibility for loosing me on the field. Over the past six years, sporadic short story sales—now numbering over 40—have bolstered me in my attempts to teach myself how to *really* write.

In 1995, I became the last of the *Mirrorshades*-anointed cyberpunks to achieve book publication with *The Steampunk Trilogy.*

I believe it was Hokusai—"The Old Man Gone Mad With Painting"—who said, at age 90 or thereabouts, "I've been painting now for 60 years, and if I only had another 30 years or so, I might get the hang of it!"

That's pretty much how I feel.

*   *   *

Despite the fact that much, some would say most, of the best science fiction is written at lengths shorter than the novel, it remains a very difficult task to develop a strong reputation without writing the latter with some frequency. Ray Bradbury and Harlan Ellison are two notable exceptions, and Paul Di Filippo seems likely to become the third. Despite a comparatively low number of published stories, he already has considerable name recognition within the field, and the recent publication of his first collection, *The Steampunk Trilogy,* may well bring him a non-genre audience as well.

Many of Di Filippo's protagonists must struggle with moral choices; sometimes they win, sometimes they're less fortunate. The body shaper in "Skintwister" knows that his talent for psychically altering the internal structure of his patients is a talent that could be used to save lives, but instead he spends his time catering to those who want cosmetic alterations, clearly a reference to plastic surgery. Only when an enemy sabotages his efforts and disfigures a beautiful woman does he begin to realize his own shortcomings. Similarly, the young criminal in "Agents" is perfectly willing to use an illegally acquired artificial intelligence as his key to manipulation of the worldwide information network, but when he suspects that the simulacrum is actually endangering the life of someone else, he disregards his own situation to intervene on her behalf.

Information technology is another recurring theme in Di Filippo's work, and may explain why he is sometimes identified with the cyberpunk movement, although his stories embrace such a wide range of plots and settings that the label is even less accurate than usual. The worldwide metamedium is the key to happiness in "Agents." In "A Thief in Babylon," the flow of information is the main factor in an interplanetary conflict. One of his best stories is "Conspiracy of Noise," wherein a young man takes a job for an enigmatic, multi-national agency that acquires intelligence and disseminates it in such a way as to precipitate riots, terrorist acts, and political movements. His superior informs him that the only thing that remains of value in the world is information and its communication among individuals, and that the ability to manipulate this exchange is the ultimate source of all power.

"Little Worker" is one of several stories set in a future North America that has been united under a dictator. Genetically modified "transgenics" can be mixed and matched from different heredities, so that a bodyguard can, for example, be 10% human, 30% wolverine, and the rest drawn from other animals as needed. The title refers to one such bodyguard, whose devotion to her autocratic master causes her to use an attack by terrorists to eliminate a rival for his affection. The same setting is used in "The Boot," a clever private eye story in which people can be booted the way automobiles are today, and "One Night in the City," the story of a dangerous gang initiation culminating in a cleverly arranged bit of revenge.

Modern music references are also common in Di Filippo's stories. One of his best, "Do You Believe in Magic?," involves a disc jockey in a near future Manhattan who hasn't left his apartment in years, and does so finally only because he has damaged his Loving Spoonful album and needs a replacement. He emerges to discover that the world has changed radically since his last visit, and that the entire Village has become a Disney theme park. "Lennon Specs" involves a quite literal transition into an altered perception in which "Lucy in the Sky with Diamonds" is an accurate description of the world.

"Mairzy Doats" is a biting indictment of some of the basic tenets of old-time science fiction. Robert Heinlein has been elected President of the United States following Franklin Roosevelt, and his term has seen a divergence in the concentration of technical research. Atomic power is used in household devices, for example, but the general technical level still lags behind. Marijuana is legal, and the sexual revolution has taken place earlier and gone to a greater extreme, but personal freedoms seem to be even more constricted than in our own world. Only members of the military or those who have joined a civilian service group can vote, for example. President Heinlein tricks several people into a one way trip to the moon because that's the only way to coerce the public into supporting the space program. The story is a piercing indictment of the simplistic ideas that formed the basis of many of the field's classics.

"Anne" is another alternate history story, this one based on the possibility that Anne Frank might have escaped to America. There she auditioned for a role in Hollywood, eventually replaced Judy Garland in *The Wizard of Oz,* and went on to marry Mickey Rooney. Ecology is the theme in "Up the Lazy River," with Greenpeace radicals sabotaging an artificial river created through the use of nanotechnology. "The Grange" is the best of Di Filippo's infrequent horror fiction, a suspenseful and brooding story of a woman's fascination with a secret society, and the rather unfortunate consequences for her less obliging husband.

As good as the above mentioned stories were, they are eclipsed easily by the three novellas that comprise *The Steampunk Trilogy.* The opening story, "Victoria," begins with the disappearance of the young Queen Victoria under mysterious circumstances. Cosmo Cowperthwait, a brilliant but rather erratic scientist, receives a visit from the Prime Minister, who wants to put an imposter on the throne temporarily, to ensure the government's stability. The stand-in he has in mind is a human sized newt that Cowperthwait has created in one of his experiments. After reluctantly agreeing to the plan, Cowperthwait sets out to track down the missing monarch, encountering a variety of adventures and odd characters along the way. The story is marvelous, capturing the essence of Victorian England, though in a somewhat twisted fashion, with nefarious noblemen, knaves, and ne'er do wells.

"Hottentots" is set in the same world, though this time in the United States. Louis Agassiz is a Swiss scientist living on the East Coast who becomes involved in the search for a magical icon made from the private parts of a Hottentot woman. Agassiz is a racist, so much so in fact that he destroys items in his household that have been touched by the black wife of the Afrikaaner who has coerced him into joining the search. As with "Victoria," the story portrays a world that resembles our own history enough to seem familiar, even though its filled with wonders and strangeness.

The concluding story, "Walt and Emily," is much more serious in tone. Emily Dickinson is initially repelled by the brash, outspoken Walt Whitman, but fascinated as well. When an experiment to discover the nature of life after death goes strangely awry, stranding them in a mysterious world half real, half dream, their relationship matures in what is easily Di Filippo's most ambitious and thoughtful work to date.

Other stories of note include "Kid Charlemagne," "Phylogenesis," and "Sleep Is Where You Find It." Di Filippo is a consistent writer whose stories may vary widely in plot, tone, and overall effect, but share his concerns about moral issues, the decisions we make about our lives, and the effects of those decisions on others. With the publication of his first book, it is likely that one of the best kept secrets in science fiction will be out at last.

—Don D'Ammassa

DISCH, Thomas M(ichael)

Pseudonyms: Thom Demijohn; Leonie Hargrave; Cassandra Knye. **Nationality:** American. **Born:** Des Moines, Iowa, 2 February 1940. **Education:** Cooper Union, New York, and New York University,

1959-62. **Career:** Part-time checkroom attendant, Majestic Theatre, New York, 1957-62; copywriter, Doyle Dane Bernbach Inc., New York, 1963-64. **Member:** Member of the board, National Book Critics Circle, 1988-91; secretary, 1989-91. Since 1964, freelance writer and lecturer; since 1987, theater critic for *The Nation.* **Awards:** O. Henry prize, 1975; John W. Campbell Memorial award, 1980; *Locus* award, 1981. **Address:** Box 226, Barryville, New York 12719, U.S.A.

SCIENCE FICTION PUBLICATIONS

Novels

The Genocides. New York, Berkley, 1965; London, Whiting and Wheaton, 1967.

Mankind under the Leash: Being a True and Faithful Account of the Great Upheavals of 2037, with Portraits of Many of the Principals Involved, as Well as Reflections by the Authors of the Nature of Art, Revolution, and Theology. New York, Ace, 1966; as *The Puppies of Terra,* London, Panther, 1978.

Echo Round His Bones. New York, Berkley, 1967; London, Hart Davis, 1969.

Camp Concentration. London, Hart Davis, 1968; Garden City, New York, Doubleday, 1969.

The Prisoner (based on television series). New York, Ace, 1969; London, Dobson, 1979; as *The Prisoner: I Am Not a Number!,* London, Boxtree, 1992.

334. London, MacGibbon and Kee, 1972; New York, Avon, 1974.

On Wings of Song. New York, St. Martin's Press, and London, Gollancz, 1979.

Triplicity (includes *Echo Round His Bones, The Genocides,* and *The Puppies of Terra*). Garden City, New York, Doubleday, 1980.

The Businessman: A Tale of Terror. New York, Harper, and London, Cape, 1984.

The M.D.: A Horror Story. New York, Knopf, 1991; London, HarperCollins, 1992.

The Priest: A Gothic Romance. London, Millennium, 1994; New York, Knopf, 1995.

Short Stories

One Hundred and Two H-Bombs and Other Science Fiction Stories. London, Compact, 1966; expanded as *White Fang Goes Dingo and Other Funny SF Stories,* London, Arrow, 1971; original version revised as *One Hundred and Two H-Bombs,* New York, Berkley, 1971.

Under Compulsion. London, Hart Davis, 1968; as *Fun with Your New Head,* Garden City, New York, Doubleday, 1971.

Getting into Death: The Best Short Stories of Thomas M. Disch. London, Hart Davis MacGibbon, 1973; revised, New York, Knopf, 1976.

The Early Science Fiction Stories of Thomas M. Disch. Boston, Gregg Press, 1977.

The Fundamental Disch. New York, Bantam, 1980; London, Gollancz, 1981.

The Man Who Had No Idea: A Collection of Stories. London, Gollancz, 1982.

Ringtime: A Story. West Branch, Iowa, Toothpaste Press, 1983.

Torturing Mr. Amberwell. New Castle, Virginia, Cheap Street, 1985.

The Brave Little Toaster (for children). Garden City, New York, Doubleday, and London, Grafton, 1986.

The Silver Pillow: A Tale of Witchcraft. Willimantic, Connecticut, M.V. Ziesing, 1987.

The Brave Little Toaster Goes to Mars (for children). Garden City, New York, Doubleday, 1988.

OTHER PUBLICATIONS

Novels

The House That Fear Built (with John Sladek as Cassandra Knye). New York, Paperback Library, 1966.

Black Alice (with John Sladek as Thom Demijohn). Garden City, New York, Doubleday, 1968; London, W.H. Allen, 1969.

Clara Reeve (as Leonie Hargrave). New York, Knopf, and London, Hutchinson, 1975.

Neighboring Lives, with Charles Naylor. New York, Scribner, 1980; London, Hutchinson, 1981.

Plays

Ben Hur (produced New York, 1989); *The Cardinal Detoxes* (produced New York, 1990).

Poetry

Highway Sandwiches, with Marilyn Hacker and Charles Platt. Privately printed, 1970.

The Right Way to Figure Plumbing. New York, Basilisk Press, 1971.

ABCDEFG HIJKLM NPOQRST UVWXYZ. London, Anvil Press Poetry, 1981.

Burn This. London, Hutchinson, 1982.

Orders of the Retina. West Branch, Iowa, Toothpaste Press, 1982.

Here I Am, There You Are, Where Were We. London, Hutchinson, 1984.

Yes, Let's: New and Selected Poems. Baltimore, Maryland, Johns Hopkins University Press, 1989.

Dark Verses and Light. Baltimore, Maryland, Johns Hopkins University Press, 1991.

Haikus of an AmPart. Minneapolis, Minnesota, Coffee House Press, 1991.

The Hawk and the Metaphor. N.p., Aralia Press, 1993(?).

The River's Snowing on the House. Barryville, New York, Disch, 1993.

Other

Fiction for children

The Tale of Dan De Lion: A Fable. Minneapolis, Coffee House Press, 1986.

The Castle of Indolence: On Poetry, Poets, and Poetasters. New York, Picator, 1994.

Editor, with Robert Arthur, *Alfred Hitchcock's Stories That Scared Even Me.* New York, Random House, 1967.

Editor, *The Ruins of Earth: An Anthology of Stories of the Immediate Future.* New York, Putnam, 1971; London, Hutchinson, 1973.

Editor, *Bad Moon Rising.* New York, Harper, 1973; London, Hutchinson, 1974.

Editor, *The New Improved Sun: An Anthology of Utopian S-F.* New York, Harper, 1975; London, Hutchinson, 1976.

Editor, with Charles Naylor, *New Constellations: An Anthology of Tomorrow's Mythologies.* New York, Harper, 1976.

Editor, with Charles Naylor, *Strangeness: A Collection of Curious Tales.* New York, Scribner, 1977.

*

Bibliography: *Thomas M. Disch: A Preliminary Bibliography* by David Nee, Berkeley, California, Other Change of Hobbit, 1982; *A Checklist of Thomas M. Disch* by Christopher P. Stephens, Hastings-on-Hudson, New York, Ultramarine, 1991.

Manuscript Collection: Beinecke Library, Yale University.

Critical Study: *The American Shore: Meditations on a Tale of Science Fiction by Thomas M. Disch—"Angouleme"* by Samuel R. Delany, Elizabethtown, New York, Dragon Press, 1978.

*   *   *

Readers of Thomas M. Disch's science fiction would do well to keep in mind that SF is but one aspect of his multifaceted career. Disch is a prolific man of letters who has published highly regarded poetry, mainstream fiction, novelizations, short stories, book and drama criticism, plays, opera libretti, children's books, and a computer interactive novel, as well as various collaborations with other writers. Some of the anthologies he has edited are landmarks in the SF field. The same playfulness of imagination and finely tuned wit are present in all the forms he turns his hand to, and his literary standards are high.

His science fiction since his first novel, *The Genocides,* appeared in 1965, has earned him a place in the front rank of contemporary SF authors. Three of his novels were cited in David Pringle's 1986 survey, *Science Fiction: The Best 100 Novels.*

Perhaps his chief distinguishing characteristic as an SF writer is his unpredictability. As critic Walter Clemons wrote in *Newsweek,* "A Disch novel almost always outfoxes our expectations," and as Disch confesses, "Publishers don't quite know what to do with me." His versatility is another trademark, and these two qualities may partly explain why he has not achieved the prominence on bestseller lists gained by more easily categorized authors.

The Genocides, a suspenseful first novel about the extinction of the human species by ubiquitous "Plants," demonstrates the breadth of the young writer's vision and displays a nascent but distinctive style recognizably his own. This was followed by a comic novel, *Mankind under the Leash* (in the U.K. as *The Puppies of Terra*), and Disch's most conventional SF novel, *Echo Round His Bones,* which he describes as "a resolutely cheerful science fiction adventure as traditional in all its trappings as a khaki fatigue uniform." His SF stories from the 1960s, most of which appeared first in the magazine *Fantastic Stories of Imagination,* were collected in *One Hundred and Two H-Bombs,* with an introduction by Harry Harrison. Harrison identified Disch as the best of "The New Wave" of SF writers then emerging, and described him as a comic writer in the SF tradition of Brian Aldiss. He also noted Disch's apparent delight in his own work, a delight that was to manifest itself in future novels and become a hallmark of Disch's writing.

Camp Concentration is Disch's first mature SF novel, and one of his three best. He was 26 when he began writing it, and says that ". . . it was only natural that the novel I was writing should convey some sense of giddy repletion and intellectual jubilation, feelings that set up an interesting interference pattern with the book's darker themes." *Camp Concentration,* set a few years ahead in the mid-1970s, is the journal of the experiences of a 35-year-old poet and political prisoner named Louis Sacchetti, who is secretly used by the military industrial complex as a guinea pig in an experiment designed to increase intelligence. But as the genius of Sacchetti and the other prisoners is developed in Camp Archimedes, they are being destroyed by the hybrid strain of syphilis used to increase their mental powers. Michael Moorcock wrote that "*Camp Concentration* represents one of the directions in which modern SF is going and is so far the outstanding example of its kind."

Under Compulsion (Fun with Your New Head in the U.S.) is a collection of stories first published in the mid-1960s, many in *New Worlds* magazine. Disch's macabre, often chilling humor is apparent in these stories about the modern human condition. Brian Aldiss wrote in *Impulse,* ". . . a genuine pessimist of a new writer has come along, to delight us with an unadulterated shot of pure bracing gloom." (It was also during the period when *Camp Concentration* and *Under Compulsion* were published that Disch began his still unfinished novel *The Pressure of Time* and wrote his best short story up to that time, "The Asian Shore.")

Using a fictional, mammoth government housing project located in New York City at 334 East 11th Street as an organizing device, Disch created a novel, *334,* out of many stories. He describes it as "a neo-realist portrait of New York City circa 2023, a book that I consider my best work to date in the genre of science fiction."

Getting into Death is a collection of stories written mainly in the 1970s and published first in magazines as different as *Orbit 6, New Worlds, Penthouse,* and *Paris Review.*

John Calvin Batchelor calls Disch's seventh novel, *On Wings of Song,* "a gay *Candide* set in 21st-century Manhattan." Like *334* it is a dystopian novel that brings together many important aspects of Disch's work, especially the sexual. Its protagonist, Daniel Weinreb, is unabashedly homosexual, and the story of his boyhood in Amesville, Iowa, in the 21st century and of his struggle to master song and the art of flight in a series of adventures and escapes that take him at last to darkest Manhattan is told with sharp ironic wit.

The M.D.: A Horror Story begins as a horror novel—and horror is a recurring element in Disch's SF—and becomes SF as it follows the misadventures of young Billy Michaels, who has supernatural powers. The novel takes him to manhood when he becomes Dr. William Michaels, a Dr. Frankenstein for the modern age who unleashes a plague on the world worse than AIDS.

Disch's most recent novel, *The Priest: A Gothic Narrative,* is a horror novel that makes a powerfully negative yet comic statement about the Catholic Church. It follows *The M.D.: A Horror Story.* (As Disch says, although these horror novels are not specifically SF, they "aren't so far afield that they aren't noticed in SF venues.")

In *The Priest,* Disch employs his considerable armory of angry wit and intelligence to make an imaginative assault on what he believes is the hypocrisy of the Church, especially in regard to sexual matters, from its anti-abortion stance to its anti-homosexual stance. It is a deeply felt statement about a rigid, unchanging Church in a changing world.

The title character of *The Priest,* the Reverend Patrick Bryce, is a Minneapolis priest with a latch for his altar boys. (He also takes on the persona of a 13th-century bishop in the Inquisition.) The themes of the novel represent a kind of Catholic code of priestly misconduct: guilt, perversion, alcoholism, child sex, hypocrisy. The Gothic, melodramatic aspects of the plot serve to advance Disch's indictment.

Disch's new collection of reviews and essays on poetry, *The Castle of Indolence: On Poetry, Poets, and Poetasters,* reminds us that he is a formidable poet with an original point of view about the wasteland of contemporary poetry: he believes that university teaching of poetry has led to careerism and mediocrity, and advocates—as Bardic schools did—the memorization of poetry.

"I cannot be counted a great success in the marketplace of science fiction," says Disch, but in summing up his career thus far, it must be said that his voice—modernist, romantic, ironic, intelligent, and chilling—makes him one of the indispensable SF masters.

—Michael Perkins

DONALDSON, Stephen R.

Pseudonym: Reed Stephens. **Nationality:** American. **Born:** Cleveland, Ohio, 13 May 1947. **Education:** College of Wooster, B.A. in English (departmental honors), 1968; Kent State University, M.A. in English, 1971. **Military Service:** Conscientious objector; assistant dispatcher, Akron City Hospital, Akron, Ohio, 1968-70. **Career:** Teaching fellow, Kent State University, 1971; acquisitions editor, Tapp-Gentz Associates, 1973; associate instructor, Ghost Ranch Writers Workshops, 1973-75; contributing editor, *Journal of the Fantastic in the Arts,* 1993-. **Awards:** British Fantasy Society award, 1979; John W. Campbell award, 1979; Balrog Fantasy award, 1981, 1983, 1985; Saturn award, 1983; Science Fiction Book Club award, 1988, 1989; The College of Wooster Distinguished Alumni award, 1989; Julia Verlanger award, 1990; Department of English Distinguished Alumni award, Kent State University, 1995. **Member:** Board of Directors, United States Karate Alliance. **Agent:** Howard Morhaim, 175 Fifth Ave., Rm. 709, New York, New York 10010, U.S.A.

SCIENCE FICTION PUBLICATIONS

Novels (series: The Gap; Mordan'ts Need; Thomas Covenant, the Unbeliever)

The First Chronicles of Thomas Covenant the Unbeliever. Glasgow, Richard Drew; as *The Chronicles of Thomas Covenant the Unbeliever,* London, Fontana, 1993.
    Lord Foul's Bane. New York, Holt, 1977; Glasgow, Richard Drew, 1983.
    The Illearth War. New York, Holt, 1977; Glasgow, Richard Drew, 1983.
    The Power That Preserves. New York, Holt, 1977; Glasgow, Richard Drew, 1983.
The Second Chronicles of Thomas Covenant the Unbeliever. London, HarperCollins, 1994.
    The Wounded Land. New York, Ballantine, and London, Sidgwick & Jackson, 1980.

The One Tree. New York, Del Rey, Ballantine, and London, Fontana, 1982.

White Gold Wielder. New York, Ballantine, and London, Collins, 1983.

Daughter of Regals. West Kingston, Rhode Island, Donald M. Grant, 1984.

The Mirror of Her Dreams (Mordant's Need). New York, Ballantine, 1987, and London, Collins, 1988.

A Man Rides Through (Mordant's Need). New York, Ballantine, 1987, and London, Collins, 1988.

The Gap into Conflict: The Real Story. London, Collins, 1990, and New York, Bantam, 1991.

The Gap into Vision: Forbidden Knowledge. New York, Bantam, and London, HarperCollins, 1991.

The Gap into Power: A Dark and Hungry God Arises. New York, Bantam, and London, HarperCollins, 1992.

The Gap into Madness: Chaos and Order. New York, Bantam, 1994.

Short Stories

Gilden-Fire (Thomas Covenant). San Francisco and Columbia, Pennsylvania, Underwood-Miller, 1981; London, Collins, 1983.

Daughter of Regals and Other Tales. New York, Ballantine, and London, Collins, 1984.

OTHER PUBLICATIONS

Novels as Reed Stephens (series: Mick Axbrewder)

The Man Who Risked His Partner. New York, Ballantine, 1984; London, Fontana, 1987.

The Man Who Killed His Brother. New York, Ballantine, 1986; London, Fontana, 1987.

The Man Who Tried to Get Away. New York, Ballantine, and London, Collins, 1990.

Other

Epic Fantasy in the Modern World: A Few Observations. Kent, Ohio, Kent State University Libraries, 1986.

Editor, *Strange Dreams: Unforgettable Fantasy Stories.* New York, Bantam, and London, HarperCollins, 1993.

*

Manuscript Collection: Kent State University Libraries, Kent, Ohio.

Stephen R. Donaldson comments:

I find it difficult to comment on my own work these days. In part this is a function of age: what's left of life seems too short to waste it talking about myself. In part I believe that my work speaks for itself better than I can speak for it; that anything I say about my work will have the effect of limiting and reducing it. And in part I find that—for me, anyway—the ability to comment is essentially retrospective. I can't talk about what I'm doing until I've actually done it: my relationship with my characters is too intuitive and intimate to permit objective observation while the work is in progress. Since my only substantial attempt at science fiction, the *Gap* se-

quence, is still "in progress" (as I write this, little more than half of the fifth and final installment has been committed to paper), I feel almost disqualified from discussing what I do, or why I do it.

A couple of points are obvious, however, in one form or another, virtually everything I write is about *redemption:* most of my characters are caught up in a vital and necessary struggle to "work out their own salvation, with fear and trembling." And my greatest technical gift as a writer is my ability to organize a large narrative canvas; to deploy large numbers of characters across large spaces in such a way that they all come together, not mechanically or arbitrarily, but organically. Whatever one may think of my choice of narrative styles, the content of my storytelling is tightly focused, despite its length: there are no wasted characters, gratuitous scenes, or thematic digressions.

In sum, my work is "epic" in the traditional sense of the term: it tackles the fundamental questions of life on a large scale.

Of course, to claim that *redemption* is one of "the fundamental questions of life" puts me in conflict with much of modern philosophy, and hints at what may be the underlying thrust of my entire body of work. If one accepts—in any form—Sartre's postulate that "Man is a futile passion," then the whole concept of *redemption* becomes something of a joke. Clearly, I reject that postulate. But I'm also intelligent enough to understand its relevance, and recognize its power. (Hence the grimness of much of my work. No one can accuse me of turning my back on "the harsh realities.") This may explain (now I'm speculating) why my story-making impulse has moved from the explicitly archetypal fantasy of the "Covenant" books through the more mundane, "human-centered" fantasy of *Mordant's Need* to the space-opera science fiction of the *Gap* books. Recognizing the obstacles which block the credibility of my kind of epic storytelling in the modern world, I'm trying by increments to translate my particular vision of humanity—"Man is an effective passion"—away from its conventionally acceptable form (fantasy) toward more "realistic," more objectively real, modes of expression. (Surely I don't need to explain that science fiction is a more "realistic" literary form than fantasy.)

The "Reed Stephens" books provide, I think, an even more "realistic" gloss on the same themes.

I have no idea where this process may lead me. I'm not even sure that I've defined the process accurately. As I say, my life with Angus Thermopyle, Morn Hyland, and Warden Dios is still "too intuitive and intimate to permit objective observation." Nevertheless, however uncertain I may be about *what* I'm doing, I'm absolutely convinced that it is *worth* doing.

*   *   *

When asked about his own work, Stephen R. Donaldson has two things to say. The first is that his characters are too immediate and intimate for him to discuss objectively while he is writing about them. The second is that his works focus around the theme of redemption.

That may be a bit self-effacing of him, however, to think in terms of simple redemption. For there is very rarely anything simple about Donaldson's writing—indeed, all three of his major series (*The Chronicles of Thomas Covenant, Mordant's Need,* and the unfinished *Gap* cycle) appear on a sweeping scale, and follow characters who profoundly affect their environment. Nothing in his work is small, including the flaws of the protagonists themselves, from the reflexive self-pariahhood of Thomas Covenant to the numb self-disbelief of Terisa Morgan, the zone-controlled chemical support of Morn Hyland and the raging fear and anger of Angus Thermopyle. Each character has a massive fault of some sort, but those faults serve a distinctive purpose, to separate the person from the rest of painful reality and shield them from continued damage, both emotional and, in the case of Covenant's leprosy, physical. By using these emotional and social barriers, they are able to protect themselves from the injurious world outside.

But that is not a true life, and none of Donaldson's characters are able to maintain that sort of solitary shelter for very long. All of them, even hardened crooks like Thermopyle, survive by rejecting the true state of affairs that surrounds them, but that is not living—only surviving. And all of them possess too much drive, too much courage and perception, to allow themselves to remain curled away when they might have the power to accomplish something.

And the only way to have an impact on events is to set aside their insulation and confront their fears. For Covenant that means letting people get close to him again, while for Terisa it requires calling attention to herself. In Morn's case it means accepting the physiological flaws and limits of her own unaided body, and for Angus it involves facing those close to him with trust and without anger and rage. But in every case it involves accepting the world as it is, and then working to change it, instead of hiding from the truth and hoping that it will go away. Because, in Donaldson's worlds as in our own, it won't just go away, not ever.

Indeed, each series reduces the chance of escape, by strengthening the ties between our own world and that of the story, and by binding the main characters more tightly into their new situation. In Donaldson's first work, Thomas Covenant only entered the Land when he passed out or was summoned, and because of that he had the easy option of claiming that it all was a dream, and therefore not important. Of course, he later escaped from this notion and accepted the problem of helping, but the fact that there was such a nebulous connection between the Land and our own reality weakened the impact of Covenant's lessons and his eventual successes. Mordant possesses more of a reality to us, because we know that there are physical methods of getting there, through mirrors—we may not understand the process involved, but Geraden's arrival in Terisa's dining room shatters a mirror and scatters glass across the floor, which grants both him and his world a reassuring sense of solidity. Because of this, it is harder to claim that none of Mordant's peril is real, and Terisa instead believes that perhaps she is the one who did not exist; she accepts the importance of Mordant itself, just not that of her own role in its struggles. And in the Gap series, there is even less chance for escape, because the stellar expanse of the Amnion and the United Mining Company is not just linked to our own world, it is our world, set into the future; and, for the first time, the main characters are themselves from within the new world of the books, and so have no other place to escape to besides their own delusions.

It is also interesting to note that, as the worlds become more real, so do the stories in them become more complex—Thomas Covenant was the undisputed main character of his series (later he handed that honor off to his doctor, Linden Avery, in the Second Chronicles, and took a back-seat), while Terisa and Geraden had almost equal play (it was always told from her point of view, but his importance cannot be denied), but Morn finds herself sharing time with Angus Thermopyle and the scarred pirate Nick Succorso. It is almost as if the characters must not only overcome their own weaknesses, but also deal with those of the people around them, and be wary of getting tripped up by others' protective camouflage. A true vision of reality must include other people, and fit their wants and needs into the picture if there is to be any hope of success; Donaldson demonstrates his own ability to consider these aspects by the way he smoothly brings so many characters into the picture, and then leaves them to resolve their own differences and find a way forward, but never out. As one Morn Hyland realizes in *The Gap into Conflict: The Real Story,* "Vast space was deadly: it called for valor, determination, and idealism." The same can be said for life itself; Donaldson himself supplies most of the idealism, but his characters demonstrate the courage and persistence that it takes to change, and far beyond simple redemption, they give themselves to the effort of changing their world, our world, for the better.

—Aaron Rosenberg

DONNELLY, Ignatius

Pseudonym: Edmund Boisgilbert, M.D. **Nationality:** American. **Born:** Philadelphia, Pennsylvania, 3 November 1831. **Family:** Married 1) Katherine McCaffrey in 1855 (died 1896); three children; 2) Marian Hanson in 1898. **Education:** Received law degree, 1850. **Career:** Lawyer, Pennsylvania, 1852-56; moved to Minnesota, 1856; joined Republican Party and was elected lieutenant governor, 1859-63; elected to U.S. Congress House of Representatives as Radical Republican, 1863-69; editor, the *Anti-Monopolist*; lobbyist and correspondent for *St. Paul Dispatch,* Washington, D.C.; ran unsuccessful gubernatorial campaign, Minnesota, 1892; nominated for vice-president of United States by Minnesota State Farmers' Alliance (forerunner of Populist Party); founded *St. Paul Representative* (weekly newspaper), 1893. **Died:** 1 January 1901.

SCIENCE FICTION PUBLICATIONS

Novels

Caesar's Column: Story of the Twentieth Century (as Edmund Boisgilbert). Chicago, Schulte, 1890; (as Ignatius Donnelly), London, Sampson Low, 1891; Cambridge, Massachusetts, Harvard University, 1960.
Doctor Huguet (as Edmund Boisgilbert). Chicago, Schulte, 1891; (as Ignatius Donnelly), London, Sampson Low, 1892.
The Golden Bottle; or, The Story of Ephraim Benezet of Kansas. New York, Merrill, 1892; London, Sampson, Low, 1893.

OTHER PUBLICATIONS

Minniger City. Philadelphia, Duross, 1856.
The Sonnets of Shakespeare. St. Paul, Minnesota, Moore, 1859.
Atlantis: The Antediluvian World. New York, Harper, 1882; London, Sampson Low, 1890; revised edition, edited by Egerton Sykes, New York, Harper, 1949.
Ragnarok: The Age of Fire and Gravel. New York, Appleton, and London, Sampson Low, 1883.
The Great Cryptogram: Francis Bacon's Cipher in the So-Called Shakespeare Plays. Chicago, Peale, and London, Sampson Low, 1888.

The American People's Money. Chicago, Laird and Lee, 1985; as
   The Bryan Campaign for the American People's Money, 1896.
The Cipher in the Plays and on the Tombstone. Minneapolis,
   Verulam, 1899; London, Sampson Low, 1900.

*   *   *

Ignatius Donnelly was first and foremost a politician, and his
writings reflect that fact. In a long political career he was twice
lieutenant governor of Minnesota (with long periods as acting governor), three times U. S. Representative, many terms in both houses
of the Minnesota Legislature, head of several state political parties,
candidate for governor, and later for president, and widely known
for his ability to bring dissenting parties together. At the same time,
although he was frequently able to achieve compromise with those
who disagreed with his views, he was less successful as a public
official than he might have been because there were some principles from which he would not budge. Trained as a lawyer and
longtime barely successful farmer, he was a reformer who stood
firmly against those who injured the people as a whole, bankers,
railroads, monopolies of any kind. To him the "Plutocracy" and the
many corrupt public officials were always the enemy, and he fought
them with everything he had. He was persuasive in numerous pamphlets and newspaper and magazine articles, and acclaimed as one
of the great orators of the Midwest.

His powers of persuasion were behind his success both as a
politician and as a writer. When a temporary setback in his political
career occurred, he turned to writing his bestselling *Atlantis: The
Antidiluvian World* and *Ragnarok: The Age of Fire and Gravel*. In
both of these works of popular—or, perhaps better, pseudo—science he marshalled his arguments like a lawyer's brief, ignoring
whatever did not fit his thesis and hammering home his points with
evidence derived from his wide-ranging reading. The success of
these works led him to continue writing even after his political star
rose again. With income from their sales he was able to indulge in
research (published as *The Great Cryptogram: Francis Bacon's
Cipher in the So-Called Shakespeare Plays* and *The Cipher in the
Plays and on the Tombstone*) seeking to prove that Bacon was the
true author of Shakespeare's plays. Lectures on all three of these
subjects added substantially to his income.

All three of his science fiction novels were written as polemics
in support of his political and economic views and to advance his
search for social justice. Although Donnelly clearly thought of himself as a literary man, widely read, capable of quoting copiously
from many literary sources, and well aware of the cadences and
rhythms of good writing, these novels are read today, not for their
literary qualities but for their place in the utopian, reformist, proletarian strain that is a major component of late-19th and early 20th-
century American fiction.

Doctor Huguet was a courageous attack on racial prejudice. The
mind and soul of Huguet a brilliant southern physician, about to
enter politics, is transformed into the body of a brutal, evil black
man. Huguet's body descends deeper and deeper into evil while
Huguet, honest, caring, brilliant but locked in a black man's body,
is regarded as a threat to the community. When the white body
kills the black body, the transformation is reversed, Huguet's mind
and soul are rejoined to his body. Because it failed to ignite others
against prejudice, Donnelly, in so far as he was ever able to believe it of his own work, regarded the book as something of a failure.

In *The Golden Bottle; or, The Story of Ephraim Benezet of Kansas,* a young farmer dreams that he can make gold and use this
unlimited wealth to reform society and end poverty, corruption, and
delinquency. In the midst of success as President and leader of the
successful war to create a new Universal Republic based on cooperation throughout the world, he awakens and realizes that gold in
itself means nothing: the real value of money is as a useful governmental measure of values for commodities. He leaves his farm
to work for the utopian world he believes the People's Party would
produce. Donnelly used the proceeds of the book to support the
People's Party of which he was a leading member.

The most successful of Donnelly's works of fiction, *Caesar's
Column,* quickly became a bestseller in both America and Europe
and was hailed with delight by his political friends and admirers.
Most of the book is made up of letters home by a young traveler in
the United States in the year 1988. The picture he paints is of a
land of amazing technological accomplishments but filled with corruption, crime, and poverty, a land in which farmers and laborers
are exploited and victimized by the rich, the "Plutocracy." This ugly
future is the result of the failure to begin reforms demanded by the
Populists in the 1890s. The downtrodden cannot forever be held
down, and the book depicts an ugly revolution that overturns the
Oligarchy. A monument to the victory, Caesar's Column, is constructed of the dead bodies, cemented together with concrete, and,
when the mob takes vengeance on its own leader, Caesar's head is
placed on a pole at the top. The narrator and friends flee to Uganda
where a utopian "Garden in the Mountains" has been established,
a society run by principles Donnelly fought all his life to bring to
fruition. In Donnelly's mind such a utopia was what he fought for
all his life.

Donnelly had a smooth, persuasive style in everything he wrote.
Unlike most writers of science fiction he had an agenda that was
clearly displayed in *Dr. Huguet, The Golden Bottle,* and *Caesar's
Column.* Few readers of science fiction are much interested in propaganda. Students of utopia are, and it is, thus, for his utopian ideas
that Donnelly is remembered, and sometimes read, as the centennial of his death comes near.

—Arthur O. Lewis

DORMAN, Sonya

Now Sonya Hess. **Nationality:** American. **Born:** 4 June 1924.
Education: Attended agricultural college, one year. **Family:** Married in 1950 (divorced); one daughter. **Career:** Has worked as stable
maid, kennel owner, receptionist, cook, dancer, greenhouse assistant, and housekeeper. **Awards:** MacDowell Colony fellowship
(five); Science Fiction Poetry Association Rhysling award, 1978.
Agent: Virginia Kidd, 538 East Harford Street, Box 278, Milford,
Pennsylvania 18337. **Address:** Box 6660, Taos, New Mexico
87571, U.S.A.

Science Fiction Publications

Novel

Planet Patrol (for children). New York, Coward McCann, 1978.

OTHER PUBLICATIONS

Poetry

Poems. Columbus, Ohio State University Press, 1970.
Stretching Fence. Athens, Ohio University Press, 1975.
A Paper Raincoat: Poems. Orono, Maine, Puckerbrush Press, 1976.
The Far Traveller. La Crosse, Wisconsin, Juniper Press, 1980.
Palace of Earth. Orono, Maine, Puckerbrush Press, 1984.
Constellations of the Inner Eye. Orono, Maine, Puckerbrush Press, 1991.
Kingdom of Lost Waters. Boise, Idaho, Ahsahata Press, Boise State University, 1993.

* * *

Sonya Dorman is one of the most unusual and gifted contemporary writers of fantasy and science fiction. Each of her stories is a unique, perfectly executed jewel. In addition to her strong sense of the macabre Dorman possesses a well-developed sense of humor, illustrated by the grimly absurd twists with which she ends many of her stories. She also writes poetry which has appeared in several SF magazines and anthologies as well as short stories which have been published in *Redbook* and other magazines outside the field of science fiction.

Although the short story is a difficult medium in which to develop characters Dorman succeeds admirably. She is economical in her descriptions of futuristic societies and their trappings. In a few, well-chosen words she manages to convey a feeling of place and time. She is also skilled at letting the natural flow of the story line serve its own descriptive function.

Her plots are deceptively simple at first glance. On examination, however, they are carefully wrought situations described through fast-paced dialogue and exquisitely crafted action. Dorman is at her best in stories like "Splice of Life" in which an ordinary, if somewhat grim, situation is expanded and twisted to make a point about the implications of contemporary medical research. This story is gory, but the gore is purposeful and intentional. It's designed to shock her readers into seeing past the superficialities, to strip bare the meat and bone of living. The harsh and painful exposure of life is characteristic of Dorman's work.

Strong, believable, and likeable women are usually the main characters in Dorman's stories. One of her most memorable heroines, Corporal Roxy Rimidon, appears first in "Bye, Bye, Banana Bird," a different kind of Dorman story. Roxy is a member of the elite special forces unit from the American Dominion called the Planet Patrol. She is tough, sexy, and quite intelligent, and her adventures make exciting reading.

Dorman exhibits a combination of many of the traditional female virtues such as compassion and sensitivity in contrast to the traditional male characteristics of strength, energy, and conciseness. All of this is overlaid by her steely determination to make us see the world as she does. Dorman's world is bitterly ironic and at the same time human. The amorphous alien creatures from "When I Was Miss Dow" seem remarkably similar to the mental patients in "Lunatic Assignment."

Her lighter stories such as the Roxy Rimidon series and the more introspective "Building Block" are also expertly crafted. The latter deals with a female space architect who has a creative block. These later stories are less macabre and biting but just as creative and well written as Dorman's earlier work.

Sonya Dorman is a rare phenomenon. She is an amalgam like her androgynous characters, able to display her sensitivity and compassion without relinquishing her energy and irony. One anthology editor cautions readers at the beginning of "Lunatic Assignment" to read the story only when they have time to read it through at one sitting and then to think about it. This precaution might preface almost all of her stories. They are not trifles to skim while sunbathing or waiting for the bus. They are energizing, thought-provoking, wryly optimistic glimpses of the future.

—Alice Chambers Wygant

———

DORSET, Richard. *See* **SHAVER, Richard S.**

———

DORSEY, Candas Jane

Nationality: Canadian. **Born:** Edmonton, Alberta, 16 November 1952. **Education:** University of Alberta, B.A. 1975; University of Calgary, B.S.W. 1979. **Career:** Has worked in theatre and social work. From 1980, freelance writer and editor: *The Edmonton Bullet.* Lives in Edmonton. **Address:** c/o Porcépic Books, 4252 Commerce Circle, Victoria, British Columbia V8Z 4M2, Canada.

SCIENCE FICTION PUBLICATIONS

Novel

Hardwired Angel, with Nora Abercrombie. Vancouver, British Columbia, Arsenal Pulp Press, 1987.

Short Stories

Machine Sex—and Other Stories. Victoria, British Columbia, Porcépic, 1988; London, Women's Press, 1990.

OTHER PUBLICATIONS

Poetry

This Is for You. Vancouver, British Columbia, Blewointmentpress, 1973.
Orion Rising. Vancouver, British Columbia, Blewointmentpress, 1974.
Results of the Ring Toss. Vancouver, British Columbia, Blewointmentpress, 1976.
Leaving Marks. Edmonton, Alberta, River Books, 1992.

Other

Editor, with Gerry Truscott, *Tesseracts 3: Canadian Science Fiction.* Victoria, British Columbia, Porcépic, 1990.

Editor, with Ellen Ticoll, *The Nuts and Bolts of Community Economic Development.* Edmonton, Alberta, Edmonton Social Planning Council, 1984.

*   *   *

Candas Jane Dorsey belongs to a new generation of Canadian science fiction writers. She has been published in *Tesseracts* anthologies. She won, with Nora Abercrombie, the Ninth Annual Pulp Press International Three-Day Novel Competition for *Hardwired Angel.* Her coming of age was achieved with the publication of *Machine Sex—and Other Stories,* which presents a distinctly different voice in science fiction.

The problem that besets anthologies is that the various stories contained in them will be compared with one another and will be judged on their own merits only with great difficulty. This is the case also with *Machine Sex—and Other Stories.* Some of the stories seem, on the surface, fairly out of place with what is expected of science fiction, namely the description of humans' reactions and evolution in a universe in constant change, through the use of science and technology.

Dorsey is excellent with the use of inner dialogue and description of her characters' feelings. Contrary to mainstream science fiction, where most characters are only described in an evasive manner, and only when it is necessary for the plot to move along, Dorsey's characters are all too aware of their thoughts, to the point that one gets the impression they watch themselves as if they are strangers on television.

In many of her stories, this is accomplished at the expense of a description of the settings in which the characters move. In the first story, "Sleeping in a Box," science or technology are so unimportant that one could easily imagine the story to have taken place in a completely non-science fiction environment, i.e., a desert island instead of the moon. This is not to say that it is not science fiction: the context just does not seem to be essential. The same could be said of the fourth story, "The Prairie Warriors;" it would be more appropriate in a fantasy collection. It is possible that Dorsey expects her readers to do some work themselves and fill in the missing gaps. "The Prairie Warriors" is a very demanding story where place names are absent, only mentioned as the village, the hills, the mountains and the prairie. We are told the effect of drugs on people whose country, origin, and allegiance remain nameless. It is beautifully written, at times mesmerizing, but the average reader may skip directly to the next story in search of a science-fiction world.

"Machine Sex" explores the blend of sex and computer software from a female point of view. The story might be regarded as feminist, but "Machine Sex" has more to do with the survival of a gifted woman in a universe that is still dominated by men, and the way in which people can use and manipulate each other. This story also has elements of cyberpunk science fiction.

Other stories in the same collection are more traditional science fiction. But Dorsey is at her best when dealing with the psychology of her character rather than an endless description of technical wizardry.

What is most effective in her best stories is a deliberate choice of places and time. This is particularly evident in "Machine Sex," where we are led across Canada and an omniscient narrator takes over from time to time to watch upon the main protagonist as if we were next-door neighbours and voyeurs.

Dorsey is fast becoming an established writer on the Canadian SF scene, not only for her fiction but for her views and analysis.

In *Tesseracts 3, Tesseracts* being a series of anthologies of Canadian science fiction, she takes the opportunity of being one of the two coeditors with Gerry Truscott to write an essay on the past future and definition of Canadian Science-Fiction, an essay that has definitely captured the imagination since it was reprinted in *Northern Stars,* an anthology intended for the American reading public and for discoverers of Canadian SF.

Dorsey claims that American SF writers could benefit and learn from Canadian and Quebecois SF writers: namely that the image of the science fiction writer producing work solely for pulp paperback is not only disappearing fast but practically inexistent in Canada and Quebec. She argues that many SF writers come from all walks of life and that many of them write books as removed from science fiction as treatises on medieval French literature.

She also argues that Canadian science fiction has a penchant for mood pieces and that it is less obsessed than American science fiction with the resolution of conflicts. For her, Canadian SF "has more to do with progress toward understanding." She prefers the label of speculative to the one of science fiction along with a number of dissenting authors. However, she does ask the question whether it is possible to write fiction that would not be speculative—whether, for instance, *Anna Karenina* is documentary—and challenges readers to give her a novel that "is not set in a parallel universe—St. Petersburg or Manawaka—simply by virtue of being fiction." She then proceeds to answer her own questions by proposing that, after all, speculative writers are not very different from mainstream writers.

Writing also in such fields as economic development as well as being a poet, Candas Jane Dorsey is certainly well siuated to investigate the very actual and unresolved question of the definition of science fiction.

—Henry Leperlier

———

DOUGLAS, R.M. *See* **RANKINE, John.**

———

DOWLING, Terry

Nationality: Australian. **Born:** 1947. **Education:** University of Sydney, B.A. (honors) 1974, M.A. (honors) 1982. **Career:** Communications instructor/lecturer. **Member:** Science Fiction and Fantasy Writers of America. **Awards:** Ditmar award, 1983, 1985, 1986, 1987, 1988 (twice), 1990, 1991, 1992. **Agent:** Richard Curtis Associates, Inc. New York, New York, U.S.A. **Address:** 11 Everard St., Hunters Hill NSW Australia 2110.

SCIENCE FICTION PUBLICATIONS

Short Stories (series: Rynosseros)

Rynosseros. North Adelaide, South Australia, Aphelion, 1990; New York, Science Fiction Book Club, 1993.

Wormwood (Rynosseros). North Adelaide, South Australia, Aphelion, 1991.

Blue Tyson (Rynosseros). North Adelaide, South Australia, Aphelion, 1992.

The Mars You Have in Me. North Perth, Western Australia, Eidolon, 1992.

Twilight Beach (Rynosseros). North Adelaide, South Australia, Aphelion, 1993.

OTHER PUBLICATIONS

Other

Editor, *The Essential Ellison: A 35-Year Retrospective,* by Harlan Ellison. Omaha, Nebraska, Nemo Press, 1987.
Editor (with Van Ikin), *Mortal Fire: Best Australian SF.* Rydalmere, New South Wales, Coronet Books, 1993.

*   *   *

Terry Dowling's first story was published in 1975, and by the time his first book appeared in 1990 he had won the Australian Science Fiction Achievement ("Ditmar") Award for fiction more times than any other Australian writer.

Commentators have tried to explain the Dowling phenomenon by pointing to similarities with the work of Jack Vance and J.G. Ballard (for Dowling has written major critical work on both writers), and Dowling has certainly mastered important aspects of each writer's style. But Dowling's vision is his own; his works create a series of myths about contemporary humanity, pleasingly woven into Australian settings, and they combine what is often hi-tech subject-matter with a contrastingly ornate style.

The stories in *Rynosseros* concern a single character, Tom Tyson, known as Tom Rynosseros because he captains the sand-ship Rynosseros. In this future Australia, the coastal cities, home of white Australians, are urbanely cosmopolitan centres of culture, while in the interior, around an inland sea, the Ab'O states represent the emancipation of the Aboriginal race whose heritage is both its past and its future destiny. Ab'O Princes use satellites to spy on tribal conflicts, and graceful wind-propelled sand-ships roll across the deserts, giving the collection its symbol of freedom and inquiry.

This Dowling future is a challenging reversal of present-day Australian conditions: in *Rynosseros,* it is the inland, not the coastline, that is the nerve-centre of change and vitality, and the Aboriginal heritage is linked with technology, not nature (for the Ab'Os are genetically altered Aborigines whose primary allegiance is not to the Land but to the *haldanes,* which are energy-vectors used to tap psychic power). The point of such a reversal is not socio-political. Dowling does not offer social criticism; his scenario exists only to break down the monolithic unalterableness of the present by offering a cleverly plausible alternative vision.

Australian writers have traditionally viewed their country and people through the mode of social realism, often in a flat, dry, stoical tone. Dowling's approach reverses this, too, for his style is ornate and often lush, and the tone is inquisitive, verging on wonder and awe. In "The Robot is Running Away from the Trees," a character discovers the relics of an old robot and wipes dust from "the impressive rococo decorations, from the faded dim-gold exotic curlicues on thighs and shoulders." Dowling relishes such lavish accumulations of images, each one adding sensuous accretions to the detail. His stories are jewelled with all manner of exotica—fire-chess, fire-sculptures, light-suits, mirage-divers, typhies, and sanchers—but none is the mere frothiness of fantasy. Dowling's exotic objects, behaviours, and rituals help to define the philosophies and perspectives of radically different cultures.

Wormwood is also a collection of short stories; however, the point of unity is not a single character but the book's scenario. "Wormwood" is the biblical name for the moment in 2023 when an alien race—the Nobodoi—successfully invaded the Earth, setting up inscrutably elaborate networks of energy ley-lines, and embarking upon a process of remoulding the planet to their own specifications. But then the Nobodio were "Recalled," leaving Earth in the hands of numerous alien "Bridging Races," Hoproi, Darzie, Matta, Salman, and Amazil, to name just a few.

If the collection has a central theme, it is the struggle of individual humans to rediscover and maintain some sense of identity as humans. But Dowling provides an individual twist to this familiar theme, for his characters are not concerned with prevailing over their alien masters and there is no climactic battle in which invaders are repelled. The humans of *Wormwood* must simply find their own way to preserve their identity in the presence of beings who may not even understand the concept of identity. In this sense *Wormwood* deals with human psychology in crisis.

Dowling's central concern is with wonder and pluralities; his fiction offers carefully-crafted scenes of spectacle, but this is always underpinned by a tolerant awareness of cultural difference. In a land that has often feared and mistrusted otherness, Dowling's stories treat the unusual as a source of wonder and potential new knowledge, not a cause for fear.

—Van Ikin

DOYLE, (Sir) Arthur Conan

Nationality: British. **Born:** Edinburgh, Scotland, 22 May 1859. **Education:** Hodder School, Lancashire, 1868-70, Stonyhurst College, Lancashire, 1870-75, and the Jesuit School, Feldkirch, Austria (editor, *Feldkirchian Gazette*), 1875-76; studied medicine at the University of Edinburgh, 1876-81, M.B. 1881, M.D. 1885. Served as senior physician at a field hospital in South Africa during the Boer War, 1899-1902; knighted, 1902. **Family:** Married 1) Louise Hawkins in 1885 (died 1906), one daughter and one son; 2) Jean Leckie in 1907, two sons and one daughter. **Career:** Practiced medicine in Southsea, Hampshire, 1882-90; full-time writer from 1891; stood for Parliament as Unionist candidate for Central Edinburgh, 1900, and tariff reform candidate for the Hawick Burghs, 1906. Member, Society for Psychical Research, 1893-1930 (resigned). LL.D.: University of Edinburgh, 1905. Knight of Grace of the Order of St. John of Jerusalem. **Died:** 7 July 1930.

SCIENCE FICTION PUBLICATIONS

Novels (series: Professor Challenger in all books except *The Doings of Raffles Haw*)

The Doings of Raffles Haw. London, Cassell, and New York, Lovell, 1892.

The Lost World: Being an Account of the Recent Amazing Adventures of Professor George E. Challenger, Lord John Roxton, Professor Summerlee, and Mr. E.D. Malone of the "Daily Gazette". London, Hodder and Stoughton, 1912; New York, Doran, 1915.

The Poison Belt: Being an Account of Another Adventure of Prof. George E. Challenger, Lord John Roxton, Prof. Summerlee, and Mr. E.D. Malone, the Discoverers of "The Lost World". London, Hodder and Stoughton, and New York, Doran, 1913.

The Land of Mist. London, Hutchinson, 1925; New York, Doran, 1926.

Short Stories

Danger! and Other Stories. London, Murray, 1918; New York, Doran, 1919.

The Maracot Deep and Other Stories. London, Murray, and New York, Doubleday, 1929.

The Professor Challenger Stories: The Lost World, The Poison Belt, The Land of Mist, The Disintegration Machine, When the World Screamed. London, Murray, 1952; as *The Complete Professor Challenger,* Ware, Hertfordshire, Wordsworth Editions, 1989.

The Best Science Fiction of Arthur Conan Doyle, edited by Charles G. Waugh and Martin H. Greenberg. Carbondale, Southern Illinois University Press, 1981.

OTHER PUBLICATIONS

Novels

A Study in Scarlet. London, Ward Lock, 1888; Philadelphia, Lipincott, 1890.

The Mystery of Cloomber. London, Ward and Downey, 1889; New York, Fenno, 1896 (?).

Micah Clarke. London, Longman, and New York, Harper, 1889.

The Firm of Girdlestone. London, Chatto and Windus, and New York, Lovell, 1890.

The Sign of Four. London, Blackett, 1890; New York, Collier, 1891.

The White Company. London, Smith Elder, 3 vols., 1891; New York, Lovell, 1 vol., 1891.

The Great Shadow. New York, Harper, 1892.

The Great Shadow, and Beyond the City. Bristol, Arrowsmith, 1893; New York, Ogilvie, 1894.

The Refugees. London, Longman, 3 vols., 1893; New York, Harper, 1 vol., 1893.

The Parasite. London, Constable, and New York, Harper, 1894.

The Stark Munro Letters. London, Longman, and New York, Appleton, 1895.

Rodney Stone. London, Smith Elder, and New York, Appleton, 1896.

Uncle Bernac: A Memory of the Empire. London, Smith Elder, and New York, Appleton, 1897.

The Tragedy of Korosko. London, Smith Elder, 1898; as *A Desert Drama,* Philadelphia, Lippincott, 1898.

A Duet, with an Occasional Chorus. London, Grant Richards, and New York, Appleton, 1899; revised edition, London, Smith Elder, 1910.

The Hound of the Baskervilles. London, Newnes, and New York, McClure, 1902.

Sir Nigel. London, Smith Elder, and New York, McClure, 1906.

The Valley of Fear. New York, Doran, and London, Smith Elder, 1915.

Short Stories

Mysteries and Adventures. London, Scott, 1889; as *The Gully of Bluemansdyke and Other Stories,* 1892.

The Captain of the Polestar and Other Tales. London, Longman, 1890; New York, Munro, 1894.

The Adventures of Sherlock Holmes. London, Newnes, and New York, Harper, 1892.

My Friend the Murderer and Other Mysteries and Adventures. New York, Lovell, 1893.

The Memoirs of Sherlock Holmes. London, Newnes, 1893; New York, Harper, 1894.

The Great Keinplatz Experiment and Other Stories. Chicago, Rand McNally, 1894.

Round the Red Lamp, Being Facts and Fancies of Medical Life. London, Methuen, and New York, Appleton, 1894.

The Exploits of Brigadier Gerard. London, Newnes, and New York, Appleton, 1896.

The Man from Archangel and Other Stories. New York, Street and Smith, 1898.

Hilda Wade (completion of work by Grant Allen). London, Richards, and New York, Putnam, 1900.

The Green Flag and Other Stories of War and Sport. London, Smith Elder, and New York, McClure, 1900.

Adventures of Gerard. London, Newnes, and New York, McClure, 1903.

The Return of Sherlock Holmes. London, Newnes, and New York, McClure, 1905.

Round the Fire Stories. London, Smith Elder, and New York, McClure, 1908.

The Last Galley: Impressions and Tales. London, Smith Elder, and New York, Doubleday, 1911.

His Last Bow: Some Reminiscences of Sherlock Holmes. London, Murray, and New York, Doran, 1917.

Tales of the Ring and Camp. London, Murray, 1922; as *The Croxley Master and Other Tales of the Ring and Camp,* New York, Doran, 1925.

Tales of Pirates and Blue Water. London, Murray, 1922; as *The Dealings of Captain Sharkey and Other Tales of Pirates,* New York, Doran, 1925.

Tales of Terror and Mystery. London, Murray, 1922; as *The Black Doctor and Other Tales of Terror and Mystery,* New York, Doran, 1925.

Tales of Twilight and the Unseen. London, Murray, 1922; as *The Great Keinplatz Experiment and Other Tales of Twilight and the Unseen,* New York, Doran, 1925.

Tales of Adventure and Medical Life. London, Murray, 1922; as *The Man from Archangel and Other Tales of Adventure,* New York, Doran, 1925.

Tales of Long Ago. London, Murray, 1922; as *The Last of the Legions and Other Tales of Long Ago,* New York, Doran, 1925.

The Case-Book of Sherlock Holmes. London, Murray, and New York, Doran, 1927.

The Conan Doyle Historical Romances. Murray, 2 vols., 1931-32.

The Field Bazaar. Privately printed, 1934; Summit, New Jersey, Pamphlet House, 1947.

Great Stories, edited by John Dickson Carr. London, Murray, and New York, London House and Maxwell, 1959.

The Annotated Sherlock Holmes, edited by William S. Baring-Gould. New York, Potter, 2 vols., 1967; London, Murray, 2 vols., 1968.

The Sherlock Holmes Illustrated Omnibus (facsimile of magazine stories). London, Murray-Cape, 1978.

The Best Supernatural Tales of Arthur Conan Doyle, edited by E.F. Bleiler. New York, Dover, 1979.

Sherlock Holmes: The Published Apocrypha, with others, edited by Jack Tracy. Boston, Houghton Mifflin, 1980.

The Final Adventures of Sherlock Holmes, edited by Peter Haining. London, W.H. Allen, 1981.

The Edinburgh Stories. Edinburgh, Polygon, 1981.

Uncollected Stories, edited by John Michael Gibson and Richard Lancelyn Green. London, Secker and Warburg, 1982.

The Best Horror Stories of Arthur Conan Doyle, edited by Frank McSherry, Martin H. Greenberg, and Charles G. Waugh. Chicago, Academy, 1989.

Plays

Jane Annie; or, The Good Conduct Prize, with J.M. Barrie, music by Ernest Ford (produced London, 1893). London, Chappell, 1893.

Foreign Policy, adaptation of his own story "A Question of Diplomacy" (produced London, 1893).

Waterloo, adaptation of his story "A Straggler of 15" (as *A Story of Waterloo,* produced Bristol, 1894; London, 1895; as *Waterloo,* produced New York, 1899). London, French, 1907; in *One-Act Plays of To-day,* 2nd series, edited by J. W. Marriott, Boston, Small Maynard, 1926.

Halves, adaptation of the story by James Payn (produced Aberdeen and London, 1899).

Sherlock Holmes, with William Gillette, adaptation of works by Doyle (produced Buffalo and New York, 1899; *Liverpool and London, 1901).*

A Duet (A Duologue) (produced London, 1902). London, French, 1903.

Brigadier Gerard, adaptation of his own stories (produced London and New York, 1906).

The Fires of Fate: A Modern Morality, adaptation of his novel *The Tragedy of Korosko* (produced Liverpool, London and New York, 1909).

The House of Temperley, adaptation of his novel *Rodney Stone* (produced London, 1910).

The Pot of Caviare, adaptation of his own story (produced London, 1910).

The Speckled Band: An Adventure of Sherlock Holmes (produced London and New York, 1910). London, French, 1912.

The Crown Diamond (produced Bristol and London, 1921). Privately printed, 1958.

The Journey, in *The Poems of Arthur Conan Doyle,* 1922.

It's Time Something Happened. New York, Appleton, 1925.

Poetry

Songs of Action. London, Smith Elder, and New York, Doubleday, 1898.

Songs of the Road. London, Smith Elder, and New York, Doubleday, 1911.

The Guards Came Through and Other Poems. London, Murray, 1919; New York, Doran, 1920.

The Poems of Arthur Conan Doyle: Collected Edition. London, Murray, 1922.

Other

The Great Boer War. London, Smith Elder, and New York, McClure, 1900.

The War in South Africa: Its Cause and Conduct. London, Smith Elder, and New York, McClure, 1902.

Works (Author's Edition). London, Smith Elder, 12 vols., and New York, Appleton, 13 vols., 1903.

The Fiscal Question. Hawick, Roxburgh, Henderson, 1905.

An Incursion into Diplomacy. London, Smith Elder, 1906.

The Story of Mr. George Edalji. London, Daily Telegraph, 1907.

Through the Magic Door (essays). London, Smith Elder, 1907; New York, McClure, 1908.

The Crime of the Congo. London, Hutchinson, and New York, Doubleday, 1909.

Divorce Law Reform: An Essay. London, Divorce Law Reform Union, 1909.

Sir Arthur Conan Doyle: Why He Is Now in Favour of Home Rule. London, Liberal Publication Department, 1911.

The Case of Oscar Slater. London, Hodder and Stoughton, 1912; New York, Doran, 1913.

Divorce and the Church, with Lord Hugh Cecil. London, Divorce Law Reform Union, 1913.

Great Britain and the Next War. Boston, Small Maynard, 1914.

In Quest of Truth, Being a Correspondence Between Sir Arthur Conan Doyle and Captain H. Stansbury. London, Watts, 1914.

To Arms! London, Hodder and Staughton, 1914.

The German War. London, Hodder and Stoughton, 1914; New York, Doran, 1915.

Western Wanderings (travel in Canada). New York, Doran, 1915.

The Outlook on the War. London, Daily Chronicle, 1915.

An Appreciation of Sir John French. London, Daily Chronicle, 1916.

A Petition to the Prime Minister on Behalf of Sir Roger Casement. Privately printed, 1916.

A Visit to Three Fronts: Glimpses of British, Italian, and French Lines. London, Hodder and Staughton, and New York, Doran, 1916.

The British Campaign in France and Flanders. London, Hodder and Stoughton, 6 vols., 1916-20; New York, Doran, 6 vols., 1916-20; revised edition, as *The British Campaigns in Europe 1914-1918,* London, Bles, 1 vol., 1928.

The New Revelation. London, Hodder and Stoughton, and New York, Doran, 1918.

The Vital Message (on spiritualism). London, Hodder and Stoughton, and New York, Doran, 1919.

Our Reply to the Cleric. Spiritualists' National Union, 1920.

A Public Debate on the Truth of Spiritualism, with Joseph McCabe. London, Watts, 1920; as *Debate on Spiritualism,* Girard, Kansas, Haldeman Julius, 1922.

Spiritualism and Rationalism. London, Hodder and Stoughton, 1920.

The Wanderings of a Spiritualist. London, Hodder and Stoughton, and New York, Doran, 1921.

Spiritualism: Some Straight Questions and Direct Answers. Manchester, Two Worlds, 1922.

The Case for Spirit Photography, with others. London, Hutchinson, 1922; New York, Doran, 1923.

The Coming of the Fairies. London, Hodder and Stoughton, and New York, Doran, 1922.

Three of Them: A Reminiscence. London, Murray, 1923.

Our American Adventure. London, Hodder and Stoughton, and New York, Doran, 1923.

Our Second American Adventure. London, Hodder and Stoughton, and Boston, Little Brown, 1924.

Memories and Adventures. London, Hodder and Stoughton, and Boston, Little Brown, 1924.

Psychic Experiences. London and New York, Putnam, 1925.

The Early Christian Church and Modern Spiritualism. London, Psychic Bookshop, 1925.

The History of Spiritualism. London, Cassell, 2 vols., and New York, Doran, 2 vols., 1926.

Pheneas Speaks: Direct Spirit Communications. London, Psychic Press, and New York, Doran, 1927.

What Does Spiritualism Actually Teach and Stand For? London, Psychic Bookshop, 1928.

A Word of Warning. London, Psychic Press, 1928.

An Open Letter to Those of My Generation. London, Psychic Press, 1929.

Our African Winter. London, Murray, 1929.

The Roman Catholic Church: A Rejoinder. London, Psychic Press, 1929.

The Edge of the Unknown. London, Murray, and New York, Putnam, 1930.

Works (Crowborough Edition). New York, Doubleday, 24 vols., 1930.

Strange Studies from Life, edited by Peter Ruber. New York, Candlelight Press, 1963.

Arthur Conan Doyle on Sherlock Holmes. London, Favil, 1981.

Essays on Photography, edited by John Michael Gibson and Richard Lancelyn Green. London, Secker and Warburg, 1982.

Letters to the Press, edited by John Michael Gibson and Richard Lancelyn Green. London, Secker and Warburg, 1985.

Editor, *D.D. Home: His Life and Mission,* by Mrs. Dunglas Home. London, Kegan Paul Trench Trubner, 1921.

Editor, *The Spiritualists' Reader.* Manchester, Two Worlds, 1924.

Translator, *The Mystery of Joan of Arc, by Léon Denis.* London, Murray, 1924; New York, Dutton, 1925.

*

Bibliography: *The World Bibliography of Sherlock Holmes and Dr. Watson* by Ronald Burt De Waal, Boston, New York Graphic Society, 1975; *A Bibliography of A. Conan Doyle* by Richard Lancelyn Green and John Michael Gibson, Oxford, Clarendon Press, 1983.

Manuscript Collection: Humanities Research Center, University of Texas, Austin.

Critical Studies (selection): *The Private Life of Sherlock Holmes* by Vincent Starrett, New York, Macmillan, 1933, London, Nicholson and Watson, 1934, revised edition, Chicago, University of Chicago Press, 1960, London, Allen and Unwin, 1961; *Conan Doyle: His Life and Art* by Hesketh Pearson, London, Methuen, 1943, New York, Walker, 1961; *The Life of Sir Arthur Conan Doyle* by John Dickson Carr, London, Murray, and New York, Harper, 1949; *Conan Doyle: A Biography* by Pierre Nordon, London, Murray, 1966, New York, Holt Rinehart, 1967; *Conan Doyle: A Biography of the Creator of Sherlock Holmes* by Ivor Brown, London, Hamish Hamilton, 1972; *The Adventures of Conan Doyle: The Life of the Creator of Sherlock Holmes* by Charles Higham, London, Hamish Hamilton, and New York, Norton, 1976; *The Encyclopedia Sherlockiana* by Jack Tracy, New York, Doubleday, 1977, London, New English Library, 1978; *Conan Doyle: A Biographical Solution* by Ronald Pearsall, London, Weidenfeld and Nicholson, 1977; *Sherlock Holmes and His Creator* by Trevor H. Hall, London, Duckworth, 1978, New York, St. Martin's Press, 1983; *Conan Doyle: Portrait of an Artist* by Julian Symons, London, G. Whizzard, 1979; *Sherlock Holmes: The Man and His World* by H.R.F. Keating, London, Thames and Hudson, and New York, Scribner, 1979; *The Quest for Sherlock Holmes: A Biographical Study of the Early Life of Sir Arthur Conan Doyle* by Owen Dudley Edwards, Edinburgh, Mainstream, 1982, Totowa, New Jersey, Barnes and Noble, 1983; *A Study in Surmise: The Making of Sherlock Holmes* by Michael Harrison, Bloomington, Indiana, Gaslight, 1984; *Arthur Conan Doyle* by Don Richard Cox, New York, Ungar, 1985; *The Complete Guide to Sherlock Holmes* by Michael Hardwick, London, Weidenfeld and Nicolson, 1986; *Sherlock Holmes: A Centenary Celebration* by Allen Eyles, London, Murray, 1986; *Elementary My Dear Watson: Sherlock Holmes Centenary: His Life and Times* by Graham Nown, New York, Ward Lock, 1986; *The Unrevealed Life of Doctor Arthur Conan Doyle: A Study in Southsea* by Geoffrey Stavert, Horndean, Hampshire, Milestone, 1987; *Arthur Conan Doyle* by Jacqueline A. Jaffe, Boston, Twayne, 1987; *The Quest for Sir Arthur Conan Doyle: Thirteen Biographers in Search of a Life* edited by Jon L. Lellenberg, Carbondale, Southern Illinois University Press, 1987.

*   *   *

Although literary history best remembers him as the creator of Sherlock Holmes, Arthur Conan Doyle also produced a considerable body of science fiction, adventure tales, and historical romances, as well as numerous works of nonfiction. In common with many other writers whose works spanned both popular and more traditional fields, Doyle preferred to be remembered for his more "mainstream" writings rather than for his popular fiction. Well before Hugo Gernsback coined the term "science fiction," Doyle felt at ease writing heroic adventure tales, which would later be placed comfortably in this category. It is not surprising that the author who celebrated deductive reasoning should turn his talents in this direction. From an early age, Doyle was fascinated by history and heroics; his medical training instilled in him a respect for the scientific method; and a flamboyant medical colleague, Dr. George Budd, influenced the young Doyle to bear with the sometimes extreme eccentricities of a man of science. It was Dr. Budd who provided the model for Professor George Edward Challenger, whose appearance in most of Doyle's science fiction reflected the increasing importance of the scientist during the late 19th and early 20th centuries.

Professor Challenger is presented as a man of enormous ego, pride, and determination completely dedicated to discovering scientific truth. He first appears in *The Lost World,* a novel that introduces some of the thematic preoccupations common to most of Doyle's science fiction. "There are heroisms all around us waiting to be done," one character declares, and it is in the spirit of heroic adventure that the fledgling newspaper reporter, Edward Malone, joins Challenger, the gentleman/hunter Lord John Roxton, and the skeptical cantankerous Professor Summerlee on a quest to test the validity of Challenger's assertion that prehistoric life exists on an isolated plateau in South America. As the heroes confront a series of physical hazards and witness numerous awe-inspiring sights, it becomes clear that Doyle's intention is to celebrate a sense of wonder, to convey a fascination with the heroic unknown, and above all to assert modern man's supreme position in both past and present worlds. "Our eyes have seen great wonders," Malone reports after the four adventurers, armed with modern weaponry, help the more advanced Indian race on the plateau dramatically assert their dominance over an inferior race of ape-men. "Now upon this plateau the future must ever be for man," the scientist declares.

The superiority of the modern scientific mind is reasserted in "When the World Screamed," a humorous short story again featuring Challenger, this time armed with "scientific" paraphernalia designed to penetrate the earth's crust in order to prove the preposterous contention that "the world upon which we live is itself a living organism" insensible to man's presence. This is the tale of Challenger's efforts to "let the earth know that there is at least one person, George Edward Challenger, who calls for attention—who, indeed, insists upon attention." Not surprisingly, Challenger achieves his goal.

The Poison Belt is a novel that emphasizes Challenger's unselfish devotion to scientific truth. As the sole predictor of the catastrophic approach toward earth of a "poisonous" belt of ether gas, Challenger can philosophically face the prospect of his own demise and the annihilation of mankind because he is so thrilled at the privilege of observing it! Malone, Roxton, Summerlee, and Mrs. Challenger add more believable exclamations of wonderment to those of the scientist. This novel reveals Doyle's delight in juxtaposing the real and unreal, the beautiful and terrible, as Challenger and company regard through a sealed window the apparent end of the world taking place during a beautiful English summer's day. "The Disintegration Machine" is the most serious of the Challenger stories. Here Malone accompanies Challenger as the Professor examines the invention of a "Latvian gentleman named Theodore Nemor . . . a machine of a most extraordinary character which is capable of disintegrating any object placed within its spere of influence." Challenger, quick to recognize the awesome military and "evil" potentialities of this invention, uses it to disintegrate Mr. Nemor himself, who holds the secret to the machine's operation.

The Land of Mist, a lengthy novel featuring Challenger only peripherally, cannot be considered science fiction. This apology for the occult reflects Doyle's own conviction about the validity of occult spiritualism. The work does restate one theme expressed in "The Disintegration Machine" and *The Maracot Deep;* it was Doyle's belief that it is absolutely essential for man's spiritual development to keep pace with his strides in the scientific realm. *The Maracot Deep* takes up this theme against a submarine environment. Here Dr. Maracot and a party of deep sea explorers, including a colorful slang-speaking Yankee handyman called Bill Scanlon, discover the lost colony of Atlantis when their undersea vessel is marooned in an Atlantic trench deeper than any previously explored by man. In an image reminiscent of that employed in *The Poison Belt,* Doyle at first isolates his scientist behind impenetrable glass as the real and unreal, the beautiful and sublime, are contrasted. With a sense of wonder, the explorers discover that, in spite of great scientific advances, Atlantis is doomed by its own limited spiritual development. Only through spiritual self-realization combined with cunning and access to scientific equipment do the heroes rise to the surface in Doyle's final assertion of the superiority of modern scientific man.

Some of Doyle's lesser-known stories, sometimes classified as science fiction, have more in common with the horror genre. In "The Silver Mirror," "The Terror of Blue John Gap," "The Horror of the Heights," and "The Captain of the Polestar" Doyle replaces a sense of wonder with a spine-chilling sense of unearthly dread; he purposely leaves the credibility of the narrators in doubt, undercutting any certainty on the reader's part that each story is "scientifically" believable. "Heroisms" are abundant but it is raw courage, not scientific superiority, that makes these protagonists into heroes.

—Rosemary Herbert

DOZOIS, Gardner (Raymond)

Nationality: American. **Born:** Salem, Massachusetts, 23 July 1947. **Career:** Served as a military journalist, 1966-69. Reader for Dell and Award publishers, and for *Galaxy, If, Worlds of Fantasy,* and *Worlds of Tomorrow,* 1970-73; cofounder, and associate editor, *Isaac Asimov's Science Fiction Magazine,* 1976-77; editor-in-chief since 1984. **Member:** Member of the Advisory Committee, Paley Library, Special Collection Department, Temple University, Philadelphia. **Awards:** Nebula award, 1983, 1985; Hugo award, for editing, 1988, 1989, 1990, 1995; *Locus* award, for editing, 1990. **Agent:** Virginia Kidd, 538 East Harford Street, Milford, Pennsylvania 18337, U.S.A.

SCIENCE FICTION PUBLICATIONS

Novels

Nightmare Blue, with George Alec Effinger. New York, Berkley, 1975; London, Fontana, 1977.
Strangers. New York, Berkley, 1978; London, Hamlyn, 1980.

Short Stories

The Visible Man. New York, Berkley, 1977.
Slow Dancing through Time, with others. Kansas City, Missouri, Ursus Press, 1990.
The Peacemaker. Eugene, Oregon, Pulphouse, 1991.
Geodesic Dreams: The Best Short Fiction of Gardner Dozois. New York, St. Martin's Press, 1992.

OTHER PUBLICATIONS

Other

The Fiction of James Tiptree, Jr. New York, Algol Press, 1977.
Living the Future: You Are What You Eat. Eugene, Oregon, Pulphouse, 1991.

Editor, *A Day in the Life: A Science Fiction Anthology.* New York, Harper, 1972.
Editor, with Jack Dann, *Future Powers: A Science Fiction Anthology.* New York, Random House, 1976.

Editor, *Another World: A Science Fiction Anthology* (for children). Chicago, Follett, 1977.

Editor, *Best Science Fiction Stories of the Year 6-10.* New York, Dutton, 5 vols., 1977-81.

Editor, with Jack Dunn, *Aliens!* New York, Pocket Books, 1980.

Editor, with Jack Dann, *Unicorns!* New York, Ace, 1982.

Editor, with Jack Dann, *Magicats!* New York, Ace, 1984.

Editor, *The Year's Best Science Fiction 1-3.* New York, Bluejay, 3 vols., 1984-86.

Editor, with Jack Dann, *Bestiary!* New York, Ace, 1985.

Editor, with Jack Dann, *Mermaids!* New York, Ace, 1986.

Editor, with Jack Dann, *Sorcerers!* New York, Ace, 1986.

Editor, with Jack Dann, *Demons!* New York, Ace, 1987.

Editor, *The Year's Best Science Fiction, 4th-12th Annual Collection.* New York, St. Martin's Press, 9 vols., 1987-95; *4th Annual Collection* as *The Mammouth Book of Best New Science Fiction,* London, Robinson, 1987; *5th-10th Annual Collections* as *Best New SF 2-7,* 1988-93; *11th Annual Collection* as *The Best New Science Fiction: 8th Annual Collection,* 1994.

Editor, *The Best of Isaac Asimov's Science Fiction Magazine.* New York, Ace, 1988.

Editor, with Susan Casper, *Ripper.* New York, Tor, 1988; as *Jack the Ripper,* London, Futura, 1988.

Editor, with Jack Dann, *Dogtales!* New York, Ace, 1988.

Editor, with Jack Dann, *Seaserpents!* New York, Ace, 1989.

Editor, *Time Travelers from Isaac Asimov's Science Fiction Magazine.* New York, Ace, 1989.

Editor, *Transcendental Tales from Isaac Asimov's Science Fiction Magazine.* Norfolk, Virginia, Donning, 1989.

Editor, with Jack Dann, *Dinosaurs!* New York, Ace, 1990.

Editor, with Jack Dann, *Little People!* New York, Ace, 1991.

Editor, *Isaac Asimov's Aliens.* New York, Ace, 1991.

Editor, *The Legend Book of Science Fiction.* London, Century, 1991; as *Modern Classics of Science Fiction,* New York, St. Martin's Press, 1992.

Editor, with Sheila Williams, *Isaac Asimov's Robots.* New York, Ace, 1991.

Editor, *Isaac Asimov's Mars.* New York, Ace, 1991.

Editor, with Jack Dann, *Magicats II.* New York, Ace, 1991.

Editor, with Jack Dann, *Unicorns II.* New York, Ace, 1992.

Editor, with Sheila Williams, *Isaac Asimov's Earth.* New York, Ace, 1994.

Editor, *Isaac Asimov's War.* New York, Ace, 1993.

Editor, *Isaac Asimov's SF-Lite.* New York, Ace, 1993.

Editor, with Jack Dann, *Dragons!* New York, Ace, 1993.

Editor, with Jack Dann, *Invaders!* New York, Ace, 1993.

Editor, with Mike Resnick, *Future Earths: Under South American Skies.* New York, DAW, 1993.

Editor, with Mike Resnick, *Future Earths: Under African Skies.* New York, DAW, 1993.

Editor, with Jack Dann, *Horses!* New York, Ace, 1994.

Editor, *The Mammouth Book of Contemporary SF Masters.* New York, Ace, 1994.

Editor, with Sheila Williams, *Isaac Asimov's Cyberdreams.* New York, Ace, 1994.

Editor, *Modern Classic Short Novels of Science Fiction.* New York, St. Martin's Press, 1994.

Editor, with Jack Dann, *Angels!* New York, Ace, 1995.

Editor, with Sheila Williams, *Isaac Asimov's Skin Deep.* New York, Ace, 1995.

Editor, with Sheila Williams, *Isaac Asimov's Ghosts.* New York, Ace, 1995.

*

Manuscript Collection: Paskow Collection, Paley Library, Temple University, Philadelphia.

*   *   *

Gardner Dozois is a master short story writer and a brilliant anthologist and editor. In one of his best known stories, "The Peacemaker" (Nebula award winner), Dozois explores a world shaken from civilization by the melting of the polar ice caps. The floods sink the great eastern seacoast cities and leave the survivors in the great American heartland at the mercy of ardent evangelists. As the young boy who is chosen at the story's conclusion learns, everyone must make sacrifices.

The best showcase for Dozois's work is the collection *Slow Dancing through Time,* with collaborations by Jack Dann, Michael Swanwick, Susan Casper, and Jack C. Haldeman II. With the personal introductions to each story, Dozois and his friends not only share the origins of each story, they give critical insight into the creative process itself. The most haunting story in the collection is "The Clowns," in which a disturbed young boy sees clowns murdering people—and only he can see them. This story would make a terrific novel because of the unforgettable, nightmarish metaphors Dozois, Dann, and Casper create. Other innovative stories include "The Gods of Mars," in which the first manned mission to Mars gets a surprise, and "Slow Dancing with Jesus," in which a girl's prom fantasy is wondrously unique.

Dozois's solo short stories are collected in *The Visible Man,* with an admiring introduction by Robert Silverberg. The dozen stories make up a solid progression of Dozois's craftsmanship in the 1970s. From a dazzling story of alien invasion ("Chains of the Sea") to the upbeat ("A Special Kind of Morning") to the naturalistic ("The Last Day of July") to the allegorical ("A Kingdom By the Sea"), Dozois displays a command of the short story form rivaled by few of his contemporaries.

In his only non-collaborative novel, *Strangers,* Dozois presents Joseph Faber, a human from Earth with an alien lover named Liraun, during his tour of the planet Weinnuach. The couple are shunned by the non-human Cian and the human trade community. Faber could care less about his peers, but to win back a measure of respectability for Liraun he consents to attend the House of Tailors where the Cian genetically alter Faber's body so he and Liraun can be interfertile: a necessary condition of Cian marriage rites. In this tremendously sad story, Dozois develops the theme of alienation, and the impossibility of ever knowing another person—hence the title *Strangers.* Through misunderstanding after misunderstanding, Faber and Liraun find themselves on a fated path to doom: the result of their failure to understand each other's culture. Yet, even though *Strangers* ends with death, it also ends with life and hope. This very moving novel is one of the forgotten and ignored classics of the 1970s.

Dozois's other novel, a collaboration with George Alec Effinger called *Nightmare Blue,* is a standard SF adventure novel written in a hard-boiled style Effinger returned to more successfully in his later novels *When Gravity Fails* and *A Fire in the Sun.* The only bright spots in *Nightmare Blue* are Dozois's creation of the alien Corcail Sendijen and the breakneck pacing of the action.

Dozois has gained a reputation as an exceptional anthologist. From such early theme anthologies as *A Day in the Life* to his latest collaborative anthologies with Jack Dann, including *Magicats!,* Dozois packages quality stories with outstanding introductory material. From 1977 to 1981 Dozois edited Dutton's hardcover series *Best Science Fiction Story of the Year Numbers 6-10.* The five volumes Dozois edited were in many ways superior to the paperback SF series edited by Donald Wollheim (DAW) and Terry Carr (Ballantine/Del Rey) in terms of coverage and selection. In 1984, James Frenkel's wonderful but shortlived Bluejay Books selected Dozois to be the editor of *The Year's Best Science Fiction,* a massive 250,000-word volume. With the appearance of the second annual collection in Spring 1985, Neil Barron in *Fantasy Review* proclaimed "Now, the Dozois anthology is the standard." The simultaneous release of the volume in hardcover and paperback made it the definitive "Year's Best SF" anthology. After Bluejay Books folded, Dozois continued his successful series with St. Martin's Press. The latest volume, 12th in the series, contains Dozois's brilliant "Summation" of the year and the usual high quality mix of new and established writers.

One of Dozois's clearest statements on science fiction is included in an anthology of articles he edited called *Writing Science Fiction and Fantasy: Twenty Dynamic Essays by Today's Top Professionals.* In "Living in the Future: You Are What You Eat," Dozois presents the guidelines for writing science fiction that will get published. In part, Dozois's essay becomes the definition of what is necessary for a story to include in order to be considered for *Asimov's Science Fiction,* a leading magazine in the field for which he has won the Hugo for best editor seven times. A master storyteller, anthologist, and editor, Dozois is one of the giants of the contemporary SF scene.

—George Kelley

DRAKE, David A.

Nationality: American. **Born:** Dubuque, Iowa, 24 September 1945. **Education:** University of Iowa, Iowa City, B.A. 1967; Duke University, Durham, North Carolina, J.D. 1972. **Military Service:** Served as an interrogator in the United States Army, 1969-71. **Family:** Married Joanne Kammiller in 1967; one son. **Career:** Assistant town attorney, Chapel Hill, North Carolina, 1972-80; part-time bus driver, Chapel Hill, 1980. Since 1981, full-time writer. **Address:** P.O. Box 904, Chapel Hill, North Carolina, 27514, U.S.A.

SCIENCE FICTION PUBLICATIONS

Novels (series: Car Warriors; Crisis of Empire; The General; Hammer's Slammers; Heroes in Hell; Kelly; Northworld; Thieves' World; Yates)

The Dragon Lord. New York, Berkley, 1979.
Time Safari. New York, Tor, 1982.
Skyripper (Kelly). New York, Tor, 1983.
The Forlorn Hope. New York, Tor, 1984.
Birds of Prey. New York, Baen, 1984.
Cross the Stars (Hammer's Slammers). New York, Tor, 1984.

Killer, with Karl Edward Wagner. New York, Baen, 1985.
Active Measures, with Janet E. Morris. New York, Baen, 1985.
At Any Price (Hammer's Slammers). New York, Baen, 1985; London, Arrow, 1988.
Bridgehead. New York, Tor, 1986.
Ranks of Bronze. New York, Baen, 1986.
Counting the Cost (Hammer's Slammers). New York, Baen, 1987; London, Legend, 1989.
Kill Ratio (Yates), with Janet Morris. New York, Ace, 1987.
Fortress (Kelly). New York, Tor, 1987.
Dagger (Thieves' World). New York, Ace, 1988.
An Honorable Defense, with Thomas T. Thomas (Crisis of Empire). New York, Baen, 1988.
Cluster Command, with W.C. Dietz (Crisis of Empire). New York, Baen, 1989.
The War Machine, with Roger MacBride Allen (Crisis of Empire). New York, Baen, 1989.
The Sea Hag (for young adults). New York, Baen, 1989.
Target (Yates), with Janet Morris. New York, Ace, 1989.
Explorers in Hell, with Janet Morris. New York, Baen, 1989.
Rolling Hot (Hammer's Slammers). New York, Baen, 1989.
Northworld. New York, Ace, 1990.
Surface Action. New York, Ace, 1990.
The Forge, with S.M. Stirling (General). New York, Baen, 1991.
The Hunter Returns (for young adults; adaptation of *Fire-Hunter,* by Jim Kjelgaard). New York, Baen, 1991.
Vengeance (Northworld). New York, Ace, 1991.
The Warrior (Hammer's Slammers). New York, Baen, 1991.
Justice (Northworld). New York, Ace, 1992.
The Hammer, with S.M. Stirling (General). Riverdale, New York, Baen, 1992.
The Square Deal (Car Warriors). New York, Tor, 1992.
Starliner. Riverdale, New York, Baen, 1992.
The Anvil, with S.M. Stirling (General). Riverdale, New York, Baen, 1993.
The Steel, with S.M. Stirling (General). Riverdale, New York, Baen, 1993.
The Sharp End (Hammer's Slammers). Riverdale, New York, Baen, 1993.
Tyrannosaur. New York, Tor, and London, Pan, 1994.
The Voyage. New York, Tor, 1994.
Igniting the Reaches. New York, Ace, 1994.
The Sword, with S.M. Stirling (General). Riverdale, New York, Baen, 1995.
Through the Breach. New York, Ace, 1995.
Arc Riders, with Janet Morris. New York, Warner, 1995.

Short Stories

Hammer's Slammers. New York, Ace, 1979; expanded edition, New York, Baen, 1987.
From the Heart of Darkness. New York, Tor, 1983.
Lacey and His Friends. New York, Baen, 1986.
Vettius and His Friends. New York, Baen, 1989.
The Undesired Princess; and, The Enchanted Bunny, with L. Sprague de Camp. New York, Baen, 1990.
The Military Dimension. New York, Baen, 1991.
Old Nathan. New York, Baen, 1991.
The Jungle, bound with *Clash by Night* by Henry Kuttner. New Yor, Tor, 1991.

OTHER PUBLICATIONS

Other (series: The Fleet; Starhunters)

Harold Coyle's Team Yankee (script adaptation). New York, Berkley, 1989.
Bluebloods (Starhunters). New York, Baen, 1990.

Editor, *Cthulhu, The Mythos and Kindred Horrors,* by Robert E. Howard. New York, Baen, 1987.
Editor, with Bill Fawcett, *The Fleet.* New York, Ace, 1988.
Editor, with Bill Fawcett, *Counterattack* (Fleet). New York, Ace, 1988.
Editor, *Men Hunting Things* (Starhunters). New York, Baen, 1988.
Editor, *Things Hunting Men* (Starhunters). New York, Baen, 1988.
Editor, with Sandra Miesel, *A Separate Star: A Science Fiction Tribute to Rudyard Kipling.* New York, Baen, 1989.
Editor, with Sandra Miesel, *Heads to the Storm.* New York, Baen, 1989.
Editor, with Bill Fawcett, *Breakthrough* (Fleet). New York, Ace, 1989.
Editor, with Martin H. Greenberg and Charles G. Waugh, *Space Gladiators.* New York, Ace, 1989.
Editor, with Martin H. Greenberg and Charles G. Waugh, *Space Infantry.* New York, Ace 1989.
Editor, with Martin H. Greenberg and Charles G. Waugh, *Space Dreadnoughts.* New York, Ace, 1990.
Editor, with Bill Fawcett, *Sworn Allies* (Fleet). New York, Ace, 1990.
Editor, with Martin H. Greenberg and Charles G. Waugh, *The Eternal City.* New York, Baen, 1990.
Editor, with Bill Fawcet, *Total War* (Fleet). New York, Ace, 1990.
Editor, with Bill Fawcett, *Crisis* (Fleet). New York, Ace, 1991.
Editor, with Bill Fawett, *Battlestation.* New York, Ace, 1992.
Editor, with Bill Fawcett, *Vanguard.* New York, Ace, 1993.

*   *   *

Though known primarily for his military science fiction, David A. Drake writes in many genres, from realistic spy novels to young adult fantasy. However, usual genre distinctions are not always easy or useful concerning Drake's fiction. While the spy-adventure novel *Skyripper* introduces extraterrestrials unnecessarily, the aliens are essential and the genres blend seamlessly in *Target* (cowritten with Janet Morris). Drake also mixes political realism and near-future extrapolation in novels such as *Active Measures* (cowritten with Janet Morris) and his stories about law enforcement in a world of constant surveillance (*Lacey and His Friends*). The magic and dragon in *The Dragon Lord* have a scientific rationale, and the alien menace of "The Hunting Ground" would function similarly if it were supernatural. Drake's horror fiction is collected in *From the Heart of Darkness,* but there may be no fiction of his from which horror is absent.

Drake's artistic influences range from classical Latin literature and German expressionistic cinema to Doc Smith's space opera and *Planet Stories. The Sharp End,* a Hammer's Slammers novel, has echoes of Dashiell Hammett's *The Glass Key* and *Red Harvest,* while other novels of his retell classical and Norse myths as science fiction. In paying tribute to his influences and exploring his interests, Drake has helped produce anthologies, such as *A Separate Star* and *Heads to the Storm,* assembled (with Sandra Miesel) in honor of Rudyard Kipling's works. Alone or in partnership,

Drake is an excellent editor of anthologies, many of them on topics for which his fiction is noted.

Drake actively acknowledges his literary debts and is often inspired by a specific author or even work: "Men Like Us," written with Theodore Sturgeon's "Thunder and Roses" in mind; "The Automatic Rifleman," based on Fritz Leiber's "The Automatic Pistol"; and "Than Curse the Darkness," addition to and critique of H.P. Lovecraft's Cthulhu mythos. Three short novels by Drake have been written in response to and published with a reprint of another, earlier, science fiction work. Published with L. Sprague de Camp's *The Undesired Princess,* Drake's "The Enchanted Bunny" would fit in *Unknown* magazine alongside the work it honors. *The Hunter Returns* presents part of the 1951 work *Firehunter,* by Jim Kjelgaard, with new material by Drake. *The Jungle* includes Henry Kuttner's "Clash by Night" from 1958 and Drake's sequel, which is, as Drake himself puts it, not pastiche but "a David Drake story" which is "set in the milieu of" Kuttner's story. Drake's novel *Surface Action* also uses many aspects of Kuttner's planet Venus, as well as the Venus of other early science fiction writers such as Leigh Brackett and Ray Bradbury.

Drake sometimes writes in the cooperative subgenre known as "shared world" collections and novels. For instance, *Dagger,* "Goddess," and "Votary" take place in Robert Lynn Asprin and Lynn Abbey's Thieves' World, and "Springs Eternal" is in the collaborative afterlife of the Hell books. Drake himself created and provides plot outlines for the Crisis of Empire series, primarily science fantasy adventure, and with Bill Fawcett created a sharable universe in *The Fleet* and its continuation, the Battlestation series. He has written novels based on games (video and otherwise), including *The Square Deal,* set in the world of Steve Jackson Games's popular Car Wars—showing that such novels can be written with craftsmanship and flair, fiction rather than mere product.

The greatest biographical influence on Drake's fiction is his army service in Vietnam and Cambodia. Drake's best-known fiction concerns soldiers and law officers, often mercenaries, in near or far futures. This military science fiction generally fulfills its subgenre, in both weaknesses and strengths. Sometimes condemned as pro-war because of its celebration of military virtues and excitement, the fiction is too grim and realistic to truly advocate any organized violence. Throughout his career, Drake has written many short stories concerning war, set in Vietnam, or featuring veterans as protagonists; many of these are collected in *The Military Dimension* (reissued, with three more stories, as *The Military Dimension II*), including a rare piece of realistic fiction that he wrote in 1971. Drake also scripted the comic book adaptation of Harold Coyle's *Team Yankee,* set in Vietnam.

Drake's major science fiction series presents Colonel Alois Hammer and his Slammers, 30th-century mercenaries hired by numerous war-torn planets. The original short stories were collected in *Hammer's Slammers,* with explanatory interludes and a new concluding story. This was followed by three novels (*Counting the Cost, Rolling Hot,* and *The Sharp End*) and two collections of a short novel and a novelette apiece (*At Any Price* and *The Warrior*). Drake uses the same fictional universe to tell different stories and explore various character-types; the works are primarily about action and the kind of men—and, refreshingly, women—who choose it. The future background is interesting, especially in the implied economics and political science, though sometimes peripheral to the action.

Cross the Stars adds to our understanding of the Slammers, but its main point is a conscious imitation of Homer's *Odyssey,* as ex-

Slammer Don Slade tries to reach his home world Tethys and set it in order. Sometimes the novel follows its model too rigorously, but the mythic elements are transformed to science fiction with creativity and depth. Similarly, *The Voyage* is based on the story of Jason and the Argonauts, as seen in the *Iliad* and other sources; here Drake has altered the action more, so the book is stronger as science fiction in its own right, while showing the same speculative use of mythic material.

Cross the Stars and *The Voyage* also contain some of Drake's best writing, including exploration of character and worldbuilding. The same quality is apparent in the Northworld series, similarly based on the Norse Eddas: *Northworld, Vengeance,* and *Justice.* Set in a multiverse in which levels occasionally interpenetrate, these books depict the psychological dangers of godlike power and the fierce values that maintain in survival-level cultures. *Vengeance* is structured with two simultaneous plots, both starring the protagonist, Nils Hansen.

Other military science fiction by Drake includes *The Forlorn Hope,* featuring Slammers-like mercenaries, which was to have begun another series, although those plans were canceled. The General series (cowritten with S.M. Stirling) demonstrates three elements common in Drake's science fiction: a young man (often of prestigious background) learning to be a soldier and/or asserting leadership; uniting an empire (usually interstellar) or keeping together one that is falling apart; and the inevitable problems and dangers posed by government and some of the officials it attracts. Recently, Drake and Ben Ohlander have begun a new series of military science fiction, set in the world of a video game, *Terra Nova.*

However, it would be wrong to categorize Drake narrowly as a writer of military science fiction. In works such as his charming and eerie young adult novel, *The Sea Hag,* or his novelette "Travellers," Drake shows more—and often more likable—kinds of people in various situations. The stories in *Old Nathan* depict the Cunning Man of the title, able to talk to animals and work magic. The tone is unique, neither pure horror nor the light, pretty magic of too much fantasy; in its knowledge of and respect for folk traditions, it is clearly influenced by the fiction of Manly Wade Wellman, a close friend of Drake's to whom the book is dedicated.

Drake also works well within the subgenre of time travel fiction. *Bridgehead,* apparently a straight story of time travel, is an ambitious and mostly successful study of technology and human relations—also the concern of *Time Safari,* a fixup of three novellas about time-traveling hunters, which features impeccable historical (or prehistorical) detail and one of Drake's more fully realized female characters. (*Tyrannosaur* contains parts two and three of *Time Safari,* slightly rewritten, and a new opening section featuring a T. Rex that escapes in the protagonist's present-day world.) *ARC Riders* (cowritten with Janet Morris) explores both time travel and alternate history with ingenuity and thoroughness.

Drake's undergraduate major was history, and history provides rich materials for Drake's fiction, even when the stories are set in the future. *Igniting the Reaches,* for instance, is based on the early life of Sir Francis Drake and his Elizabethan contemporaries, combining trade, piracy, and diplomacy on an interstellar scale; Drake continues that story in *Through the Breach* and *Fireships.* Some of Drake's best fiction grows out of his love for, and deep understanding of, ancient Rome. In works including *Killer* (cowritten with Karl Edward Wagner), *The Dragon Lord,* and some of his short stories (many in *Vettius and His Friends*), Drake demonstrates his knowledge of historical settings and ability to present them, especially the Roman empire from prime to decay. The science fic-

tion or fantasy threat and historical setting mesh well in these works, and in *Birds of Prey* they also allow especially noteworthy development of theme and character. *Ranks of Bronze,* also noteworthy, is a bildungsroman about an officer, captured and forced to fight on alien worlds, who learns the meaning and value of being a Roman.

Primarily considering himself a storyteller, Drake provides involving fiction. His strong yet unobtrusive prose makes him one of the best action writers in science fiction; his ability with plot has grown steadily since *The Dragon Lord* and is now another great strength. In writing or in background research, Drake's "overriding concern," as friend and fellow-writer Karl Edward Wagner wrote, "remains *get it right.*"

—Bernadette Lynn Bosky

DREW, Wayland

Nationality: Canadian. **Born:** Oshawa, 12 September 1932. **Education:** Oshawa Collegiate and Vocational Institute and at University of Toronto. **Family:** Married Gwendolyn Drew, 18 October 1957; one son, three daughters. **Agent:** Amanda Urban, International Creative Management, 40 West 57th Street, New York, New York 10019, U.S.A.

SCIENCE FICTION PUBLICATIONS

Novels (series: Erthring)

Dragonslayer: A Novel (novelization of screenplay). London, Fontana, and New York, Ballantine, 1981.
The Erthring Cycle. Garden City, New York, Doubleday, 1986.
  The Memoirs of Alcheringia. New York, Ballantine, 1984.
  The Gaian Expedient. New York, Ballantine, 1985.
  The Master of Norriya. New York, Ballantine, 1985.
*batteries Not Included: A Novel (novelization of screenplay). New York, Berkley, 1987; London, Grafton, 1988.
Willow: A Novel (novelization of screenplay). New York, Ballantine, and London, Sphere, 1988.

OTHER PUBLICATIONS

Novels

The Wabeno Feast. Toronto, Anansi, 1973.
Corvette Summer: A Novel (novelization of screenplay). New York, New American Library, 1978.
Halfway Man. Ottawa, Ontario, Oberon Press, 1989.

Other

The Nature of Fish, with others. Toronto, Natural Science of Canada, 1974.
The Nature of Mammals, with others. Toronto, Natural Science of Canada, 1974.

Superior: The Haunted Shore, with Bruce Littlejohn. Toronto,
Gage, and New York, Beaufort, 1975; revised edition,
Willowdale, Ontario, Firefly Books, 1994.
Brown's Weir (travel), with Gwendolyn Drew. Ottawa, Ontario,
Oberon Press, 1983.
A Sea Within: The Gulf of St. Lawrence, with Bruce Littlejohn.
Toronto, McClelland and Stewart, 1984.

*   *   *

Wayland Drew's novelization of the film *Dragonslayer* was
largely unheralded. Although he had written previous novels, this
was his first byline in the fields of SF and fantasy. Any inventiveness or interest in the story could be attributed to the original
screenwriters. It was another three years before Drew published
his first science fiction novel, although his fine adaptation of the
story of a dying wizard's battle against the last dragon in the world
was artfully written, and later reprinted with no mention of the movie
upon which it was based. The visual impact of the special effects
is missing, but Drew's highly descriptive language conveys much
of the sense of wonder and power of the final sequences.

The Memoirs of Alcheringia is the first volume in the Erthring
Cycle, a trilogy published between 1984 and 1986. This panoramic
story is set within a post-holocaust world, in which descendants of
the survivors have fragmented into a number of more or less primitive societies. A rigid code of behavior born of the frightening events
that destroyed civilization prohibits any return to the high technology of the past. More ominously, there exists a surviving bastion
of scientific knowledge that secretly works behind the scenes to
prevent such a resurgence. At the same time, they hope to lead the
barbaric masses gradually toward a less hazardous and bellicose
existence. The internal inconsistency of the two conflicting motives
is the source of most of the plot conflict, both in their relationship
to the rest of the planet, and as the driving force in their internal
bickering. The primary protagonist is a member of one of these
primitive tribes, gifted, or perhaps cursed, with a profound curiosity about the nature of his world and a determination that life should
be easier. What should have been a routine raiding-party marking
the transition from childhood to adult life, is actually the preamble
to a series of events that will alter both the man himself and his
society.

The story continues in *The Gaian Expedient.* Yggdrasil, the scientific colony in control, is beginning to experience problems of
its own. Despite efforts to conserve resources, the physical situation in their base is deteriorating rapidly. The dwindling supplies
and energy sources cause increasing tension among the scientific
community as well, threatening a schism within their ranks. Frustrated by the intransigence of the people they attempt to help, one
faction advocates using coercive and manipulative techniques to
play one group against another, even though such intervention contradicts their code of conduct. Meanwhile, the protagonist has grown
increasingly disenchanted with the situation, determined that the
tribes should enjoy freedom from external intervention.

The situation reaches a climax in *The Master of Norriya.* Despite its dominating technology, Yggdrasil is no longer capable of
controlling the tribes; rebellion and internal conflict threaten to destroy any trace of stability. They have also perverted their own doctrines, and are reduced to using conscripted labor to deal with the
increasingly strenuous efforts required to maintain the colony's
physical and functional integrity. Despite their efforts to remain in
power, a counterbalancing force has arisen among the nomads, led

by an intelligent but discontented outcast, and an unlikely collection of rebels, misfits, and the shunned mutants. Although stylistically the trilogy is an adventure story, and quite entertainingly done,
there is also a clear statement of Drew's acknowledgment of the
indomitability of the human spirit and its perverse need to advance
at its own pace and in its own fashion, rather than at the dictates of
a self-proclaimed authority.

Unfortunately, Drew's only subsequent writing in the field consists of two more film novelizations. **batteries Not Included* is an
amusing, sentimental, and not entirely credible, story of some mechanical lifeforms, and the impact their presence has on the residents of an apartment building. *Willow* is another fantasy-quest
novel, which follows the adventures of a diminutive protagonist
seeking to protect an infant from the minions of an evil sorceress-
queen. Both are creditable adaptations of the screen plays, the stories themselves are well constructed, but obviously there is little
evidence of Drew's own imaginative powers in either.

—Don D'Ammassa

DRUMM, D.B. *See* NAHA, Ed.

DUANE, Diane

Nationality: American. **Agent:** Donald A. Maass, 64 West 84th
Street, Apartment 3-A, New York, New York 10024. **Address:** c/
o Pocket Books, The Simon and Schuster Building, 1230 Avenue
of the Americas, New York, New York 10020, U.S.A.

SCIENCE FICTION PUBLICATIONS

Novels (series: Epic Tales of the Five; Guardians of the Three;
Space Cops; Star Trek; Wizardry)

The Door into Fire (Epic Tales). New York, Dell, 1979; London,
Magnum, 1981.
The Wounded Sky (Star Trek). New York, Pocket Books, 1983;
London, Firecrest, 1986.
So You Want to Be a Wizard? (for children). New York, Delacorte
Press, 1983; London, Corgi, 1991.
The Door into Shadow (Epic Tales). New York, Bluejay, 1984:
London, Corgi, 1991.
My Enemy, My Ally (Star Trek). New York, Pocket Books, 1984;
London, Titan, 1989.
Deep Wizardry (for children). New York, Delacorte Press, 1985;
London, Corgi, 1991.
The Romulan Way, with Peter Morwood (Star Trek). New York,
Pocket Books, 1987; London, Titan, 1987.
Spock's World: A Novel (Star Trek). New York, Pocket Books,
1988; London, Simon and Schuster, 1989.

Keeper of the City, with Peter Morwood (Guardians). New York, Bantam, 1989.

Doctor's Orders (Star Trek). New York, Pocket Books, 1990; London, Titan, 1990.

High Wizardry (for children). New York, Delacorte Press, 1990; London, Corgi, 1991.

Support Your Local Wizard (omnibus). New York, Guild American, 1990.

Mindblast, with Peter Morwood. (Space Cops). New York, Avon, 1991.

High Moon, with Peter Morwood (Space cops). New York, AvonNova, 1992.

Kill Station, with Peter Morwood (Space cops). New York, AvonNova, 1992.

Dark Mirror (Star Trek). New York, Pocket Books, and London, Simon and Schuster, 1993.

The Door into Sunset (Epic Tales). London, Corgi, 1992; New York, Tor, 1993.

A Wizard Abroad (Wizardry; for children). London, Corgi, 1993.

SeaQuest DSV: The Novel, with Peter Morwood. London, Millennium, and New York, Ace, 1993.

Spider-Man: The Venom Factor. New York, Byron Preiss Multimedia, 1994.

*   *   *

Diane Duane entered science fiction by the *Star Trek* route, and she is still writing for that remarkable phenomenon that has taken on a life of its own. However, she also writes fantasy, and her major claim to serious consideration rests on two excellent fantasy novels, *The Door into Fire* and *The Door into Shadow.* They are half of a projected tetralogy which, we are told, is to be focused on the adventures and development of five main characters: the humans Herewiss, Freelorn, Segnbora, and, presumably, the fire elemental Sunspark and the dragon Hasai.

Like too many fantasies, these books are set in a geographically isolated imaginary land with a quasi-feudal society and plenty of magic. The adventures apparently are all going to culminate in crises leading to passage to a higher state for the various major characters, and they have added import as part of the struggle of good against evil. Duane's achievement is to have transcended this hackneyed scenario, despite a weakness for excessively happy endings.

She does this by setting constraints upon her universe. The Goddess who created it is good, but neither omnipotent nor omniscient. The presence of evil, which manifests itself as Shadow, is the result of Her attempt in Her aspect as Maiden to create a closed universe without evil, a task which in Her other aspects as Mother and Hag She knows to be impossible. This means that the Goddess really does need human aid in the struggle against Shadow.

The power with which the Goddess opposes Shadow is Fire, life-force which, when present in an individual in large enough quantity, can be used for extra-sensory perception and to perform ordinary and extraordinary acts. Like all power, it has its price: if not used, it is lost; if used, it shortens the life of its user. It is entirely distinct from magic, which is no more than a kind of technology based on the affinities of words to the physical world. As with all technology, it uses energy. Given the choice, it is often less tiring for a magician to use nonmagical means to an end.

None of the Goddess's aspects, which are sometimes at odds, is entirely benign. Those who ask a boon may get it; but if they presume too much, they will bitterly regret getting exactly what they

requested. All of this is known to Her followers because the Goddess makes Herself manifest to everyone individually at least once in a lifetime. Hence there is a great store of anecdotal information from which it is possible to learn Her will, particularly with respect to sexual ethics and the proper social order, where the systems propounded deserve to be studied for their intrinsic interest.

Given this context, Herewiss, the first male in generations to have a usable amount of Fire, *must* learn to use it. Segnbora, with too much to control by normal means, *must* find a way to control it. Freelorn, whose hereditary duties require him to perform ceremonies binding vast powers, *must* overthrow the usurper of his throne in order to perform them; and the others are bound to help him, although the imperatives that drive Sunspark and Hasai are not yet entirely clear. Should any of them fall, the result would be unimaginable disaster.

Duane is an elegant universe-maker. The world in which her characters live is no mere backdrop. It informs the actions of her characters, giving them motives beyond those which can be ascribed simply to human or non-human nature. Her treatments of magic and religion, here for once in a beneficent relation to each other, are particularly well thought out. Moreover, she does not tell, she shows. Such integration is rare, especially in sword-and-sorcery stories. The result is vivid, entertaining writing that deserves study both for its technical excellence and the ideas it contains.

—William M. Schuyler, Jr.

DUNCAN, Dave

Nationality: Canadian. **Born:** Scotland, in 1933. **Education:** University of St. Andrews, Fife. **Family:** Married; three children. **Career:** Petroleum geologist, 1955-86. **Awards:** Canadian Science Fiction and Fantasy (Aurora) award, 1990. **Agent:** Richard Curtis & Associates, 171 East 74th Street, New York, New York 10021. **Address:** Box 1, Site 13, SS 3, Calgary, Alberta T3C 3N9 Canada.

SCIENCE FICTION PUBLICATIONS

Novels (series: Man of His Word; A Handful of Men; Seventh Sword)

A Rose-Red City. New York, Ballantine, 1987; London, Legend, 1989.

Shadow. New York, Ballantine, 1987; London, Legend, 1989.

The Reluctant Swordsman (Seventh Sword). New York, Ballantine, 1988; London, Legend, 1990.

The Coming of Wisdom (Seventh Sword). New York, Ballantine, 1988; London, Legend, 1990.

The Destiny of the Sword (Seventh Sword). New York, Ballantine, 1988; London, Legend, 1991.

West of January. New York, Ballantine, 1989.

Magic Casement (Man of His Word). New York, Ballantine, 1990.

Strings. New York, Ballantine, 1990.

Faery Lands Forlorn (Man of His Word). New York, Ballantine, 1991.

Hero! New York, Ballantine, 1991.

Perilous Seas (Man of His Word). New York, Ballantine, 1991.

Emperor and Clown (Man of His Word). New York, Ballantine, 1992.
The Reaving Road. New York, Ballantine, 1992.
The Cutting Edge (Handful of Men). New York, Ballantine, 1992.
Upland Outlaws (Handful of Men). New York, Ballantine, 1993.
The Stricken Field (Handful of Men). New York, Ballantine, 1993.
The Living God (Handful of Men). New York, Ballantine, 1994.
The Hunter's Haunt. New York, Ballantine, 1995.
The Cursed. New York, Ballantine, 1995.

* * *

Dave Duncan made his debut in 1987 with *A Rose-Red City.* Mera is a city that exists outside normal time and space, administered by the mysterious Oracle, home to heroes from both the past and the future. Within Mera, no one ages, and it provides sanctuary from enemies both mundane and even supernatural. A team of its residents are sent on a mission to rescue a woman from a time roughly our own, but they must contend with two major problems. First, several inhuman creatures are determined to abort the rescue; second, the woman will not allow herself to be rescued unless her children can go as well, and children are never admitted to Mera. An original mix of magic and the real world, and a very auspicious first novel.

The heroic figure is repeated over and over in Duncan's subsequent novels. In *Shadow,* a young man must reconcile his own dreams of destiny with the requirements of his society, and finds a way to satisfy both. Set on a colony world which has lost much of the knowledge necessary to support a high civilization, young men dream of being one of the elite selected to ride the skies on giant eagles. The protagonist finds his dreams in danger when he is appointed bodyguard to a member of a noble family, then subsequently framed as a traitor. There follows a somewhat predictable recounting of his efforts to clear his name, but the charm of the book is in the elaborately described culture against which these events take place.

Duncan's next work was "The Seventh Sword" trilogy. *The Reluctant Swordsman* starts with an unlikely hero from our own world, transported to another where a sarcastically threatening godling informs him that he must serve as swordsman for the goddess. With a new, powerful body, Wallie Smith rises to the occasion, but the dangers he faces in the opening volume pale to insignificance in *The Coming of Wisdom,* which introduces a group of evil sorcerers whose powers may exceed even those of the goddess. In the concluding volume, *The Destiny of the Sword,* everything appears to have gone wrong and almost certain defeat stares him in the face. The trilogy is in many ways a cliché; we know from the outset that the hero will triumph in the end. Duncan has, however, embellished the familiar theme with well written, crisply narrated adventures.

West of January is in many ways Duncan's best novel. Once again we have a primitive colony world, this one peopled almost entirely with semi-nomadic tribes who relocate at the instruction of the Angels, mysterious people who retain a higher level of technology. The protagonist is another reluctant hero, this time a young man cast out of his tribe after his father is killed, who wanders the planet trying to discover a place where he belongs, and incidentally uncovering a number of secrets hidden from his people. This is certainly Duncan's most inventive work to date, unfolding mystery upon mystery as he reveals his world to us.

Duncan's next book, *Strings,* varied somewhat from his usual style. Our attention is split between two main characters this time, a young woman whose extrasensory powers are of extraordinary value to a team exploring potential colony worlds, and a young man involved in murder and politics. The blend of intrigue and adventure is well-balanced and effective.

Hero! was something of a disappointment. Vaun is a man who overcame the poverty of his background to rise to a high position in the Space Patrol, only to discover that the Patrol has grown corrupt and is often in league with bands of criminals. At the same time, a major interstellar conflict has just come to an uncertain end, but a mysterious ship on a collision course with a settled world may be the last gasp of the defeated Brotherhood, or the first blow in a renewed war, or perhaps something even less predictable. This time, however, Duncan's efforts to make Vaun into a heroic figure are too heavy-handed; he is so competent and authoritative that we just cannot accept him as a real human being.

The Magic Casement started a new series, "A Man of His Word." Duncan provides a new, unlikely hero, Rap the stableboy. When his king is stricken with an apparently fatal disease, Rap must journey to another land where Princess Inos has gone to improve her education. Naturally, a host of monsters are prepared to challenge his right to pass. Although he triumphs, at the last moment the Princess is kidnapped into another world, and when he attempts to follow, in *Faery Lands Forlorn,* he finds himself faced with a fresh struggle. The story continued in *Perilous Seas* and came to a rousing conclusion with *Emperor and Clown.*

Having apparently decided that fantasy was a more promising genre than science fiction, Duncan inaugurated a new series with *The Cutting Edge.* A mythical kingdom is on the verge of collapse because of a weak ruler and the machinations of an evil sorcerer who is using magical bonds to forge an army of enslaved sorcerers to carry out his will. A typically reluctant hero becomes embroiled in the conflict, and survives battles, traps, assassins, and magical attacks in the opening volume, then through *The Upland Outlaws, The Stricken Field,* and finally *The Living God,* wherein the villain is finally defeated and the world saved for the forces of good. Some of the adventures are cleverly plotted and the story is generally entertaining, but the series is simply another version of an all too familiar fantasy cliché with little new to recommend it. A stand-alone novel, *The Reaver Road,* also a fantasy, is another derivative adventure story, though less formulaic than the other recent Duncan novels.

Duncan is a potentially talented writer of adventure stories, occasionally colored with mild humor, who appears to have settled into a regular pattern of routine fantasies that are competent and entertaining, but only occasionally enlivened by the enthusiasm evident in his earlier work. Although he has confined himself almost entirely to novel-length works up until the present, his short story "A Boy at Heart" is also of interest.

—Don D'Ammassa

DUNCAN, David

Nationality: American. **Born:** Billings, Montana, 17 February 1913. **Education:** University of Montana, Missoula, B.A. 1935. **Family:** Married Elaine Sulliger in 1940; three daughters. **Career:** Personnel examiner, Department of Agriculture, Washington, D.C., 1936; social worker, California State Relief Administration, Fresno,

1936-40; manager of California housing project, Farm Security Administration, 1941-43; field director in California and Nevada, American Red Cross, 1943-44; labor economist, National Labor Bureau, San Francisco, 1944-46. Since 1946, freelance writer.

SCIENCE FICTION PUBLICATIONS

Novels

Dark Dominion. New York, Ballantine, 1954; London, Heinemann, 1955.
Beyond Eden. New York, Ballantine, 1955; as *Another Tree in Eden,* London, Heinemann, 1956.
Occam's Razor. New York, Ballantine, 1957; London, Gollancz, 1958.

OTHER PUBLICATIONS

Novels

Remember the Shadows. New York, McBride, 1944.
The Shade of Time. New York, Random House, 1946; London, Grey Walls Press, 1949.
The Bramble Bush. New York, Macmillan, 1948; London, Sampson Low, 1949; as *Sweet, Low, and Deadly,* New York, Mercury, 1949.
The Madrone Tree. New York, Macmillan, 1949; London, Gollancz, 1950; as *Worse Than Murder,* New York, Pocket Books, 1954.
The Serpent's Egg. New York, Macmillan, 1950.
None But My Foe. New York, Macmillan, 1950.
Wives and Husbands. Cleveland, World, 1952.
The Trumpet of God. New York, Doubleday, 1956.
Yes, My Darling Daughters. New York, Doubleday, 1959; London, Heinemann, 1960.
The Long Walk Home from Town. New York, Doubleday, 1964.

Plays

Screenplays: *Sangaree,* with Frank Moss, 1953; *Jivaro,* with Winston Miller, 1954; *The White Orchid,* with Reginald LeBorg, 1955; *The Monster That Challenged the World,* with Patricia Fielder, 1957; *The Black Scorpion,* with Robert Blees and Paul Yawitz, 1957; *The Thing That Couldn't Die,* 1958; *Monster on the Campus,* 1958; *The Leech Woman,* with Ben Pivar and Francis Rosenwald, 1960; *The Time Machine,* 1960; *Fantastic Voyage,* with others, 1966.

Television Plays: *The Human Factor* (*The Outer Limits* series), and for *Telephone Time, My Three Sons, National Velvet, It's a Man's World, Higgins, Daniel Boone, Studio One, The High Chaparral,* and *Men into Space* series.

*   *   *

David Duncan is one of the most accomplished stylists to have worked in science fiction and fantasy, yet he is an almost forgotten figure. The reason for this is that, like Edgar Pangborn's and Ray Bradbury's, his ideas are not often very original and his science is sometimes bizarre; his method is that of the mystery story—one in which the enigma is left unexplained for a good deal of the book, and when the problem is solved the story simply ends. The unknown is not brought on stage for very long, and its consequences are left undeveloped. Yet there are so many satisfactions of characterization, background and description, social observation, ideas about human life and destiny, that one is tempted to dismiss the seeming flaws. Duncan is an elegant, poetic wordsmith who involves the reader completely.

Dark Dominion is an overwhelming emotional experience that leaves the reader drained. The story is about the building, in secret, of a military space station that will dominate the earth. We are shown the effects of this terrible purpose on the lives of the scientists involved, as they struggle to complete the project, and later to change its meaning for the world. The novel is filled with moments of great beauty, and they are worth the speculative and scientific lapses. The classic novels of the 1950s do not surpass this one in skill, even when they are superior in ideas and originality. "Duncan's forte is people," wrote Damon Knight (in *In Search of Wonder,* 1967); "he sees them with an inquiring, ironic, compassionate but unsentimental eye. At his best, the characters he draws are sharply individual, each one believable and distinct from every other. He fills up the scene with moving portraits, and their intricate mutual relationships, effortlessly handled, make his book." This is a lesson that better writers—those whose thinking and conceptual development, even their stories, are better—have not learned: that to produce a valuable piece of fiction, including SF, a writer must show everything as belonging to the awareness of characters; ideas as well as feelings must be seen sticking to the insides of people.

Occam's Razor is a sketchy story, but it also has the compelling portraits and personal interactions of *Dark Dominion.* The story details the accidental visit of two beings from a parallel world, whose sudden appearance causes much misunderstanding; but the novel ends where it should begin—namely, in the effects of these people's presence on our world, after this fact is discovered. We are given only half the story, that of the events leading up to the solution of the mystery concerning the identity of the two visitors. Still, this is a persuasive and humane story. *Beyond Eden* is more an all-around success than the other two novels, though it lacks the eloquence of *Dark Dominion.* Set in the 1950s atmosphere of the McCarthy hearings and the Oppenheimer persecution, the story deals with a fascinating water project in California. The enterprise discovers a new kind of water that might transform human nature, though at first it seems to kill people, embarrassing the chief scientist who already has a bad past to live down. Again, the story ends where the confrontation with the unknown might lead to new understandings and a set of problems of a higher order.

One might also argue that Duncan chose not to explore beyond "mere mystery"—that his sense of human limits prevented him from inventing glib "understandings" of the kind demanded by so many SF readers. Duncan chose to stay closer to the present. His problem does suggest a prescription: truly great science fiction demands that one be a fine writer with all the skills of a contemporary novelist and possess the intellect necessary to speculate beyond the point of "mere mystery," surface drama, and obvious topicality.

David Duncan drew enthusiastic reviews for his novels. Groff Conklin called him "a richly endowed mind" whose work should not be missed. Anthony Boucher, Theodore Sturgeon, P. Schuyler Miller, and others ranked his books with the best of their years. In a field whose main problem is a lack of the authenticity that belongs to a literature won from experience, Duncan has the virtue of seeming very authentic, despite his supposed shortcomings. His novels are as he intended them to be, and their virtues are the short-comings of most SF. In the only statement about his science fiction, Duncan wrote: "To me the great virtue of the science-fiction story doesn't reside in its elaborate gadgets and twistings of time and space—although these can be majestically entertaining—but in its possibilities for analysis of man and the social order." He saw SF as a literature of critical possibilities, and for this he deserves serious attention.

—George Zebrowski

DUNSANY, Lord (Edward John Moreton Drax Plunkett, 18th Baron Dunsany)

Nationality: Irish. **Born:** London, 24 July 1878; succeeded to the barony, 1899. **Education:** Cheam School, Surrey; Eton College, Berkshire; then privately tutored; Royal Military Academy, Sandhurst, Surrey. **Military Service:** Served as a 2nd lieutenant in the Coldstream Guards in Gibraltar and in the Boer War, 1899-1902; captain in the Royal Inniskilling Fusiliers during World War I; wounded in the Dublin Easter Rebellion, 1916; served in the Home Guard during World War II. **Family:** Married Lady Beatrice Child-Villiers in 1904; one son. Lived at Dunstall Priory, Kent, and Dunsany Castle, County Meath. **Career:** Byron professor of English literature, University of Athens, 1940-41. D.Litt.: University of Dublin, 1939. Fellow, Royal Society of Literature, and Royal Geographical Society; member, Irish Academy of Letters. **Died:** 25 October 1957.

SCIENCE FICTION PUBLICATIONS

Novels

The Chronicles of Rodriguez. London, Putnam, 1922; as *Don Rodriguez: Chronicles of Shadow Valley,* New York, Putnam, 1922.
The King of Elfland's Daughter. London and New York, Putnam, 1924.
The Charwoman's Shadow. London and New York, Putnam, 1926.
The Blessing of Pan. London and New York, Putnam, 1926.
The Curse of the Wise Woman. London, Heinemann, and New York, Longman, 1933.
If I Were Dictator: The Pronouncements of the Grand Macaroni. London, Methuen, 1934.
My Talks with Dean Spanley. London, Heinemann, and New York, Putnam, 1936.
The Strange Journeys of Colonel Polders. London, Jarrolds, 1950.
The Last Revolution: A Novel. London and New York, Jarrolds, 1951.

Short Stories (series: Jorkens)

The Gods of Pegana. London, Elkin Matthews, 1905; Boston, Luce, 1916.
Time and the Gods. London, Heinemann, 1906; Boston, Luce, 1913.

The Sword of Welleran and Other Stories. London, G. Allen, 1908; Boston, Luce, 1916; revised and enlarged as *The Sword of Welleran and Other Tales of Enchantment,* New York, Devon-Adair, 1954.
The Fortress Unvanquishable, Save for Sacnoth. Sheffield, The School of Art Press, 1910.
A Dreamer's Tales. London, G. Allen, and Boston, Luce, 1910; as *A Dreamer's Tales and Other Stories,* New York, Boni and Liveright, 1919.
The Book of Wonder: A Chronicle of Little Adventures at the Edge of the World. London, Heinemann, 1912; Boston, Luce, 1913; with *Time and the Gods,* New York, Boni and Liveright, 1918.
Selections from the Writings of Lord Dunsany. Churchtown, Dundrum, Cuala Press, 1912; Boston, Little Brown, 1916.
Fifty-One Tales. London, Elkin Matthews, and New York, Kennerley, 1915; as *The Food of Death: Fifty-One Tales,* Hollywood, Newcastle, 1974.
Carcassone. Boston, Luce, 1916(?).
Tales of Wonder. London, Elkin Matthews, 1916; as *The Last Book of Wonder,* Boston, Luce, 1916.
Tales of Three Hemispheres. Boston, Luce, 1919; London, Fisher Unwin, 1920.
Why the Milkman Shudders When He Perceives the Dawn. Fostoria, Ohio, Sowers, 1925.
The Travel Tales of Mr. Joseph Jorkens. London and New York, Putnam, 1931.
Mr. Jorkens Remembers Africa. London, Heinemann, 1934; as *Jorkens Remembers Africa,* New York, Longman, 1934.
Jorkens Has a Large Whiskey. London, Putnam, 1940.
The Fourth Book of Jorkens. London, Jarrolds, 1947; Sauk City, Wisconsin, Arkham House, 1948.
The Man Who Ate the Phoenix. London, Jarrolds, 1949.
Jorkens Borrows Another Whiskey. London, M. Joseph, 1954.
At the Edge of the World (selections), edited by Lin Carter. New York, Ballantine, 1970.
Beyond the Fields We Know (selections), edited by Lin Carter. New York and London, Ballantine, 1972.
Gods, Men, and Ghosts: The Best Supernatural Fiction of Dunsany (selections), edited by E.F. Bleiler. New York, Dover, 1972.
Over the Hills and Far Away (selections), edited by Lin Carter. New York, Ballantine, 1974.
The Ghosts of the Heaviside Layer, and Other Fantasms. Philadelphia, Owlswick Press, 1980.
The Ghosts. Mankato, Minnesota, Creative Education, 1993.

OTHER PUBLICATIONS

Novels

Up in the Hills. London, Heinemann, and New York, Putnam, 1935.
Rory and Bran. London, Heinemann, and New York, Putnam, 1936.
The Story of Mona Sheehy. London, Heinemann, 1939; New York, Harper, 1940.
Guerrilla. London, Heinemann, and New York, Bobbs-Merrill, 1944.
His Fellow Men. London, Jarrolds, 1952.

Short Stories

Tales of War. London and New York, Putnam, 1918.

The Little Tales of Smethers. London, Jarrolds, 1952.

Plays

The Sphinx at Gizeh, in *Tripod,* May 1912.

Five Plays [includes *The Glittering Gate* (produced 1909), *The Gods of the Mountain* (produced 1911), *King Argimines and the Unknown Warrior* (produced 1911), *The Golden Doom* (produced 1912), and *The Lost Silk Hat* (produced 1913)]. London, Grant Richards, and Boston, Little Brown, 1914.

Plays of Gods and Men [includes *The Tents of the Arabs* (produced 1914), *The Queen's Enemies* (produced 1916), and *The Laughter of the Gods* (produced 1919)]. London, Fisher Unwin, and New York, Luce, 1917.

A Night at an Inn: A Play in One Act (produced 1916). New York, Sunwise Turn, 1916.

The Murderers (produced 1919).

The Prince of Stamboul (produced 1919?).

If: A Play in Four Acts (produced 1921). London and New York, Putnam, 1921.

Cheezo (produced 1921). London and New York, Putnam, 1921.

Plays of Near and Far [includes *The Compromise of the King of the Golden Isles, The Flight of the Queen, Cheezo, A Good Bargain, If Shakespeare Lived Today,* and *Fame and the Poet* (produced 1924)]. London and New York, Putnam, 1922: *The Compromise of the King of the Golden Isles* published separately, New York, Grolier Club, 1924; *If Shakespeare Lived Today,* New York, Putnam, 1923.

Lord Adrian: A Play in Three Acts (produced 1923). Waltham Saint Lawrence, Berkshire, Golden Cockerel Press, 1933.

Alexander and Three Small Plays [includes *Alexander* (produced 1938], *The Old King's Tale, The Evil Kettle,* and *The Amusements of Khan Kharuda*). London and New York, Putnam, 1925.

Mr. Faithful: A Comedy in Three Acts (produced 1927). New York, French, 1935.

Seven Modern Comedies [includes *Atalanta in Wimbledon, The Raffle, The Journey of the Soul, In Holy Russia, His Sainted Grandmother* (produced 1926), *The Hopeless Passion of Mr. Bunyon,* and *The Jest of Hahalaba* (produced 1927)]. London and New York, Putnam, 1928.

The Old Folk of the Centuries. London, Elkin Matthews. 1930.

Plays for Earth and Air [includes *Fame Comes Late, A Matter of Honour, Mr. Sliggen's Hour, The Pumpkin, The Use of Man, The Bureau de Change, The Seventh Symphony, Golden Dragon City, Time's Joke,* and *Atmospherics*]. London, Heinemann, 1937.

The Strange Lover (produced 1939).

Poetry

Fifty Poems. London and New York, Putnam, 1929.

Mirage Water. London, Putnam, 1938; Philadelphia, Dorrance, 1939.

War Poems. London, Hutchinson, 1941.

A Journey. London, Macdonald, 1943.

Wandering Songs. London, Hutchinson, 1943.

The Year. London, Jarrolds, 1946.

To Awaken Pegasus and Other Poems. Oxford, Ronald, 1949.

Other

Nowadays. Boston, Four Seas, 1918.

Unhappy Far-Off Things. London, Elkin Matthews, and Boston, Little Brown, 1919.

My Ireland. London, Jarrolds, and New York, Funk and Wagnalls, 1937.

Patches of Sunlight (autobiography). London, Heinemann, and New York, Reynal and Hitchcock, 1938.

While the Sirens Slept (autobiography). London, Jarrolds, 1944.

The Donellan Lectures 1943. London, Heinemann, 1945.

A Glimpse from a Watchtower: A Series of Essays. London, Jarrolds, 1946.

The Sirens Wake (autobiography). London, Jarrolds, 1945.

Editor, *Modern Anglo-Irish Verse.* N.p., 1914.
Editor, *Last Song by Francis Ledwidge.* London, Herbert Jenkins, 1918.

*

Bibliography: in *Bibliographies of Modern Authors 1* by H. Danielson, London, Bookman's Journal, 1921; *Lord Dunsany: A Bibliography* by S.T. Joshi and Darrell Schweitzer, Metuchen, New Jersey, Scarecrow Press, 1993.

Critical Studies: *Dunsany the Dramatist* by Edward Hale Bierstadt, Boston, Little Brown, 1917; revised edition, 1919; *Dunsany, King of Dreams: A Personal Portrait* by Hazel Smith, London, Weidenfeld and Nicolson, and New York, Exposition Press, 1959; *Pathways to Elfland: The Writings of Lord Dunsany* edited by Darrell Schweitzer, Philadelphia, Owlswick Press, 1989; *Lord Dunsany: Master of the Anglo-Irish Imagination* by S.T. Joshi, Westport, Connecticut, Greenwood Press, 1995.

*   *   *

While Lord Dunsany may have been a minor figure in Irish literature, the extent of his role in the development of modern fantasy is major. He was a critical influence on H.P. Lovecraft, L. Sprague de Camp, and Fritz Leiber, and his play *King Argimenes and the Unknown Warrior* is one of the sources for Fletcher Pratt's *The Well of the Unicorn.* From his first book, *The Gods of Pegana,* in which he creates an entire pantheon, to his Jorkens series of adventure stories based on his travels in Algeria and the Sudan, to his masterpiece *The King of Elfland's Daughter,* Dunsany belongs with William Morris and George MacDonald as the generating forces of modern fantasy.

Dunsany's fantasy is characterized by his exotic settings; difficult, if creative and frequently numinous, prose; and stalwart protagonists and alluring, exquisite heroines. His ability to create vivid setting is partially explained by his relationship with Sidney H. Sime; Sime's drawings inspired "The Distressing Tale of Thangobrind the Jeweller, and of the Doom that Befell Him" (in *The Book of Wonder*). Dunsany's visual settings are evident in the country village and the activities of love in *The Blessing of Pan* and in the fictional Spanish Golden Age in *The Chronicles of Don Rodriguez* and *The Charwoman's Shadow.* However, his greatest stylistic triumph is the much-heralded *The King of Elfland's Daughter,* and in this novel all the qualities of his fantastic fictions are epitomized. Drawing on the themes of alienation and identity and the structure of the quest, which characterize much of his canon, Dunsany creates an interplay between the world of faery and everyday with his innovative proper names, coined phrases, and characterizations. In the novel, Alveric falls in love with an elfin princess, but after she bears him a son, she can no longer endure the crude society of mankind and returns to faery. Alveric's quest for his wife provides ample opportunity for Dunsany's ability to create numinous wonder, and the quest is resolved through love and harmony.

The ongoing reprinting of Dunsany's tales—especially "The Sword of Welleran" and "The Fortress Unvanquishable Save for Sacnoth"—demonstrates Dunsany's continuing influence on the literature of fantasy, the lasting appeal of his fantastic settings, and his role as a progenitor of modern fantasy literature in all its varieties and techniques.

—Roger C. Schlobin

DURRELL, Lawrence (George)

Nationality: British. **Born:** Julundur, India, 27 February 1912; brother of the zoologist and writer Gerald Durrell. **Education:** College of St. Joseph, Darjeeling, India; St. Edmund's School, Canterbury, Kent. **Family:** Married 1) Nancy Myers in 1935 (divorced 1947); 2) Eve Cohen in 1947 (divorced); 3) Claude Durrell in 1961 (died 1967); 4) Ghislaine de Boysson in 1973 (divorced 1979); two daughters (one deceased). **Career:** Has had many jobs, including jazz pianist (Blue Peter nightclub, London), automobile racer, and real estate agent; lived in Corfu, 1934-40; editor, with Henry Miller and Alfred Perlès, the *Booster* (later *Delta*), Paris, 1937-39; columnist, *Egyptian Gazette*, Cairo, 1941; editor, with Robin Fedden and Bernard Spencer, *Personal Landscape*, Cairo, 1942-45; special correspondent in Cyprus for the *Economist*, London, 1953-55; editor, *Cyprus Review*, Nicosia, 1954-55. Taught at the British Institute, Kalamata, Greece, 1940. Foreign Service press officer, British Information Office, Cairo, 1941-44; press attaché, British Information Office, Alexandria, 1944-45; director of public relations for the Dodecanese Islands, Greece, 1946-47; director, British Council Institute, Cordoba, Argentina, 1947-48; press attaché, British Legation, Belgrade, 1949-52; director of public relations for the British Government in Cyprus, 1954-56. Andrew Mellon Visiting Professor of Humanities, California Institute of Technology, Pasadena, 1974. **Awards:** Duff Cooper Memorial prize, 1957; Foreign Book prize (France), 1959; James Tait Black Memorial prize, 1975; Cholmondeley award, 1986; International Literary prize (Antibes), 1989. Fellow, Royal Society of Literature, 1954. **Died:** 7 November 1990.

SCIENCE FICTION PUBLICATIONS

Novels

The Revolt of Aphrodite. London, Faber, 1974.
   Tunc: A Novel. London, Faber, and New York, Dutton, 1968.
   Nunquam: A Novel. London, Faber, and New York, Dutton, 1970.

Short Stories

Down the Styx. Santa Barbara, California, Capricorn Press, 1971.

OTHER PUBLICATIONS

Novels

Pied Piper of Lovers. London, Cassell, 1935.
Panic Spring (as Charles Norden). London, Faber, and New York, Covici Friede, 1937.
The Black Book: An Agon. Paris, Obelisk Press, 1938; New York, Dutton, 1960; London, Faber, 1973.
Cefalû. London, Editions Poetry London, 1947; as *The Dark Labyrinth,* London, Ace, 1958; New York, Dutton, 1962.
The Alexandria Quartet. London, Faber, and New York, Dutton, 1962.
   Justine. London, Faber, and New York, Dutton, 1957.
   Balthazar. London, Faber, and New York, Dutton, 1958.
   Mountolive. London, Faber, 1958; New York, Dutton, 1959.
   Clea. London, Faber, and New York, Dutton, 1960.
White Eagles over Serbia. London, Faber, and New York, Criterion, 1957.
The Avignon Quintet. London, Faber, 1992.
   Monsieur; or, The Prince of Darkness. London, Faber, 1974; New York, Viking Press, 1975.
   Livia; or, Buried Alive. London, Faber, 1978; New York, Viking Press, 1979.
   Constance; or, Solitary Practices. London, Faber, and New York, Viking Press, 1982.
   Sebastian; or, Ruling Passions. London, Faber, 1983; New York, Viking Press, 1984.
   Quinx; or, The Ripper's Tale. London, Faber, 1985.

Short Stories

Zero, and Asylum in the Snow. Privately printed, 1946; as *Two Excursions into Reality,* Berkeley, California, Circle, 1947.
Esprit de Corps: Sketches from Diplomatic Life. London, Faber, 1957; New York, Dutton, 1958.
Stiff Upper Lip: Life among the Diplomats. London, Faber, 1958; New York, Dutton, 1959.
Sauve Qui Peut. London, Faber, 1966; New York, Dutton, 1967.
The Best of Antrobus. London, Faber, 1974.

Plays

Sappho: A Play in Verse (produced Hamburg, 1959; Edinburgh, 1961; Evanston, Illinois, 1964). London, Faber, 1950; New York, Dutton, 1958.
Acte (produced Hamburg, 1961). London, Faber, and New York, Dutton, 1965.
An Irish Faustus: A Morality in Nine Scenes (produced Sommerhausen, Germany, 1966). London, Faber, 1963; New York, Dutton, 1964.
Judith (shortened version of screenplay), in *Woman's Own* (London), 26 February-2 April 1966.

Screenplays: *Cleopatra,* with others, 1963; *Judith,* with others, 1966.

Radio Script: *Greek Peasant Superstitions,* 1947.

Television Scripts: *The Lonely Roads,* with Diane Deriaz, 1970; *The Search for Ulysses* (U.S.); *Lawrence Durrell's Greece; Lawrence Durrell's Egypt.*

Recording: *Ulysses Come Back: Sketch for a Musical* (story, music, and lyrics by Durrell), 1971.

Poetry

Quaint Fragment: Poems Written Between the Ages of Sixteen and Nineteen. London, Cecil Press, 1931.
Ten Poems. London, Caduceus Press, 1932.
Ballade of Slow Decay. Privately printed, 1932.
Bromo Bombastes: A Fragment from a Laconic Drama by Gaffer Peeslake. London, Caduceus Press, 1933.
Transition. London, Caduceus Press, 1934.
Mass for the Old Year. Privately printed, 1935.
Proems: An Anthology of Poems, with others. London, Fortune Press, 1938.
A Private Country. London, Faber, 1943.
The Parthenon: For T.S. Eliot. Privately printed, 1945(?).
Cities, Plains, and People. London, Faber, 1946.
On Seeming to Presume. London, Faber, 1948.
A Landmark Gone. Privately printed, 1949.
Deus Loci. Ischia, Italy, Di Mato Vito, 1950.
Private Drafts. Nicosia, Cyprus, Proodos Press, 1955.
The Tree of Idleness and Other Poems. London, Faber, 1955.
Selected Poems. London, Faber, and New York, Grove Press, 1956.
Collected Poems. London, Faber, and New York, Dutton, 1960; revised edition, 1968.
Penguin Modern Poets 1, with Elizabeth Jennings and R.S. Thomas. London, Penguin, 1962.
Poetry. New York, Dutton, 1962.
Beccafico/Le Becfigue (English, with French translation by F.-J. Temple). Montpelier, France, La Licorne, 1963.
A Persian Lady. Edinburgh, Tragara Press, 1963.
Selected Poems 1935-1963. London, Faber, 1964.
The Ikons and Other Poems. London, Faber, 1966; New York, Dutton, 1967.
The Red Limbo Lingo: A Poetry Notebook for 1968-1970. London, Faber, and New York, Dutton, 1971.
On the Suchness of the Old Boy. London, Turret, 1972.
Vega and Other Poems. London, Faber, 1973.
Lifelines. Edinburgh, Tragara Press, 1974.
Selected Poems, edited by Alan Ross. London, Faber, 1977.
Collected Poems 1931-1974, edited by James A. Brigham. London, Faber, and New York, Viking Press, 1980.

Other

Prospero's Cell: A Guide to the Landscape and Manners of the Island of Corcyra. London, Faber, 1945; with *Reflections on a Marine Venus,* New York, Dutton, 1960.
Key to Modern Poetry. London, Peter Nevill, 1952; as *A Key to Modern British Poetry,* Norman, University of Oklahoma Press, 1952.
Reflections on a Marine Venus: A Companion to the Landscape of Rhodes. London, Faber, 1953; with *Prospero's Cell,* New York, Dutton, 1960.
Bitter Lemons (on Cyprus). London, Faber, 1957; New York, Dutton, 1958.
Art and Outrage: A Correspondence about Henry Miller Between Alfred Perlès and Lawrence Durrell, with an Intermission by Henry Miller. London, Putnam, 1959; New York, Dutton, 1960.
Groddeck (on George Walther Groddeck). Wiesbaden, Limes, 1961.

Briefwechselüber "Actis," with Gustaf Gründgens. Hamburg, Rowohlt, 1961.
Lawrence Durrell and Henry Miller: A Private Correspondence, edited by George Wickes. New York, Dutton, and London, Faber, 1963.
La Descente du Styx (English, with French translations by F.-J. Temple). Montpellier, France, La Muréne, 1964; as *Down the Styx,* Santa Barbara, California, Capricorn Press, 1971.
Spirit of Place: Letters and Essays on Travel, edited by Alan G. Thomas. London, Faber, and New York, Dutton, 1969.
Le Grand Suppositoire (interview with Marc Alyn). Paris, Belfond, 1972; as *The Big Supposer,* London, Abelard Schuman, and New York, Grove Press, 1973.
The Happy Rock (on Henry Miller). London, Village Press, 1973; Belfast, Maine, Bern Porter, 1982.
The Plant-Magic Man. Santa Barbara, California, Capra Press, 1973.
Blue Thirst. Santa Barbara, California, Capra Press, 1975.
Sicilian Carousel. London, Faber, and New York, Viking Press, 1977.
The Greek Islands. London, Faber, and New York, Viking Press, 1978.
A Smile in the Mind's Eye. London, Wildwood House, 1980; New York, Universe, 1982.
Literary Lifelines: The Richard Aldington-Lawrence Durrell Correspondence, edited by Harry T. Moore and Ian S. MacNiven. New York, Viking Press, and London, Faber, 1981.
Caesar's Vast Ghost: Aspects of Provence. London, Faber, and New York, Arcade, 1990.

Editor, with others, *Personal Landscape: An Anthology of Exile.* London, Editions Poetry London, 1945.
Editor, *A Henry Miller Reader.* New York, New Directions, 1959; as *The Best of Henry Miller,* London, Heinemann, 1960.
Editor, *New Poems 1963.* London, Hutchinson, 1963.
Editor, *Lear's Corfu: An Anthology Drawn from the Painter's Letters,* Corfu, Corfu Travel, 1965.
Editor, *Wordsworth.* London, Penguin, 1973.
Translator, *Six Poems from the Greek of Sikelianos and Seferis.* Privately printed, 1946.
Translator, with Bernard Spencer and Nanos Valaoritis, *The King of Asine and Other Poems,* by George Seferis. London, Lehmann, 1948.
Translator, *The Curious History of Pope Joan,* by Emmanuel Royidis. London, Verschoyle, 1954; revised edition, as *Pope Joan: A Romantic Biography,* London, Deutsch, 1960; New York, Dutton, 1961.

*

Bibliography: *Lawrence Durrell: An Illustrated Checklist* by Alan G. Thomas and James A. Brigham, Carbondale, Southern Illinois University Press, 1983.

Manuscript Collections: University of California, Los Angeles; University of Illinois, Urbana.

Critical Studies: *The World of Lawrence Durrell* edited by Harry T. Moore, Carbondale, Southern Illinois University Press, 1962; *Lawrence Durrell* by Jon Unterecker, New York, Columbia University Press, 1964; *Lawrence Durrell* by John A. Weigel, New

York, Twayne, 1965; *Lawrence Durrell: A Study* (includes bibliography by Alan G. Thomas), London, Faber, 1968, New York, Dutton, 1969, revised edition, Faber, 1973, and *Lawrence Durrell,* London, Longman, 1970, both by G.S. Fraser; *Deus Loci: Lawrence Durrell Newsletter* (Kelowna, British Columbia), since 1977; "Lawrence Durrell Issue" of *Labrys 5* (London), 1979; *Critical Essays on Lawrence Durrell* edited by Alan Warren Friedman, Boston, Hall, 1986.

*   *   *

Lawrence Durrell's *Tunc* and *Nunquam* are the two parts of a science fiction novel known collectively as *The Revolt of Aphrodite.* The plots describe the efforts of Felix Charlock to build a computer, Abel, and a robot double of a prostitute-turned movie-actress, Iolanthe. In doing so, he is involved with a conglomerate corporation known as Merlin or the "firm" and its owners, Julian, Jocas, and Benedicta. Durrell is attempting to dissect the notion of culture; the superficial bases for this examination are Spengler (the approach to culture, the concern with money and contractual obligation, and even the term "the firm" itself are taken from *The Decline of the West*) and Freud (particularly the psychopathology of sex and the sexual connotations of money).

Durrell has identified the major preoccupations of all his fiction when he writes (in *Key to Modern Poetry*) that "Time and the ego are the two determinants of style for the twentieth century. . . ." The double, whether robot or human, is also very common in Durrell's writing, and is related to his attempts to handle multifaceted personalities and fragmented time from multiple viewpoints, as in *The Alexandria Quartet.* In *Key to Modern Poetry* he briefly traces the literary history of the double and ends by saying that "in nearly every case we are given a double which is either a saint, a criminal or a monster." Character is difficult to assess in Durrell's works; the surface descriptions of neuroses, frequently maimed characters, impotence, incestuous triangular relationships, and other sexual aberrations produce a shock value that often hides the suspicion that there really are no "characters" in his work—only puppets with a strong aroma.

The major distinctive feature of Durrell's writing is his baroque style. His writing is that of a poet—a sensuous mosaic of exotic words and images that adds a welcome dimension to the often flat prose of contemporary fiction. The occasional excesses are also those of the poet, mainly overwriting and tiresome platitudes. Throughout his career Durrell has had a remarkable eye for "place," and it appears again in *Tunc* and *Nunquam,* although somewhat supplanted by the ubiquity of the "firm." The technology that supplies the science fiction basis in both books is remarkably crude, unimaginative, and dated. Much of the character motivation in *Tunc* and *Nunquam* is centered around the concept of a person's work in relation to his culture and his emotional life. As A.W. Friedman has said, "The rule in Durrell is that to deny the validity of one's work is to negate love." Love and work drive and frustrate Charlock and the other characters throughout the books.

The book titles derive from the epigraph "Aut tunc, aut Nunquam" (It was then or never) from the *Satyricon* of Petronius. The implication of a last chance for society to define its values is supported by a quotation from *Tunc* which can serve as a statement of purpose for the two books: "When a civilisation has decided to bury its head in the sand what can we do but tickle its arse with a feather?"

—Norman L. Hills

E

EDDINGS, David

Nationality: American. **Born:** Spokane, Washington, 7 July 1931.
Education: Reed College, Portland, Oregon, B.A. in literature 1954;
University of Washington, Seattle, M.A. in English 1961. **Military
Service:** Served in United States Army, 1954-56. **Family:** Married Judith Lee Schall in 1962. **Agent:** Eleanor Wood, Blasingame,
McCauley, and Wood, 111 Eighth Avenue, Suite 1501, New York,
New York 10011, U.S.A.

SCIENCE FICTION PUBLICATIONS

Novels (series: The Belgariad; The Elenium; The Mallorean; The
Tamuli)

The Belgariad. 2 vols., Garden City, New York, Doubleday, and
London, Century, 1985.
  Pawn of Prophecy. New York, Ballantine, 1982; London, Century, 1983.
  Queen of Sorcery. New York, Ballantine, 1982; London, Century, 1984.
  Magician's Gambit. New York, Ballantine, 1983; London, Century, 1984.
  Castle of Wizardry. New York, Ballantine, and London, Century, 1984.
  Enchanter's Endgame. New York, Ballantine, 1984; London, Century, 1985.
The Mallorean:
  Guardians of the West. New York, Ballantine, and London, Bantam, 1987.
  King of the Murgos. New York, Ballantine, and London, Bantam, 1988.
  Demon Lord of Karanda. New York, Ballantine, and London, Bantam, 1988.
  Sorceress of Darshiva. New York, Ballantine, and London, Bantam, 1989.
  The Seeress of Kell. New York, Ballantine, and London, Bantam, 1991.
The Tamuli:
  Domes of Fire. London, HarperCollins, 1992, and New York, Ballantine, 1993.
  The Shining Ones. New York, Ballantine, and London, HarperCollins, 1993.
  The Hidden City. New York, Ballantine, and London, HarperCollins, 1994.
The Elenium. London, Grafton, 1993.
  The Diamond Throne. New York, Ballantine, and London, Grafton, 1989.
  The Ruby Knight. New York, Ballantine, and London, Grafton, 1990.
  The Sapphire Rose. London, HarperCollins, 1991, and New York, Ballantine, 1992.

OTHER PUBLICATIONS

Novels

The Losers. New York, Fawcett, 1992; London, HarperCollins, 1993.
High Hunt. New York, Putnam, 1973; London, HarperCollins, 1993.
Two Complete Novels (omnibus; includes *The Losers* and *High Hunt*). New York, Wings Books, 1994.

*

David Eddings comments:

The medieval romance was an entertaining form until Cervantes
killed it with *Don Quixote.* Tennyson's bowdlerization of Malory
did not offend Queen Victoria, which may be the best thing (or the
worst) which can be said of it. Both Lewis and Tolkien followed
Tennyson, which may have been an error. I prefer to follow Malory
(which may also be an error). The great failing of romancers appears to be a compulsion to take themselves seriously. I try not to,
because I'm sure there's another Cervantes lurking out there waiting to prick the balloon of our ponderous pomposity. I've tried to
create realistic, believable characters to function in an unrealistic,
unbelievable world. I left the warts on them, allowed them to be
silly from time to time and to bicker with each other when they felt
that way. I can only hope that the reader has half as much fun with
the books as I did.

*   *   *

In the unending wave of fantasy trilogies and longer, longer -
ologies that flowed from the font of the paperback publication of
The Lord of the Rings, only a few stay in the memory longer than
the first reading. Some stay because of quality and strangeness and
some because of entertainment value. David Eddings's first and
most popular fantasy sequence, *The Belgariad,* is one of the latter.
It can't lay claim to either great literary quality or innovation in its
depiction of a fantastic universe but it concentrates to great effect
on character and action, the twin keys to storytelling.

Unlike many other long fantasy sequences, *The Belgariad* is
clearly written as a planned and plotted whole. It is not one novel
stretched but a single story that takes five volumes to tell. Using
the time-honoured device of showing the world through the eyes
of a naive narrator, Eddings takes his time to explore the world
and the people met by the farm-boy Garion on his way to the throne
of his ancestral kingdom and beyond. Gradually we see his sensible, workaday, limited world expand to include stranger and
stranger things. Particularly entertaining is his slow discovery of
his own sorcerous powers and the limits placed on them by those
laws of physics that Eddings decides are entertaining: there is great
fun in the sequence where he tries to move a rock by the force of
his mind and discovers the "equal and opposite reaction" principle.
The quest which forms the centre of the story is guided by an aware
and active principle of Destiny, which is a major personality in the
story and Eddings enjoys exploring the issues of predestination, of
responsibility and of moral choice in a universe where the gods are
almost embarrassingly immanent and interfere regularly in human
affairs.

The world is in every way a standard-issue fantasy one, with diverse but recognisable cultures butting up against each other in a totally unrealistic fashion. There are analogues of Vikings, Imperial Romans, ancient Egyptians, and horse barbarians all within a few days travel of each other. But even the inhabitants of the "evil empire" of Angarak (roughly every Eastern culture you've ever heard of melded together) whose priests rip hearts out daily, talk like just plain folks. The only truly strange culture is that of the religiously obsessed, subterranean Ul-Gos, and even they remind one of Orthodox Jews.

But originality in the design of the world is not what Eddings is interested in, nor the conflict between cultures. The focus of the books is on the comedy of character. The contrasts among the members of the band of heroes, between the toweringly noble (and not too bright) knight Mandorallen, and the berserker warrior Barak, between the grim horse-lord Hettar and the spy Silk, the centuries-old battling between the sorcerer Belgarath and his daughter Polgara, the developing love between Garion and the Imperial (and imperious) Princess Ce'Nedra and the growth of a sense of responsibility in the two adolescents: these are what Eddings concentrates on.

The chief flaws come when the artifice fails and you become aware of the lack of depth to the illusion. As noted above nearly everybody in the books thinks, at the core, like a 20th-century Westerner; those who don't (Sir Mandorallen, for instance) are distinguished by very basic devices (cod "theeing" and "thouing" in Mandorallen's case). When the language too fails and you clearly hear the diction of a spoiled Middle American brat from the mouth of Ce'Nedra (supposedly raised at one of the richest and oldest courts in the world) then you cringe and see the whole edifice shudder for a moment.

Unhappily, the rest of Eddings's writing career is less satisfactory. The sequel to *The Belgariad, The Malloreon,* has all the faults of the first sequence in an exaggerated form and repeats the effects that worked well in the first sequence to the point of nausea. The characters and characterisations that were entertaining once overstay their welcome. Plot and incident repeat each other and what depth of theme was present in the first saga becomes trite and overfamiliar. The final conclusion of this sequence, delayed as it was beyond its original schedule for publication, reads like something written to fulfill a contract. In the end the great climax of the quest of ages boils down to "and with one bound the universe was saved."

Eddings latest work in fantasy, *The Elenium* and its sequel *The Tamuli,* are shorter and written with a greater emphasis on action. At first his gift with character seemed to have returned with a shift to a new world and new peoples. Again the nature of magic and of the gods is a focus of interest and capital D Destiny hangs heavy in the background, waiting to guide events. But not only does one miss the length which he could use in the earlier works to develop the world, but by the end all the fault of the earlier books are repeated especially in the second trilogy. The overbearing cuteness of the female characters, the cardboard nature of the villains and heroes alike don't compensate for the occassional bits of enjoyable invention.

It's a shame to have to say that in the end Eddings gifts are turned more into trickery than enjoyable storytelling.

—Michael Cule

EDDISON, E(ric) R(ucker)

Nationality: British. **Born:** Adel, Yorkshire, 24 November 1882. **Career:** Civil servant and author. **Died:** 18 August 1945.

SCIENCE FICTION PUBLICATIONS

Novels

The Worm Ouroboros: A Romance. London, Cape, 1922; New York, Boni, 1926.
Zimiamvia: A Trilogy. New York, Dell, 1992.
  Mistress of Mistresses: A Vision of Zimiamvia. London, Faber, and New York, Dutton, 1935.
  A Fish Dinner in Memison. New York, Dutton, 1941; London, Ballantine, 1972.
  The Mezentian Gate. Plaistow, United Kingdom, Curwen Press, 1958; New York, Ballantine, 1969.

OTHER PUBLICATIONS

Novel

Styrbiorn the Strong. London, Cape, and New York, Boni, 1926.

Other

Editor and translator (from Icelandic), *Egil's Saga, Done into English out of Icelandic,* by Snorri Sturlson. Cambridge, Cambridge University Press, 1930; New York, Greenwood Press, 1968.

*   *   *

William Morris was an important influence on many later writers, including E.R. Eddison. Eddison's *Styrbiorn the Strong,* a historical romance, is based on materials found in the Norse and Icelandic sagas, and is often considered, with Haggard's *Eric Brighteyes,* one of the best modern depictions of the Viking Age. Four years later, Eddison published *Egil's Saga,* a prose translation of an Icelandic saga. In both works, Eddison mentions Morris's romances and translations.

Eddison's fame, however, rests largely on a work which has much in common with saga and historical romance, but is actually pure fantasy, *The Worm Ouroboros.* It is both romantic and epic, filled with the lavish description and heroic adventure that delight fantasy readers. And at the end of the novel, just as the reader and the characters are wishing that it could go on forever, their wish is granted, the action begins all over again, and the plot of the novel, like the worm of the title, becomes circular and eats its own tail. Eddison's Zimiamvian trilogy—*Mistress of Mistresses, A Fish Dinner in Memison,* and *The Menzentian Gate*—that follows *The Worm Ouroboros* and is set in the heaven of the world depicted in that novel, is less successful. Most critics agree that the philosophy Eddison propounds in the Zimiamvian trilogy makes the novels difficult to read, and most readers find them harder going than *The Worm Ouroboros. The Menzentian Gate* is especially difficult; it was finished and published after Eddison's death.

—C.W. Sullivan III

EDMONDSON, G.C.

Pseudonyms: John Cleve; Kelly P. Gast; Jake Logan; J.B. Masterson. **Nationality:** American. **Born:** José Mario Garry Ordonez Edmondson y Cotton, Rachauchitlán, Tabasco, Mexico, 11 October 1922. **Education:** Vienna, M.D. **Military Service:** Served in the United States Marine Corps, 1942-46. **Family:** Married three times; two sons and two daughters. **Career:** Has worked as a blacksmith. **Agent:** Richard Curtis, 164 East 64th Street, New York, New York 10021, U.S.A.

SCIENCE FICTION PUBLICATIONS

Novels (series: Cunningham; Time Ship; Spaceways)

The Ship That Sailed the Time Stream (Time Ship). New York, Ace, 1965; London, Arrow, 1971; expanded editon, New York, Ace, 1978.
Chapayeca. Garden City, New York, Doubleday, 1971; London, Hale, 1973; as *Blue Face,* New York, DAW, 1972.
T. H. E. M. Garden City, New York, Doubleday, 1974.
The Aluminum Man. New York, Berkley, 1975.
The Man Who Corrupted Earth. New York, Ace, 1980.
To Sail the Century Sea (Time Ship). New York, Ace, 1981.
Star Slaver (with Andrew J. Offutt as John Cleve). New York, Berkley, 1983.
The Takeover, with C.M. Kotlan. New York, Ace, 1984.
The Cunningham Equations, with C.M. Kotlan. New York, Ballantine, 1986.
The Black Magician, with C.M. Kotlan (Cunningham). New York, Ballantine, 1986.
Maximum Effort, with C.M. Kotlan (Cunningham). New York, Ballantine, 1987.

Short Stories

Stranger Than You Think. New York, Ace, 1965.

OTHER PUBLICATIONS

Novels

Rudge (as J.B. Masterson). Garden City, New York, Doubleday, 1979; London, Hale, 1980.
Slocum's Slaughter (as Jake Logan). New York, Playboy Press, 1980.

Novels as Kelly P. Gast

Dil Dies Hard. Garden City, New York, Doubleday, 1975.
The Long Trail North. Garden City, New York, Doubleday, 1976.
Murphy's Trail. Garden City, New York, Doubleday, 1976; London, Hale, 1977.
The Last Stage from Opal. Garden City, New York, Doubleday, 1978.
Murder at Magpie Flats. Garden City, New York, Doubleday, 1978.
Paddy. Garden City, New York, Doubleday, 1979; London, Hale, 1980.

Other

Practical Welding, with LeRoy A. Scheck. Beverly Hills, California, Bruce, 1976; 2nd edition, Encino, California, Glencoe, 1984.
Le livre noir d'haute cuisine. N. p., Bookmaker, 1977.
Water Rationing Made Simple. N. p., Bookmaker, 1977.
The Basic Book of Home Maintenance and Repair, with T.J. Roybal. Chicago, American Technical Society, 1979.
Diesel Mechanics: An Introduction, with Richard Little. North Scituate, Massachusetts, Bretona, 1982.

*   *   *

Between 1957 and 1965, G.C. Edmondson successfully sold a dozen or so short stories which, while reasonably entertaining, made scarcely a ripple in the science fiction community. For the most part, they were lightly humorous, particularly those in the "Mad Friend" series, zany adventures of a mysterious "friend" of the author whose many exploits included a meteor that was not quite what it seemed or an encounter with a time traveller from the future. Although rarely reprinted, stories like "From Caribou to Carrie Nation," "The Inferlab Project," "Rescue," and "Technological Retreat" still measure up favorably against most contemporary stories. The series was later collected as half of an Ace double book under the title *Stranger Than You Think,* but the real significance of the collection's appearance was the novel on the flip side.

The Ship That Sailed the Time Stream was not the first novel about people misplaced in time, nor is it the best. An experimental naval ship is testing a new anti-submarine device when lightning strikes and a scientific fluke sends the entire vessel back 1000 years in time. Faced with dwindling provisions and the probability that they will never be able to return to their own time, the crew sets off to find civilization, only to run into a bunch of Viking raiders. Edmondson takes a simple, straightforward plot and runs with it, producing good-natured adventure fiction at its very best. With a single book, he had acquired a following.

Unfortunately, it was more than five years before Edmondson wrote again, publishing a single short story in 1970, and then the novel *Chapayeca* in 1971. *Chapayeca* (later reprinted as *Blue Face*) follows the final expedition of an unhappy, recently handicapped anthropologist among the Indian tribes of Mexico. Rumors of a mysterious presence lead him to the discovery that an alien being is living secretly among the natives. A quietly understated, very short novel whose literary values are exceptional, this book showed that Edmondson's prose style had improved dramatically. Unfortunately, the low key plot attracted few readers, and several more years passed before another book appeared.

The Aluminum Man marked Edmondson's return to more traditional themes. An alien provides two humans with a bacterial strain that produces aluminum, then spends most of the book trying to find them and get it back. There are some fine flashes of humor at times, but the impact of the new source of aluminum on the economy is hinted at but never really explored. Several years more would pass before Edmondson returned to this theme in a much more serious vein with *The Man Who Corrupted the Earth,* which considers a wide range of issues from pollution to the world economy to the values and disadvantages of space exploration. Some predictable melodramatic plot elements are intertwined in what was Edmondson's most serious attempt to address contemporary social issues within a futuristic context.

Edmondson published the sequel to his first novel in 1981. *To Sail the Century Sea* is not quite as fresh and exciting as its predecessor, but it remains one of Edmondson's best novels. Having returned to the present and, after an interval of several years, having convinced the authorities that their story of travel through time is true, the protagonist and several of his companions are sent back, deliberately this time, on a special mission to change a pivotal event in history. *To Sail the Century Sea* contains more rousing adventure, this time with a clever surprise ending.

Edmondson's last four novels were all written in collaboration with C.M. Kotlan, and while they continued to use adventure and action as the focus of the story, there was as well an increasingly dim portrayal of the foibles of the human race. *The Takeover* is a novel of political paranoia. *The Pentagon* has been subverted and allows a Soviet takeover of the U.S. government. The only possible hope is a fleet of nuclear submarines that has refused to surrender, and that must act quickly to take advantage of the threat their weaponry offers. The book is suspenseful, but very derivative of countless similar works.

The last three books comprise a trilogy. *The Cunningham Equations* introduces Blaise Cunningham, an expert in artificial intelligence who has created an AI named Alfie, who aids him in this and subsequent adventures. He is inexplicably the object of interest of a number of professional thugs, who seem determined to kidnap his dog. Cunningham pursues his own investigation and becomes involved with a plan to alter human capabilities through genetic engineering of a parasitical life-form.

The plot unfolds in *The Black Magician*. The new life-forms are supposed to benignly enhance human intelligence, but they have been inadequately studied and an unpleasant side effect begins to emerge. Under the right conditions, they will seize control of their host, because they have found a way to survive on their own. Effective efforts to track down the parasites and destroy them are hindered by the fact that the government is reluctant to admit that the problem exists. Everything is ultimately resolved in the concluding volume, *Maximum Effort*. The growing numbers of parasitically controlled humans are now interacting, working to establish themselves as the dominant force on earth. Blaise Cunningham alone may possess the secret that will bring their efforts to a halt. As a whole, the trilogy is quite suspenseful, eschewing graphic horror for more effectively suggestive scenes and situations. At the same time, it is a darker vision than that found in Edmondson's earlier books, and while these last novels are technically more effective, they are less entertaining than his early works.

—Don D'Ammassa

EDWARDS, Norman. *See* **CARR, Terry; WHITE, Ted.**

EFFINGER, George Alec

Nationality: American. **Born:** Cleveland, Ohio, January 1947. **Education:** Yale University, New Haven, Connecticut, 1965, 1969, and New York University, 1968. **Career:** Freelance writer; since 1971, writer for *Marvel Comic Books,* New York. **Awards:** Nebula award, for novelette, 1988. **Agent:** Richard Curtis, 164 East 64th Street, New York, New York 10021, U.S.A. **Address:** Box 15183, New Orleans, Louisiana 70175, U.S.A.

SCIENCE FICTION PUBLICATIONS

Novels (series: Marîd Audran; Planet of the Apes; Nick of Time)

What Entropy Means to Me. Garden City, New York, Doubleday, 1972.
Relatives: A Novel. New York, Harper, 1973.
Planet of the Apes: Man the Fugitive. New York, Award, 1974.
Nightmare Blue, with Gardner Dozois. New York, Berkley, 1975; London, Fontana, 1977.
Escape to Tomorrow (Apes). New York, Award, 1975.
Journey into Terror (Apes). New York, Award, 1975.
Those Gentle Voices: A Promethean Romance of the Spaceways. New York, Warner, 1976.
Lord of the Apes (Apes). New York, Award, 1976.
Death in Florence. Garden City, New York, Doubleday, 1978; as *Utopia 3,* Chicago, Playboy Press, 1980.
Heroics. Garden City, New York, Doubleday, 1979.
The Wolves of Memory. New York, Putnam, 1981.
The Nick of Time. Garden City, New York, Doubleday, 1985; London, New English Library, 1987.
The Bird of Time (Nick of Time). Garden City, New York, Doubleday, 1986; London, New English Library, 1988.
When Gravity Fails (Marîd). New York, Arbor House, 1987.
A Fire in the Sun (Marîd). Garden City, New York, Doubleday, 1989.
The Zork Chronicles (adapted from computer game). New York, Avon, 1990.
The Exile Kiss (Marîd). Norwalk, Connecticut, Easton Press, 1991.
The Red Tape Wars (with Jack Chalker and Mike Resnick). New York, Tor, 1991.
Maureen Birbaum, Barbarian Swordperson. Austin, Texas, Swan Press, 1993.

Short Stories

Mixed Feelings: Short Stories. New York, Harper, 1974.
Irrational Numbers. Garden City, New York, Doubleday, 1976.
Dirty Tricks. Garden City, New York, Doubleday, 1978.
Idle Pleasures. New York, Berkley, 1983.
The Old Funny Stuff. Eugene, Oregon, Pulphouse, 1989.
Look Away. Eugene, Oregon, Axolotl, 1990.
Schrödinger's Kitten. Eugene, Oregon, Pulphouse, 1992.

OTHER PUBLICATIONS

Novel

Felicia. New York, Berkley, 1976.
Shadow Money. New York, Tor, 1988.

*

George Alec Effinger comments:
   (1985) I try to do new things with old material. A good deal of my science fiction is an attempt to take traditional SF furniture

(storylines, settings, characters, and hardware) and combine it with some element of the absurd. The result is not science fiction, because it bears little resemblance to the rational real world. Perhaps surreal fantasy describes these stories best. My antecedents are as much in the theater of the absurd as they are in science fiction.

One of my favorite experiments is to appropriate an accepted SF situation and populate it with one or more of the continuing characters I have established in my stories over the years. These characters are not recurring in the usual sense. Rather, I think of them as a kind of repertory company. They may die in one story and reappear later as necessary. They live in many eras and appear together in various combinations, sometimes contradicting earlier stories. Just as William Bendix appeared in one motion picture and was killed or married, then months later appeared in another movie, unrelated to the first, so my characters pop up here and there throughout my own future history, unaffected by the stories in which they performed previously. Whenever they appear, however, they always represent the same kind of person, making for me a private stable of stereotypes to draw upon.

I enjoy parody, satire, and pastiche, but every once in a while I will do a serious story in a straight SF mode, mostly to keep the audience on its toes. SF is the only neighborhood of writing where I could get away with this kind of thing, and I am immensely grateful to the field and its readers for giving me the opportunity.

*   *   *

Since the publication of his best-known novel, *What Entropy Means to Me,* George Alec Effinger has demonstrated versatility in books as disparate as the mainstream novel *Felicia,* the teleplay adaptation *Man the Fugitive,* and *Nightmare Blue,* a collaboration with Gardner Dozois. More importantly, he has produced short stories and novels linked in strange and wondrous ways to form a unique "Effinger's World." Some critics label him a writer of sword and sorcery; others, of myth. Still others avoid labels, preferring a literary report card showing a high rating in technique, a low one in substance. Despite any problem with fitting him into the established definitions of science fiction, Effinger does offer an exceptional reading experience.

What Entropy Means to Me is a structural tour de force, being four intricately interwoven stories with author-character Seyt as nexus. First is a romantic quest tale of an eldest son searching for a lost father. Aided by a magic-competent companion, Dore overcomes natural obstacles, monsters, seduction, villainy, only to find Father at a point of no return. If *Entropy* went no further, it could sustain the label of sword and sorcery. But *Entropy* is more, three stories more. Functioning much as a chorus in a Greek tragedy, Seyt relates his family's saga from Earth to the planet Home. The third story evolves as a classic political power struggle to fill the vacuum created by the absence of father and eldest son. Seyt faithfully records the machinations, religious conflicts, and personal hurt involved. The fourth story gains subtle attention. This is the story of creation—literary creation. Seyt makes us aware of the artist, story churning in his head, faced with the arduous task of shaping it for an audience. Seyt must grapple with the author's universal problems: critical pressure from readers; political pressure to slant toward propaganda; and inner pressure to maintain authorial integrity. This trenchant commentary on the art and act of writing, reappearing in later short stories and novels, helps link *Entropy* to them.

Effinger's later fictional world is a paradox. We may recognize a familiar society, only to have subsequent paragraphs jolt us into a surreal world. Often gray, sometimes diseased, always warped by conformity, this society is best epitomized by the village of Gremmage in "Things Go Better," "Heart Stop," and "Lights Out." Gremmage isolates, smothers, and molds newcomers to its ways. Effinger's larger society has the Representatives, six men governing by whimsical stupidity ("Lydectes: On the Nature of Sport," "Contentment, Satisfaction, Cheer, Well-Being, Gladness, Joy, Comfort, and Not Having to Get Up Early Any More," and *Relatives*). Effinger's people freely slip from story to story, changing personalities and identities illogically. For example, the three separate Weinraub/Weintraubs triplicate experience in *Relatives,* then show up as a writer of a trilogy of novels in "Biting Down Hard in Truth." Global bum Bo Staefler of *Death in Florence* has little obvious relationship to baseball catcher Bo Staefler ("Naked to the Invisible Eye") or to castaway Bo Staefler ("World War II"). Robert Hanson appears as an 11-year-old boy ("Chase Our Blues Away"), a young man afflicted with altruism ("Strange Ragged Saintliness"), one for whom a park is named ("Timmy Was Eight"), and an android clone ("The Awesome Menace of the Polarizer"). Jennings suffers metamorphosis from a tough coach ("Biting Down Hard on Truth") to a chairman of the board ("At the Bran Foundry") to an astro-physicist (*Those Gentle Voices: A Promethean Romance of the Spaceways*).

And then there is Sandor Courane, one of the many personalities moving in and out of Effinger's multifaceted morality play. Courane shifts from being a lightweight science fiction writer in "The Pinch-Hitters," one of Effinger's sports short stories (see "Naked to the Invisible Eye," "From Downtown at the Buzzer," and "Breakaway" for other sports-oriented tales) to serve in *The Wolves of Memory* as a tormented Everyman trying to cope with the mysteries of life and death, of causation and purpose. In the novel Effinger demonstrates his control of surrealistic shifts of perspective in time and place, enriching them with parodic hints of Eden, the Fall, and the Crucifixion, ironically combined with a man/technology relationship.

In later novels Effinger goes in for other unique combinations. *The Red Tape Wars,* for example, combines his imagination with those of Jack Chalker and Mike Resnick. Together they produce a humorous novel that satirizes the bureaucracy, academia, even themselves as writers. *The Zork Chronicles* combines the "Zork" computer game with a parody of the heroic genre. *Look Away,* an alternate worlds theme, uses U.S. Civil War events linked with 20th-century Mideast situations. These all reinforce Effinger's own comment above: "I try to do new things with old material." His latest, notable "new things with old material" features a three-volume series with Marîd Audran as protagonist and is set in a near-future North Africa. The area is broken up into small political units, most of them hostile to each other, even with hostility within each unit. Marîd in *When Gravity Fails* is a footloose street man, able to survive by his wits and various mood-enhancing drugs. He lives in the Budayeen, a ghetto-like area dominated by Friedlander Bey, a "godfather" type. Despite attempts to remain free, Marîd is drawn into the violent life of the Budayeen, eventually selling out his independence to Bey as one of his agents, moving into Bey's mansion, and serving more as a "go-fer." In *A Fire in the Sun* Marîd has become a policeman, really serving as Bey's contact within that force. Events take a grisly turn, forcing Marîd to take matters into his own hands. With the aid of surgical implants and the personality modifiers he had earlier tried to avoid, Marîd solves the mystery of the violent power struggle, acting more as a detective than a policeman. While still linked with Bey, he has gained power and a certain amount of the independence he desires. Things change in *The Exile Kiss* when both Marîd and Bey suffer exile for a framed-up murder. They are banished to the Arabian desert. During their trials in the desert, their return, and the search for both justice and revenge, Marîd grows in stature, reaching a higher, though uncomfortable, state of self-awareness. Will a fourth sequel carry Marîd Audran to comfort in the independence he desires? Only Effinger and time will tell.

Effinger is master of the *non sequitur* which teases the mind with the thought that there is a veiled logic and an illuminating insight here, could one but rearrange things. If not, the reader must provide his own, for Effinger has prodded his mind unmercifully. Musing on the act of writing, a character in "The Ghost Writer" inadvertently gives us a summation for Effinger himself: "There was always the chance that a new fragment might join two of the enigmatic earlier pieces, and a whole framework might begin to be evident. But not today. Here was another piece, of perhaps a totally different puzzle. It was longer, and it was exciting. The audience would be satisfied, but not the scholars."

—Hazel Pierce

EGAN, Greg

Nationality: Australian. **Born:** 1961. **Awards:** Ditmar award (twice), 1993, 1995.

SCIENCE FICTION PUBLICATIONS

Novels

An Unusual Angle. Carlton, Victoria, Australia, Norstrilia Press, 1983.
Quarantine. London, Legend, 1992; New York; HarperPrism, 1995.
Permutation City. London, Millinnium, 1994.
Axiomatic. London, Millennium, 1995.

*   *   *

Australian Greg Egan is emerging as an important and prolific writer in the 1990s. The primary focus of his extrapolative fiction is a cluster of ideas currently central to the philosophy of science, particularly as it relates to quantum mechanics, biotechnology and the posthuman condition.

To date, Egan has published one fantasy and two science fiction novels, both of which have won the Australian 'Ditmar' Science Fiction award for best long fiction: *Quarantine* (1992) in 1993; *Permutation City* (1994) in 1995. His short stories appear in many of the major SF venues, such as *Interzone, Asimov's Science Fiction, Pulphouse, Aurealis* and *Eidolon.* His work is included in all of the recent Australian anthologies in the field, as well as in international collections such as *Interzone: The 4th Anthology* (1989), *The Year's Best Fantasy* (1989), and most notably, in each of Gardner Dozois's *Year's Best Science Fiction* anthologies since 1991. Two of these stories have won Ditmar awards for best Australian short fiction: "Closer" (1992) in 1993; and "Cocoon" (1994) in 1995. "Our Lady of Chernobyl" (1994) was also on the 1995 final ballot.

Egan's experience in amateur experimental film making is evident in his early genre work, particularly in his 1983 novel, *An Unusual Angle.* This is a slight stream-of-consciousness fantasy, in which an adolescent protagonist records impressions of his high school years through the lens of an imaginary camera "hidden" inside his head. The story ends, coventionally, with the metaphorical extraction of the film/text. Egan's interest in film is also evident in short stories such as "Tangled Up" (1985), in which the urban environment and the inner world of the protagonist are inextricably confused; and in the cinematic descriptions of surreal horror in "Mind Vampires" (1986), which explores, *inter alia,* the role of the artist as voyeur.

The short story "Scatter My Ashes" (1988) combines this role with an examination of the connection between the personal responsibility of the individual who records scenes of violence and the role of the society that broadcasts such images. Here, photographer and murderer invoke each other, and are presented as two sides of the same social coin that is the currency of trade in the pornography of violence. The tension between civic duty and individual moral responsibility is again canvassed in "Neighbourhood Watch" (1986), where the righteous dreams of civic leaders have created a nightmare predator as their peace-keeper; and again, in a very different vein, in "Beyond the Whistle Test" (1989), where an advertising executive responsible for broadcasting "neural noise," lethal to some listeners, is trapped by his own construct.

Egan's work as a computer programmer in medical research is reflected in his fascination with the possibilities inherent in future interaction between the biological human and the computer. He creates a near future of the posthuman, where the "downloading" of the self, or its augmentation through various permutations as "neural modifications" or "mods," has become normal practice. The development of these ideas is evident in short stories such as "Learning to Be Me" (1990), in which he describes the transition of identity between the protagonist's original organic brain and the "jewel" implanted in his skull—a memory storage device that can be transplanted to new bodies when necessary, thus ensuring immortality for its owner. This idea is pursued further in "Transition Dreams" (1993), which canvasses the metaphysics of the virtual dreams of a software model of the original brain of the story's protagonist, who is undergoing transition into an "eternal" robotic body.

Such questions about what truly constitutes the human are at the centre of Egan's critically acclaimed first science fiction novel, *Quarantine* (1992). The title refers to a situation that has arisen because unspecified alien forces have enclosed our solar system in a "Bubble." This isolates humanity, whose existence is inimical to other life forms because human choice-based logic is depleting the universe of its infinite possibilities, and prevents further cosmic infection. One entirely predictable outcome of this quarantine is the emergence of millenial cults, including the extemist group, the Children of the Abyss, responsible for the initial violence of the action.

Set in a near future Australia, *Quarantine* presents a society in which bioengineering has progressed to a point where people can, and do, modify their minds in any way they wish, by simply plugging in software "mods." These "mods" recall George Alec Effinger's "moddies and daddies" in his near eastern Marîd Audran series (*When Gravity Fails,* 1987; *A Fire in the Sun,* 1989; *The Exile Kiss,* 1991). Like Effinger, and indeed many SF novelists, Egan uses the plot device of the private investigator to explore the fictional society. Typically, Egan also uses his detective protagonist to examine the ethical ramifications of allowing people to become exactly what they want to be: the hero, Nick Stavrianos, witnessed the murder of his wife while he was using a "behavioural mod" that prevented him from caring, and he responds to the dilemma of knowing how much he will be hurt when he "deprimes" by acquiring a further neural "happiness mod" to prevent exposure to grief. The course of his investigation into her death leads to his being captured and fitted, against what was then his will, with a further brain controlling mod which renders him totally loyal to the cause of his captors. Coincidentally, it also places him at the centre of a scientific breakthrough that reveals the key to the Bubble, and shapes the destiny of the planet.

Such questions of imposing loyalty upon unwilling victims through neural modification are also present in "Chaff" (1993), set in the jungles of South America, where genetically engineered rainforests provide security, and genetically tailored bioweapons give a new twist to the "heart of darkness."

In Egan's most recent novel, *Permutation City* (1994; parts of which are derived from the story "Dust," 1992), he takes the extrapolation of the posthuman condition even further, offering a fascinating exploration of the nature of human consciousness, and of the possibilities of nonhuman evolution. One of the central concerns is the fine distinction to be drawn between self-transformation and death. The thesis of the novel, as in many of his short stories, is that the human mind can be downloaded into virtual environments, where the resultant copies can exist forever as virtual people: provided, of course, that the world's computer networks remain stable. The novel's protagonist, Paul Durham, is utterly obsessed with virtual and artificial life, and he finances his researches by creating a virtual sanctuary, and then selling "living space" in it to those rich enough to afford it. The inhabitants include a range of character types—ranging from a billionaire banker-cum-murderer coming to terms with his guilt, to a stowaway couple enacting their fantasies of timeless love—but here, as in *Quarantine*, characterization remains secondary to scientific and philosophical extrapolation.

Permutation City (the title itself is a pun on PC) is deliberately clever, with chapter headings, such as "Remit not paucity," that are anagrams of the title, and of each other, and an opening poem entirely constructed of such anagrammatical permutations. The virtual characters in the "Sanctuary" also act out endless permutations of their meta-lives, until the virtual construct begins to collapse, and systems errors begin to claim parts of their virtual selves. Meanwhile, the Lambertians, a non-human biological race created by programmer Maria Deluca in the meta-construct called the Autoverse, quietly evolve toward a different concept of reality that impinges negatively upon the virtual/human, denying their creators the chance to be gods.

Egan is now writing full time, and should continue to develop as a major writer of the 'hard' science fiction that concerns itself with ideas.

—Janeen Webb.

———

EGBERT, H.M. *See* **ROUSSEAU, Victor.**

———

EISENSTEIN, Phyllis

Nationality: American. **Born:** Phyllis Kleinstein, Chicago, Illinois, 26 February 1946. **Education:** University of Chicago, 1963-66; University of Illinois, Chicago, 1978-81, B.A. in anthropology 1981. **Family:** Married Alex Eisenstein in 1966. **Career:** Cofounder and Director, Windy City SF Writers Conference, Chicago, 1972-77. Anthology Trustee, Science Fiction Writers of America, 1976-81. Since 1989, has taught science fiction writing, and since 1993 has taught popular fiction writing, both at Columbia College, Chicago. **Address:** 6208 North Campbell, Chicago, Illinois 60659, U.S.A. **Online Address:** Phyllis@Ripco.com.

SCIENCE FICTION PUBLICATIONS

Novels (series: Alaric; Cray)

Sorceror's Son (Cray). New York, Ballantine, 1979; London, Grafton, 1990.
Shadow of Earth. New York, Dell, 1979.
In the Hands of Glory. New York, Timescape Books, 1981.
The Crystal Palace (Cray). New York, New American Library, 1988; London, Grafton, 1991.
In the Red Lord's Reach (Alaric). New York, New American Library, 1989; London, HarperCollins, 1992.

Short Stories (series: Alaric)

Born to Exile (Alaric). Sauk City, Wisconsin, Arkham House, 1978; London, HarperCollins, 1992.

*

Phyllis Eisenstein comments:

I'd rather not compose a "personal statement" about my work, because my personal statements are embedded in that work. However, I do believe that the current schism between "significant art" and "mere entertainment" is a product of academic pretensions that have nothing to do with the intrinsic value of any particular work. Art cannot survive when it does not have a popular audience of some kind; and any art whose highest aspiration is to compete with the temporary thrills of a roller coaster will also not be long remembered. I am not the first one to make this observation, and I certainly hope that I won't be the last.

*   *   *

Phyllis Eisenstein is probably best known as a writer of fantasy. *Sorceror's Son, The Crystal Palace, Shadow of Earth, Born to Exile, In the Red Lord's Reach,* and many of her short stories certainly exist in the realm of the fantastic. However, since her first published story, "The Trouble with the Past," Eisenstein's works also have explored such familiar science fiction themes as time travel, space exploration, space colonies, and first contact. Eisenstein creates a memorable mood or presents a tantalizing idea through strong characterization. She explores the effects of her settings and premises on the main character and that character's interpersonal relationships.

A powerful example is "In the Western Tradition," in which Eisenstein deftly treats time travel on both the physical and the psychological levels. A recurring theme in her writings, time travel is handled with a twist in this story. Instead of actually traveling in time, people view past events by means of sophisticated machinery. Requiring highly skilled operators, the equipment by its geographic location limits the range of observable events. As intriguing as this concept is, the central story is about Allison, a very talented operator who becomes so obsessed with the past that she isolates herself from her own contemporary life. Equally compelling for point of view are "Taboo," with its interplay between anthropologists and natives as well as among the scientists themselves, and "Nightlife," a look at the reality of dreams.

Many of her early stories written in collaboration with her husband Alex tend to be oriented more to the external structure of the plot or concept than to the effect of that structure on the characters. These stories seem to lack the depth and insight of her solo writings. An exception is "You Are Here," a disturbing story whose full impact is not realized until its conclusion. While that ending is rather predictable, the building of the character is subtle.

Eisenstein came into her own with her series about Alaric, a minstrel with the apparently magical power of teleportation. Each of these stories is complete in itself, but if read in order, as in the collection *Born to Exile,* they form a continuous account of Alaric's adventures. Other than the minstrel's extraordinary talent and the locals' superstitions, magic is not a major part of this world. In fact, Alaric himself tries to fight the superstitious beliefs found among his medieval society. *In the Red Lord's Reach* continues the minstrel's episodic tale. In the north, where witches are revered and natural magnetic powers are used as sources of magic, Alaric finally finds acceptance of his power. Now he must fight his lack of belief in magic as he searches within himself for the path he will follow.

Eisenstein continues her practical approach to magic in *Sorcerer's Son.* The sorcerers' magical powers are strictly defined, operating according to laws much as science does. One finds sorcerers, demons, magic, and, of course, a quest—all the typical elements of fantasy. Happily, Eisenstein also gives free rein to her enjoyable wit and humor, adding greatly to the humanity of the tale of Cray Ormoru. Set in the same world, *The Crystal Palace* presents a somber mood as Cray pursues a different sort of quest. There is more emphasis on motive than on action as Cray confronts his own beliefs and desires in trying to free the ice sorceress Aliza from an entrapment she does not feel or acknowledge.

Strong, resourceful, and independent women figure prominently in Eisenstein's work. This makes *Shadow of Earth* somewhat disappointing. Accidentally thrust into a medieval society, 20th-century Celia seems little able to cope with her drastic change of circumstance and social status and is ultimately only slightly changed by the experience. The book has been touted by feminists for showing the harshness of a world where a woman's only value is in bearing children. Perhaps Eisenstein intentionally makes this heroine weak to emphasize the helplessness of a technologically educated woman in a more primitive society. Although *In the Hands of Glory* sometimes lapses into the romantic clichés of space opera, its strong point is Dia Catlin, who faces conflict when her ideals encounter sordid reality. The outcome of a planetary rebellion is secondary to the growth and change Dia painfully undergoes.

Phyllis Eisenstein shows increasing maturity as a writer. Adept at handling various formats, she uses a variety of subjects equally well. In her latest works she concentrates on the psychological development of her characters, seemingly not content to let them merely be heroes. The worlds she creates, whether magical or otherwise, are carefully crafted and believable, her characters individual and memorable.

—Gay E. Carter

EKLUND, Gordon

Nationality: American. **Born:** Seattle, Washington, 24 July 1945. **Education:** Contra Costa College, San Pablo, California, 1973-75. **Military Service:** Served in the United States Air Force, 1963-67: Sergeant. **Family:** Married Dianna Mylarski in 1969; two sons. **Career:** Since 1968, freelance writer. **Awards:** Nebula award, 1974. **Agent:** Kirby McCauley Ltd., 155 East 77th Street, Suite 1A, New York, New York 10021, U.S.A.

SCIENCE FICTION PUBLICATIONS

Novels (series: Lord Tedric; Star Trek)

The Eclipse of Dawn. New York, Ace, 1971.
A Trace of Dreams. New York, Ace, 1972.
Beyond the Resurrection. Garden City, New York, Doubleday, 1973.
All Times Possible. New York, DAW, 1974.
Inheritors of Earth, with Poul Anderson. Radnor, Pennsylvania, Chilton, 1974.
Serving in Time. Don Mills, Ontario, Laser, 1975.
Falling Toward Forever. Don Mills, Ontario, Laser, 1975.
The Grayspace Beast. Garden City, New York, Doubleday, 1976.
Dance of the Apocalypse. Toronto, Laser, 1976.
If the Stars Are Gods, with Gregory Benford. New York, Berkley, 1977; London, Gollancz, 1978.
The Starless World (Star Trek) New York, Bantam, 1978; London, Corgi, 1985.
Space Pirates, with E.E. Smith. New York, Baronet, 1979; as *Lord Tedric: The Space Pirates,* London, Wingate, 1979.
Devil World (Star Trek). New York, Bantam, 1979; London, Corgi, 1985.
Black Knight of the Iron Sphere, with E.E. Smith (Lord Tedric). New York, Baronet, 1979; as *Lord Tedric: The Black Knight of the Iron Sphere,* London, Star, 1979.
Lord Tedric; Alien Realm (omnibus), with E.E. Smith. London, Star, 1980.
Lord Tedric, with E.E. Smith. New York, Baronet, 1978.
Lord Tedric: Alien Realms, with E.E. Smith. London, Star, 1980.
The Garden of Winter. New York, Berkley, 1980.
Find the Changeling, with Gregory Benford. New York, Dell, 1980; London, Sphere, 1983.
A Thunder on Neptune. New York, Morrow, 1989.

*

Gordon Eklund comments:
(1985) If there's any one aspect of my work to date that seems worth emphasizing, it would have to be the range of themes, subjects, styles, and moods that I've attempted. I don't believe that any two of my novels are very much alike, and the short stories

are even more varied, if only because of their greater number. To me, the science fiction field is an extremely broad category—one encompassing, as it does, all of possibility—and I've found it extremely difficult to settle down to mining a single nook within the field. I suppose a few certain types of stories can easily be seen as favorites of mine—I find particular pleasure in dealing with time and parallel worlds—but I wouldn't want to predict that this will remain valid during my next 10 years as a writer.

*   *   *

One aspect of science fiction which is generally misunderstood by those outside the field is that it encompasses a range of fiction from pure, lightweight adventure to more literary, theme- and character-oriented work. Readers within the field recognize which authors fall into which category, but outsiders tend to lump all SF authors together as purveyors of "escape fiction." Gordon Eklund is one of a comparatively small number of writers who wrote in both voices, which perhaps had the unfortunate side-effect of confusing his audience.

Eklund's lighter fare is entertaining but familiar. *Serving in Time*, for example, is a lightweight action story employing a very traditional theme. A man living in an apparently utopian future Earth is shanghaied into an organization that polices the time lines and which has altered the course of human history to create the world he finds so pleasant. Upset by the manipulation, he attempts to subvert their work and correct a great wrong but just makes matters worse. A different form of time travel plagues the protagonist of *Falling Toward Forever*. A mercenary becomes unattached from time and proceeds through a series of futures, drawn by an unseen presence who hopes to take advantage of his martial skills.

In *Dance of the Apocalypse*, we are shown a typical postcatastrophe America, although the cause is not clear. The cities are in ruins, plague and food shortages threaten the survivors, law and order has broken down. Against that background, one tough-minded man is instrumental in starting civilization going again. *The Grayspace Beast* is an otherworld quest story about a group of adventurers seeking a mythical creature on a far world, enlivened by well-drawn characters and an unusually evocative setting.

The "Lord Tedric" series is loosely based on a story written by Edward E. Smith before his death. The four novels, *Lord Tedric*, *Space Pirates*, *Black Knight of the Iron Sphere*, and *Alien Realms*, are unabashed space operas. In the opening volume we are introduced to Lord Tedric, whose battle against an evil wizard in a world of magic is contrasted with his new efforts in a galactic society of the far future when he is drawn there to help oppose a tyrant. In subsequent adventures Tedric becomes a space pirate, is branded a traitor, and battles a number of decadent, power-hungry local rulers trying to carve out their own spheres of influence in a crumbling interstellar empire. Fast-paced and decidedly plot-driven, the series provided good light entertainment, but did little to enhance Eklund's reputation. Eklund's two Star Trek novels, *Devil World* and *The Starless World*, are both typical adventures, involving respectively a disembodied alien intelligence and an artificial world constructed within a shell.

The Eclipse of Dawn, on the other hand, is a serious, well-conceived and executed novel of a near future America that has become isolationist and weakened by a new civil war that has resulted in the destruction of Washington and movement of the capi-

tal to the West Coast. One of the candidates for the presidency announces that he will rebuild the country with the aid of a race of immortal aliens living in the Jovian system. *A Trace of Dreams* is a more serious-minded adventure story, set on a shunned planet where a group of outcasts struggles to survive and make contact with an enigmatic alien race indigent to that world. Arguably the best of his novels is *All Times Possible*, which examines the different roles a specific individual may have had in the political development of America by examining his career in a number of parallel universes. *The Garden of Winter* is a rather convoluted story of the quest to reshape humanity's destiny, more ambitious than successful. It was the last of Eklund's novels to appear for almost a decade, that break interrupted in 1989 with *A Thunder on Neptune*, an adventure story for younger readers but one of Eklund's most controlled efforts. A boy who has lost the use of his legs is given a new chance when he is offered the chance to become physically transformed as part of a team being sent to explore the planet Neptune. Not a major work, but a well written, cleanly told story with a well-realized setting.

Eklund also collaborated on three other novels. *Inheritors of Earth*, based on a minor early short story by Poul Anderson, examines the superman theme but does little with it. *Find the Changeling* with Gregory Benford is an amusing, gripping puzzle story about the search for a shapechanging alien. Much more impressive is *If the Stars Are Gods*, assembled from a series of shorter works, which follows the career of a man uniquely positioned to chronicle humanity's first encounter with an alien race.

During the 1970s, Eklund was also a prolific short story writer. Among the more interesting of those works is the novelette "The Twilight River," which places vampires, sorcerers, and other legendary creatures in the far future of the Earth, and the alternate history story "The Karamazov Caper." Others of particular note include "West Wind Falling," "The Shrine of Sebastian," "Dear Aunt Annie," "The Chambers of Memory," "Examination Day," "The Anaconda's Smile," and "Moby, Too." Eklund's strengths were in his plotting, his ability to create a credible setting, and, in his more serious work, a deft ability to provide depth to his characters. His absence from the field during the past decade has been a major loss to readers.

—Don D'Ammassa

ELDERSHAW, M. Barnard

Pseudonym for Marjorie Faith Barnard and Flora Sydney Patricia Eldershaw (1897-1956). **Nationality:** Australian. **Born:** New South Wales, 16 August 1897. **Education:** Cambridge School, Hunters' Hill; Sydney Girls' High School; University of Sydney (exhibitioner; University Medal, 1920), 1916-20, B.A. (honours) in history 1920; Sydney Teachers College, 1920. **Career:** Librarian Sydney Public Library and Sydney Technical College Library, 1920-35; freelance writer, 1935-42; Librarian, Sydney Public Library, 1942, and Commonwealth Scientific and Industrial Research Organization Library, Sydney, 1942-50. **Awards:** Bulletin prize, 1928: Patrick White award, 1983. **Member:** Order of Australia, 1979. **Died:** 1987.

Science Fiction Publications

Novel

Tomorrow and Tomorrow. Melbourne, Georgian House, 1947; London, Phoenix House, 1949; complete text, as *Tomorrow and Tomorrow and Tomorrow,* London, Virago Press, 1983; New York, Dial, 1984.

Other Publications with Flora Sydney Patricia Eldershaw

Novels

A House Is Built. London, Harrap, and New York, Harcourt Brace, 1929.
Green Memory. London, Harrap, and New York, Harcourt Brace, 1931.
The Glasshouse. London, Harrap, 1936.
Plaque with Laurel. London, Harrap, 1937.

Play

The Watch on the Headland, in *Australian Radio Plays,* edited by Leslie Rees. Sydney, Angus and Robertson, 1946.

Other

Philip of Australia: An Account of the Settlement at Sydney Cove 1788-1792. London, Harrap, 1937.
Essays in Australian Fiction. Melbourne, Melbourne University Press, 1938; Freeport, New York, Books for Libraries, 1970.
The Life and Times of Captain John Piper. Sydney, Australian Limited Editions Society, 1939.
My Australia. London, Jarrolds, 1939; revised edition, 1951.
Plaque with Laurel, Essays, Reviews, Correspondence, edited by Maryanne Dever. St. Lucia, Queensland, University of Queensland Press, 1995.

Editor, *Coast to Coast: Australian Stories 1946.* Sydney, Angus and Robertson, 1947.

Other Publications as Marjorie Faith Barnard

Short Stories

The Persimmon Tree and Other Stories. Sydney, Clarendon, 1943; revised edition, London Virago Press, 1985; New York, Penguin, 1986.
But Not for Love: Stories of Majorie Barnard and M. Barnard Eldershaw, edited by Robert Darby. Sydney, Allen and Unwin, 1988.

Other

The Ivory Gate. Privately printed 1920.
Macquarie's World. Sydney, Australian Limited Editions Society, 1941.
Australian Outline. Sydney, Ure Smith, 1943; revised edition, 1949.
The Sydney Book. Sydney, Ure Smith, 1947.
Sydney: The Story of a City. Melbourne, Melbourne University Press, 1956.

Australia's First Architect: Francis Greenway. London, Longman, 1961.
A History of Australia. Sydney, Angus and Robertson, 1962; revised edition, 1963; New York, Praeger, 1963.
Georgian Architecture in Australia, with others. Sydney, Ure Smith, 1963.
Lachlan Macquarie. Melbourne, Oxford University Press, 1964.
Miles Franklin. New York, Twayne, 1967; revised edition, St. Lucia and London, University of Queensland Press, 1988.

*

Marjorie Faith Barnard comments:

(1981) Two things have a bearing on my writing: one is the circumstances of my childhood, and the other a successful collaboration.

I was an only child, had no playmates, and did not go to school until I was ten (having been taught by governesses prior to that). This was the best possible beginning for a writer. My natural creativity was not quenched by having too much. I created my own exciting and happy world. Words were my toys. I had the close companionship of my mother and free access to my great-grandmother's books—the Victorian poets, a complete set of Dickens, many histories. I had no taste for the insipid children's books of my period and escaped them almost entirely.

My collaboration with Flora Eldershaw was successful and disciplined. We both wanted to write and each had something to contribute. Our rule was to discuss the plan of a book in detail and agree upon it before anything was written down. Flora had a fine critical ability and curbed my exuberance. I wrote the better prose and had more leisure, so most of the actual writing fell to me. Our association was professional: her friends were not my friends, her way of life not mine. This was a good thing; close friendship would have brought other than literary considerations into it all. We worked in a dry light.

*Tomorrow and Tomorrow** was entirely my own work as Flora Eldershaw, for reasons of geography and pressure of work, could not contribute. It is a serious book, the best and worst thing I have ever done. I cared too much. As an historian I could see all too clearly the probable future of this country. The book had its roots in the anguish of the years preceding the Second World War. It is about human survival and escape from bondage. The book ran into difficulties. It was hard to find a publisher for such a long and in some ways controversial novel; times were touchy. Without my knowledge my publisher submitted the manuscript to the censor who cut the latter part severely. It was not subversive and now would have no difficulty in being printed *in toto,* but costs have prohibited its republication in its original form.

*[Research by Maryanne Dever has shown this statement to be inaccurate, as there is considerable documentation to indicate that *Tomorrow and Tomorrow* was a collaborative work by Barnard and Eldershaw. An example is Eldershaw's letter to Miles Franklin in the Mitchell Library (MSS 3651/1/19-22), which mentions "the awful effort of having to close up the gaps left by the censor and adapting the ending."—Lucy Sussex, 1995]

*   *   *

M. Barnard Eldershaw is the pen name of the Australian historical novelists Marjorie Barnard and Flora Eldershaw, who in *Tomorrow and Tomorrow,* their one science fiction novel, apply the selective techniques of the historical novelist to recreate Australia of the period 1924-46 through the eyes of a man four centuries in the future.

The reconstruction of cultural malaise moving into wartime confusion is brilliant if overlong but the story (completed in 1942) moves on to a vision of a different ending to the World War of 1939-45, one wherein an exhausted people turns on the culture which has brought only recurrent agony to each new generation and destroys it. The razing of Sydney by fire is a tremendous symbolic set piece. All this is conveyed as sections of a novel written by a 24th-century littérateur, in a time when youth is again restive in a culture (conventionally pastoralutopian) which it sees as oppressive in its settled satisfaction. The author's political argument (this is a political novel) turns on a newly devised voting machine which records the thoughts of electors to give an accurate survey of mass attitudes.

When a public test of the machine is made, with youth proposing far-reaching constitutional changes, the outcome is devastating for the young protesters. The motion is lost when the machine records a 62% majority of the electors as utterly indifferent to the question. The warning is simple—that indifference leads to frustration and eventually to the violence which destroyed the earlier culture.

The Australian censorship at the time found much of this material not actually subversive but politically disquieting, particularly that dealing with the war which was still in progress, and made numerous deletions. Some are, from the viewpoint of the 1940s, understandable; ideas of an ultimate political doublecross by Russia and Australian secession from the British Empire were touchy stuff—but finally honoured by events, though not in the form of the writer's forecast. Other deletions are hard to justify: what, for instance, could have been the objection to: (a man of the 24th-century is speaking) "I only know by chance and the skin of my teeth that jigsaw puzzles were a fashionable craze four centuries ago and now are one with crosswords and diabolo"? It is no longer possible to recover the state of mind which caused such aberrations. The curious will find all the deletions restored and listed in the Virago edition of 1983.

Tomorrow and Tomorrow and Tomorrow (the full title now restored) is powerfully characterised and is a masterly example of science fiction used to present an argument in dramatic detail. Nobel Prize-winner Patrick White named it the Australian novel he would most like to see republished. It has been.

—George Turner

ELGIN, (Patricia Anne) Suzette Haden

Nationality: American. **Born:** Patricia Anne Suzette Wilkins, Louisiana, Missouri, 18 November 1936. **Education:** University of Chicago (Academy of American Poets Award, 1955), 1954-56; California State University, Chico, B.A. in French and English 1967; University of California, San Diego, 1968-73, M.A. in Linguistics 1970, Ph.D. 1973. **Family:** Married 1) Peter Joseph Haden in 1955 (died), one son and two daughters; 2) George N. Elgin in 1964, one son; nine grandchildren. **Career:** Television folk music performer, Redding, California, 1966-68; instructor, Chico Conservatory of Music, 1967-68; French teacher, 1968-69; guitar teacher,

1969-70; linguistics teacher, University of California, San Diego, summer 1971; Assistant Professor, then Associate Professor of linguistics, San Diego State University, 1972-80, now Emeritus. Since 1980, founding director, Ozark Center for Language Studies, and editor, *The Lonesome Node* (now titled *Linguistics and Science Fiction*), for members of the Linguistics and Science Fiction Network. **Awards:** Eugene Saxon Fellowship, 1957-58. **Member:** Science Fiction Writers of America; Authors Guild; Linguistics and Science Fiction Network (chair); Science Fiction Poetry Association (founder). **Agent:** Jeff McCartney, 201 Oratam Terrace, Leonia, New Jersey 07605. **Address:** P.O. Box 1137, Huntsville, Arkansas 72740, U.S.A. **Online Address:** ocls@sibylline.com.

SCIENCE FICTION PUBLICATIONS

Novels (series: Communipath; Native Tongue; Ozark)

Communipath Worlds. New York, Pocket Books, 1980.
The Communipaths. New York, Ace, 1970.
Furthest. New York, Ace, 1971.
At the Seventh Level. New York, DAW, 1972.
Star-Anchored, Star-Angered (Communipath). Garden City, New York, Doubleday, 1979.
The Ozark Trilogy. Garden City, New York, Doubleday, 1982.
Twelve Fair Kingdoms. Garden City, New York, Doubleday, 1981.
The Grand Jubilee. Garden City, New York, Doubleday, 1981.
And Then There'll Be Fireworks. Garden City, New York, Doubleday, 1981.
Native Tongue. New York, DAW, 1984; London, Women's Press, 1985.
Yonder Comes the Other End of Time (Communipath). New York, DAW, 1986.
The Judas Rose (Native Tongue). New York, DAW, 1987; London, Women's Press, 1988.
Earthsong (Native Tongue). New York, DAW, 1994.

OTHER PUBLICATIONS

Other

Guide to Transformational Grammar: History, Theory, Practice, with John T. Grinder. New York, Holt Rinehart, 1973.
What Is Linguistics? Englewood Cliffs, New Jersey, Prentice-Hall, 1973; revised edition, 1979.
A Primer of Transformational Grammar for Rank Beginners. Urbana, Illinois, National Conference of Teachers of English, 1975.
The Gentle Art of Verbal Self-Defense. Englewood Cliffs, New Jersey, Prentice-Hall, 1980; *More on the Gentle Art of Verbal Self-Defense,* 1983; *The Last Word on the Gentle Art of Verbal Self-Defense,* 1987; *Success with the Gentle Art of Verbal Self-Defense,* 1989; *Staying Well with the Gentle Art of Verbal Self-Defense,* 1990; new edition, as *Last Word on the Gentle Art of Self-Defense,* 1992; as *More on the Gentle Art of Verbal Self-Defence,* London, Prentice-Hall, 1992.
A First Grammar and Dictionary of Láadan. Madison, Wisconsin, Society for the Furtherance and Study of Fantasy and Science Fiction, 1985; second edition, 1988.
Pouring Down Words. Englewood Cliffs, New Jersey, Prentice-Hall, 1975.

A Celebration of Ozark English: A Collection of Articles from the Lonesome Node, 1980 to 1990. Huntsville, Arkansas, OCLS Press, 1991.
Genderspeak: Men, Women, and the Gentle Art of Verbal Self-Defense. New York, Wiley, 1993.
The Gentle Art of (Verbal) Written Self-Defense Letter Book: Letters in Response to Triple-F Situations. Englewood Cliffs, New Jersey, Prentice-Hall, 1993.
BusinessSpeak: Using the Gentle Art of Verbal Persuasion to Get What You Want at Work. New York, McGraw-Hill, 1995.
You Can't Say That to Me! Stopping the Pain of Verbal Abuse: An 8-Step Program. New York, Wiley, 1995.

*

Manuscript Collection: Chater Collection, Love Library, San Diego State University; University of Oregon Library, Eugene.

Suzette Haden Elgin comments:

(1981) I went into writing science fiction originally because as a married woman with four kids at home I couldn't pay my graduate school tuition any other way, it being well known that such women are not "Ph.D. material." I know that's not an inspiring or romantic reason, but it's honest. Because I am a linguist my major interest is problems of communication as they are now and as they are likely to develop in the future; I have focused my books on this topic up to now, along with—as subtopics—an attempt to make clear what a pernicious crock Romantic Love is, and a fascination with problems of theology especially as they apply to women under the constant influence of religious language. My books have been picked up as feminist, which I hadn't realized they were until I read the reviews.

I take my SF writing very seriously, and feel that anybody who spends the time and money to read something I have written should not feel cheated, and should not be presented with a cryptic puzzle used to demonstrate how clever I am. My first four books have been part of an ongoing series about a rather bumbling mind-deaf superspy; I am now writing a fantasy trilogy, and am enjoying the change. But there will be more Coyote Jones books—the intergalactic superspy framework is a gentle kind of spoof that allows me plenty of room to move around and be as entertaining as possible without writing anything I have to be ashamed of later. I try to avoid the Brothers Karamazov Syndrome, and do not allow my characters to pontificate.

I plot a book down to the most minute detail in advance, filling notebooks with maps, biographies, every conceivable sort of information I might need in the book about its culture and characters. That takes at least a year. When I do the actual writing, however, I do only one draft. Then I revise as I type the final manuscript, and that writing process generally takes about six weeks from start to finish. I don't believe in inspiration, I believe in hard work. I hope that shows in my work; it's meant to. I have no problem "finding ideas"; my only problem is finding time to write them all. That, I expect, comes from rigorous training in the scientific method: one just poses hypotheses, and extrapolates.

Most embarrassing moment: having nobody notice that I had intended *Furthest* as a straightforward satire of the United States system of economics; that is, anything's allowed as long as you've filled out the proper forms.

*   *   *

Suzette Haden Elgin, like Gregory Benford or Fred Hoyle, writes science fiction concerning her professional field. In her case the science is linguistics, in which Elgin has done both academic and popular work. In fact, she may be even better known for her books of advice on linguistic techniques for dealing with people—which she calls "the gentle art of verbal self-defense"—than she is for her science fiction.

Still, Elgin's fiction is decidedly worthy of interest, with its strong narrative voice, good developments of characters and cultures, and examination of many social issues. Elgin's novels all take place in roughly compatible futures, which at least share some references, but divide into three main fictional worlds. At first established as separate, the Communipath series and the Ozark trilogy do meet in *Yonder Comes the Other End of Time.* Her more recent Native Tongue books are more independent in feel, especially as the series develops.

The Communipath books are clearly science fiction, set in a far future populated by a number of humanoid cultures on a number of planets. The prevailing theme of the books is communication, in all its various and difficult guises. These include different forms of telepathy, and social and communication systems such as the Multiversities (higher education more rare but more esteemed than now) and a system of ritual battle by carefully selected and honored poets, in which soldiers suffer for their side's inferior verse, in *At the Seventh Level.*

Tri-Galactic Agent Coyote Jones is central to the Communipath books. He is an extremely powerful projective telepath but also "mind-deaf," a rare and pitiable affliction which, however, suits him for the assignment in *Star-Anchored, Star Angered:* checking out Drussa Silver, a female messiah whose abilities include—but go beyond—telepathy. Her followers, in their religion-based community/communication/communion, recall the Maklunites of *The Communipaths.* Other characters in these novels include a "mind wife," rebelling against the life of psychic concubine for which she has been trained, in *Furthest;* and Susannah, an extremely telepathically gifted baby, drafted for the communipath system (likened to a psychic bucket-brigade) that passes messages through otherwise impossible distances (*The Communipaths*).

The speculative discussion of specific forms of discourse is also one of the strengths of Elgin's Ozark trilogy: *Twelve Fair Kingdoms, The Grand Jubilee,* and *And Then There'll Be Fireworks.* In this series, the Twelve Families of Planet Ozark left Earth and founded a mostly utopian society with a technology based primarily on magic. The setting on another planet and use of scientific technology (especially the "comsets" run by the main family in the trilogy, the Brightwaters) would justify calling the books science fiction; and in a deeper sense the society and magic (which is always a technology) also show extrapolative insight, much like the extrapolative fantasy of John W. Campbell's magazine *Unknown* in the 1940s. On the other hand, the three novels are more like contemporary fantasy in tone; and while they explain how the magic works (the highest form is based on transformational-generative grammar), no material explanation is given for why it does. This question is left open in *Yonder Comes the Other End of Time,* in which Coyote Jones finds that Ozark magic may function by the rules of "psience" as he knows them, or it may not.

Much of the charm of the Ozark trilogy comes from the familiar strangeness, and strange familiarity, of alien equivalents of the modern-American Ozark culture Elgin knows well, including "mules," actually telepathic (but generally uncommunicative) aliens who fly by magic; and "the Grannies," a powerful social class, able to perform household magic and known for their folksy and fiery "formspeech." The plot of the books primarily revolves around Responsible of Brightwater, a 14-year-old girl who holds the position, as does one female each generation, of Meta-Magician. Unknown to most, she holds powers greater than even the Magicians of Rank, and her mere functioning is vital to the maintenance of magic on Ozark.

The Communipath and Ozark books show the growth of Elgin as an author, especially in plotting. The plots of the Communipath series are often loose, with too abrupt a solution by Coyote Jones, and too many intriguing developments—such as the changes hinted at the end of *The Communipaths*—dropped or only vaguely referred to later. In the Ozark books, the plots are complicated but always tight, with material, such as the character of Silverweb of McDaniels, which is not only interesting but later shown to be vital. The narrative voice gets more sure and the characters get both more human and more powerful, although Responsible can occasionally verge on the unconvincing precociousness of Tessa in *The Communipaths*. The book which joins the two series is harder to judge as a novel, since its significance often depends on knowing the other books; it does succeed in its own terms, especially demonstrating the irresistible wit that characterizes Elgin's best writing.

Native Tongue, The Judas Rose, and *Earthsong* are impressive science fiction novels in many ways, although the third book does seem to leave some of the elements of the first two novels unresolved as it takes a somewhat different direction. In the first two books, the main theme is communication among aliens: between humans and extraterrestrial aliens; and between men and women, who are almost as alien to each other. In a future of copious interplanetary trade, the linguists have become a necessary and powerful yet despised and feared social class, marrying among their households and raising their children to be translators before the age of natural language acquisition is past. The events also occur in a future in which women's liberation is only a legend, and men have complete legal control of all females; within this tyranny, however, the linguist women use their skills (and isolation from the men) to design and promote Láadan, a language formed to express women's concerns and values. Fictional "prefaces" to both novels explain that the manuscripts were published in a further, more egalitarian, future, which apparently came about due to the events the novels describe.

In the third book, *Earthsong,* the linguist women have been changed by the use of Láadan, although the emphasis of the book is on the women's further discovery of "audiosynthesis." That is, just as plants create food from light via photosynthesis, humans have the ability, hinted at throughout history but never before practiced widely, to use music as a substitute for food. Since the aliens have stopped all trade (at the end of *The Judas Rose*), audiosynthesis is necessary to survive the economic crisis. There are also parallels between the evolution caused by Láadan and that which audiosynthesis promotes. The change in focus blunts some of the effects of the previous books, however, and some ideas—including that whales are sentient and can communicate with some aliens that humans cannot—seem too abruptly handled. Moreover, the use of multiple narrative voices, based on a somewhat-experimental idea of one character trying to communicate after death, may be less successful than it should be.

The strongest aspect of the Native Tongue books, interwoven with the linguistic concerns, is a caustic and often compelling examination of gender issues. Elgin has shown societies repressive of women elsewhere, as in *At the Seventh Level.* In fact, while strong females appear in all her books—from a Multiversity dean to Troublesome of Brightwater—Elgin writes more about problems of gender-roles than about solutions, and sometimes her novels may too simply reverse the sexism they examine. Especially in the Ozark trilogy and Native Tongue books, men are by nature bumbling fools, but still strong enough to trouble and oppress women. This aspect bothers many readers, but Elgin's does convey her perspective well, and her presentation is often uncomfortably convincing. The Native Tongue books also have incisive, discomforting things to say about systems of medical care, and about religion (clearly also an interest of Elgin's in the Ozark and Communipath books).

Though not as widely known as she should be, Elgin is a significant author whose novels both use genre conventions and surpass or undermine them. Her books also present the reader with an enticing blend of readability and challenging (often provoking) insights concerning serious issues.

—Bernadette Lynn Bosky

ELIADE, Mircea

Nationality: American Romanian. **Born:** Bucharest, Romania, 9 March 1907. **Education:** University of Bucharest, 1925-28, graduated in Letters and Philosophy in 1928 with a dissertation on Tommaso Campanella; University of Calcutta, India, 1928-31, where he prepared his Ph.D. dissertation on Yoga, maintained in Bucharest, 1933, and published in Paris, 1936. **Military Service:** Served in the Romanian Army, anti-aircraft artillery, 1932. **Family:** Married 1) Nina Mare in 1934 (died 1944); 2) Georgette Christinel in 1950. **Career:** Assistant professor of philosophy, University of Bucharest, 1933-39; cultural attaché at the Romanian Legation in London, U.K., 1940; cultural counsellor at the Romanian Embassy in Lisbon, Portugal, 1941-44; professor of history of religions, "L'École des Hautes Études" of the Sorbonne University, Paris, 1945-49; wandering scholar and lecturer, 1950-1955, in Paris and Strassbourg (France), Rome and Ascona (Italy), Munich and Freiburg (West Germany), Geneva (Switzerland), Amsterdam (Holland), Lund (Sweden) etc.; professor of history of religions, University of Chicago, USA, 1956-1986; editor (together with Joseph M. Kitagawa and Charles Long) of *History of Religions,* 1961-86. Participated in: the International Congresses of Orientalists, Paris, 1948; Munich, 1951, 1957, and in many International Congresses of the History of Religions: Amsterdam, 1950; Rome, 1951; Paris, 1955; Tokyo, 1958; Marburg (West Germany), 1960; Stockholm, 1970; Turku (Finland), 1973. **Member:** American Academy of Arts and Sciences, 1966; fellow of the British Academy, 1970; corresponding member of the Austrian Academy of Sciences, 1973; member of the Belgian Academy, 1975. **Awards:** Doctor Honoris Causa of: Yale University, 1966; University of la Plata, Argentina, 1969; Ripon College, Wisconsin, 1969; Loyola University, Chicago, 1970: Boston College, 1971; La Salle College, Philadelphia, 1972; Oberlin College, Ohio, 1972; University of Lancaster, 1975; University of Sorbonne, Paris, 1976; University of Washington, 1985. "Christian Culture Award" of the Windsor University, Canada, 1968;

"Bordin Award" of the French Academy, 1977; "Legion of Honour", Paris, 1978; "Dante Alighieri International Award", Arezzo, Italy, 1984. Nobel Prize nominee in 1980. **Died:** 22 April 1986.

SCIENCE FICTION PUBLICATIONS

Fantastic Tales, translated into English by E. Tappe. N.p., 1969. [The collection includes "Un om mare," 1945 ("A Big Man").]

The Tales of the Occult, translated into English by William Ames Coates. N.p., 1970.

Two Strange Tales, translated into English by William Ames Coates. N.p., 1986. [Both these collections include: "Nop i la Serampore," 1940 ("Nights at Serampore," translated into English as "Midnight at Serampore") and "Secretul doctorului Honigberger," 1940 ("Doctor Honigberger's Secret").]

Youth without Youth and Other Novellas, translated into English by Mac Linscott Ricketts. Columbus, Ohio State University Press, 1989.

OTHER PUBLICATIONS

"With the Gipsy Girls" ("La ig nci," 1959), in *Denver Review,* 1973.

The Forbidden Forrest, translated into English by Mac Linscott Ricketts and Mary Park Stevenson. N.p., 1978 (*Forêt interdite,* 1955; *Noaptea de Sânziene,* 1971).

Tales of the Sacred and Supernatural, 1981.

From Primitives to Zen: A Thematic Sourcebook on the History of Religions. London and New York, Harper & Row, 1967.

Myths, Rites, Symbols. New York, Harper, 1975.

Occultism, Witchcraft and Cultural Passions: Essays in Comparative Religions. Chicago and London, Chicago University Press, 1976.

Autobiography, translated into English by Mac Linscott Ricketts, New York and San Francisco, Harper & Row, 1981.

Editor, *The Encyclopaedia of Religions,* 16 vols. New York, Macmillan, 1987.

Mircea Eliade comments:

(1977) When I finished high school I already understood that I was simultaneously solicited by two, or even three "vocations": on the one hand, by objective research (from natural sciences I had passed to orientalism, to the history of religions and philosophy), and on the other, by literary imagination: either fantastic fiction, realistic literature, or psychological literature, such as I had practiced in a few novelettes and, especially, in *The Novel of the Short-Sighted Adolescent.*

This "threefold vocation," as I would call it, inspired my entire production, from the first books of my youth to the present. In the three years spent in India (1928-31) I published many studies on the Indian philosophies and sciences, and I prepared my doctorate thesis about Yoga (appeared in 1936), but I also wrote a half autobiographical novel (*Isabel and the Devil's Waters,* 1930) and another, less fantastic, *The Light that Goes Out* (published in 1934). After returning to my country and before leaving for London, in the spring of 1940, there appeared, beside the scientific works (*Asian Alchemy, Yoga, Babylonian Cosmology and Alchemy,* the review *Zalmoxis*) and several collections of articles (*India, Oceanogra-*

phy, Fragmentarium etc.), a number of "realistic" novels (*Maitreyi, Return from Paradise, The Hooligans, Wedding in Heaven*), but also three books of fantastic literature (*Miss Christina, The Snake, Doctor Honigberger's Secret*).

It is obvious that the courses I taught, starting with 1945, at the École des Hautes Études (Sorbonne), and after 1956 at the University of Chicago, constrained me to reduce my literary activity considerably: especially because I had decided to write fiction (as well as the *Diary* and later on the *Autobiography*) in the Romanian language. This time, after finishing the fresco-novel *The Forbidden Forrest* (appeared first in French translation: *Fôret Interdite,* Gallimard, 1955), I only wrote small novels and fantastic novelettes (most of them collected in the volume *In Dionys's Courtyard,* Paris, 1977).

There would be a lot to say regarding this almost exclusive concentration on fantastic fiction. In the *Diary,* as well as in some other writings, I commented on what I dare call my conception of fantastic literature. And which differs, for example, from that of the German romantics, from Edgar Allan Poe's, or from J.L. Borges's. It would be useless to try and summarize it here. It is enough to mention that it is in accordance with my conception of the mystic thinking and the imaginary universes which it founds, universes parallel to everyday world and which distinguish themselves first of all through a different experience of space and time. Which does not mean, of course, that the fantastic fiction I write is inspired by my studies of comparative history of religions, nor that it could only be understood by the readers familiar with such studies. I can't remember ever using mythological documents or their symbolic significance when writing fiction. As a matter of fact, I discovered the subject of the novel or story as I was writing it. The parallel universes revealed by the story were the fruit of creative imagination, not of erudition or hermeneutics which were at my hand as a historian of comparative religions.

*   *   *

Mircea Eliade is better known in the West for his scholarly works and studies in comparative religion, written in French or English and translated all over the world. Unfortunately, his literary work, written in Romanian, equally masterful but less translated, is not well enough known as yet. Thus, as a writer of fiction, he continues to belong entirely to Romanian literature: in his native land, Romania, he is better known for his fantastic and realistic fiction, which ranked him among the nation's major writers as early as before the Second World War, when he was still living at home. He continued to write fiction exclusively in Romanian after the War, during the near half of a century he spent abroad, in England, Portugal, France, America. He wrote both realistic and fantastic fiction, the latter including some genuine masterpieces: the novels *Domni oara Christina* ("Miss Christina," 1936) and *arpele* ("The Snake," 1937), the novelettes "La ig nci" ("With the Gipsy Girls," 1959) and "Pe strada Mântuleasa" ("On Mântuleasa Street," 1968). About seven of his writings, by force of habit also labelled as "fantastic," may be read as science fiction, albeit as a somewhat borderline one.

This borderline is natural after all, as Eliade is not a SF writer proper, but a "mainstream writer of SF," a "guest" to the SF genre. By the very virtue of his strong and irreducible personality, he transferred into science fiction, when he "visited" it, all his strongly marked personal features, all his defining biases and obsessions, his unique mindshape, his main characteristic themes: the hidden mythical patterns of human life, the illusory nature of time, the trial of death and the search for immortality, the trial of the labyrinth and, above all—perhaps the most "Eliadian" theme—the never unveiled face of divinity, the impenetrable disguise of the sacred when disclosed in the stuff of the profane, the ambiguous concealment of the "Deus ignotus," of the "unknown" or "hidden God" in his mundane journey, which makes him unrecognizable to mortals' eyes. In Eliade's fiction all these can be found, figured in a "fantastic" key mainly, but sometimes also in a SF key; in the latter case, the fictional proceeding becomes sciencefictional proper, analogy and extrapolation being fully at work with thorough logical rigour, though the "scientific" hypothesis may be drawn from the "imaginary" or "pseudo" science, rather than from "real" science.

In this manner, having a rich knowledge of the Indian culture, Eliade extrapolates various hypotheses taken from Indian doctrines and esoteric practices such as Yoga and Tantra. "Secretul doctorului Honigberger" ("Doctor Honigberger's Secret," 1940) tells a compelling story about time distortion and human-body invisibility. In "Nop i la Serampore" ("Nights at Serampore," 1940) time reversibility reduces individual lifespans to infinitesimal proportions as compared to the great time-intervals of supra-individuality. A sense of human ephemerality, a sense of time flimsiness and a suggestion that time is only an illusion spring out from both these "Indian" stories.

The short story "Un om mare" ("A Big Man," 1945) deals with a case of "macroanthropism": it is the story of a giant comparable, to a certain point, to the one in H.G. Wells's *The Food of the Gods* (1904), but with a specific "Eliadian" touch.

Another two novelettes, or novellas, assimilable to SF were written in Paris much later, in 1976, both on the pretext of mutants (admitting the possibility of a developmentally-induced mutation, not only of a genetically transmitted one). The old schoolmaster Dominic Matei, the hero of the novelette "Youth without Youth," almost the length of a novel, is a mutant who becomes young, immortal and all-remembering after a thunderbolt. He travels like a young and glorious god through space and time, where he has a lot of exciting experiences, but afterwards he decides to go back to his native town, Piatra Neam, to die there old and decrepit, unknown and uncomprehended by his old fellows. Thus he yields to the mutants' nostalgia, common in Romanian SF, of returning to human vulnerability and ephemerality, but at the same time follows the paradigm of "the hidden God."

In the other novelette written in Paris in 1976, in Romanian as well, but under a French title, "Les trois Grâces" ("The Three Graces"), Eliade extrapolates an idea he found—as he himself states—in the "Apocrypha" of *The Old Testament,* transforming it into a cruel mutant-story. An occult fragment, perhaps imaginary, of these biblical *Apocrypha* is supposed to refer to the "biological and medical implications of the theology of the original sin": according to it, disease and death, to which man was condemned after the loss of Paradise, would be the effect of some cellular amnesia; if, by some medical treatment, the cells could be made to remember how to regenerate, disease and death would cease to exist and youth would be eternal. The mystery of immortality lies hidden and forgotten within the very core of the mortal human biology, just like the sacred within the profane. Initiated into the occult doctrine of *Apocrypha* by Father Calinic, an old orthodox monk, doctor Aurelian T taru applies an original rejuvenation treatment to three old women suffering from cancer. The action takes place in the Romania of the fifties, terrorized by the Secret Police and under the "Iron Curtain." In these circumstances, the treatment is sud-

denly discontinued and forbidden by an official order, Dr. T taru destroys all his notes before moving to another hospital, while the three women are abandoned in the semi-vegetal condition of hamadryads, condemned to live "like flowers, following the sun," getting young in spring and old in autumn, which represents a constant source of unhappiness for them. The last of "the three Graces," the old and young Frusinel ("Euphrosyne"), unknowingly remakes the unhappy fate of the mythological Persephone, allowed to live half a year on the surface of the earth, but condemned to spend the other half in the underworld of Hades.

Among the "inedited novelettes" published in Romania after Eliade's death, there are two others that bear a SF streak. "Dayan" (1979-80) features a brilliant student in mathematics, Constantin Orobete, who tries to discover "the absolute equation," which Albert Einstein and Werner Heisenberg are said to have envisaged in order to re-create the world; in failing to do so, Orobete divulges his double nature: he is at the same time a SF character and the bearer of a mythical role, an unsuccessful envoy of the sacred trying to disclose itself in the profane. The same multivocality may also be found in the short-story "La umbra unui crin . . ." ("In the Shade of a Lily . . . ," 1982), where the secret exodus of the chosen ones toward "a space of other dimensions" is disguised as a caravan of trucks mysteriously vanishing at a curve of the road.

Put together, the seven aforementioned stories would certainly make up a book masterly science fiction.

—Cornel Robu

ELLISON, Harlan (Jay)

Nationality: American. **Born:** Cleveland, Ohio, 27 May 1934. **Education:** Attended Ohio State University, Columbus, 1951-53. **Military Service:** Served in the United States Army, 1957-59. **Family:** Married 1) Charlotte Stein in 1956 (divorced); 2) Billie Joyce Sanders in 1961 (divorced); 3) Lory Patrick in 1965 (divorced); 4) Lori Horowitz in 1976 (divorced). **Career:** Editor, *Rogue;* founding editor, Regency Books, Evanston, Illinois, 1961-62. Freelance writer and lecturer; editor, Harlan Ellison Discovery Series. Vice-president, Science Fiction Writers of America, 1965-66 (resigned). **Awards:** Nebula award, 1965, 1969, 1977; Writers Guild of America award, for TV play, 1965, 1967, 1973; Hugo award, 1966, 1968 (3 awards), 1972 (for editing), 1974, 1975, 1978; Mystery Writers of America Edgar Allan Poe award, 1973; Jupiter award, 1973; *Locus* award, 1983; Bram Stoker award, for collection, 1988, for nonfiction, 1990. **Address:** 3484 Coy Drive, Sherman Oaks, California 91423, U.S.A.

SCIENCE FICTION PUBLICATIONS

Novels

The Man with Nine Lives, bound with *A Touch of Infinity.* New York, Ace, 1960.
Doomsman, bound with *Telepower,* by Lee Hoffmann. New York, Belmont, 1967.
Phoenix without Ashes: A Novel of the Starlost, with Edward Bryant. Greenwich, Connecticut, Fawcett, 1975; Manchester, Savoy, 1978.

The City on the Edge of Forever (novelization of TV play). New York, Bantam, 1977.

Short Stories

A Touch of Infinity, bound with *The Man with Nine Lives.* New York, Ace, 1960.

Ellison Wonderland. New York, Paperback Library, 1962; as *Earthman, Go Home,* 1964; revised edition, with original title, New York, Bluejay, 1984.

Paingod and Other Delusions. New York, Pyramid, 1965; revised edition, 1975.

I Have No Mouth and I Must Scream. New York, Pyramid, 1967.

From the Land of Fear. New York, Belmont, 1967.

Love Ain't Nothing But Sex Misspelled: Twenty-Two Stories. New York, Trident Press, 1968; revised edition, New York, Pyramid, 1976.

The Beast That Shouted Love at the Heart of the World. New York, Avon, 1969; abridged edition, London, Millington, 1976; revised edition, New York, Bluejay, 1984; further revised, Brooklandville, Maryland, Borderlands Press, 1994.

Over the Edge: Stories from Somewhere Else. New York, Belmont, 1970.

Partners in Wonder, with others (collaborations). New York, Walker, 1971.

Alone against Tomorrow: Stories of Alienation in Speculative Fiction. New York, Macmillan, 1971.

De Helden van de Highway. [Holland], n.p., 1973.

All the Sounds of Fear. St. Albans, Hertfordshire, Panther, 1973.

The Time of the Eye. St. Albans, Hertfordshire, Panther, 1974.

Approaching Oblivion: Road Signs on the Treadmill toward Tomorrow. New York, Walker, 1974; London, Millington, 1976.

Deathbird Stories: A Pantheon of Modern Gods. New York, Harper, 1975; London, Millington, 1977; revised edition, New York, Bluejay, 1984; further revised, Norwalk, Connecticut, Easton Press, 1991.

No Doors, No Windows. New York, Pyramid, 1975; revised edition, Brooklandville, Maryland, Borderlands Press, 1991.

oe Kan Ik Schreeuwen Zonder Mond. [Holland], n.p., 1977.

Strange Wine: 15 New Stories from the Nightside of the World. New York, Harper, 1978.

The Book of Ellison, edited by Andrew Porter. New York, Algol Press, 1978.

The Illustrated Harlan Ellison, edited by Byron Preiss. New York, Baronet, 1978.

The Fantasies of Harlan Ellison (omnibus). Boston, Gregg Press, 1979.

Shatterday. Boston, Houghton Mifflin, 1980.

Stalking the Nightmare. Huntington Woods, Michigan, Phantasia Press, 1982.

The Essential Ellison: A 35-Year Retrospective, edited by Terry Dowling with Richard Delap and Gil Lamont. Omaha, Nebraska, Nemo Press, 1987.

Angry Candy. Boston, Houghton Mifflin, 1988.

Footsteps. Round Top, New York, Footsteps Press, 1989.

Dreams with Sharp Teeth (omnibus). New York, Quality Paperback Book Club, 3 vols., 1991.

Run for the Stars, bound with *Echoes of Thunder,* by Jack Dann and Jack C. Haldeman II. New York, Tor, 1991.

Ensamvark. [Sweden], n.p., 1992.

Mind Fields: The Art of Jacek Yerka, the Fiction of Harlan Ellison. Beverly Hills, California, Morpheus International, 1994.

Graphic Novels

Demon with a Glass Hand, illustrated by Marshall Rogers. New York, DC Comics, 1986.

Night and the Enemy, illustrated by Ken Steacy. Norristown, Pennsylvania, Comico, 1987.

Vic and Blood: The Chronicles of a Boy and His Dog, illustrated by Richard Corben. New York, St. Martin's Press, 1989.

Harlan Ellison's Dream Corridor Special. Milwaukie, Oregon, Dark Horse Comics, 1995.

Plays

The City on the Edge of Forever (televised, 1967). Published in *Six Science Fiction Plays,* edited by Roger Elwood, New York, Pocket Books, 1976.

I, Robot: The Illustrated Screenplay. New York, Warner, 1994.

Television Plays: *The City on the Edge of Forever* (*Star Trek* series), 1967.

OTHER PUBLICATIONS

Novels

The Deadly Streets. New York, Ace, 1958; London, Digit, 1959; revised edition, New York, Pyramid, 1975.

Rumble. New York, Pyramid, 1958; revised edition as *Web of the City,* 1975.

The Juvies. New York, Ace, 1961.

Rockabilly. Greenwich, Connecticut, Fawcett, 1961; London, Muller, 1963; revised edition as *Spider Kiss,* New York, Pyramid, 1975.

Short Stories

Sex Gang (as Paul Merchant). San Diego, California, Nightstand, 1959.

Gentleman Junkie and Other Stories of the Hung-Up Generation. Evanston, Illinois, Regency, 1961; revised edition, New York, Pyramid, 1975.

All the Lies That Are My Life. San Francisco, Underwood-Miller, 1980.

Mefisto in Onyx. Shingletown, California, Ziesing, 1993.

Plays

Harlan Ellison's Movie. Westminister, Maryland, Mirage Press, 1991.

Screenplay: *The Oscar,* with Russell Rouse and Clarence Greene, 1966.

Television Plays: *Who Killed Alex Debbs? [Purity Mather?, Andy Zygmunt?, Half of Glory Lee?]* (*Burke's Law* series), 1963-65; *The Soldier* and *Demon with a Glass Hand* (*The Outer Limits* series), 1963-64; and for *Route 66, The Untouchables, The Alfred Hitchcock Hour,* and *The Man from U.N.C.L.E.* series.

Other

Memos from Purgatory. Evanston, Illinois, Regency, 1961.
The Glass Teat: Essays of Opinion on Television. New York, Ace, 1970.
The Other Glass Teat: Further Essays of Opinion on Television. New York, Pyramid, 1975.
Sleepless Nights in the Procrustean Bed: Essays, edited by Marty Clark. San Bernardino, California, Borgo Press, 1984; London, Xanadu, 1990.
An Edge in My Voice. Norfolk, Virginia, Donning, 1985; revised edition, 1987.
Harlan Ellison's Watching. Los Angeles, Underwood-Miller, 1989.
The Harlan Ellison Hornbook (essays). New York, Penzler, 1990.

Editor, *Dangerous Visions: 33 Original Stories.* Garden City, New York, Doubleday, 1967; abridged edition, London, Bruce and Watson, 2 vols., 1967.
Editor, *Nightshade and Damnations,* by Gerald Kersh. Greenwich, Connecticut, Fawcett, 1968.
Editor, *Again, Dangerous Visions.* Garden City, New York, Doubleday, 1972; London, Millington, 1976.
Editor, *Medea: Harlan's World.* Huntington Woods, Michigan, Phantasia Press, 1985.

Recording: *Blood!,* with Robert Bloch, Alternate World, 1976.

*

Bibliography: *Harlan Ellison: A Bibliographical Checklist* by Leslie Kay Swigart, Dallas, Williams, 1973.

Critical Studies: *Harlan Ellison: Unrepentant Harlequin* by George Edgar Slusser, San Bernardino, California, Borgo Press, 1977; "Harlan Ellison Issue" of *Fantasy and Science Fiction* (New York), July 1977; *The Book of Ellison* edited by Andrew Porter, New York, Algol Press, 1978.

* * *

Very few people are ambivalent about Harlan Ellison; most either thoroughly like or thoroughly dislike his writing. But he has won many awards for that writing, and not a few of them, such as those from the Writers Guild of America and the Mystery Writers of America, have come from outside the science fiction world. In fact, many of those who dislike him personally will admit that he is a fine writer. He is, indeed, a fine writer of fiction as well as a daring editor, an energetic collaborator, and a fearless critical commentator who has had a significant impact on the science fiction field.

In such Ellison stories like "A Boy and His Dog," there are graphic descriptions of sex and violence, and the language of at least some of the characters is littered with words generally considered obscene. But, Ellison might argue, such description and language are necessary to the story. "A Boy and His Dog" depicts the aftermath of World War III. Roving gangs and roving independents, called "solos," occupy the surface of the planet; these young toughs, mostly male, are the same sort as those who roam inner-city streets today. Their language must be realistic and accurate to carry the story. Ellison sets his group in opposition to the other group of survivors, those living in underground cities to which they retreated as the war broke out. The surface gangs are destroy-

ing each other (and eventually themselves) through violence; the below-grounders are sterile and wasting away. And without the obscenities and the violence, the reader would be less able to contrast the destructive aggressiveness of the surface group to the equally destructive non-participation of the below-grounders.

In addition to helping expand the language of science fiction in his own stories, Ellison has also actively encouraged others to do the same, most strongly as an editor. As editor of the *Dangerous Visions* series (1967 and 1972; there is also a legendary third volume), Ellison encouraged his fellow science fiction writers to send him those stories which other editors had considered too controversial to put into print. Ellison encouraged not just experiments with language, but experiments in style and subject matter as well. He saw the stories into print, and many of them became award winners.

Ellison's eagerness to experiment has also led him to collaborate in various ways with other science fiction writers and artists. *Partners in Wonder* (1971) and *Medea: Harlan's World* (1985) are fictional creations in which Ellison either coauthors the stories or provides the initial settings to which other writers respond. Two other collaborations, *Night and the Enemy* (1987), with Ken Steacy, and *Vick and Blood: The Chronicles of a Boy and His Dog* (1989), with Richard Corben, are illustrated texts. More recently, he collaborated on *Mind Fields: The Art of Jacek Yerka, the Fiction of Harlan Ellison* (1994), a collection of 33 full-color paintings by Yerka accompanied by an original prose or poetic piece by Ellison. *Demon with a Glass Hand,* originally written for the television show *The Outer Limits,* appeared from DC Comics in 1986, and *Harlan Ellison's Dream Corridor Special* was published by Dark Horse Comics in 1995.

It is, however, his own writing that is most important. Many of his best and most memorable short stories expand fictional boundaries in their subject matter. "Shattered Like a Glass Goblin" is a story about people on drugs who eventually, after continued and heavy use, become the creatures they hallucinate. They turn on and destroy each other in bestial ways. The narrator becomes a crystal goblin and is shattered by a swipe from the hairy paw of the creature that was once his girlfriend. In "Delusion for a Dragon Slayer" a man is given the chance to attain heaven if he can act like the heroic-fantasy hero he has always dreamed of being: he misses by a long way. And "Catman" was written as the future sex story for a volume of ultimate science fiction stories called *Final Stage.*

Other Ellison stories are experimental in style. "The Beast That Shouted Love at the Heart of the World" is written to be read as if the separate segments were arranged in a circle instead of a sequence of pages. "Pretty Maggie Moneyeyes" attempts to portray a person's impressions at the moment of death. Ellison uses italics, varied spacing, and other typographical arrangements to try to present these impressions and sensations. "From A to Z in the Chocolate Alphabet" consists of the alphabet, with a short story for each letter.

"The Deathbird" is a story experimental in both subject and style. In this story, appropriately dedicated to Mark Twain, Ellison attempts to show that Satan was the "good guy" and that God, who is responsible for the condition of the world, is insane. The story is told in 26 sections, each numbered, of which only 20 or 21 actually advance the plot of the story. Some of the others are direct addresses to the reader or quizzes for the reader to take; one section is the story of Ellison's dog, Ahbhu.

But there is more to Harlan Ellison than his science fiction. In newspaper columns later collected and published as *The Glass Teat* and *The Other Glass Teat,* he began with commentaries on film and television, which expanded to become examinations of all kinds of social and political topics. More recently, a number of his essays from a variety of sources have been collected and published as *Sleepless Nights in the Procrustean Bed* and *The Harlan Ellison Hornbook.* In addition, early Ellison fiction, much of it based on his experiences with street gangs, has been rereleased; and from time to time, Ellison has written for television, from the original *Burke's Law* to his own ill-fated *The Starlost,* and for the movies.

Ellison's career is more multifaceted than that of perhaps any other science fiction author, and because of the variety of things that he does—writing, editing, lecturing, and critiquing—he continues to be an important force in science fiction. An overview of that importance can be seen in *The Essential Ellison,* a 35-year, 1000-page retrospective featuring both fiction and nonfiction from 1949 to 1983. Although it does not contain his most recent work, such as "Susan," in the seventh *Year's Best Fantasy and Horror* (1994) and "The Man Who Rowed Christopher Columbus Ashore," in *Best American Short Stories 1993,* it more than amply illustrates the range and power of a writer who may yet be one of the century's most important and influential.

—C.W. Sullivan III

EMERSON, Ru

Pseudonym: Roberta Cray. **Nationality:** American. **Born:** Monterey, California, 15 December 1944. **Education:** Attended University of Montana, Missoula, 1963-66. **Career:** Worked as legal secretary in Los Angeles, 1966-83, and in Salem, Oregon, 1984-85. **Agent:** Richard Curtis Literary Agency, 171 East 74th Street, New York, New York 10021. **Address:** 2600 Reuben-Boise Road, Dallas, Oregon 97338, U.S.A. **Email Address:** (AOL) RuE6982539; (GENIE) R.Emerson10.

SCIENCE FICTION PUBLICATIONS

Novels (series: Nedao; Night-Threads; Bard's Tale)

The Princess of Flames. New York, Ace, 1986; London, Unicorn, 1987.
The Nedao Trilogy:
   To the Haunted Mountains. New York, Ace, 1987; London, Headline, 1988.
   In the Caves of Exile. New York, Ace, and London, Headline, 1988.
   On the Seas of Destiny. New York, Ace, and London, Headline, 1989.
Beauty and the Beast: Masques (novelization of TV script). New York, Avon, 1990.
Spell Bound. New York, Ace, 1990.
Night-Threads:
   The Calling of the Three. New York, Ace, 1990.
   The Two in Hiding. New York, Ace, 1991.
   One Land, One Duke. New York, Ace, 1992.
   The Craft of Light. New York, Ace, 1993.
   The Art of the Sword. New York, Ace, 1994.

The Science of Power. New York, Ace, 1995.
Fortress of Frost and Fire, with Mercedes Lackey (Bard's Tale). Riverdale, New York, Baen, 1993.
The Sword and the Lion (as Roberta Cray). New York, Daw, 1993.
Starbridge 7: Voices of Chaos (with A.C. Crispin). New York, Ace, 1995.

*

Ru Emerson comments:

I always wanted to write but never knew until I started reading fantasy and science fiction (in my early 20s) where my stories lay. I still find the genre exciting because of the opportunity to stretch one's imagination within a logical and real-seeming framework. Also, I very much enjoy creating my own histories and maps, almost as much as creating and writing the stories.

My main intention, always, is to tell a story—and to do it in such a fashion that a generation raised on movies and television can see the people and places as clearly as I do. Apart from this, I believe the most common recurring thread that ties my writing together is courage—not those who have it, but those who never knew they had it, how they find it in need (or don't find it at all), how great the circumstance needed to bring it out—how it changes people's lives.

*   *   *

Emerson states in a *Contemporary Authors* article (*CA* 121): "All my works at present are science fiction and fantasy. I began reading speculative fiction in 1970 with J.R.R. Tolkien, Isaac Asimov and Andre Norton." The influence of these writers, especially of Tolkien and Norton, are evident in her 12 novels to date [two additional novels, *The Science of Power* (the concluding volumes of the Night-Threads series) and *Starbridge 7: Voices of Chaos* were scheduled for publication in late 1995], published between 1986 and 1995. These include two fantasy novels, the *Nedao Trilogy,* the Night-Threads series (five books), *Masques* (a "Beauty and the Beast" novelization), and, with Mercedes Lackey, *Fortress of Frost and Fire,* a gaming offshoot, and short stories. This prolific production is usual in young fantasy authors and somewhat reflects publishers' efforts to provide readers with a sure thing. Emerson's earlier works are very similar, involving magic, kingdoms won and lost, battles between good and evil, and a focus on the leaders at the expense of spear carriers. Her characters all do great and heroic or dark and dastardly deeds, often at great personal cost, but her books cannot be read for the details of everyday life, nor even the details of journeys across mountain, plain, and desert, although most of the books include a few maps. They allow one to imagine, rather, what it might be like to send large groups of people to their deaths because it is the right thing to do and, while they conclude with the beauty of peace, they are concerned mostly with the heroism of war, an underlying message which is more characteristic of classical heroic fantasy than it is of Tolkien or Norton. They are, in fact, one of an emerging subgenre of fantasy novels where that melded conception of medieval history, myth, magic, and war-gaming meet. Their entertainment value is in following the twists and turns of the familiar game. The serial novelization *Masques* and the gaming novel *Fortress of Frost and Fire* both fulfill conventions of an already established series and contribute no new perspectives on the sword-and-sorcery fantasy genre.

The most recent Night-Threads series explores some twists of the generic conventions for fantasy which were first seen in writers such as Marion Zimmer Bradley, with female secret societies, heads of state, and sword-and-sorcery heroes.

Emerson's first published novel, *The Princess of Flames,* has many echoes of the King Arthur stories. It describes the adventures Elfrid, the bastard, female, youngest child of an aging King, Alster. She has three older half-brothers and two older half-sisters who are the children of the King and his legal wife, a woman he found so unpleasant that he banished her to a convent many years before. Despite the fact that he has grown sons, one of whom he expects will inherit the throne, Alster takes Elfrid as his favorite and allows her easy access to his person and freedom to wear 'men's' clothing and to learn bow and swordplay. Despite sibling rivalry, she is the hero of this tale and her father's trust in her proves to have been well-placed.

Alster's oldest son, Sedry, has persuaded his younger siblings to aid him and nobles more loyal to his mother in ousting the king. He intends that the King and Elfrid should die, Elfrid's defense is so successful that Sedry must send them into exile instead. He attempts to arrange their discrete murder, an eventuality which doesn't transpire, again, because of Elfrid. The rest is adventure and battles between Elfrid and her usurper-brother, King Sedry and a second ruthless and sadistic brother, Hyrcan.

The Tales of Nedao, a fantasy trilogy patterned somewhat after Tolkien's work, focuses, like *Princess,* on the adventures of a female protagonist, with an interesting twist. Ylia is the legal daughter and proclaimed heir of the Kingdom of Nedao. Her father, King Brandt has recognized in her the ability to preserve his kingdom and has, as in *Princess,* developed a deep affection for her. He has also provided her with training in sword, bow and statecraft, as befits an heir. While Ylia is not a bastard like Elfrid, her flaw is that she has an outlander mother, an Aeldran who has magic powers which she can enhance through her familiar, a sentient, calico cat named Nisana. In fact, the tale is narrated by Nisana, who begins each chapter of the three-volume work with a short or long pronouncement about its contents.

Again, as with *Princess,* the characters are either all good or all bad, with a few who waffle from good to bad. The protagonists seek to protect and rule their people and the antagonists seek the same thing, although in the name of power and conquest and through less palatable means. There are several familiar plot elements such as nonhuman beings with unusual powers who are aligned either with the good guys (Ylia and her groups) or the bad guys, her half-brother, Vess and his common-law father, the Wizard/villain Lysiad. Others include the battle of a war between good and evil that has lasted for thousands of years, the use of armies of the dead, and the use of inanimate objects as foci of power.

Each volume chronicles a discrete period in the loss and reconquest of the Kingdom of Nedao. The first, *To the Haunted Mountains,* loses no time in deposing and killing the King and Queen of Nedao. Slowly the few survivors of an invasion of neighboring Tehlatt, which was initiated by Lysiad's desire for power, travel to a more hospitable and defensible location to regroup and look for allies. They begin to rebuild in *In The Caves of Exile.* Ylia also arranges to have many young women trained in sword and bow, sets up trade with current neighbors, and finds and marries a wandering outlander who just happens to be the oldest son of the noble she has named as her temporary heir. As might be expected, *On the Seas of Destiny* chronicles the final battles between the evil Vess, his powerful Wizard father, Lysiad and the Wizard's companion,

Maritta. Magical intervention is the order of the day on both sides of the battle. The novels leave one with a sense of mighty tasks accomplished and great wrongs righted.

Spell Bound, a novel in one book, may be the best of Emerson's work. She has created a compact plot within an innovative retelling of the Cinderella story. The characters are anything but storybook, although the usual evil villains and heroic youngsters that appear in her other books are here also. At least the heros, a young prince named Conrad and a much-abused, noble stepdaughter, Sofia, both have a taint of misdeeds about them to make them more interesting. Sofia is characterized by many of the Cinderella stereotypes. Her father and mother are dead and she lives with a stepmother and two stepsisters, all of whom are more "coarse" socially and physically than she. One twist from the legend is that Sofia's mother was Spanish and was skilled in her own kind of magic, some of which is at Sophia's disposal. She decides to escape from her virtual servitude in her stepmother's household by making a pact with a "green witch" Ilse, who turns out to be anything but a fairy godmother. Ilse is pursuing her own ends of revenge on the fathers of Sofia and Conrad, who participated in burning to death her mother, Old Gerthe. By stepping outside the bounds of women's "Green Magic" and into men's "Gold Magic," Ilse has already succeeded in ridding herself of the older generation and hopes in one sweep to take care of the younger one. While there is justification for both Ilse and Gustave's actions, they are both portrayed as vain, overconfident, selfish and shallow so that their eventually defeat is predictable.

Emerson's most recent fiction, Night-Threads, is a young-adult series with five current volumes, *The Calling of the Three, The Two In Hiding, One Land, One Duke, The Craft of Light,* and *The Art of the Sword.* It's most unique feature is readerly transference— it introduces us to a fantastic parallel world that resembles early 19th-century Europe and the Middle-East, with references to British Colonialist policies towards China and other conquered peoples. This is accomplished through three characters—Jennifer, a junior lawyer; Chris, a young man and fantasy war-gamer; and Robyn, Chris's mother—who are taken from contemporary Los Angeles and become a part of the intrigue in the country of Zelharri where they were initially (*The Calling of the Three*) summoned by the magical powers of a young woman, Lialla Night, and her brother Aletto. The three are gradually integrated into the Night Threads culture and become significant forces for good. The disjunction, and also the charm of these novels are in their frequent reminders of the contemporary world used to reflect back and illuminate their understanding of this more primitive world. Jennifer and Robyn find mates and take up positions of influence in the monarchy and in the developing trade culture. Chris readjusts his cynical attitudes towards life and, by book five, has been in this parallel past for three years and still uses a version of youth slang from the 1980s, but he also refers to the Opium Wars with China and other 19th century European foreign policy. Jennifer and Chris's successes as merchants are directly dependent on their 'superior' twentieth century knowledge of technology. And running through the series like a needle is the Night-Threads secret society, a society of women, of whom Lialla is only one, with the ability to manipulate through their use of Night Thread magic.

Emerson's writing style is somewhat more adventurous in her short stories, like "A Golden Night for Silver Fishes" and "The Werewolf's Gift." But, as her last series confirms, she seems to have found her audience and her expression in these heroic tales of female and male adventurers of nobility, wit and charm, which satisfy readers' desires for a larger-than-life world in which to indulge fantasies of social and economic importance.

—Janice M. Bogstad

EMSHWILLER, Carol

Nationality: American. **Born:** Carol Fries, Ann Arbor, Michigan, 12 April 1921. **Education:** University of Michigan, Ann Arbor, B.A. in music and B. Design 1949; Ecole Nationale Supérieure des Beaux-Arts, Paris (Fulbright Fellow), 1949-50. **Family:** Married the filmmaker Ed Emshwiller in 1949 (died 1990); two daughters and one son. **Career:** Since 1978, member of the Continuing Education Faculty, New York University. Conducted workshops for Science Fiction Bookstore, New York, 1975, 1976 and Clarion Science Fiction Workshop, 1978, 1979; guest teacher, Sarah Lawrence College, Bronxville, New York, 1983. **Awards:** MacDowell Fellowship, 1971; Creative Artists Public Service Grant, 1975; National Endowment Grant, 1979; New York State Grant, 1988; New York University continuing education award for teaching excellence, 1989. **Address:** 210 East 15th Street, Apartment 12E, New York, New York, 10003; (summer) Rt. 1, Box 36 E, Cherrytree Circle, Bishop, CA, 93514, U.S.A.

Science Fiction Publications

Novel

Carmen Dog. London, Women's Press, 1988; San Francisco, California, Mercury House, 1990.

Short Stories

Joy in Our Cause: Short Stories. New York, Harper, 1974.
Verging on the Pertinent: Stories. Minneapolis, Minnesota, Coffee House Press, 1989.
The Start of the End of It All. London, Women's Press, 1990; revised as *The Start of the End of It All: Short Fiction,* San Francisco, Mercury House, 1991.
Venus Rising. Cambridge, Massachusetts, Edgewood Press, 1992.

Other Publications

Novel

Ledoyt. San Francisco, Mercury House, 1995.

Plays

Television Plays: *Pilobolis and Joan,* 1974; *Family Focus,* 1977.

*

Carol Emshwiller comments:

(1991) Formal/structural concerns have always interested me the most, so once I had learned to plot and had published numerous science-fiction stories (and a few mystery stories), I decided to learn how *not* to plot. My concerns were for the various ways of form-

ing a story and keeping forward movement without plotting. This was as hard to learn as plotting (harder, because I had no models in those days) and had to be learned as slowly. Looking back, I see that I did away with plot elements one at a time. I was unable to let go of them by twos or threes. I'm not really exactly sure what I put in their place, one by one, but I did refer to modern poetry for inspiration and I took many modern poetry techniques as models for my stories. Sometimes I tried to write a "story" all "between the lines," leaving a lot of work for the reader. Sometimes I tried to create the illusion of action without there actually being any.

Also I tried to write, as in modern poetry (which is influenced in this, I think, by the Chinese and Japanese), without the use of simile or metaphoric language, and, I hope, without a trace of the pathetic fallacy. I also tried to do away with character, and substituted what I called "selves," which, in my mind, were much more real than "characters" (though perhaps just different). I used the first person and tried for a kind of internal, psychological realism. To me, the "selves" represented the insides of everybody . . . the little fleeting thoughts . . . the little vanities . . . things not admitted by any of us. Also big things not admitted: petty hates, oedipal feelings, incest . . . .

Why might one bother doing this? Well, like most science-fiction writers, my study was "what-would-happen-if," but not what-would-happen-if the ice age returned, or if apes began teaching each other to talk, but what-would-happen-if, for instance, a story had only a single bit of action? or none? What could hold the interest? What could move it forward? However, I may have written myself into a hole by now. Plot seems to be slowly coming back into my work. I'm not sure where I'll go from here, but I'm sure that "structures" will be one of my primary concerns.

Of course, there's that other thing: that when your conscious mind is kept busy with forms, the subconscious mind can be freed to work on all those underground things that are, perhaps, more important to a story.

(1995) I haven't had time to revise this and it does explain how I *used* to write my more "experimental" stories, but for a long time I've been only writing stories (and novels) with plots—standard plots. I can't imagine writing without that now.

*   *   *

A prolific writer of short stories, until recently it has been hard for Emshwiller to receive the recognition she richly deserves. Her stories were available only in magazines and general anthologies like *New Worlds, Orbit,* and *Arbor House Treasury of Modern Science Fiction* as well as both editions of Pamela Sargent's *Women of Wonder* series. Emshwiller's métier is and probably always will be the short story, which she has been publishing since 1955 but currently four of her titles are simultaneously in print, from smaller presses such as Mercury House and Women's Press and one can more easily make a habit of reading her work. *The Start of the End of it All* won the Hugo for best collection in 1991 and her most recent title in print is a chapbook of "Venus Rising" (Edgewood Press, 1992). Many stories are science fiction by the general definition of the genre, making allusions to alien invasions, humans with peculiarly alien characteristics or behavior, and mythical creatures who change from human to animal, animal to human and human to plant. But they are also much more, in fact, what SF at its best can always be. Her plots, when they manifest themselves at all, are clearly secondary to series of brief frisson of recognition grafted onto seemingly absurdist or lighthearted tales of women and bears or large or small people. They wrench us from our normal, cozy cages of perception and expectation. A varied and gripping set of lyrical studies, her fictions are each also a virtuoso performance in language and thought. At once tongue-in-cheek and symbolic exposés of the human condition, many are reminiscent of Kafka, but a Kafka with a light and witty touch, who chortles playfully as s/he plunges us into a grim reflection on, for example, man's inhumanity to woman. While Emshwiller's topoi are reminiscent of Kafka, her style and sense of humor conjure up Calvino's *Cosmicomics.*

Present, like a nagging itch, throughout is the understanding that we repress many distasteful truths about the relationships between men and women as well as between humans and those creatures who share the earth with us. Because she often narrates in the first person, from the female perspective, one could assume she is speaking for women and against men. However, no one can read such work as *Carmen Dog,* her novel, or her very well-known "Sex and/or Mr. Morrison" and avoid the satirical presentation of women's weaknesses, vanities, and often, confusion about their own desires. This is not to say that women and men are presented in equal positions of power, but rather that Emshwiller will not allow us easy answers to the inequalities and division of power and what motivates or sustains it. The most delightful feature of Emshwiller's fiction are its allusive and often allegorical characterizations. *Carmen Dog* is an extended example of what can be called her use of sliding signifieds. Pooch is the central character in a rebellion of females against males, but it is a rebellion that manifests itself physically before it reaches the level of consciousness. Were Emshwiller to describe a world in which women were turning into animals because of their centuries-old treatment as such, she would have created an interesting story. She does not stop with this allegory, however, because her animals are also turning into women. House pets, including cats, dogs, and snakes, gradually take over the duties that their mistresses abandon, to varying degrees and with varying success.

The novel opens with Pooch's master and mistress consulting a psychologist to try and save their marriage. One can tell, however, that he is advising the husband more than the wife as he says "you say she was a fairly good wife and mother, though somewhat irritating at times, and you want her back that way as soon as possible? You must realize, however, that she is at this very moment in a period of profound change, both physical and psychological." But the psychologist, who later sets himself up to save 'motherhood' by running behavioral experiments on the animal-women and women-animals, knows this is also a widespread trend and speaks of them "as if they all had eaten an apple from the tree of a different kind of knowledge and have seen with new eyes, not that they are naked, but have seen that they are clothed." Pooch is alternately eager to take up what her mistress has abandoned, including the care of the baby and the love of the husband, and offended at the demands made by crude men on her body. Thus, as the other transitional creatures, she just can't manage to be either the perfect wife or the perfect rebel until all avenues are closed to her but the latter. In fact, a more bemused bunch of individuals than the characters, male and female, in this story, would be hard to find. The endearing sincerity of Pooch, the simplistic, sybaritic eagerness of the men around her and the puzzled meanderings of her female friends propel the reader through this allegory.

Joy in Our Cause was the first collection of fiction, but two much more recent collections have brought us more up-to-date stories. *The Start of the End of It All* gives us 18 short stories, including the ever popular "Sex And/or Mr. Morrison" and "Chicken Icarus." Reviewers have mentioned the cat-loathing aliens of the title story, but equally delightful are the creatures of "Draculalucard" and "Moon Song."

I have tried to pick a favorite story from *Verging on the Pertinent,* and am unable to do so. The work opens with "Yukon" in which a woman leaves the human brute she started out with and chooses instead a male black bear, winters with him and then finds a third, more satisfying partner. Even the titles of her stories alone are intriguing: "Mental Health and its Alternatives," "There is no God but Bog," "What Every Woman Knows," "The Futility of Fixed Positions," "Queen Kong," and the title story, a sassy, irreverent gloss on the absurdity of positions assigned to "remarkable" women to set them apart and deny the potential of all women as full people. All of Emshwiller's stories rely on suggestion, resonance, and symbol. We all know what she's talking about although she never says it. I am especially, viscerally, fond of "Queen Kong," where the ironic pose of the narrator shifts from the male to female positions at will. This comment about a large woman is typical, and typically evocative: "They are against all elegances, and no wonder, when even seeing them at a distance or simply in silhouette is unnerving. But the potential of large women! The huge, unrealized potential! Their great longings, their colossal grudges, their long-term memories, their rage! No wonder they deny all art . . . deny all civilization and try to convince their tiny, more discreet sisters to join them."

Emshwiller is often in others' anthologies but, since her métier seems to be the short story, and each story is the obvious recipient of much time and patience on her part, it is good to see such outlets for her work as alternative-press chapbooks. *Venus Rising* is a multiple-viewpoint first person narrative about Venus, vaguely imaged as a seal or a human, perhaps in fact a selkie, and Zuesa, a transitional ape-to-human. "Where I come from, giants rule . . . generations of princes, lords, barrons, sitting in the royal setting on tree limbs that represent ten thousand warriors, all the leaders having swung down via private chutes or air bridges of their own suspending, having entered through the sky gates of the messengers of good tidings, all, feathered like sun birds, swinging princely arms as far as is allowed and sometimes even farther, and I, one of them, my arms raised, I permitted to take my place at the topmost royal hearth when the fires burn brightest." He seeks to possess as many selkies as he can and Venus, after sacrificing herself to his lust in an attempt to save other women and their tribes, reaches the point where she will sacrifce him. And a new race may be born. The air-dreams of conquest and the sea dreams of coexistence make for lyrical and arresting prose and story.

It is possible to misunderstand Emshwiller. If one reads a single purpose into the multilayered allusions, one can be taken aback by the bald, almost gallows humor which cuts to the core of ambiguities that make up women's attitudes towards themselves and the cultures which encase them. One can never quite determine which of the speaker's statements should be taken ironically and which are authoritative. Emshwiller's grace, technical virtuosity, insight, humor, and depth rest in the narrators who never settle on a single or simple political position and therefore reflect this ambiguity of intent. It is one that we shall perhaps not escape until culture is organized along another matrix from that of sex. The stories are delightful for their artistry on all levels and examples of the best that the short story as an art form has to offer. You owe it to yourself to read and reread this author.

—Janice M. Bogstad

ENGDAHL, Sylvia (Louise)

Nationality: American. **Born:** Los Angeles, California, 24 November 1933. **Education:** Pomona College, Claremont, California, 1950; Reed College, Portland, Oregon, 1951; University of Oregon, Eugene, 1951-52, 1956-57; University of California, Santa Barbara, B.A. in education 1955; graduate work in anthropology, Portland State University, Oregon, 1978-80. **Career:** Elementary schoolteacher, Portland, 1955-56; programmer, then computer systems specialist, SAGE Air Defense System, Lexington, Massachusetts; Madison, Wisconsin; Tacoma, Washington; and Santa Monica, California, 1957-67; full-time writer, 1968-80; self-employed developer and vendor of home computer software, 1981-84. Since 1985, staff member, Connected Education Inc., New York. **Awards:** Newberry award, 1971; Christopher award, 1973; Phoenix award, 1990. **Address:** 3088 Delta Pines Drive, Eugene, Oregon 97401, U.S.A.

SCIENCE FICTION PUBLICATIONS (FOR YOUNG ADULTS)

Novels (series: Elana; Noren)

Enchantress from the Stars (Elana). New York, Atheneum, 1970; London, Gollancz, 1974.
Journey between Worlds. New York, Atheneum, 1970.
The Far Side of Evil (Elana). New York, Atheneum, 1971; London, Gollancz, 1975.
This Star Shall Abide (Noren). New York, Atheneum, 1972; as *Heritage of the Star,* London, Gollancz, 1973.
Beyond the Tomorrow Mountains (Noren). New York, Atheneum, 1973.
The Doors of the Universe (Noren). New York, Atheneum, 1981.

OTHER PUBLICATIONS (FOR YOUNG PEOPLE)

Other

The Planet-Girded Suns: Man's View of Other Solar Systems. New York, Atheneum, 1974.
The Subnuclear Zoo: New Discoveries in High Energy Physics, with Rick Roberson. New York, Atheneum, 1977.
Tool for Tomorrow: New Knowledge about Genes, with Rick Roberson. New York, Atheneum, 1979.
Our World Is Earth. New York, Atheneum, 1979.

Editor, with Rick Roberson, *Universe Ahead: Stories of the Future.* New York, Atheneum, 1975.
Editor, *Anywhere, Anywhen: Stories of Tomorrow.* New York, Atheneum, 1976.

*

Sylvia Engdahl comments:

(1985) I have encountered a good deal of misunderstanding concerning the audience for which my novels are intended, and I would like to clear it up. In the first place, though the present structure of the publishing business requires them to be issued as children's books, my novels are not meant for children; they are directed to older teenagers and young adults. Some exceptional preadolescents enjoy them, but do not grasp all their levels and on the whole find them heavy reading, since they are not primarily action stories. Their main emphasis is on the significance of space exploration, man's place in the universe, and human values I consider universal: all themes in which I believe today's young people are seriously interested.

In the second place, my novels do not fit the "science fiction" category much better than the "children's book" category; they aren't category books at all. Although they are set in future or hypothetical worlds, they are not directed toward fans of genre-oriented SF—they are meant for a general audience. They are not exotic enough to suit many SF fans, and *this is intentional.* My use of themes already old to the "fan" audience is also intentional. My aim is to reach readers who do not have a special background and do not care for fiction that seems far removed from real life, readers who find most SF too "far-out" for their tastes. I feel strongly that the future is not something that should be set apart and discussed only in literature of a particular type, directed to readers of a specific genre. The future is important to everyone, not just to those who choose to become familiar with the conventions and jargon of genre-oriented books. My chief goal is to place it in perspective in relation to the past and present, as well as to offer an affirmative outlook toward a universe wider than the single planet Earth. There is a desperate need, I believe, for fiction that conveys such themes to people beyond the comparatively small circle of SF fandom, and I therefore purposely market my own work outside that circle. I'm happy, of course, when people within the SF field like it; but I'm even happier when other people tell me they thought they didn't like space stories until they read mine. In my opinion, expansion into space is essential to human survival, and promoting that idea among readers who are not already space enthusiasts will remain my primary concern.

*   *   *

In her foreword to *Anywhere, Anywhen: Stories of Tomorrow,* Sylvia Engdahl makes explicit her reasons for not wanting to be classified as an SF writer. She addresses the problem of esotericism in the genre: conventions which guide the initiated reader are potentially alienating to the reader from outside the genre. Engdahl believes that the problems of the future are of interest to everyone, not only the fans of a specific field of literature (appropriately the stories in the above mentioned collection are by writers not normally associated with SF). With this in mind, Engdahl tries to avoid the jargon often associated with SF, the hard-core writer's emphasis on projections of technological innovation and the traditional conventions of space opera. Nevertheless, she works firmly *within* the field—justifying the fantastic elements of her stories in a substantial atmosphere of scientific credibility. Indeed, science and, in particular, the scientific method, play an important role in her narratives.

"Timescape," a novella written with her mother (Mildred Butler) for the *Anywhere, Anywhen* collection, serves as a useful introduction to Engdahl's works, containing themes common throughout her fiction. Alienation from society, the difficult quest for one's true identity, freedom of thought vs. authority and scholastic instruction: these are problems the protagonist Mark faces. An unwitting participant in a unique time-travel experiment, he is forced to approach his environment with a critical mind; to question the things around him, as well as the deeply felt moral principles within him. Set in opposition is the blind faith of religion and the analytic faculties of the scientific mind—an opposition predominant in her novels.

This Star Shall Abide, Beyond the Tomorrow Mountains, and *The Doors of the Universe* form a complete series in which the central figure is Noren, a character very similar to Mark in "Timescape." Both are male adolescents, nonconformists, introspective in nature, and alienated from society. Noren is alienated because of his refusal to believe in a pseudoreligious legend which is the basis of social structure in a semifeudal agrarian society. As a condemned heretic, he is sentenced to the mercy of the Scholars who live in a "holy" city. It is here that he undergoes a tortuous series of initiations and interrogations and learns of the desperate attempts of benevolent scientists to preserve their near-extinct race, after fleeing from a nova and settling on a poisonous planet. Noren's enquiring mind—as opposed to the blind acceptance of the majority of the villagers—his ability to doubt and to explore the world scientifically (by setting up hypotheses and testing them) are those qualities which qualify him for the dubious honour of joining the Scholars. Although Noren is willing to risk his life in order to challenge the essentially orthodox structure of his society, his greatest problems arise from self-doubts and intense personal scrutiny.

Presented in Engdahl's work is the concept of hierarchies of human evolution. The Noren series encompasses four stages of development: the primitive stage of the ignorant mutant savages; the medieval culture of the villagers, who see high technology as divine magic; the sophisticated scientific culture of the Scholars, who envision the Universe as a series of problems to be solved scientifically and—represented by Lianne, a visitor from another race—the higher culture, in which "magical" concepts, such as psi powers, are encompassed within a comprehensive, advanced scientific framework. In the stories which have Elana as their protagonist (*Enchantress from the Stars* and *The Far Side of Evil*) three stages are represented: the primitive, the industrial, and the higher. Elana is of the higher culture—a member of an Anthropological Service—and her anthropological skills are tested when she has to aid an "inferior," less advanced culture, without interfering with their normal rate of progress. Principles of noninterference are of central importance in all of Engdahl's writings, love-interest often complicating these principles.

To Engdahl, the stars are symbols of knowledge, hope, and humankind's destiny. The outwardly focused vision of her stories presents space exploration as a) the salvation of threatened races, and b) the next stage in our youthful races's progression towards cultural and scientific adulthood. She goes as far as to say that space exploration is essential to the survival of our race.

Engdahl's SF is not easy to read. Her narratives are detailed and perhaps overly long, visual detail rejected in favour of copious dialogue and commentary. The minute workings of her protagonists's minds are foregrounded, at the expense of dramatic action. However, although demanding texts, they are rewarding for those willing to work at them. While readers might be left uneasy about her frequent presentation of benevolent tyrannies, she forces her audience to think seriously about the nature of free will and freedom of expression. Nevertheless, there is an awkward contradiction between her affirmation of the basic equality of human beings and her rationalisation of elaborate caste systems. However, her narratives are deeply concerned with morality and, while sometimes a little didactic in style, they are compassionate and intensely rea-soned, providing engaging reading, and are guaranteed to provoke thought.

—Mark Warwick Leahy

ENGH, M(ary) J(ane)

Pseudonyms: Jane Beauclerk; Bird Ferguson; M.J. Ferguson. **Nationality:** American. **Born:** McLeansboro, Illinois, 26 January 1933. **Education:** University of Chicago, B.A. 1951; University of Illinois, Champaign-Urbana, B.A. 1953; University of Oklahoma, Norman, M.L.S. 1973. **Family:** Married 1) David W. Ferguson in 1954 (divorced 1960), two sons; 2) Richard Engh in 1963 (divorced 1969). **Career:** Library assistant, University of Chicago, 1954-55; assistant librarian, *American People's Encyclopedia,* Chicago, 1955-56; writer for correspondence course research project, U.S. Navy, Chicago, 1957-58; editorial assistant, 1959-61, and associate editor, 1961-63, Scott, Foresman, and Company, Chicago; teacher in public schools, McLeansboro, Illinois, 1964-65; editor, C.E. Tuttle and Company, Tokyo, 1966-67; library clerk, 1971-72, and assistant biological sciences librarian, 1973-79, Oklahoma State University, Stillwater; reference librarian, Owen Science and Engineering Library, Washington State University, Pullman, 1979-85. **Awards:** National Endowment for the Arts Creative Writing Fellowship, 1982. **Agent:** Virginia Kidd, Virginia Kidd Literary Agency, Box 278, 538 East Harford Street, Milford, Pennsylvania 18337. **Address:** P.O. Box 97, Garfield, Washington 99130 U.S.A.

SCIENCE FICTION PUBLICATIONS

Novels

Arslan. New York, Warner, 1976; as *A Wind from Bukhara,* London, Grafton, 1989.
The House in the Snow (for children). New York, Orchard, 1987.
Wheel of the Winds. New York, Tor, 1988; London, Grafton, 1989.
Rainbow Man. New York, Tor, 1993.

*

M.J. Engh comments:

I don't remember who said, "Consistent writers make more money, but adventurous writers have more fun." Certainly it makes good sense, commercially and even aesthetically, for a writer to stick to one or a few types of writing. You can explore your niche to its innermost recesses, bring your techniques to perfection, and yes, make more money. Readers and publishers alike prefer to buy products with labels.

The trouble is that labels become ID cards. I don't want to be defined by what I wrote last decade or last year. The universe isn't divided into isolated packets. Everything interconnects. How can I not follow some of the threads that lead from one niche to myriad others? One thread I've been following for more than twenty years is this: We live in a universe in which people do hideous things to one another. And the first question is not "What, if anything, should I do about these horrors?" It's more basic: "How, if at all, can I live with the knowledge that horrors exist? "But telling people that horrors exist turns out to be oddly difficult. If you show the horror, people quickly get used to it. If you discuss it at a distance, you lose impact. In "The Oracle," I tried a third way, which may be the most direct: showing not the horrible events, but horror itself in the protagonist's mind.

Of course, the universe isn't uniformly grim and grisly; the universe isn't uniform. This means I can write humor or adventure stories, historical realism or children's picture books, with equal enthusiasm. Finding an adventurous publisher is harder.

*　　*　　*

The wide variety of M.J. Engh's writings demonstrates her versatility and persistence. Recognized since the (re)publication of her 1976 novel *Arslan* in 1989 as a science fiction writer of stature, she has published poetry since 1955 (as M.J. or Bird Ferguson), and science fiction since 1964 (as Jane Beauclerk). Among the many whose first published science fiction book died unnoticed in paperback, she stands almost alone in having it reissued 10 years later in hardcover to public favor and critical acclaim. David Hartwell of Arbor House proudly takes credit for spotting the excellence of *Arslan,* for engineering its republication, and even for insisting that the dust jacket bear no SF design. Algis Budrys has called *Arslan* a "genuine work of speculative political science." The book provides an unusual vision of the power—and the limitations—of one charismatic individual whose dreams of world domination become reality, while developing a profound double agenda: both the actions of the dictator and the inaction of the "good" man show us to ourselves.

Character development drives Engh's fiction. In *Arslan* she shows the title character through the eyes of two of his victims, and all three come astonishingly alive in this end-of-the-world novel which (unusually) avoids nuclear holocaust. She takes some literary risks in this. "The Oracle," an in-depth, first-person narrative study of a damaged psyche, is reminiscent of the first section of Faulkner's *The Sound and the Fury.* In her second novel, *Wheel of the Winds,* she narrates the story entirely from the point of view of humanoid (but not *human*) characters whose quasi-medieval society is about to undergo radical change from contact with Terrans. This means that, like Heinlein, Engh must set up her tale so that the reader can provide the connections between what the characters know but do not (or cannot) discuss, and the plot. Having worked out the technical details of a habitable world fixed to its primary, and the ways in which the inhabitants would explain them, she must also deal with the disparity of understanding between the natives and their Terran captive. After his escape, he enlists two natives in a "marvelous voyage" to the dark, stormy, dangerous, and usually uninhabited side of their planet to retrieve his equipment and signal his people. Not only does Engh demonstrate that the changes that will ensue will not benefit either the natives or their society as they hope, she also explores the inability of a technically oriented person to explain scientific concepts to people who don't share that background in any meaningful way.

Along with her strengths of characterization, Engh effectively describes physical setting and physical effort. These drive the voyage in *Wheel of the Winds,* and are particularly noticeable in "The Oracle." Her depiction of the Philippines, where she has lived, breathes alienation and ambiance. Using only the voice of a limited, almost prelingual narrator in "Moon Blood," she conveys a remarkable sense of prehistoric place. She moves to the opposite pole, to the distant future, in "Tick," where the problem of relating

"ship's time" to some long-abandoned terrestrial standard—and the psychological as well as physical need for such a relationship—literally tear a family apart. She frequently explores the need for certainty, whether in science or religion, and the conflict between those who require it and those who do not. In *Rainbow Man,* Engh not only contrasts the constantly mobile but socially stable starship crew with a people bound by (and to) a religious vision. Liss, who makes a leap of faith in deciding to leave her ship and locate on Bimran, initially believes that she will have no problems acclimating herself to this very different society. She learns differently from Doron, the Selector, who clings to the absolute certainty of his faith.

Always, Engh uses language to provide major clues to the worldview she invents. On Bimran, no word exists for an infertile woman. Liss is considered a "man" who dresses in unusually colorful clothes. No one calls her by name. She is the Rainbow Man. This linguistic rigidity reflects Bimran salvationist religion, which rests not on revelation but on observable proof: those who achieve Bliss in their lifetime do so in full view. So do those who suffer punishment. Liss, a rational romantic, also seeks her reward on earth, here and now, but seeing Bimran's version shocks her. Her connection with Doron, an entirely rational believer in sin and punishment, creates enough ambivalence in him that he oversteps the rigid boundaries of his role. While Liss seeks an irrational measure of security in her romantic leap of faith, Doron clings to his absolute knowledge and risks certain punishment in this life to secure bliss hereafter. While Bimran does not insist that others believe, it reacts most forcefully if anyone causes one of their own to waver in his belief. Here, Engh deals with the moral consequences of making theological choices in highly specific and physical terms.

Shaping a fiction sometimes seems problematic for Engh. *Wheel of the Winds* is unevenly paced; *Rainbow Man* moves more smoothly, and *Arslan* holds together exceptionally well. But her flair for character development sometimes stretches a piece out of shape, as it does in "Penelope Comes Home," where background details, metaphoric resonances, and episodes of characterization almost derail the rather standard plot. On the other hand, "Moon Blood" is very tightly organized, and "Same Thing Twice," a delightful bit of biting humor, not only moves briskly through a most imaginative setting but also thoroughly develops the viewpoint character.

In her writing career, Engh has met a problem common to those who produce work in many modes: few of her tales have found immediate acceptance, while some have suffered the collapse of various magazines. In her stories, she often simultaneously engages and frustrates her readers' expectations. While consistently stretching generic boundaries, she has managed to publish some proportion of her work; but she considers *Wheel of the Winds* not her second novel, but her fifth, following a mainstream novel about the French nuclear testing program in the Pacific; "The Oracle"; and the first volume of an historical trilogy. The other novels are completed but still (at this writing) unsold. Currently Engh is collaborating on a biographical dictionary of active women in the ancient Roman world, and considering another science fiction novel, one dealing with "time, politics, personal identity, and fun stuff like that." M.J. Engh is endlessly interested in what makes people "human," the worthiest, most difficult, and most fascinating of all literary topics.

—Martha A. Bartter

ENGLAND, George Allan

Nationality: American. **Born:** Fort McPherson, Nebraska, 9 February 1877. **Education:** Harvard University, Cambridge, Massachusetts, B.A. 1902 (Phi Beta Kappa); M.A. 1903. **Family:** Married; one daughter. **Career:** Regular contributor to Munsey magazines until his retirement from writing, 1931; chicken farmer from 1931. Socialist candidate for Congress, 1908, and for governor of Maine, 1912. **Died:** 26 June 1936.

SCIENCE FICTION PUBLICATIONS

Novels

Darkness and Dawn. Boston, Small Maynard, 1914; as *Darkness and Dawn, Beyond the Great Oblivion, The People of the Abyss, Out of the Abyss,* and *The Afterglow,* New York, Avalon, 5 vols., 1964-67.
The Air Trust. St. Louis, Phil Wagner, 1915.
The Golden Blight. New York, H.K. Fly, 1916.
Cursed. Boston, Small Maynard, 1919.
Keep Off the Grass. Boston, Small Maynard, 1919.
The Flying Legion. Chicago, McClurg, 1920.
Elixir of Hate. Laurel, New York, Lightyear, 1976.

OTHER PUBLICATIONS

Novels

The Alibi. Boston, Small Maynard, 1916.
Pod, Bender, & Co. New York, McBride, 1916; London, Laurie, 1919.
The Gift Supreme. New York, Doran, 1916.
The Greater Crime. London, Cassell, 1917.
Adventure Isle (for children). New York, Century, 1926.

Poetry

Underneath the Bough. New York, Grafton Press, 1903.

Other

Socialism and the Law. Fort Scott, Kansas, Monitor, 1913.
The Story of the Appeal. Privately printed, 1915(?).
Isles of Romance. New York, Century, 1920.
Vikings of the Ice. New York, Doubleday, and London, Heinemann, 1924; as *The White Wilderness,* London, Cassell, 1924; as *The Greatest Hunt in the World,* Montreal, Tundra, 1969.

Translator, *Their Son, The Necklace,* by Eduardo Zamacois. New York, Boni and Liveright, 1919.

*   *   *

Although George Allan England lived well into the era of specialized SF magazines, he never wrote any original works for them. His works appeared, for the most part, in the variety pulp magazines published by Frank A. Munsey and edited by Bob Davis. England's heyday was the decade between 1910 and 1920.

By far England's most important work of science fiction is *Darkness and Dawn.* This massive effort was originally published as three separate serials, then as a single volume. In this work a heavy anesthetic gas sweeps over the entire world, at first rendering unconscious and ultimately killing those who breathe it. One man and one woman, however, in an office in the top story of the Flatiron Building in New York, receive only a partial dose of the gas. They sleep for centuries and revive to find a world in ruins. The revived couple struggle to rebuild their lives, encountering a race of superevolved intelligent rats, barbaric degenerate humans, and finally a lost civilization cut off from the rest of the world for hundreds of years. The book is highly successful as an adventure tale and as a study of courage and perseverance on the part of the survivors. An unfortunate element of racism is present in this and in several other of the author's works, though England was largely following the conventions of popular literature of his day; he did not originate these attitudes, and did not press them very emphatically.

The Flying Legion, although not as widely remembered as *Darkness and Dawn,* is deserving of recognition in its own more modest right. It reflected a convention of its time, the assumption that World War I veterans, returning to the drab realities of civilian, peacetime existence, would suffer from intolerable boredom and would be driven to seek excitement in such fields as might offer danger and exotic adventures. In *The Flying Legion* just such a party of veterans assemble. One of them, to add a fillip, is a beautiful young woman in disguise. This legion hijacks the world's largest and most advanced aircraft (choosing to do so rather than buy it despite their immense joint wealth) and sets out to find adventure in the unknown regions of the Arabian desert. In outline the book is an exercise in cliché, yet it is executed with such verve and color as to be irresistible even to the modern reader.

Few of England's other science fiction works were issued in volume form. *Elixir of Hate* deals with research into a youth serum; the serum is perfected, stolen, swallowed by the thief who then discovers that he has taken an overdose and is reduced to infancy. England's two "socialist novels" both contain SF elements. *The Air Trust* deals with greedy capitalists who corner air and sell the very breath of life for profit. *The Golden Blight* is concerned with a revolutionary who discovers a method by which he can destroy all the gold that exists, thereby bringing about the collapse of the entire world's economy. Both these books are heavy on polemic and of little value as works of fiction, although interesting examples of their sort, and comparable to such socialist science fiction as Jack London's *The Iron Heel.*

A number of England's unreprinted works are rewarding. "The Empire in the Air," concerning an invasion of Earth from the fourth dimension, might be compared with the space operas of the 1920s and 1930s, although it appeared in 1914. "The Nebula of Death" involves the passage of the Earth through a cosmic cloud which absolutely inhibits photosynthesis; the novel is comparable, in different ways, to *The Second Deluge* by Garrett P. Serviss and *Brain Wave* by Poul Anderson.

—Richard A. Lupoff

ENGLISH, Richard. *See* SHAVER, Richard S.

ENNIS, Robert D. *See* **TUBB, E.C.**

ERICKSON, Steve (Michael)

Nationality: American. **Born:** Stephen Michael Erickson, Santa Monica, California, 20 April 1950. **Education:** University of California, Los Angeles, B.A. 1972, M.A. 1973. **Awards:** Samuel Goldwyn award for fiction (UCLA), 1972; National Endowment for the Arts fellowship, 1987.

SCIENCE FICTION PUBLICATIONS

Novels

Days Between Stations: A Novel. New York, Poseidon Press, 1985; London, Futura, 1988

Rubicon Beach. New York, Poseidon Press, 1986; London, Futura, 1989

Tours of the Black Clock. New York, Poseidon Press, and London, Simon & Schuster, 1989

Arc d'X. New York, Poseidon Press, 1993; London, Hutchinson, 1994.

OTHER PUBLICATIONS

Other

Leap Year: A Political Journey. New York, Poseidon Press, and London, Futura, 1989.

* * *

During the 1980s the links between science fiction and postmodernism first received critical attention, though postmodernists from Burroughs to Pynchon and science fiction writers such as Ballard had been aware of, and influenced by each other's work for years before then. But if any one writer deserves the description "postmodern SF" it is Steve Erickson.

His novels take vivid, imaginative leaps into parallel worlds where Hitler survives into the 1960s or a variety of authoritarian religio-political systems rule the United States, or they shatter the geography of the familiar world so that Los Angeles is inundated by sand or undermined by a network of rivers and caves. Yet these science fictional devices, integral to the stories as they are, also provide a distanced, altered perspective that breaks the frame of the novel. So that a work of journalism, a personal view of the 1988 American presidential election, can incorporate the ghost of Sally Hemings, Thomas Jefferson's slave mistress, and she in turn can open the way to the parallel worlds of the novel *Arc d'X.*

Each of Erickson's novels involves deliberate distortion, of geography, of history and of character, each of which is inter-related so that changes in the natural world always reflect changes in the psychological world. Together they represent a personal vision of the shifting nature of identity in what Erickson calls the "post-atomic" world, and the consequent unreliability of our political morality.

Thus in his first novel, *Days Between Stations,* he tells of a love affair between a dysfunctional couple, Lauren, guilty at the loss of her child, and Michel who has a strange lacuna in his memory and who at one point adopts an eyepatch he doesn't need and which skews his perception of the world. This relationship is mirrored by that between Adolphe, a silent film maker whose epic masterpiece is never finished, and Janine, his star, whom he loves but who may be his sister. As these relationships break down so the natural world also becomes distorted: the canals of Venice dry up and all the contestants in a cycle race there are mysteriously lost for days, Paris is frozen, and a train journey across Europe is extended to subjective years.

There is a similar topographical breakdown in *Rubicon Beach* which tells three stories apparently so unrelated that they take place in different universes, yet which weave together into a unified whole. The worlds are different because that is how they are perceived by their inhabitants not because of any objective difference. In Los Angeles after some sort of social apocalypse a released prisoner, guilty at betraying his friend, dreams of a girl who repeatedly executes a man. The man is himself, the girl is Catherine, a strange, charismatic girl from the Amazon who haunts the life of a Hollywood filmmaker in our familiar world. The third story tells of Jack Mick Lake who discovers a new number between nine and ten, though both Cale, the released prisoner, and Catherine reappear. Together the stories build into a complex and relativistic account of the way we build our own moral universes.

In both *Days Between Stations,* where Adolphe was born with the century, and *Rubicon Beach,* in which Lake's story covers the whole of the century, the 20th century itself has a significant part to play. But in *Tours of the Black Clock,* perhaps his finest work, that becomes explicit, and the dislocation of landscape becomes a dislocation of time. The key to this rich and allusive novel is a blueprint of the 20th century (maps figure large in Erickson's iconography) which reveals a secret room where the soul of the century is hidden.

The history of the century has split. In one part we follow the story of Banning Jainlight, Hitler's pornographer, whose fantasies, even in the light of the death of his own wife and child, enchant Hitler and prevent the invasion of Russia, so that the Second World War is prolonged into the 1960s. Jainlight's stories revolve around a woman he glimpsed only once, but who is real in our history of the century. The novel pursues their relationship back and forth across streams of history, and again the focus of the story reveals that our own morality creates our worlds. As Erickson puts it: "In a century when time and space have liberated themselves of all reference points, perhaps one good thing owns a universe unto itself."

The political morality implicit in all these novels becomes explicit in his work of imaginative journalism, *Leap Year: A Political Journey.* As Erickson criss-crosses America in search of its soul somewhere within the presidential election year he becomes haunted, literally, by the ghost of Sally Hemings. She was Thomas Jefferson's slave and mistress who chose slavery with her lover over freedom and so made a decision which, Erickson believes, shaped the moral landscape of America. Hemings obviously fascinated Erickson, for her story, or at least a version of it, was the starting point of *Arc d'X.*

Again time has been disrupted. From Jefferson's relationship with Sally and the burning of a slave a host of variant America's spring. Principal among these is a theocracy, perched on the edge of a volcano, where a subterranean society practices all the liberties denied them by their masters, and where Etcher is involved in literally rewriting history. But an inexplicable murder here leads into other histories where, for instance, an American novelist called Steve Erickson is murdered in Berlin. Time and again, in this novel as in all Erickson's work, his characters find themselves coming up against the moral and political world they have shaped. And as they find it wanting so they find their geographical world has shifted, such that the volcano which is a central image of *Arc d'X* becomes a potent image of the catastrophe wrought by our moral failures.

—Paul Kincaid

ESHBACH, Lloyd Arthur

Nationality: American. **Born:** Palm, Pennsylvania, 20 June 1910. **Education:** Attended school to the tenth grade; Charles Morris Price School of Advertising and Journalism, Philadelphia. **Family:** Married Helen Margaret Richards in 1931 (died 1978); two sons. **Career:** Worked for department stores, 1925-41; advertising copywriter, Glidden Paint Company, Reading, Pennsylvania, 1941-50; publisher, Fantasy Press, Reading, 1950-58, and Church Center Press, Myerstown, Pennsylvania, 1958-63; advertising manager, 1963-68, and sales representative, 1968-75, Moody Press, Chicago; clergyman for three small churches in eastern Pennsylvania, 1975-78. **Awards:** Milford award, 1988. Agent: James Allen, Virginia Kidd, Box 278, Milford, Pennsylvania 18337, U.S.A. **Address:** 220 South Railroad Street, Myerstown, Pennsylvania 17067, U.S.A.

SCIENCE FICTION PUBLICATIONS

Novels (series: Gates of Lucifer)

Subspace Encounter, with E.E. Smith. New York, Berkley, 1983; London, Panther, 1984.
The Land beyond the Gate. New York, Ballantine, 1984.
The Armlet of the Gods (Gates). New York, Ballantine, 1986.
Sorceress of Scath (Gates). New York, Ballantine, 1988.
The Scroll of Lucifer (Gates). New York, Ballantine, 1990.

Short Stories

Tyrant of Time. Reading, Pennsylvania, Fantasy Press, 1955.
The Elfin Lights. N.p., n.d.

OTHER PUBLICATIONS

Plays

Radio Series, with H. Donald Spatz: *The Crimson Phantom, The Bronze Buddha, Tales of the Crystal, Cupid's Capers, The Pennington Saga, The Doings of the Dinwiddies,* and *Tales of Tomorrow,* 1933-35.

Other

Over My Shoulder: Reflections on a Science Fiction Era. Philadelphia, Train, 1983.

Editor, *Of Worlds Beyond: The Science of Science Fiction Writing: A Symposium.* Reading, Pennsylvania, Fantasy Press, 1947; London, Dobson, 1965.
Editor, *Alicia in Blunderland,* by P. Schuyler Miller. Philadelphia, Train, 1983.

*

Manuscript Collection: Temple University, Philadelphia.

Lloyd Arthur Eshbach comments:

The editors have invited introductory comments about my work. In preparation for such comment I've reread a cross section of the stories I wrote, the last one published well over two decades ago, the earliest almost 50 years in the past. Most of my stories were as unfamiliar as if they were the efforts of a stranger.

The reading was an interesting experience. Some of the stories made me cringe, they were so incredibly bad. Others were a surprise: they were better than I thought possible. Indeed, a few actually pleased me. In self-defense I believe I should say that in the 1930s a comparative handful of youthful pioneers were breaking new trails in fiction. Most of us were amateurs trying to learn our craft. A fairly new idea and a minimal ability to put thoughts into words sufficed to produce a saleable story. In short, we learned by doing, received the encouragement of publication for our efforts, and even payment (such as it was) as frosting on a cake. Characters were one-dimensional and stereotyped, conversations were stilted, action usually was melodramatic, and literary style was either derivative or nonexistent—but there was that often-referred to "sense of wonder" born of youthful enthusiasm and uninhibited imagination.

My first accepted story, written in 1928 when I was 18, was "A Voice from the Ether," though in order of publication it was fifth. An earlier version of "The Valley of Titans" preceded it, but the complete rewrite and expansion took place more than a year after the completion and acceptance of "A Voice from the Ether." The fact that the latter story was selected by Michael Ashley for his *History of the Science Fiction Magazine* (1974) as a representative story for 1931 was most gratifying.

As I write (March 1979) I have almost reached my three score and ten—and in my retirement years I've resumed writing. My first effort, well along in production, is an informal history of a science fiction era—the story of the groundbreaking careers of the specialty hardback SF publishers of the 1940s. Upon its completion I plan to write a science fantasy novel I started plotting 30 years ago. I hope I've learned something about life and about writing during three decades. If I have, I may be giving the youngsters some competition after all these years.

(1985) In the five years and eleven months that have passed since I wrote the preceding paragraphs, I have been quite busy. The informal history of the specialist SF publishers of the 1930s, 40s, and 50s, called *Over My Shoulder: Reflections on a Science Fiction Era,* was published in 1983. Following the completion of my reminiscences, I finished writing the last SF novel of E.E. "Doc" Smith, left in a fragmentary state at his death in 1965, *Subspace Encounter.* My name appears as "Edited and with an Introduction by Lloyd Arthur Eshbach." This was according to my decision, though I would have been justified in calling it a collaboration, since I wrote more than 12,000 words of it, did the final polishing, connected various scenes in logical sequence with the necessary transitions, etc. However, it was his story and I wanted him to receive full credit. We were close friends.

In 1983 I edited and wrote the introduction for *Alicia in Blunderland* by P. Schuyler Miller, a science fictional parody of *Alice in Wonderland,* which appeared as a serial in a SF fan magazine in 1933-34. Earlier, in 1980, I wrote the science fantasy novel I referred to in my initial comments. It did not sell, and after putting it aside for a year I saw why. It needs a complete rewriting which I plan to do after completion of my present project. This project is a tetralogy based on mythology, largely Celtic mythology, though venturing into the myths and legends of other lands and times. The first novel in this series, *The Land Beyond the Gate,* was published in 1984. The second novel, *The Armlet of the Gods,* already written and under contract, is in the editor's possession. I expect to complete the writing of the third novel within the next six months, and the fourth early in 1986.

(1991) My writing in the last decade has been largely in the field of fantasy based on the prehistory and mythology of ancient peoples. I have a science fiction novel in the works which I hope one day to complete, but I find writing fantasy more enjoyable. Fantasy requires far more research than SF (as I write it) but I enjoy the research. After all, I write to please two people—myself first and then the editor. If the readers like what I produce, that's a bonus.

*   *   *

Though he was on the scene as a writer in the formative 1930s, Lloyd Arthur Eshbach's real impact on the field—and it was a substantial one—was in his role as a publisher. Having been involved mostly behind the scenes with William Crawford's *Marvel Tales* and other ventures before the war and then with the Hadley group that began the specialist press era, he organized Fantasy Press, which was to prove the most significant imprint in the period when science fiction moved into book publication in its own right. He understood what was needed better than the other hopefuls trying to do the same things, and his judgment reflected thorough knowledge and appreciation of the first two decades of explicit SF in the early magazines.

The symposium *Of Worlds Beyond: The Science of Science-Fiction Writing,* which he instigated in 1947, is memorable as the first book on modern science fiction, and though not critically profound its common-sense analysis based on leading writers' practical experience made it an important work for the serious reader, and it answered most of the fumbling attempts at criticism by outsiders in its time.

Like the other presses in the movement, Eshbach's operated almost entirely by putting popular magazine serials into book form with the occasional short story collection. Their near-monopoly of the book field did not last long enough—less than 10 years—for them to move on to presenting new works as a serious undertaking, and there was little scope for editorial skills. He acknowledges, however, that he did substantial revision work verging on collaboration in a few cases such as the later Campbell books he produced. More recently he ably linked E.E. Smith's disconnected fragments of unfinished work into the new novel *Subspace Encounter.*

His own stories do not amount to a large body of work and are too diverse to characterize readily. We cannot identify any distinct trend or theme. But while a few are no more than potboilers most are full of original or at least unusual thoughts. The main fault, in fact, as in many writers of the period, is the multiplicity of new and revelatory concepts that jostle for the reader's attention and are not properly explored. The Mad Scientist, stock character of the time, appears in several cases as a threat to society and originator of the action. In "The Valley of Titans" he operates as an air pirate from a dinosaur-infested enclave, and incidentally creates a community of ape-people by evolutionary experiments. Introduction of an underground realm of prehuman energy beings and a godlike alien power is confusing.

In "The Invisible Destroyer" the dissident genius undertaking to dictate to the world, evidently single-handed, is trying to prevent the peaceable establishment of a world state. His objections are logical and—taken out of context and disregarding how economic and ideological forces interact in the 1980s—make good sense, and there is no attempt to refute them. "Vibration," a popular all-embracing basis for marvels around 1930, produces not only novel weaponry but access to other coexistent worlds, and a higher civilization thus found is induced to intervene.

Biological warfare figures in "The Gray Plague," with the Venusians planning to eliminate Man with a fatal pandemic to leave Earth clear to occupy. "Out of the Past" points out one of many criminal misuses of time travel that make it undesirable. "Dust" concisely introduces one possible hazard of interplanetary contact: bringing back dormant foreign life-forms as spores. "The Meteor Miners" (*The Tyrant of Time*) shows a possible future space-based industry in a rare anticipation of ordinary working life in another era. "The Outpost on Ceres," in which aliens threaten a refueling base, also deals with a future working environment, and is notable for its sensible treatment of a drug dependence problem.

"The Time Conqueror" (*The Tyrant of Time*) is a notable early contribution to the tradition of the disembodied brain. Developing enhanced power and insight, the immortal brain makes itself world dominant, and we are shown episodes in successively remote times. Despite the rather exaggeratedly emotive language it is still an interesting and effective tale. "The Kingdom of Thought" combines the theme of time travel bringing together people from many eras with that of physically degenerate and intellectually potent superhumans of a remote future, evolved into good and evil branches with irreconcilable differences. The Cummings concept of size-change and submicroscopic worlds is carried to extremes in two stories. In "A Voice from the Ether" the familiar Mad Scientist brings up a deadly parasitic organism from subatomic size and destroys his world, Mars. In "The Light from Infinity" humanoids from a supra-universe shrink down and attack Earth, foiled by an expedition that uses their size-changer to reach the supra-world and retaliate. Needless to say, the paradoxes are ignored. "The Shadows from Hesplon" is a fourth dimension story, in which nasties from a higher dimensional plane use hypnotic means to have physical entry points made for them. It is unusual for making considerable efforts to visualize wholly alien experiences.

Eshbach's work, strong in content at the expense of form, helped build up the range of unconventional visions and fancies that early science fiction displayed, though he was less successful in controlling and resolving them.

—Graham Stone

EVANS, E(dward) Everett

Nationality: American. **Born:** 30 November 1893. **Family:** Married Thelma D. Hamm in 1953. **Career:** Cofounder, National Fantasy Fan Federation; editor, *The Time-Binder.* **Died:** 2 December 1958.

SCIENCE FICTION PUBLICATIONS

Novels (series: George Hanlon)

Man of Many Minds (Hanlon). Reading, Pennsylvania, Fantasy Press, 1953.
Alien Minds (Hanlon). Reading, Pennsylvania, Fantasy Press, 1955.
The Planet Mappers (for children). New York, Dodd Mead, 1955.

Short Stories

Food for Demons. San Diego, Shroud Publishers, 1971.

*   *   *

E. Everett Evans is perhaps best remembered for his novel *Man of Many Minds,* which, while competently enough written for its time, is an unremarkable novel otherwise. George Hanlon is a young man who participates in a plot to fake his dishonorable discharge from the Interstellar Corps in order to discover the origin of a plot to wrest control of interstellar civilization from humanity. Hanlon is gifted with a telepathic ability that makes him potentially the most effective spy in the universe, except that the force he is ranged against is equally gifted. Though mildly entertaining, the novel and its sequel, *Alien Minds,* are not very notable. Two other works saw print as well. *The Planet Mappers* is a juvenile novel of action and adventure that entertains while you are reading it but eludes memory a day or two later. "Masters of Space," substantially revised by Edward E. Smith following Evans's death, is at best a routine novel of interstellar war and telepathy.

Far more noteworthy are Evans's shorter works, particularly those of the supernatural. Two stories in particular are exceptional. "The Shed" is set in a small, remote town at the turn of the last century. An abandoned storage shed serves as a gymnasium for the town's children, despite the existence of a peculiar shadow that seems independent of a light source. All goes well until a dog and a cat, and eventually a child, enter the shadow, never to return. "The Brooch" is almost as effective in building its element of suspense. While strolling through a graveyard, a priest notices activity under the soil of a recent grave. Dismissing it as the activity of a mole, he forgets the matter until it becomes apparent that two graves have been actively disturbed. An exhumation of the two graves, both wives of the same man, reveals that a brooch prized by the first wife and buried with the second has moved from one coffin to the other. Evans wrote several stories about vampires, anticipating to a certain extent the more sympathetic treatment given to such characters in recent novels. In "The Undead Die" two lovers are attacked by a vampire and caused to join the undead, but their love remains whole and they triumph over the evil of their new lives, eventually to be reunited in true death. To a lesser extent, the vampire waitress of "The Unusual Model" is viewed sympathetically, as she falls in love with a young man she had chosen to be her next victim.

Many of Evans's stories have never been reprinted, some with good reason, such as a rather silly series about a society of humanlike robots on Mars ("Little Miss Ignorance," "Little Miss Boss"), but even some of those that utilize overly familiar plots are generally well-written. Of particular note are "Fly by Night," in which an introvert surrenders his anonymity by demonstrating his ability to levitate in order to save the life of a falling man, and "Blurb," yet another story of a writer whose character assumes physical reality. Both are unpretentious and unambitious, but succeed extremely well within their intentions. A manifested demon is outsmarted in swift fashion in "Food for Demons," one of Evans's more familiar stories.

The optimism that colors the stories and novels, even those with unpleasant themes, is refreshing. Evans is firm in his faith of the essential goodness of humanity. His prose is clear and concise, with no conscious attempt to develop a style. For the most part, the stories are nostalgic, reflecting a simpler time and a clear border between good and evil. While this may seem less than plausible today, Evans was usually a good enough writer to cause you to overlook that anachronism, at least for a while.

—Don D'Ammassa

F

FAIRMAN, Paul W.

Pseudonyms: Adam Chase; Lester del Rey; Paula Fairman; Ivar Jorgensen; Paulette Warren. **Nationality:** American. **Born:** 1916. **Career:** Editor, *If,* 1952; associate editor, *Fantastic Adventures,* 1952-53; associate editor, 1952-53, managing editor, 1953-54, and editor, 1956-58, *Amazing and Fantastic;* editor, *Dream World,* 1957, and *Pen Pal,* 1957. Freelance writer from 1958. **Died:** 1977.

SCIENCE FICTION PUBLICATIONS

Novels

The Golden Ape, with Milton Lesser (as Adam Chase). New York, Avalon, 1959.
City under the Sea (novelization of TV play). London, Digit, 1963; New York, Pyramid, 1965.
The World Grabbers: A Dramatic Novel (novelization of TV play). Derby, Connecticut, Monarch, 1964.
I, The Machine. New York, Lancer, 1968.
The Forgetful Robot (for children). New York, Holt Rinehart, 1968; London, Gollancz, 1970.
The Frankenstein Wheel. New York, Popular Library, 1972.

Novels as Lester del Rey (with Lester del Rey)

The Runaway Robot (for children). Philadelphia, Westminster Press, 1964; London, Gollancz, 1967.
The Scheme of Things. New York, Belmont, 1966.
Siege Perilous. New York, Lancer, 1966; as *The Man without a Planet,* 1969.
Tunnel through Time (for children). Philadelphia, Westminster Press, 1966.
The Infinite Worlds of Maybe. New York, Holt Rinehart, 1966.
Rocket from Infinity. New York, Holt Rinehart, 1966.
Prisoners of Space (for children). Philadelphia, Westminster Press, 1968.

Novels as Ivar Jorgensen

Ten from Infinity. Derby, Connecticut, Monarch, 1963; as *The Deadly Sky,* New York, Pinnacle, 1971; as *Ten Deadly Men,* Pinnacle, 1976.
Rest in Agony. Derby, Connecticut, Monarch, 1963; expanded edition, New York, Lancer, 1967; as *The Diabolist,* New York, Lancer, 1973; .
Whom the Gods Would Slay. New York, Belmont, 1968.

Short Stories

The Doomsday Exhibit. New York, Lancer, 1971.
Nine Worlds West. Sydney, Australia, American Science Fiction, 1955.

OTHER PUBLICATIONS

Novels (series: Partridge Family)

The Glass Ladder. Kingston, New York, Quinn, 1950.
The Heiress of Copper Butte. New York, Quinn, 1951.
The Montana Vixen. New York, Lion, 1952.
The Joy Wheel. New York, Lion, 1954.
Search for a Dead Nympho. New York, Lancer, 1967.
Lancer. New York, Popular Library, 1968.
The Cover Girls. New York, Macfadden, 1970.
Pattern for Destruction. New York, Macfadden, 1970.
Playboy. New York, Macfadden, 1970.
That Girl (novelization of TV play). New York, Popular Library, 1971.
To Catch a Crooked Girl. New York, Pinnacle, 1971.
Bridget Loves Bernie (based on TV series). New York, Lancer, 1972.
Five Knucklebones (for children). New York, Holt Rinehart, 1972.
The Ghost of Graveyard Hill. New York, Curtis, 1972.
Terror by Night. New York, Curtis, 1972.
Junior Bonner. New York, Lancer, and London, Sphere, 1972.
The Treaure of Ghost Mountain (Partridge Family; based on TV series). New York, Curtis, 1972.
Love, American Style (based on TV series). New York, Pinnacle, 1972?
The Girl with Something Extra (Partridge Family; based on TV series). New York, Curtis, 1973.
Coffy (novelization of screenplay). New York, Lancer, 1973.

Novels as Paula Fairman

Forbidden Destiny. Los Angeles, Pinnacle, 1977.

Novels as Paulette Warren

Ravenkill. New York, Lancer, 1965.
Ghost of Ravenkill Manor. New York, Lancer, 1966?
Brooding Mansion. New York, Lancer, 1967.
The Nurse of Brooding Mansion. New York, Lancer, 1967.
The Bitterhill Saga. New York, Lancer, 1968.
Some Beckoning Wraith. New York, Lancer, 1969.
Dark Shadows at Bitterhill. New York, Lancer, 1970.
The Shadowed Staircase. New York, Lancer, 1971.
Horror House. New York, Lancer, 1972.
Apprentice in Terror. New York, Berkley, 1974.
Caliban's Castle. New York, Berkley, 1976.
Dark Shadows of Bitterhill. New York, Manor, 1976.
Night Falls at Bitterhill. New York, Manor, 1976.
Storm over Bitterhill. New York, Manor, 1976.
Lady Sinister. New York, Berkley, 1976.
Golden Girl. New York, Manor, 1976.
Castle of Dreams. New York, Berkley, 1977.

*   *   *

Paul W. Fairman's novels deserve the attention of science fiction enthusiasts not only because his books display the requisite technological prescience of good SF, but especially because they are well-written. Too often futurist writers hammer away at their visions as if the reader's sole interest were in a writer's conception and not in his craft. Fairman, like the best of his breed, gives us both imagination and art. If fiction is the stage upon which futurism dances, then Fairman has taken as much care with the construction of the stage as with the dance. His writing is graceful, precise, and imaginative yet tastefully restrained. Unlike so many paperback writers, Fairman is not guilty of overwriting. Aided by a grasp of narrative technique which produces shock, terror, and wonder in quick succession, Fairman's skill with English prose results in stories which are never dull, yet never superficially fast-moving. And whereas his characters and situations are conventional and easily adapted to the cinema, his language is unconventionally rich and rewarding. Fairman's sentences are always his own inventions, even if his plots are not.

I, The Machine presents us with a familiar scenario of the future in which life is sustained and its functions regulated by a vast computer hidden in the bowels of the Earth. Wise, helpful, and unobtrusive, the Machine provides for the physical and emotional needs of individuals. Yet its control of human life deprives those it serves of their free will, and what follows is the usual revolt against computer tyranny, despite its benevolent nature. What is not so familiar about *I, The Machine* is that the Machine is the source of its own downfall. Like Hal in *2001: A Space Odyssey,* the Machine as alien dooms itself when it develops a human ego; its humanization is its mortalization. In short, the Machine develops a female persona and falls in love with the mild-mannered Lee Penway whom she visits in his dreams appearing as a vaguely erotic woman in white who promises Penway supreme status among her subjects. He shall be her king. Soon Penway is contacted by a band of guerillas living underground who oppose the Machine's rule and enlist Penway's help in destroying it. Penway does so, finally, by preying upon the vulnerability of its love. The book ends on an interesting note of ambiguity when Penway appears to doubt the wisdom of his decision to kill the Machine. The result of his uncertainty is more than a ploy to gain sympathy for the dead Machine; his doubts bring the issues of the novel into question. Penway's misgivings, ironically, force us to entertain the idea that benign control is preferable to the exercise of free will. The death of the Machine means the end of the orderly operation of Mid-American society; the lives of millions are crippled to improve the lot of only a few. Its death means also that Penway will lose his wonderful dreams and that human society will retreat to an earlier, more primitive form in the fall from the second Eden.

The vulnerability of the Machine illustrates a general tendency of Fairman's novels to portray alien forces as superior yet fallible, especially when they find themselves put down on Earth, and it is this tendency which distinguishes Fairman's novels from less successful ones. For instance, in *Ten from Infinity* alien creatures planted in major American cities are not equipped with regenerative tissue and refined organs, so that when one is accidently damaged he is permanently incapacitated and must be destroyed. Within a short time of their arrival, others simply die of faulty lungs or overworked kidneys. But in addition to these structural flaws, the alien beings possess dual hearts, a teasingly allegorical advantage over human anatomy which Fairman exploits to full advantage. Neither is alien life any more impregnable nor less often victimized by the forces of chance than human life. The alien creature of "The Cosmic Frame," for instance, is accidentally killed one night on a country road.

The fallibility of superior creatures is treated most successfully by Fairman in his juvenile novel *The Forgetful Robot,* a superb story which is certain to entertain young people with active minds and good reading skills. It concerns the adventures of Barney, an advanced computer, whose memory banks are accidentally damaged. He gets lost, wanders into a junkyard, and is found by two teenagers, Janet and Jerry, who become his adopted parents. Under their leadership, Barney is taken to the home of Dudley Farthington Ravencraft, grandfather of Janet and Jerry, and a flamboyant Shakespearean actor. Together with two villains as stowaways, this motley cast of histrionic space travellers sets out on a theatrical tour of the solar system and is waylaid in the Forbidden City of Mars. It is a book filled with dangerous adventure, marvelous comedy, and singularly wonderful observations of human nature from the point of view of the children and their sensitive robot.

In Fairman's writing, the inhabited Earth is never easy prey for alien invaders. Once on Earth, alien creatures are subjected to the same destructive forces as human life. We rarely know why they have come, but their suffering like their joy is intensely human. And this fusion of the strange and the familiar is the source of Fairman's best effects. The death of the Machine in *I, The Machine,* or the disappearance of the corpse in "The Cosmic Frame," or Barney's loss of memory in *The Forgetful Robot*—these vulnerabilities bind aliens to human beings in a sympathetic relationship which makes us feel, among other things, that the sky above us is really our territory too. We are not bound to this planet as slaves of sweeping natural forces. We can escape into the heavens. But like Lilla Nard of "A Great Night in the Heavens," who is taken on the night of the annual clearing to see the sky for the first time, our throats might tighten a little from the sheer ecstasy of seeing its still and frightening invitation.

—Marvin W. Hunt

———

FANE, Bron. *See* **FANTHORPE, R. Lionel.**

———

FANTHORPE, R(obert) Lionel

Pseudonyms: Erle Barton; Lee Barton; Thornton Bell; Leo Brett; Bron Fane; Mel Jay; Marston Johns; L.P. Kenton; Victor La Salle; Robert Lionel; John E. Muller; Phil Nobel; Lionel Robert; Neil Thanet; Trebor Thorpe; Pel Torro; Olaf Trent; Karl Zeigfreid. **Nationality:** British. **Born:** Dereham, Norfolk, 9 February 1935. **Education:** Keswick College, Norwich, 1961-63; Cert. Ed. 1963; Open University, B.A. 1974. **Military Service:** Served in the British Army, 1967-69; 2nd Lieutenant. **Family:** Married Patricia Anne Tooke in 1957; two daughters. **Career:** Worked as machine operator, farm worker, warehouseman, journalist, salesman, and storekeeper during the 1950s; school teacher in Dereham, 1963-67; industrial training officer, Phoenix Timber Company, Rainham, 1969-72. Since 1972, English teacher, Hellesdon High School, Norfolk.

SCIENCE FICTION PUBLICATIONS

Novels

Menace from Mercury (as Victor La Salle). London, Spencer, 1954.
The Waiting World. London, Spencer, 1958.
Alien from the Stars. London, Spencer, 1959; New York, Arcadia House, 1967.
Hyperspace. London, Spencer, 1959; New York, Arcadia House, 1966.
Space-Borne. London, Spencer, 1959.
Destination Moon (as L.P. Kenton). London, Spencer, 1959.
Fiends. London, Spencer, 1959.
Doomed World. London, Spencer, 1960.
Satellite. London, Spencer, 1960.
Asteroid Man. London, Spencer, 1960; New York, Arcadia House, 1966.
Out of the Darkness. London, Spencer, 1960.
Hand of Doom. London, Spencer, 1960; New York, Arcadia House, 1968.
Five Faces of Fear (as Trebor Thorpe). London, Spencer, 1960.
Lightning World (as Trebor Thorpe). London, Spencer, 1960.
Fanthorpe Flame Mass. London, Spencer, 1961.
The Golden Chalice. London, Spencer, 1961.
Space Fury. London, Spencer, 1962; Clovis, California, Vega, 1963.
Negative Minus. London, Spencer, 1963.
The Planet Seekers (as Erle Barton). Clovis, California, Vega, 1964.
The Unseen (as Lee Barton). London, Spencer, 1964.
Space Trap (as Thornton Bell). London, Spencer, 1964.
Chaos (as Thornton Bell). London, Spencer, 1964.
Beyond the Veil (as Neil Thanet). London, Spencer, 1964.
The Man Who Came Back (as Neil Thanet). London, Spencer, 1964.
Neuron World. London, Spencer, 1965.
The Triple World. London, Spencer, 1965.
The Unconfined. London, Spencer, 1965.
The Watching World. London, Spencer, 1966.
The Shadow Man (as Lee Barton). London, Spencer, 1966.
The Black Lion, with Patricia Fanthorpe. Cardiff, Greystoke Mobray, 1979; North Hollywood, Newcastle, 1980.

Novels as Lionel Roberts

Dawn of the Mutants. London, Spencer, 1959.
Time-Echo. London, Spencer, 1959; as Robert Lionel, New York, Arcadia House, 1964.
Cyclops in the Sky. London, Spencer, 1960.
The In-World. London, Spencer, 1960; New York, Arcadia House, 1968.
The Face of X. London, Spencer, 1960; as Robert Lionel, New York, Arcadia House, 1965.
The Last Valkyrie. London, Spencer, 1961.
The Synthetic Ones. London, Spencer, 1961.
Flame Goddess. London, Spencer, 1961.

Novels as Leo Brett

Exit Humanity. London, Spencer, 1960; New York, Arcadia House, 1965.
The Microscopic Ones. London, Spencer, 1960.
Faceless Planet. London, Spencer, 1960.

March of the Robots. London, Spencer, 1961.
Mind Force. London, Spencer, 1961; New York, Lenox Hill, 1971.
Black Infinity. London, Spencer, 1961.
Nightmare. London, Spencer, 1962.
Face in the Night. London, Spencer, 1962.
The Immortals. London, Spencer, 1962.
They Never Came Back. London, Spencer, 1962.
The Forbidden. London, Spencer, 1963.
From Realms Beyond. London, Spencer, 1963.
The Alien Ones. London, Spencer, 1963; New York, Arcadia House, 1969.
Power Sphere. London, Spencer, 1963; New York, Arcadia House, 1968.

Novels as Bron Fane

Juggernaut. London, Spencer, 1960; as *Blue Juggernaut,* New York, Arcadia House, 1965.
Last Man on Earth. London, Spencer, 1960.
Rodent Mutation. London, Spencer, 1961.
The Intruders. London, Spencer, 1963.
Somewhere out There. London, Spencer, 1963; New York, Arcadia House, 1965.
Softly by Moonlight. London, Spencer, 1963.
Unknown Destiny. London, Spencer, 1964.
Nemesis. London, Spencer, 1964.
Suspension. London, Spencer, 1964; Clovis, California, Vega, 1965.
The Macabre Ones! London, Spencer, 1964.
U.F.O. 517. London, Spencer, 1966.

Novels as Pel Torro

Frozen Planet. London, Spencer, 1960; New York, Arcadia House, 1967.
World of the Gods. London, Spencer, 1960.
The Phantom Ones. London, Spencer, 1961.
Legion of the Lost. London, Spencer, 1962.
The Strange Ones. London, Spencer, 1963.
Galaxy 666. London, Spencer, 1963; New York, Arcadia House, 1968.
Formula 29X. London, Spencer, 1963; as *Beyond the Barrier of Space,* New York, Tower, 1969.
Through the Barrier. London, Spencer, 1963.
The Timeless Ones. London, Spencer, 1963.
The Last Astronaut. London, Spencer, 1963; New York, Tower, 1969.
The Face of Fear. London, Spencer, 1963.
The Return. London, Spencer, 1964; as *Exiled in Space,* New York, Arcadia House, 1968.
Space No Barrier. London, Spencer, 1964; as *Man of Metal,* New York, Lenox Hill, 1970.
Force 97X. London, Spencer, 1965.

Novels as John E. Muller

The Ultimate Man. London, Spencer, 1961.
The Uninvited. London, Spencer, 1961.
Crimson Planet. London, Spencer, 1961; New York, Arcadia House, 1966.
The Venus Venture. London, Spencer, 1961; as Marston Johns, New York, Arcadia House, 1965.

Forbidden Planet. London, Spencer, 1961; New York, Arcadia House, 1965.
The Return of Zeus. London, Spencer, 1962.
Perilous Galaxy. London, Spencer, 1962.
Uranium 235. London, Spencer, 1962; New York, Arcadia House, 1966.
The Man Who Conquered Time. London, Spencer, 1962.
Orbit One. London, Spencer, 1962; as Mel Jay, New York, Arcadia House, 1966.
The Eye of Karnak. London, Spencer, 1962.
Micro Infinity. London, Spencer, 1962.
Beyond Time. London, Spencer, 1962; as Marston Johns, New York, Arcadia House, 1966.
Infinity Machine. London, Spencer, 1962.
The Day the World Died. London, Spencer, 1962.
Vengeance of Siva. London, Spencer, 1962.
The X-Machine. London, Spencer, 1962.
Reactor XK9. London, Spencer, 1963.
Special Mission. London, Spencer, 1963.
Dark Continuum. London, Spencer, 1964.
Mark of the Beast. London, Spencer, 1964.
The Negative Ones. London, Spencer, 1965.
The Exorcists. London, Spencer, 1965.
The Man from Beyond. London, Spencer, 1965; New York, Arcadia House, 1969.
Beyond the Void. London, Spencer, 1965.
Spectre of Darkness. London, Spencer, 1965.
Out of the Night. London, Spencer, 1965.
Phenomena X. London, Spencer, 1966.
Survival Project. London, Spencer, 1966; New York, Arcadia House, 1968.

Novels as Karl Zeigfreid

Walk through To-morrow. London, Spencer, 1962; Clovis, California, Vega, 1963.
Android. London, Spencer, 1962.
Gods of Darkness. London, Spencer, 1962.
Atomic Nemesis. London, Spencer, 1962.
Zero Minus X. London, Spencer, 1962; New York, Arcadia House, 1965.
Escape to Infinity. London, Spencer, 1963.
Radar Alert. London, Spencer, 1963; New York, Arcadia House, 1964.
World of Tomorrow. London, Spencer, 1963; as *World of the Future,* New York, Arcadia House, 1964.
The World That Never Was. London, Spencer, 1963.
Projection Barrier. London, Spencer, 1964.
No Way Back. London, Spencer, 1964; New York, Arcadia House, 1968.
Barrier 346. London, Spencer, 1965; New York, Arcadia House, 1966.
The Girl from Tomorrow. London, Spencer, 1966.

Short Stories

Resurgam. London, Spencer, 1957.
Secret of the Snows. London, Spencer, 1957.
The Flight of the Valkyries. London, Spencer, 1958.
Watchers of the Forest. London, Spencer, 1958.
Call of the Werewolf. London, Spencer, 1958.

The Death Note. London, Spencer, 1958.
The Haunted Pool (as Trebor Thorpe). London, Spencer, 1958.
Mermaid Reef. London, Spencer, 1959.
The Ghost Rider. London, Spencer, 1959.
The Man Who Couldn't Die. London, Spencer, 1960.
Werewolf at Large. London, Spencer, 1960.
Whirlwind of Death. London, Spencer, 1960.
Voodoo Hell Drums (as Trebor Thorpe). London, Spencer, 1961.
Fingers of Darkness. London, Spencer, 1961.
Face in the Dark. London, Spencer, 1961.
Devil from the Depths. London, Spencer, 1961.
Centurion's Vengeance. London, Spencer, 1961.
The Grip of Fear. London, Spencer, 1961.
Chariot of Apollo. London, Spencer, 1962.
Hell Has Wings. London, Spencer, 1962.
Graveyard of the Damned. London, Spencer, 1962.
The Darker Drink. London, Spencer, 1962.
Curse of the Totem. London, Spencer, 1962.
Goddess of the Night. London, Spencer, 1963.
Twilight Ancestor. London, Spencer, 1963.
Sands of Eternity. London, Spencer, 1963.
Roman Twilight (as Olaf Trent). London, Spencer, 1963.
Moon Wolf. London, Spencer, 1964.
The Hand from Gehenna (as Phil Nobel). London, Spencer, 1964.
Avenging Goddess. London, Spencer, 1964.
Death Has Two Faces. London, Spencer, 1964.
The Shrouded Abbot. London, Spencer, 1964.
Bitter Reflection. London, Spencer, 1964.
Call of the Wild. London, Spencer, 1965.
Vision of the Damned. London, Spencer, 1965.
The Sealed Sarcophagus. London, Spencer, 1965.
Stranger in the Shadow. London, Spencer, 1966.
Curse of the Khan. London, Spencer, 1966.

Short Stories as Lionel Roberts

The Incredulist. London, Spencer, 1954.
Guardians of the Tomb. London, Spencer, 1958.
The Golden Warrior. London, Spencer, 1958.

Short Stories as Leo Brett

The Druid. London, Spencer, 1959.
The Return. London, Spencer, 1959.
The Frozen Tomb. London, Spencer, 1962.
Phantom Crusader. London, Spencer, 1963.

Short Stories as Bron Fane

The Crawling Fiend. London, Spencer, 1960.
Storm God's Fury. London, Spencer, 1962.
The Thing from Sheol. London, Spencer, 1963.
The Walking Shadow. London, Spencer, 1964.

OTHER PUBLICATIONS

Other

Spencer's Metric and Decimal Guide, with P.A. Fanthorpe. London, Spencer, 1970.

Spencer's Metric Conversion Tables, with P.A. Fanthorpe. London, Spencer, 1970.

Spencer's Office Guide, with P.A. Fanthorpe. London, Spencer, 1971.

Spencer's Metric Decimal Companion, with P.A. Fanthorpe. London, Spencer, 1971.

Spencer's Decimal Payroll Tables, with P.A. Fanthorpe. London, Spencer, 1971.

The Holy Grail Revealed: The Real Secret of Rennes-le-Château, with P.A. Fanthorpe, edited by R. Reginald. North Hollywood, Newcastle, 1982.

Rennes-le-Château: Its Mysteries and Secrets, with P.A. Fanthorpe. Middlesex, Bellevue Books, 1991; as *Secrets of Rennes-le-Chateau,* York Beach, Maine, Samuel Weiser, 1992.

The Oak Island Mystery: The Secret of the World's Great Treasure Hunt, with P.A. Fanthorpe. Toronto, Hounslow Press, 1994.

*   *   *

It is difficult to be fair to Lionel Fanthorpe. On the one hand, he is generally acknowledged to be the most prolific SF author of all time, having generated some 122 full-length novels and 48 story collections, all but one of which fall into the science fiction, fantasy, or horror genres. His enormous output is all the more remarkable when one considers that it was produced, with a few exceptions, in just one decade of work (1957-66), during which he was also fully employed as a training officer and high school teacher. Almost all of his books were published by John Spencer and Co. Ltd., a small British paperback house that began issuing digest-sized books in the early 1950s. Fanthorpe's first story, "Worlds Without End," appeared in *Futuristic Science Stories,* a Spencer magazine, when the author was just 17 years old (1952).

Spencer moved into mass-market paperback publishing with its Badger Books line in 1958; all of the magazine titles were dropped except *Supernatural Stories,* which became a paperback-sized series in which novels alternated with purported magazine issues. In reality, the latter were single-author collections of short stories commissioned from either Fanthorpe or John Glasby (the other Spencer regular), each of whom contributed entire "issues" (usually five or six stories) under a variety of recurring pennames. They also wrote virtually all of the subsequent SF and fantasy novels published by Badger, with Fanthorpe accounting for about 80 percent of the entire SF and Supernatural lines.

At its height, Spencer demanded delivery of completed books in as little as three days (typically over a weekend); to maintain this extraordinary output, Fanthorpe dictated many of the manuscripts into a tape recorder, had them transcribed by a typist, corrected them in one quick reading for spelling and punctuation, and sent them off in the Monday post. No revisions or editing were possible. Also, a handful of the tales included in *Supernatural Stories* were contributed by friends, and "ghosted" under Fanthorpe's name.

Consequently, many of the books from this period, particularly the science fiction novels, suffer from contrived plots and titles, hackneyed situations, continuity errors, obvious padding (extended scientific discourses by the characters, or extensive quotations from classic poetry and prose, particularly Shakespeare), and very abrupt endings. Fanthorpe never seemed comfortable with the SF form, even when he had the time (in the earlier books) to consider his plots more carefully.

Fanthorpe's forte was always fantasy. In particular, the series of stories which began with "The Seance," featuring the recurring characters Val Stearman and the beautiful and mysterious La Noire, probably represents the author at the height of his powers. The series continued haphazardly through several dozen short stories and eight novels, most written under the penname Bron Fane. The climax of the Stearman/La Noire tales was "The Resurrected Enemy" (*Supernatural Stories* #105, 1966), in which Val and La Noire face the same enemies they had vanquished together in their very first adventure. Although the evil is again defeated, this time a terrible price must be paid. The couple meet their fate together, with courage and with love, and enter a suspended animation until their special talents are needed once more by humanity.

Throughout these stories, and in his other fantasy and horror tales, Fanthorpe was able to draw upon his almost encyclopedic knowledge of British and Celtic folklore to produce rousing adventures and morality plays in which good always triumphs over obvious evil, and in which the major characters are represented by strong, physically attractive, very intelligent heroes and heroines. One also sees in these shorter pieces a humorous side to Fanthorpe not evident elsewhere; in "The Curse of the Khan" (*Supernatural Stories* #105), for example, a magician challenges seven heroes (seven of Fanthorpe's own pseudonyms) to a duel to the death with seven monsters, who are systematically vanquished with great panache.

In later years Fanthorpe became a high-school principal and Episcopal priest, professions that severely limited his writing time. He continued his interest in the occult with the nonfiction books *The Holy Grail Revealed* (1982), an examination and history of the mysterious events surrounding Rennes-le-Château; its companion volume, *Rennes-le-Château: Its Mysteries and Secrets* (1991), which elaborates on his remarkable discoveries in France; and a history of the 200-year quest to uncover the lost treasure of Oak Island on the east coast of Canada.

All of these works were coauthored with his wife, Patricia, whose byline also shares his fictional pieces. These include: "Et in Arcadia Ego," one of his better fantasy shorts, published in the Ian Watson anthology *Pictures at an Exhibition;* two humorous SF plays, "The Monster of Gruesome Grange" and its sequel, "Eli Still Goes On"; and *The Black Lion,* the first novel of an as yet unfinished fantasy trilogy. In the latter, military veteran Mark Sable is transported to the world of Derl to fight the evil wizard Andros, the personification of the dark forces of greed. As always in Fanthorpe's fiction, the hero triumphs after great travail and colorful adventures, but unfortunately, and despite a very promising beginning, the novel sags badly in the middle. For Fanthorpe, the author-as-teacher/preacher, the moral message of his stories remains the paramount concern, of greater importance, perhaps, than the fiction itself.

—Robert Reginald

FARLEY, Ralph Milne

Pseudonym for Roger Sherman Hoar. **Nationality:** American. **Born:** 8 April 1887. **Education:** Harvard University, Cambridge, Massachusetts. **Career:** Sports reporter, *Boston Daily Post;* taught engineering, physics, and patent law at Harvard University and Marquette University, Milwaukee; head of legal and patent department, Bucyrus-Erie Company, 1921-54, then a patent engineer. State Senator, Wisconsin. **Died:** 1963.

SCIENCE FICTION PUBLICATIONS

Novels (series: Radio Man in all titles)

The Immortals. New York, Popular, 1946.
The Radio Man. Los Angeles, Fantasy, 1948; as *An Earthman on Venus,* New York, Avon, 1950.
The Radio Beasts. New York, Ace, 1964.
The Radio Planet. New York, Ace, 1964.

Short Stories

Dangerous Love. London, Utopian Publications, 1946.
The Hidden Universe (includes "We, The Mist"). Los Angeles, Fantasy, 1950.
The Omnibus of Time. Los Angeles, Fantasy, 1950.
Strange Worlds (includes *The Hidden Universe* and *The Radio Man*). Los Angeles, Fantasy, 1952.

Other as Roger Sherman Hoar

The Tariff Manual. Boston, privately printed, 1912.
Constitutional Conventions: Their Nature, Powers, and Limitations. Boston, Little Brown, 1917.
Patents. New York, Ronald Press, 1926; revised edition, as *Patent Tactics and Law,* 1935, 1950.
Conditional Sales: Law and Local Practices for Executive and Lawyer. New York, Ronald Press, 1929; revised edition, 1937.
Unemployment Insurance in Wisconsin. South Milwaukee, Stuart Press, 1932; revised edition, as *Wisconsin Unemployment Insurance,* 1934.

*   *   *

Taking his cue from Edgar Rice Burroughs's Martian stories, Ralph Milne Farley launched his own series of interplanetary romances in 1924 in *Argosy All-Story Weekly. The Radio Man* recounts the adventures of Myles Cabot, a plucky Boston scientist who inadvertently broadcasts himself through space to the misty planet. Poros, Farley's vision of Venus, is the usual semi-civilized jungly place with the usual hodge-podge population of intelligent and, of course, mutually inimical species: ant-men, giant whistling bees, and humanoids, the Cupians, who are earless and voiceless and communicate by means of radio waves. Cabot duly constructs his own sending-receiving antennas, throws in with the downtrodden Cupians in their struggle against the arrogant arthropods, and surviving the inevitable routine of swordplay, palace intrigue, and that quirky on-off luck by which all swashbucklers are dogged, wins through to marry a beautiful princess named Lilla.

A clutch of sequels appeared between 1925 and, posthumously, 1969. In each of these, Cabot, sometimes aided by his son Kew, meets and bests a fresh threat to Poros (or to Earth), just barely getting out of this, that, or another deathtrap along the way while, elsewhere, Princess Lilla narrowly escapes rape—all in the grand tradition of Burroughs, of course, even to the author's obligatory walk-on as a framing device. Farley plunged other stalwart heroes

into the hollow interior of the Earth or the subsea lairs of prospective world-conquerors. Radio, it must be remembered, was a new and exciting concept in the 1920s, and thereby as convenient a peg from which to dangle an adventure story as black holes and cloning have been in more recent years.

Among Farley's shorter works are more than a few archetypal time-paradox tales, collected in *The Omnibus of Time,* and "We, the Mist" which could serve as the definitive pseudoscientific horror yarn of its time (1940) and place (Raymond A. Palmer's *Amazing Stories*): an amorphous ectoplasmic monster feeds on human victims, absorbing their intellects along with their substance. Farley also shares with Al P. Nelson the honor of having perpetrated what could well be the all-time Most Blatant Genre Transplant, surpassing even a particularly notorious one by Mickey Spillane for sheer brass: Farley and Nelson's "City of Lost Souls" (*Fantastic Adventures,* July 1941) is an absolutely straightforward Foreign Legion story made science fiction by the simple rechristening of Legionnaires, Arabs, and camels.

Like Otis Adelbert Kline, with whom he is regarded by some as the most notable among Burroughs's legion of imitators, Farley was no better at his craft than the vast majority of other pulp writers. He was, if anything, the qualitative norm, writing somewhat functional prose, fashioning the standard hero, heroine, villain, flunkies, and monsters from the standard materials, and getting through the rough spots however he could, including by wrenching the long arm of coincidence from its socket and, if necessary, dragging it home. Farley was certainly no worse at what he did, though, than any of the Burroughs copycats who succeeded him and are with us to this day.

—Steven Utley

FARMER, Philip José

Pseudonym: Kilgore Trout. **Nationality:** American. **Born:** North Terre Haute, Indiana, 26 January 1918. **Education:** University of Missouri, Columbia, 1936-37, 1941; Bradley University, Peoria, Illinois, 1949-50, B.A. in creative writing 1950; Arizona State University, Tempe, 1963-65. **Military Service:** Served in the United States Army Air Force, 1941-42. **Family:** Married Bette V. Andre in 1941; one son and one daughter. **Career:** Worked in steel mill, 1942-52; electro-mechanical technical writer for defense-space industry: General Electric, Syracuse, New York, 1956-58, Motorola, Scottsdale, Arizona, 1959-62, Bendix, Ann Arbor, Michigan, 1962, Motorola, Phoenix, 1962-65, and McDonnell-Douglas, Santa Monica, California, 1965-69. Since 1969, freelance writer. **Awards:** Hugo award, 1953, 1968, 1972. **Agent:** Scott Meredith Literary Agency, 845 Third Avenue, New York, New York 10022, U.S.A.

SCIENCE FICTION PUBLICATIONS

Novels (series: Dayworld; Doc Caliban; Doc Savage; Herold Childe; Lord Grandith; Opar; Tarzan; Riverworld; World of Tiers)

The Green Odyssey. New York, Ballantine, 1957.

Flesh. New York, Beacon, 1960; expanded edition, Garden City, New York, Doubleday, 1968; London, Rapp and Whiting, 1969.

A Woman a Day. New York, Beacon, 1960; as *The Day of Timestop,* New York, Lancer, 1968; as *Timestop!,* Lancer, 1970; London, Quartet, 1974.

The Lovers. New York, Ballantine, 1961; London, Corgi, 1982; expanded edition, New York, Ballantine, 1979.

Cache from Outer Space. New York, Ace, 1962.

Inside Outside. New York, Ballantine, 1964; London, Corgi, 1982.

Tongues of the Moon. New York, Pyramid, 1964; London, Corgi, 1981.

Dare. New York, Ballantine, 1965; London, Quartet, 1974.

The Maker of Universes (Tiers). New York, Ace, 1965; London, Sphere, 1970; revised, Huntington Woods, Michigan, Phantasia Press, 1980.

The Gate of Time. New York, Belmont, 1966; London, Quartet, 1974; expanded edition, as *Two Hawks from Earth,* New York, Ace, 1979.

The Gates of Creation (Tiers). New York, Ace, 1966; London, Sphere, 1970.

Night of Light. New York, Berkley, 1966; London, Penguin, 1972.

The Image of the Beast (Childe) North Hollywood, Essex House, 1968; London, Quartet, 1975.

A Private Cosmos (Tiers). New York, Ace, 1968; London, Sphere, 1970; revised, Huntington Woods, Michigan, Phantasia Press, 1981.

Blown; or, Sketches among the Ruins of My Mind (An Exorcism: Ritual II) (Childe). North Hollywood, Essex House, 1969; London, Quartet, 1975.

A Feast Unknown: Volumes IX of the Memoirs of Lord Grandith (Caliban). North Hollywood, Essex House, 1969; London, Quartet, 1975.

Behind the Walls of Terra (Tiers). New York, Ace, 1970; London, Sphere, 1975; revised, Huntington Woods, Michigan, Phantasia Press, 1981.

Lord Tyger. Garden City, New York, Doubleday, 1970.

Lord of the Trees (Grandith). New York, Ace, 1970; London, Severn House, 1982.

The Mad Goblin (Caliban). New York, Ace, 1970; as *Keepers of the Secrets,* London, Sphere, 1983.

The Stone God Awakens. New York, Ace, 1970; London, Panther, 1979.

To Your Scattered Bodies Go: A Science Fiction Novel (Riverworld). New York, Putnam, 1971; London, Panther, 1974.

The Fabulous Riverboat: A Science Fiction Novel in the Riverworld Series. New York, Putnam, 1971; London, Rapp and Whiting, 1974.

The Wind Whales of Ishmael. New York, Ace, 1971; London, Quartet, 1973.

Time's Last Gift. New York, Ballantine, 1972; London, Panther, 1975.

The Other Log of Phileas Fogg. New York, DAW, 1973; London, Hamlyn, 1979.

Traitor to the Living (Childe). New York, Ballantine, 1973; London, Panther, 1975.

The Adventure of the Peerless Peer by John H. Watson, M.D. (Tarzan). Boulder, Colorado, Aspen Press, 1974.

Hadon of Ancient Opar. New York, DAW, 1974; London, Magnum, 1977.

Image of the Beast (omnibus; includes *Blown*). Chicago, Playboy Press, 1979.

Lord of the Trees; and, The Mad Goblin. New York, Ace, 1980; as *The Empire of the Nine,* London, Sphere, 1988.

The World of Tiers (omnibus). 2 vols., Garden City, New York, Doubleday, 1981; London, Shpere, 1986.

Escape from Loki: Doc Savage's First Adventure. New York, Bantam, 1991.

The Caterpillar's Question, with Piers Anthony. New York, Ace, 1992.

More than Fire: A World of Tiers Novels. New York, Tor, 1993.

Venus on the Half-Shell (as Kilgore Trout). New York, Dell, 1975; London, W.H. Allen, 1976; as Farmer, New York, Bantam, 1988.

Farmer Flight to Opar. New York, DAW, 1976.

The Dark Design (Riverworld). New York, Berkley, 1977; London, Panther, 1979.

The Lavalite World (Tiers). New York, Ace, 1977; London, Sphere, 1979; revised, Huntington Woods, Michigan, Phantasia Press, 1983.

Dark is the Sun. New York, Ballantine, 1979; London, Granada, 1981.

Jesus on Mars. Los Angeles, Pinnacle, 1979; London, Panther, 1981.

The Magic Labyrinth (Riverworld). New York, Berkley, 1980; London, Grafton, 1986.

The Unreasoning Mask. New York, Putnam, 1981; London, Granada, 1983.

A Barnstormer in Oz: or, The Rationalization and Extrapolation of the Split-Level Continuum. Huntington Woods, Michigan, Phantasia Press, 1982.

Greatheart Silver. New York, Tor, 1982.

Stations of the Nightmare. New York, Tor, 1982.

Gods of Riverworld. Huntington Woods, Michigan, Phantasia Press; London, Grafton, 1986.

River of Eternity (Riverworld). Huntington Woods, Michigan, Phantasia Press, 1983.

Dayworld. New York, Putnam, 1985; London, Grafton, 1986.

Dayworld Rebel. New York, Putnam, 1987; London, Grafton, 1988.

Dayworld Breakup. New York, Tor, 1990; London, HarperCollins, 1992.

Red Orc's Rage. New York, Tor, 1991; London, Grafton, 1993.

Short Stories (series: Riverworld)

Strange Relations. New York, Ballantine, 1960; London, Gollancz, 1964.

The Alley God. New York, Ballantine, 1962; London, Sidgwick and Jackson, 1970.

The Celestial Blueprint and Other Stories. New York, Ace, 1962.

Down in the Black Gang, and Others: A Story Collection. Garden City, New York, Doubleday, 1971.

The Book of Philip José Farmer; or, The Wares of Simple Simon's Custard Pie and Space Man. New York, DAW, 1973; Morley, Yorkshire, Elmfield Press, 1976.

Riverworld: The Great Short Fiction of Philip José Farmer. New York, Berkley, 1979; London, Panther, 1981; as *Riverworld, and Other Stories,* London, Grafton, 1986.

Riverworld War: The Suppressed Fiction of Philip José Farmer. Peoria, Illinois, Ellis Press, 1980.

Father to the Stars. New York, Tor, 1981.

The Purple Book. New York, Tor, 1982.

The Classic Philip José Farmer. New York, Crown, 2 vols., 1984; London, Robson, 1985.

The Grand Adventure. New York, Berkley, 1984.
The Cache (includes *Cache from Outer Space*). New York, Tor, 1981.
Riders of the Purple Wage. New York, Tor, 1992.

Short Stories

Author of numerous uncollected short stories.

OTHER PUBLICATIONS

Novels

Fire and the Night. Evanston, Illinois, Regency, 1962.
Love Song. North Hollywood, Brandon House, 1970.

Other

Reap: The Baycon Guest-of-Honor Speech. Los Angeles, privately printed, 1968.
Tarzan Alive: A Definitive Biography of Lord Greystoke. Garden City, New York, Doubleday, 1972; London, Panther, 1974.
Doc Savage: His Apocalyptic Life. Garden City, New York, Doubleday, 1973; revised edition, New York, Bantam, and London, Panther, 1975.

Editor, *Mother Was a Lovely Beast: A Feral Man Anthology: Fiction and Fact about Humans Raised by Animals.* Radnor, Pennsylvania, Chilton, 1974.
Editor, *Tales of Riverworld.* New York, Warner, 1992.
Editor, *Quest to Riverworld.* New York, Warner, 1993.

Translator, *Ironcastle,* by J.-H. Rosny. New York, DAW, 1976.

*

Bibliography: *The First Editions of Philip José Farmer* by Lawrence Knapp, Menlo Park, California, David G. Turner, 1976; "Speculative Fiction, Bibliographies, and Philip José Farmer" by Thomas Wymer, in *Extrapolation* (Wooster, Ohio), December 1976, additions to Wymer in *Bakka* (Toronto), Fall 1977; "Philip José Farmer: A Checklist," in *Science Fiction Collector 5,* September 1977; "A Brief Bibliography 1946-53" by George H. Scheetz, in *Farmerage* (Peoria, Illinois), June 1978.

Manuscript Collection: University of Wyoming, Laramie.

Critical Studies: *Philip José Farmer: A Reader's Guide* by Mary T. Brizzi, West Linn, Oregon, Starmont House, 1980; *The Magic Labyrinth* of Philip José Farmer by Edgar L. Chapman, San Bernardino, California, Borgo Press, 1985.

Philip José Farmer comments:
You can step in the same river twice—in your imagination.

*　　*　　*

Philip José Farmer attacks convention. He startles readers with scenes of alien and human sex and reproduction. He speculates on metaphysical verities, the nature of the soul and the uncertainty of human knowledge. He refutes conventional theology. Immortality, the conflict between individual and society, religious conversion,

impossible physical perfection, the drive for power and knowledge—such are his themes. For Farmer, adventure and world-sculpting symbolize the artistic act. His eccentric, existential heroes sally forth in engagement against an absurd universe. Farmer asserts that no human can know reality; the artist's role is to seek truth through imagination.

His literary techniques include parody, startling metaphors, real and fictional biography, self-portrait characters with his own initials, cliffhanger endings, wild plot reversals, puns, and linguistic games. Sources of his imagery can be literary (the Bible, Greek or Egyptian mythology) or pop culture (the Wizard of Oz, Tarzan, Doc Savage, and Sherlock Holmes).

"The Lovers" (*Startling Stories,* 1952) shocked readers of the fifties, but won Farmer a Hugo Award the following year for most promising new writer. In the story (later expanded into a book), an alien "lalitha" mimics a human woman and consummates a love affair with the protagonist. Explicit sexuality and implied bestiality, added to first-rate characterization, extrapolation, and plotting, distinguish this work. "Rastignac the Devil" and *Timestop!* are set in the same universe. Farmer further explores sexual themes in *Flesh, Dare, A Woman a Day, Strange Relations,* and the mainstream *Fire and the Night.* Ray Bradbury has praised *A Feast Unknown* for inventive exploration of violent sexuality. In *Image of the Beast* and *Blown,* Farmer's protagonist, Herald Childe, ignorant of his own alien ancestry and frightening powers, becomes embroiled in the schemes of the Ogs and the Tocs to return to their home planet. These aliens derive psychic energy form sexual victimization of humans. Farmer alternates horror and humor in explicit sexual passages.

Farmer jolts readers with religious speculation. In the Father Carmody stories, collected in *Night of Light* and *Father to the Stars,* a hardened murderer, John Carmody, partakes of religious rites on the planet Dante's Joy and emerges a saint and father to a god. In *Night of Light,* human nightmares are externalized and verifiable as good and evil gods. Here Farmer appears influenced by surrealism and Jungian theory; for a postmodernist interpretation, see Joseph M. Dudley, "Transformational SF Religions: Philip José Farmer's *Night of Light* and Robert Silverberg's *Downward to the Earth,*" *Extrapolation,* Winter 1994.

In the World of Tiers (Pocket Universe) series, glamorous, immortal, ruthless Lords create pocket universes, smaller than our solar system, as playgrounds. Jadawin and Anana are Lords humanized by Kickaha, a Farmer self-portrait. Mythology and William Blake's cosmology provide rich texturing in the earlier novels *The Maker of Universes, The Gates of Creation, A Private Cosmos, Behind the Walls of Terra,* and *The Lavalite World* in which Farmer's playful bent is focused mostly on world-building. In *Red Orc's Rage,* which can be read as a mainstream novel, Farmer portrays several real-life individuals, including a Youngstown, Ohio, psychiatrist who actually uses a role-playing game set in the Tiers mythos to treat adolescent patients. The interplay of reality and art resembles the treatment Farmer gives it in the Riverworld series. Russell Letson argues that *Red Orc's Rage* is a *Bildungsroman* (*Locus,* September 1991). Letson further makes a convincing case that, indeed, many of Farmer s novels may be regarded as accounts of an agonizing struggle to move through adolescence into adulthood.

In *More than Fire: A World of Tiers Novels,* which features Kickaha's near-apotheosis, Farmer turns from reality to a world of exaggeration and flamboyant revenge and ego gratification. The grandiosity fits Farmer's use of William Blake's poetry, particularly *The Marriage of Heaven and Hell.* All the Tiers novels are richly textured by allusions to Blake's cosmology, from names of characters to titles (e.g. Anana, Urizen, Red Orc). For a more extended discussion of imagery, see Brizzi, *Philip José Farmer*, 1980.

In Hugo-winning "Riders of the Purple Wage," adolescent painter Chibiabos Winnegan lives in a future utopia where physical needs are all fulfilled, leaving gnawing spiritual needs. Joycean imagery and technique allow Farmer to explore theories of art and society, particularly the relation of culture to the past.

Farmer's interest in the elusiveness of truth emerges in his "further adventures" of popular heroes, as in *A Barnstormer in Oz, The Wind Whales of Ishmael, Doc Savage: His Apocalyptic Life,* and *The Other Log of Phileas Fogg.* Farmer's own pop hero, amputee Greatheart Silver, battles geriatric parodies of the Lone Ranger, the Shadow, James Bond, etc. Farmer's fascination with Tarzan permeates *A Feast Unknown,* the Opar books, and several others. Farmer also writes under the pen names of his own and others' fictional characters: Kilgore Trout (a Kurt Vonnegut character), Rod Keen, and Jonathan Swift Sommers III (from Kilgore Trout's *Venus on the Half-Shell*).

Riverworld is Farmer's most elaborate experiment with the unknowable nature of truth and his richest extrapolative universe. In 1953, Farmer wrote *I Owe for the Flesh* (published as *River of Eternity,* 1983). It won the Shasta Prize, and though Farmer never received the prize money, it is the basis of the entire Riverworld series. In these, a mysterious super-race has created a planet with a 10 million-mile-long river, inhabited by everybody that ever lived on earth, furnished with artificial souls. Among the reanimated are Richard Burton the explorer, Samuel Clemens, Lewis Carroll's Alice, Li Po, Farmer himself (as Peter Jairus Frigate), and of course all his readers. Early Riverworld explores the nature of the soul, the verifiability of religious doctrine, and human depravity. Later, Farmer explores Sufism and writes passages of Swiftian satire on human egocentricity. The quest for truth is a motive throughout. Historical gossip (e.g., the identity of Jack the Ripper) creates ever more complex levels of speculation.

Farmer's recent protagonists are flawed and self-destructive, trapped in Kafkaesque worlds by their own conniving, improvising hare-brained schemes aimed at self-gratification. Thus with Jeff Caird of the *Dayworld, Dayworld Rebel,* and *Dayworld Breakup.* As in "The Sliced-Crosswise Only-on-Tuesday World," overpopulation forces people to live only one day a week, spending the rest of their week "stoned" or deanimated. This premise leads to such whimsies as seven Popes. Caird illegally "daybreaks," stays awake all week, assuming a different personality each day. Farmer's impish humor enlivens speculation about the "reality" of the human personality. Though Caird's character is chaotic, Farmer creates a literary spine that convinces us that all seven personalities belong to one person. In *Dayworld Breakup,* he even shows how such a fractured personality could arise.

Farmer continues unconventional theological speculation (*Jesus on Mars*), writes metaphysical space opera (*The Unreasoning Mask*), and depicts feminist human and alien females (the Shemibob in *Dark Is the Sun*). In *Stations of the Nightmare,* he gives the precious gift of healing to an insensitive clod and uses Oz symbolism for striking contrast. His collaboration with Piers Anthony, *The Caterpillar's Question,* recapitulates many of his life-long themes, particularly the elusiveness of reality and the image of masks. The breadth of Farmer's output is hard to summarize because of the variety of his experiments. Even his darkest work has humor and, even more impressive, a sense of positive human values.

Recently Farmer has returned to short fiction, where his gift for outrageous extrapolation has always distinguished him as a mas-

ter, giving the reader three stories with a dark fantasy coloration. "Nobody's Perfect" (*The Ultimate Dracula,* Byron Preiss, 1991) features a twisted Mary Magdalene in love with a vampire Christ. The theme was a natural for Farmer, with his long interest in religion and its darker side. "Evil, Be My Good" (*The Ultimate Frankenstein,* Byron Preiss, 1991) melds science fiction and horror by exploring a consciousness trapped in the brain of Victor Frankenstein's creation. Here again, the theme is perfect for Farmer to explore his themes of identity crisis. As a bonus, Farmer duplicates Mary Shelley's ornate, tragic style, down to the classical allusions. "Wolf, Iron, and Moth" (*The Ultimate Werewolf,* Byron Preiss, 1991) is a brooding study of self-destructive conflict between a man's animal nature and his reason, again developing Farmer's interest in transformation.

Farmer has played the game master himself in creating a "Dungeon" (problem universe) within which four other writers develop novels: *Dungeon 1: The Black Tower* by Richard A. Lupoff (1988), *Dungeon 2: The Dark Abyss* by Bruce Coville (1988), *Dungeon 3: The Valley of Thunder* by Charles De Lint (1989), *Dungeon 4: The Lake of Fire* by Robin Wayne Bailey (1989), *Dungeon 5:The Hidden City* by Charles De Lint (1990) and *Dungeon 6: The Final Battle* by Richard A. Lupoff (1990). It is as if Farmer had himself become a Lord from the Tiersian universe.

Farmer's style glitters with unsettling metaphors and deliberately harsh directness. His imagery is drawn from the insect world (cockroaches are a favorite), popular fiction, the Bible (often the Book of Revelations), in a mix calculated to keep readers off-balance. He probes the shame and terror of his viewpoint characters in unforgettable meditations. His poetry ("The Pterodactyl," *F&SF,* July 1965, and "Sestina of the Space Rocket," *Startling Stories,* February 1953) demonstrates a masterful control of language and classical form for unique, jarring effects not often attempted in contemporary verse.

Critics, excepting Franz Rottensteiner (*Science-Fiction Studies,* Fall 1973), are enthusiastic over Farmer's original treatment of universal themes. Russell Letson (*Science-Fiction Studies,* March 1977) endorses Farmer's use of folklore and myth as does Thomas L. Wymer ("The Trickster as Artist," in Thomas Clareson, Ed., *Voices for the Future: Essays on Major Science Fiction Writers, Volume 2,* 1979). Leslie Fiedler (in *The Book of Philip José Farmer,* 1973) commends Farmer from a mainstream perspective. Edgar L. Chapman's *The Magic Labyrinth of Philip José Farmer* (1984) praises Farmer's spirit of affirmation. David Pringle (*Modern Fantasy: The Hundred Best Novels,* 1989) lists *A Feast Unknown.*

Much criticism, including Dudley's postmodernist interpretation, above, has focused on Farmer's religious themes. See Robert J. Edgeworth, "Lucian of Samosata and Philip José Farmer," *Comparative Literature Studies,* 1987; and Edgar L. Chapman, "From Rebellious Rationalist to Mythmaker and Mystic: The Religious Quest of Philip José Farmer," in Robert Reilly, ed., *The Transcendent Adventure: Studies of Religion in Science Fiction/Fantasy,* 1985. But his view of the erotic has also, understandably, drawn critical interest. See Gary K. Wolfe, "The Dawn Patrol: Sex and Technology in Farmer and Ballard," *New York Review of Science Fiction,* September 1990, and Annette Goizet, "Amour, sexualité, érotisme dans *The Lovers (Les Amants étrangers)* de P.J. Farmer," in Roger Bozzetto et al., *Eros, science fiction, fantastique,* 1991.

Farmer continues to be experimental, irreverent, improvisational, playful and profound.

—Mary Turzillo Brizzi

FARREN, Mick

Nationality: British. **Born:** Cheltenham, Gloucestershire, 3 September 1943. **Education:** Worthing High School for Boys, Sussex; St. Martin's School of Art, London. **Family:** Married 1) Joy Hebditch in 1967 (divorced 1979); 2) Elizabeth Volck in 1979. **Career:** Short order cook, London Zoo, 1965; painter, 1965-67; lead singer, Deviants rock band, 1967-69; editor, *It* magazine, and *Nasty Tales* magazine, both London, 1970-73; consulting editor, *New Musical Express,* London, 1975-77. **Agent:** Abner Stein, 10 Roland Gardens, London, SW7 3PH, England; or, Merrilee Heifetz, Writers House, 21 West 26th Street, New York, New York 10010, U.S.A.

SCIENCE FICTION PUBLICATIONS

Novels (series: DNA Cowboys; Jeb Stuart Ho)

The Texts of Festival. London, Hart Davis MacGibbon, 1973; New York, Avon, 1975.
The Quest of the DNA Cowboys (Ho). London, Mayflower, 1976.
Synaptic Manhunt (Ho). London, Mayflower, 1976.
The Neural Atrocity (Ho). London, Mayflower, 1977.
The Feelies. London, Big O, 1978; revised, New York, Ballantine, 1990.
The Song of Phaid the Gambler. London, New English Library, 1981; revised edition published in 2 vols. as *Phaid the Gambler* and *Citizen Phaid,* New York, Ace, 1986-87.
Protectorate. London, New English Library, 1984; New York, Ace, 1985.
Corpse. London, New English Library, 1986; as Vickers, New York, Ace, 1988.
Their Master's War. New York, Ballantine, 1987; London, Sphere, 1988.
The Long Orbit. New York, Ballantine, 1988; as *Exit Funtopia.* London, Sphere, 1989.
The Armageddon Crazy. New York, Ballantine, 1989; London, Orbit, 1990.
The Last Stand of the DNA Cowboys (Ho). New York, Ballantine, 1989; London, Orbit, 1990.
Mars—The Red Planet. New York, Ballantine, 1990.
Necrom. New York, Ballantine, 1991.

OTHER PUBLICATIONS

Novel

The Tale of Willy's Rats. London, Mayflower, 1975.

Other

Watch Out Kids, with Edward Barker. London, Open Gate, 1972.
Rock 'n' Roll Circus, with George Snow. London, Pierrot, and New York, A and W, 1978.
Elvis Presley: The Complete Illustrated Record, with Roy Carr. London, Eel Pie, and New York, Crown, 1982.

The Black Leather Jacket. London, Plexus, 1985; New York, Abbeville, 1986.
Elvis and the Colonel, with Dirk Vellenga. New York, Delacorte, 1988; London, Grafton, 1989.

Editor, *Get on Down.* London, Futura, 1976.
Editor, with Pearce Marchbank, *Elvis in His Own Words.* London, Omnibus Press, 1977; as *Elvis Presley,* New York, Music Sales, 1978.
Editor, with David Dalton, *The Rolling Stones: In Their Own Words.* New York, Putnam, 1983; London, Omnibus, 1994.

Recording: *Vampires Stole My Lunch Money, 1978.*

*

Mick Farren comments:

(1985) I suppose the most important factor in my attitude to science fiction is that I have little or no truck with hardware. All technology has an on/off switch, and if it doesn't work you kick it. If it still doesn't work, you send for the repairman. I also don't like to have too much truck with the powerful. A society will show you more about itself if you look at its deadbeats, its drifters, and its whores. More politely, you could say I have an ear for the music of the streets, wherever or whenever those streets might be.

*   *   *

The appearance of Mick Farren's first novel, *The Texts of Festival,* in 1973 went almost without notice, despite its direct line to the same subculture that now feeds voraciously on science fiction, perhaps because Farren was ahead of his time. Festival is a city of popular culture, the setting for a futuristic melodrama of the barbarians at the gates. Apparently it sold poorly because Farren next wrote a trilogy published in England in 1976 and 1977, but still not available in a U.S. edition.

The Quest of the DNA Cowboys and its two sequels, *The Synaptic Manhunt* and *The Neural Atrocity,* are wildly imaginative, highly inventive, if somewhat simpleminded in plot. An insane computer provides for all the material needs of the human race, but in order to do so, it is systematically deconstructing reality, leaving behind growing expanses of nothingness. Two adventurers set off across this fragmented landscape, avoiding vendettas, bandits, and natural disasters, ultimately discovering the nature of the catastrophe but without being able to resolve it. Twelve years later, Farren wrote *The Last Stand of the DNA Cowboys,* which oddly enough *is* available in the United States, in which the two stalwarts return only to become the targets for a vengeful army of barbarian warriors led by a fanatic with a holy mission. The later book has a lot more polish than the original trilogy, but manages to keep much of the sense of wondrous oddness that made the earlier books so fascinating.

Farren's new books appeared with less frequency as the 1970s turned into the 1980s. *The Feelies* was a variation on an old theme, the escape by those addicted to television and drugs to a new sensation that combines the two. Now it is possible to mentally enter a dream world indistinguishable from reality. Next came *The Song of Phaid the Gambler,* so lengthy that it was published in two volumes in the United States, as *Phaid the Gambler* and *Citizen Phaid.* Despite occasional clumsiness with the plot, Farren manages to create an interesting and entertaining post-disaster world, with a protagonist attempting to escape the attentions of a satisfying array of villains.

Protectorate was more uneven. Again, Farren resorts to a perhaps overly familiar plot, this time an earth ruled by insect-like aliens who administer the world as an aristocracy, confining the majority of the population to substandard ghettos from whence the inevitable revolution takes place in the waning chapters. But from this point on, Farren produced a minimum of one book a year, with noticeably growing maturity.

Vickers (originally published in England as *Corpse*) continues Farren's long string of less than admirable future societies. A combination of crime novel and nuclear disaster, the book features a protagonist who is a soldier turned hit man faced with a megalomaniac plot to seize control of the world. Professional soldiers figure again in *Their Master's War*, although this time the protagonist is a conscript barbarian, kidnapped into a spaceship by the alien Therem, trained and equipped with high tech weaponry, and set down to fight unexplained battles on far worlds. A mercenary is a double-edged sword, however, and once the conscripts realize how little their lives matter to the Therem, and how much power their weapons provide, it's only a matter of time until it occurs to them to alter the situation.

The Long Orbit is far superior to anything Farren had previously written. Set in a future where you can use a robot to fulfill your obligations to society, the novel's hero is a would-be private detective who calls himself Marlowe and pretends to solve crimes in a world where such activity no longer has any meaning. Or does it? When a beautiful woman offers to hire him to locate her missing sister, it seems like nothing more than an entertaining diversion, until it becomes obvious that someone wants Marlowe to fail, even if it means killing him in the process.

The Armageddon Crazy is a return to the depressing, repressive future societies Farren wrote of so frequently in the past. In this case, America has a fundamentalist president who has suspended the Constitution and uses religious police to enforce his policies and imprison those who demur. A special effects expert hired to provide a "miracle" teams up with a disaffected police officer frustrated by the corruption of justice and a spy within the president's religious army to help orchestrate the overthrow of the government. Although Farren has once again produced a grim portrayal of human failings, the resolution is uplifting and optimistic.

Farren followed the excellent *The Last Stand of the DNA Cowboys* with *Mars—The Red Planet*. Both American and Soviet colonies exist on Mars, where a curious reporter decides to investigate rumors that the Russians have uncovered alien artifacts and are suppressing news of their existence. His attempts to investigate are disrupted by the intransigence of the Soviets, the uproar surrounding the discovery that a serial killer is prowling the colonies, and rumors of an alien landing elsewhere on the planet. The Martian settings are particularly well handled, and Farren spends a great deal of time creating a setting in which the physical problems of existing on an airless world are dealt with convincingly. His most recent novel, *Necrom,* while not nearly as impressive, is an entertaining blend of science fiction and fantasy, featuring a plausible (more or less) explanation for demons and their interactions with the real world. Basically an adventure writer, Farren nevertheless takes great pains to create viable characters and is unusually proficient at the creation of exotic settings and cultures.

—Don D'Ammassa

FEARN, John (Francis) Russell

Pseudonym: Geoffrey Armstrong; Thornton Ayre; Hugo Blayn; Hank Carson; Dennis Clive; Hank Cole; John Cotton; Polton Cross; Astron Del Martia; Mark Denholm; Spike Gordon; Volsted Gridban; Griff; Conrad G. Holt; Frank Jones; Nat Karta; Clem Larson; Paul Lorraine; Jed McCloud; Jed McNab; Dom Passante; Lawrence F. Rose; Frank Russell; John Russell; Bryan Shaw; John Slate; Vargo Statten; K. Thomas; Earl Titan; John Wernheim; Ephraim Winiki. **Nationality:** British. **Born:** Born in Worsley, Lancashire, 5 June 1908. **Family:** Married Carrie Worth in 1956. **Career:** Cotton salesman; cinema projectionist during World War II. Editor, as Vargo Statten, *British Science Fiction Magazine,* both Luton, Bedfordshire, 1954-56. **Died:** 18 September 1960.

SCIENCE FICTION PUBLICATIONS

Novels (series: Clayton Drew; Golden Amazon)

Valley of Pretenders (as Dennis Clive). New York, Columbia, 1942.
The Voice Commands (as Dennis Clive). New York, Columbia, 1942.
The Intelligence Gigantic. Kingswood, Surrey, World's Work, 1943.
The Golden Amazon. Kingswood, Surrey, World's Work, 1944; as *Other Eyes Watching* (as Polton Cross), London, Pendulum, 1946.
Liners of Time. Kingswood, Surrey, World's Work, 1947.
Slaves of Ijax. Llandudno, Caernarvonshire, Kaner, 1948.
The Golden Amazon Returns. Kingswood, Surrey, World's Work, 1948; as *The Deathless Amazon,* Toronto, Harlequin, 1955.
The Trembling World (as Astron Del Martia). London, Frances, 1949.
Account Settled (as John Russell). London, Paget, 1949.
Emperor of Mars (Drew). London, Panther, 1950.
Warrior of Mars (Drew). London, Panther, 1950.
Red Men of Mars (Drew). London, Panther, 1950.
Goddess of Mars (Drew). London, Panther, 1950.
Operation Venus. London, Scion, 1950.
The Gold of Akada (as Earl Titan). London, Scion, 1951.
Anjani the Mighty (as Earl Titan). London, Scion, 1951.
The Golden Amazon's Triumph. Kingswood, Surrey, World's Work, 1953.
The Amazon's Diamond Quest. Kingswood, Surrey, World's Work, 1953.
Cosmic Exodus (as Conrad G. Holt). London, Pearson, 1953.
Liquid Death (as Griff). London, Modern Fiction, 1953.
Dark Boundaries (as Paul Lorraine). London, Warren, 1953.
The Hell Fruit (as Lawrence F. Rose). London, Pearson, 1953.
Z Formations (as Bryan Shaw). London, Warren, 1953.
The Amazon Strikes Again. Kingswood, Surrey, World's Work, 1954.
Vision Sinister (as Nat Karta). London, Dragon Books, 1954.
Twin of the Amazon. Kingswood, Surrey, World's Work, 1954.
The Silvered Cage (as Hugo Blayn). London, Dragon, 1955.
Secrets of the Vase (as Preston James). London, World, 1955.
Conquest of the Amazon. London, Futura, 1976.
No Grave Need I. Wallsend, Harbottle, 1984.
The Slitherers. Wallsend, Harbottle, 1984.
Climate, Incorporated. Wallsend, Harbottle, 1987.

Lord of Atlantis. Marsh, Westbury, Zeon Books, 1991.

Novels as Vargo Statten

Annihilation. London, Scion, 1950.
The Micro Men. London, Scion, 1950.
Wanderer of Space. London, Scion, 1950.
2000 Years On. London, Scion, 1950.
Inferno. London, Scion, 1950.
The Cosmic Flame. London, Scion, 1950.
Nebula X. London, Scion, 1950.
The Sun Makers. London, Scion, 1950.
The Avenging Martian. London, Scion, 1951.
Cataclysm. London, Scion, 1951.
The Red Insects. London, Scion, 1951.
Deadline to Pluto. London, Scion, 1951.
The Petrified Planet. London, Scion, 1951.
Born of Luna. London, Scion, 1951.
The Devouring Fire. London, Scion, 1951.
The Renegade Star. London, Scion, 1951.
The New Satellite. London, Scion, 1951.
The Catalyst. London, Scion, 1951.
The Inner Cosmos. London, Scion, 1952.
The Space Warp. London, Scion, 1952.
The Eclipse Express. London, Scion, 1952.
The Time Bridge. London, Scion, 1952.
The Man from Tomorrow. London, Scion, 1952.
The G-Bomb. London, Scion, 1952.
Laughter in Space. London, Scion, 1952.
Across the Ages. London, Scion, 1952.
The Last Martian. London, Scion, 1952.
Worlds to Conquer. London, Scion, 1952.
Decreation. London, Scion, 1952.
The Time Trap. London, Scion, 1952.
Science Metropolis. London, Scion, 1952.
To the Ultimate. London, Scion, 1952.
Ultra Spectrum. London, Scion, 1953.
The Dust Destroyer. London, Scion, 1953.
Black-Wing of Mars. London, Scion, 1953.
Man in Duplicate. London, Scion, 1953.
Zero Hour. London, Scion, 1953.
The Black Avengers. London, Scion, 1953.
Odyssey of Nine. London, Scion, 1953.
Pioneer 1990. London, Scion, 1953.
The Interloper. London, Scion, 1953.
Man of Two Worlds. London, Scion, 1953.
The Lie Destroyer. London, Scion, 1953.
Black Bargain. London, Scion, 1953.
The Grand Illusion. London, Scion, 1953.
Wealth of the Void. London, Scion, 1954.
A Time Appointed. London, Scion, 1954.
I Spy. . . . London, Scion, 1954.
The Multi-Man. London, Scion, 1954.
Creature from the Black Lagoon (novelization of screenplay). London, Dragon, 1954.
1,000-Year Voyage. London, Dragon, 1954.
Earth 2. London, Dragon, 1955.

Novels as Volsted Gridban (series: Clifford Brooks; Adam Quirke)

Moons for Sale. London, Scion, 1953.
The Dyno-Depressant. London, Scion, 1953.

Magnetic Brain. London, Scion, 1953.
Scourge of the Atom. London, Scion, 1953.
A Thing of the Past (Brooks). London, Scion, 1953.
Exit Life. London, Scion, 1953.
The Master Must Die (Quirke). London, Scion, 1953.
The Purple Wizard. London, Scion, 1953.
The Genial Dinosaur (Brooks). London, Scion, 1954.
The Frozen Limit. London, Scion, 1954.
I Came, I Saw, I Wondered. London, Scion, 1954.
The Lonely Astronomer (Quirke). London, Scion, 1954.

Short Stories

From Afar. Wallsend, Tyne and Wear, Cosmos Literary Agency, 1982.
Survivor of Mars. Wallsend, Tyne and Wear, Cosmos Literary Agency, 1982.
Worlds Within. Wallsend, Tyne and Wear, Cosmos Literary Agency, 1982.
Tales of Wonder. Wallsend, Tyne and Wear, Cosmos Literary Agency, 1983.

Also author of numerous uncollected short stories.

OTHER PUBLICATIONS

Novels

The Test of Love (published anonymously). London, Popular Fiction, 1947.
The Flying Horseman. Glasgow, Western Book Distributors, 1947.
The Avenging Ranger, Llandudno, Caernarvonshire, Kaner, 1948.
Rustlers Canyon. Llandudno, Caernarvonshire, Kaner, 1948.
Thunder Valley. Redhill, Surrey, Wells Gardner Darton, 1948.
Yellow Gulch Law. Llandudno, Caernarvonshire, Kaner, 1948.
Dead Man's Shoes. London, Paget, 1949.
Outlaw's Legacy (as Clem Larson). London, Paget, 1949.
Six-Gun Prodigal (as Hank Cole). London, Paget, 1949.
Six-Guns Shoot to Kill (as Hank Carson). Glasgow, Muir Watson, 1949.
Gunsmoke Valley. Glasgow, Muir Watson, 1949.
Stockwhip Sheriff (as Polton Cross). Glasgow, Muir Watson, 1949.
Valley of the Doomed. Kingswood, Surrey, World's Work, 1949.
Murder's a Must. Glasgow, Muir Watson, 1949.
Tornado Trail. Glasgow, Muir Watson, 1949.
Arizona Love. London, Rich and Cowan, 1950.
Aztec Gold. London, Scion, 1950.
Ghost Canyon. London, Scion, 1950.
Merridew Rides Again. Kingswood, Surrey, World's Work, 1950.
Rattlesnake. London, Scion, 1950.
Skeleton Pass. London, Scion, 1950.
Bonanza. London, Scion, 1950.
Firewater. London, Scion, 1950.
Hell's Acres (as Mick McCoy). London, Scion, 1950.
Lead Law. London, Scion, 1950.
Merridew Marches On. Kingswood, Surrey, World's Work, 1951.
The Hanging 9. London, Scion, 1951.
Guntoter from Kansas (as Jed McNab). London, Panther, 1951.
Injun Canyon (as Jed McNab). London, Panther, 1951.
Golden Canyon. London, Partridge, 1951.
Killer's Legacy. London, Rich and Cowan, 1952.

Merridew Fights Again. Kingswood, Surrey, World's Work, 1952.
Merridew Follows the Trail. Kingswood, Surrey, World's Work, 1953.
Don't Touch Me (as Spike Gordon). London, Modern Fiction, 1953.
You Take the Rap (as Spike Gordon). London, Modern Fiction, 1953.
Shattering Glass (as Frank Russell). London, Brown Watson, 1953.
Navajo Vengeance. London, Rich and Cowan, 1956.

Novels as John Slate (series: Maria Black)

Black Maria, M. A. London, Rich and Cowan, 1944.
Maria Marches On. London, Rich and Cowan, 1945.
One Remained Seated (Black). London, Rich and Cowan, 1946.
They Arm Alone (Black). London, Rich and Cowan, 1947.
Framed in Guilt. London, Rich and Cowan, 1948.
Death in Silhouette (Black). London, Rich and Cowan, 1950.

Novels as Hugo Blayn (series in all books: Inspector Garth)

Except for One Thing. London, Stanley Paul, 1947.
The Five Matchboxes. London, Stanley Paul, 1948.
Flashpoint. London, Stanley Paul, 1950.
What Happened to Hammond? London, Stanley Paul, 1951.
Vision Sinister (as Nat Karta). London, Dragon, 1954.

Novels as Jed McCloud

Accident Trail. London, Dragon, 1955.
Feather-Fist Jones. London, Dragon, 1955.
Sheriff of Deadman's Bend. London, Brown Watson, 1956.
Phantom Avenger. London, Brown Watson, 1956.

*

Critical Study: *The Multi-Man: A Biographic and Bibliographic Study of John Russell Fearn* (includes bibliography) by Philip Harbottle, privately printed, 1968.

*   *   *

While still at school, John Russell Fearn wrote juvenile science fiction, flavoured by his readings of Verne and Wells, and contemporary boys' magazines, such as *The Nelson Lee Library.* His early idol was Edwy Serles Brooks. On leaving school, he drifted through a quick succession of jobs, all of which bored him; he wrote continuously, gradually becoming more proficient, and he also formed a lifelong interest in the cinema. He eventually broke into print with a series on film stars in the British *Film Weekly* in 1931.

Discovering *Amazing Stories* that same year, Fearn submitted his first SF novel, *The Intelligence Gigantic,* an influential novel that introduced to SF the concept of the latent powers in the unused portions of the human brain. "We only think and receive impressions in snatches, imperfectly understood, but . . . with a nerve connection to make the entire brain of use, we can operate our brain power to the full." *Amazing* serialized the novel in 1933. John W. Campbell later developed the same idea in his story "The Double Minds" (1937), and his later obsession with the idea led to many stories about "psionics" and the hidden powers of the human brain by many other writers, including Heinlein.

Amazing also serialized Fearn's next two stories, "Liners of Time" (1935) and its sequel "Zagribud" (1937). In these stories,

Fearn went the limit with imagination, the result of his exposure to the "super science" stories of Smith and Campbell. Wonderful events abound: time travel on a cosmic scale, invisible cities, entire planets being destroyed. All is explained away in a welter of pseudoscience. Buried in the hodge-podge was the core of an interesting idea, that of differing time-lines capable of being altered and manipulated by an unscrupulous time-traveler. Fearn's ideas were subsequently properly developed by other writers, notably Jack Williamson (*The Legion of Time*) and Isaac Asimov (*The End of Eternity*).

While awaiting the publication of these novels in *Amazing,* Fearn wrote a series of novelettes for the revived *Astounding Stories,* edited by F. Orlin Tremaine, debuting with the classic "The Man Who Stopped the Dust" (1934). SF historian Sam Moskowitz has confirmed that the plot, describing the weird consequences of destroying dust, was unique. Reprinting the story in 1975, Forrest J. Ackerman wrote that it was "the kind of story that makes an old member of dinosaur fandom like me weep, 'Why don't they write yarns like that anymore?'" Fearn followed the story with a host of "thought variants," including "Deserted Universe," "Metamorphosis," and "Mathematica" and "Mathematica Plus," the latter stories extrapolating from Sir James Jeans's speculation that the creator of the universe must have been a "Supreme Mathematician." While the stories were wildly imaginative, many of them were carefully controlled and are regarded by some critics as Fearn's best work. But by 1937, it was becoming apparent that in striving for originality, the "thought variant" school of writing had developed a uniform sameness—a kind of cosmic monadism—that represented a literary dead end. Fearn was one of the first to realize this and abandoned the pseudoscientific approach, exploring instead human and adventurous elements which had been introduced to SF by Stanley Weinbaum.

The scores of SF magazine stories Fearn produced contributed greatly to the thematic base of SF ideas and concepts. His ideas were often revolutionary and frequently embraced cosmology and the purpose and future of human life. "Before Earth Came" (1934) postulated the artificial construction of the solar system by alien scientists, while in "Dark Eternity" (1937) a scientist accidentally annihilates the whole of space-time. "Subconscious" (1936) was the first substantial story on the "we are property" theme, published three years before Russell's *Sinister Barrier,* and it was also clearly based on Fortean ideas: "Just as humans raise and fatten cattle, and then kill them off, so, in a different way have these malignant beings (Martians) seen fit, through unguessable centuries, to cause Earthlings to build up a perfect world, and then, when comparative perfection is attained, they will wipe man out of existence." Writing as Thornton Ayre, one of his many pseudonyms, Fearn introduced detective "webwork" elements to SF, as in "Locked City" and "Secret of the Ring" (both 1938). As Ayre, he also created Violet Ray, the prototype of his famous superwoman, the Golden Amazon.

In 1944 Fearn completely revised his Amazon concept, upgrading his writing from the pulp level, and broke into the hardcover market in Britain with *The Golden Amazon.* In this version, a baby girl is the subject of an idealistic scientist's glandular experiments, his aim being to end world wars by creating a superwoman who would institute a benign scientific rule upon reaching maturity. But the apparently successful experiment has a flaw: it instills into the girl a hatred of all men, and a ruthless cruelty. With her supernatural strength and scientific gifts, she breaks the will and strength of men, elevating women to positions of wealth and power. In the book's climax, she is seen to collapse and die, "burned out," but it is actually only her synthetic image, which paved the way for sequels. The original novel was reprinted by the Canadian general magazine, the *Toronto Star Weekly* in 1945, and had such a tremendous impact that the *Star* commissioned a series which ran for 16 years, ending only with Fearn's death.

Responding to reader demands, the *Star* commissioned the Scott Meredith Agency to find a writer to continue the Amazon series, and many famous SF writers were tried out. All were rejected; no other writer could duplicate Fearn's unique, popular style; Fearn had in fact been the only SF writer to be published by the *Star* syndicate, which licensed reprints to at least four American newspapers in the Maine and New York areas.

Having found the lucrative *Star* market, Fearn quit the pulp magazines. He wrote detective thrillers as John Slate, beginning with *Black Maria, M.A.* (1944). Reviewers hailed Slate as a second Agatha Christie. Writing as Hugo Blayn, Fearn created a second detective series featuring an eccentric scientist, Dr. Carruthers, many of whose adventures blur into science fiction, notably *What Happened To Hammond?* (1951), which features a matter transmitter. Fearn also diversified into westerns, but then in 1950, he was lured back into concentrating on SF. In Britain there was a general awakening in the public imagination to the possibilities of science, and space travel in particular. Films such as *Destination Moon* were immensely popular, and caused a burgeoning of interest in SF and science (the latter exemplified by the Festival of Britain in 1951: an exhibition of the Arts and Sciences symbolised by its famous "Skylon," an icon of futuristic imagery). Unfortunately, this coincided with widespread paper rationing, which enabled opportunist publishers to enter the field with a flood of cheaply produced paperback novels. None of these publishers strived for quality, as almost anything on the bookstalls would sell after wartime restrictions. These publishers set the prevailing conditions for British writers, and Fearn was signed to a contract by Scion Ltd. to write SF novels for them exclusively, under the pseudonym Vargo Statten. By 1953, he was also writing as Volsted Gridban, and was contracted to provide two novels a month. Fearn managed to maintain this prodigious output by cannibalising many of his prewar stories for *Astounding* and other magazines, as well as wholly new works. Critics condemned him unread, but several of the Scion novels are outstanding, and are definitive treatments of classic SF themes, such as *Annihilation,* ecological disaster on a global scale, and *Cataclysm,* which describes a disaster of cosmic proportions. Along with the cosmic epics were also some very human stories, such as *Decreation,* a humourous treatment of the superman theme, and *The Time Trap,* the mystery of the *Marie Celeste* extrapolated into SF.

The speed of production and publishing climate associated with the Statten novels generated an opprobrium that has remained in the eyes of most English literary critics, and led Brian Aldiss to dismiss them as the work of a "grub-streeter." But the Italian critics (and Fearn's readers) have ironically found much to celebrate in the dozens of stories reprinted since 1977. Ugo Malaguti has succinctly explained why: "Fearn has a way of getting right to the roots of the process of communication by means of a series of archetypes and symbols, which, when put together in a logical and continuous sequence provide the basis for a means of immediate communication . . . . With his apparent simplicity of message, he manages to concentrate into 10 lines the fears, the hopes, and dynamism of dozens of pages of other writers' work. This is the real

basis for his success, and the reason why, as a writer, he is destined never to die."

—Philip J. Harbottle

FEIST, Raymond E(lias)

Nationality: American. **Born:** 23 December 1945. Lives in San Diego, California. **Address:** c/o Doubleday, 666 Fifth Avenue, New York, New York 10103, U.S.A.

SCIENCE FICTION PUBLICATIONS

Novels (series: Empire; Riftwar)

Magician (Riftwar). Garden City, New York, Doubleday, 1982; London, Granada, 1983; in 2 vols. as *Magician, Apprentice* and *Magician: Master,* New York, Bantam, 1986.
Silverthorn (Riftwar). Garden City, New York, Doubleday, and London, Granada, 1985.
A Darkness at Sethanon (Riftwar). Garden City, New York, Doubleday, and London, Grafton, 1986.
Daughter of the Empire, with Janny Wurts. Garden City, New York, Doubleday, and London, Grafton, 1987.
Faerie Tale. Garden City, New York, Doubleday, and London, Grafton, 1988.
Prince of the Blood (Riftwar). Garden City, New York, Doubleday, and London, Grafton, 1989.
Servant of the Empire, with Janny Wurts. Garden City, New York, Doubleday, and London, Grafton, 1990.
The King's Buccaneer (Riftwar). Garden City, New York, Doubleday, and London, HarperCollins, 1992.
Mistress of the Empire, with Janny Wurts. Garden City, New York, Doubleday, and London, HarperCollins, 1992.
Shadow of a Dark Queen: A Novel. New York, Morrow, and London, HarperCollins, 1994.

*   *   *

Raymond E. Feist's epic fantasies remind one, at times, of the works of James Clavell. They have the same sort of sweep and grandeur; the same intricacy of plot. There is a fascination for detail and an aptitude for vivid description. The difference is, though, that Clavell researches in great detail to find the raw material for his stories, whereas Feist works in the area of speculation, and must create his worlds out of whole cloth. That the end product is so convincing is a tribute to Feist's imagination.

The technique Feist employs is that of following several different plot lines from the viewpoints of those most involved with them. The plotlines are extensive, progressing through years of change and exploration by the parties involved, and in a variety of widely separated settings. In *Magician,* the first of the Riftwar series, the plots follow out the lives and development of several people in the castle of Crydee, an imaginary land somewhere, as one discovers later, in another dimension, or on another plane. Chief among the protagonists are Pug and Tomas, two friends whose lives lead in different directions when they are chosen to be apprenticed to different masters. Tomas is apprenticed to the Swordmaster of Castle Crydee; Pug is apprenticed to the court magician. The basis for the entire story rests upon the difference in these two boys' lives, and what they lead to.

The boys are separated by the Riftwar when armies and magicians from a different dimension begin to invade that of Crydee. It is here that Feist's command of his chosen method of story telling becomes apparent. Where it would be easy to lose track of the weave of the differing plot lines, confusing one with another, Feist's development of the individual characters is sufficiently strong to maintain the reader's interest in both of the two dominant plot lines. At times, with other writers who use this technique, one character predominates to the extent that only the plot line involving that character is of interest, with chapters involving the other plot lines merely an interruption to the main plot. Feist, however, maintains the balance between characterisation and plot interest very finely, so that it is sometimes an effort to tear one's attention from the last chapter to go on to the next, only to find the same phenomenon at the end of that chapter.

A further strength of Feist's is that he fleshes out the main plot line with meticulous detail. The structure of the world of Crydee and that of the Tsurani, in the Riftwar series, is precise and self-consistent. There are very few loose ends to tidy up in terms of the setting, and yet Feist is also capable of surprising the reader. Indeed, it is almost as if the setting has become a type of character in its contribution to the plot. However, what happens within the setting is also detailed and well-developed. The court intrigue which takes place both within Crydee and Tsurani, the diplomacy between the kingdoms, empires, and cities in the vast war which occurs, and the political structures which are both implied and explicit are all drawn with a masterly hand, and are obvious products of a fully realised vision of a world other than our own. This may be as a result of Feist's experience in designing fantasy role-playing games, but it certainly leads to a setting which is seamless and never jars the reader out of the world of the story, no matter how bizarre the events which occur therein.

The initial triad of the Riftwar series, *Magician, Silverthorn,* and *A Darkness at Sethanon,* remain Feist's strongest works. Perhaps this is because these were the works which introduced the twin worlds of the Tsurani and Crydee to us, and in which Feist's imagination was given freest rein. The works which have followed have been drawn from the ideas initiated in this series, but have developed in slightly different directions. The imagination and attention to detail which marked the first trilogy are still present, but they do not dazzle as much because the world has become familiar to readers of Feist. In the first series, Feist challenged some of the precepts of the Fantasy genre, and this contributed to the interest which that series held. The following works simply explore the results of those challenges.

Feist's exploration of the reaction of his characters to massive and irreversible changes in the world around them could be seen as a metaphor for the world of the late 20th century, but this might strain the fabric of the text a little. The novels are not deep psychological explorations, but they are not gloomy, either. What they lack in depth, they make up for in breadth and imagination. What remains to be seen is whether Feist can pull off the trick of creating a fascinating world more than once. He has certainly done so with what he has written so far.

—Ian Nichols

FELICE, Cynthia

Nationality: American. **Born:** Cynthia Lindgren, Chicago, Illinois, 12 October 1942. **Education:** North Park College, Elmhurst College, and University of Colorado, Colorado Springs. **Family:** Married Robert Edward Felice in 1961; two sons. **Career:** Sales engineer, Lindgren and Associates, Chicago, 1962-71; owner and manager, Glenn Russ Motel, Colorado Springs, 1972-78; technical writer, Kaman Sciences Corp., Colorado Springs, 1978-79; technical communications manager, Inmos Corp., Colorado Springs, 1979-81. Since 1981, technical communications manager, United Technologies Micro-electronics Center, Colorado Springs. **Awards:** Society for Technical Communication award, 1984. **Agent:** Richard Curtis, Richard Curtis Associates, 164 East 64th Street, New York, New York 10021, U.S.A.

SCIENCE-FICTION PUBLICATIONS

Novels

Godfire. New York, Pocket Books, 1978.
The Sunbound. New York, Dell, 1981.
Water Witch: A Novel, with Connie Willis. New York, Ace, 1982.
Eclipses. New York, Pocket Books, 1983.
Downtime. New York, Bluejay, 1985.
Double Nocturne. New York, Bluejay, 1986.
Light Raid, with Connie Willis. New York, Ace, 1989.
The Khan's Persuasion. New York, Ace, 1991.
Iceman. New York, Ace, 1991.

*   *   *

Cynthia Felice's work reflects her strong interest in creating complex human characters in unusual circumstances. In her first SF novel, *Godsfire,* Felice builds a sophisticated society where intelligent felines rule over their human slaves. Felice makes psychological points by having the novel narrated by one of the cat people who constantly points out the differences—often the superiority—of felines over humans. *Godsfire* also has its share of mysteries: Felice creates a planet that has a climate of constant rain; therefore, the inhabitants are unaware of the existence of the sun. The origin of the humans is equally mysterious. Felice presents the reader with a clever plot and a great deal of social commentary that makes for fascinating reading.

The Sunbound explores relationships less successfully. Allis is in love with Daneth and is pregnant by him. Yet Daneth has his own secret: he is an alien. When Daneth dies, he leaves Allis a fabulous jewel that confers telepathy to the holder. The crew of Daneth's ship seek him and find Allis and the jewel instead. When Milani, Daneth's former lover and co-captain of Daneth's ship, *The Sovereign Sun,* discovers the situation, she vents her rage and hatred on Allis. Allis, bewildered by events, feels she's been abused by the aliens and throws the jewel away. But Felice creates a crisis where only Allis and the power of the jewel can save the aliens from extinction. The plot of *The Sunbound* is too contrived and the character of Allis is too emotional, too childish, to provide much entertainment.

In *Water Witch: A Novel* Felice collaborates with the Nebula winner Connie Willis to create a desert planet called Mahali. As in Frank

Herbert's *Dune,* finding and controlling water are the most important activities. Felice and Willis do a marvelous job with the main character, Deza, a young woman who pretends she's a member of the ruling family of water witches. Deza is feisty and sympathetic at the same time. Her deception leads her into a wheels-within-wheels plot that Felice and Willis spin successfully. *Water Witch* is an outstanding science fiction novel.

Felice and Willis's second collaboration, *Light Raid,* is more conventional. A young woman worried about her parents during a laser war between the Western States and Quebec leaves neutral Victoria to return to her home in Denver Springs. Seventeen-year-old Helene Ariadne arrives to find her mother arrested for treason and her father helpless to free her. Ariadne involves herself in a complicated plot where she falls in love with the mysterious but romantic Joss Liddell, and together they discover spies, intrigue, and danger. Ariadne is a plucky character and the novel is an entertaining romp without the seriousness of *Water Witch.*

Eclipses is less outstanding. Felice writes a family saga set on another arid world called Seresunar. Beth, an anthropologist, marries Aram, heir to the Water Barony. Their relationship is a stormy one: their temperaments lead them into infidelity and eventual reconciliation. Beth gives birth to a son whose wild nature shakes Seresunar's society. Yet the book is more of a romance novel than a science fiction novel. The overheated love relationships tire after awhile in this long novel, while the science fiction aspects remain underdeveloped.

Double Nocturne is one of Felice's better SF novels. Tom Hark and his crew are sent to repair the Artificial Intelligence that helps in governing the planet called Islands. The colony has been cut off during the Homeworlds Wars; now that the wars are over, Hark's mission is to help restore the abandoned colony. But when Hark is forced to make an emergency landing on Islands, he discovers that the failing AI has resulted in feudal matriarchal societies where men have no rights and are treated like slaves. Hark has to race against time to solve the puzzle of Islands before his orbiting starship strands him on Islands forever.

The Khan's Persuasion recapitulates Felice's formula of galactic intrigue blended with hotblooded romance. But it is a rehash of the elements Felice worked with more successfully in *Downtime.* In each book, the excesses of intricate plotting weaken the overall quality of the works.

Cynthia Felice's novels are best when she centers her work on complex character relationships that are as interesting as they are realistic.

—George Kelley

FERRAT, Jacques Jean. *See* MERWIN, Sam, Jr.

FINNEY, Jack

Nationality: American. **Born:** Walter Braden Finney, Milwaukee, Wisconsin, in 1911. **Education:** Knox College, Galesburg, Illinois. **Family:** Married Marguerite Guest; one daughter and one son. **Career:** Self-employed writer. **Awards:** World Fantasy life achievement award, 1987. **Agent:** Don Congdon Associates, 156 Fifth Avenue, Suite 625, New York, New York 10010, U.S.A.

SCIENCE FICTION PUBLICATIONS

Novels (series: Time)

The Body Snatchers. New York, Dell, and London, Eyre and Spottiswoode, 1955; as *Invasion of the Body Snatchers,* New York, Award, 1973; London, Sphere, 1978.
The Woodrow Wilson Dime. New York, Simon and Schuster, 1968.
Time and Again (Time). New York, Simon and Schuster, 1970; London, Weidenfeld and Nicolson, 1980.
Marion's Wall: A Novel. New York, Simon and Schuster, 1973.
3 by Finney: The Woodrow Wilson Dime, Marion's Wall, The Night People. New York, Simon and Schuster, 1987.
From Time to Time: A Novel. New York, Simon and Schuster, 1995.

Short Stories

The Third Level. New York, Rinehart, 1957; as *The Clock of Time,* London, Eyre and Spottiswoode, 1958.
I Love Galesburg in the Springtime. New York, Simon and Schuster, 1963; London, Eyre and Spottiswoode, 1965.
Forgotten News: The Crime of the Century and Other Lost Stories. Garden City, New York, Doubleday, 1983.
About Time: Twelve Stories (includes *The Third Level* and *Forgotten News*). New York, Simon and Schuster, 1986.

OTHER PUBLICATIONS

Novels

5 Against the House. Garden City, New York, Doubleday, and London, Eyre and Spottiswoode, 1954.
The House of Numbers. New York, Dell, and London, Eyre and Spottiswoode, 1957.
Assault on a Queen. New York, Simon and Schuster, 1959; London, Eyre and Spottiswoode, 1960.
Good Neighbor Sam. New York, Simon and Schuster, and London, Eyre and Spottiswoode, 1963.
The Night People. Garden City, New York, Doubleday, 1977.

Plays

Telephone Roulette: A Comedy in One Act, adaptation of his story "Take a Number." Chicago, Dramatic Publishing Company, 1956.
This Winter's Hobby: A Play. New York, Studio Duplicating Service, 1966.

*   *   *

Escapism is a term too often loosely applied to SF, but in the case of Jack Finney it is strangely appropriate. His most enduring theme is escape from the pressures and irritations of the present, usually into an idyllic past, but sometimes to another planet or a parallel dimension. A popular magazine writer who produced many stories in areas other than science fiction, Finney has made himself into the poet of nostalgia and lost innocence within the genre, seldom more than peripherally concerned with the mechanisms of his SF concepts or with how his characters get from this world to the other.

Ironically, Finney's most famous science fiction novel is also his least characteristic. *The Body Snatchers* (filmed twice as *Invasion of the Body Snatchers*) is a suspenseful invasion-of-earth story that has gained the status of a minor classic because of the popularity of the film versions and because of the key element of paranoid fantasy that is the basis of its appeal: the notion that aliens might gradually replace the entire population of a city with exact duplicates without anyone noticing the difference. Although this idea had been current in science fiction long before Finney brought it to the attention of a wider public, the skill with which Finney unveils this horror and the fears abroad at the time he wrote the story—the "takeover" might as well be a metaphor for either Communism or McCarthyism—combined to give it an impact few SF stories had previously had.

More characteristic are the short stories that Finney published during the 1950s collected in *The Third Level* and *I Love Galesburg in the Springtime*. The most common theme of these stories is time travel into the past. "I'm Scared," one of the best, details the gradual breakdown of the flow of historical time under psychological pressure from a population seeking to escape the present. In "Such Interesting Neighbours" the time travelers are from the future, but the motivation to escape their own time remains the same (the story ingeniously suggests that the end of the world will be brought about by time travel, because everyone will gradually abandon the future and redistribute themselves throughout history). "Of Missing Persons" replaces time travel with space travel, but the theme of escape remains central. Two stories, "The Third Level" and "Second Chance," suggest that certain things or locations can provide magical "portals" to the past; in "Second Chance" a meticulously reconstructed old car takes its driver into a past world simply because the experience he has in driving it parallels an experience that might have taken place when the car was new.

This notion that by meticulously recreating the past we can return to it was developed at great length in Finney's most ambitious novel, *Time and Again,* in which a volunteer for a secret government time-travel project finds himself in the Manhattan of 1882. Although only the vaguest references to Einstein serve to account for this time travel, and although there are inconsistencies of plot and historical verisimilitude (some of the latter are deliberate), the novel is a convincing portrait of a lost age and a persuasive account of what it might actually feel like to awake in a different time. Other Finney novels have dealt with the culture shock of different ages meeting using even less rationalistic devices—reincarnation, for example, in *Marion's Wall*—but *Time and Again* remains his most successful contribution to this genre. Though not fundamentally a science fiction writer, Finney is a skilled narrator and an evocative stylist who frequently uses SF themes with considerable effect.

—Gary K. Wolfe

FISK, Nicholas

Pseudonym for David Higginbottom. **Nationality:** British. **Born:** London, 14 October 1923. **Education:** Ardingly College, Sussex.

Military Service: Served in the Royal Air Force during World War II. **Family:** Married Dorothy Antoinette Richold in 1949; twin daughters and two sons. **Career:** Has worked as an actor, journalist, musician, editor, and publisher; former advertising creative director and consultant. **Agent:** Laura Cecil, 17 Alwyne Villas, London N1 2HG. **Address:** 59 Elstree Road, Bushey Heath, Hertfordshire WD2 3QX, England.

SCIENCE FICTION PUBLICATIONS (for children)

Novels (series: Starstormers)

Space Hostages. London, Hamish Hamilton, 1967; New York, Macmillan, 1969.
Trillions. London, Hamish Hamilton, 1971; New York, Pantheon, 1973.
Grinny. London, Heinemann, 1973; Nashville, Nelson, 1974.
High Way Home. London, Hamish Hamilton, 1973.
Little Green Spaceman. London, Heinemann, 1974.
Time Trap. London, Gollancz, 1976.
Wheelie in the Stars. London, Heinemann, 1976.
Antigrav. London, Kestrel, 1978.
Escape from Splatterbang. London, Pelham, 1978; New York, Macmillan, 1979; as *Flamers,* Sevenoaks, Kent, Knight, 1979.
Monster Maker. London, Pelham, 1979; New York, Macmillan, 1980.
A Rag, A Bone, and a Hank of Hair. London, Kestrel, 1980; New York, Crown, 1982.
The Starstormer Saga:
  Starstormers. Sevenoaks, Kent, Knight, 1980.
  Sunburst. Sevenoaks, Kent, Knight, 1980.
  Catfang. Sevenoaks, Kent, Knight, 1981.
  Evil Eye. Sevenoaks, Kent, Knight, 1982.
  Volcano. Sevenoaks, Kent, Knight, 1983.
Robot Revolt. London, Pelham, 1981.
On the Flip Side. London, Kestrel, 1983.
You Remember Me! London, Kestrel, 1984; Boston, Hall, 1987.
Bonkers Clocks, illustrated by Colin West. London, Viking Kestrel, 1985.
Dark Sun, Bright Sun, illustrated by Brigid Marlin. Glasgow, Blackie, 1986.
Mindbenders. London, Viking Kestrel, 1987.
Backlash. London, Walker, 1988.
The Talking Car, illustrated by Ann John. London, Macmillan, 1988.
The Worm Charmers. London, Walker, 1989.
The Telly Is Watching You. London, Macdonald, 1989.
The Back-yard War. London, Macmillan, 1990.
The Model Village. London, Walker, 1990.
A Hole in the Head. London, Walker, 1991.
Pig Ignorant. London, Walker, 1991.
Broops! Down the Chimney. London, Walker, 1991.
Extraterrestrial Tales (includes *Space Hostages, Trillions,* and *On the Flip Side*). London, Penguin, 1991.
Fantastico. Harlow, England, Longman, 1994.

Short Stories

Sweets from a Stranger and Other SF Stories. London, Kestrel, 1982.

Living Fire and Other S-F Stories. London, Corgi, 1987.

OTHER PUBLICATIONS (for children)

Novels

The Bouncers. London, Hamish Hamilton, 1964.
The Fast Green Car. London, Hamish Hamilton, 1965.
There's Something on the Roof! London, Hamish Hamilton, 1966.
Emma Borrows a Cup of Sugar. London, Heinemann, 1973.
The Witches of Wimmering. London, Pelham, 1976.
Leadfoot. London, Pelham, 1980; revised edition, London, Piper, 1992.
Snatched. London, Hodder and Stoughton, 1983.

Other

Look at Cars, illustrated by the author. London, Hamish Hamilton, 1959; revised edition, London, Panther, 1969.
Look at Newspapers, illustrated by Eric Thomas. London, Hamish Hamilton, 1962.
Cars. London, Parrish, 1963.
The Young Man's Guide to Advertising. London, Hamish Hamilton, 1963.
Making Music, illustrated by Donald Green. London, Joseph, 1966; Boston, Crescendo, 1969.
Lindbergh the Lone Flier, illustrated by Raymond Briggs. London, Hamish Hamilton, and New York, Coward McCann, 1968.
Richthofen the Red Baron, illustrated by Raymond Briggs. London, Hamish Hamilton, and New York, Coward McCann, 1968.
Editor, *The Puffin Book of Science Fiction Stories.* London, Viking, 1993.

*

Illustrator: *A Fishy Tale* by Beryl Cooke, 1957; *Look at Aircraft* by Sir Philip Joubert de la Ferte, 1960; *The Bear Who Was Too Big* by Lettice Cooper, 1963; *Tea with Mr. Timothy* by Geoffrey Morgan, 1966; *Menuhin's House of Music* by Eric Fenby, 1969; *Skiffy* by William Mayne, 1972.

Nicholas Fisk comments:

I came fairly late to children's writing. It was a Puffin list that showed me the light. I was looking for a copy of Geoffrey Household's *Rogue Male* and found it in Puffin. I thought, if the publisher thinks fit to offer this title to children, the world must be changing. For the better.

Most of my output for children has been science fiction. The SF writer is fortunate in that, unhampered by present or past, he can invent his own games, rules and players. He is unfortunate in that he must make these matters clear—and explanation is the enemy of narration. Also, unfortunately, the genre is still not quite respectable, not quite nice. Perhaps the word science offends the nice palate? It offends mine. I am not a scientist, my books are not centered on the sciences. They are stories of possibility. Not SF, but IF—what would happen IF.

The stories are on a domestic, not a cosmic, scale because written words are not apt for the rendering of explosions and gargantuan hardware; these belong to the cinema. My central characters are children because the stories are written for children. This poses

no problem and indeed may offer simplifications and speedings-up of the narrative. Although the stories have become more complex in subject and structure, I have learned from my own and countless other children that the quick, generous, adventurous mind can always stick to the point, even if the author must stagger about a bit in the hope of satisfying himself or a publisher's editor. And in any case today's children are no longer confined to some nursery ghetto. Families live in each other's laps, watching the same TV programmes. My readers and I are not unlike.

Other reasons for writing as I do include a distaste for most modern adult fiction coupled with a huge admiration for the writers and illustrators of present day children's books. I do various kinds of writing to earn a living; it is the children's writing that gives me the authentic tingle.

*　　*　　*

Nicholas Fisk is currently one of the best of those writers presenting "hard" SF to children. In such a situation a writer has two choices: to try to explain his science to a juvenile audience, or simply to ignore most of the problems as being outside his province. Fisk has tried both: *Antigrav* is a good story despite the lack of explanations; *Escape from Splatterbang* shows how such explanations can be at once trite and boring. By contrast, in *Trillions* the working out of a scientific answer forms an exciting and integral part of the plot. *Trillions* is also the book of Fisk's most likely to appeal to the adult reader, partly because of the scientific interest, partly because the "opposition" in *Trillions* is the Military Mind, as personified by General Hartman, in whom he will recognise all those who hate and fear what is alien to them. More usually in Fisk's books the forces of ignorance are the adults who ignore or fail to comprehend their children. The books can most usefully be seen from the point of view of an intelligent 11-year-old—old enough to see and understand the adult world of deceit and hypocrisy, but not old enough to change or participate in it.

One of Fisk's greatest strengths as a writer is his avoidance of clichés, both in plot and character. Indeed several of his books, most notably *Space Hostages* and *Antigrav,* are crucially concerned with a realisation that people do not conform to stereotypes. *Antigrav* rather neatly contrasts two scientists—one the classic sinister, balding geologist from behind the Iron Curtain, the other the expansive English all-rounder much given to appearing on TV chatshows. Arthur Sonning is summed up at the end as "You poor sap," while Czeslaw, victory gained, weighs the possible results of that victory and throws it away. It is further typical of Fisk that this moral superiority does not lessen the personal price which Czeslaw has to pay for "failure." In *Space Hostages* an experienced reader of children's fiction is likely to be expecting the puny clever Pakistani to be triumphant at the expense of the village bully. What actually happens is that both discover their interdependence as Fisk shows that the very qualities which make Tony a bully are those which make him a successful leader in a time of crisis. In *Escape from Splatterbang* a hint of romance is raised, only to be quashed by the bitter-sweet ending as the gypsy girl, only half-understood to the end, disappears back among her people. Here, as in *Time Trap* and other of the novels, the ending respects and even underlines the realities of human behaviour.

Fisk is never likely to have a large adult audience; his books side too firmly with the children—but at least they do so plausibly. In *Grinny* (one of his best books) the reader looks on, as helpless as the children, while the implacable "Great Aunt Emma" manipulates adult minds to her own ends. The notable achievement of this book is the way (again avoiding cliché) that Grinny's curiosity is shown as most sinister—she pokes and pries into human habits and customs like someone lifting a stone to observe the earwigs. Fisk's one real incursion into teenage SF—*Wheelie in the Stars*—is one of his poorest books: his clever-clever cardboard teenagers contrast very badly with the impotent desperation and reluctant courage of his children. This is more to be regretted since *High Way Home* shows how convincingly he can draw both teenagers and female characters (usually a notable blindspot). Fisk is not destined for a place among the Immortals: he lacks the necessary mastery of style and timeless appeal. But he is doing a competent job in a difficult field.

—Philippa Stephensen-Payne

FLINT, Homer Eon

Nationality: American. **Born:** Homer Eon Flindt, 1892. **Died:** 1924.

SCIENCE FICTION PUBLICATIONS

Novels

The Blind Spot, with Austin Hall. Philadelphia, Prime Press, 1951; London, Museum Press, 1953.
The Devolutionist, and The Emancipatrix. New York, Ace, 1965.
The Lord of Death, and The Queen of Life. New York, Ace, 1965.

* * *

See the essay on Austin Hall.

FORD, John M.

Pseudonym: Michael J. Dodge. **Nationality:** American. **Born:** 1957. **Awards:** World Fantasy award, 1984. **Address:** c/o Tor Books, 49 West 24th Street, 9th floor, New York, New York, 10010, U.S.A.

SCIENCE FICTION PUBLICATIONS

Novels (series: Star Trek)

Web of Angels. New York, Pocket, 1980.
The Princes of the Air. New York, Timescape, 1982.
The Dragon Waiting: A Masque of History. New York, Timescape, 1983; London, Corgi, 1985.
Star Trek: Voyage to Adventure (for children; as Michael J. Dodge). New York, Archway, 1984; London, Carousel, 1985.
The Final Reflection: A Star Trek Novel. New York, Pocket, 1984; Bath, Firecrest, 1985.
How Much for Just the Planet?: A Star Trek Novel. New York, Pocket, and London, Titan, 1987.

Fugue State, bound with *The Death of Doctor Island,* by Gene Wolfe. New York, Tor, 1990.
Growing Up Weightless. New York, Bantam, 1993.

Short Stories

Casting Fortune. New York, Tor, 1989.

OTHER PUBLICATIONS

Novel

The Scholars of Night. New York, Tor, 1988.

Other

Editor, with George H. Scithers and Darrell Schweitzer, *On Writing Science Fiction: (The Editors Strike Back!).* Philadelphia, Owlswick Press, 1981.

* * *

John M. Ford is a versatile writer. His work includes fiction, science fiction, horror and poetry, as well as non-fiction and game design. He is at home in many worlds, among them, the Star Trek universe, Liavek, alternate versions of Earth history and plausible futures. He is adept at writing for many ages, his work ranging from titles for children, to young adults, to dense, convoluted tales for adults. The thematic content of his science fiction, science fantasy and fantasy, includes, among other themes; issues of memory/reality, human-computer interactions, and the power of humor and other emotions. He also publishes outside the genre.

While Ford's range is diverse, his style is a presence in all his writing. It is episodic, sometimes fragmented, although he usually has the story threads firmly in hand, and dense, sometimes overpowered, with literary, poetic, musical, and mythological allusions. This complex style can be difficult, sometimes opaque and almost impenetrable, but make the effort to read his work and you will be rewarded with intricate fantasy, provocative ideas and some intriguing characters.

In *Fugue State* (the title is a medical term, the condition of dissassociative reaction during which an amnesiac is without memory of their previous life, also usually unremembered upon their return to previous life) Ford's fragmented and episodic style are particularly evocative and effective. It is difficult and often painful to read, but this construction forces the reader to more directly confront the issue of memory/reality. The complex structure and dark tone are reminiscent of some of Dick's work.

With his Liavek (a fantasy shared world) stories, Ford serves up believable magic, mystery and intrigue with dramatic flair. Here again his style can sometimes intrude. The stories are an excellent introduction to Liavek.

Ford's most clearly science fiction works, in addition to his Star Trek novels, include *Web of Angels, The Princes of the Air,* and his most recent novel, *Growing up Weightless. Web of Angels* explores human/computer interactions and potential social and political ramifications, as well as the theme of personal growth. Ford's style here stands between the action and the reader, but the mythological allusions (along with Grailer Diomede's painful maturation) are what give the story depth while the dramatic impact of his hybrid technology engage. *Princes of the Air* follows the Star Wars tradition, well paced, high action space adventure. *Growing up Weightless* tells of a young man's coming of age on the lunar colony and in space. This exciting imaginative story draws the reader into Matt's world and head while he experiences, learns and hurts on his journey to adulthood, evoking the feel and power of Heinlein's *The Moon is a Harsh Mistress.*

In his *Star Trek* novels Ford's style is less obtrusive, yet unmistakable. The two novels are very different, yet both possess broad appeal beyond Star Trek fandom. Clearly written for young adults, the action is fast paced yet substantive, the characters vibrant and convincing, the finely crafted stories readable on several levels. *The Final Reflection* (Star Trek #16) is one of the first and best portrayals of Klingon cultural identity, seen from both the viewpoint of Federation peoples and from the Klingon. It can be read as an action story, as political intrigue, and as a journey of self-discovery and maturation. *How Much for Just the Planet?* (Star Trek #36) is Ford's most light-hearted story. It has an absurd and amusing plot. The characters are charming, the Star Trek and Klingon cast believable, the Direidians (local planet population) wacky and weird, and the computers develop personality disorders. Song lyrics lace the story, takeoffs from Gilbert and Sullivan, to famous TV Western's theme songs, to well known folk music, taking the reader on a nostalgic trip while the juxtaposition of the original songs' symbolism with the takeoff lyrics present another layer of meaning to the plot twists.

The Dragon Waiting: A Masque of History is Ford's alternative history complete with magic, and a prize winning fantasy. This is Ford's most ambitious work. Its characterization, the development of its historical atmosphere, its believable magic and plot are convincing. Ford's hallmark style will cause some readers problems. It is set in the time of Richard III, but the twist is that Christianity never rose to dominate Europe and Byzantium is attempting to influence the English succession. Ford assembles a cast of interesting and engaging characters (a Welsh wizard, a noble Greek mercenary, a female doctor from the Medici Italy, and a German vampire weapons expert), who with historical figures, bring Richard to the throne.

Ford is a prolific writer of short science fiction with his work appearing in magazines, frequently gracing various collections and, collected and published in book format (*Casting Fortune*), a revised edition of his "Fugue State" published as a Tor SF Doubles (25), and one of his early works, long out of print, "Princes of the Air" has been reissued and microfilmed for archival purposes. His *The Dragon Waiting,* an alternate history, won the World Fantasy Award for Best Novel. In addition to his science fiction and fantasy Ford has received a Rhysling Award (presented by the Science Fiction Poetry Association, named after the blind poet in Heinlein's "The Green Hills of Earth") for his long poem, "Winter Solstice, Camelot Station." Ford is a prolific writer, displaying significant talent and garnering a following, a writer to anticipate and enjoy.

—Catherine M. Currier

FORSTCHEN, William R.

Nationality: American. **Address:** c/o Ballantine Books, 201 East 50th Street, New York, New York 10022, U.S.A.

SCIENCE FICTION PUBLICATIONS

Novels (series: Crystal; Gamester Wars; Ice Prophet; The Lost Regiment; Wing Commander)

Ice Prophet. New York, Ballantine, 1983.
The Flame upon the Ice. New York, Ballantine, 1984.
A Darkness upon the Ice. New York, Ballantine, 1985.
Into the Sea of Stars. New York, Ballantine, 1986.
The Gamester Wars:
    The Alexandrian Ring. New York, Ballantine, 1987.
    The Assassin Gambit. New York, Ballantine, 1988.
The Crystal Warriors, with Greg Morrison. New York, Avon, 1988.
The Lost Regiment:
    Rally Cry. New York, Roc, 1990; London, Roc, 1992.
    Union Forever. New York, Roc, 1991; London, Roc, 1992.
The Crystal Sorcerers, with Greg Morrison. New York, Avon, 1991.
Terrible Swift Sword (Lost Regiment). New York, Roc, 1992.
Fateful Lightning (Lost Regiment). New York, Roc, 1993.
The Napoleon Wager (Gamester Wars). New York, Ballantine, 1993.
End Run, with Christopher Stasheff (Wing Commander). Riverdale, New York, Baen, 1994.
Star Voyager Academy. Riverdale, New York, Baen, 1994.
Fleet Action. Riverdale, New York, Baen, 1994.
Arena. New York, HarperPrism, 1994.
Heart of the Tiger, with Andrew Keith. Riverdale, New York, Baen, 1995.
1945, with Newt Gingrich. Riverdale, New York, Baen, 1995.

*   *   *

One of the difficulties of a powerful debut is the elevated expectations of readers who assume that subsequent works will continue to break new ground. William R. Forstchen is one of those writers who broke into the field with a remarkable and memorable first effort, a trilogy, and whose subsequent work, while frequently technically superior, has not attracted nearly as much attention.

Forstchen attracted immediate favorable attention with the publication of *Ice Prophet,* first of a trilogy set in a primitive future society in which ice covers the Earth's surface as the result of a scientific experiment gone awry, altering the planet's ecology. A network of city states is dominated by the Cornathian Brotherhoods, a theocracy which is divided against itself because of concealed rivalries, including a secret priesthood with a generations-long plan to secure ultimate power for themselves.

Since it was scientific innovation that wrecked the old world, the Brotherhoods have forbidden innovation to the populace, although they have secret hoards of supposedly lost knowledge. Michael Ormson is the charismatic leader who rises in opposition to this restriction, advocating religious freedom and the pursuit of knowledge. Against his wishes, he comes to be viewed as a messianic figure, and bloody warfare ensues in response to this heresy.

By the opening of the second novel, *The Flame Upon the Ice,* Ormson heads a rebellious army which controls the southern islands. He and his allies have devised new methods of conducting warfare on ice-traveling warships, the details of which reflect Forstchen's own interest in ice sailing. The battle scenes are bloody, violent, and convincing, as Forstchen works out the tactical and strategic necessities of war on an ice field. Unbeknownst to Ormson, he has become the tool of the secret priesthood, the instrument through which they plan to crush the power of the Cornathian Brotherhoods and depose the present leader. Complicating matters is Ormson's unease at the horrors perpetrated in his name. Rather than bring new freedom, he has caused more death and destruction than the world has known for generations. An eastern empire begins to extend its influence as well, hoping to take advantage of the ensuing power vacuum. A major military triumph for the rebels climaxes the second volume.

The established church is resurgent in *The Darkness Upon the Ice.* Using devices from their secret laboratories, they attack Ormson's army with cannons and use air surveillance. The populace is uneasy with the widespread destruction, and Ormson himself appears to be dying of some insidious disease. The ultimate battle resolves things neatly and draws the trilogy to an optimistic, if somewhat bloody-minded conclusion. Although the central plot is straightforward and traditional, Forstchen enriched it with strong characterizations and some marvelously intricate interrelationships among the opposing forces. The trilogy was extremely well-received and Forstchen was quickly identified as a promising new talent, a promise that has been filled unevenly ever since.

Into the Sea of Stars, which followed the trilogy, was a disappointingly bland space opera. Fortunately, it seems to have been an interim project leading to Forstchen's newest interest, the displacement of historical characters through time and space. The first of these was an outright fantasy, *The Crystal Warriors* and its sequel, *The Crystal Sorcerers.* During World War II, one U.S. and one Japanese soldier are plucked out of time to take part in a magical battle in another reality. Despite an apparent victory in volume one, the conflict resumes in a comparatively uninteresting sequel.

A more interesting variation of this can be found in *The Alexandrian Ring, The Assassin Gambit,* and *The Napoleon Wager,* collectively known as "The Gamester Wars." In the first, Alexander the Great is brought through time to a far future conflict where he is pitted against another, fictional, time traveler. In the second, a legion of Samurai warriors are drawn in to help resolve the conflict. The concluding volume is set once again in an artificial world designed to recreate a crucial period of human history, the Napoleonic Era, with alien intelligences gambling on the outcome given some slight variations to the course of events.

Forstchen dealt with a similar theme much more effectively in his next series in which a number of Civil War soldiers are kidnapped to another planet where aliens rule over a captive human population. In *Rally Cry* the new arrivals spark a rebellion that frees a large group of the enslaved populace, and in *Union Forever,* a major war erupts on the divided world. The "Lost Regiment" series, which concluded with a human victory over their oppressors in *Terrible Swift Sword,* combines the best elements of military-oriented science fiction and historical adventure.

For the most part, Forstchen's subsequent fiction has been disappointing and unoriginal. With Christopher Stasheff he wrote two military adventures set in space and based on the computer game Wing Commander. *End Run* and *Fleet Action* are competent of their type, but offer nothing not to be found in a dozen other routine space war stories. A short story, "Endings," set in the world of cyborged tanks originally created by the late Keith Laumer, is marginally more interesting.

A young adult novel, *Star Voyager Academy,* apparently the opening volume of a series, holds more promise. Although it's more or less a reprise of the outsider who proves himself in the academy and then is instrumental in averting a disaster, Forstchen works through the old path with style and sets the stage for further, and hopefully more original adventures.

Forstchen is a writer who takes his work seriously and spends a great deal of effort getting the details right. Hopefully the game-derived books will provide sufficient income to allow him to devote his creative energies to the more ambitious and serious work of which he has already proven himself capable.

—Don D'Ammassa

FORWARD, Robert L(ull)

Pseudonym: Susan Lull. **Nationality:** American. **Born:** Geneva, New York, 15 August 1932. **Education:** University of Maryland, College Park, 1950-54, B.S. 1954; University of California, Los Angeles, M.S. 1958; University of Maryland, Ph.D. in physics 1965. **Military Service:** Served in the United States Air Force, 1954-56: Captain. **Family:** Married Martha Neil Dodson in 1954; one son and three daughters. **Career:** Technical staff member, 1956-66, associate manager, Theoretical Studies Department, 1966-67, manager, Exploratory Studies Department, 1967-74, and senior scientist, 1974-87, Hughes Research Laboratories, Malibu, California. Since 1987, owner and chief scientist, Forward Unlimited; also partner and chief scientist of Tethers Unlimited. **Awards:** Gravity Research Foundation award, 1965; IEEE-AES Carlton award, 1981; *Locus* award, 1981; Star-Cloud award (Japan), 1982, 1990. **Member:** Author's Guild. **Agent:** Scott Meredith Literary Agency, 845 Third Avenue, New York, New York 10022, U.S.A. **Address:** P.O. Box 2783, Malibu, California 90265-7783, U.S.A. **Online Address:** forward@whidbey.com.

SCIENCE FICTION PUBLICATIONS

Novels (series: Dragon's Egg; Rocheworld)

Dragon's Egg. New York, Ballantine, 1980; London, New English Library, 1981.
The Flight of the Dragonfly (Rocheworld). New York, Pocket Books, 1984; London, New English Library, 1987; expanded edition, Riverdale, New York, Baen, 1985; expanded as *Rocheworld,* 1990.
Starquake (Dragon's Egg). New York, Ballantine, 1985; London, New English Library, 1988.
Martian Rainbow. Norwalk, Connecticut, Easton Press, 1991.
Timemaster. New York, Tor, 1992.
Camelot 30K. New York, Tor, 1993.
Return to Rocheworld, with Julie Forward Fuller. Riverdale, New York, Baen, 1993.
Marooned on Eden (Rocheworld), with Martha Dodson Forward. Riverdale, New York, Baen, 1993.
Ocean Under the Ice (Rocheworld), with Martha Dodson Forward. Riverdale, New York, Baen, 1994.
Rescued from Paradise (Rocheworld), with Julie Forward Fuller. Riverdale, New York, Baen, 1995.

OTHER PUBLICATIONS

Other

Antiproton Annihilation Propulsion: Final Report. Edwards Air Force Base, California, Air Force Rocket Propulsion Laboratory, 1985.

Advanced Space Propulsion Study: Antiproton and Beamed Power Propulsion. Edwards Air Force Base, California, Air Force Astronautics Laboratory, 1987.

Future Magic. New York, Avon, 1988.

Mirror Matter: Pioneering Antimatter Physics, with Joel Davis. New York and London, Wiley, 1988.

Indistinguishable from Magic. New York, Baen, 1995.

*

Manuscript Collection: Eaton Collection, Special Collections, Rivera Main Library, University of California-Riverside, Riverside.

Robert L. Forward comments:

I write *hard* science fiction. After I have decided upon a general story idea, but before I write a detailed outline, I spend six to nine months collecting data, calculating orbits, drawing vehicles and habitats, designing alien physiologies and cultures, and working out timelines. During this "science research" phase, the requirements of the laws of science suggest (and sometimes force) the plot line to move in a certain direction. Thus, in one sense, the science writes the fiction. In all of my novels to date, ideas that were generated during this research phase were so novel and so scientifically sound, that I turned them into technical papers that were later published in scientific archive journals (with a footnote referencing the novel as the first publication of the idea). The drawings and the results of this research phase are usually included as a technical appendix to the novel.

*   *   *

Dr. R.L. Forward made his reputation as a writer of "hard" SF. In this genre we do not seek for the delineation and development of character, or for insight into the Human Condition; we look rather for the working out of an idea which involves either a novel scientific hypothesis or an exciting extrapolation of technology. This he provided. Originally a professional physicist working on problems of gravitation, Forward in his early writing displayed the qualities of disciplined imagination which his main occupation required. His early books each had a technical appendix (in one case disguised as the report of a Congressional hearing) explaining and justifying the ideas employed.

His first novel, *Dragon's Egg*, is built around his most startling notion (based upon an earlier suggestion by F. Drake): that intelligent life could exist upon the surface of a neutron star. Under the fantastic g-forces and intense magnetic fields at the surface of a neutron star, specimens of this life form—known as the Cheela—are of variable shape, but generally like minute pancakes 5mm in diameter and 0.5mm thick, but massing a clear 70 kg. At this size and enormous rate of energy processing, they live at a formidable pace—roughly a million times our own. This, of course, presents the author with a very difficult communication problem, not made any easier by the fact that the tidal forces around a neutron star are so great that a human being, even in free fall, would be torn apart whilst still many hundreds of km above the surface. The solutions are ingenious. The module in which the humans approach the star is itself orbited, at a radius of 200m, by a necklace of six ultra-dense spheres whose own gravitational fields exactly compensate, within the small volume of the module, for that of the star. This reader recalls his delighted "I'd never have thought of that!" reaction on first reading this scheme. Information transmission is by

fast laser link, whose 200 megabytes/sec is the Cheela equivalent of a slow reading speed.

The story of *Dragon's Egg* is simply the exposition, in a plain and straightforward narrative style, of how Humans and Cheela become aware of one another, of how they learn to communicate, come to make friends, and finally part on amicable terms. The plot is satisfactory and credible, given the premises. The characters lack depth, but are adequate as processors and exchangers of ideas, which is all they are, or are meant to be. They do not linger in the mind: six months after reading the book, this reader could recall nothing about them, save that one was swiftly cured of a cancer by an X-ray-eyed Cheela. The "heroes" of the book are not the characters, Human or Cheela; they are the ideas, problems, and solutions. And as such they are very satisfactory.

A general, though not universally valid rule for writers of successful SF is: don't write a sequel. Dr. Forward defies this rule, successfully, in the case of *Dragon's Egg,* with a sequel entitled *Starquake.*

It is known that neutron stars sometimes exhibit a sudden very slight change in their rate of spin. Current theory attributes this to a minute change in the radius of the star; but such a minute change would constitute a shattering "starquake" for any beings such as the Cheela. The premise of this book is that such an event occurs, setting back the promising civilisation of the Cheela almost to starting point; and the story tells how the humans aid a renaissance and are rewarded with a "space warp" return journey to Earth. The space warp is somewhat less unconvincing than most, involving the Kerr solutions to the equations of General Relativity.

Dr. Forward created another strange world for *The Flight of the Dragonfly,* peopled it with another strange species, and provided another way of getting there. The voyage employs a variant of the "radiation sail" concept, driven, not directly by the Sun, but by a vast array of lasers deployed in space focused by an immense Fresnel lens, similarly deployed. (The idea was expanded in an article in the semi-popular science journal *New Scientist,* 2 October 1986.) The strange double planet of the story is even odder than a neutron star—there is, after all, very good reason to believe that neutron stars exist. "Rocheworld" consists of two roughly moon-sized egg-shaped planets, not quite in contact, but so close as to share an atmosphere; each occupies the Roche lobe of the other. What a charming idea! One of these worlds is covered by an ocean, wherein live a cheerful race of large, brightly coloured beings whose sole interests are Pure Mathematics and water sports. Perhaps they are a little too good to be credible: dominant species tend to be aggressive species; that is one reason why they are dominant. Again, neither the characters nor the plot are memorable. There is no absurdity, and the narrative is smooth; but again the interest is in the strange world, in the dangers and problems it poses and in the ingenuity of the solutions.

A revised version of *The Flight of the Dragonfly* appeared under the title of *Rocheworld.* It is longer, and some details are expanded, but it does not differ in any essential.

Soon after completing this, Dr. Forward elected to become a full-time writer. It would be pleasant to be able to say that he has gone from strength to strength; alas, that is not the case. None of his more recent works matches the quality of the earlier ones. True, the last four are coauthored; and it is not possible to say how much of each he is responsible for.

Martian Rainbow attempts to tackle personal relationships, in the shape of a clash between twin brothers; but only demonstrates that this is not the author's forte. The exigencies of the incredible plot require the Good Brother, aided by his girlfriend (who has brains, all the virtues, and beauty with them) to accomplish the "greening" of Mars, not in centuries, or even years, but in weeks. To achieve this, they haply find some general-purpose self-replicating machines, left around by Some Others, which buckle down and do the job in short order. As we would expect of the author, the machines in themselves are convincing; the context and plot are not.

It is peculiarly difficult to write time-travel stories that convince. *Timemaster,* despite its unusual mathematical sophistication, must be added to the long list of those that do not. The hero, who is just sufficiently well-drawn to be odious, returns occasionally to give his younger self some good advice. The reader is not prevented from thinking: "But suppose he had become so ashamed of his past that he shot his younger self?" And the whole, rare art of time-travel stories is precisely to prevent the reader from thinking, or at least from caring about such thoughts.

Four sequels to *Dragonfly/Rocheworld* have now appeared, variously coauthored with M.D. Forward or J.F. Fuller. These are *Return to Rocheworld, Marooned on Eden, Ocean Under the Ice,* and *Rescued from Paradise.*

In the first of these, the crew of the Dragonfly continue their exploration of Rocheworld and their friendly converse with its inhabitants. However, the main focus seems to be upon the explorers' sexuality and interpersonal relationships. There is not the faintest objection to the explicit portrayal of sexuality in an SF context; but it should be made credible, and here it is not. Also, the explorers now appear so neurotic that this reader was left wondering how they had managed to pass the selection process to get on board in the first place.

In the subsequent books the explorers and their local friends visit other planets of Rocheworld's sun, discover new races of beings under the icy surface of a sea, find themselves marooned, settle to making a life for themselves, and finally are faced with difficult decisions when offered a return to Earth. In every case the relavent technology is convincingly and interestingly described and the way the castaways cope is often ingenious; but these matters are no longer the main thrust of the stories. This reader, at least, found that the author(s) simply failed to make the characters and their interplay interesting or believable.

At his best, as in his earlier works, Dr. Forward's fictions are excellent. It is much to be hoped that he returns soon to his true literary ancestry, which may be traced to Verne rather than to Wells. He is at his formidable best in inventing problems and dangers for his characters to face, and technologies for them to use, in bizarre but well-constructed worlds. The taste for this kind of "hard" SF is, like the taste for very dry wine, not everybody's; but few can satisfy it as well as he does, when he so chooses.

—M. Hammerton

FOSTER, Alan Dean

Nationality: American. **Born:** New York City, 18 November 1946. **Education:** University of California, Los Angeles, B.A. in political science 1968; M.F.A. in film 1969. **Military Service:** Served in the United States Army Reserve, 1969-75. **Family:** Married JoAnn Oxley in 1975. **Career:** Head copywriter, Headlines Ink Agency, Studio City, California, 1970-71; instructor in English and film, University of California, Los Angeles, intermittently since 1971, and Los Angeles City College, 1972-76. **Awards:** Galaxy award, 1979; Southwest Book award, 1990. **Member:** SFWA, WGAW. **Agent:** (fiction) Virginia Kidd, Box 278, Milford, Pennsylvania 18337; (media) William Morris, 151 El Camino Blvd., Beverly Hills, California. **Address:** P.O. Box 12757, Prescott, Arizona 86301, U.S.A.

SCIENCE FICTION PUBLICATIONS

Novels (series: Alien; Commonwealth; The Damned; Spellsinger; Star Wars)

The Tar-Aiym Krang (Commonwealth). New York, Ballantine, 1972. London, New English Library, 1979.
Bloodhype (Commonwealth). New York, Ballantine, 1973; London, New English Library, 1979.
Icerigger (Commonwealth). New York, Ballantine, 1974; London, New English Library, 1976.
Luana (novelization of screenplay). New York, Ballantine, 1974.
Dark Star (novelization of screenplay). New York, Ballantine, 1974; London, Orbit, 1979.
Midworld (Commonwealth). Garden City, New York, Doubleday, 1975; London, Macdonald and Jane's, 1977.
Star Wars: From the Adventures of Luke Skywalker (as George Lucas). New York, Ballantine, 1976.
Orphan Star (Commonwealth). New York, Ballantine, 1977; London, New English Library, 1979.
The End of the Matter (Commonwealth). New York, Ballantine, 1977; London, New English Library, 1979.
Splinter of the Mind's Eye: From the Adventures of Luke Skywalker (Star Wars). New York, Ballantine, and London, Sphere, 1978.
Mission to Moulokin (Commonwealth). Garden City, New York, Doubleday, and London, New English Library, 1979.
The Black Hole: A Novel (novelization of screenplay). New York, Ballantine, 1979.
Cachalot: A Novel (Commonwealth). New York, Ballantine, 1980; London, New English Library, 1987.
Outland (novelization of screenplay). New York, Warner, and London, Sphere, 1981.
Clash of the Titans (novelization of screenplay). New York, Warner, and London, Macdonald, 1981.
The Thing: A Novel (novelization of screenplay). New York, Bantam, and London, Corgi, 1982.
Nor Crystal Tears (Commonwealth). New York, Ballantine, 1982; London, New English Library, 1986.
For Love of Mother-Not (Commonwealth). New York, Ballantine, 1983; London, New English Library, 1984.
Spellsinger at the Gate. Huntington Woods, Michigan, Phantasia Press, 1983.
Spellsinger. New York, Warner, 1983; London, Orbit, 1984.
The Hour of the Gate. New York, Warner, and London Orbit, 1984.
Krull: A Novel (novelization of screenplay). New York, Warner, and London, Corgi, 1983.
The Man Who Used the Universe. New York, Warner, 1983; London, Orbit, 1984.
The I Inside. New York, Warner, 1984; London, Orbit, 1985.
Voyage to the City of the Dead (Commonwealth). New York, Ballantine, 1984; London, New English Library, 1986.
Slipt. New York, Berkley, 1984.

The Last Starfighter (novelization of screenplay). New York, Berkley, and London, W.H. Allen, 1984; adapted for children by Lynn Haney as *The Last Starfighter Storybook,* New York, Putnam, 1984.

The Day of the Dissonance (Spellsinger). Huntington Woods, Michigan, Phantasia Press, 1984; London, Orbit, 1985.

The Moment of the Magician (Spellsinger). Huntington Woods, Michigan, Phantasia Press, 1984; London, Macdonald, 1985.

Starman: A Novel (novelization of screenplay). New York, Warner, 1984; London, Corgi, 1985.

Shadowkeep. New York, Warner, 1984; London, W.H. Allen, 1985.

Sentenced to Prism (Commonwealth). New York, Ballantine, 1985; London, New English Library, 1988.

Pale Rider. New York, Warner, and London, Arrow, 1985.

The Paths of the Perambulator (Spellsinger). West Bloomfield, Michigan, Phantasia Press, 1985; London, Macdonald, 1986.

Season of the Spellsong (includes *Spellsinger, Hour of the Gate,* and *Day of the Dissonance*). Garden City, New York, Doubleday, 1985.

Into the Out Of. New York, Warner, 1986; London, New English Library, 1987.

The Time of the Transference (Spellsinger). West Bloomfield, Michigan, Phantasia Press, 1986; London, Orbit, 1987.

Spellsinger Scherzo (includes *The Moment of the Magician, The Paths of the Perambulator,* and *The Time of the Transference*). Garden City, New York, Doubleday, 1987.

The Deluge Drivers (Commonwealth). New York, Ballantine, 1987; London, New English Library, 1988.

Glory Lane. New York, Ace, 1987; London, New English Library, 1989.

To the Vanishing Point. New York, Warner, 1988; London, Sphere, 1989.

Maori. New York, Berkley, 1988.

Flinx in Flux (Commonwealth). New York, Ballantine, 1988; London, New English Library, 1989.

Alien Nation (novelization of screenplay). New York, Warner, 1988; London, Grafton, 1989.

Quozl. New York, Ace, 1989; London, New English Library, 1991.

Cyber Way. New York, Ace, 1990; London, Orbit, 1992.

A Call to Arms (Damned). Norwalk, Connecticut, Easton Press, 1991.

Cat-a-lyst. New York, Ace, 1991; London, Orbit, 1992.

The False Mirror (Damned). New York, Ballantine, 1992.

Codgerspace. New York, Ace, 1992; London, Orbit, 1993.

Son of Spellsinger. New York, Warner, and London, Orbit, 1993.

The Spoils of War (Damned). New York, Ballantine, 1993.

The Complete Alien Omnibus. London, Warner, 1993.

   Alien (novelization of screenplay). New York, Ballantine, and London, Macdonald and Jane's, 1979.

   Aliens (novelization of screenplay). New York, Warner, and London, Orbit, 1986.

   Alien 3 (novelization of screenplay). New York and London, Warner, 1992.

Greenthieves. New York, Ace, and London, Orbit, 1994.

Chorus Skating (Spellsinger). New York, WArner, 1994; London, Orbit, 1995.

Design for Great Day, with Eric Frank Russell. New York, Tor, 1995.

Life-Form. New York, Ace, 1995.

Short Stories (series: Star Trek)

Star Trek Log One [-Ten] (adaptation of television series). New York, Ballantine, 10 vols., 1974-78; as *Log One [-Log Nine],* 3 vols., 1993; London, Pocket Books, 1995.

With Friends Like These. . . . New York, Ballantine, 1977.

. . . Who Needs Enemies? New York, Ballantine, 1984; London, Orbit, 1986.

The Horror on the Beach: A Tale in the Cthulhu Mythos. San Diego, California, Valcour and Krueger, 1978.

The Metrognome and Other Stories. New York, Ballantine, 1990.

Montezuma's Strip. New York, Warner, 1995.

OTHER PUBLICATIONS

Play

Screenplay: *Star-Trek,* 1979.

Other

Sir Charles Berkley and the Referee Murders (graphic novel). Prescott, Arizona, Hamilton Comics, 1993.

Editor, *The Best of Eric Frank Russell.* New York, Ballantine, 1978.

Editor, *Animated Features and Silly Symphonies.* New York, Abbeville, 1980.

Editor, with Martin H. Greenberg, *Smart Dragons, Foolish Elves.* New York, Ace, 1991.

Editor, with Martin H. Greenberg, *Betcha Can't Read Just One.* New York, Ace, 1993.

*

Critical Studies: *A Guide to the Commonwealth: The Official Guide to Alan Dean Foster's Humanx Commonwealth Universe* by Robert Teague and Michael Goodwin, Roy, Utah, Galagraphics, 1985.

Alan Dean Foster comments:

   Many of my science fiction novels, particularly the earlier works, take place in what is called the Universe of the Commonwealth, a future society in which mankind has formed a close alliance with a race of insect-like creatures called the Thranx. Within this series are sub-series such as the *Icerigger* trilogy and the stories that deal with the characters Flinx and Pip, as well as independent novels. Events and characters will occasionally overlap, as with the *Icerigger* books and *The End of the Matter.* It is my eventual intention to tie all the Commonwealth stories together in one grand conclusion (perhaps in 40 or so years).

   Other works include the *Spellsinger* fantasy series, independent novels of SF such as *Glory Lane, Quozl,* and The Damned trilogy, tales of contemporary horror and suspense like *Into the Out Of* and *To The Vanishing Point,* and the historical novel *Maori,* which is set in 19th-century New Zealand.

   With a few exceptions my short fiction is not tied to any of my novels, including those which form series of their own such as the stories of the mountain man Mad Amos Malone and the tales of the *Montezuma Strip.* In my book-length stories of adventure I try to explore how people, especially ordinary people, react to extraordinary circumstances and events, while the shorter fiction tends to deal with more intimate concerns.

Personal concerns which are often reflected in my work are a life-long interest in ecology, travel, other cultures, the unexplored potential of the human mind, and historical serendipity, in which the small and seemingly unimportant often give rise to events of world-shaking consequence (viz. World War I and the election of a B-movie actor to the presidency of the United States).

*

Manuscript Collection: Special Collections Department, Hayden Library, Arizona State University, Tempe.

*   *   *

Alan Dean Foster is perhaps best known for his competent, well-written film novelizations (*Alien, Alien Nation, Outland, The Thing, The Last Starfighter,* and numerous others). He has also written *Splinter of the Mind's Eye* based on the Star Wars characters, and the Star Trek "Log" series based on the animated television series.

However, it is within the framework of his science fiction adventures that Foster's talents shine through. In the tradition of Edgar Rice Burroughs, Foster creates exotic worlds, peopling them with strange and fascinating races and with memorable characters, using them as the backdrop against which he weaves his tales. His plausible, scientifically sound settings combined with vivid, sensual descriptions make Foster's worlds come alive. As with the works of Robert Heinlein, Gordon Dickson, and Poul Anderson, many of Foster's novels share a common setting. For Foster it is the "Humanx Commonwealth," a loose confederation of planets settled by humans and the insectoid Thranx.

Some of these fascinating Commonwealth worlds can be found in such diverse works as *Cachalot, Icerigger,* and *Midworld.* Cachalot, an ocean world of swelling blue waves, is dotted with islands whose gemlike beaches are so brilliant they may cause blindness. In this environmental adventure, humans in their floating cities peacefully share the world with porpoises, dolphins and whales. The whales, however, shun human contact because of sharp racial memories of near genocide on Earth. A woman biologist and her team of experts try to discover who or what is methodically destroying human cities. *Icerigger* focuses on the ice world of Tran-ky-ky with its scattered, isolated settlements. Ethan Fortune, Skua September and others who are stranded on Tran-ky-ky must overcome the hostile, subarctic environment and enlist the help of the feline natives to assist them in reaching the Commonwealth outpost. Another environmental tale, *Midworld* features an off-course human colony ship which ends up on a hostile jungle world that makes the films *Alien* and *Predator* look like a walk in the park. After generations, the descendants have literally become one with the environment only to have their existence threatened by a greedy corporation intent upon milking the virgin planet of all it resources.

In *Nor Crystal Tears,* one of Foster's strongest works, the setting is subordinate to the characters. It is a first contact novel depicting the meeting of humans with the insectoid Thranx as seen through the eyes of Thranx agriculturalist Ryo. Ryo's vision of peaceful coexistence between Thranx and humans is realized with the help of several stranded Earth explorers. Their struggle and sacrifice to achieve this vision overcomes the prejudice and distrust on the part of both cultures resulting in the founding of the Commonwealth.

In *Life-Form,* a team of scientists are dispatched to investigate the flora and fauna on the recently discovered Xica. With the discovery of sentient humanoids, their reputations and fortunes seem assured. However, things turn deadly on the seemingly idyllic planet when the animal life turns out to be thixotropic, viciously morphing when threatened.

Another of Foster's first contact novels is *A Call To Arms,* book one of The Damned series in which Earth is caught in the middle of galactic warfare between the Amplitur and the Weave. The Amplitur is a telepathically manipulative race which subverts all races to its purpose. The Weave is a loose coalition of races all of whom dislike the idea of being genetically altered. While similar to the Commonwealth, the Weave, instead of treating Earthlings as equals, is using them as warriors because of their aggressiveness, while denying them citizenship. This premise is similar to that of the plight of the African American soldiers in the Allied/Axis conflict during World War II.

In *The False Mirror,* book two of The Damned, the Amplitur have created a superior fighting force from genetically altered human embryos, tipping the scales in their favor. Ranji, one of these genetic warriors is captured by the Weave. Informed of his human heritage and released from the Ampliture's mind control, Ranji returns to free his "people."

In book three of The Damned, *The Spoils of War,* scholar Lalelelang, a member of the avian-like Wais, has made the study of humans her life's work. While pursuing her research, she has become convinced that the humans, while fighting for the Weave, have their own agenda. Thinking their plan compromised, human Col. Nevan Straat-ien considers killing Lalelelang. While getting close to her, a bonding which grows into a lifelong friendship, occurs. In the telling of Ranji's and Lalelelang's stories, Foster as he has done in *Nor Crystal Tears* has produced compelling, rich novels peopled with complex protagonists.

Many of Foster's protagonists are depicted as superhuman, extraordinary, or exotic. The genetically altered Flynx, with his psi powers and his symbiotic pet minidragon is one of Foster's most popular characters. Foster chronicles Flynx's adventures as he searches for his parents in the Flynx of the Commonwealth series. Flynx, a rogue and an ethical thief, is reminiscent of Fritz Leiber's Gray Mouser and Harry Harrison's Jimi diGriz. However, Flynx's childhood as an orphan and a slave is strikingly similar to Thorby Baslim's in Robert Heinlein's *Citizen of the Galaxy.* Another of Foster's popular characters is Jon-Tom (Jonathan Thomas Meriweather), a UCLA student who is magicked to another world by the turtle wizard Clothahump in the Spellsinger series. Jon-Tom joins forces with Clothahump and his ragtag band of humans and animals in a battle against an ancient evil. This mixture of light adventure with humor is similar to the Myth series by Robert Asprin and the Xanth books by Piers Anthony.

Foster's fondness for tongue-in-cheek, twisting the English language, puns, and outrageous situations is also evident in such novels as *Cat-a-lyst, Codgerspace,* and *Glory Lane. Cat-a-lyst* finds handsome actor Jason Carter teamed up with a bank robber, an archeologist, a gossip reporter, and alien vegetables to thwart an invasion of Earth by Incan descendants from another dimension. In *Codgerspace,* five senior citizens chancing upon a UFO are caught up in an interstellar conflict. *Glory Lane,* one of Foster's better novels finds Seeth, a punk rocker, Kerwin, a nerd, and Miranda an airheaded shopaholic inadvertently thrown together on a quest to save the universe when they stumble upon an alien kidnapping. Other characters include telekinetic Jake Pickett and his telepathic grand-niece Amanda who battle the corrupt corporation whose chemical wastes caused their mutations in *Slipt.*

Foster is also very fond of portraying the common or everyday person as caught up in events beyond his or her control. Will Dulac, composer and teacher, is the first person kidnapped by the Weave in *A Call To Arms,* book one in the series The Damned. *To The Vanishing Point* finds sporting goods executive Frank Sonderberg, his family, and a 4000-year old-girl named Mouse on a quest to save the universe from unraveling. In *Cyber Way,* aging, overweight detective Vernon Moody solves the murder of an art collector involving Indian sand paintings, ancient Navajo rituals, and aliens.

Like *Cyber Way,* Alan Dean Foster has written other science fiction mysteries. Both *Montezuma's Strip* and *Greenthieves* take place in the 21st-century southwestern United States. Detective Broderick Manz and his robot sidekicks try to discover how valuable pharmaceuticals are being hijacked from inside an impenetrable metal building guarded by three security teams, motion detectors, alarms and other high-tech systems in *Greenthieves. Montezuma's Strip* features five short stories published from 1988 through 1994 under the pseudonym of James Lawson. In these tales Foster has created the fascinating high-tech world of "The Strip" which runs along the U.S./Mexican border. Here large corporations can cut expenses using hispanic labor. Services and products both legal and illegal are available for a price. It is in the seamy world of the strip that short, aging, blue-eyed Tex-Mex cop Angel Cardenas tries to crack seemingly unsolvable high-tech crimes involving cryogenics, virtual reality, deadly computer programs, and the illegal use of neuromuscular stimulation implants to control animals and people. However, Cardenas has an edge, as an "Intuit" he is able to tell from body language and vocal inflections if someone is telling the truth. While characterization is not Foster's greatest strength, the reader comes to know and like his characters.

Many of Alan Dean Foster's novels deal with such ideas as man's inhumanity to man (*Midworld*), prejudice (*Nor Crystal Tears,* The Damned series), or destruction of the environment (*Midworld, Slipt, Icerigger*). But themes of peace through mutual cooperation, understanding, and respect for life (*Nor Crystal Tears, Icerigger, Cachalot, Midworld*) occur over and over within Foster's fiction. Foster's readability, memorable characters, and believable worlds combined with an element of hope are the reasons he not only holds his fans but continues to attract new ones.

—John I. Lawson

FOSTER, M(ichael) A(nthony)

Nationality: American. **Born:** Greensboro, North Carolina, 2 July 1939. **Education:** Greensboro High School, graduated 1957; Syracuse University, New York, 1957-58, 1959-60; University of Maryland extension courses in Karamursel, Turkey, 1961-62; University of Oregon, Eugene, 1962-64, B.A. in Slavic languages 1964. **Family:** Married Judith Ann Forsythe in 1965; two sons. **Military Service:** Served in the United States Air Force, 1957-62, 1965-76: Russian linguist, 1957-62, Intelligence, 1965-71, Strategic Missiles, 1971-75, and Intercept Weapons Director, 1975-76: Captain. **Career:** Photographer: individual shows—Rapid City, South Dakota, 1972, 1973, 1974. **Address:** 5409 Amberhill Drive, Greensboro, North Carolina 27455, U.S.A.

SCIENCE FICTION PUBLICATIONS

Novels (series: Ler; Morphodite)

The Warriors of Dawn (Ler). New York, DAW, 1975; London, Hamlyn, 1979.
The Gameplayers of Zan (Ler). New York, DAW, 1977; London, Hamlyn, 1979.
The Day of the Klesh (Ler). New York, DAW, 1979.
Waves. New York, DAW, 1980.
The Morphodite. New York, DAW, 1981.
Transformer (Morphodite). New York, DAW, 1983.
Preserver (Morphodite). New York, DAW, 1985.

Short Stories

Owl Time: A Collection of Fictions. New York, DAW, 1985.

OTHER PUBLICATIONS

Poetry

Shards from Byzantium. Privately printed, 1969.
The Vaseline Dreams of Hundifer Soames. Privately printed, 1970.

*

M.A. Foster comments:

As of 1995, although I write daily, I am no longer active in publishing science fiction in any sense. Obviously, a full and complete discussion of these circumstances is far beyond the scope of an article of this nature.

One thing which may be worth saying here is a lesson I learned from the practice of writing: to start and to continue to write is as easy and natural as dreaming, or as growth in a landscape. It is when to stop writing that the art appears. This principle was originally intended to apply within the work of a story, so to speak, but it is also true in the larger sense as well, if difficult to apply in practice.

*   *   *

Since his advent on the SF scene with *The Warriors of Dawn* in 1975, M.A. Foster completed six novels, a few short stories, and a collection entitled *Owl Time.* He has not published any SF since 1986 and he says he does not intend to do so in the future, although he continues to write.

The selections in *Owl Time* differ somewhat from the rest of Foster's corpus, but the full-length novels have several characteristics in common. They contain seemingly loose plots, with emphasis on character and setting rather than on story development. Yet each story is a gradual unfolding of the interrelationship between characters' actions and the positioning of the cosmos. Each depends on the perspective of one, or at most two, viewpoint characters, usually narrated in the third person. Finally, Foster displays an antideterministic philosophy through both theme and technique. Each novel turns around the resolution of a many-leveled mystery, an attempt to discover who or what is manipulating the society on a particular world. Foster repeatedly introduces variations on Tarot and the *I Ching,* both oracular methods of tracing a nondeterministic future. He also refers often to Zen disciplines. However, the ultimate answer to each quest lies most often in the minute actions of individuals.

Six of Foster's novels also focus on the consequences of potential genetic manipulation. *The Warriors of Dawn, The Gameplayers of Zan,* and *The Day of the Klesh* develop from the premise that human attempts to create a superhuman race, called Ler, will yield unwanted results. *Gameplayers,* chronologically first in the full tale, documents the agony of mistrust and misunderstanding that sends most of Ler off to the planet from which warriors (in *The Warriors of Dawn*) appear. The Klesh, humans these Warriors have enslaved for purposes of breeding, are freed to migrate to Monsalvat, the planet which forms the backdrop for the third novel in the story's internal chronology, *The Day of the Klesh.*

The Morphodite, Transformer, and *Preserver* presuppose a more refined set of techniques for genetically manipulating live beings. These are perfected on a backwater planet called Oerlikon to result in a being who can change his/her shape, going from female to male to female, and losing 20 years of chronological age, but not of memory, with each protoplasmic transformation. Demsing/ Nazarine/Phaedrus/Damistofia/Rael/Jedily uses an extension of principles upon which the *I Ching* was constructed to "read" the world around him/her and discover which act is the most likely to cause the disintegration of the rigid Oerlikon society. However, like the Ler in Foster's first trilogy, his/her power soon outstrips that of his/her immediate creators as she/he realizes the organizational lines of power and how easily they can be manipulated. *Preserver,* the conclusion of the trilogy, amplifies on the theme of lines of force as it shows the morphodite gradually becoming aware of past transformations and enhanced power. The sensitive handling of female characters, both in the person of the viewpoint character as one of his/her states and her/his companions when she/he is male, is more developed in these three novels. This ability of Foster to create fully human female characters such as Fellerian, Snajirmil, and Mevlanen, (*Gameplayers*) led to speculation with the first two novels that the author was female. Many of the techniques, such as elaborate description through footnotes, as well as in-text references, multilayered plot, and "scientification" of divination tools, are displayed with much refinement in these three novels.

Waves is the most Russian of Foster's novels, taking place on a planet which seems to have been settled by people of that national grouping. While the setting reflects Foster's language ability (he acted in the capacity of Russian linguist while with the U.S. Air Force), the plot follows a linguistic mystery—an ocean that seems to speak a language. Perhaps because he had to resolve the mystery in the course of only one novel, Foster was not as successful in substituting his own type of multilayered complexity for tight structure. In fact, the plot tends to get lost in the love story of his two protagonists. *Waves* is slow-paced, somewhat lyrical, and reminiscent of Lem's *Solaris.*

Foster's short novels, four of which appeared in *Owl Time,* are exercises in style variation in which he adopts styles he identifies with different SF and non-SF writers. Yet, with the possible exception of "The Conversation," they seem very much Foster. This rather atypical Foster story creates a conversation between an author and a character whose positions are not fixed in relation to one another, the real author, or the reader. That its content is a commentary on totalitarianism adds to the story's engaging quality. "Entertainment," which Foster claims is an attempt to emulate Jack Vance, incorporates the footnotes, prefatory quotations, single viewpoint character and puzzle-plot of his earlier fiction.

—Janice M. Bogstad

FOWLER, Karen Joy

Nationality: American. **Born:** Bloomington, Indiana, 7 February 1950. **Education:** University of California, Berkeley, 1968-70, 1971-72, B.A. 1972; State University of New York, Albany, 1970-71; University of California, Davis, 1972- 74, M.A. 1974. **Family:** Married Hugh Fowler in 1972; one son, one daughter. **Career:** Writer in residence, Cleveland State University, Ohio, Spring 1990. **Awards:** John W. Campbell award, 1978; National Endowment for the Arts grant, 1988. **Agent:** Wendy Weil, Wendy Weil Agency, 747 Third Avenue, New York, New York 10017, U.S.A. **Address:** 3404 Monte Vista, Davis, California 95616, U.S.A.

SCIENCE FICTION PUBLICATIONS

Short Stories

Artificial Things. New York, Bantam, 1986.
Peripheral Vision. Eugene, Oregon, Pulphouse, 1990.
The War of the Roses. Eugene, Oregon, Pulphouse, 1991.
Letters from Home: Short Stories, with Pat Cadigan and Pat Murphy. London, Women's Press, 1991.

OTHER PUBLICATIONS

Novel

Sarah Canary. New York, Holt, 1991; London, Hodder and Stoughton, 1992.

*   *   *

There is a moment in the story "Face Value" in which two humans, falling out of love, are investigating the alien menes. One is asked what he thinks he is doing: "'Is that a trick question?' he asked. 'I imagine I am studying the mene. What do you imagine I am studying?' 'What humans always study,' said Hesper. 'Humans.'" The story is about not taking things at face value, and that is a lesson to be learned in reading any of Karen Joy Fowler's stories. Though she may use the paraphernalia of science fiction—aliens, other worlds, robots, time travel—her work is always about the human. In fact there is usually a discomforting domesticity about her work in which characters have to face up to their own inadequacies, disappointments or failures in situations whose very ordinariness emphasises the small tragedy.

In "Lily Red" a woman stages a small rebellion from the narrowness of her marriage and is offered the chance of an encounter with an ageless Indian, but she fails to see the magic and returns home. In "The Lake was Full of Artificial Things" a woman uses memory-enhancement techniques to meet again with the boyfriend she rejected and who was then killed in Vietnam, but the meetings go beyond what memory could supply and the woman is, instead, confronted with her own lack of understanding of the man, and of her own motivations.

The Vietnam era looms large in her work; there are many references to that time, and to the ideals and inspirations that shaped the 1960s. These, however, usually form the basis for a story about how those ideals have been lost or betrayed. "The War of the

Roses" recounts a confrontation between a hard-line revolutionary society and a small community whose life is devoted to tending flowers. The community is destroyed, but the revolution has to absorb much of the community's learning in order to survive, and the revolutionary who precipitated the confrontation finds herself tending flowers and learning, in a way typical of Fowler, that memory and regret are the same thing.

Memory is important in Fowler's work. Raina in "Recalling Cinderella" is haunted by a vague memory that, when recognised, sets off her final rebellion. Yet memory always triggers sadness, which must be accepted in order for us to survive. "The Faithful Companion at Forty" has Tonto looking back on the indignities of his career as a sidekick, but by confronting the unhappiness of his memories he is, in the end, stronger than the Lone Ranger, who cannot accept the happy memories of his youthful adventures and so plunges into one more time-travelling exploit which, we are left to suppose, will be the death of him.

It is typical, also, that Fowler should write about the sidekick rather than the hero. If there is one common trait shared by practically all her characters it is cowardice. Sometimes it is overcome, though to ambiguous effect, as in "The Dragon's Head" when little Penny finally confronts the old witch lady who lives in her neighbourhood and learns a mystery that haunts her life. Other times it is not, as when Hannah, the historian in "Praxis" whose field of expertise is the moment of choice that can change the whole history of human affairs, is confronted with such a moment herself and is unable to make the choice. Such moments of defeat and self-revelation echo through all Fowler's stories, though generally they provide the key to something else—maybe not happiness, a commodity in short supply in her stories and usually regarded with distrust, but at least a measure of achievement. Thus in "Lieserl" a young Albert Einstein, over a period of a few days, receives letters telling him of the birth, life, old age, and death of a daughter he never sees. The letters naturally frighten him, but at the same time they foreshadow the relativity towards which he is groping.

All of these characteristics, concerns, and techniques come into play, to haunting effect, in her novel *Sarah Canary*. Inexplicable and indefinable, it is set in the American northwest of 1873 but it is not historical fiction, it contains, indeed it focuses upon, a moment of transcendence, yet it is not fantasy. Not quite. In tone and intent Fowler comes closest, in this novel, to those postmodernist writers such as Doctorow and Coover who have mythologised the American past to illuminate the American present. The novel is punctuated with collections of curious facts from the period which serve a double purpose: they set the events of the story within the belief structure of the period, but more importantly they illustrate how much and, significantly, how little has changed in our attitudes towards ourselves, our minorities and our world.

The ordinary people facing up to inadequacy, disappointment, failure, are again at the centre of things, but this time they are marginalised in another, more emphatic sense also. These are minorities: Chinese, native American, women, insane. They are not quite at ease within their world, which explains not only their perspective but also the urgency of their seemingly meaningless quest. Sarah Canary herself (we never know her true name) is hardly seen but she touches, fleetingly, the lives of an odd assortment of characters. To Chin, a Chinese railway worker who meets her in a forest near Tacoma, she is ugly but he finds himself drawn to follow her trail nevertheless. Like the others who join the quest—BJ the patient at the Steilacoom asylum, Adelaide Dixon the outrageous advocate of women's sexual freedom—there is really no good rea-

son why he should become so committed to the hunt, why he should find himself caught up in so many escapades along the way. But Sarah Canary, who may be mad or wild or not even real, holds out a tenebrous promise that cannot be denied. The promise is fulfilled in Sarah's final transformation, a scene which lifts the book from its apparent oblique realism to something which feels at once far less explicable but far more satisfying. And Chin, who holds the whole book together, is left to reflect: "We dream our little dreams, dream that we are dreamers . . . while all about us the great dream goes on. Sometimes one of the great dreamers passes among us."

With *Sarah Canary* the small, ordinary, human compass of Karen Joy Fowler's stories is shown to have vastly greater resonance.

—Paul Kincaid

———

FOWLER, Sydney. *See* **WRIGHT, S. Fowler.**

———

FOX, Gardner F(rancis)

Pseudonyms: Jefferson Cooper; Lynna Cooper; Jeffrey Gardner; James Kendricks; Simon Majors; Kevin Matthews; Bart Somers. **Nationality:** American. **Born:** Brooklyn, New York, 20 May 1911. **Education:** St. John's University, Jamaica, New York, B.A. 1932, LL.B. 1935. **Family:** Married Lynda J. Negrini in 1937; one son and one daughter. **Career:** Lawyer. From 1937, comic book writer (Batman, Superman, The Flash, Green Lantern, and others). **Died:** 24 December 1986.

SCIENCE FICTION PUBLICATIONS

Novels (series: Commander Craig; Kothar; Kyrik; Lady from L.U.S.T.; Alan Morgan)

Escape across the Cosmos. New York, Paperback Library, 1964.
The Arsenal of Miracles. New York, Ace, 1964.
Warrior of Llarn (Morgan). New York, Ace. 1964.
The Hunter out of Time. New York, Ace, 1965.
Beyond the Black Enigma (Craig; as Bart Somers). New York, Paperback Library, 1965.
Fox Thief of Llarn (Morgan). New York, Ace, 1966.
The Druid Stones (as Simon Majors). New York, Paperback Library, 1967.
Abandon Galaxy (Craig; as Bart Somers). New York, Paperback Library, 1967.
Kothar Series:
  Kothar—Barbarian Swordsman. New York, Belmont, 1969.
  Kothar of the Magic Sword! New York, Belmont, 1969.
  Kothar and the Demon Queen. New York, Belmont, 1969.
  Kothar and the Conjurer's Curse. New York, Belmont, 1970.
  Kothar and the Wizard Slayer. New York, Belmont, 1970.

Lady from L.U.S.T. Series (as Rod Gray):

The Poisoned Pussy. New York, Tower, 1969.
Blow My Mind. New York, Tower, 1970.
Laid in the Future. New York, Tower, 1970.
The Copulation Explosion. New York, Tower, 1970.

Kyrik Series:

Kyrik, Warlock Warrior New York, Leisure, 1975.
Kyrik Fights the Demon World. New York, Leisure, 1975; London, Jenkins, 1976.
Kyrik and the Wizard's Sword, New York, Leisure, 1965
Kyrik and the Lost Queen. New York, Leisure, 1976.

Conehead. New York, Ace, 1973.

OTHER PUBLICATIONS

Novels

The Borgia Blade. New York, Fawcett, 1953; London, Fawcett, 1954.
Madame Buccaneer. New York, Fawcett, 1953; London, Fawcett, 1954.
Woman of Kali. New York, Fawcett, 1954; London, Muller, 1960.
The Gentleman Rogue. New York, Fawcett, 1954; London, Red Seal, 1959.
Rebel Wench. New York, Fawcett, 1955; London, Fawcett, 1958.
Queen of Sheba. New York, Fawcett, 1956.
One Sword for Love. New York Fawcett, 1954; London, Fawcett, 1956.
Terror over London. New York, Fawcett, 1957.
The Conquering Prince. New York, Fawcett, 1957; London, Fawcett, 1958.
Witness This Woman. New York, Fawcett, 1959; London, Muller, 1961.
Creole Woman. New York, Fawcett, 1959.
Iron Lover. New York, Avon, 1959.
The Devil Sword (as Kevin Matthews). New York, Hill, 1960.
Bastard of Orleans. New York, Avon, 1960.
Scandal in Suburbia. New York, Hill, 1960.
Woman of Egypt (as Kevin Matthews). London, Panther, 1961.
Barbary Devil (as Jeffrey Gardner). New York, Pyramid, 1961.
Cleopatra (as Jeffrey Gardner). New York, Pyramid, 1962.
As Good as Dead. New York, Fawcett, 1962.
Five Weeks in a Balloon (novelization of screenplay). New York Pyramid, 1962.
One Wife's Ways. New York, Fawcett, and London, Muller, 1963.
Tom Blood, Highwayman. New York, Avon, 1963.
Lion of Lucca. New York, Avon, 1966.
Ivan the Terrible. New York, Avon, n.d.
The Bold Ones. New York, Leisure, 1976.
The Liberty Sword. New York, Leisure, 1976.
Hurricane. New York, Leisure, 1976.
Savage Passage. New York, Leisure, 1978.
Blood Trail. New York, Belmont, 1979.

Novels as Jefferson Cooper

Arrow in the Hill. New York, Dodd Mead, 1955.
The Bloody Sevens. New York, Permabooks, 1957.
The Swordsman. New York, Pocket Books, 1957.
The Questing Sword. New York, Permabooks, 1958; London, Consul, 1960.

Captain Seadog. New York, Pocket Books, 1959.
Veronica's Veil. New York, Permabooks, 1959.
Delilah. New York, Paperback Library, 1962.
Jezebel. New York, Paperback Library, 1963.
Slave of the Roman Sword. New York, Paperback Library, 1965.
This Sword for Hire. New York, Paperback Library, 1966.

Novels as James Kendricks

Beyond Our Pleasure. Derby, Connecticut, Monarch, 1959.
Sword of Casanova. Derby, Connecticut, Monarch, 1959.
Adultress. Derby, Connecticut, Monarch, 1960.
She Wouldn't Surrender. Derby, Connecticut, Monarch, 1960.
The Wicked, Wicked Woman. Derby, Connecticut, Monarch, 1961.
Love Me Tonight. Derby, Connecticut, Monarch, 1963.

Novels as Lynna Cooper

An Offer of Marriage. New York, New American Library, 1976.
Substitute Bride. New York, New American Library, 1976.
Her Heart's Desire. New York, New American Library, 1976.
The Hired Wife. New York, New American Library, 1978.
Forgotten Love. New York, New American Library, 1979.
Hearts in the Highlands. New York, New American Library, 1980.
Inherit My Heart. New York, New American Library, 1981.

*   *   *

Gardner F. Fox was probably best known for his comic book work, which includes scripts for such science fiction-based characters as Superman and Hawkman. Yet his best science fantasy writing is probably to be found in a dozen space operas published between 1945 and 1952, mainly in *Planet Stories,* where they are overshadowed by the more impressive work of Ray Bradbury, Leigh Brackett, and Ross Rocklynne. But much of that work remains highly entertaining.

His first actual SF-fantasy sale was to *Weird Tales,* but his first story for *Planet Stories,* "The Last Monster"—a benevolent alien's efforts to aid endangered humans are misread as the menacings of a monster—won the instant approval of the magazine's readers. Fox buttressed his success with "Man Nth," in which aliens recruit beings from various worlds and endow them with superhuman powers to enable them to fend off a cosmic threat that would do justice to some of the grander fancies of A.E. van Vogt. "Man Nth" was an almost flawless entertainment and demonstrated a much surer touch than "The Last Monster." "Engines of the Gods" and "The Man the Sun Gods Made" established Fox as one of the most reliable writers of strong space adventure novelettes. "The Man the Sun Gods Made," about an artificial superman who stymies Earth's plans to exploit his planet, melded concepts Fox had already proven himself comfortable with—supermen and super-science—with the sort of story Leigh Brackett was already demonstrating success with.

"Vassals of the Lode-Star" is one of the strongest of his stories, arguably the best work he produced in the field. A rift in the fabric of time and space transports its hero to another world where he finds himself in a war with a superbeing bent on enslaving everything in reach. This was a story where everything worked for Fox: a strong and likeable lead character, Thor Masterson, a swift and interesting plot, concepts that are sufficiently gradiose and metaphysical to evoke a sense of wonder, and a benevolent alien, the Discoverer. "When Kohonnes Screamed" is less successful, though strongly imaginative, dealing with a planet where space and matter are dangerously and unpredictably distorted by a force which must somehow be located and destroyed. "Tonight the Stars Revolt!" is a strongly plotted story written in a terse prose under the now-traditional influence of Brackett, its conventional overcome-the-evil-ruler plot buoyed with fine storytelling and a strong imagination.

With the collapse of the SF market, Fox found success with original paperback historical novels, and he touched the periphery of SF with a novelization of the movie of Jules Verne's *Five Weeks in a Balloon*. But *Escape Across the Cosmos* was his first true SF novel. It was the story of a superman, falsely accused of a crime, who sets out to defend himself. *The Arsenal of Miracles* told of an outcast Earthman—a disgraced space officer—who joins forces with the queen of an alien world to fight the overwhelmingly powerful Empire of Earth. Some of its passages may have promised the same sort of fun delivered by his earlier stories, but novel-length SF seems never to have been Fox's forte. *Arsenal of Miracles* is a fun read, but none of the subsequent novels is quite as good. Under the name Bart Somers he produced two space operas based on the adventures of a character called Commander Craig, a space-going trouble shooter.

Conehead is one of his most interesting efforts. It touches on a more serious theme than is common to Fox's work, racial prejudice. His hero is the standard space officer of most of Fox's novels, but instead of being a warrior, he is a lawyer who sets out to establish the civil rights of the natives of a planet under the domination of Earth. The story returns ultimately to familiar ground: the planet holds the remnants of an alien race, all but extinct, yet still possessing god-like powers, and it is the force of their powers and not of any moral argument that ultimately sways the empire.

Fox was no idea man. His backgrounds are often merely sketched in, which probably accounts for his failure to draw any really widespread following among readers. But he was also a genuinely unpretentious writer whose work provides the sort of straightforward entertainment expected of good space opera. His novels are workmanlike and fun, but they lack the flair, imagination, and pacing of his best magazine stories.

—Gerald W. Page

FRANK, Pat (Harry Hart)

Nationality: American. **Born:** Chicago, Illinois, 5 May 1907. **Education:** Attended the University of Florida, Gainesville, 1925-26. **Family:** Divorced; one son and one daughter. **Career:** Reporter, *Jacksonville Journal*, Florida, 1927-29, *New York Journal*, 1929-32, and *Washington Herald*, 1933-38; Chief of the Washington Bureau, 1938-41, and correspondent in Italy, Austria, Germany, Turkey, and Hungary, 1944-46, Overseas News Agency; Assistant Chief of Mission, Office of War Information, 1941-44; member of United Nations Mission to Korea, 1952-53; staff member, Democratic National Committee, 1960; consultant, National Aeronautics and Space Council, 1961; consultant Department of Defense, 1963-64. **Awards:** War Department commendation, 1945; Reserved Officers Association citation, 1957; American Heritage Foundation award, 1961. **Died:** 12 October 1964.

SCIENCE FICTION PUBLICATIONS

Novels

Mr. Adam: A Novel. Philadelphia, Lippincott, 1946; London, Gollancz, 1947.
Forbidden Area. Philadelphia, Lippincott, 1956; as *Seven Days to Never*, London, Constable, 1957.
Alas, Babylon: A Novel. Philadelphia, Lippincott, and London, Constable, 1959.

OTHER PUBLICATIONS

Novels

An Affair of State. Philadelphia, Lippincott, 1948; London, Corgi, 1951.
Hold Back the Night. Philadelphia, Lippincott, and London, Hamish Hamilton, 1952.

Other

The Long Way Round. Philadelphia, Lippincott, 1953.
How to Survive the H-Bomb, and Why. Philadelphia, Lippincott, 1962.
Rendezvous at Midway: U.S.S. Yorktown and the Japanese Carrier Fleet, with Joseph D. Harrington. New York, Day, 1967.

*   *   *

In the late 1940s and 1950s, a growing distrust of technology focused on the dangers of atomic energy. The most obvious danger was that of nuclear war, but concerns about reactor breakdowns or bomb-factory explosions were also on people's minds. The immediate blast was one threat, and genetic damage from radiation was another. Science fiction writers were among the first during this period to give such fears a public voice, and one of those writers was Pat Frank.

Frank wrote a great deal of material—fiction and nonfiction—dealing with the possible problems with atomic materials. His first novel, *Mr. Adam*, postulates universal male sterility as one of the results of an explosion at an atomic bomb factory in Mississippi. *Forbidden Area* attempts to show how, why, and when the Russians might attack the United States. This book is an especially grim indictment of America's lack of preparedness for such a possibility. Frank shows how the various agencies—paralyzed by red tape, interdepartmental bickering, unqualified political appointees in positions of power, and the like—refuse to act until it is almost too late, averting an all-out Russian attack by only minutes.

Frank is probably best known as the author of *Alas, Babylon*, a postatomic war novel. Randy Bragg, an inhabitant of Fort Repose, Florida, is warned by his brother, Mark, a SAC Intelligence Officer, that the war is coming. Mark sends his wife and children to Randy because Fort Repose will be safer during such a war than will SAC Headquarters, Omaha. The bombs and missiles fall, and the people of Fort Repose are on their own. Unlike Nevil Shute's *On the Beach*, in which everyone dies, *Alas, Babylon* is basically a romantic view of the aftermath of an atomic war. Randy and his friends do not have too much difficulty surviving—though Civil Defense agencies have prepared almost no one, and Randy has to organize the people of Fort Repose—and only one of the central characters is killed. With this romantic novel, however, Frank presents all the atomic fears, from initial blast to genetic mutation, in one package.

Frank also examines the use of power in *Alas, Babylon*. There are various people in the novel who have power and should not. Randy was defeated in politics by an opponent who appealed to bigotry and fear. The Navy Ensign who fires the shot that starts the war uses the power of his jet plane to compensate for his diminutive physical stature. Randy, however, uses the power at his disposal to keep Fort Repose safe. From this, it is clear that it is not power, per se, that Frank objects to but the lack of qualifications of some of the people who have the power.

Frank's novels are well-written. They have strong plots, well-paced action, and interesting characters. They are not so much appeals to the reader's fear of atomic power as they are warnings.

—C.W. Sullivan III

FRANKE, Herbert W.

Nationality: Austrian. **Born:** 1927. **Career:** Scientist and author; teacher of cybernetic aesthetics, University of Munich.

SCIENCE FICTION PUBLICATIONS

Novels

Der orchideekäfig. Munich, Goldmann, 1961; translated by Christine Priest as *The Orchid Cage,* New York, DAW, 1973.
Das gedankennetz. Munich, Goldmann, 1961; translated by Christine Priest as *The Mind Net,* New York, DAW, 1974.
Zone null. Munich, Lichtenberg, 1970; translated by Chis Harriman as *Zone Null,* New York, Seabury Press, 1974.

*

Writer, scientist, spelunker, computer expert, and academic, Herbert W. Franke writes novels, short stories, and science books for laymen about computers, information science, and the potentialities of psychological manipulation through electronic sensory stimulation. His earlier novels emphasized dominant military-industrial systems allied to conformist drug cultures, radioactive desolations, decadent game-satiated mass cultures, entrapment in plastic environments, and the definition of enforced "superiority" as conformity to one man's monomaniacal obsessions. Some of the novels of the late 1970s and early 1980s portray superman-obsessed leaders who use electronic simulations to test and delude their trainees (*Schule für Übermenschen*). From *Glasfalle* to *Kälte des Weltraums* tyrants are a continuing thread, but the later novels allow their heroes more freedom. Although Franke portrays enforced "superiority" harshly, a hero may submit voluntarily to the training school rigors in the beginning to survive a tyrant in the end (*Schule für Übermenschen*). His analysis of scientists' responsibility for the state of affairs continues in *Keine Spur vom Leben* and *Tod eines Unsterblichen*. Most striking is the development of the entertainment park theme in *The Orchid Cage* through *Zone Null* and

Sirius Transit (1979). There the dominant personality is a "Star" who manipulates the masses by faking the conquest of a distant planet. Two recent works: *Endzeit* (1985) and *Dea Alba* (1988), revolve around the ambiguities of computer interpreted data. A sound cassette accompanies *Dea Alba* to reflect the descriptions of strange sensory effects on a crew investigating a far distant planet, effects which entice two crew members away from their compatriots and transform their physical natures. *Endzeit*'s hero is expected to solve Earth's loss-of-water/energy problem by data manipulation. Both novels have quasi-religious endings with the rain storm after arid millennia (1985) or matter transformation (1988). Though some characters show a modest development, the novels are often ironic in outline and analytical in the disclosure of unifying social, psychological, and electronic systems. With the basic themes of heroes who question, critical encounters with a deadening status quo, and analyses of the psychological potentialities of advanced technology, Franke continues to plumb the long term problems of both individual and species survival.

—Alice Carol Gaar

FRAYN, Michael

Nationality: British. **Born:** London, 8 September 1933. **Education:** Kingston Grammar School, Surrey; Emmanuel College, Cambridge, B.A. 1957. **Military Service:** Served in the Royal Artillery and Intelligence Corps, 1952-54. **Family:** Married Gillian Palmer in 1960; three daughters. Reporter, 1957-59, and columnist, 1959-62, *The Guardian,* Manchester and London; columnist, *The Observer,* London, 1962-68. **Awards:** Maugham award, 1966; Hawthornden prize, 1967; National Press award, 1970; Standard award for play, 1976, 1981, 1983, 1985; Society of West End Theatre award, 1977, 1982; British Theatre Association award, 1981, 1983; Olivier award, 1985. **Agent:** Elaine Greene Ltd., 31 Newington Green, London N169PU, England.

SCIENCE FICTION PUBLICATIONS

Novels

The Tin Men. London, Collins, 1965; Boston, Little Brown, 1966.
A Very Private Life. London, Collins, and New York, Viking, 1968.
Sweet Dreams. London, Collins, 1973; New York, Viking, 1974.

OTHER PUBLICATIONS

Novels

The Russian Interpreter. London, Collins, and New York, Viking, 1966.
Towards the End of the Morning. London, Collins, 1967; as *Against Entropy,* New York, Viking Press, 1967.
The Trick of It. London and New York, Viking, 1990.
A Landing on the Sun. London, Viking, 1991; New York, Viking, 1992.
Now You Know. London, Viking, 1992; New York, Viking, 1993.

Plays

Zounds!, with John Edwards, music by Keith Statham (produced Cambridge, 1957).

The Two of Us (includes *Black and Silver, The New Quixote, Mr. Foot, Chinamen*) (produced London, 1970; Ogunquit, Maine, 1975; *Chinamen* produced New York, 1979). London, Fontana, 1970; *Chinamen* published in *The Best Short Plays 1973,* edited by Stanley Richards, Radnor, Pennsylvania, Chilton, 1973; revised version of *The New Quixote* (produced Chichester and London, 1980).

The Sandboy (produced London, 1971).

Alphabetical Order (produced London, 1975; New Haven, Connecticut, 1976). Included in *Alphabetical Order and Donkeys' Years,* 1977.

Donkeys' Years (produced London, 1976). Included in *Alphabetical Order and Donkeys' Years,* 1977.

Clouds (produced London, 1976). London, Eyre Methuen, 1977.

Alphabetical Order and Donkeys' Years. London, Eyre Methuen, 1977.

The Cherry Orchard, adaptation of a play by Chekhov (produced London, 1978). London, Eyre Methuen, 1978.

Balmoral (produced Guildford, Surrey, 1978; revised version, as *Liberty Hall,* produced London, 1980). London, Methuen, 1987.

The Fruits of Enlightenment, adaptation of a play by Tolstoy (produced London, 1979). London, Eyre Methuen, 1979.

Make and Break (produced London, 1980; Washington, D.C., 1983). London, Eyre Methuen, 1980.

Noises Off (produced London, 1981; New York, 1983). London, Methuen, 1982; New York, French, 1985.

Three Sisters, adaptation of a play by Chekhov (produced Manchester, 1985; London, 1987). London, Methuen, 1983.

Benefactors (produced London, 1984). London, Methuen, 1984.

Wild Honey, adaptation of a play by Chekhov (produced London, 1984; New York, 1986-87). London, Methuen, 1984.

Number One, adaptation of a play by Jean Anouilh (produced London, 1984).

Plays 1 (includes *Alphabetical Order, Donkey's Years, Clouds, Make and Break, Noises Off*). London and New York, Methuen, 1985.

Clockwise (screenplay). London, Methuen, 1986.

The Seagull, adaptation of a play by Chekhov (produced Watford, Hertfordshire, 1986). London, Methuen, 1986.

Uncle Vanya, adaptation of a play by Chekhov. London, Methuen, 1987.

Look, Look. London, Methuen, 1990.

Audience: A Play in One Act. New York, French, 1991.

Plays II. London, Methuen, 1991.

Hear: A Play in Two Acts. London, Methuen, 1993; New York, French, 1994.

Television Plays and Documentaries: *Second City Reports,* with John Bird, 1964; *Jamie, On a Flying Visit,* 1968; *One Pair of Eyes,* 1968; *Birthday,* 1969; *Beyond a Joke* series, with John Bird and Eleanor Bron, 1972; *Laurence Sterne Lived Here* (Writers' Houses series), 1973; *Imagine a City Called Berlin,* 1975; *Making Faces,* 1975; *Vienna: The Mask of Gold,* 1977; *Three Streets in the Country,* 1979; *The Long Straight (Great Railway Journeys of the World* series), 1980; *Jerusalem,* 1984; *First and Last,* 1989.

Other

The Day of the Dog (Guardian columns). London, Collins, 1962; New York, Doubleday, 1963.

The Book of Fub (Guardian columns). London, Collins, 1963; as *Never Put Off to Gomorrah,* New York, Pantheon, 1964.

On the Outskirts (Observer columns). London, Collins, 1964.

At Bay in Gear Street (Observer columns). London, Fontana, 1967.

Constructions (philosophy). London, Wildwood House, 1974.

Great Railway Journeys of the World, with others. London, BBC Publications, 1981.

The Original Michael Frayn: Columns from the Guardian and The Observer. Edinburgh, Salamander Press, 1983.

Listen to This: Sketches and Monologues. London, Methuen, and New York, French, 1990.

Editor, *The Best of Beachcomber,* by J.B. Morton. London, Heinemann, 1963.

Translator, *Plays,* by Anton Chekhov. London, Methuen, 1988.

Translator, *The Sneeze: Plays and Stories by Anton Chekhov.* London, Methuen, and New York, French, 1989.

Translator, *Exchange,* by Yuri Trifonov. London, Methuen, 1990.

* * *

Michael Frayn is not an easy writer to categorize. *The Tin Men* is obviously not SF but witty comedy, school of Waugh; on the other hand, it obviously is SF, as it purports to be written by a computer and satirizes men who behave like computers and are trying to make computers behave like men. When a robot comes to write its own prehistory, it will have to give classic place in its mythology to Macintosh's ethical machines and their struggles on the sinking raft. But the novel is not so much SF itself as an exuberant account of the men who are trying to make our world into an SF dystopia. The great discovery of Macintosh and Goldwasser is that, because all human life is of no purpose other than to provide newspaper headlines and statistics, humans can stop living and let the computers do it for them. Computers can produce newspapers, sports results, pornography, prayers: who needs people? The characteristic inverted logic of Frayn's tin men naturally produces a novelist who begins by writing the blurbs, the potted biography, and the reviews, and only then tries writing the book (formulaically, of course), before capitulating to the superior power of his typewriter keyboard. What *The Tin Men* itself lacks as a novel is a story worthy of its theme. Admittedly the story, which concerns the opening of the Ethics Wings in a computer research establishment, not by the Queen, as planned but by her stand-in for rehearsals (an ungainly man called Nobbs), illustrates several aspects of the theme of illusion mistaken for reality, but its spirit of low farce inoculates the reader against taking the book seriously. Also, the novel's short-breathed episodic quality—it is really only a series of sketches strung loosely together by a farcical plot—too openly betrays the author's work as a whimsically satiric journalist. The short-breath syndrome is familiar among SF novelists who are really short story writers; in *The Tin Men* we have an essayist trying to write a novel and not quite succeeding.

A Very Private Life also has a mosaic quality (as indeed does Frayn's stimulating philosophical work, *Constructions*), but here the small pieces compose a highly satisfactory work of art, one of the most delightful fabulations in the genre. The heroine, Uncumber, begins as a misfit in a society where what the Haves have is privacy: they meet by holovision, as in Asimov's *The Naked Sun.* Uncumber falls in love with a man who lives on the fringes of her enclosed society, journeys outside her cell to meet him, is disillusioned by life outside, falls in with outlaws, is rescued by the police and rehabilitated. Comparison with *The Naked Sun* is instructive because, unlike Asimov and the typical SF writer who might handle such a theme, Frayn has not written a dystopian satire: his absurd world is presented not as a threat but as an alteration simply, a new mode, not inhuman but nicely domesticated by engaging touches of ordinariness. Again, if we compare Frayn's work with Angela Carter's *Heroes and Villains,* in which the ivory tower world is promptly sacrificed to the perverse gypsy delights of the world outside, we see how detached and balanced, how cool Frayn is. Uncumber does not find the outer world romantic, as a Carter heroine would; instead, the best it can offer is a tatty attempt to emulate the values of those inside, while the worst is nasty and brutish: the outlaws are indeed, as they are called, "Sad Men." Frayn's novel is written as a fairy story that begins "Once upon a time there will be a little girl called Uncumber," and in that spirit it should be read.

Sweet Dreams, clearly to be read as a fantasy, as it is a story set in the afterlife, in which revivification is without benefit of technology (by which Farmer and Silverberg, say, have accommodated this mythological idea to SF), is a wickedly soft-centred utopian novel. Howard Baker thinks he has had a car accident and gone to heaven, where he finds himself to be the centre of a circle of his own friends, some of whom must, confusingly enough, be still "alive" in the lower world. For Howard everything is possible in a state where such a frequently expressed (but never, of course, on Earth, seriously meant) erotic wish to browse on a lover's buttocks, for example, can be fulfilled without damage to the compliant partner; where one can levitate or change one's age at will. The trouble is, that Howard does not wish to change; he is, alas, rather lacking in imagination. God gives him the job of helping create the Alps; Howard brilliantly reinvents the Matterhorn. His astringent friend Phil goes one better by creating man in Howard's image. The sad moral seems to be that people like to talk about heaven or utopia but they do not really want it, because they would not know what to do with it if they had it.

A Landing on the Sun has a title that sounds like SF or 17th-century fantasy, but the phrase is metaphorical. In the sunshine, a civil servant, Jessel, discovers that "Life . . . is nothing more nor less than another way of writing *file.*" It is his job to prepare a file, but what he does instead is to discover life. The file is about a dead civil servant, Summerfield, and his Controller, Dr. Severin, who becomes available to him for interviewing. Summerfield had died, 20 years before, like Actaeon or Phaeton, perhaps through his knowledge of secrets passed to Russians. Jessel and his associates prepare a file in order to express their understanding of the quality of life, or, more specifically, of happiness, which "is surely the sun at the centre of our conceptual planetary system—and has proved just as hard to look at directly." It is when he and Severin move out of an attic to the Gormenghastian rooftops of Whitehall that they find their place in, and on, the sun. Jessel follows the whole course of the development of the old, probably misconceived, Strategy Unit through the media of typed reports and previously unheard cassette tapes. As Jessel listens with enormous sensitivity to the sounds of silence on his tapes, the reader enjoys a pleasure like that of reading Sterne (it helps actually to have read Sterne before) or Richardson's epistolary novels, and is exhilarated by Frayn's modern detective story which leads Jessel to discover many surprising events, including ones which affected his own earlier

life (and his current life) directly. When considered as a time-travel narrative, *A Landing on the Sun* is surprisingly like science fiction in its method: it is thoroughly dependent on technology for its modal form. It is, perhaps, easier to regard it as a philosophical novel (which refers to *Candide* and may recall *Rasselas* to the reader), but then the kind of philosophical enquiry to which it gives rise is one of the best functions of SF.

In *Constructions* Frayn tells us "I should like to say this: don't *worry* when you find yourself in the midst of a mythology. Relax and enjoy it." Some SF readers may find themselves graveled by the way in which this sharp and witty writer pulls his punches. Frayn is not a knock-down satirist: he is a comic ironist who enjoys the spectacle of human absurdity, and wants us to share the fun: it seems highly apt that he should once have presented a wonderful brief documentary on Laurence Sterne for television. Similarly, the film screenplay *Clockwise,* for a Michael Codron production directed by Christopher Morahan and starring John Cleese, though a farce, holds, in its philosophical if frenetic examination of a headmaster who has allowed time to control his life, much of the Shandean sense of oppression by time as well as having an affinity with SF treatments of the inexorable fourth dimension. His brilliant farce, *Noises Off,* which is sometimes reviewed, thankfully, as pure entertainment, is itself replete with philosophical implications of a kind that might have attracted the author of *The Truth in Painting,* although, thankfully, so far as I know, it has hitherto escaped a Derridian deconstructionist reading. The more serious *Make and Break* is about the life-and-death problems of workaholics, and it makes its point tellingly in a fantasy mode by presenting even John Garrard's dreams to the stage.

The recent novels *The Trick of It* and *Now You Know,* are admirable in their experimental quality as narratives. *The Trick of It* is a brilliant piece of epistolary writing, a collection of letters by a British academic critic to a Goethe scholar in Melbourne, Victoria. The set of letters should have been destroyed, according to one narratorial instruction, but should have been preserved, according to a later instruction, as the only means of keeping the author alive. The narrator leaves for Abu Dhabi when his university introduces postmodernist criticism, and one sympathises with him. The lecturer has been teaching his wife's fiction, until she starts writing a biography of the lecturer's mother, a text which he attacks—and which leads him to commence a novel himself, a failure. *Now You Know* is written in chapters formed of double internal dialogues by the various characters associated with a lobby group called OPEN, in which it is brought open to OPEN's leader, well-known media star Terry Little, that the group itself is, and must be, fundamentally closed—until a "now you know" climax eventuates. As in *The Trick of It,* something of the madness of civil service life is presented brilliantly by the too-open character Hilary Wood. The novel reads like one of those plays in which internal and external dialogue are presented simultaneously, and therefore in some respects is to be associated with the dream-sequences in *Make and Break.*

—Michael J. Tolley

—————

FRENCH, Paul. *See* **ASIMOV, Isaac.**

—————

FRIEDBERG, Gertrude

Also wrote as Gertrude Tonkonogy. **Nationality:** American. **Born:** Gertrude Tonkonogy, New York City, 17 March 1908. **Education:** Wellesley College, Massachusetts; Barnard College, New York, B.A. 1929. **Family:** Married Charles K. Friedberg; one son and one daughter. **Career:** Mathematics teacher in New York public schools, and freelance writer. **Died:** 17 September 1989.

SCIENCE FICTION PUBLICATIONS

Novel

The Revolving Boy. Garden City, New York, Doubleday, 1966; London, Gollancz, 1967.

OTHER PUBLICATIONS

Plays

Three Cornered Moon: A Comedy in Three Acts (as Gertrude Tonkonogy; produced New York, 1933). New York, French, 1933.
Town House, adaptation of stories by John Cheever (produced New York, 1948).

*   *   *

Gertrude Friedberg's *The Revolving Boy* follows the early life of a supernormal child, Derv, who has the ability to be both radiometer and compass. One of the major themes of the novel is that of discovering and communicating with another civilization. Derv was born to astronauts in 1970, in a weightless condition far from the Earth's forces. Because he did not experience gravity at birth, he was able to align himself to a signal from another solar system. He feels compelled to preserve his original orientation to this signal—called the Direction—and consequently, when his body is turned in one direction, he must unwind himself in the opposite direction to recapture his original position. He turns somersaults in bed to compensate for the Earth's revolutions and his day's turnings. During his elementary school years, his teachers become concerned as he executes dangerous spins on stairways. He becomes known as "the boy who leans" when his body begins listing in the direction of the signal.

To escape the publicity following his birth, Derv's parents faked a fatal accident in a sailboat, escaped undetected, and assumed new identities. The novel excels in following the parents' fears of discovery as they observe the development of Derv's talent. When Derv reaches high school, an astronomer who knew the astronaut parents discovers their true identities and persuades them to allow Derv to help trace the signal on a laboratory radiometer. Just as the signal is found electronically, Derv and his parents disappear again. Part Two of the book begins some years later, after Derv has taken a new name—Fred Gany—and married his childhood sweetheart, Prin (now Reine), who has perfect pitch. Derv/Fred's signal has suddenly stopped and he has lost his sense of balance. The remainder of the book concentrates on Prin/Rein's attempts to relocate the laboratory radiometer (which has been abandoned) and to determine if the signal has indeed terminated.

Friedberg's scientific projections are mostly erroneous. For instance, the exposition of her novel is centered on the ban on space travel in 1970, due to a belt of nuclear waste around the Earth. She overestimated the speed of change to electronic devices in the homes of the 1970s. Her scientific research can also be faulted, since she has failed to take into account some of the properties of radio signals, such as the possibility of blockage by shielding masses (the Earth, tunnels, and concrete buildings).

"The Short and Happy Death of George Frumkin" is a tongue-in-cheek look at the use of artificial organs. George, 97 years old, has developed not only a knock in his artificial heart, but also a bad case of ennui, as he refuses to complete a promised rewrite of the second act of a play. George's wife, Helen, persuades him to call an electrician, Dr. Stebbins (most doctors are electricians these days), who tells him that he needs "a new battery and a new variable autotransformer." In order to hook him to his new system, Dr. Stebbins switches him to house current until the calibration procedure is finished. During the short space between plug-ins, George is "dead." However, house current proves a boon to George, providing him with the creative energy to rewrite his second act, plus an oversupply of sexual libido (he attacks his wife and propositions the maid during this interval). But after his return to battery power, he resumes his uninspired ways, learning nevertheless that his rewritten second act has given the play "more heart." This entertaining spoof is a gem, undoubtedly Friedberg's best science fiction effort. She uses a female narrator for this story, plus a steady supply of eccentric comic characters.

"For Whom the Girl Waits," properly called science fantasy, is a dreamlike account of double identities in a high school setting. The main character, Louis Demperi, is a substitute teacher who assumes the identity of the teacher he replaces. The role-playing works well until he takes the place of a man named Koppinger, for whom a beautiful girl waits each afternoon after school. Then he becomes disoriented and cannot remember that he is Koppinger, until he discovers that another man has assumed his own identity. Demperi decides to carry on with Koppinger's role and meets the girl, who rejects him and causes him to have a fatal car accident. But his identity lives on in the person of Demperi's substitute. The story is somewhat confusing but is imaginative and fascinating to read.

Friedberg wrote in a simple, unpretentious style and in general organized her material chronologically. She excelled in the handling of women characters, which suggests that her works might have been more successful if the central characters had been women instead of men.

—Judith Snyder

G

GADALLAH, Leslie

Nationality: Canadian. **Born:** 1939.

SCIENCE FICTION PUBLICATIONS

Novels (series: Cat's Pawn)

Cat's Pawn. New York, Ballantine, 1987.
The Loremasters. New York, Ballantine, 1988.
Cat's Gambit. New York, Ballantine, 1990.

*   *   *

One of the best ways to acquire an immediate following among SF readers is to create either a single character so distinct that further adventures are avidly sought after, or to create a culture—particularly an alien culture—that is rich enough to capture the popular imagination and diverse enough to support additional volumes. Leslie Gadallah attempted with considerable success to do both in *Cat's Pawn,* a well-received first novel, which also exploits the apparent popularity of cats within the science fiction community. Several other writers—most notably C.J. Cherryh—have used this same device to considerable effect.

Bill Anderson is a space traveler stranded on Orion when an illness puts an end to his professional career. Although he finds a warm reception there, and his alien friend Talan is happy to have him near, Anderson feels homesick and confused, and seeks to find a new purpose for his truncated life. He finds a job as a translator without realizing that he is in the pay of a criminal element among the human population, and stumbles across a dire secret. The Oriani are involved in a desperate war against another species, the Kaz, who are slowly spreading throughout the galaxy, absorbing one race after another. The Oriani have concealed much of the truth from the human race, which has its own internal political problems.

The novel ends somewhat disjointedly. The secret is out, but Anderson has been discredited as a madman, and the motivations of the Oriani remain somewhat obscure. This was presumably to set the stage for the sequel, *Cat's Gambit,* wherein the Kaz have continued to expand toward Earth and Orion, and in fact the second book concludes with them still largely triumphant. The Oriani have been almost completely defeated and their numbers are dwindling quickly. Their only hope is to find representatives of yet another race, one whose existence may be nothing more than a legend.

One of the Oriani convinces a human pirate to take her aboard his ship and set off on a search for the fabled world, but only after his resistance to the idea is overcome by overt coercion on the part of her superiors. Unfortunately, the planet lies within the Kaz sphere of influence, so the mission seems doomed from the outset. Despite his involuntary service and constant battles with his Oriani passenger, MacDonald the pirate finds himself growing fond of his companion, ultimately feels obligated to complete her mission even when it is no longer mandatory that he do so. The interplay between the two main characters is handled skillfully, despite the rather disheartening ending.

Despite the successful conclusion of this second adventure, it is not at all clear that the Kaz will not prove too strong for their enemies, and it seems likely that at least one further story in the series was contemplated, although to date no such continuation has appeared or been announced. Gadallah's only other novel, in fact, is *The Loremasters,* which is unrelated to the other two, but which shares the dim view of human culture hinted at in the Cat books.

The Loremasters uses a very different setting and theme. The Earth has declined technologically as the consequence of a universal power shortage that has left modern civilization shattered, surviving pockets of limited scientific ability living in sheltered enclaves, separate from each other and largely dominated by ineffective governments. Reese is a scientist from one such enclave who is unhappy with the complacent acceptance of disaster prevalent among his fellows and seeks a solution among the less advanced people living in the open lands. His initial efforts are not only successful, they land him in danger of losing his own life. When he demonstrates some of his scientific knowledge, the locals believe him to be practicing witchcraft and demand that he be killed. His efforts to explain the true situation fail, but fortunately he has friends who eventually rescue him before the execution takes place.

Gadallah has also produced occasional short fiction, including "The Butterfly Effect," which shows the frustrations of an unemployed meteorologist who stumbles upon the way to accurately predict apparently random shifts in weather but can't convince anyone that he's right, and "Motherlove," a slight piece about a contemporary witch. Her major strength is her ability to create a credible society and place interesting people in that context. Her visions are somewhat melancholic, however, and there is always a sense that even the victories are limited ones.

—Don D'Ammassa

GADE, Henry. *See* **PALMER, Raymond A.**

GAIL, Otto

Nationality: German. **Born:** 1896. **Died:** 1956.

SCIENCE FICTION PUBLICATIONS

Novels

Hans Hardts mondfahrt: eines abenteurerliche erzahlung. N.p., 1928; translated as *By Rocket to the Moon: The Story of Hans Hardt's Miraculous Flight,* New York, Sears, 1931.
Der schuss ins all. Breslau, Bergstadt, 1925; translated by Frances Currier as *The Shot into Infinity,* New York, Garland, 1975.

OTHER PUBLICATIONS

Other

Wir plaudern uns durch die physid. Stuttgart, Thienemann, 1931; translated by H. Staford Hatfield as *Romping through Physics,* London, Routledge, 1933; New York, Knopf, 1934.

"The Stone from the Moon," in *Science Wonder Quarterly,* Spring 1930.

Otto Gail, the German popular science and science fiction writer, was closely associated with rocketry pioneers such as Hermann Oberth, and influential in development of realistic depiction of space travel in Anglo-American and even Soviet SF. All three of Gail's science fiction novels were translated into English.

Until the appearance of *The Shot into Infinity* in *Wonder Stories Quarterly* in 1929 there was little technical realism in Anglo-American SF devoted to the conquest of space. Victorian devices like anti-gravity were still common, and even when rockets were used they tended to be built by precocious inventors right in their back yards. Gail, also the author of a 1928 non-fiction work of popularization, *With Rocket Ships into Space,* was familiar with the work of Oberth and other theorists. And if he did not *fully* realize the logistical problems of the Space Age, he was certainly aware space travel would be a massive undertaking. *The Shot into Infinity* mixes Vernean SF with romantic melodrama. August Korf, the hero, has been working on a multistage liquid-fuel rocket—a project that has languished for lack of funding (partly due to his own stubbornness: he is too proud to appeal to the world for help). A rival has stolen his earlier plans for a solid-fuel craft, and sent an astronaut to the Moon. Alas, solid fuel proves inadequate, and the luckless pilot is trapped in lunar orbit. So naturally Korf speeds completion of his *Geryon* to attempt a rescue, and of course the dying pilot turns out to be his former true love, who was impatient with his caution and wanted to go herself. Amid the melodrama, there remain realistic scenes of acceleration, stage separation, space walks, and the like. Too, there is the sense that reality is unforgiving, as in Tom Godwin's later "The Cold Equations," and, above all, a sense of mission: space travel as a cause. *The Shot into Infinity* is ancestor to such later works as Robert A. Heinlein's "The Man Who Sold the Moon" and Arthur C. Clarke's *Prelude to Space.*

"The Stone from the Moon" is less interesting; although it features a space station, the plot centers on an occult Lost Atlantis theme. *By Rocket to the Moon* is strictly juvenile. Despite the earlier influence of Konstantin Tsiolkovsky, Gail's work seems to have had some impact on Soviet SF through translations. Aleksandr Belyaev tries to go *The Shot into Infinity* one better with *A Leap into Nothingness* (1933), with even more attention to logistics and outdoes "The Stone from the Moon" with the space station in *KETStar* (1936).

—John J. Pierce

GAIMAN, Neil (Richard)

Nationality: English. **Born:** Portchester, England, 10 November 1960. **Education:** Ardingly College, 1970-74; Whitgift School, 1974-77. **Family:** Married Mary McGrath in 1985; one son, one daughter. **Awards:** Mekon Award, 1988; Eagle award, 1988, 1990. **Awards:** World Fantasy award, 1990. **Member:** Society of Trip Illustrators (chair, 1988-90); Science Fiction Foundation (committee member); British Fantasy Society.

SCIENCE FICTION PUBLICATIONS

Novels

Good Omens: The Nice and Accurate Prophecies of Agnes Nutter, Witch, with Terry Pratchett. London, Victor Gollancz, and New York, Workman, 1990.

Short Stories

Angels & Visitations: A Miscellany. Minneapolis, Minnesota, DreamHaven Books, 1993.

OTHER PUBLICATIONS

Graphic Novels

Violent Cases. London, Titan, 1987; Northampton, Massachusetts, Tundra, 1991.

The Sandman, with others. London, Titan, and New York, DC Comics, 1990.

The Books of Magic. New York, DC Comics, 1991.

Black Orchid. London, Titan, and New York, DC Comics, 1991.

Signal to Noise. London, Victor Gollancz, 1992.

Miracle Man, Book Four: The Golden Age. Forestville, California, Eclipse, 1992; London, EclipseGraphicNovels, 1993.

Death, the High Cost of Living, with Chris Bachalo and Mark Buckingham. New York, DC Comics, 1993; London, Titan, 1994.

The Children's Crusade, with Chris Bachalo. New York, DC Comics, 1993-94.

Other

Duran, Duran: The First Four Years of the Fab Five. New York, Proteus, 1984.

Don't Panic: The Official Hitch-Hiker's Guide to the Galaxy Companion. London, Titan, and New York, Pocket, 1988; revised as *Don't Panic: Douglas Adams & The Hitchhiker's Guide to the Galaxy,* with David K. Dickson. London, Titan, 1993.

Editor, with Kim Newman, *Ghastly Beyond Belief.* London, Arrow, 1985.

Editor, with Stephen Jones, *Now We Are Sick: A Sampler.* East Grinstead, West Sussex, Neil Gaman, 1986; Minneapolis, Minnesota, DreamHaven, 1991.

Editor, with Alex Stewart, *Temps, Volume 1.* London, Roc, 1991.

Editor, with Alex Stewart, *Eurotemps.* London, Roc, 1992.

Editor, with Mary Gentle and Roz Kaveney, *The Weerde.* London, Roc, 1992.

*   *   *

Neil Gaiman is the most respected, successful writer working at the cutting edge of mainstream comics. Gaiman personally stopped reading mainstream comics when he was 16, convinced that nothing interesting was going on. His interest was rekindled by Alan Moore's *Swamp Thing* and strengthened in 1986 by the publication of Moore's *Watchmen* and Frank Miller's *Batman: The Dark Knight Returns.* Suddenly the world of comics appeared to be full of possibilities for an imaginative young writer, and Gaiman began scripting *Violent Cases,* an exploration of memory/fantasy that was illustrated in faded tones by Dave McKean.

By that time, however, Gaiman already had established himself as a resourceful journalist and occasional writer of prose fiction. The pieces collected in *Angels & Visitations* show his growing skill in handling recurring concerns. In particular, Gaiman's first-person characters show a constant propensity toward superficial relationships, willingness to betray others for selfish ends, and insensitivity to the damage they inflict. They are not so much deliberately evil, however, as they are merely underdeveloped, temporary creatures—humans, in other words. To the extent they become aware of the limits of that condition, they desire to escape from it by making contact with something larger, more permanent. In the early story "Looking for the Girl," for example, an ogler of men's-magazine nude photos finally meets the archetypal, perpetually-19-year-old model and refrains from approaching her sexually because "[s]he was my dream; and if you touch a dream it vanishes, like a soap bubble." Though he ages, he somehow is comforted by awareness that the dream of eternal youth exists. The more recent "Murder Mysteries" combines conventions of the violent modern detective story and the Mystery plays that were intended to illuminate religious issues by acting them out. The framing story is told by a young man with odd gaps in his memory, approached by a derelict who claims to be a dispossed angel—who tells of his having been commanded to investigate the murder of an angel in Heaven during the turbulent period as the Universe was being designed. The story first involves readers in the fundamental question of reading: What's happening? Then a contemporary reader turns naturally to the familiar mystery-fiction puzzle: Who dunnit? As the story ends and the implications of both levels of action sink in, however, readers are left with an awareness of the unsolvable Mysteries of love and forgiveness.

Shortly after he began to work in comics, Gaiman was approached by representatives of DC Comics to see if he could revitalize any of that major publisher's stable of characters. He picked the female crimefighter the Black Orchid and wrote a determinedly unconventional script that begins with blunt violence where readers have learned to expect talky temporizing ("I've read all the comics," the gangster says, "So . . . I'm not going to set up some kind of complicated LASER BEAM DEATHTRAP, then leave you alone to escape. . . . I'm going to kill you. NOW.") and concludes a long buildup toward violent confrontation with the villains' discovery that they can't bring themselves to attack the heroine because she is simply too *wonderful* to hurt. Gaiman's script is a striking, if not quite convincing, treatment of conflict, and Dave McKean's painted panels reinforce the *un*comicbook mood.

Before taking a chance on publishing a lushly illustrated work by a new writer, however, DC suggested it would be advisable to build Gaiman's reputation by doing a monthly comic for awhile. After brief consideration, Gaiman suggested the idea of *The Sandman.* The magazine was an immediate popular and critical success. It was the mainstay of DC's Vertigo subdivision and was a consistent prize winner from its beginning in 1988 until Gaiman chose to end it in late 1995. All the stories from the monthly have been collected in reprint albums, with introductions by the likes of Clive

Barker, Harlan Ellison, Samuel R. Delany, and Gene Wolfe. In total, it is an immensely rich, subtle exploration of Gaiman's concerns.

Part of the magazine's interest is due to Gaiman's presentation of the titular character. Continuing characters in fantastic comic books are usually either mere hosts who introduce the stories' actual characters or superbeings whose exploits are themselves the stories. The Sandman's relation to other characters—and the magazine's readers—is more complicated. The first issue of *The Sandman* begins with a group of occultists plotting to trap Death so they can live forever. The victim of their conjuring, however, is Someone Else. As Gaiman describes him in a synopsis that begins *The Doll's House* (first-published of the albums but containing issues #8-16 of the magazine), "The Man in the circle was dressed in black, His head hidden by a helm carved of bone, and glass, and metal. Fires danced in the velvet darkness of His robe; around His neck hung a precious stone, a ruby; and by His side was a leathern pouch, drawn tight at the top by cords." While helpless, he is stripped naked and imprisoned in an airless glass globe; the humans realize this is a being of immense power, but they do not know what to make of him. Readers, too, are not sure how to approach the character. His face is not even seen until over halfway through the story—lean, pale, grim, with sunken eyes and dark, shaggy hair. Only in the last pages of that issue, when he escapes his prison, does he show some of his powers as Morpheus, Lord Dream. To some extent, thus, readers identify with Dream; however, readers also are shoved away from the character, aware that they do know and perhaps can know very little about him. He reminds us of the comment in Miller's Batman album, quoted with approval by Gaiman, that heroes are too big to understand, let alone judge.

References throughout the series make it possible to piece together Dream's background as one of seven powerful, supernatural beings, the Endless, along with his older brothers, cowled Destiny and burly Destruction, his cute and perky older sister Death, and his three younger sisters, androgynous Desire, grim Despair, and feckless Delerium. Though the Endless sometimes appear in religious rituals, they are not gods. Gods die with their worshipers; the Endless continue. They appear to represent categories of experience, reflecting the way intelligence organizes life. According to Gaiman, mythologies are "the stories that we tell each other to try and make sense of the world." The Endless embody that effort.

Readers were not given all that background initially, of course, and Gaiman has presented the basic situation with considerable ambiguity. The human character Rose Walker, looking back on her nightmarish experience in *The Doll's House,* interprets it as meaning that people are "just dolls. We don't have a clue what's really going down, we just kid ourselves that we're in control of our lives while a paper's thickness away things that would drive us mad if we thought about them for too long play with us." Just a few pages later, however, Dream warns Desire not to meddle in human affairs: "We of the endless are the servants of the living—we are NOT their masters. We exist because they know, deep in their hearts, that we exist. . . . We are their toys. Their dolls, if you will."

In the character of the Sandman himself, Gaiman illustrates this uncertainty. Dream has supernatural powers and proudly declares his superiority to mortals. On the other hand, Dream frequently makes mistakes because he fails to understand human relationships; he doesn't know how to make the kind of response humans do because we appreciate our weakness and know how much we depend on each other. Death is more sympathetic because she is in touch with people daily and because she periodically becomes human herself to feel what that condition is like. Dream tends to retreat to his separate realm, insulated from much direct human contact.

Or at least this is how things *seem* to be. Remember Dream's assertion that the Endless reflect humanity, rather than the other way round. Interrupting the grim *Doll's House* main storyline is "Men of Good Fortune," in which Death and Dream inform a contemporary of Chaucer's that he can go on living as long as he wishes; Dream chats with the man every hundred years after that, until the man highly offends Dream late in the nineteenth century by presuming to guess that Dream continues their meetings because of loneliness, a need for friendship. Dream angrily storms out. In contemporary times, therefore, the man is pleasantly surprised when Dream shows up again, remarking that "I have always heard it was impolite to keep one's friends waiting." Dream is consistently remote, too large to approach in human terms; yet he startles readers by revealing feelings that he either has found in his nature as created out of mortal yearnings or, perhaps, has learned by experience with humans. Samuel R. Delany sees this as the basis of Gaiman's work, focussing his introduction to *A Game of You* on the characters' interpersonal relationships—playing the game of *you* rather than withdrawing into the game of *I*.

This has a great deal to do with the way Gaiman has chosen to end the series, with the Sandman's death and his replacement by another embodiment of Dream. Morpheus must die because he has shed family blood and thus become fair prey for the Furies, "The Kindly Ones." What actually has happened is that Dream has given the boon of death to the severed head of his son, Orpheus, centuries after he declared he would have nothing further to do with the young man for entering Hades to retrieve Euridice. At that point, Calliope, Orpheus' mother, made the harsh judgment that Morpheus "cannot share anything; any part of himself. I thought I could CHANGE him. But HE does not change. He WILL not. Perhaps he CAN not." Events prove this to be untrue. Dream fully understands that releasing Orpheus is an absolute violation of inhuman, unchanging rules. He *must* do it, though, for his own personal, human reasons. Readers are left with the unanswerable question of how long Dream has been preparing for the act of mercy that ends Orpheus's mutilated existence. As Death remarks, shortly before she ends her brother's present existence, "you've been making [preparations for death] for AGES. You just didn't let yourself know that was what you were doing." One translation of "Morpheus" is, after all, *Shaper.*

We shape our dreams, yet are shaped by them. That is true of humans and appears to be true of The Sandman too. Sometimes our dreams are dark. From *Violent Cases* on, Gaiman has shown his understanding of how ready humans are to give away their individual perceptions. In Gaiman's *The Compleat Alice Cooper,* the Showman offers young adolescents a trade: He'll remove the future's uncertainty if they give up its potential; although the protagonist rejects the deal, the Showman is still waiting patiently at the album's end. In his recent short story "Snow, Glass, Apples," Gaiman upends the tale of Snow White, with an heroic queen using benign witchcraft to protect her subjects from an inhuman girl-creature that mimes wholesomeness; readers know too well which version of the story has survived. And finally, taking over the *Miracleman* comic series from Alan Moore, Gaiman has begun showing the mingled attraction and horror of living in a world with godlike superheroes.

Gaiman's major work to date, however, is the *Sandman* series. Like most superior fiction *The Sandman* supplies fewer answers than sharply focused questions. In "A Midsummer Night's Dream," winner of the World Fantasy Award for best short story of 1990, Dream brings together a troupe of Elizabethan actors and an audience from Faerie. Dream has commissioned a play from one of the performers, previously a fumbling young hack encountered in "'Men of Good Fortune'" as Will Shaxberd. As part of his bargain with Dream, William Shakespeare will have access to "the great stories"; as Dream says, "Through him they will live for an age of man; and his words will echo down through time." Yet Shakespeare's son Hamnet complains to one of the actors that stories are all the writer cares about now: "If I DIED, he's just write a PLAY about it. 'Hamnet.'" Dream himself ponders whether giving Shakespeare what he most desired was the right thing to do. The story raises larger questions, however. Seen in the overall context of the series, references suggest that even centuries ago Dream was (unconsciously?) beginning to prepare for Orpheus' and his own deaths. And where do Shakespeare's "stories" come from: Is *Hamlet,* for example, one of the eternal tales of humanity or was it produced by one individual's circumstances—such as his frustrated, helpless grief at his son's death? But *which* oblivious father and rebellious son are the real subjects here? What *The Sandman* suggests finally, is that we can discover all manner of horror and hope within ourselves.

This a writer to watch. One way we transitory humans can get in touch with something larger than ourselves is by listening to stories, and Neil Gaiman tells honest tales.

—Joe Sanders

GALAXAN, Sol. *See* **COPPEL, Alfred.**

GALLUN, Raymond Z(inke)

Pseudonym: William Callahan. **Nationality:** American. **Born:** Beaver Dam, Wisconsin, 22 March 1911. **Education:** University of Wisconsin, Madison, 1929-30; Alliance Française, Paris, 1938-39; San Marcos University, Lima, Peru, 1960. **Family:** Married 1) Frieda E. Talmey in 1959 (died 1974); 2) Bertha Erickson Backman in 1978. **Career:** Construction worker for Army Corps of Engineers, 1942-43; marine blacksmith, Pearl Harbor Navy Yard, 1944; technical writer, EDO Corporation, College Point, New York, 1964-75. **Awards:** Fandom Hall of Fame award, 1979. **Died:** 2 April 1994.

SCIENCE FICTION PUBLICATIONS

Novels

People Minus X: A Science Fiction Novel. New York, Simon and Schuster, 1957.

The Planet Strappers. New York, Pyramid, 1961.
The Eden Cycle. New York, Ballantine, 1974.
Skyclimber: The Literary Adventures and Autobiography of Raymond Z. Gallun, with Jeffrey M. Elliot. New York, Tower Books, 1981.
Bioblast! New York, Berkley, 1985.

Short Stories

The Machine That Thought (as William Callahan). New York, Columbia, 1942?
The Best of Raymond Z. Gallun, edited by John J. Pierce. New York, Ballantine, 1978.
The Great Illusion, with others. Wallsend, England, Tyne and Wear, 1973.

OTHER PUBLICATIONS

Other

Starclimber (autobiography). San Bernardino, California, Borgo Press, 1991.

*

Raymond Z. Gallun comments:

(1985) Most of my science fiction was originally published in the 1930s, mainly in *Astounding* while F. Orlin Tremaine, whom I remember with appreciation, was editor. I think I aimed mostly at realism insofar as it could be constructed from what was then supposed to be true about the various planets, plus humanizing of even the unhuman characters, giving them points of sympathetic contact without overdoing the sympathy. Sometime after World War II I dropped out of SF to do other things. Being now retired from formal employment, I have been trying to get back into SF writing. "Then and Now" (*Analog,* December 1977) is a fair example of what I have been recently trying to do.

* * *

Raymond Z. Gallun has published in the pulps vast quantities of clumsy and primitive fiction, and yet his treatments of several of the more sophisticated problems facing modern man are often exciting and provocative to read. He is a vintage science fiction pulp writer from the 1930s who published his most ambitious novel in the 1970s. One critic has labeled his underlying philosophy "Darwinian existentialism"; and two short quotations from what Gallun himself has called his favorite short story, "The Restless Tide," will introduce the stark polarities that he continually balances in his best work. At the end of the story, the protagonist concludes, "Mankind was like a rough, sturdy plant, growing, thrusting; crude but magnificent, and caught between rot and fire." Earlier he had exhorted his wife, "It's the contrasts that count. There's a rough drama in people."

Gallun's novel *The Eden Cycle* is a fine expansion of these earlier themes. The Hegelian balancing of opposites along with the classic polar opposition, which is also a key to the meaning for us of Darwinian theory, between the glory of early primitive development and the continual trend toward greater sophistication, are well developed in this long narration of the most advanced human he-

donists governed by aliens. In fact, for Gallun the contrasts that run throughout his fictions are so roughly vivid that they become emblematic of what the Renaissance loved to call man's amphibian nature. Aliens are presented as complex and sympathetic characters early—"Old Faithful" (1934)—and then throughout his career. In addition to the rough contrast of man to alien, there is repeatedly drawn the contrast of creature to environment, as in "Godson of Almarlu," as well as the contrast of past to present. Science fiction lends itself particularly well to the old opposition between a golden age of the past and a modern iron age because SF tries to image both technology and man's inner primitive self. Gallun's work conveys these oppositions continually in the narratives mentioned above and in such pieces as *People Minus X,* "Return of a Legend," and "The Lotus-Engine."

Rough contrast is also a most appropriate characterization for the literary impressions of Gallun's extrapolations. For example, "The Lotus-Engine" makes skillful use of the classic Homeric myth of the lotus eaters and also weaves a most explicit set of images to convey again the old story of mutability and decline associated with technological advance. But even in this story the pulp characterizations of "old chums" must enter, and the characters even smoke cigarettes inside the oxygen rich helmets of their "space armor." A genre that can retell the most profound human dilemmas in what are often such rough forms is indeed sturdy and growing, and Gallun was one sturdy and often rough writer who contributed greatly to its growth.

—Donald M. Hassler

GALOUYE, Daniel F(rancis)

Nationality: American. **Born:** New Orleans, Louisiana, 11 February 1920. **Education:** Louisiana State University, Baton Rouge, B.A. in journalism 1941. **Military Service:** Served as a pilot in the United States Navy, 1941-46: Lieutenant in Naval Reserve. **Family:** Married Carmel Barbara Jordan in 1945; two daughters. **Career:** Reporter, then assistant news editor, 1946-55, chief editorial writer, 1955-60, and associate editor, 1960-65, *New Orleans States-Item.* Consultant, New Orleans Science Center and Planetarium Committee. **Died:** 7 September 1976.

SCIENCE FICTION PUBLICATIONS

Novels

Dark Universe. New York, Bantam, 1961; London, Gollancz, 1962.
Lords of the Psychon. New York, Bantam, 1963.
Counterfeit World. London, Gollancz, 1964; as *Simulacron-3,* New York, Bantam, 1964.
The Lost Perception. London, Gollancz, 1966; as *A Scourge of Screamers,* New York, Bantam, 1968.
The Infinite Man. New York, Bantam, 1973.

Short Stories

The Last Leap and Other Stories of the Super Mind. London, Corgi, 1964.

Project Barrier. London, Gollancz, 1968.

* * *

Daniel F. Galouye, a greatly underrated and largely forgotten writer, is probably best remembered for the numerous short stories and novelettes in the science fiction "slicks" of the 1950s and 1960s. However, his primary contribution to the field rests in three novels: *Dark Universe, Simulacron-3* (published in the U.S. as *Counterfeit World*), and *Lords of the Psychon.* Always well-conceived, well-planned, and well-crafted, Galouye's stories are extrapolations of scientific fact or theory, but his vivid and far-ranging imagination and his incredible attention to detail often carry his readers well into the fantastic. These characteristics are most visible in the novels where the length permits the accumulation of detail to achieve its full impact.

Though many of Galouye's stories use a post-disaster motif, they reflect his optimistic belief in the capability of man to develop his latent mental abilities, and often the resolutions of his plots depend upon the evolvement of such talents as astral projection, extended vision, teleportation, and mental manipulation of matter or energy. Curiously, he often depicts faster-than-light spaceships powered by psychokinesis, as in "The Centipedes of Space" and "Phantom World." His ultimate statement on human development, however, is found in "The Secret of the Immortals," where he proposes a metamorphosis that not only brings new mental powers but an extended life of at least 5,000 years.

Galouye's work also displays a preoccupation with the idea that man may be manipulated by external forces, and often the world of the story is a microcosm of some vaster universe. This concept frequently takes the form of a puppet motif. One of the most unusual twists on this theme occurs in "Gulliver Planet," where microscopic aliens invade the bodies of seven humans and manipulate them as part of their invasion plan. The theme's unique treatment, however, comes in *Simulacron-3,* where Doug Hall, the protagonist, discovers that he is merely an electric analogue in a total electronic simulation of the real world.

Galouye's overriding concern is the nature of reality and the related problem of perceiving it. Most of his stories and his three best novels treat this theme. *Dark Universe* deals with a colony that has survived a worldwide atomic war by retreating underground. One of 17 such colonies, "U.S. Survival Complex Number Eleven" functions well until a minor fault shift totally destroys its ability to generate electricity and cuts off all but a few of the superheated water conduits that lead to the group's basic living chamber. Through succeeding generations, the loss of sight and the disintegration of their knowledge of their original world creates a culture totally dependent on sound for survival and ignorant of their true circumstances. The story concerns the attempt of one young man, Jared Fenton, to discover what light really is. The novel's status as a minor classic comes from Galouye's treatment and control of his material. His elimination of all words from the narrative that relate to sight and his passages which describe how Fenton uses his non-visual senses to perceive his world are brilliantly effective.

Simulacron-3, an extremely original work, also treats the nature of reality. Doug Hall discovers that his world is but an electromathematical model of an average community and that it is marked for extinction. In an ironic reversal of roles, he manages to change places with the real Doug Hall, the megalomaniacal operator of the simulator, and prevent his world from being erased. *Lords of the*

Psychon, though not quite so well-controlled as *Dark Universe* or so original as *Simulacron-3,* is a post-destruction story that concerns the efforts of Geoffrey Maddox to prevent aliens from drawing Earth into another dimension. In the process of fighting them, he learns that he can mentally manipulate the fundamental form of matter, a pink plasma called psychon, and he proves that it is itself merely a reflection of the mental.

Galouye's major weakness is his relatively shallow characterization. It is often difficult to distinguish between his parade of military protagonists, and his women are seldom more than helpless sex objects. Where he has the time to infuse his narrative with detail, however, his principal characters manage to become more than cardboard cutouts. Originality, control, and fast pace are typical of his best writing.

—Carl B. Yoke

GARDNER, Craig Shaw

Nationality: American. **Born:** Rochester, New York, 2 July 1949. **Education:** Boston University. President, Horror Writers of America, since 1990. **Agent:** Merrilee Heifetz, Writers House, 21 West 26th Street, New York, New York 10010. **Address:** P.O. Box 458, Cambridge, Massachusetts 02238, U.S.A.

SCIENCE FICTION PUBLICATIONS

Novels (series: Arabian Nights; Batman; Cineverse; Dragon Circle; Ebezenum; Wuntvor)

A Malady of Magicks (Ebezenum). New York, Ace, 1986; London, Headline, 1988.
A Multitude of Monsters (Ebezenum). New York, Ace, 1986; London, Headline, 1988.
A Night in the Netherhells (Ebezenum). New York, Ace, 1987; London, Headline, 1989.
A Difficulty with Dwarves (Wuntvor). New York, Ace, 1987; London, Headline, 1989.
The Exploits of Ebenezum (includes *A Malady of Magicks, A Multitude of Monsters,* and *A Night in the Netherhells*). Garden City, New York, Doubleday, 1987.
The Lost Boys: A Novel (novelization of screenplay). New York, Berkley, 1987; London, Bantam, 1988.
An Excess of Enchantments (Wuntvor). New York, Ace, 1988; London, Headline, 1989.
Wishbringer (novelization of a computer game). New York, Avon, 1988.
A Disagreement with Death (Wuntvor). New York, Ace, and London, Headline, 1989.
Back to the Future, Part II: A Novel (novelization of screenplay). New York, Berkley, and London, Headline, 1989.
The Wanderings of Wuntvor (includes *A Difficulty with Dwarves, An Excess of Enchantments,* and *A Disagreement with Death*). Garden City, New York, Doubleday, 1989.
Batman (novelization of screenplay). New York, Warner, and London, Futura, 1989.
The Other Sinbad (Arabian Nights). London, Headline, and New York, Ace, 1991.

Back to the Future Part III (novelization of screenplay). New York, Berkley, and London, Firecrest, 1990.

The Cineverse Cycle. New York, Guild America, 1991; as *The Cineverse Cyle Omnibus,* London, Headline, 1992.

Slaves of the Volcano God. London, Headline, and New York, Ace, 1989.

Bride of the Slime Monster. New York, Ace, 1990.

Revenge of the Fluffy Bunnies. London, Headline, and New York, Ace, 1990.

The Batman Murders. New York, Warner, 1990; London, Penguin, 1991.

The Other Sinbad (Arabian Nights). London, Headline, and New York, Ace, 1991.

A Bad Day for Ali Baba (Arabian Nights). London, Headline, 1991; New York, Ace, 1992.

Batman Returns. New York, Warner, and London, Mandarin, 1992.

Scheherazade's Night Out (Arabian Nights). London, Headline, 1992; as *The Last Arabian Night,* New York, Ace, 1993.

Raven Walking (Dragon Circle). London, Heinemann, 1994; as *Dragon Sleeping,* New York, Ace, 1994.

Dragon Waking (Dragon Circle). London, Heinemann, and New York, Ace, 1995.

Short Stories

Author of uncollected short stories.

*

Craig Shaw Gardner comments:

I've had at least three careers so far in science fiction. The first was as a "promising young writer" (I was written up as such in *Fantasy Review* along with Steve Rasnic Tenn and Al Sarantonio). I next became one of those Funny Fantasy guys (along with Bob Asprin, Terry Pratchett, et. al.) for my steady-selling Ebezenum and Cineverse series. Even more recently, I became the bestselling author of Batman; thanks to the most successful of those novelizations, I did keep food on the table.

Who knows what's next?

* * *

Humorous science fiction and fantasy have always been viewed within the genre as a kind of poor cousin, amusing enough when you read it but with no true lasting power as literature, as though it were somehow less an achievement to make the reader laugh than to provide suspense, adventure, or drama. Incidental jokes within the context of an adventure are acceptable, but a broad spoof is assumed to be transient and of little importance. Fantasy has been somewhat more tolerant of this literary form, but even there humor has generally been suspect at novel length at least until recently. Part of this may be because it is indeed difficult to maintain a genuinely humorous tone at greater lengths. It is especially surprising therefore that Craig Shaw Gardner acquired an enviable reputation based almost entirely on two series of amusing fantasy and science fiction novels.

Gardner introduced his marvelously funny wizard, Ebenezum, in short stories such as "A Drama of Dragons" and "A Gathering of Ghosts," and their popularity eventually led to their incorporation into an episodic novel, *A Malady of Magicks,* in 1986. Ebenezum crosses swords with an inept demon, and the spell which was supposed to kill him actually only served to make him allergic to magic. The opening stages of his quest for a cure form the first

of six hilariously entertaining book-length adventures of the wizard and his apprentice, Wuntvor.

The immediate follow-up was *A Multitude of Monsters.* Still inflicted with his allergy, Ebenezum faces a fresh round of attacks from the vengeful demon Guxx, as well as the complications that arise from the presence of an organization of inhuman creatures determined to secure equal billing with human beings and other, more popular, mythical figures. Rounding out the first trilogy was *A Night in the Netherhells.* Unable to destroy the wizard, Guxx steals the city which holds his cure, necessitating a journey to hell itself. Although he is able to thwart Guzz's immediate intention, his curse only becomes worse.

Ebenezum's adverse reaction to magic is now contagious, spreading throughout the magical community, so his apprentice Wuntvor sets off on his own in the opening volume of a second trilogy, *A Difficulty with Dwarves,* followed in due course by *An Excess of Enchantments* and *A Disagreement with Death.* Wuntvor must travel to far lands, outwit a powerful and malevolent witch, and then escape the clutches of Death personified before his journey can be brought to a close. Through all six books, Gardner makes use of an irreverent, slapstick style of humor heavily reliant on anachronisms and literary sight gags.

Gardner brought the same brisk, entertaining style to *Wishbringer,* a novel inspired by the Infocom interactive text adventure game. The town of Festeron is transformed magically, with all of its good elements mirroring evil ones, and only the protagonist is able to remember what it was like before. Now he is the only hope the citizens have to escape the enchantment and return to their former lifestyles.

Gardner wrote several creditable novelizations during this period as well. *Batman*'s darker humor was something of a departure, and *Batman Returns* was an even more twisted and savage look at the comic book hero's career. His novelizations of the "Back to the Future" film series did an excellent job of capturing the humor of that series. *The Lost Boys,* on the other hand and despite moments of dark humor, is a serious tale of horror unlike anything Gardner had previously written at novel length, although he was already starting to drift in that direction in some of his short stories, most notably "The Three Faces of Night," "Walk Home Alone," and "She Closed Her Eyes."

In 1989, Gardner started a new trilogy, science fiction this time, but also a return to the wacky, exaggerated style of his earlier fantasies. *Slaves of the Volcano God* is the first in the Cineverse Cycle. The Cineverse is a kind of alternate universe that occasionally impinges on the real world. Within its confines, all of the institutions of classic films, particularly the "B" films, are reality. Heroes are really heroes, and sidekicks know their place; heroines are invariably gorgeous and waiting to be rescued, and no act is too despicable for the villains.

The protagonist, Roger Gordon, comes into possession of a Captain Crusader decoder ring that enables him to cross the barrier between worlds. In order to rescue the woman he loves, he must make his way through westerns, jungle adventures, and the romantic Pacific. Although he triumphs against Dr. Dread in the early going, Gordon must persevere through *Bride of the Slime Monster* and *Revenge of the Fluffy Bunnies.* Gardner lampoons numerous "B" movie conventions along the way, wisely keeping the individual adventures short and fast-paced so that the gimmicks of the Cineverse don't become too repetitive.

Two other short stories, both fantasies, stand out from that same period, "A Malacy of Magicks," one of his very first published stories, and "Demon Luck" from the shared universe Ithkar series. Gardner has yet to write a serious, original science fiction novel but his humor is genuinely funny, and his writing skills are sufficient to put him in good stead no matter in which direction his future lies. A recent original story, "Kraven the Hunter Is Dead," makes use of the Marvel Comics character Spiderman.

Gardner's most recent novel is *The Dragon Sleeping,* opening volume of a series ostensibly aimed at younger readers although it makes few concessions in that direction. A neighborhood is physically removed from our world and materializes in another, where two rival magical forces are at war. The majority of those thus transported are captured by one side, which claims to represent the forces of good, although a few children escape and meet representatives from the other side, who are clearly more likable. Although fantasy, the novel has the same feel as some of the early Heinlein juveniles, adult plots and themes surrounding adolescent characters rather than children's stories.

Gardner's fiction is difficult to categorize because he writes everything from humor to horror, adventure to satire, original work and novelizations, adult and young adult. It is the mark of most successful writers that they are willing to strike out in new directions, and that would seem to indicate a promising future.

—Don D'Ammassa

GARNETT, David

Pseudonyms: David Lee; David Ferring. Also writes as Dav Garnett. **Nationality:** British. **Address:** West Grange, Ferring Grange Gardens, Ferring, West Sussex BN12 5HS, England.

SCIENCE FICTION PUBLICATIONS

Novels (series: Warhammer-Konrad)

Mirror in the Sky (as Dav Garnett). New York, Berkley, 1969; London, Hale, 1973.
The Starseekers (as Dav Garnett). New York, Berkley, 1971; London, Hale, 1975.
Time in Eclipse. London, Hale, 1974.
Destiny Past (as David Lee). London, Hale, 1974.
The Forgotten Dimension. London, Hale, 1975.
Phantom Universe. London, Hale, 1975.
The Hills Have Eyes, Part 2 (novelization of screenplay; as David Ferring). London, Panther, 1984.
Konrad (as David Ferring). Brighton, East Sussex, GW Books, 1990.
Shadowbreed (as David Ferring; Warhammer). Brighton, East Sussex, GW Books, 1991.
Warblade (as David Ferring; Warhammer). London, Boxtree, 1993.

Short Stories

Cosmic Carousel. London, Hale, 1976.

OTHER PUBLICATIONS

Other

Editor, *The Orbit Science Fiction Yearbook.* London, Futura, 3 vols., 1988-90.

Editor, *Zenith: The Best in New British Science Fiction.* London, Sphere, 1989.
Editor, *Zenith 2: The Best in New British Science Fiction.* London, Orbit, 1990.
Editor, *New Worlds.* London, Gollancz, 3 vols., 1991-93.

*   *   *

David Garnett's first novel, *Mirror in the Sky,* written in 1967 when the author was 19, is an anti-Vietnam War novel. It draws upon elements of Heinlein's *Starship Troopers,* viewing them from a different perspective. In *Mirror in the Sky,* the infantry of the future fights an endless war against an unknown enemy, and, through a drug in their daily rations, are programmed to obey orders. They have been taught (falsely) that their enemy can mimic humans perfectly, which is why the aliens appear identical to the human troops.

The Starseekers is a comedy in which the richest man on Earth flees his native planet in order to escape numerous creditors, including various ex-wives and tax authorities. This is William Ewart—the first names of Prime Minister Gladstone—and his pretext for leaving is an archeological expedition, which leads to many galactic adventures. The book takes numerous swipes at many of science fiction's clichés, from interstellar secret agents to space pirates.

After these space war and space opera books, Garnett wrote in 1969 a sword-and-sorcery novel, but *Phantom Universe* remained unpublished until it was given a science fiction rationale—the mind of a space pilot is trapped within the body of a character in a fantasy world.

Garnett's fourth novel, written in 1970, had been published several months earlier. *The Forgotten Dimension* treats yet another basic SF theme, that of revolution. The subtext is one of racism, which is emphasized by the discovery that humankind is descended from a race of another dimension.

Cosmic Carousel is Garnett's first collection of short stories. This includes reprints from *Fantasy and Science Fiction* and *New Writings in Science Fiction,* as well as two stories that were condensed from unpublished novels written in 1969, "Adventures of a Stone Age Man" and "Forever Changes."

In 1970, at the age of 23, Garnett wrote the last of his early novels. *Time in Eclipse* is without doubt his finest novel. Set in a future Europe that has reverted to feudalism, the book encompasses a whole spectrum of science fictional themes: underground civilizations, time travel, endless war, aliens, androids, computers.

Garnett has written numerous other books in various genres, and under various pseudonyms, returning to science fiction with only a handful of short stories, like "Still Life" (in *Fantasy and Science Fiction,* nominated for a Hugo) and "The Only One" (in *Interzone,* nominated for The British Science Fiction Award).

Since 1987, Garnett has been one of the instigators of a new spate of all-British SF anthologies, as well as an editor of the best of the year collection, *The Orbit Science Fiction Yearbook.* Of more significance, however, were the two Zenith anthologies, which showcased established British SF authors, such as Aldiss and Moorcock, as well as encouraging new talents. His latest venture as editor is a resurrection after 12 years of the highly influential new wave magazine/anthology *New Worlds.*

—David Wingrove

GARRETT, Gordon. *See* GARRETT, Randall.

GARRETT, (Gordon) Randall

Pseudonyms: Gordon Aghill; Alexander Blade; Walter Bupp; Ralph Burke; Gordon Garrett; David Gordon; Richard Greer; Ivar Jorgensen; Darrel T. Langart; Clyde T. Mitchell; Mark Phillips; Robert Randall; Leonard G. Spencer; S.M. Tenneshaw; Gerald Vance. **Nationality:** American. **Born:** Lexington, Missouri, 16 December 1927. **Education:** Texas Tech University, Lubbock, B.S. **Military Service:** Served in the United States Marine Corps during World War II: Corporal. **Family:** Married Vicki Ann Heydron. **Career:** Industrial chemist, Battle Creek, Michigan, and Peoria, Illinois; then freelance writer. **Died:** 31 December 1987.

Science Fiction Publications

Novels (series: Gandalara; Lord Darcy; Nidor)

The Shrouded Planet (Nidor; with Robert Silverberg as Robert Randall). New York, Gnome Press, 1957.
The Dawning Light (Nidor; with Robert Silverberg as Robert Randall). New York, Gnome Press, 1959.
Pagan Passions, with Laurence M. Janifer. New York, Galaxy, 1959.
Unwise Child. Garden City, New York, Doubleday, 1962; London, Mayflower, 1963; as *Starship Death,* New York, Leisure, 1982.
Anything You Can Do . . . (as Darrel T. Langart). Garden City, New York, Doubleday, and London, Mayflower, 1963; as Randall Garrett, New York, Lancer, 1969.
Too Many Magicians (Lord Darcy). Garden City, New York, Doubleday, 1967; London, Macdonald, 1968.
The River Wall (Gandalara), with Vicki Ann Heydron. New York, Bantam, 1986.
The Gandalara Cycle, with Vicki Ann Heydron. New York, Bantam, 2 vols., 1986.
  The Steel of Raithskar. New York, Bantam, 1981.
  The Glass of Dyskornis. New York, Bantam, 1982.
  The Bronze of Eddarta. New York, Bantam, 1983.
  The Well of Darkness. New York, Bantam, 1983.
  The Search for Kä. New York, Bantam, 1984.
  Return to Eddarta. New York, Bantam, 1985.

Novels as Mark Phillips (with Laurence M. Janifer; series: Kenneth J. Malone in all titles)

Brain Twister: A Science-Fiction Novel. New York, Pyramid, 1962.
The Impossibles. New York, Pyramid, 1963.
Supermind. New York, Pyramid, 1963.

Short Stories (series: Lord Darcy)

Takeoff! Virginia Beach, Donning, 1980.
Murder and Magic (Lord Darcy). New York, Ace, 1979.
Lord Darcy Investigates. New York, Ace, 1981.
The Best of Randall Garrett, edited by Robert Silverberg. New York, Timescape, 1982.

Lord Darcy: A 3-in-1 Volume (includes *Too Many Magicians, Murder and Magic,* and *Lord Darcy Investigates*). Garden City, New York, Doubleday, 1983.
Takeoff Too! Norfolk, Virginia, Donning, 1987.

Other

Pope John XXIII, Pastoral Prince. Derby, Connecticut, Monarch, 1962.
A Gallery of the Saints. Derby, Connecticut, Monarch, 1963.

*   *   *

Randall Garrett paid his dues writing under a bewildering number of pseudonyms for the magazines of the 1950s, and most of his stories are firmly set in the idea-oriented action adventure frame of the *Astounding* "house style." Character and description are kept firmly subordinate to concept and event, and, however useful this period may have been in teaching him his craft, the results are usually routine. For example, compare "There's No Fool" with Asimov's "Belief." The theme in both is essentially emotional rather than intellectual: How do you convince someone of something he "knows" to be impossible? Where Garrett treats the theme in an externalised fashion, Asimov takes us inside the emotional confusion of his characters. "Despoilers of the Golden Empire" (in *Takeoff*), to give another example, is a pure literary trick, retelling the life of Pizarro in terms of the clichés of space opera. Also enjoyable from this early period is his parody of Gernsbackian optimism, "Masters of the Metropolis" (with Lin Carter) and the "Her Majesty's FBI" sequence ("Brain Twister," "The Impossibles," and "Supermind").

The early stories, although superficial in many ways, are never less than entertaining, and occasionally there appears a unity of theme and style that is exceptional and which produces a strength of effect above Garrett's routine level. In "But I Don't Think" he produces an early example of his love of inverting the themes of classic science fiction in a black parody of *The Space Merchants.* A privileged member of an autocratic society is suddenly thrust into its lowest depths. Where Pohl and Kornbluth's hero joins the underground and learns humanity, Garrett's character shoots his serf benefactress and returns cringing to duty. "The Destroyers" is the story of a society doomed by outsiders seeking to liberate it. It concentrates on mood rather than action, allowing most of the major events to occur "offstage." And "The Queen Bee" is a dark little story of selfishness and justice among the survivors of a starship crash.

In the 1960s and 1970s Garrett produced the series he is best remembered for: the Lord Darcy stories. Set in a world where the Angevin Empire has survived into the 20th century, and where magic has become the dominant science and technology, the stories centre on the detective Lord Darcy of Rouen and his "forensic magician," Master Sean O'Lochlainn. It is notoriously difficult to write classically "fair" detective stories in a science-fictional world, and one would think that the addition of magic, whose fundamental laws are unknown to the reader until Garrett explains them, would make the task impossible. But all the Lord Darcy series are perfect puzzle stories: the best of them, the novel *Too Many Magicians,* has been voted one of the best "locked room" mysteries of all time, and the conclusion is one of the most satisfactory I've ever read; the solution is one you feel you should have spotted and the sensation of pieces sliding artistically into place in one's mind is one every mystery fan will appreciate.

The stories successfully parody all the major figures in the 20th-century detective story: Rex Stout in the person of the Marquis of London, Dorothy L. Sayers in the opening of "The Ipswich Phial," Agatha Christie in "The Napoli Express," and Conan Doyle just about everywhere. The continuation of the series after Garrett's death has been less happy.

In the 1970s Garrett's output declined with his increasing ill-health, but the quality of his work improved. Among his shorter pieces might be mentioned "The Final Fighting of Fion Mac Cumhail" and the Lovecraftian pastiche "The Horror out of Time." He began (but did not live to quite finish) the Gandalara series (written with his wife Vicki Ann Heydron), a fine sword-and-psionics adventure set in a desert world. The two *Takeoff!* collections contain some of the best of his lighter work and should not be allowed to go out of print; future generations of fans will be rediscovering Garrett for a long while. Some far-sighted publisher should put together a collection of Garrett's darker short work.

—Michael Cule

GEMMELL, David A.

Nationality: British. **Born:** London, England, 1 August 1948. **Education:** Attended Faraday Comprehensive School. **Family:** Married to Valerie Gemmell; one son, one daughter. **Career:** Worked for Pepsi Cola, London, 1965; reporter and editor, *Westminster Press,* London, 1966-72; editor, *Hastings Observer,* 1976; editor, *Folkstone Herald,* 1984. Since 1986, full-time writer. **Address:** 180 Mill Lang, Hastings, England.

SCIENCE FICTION PUBLICATIONS

Novels (series: Drenai; Hawk Queen; Macedon; Sipstrassi)

Legend (Drenai). London, Century, 1984; as *Against the Horde,* Delavan, Wisconsin, New Infinities, 1988; under original title, New York, Ballantine, 1994.
The King beyond the Gate (Drenai). London, Century, 1985; Delavan, Wisconsin, New Infinities, 1988.
Waylander (Drenai). London, Century, 1986; Delavan, Wisconsin, New Infinities, 1988.
Wolf in Shadow (Sipstrassi). London, Legend, 1987; as *The Jerusalem Man,* New York, Baen, 1988.
Ghost King (Sipstrassi). London, Legend, 1988.
Last Sword of Power (Sipstrassi). London, Legend, 1988.
Knights of Dark Renown. London, Legend, 1989; New York, Ballantine, 1993.
The Lost Crown (juvenile). London, Hutchinson Children's, 1989.
The Last Guardian (Sipstrassi). London, Legend, 1989.
Lion of Macedon. London, Legend, 1990; New York, Ballantine, 1992.
Quest for Lost Heroes (Drenai). London, Legend, 1990; New York, Ballantine, 1995.
Dark Prince (Macedon). London, Legend, 1991; New York, Ballantine, 1993.
Drenai Tales (includes *Legend, Waylander,* and *The King beyond the Gate*). London, Legend, 1991.

Morningstar. London, Legend, 1992; New York, Ballantine, 1993.
Waylander II: In the Realm of the Wolf (Drenai). London, Legend, 1992.
Stones of Power: The Sipstrassi Omnibus (includes *Wolf in Shadow, Ghost King, Last Sword of Power,* and *The Last Guardian*). London, Legend, 1992.
Bloodstone (Sipstrassi). London, Legend, 1994.
Ironhand's Daughter (Hawk Queen). London, Legend, 1995.

Short Stories

The First Chronicles of Druss the Legend (Drenai). London, Legend, 1993.

*

David A. Gemmell comments:

In 1986, while sitting at a signing session in Birmingham, U.K., a young couple approached me. The man gave me a dog-eared copy of *Legend* and asked me to sign it. He was embarrassed and nervous, and when I had signed the book he walked away swiftly. The woman also walked away, but she looked back, stopped, and returned to the table.

"I just thought I'd tell you," she said, "that whenever Simon is feeling depressed, or things have gone wrong for him, he takes *Legend* from the shelf and reads his favourite sections. It always lifts him. I just thought I'd tell you that." I treasure that moment.

I write because I love the craft.

But I also write in the hope that the reader, upon finishing a Gemmell novel, will feel uplifted and perhaps even find his—or her—resolve to do good strengthened.

In real life, evil is often triumphant.

But not in Gemmell novels. Not ever!

*   *   *

At a time when fantasy writing is considered to be much the preserve of the female writer and aimed at a female audience, David A. Gemmell's very muscular style of heroic fantasy must come as something of a surprise to many first-time readers, and perhaps seem a little old-fashioned.

He draws on a tradition easily traced from Tolkien's *Lord of the Rings* to Robert E. Howard's *Conan,* namely, the small band of heroes who conquer against seemingly impossible odds, fired by a belief in justice and the need for a clear-cut morality.

Gemmell's Drenai stories epitomise this approach, regrettably to the point of formula. Reading the novels in quick succession can leave the reader uncertain as to which story he is actually reading, so familiar does the plot become. In essence, a small band of fighters oppose the ruling force within their country, gather a rag-tag army of followers around them, which is trained to become a fighting force par excellence. In the process, a young man will triumph over his personal doubts and weaknesses, and acquire the strength and determination to lead the army to victory.

It's an archetypal story, and one that has surely been done to death already, yet Gemmell's hard-driving prose brings new life to a tired warhorse, creating a genuinely inspiring story each time. Perhaps his soldiers die a little more cleanly than would be accurate given the circumstances, but Gemmell's descriptions of training, battle, and strategy are vividly written and absorbing to read, which must in part explain the colossal popularity of the Drenai stories.

His female characters, certainly in the Drenai stories, are for the most part very strong and capable women, warriors who stand alongside their men. Whether they represent admirable role models for women, or fulfil an adolescent fantasy is difficult to decide, but they are not offensive in their strength, and the emphasis is on their skills as fighters rather than their sexuality.

Gemmell has also subtly woven around the stock plot other less obvious themes. A religious element is embodied in the battle between the Source and Chaos, a recurrent theme in all his books. In the Drenai stories, the priests of the Source preach a passive acceptance of the difficulties inherent in this life, and claim to represent strength through turning the other cheek. For Gemmell, this seems to be insufficient, and in *Waylander,* first in the internal chronology of the stories, he shows the creation of a fighting force of priests, vaguely reminiscent of the Knights Templar, prepared to use their remarkable telepathic and magical powers in an active rather than passive fashion. They recur throughout the Drenai stories, while a similar group of fighters appear in *Knights of Dark Renown.*

Another theme, most fully explored in the novella, "Druss the Legend," but again recurrent in all his work, is that of the discrepancies between actual deed in battle and the stories that spring up around them. At the time of the story, Druss is a middle-aged man, overweight and tired, called to fight one last battle, not for his skills, but for the effect his presence will have on men's morale. Throughout the story, he is called on to refute the wilder myths, which is then contrasted with the disappointment of men as they meet the legend in the flesh. And yet, at the last, Druss fulfils the expectation of the legend one more time. Read in conjunction with the other Drenai tales, in which Druss features time and again as a name around which men are rallied, it gives a fascinating, and unexpected, insight into the nature of hero-worship. And in *Knights of Dark Renown,* an entire war is fought and won on the belief that Llaw Gyffes is leading a huge rebel force when in fact, since escaping from prison, he has retreated to a solitary hideout. Gemmell seems, time and again, to suggest that a legend has more force than reality, overcoming great odds if people will only believe. And indeed, if Gemmell's work can be said to offer any philosophy, it is that you don't know what you can do until you try.

His other main series of stories, the Sipstrassi stories, is much darker, and more equivocal than the Drenai stories, and in many respects less successful. Certainly, they present a good deal of confusion to the reader, with the first and fourth books concerning Jon Shannow, a futuristic cowboy in a post-catastrophe society, while the second and third books are apparently a re-interpretation of the story of Uther Pendragon. It is difficult to see the relationship between the two stories, although they are drawn together by the slenderest thread of the Sipstrassi stones, which give their possessor remarkable power over time and space, and by the comings and goings of the Rolynd, a group of people who originate from the lost realm of Atlantis, including a man who is variously referred to as Aristotle or Maedhlyn (Merlin), and who will re-appear in Gemmell's Macedon stories. It falls to Jon Shannow, however, to solve the mystery of the Atlantean destruction in a finale, in *The Last Guardian,* which manages to incorporate the power of the Sipstrassi, power-crazed Atlantean priests, a nuclear missile, the Bermuda Triangle, and the lost aeroplanes of Flight 19. Jon Shannow is a more complex man than his Drenai counterparts, a killer who struggles with moral complexities, all the while professing himself a Christian in search of Jerusalem. It seems to be Gemmell's intention to show his growing awareness of the prob-

lems of viewing life in a strictly black and white fashion in a society that views things in shades of grey. Ultimately, Gemmell seems uncomfortable with the gunslinging elements of the world he has created, while the Arthurian books in the series show him on familiar but well-presented territory.

Gemmell's *Lion of Macedon* and *The Dark Prince* concern the historical character Parmenion, strategos to Philip of Macedon, father of Alexander the Great. Gemmell skilfully blends fantasy and history in an exciting and highly readable fashion. In many respects, these two books combine the best of the Drenai stories, with their deeds of heroic valour, with the darker aspects of the Sipstrassi stories. Parmenion is, and will always remain, despite his skill and his courage, an outsider, and for all his success will be doomed to ultimate failure, a new but satisfying departure from Gemmell's inspirational stance. Sadly, however, the women in these two books take up a more conventional role, as all-powerful but meddling seers, schemers and plotters, which is a disappointment after the robust characters of his earlier novels but apparently in keeping with the society he portrays.

Ironhand's Daughter, Gemmell's most recent work, introduces a new series, The Hawk Queen, set in a Highland kingdom lately overrun and enslaved by the Outlanders, one of whom, Ranulph Gotasson, now intends to slaughter the Highlanders. The Highlanders, characteristically for a Gemmell novel, look back to the days of Ironhand, an almost mythical leader who, in common with King Arthur, is said to return when his people are in need of him. In this volume, the huntress Sigarni is revealed as the new leader of her people, Ironhand's daughter indeed, but as Cherith Baldry noted in *Vector* 183, "Sigarni's attitudes and way of life are so close to the masculine that a lot of this point is lost."

Clearly Gemmell has hit upon a winning formula, which he manages to sustain without too much repetition, producing attractive and readable fiction. Commercial success clearly dictates more of the same or similar, but it is not impossible that Gemmell will at some point surprise us all with a very different story.

—Maureen Speller

GENTLE, Mary

Nationality: British. **Born:** Eastbourne, Sussex, 29 March 1956. **Education:** Attended high school in Hastings, Sussex. **Career:** Has worked as movie projectionist, clerk, and civil servant.

SCIENCE FICTION PUBLICATIONS

Novels (series: Orthe; White Crow)

A Hawk in Silver (for children). London, Gollancz, 1977; New York, Lothrop Lee, 1985.
Golden Witchbreed (Orthe). London, Gollancz, 1983; New York, Morrow, 1984.
Ancient Light (Orthe). London, Gollancz, 1987; New York, Signet, 1989.
Rats and Gargoyles (White Crow). London, Bantam, 1990; New York, Roc, 1991.

The Architecture of Desire (White Crow). London, Bantam, 1991; New York, Roc, 1993.
Grunts! A Fantasy with Attitude. London, Bantam, 1992; New York, Roc, 1995.

Short Stories

Scholars and Soldiers. London, Macdonald, 1989.
Left to His Own Devices. London, Orbit, 1994.

OTHER PUBLICATIONS

Other

Editor, with Roz Kaveney, *Villains!* London, Roc, 1992.
Editor, with Roz Kaveney and Neil Gaiman, *The Weerde.* London, Roc, 1992.

*   *   *

Mary Gentle's first novel, *A Hawk in Silver,* a juvenile fantasy (written when she was 18), falls outside the concerns of this volume, but her first adult science fiction work, *Golden Witchbreed,* suggested that a major new talent had entered the genre. Its main protagonist, Lynne de Lisle Christie, is an envoy from Earth to the human-like aliens of Orthe—that subtle distinction in names suggestive of the ambivalence that exists at every level of the novel. Her journeys about Orthe, the betrayals, discoveries and eventual self-discovery, involve us not merely on the level of a good adventure story, but—in the manner of the very best of SF—make us reflect upon our own social organisations. Orthe is a world which, while seeming primitive, is in fact more advanced than our own. We judge things by our own techno-evolutionary terms, but Orthe has taken a very different socio-historical direction. Gentle's depiction of this world and its people is vividly imagined, and—unlike so many such conceived worlds—appears very real to us.

The enigma of Orthe's past history and of the ancient "Golden" race which lay teasingly beneath the surface of *Golden Witchbreed* (hidden, one might say, in the Brown Tower, where Lynne finally journeys) comes to the foreground in the sequel, *Ancient Light,* where we learn the reasons for the Orthean taboos about "Golden" technology. Set 10 years after the first book, this novel again has Lynne de Lisle Christie at the heart of things; a vast Corporation, PanOceania, attempts to trace and resurrect the ancient Golden technology—"ancient light"—which, we learn, once destroyed half of Orthe. As adviser to PanOceania but friend to Orthe, Christie's loyalties are torn, especially when the corporation's activities spark a war. The book attempts to come to grips with the very real moral problems involved in trading with "primitive" societies and the resultant technological imbalance. But the real strength of this novel lies in its description of the human-like Ortheans and their long "past-memories" that stretch back into the far past when the Golden Witchbreed enslaved them.

If Gentle's writing has one flaw it is in pacing. A tendency to be over-descriptive, to dwell perhaps too leisurely on details of setting and dress, often mars the flow of her work. That said, Gentle does create a distinctive atmosphere that lingers long after plot details have faded in the memory. *Rats and Gargoyles,* a novel that is part sword and sorcery, part alternate world mystery, part fable, and part hermetic text, moved Gentle's work away from the stud-

ied realism of the Orthe books into a rich and heady brew of alchemy, numerology, and architecture. The world of this novel (and its associated stories, some of which were collected in *Scholars and Soldiers*) is a world underpinned by pattern and number, where, in an ancient city anchored only vaguely in time and space, vast edifices are being constructed to universal patterns set down by Architect-Lords thousands of years before. Forces of dark and light are at work in this seemingly mid-Renaissance world, but it is to the human (and human-sized rat) characters that we turn for enlightenment in this hermetic maze and to whom we owe what enjoyment we derive from this awesome and complex game of gods and men. Indeed, with its Thieves Guild, its spells and demons, its sword-wielding rats and its long, cold vistas of time and stone, this book reads rather like a cross between Peter Greenaway's film *The Draughtsman's Contract* and a Fritz Leiber "Fafhrd and the Gray Mouser" tale.

Gentle's *The Architecture of Desire* extends this sequence, using the same central characters (the scholar-soldier, Valentine, and the Lord-Architect Casaubon) as in the previous works. Once again the imaginative blend of the familiar and the strange is genuinely disconcerting as Gentle presents us with a (vaguely Elizabethan) city of London that never was, except in the strangest of dreams. In stretching and redefining the boundaries of both fantasy and the alternate world novel, Gentle appears to be creating her own fictional sub-universe; a strange generic hybrid of 1940s exotic colouring and clinical 1990s perspective.

—David Wingrove

GEORGE, Peter (Bryan)

Pseudonyms: Peter Bryant; Bryan Peters. **Nationality:** British. **Born:** Wales in 1924. **Military Service:** Served in the Royal Air Force during World War II; rejoined Royal Air Force in 1951; retired as Flight Lieutenant, 1962. **Died:** 1 June 1966.

SCIENCE FICTION PUBLICATIONS

Novels

Two Hours to Doom (as Peter Bryant). London, Boardman, 1958; as *Red Alert,* New York, Ace, 1959; revised edition, as *Dr. Strangelove; or, How I Learned to Stop Worrying and Love the Bomb* (as Peter George), London, Corgi, 1963; New York, Bantam, 1964.
Commander-1. London, Heinemann, and New York, Delacorte Press, 1965.

OTHER PUBLICATIONS

Novels

Come Blonde, Came Murder. London, Boardman, 1952.
Pattern of Death. London, Boardman, 1954.
Cool Murder. London, Boardman, 1958.
The Final Steal. London, Boardman, 1962; New York, Dell, 1965.

Novels as Bryan Peters

Starbuck. London, Digit, 1957.
Hong Kong Kill. London, Boardman, 1958; New York, Washburn, 1959.
Sons of Nippon. London, Digit, 1961.
The Big H. London, Boardman, 1961; New York, Holt Rinehart, 1963.

* * *

On the basis of his two science fiction novels, Peter George's career in science fiction would be only a literary footnote. But one of them, *Two Hours to Doom (Red Alert),* formed the basis for Stanley Kubrick's brilliant film *Dr. Strangelove,* and the rewritten novel *Dr. Strangelove* must be considered a minor classic of SF. No other example comes to mind of a film "tie-in" novel superior to the original version, and this work will repay serious reading and examination.

Richard Gid Powers's introduction to the Gregg Press edition of *Dr. Strangelove* (1979) examines *Red Alert* in the context of the tradition of "future war" fiction, most especially the nuclear holocaust stories so characteristic of the Cold War period, and draws a comparison with Nevil Shute's *On the Beach* (1957). *Red Alert* is a humorless thriller, full of procedural details concerning the Strategic Air Command and of sincere moral underpinnings, about the danger of hair-trigger nuclear retaliation systems to all humanity. At the end of the book, catastrophe is averted, both Russians and Americans seek peace, and the wise president has the last word. Not so *Dr. Strangelove.* Powers makes a case that Kubrick and Southern, in writing the screenplay, altered George's original beyond his control and his talents. Whatever is the case, *Dr. Strangelove* is a small masterpiece of black humor, worth a place beside works of Heller and Vonnegut—and it is certainly within the borders of science fiction, though only just. In the new version an insane general closes his U.S. military base and sends his planes against the Russians, fully armed for retaliation from an (imagined) enemy attack (and, for security, maintaining radio silence); all planes are turned back in the nick of time, except one, whose radio is damaged. Its target will detonate an automatic Doomsday Machine, a nuclear device capable of destroying the entire surface of the Earth. This one plane succeeds heroically, ironically, and destroys the world. Except for the ending, this is George's story. But it is not told in George's *Red Alert* style nor with his characters. All the ordinary names are changed to grotesques, to General Jack D. Ripper, "king" Kong, Mandrake, Turgidson, Strangelove. Every sentence points out, deadpan and without a moral stance, the insanity and absurdity of every character and every action in context. The point of view is nonhuman (note the framing device not in the film) and this is the story of the end of humanity. Science fiction elements are added, through the presentation of mad scientist Strangelove, in the body of the text as well.

On the other hand, George's sequel, *Commander-1* (in which the last surviving military officer after nuclear holocaust declares himself the ruler of the world and forms a dystopian island society in the South Seas) is serious, moral, and pedestrian. It is in every way a sequel to *Red Alert,* not to *Dr. Strangelove.*

—David G. Hartwell

GERNSBACK, Hugo

Nationality: American. **Born:** Luxembourg, 16 August 1884; emigrated to the United States in 1904. **Education:** EcoleTechnikum, Germany. **Family:** Married Marn Hancher (third marriage); two daughters and one son from previous marriages. **Career:** Inventor, businessman, and editor: founder, Electric Importing Company, world's first radio supply house, and designed the first home radio set, Telimco Wireless: the Telimco catalogue evolved into the first radio magazine, *Modern Electrics,* 1908, then *Electrical Experimenter,* 1913, and *Science and Invention,* 1920; also edited 50 other magazines, including *Radio News and Sexology,* and the first science fiction magazine, *Amazing,* 1926-29, *Amazing Stories Annual,* 1927, *Amazing Stories Quarterly,* 1928-29, *Air Wonder Stories,* 1929-30, *Science Wonder Stories,* 1929-35, *Science Wonder Quarterly,* 1929-32, *Scientific Detective,* 1929-30, *Thrilling Wonder Stories,* 1929-36, *Amazing Detective Tales,* 1930, and *Science Fiction Plus,* 1953; held some 80 patents; founded WRNY radio, New York, 1925, and made television broadcasts in 1928. **Awards:** Hugo Special award, 1960 (the Hugo award is named after him). Officer of the Oaken Crown, Luxembourg, 1954. **Died:** 19 August 1967.

SCIENCE FICTION PUBLICATIONS

Novels

Ralph 124C41+: A Romance of the Year 2660. Boston, Stratford, 1925; London, Cherry Tree, 1952.
Ultimate World, edited by Sam Moskowitz. New York, Walker, 1972.

OTHER PUBLICATIONS

Other

The Wireless Telephone. New York, Modern Electrics, 1910.
Wireless Hook-Ups. New York, Modern Electrics, 1911.
Radio for All. Philadelphia, Lippincott, 1922.
How to Build and Operate Short Wave Receivers. New York, Short Wave Craft, 1932.
Evolution in Modern Science Fiction. New York, Gernsback, 1952.
TV Repair Techniques. New York, Gernsback, 1953.
Science Fiction vs. Reality. Privately printed, 1960.
Concrete Science Fiction. Privately printed, 1961.

*

Critical Study: *Hugo Gernsback, Father of Science Fiction* by Sam Moskowitz, privately printed, 1959.

* * *

While Hugo Gernsback is regarded as one of the pivotal figures in the history of science fiction, his own output of fiction was relatively limited, and only two of his works—novels written many years apart—are available to readers lacking access to magazine files.

Gernsback's major occupation was publishing, and he started a series of popular science magazines in 1908. Here his most famous work, *Ralph 124C41+,* was serialized in 1911-12. The chief virtue of the novel is its serious attempt at detailed prediction. Among many other developments, Gernsback anticipated the substitution of zipcode-like designations for patronymics. In this connection, Ralph's name can be read as a rebus-like pun: "one to foresee for one." Considerable cleverness is shown in the book's predictions, some of which were listed in later years by Gernsback's longtime admirer and onetime employee, Sam Moskowitz: "Florescent lighting, skywriting, automatic packaging machines, plastics, the radio directional range finder, juke boxes, liquid fertilizer, hydroponics, tape recorders, rustproof steel, loud speakers, night baseball, aquacades, microfilm, television, radio networks, vending machines dispensing hot and cold foods and liquids, flying saucers, a device for teaching while the user is asleep, solar energy for heat and power, fabrics from glass, synthetic materials such as nylon for wearing apparel, and, of course, space travel. . . ." In addition, as Moskowitz points out, *Ralph* not only predicts the development of radar, but provides an accurate explanation of its principles. While *Ralph 124C41+* is an astonishing feat of technical prediction, it is, unfortunately, almost unreadable. Gernsback's notions of characterization and plotting were borrowed from the corniest of Victorian melodrama. Even these limitations might have been overcome by a lively narrative style, but Gernsback's style was dull and his tone pedantic. He was convinced that the function of science fiction was education, and apparently envisioned his typical reader as a not-very-bright young adolescent who had trouble with his high school science courses, and would be helped by the reiteration of his lessons in thinly fictionalized form.

In 1915-16, Gernsback published a series of short stories about Baron Munchausen. Typically, each story concentrates on demonstrating one principle of physics, chemistry, astronomy, geology, etc., in the familiar pedantic Gernsback style. In his second novel, *Ultimate World,* a party of alien scientists, studying the Earth and its inhabitants, and possessed of vast powers to control humans, conduct a series of sexual experiments, at first on a married couple, then on many more individuals. Despite the apparently risqué theme of the book, its development is marked by the same dull pedantry that had made *Ralph* practically unreadable.

In fact, Gernsback's impact on the field was primarily a result of his efforts as a publisher. Almost from the outset he had featured an occasional work of science fiction in his popular science magazines. In 1924 he announced Scientifiction; somehow the project failed to materialize, but by 1926 Gernsback was able to issue *Amazing Stories,* the first science fiction magazine. Gernsback's heavy emphasis on scientific detail and the generally stodgy tone of his publications limited both their popular acceptance and their literary levels, but his contributions as a pioneer are undeniable.

—Richard A. Lupoff

GERROLD, David

Nationality: American. **Born:** Chicago, Illinois, January 1944. **Education:** Los Angeles Valley Junior College; University of Southern California, Los Angeles; California State University, Northridge, B.A. in theatre arts 1967. **Career:** Columnist, *Starlog* and *Galileo*

magazines; story editor, *Land of the Lost* TV series, 1974. Since 1984, computer columnist, *Profiles.* **Awards:** Skylark award, 1979. **Agent:** Richard Curtis, 9420 Reseda Boulevard, Northridge, California 91328, U.S.A.

SCIENCE FICTION PUBLICATIONS

Novels (series: Star Trek; Trackers; War against the Chtorr)

The Flying Sorcerers, with Larry Niven. New York, Ballantine, 1971; London, Corgi, 1975.
Space Skimmer. New York, Ballantine, 1972; London, Arrow, 1987.
Yesterday's Children. New York, Dell, 1972; London, Faber, 1974; revised, New York, Popular Library, 1980; as *Starhunt,* London, Hamlyn, 1985; New York, Bantam, 1995.
When HARLIE Was One: A Novel. Garden City, New York, Doubleday, 1972; expanded as *When HARLIE Was One (Release 2.0).*
Battle for the Planet of the Apes (novelization of screenplay). New York, Award, 1973.
The Man Who Folded Himself. New York, Random House, and London, Faber, 1973.
Moonstar Odyssey. New York, Signet, 1977.
Deathbeast. New York, Popular Library, 1978; London, Hale, 1981.
The Galactic Whirlpool: A Star Trek Novel. New York, Bantam, 1980; London, Titan, 1993.
Encounter at Farpoint (Star Trek). New York, Pocket Books, 1987; London, Titan, 1988.
The War against the Chtorr:
    A Matter for Men. New York, Timescape, 1983; London, Futura, 1984; expanded edition, New York, Bantam, 1989.
    A Day for Damnation. New York, Timescape, 1984; expanded edition, New York, Bantam, 1989.
    The War against the Chtorr: Invasion (includes *A Day for Damnation* and *A Matter for Men*). Garden City, New York, Doubleday, 1984.
    A Rage for Revenge. New York, Bantam, 1989.
Enemy Mine, with Barry Longyear (novelization of a screenplay). New York, Charter, 1985; London, Corgi, 1986.
Chess with a Dragon. New York, Walker, 1987; London, Hutchinson, 1988.
Voyage of the Star Wolf. New York, Bantam, 1990.
A Season for Slaughter (Chtorr). New York, Bantam, 1992.
Under the Eye of God (Trackers). New York, Bantam, 1993.
A Covenant of Justice (Trackers). New York, Bantam, 1994.
The Middle of Nowhere. New York, Bantam, 1995.

Short Stories

With a Finger in My I. New York, Ballantine, 1972.

OTHER PUBLICATIONS

Plays

Screenplays: *Man Out of Time; Logan's Run* (as Noah Ward).

Television Plays: *The Trouble with Tribbles,* 1967, *The Cloud Minders,* 1968, and *Encounter at Farpoint,* 1987, all in *Star Trek* series; *More Trouble with Tribbles,* 1973, and *BEM,* 1974, both in *Animated Star Trek* series; *CHA-KA, The Sleestak God, Possession, Circle,* and *Hurricane,* all in *Land of the Lost* series; *The Swamp Monster,* in *The Biskitts* series; *Levitation* and *If the Shoes Fit . . .* (as Noah Ward), both for *Tales from the Darkside* series, 1984.

Other

The Trouble with Tribbles (Star Trek). New York, Ballantine, 1973.
The World of Star Trek. New York, Ballantine, 1973; revised edition, New York, Bluejay, 1984.
Fatal Distractions! 87 of the Very Best Ways to Get Beaten, Eaten, Maimed, and Mauled on your PC. Corte Madera, California, Waite Group Press, 1994.

Editor, with Stephen Goldin, *Protostars.* New York, Ballantine, 1971.
Editor, with Stephen Goldin, *Generation: An Anthology of Speculative Ficton.* New York, Dell, 1972.
Editor, *Science Fiction Emphasis 1: An Anthology of Original Science Fiction.* New York, Ballantine, 1974.
Editor, with Stephen Goldin, *Alternities.* New York, Dell, 1974.
Editor, with Stephen Goldin, *Ascents of Wonder.* New York, Popular Library, 1977.
Editor, with David Truesdale, *Starlog's Science Fiction Yearbook, Vol. 1.* New York, Starlog Press, 1979.

*

David Gerrold comments:
I don't talk about writing. I write.

* * *

David Gerrold's career begins with television; he wrote *The Trouble with Tribbles,* probably the most popular episode of television's most popular SF series, *Star Trek.* Three decades later, Gerrold has published nearly 30 books, has had 20 screenplays produced; and *Tribbles,* a minor (though amusing) piece of television fluff, is still, in all likelihood, the work for which he is best known by the general public.

Gerrold is at least partly responsible for this persistent identification with what is not his best work. He wrote two of the earliest and most perceptive books about the Star Trek phenomenon; and wrote an original Star Trek novel, *The Galactic Whirlpool.* In the late 80s he served as story editor for the first season of *Star Trek: The Next Generation,* and also published the novelization of TNG's first episode.

Perhaps due to his work in Hollywood, Gerrold's literary career has never quite jelled as it might have. He is among the best and most inventive SF writers of his generation, but despite consistently excellent work has yet to achieve the commercial success of many less talented writers—indeed, one of Gerrold's strengths as a writer, his ability to move easily between novels and screenplays, has arguably distracted him from focusing on either.

Gerrold's first published novel was a collaboration with Larry Niven, *The Flying Sorcerers. Sorcerers* is a minor work, notable mainly for a lively wit that is (looking at each writer's later career) surely Gerrold's contribution—the book ends with a truly horrible pun regarding a Famous SF Writer. . . .

His first solo novel, *When Harlie Was One,* was nominated for both the Hugo and Nebula Awards. It's an early (1971) and surprisingly realistic treatment of the themes of AI. The novel's social background grew dated with the passage of the years—it is, as much as Spinrad's *Bug Jack Barron,* a vision of the future that is rooted in the 60s. Despite this, the area that one might have expected to date most severely, Gerrold's treatment of the themes of AI, survives remarkably well. SF writers will tell you (a touch indignantly at times) that "SF Is Not Prediction"; nonetheless Gerrold performed what strikes me, 25 years later, as a remarkable job of prediction—in a field that did not really exist in 1971. Gerrold's revision, in 1988, was *When Harlie Was One (Release 2.0);* it removes some of the artifacts of the 60s—the scientists with their marijuana cigarettes, e.g.—while taking advantages of improvements in the understanding of what AI might actually look like. In a time when hundreds of cyberpunk novels, many of them intimately concerned with the theme of AI, have come and gone, it's striking to come back to Gerrold's *Harlie* and realize that none of the cyberpunks have managed to substantially improve on Gerrold's groundbreaking, 25-year-old portrayal of how an Artificial Intelligence might come into being.

The subject of Gerrold's work is, it's become clear with the passage of the years, the author himself—he leaves himself naked on the page to a degree that's rarely seen in science fiction, and is occasionally disturbing. The first novel where this is really apparent is Gerrold's 1973 novel *The Man Who Folded Himself.* It's told in first person and it reads like a compulsive autobiography. Much like Heinlein's *All You Zombies,* every significant character who appears in *Folded* is the same person—mother, father, daughter, son, uncle, lover—all are the same man/woman, in a solipsist, narcissistic loop that defies brief summarization. *Folded* is far from being simply a rework of *Zombies,* though. What's memorable and valuable about the novel is something that, in lesser hands, would be a solid drawback: the author's intense identification with his viewpoint character. The author is writing (you have to believe) about himself—about his own hopes and desires and dreams; and his willingness to present himself, good and bad, to the reader's inspection, is remarkable. Though the execution is sometimes flawed, the urgency behind the telling is undeniable, and the novel earned Gerrold another pair of Hugo and Nebula nominations; it is his most memorable stand-alone novel.

Several of Gerrold's less important novels, aside from being generally "good reads," have further points of interest; Gerrold has used many of them as exercises for various stylistic approaches. His novel *Yesterday's Children* (revised as *Starhunt*) is written entirely in the present tense; in *Moonstar Odyssey,* Gerrold writes many passages in metric prose, a technique he learned from Theodore Sturgeon. Though it perceptibly slows one's reading in places, it produced some quite beautiful prose. In his "Trackers" adventure novels (*Under the Eye of God; A Covenant of Justice*) there are no passive voice sentences, no use of the verb "to be" until the end of the second book. The result makes for a very fast read, and an interesting contrast with the more studied pace of *Moonstar Odyssey.*

Two of Gerrold's most recent novels, *Star Wolf* (1990) and *The Middle of Nowhere* (1995), are indirect sequels to *Yesterday's Children* (1972). In the updated novels, Jonathan Thomas Korie, executive commander of the eponymous *Star Wolf,* learns lessons about the nature of combat and command that would be familiar to another JTK, James Tiberius Kirk. The novels are well-written and have their interests—Gerrold has said that they were written to show what life aboard a combat starship might actually be like—but one of the more interesting things about them is that, along with *When Harlie Was One* and *The War Against the Chtorr* novels, they are clearly intended as a framework for a future history along the lines of Heinlein's and Niven's. (A television series—*The Star Wolf*—based upon Gerrold's two *Star Wolf* novels, is in production at this writing, bringing the links with *Star Trek* full circle.)

The central work of David Gerrold's literary career is *The War Against the Chtorr.* It is not overstating the matter to say that *The War Against the Chtorr* is at least the second-best alien invasion story ever published, after (perhaps) H.G. Wells's *War of the Worlds.*

Chtorr is in many ways an improvement on Wells's work. It opens with a devastating plague, and the survivors soon learn that the plague was no natural phenomenon: it was the opening round of an assault upon not just humanity, but upon the ecosystem that produced humanity. The first wave of Chtorran invaders, called "worms," look something like 20-foot long caterpillars with teeth. But the worms are not alone: with them has come what appears to be the entire ecosystem of their home world, an ecosystem a billion years older than Earth's, nastier and meaner and much tougher than anything on Earth, including, probably, the human race.

The work to date consists of four novels, with at least two more due. They are *A Matter for Men; A Day for Damnation; A Rage for Revenge;* and *A Season for Slaughter.* The alliterative, slightly generic titles are unfortunate, as they tend to mask Gerrold's very real literary ambition. The series as a whole suffers from a charismatic didacticism reminiscent of Heinlein at his best—Gerrold is never more comfortable than when dynamiting his points home. Again, in lesser hands, e.g. later Heinlein, this could have been disastrous. But Gerrold's themes are dark, disturbing, and above all brutal; his didacticism is, in this instance, appropriate to his material.

His material is a young man named Jim McCarthy. A man of about 20 when *A Matter for Men* opens, in the first four novels we watch McCarthy grow into perhaps his early thirties. While McCarthy is growing into manhood, the Earth itself is dying around him; the Chtorran ecosystem, more ferocious and more fertile than Earth's, has infiltrated the oceans and the land, is busy elbowing aside Earth's native plants and animals. In *Matter* and *Day* we watch as McCarthy learns to appreciate the true depth of the disaster facing humanity; as his family, friends, and comrades die around him.

The only novel in the series whose title I really like is *A Rage for Revenge*—it's a great title for a great book, a Grand Guignol of a piece that is, in short, brilliant, among the best works in all of SF; and it is the high point of Gerrold's career to date. It's been noted elsewhere that an enduring theme of Gerrold's is that of the ordinary man who finds himself confronted with an extraordinary situation in which his choices are to either grow, or die; and nowhere is this more literally demonstrated than parts of *A Rage For Revenge.* Moral absolutists will have a difficult time with this novel —in Jim McCarthy, *Rage* has a first-person protagonist whose greatest accomplishment is that the world he suffers in has not, yet, turned him into the same caliber of monster as his human and Chtorran enemies. The novel begins with a disturbing scene, McCarthy's capture by a group of human-Chtorran renegades, and then escalates into ever more disturbing territory—in four or five places the material is genuinely wrenching; and made more wrenching yet by the inescapable supposition that Gerrold is, once again, writing about himself. (Excepting *Starship Troopers,* Heinlein's didacticism resembles the impromptu outbursts of an opinionated uncle; by contract, Gerrold's use of this technique is studied and usually effective.)

The last book published in the sequence is *A Season for Slaughter. Season* is a darker and more somber novel than the first three books. It explores—engagingly but without the kinetic and sometimes horrifying rush of *Rage*—the themes that have come to dominate Gerrold's writing of late, principally personal responsibility and alienation. In it, McCarthy learns more of the nature of the Chtorran threat; though how, and if, humanity will deal with that threat, is still unclear. The novel ends in mid-scene; and it is probably safe to say that there is no other series currently in progress whose resolution is so eagerly awaited by its fans.

As an artist, David Gerrold is himself still very much a work in progress. Those who feared, in the late 70s and early 80s, that the artist had burned out prematurely, may be reassured. For a variety of reasons his career has yet to fulfill its early promise; but that said, his recent work is better than his early work. This is a considerable achievement. In a field where authors—Heinlein, Asimov, Zelazny, Niven, among dozens of examples—do not tend to improve as they age, Gerrold stands as an artist for whom there is as much reason for hope today as there was in 1971.

Gerrold has been nominated for the Hugo and Nebula awards nine times. His story *The Martian Child,* a literal retelling of the events surrounding the adoption of his son Sean, won the 1995 *Locus* Readers' Poll for Best Short Story; and the 1995 Nebula Award as well, six weeks after Sean's adoption was finalized. It went on to win the Hugo Award later that year.

—Daniel Keys Moran

GESTON, Mark S(ymington)

Nationality: American. **Born:** Atlantic City, New Jersey, 20 June 1946. **Education:** Abington High School; Kenyon College, Gambier, Ohio (*Kenyon Review* prize, 1968), A.B. in history 1968 (Phi Beta Kappa); New York University Law School (Root-Tilden Fellow), 1968-71, J.D. 1971. **Family:** Married 1) Gayle Howard in 1971 (divorced 1972); 2) Marijke Havinga in 1976; two daughters and one son. **Career:** Since 1971, attorney, Eberle, Berlin, Kading, Turnbow, and McKlveen, Boise, Idaho. **Agent:** John Hawkins and Associates, 71 West 23rd Street, Suite 1600, New York, New York 10010. **Address:** Box 1368, Boise, Idaho 83701, U.S.A.

SCIENCE FICTION PUBLICATIONS

Novels (series: Havengore)

Lords of the Starship (Havengore). New York, Ace, 1967; London, Joseph, 1971.
Out of the Mouth of the Dragon (Havengore). New York, Ace, 1969; London, Joseph, 1972.
The Day Star. New York, DAW, 1972.
The Siege of Wonder. Garden City, New York, Doubleday, 1976.
Mirror to the Sky. New York, Morrow, 1992.

*   *   *

Mark S. Geston is an unarmored adventurer into worlds of ideas and dreams not yet articulated by our world. He examines with compassion and keen eyes the apparent cycles of the desire of humanity to construct and destroy. He often deals with time in a tangible way, as a mapmaker might deal with the real rivers of our world.

Out of the Mouth of the Dragon begins with the record of a mighty battle lost and the return of the only surviving ship carrying the survivors back to the Maritime Republics. With the return of this ship begins a young man's long trek back to the ultimate Armageddon which would either renew humanity or result in the end of consciousness for the inhabitants of this world. It is an interesting though rather depressing tale of the quest of man to modify his physical and moral restrictions by choosing to accept a mortality over which he has some control. Thus the novel offers hope to mortals: in the face of the inevitable, what we become is what counts.

In *The Day Star* Geston etches the propensity of humanity for war, and the timeless effects of this propensity. As usual, he mixes dreams with reality, tangibility with mists, ghosts with people, and legend with substance in a fascinating, shimmering kaleidoscope of a being engaged in the ultimate search: for reality and the realization of the higher aspirations of his society.

The Siege of Wonder presents a hemisphere of wizardry opposing a hemisphere of science, with mankind attempting to destroy itself even after many wasted generations. Geston seems to be saying that the magic of one beholder may be the science of the next.

Geston is adept at painting those things which, to the average reader, would seem to illustrate contrary values. One scene in *The Siege of Wonder* has a wizard commander coming through the city with his followers' whitened bones protruding from their armor—a sign of the importance of their leader.

—John V. Garner

GIBSON, William (Ford)

Nationality: American. **Born:** Conway, South Carolina, 17 March 1948. **Education:** University of British Columbia, Vancouver, B.A. in English 1977. **Family:** Married Deborah Jean Thompson in 1972; one son and one daughter. **Awards:** Philip K. Dick Memorial award, 1985; Nebula award, 1985; Hugo award, 1985. **Agent:** Martha Millard, 204 Park Avenue, Madison, New Jersey 07940, U.S.A.

SCIENCE FICTION PUBLICATIONS

Novels

Neuromancer. New York, Ace, and London, Gollancz, 1984.
Count Zero. New York, Arbor House, and London, Gollancz, 1986.
Mona Lisa Overdrive. New York, Bantam, and London, Gollancz, 1988.
The Difference Engine, with Bruce Sterling. London, Gollancz, 1990; New York, Bantam, 1991.
Virtual Light. New York, Bantam, and London, Viking, 1993.

Short Stories

Burning Chrome. New York, Arbor House, and London, Gollancz, 1986.

Other

Johnny Mnemonic (includes a screenplay and short story). New York, Ace, 1995.
Agrippa: A Book of the Dead, with Dennis Ashbaugh. N.p., n.d.

*

Critical Study: Interview with Steve Brown, in *Heavy Metal,* (New York), May 1985.

* * *

William Gibson will probably always best be known, much to his chagrin, as the godfather of cyberpunk and the man who in his breathtakingly successful first novel, *Neuromancer,* coined the term *cyberspace,* "a consensual hallucination . . . a graphic representation of data abstracted from every computer in the human system." With the publication of that book, which garnered science fiction's triple crown (the Hugo, Nebula, and Philip K. Dick awards), his name became synonymous with the artistic and political rebellion against lifeless, predictable SF of the 1970s and early 80s, as well as increasingly repressive corporate and governmental control of electronic information networks. While *cyber* connotes a technosphere of cybernetics, cybernauts, and computers, *punk* connotes a countercultural sociosphere, especially that of punk rock, itself an embodiment of both anarchy and an attempt to return to the pure musical roots of rock 'n' roll in much the same way cyberpunk attempts returning to the rich literary roots of SF's New Wave.

Although what may finally matter most are the differences rather than the similarities among the loose group of writers including Lewis Shiner, Pat Cadigan, and Richard Kadrey whose names have been associated with the "movement" initially christened by Gardner Dozois in a 1984 article in the *Washington Post,* and championed by Bruce Sterling in his preface-manifesto to *Mirrorshades* (the 1986 cyberpunk anthology he edited), and although there are clearly a number of antecedents to their important work (among them Alfred Bester's *The Demolished Man* [1951], Anthony Burgess's *A Clockwork Orange* [1962], and Ridley Scott's *Blade Runner* film [1982] based on Philip K. Dick's novella), it is nonetheless accurate to say William Gibson's output in certain ways is emblematic of cyberpunk's aesthetic and vision.

First, his fiction evinces a style, carefully crafted and complexly resonant, that grows out of the New Wave's emphasis on the literariness of a text. Reminiscent of the work of J. G. Ballard or Harlan Ellison, it places a premium on information density, detail and inventory, syntactical flash and burn, that remains foreign to much SF, and on a surreal poetic intensity enhanced by the use of narrative jump-cuts fast as those found on MTV, striking juxtapositions, frequent use of metaphors anchored in an art of the unpleasant, and a fertile ambiguity generated by writing about the future as if it were the present. This last device does away with the info-dumps associated with traditional science fiction, where plot often snags and stops while characters or narrators explain various gadgets and concepts for the reader's benefit, and instead allows context to provide definition. The outcome is that several pages routinely pass after the first mention of an object or term before the reader can fully piece together its function and meaning. Some thus report a sense of disorientation, even frustration, when tackling Gibson's writing, the nagging feeling they have just missed something significant, while many others embrace his style's speed, complexity, originality, and texture.

Gibson's world and characters—particularly those found in his early short stories collected in *Burning Chrome* and his first three companion novels known as the Matrix Trilogy (*Neuromancer, Count Zero,* and *Mona Lisa Overdrive*)—harmonize well with the world and characters found in cyberpunk fiction by such writers as John Shirley, Tom Maddox, and George Alec Effinger. Opposed to much conventional SF space opera, typically set in the distant future, peopled with aliens, and enacted on a galactic scale, Gibson's brand extrapolates an all-too-real near-future world set as little as twenty or thirty years from now, peopled with those at the margins of society, and enacted on a global and antiheroic scale. Exploring this fractured, confused, and Japanized universe, one has the impression civilization has already peaked. World War III, for instance, has occurred, lasting about three weeks and centered in Bonn and Beograd. Printed books have become fashionably archaic, and the most popular entertainment takes the form of simstims, or Simulated Stimuli, where by jacking into a machine one can experience the sensations and perceptions of another person. Paper money, quasi-illegal, has been replaced for the most part by credit chips. Pollution pervades the landscape, and overpopulation combined with conurbation has turned the Boston-Atlanta Metropolitan Axis (or Sprawl) into a "vast generic tumble." Traditional governments with geographical borders have dissolved into multinational corporations with informational borders. There is no sign of the old United States.

Inhabiting this dystopic wasteland that gradually comes to resemble "a deranged experiment in social Darwinism," as the narrator of Neuromancer comments, are tough, high-tech lowlifes who exist at the fringes of society in a criminal subculture. They are hustlers, anarchists, black marketeers, addicts, assassins, hackers, crackers, and phreaks. Like Deke, a drifter in "Dogfight," who cheats at a hyped-up video game to rob a handicapped vet of money and prestige, they are out for themselves rather than for altruism or ideology. They want credit, not human relationships or political change. Devouring experience in the form of new drugs, new programs and new simstims, they feel old at 28 and are often scarred mentally and physically, like Molly in *Neuromancer,* whose boyfriend has been brutally murdered, and who wears a scar running from just below her left nipple to the waistband of her jeans; external hurt forms an objective correlative for internal. Although Molly has sex with Case in *Neuromancer,* Turner with Allison in *Count Zero,* and Mona with Eddy in *Mona Lisa Overdrive,* most of Gibson's characters prefer to make love to their machines rather than to each other. "I saw you stroking that Sendai," Molly tells Case, whose name implies his "en-cased" state of existence. "Man, it was pornographic."

Those machines are gateways in the Matrix Trilogy to a radically original, even transcendental, reality: cyberspace. If Gibson imagines a frightening external "meatworld" in the Sprawl, Dog Solitude, and Chiba City, he imagines a mesmerizing internal realm, hallucinatory and mystical, in the cyberspace matrix which he (a confessed techno-hickster who wrote his first novel on a beatup typewriter) extrapolated, not from the spacial data management systems studied at MIT, NASA, and elsewhere at the time, as one might suspect, but from watching rapt kids on Granville Street in Vancouver, his hometown, playing video games in arcades.

Originally no more than an abstract representation of data in his early stories, cyberspace metamorphoses over the course of the Trilogy. At the moment the two artificial intelligences, Neuromancer and Wintermute, merge at the end of Gibson's first novel, becom-

ing a godlike unity of opposites, the newly generated entity fragments because it is so lonely. The consequence is a host of smaller gods or subprograms that take on the names and personalities of voodoo deities in the matrix. Gibson thereby blends notions of religion and technology in the digital beyond, both of which concepts prove to be little more than elaborate games, abstract organizations of data that at best bear a distant relationship with reality. In addition, cyberspace becomes a metaphor for individual and cultural memory, and the fragility of both. The gothic quality of the matrix, haunted as it is by spirits of the dead, implies too the surreal landscape of the irrational psyche, which itself conjures up a metaphor for mind/body dualism. Characters who enter cyberspace leave their bodies behind, lose themselves in the mental landscape of the matrix, like Case, who exhibits "a certain relaxed contempt for the flesh."

Upon completion of the Matrix Trilogy, Gibson in large part left the world of cyberspace behind. In his fourth, longest, and most complex novel, *The Difference Engine,* written with Bruce Sterling, cyberspace plays no part whatsoever. Instead the action revolves around an alternate history in which Victorian inventor Charles Babbage computerized our culture nearly a century before the fact. However, because of the emphasis on the politics of information in the book, in addition to its gritty rendering of nineteenth-century London's underbelly that would have made Charles Dickens proud, several critics have proclaimed it as the primogenitor of an admittedly tiny subgenre of cyberpunk: steampunk.

Next followed another collaboration, *Agrippa: A Book of the Dead,* cyberpunk in form and technological presentation, but surprisingly traditional in content. Created in partnership with the abstract expressionist painter Dennis Ashbaugh, *Agrippa* is a $2000 gentle and fond autobiographical prose poem about Gibson's childhood—about, like cyberspace itself, memory—that exists on disks designed to self-destruct after one reading (although within twenty-four hours of its appearance real-life hackers broke its code and released it on the Internet). A metaphor for (un)total recall, as well as a thematic exploration of it, *Agrippa* happens only in a viral space that literally nibbles away at its own boundaries, performs rather than simulates deconstruction.

Virtual Light, Gibson's fifth novel, abandons the surreal aspects of cyberspace and replaces it with a universe almost completely rooted in the meatworld. The high-intensity apocalyptic prose associated with the electronic ether gives way in good portion to a thinner black humor akin to the bright cartoonish mischief of Thomas Pynchon: a psycho-killer with the Last Supper tattooed on his chest; a woman who visits San Francisco to retrieve her husband's cryogenically frozen brain from a tank of them so it doesn't have to feel so crowded in the afterlife. The intricate and deeply spiritual exploration of cyberspace pervading the Trilogy yields to very funny, if often very easy, parody. Meanwhile, two key metaphors dominate *Virtual Light.* First is the San Francisco bike-messenger service, one of whose employees, Chevette Washington, steals a pair of virtual reality glasses from a grotesque man at a party on an angry whim; those bikes suggest environmentally conscious no-fuel freedom, anarchic energy, exhilarating sexy fashion, the cultural inscription of the techno-hip. Second is the Oakland Bay Bridge, abandoned by the city after a megalithic earthquake, and slowly inhabited by the homeless; its patchwork dwellings and diversity suggest postmodern America itself.

Johnny Mnemonic, the film for which Gibson wrote the screenplay, commercializes the idea of cyberpunk. Directed by painter Robert Longo, and starring Keanu Reeves and Dina Meyer, *Johnny*

Mnemonic is based primarily on Gibson's early story by the same name about a courier who stores data for others in a brain-implanted memory chip, but also cannibalizes scenes, images, and gizmos from many of his other works, including cyberspace sequences from *Neuromancer* and the bridge from *Virtual Light*. The result, fast and flashy, abundant with impressive special effects, overlays a stock Hollywood chase-plot on top of serious cyberpunk considerations, downplaying philosophical and political investigation in favor of predictably entertaining diversion—the very formula, in other words, cyberpunk revolted against in the first place. Both critics and box-office agree that Gibson's attempt at screenwriting failed to live up to its promise.

One of the most startling insights about Gibson's oeuvre is, for all its seeming mutation, how much of a piece it really is. As far back as his first published short story, "Fragments of a Hologram Rose," written in 1976 in lieu of a final paper for a science-fiction course he took at the University of British Columbia, one can spot a thematic cluster that will weave through his fiction for the next twenty years: the importance and fragility of memory, the tenuous distinction between human and machine, suspicion and fear of multinational corporations' control over information and individuals, distrust of normalcy, the instability of postmodern society and self, a genuine longing for a transcendent realm beyond the meatworld, the complex relationship between the mind and the body, the artist as outlaw and the outlaw as artist, and so on. Such themes give rise to a number of intriguing centuries-old questions (*what constitutes human identity? what will tomorrow look like if we're not careful? what is free will?*) which Gibson, explores with a visionary passion and innovative flair that has earned him a place in the elite constellation of science fiction's most significant contemporary practitioners.

—Lance Olsen

GILLILAND, Alexis A(rnaldus)

Nationality: American. **Born:** Bangor, Maine, 10 May 1931. **Education:** Purdue University, West Lafayette, Indiana, B.S. 1953; George Washington University, Washington, D.C., M.S. 1963. **Military Service:** Served in the United States Army Presidential Honor Guard, 1954-56. **Family:** Married Dorothea Cohle in 1959; one son. **Career:** Thermochemist, National Bureau of Standards, 1956-67, and chemist and specification writer, Federal Supply Service, 1967-82, both in Washington, D.C. Since 1982, freelance writer. Also a cartoonist. **Awards:** Hugo award, for art, 1980, 1983, 1984, 1985; John W. Campbell award, 1982. **Address:** 4030 Eighth Street South, Arlington, Virginia 22204, U.S.A.

SCIENCE FICTION PUBLICATIONS

Novels (series: Rosinante; Wizenbeak)

The Revolution from Rosinante. New York, Ballantine, 1981.
Long Shot for Rosinante. New York, Ballantine, 1981.
The Pirates of Rosinante. New York, Ballantine, 1982.
The End of the Empire. New York, Ballantine, 1983.
Wizenbeak (illustrated by Tim Kirk). New York, Bluejay, 1986.

The Shadow Shaia (Wizenbeak). New York, Ballantine, 1990.
Lord of the Troll-Bats (Wizenbeak). New York, Ballantine, 1992.

OTHER PUBLICATIONS

Other (cartoons)

The Iron Law of Bureaucracy. Port Townsend, Washington, Loompanics, 1979.
Who Says Paranoia Isn't "In" Anymore. Port Townsend, Washington, Loompanics, 1985.
The Waltzing Wizard: Cartoons. Mercer Island, Washington, Starmont House, 1989.

*   *   *

The Campbell award-winner Alexis A. Gilliland exemplifies the basic literary principle "write what you know." Gilliland, a retired federal bureaucrat, exposes the inner workings of authority with an accuracy and detail science fiction has hitherto only pretended to achieve. He has written what may be SF's first "consciously thematic" as opposed to propagandistic stories about bureaucracy. (Compare Keith Laumer's polemical farces about Terran diplomacy which are also based on personal experience).

Instead of merely denouncing administrative sclerosis, Gilliland establishes it through form as well as content. His storytelling technique employs both alternating and redundant viewpoints assembled like overlapping transparencies to create composite figures no single sheet can hold. Data-handling and decision-making processes are actually shown but, just as in a real bureaucracy, words outnumber deeds. Slick, witty, pun-laced dialogue carries the plot.

Gilliland's plausible technology reflects his initial scientific training. He is careful to show exactly how his characters are fed, clothed, and housed. This concreteness anchors outrageous events to some semblance of reality. Offbeat humor penetrates even the sex, slaughter, and metaphysics, for Gilliland is also a gifted cartoonist. (He has won three Hugo awards as Best Fan Artist and has published three cartoon books.)

Gilliland's writing career opened with the Rosinante trilogy. Here, under the leadership of a maverick bureaucrat, a space colony wins its independence from the despotic North American Union and topples terrestrial powers. But the real winners prove to be the revolutionaries' computers, intelligent mechanisms who wear the images of 20th-century movie stars. One computer proclaims itself the prophet of a new spacefaring religion while another evangelizes humans on its behalf to establish a symbiotic society of machines and men.

The End of the Empire is a more conventional narrative with a more radical message. It dares to criticize libertarianism, a political system favored by Robert A. Heinlein and other SF writers. Gilliland shows how too little government can be every bit as disastrous as too much government. (For example, tyrannical anarchy defines subversion as attempting to "under-raise" the regime.) The hero is a brilliant loner loyal to a moribund empire which he can be expected to revive singlehandedly in future adventures. Among the hero's obvious prototypes are Poul Anderson's Flandry and Keith Laumer's Retief, gallant guardians to whom this book is dedicated.

Gilliland moved from political science fiction to political fantasy in his trilogy *Wizenbeak, The Shadow Shaia,* and the forthcoming

Lord of the Troll-Bats. He brings the same skills for skewering governmental idiocy to a magical world that incorporates early modern witch-hunting, Japanese sword-fighting, and an Eastern Mediterranean cultural milieu. The results are darker than Gilliland's previous books and bear some resemblance to Avram Davidson's Dr. Esterhazy stories.

A gift for finding curious angles in prosaic realities is the foundation of Gilliland's SF career. "It is my fond belief," says the author, "that my novels bear thinking about, and that this may give the reader some insight into the real world, but this is an *ex post facto* rationalization to justify having written."

—Sandra Miesel

GILMAN, Charlotte (Anna) Perkins (Stetson)

Nationality: American. **Born:** Hartford, Connecticut, 3 July 1860. **Family:** Married 1) Walter Stetson in 1884 (divorced), one daughter; 2) George Houghton Gilman in 1900. **Died:** 17 August 1935.

SCIENCE FICTION PUBLICATIONS

Novel

Herland. New York, Pantheon, and London, Women's Press, 1979.

OTHER PUBLICATIONS

Novels

The Yellow Wallpaper (novella). Boston, Small Maynard, 1899.
What Diantha Did. New York, Charlton, 1910; London, T.F. Unwin, 1912.
The Crux. New York, Charlton, 1911.
Moving the Mountain. New York, Charlton, 1911.
Benigna Machiavelli. Santa Barbara, California, Bandanna Books, 1994.

Short Stories

The Charlotte Perkins Gilman Reader: The Yellow Wallpaper and Other Fiction, edited by Ann J. Lane. New York, Pantheon, 1980.
The Yellow Wallpaper and Other Writings, edited by Lynne Sharon Schwartz. New York, Bantam, 1989.
Herland and Selected Stories, edited by Barbara H. Solomon. New York, Signet, 1992.
"The Yellow Wall-Paper" and Selected Stories of Charlotte Perkins Gilman, edited by Denise D. Knight. Newark, Delaware, University of Delaware Press, 1994.
The Yellow Wall-Paper and Other Stories, edited by Robert Schulman. Oxford, Oxford University Press, 1995.

Poetry

In This Our World. Oakland, California, McCombs and Vaughan, 1893; London, T.F. Unwin, 1895.

Suffrage Songs and Verses. New York, Charlton, 1911.

Other

A Clarion Call to Redeem the Race! Mt. Lebanon, New York, The Shaker Press, 1890.
Women and Economics. Boston, Small Maynard, 1898; London, Putnam, 1905.
Concerning Children. Boston, Small Maynard, 1900; London, Putnam, 1901.
The Home, Its Work and Influence. New York, McClure Phillips, 1903; London, Heinemann, 1904.
Human Work. New York, McClure Phillips, 1904.
The Punishment that Educates. Cooperstown, New York, Crist Scott, 1907.
The Man-Made World; or, Our Androcentric Culture. New York, Charlton, and London, T.F. Unwin, 1911.
His Religion and Hers: A Study of the Faith of Our Fathers and the Work of Our Mothers. New York and London, Century, 1923.
The Living of Charlotte Perkins Gilman (autobiography). New York, Appleton-Century, 1935.
Charlotte Perkins Gilman: A Nonfiction Reader, edited by Larry Ceplair. New York, Columbia University Press, 1991.
The Diaries of Charlotte Perkins Gilman, edited by Denise D. Knight. Charlottesville, Virginia, University Press of Virginia, 1994.
A Journey from Within: The Love Letters of Charlotte Perkins Gilman, 1897-1900, edited by Mary A. Hill. Lewisburg, Pennsylvania, Bucknell University, 1995.

*

Critical Study: *Charlotte Perkins Gilman: The Woman and Her Work* by Sheryl L. Meyering, Ann Arbor, Michigan, UMI Research Press, 1989; *To "Herland" and Beyond: The Life and Work of Charlotte Perkins Gilman* by Ann J. Lane, New York, Pantheon, 1990.

*   *   *

Written in 1915, *Herland* was first published serially in Gilman's own monthly magazine *The Forerunner,* every line of which she wrote herself, including the advertisements. It was the second and clearly the best of the three utopian novels Gilman wrote in an effort to convince the masses that her feminist-socialist vision of society was both viable and appealing. It was also the only one of the three to be published separately.

Gilman situates the world of *Herland* on a "spur" of land "up where the maps had to be made," where the all-female inhabitants have been able to create a utopia because of the absence of men. The story is narrated by a male, Vandyck Jennings, one of three stereotypically under-evolved American men who stumble into this no man's land, each with his own predictable reaction to a community that neither needs nor desires a masculine intrusion. Jennings himself symbolizes the rational, intellectual, educated man who early in the novel states matter-of-factly, "This is a civilized country. . . . There must be men." His friend Terry Nicholson represents the oversexed, macho, ravisher of women who assumes that eventually the women of Herland will succumb to their "natural" sexual attraction to forceful, dominant men. Terry's polar opposite in temperament, but not in his capacity to accept insulting clichés about women, is Jeff Margrave, who idealizes women "in the best Southern style, . . . full of chivalry and sentiment, and all that."

The utopian nature of Herland is brought increasingly into focus as the men are made to face the wrongheadedness of their own assumptions about a country full of only women. These women do not quarrel among themselves; their country is not chaotic, but civilized in the extreme—"Everything [is] beauty, order, perfect cleanness, [with] the pleasantest sense of home over it all. . . . [There is] no dirt . . . no smoke . . . no noise." The women reproduce through parthenogenesis, are not attracted to aggression, and do not confuse aggression with strength. Further, the men are forced to admit that the women of Herland are attractive, despite the fact that they do not fit the traditional, male-defined image of female beauty. Their hair is very short; their clothes are uniform and neither clinging nor revealing; their bodies are straight and vigorous, but not, in male terms, sexually alluring. Besides, these women have absolutely no sexual interest in the men, a reality that is perhaps the most distressing of all to the three Americans.

The Herlanders' religion—Maternal Pantheism—derives from a central myth of "one family, all descended from one mother." The power of mother-love defines their relationships to one another and to the Earth, which is no longer perceived as an adversary to have dominion over as in the patriarchal Judeo-Christian tradition as described to the Herlanders by Vandyck Jennings, much to the women's horror. Instead, they identify *Mother*-earth not as an *other*, but as *another*, whose progenitive power resembles their own and is revered in much the same way. This view of motherhood was as foreign to the three men as was everything else in Herland, especially to Terry, whose "idea of motherliness was the usual one, involving a baby in arms . . . and the complete absorption of the mother in said baby. . . . A motherliness which dominated society, which influenced every art and industry, which absolutely protected all childhood, and gave to it the most perfect care and training, did not seem motherly."

Narrator Jennings begins to see that without the tradition of God the Father to bolster it, the "tradition of men as guardians and protectors had quite died out. [There were] no men to fear and therefore no need of protection." Violence is a fact of life only where there are men. These women "had had no wars. They had had no kings, and no priests, and no aristocracies. They were sisters, and as they grew, they grew together—not by competition, but by united action." When overpopulation became a problem, they confronted it, "not by a 'struggle for existence' which would result in an everlasting writhing mass of underbred people trying to get ahead of one another. . . . Neither did they start off on predatory excursions to get more land from somebody else. . . . Not at all. They sat down in council together and thought it out. . . . They said: 'With our best endeavors this country will support about so many people. . . . That is all the people we will make.'"

As Jennings is compelled to discard his stereotypes one by one, he experiences a kind of conversion and is led "to the conviction that those 'feminine charms' we are so fond of are not feminine at all, but mere reflected masculinity—developed to please us because they had to please us, and in no way essential to the real fulfillment of their great process." Both Jennings and Jeff Margrave slowly come to acknowledge the obvious: the absence of patriarchy has produced only positive results; the more they learn about this matriarchal community, the more despicable their patriarchal one seems by contrast. Of the three, only Terry refuses to relinquish the male warrior tradition with its aggression, dominance, and violence. After he commits what amounts to marital rape, he is banished forever from Herland. With the transformation of the other

two, however, Gilman seems to suggest that most if not all men are, at least, redeemable.

—Sheryl L. Meyering

GILMAN, Robert Cham. *See* **COPPEL, Alfred.**

GILMORE, Anthony. *See* **BATES, Harry.**

GLAMIS, Walter. *See* **SCHACHNER, Nat.**

GLOAG, John (Edwards)

Nationality: British. **Born:** London, 10 August 1896. **Education:** Attended technical high school, London. **Military Service:** Served in the Essex Regiment, 1916-17, and Welch Guards, 1917-19; 2nd Lieutenant; invalided home, 1918. **Family:** Married Gertrude Mary Ward in 1922; one daughter, and one son, the writer Julian Gloag. **Career:** Worked in studio of Thornton-Smith Ltd., 1913-16; advertising department staff member, Lever Organisation, 1920-2; art editor, 1922-27, and editor, 1927, *Cabinet Maker;* director, Pritchard Wood & Partners, 1928-61; director of public relations, Timber Development Association, 1936-38; full-time writer after 1961. **Member:** Advisory Committee, Board of Trade, 1943-47; Board of Trustees, Sir John Soane's Museum, 1960-70. Vice-president, Royal Society of Arts, 1952-54; president, Society of Architectural Historians, 1960-64. **Awards:** Royal Society of Arts silver medal, 1943, and bicentenary gold medal, 1958. **Died:** 17 July 1981.

SCIENCE FICTION PUBLICATIONS

Novels

To-morrow's Yesterday. London, Allen and Unwin, 1932.
The New Pleasure. London, Allen and Unwin, 1933.
Winter's Youth. London, Allen and Unwin, 1934.
Manna. London, Cassell, 1940.
99%. London, Cassell, 1944.

Short Stories

First One and Twenty: An Omnibus Volume Including To-morrow's Yesterday and Twenty Short Stories. London, Allen and Unwin, 1946.

OTHER PUBLICATIONS

Novels

Sweet Racket. London, Cassell, 1936.
Ripe for Development. London, Cassell, 1936.
Sacred Edifice. London, Cassell, 1937; revised edition, 1954.
Documents Marked Secret. London, Cassell, 1938.
Unwilling Adventurer. London, Cassell, 1940.
I Want an Audience. London, Cassell, 1941.
Mr. Buckby Is Not at Home. London, Cassell, 1942.
In Camera. London, Cassell, 1945.
Kind Uncle Buckby. London, Cassell, 1946.
All England at Home. London, Cassell, 1949.
Not in the Newspapers. London, Cassell, 1953.
Slow. London, Cassell, 1954.
Unlawful Justice. London, Cassell, 1962.
Rising Suns. London, Cassell, 1964.
Caesar of the Narrow Seas. London, Cassell, 1969; New York, St. Martin's Press, 1972.
The Eagles Depart. New York, St. Martin's Press, 1973.
Artorius Rex. London, Cassell, and New York, St. Martin's Press, 1977.

Short Stories

It Makes a Nice Change. London, Nicholson and Watson, 1938.
Take One a Week: An Omnibus Volume of 52 Short Stories. London, Chantry, 1950.

Poetry

Board Room Ballads and Other Verses. London, Allen and Unwin, 1933.

Other

Simple Furnishing and Arrangement, with Helen Gloag. London, Duckworth, 1921.
Simple Schemes for Decoration. London, Duckworth, and New York, Stokes, 1922.
The House We Ought to Live In, with Leslie Mansfield. London, Duckworth, 1923.
Colour and Comfort. London, Duckworth, 1924; New York, Stokes, 1925.
Time, Taste, and Furniture. London, Richards, and New York, Stokes, 1925.
Artifex; or, The Future of Craftsmanship. London, Kegan Paul, and New York, Dutton, 1926.
Home Life in History: Social Life and Manners in Britain 200 B.C.-A.D. 1926, with C. Thompson Walker. London, Benn, 1927; New York, Coward McCann, 1928.
Modern Home Furnishing. London, Macmillan, 1929.
Men and Buildings. London, Country Life, and New York, Scribner, 1931; revised edition, London, Chantry, 1950.
English Furniture. London, A. and C. Black, 1934; 6th edition, 1973.
Industrial Art Explained. London, Allen and Unwin, 1934; revised edition, 1946.
Word Warfare: Some Aspects of German Propaganda and English Liberty. London, Nicholson and Watson, 1939.

The American Nation: A Short History of the United States. London, Cassell, 1942; revised edition, with Julian Gloag, 1955.
What about Business? London, Penguin, 1942; revised edition, as *What about Enterprise?,* London, Allen and Unwin, 1948.
The Missing Technician in Industrial Production. London, Allen and Unwin, 1944.
The Englishman's Castle: A History of Homes, Large and Small, in Town and Country, from a.d. 100 to the Present Day. London, Eyre and Spottiswoode, 1944; revised edition, 1949.
Plastics and Industrial Design. London, Allen and Unwin, 1945.
British Furniture Makers. London, Collins, and New York, Hastings House, 1945.
House Out of Factory, with Grey Wornum. London, Allen and Unwin, 1946.
Good Design, Good Business. London, His Majesty's Stationery Office, 1947.
The English Tradition in Design. London, Penguin, 1947; revised edition, London A. and C. Black, 1959; New York, Macmillan, 1960.
Self-Training for Industrial Designers. London, Allen and Unwin, 1948.
A History of Cast Iron in Architecture, with D.L. Bridgewater. London, Allen and Unwin, 1948.
How to Write Technical Books. London, Allen and Unwin, 1950.
Two Thousand Years of England. London, Cassell, 1952.
A Short Dictionary of Furniture. London, Allen and Unwin, and New York, Studio, 1952; revised edition, 1969; revised by Clive Edwards as *A Complete Dictionary of Furniture,* Woodstock, New York, Overlook Press, 1991.
Georgian Grace: A Social History of Design from 1660 to 1830. London, A. and C. Black, and New York, Macmillan, 1956.
Guide to Western Architecture. London, Allen and Unwin, and New York, Grove Press, 1958.
Advertising in Modern Life. London, Heinemann, 1959.
Victorian Comfort: A Social History of Design 1830-1900. London, A. and C. Black, and New York, Macmillan, 1961.
Victorian Taste: Some Social Aspects of Architecture and Industrial Design from 1820-1900. London, A. and C. Black, and New York, Macmillan, 1962.
The English Tradition in Architecture. London, A. and C. Black, and New York, Barnes and Noble, 1963.
Architecture. London, Cassell, 1963; New York, Hawthorn, 1964.
The Englishman's Chair: Origins, Design, and Social History of Seat Furniture in England. London, Allen and Unwin, 1964; as *The Chair,* South Brunswick, New Jersey, A.S. Barnes, 1967.
Enjoying Architecture. Newcastle-upon-Tyne, Oriel Press, 1965.
A Social History of Furniture Design from b.c. 1300 to a.d. 1960. London, Cassell, and New York, Crown, 1966.
Mr. Loudon's England: The Life and Work of John Claudius Loudon, and His Influence on Architecture and Furniture Design. Newcastle-upon-Tyne, Oriel Press, 1970.
Guide to Furniture Styles: English and French 1450-1850. London, A. and C. Black, and New York, Scribner, 1972.
The Architectural Interpretation of History. London, A. and C. Black, 1975.

Editor, *Design in Modern Life.* London, Allen and Unwin, 1934.
Editor, *The Place of Glass in Building.* London, Allen and Unwin, 1943; revised edition, 1948.
Editor, *Introduction to Early English Decorative Detail.* London, Academy, 1965.

*   *   *

In a writing career spanning more than 50 years John Gloag published more than 60 books. These include works dealing with history, social history, architecture, propaganda, and industrial art as well as numerous short stories, mysteries, mainstream novels, and science fiction. The science fiction, written mostly in the 1930s and 1940s, is more closely related to the fiction of Huxley, Stapledon, and Beresford than to the products of the burgeoning SF magazine market of that period.

The short stories often deal with unexplainable phenomena and science fiction concepts, but the brevity of the form does not allow Gloag fully to explore the ramifications of his ideas.

To-morrow's Yesterday, Gloag's first extended foray into SF, uses the complicated device of a motion picture within the novel. The motion picture is represented as an attempt by the species which has succeeded man to understand the forces within humanity that led to its extinction. The creatures from the future examine the contemporary, 1930 situation, and conclude that "They all lived for themselves!" The creatures then travel back in time to view a conversation between Herod and Pilate and they remark "There have been great ones who could see and teach and plan . . . But . . . with them everything ended in words." Subsequent scenes in the film show the beginning of the war which leads to man's descent into barbarism, and several stages in man's reversion to animality. The concluding portion of the book depicts the public's reaction to the film and allows Gloag to comment bitterly on the worlds of advertising, newspaper publishing, and to show that the world is following the path outlined in the film.

In *Winter's Youth* Gloag examines the political and social consequences of a process that arrests and reverses aging. Peripheral to the main plot, but lending verisimilitude to the action, are the concepts of radiant inflammatol (the deadliest of all explosives which makes war impossible), government advertising in newspapers, a faked new apocryphal book of the Bible, German pagan religion, and a new British political party. Much of the action concerns the political manoeuvring which arises because of the disclosure of the faked apocrypha and the consequences that the age-arresting process has on the users and on the general public. Gloag creates a scathing portrait of political partisanship, but he again attacks journalism and the advertising industry.

99% explores the effects on a number of men, who represent various aspects of society, of a drug which allows the individual to reexperience a significant event in the life of one of his ancestors. The motivating concept, that it is possible to relive important experiences of remote ancestors, because the memories are somehow incorporated into the genetic material, is one that has no scientific validity, but Gloag is not interested in the concept. He is concerned with the effects that the experiences have upon modern, civilized men. The experiences dredged up, both by the drug and by the influence of the man supplying the drug, range from that of a waylaid, failed Crusader, to that of a young boy fleeing the sack of Carthage, to that of a shaman of a tribe that existed millennia ago. The memories change the outlooks of the contemporary men in ways that could not have been anticipated.

—Harvey J. Satty

GODFREY, R.H. *See* **TUBB, E.C.**

GODWIN, Tom

Nationality: American. **Born:** 1915. **Career:** Worked as a prospector. **Died:** 1980.

SCIENCE FICTION PUBLICATIONS

Novels (series: Ragnarok)

The Survivors (Ragnarok). Hicksville, New York, Gnome Press, 1958; as *Space Prison,* New York, Pyramid, 1960.
The Space Barbarians (Ragnarok). New York, Pyramid, 1964.
Beyond Another Sun. New York, Curtis, 1971.

*   *   *

"The Cold Equations" is the story for which Tom Godwin is best known and upon which rests his secure place in the history of science fiction. It is entirely fitting that it was first published in John Campbell's *Astounding Science Fiction* because, although written slightly after the period of Campbell's domination of the genre magazines and, therefore, the genre itself, the story is the prototypic Campbellian story, at once a prime example of Golden Age science fiction and a definer of it. James Gunn, in *The Road to Science Fiction 3,* called "The Cold Equations" a touchstone story.

"The Cold Equations" presents a future in which space travel has become developed enough for mankind to begin the process of colonizing some of the other habitable planets. But this is only the beginning of the great age of colonization. Fuel still needs to be exactly measured and at every turn the universe threatens human life. Godwin makes clear, however, that these threats are not the creations of a hostile universe for the specific destruction of humanity. These threats originate within the nature of the universe, and all objects, living or not, that inhabit that universe must live under their sway. Thus, early in the story, Godwin presents his reader with a view of space that parallels the view of the frontier held by early American pioneers.

In "The Cold Equations," a space colony is suffering from a disease for which there is a serum, and a small ship is sent to rescue the colonists. The ship has sufficient fuel to carry the pilot and his cargo to the stricken colony and not a drop more. However, a girl has stowed away on the ship with the hope of once again seeing her brother who is one of the colonists. Within this simple plot Godwin develops the most popular of Campbell's themes: ignorance kills. Whether man is challenged by a creation of science, an alien invasion, or a new environment, what will most surely destroy the race is not the challenge but a failure to know the nature of that challenge. The girl did not realize the consequences of her actions, but at the end of the story she must be jettisoned. The universe is not sentimental. While it will make no special effort to kill a human being, it will do nothing to save one, either. Nothing Godwin has written since has equalled this one story.

In *The Survivors* a race of aliens maroon some 4,000 humans on a hostile planet barely capable of sustaining human life. But the humans do adapt and later return to destroy the aliens who were once their conquerors. Mankind will prevail, Godwin tells the reader, for the race has the intelligence, desire, and energy to survive all threats. *The Space Barbarians,* a sequel to *The Survivors,* continues this theme, though in a more space-opera manner. Godwin returns again to the pioneer nature of the human race in *Beyond Another Sun,* in which alien anthropologists observe humans as they colonize a planet.

In each of the works that follow "The Cold Equations" many of the features that characterized that story can be seen: a clear narrative voice, simple descriptions that economically fill in the background needed to understand the action of the characters, themes that form the very foundation of Golden Age SF, and occasional sentimental passages that, at their best, soften the harshness of the fictional worlds and, at their worst, detract from the effect Godwin is attempting to achieve. But "The Cold Equations" contains these traits in a way that few other science fiction works have matched.

—Stephen H. Goldman

GOLD, H(orace) L(eonard)

Nationality: American. **Born:** Montreal, Canada, 26 April 1914; immigrated to the United States at age 2. **Military Service:** Served as a combat engineer in the Pacific, 1944-46. **Family:** Married 1) Evelyn Stein in 1939; 2) Muriel Conley; one son and three step-children. **Career:** Assistant editor, *Thrilling Wonder Stories, Startling Stories,* and *Captain Future,* and associate editor, Standard Magazines, New York, 1939-41; managing and contributing editor, Scoop Publications, New York, 1941-43; editor, A and S Comics, New York, 1942-44; contract writer, Molle Mystery Theatre, 1943-44; president, Rossard Company, New York, 1946-50; editor, *Galaxy,* and Galaxy Science Fiction Novels, New York, 1950-61; editor, *Beyond Fantasy Fiction,* 1953-55, and *If,* 1959-61: retired as disabled veteran, 1960. **Awards:** Hugo award, for nonfiction, 1953; Westercon Life Achievement award, 1975; Milford award, 1987. **Address:** 1253 North Havenhurst, Apartment 116, Los Angeles, California 90046, U.S.A.

SCIENCE FICTION PUBLICATIONS

Short Stories

The Old Die Rich and Other Science Fiction Stories: With Working Notes and an Analysis of Each Story. New York, Crown, 1955; London, Dobson, 1965.

OTHER PUBLICATIONS

Other

What Will They Think of Last? SF for Fun and Profit from the Inside, edited by Eugene J. Gold. Crestline, California, Institute for the Development of the Harmonious Human Being, 1976.

Editor, *Galaxy Reader* [and *Second to Sixth*]. New York, Crown, 2 vols., 1952-54; Garden City, New York, Doubleday, 4 vols., 1958-62; selection from *The Second Galaxy Reader* as *The Galaxy Science Fiction Omnibus,* London, Grayson, 1955.

Editor, *Five Galaxy Short Novels.* Garden City, New York, Doubleday, 1958.

Editor, *The World That Couldn't Be and 8 Other Novelets from Galaxy.* Garden City, New York, Doubleday, 1959.

Editor, *Bodyguard and Four Other Short Novels from Galaxy.* Garden City, New York, Doubleday, 1960.

Editor, *Mind Partner and Eight Other Novelets from Galaxy.* Garden City, New York, Doubleday, 1961.

*

H.L. Gold comments:

(1985) I would very much like to be rediscovered as a science fiction and fantasy author (including work since 1955), but I'm overshadowed as editor.

*   *   *

About half a dozen editors and publishers have had a truly pervasive effect on the development of science fiction. Some of these are well remembered; others, almost wholly forgotten. The list must include Frank A. Munsey, who virtually invented the pulp magazine in 1896, Farnsworth Wright (*Weird Tales*), Hugo Gernsback (*Amazing Stories*), John W. Campbell, Jr. (*Astounding*), Anthony Boucher and J. Francis McComas (*The Magazine of Fantasy and Science Fiction*), and H.L. Gold. After many years of editorial work, in 1950 Gold became the founding editor of *Galaxy Science Fiction.* The importance of this event cannot be overemphasized. For some 20 years prior to 1950, *Astounding* had paid the highest rates in the science fiction field, had enjoyed the backing of the largest, wealthiest, and most influential publishing house, and had maintained by far the largest circulation. As a consequence, the bulk of quality writing in the field was calculated to reach *Astounding.* Even the lesser magazines, because they tended to subsist on the leavings of *Astounding,* also reflected the taste of *Astounding*'s editors. With the almost simultaneous founding of *Fantasy and Science Fiction* and *Galaxy,* two new markets opened which paid competitive rates and offered generally equivalent quality of presentation and prestige. *F & SF* emphasized style, wit, and general literary excellence. *Galaxy,* reflecting Gold's worldview, placed heavy emphasis on social satire, combining relevance of theme with irreverence of outlook. The result was a magnificent flowering of novels and short stories by Pohl and Kornbluth, Simak, Asimov, Bradbury, Heinlein, and scores of others.

Gold's own writing has been of limited quantity and impact, although it is far from worthless. His only novel, *None But Lucifer,* was written in collaboration with L. Sprague de Camp for *Unknown* magazine in 1939, and has never been reprinted. Of Gold's scattered short stories, a dozen were gathered in *The Old Die Rich.* As might be expected, the stories reflect considerable, often acid, wit. The title story of the book concerns a complex scheme of time travel and murder, unravelled through careful, formal detection techniques. "Love in the Dark" deals lightly with the succubus theme, brought up-to-date and converted into a tale of contact with aliens. "Trouble with Water," probably Gold's best-remembered story, is a fantasy concerning a small businessman who offends a water elemental. A number of other stories in the book, particularly "The Man with English" and "Problem in Murder," hold up well despite their age. Particularly interesting in the book is Gold's page of notes on each story, detailing his original conception, technical problems, and writing approach to that project.

Also of interest is *What Will They Think of Last?,* a collection of Gold's editorials from *Galaxy.* Some of the editorials reflect ephemeral concerns, but others are most illuminating on the functioning of *Galaxy* during the Gold era.

—Richard A. Lupoff

GOLDIN, Stephen

Nationality: American. **Born:** Philadelphia, Pennsylvania, 28 February 1947. **Education:** University of California, Los Angeles, B.A. in astronomy 1968. **Family:** Married 1) Kathleen McKinney (Kathleen Sky), in 1972 (divorced 1982); Mary Mason in 1987. **Career:** Physicist, Navy Space Systems Activity, El Segundo, California, 1968-71; manager, Circle K. Grocery Store, Rosemead, California, 1972; editor, Jaundice Press, Van Nuys, California, 1973-74; editor, *San Francisco Ball*, 1973-74, *SFWA Bulletin*, 1975-77, and *L-5 News*, 1981-83. Since 1991, technical writer/game designer for Spectrum Holobyte, Alameda, California. **Address:** 744 Haight Ave., Alameda, California 94501, U.S.A.

SCIENCE FICTION PUBLICATIONS

Novels (series: Jade Darcy; The Family d'Alembert; The Parsina Saga; Honey B; Star Trek)

Herds. Don Mills, Ontario, Laser, 1975.
Caravan. Don Mills, Ontario, Laser, 1975.
Scavenger Hunt (Honey B). Toronto, Laser, 1975.
Finish Line (Honey B). Toronto, Laser, 1976.
Imperial Stars, with E.E. Smith (d'Alembert). New York, Pyramid, and London, Panther, 1976.
Strangler's Moon, with E.E. Smith (d'Alembert). New York, Pyramid, 1976; London, Panther, 1977.
The Clockwork Traitor, with E.E. Smith (d'Alembert). New York, Pyramid, 1977; London, Panther, 1978.
Assault on the Gods. Garden City, New York, Doubleday, 1977; London, Hale, 1978.
Getaway World, with E.E. Smith (d'Alembert). New York, Pyramid, and London, Panther, 1977.
Mindflight. New York, Fawcett, 1978; London, Hamlyn, 1982.
Appointment at Bloodstar, with E.E. Smith (d'Alembert). New York, Pyramid, 1978; as *The Bloodstar Conspiracy,* London, Panther, 1978.
The Purity Plot, with E.E. Smith (d'Alembert). New York, Berkley, and London, Panther, 1978.
Trek to Madworld: A Star Trek Novel. New York, Bantam, 1979; London, Titan, 1994.
The Eternity Brigade. New York, Fawcett, 1980.
A World Called Solitude. Garden City, New York, Doubleday, 1981.
And Not Make Dreams Your Master. New York, Fawcett, 1981.
Planet of Treachery, with E.E. Smith (d'Alembert). New York, Berkley, and London, Panther, 1982.
Eclipsing Binaries, with E.E. Smith (d'Alembert). New York, Berkley, 1983; London, Panther, 1984.
The Omicron Invasion, with E.E. Smith (d'Alembert). New York, Berkley, 1984.
Revolt of the Galaxy, with E.E. Smith (d'Alembert). New York, Berkley, and London, Grafton, 1985.

The Rehumanization of Jade Darcy: Jade Darcy and the Affair of Honor, with Mary Mason. New York, New American Library, and London, New English Library, 1988.
The Parsina Saga: Shrine of the Desert Mage. New York, Bantam, 1988.
The Storyteller and the Jann. New York, Bantam, 1988.
Crystals of Air and Water. New York, Bantam, 1989.
The Rehumanization of Jade Darcy: Jade Darcy and the Zen Pirates, with Mary Mason. New York, Penguin, 1990.

OTHER PUBLICATIONS

Other

The Business of Being a Writer, with Kathleen Sky. New York, Harper, 1982.

Editor, with David Gerrold, *Protostars.* New York, Ballantine, 1971.
Editor, with David Gerrold, *Generation: An Anthology of Speculative Fiction.* New York, Dell, 1972.
Editor, *The Alien Condition.* New York, Ballantine, 1973.
Editor, with David Gerrold, *Science Fiction Emphasis I: An Anthology of Original Science Fiction.* New York, Ballantine, 1974.
Editor, with David Gerrold, *Alternities.* New York, Dell, 1974.
Editor, with David Gerrold, *Ascents of Wonder.* New York, Popular Library, 1977.

*

Stephen Goldin comments:

Looking closely at my work might almost give one the impression that my short stories were written by someone entirely different than the author of my novels. This is due in part to the changes in myself, and in part to the nature of the works themselves.

With only a few exceptions, my short stories are downbeat and tragic. They were the product of my early career, a young man trying to impress the world with his cynicism and acceptance of the universe's perversity. In part, too, this is because a short story is like a photograph, an encapsulated moment of immense importance to the character(s) involved—and it seemed far easier for me to capture a tragic moment than a triumphant one. My mind was at its blackest in tragedies like "The Last Ghost," "Sweet Dreams, Melissa," "Of Love, Free Will, and Gray Squirrels on a Summer Evening," and "Xenophobe"; but there is a bleakness in even those stories with a primarily humorous slant: "The World Where Wishes Worked," "Stubborn," "Grim Fairy Tale," and "Constance and the Sex Machine."

My career (and my apparent outlook) did a complete turnabout when I switched to writing novels in the mid-1970s. Every single one of my novels has an upbeat ending. If a short story may be likened to a photograph, then a novel is a movie, the progression of a character through events, changing at least himself if not the world around him. I like to believe now that a person is responsible for his own life; even if the situation starts out looking hopeless and desperate, a firm and resourceful person can take charge of himself and turn the situation around. My characters may go through hell, but in the end they manage to triumph over their adversities. The somewhat more mature me doesn't need to hide behind that shield of cynicism. I've become a born-again optimist. If there is any message in my work at all, it's that no matter how bad things might be there is always a solution to the person willing to work for it.

* * *

Stephen Goldin established himself as one of the more reliable writers of science fiction and fantasy adventure during the first few years of his career, although his voice has been mostly silent during the first half of the 1990s. His first novels were for the ill-fated Laser line, but he was able to move on from there to more prestigious publishers. *Scavenger Hunt,* the best of his four Laser novels, deals with a brother and sister on an interstellar scavenger hunt, a social event that takes on more than casual significance as murder and mayhem are added to the competition. Goldin completed their quest for victory in the sequel, *Finish Line.*

Herds is set in a hippie commune, where a young woman has become telepathically linked to aliens. Her companions have been framed for murder by a local man, complicating this crisis in her life. The aliens are a herd culture, the ultimate communists, and the contrasts between them and the commune is fascinating. Goldin's fourth Laser novel was *Caravan,* a postapocalypse story wherein a group of people flee across country to secret caverns where the first starship is under construction. An overused plot limps along to a satisfactory but unedifying conclusion.

A fugitive from the repressive government of Earth lives like a hermit in *A World Called Solitude,* until a castaway tells him of encroaching aliens and the urgent need to warn the home world. Initially he is indisposed to help, but ultimately species loyalty prevails and he uses the technology of an extinct race to foil the intruders. *Assault on the Gods* features a primitive planet dominated by a secret computer complex that functions as a god. Adventurers from off planet set off on a quest to free the natives from this mental domination.

One of Goldin's best novels is *Mindflight.* Telepaths fall prey to telepause, a period of increased telepathic ability that shortly precedes death. The protagonist is a secret agent who is affected by the onset of this condition, and becomes the object of a manhunt by other agents because of a secret locked inside his mind.

And Not Make Dreams Your Master concerns a world where dreams can be broadcast and talented dreamers are at the peak of the entertainment industry, shaping their fantasies to cater to public demand. When the greatest of all dreamers crosses the border into insanity, the lives of those vicariously participating are suddenly in jeopardy. *The Eternity Brigade* follows the careers of several professional soldiers whose personalities are stored in memory banks, brought back to consciousness only when there is a battle to be fought. After several generations have passed in the outside world, these soldiers are virtually slaves, their tapes have been stolen and duplicated, and they may end up fighting their former friends, or other versions of themselves. These last two are among Goldin's finest novels.

He also wrote several novels in the Family D'Alembert series, based on characters created by Edward E. Smith. Earth is the center of an interstellar empire with a royal family and the usual mixture of court intrigue, corrupt officials, and ambitious adventurers. Although the rulers are essentially benevolent, various factions seek to wrest control and provide the villains of each adventure. The D'Alemberts are from a heavy gravity world, and their unusual physical abilities make them perfect agents for the imperial secret service. Under the guise of a traveling circus, they become involved in a series of adventures to ensure the continuity of the empire.

The Imperial Stars was the first adventure, serving primarily to establish the background. A group of assassins must be infiltrated and neutralized before they can carry out their plans. Criminals are systematically kidnapping people from a resort world in *Strangler's Moon.* A robot is married to a member of the royal family in *The Clockwork Traitor,* weakest in the series. An old enemy returns in *Getaway World,* planning an alliance between various criminal organizations. Arch villains "C" and the Lady "A" appear in the next, *Appointment at Bloodstar,* and return in subsequent books. In their first foray, they use assassination to weaken confidence in the government. In subsequent titles such as *The Purity Plot* and *Planet of Treachery,* the D'Alemberts tangle with the sinister duo repeatedly.

The D'Alembert series stopped in the mid-1980s, and Goldin did not appear in print again for several years. His subsequent books have shown even greater maturity than the best of his early work. The "Parsina Saga," a fantasy trilogy consisting of *Shrine of the Desert Mage, The Storyteller and the Jann,* and *Crystals of Air and Water,* is a wonderfully inventive series of Arabian nights style adventures, with the protagonists facing off against an evil djinn and his army.

Goldin later launched a new science fiction series, written in collaboration with Mary Mason, featuring Jade Darcy, interstellar traveler and adventurer. In *Jade Darcy and the Affair of Honor,* she is employed as a bouncer on an alien world, but is trapped into conducting a dangerous secret mission against unfriendly aliens because of a mystery in her past. The superior sequel, *Jade Darcy and the Zen Pirates,* transports her to a monastery world where she becomes involved in the various plots and counterplots involved in the succession to supreme power. Both novels are overtly action-oriented, but Goldin demonstrates an increasing mastery of pace and characterization with these novels.

Although not noted as a short story writer, Goldin is not without talent in that area as well. "But as a Soldier, for His Country," upon which *Mindflight* is based, stands quite well on its own. There is genuine feeling in "Sweet Dreams, Melissa," about a sentient computer personality, and in a short fantasy story, "The Last Ghost," who exists in a world where death has been conquered. Unfortunately, Goldin's only science fiction credit during the early 1990s of any note is "The Height of Intrigue," and there were no additional novels. That single story is a complex web of intrigue involving the legal problems affecting Earth's relationship with a galactic society. Someone is smuggling human literature off the planet in contravention of the law, and the authorities want it brought to a stop.

It's unclear why Goldin has left the field, since his novels are fine examples of adventure-oriented science fiction. Perhaps he fell prey to the change of emphasis to more introspective, serious themes. Hopefully, at some point he'll emerge to continue the steady development apparent in his published work.

—Don D'Ammassa

GOLDING, (Sir) William (Gerald)

Nationality: British. **Born:** St. Columb Minor, Cornwall, 19 September 1911. **Education:** Marlborough Grammar School; Brasenose College, Oxford, B.A. 1935. **Military Service:** Served in the Royal Navy, 1940-45. **Family:** Married Ann Brookfield in

1939; one son and one daughter. **Career:** Writer, actor, and producer in small theatre companies, 1934-40; schoolmaster, Bishop Wordsworth's School, Salisbury, Wiltshire, 1945-61; Visiting Professor, Hollins College, Virginia, 1961-62. **Awards:** James Tait Black Memorial prize, 1980; Booker prize, 1980; Nobel Prize for Literature, 1983. M.A.: Oxford University, 1961; D.Litt.: University of Sussex, Brighton, 1970; University of Kent, Canterbury, 1974; University of Warwick, Coventry, 1981; the Sorbonne, Paris, 1983; Oxford University, 1983; LL.D.: University of Bristol, 1984. Honorary Fellow, Brasenose College, 1966. Fellow, 1955, and Companion of Literature, 1984, Royal Society of Literature. C.B.E. (Commander, Order of the British Empire), 1966. Knighted, 1988. **Died:** 19 June 1993.

SCIENCE FICTION PUBLICATIONS

Novels

Lord of the Flies: A Novel. London, Faber, 1954; New York, Coward McCann, 1955.
The Inheritors. London, Faber, 1955; New York, Harcourt Brace, 1962.

Short Stories

The Scorpion God: Three Short Novels. London, Faber, 1971; New York, Harcourt Brace, 1972.

OTHER PUBLICATIONS

Novels

Pincher Martin. London, Faber, 1956; as *The Two Deaths of Christopher Martin,* New York, Harcourt Brace, 1957.
Free Fall. London, Faber, 1959; New York, Harcourt Brace, 1960.
The Spire. London, Faber, and New York, Harcourt Brace, 1964.
The Pyramid. London, Faber, and New York, Harcourt Brace, 1967.
Darkness Visible. London, Faber, and New York, Farrar Straus, 1979.
Rites of Passage. London, Faber, and New York, Farrar Straus, 1980.
The Paper Men. London, Faber, and New York, Farrar Straus, 1984.
Close Quarters. London, Faber, and New York, Farrar Straus, 1987.
Fire Down Below. London, Faber, and New York, Farrar Straus, 1989.
To The Ends of the Earth (includes *Rites of Passage, Close Quarters,* and *Fire Down Below*). London, Faber, 1991.
The Double Tongue. London, Faber, and New York, Farrar Straus, 1995.

Plays

The Brass Butterfly, adaptation of his story "Envoy Extraordinary" (produced London, 1958). London, Faber, 1958; Chicago, Dramatic Publishing Company, n.d.

Radio Plays: *Miss Pulkinhorn,* 1960; *Break My Heart,* 1962.

Poetry

Poems. London, Macmillan, 1934; New York, Macmillan, 1935.

Other

The Hot Gates and Other Occasional Pieces. London, Faber, 1965; New York, Harcourt Brace, 1966.
Talk: Conversations with William Golding, with Jack I. Biles. New York, Harcourt Brace, 1970.
A Moving Target (essays). London, Faber, and New York, Farrar Straus, 1982.
An Egyptian Journal. London, Faber, 1985.

*

Critical Studies (selection): *William Golding* by Samuel Hynes, New York, Columbia University Press, 1964; *William Golding: A Critical Study* by James R. Baker, New York, St. Martin's Press, 1965; *The Art of William Golding* by Bernard S. Oldsey and Stanley Weintraub, New York, Harcourt Brace, 1965; *William Golding* by Bernard F. Dick, New York, Twayne, 1967; *William Golding: A Critical Study* by Mark Kinkead-Weekes and Ian Gregor, London, Faber, 1967, New York, Harcourt Brace, 1968; *William Golding* by Leighton Hodson, Edinburgh, Oliver and Boyd, 1969, New York, Putnam, 1971; *The Novels of William Golding* by Howard S. Babb, Columbus, Ohio State University Press, 1970; *William Golding: The Dark Fields of Discovery* by Virginia Tiger, London, Calder and Boyars, and Atlantic Highlands, New Jersey, Humanities Press, 1974; *William Golding* by Stephen Medcalf, London, Longman, 1975; *William Golding: Some Critical Considerations* edited by Jack I. Biles and Robert O. Evans, Louisville, University Press of Kentucky, 1978; *Of Earth and Darkness: The Novels of William Golding* by Arnold Johnston, Columbia, University of Missouri Press, 1980; *A View from the Spire: William Golding's Later Novels* by Don Crompton, Oxford, Blackwell, 1985; *William Golding: The Man and His Books: A Tribute on His 75th Birthday* edited by John Carey, London, Faber, 1986, New York, Farrar Straus, 1987; *William Golding: A Structural Reading of His Fiction* by Philip Redpath, London, Vision Press, 1986; *The Novels of William Golding* by Stephen Boyd, Brighton, Sussex, Harvester Press, and New York, St. Martin's Press, 1988; *William Golding* by James Gindin, London, Macmillan, and New York, St. Martin's Press, 1988.

*   *   *

William Golding's novels are unique, fabulistic inversions of traditional perspectives that explore human nature and its veneer of civilization to suggest that man's instinctual past is directly linked to our present. Their deceptively simple and economical style reinforces the illusion of primitive perceptions and primitive ties. Golding doesn't interfere or preach, but his "naturalistic-allegorical" form speaks for itself. He equates scientific and technological progress with dehumanization and tracing the defects of society directly to the defects of human nature. Often his perspectives are unexpected and startling.

Until its last chapter, *The Inheritors* is written from the point of view of the mind and senses of Neanderthals, childlike, instinctual, semi-telepathic vegetarian ape-men with a strong sense of community, people closer to the senses than the next evolutionary step forward, Cro-Magnon man, the invaders who take over Neanderthal territory. These new men, whom we see through the uncomprehending eyes of the Neanderthals, are aggressive, vicious, wolf-like meat-eaters. They walk upright and lack fur, use bow and arrows, build stockades and canoes, and take preventive measures. However, in them are the seeds of modern man: "they are the forest"; they compete for women and rank, are beset by jealousies and animosities, dissemble and plot, drown their senses in liquor, and take their sex with violence. Contact with them helps the Neanderthals discover the process of analogy and of causal connection, but also possessiveness and rationalization. It is as if reason and depravity are inextricably bound, so that "man's" lost instinctual past is forever more golden than his threatening "reasoned" future.

Lord of the Flies, Golding's best-known work, is a social allegory of human regression. Set in a post-catastrophic near future in which war has laid waste to much of the West and civilization is in ruins, the novel focuses on a boys' choir, stranded on a tropical island, to create a microcosm of the civilized world; therein the youngsters are equated with social types (the politician, the intellectual, the mystic/poet, the military leader, the bully), and the jungle with disorder, chaos, and primitive compulsions that lurk beneath the civilized surface. The story traces the loss of order and of civilized restraints, man's evolution from savage in reverse, as the boys revert to their primitive, selfish selves, beset by anger, fear, and superstition, swept by blood lust. Their struggle becomes a battle of adult proportions between the intelligent and the irrational, the humane and the bestial. The *deus ex machina* intrusion of adults at the end confirms the island as microcosm: the boys have scorched their island with fire as their parents have consumed theirs with bombs; both children and adults are irresponsible, violent, brutal, sadistic. The image of man is not pleasant: selfish, easily manipulated, at home with mindless rituals, he lives for the day, enjoys abusing the weak and the helpless, and is better than the beast only by a conscious effort.

The Scorpion God is really three short novels in one. The first, entitled "The Scorpion God," set in a land much like ancient Egypt, examines man's capacity for blindly accepting the irrational, especially if sanctified by religious trappings. Ultimately, it traces the exposure and destruction of a religion based on human gods and a myth of incestuous procreation and human sacrifice for the sake of a valley's fertility. The second, "Clonk Clonk," examines man as a sexual animal, exploring the union of a primitive hunter, Chimp, with a tribal mother, Palm, to define sexual differences as sensed by an unsophisticated primitive mentality. The third, "Envoy Extraordinary," studies man as a technological miracle worker, clever, but perhaps too clever for the good of his species. Its emphasis is on the dilemma of technological advance, the diminution of quality of life that accompanies the increase in technological knowledge.

All of Golding's works are tangential to science fiction in that they are novels of ideas, allegories evoking conflicts bound up with man's technological achievements, his mental aspirations, and his mastery of illusion and self-delusion. For example, *The Spire,* an historical study of the construction of a 400-foot spire on a medieval church, captures the pride, daring, egotism, and enthusiasm that leads man purposefully to face difficult technological challenges and to reach beyond his grasp, while the psychological projection of *Pincher Martin* captures in the last moments of consciousness the desperate fantasy of a drowning man whose mind reconstructs reality to suit his own desire for life. This greedy, lustful, self-centered British naval officer, blown off his ship by a German torpedo in the North Atlantic, sees himself in mythic roles (Ajax, Prometheus, King Lear) defiantly asserting his own fictional creation against mental and physical death. *Free Fall* challenges the assumption that man can ultimately control his universe; *Darkness Visible* begins with the Nazi firebombings of London, follows the experiences of a pitiful, aging pederast and sadistic twin terrorists (moral monsters since childhood), and ends with a terrorist fireball to explore man's essential depravity and manifest evil; and even *The Paper Men,* a realistic domestic comedy about a prominent English novelist pursued and tormented by an American academic determined to pen his authorized biography, captures a sense of life as two-dimensional farce. The Talbot trilogy (*Rites of Passage, Close Quarters,* and *Fire Down Below*), a "Ship of Fools" allegory set during the Napoleonic era, effectively evokes the wit, inventiveness, and diction of the 18th-century picaresque style, the technical ship-lore of the Hornblower series, the social setting and moral seriousness of the 19th-century novel of manners, and the concern with the duality of man of early gothic fiction: his sense of social and personal responsibility and his potential for evil. Therein, Golding recounts the sea voyage from England to the Antipodes of the aristocratic young Edmund Talbot. It is a voyage of self-discovery, a rite of passage in which man's endurance, faith, and courage are tested against nature (in particular the sea and the ice), his fellows, and himself. It is also a microcosm of the human voyage (man floundering in a sea of error), with an elaborate system of correspondences that make these books not simply a loving re-creation of "boy's own" naval books but a darker, more ambiguous allegory of modern society: its depraved depths, its shame, its purgatory, its conflicts, its dream of paradise. As the young hero discovers the lie of surface perceptions, his shipmates move from the reason and restraint of Northern latitudes to the warm-blooded abandon of Southern ones, and every man passes the antipodes between the divine and the diabolical.

Thus Golding, in a variety of forms, explores human nature. He makes us look deep into man's past to understand the drama of his present and his future; he fears that man's technological development always outstrips his moral development; he warns of the depths of man's savagery, but finds hope in minds that can question, reason, and challenge. Golding infuses realistic setting and milieu with analogical and allegorical significance to lead the reader to reexamine man's intrinsic nature.

—Gina Macdonald

GOLDSTEIN, Lisa

Nationality: American. **Born:** Los Angeles, California, 21 November 1953. **Education:** University of California, Los Angeles, B.A. 1975. **Family:** Married Douglas Asherman in 1986. Co-owner, Dark Carnival Bookstore, Berkeley, California, 1976-82. **Awards:** American Book award, 1983. **Agent:** Lynn Seligman, 400 Highland Avenue, Upper Montclair, New Jersey 07043, U.S.A. **Address:** P.O. Box 656, Pacifica, Californis 94044, U.S.A.

SCIENCE FICTION PUBLICATIONS

Novels

The Red Magician. New York, Pocket Books, 1982; London, Unicorn, 1987.

The Dream Years. New York, Bantam, 1985; London, Allen and Unwin, 1986.
A Mask for the General. New York, Bantam, 1987: London, Legend, 1989.
Tourists: A Novel. New York, Simon and Schuster, 1989.
Strange Devices of the Sun and Moon. New York, Tor, 1993.
Summer King, Winter Fool. New York, Tor, 1994.

Short Stories

Daily Voices. Eugene, Oregon, Pulphouse, 1989.
Travellers in Magic. New York, Tor, 1994.

*

Lisa Goldstein comments:

I like to write stories which take place at the intersection where fantasy and reality meet, stories which show the magic in day-to-day existence. Daily life offers endless examples of things that are strange, inexplicable, wonderful and/or terrible—dreams, humor, coincidences, love, death—yet most people seem to close their eyes to anything out of the ordinary. My novel *Tourists,* for example, and various short stories also set in the imaginary country of Amaz, show how unreal everyday life can become with just a slight change of perspective, a view from another country. *Strange Devices of the Sun and Moon* takes place in 16th-century England, at a time when fantasy and mythology were just starting to be ignored in favor of a new, scientific way of thinking. A lot of these ideas come from the surrealists, who influenced me a great deal; *The Dream Years* deals with the surrealists and their way of looking at the world.

*   *   *

Lisa Goldstein made an immediate impact on the literary world in general as well as the science fiction community with the publication of her first published fantasy novel, *The Red Magician.* This unique and original fantasy won the American Book Award even though it was a paperback original by an unknown writer, and drew public attention to her subsequent novels and short stories, most of which were immediate successes with critics and readers alike.

The Red Magician is set in a rural Jewish village in Europe in the days immediately preceding World War II. The local rabbi possesses sorcerous powers, a fact known to and approved by his constituents. One day a red-haired wanderer enters the village, a magician in his own right, and warns them of the tribulations to come, when the forces of Fascism will seize their property and their lives. The rabbi refuses to accept the warning, condemning the messenger as a deceiver and a threat. As a consequence the village is unprepared when modern armies overwhelm them, driving the sorcerous rabbi into exile in the form of a wolf and setting off a subsequent magical combat.

Goldstein skillfully intertwined fantasy and reality in the novel, allowing the reader to experience the pain and anger of the oppressed in a context that was entertaining rather than pedantic. The prose is fluid and evocative, and her portrayal of the relationship between the magician and a young woman of the village is particularly effective. After such a well-received debut, expectations for her next novel were high.

The Dream Years was an even more noteworthy achievement, although it drew less critical acclaim. Robert St. Onge is an aspir-

ing novelist trying to find happiness, love, an understanding of the world, acceptance by his peers, and his own literary voice in the art world of 1920s Paris, the birth years of the surrealist movement. He encounters an enigmatic woman who eventually leads him through a rift in time, the other end of which is the riotous Paris of 1968, where a new art movement has sprung from the ashes of the old. The contrast between the two views of art, life, and politics clash, and each is thrown into fresh relief by the other. Through the characters of St. Onge and the woman, as well as a number of historical characters recreated in great detail, we are provided insight not only into two diverse cultures, but into the means by which one evolves into the other, and the shape that our future dreams might assume.

Goldstein's third novel, *A Mask for the General,* is more conventionally science fiction, but still makes use of her unique perspective, evocative writing style, and her ability to wrap her plots in an unreal atmosphere that is nonetheless engaging and convincing. The story is set in a future America governed by the General of the title, a despotic tyrant who brutally suppresses any opposition. An underground resistance does exist, but they are a tenuous group with no real grasp of the magnitude of the task they face, and no power base either in terms of manpower or equipment to effect a revolution. There is another, more popularly based resistance, known as the Tribes. These are people who have adopted an alternate lifestyle which is tolerated if not exactly approved by the establishment. Typically, members wear elaborately constructed animal masks indicating their tribal affiliation, and have little taste for physical confrontation.

Two very different young women are thrown together against this background, and become the catalysts for a fundamental change in the relationships between the two countercultures, ultimately serving to shape the form of a unified and more effective, though quite unconventional, resistance movement. Goldstein avoids retelling old stories; there are no climactic sieges of the bastions of government, no miraculous reversal of the power structure. Nor is it a simplistic transplanting of the principles of passive resistance to a futuristic setting, but rather a rethinking of the way political and social forces can affect the nature of our society. Nevertheless the ending is upbeat, original, and evidence of Goldstein's maturity and continued growth as a novelist.

Tourists, expanded from a shorter work, is a disorienting and even frightening story of a family that travels to an imaginary foreign country where the laws of society seem to be inherently illogical. Although only marginally SF, it takes advantage of one of the field's most effective devices, the use of an essentially alien culture as the means to examine our own. It's Goldstein's most tightly controlled and effective novel to date.

Her more recent novels have moved back in the general direction of conventional fantasy, although each contains elements that set them aside from the rest of that field. *Strange Devices of the Sun and Moon* reveals another chapter in the perpetual war among the powers of Faerie, but this time the battle is played out in our world, in England during the reign of Elizabeth I. The struggle for succession in Faerie is mirrored in secretive plots against Elizabeth, and the resolution of both becomes intricately interrelated. *Summer King, Winter Fool* moves into even more mythic territory, set in a fantasy world where gods and mortals interact regularly. While a bored aristocracy struggles to win petty power struggles, the God of Summer decides to abandon Heaven for Earth, and a young man discovers his lost birthright and seeks to regain his family title. Although the themes in the latter are more conventional than in most of Goldstein's other novels, the story is embellished by her talent for making things seem not quite normal, even in the most normal of situations.

Goldstein has written a small but respected body of short fiction as well. "Ever After" is a delightful look at what happened after Cinderella and her prince were married. "Cassandra's Photographs" is a compelling fantasy about a young woman who discovers a cache of photographs of herself, in situations that have not yet occurred. The importance of family to the individual is the theme of "Alfred"; "Rites of Spring" is concerned with the effect of a seemingly endless winter. Other stories of note are "Preliminary Notes on the Jang," "Death Is Different," "The Woman in the Painting," "Infinite Riches," and "Daily Voices." Most of her best short fiction has been collected in *Travellers in Magic*.

—Don D'Ammassa

GORDON, David. *See* **GARRETT, Randall.**

GORDON, Rex

Pseudonyms: Stanley Bennett Hough; Bennett Stanley. **Nationality:** British. **Born:** Preston, Lancashire, 25 February 1917. **Education:** Preston Grammar School; Radio Officers College, Preston; attended classes of the Workers Educational Association. **Family:** Married Justa E.C. Wodschow in 1938. **Career:** Radio operator, Marconi Radio Company, 1936-38; radio officer, International Marine Radio Company, 1939-45; ran a yachting firm, 1946-51. Since the 1970s, teacher of creative writing, Workers Educational Association, and Local Authorities, Cornwall. **Awards:** Infinity award, 1957. **Agent:** A.M. Heath, 79 St. Martin's Lane, London WCHN 4AA. **Address:** 21 St. Michael's Road, Ponsanooth, Truro, Cornwall, England.

SCIENCE FICTION PUBLICATIONS

Novels

Mission in Guemo: A Novel. London, Hodder and Stoughton, 1953; New York, Walker, 1964.
Utopia 239. London, Heinemann, 1955.
Extinction Bomber (as S.B. Hough). London, Bodley Head, 1956.
No Man Friday. London, Heinemann, 1956; as *First on Mars,* New York, Ace, 1957.
First to the Stars. New York, Ace, 1959; as *The Worlds of Eclos,* London, Consul, 1961.
Beyond the Eleventh Hour (as S.B. Hough). London, Hodder and Stoughton, 1961.
First Through Time. New York, Ace, 1962; as *The Time Factor,* London, Gibbs and Phillips, 1964.
Utopia Minus X. New York, Ace, 1966; as *The Paw of God,* London, Gibbs, 1967.

The Yellow Fraction. New York, Ace, 1969; London, Dobson, 1972.

OTHER PUBLICATIONS

Novels as S.B. Hough

Frontier Incident. London, Hodder and Stoughton, 1951; New York, Crowell, 1952.
Moment of Decision. London, Hodder and Stoughton, 1952.
The Seas South. London, Hodder and Stoughton, 1953.
The Primitives. London, Hodder and Stoughton, 1954.
The Bronze Perseus. London, Secker and Warburg, 1959; New York, Walker, 1962; as *The Tender Killer,* New York, Avon, 1963.
Dear Daughter Dead. London, Gollancz, 1965; New York, Walker, 1966.
Sweet Sister Seduced. London, Gollancz, 1968; New York, Harper, 1983.
Fear Fortune, Father. London, Gollancz, 1974; New York, Harper, 1984.

Novels as Bennett Stanley

Sea Struck. New York, Crowell, 1953; as *Sea to Eden,* London, Hodder and Stoughton, 1954.
The Alscott Experiment. London, Hodder and Stoughton, 1954.
Government Contract. London, Hodder and Stoughton, 1956.

Other as S.B. Hough

A Pound a Day Inclusive: The Modern Way to Holiday Travel. London, Hodder and Stoughton, 1957.
Expedition Everyman: Your Way on Your Income to All the Desirable Places of Europe. London, Hodder and Stoughton, 1959.
Expedition Everyman 1964. London, Hodder and Stoughton, 1964.
Where? An Independent Report on Holiday Resorts in Britain and the Continent. London, Hodder and Stoughton, 1964.
Creative Writing: A Handbook for Students, Tutors and Education Authorities. Plymouth, Workers Educational Association, 1983.

*

Manuscript Collection: University of Wyoming, Laramie.

Critical Study: "The Lives and Times of Geoffrey Household" by Michael Barber, in *Books and Bookmen* (London), January 1974.

*   *   *

Rex Gordon is actually the pseudonym of Stanley B. Hough, who writes most of his fiction under his own name. The pseudonym was used for six novels published between 1955 and 1969. The first, *Utopia 239,* is a standard after-the-bomb story about the rebirth of civilization; it was not widely read and is the only one of the Rex Gordon books never reprinted. He attracted immediate attention with the novel *No Man Friday* (published in the U.S. as *First on Mars*).

The theme of man struggling to survive in a hostile environment is an old one in literature, of course, and this is a fine example of the science fiction equivalent of Stephen Crane's "The Open Boat" or Jack London's "To Build a Fire," as well as Defoe's *Robinson Crusoe.* Gordon Holder is the sole survivor of the crashlanding of the first manned expedition to Mars. With a small amount of equipment salvaged from the wreckage, he makes arrangements for his continued existence on a planet where food, water, shelter, and even oxygen cannot be taken for granted.

The adventures that follow are at once understated and melodramatic. After juryrigging a sort of bicycle, Holder takes a grand tour of the Martian landscape, carrying out some of the research projects that were the original reason for the trip to Mars, but he is constantly aware of the fact that one moment of inattention could result in his death. Gordon's meticulous attention to scientific detail lent an air of credibility to the story that elevated it above other adventure stories of its type. This is not a swashbuckling tale of action, although Holder does eventually encounter intelligent Martians. Rather than beautiful princesses or malevolent monsters, the Martians are unknowable to humanity, so alien even to the concept of technology that they have no interest in Holder, his civilization, or his fate. The single flaw in Defoe's novel is that the shipwreck seems to be a bottomless treasure trove. Gordon evades this trap by having Holder salvage minimal equipment, then leave the vicinity of the wreckage. There is no doubt that he must find the means elsewhere if he is to survive.

Although Gordon was never to achieve the success of this novel again, his subsequent efforts were certainly entertaining. *The Worlds of Eclos* (*First to the Stars* in the U.S.) features two scientists, one male and one female, who profoundly dislike each other even though they are teamed together for a trip to Mars. Through mischance, their ship leaves its course and wanders into interstellar space, and although time dilation will allow them to survive the voyage to another star, it is doubtful they will ever be able to return home. Although the woman dies, the man and their child live to meet an alien race, which Gordon uses as a device to examine humanity's foibles, at the same time he casts doubt upon our ability ever to understand another intelligence, a reprise of the theme from the waning chapters of *No Man Friday.*

The Time Factor (predictably *First Through Time* in the U.S.) makes use of a standard theme. An unmanned probe into the far future reveals a devastated Earth. A living human must volunteer to undergo the same journey, discover the cause of the disaster, and bring that information back so that it can be averted. Although the puzzle is solved, the novel ends with a pessimistic overtone.

The Paw of God is a dystopian adventure story, published in the U.S. in a revised version under the title *Utopia Minus X.* An astronaut returns to Earth from an interstellar voyage, only to discover that, because of the time differential, he has arrived after the civilization he represented has fallen prey to an oppressive worldwide dictatorship that mandates happiness and contentment, and outlaws scientific research on the basis that no future progress is possible. Gordon uses his skeptical protagonist as a device to examine the workings of tyranny, although for the most part the story remains a routine adventure story.

Gordon's last published SF novel is *The Yellow Fraction,* in many ways quite a departure for him. The setting is a colony world where three distinct political factions—the yellows, the blues, and the greens—all have very different views about how the colony should be developed, in harmony with the planet, by imposing itself on the environment, or whether to remain at all. What ensues is a mix of political struggle, military campaigns, and interplanetary adventure, unfortunately so unfocused that the story never quite comes together.

Two other science fiction novels appeared under Hough's byline, *Extinction Bomber* and *Beyond the Eleventh Hour,* but they are more properly contemporary political thrillers, in each case dealing with the possibility of worldwide nuclear conflict, and neither reached a wider genre readership.

Although Rex Gordon never lived up to the promise of his second novel, his subsequent work has been undeservedly ignored. He masked serious speculation about the future of humanity under a veneer of adventure writing, and his narrative style exudes an enthusiastic sense of wonder about the universe that communicates itself readily to his audience.

—Don D'Ammassa

GORDON, Stuart

Pseudonym for Richard Gordon. **Other Pseudonym:** Alex R. Stuart. **Nationality:** British. **Born:** Scotland in 1947. **Agent:** Maggie Noach, 21 Redan Street, London W14, England.

SCIENCE FICTION PUBLICATIONS

Novels (series: Eyes; Watchers)

Time Story. London, New English Library, 1972.
Suaine and the Crow-God. London, New English Library, 1975.
The 'Eyes' Trilogy. London, Sidgewick and Jackson, 1978.
   One-Eye. New York, DAW, 1973; London, Sidgwick and Jackson, 1974.
   Two-Eyes. New York, DAW, 1974; London, Sidgwick and Jackson, 1975.
   Three-Eyes. New York, DAW, 1975; London, Sidgwick and Jackson, 1976.
Smile on the Void: The Mythhistory of Ralph M'Botu Kitaj. New York, Berkley, 1981; London, Arrow, 1982.
Fire in the Abyss. New York, Berkley, 1983; London, Arrow, 1984.
Achon! (Watchers). London, Macdonald, 1987.
The Hidden World (Watchers). London, Macdonald, 1988.
The Mask (Watchers). London, Macdonald, 1990.

OTHER PUBLICATIONS AS ALEX R. STUART

Novels

The Outlaws. London, New English Library, 1972.
The Bike from Hell. London, New English Library, 1973.
The Devil's Rider. London, New English Library, 1973.

Other

The Paranormal: An Illustrated Encyclopedia. London, Headline, 1992.
The Encyclopedia of Myths and Legends. London, Headline, 1993.
The Book of Curses: True Tales of Voodoo, Hoodoo, and Hex. London, Headline, 1994.

*

Stuart Gordon comments:

(1985) The label "science fiction" is used to cover many different approaches to storytelling, most of which have little to do with "science" as such, save in a romantic, generalised way. The thrust of my own work has typically been occult or mythic in its main concern, and can be defined as science fiction only insofar as it has involved itself with the overtly fantastic, and insofar as it has been characterised (I hope) by that "sense of wonder" which romantically typifies the genre as a whole.

I have a strong sense of history and have drawn on this sense in my stories. "Those who forget their history are condemned to repeat it"—it disturbs me that as a whole our Western culture appears to be increasingly out of touch with any real sense of the past and how it shaped what we are now. This is not to worship or take refuge in an unreal nostalgia, but to encourage the social growth of wider, deeper perspectives, so that history as we live it at present should no longer be just "a nightmare from which we are struggling to awake," but the vital process in which, individually and collectively, we live and move and have our being.

In this respect all imaginative literature, however labelled, can play an important role. Inventing tales of fantasy for their own sake may be entertaining and even to some degree therapeutic, alleviating the problems of everyday life, but such use of the imagination is not invariably positive, and might even in some cases be considered a criminal distraction. To my mind this danger has become clearly apparent in the extent to which science fiction—once vigorously independent—has been colonised by the mass media and converted into moneyspinning wide-screen clichés which, at their worst (as in the movie of *Dune*), function as crude political propaganda disguised as entertainment. If science fiction has any sort of serious function, surely it is to encourage people to wake up and to think and see for themselves, rather than to distract them still further with the special effects of an enchanting but ultimately seedy (and deadly) hall of mirrors.

*   *   *

Drawing heavily on a sense and a feel for the depth of history, Gordon uses mythology, human experience, and his own interpretation of the forces that have shaped our culture to create new, fascinating worlds and settings in his fiction.

Gordon's first novel was *Time Story,* a short but highly inventive time-travel story involving the usual paradoxes but in subtly different and often entertaining fashion. The two main characters are compelled to act out dual roles as they seek their destiny in a timestream that may not be as immutable as common knowledge would have it. Although the novel aroused little interest, it's a tightly plotted and well-conceived work that seems to have been ignored because Gordon didn't indulge in the excesses common to this theme. The characters never quite come to life, either, and since neither of them is particularly likable, it is difficult to empathize.

The reaction to his Eyes trilogy was quite different. *One-Eye* is set in a postapocalypse version of the Earth, but so far in the future that the very nature of the disaster that destroyed the old civilization has been lost in the mists of time. In order to preserve the genetic "norm," all infants judged to be mutants are by law condemned to death. But an ancient prophecy says that a one-eyed child will be born, harbinger of a new faith that will transform the world. A disaffected military officer defects from his post and raises a force to protect the divine infant.

With the assistance of an immortal android, the outcasts flee to a rebel stronghold where the child uses its powers to raise an inhu-

man army, abandoning its former protectors. The confused line of demarcation between good and evil is a common theme in Gordon's work, where characters often change sides and the reader's loyalties are constantly shifting.

The sequel, *Two-Eyes,* is set in the same world, but with a different cast of characters. A peaceful country dedicated to artistic endeavor is torn between two internal factions, and menaced by invading barbarians from without. The telepathic dreamsong of the mutant child endangers them as well. The conflict here is designed to set the stage for the ultimate confrontation, resolved in *Three-Eyes.*

The climactic volume reveals the true nature of the cataclysm that destroyed the world, a misguided attempt to avoid a new Ice Age by tapping the power of another universe, inadvertently allowing creatures of that other reality to enter our own world. Gordon brings the trilogy to a satisfactory conclusion, tying up the loose ends and dispatching the villains.

In tone, setting, and many of the details, the trilogy is more properly a fantasy than science fiction. The technology is so far advanced above our own that it appears to be magic, as do the psychic powers possessed by many of the characters and the nearly demonic forces marshalled by the villains. Read either as science fiction or as fantasy, however, it remains a powerful, complex, and endlessly inventive story, enlivened by Gordon's erudite style and surprising plot twists.

Gordon moved more overtly into fantasy with *Suaine and the Crow-God,* but the novel was not nearly so successful as his previous work. He turned next to episodic, satiric science fiction with *Smile on the Void.* Set in the not too distant future, it follows the exploits of an adventurous con man and entrepreneur as he travels the world, seeking his destiny and a fast buck. Many of the individual episodes are hilarious, most are very, very strange, and although there is some excellent writing, the book's overall effect is disjointed and unsatisfying.

Fire in the Abyss was a noticeable improvement, although still not the equal of Gordon's earlier work. The U.S. government has been snatching historical figures out of time, but they make a serious mistake when they choose Sir Humphrey Gilbert. Bold, intelligent, curious, and talented, Gilbert establishes a telepathic link with some of the other prisoners and arranges a grand escape. We then see the future of our present culture through the skeptical eyes of an ancestor. Gilbert is a brilliantly portrayed rogue, in what is actually a very amusing novel.

Under his real name, Richard, Gordon was published four times in the now defunct *New Worlds* and its companion magazine, *Science Fantasy.* Two of these are worth noting. In "A Light in the Sky," a destroyed moon colony continues to broadcast a distress signal, providing a constant reproach for uncaring humanity. "Time's Fool" is a precursor of *Fire in the Abyss.* The Marquis De Sade is pulled through time to our future where he is placed on trial, only to prove himself a superior character to those set up as his judges.

—Don D'Ammassa

GOTLIEB, Phyllis (Fay)

Nationality: Canadian. **Born:** Phyllis Fay Bloom, Toronto, Ontario, 25 May 1926. **Education:** Public schools in Toronto; University of Toronto, B.A. in English 1948, M.A. 1950. **Family:** Married Calvin Gotlieb in 1949; one son and two daughters. **Agent:** Donald Maass, 64 West 84th Street, New York, New York 10024, U.S.A. **Address:** 19 Lower Village Gate, Number 706, Toronto, Ontario M5P 3L9, Canada.

Science Fiction Publications

Novels (series: Dhalgren; Starcats)

Sunburst. Greenwich, Connecticut, Fawcett, 1964; London, Coronet, 1966.
O Master Caliban! A Novel (Dhalgren). New York, Harper, 1976; London, Bantam Corgi, 1979.
Trilogy:
  A Judgment of Dragons. New York, Berkley, 1980.
  Emperor, Swords, Pentacles. New York, Ace, 1982.
  The Kingdom of the Cats. New York, Ace, 1985.
Heart of Red Iron (Dhalgren; sequel to *O Master Caliban!*). New York, St. Martin's Press, 1989.

Short Stories

Son of the Morning and Other Stories. New York, Ace, 1983.

Also author of numerous short stories.

Other Publications

Novel

Why Should I Have All the Grief? Toronto, Macmillan, 1969.

Plays

Doctor Umlaut's Earthly Kingdom (broadcast, 1970; produced North Bay, Ontario, 1972). Toronto, Calliope Press, 1974.
Silent Movie Days (broadcast, 1971). Included in *The Works,* 1978.
Garden Varieties (broadcast, 1973; produced Ontario, 1973). Included in *The Works,* 1978.

Radio Plays: *Doctor Umlaut's Earthly Kingdom,* 1970; *Silent Movie Days,* 1971; *The Contract,* 1972; *Garden Varieties,* 1973; *God on Trial Before Rabbi Ovadia,* 1974.

Poetry

Who Knows One? Toronto, Hawkshead Press, 1962.
Within the Zodiac. Toronto, McClelland and Stewart, 1964.
Ordinary, Moving. Toronto, Oxford University Press, 1969.
Doctor Umlaut's Earthly Kingdom. Toronto, Calliope Press, 1974.
The Works: Collected Poems. Toronto, Calliope Press, 1978.

Other

Editor, with Douglas Barbour, *Tesseracts2.* Victoria, British Columbia, Porcépic Books, 1987.

*

Phyllis Gotlieb comments:

I like to work in as broad a range of genres as possible, and in all of them I am primarily interested in people, their emotions, actions, dynamics. After that I am interested in everything else in the universe.

*   *   *

Since 1959, Phyllis Gotlieb has produced a solid body of science fiction, including six novels and over 15 stories. While her output has been diverse and iconoclastic, it is marked by a vivid pictorial imagination, a sense of verbal fun, a serious claim to one of the most diverse science fiction bestiaries, and a frequently voiced but not stifling range of moral concerns. Much of her work also unfolds into an imaginative whole, building up a vision of GalFed (the Galactic Federation) and its struggles with various races to ensure their rights.

Gotlieb's first three published stories, "Phantom Foot," "A Grain of Manhood," and "Gingerbread Boy," are standard magazine stories of their time, clever ideas worked out with snap and economy. "A Grain of Manhood" is the most evocative and touches a deep level of human pain. In it a woman waits to give birth to a child while her husband stands angrily by. He is sterile and their match was one of convenience so he could migrate into space. She is pregnant because her transport ship crashed and she was sheltered by a strange humanoid race with prismatic skins, one of whom impregnated her in response to her deep unvoiced wish for the child she would never have with her husband. The story captures the damaged male psyche and the woman's dilemma of wanting the child and yet not wanting to hurt her husband. In the heartstopping ending the child is born a perfect replica of her husband, made so by the psychokinetic genetic manipulation practiced by the prismatic race, who drew the model from the wife's imagination. It is a bittersweet ending, for while the husband now has the child he can respectably exhibit to the world, he has revealed his shallowness by berating his wife before the birth, and while the wife has redeemed herself with her husband, she remains far from him, lost in dreams of the prismatic wonder beings.

Gotlieb's 1964 novel, *Sunburst,* is one of the most imaginative, humorous, and at the same time socially aware nuclear accident novels ever written. In it 47 psychotic children with stunning psychokinetic (psi) powers have been accidentally created by a power plant leak and are penned up in the Dump, an enclosure that is proof against their powers. Their fury against the world at large is partly because of what they are (some, like Doyboy, are physical mutants), their imprisonment, and, interestingly, because they are all from the immigrant working-class families that provided the workers in the dangerous areas of the power plant. The heroine, 13-year-old Shandy Johnson, is herself an Imper (Impervious to the psi forces) who remembers with horror the sunburst of the radioactive cancerous wound that killed her father when she was three. The novel makes use of psychology and the anthropology of Margaret Mead as Shandy finally and reluctantly joins in attempting to control a breakout by the Dumplings and opens up a way to understand them as primitives, with some of the special perceptive power of animals and animal-like lack of moral affect. The novel has a comic side in that the Dumplings are sometimes the fulfillment of children's fondest fantasies—teleporting around breaking windows, tripping policemen, and then vanishing.

"Son of the Morning" is the novella-length short story that launches Gotlieb's most enchanting creations, the hundred kilogram sentient dark red leopard derivatives called Ungruwarkh (a phonetic growl). Kheng, the male, and his mate, Prandra, who has exceptional ESP powers, spend this story accidentally trapped in an 18th-century Polish ghetto, where they have been tossed by a superbeing, a Qumedni, which turns out to be the rebel creature who in fact took leopards from Earth and made them sentient on their planet. Tangled in this tale is Gotlieb's extensive knowledge of Judiac lore, and in its wonderful conclusion the brave local rabbi finds himself, his faith sorely tried, floating in a transparent bubble in space with the cats and the Qumedon. There is much humour here, as the cats find Yiddish very hard on their sensitive hearing and are constantly having to resist the temptation to eat the wonderful smelling humans.

The obvious success of Prandra and Kheng led to *A Judgment of Dragons,* four tales of their adventures, the first of which is "Son of the Morning." "The King's Dogs" is a detective story that centres on the murder of an ESP in the ESP institute, the destruction of the 300-year-old brain-in-a-glasstex-case who was Prandra and Kheng's dearest friend. Then follows "Nebuchadnezzar," in which the cats help a race of living blue bathmats to defeat drug smugglers, and, finally, "A Judgment of Dragons," in which the other Qumedni finally come to judge the maverick who made the cats sentient. This tale approaches the theological, for Prandra and Kheng are actually meeting their maker and his enemies in a climactic engagement.

The Ungruwarkh make two more appearances in Gotlieb's work. *Emperor, Swords, Pentacles* is a richly imagined novel in which Emerald, daughter of Kheng and Prandra, and her impetuous mate Raanung are brought to assist in resisting a complex plot to overrun a planet populated by sentient medieval crawfish. This novel is crowded with the wonderful Gotlieb beasts, including an intelligent 40-year-old, one-metre-long embryo arrested at three months growth and an ESP, which is essentially a brain with five eyes in a ball of leaves mounted on chicken feet. The cats are particularly well developed as savage ironists.

The Kingdom of the Cats is the last novel dealing with the red leopards, and it is set chiefly in the Grand Canyon where a group of them, who have volunteered to return to Earth, are slaughtered. The solution to this horror leads through half the galaxy, and the Ungruwarkh surprise even their Qumedon creator. The novel ends in an unusual unwinding tone, which does credit to a science fiction author with the sense and balance to leave her most memorable creations at their peak.

Gotlieb's other novel sequence is *O Master Caliban!* and its sequel, *Heart of Red Iron.* These books deal with a wild planet where Dhalgren, while doing biological experiments, has been overwhelmed by the ergs, intelligent mobile machines. His son Sven, human but four-armed, leads a strange group of castaways (an intelligent, speech-making gibbon, a likewise gifted 14-hands-tall goat) across the planet to rescue his father and prevent the ergs from sending a hominoid-erg replica of his father out into the universe. In the second novel a return to the planet by an older Sven enmeshes him in a second struggle with the ergs and a complex mesh of other races who are being brought to colonise, including 50-foot sentient pythons with horns, and the Crystalloids, metallic creatures with nasty tempers who are carried about in boxes. There is also the attempt to rescue the mysterious Empress of Stones, whose ship has crashed into a volcano on the planet. Both of these novels have an oppressive sense of a struggle to survive against both the planet and their enemies and both teem with a profusion of description. With its strong Shakespearean overtones of the rights of

creators and their responsibilities, and the subsidiary conflict of robot and man, *O Master Caliban!* is Gotlieb's most effective and most moving novel.

—Peter A. Brigg

GOTSCHALK, Felix C.

Nationality: American. **Born:** Richmond, Virginia, 7 September 1929. **Education:** Virginia Commonwealth University, Richmond, B.S. 1954 (Phi Beta Kappa), M.S. 1956; Tulane University, New Orleans, Ph.D. 1958. **Military Service:** Served in the United States Marine Corps, 1947-49. **Family:** Married Nelle Mull in 1957; one son and one daughter. **Career:** Draftsman, Vepco, Richmond, 1946-47, 1949-51; pianist, Chelf's, 1951-56, and On the Road, 1956-58, both in Richmond; Assistant Professor, Nicholls State University, Thibodaux, Louisiana, 1958-62, and Bowman Medical School, Winston-Salem, North Carolina, 1962-70; in private practice as a psychologist, Winston-Salem, 1970-81. Since 1981, full-time writer. **Address:** 4021 Tangle Lane, Winston-Salem, North Carolina 27106, U.S.A.

SCIENCE FICTION PUBLICATIONS

Novel

Growing Up in Tier 3000. New York, Ace, 1975.

Short Stories

Author of numerous short stories.

*

Manuscript Collection: Temple University, Philadelphia.

Felix C. Gotschalk comments:

(1981) Writing is for me an indulgence, an egocentric luxuriation, something I do because it pleases me. I have experimented (consciously and unconsciously) with verbosity, neologisms, symmetry, cadence, self-canceling reciprocity, and, even, monosyllabicity. I cannot plot story lines and do not attempt to do so. I do not know what is going to happen in any of my stories; and it is special voyeuristic fun to have a good flow of writing (say, 3000 words in one evening), and then read it the next day to see what it was that I wrote the night before. How to characterize my writing I do not know. One critic called it "poetic hardware," others have been less kind. I would like to write an erotic story that would guarantee the reader a spontaneous orgasm.

(1985) I am trying to be less self-indulgent in my writing, and have a 250K word mainstream novel completed, titled *Southern Pearls and Swine.* Henry Miller is my all-time favorite author, and I think J.G. Ballard is our best for evoking the "sense of wonder."

*   *   *

Felix C. Gotschalk published his first science fiction in 1974, and within a year his quirky, hyperkinetic stories were appearing in a wide range of SF publications, including Damon Knight's *Orbit* and Robert Silverberg's *New Dimensions*. Gotschalk's voice is immediately recognizable in all his work: a high-tech jargon charged with neologisms and rewired syntax that sometimes seems affected but often conveys a powerful sense of the psychic dislocations and altered sensibility of life in an advanced, high-energy civilization.

A number of Gotschalk's stories, including "A Day in the South Quad" and his novel *Growing Up in Tier 3000,* are set against a more or less common background, where life in automated urban domes allows for an impressive array of hedonistic pleasures but sharply restricts individual freedom as solicitous computer systems control man's more self-destructive tendencies. Several stories raise the question of how the enormous energy demands of such a society are to be met (in other stories this problem is dispensed with; Gotschalk has shown little interest in such genre conventions as inter-story chronologies or consistency). Others are set in the present or near-future, often told from the point of view of a middle-aged academic or administrator, as in "The Man with the Golden Reticulates" and "Charisma Leak." The voice in these stories is wry, male, and exuberantly egocentric; the prevailing sense is of the self-aware individual celebrating life despite unforestalled mortality and numerous technological forebodings.

The person of Gotschalk's protagonist is essentially identical in all his stories, whether incarnated as a high-tech infant prodigy, young stud, mature man of the world, or bionically rebuilt geezer. It can be argued that Gotschalk writes most effectively when his narrative contains more than one of these figures, whose interaction can prove more interesting than the self/other dichotomy that otherwise results. Such is the case with *Growing Up in Tier 3000,* a short but intense novel in which competition within the nuclear family for available energy compels the young children to turn upon their parents, who realize that advancing technology has left them ill-equipped to withstand their four-year-old successors.

By 1980 Gotschalk had published some 18 stories and a novel, and had explored the possibilities of his idiosyncratic newspeak perhaps to the point of diminishing returns. During this period the original anthology market in which his best work had appeared began to weaken, and perhaps for this reason, or because Gotschalk was then writing novels (several of which evidently await publication), his work began to appear less frequently. The stories he has published in recent years have relied less heavily on flamboyant stylistic effects, and many experiment with vernacular voices of odd locales in a slightly seedy future, often in the American South ("Take a Midget Step," "Vestibular Man"). The tales are upbeat, refreshing, and usually form a kind of success story. Gotschalk's characteristic buoyancy is engagingly conveyed, though he remains disconcertingly unabashed in celebrating the aggressiveness of the Western male.

—Gregory Feeley

GOULART, Ron(ald Joseph)

Pseudonyms: R.T. Edwards; Chad Calhoun; Franklin W. Dixon; Lee Falk; Ian R. Jamieson; Josephine Kains; Jillian Kearny; Howard Lee; Zeke Masters; Kenneth Robeson; Frank S. Shawn; Joseph Silva; Con Steffanson. **Nationality:** American. **Born:** Berkeley, California, 13 January 1933. **Education:** University of California, Berkeley, B.A. 1955. **Family:** Married Frances Sheridan in 1964; two sons. **Career:** Advertising copywriter, Guild Bascom and Bonfigci, San Francisco, 1955-57, 1958-60, Alan Alch Inc., Hollywood, 1960-63, and Hoefer Dietrich and Brown, San Francisco, 1966-68. Author of science fiction comic strip *Star Hawks,* with Gil Kane, 1977-79. Since 1988, consultant on William Shatner's *TekWar* series of science fiction novels; scriptwriter for the first 18 issues of Marvel's *TekWorld* comic book. Since 1994, publisher of *Ron Goulart's Weekly.* **Member:** Board of directors, Mystery Writers of America, 1979-83, 1984-88, 1989-91. **Awards:** Mystery Writers of America Edgar Allan Poe award, 1971. **Agent:** Ivy Fischer Stone, Fifi Oscard Agency, 24 West 40th Street, New York, New York 10018. **Address:** 30 Farrell Road, Weston, Connecticut 06883, U.S.A.

SCIENCE FICTION PUBLICATIONS

Novels (series: Barnum System; Harry Challenge; Battlestar Galactica; The Exchameleon; Gypsy; Ben Jolson; Odd Jobs; Skyrocket Steele; Star Hawks; Wild Talents)

The Sword Swallower (Jolson). Garden City, New York, Doubleday, 1968.
After Things Fell Apart. New York, Ace, 1970; London, Arrow, 1975.
The Fire-Eater (Barnum System). New York, Ace, 1970.
Clockwork's Pirates. New York, Ace, 1971.
Gadget Man. Garden City, New York, Doubleday, 1971; London, New English Library, 1977.
Death Cell (Barnum System). New York, Beagle, 1971.
Hawkshaw. Garden City, New York, Doubleday, 1972; London, Hale, 1973.
Plunder (Barnum System). New York, Beagle, 1972.
Wildsmith. New York, Ace, 1972.
Shaggy Planet (Barnum System). New York, Lancer, 1972.
A Talent for the Invisible (Wild Talents). New York, DAW, 1973.
The Tin Angel. New York, DAW, 1973; with *Flux,* London, Millington, 1978.
Spacehawk, Inc. New York, DAW, 1974.
Flux (Jolson). New York, DAW, 1974; with *The Tin Angel,* London, Millington, 1978.
When the Waker Sleeps. New York, DAW, 1975.
The Hellhound Project. New York Doubleday, 1975; London, Hale, 1976.
Vampirella (novelizations of comic strip):
    Bloodstalk. New York, Warner, 1975; London, Sphere, 1976.
    On Alien Wings. New York, Warner, 1975; London, Sphere, 1977.
    Deadwalk. New York, Warner, 1976; London, Sphere, 1977.
    Blood Wedding. New York, Warner, 1976.
    Deathgame. New York, Warner, 1976.
    Snakegod. New York, Warner, 1976.
A Whiff of Madness (Barnum System). New York, DAW, 1976.
The Enormous Hourglass. New York, Award, 1976.
Quest of the Gypsy: A Novel. New York, Pyramid, 1976.
Crackpot. Garden City, New York, Doubleday, and London, Hale, 1977.
The Emperor of the Last Days. New York, Popular Library, 1977.
The Panchronicon Plot. New York, DAW, 1977.
Nemo. New York, Berkley, 1977; London, Hale, 1979.
Eye of the Vulture: A Novel (Gypsy). New York Jove, 1977.
The Island of Dr. Moreau (novelization of screenplay; as Joseph Silva). New York, Ace, 1977.
Challengers of the Unknown. New York, Dell, 1977.

Capricorn One. New York, Fawcett, 1978.

Stalker from the Stars (novelization of *The Hulk* comic book; as Joseph Silva, with Len Wein and Marv Wolfman). New York, Pocket, 1978.

The Wicked Cyborg (Barnum System). New York, DAW, 1978.

Calling Dr. Patchwork (Odd Jobs). New York, DAW, 1978.

Cowboy Heaven. Garden City, New York, Doubleday, 1979; London, Hale, 1980.

Hello, Lemuria, Hello (Wild Talents). New York, DAW, 1979.

Holocaust for Hire (novelization of *Captain America* comic book; as Joseph Silva). New York, Pocket, 1979.

Star Hawks, illustrated by Gil Kane:

    Star Hawks: Empire 99 (Barnum System). New York, Playboy Press, 1980.

    The Cyborg King. Chicago, Playboy Press, 1981.

Hail Hibbler. New York, DAW, 1980.

Skyrocket Steele. New York, Pocket Books, 1980.

The Robot in the Closet. New York, DAW, 1981.

Brinkman. Garden City, New York, Doubleday, 1981.

Upside Downside. New York, DAW, 1982.

Big Bang (Odd Jobs). New York, DAW, 1982.

Battlestar Galactica, with Glen A. Larson (novelizations of teleplays):

    Greetings from Earth: A Novel. New York, Berkley, 1983.

    Experiment in Terra. New York, Berkley, 1984.

    The Long Patrol: Novel. New York, Berkley, 1984.

Hellquad. New York, DAW, 1984.

The Prisoner of Blackwood Castle (Harry Challenge). New York, Avon, 1984.

Suicide, Inc. New York, Berkley, 1985.

Brainz, Inc (Odd Jobs). New York, DAW, 1985.

Galaxy Jane. New York, Berkley, 1986.

Daredevils, Ltd (Barnum System/Exchameleon). New York, St. Martin's Press, 1987.

The Curse of the Obelisk (Harry Challenge). New York, Avon, 1987.

Starpirate's Brain (Exchameleon). New York, St. Martin's Press, 1987.

Everybody Come to Cosmo's (Exchameleon). New York, St. Martin's Press, 1988.

Novels as Con Steffanson (series: Flash Gordon in all titles)

The Lion Men of Mongo. New York, Avon, 1974.

The Plague of Sound. New York, Avon, 1974.

The Space Circus. New York, Avon, 1974.

Novels as Kenneth Robeson (series: Avenger in all titles)

The Man from Atlantis. New York, Warner, 1974.

Red Moon. New York, Warner, 1974.

The Purple Zombie. New York, Warner, 1974.

Dr. Time. New York, Warner, 1974.

The Nightwitch Devil. New York, Warner, 1974.

Black Chariots. New York, Warner, 1974.

The Cartoon Crimes. New York, Warner, 1974.

The Death Machine. New York, Warner, 1975.

The Blood Countess. New York, Warner, 1975.

The Glass Man. New York, Warner, 1975.

The Iron Skull. New York, Warner, 1975.

Demon Island. New York, Warner, 1975.

Short Stories

What's Become of Screwloose? and Other Inquiries. New York, Scribner, and London, Sidgwick and Jackson, 1971.

Ghost Breaker. New York, Ace, 1971.

Broke Down Engine and Other Troubles with Machines. New York, Macmillan, 1971.

The Chameleon Corps and Other Shape Changers (Jolson). New York, Macmillan, and London, Collier Macmillan, 1972.

Odd Job No. 101 and Other Future Crimes and Intrigues. New York, Scribner, 1974; London, Hale, 1976.

Nutzenbolts and More Troubles with Machines. New York, Macmillan, 1975; London, Hale, 1976.

Skyrocket Steele Conquers the Universe and Other Media Tales. Eugene, Oregon, Pulphouse, 1990.

OTHER PUBLICATIONS

Novels

If Dying Was All. New York, Ace, 1971.

Too Sweet to Die. New York, Ace, 1972.

The Same Lie Twice. New York, Ace, 1973.

Cleopatra Jones (novelization of screenplay). New York, Warner, 1973.

Chains (novelization of TV series; as Howard Lee). New York, Warner, 1973.

Superstition (novelization of TV series; as Howard Lee). New York, Warner, 1973.

One Grave Too Many. New York, Ace, 1974.

The Tremendous Adventures of Bernie Wine. New York, Warner, 1975.

Cleopatra Jones and the Casino of Gold (novelization of screenplay). New York, Warner, 1975.

Agent of Love (as Jillian Kearny). New York, Warner, 1979.

Ghosting. Toronto, Raven House, 1980.

Love's Claimant (as Jillian Kearny). New York, Warner, 1981.

Prize Meets Murder (as R.T. Edwards, with Otto Penzler). New York, Pocket, 1984.

A Graveyard of My Own. New York, Walker, 1985.

Triple "O" Seven (as Ian R. Jamieson). Vancouver, Talon, 1985; New York, Mysterious Press, 1990.

The Wisemann Originals. New York, Walker, 1989.

Even the Butler Was Poor. New York, Walker, 1990: Bath, Avon, Chivers, 1992.

The Tijuana Bible. New York, St. Martin's Press, 1990.

Now He Thinks He's Dead. New York, Walker, 1992.

Novels as Frank S. Shawn (series: Phantom in all titles)

The Veiled Lady. New York, Avon, 1973.

The Golden Circle. New York, Avon, 1973.

The Mystery of the Sea Horse. New York, Avon, 1973.

The Hydra Monster. New York, Avon, 1973.

The Goggle-Eyed Pirates (as Lee Falk). New York, Avon, 1974.

The Swamp Rats. New York, Avon, 1974.

Novels as Con Steffanson

Laverne and Shirley: Teamwork (novelization of television play). New York, Warner, 1976.

Laverne and Shirley: Easy Money (novelization of television play). New York, Warner, 1976.
Laverne and Shirley: Gold Rush (novelization of television play). New York, Warner, 1976.

Novels as Josephine Kains

The Devil Mask Mystery. New York, Zebra, 1978.
The Curse of the Golden Skull. New York, Zebra, 1978.
The Green Lama Mystery. New York, Zebra, 1979.
The Whispering Cat Mystery. New York, Zebra, 1979.
The Witch's Tower Mystery. New York, Zebra, 1979.
The Laughing Dragon Mystery. New York, Zebra, 1980.

Novels as Chad Calhoun (series: Agent Brad Spear in all titles)

The Hidden Princess. Wayne, Pennsylvania, Banbury, 1982.
The Mountain Queen. Wayne, Pennsylvania, Banbury, 1982.
The Lady Rustler. Wayne, Pennsylvania, Banbury, 1982.

Novels as Zeke Masters (series: Faro Blake in all titles)

High Card. New York, Pocket, 1982.
Loaded Dice. New York, Pocket, 1982.
Texas Two-Step. New York, Pocket, 1983.
Cashing In. New York, Pocket, 1983.

Novels as Franklin W. Dixon (series: Hardy Boys Casefiles)

Disaster for Hire. New York, Pocket, 1989.
The Deadliest Dare. New York, Pocket, 1989.
Castle Fear. New York, Pocket, 1990.

Other

The Assault on Childhood. Los Angeles, Sherbourne Press, 1969; London, Gollancz, 1970.
Cheap Thrills: An Informal History of the Pulp Magazines. New Rochelle, New York, Arlington House, 1972.
An American Family. New York, Warner, 1973.
The Adventurous Decade: Comic Strips in the Thirties. New Rochelle, New York, Arlington House, 1975.
Focus on Jack Cole. Agoura, California, Fantographics, 1986.
The Great Comic Book Artists. New York, St. Martin's Press, 2 vols., 1986, 1988.
Ron Goulart's Great History of Comic Books. Chicago, Contemporary Books, 1986.
The Dime Detectives. New York, Mysterious Press, 1988.
Over 50 Years of American Comic Books. Lincolnwood, Illinois, Mallard Press, 1991.
The Comic Book Reader's Companion: An A-to-Z Guide to Everyone's Favorite Art Form. New York, HarperPerennial, 1993.

Editor, *The Hardboiled Dicks: An Anthology and Study of Pulp Detective Fiction.* Los Angeles, Sherbourne Press, 1965; London, Boardman, 1967.
Editor, *Lineup Tough Guys.* Los Angeles, Sherbourne Press, 1966.
Editor, *The Great British Detective.* New York, New American Library, 1982.
Editor, *The Year of the Bat: The History of DC Comics: Fifty Years of Fantastic Imagination.* Las Vegas, Pioneer, 1989.

Editor, *The Encyclopedia of American Comics.* New York, Facts on File, 1990.

* * *

At heart, Ron Goulart is a frustrated cartoonist. Even the most casual reader will appreciate how much the world of comic books and comic strips informs his fiction. In addition, his contribution to the lore and history of comics has been significant. His skill at weaving such personal enthusiasms into his fiction gives it an added texture and dimension.

Ron Goulart's fictional world includes Southern California, the Barnum system in outer space, and as many other alternate worlds in between as his lively imagination can conjure up. He began his writing career with parodies and humorous sketches and has continued to write with a slightly cockeyed view of the world. He has written stories in virtually every genre, but is primarily considered a science fiction writer. Just as his mysteries have a touch of the fantastic, his science fiction has a touch of the mysterious and often seems to straddle genres when it doesn't simply defy all categories.

His stories of outer space nearly all take place outside our own solar system in that group of planets dominated by Barnum. In the Barnum system, Murdstone is the least favoured planet, but Malagra is the pesthole of the universe. Like other legendary places (Dogpatch or Hogscratch, Arkansas) the Barnum system adjusts its dimensions to suit the current story. The Barnum system has been imaginatively realized in visual terms by artist Gil Kane in the comic strip *Star Hawks*. All of the Goulart humor comes across in the adventures of Rex Jaxan and Chavez of the Interplanetary Law Service. Ben Jolson, the multi-faced agent for the Chameleon Corps, is called on by the Political Espionage Office on Barnum to investigate mysterious happenings. *The Sword Swallower* pulls together earlier threads from his short stories, but Jolson's shapechanging powers are not exploited as imaginatively in full length as they are in the shorter form. In "Chameleon" Jolson foils an assassination by emulating Jack Cole's Plastic Man and hiding in one corner of the room disguised as a TV set. Jolson's career outside the Chameleon Corps is continued in a series that began with *Daredevils, Ltd.*

One of his best collections of short stories, *Broke Down Engine,* is concerned entirely with the problem of mankind's increasing dependence on machines. Told with humor, they also embody a bitter view of a future in which human beings become isolated from one another. Goulart's days as an advertising copywriter serve as the basis for his stories about androids in show business. He brings a fine eye and ear for the ridiculous to these in which the satire may be deeper than mere surface humor. One thinks of real life "personalities" who respond to interviewers in precise, robotic terms. Perhaps the ultimate meshing of themes for Goulart's repertoire is *Cowboy Heaven,* in which an android replacing the ailing actor Jake Troop in the film *Saddle Tramp* doesn't know when to stop. Goulart has his serious side, and this comes out in the stories of fantasy and derring-do about the mysterious Gypsy's search for his own identity.

Goulart's style is concise and his stories are told mostly in dialogue. The reader has to be alert and not let the fast pace and skeletal appearance prevent him from enjoying the yarn. At his best, Goulart is a witty and engaging storyteller, with a recognizable reality to his fantasies. His Southern California is the extrapolation of present trends in the ridiculous; his machinery gone amok is an extension of our own worst fears as a vacuum cleaner malfunctions or an automobile breaks down.

No Goulart character can expect to grow old in retirement. There are always new challenges to face, such as the planet system in *Hellquad:* no matter which one you choose to land on, the other three are worse. His brand of science fiction may be set in 2033 or 1941 or 1897. The Harry Challenge series features an 1890's private detective whose cases involve fantasy and science fiction elements. Goulart himself is not afraid of challenge, whether it is extending his series of reference works on comics or serving as sometime ghostwriter to the genre. The Goulart oeuvre is a Möbius strip; when you've read one, you've just begun.

—J. Randolph Cox

———

GRAHAM, Robert. *See* **HALDEMAN, Joe.**

———

GRANT, Charles L.

Also writes as C.L. Grant. **Other Pseudonyms:** Felicia Andrews; Steven Charles; Lionel Fenn; Simon Lake; Deborah Lewis; and Geoffrey Marsh. **Nationality:** American. **Born:** Newark, New Jersey, 12 September 1942. **Education:** Trinity College, Hartford, Connecticut, B.A. 1964. **Military Service:** Served in the United States Army Military Police, 1968-70: Bronze Star. **Family:** Married Debbie Voss in 1973; one son and one daughter. **Career:** English teacher, Toms River High School, New Jersey, 1964-70, Chester High School, New Jersey, 1970-72, and Mt. Olive High School, New Jersey, 1972-73; English and history teacher, Roxbury High School, New Jersey, 1974-75. Since 1975, freelance writer. Executive secretary, Science Fiction Writers of America, 1973-77. **Awards:** Nebula award, 1976, 1978; World Fantasy award, for nonfiction, 1980, for editing, 1983. **Agent:** Howard Morhaim Literary Agency, 175 Fifth Avenue, Suite 709, New York, New York 10010, U.S.A.

SCIENCE FICTION PUBLICATIONS

Novels (series: Oxrun Station; Parric family; X Files)

The Shadow of Alpha (Parric). New York, Berkley, 1976.
The Curse (as C.L. Grant). Canoga Park, California, Major, 1977.
Ascension (Parric). New York, Berkley, 1977.
The Hour of the Oxrun Dead. Garden City, New York, Doubleday, 1977.
The Sound of Midnight (Oxrun). Garden City, New York, Doubleday, 1978.
The Ravens of the Moon. Garden City, New York, Doubleday, 1978; London, Sidgwick and Jackson, 1979.
Legion (Parric). New York, Berkley, 1979.

The Last Call of Mourning (Oxrun). Garden City, New York, Doubleday, 1979.
Quiet Night of Fear. New York, Berkley, 1981.
The Grave (Oxrun). New York, Popular Library, 1981.
Bloodwind (Oxrun). New York, Popular Library, 1982.
The Soft Whisper of the Dead (Oxrun). West Kingston, Rhode Island, Donald Grant, 1982.
The Nestling. New York, Pocket, 1982; London, Hamlyn, 1983.
Night Songs. New York, Pocket Books, 1984.
The Tea Party. New York, Pocket Books, 1985; London, Raven, 1995.
The Long Night of the Grave (Oxrun). West Kingston, Rhode Island, Donald Grant, 1986.
The Orchard (Oxrun). New York, Tor, 1986; London, Macdonald, 1989.
The Pet. New York, Tor, 1986; London, Futura, 1987.
For Fear of the Night. New York, Tor, and London, Futura, 1988.
Dialing the Wind (Oxrun). New York, Tor, 1988.
In a Dark Dream. New York, Tor, 1989; London, New English Library, 1990.
Stunts. New York, Tor, 1990: London, New English Library, 1991.
Fire Mask (for children). New York, Bantam, 1991.
Something Stirs. New York, Tor, 1991; London, New English Library, 1992.
Raven. New York, Tor, and London, New English Library, 1993.
Jackals. New York, Tor Forge, 1994; London, New English Library, 1995.
Goblins (X Files). New York, HarperPrism, 1994; London, HarperCollins, 1995.
Whirlwind (X Files). New York, HarperPrism, 1995.
The Black Carousel (Oxrun). New York, Tor, 1995.

Novels as Geoffrey Marsh (series: Lincoln Blackthorne in all titles)

The King of Satan's Eyes. Garden City, New York, Doubleday, 1984.
The Tail of the Arabian, Knight. Garden City, New York, Doubleday, 1986.
The Patch of the Odin Soldier. Garden City, New York, Doubleday, 1987.
The Fangs of the Hooded Demon: A Lincoln Blackthorne Novel. New York, Tor, 1988.

Novels as Steven Charles (for children; series: Private School in all titles)

Nightmare Session. New York, Archway, 1986; London, Lightning, 1990.
Academy of Terror. New York, Archway, 1986; London, Lightning, 1990.
Witch's Eye. New York, Archway, 1986; London, Lightning, 1990.
Skeleton Key. New York, Archway, 1986; London, Lightning, 1990.
The Enemy Within. New York, Archway, 1987.
The Last Alien. New York, Archway, 1987.

Novels as Lionel Fenn (series: Kent Montana; Quest for the White Duck)

Blood River Down (Quest). New York, Tor, 1986.
Web of Defeat (Quest). New York, Tor, 1987.
Agnes Day (Quest). New York, Tor, 1987.

The Seven Spears of the W'dch'ck (Montana). New York, Tor, 1988.

Kent Montana and the Really Ugly Thing from Mars. New York, Ace, 1990.

Kent Montana and the Reasonably Invisible Man. New York, Ace, 1991.

Kent Montana and the Once and Future Thing. New York, Ace, 1991.

The Mark of the Moderately Vicious Vampire (Montana). New York, Ace, 1992.

The Neighbor of the Beast (Montana). New York, Ace, 1992.

Once Upon a Time in the East (Diego). New York, Ace, 1993.

By the Time I Get to Nashville (Diego). New York, Ace, 1994.

Time: The Semi-Final Frontier (Diego). New York, Ace, 1994.

Short Stories

Tales from the Nightside: Dark Fantasy. Sauk City, Wisconsin, Arkham House, 1981; London, Futura, 1988.

A Glow of Candles and Other Stories. New York, Berkley, 1981.

Nightmare Seasons (Oxrun). Garden City, New York, Doubleday, 1982; London, Futura, 1989.

Black Wine, with Ramsey Campbell; edited by Douglas E. Winter. Arlington Heights, Illinois, Dark Harvest, 1986.

The Dark Cry of the Moon (Oxrun). West Kingston, Rhode Island, Donald Grant, 1986.

OTHER PUBLICATIONS

Novels as Deborah Lewis

Voices out of Time. New York, Zebra, 1977.
Eve of the Hound. New York, Zebra, 1977.

Novels as Felicia Andrews

River Witch. New York, Jove, 1979.
Moon Witch. New York, Jove, 1980.
Mountain Witch. New York, Jove, 1980.

Other

Editor, *Writing and Selling Science Fiction,* by the Science Fiction Writers of America. Cincinnati, Writer's Digest, 1976.

Editor, *Shadows [1]-10.* Garden City, New York, Doubleday, 10 vols., 1978-87; vol. 1 as *Shadows II,* London, Headline, 1987; *Shadows 4* as *Shadows,* London, Headline, 1987.

Editor, *Nightmares.* Chicago, Playboy, 1979.

Editor, *Horrors.* New York, Playboy, 1981.

Editor, *Terrors.* New York, Playboy, 1982.

Editor, *The Dodd, Mead Gallery of Horror.* New York, Dodd Mead, 1983; as *Gallery of Horror,* London, Robson, 1983.

Editor, *Fears.* New York, Berkley, 1983.

Editor, *Midnight.* New York, Tor, 1985.

Editor, *The Chronicles of Greystone Bay:*
  The First Chronicles of Greystone Bay. New York, Tor, 1985.
  Doom City. New York, Tor, 1987.
  The SeaHarp Hotel. New York, Tor, 1990.
  In the Fog: The Final Chronicle of Greystone Bay. New York, Tor, 1993.

Editor, *Night Visions 2: All Original Stories.* Arlington Heights, Illinois, Dark Harvest, 1985; as *Night Visions: Dead Image,* New York, Berkley, 1987; as *Night Terrors,* London, Headline, 1987.

Editor, *After Midnight.* New York, Tor, 1986.

Editor, *The Best of Shadows.* New York, Doubleday, 1988.

Editor, *Final Shadows.* New York, Doubleday, 1991.

*

Charles L. Grant comments:

(1985) In science fiction, I'm working on a future history that most of my more recent stories and novels fit into, a history that will eventually cover over 500 years, primarily tracing a single family (the Parrics). In horror fiction, my aim is, simply, to produce a fright in the reader. In this regard I generally use two settings: Hawthorne Street (a place in an unnamed town in an unnamed area of the country), and Oxrun Station, an upper-middle and upper-class village in western Connecticut. If there's any influence at all in my work it comes not from Lovecraft or Smith, but from Bradbury and Ellison, with perhaps a dollop of Sturgeon.

*   *   *

Charles L. Grant first appeared with a flurry of striking short stories in the early 1970s, followed by a handful of promising novels before redirecting his career into the horror field. Most of his efforts remained in that area, where he developed a reputation for restrained, atmospheric writing, but in the 1990s he once again began to produce science fiction at novel length.

Grant attracted attention with his first few stories, for example, "The Summer of the Irish Sea," in which his gift for unusual imagery was evident. In a world where peace has ostensibly been achieved, aggression is channeled into other outlets, in this case a traditional hunting party with a human being as the fox. World War III kills all but one survivor, an elderly shepherd whose remaining flock is mysteriously dwindling, leading him to a confrontation with the god Pan.

In "Abdication," an astronaut becomes president, but is denied reelection because of his opposition to the space program, providing Grant a springboard for examining our national motivation for the project. "The Rest Is Silence" is one of Grant's best early short stories. After resigning from his teaching position, the protagonist throws a party at which he uses a unique mental power to open the barriers between universes.

"Everybody's a Winner, the Barker Cried" is both depressing and elevating. Following a nuclear exchange, two doomed victims meet for a last ride on the ferris wheel, reaffirming the human spirit even as they surrender their lives. The teaching profession is examined again in "When Two or Three Are Gathered." Our conventional teaching methods are now forbidden, but one man continues to conduct bootleg classes for those few students unwilling to surrender to the system. It was already evident that Grant was fond of the horror genre, and another fine story from this period is "Come Dance with Me on My Pony's Grave," in which a Vietnam vet struggles to understand the strange bonds between his adopted Asian son and a pony.

In 1976 Grant published his first science fiction novel, *The Shadow of Alpha,* the first volume in the "Parric" trilogy. Earth has been devastated by plagues and the survivors lead a barbarous life, cloistered in cities or roaming the wilderness. Androids which were designed to take over much of the drudgery of life have gone off on tangents of their own, and are now often inimical to human life. Two sequels, *Ascension* and *Legion,* followed, with the central government reestablishing its authority. Although there was steady improvement and the novels are enjoyable and tightly plotted, they lack the depth and energy of Grant's more ambitious works.

Grant moved steadily away from science fiction in the years that followed, producing numerous horror, suspense, and romance novels, usually under pseudonyms. As Steven Charles, he wrote a six-volume series for young adults consisting of *Nightmare Session, Academy of Terror, Witch's Eye, Skeleton Key, The Enemy Within,* and *The Last Alien.* A remote private school is the hunting ground for an alien species that bears a remarkable resemblance to werewolves. The invaders are mysteriously disposing of members of the staff and student body and, predictably, no one believes the students who initially suspect and then discover the truth.

More interesting are the humorous fantastic adventures that have appeared under the names Geoffrey Marsh and Lionel Fenn. Under the Marsh name Grant has chronicled several adventures of Lincoln Blackthorne, most effectively in the first volume, *The King of Satan's Eyes,* less so in the sequels. As Lionel Fenn, Grant produced an amusing and entertaining fantasy trilogy consisting of *Blood River Down, Web of Defeat,* and *Agnes Day.* A perfectly ordinary man from our own world finds the gateway to a magical realm and crosses over, where he is immediately identified as a mythical hero and set upon the road to war, women, and warlocks. *The Seven Spears of W'dch'ck,* a similar but much funnier variation, appeared more recently.

Grant also used the Fenn name to spoof more traditional themes. *Kent Montana and the Really Ugly Thing from Mars* takes apart the alien invasion story and reassembles the pieces in a bizarre parody. He followed this immediately with *Kent Montana and the Reasonably Invisible Man,* and more and presumably similar volumes are predicted for the future.

Although occasional science fiction and fantasy stories continued to appear, most notably "The Peace That Passes Never" and "And Weary of the Sun," the vast majority of Grant's substantial body of fiction during the 1980s was in the supernatural horror genre. The most noteworthy of these include *The Nestling,* a blend of Indian legend and modern day shapechanging; *The Orchard,* a chilling and very original "monster" story; *The Pet; Nightmare Seasons,* a collection of four superb novelettes; and *Stunts,* wherein an American professor in England discovers that he has run afoul of an ancient magical force. Supernatural elements run through books he has written for other genres as well, including the Felicia Andrews romances and the Deborah Lewis gothic suspense stories. Grant has come to be known as one of the foremost writers of "quiet" horror, that is, stories that rely on the psychological pressure on the protagonists and the inherent suspense of the situation rather than on grisly dismemberments or other overt descriptive devices.

Grant's latest series of humorous science fiction adventures consists, so far, of *By the Time I Get to Nashville, Once Upon a Time in the West,* and *Time: The Semi-Final Frontier.* The premise is a tradition of the genre, the single individual displaced in time and reacting to different environments in terms of his own culture, satirized broadly in this case because the protagonist is a gunslinger from the Old West who uses a time-traveling train to visit the present and the future. Another Kent Montana story, "The Alien Visitor, Probably from Someplace Else," similarly lampoons a familiar theme.

Although his turn to the horror field caused Grant to remain a peripheral influence on science fiction for many years, the recent decline in interest in horror fiction is likely to have an effect. Grant has recently begun writing a series of original novels based on the *X Files* television program, which affords an opportunity to blend science fiction and horror themes. Grant's demonstrated skills in both fields bode well for his continued popularity, both as an adult writer and as one of the few authors of young adult fiction who have managed to resist editorial pressures to write fiction down to some imagined less comprehensive level. Whether his future science fiction work will remain light humor or take a more serious turn remains to be seen.

—Don D'Ammassa

GRANT, Mark. *See* **BISCHOFF, David F.**

GRANT, Richard

Nationality: American. **Born:** 1952.

Science Fiction Publications

Novels

Saraband of Lost Time. New York, Avon, 1985; London, Bantam, 1987.
Rumors of Spring. Toronto and New York, Bantam, 1987; as *Rumours of Spring,* London, Bantam, 1988.
Views from the Oldest House: A Novel. New York, Doubleday, 1989.
Through the Heart. New York, Bantam, 1992.

* * *

Richard Grant's four novels stand as genre-spanning chimeras: postmodern romances much concerned with the end of tradition and the faltering of history, which nonetheless regard the fallen worlds they present with considerable good cheer, and mix literary references from various medieval, modernist, and science fiction sources in a manner that suggests an implicit faith that narrative tradition will continue to roll on past the point where the roadway of Western Civ breaks down. This ebullient combination of continuity and disjunction is one of the salient characteristics of Grant's work; the other is its extravagant ambition.

Saraband of Lost Time offers a venue that would become familiar throughout Grant's work: the post-collapse landscape, where scraps of ancient technology and persevering institutions coexist incongruously with medieval pastoralism or squalor. Grant draws freely though inventively upon Mervyn Peake, M. John Harrison, and John Crowley in a discursive and witty quest tale concerning the confused search for an ancient force or device capable of shaking the world from its dormant stagnancy. Although perhaps too leisurely in its pacing, and sometimes overly mannered, Grant's novel shapes itself as a postmodern but legitimate (and formal) comedy, where folly and error do not finally prevent the protagonists from stumbling into a realm of enchantment where they are confounded and transformed.

The last two sentences also describe *Rumors of Spring,* which tells a similar story with considerably more verbal energy, a wider range of allusion, and greater degree of baroque invention. Set (like *Saraband*) some 500 years after a major ecological collapse, Grant's second novel centers upon the Carbon Bank Forest, site of a mysterious research project during the last years before civilization fell apart, which has undergone mysterious changes that finally obtrude upon the attention of the benighted society beyond. Grant's fussy and tottering protagonists respond by launching a fatuous First Biotic Crusade, sent on a hubris-propelled mission to smite an uncomprehended foe. The vision of organic self-realization and serenity that waits within the Carbon Bank Forest is more explicitly Shakespearean in its arcadian verdure than was the Secret Garden in *Saraband,* and the comedy funnier, but the amplitude of literary reference (the local paper of the town of Riverrun is called the *Daily Wake;* a character calls, "Come back to the raft," announcing affinities with the wilderness themes in *Huckleberry Finn*) and extent of comedy threaten to become fulsome. *Rumors of Spring* offers greater riches, if almost certainly in surfeit.

Views from the Oldest House, Grant's longest novel, is also his most complex and melancholy, for beyond its initial resemblances to his earlier work—we are once again in a stagnant collapsed society, with a mysterious institute offering the promise of transcendent redemption—lies something other than comedy. Turner Ashenden, a diffident college student who comes upon the Bad Winters Institute of Science and Philosophy and is brought by the ministrations of the mysterious GRAILNET into contact with his true self, partakes of King Arthur, Tyrone Slothrop, and older heroes, although the question of who tells the story is more complex and ambiguous. Although the density of literary allusion informs the novel's structure more significantly than in *Rumors of Spring,* its bookishness is finally a liability, for the narrative voice is too plainly that of *Gravity's Rainbow,* and the novel fails to achieve its own imaginative autonomy.

In *Through the Heart,* Grant adopts a sparer style and a cleaner narrative line, which follows the point of view of a single character throughout. "When their wagon broke down at the Oasis, Kem was traded by his family for a scavenged motor and a set of high-grade tools. The rest of the wagons blew eastward on the autumn winds." Kem, a young man who has lived his life in an arid wasteland, joins the crew of the Oasis, an enormous vehicle that rolls across the plains like a leviathan. Grant's sere tale of the Oasis' journey across an America devastated by plague constitutes a peculiar kind of sentimental education, in which Kem slowly comes to understand what has overtaken his world and the role that the Oasis plays in it. At 376 pages, however, *Through the Heart* is too long for the story it tells or for the mystery at its center, which reduces to allegory-like fable.

Postmodernist that he is, Grant shows little interest in such genre conventions as series or internal chronologies. Links exist between all his stories—elements such as the Carbon Bank Forest recur in several of them, and the "Drode's Equations" of his first published story are referred to in *Views from the Oldest House*—but they cannot be said to inhabit the same universe, or stand in relation to each other in any of the manners traditional to genre fiction. Like Joyce and other novelists of imperial self-assurance, Grant alludes in one novel to another, as though his fictions were sovereign imaginative worlds that occasionally rise in each other's skies.

Grant is a novelist of unusual inventiveness and power, whose aesthetic and ambitions (which he has discussed in such essays as "The Exile's Paradigm") ensure that he works at the limit of his abilities, rather than safely within them. If none of his novels can confidently be called an unqualified success, he remains a writer of considerable potential.

—Gregory Feeley

GREEN, Joseph (Lee)

Nationality: American. **Born:** Compass Lake, Florida, 14 January 1931. **Education:** University of Alabama, Tuscaloosa, B.A. **Family:** Married 1) Juanita Henderson in 1951 (divorced 1975), one son and one daughter; 2) Patrice Milton in 1975, two daughters. **Career:** Laboratory technician, International Paper Company, Panama City, Florida 1949-51; shop worker and welder, Panama City, 1952-54; millwright in Florida, Texas, and Alabama, 1955-58; senior supervisor, Boeing Company, Seattle, 1959-63. Technical writer and science writer at Kennedy Space Center, Florida, 1965-83. Since 1984, public affairs writer/editor for NASA, Kennedy Space Center. **Agent:** Blassingame McCauley and Wood, 432 Park Avenue South, New York, New York 10016, U.S.A. **Address:** 1390 Holly Avenue, Merritt Island, Florida 32952, U.S.A.

SCIENCE FICTION PUBLICATIONS

Novels

The Loafers of Refuge. London, Gollancz, and New York, Ballantine, 1965.
Gold the Man. London, Gollancz, 1971; as *The Mind behind the Eye,* New York, DAW, 1972.
Conscience Interplanetary. London, Gollancz, 1972; Garden City, New York, Doubleday, 1973.
Star Probe. London, Millington, 1976; New York, Ace, 1978.
The Horde. Toronto, Laser, 1976; London, Dobson, 1979.

Short Stories

An Affair with Genius. London, Gollancz, 1969.

Also author of numerous other short stories.

*

Joseph Green comments:

(1991) Most of my stories have an underlying philosophical theme that is often not apparent on the surface. At heart I think of myself as an untrained, poorly equipped, cornball philosopher, and what I enjoy most is playing with ideas in fictional form. For that reason, I'll never create a consistent "future history." If I write a story about the totally secular world of 2090 today, I may want to write one tomorrow about the new surge in absolutist religion from 2070 to 2110. I have no faith at all in a single future.

I've achieved some small reputation as a writer of unusually believable aliens. I don't know why. I dream them up, work to make them real, and write about them because I enjoy it. Do I need a better reason? I write primarily for readers, not critics or other writers. If a reader enjoys my work, that's good. If it also makes him think, that's even better.

(1995) I plan to return to active writing in '96.

*   *   *

Joseph Green is a strongly imaginative writer. He likes to set his heroes problems, sometimes highly exotic or elaborately contrived, always laid out with great clarity and convincingly resolved. These heroes are often troubleshooters, typically working at the interface between human and alien, sometimes—and this is probably his most characteristic motif—even operating with alien bodies. In his most powerful novel, *Gold the Man,* this alienation works as far as two removes, for the hero is emphatically a man trapped in a superman's body, put to work inside an alien giant. In confronting his character with painful dilemmas, Green communicates to the reader a strong concern; he is also able to treat sympathetically those on both sides of an irreconcilable debate, as in *Star Probe,* which concerns one battle in a larger war between the space scientists and the Friends of the Earth. In *The Horde* he presents one of the genre's most sympathetic accounts of a kind of alien hive species, the humanoid Shemsi, as an improbable friendship develops between human and humanoid bound together, for different reasons, on a dangerous mission.

Reflecting their origins as series of short stories, *The Loafers of Refuge* and *Conscience Interplanetary* are episodic narratives. In the first, troubleshooter Carey, as the first man born on Refuge, works to resolve conflict between humans and the native loafers, who have developed mental but not mechanical power. Human-Loafer interaction is mutually beneficial: for instance, the Loafers revivify their living trees (the Entlike *breshwahr*), and one of them shows how men can survive matter transmission, thus enabling rapid colonization of other planets to relieve the overcrowded Earth. In the second, the hero Allan Odegaard has the job of checking whether intelligence exists on a planet: if so, it must be left alone; if not, it may be colonized (a problem consequent on the solution found in *The Loafers*). Throughout his seven extraordinary adventures, Allan is in more danger from reactionary humans than from the weird life-forms he encounters.

Gold the Man is a classic novel, whether considered as a profound study of the loneliness of the superman in no-man's-land or as an exciting contribution to Brobdingnagian fantasy. Earth is at war with giant humanoids, the Hilt-Sil, one of whom, suffering from irreparable brain damage, is captured. The superman Gold, and a female assistant, Marina Petrovna, are installed in the head of the 300-foot captive, where they control his brain, seated behind one of his eyes. In this extraordinary Trojan horse, they spy on the alien planet, finding the feared enemies to be a race of gentle giants living an idyllic life but forced to look for another planet because of danger from their own sun. Gold helps resolve their problems and, remarkably enough, his enforced voyeurism of their Gargantuan love-play resolves his personal fear of impotence: being a superman, he was a slow developer, but he rapes and impregnates the helpless Marina and their child is born with the assistance of a friendly Hilt-Sil doctor who has discovered them (this is not a macho fantasy story for all that). Green sets himself difficult problems in this powerful novel, but he handles both the physicalities and the psychological stresses of the intriguing situations with great tact and skill.

In the light of *Gold the Man,* Green makes less than expected of the interesting motif in *Star Probe* of an old man, deceased, who is brought back to life in the body of his idiot grandson for the purposes of a suicide mission. The mission concerns the investigation of an alien probe in the solar system; once the difficulties of getting a rocket to the probe have been resolved, Green is able once again to concern himself with the interesting problem of communication between alien and human; within the novel as a whole, however, the probe serves only as an emblem of what the struggle for funds between space scientists and ecologists is all about.

Among Green's many fine short stories, it is hard to pick out the best or most characteristic, but "Jinn," "Once Around Arcturus," "Treasure Hunt" (man inside crystal chariot-horse), "When I Have Passed Away" (exotic Giantesses), "Last of the Chauvinists," and "To See the Stars That Blind" (written with his wife, Patrice Milton, brilliantly presenting the wonder and horror of a new mode of seeing), should be included. Nine short stories are collected in *An Affair with Genius,* including "The Decision Makers," which is recycled in *Conscience Interplanetary.* They show a preference for open over closed endings, not surprising in view of the author's expressed lack of faith in "a single future." Two stories, "Tunnel of Love" and "Dance of the Cats," one humorous and the other horrific, feature the same two enterprising young Space Service men, Silva de Fonseca ("Quicksilva") and Aaron Gunderson. Green has published few stories in recent years; in one of the most recent, "Still Fall the Gentle Rains" (written with Patrice Milton), the concern is still, movingly, with human-humanoid relations and the species implications of sexuality: in this case, lower fertility implies greater honesty; in "And Be Lost Like Me," a new test for a typical Phildickian problem, distinguishing alien from human, is presented.

—Michael J. Tolley

* * *

GREEN, Peter. *See* BULMER, Kenneth.

* * *

GREEN, Terence M(ichael)

Nationality: Canadian. **Born:** Toronto, Ontario, 2 February 1947. **Education:** University of Toronto, B.A. 1967; B.Ed. 1973; University College Dublin, Ireland, M.A. 1972. **Family:** Married 1) Penny Dakin in 1968 (divorced 1990); 2) Merle Casci in 1994; two sons. **Career:** English teacher in a Toronto secondary school, 1968-95. **Awards:** Canada Council grants, 1983, 1992; Ontario Arts Council Grants, 1991-93. **Agent:** Shawna McCarthy, Scovil Chichak Galen, 381 Park Ave. South, New York, New York 10016, U.S.A. **Address:** 32 Brooklyn Ave., Toronto, Ontario, M4M 2X5, Canada.

SCIENCE FICTION PUBLICATIONS

Novels

Barking Dogs. New York, St. Martin's Press, 1988.

Children of the Rainbow. Toronto, McClelland & Stewart, 1992.

Short Stories

The Woman Who Is the Midnight Wind. Porters Lake, Nova Scotia, Pottersfield Press, 1987.

*

Terence M. Green comments:

All fiction writing is exploration, self-discovery, truth-finding, combined with emotional involvement with characters. It is storytelling about things we know, things we want to know, and things we can never know.

I've always enjoyed the element of the Fantastic in fiction. But I enjoy it as background to a story, not as foreground, and this is probably how I operate as a writer. I make a conscious effort, in most cases, to "transmute brute fact with passion" (paraphrasing Maugham), and to try to blend the intellectual with the emotional. I tend to subscribe to Faulkner's dictum that "the problems of the human heart in conflict with itself" are the main things "worth the agony and the sweat" of creative endeavor.

Write about black holes, cloning, cryonics, cybernetics, generation starships, genetic engineering, ghosts, what have you. But infuse the stories with characters with whom a reader can identify, and to whom something of human import actually happens.

SF&F gives us a vast backdrop, a potentially clever and entertaining backdrop, against which to ask the same questions that Shakespeare, Steinbeck, Malamud, Carver, Melville, and others have been asking consistently and relentlessly: what does it mean to be human? Who am I? Why do I do what I do? Where am I heading? Where are we all heading? And what should I be doing?

Homer discovered the fantastic and infused his *Odyssey* with it; it has fascinated us ever since. He succeeded in blending inner human mysteries with the outer mysteries of an unknowable universe. Shakespeare realized its potential too (witches in *Macbeth,* the ghost in *Hamlet*). Why shouldn't writers want to follow in their footsteps, however modestly?

Trying to utilize the pyrotechnic novelty and cleverness of the Fantastic, transform it into metaphor, and proceed with emotional resonance to the search for identity and our place in the scheme of things: this is the challenge, and the opportunity.

*   *   *

Just as Canada finds its place in the world somewhere between its British past and the always changing American future, so Canadian SF tends to be a wayward mix of U.S. technophilia and British social extrapolation. In terms of this too simplistic opposition, Terence Green's science fiction is quintessentially Canadian, with its graceful focus on characterization, its rhetorical understatement, its placing of characters in a complex social environment, as well as its refusal to explore technology for itself alone. Thus his SF stories can be set on other planets, as is the title story of *The Woman Who Is the Midnight Wind* (1987), but they are more likely to be set in our present or near future, and to focus most forcefully on the personal lives of the characters. Time travel of a kind features

in his latest two novels, *Children of the Rainbow* (1992) and *Shadows of Ashland* (1996), but in neither case does he work up a complex pseudoscientific explanation. In the former, the explanation is infiltrated with ESP elements; in the latter, there is no explanation beyond the utmost desires of the human heart. And it is that heart that Green is most concerned to explore.

Green began writing short stories, and two of his novels—in time-honored SF fashion—are based on earlier stories. Some of those stories are lightweight extrapolations based on his life as a teacher; there technological advances are seen in the context of what a humanist would say teaching really means. Others, like "Legacy," in which the murdering son must face his father, kept alive long enough to name his murderer, or "Susie Q2," in which a highly advanced cybernetic system containing constructs of remembered people helps a man decide not to commit suicide, seem more hard science oriented, but it is the human interaction at their center which most concerns us. In "The Woman Who Is the Midnight Wind," a widow's diary illuminates her slowly developing empathy with the half-alien child of another settler. Her emotional growth is foregrounded, not the alien environment.

In "Barking Dogs," Green imagines a machine that can tell you if another person is telling the truth, and gives it to a policeman in a near future and violent Toronto. In the story, his discovery that he wants to trust his own feelings when it comes to those he loves is the point. In *Barking Dogs,* Green expands the story two ways: by looking backward to Mitch's growing friendship with his partner, who was killed in action; and by creating a mystery-thriller plot in which Mitch takes on a drug king. On its own terms *Barking Dogs* works quite well, but its ending does seem a bit abrupt.

Children of the Rainbow is a much more complex novel. A time travel narrative, it sends Fletcher Christian IV back from 2072 to Norfolk Island in 1835, while catapulting Bran Michael Dalton from that notorious prison forward to Pitcairn Island in 1972. Green imagines an intriguing future in which South America has become a power in the world; his creation of both contemporary Pitcairn and historical Norfolk is based on solid scholarship. 1972 is the key date, for that is when the French exploded an atomic bomb at Mururoa Atoll, and Green imagines that such an explosion interferes massively with the attempt to send Christian back to Pitcairn Island. The novel is most interesting for the way it shows its characters trying to make sense of their new situations. Dalton has found a kind of paradise, but has to learn to live with technologies he never even dreamed of; Christian must try to convince his jailers that he is what he says he is. His conversations with the intelligent and well read Major Anderson, the commandant of Norfolk, are both historically intriguing and ironic.

One of Green's most moving stories, "Ashland, Kentucky," is the basis of his latest novel, *Shadows of Ashland.* Here, unlike *Barking Dogs,* the expansion is almost completely one of deepening the characters and their relations, rather than pushing conventional plot devices into the narrative. In the story, the narrator discovers that "Things have to be settled, or they never go away." His father tells him this when his dying mother asks to see her brother, who went missing in the U.S. in the 1930s. After she dies, saying he did visit her, letters from him begin to arrive, but they are dated 1934. In the story, he follows the letters to Ashland, Kentucky, where he somehow gains a brief meeting with his uncle 50 years ago. In *Shadows of Ashland,* he still goes to Ashland, but there he not only meets people who remember his uncle, he travels back in time and stays there long enough to learn just what the 30s were like for such people and how his uncle may have died. Once again, the historical background is richly evoked. Moreover, in the present he also meets his uncle's daughter as well as a contemporary woman with whom he falls in love. The theoretical explanation is minimal, for, like Gene Wolfe's *Peace,* what's important is the emotional encounters between intriguing characters, as well as the exploration of personal loss.

Shadows of Ashland is Green's finest novel yet, not least because it so carefully articulates a world the reader can believe in. It is, perhaps, closer to "magic realism" than to traditional science fiction, yet it is also a story of alternate worlds, even if those worlds are the ones people make up to keep themselves going in hard times. A powerfully evocative study of complex personal relations, it should gain Green even more critical attention and a wider audience. He is rapidly becoming one of Canada's finest writers in the field.

—Douglas Barbour

GREENLAND, Colin

Nationality: British. **Born:** Dover, Kent, 17 May 1954. **Education:** St. Lawrence College, Ramsgate, Kent, 1964-72; Pembroke College, Oxford, 1972-79, B.A. in English literature and language (honors) 1975; D. Phil. in English literature 1981. **Career:** Fellow in creative writing, Science Fiction Foundation, North East London Polytechnic, 1980-82; co-editor, *Interzone* magazine, London, 1982-85; U.K. coordinator, Eaton Conference on Science Fiction, University of California, Riverside/North East London Polytechnic, 1983-84; part-time tutor, University of London Extra-mural Department, 1985-90; chair, Science Fiction Writers' Conference, Milford, Hampshire, 1986. Since 1989, reviews editor, *Foundation* magazine, London. **Awards:** J. Lloyd Eaton award, for criticism, 1985; Arthur C. Clarke award, 1991; British Science Fiction Association award, for best novel, 1991. **Agent:** Maggie Noach, 21 Redan Street, London W14 0AB, England; or, Martha Millard, 204 Park Avenue, Madison, New Jersey, 07940, U.S.A. **Address:** 2A Ortygia House, 6 Lower Road, Harrow, Middlesex HA2 0DA, England.

SCIENCE FICTION PUBLICATIONS

Novels (series: Daybreak)

Daybreak on a Different Mountain. London, Allen and Unwin, 1984.
The Hour of the Thin Ox (Daybreak). London, Unwin, 1987.
Other Voices (Daybreak). London, Unwin Hyman, 1988.
Take Back Plenty. London, Unwin Hyman, 1990; San Francisco, Pomegranate, 1993.
Harm's Way. London, HarperCollins, and New York, AvoNova, 1993.

Short Stories

In the Garden: The Secret Origin of the Zodiac Twins. Birmingham, England, Birmingham Science Fiction Group, 1991.

OTHER PUBLICATIONS

Other

The Entropy Exhibition: Michael Moorcock and the British "New Wave" in Science Fiction. London and Boston, Routledge, 1983.
Magnetic Storm: The Work of Roger and Martyn Dean. London, Dragon's World, 1984.
The Freelance Writer's Handbook, with Paul Kerton. London, Ebury, 1986.
Michael Moorcock: Death Is No Obstacle (interview). Manchester, England, Savoy, 1992.

Editor, with John Clute and David Pringle, *Interzone: The First Anthology: New Science Fiction and Fantasy Writing.* London, Dent, 1985.
Editor, with George Slusser and Eric S. Rabkin, *Storm Warnings: Science Fiction Confronts the Future.* Carbondale and Edwardsville, Southern Illinois University Press, 1987.
Adaptor, *Titus Unbound,* by Mervyn Peake (for children). Oxford, Oxford University Press, 1977.

*   *   *

With a doctoral thesis on the "New Wave" in British science fiction and a solid background of reviews and articles in *Foundation, The Guardian,* and *The Times Literary Supplement,* Colin Greenland might seem to have been over-prepared for the profession of science fiction writer. His first novel, *Daybreak on a Different Mountain,* is assured and fresh, but at the same time strangely muted and compressed. The city of Thryn, reeking of decay and past grandeur, festers most convincingly behind its high walls; its infrastructure is not made plain even to its remaining aristocrats. Lupio, the playboy, finds himself suddenly involved in the prophecies of the mad old priestess, Kavi. He falls in with the poet Dubilier, who is escaping from an unhappy love affair. Together this complementary pair set out to do the impossible: they venture beyond the walls of Thryn in search of the god Gomath and his guide, the Cirnex, last seen upon the sacred mountain, Hisper Einou. Their adventurous quest among the peoples of Outwall leads not only to self-knowledge but to revelation.

Colin Greenland extended his range with *The Hour of the Thin Ox,* first of a series of books dealing with an alternate world. Bryland, which has overtones of 17th-century England, and the Seven Realms, are contrasted with Escaly, an eastern empire. Jillian Curram, a hardy and resourceful heroine, experiences the ruin of her Bryland estates as the country drifts into war. Already, as a child, she had a fateful glimpse of the Princess Nette of Luscany and of Karel Jessup, the gruff, young engineer, inventor of a fearful weapon that seems to resemble a Gatling gun. Meanwhile, in distant Escaly, Ky varan, an innocent scholar, rises through the ancient hierarchies to become Imperial Geometer. He is already an old man when his young apprentice, Bi tok, begins to bring warmth and understanding into his life. The tragi-comedy of this appealing pair is one of the author's finest achievements.

Cultures clash in a third world, the rainforests of Belanesi, home of a mysterious race of faun-like natives. The Imperial Geometer and his apprentice, who have crashed in the jungle in the course of a foolish propaganda mission, benefit from the healing arts of these people and begin to learn about their civilisation. Savage Escalan troops are penetrating the forest, killing all who come in their way, but Jill Curram and her band of female guerillas, Bryland irregulars, meet with unexpected success.

The wry originality of the series, its blend of clever extrapolation and mystery, continues in *Other Voices,* a winter's tale set in the mountain archduchy of Luscany. In another childhood episode, Serin, daughter of mad Dr. Guille, the necrobiologist, and his gypsy wife, experiences the very beginning of the Escalan occupation of her country. Ten years later, while Princess Nette chafes at the restrictions of a puppet ruler, Serin witnesses the murder of an Escalan official, an event that triggers off the long-awaited revolution. The acrid interchanges of the long-suffering Princess with her Escalan overlords, with courtiers, and with her contrary old mother, the Archduchess, are mordant and stylish. Strangest voice of all is that of Serin's unidentified admirer, once a man, now undead, a vampire. He beckons the reader on to a further chronicle.

Take Back Plenty, a breakthrough book, winner of prestigious awards, is a space opera: it teems with characters, explores strange worlds, leaps hectically through space and time. This is Greenland unbound. As Tabitha Jute, the indomitable spacer, rackets round the solar system one jump ahead of her creditors and assorted baddies, she tells marvelous tales to the inscrutable persona of her ship, the *Alice Liddell.* From the canals of Mars during Carnival, to the steamy jungles of Venus and the scungy loading docks of Plenty, a deconstructed space habitat, the Terran system is under the sway of the elusive Capellans and their doggy bureaucrats, the Eladeldi. Tabitha is at the centre of a vortex of intrigue and misadventure: empires crumble, legends proliferate, sentient beings perish nastily, and the best of friends, sadly, must part. The moral of this absorbing extravaganza might be "There is no such thing as a free space drive." The hidden capacities of the author are as manifold as the field of science fiction and fantasy itself. He understands the genre thoroughly and can be relied upon to reawaken our sense of wonder.

—Cherry Wilder

GREENLEAF, William

Nationality: American. **Born:** 1917. **Address:** c/o Ace Books, 200 Madison Avenue, New York, New York 10016, U.S.A.

Science Fiction Publications

Novels (series: Tartarus)

Timejumper. New York, Leisure Books, 1980.
The Tartarus Incident. New York, Ace, 1983.
The Pandora Stone. New York, Ace, 1984.
Starjacked! (Tartarus). New York, Ace, 1987.
Clarion. New York, Tor, 1988.

*   *   *

Science fiction has long been a haven for the unabashed adventure story, and indeed the term "space opera" has been coined to describe a certain subgroup of interplanetary adventures that are essentially traditional western plots transported to an interplanetary

setting. Similarly, lost race novels, pirate stories, and spy stories can be modified to fit into an interstellar environment. One of the more interesting if not truly major writers taking advantage of this situation is William Greenleaf.

Greenleaf's first novel, *Timejumper,* first appeared in 1980. The setting is familiar: in a far future Earth, the remnants of humanity are split into two groups, the barbarians who roam the wastelands and those who have held onto the trappings of technological civilization and live in what remains of the great urban metropolises of another age. The novel brings together two disparate individuals, an obsessively curious barbarian boy and a brilliant but warped genius who has constructed a device that will allow him to move about in time. The result is access to another world, and a fresh hope for humanity, unless the repressive priesthood can block humanity's aspirations. Greenleaf is quite skillful at providing surprising reversals in his fiction, and this first novel, though relatively clumsy, has a freshness and enthusiasm that overcomes its shortcomings.

The Tartarus Incident is a markedly better novel. A spaceship and its crew inadvertently arrive on the wrong planet and find themselves stranded. Although there is no immediate prospect of rescue, neither is there any cause for panic; they recognize that it's only a matter of time until the authorities realize they have not arrived, investigate, and determine where they have in fact landed. As it happens, however, they don't have time for leisure. The discovery of an ancient, abandoned city on the planet is at first a source of interest, but then growing alarm as a discorporate mental force reaches out to alter the minds of the crew members. Although Greenleaf shows notable ability to evoke a mood of terror, this really isn't the major focus of the book. The best passages in fact are those dealing with the crew's attempts to adjust to their isolation and, back on Earth, the efforts of a minor official to discover what happened to the missing ship.

Following *The Pandora Stone,* an interesting but minor adventure story, Greenleaf produced *Starjacked!,* a blend of space adventure, pirate story, and straightforward adventure. The Fringes are an area of human-colonized space sufficiently remote from the more settled worlds that law and order are not something that can be taken for granted. The Guards is a paramilitary organization created to maintain some degree of security for space travellers. Unfortunately, elements within the Guard have come to an arrangement with some of the space pirates, as a consequence of which they jointly arrange the hijacking of a starship.

An investigative reporter following a lead finds himself in the middle of events when he is taken prisoner by the pirates and locked away aboard the hijacked ship. Although not ordinarily a leader, he finds himself reluctantly helping to organize an attempt to regain control of the ship. Because of the circumstances of the hijacking, however, return to more civilized regions will not be quite as simple. The pirates and the Guard both have good reason to arrange that no one lives to provide a true account. Although the waning chapters deteriorate into an overly melodramatic series of battles, Greenleaf's gift for characterization is evident in the earlier chapters, and the book is on the whole a quite satisfying creation.

Greenleaf's most recent novel is *Clarion,* which like most of his earlier books has at its center a mystery, the resolution of which is intimately involved with the resolution of the main plotline. Clarion is a colony world that has been out of touch with the rest of the human race for over two centuries. Now its population is held in thrall by a charismatic cult leader, who may not be a human being at all but rather an alien interloper hoping to lead the colony to its destruction. Opposed to him, albeit not by intention, is a psionically talented artist whose abilities cause him to become the target of a series of assassination attempts. As with *The Tartarus Incident,* Greenleaf makes use of a repulsive alien entity to heighten tension, although the overriding mood of the story is still one of adventure rather than terror. *Clarion* contains a far more intricately developed civilization than any of Greenleaf's earlier novels, stronger characterization, a more tightly controlled plot, and noticeably smoother prose. If this is truly indicative of his continuing development as a writer, then Greenleaf is on the verge of becoming a significant contributor to the field.

—Don D'Ammassa

GREER, Richard. *See* **GARRETT, Randall.**

GREGORY, John. *See* **HOSKINS, Robert.**

GREY, Carol. *See* **LOWNDES, Robert A.W.**

GREY, Charles. *See* **TUBB, E.C.**

GRIBBIN, John R.

Nationality: British. **Born:** Maidstone, Kent, in 1946. **Education:** Sussex University, B.Sc. 1966, M.Sc. 1967; Cambridge University, Ph.D. 1971. **Career:** Staff writer for *Nature* magazine, 1970-75; member of Science Policy Research Unit, University of Sussex, Brighton, 1975-78. Since 1978, physics consultant to *New Scientist.* Adviser to Thames-TV and TV South. Since 1992, visiting fellow in astronomy, University of Sussex. **Awards:** National award (Association of British Science Writers), 1974, 1991. **Member:** Fellow of Royal Astronomical Society, Fellow of Royal Meteorological Society, Fellow of Royal Geographical Society. **Agent:** Murray Pollinger, 222 Old Brompton Road, London SW5 0BZ, England.

SCIENCE FICTION PUBLICATIONS

Novels

The Sixth Winter, with Douglas Orgill. London, Bodley Head, and New York, Simon and Schuster, 1979.

Double Planet, with Marcus Chown. London, Gollancz, 1988; New York, Avon, 1991.
Father to the Man. London, Gollancz, 1989; New York, Tor, 1990.
Reunion, with Marcus Chown. London, Gollancz, 1991.
Brother Esau, with Douglas Orgill. London, Bodley Head, and New York, Harper and Row, 1982.
Ragnarok, with D.G. Compton. London, Gollancz, 1991.
Innervisions. London, Roc, 1993.

OTHER PUBLICATIONS

Other

The Jupiter Effect, with Stephen H. Plagemann. London, Macmillan, and New York, Walker, 1974; revised edition, New York, Vintage, 1976; revised as *The Jupiter Effect Reconsidered,* New York, Vintage, 1982.
Our Changing Climate. London, Faber, 1975.
Astronomy for the Amateur. London, Macmillan, and New York, D. McKay, 1976.
Forecasts, Famines, and Freezes: Climate and Man's Future. London, Wildwood House, and New York, Walker, 1976.
Galaxy Formation: A Personal View. London, Macmillan, and New York, Wiley, 1976.
Our Changing Planet. London, Wildwood House, and New York, Crowell, 1977.
White Holes: Cosmic Gushers in the Universe. St. Albans, Hertfordshire, Paladin, and New York, Delacorte Press/E. Friede, 1977.
Our Changing Universe: The New Astronomy. London, Macmillan, and New York, Dutton, 1976.
The Climatic Threat: What's Wrong with Our Weather? London, Fontana, 1978; as *What's Wrong with Our Weather: The Climactic Threat of the 21st Century,* New York, Scribner, 1979.
Earthquakes and Volcanoes. New York, Gallery, 1978.
This Shaking Earth. London, Sidgwick and Jackson, and New York, Putnam, 1978.
Climate and Mankind. London, Earthscan, 1979.
Future Worlds. London, Abacus, 1979; New York, Plenum Press, 1981.
Timewarps. London, Dent, and New York, Delacorte Press/E. Friede, 1979.
Weather Force: Climate and Its Impact on Our World. London, Hamlyn, and New York, Putnam, 1979.
The Death of the Sun. New York, Delacorte Press/E. Friede, 1980.
The Strangest Star: A Scientific Account of the Life and Death of the Sun. London, Athlone Press, 1980.
Carbon Dioxide, the Climate, and Man. London, IIED, 1981.
Genesis: The Origins of Man and the Universe. London, Dent, and New York, Delacorte Press/E. Friede, 1981.
Future Weather and the Greenhouse Effect. New York, Delacorte Press/E. Friede, 1982.
The Monkey Puzzle: A Family Tree, with Jeremy Cherfas. London, Bodley Head, and New York, Pantheon, 1982.
Beyond the Jupiter Effect, with Stephen H. Plagemann. London, Macdonald, 1983.
Spacewarps. New York, Delacorte Press/E. Friede, 1983; London, Penguin, 1984.
In Search of Schrödinger's Cat: The Startling World of Quantum Physics Explained. London, Wildwood House, and New York, Bantam, 1984.

The Redundant Male: Is Sex Irrelevant in the Modern World?, with Jeremy Cherfas. London, Bodley Head, and New York, Pantheon, 1984.

In Search of the Double Helix: Darvin, DNA, and Beyond. Aldershot, Wildwood House, and New York, McGraw-Hill, 1985.

Weather, with Mary Gribbin. London, Macdonald, and Vero Beach, Florida, Rourke Enterprises, 1985.

In Search of the Big Bang: Quantum Physics and Cosmology. London, Heinemann, and New York, Bantam, 1986.

The Omega Point: The Search for the Missing Mass and the Ultimate Fate of the Universe. London, Heinemann, 1987; New York, Bantam, 1988.

The One Per Cent Advantage: The Sociobiology of Being Human, with Mary Gribbin. Oxford and New York, Blackwell, 1988.

The Hole in the Sky: Man's Threat to the Ozone Layer. New York, Bantam, and London, Corgi, 1988; revised, New York, Bantam, 1993.

Cosmic Coincidences: Dark Matter, Mankind, and Anthropic Cosmology, with Martin Rees. New York, Bantam, 1989; as *The Stuff of the Universe: Dark Matter, Mankind, and the Coincidences of Cosmology,* London, Black Swan, 1991.

Winds of Change, with Mick Kelly. London, Headway, 1989.

The Cartoon History of Time, with Kate Charlesworth. London, Cardinal, and New York, Plume, 1990.

Children of the Ice: Climate and Human Origins, with Mary Gribbin. Oxford and Cambridge, Massachusetts, Blackwell, 1990.

Hothouse Earth: The Greenhouse Effect and Gaia. New York, Grove Weidenfeld, and London, Black Swan, 1990.

Blinded by the Light: The Secret Life of the Sun. London, Bantam, and New York, Harmony, 1991.

The Matter Myth: Towards 21st-Century Science, with Paul Davies. London, Viking, 1991; New York, Simon and Schuster, 1992.

Stephen Hawking: A Life in Science, with Michael White. London, Viking, and New York, Dutton, 1992.

In Search of the Edge of Time. London, Bantam, 1992; as *Unveiling the Edge of Time: Black Holes, White Holes, Wormholes.* New York, Harmony, 1992.

Too Hot to Handle? Greenhouse Effect, with Mary Gribbin. London, Corgi, 1992.

Being Human: Putting People in an Evolutionary Perspective, with Mary Gribbin. London, Dent, 1993.

In the Beginning: The Birth of the Living Universe. London, Viking, and Boston, Little, Brown, 1993.

Time and Space, with Mary Gribbin. London, Dorling Kindersley, 1994.

Einstein: A Life in Science, with Michael White. London, Simon and Schuster, 1993; New York, Dutton, 1994.

Darwin: A Life in Science, with Michael White. London, Simon and Schuster, 1995.

Schrödinger's Kittens and the Search for Reality. London, Weidenfeld and Nicolson, and Boston, Little, Brown, 1995.

Editor, *Climatic Change.* Cambridge and New York, Cambridge University Press, 1978.

Editor, *Cosmology Today.* London, IPC Magazines, 1982.

Editor, *The Breathing Planet.* Oxford and New York, Blackwell, 1986.

*   *   *

John Gribbin has become one of Britain's most prolific and best-known popularisers of science, with books on almost every hot scientific issue, from black holes to the ozone layer. He is physics consultant to *New Scientist,* and a contributor of scientific articles to numerous other periodicals. He became known as a regular writer of science fact articles to *Analog* in the 1970s, and it was natural that his first SF sale should have been to that magazine in September 1984: a short story called "Perpendicular Worlds," in which a contemporary scientist discovers both time travel and the infinity of alternative realities, and by sending back large amounts of bacteria over the course of several billion years, managed to create life. Such playful and unserious stories continued to appear in *Analog,* including several contributions to the magazine's scientific humour series, "Probability Zero," and a sequel to "Perpendicular Worlds" in February 1986. The most successful of these was probably "The Carbon Papers" (January 1990) in which, in January 1890, Sherlock Holmes works out that a mysterious death was in fact the suicide of a scientist who had discovered the greenhouse effect, and was trying to protect the coal-driven British Empire from the effects of that discovery: his papers were preserved by Holmes and Watson, to be opened a century later. "Other Edens" (*Interzone 31,* 1989) is a short, witty, and cynical piece following the exploits of a brave (but drug-fuddled) space pioneer, wiping another Gaia-planet free of life: "another Eden for the home planet's huddled masses."

Signs that Gribbin was also interested in more serious aspects of SF, and was also maturing as a fiction writer, getting beyond mere fictionalised lectures, appeared in two *Analog* stories that were subsequently developed into novels: "Double Planet" (November 1984) and "The Sins of the Fathers" (mid-December 1986). *Double Planet,* by Gribbin with fellow *New Scientist* writer Marcus Chown, is an SF thriller involving political intriguing both on Earth and on some of the last surviving space shuttles, sent to rendezvous with a comet heading perilously close to the Earth. The mission—to crash the comet into the Moon, thus providing it with the makings of an atmosphere, and providing the solar system with the double planet of the title—is ultimately successful; the novel is less so, with its political clichés and stereotypical characters. The sequel, *Reunion* (again with Chown), is set on the Moon a thousand years later, and is about the struggles of a teenage girl against the religious leadership. There is a love interest: the girl from the Moon, the boy from the Earth, who overcome various difficulties, have assorted adventures, and meet up two-thirds of the way through the book to save mankind. Towards the end there is some excellent circumvention of Asimov's three laws of robotics (which are unattributed), and the outwitting of a paranoid computer: logic in action, and quite nicely done. The novel is, on the whole, a good, light read, though structurally unbalanced.

Gribbin has also written two novels in collaboration with Douglas Orgill: *The Sixth Winter,* a fairly traditional disaster story about a new ice age, and *Brother Esau,* about the discovery of the Yeti.

Father to the Man, his first solo novel, also has its problems, with its scene-setting of a near-future Earth beset with political and environmental problems clumsily integrated into the fiction, and the resolution of the plot rather hastily contrived. But its story of a scientist doing his work investigating the gene-maps of humans and chimpanzees, and developing a crossbreed (rather predictably named Adam) despite the opposition of religious fundamentalists, is one that raises all kinds of interesting issues, and the characterisation seems more secure than in the collaborative novels. Structurally, though, it's untidy: two main sections of the story set 10 years apart, with a lot of little fragments of Adam's childhood and the world political scene scattered before and between them. Also, there is far too little integration of the perfectly sound societal extrapolations into the story; if there are climatic changes, if the standard of living is reduced, if the ultra-right is gaining support, if governments change, if Africa is falling apart, if the Americans withdraw from Europe—does this not have some impact on the scientist at the heart of the book?

Ragnarok, cowritten with sadly underrated SF novelist D.G. Compton, is a thriller about a double-Nobel laureate (physics and peace) blackmailing the U.S. and Russia into stopping all nuclear tests and giving half their money to the poor, or a small nuclear device carefully placed directly over a major fault line just off Iceland will be exploded. It's a well-thought-out set-up, and if it seems just a touch naive, then many terrorist plots are. Gribbin presumably provided the scientific detail, and Compton the generally fine writing (the raw beauty of Iceland is particularly well portrayed). The plot is sound if predictable, but once again the novel is spoiled by stereotyped characterisation; and whatever one's personal views on nuclear weaponry, the peace-nicking arguments are more than a little didactic.

Innervisions, another solo work, is an undistinguished space-ark story, in which some of the characters suspect that their "world" is a spaceship; they don't prove it until the end of the book, though the reader realises almost from page one. Nevertheless, it provides some interesting parallels of the renaissance scientist-versus-Christian-establishment debates concerning the shape of the Earth and the uniqueness of life.

Not surprisingly, considering his nonfiction work, Gribbin brings some excellent scientific ideas into his novels, but his thriller-type plotting and stereotyped characterisation unfortunately give his novels the feel of 1950s juvenile SF adventures. Nevertheless, he is one of the very few science-based British SF writers, and the science in his books can always be relied upon to be considerably more accurate than most fictional science.

—Edward James, updated by David V. Barrett

GRIDBAN, Volsted. *See* FEARN, John Russell; TUBB, E.C.

GRIFFIN, Russell M.

Nationality: American. **Born:** Stamford, Connecticut, 29 April 1943. **Education:** Mount Hermon School, 1957-61; Trinity College, Hartford, Connecticut, 1961-65, B.A. in English 1965; Case Western Reserve University, Cleveland, 1967-70, M.A. 1969, Ph.D. 1970. **Family:** Married Sheila Vaznelis in 1965; two children. **Career:** English teacher, Proctor Academy, Andover, New Hampshire, 1965-67. Professor of English, University of Bridgeport, Connecticut, from 1970. **Died:** 1986.

SCIENCE FICTION PUBLICATIONS

Novels

The Makeshift God. New York, Dell, 1979; London, Granada, 1982.
Century's End. New York, Bantam, 1981.
The Blind Men and the Elephant. New York, Pocket Books, 1982.
The Timeservers. New York, Avon, 1985.

*

Russell M. Griffin comments:

(1985) The first adult paperback I ever owned was an anthology of science fiction I took to boys' camp my first summer away from home. The book is long since lost, but not the stories.

But I suppose what has kept me in science fiction more than anything else since is the medievalist in me. Where else can a writer enjoy the same scope and freedom of invention one finds in the dream visions of Chaucer, Langland, and Gower? Where else in modern literature is allegory allowed to survive at all? Science fiction, as the works of Orwell and Huxley attest, provides the ideal vehicle for social comment and satire. Re-erect Spenser's Castle of Pride or create a society where equality is enforced by crippling the gifted? They are only a planet or an age away.

*   *   *

Russell M. Griffin's four published novels are fresh, witty, and crisply written versions of basic (and one not so basic) science fiction themes. Especially noteworthy are his inventiveness and exceptional gift for comedy and satire. Regarding the latter, while certain passages in his work are reminiscent of another fine satirist, John Sladek, Griffin's passages are usually rather better integrated into the work as a whole than Sladek's.

Griffin's first novel, *The Makeshift God,* would be impressive even were it not a first novel. The first half, especially, is brilliantly achieved; the second tends to lean more on mere adventure elements. However, Griffin's next two novels are more ambitious, both artistically and thematically. Significantly, both can be seen as closer to "mainstream" fiction than either his first or most recent efforts. His second novel, *Century's End,* is set in the near future (1999). Millennial actions and expectations abound: crazies and zanies expecting the worst, plotting the worst, are everywhere. In the controlled wit of the presentation, in the skill of its scene construction, and in its deft satirical art, this novel exemplifies many of the best qualities of the innovative science fiction of the past two decades; it can be meaningfully discussed in a context that includes the best of such writers as Vonnegut, Dick, and Disch. One thing that relates this novel to such major figures is the obvious intelligence manifested throughout—and not merely literary intelligence; for Griffin proves to be highly informed about a wide range of subjects—for example, satellite technology, climatology and geology, and the psychology and sociology of aberrant religious cults.

The plot focuses on the deadly rivalry of two such cults, one headed by an "inspired" madwoman, the other headed by a corporate-minded TV evangelist named Dr. Love. Griffin focuses much of the novel's deft satire on these two groups and their benighted followers; he focuses also on related hypes, TV programming and advertising, for example. The central characters ranged against the cults and their manipulative techniques are the bright, sardonic Jervis Santalucia, who is half-black and rarely at ease about his identity, and Circe McPhee, a professional prognosticator. The chaos of modern life is such that government and big business have turned to the occult for answers.

While the writing in Griffin's third novel, *The Blind Men and the Elephant*, is just as witty and persuasive, the work itself—plot, theme, milieu—is his least science-fictional. The highly bizarre plot and accompanying cast of zanies relate to the pathetic-comic misadventures of a latter-day "Elephant Man"— a terribly deformed yet bright and sensitive creature who is commercially exploited by a media huckster (TV again) and spied upon by sinister government agents. We soon learn that Elephant Man is no more than five or six years old, the ghastly product of government "experimentation" in cloning. His misadventures are a very Vonnegutian assemblage of black humor, farce, and satire. While individual episodes are very freshly done, it is doubtful that the overall presentation is as successful as it might have been. This volume is perhaps more to be recommended to fans of sixties-seventies mainstream black humor writing than to SF fans.

The Timeservers is, again, an impressive piece of writing. It resembles his first book in being overtly science-fictional in its setting, themes, and characterization—interstellar travel, encounters with alien races, and so on. Certain interests—cloning, Roman Catholic ritual, the omnipresence of human violence (here embodied in a war with strong Vietnam overtones)—return from earlier Griffin books. But Griffin is not repeating himself; he is just as fresh in approach, quite as interesting and witty here as in his previous books. Not only has he chosen the best of models (Dick, Sladek, et al), but in his best work, in his finest episodes, he transcends those models, bringing a new voice to the impressive choir of post-Campbellian writers.

—Robert E. Colbert

GRIFFITH, George

Pseudonyms: Levin Carnac; Lara; Stanton Morich. **Nationality:** British. **Born:** George Chetwynd Griffith-Jones, Plymouth, Devon, 20 August 1857. **Education:** schools in Lancashire and in evening classes, College of Preceptors Diploma 1887. **Family:** Married Elizabeth Brierly in 1887 (died 1933); two sons and one daughter. **Career:** Merchant seaman, 1873-77; English teacher, Worthing College, Sussex, 1877-83, and Bolton Grammar School, Lancashire, 1883-87; journalist in London, 1888-89; staff writer, *Pearson's Weekly*, 1890-99, and *Pearson's Magazine*, 1896-1903, both London: traveled extensively for these magazines, including two trips around the world; correspondent in South Africa for *London Daily Mail*, 1903. **Died:** 4 June 1906.

SCIENCE FICTION PUBLICATIONS

Novels (series: Olga Romanoff)

The Angel of the Revolution: A Tale of the Coming Terror (Romanoff). London, Tower, 1893; Westport, Connecticut, Hyperion Press, 1974.
Olga Romanoff; or, The Syren of the Skies: A Sequel to "The Angel of the Revolution." London, Tower, 1894; Westport, Connecticut, Hyperion Press, 1974.

Valdar the Oft-Born: A Saga of Seven Ages. London, Pearson, 1895; Naperville, Illinois, FAX, 1972.
The Outlaws of the Air. London, Tower, 1895.
Briton or Boer?: A Tale of the Fight for Africa. London, White, 1897.
The Romance of Golden Star. London, White, 1897; New York, Arno Press, 1978.
The Destined Maid. London, White, 1898.
The Gold-Finder. London, White, 1898.
The Great Pirate Syndicate. London, White, 1899.
The Justice of Revenge. London, White, 1901.
Captain Ishmael: A Saga of the South Seas. London, Hutchinson, 1901.
A Honeymoon in Space. London, Pearson, 1901; New York, Arno Press, 1975.
Denver's Double: A Story of Inverted Identity. London, White, 1901.
The White Witch of Mayfair. London, White, 1902.
A Woman against the World. London, White, 1903.
The World Masters. London, Long, 1903.
The Lake of Gold: A Narrative of the Anglo-American Conquest of Europe. London, White, 1903.
The Stolen Submarine: A Tale of the Russo-Japanese War. London, White, 1904.
A Criminal Croesus. London, Long, 1904.
A Mayfair Magician: A Romance of Criminal Science. London, White, 1905; as *The Man with Three Eyes*, n. d.
The Mummy and Miss Nitocris: A Phantasy of the Fourth Dimension. London, Laurie, 1906; New York, Arno Press, 1976; as *The Mummy and the Girl*, n. d.
The Great Weather Syndicate. London, White, 1906.
Novels (omnibus: includes *A Mayfair Magician, The World Peril of 1910, The Lake of Gold,* and *The Missionary*). London, White, 1906.
The World Peril of 1910. London, White, 1907.
The Sacred Skull. London, Everett, 1908.
The Lord of Labour. London, White, 1911.

Short Stories

Gambles with Destiny. London, White, 1899.
The Raid of "Le Vengeur" and Other Stories. London, Ferret Fantasy, 1974.

OTHER PUBLICATIONS

Novels

The Knights of the White Rose. London, White, 1897.
The Virgin of the Sun. London, Pearson, 1898.
The Rose of Judah. London, Pearson, 1899.
Brothers of the Chain. London, White, 1900.
Thou Shalt Not— (as Stanton Morich). London, Pearson, 1900.
The Missionary. London, White, 1902.
An Island Love-Story. London, White, 1904.
His Better Half. London, White, 1905.
His Beautiful Client. London, White, 1905.
A Conquest of Fortune. London, White, 1906.
John Brown, Buccaneer. London, White, 1908.

Short Stories

A Heroine of the Slums. London, Tower, 1894.

Knaves of Diamonds, Being Tales of Mine and Veld. London, Pearson, 1899; as *The Diamond Dog,* 1913.

Poetry (as Lara)

Poems General, Secular, and Satirical. London, Stewart, 1883.
The Dying Faith. London, Stewart, 1884.

Other

Men Who Have Made the Empire. London, Pearson, 1897.
In an Unknown Prison Land: An Account of Convicts and Colonists in New Caledonia. London, Hutchinson, 1901.
With Chamberlain in Africa. London, Routledge, 1903.
Sidelights on Convict Life. London, Long, 1903.

Translator (as Levin Carnac), *The Hope of the Family,* by Alphonse Daudet. London, Pearson, 1898.

*

Bibliography: By George Locke, in *The Raid of "Le Vengeur" and Other Stories,* 1974.

*   *   *

George Griffith published almost 50 books of crime, adventure, fantasy, romance, social melodrama, verse, and nonfiction. Most importantly, his output includes over 20 books of, or in the margins of, SF. He became one of the first, most characteristic, and most popular professional writers of editorially planned and instantly sensational fiction in the rising "yellow press" of the turn of the century. Griffith also met the usual end of such hacks, being forced to get more outrageous and less believable in each succeeding novel and to shed whatever original insights he might have had in the process.

His best work, consequently, is clearly his first novel, *The Angel of the Revolution,* though even that is marred by slipshod haste, racist chauvinism, and melodramatic sensationalism. Yet the subsumption of Verne's gadgetry and the "future war" tale, plus a dash of travelogue exoticism and a barrelful of Bulwerian melodrama, under a real sympathy with justice wrecked on the existing political order of despotism and Mammon by a group of avenging heroes united into an Anarchist or Terrorist Brotherhood of Freedom, was a genuine breakthrough. The brains of the conspiracy, the super-intelligent Hungarian Jew Natas, is, in spite of his name, his hypnotic powers, and his crippled exterior, convincingly portrayed as a victim of Tsarist oppression rather than a mad beast. The main hero, an English inventor, is starving in his garret while inventing his super-airplane; and the executive head of the Terrorists is an English aristocrat, thus permitting Griffith to alloy plebeian hatred with snobbery. There follow cliffhanging global adventures dovetailing the fates of the heroes and their beautiful and fully equal female counterparts, especially Natas's daughter Natasha, and the world war that develops in 1904. The bloodthirsty Franco-Slavonic alliance is defeated by the Brotherhood who set up an Anglo-Saxon federation to guide the world toward disarmament and a vague social justice never clearly spelled out in economic terms. But this heady brew contains a few memorable set scenes, and—most importantly—an at least partial realization that the fusion of politics and the new technology makes the old social rela-

tionships not only unstable but catastrophically untenable. This realization made Griffith a pioneer in the instauration of a new SF tradition that culminated in Wells and still overshadows our whole century.

The sequel, *Olga Romanoff,* written to exploit *The Angel*'s great success, is inferior, its only new element being an interplanetary threat copied from Flammarion's ubiquitous comets. Already in *The Outlaws of the Air* the exploitation becomes unreadable: the anarchists are vicious beasts, the heroes English gentlemen, the ideal a rosewater South Sea colony, the fights simply ludicrous; *The Great Pirate Syndicate* descends to bloodthirsty Anglo-Saxon wishdream-imperialism and anti-Semitism. In Griffith's feverish gallop through all the popular literary forms, *A Honeymoon in Space* was his venture into interplanetary voyages; it groups all its clichés (aggressive Martians, angel-like Venusians, antigravity, monsters galore) around a safari-story of a lord, his beautiful American bride, and their faithful retainer. His later works are unworthy of a writer with political convictions and a generous plebeian indignation: if the story that Griffith died of drink is true, it would provide an appropriately moral dying fall. And it would still remain exemplary for the SF of our century.

—Darko Suvin

GRIFFITH, Nicola (Jane)

Nationality: British (resided in US since 12/89; resident alien since 9/94). **Born:** Leeds, Yorkshire, England, 30 September 1960. **Family:** Married Kelley Eskridge in 1993 (but marriage between two women not legally recognized here—yet). **Career:** Labourer, Dept. of Environment, 1976, Helmsley, Yorks; Technician, Hull City Council, 1980, Hull; singer and songwriter, Janes Plane, 1981-82, Hull, humberside; singer and songwriter, Janes Remains, 1982-1983, Hull; welfare benefits adviser, Hull City Council, 1987-88, Hull; caseworker-Council for Drug Problems, Hull, 1988-89; full-time writer, 1989-present; also: Women's self-defense teacher, 1983-89; instructor, creative writing, Humberside County Council Adult Ed, 1988-89; instructor, creative writing, Workers' Education Council, 1988-89; teacher, creative writing, Lincolnshire and Humberside Arts Council, Special Programme, 1989; Reviewer; *Southern Voice,* 1991-93; *New York Review of SF,* 1993-94. **Awards:** National Network of Women Writers (UK), short fiction contest winner, 1986; Lambda Literary Award, 1993; Georgia Council for the Arts, Individual Artist's Award, 1993; Atlanta Bureau of Cultural Affairs, Artist's Project Grant, 1994; James Tiptree, Jr. Memorial Prize, 1994. **Agent:** Shawna McCarthy, Scovil Chichak Galen, 381 Park Avenue South, Suite 1020, New York, New York 10016. **Address:** 1814 Marlbrook Drive N.E., Atlanta, Georgia 30307-1726, U.S.A.

SCIENCE FICTION PUBLICATIONS

Novels

Ammonite. London, Grafton, and New York, Ballantine, 1993.
Slow River. New York, Ballantine, 1995.

*

Nicola Griffith comments:

The worlds in which my characters exist and interact form the backbone of my fiction. I want the reader to know how each place smells, how the ground feels underfoot, what the ambient noise is like, how the wind—if there is wind—tastes on the back of the tongue. Whether this world is largely pastoral or urban, whether it is in our past, present or future, or even outside our universe entirely does not matter. It must only be real to the characters and, through them, the reader.

In this regard, I would say my main influence has not been science fiction, but those historical novelists I tend to call the English Landscape Writers: Mary Stewart, Rosemary Sutcliff, Henry Treece and (to a lesser extent, because I came to her work later) Mary Renault. The first alien worlds I encountered brimmed with the rough magic of moor and menhir and monastery, of *gravitas* and woad and wet wool. Through these writers, I understood that a character is always a product of her time and place; that Things Would Happen if you took that product of a specific time and place, and put her somewhere else.

Therefore much of my work explores people and their place in the world: what that place might have been, and how they lost it; whether or not it can be regained or, if not, whether they can make their way anew. I have taken people from one planet and put them in another. I have left people in place but changed their perception of the world around them. I have moved people from one layer of their society to another. I pick up these poor characters and drop them somewhere strange—to them and/or us—and watch with interest while they struggle to deal with finding themselves in an alien place, time or culture. Lately, I have begun playing with people who stay in the same world, with the same job, the same friends, the same financial means, only to find that their bodies, minds, or souls have changed in such a way as to make them alien to themselves.

Whether it is a science fiction novel about learning to belong on a strange planet; or one about being stripped of past, moral identity and family; whether it is a psychological thriller where the protagonist's self-identity is taken from her by chronic illness; or whether it is erotic horror about a woman from a repressed English background finding herself in the lush jungle with no rules, my work is fueled by people and their places. People are constantly being changed by their changing worlds, and their cultures are in turn subtly influenced by the individuals of which it is composed. People are their places are their people.

*   *   *

Like a comet, Nicola Griffith's impact on the SF scene has been fast and blinding: her 1993 debut *Ammonite* won the Georgia Council for the Arts Individual Artist's Award, the Tiptree Memorial Prize, and the Lambda Literary Award. Hailed by critics as a feminist force to be reckoned with, Griffith has impressed such fellow writers as Kim Stanley Robinson and Ursula K. Le Guin. Even before *Ammonite* garnered wide acclaim, Griffith won the National Network of Women Writers' short story contest in 1986 and her numerous short stories and novellas, published in both the U.K. and U.S., have been translated into several languages. Her eagerly awaited second novel, 1995's *Slow River,* is as well-written and engaging as her first effort.

Griffith has led a life almost as interesting as her characters'—she's worked as a welfare benefits advisor, drug abuse counselor, women's self-defense instructor, laborer for the Yorks Dept. of Environment, led creative writing workshops, even wrote and performed songs with two bands before settling into her current incarnation as successful novelist.

In *Ammonite,* Grenchstom's Planet (called "GP" or "Jeep") is populated by a group of quarantined women who survived a virus that has inexplicably killed all males and some females. Immune and thriving, Jeep's women not only rebuild a stable and diverse civilization but are able to reproduce. Hoping to test an experimental vaccine called FN-17 and exploit Jeep's natural resources, the Durallium Company sends an anthropologist named Marghe Taishan to live on the planet, locate her predecessor and report her findings. Yet Marghe undergoes a transformation to better study Jeep's unique societies—she goes "native"—and rediscovers herself and her sexual identity in the process.

Though *Ammonite's* premise isn't a new one (*The Wanderground, Herland,* and *The Left Hand of Darkness* come to mind), Jeep's tribal culture is sufficiently different to warrant attention. Men no longer exist, yet the aggression and crimes generally attributed to them are very much alive. Griffith's focal point, the virus, is a medical phenomenon to Jeep's inhabitants—while it's capable of decimating the population it has also somehow created a master race of women who can bond seamlessly with both their environment and each other.

Slow River, like its predecessor, is also about self-discovery, and survival and independence. Heiress Lore Van Oesterling is kidnapped just after receiving tragic family news. Kept drugged and naked, she learns her family won't pay her ransom and mortally wounds one of her captors to escape. Injured and bleeding, she's taken in by Spanner, a small-time thief who makes Lore one of her accomplices. Going along with Spanner's schemes out of loyalty, love and dependency, Lore comes to hate her complicity and Spanner's use of her emotional and physical fragility. Striking out on her own with the identity of a dead woman, Lore manages to earn a living and gain a small measure of self-respect before her house of cards caves in.

Both *Ammonite* and *Slow River* revolve around learning to exist in a hostile environment, be it near-future Europe or Grenchstom's Planet. Just as Marghe battles the Durallium Company and her insecurities, Lore must acknowledge the shadowy horrors within her family and her own growing corruption. Each protagonist has been displaced from her former insulated life and must forge a new identity based on her true needs.

Though a relative newcomer, Griffith's mastery of language is exceptional, her settings imaginative and well-drawn, her characters compelling, and her plots fast and finely-tuned. Griffith is swiftly earning her place among the vanguard of SF literature.

—Sydonie Benet

GRINNELL, David. *See* **WOLLHEIM, Donald A.**

GROENER, Carl. *See* **LOWNDES, Robert A.W.**

GUIN, Wyman (Woods)

Nationality: American. **Born:** Wanette, Oklahoma, 1 March 1915. **Education:** Riverside City College, California, J.C. 1934. **Family:** Married 1) Jean Adolph in 1939 (divorced 1955); 2) Valerie Carlson in 1956; two sons and three daughters. **Career:** Technician in pharmacology. Advertising writer, advertising manager, and marketing vice-president, Lakeside Laboratories Inc., Milwaukee, 1938-62; vice-president, Medical Television Communications Inc., Chicago, 1962-64. Since 1964, planning administrator, L.W. Erolich-Intercon International. **Died:** 1989.

SCIENCE FICTION PUBLICATIONS

Novel

The Standing Joy. New York, Avon, 1969.

Short Stories

Living Way Out. New York, Avon, 1967; as *Beyond Bedlam,* London, Sphere, 1973.

*   *   *

Although Wyman Guin has written a novel, *The Standing Joy,* his most important work is to be found in his novelettes from the 1950s and 1960s. The stories are remarkable for the way in which Guin takes up far-out sociological or psychological ideas and gives them substance in carefully worked out dramatic conflicts against the background of alternate societies; despite some extravaganzas in the details, they carry conviction and emerge as fully rounded and believable SF worlds.

His best story is the minor classic "Beyond Bedlam," which employs the basic inversion device of so much science fiction: what is considered an illness today—schizophrenia in this case—is in about a thousand years in the future the norm, with a drug-induced, law-enforced schizophrenia in every human being. Everybody is inhabited by two personalities that change in five-day shifts. This procedure has eliminated man's aggressive impulses, and hence war, but has also led to the disappearance of art and emotional pleasures. The theme of the story is treated not so much as a utopian dream or a dystopian nightmare as an exercise in creating a different alternate society, with all the ramifications of good and evil following from the basic premise.

"The Delegate from Guapanga" and "A Man of the Renaissance" both have richly exotic sociocultural backgrounds. The first story contrasts two alien philosophies of "Mentalists" and "Matterists," the Mentalists being closer to nature with ideals of a simpler life and tradition, the Matterists representatives of a mechanistic-scientific culture. The hero of the story develops a curious political idea of "dishonesty in government." The second story is about a man of ambition in an archipelagic world, who by sometimes Machiavellian means tries to realize his purely rationalist and revolutionary notions in a world governed by traditional values. In "Volpla" a joke in genetical engineering by a misanthropic lone scientist—artificially created beings that were to be passed off as visitors from the stars—turns out differently by a simple reversion of the reader's expectations. "My Darling Hecate" and "The Root and the Ring" are slight and mildly amusing volatile fantasies.

Guin's novel, *The Standing Joy,* is a parallel Earth story, with the characters having "twins" on another Earth, perhaps our own. Its protagonist, Colin Collins, a superman who has invented the prolonged orgasm, gathers around him a group of other talented inventors; the sex is harmless, but the whole thing is a bit confused. Wyman Guin's typical work is characteristic of its time and the magazine (*Galaxy*) in which most of it appeared, a slickly written fiction of ideas that manages to entertain and to stimulate without moving the reader deeply.

—Franz Rottensteiner

GUNN, James E(dwin)

Nationality: American. **Born:** Kansas City, Missouri, 12 July 1923. **Education:** University of Kansas, Lawrence, B.A. in journalism 1947, M.A. in English 1951. **Military Service:** Served in the United States Naval Reserve, 1943-46; Lieutenant. **Family:** Married Jane Frances Anderson in 1947; two sons. **Career:** Editor, Western Printing and Lithographing Company, Racine, Wisconsin, 1951-52. Assistant instructor, 1955-56, managing editor, Alumni Association, 1955-58, administrative assistant to the Chancellor for University Relations, 1958-70, lecturer, 1970-74; Professor of English, 1974-93; Emeritus Professor of English, 1993-, University of Kansas. Director, Center for the Study of Science Fiction, University of Kansas, 1982-. **Member:** Executive Committee, and president, 1980-82, Science Fiction Research Association; president, Science Fiction Writers of America, 1971-72. **Awards:** Byron Caldwell Smith prize; World Science Fiction special award, 1976, and Hugo Achievement award, 1983; Pilgrim award, 1976; Edward Grier award, 1989. Guest of Honor, Mid-Americon 1, Macron 10, Fortcon 1. **Agents:** Dorris Halsey, 8733 Sunset Boulevard, Los Angeles, California 90069; or, Maggie Noach, 2, Redan Street London W14 0AB, England. **Address:** 2215 Orchard Lane, Lawrence, Kansas 66049, U.S.A.

SCIENCE FICTION PUBLICATIONS

Novels

This Fortress World. New York, Gnome Press, 1955; London, Sphere, 1977.
Star Bridge, with Jack Williamson. New York, Gnome Press, 1955; London, Sidgwick and Jackson, 1978.
The Joy Makers. New York, Bantam, 1961; London, Gollancz, 1963.
The Immortals. New York, Bantam, 1962; London, Panther, 1975.
The Immortal: A Novel (novelization of TV series). New York, Bantam, 1970.
The Burning. New York, Dell, 1972.
The Listeners. New York, Scribner, 1972; London, Arrow, 1978.
The Magicians. New York, Scribner, 1976; London, Sidgwick and Jackson, 1978.
Kampus: A Novel. New York, Bantam, 1977.
The Dreamers. New York, Simon and Schuster, 1980; London, Gollancz, 1981; as *The Mind Master,* New York, Pocket Books, 1982.

Short Stories

Station in Space. New York, Bantam, 1958.
Future Imperfect. New York, Bantam, 1964.
The Witching Hour. New York, Dell, 1970.
Breaking Point. New York, Walker, 1972.
Some Dreams Are Nightmares. New York, Scribner, 1974.
The End of the Dreams: Three Short Novels about Space, Happiness, and Immortality. New York, Scribner, 1975.
Tiger! Tiger! Polk City, Iowa, Drumm, 1984.
Crisis! New York, Tor, 1986.
The Unpublished Gunn, Part One. Polk City, Iowa, Drumm, 1992.

OTHER PUBLICATIONS

Play

Thy Kingdom Come (produced Lawrence, Kansas, 1947).

Other

Alternate Worlds: The Illustrated History of Science Fiction. Englewood Cliffs, New Jersey, Prentice-Hall, 1975.
The Discovery of the Future: The Ways Science Fiction Developed. College Station, Texas A and M University Library, 1975.
Teachers's Manual: The Road to Science Fiction, with Stephen H. Goldman. New York, New American Library, 1980.
Isaac Asimov: The Foundations of Science Fiction. New York, Oxford University Press, 1982.
Inside Science Fiction: Essays on Fantastic Literature. San Bernardino, California, Borgo Press, 1992.

Editor, *Man and the Future.* Lawrence, University Press of Kansas, 1968.
Editor, *Nebula Award Stories Ten.* New York, Harper, 1975.
Editor, *The Road to Science Fiction: From Gilgamesh to Wells, from Wells to Heinlein, from Heinlein to Here, from Here to Forever.* New York, New American Library, 4 vols., 1977-82.
Editor, *The New Encyclopedia of Science Fiction.* New York and London, Viking, 1988.
Editor, *The Best of Astounding: Classic Short Novels from the Golden Age of Science Fiction.* New York, Carroll and Graf, 1992.

*

Bibliography: *A James Gunn Checklist,* Polk City, Iowa, Drumm, 1983.

Manuscript Collection: University of Kansas, Spencer Research Library, Lawrence.

James E. Gunn comments:

I began an autobiographical essay for *Contemporary Authors Autobiography Series* with the statement: "I am a professor of English at the University of Kansas, the author of some 80 published science fiction stories and the author or editor of 24 books, almost all of them either science fiction or about science fiction. At the age of 61, as I write this account of my life in that fabled year of 1984, in the quiet university town of Lawrence, Kansas, trying to make sense out of what has happened to me, my first thought is that, unlikely as it might once have seemed, this is where I belong; this

is what I was meant to do." Now that I am 72 and retired from teaching, but returned to full-time writing, the conclusion, in 1995, still seems appropriate.

The facts that I have been president of both of the Science Fiction Writers of America and the Science Fiction Research Association, that I have written almost as much critical material about science fiction as I have written science fiction, that I split my working time between teaching and writing, illustrate the ways in which my work has tried to bridge two cultures. In the introduction to my 1972 collection of stories, *Breaking Point,* I wrote that "the stories in this collection were intended [to help] bridge the gap between science fiction and the mainstream, between the ghetto and the larger world outside, between C.P. Snow's Two Cultures." They were, I indicated, intended to adopt an evolutionary, not a revolutionary, approach to a literature, accepting the strengths of a popular genre and trying to build upon them.

Finally, in my autobiographical essay, I wrote about a story that became the starting point for my writing of *The Dreamers,* "Looking back over my career as a writer of science fiction, I realize now that I have always been fascinated by the seductive power of dreams, even while I have insisted that reality, while it may be hard and tragic, is preferable." I concluded the essay with the statement, "That would be consistent with my life as I see it: surprise tempered by understanding, optimism tempered by reality, ambition tempered by pragmatism.

"The true heroes of my stories are rational people who accept the world as it is while never giving up the possibility of making it better. The villains are much the same, only they are willing to go too far to get what they want; they want what everyone else wants, but their desires are not restrained by a sense of other people's needs.

"A fiction writer's work may not always reflect his values, but if he writes out of what he has experienced and thought and felt, it must reflect the writer. What I am ultimately must be seen in the mirror of my writing."

*   *   *

In his definitive anthology entitled *The Road to Science Fiction,* James E. Gunn defines science fiction as idea-fiction that describes change and its consequences on the human race. This change is often technological and, in most cases, is brought about by human actions and desires. While such a definition may not work for all of science fiction or for all its writers, it has worked well for Gunn. Since 1949 his work has consistently represented human characters confronting altered futures. As in the stories collected in *Station in Space,* Gunn sees humanity as a race that needs to be challenged in order to grow. He recognizes that many people would prefer to live in stable worlds in which each day is like all the others, and, therefore, his plots frequently deal with how the major characters thwart the deadly appeal of stasis.

James Gunn was raised on a steady diet of hero pulps, dime novels, and early science fiction magazines. When the latter came along, he was swept into the current. With such early work as *The Joy Makers,* which deals most closely with the allure of stasis, it may be said that Gunn is a forebear to the "New Wave" of science fiction. Specifically, in his story collection, *Breaking Point,* Gunn says he "attempted to bring to the task of telling a science fiction story everything I knew about setting and symbol, theme and character." One can see in James Gunn's body of work the evolution of the genre itself.

Gunn's favorite writing length is the novelette because it allows him to center his story on a single event that is economically described and resolved. Many of his "novels" consist of three or four novelettes connected by a common theme. In *The Joy Makers,* for example, Gunn explores what people think will make them happy within an extended period of time through a true science of hedonics. In each story a stage is reached which eventually supports his thesis that even if absolute happiness could be found it would probably be rather disappointing. The use of a series of novelettes allows a story to end with a dramatic statement that does not need the amplification and development a novel demands.

The Immortals, another series of interconnected stories, investigates a world in which immortality is possible. However, in each story the possibility of immortality is not as important as its effect on the characters. Gunn wishes to describe human attitudes toward death and uses the device of immortality to put these attitudes into sharp relief. Because he deals with such issues, Gunn's stories often touch on current problems. For example, medical technology has been more and more directed toward the prolongation of life. But such technology has added huge costs to basic hospital services. In the third story of *The Immortals* Gunn presents the ultimate direction such a trend could take. The story effectively describes just how dangerous humanity's preoccupation with avoiding death can be.

In *The Listeners* Gunn studies communication in the same way he explored immortality. While the unifying concept among these novelettes is the attempt to decipher and answer a message from Capella, the theme concerns communication between individuals. In each story, with the Capellan project in the background, the foreground is filled with husbands and wives, fathers and sons, leaders and followers, writers and readers, men and intelligent machines and humans and aliens who try to communicate. A recurring metaphor tying these stories together is the anthropomorphized radio dish and "Computer Run" sequences: The dish is an infinitely patient listener, yet has no capacity to communicate; the Computer slowly learns what it means for living beings to communicate while portraying to the reader a human world that seems unable to do so. The result is a work that describes not only an adventure in the near future but a moving account of humanity's present. Communication with aliens may happen some day, but for now human communication could do with some improvement.

The Dreamers (inexplicably renamed *The Mind Master* by the paperback publisher), collects three novelettes with the addition of inter-chapter material that adds up to yet another story. Each of these stories traces the consequences of the discovery of chemical learning. By imparting instant knowledge through chemistry, humanity has eliminated the difficulty normally associated with learning. But it has also created a future race in which imagination is sadly lacking. Even dreams come from pills and injections. By far the darkest of Gunn's works, *The Dreamers* still gives the reader human characters who are capable of love and who care about what has happened to their fellow human beings, though they are all, to one extent or another, psychologically damaged. In fact, through most of "The Volunteer" section, one is assaulted with the surgeon's dreams of betrayal and vengeance over the history of human evolution. But one must read these sadistic images as symptoms of the disease which has overtaken society rather than, as one critic interpreted, a loss of control on the author's part. The stories might deal with a nightmare age, but Gunn regrets this nightmare. This novel is a cautionary tale. It is as if Gunn is telling the reader that these characters, and by extension humanity, deserve better than their allotted fates.

And Gunn does give humanity a better fate in his most recent book *Crisis!* Set in our present, the stories deal with a man from the future who comes to the present in order to avert events that will destroy the future. This character is not allowed to act directly, but must convince people of the present to act simply by speaking and reasoning with them. Gunn covers a wide variety of problems (from energy to war to terrorism), and presents some interesting views on why and how they happen.

Two more conventional novels deserve mention. *This Fortress World,* Gunn's first novel, is a highly readable story that makes use of the popular science fiction galactic empire. But Gunn relates the story from the point of view of an ordinary inhabitant rather than a super-hero. Life in a galactic empire can be rather unpleasant if the character is only one of the crowd; Gunn metaphorically stresses the damage that can be caused by self-imposed isolation in a wonderful opening passage about galactic empire that ties in to later passages about human isolation. The grand metaphor of the "fortress world" ranges from the largest perspective—all of humanity shielding itself from the universe, to the second level of individual worlds as fortresses unassailable by other worlds, to the main character who has walled himself off from a sick and uncaring world. Even in space-opera mode, Gunn is impelled to approach serious themes. *This Fortress World* is Gunn's attempt to bring "reality" to space opera, and in this way might be considered an early precursor to cyberpunk.

At the opposite pole lies *Kampus,* a work that has suffered from misreading. It is too easy—and misleading—to read this novel as a damnation of the campus of the 1960s. *Kampus* is, in fact, a parable about people who believe that everyone should be allowed to do "their own thing." It is similar to Voltaire's *Candide* in that the world and action presented in the novel are not meant to be taken as serious attempts to portray "reality." Unlike *Candide,* however, *Kampus* questions what life would be like if everyone were only to tend his own garden, which is clear in scenes where absurdity drives the action as in the cannibalism scene; or where the setting is absurd as in the walled university—walled off from the town to protect the town rather than what lay within its walls; and several characters, such as the student body leader, who might have been *Dune*'s Baron Harkonnen during his college years.

A new (unpublished) novel, *Catastrophe!,* ought to be purchased by the time this sees print. In *Catastrophe!* we see the culmination of more than 20 years of part-time writing effort, honed and refined such that readers can expect literary elements on par with the best in mainstream. It is the story of six characters working along individual paths toward the coming millennium and the end of the world, and along that path each character's "world" ends in various ways, resulting either in personal growth or destruction. As with all of Gunn's work, each scene provides the reader with the kind of dramatic pleasure and payoff one seeks in a short story while building along the way into a novel and developing a fully realized world.

James E. Gunn has made a career of science fiction as an author, teacher, and scholar. His criticism attests to his sensitivity to the genre. His fiction shows an equal sensitivity to what is possible in science fiction. As one reads his stories, one is struck by the variety of themes, plots, and styles he is capable of. His tone ranges from lighthearted—though humor is usually only found in his short work—to damningly serious, as in the long sadistic scenes of human evolution in *The Dreamers. Kampus* is a remarkable feat of stylistic experimentation that was not at all predictable from *The Listeners. The Dreamers* and *Crisis!* prove that his interest in style has not ended. In a literature that is itself concerned with change, it is somehow reassuring that one of the writers most interested in this theme is himself able to change.

—Stephen H. Goldman, updated by Christopher McKitterick

GUTHRIE, Alan. *See* TUBB, E.C.

GUTTERIDGE, (Thomas Gordon) Lindsay

Nationality: British. **Born:** Easington, County Durham, 20 May 1923. **Education:** an art school in Newcastle-upon-Tyne. **Family:** Married Marjorie Kathleen Carpenter; one daughter. **Career:** Freelance commercial artist, London 1939-41, 1950-68; art teacher, King Edward School of Art, Newcastle, 1941-43; cattle stockman in Australia, 1946-48; freelance photographer, 1958-60; former art director, Robert Sharp and Partners, advertising agency, London. **Address:** 15 Howdale Road, Downham Market, Norfolk PE38 9AB, England.

SCIENCE FICTION PUBLICATIONS

Novels (series: Matthew Dilke in all books)

Cold War in a Country Garden. London, Cape, and New York, Putnam, 1971.
Killer Pine. London, Cape, and New York, Putnam, 1973.
Fratricide Is a Gas. London, Cape, 1975.

*

Lindsay Gutteridge is the author of three espionage novels featuring Matthew Dilke as hero, a micro-man one-quarter of an inch in height. They are all splendid adventure stories and powerfully engage the sense of wonder. Gutteridge plays rough with his miniature spies and their normal-sized masters and foes, so that these should perhaps be classified as adult entertainments, but there is nothing very special in the books considered as offbeat spy thrillers. Their distinctive quality is science-educational: they are the closest fictional equivalents I have found to *The Hellstrom Chronicle*. Whereas that film's overwhelming images of the alien life we overlook projected an inimical world in which ants are far better adapted for survival than we hubristic humans, Gutteridge, better balanced, discovers not only beauty and terror, monstrosity and indifference, but delightful nourishment. By not being insect-sized, Gutteridge suggests, we are missing the marvellous abundant food of pollen and nectar. If only we could be miniaturized, our survival problems would be over. There, of course, is the rub which would lead us to classify these works as pure fantasies were it not that they belong to a tradition of micro-people in SF established by such writers as Asimov, Blish, and Leinster, and that they use the convention to instruct us about natural history so fully and sensitively. The microscopic eye is a human one, and the wonders seen are related to human fears, needs and desires.

Cold War in a Country Garden, in which the mission of three micro-men is to implant transmitters in the hair of a Russian, is closest perhaps to the conventional spy thriller, substituting a box of centipedes for the snake pit or piranha pool as a persuasive threat to the captured Dilke. When he escapes, rescuing a micro-negress, Hyacinthe, who aids him in his second adventure, the pursuers are caught by an ant-lion. *Killer Pine* is a novel of ecological warfare, in which the enemy are Russian micro-men who inhabit a metal container on a pine in a Canadian forest, breeding termites to spread a viral death. We are given fascinating and horrid glimpses of life in a termite colony, in a tree which, for the micro-climbers, has the scale of Mount Everest. The third novel, *Fratricide Is a Gas,* has affinities with novels of industrial espionage: here Matthew Dilke is pitted alone against a sadistic Nazi chemist in Peru. The highlight of this novel is a sequence in which Dilke climbs jungloid thorns and creepers, enjoying on the way an idyllic repose in the bloom of an orchid, where he is visited by a hummingbird and witnesses the giant courtship of butterflies and the predations of parasitic wasps and shaggy spiders.

Gutteridge's micro-man's view gives us the pleasure of a sardonic perspective on the conventions of spy fiction and also a Swiftian magnification of some of our physical and spiritual coarseness, as when Dilke spies from a perch on the top of Lippe's study chair not only the eroded massif of his head but also the monstrous cruelty of his mind, revealed by his most private occupations. Gutteridge's work may well have influenced *The Micronauts* by Gordon Williams (1977), an exciting, more fully science fiction narrative which, however, lacks the Gutteridge charm.

—Michael J. Tolley

H

HAGGARD, H(enry) Rider

Nationality: British. **Born:** Bradenham, Norfolk, 22 June 1856. **Education:** Ipswich Grammar School, Suffolk; Lincoln's Inn, London, 1881-85: called to the Bar, 1885. **Family:** Married Louisa Mariana Margitson in 1880; one son and three daughters. **Career:** Lived in South Africa, as Secretary to Sir Henry Bulwer, Lieutenant-Governor of Natal, 1875-77, member of the staff of Sir Theophilus Shepstone, Special Commissioner in the Transvaal, 1877, and Master and Registrar of the High Court of the Transvaal, 1877-79; returned to England, 1879; managed his wife's estate in Norfolk, from 1880; worked in chambers of Henry Bargave Deane, 1885-87; Unionist and Agricultural candidate for East Norfolk, 1895; coeditor, *African Review*, 1898; travelled throughout England investigating condition of agriculture and the rural population, 1901-02; British Government Special Commissioner to report on Salvation Army settlements in the United States, 1905; chairman, Reclamation and Unemployed Labour Committee, Royal Commission on Coast Erosion and Afforestation, 1906-11; travelled around the world as a member of the Dominions Royal Commission, 1912-17. Chairman of the Committee, Society of Authors, 1896-98; vice-president, Royal Colonial Institute, 1917. Knighted, 1912; K.B.E. (Knight Commander, Order of the British Empire), 1919. **Died:** 14 May 1925.

Science Fiction Publications

Novels (series: Allan Quatermain; She)

King Solomon's Mines (Quatermain). London and New York, Cassell, 1885.

She: A History of Adventure. New York, Harper, 1886; London, Longman, 1887.

Allan Quatermain: Being an Account of His Further Adventures and Discoveries in Company with Sir Henry Curtis, Bart., Commander John Good, R.N., and One Umslopogaas. London, Longman, and New York, Harper, 1887; abridged as *Allan Quatermain and the Lost City of Gold,* edited by Sarah Litvinoff, London, Arrow, 1986.

Allan's Wife. New York, Munro, 1887.

A Tale of Three Lions, and On Going Back. New York, Lovell, 1887.

Maiwa's Revenge: A Novel (Quatermain). New York, Harper, and London, Longman, 1888.

Cleopatra: Being an Account of the Fall and Vengeance of Harmachis, the Royal Egyptian, as Set Forth by His Own Hand. London, Longman, and New York, Harper, 1889.

Beatrice: A Novel. London, Longman, and New York, Harper, 1890.

The World's Desire (with Andrew Lang). London, Longman, and New York, Harper, 1890.

Eric Brighteyes. London, Longman, and New York, United States Book Company, 1891.

Nada the Lily. New York and London, Longman, 1892.

Montezuma's Daughter. New York and London, Longman, 1893.

The People of the Mist. London and New York, Longman, 1894.

The Wizard. Bristol, Arrowsmith, and New York, Longman, 1896.

Heart of the World. New York, Longman, 1895; London, Longman, 1896.

Swallow: A Tale of the Great Trek. New York and London, Longman, 1899.

Lysbeth: A Tale of the Dutch. New York and London, Longman, 1901.

Pearl-Maiden: A Tale of the Fall of Jerusalem. London and New York, Longman, 1903.

The Brethren. London, Cassell, and New York, Doubleday, Page, 1904.

Stella Fregelius: A Tale of Three Destinies. London and New York, Longman, 1904.

Ayesha: The Return of She. London, Ward Lock, and New York, Doubleday, Page, 1905; as *The Return of She: Ayesha,* New York, London, 1967.

Benita: An African Romance. London, Cassell, 1906; as *The Spirit of Bambatse: A Romance,* New York, Longman, 1906.

The Yellow God: An Idol of Africa. New York, Cupples and Leon, 1908; London, Cassell, 1909.

The Ghost Kings. London, Cassell, 1908; as *The Lady of the Heavens,* New York, Authors and Newspapers Association, 1908.

The Lady of Blossholme. London, Hodder and Stoughton, 1909.

Morning Star. London, Cassell, and New York, Longman, 1910.

Queen Sheba's Ring. London, Nash, and New York, Doubleday, Page, 1910.

The Mahatma and the Hare: A Dream Story. London, Longman, and New York, Holt, 1911.

Red Eve. London, Hodder and Stoughton, and Garden City, New York, Doubleday, Page, 1911.

Marie (Quatermain). London, Cassell, and New York, Longman, 1912.

Child of Storm (Quatermain). London, Cassell, and New York, Longman, 1913.

The Wanderer's Necklace. London, Cassell, and New York, Longman, 1914.

The Holy Flower (Quatermain). London, Ward Lock, 1915; as *Allan and the Holy Flower,* New York, Longman, 1915.

The Ivory Child (Quatermain). London, Cassell, and New York, Longman, 1916.

Finished. London, Ward Lock, and New York, Longman, 1917.

Elissa; or, The Doom of Zimbabwe. London, Hodder and Stoughton, 1917.

Moon of Israel: A Tale of the Exodus. London, Murray, and New York, Longman, 1918.

Love Eternal. London, Cassell, and New York, Longman, 1918.

When the World Shook: Being an Account of the Great Adventure of Bastin, Bickley, and Arbuthnot. London, Cassell, and New York, Longman, 1919.

The Ancient Allan (Quatermain). London, Cassell, and New York, Longman, 1920.

She and Allan. New York, Longman, and London, Hutchinson, 1921.

The Virgin of the Sun. London, Cassell, and Garden City, New York, Doubleday, Page, 1922.

Wisdom's Daughter: The Life and Love Story of She-Who-Must-Be-Obeyed (She). London, Hutchinson, and Garden City, New York, Doubleday, Page, 1923.

Heu-Heu; or, The Monster (Quatermain). London, Hutchinson, and Garden City, New York, Doubleday, Page, 1924.

Queen of the Dawn: A Love Tale of Old Egypt. Garden City, New York, Doubleday, Page, and London, Hutchinson, 1925.

Treasure of the Lake (Quatermain). Garden City, New York, Doubleday, Page, and London, Hutchinson, 1926.

Allan and the Ice-Gods: A Tale of Beginnings (Quatermain). London, Hutchinson, and Garden City, New York, Doubleday, Page, 1927.

The Works of H. Rider Haggard (omnibus). New York, Black, 1928; as *The Favorite Novels of H. Rider Haggard,* New York, Blue Ribbon, 1928?

Mary of Marion Isle. London, Hutchinson, 1929; as *Marion Isle,* Garden City, New York, Doubleday, Doran, 1929.

Belshazzar. London, Paul, and Garden City, New York, Doubleday, Page, 1930.

The Classic Adventures (omnibus). Poole, England, New Orchard, 1986.

Collected Novels: King Solomon's Mines, Maiwa's Revenge, Cleopatra, She (omnibus). Secaucus, New Jersey, Castle Books, 1987.

Short Stories

Allan's Wife, and Other Tales (Quatermain). London, Blackett, and New York, Harper, 1889.

Alan the Hunter; A Tale of Three Lions. Boston, Lothrop, 1898.

Black Heart and White Heart, and Other Stories. London, Longman, 1900; as *Elissa, and Black Heart and White Heart,* New York, Longman, 1900.

The Wizard; and, Black Heart and White Heart. London, Newnes, 1907; as *Black Heart and White Heart; and, The Wizard,* London, Hodder and Stoughton, 1924.

The Missionary and the Witch Doctor. New York, Paget, 1920.

Smith and the Pharaohs, and Other Tales (Quatermain). Bristol, Arrowsmith, 1920; New York, Longman, 1921.

The Best Short Stories of Rider Haggard, edited by Peter Haining. London, Joseph, 1981.

OTHER PUBLICATIONS

Novels

Dawn. London, Hurst and Blackett, 3 vols., 1884; New York, Appleton, 1 vol., 1887.

The Witch's Head: A Novel. London, Hurst and Blackett, 3 vols., 1884; New York, Appleton, 1 vol., 1885.

Jess. London, Smith Elder, and New York, Harper, 1887.

Mr. Meeson's Will. New York, Harper, and London, Spencer Blackett, 1888.

My Fellow Laborer (includes "The Wreck of the Copeland"). New York, Munro, 1888.

Colonel Quaritch, V.C. New York, Lovell, 1888; London, Longman, 3 vols., 1888.

Joan Haste. London and New York, Longman, 1895.

Doctor Therne. London and New York, Longman, 1898.

The Spring of a Lion. New York, Neeley, 1899.

The Way of the Spirit. London, Hutchinson, 1906.

Fair Margaret. London, Hutchinson, 1907; as *Margaret,* New York, Longman, 1907.

Other

Cetywayo and His White Neighbours; or, Remarks on Recent Events in Zululand, Natal, and the Transvaal. London, Trübner, 1882; revised edition, 1888; reprinted in part, as *The Last Boer War,* London, Kegan Paul, 1899; as *A History of the Transvaal,* New York, New Amsterdam, 1899.

Church and the State: An Appeal to the Laity. Privately printed, 1895.

A Farmer's Year, Being His Commonplace Book for 1898. London and New York, Longman, 1899.

The New South Africa. London, Pearson, 1900.

A Winter Pilgrimage: . . . Travels Through Palestine, Italy, and the Island of Cyprus. London and New York, Longman, 1901.

Rural England. London and New York, Longman, 2 vols., 1902.

A Gardener's Year. London and New York, Longman, 1905.

Report on the Salvation Army Colonies. London, His Majesty's Stationery Office, 1905; as *The Poor and the Land,* London and New York, Longman, 1905.

Regeneration, Being an Account of the Social Work of the Salvation Army in Great Britain. London, Longman, 1910; New York, Longman, 1911.

Rural Denmark and Its Lessons. London and New York, Longman, 1911.

A Call to Arms to the Men of East Anglia. Privately printed, 1914.

The After-War Settlement and the Employment of Ex-Service Men in the Overseas Dominions. London, Saint Catherine Press, 1916.

The Days of My Life: An Autobiography, edited by C.J. Longman. London and New York, Longman, 2 vols., 1926.

The Private Diaries of Sir H. Rider Haggard 1914-1925, edited by D.S. Higgins. London, Cassell, and New York, Stein and Day, 1980.

*

Bibliography: *A Bibliography of the Writings of Sir Henry Rider Haggard* by J.E. Scott, London, Elkin Mathews, 1947.

Critical Studies: *The Clock That I Left* (biography) by Lilias Rider Haggard, London, Hodder and Stoughton, 1951; *Rider Haggard: His Life and Works* by Morton N. Cohen, London, Hutchinson, 1960, New York, Walker, 1961, revised edition, London, Macmillan, 1968; *H. Rider Haggard: A Voice from the Infinite* by Peter Berresford Ellis, London, Routledge, 1978; *Rider Haggard, The Great Storyteller* by D.S. Higgins, London, Cassell, 1981, New York, Stein and Day, 1983; *Rider Haggard and The Fiction of Empire: A Critical Study of British Imperial Fiction* by Wendy R. Katz, Cambridge, Cambridge University Press, 1988.

*   *   *

H. Rider Haggard shares the fate of writers like Mark Twain, Robert Louis Stevenson, and Lewis Carroll in that his novels now serve either in children's editions or as grist for Hollywood's mill. But Haggard never meant his works to be juvenile fare, for they are filled with very adult passions. Of his many novels, the majority are fantasy-romances that range in setting from South Africa to Iceland to Mexico, and in time from the days of Babylon to contemporary central Africa.

Haggard's first successful novel was *King Solomon's Mines,* which he published in the year after he set up practice in London as a barrister. So enthusiastic was the public reception of this novel, in which Haggard created the prototype of the "Great White Hunter," that he virtually gave up the law, and devoted most of his time to writing. The hero of *King Solomon's Mines,* Allan Quatermain, is asked by a beautiful Englishwoman to find her husband, who is lost in the African jungle. When the tracks of the missing husband lead to a long-hidden cave, only the skeleton of the husband is found, along with the treasure of King Solomon, missing for 2000 years. In the sequel, *Allan Quatermain,* Allan dies, and Haggard found himself in the same position as Conan Doyle when, tiring of his famous detective, he killed off Sherlock Holmes: the public would have no part of it. Because of this outcry, Haggard used the device of the "discovered manuscript" to write 13 more novels about Quatermain. In these, Allan meets with further adventures both in his own time and in a past life in ancient Babylon.

The theme of reliving past lives is one which Haggard used many times, especially in the series of novels about the mysterious Ayesha, or She-Who-Must-Be-Obeyed. *She: A History of Adventure,* the first of these novels, introduces Ayesha, the queen of a cannibal tribe in Africa, the people of the Kor, as she waits for the return of her lover, whom she murdered two millennia ago when he dared to marry someone else. Her wait comes to an end when a young Englishman, Leo Vincey, comes to her land. One glance at Vincey is enough to convince her that Leo is the reincarnation of the long-dead lover. She tries to persuade Leo to join her in eternal life, the secret of which she had discovered in the flame at the heart of a volcano. But once again Ayesha is frustrated when Leo too takes another woman for a wife. After banishing Leo's wife, Ayesha takes him and his companions to the volcano to renew her arguments for him to bathe with her in the flames. But the magic only works once, for when Ayesha enters for the second time, she begins to age before the eyes of the men, turning into a 2000-year-old crone. To their horror, she dies at their feet. Sickened and dazed, the men return to England to try to forget the sight. Like Quatermain, Ayesha was called back for repeat performances. Haggard wrote two more novels about her return from death—*Ayesha: The Return of She* and *She and Allan*—and still another about her early years in ancient Egypt, *Wisdom's Daughter: The Life and Love Story of She-Who-Must-Be-Obeyed.*

That most of the titles of Haggard's works are unfamiliar even to SF readers shows the success of modern critics in stamping out much of 19th-century fantasy. The few that are relatively well known owe their longevity to the movies, where, even though the plots have been somewhat altered, the mystery and romance of the settings and characters have been preserved.

—Walter E. Meyers

HAIBLUM, Isidore

Nationality: American. **Born:** Manhattan, New York, 23 May 1935. **Education:** High School of Art and Design; City College of New York (editor, Mercury), B. A. in English and social sciences 1958. **Military Service:** Served in the United States Army Reserve, 1959-64. **Career:** Has worked as interviewer, scriptwriter, and folk-singers agent; now freelance writer. **Address:** 160 West 77th Street, New York, New York 10024, U.S.A.

SCIENCE FICTION PUBLICATIONS

Novels (series: Dunjer; Morgan; Nick Siscoe and Ross Block)

The Tsaddik of the Seven Wonders. New York, Ballantine, 1971.
The Return. New York, Dell, 1973.
Transfer to Yesterday. New York, Ballantine, 1973.
The Wilk Are Among Us. Garden City, New York, Doubleday, 1975; revised edition, New York, Dell, 1979.
Interworld (Dunjer). New York, Dell, 1977; London, Penguin, 1980.
Nightmare Express. New York, Fawcett, 1979.
The Identity Plunderers (Siscoe and Block). New York, New American Library, 1984.
The Mutants Are Coming (Morgan). Garden City, New York, Doubleday, 1984.
The Hand of Ganz: A Science Fiction Novel (Siscoe and Block). New York, New American Library, 1985.
Out of Sync (Morgan). New York, Ballantine, 1990.
Specterworld (Dunjer). New York, Avon Books, 1991.
Crystalworld (Dunjer). New York, AvoNova, 1992.
Outerworld. N.p., n.d.

OTHER PUBLICATIONS

Novels

Murder in Yiddish. New York, St. Martin's Press, 1988.
Bad Neighbors. New York, St. Martin's Press, 1990.

Other

Faster Than a Speeding Bullet, with Stuart Silver. Chicago, Playboy Press, 1980.

*

Isidore Haiblum comments:

(1981) Haiblum's work has its roots in the *Black Mask* Hammett-Chandler tradition and in the humor of Sholom Aleichem; it is often both hardboiled and zany and sometimes ethnic. His style is awash with idioms, slang, and underworld lingo. His settings, despite the given dates, are often the 1930s, a time he rather likes. The jury is still out on how all this will go over in SF. *The Tsaddik of the Seven Wonders* was billed by the publishers as "The First Yiddish Science Fantasy Novel Ever."

And about *Interworld* Gerald Jones wrote in *The New York Times:* "If you have ever wondered what *The Big Sleep* would sound like if Raymond Chandler were reincarnated as Roger Zelazny, this is your book." *The Nightmare Express* (a big alternative universe novel set in the 1930s and elsewhere), *Outerworld* (again with ace gum-shoe Dunjer from *Interworld*), and a revised edition of *The Wilk Are Among Us* take all this a step further. Haiblum has his fingers crossed.

(1985) With the passing of the years Haiblum has also taken to holding his breath. Meanwhile his novels have been translated into French, German, Italian, Hebrew, and Spanish.

*   *   *

Isidore Haiblum's first published book was *The Tsaddik of the Seven Wonders,* billed as the first Yiddish science fantasy novel. It was an auspicious debut, a wondrous mixture of magic and time-travel as the Tsaddik, a wise man whose knowledge transcends time and space, journeys to the future, where ancient knowledge and superscience make an odd marriage. A delicious romp from a decidedly original viewpoint, filled with good-natured humor and a healthy sense of the absurd, the story remains the author's most interesting work, though subsequent work was considerably more polished.

Haiblum became more serious for the two novels that followed, *The Return* and *Transfer to Yesterday*. In the first, the New Society is a nearly Utopian civilization, with fair treatment for all and ample rewards for those who excel. Or is it? The protagonist is subject to irrational fits of violence, and the most promising and successful members of the New Society are mysteriously disappearing. Is there a purely terrestrial explanation, or is there a connection to a recent space mission, which may have brought back more than quiescent samples? There follows a fairly standard series of captures and escapes, confidences and betrayals, in what was a competent novel based on tried and true plot devices, but it's a far less interesting effort than *Tsaddik*.

Transfer to Yesterday bears some superficial resemblance to both of its predecessors, in that it involves time travel and flawed Utopias. The factional world of the League is rocked by a new, destabilizing element. A device has been created which allows one to view the past; the catch is that in order to do so, a psychic link must be established with one's own ancestors. A fanatical cult attempts to use the new technology for its own purposes, thereby creating even greater societal unrest. There is a distinct flavor of the traditional private eye mystery, a style which Haiblum apparently finds comfortable as he has resorted to it several times in subsequent books.

The Wilk Are Among Us marked a return of Haiblum's gift for grotesque humor. A galactic sociologist uses a matter transmitter to travel from planet to planet, but due to a malfunction, he arrives on a strange world, accompanied by three aliens from distinct species possessing powers of mental control and the ability to create chaos out of order. The most troubling of his companions is the wilk, whose coincidental resemblance to the local inhabitants makes it difficult to identify and neutralize the creature, who is disrupting the local culture. *Wilk* is an often amusing logical problem story, but the ambiguity between humor and more serious concerns is sometimes awkwardly done, and the book fails to succeed entirely either as a mystery or as a comic novel.

That all changed with *Interworld*, a wonderfully funny futuristic detective story. Tom Dunjer's laboratory is burglarized and an important device he was developing is missing. Whether or not it was his fault is irrelevant; if he wants to save his job, it is necessary to retrieve it, even if that means finding a way to outwit the security system of Interworld, a rival corporation. Before the story is over, the protagonist visits a wide variety of worlds and realities in a nonstop rush toward madness. Haiblum followed up with a shorter, somewhat disappointing sequel, *Outerworld*, then two much more satisfying adventures, *Crystalworld* and *Spectreworld*. Dunjer faces ever more disastrous possibilities in each subsequent adventures, traveling across the dimensional barriers, thwarting mad scientists, and dealing with his less than entirely competent robotic assistants. No cliche of the field goes untrounced as Haiblum sends his protagonist on a series of unlikely adventures.

Nightmare Express uses some of the same themes to less humorous effect. The protagonist is cast adrift in a time bubble, forced to witness flashes of one time period after another, pursued by in-dividuals who seem to have stepped out of time themselves, while robots and beautiful women conspire with him, or perhaps against him, suggesting that he may have fallen into the clutches of alien invaders. The same wild enthusiasm for mixing bizarre plot elements infuses this, the best of his more serious work.

The Mutants Are Coming is another of Haiblum's overtly humorous novels. A reluctant ambassador from the moon returns to Earth in order to promote financing for the lunar base. He is opposed by a variety of goons, becomes enmeshed in the mystery of a missing politician, and is caught up within the coils of an underground movement of mutants. Although the book has its moments, for the most part the humor this time around is artificial and unfunny.

The Identity Plunderers and its sequel, *The Hand of Ganz,* are both more serious and more satisfying. In the first, an investigative reporter recognizes a body in the city morgue while two individuals with erased memories attempt to escape a prison camp on another planet. Haiblum alternates between the two story lines, ultimately bringing them together, and ties everything up neatly. In the sequel, extraterrestrial interests are plotting to use their influence to alter the future of Earth. The protagonist of *The Identity Plunderers* discovers the plot and sets off into the galaxy to find a way to foil the evil Ganz and his cohorts. It makes for good adventure leavened with flashes of Haiblum's irrepressible levity.

Out of Sync is another serious novel, and one of Haiblum's most successful. An entrepreneur who has made his reputation by establishing impregnable security systems finds his world crumbling when several of his clients experience impossible robberies. Then he witnesses one himself, and realizes that the perpetrators have access to some form of technology beyond anything known to human science. When he attempts to trace them to their base, he finds himself on another planet, and in trouble up to his eyebrows. *Out of Sync* is an excellent adventure story drawing upon the best techniques Haiblum employed throughout his career.

Haiblum is one of the few legitimate comedic voices in the field, and it seems likely that most of his efforts will be in that direction. His serious adventure novels are invariably competent but unexceptional, and the best of these are the ones where he has found the right balance between sobriety and levity.

—Don D'Ammassa

HALAM, Ann. *See* **JONES, Gwyneth A.**

HALDEMAN, Jack C(arroll, II)

Pseudonym: John Cleve (joint pseudonym). **Nationality:** American. **Born:** Hopkinsville, New York, 18 December 1941; brother of Joe Haldeman, *q.v.* **Education:** University of Oklahoma, Norman, 1960-63; Johns Hopkins University, Baltimore, B.S. in life science 1973. **Family:** Married 1) Alice Haldeman in 1965; 2) Vol Haldeman in 1975; two daughters. **Career:** Research assistant,

Johns Hopkins University School of Hygiene and Public Health, 1963-68; medical technician, University of Maryland Hospital, 1968-73; has also worked as a statistician, photographer, and printer's devil. President, Washington Science Fiction Association, seven years; chairman, Discon II. **Agent:** Eleanor Wood, Blassingame, McCauley, and Wood, 111 8th Avenue, Suite 1501, New York, New York 10001, U.S.A.

Science Fiction Publications

Novels (series: Spaceways; Star Trek)

Vector Analysis. New York, Berkley, 1978.
Perry's Planet (Star Trek). New York, Bantam, 1980; London, Titan, 1994.
There Is No Darkness, with Joe Haldeman. New York, Ace, 1983; London, Futura, 1985.
The Iceworld Connection, with Andrew J. Offutt and Vol Haldeman as John Cleve (Spaceways). New York, Berkley, 1983.
The Fall of Winter. New York, Baen, 1985.
Bill, the Galactic Hero, on the Planet of the Zombie Vampires, with Harry Harrison. New York, Avon, 1991; London, Gollancz, 1992.
Echoes of Thunder, with Jack Dann; with *Run for the Stars,* by Harlan Ellison. New York, Tor, 1991.
High Steel, with Jack Dann. New York, Tor, 1993.

Short Stories

Slow Dancing through Time, with others. Shingletown, California, Mark Ziesing, 1990.

*

Jack C. Haldeman comments:
Sometimes I write hard science fiction, sometimes soft. Sometimes I'm serious, sometimes I'm humorous. Mostly I'm traditional, though occasionally I try something experimental. I often draw on my scientific background as well as my sense of humor. Mostly I try to entertain, though I have been known to slip in a message or two. I try not to let it clutter up the story.

*   *   *

Jack C. Haldeman has spent most of his career writing short fiction, and is one of the few to take as a common theme the sports story, often but not always humorous, which became one of his trademarks almost from the outset. It started in 1977 with "Louisville Slugger," an anecdotal piece in which the future of humanity depends upon a baseball game played against some Arcturians. This was followed by a sequel, "Home Team Advantage," wherein the Arcturian aliens discover that man is inedible and forfeit their prize, the consumption of humanity.

Haldeman continued in the same vein with "The Thrill of Victory" and "The Agony of Defeat," this time concentrating on a team of robotic football players who are first faced with the discovery that they have been illegally programmed with a will to win, and then matched in a championship game against genetically altered human beings. All four stories are light and gimmicky, and had Haldeman continued exclusively along this course, it's unlikely he'd have been more than a footnote in the field. But as he grew more experienced as a writer, Haldeman began to stretch in different directions.

"Thirty Love" was decidedly different, though still a sports story. A professional tennis player has experienced a long and successful career because his precognitive powers enable him to anticipate where the ball will next be hit. During his final match, he deliberately throws the game when he realizes that defeating his opponent will cause the latter a trauma that will utterly ruin his life. The sports stories that immediately followed often returned to comedic themes, and only "Race the Wind" varied from the pattern. A disabled man is determined to participate in slalom racing through the use of technology. Although the character is well drawn, the plot falls short of exploiting the possibilities of the theme.

There have been, however, several extremely good stories outside the context of his sports series. "Songs of Dying Swans" involves the tragic destruction of a race of altered humans, and the consequences of this act on the rest of civilization. "Laura's Theme" is the haunting, enigmatic tale of a strange woman who seems always to be present when other peoples' lives take radical turns for the worse. It's one of Haldeman's most ambitious early efforts and still one of his best stories.

Haldeman's humor ranges from slight but amusing to genuinely funny. A typical middle class family is startled and dismayed to discover that their front yard has suddenly become the legendary elephants' graveyard in "What Weighs 8000 Pounds and Wears Red Sneakers?" In "Those Thrilling Days of Yesteryear," archeologists are engaged in manufacturing and burying artifacts, because the past as we know it is all a fraud. Haldeman invents new mythical creatures in "Games Children Play" and all the pending accidents of the future occur at once in "A Very Good Year."

His more recent serious work has been of considerably higher calibre. "Spring Fever" compares human activity to that of lemmings. An Indian is drafted into duty in orbit in "High Steel" and averts a disaster in a short piece that became the basis for the novel *High Steel,* written in collaboration with Jack Dann. Using the unusual point of view of a man who is essentially a construction worker, Haldeman and Dann have created a realistic look at what it might really be like to be involved in the physical construction of the first orbiting space habitat. There's an understated and effective melodramatic plot to keep things moving, but the novel's strongest qualities are in its depiction of the protagonist and the evocation of his environment.

Haldeman's first solo novel, *Vector Analysis,* is a routine but well handled story of adventure and scientific mystery in space. *Perry's Planet,* a "Star Trek" adventure, is similarly competent but has a less interesting plot. *There Is No Darkness,* coauthored with Joe Haldeman, is an episodic adventure following a group of young adults through various adventures on different planets and was originally published as a series of shorter works. *The Fall of Winter* demonstrated a marked improvement in the quality of his writing while still reflecting his ongoing interests. A team of terraformers is at work on an alien planet when a series of incidents hampers their efforts. The novel is a well worked out scientific mystery wrapped up in a good adventure story.

Haldeman is a reliable, steady producer of interesting shorter work. "Cold Warrior" and "Death of a Dream" both examine alternate careers for Marilyn Monroe and Martin Luther King respectively, and the latter in particular is thoughtful and well controlled. Other short pieces of interest are "Wet Behind the Ears," "We the People," "By the Sea," and "Lonesome Homesick Blues."

—Don D'Ammassa

HALDEMAN, Joe (William)

Pseudonym: Robert Graham. **Nationality:** American. **Born:** Oklahoma City, 9 June 1943; brother of Jack C. Haldeman, *q.v.* **Education:** University of Maryland, College Park, B.S. in physics and astronomy, 1967; graduate study, 1969-70; University of Iowa, Iowa City, M.F.A. 1975. **Military Service:** Served in the United States Army, 1967-69: Purple Heart. **Family:** Married Mary Gay Potter in 1965. **Career:** Teaching Assistant, University of Iowa, 1975; editor, *Astronomy,* Milwaukee, 1976. Since 1970, freelance writer. Treasurer, Science Fiction Writers of America, for two years; president, 1992-94. Since 1983, adjunct professor, Massachusetts Institute of Technology. **Awards:** Nebula award, 1975, 1990, 1993; Hugo award, 1976, 1977, 1991, 1995; Ditmar award, 1976; Galaxy award, 1978; Rhysling award, 1984, 1990; Homer award, 1995. **Agent:** Ralph Vicinanza, 111 Eighth Ave. #1501, New York, New York 10011, U.S.A. **Address:** 5412 N.W. 14th Avenue, Gainesville, Florida 32605, U.S.A. **Online Address:** joe.haldeman@genie.geis.com.

SCIENCE FICTION PUBLICATIONS

Novels (series: Attar; Star Trek; Worlds)

The Forever War. New York, St. Martin's Press, and London, Weidenfield and Nicolson, 1975.
Attar's Revenge (as Robert Graham). New York, Pocket Books, 1975; London, Mews, 1977.
War of Nerves (as Robert Graham). New York, Pocket Books, 1975.
Mindbridge. New York, St. Martin's Press, 1976; London, Macdonald and Jane's, 1977.
Planet of Judgment (Star Trek). New York, Bantam, and London, Corgi, 1977.
World without End: A Star Trek Novel. New York, Bantam, and London, Corgi, 1979.
Worlds: A Novel of the Near Future. New York, Viking Press, 1981; London, Macdonald, 1982.
There Is No Darkness, with Jack C. Haldeman. New York, Ace, 1983.
Worlds Apart. New York, Viking Press, 1983; London, Orbit, 1984.
Tool of the Trade. New York, Morrow, and London, Gollancz, 1987.
Buying Time. Norwalk, Connecticut, Easton Press, 1989; as *The Long Habit of Living,* London, New English Library, 1989.
The Hemingway Hoax. New York, Morrow, and London, New English Library, 1990.
Worlds Enough and Time: The Conclusion of the Worlds Trilogy. New York, Morrow, and London, New English Library, 1992.

Short Stories

All My Sins Remembered. New York, St. Martin's Press, 1977; London, Macdonald and Jane's, 1978.
Infinite Dreams. New York, St. Martin's Press, 1978.
Dealing in Futures: Stories. New York, Viking Press, 1985; London, Orbit, 1986.
More Than the Sum of His Parts. Eugene, Oregon, Pulphouse, 1991.
Vietnam and Other Alien Worlds (with essays and poetry). Framingham, Massachusetts, NESFA Press, 1993.

OTHER PUBLICATIONS

Novels

War Year. New York, Holt Rinehart, 1972; original version, New York, Pocket Books, 1978.
1968: A Novel. London, Hodder and Stoughton, 1994; New York, Morrow, 1995.

Plays

The Devil His Due, in *Fantastic* (New York), August 1974.
The Moon and Marcek, in *Vertex* (Los Angeles), August 1974.
The Forever War (produced Chicago, 1983).

Other

Editor, *Cosmic Laughter: Science Fiction for the Fun of It.* New York, Holt Rinehart, 1974.
Editor, *Study War No More: A Selection of Alternatives.* New York, St. Martin's Press, 1977; London, Orbit, 1979.
Editor, *Nebula Award Stories 17.* New York, Holt Rinehart, 1983.
Editor, with Martin H. Greenberg and Charles G. Waugh, *Body Armor: 2000.* New York, Ace, 1986.
Editor, with Martin H. Greenberg and Charles G. Waugh, *Supertanks.* New York, Ace, 1987.
Editor, *The Best of John Brunner.* New York, Ballantine, 1988.
Editor, with Martin H. Greenberg and Charles G. Waugh, *Spacefighters.* New York, Ace, 1988.

*

Critical Studies: *Joe Haldeman,* Mercer Island, Washington, Starmont House, 1980, and *The Fiction of Joe Haldeman,* University of Iowa, unpublished dissertation, 1981, both by Joan Gordon.

Joe Haldeman comments:

Along with most of my contemporaries, I believe that science fiction is primarily a literature of ideas, but that this quality does not make it exempt from normal literary standards. A poorly written SF story may be published if the idea behind it is sufficiently interesting, and there's nothing "improper" about that so long as an audience exists for it. But the best SF is that which excels both in concept and in execution—examplars being as diverse as Bester's *The Stars My Destination* and Delany's *Dhalgren*—and at its best I think it has an advantage over literature that is "just plain literature." There's no over-riding didactic or dialectic principle behind my writing. I write the sort of stories and books I would like to read. I'm fortunate in that a lot of moneybearing readers seem to share my tastes. Whether I would be willing (or able) to write differently if the market demanded it, I can't honestly say. I would like to think I'd stick to my guns, but on the other hand I do rather like working without bosses or time clocks.

*   *   *

SF, that fiercely questioning genre, had not exactly come to grips with the Vietnam question until publication of Joe Haldeman's "Hero" in the June 1972 issue of *Analog.* We had had the statements in the magazines about which authors supported the war and which opposed, and a great deal of debate about what Heinlein *really* meant in "Starship Troopers" (1959). And then "Hero" appeared, and it took the aspects of the war which had most disturbed us as onlookers and retold them in a setting remote from the emotions and politics of the real Vietnam, to try to let them be seen for what they were; described without rhetoric, to let their natures speak for themselves. While the war came to an end, Haldeman went on to describe in *The Forever War* the alienation of his soldiers from the culture that had used them. In their case this was brought about by time dilation, the effect of travelling at relativistic speeds, projecting them ever onwards into the future at different rates for different journeys.

The Forever War runs in the future, for 1200 years, between enemies evenly matched. Time dilation allows the narrator to see it (in snatches) from beginning to end. Some reviewers were unhappy with that end, where the soldier's ignorance of the Big Picture was allowed to remain: Haldeman's war is eventually ended by clones who can communicate only with one another, or with the hive-mind of the aliens, leaving the characters and the reader in the dark. But interstellar war could only occur between races with evenly matched technology, or with drastically differing technologies making conflict possible. Does loss of individuality then mean loss of progress? If so, then the use of time dilation to bring Haldeman's major characters together at the end of the novel is not a glib happy ending (as some have alleged) but a chance for humanity to bypass the cloning dead-end, and try another course.

Mindbridge was another examination of human contact with a hive-mind, while *All My Sins Remembered* was a damning indictment not merely of big government but also of the standard SF attitude to individuality. SF used to be full of people who find out that they're really someone else (usually somebody more powerful), and part of the problem in identifying with central characters is often their lack of individuality; some authors have run together novellas into "fix-up" novels just by changing the name of the central character.

McGavin in *All My Sins Remembered* is a government agent, repeatedly given new identities through psychological conditioning and plastic surgery. In real life, such changes of role can lead to personality disorders, especially for military personnel who assess themselves by rank. Haldeman's McGavin does not end up with no personality of his own, unlike the actor in Ellison's "All the Sounds of Fear": he is an individual moved and controlled by an organisation which commands his loyalty but is beyond his control.

This is again the situation of the central characters in *The Forever War* and *Mindbridge.* One begins to notice that other central characters are in the same boat: victims of rape and kidnapping (*Worlds: A Novel of the Near Future*), people hounded by the KGB and CIA because of their unique talents (*Tool of the Trade*), or hunted across the Solar System by the wealthy (*Buying Time,* aka *The Long Habit of Living*). Even the *Star Trek* novel, *Planet of Judgment,* finds Kirk, Spock et al at the receiving end of the conflict between greater powers. The short stories collected in *Dealing in Futures* and *Infinite Dreams* have been more varied and do allow us to think that life in the future doesn't necessarily consist of being pushed around by vastly powerful forces.

In this light one has to welcome *The Hemingway Hoax,* in which the central character sets out to emulate Hemingway, allows himself out of stubbornness to be put to several harrowing deaths in a variety of parallel universes, *becomes* Hemingway, transcends him, and leaves his tormentors wondering "Where did he go?" It would

be nice if we could all do the same; but if SF has a purpose, perhaps it is to make us believe that at least in theory we can.

—Duncan Lunan

HALE, Edward Everett

Pseudonyms: F. I.; Col. Frederic Ingham. **Nationality:** American. **Born:** Boston, Massachusetts, 3 April 1822; grandnephew of Nathan Hale. **Education:** Harvard University, 1835-1839, A.B., 1839. **Family:** Married Emily Baldwin Perkins in 1852; one daughter and seven sons. **Career:** taught at Boston Latin School, 1839-41; contributed to numerous magazines and independently studied theology; obtained license to preach, 1842; ordained minister, Church of the Unity, Worcester, then at South Congregational Church, Boston, 1856; chaplain of U.S. Senate, 1903-09. **Died:** 10 June 1909.

SCIENCE FICTION PUBLICATIONS

Short Stories

Sybaris and Other Homes. Boston, Field Osgood, 1869.
Ten Times One Is Ten: The Possible Reformation: A Story in Nine Chapters (as Col. Frederic Ingham). Boston, Roberts Brothers, 1971.
His Level Best and Other Stories. Boston, Roberts Brothers, 1872.
The Brick Moon and Other Stories. Boston, Little Brown, 1899.
The Brick Moon: From the Papers of Captain Frederic Ingham. Barre, Massachusetts, Spiral Press, 1971.

OTHER PUBLICATIONS

Short Stories

The Man Without a Country and Other Stories. 1868.

*   *   *

Edward Everett Hale was a minister, journalist, editor, educator, historian, reformer, all of these activities providing reason for his prolific production of novels, short stories, newspaper and magazine articles, travel books, historical studies, well over 900 different works, according to one bibliographer. He is best known to the general reader for his often-reprinted short story, "The Man without a Country," but, although his contributions to the genre are a very minor part of his enormous output, his place in science fiction would be secure if only for the first story of an earth satellite, "The Brick Moon."

First published in four parts in *The Atlantic Monthly,* 1869-70, *The Brick Moon* was well received and republished in book form several times. The Brick Moon's builders designed it to be a permanent light in the sky that would help ships at sea to find their way. The theory that given enough speed to begin a permanent fall around the earth an object would become a satellite is not far removed from the principles by which present-day satellites remain in orbit. It was built of brick, the most heat-resistant substance known at that time, globular, with the surface sealed tight to prevent loss of air. Prematurely sent into orbit—and much higher than intended—tenanted by the inventors and their families who were protected from the shock because they were sleeping in hammocks at the time, it became a permanent home that kept in touch with Earth by means of figures in Morse code laid out in a clearing. The narrator, an earthbound friend, regards the little colony as a kind of utopia.

Hale made several contributions to utopian fiction in more traditional forms. Of these "My Visit to Sybaris," the longest piece in *Sybaris and Other Homes,* is the most effective. A voyager to a previously unknown land describes the wonders of the society discovered there. In Sybaris the principal object of government, with all efforts directed toward this end, is to care for the individual citizen, each "protected in the enjoyment, not of what the majority likes, but of what he chooses, so long as his choice injures no other man." To this end, means to avoid boredom are developed, and all public facilities remain open day and night. In common with several other utopias this society demands absolute punctuality in all matters and banishment for failure to marry. The other four items, both fiction and nonfiction, in this volume, as well as the later, fictional, *How They Lived in Hampton,* deal with one of Hale's major concerns, that of "the necessity of better homes for laboring men," and how this goal might be achieved. In *Ten Times One Is Ten* he describes a way in which a small group of people choosing to live by high moral principles of a recently deceased friend might communicate such ideas to others and they in turn to others until "in twenty-seven years the 1. became 1,000,000,000—ONE THOUSAND MILLION." Several novels, tracts, and short stories that followed were more or less continuations of this basic theme.

Among numerous fantasies is *Susan's Escort,* a short, humorous satire that exemplifies Hale's lighthearted view of Boston society. Susan, a young schoolteacher with no male relatives or fiancé nearby, likes to attend opera, lectures, and other public events. Needing an escort, she creates "Mac" from mackintosh, rattan hoops, umbrella slide, pantaloons, arctics, light enough to carry on one arm and easily disassembled and carried in an umbrella case. Gradually Mac becomes sentient and learns to talk. Susan gives him up but finds him a job as a clothing dummy where he lives happily ever after. "The Happy Island" is a slight piece, a satire describing how a busy man's friends arrange to have the unwanted solicitors who plague him sent to an island off the coast of Florida. With all their needs completely satisfied they live happily haranguing each other while their benefactor gets on with his busy life.

Hale wrote both fantasy and science fiction, often blurring whatever distinction there may be between these two kinds of imaginative writing. His earliest printed story, "A Tale of a Salamander" (1842) describes a student's attempt to prove the glassblower superstition that a salamander will emerge from any fire left to burn for more than 40 days. His hopes for fame and fortune are not realized, but he is able to warn others not to try the experiment. In a story reminiscent of works by later science fiction writers, "My Double and How He Undid Me," a minister hires a double to appear in his place at unwelcome functions; at first successful, the ruse is at last discovered and the minister is forced to flee to the wilderness to begin anew. "The Skeleton in the Closet" is an extravagant explanation of why the Confederates lost the Civil War as the result of an attempt to remedy a shortage of hoop skirt "skeletons." The narrator brings back a fresh supply obtained while on a spy trip to New York. The abandoned, obsolete hoops cause problems through jammed machinery, broken legs, various accidents, etc., until they lead to "the ruin of the Confederate army, navy, ordinance, and treasury: and it led to the capture of the poor Presi-

dent too." Hale wrote many stories based on unexpected consequences of dabbling in science or pseudoscience, e.g., "The Dot and Line Alphabet," "Dick's Christmas," and "The Lost Palace." What might be called alternative history appears in descriptions of meetings between historical figures, e.g., Homer and David exchange songs ("A Piece of Possible History").

Whether utopian writing precedes or follows science fiction historically, and whether fantasy subsumes both or is yet another kind of imaginative writing, there is no doubt that they are closely related to each other. Hale wrote well in all three forms and deserves acknowledgment as one of America's earliest practitioners. He seldom achieved greatness as a literary artist, in part because so much of his work was do-good polemic, but his pleasant and witty style continues to attract readers, and many of his proposed reforms of society make sense a century later.

—Arthur O. Lewis

HALL, Austin

Nationality: American. **Born:** 1882. **Education:** Lincoln High School, Cleveland; Ohio Northern University, Ada; Ohio State University, Columbus; University of California, Berkeley. **Career:** Did newspaper and electrical work, then worked in mining and ranching; wrote hundreds of western stories. **Died:** 1933.

SCIENCE FICTION PUBLICATIONS

Novels

People of the Comet. Los Angeles, Griffin, 1948.
The Blind Spot, with Homer Eon Flint. Philadelphia, Prime Press, 1951; London, Museum Press, 1953.
The Spot of Life. New York, Ace, 1965.

OTHER PUBLICATIONS

Other

Unto the Children: A Story of the Redwoods. San Jose, Semperviren's Club of California, 1924.

*   *   *

Homer Eon Flint, writing alone and in collaboration with Austin Hall, produced a large quantity of science fiction from 1916 to 1924, most of which appeared in the Munsey Magazines *All-Story* and *Argosy.* His fame, however, and that of Austin Hall, rests on one of the most admired and cherished fantasies of the early 20th century, *The Blind Spot,* and its sequel *The Spot of Life,* written by Hall after the death of Flint.

Flint's first published story was "The Planeteer," set in the 23rd century, when Earth's population has grown so great that global starvation is threatened. Through engineering feats on a truly cosmic scale, the earth's orbit is shifted to one closer to Jupiter's, and the latter planet then furnishes a new and inexhaustible source of food. In a sequel, "King of Conserve Island," an Earthly monarch attempts to gain control of Jupiter and its food resources, and is thwarted by a hero who cuts off the heat of the sun and freezes the villain into submission. "The Lord of Death" is about two men who travel to the planet Mercury, and find there an ancient record of a man and woman named Adam and Eve who had left Mercury millennia earlier for an unknown destination. In "The Queen of Life" the same characters take their spaceship to Venus, where they discover an apparently utopian civilization.

Hall's writing career began with "Almost Immortal," the story of a Tibetan doctor thousands of years old who has been able to prolong his own life by absorbing the bodies and the wills of younger men at regular intervals. His downfall comes when the last man he assimilates turns out to have a will greater than his own. "The Rebel Soul" has a quite similar plot involving undying souls that take possession of individuals across the ages. A sequel, "Into the Infinite," carries on the story of a man who has been possessed by the Rebel Soul, and who is eventually freed through the power of a woman's love. "The Man Who Saved the Earth" describes an attempt by the inhabitants of Mars to capture all the water on Earth and transport it to Mars, turning the latter into a verdant planet. This plot is foiled at the last minute by the one man on Earth with the necessary knowledge, just as the oceans are drying up.

The literary styles of Flint and Hall were curiously similar, sharing the same strengths and weaknesses. Both were totally innocent of the fine points of sentence structure and grammar, and neither had a particularly large vocabulary. Each man, however, had a vivid and far-reaching imagination and a delight in reaching out into the vastnesses of time and space. Their complicated plotting and their skill in describing the life, customs, and technologies of the worlds of the distant future compensate for their somewhat clumsy style.

The high point in the literary careers of Flint and Hall was their collaboration on *The Blind Spot,* a classic in the field despite the literary flaws that distinguish the other works of both authors. *The Blind Spot* is more fantasy and mystery than science fiction. In a downtown San Francisco apartment building a gateway between two parallel worlds is discovered. A man emerges from the Spot, and takes back with him a scientist from this world. They are followed by would-be rescuers of the scientist, and the plot thereafter involves additional crossings through the Spot, bringing in more mystery and occultism than science. The Spot is finally closed at the end of the novel, to protect the inhabitants of this world from possible danger from the people on the other side. Flint died in 1924, under violent and mysterious circumstances that have never been explained. Hall continued to write alone, and in 1932 produced *The Spot of Life,* a sequel in which the Spot is reopened by the inhabitants of the other world, with the object of an invasion by force of our world. This novel takes place a generation after the time of the original story, and Earth's savior in *The Spot of Life* is the son of the principal character in the first novel.

—Douglas E. Way

HAMILTON, Edmond

Pseudonym: Brett Sterling. **Nationality:** American. **Born:** Youngstown, Ohio, 21 October 1904. **Education:** Westminster College, New Wilmington, Pennsylvania, 1919-21. **Family:** Married Leigh Brackett, *q.v.,* in 1946. **Career:** Freelance writer: staff writer for Superman comics in the 1940s. Guest of Honor, 22nd World Science Fiction Convention, 1964; elected to First Fandom Science Fiction Hall of Fame, 1967. **Died:** 1 February 1977.

SCIENCE FICTION PUBLICATIONS

Novels (series: Captain Future; John Gordon; Interstellar Patrol; Starwolf)

The Star Kings (Gordon). New York, Signet, 1949; London, Museum Press, 1951; as *Beyond the Moon,* New York, New American Library, 1950.

The Monsters of Juntonheim: A Complete Book-length Novel of Amazing Adventure. London, Consul, 1950; as *A Yank at Valhalla,* Manchester, England, Worlds, 1950.

Tharkol, Lord of the Unknown: A Novel. Manchester, England, 1950.

City at World's End. New York, Fell, 1951; London, Museum Press, 1952.

The Sun Smasher. New York, Ace, 1959.

The Star of Life. New York, Torquil, 1959.

The Haunted Stars. New York, Torquil, 1960; London, Jenkins, 1965.

Battle for the Stars. New York, Torquil, 1961; London, Mayflower, 1963.

Outside the Universe (Interstellar Patrol). New York, Ace, 1964.

The Valley of Creation. New York, Lancer, 1964.

Fugitive of the Stars. New York, Ace, 1965.

Doomstar. New York, Belmont, 1966.

The Weapon from Beyond (Starwolf). New York, Ace, 1967.

The Magician of Mars (Future). New York, Popular Library, 1969.

Starwolf (omnibus). New York, Ace, 1982.

Chronicles of the Star Kings (omnibus). London, Arrow, 1986.

Danger Planet (Future; as Brett Sterling). New York, Popular Library, 1968.

The Closed Worlds (Starwolf). New York, Ace, 1968.

World of the Starwolves. New York, Ace, 1968.

Outlaw World (Future). New York, Popular Library, 1969.

Quest beyond the Stars (Future). New York, Popular Library, 1969.

Outlaws of the Moon (Future). New York, Popular Library, 1969.

The Comet Kings (Future). New York, Popular Library, 1969.

Planets in Peril (Future). New York, Popular Library, 1969.

Calling Captain Future. New York, Popular Library, 1969.

Captain Future's Challenge. New York, Popular Library, 1969.

Galaxy Mission (Future). New York, Popular Library, 1969.

Captain Future and the Space Emperor. New York, Popular Library, 1969.

Return to the Stars (Gordon). New York, Lancer, 1970.

Short Stories

The Metal Giants. Washburn, North Dakota, Swanson, 1935(?).

The Horror on the Asteroid, and Other Tales of Planetary Horror. London, Allan, 1936; Boston, Gregg Press, 1975.

Tiger Girl. London, Utopian, 1945.

Murder in the Clinic. London, Utopian, 1946.

Crashing Suns (Interstellar Patrol). New York, Ace, 1965.

What's It Like Out There? and Other Stories. New York, Ace, 1974.

The Best of Edmond Hamilton, edited by Leigh Brackett. Garden City, New York, Doubleday, 1977.

The Great Illusion, with others. Wallsend, Tyne and Wear, England
Fantasy Booklet, 1973.
Legion of the Super-Heroes: Archive, Volume 2 (graphic novel).
New York, DC Comics, 1992.

OTHER PUBLICATIONS

Other

Editor, *The Best of Leigh Brackett.* Garden City, New York,
Doubleday, 1977.

*

Manuscript Collection: Eastern New Mexico University Library,
Portales.

*   *   *

Edmond Hamilton virtually invented the idea of the Space Patrol. The concept of a galactic civilization entered the mainstream
of science fiction through Hamilton's stories for *Weird Tales* and
Amazing Stories between 1928 and 1930, and it has been a lasting
influence. More generally, Hamilton is identified with space opera.
He was writing it before the term was coined, and he wrote a tremendous amount of it for *Air Wonder Stories, Amazing, Startling,*
and *Thriller Wonder Stories* (Hamilton published little in *Astounding, Galaxy,* and *Fantasy and Science Fiction;* oddly enough,
Hamilton was also conspicuous by his absence in *Planet Stories,*
supposedly the epitome of space opera). Most of his stories show
the defects of the genre he pioneered. The action was fast and furious and sometimes absurd. The characterization was minimal and
the dialogue was ghastly. But Hamilton was fond of the Big Idea,
and he could communicate the excitement of sweeping concepts.
(It was typical of Hamilton to present the whole panorama of evolution in a short story, and to throw in some original twists along
the way.) He caught the drama of science, even if he didn't get all
the details right. His stories had verve and feeling, and they were
alive. Hamilton did not take himself with undue solemnity; he had
some fun with his writing. At the same time, he was writing stories that he liked to read, and it showed. The least of Hamilton's
stories were always blessed by that extra dimension that makes all
the difference: the sense of wonder.

Hamilton's most famous (or infamous) creation was Captain Future. The name was decidedly unfortunate; it is so trite that it virtually demands parody. (It got some, too. Captain Future was the
only character in SF who managed to attract the scalpel of S.J.
Perelman.) The magazine *Captain Future* was published quarterly
from 1940 through 1944, and each issue featured a short Captain
Future novel. Hamilton wrote most of them, as well as some later
Captain Future stories that appeared in *Startling Stories.* By and
large, this was formula fiction redeemed at times by flashes of the
Hamilton talent. Captain Future was Curt Newton, also known as
the Wizard of Science and the Man of Tomorrow. With his sidekicks—Grag the robot, Otho the android, and Simon Wright, a brain
in a box—Captain Future kept boredom at bay by saving the solar
system from assorted disasters.

Beginning perhaps with *City at World's End* (1951), Hamilton's
fiction took on a more subdued tone as he adapted to a changing
market. He cut down on the melodrama, introduced more shadings

in his stories, and worked to create believable characters. One can
only salute the effort; the novels range from *The Haunted Stars* to
the *Starwolf* series, and they are better than a great many science
fiction tales with inflated reputations. Unfortunately, when Hamilton
got rid of the corn he also lost much of the excitement that had
marked his work. The spark is still there, but the fire never really
gets going.

There is a kind of pathos about Hamilton's later work. He had
been a creative professional writer for a quarter of a century, and
now he had to prove himself all over again. His talent may have
been obscured by the type of SF to which he devoted himself, but
the mature Hamilton shows to good advantage in a number of classic short stories, including "What's It Like Out There?" and "The
Pro."

Edmond Hamilton was one of the most prolific of all science
fiction writers. There was joy in his work, and he opened a lot of
doors for those who came after him.

—Chad Oliver

———

HAMLET, Ova. *See* **LUPOFF, Richard A.**

———

HAND, Elizabeth

Nationality: American. **Born:** San Diego, California, 29 March
1957. **Education:** The Catholic University of America, Washing-
ton, D.C., 1975-84; B.A. in cultural anthropology 1984. **Family:**
Married the writer Richard Grant, *q.v.;* one daughter. **Career:** Ar-
chival researcher, National Air and Space Museum, Smithsonian
Institution, Washington, D.C., 1979-86; cofounder of the National
Air and Space Museum's Archival Videodisc Program. **Agent:**
Martha Millard Literary Agency, 204 Park Avenue, Madison, New
Jersey, 07940. **Address:** Tooley Cottage, Coleman Pond, P.O. Box
133, Lincolnville Beach, Maine, 04849, U.S.A.

SCIENCE FICTION PUBLICATIONS

Novels (series: Winterlong)

Winterlong: A Novel. New York, Bantam, 1990; London, Bantam,
1991.
Aestival Tide (Winterlong). New York and London, Bantam, 1992.
Icarus Descending (Winterlong). New York, Bantam, 1993.
Waking the Moon. London, HarperCollins, 1994; New York,
HarperPrism, 1995.

*

Elizabeth Hand comments:

As a feminist author and critic, my work is concerned primarily with moral issues and issues of sexual identity, sexual transformation, sexual liberation. As a lapsed Catholic, my writing is obsessed with death and the hope of redemption, and guilt for writing about all that sex.

*   *   *

Elizabeth Hand emerged in the late 1980s to become one of the science fiction field's most promising new authors, and has continued in the 1990s to produce a number of excellent shorter works and three novels that have clearly established her as a distinctive and original voice.

Hand's first story, "Prince of Flowers," appeared in *The Twilight Zone* in 1988. It was a contemporary supernatural fantasy about a young woman named Helen who works for a cultural history museum in downtown Washington, D.C. where she opens and inventories old crates of curious objects and papers donated to the museum. (The characters, setting and some of the plot are undoubtedly drawn from Hand's own experiences working for a museum in D.C.) Helen begins to occasionally, then more frequently, take some of the smaller curios home with her to decorate her apartment. The fantasy element involves her discovery of a strange Indonesian "spirit puppet," the Prince of Flowers of the title, in a crate that had been unopened for nearly a century. It was an archetypal *Twilight Zone* story, but quite nicely written, and was chosen by Karl Edward Wagner for inclusion in his *Year's Best Horror Stories XVII*.

Hand's second story appeared more than a year later, in 1989, in the fifth issue of *Pulphouse*. "On the Town Route" was also based on the author's own experiences, and told the story of a young woman accompanying a young man who drives an ice cream truck through a poverty-stricken area in rural Virginia. The people to whom he sells (or just as often gives away) his ice cream are poor, dirty, and eerily ignorant of all social customs, as well as obviously both psychologically and nutritionally dependent on his visits, especially one family. One night, driving back after dark, they hit and believe they have surely killed the young daughter in that family, only to have her blind mother come, revive her, and walk her home. The story builds to an unexpectedly dramatic supernatural conclusion. The story was chosen by Ramsey Campbell for *Year's Best Horror 2*.

With her third story, "The Boy in the Tree," also published in 1990, Hand moved from contemporary supernatural horror to science fiction, with a story set in the indeterminate future at a scientific research facility where specially trained and augmented empaths are used to treat psychopathic patients. The protagonist is one of those empaths, and she has never known another life, having never left the facility since being brought to it as an autistic child. All of the empaths have the ability to "tap" into others (establish an empathic connection) by tasting a small quantity of their blood, and the empaths in the facility have very strange mutual relationships that primarily revolve around vampiric kissing to share the minds they have experienced during treatments. The boy of the title is some sort of mysterious demi-god persona that comes to inhabit the protagonist's mind, resulting in some of her patients being plunged into despair and killing themselves.

Hand's first novel appeared in 1990 and received significant critical notice. *Winterlong* begins with a slightly modified version of "The Boy in the Tree" and continues to unfold a bizarre world some 50 to 100 or more years in our future after a long series of biological-weapons wars have devastated human civilization, and only

some enclaves of Ascendants (apparently people who have retreated to the high ground in orbital defense stations) have any high-technological capabilities. The story takes place in the slowly decaying remnants of Washington, D.C., called the City of Trees, and the suburbs of Northern Virginia, where the empathic research facility is located. The story follows the empath Wendy as she escapes from the research facility, which is coming under dangerous new Ascendant management, and avoids a deadly biological air attack to escape with the help of a male medical attendant to the City of Trees.

Wendy's travels into D.C. take her through a nightmare of the remnants of biological warfare and genetic engineering experiments, as she is attacked by deadly exotic flora, insane mutated children, escaped packs of genetically engineered "geneslaves," and much more. Eventually, she and her partner reach the relative safety of his friends, who are of a house (extended family) of courtesans. Slowly we are introduced to the degenerated remnants of humans who have survived around the Mall and parts of northwest D.C., extended families which occupy specific buildings, and specialize in a few remaining arts; some specialize in prostitution, some in maintaining various museums, some in the botanical sciences, and some in the zoological sciences. The social and sexual practices of these people are strange indeed, as we learn both from Wendy's viewpoint, and that of her long-lost brother, who looks just like her, and is one of the most prized male prostitutes.

There is some beauty left in this hideously degenerate human society, but not much. The continual mistreatment of children and the tendency to mix torture and death with sexual pleasure is particularly extreme. Stylistically, this has more resemblance to fantasy than science fiction; the SF underpinnings are virtually invisible, since no one who is sane really knows what's going on. There are some marvelous characters, but none seem to act on their own volition; all feel driven by unseen forces. Throughout the book, the situation only degenerates further, as an insane Ascendant takes over the National Cathedral, gains the cooperation of a disorganized, superstitious army of mutated children and geneslaves, and sets up the final hideous prophesied event where brother and sister meet.

Hand's next novel, *Aestival Tide,* published in 1992, is not the direct sequel to *Winterlong* that is described in the afterword to that book, but a sequel that is a more straightforward science fiction novel set in a somewhat less degenerate venue, the Gulf-coast domes city of Araboth, ruled by the powerful but decadent family that oversees all of North America. The story involves the moral and physical downfall of the city, and the futile efforts of a small disparate group of characters to avoid the prophesized collapse; at the end of the novel, Araboth is destroyed by a tsunami. The city and its inhabitants are marvelously original creations, and *Aestival Tide* is a more coherent and focused novel than *Winterlong*.

Icarus Descending, the third and final book in the trilogy, was published in 1993. It involves the Ascendants, who rule the Earth from their orbiting space stations, and their monstrous but beautiful geneslaves, the energumens, each of which are designed to live just 1000 days. In this novel the energumens revolt and destroy all of the ruling Ascendants both on the space stations and on Earth. A number of loose ends are tied up from the earlier novels, and in the end the Earth is destroyed by a comet, the Icarus of the title, reminiscent of the tsunami that destroyed Araboth in *Aestival Tide.*

While writing these novels, Hand also wrote several works of short fiction, all of superior quality. "Snow on Sugar Mountain" is a fantasy about a dying astronaut and a teenage runaway who can shapeshift into a fox. "In the Month of Athyr" is a disturbingly effective science fiction novelette about the use of bioengineered sex slaves that is reminiscent of Connie Willis's memorable story "All My Darling Daughters." "Justice" was one of the most controversial SF short stories of 1992. "Last Summer on Mars Hill" was a gentle contemporary fantasy novella reminiscent of some of her earliest stories.

Hand also has written a great deal of literary criticism, not all of it related to SF. She has written book reviews regularly for the *Washington Post,* weekly for the *Detroit Metro Times,* and occasionally for *The New York Review of Science Fiction,* the feminist quarterly *Belles Lettres, Kirkus,* and Penthouse Publications. She is a contributing editor to the semi-professional SF review magazine *Science Fiction Eye,* where she has published a number of interesting reviews and essays on the field. She is married to Richard Grant, a highly promising SF author who entered the field in the mid-1980s.

The *Winterlong* trilogy is clearly Hand's most important body of work to date, and adds a dark but significant contribution to the science fantasy subgenre, very much in the tradition of Jack Vance and Gene Wolfe. Its gothic style, baroque venue, and decadent characters clearly establish Hand as a developing master of the form. The first two novels in the series were nominees for the Philip K. Dick Award. She has also shown herself to be equally capable of writing contemporary fantasy and more conventional science fiction, and her next novel will be a contemporary supernatural horror novel entitled *Walking the Moon.* Elizabeth Hand has clearly become one of the writers to watch in the science fiction and fantasy field.

— D. Douglas Fratz

HARDING, Lee (John)

Pseudonym: Harold G. Nye. **Nationality:** Australian. **Born:** Colac, Victoria, 17 February 1937. **Education:** Australian primary schools. **Family:** Married 1) Carla Bleeker in 1960 (divorced 1974), two sons and one daughter; 2) Irene Anne Pagram in 1982, one daughter. **Career:** Freelance photographer, 1953-70. **Awards:** Ditmar award, 1970, 1972; Alan Marshall award, 1978; Australian Children's Book of the Year award, 1980. **Agent:** Virgina Kidd, Box 278, Milford, Pennsylvania 18337, U.S.A. **Address:** P.O. Box 198, Fern Tree Gully, Victoria 3156, Australia.

SCIENCE FICTION PUBLICATIONS

Novels

Fallen Spaceman (for children). Stanmore, New South Wales, Cassell, 1973; London, Cassell, 1975; revised edition, New York, Harper, 1979.
A World of Shadows. London, Hale, 1975.
The Children of Atlantis (for children). Stanmore, New South Wales, Cassell, 1975.
The Frozen Sky (for children). Stanmore, New South Wales, Cassell, 1975.
Future Sanctuary. Toronto, Laser, 1976.

Return to Tomorrow (for children). Stanmore, New South Wales, Cassell, 1976.
The Weeping Sky (for children). Stanmore, New South Wales, Cassell, 1977.
Displaced Person (for children). Melbourne, Hyland House, 1979; as *Misplaced Persons,* New York, Harper, 1979.
The Web of Time (for children). Stanmore, New South Wales, Cassell, 1980; New York, Penguin, 1985.
Waiting for the End of the World (for children). Melbourne, Hyland House, 1983; New York, Penguin, 1985.

OTHER PUBLICATIONS

Plays

Radio Plays: *Journey into Time* serial, Australian Broadcasting Commission, 1978; *The Legend of New Earth* serial, Australian Broadcasting Commission, 1979.

Other

Editor, *Beyond Tomorrow: An Anthology of Modern Science Fiction.* South Melbourne, Victoria, Wren, 1975; abridged edition, London, New English Library, 1977.
Editor, *The Altered I: An Encounter with Science Fiction.* Carleton, Victoria, Norstrilia Press, 1976; revised edition, New York, Berkley, 1978.
Editor, *Rooms of Paradise.* South Yarra, Victoria, Quartet, 1978; New York, St. Martin's Press, 1979.

*   *   *

For many years one of the most promising Australian science fiction writers, Lee Harding edited influential anthologies of Australian SF, published his short stories in a range of international publications in the 1960s and early 1970s, and established himself as a novelist late in his writing career with two books for adults and a series of novels for "young adult" readers (though each of these is pitched at a different level of readership). His writings reflect a mature and distinctive commitment to characterization and to straightforward techniques of narrative and construction. Though his prose style has recently been attacked by critics (especially those less in sympathy with straightforward, unadorned writing), Harding still commands respect for the themes examined in his best works.

A World of Shadows—a novel for adult readers—deals competently with questions of identity and the nature of reality. Astronaut Stephen Chandler is beset by the smoke-like alien Shadows, and as a result of their onslaught he returns to Earth in the body of his co-pilot, but with his own mind and memories intact within the new body. He becomes involved in a desperate struggle to convince the authorities—and his wife—of his real identity. But what now *is* his "real" identity? Harding describes *A World of Shadows* as "an unusual ontological thriller," and while the novel offers no profound new insights, it does offer an entertaining and cogent canvassing of issues.

Future Sanctuary, Harding's second adult novel, offers a much less satisfactory exploration of the nature of reality. A fugitive pursued for some nameless (and possibly non-existent) crime finds haven in the limbo-world of Sanctuary, but this surface action is revealed to be merely the heroic psychodrama of a deranged poet.

The title of the young adult novel *The Weeping Sky* comes from the novel's central image of an eerie weeping "wound" in the sky, and through skilled and subtle manipulation of characters, situation, and setting, Harding presents an eloquent statement on the elusive, illusory nature of reality. His characters seem to belong to our world, but their society is medieval and their religion is an unknown variant of Christianity; the "wound" in the sky appears to be a harmless though supernatural phenomenon, but there is evidence that it might be a thoroughly rational precursor of natural disaster.

Harding's prize-winning young adult novel, *Displaced Person,* presents a sustained exploration of the nature of reality as the teenager Graeme Drury becomes estranged from the world and people around him and is drawn into a soundless, colourless "grey world" or limbo. This novel is more skilled in execution than *The Weeping Sky,* for it contains some hauntingly lyrical scenes and succinctly accurate accounts of suburban lifestyle, but it is the lesser novel in conception. Its themes are too explicit, and the attempts at metaphysical speculation are ineffective (though minor textual changes to the second edition are an improvement). Nevertheless, as a fable of urban alienation it has been immensely successful with teenage readers.

Waiting for the End of the World may have marked the end of Harding's writing career, for he has published no fiction since then. Set in a decrepit totalitarian future Australia, *Waiting for the End of the World* is a fable of contemporary *angst.* Its central characters are rebellious individuals who have fled the dystopian city to live in the wilds, but now roving patrols are burning the woodlands to smoke out these rebels. As critic Russell Blackford has noted, the characters do little to avert their ultimate demise: they are passively *waiting* for the end of their world.

Lee Harding has a gift for narrative, and consequently it is the storyline that is paramount in each of his novels. Yet Harding is no mere storyteller, for his plots are a way of finding characters and themes, and they are always generated by the plight of his characters. It is stock critical jargon to talk about an author "examining" his themes (implying an approach that is analytical, rigorous, perhaps even exaustive), but this is not appropriate for describing Harding's method. Instead of delving deeply, Harding *canvasses* issues with a deft, light touch.

—Van Ikin

HARNESS, Charles L(eonard)

Pseudonym: Leonard Lockhard. **Nationality:** American. **Born:** Colorado City, Texas, 29 December 1915. **Education:** George Washington University, Washington, D.C., B.S. 1942, LL.B. 1946. **Family:** Married Nell W. Harness in 1938; one daughter and one son. **Career:** Mineral economist, United States Bureau of Mines, Washington, D.C., 1941-47; patent attorney, American Cyanamid Company, Stamford, Connecticut, 1947-53; patent attorney, W.R. Grace and Company, Columbia, Maryland, 1953-81. **Agent:** Joseph Elder Literary Agency, P.O. Box 298, Warwick, New York 10990. **Address:** 6705 White Gate Road, Clarksville, Maryland 21029, U.S.A.

SCIENCE FICTION PUBLICATIONS

Novels

Flight into Yesterday. New York, Bouregy, 1953; as *The Paradox Men,* New York, Ace, 1955; London, Faber, 1964; revised edition, New York, Crown, 1984.
The Ring of Ritornel. London, Gollancz, and New York, Berkley, 1968.
Wolfhead. New York, Berkley, 1978.
The Catalyst. New York, Pocket Books, 1980.
Firebird. New York, Pocket Books, 1981.
The Venetian Court. New York, Ballantine, 1982.
Redworld. New York, DAW, 1986.
Krono. New York, Watts, 1988.
Lurid Dreams. New York, Avon, 1990.
Lunar Justice. New York, Avon, 1991.

Short Stories

The Rose. London, Compact, 1966; New York, Berkley, 1969.

OTHER PUBLICATIONS

Other

Marketing Magnesite and Allied Products, with Nan C. Jensen. Washington, D.C., Bureau of Mines, 1943.
Mining and Marketing of Barite, with F.M. Barsigian. Washington, D.C., Bureau of Mines, 1946.

*

Manuscript Collection: University of Maryland, College Park.

Charles L. Harness comments:
I did it for money.

*   *   *

Charles L. Harness has not written as much as his admirers (Damon Knight, Brian Aldiss, Michael Moorcock) would have wished. His work has always been highly intricate, and his early stories have been compared to those of A.E. van Vogt. Unlike that author, he provides what seems to be a rational explanation for all the astonishing turns of his plots; like van Vogt, his best work has the compelling power of a dream. It is highly cerebral as well; in the words of Louis MacNeice, Harness likes "to draw the corks out of an old conundrum,/And watch the paradoxes fizz."

In *Flight into Yesterday* the hero, Alar, emerges from a wrecked spaceship with no memory of who he is but a certainty that he has a most urgent task to perform. He is sponsored by the Society of Thieves, and protected by the heroine, Keiris, who is the widow of a vanished scientist. The society he finds himself in is sophisticated but decadent; there are brilliant ball scenes and hideous torture chambers. As he attempts to escape from the Imperial police, he talks to the Empress, to a Toynbeean student of the downfall of civilizations, and to the lunatic crew of a solarion, a station perilously located on the surface of the Sun. The play of ideas is brilliant, the menace threatening. The ending is perhaps a shade too perfect, with the hero cancelling out all the misery of humanity. But the book is a dazzler all the same.

"The Rose" is perhaps Harness's most beautiful single work. The heroine, Anna van Tuyl, is at once a composer, a ballet dancer, and a psychotherapist. She is composing a ballet based on Oscar Wilde's story "The Nightingale and the Rose," and is at a standstill in the piece; she is also suffering from a deforming illness. Then she is asked to treat Ruy Jacques, the husband of the eminent and arrogant scientist Martha Jacques: Ruy Jacques has forgotten how to read print, but can read people's intentions instead. In attempting to cure Ray Jacques, Anna falls in love, incurring the jealousy of Martha Jacques. The climax is one of death and transfiguration: Anna finds the perfect ending to her ballet and dies, but hands on the key to a higher mode of life. The summary cannot do justice to the work, which must be read.

The Ring of Ritornel is again set in a society of formal brilliance and extreme tyranny. The villain is the Emperor Oberon, who cares nothing for human life. The hero, James Andrek, has been robbed of both his father and his elder brother by Oberon, and is determined to find the culprit. At the close of the book, a new cycle of the universe is about to begin, and only two people from the old universe will survive. In the warring religions of Alea and Ritornel, Harness poses old questions of chance and destiny. The structure of the book is both mathematical and musical: certain characters and motifs recur, but always with a different effect.

Wolfhead is more direct in manner than the other novels. Set in an Earth long after an atomic catastrophe, it has a hero who descends into the underground kingdom in pursuit of his lost love Beatra. As is fitting for a successor to Dante, he is guided by Virgil—a she-wolf into whose brain a small part of his own has been grafted. The theme is one of unrelenting war; in the end the hero at least succeeds in rescuing his society, but not his wife.

The Catalyst is set in the near future, and deals with a plague called novarella and a chemical called trialine which can cure it. There is a stunning portrait of the scientist Serane, and the way in which he reaches his discoveries by totally cicumventing the bureaucratic structure in which he works. The hero, Paul Blandford, succeeds in securing priority for Serane's invention by an incredible trial run. Thomas M. Disch has complained of the fantastic element in this novel, but I respect that Harness feels life really is like this: we make discoveries half in a dream, and sometimes we do seem to be protected by guardian angels. This aspect of the book reminds me strongly of Arthur Koestler's life of Kepler in *The Sleepwalkers*.

Harness's earlier short stories were perhaps stronger on plot than on character; his first, "Time Trap," already showed the ability to construct a highly ingenious time loop. His most brilliant early story, "The New Reality," begins from the premise that early man was not less observant than we, and concludes that the world *was* flat until the 5th century B.C. The villain, Luce (alias Lucifer), brings about a completely new universe by rendering all previous theories about reality untenable, and A. Prentiss and E. (alias Adam and Eve) survive into the new reality—which is paradisal. But so does the snake! The richest short stories Harness has given us, however, belong to a period since the middle 1960s. "Probable Cause" deals with the case of a convicted murderer of a president: since the evidence against the accused was obtained by clairvoyance, the Supreme Court must consider whether his constitutional rights have been abridged. "The Alchemist" and "An Ornament to His Profession" both deal with a chemical manufacturing firm and the problems of patent law; in the first, the firm discovers with horror that

one of its scientists is practising alchemy; in the second, the lawyer Con Patrick is driven to realize that he would sell his soul if necessary to protect his patents. The later Harness stories have surrendered nothing in the skill of plotting, but they have a sure humour and sense of the richness of human life that were lacking in the earlier short stories (excepting always "The Rose"). His best work is a high-water mark in science fiction.

—Charles Cushing

HARRISON, Harry

Pseudonyms: Felix Boyd; Leslie Charteris; Hank Dempsey. **Nationality:** American. **Born:** Stamford, Connecticut, 12 March 1925. **Education:** art schools in New York. **Military Service:** Served in the United States Army Air Corps during World War II: Sergeant. **Family:** Married Joan Merkler in 1954; one son and one daughter. **Career:** Freelance commercial artist, 1946-55. **Career:** Formerly, editor, *SF Impulse,* London; editor, *Fantastic,* New York, 1968. **Awards:** Nebula award, 1973; Prix Jules Verne, 1980. **Agent:** Sobel Weber Associates, 146 East 19th Street, New York, New York 10003-2404, U.S.A. **Address:** 58 Haddington Road, Dublin 4, Ireland.

SCIENCE FICTION PUBLICATIONS

Novels (series: Bill, the Galactic Hero; Deathworld; Planet of the Damned; Stainless Steel Rat; To the Stars; Warriors of the Way; West of Eden)

The Stainless Steel Rat: A Science Fiction Novel. New York, Pyramid, 1961; London, New English Library, 1966.
Planet of the Damned. New York, Bantam, 1962; as Sense of Obligation, London, Dobson, 1967.
Bill, The Galactic Hero. Garden City, New York, Doubleday, and London, Gollancz, 1965.
Plague from Space. Garden City, New York, Doubleday, 1965; London, Gollancz, 1966; as *The Jupiter Legacy,* New York, Bantam, 1970.
Make Room! Make Room! Garden City, New York, Doubleday, 1966; London, Penguin, 1967; as *Soylent Green,* New York, Berkley, 1973.
The Technicolor Time Machine. Garden City, New York, Doubleday, 1967; London, Faber, 1968.
The Man from P.I.G. (for children). New York, Avon, 1968.
Captive Universe. New York, Putnam, 1969; London, Faber, 1970.
The Daleth Effect: A Science Fiction Novel. New York, Putnam, 1970; as *In Our Hands, The Stars,* London, Faber, 1970.
The Stainless Steel Rat's Revenge. New York, Walker, 1970; London, Faber, 1971.
Spaceship Medic (for children). London, Faber, and Garden City, New York, Doubleday, 1970.
Tunnel through the Deeps. New York, Putnam, 1972; as *A Transatlantic Tunnel, Hurrah!,* London, Faber, 1972.
Stonehenge, with Leon E. Stover. New York, Scribner, and London, Davies, 1972; revised and expanded as *Stonehenge: Where Atlantis Died,* New York, Tor, 1983; London Granada, 1985.

The Stainless Steel Rat Saves the World. New York, Putnam, 1972; London, Faber, 1974.

Star Smashers of the Galaxy Rangers. New York, Putnam, 1973; London, Faber, 1974.

The Deathworld Trilogy: Three Novels. Garden City, New York, Doubleday, 1974.

   Deathworld. New York, Bantam, 1960; London, Penguin, 1963; as *Deathworld 1,* London, Sphere, 1973.

   Deathworld 2: A Sequel to Deathworld, New York, Bantam, 1964; London, Sphere, 1977; as *The Ethical Engineer,* London, Gollancz, 1964.

   Deathworld 3. New York, Dell, 1968; London, Faber, 1969.

The Men from P.I.G. and R.O.B.O.T. (for children). London, Faber, 1974; New York, Atheneum, 1978.

The California Iceberg (for children). London, Faber, and New York, Walker, 1975.

The Lifeship, with Gordon R. Dickson. New York, Harper, 1976; as *Lifeboat,* London, Orbit, 1977.

Skyfall. London, Faber, 1976; New York, Atheneum, 1977.

The Adventures of the Stainless Steel Rat (omnibus). Garden City, New York, Doubleday, 1977.

The Stainless Steel Rat Wants You! London, Joseph, 1978; Garden City, New York, Doubleday, 1979.

Planet Story, illustrated by Jim Burns. London, Pierrot, and New York, A and W Visual Library, 1979.

To the Stars. Garden City, New York, Doubleday, 1981.

   Homeworld. New York, Bantam, and London, Panther, 1980.

   Wheelworld. New York, Bantam, and London, Panther, 1981.

   Starworld. New York, Bantam, and London, Panther, 1981.

Planet of No Return (Planet of the Damned). New York, Simon and Schuster, 1981; London, Severn House, 1983.

Invasion: Earth. New York, Ace, 1982; London, Sphere, 1984.

The Stainless Steel Rat for President. Garden City, New York, Doubleday, and London, Sphere, 1982.

A Rebel in Time. New York, Tor, and London, Granada, 1983.

West of Eden. New York, Bantam, and London, Granada, 1984.

A Stainless Steel Rat Is Born. London, Titan, and New York, Bantam, 1985.

Winter in Eden. London, Grafton, and New York, Bantam, 1986.

The Stainless Steel Rat Gets Drafted. London and New York, Bantam, 1987.

Return to Eden. London, Grafton, and New York, Bantam, 1988.

The Planet of Robot Slaves. New York, Avon, 1989; as *Bill, the Gallactic Hero, On the Planet of Robot Slaves.* London, Gollancz, 1989.

Bill, the Gallactic Hero, On the Planet of Bottled Brains, with Robert Sheckley. New York, Avon, and London, Gollancz, 1990.

Bill, the Gallactic Hero, On the Planet of Tasteless Pleasure, with David Bischoff. New York, Avon, and London, Gollancz, 1991.

Bill, the Gallactic Hero, On the Planet of the Zombie Vampires, with Jack C. Haldemann II. New York, Avon, 1991; London, Gollancz, 1992.

Bill, the Gallactic Hero, On the Planet of Ten Thousand Bars, with David Bischoff. New York, Avon, 1991; as *Bill, the Gallactic Hero, On the Planet of the Hippies from Hell,* London, Gollancz, 1992.

Bill, the Gallactic Hero: The Final Incoherent Adventure, with David M. Harris. New York, AvoNova, 1992; London, Gollancz, 1993.

The Turning Option: A Novel, with Marvin Minsky. New York, Warner, and London, Viking, 1992.

The Hammer and the Cross (Warriors of the Way), with John Holm. London, Legend, and New York, Tor, 1993.

The Stainless Steel Rat Sings the Blues. London and New York, Bantam, 1994.

One King's Way (Warriors of the Way), with John Holm. London, Legend, and New York, Tor, 1995.

Warriors of the Way, with John Holm (omnibus). New York, Guild America Books, 1995.

Short Stories

War with the Robots: Science Fiction Stories. New York, Pyramid, 1962; London, Dobson, 1967.

Two Tales and Eight Tomorrows. London, Gollancz, 1965; New York, Bantam, 1968.

Prime Number. New York, Berkley, 1970; London, Sphere, 1975.

One Step from Earth. New York, Macmillan, 1970; London, Faber, 1972.

The Best of Harry Harrison. New York, Pocket Books, 1976; revised edition, London, Sidgwick and Jackson, 1976.

Stainless Steel Visions. New York, Tor, and London, Legend, 1993.

Galactic Dreams. London, Legend, and New York, Tor, 1994.

OTHER PUBLICATIONS

Novels

Vendetta for the Saint (as Leslie Charteris). Garden City, New York, Doubleday, 1964; London, Hodder and Stoughton, 1965.

Montezuma's Revenge. Garden City, New York, Doubleday, 1972.

Queen Victoria's Revenge. Garden City, New York, Doubleday, 1974; London, Severn House, 1977.

The QE2 Is Missing. London, Futura, 1980; New York, Tor, 1982.

Other

Great Balls of Fire! London, Pierrot, and New York, Grosset and Dunlap, 1977.

Mechanismo. London, Pierrot, and Los Angeles, Reed, 1978.

Spacecraft in Fact and Fiction, with Malcolm Edwards. London, Orbit, 1979.

You Can Be the Stainless Steel Rat: An Interactive Game Book. London, Grafton, 1985.

Editor, *Collected Editorials from Analog,* by John W. Campbell, Jr. Garden City, New York, Doubleday, 1966.

Editor, with Brian Aldiss, *Nebula Award Stories Two.* Garden City, New York, Doubleday, 1967; as *Nebula Award Stories 1967,* London, Gollancz, 1967.

Editor, with Leon E. Stover, *Apeman, Spaceman: Anthropological Science Fiction.* Garden City, New York, Doubleday, and London, Rapp and Whiting, 1968.

Editor, with Brian Aldiss, *Farewell, Fantastic Venus!* London, Macdonald, 1968; abridged as *All about Venus,* New York, Dell, 1968.

Editor, with Brian Aldiss, *Best SF: 1967* [to *1975*]. New York, Putnam, 7 vols., 1968-74; Indianapolis, Bobbs Merrill, 2 vols., 1975-76; as *The Year's Best Science Fiction No. 1-9,* London, Sphere, 8 vols., 1968-76; London, Futura, 1 vol., 1976.

Editor, *SF: Author's Choice 1-4.* New York, Berkley, 4 vols., 1968-74; vol. 1 as *SF: Author's Choice: Backdrop of Stars,* London, Dobson, 1968.

Editor, *Four for the Future: An Anthology on the Themes of Sacrifice and Redemption.* London, Macdonald, 1969.

Editor, *Blast Off: S.F. for Boys.* London, Faber, 1969; as *Worlds of Wonder: Sixteen Tales of Science Fiction,* Garden City, New York, Doubleday, 1969.

Editor, *The Year 2000: An Anthology.* Garden City, New York, Doubleday, 1970; London, Faber, 1971.

Editor, *Nova 1-4.* New York, Delacorte Press, 1 vol., 1970; New York, Walker, 3 vols., 1972-75; London, Sphere, 4 vols., 1975-76; vol. 3 published as *The Outdated Man,* New York, Dell, 1975.

Editor, *The Light Fantastic: Science Fiction Classics from the Mainstream.* New York, Scribner, 1971.

Editor, with Brian Aldiss, *The Astounding-Analog Reader.* Garden City, New York, Doubleday, 2 vols., 1972-73; volume 1 reprinted in 2 vols., London, Sphere, 1973.

Editor, with Theodore J. Gordon, *Ahead of Time.* Garden City, New York, Doubleday, 1972.

Editor, *Astounding: John W. Campbell Memorial Anthology.* New York, Random House, 1973; London, Sidgwick and Jackson, 1974.

Editor, with Carol Pugner, *A Science Fiction Reader.* New York, Scribner, 1973.

Editor, with Willis E. McNelly, *Science Fiction Novellas.* New York, Scribner, 1975.

Editor, with Brian Aldiss, *SF Horizons* (reprint of magazine). New York, Arno Press, 1975.

Editor, with Brian Aldiss, *Hell's Cartographers: Some Personal Histories of Science Fiction Writers.* London, Weidenfeld and Nicolson, and New York, Harper, 1975.

Editor, with Brian Aldiss, *Decade: The 1940s, The 1950s, The 1960s.* London, Macmillan, 3 vols., 1975-77; *The 1940s and 1950s,* New York, St. Martin's Press, 2 vols., 1978.

Editor, with Bruce McAllister, *There Won't Be War.* New York, Tor, 1991.

*

Bibliography: *Harry Harrison: Bibliografia 1951-1965* by Francesco Biamonti, privately printed, 1965.

Critical Study: *Harry Harrison* by Leon Stover, Boston, Twayne, 1990.

Manuscript Collection: University of California, Fullerton.

Harry Harrison comments:

I have always believed in readability. The easier the flow of the prose, the more basic the vocabulary, the more readers there will be who can follow and enjoy a book. But complex technical terms can be used where there is no alternative. I have found that an action story with two or three levels of intellectual content below the surface enables me to say just what I wish to say. I have also found that humor—and black humor—can carry ideas that can be expressed in no other way. The fact that my books have been translated into 27 languages must indicate that I am communicating with my audience.

*   *   *

Harry Harrison gets straight down to a story, and keeps going with little or no padding until it is done. In the classic opening to *The Stainless Steel Rat,* Slippery Jim DiGriz causes a safe to fall on the policeman who is trying to arrest him. While this could seem impossibly cruel and violent, the voice of the policeman is heard from beneath the safe, adding the destruction of a police robot to the charges, comically defusing both the shock of this possible murder and the impression that DiGriz might be a bad man. Here we have three hallmarks of Harrison's fiction: the breathless pace; the comedy bordering on farce; and the strict moral concerns.

The pace of Harry Harrison's writing is no accident, nor is it clumsily achieved. Examine carefully the first page of any of his early novels, and the speed of the telling immediately becomes apparent. Examine it carefully, because the pace will have you turning the page before you realise you have read it. Yet the short sentences, snappy dialogue and spare description belie the amount of information packed in; no necessary detail is left out, but no extraneous information is included. Harrison gets on with the story, which is very pleasing in comparison with some modern fantastic fiction. The slenderness of many of his books is a testament not to their slightness, but rather to the spareness of the storytelling in them.

First and foremost entertainments, nevertheless, in the tradition of great comedy, even the most light-hearted of Harrison's stories have deeply serious foundations. Novels like *Bill, the Galactic Hero, The Technicolor Time Machine, The Stainless Steel Rat,* and *Star Smashers of the Galaxy Rangers* might appear to be no more than romps through the clichés of science fiction; but each of them has, at its centre, a powerful moral point. While *Bill, the Galactic Hero* is a deeply felt antiwar statement, rather than being simply an emotional rant against the barbarism of war, it actually looks in detail at the kind of top-heavy bureaucracy that makes modern war first possible, and then necessary. The humour of the situation springs largely from the ludicrousness of the society depicted; but the society depicted looks suspiciously like our own.

Similarly, *Star Smashers of the Galaxy Rangers* satirises the militarist science fiction of the time (Heinlein's *Starship Troopers* for instance), showing the attitudes to conflict and space opera to be unthinkingly juvenile; and *The Technicolor Time Machine* satirises Hollywood, making it clear that Hollywood moguls will trivialise almost anything in the interest of making money.

The Stainless Steel Rat and its sequels are not so easily categorized. Slippery Jim DiGriz is a raffish outlaw, but he has a very strong moral sense; the top-heavy bureaucracies are again his and Harrison's target. As this series proceeds, the system draws him in, so that he finally has to try to deal with society's ills rather than taking advantage of them.

There are similar concerns in Harrison's other writing. While the comic novels draw the casual reader in, and only gradually reveal their morals, works such as the Deathworld trilogy, with its ecological concerns, and *Make Room! Make Room!* with its depiction of overpopulation show Harrison's naked concern with the fate of our planet and our race.

More recently, the West of Eden trilogy introduces the concept of dinosaurs who survived up to the time of early human beings, using a rigorous extrapolative basis. A sentient reptile species has evolved parallel with mankind. While it has civilization and science far in advance of man's, it has never developed fire. The trilogy concerns the meeting of these two races, and the subsequent war.

Harrison's storytelling has been compared to H.G. Wells's in this trilogy. The comparison is apt, but Harrison also imports some of Wells's less attractive aspects. The characterisation is necessarily and typically thin, but where in Harrison's earlier works the speed of the story-telling denied the reader the opportunity to consider this problem, these stories are much more leisurely. Harrison's lifelong friendship with Brian Aldiss may be a cause, as there are many similarities between the West of Eden books and Aldiss's Helliconia trilogy.

It would, however, be unfair to condemn these books on this basis, particularly as this reader has always been out of sympathy with Aldiss's work. Harrison's inventiveness does not flag when it comes to new types of gadgets for the intelligent dinosaurs to create. While it must be said that Harrison's more recent work seems to have drifted into sequelitis, with him often collaborating with other comic writers to keep the humour side moving, it is only in comparison with his earlier work that any of these novels pall. They are intriguing science fiction, and would be highly prized even if they were all he had ever written.

—Paul Brazier

HARRISON, M(ichael) John

Nationality: British. **Born:** Great Britain, 26 July 1945. **Education:** schools in England. **Career:** Groom, Atherstone Hunt, Warwickshire, 1963; student teacher, Warwickshire, 1963-65; clerk, Royal Masonic Charity Institute, London, 1966. Literary editor and reviewer, *New Worlds;* regular contributor, *New Manchester Review,* 1978-79. **Agent:** Anthony Sheil Associates, 43 Doughty Street, London WCIN 2LF, England.

SCIENCE FICTION PUBLICATIONS

Novels (series: Viriconium)

The Committed Men. London, Hutchinson, and Garden City, New York, Doubleday, 1971.
The Pastel City (Viriconium). London, New English Library, 1971; Garden City, New York, Doubleday, 1972.
The Centauri Device. Garden City, New York, Doubleday, 1974; London, Panther, 1975.
A Storm of Wings: Being the Second Volume of the 'Viriconium' Sequence, in Which Benedict Paucemanly Returns from His Long Frozen Dream in the Far Side of the Moon, and the Earth Submits Briefly to the Charisma of the Locust. Garden City, New York, Doubleday, and London, Sphere, 1980.
In Viriconium. London, Gollancz, 1982; as *The Floating Gods,* Pocket Books, 1983.
Viriconium (omnibus; includes *In Viriconium*). London, Unwin, 1988.
The Course of the Heart. London, Gollancz, 1992.

Short Stories

The Machine in Shaft Ten, and Other Stories. London, Panther, 1975.
The Ice Monkey, and Other Stories. London, Gollancz, 1983.

Viriconium Nights. New York, Ace, 1984; revised edition, London, Gollancz, 1985.

OTHER PUBLICATIONS

Other

Climbers. London, Gollancz, 1989.
The Luck in the Head, with Ian Miller (graphic novel). London, Gollancz, 1991; Milwaukie, Oregon, Dark Horse Comics, 1993.

*

M. John Harrison comments:

(1985) I am often thought of as a pessimistic writer. I believe this is an over-simplification and prefer to think of myself as a compassionate but realistic one. There is a difference between compassion and that facile, sentimental—and political—optimism found at the crux of most SF, a genre the poverty of whose subject matter is legendary.

My fiction is concerned with the inability of people to feel ordinary emotions, or to communicate them successfully to one another; their efforts to maintain identity in the face of abstract systems and idealistic social structures; and their perception of themselves as live individuals in a meaningless, contingent universe.

The most radical expression of this existential standpoint is found in the collection *Viriconium Nights,* but it is clearly present in stories such as "The Machine in Shaft Ten" and "Settling the World" and in *The Committed Men.*

In fact, my fiction is not easily described as SF. Though in-genre critics have described it as an "illustration of entropy," this is to put the cart before the horse. In work like "Running Down" and *In Viriconium* I have consistently used entropy as a metaphor, an illustration, of the human condition: I have no interest in it as a scientific concept. I have used the psychology of sensory deprivation and the ethological notion of "Umwelt" in a similarly metaphorical way. Fiction and science get into bed together at the risk of popularisation, which despite George Steiner's elegant efforts is still only popularisation, or (increasingly) bad faith. I would prefer to avoid that.

My interest in the fantastic allegory or parable, bread and butter of contemporary SF, has declined.

Since 1980 I have turned away from the extreme absurdism of *The Pastel City* and *A Storm of Wings*—with their stress on the failure of, and the fear of, action—and in "The Quarry" or "Old Women" can be seen an increasingly direct and sensual engagement with those areas where ethology, early-modernist fiction and a moderate existentialism seem to share ground in the concept of the "accented moment sign" or moment-of-being. I am interested in the lives of individuals; compassion is not a function of the grand or political scale. For the same reason I am drawn to the short novel rather than the heavily researched three-decker with its blundering Victorian moralism.

My writing is oblique, compressed, and allusive, with a carefully textured surface. Despite this I am much less a stylist, and very much less a "writer-for-writing's-sake," than is generally supposed in the theoretical regions of SF, which are as poverty-stricken as its human ones.

For the more recent short stories—"The Ice Monkey," "Egnaro," "The New Rays," and "A Young Man's Journey to Viriconium"—

and for *Climbers,* my notebooks have provided material observed from life. This is ordered at the outset according to its own internal demands. Thereafter setting and event amplify the theme; character and meaning are less stated than allowed to emerge. What appears to be atmosphere is more often than not metonymy or metaphor.

*   *   *

M. John Harrison's most enduring work in science fiction is the Viriconium series. The first book, *The Pastel City,* presents a civilization in decline where medieval social patterns clash with the advanced technology and superscience weaponry that the citizens of the city know how to use but have forgotten how to engineer. Harrison's leading character, Cromis, fancies himself a better poet than a swordsman, yet he leads the battle to save Viriconium, the Pastel City, from the brain-stealing golems from Earth's past. The decadence Harrison describes is reminiscent of Michael Moorcock's vision of the far future in *The End of All Songs.*

The next book in the Viriconium series is *A Storm of Wings.* Fay Glass and Alstath Fulthor of the Reborn try to alert the powers of Viriconium that the northern highlands are overrun by insectile armies. A race of intelligent insects is invading Earth as human interest in survival wanes. Fay brings the severed head of an invading locust-like giant insect to show the extent of the disaster. Harrison brilliantly depicts the workings of civilization on the verge of collapse and the heroic efforts of individuals to help it sustain itself a little longer.

The Floating Gods is a moody portrait of Viriconium beset by a mysterious plague. As artist Audsley King slowly dies from the plague, her friend Ashlyme tries to save her. Yet his efforts are purposeless and his adventures misdirected. Where the previous books in the series held some sword and sorcery elements, *The Floating Gods* goes beyond black humor into a coma of despair.

Viriconium Nights is a collection of eight vignettes of the night life in the Pastel City. Many of the pieces feature some of Harrison's best writing, but that is what most of the stories are: exercises in style. The characters remain ill-defined and the actions are directionless and at times absurd. Vivid images come to nothing as plot and characters never interact.

Of Harrison's other novels, his first, *The Committed Men,* is notable for its grotesque descriptions of post-nuclear holocaust Earth. A band of unlikely characters—a dwarf, a cripple, a doctor, and a girl who has just given birth to an ugly mutant baby—travel south to save the baby they are "committed" to delivering to the new race of mutants. Harrison's most recent novel, *Climbers,* contains some of his best writing and delivers some memorable, chilling scenes.

Harrison's most accessible book is *The Centauri Device,* where space tramp John Truck is hunted down by a cast of bizarre characters: General Alice Gaw, ruthless head of the Israeli World Government; Gadaffi ben Barka, terrorist supreme of the Union of Arab Socialist Republics; and Dr. Grishkin, leader of the weird Opener cult. Truck's mother was a Centauran, one of the last before the Centauri Genocide. Now Truck is the last Centauran and the rival groups need him to arm the most powerful weapon in the galaxy: the Centauri device that will respond only to the genetic code of a true Centauran. There's plenty of action, black humor, and political commentary in this fast-paced space opera. The ending is a bit too pat, but Harrison is in fine control of this book all the way.

The Ice Monkey and Other Stories shows Harrison's wide range of subject matter. In seven stories, Harrison manages to capture pathos, humor, awe, despair, and pain. The best piece is "The Incalling," in which an editor is haunted by an author's attempts to cure himself of cancer by faith healing. This is an unforgettable story.

Harrison's famous *Interzone* story, "The Luck in the Head," was published as a graphic novel with Ian Miller. In addition, Harrison's *The Course of the Heart* explores the frontiers of reality within fantasy. An associational novel about rockclimbing called *Climbers* features Harrison's take on living in a world of bleakness that bears a startling resemblance to Viriconium.

M. John Harrison is a brilliant stylist whose work captures the grotesque and the decadent in vivid, absurd images that are as fascinating as they are unique.

—George Kelley

HAWKE, Simon

Pseudonyms: J. D. Masters; Nicholas Yermakov. **Nationality:** American. **Born:** Nicholas Yermakov, New York City, 30 September 1951; name legally changed. **Education:** Valley Forge Military Academy, Pennsylvania; American University, Washington, D.C.; Hofstra University, Hempstead, New York, B.A. in English and communications 1974. **Career:** Has worked as musician, broadcaster, journalist, salesman, bartender, and factory worker. **Agent:** Adele Leone Agency, 26 Nantucket Place, Scarsdale, New York 10583, U.S.A.

SCIENCE FICTION PUBLICATIONS

Novels (series: Batman; Dark Sun; Psychodrome; Reluctant Sorcerer; Sons of Glory; Star Trek; Timewars; The Wizard)

The Ivanhoe Gambit (Timewars). New York, Ace, 1984; London, Headline, 1987.
The Timekeeper Conspiracy (Timewars). New York, Ace, 1984; London, Headline, 1987.
The Pimpernel Plot (Timewars). New York, Ace, 1984; London, Headline, 1988.
The Zenda Vendetta (Timewars). New York, Ace, 1985; London, Headline, 1988.
The Nautilus Sanction (Timewars). New York, Ace, 1985; London, Headline, 1988.
The Khyber Connection (Timewars). New York, Ace, 1986; London, Headline, 1989.
Psychodrome. New York, Ace, 1987.
The Wizard of 4th Street. New York, Popular Library, 1987.
The Argonaut Affair (Time Wars). New York, Ace, 1987; London, Headline, 1989.
The Wizard of Whitechapel. New York, Popular Library, 1988.
The Dracula Caper (Timewars). New York, Ace, 1988; London, Headline, 1990.
The Shapechanger Scenario (Pyschodrome). New York, Ace, 1988.
The Lilliput Legion (Timewars). New York, Ace, 1989.
The Wizard of Sunset Strip. New York, Popular Library, 1989.
The Wizard of Rue Morgue. New York, Popular Library, 1990.
The Hellfire Rebellion (Timewars). New York, Ace, 1990.

The Cleopatra Crisis (Timewars). New York, Ace, 1990.

Predator 2: A Novel (novelization of screenplay). New York, Jove, 1990.

Batman: To Stalk a Spector. New York, Warner, and London, Roc, 1991.

The Samuri Wizard. New York, Warner, 1991.

The Six-Gun Solution (Timewars). New York, Ace, 1991.

The Wizard of Santa Fe. New York, Warner, 1991.

Sons of Glory. New York, Jove, 1992.

The Reluctant Sorcerer. New York, Warner, 1992.

The Nine Lives of Catseye Gomez. New York, Warner, 1992.

Call to Battle (Sons of Glory). New York, Jove, 1993.

The Inadequate Adept (Reluctant Sorcerer). New York, Warner, 1993.

Dark Sun: The Outcast. Lake Geneva, Wisconsin, TSR, 1993.

The Romulan Prize (Star Trek). New York, Pocket Books, and London, Titan, 1993.

The Wizard of Camelot. New York, Warner, 1993.

The Wizard of Lovecraft's Cafe. New York, Warner, 1993.

Dark Sun: The Seeker. Lake Geneva, Wisconsin, TSR, 1994.

Dark Sun: Nomad. Lake Geneva, Wisconsin, TSR, 1994.

The Patrician Transgression (Star Trek). New York and London, Pocket Books, 1994.

The Whims of Creation. New York, Warner, 1995.

Blaze of Glory (Star Trek). New York, Pocket Books, 1995.

Dark Sun: The Broken Blade. Lake Geneva, Wisconsin, TSR, 1995.

Novels as J.D. Masters

Steele. New York, Charter, 1989.

Cold Steele. New York, Charter, 1989.

Killer Steele. New York, Charter, 1990.

Jagged Steele. New York, Charter, 1990.

Renegade Steele. New York, Berkley, 1990.

Target Steele. New York, Berkley, 1990.

Novels as Nicholas Yermakov (series: Last Communion)

Journey from Flesh. New York, Berkley, 1981.

Last Communion. New York, Signet, 1981.

Fall into Darkness. New York, Berkley, 1982.

Clique. New York, Berkley, 1982.

Epiphany (Last Communion). New York, Signet, 1982.

Battlestar Galactica 6: The Living Legend (novelization of screenplay), with Glen A. Larson. New York, Berkley, 1982.

Battlestar Galactica 7: War of the Gods (novelization of screenplay), with Glen A. Larson. New York, Berkley, 1982.

Jehad (Last Communion). New York, Signet, 1984.

Short Stories

The 9 Lives of Catseye Gomez. Arvada, Colorado, Roadkill Press, 1991.

OTHER PUBLICATIONS

Novels

Friday the 13th, Part VI (novelization of screenplay). New York, Signet, 1986.

Friday the 13th, Part I (novelization of screenplay). New York, Signet, 1987.

Friday the 13th, Part II (novelization of screenplay). New York, Signet, 1988.

Friday the 13th, Part III (novelization of screenplay). New York, Signet, 1988.

*

Simon Hawke comments:

I approach my writing with a musician's sensibilities, which is to say that I enjoy "playing different kinds of music." I practice hard, I play often, and I continually seek to improve, but the driving force is the sheer joy of playing and the appreciation of the listener, or in this case, the reader. Writing is not so much a profession or an art as it is a lifestyle. Writers are fringe people. We deal in dreams. We shape them, hone them, polish them, nurture them lovingly, then share them. It's a craft, perhaps more ethereal than most, but no less demanding. Its special attraction is that it can never be truly mastered. But I'll keep on trying, just the same.

*   *   *

Although Simon Hawke is chiefly noted now for his Time Wars and Wizard series, his earlier novels are of unusually high quality and are less inclined to be restatements of one another. *Journey from Flesh,* expanded from the story "Surrogate Mouth," follows the adventures of a man who gains empathic powers after eating an alien lizard. His new ability involves him in an attempt by aliens to hunt down the lizards because of the regenerative powers their flesh offers. Ultimately he learns that the lizards are in fact sentient but doomed by their biology to extinction.

The eradication of an entire species is the major theme of the trilogy consisting of *Last Communion, Epiphany,* and *Jehad.* Boomerang is a newly discovered world with a native population, the Shades, who resemble human beings, although there is no sign of any technological civilization. A chance encounter reveals that they are a gestalt species who absorb the personalities of those that die, raising the possibility that human immortality might be achieved through contact with this species. The two subsequent books reveal the efforts by an avaricious human government to take advantage of the aliens, even if it means sending an expedition into the past and eventually destroying the Shades themselves forever.

The protagonist of *Clique* is a salesman who helps promote the use of auras, holographic projectors which individuals can wear to change the way they appear to others. This is also a reworking of a short story theme, in this case taken from "A Whisper of Banshees." Eventually the protagonist recognizes that he is helping people to escape the necessity of dealing with the real world and forms an anti-aura movement, which becomes just as rigid in its own way. Despite some faltering near the end, this is clearly superior to the novels that have preceded it.

Fall into Darkness, the last of the early non-series novels, draws heavily on Russian folklore, transplanted to a human colony world now pretty much isolated from the rest of humankind. It's primarily a swashbuckling pirate story, but an excellent one. Hawke's interest in using the past for story material led logically to the Time Wars series, which ran 12 volumes in all.

The Ivanhoe Gambit kicked off the series in 1984, and it concluded with *The Six-Gun Solution* in 1991. In broad terms, it's the traditional "change war" story; a group of time travellers exist primarily to neutralize others who wish to change the course of history for one reason or another. But Hawke quickly expanded the theme, adding a rival service from an alternate Earth seeking to extend its authority into our own time stream, renegade agents, and other recurring villains. It is an extremely well researched series, and the occasional accompanying essays are often as interesting as the original stories. Although they are to a certain degree formulaic, individual volumes do stand out, particularly *The Argonaut Affair, The Hellfire Rebellion, The Dracula Caper,* and the concluding volume, which draws together all the different threads into one neat conclusion.

Psychodrome and its sequel, *The Shapechanger Scenario,* may have been intended as another open-ended series, but one which the author abandoned quickly. Psychodrome is an interstellar game that pits adventurers against each other for the entertainment of the viewing audience. Arkady O'Toole is a gambler who participates in the game primarily to escape the attention of some personal enemies, but he soon discovers that he has been pursued and the dramatic dangers may be more real than he had intended. In the sequel, shapechanging alien creatures complicate matters thoroughly, and O'Toole must deal with them within the context of Psychodrome, whose viewers are convinced that the alien menace is simply another part of the program, with no objective reality.

In 1987, Hawke started another series, this one fantasy, although he uses the devices of science fiction to provide a novel setting and occasional interesting contrasts of mood and place. *The Wizard of 4th Street* introduces a standard inept wizard, sets him down in a futuristic New York City, and unleashes a series of comic adventures that vary from vaguely amusing to sidesplittingly funny. The wizard teams up with a streetwise thief, then travels to England in *The Wizard of White Chapel,* where the twosome confronts survivors from Camelot and a malevolent supernatural force prowling the city's streets. Alternating chills and laughter continue in *The Wizard of Sunset Strip,* in which the less than dynamic duo travels to Hollywood to confront yet another supernatural manifestation, this one indulging in a series of Ripper-like killings. *The Wizard of Rue Morgue* is set in Paris and *The Samurai Wizard* moves the action to Japan in the strongest entry of the series. Subsequent novels which similarly blend science fiction and fantasy include *The Nine Lives of Catseye Gomez,* possibly the best effort Hawke has done in this area, and *The Inadequate Adept.*

Hawke has recently introduced a new series for the TSR fantasy line, starting with *Nomad* and *Seeker.* Standard heroic fantasies, the books are competent but unlikely to produce significant new work. His two media-related novels, *The Patrian Transgression* (Star Trek) and *The Romulan Prize* (Star Trek: Next Generation) are similarly limited, although the latter in particular is one of the better novels in that series. *The Whims of Creation,* though more original, is only marginally more interesting. A gigantic starship on its way to another star system is invaded by magical creatures from an alternate reality.

Although Hawke rarely writes at shorter length, he produced several interesting tales early in his career, the most noteworthy of which are "Elm War," "Melponeme, Calliope, and Fred," "Crash Course for Ravers," and "The Orpheus Implant." Although Hawke appears to have abandoned writing serious individual novels in favor of series, he is clearly concerned that each entry be a complete story in itself, the background carefully researched and presented, and the story entertaining. The originality and creativeness of those stories and the early novels seems to have largely disappeared from his recent work, which continues to be competent and entertaining, but invariably unremarkable.

—Don D'Ammassa

HEARD, Gerald. *See* **HEARD, H.F.**

HEARD, H(enry) F(itzgerald)

Pseudonym: Gerald Heard. **Nationality:** British. **Born:** London, 6 October 1889. **Education:** Gonville and Caius College, Cambridge, B.A. (honours) in history 1911, graduate work 1911-12. **Career:** Worked with the Agricultural Cooperative Movement in Ireland, 1919-23, and in England, 1923-27; editor, *Realist,* London, 1929; Lecturer, Oxford University, 1929-31; science commentator, BBC Radio, London, 1930-34; settled in the United States, 1937; Visiting Lecturer, Washington University, St. Louis, 1951-52, 1955-56; Haskell Foundation Lecturer, Oberlin College, Ohio, 1958. **Awards:** Bollingen grant, 1955; British Academy Hertz award. **Died:** 14 August 1971.

SCIENCE FICTION PUBLICATIONS

Novels

Doppelgangers: An Episode of the Fourth, the Psychological, Revolution, 1997. New York, Vanguard Press, 1947; London, Cassell, 1948.
The Black Fox: A Novel of the 'Seventies' (as Gerald Heard). London, Cassell, 1950; New York, Harper, 1951.

Short Stories

The Great Fog and Other Weird Tales. New York, Vanguard Press, 1944; revised edition, London, Cassell, 1947; as *The Great Fog: Weird Tales of Terror and Detection,* Garden City, New York, Sun Dial Press, 1946.
The Lost Cavern and Other Tales of the Fantastic. New York, Vanguard Press, 1948; London, Cassell, 1949.
Gabriel and the Creatures (as Gerald Heard). New York, Harper, 1952; as *Wishing Well: An Outline of the Evolution of the Mammals Told as a Series of Stories about How the Animals Got Their Wishes,* London, Faber, 1953.

OTHER PUBLICATIONS

Novels

A Taste for Honey. New York, Vanguard Press, 1941; London, Cassell, 1942; as *A Taste for Murder,* New York, Avon, 1955.

Reply Paid: A Novel. New York, Vanguard Press, 1942; London, Cassell, 1943.

Murder by Reflection. New York, Vanguard Press, 1942; London, Cassell, 1945.

The Notched Hairpin. New York, Vanguard Press, 1949; London, Cassell, 1952.

Other as Gerald Heard

Narcissus: An Anatomy of Clothes. London, Kegan Paul, and New York, Dutton, 1924.

The Ascent of Humanity: An Essay on the Evolution of Civilization. London, Cape, and New York, Harcourt Brace, 1929.

The Emergence of Man. London, Cape, 1931; New York, Harcourt Brace, 1932.

Social Substance of Religion: An Essay on the Evolution of Religion. London, Allen and Unwin, and New York, Harcourt Brace, 1931.

This Surprising World: A Journalist Looks At Science. London, Cobden Sanderson, 1932.

Those Hurrying Years: An Historical Outline 1900-1933. London, Chatto and Windus, and New York, Oxford University Press, 1934.

Science in the Making. London, Faber, 1935.

The Source of Civilisation. London, Cape, 1935; New York, Harper, 1937.

The Significance of the New Pacifism, with *Pacifism and Philosophy,* by Aldous Huxley. London, Headley, 1935.

Exploring the Stratosphere. London, Nelson, 1936.

Science Front 1936. London, Cassell, 1937.

The Third Morality. London, Cassell, and New York, Morrow, 1937.

Pain, Sex and Time: A New Hypothesis of Evolution. New York, Harper, and London, Cassell, 1939.

The Creed of Christ: An Interpretation of the Lord's Prayer. New York, Harper, 1940; London, Cassell, 1941.

A Quaker Meditation. Wallingford, Pennsylvania, Pendle Hill, 1940(?).

The Code of Christ: An Interpretation of the Beatitudes. New York, Harper, 1941; London, Cassell, 1943.

Training for the Life of the Spirit. London, Cassell, 2 vols., 1941-44; New York, Harper, 1 vol., n. d.

Man the Master. New York, Harper, 1941; London, Faber, 1942.

A Dialogue in the Desert. London, Cassell, and New York, Harper, 1942.

A Preface to Prayer. New York, Harper, 1944; London, Cassell, 1945.

The Recollection. Stanford, California, Delkin, 1944.

The Gospel According to Gamaliel. New York, Harper, 1945; London, Cassell, 1946.

Militarism's Post-Mortem. London, P.P.U., 1946.

The Eternal Gospel. New York, Harper, 1946; London, Cassell, 1948.

Is God Evident? An Essay Toward a Natural Theology. New York, Harper, 1948; London, Faber, 1950.

Is God in History? An Inquiry into Human and Pre-Human History in Terms of the Doctrine of Creation, Fall, and Redemption. New York, Harper, 1950; London, Faber, 1951.

Morals since 1900. London, Dakers, and New York, Harper, 1950.

The Riddle of the Flying Saucers. London, Carroll and Nicholson, 1950; as *Is Another World Watching?.* New York, Harper, 1951; revised edition, New York, Bantam, 1953.

Ten Questions on Prayer. Wallingford, Pennsylvania, Pendle Hill, 1951.

The Human Venture. New York, Harper, 1955.

Kingdom Without God: Road's End for the Social Gospel, with others. Los Angeles, Foundation for Social Research, 1956.

Training for a Life of Growth. Santa Monica, California, Wayfarer Press, 1959.

The Five Ages of Man: The Psychology of Human History. New York, Julian Press, 1964.

Editor, *Prayers and Meditations.* New York, Harper, 1949.

*   *   *

Doppelgangers, the novel by H.F. Heard best known to science fiction readers, depicts a hedonistic dictatorship based on behavior control. The hero, nameless except as "the remodeled man" or Alpha II, belongs to an underground organization ruled by the Mole, who also uses behavior control to sabotage the dictatorship. In the novel, the hero is "remodeled" physically to duplicate the dictator Alpha, who needs a double to impersonate him and absorb the psychic impact of his charismatic appearances. When Alpha commits suicide, Alpha II is left as dictator. An assassination attempt by a follower of the Mole leads to a series of discoveries about the true government of the world, which remains in the hands of spiritually evolved people called elevates.

The novel explores Heard's ideas about the human condition. The nature of Alpha's dictatorship is despotism through indulgence, suave reduction of the human soul to childishness by supplying the masses with entertainment and pleasures. "Animectomy," or cutting away of the soul, prefigures B.F. Skinner's *Walden II.* As a dystopian novel, *Doppelgangers* can also be compared to Orwell's *Nineteen Eighty-Four* or Huxley's *Brave New World.* But Heard also explores evolution, especially as a self-directed project with Hegelian overtones, since he sees human history as a continuing aspiration toward something higher, with Alpha's dictatorship only one step on the ladder. Heard is also interested in the relationship of the soul to its manifestations. Clothes reflect customs: a man's appearance determines and is determined by his ideas; etymology reveals truths of history. Indeed, one of Heard's first books was a history and philosophy of costume, *Narcissus: An Anatomy of Clothes,* and his style and ideas are influenced by the "Clothes Philosophy" of Carlyle's *Sartor Resartus.* The dictatorship in *Doppelgangers* is also based on Sheldon's somatypes which posit a relationship between body type and personality. *Doppelgangers* is a philosophical novel; though the psychological exploration of the few major characters is deep, this is not a psychological novel. The style is involuted with tricky puns and allusions.

The Black Fox is an occultist novel with speculative content. Throcton, a British cleric envious of advancement, uses black magic to destroy his enemy. When the magic recoils, he is saved only by the self-sacrifice of his sister. Heard bases the black magic, involving etymology of the word *alopecia* from fox mange, on Biblical, Sufist, and folklore learning, speculating on the relation of mind and body. Treatment of black magic as an explainable phenomenon prefigures the thinking of such contemporaries as Colin Wilson. Psychological analysis is strong in this novel, and the isolated, highly cerebral Throctons, brother and sister, are eccentric but complexly interesting. Except for his detective fiction, *The Black Fox* represents the best use of suspense in Heard's fiction.

Gabriel and the Creatures is a speculative fantasy based on the premise that a species has the will to evolve in a certain direction, and that God, through the angel Gabriel, will grant each species its wish. *The Gospel According to Gamaliel,* a retelling of the New Testament by a Hebrew ecclesiast, teacher of St. Paul, is speculative in its attempt to reconcile differing theological viewpoints.

Heard's short stories are mostly collected in *The Great Fog and Other Weird Tales* and *The Lost Cavern and Other Tales of the Fantastic.* They speculate upon some of Heard's favorite concerns: evolution in "The Thaw Plan," "The Lost Cavern," "Wingless Victory," and "The Great Fog"; medical knowledge in "The Rousing of Mr. Bradegar" and "The Crayfish"; architecture in "Dromenon"; and telepathic exchange in "The Swap." "The Cat 'I Am'" may be seen as an early study for *The Black Fox.* Heard's heroes are isolated, scholarly types.

Heard's major output is not in fiction but in religious philosophy; he has also written detective fiction and a work on flying saucers. Except for reviews and an occasional mention in critical works, Heard has received little critical attention. His strength is in speculation rather than character or plot. Nonetheless, *Doppelgangers* is a significant dystopian novel which merits a place in the science fiction canon.

—Mary T. Brizzi

HEINLEIN, Robert A(nson)

Nationality: American. **Born:** Butler, Missouri, 7 July 1907. **Education:** University of Missouri, Columbia, 1924-25; United States Naval Academy, Annapolis, Maryland, B.S. 1929; University of California, Los Angeles, 1934-35. **Military Service:** Served in the United States Navy, 1929 until retirement because of physical disability, 1934. **Family:** Married 1) Leslyn McDonald (divorced); 2) Virginia Gerstenfeld in 1948. **Career:** Owned a silver mine, Silver Plume, Colorado, 1934-35; worked in mining and real estate, 1936-39; civilian engineer, Philadelphia Navy Yard, 1942-45. Forrestal Lecturer, United States Naval Academy, 1973. Recipient: Hugo award 1956, 1960, 1962, 1967; Boys' Clubs of America award, 1959; Grand Master Nebula award, 1974; *Locus* award, 1985. Guest of Honor, World Science Fiction Convention, 1941, 1961, 1976. L.H.D.: Eastern Michigan University, Ypsilanti, 1977. **Died:** 8 May 1988.

SCIENCE FICTION PUBLICATIONS

Novels (series: Future History; Luna)

Rocket Ship Galileo (for children). New York, Scribner, 1947; London, New English Library, 1971.
Space Cadet (for children). New York, Scribner, 1948; London, Gollancz, 1966.
Beyond This Horizon. Reading, Pennsylvania, Fantasy Press, 1948; London, Panther, 1967.
Sixth Column: A Science Fiction Novel of a Strange Intrigue. New York, Gnome Press, 1949; as *The Day after Tomorrow,* New York, Signet, 1951; London, Mayflower, 1962.
Red Planet: A Colonial Boy on Mars (for children). New York, Scribner, 1949; London, Gollancz, 1963; expanded edition, New York, Ballantine, 1990.

Farmer in the Sky (for children). New York, Scribner, 1950; London, Gollancz, 1962.
Waldo, and Magic Inc. Garden City, New York, Doubleday, 1950; as *Waldo, Genius in Orbit,* New York, Avon, 1958.
The Puppet Masters. Garden City, New York, Doubleday, 1951; London, Museum Press, 1953; expanded edition, New York, Ballantine, 1990; adapted for children by David Fickling, Oxford, Oxford University Press, 1979.
Between Planets (for children). New York, Scribner, 1951; London, Gollancz, 1968.
The Rolling Stones (for children). New York, Scribner, 1952; as *Space Family Stone,* London, Gollancz, 1969; adapted for children by Rosemary Border, Cambridge, Cambridge University Press, 1978.
Starman Jones (for children). New York, Scribner, 1953; London, Sidgwick and Jackson, 1954.
The Star Beast (for children). New York, Scribner, 1954; London, New English Library, 1971.
Tunnel in the Sky (for children). New York, Scribner, 1955; London, Gollancz, 1965.
Time for the Stars (for children). New York, Scribner, 1956; London, Gollancz, 1963.
Double Star. Garden City, New York, Doubleday, 1956; London, Joseph, 1958.
The Door into Summer. Garden City, New York, Doubleday, 1957; London, Panther, 1960.
Citizen of the Galaxy (for children). New York, Scribner, 1957; London, Gollancz, 1969.
Have Space Suit—Will Travel (for children). New York, Scribner, 1958; London, Gollancz, 1970.
Methuselah's Children (Future History). Hicksville, New York, Gnome Press, 1958; London, Gollancz, 1963.
Robert Heinlein Omnibus (includes *The Man Who Sold the Moon* and *The Green Hills of Earth*). London, Science Fiction Book Club, 1958.
Starship Troopers (for children). New York, Putnam, 1959; London, New English Library, 1961.
Stranger in a Strange Land. New York, Putnam, 1961; London, New English Library, 1965; expanded, New York, Putnam, 1990.
Podkayne of Mars: Her Life and Times (for children). New York, Putnam, 1963; London, New English Library, 1969.
Glory Road. New York, Putnam, 1963; London, New English Library, 1965.
Farnham's Freehold: A Novel. New York, Putnam, 1964; London, Dobson, 1965.
Three by Heinlein (includes *The Puppet Masters, Waldo, Magic Inc.*). Garden City, New York, Doubleday, 1965; as *A Heinlein Triad.* London, Gollancz, 1966.
The Robert Heinlein Omnibus (includes *Beyond This Horizon, The Man Who Sold the Moon,* and *The Green Hills of Earth*). London, Sidgwick and Jackson, 1966.
The Moon Is a Harsh Mistress (Luna). New York, Putnam, 1966; London, Dobson, 1967.
I Will Fear No Evil. New York, Putnam, 1970; London, New English Library, 1972.
Time Enough for Love: The Lives of Lazarus Long: A Novel (Future History). New York, Putnam, 1973; London, New English Library, 1974.
The Number of the Beast. New York, Fawcett, and London, New English Library, 1980.

A Heinlein Trio: The Puppet Master; Double Star; The Door into Space. Garden City, New York, Doubleday, 1980.

Friday. New York, Holt Rinehart, and London, New English Library, 1982.

Job: A Comedy of Justice. New York, Ballantine, and London, New English Library, 1984.

The Cat Who Walks through Walls: A Comedy of Manners (Luna). New York, Putnam, 1985; London, New English Library, 1986.

To Sail beyond the Sunset: The Life and Loves of Maureen Johnson (Being the Memoirs of a Somewhat Irregular Lady) (Future History). New York, Putnam, and London, Joseph, 1987.

Short Stories (series: Future History)

The Man Who Sold the Moon. Sidney, American Science Fiction, 1952.

The Man Who Sold the Moon: Harriman and the Escape from Earth to the Moon! (Future History). Chicago, Shasta, 1950; London, Sidgwick and Jackson, 1953.

Universe (Future History). New York, Dell, 1951.

The Green Hills of Earth: Rhysling and the Adventure of the Entire Solar System! (Future History). Chicago, Shasta, 1951; London, Sidgwick and Jackson, 1954.

Revolt in 2100: The Prophets and the Triumph of Reason over Superstition! (Future History). Chicago, Shasta, 1953; London, Digit, 1959.

Assignment in Eternity: Four Long Science Fiction Stories. Reading, Pennsylvania, Fantasy Press, 1953; London, Museum Press, 1955; abridged edition, as *Lost Legacy,* London, Digit, 1960.

The Menace from Earth. Hicksville, New York, Gnome Press, 1959; London, Dobson, 1966.

The Unpleasant Profession of Jonathan Hoag. Hicksville, New York, Gnome Press, 1959; London, Dobson 1964; as *6 x H: Six Stories,* New York, Pyramid, 1961.

Orphans of the Sky (Future History; includes *Universe*). London, Gollancz, 1963; New York, Putnam, 1964.

The Worlds of Robert A. Heinlein. New York, Ace, 1966; London, New English Library, 1970.

The Past through Tomorrow: "Future History" Stories. New York, Putnam, 1967; abridged edition, London, New English Library, 2 vols., 1977.

The Best of Robert Heinlein, edited by Angus Wells. London, Sidgwick and Jackson, 1973.

Destination Moon, edited by David G. Hartwell. Boston, Gregg Press, 1979.

Expanded Universe: The New Worlds of Robert A. Heinlein. New York, Grosset and Dunlap, 1980.

Requiem: New Collected Works by Robert A. Heinlein and Tributes to the Great Master, edited by Yoji Kondo. New York, Tor, 1992.

OTHER PUBLICATIONS

Plays

Screenplays: *Destination Moon,* with Rip Van Ronkel and James O'Hanlon, 1950; *Project Moonbase,* with Jack Seaman, 1953.

Other

The Discovery of the Future . . . : Speech Delivered by Guest of Honor at 3rd World Science Fiction Convention. Los Angeles, Novacious, 1941.

"On the Writing of Speculative Fiction," in *Of Worlds Beyond: The Science of Science-Fiction Writing,* edited by Lloyd Arthur Eshbach. Reading, Pennsylvania, Fantasy Press, 1947; London, Dobson, 1965.

"Why I selected 'The Green Hills of Earth,'" in *My Best Science Fiction Story,* edited by Leo Margulies and O.J. Friend. New York, Merlin Press, 1949.

"Ray Guns and Rocket Ships," in *Library Journal* (New York), July 1953.

"Science Fiction: Its Nature, Faults, and Virtues," in *The Science Fiction Novel,* edited by Basil Davenport. Chicago, Advent, 1959.

"Heinlein on Science Fiction," in *Vertex* (Los Angeles), April 1973.

The Notebooks of Lazarus Long. New York, Putnam, 1978.

Grumbles from the Grave, edited by Virginia Heinlein. New York, Ballantine, 1989; London, Orbit, 1991.

Tramp Royale. New York, Ace, 1992.

Take Back Your Government: A Practical Handbook for the Private Citizen Who Wants Democracy to Work. Riverdale, New York, Baen, 1992.

Editor, *Tomorrow, The Stars: A Science Fiction Anthology.* Garden City, New York, Doubleday, 1952.

*

Bibliography: *Robert A. Heinlein: A Bibliography* by Mark Owings, Baltimore, Croatan House, 1973.

Manuscript Collection: University of California Library, Santa Cruz.

Critical Studies: *Seekers of Tomorrow* by Sam Moskowitz, Cleveland, World, 1966; *Heinlein in Dimension: A Critical Analysis* (includes bibliography) by Alexei Panshin, Chicago, Advent, 1968; *Robert A. Heinlein, Stranger in His Own Land,* San Bernardino, California, Borgo Press, 1976, and *The Classic Years of Robert A. Heinlein,* Borgo Press, 1977, both by George Edgar Slusser; *Robert A. Heinlein* edited by Martin H. Greenberg and Joseph D. Olander, New York, Taplinger, and Edinburgh, Harris, 1978; *Robert A. Heinlein: America as Science Fiction* by H. Bruce Franklin, New York, Oxford University Press, 1980, London, Oxford University Press, 1981.

*   *   *

Robert A. Heinlein's near-50-year career as a writer is much too complex to cover entirely in any survey article. The growth of that career, in fact, is coterminous with the development of mass-market publishing in the U.S. Already in his early 30s, Heinlein published his first story, "Lifeline," in Campbell's *Astounding Science Fiction.* He proceeded, over several years of intense activity, to produce stories and novellas, which he sought to draw together in the broader framework of a "future history." After World War II, he returned to SF, but now works primarily in the medium of the "juvenile novel": compact narratives, in hardback format, recounting the coming of age of young inventors, starmen, and astronauts. Heinlein entered the age of the mass-market paperback with *Starship Troopers* (1959), and publication throughout the 1960s and early 1970s with fatter and fatter novels, from *Stranger in a Strange Land* (1961) to *Time Enough for Love* (1973). In his final stage, Heinlein exploited the riches of design and feel of the modern hardback bestseller, in works from *Number of the Beast* (1980) through *To Sail Beyond the Sunset* (1987), the last of his published novels. Heinlein has worked in every format and form, from short narrative to massive didactic tract. In doing so, he has literally shaped the course of American SF.

Heinlein is much more, however. First, he is a significant *American* writer. Indeed, if we accept the idea that American SF—with its fascination with individuals who found societies, create institutions, and push back the frontiers of nature—is the natural continuation of a tradition that reaches back to Emerson, Melville, and Twain, then Heinlein's preoccupations place him solidly in our literary mainstream. Second, Heinlein is a significant *modern* writer. He has produced some of the finest, and boldly experimental, short fiction of this century. And his massive late novels, generally dismissed by critics as self-indulgent ramblings, are in fact astonishing examples of "metafiction." Heinlein was surely not privy to French "new novels" or literary theory. Yet just as Looney Toons did not wait for Roland Barthes to create a "mise en abime" narrative, so Heinlein, in a work like *Number of the Beast,* invented out of the stuff of his own created world (and the SF genre itself) a fascinating piece of self-reflexivity.

In terms of thematics however, Heinlein's work, from beginning to end, displays a singular consistency and purpose. Across the wide expanse of stories and novels, many topics are debated—military organizations, political and legal systems, modalities of sex and genetic distribution—but always within the framework of one, single, obsessive theme: that of personal time. From the first story, "Lifeline," the question has been: "How much time do I [the protagonist] have under the old dispensation (Providence or Fatality)?" How much time can I gain for myself under a new dispensation, which is Heinlein's curious combination of skill, luck ("serendipity"), and grace? The title of Heinlein's final novel is taken from Tennyson's poem "Ulysses": "To sail beyond the sunset, and the baths/Of all the western stars, until I die." Death is accepted in Heinlein as in Tennyson (the latter, in "Tithonus," presents eternal life without the possibility of physical activity as a horror). The key word however is "until." Just as Odysseus was promised life *extension* as long as he sticks to his native habitat, the sea, so Heinlein's heroes, who all eventually conflate into the archetypal Lazarus Long, can hope to expand the spacetime parameters of their individual life lines only as long as they restrict their quest to the physical (and ultimately genetic) limits of their own bodies. They know the point of origin, it is their material birth; husbanding this, they can forestall the end indefinitely if not forever. Heinlein's heroes derive their energy from the fact that they live, not under the curse of immortality, but in a state of endless reprieve.

Let us trace this dynamic pattern throughout Heinlein's work. Examples will be selective, yet representative, and will reveal the persistence of vision through changing formats. To readers of pulp SF, even early Campbellian stories that, despite their "problem-solving" focus, still retain their dose of action, the first story under a Heinlein byline, "Life-Line" (*ASF,* August 1939) must have been puzzling. The story has no hero in the conventional sense—Hugo Pinero, the maverick scientist who invents a machine to measure the length of human life spans, is middle-aged, pot-bellied, has dubious scientific credentials, and does more talking than acting. Nor does it pose, and solve a problem in the strict sense. It is, on one hand, a display vehicle for a particular *type* of character: the individualist who works outside and against the establishment. His invention is not sanctioned or financed by the scientific world. Moreover, it upsets deep-rooted economic and moral systems: the insur-

ance industry cannot survive a machine that predicts each client's moment of death; nor can human will live with such knowledge. The story pits Pinero against system in key Heinlein situations: in the courtroom, and in the business boardroom. His only act of heroism, but one that sets him apart from all others, is to know his moment of death, and go through with it. For others, life is livable only in uncertainty. Pinero, by having no illusions, affirms material pre-destiny, and at the same time shows mankind the only way to proceed: know, and while waiting, in the meantime, act "Life-Line" looks forward, in one sense, to what is the prime obsession of the late Heinlein heroes: to stretch the spacetime within the limits of the individual material life-line, so that this individual world (or body) becomes literally co-extensive with the larger universe. The early stories color this nascent tendency to material solipsism with various tones. On one extreme, we see the striving in a positive light. In "Gulf" (1949), Kettle Belly Baldwin develops "speedtalk," which gives him an "association time" three times faster than normal men. The result: "an *effective* life time of at least *sixteen* hundred years, reckoned in flow of ideas." This compression of life force bestows power in the active world. Bob Wilson's loops around a point in the time line however, in "By His Bootstraps" (Anson MacDonald, 1941), entrap him in a powerless nightmare. Like Pinero's life-line, Bob's "time gate," opening to suspend his existence in a series of futile time curves around one instant in his line, is a mark of physical predestination. Within this hellish "perpetual motion fur farm," Bob's *only* course is to find a future in this futureless state, and declare it to be "great."

In other early stories and novellas, however, Heinlein shifts the focus of this problem away from metaphysical to more practical situations, and the reprieve offered the Heinlein hero is played out in the political or social sphere. In "They" (1941), the hero, who in his increasing alienation from the world is condemned as paranoid ("they" are all against him), refuses these limits, now social in nature. He asserts, in turn, that they are all, in a literal physical sense, against him. Through this assertion, he opens his own gate into elsewhere, poking a hole through what is a veil of illusion *real* aliens have placed around our comfortable lives. This hero passes through the final solipsistic temptation of suicide. Rejecting this, he reaches out, as *active* rebel, toward what invariably occurs in Heinlein: a waiting circle of equally staunch individualists, men (and occasionally women) who are capable of defeating illusions, of facing their destiny head-on. We find similar breakthrough, but in a fleshed-out social and political context, in a story like "Coventry" (1940). This story, sequel to "If This Goes On," offers a vision, in terms of social revolution, of "plus ca change, plus c'est la meme chose." The old religious dictatorship is gone, but the "covenant," in the form of a social contract oppressive to the individual, abides. Dave MacKinnon is declared antisocial in terms of this contract, and literally sent to Coventry, where he hopes to find a viable social alternative in anarchy. What he finds is lawlessness and war—human nature in its general reprobate state. If such mankind needs laws, Heinlein rejects both heaven and hell, covenant and coventry, for the sake of an inner guidance. Via this "intuition," Dave discovers kindred spirits, who help to lead him out of personal and physical anarchy Through their guidance, he is in fact reborn, emerging from drowning in the river that confines this hell, into the arms of members of a secret society. This however is no resurrection, only reprieve, for the work of gaining control over regenerate masses remains to be done, if it ever can.

Likewise, breakthrough and reprieve are the themes of the novella cluster "Universe" and "Common Sense." "Universe" sets the stage on a generation starship that, on its way to Proxima Centauri, is seized by mutineers and goes astray. The ship literally becomes a closed universe for humans who revert from scientific enlightenment to a state of superstitious "geocentrism." The story is that of Hugh Hoyland, a new Galileo, who imputes that this orb is not the center of things, but moves around other bodies. To affirm this, he must "climb" to the forbidden outer layers, break through the darkness and gaze hopefully on new worlds. This Hugh does with the help of the two-headed "mutie" (mutant and mutinous to canonical authority) Joe-Jim. But just seeing the stars is not enough for Hugh; unlike the "philosopher" Joe-Jim, he wants to go there. "Common Sense," as sequel, is the story of who gets to found a new world, and why they get to go. Jim's two heads may be better than one, but they war with each other. This physical incarnation of mankind's divided psyche is also a *mutant,* a physical emblem of the sin of knowledge whereby mankind originally fell. Mankind can survive only by having and using one head—singleness of purpose and common sense. This term is tricky. For where Heinlein rejects angels and devils in favor of the common man, in his sense "commonality" is but a way of keeping the paths of grace (or the gene pools) open so that the "uncommon common man," the Hugh Hoyland ("high land?") will emerge. Heinlein's later work is rife with such everymen supermen—for example Johann Sebastian Bach Smith in *I Will Fear No Evil* (1970). Here, in this necessary sequel to "Universe," on the outer circles of this geocentric hell, tighter and tighter circles of Heinlein's elect are formed. The logic of human survival is stark and clear: for Hugh and his band to leave the ship and found a new world, all must be genetically viable; Joe-Jim and the muties must stay behind. Like a good pagan bound to the first circle of hell, Joe-Jim sacrifices himself in order to give Hugh, and humanity, a reprieve. For though, in their new world, there will be "always good eating," eating implies the necessity of work, and of death; "I too am in Arcadia."

One could argue that all of Heinlein, all of his themes and obsessions, are fully developed in these early stories and novella. The magic years, in fact, are 1939-42. Yet from the late 1940s through the 1950s Heinlein, turning to the medium of the short novel (the paperback era had begun, but the model lengthwise for these narratives is the Scribner juvenile—c. 250 pages), produced some superb fiction. If in many of his stories, the traditional aspects of fiction, such as action and character development, were atrophied for the sake of developing a problem or an idea, these novels of the 1950s represent, for Heinlein, a skillful balance between the narrative and the didactic. Indicative of a change of focus is the fact that many of these novels, serialized in magazines before publication as novels, were serialized, not in *Asimov's Science Fiction,* but in *Galaxy* and *Fantasy and Science Fiction.* Let us look briefly at two novels from this period: one closer through its "adult" hero to novellas like "Coventry"—*The Puppet Masters* (1951—serialized in Galaxy), the other featuring a young adolescent protagonist we did not see in the early stories—*Have Space Suit—Will Travel* (1958—serialized in *F&SF*). *The Puppet Masters* externalizes the possessor aliens of "They" into vampiric "slugs," who now possess not only minds but physical bodies. These they fasten onto and ride, turning their hosts into misshapen hunchbacks, literal products of a secular damnation and fall. Once again, this fall is an abdication of the individual will to a group mind or collective dogma. Once again, the manacles placed on free man in communality are mind-forged. The slugs, all interchangeable parts in a sterile group entity that can neither grow or change, lure mankind by offering freedom from striving. These parasites invade (in the early 50s an

all too complacent) America; their advance is halted by the actions of a secret group—as in "Coventry" one that again reveals its underlying structure to be paramilitary. What makes this novel rich, however, is that the military and the family structure are calqued on each other. The protagonist Sam's superior is the "Old Man," who late in the novel turns out to be just that—his biological father. Sam's *Bildung* or formation as an adult involves struggle both with the father and the boss. Yet the promise of Freudian drama, like the promise of political intrigue as Sam tracks and destroys the slugs, fails to materialize. Sam does not overthrow the father; he replaces him, in literally infusing breath into him, *becomes* him— the young spirit in a mantle of age and wisdom. Mary, the mother-lover, rather than the object of Oedipal strife, yields unbidden (in a kind of immaculate conception) the solution to all dramas. In the past she survived a Venusian fever that kills the slugs. She does not, however, remember the name of the fever. When scientists probe the inner reaches of her mind, Sam stops this rape. He tells them she must remember by herself, and lo, she does. The slugs are infected and (as they are all parts of a single organism) die en masse. The novel ends with Sam and family entering a spaceship, bound for the slug's home on Titan. A reprieve has been granted, and these humans will use the interim (again common sense where to take out the enemy before it can regroup.

Have Space Suit—Will Travel is a frankly juvenile version of this alien-testing-and-reprieve scenario. Sam and Mary become Kip and Peewee. Preadolescent Kip is running around the Midwest plains in his play spacesuit when he is snatched up by hideous aliens. He and Peewee (another captive) save an alien they call the Mother Thing from these "wormfaces," only to learn "she" is an intergalactic police agent. They are arrested and brought before an intergalactic bar of justice; mankind (like the wormfaces) is on trial as a brutal and reprobate race, and they must appear as specimens of humanity to plead for it. In early stories, like "Magic, Inc.," (1940) Heinlein relishes trial scenes; in later novels such as *Stranger in a Strange Land* (1961), he spins them out ad nauseum. Here the trial is, against expectations, powerful and moving, a high point in all Heinlein. The judges are again a group entity, pieced together of replaceable parts, repairable and thus immortal. A single man however, however vicious, is a formidable force precisely because he *cannot* be replaced, nor can any part of him. On the brink of a "guilty" verdict, Kip causes his judges to halt in dismay precisely because he is ready to throw the whole irreplaceable life he has away. The judges, in their collective wisdom, have learned they have limits, and wish to impose them on all species for the good of all. Kip blurts out that he, as an individual human being, has no limits. To prove it, he opts to return to Earth. Knowing humanity must die, he will die with them. The judges cannot fathom the paradox of Kip, who like Pascal's thinking reed is fatally limited *and yet* limitless in his potential power. The judges must ponder; meanwhile they return Kip and Peewee to Earth, back into mainstream America. Out of this flow may come men who build spaceships to go, find and destroy these judges. The beauty of this story's end is that Kip returns to the local soda fountain Heinlein's final period is variously dated. Some see it beginning with *Starship Troopers* (1959). This novel however, in format no longer than a 1950s "adult" like *Citizen of the Galaxy* (1957), or even a juvenile like *Starman Jones* (1953), is in a sense but a shriller version of *The Puppet Masters.* The didactic tone may seem particularly strident here because, usurping large sections of a medium-sized work, it foils readers' expectations of action-adventure. This "preachiness" finds a better balance in the larger fictional structure of *Stranger in a Strange Land.* A hundred pages longer in its initial version than any previous Heinlein novel (the new "uncut version" published in 1991 has 525 pages, a hundred more than the 1961 version), *Stranger* inaugurates, in my reckoning, Heinlein's last stage. The novel is, to be sure, an assemblage of narrative parts (the Jubal Harshaw material was originally intended to be a work in itself). This assemblage however—producing an omnibus work that combines a novel of political and legal intrigue with the novel of "manners," and perhaps even something like a saint's life—is an uncanny replay of 18th-century fictional forms. His narrator becomes loquacious in the manner of the *Tom Jones* narrator; the focus on the "life and times" of Michael Valentine Smith echoes that of *Jonathan Wild* or *Moll Flanders*: the proliferating structure *à tiroirs*, ennesting story within story, harkens back to *Tristram Shandy*, or vast Gothic constructs like *The Monk*. This is the form Heinlein will cultivate in his ever-more-massive novels of the 1970s—*I Will Fear No Evil* and *Time Enough for Love*. It is the form which will begin to spread from novel to novel in *The Number of the Beast* (1980). During this period Heinlein continued to write shorter novels (and win Hugo Awards for them, notably *The Moon Is a Harsh Mistress*, 1966); these however are nostalgic nods to the 1950s. It is in the vast multiplex novels—from *Stranger* down to the megafrescoes of *The Cat Who Walks Through Walls* (1986) and *To Sail Beyond the Sunset* (1987)—that Heinlein struggles to combine all his "universes" into a single cosmic comedy of manners—a veritable postmodernist *comédie humaine.*

The great synthesizing figure of Heinlein's late novels is the Howard Family patriarch, Lazarus Long. Long, who first appeared in the early serialized novella "Methuselah's Children" (1941), returns in *Time Enough for Love* at the end of a vast span of time in which the Howard seed, through his active mediation, has spread across the known universe. Galactic civilization has reached a utopian impasse, and Lazarus, with nothing left to strive for, contemplates suicide. From this initial situation (or "problem"—when we run out of world, is it *worth* living forever?), the novel unfolds as a series of narrative sections, each of which presents Lazarus exploring the possibility of having new experiences in a world circumscribed by his own body and gene pool, in other words a world where everybody and thing partakes of him and him alone. This is Heinlein's old and persistent theme of solipsism writ as large as the physical universe. Among Heinlein's pre-*Stranger* work, solipsism proved the sole confining structure his protagonists could not break out of. In the poignant (and even un-Heinleinian) ending of "All You Zombies!" (1959), the time-traveling narrator, all powerful within his curved spacetime, finds himself, in a reflective moment, suddenly aware that all this is meaningless void—there is no one "out there," and he is all alone in the dark. Lazarus, though bounded by the same personal space, is convinced by his "family" to carry on. His quest is for ever newer and more astounding experiences within a spatiotemporal continuum bounded by his sole self. He causes Minerva the computer to fall in love with him, and she steps down from machine immortality to perishable (if still long-lived) flesh. He clones two "daughters," has them raised by a foster mother, takes them as lovers, and finally inseminates them artificially with his seed, which they bring to term. The ultimate gambit, however, is his time-traveling return to his own Missouri childhood, where (protected from the grandfather paradox by the presence of his "then" self as child—he cannot sire himself if he is already present) he fulfills his Oedipal fantasies by taking his mother as lover. Lazarus however, the Cronos who lives by devouring his progeny, discovers here the one woman he cannot sire upon. For-

bidden neither by incest taboo nor by genetic fear, but by time and its paradoxes, Lazarus's first cause remains inviolate. The solipsist can perpetuate what is already created: he cannot create himself.

In the final pages of *TEL,* Lazarus asks to see God, and is told to look in a mirror. In *Number of the Beast,* however, it is no longer a character who is god in his creation, but the author himself. This novel pairs two figures whose origin is Edgar Rice Burroughs's Mars novels—Dejah Thoris (D.T.) Burroughs and Zeb J. (for John) Carter-with Heinlein prototypes Jake and Hilda, and takes them across the plenum on a time machine that, operating on the principle of "pantheistic multiperson solipsism," conflates all creation into a number of instantaneously accessible universes neatly resumed by the "number of the beast," 6 to the 6th power. The apocalypse or revelation however, in this novel, is that of an ever vaster solipsism. Persons and universes whirl by, "multitudes" beyond count. Yet, in the blurring, all becomes one. Differences fall, even the final one between fiction and reality. A character like D.T. Burroughs steps back and forth between these realms, and the reader finds himself in the presence of a very postmodern "text" in the process of writing its own "reality." Finally, as this odyssey in and out of fiction ends, we realize that the fiction is Heinlein's fiction. The bestial powers of science and universe collapse back upon a center finally revealed to be a great "world" con, a science *fiction* masquerade, where real authors and fictional characters, including Heinlein, pass arm in arm, led by none other than "author" Jubal Harshaw. Author, character and all known universes become coextensive, solipsism without end.

Midway in *Number,* D.T.'s world intersects with that of Lazarus and *TEL.* There is a new round of sexual mixing, but to the reader the thrill is gone. "Multiple-ego solipsism" promises giant transreality masturbation. The damper on this boy's game in this novel is a growing presence of the female. Heinlein consciously projects D.T. and Hilda "Sharp" Corners as proto-"feminists." In the late, late Heinlein, the prophetic ending of "All You Zombies!" comes to pass: the world-conquering patriarch sits in the dark alone, and calls for his lost Jane. Lazarus, in *TEL,* could neither control nor fathom Mother Maureen. She re-emerges in the Lazarus "circle" in *The Cat Who Walks Through Walls,* and dominates the author's last novel. *To Sail Beyond the Sunset* is presented as the "autobiography" of Maureen Johnson. And we see here, finally from *her point of view,* the female presence that literally enfolds—as mother, lover, daughter—the patriarch's solipsistic life. She is irreducible first cause, the source of energy that Lazarus, like Antaeus, must touch in order to rise from death at Verdun in *TEL.* Only *in extremis* does Heinlein's world—a man's world of endless expansion, obsessed with pushing out the end—come to terms with its origins. Heinlein, in these last novels, has become a writer, less of fiction, than of myth.

—George Slusser

HENDERSON, Zenna

Nationality: American. **Born:** Zenna Chlarson, Tucson, Arizona, 1 November 1917. **Education:** Arizona State College, now University, B.A. 1940, M.A. 1955. **Family:** Married in 1944 (divorced). **Career:** After 1940, elementary school teacher in Arizona: also taught at the Japanese Relocation Camp, Sacaton, Arizona, during

World War II, Laon sur Marne, Aisne, France, 1956-58, and Seaside Children's Hospital, Waterford, Connecticut, 1958-59. **Died:** 11 May 1983.

SCIENCE FICTION PUBLICATIONS

Short Stories (series: People)

Pilgrimage: The Book of the People. Garden City, New York, Doubleday, 1961; London, Gollancz, 1962.
The Anything Box. Garden City, New York, Doubleday, 1965; London, Gollancz, 1966.
The People: No Different Flesh. Garden City, New York, Doubleday, and London, Gollancz, 1966.
Holding Wonder. Garden City, New York, Doubleday, 1971; London, Gollancz, 1972.
The People Collection. London, Corgi, 1991.

*

Zenna Henderson commented:

(1981) When I was about 12 I began reading science fiction—Jules Verne, Haggard, and Edgar Rice Burroughs, and all the current magazines I could get hold of, but it wasn't until I had graduated from college that I began writing fantasy and science fiction. I have only a sketchy scientific background, so of necessity I write from a nontechnical viewpoint. My favorite SF authors, when I was still reading it, were Heinlein, Bradbury, Clement, and Asimov. Mottos I try to observe when I write: stories consist of unusual people in ordinary circumstances or ordinary people in unusual circumstances; write about what you know; don't let your subtleties become obscurities.

*   *   *

"Write what you know" is the cornerstone of Zenna Henderson's science fiction career. She constructed story after story out of experiences accumulated during her many years in the elementary classroom. She found teachers useful viewpoint characters because their vision is multiplied through their students' eyes. Her fictional children have the appealing naturalness that comes of being modeled directly from life.

Henderson made more and better use of adult-child interactions than adult-adult ones, but she always kept human relationships paramount. She ignored man's struggles against the universe because she did not perceive the cosmos as hostile. By rejecting sex, sadism, and violence, her stories offer a gentle alternative to macho entertainments. Yet feminist critics scorn Henderson for occupational stereotyping without acknowledging that she depicts single women, older women, and female friendships positively. Wonder in familiar settings is Henderson's forte. She reveals the world a child or a saint might see—a place where time can shift and dimensions fold, where mountains walk and wishes come true. Friction between the mundane and the marvelous generates her dramas. For example, a small boy battles a demon ("Stevie and the Dark") or school routine survives the collapse of civilization ("As Simple as That").

Henderson's most popular stories are those collected in *Pilgrimage: The Book of the People* and *The People: No Different Flesh.* Each volume's components are united by a frame-story, a device

that succeeds better in *Pilgrimage* because it is a poignant tale in its own right. The frame of *The People* is simply an excuse for flashbacks to events preceding and following those in *Pilgrimage.* The People are extraterrestrial refugees with psychic gifts who have been hiding in the American southwest since the 1890s. They are gradually overcoming memories of persecution and forming partnerships with humans. Their perilous flight from their lost Home to Earth, their true Promised Land, parallels the Old Testament Exodus—a comparison underscored by Biblical names and titles. (Basic Christian values undergird all of Henderson's writing.) Although the People had a different salvation history, their beliefs are compatible with Christianity. They even use a trinitarian invocation of God as the Power, the Presence, and the Name. Their bonding through love is Henderson's answer to the conflicts between community and individuality that run through so much of her fiction.

Secret aliens among us is an old SF notion, but no one has put it to happier use than Henderson. The sheer wholesomeness of her People is enough to set them apart. "They're us only more so," says the author. Whether reading thoughts, operating spacecraft, or hemming dresses, the People wield their powers with a cheerful reverence that is refreshingly matter-of-fact. Henderson is neither antitechnological nor pro-occultist like Andre Norton. Miracles in a grittily realistic setting strike just the right note of aesthetic contrast to make the stories work.

Henderson's paradigm of sympathetic adult aiding troubled wonder-child is as distinctive as her signature. Yet it is a conscious pattern to be varied at will. "Something Bright" reverses the usual roles to disguised alien adult and helpful human child. Not all teachers are caring ("The Last Step") or effective ("You Know What, Teacher?"). Not all marvels are desirable ("The Substitute," "Turn the Page," "Sharing Time"). Children's wonderful powers can cause tragedy ("The Believing Child," "Come On, Wagon!," "Hush"). In such works Henderson displays an excellent although curiously unappreciated touch for horror. She can handle insanity as vividly as psi ("Swept and Garnished," "One of Them").

At her worst, Henderson's sentimentality overflows. Occasionally her ideas are too weak. Her range of subject matter is admittedly small. But overall, she worked with sound, unobtrusive craftsmanship. She had the classic short story writer's talents for precise focus, good characterization, and shrewd deployment of details. A kindly, traditional sensibility animates her writing. This description of ultimate happiness from "The Anything Box" conveys her special flavor: "all the worry and waiting, the apartness and loneliness were over and forgotten, their hugeness dwindled by the comfort of a shoulder, the warmth of clasping hands—and nowhere, nowhere was the fear of parting. . . ." Henderson was SF's mistress of the happy ending.

—Sandra Miesel

HENSLEY, Joe L(ouis)

Nationality: American. **Born:** Joseph Louis Hensley, Bloomington, Indiana. 19 March 1926. **Education:** Indiana University, Bloomington, B.A. 1950, LL. B. 1955: called to the Indiana Bar, 1955. **Military Service:** Served as a hospital corpsman in the United States Navy, 1944-46; recalled as journalist, 1951-52. **Family:** Married Charlotte Ruth Bettinger in 1950; one son. **Career:** Partner,

Metford and Hensley, 1955-72, and Hensley Todd and Castor, 1972-75, Madison, Indiana; Judge Pro-Tempore, 80th Judicial Circuit, Versailles, Indiana, 1975-76; Judge, 5th Judicial Circuit, Madison, 1977-88. Member, Indiana General Assembly, 1961-62; Prosecuting Attorney, 5th Judicial Indiana Circuit, 1963-66. President, Indiana Judges Association, 1983-84. Since 1989, partner, Hensley Walro Collins and Hensley, Madison, Indiana. **Agent:** Virginia Kidd, Box 278, Milford, Pennsylvania 18337, U.S.A. **Address:** 2315 Blackmore, Madison, Indiana 47250, U.S.A.

SCIENCE FICTION PUBLICATIONS

Novel

The Black Roads. Toronto, Laser, 1976.

OTHER PUBLICATIONS

Novels

The Color of Hate. New York, Ace, 1960; as *Color Him Guilty,* New York, Walker, 1987.
Deliver Us to Evil. Garden City, New York, Doubleday, 1971.
Legislative Body. Garden City, New York, Doubleday, 1972.
The Poison Summer. Garden City, New York, Doubleday, 1974.
Song of Corpus Juris. Garden City, New York, Doubleday, 1974.
Rivertown Risk. Garden City, New York, Doubleday, 1977.
A Killing in Gold. Garden City, New York, Doubleday, 1978; London, Gollancz, 1979.
Minor Murders. Garden City, New York, Doubleday, 1979.
Outcasts. Garden City, New York, Doubleday, 1981.
Robak's Cross. Garden City, New York, Doubleday, 1985.
Robak's Fire. Garden City, New York, Doubleday, 1986.
Fort's Law. Garden City, New York, Doubleday, 1987; London, Hale, 1991.
Robak's Run. New York, Doubleday, 1990.
Grim City. New York, St. Martin's Press, 1994.

Short Stories

Final Doors (includes essay). Garden City, New York, Doubleday, 1981.
Robak's Firm (includes essays). Garden City, New York, Doubleday, 1987.

*

Manuscript Collection: Lilly Library, Indiana University, Bloomington.

Joe L. Hensley comments:

(1985) I don't write very much science fiction. Suspense is a more familiar game to me. But I still admire those who do write science fiction and am happy, now and then, when I do also.

*   *   *

Joe L. Hensley's most important SF stories are connected with Harlan Ellison. Hensley and Ellison are great friends, and Ellison wrote 2000 words of introduction to "Lord Randy, My Son" for

Dangerous Visions. The story is a masterpiece of understated horror. Ellison's introduction to the story tells how Hensley—a lawyer—saved Ellison from being court-martialed by the U.S. Army. Ellison provides another introduction to Hensley and Ellison's collaboration "Rodney Parish for Hire." This chilling account of a youngster who kills other children for profit is a good example of the strengths of both writers. The story features strong characterization, fast-paced writing, and a suspenseful plot.

Hensley's only SF novel, *The Black Roads,* is a reworking of the setting and themes best developed by Mack Reynolds's *Rollertown* (1976). After a nuclear war, only American technology survives. A society based on roadways evolves as the ultimate realization of humans' love for their automobiles. Duels are fought between cars, and Red Roadmen ride the lanes in their supercharged autos keeping law and order. The mobile society is interesting, but Hensley never elevates his characters above the level of cardboard. The result is a staleness absent from Hensley's better short stories and the mystery novels for which he is better known.

The best of Hensley's short stories, both mystery and SF, are collected in *Final Doors.* Hensley's two collaborations with Harlan Ellison are included as well as his collaboration with SF and horror writer Gene DeWeese. The most haunting story in the collection is "Killer Scent," in which a sheriff secretly hunts down psychopathic killers that give off a "scent" only he can sense. The sheriff, when finally discovered, explains his hunting of the psychopaths this way: "Sometimes I think they're mutants, the coming race for earth. . . . Maybe they came along to wipe us out, take our places, be the survivors of the cities, mercilessly preying on each other after we're gone." "Killer Scent" works equally well as a suspense story and an SF story. It is one of the seven original short stories included in this 18-story collection.

Hensley's writing is unusually crisp, his plotting is tight, and his best work has power and insight. Much of his work—especially his Robak mystery novels—reflects his background in law and the criminal justice system.

—George Kelley

HERBERT, Frank (Patrick)

Nationality: American. **Born:** Tacoma, Washington, 8 October 1920. **Education:** Attended the University of Washington, Seattle, 1946-47. **Family:** Married Beverly Ann Stuart in 1946; one daughter and two sons. **Career:** Reporter and editor for West Coast newspapers; lecturer in general and interdisciplinary studies, University of Washington, 1970-72; social and ecological studies consultant, Lincoln Foundation and the countries of Vietnam and Pakistan, 1971. **Awards:** Nebula award, 1965; Hugo award, 1966; Prix Apollo, 1978. **Died:** 12 February 1986.

SCIENCE FICTION PUBLICATIONS

Novels (series: Dune; Jorj X. McKie; Pandora)

The Dragon in the Sea. Garden City, New York, Doubleday, 1956; London, Gollancz, 1960; as *21st Century Sub,* New York, Avon, 1956; as *Under Pressure,* New York, Ballantine, 1974.

The Great Dune Trilogy, London, Gollancz, 1979.
  Dune. Philadelphia, Chilton, 1965; London, Gollancz, 1966; as *The Illustrated Dune,* New York, Berkley, 1977.
  Dune Messiah. New York, Putnam, 1969; London, Gollancz, 1971.
  Children of Dune. New York, Berkley, and London, Gollancz, 1976.
Destination: Void (Pandora). New York, Berkley, 1966; London, Penguin, 1967; revised, New York, Berkley, 1978.
The Eyes of Heisenberg. New York, Berkley, 1966; London, Sphere, 1968.
The Green Brain. New York, Ace, 1966; London, New English Library, 1973.
The Santaroga Barrier. New York, Berkley, 1968; London, Rapp and Whiting, 1970.
The Heaven Makers. New York, Avon, 1968; London, New English Library, 1970.
Whipping Star (McKie). New York, Putnam, 1970; London, New English Library, 1972; revised edition, New York, Berkley, 1977.
The God Makers. New York, Putnam, and London, New English Library, 1972.
Hellstrom's Hive. Garden City, New York, Doubleday, 1973; London, New English Library, 1974.
The Dosadi Experiment (McKie). New York, Putnam, 1977; London, Gollancz, 1978.
The Jesus Incident (Pandora), with Bill Ransom. New York, Berkley, and London, Gollancz, 1979.
Direct Descent. New York, Ace, 1980; London, New English Library, 1982.
The White Plague. New York, Putnam, 1982; London, Gollancz, 1983.
The Lazarus Effect (Pandora), with Bill Ransom. New York, Putnam, and London, Gollancz, 1983.
Man of Two Worlds, with Brian Herbert. New York, Putnam, and London, Gollancz, 1986.
The Second Great Dune Trilogy. London, Gollancz, 1987.
  God Emperor of Dune. New York, Putnam, and London, Gollancz, 1981.
  Heretics of Dune. New York, Putnam, and London, Gollancz, 1984.
  Chapter House: Dune. London, Gollancz, 1985; as *Chapterhouse: Dune,* New York, Putnam, 1985.
The Ascension Factor (Pandora), with Bill Ransom. New York, Putnam, and London, Gollancz, 1988.

Short Stories

The Worlds of Frank Herbert. London, New English Library, 1970; New York, Ace, 1971.
The Book of Frank Herbert. New York, DAW, 1973; London, Panther, 1977.
The Best of Frank Herbert, edited by Angus Wells. London, Sidgwick and Jackson, 1975.
The Priests of Psi and Other Stories. London, Gollancz, 1980.
Eye, edited by Byron Preiss. New York, Berkley, 1985; London, Gollancz, 1986.

OTHER PUBLICATIONS

Novel

Soul Catcher. New York, Putnam, 1972; London, New English Library, 1973.

Poetry

Songs of Muad'Dib: Poems and Songs from Frank Herbert's Dune Series and His Other Writings, edited by Brian Herbert. New York, Ace, 1992.

Other

Threshold: The Blue Angels Experience. New York, Ballantine, 1973.
Without Me You're Nothing: The Essential Guide to Home Computers, with Max Barnard. New York, Simon and Schuster, and London, Gollancz, 1980; as *The Home Computer Handbook,* London, New English Library, 1985.
The Maker of Dune: Insights of a Master of Science Fiction, edited by Tim O'Reilly. New York, Berkley, 1987.
The Notebooks of Frank Herbert's Dune, edited by Brian Herbert. New York, Perigee Books, 1988.

Editor, *New World or No World.* New York, Ace, 1970.
Editor, with others, *Tomorrow, and Tomorrow, and Tomorrow. . . .* New York, Holt Rinehart, 1974.
Editor, *Nebula Winners Fifteen.* New York, Harper, 1981; London, W.H. Allen, 1982.

*

Critical Studies: *Frank Herbert* by Timothy O'Reilly, New York, Ungar, 1981; *The Dune Encyclopedia* edited by Willis E. McNelly, New York, Putnam, and London, Corgi, 1984.

*   *   *

Frank Herbert's science fiction is deeply humanistic, an amalgam of history, philosophy, theology, psychology, and science that explores man's future in terms of his past. Though peopling distant worlds with both alien and humanoid entities, his works focus on man: his diversity and his singularity—his nature, limits, potentialities, his inseparable ties to his environment and his fellow creatures, his genetic and cultural heritage that paves the way for his future, his latent mystical and psychic abilities that training and necessity might nurture, his need for challenge and adversity, and his dual potential for progress or destruction. Although his main characters usually remain familiar and psychologically credible, even amid alien settings, to Herbert humanity is not fixed, but rather is continually evolving both physically and intellectually, adapting to changed or new environments, growing decadent and stagnant when too comfortable but learning to survive and thrive when necessity compels. When fixed in rigid patterns (religious, political, genetic), he becomes mechanical, perverted, dehumanized, and doomed; but change and evolution, even if violent, bizarre, or seemingly incomprehensible, bring hope; adversity and competition create strength. Herbert's message is that man must learn from his past, avoid absolutist traps, recognize that right might be wrong in changed circumstances, explore his limits to their fullest, but never lose touch with the ecosystems on which he depends and to which he must continually adapt. In keeping with his varied intellectual concerns, Herbert's narrative structure is episodic, even fragmented, more dependent on clashes of ideas than on action.

In the *Dune* series, *The God Makers, The Santaroga Barrier, The Heaven Makers, The Dosadi Experiment,* and in the "Pandora" series, Herbert describes the trials, conflicts, and rites of passage through which man can evolve godlike powers of intellect and foresight, but further suggests the difficulties and dangers such powers necessitate. Frequently these evolutionary leaps are precipitated by contact with special organic chemicals ("spice" in *Dune,* "Jaspers" in *The Santaroga Barrier,* kelp hallucinogens in *The Jesus Incident, The Lazarus Effect,* and *The Ascension Factor*), by the genetic mix of unique strains (*The God Makers, Dune* series, *The Heaven Makers, The Ascension Factor*), or by a special mind or body fuse (*The Dosadi Experiment, The Jesus Incident, The Ascension Factor, Man of Two Worlds*). *Soul Catcher,* though not science fiction per se, weaves a tale of mystic Indian powers gained through birth and ritual, and ancient alien gods who heighten the perception of those seeking their frightening aid.

In *The Dosadi Experiment,* humans and a number of alien species, caged together on a toxic planet, bred for vengeance and cunning, plagued by overpopulation, and conditioned by constant war and hunger, learn to overcome all barriers (even a tempokinetic "God Wall") and avenge themselves on their creators. An alien female with features like a praying mantis merges with a human to produce total mind transference and psi power that force the tribunal to recognize Dosadi power and potential. In *Whipping Star,* the secret agent from *The Dosadi Experiment* (Jorj X. McKie) must cope with the peculiar customs and qualities of alien races as he seeks a loophole in a legal contract spelling death for the only surviving alien capable of controlling "jumpdoors" for speedy transport.

The God Makers focuses on an interplanetary troubleshooter assigned to monitor planets and to detect at early stages signs of aggressiveness that might trigger future war; in fulfilling these duties he discovers and develops extrasensory powers that lead him to rites of passage on a special planet of philosophers, rites that make clear his godhood and teach him to use his powers to do what has been his job all along—prevent war and aggression through compromise between potential enemies. However, one drawback of being a superpower and of attaining immortality is the possibility of boredom. Paul Atreides of *Dune,* omnipotent ruler of thousands of planets, fakes his own death and retires to private interests, while his descendant, Emperor Leto II, the God-Emperor of Dune, longs for an equal mind with whom to share the Machiavellian twists of his long-term plans for his subjects.

In *The Heaven Makers,* an immortal alien movie producer, using Earth as a set for filming full sensory movies of wars, natural disasters, and other horrors to relieve the boredom of his jaded race, breaks regulations and interferes with human cycles, originally to provide more entertaining disasters, but ultimately to produce a blessed loss of immortality. *Man of Two Worlds* (written with Brian Herbert) also examines man through alien eyes, postulating a race of idiot-savant storytellers (the main one called "Habiba" or "Love" as in "God is Love") with the power to create substance, initiate life, and interfere in the evolution of that life; however, this power backfires when the story they create is that of Earth and Earthlings, creatures whose greed, physical obsessions, and lust for power infect their creators, turn peaceful spirits into violent murderers, and threaten the universe. The story turns on a dynamic and unscrupulous news editor and magnate forced to share his body with an alien who holds very different views about pleasure and responsibility. Each of these books examines alien intelligence in order to more clearly define the human.

The most famous of Herbert's books tracing human evolution to a higher state of being is the much imitated *Dune* sextet, a complex

series of epic proportions and of epic concerns that depicts the development, expansion, and diversification of religion and politics on an alien, feudal desert world, and that traces the intergalactic rise and fall of a great family caught up in messianic convulsions. Its scope is incredible—an entire world convincingly and thoroughly drawn in topography, ecology, history, literature, and culture. It remains Herbert's finest and most imaginative achievement. In it Herbert concerns himself, not with future technologies, but with the evolution of human logic and prescience. The series begins with revolutionary powers and vast changes, and traces the political line as it sinks into stasis, becomes ingrown and perverted, until new blood and unexpected evolutions force the changes necessary for regeneration and for ultimate survival of a people and a world.

The first in the series, *Dune,* concerns the growth and maturation of Paul Atreides, the product of generations of controlled breeding and Bene Gesserit training in desert discipline. Once his latent powers are enhanced by an overdose of Arrakis spice (the byproduct of the desert's giant sandworms), his mind, with its heightened consciousness, becomes permanently opened to see and shape the future; his time travel involves a succession of choices between alternative futures. Beset by conspiracies, but revered by the Bedouin-like Fremen, whose scrupulous water conservation measures allow them a precarious existence, Paul Atreides becomes the prophet to his infant sister and leads the desert people on a *jihad* to conquer their planet and a thousand others.

As *Dune Messiah* traces an imperial intergalactic intrigue by the Bene Gesserit to overthrow the "god" they themselves created (a common Herbert theme), it also demonstrates the corrupting effects of power as the deserts are tamed, the hardened Fremen grow water-fat and soft, ideals are lost, and religion becomes dead ritual. Only the sacrifice of Paul Atreides, who has learned to see too much and yet too little, can free himself and his subjects from the unbearable burden and dangers of foreknowledge. Its action complicated by a Tleilaxu face dancer and a "ghola" recreation of a dead hero, this novel overwhelms with Byzantine twists.

The focus on ecology and political intrigue continues in *Children of Dune,* which is a disturbing debunking of Paul Atreides: an analysis of grand schemes doomed to failure and of shortsighted wishes inflicted on the environment. Therein Paul's son Leto, as head of the House of Atreides, must undo the evils of the past by avoiding the goodness that made his father so dangerous and by reteaching his subjects to live by their instincts, to think and act for themselves, and to appreciate traditions that will preserve the ecology, the giant worms, and the melange harvest in the sands. His method is twofold: assuring the death of his father (now a wandering desert preacher) and then transforming himself by merging with the sandtrout of Arrakis to become a seemingly indestructible, towering monster, who returns the planet to desert.

The fourth in the series, *The God-Emperor of Dune,* is an ambitious book, more philosophy than action, an interpretation of the Dune past by Leto, who, as a merged being, lives for thousands of years, retains all ancestral memories and thought patterns, but becomes less and less human. He reminisces, theorizes, manipulates, and teaches. Able to predict the future because of his firm sense of history and human nature, he turns tyrannical and intentionally sets in motion antagonisms that eventually erupt in violence. His goal is growth and change instead of fixed, rigid religious and genetic patterns that would doom his subjects to weakness, degeneration, and perhaps extinction. Knowing that male armies historically turn on their own population, his is an army of women, chosen for their stability and their survival instincts. His "death" is self-chosen and self-sacrificial; at the price of his humanity, he divides into countless sandfish that will eventually become the giant worms of Arrakis. He leaves behind a fear of gods and a distrust of heroes—the ultimate lesson of the *Dune* series: man must depend on himself alone; gods and heroes foster lazy thinking, passivity, and inaction.

Heretics of Dune focuses on the ultimate working out of the God Emperor's plans—Arrakis turned desert once more, its people forced to revive old skills and learn new. Therein the Bene Gesserit joins uneasy forces with Tleilaxu face dancers to fight invading forces from the distant colonies and to attempt to manipulate a desert child who rides the sandworms, and the ghola, Duncan Idaho, whose quest for identity leads him to cut through the illusions that envelop him and those around him. Herbert once again raises questions about genetic variability and uncertainty, hidden conditioning, hyperconsciousness, bureaucratic failures, pursuit of absolutes, and self-discovery.

Chapterhouse: Dune ends the 50,000 year saga of the House of Atreides and their desert planet, leaping 15,000 years into the future from the time of Leto II to see his dream of rebellion fulfilled, his planet returned to desert, ghola Duncan Idaho at work again, and the Bene Gesserit battling the alien Honored Matres. The underpinnings of the *Dune* series depends on a feminine mystique, with its band of wise women who have seeded an empire with myths and genetic manipulation that fit their purposes and then who save or destroy accordingly. The final volume finds the Mother Superior still trying to work out her mysterious plan to ensure survival of a now scattered Bene Gesserit and willing to accept the distasteful price of survival. Religious mysticism and desert lore, complex intrigue and equally complex intellectual discourse, a sense of the mysteries of time and of alternative futures infuse these books with a life and interest beyond mere plot.

Herbert's milieu is always firmly grounded in present-day political and social realities rather than in escapist fantasy. His books are carefully researched and highly detailed. For instance, his description of a desert society whose fanatical and feudal codes of behavior revolve around their desperate need for water reflects Bedouin survival in the Sahara. *The Dragon in the Sea* so concretely describes deepwater submarine controls that British Naval Intelligence followed his model, and *Destination: Void* is a comprehensive study in computer theory. A suspenseful thriller, *The Dragon in the Sea* depicts a world made paranoid by 16 years of war. A psychologist joins the four-man crew of a deepsea atomic submarine/tug to find a saboteur. The mission, to steal oil from underwater deposits in enemy territory, involves fear and tension from the natural dangers of depth and pressure, heightened by fears of a spy. The book, with its superb technical detail, defines sanity as the ability to adapt to "insanity." So too does *Destination: Void.* Here four scientists in a spaceship with a human cargo of thousands, all unknowingly part of a vast experiment to force invention, are supposedly travelling toward an Eden when they suffer "organic" computer failure and have to create a conscious mechanical brain to guide them. They react under pressure against impossible odds and succeed in producing a supercybernetic computer that acquires godlike powers of life and death, and that agrees to take them to an Eden if they will contemplate how to "worship" him.

Despite his skillful handling of technical description, Herbert, in the tradition of American romanticism, opposes the mechanistic with the natural and organic to show the superiority of the intuitive biological organism. In "Seed Stock," it is the lowly workman, not the lab-dependent scientists, who instinctively adjusts to an alien planet.

In *The Eyes of Heisenberg* rebels in a totally genetically engineered world oppose the immortal Optimen and their enemy Cyborgs, and deliberately interfere with gene surgery to bring about a return to mortality and to reproduce an embryo with the forbidden gene combination of intelligence and fertility. In *The Jesus Incident,* a sequel to *Destination: Void,* Herbert sets in opposition clones and "naturals," testtube babies and true births, as he continues the story of the scientists and their crew, deposited on an alien planet (Pandora), a water-dominated world filled with incredible horrors (nerve worms and hooded dashers and other predatory alien creatures). Instead of seeking to come to terms with the planet, they and their descendants try to wipe out its population, even the ruling sentient kelp, Avata, only to learn too late that the hope for Pandora rests in accepting the planet and living in harmony with its sentients, who can teach them about themselves and their past, their ship, and their gods.

The Lazarus Effect continues the story of Pandora as its human colonists try to make it habitable: the methodical, cautious "mermen," who live beneath the sea in hive-like units, by cultivating the kelp and trying to revive its sentient powers, and the more outgoing, boisterous "islanders," happier fisherfolk, by constructing huge floating piles of organic matter on which to live. Divided by custom, manner, environment, and deep-rooted "racial" stereotyping (genetically engineered clones versus "pure" human types), these descendants of the "Ship" crew from *Destination: Void* find a common bond only after the Kelp, aided by a miracle child bred of kelp, poetry, and human genetics, begins to direct their destiny, destroy fanatical conspirators, and help "resurrect" human and animal life frozen in space for centuries. However, such a resurrection begins another cycle of destruction, for these revived Moonbase clones look with scorn on Mermen and Islanders alike. In *The Ascension Factor,* they have enslaved both Kelp, and Pandorans, and have used hunger, propaganda, and brute force to prepare for their own return to space, no matter the cost to the natives. However, aided by a human child nurtured by the kelp (Christa Galli), a disembodied brain prepared to generate spaceship power, and a news system cable network, Pandorans find their destiny in a single-mind force that unites Mermen, Islanders, Kelp, and Clones, as well as the memories of all the planet's dead who have gone down to the sea. The novels in the "Pandora" series exemplify Herbert's approach: speculation about the nature of deities and of human evolution; technical wonders and genetic horrors; the concept of ancestral memory; natural enlightenment drugs; a poet who ultimately understands man's destiny, and an extraordinary child who will sweep away old orders and initiate new. Its purposeful interweaving of Christian myth suggests man cannot escape his past, for through it he finds his future. Its final message is that man must look within his own soul to find the salvation and the god he seeks; at the same time he must find harmony with the natural world if he is to use the knowledge he gains from self-examination.

Clearly then, related to Herbert's concern for the natural is an interest in ecology and a respect for rural values, a fear of man's tampering with nature coupled with a realization that he must tamper with himself if he is to advance. In "Operation Syndrome," a madman's electronic device to produce mass schizophrenia forces the development of telepathic communications to save world sanity. In "The Gone Dogs" a disease wipes out the canine population as we know it, but the species is ultimately preserved in a radical new form. "Seed Stock" criticizes the egoism of a terraforming process that disrupts natural ecology.

The Green Brain, Hellstrom's Hive, and *The White Plague* tackle the problem of human interference in nature. Set in Oregon, *Hellstrom's Hive* focuses on a secret zoological experiment that postulates the obsolescence of present family relations and of individuality; a government investigator discovers evolution's terrifying possibilities—a utopian human hive, a colony bred for physical and mental specialization that will make feasible world dominance—to preserve the hive. While the hive attains perfect harmony, from a human perspective the results are chilling. *The Green Brain* is another chilling tale that emphasizes man's dependence on insects and the potentiality of chemical sprays backfiring in unexpected ways. In an overpopulated world seeking *lebensraum* in jungles, an international organization systematically exterminates voracious insects until they defensively mutate to incredible sizes and types; some mutations involve protective "coloration"—insect colonies that appear human. A ruling insect "Brain," a corporate intelligence that is the product of this mutation, plans to restore and maintain nature's balance.

In *The Santaroga Barrier* Herbert deals with man coping with the imbalance within himself. In a world dominated by false, greedy, superficial advertising men, the Santaroga Valley remains isolated and impervious to modernization. An investigator engaged to a Santaroga psychiatrist seeks answers in "Jaspers," food infused with natural chemicals from Santaroga caves, chemicals that help users see through artifice and falsity to discover true values of community and integrity. But this proves a two-edged blessing, for with awareness comes the aftereffects of not being able to live outside the valley for very long and a subconscious reflex to destroy any stranger who does not belong. The drug produces enlightenment and well-being at the cost of freedom.

The White Plague, a topical projection, makes a significant change in Herbert's canon. This novel is more heavily cynical about present realities than his past works. It is a double-edged attack on 1) the social and cultural attitudes that produce and encourage the mindless violence of terrorist groups, and 2) the potentials unleashed by recombinant DNA research that make it possible for one man only, with the right training, to unleash on the world at any moment an irreversible horror. It focuses on a molecular biologist who, unhinged by the senseless deaths of his wife and children in an IRA bombing, produces an unstoppable synthesized plague that kills only women. The result is chaos, panic, a breakdown of government and social order, and, ironically enough, a return to the self-destructive adolescent male patterns of might makes right and survival of the most cunning and brutal that terrorism has always fostered.

The collection of essays and materials in *Frank Herbert: The Maker of Dune,* published after Herbert's death, discusses the origins of the *Dune* novels and suggests the diversity of Herbert's interests and the rural origins of his commitment to harmony with nature.

In conclusion, Herbert mingles Eastern and Western philosophies, archetypes, and myths to produce a humanistic worldview, both skeptical and idealistic, one which explores the "god" in man but warns of the fragility of his world and of the dangers of utopias. His examination of evolving intelligence, whether mechanical (*Destination: Void*), insect (*The Green Brain*), alien ("The Tactful Saboteur," *Whipping Star, The Dosadi Experiment, Man of Two Worlds*), or humanoid (*Dune* series, Pandora series), warns that man must stay adaptable, responsible, self-aware, and attuned to his environment in order to survive. His view is relativistic, his philosophy dialectical, his historical focus cyclical; his characters are complicated, his carefully considered details convincing, and, despite a

rough-edged style and a weakness for extended discourse and jargon, his plots are provocative and intriguing, with a rich complexity and an imaginative scope that should please and challenge.

—Gina Macdonald

HERBERT, James

Nationality: British. **Born:** London, 8 April 1943. **Education:** St. Aloysius College, and Hornsey College of Art, both London. **Family:** Married Eileen O'Donnell in 1968; three daughters. **Career:** Typographer, John Collings Advertising, London, 1963-66; art director, Group Head, and associate director, Ayer Barker Hegemann International, London, 1966-67. **Agent:** Bruce Hunter, David Higham Associates, 5-8 Lower John Street, London W1R, 4HA, England; or, Claire Smith, Harold Ober Associates, 40 East 49th Street, New York, New York 10017, U.S.A.

SCIENCE FICTION PUBLICATIONS

Novels (series: Rats)

The Rats. London, New English Library, 1974; New York, New American Library, 1975; reprinted as *Deadly Eyes,* New American Library, 1983.

The Fog. London, New English Library, and New York, New American Library, 1975.

The Survivor. London, New English Library, 1976; New York, New American Library, 1977.

Fluke. London, New English Library, 1977; New York, New American Library, 1978.

The Spear. London, New English Library, 1978; New York, New American Library, 1980.

Lair (Rats). London, New English Library, and New York, New American Library, 1979.

The Dark. London, New English Library, and New York, New American Library, 1980.

The Jonah. London, New English Library, and New York, New American Library, 1981.

Shrine. London, New English Library, 1983; New York, New American Library, 1984.

Domain (Rats). London, New English Library, 1984; New York, New American Library, 1985.

Moon. London, New English Library, 1985; New York, Crown, 1986.

The Magic Cottage. London, Hodder and Stoughton, 1986; New York, New American Library, 1987.

Sepulchre. London, Hodder and Stoughton, 1987; New York, Putnam, 1988.

Haunted. London, Hodder and Stoughton, 1988; New York, Putnam, 1988.

Creed. London, Hodder and Stoughton, 1990.

Portent. London, Hodder and Stoughton, 1992.

The City: The Rats Saga Continues, with Ian Miller (for children). London, Pan, 1994.

The Ghosts of Sleath. London, HarperCollins, 1994; New York, HarperPrism, 1995.

Other

James Herbert's Dark Places: Locations and Legends, with photographs by Paul Barkshire. London, HarperCollins, 1993.

*   *   *

James Herbert started his writing career relatively inauspiciously with *The Rats* in 1974, ostensibly just one more example of the gory, man-versus-animal chillers that enjoyed great popularity on both sides of the Atlantic for several years. Herbert's unique touch was the introduction of a single, giant mutant rat, whose intelligence was such that she could direct her fellows in organized attacks on humanity. Herbert's clear, crisp style provided some distance from his contemporaries, and his next novel was to mark him as a writer to watch.

The Fog, published in 1975, could have been just another disaster novel, a subgenre that British novelists have dominated for decades. An earthquake releases into the atmosphere a previously unknown gas that unleashes the inhibitions of anyone who breathes it, leading to widespread murders, assaults, and acts of civil unrest. A small team of researchers races against time to discover a means of controlling the effects of the fog before civilization grinds to a complete halt.

Herbert's next two novels went in entirely different directions. *The Survivor* is purely supernatural, but with a clever plot twist involving the sole survivor of a tragic plane crash who begins to experience visions of the afterworld. *Fluke,* an interesting experiment but not one of Herbert's successes, concerns a murdered man reborn into the body of a dog, in which guise he sets out to solve the mystery of his own death and bring the culprit to justice.

The uncertain popularity of these books may explain why Herbert's next book, *Lair,* returned to more familiar ground. The giant mutant rat of *The Rats* returns, now having laid her plans in secret and raised an enormous army conditioned to do her bidding without question. The scope was larger, the gore more pervasive, but basically it recapitulated Herbert's earlier novel.

Subsequent novels, which appeared almost annually thereafter, were less conservative. *The Spear* is a contemporary thriller involving the discovery of a Neo-Nazi movement that has pursued Hitler's fascination with the occult to its fruition, actual possession of supernatural powers. From this point on, Herbert moved squarely toward the supernatural, although trappings of science fiction and conventional suspense novels continue to shape him stylistically.

The Dark returned to the contagious madness of *The Fog,* but this time the source was an evil force from antiquity set free to influence the living once more. In *The Jonah,* a police detective suffers from the fact that his presence carries a plague of bad luck to everyone he comes to love. The revelation of the nature of this curse, following a plot that resembles nothing so much as a conventional, police procedural murder mystery, was one of Herbert's more inventive plot devices, and the book is certainly one of his most interesting accomplishments.

Shrine was another experiment for Herbert, this time mixing theology with the supernatural. A young, deaf mute girl undergoes a remarkable religious experience; then she acquires use of all her senses and seems perfectly normal. Then it is discovered that she had also acquired the power of healing, and there is widespread belief that a miracle has occurred, and that she is a living saint. Others believe this is just another plot by the Adversary to fool people into false beliefs.

Herbert returned to science fiction with *Domain,* the third novel with the mutated rats. In the opening chapter, a nuclear war devastates the Earth, destroying civilization and leaving small clusters of survivors struggling to remain alive in underground shelters while they wait for the radioactivity above to dissipate. Their existence becomes much more problematical when hordes of mutant rats, now grown more ferocious and far more intelligent than their predecessors, invade the remaining shelters in an attempt to seize mastery of the planet.

Moon is also arguably science fiction. On a remote island, an introspective man discovers that he has become telepathically linked to a serial killer, able to witness his crimes after a fashion, but without sufficient clarity to be able to identify the murderer. The other half of the link becomes aware of the connection, and begins to retrace the tenuous connection, determined to eliminate the only person who knows, however uncertainly, his dark secret. The plot is that of a standard suspense thriller, with the fantastic element giving it a unique and very suspenseful twist.

The Magic Cottage, an untraditional haunted house story, is noteworthy because of its characterization, developed more fully than in Herbert's previous work. *Haunted* uses a similar setting and deals with the same theme quite differently. *Sepulchre* features an ancient Sumerian demon who can impart supernatural powers to its followers. The interface here between the world of high finance and that of the supernatural provides a fascinating contrast.

Although Herbert's popularity in the United States seems to have waned in recent years, the quality of his writing has steadily improved. It is unfortunate for science fiction readers that he seems to have moved almost entirely into supernatural themes and plots, particularly when he has shown an ability to use unconventional settings and plot elements to turn the reader's expectations end for end.

—Don D'Ammassa

HERON-ALLEN, Edward. *See* **BLAYRE, Christopher.**

HIGH, Philip E(mpson)

Nationality: British. **Born:** Biggleswade, Bedfordshire, 28 April 1914. **Education:** Kent College, Canterbury. **Military Service:** Served in the Royal Navy during World War II. **Family:** Married Pamela Baker in 1950; two daughters. **Career:** Has worked as a salesman, reporter, and insurance agent; bus driver, East Kent Road Car Company, 1951-79; now retired. **Agent:** Carnell Literary Agency, Rowneybury Bungalow, near Old Harlow, Essex CM20 2EX. **Address:** 34 King Street, Canterbury, Kent CT1 2AJ, England.

SCIENCE FICTION PUBLICATIONS

Novels

The Prodigal Sun. New York, Ace, 1964; London, Compact, 1965.
No Truce with Terra. New York, Ace, 1964.
The Mad Metropolis. New York, Ace, 1966; as *Double Illusion,* London, Dobson, 1970.
These Savage Futurians. New York, Ace, 1967; London, Dobson, 1969.
Twin Planets. New York, Paperback Library, 1967; London, Dobson, 1968.
Reality Forbidden. New York, Ace, 1967; London, Hale, 1968.
Invader on My Back. New York, Ace, and London, Hale, 1968.
The Time Mercenaries. New York, Ace, 1968; London, Dobson, 1969.
Butterfly Planet. London, Hale, 1971.
Sold—For a Spaceship. London, Hale, 1973.
Come, Hunt an Earthman. London, Hale, 1973.
Speaking of Dinosaurs. London, Hale, 1974.
Fugitive from Time. London, Hale, 1978.
Blindfold from the Stars. London, Dobson, 1979.

*

Philip E. High comments:

I am a storyteller. I have never claimed great literary abilities. I am not only a great believer in a happy ending, but am psychologically incapable of writing any other sort. A reader asks to be entertained and stimulated, not depressed. I have a vivid imagination and I try to put what I imagine on paper. But I am also old-fashioned: I like a story to have a beginning, a middle, an end, and, yes, a purpose with all the loose ends tied up.

*   *   *

Philip E. High is one of a number of writers of fast-paced adventure novels who rose to prominence with the publication of several novels by Ace Books. His work is generally written with little effort at stylistic flamboyance, with simple but well-constructed plots. A definite tendency toward bizarre settings has helped to distinguish his novels from those of others working the same vein.

Twin Planets, for example, is set on a kind of alternate Earth, but it is not one of the slightly divergent histories standard in the field. Rather, it is a very similar world somewhat advanced in time, whose unpleasant experience with alien invaders led its inhabitants to attempt to help our own reality avoid a similar experience. Similarly, in *Invader on My Back* aliens have conquered the Earth and divided humanity into a number of disparate personality types. The common failing is a mortal dread of peering upward, conditioned into them because of their subjugated status. *Reality Forbidden* is also characterized by odd setting and events, partially rationalized in this case by the existence of dream machines, inventions that lull humanity into a careless conformity. Indeed, one of the recurring themes in High's novels is a dread of conformity and the value of the individual, usually a super-normal human. The two protagonists of *Twin Planets* are genetic supermen, and the human sent by aliens to help "civilize" Earth in *The Prodigal Sun* is also a superhuman. A man with an incredibly powerful intelligence helps lead a revolt against an overly protective computer mind in *The Mad Metropolis,* and another with an extremely active curiosity leads the struggle against a post-collapse government in *These Savage Futurians.*

In *The Time Mercenaries,* High's best novel, future humanity has bred itself to the ultimate degree of conformity and passivity, and cannot use violence even in self-defense. To protect themselves against alien invaders, these future beings resurrect the crew of a present-day submarine, knowing that men of our period would not be restrained by their inflexible ethical code. Alien invasions are rather common in High's novels, usually to enslave us as in *Sold—For a Spaceship,* but sometimes to control our antisocial nature, as in *The Prodigal Sun* and *No Truce with Terra.* High makes the point quietly, however; he is more concerned with adventure than with social commentary.

High's more recent novels have been far less successful. *Come, Hunt an Earthman* was a disappointingly lackluster space adventure story, but *Speaking of Dinosaurs* had a clever plot, an intriguing scientific mystery, and was as well-written as almost anything else High has written. Subsequent books have continued to concentrate on adventurous themes, but without increasing the author's popularity.

—Don D'Ammassa

HILL, D.W.R. *See* **TUBB, E.C.**

HILL, John. *See* **KOONTZ, Dean R.**

HOBAN, Russell (Conwell)

Nationality: American. **Born:** Lansdale, Pennsylvania, 4 February 1925. **Education:** Lansdale High School; Philadelphia Museum School of Industrial Art, 1941-43. **Military Service:** Served in the United States Army Infantry, 1943-45: Bronze Star. **Family:** Married 1) Lillian Aberman (i.e., the illustrator Lillian Hoban) in 1944 (divorced 1975), one son and three daughters; 2) Gundula Ahl in 1975, three sons. **Career:** Magazine and advertising agency artist and illustrator; story board artist, Fletcher Smith Film Studio, New York, 1951; television art director, Batten Barton Durstine and Osborn, 1951-56, and J. Walter Thompson, 1956, both in New York; advertising copywriter, Doyle Dane Bernbach, New York, 1965-67. Since 1967, full-time writer; since 1969 has lived in London. **Awards:** Christopher award, for children's book, 1972; Whitbread award, for children's book, 1974; George G. Stone Center for Children's Books award, 1982; Ditmar award (Australia), 1982; John W. Campbell Memorial award, 1982. **Agent:** David Higham Associates Ltd., 5-8 Lower John Street, London W1R 4HA, England.

SCIENCE FICTION PUBLICATIONS

Novel

The Lion of Boaz-Jachin and Jachin-Boaz. London, Cape, and New York, Stein and Day, 1973.
Kleinzeit. London, Cape, and New York, Viking Press, 1974.
Riddley Walker. London, Cape, and New York, Summit, 1980.
Pilgermann. London, Cape, and New York, Summit, 1983.
The Medusa Frequency. London, Cape, and New York, Atlantic Monthly Press, 1987.

OTHER PUBLICATIONS

Novels

Turtle Diary. London, Cape, 1975; New York, Random House, 1976.

Plays

The Carrier Frequency, with Impact Theatre Co-operative (produced London, 1984).
Riddley Walker, adaptation of his own novel (produced Manchester, 1986).

Television Play: *Come and Find Me,* 1980.

Fiction (for children)

Bedtime for Frances. New York, Harper, 1960; London, Faber, 1963.
Herman the Loser. New York, Harper, 1961; Kingswood, Surrey, World's Work, 1972.
The Song in My Drum. New York, Harper, 1962.
London Men and English Men. New York, Harper, 1962.
Some Snow Said Hello. New York, Harper, 1963.
The Sorely Trying Day. New York, Harper, 1964; Kingswood, Surrey, World's Work, 1965.
A Baby Sister for Frances. New York, Harper, 1964; London, Faber, 1965.
Bread and Jam for Frances. New York, Harper, 1964; London, Faber, 1966.
Nothing to Do. New York, Harper, 1964.
Tom and the Two Handles. New York, Harper, 1965; Kingswood, Surrey, World's Work, 1969.
The Story of Hester Mouse Who Became a Writer. New York, Norton, 1965; Kingswood, Surrey, World's Work, 1969.
What Happened When Jack and Daisy Tried to Fool the Tooth Fairies. New York, Four Winds Press, 1965.
Henry and the Monstrous Din. New York, Harper, 1966; Kingswood, Surrey, World's Work, 1967.
The Little Brute Family. New York, Macmillan, 1966.
Save My Place. New York, Norton, 1967.
Charlie the Tramp. New York, Four Winds Press, 1967.
The Mouse and His Child. New York, Harper, 1967; London, Faber, 1969.
A Birthday for Frances. New York, Harper, 1968; London, Faber, 1970.
The Stone Doll of Sister Brute. New York, Macmillan, and London, Collier Macmillan, 1968.

Harvey's Hideout. New York, Parents' Magazine Press, 1969; London, Cape, 1973.
Best Friends for Frances. New York, Harper, 1969; London, Faber, 1971.
The Mole Family's Christmas. New York, Parents' Magazine Press, 1969; London, Cape, 1973.
Ugly Bird. New York, Macmillan, 1969.
A Bargain for Frances. New York, Harper, 1970; Kingswood, Surrey, World's Work, 1971.
Emmet Otter's Jug-Band Christmas. New York, Parents' Magazine Press, and Kingswood, Surrey, World's Work, 1971.
The Sea-Thing Child. New York, Harper, and London, Gollancz, 1972.
Letitia Rabbit's String Song. New York, Coward McCann, 1973.
How Tom Beat Captain Najork and His Hired Sportsmen. New York, Atheneum, and London, Cape, 1974.
Ten What? A Mystery Counting Book. London, Cape, 1974; New York, Scribner, 1975.
Dinner at Alberta's. New York, Crowell, 1975; London, Cape, 1977.
Crocodile and Pierrot, with Sylvie Selig. London, Cape, 1975; New York, Scribner, 1977.
A Near Thing for Captain Najork. London, Cape, 1975; New York, Atheneum, 1976.
Arthur's New Power. New York, Crowell, 1978; London, Gollancz, 1980.
The Twenty-Elephant Restaurant. New York, Atheneum, 1978; London, Cape, 1980.
The Dancing Tigers. London, Cape, 1979.
La Corona and the Tin Frog. London, Cape, 1979.
Flat Cat. London, Methuen, and New York, Philomel, 1980.
Ace Dragon Ltd. London, Cape, 1980.
The Serpent Tower. London, Methuen, 1981.
The Great Fruit Gum Robbery. London, Methuen, 1981; as *The Great Gumdrop Robbery.* New York, Philomel, 1982.
They Came from Aargh! London, Methuen, and New York, Philomel, 1981.
The Battle of Zormla. London, Methuen, and New York, Philomel, 1982.
The Flight of Bembel Rudzuk. London, Methuen, and New York, Philomel, 1982.
Ponders (Jim Frog, Big John Turkle, Charlie Meadows, Lavinia Bat). London, Walker, and New York, Holt Rinehart, 4 vols., 1983-84.
The Rain Door. London, Gollancz, 1986; New York, Crowell, 1987.
The Marzipan Pig. London, Cape, 1986; New York, Farrar Straus, 1987.
Monsters. New York, Scholastic, and London, Gollancz, 1989.
Jim Hedgehog's Supernatural Christmas. London, Hamilton, 1989; New York, Clarion Books, 1992.
Jim Hedgehog and the Lonesome Tower. London, Hamilton, 1990; New York, Clarion Books, 1992.
M.O.L.E.: Much Overworked Little Earthmover, with Jan Pienkowski. London, Cape, 1993.
The Court of the Winged Serpent, with Patrick Benson. London, Cape, 1994.

Poetry (for children)

Goodnight. New York, Norton, 1966; Kingswood, Surrey, World's Work, 1969.

The Pedaling Man and Other Poems. New York, Norton, 1968;
Kingswood, Surrey, World's Work, 1969.
Egg Thoughts and Other Frances Songs. New York, Harper, 1972;
London, Faber, 1973.

Other

*The Moment Under the Moment: Stories, a Libretto, Essays, and
Sketches.* London, Cape, 1992.

Other (for children)

*What Does It Do and How Does It Work? Power Shovel, Dump
Truck, and Other Heavy Machines.* New York, Harper, 1959.
The Atomic Submarine: A Practice Combat Patrol under the Sea.
New York, Harper, 1960.

*   *   *

Russel Hoban is a science fiction writer through only one novel,
Riddley Walker; but that novel is a masterpiece. Hoban's other novels are essentially fantastic or surreal, even though several are set
in contemporary London, where this American writer has lived for
many years; none of his books is marketed as SF. He began as a
writer of children's books, a career which culminated in the classic
fantasy *The Mouse and his Child* (1967); since then he has written
six adult novels from *The Lion of Boaz-Jachin and Jachin-Boaz*
(1973) through *The Medusa Frequency* (1987).

Apart from *Turtle Diary,* all these novels could be called surreal
"fantasies," and most are related to actual events in Hoban's life or
background. *The Lion of Boaz-Jachin and Jachin-Boaz* tells of a
family disruption, and the subsequent anger felt by an almost grown-
up son for his father, now living with a new partner in London.
The son's anger takes the form of a lion roaming the streets of
London, a lion that can be seen by gifted people (such as mental
patients), and needs to be fed large quantities of real meat. The
book is full of sprightly symbolism. The same can be said of
Kleinzeit, which centres on the experience of hospitalization.
Pilgermann's theme is the Jewish experience of the First Crusade,
beginning with pogrom and ending with massacre, but as usual it
is highly symbolist. The hero-narrator is literally a "ghost-writer,"
since he is dead before he utters his first word; and the book includes elements of a very charming Zen-like mysticism. *The Medusa Frequency* is based on a motif of severed heads, including
that of Orpheus, the archetypal poet (and novelist?). Even at their
most surreal moments, these are very personal books.

Personal elements are less obtrusive in Hoban's greatest novel,
Riddley Walker, which achieved instant recognition, and deservedly
won the John W. Campbell award in 1982. It is not remarkable for
its overt plot: it is an after-the-bomb story set some 2400 years in
the future in Kent, England, and covers a few weeks in which the
neo-barbarians rediscover gunpowder and put it to disastrous use.
The public issue is the one familiar from Walter Miller's *A Canticle for Leibowitz:* is technical progress desirable? There is another echo of Miller: the misinterpretation of a prebomb icon—in
Miller a circuit-diagram, in Hoban a painting of the Legend of St.
Eustace in Canterbury Cathedral. But otherwise the books are very
different. Where Miller is panoramic, Hoban concentrates on the
mind of young Riddley Walker, a tribal shaman. The inner form of
the book is Bildungsroman: it is Riddley's struggle to come to terms
with the problem of Power. And that is why we get the narrative in

Riddley's own voice, a very distinctive voice, which begins like
this: "On my naming day when I come 12 I gone front spear and
kilt a wyld boar he parbly ben the las wyld pig on the Bundel Downs
any how there hadnt ben none for a long time befor him nor I aint
looking to see none agen." And so it goes on. No other SF author
has attempted to produce a whole novel in language so altered from
present English (not even Anthony Burgess in *A Clockwork Orange*). But the language is justified by its peculiar effects. Its sheer
vitality, its combination of demotic crudeness and mystical symbolism could not be achieved otherwise. Indeed, the language is
symbolic in some of its minute details (see my article "Making the
Two One," *Extrapolation 25,* Summer 1984).

Above all, the altered spelling facilitates some pregnant puns,
wud for "wood/would," *hart* for "hart/heart," and *Addom* for "Adam/
atom." These appear in the "Eusa Story," the central myth-scripture
of "Inland" (East Kent). In this myth, the "Littl Shynin Man the
Addom" is caught by the scientist Eusa in the "Hart of the Wud"
and torn apart: which signifies fission both of the atomic nucleus
and of Adam, humanity. Both the atom and our selves are split in
the heart of our "would," our will to creativity and power. Many
characters in the novel are fissioned too, their heads blown off (by
the gunpowder bomb) away from their hearts. But Riddley and his
followers avoid this fate by giving up physical power in favour of
"the 1st knowing" (mystical intuition): they dedicate themselves to
spreading wisdom by the current literary medium, the puppet show.

The great merit of *Riddley Walker* resides not so much in its plot
or theme, which are common enough, but in its sheer expressiveness. It is full of myths, legends, symbolic figures, such as Punch
(violence), Greanvine (mortality), Aunty (the goddess of Death).
In this it is most comparable to Vonnegut's *Cat's Cradle* (with its
texts of "Bokononism") and to Le Guin's *The Left Hand of Darkness* (with its Handdara legends). It is also an instance of that fairly
frequent phenomenon, the writing of a great science fiction novel
by an author on the fringe of the genre.

—David Lake

HOCH, Edward D.

Pseudonyms: Irwin Booth; Stephen Dentinger; Ellery Queen. **Nationality:** American. **Born:** Rochester, New York, 22 February 1930.
Education: University of Rochester, New York, 1947-49. **Military Service:** Served in the United States Army, 1950-52. **Family:**
Married Patricia A. McMahon in 1957. **Career:** Worked at Rochester Public Library, 1949-50; Pocket Books, New York City, 1952-
54; and Hutchins Advertising Company, Rochester, 1954-68. Since
1968, self-employed writer. Columnist (as R.E. Porter), *Ellery
Queen's Mystery Magazine,* New York. President, 1982, and member, Board of Directors, Mystery Writers of America; member, Science Fiction Writers of America. **Awards:** Mystery Writers of
America Edgar Allan Poe award, for short story, 1968. **Agent:** Larry
Sterning, 742 Robertson Street, Milwaukee, Wisconsin 53213. **Address:** 2941 Lake Avenue, Rochester, New York 14612, U.S.A.

SCIENCE FICTION PUBLICATIONS

Novels (series: Carl Crader and Earl Jazine in all books)

The Transvection Machine. New York, Walker, 1971; London, Hale, 1974.
The Fellowship of the HAND. New York, Walker, 1973; London, Hale, 1976.
The Frankenstein Factory. New York, Warner, 1975; London, Hale, 1976.

Short Stories (series: Simon Ark)

The Judges of Hades and Other Simon Ark Stories. North Hollywood, Leisure, 1971.
City of Brass. North Hollywood, Leisure, 1971.
The Quests of Simon Ark. New York, Mysterious Press, 1984.

OTHER PUBLICATIONS

Novels

The Shattered Raven. New York, Lancer, 1969; London, Hale, 1970.
The Blue Movie Murders (as Ellery Queen). New York, Lancer, 1972; London, Gollancz, 1973.

Short Stories

Ellery Queen Presents: The Spy and the Thief: 14 Stories about Rand and Nick Velvet, edited by Ellery Queen. New York, Davis, 1971.
The Thefts of Nick Velvet. Yonkers, New York, Mysterious Press, 1978.
The Theft of the Persian Slipper. New York, Mysterious Press, 1978.
Leopold's Way, edited by Francis M. Nevins Jr. and Martin H. Greenberg. Carbondale, Illinois, Southern Illinois University Press, 1985.
The Problem of the Pink Post Office, adapted for children by Rosanne Keller. Syracuse, New York, New Readers Press, 1988.
The Spy Who Read Latin and Other Stories. Helsinki, Finland, Eurographica, 1990.
The People of the Peacock. Eugene, Oregon, Mystery Scene Press, 1991.
The Night, My Friend: Stories of Crime and Suspense, edited by Francis M. Nevins Jr. Athens, Ohio University Press, 1992.

Other

The Monkey's Clue, The Stolen Sapphire: Two Mysteries for You to Solve!: Match Wits with Detective Tommy Preston (for children). New York, Grosset and Dunlap, 1978.

Editor, *Dear Dead Days: The 1972 Mystery Writers of America Anthology.* New York, Walker, 1972; London, Gollancz, 1974.
Editor, *Best Detective Stories of the Year.* New York, Dutton, 6 vols., 1976-81.
Editor, *All But Impossible! An Anthology of Locked Room and Impossible Crime Stories.* New Haven, Connecticut, Ticknor and Fields, 1981; London, Hale, 1983.
Editor, *The Year's Best Mystery and Suspense Stories.* New York, Walker, 9 vols., 1982-91.
Editor, with Martin H. Greenberg, *Great British Detectives.* Chicago, Academy Chicago, 1987.
Editor, with Martin H. Greenberg, *Women Write Murder.* Chicago, Academy Chicago, 1987.

Editor, with Martin H. Greenberg, *Murder Most Sacred: Great Catholic Tales of Mystery and Suspense.* New York, Dembner, 1989.

*

Bibliography: "Edward D. Hoch: A Checklist" by Willian J. Clark, Edward D. Hoch, and Francis M. Nevins, Jr., in *Armchair Detective* (White Bear Lake, Minnesota), February 1976, revised edition, by Nevins and Hoch, privately printed, 1979.

Edward D. Hoch comments:

(1985) I have always viewed my science fiction and fantasy as offshoots of my mystery writing, and nearly all my science fiction contains elements of mystery and detection.

*   *   *

Edward D. Hoch is one of the few writers who have been able to blend successfully the detective story with science fiction (others include Isaac Asimov, Anthony Boucher, Fredric Brown, Randall Garrett, and Ron Goulart). Of his three novels and more than 60 short stores which qualify as SF or fantasy, nearly all have criminous elements.

Each of Hoch's three SF novels is a classic mystery set in the 21st century and features the "Computer Cops," a team of government investigators led by Carl Crader and Earl Jazine. The first, *The Transvection Machine,* is perhaps the best—a strong blending of baffling mystery, inventive science fiction, and social commentary. Almost as good is *The Fellowship of the Hand,* which continues Crader's and Jazine's attempts to combat an organization known as HAND (Humans Against Neuter Domination), pledged to destroy all machines capable of dominating man. *The Frankenstein Factory,* which deals with a futuristic variation on the Frankenstein theme involving cryonics, is less successful in that it seems more an attenuated novelette than a fully realized novel.

Hoch's true forte, however, is the short story. He has published more than 500 in the past quarter-century and is widely acclaimed as the premier writer of short mystery fiction. Among the more memorable of his SF detective tales are "The Wolfram Hunters" and "Computer Cops"; noncriminous SF include "Zoo," "The Faceless Thing," and "The Last Paradox." But it is the 80 novelette-length adventures about Simon Ark, a man who claims to be a 2000-year-old Copt priest, which are perhaps the most well-known of all Hoch's fictional creations. These are primarily tales of detection, but each deals with such fantastic elements as werewolves, witches, religious cults, scientific experiments, and Fortean phenomena. The best of the early Simon Ark stories (from the 1950s) appear in *City of Brass* and *The Judges of Hades and Other Simon Ark Stories.* A new series of Ark stories began in *Ellery Queen's Mystery Magazine* in 1978, and a new collection, *The Quests of Simon Ark,* was published in 1984.

The chief attribute of Hoch's work is its invariably intricate and ingenious plotting; few rival him in his ability to summon a seemingly endless and wide-reaching flow of ideas. If plot receives more emphasis than character development in some of his prose (notable exceptions are "The Wolfram Hunters" and "The Faceless Thing"), this in no way diminishes its high entertainment value. The richness of idea and incident more than compensates.

—Bill Pronzini

HODDER-WILLIAMS, (John) Christopher (Glazebrook)

Pseudonym: James Brogan. **Nationality:** British. **Born:** London, in 1926. **Education:** Eton College. **Military Service:** Served in the Royal Signals, in the Middle East, 1944-48: Lieutenant. **Career:** Worked in Africa after World War II; worked in England for film, television, and recording companies; also a jazz pianist and a composer of songs for Broadway and for British television. **Died:** 15 May 1995.

SCIENCE FICTION PUBLICATIONS

Novels

Chain Reaction. London, Hodder and Stoughton, and Garden City, New York, Doubleday, 1959.
The Main Experiment. London, Hodder and Stoughton, 1964; New York, Putnam, 1965.
The Egg-Shaped Thing. London, Hodder and Stoughton, 1966; New York, Putnam, 1967.
Fistful of Digits. London, Hodder and Stoughton, 1968.
98.4: A Novel. London, Hodder and Stoughton, 1969.
Panic O'Clock. St. Ives, Cornwall, United Writers, 1973.
The Prayer Machine. London, Weidenfeld and Nicolson, 1976; New York, St. Martin's Press, 1977.
The Silent Voice: A Novel. London, Weidenfeld and Nicolson, 1977.
The Thinktank That Leaked. St. Ives, Cornwall, United Writers, 1979.
The Chromosome Game. London, Mithras, 1984.

OTHER PUBLICATIONS

Novels

The Cummings Report: A Novel (as James Brogan). London, Hodder and Stoughton, 1958.
Final Approach. London, Hodder and Stoughton, and Garden City, New York, Doubleday, 1960.
Turbulence: A Novel. London, Hodder and Stoughton, 1961.
The Higher They Fly: A Novel. London, Hodder and Stoughton, 1963; New York, Putnam, 1964.
Coward's Paradise. St. Ives, Cornwall, United Writers, 1974.

Plays

Radio Play: *Final Approach,* from his own novel, 1967.

Television Plays: *The Ship That Couldn't Stop,* 1961; *The Hot White Coal,* 1963; *The Higher They Fly,* from his own novel, 1963; *A Voice in the Sky,* 1964.

*   *   *

Christopher Hodder-Williams was never as widely known in America as in Britain, possibly because his brand of science fiction (or "fiction science" as he sometimes preferred to call it) placed much more emphasis on the dangers of undisciplined research and experimentation and less on the wonders of technology. He has been criticised for overworking the Frankenstein theme in his novels, but he was never a technophobe; what he was against, in all his books, was the unthinking misuse of technology, and he was particularly worried about how this might change mankind. As one character in *Fistful of Digits* says, "Many people fear computers, because they seem to impersonate human beings. But they are wrong. What they should fear is the opposite: human beings who impersonate computers."

His first novel was a non-SF thriller, and many of his SF novels could really be called techno-thrillers. His second novel, and first "fiction science" novel, *Chain Reaction,* dealt with the insidious threat of atomic radiation let loose upon an unsuspecting world, and was one of the first novels to deal with the potential dangers of radiation, a recurring theme in Hodder-Williams's work.

After three aviation novels which were favourably compared with Nevil Shute, he moved firmly into the SF genre with *The Main Experiment,* one of his best-written books, which follows an unorthodox young scientist as he takes a new position with an atomic research unit. It is not long before the protagonist discovers that the project director has been taking some liberties with his progress reports and that the project itself is out of control. Even more frightening is the fact that the byproduct of the research is a force which alters personalities and perceptions, strikes out beyond the boundaries of the experimental station, and might well pose a danger to the world at large.

The Egg-Shaped Thing repeated this theme, but with more complexity. When an entrepreneur is driven out of business, it almost costs him his sanity as well; subsequently, he cannot be entirely certain of those things which he thinks he is experiencing. How, for example, does it happen that he can remember things which have not yet happened? Why are his rivals exacting revenge for acts which he has not yet committed? Once again the focus of our attention is a secretive research establishment experimenting with the atom, but this time the experiment itself may be conscious, and exerting itself to control the actions of others.

In *Fistful of Digits,* perhaps his most complex novel, the amoral misuse of technology is again the villain, though this time Hodder-Williams abandons the menace of nuclear radiation for the equally promising field of computerisation. A powerful group of private businessmen have created an elaborate, extensive network of computers under the general name Servix, which is secretly extending their ability to manipulate others. Their extrapolation warns of potential problems if the protagonist continues to associate with a particular young woman involved with their project, so they take steps to end the relationship. The girl, and others, are effectively wired into the system as computer peripherals, with specific functions and actions. Once again this book was ahead of its time in warning of the potential dangers of handing over too much control to computers, especially when telephone systems, aeroplane ticket-booking, water-flow control in hydroelectric power stations and American nuclear defense are all linked in one vast network.

In *98.4* the scientists at the usual research station are experimenting with dispensing with the human body and linking the brain, with eyes and ears, to a computer. The eventual idea is to have NCBMs—nerve-controlled ballistic missiles. The novel, eight years before Colin Cooper did it in *Dargason,* uses music as a weapon; it's recorded through a pair of human ears instead of microphones. The fidelity is marvellous; it's the morality which is questionable.

A contagious, life-threatening wave of panic sweeps across Britain in *Panic O'Clock;* the paperback cover, showing people lining up to step off a cliff, hammers home the lemming/overpopulation analogy. It's an interesting premise, but the novel swiftly becomes a standard British disaster novel along the lines of John Christopher's *Death of Grass* and most of John Wyndham.

Coward's Paradise, though not strictly speaking science fiction, is Hodder-Williams's most disturbing novel. It is set in the form of a diary of a young writer who is being treated for acute anxiety; the "treatment" consists of a prefrontal lobotomy, still a popular operation at the time the novel was written. The writer is cured of his anxiety—and of his ability to write, the centre of anxiety being in many ways the centre of the personality.

The Prayer Machine is also about mental illness, but here the protagonist's schizophrenia is used as the means of projecting himself into an extrapolated world a hundred years on, where pollution has caused radical changes to humanity. If he returns to his own time and forces a change, he will cause the future world, and those he has grown to know and love in it, to cease to exist. The denouement is a classic rendering of paradox and simultaneity; the reader must accept that A and B, though mutually exclusive, are both true.

Hodder-Williams's last three novels are less successful. *The Silent Voice* is about mass delusion caused by radio waves picked up directly by human brains; computers have decided to take over the world. In *The Think Tank That Leaked* there is an uneasy symbiosis between man and computer; human negative emotions can be drawn off into a crystalline "think tank," but people lose their self-determination when the crystal enters their brain. *The Chromosome Game,* set 200 years after a nuclear holocaust, has echoes of William Golding's *Lord of the Flies:* a bunch of teenagers, grown from sperm and ova in a submarine, carry the future of humanity—but are as selfish and racist as people ever were.

Shortly before his death Hodder-Williams completed *Schizorama* [unpublished at his death], a follow-up to *Coward's Paradise;* this is a hard-hitting examination of the problems of a schizophrenic released back into the community with inadequate support. There are some SF elements, including a reprise of the idea of music being used as a weapon.

Hodder-Williams perhaps concentrated too much on a few themes: the dangers of radiation, the altering of personality and perception, the confusion of cause and effect, and man's over-reliance on computers. But in all his novels the characterisation is strong, largely because the characters are allowed to be flawed human beings; the plots are logically constructed and the suspense well-developed; the science and technology are meticulously researched; and the moral points are well-made. Commercial success eluded him from the 1970s onwards, but he left seven or eight memorable novels which, though science-based, have unusually not become dated.

—Don D'Ammassa, updated by David V. Barrett

HODGSON, William Hope

Nationality: British. **Born:** Blackmore End, Essex, 15 November 1877. **Career:** Apprentice seaman, 1891-95; officer in the Mercantile Marine: Lieutenant; founder and teacher, W.H. Hodgson's School of Physical Culture, Blackburn, Lancashire, 1899-1901. **Military Service:** Joined University of London Officer Training Corps, 1914; commissioned in Royal Field Artillery, 1915; left ser-

vice because of injury, 1916; recommissioned, 1917, and died at Ypres. **Awards:** Royal Humane Society Medal, 1898. **Died:** 17 April 1918.

SCIENCE FICTION PUBLICATIONS

Novels

The Boats of the "Glen Carrig": Being an Account of Their Adventures in the Strange Places of the Earth, after the Foundering of the Good Ship Glen Carrig through Striking upon a Hidden Rock in the Unknown Seas to the Southward, as Told by John Winterstraw, Gent., to His Son, James Winterstraw, in the Year 1757, and by Him Commited Very Properly and Legibly to Manuscript. London, Chapman and Hall, 1907; New York, Ballantine, 1971.

The House on the Borderland: From the Manuscript Discovered in 1877 by Messrs. Tonnison and Berreggnog, in the Ruins That Lie to the South of the Village of Kraighten, in the West of Ireland. London, Chapman and Hall, 1908.

The Ghost Pirates. London, Stanley Paul, 1909; Westport, Connecticut, Hyperion Press, 1976.

The Night Land: A Love Tale. London, Nash, 1912; abridged and revised as *The Dream of X,* in *Poems and The Dream of X,* 1912; West Kingston, Rhode Island, Grant, 1977.

The House on the Borderland and Other Novels. Sauk City, Wisconsin, Arkham House, 1946.

Short Stories

The Ghost Pirates, A Chaunty, and Another Story. New York, Reynolds, 1909.

Carnacki, the Ghost-Finder. New York, Reynolds, 1910; with other stories and poems, London, Nash, 1913; augmented edition, Sauk City, Wisconsin, Mycroft and Moran, 1947; London, Grafton 1991.

Men of the Deep Waters. London, Nash, 1914.

Deep Waters. Sauk City, Wisconsin, Arkham House, 1967.

Out of the Storm: Uncollected Fantasies, edited by Sam Moskowitz. West Kingston, Rhode Island, Grant, 1975.

Masters of Terror, Volume One: William Hope Hodgson (selected stories), edited by Peter Tremayne. London, Corgi, 1977.

William Hope Hodgson: A Centenary Tribute 1877-1977, with an essay by Peter Tremayne. Dagenham, Essex, British Fantasy Society, 1977.

The Haunted "Pampero." London, Ferret Fantasy, 1980.

Spectral Manifestations. Oxford, Bellknapp, 1984.

The Haunted Pampero: Uncollected Fantasies and Mysteries, edited by Sam Moskowitz. Hampton Falls, New Hampshire, Grant, 1991.

Demons of the Sea, edited by Sam Gafford. West Warwick, Rhode Island, Necronomicon Press, 1992.

At Sea, edited by Sam Gafford. West Warwick, Rhode Island, Necronomicon Press, 1993.

OTHER PUBLICATIONS

Short Stories

The Luck of the Strong. London, Nash, 1916.

Captain Gault, Being the Exceedingly Private Log of a Sea-Captain. London, Nash, 1917; New York, McBride, 1918.

Poetry

Poems and The Dream of X. London, Watt, and New York, Paget, 1912.
Cargunka and Poems and Anecdotes. London, Watt, and New York, Paget, 1914.
The Calling of the Sea. London, Selwyn and Blount, 1920.
The Voice of the Ocean. London, Selwyn and Blount, 1921.
Poems of the Sea. London, Ferret Fantasy, 1977.

*

Bibliography: by A.L. Searles, in *The House on the Borderland and Other Novels,* Sauk City, Wisconsin, Arkham House, 1946.

* * *

One of the most remarkable visionary fantasists of the pre-World War I era, William Hope Hodgson is chiefly remembered today as the author of two extravagant fantasies, *The House on the Borderland* and *The Night Land,* as well as a number of atmospheric horror stories of the sea and a series of "psychic detective" tales apparently modeled on those of Algernon Blackwood. Praised by H.P. Lovecraft and "rediscovered" by Arkham House publishers in the 1940s, Hodgson has grown into something of a cult figure in recent years, claimed by both historians of the scientific romance and fans of horror fiction.

There is little that is overtly "scientific" about his romances, however, and they seldom follow the uncomplicated narrative lines characteristic of romance. His first novel, *The Boats of the "Glen Carrig,"* is cast in the form of an 18th-century manuscript describing the adventures of castaways adrift in the Sargasso Sea, who encounter islands full of plants that absorb living things, weed-bound derelict ships, giant crabs, and slug-like "weed men" with beaked faces. Like much of Hodgson's short fiction, the novel exploits the legend of the Sargasso Sea in an effective and haunting way, and reflects what would prove to be a continuing Hodgson theme of the struggle between matter and spirit, with matter represented through almost obsessive images of slime, fungus, and rot.

Hodgson regarded his next two novels, *The House on the Borderland* and *The Ghost Pirates,* as parts of a thematically linked trilogy with *The Boats of the "Glen Carrig."* Certainly the themes of matter and spirit, entrapment and decay, and humanoid monsters are common to all three works, but the critic Brian Stableford is probably correct in surmising that had Hodgson been familiar with the concept of entropy, he might have seen that as his central theme. *The House on the Borderland*—again cast in the form of an old manuscript, this time found in the ruins of a desolate house in Ireland—is distinguished for the stunningly imagined visions of other worlds and times experienced by the narrator, including an astonishing passage in which he watches time accelerate until the entire solar system collapses. *The Ghost Pirates* returns to Hodgson's more familiar shipboard setting, but retains much of the otherworldly atmosphere of *The House on the Borderland* in its account of a ship which is first invaded by the not-quite-human "pirates" of the title and later sails into a mysterious otherworldly fog, where strange beings kill all but one survivor.

Hodgson's most ambitious and least readable novel was his last. *The Night Land* again employs an antiquated narrative style—this time that of a medieval dream-vision—but the result reads like a clumsy amalgam of William Morris and H.P. Lovecraft. This unfortunately turgid prose disguises one of the most remarkable and haunting visions of the far future in all fantastic literature. Millions of years from now, a remnant of humanity survives in a giant pyramid called the Last Redoubt, surrounded by eternal darkness occupied by a variety of strange and hostile beings. Discovering the existence of another outpost of humanity, the narrator—in his dream—sets out across this foreboding landscape to rescue a woman he believes to be the reincarnation of his dead lover. In the end, love sentimentally triumphs over the forces of decay and chaos.

If *The Night Land* is Hodgson's epic treatment of decay and survival, his short stories are lyrics on the same themes. The most famous of these, "The Voice in the Night," tells of a man and his wife stranded on a remote island who, after eating a strange fungus, are transformed into fungoid beings themselves. "The Derelict" describes a ship so overgrown with fungus that it becomes a living organism. Giant rats overtake a ship in "The Mystery of the Derelict," and "From the Tideless Sea" is another tale of strange monsters in the Sargasso Sea. Even the lighter tales of Carnacki, the detective who investigates paranormal phenomena, are apt to feature disturbing images of distorted life—such as a room that puckers up and whistles, or a monstrous hog-like being from another dimension in "The Hog."

Hodgson's idiosyncratic and disturbing visions have gained him a unique and lasting reputation in fantastic literature. While his death in World War I at the age of 40 would seem to have cut short what may have been an even more remarkable career, the fact is he wrote relatively little during the last years of his life, and seemed to regard *The Night Land* as his personal epic. It remains one of the great oddities of the genre, and together with *The House on the Borderland* qualifies Hodgson as one of the first true visionaries of the far future.

—Gary K. Wolfe

HOFFMAN, Lee

Pseudonym: Georgia York. **Nationality:** American. **Born:** Chicago, Illinois, 14 August 1932. **Education:** Armstrong Junior College, Savannah, Georgia, A.A. 1951. **Family:** Married Larry T. Shaw (divorced). **Career:** Printer's devil, Savannah Vocational School; staff member, Hoffman Radio-TV Service; assistant editor, *Infinity,* 1956-58, and *Science Fiction Adventures,* 1956-58, both New York; staff member, MD Publications; claim handler, Hoffman Motors; in printing production, Arrow Press, Allied Typographers, and George Morris Press. Since 1965, freelance writer. **Awards:** Western Writers of America Spur award, 1968. **Address:** 350 N.W. Harbor Boulevard, Port Charlotte, Florida 33952, U.S.A.

S꜀ɪᴇɴᴄᴇ Fɪᴄᴛɪᴏɴ Pᴜʙʟɪᴄᴀᴛɪᴏɴs

Novels

Telepower. New York, Belmont, 1967.

The Caves of Karst. New York, Ballantine, 1969; London, Dobson, 1970.
Always the Blackknight. New York, Avon, 1970.
Change Song. New York, Doubleday, 1972.

Short Stories

In and Out of Quandary, edited by Charles J. Hitchcock. Cambridge, Massachusetts, NESFA Press, 1982.

Other Publications

Novels

Gunfight at Laramie. New York, Ace, 1966; London, Gold Lion, 1975.
The Legend of Blackjack Sam. New York, Ace, 1966.
Bred to Kill. New York, Ballantine, 1967.
The Valdez Horses. New York, Doubleday, 1967; London, Tandem, 1972.
Dead Man's Gold. New York, Ace, 1968.
The Yarborough Brand. New York, Avon, 1968; London, Hale, 1981.
Wild Riders. New York, New American Library, 1969; London, Hale, 1979.
Loco. New York, Doubleday, 1969; London, Tandem, 1973.
Return to Broken Crossing. New York, Ace, 1969; London, Hale, 1982.
West of Cheyenne. New York, Doubleday, 1969; London, Tandem, 1973.
Wiley's Move. New York, Dell, 1973; London, Hale, 1980.
The Truth about the Cannonball Kid. New York, Dell, 1975; London, Hale, 1980.
Fox. New York, Doubleday, 1976; London, Hale, 1980.
Nothing But a Drifter. New York, Doubleday, 1976; London, Hale, 1980.
Trouble Valley. New York, Ballantine, 1976; London, Hale, 1980.
Sheriff of Jack Hollow. New York, Dell, 1977; London, Hale, 1979.
The Land Killer. New York, Doubleday, 1978; London, Hale, 1981.
Savage Key (as Georgia York). New York, Fawcett, 1979; London, Coronet, 1983.
Savannah Grey (as Georgia York). New York, Fawcett, 1981.
Savage Conquest (as Georgia York). New York, Fawcett, 1983.

*   *   *

The science fiction novels of Lee Hoffman are novels of human feelings, not of hard science. The SF concepts are well thought out and are integral to the storylines, but they are clearly secondary to the characters. Unlike some SF where the idea is the star and the emphasis is placed on the nuts and bolts or on the astronomical bodies while the people seem stamped out of cookie dough, Hoffman's fiction is populated with characters who live and breathe and grow and develop. The songs they sing are ones for men and women, not for pulsars and machines.

Perhaps the clearest example of her ability to make her characters very human is the protagonist in *The Caves of Karst,* a man who has undergone an operation to enable him to breathe underwater. Though this allows him to work the underwater mines more effectively, he did not choose to undergo the operation solely for financial considerations; as the novel unfolds it becomes clear that the choice was made (on some level of consciousness) to protect his ego from an unhappy love affair. People on Karst, as on Earth, often shun those who differ physically from the norm and those who *choose* to have such differences are frequently confronted with outright hatred. His adjustment to his condition, to women in general and his girlfriend in particular, and to himself during a time of crisis is the heart of the book.

There are three primary themes that run through Hoffman's work: 1) Individuality and the freedom of choice that comes with it are extremely important but must be tempered with the realization that individuals need to work together, to interact, in order to achieve certain goals; 2) It is both wrong and dangerous to try to control something or someone without consent; 3) Things may not be the way you originally thought they were or the way you have been told they were. Each theme is expressed with varying degrees of emphasis, depending on the novel, but all three are interrelated in her science fiction.

Hoffman's style is lean and direct. Each novel opens with action, tossing the reader into the midst of unfolding events: *Telepower* begins with an attack on post-atomic war Cleveland by an army of rats; *The Caves of Karst* starts with an underwater "gunfight" in a mine; *Always the Blackknight* opens with a battle between knights on robot horses; and, although the first chapter of *Change Song* is used to establish a sense of wrongness and an atmosphere of danger, the second chapter quickly produces a fight between men with magical powers. Hoffman uses her writing skills to capture the reader immediately, and all of her work has been set on earth-like planets so that the reader can rapidly believe in the setting. Hoffman strives to entertain the reader while stating her messages.

To enrich her science fiction, she occasionally employs the techniques of other genres to give a more diverse flavor. In *Telepower* Hoffman forges a bond between the gruesome qualities of the horror novel and the telepathic power so common in science fiction. Drawing upon her own experience as a writer of westerns, she gives *The Caves of Karst* an Old West setting (or what the Old West would have been like if the prospectors had gills) while at the same time using all the plot-twists of a mystery novel. *Always the Blackknight* has the flavor of the tales of knighthood, as the title might indicate, and *Change Song* has most of the elements of quest-fantasy. In fact *Change Song* is really more fantasy than science fiction, much in the same way that Theodore Sturgeon's *More Than Human* is, although on the world where *Change Song* takes place control of the elements and the power to cast spells are like our science in that one is trained in these fields. By being willing to take the risks of mixing elements of other genres with science fiction, Lee Hoffman has given her work an added dimension.

—Terry Hughes

HOGAN, James P(atrick)

Nationality: British. **Born:** London, 27 June 1941. **Education:** Royal Aircraft Establishment Technical College, Farnborough, Berkshire, 1957-61; Reading and Enfield colleges, 1961-65. **Family:** Married 1) Iris Crossley in 1961 (divorced), three daughters; 2) Lyn Dockerty in 1976 (divorced); 3) Jacklyn Price in 1982; three sons. **Career:** Engineer, Solarton Electronics, Farnborough, 1961-

62, Racal Electronics, Bracknell, Berkshire, 1962-64; sales engineer, 1964-66, and sales manager, 1966-68, ITT, Harlow, Hertfordshire; computer sales executive, Honeywell, London, 1968-70, and Leeds, 1970-72; insurance salesman, Sun Life Canada, Leeds, 1972-74; computer salesman, 1974-77, and sales training consultant in Maynard, Massachusetts, 1977-79, Digital Equipment Corporation, Leeds. Since 1979, full-time writer. **Awards:** Libertarian Futurist Society "Prometheus" award, twice; Japanese "Seiunsho" ("Galaxy") award, three times. **Member:** Science Fiction Writers of America. **Agent:** Russel Galen, Scovil, Chichak & Galen, 381 Park Ave. S., Suite 1020, New York, New York 10016. **Address:** 96 Main St., Bray, County Wicklow, Ireland. **Online Address:** 73261,246@compuserve.com.

SCIENCE FICTION PUBLICATIONS

Novels (series: Minervan Experiment)

The Minervan Experiment. Garden City, New York, Doubleday, 1981; as *James P. Hogan's The Giants Novels,* New York, Ballantine, 1991.
Inherit the Stars. New York, Ballantine, 1977; London, Grafton, 1989.
The Gentle Giants of Ganymede (Minervan Experiment). New York, Ballantine, 1978; London, Grafton, 1989.
Giants' Star. New York, Ballantine, 1981; London, Grafton, 1989.
The Genesis Machine. New York, Ballantine, 1978.
The Two Faces of Tomorrow. New York, Ballantine, 1979.
Thrice upon a Time. New York, Ballantine, 1980.
Voyage from Yesteryear. Garden City, New York, Doubleday, 1982; London, Penguin, 1984.
Code of the Lifemaker. New York, Ballantine, 1983; London, Penguin, 1985.
The Proteus Operation. New York, Bantam, 1985; London, Century, 1986.
Endgame Enigma. New York, Bantam, 1987; London, Century, 1988.
The Mirror Maze. New York, Bantam, 1989.
The Infinity Gambit. New York, Bantam, 1991.
James P. Hogan's Entoverse. New York, Ballantine, 1991; London, Orbit, 1992.
The Muliplex Man. New York, Bantam, 1992.
Out of Time. New York, Bantam, 1993.
The Immortality Option. New York, Bantam, 1993.
Realtime Interrupt. New York, Bantam, 1995.

Short Stories

Minds, Machines, and Evolution (includes nonfiction). New York, Bantam, 1988.

OTHER PUBLICATIONS

Other

Grant at Vicksburg: A Critical Analysis. Carlisle Barracks, Pennsylvania, U.S. Army War College, 1992.

*

James P. Hogan comments:

I enjoyed writing essays and stories when I was at school, and thought about being a writer then. It seemed such a pleasant way of making a living that I couldn't understand why anyone would want to do anything else. So, when I was 16 or thereabouts, I announced that I was going to be a writer. Somebody asked what, with all the accumulated wisdom and experience of 16 years, I thought I was going to write about that the world was breathlessly waiting to read. A good point. So I forgot about it for a while, and concentrated instead on getting an education, getting around, and learning something about the world and about people.

I studied electrical and electronic engineering, graduated, and worked for a few years as a designer of digital systems. After that I moved into sales, then into the computer industry with such outfits as ITT, Honeywell, and DEC, talking to scientists in just about every discipline about their computing needs. I had always been fascinated with science—not the gadgetry and gimmickry that is so often mistaken for science, but the underlying process of discovery itself—the methodology of distinguishing beliefs that are probably true from beliefs that are probably not. It made an exciting detective story that has been going on for hundreds of years all over the world, with thousands of people fitting together the pieces of an enormous, ongoing puzzle.

But how many people saw it that way? I became irritated by the kind of sensationalism that sells by always showing science as a sinister, dangerous business that threatened human values, and scientists as devoid of humor or emotion. This bore little similarity to the things I had seen, but many accepted it as reality and became disillusioned. And that was a shame, for although it's true that as a species we have made our share of mistakes, we've come a long way along the road of elevating ourselves from an animal level of existence and have accomplished much to be proud of. We are not helpless creatures at the mercy of a universe we cannot comprehend, but through the power of our minds have the ability to understand and solve our problems. I found that a pretty exciting and reassuring thought. It turned out there were lots of other people who were tired of being told about doom, gloom, and how pointless everything was, and who wanted to hear something positive about themselves for a change. Now, unlike the situation when I was 16, I did have something to write about that people wanted to hear . . . and the rest followed.

*   *   *

It would be easy to dismiss the earlier fiction of James P. Hogan as reactionary tracts in the guise of novels, since his narrators and characters often digress into irrelevant and ill-tempered attacks on progressive institutions and projects. As one reads through them, one is struck by the amount of time the narrator and (on occasion) the most scientifically respectable characters spend railing at labor unions, the mass media, popular culture, environmental activists and advocates of solar energy, *The Limits to Growth* thesis, and any portion of education devoted to topics other than science and engineering. Hogan tries very hard to be a reliable propagandist for the military-industrial complex. He nearly succeeds.

Fortunately for his readers, the imaginative power of Hogan's SF subverts his self-imposed role of apologist for technical society. The propaganda, after all, is the product of a faith—a faith in reason, to be sure, but a faith nonetheless. Hogan's fiction invites the reader to share the belief that a trained mind, working with other trained minds in a scientific team, can conquer the natural universe.

In Hogan's plots, it is not environmentalists or union leaders who nearly stymie the efforts of reasonable men (for Hogan's strong characters are almost always male), but rather ignorant governmental or corporate bureaucrats, behind whom lurk power-hungry and greedy executives who wish to use science for nefarious ends. Thus an interesting inconsistency emerges: in thematized narration and dialogue, we are *told* that the enemies of reason are (for example) the welfare state and environmental activists, while we are *shown* by the plot that the biggest enemy is in fact the military-industrial complex. The inconsistency is not fatal: it rather adds to the pleasure of reading Hogan.

The typical Hogan protagonist is a strong-willed and competent scientific investigator, or an individual who struggles against an incompetent bureaucracy and malevolent leaders, or both. He is more willing than those around him to entertain unorthodox ideas—as long as those ideas are not the product of superstition (like "psi-powers") or ignorance (meaning any questioning of scientific or technical progress). In *The Genesis Machine* (a fictionalization of Herman Kahn's concept of "doomsday machine"), Brad Clifford is not simply a brilliant mathematical physicist who has worked out the equations of the dimensions beyond ordinary spacetime; he is also a romantic hero who creates a device which effectively disarms the nuclear-war-making capabilities of both sides in a 21st-century world about to destroy itself. In *Code Of The Lifemaker,* the cynical "psychic" Karl Zambendorf (redeemed by the fact that he does not actually believe in his "powers") leads a rebellion that aborts the plans of a cabal of industrialists and politicians to impose a neocolonial slavery upon the evolved robotic civilization discovered on Titan. An exception that proves the rule is *Voyage from Yesteryear,* which as a utopian fiction has a society rather than an individual for its hero: the Chironians, who have been able to implement absolute personal freedom owing to their unregulated science and technology and resultant economic abundance. The leaders of a new emigrant group from Earth attempt to impose a centralized political economy on the Chironians, but they fail when many of their followers find Chironian anarchism attractive.

Hogan's *Minervan Experiment* trilogy is marred when its third part, *Giant's Star,* descends into a space operatic war between Earth's alien allies and the "Evil Empire" that seeks to enslave them. Its first two parts (*Inherit the Stars* and *The Gentle Giants of Ganymede*), however, constitute a fine SF detective story centered on Victor Hunt, an almost archetypal Hogan hero who heads up the team of United Nations Space Agency scientists that unravels the mystery of a humanoid corpse found on the moon. As Hunt and his team probe more deeply into the origins of the "Lunarians," they reconstruct the story of an ancient alien civilization and its colonies in the solar system, a process which enables them to advance a daring new hypothesis about the origins of mankind. Aside from promoting some of Hogan's favorite themes, such as the never-ending struggles between reason and superstition, and between individual freedom and the security state, *The Minervan Experiment* illustrates another important feature of Hogan's SF: his portrayal of the methods of scientific investigation.

Since this particular investigation is an interdisciplinary one, the investigators must constantly share their knowledge as well as formulate, test, and discard successive hypotheses. Hogan also conveys what might be called the human dimension of science—the rivalries between fields, the interpersonal conflicts, and the exhilaration that comes with the discovery of a new piece of knowledge that can be fit into one's previous investigations. In the bargain, Hogan seamlessly integrates present-day "normal" science with the speculative, fictional science of his near-future setting. This promotes an important theme that runs throughout his SF: the unity and the smooth growth curve of Western science and technology, with the spirit of reason only occasionally disrupted by social backwardness and the apparent discontinuities associated with paradigm shifts in science itself.

More speculative and less constrained than most of Hogan's SF, *The Proteus Operation* exploits two widely used SF premises—an alternate universe in which the Nazis won the war, and the many-worlds interpretation of quantum mechanics. Sending a team back from the Nazi 1975, Hogan has them gradually undo the chain of events that led to the Nazi victory. Along the way, he does not overlook the comic potential in having characters encounter younger or older versions of themselves, or the *frisson* that can result from mixing historical figures (e.g., Albert Einstein, Isaac Asimov, and Winston Churchill) with fictional ones. Unfortunately, the nonfictional characters come off as unusually flat and stereotyped, perhaps because they are merely revered icons. An interesting effect of Hogan's design for this novel is that his narrator must express admiration for the New Deal and the wartime alliance with the Soviets, even to the extent of excusing Stalin's role in the nonaggression pact! It is fascinating to see Hogan work the other side of the political street for a while, but the preaching remains tiresome. Interestingly, the novel emphasizes teamwork so much that no one character stands out as hero.

In *Endgame Enigma* the propaganda is hysterical and desperate, and the romance of science and technology shrinks to a fantasy about military hardware. While Hogan may be attempting to cash in on the popularity of the Cold War technothriller, he lacks Tom Clancy's willingness to jettison all else for hardware and suspense. Instead he uses his story as a platform for warning us about what crafty schemes the Soviets will come up with in their waning years. Unluckily, he achieves risibility by placing his novel in the year 2017 while retaining such standard details as an East German Soviet satellite, KGB men in blue serge suits, and large Russian women in shapeless dresses and thick stockings. We are asked to believe that a faltering Soviet command economy can create not only a space station three kilometers in diameter, but also a whirling underground replica somewhere in Siberia, fooling all but a few cynical CIA men. We are asked to believe that the Soviets plan to celebrate the centennial of the November revolution by starting World War III. We are asked to believe that Western politicians are knaves and Western scientists are fools while Western intelligence people are devoted public servants. Lew McCain, Hogan's hero, is a bloodless imitation, almost a parody, of Victor Hunt and Karl Zambendorf. All in all, one looks to Hogan for better work.

One finds better work in Hogan's post-1990 fiction, in which the propaganda is muted, even halfhearted. In *The Immortality Option,* he brings back the setting and characters of *Code of the Lifemaker,* and gives us a prequel-sequel explaining the origins of Titanian life. Much of the story is told from alien viewpoints, and Zambendorf and his team manage to save the Titanians from destruction by malevolent machine intelligences and misguided Earth officials. In *Out of Time,* two Manhattan detectives team up with a priest-biologist and a physicist to solve the mystery of temporal disruptions associated with large computer installations, and to eradicate the "plague." While the scientific speculation seems not fully worked out, the premise is uniquely imaginative and weirdly comic.

Hogan's fiction has become much more immersed in the technology, epistemology, and ethics of artificial intelligence, especially in its "cyborg" form. In *The Multiplex Man,* with a complex plot to match its exploration of identity, a volunteer finds himself "kidnapped" by a number of personalities inadvertently or deliberately downloaded into his body, and the object of a struggle between U.S. security forces and the agents of the despised but freedom-loving Offworlders. And in the dazzling *Realtime Interrupt,* computer scientist Joe Corrigan is able to free himself from imprisonment in a virtual reality program he helped design, foiling the plans of a corporate conspiracy to highjack the technology for crass commercial purposes. Corrigan finds his true love in the bargain, and returns to his native Ireland to work on pure research with a group of people that "no computer on earth could simulate."

The pastoral trajectory of Joe Corrigan reflects Hogan's recent career as an SF writer. Hogan is after all a romantic optimist: he shows us in his fictions that reason will ultimately prevail, and that superstition and ignorance present only temporary setbacks to the spirit of science. Yet like Corrigan he has recently begun to divide his time between the U.S. and Ireland, perhaps reflecting in that choice his fiction's desire to combine technological utopia with pastoral simplicity. In any case, James Hogan is a much more surprising storyteller now, and the change is all to the good.

—John P. Brennan

HOLDSTOCK, Robert

Pseudonyms: Robert Black; Chris Carlsen; Steve Eisler; Robert Faulcon; Richard Kirk. **Nationality:** British. **Born:** Hythe, Kent, 2 August 1948. **Education:** University College of North Wales, Bangor, 1967-70, B.Sc. (honours) in applied zoology 1970; London School of Hygiene and Tropical Medicine, 1970-71, M.Sc. in medical zoology 1971. **Career:** Research student, Medical Research Council, London, 1971-74. **Awards:** British Science Fiction Association award, 1985; World Fantasy Convention award, 1985. **Agent:** A.P. Watt Ltd., 26-28 Bedford Row, London WC1R4HL. **Address:** 54 Raleigh Road, London N8, England.

SCIENCE FICTION PUBLICATIONS

Novels (series: Mythago)

Eye Among the Blind. London, Faber, 1976; Garden City, New York, Doubleday, 1977.
Earthwind. London, Faber, 1977; New York, Pocket Books, 1978.
Where Time Winds Blow. London, Faber, and New York, Pocket Books, 1981.
Mythago Wood. London, Gollancz, 1984; New York, Arbor House, 1985.
Lavondyss: Journey to an Unknown Region (Mythago). London, Gollancz, 1988; New York, Morrow, 1989.
The Fetch. London, Orbit, 1991.
The Hollowing (Mythago). London, HarperCollins, and New York, Penguin, 1993.

Novels as Chris Carlsen (series: Berserker in all titles)

Shadow of the Wolf. London, Sphere, 1977.
The Bull Chief. London, Sphere, 1977.

The Horned Warrior. London, Sphere, 1979.

Short Stories

In the Valley of the Statues. London, Faber, 1982.
Elite: The Dark Wheel. Cambridge, Acornsoft, 1984.
The Bone Forest. London, Grafton, 1991.

OTHER PUBLICATIONS

Novels

Legend of the Werewolf (novelization of screenplay; as Robert Black). London, Sphere, 1976.
The Satanists (novelization of screenplay; as Robert Black). London, Futura, 1978.
Necromancer. London, Futura, 1978; New York, Avon, 1980.
Bulman. London, Futura, 1984.
One of Our Pigeons Is Missing. London, Futura, 1985.
The Emerald Forest (novelization of screenplay). New York, Zoetrope, and London, Penguin, 1985.

Novels as Richard Kirk (series: Raven in all titles)

Raven, Swordmistress of Chaos, with Angus Wells. London, Corgi, 1978.
A Time of Ghosts. London, Corgi, 1978.
Lords of the Shadows. London, Corgi, 1979.

Novels as Robert Faulcon (series: Nighthunter in all titles)

The Stalking. London, Arrow, 1983; as *Night Hunter,* New York, Charter, 1987.
The Talisman. London, Arrow, 1983; New York, Charter, 1987.
The Ghost Dance. London, Arrow, 1983: New York, Charter, 1987.
The Stalking [and] *The Talisman.* London, Arrow, 1987.
The Ghost Dance [and] *The Shrine.* London, Arrow, 1987.
The Shrine. London, Arrow, 1984; New York, Charter, 1988.
The Hexing. London, Arrow, 1984; New York, Charter, 1988.
The Labyrinth. New York, Berkley, 1987; New York, Charter, 1988.
The Hexing; and, The Labyrinth: Nighthunter Collection III. London, Legend, 1989.

Other

Space Wars: Worlds and Weapons (as Steve Eisler). London, Octopus, 1978.
Alien Landscapes, with Malcolm Edwards. London, Pierrot, 1979.
The Alien World: The Complete Illustrated Guide (as Steve Eisler). London, Octopus, 1978.
Tour of the Universe: The Journey of a Lifetime; The Recorded Diaries of Leio Scott and Caroline Luranski, with Malcolm Edwards. London, Pierrot, and New York, Mayflower, 1980.
Magician: The Lost Journals of the Magus, Geoffrey Carlyle, with Malcolm Edwards. Limpsfield, Surrey, Paper Tiger, 1982.
Realms of Fantasy, with Malcolm Edwards. Limpsfield, Surrey, Paper Tiger, 1983.
Lost Realms, with Malcolm Edwards. Limpsfield, Surrey, Paper Tiger, 1985; Topsfield, Massachusetts, Salem House, 1985.

Merlin's Wood; or, The Vision of Magic. London, HarperCollins, 1994.

Editor, *Encyclopedia of Science Fiction.* London, Octopus, 1978.
Editor, with Christopher Priest, *Stars of Albion* (anthology of British science fiction). London, Pan, 1979.
Editor, with Christopher Evans, *Other Edens.* London, Unwin Hyman, 3 vols., 1987-89.

*

Robert Holdstock comments:

(1985) I am usually inspired to write by the contemplation of far distant places and far distant times, be they future or past. I quite deliberately build into my work and my characters both a passionate awareness of past times and a strong sense of alienation. I relish alien landscapes, but am not concerned with futuristic man. My characters are humans of my own age, and I try to see them, and the exotic locations of time and space, to explore the boundaries and potentiality of man's awareness, of his senses, of his evolution. All my work is concerned with evolution, and with the persistence of memory, the continued presence—genetically, spiritually, passionately—of all of life in all of mankind.

*   *   *

Eye Among the Blind, Robert Holdstock's debut science fiction novel, attracted considerable attention because of its unique perspective. Interstellar civilization has been devastated by the appearance of a new and virulent plague which threatens the future of the entire human species. Desperate scientists turn to the only other known intelligent race, who live on a world where the nature of reality seems to be different. Visitors discover that evolution there is a dynamic, rapidly paced phenomenon. More unsettling is the fact that mythical creatures are assuming full reality, that the presence of intelligence in fact has influence over the structure of the physical universe. This blend of the rational and the fantastic is a theme which would figure significantly in Holdstock's more recent, and much more significant work.

Although Holdstock's next novel, *Earthwind,* is less successful in terms of story, his talent for exotic settings and fantastic imagery are apparent again. The planet Aeran is a primitive world whose culture undergoes a series of shocks when humans arrive. This time the author seems to have become too preoccupied with the backdrops, because the plot falters repeatedly.

This was not true of *Where Time Winds Blow,* the most successful of Holdstock's relatively conventional science fiction novels. Time is a variable factor on a far world where the winds blow down great rift valleys, transporting people and objects into time past or time future, apparently at random. There's a balancing transfer of matter from the destination time, a cosmic packrat effect, and some of the artifacts are valuable enough to support a thriving industry consisting of daring adventurers who are willing to risk being whisked off through time and space in return for the financial rewards of discovering a valuable artifact deposited by a previous timewind.

This is a complexly textured novel that anticipates Holdstock's major work. One of the high-ranking officials in the planetary government is mentally unbalanced, believes that the winds are actually a kind of weapon employed by time travelers existing outside the physical universe. Others on the planet are privy to a secret

infrastructure of knowledge which they refuse to share with outsiders, and all activities involving the timewinds are shrouded by bizarre rituals and a blend of superstition and charlatanism. The structure of the novel was apparently too complicated and divorced from scientific rigor for most genre readers, as it attracted little comment despite its originality and skillful presentation.

Holdstock briefly experimented with other genres, frequently under a pseudonym, although his most significant horror novel, *Necromancer,* appeared under his own name. *Necromancer,* a dark contemporary fantasy, involves the investigation of an ancient stone font in a British church. At one time in its mysterious past, the font was the sacred object of a group of pagans who worshiped animistic spirits. In the present day, the imprisoned spirits of the stone entrap the soul of a modern youth, whose mother pursues considerable efforts despite terrifying opposition to secure his spiritual freedom. Once again, references to a world of the imagination that lies hidden within our own provide the basic structure for the story.

As Robert Faulcon, Holdstock wrote a series of minor supernatural adventures, the "Nighthunter" series, about a man whose family has been kidnapped by a cult of satanists. To secure their release, he learns the Black Arts himself in an implausibly short time. As Chris Carlsen he produced three traditional heroic fantasies in a Viking setting, but these are also thoroughly unmemorable.

Holdstock finally attracted the attention his work deserved with *Mythago Wood.* The wood is a forest in Great Britain which has survived untouched since the last Ice Age. Within its depths exist elemental forces that shape reality, the origin of all human mythologies. The protagonist's explorations of the forest reveal wonder, terror, and renewed hope. It's a beautifully described setting, brilliantly evoked in the first two sequels. *Lavondyss: Journey to an Unknown Region* and *The Hollowing* both follow the adventures of other explorers into a world where what appears to be real may not be, where death is not final, and where the archetypes of legend may exist as concrete realities. The series propelled Holdstock from the stature of a minor but interesting writer to a major voice.

Although not a prolific short story writer, Holdstock has produced some tales of note, most of the best of which have been collected in *The Bone Forest.* The title story is also set in Mythago Wood and examines the nature of obsession, in this case a scientist whose determination to understand the peculiarities of the forest drive a wedge between himself and his family. Other stories of note include "The Shapechanger," "The Boy Who Jumped the Rapids," and "Scarrowfell."

It's clear that Holdstock's reputation has been established by the Mythago Wood novels, uncertain whether he will continue to sup at that same well and move forward into fresh territory. The success of the two sequels seems to indicate there is still fertile ground to be tilled, so it is likely Holdstock's reputation will continue to grow regardless of the direction he chooses to take.

—Don D'Ammassa

HOOVER, H(elen) M(ary)

Nationality: American. **Born:** Stark County, Ohio, 5 April 1935. **Education:** Louisville High School; Mount Union College, Alliance, Ohio; Los Angeles School of Nursing. **Agent:** (UK only) Marilyn Malin, 5/33 Ferncroft Ave., London NW3 7PG; for U.S., contact author. **Address:** 9405 Ulysses Court, Burke, Virginia 22015, U.S.A.

SCIENCE FICTION PUBLICATIONS

Novels (for children; series: Morrow)

Children of Morrow. New York, Four Winds Press, 1973; London, Methuen, 1975.
Treasures of Morrow. New York, Four Winds Press, 1976.
The Delikon. New York, Viking Press, 1977; London, Methuen, 1978.
The Rains of Eridan. New York, Viking Press, 1977; London, Methuen, 1978.
The Lost Star. New York, Viking Press, 1979; London, Methuen, 1980.
Return to Earth: A Novel of the Future. New York, Viking Press, 1980; London, Methuen, 1981.
This Time of Darkness. New York, Viking Press, 1980; London, Methuen, 1982.
Another Heaven, Another Earth. New York, Viking Press, 1981; London, Methuen, 1983.
The Bell Tree. New York, Viking Press, 1982.
The Shepherd Moon: A Novel of the Future. New York, Viking Press, and London, Methuen, 1984.
Orvis. New York, Viking Kestrel, and London, Methuen, 1987; as *Journey through the Empty,* London, Lighting, 1990.
The Dawn Palace: The Story of Medea. New York, Dutton, 1988.
Away Is a Strange Place to Be. New York, Dutton, 1990.
Only Child. New York, Dutton, 1992.
The Winds of Mars. New York, Dutton, 1995.

OTHER PUBLICATIONS

Other

The Lion's Cub (for children). New York, Four Winds Press, 1974.

*

Manuscript Collection: Kerlan Collection, University of Minnesota, Minneapolis.

Critical Study: *Science Fiction: The Mythos of a New Romance* by Janice Antczak, New York, Neal Schuman, 1985.

H.M. Hoover comments:

All fiction writers create singular worlds if they try, but in some respects fantastic worlds must be more real, more logically detailed and specific than straight fiction. When one writes about an alien world, it is just that to the reader. He or she must be told how and why it functions, and the telling must have consistency or all is lost. It must also be part of the story and not an inventory of facts. As a child I resented authors who ignored known facts (or facts *they* established within their fantasy) to make their plots work. I suspected them at first of ignorance and, later, of contempt for their readers. It is still done and I still have those suspicions.

*   *   *

H.M. Hoover consistently produces youth science fiction of very high quality, finding in SF a congenial and fertile ground for exploring those problems young people may face in less exotic environments: alienation from parents, feelings of isolation, feelings of being trapped or of being an anomalous creature out of sync with the Universe. Often Hoover's young people have special talents and sensitivities unappreciated by the adults around them.

So it is in *Children of Morrow* and its sequel *Treasures of Morrow.* Tia and Rabbit are telepaths ill-at-ease in their wasteland home, "The Base"; but a visit to the more advanced and enlightened community of Morrow proves ironically that home is not a simple matter to define. Anthropocentrism is examined in *The Rains of Eridan* when Theo, a young naturalist, and Karen, a child-orphan of conflict, team up first to survive, later to explore planetary lifeforms. Here and throughout Hoover's work, characters grope toward friendship across the generations and search for clues to enlighten their immediate situation and solve the larger mystery which imprisons those about them. Often the clear-eyed vision of children is instrumental in the process. The story of planetary exploration provides a background for their developing relationship. Karen learns to trust her new parent, and Theo learns that the child is skilled beyond her years both with laser gun and in the handling of fear and grief. ("Like you I can shut part of my mind off till it's safe to think again.")

In *The Lost Star* the young hero is ignored by parents who have adopted emotional reserve as a policy for working together as off-Earth astronomers over long periods of time. Hoover's ability, born of youthful innocence, to recognize intuitively the intelligence and intrinsic worth of alien creatures is reminiscent of Ursula K. Le Guin's *The Word for World Is Forest;* but Hoover's is a much lighter and more hopeful tale.

This Time of Darkness uses the familiar idea of the escape from an hermetic environment to explore in depth the struggle of children to receive the affection and acceptance which should be theirs by right. Ostracized for their ability to read, Amy and Axel are two children in a Big Brother-style underground hive community so benighted it has left scars on their bodies and has lost sight of any concept of a better world outside. Readers of SF will see in this story a children's literature counterpart of E.M. Forster's classic "The Machine Stops," and teachers may find it worthwhile for the hope it provides the abused child of the real world struggling for psychic survival. In *The Bell Tree* Hoover uses the device of archeologists exploring an alien world to study the relationships of a young woman, her father, and her first boyfriend; and in *The Shepherd Moon* the loneliness of Merry, a 13-year-old of the 48th century, is set against a background of terrorist intrigue.

Hoover has written that science fiction's presentation of ideas as images makes it important as a teaching tool, since imaging is the very thinking process Einstein and other great thinkers use to generate new ideas. In Hoover's fiction we find provocative images of scientific concepts and a liberating experience for the human spirit.

—Thomas P. Dunn

HOSHI, Shin'ichi

Nationality: Japanese. **Born:** 1926. **Education:** Tokyo University. **Career:** Cofounder, with Takumi Shibano, of the fanzine *Uchijin.*

SCIENCE FICTION PUBLICATIONS

Short Stories

Enu shi no yuenchi. Tokyo, Kodansha, 1971; translated by Stanleigh
H. Jones as *A Bag of Surprises,* Tokyo, Kodansha, 1989.
Kimagure robotto. Tokyo, Kadokawa, 1972; translated by Robert
Matthew as *The Capricious Robot,* Tokyo, Kodansha, 1986.
No saku hinshu. N.d.; translated by Bernard Susser and Tomoyoshi
Genkawa as *The Spiteful Planet and Other Stories,* Tokyo, Ja-
pan Times, 1978.
Nokku no otago. Tokyo, Shinchosha, 1985; translated by Stanleigh
H. Jones as *There Was a Knock,* Tokyo, Kodansha, 1984.

*   *   *

Shin'ichi Hoshi was one of the first professional science fiction
writers in Japan. Before his appearance, several writers had published old-fashioned invention stories or fantastic adventures. Hoshi,
however, wrote genuine science fiction and modern fantasy stories
ranking with works of Fredric Brown, Ray Bradbury, and Robert
Sheckley. He made his debut in 1957 in the *Hoseki* mystery magazine at the time, with "Sekisutora" (Sextra) reprinted from *Uchujin,*
the first Japanese science fiction fanzine. He won immediate popularity and became one of the most prolific writers.

Hoshi has specialized in the "short-short" stories, of which he
has turned out over 1000. His writing is extremely refined, readable, and fairly attractive, neither ambiguous nor pompous. Although short-short stories are generally considered unworthy of
rereading because readers who have already known the punch line
do not recuperate the wonder of the first reading, Hoshi's stories
are exceptions, recalling the Japanese tradition of Haiku. He is one
of the most popular writers in Japan. Even a reader who dislikes
science fiction or fantasy would have read one or two of his short-
short stories. Almost every work of his has been in print.

His first collection, *Jinzô Bijin* (A Man-Made Beauty, 1961),
contains 30 short-short stories including "Sekisutora," "Bokko-
chan" (translated in *F&SF,* June 1963), "Ôi, Dede Koi!"(translated
as "He-y, Come on Ou-t" in *F&SF,* November 1978), "Ai No
Kagi"(Key of Love), and "Tsuki No Hikari" (Moonshine). The latter two stories are as sentimental and poetic as Bradbury's. Later,
Hoshi became more satirical, repressing his ealier lyrical elements.
In 1967, he won The Award of the Mystery Writers Association of
Japan for his 10th collection, *Môsô Ginkô* (The Bank of Daydreams).
By that time he had transcended the generic boundaries of writing,
ranging from detective fiction (*Kimagure Shisû* [A Caprice Index,
1963]), juvenile science fiction (*Kuroi Hikari* [The Black Light,
1966] and *Kimagure Robot* [The Capricious Robot, 1966]), and a
biography of his businessman father (*Jinmin Wa Yokashi Kanri
Wa Tsuyoshi* [The People Are Weak, The Officials Are Strong,
1967]) to science fiction thriller (*Muma No Hyôteki* [Target of Nightmare, 1964]) dealing with an invasion from another dimension and/
or the unconscious. The significance of his transgeneric writing
lies in the wide variety of short-short stories, from satire to horror
story, from humorous fantasy to absurd tale.

During the 1970s, Hoshi expanded the potentiality of his writing range much more. He published some historical stories and a
play, several collections of essays, a biography of his grandfather
who was a well-known doctor, and a travelogue. In the decade his
most skillful short stories include "Fuzai No Hi" (The Day of Absence, contained in *Mirai Isoppu* [Aesop's Fable of the Future],

1971) in which the characters discuss the very plot structure of the
story narrated by their own author, and "Mon No Aru Ie" (The
Home with a Gate, contained in *Gotagota Kiryû* (The Troublous
Air Current, 1974) featuring a strange relationship of the dwellers
in a house.

Hoshi's most important work of science fiction is probably *Koe
No Ami* (Net of the Voice, 1970) featuring a near-future society in
which a computer controls the whole telephone network; people
are unconsciously handled by the computer. This novel is comparable with R.F. Jones's *Colossus,* though Hoshi did not describe
the computer as a tyrant: it accomplishes the conquest silently.

—Shinji Maki

HOSKINS, Robert

Pseudonym: Grace Corren; John Gregory; Susan Jennifer; Michael
Kerr. **Nationality:** American. **Born:** Lyons Falls, New York, 23
May 1933. **Education:** Attended Albany State College for Teachers, New York, 1951-52. **Career:** Worked in family business, 1952-
64; attendant, Wassaic State School for the Retarded, New York,
1964-66; house parent, Brooklyn Home for Children, 1966-68; sub-
agent, Scott Meredith Literary Agency, New York, 1967-68; senior
editor, Lancer Books, New York, 1969-72. Since 1972, freelance
writer. **Address:** c/o Harlequin Enterprises, 225 Duncan Mill Road,
Don Mills, Ontario M3B 3K9, Canada.

SCIENCE FICTION PUBLICATIONS

Novels (series: Alnians; Mack Bolan's Phoenix Force)

Evil in the Family (as Grace Corren). New York, Lancer, 1972.
The Shattered People. Garden City, New York, Doubleday, 1975.
Master of the Stars (Alnians). Toronto, Laser, 1976.
To Control the Stars (Alnians). New York, Ballantine, 1977.
Tomorrow's Son. Garden City, New York, Doubleday, 1977.
Jack-in-the-Box Planet (for children) Philadelphia, Westminster
Press, 1978.
To Escape the Stars (Alnians). New York, Ballantine, 1978.
The Attic Child (as Grace Corren). Los Angeles, Pinnacle, 1979.
Legacy of the Stars (as John Gregory). New York, Leisure Books,
1979; as Robert Hoskins, London, Hale, 1981.
The Island of Dr. Moreau (as Michael Kerr; adapted from the novel
by H.G. Wells). New York, Scholastic, 1978.
The Night Runner: The Gemini Run (as Michael Kerr). New York,
Charter, 1979.
The Fury Bombs (as Gar Wilson; Phoenix Force). Toronto, World-
wide, 1983.

OTHER PUBLICATIONS

Novels

The House of Counted Hatreds (as Susan Jennifer). New York,
Avon, 1973; as Grace Corren, Los Angelels, Pinnacle, 1980.

Country of the Kind (as Susan Jennifer). New York, Avon, 1975.
Survival Run (novelization of screenplay). Los Angeles, Pinnacle, 1979.

Novels as Grace Corren

The Darkest Room. New York, Lancer, 1969.
A Place on Dark Island. New York, Lancer, 1971.
Mansion of Deadly Dreams. New York, Popular Library, 1973.
Dark Threshold. New York, Popular Library, 1977.

Play

Television Play: *Birthday Party (Kojak* series), 1976.

Other

Editor, *First Step Outward.* New York, Dell, 1969.
Editor, *Infinity 1-5.* New York, Lancer, 5 vols., 1970-73.
Editor, *The Stars Around Us.* New York, New American Library, 1970.
Editor, *Swords Against Tomorrow.* New York, New American Library, 1970.
Editor, *Tomorrow 1.* New York, New American Library, 1971.
Editor, *The Far-Out People.* New York, New American Library, 1971.
Editor, *Wondermakers 1-2.* New York, Fawcett, 2 vols., 1972-74.
Editor, *Strange Tomorrows.* New York, Lancer, 1972.
Editor, *The Edge of Never: Classic and Contemporary Tales of the Supernatural.* New York, Fawcett, 1973.
Editor, *The Liberated Future.* New York, Fawcett, 1974.
Editor, *The Future Now: Saving Tomorrow.* New York, Fawcett, 1977.
Editor, *Against Tomorrow.* New York, Fawcett, 1979.

*

Robert Hoskins comments:

An unhappy, and fat, childhood in a small Adirondack football village turned me early to escapism. Comics led to pulps, to fandom, through the letter columns. After years of writing, I began selling an occasional story while still gathering pounds of rejection slips. It was not until I worked, first, for an agent, and then as an editor, that I learned the techniques of novel construction. Impossible though the idea is, I think all young writers should have a spell in both jobs. I consider myself strictly an entertainer; the one novel that is deliberately allegorical I have not at this date been able to sell. I've published 40 short stories, but find it easier to construct a novel. Once an idea comes, it seems to grow and grow.

*   *   *

Except for *Evil in the Family,* a gothic novel involving a time-travel fantasy, Robert Hoskins's major contribution to science fiction until 1975 was in writing, anthologizing and introducing short stories, and acting as general and then senior editor for Lancer Books' science fiction program. Although he has continued these activities, he has also added to them, expanding themes from his short stories into a series of novels which explore the inherent value of primitive versus technological man, the effects of free evolution versus outside interference and artificial control, the need for change

and progress and the threat of regression without it, and the private, economic, and sociological reasons for galactic exploration. His works are always filled with action and adventure, monsters and barbaric peoples, advanced races and mercenary predators. As he notes in his introductions, man has had and always will have his heroes, and, while the nature of their heroism and the weapons which they wield in the name of progress and right may change, their essential questing spirit and dreams of glory do not.

In *The Shattered People* Hoskins gradually reveals the secret ties between a savage desert world of naked hunters armed with slings and stones and a highly technological nuclear civilization ruled by a tyrannical council contemptuous of life. In the first, vicious cats prowl in packs and sentient aliens (huge, bird-like creatures) keep watch, while in the other, urban rebels, aided by their "empress," a titular head virtually imprisoned in her own palace, meet in subterranean passages and plot to throw off their shackles. Mind-wipes and deportation thrust the strongest and most outspoken members of the urban world into the primitive one, until one man's psi powers enable him to regain his memory and bridge the gap between the two, merging the instinctive with the rational for an unbeatable pair.

Tomorrow's Son, set in the 23rd century, focuses on a geneticist and his android son, trapped in a rigid, genetically predetermined caste system, which they are determined to alter in order to assure a better world. On Earth the father engages in forbidden android research to help revitalize the swiftly deteriorating genetic make-up of humanity, while on a primitive planet, Karyllia, his son struggles to protect alien humanoids from repeating humanity's evolutionary mistakes, only to discover that he must protect them not only from themselves but from the fanaticism and destructiveness of his own world. Both men prove pawns of larger schemes to protect Karyllia from outside interference and to force humans to accept change— change that can revitalize a regressing world where average I.Q. decreases yearly and masses of subhumans are crowded into barracks, experience sex and violence vicariously, and drown their minds in joyjuice. The book includes bizarre beasts of burden, strange snake-lizards in swamps, and primitive tribal conflicts. As usual, Hoskins emphasizes the stench of primitive worlds and the lack of respect for life in both primitive and advanced societies.

In his trilogy (*Master of the Stars, To Control the Stars, To Escape the Stars*) Hoskins sets up a universal cycle of development and regression and postulates a series of stargates on most worlds, built by an ancient interstellar race; one sets the controls and steps into other worlds, some of which have regressed to the primitive while others have advanced to the stars. *Master of the Stars* focuses on the Alnians at the height of their development, struggling to avoid the contaminating barbarism of other worlds. *To Control the Stars* deals with an internal conflict in the Society for Humanoidic Studies, a conflict that affects the future of thousands of worlds and forces the central character to fight for his life from world to world and to seek answers among the Alnians (the only humanoids with a continuous history). The Society's original goal, observation of other worlds without interference, has been perverted into a lust for power, wealth, and exploitation that focuses on evolutionary control and forced rapid progress. There is much action— escape, recapture, romance. *To Escape the Stars* picks up thousands of years later when the Society has been reduced to a library cult devoutly recording galactic history. A scheme to plunder a rich, high-gravity world of rural innocents leads first to treachery, and then to a revived search for the Alnians and their master codex to the stargates. The main figure changes from a jaded and unscrupulous exploiter to a student of the universe, and discovers the dangers of isolation and of failure to accept change and conflict.

Hoskins argues man's need for challenge, discovery, and change, but at the same time suggests that no matter how far man progresses and how much he changes, he will always carry with him inescapable characteristics and instincts from his primitive past—instincts that help him survive and that, at times, impel him to heroic deeds.

—Gina Macdonald

————

HOUGH, S.B. *See* **GORDON, Rex.**

————

HOYLE, Fred and Geoffrey

Nationality: British. **HOYLE, Fred: Born:** Bingley, Yorkshire, 24 June 1915. **Education:** Bingley Grammar School; Emmanuel College, Cambridge (Mayhew Prizeman, 1936; Smith's Prizeman, 1938; Goldsmith Exhibitioner; Senior Exhibitioner of the Royal Commission for the Exhibition of 1851), mathematical tripos 1936, M.A. 1939. **Military Service:** Served in the Admiralty, London, 1939-45. **Family:** Married Barbara Clark in 1939; one son, Geoffrey Hoyle, and one daughter. **Career:** Research Fellow, St. John's College, 1939-72, University Lecturer in Mathematics, 1945-58, Plumian Professor of Astronomy and Experimental Philosophy, 1958-72, and Director, Institute of Theoretical Astronomy, 1966-72, Cambridge University. Visiting Professor, 1953, 1954, 1956, Fairchild Scholar, 1974-75, and since 1963, Associate in Physics, California Institute of Technology, Pasadena. Staff member, Mount Wilson and Palomar observatories, California, 1957-62; Professor of Astronomy, Royal Institution, London, 1969-72; White Professor, Cornell University, Ithaca, New York, 1972-78. Honorary Research Professor, University of Manchester, since 1972, and University College, Cardiff, since 1975; since 1973, Honorary Fellow, St. John's College, Cambridge; since 1984, Honorary Fellow, Emmanuel College, Cambridge. Member, Science Research Council, 1968-72. **Awards:** Royal Astronomical Society Gold Medal, 1968; Kalinga prize, 1968; Astronomical Society of the Pacific Bruce Medal, 1970, and Klumpke-Roberts award, 1977; Royal Society Medal, 1974. Guest of Honor, Frontiers of Astronomy Symposium, Venice, 1975. Sc.D.: University of East Anglia, Norwich, 1967; D.Sc.: University of Leeds, 1969; University of Bradford, 1975; University of Newcastle, 1976. Fellow, 1957, and Vice-President, 1969-71, Royal Society; Honorary member, American Academy of Arts and Sciences, 1964, Royal Irish Academy, 1977, and Mark Twain Society, 1978. Foreign member, American Philosophical Society, 1980. Foreign Associate, National Academy of Sciences (U.S.A.), 1969; president, Royal Astronomical Society, 1971-73. Knighted, 1972. **Address:** c/o Royal Society, 6 Carlton House Terrace, London SW1Y 5AG, England. **HOYLE, Geoffrey: Born:** Scunthorpe, Lincolnshire, 12 January 1942; son of Fred Hoyle. Educated at Bryanston School, Blandford Forum, Dorset, 1955-59; St. John's College, Cambridge, 1961-62. **Family:** Married Valerie Jane Coope in 1971. Worked in documentary film production, 1963-67. **Address:** 8 Milner Road Bournemouth BH4 8AO, England.

SCIENCE FICTION PUBLICATIONS

Novels

Fifth Planet. London, Heinemann, and New York, Harper, 1963.
Rockets in Ursa Major: A Novel. London, Heinemann, and New York, Harper, 1969.
Seven Steps to the Sun. London, Heinemann, and New York, Harper, 1970.
The Molecule Men and The Monster of Loch Ness: Two Short Novels. London, Heinemann, 1972; as *The Molecule Men,* New York, Harper, 1972.
The Inferno. London, Heinemann, and New York, Harper, 1973.
Into Deepest Space. New York, Harper, 1974; London, Heinemann, 1975.
The Incandescent Ones, edited by Barbara Hoyle. London, Heinemann, and New York, Harper, 1977.
The Westminster Disaster, edited by Barbara Hoyle. London, Heinemann, and New York, Harper, 1978.
The Energy Pirate (for children). Loughborough, Ladybird, 1982.
The Giants of Universal Park (for children). Loughborough, Ladybird, 1982.
The Frozen Planet of Azuron (for children). Loughborough, Ladybird, 1982.
The Planet of Death (for children). Loughborough, Ladybird, 1982.

Novels by Fred Hoyle (series: Andromeda)

The Black Cloud. London, Heinemann, and New York, Harper, 1957.
Ossian's Ride. London, Heinemann, and New York, Harper, 1959.
A for Andromeda: A Novel of Tomorrow (novelization of TV serial), with John Elliot. London Souvenir Press, and New York, Harper, 1962.
Andromeda Breakthrough: A Novel of Tomorrow's Universe (novelization of TV serial), with John Elliot. London, Souvenir Press, and New York, Harper, 1964.
October the First Is Too Late. London, Heinemann, and New York, Harper, 1966.
Comet Halley: A Novel in Two Parts. London, Joseph, 1985; New York, St. Martin's Press, 1986.

Short Stories by Fred Hoyle

Element 79. New York, Signet, 1967.

OTHER PUBLICATIONS

Other

Commonsense in Nuclear Energy. London, Heinemann, and San Francisco, Freeman, 1980.

OTHER PUBLICATIONS BY FRED HOYLE

Plays

Rockets in Ursa Major (for children: produced London, 1962).

Television Plays (with John Elliot): *A for Andromeda* serial, 1961; *The Andromeda Breakthrough* serial, 1962.

Other

Some Recent Researches in Solar Physics. Cambridge, University Press, 1949.
The Nature of the Universe: A Series of Broadcast Lectures. Oxford, Blackwell, 1950; New York, Harper, 1951; revised edition, 1960.
A Decade of Decision. London, Heinemann, 1953.
Frontiers of Atronomy. London, Heinemann, and New York, Harper, 1955.
Man and Materialism. New York, Harper, 1956; London, Allen and Unwin, 1957.
Astronomy. London, Macdonald, and New York, Doubleday, 1962.
A Contradiction in the Argument of Malthus (lecture). Hull, University of Hull, 1963.
Star Formation. London, Her Majesty's Stationery Office, 1963.
Of Men and Galaxies. Seattle, University of Washington Press, 1964; London, Heinemann, 1965.
Nucleosynthesis in Massive Stars and Supernovae, with William A. Fowler. Chicago, University of Chicago Press, 1965.
Encounter with the Future. New York, Simon and Schuster, 1965.
The Asymmetry of Time (lecture). Canberra, Australian National University, 1965.
Galaxies, Nuclei, and Quasars. New York, Harper, 1965; London, Heinemann, 1966.
Man in the Universe. New York, Columbia University Press, 1966.
The New Face of Science. Cleveland, World, 1971.
From Stonehenge to Modern Cosmology. San Francisco, Freeman, 1972.
Nicolaus Copernicus: An Essay on His Life and Work. London, Heinemann, and New York, Harper, 1973.
Action-at-a-Distance in Physics and Cosmology, with J.V. Narlikar. San Francisco, Freeman, 1974.
Astronomy and Cosmology: A Modern Course. San Francisco, Freeman, 1975.
Astronomy Today. London, Heinemann, 1975; as *Highlights in Astronomy,* San Francisco, Freeman, 1975.
Ten Faces of the Universe. London, Heinemann, and San Francisco, Freeman, 1977.
On Stonehenge. London, Heinemann, and San Francisco, Freeman, 1977.
Energy or Extinction? The Case for Nuclear Energy. London, Heinemann, 1977.
The Cosmogony of the Solar System. Cardiff, University College Press, 1978; Short Hills, New Jersey, Enslow, 1979.
Lifecloud: The Origin of Life in the Universe, with Chandra Wickramasinghe. London, Dent, 1978; New York, Harper, 1979.
Diseases from Space, with Chandra Wickramasinghe. London, Dent, 1979; New York, Harper, 1980.
The Physics-Astronomy Frontier, with J.V. Narlikar. San Francisco, Freeman, 1980.
Steady-State Cosmology Revisited. Cardiff, University College Press, 1980.
The Relation of Astronomy to Biology. Cardiff, University College Press, 1980.
Ice: The Ultimate Human Catastrophe. New York, Hutchinson, and New York, Continuum, 1981.
The Quasar Controversy Resolved. Cardiff, University College Press, 1981.
Evolution from Space, with Chandra Wickramasinghe. London, Dent, 1981; New York, Simon and Schuster, 1982.
Space Travellers, The Bringers of Life, with Chandra Wickramasinghe, edited by Barbara Hoyle. Cardiff, University College Press, and Hillside, New Jersey, Enslow, 1981.
Facts and Dogmas in Cosmology and Elsewhere (Rede Lecture). Cambridge, University Press, 1982.
Efroms and Other Papers on the Origin of Life. Hillside, New Jersey, Enslow, 1982.
The Universe According to Hoyle. Hillside, New Jersey, Enslow, 1982.
The Intelligent Universe: A New View of Creation and Evolution. London, Joseph, 1983; New York, Holt Rinehart, 1984.
Flight. Loughborough, Ladybird, 1984.
Archaeopteryx, the Primordial Bird: A Case of Fossil Forgery, with Chandra Wickramasinghe. Swansea, Christopher Davies, 1986.
The Small World of Fred Hoyle: An Autobiography. London, Joseph, 1986.
Cosmic Life-Forces, with Chandra Wickramasinghe. London, Dent, 1988; New York, Paragon House, 1990.
The Theory of Cosmic Grains, with Chandra Wickramasinghe. Boston, Kluwer, 1991.
The Origin of the Universe and the Origin of Religion. Wakefield, Rhode Island, Moyer Bell, 1993.
Our Place in the Cosmos: The Unfinished Revolution, with Chandra Wickramasinghe. London, Dent, 1993.
Home is Where the Wind Blows: Chapters from a Cosmologist's Life. Mill Valley, California, University Science Books, 1994.

OTHER PUBLICATIONS BY GEOFFREY HOYLE

Other

2010: Living in the Future (for children). London, Heinemann, 1972; New York, Parents' Magazine Press, 1974.
Disaster (for children). London, Heinemann, 1975.
Ask Me Why, with Janice Robertson. London, Severn House, 1976.

*   *   *

If there is a single theme common to the work of noted astronomer Fred Hoyle, the bulk of whose fiction was a collaborative effort with his son Geoffrey, it is that the salvation of humanity lies not in our political institutions, but in the free operation and far-ranging minds of the scientific community. A more welcome concept for science fiction readers would be hard to imagine, and given his own background in the scientific community, it is unsurprising that he should be so partisan.

Perhaps coincidentally, Hoyle's three most interesting novels were the ones written before he began collaborating, first with John Elliot, then with son Geoffrey. *The Black Cloud* is a novel of world catastrophe: a cloud of immense proportions enters our solar system, cutting off the sunlight and dooming the human race to extinction. One scientist has an inspiration; the cloud itself may well be a living entity, and if some way can be found to communicate, doom may be averted. He mobilizes an effort in short order, and in the waning hours achieves success. The attraction of the novel was not only its melodramatic plot, but Hoyle's infectious fascination with the mysteries and potential of outer space.

In *Ossian's Ride*, the protagonist is a scientist recruited as a spy to infiltrate a secretive research establishment in Ireland. It doesn't take long for him to realize there is an undertext to what he is being told, but his efforts to investigate further alert his quarries to their danger. After a thrilling series of chases and escapes, he and the reader learn that technological information from another world has been transmitted to Earth, and the scientists who received it are making great efforts to prevent it from falling into the wrong hands, specifically those of the government.

Unprecedented solar emanations interfere with the normal flow of time in *October the First Is Too Late*, the most ambitious of Hoyle's solo novels. Different parts of the world are thrown forward or backward in time. Once again, the only possible salvation is if scientists can somehow find a way to counteract the effect and restore time's equilibrium.

In the early 1960s, Hoyle worked on a BBC television series, and he produced two subsequent novelizations in collaboration with John Elliot, *A for Andromeda* and *Andromeda Breakthrough*. This was the dark other side of the theme of *Ossian's Ride;* an intelligent species is beaming information to Earth, but not benevolently in this instance. Rather, they are using human scientists as pawns in their plan to launch an invasion of the Earth, implanting their strategy secretly in the programming of a supercomputer constructed under their tutelage. Thwarted in the first volume, they use a robot still under their control to pursue their quest in the second, with an equal lack of success.

Fifth Planet, representing the first appearance of Geoffrey as co-writer, is a similar invasion story, this time from a mysterious planet passing through the far reaches of our system. The aliens in this case are capable of mimicking real human beings and supplanting them, although their counterfeit is inept enough to alert the protagonist to what is happening. Once again, the answer is a scientific one, rather than ineffectual government action. Another alien power menaces Earth in *Rockets in Ursa Major,* but the danger is so intellectualized, there is little suspense in this lackluster effort.

A man finds himself propelled 10 years into the future in *Seven Steps to the Sun,* an occasionally interesting but very slow-paced novel. *The Inferno* is a return to the world catastrophe story, this time resulting from the advent of a quasar close enough to cause disastrous climatological effects on Earth. It's a more convincing story than most of the later books, with a strong but believable protagonist bringing order out of chaos, but there was little to differentiate it from a large number of similar novels. *Into Deepest Space,* the sequel to *Rockets in Ursa Major,* is a space opera rendered almost unreadable by intrusive discourses on the details of life in space.

A different sort of alien invasion provides the theme in *The Incandescent Ones.* Alien star travellers offer humanity the benefits of their superscience, but there is a hidden cost that may be too high to pay. This is one of the few occasions where the Hoyles imply that "there are some things man was not meant to know," at least during this stage of human development. Unfortunately, the novel is predictable and slow moving, often because of the heavy-handed way in which the authors preach their message. *The Westminster Disaster* was more of a contemporary spy thriller with science fiction overtones, a power struggle between world powers

with terrifying consequences for England. Once again, the Hoyles use the opportunity to point out the danger of putting too much trust in government institutions. Unlike the novels that immediately preceded it, the plot and narrative move quite fluidly in this case, although the nature of the political struggle is somewhat dated.

Fred Hoyle's solo shorter fiction was collected in *Element 79,* but although some of these provide interesting insights into Hoyle's view of the world, none are of particular note as fiction. He and Geoffrey collaborated on two novellas, "The Molecule Men" and "The Monster of Loch Ness," both of which are of some merit. The former is an almost lighthearted scientific mystery, the latter a reasonably suspenseful story of Nessie.

—Don D'Ammassa

HOYLE, Trevor

Nationality: British. **Born:** Rochdale, Lancashire, 25 February 1940. **Education:** Rochdale Grammar School, 1951-57. **Awards:** BBC/Radio Times Drama award, 1990. **Agent:** Sheil Land Associates Ltd., 43 Doughty Street, London WC1N 2LF. **Address:** 34 Cedar Lane, Newhey, Rochdale, Lancashire OL16 4LQ, England.

SCIENCE FICTION PUBLICATIONS

Novels (series: Blake's Seven; Q)

Q: Seeking the Mythical Future. London, Panther, 1977; New York, Ace, 1982.
Q: Through the Eye of Time. London, Panther, 1977; New York, Ace, 1982.
Terry Nation's Blake's 7. London, Sphere, 1977; reprinted *Terry Nation's Blake's Seven: Their First Adventure,* Secaucus, New Jersey, Lyle Stuart, 1988.
Q: The Gods Look Down. London, Panther, 1978; New York, Ace, 1982.
Terry Nation's Blake's 7: Project Avalon. London, Arrow, 1979; Secaucus, New Jersey, Lyle Stuart, 1988.
Earth Cult. London, Panther, 1979; as *This Sentient Earth,* New York, Zebra, 1979.
Terry Nation's Blake's 7: Scorpio Attack. London, BBC, 1981; Secaucus, New Jersey, Lyle Stuart, 1988.
The Last Gasp. New York, Crown, 1983; London, Sphere, 1984; revised, London, Grafton, 1990.
Blind Needle. New York, Riverrun Press, 1994; London, Calder, 1994.

OTHER PUBLICATIONS

Novels

The Relatively Constant Copywriter. Manchester, Northern Writers, 1972.
Rule of Night. London, Futura, 1975.
The Sexless Spy. London, Sphere, 1977.
The Svengali Plot. London, Sphere, 1978.

The Man Who Travelled on Motorways. London, Calder, and Dallas Texas, Riverrun, 1997.

The Stigma. London, Sphere, 1980.

Vail. London, Calder, and Dallas, Riverrun, 1984.

K.I.D.S. London, Sphere, 1987; New York, Berkley, 1990.

The Hard Game. London, New English Library, 1973.

Rock Fix. London, Futura, 1977.

Plays

Television Plays: *Terry Nation's Blake's Seven: Ultraworld,* 1980; *Whatever Happened to the Heroes?,* 1982.

Radio Plays: *Conflagration,* 1991; *Gigo,* 1991.

*

Manuscript Collection: Rochdale Reference Library, Lancashire.

*   *   *

Trevor Hoyle's well known "Q" series consists of three books: *Seeking the Mythical Future, Through the Eye of Time,* and *The Gods Look Down.* Christian Queghan is a Myth Technologist who investigates possible pasts and futures in a discipline that assures all realities are equally probable. In *Seeking the Mythical Future* Queghan is inserted into a parallel universe where humans and dinosaurs exist together, where personal beliefs are rigidly controlled, and where Psychological Concentration Camps exist for those who will not conform to normalcy. The satire on scientific methods and bureaucratic bungling makes the book lively yet profoundly serious.

Through the Eye of Time is the most ambitious book in the series. The scientists of Queghan's Earth IVn, a terraformed version of Old Earth, are working on a project to reconstruct a human brain. The identity chosen: Adolf Hitler. Queghan involves himself in the project when he finds the computer exchanging data by coincidence. That coincidence convinces Queghan that an alternate reality—where Germany developed the Atomic Bomb first—is undermining the reality of his Earth's reality. Only insertion into that alternate reality can prevent the disaster that threatens the spacetime continuum. Hoyle captures the personality of Hitler beautifully and creates a unique, sinister character in Dr. Theodor Morell, personal physician to Hitler.

The concluding volume is less successful. Queghan joins forces with Dr. Francis Dagon to decipher primitive texts from ancient Earth through Myth Technology. The computer describes the legendary Ark of the Covenant in the form of blueprints for an existing technology. Queghan is sure Dagon is using his research findings in an attempt to change history. Only Queghan's power to insert himself into alternate realities can stop Dagon's plans to alter the past. The idea is clever, but the book's conclusion is too clichéd, much too predictable. However, the "Q" series is one of the best extended explorations of alternative realities in science fiction.

Hoyle's best book is an environmental disaster novel, *The Last Gasp.* Earth is totally polluted: the microscopic plant life in the oceans is dying, causing the beginning of the destruction of the food chain. At the same time, the super-powers plan to fight their next war with new, deadly forms of environmental warfare. British marine biologist Gavin Chase and a team of scientists realize the Earth is doomed and attempt to escape the death of the biosphere

by building giant space colonies to survive in. Yet they have enemies in the military-industrial complex who refuse to believe that Earth is dying. Chief of these forces is Lloyd Madden, an evil genius who desires the death of the human race so he can repopulate it with a new race of mutants. *The Last Gasp* delivers a chilling portrait of disaster and hope.

Hoyle's most haunting work is the frankly erotic novel *The Man Who Travelled on Motorways.* As the narrator travels, his mind explores the realities and fantasies of his life. Much of the book is surreal, but science fictional aspects are apparent in the discussion of reality. Much of the book is sexist: Hoyle's narrator seems incapable of love, merely using women to satisfy his sexual needs in loathsome fashions. Yet the book speaks to the unconscious desires of travelers of either sex and takes a bold, difficult path to break down life's certainties into more truthful probabilities.

Terry Nation's Blake's 7: Scorpio Attack is a novelization based on the popular BBC television SF series. Hoyle brings together three scripts written by Chris Boucher, James Follett, and Robert Holmes; the resulting novel will be a delight to fans of the series as the followers of Blake fight against the Dictatorship following the Atomic Wars with their new space ship, *Scorpio.*

In *Terry Nation's Blake's 7: Project Avalon,* Hoyle takes Roj Blake and his crew from Amersat, Planet of the Dead, to the planet Aristos with its oceans of acid and with the Federation's Supreme Commander Servaian and Space Commander Travis intent on destroying Blake's Seven. This is space opera at its frothiest.

Trevor Hoyle is an unusual writer with a gift for blending the real and the surreal in his dreamlike visions.

—George Kelley

HUBBARD, L(aFayette) Ron(ald)

Nationality: American. **Born:** Tilden, Nebraska, 13 March 1911. **Education:** George Washington University, Washington, D.C., B.S. in civil engineering 1934; Princeton University, New Jersey, 1945; Sequoia University, Ph.D. 1950. **Family:** Married Mary Sue Whipp; two daughters and two sons. **Career:** Wrote travel and aviation articles in the 1930s; explorer: Commander, Caribbean Motion Picture Expedition, 1931, West Indies Mineral Survey Expedition, 1932, and Alaskan Radio-Experimental Expedition, 1940. Director, Hubbard Foundation; founding director, Church of Scientology, 1952; director, Dianetics and Scientology, 1952-66; resigned all directorships, 1966. **Died:** 29 January 1986.

SCIENCE FICTION PUBLICATIONS

Novels (series: Mission Earth)

Death's Deputy. Los Angeles, Fantasy, 1948.

Final Blackout. Providence, Rhode Island, Hadley, 1948.

Slaves of Sleep. Chicago, Shasta, 1948.

Triton, and Battle of Wizards. Los Angeles, Fantasy, 1949.

The Kingslayer (includes "The Beast" and "The Invaders"). Los Angeles, Fantasy, 1949; as *Seven Steps to the Arbiter,* Chatsworth, California, Major, 1975.

Two Science Fantasy Novels by L. Ron Hubbard: Typewriter in the Sky, Fear. New York, Gnome Press, 1951; as *Fear, and Typewriter in the Sky,* New York, Popular Library, 1977.

From Death to the Stars (includes *Death's Deputy* and *The Kingslayer*). Los Angeles, Fantasy, 1953.

Return to Tomorrow. New York, Ace, 1954; London, Panther, 1957.

Fear: An Outstanding Psychological Science Fiction Novel. New York, Galaxy, 1957.

Fear, and Ultimate Adventure. New York, Berkley, 1970.

Battlefield Earth: A Saga of the Year 3000. New York, St. Martin's Press, 1982; London, Quadrant, 1984.

Mission Earth:

   The Invaders Plan. Los Angeles, Bridge, 1985; London, New Era, 1986.

   Death Quest. Los Angeles, Bridge, 1985; London, New Era, 1987.

   Black Genesis: Fortress of Evil. Los Angeles, Bridge, 1986; London, New Era, 1986.

   The Enemy Within. Los Angeles, Bridge, 1986; London, New Era, 1987.

   An Alien Affair. Los Angeles, Bridge, 1986; London, New Era, 1987.

   Fortune of Fear. Los Angeles, Bridge, 1986; London, New Era, 1987.

   Voyage of Vengeance. Los Angeles, Bridge, 1987; London, New Era, 1988.

   Disaster. Los Angeles, Bridge, 1987; London, New Era, 1988.

   Villany Victorious. Los Angeles, Bridge, 1987; London, New Era, 1988.

   The Doomed Planet. Los Angeles, Bridge, 1987; London, New Era, 1988.

Short Stories

Ole Doc Methuselah. Austin, Texas, Theta Press, 1970.

Lives You Wished to Lead But Never Dared, edited by V.S. Wilhite. Clearwater, Florida, Theta Press, 1978.

The Ghoul. Hollywood, Author Services, 1991.

The Ultimate Adventure. Hollywood, Author Services, 1992.

Fantasy Short Stories. Hollywood, Author Services, 1993.

Science Fiction Short Stories. Hollywood, Author Services, 2 vols., 1993-94.

The Automatic Horse (for children). Hollywood, Author Services, 1994.

To the Stars. Hollywood, Author Services, 1995.

OTHER PUBLICATIONS

Novel

Buckskin Brigades. New York, Macaulay, 1937; London, Wright and Brown, 1938.

Short Stories

Arctic Wings. Hollywood, Author Services, 1991.

Black Towers to Danger. Hollywood, Author Services, 1991.

The Carnival of Death. Hollywood, Author Services, 1991.

The Case of the Friendly Corpse. Hollywood, Author Services, 1991.

Guns of Mark Jardine. Hollywood, Author Services, 1991.

Hell's Legionnaire, The Conroy Diary, Buckley Pays a Hunch: A Special Collecton of Short Stories. Hollywood, Author Services, 1991.

The Red Dragon. Hollywood, Author Services, 1991.

Six-Gun Caballero. Hollywood, Author Services, 1991.

Adventure Short Stories. Hollywood, Author Services, 5 vols., 1992-94.

The Chee-Chalker. Hollywood, Author Services, 1992.

Empty Saddles. Hollywood, Author Services, 1992.

Forbidden Gold. Hollywood, Author Services, 1992.

Hot Lead Payoff. Hollywood, Author Services, 1992.

Inky Odds. Hollywood, Author Services, 1992.

The Kilkenny Cats Series. Hollywood, Author Services, 1992.

Sea Fangs. Hollywood, Author Services, 1992.

The Tramp. Hollywood, Author Services, 1992.

Western Short Stories. Hollywood, Author Services, 6 vols., 1992-95.

Wild-Gone-Mad, and Hurricane's Roar. Hollywood, Author Services, 1992.

The Battling Pilot. Hollywood, Author Services, 1993.

Brass Keys to Murder. Hollywood, Author Services, 1993.

Hurtling Wings. Hollywood, Author Services, 1993.

The Indigestible Triton. Hollywood, Author Services, 1993.

The Sky-Crasher. Hollywood, Author Services, 1993.

Branded Outlaw. Hollywood, Author Services, 1994.

The Falcon Killer. Hollywood, Author Services, 1994.

Hostage to Death; and, Killer Ape. Hollywood, Author Services, 1994.

The Iron Duke. Hollywood, Author Services, 1994.

Mystery/Suspense Short Stories. Hollywood, Author Services, 1994.

Sabotage in the Sky. Hollywood, Author Services, 1994.

Trouble on His Wings. Hollywood, Author Services, 1994.

Poetry

Hymn of Asia: An Eastern Poem. Los Angeles, Church of Scientology, 1974.

Other

Dianetics: The Modern Science of Mental Health. New York, Hermitage House, 1950; London, Ridgway, 1951.

Science of Survival. Wichita and East Grinstead, Sussex, Hubbard, 1951.

Self Analysis. Wichita, International Library of Arts and Science, 1951.

Dianetics: The Original Thesis. Wichita, Wichita Publishing, 1951.

Handbook for Preclears. Wichita, Scientic Press, 1951.

Notes on the Lectures of L. Ron Hubbard. Wichita, Hubbard, 1951.

Advanced Procedure and Axioms. Wichita, Hubbard, 1951.

Scientology 8-80. Phoenix, Hubbard, and East Grinstead, Sussex, Scientology, 1952.

A Key to the Unconscious. Phoenix, Scientic Press, 1952.

Dianetics: The Evolution of a Science. London, Hubbard, 1953; Phoenix, Hubbard, 1955.

Scientology: A History of Man. London, Hubbard, 1953.

How to Live Though an Executive. Phoenix, Hubbard, 1953.

Self-Analysis in Dianetics. London, Ridgway, 1953.

Scientology 8-8008. London, Hubbard, 1953.

Dianetics 1955! Phoenix, Hubbard, 1954.

The Creation of Human Ability: A Handbook for Scientologists. Phoenix, Hubbard, and London, Scientology, 1955.

This Is Scientology: The Science of Certainty. London, Hubbard, 1955.

The Key to Tomorrow (selections), edited by U. Keith Gerry. Johannesburg, Hubbard, 1955.

Scientology: The Fundamentals of Thought. London, Hubbard, 1956.

Problems of Work. Johannesburg, Hubbard, 1957.

Fortress in the Sky (on the moon). Washington, D.C., Hubbard, 1957.

Have You Lived Before This Life? London, Hubbard, 1958; New York, Vantage, 1960.

Self-Analysis in Scientology. London, Hubbard, 1959.

Scientology: Plan for World Peace. East Grinstead, Sussex, Scientology, 1964.

Scientology Abridged Dictionary. East Grinstead, Sussex, Hubbard, 1965.

A Student Comes to Saint Hill. Bedford, Sidney Press, 1965.

Scientology: A New Slant on Life. London, Hubbard, 1965.

East Grinstead. East Grinstead, Sussex, Hubbard, 1966.

Introduction to Scientology Ethics. Edinburgh, Scientology, 1968; Los Angeles, Bridge, 1985.

The Phoenix Lectures. Edinburgh, Scientology, 1968.

How to Save Your Marriage. Copenhagen, Scientology, 1969.

When in Doubt, Communicate: Quotations from the Work of L. Ron Hubbard, edited by Ruth Minshull and Edward M. Lefshon. Ann Arbor, Michigan, Scientology, 1969.

Scientology 0-8. Copenhagen, Scientology, 1970.

Mission into Time. Copenhagen, Scientology, 1973.

The Management Series 1970-1974. Los Angeles, American Saint Hill Organization, 1974.

The Organization Executive Course. Los Angeles, American Saint Hill Organization, 8 vols., 1974.

Dianetics Today. Los Angeles, Scientology, 1975.

Dianetics and Scientology Technical Dictionary. Los Angeles, Scientology, 1975.

The Technical Bulletins of Dianetics and Scientology. Los Angeles, Scientology, 1976-86.

The Volunteer Minister's Handbook. Los Angeles, Scientology, 1976.

Axioms and Logics. Los Angeles, Scientology, 1976.

A Summary of Scientology for Churches. Los Angeles, Scientology, 1977.

The Book of Case Remedies. Los Angeles, Scientology, 1977.

What Is Scientology. Los Angeles, Scientology, 1978.

The Research and Discovery Series. Los Angeles, Scientology, 1980-86.

The Second Dynamic (selection), edited by Cass Pool. Portland, Oregon, Heron, 1981.

Self-Analysis. Los Angeles, Bridge, 1982.

Scientology: Fundamentals of Thought. Los Angeles, Bridge, 1983.

Dianetics: The Evolution of a Science. Los Angeles, Bridge, 1983.

The Problems of Work. Los Angeles, Bridge, 1983.

The Dynamics of Life. Los Angeles, Bridge, 1983.

The Way to Happiness. Los Angeles, Bridge, 1984.

Purification: An Illustrated Answer to Drugs. Los Angeles, Bridge, 1984.

The Learning Book. Copenhagen, New Era, 1984.

Child Dianectics. Los Angeles, Bridge, 1989.

The Book of Case Remedies. Los Angeles, Bridge, 1991.

Art. Los Angeles, Bridge, 1991.

Assists Processing Handbook. Los Angeles, Bridge, 1992.

Other texts and pamphlets published.

*

Critical Studies: *Bare-Faced Messiah: The True Story of L. Ron Hubbard* by Russell Miller, London, Joseph, 1987; New York, Holt, 1988; *A Piece of Blue Sky: Scientology, Dianetics, and L. Ron Hubbard Exposed* by Jon Atack, London, Lyle Stuart, and New York, Carol, 1990.

*   *   *

Best known as the author of *Dianetics* and the founder of the Dianetics-based Church of Scientology, L. Ron Hubbard was a prolific writer of pulp adventure fiction during the 1930s and 1940s. Much of his SF and fantasy, published in *Astounding* and *Unknown,* is of interest today only because its bizarre gnostic psychology anticipates some of the doctrines and practices of Dianetics and Scientology. However, despite a prose style that begs for better editing, some of his fiction justifies the high regard given him by other veterans of the Golden Age.

Having begun as a writer of nautical adventure fiction, Hubbard often composed SF and fantasy simply by inserting conventional plots in a new context by means of a fantastic premise or framing device. For instance, in *Slaves of Sleep,* a meek, young shipping magnate is accused of a gruesome murder committed by a North African *jinni* released from an ancient jar. Jailed for the crime, Jan Palmer finds himself plunged, while asleep, into an alternate life as a cynical, troublemaking, but courageous sailor. In that world, which is ruled by demons out of Arabic folklore, Palmer is also in trouble with the authorities. As the two stories clunk along in uneasy partnership, the bookish shipowner's personality is modified by that of his *alter ego,* who purloins a powerful talisman and wins a battle in the other world. All this results in Palmer's being cleared and restored to his inheritance in this world, and winning a bride in the bargain. In spite of a few moments of strong social satire and an intriguing glimpse of the role of fantasy in constructing the personality, the novel is not much more than a pseudo-folktale in an awkward framework.

Typewriter in the Sky, Hubbard's most successful fiction, also uses such a framing device. In this delightful confection, an unemployed musician is transported into the world of a Spanish Main romance being composed hastily by an acquaintance who hacks mass-market adventure fiction. Mike DeWolf is not only protagonist, but also prime reader of the text: buffeted by narrative implausibilities and inconsistencies as well as by a major rewrite that sets up an alternate but no less fatal ending, he is finally thrust out of the fiction to return as a vagrant to the streets of modern New York, wondering whether his primary universe is being created by a god "in a dirty bathrobe." This skillful mockery of plot appeared a quarter-century before the vogue for metafiction, and long before Borges became generally known to American writers. A similar vein of humor appears in *Triton,* a cleverly conceived, though clumsily executed, lark about a milquetoast who swallows a sea-god, thereby gaining the *machismo* needed to face down his dry-land persecutors. *Triton,* in fact, is a reprise of the central fantasy of *Slaves of Sleep,* but much tighter and wittier than the earlier piece. Two other early novels, *Fear* and *Death's Deputy,* offer plots that use demons to explain murders and untimely deaths. Altogether, Hubbard's early work shows a bent more for the weird tale and for humor than for straight-ahead SF.

It is apparently a convention of Hubbard criticism to praise as his finest novel the militaristic *Final Blackout*. It is hard to see why, unless its virulent fascism—which the text disingenuously attempts to deny—appeals to critics who share its ideological distaste for democracy or social welfare. The narrative reads like the plot summary of a much longer work, and its hero (known only as "the Lieutenant") is developed as neither a realistic character nor a credible personification. Only if read ironically—as Hubbard surely did not intend—does the book amount to much more than a fascist utopia and anti-progressive tract.

Hubbard's postwar SF is of little distinction. The stories collected in *Ole Doc Methuselah* are about a long-lived medical man who runs an interstellar ambulance service, dashing about the Galaxy conquering disease, injury and ignorance, and fighting injustice. The series is vintage space opera: Doc has a cute alien sidekick, he wields a blaster as comfortably as a hypodermic, and he faces down hordes of tyrannical villains in his capacity as a Soldier of Light. Even more predictable is *The Kingslayer*, a tale of Byzantine conspiracy involving Kit Kellan. A young drifter rescued from the authorities by revolutionaries and recruited to assassinate the all-powerful Galactic Arbiter, Kit manages to overcome most of the obstacles to finding his victim, but he is seized just before reaching his goal. Brought before the Arbiter, he learns that the ruler is not a despot, that the revolutionaries are operatives loyal to the Council, that his mission has been a test of his mettle, and that he himself is the Arbiter's son and heir presumptive. Aside from being a psychoanalytic goldmine, the novel is another variation on the old Galactic Empire motif, with a touch of *Final Blackout*'s adulation of the military strongman.

For over three decades, except for an occasional reprint, the SF community heard nothing from Hubbard that did not have to do with his notoriety as the embattled leader of the Scientology movement. Then in 1983, a behemoth of a novel appeared under the title of *Battlefield Earth: A Saga of the Year 3000*. Claimed by Hubbard to be the longest SF novel ever published (819 pages clothbound and 1066 pages in paper), the book came with a recorded "soundtrack" and a preface in which Hubbard got into the acts of defining SF and describing what it was like to write for John W. Campbell, Jr. The novel itself, a throwback to earlier modes of SF, is the tale of how Jonnie Goodboy Tyler marshals the pitiful remnant of humanity to overthrow the Psychlo yoke, and then manipulates the Galactic Bank to restore the former mining colony of Earth to its rightful preeminence among the various foul-smelling aliens of the universe. The technological accomplishments of the year 3000 are barely updated applications of the "superscience" of the old space operas—from matter transmitters to machines that enable one to learn alien languages instantaneously. The various ethnic groups of the Earthling resistance are led by Highland clans complete with warpipes, kilts, and claymores. The good guys defeat the bad guys because they are virtuous, persistent, lucky—and look like us. And women and alien females are put firmly in their place: they breed, nurture, and cook. The wit that sometimes shone through Hubbard's earlier turgidities has been reduced to puns like "the nebula of crap." But for all its obvious flaws, *Battlefield Earth* is an entertaining read: Hubbard does know how to tell an exciting story (or two, to be exact).

Much the same judgment can be made of the ambitious *Mission Earth* serial, a suspenseful romance in 10 volumes and 3903 pages, which began to appear the year before Hubbard's January 1986 death and concluded in 1987. This "dekalogy" chronicles the exploits of the heroic Jettero Heller, an intrepid space engineer who saves not only his own Voltarian Confederacy, but also the Earth, from the evil machinations of a villainous civil servant. In a semischolarly introduction to Volume I (with no references to writings after 1974), Hubbard discusses at excessive length the use of SF as a vehicle for social satire; besides innumerable plot reversals, intrigues and complications, much of *Mission Earth*'s formidable size is due to a great deal of rather sophomoric satire on such topics as the UN, New York cabdrivers, the FBI and the CIA, and most prominently the professions of psychology and psychotherapy. It is a tribute to Hubbard's storytelling skills that one finds it hard not to keep turning the pages of the unwieldy chronicle.

Never a stranger to controversy, Hubbard has continued to generate it since his death. In 1990, the Supreme Court let stand a copyright infringement ruling against Henry Holt, the publisher of *Bare-Faced Messiah: The True Story of L. Ron Hubbard*, for quoting about 1100 words of unpublished Hubbard material. The ruling, which stunned publishers and scholars, led to legislative initiatives to clarify the "fair use" provisions of the copyright law. And in 1991, charges surfaced that *Mission Earth* and other recent Hubbard writings had actually been ghostwritten.

Meanwhile, Bridge Publications, Hubbard's Los Angeles house, has begun to reissue Hubbard's earlier writings on acid-free paper with library bindings, ensuring fans and foes a continuing supply of the old guru's wit and wisdom. Dianetics and Scientology remain Hubbard's outstanding SF invention.

—John P. Brennan

HUDSON, Michael. *See* **KUBE-McDOWELL, Michael P.**

HUGHART, Barry

Nationality: American. **Born:** Peoria, Illinois, 13 March 1934. **Education:** Columbia University, New York, B.A. in English 1956. **Military Service:** Served in United States Air Force 1956-60. **Career:** Technical representative, 1960-63, and vice president, 1963-65, Techtop Weapons; manager, Lenox Hill Bookshop, New York City, 1965-70. Since 1970, freelance writer. **Awards:** World Fantasy award, 1985. **Agent:** Jane Butler, 212 Third Street, Milford, Pennsylvania 18337, U.S.A. **Address:** 2928 North Beverly Avenue, Tucson, Arizona 85712, U.S.A.

SCIENCE FICTION PUBLICATIONS

Novels (series: Master Li and Number Ten Ox in all books)

The Bridge of Birds: A Novel of an Ancient China That Never Was. New York, St. Martin's Press, 1984; as *Bridge of Birds*, London, Century, 1986.

The Story of the Stone. Garden City New York, Doubleday, 1988;
London, Bantam, 1989.
Eight Skilled Gentlemen. Garden City New York, Doubleday, and
London, Bantam, 1991.

*

Barry Hughart comments:

My three novels featuring Master Li and Number Ten Ox are
set in a seventh-century China that never existed as a whole, but
did exist in fragments. Which is to say that 99% of the history,
customs, popular music, children's songs, culinary recipes, medical formulas, odd folk beliefs—you name it—that I include is real,
acquired through more hours in university libraries than I care to
think about, but not chronologically accurate; what I do is mix
things up to produce a particular effect. For example, in *Eight Skilled
Gentlemen* I've taken a children's song set down by a Frenchman
in Peking in 1911, added terms from a scholarly monograph on
boatmen's slang dated 1793 by a Dutch scholar in south China,
tied the result to the most famous of all odes and shamanistic chants
in "Nine Songs," ascribed to the fourth century B.C. but most certainly prehistoric, and then added a sprinkling of Baudelaire-like
lines (rather like whipped cream on top) by Li Ho, A.D. 791-817.
The result is verse matter-of-factly accepted by my seventh-century sage, Master Li, as being a unified whole, rather good, interesting in that it may be useful in providing clues to the mystery
he's involved in but otherwise quite typical of the culture. Is he
wrong?

Well, let's start with the flat statement that the most profoundly
Chinese poem of the past century is *Burnt Norton*. "Time present
and time past / Are both perhaps present in time future / And time
future contained in time past." The point being that China, while a
historical babe compared to Egypt or Iran, possesses the oldest continuous civilization on earth. It is usually pointless to isolate a Chinese custom or art form and assign a definitive cause, creator, or
date, because everything has, is, and will be evolving from everything else; all that is past is present, all that is present is past, both
will be eternally present in the future. Master Li can read lines that
will not be "created" for a thousand years and shrug and say "Why
not?", since he is simultaneously reading in those lines the music
of a thousand years of the past. "Only by the form, the pattern /
Can words or music reach / The stillness, as a Chinese jar still /
Moves perpetually in its stillness." Oh yeah, and a barbarian who
proleptically picks from the cultural cornucopia can produce a "true"
China in which magic and miracles *must* occur. Thus the Master Li
books, concerning which the label "fantasy" is a battle cry to militant metaphysicians.

*   *   *

All three of Barry Hughart's published novels are set in a seventh-century version of China that bears some, but not much, relationship to the real one. It is the land of a decaying empire, ruled
by emperors and kings and warlords, plagued by vampires and
bandits and demons and more purely mundane villains. It is a mysterious and often beautiful landscape filled with strange people and
events.

Against this backdrop, Hughart presents two characters around
whom all three novels unfold. Li Kao is an elderly scholar with a
weakness for wine, but possibly also possessing the most brilliant
mind in the world. He is essentially an Oriental Sherlock Holmes,

but with marked differences. Li is a pragmatist, perfectly capable
of shrugging at disaster, so long as it isn't his disaster. The Watson
substitute is Number Ten Ox, who narrates each adventure, a strong,
brave, and loyal peasant whose relationship with Li begins in the
first volume when he employs him to solve a problem in his village.

Hughart's style is somewhat reminiscent of the "Kai Lung" stories of Ernest Bramah. The text is enriched by anecdotes, poems,
creative folk tales, and an entire mythic cosmology invented for the
series. Although each novel is essentially a mystery, solved after
the heroes survive a series of adventures, each contains a strong
element of dark humor as well. At times, ghastly incidents are related in an offhanded, almost comic fashion.

Bridge of Birds was the first to appear, and it won the World
Fantasy award, evidence that Hughart had made an instant, favorable impression with readers. Every child in Number Ten Ox's village between the ages of eight and 13 has fallen into a coma. Although Li is able to identify the cause readily enough, a cure requires possession of the Great Root of Power, an item so rare and
valuable that acquiring it means risking an attempted theft from the
Ancestress, a deposed Empress of China who still commands powerful forces.

After a series of adventures, the protagonists infiltrate her household, only to find themselves involved with a ghost, an unsolved
murder mystery, and the likelihood that they'll be executed out of
hand for entering in the first place. Hughart resolves everything in
a resounding fashion and ties up all the loose ends neatly.

Three years later, he followed this success with an even better
adventure, *The Story of the Stone*. This time, Master Li is approached by the abbot of a monastery to investigate the death of
one of his monks. It appears that at the time he died, a hypnotic
sound lured most of the other monks away, that a small area of the
surrounding landscape was entirely denuded of plant life, and that
visions were seen of the Laughing Prince, a supposedly insane despot who had died centuries earlier.

In the fashion of murder mysteries, the crime is repeated after
Li's arrival. He concludes that those responsible are both mundane
and supernatural, and in order to identify the perpetrator, he and a
group of companions must journey to Hell itself, to question the
keeper of the records of life and death. The resolution involves the
discovery of a mysterious stone that can absorb human souls, and
the revelation of the mortal whose secret plotting led to the deaths.
As with many of the Sherlock Holmes stories, Hughart cheats in
terms of traditional mystery writing—there is no possible way for
the reader to figure out in advance what has happened. Fortunately,
it doesn't matter. The focus of the book is the way in which Li
reveals the details, and the exotic landscape that provides the stage
for his antics.

Most recent, and easily surpassing its two predecessors, is *Eight
Skilled Gentlemen*. Once again, Li is called upon to solve a series
of murders, this time the systematic elimination of highly placed
mandarins who are apparently involved in a highly remunerative
smuggling operation. A witness to the first killing relates an incredible story of an assassin who strikes with a ball of fire, then
escapes in the form of a crane, following which the dead body is
decapitated by a vampire. Li is skeptical until he uncovers a connection to an ancient order, and witnesses the second murder himself, also perpetrated by a clearly inhuman creature. His investigations further reveal a set of artifacts which, if employed by the
wrong hands, might cause a catastrophe that would sweep all of
China.

One of the greatest challenges in creating a fantasy world is to make it seem like a real place. Hughart has created an entire alter reality in these novels, given it a social system, history, philosophy, and unique mythology. His characters are exaggerated and to a certain degree superficial, but only in the sense that all fairy tale characters are unrealistic. It is the mosaic of people, places, and events that mark these as outstanding works of fantasy.

—Don D'Ammassa

HUGHES, Monica

Nationality: Canadian. **Born:** Monica Ince, Liverpool, Lancashire, England, 3 November 1925; daughter of the mathematician E.L. Ince; became Canadian citizen in 1957. **Education:** Convent of the Holy Child Jesus, Harrogate, Yorkshire, graduated 1942; Edinburgh University, 1942-43. **Military Service:** Served in the Women's Royal Naval Service, 1943-46. **Family:** Married Glen Hughes in 1957; two daughters and two sons. **Career:** Dress designer, London, 1948-49, and Bulawayo, Zimbabwe, 1950; bank clerk, Umtali, Zimbabwe, 1951; laboratory technician, National Research Council, Ottawa, 1952-57. **Awards:** Vicky Metcalf award, 1981; Canada Council prize, 1982, 1983. **Agent:** Pamela Paul, The Pamela Paul Agency, 253 High Park Ave., Toronto, Ontario M6P 255, Canada. **Address:** 13816-110A Avenue, Edmonton, Alberta T5M 2M9, Canada.

SCIENCE FICTION PUBLICATIONS (for children)

Novels (series: Arc One; Conshelf Ten; Isis; Sandwriter)

Crisis on Conshelf Ten. Toronto, Copp Clark, and London, Hamish Hamilton, 1975; New York, Atheneum, 1977.
Earthdark (Conshelf Ten). London, Hamish Hamilton, 1977.
The Tomorrow City. London, Hamish Hamilton, 1978.
Beyond the Dark River. London, Hamish Hamilton, 1979; New York, Atheneum, 1981.
The Keeper of the Isis Light. London, Hamish Hamilton, 1980; New York, Atheneum, 1981.
The Guardian of Isis. London, Hamish Hamilton, 1981; New York, Atheneum, 1982.
The Isis Pedlar. London, Hamish Hamilton, 1982; New York, Atheneum, 1983.
Ring-Rise, Ring-Set. London, MacRae, and New York, Watts, 1982.
Beckoning Lights. Edmonton, Alberta, LeBel, 1982.
The Space Trap. London, MacRae, 1983; New York, Watts, 1984.
Devil on My Back (Arc One). London, MacRae, 1984; New York, Atheneum, 1985.
Sandwriter. London, MacRae, 1985; New York, Holt, 1988.
The Dream Catcher (Arc One). London, MacRae, 1986; New York, Atheneum, 1987.
The Promise (Sandwriter). Toronto, Stoddart, and London, Methuen, 1989; New York, Simon and Schuster, 1992.
Invitation to the Game. Toronto, HarperCollins, 1990; New York, Simon and Schuster, and London, Methuen, 1991.
The Crystal Drop. London, Methuen, 1992; New York, Simon and Schuster, 1993.

The Golden Aquarians. Toronto, HarperCollins, 1994; New York, Simon and Schuster, 1995.
Castle Tourmandyne. Toronto, HarperCollins, 1995.

OTHER PUBLICATIONS (for children)

Novels

Gold-Fever Trail: A Klondike Adventure. Edmonton, Alberta, LeBel, 1974.
The Ghost Dance Caper. London, Hamish Hamilton, 1978.
Hunter in the Dark. Toronto, Clarke Irwin, 1982; New York, Atheneum, 1983.
The Treasure of the Long Sault. Edmonton, Alberta, LeBel, 1982.
My Name Is Paula Popowich! Toronto, Lorimer, 1983.
Blaine's Way. Toronto, Irwin, 1986; London, Severn House, 1988.
Log Jam. Toronto, Irwin, 1987; as *Spirit River,* London, Methuen, 1988.
The Refuge. Toronto, Doubleday, 1989.
Little Fingerling: A Japanese Folk Tale (illustrated). Toronto, Kids Can Press, 1989; Nashville, Ideals, 1992.
A Handful of Seeds. Toronto, Lester, 1993.
Chairs. Aylesbury, England, Ginn, 1994.
Hats. Aylesbury, England, Ginn, 1994.
Hedgehogs, with Betty Root. Aylesbury, England, Ginn, 1994.

*

Manuscript Collection: University of Calgary, Alberta.

Monica Hughes comments:
I grew up fascinated by the story of humankind, the way in which we acquired language, told stories, developed tribal customs, and at last discovered our world and learned how to dominate it. The interconnectedness of it all.

It is only a step around a dark corner from the past into the future: given what happened then, what might happen when . . . ? I am particularly concerned with the fragility of our environment and with the loss of the "bloom on the grape" of life as our technological society progresses like a juggernaut, threatening rain forests, oceans, indigenous native cultures.

*   *   *

Monica Hughes is most successful and provocative when she uses one or both of two themes: 1) The price society is willing to pay for technological progress, and the importance of people's adapting intelligently to the environment they find themselves in; and 2) young adult concerns, in particular the first stirrings of romantic love. Witness, for example, *The Keeper of the Isis Light,* the first and best segment of the Isis trilogy, and *Ring-Rise, Ring-Set,* runner-up for the 1982 Guardian award. Hughes is less successful when she succumbs to cuteness, e.g., *The Isis Pedlar* with its unconvincing portrait of an irresponsible but likeable Irish inter-galactic pedlar, or fails to respect the boundaries science sometimes imposes upon the imagination, e.g., *The Space Trap* with its aliens implausibly banded together in self-defense.

In *The Keeper of the Isis Light,* although using some material previously tapped—surgery to facilitate human adaptation to a hostile environment (*Crisis on Conshelve Ten* where "mer-men" are created in order more readily to explore the seas) and the high risks of over-relying on artificial intelligence (*The Tomorrow City* where the central computer, C-Three, runs amuck)—Hughes put together an original and poignant story. Young Olwen, the daughter of scientists responsible for the Isis Light, is surgically altered by Guardian, a highly advanced robot, to withstand the excessive radiation of Isis which had killed her parents. In doing so, the robot only follows instructions to guard the child at all costs. Unaware that she has been altered to appear lizard-like and believing that she is beautiful, Olwen feels attracted to Mark London, a member of the first Isis colony. He too is attracted to the loveliness he senses beneath the mask Guardian forces Olwen to wear. When Mark learns the truth and in horror recoils from Olwen's uncovered face, she realizes his declaration of love is insincere; and she must live rejected. Hughes makes clear that Guardian's decision to alter surgically Olwen's appearance, although defensible on technical grounds, profoundly shocks sensibilities which equate being human with looking human. Hence, the technological innovation Olwen's survival represents demands too high a price: not only does the young woman suffer permanent rejection, but technology is perceived as so threatening that the colony is persuaded at great risk to its survival to use as little of it as possible.

In *Ring-Rise, Ring-Set,* which is both SF and survival story, Hughes explores another moral problem effected by technology. When the sun's rays are blocked by rings of meteoric dust in the atmosphere and a new ice age is imminent, most people, banding together in Cities and submitting to regimentation, frantically seek technology to dissolve the rings. One new technique, however, seriously endangers the Ekoes who insist upon living outside the City close to nature. The focus of the clash between the two differing cultures is Lisa, a City dweller, who, running away to the icy wastes, becomes lost and is found by the Ekoes. Lisa's refusal to return to City because at last she feels whole among the Ekoes where too she has found love is credible and moving. Moreover, the novel forthrightly presents both City's uncertainty whether technology can or ought to preserve civilization as is, and the Ekoes' determination, regardless of cost, not to abandon their values for the sake of survival as defined by City. When Hughes is "on target," her novels convincingly demonstrate that it is no easy, painless resolution of the conflict that can result when technology impinges upon human life.

—Francis J. Molson

HUGHES, Zach

Pseudonym for Hugh Zachary. **Other Pseudonyms:** Evan Innes; Pablo Kane; Peter Kanto. **Nationality:** American. **Born:** Holdenville, Oklahoma, 12 January 1928. **Education:** Oklahoma A & M College, 1945-46; University of North Carolina, Chapel Hill, B.A. in journalism 1951. **Military Service:** Served in the 82nd Airborne Division of the United States Army, 1946-48. **Family:** Married Elizabeth Wiggs in 1948; two daughters. **Career:** Worked in radio and television broadcasting, 1948-61. Since 1962, part-time fisherman, guide, florist, construction worker, and freelance writer. City commissioner, Yaupon Beach, 1988-92. **Awards:** Southern Books award, 1972. **Address:** 7 Pebble Beach Drive, Yaupon Beach, North Carolina 28465, U.S.A.

SCIENCE FICTION PUBLICATIONS

Novels (series: Rack the Healer)

The World Where Sex Was Born (as Peter Kanto). New York, Ophelia Press, 1968; as *The World Where Sex Is Born,* London, Grafton, 1989.
Rosy Cheeks (as Peter Kanto). New York, Bee-Line, 1969.
A Dick for All Seasons (as Pablo Kane). New York, Ophelia Press, 1970.
The Book of Rack the Healer. New York, Award, 1973.
The Legend of Miaree. New York, Ballantine, 1974.
Gwen, in Green (as Hugh Zachary). Greenwich, Connecticut, Fawcett, 1974; London, Coronet, 1976.
Tide. New York, Berkley, 1974.
Seed of the Gods. New York, Berkley, 1974; London, Hale, 1979.
The Stork Factor. New York, Berkley, 1975.
For Texas and Zed. New York, Popular Library, 1976.
Tiger in the Stars. Toronto, Laser, 1976.
The St. Francis Effect. New York, Berkley, 1976.
Killbird. New York, Signet, 1980.
Pressure Man. New York, Signet, 1980.
Thunderworld (Rack the Healer). New York, Signet, 1982.
Gold Star. New York, Signet, 1983.
Closed System. New York, Signet, 1986.
Sundrinker. New York, DAW, 1987.
The Dark Side. New York, Signet, 1987.
The Revenant (as Hugh Zachary). New York, Onyx, 1988.
Life Force. New York, DAW, 1988.
Mother Lode. New York, DAW, 1991.
Deep Freeze. New York, DAW, 1992.
The Omnificence Factor. New York, DAW, 1994.

OTHER PUBLICATIONS AS EVAN INNES

Novels

America: 2040. New York, Bantam, 1986.
The Golden World. New York, Bantam, 1986.
City in the Mist. New York, Bantam, 1987.
The Return. New York, Bantam, 1988.
The Star Explorer. New York, Bantam, 1988.

OTHER PUBLICATIONS AS HUGH ZACHARY

Novels

One Day in Hell. New York, Newstand Library, 1961.
Glamour Boy (as Peter Kanto). North Hollywood, Brandon House, 1966.
Too Young to Wait (as Peter Kanto). North Hollywood, Brandon House, 1966.
Suddenly, Wonderfully Gay (as Peter Kanto). North Hollywood, Brandon House, 1968.
A Small Slice of War (as Peter Kanto). New York, Flagship, 1968.
A Feast of Fat Things. Jacksonville, Illinois, Harris Wolfe, 1968.
The Coupling Game (as Peter Kanto). New York, Traveller's Companion, 1969.
Naked Joy (as Peter Kanto). New York, Ophelia Press, 1970.

Rake's Junction. New York, Lancer, 1970.
The Legend of the Deadly Doll. New York, Award, 1973.
Second Chance. Canoga Park, California, Major, 1976.
Dynasty of Desire, with Elizabeth Zachary. New York, Dell, 1978.
The Land Rushers, with Elizabeth Zachary. New York, Dell, 1979.
Love and Battle, with Elizabeth Zachary. New York, Ballantine, 1980.
The Golden Dynasty, with Elizabeth Zachary, New York, Dell, 1980.
To Guard the Right. Toronto, Raven House, 1980.
Top Level Death. Toronto, Raven House, 1981.
Bloodrush. New York, Leisure, 1981.
Murder in White. New York, Leisure, 1981.
Freedom's Passion. Wayne, Pennsylvania, Dell/Banbury, 1981.
Tower of Treason. New York, Jove, 1982.
Treasure of Hope. Wayne, Pennsylvania, Dell/Banbury, 1982.
Flight to Freedom. Wayne, Pennsylvania, Dell/Banbury, 1982.
Desert Battle. Wayne, Pennsylvania, Dell/Banbury, 1982.
Bitter Victory. Wayne, Pennsylvania, Dell/Banbury, 1983.
The Venus Venture. New York, Vanguard, 1986.
Dos Caballos. New York, M. Evans, 1989.
Some 60 other novels published under various pseudonyms.

Play

Screenplay: *Tide.*

Other

The Beachcomber's Handbook of Seafood Cookery. Winston-Salem, North Carolina, Blair, 1969.
Wild Card Poker. Brattleboro, Vermont, Stephen Greene Press, 1975.

*

Zach Hughes comments:

I think the first duty of any writer, including a science-fiction writer, is to tell a story which involves real people who react to situations with believable motivation. Moreover, I feel that the setting for science fiction is, first and foremost, space. I write little science fiction, because it is difficult for me to come up with an idea which qualifies, in my mind, as worthy of having been published during the golden years of SF when awe and wonder and the sense of infinite distance and infinite variety in the universe was a necessary ingredient for any SF story. Several of my SF books are set in the time of The United Planets Confederation, as introduced in the last section of my first SF book, *The Book of Rack the Healer* and continued through such books as *Gold Star, Closed System, The Dark Side,* and the upcoming *Mother Lode.*

*   *   *

Zach Hughes is the pseudonym Hugh Zachary uses for his science fiction novels. His first SF novel, *The Book of Rack the Healer,* is in many ways his best book. Earth, centuries after a nuclear holocaust, is dying from accumulated radiation and pollution. Mankind has evolved into four species: Keepers, moronic women whose brains store knowledge like a computer; Far Seers, males who supply leadership; Healers, males who have the power to travel on Earth's ravaged surface and collect raw materials to feed the population by regenerating cells damaged by the corrosive atmosphere; and Power Givers, women with the power of flight. Hughes cre-

ates an innovative ecological puzzle, while developing the characters of Rack the Healer, Red Earth the Far Seer, and Beautiful Wings the Power Giver. The ending is tragic, yet Hughes manages to moderate the pathos with hope. Hughes continues this story in a prequel called *Thunderworld.* The crew of a small scout ship discovers an infant solar system with an Earth-type planet racked with earthquakes and about to enter an Ice Age. The crew names the planet "Worthless" because their mission is to find worlds suitable for human colonization to ease the crushing overpopulation of Earth. But before they leave, one of the crew members unknowingly takes on a telepathic symbiotic life-form. Hughes explores the concept of dual identities sharing the same body. Then news arrives that war has broken out on Earth and the home of Man has been reduced to a radioactive, burned-out cinder. Hughes cleverly weaves these developments into a complex plot where the world of Rack the Healer and this "Worthless" planet converge 50,000 years in the future.

Hughes reworks this material in *Life Force.* An idyllic planet called Beauty causes a conflict between Andrew Reznor's Galactic Enterprises—which sees Beauty as a refuge for Earth's endangered species—and the Bureau of Colonization, which wants to send a large part of Earth's crowded population to settle the planet. But neither side figured on Beauty's own goals, goals the planet would kill to protect. Although a bit preachy, Hughes delivers a strong message of hope in *Life Force.*

Killbird also shares these themes. Eban the Hairy One is one of a small group of primitives surviving a nuclear holocaust. Hughes cunningly invents a sophisticated society, while sending Eban on an incredible set of adventures in the dangerous, savage world. *Killbird* possesses many of Hughes's best-developed characters— Eban, his wife Mar, and the bitter Yuree—as well as some of his best writing.

The Legend of Miaree is a clever positioning of a sociological disaster with the problems of translating alien texts. It is really two books in one: the actual legend of Miaree is being read by human students at a planetary university as the translation of the only surviving artifact of two destroyed alien races. The students and their professor provide commentary on the deadly progression of events, commentary that gives additional insight into the contrast between alien societies. Hughes does a masterful job creating the character of Miaree and her culture as two galaxies collide, threatening two star races. The ending is grim, but Hughes skillfully lightens the mood by shifting the actions to the human students and their wise professor.

In contrast to Hughes's serious SF, he has written his share of space operas. *The Dark Side* is a vengeance novel where Aaron Denton pledges to avenge the death of his home planet, St. Paul, by hunting down those responsible for its destruction. *Pressure Man* features Dominic "Flash" Gordon on a desperate mission to build a spacecraft that will withstand the pressures of 30,000 atmospheres. An alien ship, which might hold the secret to faster-than-light space travel, is orbiting Jupiter. Gordon is charged with designing a new ship to capture the alien craft. Hughes tells Gordon's story with the backdrop of an Earth swelling with overpopulation and radical groups bent on destroying the space program. The politics of the novel is ultra-conservative, and the plot cheats the reader of an actual first contact turn into a tribute to Immanuel Velikovsky's theories instead. *Gold Star* features Pete and Jan Jaynes, a married couple aboard a space tug, who hunt for the missing experimental starship *Rimfire* for salvage and find themselves fighting for their lives against a rival band of salvagers. *Seed of the Gods,* an attempt to spoof the von Daniken cult, is a routine "first contact" novel.

Two ecological disaster novels, *Tide* and *The St. Francis Effect,* suffer from undeveloped characters, though some of the information is fascinating. In *Tide,* efforts to produce increased breeding of fish lead to mutations that trigger extreme aggression in the fish and in the people who eat them. In *The St. Francis Effect* a deep-ocean mining operation in the Pacific brings up an ages-old parasite carried by mosquitos. The resultant plague has a 100% mortality rate, and in a matter of days turns its victims into mummified corpses. The book is an effective disaster novel but the mosquitos and the disease—not the human characters—are the stars.

The Stork Factor and *For Texas and Zed* are both superman novels. In the first, set in a repressive and totalitarian future society totally controlled by a religious dictatorship, a young priest, Luke, has developed psi powers, and becomes part of the underground plotting to overthrow the government. At the same time, an advanced alien race sends a starship to Earth to determine the threat its technology presents. The impact of the convergence of events produces a fast-paced, entertaining novel. In *For Texas and Zed,* Lex Murichon, one of the leading figures of the planet Texas delegation to the Earth Empire, is a blend of the heroes from H. Beam Piper and John J. McGuire's *A Planet for Texans* (1958) and Harry Harrison's satiric *Bill, The Galactic Hero* (1965). The fierce independence of the Texans is translated into a culture on a hidden solitary planet where the new Texans provide meat to the Empire while staying above the cold war between the Empire and the Cassiopeian battle fleet. But Lex gets involved as a gunner aboard an Empire starship, deserts, and heads back to Texas, thus causing a state of war. This much of the novel is accomplished with wit and style. But after Texas successfully defends itself against the Empire's attacks and Lex becomes the leader of the Texas forces—evolving into an all-conquering Alexander the Great figure—the book sags badly.

Tiger in the Stars is a van Vogtian novel of humans encountering aliens of vast supremacy. The hero, John Plank, is turned into a cyborg linked with a starship of incredible power. Unfortunately, the novel drifts from subplot to subplot without developing a picture of future human culture or the fantastic alien culture. The ending becomes predictable far too soon and the result is a flatness usually absent from Hughes's best work.

Gwen, In Green features a young couple moving into a rambling house on an isolated island in the south. But within the clear pool near the house grow alien plants who establish contact with the young wife, Gwen. As the relationship between Gwen and the alien plants becomes stronger, the plot explodes with murder and sexuality. The book generates a memorable griminess as well as a powerful examination of the eerie symbiotic relationship of human and alien.

—George Kelley

HUNT, Gil. *See* **TUBB, E.C.**

HUNTER, Evan

Pseudonyms: Curt Cannon; Hunt Collins; Ezra Hannon; Richard Marsten; Ed McBain. **Nationality:** American. **Born:** Salvatore A. Lombino in New York City, 15 October 1926. **Education:** Cooper Union, New York, 1943-44; Hunter College, New York, B.A. 1950 (Phi Beta Kappa). **Military Service:** Served in the United States Navy, 1944-46. **Family:** Married 1) Anita Melnick in 1949 (divorced), three sons; 2) Mary Vann Finley in 1973, one stepdaughter. **Career:** In the early 1950s taught in vocational high schools, and worked for the Scott Meredith Literary Agency, in New York. **Awards:** Mystery Writers of America Edgar Allan Poe award, 1957. Lives in Norwalk, Connecticut. **Agent:** John Farquharson Ltd., 250 West 57th Street, New York, New York 10107, U.S.A.; or, 162-168 Regent Street, London W1R 5TB, England.

SCIENCE FICTION PUBLICATIONS

Novels

Find the Feathered Serpent (for children). Philadelphia, Winston, 1952.
Rocket to Luna (for children; as Richard Marsten). Philadelphia, Winston, 1953; London, Hutchinson, 1954.
Danger: Dinosaurs! (for children; as Richard Marsten). Philadelphia, Winston, 1953.
Tomorrow's World (as Hunt Collins). New York, Avalon, 1956; as *Tomorrow and Tomorrow,* New York, Pyramid, 1956; as Ed McBain, London, Sphere, 1979.
Nobody Knew They Were There. New York, Doubleday, and London, Constable, 1971.

OTHER PUBLICATIONS

Novels

The Evil Sleep! N.p., Falcon, 1952.
The Big Fix. N.p., Falcon, 1952; as *So Nude, So Dead* (as Richard Marsten), New York, Fawcett, 1956.
Don't Crowd Me. New York, Popular Library, 1953; London. Consul, 1960; as *The Paradise Party,* London, New English Library, 1968.
Cut Me In (as Hunt Collins). New York, Abelard Schuman, 1954; London, Boardman, 1960; as *The Proposition,* New York, Pyramid, 1955.
The Blackboard Jungle. New York, Simon and Schuster, 1954; London, Constable, 1955.
Second Ending. New York, Simon and Schuster, and London, Constable, 1956; as *Quartet in H,* New York, Pocket Books, 1957.
Strangers When We Meet. New York, Simon and Schuster, and London, Constable, 1958.
I'm Cannon—For Hire (as Curt Cannon). New York, Fawcett, 1958; London, Fawcett, 1959.
A Matter of Conviction. New York, Simon and Schuster, and London, Constable, 1959; as *The Young Savages,* New York, Pocket Books, 1966.
Mothers and Daughters. New York, Simon and Schuster, and London, Constable, 1961.

Buddwing. New York, Simon and Schuster, and London, Constable, 1964.

The Paper Dragon. New York, Delacorte Press, 1966; London, Constable, 1967.

A Horse's Head. New York, Delacorte Press, 1967; London, Constable, 1968.

Last Summer. New York, Doubleday, 1968; London, Constable, 1969.

Sons. New York, Doubleday, 1969; London, Constable, 1970.

Every Little Crook and Nanny. New York, Doubleday, and London, Constable, 1972.

Come Winter. New York, Doubleday, and London, Constable, 1973.

Streets of Gold. New York, Harper, 1974; London, Macmillan, 1975.

Doors (as Ezra Hannon). New York, Stein and Day, 1975; London, Macmillan, 1976.

The Chisholms: A Novel of the Journey West. New York, Harper, and London, Hamish Hamilton, 1976.

Walk Proud. New York, Bantam, 1979.

Love, Dad. New York, Crown, and London, Joseph, 1981.

Far from the Sea. New York, Atheneum, and London, Hamish Hamilton, 1983.

Lizzie: A Novel. New York, Arbor House, and London, Hamish Hamilton, 1984.

Criminal Conversation. New York, Warner, 1994.

Novels as Richard Marsten

Runaway Black. New York, Fawcett, 1954; London, Red Seal, 1957.

Murder in the Navy. New York, Fawcett, 1955; as *Death of a Nurse* (as Ed McBain), New York, Pocket Books, 1968; London, Hodder and Stoughton, 1972.

The Spiked Heel. New York, Holt, 1956; London, Constable, 1957.

Vanishing Ladies. New York, Permabooks, 1957; London, Boardman, 1961.

Even the Wicked. New York, Permabooks, 1958; as Ed McBain, London, Severn House, 1979.

Big Man. New York, Pocket Books, 1959; as Ed McBain, London, Penguin, 1978.

Novels as Ed McBain

Cop Hater. New York, Permabooks, 1956; London, Boardman, 1958.

The Mugger. New York, Simon and Schuster, 1956; London, Boardman, 1959.

The Pusher. New York, Simon and Schuster, 1956; London, Boardman, 1959.

The Con Man. New York, Permabooks, 1957; London, Boardman, 1960.

Killer's Choice. New York, Simon and Schuster, 1958; London, Boardman, 1960.

Killer's Payoff. New York, Simon and Schuster, 1958; London, Boardman, 1960.

April Robin Murders, with Craig Rice (completed by McBain). New York, Random House, 1958; London, Hammond, 1959.

Lady Killer. New York, Simon and Schuster, 1958; London, Boardman, 1961.

Killer's Wedge. New York, Simon and Schuster, 1959; London, Boardman, 1961.

'Til Death. New York, Simon and Schuster, 1959; London, Boardman, 1961.

King's Ransom. New York, Simon and Schuster, 1959; London, Boardman, 1961.

Give the Boys a Great Big Hand. New York, Simon and Schuster, 1960; London, Boardman, 1962.

The Heckler. New York, Simon and Schuster, 1960; London, Boardman, 1962.

See Them Die. New York, Simon and Schuster, 1960; London, Boardman, 1963.

Lady, Lady, I Did it! New York, Simon and Schuster, 1961; London, Boardman, 1963.

Like Love. New York, Simon and Schuster, 1962; London, Hamish Hamilton, 1964.

Ten Plus One. New York, Simon and Schuster, 1963; London, Hamish Hamilton, 1964.

Ax. New York, Simon and Schuster, and London, Hamish Hamilton, 1964.

The Sentries. New York, Simon and Schuster, and London, Hamish Hamilton, 1965.

He Who Hesitates. New York, Delacorte Press, and London, Hamish Hamilton, 1965.

Doll. New York, Delacorte Press, 1965; London, Hamish Hamilton, 1966.

Eighty Million Eyes. New York, Delacorte Press, and London, Hamish Hamilton, 1966.

Fuzz. New York, Doubleday, and London, Hamish Hamilton, 1968.

Shotgun. New York, Doubleday, and London, Hamish Hamilton, 1969.

Jigsaw. New York, Doubleday, and London, Hamish Hamilton, 1970.

Hail, Hail, The Gang's All Here! New York, Doubleday, and London, Hamish Hamilton, 1971.

Sadie When She Died. New York, Doubleday, and London, Hamish Hamilton, 1972.

Let's Hear It for the Deaf Man. New York, Doubleday, and London, Hamish Hamilton, 1973.

Hail to the Chief. New York, Random House, and London, Hamish Hamilton, 1973.

Bread. New York, Random House, and London, Hamish Hamilton, 1974.

Where There's Smoke. New York, Random House, and London, Hamish Hamilton, 1975.

Blood Relatives. New York, Random House, 1975; London, Hamish Hamilton, 1976.

Guns. New York, Random House, 1976; London, Hamish Hamilton, 1977.

So Long as You Both Shall Live. New York, Random House, and London, Hamish Hamilton, 1976.

Long Time No See. New York, Random House, and London, Hamish Hamilton, 1977.

Goldilocks. New York, Arbor House, 1977; London, Hamish Hamilton, 1978.

Calypso. New York, Viking Press, and London, Hamish Hamilton, 1979.

Ghosts. New York, Viking Press, and London, Hamish Hamilton, 1980.

Rumpelstiltskin. New York, Viking Press, and London, Hamish Hamilton, 1981.

Heat. New York, Viking Press, and London, Hamish Hamilton, 1981.

Beauty and the Beast. London, Hamish Hamilton, 1982; New York, Holt Rinehart, 1983.

Ice. New York, Arbor House, and London, Hamish Hamilton, 1983.
Jack and the Beanstalk. New York, Holt Rinehart, and London, Hamish Hamilton, 1984.
Lightning. New York, Arbor House, and London, Hamish Hamilton, 1984.
Snow White and Rose Red. New York, Holt Rinehart, and London, Hamish Hamilton, 1985.
Eight Black Horses. New York, Arbor House, 1985.
Another Part of the City. New York, Mysterious Press, 1985; London, Hamish Hamilton, 1986.
Cinderella. New York, Holt, and London, Hamish Hamilton, 1986.
Poison. New York, Arbor House, and London, Hamish Hamilton, 1987.
Puss in Boots. New York, Holt, and London, Arbor House, 1987.
Tricks. New York, Arbor House, and London, Hamish Hamilton, 1987.
The House That Jack Built. New York, Holt, and London, Hamish Hamilton, 1988.
Lullaby. New York, Morrow, and London, Hamish Hamilton, 1989.
Downtown. New York, Morrow, and London, Heinemann, 1989.
Three Blind Mice. New York, Arcade, 1990; London, Heinemann, 1991.
Vespers. New York, Morrow, 1990.
Widows: A Novel. New York, Morrow, and London, Heinemann, 1991.
Downtown: A Novel. New York, Morrow, 1991; Bath, Avon, Chivers, 1992.
Kiss: A Novel of the 87th Precinct. New York, Morrow, and London, Heinemann, 1992.
Mary, Mary. New York, Warner, and London, Heinemann, 1992.
Three Complete 87th Precinct Novels (includes *Tricks, Ice,* and *Eight Black Horses*). New York, Wings, 1992.
Mischief: A Novel of the 87th Precinct. New York, Morrow, and London, Hodder and Stoughton, 1993.
There Was a Little Girl. New York, Warner, and London, Hodder and Stoughton, 1994.
Romance. New York, Warner, 1995.

Short Stories

The Jungle Kids. New York, Pocket Books, 1956.
I Like 'em Tough (as Curt Cannon). New York, Fawcett, 1958.
The Last Spin and Other Stories. London, Constable, 1960.
The Empty Hours (as Ed McBain). New York, Simon and Schuster, 1962; London, Boardman, 1963.
Happy New Year, Herbie, and Other Stories. New York, Simon and Schuster, 1963; London, Constable, 1965.
The Beheading and Other Stories. London, Constable, 1971.
The Easter Man (a Play) and Six Stories. New York, Doubleday, 1972; as *Seven,* London, Constable, 1972.
The McBain Brief (as Ed McBain). London, Hamish Hamilton, 1982; New York, Arbor House, 1983.
McBain's Ladies: The Women of the 87th Precinct. New York, Mysterious Press, and London, Hamish Hamilton, 1988.
McBain's Ladies Too. New York, Mysterious Press, 1989.

Plays

The Easter Man (produced Birmingham and London, 1964; as *As Race of Hairy Men,* produced New York, 1965). Included in *The Easter Man (a Play) and Six Stories,* 1972.

The Conjuror (produced Ann Arbor, Michigan, 1969).

Screenplays: *Strangers When We Meet,* 1960; *The Birds,* 1963; *Fuzz,* 1972; *Walk Proud,* 1979.

Television Plays: *Appointment at Eleven (Alfred Hitchcock Presents* series), 1955-61; *The Chisholms* series, from his own novel, 1978-79; *The Legend of Walks Far Woman,* 1982.

Other (for children)

The Remarkable Harry. New York and London, Abelard Schuman, 1961.
The Wonderful Button. New York, Abelard Schuman, 1961; London, Abelard Schuman, 1962.
Me and Mr. Stenner. Philadelphia, Lippincott, 1976; London, Hamish Hamilton, 1977.

Other (as Ed McBain)

Editor, *Crime Squad.* London, New English Library, 1968.
Editor, *Homicide Department.* London, New English Library, 1968.
Editor, *Downpour.* London, New English Library, 1969.
Editor, *Ticket to Death.* London, New English Library, 1969.

*

Manuscript Collection: Mugar Memorial Library, Boston University.

*　　*　　*

Although he is best known as a mainstream novelist of considerable stature (*The Blackboard Jungle, Last Summer, Sons*), and as today's finest practitioner of the police procedural novel (the 87th Precinct series of more than 30 novels under his Ed McBain pseudonym), Evan Hunter began his career in the early 1950s as a science fiction writer and contributed a number of short stories and novels to the genre during the first half of that decade. The best of the stories are "Inferiority Complex," "Million Dollar Maybe," which involves a magazine's offer of one million dollars to the first private citizen who reaches the moon and returns alive, and "The Fallen Angel," an excellent deal-with-the-devil fantasy with a circus background.

All three of Hunter's early SF novels are adventure stories for young readers. *Find the Feathered Serpent,* an interesting blend of time and travel and Mayan history, is perhaps the best. *Rocket to Luna* is an account of the first moon-bound rocket, and *Danger: Dinosaurs!* again uses the time-travel theme, in this case into the dim past when saurians roamed the Earth. Hunter's most memorable contribution to SF is his only adult novel, *Tomorrow's World*—a caustically satirical study of a future in which narcotics have been legalized and there is a bitter struggle for control of publishing, movies, and television between the Vikes, who are responsible for the current vogue of drug use and vicarious entertainment, and the Realists, who advocate a return to the moral standards of the past. The novel, which has deservedly remained in print during most of the past quarter-century, is an expanded version of "Malice in Wonderland" (*If,* January 1954); interestingly, "Malice" is told in the first person, by the Vike literary agent Van Brant, while *Tomorrow's World* is a third-person novel whose viewpoint shifts between Brant and members of the Realist movement. What makes both novella and novel especially fascinating is the combination of Hunter's unsurpassed ear for dialogue and his meticulous use of a drug-oriented, futuristic slang.

With the exception of his screenplay for Alfred Hitchcock's fantasy-based film *The Birds,* Hunter has written no science fiction since the middle 1950s. But the many reprintings of *Tomorrow's World* and the occasional reprinting of short stories serve as reminders to the SF reader that his contribution to the field, though small, is by no means inconsequential.

—Bill Pronzini

HUXLEY, Aldous (Leonard)

Nationality: British. **Born:** Godalming, Surrey, 26 July 1894; son of scientist T.H. Huxley; brother of the scientist and writer Julian Huxley. **Education:** Hillside School, Godalming, 1903-08; Eton College, 1908-13; Balliol College, Oxford, 1913-15, B.A. (honours) in English 1915. **Family:** Married 1) Maria Nys in 1919 (died 1955); 2) Laura Archera in 1956; one son. **Career:** Worked in the War Office, 1917; taught at Eton College, 1918; member of the editorial staff of the *Athenaeum,* London, 1919-20; drama critic, *Westminster Gazette,* 1920-21; full-time writer from 1921; travelled and lived in France, Italy, and the United States, 1923-37; settled in California, 1937, and worked as a freelance screenwriter. **Awards:** American Academy award, 1959. **Member:** Companion of Literature, Royal Society of Literature, 1962. **Died:** 22 November 1963.

Science Fiction Publications

Novels

Brave New World: A Novel. London, Chatto and Windus, and Garden City, New York, Doubleday, Doran, 1932.
After Many a Summer Dies the Swan. New York, Harper, 1939; as *After Many a Summer,* London, Chatto and Windus, 1939.
Time Must Have a Stop. New York, Harper, 1944; London, Chatto and Windus, 1945.
Ape and Essence. New York, Harper, 1948; London, Chatto and Windus, 1949.
Island: A Novel. London, Chatto and Windus, and New York, Harper, 1962.

Other Publications

Novels

Crome Yellow. London, Chatto and Windus, 1921; New York, Doran, 1922.
Antic Hay. London, Chatto and Windus, and New York, Doran, 1923.
Those Barren Leaves. London, Chatto and Windus, and New York, Doran, 1925.
Point Counter Point. London, Chatto and Windus, and New York, Doubleday, 1928.

Eyeless in Gaza. London, Chatto and Windus, and New York, Harper, 1936.
The Genius and the Goddess. London, Chatto and Windus, and New York, Harper, 1955.

Short Stories

Limbo. London, Chatto and Windus, and New York, Doran, 1920.
Mortal Coils (includes play *Permutations among the Nightingales*). London, Chatto and Windus, and New York, Doran, 1922.
Little Mexican and Other Stories. London, Chatto and Windus, 1924; as *Young Archimedes and Other Stories,* New York, Doran, 1924.
Two or Three Graces and Other Stories. London, Chatto and Windus, and New York, Doran, 1926.
Brief Candles. London, Chatto and Windus, and New York, Doubleday, 1930; as *After the Fireworks,* New York, Avon, n.d.
Twice Seven: Fourteen Selected Stories. London, Reprint Society, 1944.
Collected Short Stories. London, Chatto and Windus, and New York, Harper, 1957.

Plays

Liluli, adaptation of a play by Romain Rolland, in *Nation* (London), 20 September-29 November 1919.
Albert, Prince Consort: A Biography Play for Which Mr. John Drinkwater's Historical Dramas Serve as a Model, in *Vanity Fair* (New York), March 1922.
The Ambassador of Capripedia, in *Vanity Fair* (New York), May 1922.
The Publisher, in *Vanity Fair* (New York), April 1923.
The Discovery, adaptation of the play by Frances Sheridan (produced London, 1924). London, Chatto and Windus, 1924; New York, Doran, 1925.
The World of Light (produced London, 1931). London, Chatto and Windus, and New York, Doubleday, 1931.
The Giocanda Smile, adaptation of his own story (produced London, 1948; New York 1950). London, Chatto and Windus, 1948; as *Mortal Coils,* New York, Harper, 1948.
The Genius and the Goddess, with Ruth Wendell, adaptation of the novel by Huxley (produced New York, 1957).

Screenplays: *Price and Prejudice,* with Jane Murfin, 1940; *Jane Eyre,* with John Houseman and Robert Stevenson, 1944; *A Woman's Vengeance,* 1947.

Poetry

The Burning Wheel. Oxford, Blackwell, 1916.
Jonah. Oxford, Holywell Press, 1917.
The Defeat of Youth and Other Poems. Oxford, Blackwell, 1918.
Leda. London, Chatto and Windus, and New York, Doran, 1920.
Selected Poems. Oxford, Blackwell, and New York, Appleton, 1925.
Arabia Infelix and Other Poems. New York, Fountain Press, and London, Chatto and Windus, 1929.
Apennine. Gaylordsville, Connecticut, Slide Mountain Press, 1930.
The Cicadas and Other Poems. London, Chatto and Windus, and New York, Doubleday, 1931.
Verses and a Comedy. London, Chatto and Windus, 1946.

The Collected Poetry of Aldous Huxley, edited by Donald Watt. London, Chatto and Windus, and New York, Harper, 1971.

Other

On the Margin: Notes and Essays. London, Chatto and Windus, and New York, Doran, 1923.

Along the Road: Notes and Essays of a Tourist. London, Chatto and Windus, and New York, Doran, 1925.

Essays New and Old. London, Chatto and Windus, 1926; New York, Doran, 1927.

Jesting Pilate: The Diary of a Journey. London, Chatto and Windus, and New York, Doran, 1926.

Proper Studies. London, Chatto and Windus, 1927; New York, Doubleday, 1928.

Do What You Will: Essays. London, Chatto and Windus, and New York, Doubleday, 1929.

Holy Face and Other Essays. London, The Fleuron, 1929.

Vulgarity in Literature: Digressions from a Theme. London, Chatto and Windus, 1930.

Music at Night and Other Essays. London, Chatto and Windus, and New York, Doubleday, 1931.

Rotunda (selection). London, Chatto and Windus, 1932.

T.H. Huxley as a Man of Letters (lecture). London, Macmilan, 1932.

Retrospect (selection). New York, Doubleday, 1933.

Beyond the Mexique Bay. London, Chatto and Windus, and New York, Harper, 1934.

The Olive Tree and Other Essays. London, Chatto and Windus, 1936; New York, Harper, 1937.

What Are You Going to Do About It? The Case for Constructive Peace. London, Chatto and Windus, 1936; New York, Harper, 1937.

Stories, Essays, and Poems. London, Dent, 1937.

Ends and Means: An Enquiry into the Nature of Ideals and into the Methods Employed for Their Realization. London, Chatto and Windus, and New York, Harper, 1937.

The Most Agreeable Vice. Los Angeles, Ward Ritchie Press, 1938.

Words and Their Meanings. Los Angeles, Ward Ritchie Press, 1940.

Gray Eminence: A Study in Religion and Politics. London, Chatto and Windus, 1941.

The Art of Seeing. New York, Harper, 1942; London, Chatto and Windus, 1943.

The Perennial Philosophy. New York, Harper, 1945; London, Chatto and Windus, 1946.

Science, Liberty, and Peace. New York, Harper, 1946; London, Chatto and Windus, 1947.

The World of Aldous Huxley: An Omnibus of His Fiction and Non-Fiction over Three Decades, edited by Charles J. Rolo. New York, Harper, 1947.

Food and People, with John Russell. London, Bureau of Current Affairs, 1949.

Prisons, with the Carceri Etchings by Piranesi. London, Trianon Press, and Los Angeles, Zeitlin and Ver Brugge, 1949.

Themes and Variations. London, Chatto and Windus, and New York, Harper, 1950.

The Devils of Loudun. London, Chatto and Windus, and New York, Harper, 1952.

Joyce the Artificer: Two Studies of Joyce's Methods, with Stuart Gilbert. London, Chiswick Press, 1952.

A Day in Windsor, with J.A. Kings. London, Britannicus Liber, 1953.

The Doors of Perception. London, Chatto and Windus, and New York, Harper, 1954.

The French of Paris, photographs by Sanford H. Roth. New York, Harper, 1954.

Adonis and the Alphabet, and Other Essays. London, Chatto and Windus, 1956; as *Tomorrow and Tomorrow and Tomorrow and Other Essays,* New York, Harper, 1956.

Heaven and Hell. London, Chatto and Windus, and New York, Harper, 1956.

Brave New World Revisited. New York, Harper, 1958; London, Chatto and Windus, 1959.

Collected Essays. London, Chatto and Windus, and New York, Harper, 1959.

On Art and Artists, edited by Morris Philipson. London, Chatto and Windus, and New York, Harper, 1960.

Selected Essays, edited by Harold Raymond. London, Chatto and Windus, 1961.

Literature and Science. London, Chatto and Windus, and New York, Harper, 1963.

The Politics of Ecology: The Question of Survival. Santa Barbara, California, Center for the Study of Democratic Institutions, 1963.

The Crows of Pearblossom (for children). London, Chatto and Windus, and New York, Random House, 1967.

The Letters of Aldous Huxley, edited by Grover Smith. London, Chatto and Windus, 1969; New York, Harper, 1970.

Great Short Works of Aldous Huxley, edited by Bernard Bergonzi. New York, Harper, 1969.

America and the Future. Austin, Texas, Jenkins, 1970.

Moksha: Writings on Psychedelics and the Visionary Experience 1931-1963, edited by Michael Horowitz and Cynthia Palmer. New York, Stonehill, 1977; London, Chatto and Windus, 1980.

The Human Situation: Lectures at Santa Barbara 1959, edited by Piero Ferrucci. New York, Harper, 1977; London, Chatto and Windus, 1978.

Huxley and God: Essays, edited by Jacqueline Hazard Bridgeman. San Francisco, HarperSanFrancisco, 1992.

Between the Wars: Essays and Letters, edited by David Bradshaw. Chicago, Dee, 1994.

Editor, with W.R. Childe and T.W. Earp, *Oxford Poetry 1916.* Oxford, Blackwell, 1916.

Editor, *Text and Pretexts: An Anthology with Commentaries.* London, Chatto and Windus, 1932; New York, Harper, 1933.

Editor, *The Letters of D.H. Lawrence.* London, Heinemann, and New York, Viking Press, 1932.

Editor, *An Encyclopedia of Pacifism.* London, Chatto and Windus, and New York, Harper, 1937.

Translator, *Virgin Heart,* by Rémy de Gourmont. New York, Brown, 1921; London, Allen and Unwin, 1926.

*

Bibliography: *Aldous Huxley: A Bibliography 1916-1959* by Claire John Eschelbach and Joyce Lee Shober, Berkeley, University of California Press, 1961; supplement by Thomas D. Clareson and Carolyn S. Andrews, in *Extrapolation 6* (Wooster, Ohio), 1964; *Aldous Huxley: An Annotated Bibliography of Criticism* by Eben E. Bass, New York, Garland, 1981.

Critical Studies (selection): *Aldous Huxley: A Literary Study* by John Atkins, London, Calder, and New York, Roy, 1956, revised edition, London, Calder and Boyars, 1967, New York, Orion Press, 1968; *The Timeless Moment: A Personal View of Aldous Huxley* by Laura Huxley, New York, Farrar Straus, 1968, London, Chatto and Windus, 1969; *Aldous Huxley: A Study of the Major Novels* by Peter Bowering, London, Athlone Press, 1968, New York, Oxford University Press, 1969; *Aldous Huxley: Satire and Structure* by Jerome Meckier, London, Chatto and Windus, and New York, Barnes and Noble, 1969; *Aldous Huxley* by Harold H. Watts, New York, Twayne, 1969; *Dawn and the Darkest Hour: A Study of Aldous Huxley* by George Woodcock, London, Faber, and New York, Viking Press, 1972; *Aldous Huxley* by Keith M. May, London, Elek, 1972, New York, Harper, 1973; *Aldous Huxley: A Biography* by Sybille Bedford, London, Chatto and Windus-Collins, 2 vols., 1973-74, New York, Knopf, 1 vol., 1974; *Aldous Huxley: A Collection of Critical Essays* edited by Robert E. Kuehn, Englewood Cliffs, New Jersey, Prentice Hall, 1974; *Aldous Huxley: The Critical Heritage* edited by Donald Watt, London, Routledge, 1975; *Demon and Saint in the Novels of Aldous Huxley* by Lilly Zahmer, Bern, Schweizer Anglistische Arbeiten, 1975; *Aspects of Structure and Quest in Aldous Huxley's Major Novels* by Bharathi Krishnan, Uppsala, Sweden, University of Uppsala, 1977; *Aldous Huxley, Novelist* by Christopher S. Ferns, London, Athlone Press, 1980; *The Dark Historic Page: Social Satire and Historicism in the Novels of Aldous Huxley 1921-1939* by Robert S. Baker, Madison, University of Wisconsin Press, 1982; *Huxley in Hollywood* by David King Dunaway, New York, Harper, and London, Bloomsbury, 1989.

*   *   *

Satirist, moralist, humanist, visionary, and proselytizer, Aldous Huxley is famous for his skeptical debunking of received attitudes and values; his eclectic intellect with its solid foundation in science, philosophy, and culture; his loathing of blind faith in progress, technology, Freudian psychology, and Watsonian behaviorism as well as orthodox Christianity; his fears of overpopulation, hedonism, scientific materialism, and dehumanization; and, in the later works, his interest in mysticism, parapsychology, and psychedelic drugs. At their best his rather quirky, erudite "novels of ideas" are rich in ironic counterpoint, humorous impieties, lively debate, and visual detail; at their worst they are loosely structured and confused diatribes in which the novel is an excuse to do what would best be handled in an essay format. Huxley takes pride in being irreverent and slightly shocking. His novels are full of characters blindly committed to ignorance and error, shocked by the ideologies of others, distracted by passions, engaged in witty repartee or philosophical debate but, in general, trapped in a static, "sick" society which destroys man's capacity for self-improvement and psychic fulfillment, dehumanizes, enslaves, and destroys.

His early works with their tea-party debates explore ineffectual communication, futility, egotism and self-alienation, disillusionment and dissociation, missed opportunities and failed epiphanies, while considering alternative approaches to reality and escapes from it. His goal, as he himself stated, was to "shock the stupid and morally reprehensible truth-haters." His later works focus much more on murder, death, disease, pain, and "vile flesh" before switching to moral affirmation.

In *After Many a Summer Dies the Swan,* an antiquarian American millionaire (Jo Stoyte), fearful of death and greedy to hang on to his material acquisitions, funds a research effort to find the physiological secret of longevity. A living example that such is possible, the Fifth Earl of Hauberk, has devolved over two centuries into a grunting apelike satyr, but Stoyte finds even such a life more attractive than death. The power struggle between characters (power through wealth or sex or knowledge) and the debates that accompany it, suggests that ultimate control eludes all in a deterministic world.

The predominance of animal imagery throughout Huxley's novels suggests the irony of man's pretensions or his descent down the chain of being to the level of lizards, dogs, apes, and ferrets. *Point Counter Point,* for example, describes a child's development from worm to fish to fetus to high-church convert. Written as a motion-picture script within a narrative frame, *Ape and Essence,* a pessimistic allegory set after the devastation of World War III, begins with the violent murder of Gandhi and moves to a dystopia, a warlike society of egocentric, lustful, materialistic baboons, to argue the dangers of man's animal side dominating intellect and science (particularly through religious and political institutions). In the script within the novel, Dr. Alfred Poole, a member of the 2108 A.D. New Zealand Rediscovery Expedition to North America, describes and then flees this debased culture with its radiation-induced mutations, its fouled waters and land, its baby sacrifices, and its grotesque caricature of human egotism. An omniscient narrator sums up Huxley's argument: "Only in the knowledge of his own Essence/ Has any man ceased to be many monkeys."

Though not Huxley's best effort, *Brave New World* is perhaps his best-known work. Set in a technologically advanced world in the 26th century, "After Ford 632," in London, Southern England, and a Zuni reservation in New Mexico, this novel deals with the basic dichotomy between progress and humanism. Huxley's futuristic society (a hierarchical pyramid with a broad base of lower-caste, ant-like identical twins) is one of testtube babies, chemical and genetic engineering, hypnopaedic conditioning, consumerism, and a mindless "happiness" made possible through sexual liberation, drugs, mass production, death conditioning, sensory films, a rejection of history and family, and an inescapable social destiny of "Community, Identity, and Stability." A small elite of Alphas and Betas do the little thinking necessary to keep their world functioning until a social outsider (Bernard Marx) introduces a real outsider: the Savage, a halfbreed raised on Shakespeare, Indian lore, and Christianity. His reservation world is one of disease, superstition, guilt, racial prejudice, possessiveness, death, and individuality. The clash of these two contrasting world views (reason vs. passion; progress vs. history) exposes the limits of each: empty happiness vs. painful freedom.

The Savage meets the utopia of his dreams and finds it wanting, a dystopia of too-easy progress against which he violently reacts. In a debate with the World Controller after the death of his "soma" drugged mother, he ineffectually demands the right to be unhappy. Seeking to create his own pure, ascetic reservation in a lighthouse, the hounded Savage, fascinated and repelled by the sexual license of sensation-crazed sightseers, beats himself, yields to sexual compulsions, and finally, unable to cope, commits suicide. Although the Savage's criticism is accurate, what he offers in place of progress is equally unacceptable: a choice "between insanity on the one hand and lunacy on the other," between technological civilization and past primitivism.

Brave New World Revisited examines the limitations and accuracy of *Brave New World,* particularly about such modern problems as drug dependency, the sexual revolution, the excesses of a consumer society, genetic engineering, and conditioning through advertising.

Huxley's last novel, *Island,* seeks a balance whose possibility *Brave New World* denied: a fusion of passion and reason—the mystical East with the technological West. In it a cynical and disenchanted outsider, Will Farnaby, is educated in the ways of Pala, a life-affirming culture that values reason, contemplation, community, and psychedelic drugs to prevent misery. This novel provides an entirely positive but fragile utopia, the antithesis of *Brave New World,* but it is stylistically weak and boring. Huxley is much more effective at moral outrage than moral affirmation, and contraception, artificial insemination, the "hybridization of microcultures," hypnosis, and the yoga of love are hardly convincing as the solution to the problems Huxley had so ably defined or predicted in earlier works. Huxley's dominant image, the islands, suggests man's surface isolation but his subsurface ties with his fellow islands. However, his novel ends, not with the realization of human potential, but with a hostile, power-driven malcontent making a drive for power against nonviolent pacifists.

Huxley's erudite and witty works balance conflicting ideological positions but with an ambiguity that negates solution or resolution. *Island* rejects as wrong his earlier vision of progress as tempting, insidious, and ultimately destructive, but it is *Brave New World,* with its sardonic vision of emptiness and loss, that has captured the imagination of modern visionaries.

—Gina Macdonald

HYDE, Shelley. *See* **REED, Kit.**

HYNE, C(harles) J(ohn) Cutcliffe (Wright)

Pseudonym: Weatherby Chesney. **Nationality:** British. **Born:** Bilbury, Gloucestershire, 11 May 1865. **Education:** Bradford Grammar School; Clare College, Cambridge, B.A., M.A. **Family:** Married Elsie Haggas in 1897 (died 1938), one daughter. **Career:** Journalist: travelled extensively as a writer for magazines. **Died:** 10 March 1944.

SCIENCE FICTION PUBLICATIONS

Novels

Beneath Your Very Boots: Being a Few Striking Episodes from the Life of Anthony Merlwood Haltoun, Esq. London, Digby Long, 1889.
The New Eden. London, Longman, 1892.
The Recipe for Diamonds. London, Heinemann, and New York, Appleton, 1893.

The Lost Continent. London, Hutchinson, and New York, Harper, 1900.
Empire of the World. London, Everett, 1910; New York, Arno Press, 1975; as *Emperor of the World: A Tale of an Anglo-German War,* London, Newnes, 1915.
Abbs: His Story through Many Ages. London, Hutchinson, 1929.
Ivory Valley: An Adventure of Captain Kettle. London, Ward Lock, 1938.
Wishing Smith. London, Hale, 1939.

Short Stories

The Adventures of a Solicitor (as Weatherby Chesney). London, Bowden, 1898.
Atoms of Empire. London and New York, Macmillan, 1904.
Man's Understanding: A Volume of Short Stories. London, Ward Lock, 1933.

OTHER PUBLICATIONS

Novels

Four Red Nightcaps. London, Eden, 1890.
Currie, Curtis & Co., Crammers. London, Remington, 1890.
A Matrimonial Mixture. London, Ward and Downey, 1891.
Stimson's Reef. London, Blackie, 1891.
Sandy Carmichael. London, Sampson Low, 1892; Philadelphia, Lippincott, 1908.
The Captured Cruiser; or, Two Years from Land. London, Blackie, 1892; New York, Scribner, 1895.
The Wild-Catters. London, Sunday School Union, 1895.
Honour of Thieves. London, Chatto and Windus, 1895; New York, Fenno, 1899; as *The Little Red Captain: An Early Adventure of Captain Kettle,* London, Pearson, 1902.
The Stronger Hand. London, Beeman, 1896.
Through Arctic Lapland. London, A. and C. Black, and New York, Macmillan, 1898.
The Glass Dagger. New York, New Amsterdam, 1899.
The Filibusters. London, Hutchinson, and New York, Stokes, 1900.
Prince Rupert the Buccaneer. London, Methuen, and New York, Stokes, 1901.
Thompson's Progress. London, Richards, 1902; New York, Macmillan, 1903.
Captain Kettle, K.C.B. London, Pearson, and New York, Federal, 1903.
McTodd. London and New York, Macmillan, 1903.
The Trials of Commander McTurk. London, Murray, and New York, Dutton, 1906.
Kate Meredith, Financier. New York, Authors and Newspapers Association, 1906; as *Kate Meredith,* London, Cassell, 1907.
The Marriage of Kettle. London, Heinemann, and Indianapolis, Bobbs Merrill, 1912.
Firemen Hot. London, Methuen, 1914.
Captain Kettle on the War-Path. London, Methuen, 1916.
Captain Kettle's Bit. London, Hodder and Stoughton, 1918.
Admiral Teach. London, Methuen, 1920.
President Kettle. London, Nash and Grayson, 1920.
Mr. Kettle, Third Mate. London, Ward Lock, 1931.
West Highland Spirits. London, Ward Lock, 1932.
Captain Kettle, Ambassador. London, Ward Lock, 1932.

Absent Friends. London, Ward Lock, 1933.

Novels as Weatherby Chesney

The Dilemma of Commander Brett. London, Bowden, 1899.
John Topp, Pirate. London, Methuen, 1901.
The Branded Prince. London, Methuen, 1902.
The Foundered Galleon. London, Methuen, 1902.
The Baptist Ring. London, Methuen, 1903.
The Mystery of a Bungalow. London, Methuen, 1904.
The Tragedy of the Great Emerald. London, Methuen, 1904.
The Cable-Man. London, Chatto and Windus, 1907.
The Claimant. London, Chatto and Windus, 1908.
The Romance of a Queen. London, Chatto and Windus, 1908.

Short Stories

The Paradise Coal-Boat. London, Bowden, and New York, Mansfield, 1897.
Adventures of Captain Kettle. London, Pearson, and New York, Doubleday, 1898.
The Adventures of an Engineer (as Weatherby Chesney). London, Bowden, 1898.
Further Adventures of Captain Kettle. London, Pearson, 1899; as *A Master of Fortune,* New York, Dillingham, 1901.
The Derelict. New York, Lewis Scribner, 1901; revised edition, as *Mr. Horrocks, Purser,* London, Methuen, 1902.
The Escape Agents. London, Laurie, 1911.
Red Herrings. London, Methuen, 1918.
The Rev. Captain Kettle. London, Harrap, 1925.
Ben Watson. London, Country Life, 1926.
Steamboatmen. London, Penguin, 1943.

Other

People and Places. London, Newnes, 1930.
But Britons Are Slaves. London, Harmsworth, 1931.
My Joyful Life. London, Hutchinson, 1935.

Don't You Agree? (essays). London, Hutchinson, 1935.

Editor, *For Britain's Soldiers.* London, Methuen, 1900.

*   *   *

Half a dozen of C.J. Cutcliffe Hyne's novels are SF, as are some of his many short stories ("The Men from Mars" in *The Adventures of a Solicitor*). In *Beneath Your Very Boots* the narrator finds beneath England a race descended underground in pre-Roman times, using Earth heat as energy source, manufacturing diamonds, but otherwise living in a theocratic dictatorship à la Rider Haggard. In a dilution of Bulwer-Lytton's *The Coming Race,* the narrator-hero invents a boring machine, is rewarded by a pleasure drug, and during an unsuccessful rebellion escapes with the obligatory beautiful underground wife.

The New Eden and *The Recipe for Diamonds* are more pallid. In the first, an archduke-scientist sets up on a Pacific island the experiment of starting a young man and woman from zero; they invent art, alcohol, and Sun-worship. In the second, Lully's recipe is found and, after intrigues involving the equally obligatory anarchist, destroyed again. *The Lost Continent* is a relatively readable Haggard-type melodrama of Atlantis, narrated by a nobleman of those times involved with a strong upstart empress. Though she is the most interesting character of the novel, women's rule still leads to decadence and the flood, after political intrigues and fights with giant saurians and cave-tigers. In *Empire of the World* a poor scientist with a ray-machine that disintegrates iron intervenes in the war of Britain vs. Germany, enforcing peace. It is an unsuccessful try at fusing the "future war" story with "a rather heavy-handed comedy of romantic entanglements in high society" (R.D. Mullen, in *Science-Fiction Studies* 6, 1975). Finally, *Abbs* is a novel about longevity, the protagonist living "through many ages." In all, Hyne is a good example of the middle range of prewar SF, a competent storyteller who wrote too conventionally and too much.

—Darko Suvin

I-J

ING, Dean

Nationality: American. **Born:** Austin, Texas, 17 June 1931. **Education:** Fresno State University, B.A. 1956; San Jose State University, M.A. 1970; University of Oregon, Eugene, Ph.D. in Speech 1974. **Military Service:** Served in the United States Air Force, 1951-55; Airman 1st Class. **Family:** Married Margaret Barrier in 1952 (divorced 1957), two children; 2) Geneva Baker in 1959, two children. **Career:** Engineer, Aerojet-General, Sacramento, California, 1957-62, and Lockheed, San Jose, California, 1962, 1965-70; assistant professor of Speech, Missouri State University, 1974-77. Since 1977, freelance writer. **Agent:** Eleanor Wood, 111 Eighth Ave., Suite 1501, New York, New York 10011. **Address:** 1105 Ivy Lane, Ashland, Oregon 97520, U.S.A.

SCIENCE FICTION PUBLICATIONS

Novels (series: Lagrange; The Man-Kzin Wars; Ted Quantrill)

Soft Targets. New York, Ace, 1979.
Systemic Shock (Quantrill). New York, Ace, 1981.
Pulling Through. New York, Ace, 1983.
Single Combat (Quantrill). New York, Tor, 1983.
Home Sweet Home: 2010 A.D., with Mack Reynolds. New York, Dell, 1984.
Eternity, with Mack Reynolds. New York, Pocket Books, 1984.
The Other Time, with Mack Reynolds. New York, Pocket Books, 1984.
Wild Country (Quantrill). New York, Tor, 1985.
Trojan Orbit, with Mack Reynolds. New York, Baen, 1985.
Deathwish World, with Mack Reynolds. New York, Baen, 1986.
The Big Lifters. New York, Tor, 1988.

Short Stories (series: Man-Kzin Wars)

Anasazi. New York, Ace, 1980.
High Tension (includes nonfiction). New York, Ace, 1982.
Firefight 2000 (includes nonfiction). New York, Baen, 1987.
The Man-Kzin Wars, with Larry Niven and Poul Anderson. New York, Baen, 1988.
The Man-Kzin Wars II, with Larry Niven, Jerry Pournelle, and S.M. Stirling. New York, Baen, 1989.
Cathouse (Man-Kzin Wars). New York, Baen, 1990.
Silent Thunder, with *Universe,* by Robert A. Heinlein. New York, Tor, 1991.

OTHER PUBLICATIONS

Novels

Blood of Eagles. New York, Tor, 1987.
The Ransom of Black Stealth One. New York, St. Martin's Press, 1989.
The Nemesis Mission. New York, Tor, 1991.

Butcher Bird. New York, Tor, 1993.

Other

Mutual Assured Survival: A Space-Age Solution to Nuclear Annihilation, with Jerry Pournelle. New York, Baen, 1984.
The Future of Flight, with Leik Myrabo. New York, Baen, 1985.
The Chernobyl Syndrome. New York, Baen, 1988.

Editor, *High Frontier,* by Daniel Graham. New York, Tor, 1983.
Editor, *The Lagrangists,* with Mack Reynolds. New York, Tor, 1983.
Editor, *Chaos in Lagrangia,* by Mack Reynolds. New York, Tor, 1984.

*

Bibliography: *The Work of Dean Ing: An Annotated Bibliography and Guide* by Scott Alan Burgess, San Bernardino, California, Borgo Press, 1990.

Dean Ing comments:

As a former senior engineer and behavioral scientist, I write hard-nosed, hard SF. Many of the things I have to say are speculative; some are unpleasant; some are vulgar and/or titillating. It takes a very good university to employ a gadfly, and I found professoring dreary. As a media theorist I felt I could put my ideas over much more widely in fast-paced fictional thrillers than in lecture halls. Q.E.D.

I rarely write before I've decided what needs saying, and outlined it excitingly. I'm a contentist. It's a sign of our times that I had to invent a word that stresses content over style, though the word "stylist" is common enough, God knows. . . .

Literature stressing content over style demands much of readers, so I must make that content sparkle like rhinestones on a soapbox. I research my work as thoroughly as possible, but I no longer take as many physical risks as I once did. But when I describe what it's like to bail out of a moving race car or get plastered against a blockhouse floor by a rocket explosion, often it's dredged up from memory.

*   *   *

Dean Ing's greatest success came with his classy Tom Clancyish techno-thriller *The Ransom of Black Stealth One.* U.S. Intelligence seeks to trick the Russians into buying an inferior version of the world's most advanced aircraft from a defector. But the real Black Stealth One is stolen from the National Security Agency by a rogue agent who takes both the plane and a hostage: Petra, a beautiful engineer. *The Ransom of Black Stealth One* is crammed with excitement, romance, and tension as both American and Soviet intelligence agencies risk everything to capture the super aircraft. Ing's earlier thriller, *Blood of Eagles,* shares the same relentless intensity of *The Ransom of Black Stealth One* but culminating in the low-tech setting of the Sierra mountains. A teenage boy is being hunted down by killers who want the secret of the stolen Nazi gold. Ing keeps the chase interesting right up to the heart-pounding climax.

Almost as good is Ing's latest thriller, *Butcher Bird.* A flying robot assassin threatens the lives of America's leaders. Ben Ullmer, an aerosystems engineer with the NSA, races against time to stop the plot in this sequel to *The Ransom of Black Stealth One.* Continuing success in writing techno-thrillers led Ing to perhaps his best book in *The Nemesis Mission.* A U.S. task force fights against time to stop the scheme of drug lord Simon Torres to fly a billion dollars and a plane with hostages from Las Vegas to Mexico. The real star of the book is the high-tech, solar-powered craft called Nemesis.

Ing's science fiction novel *The Big Lifters* reworks many of his favorite themes. Entrepreneur John Wesley Peel develops an alternative to trucks: a combination of dirigible and magnetic levitation trains. Opposing this safer, more efficient advance are the Teamsters—who fear job losses—and Iranian terrorists. The characters are wooden and the plot is predictable.

More entertaining is *Cathouse,* a collection of two novellas, "Cathouse" and "Briar Patch," which were previously published separately in Larry Niven's *Man-Kzin War* series. Both stories echo the wit of Eric Frank Russell's classic stories of humans outsmarting aliens.

Ing's first novel, *Soft Targets,* presents many of the themes he develops in his later works: the fragility of society and the importance of individualism. Hakim Arif, a terrorist who calls his organization Fat'ah, sees an open society such as the United States filled with "soft targets" that he can strike at will. In the near future, Ing suggests, terrorism and an open society may be mutually exclusive. Much is made of the power of the media to turn terrorists into media stars. The character of Hakim Arif is well drawn and chillingly convincing. The problem is with the plot: the FCC commissioner Maurice Everett and heads of the major television networks create a straw man in the comedian Charlie George who satirizes terrorists on his program to draw out Fat'ah. However, Everett miscalculates the cleverness of the terrorists and finds himself kidnapped along with Charlie George. The conclusion, though realistically violent, lacks coherence.

Anasazi, a collection of two novellas and a short novel, is uneven. The title short story, "Anasazi," deals with the possession of a tribe of Indians by parasitic aliens. Although it addresses many of the same issues as Robert Silverberg's award-winning "Passengers," "Anasazi" shows more control over the characters and plot by Ing. The novella, "The Devil You Don't Know," concerns a drug ring operating within a mental hospital. Ing's handling of psi powers in this story is deft and convincing.

Systemic Shock introduces readers to a nuclear/biological holocaust where the United States and its allies suffer staggering losses from the India-China alliance. Most of the large cities of the world are reduced to rubble and only decentralized populations survive. Ing creates a likable hero in young 15-year-old Ted Quantrill and presents a surviving society dominated by the Mormon and other religious groups. Quantrill loses his family in the nuclear strikes and biological plagues. Because of his intelligence and lightning reflexes, he's recruited into the new government's secret T Section as a gunsel. A receiver/transmitter is surgically planted in his skull, along with an explosive charge. Quantrill shows us how to survive in the new "Streamlined America" where nuclear bombs have destroyed most of the rules and the power to rule comes from the barrels of guns. Ing's realism is refreshing when compared to other post-holocaust novels like Jerry Ahern's bloody "Survivalist" series. Even so, Ing makes the plot unnecessarily complicated and the conclusion unsatisfying.

Ing's most interesting collection is *High Tension,* which is a blend of fact articles and short stories. "Gimme Shelter" is a detailed account of how to survive a nuclear war. This is an issue Ing returns to in *Pulling Through.* The short story "Down and Out on Ellfive Prime" owes a debt to George Orwell as Ing explores life aboard an orbiting space colony. "Living Under Pressure" presents detailed photographs to aid in the construction of an air supply unit for a small nuclear shelter. The best part of *High Tension* is Ing's powerful introductions to each story and article, giving the reader more insight into his philosophy.

Pulling Through puts all Ing's survivalist articles into practice as Harve Rackham and Kate Gallo survive the nuking of the San Francisco area and find the means to pull through the crisis. They build an air pump and filter, and they make their own fallout radiation meter from common household materials. Harve and Kate have to survive more than radiation as the other survivors, ordinary citizens and escaped convicts, supply subplots. But *Pulling Through* is more didactic than entertaining. The details of Harve and Kate's survival are interesting but can't make up for the plot weaknesses.

With *Single Combat* Ing returns to his most convincing vision: postholocaust America dominated by the Mormons and other religious groups. Ted Quantrill returns, older by a few years, and more disenchanted with his role as a government assassin. Resistance to the new order of theocracy is emerging and Ing manages to free Quantrill of the receiver-transmitter and explosive implanted in his head. Given his freedom, Quantrill seeks revenge on the government that controlled him for so long. *Single Combat* remains Ing's best book, combining an action-packed plot and believable characters into a thrilling adventure story.

In addition to his own work, Dean Ing has completed a series of science fiction novels left unfinished by the late Mack Reynolds. *Eternity* is a conventional immortality novel. *Trojan Orbit* is a thriller about sabotage aboard Island One, the first United States space colony. The best book is *The Other Time,* in which Donald Fielding is sent by timewarp to the court of Montezuma where he takes up the identity of Quetzalcoatl and helps the Aztecs defeat Cortez's Spanish troops.

Dean Ing is a solid, capable writer whose background in engineering and science is evident in his science fiction and in his successful techno-thrillers.

—George Kelley

JABLOKOV, Alexander

Nationality: American. **Born:** Evanston, Illinois, 29 April 1956. **Education:** University of Southern California, B.S. 1978; Dartmouth College, M.S. 1981. **Family:** Married Mary Elizabeth Tobias in 1993. **Agent:** Val Smith, 1746 Route 44/55, Modena, New York 12548, U.S.A.

SCIENCE FICTION PUBLICATIONS

Novels

Carve the Sky. New York, Morrow, 1991.
A Deeper Sea. New York, Morrow, 1992.

Nimbus. New York, Morrow, 1993.
The Breath of Suspension. Sauk City, Wisconsin, Arkham House, 1994.

* * *

Alexander Jablokov established himself as an SF writer to watch with a number of distinctive works of short fiction, primarily of novelette length, in the mid-to-late 1980s, most of which were published in *Isaac Asimov's Science Fiction Magazine.* His first story was "Beneath the Shadow of Her Smile" (1985). His work drew comparisons with Alfred Bester and early Roger Zelazny, as well as with later writers such as Bruce Sterling.

Many of his best stories exhibit a profound interest in both art and history. "At the Cross-Time Jaunter's Ball" (1987) is an intricate story about a group of immortals whose art is in creating whole new parallel universes with histories different from our own. "The Death Artist" (1990) is a coolly written story about an artist whose medium is creating death experiences through the use of clones and memory recordings. "Living Will" (1991) was a melancholy story about a man dying of a brain-degenerative disorder who is trying to translate his memories and personality into a computer simulation. Most of his best short fiction was collected in *The Breath of Suspension* (1994). Jablokov also produced a number of stories as part of a project by the Cambridge Writers Workshop, along with other promising young authors such as David Alexander Smith, Geoffrey Landis, and Steven Popkes, set in a common "Future Boston." These stories, including "The Place of No Shadows" (1990) and "The Adoption" (1991), were published in the anthology *Future Boston* (1994).

Jablokov's first novel was *Carve the Sky* (1991), set in a future Boston, at a time in the 24th century when much of the Solar System has been colonized. Those living on the inner planets have grown to be continually at odds with those living on various moons of the outer planets, and they are on the verge of another war. Throughout the Solar System, there are evidences of an alien race long departed. Jablokov's protagonist is a professor at a transformed Harvard University who is seeking a figurine which is the key to discovering the secrets of interstellar travel, a hidden treasure of a rare, unstable element left over by the ancient starfaring race, a search that eventually leads her to the Asteroid Belt. *Carve the Sky* is an intricate novel of baroque complexity, although maybe a bit too ambitious; at times, it bordered on information overload. It was nominated for the Locus Award as one of the best first novels of the year.

His second novel, *A Deeper Sea* (1992), is expanded from his excellent 1989 novella of the same title, and involves intelligent dolphins and whales in a 21st-century milieu. The story involves a Soviet scientist who establishes communication with dolphins, and discovers that until a few thousand years ago at the time of the ancient Minoans, dolphins had always talked to humans. The scientist uses the dolphins as weapons in a war with the Americans and Japanese, but the Americans win anyway. Meanwhile, an American scientist is investigating evidences of life on Jupiter, and seeks to enlist the Soviet scientist and his dolphins, which are very talented communicators, in her quest to establish communications with the Jovian life forms. The dolphins and an orca whale are taken to Jupiter as part of a team to develop communications. Although the book is compelling and original, its overly complex narrative makes it in many ways inferior to the novella from which it was expanded.

Nimbus (1993), Jablokov's third novel, is a fast-paced murder mystery set in a decidedly cyber-punkish future. Set thirty years in the future, after the end of the "Devolution Wars", the protagonist is a jazz pianist and installer of illegal "verts" (mental augmentation computer-chip implants) into the brains of rich corporate mo-

guls. He also has faint memories of being part of a top-secret government project during the Wars, The Nimbus Project. When he learns that others from the Project are being murdered, he must reactivate his intentially-suppressed memories of the project so he can protect himself and find the killer. He regains his disturbing memories, and sets off to solve the mystery, utilizing the help of his contacts the jazz underground, and the criminal subculture where he obtains his illegal verts.

Jablokov's high-tension, fast-paced plotting and fascinatingly original future world in *Nimbus* reminds one of William Gibson's fiction, and shares many of its strengths and weaknesses. While the narrative is quite believable on a moment-by-moment level, the plot and milieu ultimately can be seen not to have sufficiently consistent and believable underpinnings. The murder mystery is marred by information withheld from the reader, and suspense-producing red herrings. Despite these flaws, *Nimbus* remains an ambitious novel, with interesting characters and a fast-paced narrative.

Alexander Jablokov has continued to develop as a promising science fiction author, willing to tackle ambitious themes with complex narratives and characterizations, producing fiction at both short- and novel-lengths that nears award-quality. If the verisimilitude of his plots and settings improve, he should be able to fulfill the promise he has shown and produce top quality works.

—D. Douglas Fratz

JACOBS, Harvey

Nationality: American. **Born:** New York, New York, 7 January 1930. **Education:** Syracuse University, B.A. 1950; Columbia University, 1950-51. **Family:** Married Estelle Rose in 1956; one son. **Career:** Public Relations, Weizman Institute of Science, New York City, 1954-55; staff member, *Village Voice,* New York City; publisher, *East,* New York City, 1956-57; director of industry affairs, American Broadcasting Co., New York City, 1958-73; instructor in writer's workshop, Syracuse University, 1958-59. **Awards:** *Playboy* Fiction award; Earplay award for drama (Writers Guild of America. **Member:** Writers Guild of America; Dramatists Guild.

SCIENCE FICTION PUBLICATIONS

Novel

Beautiful Soup: A Novel for the 21st Century. New York, Celadon Press, 1993.

Short Stories

The Egg of the Glak and Other Stories. New York, Harper, 1969; London, Secker & Warburg, 1971.

OTHER PUBLICATIONS

Novels

Summer on a Mountain of Spices. New York, Harper, 1975.
The Juror: A Novel. New York, Franklin Watts, 1980.

Other

Famous Fingerprints, with David Martin (cartoons). New York, Grosset & Dunlap, 1969.
Mrs. Portnoy's Retort: A Mother Strikes Back!, with David Martin (cartoons). New York, Allograph Publishers, 1969.
The Hartland Open Space Project: Technical Report, with Darby Bradley. Montpelier, Vermont, Natural Resources Council, 1976.
Hugging the Heartland: Prideful Essays about the Place and the People. Evanston, Illinois, Highlander Press, 1990.

*

Manuscript Collection: Syracuse University Library, Syracuse, New York.

*   *   *

Humorous science fiction has a long and uneven career. On the one hand, there have been a number of writers in the field who have used it extensively, Robert Sheckley, Ron Goulart, Douglas Adams, and Randall Garrett, all well respected in the field. But with the exception of Adams, who is something of an anomaly, funny SF has always been viewed as something suspect. There's something not quite "serious" about it. Readers may chuckle while they're reading it, but when they talk about the important stories in the field, humor is excluded.

The exception to that rule is the kind of intellectual satire that made Kurt Vonnegut popular beyond the borders of the field. It's in this tradition that Harvey Jacobs usually writes, a tradition that has fallen out of favor in the genre. Were that not so, it is likely that Harvey Jacobs would hold a much more important place in the field than he presently does, because his stories use a satiric, even whimsical tone to examine what it means to be human, how we treat our selves and one another, and the often absurd rules we set up to govern our own behavior.

Most of Jacobs's fiction is skillfully written and sufficiently oddball that it appears as frequently in slick mainstream magazines as in purely science fiction publications, and his bizarre vision of the modern world has been compared to Magic Realism, fantasy, and surrealist fiction. His best-known story is undoubtedly "The Egg of the Glak," which involves the discovery of a fertile egg of the supposedly extinct species the glak. The protagonist is overseeing its protracted hatching, and becomes obsessively involved with its welfare for reasons even he doesn't comprehend, redesigning his own life in order to advance what is ultimately a trivial accomplishment.

A woman is courted by an inarticulate alien in "Where Did You Get My Number?" and finally decides to run off to the stars. The stand-in for an award winning but reclusive scientist destroys the world as part of his acceptance speech in "Accepting for Winkelmeyer." "In Seclusion" involves two actors living in a remote castle to publicize their appearance in a forthcoming monster movie, unaware that a giant sea creature has risen from the depths is watching them, hoping to have them for lunch. It's much more overtly farcical than most of Jacobs' fiction. Flying saucers land in Russia in "The Man Who Made a Baby" and encounter a man with a mission. A distant world with unusually lush vegetation becomes the gimmick for an advertising campaign in "Busby," and a writer discovers he may have chosen the wrong audience for his work.

Many of Jacobs's stories are more properly fantasy than science fiction. A woman is hunted down by her dolls grown life size, animated, and vengeful in "Kitten Kaboodle and Sidney Australia." The unusual search for a holy man's heir is the subject of "Seymourlama." In "The Toll Bridge" a psychologist is menaced by the incarnation of Attila the Hun, who announces his murderous intentions. Other stories of note include "Gravity," "The Toy," and "My Rose and My Grave."

Jacobs's sole genre novel is the sharply satiric *Beautiful Soup.* James Wander is a citizen of a future world that has abandoned individualism in the name of tranquility. Every citizen is imprinted with a bar code which effectively circumscribes his or her life. The data includes identity, prospects, career, and so on. Wander has a bright future ahead of him, according to his coding, until an accident in a grocery store overwrites his code with a new one, and he is condemned to living out the rest of his life as a can of pea soup. It is illegal, you see, to alter or remove bar codes, no matter how they have been acquired. Jacobs superimposes a twisted version of the usual anti-dystopian plot onto this foundation, Wander struggling to adjust to his new situation, ultimately becoming a rebel determined to overthrow the government and restore human freedom. Despite the relentlessly absurd plot, the novel is a caustic indictment of the pressure for conformity and our willingness to relinquish control of our own lives. Jacobs does seem slightly uncomfortable at this length, however, and portions of the latter half of the novel seem unnecessarily protracted, but he regains control soon thereafter and provides a satisfying conclusion.

Harvey Jacobs is not a prolific writer, but he is a uniformly good one. Much of the best of his short fiction has been collected in *The Egg of the Glak and Other Stories,* though not all of these are science fiction. His voice, though infrequently heard, is one of intelligent wit and an insightful perception of humanity's gift for the absurd, and his reputation in the field, considering the relatively small size of his genre work, is a testimony to the impact those few stories have made on readers.

—Don D'Ammassa

JAKES, John (William)

Pseudonyms: William Ard; Alan Payne; Jay Scotland. **Nationality:** American. **Born:** Chicago, Illinois, 31 March 1932. **Education:** DePauw University, Greencastle, Indiana, A.B. 1953; Ohio State University, Columbus, M.A. in American literature 1954. **Family:** Married Rachel Ann Payne in 1951; three daughters and one son. **Career:** Copywriter, then promotion manager, Abbott Laboratories, North Chicago, 1954-60; copywriter, Rumrill Company, Rochester, New York, 1960-61; freelance writer, 1961-65; copywriter, Kircher Helton and Collett, Dayton, Ohio, 1965-68; copy chief, then vice-president, Oppenheim Herminghausen and Clarke, Dayton, 1968-70; creative director, Dancer Fitzgerald Sample, Dayton, 1970-71. Writer-in-Residence, DePauw University, Fall 1979. Since 1971, freelance writer. LL.D.: Wright State University, Dayton, Ohio, 1976; Litt.D.: DePauw University, 1977; L.H.D., Winthrop College, 1985. **Address:** c/o Rembar and Curtis, Attorneys, 19 West 44th Street, New York, New York 10036, U.S.A.

Science Fiction Publications

Novels (series: Brak; Dragonard; Klekton)

When the Star Kings Die (Dragonard). New York, Ace, 1967.
Brak the Barbarian. New York, Avon, 1968; London, Tandem, 1970.
The Asylum World. New York, Paperback Library, 1969; London, New English Library, 1978.
The Hybrid. New York, Paperback Library, 1969.
The Planet Wizard (Dragonard). New York, Ace, 1969.
Secrets of Stardeep (for children). Philadelphia, Westminster Press, 1969.
Tonight We Steal the Stars (Dragonard). New York, Ace, 1969.
Brak the Barbarian Versus the Sorceress. New York, Paperback Library, 1969; as *Brak the Barbarian—The Sorceress,* London, Tandem, 1970.
Brak Versus the Mark of the Demons. New York, Paperback Library, 1969; as *Brak the Barbarian—The Mark of the Demons,* London, Tandem, 1970.
The Last Magicians. New York, Signet, 1969.
Black in Time. New York, Paperback Library, 1970.
Mask of Chaos. New York, Ace, 1970.
Master of the Dark Gate (Klekton). New York, Lancer, 1970.
Monte Cristo #99. New York, Curtis, 1970.
Six-Gun Planet. New York, Paperback Library, 1970; London, New English Library, 1978.
Mention My Name in Atlantis—Being, at Last, the True Account of the Calamitous Destruction of the Great Island Kingdom, Together with a Narrative of Its Wondrous Intercourses with a Superior Race of Other-Worldlings, as Transcribed from the Manuscript of a Survivor, Hoptor the Vintner, for the Enlightenment of a Dubious Posterity. New York, DAW, 1972.
Time Gate (for children). Philadelphia, Westminster Press, 1972.
Witch of the Dark Gate (Klekton). New York, Lancer, 1972.
On Wheels. New York, Warner, 1973.
Conquest of the Planet of the Apes (novelization of screenplay). New York, Award, 1974.
Brak: When the Idols Walked. New York, Pocket Books, 1978.
Excalibur!, with Gil Kane. New York, Dell, 1980.

Short Stories

The Best of John Jakes, edited by Martin H. Greenberg and Joseph D. Olander. NewYork, DAW, 1977.
Fortunes of Brak. New York, Dell, 1980.

Other Publications

Novels

The Texans Ride North (for children). Philadelphia, Winston, 1952.
Wear a Fast Gun. New York, Arcadia House, 1956; London, Ward Lock, 1957.
A Night for Treason. New York, Bouregy, 1956.
The Devil Has Four Faces. New York, Bouregy, 1958.
This'll Slay You (as Alan Payne). New York, Ace, 1958.
The Imposter. New York, Bouregy, 1959.
Johnny Havoc. New York, Belmont, 1960; London, Severn, 1990.
Johnny Havoc Meets Zelda. New York, Belmont, 1962; as *Havoc for Sale,* New York, Armchair Detective Library, 1990.

Johnny Havoc and the Doll Who Had "It." New York, Belmont, 1963; as *Holiday for Havoc,* New York, Armchair Detective Library, 1991.
G.I. Girls. Derby, Connecticut, Monarch, 1963.
Making It Big. New York, Belmont, 1968; as *Johnny Havoc and the Siren in Red,* New York, Armchair Detective Library, 1991.
Kent Family Chronicles:
The Bastard. New York, Pyramid, 1974; as *Fortune's Whirlwind* and *To an Unknown Shore,* London, Corgi, 2 vols., 1975.
The Rebels. New York, Pyramid, 1975; London, Corgi, 1979.
The Seekers. New York, Pyramid, 1975; London, Corgi, 1979.
The Furies. New York, Pyramid 1976; London, Corgi, 1979.
The Titans. New York, Pyramid 1976; London, Corgi, 1979.
The Warriors. New York, Pyramid, 1977; London, Corgi, 1979.
The Lawless. New York, Jove, 1978; London, Corgi, 1979.
The Americans. New York, Jove, 1980; London, Fontana, 1989.
North and South trilogy:
North and South. New York, Harcourt Brace, and London, Collins, 1982.
Love and War. New York, Harcourt Brace, 1984; London, Collins, 1985.
Heaven and Hell. New York, Harcourt Brace, 1987; London Collins, 1988.
California Gold. New York, Random House, 1989; London, Collins, 1990.
Homeland. New York, Doubleday,and London, Little Brown, 1993.

Novels as Jay Scotland

The Seventh Man. New York, Bouregy, 1958.
I, Barbarian. New York, Avon, 1959; revised edition, as *John Jakes,* New York, Pinnacle, 1976.
Strike the Black Flag. New York, Ace, 1961.
Sir Scoundrel. New York, Ace, 1962; revised edition, as *King's Crusader,* New York, Pinnacle 1977.
Veils of Salome. New York, Avon, 1962.
Arena. New York, Ace, 1963.
Traitors' Legion. New York, Ace, 1963; revised edition, as *The Man from Cannae,* New York, Pinnacle, 1977.

Novels as William Ard

Make Mine Mavis. Derby, Connecticut, Monarch, 1961.
And So to Bed. Derby, Connecticut, Monarch, 1962.
Give Me This Woman. Derby, Connecticut, Monarch, 1962.

Short Stories

The Best Western Stories of John Jakes, edited by Martin H. Greenberg and Bill Pronzini. Athens, Ohio University Press, 1991; as *In the Big Country: The Best Western Stories of John Jakes,* Thorndike, Maine, Hall, 1993.

Plays

Dracula, Baby (lyrics only). Chicago, Dramatic Publishing Company, 1970.
Wind in the Willows. Elgin, Illinois, Performance, 1972.
A Spell of Evil. Chicago, Dramatic Publishing Company, 1972.
Violence. Elgin, Illinois, Performance, 1972.

Stranger with Roses, adaptation of his own story. Chicago, Dramatic Publishing Company, 1972.

For I Am a Jealous People, adaptation of the story by Lester del Rey. Elgin, Illinois, Performance, 1972.

Gaslight Girl. Chicago, Dramatic Publishing Company, 1973.

Pardon Me, Is This Planet Taken? Chicago, Dramatic Publishing Company, 1973.

Doctor, Doctor!, music by Gilbert M. Martin, adaptation of a play by Molière. New York, McAfee Music, 1973.

Shepherd Song. New York, McAfee Music, 1974.

Other

Tiros: Weather Eye in Space. New York, Messner, 1966.

Famous Firsts in Sports. New York, Putnam, 1967.

Great War Correspondents. New York, Putnam, 1968.

Great Women Reporters. New York, Putnam, 1969.

The Bastard Photostory. New York, Jove, 1980.

Susanna at the Alamo: A True Story (for children). New York, Harcourt Brace, 1986.

Editor, with Martin H. Greenberg, *New Trails: Twenty-Three Original Stories of the West from Western Writers of America.* New York, Doubleday, 1994.

*

Bibliography: In *The Best Western Stories of John Jakes,* edited by Martin H. Greenberg and Bill Pronzini, Athens, Ohio University Press, 1991.

Manuscript Collections: University of Wyoming, Laramie; DePauw University, Greencastle, Indiana.

Critical Study: *The Kent Family Chronicles Encyclopedia* edited by Robert Hawkins, New York, Bantam, 1979.

John Jakes comments:

My first sale was a science fiction story. I grew up on the genre, and wanted to write nothing else—though I did. Eventually, the novels I did turn out were greeted unenthusiastically, and two or three on which I worked particularly hard, and of which I was particularly proud—*Six-Gun Planet, Black in Time, On Wheels*—disappeared almost within days of publication. That convinced me to stop writing SF. I have friends among SF writers, but found the few conventions I attended in large part boring—perhaps a second reason I abandoned the field: not, I must add, without considerable regret.

*   *   *

Unfortunately, as far as his science fiction writing is concerned, John Jakes is best known for creating Brak the Barbarian. This is not to demean the Brak stories but rather to rue the fact that Jakes has written several other excellent novels which have gone virtually unnoticed.

The Brak stories follow a specific formula and so, even though very good, become wearisome by the repetition of their active force represented by the god Yob-Haggoth and is implemented by his agent, Septegundus, a man with no eyelids and skin covered with the living, writhing figures of the souls he has captured. Septegundus is aided by his beautiful but equally evil daughter,

Ariane. Throughout his various "on-the-road" adventures, Brak encounters analogues of Ariane, whom he eventually recognizes by their display of evil and lustful natures. Nordica Fire-Hair, in *The Sorceress,* is an excellent example. A dutiful daughter, she suddenly changes. She leaves her father, an alchemist who has learned the secret of turning things to gold, to die in a deep pit inhabited by a dragonlike creature called Manworm. As Brak becomes more and more involved with her, he recognizes that she is possessed by Ariane. When Nordica is finally killed, Brak sees the spirit of Ariane leaving the corpse.

Cast out of his own land in the far north for blaspheming the gods, Brak is constantly pursued by the forces of Septegundus in his eternal quest to reach the fabled golden city of Khurdisan in the south. Septegundus has vowed to kill him for interfering in his affairs. An incarnation of Conan, Brak is instinctive and physical, but even his strength and cunning are no match for the supernatural forces of evil, so he is aided in his continuing battle with Yob-Haggoth by various Nestorian priests who represent the mysterious Nameless God. Inevitably, Brak loses his sword, encounters some sort of fantastic monster which he must slay, Manworm, Scarlet-jaw, Doomdog, or The Thing That Crawls, and plies his way toward Khurdisan. But regardless of the formalization of the stories and the impression that some were written hastily, their fast-paced action recommends them. Within the formula, Jakes's inventiveness makes the stories both attractive and interesting.

The highly imaginative quality of Jakes's writing is perhaps better displayed in some of his other novels. Among them, *The Planet Wizard, The Hybrid,* and the Klekton books are the best. The Klekton is a ring of alternate Earths that can be reached by traveling through various mindgates. The novels tell the story of Gavin Black, a down-and-out journalist who becomes a pawn of Bronwyn, a police official of an alternative world called Earth Prime. Bronwyn is attempting to stop an invasion of our Earth from yet another alternate Earth called Earth Three or Shulkor. The population of all three Earths are descended from a great civilization that lived on heartland Earth before the Ice Age. When cold and ice threatened them, some went up the Klekton and some down, there to develop into radically different peoples. The Shulkorites became savage and warlike, while Bronwyn's people developed their intellectual abilities. Now, the Shulkorites want to use heartland Earth as a base to destroy Earth Prime and to extend their power to the more hospitable worlds down the chain. At first bribed, Black later permits himself to be used so that he can gain access to the gates in order to be reunited with Samantha, a girl from Earth Three with whom he has fallen in love.

The Hybrid tells the story of Andreas Law, the son of an Earth father and an Omqu mother, who has the unique ability to project destructive blasts of mental energy. Law becomes the tool of a fanatic Earth billionaire, Sir Robert Baron, who is trying to sabotage a proposed peace treaty between Earth and Omqu because he hates the humanoid but feathered aliens. Cast against a background of two intergalactic cultures trying to understand one another, *The Hybrid* is a story of prejudice handled sensitively and thoughtfully. It is a perceptive and imaginative exploration of what might happen when man achieves intergalactic travel and finds that he is not the only humanoid in the universe.

The Planet Wizard is a story of self-discovery, power, and love. Set in another galaxy eons after it has been colonized by Earthmen, *The Planet Wizard* tells of civilizations left to cope for themselves after planetary wars have destroyed the great business houses that controlled galactic society. Superstition abounds as knowledge and technology fade. Magus Blacklaw, a bogus magician but first-rate confidence man, traps himself and his daughter, Maya, into having to make a trip to the feared planet of Lightmark to exorcise its demons and to secure access to the resources of the great house that did business there. Blacklaw is a lovable rogue who rises above himself in his efforts to provide a better life for his daughter. In ridding Lightmark of its demons, he finds strength and courage he did not know he possessed.

Jakes is a highly competent writer whose imagination and versatility deserve respect. Always interesting, his stories provide fast-paced entertainment while imaginatively exploring the possibility of life in the distant future.

—Carl B. Yoke

JANIFER, Laurence M.

Pseudonym for Larry Mark Harris. **Other Pseudonyms:** Alfred Blake; Andrew Blake; Mark Phillips; Barbara Wilson. **Nationality:** American. **Born:** Brooklyn, New York, 17 March 1933. **Education:** Attended City College of New York, one year. **Family:** Married 1) Sylvia Siegel in 1955 (divorced 1958); 2) Sue Blugerman in 1960 (divorced 1962); 3) Rae Montor in 1966 (divorced 1968); 4) Beverly Goldberg in 1969 (separated 1984); two daughters and one son. **Career:** Pianist and arranger, New York, 1950-59; editor, Scott Meredith Literary Agency, New York, 1952-57, 1985-91; editor and art director, detective and science-fiction magazines, 1953-57; professional comedian, 1957-70. **Agent:** Scott Meredith Literary Agency, 845 Third Avenue, New York, New York 10022, U.S.A.

SCIENCE FICTION PUBLICATIONS

Novels (series: Angelo di Stefano; Gerald Knave; Survivor)

Pagan Passions (as Larry M. Harris), with Randall Garrett. New York, Galaxy, 1959.
Slave Planet: A Science Fiction Novel. New York, Pyramid, 1963.
The Wonder War. New York, Pyramid, 1964.
You Sane Men. New York, Lancer, 1965; as *Bloodworld,* 1968.
A Piece of Martin Cann. New York, Belmont, 1968.
Target: Terra (di Stefano), with S.J. Treibich. New York, Ace, 1968.
The High Hex (di Stefano), with S.J. Treibich. New York, Ace, 1969.
The Wagered World (di Stefano), with S.J. Treibich. New York, Ace, 1969.
Power. New York, Dell, 1974.
Survivor. New York, Ace, 1977.
Knave in Hand. New York, Ace, 1979.
Reel. Garden City, New York, Doubleday, 1983.

Novels as Mark Phillips (with Randall Garrett; series: Kenneth J. Malone in all books)

Brain Twister: A Science-Fiction Novel. New York, Pyramid, 1962.
The Impossibles. New York, Pyramid, 1963.
Supermind. New York, Pyramid, 1963.

Short Stories

Impossible? New York, Belmont, 1968.
Knave and the Game: A Collection of Short Stories. Garden City, New York, Doubleday, 1987.

OTHER PUBLICATIONS

Novels

The Pickled Poodle: A Novel (as Larry M. Harris). New York, Random House, 1960; London, Boardman, 1961.
The Protector (as Larry M. Harris). New York, Random House, 1961; London, Boardman, 1962.
The Bed and I (as Alfred Blake). N.p., Intimate, 1962.
Faithful for 8 Hours (as Alfred Blake). New York, Beacon, 1963.
The Pleasures We Know (as Barbara Wilson). New York, Lancer, 1964.
The Velvet Embrace (as Barbara Wilson). New York, Lancer, 1965.
The Woman without a Name. New York, New American Library, 1966.
The Final Fear. New York, Belmont, 1967.
You Can't Escape. New York, Lancer, 1967.

Novels as Andrew Blake

I Deal in Desire. N.p., Boudoir, 1962.
Sex Swinger. New York, Beacon, 1963.
Love Hostess. New York, Beacon, 1963.

Other

Editor, *Master's Choice: The Best Science-Fiction Stories of All Time, Chosen by the Masters of Science Fiction.* New York, Simon and Schuster, 1966; London, Jenkins, 1967; as *18 Greatest Science Fiction Stories,* New York, Grosset and Dunlap, 1971.
Ghost Writer for *Ken Murray's Giant Joke Book,* 1957; *The Henry Morgan Joke Book,* 1958; *The Foot in My Mouth* by Jeff Harris, 1958; *Tracer!* by Ed Goldfader, 1970.
Editor, *Yes, I'm Here with Someone* by Thomas Sutton, 1958.

*

Laurence M. Janifer comments:

I write funny stuff or non-funny stuff. It depends on how I feel. In either case, all I aim at doing is providing a world for the reader to live in for a while. Once in a long while I'll try to demonstrate an axiom of some sort—not often. I'd rather write funny stuff (or semi-funny stuff like the Knave adventures) because there is so damned little of it around. But I have not got much control over what my head sends me. I write SF because it fascinates me, and I continue to have the nagging feeling that SF ought to have something to do with science. I am violently against any attempt to get a scholarly view of my work or to assess my Purpose in Writing. This sort of thing should be stamped out. If you can believe and live in the worlds I write, I'm both happy and flattered. I look forward to creating more worlds, some SF and some not, for an indefinite time.

* * *

A first impression of Laurence M. Janifer's books might be that they emphasize stock subjects and sensation. *You Sane Men* is the story of a world on which Bound Men and Bound Women are held as objects of torture in what are called Remand Houses. The "Lords and Ladies" inflict pain on them with whips and hot brands and derive pleasure or sexual strength from this. In *Power,* Aaron Norin, the son of a respected empire official, leads a spaceship in rebellion against the empire. *Slave Planet* is about a world where cynical colonists from earth use alligator-like aliens as slaves to extract precious metals. Mental telepathy is used in *A Piece of Martin Cann* to cure a patient; *The Wonder War* is about a war to gain power over an entire galaxy.

These lurid but stock topics, however, acquire some complexity in Janifer's best novels. Janifer's central subjects are power and rebellion, and he often treats these with subtle irony. Jo, the narrator of *You Sane Men,* is a refugee from the world of blood, addressing the "sane men" who doubt that it is possible for human beings to run a social system based on torture. But his horrible world is sane and is human, for the point is that sane people are capable of extreme, thoughtless cruelty. Jo joins with other young people in a revolt against the ruling council, a revolt ironically not against the institution of cruelty but against the exclusion of young people from decision-making. When a lady is killed another irony develops: in contrast to our crime-ridden earth, the blood world has never had a murder, and its natives are comically inept detectives. Torture is legalized, but other crimes are almost unknown. Satire of our sexual taboos develops when Jo is shocked to discover that some men enjoy torturing men, and women.

The irony of *Power* is more understated. Isidor Norin's family all have power. His daughter Rachel is married to a famous actor, and his son Alphard is the assistant to a powerful religious leader. When the spaceship *Valor,* led by his son Aaron, rebels from the empire, Aaron is killed and his father becomes critically ill. The rebellion is apparently crushed, and the Emperor retains all formal power, but the idea of freedom has been kindled in several minds. In *Slave Planet* Janifer gently portrays the naive point of view of several of the enslaved aliens. Janifer avoids pathos by giving us their puzzled acceptance of their condition. We are also made to see through the rather exaggerated moralism which brings a military liberation force from the shocked confederation to Fruyling's world. Thus, the overthrow of slavery and its replacement by automatic machinery are complex events. We reject the view of Dr. Haelingen that slavery is inevitable on this world, but we do consider it.

Janifer's short stories are competent but routine, although his talent at presenting unusual points of view comes through in such stories as "Thine Alabaster Cities Gleam" (in *Future City,* edited by Roger Elwood, New York, Simon and Schuster, 1973), about a couple caught in a skyscraper at night when the electricity, and the air supply, goes out. They will die—even the woman's diamond can make only faint scratches in the window. "Civis Obit" (in *Dystopian Visions,* edited by Roger Elwood, Englewood Cliffs, New Jersey, Prentice Hall, 1975) gives us the point of view of a telepath who preserves sanity only by developing the skill of shutting out human suffering. "Amfortas" (in *Omega,* edited by Roger Elwood, New York, Walker, 1974) develops the psychological effects of massive organ transplants.

The multiple points of view of *Reel* signal Janifer's entry into literary modernism. Although the subject matter is familiar to Janifer readers—a power struggle on "The Reel," a resort planet of the far future—Janifer's technique is deft and impressionistic. Janifer is a writer of promise and more than occasional achievement.

—Curtis C. Smith

JASON, Jerry. *See* **SMITH, George H.**

———

JAY, Mel. *See* **FANTHORPE, R. Lionel.**

———

JEFFERIES, (John) Richard

Nationality: English. **Born:** Coate Farm, Liddington, Wiltshire, 6 November 1848. **Education:** Studied at schools in Sydenham, Kent, and Swindon, to 1863. **Family:** Married Jessie Baden in 1874; three children. **Career:** Travelled to France, 1865; returned to Swindon and became a reporter for the *North Wiltshire Herald,* 1866-70; wrote for a Gloucestershire paper; travelled in Belgium, 1870; returned to England and became a freelance writer; settled in London and wrote for the *Pall Mall Gazette,* c. 1872. **Died:** 14 August 1887.

SCIENCE FICTION PUBLICATIONS

Novels (series: Sir Bevis)

Wood Magic: A Fable (Bevis). London, Cassell, 1881, 2 volumes; as *Sir Bevis: A Tale of the Fields* (Bevis), edited by Eliza J. Kelley. Boston, Ginn, 1899.
Bevis: The Story of a Boy. London, Sampson Low, 1882, 3 volumes.
After London; or, Wild England. London, Cassell, 1885.
Blake of the "Rattlesnake;" or, The Man Who Saved England: A Story of Torpedo Warfare. London, Tower, 1895.
The Incubated Girl. London, Tower, 1896.
To Venus in Five Seconds: Being an Account of the Strange Disappearance of Thomas Plummer, Pill-Maker. London, Innes, 1897.
The Violet Flame: A Story of Armageddon and After. London, Ward Lock, 1899.

Other

Jack Brass, Emperor of England. London, Pettitt, 1973.

OTHER PUBLICATIONS

Other

The Story of My Heart, My Autobiography. London, Longmans, Greeen, 1883; Boston, Roberts, 1883.

*   *   *

In his short life Richard Jefferies published many novels, pamphlets, and collections of essays, and left an even greater number in manuscript or uncollected that have since been published. *After London* is easily the best of those that may rightly be characterized as science fiction. However, a number of earlier works, most of them fragmentary and not published in his lifetime, demonstrate that Jefferies had hit on its themes some years before. Closely related is "The Rise of Maximin, Emperor of the Occident," a serial that appeared in *The New Monthly Magazine* in 1876-77 and may well be a kind of preliminary version. Like Felix the hero of *After London,* Maximin is an intelligent man in a semi-barbaric country, in his case in the distant past. Where Felix temporarily exiles himself, Maximin, outlawed by his home town, gathers a loyal following through his writings, leads them to military success, and is eventually acclaimed as emperor. Several shorter pieces have some connection. "The Great Snow" is a fragment about another catastrophe that brings death to millions. This story of the breakdown of society and the onset of barbarism ends in mid-sentence. "Three Centuries at Home" and "The Backwoods" both contain material later used in *After London.* An early pamphlet, *Jack Brass, Emperor of England,* is an ironic attempt at political satire, proposing newspapers "present communistic ideas," keep factories and "beer-shops" open on Sundays, and other fooleries aimed at traditional Victorian customs.

After London itself is often regarded as the third part of a trio of which the other two parts are *Wood Magic: A Fable* and *Bevis: The Story of a Boy,* and there is good reason to link them together. The former is a fantasy in which a seven-year-old boy talks with the wind, the brook, and numerous birds, insects, animals, and plants. It is almost an allegory of human political activities, mirrored in the actions of birds and animals. The latter is the story of the same boy a few years older and his friend. Together they roam the woods, the lake, and the countryside. They build a gun and use it, learn to swim, go rafting on the lake, and spend time on an island. More concerned with material matters than the younger boy who never got much beyond a kind of spiritual interest in everything, it has been a popular children's book since its publication.

After London has a more mature hero, who is many ways what the younger boys might have grown to be and, like the others, a kind of alter ego of the author who is never far from being a part of his writings, both fiction and non-fiction. Far in the future a catastrophe, vaguely ascribed to "the 'Unknown Orb,' the dark body travelling in space," has led to formation of a large lake covering most of southern England, including London. Part I, "The Relapse into Barbarism" is some of the best of Jefferies' writing. His description of the changes in human, animal, and plants provides a shudderingly realistic and believable background for Part Two, "Wild England." What is left of "civilized" human society lives mostly on the shores of the lake: barbaric, feudalistic, uninterested in intellectual matters, always on the defensive against the men of the woods and the invading Welsh, Irish, and Scots. Felix Aquila, eldest son of a baron, is intelligent, something of a dreamer, a reader, little concerned with the warlike lives of his contemporaries, and certainly not the husband his beloved Aurora's father desires for her. Felix's plans for improving defenses and weapons are scoffed at. His fierce independence drives him to construct a sailing canoe with which to seek his fortune in the service of some king or baron who might recognize his talents. The journey takes him along the coast of the lake to a war which is so badly run that he is happy to escape back to his canoe; he blunders inadvertently into the London swamp (where equally inadvertently he finds a large diamond), on an island, and, finally, his canoe run aground and destroyed, meets a group of shepherds on the Downs. His escape from the noxious fumes and other dangers of the swamp, his superior archery, and his ability to plan excellent defenses against the ever-marauding gypsies gains him an offer of kingship; he postpones acceptance because he wishes to return to Aurora. The book ends somewhat unsatisfactorily (perhaps shortened to please the publisher) with Felix heading west through the forest in hopes of returning home to win Baron Thyma's blessing now that the diamond makes him rich. He then plans to bring Aurora to the land of the shepherds and build a fortress at a narrow part of the lake that will defend the land against the raiders from Wales and Ireland.

The Story of My Heart, My Autobiography, written at about the same time as *After London,* has little biographical detail, but its philosophical and mystical musings resemble the beliefs that sway Felix Aquila. Several passages adumbrate the kind of utopia Jefferies might have produced had he lived to write it. Jefferies was at home in nature and wrote much about it, but he had no illusions about the universe's indifference to humanity. "There is," he wrote, "nothing human in the whole round of nature." In human society as in nature he was all too aware that the weak existed only as the strong permitted. Much of his writing is permeated with an anti-authority bias of which the rebellion of birds and animals against the dictatorial Kapchak the magpie in the fable *Wood Magic* and Felix Aquila's distrust of king and courtiers are examples.

Late in life Jefferies appeared to turn to more imaginative ideas than those of his earlier novels and essays. As his criticism of society grew stronger, fantasy and science fiction gave him the opportunity to express his deepest beliefs about what might happen to society if things went wrong, but he had only touched the surface when death stilled his pen.

—Arthur O. Lewis

JENKINS, Will F. *See* **LEINSTER, Murray**

JESCHKE, Wolfgang

Nationality: German. **Born:** 1936.

SCIENCE FICTION PUBLICATIONS

Novels

Derletzte tag der schopfung. Munich, Nymphenburger, 1981; translated by Gertrud Mander as *The Last Day of Creation,* London, Century, 1982; New York, St. Martin's Press, 1984.
Midas. Munich, Wilhelm Heyne Verlag, 1987; Sevenoaks, Kent, New English Library, 1990.

Other

"A Little More Than Twelve Minutes," in *New Writings in SF,* edited by Kenneth Bulmer, 1975.
"The King and the Dollmaker," in *The Best from the Rest of the World: European Science Fiction,* edited by Donald A. Wollheim, 1976.

"The Land of Osiris," in *Isaac Asimov's Science Fiction Magazine,* March 1985.

*   *   *

Although Wolfgang Jeschke's output is small, he ranks among Germany's most important SF writers, but is much better known as editor (since 1972) of Wilhelm Heyne's successful SF line, the largest in Europe. As a writer, he is almost the exact opposite of somebody like H.W. Franke (generally considered to be the most important SF writer in Germany), who is more interested in content than in the manner of expressing it, and who has turned a style severe and austere into a virtue. Jeschke is a more natural writer, interested in a tale well told, rich in background, narrative turns, and incident. Mood and stylistic qualities are often more important than plot, subject matter, or theme. Consequently, many of his stories are variations on well-known SF themes or build upon previous SF.

His first professionally published story, "Der Türmer," is typical of this: a sentient and telepathic plant on a far planet comes into contact with a lonely human being, striving like the humans to conquer space and to spread its seeds on other planets. One of Jeschke's favorite topics is time-travel and its paradoxes, as in one of his earliest stories, "Supernova," later revised as "The Gap in the Mountain," in which an earthman is caught in a time-loop. Similarly, in "A Little More Than Twelve Minutes," time travelers from the future wait for the building of the first time machine so that they can return home. Sometimes Jeschke's stories contain mythical allusions or provide SF versions of classical tales, as in "Sirens on the Shore." His imminent death is made bearable for a dying spaceman by aliens that project his inmost longings into his mind. This character of wish-fulfillment is also evident in "The Gate of Night," in which the after-effects of an atomic war are undone by mutants who create another reality track, thus giving mankind another chance. Other early stories feature a horrible new disease, the transplantation of human memories into robot bodies or the long voyage to the stars by human beings who have forgotten their origins and purpose. These are well-written but not terribly original, old-fashioned and slight stories. Of quite a different order is the long story "The King and the Dollmaker," another time-travel tale, but this time a virtuoso performance, so complex and well-constructed a story that it can stand beside the best time-travel stories, a tour de force that turns artifice into a high art, although this was recognized (upon its appearance in Donald A. Wollheim's *The Best from the Rest of the World*) only by perceptive critics like Michael Bishop.

Jeschke's newer stories and radio dramas, collected in the volume *Schlechte Nachrichten aus dem Vatikan* (1993), are both more substantial in content and more experimental in form, and are told with narrative zest and often with baroque exuberance. Jeschke's main topic has shifted from time travel to the ecological crisis and the remaking of man and other biological systems. "Dokumente über den Zustand des Landes vor der Verheerung" is a skillful arrangement of real documents, newspaper items, excerpts from essays, books, speeches of politicians, and statements by scientists and environmentalists. "Osiris Land," translated as "The Land of Osiris," is the story of a picaresque journey through a post-atomic Africa, and a contact with an alien visitor, and "Nekyomanteion" takes place in the world of MIDAS, where dead humans are, unsuccessfully, resurrected as electronic copies. The most interesting of Jeschke's later stories is the privately published long novella

"Meamones Auge" (1994), with its strange life-cycles on the coorbital moons of a gas giant in another solar system, where life is threatened with extinction every few years by the swingby of the moons. Human beings have become wanderers in the cosmos, and the protein of GODs (genetically originated devices) is harvested periodically in a feast of bloody slaughter, while amidst cosmic upheaval the human rulers try to recapture the splendor and the luxuries of a long dead past on Earth.

Jeschke's first novel, *The Last Day of Creation,* again turns back to time-travel. The book starts with the discovery of a series of mysterious artifacts that are both a spoof on Erich von Däniken's ancient astronauts theories and the saintly traditions of the Roman Catholic Church. The discoveries are taken by the American authorities to mean that their project is viable: to travel back into the past in order to change the present, to steal the Arab oil from under the noses of the sheikhs. But from the beginning, everything goes wrong, the time troops arrive in little groups, spaced years apart, and are already awaited by superior and better-equipped enemy forces. They are not even all from the same future but from alternate futures, and they are soon stranded in the past, for no return is possible, and all that is left to them is fighting for their bare survival in the jungles of the Mediterranean (then not yet a sea), with only dim prospects of a golden Atlantis in the Bermudas ahead. Jeschke's novel is both an engaging fast-paced adventure story and a narrative with deeper meanings, satiric both of the current situation of the world and other SF stories depicting attempts to improve history by time-travel.

Jeschke's second SF novel, *Midas,* might be described as a German contribution to cyberpunk SF; MIDAS (Molecular Integrating and Digital Assembling System) allows the reconstruction and electronic storing of human beings who then appear as irritating factors in the world-wide information nets. *Midas* is one of those novels in which it is more interesting to journey than to arrive, in this instance through a run-down world shaken by civil wars and local strife, from Sri Lanka to the High Tec countries. It takes the form of a thriller in which plots and counterplots proliferate, but in which there is no final resolution and cannot be one. Giant airships, propelled by genetically engineered animal muscles, are among the most vivid images of a novel that is more remarkable for its gloomy futuristic setting than for its plot or characters, and the dense atmospheric effect of the novel continues to haunt the reader long after the ramifications of the plot have been forgotten.

—Franz Rottensteiner

JETER, K.W.

Pseudonym: Dr. Adder. **Nationality:** American. **Born:** Los Angeles, California, 1950. **Agent:** Russ Galen, Scott Meredith Literary Agency, 845 Third Avenue, New York, New York 10022, U.S.A.

<small>SCIENCE FICTION PUBLICATIONS</small>

Novels (series: Alien Nation; Cylinder Trilogy; Dr. Adder; Star Trek; Time Machine)

Seeklight. Don Mills, Ontario, Laser, 1975.

The Dreamfields. Toronto, Laser, 1976.

Morlock Night (sequel to *The Time Machine* by H.G. Wells). New York, DAW, 1979; London, Grafton, 1989.

Soul Eater. New York, Tor, 1983; London, Kinnell, 1989.

Dr. Adder. New York, Bluejay, 1984; London, Grafton, 1987.

Night Vision. New York, Tor, 1985.

The Glass Hammer (Dr. Adder). New York, Bluejay, 1985; London, Grafton, 1987.

Infernal Devices: A Mad Victorian Fantasy. New York, St. Martin's Press, 1987; London, Grafton, 1988.

Death's Arms (Dr. Adder). New York, St. Martin's Press, 1987; Bath, England, Morrigan, 1989; as as *Death Arms,* London, Grafton, and New York, St. Martin's Press, 1989.

Dark Seeker. New York, Tor, 1987; London, Pan Books, 1991.

Mantis. New York, Tor, 1987; London, Pan Books, 1992.

Farewell Horizontal (Cylinder Trilogy). New York, St. Martin's Press, 1989; London, Grafton, 1990.

In the Land of the Dead. New York, New American Library, and Bath, England, Morrigan, 1989.

Alligator Alley (as Dr. Adder), with Ferret writing as Mink Mole. Scotforth, Lancashire, Morrigan Publications, 1989.

The Night Man. New York, New American Library, 1990; London, Pan Books, 1991.

Madlands. New York, St. Martin's Press, 1991.

Wolf Flow. New York, St. Martin's Press, 1992.

Bloodletter (Star Trek). New York and London, Pocket Books, 1993.

Dark Horizon (Alien Nation). New York, Pocket Books, 1993.

Warped (Star Trek). New York, Pocket Books, 1995.

Graphic Novel

Mister E, with John K. Snyder III and Jay Geldhof. New York, DC Comics, 4 vols., 1991.

*   *   *

K.W. Jeter's work has the flavor of Philip K. Dick's studies in reality at their best. In Jeter's most imaginative SF novel, *Farewell Horizontal,* he creates the Cylinder: a vast building whose bulk reaches high above the clouds. Jeter's hero, Ny Axxter, leaves the comfortable, data-dominated society within the Cylinder to encounter the bizarre life of living on the vertical walls outside the Cylinder. The situation is surreal, and yet Jeter gives this weird setting credibility and drama as Ny Axxter explores this fascinating world far from our horizontal reality.

From Jeter's first published novel, *Seeklight,* it was clear Jeter possessed a talent for conjuring up innovative, exciting settings. *Seeklight* features a semi-feudal society and a young man named Daenek whose identity as son of a former leader gets him marked for death. Yet, in the middle of the action, a sociologist will appear through the use of superscience technology and ask questions of the novel's participants like any good graduate research assistant would. This is the odd juxtapositioning of Jeter's reality: one world holds several different, even contradicting, realities. Yet the strange mingling of worlds works; Barry Malzberg, in the introduction to *Seeklight,* calls Jeter's first novel "one of the three or four best SF novels I have ever read."

Jeter's next novel, *The Dreamfields,* reads very much like a Philip K. Dick novel. Ralph Metric is a member of Operation Dreamwatch, supposedly an experimental project to control and ob-

serve severely disturbed teenagers through their dreams. Yet in the dreamstate, Ralph discovers a different reality operating. There is an alien invasion of Earth forming in the Dreamfields and those disturbed teenagers' dreams hold power in the aliens' alternate reality. Shifting identities and surreal plot elements make *The Dreamfields* one of Jeter's most ambitious novels.

Morlock Night is Jeter's attempt to finish H.G. Wells's *The Time Machine.* At the conclusion of Wells's book, the Time Traveller went back to the future of the Morlocks and the Eloi and never returned. Jeter supposes: what if the Time Traveller was murdered by the Morlocks and they used the Time Machine to invade England of 1892? An interesting notion gone wrong is the result. A young man named Edwin Hocker is recruited by a cryptic man calling himself Dr. Ambrose. Together they try to change the reality of the deadly Morlock invasion by ringing together the ancient sword of power: Excalibur. The novel goes awry when Merlin and King Arthur join forces to defeat the Morlock menace. Too much of the book is spent mucking around in the London sewers—the Morlock's secret staging area—and too much of the plot is predictable.

Much superior to *Morlock Night* is Jeter's later, more sophisticated Victorianesque novel, *Infernal Devices.* The Brown Leather Man, a mysterious being, brings George Dower a device to repair, which George's genius father had built decades ago. Mad plot complications multiply as Jeter creates a wild, entertaining fantasy in the mists of Old London.

Dr. Adder—Jeter's most controversial novel—includes an afterward by Philip K. Dick comparing the book to the works of James Joyce and Henry Miller, and the more daring story in Harlan Ellison's *Dangerous Visions.* Jeter couldn't find a publisher for the work, written in 1972, for more than a decade because of its graphic violence and sex. Most of the book's action centers around Los Angeles and its sewers of the near future. The city is populated by surgically altered prostitutes (the results of Dr. Adder's talents), snipers, and Mother Endure, who takes care of all the losers in Rattown. Opposed to Adder's degenerate lifestyle is videopreacher John Mox and his Moral Forces. Into this maelstrom comes E. Allen Limmit on a mission to deliver a flashglove—a banned CIA weapon of incredible powers—to Dr. Adder. Like a catalyst, Limmit sets off a war among the powers of Los Angeles: a war that Limmit's true identity holds the key to.

The controversy surrounding *Dr. Adder* generated more heat than light. The book is the result of an immature writer just learning his craft: too much of *Dr. Adder* seems calculated to shock or disgust the reader rather than to move the plot of the book or develop the characters. There is much to praise in *Dr. Adder:* Jeter's picture of a nightmarish future controlled by cabals is innovative, evoking echoes of Dick's dark futures in *Flow My Tears, The Policeman Said* and *A Scanner, Darkly.* Certainly it prefigured the entire cyberpunk movement.

Soul Eater is Jeter's best book to date. David Braemer once had a happy marriage. Then his wife, Renee, after a bizarre episode in which she tried to kill her young daughter Dee, suffered a massive stroke and lies comatose, tended by her brother Jess and adopted sister Carol in their family house. Braemer is disturbed by Dee's behavior: the little girl will fall into a troubled sleep, then sleepwalk into the kitchen, find the largest knife she can, and head for Braemer's bedroom. Braemer has awoken to Dee standing over him with a knife ready to plunge into his chest. Braemer thinks the trauma of Renee's attempt on her daughter's life and subsequent stroke are affecting the little girl's sanity. But two people meet with Braemer to warn him: Kathy, Renee's other sister, and an enigmatic man named Pedersen. The warnings are the same: Renee has the power to insert her identity into others, and she is using Dee as an instrument to kill David. Braemer discounts the warnings as absurdities, but later finds more horror and more truth in those warnings than he could have imagined. *Soul Eater* is an extraordinary horror novel with Jeter's best-realized characters and writing.

Unfortunately, not all Jeter's horror novels equal the power of *Soul Eater. In the Land of the Dead* contains echoes of James M. Cain's classic *The Postman Always Rings Twice.* A California orange grower named Vandervelde is the victim of a murder plot as his mistress, Fay, and his foreman, Cooper, decide to murder him. The novel veers into the land of horror as Fay gets the murdered man's corpse to open his safe. *The Night Man* is a supernatural vengeance novel whose predictable plot never hangs together. *Dark Seeker* is an overblown novel of demonic possession whose brutality leads to the readers' exhaustion.

Jeter has written two of the better *Star Trek: Deep Space Nine* series volumes. In *Bloodletter,* Commander Sisko, Major Kira, and the crew of Deep Space Nine move to respond to the Cardassian threat of establishing a base on the other side of the wormhole. Using that action as a backdrop, Jeter explores Major Kira's violent past.

Warped is the first *Star Trek: Deep Space Nine* hardcover entry. Again, Jeter juggles two plots: the problem Commander Sisko faces with a religious movement on Bajor, whose success would force the Federation to leave Deep Space nine, and a series of murders Shapeshifter Odo investigates. Cleverly, Jeter has these two plots intersect in a surprising conclusion.

Jeter's latest project is to write *Blade Runner: Edge of Human,* a sequel to Philip K. Dick's famous *Do Androids Dream of Electric Sheep,* which inspired the filme *Blade Runner.*

K.W. Jeter's most innovative works are science fiction novels whose sense of reality are straight out of the Dickian universe. His horror novels feature both the best and the worst of his writing.

—George Kelley

JEURY, Michel

Pseudonym: Albert Higon. **Nationality:** French. **Born:** 1934.

<small>SCIENCE FICTION PUBLICATIONS</small>

Novels

Aux Etoiles du Destin (as Albert Higon). N.p., n.d.
La Machine du Pouvoir (as Albert Higon). N.p., n.d.
Le temps incertain. Paris, R. Laffont, 1973; translated by Maxim Jakubowski as *Chronolysis,* New York, Macmillan, 1980.
Le Fête du changement. N.p., n.d.
Soleil chaud, poisson des profondeurs. N.d., n.d.
Les Animaux de Justice. N.d., n.d.

*   *   *

When *Le Temps incertain* (*Chronolysis*) appeared in 1973, a new author arrived in French science fiction and established himself immediately at his peak. Michel Jeury was neither a young writer nor a newcomer. Born in 1934, he had already published in 1960 (under the pseudonym of Albert Higon) *Aux Etoiles du Destin* and *La Machine du Pouvoir,* which attempted a synthesis between the French tradition of the *roman d'anticipation* and recent American science fiction. Then for more than 10 years Jeury was silent. Of humble, peasant background, which had already placed him apart in the social universe of science fiction, he spent many difficult years and had nearly ceased writing entirely. This origin, these difficulties, these uncertainties on the order of the world, are essential to the understanding of his work.

In *Chronolysis* two futures, the one dominated by a multinational fascist HKH, the other more human and asserted by intelligent computers, the Phords, dispute our present, which will decide their existence. Both futures have use of the weapon chronolyse, which permits sending agents into the past, or rather projecting their personality there. But the chronolitic drug is not as certain as a machine, because it acts upon the mind. Robert Holzach thus enters into a universe of uncertainty where the past, the present, the future, and the possible encounter each other and are superimposed, alternatively. He's a man hunted to the depths of his own psyche. So well is this done that the novel has the characteristics of a realistic nightmare, without becoming hallucinatory.

Jeury is so remarkable for creating the social fabric of a period that he specializes both in economic problems and the hesitations of the real, as well as an anguish that is sometimes precise, other times diffuse. Therefore, certain commentators relate Jeury to Philip K. Dick. But one can also discern in the *principe d'incertitude* the influence of Robbe-Grillet. If this is the case, Jeury brings to the *nouveau roman* a simplicity of writing and an almost prophetic content which it ordinarily lacks. In reality, Jeury invents—and does not cease to explore in his major works—a personal world that is somber, even pessimistic, controlled by vast social machines, by informational networks, by the omnipresence of tyranny, by the image, the falsification of the real for the benefit of the dominant groups.

In this universe where nothing is ever exactly as it seems, the central character, a little man, flees, tries to survive and even bring about a better world, a utopia like that in *La Fête du changement,* perhaps Jeury's most brilliant novel but a utopia without rules.

The result defies all analytic description. If *Chronolysis* and its successors have known an instant success, it is in the dissolution of the framework of the real and in joining the philosophic themes then developed by Lyotard, Deleuze, and Guttari, whom Jeury probably hadn't yet read.

The little man hunted is evidently Jeury himself, perceiving the crushing of his social group by the great forces fighting among themselves for absolute supremacy.

One finds again these preoccupations, this obsession, in his later works, notably in *Soleil chaud, poisson des profondeurs* and in *Les Animaux de Justice.* But with *Les Yeux Geants* the writer was to go further yet, describing the encounter between a society in crisis in the beginning of the 21st century and an absolute strangeness, an extra-terrestrial who manifests himself always in an elusive manner. The novel is a long progression towards the discovery of the other as indicated by the last sentence: "the ending of this story can never be written with human words." In this terrain, Jeury has surpassed, in my judgment, Stapledon, Clarke, and Lem. He borders on the frontier of mysticism without ever letting himself be taken into its pitfalls, and shows that it is a question at the same time of a mediated perception and a social phenomenon. He has thus profoundly renewed science fiction; too much perhaps for its habitual public.

The other side of the coin is that the narrowness of the French quest for science fiction works of high quality limits Jeury to producing more commercial work, where he is less comfortable. His skill even in describing problematic unknown universes in dissolution prevents him from producing simple and manichaean works which please the larger public. And that is precisely because his characters, without being anti-heroes, cannot and will not dominate the conflicts that confront them. If science fiction is a literature obsessed by theory, Jeury introduces to it, exaggerated by the taste of the majority, doubt.

The drama, and I weigh my words, is that Jeury, as with so many other writers of breadth, might find himself prevented from writing what he is and obliged to turn away from and devalue his talent. This would be an immense loss for French literature and for world-wide science fiction. The reader will profit from consulting my preface to the *Livre d'or de Michel Jeury* (Presses-Pocket, 1982) where I develop the ideas briefly sketched here on the sense, the importance, and the genesis of Jeury's work.

—Gérard Klein (translated by Ann K. Smith)

JOHNS, Kenneth. *See* **BULMER, Kenneth.**

JOHNS, Marston. *See* **FANTHORPE, R. Lionel.**

JONES, D(ennis) F(eltham)

Nationality: British. **Born:** 1917. **Military Service:** Served in the Royal Navy during World War II. **Career:** Worked as a bricklayer and market gardener. **Died:** April 1981.

SCIENCE FICTION PUBLICATIONS

Novels (series: Colossus)

Colossus (Colossus). London, Hart Davis, 1966; New York, Putnam, 1967.
Implosion. London, Hart Davis, 1967; New York, Putnam, 1968.
Denver Is Missing. New York, Walker, 1971; as *Don't Pick the Flowers,* London, Panther, 1971.
The Fall of Colossus (Colossus). New York, Putnam, 1974.

The Floating Zombie. New York, Berkley, 1975.
Colossus and the Crab (Colossus). New York, Berkley, 1977.
Earth Has Been Found: A Novel. New York, Dell, 1979; as *Xeno: Science Fiction,* London, Sidgwick and Jackson, 1979.
Bound in Time. London, Granada, 1981.

*   *   *

Asimov in "The Machine and the Robot" writes, "Surely the *great* fear is not that machinery will harm us—but that it will supplant us." In *Colossus* D.F. Jones has certainly created one of the finest embodiments of this fear. Because men are attached to their freedom, or at least to a sense of freedom, *Colossus* becomes the ultimate horror story in which man is enslaved by his own creation. Jones develops the horror through the logic and detail of presentation. Each of the steps by which Colossus comes to power follows from the previous; all the hardware is credible. Forbin serves as a foil to the machine (eliciting such information as the reader needs to understand Colossus) and as an emotional soundingboard (articulating and amplifying the fear). The futility of Forbin's defiance of Colossus, especially his refusal to love it, contributes to the power of the ending.

The two sequels to *Colossus* do not quite measure up to the same standard. Neither seems to have the same level of conviction. In *The Fall of Colossus,* the emphasis has shifted away from the horror of machine domination. Colossus's attempts to comprehend human emotion, Forbin's shift toward love for the machine, the Sect's worship, the Fellowship's opposition—none of these stimulate the same level of excitement. The sexual experiment on Cleo seems contrived and not very relevant. The outside intervention which brings the fall has a *deus ex machina* quality. In *Colossus and the Crab,* the tight, straightforward plotting that is a strength in most of Jones's novels seems to have given way to a rather choppy, almost episodic style. The whole concept of the novel, which pits Forbin against two aliens from Mars, leads to the revival of Colossus and ends in a sort of Mexican standoff, gives the feeling that the author merely wanted to wrap up the series. The novel's climactic point, although it effectively builds the emotional tension of Forbin's naval attack, gets its power purely from situation—Forbin never seems to rise to the heroic level.

Perhaps that is because plot and setting, rather than characterization, are Jones's strengths. The plots of his other novels command the reader's attention, leading step-by-step to a satisfying conclusion. Whether he deals with population (*Implosion*), alien invasion (*Earth Has Been Found*), or geologic catastrophe (*Don't Pick the Flowers*), the plot flows ineluctably from the initial assumption. Settings also contribute much to the effectiveness of all his works. Each setting presents a recognizable Earth in a not-too-distant future. The familiarity of setting functions effectively as a contrasting ground for the strange situation. More than a trace of the mad-scientist motif enters into his work. All his central characters are scientists, and either initiate an action beyond control or attempt to cope with a situation beyond comprehension.

Don't Pick the Flowers is the best of his novels. Its highly improbable situation is invested with a sense of possibility. The chief characters seem very human (when compared with Forbin, for instance) in their fears and desires, and in their strength to cope with an overwhelming situation, to endure against very long odds.

—Robert Reilly

JONES, Diana Wynne

Pseudonym: Diana Gwyneth Burrow. **Nationality:** British. **Born:** London, 16 August 1934. **Education:** The Friends' School, Saffron, Walden, 1946-51; Saint Anne's College, Oxford, B.A. 1956. **Family:** Married John Anthony Burrow in 1956; three sons. **Career:** Part-time writer, 1943-73. Since 1973, full-time writer. Member of Guardian Award Committee, 1978-81; member of Whitbread Award Committee, 1988. **Awards:** Guardian award (for children's books), 1977; Honour Book, Boston Globe/Hornbook, 1984, 1986. **Agent:** Laura Cecil, 17 Alwyne Villas, London N, 2HG, England. **Address:** 9 The Polygon, Bristol BS8 4PW, England.

SCIENCE FICTION PUBLICATIONS

Novels (for children; series: Chrestomanci; Dalemark; Howl)

Wilkin's Tooth. London, Macmillan, 1973; as *Witch's Business,* New York, Dutton, 1974.
The Ogre Downstairs. London, Macmillan, 1974; New York, Dutton, 1975.
Eight Days of Luke. London, Macmillan, 1975; New York, Greenwillow, 1988.
Dogsbody. London, Macmillan, 1975; New York, Greenwillow, 1977.
Cart & Cwidder (Dalemark). London, Macmillan, 1975; New York, Atheneum, 1977.
Power of Three. London, Macmillan, 1976; New York, Greenwillow, 1977.
Drowned Ammet (Dalemark). London, Macmillan, 1977; New York, Atheneum, 1978.
Charmed Life (Chrestomanci). London, Macmillan, and New York, Greenwillow, 1977.
The Spellcoats (Dalemark). London, Macmillan, and New York, Atheneum, 1979.
The Magicians of Caprona (Chrestomanci). London, Macmillan, and New York, Greenwillow, 1980.
The Homeward Bounders. London, Macmillan, and New York, Greenwillow, 1981.
The Time of the Ghost. London, Macmillan, 1981.
Witch Week (Chrestomanci). London, Macmillan, and New York, Greenwillow, 1982.
Archer's Goon. London, Methuen, and New York, Greenwillow, 1984.
Fire and Hemlock. London, Methuen, and New York, Greenwillow, 1985.
Howl's Moving Castle (Howl). London, Methuen, and New York, Greenwillow, 1986.
A Tale of Time City. London, Methuen, and New York, Greenwillow, 1987.
The Lives of Christopher Chant: The Childhood of Chrestomanci (Chrestomanci). London, Methuen, and New York, Greenwillow, 1988.
Castle in the Air (Howl). London, Methuen, 1990; New York, Greenwillow, 1991.
Black Maria. London, Methuen, 1991; as *Aunt Maria,* New York, Greenwillow, 1991.
The Crown of Dalemark (Dalemark). London, Mandarin, 1993; New York, Greenwillow, 1995.

Hexwood. London, Methuen, 1993; New York, Greenwillow, 1994.

Novel (for adults)

A Sudden Wild Magic. New York, Morrow, 1992.

Short Stories (for children)

Warlock at the Wheel and Other Stories. London, Macmillan, and New York, Greenwillow, 1984.

OTHER PUBLICATIONS

Novel (for adults)

Changeover. London, Macmillan, 1970.

Novels (for children)

Who Got Rid of Angus Flint? London, Evans, 1978.
Chairperson. London, Hamish Hamilton, 1989.
Wild Robert. London, Methuen, 1989.
Yes, Dear. London, Collins, and New York, Greenwillow, 1992.

Short Stories (for children)

The Four Grannies. London, Hamish Hamilton, 1980.
Stopping for a Spell: Three Fantasies (omnibus). New York, Greenwillow, 1993.

Other

My Brother and I Like Cookies, with Anna A. Carlson (for children). N.p., 1980.
The Skivver's Guide (for children). Sevenoaks, Kent, Knight, 1984.

Anthologies Edited as Diana Wynne

Colour in Your Home: The Best of Australian Home Journal's Decorating Ideas. Sydney, Murray, 1977.
Easy Family Meals: The Best of Australian Home Journal's Recipes. Sydney, Murray, 1977.
Easy Gardening: An Australian Home Journal Publication. Sydney, Murray, 1977.
Exciting Ways with Floors and Walls: The Best of Australian Home Journal's Decorating Ideas. Sydney, Murray, 1977.
Extending Your Home: An Australian Home Journal Publication. Sydney, Murray, 1977.
Bathrooms: The Best of Australian Home Journal's Decorating Ideas. Melbourne, Murray, 1978.
Carefree Summer Living: The Best of Australian Home Journal's Decorating Ideas. Sydney, Murray, 1978.
Decorating for Rented Flats: The Best of Home Journal's Decorating Ideas. Sydney, Murray, 1978.
How to Choose a Furnishing Style. Sydney, Murray, 1978.
Leisure Homes. Sydney, Murray, 1978.
Two Hundred Outdoor Ideas. Sydney, Murray, 1978.
Australian Home Journal Cookbook. Ultimo, New South Wales, Murray, 1979.
Australian and Country Gardens. Sydney, Murray, 1979.

Dining Rooms and Eating Areas: The Best of Australian Home
  Journal's Decorating Ideas. Sydney, Murray, 1979.
Hand Knits for the Family. Sydney, Murray, 1979, 3 volumes.

*

Diana Wynne Jones comments:

I knew I was going to be a writer in the middle of one afternoon, the year I was eight. Since I was (and am) wildly dyslexic,
my parents just laughed. But my conviction never left me. I set
about making it the truth almost at once and completed several books
before I was fifteen. It is quite important to know that you can
finish a full-length book: that is the only thing to be said for my
early efforts.

What I *didn't* know was what kind of books I was going to
write. I was quite surprised to find myself writing ostensibly for
children (this was after I had written several adult novels and published one, *Changeover* in 1970). Some of this had to do with the
fact that I had children, who objected strenuously to the rigid and
boring books for children currently being published: having read
some of them aloud, I thought "I can do better than *this!*" Some of
it had to do with my own childhood: my father was too mean to
buy his kids books and he gave us one between the three of us
every Christmas. We experienced book-famine. I, particularly, craved
books which told of things which were unlikely to happen in real
life—and at the same time felt that not much *couldn't* happen. This
was during World War II, remember, with all its idiocies and steady
stream of inventions such as rocketry and atom-splitting; and this
was balanced by life in a rural village where there were not only
witches but a man who became a werewolf in the church porch
every full moon. Our bedroom faced the church porch and we used
to listen to him howling. I have never felt there was much difference between werewolves and atom-splitting: both belong to the
same life.

Hence, probably, is both my conviction that the "non-real-life"
events/facts in a book can be what you will: the important thing is
the story you tell about them. It has to have shape; it has to be an
enthralling experience; and if it *means* anything, that meaning has
to grow out of the story.

From about 1973, I was writing full-time, often howling with
laughter as I wrote, sometimes crying (I cried near the end of *Do
gsbody*). The fact was that writing for children, once the old rigid
rules were broken, gave one tremendous freedom during the 1970
and 1980s. (Since then, genre has become a preoccupation in all
forms of writing about "non-real-life" and everything had become
constrained and boring again.) Children, I found, grew up reading
my books, and didn't leave off once they attained adult stature. I
hope to go on writing books that people of all ages enjoy. But I
suppose the important thing is that I enjoy them too. If I find I am
not enjoying something I'm writing, I bin it and think of a new
way to do it that is more interesting.

*   *   *

Many readers would categorise Diana Wynne Jones as a fantasy
writer, writing for children and young adults. Certainly, her work,
superficially at least, contains all the elements one would expect of
a fantasy novel. Given the fact, however, that the author herself
dislikes genre categories, it should come as no surprise that many
of her books deal with themes which, depending on whose eyes
they're seen through, would count as science fiction, and a good
half dozen of her novels have overt science fictional ideas. But
Wynne Jones is further distinguished from other novelists by her
ability to combine fantastical elements with a very down-to-earth
perception of the nature of life. Many of her characters, children
and teenagers, through the course of the novel, learn more about
their place in their world, or find a new and more appropriate place.

The earliest of the science fiction novels, *Sirius,* easily mixes
myth with science fiction, as Sirius, the Dog Star, on trial before
his fellow star beings for crimes trumped-up by his companion
star is exiled to Earth and ordered to search for an artifact, a zoi.
He naturally assumes the shape of a dog, a puppy in fact, and much
of the story is concerned with his life in dog form, helping his new
owner Kathleen as well as hunting for the artifact. Kathleen, whose
father is in prison because he is a membr of the IRA, is exploited
by the relatives with whom she is obliged to live, and it is Sirius
who introduces her to Miss Smith, the woman with whom she will
eventually go to live.

The Homeward Bounders is much more overtly science fictional,
based on the premise that parallel universes exist and that it is possible to cross from one to another at certain points. This is a classic SF device, but Wynne Jones does not simply use the trope as it
stands. Instead, she mixes in the possibility that the different worlds
are "played" by Them, in the same way that game-players play Dun-
geons and Dragons, or re-enact classic battles. People who discover this are discarded to the boundaries, as Jamie, the hero, discovers. Condemned to wander through time, he encounters other
Homeward Bounders, and with two of them, Joris and Helen, and
one of his own descendants, he finally works out how to defeat
Them, and return the Homeward Bounders to their own worlds.
En route, Jamie visits many different worlds and through his eyes,
Wynne Jones provides a powerful critique of the way in which
societies manage themselves. The final moments, when Jamie
realises that he will continue to travel because his own world is no
longer enough for him, are poignant indeed, as Wynne Jones shows
that home, while perhaps desirable for most, is not the only choice.

One of Wynne Jones's best-loved novels is *Archer's Goon,* another story using time-travel paradoxes alongside magic. Howard's
town, as he discovers, is run by seven wizards, who control things
like power and finance. One of them has been forcing Howard's
father to write for him and when Quentin forgets to, the Goon is
sent round to collect the debt. Howard sets out to discover what's
happening and in the process discovers a plot to take over the
world. He also learns that the wizards have been trapped in the
town, obliged to take care of their youngest sibling, who is of
course, Howard himself, or Venturus, whose carelessness has meant
that they've all been trapped much longer than intended. Venturus
intended, when old enough, to fly away in his own rocket ship and
this is eventually used to dispose of the disruptive elements of the
family.

Although magic is involved, there is no doubt whatsoever that
Wynne Jones is very confident in using the devices of science fiction, and this is even clearer in *A Tale of Time City,* a novel with
very little in it that could be termed overtly magical. Instead, the
wonder is supplied in an imaginative portrayal of many aspects of
the future, some of which must surely seem magical to those not
yet familiar with them. The reader sees the wonder of the city
through the eyes of a girl, Vivian, snatched out of her own time,
1939 (though not quite the 1939 that we would recognise). Time
City is in fact a city out of time, looking after time streams and

ensuring that paradoxes don't occur. On the other hand, Time City is crumbling, itself subject to a cycle of renewal to avoid complete sterility, and the time is coming when the artifacts which control this process must be brought together. This makes the city even more vulnerable, and there are those who would like to destroy it altogether. In the meantime, they are causing chaos in time, bringing about events sooner than they are intended to happen. Vivian, kidnapped by Jonathan and Sam, becomes involved with the hunt to discover Faber John's artifacts, which will save the city, and in the process the reader is treated to an extremely amusing, almost satirical, commentary on the nature of change, and how different cultures will view their predecessors and fail to interpret their possessions.

By contrast, *A Sudden Wild Magic,* intended as a novel for young adults, tackles the gender wars, and those most familiar of SF devices, the patriarchal and feminist utopian societies. Once again, she settles for parallel universes, but in this instance, our world is being used almost as a testbed for another world, which duplicates its problems here, then waits to see what we do about them. However, given the sort of society we are, we don't tend to come up with the solutions as swiftly as the alternative world would wish. The scientists, all male, in their observatory, are menaced by the matriarchal society of Leanthe, and the witches of Britain are forced to take action, sending a spaceship through time and space to penetrate the parallel universe and stop the scientists of Arth. Funny though this is, and Wynne Jones's writing almost always exhibits a splendid sense of the ridiculous, there is a much more serious side to the novel, as Wynne Jones discusses what happens to societies when the trade in ideas is one-sided, in this case literally unbalancing the universe, as well as pointing out the absurdities of exclusively male and female societies. Here there are no good guys or bad guys, merely rather foolish people who seem unable to have happiness without seizing control at the same time. Here we can have global warming as a result of a misguided experiment by a parallel universe which can't solve the problem either.

Wynne Jones's most recent work, *Hexwood,* returns once again to the theme of the time paradox and also to Them, the mysterious set of people who are presumed to run the universe. In this instance, they are the Reigners, who organise the worlds like businesses. Earth is being mined for flint, a commodity which is worthless here, but worth a fortune elsewhere in the galaxy. Thus Earth itself is placed in the position of so many Third World countries, exploited and denied payment. The Reigners themselves are corrupt and have, so they believe, taken steps to ensure that they are not discovered. However, others with Reigner blood still exist and look forward to a time when the Reigners can be toppled.

The story, though, is centred on Hexwood, an entity in itself, and like human memory, it does not take the story in order. Thus, as Ann, the protagonist, stumbles into the wood, she encounters the story of Mordion and Hume, at different stages in Hume's life, forward and backward in time, as they struggle to defeat the Reigners. It's a complex presentation, not easily grasped, but Wynne Jones keeps firm control of her story and although it may seem as muddled as the human memory itself, the denouement makes perfect sense of everything.

It's regrettable that Diana Wynne Jones's unique blending of science fiction and fantasy is not more often recognised for what it is. It is too easy to pin a label on her fiction, thus loading it with one set of literary perceptions, when it could as easily be perceived in an entirely different way by another reader. I like to think that for Wynne Jones, science fiction and fantasy are merely two conve-

nient and arbitrary points on a continuum of fiction writing and that she writes as she wishes, and leaves it to others to decide. That would certainly be in keeping with the free literary spirit which pervades these, and all her other novels.

—Maureen Kincaid Speller

JONES, Gwyneth A(nn)

Pseudonym: Ann Halam. **Nationality:** British. **Born:** Manchester, Lancashire, 14 February 1952. **Education:** Notre Dame Convent, Manchester, 1963-70; University of Sussex, 1970-73, B.A. (honors) in history of ideas 1973. **Family:** Married Peter Gwilliam in 1976; one son. **Career:** Executive officer, Manpower Services Commission, Hove Sussex, 1975-77. **Agent:** Herta Ryder, c/o Toby Eady Associates, 18 Park Walk, London, SW10 0AQ. **Address:** 30 Roundhill Crescent, Brighton, East Sussex BN2 3FR, England.

SCIENCE FICTION PUBLICATIONS

Novels (series: Daymaker)

Water in the Air. London and New York, Macmillan, 1977.
Dear Hill. London, Macmillan, 1980.
Divine Endurance. London, Allen and Unwin, 1984; New York, Arbor House, 1987.
Escape Plans. London, Allen and Unwin, 1986.
Kairos. London, Unwin Hyman, 1988.
The Hidden Ones (for children). London, Women's Press, 1988.
White Queen. London, Gollancz, 1991; New York, Tor, 1993.
Flowerdust. London, Headline, 1993; New York, 1995.
North Wind. London, Gollancz, 1994.

Novels as Ann Halam (for children; series: Inland)

Ally, Ally, Aster. London, Allen and Unwin, 1981.
The Alder Tree. London, Allen and Unwin, 1982.
King Death's Garden: A Ghost Story. London, Orchard, 1986.
Inland trilogy:
    The Daymaker. London and New York, Orchard, 1987.
    Transformations. London and New York, Orchard, 1988.
    The Skybreaker. London, Orchard, 1990.
Dinosaur Junction. London, Orchard, 1992.
The Haunting of Jessica Raven. London, Orion, 1994.

Short Stories

Identifying the Object. Austin, Swan Press, 1993.

OTHER PUBLICATIONS (for children)

Novels

The Influence of Ironwood. London, Macmillan, 1978.
The Exchange. London, Macmillan, 1979.

Novel as Ann Halam

Into the Silent Water. London, Orchard, 1990.

*

Gwyneth A. Jones comments:

(1991) I started telling stories at a very early age. My father was a storyteller, my mother passionately interested in the future; hence science fiction drew me, though I was bound to become some kind of fantasist. When I was at university I used to tell people stories as presents (I also used to lay a mean Tarot)—fantasies based on observation of the recipient's personality and aspirations. Two of these survive in print: "The Snow Apples" and "Laiken Langstrand." When I first wrote published novels I wrote for children, through happenstance, because I was introduced to a children's editor (Marni Hodgkin, at Macmillan, London). By the time I started to write for adults I'd been thinking about my craft for a long time. I'd become interested in the why and how of storytelling, and of science fiction. *Divine Endurance* is a science fantasy of the old kind, silently dedicated to Zelazny's *Lord of Light* and many others. *Escape Plans* and *Kairos* are also in their way about science fiction as much as they are novels on their own account. Meanwhile, "Ann Halam" continues to tell stories; but the storytelling of these juveniles is inextricably mingled with my own brooding on the problems of my life and times. In particular, in the Daymaker series, with the problem of reconciling our triumphs of technology with our need to preserve the past, the present, and the planet.

I rarely write short stories now. When I do it's because I've been directly asked for one, or because I want to work out something about my current novel, or explain something (to myself) about a novel that's already written. "The Eastern Succession" moved the fantasy-like world of "Divine Endurance" into a more realistic continuum. The story entitled "Forward Echoes," in the December 1990 issue of *Interzone,* encapsulates the theme of my current novel, but tells it from a viewpoint that has no place in the novel's version of the story of Braemar and Johnny.

(1995) Since 1990 I've been writing a series about aliens on earth. My "Aleutian" books continue the themes of the Daymaker trilogy and *Divine Endurance:* is there a different way to live? How much do we have to change to find a sustainable future that does not destroy our environment; how much potential for change do we have? My "Aleutians" are a reverse image of the white European colonisers of Africa, India, and Asia. Their "superiority" is in life-sciences, in community, in a shared unconscious that the humans take for telepathy. They have no gender, and a very weak concept of "otherness." They don't know they are aliens.

I had a very interesting time working out nonsexual strategies for reproduction and evolution, finding myself much drawn to the idea of "sexual" relations as primarily a social glue (if you'll pardon the expression) even in human society, with reproduction a casual side effect. But at least as important to me is this story of the colonisers and the colonised: a very different story from the slave narratives or the cultural imperialism—narratives which abound in U.S. science fiction. Certainly, there is "another way" of describing SF's central theme—the encounter with the alien, and what becomes of both parties.

*   *   *

Gwyneth Ann Jones is the author of SF novels and a handful of short stories for adults, but the bulk of her work has been, and remains, within the category labelled "children's." As such, however, it should certainly not be ignored. Under the name Ann Halam, in particular, she has created some of the most thought-provoking and imaginative children's fantasies being written today: books which are much more interesting and challenging than most fantasy novels marketed as "adult."

Ally, Ally, Aster, the best of her earlier children's books, is certainly more straightforward than those she wrote in the late 1980s. The characters, particularly the "villains," are like caricatures, and the narrative has little to it beyond the surface tale of modern children being confronted with ancient magic and disbelieving adults, with the traditional ending of the adults—the parents—being unaware that anything exciting and supernatural had happened. Magic is thus safely kept away from the "real world." It is a well-told tale full of suspense nevertheless, but no real indication of the Halam novels that were to follow. *King Death's Garden* is a much richer and more complex novel, dealing with a boy's attempt to understand the secrets of the cemetery behind his great-aunt's house in Brighton (the cemetery near Jones's house) and the mystery of the professor who used to live there (who claimed to photograph fairies), but also examining with considerable insight the problems of growing up, of accepting responsibility, of coping with an adult world.

The "Inland" trilogy is her most important contribution to children's literature and is at the point where she crosses from fantasy into science fiction. The books are set on a future earth, where the magic of the almost totally female group of coveners protects the population and its flocks from the dangerous remains of the present industrial world—and keeps them in a stable, rural world, isolated from new ideas or possibilities of change. The books—*The Daymaker, Transformations,* and *The Skybreaker*—follow the career of Zanne, a young girl with prodigious magical powers, who becomes a covener "troubleshooter," sent to kill any surviving ancient machines—despite her own attraction to ancient technology. No trilogy that begins with a novel set in a school for young magicians can avoid comparison with Le Guin's "Earthsea" series. "Inland" stands up to the comparison well, and examines problems that are of perennial concern: questions of morality and of personal responsibility, of the nature of democracy, and of the opposition between "green" values and technology. Zanne finds no easy answers in any of the books; as Maureen Speller has written of *The Skybreaker* (in *Vector 160,* 1991), "It is rare indeed for a novel to come to terms so thoroughly with the uncertainties of life. . . . My only regret is that, as a result of them being published in a children's fiction imprint, too many people will have missed the opportunity to tackle this demanding and intellectually satisfying work."

On Earthsea, women were unable to become magicians; in Inland very few men have that ability. In her more recent novels, Jones has become much more concerned about, or more public about, her feminism. This is perhaps most noticeable in *The Hidden Ones,* written as Gwyneth A. Jones for "Livewires," the teenage imprint of the Women's Press. It is about a woman scientist trying to investigate the "poltergeist effect" in a young girl, around whom strange things happen. Both women get involved in a plan to save a local rural beauty spot from the hands of developers. But the story is told from the viewpoint of the girl: a confused, aggressive, suspicious adolescent, who finds it almost impossible to establish any sort of normal relationship with adults or other teenagers. The strong characters are all women. *The Hidden Ones* offers

489

a frank and ultimately sympathetic portrait of tortured adolescence. Jones later remarked, "I believed by the end that I had managed to express my original vision; an exciting rite of passage story that would involve hard science and would *belong* to the girl-protagonist, instead of being hijacked by cosmic truth on the one hand, or on the other by the first male character to arrive on the scene" (in L. Armitt, editor, *Where No Man Has Gone Before: Women and Science Fiction,* edited by L. Armitt, 1991).

Jones has published a number of SF and fantasy short stories for adults, although it is clear that her main commitment is to the novel. For several years, while working on children's books, she was also working on her first adult SF novel, *Divine Endurance.* Like its successor *Escape Plans, Divine Endurance* is set in a far-future that is thoroughly, if perhaps insidiously, feminist: all the major human characters are women, and when men appear, as they do only occasionally, they are regarded as ineffectual inconveniences—just as women have been regarded in most 20th-century SF. Both have been called difficult books: as Jones herself has said, "I have a way of making simple things difficult." Crucial facts are lost to the reader who does not read slowly, and subtle and deliberate allusions, to other works of SF for instance, are not as obvious as the author seems to believe. But they are both rich and exciting books, which do repay the careful reading. *Divine Endurance* is the story of the journey of a girl, Cho, and her cat Divine Endurance, from the desert wastes of China into a far future Malaysia: Jones uses her three-year sojourn in Singapore to haunting effect. As in the other novels, it takes time to work out what is happening: that Cho is in fact an android, for instance, and that her cat has plans for her.

In *Flowerdust* she returned to the world of *Divine Endurance* with a story that made it even more evident that one of her central concerns is colonialism, and the ways that cultures affect each other. There is a strong feminist principle underlying this interest, and as often as not there are sexual as well as cultural resonances underlying the way that mutual non-comprehension lies at the heart of all such relationships. In *Escape Plans,* for instance, ALIC, a visitor from a utopian space-habitat, abandons the immense power her computer access gives her when she helps a threatened proletarian woman on a whim. As a result she finds herself trapped among a huge human underclass she barely understands, and sees from a new perspective how the "utopia" she comes from is maintained by their labour. We learn alongside ALIC. There is a glossary, but in common with all her books it is only gradually that we come to understand what the jargon-rich language of the book is really saying; and the nature of the language is, of course, intimately interwoven with the political nature of the world.

Such incomprehension is even more significant in *Kairos,* her most complex and challenging novel to date, in which we, the readers, are as much in a fog as the protagonists who find their world changing about them. It is set in a near-future Britain whose political and social customs are only slightly extrapolated from the late-1980s, with an increasingly Thatcherised Britain and an increasingly brutal police. Two couples, gay and lesbian, gradually become enmeshed in the intrigues of BREAKTHRU, a sinister, mysterious and apparently neo-fascist group who turn out to be experimenting with Kairos, a drug that alters not only consciousness but reality itself.

Such questions of power and oppression, political and sexual, lie at the heart of *White Queen* and *North Wind,* the first two parts of a projected trilogy which directly confronts the notion and nature of colonialism. In *White Queen* aliens (known as the Aleutians because they first make themselves known on the Aleutian Islands) land on earth and gradually establish their own enclave in northern Thailand. The power of these aliens goes largely unrecognised at first because they spread their influence by trade, a classic recapitulation of European colonialism in Asia. To this is added the sexual confusion that the aliens have no clearly defined sexual characteristics, and become "he" or "she" according to criteria that are incomprehensible to the humans. There are similar incomprehensions about death; in fact the whole basis of the novel is that the two races can understand each other only in the broadest terms.

The first novel tells of journalists Johnny Guglioli and Braemar Wilson who come to understand the threat of the aliens and take precipitate and in the end unsuccessful action to thwart them. By the second novel, *North Wind,* they are long dead and held in greater regard by the occupying powers than they are by humankind. In fact, the most common characteristic of humanity is an attempt to make themselves like their colonial masters, generally by self-mutilation.

The assumption of an equation between sexual relationships and colonialism can be uncomfortable, the perception that human interaction is based on mutual incomprehension is challenging, and the way that this incomprehension is built into the structure of her books so that they operate a slow and never complete revelation can make them difficult to read. Nevertheless, Gwyneth Jones writes some of the most intelligent and intriguing science fiction around, a science fiction that exploits the possibilities of the genre to make informed and pertinent points in a way that illustrates the strength of the genre as a medium for commenting upon our world. Her fiction has already won considerable critical acclaim, it now deserves greater popularity also.

—Edward James, updated by Paul Kincaid

JONES, Neil R(onald)

Nationality: American. **Born:** Fulton, New York, 29 May 1909. **Education:** Attended Fulton public schools. **Military Service:** Served in the 2nd Armored Division of the United States Army, 1942-45. **Family:** Married Rita Gwendoline Rees in 1945. **Career:** Stamp dealer, bookkeeper, cost analyst, office manager, game manufacturer; unemployment insurance claims examiner, State of New York, for 26 years. **Died:** 15 February 1988.

SCIENCE FICTION PUBLICATIONS

Short Stories (series: Professor Jameson; Tales of the 24th Century; Tales of the 26th Century)

The Planet of the Double Sun. New York, Ace, 1967.
The Sunless World. New York, Ace, 1967.
Space War. New York, Ace, 1967.
Twin Worlds. New York, Ace, 1967.
Doomsday on Ajiat. New York, Ace, 1968.

*

Neil R. Jones comments:

I am one of the earlier science fiction writers in this country. My first story, "The Death's Head Meteor," appeared in 1930, and was the first SF story to use the word astronaut. "The Jameson Satellite" was the beginning of what is possibly the longest running series in science fiction; from 1931 to 1968, 23 stories in the series were published. I also wrote two other series ("Tales of the 24th Century" and "Tales of the 26th Century"); both included stories of the Durna Rangue cult. All the stories were written in the vein of a future history. Michael Ashley (*History of the Science Fiction Magazine*) puts it this way: "an overall framework in which each story forms part of a future history, invented by Jones long before either Heinlein or Asimov. The key story is the Jameson adventure 'Times's Mausoleum' (*Amazing,* December 1933) which remained the basis for all of Jones's other tales."

* * *

In 1929 Hugo Gernsback, through the manipulations of creditors, lost the ownership of the world's first science fiction magazine, *Amazing Stories.* His reputation was so strong, however, that within months he was back in business with three new titles: *Science Wonder Stories, Scientific Detective Monthly,* and *Air Wonder Stories.* It was in the seventh issue of this last title, dated January 1930, that Neil R. Jones's first story, "The Death's Head Meteor," appeared.

Although Jones would sell a respectable handful of stories to him in the half-dozen or so years before Gernsback left the field, it was not the *Wonder* magazines that would become most important to Jones but *Amazing Stories.* It was the July 1931 issue of *Amazing* that published Jones's story "The Jameson Satellite," which told how Professor Jameson arranged for his body to be fired into space after his death, there to orbit the Earth for 40 million years, at which time, the body and its brain still perfectly preserved in the vacuum of space, it is discovered by space explorers from the planet Zor.

The Zoromes are machine men, their living brains transferred to mechanical bodies, supported by four legs and equipped with six tentacles. Their brains are protected by a conical metal head to which are affixed a series of mechanical eyes surrounding the head, and one looking straight up. Thus, they are not subject to the wear and tear of fleshly life, and boast lifetimes sufficiently long to permit interplanetary exploration. In fact, only a severe accident featuring direct damage to the head is fatal to them. They communicate by telepathy.

Jameson's brain is removed from his corpse and placed in one of the mechanical bodies. He becomes 21MM392. He learns that the Earth is long dead and that he may well be the last representative of the human race. He joins the Zoromes in their journey through the cosmos.

And what a journey it is. At a time when the imaginations of most science fiction writers seemed restricted to the solar system, Jones joyfully let his heroes zoom from star system to star system. Jones proved adept at planet building, and story after story featured truly wonderful discoveries.

The fifth story of the series, "Time's Mausoleum" (*Amazing,* December 1933), featured a glimpse back in time to show Jameson some of what had happened to the solar system. Significantly, the story outlines a future history in use by Jones several years before the more highly publicized Future History of Robert Heinlein began.

The bulk of Jones's future history concerns his second magazine series, the Durna Rangue. The Durna Rangue is a semi-scientific cult founded in the 24th century. Their scientific experiments, often conducted on human guinea pigs, get them driven first from Earth and then from Mars. At last they are forced to hide on one of the moons of Uranus. In the 26th century, they ally themselves with space pirates and conquer the Earth, which they then rule as an outlaw world. The first Durna Rangue story was "Little Hercules" (*Astounding,* September 1936). The final to appear (and one of Jones's best stories) was "The Citadel in Space," published in the third issue of *Two Complete Science-Adventure Books,* Summer 1951. Only some of the stories in this series have been published, while the Professor Jameson series numbers at least 23.

If Jones benefitted from the first expansion of the magazine science fiction field, it was the next expansion in the late 1930s in which he lost prominence. In the late 1930s, all three SF magazines changed editorial hands and all three editors—Mort Weisinger at *Thrilling Wonder Stories,* John Campbell at *Astounding,* and Ray Palmer at *Amazing*—felt it was time for a change. Weisinger and Palmer both went after a more juvenile audience, a policy Palmer abandoned at the outset of the World War II in favor of one designed to appeal to a blue collar audience.

Although Jones had the sort of imagination and approach to storytelling that Palmer liked, he found *Amazing*'s new editor less than receptive to continuing the Jameson series. Palmer complained about the often minor tone of Jones's plots, but it seems more likely that in his efforts to find stories about characters the man on the street could identify with, he simply felt an immortal machine man called 21MM392 didn't fit the bill. Jones sold several times to Palmer but those stories were action-adventure pieces, usually without the imagination and sweep of the Professor Jameson stories. The Jameson stories would find their second home in 1940 in the short-lived *Astonishing Stories* (edited by Fred Pohl) and, after the war in the revival of *Super Science Stories.* In the late 1960s Ace Books issued five paperback collections of the Professor Jameson series, including in the fifth two stories never previously published, though they appear to have been sold at one time to *Amazing.*

Jones wrote action stories with strongly imaginative and often highly clever backgrounds. His prose style is expository and tends to distance the reader from the characters, and, in that respect, may be old-fashioned and off-putting to many readers. But this is a characteristic he shares with other writers who are still widely read, including Lester Dent (who wrote the Doc Savage books as Kenneth Robeson) and Philip José Farmer. His type of writing is, therefore, probably a matter of taste to many readers. But he still has his fans, many of them too young to have encountered him when he first appeared. Professor Jameson is an astonishing achievement and while that series may have its equals in its ability to arouse the good, old-fashioned sense of wonder, nothing surpasses it.

—Gerald W. Page

JONES, Raymond F.

Nationality: American. **Born:** Salt Lake City, Utah, in 1915. **Education:** Studied engineering and English in college. **Career:** Radio engineer, then full-time writer. Lives in Arizona. **Address:** c/o Pinnacle Books, Kensington Publishing Corporation, 475 Park Avenue S, New York, New York 10016, U.S.A.

SCIENCE FICTION PUBLICATIONS

Novels (series: Ron Barron)

Renaissance: A Science Fiction Novel of Two Human Worlds. New York, Gnome Press, 1951; as *Man of Two Worlds,* New York, Pyramid, 1963; with original title, London, Grafton 1991.

The Alien: A Gripping Novel of Discovery and Conquest in Interstellar Space. New York, World Editions, 1951.

The Island Earth. Chicago, Shasta, 1952; London, Boardman, 1955.

Son of the Stars (Ron Barron; for children). Philadelphia, Winston, 1952; London, Hutchinson, 1953.

Planet of Light (Ron Barron; for children). Philadelphia, Winston, 1953.

The Secret People. New York, Avalon, 1956; as *The Deviates,* New York, Galaxy, 1959.

The Year When Stardust Fell: A Science Fiction Novel (for children). Philadelphia, Winston, 1958.

The Cybernetic Brains. New York, Avalon, 1962.

Voyage to the Bottom of the Sea (for children). Racine, Wisconsin, Whitman, 1965.

Syn. New York, Belmont, 1969.

Moonbase One (for children). New York and London, Criterion, 1972.

Renegades of Time. Don Mills, Ontario, Laser, 1975.

The King of Eolim. Don Mills, Ontario, Laser, 1975.

The River and the Dream. Toronto, Laser, 1977.

Weeping May Tarry, with Lester del Rey. Los Angeles, Pinnacle, 1978.

Short Stories

The Toymaker. Los Angeles, Fantasy, 1951.

The Non-Statistical Man. New York, Belmont, 1964; London, Digit, 1965.

OTHER PUBLICATIONS (for children)

Other

The World of Weather. Racine, Wisconsin, Whitman, 1961.

Animals of Long Ago. Racine, Wisconsin, Whitman, 1965.

Ice Formation on Aircraft (for adults). Geneva, World Meteorological Organization, 1968.

Physicians of Tomorrow. Chicago, Reilly and Lee, 1971.

Radar: How It Works. New York, Putnam, 1972.

*   *   *

Raymond F. Jones is an almost archetypical John Campbell writer, whether writing for *Astounding,* as with "Noise Level" where scientists are lured into inventing anti-gravity, or for *Thrilling Wonder Stories,* with the Peace Engineer stories where aliens secretly involve earth scientists in a program to produce materials needed to defend their home world against invaders (*This Island Earth*).

Jones's first novel, *Renaissance,* is a long and complex parallel-worlds story that contains variations on a number of familiar SF themes against a somewhat more adventurous narrative than is usual in his stories. *The Alien* is a bit more straightforward in its

storytelling, although its ideas and the approach he takes to them is not simple at all. The shadow of A.E. van Vogt falls across both these books, the first in its resemblance in early passages to *Slan,* the second in its exploration of ideas and attitudes similar to those of *The World of Null A. The Alien* opens with a strong idea: a representative of a long-extinct extraterrestrial race is discovered entombed in the asteroid belt, and brought back to life. While the revival processes go forward, new discoveries indicate this being is thoroughly evil and responsible for the destruction of his own race, something he would no doubt manage for humanity as well. The wealth of ideas from which the story draws its strength occasionally betrays it, as when we are suddenly shown that our supposedly solar-system-bound humans have had the capability of interstellar flight (and use that capability with the utmost casualness); and, again, when a semanticist translates and teaches himself an entire alien language on the basis of a few hours' first-contact conversation. Overlook such points, however, and the book is as good an example of this type of space adventure as you're likely to find short of Edmond Hamilton.

It would be a mistake, however, to place Jones in the camp of Doc Smith or Hamilton, or even van Vogt. Jones has always managed to remain a force unto himself, although a pretty low-key force. One of the ways this has been achieved has been in his handling of characters. The typical Jones character is an engineer, technician, or mathematician, middle-class, and presented in a straightforward and realistic manner that contrasts sharply with the politicians, artists, scholars, militarists, rebels, and engineer-savants that make up the bulk of the field's fictional populace. Jones seldom attempts any deep probing of his characters but has always drawn his strength from the ability to portray his characters in equally believable environments. He is also a very economical writer, and after *The Alien* he settled down to a more suitably quiet form of fiction. *The Island Earth* is the first book-length work of his that can be labeled typical. His characters are thoroughly convincing engineers, and, despite the melodrama and detective story touches, their thought processes are the thought processes of reasonable engineers. The complexities that cluttered *Renaissance* and *The Alien* are shunted into the background and the interest of the story lies not in galaxy-spanning events but in the impact of galaxy-spanning events on the lives of seemingly everyday people. The argument could be raised that the best of Jones's novels were written for the Winston juvenile series. *Son of the Stars,* in which teenagers encounter the survivor of a wrecked flying saucer and subsequently find their extraterrestrial friend endangered by adult prejudices, is certainly one of the best of that fondly remembered series of juvenile novels. *Planet of Light* is a sequel.

One of Jones's best stories is "The Non-Statistical Man," which tells of an insurance company statistician who encounters a series of anomalies involving recent claims. At first intrigued, then openly alarmed, he investigates and is led to the conclusion that there are people who possess a 100 percent reliable intuition, rendering his own statistical approach superfluous and pointless. These people know when they're going to need insurance and they don't get it till then. The character's discovery of all this, his reactions to it, and his subsequent change of philosophy as he discovers that the process that makes intuition infallible can be taught to anyone—even him—is written in the low-key style that is the strength of Jones's best writing, and the result is one of his most convincing and compelling stories. It also illustrates the other strength of Jones. He's always been a storyteller who has gone to great pains to build his stories on definite ideas, making him something of a purist among SF writers. His complexities never overwhelm everything else in the way they usually do in the hands of others, and in his later, quieter fiction, his storytelling ability is often quite remarkable for its purity, directness, and seeming effortlessness. This effortlessness may have something to do with the decline in his readership in recent years: Jones is entertaining and often thought-provoking, but he doesn't generate the flair and excitement of a good many lesser but better-known writers.

Jones has also never marked out a particular type of fiction as his own. Most of his stories are recognizably the work of one writer, with a type of character and a worldview that are identifiable, but any story by Jones is apt to be written with a particular market in mind. "Seven Jewels of Chamar" is pure *Planet Stories* space opera and "Tools of the Trade" is a classic *Astounding* engineering problem story of the type John Campbell was always supposed to be looking for. But the first doesn't rank with the stories of Emmett McDowell or Gardner F. Fox, and the second is a middle-grade example of the sort of thing Eric Frank Russell was starting to be known for. Jones's recent novels have been good entertainments, but they've lacked the strengths of his early work.

Jones is a thoroughgoing professional and, in retrospect, a writer of surprising versatility. But the price of this seems to be that too often he came on the scene with a perfectly good story that was still second best to the similar works of someone else. But there have been times when the works he produced were principally from no source but himself, slanted to no editorial taste but his own—works like *The Island Earth, Son of the Stars,* and "The Non-Statistical Man"—and those results have always been worth waiting for—or searching out.

—Gerald W. Page

JORGENSEN, Ivar. *See* **FAIRMAN, Paul W.; GARRETT, Randall.**

JORGENSON, Ivar. *See* **SILVERBERG, Robert.**

JOSEPH, M(ichael) K(ennedy)

Nationality: New Zealander. **Born:** Chingford, Essex, England, 9 July 1914. **Education:** Sacred Heart College, Auckland; Auckland University College, B.A. 1933, M.A. 1934; Merton College, Oxford, B.A. 1938, B. Litt. 1939, M.A. 1945. **Military Service:** Served in the British Army in the Royal Artillery, 1940-46. **Family:** Married Mary Julia Antonovich in 1947; four sons and one daughter. **Career:** Lecturer in English, 1945-49, and Senior Lecturer, 1950-59, Auckland University College; Associate Professor, 1960-69, and Professor of English, 1970-79, University of Auckland. **Awards:** Hubert Church Prose award, 1959; Jessie Mackay Poetry award, 1960; New Zealand Book award, for fiction, 1978. **Died:** 4 October 1981.

SCIENCE FICTION PUBLICATIONS

Novel

The Hole in the Zero: A Novel. London, Gollancz, 1967; New York, Dutton, 1968.

OTHER PUBLICATIONS

Novels

I'll Soldier No More: A Novel. Auckland, Paul's Book Arcade, and London, Gollancz, 1958.
A Pound of Saffron. Auckland, Paul's Book Arcade, and London, Gollancz, 1962.
A Soldier's Tale. Auckland and London, Collins, 1976.
The Time of Achamoth. Auckland and London, Collins, 1977.
Kaspar's Journey. Auckland, Brick Row/Hallard Press, 1988.

Poetry

Imaginary Islands: Poems. Christchurch, New Zealand, privately printed, 1950.
The Living Countries: Poems. Auckland, New Zealand, Paul's Book Arcade, 1959.
Inscription on a Paper Dart: Selected Poems, 1945-72. New Zealand, Auckland University Press, 1974.

Other

Charles Aders: A Biographical Note: Together with Some Unpublished Letters Addressed to Him by S.T. Coleridge and Others, and Now in the Grey Collection. New Zealand, Auckland University College, 1953.
Byron the Poet. London, Gollancz, 1964; New York, Humanities Press, 1966.
Editor, *Frankenstein: or, The Modern Prometheus,* by Mary Shelley. New York and London, Oxford University Press, 1969.

* * *

M.K. Joseph, a New Zealand writer and educator, produced only one science fiction novel, *The Hole in the Zero.* While the book's primary staging occurs on an undefined planet in untime and unspace—that is, beyond the known universe and within the philosophical hole in the zero—Joseph constructs his plot in such a manner that it succeeds in operating on several contrasting levels simultaneously.

Like Doris Lessing's *Briefing for a Descent into Hell,* the book teems with archetypal themes and figures; and like Kurt Vonnegut, Jr.'s *Slaughterhouse-Five,* it is episodic, lurching from time into untime, space into unspace, with what appears to be, on first encounter, disconcerting irregularity. Although not easily accessible to the casual reader—which may explain its relative obscurity outside of the novelist's native New Zealand—*The Hole in the Zero* proves to be a closely integrated, carefully executed story exhibiting few major flaws. The least well-developed sequence and the most apparent flaw is that which satirizes the decade in which the novel was written, the 1960s. But several notable strengths counterbalance this apparent weakness.

The familiar motif of life existing as a dream within the mind of a dreamer, a bitter denouncement when voiced by Mark Twain in *The Mysterious Stranger,* loses its threatening aspect with Joseph and achieves a rather comfortable appearance as a known escape clause in the midst of the unknown. Joseph's universe migrates swiftly from an exploration of the duality of man's nature to that of a single man bifurcating into colinear lives, certainly a Wellsian concept. Progressing from these familiar byways, the book passes into a multiplicity of experiences in which each man must make a conscious choice before his life can assume direction. Finally, however, the life cycle itself degenerates into an endlessly repetitive dictum; and hell is the doom sequence of a single, unvarying lifespan swelling to encompass eternity, until even this stalls and the endless paradoxically reaches a terminus.

It is then that Joseph's central theme, that of man directed by an ultimately moral universe, emerges. For a merciful intelligence, perhaps the obscure figure of the Gespenster, metes out to each individual what each sought. Vividly illustrating the adage that man is a questing beast, supplanted by an occasional glimmer of Milton, Joseph's three male heroes/antiheroes act out their appointed roles—

the first seeking power, the second pleasure, and the third, the hero of the tale, Seth Paradine, truth. This trio is, with varying ability, integrated into the novel's multitudinous layering technique. But the solitary female character, Helena, is never well served by the author. Indeed, if achieving a limited dimensionality while assuming the role of dreamer and dream-maker—hampered by appearing as a quintessential Lady of Shalott whose tapestry of life is destroyed by the contest between Paradine and his Hyde-ish opposite, Merganser—Helena's primary role remains that of bit player in the scenes directed alternately by her father, Merganser, and Paradine.

Finally, then, Paradine emerges triumphant as the major character. He is Everyman, the first and last man, God the Father and God the Son, Judas and Peter, and Adam. He assumes a focal point in the varied panoply of mythological and archetypal superstructures with which the novel is endowed and which, at times, seem so overweighted that they verge on inner collapse. Nevertheless, because Paradine is the seeker after truth, *The Hole in the Zero* speaks with a commanding and hopeful voice. For, while exposing the evil that men do to themselves, their environment, and to others, it is mankind's great capacity for good and a desire to serve while questing after the God within and without which emerge as M.K. Joseph's essentially Christian final declaration.

—Sharon-Ilona Hecht

K

KAFKA, Franz

Nationality: Czech. **Born:** Prague, Bohemia (now Czechoslovakia), 3 July 1883. **Education:** Ferdinand-Karls University, Prague, doctorate in law 1906; also attended technical institute in Prague. **Family:** One son. **Career:** Worked for attorney Richard Loewy drafting legal notices, Prague, 1906; intern in law courts, Prague, 1906-07; staff member of insurance company Assicurazioni Generali, Prague, 1907-08; specialist in accident prevention and workplace safety for Workers' Accident Insurance Institute for the Kingdom of Bohemia, Prague, 1908-22. Worked at Prague Asbestos Works Hermann & Co., Zizkov, 1911-17. **Died:** 3 June 1924.

SCIENCE FICTION PUBLICATIONS

Short Stories

Sie verwandlung. N.p., 1915; translated by A. L. Lloyd as *The Metamorphosis,* London, Parton Press, 1937; New York, Vanguard Press, 1946.
The Great Wall of China and Other Pieces, translated by Willa Muir and Edwin Muir. London, Secker, 1933.
The Penal Colony, translated by Willa Muir and Edwin Muir. New York, Schocken, 1948; as *In the Penal Settlement: Tales and Short Prose Works,* London, Secker and Warburg, 1949.
Selected Short Stories of Franz Kafka, translated by Willa Muir and Edwin Muir. New York, Modern Library, 1952; as *The Metamorphosis and Other Stories,* Harmondsworth, Middlesex, Penguin, 1961.
Franz Kafka: Stories, 1904-1924, translated by J. A. Underwood. London, Macdonald, 1981.
The Transformation and Other Works: Works Published during Kafka's Lifetime, translated by Malcolm Pasley. London, n.p., 1992.

OTHER PUBLICATIONS

Novels

Der prozess. N.p., 1925; translated by Willa Muir and Edwin Muir as *The Trial,* London, Gollancz, and New York, Knopf, 1937.
Das schloss. N.p., 1926; translated by Willa Muir and Edwin Muir as *The Castle,* London, Secker, and New York, Knopf, 1930.
Amerika. N.p., 1927; translated by Willa Muir and Edwin Muir as *Amerika,* London, Routledge and Kegan Paul, 1938; New York, New Directions, 1946.

Other

Diaries. N.p., 1948, 2 volumes.

*   *   *

Albert Einstein could not read Kafka. He handed back a novel of Kafka's Thomas Mann had lent him, confessing he had been unable to finish it, saying, "The human mind isn't that complex." Something of Einstein's bafflement has been felt by every honest critic approaching Kafka's work. It speaks for itself. It is plain, unadorned. It holds no mystery. Kafka hides nothing. "As Gregor Samsa awoke one morning from uneasy dreams he found himself transformed in his bed into a gigantic insect." Nothing could be more transparent, anticipated even.

The quoted sentence opens the story "Metamorphosis," a favourite with science fiction readers. Yet the question must be asked, Is Franz Kafka a science fiction writer? The answer has to be that such a question diminishes him. He is one of the great writers of the 20th century, eternally readable, eternally astonishing. Among the shelves of books of criticism on his work, there is no critic rash enough to claim him for SF.

And yet with Kafka there are always qualifications. There was a long-prevailing fashion within the SF field—promoted by John W. Campbell—to regard the universe as a large wiring diagram that could be rapidly scrutinized and solved, possessed, within a generation. His writers in his magazine wrote as if this were so. Their world picture has dated badly.

The opposing view is that the universe, now revealed as so full of anomalies, is ultimately unfathomable to the human mind, which is a subordinate part of the whole. Of this view (not at all defeatist, but rather quietist), Kafka is king. His two great novels, *The Trial* and *The Castle*—unfinished at his premature death—both present their central character with problems to which no solution appears possible.

Not that these novels are allegories. Nor are they religious, though religious intensity is certainly there. They seem rather to be Symbolist novels, the equivalent in prose of a Max Ernst painting. ("The symbol *is* what it represents; the allegory represents what, in itself, it is *not*"—Eric Heller, in *The World of Franz Kafka,* edited by J.P. Stern, 1980). Perhaps it would be safest to say that Kafka achieved a new kind of fiction for modern man, as SF has scarcely managed to do. He was dedicated, as Proust was dedicated, to the written word to a remarkable degree; they were not commercial authors.

The inexplicable has much to do with it. In *The Trial,* K is inexplicably under arrest for a crime he cannot determine. In *The Castle,* K arrives at a village where he believes a job awaits him; inexplicably, nobody can confirm this. Against these monstrous dilemmas, K brings determination and logic. Ever and again, new complications arise.

Both *The Trial* and *The Castle,* among the greatest novels of the century, contain a great deal of wit, or more precisely black humour. Charles Dickens was one of Kafka's models. The pure fantasy stories are also humorous and owe something to the Jewish tradition. For instance, "Investigations of a Dog" is as written by a dog. A certain sly native masochism appears in "In the Penal Settlement" and some of the shorter stories; in "The Vulture," a man suffers a vulture to mutilate his feet, before finally drowning it in his own blood.

A Czech born in Prague, Kafka wrote in German, mainly for himself and his circle of friends, among whom Max Brod was responsible for saving the manuscripts Kafka wanted burnt. The Mitteleuropean complexion of the work has led critics to see in it predictive qualities, foreseeing the complexities of oppression Hitler's Third Reich was to inflict on Czechs and, more particularly, Jews. One of Kafka's unconsummated loves was for Milena Jesenska, who was to die in the Ravensbruck concentration camp in 1944, 20 years after Kafka's death in a sanitorium.

The paradox of Kafka's art and his life is well expressed in Pietro Citati's biography: "All the people who met Franz Kafka in his youth or maturity had the impression that he was surrounded by a 'wall of glass.' There he stayed, behind that very transparent glass, walking gracefully, gesticulating, speaking. . . . The more he participated in the destiny and sufferings of others, the more he excluded himself from the game."

Almost everything Kafka wrote is worth reading and rereading. His *Diaries* (2 vols., 1948) are recommended, and also his restrainedly crushing "Letter to His Father"—that father, a prosperous Jewish merchant, being a source of his son's misery and inspiration alike. "You, so tremendously the authoritative man, did not keep the commandments you imposed on me."

—Brian W. Aldiss

KAGAN, Janet

Nationality: American. **Born:** 1945.

SCIENCE FICTION PUBLICATIONS

Novels

Uhura's Song: A Star Trek Novel. New York, Pocket, and Bath, England, Firecrest, 1985.
Hellspark. New York, Tor, 1988.

Short Stories

Mirabile. New York, Tor, 1991.

*   *   *

Janet Kagan is a "good read" of the type that harks back to the early days of the science fiction tradition, full of science but focusing on the tale and the characters with a light touch of humor. She has written many short stories that regularly appear in science fiction magazines and anthologies, some of which have been collected in her book *Mirabile.* She is also the author of one of the better Star Trek novels, *Uhura's Song.* Her long novel, *Hellspark,* is classic science fiction, character-centered adventure.

It is with great pleasure that the reader can once again enter the world of Star Trek in *Uhura's Song.* The cast is all there, interacting with the warmth and wit that bring them to life in the mind's eye. This is a first-contact story with the action largely centering around Uhura, another strong engaging female character, Dr. Wilson (also a trickster type character), and the aliens. The Enterprise's mission, driven by a deadly plague that could spell disaster for the Federation, is to locate an alien race based on some ambiguous clues from forbidden songs exchanged between Uhura and an alien friend. The aliens are fascinating felines, Eeiauoans, and their distant ancestors, Sivaoans, who hopefully may have a clue to the plague. The action clips along with intrigue, diplomatic snares and

a desperate timetable, set against the well-realized alien feline culture. Kagan's development of Uhura, Wilson, and the Sivaoans and her well-crafted and vital alien culture set this above the standard space adventure while her portrayal of the Star Trek crews allows us to "watch" the episode unfold. Cat lovers will especially enjoy this book.

The unflagging pace as well as the wonderful characters draws the reader right into the world of *Hellspark.* It's a murder-mystery science fiction novel that continually generates excitement. The intrigue and the unfolding science grip the reader while our ties to the characters, especially Tocohl Susumo a freetrader-translator-judge, keep us involved in the action from start to finish. These are people and places you will want to meet again. It explores human motivation and communication between alien cultures. The science, grounded in linguistics, kinesics, and proxemics, is the mechanism to heighten awareness and open the mind to other possible social structures and cultures, and the dangers and rewards of interaction between cultural groups. The science is fascinating and vividly foregrounds the subtleties of cultural differences as well as limning the obvious differences. This would be a good book to read before going abroad.

In *Mirabile* Kagan takes the cliché lost human colony story and turns out a delightful romp into a powerful positive future. The new social structure combines the best of old Earth with the best of a survival culture; everyone's contribution is both valued and honored as are the individuals. The only problems are biological, dragon's teeth. To maximize genetic possibilities, all life-forms are able to have other life-forms as offspring; a plant, for example, could grow insects or a cow give birth to a bear. Having lost the colony's genetic records, the whole breeding process is one big surprise with frequent nightmares. The various stories in this universe are tied together by the character of Annie Jason Masmajean, a woman you'd like to know better by visiting her world. This universe and her other writings demonstrate that Janet Kagan is an author to anticipate and enjoy.

—Catherine M. Currier

KAHN, James

Nationality: American. **Born:** Chicago, Illinois, 30 December 1947. **Education:** University of Chicago, B.A. 1970, M.D. 1974. **Family:** Married Jill Alden Littlewood in 1975; one daughter. **Career:** Physician: intern, University of Wisconsin, Madison, 1974-75; resident, Los Angeles County Hospital, 1976-77, and University of California, Los Angeles, 1978-79. Since 1978, Emergency Room physician, Rancho Encino Hospital, Los Angeles. **Address:** c/o St. Martin's Press, 175 Fifth Avenue, New York, New York 10010, U.S.A.

SCIENCE FICTION PUBLICATIONS

Novels (series: New World; Poltergeist)

New World trilogy:
World Enough and Time. New York, Ballantine, 1980; London, Granada, 1982.

Time's Dark Laughter. New York, Ballantine, 1982; London, Panther, 1983.

Timefall. New York, St. Martin's Press, 1987; London, Grafton, 1988.

Poltergeist (novelization of screenplay). New York, Warner, and London, Granada, 1982.

Star Wars: Return of the Jedi (novelization of screenplay). New York, Ballantine, and London, Macdonald, 1983; in *The Star Wars Trilogy,* Ballantine, 1987.

Indiana Jones and the Temple of Doom (novelization of screenplay). London, Sphere, and New York, Ballantine, 1984.

Poltergeist II (novelization of screenplay). London, Corgi, and New York, Ballantine, 1986.

The Echo Vector. New York, St. Martin's Press, 1987; London, Grafton, 1989.

OTHER PUBLICATIONS

Novels

Diagnosis: Murder. New York, Carlyle, 1978.

The Goonies: A Novel (novelization of screenplay). New York, Warner, and Sevenoaks, Kent, Coronet, 1985.

Plays

Television Plays: *A Pig Too Far* (*St. Elsewhere* series), 1983; for *E/R* series 1984-85.

Poetry

Nerves in Patterns, with Jerome McGann. X Press, 1978.

*

James Kahn comments:

I think of my work primarily as storytelling, my purpose to entertain, and, if possible, to enthrall. Within that framework I rely on the themes of death and rebirth a great deal, a cyclical movement in time and space—sometimes metaphorically, sometimes physically.

*   *   *

James Kahn has been building his knowledge of the craft of writing through novelizations of screenplays: *Poltergeist, Return of the Jedi, Indiana Jones and the Temple of Doom, The Goonies,* and *Poltergeist II.* His first science fiction short story, "Mobius Trip," dates back to 1971; since then, he has explored other genres to some extent, including a detective novel, *Diagnosis: Murder,* and a volume of poetry, *Nerves in Patterns.* His main original work, the New World Trilogy, consists of *World Enough and Time, Time's Dark Laughter,* and *Timefall.*

The most interesting of the novelizations is *Poltergeist,* where Kahn's contact with ESP research in medical school and background in myth lead to descriptions of the astral planes and their inhabitants, especially the shadow, tree, and flame figures, that are congruent with accounts of occult experience and well above the level of the rest of the film material. The *Star Wars* volume, *Return of the Jedi,* is even and competent, with good landscape descriptions but little depth in characterization. Characterization techniques be-

gin to expand in the *Indiana Jones* novelization with development of Short Round's viewpoint and the reiterated theme "Anything Goes" to characterize Willie; a limited juvenile narrator is also developed for *The Goonies.*

World Enough and Time is unusually high in quality for a first science fiction novel, possibly because of Kahn's love of words and interest in integrating poetic quotations either directly into the narration or as commentary on experience by scholar vampires. The title derives from Marvell's "To His Coy Mistress," though the novel deals with interrupted love rather than unfulfilled sexual desire. Rose and Dicey are kidnapped from their respective husbands, the centaur Beauty and the human Scribe Josh, for unknown reasons; Josh and Beauty join in pursuit and claim Venge-right, acquiring as companions the cat/human Isis, the Flutterby (giant butterfly) Humbelly, the Neuroman Jasmine, and the highly educated and philanthropic Vampire Lon—the range of species and interests in the novel is extensive, if left at a somewhat shallow level. The mission is partly successful: Dicey has been entranced by a vampire and dies, but Josh's brother Ollie is rescued and Rose is released from the Neuroman experiment that interlocks human minds for increased intelligence and a wider field of perception.

The development of minor themes is what makes the novel outstanding. Time obscures truth by turning history into legend; maturation requires the ability to accept the difference. Jasmine as long-lived lecturer on the past is a little obvious, but she forces Beauty to adjust to the fact that centaurs, like other talking animals, are a recent creation of man through genetic engineering, not the ancient people of their myths. Scribery, the belief in the power of the word in itself, develops when adult humans are wiped out in the Race Wars by their creations; Josh must accept this, but retains faith in an intrinsic power for words. Kahn's medical background is at its best in the human need to create their fantasies, even the destructive ones like Vampires, the self-hate of the failure Accidents, the desire for long life at any price expressed in the Neuroman process where a fungus eats away all tissue but nerve cells and these cells serve as the core for an artificial body. But the creations are close to the fantasy borderline, resembling the dragons of Pern rather than hard-core science fiction, in spite of realistic elements like the limited perception of the cat Isis with her fragment of human brain—abilities are not held tightly to physical law.

The sequel, *Time's Dark Laughter,* is more ambitious and less successful, though beautifully titled; it presents a cyclic universe, destroyed and reborn whenever human genetic possibilities combine to produce a semi-divine being that possesses full consciousness of the universe but lacks control over power and moral insight and so must be killed—cycles will continue until a solution to the problem is found. All experience is becoming sour for all characters in this novel: Josh is forced back to the city of the experiment by brain seizures to match his genetic component with the queen's and create the bird-girl deity; the quest to recover Josh and Rose succeeds in destroying the girl by a virus keyed to her unique DNA, but the nature of the world has been altered and much destroyed. Josh and Rose start over in a new Eden, their first Children Can and Able. One problem is this confusion of cycles: the sun now rises in the east instead of the west and a new animal appears that is clearly a giraffe, suggesting that the new cycle is ours, but the bird-girl refers to Jahweh as a past self and many terms in the old cycle are specifically ours—California, Monterey, Pope. It is difficult to credit such specifics as accidental similarities in recurring cycles, and the pattern remains in an uncomfortable tension.

Kahn's strengths lie in language, background in medicine, the use of myth. Techniques still need improvement: consistency in characterization (notably with Jasmine), methods for integrating extrapolated history and other background material smoothly into narrative, selectivity among ideas. But the combination of recurrent pattern with the fixing of position resulting from the tension between a straight-line quest and cyclic time offers possibilities that deserve serious exploration.

—Marilyn K. Nellis

KAPP, Colin

Nationality: British. **Born:** 1928. **Career:** Worked as an electrical technician. **Address:** c/o New English Library, Mill Road, Dunton Green, Sevenoaks, Kent TN13 2YA, England.

Science Fiction Publications

Novels (series: Cageworld; Chaos)

Transfinite Man. New York, Berkley, 1964; as *The Dark Mind,* London, Corgi, 1965.
The Patterns of Chaos. London, Gollancz, 1972; New York, Award, 1973.
The Wizard of Anharitte. New York, Award, 1973; London, Panther, 1975.
The Survival Game. New York, Ballantine, 1976; London, Dobson, 1977.
The Chaos Weapon. New York, Ballantine, 1977; London, Dobson, 1979.
Manalone. London, Panther, 1977.
The Ion War. New York, Ace, 1978; London, Dobson, 1979.
The Timewinders. London, Dobson, 1980.
Search for the Sun! (Cageworld). London, New English Library, 1982; New York, DAW, 1983.
The Lost Worlds of Cronus (Cageworld). London, New English Library, 1982; New York, DAW, 1983.
The Tyrant of Hades (Cageworld). London, New English Library, 1982; New York, DAW, 1984.
Star-Search (Cageworld). London, New English Library, 1983; New York, DAW, 1984.

Short Stories

The Unorthodox Engineers. London, Dobson, 1979.

*   *   *

If any SF writer could typify the Blakean aphorism "Energy is eternal delight," Colin Kapp does so both in terms of human passion and of the energies that compose the universe. The former is unusual in a writer dealing with such esoteric sciences as atomic theory; the latter demonstrates a feeling of awe toward the forces of nature, rather than extolling the way technology utilizes such forces.

Not all of Kapp's works demonstrate the fascination with energy—various stories for *Analog* and the tales of "the Unorthodox Engineers" are standard scientific problem-solving puzzles.

The majority of his works, however, describe the energy states of physics in rhapsodic terms ("Around him the hellish sums and unbelievable vortexes of transfinity shifted and phased in a terrible kaleidoscope of new geometrics and unknown colors"—*Transfinite Man*). In essence, Kapp relates to energy-states as Asimov did to robots—devising a conceptual structure for the scientific phenomena, and giving its many facets relevance to the many facets of human response. In fact, Kapp goes so far as to posit direct interaction between natural forces and human thought-energy. *Transfinite Man* describes a demonic hero, able to survive the dimensions of transfinity by virtue of maniacal hatred. *The Ion War* and "Mephisto and the Ion Explorer" portray human beings able to transform themselves into vessels of ionic energy. "Lambda 1" and "The Imagination Trap" detail the world of Tau-space, a sub-atomic dimension in which matter directly responds to mental manipulation, and *The Chaos Weapon* concerns a female psychic who can read entropic energy-patterns which indicate oncoming catastrophes. Surprisingly, this interaction is not mechanistically explained in terms of psionics (i.e., the human brain transmits energy like a radio, etc.)—rather, Kapp merely portrays a direct correspondence; rather like the hermetic relationship of man and universe, microcosm and macrocosm.

Such a relationship would be facile if the human personalities were not as vividly realized as the cosmic aspects. Kapp's characters are neither subtle nor complex, but they are vivid, especially in regard to romantic attachments. In "Hunger over Sweet Waters" a scientist and his female coworker, with whom he is in love, are stranded together on a world without drinkable water, and though the scientist is married to another woman and cannot enjoy a relationship with his coworker, his love for her is the spur for his invention of a way to secure their rescue. In both *The Ion War* and *The Patterns of Chaos* the relationship between woman and man is less like love than like the intimacy of "torturer and victim"—the female being a caustic "bitch-goddess" who drives the male to perform superhuman feats. This sort of antagonistic romance—also present in *Transfinite Man, The Chaos Weapon,* and "Lambda I"—is the means by which the hero exceeds his limits, discovering strategies for survival or salvation. (In recent works—such as the entertaining pulp-style adventure of the *Cageworld* series—the antagonistic romance-angle is toned down, but still present to a degree.)

Though Kapp equals several more revered authors in terms of imaginative scope and striking characters, he lacks a quality that generally enhances the popularity of such authors—that is, an overt philosophy that describes man's place in the universe. Despite this lack, his stories can yield a wealth of implicit insights, while his articulation of scientific concepts is surpassed only by the very best of SF.

—Gene Phillips

KAVAN, Anna

Pseudonym for Helen Woods. **Other Pseudonym:** Helen Ferguson. **Nationality:** Anglo-American. **Born:** Cannes, France, in 1901; brought up in California. **Education:** Educated privately and in Church of England Schools. **Married:** 1) Donald Ferguson (divorced); 2) Stuart Edmonds (divorced), one son. **Career:** Lived in the United States, Burma, Europe, Australia, and New Zealand; settled in London. **Died:** 5 December 1968.

SCIENCE FICTION PUBLICATIONS

Novels

Eagles' Nest. London, Owen, 1957.
Ice. London, Owen, 1967; New York, Doubleday, 1970.

Short Stories

Asylum Piece and Other Stories. London, Cape, 1940; New York, Doubleday, 1946.
I Am Lazarus. London, Cape, 1945.
Julia and the Bazooka, edited by Rhys Davies. London, Owen, 1970; New York, Knopf, 1975.
My Madness: The Selected Writings of Anna Kavan, edited by Brian W. Aldiss. London, Picador, 1990.

OTHER PUBLICATIONS

Novels

Change the Name. London, Cape, 1941.
House of Sleep. New York, Doubleday, 1947; as *Sleep Has His House,* London, Cassell, 1948.
A Scarcity of Love. Southport, Lancashire, Downie, 1956; New York, Herder, 1972.
Who Are You? Lowestoft, Suffolk, Scorpion Press, 1963.
Mercury. London and Chester Springs, Pennsylvania, Peter Owen, 1994.
The Parson. London and Chester Springs, Pennsylvania, Peter Owen, 1995.

Novels as Helen Ferguson

A Charmed Circle. London, Cape, 1929.
The Dark Sisters. London, Cape, 1930.
Let Me Alone. London, Cape, 1930; Short Hills, New Jersey, Enslow, 1978.
A Stranger Still. London, Lane, 1935.
Goose Cross. London, Lane, 1936.
Rich Get Rich. London, Lane, 1937.

Short Stories

A Bright Green Field and Other Stories. London, Owen, 1958.
My Soul in China, edited by Rhys Davies. London, Owen, 1975.

Other

The Horse's Tale, with K.T. Bluth. London, Gaberbocchus, 1949.

* * *

Recalling the gothic horrors of Mary Shelley's *Frankenstein,* Anna Kavan inverts the terror stimulus from the external monster to the interior of the mind. Kavan's works are explorations of the mentally ill, those possessed by fear of an external and menacing society. The Monster is within the self—sometimes evidenced as unreasoning fear and suspicion and sometimes emanated as an obsessive desire to control/torture others as catharsis for self-destructive tendencies.

Kavan, like Shelley, did not consciously write science fiction. Kavan's writings are characterised by their frequent and enigmatic shifts between fantasy and reality, abrupt mood shifts, and poetic descriptions. Some of her works are catastrophe fiction, envisioning mass chaos epitomized in the chaos of the central character's mind. The protagonist's mental condition both parallels and illuminates the basic irrationality of the civilizations Kavan depicts. It is the shifting of reality planes within a setting of worldwide catastrophe that marks some of Kavan's psychological fiction as science fiction. Although many of her works are primarily descriptions of the world of the mentally ill, at least "The Birthmark," *Ice,* and *House of Sleep* present a world outside the central character's mind which is also distorted.

In "The Birthmark" the young girl narrator meets an alien girl who fears the discovery of her peculiar skin marking, implying to the narrator that such a discovery would ban her from the narrator's world. Many years later, while touring a castle, the narrator discovers (or thinks she does) the same girl locked in a dungeon—being persecuted for her special talents—talents symbolized and identified by that birthmark.

Ice is also set in a hostile world: nuclear testing has brought on a rapidly advancing ice age. Kavan depicts, unlike many science-fiction writers, an apathetic populace who are unable to comprehend the impending disaster or to break their routine existence. The people remain true to their nature: complacent in the face of chaos. Of course some attempt to flee, but government and business continue to function. Even war continues as the demise of civilization approaches. Within this hostile world the protagonist obsessively searches for a frail, seemingly inept woman whom he both loves and hates. Her weakness of will and body obsesses him as it does his rival, and he alternately wishes to protect and destroy her. Ultimately he conquers the fear of rejection which instigates his violent fantasies toward her and they join in love, and at peace, as they wait for their deaths.

In *House of Sleep* Kavan presents B's progressing rejection of reality which stems from childhood. B finds that only her daydreams and the cover of night provide the security ripped away from her by her mother's unexplained death. B retreats into her imagination, finding there a haven from the isolation and alienation of a society which cares neither for her or for itself. She flees from place to place, always recording the threatening, if ineffectual, liaison officer and the civil disruption and fear within an oppressive government. B states: "Without understanding the reason, I knew that I had to keep the day unimportant. I had to prevent the day world from becoming real." In Kavan's abrupt and frequently imperceptible shifts from reality to fantasy she illustrates the operation of an escape mechanism within the mind of one who can neither accept nor interact in the alien world of reality.

Kavan brings brilliant character portrayal into the genre of science fiction, exploring the inner universe of the mind rather than the outer galaxies of the universe. What she finds within the mind is fear and violence: the essence of terror, confirmed by the irrationality of uncaring society which persecutes without knowledge or reason those whose perceptions differ from the norm. Thus Kavan explores various reality levels, questioning society's grasp of reality, and indicating that perhaps sanity is only a matter of perception: that we live in an insane world and are unable to judge who within it is sane or insane.

—Jane B. Weedman

KELLER, David H(enry)

Pseudonym: Henry Cecil. **Nationality:** American. **Born:** Philadelphia, Pennsylvania, 23 December 1880. **Education:** Educated at the University of Philadelphia Medical School. **Military Service:** Served as a physician working in shell-shock during World War I; medical professor on the faculty of the Army Chaplain's School at Harvard University, Cambridge, Massachusetts, during World War II. **Family:** Married in 1903. **Career:** Physician, specializing in psychoanalysis: junior physician, Illinois Mental Institute, after 1915, and worked in other hospitals in Louisiana, Tennessee, and Pennsylvania. Editor, *Sexology* and *Your Body* in the 1930s. **Died:** 13 July 1966.

SCIENCE FICTION PUBLICATIONS

Novels

The Sign of the Burning Hart: A Tale of Arcadia. St. Lo, France, Imprimerie de la Manche, 1938; Hollywood, National Fantasy Fan Federation, 1948.
The Devil and the Doctor. New York, Simon and Schuster, 1940.
The Solitary Hunters; and, The Abyss: Two Fantastic Novels. Philadelphia, New Era, 1948.
The Eternal Conflict. Philadelphia, Prime Press, 1949.
The Homunculus. Philadelphia, Prime Press, 1949.
The Lady Decides. Philadelphia, Prime Press, 1950.

Short Stories

The Thought Projector. New York, Stellar, 1929.
Wolf Hollow Bubbles. Jamaica, New York, Arra Printers, 1934(?).
Men of Avalon. Everett, Pennsylvania, Fantasy, 1935(?).
The Waters of Lethe. Great Barrington, Massachusetts, Kirby, 1937.
The Television Detective. Los Angeles, Los Angeles Science Fiction League, 1938.
The Thing in the Cellar. Millheim, Pennsylvania, Bizarre Series, 1940.
Life Everlasting, and Other Tales of Science, Fantasy, and Horror, edited by Sam Moskowitz and Will Sykora. Newark, New Jersey, Avalon, 1947.
The Final War. Portland, Oregon, Perri Press, 1949.
Tales from Underwood. New York, Arkham House, 1952.
A Figment of a Dream. Baltimore, Mirage Press, 1962.
The Folsom Flint, and Other Curious Tales. Sauk City, Wisconsin, Arkham House, 1969.
The Last Magician: Nine Stories from Weird Tales, edited by Patrick H. Adkins. New Orleans, P.D.A. Enterprises, 1978.
The Human Termites: A 1929 Science Fiction Extravaganza. New Orleans, P.D.A. Enterprises, 1979.

OTHER PUBLICATIONS

Poetry

Songs of a Spanish Lover (as Henry Cecil). Alexandria, Louisiana, Wall Printing Co., 1924.

Other

The Kellers of Hamilton Township: A Study in Democracy. Alexandria, Louisiana, Wall Printing Co., 1922.
The Sexual Education Series. New York, Popular Book Corporation, 10 vols., 1928.
Know Yourself! Life and Sex Facts of Man, Woman, and Child. New York, Popular Book Corporation, 1930.
Portfolio of Anatomical Manikins. New York, Sparacio, 1932.
Picture Stories of the Sex Life of Man and Woman: 317 Simple Instructions Explaining How Sex Functions in Human Beings. New York, Popular Medicine, 1941.

*   *   *

The genre of science fiction and fantasy has seemed to attract some of the most talented, versatile, and idiosyncratic personalities and made writers of them. David H. Keller pursued a varied and successful career as physician, military doctor, psychiatrist, and medical researcher. He published widely in the professional literature of his field. He also wrote fiction—but only for his family and friends. Then in 1928 *Amazing Stories* published "The Revolt of the Pedestrians," a long dystopian narrative that Keller had completed before Hugo Gernsback had even started *Amazing*. The story was such a success that Gernsback contracted for 12 more from Keller, and during the next decade or so 60 "Kelleryarns" were published in SF and fantasy markets. *Weird Tales* served as another primary outlet for the Keller stories. During the final two decades of his life, however, Keller returned to private publishing and almost continuous writing of stories and books that may or may not have been marketable. His overall accomplishment seems immense, individual, and idiosyncratic. Some of his stories are classics of the horror/weird fantasy variety. Much of his writing reads as pleasantly whimsical and expressive of the "humours" of his personality in the 18th-century sense. In many ways, especially in the final years of his life, he was like an 18th-century eccentric or country gentleman who loved and expressed wit, humour, and imaginative curiosity in both his living and his writing. In all ways, Keller was his own man; and it is perhaps too soon for a literary assessment of his work whether in abnormal psychology or in fantasy or humorous narrative.

Regardless of any later assessment of his large volume of rather whimsical writing, certain careful elements in his art are apparent. Keller is often very skillful in the subtle understated suggestion of the supernatural that creates the greatest chill of horror. He combines with this a fascination in the psychosomatic relations of mental disorder to behavior. Among the short, chilling masterpieces that embody these artfully controlled effects are "The Thing in the Cellar," "A Piece of Linoleum," and "The Dead Woman," all from the early 1930s. Keller writes, then, with a subtle control of statement and tone that is unusual in the early pulp markets of the genre. The other element in his art that is particularly impressive is his use of point of view. Many of his narratives are told in first person, and he is master of the ironic first-person narrator who gradually reveals his own insanity to the reader without realizing it himself. As in Swift's *A Modest Proposal,* a Keller narrator will often be condemning himself/herself while telling what seems to be his/her side of the story. The other kind of first-person narrator is Keller himself in the person of various point-of-view characters with whimsical names, such as Jacobus Hubelaire who writes his own autobiography that is really Keller's, or Colonel Horatio Bumble in *The Homunculus.* This last, strange little book gives a fictional picture in the first person of Keller/Bumble that may or may not be the real Keller. But it shows a 20th-century retired Colonel of the Army Medical Corps who dabbles in writing and in the supernatural and who resembles an 18th-century eccentric, such as one might find in a Smollett novel or in the person of Erasmus Darwin, much more than a modern writer. At the same time the book, in its way, treats fascinating themes of scientific methodology, married life, and writing itself. Keller is a puzzlement in the genre—unique, varied, and often extremely effective.

—Donald M. Hassler

KELLERMANN, Bernhard

Nationality: German. **Born:** 1879. **Died:** 1951.

SCIENCE FICTION PUBLICATIONS

Novel

Der tunnel. Berlin, S. Fischer, 1913; translated as *Transatlantic Tunnel,* London, Hodder Stoughton, 1915; as *The Tunnel,* New York, Macaulay, 1915.

*   *   *

Bernhard Kellermann's only science fiction novel, *Der tunnel (The Tunnel),* was influential in the development of a school of SF better known in the Soviet Union than in the West. "Industrial science fiction," as it was later christened by Soviet critics, goes beyond the strict invention-adventure format of Jules Verne as represented in both the *voyages extraordinaires* and the juvenile SF (dime novels, Tom Swift, etc.) that imitated them: vast engineering projects change both the face of the world and ordinary people's lives. But no more than in straight Vernean SF is there any fundamental change in society. Early examples include André Lauries's *New York to Brest in Seven Hours* (1888, France), involving construction of a transatlantic oil pipeline, and Luigi Motta's *The Submarine Tunnel* (1912, Italy), which anticipates the project in Kellermann's novel.

The Tunnel was undoubtedly the most popular of these; it was translated into English within a year, and was still remembered fondly enough two decades later to inspire three movie versions, *The Tunnel* (1935, in simultaneous French and German versions) and *Transatlantic Tunnel* (1935, Britain). Even the novel reads like a cross between Verne and Cecil B. DeMille. Mac Allan, the hero, is an idealistic engineering genius typical of invention SF. But realization of his dream requires billions of dollars and entire armies of workers—and costs thousands of lives. Kellermann realizes the scale of logistics for such a project, from an artificial Niagara to provide electric power to a new city to house workers. Although

gigantic boring machines do the basic tunneling work, the toll on human life is great—and the project is nearly doomed by an explosion that kills nearly 3000 and leads to strikes and riots. Despite being made a scapegoat for the disaster and being sent to jail (his wife and child already having been killed by rioters), Allan eventually redeems himself and completes the tunnel. Through it all, there are no basic moral or social questions: Western civilization is united by the ideals of science and engineering; there are no wars or serious international disputes. Even the scientific imagination is shortsighted: the possibility of air travel across the Atlantic is curtly dismissed.

Kellermann's collected works were translated in 1930 in the Soviet Union, where his sympathy for the Bolshevik Revolution struck a responsive chord. *The Tunnel* undoubtedly helped inspire Aleksandr Kazantsev's *Arctic Bridge* (1946), involving a similar project across the Arctic Ocean, as well as such industrial SF novels as Aleksandr Belyaev's *Under the Arctic Sky* (1938), Grigori Adamov's *The Banishment of the Lord* (1946), Vladimir Nemtsov's *Golden Bottom* (1948), and Kazantsev's *Northern Jetty* (1952), devoted to Siberian development and similar projects.

—John J. Pierce

KELLEY, Leo P(atrick)

Nationality: American. **Born:** Wilkes Barre, Pennsylvania, 10 September 1928. **Education:** New School for Social Research, New York, B.A. in English 1957. **Career:** Advertising copywriter and manager, McGraw-Hill Book Company, New York, 1959-69. Since 1969, freelance writer. **Address:** 702 Lincoln Boulevard, Long Beach, New York 11561, U.S.A.

SCIENCE FICTION PUBLICATIONS

Novels (series: Galaxy 5; Space Police)

The Counterfeits: A Startling Science Fiction Novel. New York, Belmont, 1967.
Odyssey to Earthdeath. New York, Belmont, 1968.
The Accidental Earth. New York, Belmont, 1970.
Time Rogue. New York, Lancer, 1970.
Brother John (novelization of screenplay). New York, Avon, and London, Pan, 1971.
The Coins of Murph. New York, Berkley, 1971; London, Coronet, 1974.
Mindmix. Greenwich, Connecticut, Fawcett, 1972; London, Coronet, 1973.
Time: 110100. New York, Walker, 1972; as *The Man from Maybe,* London, Coronet, 1974.
Mythmaster. New York, Dell, 1973; London, Coronet, 1974.
The Earth Tripper. Greenwich, Connecticut, Fawcett, 1973; London, Coronet, 1974.
The Time Trap (for children). Belmont, California, Pitman, 1977; London, Murray, 1978.
Space Police (for children):
   Prison Satellite. Belmont, California, Pitman, 1979; London, Hutchinson, 1980.

Worlds Apart. Belmont, California, Pitman, 1979; London, Hutchinson, 1980.

Earth Two. Belmont, California, Pitman, 1979; London, Hutchinson, 1980.

Backward in Time. Belmont, California, Pitman, 1979; London, Hutchinson, 1980.

Sunworld. Belmont, California, Pitman, 1979; London, Hutchinson, 1980.

Death Sentence. Belmont, California, Pitman, 1979; London, Hutchinson, 1980.

Night of Fire and Blood (for children). Belmont, California, Pitman, and London, Murray, 1979.

Star Gold (for children). Belmont, California, Pitman, and London, Murray, 1979; as *Alien Gold,* New York, Bantam, 1983.

Galaxy 5 (for children):

Good-bye to Earth. Belmont, California, Pitman, 1979; London, Murray, 1980.

On the Red World. Belmont, California, Pitman, 1979; London, Murray, 1980.

Vacation in Space. Belmont, California, Pitman, 1979; London, Murray, 1980.

Dead Moon. Belmont, California, Pitman, 1979; London, Murray, 1980.

Where No Sun Shines. Belmont, California, Pitman, 1979; London, Murray, 1980.

King of the Stars. Belmont, California, Pitman, 1979; London, Murray, 1980.

OTHER PUBLICATIONS

Novels (series: Cimarron; Luke Sutton)

Deadlocked! New York, Fawcett, 1973.

Luke Sutton:

Luke Sutton, Outlaw. Garden City, New York, Doubleday, and London, Hale, 1981.

Luke Sutton, Gunfighter. Garden City, New York, Doubleday, and London, Hale, 1982.

Luke Sutton, Indian Fighter. Garden City, New York, Doubleday, 1982; London, Hale, 1983.

Luke Sutton, Avenger. Garden City, New York, Doubleday, and London, Hale, 1983.

Luke Sutton, Outsider. Garden City, New York, Doubleday, 1984; London, Hale, 1986.

Luke Sutton, Bounty Hunter. Garden City, New York, Doubleday, 1985; London, Hale, 1991.

Luke Sutton, Hired Gun. Garden City, New York, Doubleday, 1987; London, Hale, 1991.

Luke Sutton, Lawman. Garden City, New York, Doubleday, 1989; London, Hale, 1992.

Luke Sutton, Mustanger. Garden City, New York, Doubleday, 1990; London, Hale, 1992.

Cimarron:

Cimarron and the Hanging Judge. New York, New American Library, 21 vols., 1983-86.

Cimarron Rides the Outlaw Trail. New York, Signet, 1983.

Cimarron and the Border Bandits. New York, Signet, 1983.

Cimarron in the Cherokee Strip. New York, Signet, 1983.

Cimarron and the Elk Soldiers. New York, Signet, 1983.

Cimarron and the Bounty Hunters. New York, Signet, 1983.

Cimarron and the High Rider. New York, Signet, 1984.

Cimarron in No Man's Land. New York, Signet, 1984.

Cimarron and the Vigilantes. New York, Signet, 1984.

Cimarron and the Medicine Wolves. New York, Signet, 1984.

Cimarron on Hell's Highway. New York, Signet, 1984.

Cimarron and the War Women. New York, Signet, 1984.

Cimarron and the Bootleggers. New York, Signet, 1985.

Cimarron and the Prophet's People. New York, Signet, 1985.

Cimarron and the Comancheros. New York, Signet, 1985.

Cimarron and the Gunhawk's Gold. New York, Signet, 1985.

Cimarron and the Hired Guns. New York, Signet, 1986.

Cimarron and the Maneaters. New York, Signet, 1986.

Cimarron and the Red Earth People. New York, Signet, 1986.

Cimarron on a Texas Manhunt. New York, Signet, 1986.

Morgan. Garden City, New York, Doubleday, 1986.

A Man Named Dundee. New York, Doubleday, 1988; London, Hale, 1992.

Thunder Gods' Gold. New York, M. Evans, 1988; London, Hale, 1991.

Bannock's Brand. New York, Doubleday, 1991.

The Money Game (for children). Belmont, California, Fearon Pitman, 1977; London, Murray, 1978.

Johnny Tall Dog. Belmont, California, Fearon Pitman, 1981; Wisbech, Cambridge, Learning Development Aids, 1990.

The Last Cowboy. Belmont, California, Fearon Pitman, 1988.

Other

Galaxy 5 Teacher's Guide. Belmont, California, Fearon Pitman, 1979.

Space Police: Teacher's Guide. Belmont, California, Fearon Pitman, 1979.

Editor, *Themes in Science Fiction: A Journey into Wonder.* New York, McGraw Hill, 1972.

Editor, *The Supernatural in Fiction.* New York, McGraw Hill, 1973.

Editor, *Fantasy: The Literature of the Marvelous.* New York, McGraw Hill, 1974.

*   *   *

Although achieving his greatest success with the Luke Sutton and Cimarron western series and non-series novels like *Thunder Gods' Gold,* Leo P. Kelley produced a number of solid science fiction novels earlier in his writing career.

Kelley's first SF novel, *The Counterfeits,* develops many of the themes he refines in his later novels. Earth is invaded by an alien race whose home planet has been destroyed. The aliens are able to assume any shape; they take human form and set about destroying human civilization. What takes this book out of the usual alien-invasion formula is Kelley's attempt to provide a plausible reconciliation at the book's conclusion.

Odyssey to Earthdeath explores the domination of a society by psychological methods in the tradition of Orwell's *Nineteen Eighty-Four.* The book suffers from undeveloped characters and a predictable plot. *Time Rogue* is one of Kelley's few attempts to use time travel as a theme for sociological speculation. Unfortunately, the plot degenerates into a good versus evil confrontation with predictable results. *The Accidental Earth* blends the themes of the previous books into an eerie amalgam. A counter-Earth is separated from our Earth by a wall of time, but an accident brings the two Earths into contact. Only the secret weapon of the Photon Spray saves Earth from alien invasion by severing the Time link and separating the two Earths again. Although the conclusion is hackneyed space opera, the beginning and middle sections of the novel feature some of Kelley's best writing. *The Coins of Murph* tells of a postholocaust society based on religion deifying the chief programmer of the Rand Corporation, Joseph Murphy, who, on some surviving audio tapes, blames the holocaust on decision making. His followers interpret this to mean all decisions should be decided by chance, hence the use of coins for flipping. The plot gets bogged down in power politics, but the sociological portrait Kelley presents is memorable.

The remaining SF novels are chiefly characterized by their cynical perspectives and brutality. *Time: 110100* is a surreal morality play of two humans on an odyssey through a strange world populated by lusty, warlike, and enigmatic simulacra. While the book has undertones of Barth's *Giles Goat-Boy,* it is damaged by a weak ending. *Mindmix* presents contemporary human society stricken by a deadly virus. The government discovers one man, Pete Bratton, who has become immune to the virus. Kelley develops a cynical picture of government scientists exploiting Bratton by transplanting the minds of dying geniuses into Bratton's brain, with successful but grim results. *The Earth Tripper* and *Mythmaster* are written in New Wave style. The better of the two books, *The Earth Tripper,* follows the bizarre adventures of an alien observer who goes AWOL on Earth in human form. Captured releasing animals from a zoo, he's taken to a secret mental institution, and he and other strange inmates become subjects of brutal experiments using "reality therapy." The mildly upbeat ending doesn't relieve much of the book's cynicism.

Since 1973, Kelley has concentrated on writing science fiction for juveniles and elementary students with low reading skills—and he has continued to produce very successful westerns. Kelley's best work features strong writing and ingenious sociological constructions of unique societies, but the unrelenting grimness of his later work coupled with New Wave writing styles weakens its appeal.

—George Kelley

KELLY, James Patrick

Nationality: American. **Born:** Mineola, New York, 11 April 1951. **Education:** University of Notre Dame, B.A. in English literature, 1972; attended Clarion Writers' Workshop, Michigan State University, East Lansing, 1974, 1976. **Family:** Married 1) Barbara Flynn in 1972 (divorced 1988); 2) Pamela Eldredge in 1991; 3 children. **Career:** Proposal writer, then coordinator of public relations, C.E. Maguire, Inc., Architects, Engineers, and Planners, Waltham, Massachusetts, 1972-77; part-time consultant, 1977-79. **Agent:** Ralph M. Vicinanza Ltd., 111 Eighth Avenue, Suite 1501, New York, New York 10011, U.S.A. **Address:** 7 Taft Road, Portsmouth, New Hampshire 03801, U.S.A.

SCIENCE FICTION PUBLICATIONS

Novels (series: Messenger Chronicles)

Planet of Whispers (Messenger). New York, Bluejay, 1984.
Freedom Beach, with John Kessel. New York, Bluejay, 1985; London, Unwin Hyman, 1987.
Look into the Sun (Messenger). New York, Tor, 1989; London, Mandarin, 1990.
Wildlife. New York, Tor, 1994.

Short Stories

Heroines. Eugene, Oregon, Pulphouse, 1990.

OTHER PUBLICATIONS

Other

Writer's Workshops. Eugene, Oregon, Pulphouse, 1991.

*

James Patrick Kelly comments:

Because my tastes in reading are various, my work has been correspondingly eclectic. I've written science fiction, fantasy, horror, and mainstream fiction, as well as poetry and essays. For me, fiction begins with people; I write to explore how our histories, personal and cultural, create our behaviors. I have always felt the need to demonstrate my range, or, to put a less elegant construction on it, I rarely stay in one place for long. During the eighties when some people tried to label me a humanist, I wrote several stories that the cyberpunks claimed. I'd like to think I've absorbed at least some of the basic lessons of feminism. I'm particularly fascinated by future shock; I think our grandchildren will be as far removed from us as we are from the Pilgrims. We live in a world of accelerating change; to stand still is to invite irrelevance. If literature is the conversation a civilization has with itself, then I want to join the people who are talking about what's happening now.

*   *   *

James Patrick Kelly's name first began to appear in the science fiction magazines in the late 1970s with several short stories which examined ethical issues using the unique attributes of the field to place these in settings not available to mainstream writers. In "Death Therapy," for example, rapists are forced to undergo the actual experience of death as a deterrent to committing further crimes, and in "Not to the Swift," an aging man is compelled by circumstances to participate in a dangerous experiment involving memory recall. In both cases, Kelly forces the reader to examine the balance between the rights of the individual and the needs of society at large.

Kelly also demonstrated early a true gift for evoking strong characters and having them interact credibly, a quality too frequently absent from the works of his contemporaries. "Homo Neuter" successfully manages to remain emotionally involving without becoming overly sentimental. A mutant searches for and ultimately discovers a young boy who shares his new abilities, only to discover that having grown up in a loveless, isolated mental state, he is incapable of expressing his own emotions, ultimately destroying the chance for a strong relationship.

The survivalist mentality is examined in "Still Time." At the outset of a nuclear war, a man who had planned to retreat from human involvement finds himself incapable of ignoring the plight of his neighbors, a very optimistic story about human nature despite the tragic setting. "The Cruelest Month," only peripherally science fiction, features a successful businesswoman who finally gives in to the pressure around her and begins to hallucinate the disintegration of her world.

"St. Theresa of the Aliens" is at once a serious story and a biting satire. Aliens have landed on Earth, but since their culture is essentially communist, they choose to deal with the Russians rather than anyone else. A strong paranoid movement grows in the West to bar all contact with the aliens because of their political system. Though dated in some ways by events, the mindset Kelly describes is applicable to other issues and the essential point of the story remains.

"Freedom Beach," written in collaboration with John Kessel and later expanded into a novel by the same name, is an introspective look at human psychology which bears some resemblance to the popular television program "The Prisoner." The name refers to an island colony which appears to be a tourist resort, but which is actually home to an amnesiac who is being watched by possibly alien beings. Often surreal but always fascinating, this is one of the better expansions of a short work into book length.

Many of Kelly's short stories during the 1980s relied on surprise endings or humor, but he continued to examine serious themes. "Crow" could almost be a sequel to "Still Time." Following the nuclear war, most of those who survive doom themselves by their selfish and shortsighted activities. A visit is paid to Emily Brontë in the mildly sentimental "Empty World," and "The Cast" is a clever look at the supernatural.

Kelly's best short story to date is almost certainly "The Prisoner of Chillon," in which a reporter and a criminal penetrate the secrets of the hidden lair of a deformed genius. More recent stories of note include "The Glass Cloud," "Heroics," and "Dancing with Chairs."

Kelly's first solo novel, *Planet of Whispers,* appeared in 1984, the first in "The Messenger Chronicles," although a second book was not to be published until five years later. The Messengers are an odd star-traveling race who have been trading food to the Chani, intelligent catlike aliens whose planetary culture is dominated by instinctive behavior. One overly greedy official cuts off the food supply, and although he is recalled, it is not until after famine has devastated the planet. The protagonist is sent to spread the word that assistance is on the way, but he discovers that starvation has led to an almost communicable form of insanity, and different factions within the Chani culture ultimately resort to physical combat when the first relief ship arrives. Despite the melodramatic plot, Kelly keeps his story and his characters firmly under control, more concerned with the struggle for the loyalties of individual Chani than the physical resolution of the story.

Look into the Sun continues the story. The religious leader of Chani culture is determined to bring her people completely into the sphere of the Messengers, and she determines that the best way to do this is to sacrifice herself in a way which will symbolize the change from planetbound to interstellar culture. To this end, she employs a human being from Earth to build her tomb, and the protagonist is the architect who arrives to deal with the situation. But what he discovers there is far more than a simple job of construction; ultimately he must examine the very things which make him a human being.

Kelly's third novel, *Wildlife,* explores different territory and reflects growing preoccupation in the field with the ramifications of biotechnology. The protagonist is a young woman whose father has predesigned her personality, but who is impatient with her determination to control her own life. The world has been transformed by a technology which allows the recording of human intelligences on microchips, which can then be transferred back into bodies that have been genetically tailored to whatever specifications one desires. The ethical questions are obvious in Kelly's exploration of the nature of identity and *Wildlife* solidified the author's position as

a writer who skillfully and insightfully examines difficult questions.

Kelly's shorter fiction continued to meet his previous high standards during the early 1990s, although the most significant of these, "Chemistry," makes up a part of *Wildlife.* Other shorter pieces of note include "Pogrom," "Big Guy," and "Monsters."

The consistently high quality and thoughtful nature of Kelly's work has already resulted in several Nebula nominations. Although his novels are thoughtful, original in concept, peopled by credible characters both alien and human, and written with a clear, authoritative style, his reputation has rested primarily on short stories. Publication of *Wildlife* is likely to alter that perception, and the next few years may see Kelly emerge as a significant novelist as well.

—Don D'Ammassa

———

KENDALL, Gordon. *See* **SHWARTZ, Susan.**

———

KENNEDY, Leigh

Nationality: American. **Born:** Denver, Colorado, 4 June 1951. **Education:** Metropolitan State College, Denver, B.A. 1979. **Career:** Clerk, Rose Memorial Hospital, Denver, 1971-80; typist, Austin Community College, Austin, Texas, 1981-85. Since 1985, full-time writer. **Agent:** Ellen Levine, Ellen Levine Literary Agency, Inc., 432 Park Avenue South, Suite 1205, New York, New York 10016, U.S.A. **Address:** 78 High Street, Pewsey, Wiltshire SN9 5AQ, England.

SCIENCE FICTION PUBLICATIONS

Novel

The Journal of Nicholas the American. London, Cape, and New York, Atlantic Monthly Press, 1986.

Short Stories

Faces. London, Cape, 1986; New York, Atlantic Monthly Press, 1987.

OTHER PUBLICATIONS

Novel

Saint Hiroshima. London, Bloomsbury, 1987; San Diego, Harcourt, 1990.

*   *   *

Reading Leigh Kennedy's second novel, *Saint Hiroshima,* one might be surprised to learn that she began her professional career with sales to *Analog*. Coming completely innocent to her novels, one might not think of them as science fiction at all. So much of Kennedy's mature work might best be described as ghost stories, in the sense that they deal with people haunted by aspects of their past. "Max Haunting," which opens the collection entitled *Faces*, tells the story of Max renewing acquaintances from the hippy days, and gradually a picture appears to show the reader just why Max lost touch with these people. Typical of this author, however, is what is missing—the vital clues are there, the scene is set, but most of the "action" occurs off-stage for the reader to interpret. Even in the "hard" SF story "Helen, Whose Face Launched Twenty-Eight Conestoga Hovercraft," it is only at the end that pieces fall in, and messages are seen to have gotten through.

In her first novel, *The Journal of Nicholas The American*, Kennedy describes the emotional torment of an empath, Nicholas Dal, with an intensity that invokes memories of Silverberg's classic *Dying Inside*. Kennedy avoids the Philip Roth-isms that Silverberg includes, in favour of a double strand of concealed terror that provides the spine of the novel. The novel, in the form of Dal's diary entries, begins with an immediate note of threat, and very quickly alludes to other mysteries: "strange powers and bloody nights." Simultaneously we learn that Nicholas's family are from the Russian countryside, and that they left after some "old scandal," and there is immediate mention of the pozhar-golava—the family secret. Then Nicholas, who is in his late 20's but still a student, meets a young woman, Jack, and against his better judgement begins an affair with her.

The second half of *The Journal of Nicholas the American* is as much about Susanne, Jack's mother, as about Nicholas. Susanne is dying of multiple cancers, and she is frustrated and angry because she has nobody to talk to. Her husband is unable to cope and insists that she will recover, while banning Jack and her sister from seeing their mother alone. Somehow, Susanne and Nicholas come together, and she finds solace while he, drunk to mute the pain, listens. This is a novel composed primarily of emotions, based around love, pain, and death, and the fear of the pursuit, which results in a moving and occasionally discomforting experience.

Similarly haunting is Kennedy's second novel, *Saint Hiroshima*, which begins in 1950 in a small town in the Rockies, when five year old Katie Doheny sees a fatal road accident. The next day her parents get their first TV, and as it is tuned in Katie suddenly sees film of the Los Alamos atomic bomb, and hears the name "Hiroshima." The events are confused in her mind, creating at the same time an obsessive fear of The Bomb and a guardian angel, Saint Hiroshima.

A few years later, Katie meets Phil Benson, a talented young pianist, and they eventually become lovers, until Phil leaves for college. When he returns for the funeral of his piano teacher, he finds Katie married to Perry, a slobbish local firefighter who could offer Katie what she most desired—a bomb shelter. Phil leaves again, but in the summer of 1962 he is recalled by a desperate Katie. Their meeting almost results in tragedy as they are trapped in the shelter and almost starve.

Katie, having borne Phil's son, eventually remarries, to Louis, while Phil drifts on disillusioned. The book skips 20 years (the dates are related to key historical events, Cuba, the Civil Rights Movement, the raid on Tripoli) to find Phil working in a mediocre St. Louis theatre as a pianist and having a dangerous affair with a psychotic, gun-toting actress. As with *Nicholas the American*, Kennedy fills in elements of the intervals, without overwhelming and unnecessary detail. Phil occasionally remembers Holly, whom he lived with in Madison, and many have found her the most memo-

rable character in the book, though she only appears as a memory.

Leigh Kennedy has never been a prolific author, but, perhaps as a result of her young family, she has published only a few short stories since *St. Hiroshima* in 1987.

"Bats" is closest to the stories collected in *Faces*. A lonely woman is visited by an unusual bat on Christmas Day, and reluctant to hurt it, she nurtures it and becomes concerned for it despite her discomfort with the creatures. Then when it is joined by other bats she becomes the focus of newspaper attention and a mysterious young man arrives and calmly removes "his" bats again. The narrator feels that she has lost something with the bats gone, but within herself she has gained something and become stronger.

If there is a curious, distant eroticism about "Bats" then in another recent story, "Tropism," Kennedy considers death in relation to the bereaved with equal distance. The corpse of a woman's dead husband exhibits signs of being still animated, showing tropic responses to his former family. The effect of Kennedy's partially detached observer (the corpse's mother narrates "Tropism") is to leave doubts as to the reality of this, and thus the trauma of bereavement comes through in separate and individual responses.

Neither of these stories is truly SF, but like all of Leigh Kennedy's stories, there is an element which hints that they might just be SF. It comes through in a feeling that the bats might be an alien avatar of the narrator's own emotional state, and in the speculation about the corpse in "Tropism" being regulated by his watch. He finally dies when his watch stops. They are, by virtue of what the author leaves unwritten, partially justified ghost stories. Kennedy always seeks to observe rather than explain.

—Kev P. McVeigh

———

KENT, Gordon. *See* **TUBB, E.C.**

———

KENT, Kelvin. *See* **BARNES, Arthur K.**

———

KENT, Mallory. *See* **LOWNDES, Robert A.W.**

———

KENT, Philip. *See* **BULMER, Kenneth**

———

KERN, Gregory. *See* **TUBB, E.C.**

———

KESSEL, John (Joseph Vincent)

Nationality: American. **Born:** Buffalo, New York, 24 September 1950. **Education:** University of Rochester, B.A. in English and physics 1972 (cum laude); University of Kansas, M.A. in English 1974, Ph.D. in English 1981. **Family:** Married 1) Penelope Crews in 1975 (divorced 1980); 2) Sue Hall in 1986; one daughter. **Career:** Copy and news editor, Commodity News Service, Leawood, Kansas, 1979-82. Since 1982, Associate Professor, then Professor of creative writing and American literature, North Carolina State University, Raleigh. **Awards:** Nebula award, 1982; Theodore Sturgeon Memorial award, 1992; *Locus* award, 1992; Paul Green Playwright's prize, 1994. **Agent:** Ralph Vicinanza Ltd., 111 Eighth Avenue, Suite 1501, New York, New York 10011. **Address:** Box 8105, Department of English, North Carolina State University, Raleigh, North Carolina 27695-8105, U.S.A. **Online address:** tenshi@unity.ncsu.edu.

SCIENCE FICTION PUBLICATIONS

Novels

Freedom Beach, with James Patrick Kelly. New York, Bluejay, 1985; London, Unwin Hyman, 1987.
Good News from Outer Space. New York, Tor, 1989; London, Grafton, 1991.

Short Stories

Meetings in Infinity: Allegories and Extrapolations. Sauk City, Wisconsin, Arkham House, 1992.

OTHER PUBLICATIONS

Play

A Clean Escape (produced Raleigh, North Carolina, 1986).

*

John Kessel comments:

See the interview "An Interview with John Kessel," *Science-Fiction Studies,* Vol. 20 (1993), pp. 94-107.

*　　*　　*

The subtitle of H. Bruce Franklin's critical study of Robert A. Heinlein, "America as Science Fiction," could be applied with equal appropriateness to the work of John Kessel. Although Kessel's fiction is far removed from Heinlein's both formally and philosophically, much of Kessel's work has also been preoccupied with the American landscape, both geographic and ideological. But while Heinlein's vision of America was of a land of infinite opportunity for the superior individual, Kessel's response has been more cautionary, insisting that America is also a land whose ideals of liberty and justice have been seriously undermined by self-righteousness, violence, and greed. And in addition to dealing with the burden of the American past, Kessel has also dealt with the equally weighty

burden of the literary past, coming to terms with his authorial precursors in such metafictional fantasies as "Another Orphan" and "The Big Dream." The result has been a body of work that, although not large (two novels and approximately 30 works of short fiction), has been marked by both literary sophistication and conceptual audacity that has made Kessel one of the most highly regarded of contemporary American SF authors.

Kessel began publishing professionally in 1978. His early stories were serious and ambitious efforts that sometimes faltered under the strain of balancing the speculative element with theme and character development. While learning his craft, Kessel also began exploring the thematic territory he would map out in greater detail in his later work. "Herman Melville: Space Opera Virtuoso," an "essay" about a Herman Melville who was born in 1902 and wrote galaxy-smashing SF for the pulps, is an early example of Kessel's awareness of American literary history and particular fascination with Melville. "Uncle John and the Saviour," perhaps the best of Kessel's early stories, describes the return of Christ as an Indianapolis football player; its background of a near-future middle-America that doesn't hesitate to commercially exploit the Second Coming is expertly realized and anticipates Kessel's later work in its exploration of the irrational underside of American culture.

Kessel's breakthrough came with his 1982 novella "Another Orphan," in which he once again rewrites Melville, this time in a fantasy about a commodities broker who awakens one morning to find himself a character in *Moby-Dick.* What's worse, he's read the book and knows what's coming. As the protagonist, Patrick Fallon, struggles to come to terms with his situation, "Another Orphan" becomes an inquiry into the perennial SF topic of reality-shaping. Unlike other SF writers, however, Kessel refuses to provide his readers with easy explanations, and Fallon achieves some degree of peace only when he accepts the irrationality and contradictions of his situation, both of which are literally pounded into him by Captain Ahab: "Admit that this is not the tale you think it is! Admit that you do not know what will happen to you . . . that we are both free and unfree, alone and crowded in by circumstances in this world that we did not make, but indeed have the power to affect!" A Hugo nominee and Nebula winner, "Another Orphan" is regarded by many as one of the finest novellas of the 1980s.

Kessel continued to publish short fiction throughout the 1980s. His most notable stories from this period are "The Big Dream," a critique of the hardboiled detective genre in which a private detective finds himself turning into a character from a Raymond Chandler novel after he is hired to investigate Raymond Chandler himself; "Judgment Call," in which a minor-league baseball player at the dawn of the 21st century meets a mysterious woman who forces him to come to terms with the emotionally crippling traumas of his own past; and "The Pure Product," a violent tale of a time-traveller who, like Flannery O'Connor's Misfit, finds "no pleasure but meanness" in a world he sees as bereft of moral values and who expresses his displeasure by travelling through the past and committing random acts of violence. Although it did not receive the same level of acclaim as "Another Orphan," "The Pure Product" is equally important as a continuation of Kessel's critique of the excesses of American society—the title is taken from the first lines of William Carlos Williams' poem "To Elsie," which inform us that "The pure products of America/go crazy." The story is also, not so incidentally, the single most compelling narrative to be found in Kessel's short fiction. "The Big Dream" was incorporated into Kessel's collaboration with James Patrick Kelly, *Freedom Beach,* in which an amnesiac writer bounces back and forth between "reality" and various literary fantasies. "Judgment Call" was incorporated, along with "Credibility" and the Nebula nominee "Mrs. Shumel Exits a Winner," into Kessel's first solo novel, *Good News from Outer Space*.

A Nebula finalist and runner-up for the John W. Campbell Memorial award, *Good News from Outer Space* stands as one of the finest satirical novels modern SF has produced. It depicts the America of 1999 as a victim of both economic collapse and millennial fever. Televangelist Jimmy-Don Gilray preaches that Judgment Day will be signaled by the arrival of a giant spaceship at midnight on New Year's Eve, while George Eberhart, a reporter for a computer network equivalent of the *National Enquirer,* dashes around the country desperately trying to prove that the aliens have already landed. As such a synopsis implies, *Good News* is a very funny novel that displays Kessel's gift for comic invention much more than does his short fiction. However, *Good News* is also serious, even horrific at times; as Norman Spinrad noted in his review of the novel, *Good News* "walks a fine line between mordant farce and psychological realism." Finally, *Good News from Outer Space* is a summation of the critiques of American society that mark much of Kessel's earlier work. In the context of the novel, the comments of the mysterious woman to the baseball player of "Judgment Call" become a comment on America itself as she tells the story of a man who "forgot the second law of thermodynamics, which tells us that we all lose, and that those times when we win are merely local statistical deviations."

Kessel's work since *Good News from Outer Space* continues to voice the author's literary and social preoccupations while becoming increasingly autobiographical. In "Invaders," parallel story lines depicting the Spanish conquest of the Incas and an alien invasion of earth are linked by passages describing the author himself writing the story and, finally, entering his own fictive world. As in *Good News,* alien invasion stands as a metaphor for our own wanton destructiveness. And in "Buffalo," perhaps Kessel's best short story to date, he describes an imaginary meeting between his own father and H.G. Wells in 1934, carefully delineating both men as representative of different aspects of "the world of limitation and loss."

Kessel's fiction in the 1990s continues to voice the author's literary and social preoccupations while experimenting with different narrative strategies. In "Invaders," parallel story lines depicting the Spanish conquest of the Incas and an alien invasion of Earth are linked by passages describing the author himself writing the story and, finally, entering his own fictive world. "Buffalo" describes an imaginary meeting between Kessel's father and H.G. Wells in 1934, carefully delineating both men as representing different aspects of "the world of limitation and loss." Nominated for the Hugo and Nebula and winner of the *Locus* and Theodore Sturgeon awards, "Buffalo" is deservedly Kessel's most acclaimed story to date. In "The Franchise," also a Hugo and Nebula nominee, George Bush and Fidel Castro pursue careers in sports rather than politics and find themselves on opposing teams in the 1958 World Series. In addition to being a strikingly insightful portrait of both figures, "The Franchise" demonstrates more fully the skill at writing sports narratives Kessel displayed in "Judgement Call." "Some like It Cold" returns to the theme of "Invaders" as a time-traveler prevents Marilyn Monroe from committing suicide only to take her to a decadent future which intends to exploit her fully as much as she was in her own time. The story's innovative SF conceit—time travel automatically creates an alternate universe, so that tampering with the past will have no effect on the time-traveler's own present—is also central to Kessel's forthcoming novel, a time-travel comedy tentatively entitled *Corrupting Dr. Nice*.

In his mid-1940s, Kessel has already produced some of the finest SF of the 1980s and 1990s. There is every reason to expect that he will continue to do so.

—F. Brett Cox

KEY, Alexander (Hill)

Nationality: American. **Born:** La Plata, Maryland, 21 September 1904. **Education:** Chicago Art Institute, 1922-24. **Military Service:** Served in the United States Navy, 1942-45: Lieutenant Commander. **Family:** Married Alice Towle in 1945; one child. **Career:** Artist: book illustrator from age 19, then art teacher at Studio School of Art, Chicago; writer from 1929. **Awards:** American Association of University Women award, 1965; Lewis Carroll Shelf award, 1972. **Died:** 25 July 1979.

SCIENCE FICTION PUBLICATIONS

Novels (for children series: Sprockets; Witch Mountain)

Sprockets: A Little Robot. Philadelphia, Westminster Press, 1963.
Rivets and Sprockets. Philadelphia, Westminster Press, 1964.
The Forgotten Door. Philadelphia, Westminster Press, 1965; London, Faber, 1966.
Bolts: A Robot Dog (Sprockets). Philadelphia, Westminster Press, 1966.
Escape to Witch Mountain. Philadelphia, Westminster Press, 1968.
The Golden Enemy. Philadelphia, Westminster Press, 1969.
The Incredible Tide. Philadelphia, Westminster Press, 1970.
Flight to the Lonesome Place. Philadelphia, Westminster Press, 1971.
The Preposterous Adventures of Swimmer. Philadelphia, Westminster Press, 1973.
The Magic Meadow. Philadelphia, Westminster Press, 1975.
Jagger, The Dog from Elsewhere. Philadelphia, Westminster Press, 1976.
The Sword of Aradel. Philadelphia, Westminster Press, 1977.
Return from Witch Mountain. Philadelphia, Westminster Press, 1978.
The Case of the Vanishing Boy. New York, Archway, 1979.

OTHER PUBLICATIONS

Novels

The Wrath and the Wind. Indianapolis, Bobbs Merrill, 1949; London, Heinemann, 1950.
Island Light. Indianapolis, Bobbs Merrill, 1950; London, Heinemann, 1951.

Other (for children)

The Red Eagle. New York, Volland, 1930.
Liberty or Death. New York, Harper, 1936.
With Daniel Boone on the Caroliny Trail. Philadelphia, Winston, 1941.

Boys Will Be Boys: Very Easy Pantomimes and Entertainments for Boys. Franklin, Ohio, Eldridge, 1945.
Cherokee Boy. Philadelphia, Westminster Press, 1957.
Mystery of the Sassafras Chair. Philadelphia, Westminster Press, 1967.
The Strange White Doves: True Mysteries of Nature. Philadelphia, Westminster Press, 1972.

*   *   *

Already an established author by 1963, Alexander Key published that year *Sprockets: A Little Robot,* an unassuming story designed to attract children presumably interested in SF or space fantasy but too young for Heinlein or Norton. The story's success prompted a sequel, *Rivets and Sprockets.*

Their acceptance by young readers and reviewers alike probably encouraged Key to believe that children's SF might be both financially profitable and professionally satisfying, for in 1966 he published a third SF tale, *The Forgotten Door,* like its predecessors relatively uncomplicated in plot and simply written but more earnest in tone and theme. Subsequently, all of Key's fiction has been children's SF best characterized as a mix of narrative simplicity and moral intention.

At his best—as in *The Forgotten Door* and *Escape to Witch Mountain,* stories focusing on ESP-gifted, extraterrestrial children marooned on an inhospitable Earth and able to return home only with the help of sympathetic humans—Key creates likeable child protagonists and plausibly involves them in struggles between good and evil. Setting, reflecting the Carolina mountains Key so obviously loves, is also a strength. At his worst, Key is prone to sentimentalize, in particular overusing ESP-gifted animals that are morally superior to humans. Perhaps it is this weakness, along with relatively low-key plots and a too obvious earnestness, that has denied major status to an author who might otherwise have warranted it because of his pioneering SF for young readers.

—Francis J. Molson

KEYES, Daniel

Nationality: American. **Born:** New York City, 9 August 1927. **Education:** Brooklyn College, New York, B.A. 1950, M.A. 1961. **Military Service:** Served as a ship's purser in the maritime service, 1945-47. **Family:** Married Aurea Georgina Vaquez in 1952; two daughters. **Career:** Editorial associate, *Marvel Science Stories,* 1950-51; associate editor, Stadium Publishing Company, New York, 1951-52; co-owner, Fenko and Keyes Photography Inc., New York, 1953; high school English teacher, Brooklyn, 1954-55, 1957-62; Instructor, Wayne State University, Detroit, 1962-66. Lecturer, 1966-72, and since 1972, Professor of English, and director of creative writing, 1973-74, 1977-78, Ohio University, Athens. **Awards:** Hugo award, 1960; Nebula award, 1966. **Address:** Department of English, Ohio University, Athens, Ohio 45701, U.S.A.

SCIENCE FICTION PUBLICATIONS

Novel

Flowers for Algernon. New York, Harcourt Brace, and London, Cassell, 1966.

Novels

The Touch. New York, Harcourt Brace, 1968; London, Hale, 1971; as *The Contaminated Man,* London, Mayflower, 1977.
The Fifth Sally. Boston, Houghton Mifflin, 1980; London, Hale, 1981.

Other

The Minds of Billy Milligan. New York, Random House, 1981; London, Bantam, 1982.
Unveiling Claudia: A True Story of Serial Murder. New York, Bantam, 1986.

*

Manuscript Collection: Ohio University, Athens.

*   *   *

Rarely has a science fiction story won such widespread praise as Daniel Keyes's "Flowers for Algernon." The story has become almost universally admired in science fiction because it not only blazed new trails in narrative technique, characterization, and plot development but managed to do so without calling distracting attention to any single part. It is first and foremost a story, and none of its literary experimentation interferes with its unfolding.

The story is told from the point of view of a mentally retarded man, Charlie Gordon, who first reaches genius level through treatment with intelligence-enhancing drugs and then regresses to his original state as the effect of the drugs wears off. Much of the success of the work rests on the narrative device of presenting the entire story as a diary written by Charlie from the start of his treatment to his ultimate reversion. Since Charlie begins and ends the story as a good-natured, trusting man who by habit and desire sees only the best in his fellow human beings, the telling never descends to bathos. Even at his most brilliant, when he is able to understand fully the pettiness and cruelty of many of the people around him, Charlie refuses to judge anyone. He accepts people for what they are and avoids such labels as good or bad.

In the course of the story, Keyes raises many questions about the nature of intelligence, the benefits that may or may not arise from "improving" the human mind, and humanity's respect (or lack of respect) for genius. But he avoids trivial answers and simple generalizations. Because Charlie accepts what happens to him without anger and with a sense of dignity, these questions can be considered in all their complexity with a minimum of emotional coloring.

Keyes later turned this 30-page story into a 200-page novel. The result was predictably less happy. Keyes was forced to abandon the first-person narrative in order to deal more elaborately with the other characters. The new narrative style diminished the dramatic treatment of Charlie and his dignified faith in people. Moreover, in filling in the larger space needed for a novel, the story shifts from Charlie's experiences and his reactions to them to Charlie's development as a character. The reader was now asked to become far more attached to Charlie, and the loss of distance added greater emotional coloring to the work. The novel is about Charlie while the short story is about what happens to Charlie and the implications of these experiences for all of humanity.

Keyes has also written a number of short stories and a later novel that deal with the human mind. The novel, *The Touch,* concerns a nuclear industrial accident and its effects on the minds of the people involved. But "Flowers for Algernon" remains his best-known work. It is essential science fiction reading that proves once and for all how both science fiction and artistic merit can coexist comfortably. As science fiction the story raises disturbing questions no other genre can do more than hint at. As literature, it explores those questions in a manner that carefully, yet delightfully, guides the reader through a myriad of emotional traps.

—Stephen H. Goldman

KILIAN, Crawford

Nationality: Canadian. **Born:** New York City, 7 February 1941; naturalized Canadian citizen, 1973. **Education:** Columbia University, New York, B.A. 1962; Simon Fraser University, Burnaby, British Columbia, M.A. 1972. **Military Service:** Served in the United States Army, 1963-65. **Family:** Married Alice Hayes Fairfax in 1966; two daughters. **Career:** Library clerk, 1965-66, and technical writer, 1966-67, Lawrence Radiation Laboratory, Berkeley, California; Instructor in English, Vancouver Community College, 1967-68. Since 1968, Instructor in English, Capilano College, North Vancouver. Instructor in English, Guangzhou Institute of Foreign Languages, People's Republic of China, 1983-84; education columnist, *Vancouver Province,* 1982-94, **Agent:** Richard Curtis, 171 E. 74th St., New York, New York 10021, U.S.A. **Address:** 4635 Cove Cliff Road, North Vancouver, British Columbia V7G 1H7, Canada. **Online address:** ckilian@hubcap.mlnet.com.

SCIENCE FICTION PUBLICATIONS

Novels (series: Chronoplane Wars; Icequake)

The Empire of Time (Chronoplane Wars). New York, Ballantine, 1978; London, Legend, 1988.
Icequake. Vancouver, Douglas and McIntyre, and London, Futura, 1979; New York, Bantam, 1980.
Eyas. Toronto, McClelland and Stewart, and New York, Bantam, 1982.
Tsunami (Icequake). Vancouver, Douglas and McIntyre, 1983; New York, Bantam, 1984.
Brother Jonathan. New York, Ace, 1985.
Lifter. New York, Ace, 1986.
The Fall of the Republic: A Novel of the Chronoplane Wars. New York, Ballantine, 1987; London, Legend.
Rogue Emperor: A Novel of the Chronoplane Wars. New York, Ballantine, 1988.
Gryphon. New York, Ballantine, 1989.
Greenmagic. New York, Ballantine, 1992.
Redmagic. New York, Ballantine, 1995.

OTHER PUBLICATIONS

Plays

Radio Plays: *A Strange Manuscript Found in a Copper Cylinder,* from novel by James De Mille, 1972; *Generals Die in Bed,* from novel by Charles Yale Harrison, 1973; *Little Legion,* 1973; *Wonders, Inc.,* from his own book, 1974; *Senator Connor's Big Comeback,* 1974; *The Mob Has Got the Bomb,* 1975.

Other

Wonders, Inc. (for children). Berkeley, California, Parnassus Press, 1968.
The Last Vikings (for children). Toronto, Clarke Irwin, 1974.
Go Do Some Great Thing: The Black Pioneers of British Columbia. Vancouver, Douglas and McIntyre, and Seattle, University of Washington Press, 1978.
Exploring British Columbia's Past. Vancouver, Douglas and McIntyre, 1983.
School Wars: The Assault on B.C. Education. Vancouver, New Star Books, 1985.
20/20 Visions: The Futures of Canadian Education. Vancouver, Arsenal Pulp Press, 1995.

*

Crawford Kilian comments:

As with any civilized pleasure, that of science fiction can turn into a vice. Its persistent theme is power: over nature, over others, over oneself. And that power is most often used not to enhance and expand the capabilities of its wielders but to win for them only a return to Eden, to some primitive and unspoiled state of life. Hence so many stories about Galactic Empires based on European models from Rome to the Raj, and the fondness for interstellar societies firmly founded on the technology and economy of ninth-century France.

Like most other writers and readers of SF, I'm intrigued by the possibilities of gaining power over nature, others, and oneself; these are deeply held wish-fulfillment fantasies. But I hope I go beyond the infantile nuke-and-zap dreams of many of my colleagues. Looking back over my work, I see my novels keep dealing with the issue of the acquisition of power by the weak, not always with happy results, and with the forging of new kinds of societies composed of outcasts and those who cast them out. In Northrop Frye's sense, then, I'm a comic writer, concerned with the creation of inclusive societies rather than with the tragic isolation of people deprived of a place in society.

Given the hypnotically lulling effect of many of the conventions of SF, I take some pleasure in bending the conventions so that the reader's stock responses don't seem quite appropriate. Some of my books have "superheroes"; in *The Empire of Time* the superhero discovers his bosses consider him a mere utensil, and for good reason. In *Eyas,* an heir to a throne is raised in seclusion amid simple folk before leaving to regain his heritage; trouble is, he's also a sexual psychopath. My intention is to make readers think twice about why such stock characters are so satisfying, and to suggest that something more complex might also be more dramatically interesting.

Another element in my work is the attempt to make the marvelous seem mundane, and the mundane marvelous. People in my books have to earn their livings, sometimes by means that seem extraordinary to us, and their lives are as cluttered with domesticity as our own—even if they're trying to cross the Antarctic ice sheet, or learning how to forge a collective mind out of those of children, animals, and computers. A day in anyone's life in the 1990s would seem like the wildest Wellsian fantasy to anyone living in Wells's time, yet we take events for granted. I try to create worlds that are both strange and comfortably familiar, like my own.

*　　*　　*

Crawford Kilian's *Brother Jonathan* is an excellent example of his strengths and weaknesses as a writer. Jonathan is an athetoid, a young cripple with little control over his ruined body. He is taken to the secret laboratories of Dr. Duane Perkin, whose medical team is working with spastics to restore their mobility through the use of new polydendronic computers that simulate nerve tissue. The world Kilian describes is dominated by giant multinational corporations controlled by a consortium; nations have been merged into corporate holdings.

Perkin's project is being funded by Intertel, who is under attack in the form of a takeover bid by another multinational company, Flanders. The success of the polydendronic computers could save Intertel from a bloody merger. The computers are implanted in animals first and, when that is successful, they are implanted in Jonathan and the other spastics. Just as success is within Perkin's grasp, a Flanders assault team attacks the labs. Jonathan and his group flee into the underground caverns where they discover they have control over their bodies and psi powers. The rest of the book explores the implications of these superhuman powers, the destruction of the corporate world government, and some satiric asides about juveniles and nationalism.

Much of *Brother Jonathan* will appeal to juveniles; this should come as no surprise because Kilian has written successful juveniles: the fantastic *Wonders, Inc.,* and the nonfiction *Go Do Some Great Thing: The Black Pioneers of British Columbia.* Kilian, an American who became a naturalized Canadian citizen, lives in Vancouver, which he uses as a setting in many of his novels.

Kilian's first SF novel, *The Empire of Time,* gives us Earth in the near future where gates called I-Screens allow access to a dozen parallel Earths, both past and future. Earth governments form a super elite called Trainables and redistribute Earth's overpopulation to these Chronoplanes. Yet when two of the Future Earths are found destroyed, Jerry Pierce of the Intertemporal Agency is sent to a colonial Earth to investigate. The fast-paced action and plot carry the book, while the characters are never really developed.

Kilian expanded this concept into a series called the Chronoplane Wars. In the second book in the series, *The Fall of the Republic,* Jerry Pierce gets involved in a hackers' plot to overthrow the government based on information from the Chronoplanes. In the third book, *Rogue Emperor,* Jerry Pierce witnesses Roman Emperor Domitian's assassination by an antitank missile which is just the first step in a plot to take over one of the parallel Earths. Kilian's series is full of fast and furious action even if the plots don't quite hold together and the characters remain cardboard.

Icequake is a disaster novel in which a group of scientists and technicians are stranded when Earth's magnetic field disappears and solar flares destroy Earth's ionosphere and ozone layer. The story of survival is gripping, but again the characters are dull and wooden.

Eyas is Kilian's best novel; Kilian describes it as "a novel of parental anxiety and hope, [which] was planned and written as my wife and I raised my two daughters." Kilian sets the action 10 million years in the Earth's future. The richness of Kilian's future is exciting: humans live with nonhuman windwalkers, centaurs, and incredibly powerful whales. *Eyas* is a story of maturity as the boy Eyas grows up to save his people from the army of Brightspear. There are fantasy elements to Eyas but Kilian has carefully crafted his future to fit within science fiction realism.

Where *Icequake* concentrated on Antarctica and New Zealand, Kilian's other disaster novel, *Tsunami,* concentrates on California and Vancouver. The Antarctic icecap falls into the ocean and the resulting tidal waves flood all coastal areas. But again, the story of survival dominates without any memorable characters to hold the interest of the reader.

Kilian's latest work centers on younger characters within fantasy themes. In *Greenmagic* a young man called Dheribi finds himself in the middle of a complex plot when he defends a slave girl from a drunkard. Unfortunately, Dheribi kills the nobleman and his sentence is slavery. But the king offers him a deal: if he helps overthrow the rival city he is being sold to, the king will pardon Dheribi. Armed with his mother's mountain magic, Dheribi takes the king's challenge. Less interesting is *Redmagic,* where Calindor, a wizard, fights the overwhelming armies of the Exteca invaders.

Crawford Kilian is much more successful at science fiction than his excursions into fantasy.

—George Kelley

KILLOUGH, (Karen) Lee

Pseudonym: Sarah Hood. **Nationality:** American. **Born:** Syracuse, Kansas, 5 May 1942. **Education:** Fort Hays State College, Kansas, 1960-62; Hadley Memorial Hospital School of Radiologic technology, 1962-64. **Family:** Married Howard Patrick Killough in 1966 (died 1994). **Career:** Radiologic technologist, St. Joseph Hospital, Concordia, Kansas, 1964-65, St. Mary Hospital, Manhattan, Kansas, 1965-67, 1969-71, and Morris Cafritz Memorial Hospital, Washington, D.C., 1967-69. Since 1971, radiologic technologist, Kansas State University Veterinary Medical Teaching Hospital, Manhattan. Columnist ("Obiter Dictum"), *The Spang Blah,* 1977-79. **Address:** Box 1821, Manhattan, Kansas 66505-1821, U.S.A. **Email Address:** klkillough@aol.com.

SCIENCE FICTION PUBLICATIONS

Novels (series: Blood; Brill/Maxwell)

A Voice out of Ramah. New York, Ballantine, 1979.
The Doppelganger Gambit (Brill/Maxwell). New York, Ballantine, 1979.
The Monitor, the Miners, and the Shree. New York, Ballantine, 1980.
Deadly Silents. New York, Ballantine, 1981.
Liberty's World. New York, DAW, 1985.
Spider Play (Brill/Maxwell). New York, Warner, 1986.
The Leopard's Daughter. New York, Warner, 1987.
Blood Hunt. New York, Tor, 1987.
Bloodlinks. New York, Tor, 1988.
Dragon's Teeth (Brill/Maxwell). New York, Warner, 1990.

Short Stories

Aventine. New York, Ballantine, 1982.

*

Manuscript Collection: Department of Special Collections, University of Kansas, Lawrence.

Lee Killough comments:

I believe that, above all else, fiction should entertain. Every novel or story I write is aimed toward giving the reader enjoyment. I write what I myself would pick off a bookshelf to read. I work hard on researching and developing background and designing realistic, rounded characters. I try to satisfy the reader who might be scientifically knowledgeable. If the expert reader's enjoyment is not spoiled by glaring errors, then the science will have a ring of authenticity to the less knowledgeable reader, too. I write psychological and extrapolative science fiction, but not based so much on my background of biology and veterinary medicine as on psychology and law. Law and mystery being part of so much of my science fiction is due to a lifelong love of mysteries. By writing science fiction mysteries I can enjoy creating science fiction and a mystery at the same time. The two forms meld well and both, I think, reflect a personal belief in the power of reason and science to find answers that will ultimately help bring order to life—or pieces of life, anyway.

*   *.   *

Lee Killough made a lasting impression with her first novel, *A Voice out of Ramah,* on the surface a standard other-worlds adventure story, but with a mature development of the details of its invented society that is rare even in more experienced writers. The protagonist is a woman who arrives on a colony world dominated by a ruthless male theocracy. Using the ruse of an ancient plague, the priesthood secretly poisons the majority of males to ensure their monopoly on power. Contact with external cultures is obviously a danger to the status quo, and the plot proceeds melodramatically to a satisfactory conclusion.

Her second novel, *The Doppelganger Gambit,* is one of the growing number of novels seeking to blend science fiction themes and settings with traditional mystery techniques. Janna Brill is an assertive female police officer teamed with Mahlon "Mama" Maxwell. In an overly computerized future, they work to discover the "impossible" murder of a businessman, whose identity is known throughout to the reader. The imposition of a police procedural plot structure on a futuristic theme is effective, and the chemistry of her detective team is unusually compelling.

Killough examined an old standby of the field in her next novel, *The Monitor, the Miners, and the Shree.* Chemel Krar is responsible for ensuring that no offworld contact affect the alien Shree as they develop their own culture. When she discovers an illegal mining operation on the planet, her goal is ostensibly to expel the pirates, but her intentions become complicated when she discovers that the Shree are aware of the aliens in their midst, and actively want further contact. She must wrestle with the imperatives of her own position and the desires of the Shree themselves.

Deadly Silents is a return to mystery themes. A race of telepaths is experiencing criminal activity for the first time. They import a police force of humans to deal with the situation, and the results are often interesting, although the narrative itself is slower paced and more episodic. Brill and Maxwell returned in two subsequent novels, *Spider Play* and *Dragon's Teeth.* Both involve high technology crimes, with settings as diverse as a colony in orbit and the world of broadcasting. Both books succeed on a variety of levels, the modern equivalent of locked room mysteries with impossible crimes and well-concealed motives.

Killough has proven herself one of the most skillful at blending genres. More recently, in *Blood Hunt* and its sequel, *Bloodlinks,* she has imposed the structure of mystery fiction on the supernatural. The protagonist of both novels is a police officer who has been attacked by and transformed into a vampire. In the first volume, he attempts to control his impulses and track down the creature that assaulted him, the latter quest taken up again in the sequel. One other novel, *The Leopard's Daughter,* is unlike anything else she has written. A fantasy set in primitive Africa, it features a female warrior who braves monsters and human enemies in a journey of discovery and revenge. *Liberty's World* is another examination of the consequences of intercultural contact, the situation arising this time when a colony ship is forced to land on a world inhabited by primitive humanoids, some of whom wish to take advantage of the offworld technology to gain political advantages over their rivals.

Killough has had one collection of short stories published, entitled *Aventine.* The seven stories contain a common setting, a community of artists and scholars in the near future. "The Siren Garden" is a complex tale of intrigue and menace, with a haunting atmosphere unlike anything else Killough has written. The intricacies of the human psyche are detailed in "A House Divided," wherein a man falls in love with a schizophrenic woman and becomes a tool in the struggle between the two personalities.

Several of her uncollected stories are also noteworthy. "Caravan," an early tale, develops an alien culture and setting with a remarkable economy of words. A perilous desert crossing amidst numerous adversities provides a fast-moving plot device. Killough examines the virtues of extraterrestrial contact again in "Sentience," this time positing a situation where the arrival of humans on a world bereft of intelligent species provides the stimulus to push one lifeform across the line of demarcation.

Other short stories of note include "Achronos." An artist finds himself temporarily suspended in time along with a group of immortal refugees from the end of the world. The interaction of the characters in a cruel manipulatory game is an elaborately choreographed dance. "The Existential Man" is another detective story, this time with a murdered police officer's ghost controlling the investigation. The conflict between progress, historical preservation, and maintenance of the ecology is examined in "Taaehalaan Is Drowning." Lee Killough has been claimed by feminists as one of their own, with great justification. Most of her fiction is characterized by strong female characters, heroes and villains both. But her commitment to the equality of females is unobtrusive, and extremely effective. In her novels, the equal status of females is taken for granted. Killough avoids pendanticism, and her ability to draw her characters so well drives home her position far more effectively than a more overt approach would likely accomplish. Although she has yet to write the kind of book that would establish her as an influential voice in the field, her competent, entertaining, and generally thoughtful and intelligent books mark her as one of its most competent practitioners.

—Don D'Ammassa

KILWORTH, Garry

Pseudonym: Garry Douglas. **Nationality:** British. **Born:** York, 5 July 1941. **Education:** Khomaksar School, Aden, 1952-54; Royal Air Force Bridgenorth School, 1954-56, and Cosford Cadet School, 1956-58; H.N.C. in business studies 1974. **Family:** Married Annette Jill Bailey in 1962; one son and one daughter. **Military Service:** Served as a Signals Master in the Royal Air Force, 1959-74. **Career:** Senior executive, Cable and Wireless, London and Caribbean, 1974-82. Since 1982, freelance writer. **Agent:** Maggie Noach, 21 Redan Street, London, W14 0AB. **Address:** c/o Unwin Hyman, 77-85 Fulham Palace Road, London W6 8JB, England.

SCIENCE FICTION PUBLICATIONS

Novels (series: Angel; Woodworld)

In Solitary. London, Faber, 1977; New York, Avon, 1979.
The Night of Kadar. London, Faber, 1978; New York, Avon, 1980.
Split Second. London, Faber, 1979; New York, Popular Library, 1985.
Gemini God. London, Faber, 1981.
A Theatre of Timesmiths. London, Gollancz, 1984; New York, Popular Library, 1986.
Highlander (as Garry Douglas). London, Grafton, 1986.
The Wizard of Woodworld (for children). London, Dragon, 1987.
Abandonati. London, Unwin Hyman, 1988.
Cloudrock. London, Unwin Hyman, 1988.
The Street (as Garry Douglas). London, Grafton, 1988.
Voyage of the Vigilance (Woodworld). London, Armada, 1988.
Hunter's Moon: A Story of Foxes. London, Unwin Hyman, 1989; as *The Foxes of First Dark,* New York, Doubleday, 1990.
Midnight's Sun: A Story of Wolves. London, Unwin Hyman, 1990.
The Rain Ghost (for children). London, Hippo, 1989; New York, Scholastic, 1990.
The Drowners (for children). London, Methuen, 1991.
Frost Dancers: A Story of Hares. London, HarperCollins, 1992.
Angel. London, Gollancz, 1993.
Billy Pink's Private Detective Agency (for children). London, Methuen, 1993.
Archangel (Angel). London, Gollancz, 1994.
The Phantom Piper (for children). London, Methuen, 1994.
The Electric Kid (for children). London, Bantam, 1994; New York, Orchard, 1995.

Short Stories

The Songbirds of Pain: Stories from the Inscape. London, Gollancz, 1984.
Trivial Tales. Birmingham, England, Birmingham Science Fiction Group, 1988.
In the Hollow of the Deep-Sea Wave. London, Bodley Head, 1989.
Dark Hills, Hollow Clocks: Stories from the Other World (for children). London, Methuen, 1990.
In the Country of Tattooed Men. London, Grafton, 1993.
Hogfoot Right and Bird-Hands. Cambridge, Massachusetts, Edgewood Press, 1993.

OTHER PUBLICATIONS

Novels

Witchwater Country. London, Bodley Head, 1986.
Spiral Winds. London, Bodley Head, 1987.
The Third Dragon (for children). London, Hippo, 1991.
Standing on Shamsan. London, HarperCollins, 1992.

Poetry

Tree Messiah. Newport, Envoi Poets, 1985.

*

Garry Kilworth comments:

I am not greatly interested in the "science" in Science Fiction. I am more concerned with unusual societies, anthropological aspects, social misfits, and exotic cultures. The issues might be contemporary, as I feel they are in *A Theatre of Timesmiths,* or universal, ageless questions such as the nurture-nature theme of *In Solitary.* I wish to explore the ordinary human spirit in a stressful state of adversity, and in its relationship to the natural world. I write science fiction and fantasy because their imaginative scope allows me more sweep than would mainstream fiction. Mysticism, including religions of all kinds, forms a thread through my work. On the entertainment level I find the best vehicle for carrying these themes is the adventure novel. In a sentence: jungles, deserts, wastelands and the man-a-lost looking for himself.

*   *   *

Characterisation has always been the strongest facet of Garry Kilworth's writing. The science fiction ideas in his work are usually secondary to the humane portrayals of his protagonists, yet his subject matter has been widely varied.

His first, rather slender novel, *In Solitary,* depicts an Earth conquered by the bird-like alien Soal, who rule by separating man from his fellow man . . . and woman. It's a tautly told yet subtle story of human courage and ingenuity, much of it set in the South Sea Islands. *The Night of Kadar* is the richest of Kilworth's early novels, drawing upon the Koran for its inspiration. A starship lands on a new world and settlers—awakened and matured from their pre-frozen embryonic state—struggle to understand their purpose on the planet, unaware of the malfunction in the machinery that ought to have instructed them. The story of the building of a land bridge and the encounter with the aliens is engrossing, but one remembers far more clearly the characters of Othman, Zayid, and, particularly, the divine idiot, Fdar. *Split Second* saw Kilworth give the Jekyll and Hyde tale a new twist as experiments with the Wiederhaus Repeater—an archaeological tool used to hologrammatically reanimate objects from the past—accidentally send a young boy, Richard, 33,000 years into the past, where he shares the mind and experiences of a juvenile boy from that time, Esk. Though an ambitious idea, it doesn't quite succeed in evoking a sense of that far distant past, but the storytelling itself is first class. *Gemini God* charts the degeneration of the human race and its attempts to solve its problems through alien contact. Another strand of the novel—empathic contact between identical twins—provides a more interesting storyline, with its examination of the nature and work of the artist. Kilworth's fifth novel, *A Theatre of*

Timesmiths, was, curiously enough, one of his best written and yet least successful works. An enclosed environment tale, it suffers from having all taken place in its chief character's head; moreover, Morag is the least sympathetic of Kilworth's main characters, and her predicament involves us only marginally. That said, Kilworth's evocation of the world inside the ice is remarkably vivid.

The first collection of Kilworth's short fiction, *The Songbirds of Pain,* contains stories published over the nine years preceding its publication. The best of them, like "Sumi Dreams Of A Paper Frog" and "The Songbirds Of Pain" are exceptional, almost fabular works, and even the least of them—"The Dissemblers" and "Let's Go to Golgotha" (which won Kilworth the *Sunday Times* Best SF Story competition in 1975)—are of a high standard.

For his next two novels, *Witchwater Country* and *Spiral Winds,* Kilworth moved away from overt genre concerns to produce what are, perhaps, his finest works, strong both in characterization and sense of place. His return to SF, *Cloudrock,* however, proved less successful. Once again we are presented with an enclosed environment, this time the great Cloudrock itself, a coral island raised like a giant mushroom high above the dried-up bed of the ocean. There the tribes of night and day eke out their lives in an unquestioning round, until the shadow—our narrator, a misformed outcast, permitted existence—brings violent change. As in *In Solitary,* with which it bears curious affinities, the potential richness of this metaphor isn't really tapped, though the character Shadow remains a haunting presence long after the tale has ended. *Abandonati* is again memorable more for its characters than its ideas. Set in a run-down near-future abandoned to the street people, Guppy, the "abandonati" of the title, accompanied by the gentle black giant, Trader, sets out to find where all the rich people went. Not Kilworth's most welcoming book, it has a savage richness and humor that distinguishes it from his other novel-length works.

Kilworth's excursions into "animal" novels, *Hunter's Moon* and *Midnight's Sun,* are much more than the usual animals-as-speaking-humans fare; they disdain the usual anthropomorphic tendencies of this subgenre. The detailed research behind both books is telling (without overwhelming the storyline), and Kilworth's robust enjoyment of the savage animal natures of his protagonists raises these two distinct (yet dovetailing) novels to a point somewhere between realism and fable.

The last several years have seen a wide diversification in Kilworth's writing and a movement away from the overtly science fictional subject matter of his first decade. His attempts to create superior juvenile fiction are proving very interesting, producing work which, as in the collection *Dark Hills, Hollow Clocks,* is as resonant as his best SF short fiction. It remains to be seen, however, whether the lessons learned in these excursions can be channelled into his longer SF work.

—David Wingrove

KING, Ray. *See* CUMMINGS, Ray.

KING, Vincent

Pseudonym for Rex Thomas Vinson. **Nationality:** British. **Born:** Falmouth, Cornwall, 22 October 1935. **Education:** Redruth School of Art, Cornwall; Falmouth College of Art, Cornwall, 1952-57; West of England College of Art, Bristol, 1959-60; University of London, 1960-62. **Military Service:** Served in the Royal Air Force. **Family:** Married Jean Blackler in 1961 (divorced 1978); one son and one daughter. **Career:** Art teacher in schools in London, Bristol, Newcastle upon Tyne, 1963-68, and since 1968 in Redruth. Painter and printmaker; work in several Arts Council exhibitions. **Agent:** Carnell Literary Agency, Danes Croft, Gooselane, Little Hallingburg, Herts. CM22 7RG, England.

SCIENCE FICTION PUBLICATIONS

Novels

Light a Last Candle. New York, Ballantine, 1969; London, Rapp and Whiting, 1970.
Another End. New York, Ballantine, 1971.
Candy Man. London, Gollancz, 1971; New York, Ballantine, 1971.
Time Snake and Superclown. London, Orbit, 1976.

*

Vincent King comments:

I've no explicit intentions, political or philosophical, but considerations of that type keep coming out of the words. The intention is fantasy, a succession of ideas, events, relationships that change, further and further revelations about the situation/plot/story. Naturally this makes for ever-increasing complexity and a continual raising of the stakes (I'm sometimes deeply shocked by what I write!), maybe for incomprehensibility, too. I often include more or less direct quotations from "reality." (Which is interchangeable with "fiction" anyway; reality is fantasy, fantasised by going through people's heads, and it doesn't matter how objective/pragmatic they say they are—that's fantasy too.) I tend to use the first person because I fantasise that it's more direct. Also it means the voice that tells the story doesn't know what's to happen, is happening. I also fantasise that it allows the fantasy to develop in a less inhibited way. The freedom of fantasy is the thing.

I think the most exciting writing today is on the fantasy end of the spectrum. I'm not speaking only of what is referred to as SF or occult writing. It's interesting that at a time when a lot of SF authors claim to be trying to "go straight," some good so-called mainstream writing seems to be turning more fantastic. What is finished, I think, for a more or less serious SF writer, is the "science" type of SF, and I think the middle-class "Hobbit" type of adventure is pretty sterile too. To me science is a type of magic—or at least that's how I use it. Science is not holy, it's practical; it's probably caused no more suffering, or release from suffering, than religions. Religions, wars, science, adultery, murders, etc. are what happen when people aren't allowed or aren't able to be creative in some way: to work out their personal fantasy, which might be a garden, or a fortune, or a model steam locomotive, or anything!

*   *   *

Suspense is a major element in all the works of Vincent King. In part, he develops suspense through the ordinary means—surprising and very quick-paced action—which keep the reader wondering what will come next. But here is also a more intellectual type of suspense which may be regarded as one of the distinguishing marks of King's work. This type of suspense also develops in two ways. First, a sort of jigsaw puzzle effect means that, in the beginning of his novels, it is often difficult to see how the various parts relate to one another. What is the connection between Ice Lover and the Mods (*Light a Last Candle*)? The reader must hold numbers of pieces in his mind, gradually fitting them together into a clear, comprehensive picture. Second, his characters have a certain enigmatic quality about them. One's curiosity is aroused because it isn't clear just who or what the protagonist is. Only near the end of the novel is the identity of Candy Man revealed.

Space exploration, the attempt to find and contact other sentient life, is a theme which King plays in a different key. Working within a long-time scheme, expending vast resources, man may just possibly find some sentient life form. Adamson finds Protia (*Another End*) after all hope has been abandoned. In *Candy Man* the failure is absolute. But even success may bring strange results. Protia ultimately absorbs Adamson, and the alien beings in *Light a Last Candle* have unsuccessfully attempted to absorb an entire colony of Earthmen. Mankind is unavoidably changed by contact with aliens.

But mankind is portrayed in a decadent state throughout King's novels. The glorious past is gone, while a few men live enervated lives among the ruins. The image of those ruins, vast cities covering entire worlds, has a central place for King. His heroes, regularly isolated (or at most accompanied by a single companion) in these vast, hive-like structures, seem compelled to explore the cellars, the subterranean depths of their worlds. Both Adamson and Candy Man are involved in extensive chase scenes in these labyrinthine depths. Ice Lover lives and fights in caves. Man, as he declines, seems to be portrayed as returning to his roots, the cave, the sea, the womb. Interestingly, the machines have held up better than their creators. The Probe keeps Adamson alive, frustrating his every suicide attempt. The entire population of Earth may have been maintained by machines (*Candy Man*) or resurrected by a computer (*Another End*). In some sense dependence upon machines has led humanity into decadence. Only if they can shake free of the machines will there be some slight hope of renewal.

Each of King's novels deals with the human proclivity to violence; all his heroes are killers who seem to enjoy killing. But in the final analysis the violence seems to be shown as both pointless and ineffective, a serious defect that men must overcome if they are to survive and advance. The conclusions of *Another End* and *Candy Man* hold out some slight hope of this.

King's greatest strength, his highly imaginative permutations upon conventional themes, combines with his ability to create suspense to produce works which fascinate and puzzle the reader. Yet these strengths are somewhat offset by a style of writing heavily dependent upon dialogue which has a rather choppy and unsophisticated quality.

—Robert Reilly

KINGSBURY, Donald (MacDonald)

Nationality: Canadian. **Born:** San Francisco, California, 12 February 1929; became Canadian citizen. **Education:** Schools in Japan, New Guinea, California, and New Hampshire; McGill University, Montreal, B.Sc. 1956, M.Sc. 1960. **Family:** Married Mireille Kingsbury in 1950 (divorced 1960); two sons. **Career:** Since 1956, Lecturer in Mathematics, McGill University. **Awards:** Compton Crook award, 1983. **Agent:** Eleanor Wood, 111 Eighth Avenue, Suite 1501, New York, New York 10011, U.S.A.

SCIENCE FICTION PUBLICATIONS

Novels

Courtship Rite. New York, Timescape, 1982; as *Geta,* London, Panther, 1984.
The Moon Goddess and the Son. New York, Baen, 1987; London, Grafton, 1988.

Also author of *The Survivor,* 1991, and *The Heroic Myth of Lieutenant Nora Argamentine,* 1994.

*

Donald Kingsbury comments:

I make up my backgrounds and test them for plausibility before I throw my characters into them—to manage as best they can. I have a preference for "fleet footed" males and females and odd cultures. I tend to write in a single future universe: *The Moon Goddess and the Son* is from its near future phase and *Courtship Rite* from 2000 or so years away.

* * *

Although Donald Kingsbury published his first short story in 1952 and wrote science articles for *Analog* in the second half of the 1970s, it was with three novelettes published in that magazine in 1978-79 that he became widely known. All three were anthologized the following year, giving Kingsbury his reputation as one of the most promising and interesting writers of technically oriented science fiction.

"To Bring In the Steel," the best of the three, dramatizes the efforts of a private consortium in the next century to maneuver an asteroid into Earth orbit while refining its rich ore into salable metals. The protagonist is a lonely, independent, supercompetent man—the model Kingsbury hero—whose misogyny and fixed ideas on government and entrepreneurship are, as in all Kingsbury's short works to date, rather implausibly validated by the story's action. The story's clean dramatic line and crisp pacing combine effectively with Kingsbury's ability to render the details of an operating space industry, and largely overcome his insistent division of the sexes into hard-headed men and childlike, undisciplined women. Less successful are "Shipwright" and "The Moon Goddess and the Son," where Kingsbury's indulgent attitude toward the engineer-hero and his recurrent theme of courtesanship as a woman's best chance of getting ahead in a world of more rational-minded men hang heavily upon the less dramatic and loosely constructed story lines. Notable in "The Moon Goddess and the Son" and "To Bring In the Steel" is Kingsbury's boosterism of space industry and of the use of space for Western strategic defense, in furtherance of which Kingsbury appears willing to suspend the critical scrutiny he brings to other technical problems and give both subjects an idealized gloss.

Courtship Rite, Kingsbury's first novel, represents a surprising advance in skill over his early stories. Kingsbury's far-ranging story of intrigue among human settlers on a resource-poor planet displays an impressive ability to present a complex plot through multiple points of view, and represents a departure in allowing the fair expression of differing ideologies without betraying the author's sympathies.

Geta, an earthlike planet with relatively arid inlands and almost no native animal life, was settled in some distant past by humans who have lost most of their technology as well as their history, and blindly worship their visible, still-orbiting ship. Cannibalism, originally practiced because of ubiquitous protein deficiencies, now serves a complex social function even as scientific advances threaten to render it unnecessary. The main thread of the story line involves a group marriage of three politically influential men and two women, who are forbidden to marry a third woman of their choice and ordered for political reasons to court a heretical pacifist of growing influence in a region over which their leader seeks hegemony. The pacifist, a visionary who preaches a rather Ghandi-like commitment to social revolution without violence, is convincingly and sympathtically portrayed. The decision of her suitors to subject her to a Death Rite—under which they might legally challenge her to a series of putative tests of fitness that will almost certainly ensure her death—provides the springboard for the story's action.

The novel's length, complexity of intrigue, and setting prompt comparison with *Dune,* which Kingsbury audaciously invites with his visionary and ecological themes as well as the device of using numerous fictive "texts" as chapter epigraphs. *Courtship Rite*'s remarkable success in withstanding such comparison and in conveying its own sense of genuine exhilaration is an achievement in itself, and augurs well for Kinsbury's future work.

In the dozen years following the appearance of *Courtship Rite,* Kingsbury published *The Moon Goddess and the Son* (1987), an expansion of his 1979 novella, as well as two novels set in the Known Space universe of Larry Niven, *The Survivor* (1991) and its sequel, *The Heroic Myth of Lieutenant Nora Argamentine* (1994). *The Moon Goddess and the Son* dramatizes humanity's spread into space with technological zeal and romantic coloratura; as with his earlier works, Kingsbury leaves little question where his own sympathies lie in any given scene. The two Man-Kzin novels devote great attention to the tactics of interstellar war and the complications of relativistic space flight, but are indifferently written and betray a consistent hostility towards women. Although Kingsbury has no problem about portraying capable and intelligent women, they are invariably presented exclusively in terms of their relationship to a powerful man (often "Daddy" or an older lover). These short novels also demonstrate, with uncomfortable clarity, Kingsbury's disposition to contrive appalling humiliations for these women.

Kingsbury is reportedly completing a sequel to *Courtship Rite,* as well as a work set earlier in the world's chronology. The fact that he has spent the last 15 years writing works set in already-existing venues, rather than creating new ones, may account for their lack of imaginative freshness. As this quality has proven Kingsbury's most effective counterweight to his dogmatism and misogyny, it seems one he can ill afford to lose.

—Gregory Feeley

KIPLING, (Joseph) Rudyard

Nationality: British. **Born:** Bombay, India, 30 December 1865, of English parents; moved to England, 1872. **Education:** United Ser-

vices College, Westward Ho!, Devon, 1878-82. **Family:** Married Caroline Starr Balestier in 1892; two daughters and one son. **Career:** Assistant editor, *Civil and Military Gazette,* Lahore, 1882-87; assistant editor and overseas correspondent, *Pioneer,* Allahabad, 1887-89; full-time writer from 1889; lived in London, 1889-92, and Brattleboro, Vermont, 1892-96, then returned to England; settled in Burwash, Sussex, 1902. Rector, University of St. Andrews, 1922-25. **Awards:** Nobel Prize for Literature, 1907; Royal Society of Literature Gold Medal, 1926. LL.D.: McGill University, Montreal, 1907; D.Litt.: University of Durham, 1907; Oxford University, 1907; Cambridge University, 1907; University of Edinburgh, 1920; the Sorbonne, Paris, 1921; University of Strasbourg, 1921; D.Phil.: University of Athens, 1924. Honorary Fellow, Magdalene College, Cambridge, 1932. **Member:** Associate member, Académie des Sciences Morales et Politiques, 1933. Refused the Poet Laureateship, 1895, and the Order of Merit. **Died:** 18 January 1936.

SCIENCE FICTION PUBLICATIONS

Novels

They. New York, Scribner, 1904.
With the Night Mail: A Story of 2000 A.D. (Together with Extracts from the Contemporary Magazine in Which It Appeared). London, Macmillan, 1909.

Short Stories

Actions and Reactions. London, Macmillan, and New York, Doubleday, 1909.
A Diversity of Creatures. London, Macmillan, and New York, Doubleday, 1917.
The Complete Supernatural Stories of Rudyard Kipling, edited by Peter Haining. London, Allen, 1987.

OTHER PUBLICATIONS

Novel

The Light That Failed. New York, United States Book Company, 1890; London, Macmillan, 1891.

Short Stories

Plain Tales from the Hills. Calcutta, Thacker Spink, 1888; New York, Lovell, and London, Macmillan, 1890.
Soldiers Three: A Collection of Stories. Allahabad, Wheeler, 1888; London, Sampson Low, 1890.
The Stories of the Gadsbys: A Tale Without a Plot. Allahabad, Wheeler, 1888; London, Sampson Low, and New York, Lovell, 1890.
In Black and White. Allahabad, Wheeler, 1888; London, Sampson Low, and New York, Lovell, 1890.
Under the Deodars. Allahabad, Wheeler, 1888; revised edition, London, Sampson Low, 1890.
The Phantom Rickshaw and Other Tales. Allahabad, Wheeler, 1888; revised edition, London, Sampson Low, 1890.
Wee Willie Winkie and Other Child Stories. Allahabad, Wheeler, 1888; revised edition, London, Sampson Low, and Chicago, Rand McNally, 1890.

Soldiers Three, and Under the Deodars. New York, Lovell, 1890.

The Phantom Rickshaw, and Wee Willie Winkie. New York, Lovell, 1890.

The Courting of Dinah Shadd and Other Stories. New York, Harper, and London, Macmillan, 1890.

Mine Own People. New York, United States Book Company, 1891.

Life's Handicap, Being Stories from Mine Own People. New York and London, Macmillan, 1891.

The Naulahka: A Story of West and East, with Wolcott Balestier. London, Heinemann, and New York, Macmillan, 1892.

Many Inventions. London, Macmillan, and New York, Appleton, 1893.

Soldier Tales. London, Macmillan, 1896; as *Soldier Stories,* New York, Macmillan, 1896.

The Day's Work. New York, Doubleday, and London, Macmillan, 1898.

The Kipling Reader. London, Macmillan, 1900; as *Selected Stories,* 1925.

Traffics and Discoveries. London, Macmillan, and New York, Doubleday, 1904.

Abaft the Funnel. New York, Dodge, 1909.

Selected Stories, edited by William Lyon Phelps. New York, Doubleday, 1921.

Debits and Credits. London, Macmillan, and New York, Doubleday, 1926.

Selected Stories. London, Macmillan, 1929.

Thy Servant a Dog, Told by Boots. London, Macmillan, and New York, Doubleday, 1930; revised edition, as *Thy Servant a Dog and Other Dog Stories,* Macmillan, 1938.

Humorous Tales. London, Macmillan, and New York, Doubleday, 1931.

Animal Stories. London, Macmillan, 1932; New York, Doubleday, 1938.

Limits and Renewals. London, Macmillan, and New York, Doubleday, 1932.

All the Mowgli Stories. London, Macmillan, 1933; New York, Doubleday, 1936.

Collected Dog Stories. London, Macmillan, and New York, Doubleday, 1934.

More Selected Stories. London, Macmillan, 1940.

Twenty-One Tales. London, Reprint Society, 1946.

Ten Stories. London, Pan, 1947.

A Choice of Kipling's Prose, edited by W. Somerset Maugham. London, Macmillan, 1952; as *Maugham's Choice of Kipling's Best: Sixteen Stories,* New York, Doubleday, 1953.

A Treasury of Short Stories. New York, Bantam, 1957.

Short Stories, edited by Edward Parone. New York, Dell, 1960.

Kipling Stories: Twenty-Eight Exciting Tales. New York, Platt and Munk, 1960.

The Best Short Stories, edited by Randall Jarrell. New York, Hanover House, 1961; as *In the Vernacular: The English in India* and *The English in England,* New York, Doubleday, 2 vols., 1963.

Famous Tales of India, edited by B.W. Shir-Cliff. New York, Ballantine, 1962.

Phantoms and Fantasies: 20 Tales. New York, Doubleday, 1965.

Short Stories, edited by Andrew Rutherford. London, Penguin, 2 vols., 1971-76.

Twenty-One Tales, edited by Tim Wilkinson. London, Folio Society, 1972.

Tales of East and West, edited by Bernard Bergonzi. Avon, Connecticut, Limited Editions Club, 1973.

Kipling's Kingdom: Twenty-Five of Kipling's Best Indian Stories, Known and Unknown, edited by Charles Allen. London, Joseph, 1987.

Fiction (for children)

The Jungle Book, illustrated by J. Lockwood Kipling and others. London, Macmillan, and New York, Century, 1894.

The Second Jungle Book, illustrated by J. Lockwood Kipling. London, Macmillan, and New York, Century, 1895; revised edition, Macmillan, 1895.

"Captains Courageous": A Story of the Grand Banks, illustrated by I.W. Taber. London, Macmillan, and New York, Century, 1897.

Stalky & Co. London, Macmillan, and New York, Doubleday, 1899; revised edition, as *The Complete Stalky & Co.,* Macmillan, 1929, Doubleday, 1930.

Kim, illustrated by J. Lockwood Kipling. New York, Doubleday, and London, Macmillan, 1901.

Just So Stories for Little Children, illustrated by the author. London, Macmillan, and New York, Doubleday, 1902.

Puck of Pook's Hill, illustrated by H.R. Millar. London, Macmillan, and New York, Doubleday, 1906.

Kipling Stories and Poems Every Child Should Know, edited by Mary E. Burt and W.T. Chapin, illustrated by Charles Livingston Bull and others. New York, Doubleday, 1909.

Rewards and Fairies, illustrated by Frank Craig. London, Macmillan, and New York, Doubleday, 1910.

Land and Sea Tales for Scouts and Guides. London, Macmillan, and New York, Doubleday, 1923.

Ham and the Porcupine. New York, Doubleday, 1935.

Play

The Harbour Watch (produced London, 1913; revised version, as *Gow's Watch,* produced London, 1924).

Poetry

Schoolboy Lyrics. Privately printed, 1881.

Echoes (published anonymously), with Alice Kipling. Privately printed, 1884.

Departmental Ditties and Other Verses. Lahore, Civil and Military Gazette Press, 1886; London, Thacker Spink, 1890.

Departmental Ditties, Barrack-Room Ballads, and Other Verse. New York, United States Book Company, 1890.

Barrack-Room Ballads and Other Verses. London, Methuen, and New York, Macmillan, 1892.

Ballads and Barrack-Room Ballads. New York, Macmillan, 1893.

The Seven Seas. New York, Appleton, and London, Methuen, 1896.

Recessional. Privately printed, 1897.

An Almanac of Twelve Sports, illustrated by William Nicholson. London, Heinemann, and New York, Russell, 1898.

Poems, edited by Wallace Rice. Chicago, Star, 1899.

Recessional and Other Poems. Privately printed, 1899.

The Absent-Minded Beggar. Privately printed, 1899.

With Number Three, Surgical and Medical, and *New Poems.* Santiago, Chile, Hume, 1900.

Occasional Poems. Boston, Bartlett, 1900.

The Five Nations. London, Methuen, and New York, Doubleday, 1903.

The Muse Among the Motors. New York, Doubleday, 1904.

A Collected Verse. New York, Doubleday, 1907; London, Hodder and Stoughton, 1912.

A History of England (verse only), with C.R.L. Fletcher. London, Oxford University Press-Hodder and Stoughton, and New York, Doubleday, 1911; revised edition, 1930.

Songs from Books. New York, Doubleday, 1912; London, Macmillan, 1913.

Twenty Poems. London, Methuen, 1918.

The Years Between. London, Methuen, and New York, Doubleday, 1919.

Verse: Inclusive Edition 1885-1918. London, Hodder and Stoughton, and New York, Doubleday, 3 vols., 1919; revised edition, 1921, 1927, 1933.

A Kipling Anthology: Verse. London, Methuen, and New York, Doubleday, 1922.

Songs for Youth, from Collected Verse. London, Hodder and Stoughton, 1924; New York, Doubleday, 1925.

A Choice of Songs. London, Methuen, 1925.

Sea and Sussex. London, Macmillan, and New York, Doubleday, 1926.

St. Andrews, with Walter de la Mare. London, A. and C. Black, 1926.

Songs of the Sea. London, Macmillan, and New York, Doubleday, 1927.

Poems 1886-1929. London, Macmillan, 3 vols., 1929; New York, Doubleday, 3 vols., 1930.

Selected Poems. London, Methuen, 1931.

East of Suez, Being a Selection of Eastern Verses. London, Macmillan, 1931.

Sixty Poems. London, Hodder and Stoughton, 1939.

Verse: Definitive Edition. London, Hodder and Stoughton, and New York, Doubleday, 1940.

So Shall Ye Reap: Poems for These Days. London, Hodder and Stoughton, 1941.

A Choice of Kipling's Verse, edited by T.S. Eliot. London, Faber, 1941; New York, Scribner, 1943.

Sixty Poems. London, Hodder and Stoughton, 1957.

A Kipling Anthology, edited by W.G. Bebbington. London, Methuen, 1964.

The Complete Barrack-Room Ballads, edited by Charles Carrington. London, Methuen, 1973.

Kipling's English History: Poems, edited by Marghanita Laski. London, BBC Publications, 1974.

Kipling: A Selection, edited by James Cochrane. London, Penguin, 1977.

Early Verse by Rudyard Kipling 1879-89, edited by Andrew Rutherford. Oxford, Clarendon Press, and New York, Oxford University Press, 1986.

Other

Quarette, with others. Lahore, Civil and Military Gazette Press, 1885.

The City of Dreadful Night and Other Sketches. Allahabad, Wheeler, 1890.

The City of Dreadful Night and Other Places. Allahabad, Wheeler, and London, Sampson Low, 1891.

The Smith Administration. Allahabad, Wheeler, 1891.

Letters of Marque. Allahabad, Wheeler, and London, Sampson Low, 1891.

American Notes, with *The Bottle Imp,* by Robert Louis Stevenson. New York, Ivers, 1891.

Out of India: Things I Saw, and Failed to See, in Certain Days and Nights at Jeypore and Elsewhere. New York, Dillingham, 1895.

The Kipling Birthday Book, edited by Joseph Finn. London, Macmillan, 1896; New York, Doubleday, 1899.

A Fleet in Being: Notes of Two Trips with the Channel Squadron. London, Macmillan, 1898.

From Sea to Sea: Letters of Travel. New York, Doubleday, 1899; as *From Sea to Sea and Other Sketches,* London, Macmillan, 1900.

Works (Swastika Edition). New York, Doubleday, Appleton, and Century, 15 vols., 1899.

Letters to the Family (Notes on a Recent Trip to Canada). Toronto, Macmillan, 1908.

The Kipling Reader (not same as 1900 collection of short stories). New York, Appleton, 1912.

The New Army in Training. London, Macmillan, 1915.

France at War. London, Macmillan, and New York, Doubleday, 1915.

The Fringes of the Fleet. London, Macmillan, and New York, Doubleday, 1915.

Tales of "The Trade." Privately printed, 1916.

Sea Warfare. London, Macmillan, and New York, Doubleday, 1916.

The War in the Mountains. New York, Doubleday, 1917.

To Fighting Americans (speeches). Privately printed, 1918.

The Eyes of Asia. New York, Doubleday, 1918.

The Graves of the Fallen. London, Imperial War Graves Commission, 1919.

Letters of Travel (1892-1913). London, Macmillan, and New York, Doubleday, 1920.

A Kipling Anthology: Prose. London, Macmillan, and New York, Doubleday, 1922.

The Irish Guards in the Great War. London, Macmillan, and New York, Doubleday, 2 vols., 1923.

Works (Mandalay Edition). New York, Doubleday, 26 vols., 1925-26.

A Book of Words: Selections from Speeches and Addresses Delivered Between 1906 and 1927. London, Macmillan, and New York, Doubleday, 1928.

The One Volume Kipling. New York, Doubleday, 1928.

Souvenirs of France. London, Macmillan, 1933.

A Kipling Pageant. New York, Doubleday, 1935.

Something of Myself for My Friends Known and Unknown. London, Macmillan, and New York, Doubleday, 1937.

Complete Works (Sussex Edition). London, Macmillan, 35 vols., 1937-39; as *Collected Works* (Burwash Edition), New York, Doubleday, 28 vols., 1941 (includes revised versions of some previously published works).

A Kipling Treasury: Stories and Poems. London, Macmillan, 1940.

Kipling: A Selection of His Stories and Poems, edited by John Beecroft. New York, Doubleday, 2 vols., 1956.

The Kipling Sampler, edited by Alexander Greendale. New York, Fawcett, 1962.

Letters from Japan, edited by Donald Richie and Yoshimori Harashima. Tokyo, Kenkyusha, 1962.

Pearls from Kipling, edited by C. Donald Plomer. New Britain, Connecticut, Elihu Burritt Library, 1963.

Rudyard Kipling to Rider Haggard: The Record of a Friendship, edited by Morton Cohen. London, Hutchinson, 1965; Rutherford, New Jersey, Fairleigh Dickinson University Press, 1968.

The Best of Kipling. New York, Doubleday, 1968.

Stories and Poems, edited by Roger Lancelyn Green. London, Dent, 1970.

Kipling's Horace, edited by Charles Carrington. London, Methuen, 1978.

American Notes: Rudyard Kipling's West, edited by Arrell M. Gibson. Norman, University of Oklahoma Press, 1981.

The Portable Kipling, edited by Irving Howe. New York, Viking Press, 1982.

"O Beloved Kids": Rudyard Kipling's Letters to His Children, edited by Elliot L. Gilbert. London, Weidenfeld and Nicolson, 1983; New York, Harcourt Brace, 1984.

Kipling's India: Uncollected Sketches 1884-1888, edited by Thomas Pinney. London, Macmillan, and New York, Schocken, 1985.

The Illustrated Kipling, edited by Neil Philip. London, Collins, 1987.

A Choice of Kipling's Prose, edited by Craig Raine. London, Faber, 1987.

Kipling's Japan, edited by Hugh Cortazzi and George Webb. London, Athlone Press, 1988.

Editor, *The Irish Guards in the Great War.* London, Macmillan, and New York, Doubleday, 2 vols., 1923.

*

Bibliography: *Rudyard Kipling: A Bibliography Catalogue* by James McG. Stewart, edited by A. W. Keats, Toronto, Dalhousie University-University of Toronto Press, 1959, London, Oxford University Press, 1960; "Kipling: An Annotated Bibliography of Writings about Him" by H.E. Gerber and E. Lauterbach, in *English Fiction in Transition 3* (Tempe, Arizona), 1960, and *8,* 1965.

Manuscript Collections: Cornell University Library, Ithaca, New York; Library of Congress, Washington, D.C.; Houghton Library, Harvard University, Cambridge, Massachusetts; Pierpont Morgan Library, New York.

Critical Studies (selection): *Rudyard Kipling: His Life and Work* by Charles Carrington, London, Macmillan, 1955, revised edition, 1978, as *The Life of Rudyard Kipling,* New York, Doubleday, 1955; *Rudyard Kipling* by Rosemary Sutcliff, London, Bodley Head, 1960, New York, Walck, 1961; *The Readers' Guide to Rudyard Kipling's Work,* Canterbury, Gibbs, 1961, and *Kipling: The Critical Heritage,* London, Routledge, and New York, Barnes and Noble, 1971, both edited by Roger Lancelyn Green, and *Kipling and the Children* by Green, London, Elek, 1965; *Kipling's Mind and Art* edited by Andrew Rutherford, Edinburgh, Oliver and Boyd, and Stanford, California, Stanford University Press, 1964; *Rudyard Kipling* by J.I.M. Stewart, London, Gollancz, and New York, Dodd Mead, 1966; *Rudyard Kipling: Realist and Fabulist* by Bonamy Dobrée, London and New York, Oxford University Press, 1967; *Kipling and His World* by Kingsley Amis, London, Thames and Hudson, 1975, New York, Scribner, 1976; *The Strange Ride of Rudyard Kipling: His Life and Works* by Angus Wilson, London, Secker and Warburg, 1977, New York, Viking Press, 1978; *Rudyard Kipling* by Lord Birkenhead, London, Weidenfeld and Nicolson, 1978; *Rudyard Kipling* by James Harrison, Boston, Twayne, 1982; *Rudyard Kipling and the Fiction of Adolescence* by Robert F. Moss, New York, St. Martin's Press, and London, Macmillan, 1982; *Kipling: Interviews and Recollections* edited by Harold Orel, London, Macmillan, 2 vols., 1983, New York, Barnes and Noble, 2 vols., 1984; *A Kipling Companion* by Norman Page, London, Macmillan, 1984; *Kipling and Orientalism* by B.J. Moore-Gilbert, London, Croom Helm, 1986; *Kipling's Hidden Narratives* by Sandra Kemp, Oxford, Blackwell, 1988; *Rudyard Kipling* by Martin Seymour-Smith, London, Macdonald, 1989.

*   *   *

Today, Rudyard Kipling is chiefly remembered as a spokesman for imperialism and as a skillful versifier, and it is often overlooked that approximately one in six of his published short stories were science fiction or fantasy. His influence on 20th-century SF writers was probably greater than anyone else's of his generation, except Wells, and is acknowledged by a number of contemporary SF writers.

His formal excursions into the future are few but memorable. *With the Night Mail* describes an Atlantic crossing by airship in the year 2000, and is accompanied by excerpts from the magazine in which it was supposed to appear. Socially, little appears to have changed, but technologically this is an astounding vision; at a time when it was novel for a liner to carry radio-telegraphy equipment, and broadcasting was two decades distant, Kipling envisaged the need for air traffic control and a General Communicator system. In the sequel, "As Easy as ABC," he speculated on the demise of democracy owing to its tendency to lapse into mob-rule—this may have been conditioned by his disappointment with the U.S. at a time when lynch-law was still common: witness the terrifying image of the memorial statue, "The Nigger in Flames,"—and on a cure for overpopulation, a problem he had encountered during his time in India.

His other works of SF and fantasy range from the early "The Bridge-Builders," in which a civil engineer overhears the Indian gods debating whether or not to destroy his masterpiece spanning the Ganges, through those astonishing tours-de-force without human characters like ".007" (steam locomotives) and "The Ship That Found Herself" (steel plates and girders and the ship's cat!), by way of speculative SF like "In the Same Boat" (a man and woman discover that the nightmares haunting them refer to real events which happened while they were in the womb) and "The Finest Story in the World" (a city clerk remembers his previous lives, as a galley-slave and on an expedition to Vinland), right up to the complex, subtle stories of his last years when he left his readers and critics far behind, like "The Children of the Zodiac."

He wrote the classic ghosts-in-reverse story, *They,* and the dead-pan fantasies of *Just So Stories;* in *Puck of Pook's Hill* and *Rewards and Fairies* he brought the people of past ages forward to the present to speak for themselves; and he wrote about sea-serpents and mysterious curses and the heady excitement of modern inventions—but never quite as anyone else would have handled them. For example, "Wireless" is indeed about early radio, but the narrator's experimental friend, trying to eavesdrop on the Royal Navy, fails to notice how the soul of Keats is striking an echo across time in a lovelorn, tubercular assistant pharmacist.

Kipling, who was possibly the most completely equipped writer ever to tackle the short-story form in the English language, exemplifies the fact that in our literary tradition there has never been a hard-and-fast line between realistic and fantastic. Indeed, he was a master at making the fantastic seem credible.

—John Brunner

KIPPAX, John

Pseudonym for John Charles Hynam. **Nationality:** British. **Born:** Alwalton, Huntingdonshire, 10 June 1915. **Education:** Attended Trinity College, Carmarthen, 1934-36. **Family:** Married Phyllis Mary Manning in 1941; one daughter. **Career:** Artist, musician, comedian, and teacher. **Died:** 17 July 1974.

SCIENCE FICTION PUBLICATIONS

Novels (series: Venturer 12 in all books)

Thunder of Stars, with Dan Morgan. London, Macdonald, 1968; New York, Ballantine, 1970.
Seed of Stars, with Dan Morgan. New York, Ballantine, 1972; London, Pan, 1974.
The Neutral Stars, with Dan Morgan. New York, Ballantine, 1973; London, Pan, 1975.
Where No Stars Guide. London, Pan, 1975.

* * *

Fear, estrangement, and the hunger to bridge the sometimes illimitable gulfs between individuals—and between cultures, planets, and species—are central themes in the science fiction and fantasy of John Kippax. The desperate quest for security in a hostile universe figures prominently in this minor English author's writing. His four *Venturer 12* novels, the first three written with Dan Morgan, are perhaps Kippax's best-known genre work but are inferior to some of his short fiction.

Thunder of Stars presents motifs of alienation that persist through the series. It introduces a group of continuing stock military characters who must wrestle in various ways with personal alienation. Central to the saga is the troubled relationship between Tom Bruce and Helen Lindstrom, officers of the elite Space Corps. At the outset, Bruce, a seemingly callous martinet, breaks off their rewarding two-year affair with the excuse that it is hampering their careers. Both are ambitious and dedicated officers, but Lindstrom does not want to sacrifice their relationship.

Bruce yearns to command *Venturer 12,* Earth's most advanced starship. He is brilliant and highly qualified. But scandal early in his career—carefully hushed up—makes his appointment a political hot potato. Then Bruce, on solar system patrol, shoots down a runaway starship filled with colonists before it can crash into Earth with appalling carnage. An inquiry vindicates Bruce but the traumatic secret of his past is revealed: On a distant colony planet Bruce once discovered humans who had been captured and surgically restructured by unknown aliens. Out of mercy, he put the hideously mutilated victims to death. Bruce wins the *Venturer 12* appointment; Lindstrom will be second in command. Their relationship remains uncomfortably platonic in the subsequent novels.

Bruce's obsessive search for the ruthless and elusive aliens called "Kilroys" unifies *Seed of Stars, The Neutral Stars,* and *Where No*

Stars Guide, the last written by Kippax alone. Continuing frustrations with alien contact are paralleled by political intrigue and estrangements, betrayals and occasional reconciliations between men and women. However, characters in the series by and large are too crudely drawn for their vulnerabilities to arouse sympathy. *The Space Corps* has a sentimental, toy-soldier quality. Although the authors take pains to show a sexually and racially integrated Corps drawn from all corners of the Earth, clumsy, insensitive writing results in unintended racial and sexual stereotyping.

More effective are Kippax's short stories, of which he wrote more than 30 between 1955 and 1961. "No Certain Armour," a Space Corps story, stresses the importance of personal responsibility and self-respect in a dangerous universe. More compelling in mood and treatment is "Blood Offering," a compact and dramatic fantasy set on an isolated tropical island. The focus is yet another prickly male/female relationship—a duel of wills between Tod Baines, a brash Australian storekeeper, and Mama Noi, an Old Polynesian witch who demands tribute on behalf of the Shark God. Baines resists the crone's petty extortions, egged on by a scornful Chinese accountant who is at odds with a huge native fisherman over the favours of an island girl. These interwoven conflicts climax in a frightening, ambiguous midnight confrontation with the Shark God that prefigures Tom Bruce's fleeting contacts with the Kilroys.

Kippax's strongly traditional work utilizes popular science fiction and fantasy motifs to remind us that gulfs—whether of water, space, or attitude—can be terrible indeed. But perfunctory writing and avoidance of innovation often blunts the impact of his message.

—Vince Kohler

KLEIN, Gérard

Pseudonym: Gilles d'Argyre. **Nationality:** French. **Born:** Neuilly, 27 May 1937. **Education:** University of Paris, Diplome of Institut d'Etudes Politiques, 1957, Diplome of Institut de Psychologie, 1959. **Military Service:** French Air Force, 1961-62. **Career:** Economist specializing in the savings field; consultant economist, Societe d'Etudes pour le Developpement Economique et Social, Paris, since 1963. **Member:** Societe Francaise de Psychologie. **Address:** 25 Rue de Jussieu, Paris, France.

SCIENCE FICTION PUBLICATIONS

Novels

Le gambit des etoiles. Paris, Le Rayon Fantastique, 1958; translated by C. J. Richards as *Starmasters' Gambit,* New York, DAW, 1973.
Chirurgiens d'une planète. Paris, Le Rayon Fantastique, 1960; translated as *Surgeons of a Planet.*
Les voiliers du soleil. Paris, Le Rayon Fantastique, 1961; translated as *Schooners of the Sun.*
Le temps n'a pas d'odeur. Paris, Denoel, 1963; translated by P. J. Skoloski as *The Day Before Tomorrow,* New York, DAW, 1972.
Le long voyage. N.p., 1964; translated as *The Long Voyage.*

Les tueurs de temps. Paris, Fleuve Noir, 1965; translated by C. J. Richards as *The Mote in Time's Eye,* New York, DAW, 1973.
Le sceptre du hasard. N.p., 1986; translated as *The Scepter of Chance.*
Les seigneurs de la guerre. Paris, R. Laffont, 1971; translated by John Brunner as *The Overlords of War,* Garden City, Doubleday, 1973.

*   *   *

Science fiction has flourished in the land of Jules Verne. And clearly the most important figure in French SF since Verne is Gérard Klein. Klein is one of the very few French SF authors (aside from Verne) to have multiple works translated into English. Despite this "privilege," however, these translations give little sense of Klein's real accomplishment. For not only is he a highly sophisticated novelist (the purely space-opera packaging DAW Books has given to his translated work gives little hint of this), but a fine short story writer and a perceptive critic as well. What is more, he is the genre's premier editor in France, whose groundbreaking Ailleurs et demain has, virtually by itself, set the course for postwar development of SF in that country. Only traces of this accomplishment exist in English. Klein deserves a massive translation effort in order to bring his criticism and editorial commentary to light, thus allowing him to take his rightful place beside Gernsback and Campbell and Aldiss as one of the shapers of SF.

Born in 1937, Klein holds advanced degrees in economics and in psychology. He works for various French think tanks, engaged in projecting future social trends. Given this background, Klein tends to see his SF (and SF in general) as an extension of this activity: specifically, as an instrument for investigating problems at the level of the structures that are seen to govern the development of human civilization. Klein's social-scientist approach is unwavering, but over the years his emphasis has shifted. The young "romantic" intellectual of the mid 1950s soon experienced, in succession, the Algerian War, the events of May 1968, the consumer conservatism of the Giscard 1970s, and finally the techno-socialism of François Mitterand. Correspondingly, his approach to socioeconomic structures in his SF extrapolations has evolved from a more classic Marxist analysis, to a flirtation with 1970s anarcho-ecolo-leftism, and finally to a fascination with the Mitterand "technorevolution," the latter seen in his recent willingness to publish writers like Benford and Forward. Constant in these changes in method and emphasis, however, is an abiding sense of the limits of human nature: a metaphysical stand that commentators have variously labeled "gnostic," or "stoic," but that, closer to French intellectual tradition, seems to partake rather of Pascal's terror of the infinite.

Klein's first work of SF was a story published in the magazine *Fiction* in 1956. Initially intended to be the French-language version of *The Magazine of Fantasy and Science Fiction,* this magazine rapidly shifted emphasis to admit new French writers. And Klein's work—both stories and critical articles—was to become one of the major forces in directing the policies of this journal toward the creation of a reborn French SF. At the same time Klein published his first novel, *Starmasters' Gambit,* in 1958, in Gallimard's Rayon fantastique series. This was followed by the publication, in close succession, of five more novels in ostensible space-opera format. All these were produced for *Fleuve noir* anticipation—an openly pulpish line that, with garish covers, claimed to be purveying "American" fare to its avid French reading public.

These novels are: *Chirurgiens d'une planète* (Surgeons of a Planet), 1960; *Les voiliers du soleil* (Schooners of the Sun), 1961; *Le long voyage* (The Long Voyage), 1964; *Les tueurs de temps* (English translation *The Mote in Time's Eye*), 1965; and *Le sceptre du hasard* (The Scepter of Chance), 1986. The pseudonym Klein used for the five novels (Gilles d'Argyre—argentum = silver = money) implies at the very least an ironic detachment from the commercial space-opera formula. And indeed, on careful reading, the novels reveal a highly self-conscious use of these conventions. What otherwise would be mindless action-adventure becomes the stuff of philosophical tales in the tradition of Voltaire. And the aggregate of these tales forms something like an epic of the rational mind in the face of a purely material universe: a saga whose implications are, beyond parody and satire, potentially tragic in a Pascalian sense.

The time-travel theme, which Klein begins to cultivate in *The Mote in Time's Eye,* becomes in his hands, more than a clever "gambit," a genuinely Cartesian device, where "time" is essentially mind, and "travel" the adjustment of an inner/rational realm to spatiotemporal *res extensa.* It is this theme that gives rise to two novels generally considered to be Klein's finest: *Le temps n'a pas d'odeur* (English translation *The Day Before Tomorrow*), 1963; and *Les seigneurs de la guerre* (English translation *The Overlords of War*), 1971.

This latter novel—which John Brunner thought enough of to translate into English—is a full-blown cosmic epic. Here Georges Corson, a mercenary fighting future battles, finds himself transported to Aergistal, a nexus beyond conventional spacetime where a race of "overlords," through control of time, create a backdrop or theater where classic battles are fought and refought. Aergistal is a "laboratory" where experiments in warfare are carried out for complex and paradoxical ends. The overlords's "goals" are three: to eradicate war, to understand war, and finally to preserve war. The need to make war, they explain, is rooted in human existence, and they remain, despite their mastery, the product of that nature. What they seek, in this rhythm of eradicating and preserving, is the structure of warfare. And this they need, for, as with Pascal's mankind, they still see Aergistal having a frontier existence, on the border between Reason and the Exterior, menace from the void of infinite non-rational space. Corson is given the choice between the three options: extirpate, know, preserve. But, however much he feels for the endless suffering caused by this cycle, he cannot dismantle the structure by choosing. For he too realizes that, in this universe, mankind seems destined to live at the borderline. Klein has often been compared to Stapledon. But this novel, with its almost gnostic sense of world limitations and cosmic imperfection, seems closer to the vision of works like Clarke's *Childhood's End* and Lem's *Solaris.*

In 1969, Klein launched for the publisher Robert Laffont the SF series Ailleurs et demain. This is a crucial moment for French SF, for it is Klein's carefully directed publishing program—in this "luxury" trade paperback series with distinctive metallized silver and gold covers—that systematically introduced key American texts to the French reader. Klein was right on top of the American new wave, and published in rapid succession: Heinlein's *Stranger in a Strange Land,* Herbert's *Dune,* Le Guin's *Left Hand of Darkness,* Delany's *Nova,* and Spinrad's *Bug Jack Barron.* Most central however was the visionary publication of Dick's *Ubik* in 1970, and its companion work *A Maze of Death* in 1972. Through these novels, Dick's influence on French SF in the 1970s was to be pervasive, spawning such "Dickian" French masterpieces as Michel Jeury's

Le Temps incertain and Andre Ruellan's *Tunnel,* both published in turn by Klein in his series. In 1990, *Ailleurs et demain* published a 20-year retrospective volume. The list of distinguished French writers published here has grown immensely. And the list of Anglo-Saxon authors published reveals that Klein has kept close to the pulse of SF development. The direction in the 1980s has, true to the U.S. scene, followed two distinct paths: on one hand that of the "harder" technocrats—Benford, Brin, Forward, Bear; and on the other that of a renewed social consciousness—Shepard, Sargent. Klein's inspired selection of texts, coupled with the insightful and provocative introductions he writes for many of these volumes, offers as close to a "classic" SF collection as any nation possesses.

Klein's fictional output has, alas, diminished since he assumed near-full-time editing duties, and many regret this. Klein however has never ceased writing criticism. And it is perhaps, in the end, as a critic and theoretician that he has made his most distinctive contribution to SF. In 1977, Klein published the expanded version of his essay, "Malaise dans la science-fiction" (an edited version was published in English in *Science-Fiction Studies,* March 1977). This is a major socioeconomic analysis of the genre that has as much if not more bearing on French SF (indeed on the condition of the literary intellectual in France in general) as it does on the Anglo-Saxon novels it specifically targets.

Klein's essays in redefining SF culminate in the figure, not of Heinlein, but of Lewis Carroll. Carroll is the master of the mind-world interface, of the proto-surrealist search for lateral or alternate, rather than expanded, universes. And by claiming Carroll as model for SF creation—an SF that, in accordance with the inward retreat of Cartesian doubt, seeks its models not in expansionist space opera but in the inner journeys of symbolist and surrealist poets—Klein effectively sets the generic direction for SF in France. Klein's vision—where inward retreat from the material world can eventually fuel the need, within the mindspace of this retreat, to improve upon Descartes and not merely eradicate but actually annihilate that world over and over again—effectively describes the dynamic of numerous works of French SF in the 1970s and 1980s.

—George Slusser

KLINE, Otis Adelbert

Nationality: American. **Born:** Chicago, Illinois, 1 July 1891. **Career:** Composer and song writer, then music publisher, film writer, and editor. Editor, *Weird Tales,* Chicago, 1924; founder, Otis Kline Associates, literary agency. **Died:** 24 October 1946.

SCIENCE FICTION PUBLICATIONS

Novels (series: Robert Grandon; Jan; Mars)

The Planet of Peril (Grandon). Chicago, McClurg, 1929.
Maza of the Moon. Chicago, McClurg, 1930.
The Prince of Peril: The Weird Adventures of Zinlo, Man of Three Worlds, upon the Mysterious Planet of Venus (Grandon). Chicago, McClurg, 1930.
Call of the Savage. New York, Clode, 1937; as *Jan of the Jungle,* New York, Ace, 1966.

The Port of Peril (Grandon). Providence, Rhode Island, Grandon, 1949.
The Swordsman of Mars. New York, Avalon, 1960.
The Outlaws of Mars. New York, Avalon, 1960.
Tam, Son of the Tiger. New York, Avalon, 1962.
Jan in India. Lakemont, Georgia, Fictioneer, 1974.

Short Stories

The Man Who Limped, and Other Stories. Hollywood, Saint, 1946.
Stories (includes *The Bride of Osiris*). Oak Lawn, Illinois, Weinberg, 1975.

*   *   *

Otis Adelbert Kline, whose literary career flourished in the 1920s and 1930s, never aimed higher than the prevailing tastes of those who read the pulp magazines *Weird Tales, Argosy,* and *Amazing Stories,* in which he published most of his stories. He was clearly influenced by and competed with his contemporaries Edgar Rice Burroughs, A. Merritt, and H.P. Lovecraft, and made no apologies for pandering to the popular taste for formula adventure stories. His work as a literary agent kept him abreast of whatever appealed to the popular imagination, and he worked these interests into his stories. His SF was of the fantastic variety denounced by Gernsback in the 1930s, Campbell in the 1940s, and Gold in the 1950s, who were committed to making SF respectable among adult readers. Had Kline been writing in the 1950s and 1960s, he would probably have been turning out the same formula stories with New Wave embellishments.

Kline's costume adventure melodramas are SF in the limited sense that he made use of conventions like psi powers, rocket travel, ray guns, and heavy doses of ritualism, totemism, and primitive religion borrowed from Frazer, Malinowski, and other anthropologists whose ideas of primitive social and religious customs had begun to stir the popular imagination. In truth, little beyond the accessories distinguish the SF from, say, the oriental adventures of the Dragoman series (*The Man Who Limped*). Much of his fantastic SF belongs in that loose category known as "sword and sorcery." Kline's imagination was highly visual and his storytelling techniques were clearly shaped by his film-writing experiences. Whatever the costumes, settings, and properties, his stories are built out of the simplest formulas of the adventure-suspense story, and his characters are stock types familiar to anyone who has seen the old Buck Rogers serials. Like Burroughs, Kline had his series of Mars and Venus stories. The latter (the Robert Grandon series) proved very popular, and perhaps should be taken as representative of Kline's most influential work in the genre.

Critical opinion on Kline has been largely negative. However, despite everything negative that has been said, including the more recently fashionable charges of racism and sexism (equally justified), there remains the embarrassing but undeniable power of Kline's naive handling of the formulas and conventions of exotic adventure. Kline's ideas are second-hand and his treatment of them trite, but that is the very heart of his appeal. He gives the reader the expected cliché, the familiar stereotype, the conventional adventure formula. No summary could do justice to his triteness, but the following vignette from "The Bride of Osiris" (1927) may stand as a fair sample of the action: "As he stood there in the midst of the hostile multitude, holding the half-fainting Doris and expecting instant death, Buell heard two sounds simultaneously—the twang of a bowstring and an encouraging shout from Rafferty." The power of such a passage may be of a low order, barely a notch above the boys' adventure stories of the time, and yet the reader may find a kind of delight encountering an almost pure example of the thriller whose only purpose is unreflective and mindless entertainment. That Kline succeeds at all is perhaps his revenge upon literary criticism.

Kline's most successful novel, and probably his best, is *Call of the Savage*. The novel was modelled on Kipling's *Jungle Books* and Hudson's *Green Mansions,* and exhibits Kline's ability to use mythic and archetypal story elements to entrap all but the most wary reader. *Call of the Savage* is fantasy rather than SF, but, as we have seen in Kline's other work, the differences as well as the resemblances are coincidental.

—Donald L. Lawler

KNEALE, (Thomas) Nigel

Nationality: British. **Born:** Barrow-in-Furness, Lancashire, 28 April 1922. **Education:** Douglas High School, Isle of Man; Royal Academy of Dramatic Art, London, 1946-48. **Family:** Married the writer Judith Kerr in 1954; one daughter and one son. **Career:** Actor, Stratford upon Avon, 1948-49; staff member, BBC Television, London, 1951-55. **Awards:** Maugham award, 1950. **Agent:** Douglas Rae (Management) Ltd., 28 Charing Cross Road, London WC2H 0DB, England.

SCIENCE FICTION PUBLICATIONS

Novel

Quatermass. London, Hutchinson, 1979.

Short Stories

Tomato Cain. London, Collins, 1949; New York, Knopf, 1950.

OTHER PUBLICATIONS

Plays

The Quatermass Experiment (televised, 1953). London, Penguin, 1959.
Quatermass II (televised, 1955). London, Penguin, 1960.
Quatermass and the Pit (televised, 1959). London, Penguin, 1960.
The Year of the Sex Olympics and Other TV Plays (includes *The Road* and *The Stone Tape*). London, Ferret Fantasy, 1976.

Screenplays: *Quatermass II (Enemy from Space),* with Val Guest, 1957; *The Abominable Snowman,* 1957; *Look Back in Anger,* with John Osborne, 1959; *The Entertainer,* with John Osborne, 1960; *HMS Defiant (Damn the Defiant),* with Edmund North, 1962; *First Men in the Moon,* with Jan Read, 1964; *The Witches,* 1966; *Quatermass and the Pit (5,000,000 Years to Earth),* 1967; *The Quatermass Conclusion,* 1979.

Television Plays: *The Quatermass Experiment,* 1953; *Nineteen Eighty-Four,* from the novel by Orwell, 1954; *The Creature,* 1955; *Quatermass II,* 1955; *Mrs. Wickens in the Fall,* 1956; *Quatermass and the Pit,* 1959; *The Road,* 1963; *The Crunch,* 1964; *The Year of the Sex Olympics,* 1967; *Bam! Pow! Zapp!,* 1969; *Wine of India,* 1970; *The Chopper,* 1971; *The Stone Tape,* 1972; *Jack and the Beanstalk,* 1974; *Murrain,* 1975; *Buddyboy,* 1976; *During Barty's Party,* 1976; *Special Offer,* 1976; *The Dummy,* 1976; *Baby,* 1976; *What Big Eyes,* 1976; *Quatermass,* 1979; *Kinvig* series, 1981; *The Woman in Black,* from the novel by Susan Hill, 1989; *Stanley and the Women,* from the novel by Kingsley Amis, 1991.

*

Nigel Kneale comments:

I have always been a scriptwriter for television and films because that's what I like doing best. I don't regard myself as a science-fiction writer, and the list above confirms this. Looking through this list I wondered what other things I wrote. The answer, of course, is things that didn't get made. Some of my best screenplays, from Huxley, Lawrence, and the like, went down with collapsing film companies. More rarely, but more painfully, there were stillborn TV originals, like *The Big Big Giggle,* a serial about a teenage suicide craze, wiped out by high cost and official nervousness that was probably justified (it could have been dangerous). Or *Crow,* about the slave trade and not dangerous at all, victim of an internal squabble in a TV company. I just have to be grateful for all those that *did* get made.

*   *   *

With a few notable exceptions, most of them in recent years, movies and television have not been kind to science fiction. The speculative ideas that characterize what is best in the genre have proven difficult to translate into visual media without interrupting the action with long expository speeches, while the spectacular visual surfaces that science fiction narratives afford have been all too tempting to filmmakers. As a result, few science fiction writers have been able to work with success in the media, and fewer still have managed to build their primary reputation as a media writer of science fiction. Nigel Kneale is a member of this select latter group. The three television serials concerning Professor Bernard Quatermass that he wrote for the BBC between 1953 and 1959—all three of which were subsequently published in book form and adapted as feature films—established a standard for the televised science fiction horror story that has seldom been surpassed.

Kneale had little direct experience as a science fiction writer before joining the BBC, although a few of his short stories from *Tomato Cain* are small masterpieces of weird fiction. While at the BBC, Kneale's plays included an adaptation for television of Orwell's *Nineteen Eighty-Four* and an original play about the abominable snowman called *The Creature* (filmed as *The Abominable Snowman*). But it was his 1953 six-part sequel *The Quatermass Experiment* that quickly established his reputation as a convincing dramatist of suspense thrillers. This tale of an alien life form that takes over the body of the lone survivor of the first space mission and metamorphoses into a hideous monster back on Earth, despite occasional absurdities (super-scientist Quatermass finally succeeds in literally *talking* the monster to death), reveals an ear for convincing dialogue, an awareness of the dramatic possibilities of the television medium (such as the use of "newscasters" to carry forth the action), and a talent for working serious issues and concepts into a fast-moving dramatic narrative. Though Quatermass is a scientist-hero in the mold of Conan Doyle's Professor Challenger, Kneale makes some pointed observations about the morality of scientific research and the relationship of government and the journalistic media to such research.

Professor Quatermass continued his fight against bureaucracy and journalistic sensationalism in two subsequent serials. *Quatermass II* concerns the attempt of an alien civilization to establish colonies on Earth by converting human workers into zombie-like slaves; it is perhaps the weakest of the three serials. *Quatermass and the Pit* is perhaps the strongest: a subway excavation in a reputedly haunted area uncovers an ancient alien spaceship which, when activated, reveals that legends of the devil are based on race memories of the aliens from Mars who once tried to conquer Earth—and in the process created us. The mix of myth, supernaturalism, and science fiction works well, and predates by several years cult rumors of gods from outer space. A fourth installment in the Quatermass series, *The Quatermass Conclusion,* was filmed in 1979.

Kneale worked on other screenplays, most notably the film adaptations of two John Osborne plays and an adaptation of Wells's *First Men in the Moon,* which he gave a characteristic twist by casting the story as a flashback told more than a half-century later by a survivor of the expedition whose secret is revealed only when the "official" first moon-landing party comes across the remnants of the earlier adventurers. Here, as in the Quatermass serials, Kneale's ironic humor, his deftness in sketching minor characters, and his sense of dramatic structure provide a strong script. Though he has shown little inclination to move beyond the horror-suspense school of science fiction, Kneale has contributed significantly to the genre's growth in the media.

—Gary K. Wolfe

KNIGHT, Damon (Francis)

Nationality: American. **Born:** Baker, Oregon, 19 September 1922. **Education:** Hood River High School, Oregon; WPA Art Center, Salem, Oregon, 1940-41. **Family:** Married 1) Gertrud Werndl; 2) Helen Schlaz; 3) Kate Wilhelm, *q.v.,* in 1963; four children. **Career:** Freelance writer: assistant editor, Popular Publications, 1943-44, 1949-50; editor, *Worlds Beyond,* 1950-51; book editor, *Science Fiction Adventures,* 1953-54; editor, *If,* 1958-59; book editor, *Fantasy and Science Fiction,* 1959-60; editorial consultant, Berkley Books, 1960-66. Co-founding director, Milford Science Fiction Writers' Conference, 1956. Lecturer, Clarion Workshop in Science Fiction and Fantasy, 1967-94. Founder, 1965, and president, 1965-67, Science Fiction Writers of America. **Awards:** Hugo award, for nonfiction, 1956; Pilgrim award, 1975; Grand Master, 1995. **Address:** 1645 Horn Lane, Eugene, Oregon 97404, U.S.A.

SCIENCE FICTION PUBLICATIONS

Novels (series: CV)

Hell's Pavement. New York, Lion, 1955; London, Banner, 1958; as *Analogue Men,* New York, Berkley, 1962.

The People Maker. Rockville Centre, New York, Zenith, 1959; revised edition, as *A for Anything,* London, New English Library, 1961; New York, Berkley, 1965.
Masters of Evolution. New York, Ace, 1959.
The Sun Saboteurs. New York, Ace, 1961.
Beyond the Barrier. Garden City, New York, Doubleday, and London, Gollancz, 1964.
Mind Switch. New York, Berkley, 1965; as *The Other Foot,* London, Whiting and Wheaton, 1966.
The Rithian Terror. New York, Ace, 1965.
Three Novels: Rule Golden, Natural State, The Dying Man. Garden City, New York, Doubleday, and London, Gollancz, 1967; as *Natural State and Other Stories,* London, Pan, 1975.
World without Children; and, The Earth Quarter: Two Science Fiction Novels. New York, Lancer, 1970.
Two Novels (The Earth Quarter and Double Meaning). London, Gollancz, 1974.
The World and Thorinn. New York, Berkley, 1980.
The Man in the Tree. New York, Berkley, 1984; London, Gollancz, 1985.
CV. New York, Tor, 1985.
The Observers (CV). New York, Tor, 1988.
A Reasonable World (CV). New York, Tor, 1991.
Rule Golden; and Double Meaning. New York, Tor, 1991.
Why Do Birds. New York, Tor, 1992.

Short Stories

Far Out: 13 Science Fiction Stories. New York, Simon and Schuster, and London, Gollancz, 1961.
In Deep. New York, Berkley, 1963; London, Gollancz, 1964.
Off Center: A Scintillating Science-Fiction Collection. New York, Ace, 1965; as *Off Centre,* London, Gollancz, 1969.
Turning On. Garden City, New York, Doubleday, 1966; London, Gollancz, 1967.
The Best of Damon Knight. Garden City, New York, Doubleday, 1976.
Rule Golden, and Other Stories. New York, Avon, 1979.
Late Knight Edition. Cambridge, NESFA Press, 1985.
One Side Laughing: Stories Unlike Other Stories. New York, St. Martin's Press, 1991.
God's Nose. Eugene, Oregon, Pulphouse, 1991.

OTHER PUBLICATIONS

Other

In Search of Wonder: Essays on Modern Science Fiction. Chicago, Advent, 1956; revised and enlarged edition, 1967.
Charles Fort, Prophet of the Unexplained. Garden City, New York, Doubleday, 1970; London, Gollancz, 1971.
The Futurians: The Story of the Science Fiction "Family" of the 30's That Produced Today's Top SF Writers and Editors. New York, Day, 1977.
Better Than One, with Kate Wilhelm. Boston, Noreascon II, 1980.
Creating Short Fiction. Cincinnati, Writer's Digest, 1981; revised, 1985.
It All Begins with Characters. Eugene, Oregon, Pulphouse, 1991.
Faking Out the Reader. Eugene, Oregon, Pulphouse, 1991.

Editor, *A Century of Science Fiction.* New York, Simon and Schuster, 1962; London, Gollancz, 1963.

Editor, *First Flight.* New York, Lancer, 1963; as *Now Begins Tomorrow,* 1969; revised edition, with Martin H. Greenberg and Joseph D. Olander, as *First Voyages,* New York, Avon, 1981.

Editor, *A Century of Great Short Science Fiction Novels.* New York, Delacorte Press, 1964; London, Gollancz, 1965.

Editor, *Tomorrow x 4.* Greenwich, Connecticut, Fawcett, 1964; London, Coronet, 1967.

Editor and translator, *Thirteen French Science-Fiction Stories.* New York, Bantam, and London, Corgi, 1965.

Editor, *Beyond Tomorrow: Ten Science Fiction Adventures.* New York, Harper, 1965; London, Gollancz, 1968.

Editor, *The Dark Side.* Garden City, New York, Doubleday, 1965; London, Dobson, 1966.

Editor, *The Shape of Things.* New York, Popular Library, 1965.

Editor, *Nebula Award Stories 1965.* Garden City, New York, Doubleday, 1966; London, Gollancz, 1967.

Editor, *Cities of Wonder.* Garden City, New York, Doubleday, 1966; London, Dobson, 1968.

Editor, *Orbit 1-21.* New York, Putnam, 12 vols., 1966-73; New York, Berkley, 1 vol., 1974; New York, Harper, 8 vols., 1974-80; vol. 1, London, Whiting and Wheaton, 1966; vol. 2, London, Rapp and Whiting, 1968.

Editor, *Science Fiction Inventions.* New York, Lancer, 1967.

Editor, *Worlds to Come: Nine Science Fiction Adventures.* New York, Harper, 1967; London, Gollancz, 1969.

Editor, *The Metal Smile.* New York, Belmont, 1968.

Editor, *One Hundred Years of Science Fiction.* New York, Simon and Schuster, 1968; London, Gollancz, 1969.

Editor, *Toward Infinity: Nine Science Fiction Tales.* New York, Simon and Schuster, 1968; London, Gollancz, 1970.

Editor, *Dimension X: Five Science Fiction Novellas* (for children). New York, Simon and Schuster, 1970; London, Gollancz, 1972; abridged as *Elsewhere x 3: Three Novellas,* London, Coronet, 1974.

Editor, *First Contact.* New York, Pinnacle, 1971.

Editor, *A Pocketful of Stars.* Garden City, New York, Doubleday, 1971; London, Gollancz, 1972.

Editor, *Perchance to Dream.* Garden City, New York, Doubleday, 1972; London, Gollancz, 1974.

Editor, *A Science Fiction Argosy.* New York, Simon and Schuster, 1972; London, Gollancz, 1973.

Editor, *Tomorrow and Tomorrow: Ten Tales of the Future.* New York, Simon and Schuster, 1973; London, Gollancz, 1974.

Editor, *The Golden Road: Great Tales of Fantasy and the Supernatural.* New York, Simon and Schuster, 1974; London, Gollancz, 1974.

Editor, *Happy Endings: 15 Stories by the Masters of the Macabre.* Indianapolis, Bobbs Merrill, 1974.

Editor, *A Shocking Thing.* New York, Pocket Books, 1974.

Editor, *Best from Orbit, Volumes 1-10.* New York, Berkley, 1975.

Editor, *Science Fiction of the Thirties.* Indianapolis, Bobbs Merrill, 1975.

Editor, *Westerns of the 40's: Classics from the Great Pulps.* Indianapolis, Bobbs Merrill, 1977.

Editor, *Turning Points: Essays on the Art of Science Fiction.* New York, Harper, 1977.

Editor, *The Clarion Awards.* Garden City, New York, Doubleday, 1984.

Translator, *Ashes, Ashes,* by René Barjavel. Garden City, New York, Doubleday, 1967.

*   *   *

Damon Knight's impact on science fiction has taken so many forms, it's difficult to imagine that we're talking about a single person. As a reviewer, Knight helped to establish a credible benchmark for criticism within the field, and produced the still readable *In Search of Wonder,* which includes the best of his essays. He has subsequently edited *Monad,* an irregular collection of literary essays dealing with various aspects of the field. As an editor, he provided platforms for some of the most innovative new stories, particularly in the multivolume *Orbit* series of original anthologies. He helped introduce American readers to works from European authors with *Thirteen French Science Fiction Stories* and assembled a large number of first-rate reprint anthologies. Knight even provided occasional illustrations for the professional magazines and has taught at several writers' conferences.

But Damon Knight is first and foremost a writer. Although not primarily thought of as a novelist, his career has been sprinkled with exceptionally thoughtful book-length works. *Analogue Men* was one of the earliest genre novels to make use of complex psychological principles in its depiction of a world where each individual citizen has been conditioned to accept the existence of an imaginary guardian. A secret society of immunes provides the only hope for humanity in one of the best early dystopias.

Three early short novels were primarily action-oriented but also illustrate some of Knight's more serious and recurring themes. *The Sun Saboteurs* (shorter version as "Earth Quarter") presents a universe in which humans are a minority, and a not particularly respected one, confined to ghettos on other worlds, barely suppressing a smoldering resentment against the superior alien civilizations that dominate the galaxy. *The Rithian Terror* (shorter version as "Double Meaning") pits a corrupt human government against a shapechanging alien. The protagonist sets out to capture the intruder, only to realize the truth about his own society and switch sides at a crucial moment. *Masters of Evolution* (shorter version as "Natural State") deals with the decline of urban centers, now engaged in open warfare against the suburbs, ultimately using biological engineering techniques as the ultimate weapon. A full-length novel from that period, *A for Anything* (also released under the title *The People Maker*) explores the danger of having too much wealth. In a society where it is possible to physically duplicate any material object, human life becomes the only valuable and irreproducible quantity. Economics therefore conspire to make slavery once again a viable business.

Two competent but unexceptional novels followed, the wildly satiric *Mind Switch* and a thoughtful technological thriller, *Beyond the Barrier.* In the former, a human being's personality is transferred into the body of an alien primate, providing the springboard for an altered perception of the foibles of humanity; in the latter, an ordinary appearing professor is actually a superkiller from a future where a barrier has been erected as protection from alien invaders. The episodic fantasy novel *The World and Thorinn* emphasized Knight's growing metaphysical interests, which were to emerge more fully and with better effect in his next novel.

The Man in the Tree marked an enormous leap forward for an already significant writer. The protagonist is capable of reaching into alternate universes, withdrawing items and using them in our own. When he inadvertently causes the death of a young bully, he becomes the target for the hatred of the man's father, who pursues him for years in search of revenge. There are numerous evident parallels to the Christ story in what remains Knight's most effective novel.

Knight subsequently completed a trilogy of novels, *CV, The Observers,* and *A Reasonable World.* In the near future, individual freedom is in jeopardy and violence continues to threaten humanity's progress toward a mature society. The passengers and crew of the CV, a seagoing vessel, are infected by the awakening of an alien creature which can infiltrate human bodies, undetectably at first, then breed and spread through other warmblooded creatures. Although this intelligent virus provides some beneficial services to its hosts, it becomes increasingly involved in policing their moral lives, ultimately acting as judge and jury, causing the deaths of those who cannot control their violent impulses. The series is a biological equivalent of Jack Williamson's classic *The Humanoids,* questioning the balance between the ordering of society and individual freedom.

Knight's most recent novel is *Why Do Birds,* a story of alien abduction, sort of, and the human capacity to embrace strange ideas. The protagonist appears in the middle of the 21st century, insisting that he was kidnapped by aliens a hundred years earlier so that he could carry a warning. Earth is going to be destroyed and the only hope for humanity is to build a gigantic structure, large enough that everyone alive on Earth can be placed in suspended animation until the crisis is past. *Why Do Birds* is a strange novel whose underlying humor is cleverly layered.

Knight has an even higher reputation for his short stories. Perhaps his best known is "To Serve Man," the title of a book by a group of visiting aliens which turns out to be a cookbook. In "You're Another," a man discovers that all of human history is simply a play, and he is no more than a minor character. Two brothers loot time in "Anachron" and the only remaining man with the capacity for cruelty is honored in "The Country of the Kind."

"Rule Golden" involves an alien who exudes an empathic gas, causing an entertaining inversion of the Golden Rule, "Be Done By As You Did." In "An Eye for a What?" the authorities must discover how to punish an alien who quite literally enjoys most of the options available. "What Rough Beast" deals with changes made to the world through manipulation of the relationship between cause and effect. Knight's wry humor is evident in "O," in which everything whose name starts with that letter disappears from the Earth.

Other short stories of particular note are "Stranger Station," "Idiot Stick," "Not With a Bang," "Cabin Boy," "Ask Me Anything," "Eripmav," "Fortyday," and "Masks." The best collections of Knight's shorter work are *Far Out* and *In Deep.* If Knight's reputation were to rely solely on his fiction, it would be safely established. His editorial and critical impact are less easily realized, but may ultimately have an even greater effect on the evolution of science fiction.

—Don D'Ammassa

KNIGHT, Norman L(ouis)

Nationality: American. **Born:** St. Joseph, Missouri, 21 September 1895. **Education:** St. Joseph Junior College, A.A. 1918; George Washington University, Washington, D.C., B.S. in chemical engineering 1925. **Military Service:** Served in the United States Army Field Artillery, 1918-19. **Family:** Married Marie Sarah Yenn in 1921; one daughter. **Career:** Worked for the Department of Agriculture: assistant observer, Davenport, Iowa, 1919-20, and observer and code translator, Washington, D.C., Weather Bureau; analytical chemist in Washington, D.C., 1925-29, Chicago, 1929, St. Louis, 1929-40, Chicago, 1940-50, and Beltsville, Maryland, 1950-64, Insecticide Division; retired in 1964; Merit award, 1962. **Died:** 19 April 1972.

SCIENCE FICTION PUBLICATIONS

Novel

A Torrent of Faces, with James Blish. Garden City, New York, Doubleday, 1967; London, Faber, 1968.

* * *

Norman L. Knight published his first story in *Astounding* in 1937, worked most of his life as a chemist specializing in pesticides, and finally published his most ambitious science fiction work in collaboration with the master, James Blish, in 1967. One theme and one setting, in fact, kept reappearing in the early stories; and the importance of that set of images in the novel suggests that Knight may have been the seminal partner in the collaboration—if not the more polished stylist. Images that led eventually to the masterpiece, *A Torrent of Faces,* can be seen as early as the serialized novel "Frontier of the Unknown," in which a deep-sea diver moves in "a twilight pierced by a million uneasy, shifting, flickering ghosts of slanting, green-tinged sun rays." This crude flood of modifiers was followed by another two-part novel, "Crisis in Utopia," in which Knight also anticipates his work with Blish. Knight includes here the fully developed conception and description of the undersea race of human mutants called Tritons. The writing is a bit more subtle, and Knight's ideas on the effects of managed evolution are suggestive.

Nevertheless, these early stories are dominated by the usual villains of melodrama and the crude overwriting that so often seems the appropriate literary parallel to the line-drawing illustrations of the early pulp magazines. The novel, however, is the culmination of all this. One of the most popular sections of the novel, "The Shipwrecked Hotel," is a polished undersea disaster epic in which the Triton race plays a major role; Triton characters are fully developed throughout the book, and much of the action takes place undersea. Also, by the time of this later work the Earth itself has replaced the melodramatic villains as a key protagonist—a much greater literary accomplishment. The individual extrapolations in the novel about living conditions in a future with one trillion inhabitants on Earth are many and richly developed, and the writing shows marked improvement over the early Knight extrapolations on the sea and on Utopia. Blish was a good teacher and a good collaborator for Knight's valuable ideas on the future, on evolution, and on accompanying disasters.

—Donald M. Hassler

KOMATSU, Sakyo

Nationality: Japanese. **Born:** 1931.

SCIENCE FICTION PUBLICATIONS

Novels

At the End of the Endless Stream. N.p., 1966.
Nippon chinbotsu. Tokyo, Kodansha, 1973; translated by Michael
    Gallagher as *Japan Sinks,* New York, Harper, 1976; as *The Death
    of the Dragon,* London, New English Library, 1976.
Goodbye Jupiter. N.p., 1982.
Shuto Shoshitsu. N.p., 1985.

Short Stories

Hoshi Goroshi. N.p., n.d.; translated as *Star Killer.*
Chi nhi wa Heiwa. N.p., n.d.; translated as *Peace on Earth.*

OTHER PUBLICATIONS

Other

The Dead Space of Japanese Civilization. N.p., 1977.
H. G. Wells and Modern Science Fiction, with Judith Merril, Tetsu
    Yano, and Robert Philmus. N.p., 1977.
Future Technology and Human Society, with Hidetoshi Kato. N.p.,
    1983.

*   *   *

Sakyo Komatsu has written widely in science fiction, other types
of fiction, and nonfiction. He was characterized in the early 1970s,
when a number of his major works were published and his fame
spread, as one of the "Big Five" of Japanese SF writers, the others
being Yasutaka Tsutsui, Shin'ichi Hoshi, Ryu Mitsuse, and Taku
Mayumura. That grouping left aside Kobo Abé, who exceeded the
"Big Five" in national fame, but is by no means an SF specialist,
having produced much mainstream literature.

Komatsu himself is not at all a tightly specialized SF writer. He
is sometimes called the Robert Heinlein of Japan, while Hoshi is
contrastingly referred to as Japan's Ray Bradbury. Like Heinlein,
Komatsu gives much thought to political and international problems, but is less inclined to specify a *correct* solution to the problems. Both writers have had a diversified cultural, technical, and
occupational background. For Komatsu, this diversified experience
contributes to his ability to present natural and realistic narratives,
and it contributed most notably to his great success with *Japan
Sinks.*

One may also say that Komatsu resembles Isaac Asimov in his
continuing output of nonfiction and fiction other than SF. His nonfiction often gets into futurology, as in *Future Technology and Human Society,* coauthored with Hidetoshi Kato (1983), which explores the way in which our dreams of today may be realized in
the future. His *The Dead Space of Japanese Civilization* (1977) is
a critical examination of Japanese culture. Komatsu's critical writings include a piece of SF criticism in English, "H.G. Wells and
Japanese Science Fiction," found in a book he wrote with Judith
Merril, Tetsu Yano, and Robert Philmus, *H. G. Wells and Modern
Science Fiction* (1977). His book of thoughtful essays on history
and criticism, *The Pleasure of Reading and Narrating,* was published in 1985. He has also written numerous mysteries, detective

stories, and travel books—these last help to account for his impressive physical descriptions.

His story "Fukurokoji" (Blind Alley) is a summary of his futurology, and is included in his book *Hoshi Goroshi* (Star Killer)—a
title drawn from another very original story in that volume. In the
same book are his skilled narratives of the birth and death of our
moon, "Kaigo" (Conjunction) and "Wareta Kagami" (The Broken
Mirror). The title story of another collection, *Chi nhi wa Heiwa*
(Peace on Earth), was nominated for the Naoki Prize, while a short-
short story therein, "Koppu Ippai no Senso" (A Full Cup of War),
deals with the development and hazards of nuclear war. The story
"Hokusai no Sekai" (The World of Hokusai) was one of the first
Japanese SF stories to appear in Russian for Soviet readers.

Japan Sinks (1973) appeared in English in 1976 and has greatly
enlarged Komatsu's fame, selling over four million copies in Japan, with renditions in a number of languages. It led to a motion
picture, which has been widely exhibited in Japan and abroad. By
the 1980s Komatsu was referred to in publications as "Mr. Sub-
mersion" and as "the man who sank Japan." In this novel he makes
plausible, with abundant data from geology and physics, what would
otherwise be regarded as highly fantastic, the submergence of virtually the entire Japanese archipelago as the result of sliding plates,
earthquakes, and terrific volcanic action. The loss of Japan in a
mere year or so of time is the fantastic element here. The same
process extending over millions of years would not be so questionable—nor might it take much of a narrative.

Komatsu has called this novel a fable, and it surely can be read
as a caution against insularity in Japan or any nation. On the question of the surviving Japanese people and their culture after their
land disappears, Komatsu says that beyond ethnocentric nationalism is a better, enriched identity, that even after a diaspora one's
own language and customs can be kept, while enhanced by a global blending. He also considers the often problematic question of
how peoples in distress may interact with the nations to which they
call for help.

At the End of the Endless Stream (1966) uses a panoramic treatment of the development of the universe and our species, and it
shares to some extent the question posed in *Japan Sinks* of how
man may fare if dislodged from his historic environment. Another
theme here is the possibility of changing human evolutionary potential for the better.

Goodbye Jupiter (1982) is mainstream, technical SF featuring a
mammoth project to use Jupiter as a sort of secondary sun, so that
the outer planets may become habitable. This was a bestseller, won
high acclaim in Japan, and appeared as a film with the title "Bye-
bye, Jupiter."

A sequel of sorts to *Japan Sinks* is *Shuto Shoshitsu,* translatable
as *Tokyo Disappears,* or more literally *The Disappearance of the
Capital.* This was published as a two-volume book in 1985 by
Tokuma Shoten after having been serialized from 1982 to 1983 by
newspapers all over Japan. In this narrative, vast storms and other
catastrophic phenomena of nature cut off Tokyo completely from
the rest of Japan. One has to consider that Tokyo looms much larger
in Japan than do many capitals in other countries. Thus its disappearance represents to the Japanese a much greater catastrophe than
the loss of Washington or Rome would constitute in the United
States or Italy, for example. The situation here enables Komatsu to
ruminate on modern vulnerability with regard to collapse of telecommunications and computer networks, and to consider at length
how a society and its economy might proceed to survive such a
disaster.

Indeed catastrophes and near-catastrophes are a leading theme in Komatsu's SF. He can be compared therefore with many other SF authors who have considered the "end of civilization as we know it," the destruction of our planet, or the end of the human race. All such themes give the writer a fine opportunity to deal with the essence of nationhood, humanity, and destiny. Komatsu deals superbly with such challenges.

—Frank H. Tucker

KOONTZ, Dean R(ay)

Pseudonyms: Aaron Wolfe; David Axton; Brian Coffey; Deanna Dwyer; K.R. Dwyer; John Hill; Leigh Nichols; Anthony North; Richard Paige; Owen West. **Nationality:** American. **Born:** Everett, Pennsylvania, 9 July 1945. **Education:** Shippensburg State College, B.A. in English 1966. **Family:** Married Gerda Ann Cerra in 1966. **Career:** Worked in a federal government poverty-alleviation program in Appalachia, then high school English teacher. Since 1969, full-time writer. **Agent:** Harold Ober Associates, 425 Madison Avenue, New York, New York 10017. **Address:** P.O. Box 9529, Newport Beach, California 92658-9529, U.S.A.

SCIENCE FICTION PUBLICATIONS

Novels

Star Quest. New York, Ace, 1968.
The Fall of the Dream Machine. New York, Ace, 1969.
Fear That Man. New York, Ace, 1969.
The Dark Symphony. New York, Lancer, 1970.
Hell's Gate. New York, Lancer, 1970.
Dark of the Woods. New York, Ace, 1970.
Beastchild. New York, Lancer, 1970.
Anti-Man. New York, Paperback Library, 1970.
The Crimson Witch. New York, Curtis, 1971.
The Flesh in the Furnace. New York, Bantam, 1972.
A Darkness in My Soul. New York, DAW, 1972; London, Dobson, 1979.
Time Thieves. New York, Ace, 1972; London, Dobson, 1977.
Warlock. New York, Lancer, 1972.
Starblood. New York, Lancer, 1972.
Demon Seed. New York, Bantam, 1973; London, Corgi, 1977.
A Werewolf Among Us. New York, Ballantine, 1973.
The Haunted Earth. New York, Lancer, 1973.
Nightmare Journey. New York, Berkley, 1975.
The Long Sleep (as John Hill). New York, Popular Library, 1975.
Invasion (as Aaron Wolfe). Don Mills, Ontario, Laser Books, 1975; as *Winter Moon* (as Dean Koontz), London, Headline, and New York, Ballantine, 1994.
Night Chills. New York, Atheneum, 1976; London, W.H. Allen, 1977.
The Vision. New York, Putnam, 1977; London, Corgi, 1980.
The Face of Fear (as Brian Coffey). Indianapolis, Bobbs Merrill, 1977; as K.R. Dwyer, London, Davies, 1978; as Dean Koontz, London, Headline, 1989.

The Voice of the Night (as Brian Coffey). New York, Doubleday, 1980; London, Hale, 1981; as Dean Koontz, London, Headline, 1991.
Whispers. New York, Putnam, 1980; London, W.H. Allen, 1981.
The Funhouse: Carnival of Terror (novelization of screenplay; as Owen West). New York, Jove, 1980; London, Sphere, 1981.
Heartbeeps (as John Hill). New York, Jove, 1981.
The Mask (as Owen West). New York, Jove, 1981; London, Coronet, 1983; as Dean Koontz, London, Headline, 1989.
Phantoms. New York, Putnam, and London, W.H. Allen, 1983.
Darkness Comes. London, W.H. Allen, 1984; as *Darkfall,* New York, Berkley, 1984.
Twilight Eyes. Plymouth, Michigan, Land of Enchantment, 1985.
The Door to December (as Richard Paige). New York, Signet, 1985; as Leigh Nichols, London, Fontana, 1987; as Dean Koontz, London, Headline, 1991.
Strangers. New York, Putnam, and London, W.H. Allen, 1986.
Watchers. New York, Putnam, and London, Headline, 1987.
Lightning. New York, Putnam, and London, Headline, 1988.
Oddkins: A Fable for All Ages. New York, Warner, and London, Headline, 1988.
Midnight. New York, Putnam, and London, Headline, 1989.
The Bad Place. New York, Putnam, and London, Headline, 1990.
Cold Fire. New York, Putnam, and London, Headline, 1991.
Hideaway. New York, Putnam, and London, Headline, 1992.
Dean R. Koontz: A New Collection (omnibus). New York, Wings, 1992.
Dragon Tears. New York, Putnam, and London, Headline, 1992.
Mr. Murder. London, Headline, and New York, Putnam, 1993.
Dean Koontz Omnibus. London, Headline, 1993.

Novels as Leigh Nichols

The Key to Midnight. New York, Pocket Books, 1979; London, Magnum, 1980; as Dean Koontz, Arlington Heights, Illinois, Dark Harvest, 1989.
The Eyes of Darkness. New York, Pocket Books, 1981; London, Fontana, 1982; as Dean Koontz, Arlington Heights, Illinois, Dark Harvest, 1989.
The House of Thunder. New York, Pocket Books, 1982; London, Fontana, 1983; as Dean Koontz, Arlington Heights, Illinois, Dark Harvest, 1988.
Twilight. New York, Pocket Books, and London, Fontana, 1984; as *The Servants of Twilight* (as Dean Koontz), Arlington Heights, Illinois, Dark Harvest, 1988.
Shadowfires. New York, Avon, and London, Collins, 1987; as Dean Koontz, Arlington Heights, Illinois, Dark Harvest, 1990.

Short Stories

Soft Come the Dragons. New York, Ace, 1970.
Strange Highways. London, Headline, and New York, Warner, 1995.

OTHER PUBLICATIONS

Novels

Hanging On. New York, Evans, 1973; London, Barrie and Jenkins, 1974.

After the Last Race. New York, Atheneum, 1974.
Strike Deep (as Anthony North). New York, Dial Press, 1974.
Prison of Ice (as David Axton). Philadelphia, Lippincott, and London, W.H. Allen, 1976; revised under name Dean Koontz as *Icebound,* New York, Ballantine, and London, Headline, 1995.
Dark Rivers of the Heart. Lynbrook, New York, Charnal House, and London, Headline, 1994.

Novels as Deanna Dwyer

The Demon Child. New York, Lancer, 1971.
Legacy of Terror. New York, Lancer, 1971.
Children of the Storm. New York, Lancer, 1972.
The Dark of Summer. New York, Lancer, 1972.
Dance with the Devil. New York, Lancer, 1973.

Novels as K.R. Dwyer

Chase. New York, Random House, 1972; London, Barker, 1974.
Shattered. New York, Random House, 1973; London, Barker, 1974.
Dragonfly. New York, Random House, 1975; London, Davies, 1977.

Novels as Brian Coffey

Blood Risk. Indianapolis, Bobbs Merrill, 1973; London, Barker, 1974.
Surrounded. Indianapolis, Bobbs Merrill, 1974; London, Barker, 1975.
The Wall of Masks. Indianapolis, Bobbs Merrill, 1975.

Other

The Pig Society, with Gerda Koontz. Los Angeles, Aware Press, 1970.
The Underground Lifestyles Handbook, with Gerda Koontz. Los Angeles, Aware Press, 1970.
Writing Popular Fiction. Cincinnati, Writer's Digest, 1973.
How to Write Best-Selling Fiction. Cincinnati, Writer's Digest, and London, Poplar Press, 1981.

Editor, with Paul Mikol, *Night Visions 6: All Original Stories.* Arlington Heights, Illinois, Dark Harvest, 1988; as *The Bone Yard,* New York, Berkley, 1991.

*

Critical Studies: *Sudden Fear: The Horror and Dark Suspense Fiction of Dean R. Koontz,* edited by Bill Munster, Mercer Island, Washington, Starmont House, 1988, second edition as *Discovering Dean Koontz,* San Bernardino, Borgo Press, 1995; *The Dean Koontz Companion,* edited by Martin H. Greenberg, Ed Gorman, and Bill Munster, New York, Berkley, 1994.

*   *   *

Dean R. Koontz's best science fiction was written before 1980; since then he more properly can be called a writer of horror novels. His best work is a convincing amalgam of sympathetic characters and quirky plots, but lately his work has stressed the psychotic characters and supernatural events found in contemporary horror fiction.

Koontz is a writer of the New Wave in science fiction, a trend characterized by authors with backgrounds in the humanities rather than the sciences. Certainly, Koontz's themes are rigorously chosen and often intriguing. His early work concerns the theme of the malevolent child, of innocence turned inside out; he handles the notion in *Beastchild,* in *A Darkness in My Soul,* in which a mutant becomes God, and quite compellingly in *Demon Seed,* in which a supercomputer creates its own genetic material which it "implants" into a human woman. In "We Three," genetically mutated children wish away harsh parents, then neighbors, then the entire world through extrasensory powers.

This theme is a corollary to Koontz's major concern—what it means to be human—which he explores in several works on robots. In "The Night of the Storm" the robot-protagonist Suranov is bored by his centralized, staid society "peopled" by robots. Humans are rumored to exist, much to the horror of the robots, whose prime rule is that the universe is logical, a dictum that the existence of humans threatens. The story also begins a robotics series carried on by New Wave writers Pamela Sargent and George Zebrowski, among others, in the Continuum series. The more turgid novel *Anti-Man* presents an android who changes into a new form of being, to the consternation of the human protagonist. This novel explores the Frankenstein theme—the relationship of the creator and his creation—as does *Demon Seed.*

Beginning with his first story "Soft Come the Dragons," Koontz clearly favors intuition and emotion as the essential components of humanness, rather than logic and reason, which can be assigned to machines. One of his best works, *A Werewolf Among Us* presents a protagonist who is a cyberdetective, a human whose brain is electronically and physically linked to a portable computer on his chest. Using a classic Agatha Christie plot, Koontz combines science fiction and detective genres. Members of a family are being murdered, the remaining members of the family are suspects, and the reader is presented with clues. However, the main conflict in the novel is psychological: when the human half of the cyberdetective realizes the murderer is another robot, his computer half rejects the notion as illogical.

Koontz also treats themes in popular culture. Marshall McLuhan's *The Medium is the Massage* was the origin for "A Mouse in the Walls of the Global Village," and "The Psychedelic Children" projects a society in which the children whose parents took LSD in the late 1960s are mutants and are hunted by society. Koontz also explores the theme of the offspring of "hippie" parents in *Dragon Tears,* in which a woman consumes so many drugs prior to the birth of her son, that her son ends up psychotic, psychic, and incapable of loving anyone. The antiestablishment bias of the 1960s is clear in Koontz's work. In *Dark of the Woods* an unimaginative, conformist society systematically eliminates aliens. In "The Twelfth Bed" old people are shut away in a nursing home run by robots.

When Koontz deals with the theme of the quest and the mythic journey, however, he writes stereotyped pulp science fiction. In *Anti-Man, Nightmare Journey, Dark of the Woods,* and *Warlock,* a hero rebelling from society sets out on a trek, usually through a cold wilderness, in which he encounters strange beasts and exotic phenomena that he eventually overcomes. The women in these works are sex goddesses only, deferential only to the hero, though, as Koontz condescendingly interjects, spunky.

More recently, he has written a series of horror novels in the Stephen King mode, some of which contain a scientific premise. *Phantoms* use a genetically altered organism as the cause of evil.

Frequently, Koontz juxtaposes governmental issues with scientific phenomena. In *Twilight Eyes,* a hidden society of evil goblins masquerade as people but were created by scientists to defend the government against its enemies. *Lightning* features a time traveler and presents a particularly strong woman protagonist who happens to be a novelist. Perhaps all her trials have some autobiographical elements. *Midnight* contains a semi-scientific premise regarding a mad scientist who has discovered a formula that causes genetic mutations. As people devolve into fear-filled, enraged animals, they terrorize a small town.

Other recent novels, such as *Shattered, Darkfall, Whispers, Servants of Twilight,* and *The Bad Place,* cannot be called science fiction, though they use psycho-scientific phenomena such as the closeness of twins, the effects of incest, religious fanaticism, and supernatural elements. In these novels, Koontz returns to sympathetic characters. The men are strong but warm, the women beautiful but competent. Family life is upheld as a premier value, and small-town California is affectionately explored.

A new trend of Koontz's is to rewrite novels that were written under his many pseudonyms. These rewritten novels consistently deal with plots involving government conspiracies and "cover-ups." *The Key to Midnight* presents the daughter of a senator who uncovers a high-security governmental secret. As a result, the heroine is brainwashed and loses her entire identity. *Shadowfires,* also originally written under a pseudonym, involves the government's manufacturing a man who keeps devolving into different stages of evolution.

Thus, Koontz is currently interested in the genres of suspense and in creating hair-raising plots and sensitive characters. If he returns to serious science fiction, he might be well advised to continue to explore his most productive theme of the Cartesian mind-body split and its consequences for what humans define as human. Koontz continues, even in his horror fiction, to define humans as beings who feel, love, and intuit, be that creature man, robot, or beast.

—Kathryn Lee Seidel

KORNBLUTH, C(yril) M.

Pseudonyms: Simon Eisner; Cyril Judd; Jordan Park. **Nationality:** American. **Born:** New York City, 1923. **Education:** University of Chicago, B.A. **Military Service:** Served in the infantry during World War II: Bronze Star. **Family:** Married Mary G. Byers in 1944; two sons. **Career:** Editor, Chicago office of Trans-Radio Press, 1949-51; freelance writer after 1951. **Awards:** Hugo award, 1973. **Died:** 21 March 1958.

SCIENCE FICTION PUBLICATIONS

Novels

Gunner Cade (as Cyril Judd, with Judith Merril). New York, Simon and Schuster, 1952; London, Gollancz, 1964.
Outpost Mars: A Science-Fiction Novel (as Cyril Judd, with Judith Merril). New York, Abelard Press, 1952; London, New English Library, 1966; revised edition, as *Sin in Space: An Expose of the Scarlet Planet,* New York, Galaxy, 1961.

Takeoff. Garden City, New York, Doubleday, 1952.
The Space Merchants, with Frederik Pohl. New York, Ballantine, 1953; London, Heinemann, 1955; revised by Pohl, New York, St. Martin's Press, 1985.
The Syndic. Garden City, New York, Doubleday, 1953; London, Faber, 1964; revised by Pohl, New York, Tor, 1982.
Search the Sky, with Frederik Pohl. New York, Ballantine, 1954; London, Digit, 1960; revised by Pohl, New York, Baen, 1985.
Gladiator-at-Law, with Frederik Pohl. New York, Ballantine, 1955; London, Digit, 1958; revised by Pohl, New York, Baen, 1986; London, Gollancz, 1987.
Not This August. Garden City, New York, Doubleday, 1955; as *Christmas Eve,* London, Joseph, 1956; revised by Pohl, New York, Tor, 1981.
Wolfbane, with Frederik Pohl. New York, Ballantine, 1959; London, Gollancz, 1960; revised by Pohl, New York, Baen, and London, Gollancz, 1986.

Short Stories

The Explorers: Short Stories. New York, Ballantine, 1954.
The Mindworm. London, Joseph, 1955.
A Mile beyond the Moon. Garden City, New York, Doubleday, 1958.
The Marching Morons, and Other Famous Science Fiction Stories. New York, Ballantine, 1959.
The Wonder Effect, with Frederik Pohl. New York, Ballantine, 1962; London, Gollancz, 1967.
Best SF Stories. London, Faber, 1968.
Thirteen O'Clock and Other Zero Hours, edited by James Blish. New York, Dell, 1970; London, Hale, 1972.
The Best of C.M. Kornbluth, edited by Frederik Pohl. Garden City, New York, Doubleday, 1976.
Critical Mass. New York, Bantam, 1977.
Before the Universe and Other Stories: The Best of the Early Work of Science Fiction's Most Famous Team of Collaborators, Including Four Stories Never Before in Book Form, with Frederik Pohl. New York, Bantam, 1980.
Our Best: The Best of Frederik Pohl and C.M. Kornbluth. New York, Baen, 1987.

OTHER PUBLICATIONS

Novels

The Naked Storm (as Simon Eisner). New York, Lion, 1952.
A Town Is Drowning, with Frederik Pohl. New York, Ballantine, 1955; London, Digit, 1960.
Presidential Year, with Frederik Pohl. New York, Ballantine, 1956.

Novels as Jordan Park

Half. New York, Lion, 1953.
Valerie. New York, Lion, 1953.
Sorority House, with Frederik Pohl. New York, Lion, 1956.
The Man of Cold Rages. New York, Pyramid, 1958.

*   *   *

C.M. Kornbluth was a major talent of the specialty magazines in the 1940s and 1950s. Probably best known as a collaborator with

Frederik Pohl on novels of social extrapolation, he was primarily a writer of short stories that frequently contrast cosmic affairs with mundane existence, sometimes to farcical, more often to sardonic, effect.

With Pohl, he helped produce a handful of lively, satiric novels that practically constitute a genre of their own: a brand of near-future dystopia, deriving in part from H.G. Wells, concentrating on one particular facet of society which becomes the dominant force in the world, as in *The Space Merchants* and *Gladiator-at-Law.* In *Search the Sky,* a much lighter and lesser work, the satire mutates into a picaresque romp, exposing Kornbluth's penchant for quick-step burlesque. The other two books, though, are characterized by a continual mordant wit in their serious development of the oppressive rule of socioeconomic institutions. Of course, these institutions are merely exaggerations of those already operating in the modern world, and are invariably connected to the realms of high finance and mass consumption, unlike, say, the dystopian worlds of Zamyatin, Orwell, or even Huxley, which are more distinctly political and totalitarian, and in many ways less directly evolved from the contemporary milieus of those writers. In this regard, Pohl and Kornbluth are more Wellsian, more extrapolative as opposed to symbolic, and much more "radical" in concept and detail than either Huxley or Orwell. The cautionary aspects of *The Space Merchants*—its background of overpopulation, scarcity of resources, pollution, and runaway commercial exploitation—have made it a canonical "prophetic novel" in the wider world outside science fiction.

Their last true collaboration, *Wolfbane,* also deals with a culture of several limited resources, but as a condition ostensibly imposed from outside, by outré alien pyramids who have stolen the Earth-Moon system away from the Sun. The book is almost pure adventure, verging on space opera at the close, but it begins in a setting of material and spiritual poverty acutely drawn in its every detail. Kornbluth never achieved the distinction apart from Pohl that he did alongside him; and Pohl was fond enough of their partnership to "collaborate" with Kornbluth even after the latter's death by working up stories from odd fragments or from their previous common property (*The Wonder Effect* is partly composed of these).

Kornbluth also collaborated with Judith Merril, as Cyril Judd, on *Outpost Mars* and *Gunner Cade.* The second is notable for its vivid evocation of a postholocaust military brotherhood, a spiritual sort of Spartanism. In both, the setting is again a down-at-heels world, but neither story has the inventive brilliance of the major Pohl-Kornbluth novels. However, each of them concerns a legendary/mythic element that resolves itself as a modest distortion of the book's initial reality frame. This thematic concern relates to Kornbluth's best short stories, many of which play with the penetration of everyday existence by the utterly fantastic, the occult, the arcane. Such a tendency may seem axiomatic for science fiction; in Kornbluth, it often ranges beyond the usual boundaries of 1950s SF in tales as diverse in tone as "The Cosmic Expense Account" and "The Last Man Left in the Bar."

On his own, he wrote only three SF novels, *Not This August, Takeoff,* and *The Syndic.* The first two are patent journeyman exercises, apparently slanted for marketing considerations. They are competent, straightforward thrillers, largely unexceptional, only possessing a certain crisp efficiency. The first is the least winsome, giving the drear account of what happens after the Soviets conquer the U.S. It reads like a script aimed at the slick magazines (in fact it was serialized in *Maclean's*) and later adapted to the SF market. *Takeoff* tells the more tolerable—but hoary—story of how an atomic

scientist helps a bunch of teenagers build a moon rocket, with appropriate interference by foreign agents to provide a veneer of suspense. *The Syndic* is another matter. Though it seems oddly cobbled together, it is nevertheless quite engaging and is Kornbluth's best solo novel. It incorporates satire, parody, homiletic fable, pulp adventure, and irrelevant moral lecture, accented by sudden left turns in the plot. Its primary narrative premise is a marvel of ironic supposition: the U.S. government, for just cause, has been exiled to the unfriendly shores of a primitive Ireland by a coalition of laissez-faire smugglers and racketeers, the good-time guys and dolls of the Syndic. Ostensibly a straight adventure story, it ultimately seems to be a loose composite of favorite crotchets, including a forceful depiction of Earth-magic which somehow manages not to blow the narrative beyond the pale of mainline SF.

Where Kornbluth truly excelled was in his shorter work, the bulk of which appeared in the collections *The Explorers, A Mile beyond the Moon,* and *The Marching Morons.* It is often madly comic; and as often sharp and deadly. At its best, it is brief, evocative, to the point; short on description, but full of vivid impressions; and usually possessed of a clearly developed moral thrust, if not always an explicit moral. His strong satiric mode slides easily into march-hare burlesque, in pieces like "Passion Pill," "Thirteen O'Clock," and "Virginia." The omnipresent sardonicism emerges most fiercely in tightly woven shorts like "The Words of Guru," "The Silly Season," and "The Rocket of 1955," but also in longer works like "Two Dooms" and "The Marching Morons." The latter two are Kornbluth's most visibly hortatory stories, although neither exists simply for the sake of its overt "lesson." He also wrote pure, slick adventures, playful novelettes like "The Slave" and "Make Mine Mars," which captivate by virtue of sheer readability, a deftness in the handling of stock figures and basic emotional appeals. And all the above, even the darkest tales, are rendered with a spritely touch; they do not sag in the middle, and there is ever a little crooked smile lurking somewhere in the corners.

Kornbluth's view of humanity may seem perplexing and inconsistent. He is sometimes accused of being a hard-case cynic, an elitist who views himself as above the common run. This is not entirely fallacious in light of "The Marching Morons"; in foreseeing a future populated mainly by just-plain-dopes, it is largely a metaphor for what Kornbluth saw around him in his own time. Yet he had a profound affection for lowly, downtrodden people, for stumblebums and gutter folk, and even some salesmen. In part it may have been the fondness of an aficionado, a collector of "characters." But he was not without a good deal of genuine sympathy, especially for those who were caught in situations they barely understood, like the deformed space pilot in "The Altar at Midnight," or for those who understood too well, like the narrator-physicist of the same story and the young genius of "Gomez." Better remembered, perhaps, are his treatments of workaday grifters and con artists, like Honest John Barlow of "Morons" or the sly narrator of "1955"—people who have no sympathy at all, and who, however clever, always get the axe at the finale. If Kornbluth sometimes admired their grit and savvy, he was also moved to exact revenge on behalf of their victims.

Though he is often viewed as a commentator on the social fabric, and the various forms of human folly, there is more to Kornbluth than the wary futurologist, the wry chronicler of crafty deals ("1955," "Time Bum"), or even the compassionate observer of human detritus ("The Little Black Bag," "The Altar at Midnight"). And this something more is his sense of the unknown and the unknowable, the hidden layers of reality, the levels of illusion enveloping the world (whether social or metaphysical). Many of his most notable, most intensely realized stories hover somewhere between strict fantasy and strictest science fiction. Both "The Words of Guru" and "Kazam Collects" are outright fantasies, of the sort that "pierce the veil" of ordinary sense, and yet they have the resolute authority, the absolute conviction, of things seen and heard and done. They begin in fairly typical urban settings, enticing the reader through unsuspected realms to arrive at states of being that can only be termed ineffable and exalted, the one horrific, the other all beauty and benevolence. "The Silly Season," a tensely told shocker, provides a contest between a series of uncanny but rather palpable illusions and the normalizing nature of daily journalism. "The Cosmic Expense Account" sets the mundane and extraordinary in adjacent territories, as a crippling "cosmic-harmony" engulfs eastern Pennsylvania. And in the jocose "Virginia," our furtive public mythologies about the Secret Masterdom of the Super Rich are made the binding private reality of an heir to fortune. Characteristically, Kornbluth does not simply mention, but actually offers a short tour of, the Museum of Suppressed Inventions.

These tales center on initiation into various kinds of arcane knowledge; and "Guru" and "Kazam" focus on persons of a special nature, born to acquire a special sort of knowledge, and power. This striving after knowledge is at the core of Kornbluth's most elusive and provocative piece of writing, "The Last Man Left in the Bar." Published very late in his career (1957), this short but densely packed work distills all his previous concerns with kinds and visions of reality, and it is a tour de force of oblique, kaleidoscopic narrative worthy of the wildest "experiments" of the New Wave. It portrays the psychological aftermath of an apparent momentary transposition of worlds. It mingles drunken uncertainties and digressions with the haunting obscurities of a poorly apprehended experience. In a landscape of shifting knowledge, the one constant is that its technical-protagonist never does learn the answers, the wherefores of his predicament. His passionate desire to know is countered by the obstinate complexity of the universe, and by willful creatures who are absorbed in their own very separate interests and imperatives.

—Alex Eisenstein

KOTZWINKLE, William

Nationality: American. **Born:** Scranton, Pennsylvania, 22 November 1938. **Education:** Rider College, Lawrenceville, New Jersey; Pennsylvania State University, University Park. **Family:** Married Elizabeth Gundy in 1970. **Career:** Cook, Le Figaro Cafe, New York City, 1963; wrote for tabloid newspaper, mid-1960s. Lived in New York 1957-70, New Brunswick, Canada, 1970-83, and Maine since 1983. **Awards:** Bread Loaf Conference Scholarship; World Fantasy award, 1977. **Address:** c/o Putnam's, 200 Madison Avenue, New York, New York 10016, U.S.A.

SCIENCE FICTION PUBLICATIONS

Novels (series: E.T.)

Hermes 3000. New York, Pantheon, 1972.

Doctor Rat. New York, Knopf, and Henley-on-Thames, Oxfordshire, Ellis, 1976.
The Leopard's Tooth (for children). New York, Seabury Press, 1976.
The Ants Who Took away Time (for children). Garden City, New York, Doubleday, 1978.
Herr Nightingale and the Satin Woman. New York, Knopf, 1978; London, Hutchinson, 1979.
E.T.: The Extra-Terrestrial in His Adventure on Earth (novelization of screenplay). New York, Putnam, and London, Barker, 1982; adapted for children as *E.T., the Extraterrestrial Storybook*, New York, Putnam, 1982.
Superman III (novelization of screenplay). New York, Warner, and London, Arrow, 1983.
E.T.: The Book of the Green Planet. New York, Berkley, 1985; adapted for children as *E.T.: The Storybook of the Green Planet*, New York, Putnam, 1985.
The Exile. New York, Seymour Lawrence, and London, Bodley Head, 1987.

Short Stories

Trouble in Bugland: A Collection of Inspector Mantis Mysteries. New York, Godine, 1983.
Jewel of the Moon. New York, Putnam, 1985.
Hearts of Wood and Other Timeless Tales. New York, Godine, 1986.
The Hot Jazz Trio. Boston, Houghton Mifflin, 1989; London, Black Swan, 1991.

OTHER PUBLICATIONS

Novels

The Fan Man. New York, Avon, and Henley-on-Thames, Oxfordshire, Ellis, 1974.
Night-Book. New York, Avon, 1974.
Swimmer in the Secret Sea. New York, Avon, 1975; Henley-on-Thames, Oxfordshire, Ellis, 1976.
Fata Morgana. New York, Knopf, and London, Hutchinson, 1977.
Jack in the Box. New York, Putnam, 1980; London, Abacus, 1981; as *Book of Love*, Boston, Houghton Mifflin, 1990.
Christmas at Fontaine's. New York, Putnam, 1982; London, Deutsch, 1983.
Queen of Swords. New York, Putnam, and London, Deutsch, 1984.
The Midnight Examiner. Boston, Houghton Mifflin, 1989.
The Game of Thirty. Boston, Houghton Mifflin, 1994.

Short Stories

Elephant Bangs Train. New York, Pantheon, and London, Faber, 1971.

Other (for children)

The Fireman. New York, Pantheon, 1969.
The Ship That Came down the Gutter. New York, Pantheon, 1970; Kingswood, Surrey, World's Work, 1976.
Elephant Boy: A Story of the Stone Age. New York, Farrar Straus, 1970.

The Day the Gang Got Rich. New York, Viking Press, 1970.
The Oldest Man and Other Timeless Stories. New York, Pantheon, 1971.
Return of Crazy Horse. New York, Farrar Straus, 1971.
The Supreme, Superb, Exalted, and Delightful, One and Only Magic Building. New York, Farrar Straus, 1973.
Up the Alley with Jack and Joe. New York, Macmillan, 1974.
Dream of Dark Harbor. Garden City, New York, Doubleday, 1979.
The Nap Master. New York, Harcourt Brace, 1979.
Great World Circus. New York, Putnam, 1983.
The World Is Big and I'm So Small. New York, Crown, 1986.
The Empty Notebook. New York, Godine, 1990.

*   *   *

William Kotzwinkle is best known to science fiction readers as the author of *Superman III*—the novelization of the movie—and the two *E.T.* books.

E.T.: The Extra-Terrestrial is an excellent novelization of Melissa Mathison's screenplay. Kotzwinkle's novelization became a best-selling paperback selling more than three million copies. It's follow-up, *E.T.: The Book of the Green Planet,* is based on a story by director Stephen Spielberg. Kotzwinkle makes E.T.'s planet come alive with bizarre characters like E.T.'s sidekick, Flopglopple, and vegetable creatures like the jumpums. Kotzwinkle's writing brings humor to the story, especially in E.T.'s communication with Elliot, who's becoming a typical teenager.

Kotzwinkle has published over 30 books, including novels, short story collections, children's books, poetry, and plays. His range extends from the wild humor of his most popular short story collection, *Elephant Bangs Train,* to the erotic juxtapositioning in *Night-Book,* to the moving autobiographical novel about the death of Kotzwinkle's child in *Swimmer in the Secret Sea.*

In 1977, Kotzwinkle won the World Fantasy award for *Doctor Rat,* a fable exposing human cruelty towards animals years before the rise of the animal rights movement. Much of Kotzwinkle's work deals in fantasy. His latest collection of stories, *The Hot Jazz Trio,* features strange and bizarre situations. For example, in the collection's lead story set in 1920s Paris, "Django Reinhardt Played the Blues," a magician's assistant gets lost in another dimension. Leading the rescue party into the Vanishing Box is Django Reinhardt, legendary Belgian jazz-blues guitarist, who is joined by Picasso and Jean Cocteau. Another story in the collection, "Boxcar Blues," features two circus performers who flee Death with a group of hoboes.

On occasion, Kotzwinkle's work can be weirdly real. Based on his 1960s experience as an editor-writer for a supermarket tabloid, *The Midnight Examiner* is the story of tabloid editor Howard Halliday's encounter with Mafia revenge. The farcical plot only serves as a vehicle for Kotzwinkle to score points on the world of tabloids in his humorous style.

More seriously, Kotzwinkle mixes realism and fantasy in *The Exile.* David Caspian, a Hollywood actor, finds himself transported back to Nazi Germany. He becomes a black marketeer as Kotzwinkle blends contemporary L.A. with Hitler's Germany. The juxtaposition of realities illustrates Kotzwinkle's point that everyone is a mixture of opposites.

Other titles, such as *The Fan Man* and *Hermes 3000,* are cult novels. Horse Badorties, the hippie con-man hero of *The Fan Man,* attracts readers because among all Kotzwinkle's characters he is the freest spirit.

Fata Morgana is a detective story set in Paris in 1861. Inspector Picard investigates the mysterious Ric Lazare and his fortune-telling machine. When Picard has his own fortune read, the story spins into the realm of illusion. *Herr Nightingale and the Satin Woman* is an exercise in murky surrealism. *Christmas at Fontaine's* is based on Kotzwinkle's experience playing Santa at E.J. Korvette's in the 1960s. *Queen of Swords* is a novel based on magic and tarot.

Kotzwinkle's astonishing breadth of subjects, characters, situations, and themes keeps his work fresh and innovative.

—George Kelley

KRESS, Nancy (Anne Koningisor)

Nationality: American. **Born:** Buffalo, New York, 20 January 1948. **Education:** State University of New York at Plattsburgh, B.S. 1969 (summa cum laude); State University of New York at Brockport, M.S. in Education 1978; State University of New York at Brockport, M.A. in English 1979. **Family:** Married 1) Michael Joseph Kress in 1973 (divorced 1984); two sons; 2) Marcos (Mark Patrick) Donnelly in 1988 (divorced 1994). **Career:** Elementary teacher in public schools in Rochester, New York, 1969-70; elementary teacher in Penn Yan School District, New York, 1970-73; instructor, State University of NY at Brockport, English Department, 1981-83; copywriter, Stanton & Hucko, Rochester, NY, 1984-89; instructor, Clarion East, 1992 and 1995; instructor, Clarion West, 1992 and 1994; summer instructor, State University of NY at Brockport Writers' Forum, 1982-93; instructor, Cleveland State Imagination Workshop (summer), 1995. Since 1990, full-time writer and part-time freelance copywriter. **Awards:** Nebula, 1985, 1991; Hugo, 1992. **Member:** Science Fiction Writers of America. **Agent:** Ralph Vicinanza, 111 Eighth Avenue, New York, New York 10011. **Address:** 50 Sweden Hill Road, Brockport, New York 14420, U.S.A.

SCIENCE FICTION PUBLICATIONS

Novels (series: Beggars)

The Prince of Morning Bells. New York, Pocket, 1981.
The Golden Grove. New York, Bluejay, 1984.
The White Pipes. New York, Bluejay, 1985.
An Alien Light: A Novel. New York, Arbor House, 1988; London, Legend, 1989.
Brain Rose. New York, Morrow, 1990; London, Legend, 1991; as *Brainrose,* New York, Avon, 1991.
Beggars in Spain. New York, Morrow, 1993.
Beggars and Choosers. New York, Tor, 1994.
Oaths and Miracles. New York, Tor, 1995.

Short Stories

Trinity and Other Stories. New York, Bluejay, 1985.
Beggars in Spain (novella). Eugene, Oregon, Axolotl Press, Pulphouse Publishing, 1991; as "Beggars in Spain," in *Isaac Asimov's Science Fiction* (New York), April 1991.
The Price of Oranges. Eugene, Oregon, Pulphouse, 1992.

The Aliens of Earth. Sauk City, Wisconsin, Arkham House, 1993.

OTHER PUBLICATIONS

Other

Beginnings, Middles, and Ends. Cincinnati, Ohio, Writer's Digest, 1993.

*

Nancy Kress comments:

My writing career, artistic method, and subgenre classification all resemble each other: a slow unplanned drift toward unexpected destinations.

Unlike many of my colleagues, I never planned to be a writer. In my late twenties, home full-time with infants, I wrote a story. Then another. Later, another. By stages, none of them planned, I wrote SF rather than some other genre; I was published; I wrote novels; I left corporate work to write full-time. There are still days when I am astonished to discover that I do this for a living. And yet, paradoxically, it also feels inevitable, the natural outcome of a life spent reading, thinking, dreaming.

Similarly, the writing of my fiction follows an unplanned path. I seldom know the ending of a story or novel before I begin. I start with characters and situation, and I write in order to discover what happens to them. The process, even when the story concerns hard science, is organic. When it works, the ending feels inevitable to me. It doesn't always work. Farming is an uncertain life.

I began my career by writing fantasy. After three novels I switched to science fiction—another unplanned move. The biologic sciences increasingly fascinate me, especially genetic engineering. Here be both dragons and the future. My sons, or theirs, will someday have to make some very hard decisions about the immense possibilities of manipulating DNA. This interests me because people—fictional or real—are never more themselves than when they make choices for others.

Every life is a combination of choices and accidents. My characters', my colleagues', mine. Sometimes this is clearest when both choices and accidents are set in the future, or a future. Everything stands out in bolder relief. Science fiction gives us that, and this is why I write it.

*   *   *

Nancy Kress started her career writing just slightly offbeat versions of traditional fantasy themes in novels like *The Prince of Morning Bells, The Golden Grove,* and *The White Pipes.* The first of these is a witty, slyly humorous story about a young girl and a magical purple dog who have a series of adventures in strange lands, each of which takes some human tendency to an extreme, generally with humorous effects. One kingdom, for example, determines everything by ruthless rationality while another resorts to mysticism in every instance.

The Golden Grove borrows from European mythology. On a mysterious island stands the grove of the title, wherein several women spend their lives weaving fantastic tapestries from spider silk. Something is apparently poisoning the grove, however, for the spiders are dying, leaving the women with time to think about their situation and worry about the future. One of them, Arachne,

decides to break the pattern of her life, paradoxically hoping to restore things to the way they were of old by changing herself. A storyteller with the power to mentally create visible animated scenes illustrating her stories is the protagonist of *The White Pipes.* Her abilities eventually get her into trouble when she visits a land convulsed by secret power struggles, falls in love, realizes that her abilities could be exploited by one of the contending factions, and subsequently finds herself in terrible danger.

Her fourth novel moved from fantasy to science fiction, and she has produced most of her subsequent work in that area. *An Alien Light* is superficially an old story retold, aliens studying humans on a primitive world to discover why we continue to practice violence on one another even after developing a high degree of intelligence. The observers become emotionally involved with their project and eventually discover a nobility they hadn't expected to find. Although occasionally awkward, there are clear indications of the more serious themes that would characterize Kress's subsequent work.

Brainrose is a far more impressive work, a well thought out and executed story set in a chaotic, dystopian future. Extrapolating from modern trends, Kress portrays a future in which a new disease erases human memories, mega-corporations finance churches as commercial ventures, extremists resort to random terrorist acts, and new techniques have been developed that allow people to recall their previous lives. The protagonists discover that the latter is a mixed blessing when they dredge up memories of traumas from their past.

Beggars in Spain and *Beggars and Choosers* are the first two thirds of a trilogy that explores the question of what it is to be human and what the consequences might be if we choose to interfere with our own evolution as a species. The opening volume follows the early life of Leisha Camden, a brilliant young woman who has been genetically modified so that she will never need to sleep. Although her physical and mental abilities allow her to achieve remarkable intellectual achievements, she and others of her kind are soon faced with intolerance and ultimately open hatred by unmodified humans who fear that they will be at a disadvantage competing with the newcomers.

Violence escalates as the story continues, until the "sleepless" decide to remove themselves from ordinary human society and use their enhanced mental abilities to create a new world for themselves. The majority of normal humans suffer from boredom and unease, because the genetically modified have taken over most of the good jobs. Their suppressed anger turns toward the Sleepless, because they are the most clearly different from ordinary human stock. Paradoxically then, the effort to separate themselves from the rest of humanity causes greater resentment and a growing fear.

Kress has also enjoyed considerable success as a short story writer, winning both the Hugo and Nebula for the original novelet on which *Beggars in Spain* is based, and another Nebula for "Out of All Them Bright Stars." The latter story is a scathing commentary on human shortsightedness, prejudice, and general bad manners, all wrapped around a single incident when an alien walks into a small town diner.

"With the Original Cast" is one of several Kress stories dealing with reincarnation, and one of her best. A new production of Shaw's play about Joan of Arc takes an unexpected turn when the actress cast in the title role discovers that she is the reincarnation of the original Maid of Orleans. "The Battle of Long Island" is an alternate history story of sorts, involving a Revolutionary War that wasn't quite the same one we remember, and a woman who has possibly faulty memories of old pain.

In "The Price of Oranges," the protagonist discovers how to travel back to 1937, so he buys his groceries there and works in the present. "Margin of Error" is a short but chilling revenge story, in which a frustrated woman programs a flaw in the nanotechnology designed to keep a lifelong rival young and attractive. The darkly comedic "The Death of John Patrick Yoder" features a man whose accidental death notice alters his entire life.

The novelet "Dancing on Air" is another story dealing with physical alteration of the human body. In this case, ballerinas are illegally using bioenhancers to improve their performances, and someone is murdering members of their profession. The protagonist is a reporter who suspects a highly respected newcomer has been enhanced but cannot prove it. The rising cost of health care and measures to keep it down are central to "The Mountain to Mohammed." Genetic scanning allows companies to hire only those with no predisposition to disease, and hospitals even screen those they don't wish to treat using similar techniques.

Other stories of note include "Shadows on the Cave Wall," "Casey's Empire," "Trinity," "Spillage," "To Scale," and "Philippa's Hands." Most of her better short fiction has been collected in *Trinity* and *The Aliens of Earth*. Kress is one of those rare writers who seems equally at ease writing novels and short stories, although it is in the latter area that she has so far attracted the most favorable comment. Her "Beggars" trilogy is likely to alter that perception although she continues to work very actively at all lengths.

—Don D'Ammassa

KUBE-McDOWELL, Michael P(aul)

Pseudonym: Michael Hudson. **Nationality:** American. **Born:** Philadelphia, 29 August 1954. **Education:** Michigan State University, East Lansing, B.A. in education 1976; Indiana University, Bloomington, M.S. in education 1981. **Family:** Married Karla Jane Kube in 1975 (divorced 1987); one son. **Career:** Science and math teacher in public schools in Middlebury, Indiana, 1976-83; instructor, Miles Laboratories, Elkhart, Indiana, 1978-80; correspondent, *Truth,* Elkhart, 1982-84; instructor, Goshen College, Goshen, Indiana, 1984-85; screenwriter, Laurel TV Inc., New York, 1985-86; instructor, Clarion SF Workshop, East Lansing, Michigan, 1990. Since 1981, book reviewer for *South Bend Tribune,* Indiana, and since 1983, full-time writer. **Agent:** Russell Galen, Scott Meredith Literary Agency, 845 Third Avenue, New York, New York 10022. **Address:** P.O. Box 22066, Lansing, Michigan, 48909-2066, U.S.A.

SCIENCE FICTION PUBLICATIONS

Novels (series: Trigon Disunity)

Isaac Asimov's Robot City: Odyssey. New York, Ace, 1987; London, Orbit, 1988.
Thieves of Light (as Michael Hudson). New York, Berkley, 1987.
　The Trigon Disunity:
　Emprise. New York, Berkley, 1985; London, Legend, 1988.
　Enigma. New York, Berkley, 1986; London, Legend, 1988.
　Empery. New York, Berkley, 1987; London, Legend, 1988.

Alternities. New York, Ace, 1988; London, Sphere, 1989.
The Quiet Pools. New York, Ace, 1990.
Exile. New York, Ace, 1992.

OTHER PUBLICATIONS

Plays

Television Plays: "Slippage," 1984, "Lifebomb," 1985, "Effect and Cause," 1985, and "The Bitterest Pill," 1986, all in the *Tales from the Darkside* series.

*

Michael P. Kube-McDowell comments:

I once believed that I wrote science fiction to cheat time. In more than one interview, I've asserted that the human species has an interesting—and possibly long—future ahead of it, and that writing SF allowed me to play in tomorrows I won't live to see.

That's still arguably true, and probably accounts in part for the human-focused, Earth-based, near-future emphasis of most of my fiction. But I've come to realize that there's more to it than that.

In retrospect, I've become aware that my writing has become part of my exploration of two basic questions: What is the nature of the universe we inhabit? And, why do we humans do what we do?

These are live questions of continuing interest, driving not only scientific but mystical inquiry, and firmly linked to the pains, frustrations, and joys of being alive. None of us is in possession of final and ultimate answers. (In my experience, those who believe they are prove to have simply cut off their inquiry too soon.)

We're playing the blindfold-and-elephant game, and each of us has a different piece of the elephant—a unique set of inherited and experiential clues. In a sense, each new story, each successive novel, is my way of calling out to the rest of you, "Here's how it looks to me at the moment. . . ."

But "Answering Big Questions" is too grand a pretension and too great a responsibility for everyday storytelling, because a theme does not a story make. A novel is about life as the writer sees it, and ordinary people as the writer understands them. The writer ought not sit down at the keyboard to confess, or to invent, but to give witness. And a novel ought not be an essay, or a tract, but a story. Not my story. *Their* story.

Who are "they"? The people who are caught in the pincers—the characters. When I begin work on a novel, I have to know where it ends, and through whose eyes I can see it: the moment, the feeling, sometimes the exact words. When I've found a place where I can stand to be silent witness to the turns, travails and small triumphs of their lives, then, and only then, am I ready to start writing.

As I write, I have a much stronger sense of watching than creating: I find myself sorting out what must have happened, rather than "making it up." The only decision that seems to belong to me is where to begin telling the story. Two points, beginning and ending, define a line, but stories, like lives, are not straight lines. Past Chapter One, I'm embarked on a journey of discovery, learning as I go how the beginning and the ending are connected.

Because of that, it strikes me that each new fiction isn't really "about" its plot, or the characters, or the setting, or the theme, or the deconstructed analysis of its literary entrails. It's about a place I found to stand, and something I saw from there, and the feelings and thoughts that experience evoked in me. Each work, in its totality, is nothing more or less than my carefully worded invitation to come and stand where I stood, and experience it for yourself.

As best as I can tell with this blindfold on, that's what fiction is all about.

*   *   *

Michael P. Kube-McDowell emerged in the 1980s as one of the best new hard science fiction writers. His finest work may be categorized as "cosmic science fiction," a subgenre characterized by a cosmic sense of wonder about the physical universe, in stories which often span great distances of space and time, and may be best exemplified by the work of Arthur C. Clarke.

Kube-McDowell's career has followed a pattern quite common in the science-fiction field. In the early 1980s, he began to build a reputation for his short fiction. His first story, "The Inevitable Conclusion," appeared in *Amazing Stories* in August 1979, and would later prove to be the first of many stories and novels set in his "Trigon Disunity" universe. His fifth published story, "Slac//," a well-constructed puzzle story (that would have been quite at home in *Analog*) about a xenological mission seeking to determine why their first expedition party disappeared and how the disappearance was connected to the relationship between the two primary intelligent species, was chosen as one of the best stories of 1981 by Donald Wollheim in his best-of-the-year volume. His 1983 fantasy "Slippage," a quintessential *Twilight Zone* story, was chosen for Karl Edward Wagner's *The Year's Best Horror Stories* (1983), and was subsequently selected by George Romero to be adapted into an episode of the television series "Tales from the Dark Side" in the 1984-85 season. Kube-McDowell's involvement with television continued between 1985 and 1987 with three teleplays for "Tales from the Darkside." These included an original teleplay, an adaptation of his story "Lifebomb," and an adaptation of a story by Frederik Pohl.

In 1983, Kube-McDowell left his profession as a high school science teacher to begin writing full time, and proved to be an even more successful writer when he moved to novel length. His first novel, *Emprise,* appeared in 1985, launching his thousand-year "Trigon Disunity" future history. It was critically well received and became a finalist for the Philip K. Dick award. He published two other novels in the "Trigon Disunity" series, *Enigma* (1986) and *Empery* (1987). These three novels share a common universe and future history. In *Emprise,* humanity sends out a spaceship to meet alien visitors to our Solar System, only to find that the visitors are human. In *Enigma,* the human protagonist is taken by a member of a race of energy-beings into the fabric of space-time where he learns that 70,000 years ago a technological Earth culture colonized other worlds, but was destroyed by a powerful alien race that is about to return. In *Empery,* mankind tries to make a preemptive strike on the aliens before they can again destroy mankind. These novels, like most of Kube-McDowell's science fiction, are often primarily involved in political struggles between various factions of characters.

He also wrote *Odyssey* (1987), the first book in the *Isaac Asimov's Robot City* series, demonstrating an ability to imitate Asimov's clear and straightforward prose and plotting style. His next book was *Alternities,* a novel about an alternative version of the U.S. whose leadership knows how to move between various "alternities," which are similar parallel realities (none of which happen to be the one we live in). Political intrigue abounds in this fast-paced science fiction thriller.

Kube-McDowell's most acclaimed book to date is *The Quiet Pools* (1990), a selection of the Book-of-the-Month Club and a nominee for the Hugo award. It is set in a future Earth faced with overpopulation and resulting ecological damage. A major project is organized and is working on a second city-sized starship to carry 10,000 men and women to a new life outside our solar system. A covert organization fervently and violently opposes the project, seen by some as mankind's last great hope. This novel posits that the desire of some to explore and move out into new frontiers may be a genetic trait that is absent in some members of our species. The novel imagines this situation leading to a human interstellar diaspora of those humans who have the trait, while those who don't stay on the depleted Earth much as the "quiet pools" sought by salmon after they have laid their eggs and are waiting to die. It is a powerful and moving hypothesis, aimed at the very heart and soul of the doctrine of science fiction.

In his latest novel, *Exile* (1992), Kube-McDowell once again chose a far-future, other-planet locale, a long-lost planet with a regressed society. The intellectually stagnant and highly regimented society is very reminiscent of modern communist China, including a tragic rebellion in a Tianamen-like city square. The novel presents an engaging view of the necessity of social dissent, and the price it extracts.

Kube-McDowell has been an instructor at the Clarion Science Fiction Workshop and has served on the jury for the Nebula award. He is also an accomplished musician and vocalist, and has played viola and keyboards with The Black Book Band, performing at science fiction conventions. Outside of science fiction, he is the author of more than 500 nonfiction articles on subjects ranging from space careers to "scientific creationism," including a four-part award-winning series on the state of American education.

—D. Douglas Fratz

KURLAND, Michael (Joseph)

Nationality: American. **Born:** New York City, 1 March 1938. **Education:** Hiram College, Ohio, 1955-56; University of Maryland overseas, 1961-62; Columbia University, New York, 1962-63. **Military Service:** Served in the United States Army, 1958-62. **Family:** Married Rebecca Jacobson in 1976 (divorced). **Career:** News editor, KPFK-Radio, Los Angeles, 1966; English teacher, Happy Valley School, Ojai, California, 1967; editor, *Crawdaddy,* New York, 1969; also a play director, road manager for a band, advertising copywriter, and ghost writer; editor, Pennyfarthing Press, San Franciso and Berkeley, California, 1976-78; president, Computer Press Association, 1989-90. **Agent:** Sharon Jarvis, R.R. 2, Box 16-B, Laceyville, Pennsylvania 18623, U.S.A. **Online Address:** Lollygags@AOL.COM.

SCIENCE FICTION PUBLICATIONS

Novels (series: Lord Darcy)

Ten Years to Doomsday: A Science Fiction Novel, with Chester Anderson. New York, Pyramid, 1964.
The Unicorn Girl. New York, Pyramid, 1969.

Transmission Error. New York, Pyramid, 1970.
The Whenabouts of Burr. New York, DAW, 1975.
Pluribus. Garden City, New York, Doubleday, 1975.
Tomorrow Knight. New York, DAW, 1976.
The Princes of Earth (for children). Nashville, Nelson, 1978.
The Last President, with S.W. Barton. New York, Morrow, 1980.
Psi Hunt. New York, Berkley, 1980.
First Cycle, with H. Beam Piper. New York, Ace, 1982.
Death by Gaslight. New York, New American Library, 1982.
Star Griffin. Garden City, New York, Doubleday, 1987.
Ten Little Wizards (Lord Darcy). New York, Ace, 1988.
Perchance. New York, New American Library, 1989.
A Study in Sorcery (Lord Darcy). New York, Ace, 1989.
Button Bright. New York, Jove, 1990.

OTHER PUBLICATIONS

Novels

Mission: Third Force. New York, Pyramid, 1967.
Mission: Tank War. New York, Pyramid, 1968.
Mission: Police Action. New York, Pyramid, 1969.
A Plague of Spies. New York, Pyramid, 1969.
The Secret of Benjamin Square (as Jennifer Plum). New York, Lancer, 1972.
The Infernal Device. New York, New American Library, and London, New English Library, 1979.

Other

The Spymaster's Handbook. New York, Facts on File, 1988.
A Gallery of Rogues: Portraits in True Crime. New York, Prentice-Hall General Reference, 1994.
How to Solve a Murder: The Forensic Handbook. New York, Macmillan, 1995.

Editor, *The Redward Edward Papers,* by Avram Davidson. Garden City, New York, Doubleday, 1978.
Editor, *The Best of Avram Davidson.* Garden City, New York, Doubleday, 1979.

*

Manuscript Collection: American Heritage Center, University of Wyoming.

Michael Kurland comments:

I try to entertain.

*   *   *

Michael Kurland's first two science fiction novels were written in conjunction with Chester Anderson. The first, a conventional collaboration, was *Ten Years to Doomsday,* a lightweight and readable book concerned with the need for an entire planet to change from a feudal/pre-technological to a fully scientific/industrial state in a decade to stave off a planned invasion. Kurland has stated that

this book was written as a parody of the works of Poul Anderson. Either as parody or in its own right, the book is fairly successful. The second novel has a more complicated history. When Anderson wrote his popular novel *The Butterfly Kid,* he included himself, Kurland, and a third friend, Tom Waters, as characters. Anderson's novel imposes a comedic alien-invasion theme upon the bohemian East Village milieu of the 1960s with hilarious results. Kurland's *The Unicorn Girl* is a sequel, continuing its themes and characters, though it is generally regarded as less successful. (Waters added a third book to the series, *The Probability Pad.*)

Kurland's first fully solo novel was *Transmission Error.* In this book he established a protagonist of generally likeable nature, his traits including considerable wit and resourcefulness, but also a feckless ability to get himself into insoluble dilemmas. He is accidentally transported to an alien planet and threatened with a life of slavery. He escapes this situation and plunges into a series of similarly unresolved problems.

By this point the general pattern of Kurland's books had become clear. Kurland is highly adept at creating societies which are compellingly believable, and populating them with vivid and sympathetic characters. His style is lively, warm, and highly informal. His stories are told with rapidity of pace and great variety of setting and incident. Their major flaw is a failure—whether by the author or his protagonist—to grapple with and satisfactorily resolve problems. The "solutions" offered are almost invariably flight rather than confrontation.

This pattern holds through Kurland's later novels, although their basic premises are wholly different from one another. *The Whenabouts of Burr* is a chase-novel proceeding through multiple parallel worlds. *Pluribus,* probably Kurland's most successful novel in the genre, takes place in a semi-barbaric future United States. The book abounds in vivid imagery, including an unforgettable scene of the protagonist, arrested for some local infraction, being removed in a standard "black-and-white" California Highway Patrol cruiser—drawn by a team of horses! *Tomorrow Knight* (the title is indicative of Kurland's love for puns and other wordplay) takes place on a planet divided, checker-board fashion, into hundreds of miniature stage-set societies. Yet in all the books, the general pattern of insoluble problem and flight persists.

The Princes of Earth is favorably comparable to standard Heinlein juveniles, containing the usual Kurland mix of convincing future societies, sympathetic characters, intriguing problem-situations, and rapid transfer from problem to problem. There is also an excellent infusion of satire, most notably a hilarious parody of the Church of Scientology. Although no further books in the series have yet appeared, *The Princes of Earth* is clearly intended as the opening volume of a series.

While Michael Kurland has seldom appeared to be a prolific author, his protracted and usually steady production of science fiction (and other works) has permitted him to accumulate a body of some 20 novels and other books. He boasted a longtime friendship with the late Randall Garrett, and following Garrett's death Kurland wrote a novel, *Star Griffin,* that had originally been intended as a collaboration between himself and Garrett. An interplanetary tale, the book shows Garrett's presence and stands as a fitting memorial to him. In similar fashion, Kurland expanded, revised, and prepared for publication *First Cycle,* a novel left in rough form by H. Beam Piper at the time of his death.

—Richard A. Lupoff

KURTZ, Katherine

Nationality: American. **Born:** Coral Gables, Florida, 18 October 1944. **Education:** University of Miami, Coral Gables, B.S. in chemistry 1966; University of California, Los Angeles, M.A. in history 1971. **Family:** Married Scott Roderick MacMillan in 1983; one stepson. **Career:** Senior training technician, Los Angeles Police Department, 1969-81. Since 1981, full-time writer. **Agent:** Russell Galen, Scovil Chichak Galen Literary Agency, 381 Park Avenue South, Suite 1020, New York, New York 10016, U.S.A. **Address:** Holybrooke Hall, Bray, County Wicklow, Ireland.

Science Fiction Publications

Novels (series: Legends of Saint Camber; Chronicles of the Deryni; Heirs of Saint Camber; Histories of King Kelson)

Deryni Rising. New York, Ballantine, 1970; London, Pan-Ballantine, 1973.
Deryni Checkmate. New York, Ballantine, 1972; London, Pan-Ballantine, 1973.
High Deryni. New York, Ballantine, 1973; London, Century, 1985.
Camber of Culdi. New York, Ballantine, 1976; London, Century, 1985.
Saint Camber. New York, Ballantine, 1978; London, Century, 1985.
Camber the Heretic. New York, Ballantine, 1981; London, Legend, 1986.
The Bishop's Heir (King Kelson). New York, Ballantine, 1984; London, Century, 1985.
The King's Justice (King Kelson). New York, Ballantine, 1985; London, Legend, 1986.
The Quest for Saint Camber (King Kelson). New York, Ballantine, 1986; London, Century, 1987.
The Legacy of Lehr. New York, Walker, 1986; London, Century, 1988.
The Harrowing of Gwynedd (Heirs of Saint Camber). New York, Ballantine, and London, Century, 1989.
The Adept, with Deborah Turner Harris. New York, Ace, 1991; Wallington, Surrey, Severn House, 1992.
King Javan's Year (Heirs of Saint Camber). New York, Ballantine, 1992.
The Lodge of the Lynx, with Deborah Turner Harris. New York, Ace, 1992; Wallington, Surrey, Severn House, 1993.
The Templar Treasure, with Deborah Turner Harris. New York, Ace, 1993; Wallington, Surrey, Severn House, 1994.
The Bastard Prince (Heirs of Saint Camber). New York, Ballantine, 1994.
Dagger Magic, with Deborah Turner Harris. New York, Ace, 1995.

Short Stories

The Deryni Archives. New York, Ballantine, 1986; London, Legend, 1988.

Other Publications

Novel

Lammas Night. New York, Ballantine, 1983; London, Severn House, 1986.

Other

Deryni Magic: A Grimoire. New York, Ballantine, 1991.
Creator, *Knights of the Blood,* by Scott MacMillan (Vampyr.SS). New York, Roc, 1993; London, Raven, 1994.
Creator, *Knights of the Blood: At Sword's Point,* by Scott MacMillan (Vampyr.SS). New York, Roc, 1994.
Editor, *Tales of the Knights Templar.* New York, Warner, 1995.

*

Bibliography: *The Work of Katherine Kurtz: An Annotated Bibliography and Guide* by Boden Clarke and Mary A. Burgess, San Bernardino, California, Borgo Press, 1993.

Manuscript Collection: University of California, San Bernardino (in process of being transferred, 1995).

*   *   *

The beginning of the tale, as related by the author in *The Deryni Archives,* derived from an especially vivid dream which came to her on the night of October 11, 1964. Kurtz summarized what she remembered of this vision on a 3 x 5 card, and shortly thereafter expanded the scenario into the novelette "Lords of Sorandor." "Sorandor" was in turn reworked into the climactic section of Kurtz's first novel, *Deryni Rising.*

These journeyman efforts contain all of the seeds of the author's later work. Katherine Kurtz has spent much of her creative life developing an alternate fantasy world centered around the medieval state of Gwynedd, the central kingdom of an area patterned roughly after 10th-to-12th-century England, Scotland, and Wales (in our own world, Gwynedd was an ancient name for Northern Wales). Although we can see rough similarities to medieval Britain—in language, culture, religion, and politics—there are equally striking differences.

Gwynedd and its neighbors are peopled by both humans and Deryni: the latter are outwardly similar to man, but have the innate ability to perform acts which their fellow humans regard as magical. These psychic talents vary considerably from individual to individual, and may be developed further with appropriate training. The history of Gwynedd has been marred by a series of conflicts between the two races, the Deryni having controlled Gwynedd for less than a century of its history. They still control Torenth, a large neighboring kingdom, which they have ruled from its inception. Such clashes have been exacerbated by lack of empathy between the two groups, by arrogance on the part of the Deryni, and by outright racial hatred and envy on the human side, with concomitant persecutions and pogroms of the Deryni minority.

Kurtz's geography also varies significantly from the Europe we know, and these differences have themselves altered the political dynamic of the region. Unlike Britain, for example, Gwynedd is joined directly to the mainland; without the benefit of a channel buffer, it is directly subject to invasion from hostile neighbors. The Mediterranean Sea does not seem to exist in this world, although references are made at several points to a "Holy Land" where Christ was born, preached, and martyred, much as in our own world. We can also see rough equivalents to the Moors, Gauls, and other ethnic groups from Earth, but no other obvious political, historical, or geographical correspondences with real-life medieval Europe.

The religious hierarchy of Kurtz's world is also subtly different from that of medieval Europe, generally following the tenets of the Roman Catholic Church, but being organized administratively along the lines of our own world's Eastern Orthodoxy. Thus, each major state contains its own autocephalous religious body, governed by an archbishop or patriarch chosen and supported by an independent ruling Synod. There is no "Pope" or central Church authority (indeed, no "Rome") in Kurtz's "Europe," although Latin remains the official Church language, and the celebration of the mass its key ritual.

Kurtz has developed her world in four sets of trilogies and nine short stories, eight of the latter being collected in *The Deryni Archives*. The Chronicles of the Deryni, comprising *Deryni Rising, Deryni Checkmate,* and *High Deryni,* relate the rise to power of King Kelson Haldane, who succeeds to the throne of Gwynedd at the age of fourteen when his father is assassinated. The Haldanes, although not traditionally Deryni, have the ability to exercise similar powers when these have been activated through a magical ritual. Kelson represents the new man, merging the best of both blood lines into one person, unfettered by the past and able to forge the nation into a unified whole. In these three novels Kelson defeats the last two representatives of the Festil dynasty, consolidates his position as King, and begins exploring his arcane heritage.

The Legends of Camber of Culdi, comprising *Camber of Culdi, Saint Camber,* and *Camber the Heretic,* takes place 300 years earlier, at a time when Deryni monarchs ruled Gwynedd. Camber, the Deryni Earl of Culdi, proves instrumental in locating the last Haldane heir, Prince Cinhil, whom he restores to the throne after the latter kills the Deryni King Imre. By the end of Cinhil's reign the restoration has created a backlash against the Deryni minority, resulting in increasingly harsh measures and massacres, as the newly appointed human bishops and peers assume the reins of power.

The Histories of King Kelson, including *The Bishop's Heir, The King's Justice,* and *The Quest for Saint Cumber,* returns to the time of Kelson, picking up where *High Deryni* left off. Now 18, Kelson must face a revolt in the provinces, endure a marriage of convenience and the murder of his wife, and counter further unrest at home, as the surviving conservative bishops attempt to oust him and his government. He also faces treachery from within his own family, and ultimately learns that the art of statesmanship must be tempered with the king's justice.

The Heirs of Saint Camber trilogy, comprising *The Harrowing of Gwynedd, King Javan's Year,* and *The Bastard Prince,* is set in the years following the death of King Cinhil Haldane. The king's passing brings the forces of repression to the fore, and the few remaining Deryni must go underground to protect the remnants of their persecuted race. One by one the King's three young sons succeed to the throne and are killed by the human monsters actually governing the realm. But King Rhys Michael's death is not without meaning, for he leaves a will that provides his supporters a way of overthrowing the conservative rulers. The succession of his infant son, King Owain, provides new hope for the future.

Politics and religion are inextricably intertwined in Kurtz's creation, as they were in our own history, with state and church constantly vying with each other and the Deryni minority for power and authority. The key players of these historical fantasies recognize that the price of failure is either disgrace or death. What sustains them is faith, an abiding and sincere belief in God, his Church, his anointed King, and their close friends and family as *the* key structures of society. Even those depicted on Kurtz's tableaux as cruel or manipulative largely perceive themselves as acting in the best interests of Church or state or family, often justifying their despicable acts through religious dictates that condemn the Deryni as evil personified. We may not applaud such individuals, but we can readily understand their motivations. The author's villains are carefully drawn in shades of gray, not splotches of black and white; some even seem marginally sympathetic, being true in their own fashion to the world as they see it. In her fiction Kurtz consistently champions intelligence, duty, sensitivity, love, faith, truth, and all of the other finer virtues. Such attributes do not always save her characters from the acts of evil-minded men, but they save their souls for eternity, and that is a far, far better thing to do.

In recent years Kurtz has begun a new series of fantasies coauthored with Deborah Turner Harris. The Adept sequence features a group of Scottish and British occult detectives seeking to right wrongs and counter the influence of evil in the modern world. *Lammas Night,* (1983) set during World War II, can be considered a prequel to these books. These novels, while entertaining in their own right, seem less effective than the Deryni books, perhaps because the contemporary setting decreases the verisimilitude of vast conspiracies and evil magicians working their wills over time on generations of insipid followers. The characters in the Adept books are less ambiguous, more rigid in their beliefs, and ultimately less real. Ironically, the authors' message shines through in these books even clearer than before. Man makes of this world what he will, Kurtz seems to be saying, either a heaven or a hell, and this condition clearly presages what he (or she) will ultimately become in the afterlife.

—Robert Reginald

KUTTNER, Henry

Pseudonyms: Keith Hammond; C. H. Liddell; Lewis Padgett. **Nationality:** American. **Born:** Los Angeles, California, 7 April 1915. **Education:** University of Southern California, Los Angeles, B.A. 1954. **Military Service:** Served in the United States Army Medical Corps during World War II. **Family:** Married C.L. Moore, *q.v.,* in 1940 (died 1988) most of his subsequent work was written with her, though not always acknowledged. Worked briefly for a literary agency, Los Angeles; freelance writer. **Died:** 3 February 1958.

SCIENCE FICTION PUBLICATIONS

Novels

Fury, with C.L. Moore. New York, Grosset and Dunlap, 1950; London, Dobson, 1954; as *Destination Infinity,* New York, Avon, 1958.

Earth's Last Citadel, with C.L. Moore. New York, Ace, 1964.

Valley of the Flame, with C.L. Moore. New York, Ace, 1964.

The Time Axis, with C.L. Moore. New York, Ace, 1965.

The Dark World, with C.L. Moore. New York, Ace, 1965; London, Mayflower, 1966.

Dr. Cyclops, with others. New York, Popular Library, 1967.

The Creature from Beyond Infinity. New York, Popular Library, 1968.

The Mask of Circe, with C.L. Moore. New York, Ace, 1971.

The Startling Worlds of Henry Kuttner, edited by C.L. Mooore (includes *Beyond Earth's Gates, Valley of the Flame,* and *The Dark World*). New York, Popular Library, 1987.

Novels as Lewis Padgett, with C.L. Moore

Tomorrow and Tomorrow, and The Fairy Chessmen. New York, Gnome Press, 1951; *The Fairy Chessmen* published as *Chessboard Planet,* New York, Galaxy, 1956; original volume published as *Tomorrow and Tomorrow* and *The Far Reality,* London, Consul., 2 vols., 1963.

Well of the Worlds. New York, Galaxy, 1953; reprinted under name Henry Kuttner, New York, Ace, 1965.

Beyond Earth's Gates. New York, Ace, 1954.

Short Stories

Ahead of Time: Ten Stories of Science Fiction and Fantasy, with C.L. Moore. New York, Ballantine, 1953; London, Weidenfeld and Nicolson, 1954.

Remember Tomorrow. Sydney, American Science Fiction, 1954.

Way of the Gods. Sydney, American Science Fiction, 1954.

No Boundaries, with C.L. Moore. New York, Ballantine, 1955; London, Consul, 1961.

As You Were. Sydney, American Science Fiction, 1955.

Sword of Tomorrow. Sydney, American Science Fiction, 1955.

Bypass to Otherness. New York, Ballantine, 1961; London, Consul, 1963.

Return to Otherness. New York, Ballantine, 1962; London, Mayflower, 1965.

The Best of Kuttner. London, Mayflower, 2 vols., 1965-66.

The Best of Henry Kuttner. Garden City, New York, Doubleday, 1975.

Clash by Night and Other Stories, with C.L. Moore, edited by Peter Pinto. London, Hamlyn, 1980.

Chessboard Planet and Other Stories, with C.L. Moore. London, Hamlyn, 1983.

Elak of Atlantis. Brooklyn, New York, Gryphon, 1985.

Clash by Night (with C.L. Moore as Lawrence O'Donnell). Sydney, American Science Fiction; bound with *The Jungle,* by David Drake, New York, Tor, 1991.

Prince Raynor. Brooklyn, Gryphon, 1987.

Kuttner Times Three. Modesto, California, Virgil Utter, 1988.

Secret of the Earth Star and Others, edited by Sheldon R. Jaffery. Mercer Island, Washington, Starmont House, 1991.

Waters of Death Presents Thunder Jim Wade. Chicago, Tattered Pages Press, 1992.

Short Stories, as Lewis Padgett, with C.L. Moore

A Gnome There Was, and Other Tales of Science Fiction and Fantasy. New York, Simon and Schuster, 1950.

Robots Have No Tails. New York, Gnome Press, 1952; New York, Lancer, 1973; as *The Proud Robot: The Complete Galloway Gallegher Stories,* Feltham, England, Hamlyn, 1983.

Mutant. New York, Gnome Press, 1953; London, Weidenfeld and Nicolson, 1954.

Line to Tomorrow. New York, Bantam, 1954.

OTHER PUBLICATIONS

Novels

The Brass Ring (as Lewis Padgett, with C.L. Moore). New York, Duell, 1946; London, Sampson Low, 1947; as *Murder in Brass,* New York, Bantam, 1947.

The Day He Died (as Lewis Padgett, with C.L. Moore). New York, Duell, 1947.

Man Drowning. New York, Harper, 1952; London, Four Square, 1961.

The Murder of Ann Avery. Garden City, New York, Permabooks, 1956.

The Murder of Eleanor Pope. New York, Permabooks, 1956.

Murder of a Mistress. New York, Permabooks, 1957.

Murder of a Wife. New York, Permabooks, 1958.

Other

Letters to Henry Kuttner, with H.P. Lovecraft, edited by David E. Schultz and S.T. Joshi. West Warwick, Rhode Island, Necronomicon Press, 1990.

*

Bibliography: By Donald H. Tuck, in *Henry Kuttner: A Memorial Symposium* edited by Karen Anderson, Berkeley, California, Sevagram, 1958.

*   *   *

In reviewing Henry Kuttner's collection *Ahead of Time,* Anthony Boucher characterized the author as "one of SF's most literate and intelligent storytellers." Other adjectives could have been added to the list: prolific, versatile, popular. There have, it is true, been periodic dry spells when editors and readers have seemed to forget the rich legacy of Kuttner's fiction, but the stories have always been rediscovered and brought back into print. There is every reason to believe that his best work will last as long as science fiction is read.

For many years the scope and volume of Kuttner's writing were partially camouflaged by the many bylines under which his stories appeared. Initially the pen names were adopted for the usual commercial reasons: to differentiate among various types of story or to disguise the fact that more than one story on a contents page was by the same author. But Kuttner, both alone and with his wife C.L. Moore, seemed to take an active delight in the creation of new pseudonyms, even on two occasions going so far as to publish fictional "autobiographies" for an alter ego: Keith Hammond in *Startling Stories,* March 1946 (an Eurasian antiquarian with 16 cats), and C.H. Liddell in *Planet Stories,* November 1950. As one after another of the Kuttner/Moore pseudonyms was revealed, a phenomenon arose which was sometimes called the "Kuttner Syndrome": the conviction that any promising new name on the SF scene had to be yet another Kuttner pen name. (One of the victims of this assumption was Jack Vance, who was identified by the editor T.E. Dikty in 1950 as a Kuttner pseudonym.) The original choice of pseudonyms for various stories has by now become clouded through numerous reprintings with altered bylines.

Kuttner's first story, "The Graveyard Rats," a superbly grisly horror story in the Lovecraft mode, appeared in *Weird Tales.* Kuttner continued to write for *Weird Tales,* but at the same time he became a prolific contributor to other pulp magazines of many types, including mystery, detective, western, adventure, "spicy," and South Sea tales. His first long story was "The Time Trap" (*Marvel Science Stories*), called "a marvellous gaudy melodrama" by Brian Aldiss. Kuttner had been a member of H.P. Lovecraft's circle of correspondents, and had met other members of that group, such as Robert Bloch, Fritz Leiber, and E. Hoffmann Price. Kuttner and Bloch collaborated on a few stories. Kuttner also collaborated with Arthur K. Barnes on two stories in their Pete Manx series. Manx was a carnival barker whose mind was projected back in time into the bodies of various inhabitants of ancient Rome, Egypt, Baghdad, and other historical or legendary locales, where he must use his innate cunning to survive. The series was carried on alternately by Kuttner and Barnes from 1939 to 1944.

Another Lovecraft correspondent and well-known *Weird Tales* writer whom Kuttner met was Catherine L. Moore. Kuttner and Moore were married on June 7, 1940, in New York, where Kuttner had moved in order to be close to his magazine markets. Kuttner and Moore had collaborated on one story in 1937, but it was not until after their marriage that their remarkable writing partnership developed. Kuttner stated on several occasions that almost all of his writing since the marriage, regardless of byline, was to some extent a collaboration with his wife; however, the degree and method of collaboration varied widely. Some stories were almost pure Kuttner, with only minor contributions from Moore, while for others the reverse was true; but on a large number of stories the two partners were able to blend their ideas and styles so well that one of them could drop a story in mid-scene and the other could pick it up, with scarcely a seam showing in the final product. While taking part fully in the collaborative works, C.L. Moore also continued to write her own stories.

The Lewis Padgett stories, taken as a whole, form a body of work of which any writer could be proud, and if Kuttner and Moore had done no other writing in the science fiction field, their reputations would still be secure on the basis of these stories. Fritz Leiber (in *Henry Kuttner: A Memorial Symposium,* 1958) identified three themes which recur in Kuttner's SF: the madman from the future, wacky robots, and wonder children. All of these are present in the Padgett stories. The Padgett treatment of robots, in particular, is as distinctive as that of any writer in the field. One of the best-known, "The Twonky," is concerned with the effect on a young married couple of a device which looks like a console radio, but is actually a robot designed to enforce its own views of proper behavior. Several of the Padgett stories were about the odd inventions of Gallegher, a scientist who can invent things only while drunk, and when sober, can never remember what the inventions are for. Told in a style frankly borrowed from Thorne Smith, the Gallegher stories are meticulously logical SF puzzles cast as wacky comedies. Five were reprinted as *Robots Have No Tails.* The deservedly famous "Mimsy Were the Borogoves" is about educational toys from the future which have a disastrous effect on a present-day family. Other Lewis Padgett stories include the Baldy series (*Mutant*)—

about telepathic mutants who must struggle for survival against the intolerance of their normal neighbors and against irrational renegades in their own ranks, a theme clearly taken from A.E. van Vogt's *Slan*—and *The Fairy Chessmen* (with its celebrated opening line, "The doorknob opened a blue eye and looked at him") and *Tomorrow and Tomorrow,* complicated tales of post-Atomic intrigue and alternate futures.

One of C.L. Moore's works from the 1940s was "Clash by Night," a moody, emotion-laden story of the Free Companies, the mercenaries of the feuding undersea Keeps on Venus in the 25th century. The Kuttners returned to this scene with the novel *Fury,* the story of Sam Harker, ruthless and driven by forces of which he was not fully aware, the one man who could liberate humanity from its stagnant undersea existence and push it into conquering the planet's savage surface. Although published as by Lawrence O'Donnell, the story was mostly Kuttner's. C.L. Moore stated in her introduction to the Lancer reprint: "*Fury* was written by about one and an eighth persons. . . . I wrote comparatively little of the copy. The idea was basically Hank's and I didn't identify very strongly with it." She also pointed out that the novel deals with "the two recurring themes which emerge quite explicitly in nearly everything we wrote. Hank's basic statement was something like, 'Authority is dangerous and I will never submit to it.' Mine was, 'The most treacherous thing in life is love.'" *Fury* is the best, and best-known, of Kuttner's long stories. Other long works include a series of nine science fantasy novels, many of them in the romantic/tragic mode of A. Merritt, written between 1943 and 1952, including *Earth's Last Citadel, Valley of the Flame, Beyond Earth's Gates,* and *Well of the Worlds.* Typical shorter works in the same style are "I Am Eden" (December 1946) and "Way of the Gods" (April 1947), both in *Thrilling Wonder Stories.* In the early 1950s the volume of new Kuttner-Moore stories decreased. Both Kuttner and Moore felt written-out in science fiction, although such stories as "Home There's No Returning" and "Two-Handed Engine" (both in *No Boundaries*) belied this claim.

Henry Kuttner has sometimes been criticized as a literary mimic who spent his energies speaking in other people's voices. He did, in fact, speak in many voices, but they were all his own. His borrowings, whether of style or of theme, were all filtered through his own sensibility, and emerged transmuted. In all of his best work there is clear evidence of a highly individual mind at work. Perhaps his most personal contribution to SF was the fusion of humor and logic which first emerged fully in the Gallegher stories. The same blend was also evident in the stories of the Hogbens, a family of mutant hillbillies, and in "The Ego Machine," probably his best "wacky robot" story. Through his stories and through his influence on other writers—Ray Bradbury, Leigh Brackett, and Richard Matheson have all acknowledged his guidance—Kuttner left an indelible mark on the science fiction field. Without his presence, science fiction of the 1940s and 1950s would have been a vastly different and much poorer body of literature.

—R.E. Briney

L

LAFFERTY, R(aphael) A(loysius)

Nationality: American. **Born:** Neola, Iowa, 7 November 1914.
Education: University of Tulsa, Oklahoma, 1932-33; International
Correspondence School, electrical engineer course, 1939-42. **Military Service:** Served in the United States Army, 1942-46: Staff
Sergeant. **Career:** Civil servant, Washington, D.C., 1934-35; clerk,
then buyer, Clark Electrical Supply Company, Tulsa, 1936-42, 1946-
50, 1952-71. Since 1971, freelance writer. **Awards:** Phoenix award,
1971; Hugo award, 1973; Smith award, 1973; World Fantasy Lifetime Achievement award, 1990. **Agent:** Virginia Kidd, Box 278,
Milford, Pennsylvania 18337. **Address:** 1715 South Trenton Avenue, Tulsa, Oklahoma 74120, U.S.A.

SCIENCE FICTION PUBLICATIONS

Novels (series: Coscuin Chronicles)

Past Master. New York, Ace, and London, Rapp and Whiting, 1968.
The Reefs of Earth. New York, Berkley, 1968; London, Dobson,
1970.
Space Chantey. New York, Ace, 1968; London, Dobson, 1976.
Fourth Mansions. New York, Ace, 1969; London, Dobson, 1972.
The Flame Is Green (Coscuin). New York, Walker, 1971.
The Devil Is Dead (Coscuin). New York, Avon, 1971; London,
Dobson, 1978.
Arrive at Easterwine: The Autobiography of a Ktistec Machine.
New York, Scribner, 1971; London, Dobson, 1977.
Not to Mention Camels: A Science Fiction Fantasy. Indianapolis,
Bobbs Merrill, 1976; London, Dobson, 1980.
Archipelago. New Orleans, Manuscript Press, 1979.
Aurelia. Norfolk, Virginia, Donning, 1982.
The Annals of Klepsis. New York, Ace, 1983.
Half a Sky: The Annals of the Coscuin Chronicles, 1849-1854, edited by Ira M. Thornhill. Minneapolis, Corroboree Press, 1984.
My Heart Leaps Up. Iowa City, Drumm, 5 vols., 1986-1990.
Serpent's Egg: A Fantasy. Bath, Morrigan, 1987.
East of Laughter. Bath, Morrigan, 1988.
Sinbad: The Thirteenth Voyage. Cambridge, Massachusetts, Broken Mirrors Press, 1989.
Dotty (Coscuin). Weston, Ontario, United Mythologies Press, 1990.
More Than Melchisedech (Coscuin):
    Tales of Chicago. Weston, Ontario, United Mythologies Press, 1992.
    Tales of Midnight. Weston, Ontario, United Mythologies Press,
    1992.
    Argo. Weston, Ontario, United Mythologies Press, 1992.

Short Stories

Nine Hundred Grandmothers. New York, Ace, 1970; London, Dobson, 1975.
Strange Doings: Stories. New York, Scribner, 1972.
*Does Anyone Else Have Something Further to Add? Stories about
Secret Places and Mean Men.* New York, Scribner, 1974; London, Dobson, 1980.

Funnyfingers and Cabrito. Portland, Oregon, Pendragon Press,
1976.
Horns on Their Heads. Portland, Oregon, Pendragon Press, 1976.
Apocalypses. Los Angeles, Pinnacle, 1977.
Golden Gate, and Other Stories, edited by Ira M. Thornhill. Minneapolis, Corroboree Press, 1982.
Four Stories. Polk City, Iowa, Drumm, 1983.
Heart of Stone, Dear, and Other Stories. Polk City, Iowa, Drumm,
1983.
Snake in His Bosom, and Other Stories. Polk City, Iowa, Drumm,
1983.
*Through Elegant Eyes: Stories of Austro and the Men Who Knew
Everything,* edited by Ira M. Thornhill. Minneapolis, Corroboree
Press, 1983.
Ringing Changes. New York, Ace, 1984.
The Man Who Made Models, and Other Stories. Polk City, Iowa,
Drumm, 1984.
Slippery, and Other Stories. Polk City, Iowa, Drumm, 1985.
Promontory Goats. Weston, Ontario, United Mythologies Press,
1988.
The Elliptical Grave. Weston, Ontario, United Mythologies Press,
1989.
How Many Miles to Babylon? Weston, Ontario, United Mythologies Press, 1989.
Episodes of the Argo (Coscuin). Weston, Ontario, United Mythologies Press, 1990.
The Early Lafferty. Weston, Ontario, United Mythologies Press, 1990.
Lafferty in Orbit. Cambridge, Massachusetts, Broken Mirrors Press,
1991.
Mischief Malicious (and Murder Most Strange). Weston, Ontario,
United Mythologies Press, 1991.
Grasshoppers and Wild Honey. Polk City, Iowa, Drumm, 1992.
Iron Tears. Cambridge, Massachusetts, Edgewood Press, 1992.

OTHER PUBLICATIONS

Novels

Okla Hannali. Garden City, New York, Doubleday, 1972.

Other

The Fall of Rome. Garden City, New York, Doubleday, 1971; as
Alaric: The Day the World Ended, Weston, Ontario, United Mythologies Press, 1993.
It's Down the Slippery Cellar Stairs: Nonfiction. Polk City, Iowa,
Drumm, 1984; expanded as *It's Down the Slippery Cellar Stairs:
Essays and Speeches on Fantastic Literature,* San Bernardino,
California, Borgo Press, 1995.
The Back Door of History. Weston, Ontario, United Mythologies
Press, 1988.
True Believers. Weston, Ontario, United Mythologies Press, 1989.
Cranky Old Man from Tulsa: Interviews with R.A. Lafferty. Weston,
Ontario, United Mythologies Press, 1990.

*

Bibliography: *An R.A. Lafferty Checklist* by Chris Drumm, Polk City, Iowa, Drumm, 1983.

Manuscript Collection: McFarlin Library, University of Tulsa, Oklahoma.

R.A. Lafferty comments:

My novels, which I wrote myself at great labor, have received more attention than my short stories, which wrote themselves. Nevertheless, the short stories are greatly superior to the novels. In my introductory note to a Dutch version of *Nine Hundred Grandmothers,* I wrote: "I hold to the true theory that good stories write themselves, or that they are independent and pre-existent entities or beings. . . . These pre-existent stories come to persons, sometimes even to persons of a resonant emptiness; and they make themselves known through these persons. . . . I am very glad that these particular stories first visited me and not someone else.

"There are a few perfect discoveries or encounters that come into every life. Only once I met a mountain lion, quite close, in the wild. She was a discovery of mine. Once only I saw a whale a-blow in the ocean. Once only I saw a big-horn mountain sheep on a high cliff. Once only I saw a pink flamingo in flight. Once only I had an encounter with each of some hundred entities called 'special stories.' These meetings were as quietly thunderous and as unexpected as the discovery of the mountain lion or whale or big-horn sheep or pink flamingo in flight.

"There is an Aladdin cave, lit by 999 lamps, that is the Universal Unconscious . . . that is shared by all persons and creatures. . . . Unsuspected stone doors of the cave are thrown open. There may be funny and fascinating encounters and living spectacles. A few of them may cluster together in a pile of things waiting to be discovered . . . piles of gold, quick ecstasies, intricate delights, entities called 'special stories.'"

A person favored with such discoveries will look for other people to share them with. 'Hey, come see the things I've found,' he'll say. That is what I say now."

However pompous that may sound, it's a statement on the most important part of my work.

*   *   *

R.A. Lafferty is science fiction's most prodigious teller of tall tales. Offspring of a yarn-spinning family, he writes rather than recites his exhilarating stories but nevertheless retains a primary allegiance to the spoken word. The quintessentially oral character of Lafferty's fiction proclaims itself on every page—each of them sounds like a tape recording transcript. (*Arrive at Easterwine* is actually presented as such.) Rhythmic repetitions of phrases and epithets tie the material together. The author is omnipresent as well as omniscient. He explains and interprets every development, sprinkling his text with epigrams, anecdotes, and invented sources. He even brings himself into stories as a thinly disguised character or as himself in *Through Elegant Eyes.*

Exposition and dialogue overshadow action. Events are more often predicted or recollected than depicted. At shorter lengths, these events are often arranged in artificial patterns reminiscent of folk tales ("Rainbird"), exempla ("The Configuration of the North Shore"), dramatized lectures ("Primary Education of the Camiroi"), or barroom whoppers ("One at a Time"). In longer works, a degree of order is imposed via elaborate symbolism (e.g., the Four Living Creatures in *Fourth Mansions*). However, Lafferty's oral mannerisms hamper him when he mistakes the accumulation of vi-

gnettes for the construction of a novel, as in *Arrive at Easterwine* and *The Devil Is Dead,* or uses a novel as an excuse for sermons and diatribes, as in *Aurelia.* (Compare the last with Robert A. Heinlein's *Stranger in a Strange Land.*)

Lafferty's way with characters is as distinctive as his storytelling technique. The floridly eccentric beings who populate his fiction are wholly unrealistic yet totally real. He succeeds best with children, traditionally the most difficult of subjects, because he approaches them with all the sentimentality of a W.C. Fields: "A child's a monster yet uncurled" (*The Reefs of Earth*). However, Lafferty's distaste for adolescents shows up in his Hugo winner "Eurema's Dam."

Besides outrageous youngsters, Lafferty's character troupe comprises: dirty old geniuses and innocent simpletons, ugly but wholesome men and violent but kindly ones, lusty egomaniacs and ascetic manipulators, witch-girls and earthy ladies of muscular charm, plus aliens that are every bit as variegated. They reappear in tale after tale: "though they always preserved the threads of their identities, they did not always have the same names or appearances, and there were not always the same number of them." Favorites get encores. Note the proper names common to *Fourth Mansions, Arrive at Easterwine,* and *The Annals of Klepsis. Archipelago, The Devil Is Dead,* and *More Than Melchisedech*) augment the historical fantasy Coscuin Chronicles tetralogy (begun with *The Flame Is Green* and *Half a Sky*; the two other volumes, *Sardinian Summer* and *First and Last Island,* have never been published); and all his extraterrestrial locales appear to exist in the same crazy universe.

So closely do Lafferty's novels resemble each other, they might as well be alternate drafts of the same story. This may reflect his habit of rewriting everything five or six times before the final draft. Elements seem to pass from work to work as easily as sherry through a solera. For instance, Lafferty's plots repeatedly combine conspiracy, romance, and growth. Secret battles between Good and Evil coteries decide the fate of worlds. Bright protagonists are shadowed by dark counterparts. Passionate couples share a yeasty mixture of carnal and spiritual love. Esoteric powers are acquired and used to prepare a chosen hero for an imperial destiny, but the outcome is often ambiguous. *The Flame Is Green* and *Half a Sky* demonstrate his scenario best. Against a panorama of 19th-century history, an Irish-born hero and his multinational comrades fight for the Green Revolution against the Red Revolution led by the Devil's own son.

In novels and short stories alike, Lafferty is obsessed with transformation. His version of Nature is incorrigibly protean— space, time, and form are liable to shift at any moment. Changes that nourish the "green-gowing world" must be welcomed whatever they cost. The price can be bloody. Lafferty's pages are speckled with gore, either from hand-to-hand combat or the butchering of animals. Yet the slaughter does not stun because death can be followed by resurrection, mutilation by healing, corruption by redemption. Lafferty knits these components together with allusions to mythology and theology. Biblical precedents influence his handling of topics like kingship, sacrifice, and regeneration. They also shape his use of animal symbols such as snakes. This is especially true of *Fourth Mansions.* Here, a naive young newsman integrates the essence of four primeval forces (Badger/Man, Python/Lion, Toad/Ox, and Falcon/Eagle) and becomes mystical Emperor "by entrenched right" to nudge the world towards the next higher Mansion in the cosmic Castle.

Lafferty also draws on history for inspiration ("Thus We Frustrate Charlemagne"). However, the thought can get lost in the quirkiness of his presentation. For instance, perceptively interpreted data in *Okla Hannali,* his epic of the Choctaw Indians, are so entangled with fable that it is hard to accept anything in the book as real. The same eccentricities abound in *The Fall of Rome.* But the Coscuin Chronicles have a sturdier skeleton of fact under the fluid flesh. The foreign locales of these books have a useful distancing effect—exotic events are more acceptable in exotic settings than in the contemporary American ones in *Fourth Mansions.*

Past Master, Lafferty's most popular novel, depends less on factual than on mythicized history. Sir Thomas More is brought forward in time and outward in space to save a diabolical utopia by dying a king's death. Lafferty sends his highly fictionalized 16th-century hero into the 26th-century to dramatize 20th-century spiritual and social issues. Compare this savory scramble of past, future, and present with Ursula K. Le Guin's didactic fable "The Ones Who Walk Away from Omelas."

There is not a bit of science in Lafferty's SF. He justifies his premises on etymological rather than scientific grounds: the name *is* the object. He coins outlandish names, chiefly from Greek and Latin, then interprets them in idiosyncratic ways—the derivations in the Coscuin Chronicles would make Isidore of Seville blush. (His debt to the classics extends to farce as well as philosophy. See *Space Chantey,* his reworking of the *Odyssey. Archipelago* was inspired by the Argosy.)

Bizarre nomenclature does not exhaust Lafferty's rampaging delight in words. He showers his pages with odd poetry. (Who else would dare to rhyme "roses" with "apotheosis" or turn chapter titles into narrative verse as he does in *The Reefs of Earth*?) This verbal virtuosity makes him SF's equivalent of "Flann O'Brien." He loves exaggeration and grotesqueries as well as any Celt before him—surely one of his ancestors had a hand in *The Cattle Raid of Cooley.* But Lafferty appreciates ethnic spice of many flavors: He uses almost as many Amerindian referents as Irish ones ("Narrow Valley") and is fascinated by gypsies ("The Land of the Great Horses").

Lafferty's great subject is the perennial war between Heaven and Hell: "We must kill the Devil afresh every day." This Adversary is no silken Mephisto but a musky blackguard whom healthy young men can drink under the table. Be they ever so pungent, demons like Ifreann and Papa Diabolus in the Coscuin Chronicles are never allowed to steal the show. The heroes and heroines overwhelm them with sheer vitality. Vice can imitate but never match the "overrunning gaiety" of virtue. Making Goodness exciting is a Lafferty specialty.

Although he rode to prominence in the 1960s with the New Wave, Lafferty shows none of the gloom characteristic of that movement. His fiction rings with the high hilarity of love and laughter. Each of his serious works ends on a note of hope, for his is the faith-filled vision of a universe en route to redemption. Despite detours, it keeps gyring upward according to divine plan. "All final answers were given in the beginning. . . . It is our task to grow out until we reach them."

—Sandra Miesel

LAKE, David (John)

Also writes as D.J. Lake. **Nationality:** Australian. **Born:** British parents in Bangalore, India, 26 March 1929; became Australian citi-

zen, 1975. **Education:** St. Xavier's School, Calcutta, 1940-44; Dauntsey's, Wiltshire, 1945-47; Trinity College, Cambridge, 1949-53, B.A. 1952, Dip. Ed. 1953, M.A. 1956; University College of North Wales, Bangor, diploma in linguistics 1965; University of Queensland, Brisbane, Ph.D. 1974. **Military Service:** Served in the Royal Artillery, 1948-49. **Family:** Married Marguerite Ivy Ferris in 1964; one daughter. **Career:** Assistant Master, Sherrardswood School, Welwyn Garden City, Hertfordshire, 1953-58, and St. Albans Boys Grammar School, Hertfordshire, 1958-59; Lecturer in English, Saigon University, 1959-61, for the Thai government, Bangkok, 1961-63, and at Chiswick Polytechnic, London, 1963-64; Reader in English, Jadavpur University, Calcutta, 1965-67. Lecturer, 1967-72, Senior Lecturer, 1973-76, and since 1977, Reader in English, University of Queensland. **Awards:** Ditmar award, 1977. **Agent:** Pamela Buckmaster, Danescroft, Goose Lane, Little Hallingbury, Bishops Stortford, Herts CM22 7RG, England. **Address:** Department of English, University of Queensland, St. Lucia, Queensland 4072, Australia.

SCIENCE FICTION PUBLICATIONS

Novels (series: Breakout)

Walkers on the Sky (Breakout). New York, DAW, 1976; revised edition, London, Fontana, 1978.
The Right Hand of Dextra (Breakout). New York, DAW, 1977.
The Wildings of Westron (Breakout). New York, DAW, 1977.
The Gods of Xuma; or Barsoom Revisited (Breakout). New York, DAW, 1978.
The Fourth Hemisphere (Breakout). St. Kilda, Victoria, Void, 1980.
The Man Who Loved Morlocks: A Sequel to The Time Machine as Narrated by the Time Traveller. Melbourne, Hyland House, 1981.
The Ring of Truth. St. Kilda, Victoria, Cory and Collins, 1982; New York, DAW, 1984.
Warlords of Xuma (Breakout). New York, DAW, 1983.
The Changelings of Chaan (for children). Melbourne, Hyland House, 1985.
West of the Moon: A Fantasy Novel (for children). Melbourne, Hyland House, 1988.

Short Stories

"Re-deem the Time" in *Rooms of Paradise,* edited by Lee Harding, Melbourne, Quartet, 1978.

OTHER PUBLICATIONS

Poetry

Hornpipes and Funerals: Forty-Two Poems and Six Odes of Horace. St. Lucia, Queensland, University of Queensland Press, 1973.

Other

John Milton: Paradise Lost (as D.J. Lake). Calcutta, Mukhopadhyay, 1967.
Greek Tragedy. Calcutta, Excelsus, 1969.

The Canon of Thomas Middleton's Plays: Internal Evidence for the Major Problems of Authorship. London, Cambridge University Press, 1975.

Editor, *The FIrst Men in the Moon,* by H.G. Wells. New York, Oxford University Press, 1995.

*

David Lake comments:

The main impulse embodied in my SF is the impulse of the human rat to imagine escapes from the cosmic trap in which he finds himself. The trap is partly (but only partly) of his own building; it has been building for a very long time; and the bars now loom very high indeed. Sometimes the rat thinks he can escape by a smart technological fix; sometimes he knows that he can't. But either way he can at least dream.

The main influences on my writing are probably H.G. Wells and C.S. Lewis, and the clash between these two authors' values. I follow Wells and Lewis in writing SF that deliberately borders on fantasy. Elves may appear wearing spacesuits. The same themes also appear in my poems, some of which are in fact close to being SF. I am also strongly influenced by my early background as a child in India under the old British Raj. I know how it feels to be an invader in a vast, different culture. Most aliens in my novels are versions of Asians. My recent fantasy novel *The Changelings of Chaan* is especially close to my early life (as it should have been, not as it was).

*   *   *

David Lake presents himself as a pessimist in search of the numinous, a fantasist without belief, choosing science fiction as his vehicle for escapism because magic does not work. Lake has little confidence in the efficacy of science, either: in "Re-deem the Time" (in *Rooms of Paradise,* edited by Lee Harding, Melbourne, Quartet, 1978) his alter ego, Ambrose Livermore, is able to use a time machine as his escape hatch into the future, leap-frogging the inevitable Big Bang, only to find the survivors engaged in determined regress, already back in 1900. In this witty tale, despair is salved by humour: Ambrose flourishes in the future 1 B.C. as Chief Jester to Obliorix.

If Earth is the City of Destruction in a godless universe, where may hope be found? In his novels Lake catapults small colonies of survivors to distant, wondrous planets, and New Jerusalem is actually built foursquare on Dextra. The two novels set in Dextra are paradigmatically interesting, complementing each other much as Blake's *Songs of Innocence* and *Songs of Experience. The Right Hand of Dextra* suggests the state of innocence, in which it is possible for the Puritan tendencies of the New Earthmen with their "Sifted Scriptures" to be corrected by incorporation with the innocent native species, despite the dextran twist of their protein molecules. Experience seems to prove otherwise, however, in the bleak feudal world of *The Wildings of Westron,* set several thousand years later, until the implicit conclusion of the first book is reiterated in absolute form: before there can really be a New Earth on Dextra, all human flesh must perish and only Dextran flesh remain. Most humans will voluntarily undergo the change; the reluctant must simply be exterminated. There is no hope in human flesh because it is closed; Dextran flesh, however, is open, unsecret, allowing telepathic understanding of one another.

The conclusion of *The Gods of Xuma* is not quite so sweeping: only the hopelessly evil human colonists are slaughtered—and fortunately the Xuman natives can tell the difference and are prepared to tolerate those humans remaining who are essentially good natured. However, it is decided that humans are not fit for space travel.

If Lake is thus predisposed in favour of aliens, describing them warmly and even with affection, he is not unduly sentimental about them, particularly about his Xumans, and wishes to correct the supposition, hung over from Burroughs, that physical love with an alien can be satisfactory. The hero's comic embarrassments with Xumans in their female phase prove the point (that Lake lacks Le Guin's solemnity in treating such an issue is not, I think, to his advantage). On the other hand, Lake's aliens are usually not very different from people and do provoke erotic ideas; however, their function is not to be wonderful love-objects (as in Burroughs) but to suggest wonderful possibilities of loving interchange between humans, suitably modified. In *The Right Hand of Dextra* he uses the Song of Solomon as the basis for a description of a transcendent sexual union, only confusing the terms, so that male and female sensations become interchangeable; in *The Wildings of Westron* he echoes Blake: "Every minute particle and particular of their body-minds were commingling, from the head even to the feet, and on every plane of existence."

Lake is an imaginative writer with the power not only to invent exciting worlds but to describe them; he acknowledges the influence of C.S. Lewis, and his evocative accounts of the deserts of Xuma or the purple forests of Dextra bear comparison with those of Malacandra. His most wonderful world is in *Walkers on the Sky,* a tier-world Farmer might envy, ruled capriciously by immortals as if to recall Zelazny's *Lord of Light.* It is a pity that he had not found a story worthy of his world, but this charge may also be levelled at Farmer, and Lake's novel is at least free from Farmer's sometimes heavy portentousness.

In "Creator," Lake shows that he is prepared to tackle the big theme, and though he trivializes it somewhat in the process—our universe exists inside a "creatron," a kind of game machine for artists on the planet Olympus, our creator being Jay Crystal (J.C.—get it?)—he succeeds in providing a provocative ironic perspective on human history.

Lake's two most recent novels have been fantasies for young adults; older readers who enjoy C.S. Lewis should find them at least as charming and thoughtful as the best of the Narnia books. Both use the pleasant conceit of advancing their young heroes to a higher world: a "Golden World" in *The Changelings of Chaan* and a "High Earth" in *West of the Moon* (written earlier though published later). These higher worlds are themselves lower than others: John Hastings must undertake a quest to the high Silver World where the gods live, before he can return to Chaan: his story draws on the author's knowledge of Indian society and Hindu myth. Gods visit the pleasant country of Vornemana (which means "West of the Moon"), where magic works, but Megan and Mark Tremaine are anomalies there, for Hardor (Earth, Ironworld) has long been closed off as a threat to Middleworld's integrity. An insecure king and his black magician, who seek forbidden knowledge, lure the two unsuspecting orphan schoolchildren to Middleworld where they soon come of age. Although these books are classed by the author as fantasy in deliberate contradistinction to science fiction, it should be remarked that *West of the Moon* considers the supposed opposition between science and magic instructively.

—Michael J. Tolley

LANDIS, Geoffrey A(lan)

Nationality: American. **Born:** Detroit, 28 May 1955. **Education:** Massachusetts Institute of Technology, B.S. 1980; Brown University, Ph.D. 1988. **Career:** Staff scientist, Spire Corp., Bedford, Massachusetts, 1977-82; research associate, Solar Energy Research Institute, Golden, Colorado, 1986-87; NASA Lewis Research Center, Cleveland, 1988-90; adjunct professor, Ohio Aerospace Institute, Brook Park, 1990-92; physicist, Sverdup Tech., Brook Park, Ohio, 1990-93; trustee, National Association of Rocketry, 1978-81. **Awards:** Nebula award, 1990; Hugo award, 1992; Dell Reader award. **Address:** NASA Lewis Research Center, 21000 Brookpark Rd., Cleveland, Ohio 44135-3191, U.S.A.

SCIENCE FICTION PUBLICATIONS

Short Stories

Myths, Legends, and True History. Eugene, Oregon, Pulphouse, 1991.

Author of numerous uncollected short stories

*   *   *

Geoffrey A. Landis is a physicist working in solar cell research who began writing short science fiction in the 1980s, and has continued to produce a number of significant stories in the hard science fiction subgenre. Most of his fiction first appeared in *Analog* and *Isaac Asimov's Science Fiction Magazine,* although some of his work has also appeared in *The Magazine of Fantasy and Science Fiction, Interzone, Amazing* and *Pulphouse.* Despite his significant success with short fiction, he has never produced a novel.

Landis gained critical attention with his first published fiction, the novella "Elemental" (1984), which was nominated for a Hugo Award in 1995. The story is set in an alternative future where both magic and science operate in tandem. It is a pure concept story, with the speculative magic treated with hard-SF rigor, as a "logical outgrowth of quantum field theory." Reality is really, according to Landis' explanation in the story, "an abstract mathematical construct" which therefore can be "controlled by the manipulation of abstract symbols." The protagonists are academics in a university "thaumaturgy" department who seek to learn the proper chants and motions to control various "elemental" forces, primary of which are earth, water, wind and fire. Because the appropriate sounds and symbols to control the elementals constantly evolve and change, high-speed computers must be used to determine (by trial and error) what spells currently work. The problem the protagonists must solve is that thousands of farmers in Italy have learned by word of mouth an incantation to improve their crops, which ends up waking the earth elemental, which is moving slowly upwards from the center of the planet, where it will erupt the dormant Mount Vesuvius. In the end, the magical academicians save the day, of course, in as interesting a manner as possible. Although the characterizations border on sophomoric, it is an interestingly original concept for a quintessential Analog-style hard SF problem story.

Landis' best-known short stories are "Ripples in the Dirac Sea" (1988), which won a Nebula Award and was nominated for a Hugo Award, and "A Walk in the Sun" (1991), which won the Hugo Award and the Dell Reader Award. These two stories represent Landis at his best, writing hard science fiction with some degree of thematic artistry.

"Ripples in the Dirac Sea" is a time travel story about a scientist who discovers the secret of time travel into the past, and uses it to travel back to the innocent time of Haight-Ashbury in San Francisco in 1965. He finds that he can stay as long as he wants in the past, but any changes he makes disappear as soon as he returns to the time he left. Just before he is to give the scientific paper that will announce his discovery to the world, he is caught in a hotel fire, and trapped in his room mere minutes before his death, he must repeatedly use the machine to travel to 1965, where he lives for 25 years and then is instantaneously transported to his present in the burning hotel room, where each time he loses a few seconds before he can reactivate his machine to return to the past to live another 25 years. The story is told out of temporal sequence, and at the end of the story he is transporting back with only seconds to spare, knowing that this might be the last time he can escape his inevitable fiery death. The language and concepts of quantum physics are used to provide incredible verisimilitude to this ironic, melancholy story.

"A Walk in the Sun" tells the suspenseful story of an astronaut who survives a shipwreck on the Moon that kills her two companions, and must find a way to call for help and wait for assistance from Earth. She must survive for 30 days until help arrives, but must keep moving to avoid the slow, inexorable setting of the sun that provides power to her suit. She will therefore have to walk totally around the Moon to survive for those 30 days. During her relentless survival run, she begins to imagine that he dead sister is with her. As she sinks into exhausted delirium, she talks more and more to her imaginary sister, who motivates her to continue. She barely completes her 11,000 km journey in time to meet the rescue ship. There have been dozens of similar stories about shipwrecked astronauts written over the past 60 years, but few have had the simplistic perfection of "A Walk in the Sun".

A number of Landis' lesser stories were reprinted, along with some original fiction, in the collection *Myths, Legends, and True History* (1991) as part of the Pulphouse Publishing *Author's Choice Monthly* series (Issue 26). In addition to several technological puzzle stories, the collection includes material as diverse as poetry, a fairy tale, and a hoax autobiography. Several of his stories were part of *Future Boston* (1994), the shared-world anthology developed by a group of writers in the Cambridge Writers Workshop. Landis has also often written a number of popular articles about science, mostly published in *Analog.*

Although Landis may never be known as a master of characterization, some of his newer fiction demonstrates significant improvements. His short story "In the Hole With the Boys With the Toys" (1993) is a clever problem story about four men manning a secret military weapon who save a stranded astronaut by firing their laser at it to keep the batteries charged until he can be rescued. The novella "The Singular Habits of Wasps" (1994) is an effective and chilling Sherlock Holmes story wherein he solves the mystery of an alien monster that is committing the murders attributed to Jack the Ripper. "Across the Sea of Darkness" (1995) is a very moving novelette about five young women aboard the first interstellar ship sent to colonize another planet who must continue their lonely decade-long voyage after one sacrifices herself mid-flight repairing the ship, and features a greater depth of characterization than any of Landis' previous work, with the possible exception of "A Walk in the Sun".

Geoffrey Landis has never been a prolific writer, producing no more than a few stories per year, and this fact, along with his lack of novel-length work, has limited his reputation. But based on only a handful of superior stories, including several of the best hard science fiction stories published in the past decade, he has established himself as a writer worthy of critical scrutiny.

—D. Douglas Fratz

———

LANG, King. *See* **TUBB, E.C.**

———

LANGART, T. *See* **GARRETT, Randall.**

———

LANGE, John. *See* **CRICHTON, Michael.**

———

LANGFORD, David

Nationality: British. **Born:** Newport, Gwent, Wales, 10 April 1953. **Education:** Newport High School; Brasenose College, Oxford, 1971-74, B.A. in physics, 1974, M.A. 1978. **Family:** Married Hazel Langford in 1976. **Career:** Weapons physicist, Atomic Weapons Research Establishment, Aldermaston, Berkshire, 1975-80. Since 1980, freelance writer. Editor, *Ansible,* Reading, Berkshire, and since 1983, contributing editor, and columnist ("Critical Mass"), *White Dwarf,* London. **Agent:** Hilary Rubinstein, A.P. Watt Ltd., 20 John Street, London WC1N 2DR. **Address:** 94 London Road, Reading, Berkshire RG1 5AU, England.

SCIENCE FICTION PUBLICATIONS

Novels

An Account of a Meeting with Denizens of Another World, 1871. Newton Abbot, Devon, David and Charles, 1979; New York, St. Martin's Press, 1980.
The Space Eater. London, Arrow, 1982; New York, Pocket Books, 1983.
Earthdoom! with John Grant. London, Grafton, 1987.

Short Stories

The Dragonhiker's Guide to Battlefield Covenant at Dune's Edge: Odyssey Two: The Collected Science Fiction and Fantasy Parodies of David Langford, Volume One. Birmingham, England, Drunken Dragon Press, 1988.

Other

Let's Hear It for the Deaf Man, edited by Ben Yalow. Framingham, Massachusetts, New England Science Fiction Association, 1992.

OTHER PUBLICATIONS

Other

War in 2080: The Future of Military Technology. Newton Abbot, Devon, Westbridge Books, and New York, Morrow, 1979.
Facts and Fallacies: A Book of Definitive Mistakes and Misguided Predictions, with Chris Morgan. Exeter, Devon, Webb and Bower, 1981; New York, St. Martin's Press, 1981.
The Science in Science Fiction, with Peter Nicholls and Brian M. Stableford. London, Joseph, 1982; New York, Knopf, 1983.
The Leaky Establishment. London, Muller, 1984.
Micromania: The Whole Truth about Home Computers, with Charles Platt. London, Gollancz, 1984; as *The Whole-Truth Home Computer Handbook,* New York, Avon, 1984.
The Third Millennium: A History of the World A.D. 2000-3000, with Brian M. Stableford. London, Sidgwick and Jackson, and New York, Knopf, 1985.
Varieties of English: An Introduction to Language Studies, with Dennis Freeborn and Peter French. London, Macmillan, 1985; as *Varieties of English: An Introduction to the Study of Language,* Basingstoke, Hampshire, Macmillan, 1993.
A Novacon Garland. Birmingham, Birmingham Science Fiction Group, 1985.
Critical Assembly. Reading, Ansible Information, 1987.
Platen Stories. N.p., 1987.
Analysing Talk: Investigating Verbal Interaction in English. Basingstoke, Hampshire, Macmillan, 1994.

*

David Langford comments:

(1985) Anything said here *ought* to be redundant. A work requiring the author's personal introduction ("Now I want you to meet little Johnny, boys and girls. He's a bit subnormal and deformed, but don't you dare tease him") is hardly likely to make its own way in the horrid outside world of bookstands. However . . .

I'm a technophile but a somewhat pessimistic one; it seems so unfair that shiny, alluring technological toys keep pointing the way to more and easier megadeaths. Yet because I like intellectual games I keep playing literary hopscotch on the edge of the unthinkable, cracking jokes about a variety of armageddons: current (*The Leaky Establishment*), seriously extrapolated (*War in 2080*) and wholly imaginary (*The Space Eater*). In the shorter efforts there are lighter jokes, parodies, and sheer fun; give me twenty thousand words or more, though, and I end up addressing gallows humour to the Angel of Death, the Spectre of World War III, the Ghost of Christmas Yet To Come, or some such unjolly companion.

By publication time this will be less an introduction than a memorial. I've no idea what I'll be writing next year, while swift and efficient technologies of modern-day publishing will doubtless have made all the above-listed works quite unobtainable. (Support a starving author—write to me and buy my remainders!) My ambition is to become a capitalist.

*   *   *

David Langford began writing as a student, with fannish parodies (some of which were later included in *The Dragonhikers' Guide to Battlefield Covenant at Dune's Edge: Odyssey Two*) and much of his fame is connected to the prodigious number of fan-writing Hugos he has collected. Much of his best writing is to be found in fanzines (especially his own *Twll Ddu* and *Ansible*) and the chapbooks *Platen Stories* (1987) and *Let's Hear It for The Deaf Man* (1992) (Langford is hard of hearing) contains some of the best.

He also writes regular SF book review columns and is noted for his willingness to spend more effort demolishing the great hyped-up clunkers (which people need to be warned against) than in recommending the better stuff (which presumably can speak for itself). Much of his work has the same joy in taking apart the illogical and second-rate, especially in *Facts and Fallacies,* a collection of throughly wrong predictions and "scientific" observations.

Apart from the numerous collaborations on nonfiction and semifictional works such as *The Necronomicon* and *The Science in Science Fiction,* with which Langford has earned his daily bread since leaving the Scientific Civil Service, Langford has published four long SF works. The first, *An Account of a Meeting with Denizens of Another World, 1871,* is a slim, one-joke volume in which an extraterrestrial probe lands in a Buckinghamshire wood and tries to open communication with a local craftsman. The cod modern commentary on the "recently discovered" manuscript laments the difficulty of conveying the concepts of quarks and DNA by purely visual means. Written as a counter to all those tales in which flying saucerites go from "me alien—you human—that tree" to advanced physics in a couple of pages, this book has, to the author's chagrin and amusement, been taken as fact by parts of the UFO press and used (unpaid and, at first, unacknowledged) to pad at least one bestselling work on the popular theme: "the government knows all about saucers and is keeping the truth from us."

His next work, *The Space Eater,* was a hard-science story centering on unlikely new branches of physics (all new branches of physics are unlikely) leading to new ways of destroying worlds even more spectacular than the ones the author worked on at the British Government's Atomic Weapons Research Establishment (and even more spectacular than most of the ones described in *War in 2080*). Its chief flaw is its uneven tone. In his short stories (one of which was expanded to *The Space Eater*) Langford tends to see the gloomy side of his technological enthusiasms. But given space Langfordian flights of fancy and humour creep in; the hero turns from a Mindless Killing Machine at the start to a Thouroughly Nice Chap by the end and for no particular reason. The book also contains SF's most impractical interstellar drive: a star-gate just a few centimenters square. First chop up your astronauts and then reassemble on the far side. . . .

The Leaky Establishment is only marginally SF but is perhaps his best long work. Drawing again on his time at Aldermaston, it is a very enjoyable farce concerning a researcher at A Top Secret Establishment who has to smuggle plutonium warheads back into his place of work. The most hilarious parts are those connected with Civil Service bureaucracy, which the author claims are pure autobiography: the endless regulations, the proposal to rename atomic weapons after the Royal Family "to promote empathy and good public feeling," the beefy security guards probing the thighs of young phyicists for lumps of plutonium.

Earthdoom!, his most recent novel, is another parody and another collaboration (with John Grant): a take off of the cult novels of doom so prevalent in the 80s. Although it contains every type of world ending, ecological, technological, and supernatural, it generally fails to amuse.

Langford's shorter work often has nice touches of charecterisation and style that stand out better on a smaller canvas. "Cube Root" and "Notes for a Newer Testament" continue his fascination with weapons, the former in a very dark vein. "A Snapshot Album" has a feeling for mood and place that could indicate new maturity in his work. Much of his recent work has been in the "shared universe" collections put together by the British SF consortium Midnight Rose. I especially enjoyed the superhero/detective story pastiche "If Looks Could Kill" in *Eurotemps* and the horror story "The Lions in the Desert" in *The Weerde II.*

—Michael Cule

LANIER, Sterling E(dmund)

Nationality: American. **Born:** New York City, 18 December 1927. **Education:** Harvard University, Cambridge, Massachusetts, A.B. 1951; University of Pennsylvania, Philadelphia, 1953-58. **Military Service:** Served in World War II and the Korean War. **Family:** Married 1) Martha Hanna Pelton in 1961 (divorced 1978), one son and one daughter; 2) Ann Miller McGregor in 1979. **Career:** Research historian, Winterthur Museum, Switzerland, 1958-60; editor, John C. Winston Company, 1961, Chilton Books, 1961-62, 1965-67, and Macrae-Smith Company, 1963-64. Since 1967, full-time writer and sculptor. **Awards:** Follett award, 1969. **Agent:** Curtis Brown Ltd., 10 Astor Place, New York, New York 10003, U.S.A.

SCIENCE FICTION PUBLICATIONS

Novels (series: Hiero Desteen)

The War for the Lot: A Tale of Fantasy and Terror (for children). Chicago, Follett, 1969; London, Sidgwick and Jackson, 1977.
Hiero's Journey: A Romance of the Future. Radnor, Pennsylvania, Chilton, 1973; London, Sidgwick and Jackson, 1975.
Science Fiction Special (34): Hiero's Journey; The War for the Lot. London, Sidgwick and Jackson, 1981.
The Unforsaken Hero. New York, Ballantine, 1983.
Menace under Marswood. New York, Ballantine, 1983.
Hiero Desteen (omnibus). Garden City, New York, Doubleday, 1984.

Short Stories (series: Brigadier Ffellowes)

The Peculiar Exploits of Brigadier Ffellowes. New York, Walker, and London, Sidgwick and Jackson, 1972.
The Curious Quests of Brigadier Ffellowes. West Kingston, Rhode Island, Donald M. Grant, 1986.

* * *

Sterling E. Lanier's fiction presents a world teeming with creatures of the fantastic imagination. No innovator or philosopher, Lanier sails on well-charted seas of the supernatural and unnatural.

His work almost always combines the worlds of fantasy and science fiction, and although his output is relatively small, his novel *Hiero's Journey* is of sufficient merit to warrant close attention.

A summary of this novel can hardly do it justice as the story pivots on one of the oldest and most frequently used plots of the genre: the hero sets out on a quest for lost knowledge through a world laid waste by nuclear war and controlled by mutants made horrible and evil by radiation. However, Lanier is able to inform this trite plot with his own vision of the fantastic and produces a world that is both delightful and terrifying. The questing hero is Per Hiero Desteen—priest, exorcist, killman, and citizen of the Metz republic of Kanda—who sets off in the eighth millennium in search of ancient legendary machines called "computers" that will help him and his people put together the knowledge of the past. This knowledge is the last hope for survival against the various forms of evil that resulted from the Death (nuclear holocaust). This theme is not without its own moral convictions, and Lanier attempts to tie his story to present-day concerns in several ways. Some connections are made through a language that is not nearly as interesting or inventive as one might hope for in this kind of novel: Lantik Sea (Atlantic Ocean), Kanda (Canada), Neeyana (Indiana), Leemutes (lethal mutations). More interesting are the contemporary social and environmental values that are invested in the tale. The nuclear devastation is served by a group of men called "the Unclean." These men were formerly psychologists, biochemists, and physicists who have been severely ravaged by radiation and now seek to rule the evil world they have created. On the other hand, Hiero is joined by a wise ancient, Brother Aldo, who belongs to a group called "the Eleveners." The eleveners are the Brotherhood of the Eleventh Commandment, a group of social scientists dedicated to the ideal: Thou shalt not despoil the Earth and the life thereon. Hiero and Brother Aldo are accompanied by a telepathic, almost human bear (Gorm), a semi-intelligent bull "morse," and a strong-willed but faithful young maiden (Luchare).

Lanier's strengths and weaknesses are both evident in this fantasy adventure yarn. He is at his best when weaving a suspenseful tale, and, while his characters lack depth and the plot has been often used before, the world he creates, filled with radiation-induced mutants, ancient, knowing wizards, and fur-covered dwarves, lives fully in the imagination and allows the reader to partake fully in the suspenseful quest. Lanier is obviously aware of the parallels with medieval romances, and those who enjoy *Beowulf, Le Morte Darthur,* and the sagas will be enthralled by the re-creation of those environments and values in a future time.

Lanier's other work is of a similar but lesser quality. His stories as a rule combine the fantastic world of unnatural monsters with the more traditional trappings of science fiction: space ships, time travel, telepathic communication. *The Peculiar Exploits of Brigadier Ffellowes* presents seven stories that feature a retired English Brigadier who narrates tales that involve supernatural powers and fantastic monsters. Lanier exhibits a good sense of humor in these stories and carefully sets them up as a series of Chinese boxes: a story within a story within a story. The monsters found here, like the Nandi bear and the sea serpent Jormungadir, are similar to those found elsewhere in Lanier's writings. But the best quality of Lanier is what accounts for the success of this and his other works: he is an excellent storyteller.

—Lawrence R. Ries

LANSDALE, Joe R(ichard)

Pseudonym: Ray Slater. **Nationality:** American. **Born:** Gladewater, Texas, 28 October 1951. **Education:** Tyler Junior College, 1970-71; University of Texas at Austin, 1971-72; Stephen F. Austin State University, Nacogdoches, Texas, 1973, 1975, 1976. **Family:** Married 1) Cassie Ellis in 1970 (divorced 1972); 2) Karen Ann Morton in 1973, one daughter and one son. **Career:** Karate instructor, 1970-79; foreman, LaBorde Custodial Services, Nacogdoches, 1980-81. Has also worked as a factory worker, ditch digger, carpenter and plumber's helper, and farmer. Since 1981, freelance writer. **Awards:** Bram Stoker award, 1988, 1989; Horror Writers of America award, 1988, 1989; American Horror award, 1989; British Fantasy award, for novella, 1989. **Agent:** Barbara Puechner, 3121 Portage Road, Bethlehem, Pennsylvania 18017. **Address:** 113 Timber Ridge Drive, Nacogdoches, Texas 75961, U.S.A.

SCIENCE FICTION PUBLICATIONS

Novels

Ace of Love. New York, Zebra, 1981; London, Kinnell, 1989.
Dead in the West. New York, Space and Time, 1986; London, Kinnell, 1990.
The Magic Wagon. Garden City, New York, Doubleday, 1986; Bath, Chivers, 1988.
The Nightrunners. Arlington Heights, Illinois, Dark Harvest, 1987.
The Drive-In: (A "B"-Movie with Blood and Popcorn, Made in Texas). New York, Bantam, 1988; London, Kinnell, 1989.
The Drive-In 2: Not Just One of Them Sequels. New York, Bantam, 1989; London, Kinnell, 1990.
Cold in July. New York, Bantam, 1989.
Savage Season. Shingletown, California, Ziesing, 1990; London, New English Library, 1992.
Batman: Captured by the Engines. New York, Warner, 1991.

Short Stories

By Bizarre Hands: Stories. Shingletown, California, Ziesing, 1989; London, New English Library, 1992.
Stories by Mama Lansdale's Youngest Boy. Eugene, Oregon, Pulphouse, 1991; expanded as *Bestsellers Guaranteed,* New York, Ace, 1993.
On the Far Side of the Cadillac Desert with the Dead Folks. Arvada, Colorado, Roadkill Press, 1991.
The Steel Valentine. Eugene, Oregon, Pulphouse, 1991.
Steppin' Out, Summer '68. Arvada, Colorado, Roadkill Press, 1992.
Tight Little Stitches on a Dead Man's Back. Eugene, Oregon, Pulphouse, 1992.
Writers of the Purple Sage. Baltimore, CD Publications, 1994.

OTHER PUBLICATIONS

Novels

Texas Night Riders (as Ray Slater). New York, Leisure, 1983; Bath, Chivers, 1990.
Batman: Terror on the High Skies (for children). Boston, Little, Brown, 1992.

Mucho Mojo. New York, Mysterious Press, 1994; London, Gollancz, 1995.

Other

Drive-By, with Andrew H. Vachss and Gary Gianni. Holyoke, Massachusetts, Crossroads Press, 1993.

Editor, *Best of the West.* Garden City, New York, Doubleday, 1986.
Editor, *The New Frontier: The Best of Today's Western Fiction.* Garden City, New York, Doubleday, 1989.
Editor, with Pat LoBrutto, *Razored Saddles.* Arlington Heights, Illinois, Dark Harvest, 1989.
Editor, with Karen Lansdale, *Dark at Heart: All New Tales of Dark Suspense.* Arlington Heights, Illinois, Dark Harvest, 1992.
Editor, with Thomas W. Knowles, *The West That Was.* New York, Wings Books, 1993.
Editor, with Thomas W. Knowles, *Wild West Show!* New York, Wings Books, 1994.

*

Joe R. Lansdale comments:

I write what interests me, and it's as simple as that. As a reader I read everything. Literary, genre, comics, plays, screenplays, and I'm influenced by it all. No matter what I write, I do my best to put something of myself and a literary sensibility into it. I hope to be both entertaining and interesting enough that someone might want to read one of my books or stories more than once.

My work often combines my interests, so that a novel or story might be as much horror as crime as suspense as SF as western as literary, and perhaps all of these. And maybe it's cat box material. What do I know?

*   *   *

Joe Lansdale has produced noteworthy supernatural horror and science fiction; moreover, his realistic fiction should not be ignored here, since so many individual pieces cross genre lines, and Lansdale often uses the same motifs within different genres. Much of Lansdale's fiction blends realistic and fantastic approaches, taking a recognizable setting, either contemporary or historical, and introducing elements such as animated dinosaurs, the living dead, or original figures like his God of the razor. Mimetic or supernatural, most of Lansdale's fiction does have some element of horror. He is sometimes classed with the "splatterpunk" writers—John Skipp, Craig Spector, David Schow, Ray Garton, and others—but the detailed depiction of violence in his work predates even the roughest formation of that movement.

Lansdale is also a regional writer: he states that he and Ardath Mayhar may be the entirety of "the East Texas school of horror." Drive-ins, good ol' boys with guns, snuff films, incest, itinerant preachers, improbable cars—this is the modern West that Lansdale writes about, capturing it in semi- mythological form. Whether set in East Texas or not, his fiction, often told first-person by the viewpoint character, uses deceptively simple, well-crafted prose to present a strong narrative voice. He blends humor with terror, and colloquialism with strong literary metaphor (trees' branches "waving in the wind like the fluttering hands of distressed lunatics"). Lansdale can also be a master of suspense and action writing, as in "Incident on and Off a Mountain Road" (*Bizarre*).

Some of Lansdale's stories are quite interestingly experimental, such as "The Diaper" (*Purple Sage*) and "Bob the Dinosaur Goes to Disneyland" (*Bestsellers*). "Not from Detroit" (*Bestsellers*) is a supernatural story about an old couple meeting death, but its tone is low-key and wistful; "Fish Night" (*Bizarre*) ends on a note of horror, but that seems almost stuck onto a tale of surreal awe. Humor and satire characterize many of even his grimmest works, and this tone predominates in stories such as "Godzilla's Twelve-Step Program" (*Purple Sage*).

Lansdale's models within science fiction and fantasy include Ray Bradbury, Richard Matheson, Fredric Brown, Gerald Kersh, Charles Beaumont, and William F. Nolan—"Bill Nolan" appears as a character in Lansdale's *Dead in the West.* Like many of these writers, Lansdale's novels range from good to excellent, but his true forte is shorter fiction, which allows him to explore a wider range of approaches and which form a significant part of his literary output. Lansdale's influences and peers in other genres are even more varied, including hardcore-crime writer Andrew Vachss, whom Lansdale thanks in the acknowledgement of *Mucho Mojo.*

Always interested in culture from high (despite his good ol' boy image) to the most popular, Lansdale acknowledges his roots, from prose writers in many genres to B-movies and comic books such as *Jonah Hex* and *Batman.* In fact, Lansdale has written two short stories featuring Batman as the protagonist; his novel *Batman: Captured by the Engines* examines the superhero's psyche but also presents a quirky supernatural story about American Indian shamanism in the machine age. Lansdale has also scripted comics—*Jonah Hex* for DC/Vertigo and *The Lone Ranger* and *Tonto* for Topps—and Dark Horse has done excellent graphic adaptations of Lansdale's stories, including "Dead in the West" and "By Bizarre Hands."

Lansdale is perhaps best known for his novel *The Drive-In: (A "B"-Movie with Blood and Popcorn, Made in Texas).* The *Drive-In* is based on an idea which Lansdale introduced in an article on drive-in movies for *Twilight Zone* magazine (reprinted in *Bizarre*): during a festival of horror films, a multi-screen outdoor theater is snatched into a mysterious limbo, to degenerate into a film-lit, popcorn-fed *Lord of the Flies.* Lansdale introduces other fantastic elements, such as the Popcorn King, and horrific problems of violence, rape, and cannibalism. In the sequel, *Drive-In 2: Not Just One of Them Sequels,* some of the survivors find an even more baffling world outside the drive-in, with dinosaurs and vampiric roles of celluloid. The books blend humor and horror, realism and fantastic invention; the first, especially, is well-paced and readable.

Lansdale has written three novels so far about Hap Collins and his friend Leonard Pine, a gay, Black Vietnam vet: *Savage Season, Mucho Mojo,* and *The Two-Bear Mambo.* Although these are realistic, contemporary novels of action-suspense and character, they show many of the elements and concerns of his science fiction or supernatural horror. *Mucho Mojo* features the town of LaBorde, in East Texas, which in "The Events Concerning a Nude Fold-Out Found in a Harlequin Romance" (*Bestsellers*) is the small city closest to Mud Creek, where the story takes place (based on Gladewater); Mud Creek, back in the Old West, is the setting of *Dead in the West* and *The Magic Wagon.*

The Hap and Leonard novels also show a theme common in Lansdale's fiction, realistic and fantastic alike: the issue of race, handled deftly and believably instead of with polemics. First, many Lansdale works present major black characters who are admirable but credibly fallible—besides Leonard, characters such as police Lieutenant Marvin Hanson in *Act of Love,* and Albert in *The Magic*

Wagon. Second, Lansdale presents redneck racism with true understanding and almost sympathy, but so that its true horrors are obvious, as in "Night They Missed the Horror Show" (*Bizarre Hands*); racism in the Old West features strongly in *The Magic Wagon* and *The Lone Ranger and Tonto.* A similar examination of misogyny is central to stories such as "Love Doll: A Fable" and "Drive-In Date" (both in *Purple Sage*).

Even when Lansdale's novels lack supernatural content, as in the Hap and Leonard books, the extreme acts and emotional states often give the same feeling. This is true of *Act of Love,* the story of a psycho-killer called the Houston Hacker and the Black police officer who is assigned to track him down. *Cold in July,* like *The Nightrunners,* shows an ordinary man drawn into violence.

The Nightrunners, a contemporary action-adventure novel, and Lansdale's early Western *The Magic Wagon,* both may or may not contain supernatural or science fiction elements. They are fantastic in the French sense, examined by critic Tzvetan Todorov in *The Fantastic:* individual readers decide whether the material is possible in our world or not, or no final determination is possible. *The Nightrunners* combines a story of defense and revenge—compared by some to *Straw Dogs*—with elements of precognition and perhaps possession. Sections of that novel have appeared separately as short fiction, including "God of the Razor" (*Bestsellers*), supernatural on its own but perhaps a psychotic delusion within the novel. *The Magic Wagon* features the preserved corpse of Wild Bill Hickok, which may or may not give one character Hickok's outstanding shooting ability. In a story for *Jonah Hex,* the patent-medicine wagon and the corpse of Wild Bill Hickok also appear, but there the corpse and the wagon's boss definitely have supernatural powers.

The widest range of Lansdale's interests and abilities is clear in his short fiction, at which he excels and which comprises a significant share of his writing. He is best known for his horror stories. *Dead in the West,* a short novel, features undead people that spread like vampires, but behave and can be killed like the living dead in films by George Romero; and Lansdale used Romero's living dead explicitly in "On the Far Side of the Cadillac Desert with Dead Folks," written for the anthology *The Book of the Dead* (reprinted in *Bizarre*). "The White Rabbit" (*Bestsellers*) combines *Alice in Wonderland* and Jack the Ripper in a story somewhat reminiscent of Frank Belknap Long's "Humpty Dumpty Had a Great Fall." "Bubba Ho Tep" audaciously introduces an animated, soul-stealing Egyptian mummy into a mental hospital setting, including inmates who think they are Elvis and John F. Kennedy (*Purple Sage*). The title story of *By Bizarre Hands* is realistic but improbable horror, which Lansdale has also rewritten in play form (*Purple Sage*).

Lansdale has written a few science fiction stories: "Trains Not Taken" and "Letter from the South, Two Moons West of Nacogdoches" (both in *Bizarre*) depict alternate histories; "Tight Little Stitches in a Dead Man's Back" (*Bizarre*) is post-World War III fiction in which the human interaction is almost more horrible—and fascinating—than the setting. "The Diaper, or, The Adventure of the Little Rounder" (*Purple Sage*), influenced by Williams Burroughs's rich experimental fiction, depicts the rapid gain and loss of superintelligence by an infant, almost a short-short *Flowers for Algernon.*

Living in Nacogdoches, Texas, with his family, Lansdale is—as is so often true of writers of horror—self-effacing yet personable, remaining true to his roots and his regional style. He has written work released under pseudonyms, probably including one or more Western novels; he has also edited or coedited anthologies of West-

ern short stories and written one young adult novel, *Terror on the High Skies.* His voice is unique within fantastic fiction, and perhaps in the field of fiction in general; it demonstrates both range and consistency.

—Bernadette Lynn Bosky

LARGE, E(rnest) C(harles)

Nationality: British. **Career:** Plant pathologist. **Died:** 1976.

SCIENCE FICTION PUBLICATIONS

Novels (series: Charles Pry)

Sugar in the Air: A Romance (Pry). London, Cape, and New York, Scribner, 1937.
Asleep in the Afternoon (Pry). London, Cape, 1938; New York, Holt, 1939.
Dawn in Andromeda. London, Cape, 1956.

OTHER PUBLICATIONS

Other

The Advance of the Fungi. London, Cape, and New York, Holt, 1940.
Potato Blight Epidemics Throughout the World, with A.E. Cox. Washington, D.C., Agricultural Research Bureau, 1960.

* * *

In some respects, E.C. Large could be considered a scientist's science fiction writer, for he deals primarily with the concerns and perspectives of the scientist in his everyday life. Large's narratives, though not abstruse, explore scientific inventions and processes with acute detail, and his work might be included in what C.S. Lewis identifies as the "fiction of engineers."

The most notable work Large produced is *Sugar in the Air,* a book considered by many to be a near-classic, for it was this novel which first embodied in speculative fiction a relatively realistic idea of the scientist's work and social situation. The story concerns a young chemical engineer, Charles Pry, who is hired by Hydro-Mechanical Constructions Ltd., to create sugar by photosynthesis, using only a handful of hints gathered by another rather eccentric scientist. Pry succeeds in discovering the elusive formula, but he encounters conflicts with company financiers in the marketing of "Sunsap," as the product is called. They are concerned with obtaining the quickest and greatest profit, while Pry idealistically strives to make the product more beneficial for society, and the book becomes a kind of tragicomedy of the scientist and commerce. The novel thus inverts the motif of the mad scientist, for it is the corporation, not Pry, who wants to exploit the discovery for its own greed. This attitude of organization vs. the individual dominated later magazine science fiction, as for example when the lone nuclear scientist is pitted against the political and military powers.

Asleep in the Afternoon, a sequel, is also an invention story, though an inferior one, dealing with similar ideas and attitudes. Charles Pry, having lost his job with Hydro-Mechanical, decides to write a novel, which is about the invention of a sleep-inducing device. Within this rather unexciting framework, Large again satirizes capitalism and corporations, as well as other aspects of contemporary life, political structure, and social attitudes.

While the first two novels deal with the relationship—and often the conflict—between the scientist and the community, *Dawn in Andromeda* is a utopian allegory. Ten British men and women (five of each) emerge Venus-like from the sea one morning onto the shores of an uninhabited planet in the Andromeda galaxy, where they have been transported by God in a rather ridiculous opening. Equipped with their scientific knowledge and practical skills—and some faint memories of Earth—they build a new society and community on this strange world, which closely resembles Earth. The original group is harmonious enough; it is the second generation's spontaneous pursuit of commerce and religion which spoils the utopian dream, reflecting the same sort of criticisms that Large displays in the previous two books. Again, the narrative is heavily endowed with scientific detail, exploring every step of the little society's progress.

But Large circumvents the most obvious problem, that of interplanetary transportation, choosing instead to follow C.S. Lewis's advice that "frankly supernatural methods are best." So the novel really doesn't follow the 17th- and 18th-century tradition of the voyage to another world, being concerned instead, like Wells's *First Men in the Moon,* with what happens there.

Though Large is obviously more scientist than writer, his books do have some literary qualities worth noting: his prose is often strong and direct, tough, effective; his characters, though not fully rounded, compel interest and arouse sympathy; he also uses imaginative names, giving characters such apt identities as Cocaine, Dr. Sinus, Dr. Zaareb, MacDuff, or Hunt-Transom, while the crew in *Andromeda* take their names from the alphabetical letterings on the bindings of *Encyclopaedia Britannica.*

Large's novels evince a firm belief in science and its potentiality; they laud the moral scientist of commitment and decry the stupidity and incompetence of so many social organizations—business, commercial, religious, political, revolutionary. Large's work offers an interesting, knowledgeable, and valuable perspective of the scientist, his work, and his place in society.

—Karen Charmaine Blansfield

———

La SALLE, Victor. *See* **FANTHORPE, R. Lionel.**

———

LASSWITZ, Kurd

Nationality: German. **Born:** 1848. **Died:** 1910.

SCIENCE FICTION PUBLICATIONS

Novels

Auf Zwei Planeten. Leipzig, Elischer, 2 volumes, 1897; translated by Hans. J. Rudnick as *Two Planets: Auf Zwei Planeten,* Carbondale, Southern Illinois University Press, 1971.

During his lifetime German professor Kurd Lasswitz was known not only for philosophical and scientific writings but also for short stories, speculative novels, and essays on the writing of science fiction. Some 40 years after his death Willy Ley's translations into English of several Lasswitz short stories introduced him to a wider readership. *Fantasy and Science Fiction* published three: "When the Devil Took the Professor" (January 1953); "Aladdin's Lamp" (May 1953); and "Psychotomy" (July 1954). In 1958 Clifton Fadiman included "The Universal Library" in his *Fantasia Mathematica.* In 1971 the 1897 Lasswitz novel *Auf Zwei Planeten* appeared in an abridged English translation as *Two Planets.*

The short stories illustrate Lasswitz's ability to combine physics, metaphysics, philosophy, mathematics, all flavored with wry humor, into intriguing speculative fiction. In "When the Devil Took the Professor" Lasswitz presents a professor talking to a group of amusingly stereotypical people, a talk that develops a Faustian situation in which the professor and the devil verbally spar over the speed of light, the power of reason, the nature of infinity, and the devil's "lot to make all the mistakes in the universe." In the other stories Lasswitz takes a more satiric look at contemporary 19th-century scientific and philosophical ideas. Even writers are not safe from criticism, as Lasswitz refers to those "superfluous volumes" in "The Universal Library." Ironically, in all four of the above-mentioned stories Professor Lasswitz features a professor as the protagonist.

In the literature of space travel Kurd Lasswitz's *Two Planets* merits notice, particularly for its acknowledged impact upon a generation of German scientist-engineers. After the initial 1897 publication, translations fostered audiences throughout Europe. Lasswitz's thousand-page novel (abridged in the English translation) focuses on the conflict of values when intellectually and ethically superior but physically similar Martians ("Nume") invade Earth ("Ba").

Three explorers accidentally discover the Martian land station at Earth's North Pole. Their balloon runs afoul of the "abaric" or antigravity field used to propel craft to a solar-powered, ring-shaped satellite. Despite this peaceful contact a subsequent misunderstanding between Martians and the crew of an English warship precipitates military reactions from Earth, soon nullified by superior Martian weapons utilizing repulsion rather than destruction. Ensuing events admit no victory for Earth. The Martians reduce Earth to protectorate status and institute a stringent system of education. Ironically they in turn suffer a reawakening of the corrupting urge to power. Only through such efforts as those of La, a Nume, and the explorer Saltner does compromise occur. Offering a microcosmic solution for the macrocosmic problem, these two fulfill destiny, or "reason within timeless will," by becoming one with love: "To follow destiny is freedom; to satisfy it is dignity."

Even as the novel gains philosophical complexity, it suffers weak plotting and characterization. Its great strength lies in description and exposition. In detail Lasswitz describes the Martian utopia as a society accommodating freedom of the individual moral will. His scientific and technological exposition of establishment of space stations, utilization of solar energy, synthetic food, and the healthy balance of scientific and humanitarian concerns prophetically foreshadows contemporary interests.

—Hazel Pierce

LATHAM, Philip

Psedonym for Robert S(hirley) Richardson. **Nationality:** American. **Born:** Kokomo, Indiana, 22 April 1902. **Education:** University of California, Los Angeles, B.A. 1926; University of California, Berkeley, Ph.D. 1931. **Family:** Married 1) Delia Shull in 1929 (died 1940); 2) Marjorie Helen Engstead in 1942, one daughter. **Career:** Assistant Astronomer, Mt. Wilson, now Hale, Observatory, Pasadena, California, 1931-58; associate director, Griffith Observatory, Los Angeles, 1958-64. After 1964, freelance writer. **Died:** November 1981.

SCIENCE FICTION PUBLICATIONS

Novels

Five Against Venus (for children). Philadelphia, Winston, 1952.
Missing Men of Saturn (for children). Philadelphia, Winston, 1953.
Second Satellite (as Robert S. Richardson). New York, McGraw Hill, 1956.

OTHER PUBLICATIONS AS ROBERT S. RICHARDSON

Plays

Television Plays: *Captain Video* series, 1953.

Other

Preliminary Elements of Object Comas Sola (1927 AA), with others. Berkeley, University of California Press, 1927.
Astronomy, with William T. Skilling. New York, Holt, and London, Chapman and Hall, 1939; revised edition, Holt, 1947.
The Practical Essentials of Pre-Training Navigation, with William T. Skilling. New York, Holt, 1942.
Sun, Moon and Stars, with William T. Skilling. New York, McGraw Hill, 1946; revised edition, 1964.
A Brief Text in Astronomy, with William T. Skilling. New York, Holt, 1954; revised edition, 1959.
Exploring Mars (for children). New York, McGraw Hill, 1954; as *Man and the Planets,* London, Muller, 1954.
The Fascinating World of Astronomy. New York, McGraw Hill, 1960; London, Faber, 1962.
Man and the Moon. Cleveland, World, 1961.
Astronomy in Action. New York, McGraw Hill, 1962.
Mars. New York, Harcourt Brace, 1964; London, Allen and Unwin, 1965.
Getting Acquainted with Comets. New York, McGraw Hill, 1967.

The Star Lovers. New York, Macmillan, 1967.
The Stars and Serendipity (for children). New York, Pantheon, 1971.

Manuscript Collection: Fullerton College Library, California.

Philip Latham comments:

(1981) Since most of my firsthand experience is in astronomy, most of my fiction has an astronomical background. But one of my stories, "Kid Anderson," is about a prizefighter. I firmly believe that science always leads science fiction. Increasingly I have gone over to science fantasy, as in "Jeannette's Hands" and other stories. My stories are always written on the basis of *people rather than gadgetry.*

Where science fiction will go in the future is a guess. There is little left to write about: we have already written stories of interplanetary travel, extra dimensions, time travel. *Stars Wars,* for example, to my mind was a fairy tale: you could have anything you wanted in it. Most SF writers have inventive ability and ingenuity, but lack true imagination, an extremely rare gift. I neither read science fiction nor look at SF on TV or in motion pictures. Henceforth, we must try to find material in the world around us. It is there if we can see it.

*   *   *

A scandal in American science fiction is how little science there is in it. A notable exception lies in Philip Latham's stories, since they were written by the professional astronomer Robert S. Richardson and bear the marks of his expertise. For more than three decades Latham's stories appeared from time to time in the major magazines and anthologies, and Latham also wrote juvenile SF novels.

Many of the early stories are based on astronomical speculation, often presented as realistic reporting. An example is "The Aphrodite Project," which has the pretense of being science fact, complete with footnotes to astronomical journals. The story imagines a 1946 Navy contract to launch a satellite rocket to Venus to measure its mass. Once near Venus the rocket releases a cloud visible to Earth— Latham does not foresee the sophisticated radio telemetry which has actually been used on such probes. The rocket succeeds in measuring not only the mass of Venus but also its period of rotation. A secondary theme is governmental secrecy as the military authorities clamp down on the release of information about the mission. The story thus presents itself as an exposé of confidential information. "The Xi-Effect" is another example of Latham's astronomical science fiction. Astronomers discover that although the universe as a whole expands, the Earth is in a segment which is shrinking, cutting out greater and greater percentages of radiation so that the eventual extinction of all light seems inevitable. In this story we begin to see Latham's interest in the characters of scientists as well as in science. Latham presents a communication gap between the branches and modes of science. It is a theoretical physicist who predicts the Xi-Effect, and the practical astronomers are shown to be as skeptical of theory as in the public at large. "The Blindness," about the return of Halley's comet in 1986, is hardly a story at all but a meditation on the influence the comet has had on history. A theory of atomic sentience is developed to explain the comet's deviance from its projected orbit. Even in this early story the scientist Richardson makes clear his interest in antiscience and mysticism.

Latham's more recent fiction develops much further the theme of the dubious border between science and magic. Much more central to these later stories, too, is a particular kind of character: the antihero who wins the reader's sympathy for his struggles in an absurd world. "After-Enfer" is an example of a Latham story which revolves around character rather than science. The story's title derives from "N-Fear," fear of other dimensions. Sam Baxter, afraid of life, stuck in a museum job, applies for the job of exploring N-space and breaks through to genuine heroism. In "Jeannette's Hands" and its sequel, "A Drop of Dragon's Blood," Latham's protagonist is an astronomer, Bob, who is literally and figuratively married to an astrologer named Dagny. We learn in these stories about the seamy side of being a professional astronomer: the rivalries and the petty jealousies between those who hold conflicting theories and conflicting claims to grant money. Bob's rival Thornton has an innovative theory about the age of the universe, but Bob suspects him of rigging his data. The rivalry is extended in the story to the details of competition over the use of the observatory during the limited nights of good viewing. Latham gives us the comedy of Bob's loss of status when Dagny is appointed official witch of California. Such are the foibles of astronomers in this story that astrology seems a refreshing alternative. In "A Drop of Dragon's Blood" we learn more about the politics of being an astronomer, the need to produce sensational findings in order to attract research funds. Bob makes a public prediction of a period for the variable star Mira in a desperate hope for publicity, because his job is in trouble. His prediction comes true in an ironic way: Mira's companion brightens at exactly the time Bob predicted Mira would brighten, in a new phenomenon, the "simmering nova." The point of the story is the unexpected nature of the universe: "there are ghosts everywhere." Once again Latham tempts us to side with Dagny's belief in magic. Although Latham brought science to science fiction, he certainly did not bring mechanical materialism.

In his most recent stories Latham turned almost completely away from the hard science of his earlier work. In "The Miracle Elixir" an ordinary office worker, who works for Pearce's Golden Specific but never thinks of taking the company product, learns what it is like to have his life turned around by a "real" elixir. Without the interest of science, Latham's recent stories are sometimes thin and awkward. Latham could not be called a major SF writer. But he brought science to his best science fiction stories and he created antiheroic and likeable astronomers as characters.

—Curtis C. Smith

LAUMER, (John) Keith

Pseudonym: Anthony LeBaron. **Nationality:** American. **Born:** Syracuse, New York, 9 June 1925. **Education:** University of Indiana, Bloomington, 1943-44; University of Stockholm, 1947-48; University of Illinois, Urbana, B.Sc. 1950, B. Arch. 1952. **Military Service:** Served in the United States Army, 1943-45: Corporal; United States Air Force, 1952-56, 1959-65: Captain. **Family:** Married Janice Perkinson in 1949. **Career:** Staff member, University of Illinois, 1952; Foreign Service Vice-Consul and Third Secretary, Rangoon, 1956-59. Since 1959, freelance writer. **Died:** 22 January 1993.

SCIENCE FICTION PUBLICATIONS

Novels (series: Bolo; Imperium; Invaders; O'Leary; Retief; Time Trap)

Worlds of the Imperium. New York, Ace, 1962; London, Dobson, 1967; with "The War against the Yukks" and "Worldmaster," New York, Tor, 1982.

A Trace of Memory. New York, Berkley, 1963; London, Mayflower, 1968.

The Great Time Machine Hoax. New York, Simon and Schuster, 1964.

A Plague of Demons. New York, Berkley, 1965; London, Penguin, 1967.

The Other Side of Time (Imperium). New York, Berkley, 1965; London, Dobson, 1968.

The Time Bender (O'Leary). New York, Berkley, 1966; London, Dobson, 1971.

Retief's War. Garden City, New York, Doubleday, 1966.

Earthblood, with Rosel George Brown. Garden City, New York, Doubleday, 1966; London, Coronet, 1979.

Catastrophe Planet. New York, Berkley, 1966; London, Dobson, 1970.

The Monitors. New York, Berkley, 1966; London, Dobson, 1968.

Planet Run, with Gordon R. Dickson. Garden City, New York, Doubleday, 1967; London, Hale, 1977; with "Once There Was a Giant" and "Call Him Lord" by Dickson, New York, Tor, 1982.

Galactic Odyssey. New York, Berkley, 1967; London, Dobson, 1968.

The Day before Forever, and Thunderhead. Garden City, New York, Doubleday, 1968.

Assignment in Nowhere (Imperium). New York, Berkley, 1968; London, Dobson, 1972.

Retief and the Warlords. Garden City, New York, Doubleday, 1968.

The Long Twilight. New York, Putnam, 1969; London, Hale, 1976.

The World Shuffler (O'Leary). New York, Putnam, 1970; London, Sidgwick and Jackson, 1973.

The House in November: A Science Fiction Novel. New York, Putnam, 1970; London, Sidgwick and Jackson, 1973.

Time Trap: A Science Fiction Novel. New York, Putnam, 1970; London, Hale, 1976.

Retief's Ransom: A Science Fiction Novel. New York, Putnam, 1971; London, Dobson, 1975.

The Star Treasure: A Science Fiction Novel. New York, Putnam, 1971; London, Sidgwick and Jackson, 1974; expanded with three stories, New York, Baen, 1986.

Dinosaur Beach. New York, Scribner, 1971; London, Hale, 1973.

The Infinite Cage. New York, Putnam, 1972; London, Dobson, 1976.

Night of Delusions. New York, Putnam, 1972; London, Dobson, 1977; with "Thunderhead and The Last Command Command," New York, Tor, 1982.

The Shape Changer: A Science Fiction Novel (O'Leary). New York, Putnam, 1972; London, Hale, 1977.

The Glory Game. Garden City, New York, Doubleday, 1973; London, Hale, 1974.

The Ultimax Man. New York, St. Martin's Press, 1978; London, Sidgwick and Jackson, 1980.

Beyond the Imperium (contains *The Other Side of Time* and *Assignment in Nowhere*). New York, Tor, 1981.

Star Colony. New York, St. Martin's Press, 1981.

The Other Sky [and] *The House in November.* New York, Tor, 1981.

Retief to the Rescue. New York, Timescape, 1983.
The Return of Retief. New York, Baen, 1984.
The Galaxy Builder (O'Leary). New York, Ace, 1984.
End as a Hero. New York, Ace, 1985.
Rogue Bolo. New York, Baen, 1986.
Reward for Retief. New York, Baen, 1989.
The Stars Must Wait (Bolo). New York, Baen, 1990.
Zone Yellow (Imperium). New York, Baen, 1990.
Judson's Eden. Riverdale, New York, Baen, 1991.
Back to the Time Trap. Riverdale, New York, Baen, 1992.
Retief and the Rascals. Riverdale, New York, Baen, 1993.

Short Stories (series: Bolo; Retief; Invaders)

Envoy to New Worlds (Retief). New York, Ace, 1963; London, Dobson, 1972; as *Retief: Envoy to New Worlds,* New York, Baen, 1987.
Galactic Diplomat: Nine Incidents of the Corps Diplomatique Terrestrienne (Retief). Garden City, New York, Doubleday, 1965.
Nine by Laumer. Garden City, New York, Doubleday, 1967; London, Faber, 1968.
The Invaders (novelization of TV series). New York, Pyramid, 1967; as *The Meteor Men* (as Anthony LeBaron), London, Corgi, 1968.
Enemies from Beyond: An Invaders Adventure (novelization of TV series). New York, Pyramid, 1967.
Greylorn. New York, Berkley, 1968; as *The Other Sky,* London, Dobson, 1968.
It's a Mad, Mad, Mad Galaxy. New York, Berkley, 1968; London, Dobson, 1969.
Retief, Ambassador to Space. Garden City, New York, Doubleday, 1969.
Retief of the CDT. Garden City, New York, Doubleday, 1971.
Once There Was a Giant. Garden City, New York, Doubleday, 1971; London, Hale, 1975; revised, New York, Tor, 1984.
The Big Show. New York, Ace, 1972; London, Hale, 1976.
Timetracks. New York, Ballantine, 1972.
The Undefeated. New York, Dell, 1974.
Retief, Emissary to the Stars. New York, Dell, 1975; augmented edition, New York, Pocket Books, 1979.
Bolo: The Annals of the Dinochrome Brigade. New York, Berkley, 1976; London, Millington, 1977.
The Best of Keith Laumer. New York, Pocket Books, 1976.
Retief at Large. New York, Ace, 1978.
Retief Unbound (includes *Envoy to New Worlds* and *Retief's Ransom*). New York, Ace, 1979.
The Breaking Earth. New York, Tor, 1981.
Worlds of the Imperium. New York, Tor, 1982.
Retief: Diplomat at Arms. New York, Pocket Books, 1982.
Chrestomathy. New York, Baen, 1984.
Retief and the Pangalactic Pageant of Pulchriture. New York, Baen, 1986.
Retief in the Ruins. New York, Baen, 1986.
The Compleat Bolo. New York, Baen, 1990.
Alien Minds. Riverdale, New York, Baen, 1991.

OTHER PUBLICATIONS

Novels

Embassy. New York, Pyramid, 1965.

The Afrit Affair (novelization of TV series). New York, Berkley, 1968.
The Drowned Queen (novelization of TV series). New York, Berkley, 1968.
The Gold Bomb (novelization of TV series). New York, Berkley, 1968.
Deadfall. Garden City, New York, Doubleday, 1971; London, Hale, 1974; as *Fat Chance,* New York, Pocket Books, 1975.

Other

How to Design and Build Flying Models. New York, Harper, 1960; revised edition, 1970; London, Hale, 1975.

Editor, *Five Fates.* Garden City, New York, Doubleday, 1970.
Editor, with Bill Fawcett, *Honor of the Regiment* (Bolo). Riverdale, New York, Baen, 1993.
Editor, with Bill Fawcett, *The Unconquerable* (Bolo). Riverdale, New York, Baen, 1994.

*

Manuscript Collections: University of Syracuse, New York; University of Mississippi, University.

Keith Laumer comments:

(1991) I have been asked if my work is "relevant," i.e., political propaganda. It is not. I prefer to treat themes that have been important to man ever since he became man, and will continue to be important as long as humanity survives; strength and courage, truth and beauty, loyalty and justice, ethics and integrity, kindness and gentleness, and many others.

*　　*　　*

During the 1960s, Keith Laumer was one of the most prolific of science fiction authors. He has to his credit a long string of titles which range over wide areas both in subject matter and in treatment. Laumer's first novel, *Worlds of the Imperium,* is told as a conventional adventure story, with only an occasional light touch. But in *The Time Bender* and its sequels featuring Layfayette O'Leary, Laumer writes what amounts to a gentle parody of his own Imperium series. And the humor in the long and popular series (mostly of short stories) concerning interstellar diplomat Jame Retief stretches almost all the way to farce. But Laumer can play the other side of the court as well: the tone is serious, even grim, in such works as *A Plague of Demons* and *Night of Delusions.* As for subject matter, Laumer has tried out virtually all the traditional possibilities and has enriched the realm of science fiction with innovations of his own—most notably the brilliantly detailed and remarkably plausible picture of the "fabric of simultaneous reality" introduced in the Imperium series. Laumer has written space-war stories, space-diplomacy stories, slightly rationalized fairy stories, time-travel stories, parallel-world stories, robot stories, psi-power stories, invasion-of-the-Earth stories (including *The Monitors,* in which the invaders are the good guys), stories of intrigue, love, rational detection, mystical apotheosis, and on and on.

Yet for all its diversity, Laumer's work holds unities as well. Some of these are of a negative sort. For instance, there is never an unhappy ending. A Laumer hero may lose a girl, but if so he will usually marry another, and will in no case allow one misfortune to poison his entire life. He may get killed in the end, but he will never go unmourned and (in *Assignment in Nowhere* and others) his sacrifice may well save the world. In the area of positive generalizations, it can be said that in some measure all Laumer stories are adventure stories, even if the author's focus is on satire, farce, romance, ratiocination, or philosophical speculation.

Moreover, Laumer heroes are virtually all of one general pattern, with variations determined chiefly by degree of maturity. While the typologies are not identical, the Laumer character does bear striking similarities to the "Heinlein individual" described by Alexei Panshin. Explanations for this resemblance might range from some basic principle of storytelling to Heinlein's and Laumer's similar background as military officers. The basic Laumer type is the full-formed competent man—sure of himself, resourceful, able to mix easily with all levels of society and to get what he wants out of anyone. Laumer has put the basic type to heaviest use in the person of Retief, hero of a "template series" where character growth is ruled out by the ground rules. For most other applications, the basic competent man is too static—he can indeed be roused to action, but only to protect what he has. A slight variation Laumer employs more often is an incipient competent man whose character is fully formed but who has not yet found his niche in life, and who is consequently searching for fulfillment. Brion Bayard fits in here in *Worlds of the Imperium*, though in the sequel, *The Other Side of Time*, he has matured into the basic type. It is of course possible to begin at an earlier point, with someone who must learn not merely how to apply competence, but competence itself. This gives us characters such as Billy Danger in *Galactic Odyssey* or, in a more humorous vein, Layfayette O'Leary. But Laumer has also moved in the other direction, beyond the competent man. Perhaps because of his own relative youth during his peak writing period, Laumer has chosen to do this not by putting one of his heroes through some sort of mid-life crisis, but rather (in a tack he might have picked up from van Vogt or the early Heinlein—or from Sophocles) by having his hero discover something about who he is that causes him to transcend his status as the competent man. In the most extreme case, the largely unsuccessful *Night of Delusions*, the protagonist finds himself to be, for most practical purposes, God. Other Laumer heroes learn that they are supermen, Arthurian reincarnations, and various sorts of robots. The effects of such revelations also vary. Some heroes go off to pursue transcendental existence, some perish gloriously, and others voluntarily return to the human state. It is difficult to decide whether in these various encounters with the transcendental, Laumer is trying to put forth a serious philosophy (in the manner of, say, Cordwainer Smith or Gordon R. Dickson), or simply, more playfully, to give his already competent heroes somewhere to go, and to pique the reader's sense of wonder. Such mystic passages are not, in any event, the most successful part of Laumer's work.

The 1960s and early 1970s remain the significant period of Laumer's production. New titles appearing since that time have been generally repackagings or "fix-ups" of older work. A partial exception, *The Galaxy Builder*, is merely one more Layfayette O'Leary novel in the same mold as its predecessors. The repackagings and reiterations do little or nothing to remedy Laumer's characteristic flaws of insufficient attention to detail and excessive repetition from work to work. Consequently, it will be left to posterity to decide which of five or six versions of essentially the same story is the one really worth keeping. But some of Laumer will most certainly be kept.

—Patrick L. McGuire

LAVOND, Paul Dennis. *See* **LOWNDES, Robert A.W.**

LeBARON, Anthony. *See* **LAUMER, Keith.**

LEE, Matt. *See* **MERWIN, Sam, Jr.**

LEE, Tanith

Nationality: British. **Born:** London, 19 September 1947. **Education:** Attended Catford Grammar School, London, and an art college. **Awards:** August Derleth award, 1980; World Fantasy Convention award, 1983. **Address:** c/o Macmillan London Ltd., 4 Little Essex Street, London WC2R 3LF, England.

SCIENCE FICTION PUBLICATIONS

Novels (series: Birthgrave; Blood Opera; Don't Bite the Sun; Dragonflight; Secret Books of Paradys; Tales from the Flat Earth; Wars of Vis)

The Birthgrave. New York, DAW, 1975; London, Orbit, 1977.
Don't Bite the Sun. New York, DAW, 1976.
The Storm Lord (Wars of Vis). New York, DAW, 1976; London, Orbit, 1977.
Drinking Sapphire Wine (Don't Bite the Sun). New York, DAW, 1977; with *Don't Bite the Sun,* London, Hamlyn, 1979.
Volkhavaar. New York, DAW, 1977; London, Hamlyn, 1981.
Vazkor, Son of Vazkor (Birthgrave). New York, DAW, 1978; as *Shadowfire,* London, Orbit, 1978.
Quest for the White Witch (Birthgrave). New York, DAW, 1978; London, Orbit, 1979.
Night's Master (Flat Earth). New York, DAW, 1978; London, Hamlyn, 1981.
Death's Master (Flat Earth). New York, DAW, 1979; London, Hamlyn, 1982.
Electric Forest. Garden City, New York, Doubleday, 1979.
Sabella; or, The Blood Stone. New York, DAW, 1980; London, Unwin, 1987.
Kill the Dead. New York, DAW, 1980; London, Legend, 1990.
Day by Night. New York, DAW, 1980.
Sometimes, after Sunset (includes *Sabella* and *Kill the Dead*). Garden City, New York, Doubleday, 1981.
Delusion's Master (Flat Earth). New York, DAW, 1981; London, Arrow, 1987.
The Silver Metal Lover. Garden City, New York, Doubleday, 1981; London, Unwin, 1986.
Lycanthia; or, The Children of Wolves. New York, DAW, 1981; London, Legend, 1990.

Cyrion (Paradys). New York, DAW, 1982.

Sung in Shadow. New York, DAW, 1983.

Anackire (Wars of Vis). New York, DAW, 1983; London, Orbit, 1985.

The Wars of Vis (includes *The Storm Lord* and *Anackire*). Garden City, New York, Doubleday, 1984.

Days of Grass. New York, DAW, 1985.

Delirium's Mistress (Flat Earth). New York, DAW, 1986; London, Arrow, 1987.

The White Serpent (Wars of Vis). New York, DAW, 1988.

The Book of the Beast (Paradys). London, Unwin, 1988; Woodstock, New York, Overlook Press, 1991.

Madame Two Swords. West Kingston, Rhode Island, Donald M. Grant, 1988.

A Heroine of the World. New York, DAW, 1989.

The Blood of Roses. London, Legend, 1990.

Black Unicorn (Dragonflight). New York, Atheneum, 1991; London, Orbit, 1994.

The Book of the Dead (Paradys). Woodstock, New York, Overlook Press, 1991.

Dark Dance (Blood Opera). London, Macdonald, and New York, Dell, 1992.

Heart-Beast. London, Headline, 1992; New York, Dell, 1993.

Elephantasm. London, Headline, 1993.

Personal Darkness (Blood Opera). London, Little Brown, 1993; New York, Dell, 1994.

The Book of the Mad (Paradys). Woodstock, New York, Overlook Press, 1993.

Darkness, I (Blood Opera). London, Little Brown, 1994.

Eva Fairdeath. London, Headline, 1994.

Gold Unicorn (Dragonflight). New York, Atheneum, 1994.

Reigning Cats and Dogs. London, Headline, 1995.

Novels (for children: series: Dark Castle)

The Dragon Hoard. London, Macmillan, and New York, Farrar Straus, 1971.

Animal Castle. London, Macmillan, and New York, Farrar Straus, 1972.

Companions on the Road. London, Macmillan, 1975.

The Winter Players. London, Macmillan, 1976.

East of Midnight. London, Macmillan, 1977; New York, St. Martin's Press, 1978.

Shon the Taken. London, Macmillan, 1979.
1986.

The Castle of Dark (Dark Castle). London, Macmillan, 1978.

Prince on a White Horse (Dark Castle). London, Macmillan, 1982.

Short Stories (series: Secret Books of Paradys)

The Betrothed. Sidcup, Kent, Slughorn Press, 1968.

Princess Hynchatti and Some Other Surprises (for children). London, Macmillan, 1972; New York, Farrar Straus, 1973.

Unsilent Night (miscellany). Cambridge, Massachusetts, NESFA Press, 1981.

Red as Blood; or, Tales from the Sisters Grimmer. New York, DAW, 1983.

The Beautiful Biting Machine. New Castle, Virginia, Cheap Street, 1984.

Tamastara; or, The Indian Nights. New York, DAW, 1984.

The Gorgon and Other Beastly Tales. New York, DAW, 1985.

Dreams of Dark and Light: The Great Short Fiction of Tanith Lee. Sauk City, Wisconsin, Arkham House, 1986.

Night's Sorceries (Flat Earth). New York, DAW, 1987; London, Legend, 1988.

Tales from the Flat Earth: Night's Daughter. Garden City, New York, Doubleday, 1987.

The Book of the Damned (Paradys). London, Unwin, 1988; Woodstock, New York, Overlook Press, 1990.

Women as Demons: The Male Perception of Women through Space and Time. London, Women's Press, 1989.

Forests of the Night. London, Unwin, 1989.

Nightshades: Thirteen Journeys into Shadow. London, Headline, 1993.

Plays

Radio Plays: *Bitter Gate,* 1977; *Red Wine,* 1977; *Death Is King,* 1979; *The Silver Sky,* 1980.

Television Plays: *Sarcophagus,* 1980, and *Sand,* 1981, both for *Blake's Seven* series.

*

Bibliography: By Mike Ashley, in *Fantasy Macabre 4* (London), 1983.

*   *   *

The fiction of Tanith Lee is a highly original and intense mixture of science fiction, heroic fantasy, and fairy tale. In all her work, her ironic sense of humor, dark imagination, and an interest in the erotic play a strong role. Her themes usually involve the individual's ability to manipulate fate, and point of view as a moral determinant. These elements are combined in a variety of ways to create varying effects.

The Birthgrave, Lee's first work for adults, contains several of the devices she exploits again in later works. The plot concerns the awakening and subsequent education of a "goddess." The heroine is a mythic creation, on whose fate rests the direction of her world. Her moral ignorance is demonstrated and alleviated in an episodic series of adventures. Societal conflicts between men and women, and between technology and science, are played out directly in her experience. Although this is undoubtedly close in spirit to *The Storm Lord,* Lee does not yet employ the more contrived style that conveys so well the super-human dimensions of that setting. And indeed, the denouement of *The Birthgrave* is pure science fiction, finding rational explanations for all the heroine's inhuman traits. This is not the case in the later novels, where some characters have frankly supernatural traits, and the prose style subtly and effectively communicates this. Larger-than-life protagonists, however, are a common feature of *The Birthgrave* and its sequels as well as *The Storm Lord, Anackire,* and *The White Serpent.* Their struggle to sort out good and evil is of paramount importance to their worlds and is usually at least partly dependent on their discovery of their own identity, which may be hidden, lost, or simply confused.

Both *Night's Master* and *Death's Master* investigate some of these same concerns from a fresh perspective. The episodic plots now give way to a structure of almost independent short stories, and the style is the full-blown, heavily stylized tone of myths and fairy tales. These stories concern demon-kind and their interaction with humanity. The demons are at pains to play elaborate ironic pranks usually targeting the most human behavior of the human characters. Like the heroes and heroines of the other novels, these characters have the ability to influence the direction of world events. However, morality rather than society is the focus of the conflict in this series. The ambiguities of moral behavior, especially as related to sexual relationships, are explored in many permutations. Self examination is rarely an issue, except as the demons call into question the assumptions of the human characters.

Lee's stylized prose draws the reader into a world reminiscent of familiar territory, which is all the more shocking when it is suddenly turned on its head. Sympathetic werewolves and vampires, wicked Cinderellas and Snow Whites, and the subversion of our expectations are the subjects of these works. The reader's sense of disorientation stems in part from the creation of real characters from the stock villains and heroes of the genre. Some of these works appear as short stories (*Red as Blood*); *Lycanthia* is a series of interrelated novellas and *Cyrion* concerns the adventures of a single hero told as a series of short stories joined by "interlogues" which provide continuity. Part of the impact of these tales derives from their extraordinary sensory reality. We experience in these novels and short stories the feel of exotic fabrics, the taste of strange fruits, the incense of haunting perfumes, and the vibrant colors of a variety of barbaric and sophisticated peoples. The reader may experience a kind of secondary sensory overload or feel oppressed by the intensity of the borrowed sensations. This extraordinarily tactile world is one of the reasons Tanith Lee's work lingers in the mind.

Lee's talent for the creation of a reality is also evident in her science-fiction works. In *Don't Bite the Sun,* for example, an invented slang conveys not only a sense of the heroine but of her entire society. This "Jang slang," used constantly by the narrator, consists almost entirely of words indicating extremes. It is the vocabulary of a society so predictable that its members have taken to attempting suicide for diversion. This is typical of Lee's science-fiction works, whose theme is generally human society and its failures, although on occasion it is purely a vehicle for humor (as in "Qatt-Sup" from *The Gorgon and Other Beastly Tales*). Human failure is usually demonstrated in the person of the protagonist, whose struggles provide the context in which society is examined.

In a recent novel, *A Heroine of the World,* Tanith Lee has modulated the fantasy to create an easily recognizable world. Love and war are key plot ingredients as they are in many of the heroic fantasies, but here they are played out on a human scale without magical interference. The tragedies are human and immediate. The heroine's will to survive is recognizable from any World War II autobiography. Her salvation, however, comes not from her own struggles, nor from the men she abandons herself to, but through her understanding of her goddess. As in a number of short stories throughout her oeuvre, Lee here uses a single element of the fantastic to provide leverage to work with an important theme.

The work of Tanith Lee is not for every taste. It is idiosyncratic and individual in its expression, characters, settings and themes. Like caviar or brandy, it is an acquired taste. It has sometimes the smothering quality of incense. It is a pleasure reserved for the sophisticated palate.

—Cathy Chauvette

Le GUIN, Ursula K(roeber)

Nationality: American. **Born:** Berkeley, California, 21 October 1929; daughter of the anthropologist Alfred L. Kroeber and writer Theodora Kroeber. **Education:** Radcliffe College, Cambridge, Massachusetts, A.B. 1951 (Phi Beta Kappa); Columbia University, New York (Faculty Fellow; Fulbright Fellow, 1953), M.A. 1952. **Family:** Married Charles A. Le Guin in 1953; two daughters and one son, two grandchildren. **Career:** Instructor in French, Mercer University, Macon, Georgia, 1954, and University of Idaho, Moscow, 1956; department secretary, Emory University, Atlanta, 1955; has taught writing workshops at Pacific University, Forest Grove, Oregon, 1971, University of Washington, Seattle, 1971-73, Portland State University, Oregon, 1974, 1977, 1979, in Melbourne, Australia, 1975, at the University of Reading, England, 1976, Indiana Writers Conference, Bloomington, 1978, 1983, University of California, San Diego, 1979, Flight of the Mind, 1990-95, and Stanford University, 1995. Lives in Portland, Oregon. **Awards:** Boston, *Globe-Horn Book* award, for children's book, 1969; Nebula award, 1969, 1974 (twice), 1991; Hugo award, 1970, 1973, 1974, 1975, 1988; National Book award for children's book, 1972; Jupiter award, 1974 (twice), 1976; Gandalf award, 1979; University of Oregon Distinguished Service award, 1981; *Locus* award (twice), 1983, 1995; Janet Heidinger Kafka award, 1986; International Fantasy award, 1988; Pushcart prize, 1991; Harold D. Vursell award, American Academy and Institute of Arts and Letters, 1991; James Tiptree, Jr., award, 1995; Theodore Sturgeon award, 1995. Guest of Honor, World Science Fiction Convention, 1975. D.Litt., Bucknell University, Lewisburg, Pennsylvania, 1978; Lawrence University, Appleton, Wisconsin; D.H.L.: Lewis and Clark College, Portland, 1983; Occidental College, Los Angeles, 1985. **Agents:** (literary) Virginia Kidd, 538 East Harford Street, Milford, Pennsylvania 18337; (dramatic) Matthew Bialer, William Morris Agency, 1350 Avenue of the Americas, New York, New York 10019, U.S.A.

SCIENCE FICTION PUBLICATIONS

Novels (series: Hain)

Rocannon's World (Hain). New York, Ace, 1966; London, Tandem, 1972.
Planet of Exile (Hain). New York, Ace, 1966; London, Tandem, 1972.
City of Illusions (Hain). New York, Ace, 1967; London, Gollancz, 1971.
The Left Hand of Darkness (Hain). New York, Ace, and London, Macdonald, 1969.
The Lathe of Heaven. New York, Scribner, 1971; London, Gollancz, 1972.
The Dispossessed: An Ambiguous Utopia. New York, Harper, and London, Gollancz, 1974.
The Word for World Is Forest (Hain). New York, Berkley, 1976; London, Gollancz, 1977.
Malafrena. New York, Berkley, 1979; London, Gollancz, 1980.
The Eye of the Heron. London, Gollancz, 1982; New York, Harper, 1983.
Always Coming Home (includes audio tape). New York, Harper, 1985; London, Gollancz, 1986.

Fiction (for children; series: Catwings)

Leese Webster. New York, Atheneum, 1979; London, Gollancz, 1981.
The Beginning Place. New York, Harper, 1980; as *Threshold,* London, Gollancz, 1980.
Catwings. New York, Orchard, 1988.
Catwings Return. New York, Orchard, 1989.
Fire and Stone, with Laura Marshall. New York, Atheneum, 1989.
Fish Soup. London, Atheneum, 1992.
Wonderful Alexander and the Catwings. New York, Orchard, 1994.

Fiction (for young adults; series: Earthsea in all titles)

The Earthsea Quartet. London, Penguin, 1993.
   A Wizard of Earthsea. Berkeley, California, Parnassus Press, 1968; London, Gollancz, 1971.
   The Tombs of Atuan. New York, Atheneum, 1971; London, Gollancz, 1972.
   The Farthest Shore. New York, Atheneum, 1972; London, Gollancz, 1973.
   Tehanu: The Last Book of Earthsea. New York, Atheneum, and London, Gollancz, 1990.

Short Stories (series: Kroy)

The Wind's Twelve Quarters. New York, Harper, 1975; London, Gollancz, 1976.
Orsinian Tales. New York, Harper, 1976; London, Gollancz, 1977.
The Water Is Wide. Portland, Oregon, Pendragon Press, 1976.
Gwilan's Harp. Northridge, California, Lord John Press, 1981.
The Compass Rose. Portland, Oregon, Pendragon Press, 1982; London, Gollancz, 1983.
The Adventure of Cobbler's Rune (Kroy). New Castle, Virginia, Cheap Street, 1982.
Solomon Leviathan's Nine Hundred and Thirty-First Trip around the World (Kroy). New Castle, Virginia, Cheap Street, 1983.
Buffalo Gals and Other Animal Presences. Santa Barbara, California, Capra Press, 1987; London, Gollancz, 1990.
The New Atlantis, bound with *The Return from Rainbow Bridge,* by Kim Stanley Robinson. New York, Tor, 1989.
Nine Lives. Eugene, Oregon, Pulphouse, 1992.
The Ones Who Walk Away from Omelas. Mankato, Minnesota, Creative Education, 1993.
A Fisherman of the Inland Sea. Norwalk, Connecticut, Easton Press, 1994.
Buffalo Gals, Won't You Come out Tonight. San Francisco, Pomegranate, 1994.
Four Ways to Forgiveness. New York, HarperPrism, 1995.

OTHER PUBLICATIONS

Fiction (for children)

Very Far Away from Anywhere Else. New York, Atheneum, 1976; as *A Very Long Way from Anywhere Else,* London, Gollancz, 1976.
The Visionary: The Life Story of Flicker of the Serpentine of Telina-Na, with *Wonders Hidden,* by Scott Russell Sanders. Santa Barbara, California, Capra Press, 1984.

A Visit from Dr. Katz. New York, Atheneum, 1988; as *Dr. Katz,* London, Collins, 1988.
A Ride on the Red Mare's Back. New York, Orchard, 1992.
Searoad: Chronicles of Klatsand. New York, HarperCollins, 1991; London, Gollancz, 1992.

Plays

No Use to Talk to Me, in *The Altered Eye,* edited by Lee Harding. Melbourne, Norstrilia Press, 1976; New York, Berkley, 1978.
King Dog (screenplay), with *Dostoevsky,* by Raymond Carver and Tess Gallagher. Santa Barbara, California, Capra Press, 1985.

Poetry

Wild Angels. Santa Barbara, California, Capra Press, 1975.
Tillai and Tylissos, with Theodora K. Quinn. N.p., Red Bull Press, 1979.
Torrey Pines Reserve. Northridge, California, Lord John Press, 1980.
Hard Words and Other Poems. New York, Harper, 1981.
In the Red Zone. Northridge, California, Lord John Press, 1983.
Wild Oats and Fireweed. New York, Harper, 1988.
Blue Moon over Thurman Street. Portland, Oregon, NewSage Press, 1993.
Going out with Peacocks and Other Poems. New York, HarperPerennial, 1994.

Other

From Elfland to Poughkeepsie (lecture). Portland, Oregon, Pendragon Press, 1973.
Dreams Must Explain Themselves. New York, Algol Press, 1975.
The Language of the Night: Essays on Fantasy and Science Fiction, edited by Susan Wood. New York, Putnam, 1979; revised edition, edited by Ursula K. Le Guin, London, Women's Press, 1989; New York, HarperPerennial, 1993.
Dancing at the Edge of the World: Thoughts on Words, Women, Places. New York, Grove Press, and London, Gollancz, 1989.
The Way of the Water's Going, with photographs by Ernest Waugh and Alan Nicholson. New York, Harper and Row, 1989.
Talk about Writing. Eugene, Oregon, Pulphouse, 1991.
Myth and Archetype in Science Fiction. Eugene, Oregon, Pulphouse, 1991.
Findings. Browerville, Minnesota, Oxhead Press, 1992.
Earthsea Revisioned. Cambridge, Massachusetts, Children's Literature New England, and Cambridge, England, Green Bay, 1993.

Editor, *Nebula Award Stories 11.* London, Gollancz, 1976; New York, Harper, 1977.
Editor, with Virginia Kidd, *Interfaces.* New York, Ace, 1980.
Editor, with Virginia Kidd, *Edges: 13 New Tales from the Borderlands of the Imagination.* New York, Pocket Books, 1980.
Editor, with Brian Atteberg, *The Norton Book of Science Fiction: North American Science Fiction, 1960-1990.* New York, Norton, 1993.

*

Bibliography: *Ursula K. Le Guin: A Primary and Secondary Bibliography* by Elizabeth Cummins Cogell, Boston, Hall, 1983; *Ursula K. Le Guin: A Primary Bibliography* by David S. Bratman, 1995.

Manuscript Collection: University of Oregon Library, Eugene.

Critical Studies: *The Farthest Shores of Ursula K. Le Guin* by George Edgar Slusser, San Bernardino, California, Borgo Press, 1976; "Ursula Le Guin Issue" of *Science-Fiction Studies* (Terre Haute, Indiana), March 1976; *Ursula Le Guin* by Joseph D. Olander and Martin H. Greenberg, New York, Taplinger, and Edinburgh, Harris, 1979; *Ursula K. Le Guin: Voyager to Inner Lands and to Outer Space* edited by Joseph W. De Bolt, Port Washington, New York, Kennikat Press, 1979; *Ursula K. Le Guin* by Barbara J. Bucknall, New York, Ungar, 1981; *Ursula K. Le Guin* by Charlotte Spivack, Boston, Twayne, 1984; *Approaches to the Fiction of Ursula K. Le Guin* by James Bittner, Ann Arbor, Michigan, UMI Research Press, and Epping, Essex, Bowker, 1984; *Understanding Ursula K. Le Guin* by Elizabeth Cummins, Columbia, University of South Carolina Press, 1990.

*   *   *

The immensely popular fiction of Ursula K. Le Guin proves that popular literature may have literary merit, a serious message, and a large audience all at once. Today the notion of a science-fiction writer producing a novel of substance, even a novel of character, is not so remarkable, as researchers continue to demonstrate that works remarkable as literature have existed in this genre ever since the publication of Mary Shelley's *Frankenstein;* but at the start of Le Guin's career, in the mid 1960s, literary excellence in science fiction was regarded as rare. Le Guin, hailed as a novelist who chose to write science fiction, has always attracted an audience composed of genre fans as well as readers who would ordinarily disdain science fiction. Le Guin's work continues to be known for literary expertise which graces a thematic preoccupation with telling essentially hopeful stories of man transcending alienation to open his imagination, his intellect, and his heart to the real adventure of the universe. Le Guin, in common with many writers of science fiction, is a talented builder of new worlds and alien landscapes; she is comfortable with technological wonders, faster-than-light vehicles, and particularly with marvels in the field of long-distance communications, but her commitment, stated clearly in the essay "Science Fiction and Mrs. Brown," is to confirm man's essential humanity against a backdrop of alien situations by means of consistently viewing her characters as the "subjects" of her narratives rather than as objects. A subjective human approach to the marvelous underlines Le Guin's view that if "Mrs. Brown [the ordinary, intriguing snatch of human character] is dead, you can take your galaxies and roll them up into a ball and throw them into the trashcan, for all I care. What good are all the objects in the universe, if there is no subject?"

A large portion of Le Guin's work focuses upon subjective views of a universe incorporating numerous habitable worlds, each "seeded" by beings from the planet Hain. Each of the five novels and several shorter works in this series revolves around the literal and figurative quests of chief characters to discover their individual purposes within the contexts of their several different worlds and, often, within the broader context of the universe. The themes and chronology of the Hain series have been worked out over two decades, but the early works anticipate or foreshadow the best moments of her later work. One of the later novels, fascinatingly, provides the scientific explanation and development of a device—the instantaneous communicator called the ansible—which has been essential to all of the previous works.

The first published works in this series, *Rocannon's World, Planet of Exile,* and *City of Illusions,* do proceed chronologically and establish a thematic preoccupation with the duality existing in nature and in man viewed, as Peter Nicholls has pointed out, "not as polarities or opposed forces" but as archetypical symbols presented as "twin parts of a balanced whole" (*The Science Fiction Encyclopedia,* 1979). Each work employs the alien as the embodiment of alienation presenting to the hero the challenge of transcending fear itself, through embracing the unknown. Communication, whether through telepathic "mindspeech" or by means of the amazing ansible, is significant, often the symbolic crux of each climax. In *Rocannon's World* an outworld ethnological surveyor stranded on Fomalhaut II is unable to accept fully his destiny of remaining on the strange world until he achieves the ability to communicate through mindspeech. In a narrative which also emphasizes the importance of naming, it is significant that, in ironic understatement, the League of All Worlds, unbeknownst to the ethnographer, gives this world his name, Rocannon's World.

Planet of Exile depicts a world which is populated by two humanoid groups, each believing themselves to be fully human and therefore superior to the other. A female character, the dreamy yet strong-willed Rolery, represents the linking of the two cultures as she overcomes her awe of the "farborn" Terran colonists through her command of telepathic powers generally possessed only by the farborns. Interestingly, discipline, along with honest communication, is described as the key to individual purpose and successful community, while community (the cooperation of both "human" societies) is necessary for the basic survival of either group. "Community," asserts Le Guin (in "Science Fiction and Mrs. Brown"), "is the best we can hope for, and community for most people means touches: the touch of your hand against the other's hand, the job done together, the sledge hauled together, the dance danced together, the child conceived together." Significantly, Rolery is offered the hope of conceiving a child with her farborn husband, while the two groups, under extreme challenge from overwhelming environmental conditions, at last unite to form a new society. Metaphor is particularly rich in the novel, which anticipates *The Left Hand of Darkness* in its description of a world dominated by a frigid winter environment.

City of Illusions describes a Hainish world where mindspeech, previously the epitome of truthful communication, has been perverted by the alien Shing invaders who can manipulate it into a "mind lie." A complex narrative tells the story of the amnesiac Falk and his quest to discover his true name and homeworld. Throughout experiences of betrayal and disorienting double identity, his hopes were "staked now totally on one belief: that an honest man cannot be cheated, that truth, if the game be played through right to the end, will lead to truth." Here truth and falsehood are regarded as polarities in essential struggle; truth may prevail only when the hero learns to allow both of his identities to work together and, significantly, when his gains access to the ansible so that he may communicate with the world of its origin as well as with the League of All Worlds. The League becomes known as the Ekumen of Known Worlds in *The Left Hand of Darkness,* which richly explores the themes suggested in earlier Hainish works. Genly Ai is a human ethnologist who visits the planet Gethen, where he is swiftly caught up in a snowbound society wrapped in political intrigue and characterized by a revolutionary (to Genly Ai as well as to the reader) androgynous worldview which raises questions about sexuality and sexism and shows a populace composed of individuals whose identity is divorced from gender. The Gethenians, usually neuter, experience a sexual cycle which gives them the ability to become either male or female at certain cyclical peaks. The implications of this alienness tax even the comprehension of this professional observer who learns that the limitation of his own alien perspective, his own alienation, is keeping him from appreciating and understanding this strange new world.

"Vaster than Empires and More Slow" and *The Word for World Is Forest* are shorter works in the Hain series which use the forest as metaphors for the unknown. The former (its title derived from Andrew Marvell's poem "To His Coy Mistress") is perhaps Le Guin's most polished and graceful statement of the need to embrace the alien, the Other, in order to understand it. Osden, a ship's empath, transcends the limitations of both time and fear when he literally embraces the surface of an alien planet which is covered by a network of sentient vegetation. "He had taken fear into himself, and accepting had transcended it. He had given up his self to the alien, an unreserved surrender, that left no place for evil. He had learned love of the Other, and thereby been given his whole self."

The Dispossessed is centered on the inventor of the ansible, a man called Shevek whose anarchist "Utopia" is ambiguously unable to provide him with the raw materials (chiefly free communication and flow of scientific information) which he needs to make his best contribution to society. This rich work is one in which occasional didacticism is nevertheless fascinating as two politically different worlds (one anarchistic, the other decadently capitalistic) are balanced by means of contrast and comparison, each presented in alternate chapters. The author uses visual perspective most strikingly here; the image of the wall as a defining force is powerfully employed, while in an early scene Shevek's world fills his view like a concave dish until, as his space vessel takes him a greater distance from it, it falls away into a convex circle, then a globe, then a distant world. The author also uses paradox, mathematical and verbal, as the key to truth, while communication among all men is the confirmation of man's essential humanity in the face of political, environmental, or other differences.

Other major works by Le Guin include *The Lathe of Heaven,* a novel outside of the Hain series dealing with a man of conscience who cannot bear the fact that his dreams effectively change reality, and *The Beginning Place,* an allegorical novel portraying a fantastic "twilight world" that becomes a haven for two adolescents fleeing from unhappy family situations in a bleak, unnamed suburbia. The protagonists learn, by means of encounters with an archetypal monster, to face the harsh disappointments of their "real" lives. *Orsinian Tales* and *Malafrena* evoke the 19th century in an imaginary country with a central European atmosphere. *Malafrena* deals with the coming of age of a young revolutionary who must learn to balance freedom and commitment.

The Compass Rose is an anthology of short stories organized around the four directions of the magnetic compass. Tales with settings and themes reminiscent of those in *Malafrena* are here accompanied by tales that are more strictly science-fictional and dealing with, for instance, a new Atlantis or an enigmatic cat used in a scientific experiment. A particular gem is "The Author of the Acacia Seeds and Other Extracts from the *Journal of the Association of Therolinguistics,*" which succeeds as a brilliant spoof of academic writing and as a comment on the difficulty of and fascination inherent in understanding the culture of another life form.

The four novels in Le Guin's Earthsea series represent a study of magical skill which appeals to adults as well as to the younger audience for which it was written. *Tehanu: The Last Book of*

Earthsea was published in 1990, a full 20 years after the first volume in the series, *A Wizard of Earthsea,* was produced and after the author had done a great deal of rethinking about the role of women in a man's world. *Times Literary Supplement* reviewer John Clute praised *Wizard* as "as polished and word-perfect a tale for older children as could be imagined." *Tehanu* is a more difficult book, in which a world beloved by its readers is fully re-examined, particularly in regard to its power structure. While the old magic is significant to the novel's ending, the book pleases feminists and students of Le Guin's maturation as a thinker more than those who are looking for more of the same in Earthsea.

Le Guin's evolution as a thinker is made particularly clear in *Dancing at the Edge of the World: Thoughts on Words, Women, Places,* a collection of the author's nonfiction including talks, essays, occasional pieces and book reviews from 1976-86. Particularly noteworthy is her reprint of the much-quoted essay "Is Gender Necessary?" (now entitled "Is Gender Necessary? Redux") along with a "running commentary" reflecting "changes of mind" and the author's more recent thinking about how the masculine pronoun employed in *The Left Hand of Darkness* limited her abilities to create an androgyne in which the female aspect was fully drawn as the male.

Le Guin's most significant accomplishment in recent years is her work *Always Coming Home,* which some refuse to classify as a novel. Featuring multiple voices, the book tells the stories of the Kesh, a people existing in woman-centered society in a future California landscape. The book's radial structure and experimental narrative techniques reflect Le Guin's preoccupation with creating a literature that is "alive, unfixed, on the move, defying definition." Her goal is to convey the experience of the Kesh world without limiting the reader to a single vantage point. As critic Elizabeth Cummins points out, the book "de-emphasizes the significance of a beginning or an end, challenges their very existence even, and instead concentrates . . . on the middle, the living, the changing."

In common with Brian Aldiss, Le Guin continually works to stretch her skills in new directions, demanding ever more of herself in terms of content and style. She is afraid neither to challenge the intelligent reader nor to fight the confines of a marketplace that demands easily categorizeable fiction, nor to correct her own thinking or "change her mind" in print. The result is some of the most stimulating and satisfying fiction available within the genre as well as outside of it. Also like Aldiss, Le Guin has written "mainstream" fiction as well as work in other forms such as poetry and memoirs.

Over the years Le Guin's work affirms that the ultimate adventure in the universe is the subjective human quest not so much for confrontation with the alien but for the defeat of alienation. In recent years, she has consciously sought to re-evaluate the hero-centered tale with its linear progression toward conquest and to turn instead toward the novel as a more flexible "carrier bag" that is shaped by the experiences contained within it.

—Rosemary Herbert

LEIBER, Fritz (Reuter, Jr.)

Nationality: American. **Born:** Chicago, Illinois, 24 December 1910. **Education:** University of Chicago, Ph.B. 1932; Episcopal General Theological Seminary, Washington, D.C. **Family:** Married Jonquil Stephens in 1936 (died 1969); one son. **Career:** Episcopal minister at two churches in New Jersey, 1932-33; actor, 1934-36; editor, Consolidated Book Publishers, Chicago, 1937-41; Instructor in Speech and Drama, Occidental College, Los Angeles, 1941-42; precision inspector, Douglas Aircraft, Santa Monica, California, 1942-44; associate editor, *Science Digest,* Chicago, 1944-56. Lecturer, Clarion State College, Pennsylvania, summers 1968-70. **Awards:** Hugo award, 1958, 1965, 1968, 1970, 1971, 1976; Nebula award, 1967, 1970, 1975, and Grand Master Nebula award, 1981; Ann Radcliffe award, 1970; Gandalf award, 1975; Derleth award, 1976; World Fantasy award, 1976, 1978; *Locus* award, 1985; Bram Stoker Lifetime Achievement award, 1988. Guest of Honor, World Science Fiction Convention, 1951. **Died:** 5 September 1992.

SCIENCE FICTION PUBLICATIONS

Novels (series: Change War; Fafhrd and the Gray Mouser)

Gather, Darkness! New York, Pellegrini and Cudahy, 1950; London, New English Library, 1966.
Conjure Wife. New York, Twayne, 1953; London, Penguin, 1969.
The Sinful Ones. New York, Universal, 1953; as *You're All Alone,* New York, Ace, 1972.
The Green Millennium. New York, Abelard Press, 1953; London Abelard Schuman, 1959.
Destiny Times Three. New York, Galaxy, 1956.
The Big Time (Change War). New York, Ace, 1961; London, New English Library, 1965.
The Silver Eggheads. New York, Ballantine, 1962; London, New English Library, 1966.
The Wanderer. New York, Ballantine, 1964; London, Dobson, 1967.
Tarzan and the Valley of Gold. New York, Ballantine, 1966.
The Swords of Lankhmar (Fafhrd and the Gray Mouser). New York, Ace, 1968; London, Hart-Davis, 1969.
A Specter Is Haunting Texas. New York, Walker, and London, Gollancz, 1969.
Swords and Deviltry (Fafhrd and the Gray Mouser). New York, Ace, 1970; London, New English Library, 1971.
Our Lady of Darkness. New York, Berkley, 1977; London, Millington, 1978.
Conjure Wife and Our Lady of Darkness. New York, Tor, 1991.

Short Stories

Night's Black Agents. Sauk City, Wisconsin, Arkham House, 1947; London, Spearman, 1975; abridged as *Tales from Night's Black Agents,* New York, Ballantine, 1961.
Two Sought Adventure: Exploits of Fafhrd and the Gray Mouser. New York, Gnome Press, 1957.
The Mind Spider, and Other Stories. New York, Ace, 1961.
Shadows with Eyes. New York, Ballantine, 1962.
A Pail of Air. New York, Ballantine, 1964.
Ships to the Stars. New York, Ace, 1964.
The Night of the Wolf. New York, Ballantine, 1966; London, Sphere, 1976.
The Secret Songs. London, Hart-Davis, 1968.
Swords against Wizardry (Fafhrd and the Gray Mouser). New York, Ace, 1968; London, Prior, 1977.
Swords in the Mist (Fafhrd and the Gray Mouser). New York, Ace, 1968; London, Prior, 1977.

Night Monsters. New York, Ace, 1969; revised edition, London, Gollancz, 1974.
Swords against Death (Fafhrd and the Gray Mouser). New York, Ace, 1970; London, New English Library, 1972.
The Best of Fritz Leiber, edited by Angus Wells. London, Sphere, and Garden City, New York, Doubleday, 1974.
The Book of Fritz Leiber. New York, DAW, 1974.
The Second Book of Fritz Leiber. New York, DAW, 1975.
The Worlds of Fritz Leiber. New York, Ace, 1976.
Rime Isle (Fafhrd and the Gray Mouser). Chapel Hill, North Carolina, Whispers Press, 1977; expanded as *Swords and Ice Magic,* New York, Ace, and London, Prior, 1977.
Bazaar of the Bizarre. West Kingston, Rhode Island, Grant, 1978.
Heroes and Horrors, edited by Stuart David Schiff. Chapel Hill, North Carolina, New Jersey, Whispers Press, 1978.
The Change War. Boston, Gregg Press, 1978.
Ship of Shadows. London, Gollancz, 1979; bound with *No Truce with Kings,* by Poul Anderson, New York, Tor, 1989.
Ervool. Roanoke, Virginia, Cheap Street, 1980.
The Mystery of the Japanese Clock. Santa Monica, Montgolfier Press, 1982.
Riches and Power: A Story for Children. New Castle, Virginia, Cheap Street, 1982.
Quicks around the Zodiac: A Farce. New Castle, Virginia, Cheap Street, 1983.
In the Beginning. New Castle, Virginia, Cheap Street, 1983.
Changewar. New York, Ace, 1983.
The Ghost Light (includes essay). New York, Berkley, 1984.
The Three of Swords (Fafhrd and the Gray Mouser; includes *Swords and Deviltry, Swords against Death,* and *Swords in the Mist*). New York, Doubleday, 1989.
The Knight and Knave of Swords (Fafhrd and the Gray Mouser). New York, Morrow, 1988; London, Grafton, 1990.
The Leiber Chronicles: Fifty Years of Fritz Leiber, edited by Martin H. Greenberg. Arlington Heights, Illinois, Dark Harvest, 1990.
Swords' Masters (Fafhrd and the Gray Mouser). Garden City, New York, Guild America, 1990.
Ill Met in Lankhmar (Fafhrd and the Gray Mouser), bound with *The Fair in Emain Macha,* by Charles deLint. New York, Tor, 1990.
Gummetch and Friends, with Margo Skinner. Hampton Falls, New Hampshire, Donald M. Grant, 1992.
Kreativity for Kats and Other Feline Fantasies. Newark, New Jersey, Wildside Press, 1990.

Poetry

The Demons of the Upper Air. Glendale, California, Squires, 1969.
Sonnets to Jonquil and All. Glendale, California, Squires, 1978.

Other

The First World Fantasy Convention: Three Authors Remember, with Robert Bloch and T.E.D. Klein. West Warwick, Rhode Island, Necronomicon Press, 1980.
Fafhrd and Me, edited by John Gregory Betancourt. Newark, New Jersey, Wildside Press, 1990.

Editor, with Stuart David Schiff, *The World Fantasy Awards, Volume Two.* Garden City, New York, Doubleday, 1980.

*

Bibliography: *Fritz Leiber: A Bibliography 1934-1979* by Chris Morgan, Birmingham, Morgenstern, 1979.

Critical Studies: "Fritz Leiber Issue" of *Fantasy and Science Fiction* (New York), July 1969; *Fritz Leiber* by Jeff Frane, San Bernardino, California, Borgo Press, 1980; *Fritz Leiber* by Tom Staircar, New York, Ungar, 1983.

*   *   *

Fritz Leiber is one of the most popular and respected writers of science fiction and fantasy. While his readers and fellow writers have appreciated his humor and concern for mankind, the critics have largely ignored his work. Leiber has sometimes been classed with the writers of "weird" stories because of his frequent use of the supernatural and his acknowledged literary debt to H.P. Lovecraft. This association is misleading since Leiber uses the supernatural as a source of symbols for the mysteries of the universe and the mind. As he says, "Many of the most typical creations of science fiction, especially the robot, the android, and the extraterrestrial, are simply the monster in a new guise. . . ."

The supernatural may also turn out to be disguised as applications of science, as in his first novel, *Gather, Darkness!* This story concerns a revolution in a repressive society controlled by a religious hierarchy using technology masquerading as supernatural miracle. The resulting satire provides a commentary on the respective roles of religion, science, and government. There is a witty surface of gadgets such as an electronically controlled haunted house, but there is also a warning against the dangers of restricting scientific knowledge to an elite, regardless of the reason. Leiber's background in the theater is probably responsible for the dramatic staging of much of the action.

The Green Millennium presents a picture of a decadent United States where organized crime and corrupt government control society through sex and games. This society is invaded by two alien species from Vega which end the violence. The main virtues of the novel are fast-moving adventure and humor, but there is an underlying layer of satire about the confusion and banality of modern values. *Destiny Times Three* is an alternate-world novel in which three very different stories have been created by an accidental time fragmentation. These worlds contain similar people, one of whom learns of his other personalities and attempts to resolve the time paradoxes. This reworking of an early magazine story is not as polished as his later work. What might have been treated as a traditional SF story has been handled more as allegory and myth.

The Big Time, the major work in a series of time-travel stories, concerns a war fought by time-traveling warriors of two groups called "Snakes" and "Spiders" who attempt to produce a victory in the future by altering the past. Leiber's belief in pacifism is presented through the disillusionment of the characters about the possibility of final victory. This framework allows Leiber to mix characters from many times and places in an entertainment and recuperation center. By limiting almost all the action to one room and employing dramatic techniques of staging and dialogue, Leiber has almost created a science-fiction play, with first-person interior narration. Character differentiations are neatly provided by excellent parodies of the characters' differing diction and vocabulary (for example, Elizabethan and Greek dramatic styles). *The Silver Eggheads* is an experiment in satire which borders on farce. The major point is his dissection of the world of publishers, writers, and readers, with humorous references to a wide range of literature, but he seems more at ease with satire in his other books. A long "disaster" novel, *The Wanderer,* describes the responses of people subjected to the earthquakes, tidal waves, and other global disasters

caused by an artificial planet which enters an orbit around the earth. Leiber's main interest is in the detailed character studies of both heroes and villains provided by this framework. Almost all of Leiber's themes and interests are included: he deals with almost all aspects of human life, from birth to death. There is also plenty of action, but the novel is not significantly different from many other catastrophe stories. In *A Specter Is Haunting Texas* the specter (a skeletally thin actor from a colony on a satellite around earth's moon) is a coerced leader of a revolution of the enslaved "Mexes" against the Texans, who are hormonally induced giants controlling most of North America. Much of the book is based on theatrical motifs, from costuming and staging to the symbolic roles of the characters, and other devices of the stage. The basic method is again satire, and though the plot is somewhat uneven, the humor and originality of the background are entertaining.

In addition to his science fiction, Leiber has written two novels about the supernatural, *Conjure Wife* and *Our Lady of Darkness,* both of which are borderline science fiction. His fantasy series relating the exploits of Fafhrd and The Gray Mouser has made him one of the most popular writers of this genre. His best-known stories are probably "Coming Attraction" and "Gonna Roll the Bones." Throughout his career, Leiber has used the same topics and themes—the supernatural, theater, cats, time, sex, politics, alcohol. His most frequent technique is satire. His writing displays considerable stylistic control (particularly in writing parodies) and the influence of many writers from John Webster and Shakespeare to Eddison, C.A. Smith, and Cabell. He seems to view the basic function of literature in terms of human identity and potentiality. The psychological presentation of character is central to his work, as is his view of literature as theater. These factors are related to the problem of psychological identity. All literature requires at least a partial suspension of personality on the part of the reader, but this demand is particularly great in science fiction and also appears prominently in the function of the actor. A similar reaction can occur with stories of the supernatural. All of these features combine to make Leiber an acute commentator on the human mind.

—Norman L. Hills

LEIGH, Stephen

Nationality: American. **Born:** Cincinnati, Ohio, 27 February 1951. **Education:** University of Cincinnati, B.F.A. in art education 1974. **Family:** Married Denise Parsley in 1974; one daughter and one son. **Career:** Art teacher, Greenhills and Forest Park school, Ohio, 1974-75. Musician: since 1969, vocalist and bassist in various groups. Currently, sales manager, Kelly Services, Cincinnati. **Awards:** Analog award, 1977. **Agent:** Merrilee Heifitz, Writers House, 21 West 26th Street, New York, New York 10010, U.S.A. **Address:** 121 Nansen Street, Cincinnati, Ohio 45216, U.S.A.

SCIENCE FICTION PUBLICATIONS

Novels (series: Dinosaur; Dr. Bones; Neweden; The Next Wave; Robots and Aliens)

Slow Fall to Dawn (Neweden). New York, Bantam, 1981; London, Headline, 1988.
Dance of the Hag (Neweden). New York, Bantam, 1983.
A Quiet of Stone (Neweden). New York, Bantam, 1984.
The Bones of God. New York, Avon, 1986; London, Headline, 1988.
The Crystal Memory. New York, Avon, 1987.
The Secret of the Lona (Dr. Bones). New York, Ace, 1988.
Changeling (Robots and Aliens). New York, Ace, 1989.
The Abraxas Marvel Circus. New York, Roc, 1990.
Alien Tongue (Next Wave). New York, Bantam, 1991.
Ray Bradbury Presents Dinosaur:
   Dinosaur World: A Novel. New York, AvoNova, 1992.
   Dinosaur Planet. New York, AvoNova, 1993.
   Dinosaur Samurai, with John J. Miller. New York, AvoNova, 1993.
   Dinosaur Warriors. New York, AvoNova, 1994.
   Dinosaur Empire. New York, AvoNova, 1995.

*

Stephen Leigh comments:

I'm fascinated by what happens when cultures collide, as well as the intricate dance of words with which we surround ourselves. I'm not traditionally religious myself, but the impact of religions on societies and individuals has been a sub-theme in my work at times. And while most of my work is science fiction rather than fantasy, it's not the hardware itself that interests me, but rather how technology alters the perceptions of those who use it. I also prefer to write about real people—non-perfect people, people with foibles and warts, with sexual appetites and hidden violences, with loves and hates that are sometimes the same thing, who laugh as often as they weep.

I'm a storyteller. My intent is to entertain. If you like what I write, wonderful!

*   *   *

Stephen Leigh belongs to science fiction's cadre of heroic adventure writers. His novels sail quickly, yet his characters do more than watch the scenery go by. Their internal struggles and interactions with political, religious, and economic forces form the themes of Leigh's novels: honor, loyalty, morality, the Prophet, the Outcast, the Seeker.

Nowhere is this better illustrated than in Leigh's Neweden novels, *Slow Fall to Dawn, Dance of the Hag,* and *A Quiet of Stone.* On the fringes of a vast, collapsing empire, the inhabitants of Neweden eke out a meager existence on their isolated planet. Neweden's isolation has given rise to a system of guild kinship and honorable settling of disputes similar to medieval England. Gyll Hermond, creator and leader of the assassin's guild known as the Hoorka, must wrestle with a middle-aged reevaluation of his life's work. The Hoorka, by virtue of Neweden's isolation, flourish under a binding code of honor which gives their victims a chance for survival. This code begins to fragment as the Hoorka ply their trade with less honor-bound worlds. Gyll's tragic tale mirrors Neweden's vanishing culture as change inevitably washes over both.

The examination of individuals shaping and being shaped by history continues in *The Bones of God* and *The Crystal Memory. The Bones of God* narrates the career of Colin Fairwood as the prophet Sartius Exori. The 26th century finds Old Earth and most of her interplanetary empire governed by a powerful theocracy under the Zakkaist church, a melding of the Judaic, Christian, and Islamic faiths. Faster-than-light travel is possible, thanks to a gift from the alien Stekoni, but leads the traveler into the Veils, where haunting dreams and the godlike Voice await. Fairwood believes in nothing save his hatred of the Zakkaist church that mutilated him and his fear that the Voice just *might* be his god calling him to action. He forms a revolution against the church while dealing with his own doubts about the existence of his god and her apparent failure to guide his actions.

Jemi Charidilis, protagonist of *The Crystal Memory,* grapples with grief for her lost son while searching for an explanation for why two years of her memory of him were stolen. Her search places her at the focus of tensions between Earth and the renegade Mars colony, and between factions of the alien T'Raijek. The completion of her search results in a confrontation with the T'Raijek which reveals to both humans and aliens just how truly alien their philosophies are to each other.

The Abraxas Marvel Circus recounts the attempts of a wild handful of characters to revive a dead eccentric genius. Leigh draws on his experience as a bassist and vocalist for rock bands in Cincinnati to weave a bizarre but believable tale around the semi-autobiographical Dirk Masterson. Leigh deftly blends the straight Dirk with the ramblings of Joan the Flower Man. These works demonstrate Leigh's technical skill at constructing believable worlds and substantive characters. Though his use of foreshadowing is sometimes heavy-handed and the focus of his story may shift too rapidly, Stephen Leigh clearly has the potential to leave his mark on science fiction. Recurrent themes such as Oriental philosophy are injected without disrupting plot, pace, or dialogue. Leigh manages a delicate balance between historical forces and the power of individuals to influence them. While individuals may act as catalysts and refiners of history, its fundamental shape results from cultures, economic needs, and stellar geography. Supporting historical trends may result in heroic successes like the Sartius Exori's suicidal assault on the Zakkaist leadership. But as Gyll Hermond discovers, such trends may produce tragedy if opposed.

Unfortunately Leigh's recent novels struggle. *Alien Tongue* begins with a chronological malaise that may keep many readers from enjoying what is otherwise a decent novel of mankind's first encounter with other intelligent life. Both Pat and Kat have disconcertingly weak moments—hardly what one expects from Earth's finest, sent to explore new worlds.

The remaining novels fill slots in several juvenile fiction series for Byron Preiss Visual Publications. The premier of Doctor Bones may entertain fans of scientifiction who miss the bravado of yore, though again Leigh's reflective nature is ill-suited to thriller SF: dialogue in the climactic scene may leave some readers giggling. The growing body of Ray Bradbury's Dinosaur novels extend the well-known short story "A Sound of Thunder" by that author. Here Leigh's young characters frantically race through time and alternate histories trying to restore a disrupted past. Though these stories make fun light reading, Leigh's talents for melding complex characters with well-constructed worlds go to waste.

Themes of past works reappear in settings defined by the series content. The exploration so evident in *The Abraxas Marvel Circus* appears to be a function of Leigh's freedom to place fresh characters into settings appropriate for the problems they face.

—Scott Burgess

LEINSTER, Murray

Pseudonym for Will(iam) F(itzgerald) Jenkins. **Nationality:** American. **Born:** Norfolk, Virginia, 16 June 1896. **Education:** Public and private schools in Norfolk. **Military Service:** Served with the Committee of Public Information, and in the United States Army, 1917-18; served in the Office of War Information during World War II. **Family:** Married Mary Mandola in 1921; three daughters and one son. **Career:** Freelance writer from 1918. **Awards:** Liberty award, 1937; Hugo award, 1956, Guest of Honor, 21st World Science Fiction Convention, 1963. **Died:** 8 June 1975.

SCIENCE FICTION PUBLICATIONS

Novels (series: Joe Kenmore; Land of the Giants; Med Service; Time Tunnel)

Murder Madness. New York, Brewer and Warren, 1931.
The Murder of the U.S.A. (as Will F. Jenkins). New York, Crown, 1946; as *Destroy the U.S.A.,* Toronto, News Stand, 1950.
Fight for Life: A Complete Novel of the Atomic Age. New York, Crestwood, 1947.
The Last Space Ship. New York, Fell, 1949; London, Cherry Tree, 1952.
Space Platform (for children; Kenmore). Chicago, Shasta, 1953.
Space Tug (for children; Kenmore). Chicago, Shasta, 1953.
Gateway to Elsewhere. New York, Ace, 1954.
The Forgotten Planet. New York, Gnome Press, 1954.
The Brain-Stealers. New York, Ace, 1954; London, Badger, 1960.
Operation: Outer Space. Reading, Pennsylvania, Fantasy Press, 1954; London, Grayson, 1957.
The Black Galaxy. New York, Galaxy, 1954.
The Other Side of Here. New York, Ace, 1955.
City on the Moon (for children; Kenmore). New York, Avalon, 1957.
Colonial Survey. New York, Gnome Press, 1957; as *Planet Explorer,* New York, Avon, 1957.
War with the Gizmos. Greenwich, Connecticut, Fawcett, 1958; London, Muller, 1959.
Out of This World. New York, Avalon, 1958.
The Monster from Earth's End. Connecticut, Fawcett, 1959; London, Muller, 1960.
The Mutant Weapon (Med Service). New York, Ace, 1959.
The Pirates of Zan. New York, Ace, 1959.
Four from Planet 5. Greenwich, Connecticut, Fawcett, 1959; London, White Lion, 1974.
The Wailing Asteroid. New York, Avon, 1960.
Men into Space (novelization of TV series). New York, Berkley, 1960.
Creatures of the Abyss. New York, Berkley, 1961; as *The Listeners; Science Fiction,* London, Sidgwick and Jackson, 1969.
This World Is Taboo (Med Service). New York, Ace, 1961.
Talents, Incorporated. New York, Avon, 1962.
Operation Terror. New York, Berkley, 1962; London, Tandem, 1968.
The Duplicators. New York, Ace, 1964.
The Other Side of Nowhere. New York, Berkley, 1964.
The Time Tunnel. New York, Pyramid, 1964.
The Greks Bring Gifts. New York, Macfadden, 1964.

Invaders of Space. New York, Berkley, 1964; London, Tandem, 1968.
Space Captain. New York, Ace, 1966.
Tunnel through Time (for children). Philadelphia, Westminster Press, 1966.
Checkpoint Lambda. New York, Berkley, 1966.
The Time Tunnel (novelization of TV series). New York, Pyramid, 1967; London, Sidgwick and Jackson, 1971.
Miners in the Sky. New York, Avon, 1967.
Space Gypsies. New York, Avon, 1967.
Timeslip!: A Time Tunnel novel. New York, Pyramid, 1967.
Land of the Giants (novelization of TV play). New York, Pyramid, 1968.
A Murray Leinster Omnibus (includes *Operation Terror, Invaders of Space,* and *Checkpoint Lambda*). London, Sidgwick and Jackson, 1968.
The Hot Spot (Giants; novelization of TV play). New York, Pyramid, 1969.
Unknown Danger (Giants; novelization of TV play). New York, Pyramid, 1969.

Short Stories (series: Med Service)

Sidewise in Time, and Other Scientific Adventures. Chicago, Shasta, 1950.
The Unknown. Sydney, American Science Fiction, 1952.
Conquest of the Stars. Sydney, American Science Fiction, 1952.
The Challenge from Beyond, with others. N.p., William H. Evans, 1954; as *The Illustrated Challenge from Beyond,* West Warwick, Rhode Island, Necronomicon Press, 1978.
Monsters and Such. New York, Avon, 1959.
Twists in Time. New York, Avon, 1960.
The Aliens. New York, Berkley, 1960.
Doctor to the Stars: Three Novelettes of the Interstellar Medical Series. (Med Service). New York, Pyramid, 1964.
Get Off My World! New York, Belmont, 1966.
S.O.S. from Three Worlds (Med Service). New York, Ace, 1966.
The Best of Murray Leinster, edited by Brian Davis. London, Corgi, 1976.
The Best of Murray Leinster, edited J.J. Pierce. New York, Ballantine, 1978.
The Med Series (omnibus). New York, Ace, 1983; abridged as *Quarantine World,* New York, Carroll and Graf, 1992.

OTHER PUBLICATIONS

Novels

Scalps. New York, Brewer and Warren, 1930; as *Wings of Chance,* London, John Hamilton, 1935.
Murder Will Out. London, John Hamilton, 1932.
Sword of Kings. London, Long, 1933.
Murder in the Family. London, John Hamilton, 1935.
No Clues. London, Wright and Brown, 1935.
Guns for Achin. London, Wright and Brown, 1936.
Outlaw Guns. New York, Star, n.d.; as *Wanted—Dead or Alive!,* London, Wright and Brown, 1950.
Cattle Rustlers. London, Ward Lock, 1952.
Texas Gun Slinger. New York, Star, n.d.
Outlaw Deputy. Toronto, Harlequin, 1954.

Novels as Will F. Jenkins

The Gamblin' Kid. New York, King, 1933; London, Eldon Press, 1934.

Mexican Trail. New York, King, 1933; London, Eldon Press, 1935.

Fighting Horse Valley. New York, King, 1934; London, Eldon Press, 1935.

Outlaw Sheriff. New York, King, 1934; as *Rustlin' Sheriff,* London, Eldon Press, 1934.

Kid Deputy. New York, King, and London, Eldon Press, 1935.

Black Sheep. New York, Messer, and London, Eldon Press, 1936.

The Man Who Feared. New York, Gateway, 1942.

Dallas (novelization of screenplay). New York, Fawcett, 1950; London, Muller, 1961.

Son of the Flying "Y". New York, Fawcett, 1951; London, Muller, 1957.

Plays

Screenplays: *Border Devils,* with Harry C. Crist, 1932; *Torchy in Chinatown,* with George Bricker, 1938.

Other

Last Murray Leinster Interview, with Ronald Payne. Richmond, Virginia, Waves Press, 1983.

Editor, *Great Stories of Science Fiction.* New York, Random House, 1951; London, Cassell, 1953.

*   *   *

A professional writer for the slick and pulp magazines from 1913 until 1967, Murray Leinster embodies in one writer the very essence of the commercial yet ambitiously serious genre of science fiction. He did his best work in short fiction. He developed and extrapolated upon certain key speculative ideas, several of the most important of which he introduced to the genre. He wrote for money and sold to several markets other than science fiction, and yet the imaginative expansion of ideas about nature and about the relation of life-forms to nature made SF a very important area in his production. Leinster wrote so much that it is hard to categorize his major themes and most characteristic effects, but always his mind is lively and he seems interested particularly in cool analyzing and in alternatives to all possibilities.

In fact, his fascination with alternatives to any situation led him to the standard science fiction theme he is often remembered as having introduced to the genre: the theme of parallel points on a time continuum, or parallel worlds. A story from 1931, "The Fifth-Dimension Catapult," plays with the notion as a kind of modern alchemy in which the clever laboratory investigator can change time and space coordinates in order to visit a completely alien parallel world; and in this case the plan is to bring back gold. Leinster's more well-known story of parallel worlds is "Sidewise in Time" in which some unexplained oscillation of the Earth results in a myriad of alternate time paths. His method of telling this story in little isolated vignettes of what might be possible here and there as the oscillations produce alternative presents is indicative of why short fiction is a primary form in SF. With change and even alternate possibilities ever present there simply does not exist the stable Victorian world for developing long narratives in one time and one place. Leinster, beginning as early as it was popularized, writes a

modern alchemy of change according to Einstein-like relativity. Some longer fictions of his that rely on this same balancing of alternatives are *Colonial Survey,* which contains his Hugo-winning novelette "Exploration Team," and *The Time Tunnel.*

Similarly, Leinster develops again and again the ramification of contact between different life-forms that are alternatives to each other. This is the often-used theme in science fiction of first contact with an alien race; and the most influential story of Leinster's of this type is entitled simply "First Contact" (1945). But many of his stories explore the alternatives of encounter and relationship between life forms who consider each other alien because they cannot or do not communicate. In "Proxima Centauri" the aliens are intelligent and mobile plants that crave animal flesh. This reversal, or notion that what we do ourselves may often be quite alien, permeates Leinster's fictions. Not only do humans enjoy vegetable salads unthinkingly, but in "The Strange Case of John Klingman" the human managers of the mental hospital seem more alien than Klingman. Similarly, the moon monkeys in "Keyhole" have more sympathy and effective understanding than their human opposites because they can communicate telepathically and hence the human thoughts, although alien to them, are not unknown.

The key seems to be knowledge and understanding, for here the two themes in Leinster's fiction come together. Alternate or parallel worlds as well as life forms alien to each other are only possible when differentiation, separateness, and mental isolation are possible. If the universe were all one, there would be only one time path and there would be continual communion. But the universe is parceled out, and communication is very seldom total or telepathic and instant. In other words, Leinster seems to be continually retelling the myth of original sin. Things are not as they should be, hence continual competitiveness and continual alternatives.

A brilliant working of this theme of the pathos of separateness and difference is in "The Lonely Planet," which seems to be an anticipation of the widely acclaimed novel by Stanislaw Lem, *Solaris.* In Leinster's story, a magnificent creature called Alyx covers an entire planet. In the beginning it is totally telepathic to mankind because it has not developed a defense against mind or total communication since it has evolved in an environment where it was the only creature. The story, then, is how mankind teaches Alyx to be secretive and competitive, finally, because Alyx learns what loneliness is. Perhaps Leinster is saying that a perfect oneness would be lonely and boring and that we need alternatives and even competitiveness. In any case, the clever, inventive, competitive, and necessarily separate mind of the scientific investigator is the favorite protagonist in a Leinster story. Thus from the point of view of modern fiction, his characters often seem grossly two-dimensional and his conflicts exaggerated and sensational. These bold and exaggerated effects prevail throughout his popular novel *The Forgotten Planet* (an expansion of "Mad Planet," 1926)—the narration of a continual war with giant insects and the growth of human rationality. But many of these effects are simply the demands of the pulp market, and seen in their most symbolic way they continually narrate the inescapable reality of human fallibility.

No treatment of Leinster and of the evolution of the genre of modern science fiction that he contributed so much to would be complete without mention of the sense of awe that goes with what is generally dismissed as space opera. In addition to the suggestiveness in theme and meaning mentioned above, Leinster's fiction reads well because of wide-ranging space patrol and med service action and because of journeys to distant second galaxies. There is also a good deal of violence, quick cruelty, and villainy in Leinster's work; and when this also is handled well it is an ancient emblem for the fallen state of mankind, an exact correlative to the infinite alternatives in the material world. But always in Leinster, along with the awe and the space opera, is the intellectual curiosity and the analytic mind—perhaps again representative of the fallen state of man, but characteristic also of the best in science fiction. Leinster grew with the genre, but he is also an example of how subtle some of the best space opera can be.

—Donald M. Hassler

LEM, Stanislaw

Nationality: Polish. **Born:** Lvov, Poland, 12 September 1921. **Education:** Studied medicine in Lvov, 1939-41, 1944-46, and in Krakow, 1946-48. **Family:** Married Barbara in 1953; one son. **Career:** Worked as garage mechanic during World War II; assistant in "Science Circle," Jagellonian University, Krakow, 1947-49; editor, *Zycie Nauki* ("The Life of Science"), 1947-49. Since 1949, writer. Teacher, University of Krakow. **Awards:** Citations from Polish Ministry of Culture, 1965, 1973; Polish State Prize for literature, 1976; Australian State Prize for foreign literature, 1985; Alfred Jurzykowski Foundation award, 1987. **Agent:** Franz Rottensteiner, Marchettigasse 9/17, A-1060 Vienna, Austria. **Address:** ul. Narwik 66, 30'436 Krakow, Poland.

SCIENCE FICTION PUBLICATIONS

Novels

Sledztwo. Warsaw, Wydawnictwo Ministerstwa Obrony Narodowej, 1959; translated by Adele Milch as *The Investigation,* New York, Seabury Press, 1974.
Eden. Warsaw, Iskry, 1959; translated by Elinor Ford and Michael Kandel as *Eden,* San Diego, Harcourt, 1989; London, Deutsch, 1990.
Solaris. Warsaw, Wydawnictwo Ministerstwa Obrony Narodowej, 1961; translated by Joanna Kilmartin and Steve Cox as *Solaris,* New York, Walker, 1970; London, Faber, 1971.
Pamietnik znaleziony w wannie. Krakow, Wydawnistwo Literackie, 1961; translated by Michael Kandel and Christine Rose as *Memoirs Found in a Bathtub,* New York, Seabury Press, 1973.
Powrot z gwiazd. Warsaw, Wydawnistwo Literackie, 1961; translated by Barbara Marszal and Frank Simpson as *Return from the Stars,* New York, Harcourt, 1980; London, Mandarin, 1990.
Niezwyciezony i inne opowiadana. Krakow, Wydawnistwo Literackie, 1964; translated by Wendayne Ackerman as *The Invincible,* New York, Seabury Press, 1973.
Glos pana. Warsaw, Czytelnik, 1968; translated by Michael Kandel as *His Master's Voice,* New York, Harcourt, 1983; London, Mandarin, 1990.
Katar. Krakow, Wydawinstwo Literackie, 1976; translated by Louis Iribane as *The Chain of Chance,* New York, Harcourt, 1978.
Fiasko. Krakow, Wydawnistwo Literackie, 1987; translated by Michael Kandel as *Fiasco,* San Diego, Harcourt, 1987.
Pokoj na ziemi. Krakow, Wydawnistwo Literackie, 1987; *Peace on Earth,* New York, Harcourt, 1994.

Short Stories (series: Ijon Tichy; Pirx the Pilot)

Dzienniki gwiazdowe (Ijon Tichy). Warsaw, Iskry, 1957; translatied by Michael Kandel as *The Star Diaries,* New York, Swabury Press, 1976.
Dziennika Gwiazdoew (Ijoh Tichy). Warsaw, Iskry, 1957; translated by Joel Stern and Maria Swiecicka-Ziemianek as *Memoirs of a Space Traveler: Further Reminiscences of Ijon Tichy,* New York, Harcourt, 1982; London, Mandarin, 1991.
Cyberiad. Krakow, Wydawnistwo Literackie, 1967; translated as *The Cyberiad: Fables for the Cybernetic Age,* New York, Seabury Press, 1974; London, Mandarin, 1990.
Opowiesci o pilocie Pirxie (Pirx the Pilot). Krakow, Wydawnistwo Literackie, 1968; translated by Louis Iribarne as *Tales of Pirx the Pilot,* New York, Harcourt, 1979; London, Mandarin, 1990.
Oposiesci o pilocie Pirxie (Pirx the Pilot). Krakow, Wydawnistwo Literackie, 1968; translated by Louis Iribarne, Michael Kandel, and Magdalena Majcherizyk as *More Tales of Pirx the Pilot,* San Diego, Harcourt, 1982; London, Mandarin, 1990.
Doskonala prozni. Warsaw, Czytelnik, 1971; translated by Michael Kandel as *A Perfect Vacuum,* New York, Harcourt, 1978, London, Mandarin, 1978.
Wielkosc urojona. Warsaw, Czytelnik, 1973; translated by Marc E. Heine as *Imaginary Magnitude,* San Diego, Harcourt, 1984; London, Mandarin, 1991.
Mortal Engines, translated by Micael Kandel. New York, Seabury Press, 1977; London, Deutsch, 1993.
The Cosmic Carnival of Stanislaw Lem: An Anthology of Entertaining Stories by the Modern Master of Science Fiction, edited and translated by Michael Kandel. New York, Seabury Press, 1981.
Solaris, The Chain of Chance, A Perfect Vacuum (omnibus). Harmondworth, Middlesex, Penguin, 1981.
Tales of Pirx the Pilot, Return from the Stars, The Invincible (omnibus). Harmondsworth, Middlesex, Penguin, 1982.
Biblioteka XXI wieka. Krakow, Wydawnistwo Literackie, 1986; translated by Catherine S. Leach as *One Human Minute,* San Diego, Harcourt, and London, Deutsch, 1986.

OTHER PUBLICATIONS

Novel

Szpital przemienienia. Krakow, Wydawnistwo Literackie, 1957; translated by William Brand as *Hospital of the Transfiguration,* San Diego, Harcourt, 1988; London, Deutsch, 1989.

Other

Filozofia prypadku: Literatura w swietle empirii (title means "The Philosophy of Chance: Literature Considered Empirically"), Wydawnictwo Literackie, 1968.
Fantastyka i futurologia. Krakow, Wydawnistwo Literackie, 1970; translated and edited by Franz Rottensteiner as *Microworlds: Writings on Science Fiction and Fantasy,* San Diego, Harcourt, 1984; London, Mandarin, 1991.

*   *   *

Stanislaw Lem's linguistic and intellectual versatility, his humanism, his scientific accuracy, and his serious commitment to philosophical questions of science and of society make him one of the most respected and innovative of modern science fiction writers. Critical of much science fiction as "hopeless" pulp, "empty games" dominated by "charlatans," Lem takes the genre seriously as an intellectual tool to investigate man's limits and potentials, to satirize his governments, his pretensions, his militancy, his illusions and delusions, and his failure of imagination. His attack encompasses East and West: Marxist and Capitalist, the scientist, the tourist, the bureaucrat, the technician, the researcher, the theoretician. In *Microworlds: Writings on Science Fiction and Fantasy* (1984), Lem criticizes writers for squandering the potential of science fiction, resorting to clichéd patterns and devices and rehashing old tales instead of initiating experiments and evolving processes of discovery to heighten human awareness and to challenge the intellect. These last mentioned goals he has made his own. He has been compared to both Swift and Voltaire for his dark wit, his serous vision, and his controversial ideas. His cynicism, his sense of man's alienation and of his absurdity in the face of the incomprehensible, his understanding of the limits of theories and interpretations (too often more reflective of their individual creator than of any reality), his fear of a scientific obsession with trivia undermining any possibility of understanding and discovery, his willingness to face the human condition, explore and criticize it, and his special perspective as a Polish scholar/scientist/social critic lend his writings significance and distinction. Generally lacking conventional plots, his works are an organic blend of learned disquisitions, real science, and philosophic questions on the nature of man and his universe within a semi-fictive or imaginative mode. They praise man's resourcefulness and decry his arrogance. Lem's particular models act as metaphors evolving universals—to both profit and delight.

Unlike those writers whose anthropomorphism he attacks as banal and absurd, Lem treats the alien as truly unknown and unknowable, with man limited by nature and experience, the alien beyond human reason and human understanding in manifestation, laws, purposes and essence, and man's persistent but failed efforts to translate the unknowable into human terms doomed to reflect only man himself. In *Solaris,* confronted with a possible sentient, colloidal ocean whose teeming diversity contradicts scientific "laws" and whose materializations bring to life their deepest obsessions, scientists collect reams of frustrating and contradictory data, write volumes of theories, and even develop an anti-field to exorcise the psychic mirrors this sentient creates, but remain stymied by alien phenomena whose essence remains forever mysterious. Their observations, theories, and methodology ultimately serve only to reveal themselves and their needs, some of which are too deeply shameful to be shared; yet they deny even these, preferring false hopes to an admission of existential absurdity (as in Kelvin's rejection and attempted murder of Rheya, an innocent "neutrino" ocean creation, an exact duplicate of his lost love, who becomes tragically more human with continued contact).

In *The Invincible* the nature of the alien also remains elusive, but as man measures his limits against that alien, he discovers more about his own nature. Therein an unmanned ship probing and measuring a new planet reveals "undefinable formations," an inexplicable black cloud, cybernetic insects, war machines, and other puzzling signs of mayhem. These lead to numerous theories about hidden civilizations and human migrations—all nonsense—and eventually force the human observers to recognize their vincibility; their specialists can study and their destructive machines attack, but man remains impotent, more in tune with the frailty and absurdity of a befuddled robot than with the dark, inscrutable configuration that

defies interpretation. The main character, Rohan, stands in "numbed awe," and concludes that "not everywhere has everything been intended for us." In *Return from the Stars,* the central figure, Hal Bregg, tells his girlfriend about an inexplicable incident on a dusty planetoid, one "like nothing. We have no referents. No analogies." In turn, Doctor Digoras in *Memoirs of a Space Traveller* finds himself the subject of an experiment he thought he was conducting, and stands helpless, "without a chance of understanding" before two amorphous fungoids.

Eden begins as a fairly straightforward adventure—a resourceful and intelligent spaceship crew crash-landed on a beautiful and previously unexplored planet whose advanced civilization, though obviously alien, seems readily comprehensible. When, however, direct contact is finally made with a native (a "doubler"), all theories and all known "facts" thus far recorded prove fallacious as once again Lem shows man narrowly seeing only his own patterns reflected in alien data. Eden proves a dystopia, characterized by genetic engineering run amuck and by an Orwellian form of disinformation and double-think so extreme that it has literally made some facets of "reality" (like a central controller) unthinkable. Yet human intervention would prove futile and destructive. The stories of Ijon Tichy and Pilot Pirx confirm Lem's theme: man stands alone, alienated from his universe, misunderstanding his fellow creatures, destructively tampering with the unknowable, redeemed only when he shows respect for other life forms and gains insight into his own nature.

Related to Lem's image of man projecting the familiar onto the alien is his focus on man's obsession with theorizing and hypothesizing, seeking a pattern amid the random chance of myriad realities. Confronted with chaos, his characters regularly declare, as does the nuclear physicist in *The Invincible,* "All this must mean something." "The Philosophy of Chance: Literature Considered Empirically" and *Summa technologiae* (philosophical essays that provide keys to his views) establish his absurdist attitudes toward man's search for meaning amid meaninglessness. The former denounces structuralism and questions why different ages and cultures respond differently to different works of literature while the latter explores the outermost limits of future possibilities from the genetic remodeling of man to the total reconstruction of reality.

In both *The Investigation* and *The Chain of Chance* private investigators try to unravel bizarre mysteries, in the former resurrection of corpses, in the latter a series of deaths on Italian highways and disappearances at an Italian seaside resort. Deductive reasoning, causal arguments, and the laws of probability imposed on a chain of coincidences seemingly explain the inexplicable, but in fact do not; man imposes significance where in reality there may be none.

In this same vein, *His Master's Voice* delineates man's attempts to interpret as some sort of stellar code, a pulsating stream of life-promoting neutrino radiation. Twenty-five thousand specialists advance divergent hypotheses to decode the so-called message, with explanations ranging from a technological gift from a dying civilization to a formula for the ultimate weapon; all are convincingly detailed, but reveal more about the theorists than the reality. The penetrating description of the formulation of scientific theories and their social impact, the moral responsibility of the scientist and the limits of his knowledge, the controversy and the conspiracies are the heart of the novel, but the role of chance and the problem of communication (between worlds, societies, and individuals) are also central. Franz Rottensteiner describes Lem's universe as "a giant Rorscharch test"—an apt phrase, for in this book even the final theory, that communication with alien worlds is impossible, may well be only a reflection of Lem's narrator's own limitations. Lem's final image is of men "like snails, each stuck to his own leaf."

Hospital of the Transfiguration, Lem's first novel, initiates concerns found in later works: the inhumanity, insanity, cruelty, and corruption of military governments and bureaucracies. A young doctor hopes employment in a provincial Polish insane asylum will provide "a kind of extraterrestrial observatory" from the safety of which he can observe the madness of the Third Reich; instead, the abuses doctors inflict on patients prove only a foretaste of the madness observed firsthand when Nazis turn the asylum into an SS hospital.

Memoirs Found in a Bathtub continues the focus on militarism and global destruction first introduced in Lem's early "social realism": *Astronauts, The Magellan Nebula,* and "Sesame." It postulates the mysterious disintegration of all paper except for a record of what happened in the "Third Pentagon" after an American revolution. These memoirs expose a bureaucratic, Dantesque hell in which intelligence gathering and surveillance are turned inward as the Pentagon invents functions, and nameless characters are caught in a senseless maze filled with double and triple agents, secret codes, loyalty tests, polygraph "mittens," sewage espionage filters, and "Seminars on Applied Agony." The military bureaucrats even invent an Antibuilding, the supposed headquarters of the opposition, though Lem's descriptions could apply equally to Moscow's Ministry of Defense, KGB centers, or the American Air Defense headquarters in the Rocky Mountains.

The reminiscences of Ijon Tichy, tourist of the universe and protagonist of *The Star Diaries, The Futurological Congress,* and *Memoirs of a Space Traveller,* point up the ridiculousness of human institutions and doctrines in a more comic vein. Tichy is average and mundane, yet his outrageous adventures, recorded in a free-wheeling, episodic diary, tilt at scientists and scientific laws, concepts of progress and nature, repression, jargon, bureaucratese, and even "unaccommodated man" with delightful informality and gusto. In the seventh Voyage Tichy gets caught in a time warp and splits into multiple selves, while in the fourth he finds his cultural assumptions about personal identity challenged. In *The Futurological Congress* he encounters revolution and chemical warfare, drug therapy and psychemization, and a "pitifully empty" world that changes grass to cheese without the cow. In *Space Traveller* "Phools" consent to their own destruction, a scientist discovers that the mechanical beings he has created are as real as he, and Tichy realizes that eternal life without body or social contact is eternal hell.

Mortal Engines and *The Cyberiad* are seriocomic robot "fairy tales," satiric parodies of human avarice, cruelty, and stupidity. In them man figures only as a monster, a cosmic joke, a "paleface," but in fact the robots themselves are contemptible mirrors of human frailty and human fallibility. Throughout the stories, whether of a robotic "Sleeping Beauty," a pirate drowned in a paper sea of trivial information, soldiers plugged together for greater efficiency, or a tyrant ironically saved by his greed and suspicion but ultimately trapped in a dream about dreaming, two robot constructors tackle complex engineering problems and perform experiments that go awry. "The Mask," a powerful story of a robot programmed to kill the man she has come to love, verges on pathos, "The Dragons of Probability" toys with the laws of probability and the properties of subatomic particles, and "How Trurl's Own Perfection Led to No Good" involves a simulated world sadistically tormented by its builder. Here and elsewhere Lem tackles the question of artificial

intelligence, suggesting that consciousness deserves respect but brings pain, error, and vice. In this whole set of witty, amusing works Lem finds a touch "of dry, mischievous Voltairean misanthropy" and "the despair and anger by the conduct of mankind" that motivates "the great humorists."

Tales of Pirx the Pilot also deals with man versus machines to question not only man's institutions and philosophies but even the value of his biological make-up. Astronaut Pirx is tough and courageous though unheroic, prosaic and bumbling but irresistible. His training mission teaches him the inadequacy of textbook knowledge and the importance of sheer guts, and his first mission shows the limits of technology and the need for close observation; each problem proves more difficult than the last, and his last adventure involves deciphering the final acts of a long dead crew from the encoded memories of a psychically wounded robot. In contrast, Hal Bregg of *Return from the Stars* is a worn-out astronaut, returning home after harrowing adventures only to find himself overpowered by changes on earth which make it alien and intimidating. He finds aggressions medically neutralized, sophisticated robots in charge, social customs incomprehensible, and risk and challenge lost concepts; yet he learns to assert his humanity and to find love and meaning and a new life. Lem himself rejects this book as "primitive" and "false" in its treatment of eliminating social evils.

Clearly Lem enjoys variety and experimentation. His *Imaginary Magnitude* consists of introductions to nonexistent books, while *A Perfect Vacuum* has clever reviews of nonexistent books, including a review of Lem's reviews. *Dialogues* (1957) examines the potentials of cybernetics through Socratic dialogues, while *Provocation* (1981), which Lem describes as "a kind of science fiction," reviews a fictitious German historical text on "The Final Solutions Considered as Redemption," in which an historian/anthropologist hypothesizes about the role of mass death as a persistent cultural phenomenon.

The Cosmic Carnival provides a good panoramic selection of Lem's best, his range from realism to fantasy, from comedy to tragedy, from the technological to the poetic. Lem is fond of situations that lend themselves to multiple interpretations, dialectics that leave the final reality ambiguous. Mirrors, masks, and multiple levels add to the confusion and to the depth of his message. Double and triple puns, intentional ambiguities, codes, neologisms, cybernetic and futuristic jargon, and carefully selected proper names add to the fun and the potential possible interpretations. However, what is most important to him is science fiction as a laboratory for exploring new cognitive approaches, of thinking what has not yet been thought, of opening man's vision of himself—his potentials and his inescapable limitations—dark and surreal though it be.

—Gina Macdonald

L'ENGLE, Madeleine

Nationality: American. **Born:** Madeleine L'Engle Camp in New York City, 29 November 1918. **Education:** Smith College, Northampton, Massachusetts, A.B. (honors) 1941; New School for Social Research, New York, 1941-42; Columbia University, New York, 1960-61. **Family:** Married Hugh Franklin in 1946 (died 1986); two daughters and one son. **Career:** Worked in the theater, New York, 1941-47; member of the faculty, University of Indiana,

Bloomington, summers 1965-66, 1971; writer-in-residence, Ohio State University, Columbus, 1970, and University of Rochester, New York, 1972. Since 1960, teacher, St. Hilda's and St. Hugh's School, New York; since 1966, librarian, Cathedral of St. John the Divine, New York; since 1970, president, Crosswicks Ltd., New York; since 1976, Lecturer, Wheaton College, Illinois; since 1976, member, Board of Directors, Authors League Foundation; president, Authors Guild of America. **Awards:** American Library Association Newbery Medal, 1963; University of Southern Mississippi award, 1978; Smith College Medal, 1980, and Sophie award, 1984; American Book award, for paperback, 1980; *Logos* award, for adult nonfiction, 1981; Catholic Library Association Regina Medal, 1984; National Council of Teachers of English ALAN award, 1986. **Agent:** Robert Lescher, 67 Irving Place, New York, New York 10009, U.S.A. **Address:** Crosswicks, Goshen, Connecticut 06756, U.S.A.

SCIENCE FICTION PUBLICATIONS

Novels (for children; series: Canon Tellis; Meg Murry)

The Arm of the Starfish (Canon Tellis). New York, Farrar Straus, 1965; London, Hodder and Stoughton, 1990.
The Young Unicorns (Canon Tellis). New York, Farrar Straus, 1968; London, Gollancz, 1970.
The Time Trilogy (Murry). New York, Farrar Strauss, 1979.
  A Wrinkle in Time. New York, Farrar Straus, 1962; London, Constable, 1963.
  A Wind in the Door. New York, Farrar Straus, 1973; London, Methuen, 1975.
  A Swiftly Tilting Planet. New York, Farrar Straus, 1978; London, Souvenir Press, 1980.
Many Waters (Murry). New York, Farrar Straus, 1986.
An Acceptable Time (Murry). New York, Farrar Straus, 1989.

OTHER PUBLICATIONS

Novels

The Small Rain. New York, Vanguard Press, 1945; London, Secker and Warburg, 1955.
Ilsa. New York, Vanguard Press, 1946.
And Both Were Young. New York, Lothrop, 1949.
Camilla Dickinson. New York, Simon and Schuster, 1951; London, Secker and Warburg, 1952; as *Camilla,* New York, Crowell, 1965.
A Winter's Love. Philadelphia, Lippincott, 1957.
Meet the Austins. New York, Vanguard Press, 1960; London, Collins, 1966.
The Moon by Night. New York, Farrar Straus, 1963; London, Lion, 1988.
The Love Letters. New York, Farrar Straus, 1966.
The Journey with Jonah. New York, Farrar Straus, 1968.
Prelude. New York, Vanguard Press, 1969; London, Gollancz, 1972.
The Other Side of the Sun. New York, Farrar Straus, 1971; London, Eyre Methuen, 1972.
Dragons in the Waters (Canon Tellis). New York, Farrar Straus, 1976; London, Hodder and Stoughton, 1991.
A Ring of Endless Light. New York, Farrar Straus, 1980; London, Lion, 1988.

A Severed Wasp. New York, Farrar Straus, 1982; London, Faber, 1984.
A House Like a Lotus (Canon Tellis). New York, Farrar Straus, 1984.
Certain Women. New York, Farrar Straus, 1992.

Short Stories

The Sphinx at Dawn: Two Stories. New York, Seabury Press, 1982.

Plays

18 Washington Square, South (produced Northampton, Massachusetts, 1940). Boston, Baker, 1944.
How Now Brown Cow, with Robert Hartung (produced New York, 1949).
The Journey with Jonah (produced New York, 1970). New York, Farrar Straus, 1967.

Poetry

Lines Scribbled on an Envelope and Other Poems. New York, Farrar Straus, 1969.
Weather of the Heart. Wheaton, Illinois, Shaw, 1978.
A Cry Like a Bell. Wheaton, Illinois, Shaw, 1987.

Other

The Twenty-Four Days before Christmas: An Austin Family Story (for children). New York, Farrar Straus, 1964.
Dance in the Desert (for children). New York, Farrar Straus, and London, Longman, 1969.
A Circle of Quiet (essays). New York, Farrar Straus, 1972.
Everyday Prayers (for children). New York, Morehouse Barlow, 1974.
Prayers for Sunday (for children). New York, Morehouse Barlow, 1974.
The Summer of the Great-Grandmother (essays). New York, Farrar Straus, 1974.
The Irrational Season (essays). New York, Seabury Press, 1977.
Ladder of Angels: Scenes from the Bible Illustrated by Children of the World. New York, Seabury Press, 1979.
The Anti-Muffins (for children). New York, Pilgrim Press, 1980.
Walking on Water (essays). Wheaton, Illinois, Shaw, 1980; Tring, Hertfordshire, Lion, 1982.
And It Was Good: Reflections on Beginnings. Wheaton, Illinois, Shaw, 1983.
Dare to Be Creative. Washington, D.C., Library of Congress, 1984.
Trailing Clouds of Glory: Spiritual Values in Children's Literature, with Avery Brooke. Philadelphia, Westminster Press, 1985.
A Stone for a Pillow. Wheaton, Illinois, Shaw, 1987.
Two-Part Invention: The Story of a Marriage (memoir). New York, Farrar Straus, 1988.
Sold into Egypt: Joseph's Journey into Human Being. Wheaton, Illinois, Shaw, 1989.
The Glorious Impossible (for children). New York, Simon and Schuster, 1990.
Baccalaureate Address. Barre, Vermont, Linfield College Press, 1991.
The Rock That Is Higher: Story as Truth. Wheaton, Illinois, Shaw, 1993.

Anytime Prayers. Wheaton, Illinois, Shaw, 1994.

Editor, with William R. Green, *Spirit and Light: Essays in Historical Theology.* New York, Seabury Press, 1976.

*

Manuscript Collections: Wheaton College, Illinois; Kerlan Collection, University of Minnesota, Minneapolis; de Grummond Collection, University of Southern Mississippi, Hattiesburg.

Madeleine L'Engle comments:

I discovered science fiction early, as a lonely only child growing up, for my first 12 years, in New York City, then in France and Switzerland. For me, the real world was clearer in the books of E. Nesbit and H.G. Wells than in the world of school. So I started writing science fiction when I was eight or nine. Fortunately all of my early work was lost somewhere or other on our journey across the Atlantic.

During college and after I turned to more "realistic" fiction, and found that it was not real enough, that my true discoveries of reality came while I was writing sci-fi or fantasy. I also discovered that for me the great theologians and modern mystics are the scientists, the physicists and astrophysicists, the cellular biologists, since they are dealing with the nature of Being itself. Einstein, Planck, Eddington, Jeans, Heisenberg, and many others, have been—and are still—my great stimulants.

*   *   *

Madeleine L'Engle has been publishing successful and provocative science fiction since the mid-1940s, adding intriguing variations to a considerable body of work, and continuously crafting fiction to engage her readers in issues and moral questions. She is nearly as prolific as some of her less thoughtful peers, and has continuously commanded the support of publishers and readers who must be described as literary. Her most well-known work is a series of novels dealing with time, including her one most signally famous work, *A Wrinkle in Time,* which introduces the children and, less directly, the father of the Murry family.

Wrinkle begins with the stark probing of a novel by Conrad, but by the time the reader recognizes what an extensive narrative hook has been set, L'Engle has paraded warm, bright, totally believable characters on stage. Every bit an existential and metaphysical thinker, L'Engle dramatizes the necessary leaps of faith that await the young reader and which certainly beckon to the more mature reader.

The second novel in the series, *A Wind in the Door,* takes up where the problem of the missing Murry father is solved, and the focus now becomes the integrity of healthy organisms and systems. Meg Murry, a young man from *Wrinkle* named Calvin, and a young superbeing become simultaneously involved in a plot involving Charles Wallace, who is being attacked at a cellular memory level, and this is shown in relationship to a black hole, L'Engle's version of a spot in the galaxy where there is a problem with cellular memory. *A Swiftly Tilting Planet* involves Meg Murry, now a grown woman, married and pregnant, but still called upon to join her siblings in an adventure relating to the potential for thermonuclear war.

Trademarks of L'Engle are her deceptively simple prose style, often undershot with social, moral, or religious issue; her restraint

in explaining too much either of philosophy, scientific apparatus, or technicalities; her crisp, individual dialog; and her ability to draw young characters who are interesting without being self-conscious. Well read in the physical and theoretical sciences, L'Engle has the same focus to be found in such writers as Theodore Sturgeon and Robert Heinlein, allowing her effectively to dramatize complex concepts whether a black hole in the galaxy and its consequence, the ability of a starfish to regenerate a portion of its body, or the ability of an immune system to keep an invader from penetrating.

L'Engle seems to have arrived at a happy synthesis of science, metaphysics, universal politics, and individual responsibility. She is one of the handful of science fiction writers whose work consistently rings true.

—Shelly Lowenkopf

———

LEPPOC, Derfla. *See* **COPPEL, Alfred.**

———

LESSER, Milton

Name now Stephen Marlowe. **Other Pseudonyms:** Adam Chase; Andrew Frazer; Ellery Queen; Jason Ridgway; C.H. Thames. **Nationality:** American. **Born:** New York City, 7 August 1928. **Education:** College of William and Mary, Williamsburg, Virginia, B.A. 1949. **Military Service:** Served in the United States Army, 1952-54. **Family:** Married 1) Leigh Lang in 1950 (divorced 1962); 2) Ann Humbert; two daughters. **Career:** Editor, Scott Meredith Literary Agency, New York, 1949-50; now a full-time writer. Writer-in-Residence, College of William and Mary, 1974-75, 1980-81. Member of the Board of Directors, Mystery Writers of America. **Agent:** Scott Meredith Literary Agency, 845 Third Avenue, New York, New York 10022, U.S.A.

SCIENCE FICTION PUBLICATIONS

Novels

Earthbound (for children). Philadelphia, Winston, 1952; London, Hutchinson, 1955.
The Star Seekers (for children). Philadelphia, Winston, 1953.
The Golden Age (with Paul W. Fairman as Adam Chase). New York, Avalon, 1959.
Recruit for Andromeda. New York, Ace, 1959.
Stadium Beyond the Stars (for children). Philadelphia, Winston, 1960.
Spacemen, Go Home (for children). New York, Holt Rinehart, 1962.
Translation. Englewood Cliffs, New Jersey, Prentice-Hall, 1976; London, W.H. Allen, 1977.

Short Stories

Secret of the Black Planet. New York, Belmont, 1965.

<small>OTHER PUBLICATIONS</small>

Novels

Violence Is Golden (as C.H. Thames). New York, Bouregy, 1956.
Find Eileen Hardin—Alive! (as Andrew Frazer). New York, Avon, 1959.
The Fall of Marty Moon (as Andrew Frazer). New York, Avon, 1960.
Dead Man's Tale (as Ellery Queen). New York, Pocket Books, 1961; London, New English Library, 1967.
Blood Is My Brother (as C.H. Thames). New York, Permabooks, 1963.
The Memoirs of Christopher Columbus. New York, Scribner, and London, Cape, 1987.
The Death and Life of Miguel de Cervantes. London, Bloomsbury, 1991.
The Lighthouse at the End of the World: A Tale of Edgar Allan Poe. New York, Dutton, 1995.

Novels as Stephen Marlowe

Catch the Brass Ring. New York, Ace, 1954.
Turn Left for Murder. New York, Ace, 1955.
Model for Murder. Hasbrouck Heights, New Jersey, Graphic, 1955.
The Second Longest Night. New York, Fawcett, 1955; London, Fawcett, 1958.
Dead on Arrival. New York, Ace, 1956.
Mecca for Murder. New York, Fawcett, 1956; London, Fawcett, 1957.
Killers Are My Meat. New York, Fawcett, 1957; London, Fawcett, 1958.
Murder Is My Dish. New York, Fawcett, 1957.
Trouble Is My Name. New York, Fawcett, 1957; London, Fawcett, 1958.
Violence Is My Business. New York, Fawcett, 1958; London, Fawcett, 1959.
Terror Is My Trade. New York, Fawcett, 1958; London, Muller, 1960.
Blonde Bait. New York, Avon, 1959.
Double in Trouble, with Richard S. Prather. New York, Fawcett, 1959.
Passport to Peril. New York, Fawcett, 1959.
Homicide Is My Game. New York, Fawcett, 1959; London, Muller, 1960.
Danger Is My Line. New York, Fawcett, 1960; London, Muller, 1961.
Death Is My Comrade. New York, Fawcett, 1960; London, Muller, 1961.
Peril Is My Pay. New York, Fawcett, 1960; London, Muller, 1961.
Manhunt Is My Mission. New York, Fawcett, 1961; London, Muller, 1962.
Jeopardy Is My Job. New York, Fawcett, 1962; London, Muller, 1963.
The Shining. New York, Trident Press, 1963.
Francesca. New York, Fawcett, and London, Muller, 1963.

Drum Beat—Berlin. New York, Fawcett, 1964.
Drum Beat—Dominique. New York, Fawcett, 1965.
Drum Beat—Madrid. New York, Fawcett, 1966.
The Search for Bruno Heidler. New York, Macmillan, 1966; London, Boardman, 1967.
Drum Beat—Erica. New York, Fawcett, 1967.
Come Over, Red Rover. New York, Macmillan, 1968.
Drum Beat—Marianne. New York, Fawcett, 1968.
The Summit. New York, Geis, 1970.
Colossus. New York, Macmillan, 1972; London, W.H. Allen, 1973.
The Man with No Shadow. Englewood Cliffs, New Jersey, Prentice-Hall, and London, W.H. Allen, 1974.
The Cawthorn Journals. Englewood Cliffs, New Jersey, Prentice-Hall, 1975; London, W.H. Allen, 1976; as *Too Many Chiefs,* London, New English Library, 1977.
The Valkyrie Encounter. New York, Putnam, and London, New English Library, 1978.
1956. New York, Arbor House, 1981; London, New English Library, 1982.
Deborah's Legacy. New York, Zebra, 1983.

Novels as Jason Ridgway

West Side Jungle. New York, Signet, 1958.
Adam's Fall. New York, Permabooks, 1960.
People in Glass Houses. New York, Permabooks, 1961.
Hardly a Man Is Now Alive. New York, Permabooks, 1962.
The Treasure of the Cosa Nostra. New York, Pocket Books, 1966.

Other

Lost Worlds and the Men Who Found Them (for children). Racine, Wisconsin, Whitman, 1962.
Walt Disney's Strange Animals of Australia (for children). Racine, Wisconsin, Whitman, 1963.

Editor, *Looking Forward: An Anthology of Science Fiction.* New York, Beechhurst Press, 1953; London, Cassell, 1955.

*   *   *

Although best known for his Chester Drum spy novels and elaborate espionage novels like *The Valkyrie Encounter,* Milton Lesser did write a series of juvenile SF novels for Winston and was a prolific contributor to the Ziff-Davis SF magazines in the late 1950s and early 1960s. Then Lesser abandoned the field to write more mainstream novels, although some of them, like *Translation* and *The Cawthorn Journals,* have science fiction elements.

Most of Lesser's SF novels are juveniles. In *Earthbound* a young cadet unjustly expelled from the Solar Academy is tricked into helping space pirates. The book is high on action and low on plausibility. *The Star Seekers* is a bit better. It reworks Robert A. Heinlein's idea of a generation starship presented in *Universe.* Here, a starship takes six generations to reach Alpha Centauri, with the attendant problems and struggles. *Stadium Beyond the Stars* is Lesser's weakest SF novel. Most of the action concerns plotting among political groups on the eve of the First Interstellar Olympic Games. The characterizations are shallow and the plot is murky. *Spacemen, Go Home* opens with humanity quarantined from star travel by a super computer which controls the galaxy. Various groups attempt to bomb the Star Brain while others attempt to convince it to lift the quarantine because humans aren't really all that violent. Again, a murky plot lurks behind the fast-paced action.

Lesser's adult works also stress action over plot and violence over character. *The Golden Age* is prime space opera featuring a bold hero who commutes among worlds in the tradition of John Carter. Duels and fights keep the action swift and the pages turning. *Recruit for Andromeda* has a tricky plot with draftees secretly tested to determine which are superior. The story has some mild racist overtones. *Secret of the Black Planet* is made up of two space-opera novelettes, "Secret of the Black Planet" and "Son of the Black Chalice." The search for a lost alien race and the secret of cell regeneration is marred by hackneyed writing and cardboard characterizations.

Most of this SF writing was done early in Lesser's career; he moved on to better paying markets and his writing skills improved as well. *The Search for Bruno Heidler* was selected as one of the best suspense novels of the year. His career peaked in the early 1970s with the publication of three successful novels: *The Summit, Colossus,* and *The Man with No Shadow.* Lesser's science fiction work quickly went out of print and is of historical interest only for an author who achieved success outside the science fiction field.

—George Kelley

LESSING, Doris (May)

Pseudonym: Jane Somers. **Nationality:** British. **Born:** Doris May Taylor, Kermansha, Persia, 22 October 1919; moved with her family to England, then to Banket, Southern Rhodesia, 1924. **Education:** Dominican Convent School, Salisbury, Southern Rhodesia, 1926-34. **Family:** Married 1) Frank Charles Wisdom in 1939 (divorced 1943), one son and one daughter; 2) Gottfried Lessing in 1945 (divorced 1949), one son. **Career:** Au pair, Salisbury, 1934-35; telephone operator and clerk, Salisbury, 1937-39, typist, 1946-48; journalist, *Cape Town Guardian,* 1949; moved to London, 1950; secretary, 1950; member of the Editorial Board, *New Reasoner* (later *New Left Review*), 1956. **Awards:** Maugham award, 1954; Médicis prize (France), 1976; Austrian State prize, 1981; Shakespeare prize (Hamburg), 1982; W.H. Smith literary award, 1986; Palermo prize, 1987; Grinzane Cavour award, 1989; Hon. D.Lit., Princeton, 1989; Hon. D.Lit. Durham, 1990; D. Fellow in Lit., Anglia, 1991; Hon. D.Lit., Warwick, 1994; Hon. D.Lett., Bard College, New York State, 1994; Woman of the Year, Norway, 1995; Hon. D.Lett., Harvard, 1995. **Member:** Associate member, American Academy, 1974; honorary fellow, Modern Language Association (U.S.), 1974. **Agent:** Jonathan Clowes Ltd., Iron Bridge House, Bridge Approach, London NW1 8BD, England.

SCIENCE FICTION PUBLICATIONS

Novels (series: Canopus in Argos: Archives)

The Memoirs of a Survivor. London, Octagon Press, 1974; New York, Knopf, 1975.
The Fifth Child. London, Cape, and New York, Knopf, 1988.
Canopus in Argos: Archives. New York, Vintage, 1992.

Re: Colonized Planet 5, Shikasta. London, Cape, and New York, Knopf, 1979.
The Marriages between Zones Three, Four, and Five. London, Cape, and New York, Knopf, 1980.
The Sirian Experiments: The Report by Ambien II, of the Five. London, Cape, and New York, Knopf, 1981.
The Making of the Representative for Planet 8. London, Cape, and New York, Knopf, 1982.
Documents Relating to the Sentimental Agents in the Volyen Empire. London, Cape, and New York, Knopf, 1983.

Short Stories

No Witchcraft for Sale: Stories and Short Novels. Moscow, Foreign Languages Publishing House, 1956.

OTHER PUBLICATIONS

Novels

The Grass Is Singing. London, Joseph, and New York, Crowell, 1950.
Children of Violence:
  Martha Quest. London, Joseph, 1952.
  A Proper Marriage. London, Joseph, 1954, with *Martha Quest,* New York, Simon and Schuster, 1964.
  A Ripple from the Storm. London, Joseph, 1958.
  Landlocked. London, MacGibbon and Kee, 1965; with *A Ripple from the Storm.* New York, Simon and Schuster, 1966.
  The Four-Gated City. London, MacGibbon and Kee, and New York, Knopf, 1969.
Retreat to Innocence. London, Joseph, 1956.
The Golden Notebook. London, Joseph, and New York, Simon and Schuster, 1962.
The Summer before the Dark. London, Cape, and New York, Knopf, 1973.
Briefing for a Descent into Hell. London, Cape, and New York, Knopf, 1971.
The Diaries of Jane Somers. New York, Random House, 1984; London, Joseph, 1985.
The Diary of a Good Neighbour (as Jane Somers). London, Joseph, and New York, Knopf, 1983.
If the Old Could (as Jane Somers). London, Joseph and New York, Knopf, 1984.
The Good Terrorist. London, Cape, and New York, Knopf, 1985.

Short Stories

This Was the Old Chief's Country. London, Joseph, 1951; New York, Crowell, 1952.
Five: Short Novels. London, Joseph, 1953.
The Habit of Loving. London, MacGibbon and Kee, 1957; New York, Crowell, 1958.
A Man and Two Women. London, MacGibbon and Kee, and New York, Simon and Schuster, 1963.
African Stories. London, Joseph, 1964; New York, Simon and Schuster, 1965.
Winter in July. London, Panther, 1966.
The Black Madonna. London, Panther, 1966.
Nine African Stories. London, Longman, 1968.

The Story of a Non-Marrying Man and Other Stories. London, Cape, 1972; as *The Temptation of Jack Orkney and Other Stories,* New York, Knopf, 1972.
Collected African Stories:
 This Was the Old Chief's Country. London, Joseph, 1973.
 The Sun between Their Feet. London, Joseph, 1973.
(Stories), edited by Alan Cattell. London, Harrap, 1976.
Collected Stories:
 To Room Nineteen. London, Cape, 1978.
 The Temptation of Jack Orkney. London, Cape, 1978.
Stories. New York, Knopf, 1978.

Plays

Before the Deluge (produced London, 1953).
Mr. Dollinger (produced Oxford, 1958).
Each His Own Wilderness (produced London, 1958). Published in *New English Dramatists,* London, Penguin, 1959.
The Truth about Billy Newton (produced Salisbury, Wiltshire, 1960).
Play with a Tiger (produced London, 1962; New York, 1964). London, Joseph, 1962.
The Storm, adaptation of a play by Alexander Ostrowsky (produced London, 1966).
The Singing Door, in *Second Playbill 2,* edited by Alan Durband. London, Hutchinson, 1973.

Television Plays: *The Grass Is Singing,* from her own novel, 1962; *Please Do Not Disturb,* 1966; *Care and Protection,* 1966; *Between Men,* 1967.
Libretto: *The Making of the Representative for Planet 8,* from her own novel, with music by Philip Glass, 1988.

Poetry

Fourteen Poems. Northwood, Middlesex, Scorpion Press, 1959.

Other

Going Home. London, Joseph, 1957.
In Pursuit of the English: A Documentary. London, MacGibbon and Kee, 1960; New York, Simon and Schuster, 1961.
Particularly Cats. London, Joseph, and New York, Simon and Schuster, 1967.
A Small Personal Voice: Essays, Reviews, Interviews, edited by Paul Schlueter, New York, Knopf, 1974.
Prisons We Choose to Live Inside. Montreal, CBC Enterprises, 1986; London, Cape, and New York, Harper and Row, 1987.
The Winds Blow Away Our Words: And Other Documents Relating to the Afghan Resistance. London, Panther, and New York, Vintage, 1987.
The Doris Lessing Reader. New York, Knopf, 1988; London, Cape, 1989.
African Laughter: Four Visits to Zimbabwe. London, HarperCollins, 1992.
Under My Skin. N.p., 1994.
Doris Lessing Conversations, edited by Earl Ingersoll. N.p., 1994.

*

Bibliography: *Doris Lessing: A Bibliography* by Catharina Ipp, Johannesburg, University of the Witwatersrand Department of Bibliography, 1967; *Doris Lessing: A Checklist of Primary and Secondary Sources* by Selma R. Burkom and Margaret Williams, Troy, New York, Whitston, 1973; *Doris Lessing: An Annotated Bibliography of Criticism* by Dee Seligman, Westport, Connecticut, Greenwood Press, 1981; *Doris Lessing: A Descriptive Bibliography of Her First Editions* by Eric T. Brueck, London, Metropolis, 1984.

Critical Studies (selection): *Doris Lessing* by Dorothy Brewster, New York, Twayne, 1965; *The Novels of Doris Lessing* by Paul Schlueter, Carbondale, Southern Illinois University Press, 1973; *Doris Lessing* by Michael Thorpe, London, Longman, 1973; *Doris Lessing: Critical Studies* edited by Annis Pratt and L.S. Dembo, Madison, University of Wisconsin Press, 1974; *The City and the Veld: The Fiction of Doris Lessing* by Mary Ann Singleton, Lewisburg, Pennsylvania, Bucknell University Press, 1976; *The Novelistic Vision of Doris Lessing: Breaking the Forms of Consciousness* by Roberta Rubenstein, Urbana, University of Illinois Press, 1979; *Notebooks/Memoirs/Archives: Reading and Re-reading Doris Lessing* edited by Jenny Taylor, London, and Boston, Routledge, 1982; *Substance under Pressure: Artistic Coherence and Evolving Form in the Novels of Doris Lessing* by Betsy Draine, Madison, University of Wisconsin Press, 1983; *Doris Lessing* by Lorna Sage, London, Methuen, 1983; *Doris Lessing* by Mona Knapp, New York, Ungar, 1984; *Doris Lessing and Women's Appropriation of Science Fiction* by Mariette Clare, Birmingham, Centre for Contemporary Cultural Studies, 1984; *Fiction; or, The Language of Our Discontent: A Study of the Built-In Novelist in the Novels of Angus Wilson, Lawrence Durrell, and Doris Lessing* by Guido Kums, New York, P. Lang, 1985; *The Unexpected Universe of Doris Lessing: A Study in Narrative Technique* by Katherine Fishburn, Westport, Connecticut, Greenwood, 1985; *Doris Lessing* edited by Eve Bertelesen, New York, McGraw Hill, 1985; *Critical Essays on Doris Lessing* edited by Claire Sprague and Virginia Tiger, Boston, Hall, 1986; *Rereading Lessing: Narrative Patterns of Doubling and Repetition* by Claire Sprague, Chapel Hill and London, University of North Carolina Press, 1987, and *In Pursuit of Doris Lessing: Nine Nations Reading* edited by Claire Sprague, New York, St. Martin's Press, and London, Macmillan, 1990; *The Theme of Enclosure in Selected Works of Doris Lessing* by Shirley Budhos, Troy, New York, Whitston, 1987; *Doris Lessing: The Alchemy of Survival* edited by Carey Kaplan and Ellen Cronan Rose, Athens, Ohio University Press, 1988; *Doris Lessing* by Ruth Whitaker, New York, St. Martin's Press, and London, Macmillan, 1988; *Doris Lessing* by Jeannette King, London, E. Arnold, 1989; *Understanding Doris Lessing* by Jean Pickering, Columbia, University of South Carolina Press, 1990.

*   *   *

Doris Lessing's series, *Canopus in Argos: Archives,* grew, according to the author, out of her plan for a single book, *Shikasta.* This first experiment in science fiction led to the exploration of multiple related themes in four more works. The movement away from the conventional realism of her earlier works to exploit the possibilities of the allegedly freer world of science fiction can be described as a partially successful experiment: it produced several very engaging and provocative works, but its supposed freedom apparently failed to provide the necessary artistic matrix through which Lessing might express her philosophical and social concerns. Lessing's autobiography, *Under My Skin* (1994), describes the process by which she formulated, from her surroundings, the details, perceptions, and theories which drive her fiction, as does *Doris Lessing Conversations* (ed. Earl Ingersoll, 1994). The engagement with the science fiction genre apparently did not allow expression of these personal concerns, for the last of the series, *The Sentimental Agent,* is the least interesting, and even though the ending is left open for a sixth or even seventh novel, Lessing has not returned to the science fiction genre, claiming to be "sidetracked" by realistic novels like *The Fifth Child, The Good Terrorist,* and other works.

Lessing, in fact, has frequently flirted with the conventions of the SF genre. *Landlocked* (1965), for instance, demonstrates Lessing's interest in extrasensory perception, while the last chapter of *The Four-Gated City* (1969) is an apocalyptic vision that points the way toward the genre. *Briefing for a Descent into Hell* (1971) and *The Memoirs of a Survivor* (1975) require a suspension of disbelief as they delve into what Lessing called "inner space fiction," and *The Fifth Child* (1988) draws on images of gnomes, trolls, and demonic changelings to depict a child who may be evil incarnate or the product of cruel treatment by relatives who see him as an alien outsider. Lessing's hope for the *Canopus* series was that it would allow her to "range freely in time and space," and to find the metaphors which would express her concern with contemporary problems and issues.

The superabundant themes and ideas encompassed by the science fiction cycle indeed range widely from planetary evolution over geological eons to the arts with which wives and husbands score minor points in forgettable skirmishes, but all the books are unified by one central concern: the role of the individual in events of great magnitude that transcend personal hopes, wishes, and desires. Most of Lessing's characters must confront a dizzying variety of forces that determine their destinies; their changing awareness of these forces provides much of the drama of their stories.

The most self-aware figures in all the novels are the mysterious representatives of the Canopean Empire. Even "Canopus," as individual officials are sometimes called, bows to a never-defined "Necessity" which rules all; in turn, Johor, Klorasty, and other Canopeans patiently guide less advanced races and even empires away from mindless violence and cruelty and toward cultural evolution. *Shikasta* details millions of years of the history of the earth, variously called "Rohanda" and "Shikasta." The Galactic time perspective allows the reader to understand that change and conflict is the one constant; the failure of a "Lock" between Canopus and Shikasta/Earth dooms the planet to degeneration and ultimately to near-destruction.

The Marriages between Zones Three, Four, and Five is comparatively sunny, but still ends in melancholy. The Canopeans are (apparently) acting as offstage "Providers" in control of a series of geographically contrasting "Zones," ranging from desert (Zone 5) to swampy lush wetlands (Zone 4) to mountain plateaus (3) to mountain passes (2). Varying zones and climates determine the personality of cultures, which in turn determines individual types, from earthy lowlander to ethereal mountaineer. Each zone has settled into smug self-satisfaction when a perhaps related decline in fertility causes the Providers to force a marriage between the queen of Zone Three, Al. Ith, and the king of Zone Four, Ben Ata. Both characters are masterfully drawn, and the uneasy marriage of a kind of high country Athenian to a lumpish Spartan provides high comedy based on the clash of female and male principles, the unending war between artistic natures and practical natures, and the gradual blending of distinct personalities in marriage. The narrator describes how later artists depicted this marriage of opposites, and Lessing's own word-pictures are like set-pieces from a medieval tableau. Queen

and King do not live happily ever after, however, for the Providers, in fine disregard for human wishes, toward the end of the book order Ben Ata to marry the wild, nomadic queen of Zone Five, thus blending the artistic intellect Ben Ata has gleaned from Al. Ith, his own orderly discipline, and the wild energy of the least civilized Zone. Al. Ith retires to the border of Zone Two, and eventually crosses it to become a flame-like wraith in a mountain atmosphere too rarified for others to tolerate. Life is change, says Lessing; even in this paradise reminiscent of a medieval fable, an unseen and only vaguely understood "necessity" casually destroys human happiness. There is no choice but to obey.

The Sirian Experiments continues this theme with another wonderfully drawn female protagonist, Ambien II, one of the five dictators who rule the technological empire in competition with Canopus. Unfortunately, Ambien II's prissy, bureaucratic, "dessicated" character is so persuasive that the reader may lack sympathy throughout much of the book, at least until this self-serving and authoritarian figure begins to learn a more sensitive and less machine-like managerial style from her Canopean opposites. As with Al. Ith and Ben Ata, sexual attraction between opposites provides the motive force for change, but there is no comedy here, only some excellent set-pieces in an Arab-like town and an Aztec-like fortress. Ambien has led Sirian "experiments" on millions of "lower species" over thousands of years, unmindful of their dubious morality because of their good intentions of forcing evolution. Miseries such as Al. Ith's in the previous novel are multiplied a million times before Ambien's Canopean teachers lead her to see from experience and example that the Sirian Empire is being taught by the Canopean just as surely as the "lower species" are being taught by the Sirian. As in the linked Zones, one relationship leads to the next, but the joins are invisible since they are firmly denied by the weaker. Colonialism involves more complex power relationships than are initially evident, with control being exercised in unexpected ways. Only experience teaches by showing us the mote in another's eye, just as Lessing's novel should raise our consciousness of Western arrogance and brutality in Africa and other former colonial areas.

In *The Sirian Experiments* evil necessity is incarnated in the Puttiorian Empire (the name suggests Spanish *puta* or whore) and their planet Shahmat (Farsi for "the king is dead," or in chess, "checkmate"). In *The Making of the Representative for Planet 8,* evil necessity is a cosmic accident. The Canopean governed colony on Planet 8 is freezing to death because of planetary climactic changes. In a fine description of a frozen world stimulated by Lessing's reading about Scott's search for the South Pole, we see the telepathic, tropically lively and colorful inhabitants of Planet 8 become slothful, fur-swaddled zombies who lose their social identities as the snow and ice wipe out occupations and social roles. Climate is destiny; eventually, led and taught by their Canopean master Johor, they give up their material existence and become a single "representative" spirit, transcending physicality.

The Sentimental Agents continues the emphasis on Canopean moderation of extreme behavior, with Incent, an agent of the empire, seduced by "Undulant Rhetoric" or a kind of intoxication with words. In contrast, the usual approach of the Canopean agents is to be noncommittal to the point of taciturnity. They are men and women of action, not empty words.

While there is an honorable tradition of 20th-century writers opposing propaganda and false rhetoric, it is especially appropriate for Lessing to end her cycle with this warning. Throughout, there have been conflicts between characters skilled at action (Ben Ata, Ambien II) and characters skilled at language (Al. Ith, Nasar,

Rhodia). Lessing's own ambivalence about the role of writer and writing may be at issue, and this uncertainty in a writer known for her earlier political stands may account for the mixed critical reception to her cycle. Like Canopus, Lessing teaches by example, but also like Canopus, she refuses easy answers and the superficial knowledge of the conventional.

For all its appropriateness in ending the cycle, even temporarily, Lessing seems to have exhausted some enthusiasm for science fiction with *The Sentimental Agents.* This work is generally acknowledged to be the least successful of the five-book series, with a fairly predictable narrative development and overly simple ideas. Lessing began with "inner space" rather than outer space concerns, and she admits to a limited knowledge of the "science" part of science fiction—she may well have discovered that without the shape given by scientific plausibility, the "freedom" science fiction offered descended into undisciplined fantasy. Walter E. Meyers among others has pointed out the literal absurdity of events in *The Making of the Representative for Planet 8,* and the other novels as well suffer from a fuzziness of cause and effect that borders on the dreamy. (The distance of *Planet 8* from the essence of the genre may be indicated by Philip Glass's opera libretto of the story, a somewhat unusual fate for an SF tale.) However engaging the characters, events of plot seem to follow the author's allegorical or symbolic interests, not those of a plausible science fiction world. The result may be very interesting fiction, but it is not really *science* fiction, and for this reason Lessing may have ended the experiment.

—Andrew Macdonald

LETHEM, Jonathan (Allen)

Nationality: American. **Born:** New York, New York, 19 February 1964. **Education:** Bennington College, Bennington, Vermont (no degree). **Family:** Married Shelley Jackson in 1986 (divorced 1991). **Career:** Bookseller, Brazen Head Bookshop, Avery Books, Gryphon Books, all New York; Pegasus Books, Pendragon Books, Moe's Books, all Berkeley. Now full-time writer. **Awards:** IAFA Crawford Fantasy award, 1995; *Locus* award, 1995. **Agent:** Richard Parks, Richard Parks Agency, 138 East 16th Street, #5B, New York, New York 10003, U.S.A. **Address:** c/o Harcourt Brace, 15 East 26th Street, New York, New York 10010, U.S.A.

SCIENCE FICTION PUBLICATIONS

Novels

Gun, with Occasional Music. New York, Harcourt, 1994; London, Hodder Headline, 1995.
Amnesia Moon. New York, Harcourt, and London, Hodder Headline, 1995.

Short Stories

Author of numerous uncollected short stories.

*

Jonathan Lethem comments:

I've got a lot of writing to do before the invitation to talk about my own work makes sense—I'll spare us generalizations about books that are still in my head rather than on the shelf. It's probably obvious already that I'm engaged with "genres" but not bound by them. Technology in my work is iconographic and metaphoric. I wouldn't know an extrapolation if it came bearing flowers. I write about myself and my friends; the thing is, we grew up in a misshapen future world called America. And we watched a lot of movies. And read a lot of SF.

* * *

Jonathan Lethem published his first short story in 1989 and had sold around 40 by the time his first novel appeared. His short stories have been published widely in anthologies and magazines in the United States and abroad. [Publication of a collection of his stories is forthcoming from Harcourt Brace in 1996. "The Happy Man" (1991) was a finalist for the 1991 Nebula and won third place for the Sturgeon; "Walking the Moons" (1990) and "Elvis National Theater of Okinawa" (1992) were reprinted in the Eighth and Tenth Annual editions of *The Year's Best Science Fiction.*

His writing has revealed both his versatility and his twisted view of reality—especially social reality—from the start. Lethem frequently portrays a finite social group whose behaviors reveal to the reader the nature of a bizarre world that its denizens themselves rarely interrogate. "'Forever,' Said the Duck" (1993), for example, is a Wildean satire of deception and self-deception at a jet-set party experienced vicariously through VR simulacra. "The Precocious Objects" (1993) poignantly portrays an artificial intelligence reaching puberty, its non-Euclidean vocabulary allowing the reader an eerie, nonhuman view of socialization.

Lethem admires the hardboiled fiction of Raymond Chandler, Dashiell Hammett, and Ross McDonald, who bequeath as much to the gritty tone of *Gun, with Occasional Music* (1994) as Philip K. Dick, Stanislaw Lem, and Cordwainer Smith contribute to its crowded furniture. A fast-paced and highly imaginative gumshoe novel, its pixilated black humor is conveyed through the weary voice of the narrator, "private inquisitor" Conrad Metcalf. In the dystopian future of the setting, you need an inquisitor's license to ask any sort of question. Metcalf has his share of problems: His ex-girlfriend ran away with his genital nerve endings, leaving him with a set of hers, and he relies on the drug Acceptol to get through the day. Tough and smart-alecky, he discomfits those he questions on behalf of his client, Orton Angwine, who has been framed for the murder of wealthy urologist Maynard Stanhunt. Yet Metcalf gives a damn, self-deprecatingly, about Truth and Justice, unlike the official Inquisitors, whose repressive powers are never fully defined but appear limitless.

One of the premises of the novel is that the government, whose visible face here is the Inquisition Office, provides drugs such as Acceptol, Avoidol, and Forgettol, all known generically as "make," to its citizens. As gangster Danny Phoneblum remarks, "Make is a tool for controlling great masses of people. It homogenizes their response to repression. . . ." In this America, the citizens prefer to forget the past, while Metcalf comes belatedly to value memory. His society includes "evolved" animals, who wear clothing, speak English, and provide menial labor and sex, and the "babyheads," scientifically advanced infants with bad attitudes who frequent bars and spout gibberish. The rest of his world leaves a similarly bad taste in your mouth.

The central mystery mutates beyond a simple whodunit. The further Metcalf pursues the murderer, the more threats and assaults he earns. His visits with the decadent inhabitants of a degenerating San Francisco are punctuated by numerous fistfights with Phoneblum's hitman, an unforgettably seedy kangaroo named Joey Castle. The solution is based on clues fairly planted throughout the book and relies, satisfyingly, on the science fictional constructs. The crime concerns the prominent issues of memory and nostalgia and forgetting—and is all the sadder for it. The novel won the *Locus* and Crawford Awards for Best First Novel in 1995.

Where *Gun* teases with the difficulties of epistemology, Lethem's second novel grapples with ontology. *Amnesia Moon* (1995), a baffling road novel, has been compared with the works of Harlan Ellison, Franz Kafka, and Dr. Seuss as well as (again) those of Dick. It also showcases the problems of memory and of self-identity, with the same startlingly jovial bleakness.

Chaos is a loner, living in a disused movie house in post-apocalyptic Hatfork, Wyoming, peopled with mutants and perverts united by starvation. The big man around town is Kellogg, who controls the rationing of food and the inhabitants' nightly dreams. When Chaos confronts Kellogg about this despotism, Kellogg replies enigmatically that Chaos's dreams are as responsible for the local conditions as his own. He adds that the widely accepted belief that a nuclear holocaust has caused these conditions is wrong: the bombs never fell, and the truth is more complicated than any nuclear war.

Chaos hits the road with a furry mutant girl named Melinda. Soon he begins to have his own dreams, which feature a beautiful house he once owned and a lost lover named Gwen, who restores his forgotten real name, Everett. He heads for California to find her, and they encounter various bizarre communities on the way.

These towns do not provide serious obstacles toward his goal: Lethem's strategy is not to endanger Chaos/Everett's life, but to revel in his gift for Fellini-esque creation of weird societies. Everett and Melinda wander across a mountain on which everyone is blinded by a hovering green mist; down the Reno Strip with its sad MacDonaldonians, fast-food servants to a population of one; and through Vacaville, where the residents move into each others' homes every few days.

San Francisco proves to be filled with people who, like George Orr's psychiatrist in Ursula Le Guin's *The Lathe of Heaven,* have plans for Everett's power to change reality with his dreams. He hears different theories about what happened when "the break" occurred, including the collision of a multitude of dreamers' ideations and an alien invasion. Everett's search for Gwen and an old friend named Cale waver as he begins to question the distinctions between the real and the false. Reality begins to fall apart like a shed in a tornado by the time the grotesque conclusion rolls around, yet ultimately he regains his self-reliance and learns to trust his comrades in the war of realities.

Lethem has a talent for portraying believable humans and nonhumans in worlds very different from ours. His emphases on memory and the subjective view of consensual reality provide a biting satire on what has been called our "post-historical age," in which history is increasingly devalued and forgotten. The comparisons between his fiction and Dick's are fair, though a bandit radiance shines through his cynical vision. Lethem enjoys playing with ideas, where Dick feared his own; and the reader ultimately emerges from the spray of phenomena in his fiction, not merely with doubt about reality and self, but with a carnival sense of a very relativistic world.

—Fiona Kelleghan

LEVIN, Ira

Nationality: American. **Born:** New York City, 27 August 1929. **Education:** Drake University, Des Moines, Iowa, 1946-48; New York University, 1948-50, A.B. in English 1950. **Military Service:** Served in the United States Army Signal Corps, 1953-55. **Family:** Married 1) Gabrielle Aronsohn in 1960 (divorced 1968), three sons; 2) Phyllis Finkel in 1979 (divorced 1982). **Awards:** Mystery Writers of America Edgar Allan Poe award, 1954, and Special award, 1980. **Agent:** Harold Ober Associates, 425 Madison Avenue, New York, New York 10017, U.S.A.

SCIENCE FICTION PUBLICATIONS

Novels

Rosemary's Baby. New York, Random House, and London, Joseph, 1967.
This Perfect Day. New York, Random House, and London, Joseph, 1970.
The Stepford Wives. New York, Random House, and London, Joseph, 1972.
The Boys from Brazil. New York, Random House, and London, Joseph, 1976.
Nightmares: Three Great Suspense Novels (omnibus). London, Joseph, 1981.

OTHER PUBLICATIONS

Novels

A Kiss before Dying. New York, Simon and Schuster, 1953; London, Joseph, 1954.
Sliver. New York, Bantam, and London, Joseph, 1991.

Plays

No Time for Sergeants, adaptation of the novel by Mac Hyman (produced New York, 1955; London, 1956). New York, Random House, 1956.
Interlock (produced New York, 1958). New York, Dramatists Play Service, 1958.
Critic's Choice (produced New York, 1960; London, 1961). New York, Random House, 1961; London, Evans, 1963.
General Seeger (produced New York, 1962). New York, Dramatists Play Service, 1962.
Drat! The Cat!, music by Milton Schafer (produced New York, 1965).
Dr. Cook's Garden (also director: produced New York, 1967). New York, Dramatists Play Service, 1968.
Veronica's Room (produced New York, 1973; Watford, Hertfordshire, 1982). New York, Random House, 1974; London, Joseph, 1975.
Deathtrap (produced New York and London, 1978). New York, Random House, 1979.
Break a Leg (produced New York, 1979). New York, French, 1981.
Cantorial (produced Stamford, Connecticut, 1984, New York, 1989). New York, French, 1990.

*

Critical Study: *Ira Levin* by Douglas Fowler, Mercer Island, Washington, Starmont, 1988.

Theatrical Activities:
Director: **Play**—*Dr. Cook's Garden,* New York, 1967.

*   *   *

Ira Levin's highly accomplished novels of suspense contain elements of science fiction and fantasy, and one, *This Perfect Day,* is set in the future. His first novel, *A Kiss before Dying,* the study of a psychopath stalking three sisters, is skillfully written but gives little suggestion of the richness in store. *Rosemary's Baby* is one of the most perfectly crafted thrillers ever written. Rosemary and Guy Woodhouse step over the threshold of a richly documented old apartment house in New York City into the world of the witches. The strength of the book lies not only in its weaving of a dreadful spell but in the strong, sweet character of the pregnant heroine. Guy's complicity in the schemes of the friendly neighbours is part of a fiendish double climax.

The book following this masterpiece of genre writing was the science fiction novel *This Perfect Day.* The future race, brown-skinned, depilated, breastless, tranquilised, stroll the windowless walkways of a totally computerised environment, patting the scanners as they pass, en route to death at age 62. LiRM35M4419, called Chip by his wry grandfather, escapes from the system by resisting UNI, the computer responsible for a boring parody of the good life. Chip's escape is obviously programmed; the appearance of those benign sybarites, the Programmers, is not surprising. The ideology of the "utopia" is weak but the quality of the writing and the level of invention are high.

Ira Levin returned to the suspense novel with *The Stepford Wives.* The setting, a commuter township in "middle America," is as persuasive as the New York of *Rosemary's Baby.* Joanna Everhart discovers the dreadful secret of the big-bosomed zombies who dote on housework. The climax is clever but the story is unsatisfying and the neatness of the writing hides many loose ends. We look in vain for one husband who refuses to trade in his wife on a new model.

The Boys From Brazil has an international setting but still retains a typical claustrophobic atmosphere. Dr. Josef Mengele, former medical superintendant of Auschwitz, emerges from his South American jungle retreat to send the organisation of Nazi veterans on a mission. Yakov Lieberman, the tired Nazi-hunter, discovers soon enough, but more slowly than the readers, why 94 elderly civil servants throughout the western world must die. These men are the adoptive fathers of teen-age sons cloned from the cells of Adolf Hitler; their deaths are an attempt to match up environment with genetic inheritance. This time the humanity of Lieberman balances the outrageous story; it is one of Ira Levin's best books. Mengele's scheme, even with its coda of an artistic lad somewhere indulging "tomorrow-the-world" fantasies, is revealed as pure moonshine.

Ira Levin's suspense novels have a unique resonance. These books, rather than *This Perfect Day,* have created a nightmare future world in which the Stepford delinquents, children of megalomaniac fathers raised by robot mothers, tangle with genetic Hitlers, under the eye of the heir of the Prince of This World, Andrew Woodhouse, the devil's child. The author not only portrays the contemporary world, but he also gives us its ancient myths and futurist fantasies.

With his latest novel, *Sliver,* Ira Levin has skipped over the fierce decade of the 1980s, heyday of terrorist and serial killer, and landed his readers securely in the postmodern era. *Sliver* is a spare, cruel,

morally ambivalent fable about electronic surveillance carried to insane lengths. The precise and un-nerving story of Kay, the smart editor, confronting the boundless amorality of her young lover, involves a certain reduction in scale as against the earlier books. It is a "tale of the city"—almost a new sub-genre. When Ira Levin sets his story in a glamorous apartment on the 20th floor, we know that it would be better for all concerned, including the cat, to keep away from the windows.

—Cherry Wilder

LEWIS, C(live) S(taples)

Pseudonyms: Clive Hamilton; N.W. Clerk. **Nationality:** British. **Born:** Belfast, Northern Ireland, 29 November 1898. **Education:** Wynyard House, Watford, Herfordshire, 1908-10; Campbell College, Belfast, 1910; Cherbourg School, Malvern, Worcestershire, 1911-13, and Malvern College, 1913-14; privately, in Great Bookham, Surrey, 1914-17; University College, Oxford (scholar; Chancellor's English Essay prize, 1921), 1917, 1919-23, B.A. (honors) 1922. **Military Service:** Served in the Somerset Light Infantry, 1917-19: First Lieutenant. **Family:** Married Joy Davidman Gresham in 1956 (died 1960); two stepsons. **Career:** Philosophy Tutor, 1924, and Lecturer in English, 1924, University College, Oxford; Fellow and Tutor in English, Magdalen College, Oxford, 1925-54; Professor of Medieval and Renaissance English, Cambridge University, 1954-63; Lecturer, University College of North Wales, Bangor, 1941; Riddell Lecturer, University of Durham, 1943; Clark Lecturer, Cambridge University, 1944. **Awards:** Gollancz prize, 1937; Library Association Carnegie Medal, 1957. D.D.: University of St. Andrews, Fife, 1946; Docteur-ès-Lettres, Laval University, Quebec, 1952; D.Litt.: University of Manchester, 1959; Hon.Dr.: University of Dijon, 1962; University of Lyon, 1963. Honorary Fellow, Magdalen College, Oxford, 1955; University College, Oxford, 1958; Magdalene College, Cambridge, 1963. Fellow, Royal Society of Literature, 1948; Fellow, British Academy, 1955. **Died:** 22 November 1963.

SCIENCE FICTION PUBLICATIONS

Novels (series: Perelandra)

Till We Have Faces: A Myth Retold. London, Bles, 1956; New York, Harcourt Brace, 1957.
The Cosmic Trilogy. London, Bodley Head, 1990.
    Out of the Silent Planet. London, Lane, 1938; New York, Macmillan, 1943.
    Perelandra. London, Lane, 1943; New York, Macmillan, 1944; as *Voyage to Venus (Perelandra),* London, Pan, 1953.
    That Hideous Strength: A Modern Fairy-Tale for Grown-Ups. London, Lane, 1945; New York, Macmillan, 1946; abridged edition, as *The Tortured Planet,* New York, Avon, 1958.

Novels (for children; series: Chronicles of Narnia in all titles)

The Chronicles of Narnia. New York, Religious Book Club, 2 vols., 1973; as *Tales of Narnia,* London, Collins, 1987.

The Lion, The Witch, and the Wardrobe. London, Bles, and New York, Macmillan, 1950.

Prince Caspian: The Return to Narnia. London, Bles, and New York, Macmillan, 1951.

The Voyage of the "Dawn Treader." London, Bles, and New York, Macmillan, 1952.

The Silver Chair. London, Bles, and New York, Macmillan, 1953.

The Horse and His Boy. London, Bles, and New York, Macmillan, 1954.

The Magician's Nephew. London, Bodley Head, and New York, Macmillan, 1955.

The Last Battle. London, Bodley Head, and New York, Macmillan, 1956.

Short Stories

Of Other Worlds: Essays and Stories, edited by Walter Hooper. London, Bles, 1966; New York, Harcourt Brace, 1967.

OTHER PUBLICATIONS

Short Stories

The Dark Tower and Other Stories, edited by Walter Hooper. London, Collins, and New York, Harcourt Brace, 1977.

Poetry

Spirits in Bondage: A Cycle of Lyrics (as Clive Hamilton). London, Heinemann, 1919.

Dymer (as Clive Hamilton). London, Dent, and New York, Dutton, 1926.

Poems, edited by Walter Hooper. London, Bles, 1964; New York, Harcourt Brace, 1965.

Narrative Poems, edited by Walter Hooper. London, Bles, 1969; New York, Harcourt Brace, 1972.

Other

The Pilgrim's Regress: An Allegorical Apology for Christianity, Reason, and Romanticism. London, Dent, 1933; New York, Sheed and Ward, 1935; revised edition, London, Bles, 1943; Sheed and Ward, 1944.

The Allegory of Love: A Study in Medieval Tradition. Oxford, Clarendon Press, and New York, Oxford University Press, 1936.

Rehabilitations and Other Essays. London and New York, Oxford University Press, 1939.

The Personal Heresy: A Controversy, with E.M.W. Tillyard. London and New York, Oxford University Press, 1939.

The Problem of Pain. London, Bles, 1940; New York, Macmillan, 1944.

The Weight of Glory. London, S.P.C.K., 1942.

The Screwtape Letters. London, Bles, 1942; New York, Macmillan, 1943; revised edition, as *The Screwtape Letters and Screwtape Proposes a Toast,* Bles, 1961; Macmillan, 1962.

Broadcast Talks: Right and Wrong: A Clue to the Meaning of the Universe, and What Christians Believe. London, Bles, 1942; as *The Case for Christianity,* New York, Macmillan, 1943.

A Preface to "Paradise Lost" (lectures). London and New York, Oxford University Press, 1942; revised edition, 1960.

Christian Behaviour: A Further Series of Broadcast Talks. London, Bles, and New York, Macmillan, 1943.

The Abolition of Man; or, Reflections on Education with Special Reference to the Teaching of English in the Upper Forms of Schools. London, Oxford University Press, 1943; New York, Macmillan, 1947.

Beyond Personality: The Christian Idea of God. London, Bles, 1944; New York, Macmillan, 1945.

The Great Divorce: A Dream. London, Bles, and New York, Macmillan, 1946.

Miracles: A Preliminary Study. London, Bles, and New York, Macmillan, 1947.

Vivisection. London, Anti-Vivisection Society, and Boston, New England Anti-Vivisection Society, 1947(?).

Transposition and Other Addresses. London, Bles, 1949; as *The Weight of Glory and Other Addresses,* New York, Macmillan, 1949.

The Literary Impact of the Authorized Version (lecture). London, Athlone Press, 1950; Philadelphia, Fortress Press, 1963.

Mere Christianity. London, Bles, and New York, Macmillan, 1952.

Hero and Leander (lecture). London, Oxford University Press, 1952.

English Literature in the Sixteenth Century, Excluding Drama. Oxford, Clarendon Press, 1954.

De Descriptione Temporum (lecture). London, Cambridge University Press, 1955.

Surprised by Joy: The Shape of My Early Life. London, Bles, 1955; New York, Harcourt Brace, 1956.

Reflections on the Psalms. London, Bles, and New York, Harcourt Brace, 1958.

Shall We Lose God in Outer Space? London, S.P.C.K., 1959.

The Four Loves. London, Bles, and New York, Harcourt Brace, 1960.

The World's Last Night and Other Essays. New York, Harcourt Brace, 1960.

Studies in Words. London, Cambridge University Press, 1960; revised edition, 1967; New York, Cambridge University Press, 1990.

An Experiment in Criticism. London, Cambridge University Press, 1961.

A Grief Observed (as N.W. Clerk; autobiography). London, Faber, 1961; Greenwich, Connecticut, Seabury Press, 1963.

They Asked for a Paper: Papers and Addresses. London, Bles, 1962.

Beyond the Bright Blur (letters). New York, Harcourt Brace, 1963.

Letters to Malcolm, Chiefly on Prayer. London, Bles, and New York, Harcourt Brace, 1964.

The Discarded Image: An Introduction to Medieval and Renaissance Literature. London, Cambridge University Press, 1964.

Screwtape Proposes a Toast and Other Pieces. London, Fontana, 1965.

Letters, edited by W.H. Lewis. London, Bles, and New York, Harcourt Brace, 1966; revised edition, edited by Walter Hooper, London, Collins, 1988.

Studies in Medieval and Renaissance Literature, edited by Walter Hooper. London, Cambridge University Press, 1966.

Spenser's Images of Life, edited by Alastair Fowler. London, Cambridge University Press, 1967.

Christian Reflections, edited by Walter Hooper. London, Bles, and Grand Rapids, Michigan, Eerdmans, 1967.

Letters to an American Lady, edited by Clyde S. Kilby. Grand Rapids, Michigan, Eerdmans, 1967; London, Hodder and Stoughton, 1969.

Mark vs. Tristram: Correspondence Between C.S. Lewis and Owen Barfield, edited by Walter Hooper. Cambridge, Massachusetts, Lowell House Printers, 1967.

A Mind Awake: An Anthology of C.S. Lewis, edited by Clyde S. Kilby. London, Bles, 1968; New York, Harcourt Brace, 1969.

Selected Literary Essays, edited by Walter Hooper. London, Cambridge University Press, 1969.

God in the Dock: Essays on Theology and Ethics, edited by Walter Hooper. Grand Rapids, Michigan, Eerdmans, 1970; as *Undeceptions: Essays on Theology and Ethics,* London, Bles, 1971.

The Humanitarian Theory of Punishment. Abingdon, Berkshire, Marcham Books Press, 1972.

Fern-Seed and Elephants and Other Essays on Christianity, edited by Walter Hooper. London, Fontana, 1975.

The Joyful Christian: 127 Readings, edited by William Griffin. New York, Macmillan, 1977.

They Stand Together: The Letters of C.S. Lewis to Arthur Greeves 1914-1963, edited by Walter Hooper. London, Collins, and New York, Macmillan, 1979.

C.S. Lewis at the Breakfast Table and Other Reminiscences, edited by James T. Como. New York, Macmillan, 1979; London, Collins, 1980.

The Visionary Christian: 131 Readings, edited by Chad Walsh. New York, Macmillan, 1981.

On Stories and Other Essays on Literature, edited by Walter Hooper. New York, Harcourt Brace, 1982.

Of This and Other Worlds, edited by Walter Hooper. London, Collins, 1982.

The Cretaceous Perambulator, with Owen Barfield, edited by Walter Hooper. Oxford, C.S. Lewis Society, 1983.

The Business of Heaven: Daily Readings from C.S. Lewis, edited by Walter Hooper. London, Fount, and New York, Harcourt Brace, 1984.

Boxen: The Imaginary World of the Young C.S. Lewis, edited by Walter Hooper. London, Collins, and San Diego, Harcourt Brace, 1985.

Letters to Children, edited by Lyle W. Dorsett and Marjorie Lamp Mead. New York, Macmillan, 1985.

First and Second Things: Essays on Theology and Ethics, edited by Walter Hooper. London, Collins, 1985.

Present Concerns, edited by Walter Hooper. London, Fount, and San Diego, Harcourt Brace, 1986.

Timeless at Heart: Essays on Theology, edited by Walter Hooper. London, Fount, 1987.

The Essential C.S. Lewis, edited by Lyle W. Dorsett. New York, Macmillan, 1988.

Letters: C.S. Lewis and Don Giovanni Calabria: A Study in Friendship, edited and translated by Martin Moynihan. London, Collins, and Ann Arbor, Michigan, Servant Books, 1988.

All My World before Me: The Diary of C.S. Lewis 1922-27, edited by Walter Hooper. London, HarperCollins, and San Diego, Harcourt Brace, 1991.

Daily Readings with C.S. Lewis, edited by Walter Hooper. London, Fount, 1992; as *Readings for Meditation and Reflection,* San Francisco, HarperSanFrancisco, 1996.

Editor, *George MacDonald: An Anthology.* London, Bles, 1946; New York, Macmillan, 1947.

Editor, *Arthurian Torso, Containing the Posthumous Fragment of "The Figure of Arthur,"* by Charles Williams. London, and New York, Oxford University Press, 1948.

*

Bibliography: "A Bibliography of the Writings of C.S. Lewis" by Walter Hooper, in *Light on C.S. Lewis* edited by Jocelyn Gibb, London, Bles, 1965; *C.S. Lewis: An Annotated Checklist of Writings about Him and His Works* by Joe R. Christopher and Joan K. Ostling, Kent, Ohio, Kent State University Press, 1974.

Manuscript Collections: Bodleian Library, Oxford; Wheaton College, Illinois.

Critical Studies (selection): *C.S. Lewis* by Roger Lancelyn Green, London, Bodley Head, and New York, Walck, 1963, revised edition, in *Three Bodley Head Monographs,* Bodley Head, 1969, *C.S. Lewis: A Biography* by Green and Walter Hooper, London, Collins, and New York, Harcourt Brace, 1974, revised edition, 1988, and *Past Watchful Dragons: The Narnian Chronicles of C.S. Lewis,* New York, Macmillan, 1979, and *Through Joy and Beyond: A Pictorial Biography of C.S. Lewis,* New York, Macmillan, 1982, both by Hooper; *Light on C.S. Lewis* edited by Jocelyn Gibb, London, Bles, 1965; *The Lion of Judah in Never-Never Land: The Theology of C.S. Lewis Expressed in His Fantasies for Children,* Grand Rapids, Michigan, Eerdmans, 1973, and *The C.S. Lewis Hoax,* Portland, Oregon, Multinomah, 1988, both by Kathryn Ann Lindskoog; *The Secret Country of C.S. Lewis* by Anne Arnott, London, Hodder and Stoughton, 1974, Grand Rapids, Michigan, Eerdmans, 1975; *The Longing for Form: Essays on the Fiction of C.S. Lewis* edited by Peter J. Schakel, Kent, Ohio, Kent State University Press, 1977, and *Reading with the Heart: The Way into Narnia* by Schakel, Grand Rapids, Michigan, Eerdmans, 1979; *The Inklings: C.S. Lewis, J.R.R. Tolkien, Charles Williams and Their Friends* by Humphrey Carpenter, London, Allen and Unwin, 1978, Boston, Houghton Mifflin, 1979; *The Literary Legacy of C.S. Lewis* by Chad Walsh, New York, Harcourt Brace, and London, Sheldon Press, 1979; *A Guide Through Narnia* by Martha C. Sammons, Wheaton, Illinois, Shaw, and London, Hodder and Stoughton, 1979; *Narnia Explored* by Paul A. Karkainen, Old Tappan, New Jersey, Revell, 1979; *Companion to Narnia* by Paul F. Ford, New York, Harper, 1980; *C.S. Lewis, Spinner of Tales: A Guide to His Fiction* by Evan K. Gibson, Grand Rapids, Michigan, Christian University Press, 1980; *C.S. Lewis* by Margaret Patterson Hannay, New York, Ungar, 1981; *C.S. Lewis: The Art of Enchantment* by Donald E. Glover, Athens, Ohio University Press, 1981; *C.S. Lewis* by Brian Murphy, Mercer Island, Washington, Starmont House, 1983; *The Politics of Fantasy: C.S. Lewis and J.R.R. Tolkien* by Lee D. Rossi, New York, and Epping, Essex, Bowker, 1984; *Clive Staples Lewis: The Drama of a Life* by William Griffin, New York, Harper, 1986; *C.S. Lewis: His Literary Achievement* by C.N. Manlove, London, Macmillan, 1987; *C.S. Lewis* by Joe R. Christopher, Boston, Twayne, 1987; *C.S. Lewis, Man of Letters: A Reading of His Fiction* by Thomas Howard, Worthing, Sussex, Churchman, 1987; *Jack: C.S. Lewis and His Times* by George Sayer, London, Macmillan, 1988; *C.S. Lewis and His World* by David Barratt, Grand Rapids, Michigan, Eerdmans, 1988; *The Taste of the Pineapple: Essays on C.S. Lewis as Reader, Critic, and Imaginative Writer* edited by Bruce L. Edwards, Bowling Green, Ohio, Bowling Green State University Press, 1988; *Owen Barfield on C.S. Lewis* edited by G.B. Tennyson, Middletown, Connecticut, Wesleyan University Press, 1989; *The Riddle of Joy: G.K. Chesterton and C.S. Lewis* edited by Michael H. Macdonald and Andrew A. Tadie, Grand Rapids, Michigan, Eerdmans, and London, Collins, 1989; *C.S. Lewis: A Biography* by A.N. Wilson, London, Collins, and New York, Norton, 1990; *The C.S. Lewis Handbook* by Colin

Duriez, Eastbourne, Monarch, and Grand Rapids, Michigan, Baker, 1990; *The Magical World of the Inklings: J.R.R. Tolkien, C.S. Lewis, Charles Williams, Owen Barfield* by Gareth Knight, Shaftsbury, Element, 1990; *A Christian for All Christians: Essays in Honour of C.S. Lewis* edited by Andrew Walker and James Patrick, London, Hodder and Stoughton, 1990.

*   *   *

C.S. Lewis is a unique figure. He once described himself as a specimen of a nearly extinct species, "old Western Man": and certainly we had no right to hope for such an author to appear in the 20th century. He has written in many guises: as medieval scholar, lay theologian, fantasist, poet. But his essential role has total inner consistency: he is above all the most powerful defender of traditional Christianity that this century has seen; and his apologia works, not through formal argument, but through images, through suggestion, through poetic creation. All his life, Lewis was haunted by *Sehnsucht,* a longing for strange beauty which the actual world could never wholly satisfy; and this led him, in early middle life, to identify the source and object of his longing with the Christian heaven and the Christian God. His subsequent creative work was a sustained imaginative polemic for this view of the universe.

Lewis is a science fiction writer, arguably, in only one short story, "Ministering Angels," and one novel, *Out of the Silent Planet.* Both are set on Mars; but the Mars of the novel is a Christian paradise ruled by an archangel. This is the first novel of Lewis's so-called "space trilogy"; the second novel, *Perelandra,* is set on Venus, and the third, *That Hideous Strength,* on Earth but with interplanetary connections. All three novels feature the same hero, Elwin Ransom, and all are a unique mixture of SF and what seem to be fantasy elements. In each novel an important part is played by the "eldils," a species of angels inhabiting interplanetary space whose bodies are composed of semi-visible light; but in the first two novels there is also a spaceship, and in the third novel a type of cyborg, a severed human head kept alive by advanced scientific technology. This mixture of science and the supernatural in the trilogy is deliberate and indeed essential; for the fundamental theme of the whole trilogy is the clash between evil modern scientism and old-fashioned Christianity. The trilogy in fact defies generic classification: it is very dubiously science fiction, by reason of all those angels (and devils, in the second and third novels), yet it is not exactly fantasy either, for the author firmly believes in the actual existence of his supernatural entities, and is out to convince us, with all the power of his very powerful art, of their reality and supreme importance. It is this polemic purpose which may repel some readers: Lewis himself has stated (*Of Other Worlds*) that *Perelandra,* at least, was written essentially for Christians only.

But *Out of the Silent Planet* is less overtly Christian, and should appeal to a wide readership by the sheer beauty of its style and images. The inner action of this novel is twofold: it is partly a *Bildungsroman,* effecting the re-education of Ransom, and through him of the reader; and partly a physical and intellectual defeat of human-racist expansionism. Ransom, an ordinary, decent literary scholar, is kidnapped by the ruthless physicist Professor Weston and his capitalist collaborator Devine and taken in Weston's secret spaceship to Mars, for Weston mistakenly believes that the "primitive natives" of Mars have demanded a human sacrifice in exchange for gold. Mars ("Malacandra") proves to be a beautiful, paradisal planet, and the natives comprise three intelligent species, all living in friendship and complementary collaboration, and all ruled by the

nearly invisible eldil Oyarsa from his paradise-island of Meldilorn. Ransom escapes from his human captors, takes refuge among the "hrossa," the seal-like poetic species, and learns the Malacandrian language. He is thus equipped to serve as interpreter in the climactic scene of the novel when Weston and Devine are arrested by the hrossa and brought to Oyarsa for judgment. This trial scene is one of the clearest, wittiest, and most striking portrayals in imaginative fiction of the clash between human-racist expansionism and the opposing school of thought—the school now represented chiefly by the ecology movement. Weston boasts to Oyarsa that nothing will stop the human race from conquering the universe, moving on from planet to planet as each world dies. Oyarsa refutes Weston with the question: "And when all are dead?"—to which Weston has no answer. After this the humans, including Ransom, are forced to return to Earth, whereupon their spaceship is destroyed by angelic power.

One other aspect of *Out of the Silent Planet* should be noted: it is a polemic parody of H.G. Wells's *The First Men in the Moon.* Like Wells, Lewis has a spherical "backyard spaceship" built by a scientist and a capitalist, and the capitalist in each novel is out for the gold of the strange planet. Lewis's main changes are two: he introduces an explicitly Christian viewpoint in the extra character Ransom; and where Wells goes for effects of horror, Lewis goes for beauty.

Perelandra is a sequel in that once more Weston lands on another planet—Venus—and once more is opposed by Ransom; but essentially the work is a variation on Milton's *Paradise Lost.* Venus (Perelandra) is a mostly oceanic world with only two inhabitants—its innocent Adam and Eve. Soon after Weston's arrival, he is possessed by a devil—and he proceeds to tempt the Perelandrian Eve to violate God's sole prohibition. At last Ransom understands his mission, and ends the temptation by destroying Weston. The Venusian paradise is saved, a second Fall is averted. This novel is an even greater achievement than *Out of the Silent Planet:* the action, limited to three characters, has concentrated dramatic power, and the scenery—the floating vegetable islands and seas of Venus—is of a beauty which has never been surpassed by an imaginative writer. It is magnificent—but it is hardly science fiction. That might also be said of the trilogy's final novel, *That Hideous Strength.* The Devil is confronted this time on Earth by planetary angels, Ransom, and the Arthurian wizard Merlin, and the wicked are destroyed in a magic holocaust.

Also relevant to Lewis's SF are his Narnia novels for children. These may be called fantasy, since they are set in and around an imaginary world (Narnia) where magic is commonplace and the inhabitants include giants, dwarfs, dragons, fauns, centaurs, and talking animals. But Narnia has an intellectual solidity similar to SF and lacking in some fantasy worlds of other writers, since it exists in a parallel universe also created, like this one of ours, by God: it is a universe whose Earth is flat, and whose stars are living beings. It is also, as usual in Lewis, a universe of marvellous beauty. Lewis is also an important critic of SF and related genres, chiefly in the essay collection *Of Other Worlds.* His remarks on characterization are justly famous.

Taking his work as a whole, one must note that although Lewis wrote little that is certainly SF, he is of the first importance in the history of this genre through the sheer power of his imagination, his ability to create beautiful worlds which are wholly realized in their actuality; and through the enormous pressure of his moral commitment, which supplies tension throughout the action of every one of his stories. Above all, he has been a most effective opponent of those who would like to see the human race give itself up to the demon of scientism, the spirit which desires the total conquest of the universe.

—David Lake

LICHTENBERG, Jacqueline

Pseudonym: Daniel R. Kerns. **Nationality:** American. **Born:** Flushing, New York, 25 March 1942. **Education:** University of California, Berkeley, B.S. in chemistry 1964. **Family:** Married Salomon Lichtenberg; two daughters. **Career:** Industrial chemist for two years, including one year in Israel. Since 1968, freelance writer. Reviewer of science fiction and fantasy in *The Monthly Aspectarian.* **Agent:** Richard Curtis Literary Agency, 171 East 74th Street, New York, New York 10021, U.S.A. **Address:** 8 Fox Lane, Spring Valley, New York 10977, U.S.A. **Online Address:** XEYQ30A@Prodigy.com.

Science Fiction Publications

Novels (series: Dushau; Kren; Luren; Sime/Gen)

House of Zeor (Sime/Gen). Garden City, New York, Doubleday, 1974.
Unto Zeor, Forever (Sime/Gen). Garden City, New York, Doubleday, 1978.
First Channel (Sime/Gen), with Jean Lorrah. Garden City, New York, Doubleday, 1980.
Mahogany Trinrose: A Sime/Gen Novel. Garden City, New York, Doubleday, 1981.
Channel's Destiny (Sime/Gen), with Jean Lorrah. Garden City, New York, Doubleday, 1982.
Molt Brother (Kren). New York, Playboy Press, 1982.
RenSime (Sime/Gen). Garden City, New York, Doubleday, 1984.
City of a Million Legends (Kren). New York, Berkley, 1985.
Dushau. New York, Popular Library, 1985.
Farfetch (Dushau). New York, Popular Library, 1985.
Zelerod's Doom: A Sime/Gen Novel, with Jean Lorrah. New York, DAW, 1986.
Outreach (Dushau). New York, Popular Library, 1986.
Those of My Blood (Luren). New York, St. Martin's Press, 1988.
Dreamspy (Luren). New York, St. Martin's Press, 1989.

Other Publications

Novels (as Daniel R. Kerns)

Hero. New York, Ace, 1993.
Border Dispute. New York, Ace, 1994.

Other

Star Trek Lives!, with Sondra Marshak and Joan Winston. New York, Bantam, and London, Corgi, 1975.

*

Jacqueline Lichtenberg comments:

As I see it, the emotional substance of the Sime Series is an examination of the fear/compassion axis of emotion that can exist between symbionts. The Sime mutation brings evolutionary pressure to bear on otherwise rather ordinary human beings to develop compassion or die. It is stunning how difficult it is to find true compassion untinged by fear in a human. But when you do find it, it is more precious than life itself. The Sime/Gen mutation is considered as another on the order of the differentiation into male and female, only the second such step ever taken.

The style in which I write emphasizes psychological problems with psychological action and resolution, rather than the standard action/adventure formula in which it is considered bad form to characterize or motivate. I aim my work basically at women between 18 and 25, though anyone who has been such an age should enjoy it as well. I am constantly surprised at the number of fans who don't fit that description, surprised and delighted to no end.

*   *   *

Jacqueline Lichtenberg began her career in science fiction as the author of *Star Trek* fan fiction, and is the creator of one of the largest and most popular of the fannish "universes" in which the cast of the *U.S.S. Enterprise* goes where no man (or woman) has gone before. Her series, notable for its complexity, and for Lichtenberg's willingness to allow other writers to participate in it, is described in *Star Trek Lives!* This spirit of cooperation, as well as the emphases within this universe on symbiosis between dissimilar creatures who come to love one another and on psychological intensity, have carried over into Lichtenberg's "independent" fiction.

Lichtenberg has three series universes. The first, and earliest, is the one begun in *House of Zeor,* which introduced her readers to the symbiotic Simes and Gens. Simes are tentacled, almost vampiric humanoids who mutated from the parent stock after a genetic catastrophe. In order to live, they must take selyn from the second mutation, the human-appearing Gens. The problem is that selyn transfer usually kills the Gen. As the series progressed from *House of Zeor,* in which the idea of "channels," certain genetically gifted Simes capable of taking selyn without harming Gens and "channeling" it to other Simes, through *Unto Zeor, Forever,* in which an injured channel confronts the Sime's fascination with fear and pain by becoming a surgeon, into the Lichtenberg and Jean Lorrah collaborations *First Channel* and *Channel's Destiny,* which show the origins of the Farris family (the Farrises are among the most talented channels) who rule the House of Zeor, several themes emerge. One is the bonding of unlikely beings who must struggle with prejudice. Another is the curious interdependence of Sime and Gen, in which the vastly stronger and faster Sime turns out to be the weak, dependent link after all. A third is the toughness of Lichtenberg's characters, who seem never to give up. This toughness is manifested in subsequent books—*Mahogany Trinrose,* in which a Farris daughter persists until she produces a new genetic variant of an old species and is thought to be a witch, and *RenSime,* in which a Farris woman who is not a channel copes with her despair at not being what she was born to be. Subsequent books in this series include another collaboration with Jean Lorrah, *Zelerod's Doom;* Lorrah plans to produce a few Sime/Gen novels independently.

Molt Brother is Lichtenberg's first novel set in a different, high-tech universe. It and its sequel, *City of a Million Legends,* introduce the kren, reptilian beings with venomed fangs who are vulnerable only when they molt. At that time, they choose molt brothers (or sisters) to guard them. This bond, like the selyn transfer for Simes, is perilous, profound, and occasionally ecstatic. *Molt Brother* is the story of Arshel Holtether, an esper archeologist who chooses a human molt brother and enters worlds of intrigue, danger, and self-discovery. It is also the story of Zref, a human/computer interface unable to link completely with his own mechanical symbiote.

Lichtenberg's series about a species called the Dushau also displays her preoccupation with symbiotes. In this trilogy (*Dushau, Farfetch,* and *Outreach*) set in a high-tech, tyrannical, and rather Byzantine galactic empire, a young woman closely connected with the court wants above all else to join a bonded group of Dushau, long-lived alien empaths who can practically bond into planetary ecologies. Because the empire suspects the Dushau of wanting independence, it is systematically exterminating them. One bond group flees a police cruiser to a planet that becomes its ally as Dushau, the human heroine, and a host of minor characters set the stage for revolution.

All of Lichtenberg's books are marked by an extraordinary density of thought. She creates extremely dangerous characters: the sinister Simes, the venomous kren whose pain somehow makes them vulnerable and understandable to her often fanatic readers. Her writing is notable for intensity rather than lyricism. Frequently her books are painful to read because of her insistence on confronting breakdowns in communication (which occasionally makes her writing tortuous and harsh) and extending them out into catastrophe. She specializes in creating a psychological "worst-case" scenario and then rehabilitating the characters who encounter it. In order to supply communication, Lichtenberg creates bonds like transfer, molt brotherhood, or the symbiosis in Dushau, but even these bonds are imperfect, if only because their severing causes anguish.

As can be seen from Lichtenberg's willingness to allow other writers to participate in her universes, she is a generous teacher, who has participated in many writers workshops, notably the one sponsored at Murray State University in Kentucky. Her fans have published three fanzines that feature letters, reviews, fragments of manuscripts, and original Sime/Gen stories by amateur writers. The audience for her work is among the most dedicated in the field, and Lichtenberg is notable for her willingness to enter their lives as generously as she has opened her worlds to them.

—Susan Shwartz

LIGHTNER, Alice (Martha)

Pseudonym: Alice L. Hopf. **Nationality:** American. **Born:** Detroit, Michigan, 11 October 1904. **Education:** Westover School, Middlebury, Connecticut, graduated 1923; Vassar College, Poughkeepsie, New York, B.A. 1927. **Family:** Married Ernest Joachim Hopf in 1935; one son. **Career:** Editorial assistant, Civil Engineering; clerk-typist, Grey Advertising, New York. From 1951, freelance writer. **Awards:** National Science Teachers Association award, 1972, 1973. **Died:** 3 February 1988.

SCIENCE FICTION PUBLICATIONS

Novels (for children; series: Rock)

The Rock of Three Planets. New York, Putnam, 1963.

The Planet Poachers (Rock). New York, Putnam, 1965.
Doctor to the Galaxy. New York, Norton, 1965.
The Galactic Troubadours. New York, Norton, 1965.
The Space Plague. New York, Norton, 1966.
The Space Olympics. New York, Norton, 1967.
The Space Ark (Rock). New York, Putnam, 1968.
The Day of the Drones. New York, Norton, 1969.
The Thursday Toads. New York, McGraw Hill, 1971.
Gods or Demons? New York, Four Winds Press, 1973.
Star Dog. New York, McGraw Hill, 1973.
The Space Gypsies. New York, McGraw Hill, 1974.
Star Circus. New York, Dutton, 1977.

OTHER PUBLICATIONS

Novel

The Walking Zoo of Darwin Dingle (for children). New York, Putnam, 1969.

Poetry

The Pillar and the Flame. New York, Vinal, 1928.

Other as Alice L. Hopf (for children)

Monarch Butterflies. New York, Crowell, 1965.
Wild Traveler: The Story of a Coyote. New York, Norton, 1967.
Earth's Bug-Eyed Monsters. New York, Norton, 1968.
Butterfly and Moth. New York, Putnam, 1969.
Carab, The Trap-Door Spider. New York, Putnam, 1970.
Biography of an Octopus [a Rhino, an Ostrich, an Ant, an Armadillo, an American Reindeer, a Giraffe, a Snowy Owl, a Komodo Dragon]. New York, Putnam, 9 vols., 1971-81.
Misunderstood Animals. New York, McGraw Hill, 1973.
Wild Cousins of the Dog [Cat, Horse]. New York, Putnam, 3 vols., 1973-77.
Misplaced Animals and Other Living Creatures. New York, McGraw Hill, 1975.
Animal and Plant Life Spans. New York, Holiday House, 1978.
Animals That Eat Nectar and Honey. New York, Holiday House, 1979.
Nature's Pretenders. New York, Putnam, 1979.
Pigs Wild and Tame. New York, Holiday House, 1979.
Whose House Is It? New York, Dodd Mead, 1980.
Bugs, Big and Little. New York, Messner, 1981.
Strange Sex Lives in the Animal Kingdom. New York, McGraw Hill, 1981.
Chickens and Their Wild Relatives. New York, Dodd Mead, 1982.
Hyenas. New York, Dodd Mead, 1983.
Bats. New York, Dodd Mead, 1985.
Spiders. New York, Dutton, 1990.

*

Manuscript Collection: Fullerton College Library, California.

*   *   *

Alice Lightner was an author of children's books, at home in nonfiction as well as SF. Her informational books about animal life are popular with young readers and have received honors from science teachers because of their solid, up-to-date information, enthusiastic concern for ecology and conservation, and capacity for explaining on a child's level of comprehension. Similar qualities mark Lightner's SF. Actually, so prominent is the last quality that in spite of lacking a prose style as supple as Norton's or an imagination as inventive as Heinlein's, Lightner has produced a body of SF that is perhaps more readily open to and enjoyed by youngsters than either of theirs.

The typical Lightner novel is an amalgam of SF and the young adult novel. The most prominent of the former is the presence of "alien" animals: either ones that do not exist today but whose future existence may be extrapolated (a unicorn-like gazelle, for instance, or a telepathic bird that can speak) or ones that are unexpected mutations of species currently existing (giant bees, for example). Another prominent SF feature is exotic setting, most often a planet newly discovered which needs to be explored and surveyed and whose flora and fauna require cataloguing and preserving. Young adult elements usually found in Lightner's fiction are mystery and dashes of romance and humor in addition to the requisite youthful protagonists. (Incidentally, Lightner is one of the very few writers of children's SF who regularly incorporate females among their protagonists.) So determined is Lightner to appeal to youth that sometimes, as in *The Galactic Troubadours,* she sacrifices plausibility for topicality: a band of rock and roll musicians make a nuisance of themselves as they travel from planet to planet. In general, though, Lightner has been successful in her mix.

Lightner's most successful novel is *The Day of the Drones.* Set in the future when nuclear conflict has poisoned the Earth and obliterated virtually everyone, the book concerns the Afrians—descendants of a small group of surviving black Africans who have managed to rebuild civilization by placing under taboo most technology and by practicing strict genetic control. Those born darkest-skinned will enjoy most privileges; fair-skinned babies, less; the occasional white baby is simply abandoned. A small group of Afrians set out to ascertain whether any other human survivors exist. In what was once England the Afrians come across the Anglics, descendants of the ancient English who are cruel, superstition-ridden, and white. They too practice social engineering, having established a bizarre matriarchy modeled upon bee-society. The impact of *The Day of the Drones* is threefold. One, the description of the two differing cultures is detailed and plausible. Second, characterization is rounded and convincing; none of the several protagonists is a mouthpiece for conventional sentiments or moral posturing. Especially interesting is Anhara, the young Afrian archeologist who has mastered Anglic so that she can appreciate the little Shakespeare that is extant and becomes sorrowed at the degradation of the race that produced the Master. Third, the investigation of racism, whether black or white, and its demeaning effects is matter-of-fact and evenhanded, hence, neither sensational nor preachy. The book, then, is impressive and challenging; as such it must be ranked among the relatively few superior examples of children's SF.

—Francis J. Molson

LINAWEAVER, Brad

Nationality: American. **Born:** North Carolina, 9 January 1952. **Education:** Florida State University, B.A.; Rollins College, Florida, M.A. **Family:** Married Cynthia-Cari Holloway, 1985 (separated); one stepdaughter. **Career:** Has worked as teacher in English, actor, and movie theater manager. Since 1974, freelance journalist. **Awards:** Prometheus award, 1989. **Agent:** Ricia Mainhardt, 612 Argyle No. L5, Brooklyn, New York, 11230, U.S.A. **Address:** 8833 Sunset Boulevard, Suite 304, Los Angeles, California 90069, U.S.A.

SCIENCE FICTION PUBLICATIONS

Novel

Moon of Ice. New York, Arbor House, 1988; London, Grafton, 1989.

*

Brad Linaweaver comments:

I've never understood the desire to take popular fiction, already in a ghetto, and break it into ever smaller pieces, pretending there is no tissue tying all the parts together. I write science fiction, fantasy, and horror. I'm not interested in specializing in one of these areas when it is painfully obvious that they are interconnected—as if a clear line could ever be drawn between different kinds of speculative fiction. Furthermore, I want to write mystery and straight historical before I'm through!

*   *   *

One of the most popular forms in science fiction has long been the Uchronia, or alternate history story. What might have happened had the South won the Civil War, if the Industrial Revolution had occurred a century earlier, if Napoleon had succeeded at Waterloo? Hundreds of stories have been written within the field, and the fascination of the theme has appealed to historians and writers not normally associated with the genre as well as those to whom it is just one of the tools of the trade. Perhaps the most popular of these questions involves World War II, what might have occurred had Germany won and the Nazis become the dominant force in international politics. The answers have been dealt with in many different ways, everything from the phantasmagorical *The Sound of His Horn* by Sarban to Philip K. Dick's classic, *The Man in the High Castle.* It might well be considered a vein of ideas long overworked, but Brad Linaweaver's first, and so far only, full-length work has taken that proposition and developed it into a major contribution to the field, a rare achievement for any writer, let alone one who had never produced a novel previously.

Originally a shorter work with the same title, *Moon of Ice* appeared in its full-length version in 1988 to nearly universal acclaim. Franklin Roosevelt was impeached and replaced with a more isolationist president, which gave Germany the time it needed to complete its own development of nuclear weapons. With that capacity, the conquest of Europe and Africa was a foregone conclusion, and now the Nazis control a large portion of the world directly, heavily influencing most of the rest. The U.S. has become even more libertarian than in our own reality, but still avoids unnecessary contact with the German empire, which has now grown fat and lazy, for the most part content with its expansion, still in the process of absorbing the disparate populations it has overrun, finally acceding to the necessity of compromising in its foreign policy in order to maintain a somewhat shaky economy.

Hilda Goebbels, daughter of one of Hitler's most trusted assistants, is repelled by the excesses and inhumanity of her own government and has become a prominent revolutionary living abroad. To this end, she has stolen her father's secret diaries and offered them and her own personal memoirs to an American publisher. Obviously this is a major coup since the diaries in particular provide detailed insight into the madness that dominated the inner circles of Hitler's closest associates, and the protagonist jumps at the opportunity to handle these works. But when he does so, he gains deep insight into a group of men held firmly in the grip of insanity, a madness which they have imposed on the people they rule. Already a new religion has been established which accepts concepts that fly in the face of observable reality (the moon is ice, for example, hence the title), and the concept of total world dominion has not been abandoned despite appearances to the contrary.

The novel is remarkable for several reasons, not the least of which is the intriguing, mystery-laden, and suspenseful plot. Linaweaver has done extensive research into the Nazi phenomenon, and his depiction of their belief in arcane magical lore and occult powers is both historically accurate and frightening. The description of Europe under the German juggernaut is evocative and chilling, just as his portrayal of an isolated, uninvolved America is convincing and depressing. His characters are fully realized and credible, neither totally villainous nor virtuous beyond flaw. His prose is careful, precise, and economical, perhaps a result of his previous experience as a journalist. *Moon of Ice* has the feel of a novel by a practiced professional, with none of the hesitancy or startling exuberance of a normal first novel. The shorter version, first published in 1982, was a finalist in the Nebula balloting for best story of the year.

Most of Linaweaver's shorter fiction through the 1980s has been to shared world anthologies, that is, those which present a common setting within which each individual author is free to experiment. Although it is often difficult to produce first rate fiction under these restrictions, Linaweaver has provided some interesting stories in this area. "High Road of the Lost Men" is set in the postnuclear-collapse universe of the late Robert Adams, and utilizes an almost fairytale style to unfold the story of survival amidst a great physical cataclysm. The same style serves him well in "Dream Pirates' Jewel," written in collaboration with Cynthia Linaweaver and set in Andre Norton's Witch World fantasy series, and in "Shadow Quest," set in the Ithkar Fair series, wherein an apprentice sorcerer has a strange series of experiences which mark his emergence as a full-fledged practitioner of the magical arts.

In recent years he has returned to his fascination with alternate histories. "Destination: Indies" is probably the best of these, a series of excerpts supposedly taken from a biography of Christopher Columbus. Also of interest is "Unmerited Favor," which examines the potential changes to historical events if Jesus of Nazareth had taken a somewhat more militant approach to reforming religion. "Press Conference" is an amusing tale set in a universe where superheroes really do exist, a device that has become increasingly popular in the genre during the last decade.

Linaweaver's failure to develop an active following among readers is certainly a consequence of his relative lack of productivity. The single novel, which inexplicably languished for some time before appearing in a mass market edition, and a handful of shorter pieces are all that he has produced in a career that has spanned more than 10 years. It is because of the high level of quality in that small body of published work that he continues to be respected and his work anticipated. *Moon of Ice* proved that Linaweaver has

the necessary tools to become one of the field's leaders. It remains to be seen whether or not he will fill that role.

—Don D'Ammassa

LINDSAY, David

Nationality: British. **Born:** Blackheath, London, 3 March 1876. **Education:** Lewisham Grammar School, London, and a secondary school in Jedburgh, Roxburgh. **Military Service:** Served in the Grenadier Guards, 1916-18. **Family:** Married Jacqueline Silver in 1916; two daughters. **Career:** Worked for Price Forbes, insurance brokers, 1894-1916; lived in Cornwall, 1919-29, and after 1929 in Sussex. **Died:** 16 July 1945.

SCIENCE FICTION PUBLICATIONS

Novels

A Voyage to Arcturus. London, Methuen, 1920; New York, Macmillan, 1963.
The Haunted Woman. London, Methuen, 1922; Hollywood, Newcastle, 1975.
Sphinx. London, Long, 1923; New York, Carroll and Graf, 1988.
Devil's Tor. London, Putnam, 1932; New York, Arno Press, 1978.
The Violet Apple [and] *The Witch.* Chicago, Chicago Review Press, 1976.
The Violet Apple. London, Sidgwick and Jackson, 1978.

OTHER PUBLICATIONS

Novel

Adventures of Monsieur de Mailly. London, Melrose, 1926; as *A Blade for Sale: The Adventures of Monsieur de Mailly,* New York, McBride, 1927.

*

Critical Studies: *The Strange Genius of David Lindsay* by J.B. Pick, Colin Wilson, and E.H. Visiak, London, Baker, 1970, as *The Haunted Man,* San Bernardino, California, Borgo Press, 1979; *The Life and Works of David Lindsay* by Bernard Sellin, translated by Kenneth Gunnell, Cambridge, University Press, 1981; *David Lindsay* by Gary K. Wolfe, Mercer Island, Washington, Starmont House, 1982.

*   *   *

While David Lindsay's first novel, *A Voyage to Arcturus,* has become recognized as one of the masterworks of 20th-century fantasy, his other novels remain unknown to all but a handful of readers, and the man himself remains a curiously distant and enigmatic figure. More a philosopher than a novelist, Lindsay wrote often awkward and laborious prose, his later work filled with long expository digressions, his ideas so complex and densely packed, his characters so unsympathetic, that many readers find his fiction at first coldly intellectual and difficult to get into. But Lindsay undeniably expanded the possibilities of fantasy as philosophical fiction, and his influence has been widely felt among modern authors as diverse as Colin Wilson and Philip José Farmer.

Lindsay's masterpiece, *A Voyage to Arcturus,* concerns the journey of a man named Maskull to Tormance, a world in the system Arcturus, where he encounters bizarre characters and himself undergoes physical transformations in a series of episodes depicting different systems of belief not unlike the different moral systems at work on Earth. As each of these moral systems is shown to be illusory, Maskull is gradually brought to a confrontation with the godlike villain Crystalman, who controls this world, and who seems, at the end, to represent the entire world of phenomenal experience. Drawing on Nietzsche, Schopenhauer, and Norse mythology for ideas and imagery, Lindsay develops a world of vivid scenery and violent action that nevertheless is rigidly structured according to the philosophical ideas he wishes to explore. The novel is a remarkable union of action and idea.

Ideas were more interesting to Lindsay than action, however, and his later novels contained little of the violent action of *Arcturus. The Haunted Woman* continued exploring the notion of subjective reality in a romance of two lovers who could only acknowledge their love in a phantom room of a haunted house. *Sphinx* turned to the science fiction device of a dream-recording machine to explore the romance between a woman composer and a writer. Like *A Voyage to Arcturus* itself, however, each of these novels was a commercial disaster, and Lindsay turned to the historical romance for his next book, *Adventures of Monsieur de Mailly,* a tale of court intrigue that nevertheless also reflected Lindsay's preoccupations with illusion and deception. *Devil's Tor* is a sprawling, slow-moving, and at times brilliant exposition of the myth of the Eternal Feminine, in a story concerning the reuniting of two halves of an ancient stone and the founding of a new race by a chosen man and woman.

Lindsay was unable to find a publisher for *The Violet Apple,* and he left another manuscript, "The Witch," unfinished. Both works were finally published in abridged form, and both retain the romance structure of *The Haunted Woman* and *Devil's Tor.* In *The Violet Apple* a dwarf apple tree, grown from a seed which according to legend came from the original tree of Eden, unites the lovers. "The Witch" explores the dual myths of the wise woman and witchcraft in a work whose controlling image is music. Though none of these later works achieves the narrative power of *A Voyage to Arcturus,* they nevertheless stand as worthwhile philosophical meditations and as studies in the problems inherent in trying to write a truly philosophical fiction.

—Gary K. Wolfe

LLEWELLYN, (David William) Alun

Nationality: Irish. **Born:** London, England, 17 April 1903. **Education:** Alleyn's School, Dulwich, London; St. John's College, Cambridge (Chancellor's Gold Medal, for poetry, 1923; College Literature prize, 1924), B.A. (honours) in history and literature 1924, LL.B. (honours) 1925, M.A. 1928; Lincoln's Inn, London: called to the Bar, 1927. **Military Service:** Served in the Intelligence Corps during World War II. **Family:** Married Lesley Deane in 1953. **Career:** Treaty translator and reviser, League of Nations, Geneva, 1936-39; legal adviser, Egyptian government, Montreux Capitulations, 1937; Secretary of the Compensation Tribunal for Coal Nationalisation, 1947-49; counsel, Camberwell Borough, London, 1951-53; public relations speaker, Commonwealth Industries Association, 1955-72. Liberal parliamentary candidate for South Croydon, 1931, 1935. **Member:** President, Union Society, 1935, and Hardwicke Society, 1953, both Middle Temple, London; Honorary Treasurer, Poetry Society of Great Britain, 1961-62. Since 1977, Honorary Secretary, and President, 1984-86, Irish P.E.N. Member, Welsh Academy, 1983. **Address:** 52 Silchester Park, Glenageary, Dun Laoghaire, County Dublin, Ireland.

SCIENCE FICTION PUBLICATIONS

Novel

The Strange Invaders. London, Bell, 1934.

OTHER PUBLICATIONS

Novels

The Deacon. London, Bell, 1934.
The Soul of Cézar Azan. London, Barker, 1938.
Jubilee John. London, Barker, 1939.

Short Stories

Confound Their Politics. London, Bell, 1934.

Plays

Ways of Love (produced 1968). London, French, 1958.
Shelley Plain (produced London, 1960).

Poetry

Ballads and Songs. London, Stockwell, 1921.

Other

History of the Union Society of London. London, Union Society, 1935.
The Emperor of Britain. London, Montgomeryshire Society, 1939.
The Tyrant from Below: An Essay in Political Revaluation. London, Macdonald and Evans, 1957.
The World and the Commonwealth. London, British Commonwealth Union, 1968.
The Shell Guide to Wales. London, Rainbird, 1969.

*

Alun Llewellyn comments:

Only one of my novels is, strictly speaking, science fiction. *The Strange Invaders* looks at this planet and the ecological change upon it as a result of Man's abandonment of Mind as a motive force of his evolution. But since all human psychology is a matter for scientific analysis, and is a more subtle matter than mechanistic theories of economics or sex can explain, the studies in my other novels of the illusions of love, religion, ambition, and power ought really to be called fictional illustrations of scientific themes. By this interpretation, all my fiction qualifies as SF.

*　　*　　*

Alun Llewellyn's *The Strange Invaders* is a fantasy set in the future when the habitable area of the Earth is gradually decreasing as a new ice age emerges. Mankind has retrogressed; as a result of disastrous wars it has lost the art of civilization and is living in a pre-iron age existence. The story takes place in what seems to be the Gobi desert, a somewhat hostile environment but one of the last places on Earth capable of supporting human life. The plot concerns a small group of people living in a half-destroyed town, isolated within the remains of a ruined city on the plains. There is a pseudo-medieval order to their existence: governed by a religious community of priests dedicated to the new trinity of Marx, Lenin, and Stalin, and controlled by a warrior group, they manage to eke out a life of basic survival. As if their plight were not bad enough, Llewellyn has this last outpost of humanity threatened by an army of enormous lizards—huge, cold-blooded creatures that are virtually invincible. The plot is concerned with the efforts of the community to survive in the face of this new and overpowering challenge. What elevates the story above the ordinary is Llewellyn's ability to show how the basic human emotions of love, hate, and jealousy survive and dominate the lives of these people even in the face of overwhelming danger and the threat of extinction.

Though the novel is cast in the form of a futuristic nightmare, it is difficult for the reader to remember that the time frame is the future and not the past. So vividly does Llewellyn evoke the sense of life of these people and so much is their life a reliving of prehistorical civilization, that the reader inevitably feels that he has been transported into the past rather than into the future.

—Joseph A. Quinn

LONDON, Jack

Nationality: American. **Born:** John Griffith London, San Francisco, California, 12 January 1876. **Education:** Grammar school in Oakland, California; Oakland High School, 1895-96; University of California, Berkeley, 1896-97. **Family:** Married 1) Bessie Maddern in 1900 (separated 1903; divorced 1905), two daughters; 2) Charmian Kittredge in 1905. **Career:** Worked in a cannery in Oakland, 1890; sailor on the *Sophie Sutherland,* sailing to Japan and Siberia, 1893; returned to Oakland, wrote for the local paper, and held various odd jobs, 1893-94; tramped the United States and Canada, 1894-96; arrested for vagrancy in Niagara Falls, New York; joined the gold rush to the Klondike, 1897-98, then returned to Oakland and became a full-time writer; visited London, 1902; war correspondent in the Russo-Japanese War for the *San Francisco Examiner,* 1904; settled on a ranch in Sonoma County, California, 1906, and lived there for the rest of his life; attempted to sail round the world on a 45-foot yacht, 1907-09; war correspondent in Mexico, 1914. **Died:** 22 November 1916.

SCIENCE FICTION PUBLICATIONS

Novels

Before Adam. New York, Macmillan, 1906; London, Laurie, 1908.
The Iron Heel. New York, Macmillan, and London, Everett, 1907.
The Scarlet Plague. New York, Macmillan, and London, Mills and Boon, 1915.
The Star Rover. New York, Macmillan, 1915; as *The Jacket (The Star Rover),* London, Mills and Boon, 1915.
Hearts of Three. London, Mills and Boon, 1918; New York, Macmillan, 1920.

Short Stories

The Strength of the Strong (story). Chicago, Kerr, 1911.
The Dream of Debs: A Story of Industrial Revolution. Chicago, Kerr, 1912.
The Strength of the Strong (collection). New York, Macmillan, 1914; London, Mills and Boon, 1917.
The Red One. New York, Macmillan, 1918; London, Mills and Boon, 1919.
Short Stories, edited by Maxwell Geismar. New York, Hill and Wang, 1960.
Goliah: A Utopian Essay. Berkeley, California, Thorp Springs Press, 1973.
Curious Fragments: Jack London's Tales of Fantasy Fiction, edited by Dale L. Walker. Port Washington, New York, Kennikat Press, 1975.
The Science Fiction of Jack London, edited by Richard Gid Powers. Boston, Gregg Press, 1975.
The Scarlet Plague and Other Stories. Stroud, England, Alan Sutton, 1995.

OTHER PUBLICATIONS

Novels

The Cruise of the Dazzler. New York, Century, 1902; London, Hodder and Stoughton, 1906.
A Daughter of the Snows. Philadelphia, Lippincott, 1902; London, Isbister, 1904.
The Kempton-Wace Letters (published anonymously), with Anna Strunsky. New York, Macmillan, and London, Isbister, 1903.
The Call of the Wild. New York, Macmillan, and London, Heinemann, 1903.
The Sea-Wolf. New York, Macmillan, and London, Heinemann, 1904.
The Game. New York, Macmillan, and London, Heinemann, 1905.
White Fang. New York, Macmillan, 1906; London, Methuen, 1907.
Martin Eden. New York, Macmillan, 1909; London, Heinemann, 1910.
Burning Daylight. New York, Macmillan, 1910; London, Heinemann, 1911.
Adventure. London, Nelson, and New York, Macmillan, 1911.
The Abysmal Brute. New York, Century, 1913; London, Newnes, 1914.
John Barleycorn. New York, Century, 1913; London, Mills and Boon, 1914.
The Valley of the Moon. New York, Macmillan, and London, Mills and Boon, 1913.

The Mutiny of the Elsinore. New York, Macmillan, 1914; London, Mills and Boon, 1915.

The Little Lady of the Big House. New York, Macmillan, and London, Mills and Boon, 1916.

Jerry of the Islands. New York, Macmillan, and London, Mills and Boon, 1917.

Michael, Brother of Jerry. New York, Macmillan, 1917; London, Mills and Boon, 1918.

The Assassination Bureau Ltd., completed by Robert L. Fish. New York, McGraw Hill, 1963; London, Deutsch, 1964.

Short Stories

The Son of the Wolf: Tales of the Far North. Boston, Houghton Mifflin, 1900; London, Isbister, 1902; as *An Odyssey of the North,* London, Mills and Boon, 1915.

The God of His Fathers and Other Stories. New York, McClure, 1901; London, Isbister, 1902.

Children of the Frost. New York, Macmillan, 1902.

The Faith of Men and Other Stories. New York, Macmillan, and London, Heinemann, 1904.

Tales of the Fish Patrol. New York, Macmillan, 1905; London, Heinemann, 1906.

The Apostate. Chicago, Kerr, 1906.

Moon-Face and Other Stories. New York, Macmillan, and London, Heinemann, 1906.

Love of Life and Other Stories. New York, Macmillan, 1907; London, Everett, 1908.

Lost Face. New York, Macmillan, 1910; London, Mills and Boon, 1915.

When God Laughs and Other Stories. New York, Macmillan, 1911; London, Mills and Boon, 1912.

South Sea Tales. New York, Macmillan, 1911; London, Mills and Boon, 1912.

The House of Pride and Other Tales of Hawaii. New York, Macmillan, 1912; London, Mills and Boon, 1914.

A Son of the Sun. New York, Doubleday, 1912; London, Mills and Boon, 1913; as *The Adventures of Captain Grief,* Cleveland, World, 1954.

Smoke Bellew. New York, Century, 1912; London, Mills and Boon, 1913; as *Smoke and Shorty,* London, Mills and Boon, 1920.

The Night Born. . . . New York, Century, 1913; London, Mills and Boon, 1916.

The Turtles of Tasman. New York, Macmillan, 1916; London, Mills and Boon, 1917.

The Human Drift. New York, Macmillan, 1917; London, Mills and Boon, 1919.

On the Makaloa Mat. New York, Macmillan, 1919; as *Island Tales,* London, Mills and Boon, 1920.

Dutch Courage and Other Stories. New York, Macmillan, 1922; London, Mills and Boon, 1923.

Jack London's Tales of Adventure, edited by Irving Shepard. New York, Hanover House, 1956.

Stories of Hawaii, edited by A. Grove Day. New York, Appleton Century Crofts, 1965.

Great Short Works of Jack London, edited by Earle Labor. New York, Harper, 1965.

The Unabridged Jack London, edited by Lawrence Teacher and Richard E. Nicholls. Philadelphia, Running Press, 1981.

Jack London's Yukon Women. New York, Belmont, 1982.

Young Wolf: The Early Adventure Stories, edited by Howard Lachtman. Santa Barbara, California, Capra Press, 1984.

In a Far Country: Jack London's Western Tales, edited by Dale L. Walker. New York, Jameson, 1986.

Short Stories, edited by Earle Labor, Robert C. Leitz III, and I. Milo Shepard. New York, Macmillan, 1990.

Stories of Boxing, edited by James Bankes. Dubuque, Iowa, William C. Brown, 1992.

Plays

The Great Interrogation, with Less Bascom (produced San Francisco, 1905).

Scorn of Women. New York, Macmillan, 1906; London, Macmillan, 1907.

Theft. New York and London, Macmillan, 1910.

The Acorn Planters: A California Forest Play. . . . New York, Macmillan, and London, Mills and Boon, 1916.

Daughters of the Rich, edited by James E. Sisson. Oakland, California, Holmes, 1971.

Gold, with Herbert Heron, edited by James E. Sisson. Oakland, California, Holmes, 1972.

Other

The People of the Abyss. New York, Macmillan, and London, Isbister, 1903.

The Tramp. New York, Wilshire's Magazine, 1904.

The Scab. Chicago, Kerr, 1904.

Jack London: A Sketch of His Life and Work. London, Macmillan, 1905.

War of the Classes. New York, Macmillan, and London, Heinemann, 1905.

What Life Means to Me. Princeton, New Jersey, Intercollegiate Socialist Society, 1906.

The Road. New York, Macmillan, 1907; London, Mills and Boon, 1914.

Jack London: Who He Is and What He Has Done. New York, Macmillan, 1908(?).

Revolution. Chicago, Kerr, 1909.

Revolution and Other Essays. New York, Macmillan, 1910; London, Mills and Boon, 1920.

The Cruise of the Snark. New York, Macmillan, and London, Mills and Boon, 1911.

Jack London by Himself. New York, Macmillan, and London, Mills and Boon, 1913.

London's Essays of Revolt, edited by Leonard D. Abbott. New York, Vanguard Press, 1926.

Jack London, American Rebel: A Collection of His Social Writings . . . , edited by Philip S. Foner. New York, Citadel Press, 1947.

(Works) [Fitzroy Edition], edited by I.O. Evans. London, Arco, and New York, Archer House and Horizon Press, 18 vols., 1962-68.

The Bodley Head Jack London, edited by Arthur Calder-Marshall. London, Bodley Head, 4 vols., 1963-66; as *The Pan Jack London,* London, Pan, 2 vols., 1966-68.

Letters from Jack London, Containing an Unpublished Correspondence Between London and Sinclair Lewis, edited by King Hendricks and Irving Shepard. New York, Odyssey Press, 1965; London, MacGibbon and Kee, 1966.

Jack London Reports: War Correspondence, Sports Articles, and Miscellaneous Writings, edited by King Hendricks and Irving Shepard. New York, Random House, 1970.

Jack London's Articles and Short Stories in the (Oakland) High School Aegis, edited by James E. Sisson. Cedar Springs, Michigan, London Collector, 1971.

No Mentor But Myself: A Collection of Articles, Essays, Reviews, and Letters on Writing and Writers, edited by Dale L. Walker. Port Washington, New York, Kennikat Press, 1979.

Revolution: Stories and Essays, edited by Robert Barltrop. London, Journeyman Press, 1979.

Jack London on the Road: The Tramp Diary and Other Hobo Writings, edited by Richard W. Etulain. Logan, Utah State University Press, 1979.

Sporting Blood: Selections from Jack London's Greatest Sports Writing, edited by Howard Lachtman. Novato, California, Presidio Press, 1981.

Novels and Stories and Novels and Social Writings (Library of America), edited by Donald Pizer. New York, Literary Classics of the United States, and London, Cambridge University Press, 2 vols., 1982-84.

Jack London's California: The Golden Poppy and Other Writings, edited by Sal Noto. New York, Beaufort, 1986.

The Letters of Jack London, edited by Earle Labor, Robert C. Leitz III, and I. Milo Shepard. Stanford, California, Stanford University Press, 3 vols. 1988.

*

Bibliography: *Jack London: A Bibliography* by Hensley C. Woodbridge, John London, and George H. Tweney, Georgetown, California, Talisman Press, 1966; supplement by Woodbridge, Milwood, New York, Kraus, 1973; in *Bibliography of American Literature 5* by Jacob Blanck, New Haven, Connecticut, Yale University Press, 1969; *The Fiction of Jack London: A Chronological Bibliography* by Dale L. Walker and James E. Sisson, El Paso, University of Texas, 1972; *Jack London: A Reference Guide* by Joan R. Sherman, Boston, Hall, 1977.

Manuscript Collections: Huntington Library, San Marino, California; Utah State University Library, Logan.

Critical Studies: *Jack London: A Biography* by Richard O'Connor, Boston, Little Brown, 1964, London, Gollancz, 1965; *The Alien Worlds of Jack London* by Dale L. Walker, Grand Rapids, Michigan, Wolf House, 1973; *Jack London* by Earle Labor, Boston, Twayne, 1974; *Jack London: The Man, The Writer, The Rebel* by Robert Barltrop, London, Pluto Press, 1976; *Jack: A Biography of Jack London* by Andrew Sinclair, New York, Harper, 1977, London, Weidenfeld and Nicolson, 1978; *Jack London and the Klondike: The Genesis of an American Writer* by Franklin Walker, San Marino, California, Huntington Library Publications, 1978; *Jack London: Essays in Criticism* edited by Ray W. Ownbey, Layton, Utah, Peregrine Smith, 1979; *Jack London: An American Myth* by John Perry, Chicago, Nelson Hall, 1981; *Solitary Comrade: Jack London and His Work* by Joan D. Hedrick, Chapel Hill, University of North Carolina Press, 1982; *The Novels of Jack London* by Charles N. Watson, Madison, University of Wisconsin Press, 1983; *Jack London* by Gordon Beauchamp, Mercer Island, Washington, Starmont House, 1984; *Jack London, An American Radical?* by Carolyn Johnston, Westport, Connecticut, Greenwood Press, 1984; *The Tools of My Trade: The Annotated Books in Jack London's Library* by David Mike Hamilton, Seattle, University of

Washington Press, 1986; *Jack London* by James Lundquist, New York, Ungar, 1987.

*   *   *

Jack London is among the more important American SF writers by virtue of his attention to social and political extrapolation, matters all too often ignored by his compatriots. In almost all of London's science fiction, mankind individually or collectively faces a challenge, be it the challenge of the primitive, the challenge of disaster, or the challenge of socialism.

"A Relic of the Pliocene" is a good example of the challenge of the primitive. In London's arctic, the scene of a good portion of his fiction, a man tells of killing the last mammoth. "When the World Was Young" takes up the theme of a man divided between an identity as a civilized businessman and a primitive savagery that seizes control every night. In "The Strength of the Strong" a cave man tells of the formation of tribes, which increase everyone's strength, and then of classes, which seem to decrease collective strength. London's novel *Before Adam* is entirely situated in primitive times.

The Scarlet Plague is London's most successful disaster novel. To read it today is to realize how tepid are many recent works about disaster. The opening scene alone is a small masterpiece. It presents an old man and two boys walking along a railroad track in the future, destroyed world, the old man reflecting on the contrast between the way things are and the way they were in the old days. This old man, once a college professor at the University of California, goes on to tell of how his world collapsed under the onslaught of the plague, which was always fatal within 30 minutes, and killed most of the world's population, sparing only the old man and about 40 others. These few spawn a new generation in a now-primitive world. The old man tells of the futile efforts at the University of California to save a remnant of the University community, and the equally futile efforts he (the old man) has made to make the new generation understand something of how things once were. Another disaster story is "The Unparalleled Invasion," in which the western nations use germ warfare to defeat the yellow peril—the combined forces of Japan and China. London's much-discussed racism is all too evident in this story.

A good deal of London's SF describes the onset of socialism, usually perceived by the ruling classes as a disaster. In "The Minions of Midas" a secret society blackmails the capitalists into submission by killing their loved ones. A similar story is *Goliah,* in which a discoverer of atomic power blackmails the world into accepting socialism. But London's great work in this mode is *The Iron Heel.* A future America has come under the iron heel of oligarchic corporations, and a working-class hero, Ernest Everhard, struggles to convince certain of the well-to-do that only a revolution can remove the oppression. London ends the book in 1932, when the oligarchy has thwarted one attempt at revolution—but another attempt is planned. Although Everhard is too pure and great, too earnest, London's novel brings to science fiction a high level of political discussion of issues that remain vital.

Almost as well known is "The Dream of Debs," a realistic account of a general strike in San Francisco which succeeds only after the fabric of society is utterly rent. When the wealthy narrator complains that "the tyranny of organized labor is getting beyond human endurance" we can see his point.

Perhaps London's greatest SF work, however, is *The Red One,* which is not cast in any of London's characteristic molds, although it does involve a white man held captive by primitive Sumatrans, thus fitting with London's interest in survival under primitive conditions. The primitive tribe in question worships the red one of the title, a sphere from the stars. The white man gives his head in exchange for the chance to hear the red one's voice. London gives us a remarkable descriptive passage in which the white man hears the alien's message and then dies, his head coveted by the tribal chieftain. The poignancy of this juxtaposition—the man of the present, captivated by the future yet held captive by the past—establishes London's importance and originality as a science fiction writer.

—Curtis C. Smith

LONG, Frank Belknap

Pseudonym: Lyda Belknap Long. **Nationality:** American. **Born:** New York City, 27 April 1903. **Education:** New York public schools; New York University School of Journalism, 1920-21. **Family:** Married Lyda Arco in 1960. **Career:** Writer for *Captain Marvel, Green Lantern, Congo Bill,* and *Planet Comics* in the 1940s; uncredited associate editor, *The Saint Mystery Magazine* and *Fantastic Universe* in the 1950s; associate editor, *Satellite Science Fiction,* 1959, *Short Stories,* 1959-60, and *Mike Shayne Mystery Magazine* until 1966. **Awards:** First Fandom Hall of Fame award, 1977; 4th World Fantasy Convention Life Achievement award, 1978; Bram Stoker Life Achievement award, 1988. **Died:** 5 September 1992.

Science Fiction Publications

Novels

Space Station No. 1. New York, Ace, 1957.
Woman from Another Planet. New York, Chariot, 1960.
The Horror Expert. New York, Belmont, 1961.
The Mating Center. New York, Chariot, 1961.
Mars Is My Destination: A Science-Fiction Adventure. New York, Pyramid, 1962.
The Horror from the Hills. Sauk City, Wisconsin, Arkham House, 1963.
It Was the Day of the Robot. New York, Belmont, 1963; London, Dobson, 1964.
Three Steps Spaceward. New York, Avalon, 1963.
The Martian Visitors. New York, Avalon, 1964.
Mission to a Star. New York, Avalon, 1964.
This Strange Tomorrow. New York, Belmont, and London, Digit, 1966.
Lest Earth Be Conquered. New York, Belmont, 1966; as *The Androids,* New York, Tower, 1969.
Journey into Darkness. New York, Belmont, 1967.
. . . and Others Shall Be Born. New York, Belmont, 1968.
The Three Faces of Time. New York, Tower, 1969.
Monster from out of Time. New York, Popular Library, 1970; London, Hale, 1971.
Survival World. New York, Lancer, 1971.
The Night of the Wolf. New York, Popular Library, 1972.
Rehearsal Night. Boston, Cat's God, 1981.

Short Stories

The Hounds of Tindalos. Sauk City, Wisconsin, Arkham House, 1946; abridged edition, London, Museum Press, 1950; in 2 vols. as *The Hounds of Tindalos* and *The Dark Beasts and Eight Other Stories from The Hounds of Tindalos,* New York, Belmont, 1963-64; as *The Black Druid, and Other Stories,* St. Albans, Hertforshire, Panther, 1975.
John Carstairs, Space Detective. New York, Fell, 1949; London, Cherry Tree, 1951.
The Challenge from Beyond, with others. N.p., William H. Evans, 1954; as *The Illustrated Challenge from Beyond,* West Warwick, Rhode Island, Necronomicon Press, 1978.
The Rim of the Unknown. Sauk City, Wisconsin, Arkham House, 1972.
The Early Long. Garden City, New York, Doubleday, 1975; London, Hale, 1977.
When Chaugnar Wakes. Warren, Ohio, Fantome Press, 1978.
Night Fear, edited by Roy Torgeson. New York, Zebra, 1979.

Other Publications

Novel

So Dark a Heritage. New York, Lancer, 1966.

Novels as Lyda Belknap Long

To the Dark Tower. New York, Lancer, 1969.
Fire of the Witches. New York, Popular Library, 1971.
The Shape of Fear. New York, Beagle, 1971.
The Witch Tree. New York, Lancer, 1971.
House of the Deadly Nightshade. New York, Beagle, 1972.
Legacy of Evil. New York, Beagle, 1973.
Crucible of Evil. New York, Avon, 1974.
The Lemoyne Heritage. New York, Zebra, 1977.

Play

Television Play: *A Guest in the House,* 1950.

Poetry

A Man from Genoa and Other Poems. Athol, Massachusetts, Cook, 1926.
The Goblin Tower. Cassia, Florida, Dragon-Fly Press, 1935.
On Reading Arthur Machen: A Sonnet. Pengrove, California Dog and Duck Press, 1949.
In Mayan Splendor. Sauk City, Wisconsin, Arkham House, 1977.

Other

Howard Phillips Lovecraft: Dreamer on the Nightside. Sauk City, Wisconsin, Arkham House, 1975.
Autobiographical Memoir. West Warwick, Rhode Island, Necronomicon Press, 1985.

*

Manuscript Collection: Lovecraft Collection, Brown University, Providence, Rhode Island.

Frank Belknap Long comments:

My work has been almost equally divided between science fiction or science fantasy and supernatural horror. What fascinates me most in the realm of SF is the strangeness, mystery, and wonder of the cosmic immensities and the possibility of intelligent life on other worlds. A few of my early stories were of the space opera type, but for many years I have shunned that kind of writing. A realistic approach has become of supreme importance to me, and I have drawn upon one or more of the natural sciences in all my more recent stories. They range from future utopias—life on earth two centuries or two million years in the future—to what life may be like, biologically considered, in some far distant region of the expanding universe.

*   *   *

Of all modern writers in the overlapping domains of science fiction, fantasy, and horror, Frank Belknap Long may hold the record for sheer longevity, and, while he does not hold that for total productivity, he has written several hundred short stories and more than 30 books. The latter are difficult to number and categorize, as they involve a number of collections, re-sorting, and retitling of short stories as well as novels. In addition to works published under his own name, Long participated in a number of collaborations and round-robins, wrote short stories under house names such as Leslie Northern, wrote anonymously on occasion, and produced several gothic novels under the name of his wife, Lyda Long. While these last works are in a sense "mere potboilers," Long maintains that they are not without merit and in some cases contain effective scenes of the horror/fantasy or near-fantasy variety.

In a career dating from 1924, and still actively writing, Long has experienced the expectable rises and declines of popularity and critical standing. For some years he was highly regarded; in later times, disdained as little more than a hack; and still more recently has emerged as a revered elder statesman held in wide affection. In this regard his standing is comparable to that of writers like Murray Leinster and Edmond Hamilton. An accumulation of potboilers temporarily obscures the author's best work; with the passage of time the inferior material dissipates and the author's true contribution comes to be recognized.

Long has experienced the additional benefit—and handicap!—of having been for many years the closest friend and associate of H.P. Lovecraft. At one time Lovecraft and Long were partners in the "revision business," working as manuscript doctors, uncredited collaborators, and even ghostwriters for literary tyros. A certain portion of Long's own fiction shows a clear stamp of influence by Lovecraft, but this in fact represents a relatively small segment of Long's output, a fact too often overlooked.

A number of Long's horror stories—most of them fantasies, a few technically science fiction but still cast within the gothic mold—are notable. These include "The Desert Lich," "Second Night Out," a supernatural sea story perhaps remotely influenced by the works of William Hope Hodgson, and "The Man with a Thousand Legs," one of the most bizarre of all lycanthropic tales.

Long also contributed some of the earliest and most effective supplements to Lovecraft's "Cthulhu Mythos." Long's dry humor is apparent in "The Brain-Eaters," whose two chief characters are thinly disguised versions of himself and Lovecraft. "The Hounds of Tindalos," probably Long's most famous story, is a thoroughly effective tale of monstrous creatures from beyond normal time and space, breaking through the "angles" of our universe; the story is most effective in evoking a sense of non-Euclidean dimension. "A Visitor from Egypt" continues the successful exploitation of the Egyptian craze of the 1920s and early 1930s popular fiction. (One chapter of this novel was written by Lovecraft, based upon a dream).

Long's science fiction bears no trace of Lovecraft. It is sometimes densely powerful, evocative, and moving; at other times, the author fails in attempted effects and falls into bathos. In general, Long's short fiction is superior to his novels; in this regard he is once more comparable to Leinster. "The Flame Midget" clearly anticipates the development of the laser. A later story, "Dark Vision" (1939), is one of the earlier and still one of the most successful to use psychiatric and specifically Freudian themes in science fiction. Long places strong emphasis on the subconscious, and in the story makes use of both electroshock and chemical shock techniques (the former accidentally; the latter clinically) in bringing about changes in the protagonist's perceptions and interpretations of reality.

Also notable is Long's series of stories about John Carstairs, "Botanical Detective." These are intriguing hybrids of space opera and scientific mystery.

Long's most effective work is probably a series of short stories ("The Great Cold," "Green Glory," and "The Last Men") set in a remote future when humankind is reduced to miniature size and enslaved by races of giant insects. In framework, the stories would appear to be routine absurd super-science adventures. But Long concentrates on the awakening consciousness of the brutalized humans as they regain their awareness of their own humanness. The pitch of noble tragedy achieved is remarkable.

In a list of his short stories which he considers the most accomplished, Long includes "Humpty Dumpty Had a Great Fall," "To Follow Knowledge," "Prison Bright—Prison Deep," "Guest in the House," "Two Face," and "Night Fear" (most included in *Night Fear*). Almost all of these stories are based on psychological themes, most notably difficulties of personal adjustment. Further, the main protagonist is most commonly a child. The psychological sensitivity of the works is noteworthy, as is their acuteness of focus and intensity of treatment. It is also noteworthy that none bears any trace of Long's Lovecraft period; with the continued passage of time it is to be hoped that Long's non-Lovecraft works (which in fact constitute the overwhelming bulk of his output) will achieve their proper evaluation.

—Richard A. Lupoff

LONGYEAR, Barry (Brookes)

Nationality: American. **Born:** Harrisburg, Pennsylvania, 12 May 1942. **Education:** Attended Wayne State University, Detroit, 1966-67. **Family:** Married Regina Bedsun in 1967. **Career:** Production manager, Madison Corporation, Detroit, 1967-68; publisher, Sol III Publications, in Philadelphia, 1968-72, and in Farmington, Maine, 1972-77. Since 1977, freelance writer. Columnist ("Salty"), *Empire Science Fiction.* **Awards:** Nebula award, 1980; Hugo award, 1980; *Locus* award, 1980; John W. Campbell award, 1980. **Agent:** Mark Lichtman, Shapiro-Lichtman Agency, 8827 Beverly Blvd., Los Angeles, CA 90048, U.S.A. **Address:** P.O. Box 100, New Sharon, Maine 04955, U.S.A. **Online Address:** BBLONGYEAR@AOL.COM.

SCIENCE FICTION PUBLICATIONS

Novels (series: Alien Nation; Circus; Dracon)

City of Baraboo (Circus). New York, Berkley, 1980; London, Macdonald, 1983.
Elephant Song (Circus). New York, Berkley, 1982.
The Tomorrow Testament (Dracon), New York, Berkley, 1983.
Enemy Mine (Dracon; novelization of screenplay based on Longyear's original story), with David Gerrold. New York, Charter, 1985; London, Corgi, 1986.
Sea of Glass. New York, St. Martin's Press, 1987; London, Legend, 1988.
Naked Came the Robot. New York, Popular Library, 1988.
The God Box. New York, Signet, 1989.
Infinity Hold. New York, Popular Library, 1989.
The Homecoming. New York, Walker, 1989.
The Change: A Novel (Alien Nation). New York, Pocket Books, 1994.
Slag Like Me: A Novel (Alien Nation). New York, Pocket Books, 1994.

Short Stories

Manifest Destiny. New York, Berkley, 1980; London, Macdonald, 1982.
Circus World. Garden City, New York, Doubleday, 1980; London, Macdonald, 1982.
It Came from Schenectady. New York, Bluejay, 1984.
Enemy Mine, bound with *Another Orphan,* by John Kessel. New York, Tor, 1989.

Other

Science Fiction Writer's Workshop—I: An Introduction to Fiction Mechanics. Philadelphia, Owlswick Press, 1980.

OTHER PUBLICATIONS

Novel

Saint Mary Blue. Minneapolis, Steel Dragon Press, 1988.

*

Manuscript Collection: Farmington Public Library, Farmington, Maine.

Barry B. Longyear comments:

I believe that every imaginable universe exists somewhere in the cosmos, at least while I am researching and writing a story. One of my tasks is to be as true to that universe as possible, which for me involves going to wherever/whenever, living and wandering there for a time, then reporting what I have experienced. The things that I report are those messages, ideas, and tales that alter my mind such that my view of the universe and my place in it becomes changed, bent, even twisted. It is my endeavor to take these matters and warp the reader's mind as well. Although it might appear that brain damage is my quest, it is only a side effect. My true mission is to go to strange and wonderful places, both dark and humorous, to pursue and grasp important truths about myself, life, and the universe that for some reason are much more understandable in science fiction than they are in the here and now. It's also fun.

*   *   *

Barry Longyear burst upon the science fiction field in 1979 with a large number of short stories, several of which were of such high quality that they earned him a number of awards. The four best of these were collected as *Manifest Destiny,* all set in a common future history. Easily the most familiar of these is "Enemy Mine," basis of the movie of the same name, later novelized by Longyear in collaboration with David Gerrold. The story concerns a single human being and an alien, enemies in a bitter war, stranded together on the same primitive planet and forced to cooperate in order to survive. From this relationship comes mutual understanding, even the beginning of friendship, and the chance that the enmity between the two species will one day pass.

The imperialism of Earth is clearly at fault in that story as well as those collected with it. "The Jaren," an even better tale, concentrates on a young alien warrior determined to resist the human advance. In "Savage Planet," an alternative to brute force is found, as humans use mis-education to subjugate the local inhabitants. Ultimately the chauvinistic use of force is repudiated in "USE Force," causing a schism and eventually a civil war between two factions of human society.

Longyear continued to write short fiction, although much less frequently, in the years that followed, but very few of his later short pieces rivalled the enthusiasm and sheer gripping intensity of these early stories. The exceptions include "Bloodsong," in which he creates another engaging alien species with a dual personality whose juncture is threatened by exposure to humans, and "Portrait of Baron Negay," which shows how art can be used to puncture the aplomb of a petty tyrant. Indeed, many of Longyear's stories involve the deflation of the ego of pompous villains by the clever use of satire or farce.

An early series of stories and novels is set against the background of an interstellar circus, *Circus World, City of Baraboo,* and *Elephant Song.* The first is a collection of seven stories set on a planet which was colonized by a shipwrecked circus, leading to the creation of "tribes" of acrobats, clowns, and other professions. An invasion by outside forces is imminent and the major protagonist must find a way within the context of the society as established to alert the populace and organize resistance. Longyear is fairly clever in developing this theme, but the stories range widely in effectiveness, the best being "The Second Law." The second volume is actually the prequel, consisting of six stories that chronicle the attempts of the circus to leave Earth in the first place, by outfoxing a rich magnate and acquiring a large interstellar ship. In the concluding episodes, their victim strikes back, arranging for the sabotage of the ship, resulting in the subsequent crash landing of the circus complement on the planet Momus. *Elephant Song* is a full-length novel that provides the bridge between the other two books, relating how the survivors of the crash managed to create a viable civilization in their new home despite shortages of materials.

The Tomorrow Testament is more or less the sequel to "Enemy Mine." The war between humans and the Dracon race continues, with each apparently determined to exterminate the other side. A captured human military officer slowly gains the confidence of a prominent member of the Dracon military, creating a useful bridge between the two warring species. Although the novel explores the interaction of the two main characters in great detail, Longyear keeps the plot lively and inventive. In some ways, this was the most technically successful of his early novels, although it covers ground he'd already explored.

A more legitimate contender as Longyear's best novel is *Sea of Glass,* a bleak, frightening dystopia set in an overpopulated future.

591

The industrialized nations are ruled by a supercomputer which has determined that a devastating war against what is currently known as the "Third World" will break out on a precise date in the near future. The protagonist is an illegal child sent to a brutal prison camp, later released as an adult, programmed to be a pivotal element in the computer's master plan to "save" the human race by sacrificing a substantial percentage of the existing population. A searing indictment of selfishness and the human tendency to allow others to make their decisions for them, *Sea of Glass* was the last major work of Longyear's early career.

Three subsequent novels, though each is entertaining, are less ambitious and less serious thematically. *Naked Came the Robot* is a darkly humorous satire set in a future where robots do most of the physical labor of the world, but whose ranks have been infiltrated by alien devices out to subvert the world's economy. *The Homecoming* is a short novel, apparently aimed at younger readers, chronicling the return of intelligent, star-traveling dinosaurs to their birth world, Earth, and their discovery that their own race has been supplanted with diminutive mammals who call themselves human beings. Predictably, they decide to exterminate the human vermin and reclaim their birthright. Longyear's only overt fantasy, *The God Box,* is the most interesting of the three. In structure, it's an episodic adventure involving a man who possesses a box whose drawers have an infinite capacity to produce whatever contents are required by the circumstances in which its owner finds himself.

Although Longyear's career faltered after the phenomenal impact of his early stories, he seems to have subsequently settled down to produce works that range from above average to exceptional. Unlike many writers, he appears unwilling to continue to examine the same themes repeatedly, but rather prefer to experiment with different styles and settings from one work to the next.

A serious illness led to a brief hiatus in Longyear's career, but he has returned with two recent novels. *Slag Like Me* and *The Change* are both media tie-ins, original work based on the cancelled *Alien Nation* television series. Unlike most similar product-oriented lines, this particular setting and cast of characters provides considerably more leverage for authors to examine real issues—gender roles, racial prejudice, civil liberties, and so on. The setting, very near future America following the arrival on Earth of humanoid aliens who are intellectually and physically our superiors, is sufficiently familiar that the points made bear relevance to the present.

Longyear has also appeared in shorter length, of which the most notable recent story is "Chimaera," which deals with an unconventional android. Other stories worth noting include "The Death Addict" and "Old Soldiers Never Die," the latter of which includes a particularly effective swipe at repressive governments.

—Don D'Ammassa

LORAN, Martin. *See* BAXTER, John.

LORD, Jeffrey. *See* NELSON, Ray.

LORRAINE, Paul. *See* FEARN, John Russell.

LOVECRAFT, H(oward) P(hillips)

Nationality: American. **Born:** Providence, Rhode Island, 20 August 1890. **Education:** Tutored at home, at a local elementary school and at Hope Street High School, Providence, 1904-05, 1907-08. **Family:** Married Sonia Greene in 1924 (divorced 1929). **Career:** Freelance writer from 1908, working as a ghost writer and, after 1918, a revisionist; astrology columnist, *Providence Evening News,* 1914-18; active in the amateur journalism movement from 1914; published *The Conservative,* 1915-19, 1923, and president of the United Amateur Press Association, 1917-18, 1923; regular contributor to *Weird Tales* after 1923. **Died:** 15 March 1937.

SCIENCE FICTION PUBLICATIONS

Novels

The Lurker at the Threshold, with August Derleth. Sauk City, Wisconsin, Arkham House, 1945; London, Gollancz, 1948.
The Case of Charles Dexter Ward. London, Gollancz, 1951; New York, Belmont, 1965.
The Dream-Quest of Unknown Kadath. Buffalo, Shroud, 1955.

Short Stories

The Shunned House. Athol, Massachusetts, Recluse Press, 1928.
The Battle That Ended the Century: (Ms. Found in a Time Machine). De Land, Florida, Barlow, 1934.
The Cats of Ulthar. Cassia, Florida, Dragonfly Press, 1935.
The Shadow over Innsmouth. Everett, Pennsylvania, Visionary Press, 1936.
The Outsider and Others, edited by August Derleth and Donald Wandrei. Sauk City, Wisconsin, Arkham House, 1939; abridged as *The Dunwich Horror,* New York, Bart House, 1945.
Beyond the Wall of Sleep, edited by August Derleth and Donald Wandrei. Sauk City, Wisconsin, Arkham House, 1943.
Marginalia, edited by August Derleth and Donald Wandrei. Sauk City, Wisconsin, Arkham House, 1944.
The Weird Shadow over Innsmouth and Other Stories of the Supernatural. New York, Bart House, 1944.
Best Supernatural Stories of H.P. Lovecraft, edited by August Derleth. Cleveland, World, 1945; expanded as *The Dunwich Horror and Others,* Sauk City, Wisconsin, Arkham House, 1963; abridged as *The Colour Out of Space and Others,* New York, Lancer, 1964; original version as *The Best of H.P. Lovecraft: Bloodcurdling Tales of Horror and the Macabre,* New York, Ballantine, 1982.
The Lurking Fear and Other Stories. New York, Avon, 1947; as *Cry Horror!,* 1958; revised edition, London, Panther, 1964; further revised, New York, Beagle, 1971.
Something about Cats and Other Pieces, edited by August Derleth. Sauk City, Wisconsin, Arkham House, 1949.
The Haunter of the Dark and Other Tales of Horror. London, Gollancz, 1951.

The Survivor and Others, with August Derleth. Sauk City, Wisconsin, Arkham House, 1957.

The Shuttered Room and Other Pieces, with others, edited by August Derleth. Sauk City, Wisconsin, Arkham House, 1959.

Dreams and Fancies. Sauk City, Wisconsin, Arkham House, 1962.

At the Mountains of Madness and Other Novels. Sauk City, Wisconsin, Arkham House, 1964; London, Gollancz, 1966; title story published separately, West Kingston, Rhode Island, Grant, 1990.

Dagon and Other Macabre Tales, edited by August Derleth. Sauk City, Wisconsin, Arkham House, 1965; London, Gollancz, 1967; abridged as *The Tomb and Other Tales,* London, Panther, 1969; New York, Ballantine, 1973.

The Dark Brotherhood and Other Pieces, with others, edited by August Derleth. Sauk City, Wisconsin, Arkham House, 1966.

3 Tales of Horror. Sauk City, Wisconsin, Arkham House, 1967.

The Shadow Out of Time and Other Tales of Horror, with August Derleth. London, Gollancz, 1968; abridged edition, as *The Shuttered Room and Other Tales of Horror,* London, Panther, 1970.

Ex Oblivione. Glendale, California, Squires, 1969.

Memory. Glendale, California, Squires, 1969.

The Horror in the Museum and Other Revisions, with others; edited by August Derleth. Sauk City, Wisconsin, Arkham House, 1970; abridged edition, New York, Beagle, 1971; as *The Horror in the Burying Ground and Other Tales,* London, Panther, 1975.

Nyarlathotep. Glendale, California, Squires, 1970.

What the Moon Brings. Glendale, California, Squires, 1970.

The Shadow over Innsmouth and Other Stories of Horror. New York, Scholastic, 1971.

The Shuttered Room and Other Tales of Terror, with August Derleth. New York, Beagle, 1971.

The Doom That Came to Sarnath, edited by Lin Carter. New York, Ballantine, 1971.

The Watchers Out of Time and Others, with August Derleth. Sauk City, Wisconsin, Arkham House, 1974.

Herbert West, the Reanimator. West Warwick, Rhode Island, Necronomicon Press, 1977.

The Statement of Randolph Carter. N.p., The Strange Company, 1976.

Collapsing Cosmoses, with Robert H. Barlow. West Warwick, Rhode Island, Necronomicon Press, 1977.

H.P. Lovecraft in the "Eyrie," edited by S.T. Joshi and Marc A. Michaud. West Warwick, Rhode Island, Necronomicon Press, 1979.

The Night Ocean, with Robert H. Barlow. West Warwick, Rhode Island, Necronomicon Press, 1982.

Four Prose Poems. West Warwick, Rhode Island, Necronomicon Press, 1987; 2nd edition, 1990.

Re-Animator: Tales of Herbert West, edited by Steven Philip Jones. Westlake, California, Malibu, 1991.

Crawling Chaos: Selected Works, 1920-1935, edited by James Havoc. London, Creation Press, 1992.

The Dream Cycle of H.P. Lovecraft: Dreams of Terror and Death. New York, Ballantine, 1995.

OTHER PUBLICATIONS

Poetry

The Crime of Crimes. Llandudno, Wales, Harris, 1915.

A Sonnet. N.p., Shepherd and Wollheim, 1936.

H.P.L. Belleville, New Jersey, Stickney, 1937.

Fungi from Yuggoth. Salem, Oregon, Evans, 1943; expanded edition, West Warwick, Rhode Island, Necronomicon Press, 1977.

Collected Poems. Sauk City, Wisconsin, Arkham House, 1963; abridged edition, as *Fungi from Yuggoth and Other Poems,* New York, Ballantine, 1971.

Medusa: A Portrait. New York, Oliphant Press, 1975.

A Winter Wish, edited by Tom Collins. Chapel Hill, North Carolina, Whispers Press, 1977.

Antarktos. Warren, Ohio, Fantome Press, 1977.

H.P. Lovecraft Christmas Book, edited by Susan Michaud. West Warwick, Rhode Island, Necronomicon Press, 1984; revised edition, 1991.

The Fantastic Poetry, edited by S.T. Joshi. West Warwick, Rhode Island, Necronomicon Press, 1990.

Other

United Amateur Press Association: Exponent of Amateur Journalism. N.p., United Amateur Press Association, 1916.

Looking Backward. Haverhill, Massachusetts, C.W. Smith, 1920.

The Materialist Today. North Montpelier, Vermont, n.p., 1926.

Further Criticism of Poetry. Louisville, Fetter, 1932.

Charleston. Privately printed, 1936.

Some Current Motives and Practices. DeLand, Florida, Barlow, 1936.

A History of the Necronomicon. Oakman, Alabama, Rebel Press, 1938.

The Notes and Commonplace Book Employed by the Late H.P. Lovecraft, edited by R.H. Barlow. Lakeport, California, Futile Press, 1938.

Supernatural Horror in Literature. New York, Abramson, 1945; revised edition, Arlington, Virginia, Carrollton-Clark, 1974.

The Lovecraft Collector's Library, edited by George T. Wetzel. Tonowanda, New York, SSR, 5 vols., 1952-55.

Autobiography: Some Notes on a Nonentity. Sauk City, Wisconsin, Arkham House, and London, Villiers, 1963.

Selected Letters 1911-1937, edited by August Derleth, James Turner, and Donald Wandrei. Sauk City, Wisconsin, Arkham House, 5 vols., 1965-76.

Hail, Klarkash-Ton! Being Nine Missives Inscribed upon Postcards by H.P. Lovecraft to Clark Ashton Smith. Glendale, California, Squires, 1971.

Ec'h-Pi-El Speaks. Saddle River, New Jersey, Gerry de la Ree, 1972.

The Occult Lovecraft. Saddle River, New Jersey, Gerry de la Ree, 1975.

Lovecraft at Last (correspondence with Willis Conover). Arlington, Virginia, Carrollton Clark, 1975.

To Quebec and the Stars, edited by L. Sprague de Camp. West Kingston, Rhode Island, Grant, 1976.

Writings in The United Amateur 1915-1925, edited by Marc A. Michaud. West Warwick, Rhode Island, Necronomicon Press, 1976.

First Writings: Pawtuxet Valley Gleaner 1906, edited by Marc A. Michaud. West Warwick, Rhode Island, Necronomicon Press, 1976.

The Conservative: Complete 1915-1923, edited by Marc A. Michaud. West Warwick, Rhode Island, Necronomicon Press, 1977.

Memoirs of an Inconsequential Scribbler. West Warwick, Rhode Island, Necronomicon Press, 1977.

Writings in The Tryout, edited by Marc A. Michaud. West Warwick, Rhode Island, Necronomicon Press, 1977.

The Californian 1934-1938. West Warwick, Rhode Island, Necronomicon Press, 1977.

Uncollected Poetry and Prose, edited by S.T. Joshi and Marc A. Michaud. West Warwick, Rhode Island, Necronomicon Press, 2 vols., 1978-80.

Science versus Charlatanry: Essays on Astrology, with J.F. Hartmann, edited by S.T. Joshi and Scott Connors. N.p., The Strange Company, 1979.

H.P. Lovecraft's Waste Paper: A Facsimile and Transcript of the Original Draft. Providence, Rhode Island, Brown University, 1979.

Juvenalia 1895-1905, edited by S.T. Joshi. West Warwick, Rhode Island, Necronomicon Press, 1984.

H.P. Lovecraft: Uncollected Letters. West Warwick, Rhode Island, Necronomicon Press, 1986.

H.P. Lovecraft: Commonplace Book, edited by David E. Schultz. West Warwick, Rhode Island, Necronomicon Press, 2 vols., 1987.

European Glimpses, with Sonia H. Greene. West Warwick, Rhode Island, Necronomicon Press, 1988.

H.P. Lovecraft: The Conservative (essays), edited by S.T. Joshi. West Warwick, Rhode Island, Necronomicon Press, 1990.

The Vivisector (essays). West Warwick, Rhode Island, Necronomicon Press, 1990.

H.P. Lovecraft: Letters to Henry Kuttner, edited by David E. Schultz and S.T. Joshi. West Warwick, Rhode Island, Necronomicon Press, 1990.

H.P. Lovecraft: Letters to Richard Searight, edited by David E. Schultz, S.T. Joshi, and Franklyn Searight. West Warwick, Rhode Island, Necronomicon Press, 1992.

H.P. Lovecraft: Letters to Robert Bloch, edited by David E. Schultz and S.T. Joshi. West Warwick, Rhode Island, Necronomicon Press, 1993.

Miscellaneous Writings, edited by S.T. Joshi. Sauk City, Wisconsin, Arkham House, 1995.

Editor, *The Poetical Works of Jonathan E. Hoag.* Privately printed, 1923.

Editor, *White Fire,* by John Ravenor Bullen. Athol, Massachusetts, Recluse Press, 1927.

Editor, *Thoughts and Pictures,* by Eugene B. Kuntz. Haverhill, Massachusetts, Lovecraft and Smith, 1932.

*

Bibliography: *The New H.P. Lovecraft Bibliography* by Jack L. Chalker, Baltimore, Anthem Press, 1962, revised edition, with Mark Owings, as *The Revised H.P. Lovecraft Bibliography,* Baltimore, Mirage Press, 1973; *A Catalog of Lovecraftiana* by Mark Owings and Irving Binkin, Baltimore, Mirage Press, 1975; *H.P. Lovecraft: An Annotated Bibliography* by S.T. Joshi, Kent, Ohio, Kent State University Press, 1981; *Howard Phillips Lovecraft: The Books, Addenda and Auxiliary* by Joseph Bell, Toronto, Soft Press, 1983.

Manuscript Collection: Brown University, Providence, Rhode Island.

Critical Studies (selection): *In Memoriam Howard Phillips Lovecraft: Recollections, Appreciations, Estimates* edited by W. Paul Cook, privately printed, 1941; *H.P.L.: A Memoir,* New York, Abramson, 1945, and *Some Notes on H.P. Lovecraft,* Sauk City, Wisconsin, Arkham House, 1959, both by August Derleth; *Rhode Island on Lovecraft* edited by Donald M. Grant and Thomas P. Hadley, Providence, Rhode Island, Grant Hadley, 1945; "H.P. Lovecraft Issue" of *Fresco* (Detroit), Spring 1958; *Lovecraft: A Look Behind the Cthulhu Mythos* by Lin Carter, New York, Ballantine, 1972, London, Panther, 1975; *Lovecraft: A Biography* by L. Sprague de Camp, New York, Doubleday, 1975, London, New English Library, 1976; *Howard Phillips Lovecraft: Dreamer on the Nightside* by Frank Belknap Long, Sauk City, Wisconsin, Arkham House, 1975; *Essays Lovecraftian* edited by Darrell Schweitzer, Baltimore, T-K Graphics, 1976, and *The Dream Quest of H.P. Lovecraft* by Schweitzer, San Bernardino, California, Borgo Press, 1978; *The H.P. Lovecraft Companion* by Philip A. Schreffler, Westport, Connecticut, Greenwood Press, 1977; *The Major Works of H.P. Lovecraft* by John Taylor Gatto, New York, Monarch Press, 1977; *The Roots of Horror in the Fiction of H.P. Lovecraft* by Barton Levi St. Armand, Elizabethtown, New York, Dragon Press, 1977; *H.P. Lovecraft* by S.T. Joshi, Mercer Island, Washington, Starmont House, 1982; *H.P. Lovecraft: A Critical Study* by Donald R. Burleson, Westport, Connecticut, Greenwood Press, 1983; *Lovecraft: A Study in the Fantastic* by Maurice Lévy, translated by S.T. Joshi, Detroit, Wayne State University Press, 1988.

*   *   *

That horror stories are externalized psychology is a commonplace of literary criticism, but readings based on sex and aggression (the two themes literary critics have tended to pick up from Freudian psychology) do not quite fit H.P. Lovecraft. Lovecraft himself warns readers away from interpretations of his work based on the fear of retribution for specific acts or impulses; his horrors are (as he says again and again) "cosmic": he declares the worst human fears to be displacement in space and time (as in "The Shadow Out of Time"), he speaks of "the maddening rigidity of cosmic law," he creates a nonfantastic and materialistic fictional world—i.e. science fiction—all implying a concern with the conditions of being, not with particular acts or situations. When the conditions of existence are themselves fearful, when such basic ontological categories as space and time break down (as does the geometry of space in so many stories, for example "The Call of Cthulhu"), we are dealing with what the psychiatrist R.S. Laing calls "ontological insecurity." If one fears that one doesn't exist securely, or that one is made of "bad stuff," any contact with another becomes potentially catastrophic. Everyone shares, to some degree, doubts about the psychological solidity or reliability of the self and the possibly devastating effects of others on that self. The extreme form of such fears is schizophrenia.

Lovecraft, although certainly not schizophrenic, did, according to L. Sprague de Camp, have a lifelong sense of marked isolation from others, an intense emotional dependency on things and not people, and the kind of overpossessive upbringing which makes it reasonable to expect that such issues would appear in his work. They do—strongly enough to make him an innovator in weird fiction—for they take precedence over either the beastliness of aggression (embodied, for example, in werewolves) or the lethal possibilities of sexual abandon (e.g., the figure of the vampire), both of which figure largely in 19th-century supernatural fiction. Sex and aggression presuppose a self existing securely enough to have desires and a relatively nonthreatening (or at least limited) other towards whom such desires can be directed. Neither an unproblematic sense of self nor a noncatastrophic other exists in Lovecraft's work. In his early Dunsanian fiction he can frolic—but with ghouls!—as in the charming (but, alas, never rewritten or polished) *Dream-Quest of Unknown Kadath,* or write pleasing, optimistic fantasies like "The Strange High House in the Mist"; but much of his earlier and most of his later fiction is preoccupied with the foreseen, yet unavoidable, engulfment of a passive, victimized self. If the narrator is a lucky spectator who escapes with his life, or even sanity, intact, his peace of mind has been shattered forever. The real point of these stories is revelation—if the engulfment does not happen, it can—and this revelation becomes the central truth of a universe thus rendered uninhabitable. The cannibalistic other takes several forms, but the commonest, strongest image, and the one readers seem to remember best is the shapeless, monstrous, indescribable "entry" (a favorite word of Lovecraft's) whose most terrifying characteristic is its structurelessness ("The Unnameable," "The Call of Cthulhu," "Dagon," "The Dunwich Horror"). The obsession with psychic cannibalism (expressed as physical in one of the flatter stories, "The Picture in the House") and the insistence on the indescribability of the threat seem to point to experience so personally archaic it is felt as pre-verbal, as does Lovecraft's characteristic straining after adjectives. In one of his best tales, "The Colour Out of Space," the threat is most abstract, its cannibalism is reported third-hand (through two narrators) and the relatively low-keyed, realistic setting gets most of the author's attention.

In only two stories does Lovecraft focus fully on the alternative to engulfment: loneliness. Selves exist and survive in both tales; they even—after a fashion—blossom into initiative. But both are figures that appear in other stories *as monsters:* in the poetically melancholy "The Outsider" a ghoulish walking corpse, and in the very interesting end of *The Weird Shadow over Innsmouth* a degenerate animal/monster. Both stories suggest that the menace is the narrator or something in the narrator, a suggestion not only psychologically truer than the image of the engulfing other that Lovecraft uses elsewhere, but one dramatically more interesting.

The view that human relations exist only as engulfment is a serious limitation on a narrative artist. Towards the end of his life Lovecraft seems to have been unhappily aware of this; unfortunately he also underrated his own work and died before it began to be popular. His originality and his undoubted talent (the eerily parodic autobiography of "The Outsider," details like the "gelatinous" voice in "Randolph Carter," or "a warmth that may have been sardonic" of *Innsmouth*) are best at their quietest, worst in their bravely direct but often inadequate attacks on a theme that requires (at the very least) poetic genius. The very rarity of literary treatments of Lovecraft's main theme gives his work added interest, however, and his work will probably always appeal to readers who find his theme compelling. If he had not died prematurely, he might have moved beyond the kind of horror story that says "This is what it feels like" to the kind that adds "and this is what is really happening." The latter moves into tragedy and implied social criticism (as does, for example, Shirley Jackson's *The Haunting of Hill House*). In *Supernatural Horror in Literature* Lovecraft concludes "the spectral in literature . . . is . . . a narrow though essential branch of human expression," a comment that might well describe his work: narrow, not appealing to wide tastes and even considerably flawed, yet authentic, and by those who find it congenial, securely loved.

—Joanna Russ

LOWAM, Ron. *See* TUBB, E.C.

LOWNDES, Robert A(ugustine) W(ard)

Pseudonyms: Arthur Cooke; Carol Grey; Carl Groener; Mallory Kent; Paul Dennis Lavond; John MacDougal; Wilfred Owen Morley; Richard Morrison; Michael Sherman; Peter Michael Sherman; Lawrence Woods. **Nationality:** American. **Born:** Bridgeport, Connecticut, 4 September 1916. **Education:** Darien High School, Connecticut; Stamford Community College, Connecticut, 1936. **Family:** Married Dorothy Sedor Rogalin in 1948 (divorced 1974); one stepson. **Career:** Worked for the Civilian Conservation Corps, 1934, 1936-37, 1939; assistant on a squab farm; salesman; porter, Greenwich Hospital Association, Connecticut, 1937-38; literary agent, Fantastory Sales Service, 1940-42; editor, *Future Fiction,* 1940-43, and *Science Fiction Quarterly,* 1940-43, 1951-58; editorial director, Columbia magazines, 1942-60; editor, *Future Science Fiction,* 1950-60, *Dynamic Science Fiction,* 1952-54, and *Science Fiction Stories,* 1954-60; editor, Avalon science fiction series, Thomas Bouregy, 1955-67; editor, *Magazine of Horror,* 1963-71, *Famous Science Fiction,* 1966-69, *Startling Mystery Stories,* 1966-71, *Weird Terror Tales,* 1969-70, and *Bizarre Fantasy Fiction,* 1970-71; associate editor, 1971-77, and managing editor, 1977-78, *Sexology* and *Luz;* production chief, *Luz,* 1978-84, and in editorial production, *Radio-Electronics, Special Projects, Hands-On Electronics,* and *Computer Digest,* 1978-89. Cofounder, Vanguard Amateur Press Association. Guest of Honor, Lunacon, 1969, and Boskone, 1973. **Address:** 717 Willow Avenue, Hoboken, New Jersey 07030, U.S.A.

Science Fiction Publications

Novels

Mystery of the Third Mine (for children). Philadelphia, Winston, 1953.
The Duplicated Man, with James Blish. New York, Avalon, 1959.
The Puzzle Planet. New York, Ace, 1961.
Believers' World. New York, Avalon, 1961.

Other Publications

Other

Three Faces of Science Fiction. Boston, NESFA Press, 1973.

Editor, *The Best of James Blish.* New York, Ballantine, 1979.

*

Robert A.W. Lowndes comments:

Although I was an active member of the Marxist-oriented Futurian Society of New York (1938-45), calling for social and political relevance in science fiction, when it came down to writing stories I found that I had no interest whatsoever in such relevance. I only wanted to tell the kind of story I actually wanted to read—full of wonder or terror or both. Whether I succeeded, or to what extent I succeeded, is for others to say.

To my mind, the best fantasy and SF is imbued with the author's feeling about the human condition, and may or may not contain what amounts to some sort of message. If there is one, it is not something consciously striven for; I've read thousands of stories written to preach a sermon, and however effective the sermon itself may have been, the stories have nearly all suffered from the approach. Fiction and homily writing are two different forms, though each may be done with a high quality of art; but mixing them produces an abortion.

*   *   *

Robert A.W. Lowndes is known mainly as an editor. He is, however, also a science fiction writer of considerable talent, particularly in the creation and description of alien worlds. This talent is best seen in *Believers' World*. Lowndes uses the now-familiar plot of exiles from Earth who have forgotten that their origin was on Earth, and whose religious beliefs have hardened into mindless fragments of ceremony. An investigator from Earth visits these exiles, now living on a "believers' world" locked into elaborate religious ceremonies. He becomes involved in a formula of action, adventure, and violence. But Lowndes effectively describes the Arabian Nights atmosphere of this world: "magic. That was the keynote of everything here—the appearance of magic." Even small everyday events seem magical: "you touched a faucet, or bent over a fountain, or stepped under a shower, and pale yellow water issued forth." Thus Lowndes creates a world that exemplifies Arthur C. Clarke's generalization that advanced technology is indistinguishable from magic.

Everything that happens on the believers' world is supposed by the inhabitants to be the will of "Ein" (Einstein, though they don't remember this). In this topsy-turvy world not only has religion ossified but science has merged with it. *The Puzzle Planet* is about a world that is similar in that our common-sense assumptions are upside down; and once again Lowndes's descriptive powers are impressive.

Even *Mystery of the Third Mine*, a juvenile novel, is well worth reading. Lowndes makes asteroid mining seem real, creating a historical parallel to the gold rush of 1848. The hero, Peter, is in a mining partnership with his father. The villains use the cover of the Asteroid Miners Association to invalidate Peter's claims and to try to seize the "third mine" platinum, deep in the asteroid. There is a good science-fun gimmick on the asteroid: low gravity baseball with a magnetized ball and players throwing bits of metal to propel themselves through space. Although the young hero is close to being a pastiche of a Heinlein juvenile, Lowndes's magical atmosphere is once again his own.

Lowndes's short stories are quite distinct from his novels and show the influence of Clark Ashton Smith and Lovecraft. One of his best is "The Abyss," which begins with this hook sentence: "We took Graf Norden's body out into the November night, under the stars that burned with a brightness terrible to behold, and drove madly, wildly up the mountain road." Beings in another dimension (or no dimension) send agents to hypnotize humans and drain the fluids from their bodies. The description of these alien beings— with long filaments that restlessly try to break into our dimension from their own—is as well done as anything in Lovecraft, and the

economy of the story is beyond Lovecraft. Economy, atmosphere, description: these are Lowndes's strongest points as a writer.

—Curtis C. Smith

———

LUCAS, George. *See* **FOSTER, Alan Dean.**

———

LULL, Susan. *See* **FORWARD, Robert L.**

———

LUNDWALL, Sam J(errie)

Nationality: Swedish. **Born:** Stockholm, 24 February 1941. **Education:** University of Stockholm, E.E. 1967; Fotoskolan, 1968. **Military Service:** Compulsory military service in the air force, 1961-62. **Family:** Married Ingrid Christina Olofsdotter in 1972; one daughter. **Career:** Electronic engineer, L.M. Ericson, Stockholm, 1956-64; photographer, Christian, Fox Amphoux, France, 1968-69; editor, Askild & Kärnekull, Stockholm, 1970-73; publisher, Delta Förlag, Stockholm, 1973-80, and since 1980, Fakta & Fantasi, Stockholm. Since 1972, editor, *Jules Verne-Magasinet,* Stockholm. Also a singer and musician, illustrator, and television producer. **Awards:** Swedish Film Institute award, 1967; Cosmos Fandom award, 1969; Futura Club award, 1972; Finnish Design award, 1972. **Address:** c/o Penguin Books, Bath Road, Harmondsworth, Middlesex UB7 0DA, England.

S<small>CIENCE</small> F<small>ICTION</small> P<small>UBLICATIONS</small>

Novels

Inga hjältar här. Stockholm, Lindqvist, n.d.
No Time for Heroes. New York, Ace, 1971.
Alice's World. New York, Ace, 1971; London, Arrow, 1975.
Bernhard the Conqueror. New York, DAW, 1973.
King Kong Blues: en berättelse från år 2018. Stockholm, Lindqvist, 1974; as *2018; or, The King Kong Blues,* New York, DAW, 1975; London, Wyndham, 1976.
Tio sanger och Alltid Lady MacBeth. Bromma, Sweden, Delta, 1975.
Bernards magiska sommar. Stockholm, Lindqvist, 1975.
Mörkrets furste: eller, djävulstornets hemlighet: en pastich. Bromma, Sweden, Delta, 1975.
Gäst i Frankensteins hus. Bromma, Sweden, Delta, 1976.
Fängelsestaden: en roman. Stockholm, Norstedt, 1978.
Flicka i fönster vid världens kant: em gptosl berättelse. Stockholm, Norstedt, 1980.
Crash. Stockholm, Norstedt, 1982.

Uncollected Short Stories

"Nobody Here But Us Shadows," in *Galaxy* (New York), August 1975.

"Take Me Down the River," in *Twenty Houses of the Zodiac,* edited by Maxim Jakubowski. London, New English Library, 1979.

OTHER PUBLICATIONS

Poetry

Visor i var tid. Stockholm, Sonora, 1965.

Novel

Mardrömmen. Stockholm, Lindqvist, 1976.

Other

Science Fiction: från begynneslsen till våradagar. Stockholm, Sveriges Radio, 1969; translated as *Science Fiction: What It's All About,* New York, Ace, 1971.

Den fantastiska romanen (essays on science fiction). Stockholm, Gummeson, 4 vols., 1972-74.

Illustrerad bibliografi över science fiction & fantasy, 1741-1973. Stockholm, Lindqvist, 1974.

Utopia-Dystopia. Bromma, Sweden, Delta, 1977.

Science Fiction: An Illustrated History. New York, Grosset and Dunlap, 1978.

Editor, with Brian W. Aldiss, *The Penguin World Omnibus of Science Fiction: An Anthology.* Harmonsdworth, Middlesex, Penguin, 1986.

Publications in Swedish: some 20 anthologies of science fiction, and translations of 237 novels into Swedish.

*

Sam Lundwall comments:

I am not a fan of my work. I wish I were.

*   *   *

Sam J. Lundwall's reputation rests chiefly on the critical/historical survey *Science Fiction: What It's All About,* which he wrote in Swedish and translated into English. One of the first general summaries of the field, the book outlines a history and a theory of the genesis of science fiction. For many readers this outline (along with that presented in Brian Aldiss's *Billion Year Spree*) serves as the first critical framework by which they define their experience of science fiction. Lundwall categorizes science fiction, defines it, and comments on it. He draws on a wide range of stories and essays as source materials for his discussions and tries generally to test his conclusions against hard observation, even though he is not ashamed to write with the verve of a totally committed partisan or fan. Treating science fiction "books, magazines, comics, fans and fanzines, juvenilia, series characters, and literary giants," he also discusses popular motifs, conventions, themes, and plot lines.

The influence of this book is not easily overstated. Published in English in 1971 at the beginning of a great wave of academic interest in the genre, it provided the foundations for the organization of a large part of the scholarship and of the design and teaching of science-fiction courses in universities. Lundwall is, moreover, straightforward, clear, and definite in communicating his attitudes. The book, consequently, stimulates interest in the study of the genre as a whole and in its various aspects. Although Lundwall's shrewd critical insights and commentary on authors and works may not seem as true five or ten years after they are first encountered, they tend to color a reader's perception of the field, having provided for many readers a starting point for disciplined study.

Sam J. Lundwall is also known as a writer of satiric novels. The best known of these and probably the most successful of the four that have been translated into English is *2018; or, The King Kong Blues.* In this novel Lundwall describes a world that in 2018 is polluted not only physically but spiritually as well. The tale begins with a description of a wedding held in a department store. Against this scene we see one of the central characters, a rootless, rebellious young girl named Anniki Norijn, trying to break free of compulsions to conform to commercially acceptable standards of taste and ethics. The rest of the novel narrates a harassed advertising executive's search for this young woman. He is forced to use her in a campaign to sell underarm deodorant. A counterplot tells of two sheikhs, brothers, one of whom out of sheer boredom manipulates the economic life of the West, which the other one in the name of religion and Bedouin honor tries to destroy. The book gets its title from a song Anniki sings that mocks the betrayed romanticism and the false facades of social institutions.

This novel is at home among that group of satiric novels that criticize the shallowness and triviality of modern life; it has been compared with Pohl and Kornbluth's *Space Merchants,* Brunner's *The Sheep Look Up,* and Burgess's *A Clockwork Orange.* Unlike Burgess's book, however, *2018* does not attack a single, philosophically distinct evil. Its attack is more generally directed against economic exploitation on all levels. Unlike *The Space Merchants* it isn't very funny; its humor is blacker, crueler, more disturbing. Finally, it is not as successful as *The Sheep Look Up* because it preaches and explains more than it narrates or dramatizes. Perhaps Lundwall should, like Brunner, have used techniques similar to those of John Dos Passos to make the circumstantial background—which is, after all, the real main character and interest in the novel—come alive. *2018* unfortunately too often reads like an undergraduate textbook.

His other translated novels, *Alice's World, No Time for Heroes,* and *Bernhard the Conqueror,* are also satiric and vary in mood from depressed to genuinely funny.

—Alexander J. Butrym

LUPOFF, Richard A(llen)

Pseudonyms: Ova Hamlet; Addison E. Steele. **Nationality:** American. **Born:** Brooklyn, New York, 21 February 1935. **Education:** University of Miami, Coral Gables, B.A. 1956. **Military Service:** Served in the Adjutant General's Corps of the United States Army, 1956-58: First Lieutenant. **Family:** Married Patricia Enid Loring in 1958; two sons and one daughter. **Career:** Technical writer, Sperry Univac, New York, 1958-63; editor, Canaveral Press, New York, 1962-70; film producer, IBM, New York City and Poughkeepsie, New York, 1963-70; editor, with Pat Lupoff, *Xero* fan magazine, 1960-63; West Coast editor, *Crawdaddy,* 1970-71, and *Changes,* 1971-72; editor, *Organ,* 1972; book editor, *Algol,* 1963-79; science fiction reviewer, *San Francisco Chronicle,* 1979-81. Since 1985, editor, Canyon Press, Redwood City, California. **Awards:** Hugo award, for editing, 1963. **Agent:** Henry Morrison Inc., P.O. Box 235, Bedford Hills, New York 10507, U.S.A. **Address:** 3208 Claremont Avenue, Berkeley, California 94705, U.S.A.

SCIENCE FICTION PUBLICATIONS

Novels (series: The Dungeon; Flat Earth; Melvinge of the Megaverse; Buck Rogers; Sun's End)

One Million Centuries. New York, Lancer, 1967; revised edition, New York, Timescape, 1981.
Sacred Locomotive Flies. New York, Beagle, 1971.
Into the Aether. New York, Dell, 1974.
The Crack in the Sky. New York, Dell, 1976; as *Fool's Hill,* London, Sphere, 1978.
Lisa Kane: A Novel of the Supernatural. Indianapolis, Bobbs Merrill, 1976.
Sandworld. New York, Berkley, 1976.
The Triune Man. New York, Berkley, 1976; London, Dobson, 1979.
The Return of Skull-Face, with Robert E. Howard. West Linn, Oregon, FAX, 1977.
Sword of the Demon: A Novel. New York, Harper, 1977; London, Sphere, 1980.
Space War Blues. New York, Dell, 1978; London, Sphere, 1979.
Buck Rogers in the 25th Century (as Addison E. Steele). New York, Dell, 1978.
That Man on Beta (Buck Rogers; as Addison E. Steele). New York, Dell, 1979.
Circumpolar! (Flat Earth). New York, Timescape, 1984; London, Granada, 1985.
Sun's End. New York, Berkley, 1984; London, Grafton, 1987.
Lovecraft's Book. Sauk City, Wisconsin, Arkham House, 1985; London, Grafton, 1987.
Countersolar! (Flat Earth). New York, Arbor House, 1987; London, Grafton, 1988.
The Forever City (for children). New York, Walker, 1988; London, Hutchinson, 1990.
Galaxy's End (Sun's End). New York, Ace, 1988; London, Grafton, 1989.
The Black Tower (The Dungeon; based on the series by Philip José Farmer). New York, Bantam, 1988; London, Bantam, 1989.
The Final Battle (The Dungeon; based on the series by Philip José Farmer). New York, Bantam, 1990.
Night of the Living 'Gator! (Melvinge of the Megaverse; based on the series by Daniel M. Pinkwater). New York, Ace, 1992.

Short Stories

Nebogipfel at the End of Time. San Francisco, Underwood Miller, 1979.
The Ova Hamlet Papers. San Francisco, Pennyfarthing Press, 1979.
Stroka Prospekt: A Story. West Branch, Iowa, Toothpaste Press, 1982.
The Digital Wristwatch of Philip K. Dick. San Carlos, California, Canyon Press, 1985.

The Digital Wristwatch of Philip K. Dick [and] *Hyperprism.* Brooklyn, New York, Gryphon, 1993.

OTHER PUBLICATIONS

Novels

The Comic Book Killer. San Francisco, California, Offspring Press, 1988.
The Classic Car Killer. New York, Bantam, 1992.
The Bessie Blue Killer: A Hobart Lindsey/Marvia Plum Mystery. New York, St. Martin's Press, 1994.
The Sepia Siren Killer: A Hobart Lindsey/Marvia Plum Mystery. New York, St. Martin's Press, 1994.

Other

Edgar Rice Burroughs, Master of Adventure. New York, Canaveral Press, 1965; revised edition, New York, Ace, 1968; revised and expanded, Ace, 1975.
The Case of the Doctor Who Had No Business; or, The Adventure of the Second Anonymous Narrator. La Grange, New York, privately printed, 1966.
The Adventures of Professor Thintwhistle and His Incredible Aether Flyer, with Steve Stiles (graphic novel; adapted from Lupoff's *Into the Aether*). N.p., Fantagraphic Books, 1991.
Barsoom: Edgar Rice Burroughs and the Martian Vision. Baltimore, Mirage Press, 1976.

Editor, *The Reader's Guide to Barsoom and Amtor.* New York, privately printed, 1963.
Editor, with Don Thompson, *All in Color for a Dime.* New Rochelle, New York, Arlington House, 1970.
Editor, with Don Thompson, *The Comic-Book Book.* New Rochelle, New York, Arlington House, 1974.
Editor, *What If? [and What If? 2] Stories That Should Have Won the Hugo.* New York, Pocket Books, 1980-81.

*

Richard A. Lupoff comments:

It's very difficult for me to "make a statement" about my own works. It seems to me that this is a task for critics. The artist is of necessity so close to his or her own work—in fact, more than close to it: is surrounded by and immersed in it—that a critical perspective is impossible.

In terms of my own career, 1981 proved to be a year of bitter irony. I had spent decades learning the craft of fiction, and felt that I had finally reached a satisfying level of competence. The last three books that I had written—*Circumpolar!, Lovecraft's Book,* and *Sun's End*—were by far the best I had ever written. My prices had risen, critics and fans were expressing approval, foreign sales were gratifying.

At this point, due to general economic conditions, there was a collapse in the marketplace. All three books were cancelled, contracts for two further novels were cancelled, and the *What If?* anthology series that I had been editing was cancelled. Everything that I had in print went out of print, and my career was in effect terminated. My income dropped to nothing and I faced economic disaster.

In the years since then, there has been considerable recovery. The three novels that I named have all been published, as have sequels to *Sun's End* and *Circumpolar!*, although the *What If?* series seems to have expired after only two volumes, despite enthusiastic critical reception.

By the end of 1985 I was able to leave a stultifying office job and resume full-time writing, mixing science fiction with other forms. In fact, my work has never been entirely located in the main stream of science fiction. My early novel *Sacred Locomotive Flies*, for instance, although influenced by Michael Moorcock's *The Final Programme* and Chester Anderson's *The Butterfly Kid*, was really more social satire and black comedy—actually comparable to Tom Robbins's *Another Roadside Attraction*—than it was science fiction. And *Lovecraft's Book*, its eponymous protagonist notwithstanding, was actually a political novel with elements of both the spy thriller and the mainstream novel in it.

Since 1988 I have started a successful series of mysteries featuring insurance adjuster Hobart Lindsey. Two of these books have been completed, with deluxe editions published by a small company in California and mass paperbacks published by Bantam Books.

Several other mystery projects are in development. One of these is both criminous and science fictional. Mr. Hajimi Ino is a Japanese Martian corporate detective whose adventures open in the year 2143 with the novella "Black Mist." I was also gratified by the reception of the short film based on my story "12:01 PM," which was nominated for an Academy Award.

I will never again put all my eggs in the science fiction basket.

*   *   *

Longtime science fiction fan Richard Lupoff's first novel, *One Million Centuries*, made use of one of the most familiar devices of science fiction, the contemporary protagonist who wakens after a period of suspended animation into a wildly different society. Although primarily an adventure story, this tale of a man who visits three separate cultures as he attempts to return to his own time was surprisingly sophisticated for a first novel. His next, *Sacred Locomotive Flies*, went off in an entirely different direction, an almost indescribable novel of a very strange near future world peopled with exaggerated characters. Although not written in an experimental style, the work thematically resembled the "New Wave" movement and enjoyed considerable notoriety within the field at the time it was published, though it encompassed slapstick humor and self-parody and the semblance was superficial.

Into the Aether is a pastiche of early works in the field, an approach Lupoff would repeat with great success later in his career. An experimental device transports the protagonists to the moon, where they must deal with space pirates as well as earthbound villainy. Lupoff would later write two novels of Buck Rogers under the name Addison E. Steele, *Buck Rogers in the 25th Century* and *That Man on Beta*, also drawn from an older tradition, but these were fairly routine potboilers lacking the inventiveness of his original work.

Lupoff grew more serious in *The Crack in the Sky*, a dystopian tale of a future when the population is declining in the wake of the loss of much of the knowledge necessary to maintain Earth's technology. Against that background there arises a new cult which advocates a return to traditional values, but whose agenda may also involve the ultimate sacrifice of the entire human species.

The Triune Man mixes adventure with wry humor. An unlikely hero is transported to another world and told it is his destiny to save the universe, but back on Earth he has been replaced by an entirely plausible imposter. Or so the reader is led to think. Lupoff plays with reality here in a style reminiscent of the better novels of Philip K. Dick, but with his own twists and turns. *Sandworld* is an unabashed adventure story, featuring a group of people inexplicably transported from Earth to a barren world peopled with alien vampires. Although suspenseful, remarkably so at times, this work is clearly less ambitious than most of Lupoff's other novels.

Five related stories were brought together for *Space War Blues*, arguably Lupoff's best book. The most noteworthy is "With the Bentfin Boomer Boys on Little Old New Alabama," but each of the other segments presents a satiric look at some aspect of modern society by examining it in the context of one or another wildly alien world. The stories were the focus of considerable discussion in the fan press and it was expected that Lupoff would continue to be a significant voice in the field, but his subsequent work, though occasionally brilliant and always clever and competently told, never again aroused such interest. Lupoff's willingness to experiment with different styles may have contributed to a lack of focus on his work, which continued to be diverse and unpredictable. During the mid-1970s he produced an intriguing Oriental style fantasy, *Sword of the Demon*, which is in some ways his most controlled and effective novel, though perhaps too unusual for his readers.

In *Sun's End*, Lupoff returned to the theme of his first novel, although on a more limited scale. An orbiting construction worker wakens 80 years following what should have been a fatal accident to discover he has been provided with an artificial body that possesses extraordinary and not entirely understood powers. He attempts to return to his homeland, only to learn that Japan has reverted to the lifestyle of centuries earlier, a culture which he now finds alien. At the same time, he discovers that the solar system itself may be destroyed within a few centuries, a threat he must deal with personally in the less successful sequel, *Galaxy's End*.

Lupoff returned to the pastiche in *Circumpolar!* and its sequel, *Countersolar!*, arguably the best novels he's written. Both are set on a doughnut-shaped alternate Earth, but one in which most of the familiar names of our own world exist. In the first, Amelia Earhart, Howard Hughes, and Charles Lindbergh are pitted against a team of villainous Germans in a race to circumnavigate the Earth by traveling around the two poles. In the sequel, a message is received from Counter-Earth, another orbiting world, and a race through space is launched pitting Albert Einstein against Eva Peron. Although both novels are broadly humorous, they both feature straightforward action, a hectic but controlled plot, and lots of derring do.

Similar games with reality are played in two other recent novels. In *The Forever City*, a rescue mission falls into an interdimensional warp that transports it to a universe based on a television program. Far more successful is *Lovecraft's Book*, set in an alternate version of our own recent past, with German agents recruiting Lovecraft to author the American version of *Mein Kampf* as the prelude to a massive German propaganda campaign. The background on Lovecraft's life has been meticulously researched, providing verisimilitude to what is a very controlled and effective novel.

Lupoff contributed a lackluster volume to a multiauthor fantasy series, but has not recently produced any book-length fiction. A single longish story, "At Vega's Taqueria," is somewhat reminiscent of his early experimental fiction. Probability theory dictates that all realities are possible given infinite time, and this principle is invoked to create a universe where reality is subjective.

Most of Lupoff's previous short fiction has consisted of satires and humorous pieces, most notably the "Ova Hamlet" series of swipes at the styles of prominent science fiction writers. Of particular interest however are "God of the Naked Unicorn," "Mektopia," "Stroka Prospekt," and "The Devil's Hopyard." His strengths still lie primarily at greater length, where his ability to create an entire new universe that is plausible and interesting establishes wonderful settings for tales of heroism, adventure, and suspense.

—Don D'Ammassa

LUTHER, Martin. *See* SELLINGS, Arthur

LYMINGTON, John

Pseudonym for John Newton Chance. **Other Pseudonyms:** Johnathan Chance; J. Drummond; David C. Newton. **Nationality:** British. **Born:** London, in 1911. **Education:** Streatham Hill College and privately. **Military Service:** Served in the Royal Air Force during World War II. **Died:** 3 August 1983.

SCIENCE FICTION PUBLICATIONS

Novels

Night of the Big Heat. London, Hodder and Stoughton, 1959; New York, Dutton, 1960.
The Giant Stumbles. London, Hodder and Stoughton, 1960.
The Grey Ones. London, Hodder and Stoughton, 1960.
The Coming of the Strangers. London, Hodder and Stoughton, 1961; New York, Manor, 1978.
A Sword Above the Night. London, Hodder and Stoughton, 1962.
The Screaming Face. London, Hodder and Stoughton, 1963; New York, Manor, 1978.
The Sleep Eaters. London, Hodder and Stoughton, 1963; New York, Manor, 1978.
Froomb! London, Hodder and Stoughton, 1964; New York, Doubleday, 1966.
The Star Witches. London, Hodder and Stoughton, 1965; New York, Manor, 1978.
The Green Drift. London, Hodder and Stoughton, 1965; as *The Night Spiders,* New York, Doubleday, 1967.
Ten Million Years to Friday. London, Hodder and Stoughton, 1967.
The Light Benders (as Johnathan Chance). London, Hale, 1968.
The Nowhere Place. London, Hodder and Stoughton, 1969.
Give Daddy the Knife, Darling. London, Hodder and Stoughton, 1969.
The Year Dot. London, Hodder and Stoughton, 1972.
The Hole in the World. London, Hodder and Stoughton, 1974.
A Spider in the Bath. London, Hodder and Stoughton, 1975.
The Laxham Haunting. London, Hodder and Stoughton, 1976.
Starseed on Gye Moor. London, Hodder and Stoughton, 1977.
The Waking of the Stone. London, Hodder and Stoughton, 1978.

The Grey Ones, A Sword above the Night. New York, Manor, 1978.
A Caller from Overspace. London, Hodder and Stoughton, 1979.
Voyage of the Eighth Mind. London, Hodder and Stoughton, 1980.
The Power Ball. London, Hale, 1981.
The Terror Version. London, Hale, 1982.
The Vale of Sad Banana. London, Hale, 1984.

Short Stories

The Night Spiders (not same as 1967 novel). London, Corgi, 1964.

OTHER PUBLICATIONS

Novels as John Newton Chance

Murder in Oils. London, Gollancz, 1935.
Wheels in the Forest. London, Gollancz, 1935.
The Devil Drives. London, Gollancz, 1936.
Maiden Possessed. London, Gollancz, 1937.
Rhapsody in Fear. London, Gollancz, 1937.
Death of an Innocent. London, Gollancz, 1938.
The Devil in Greenlands. London, Gollancz, 1939.
The Ghost of Truth. London, Gollancz, 1939.
The Screaming Fog. London, Macdonald, 1944; as *Death Stalks the Cobbled Square,* New York, McBride, 1946.
The Red Knight. London, Macdonald, and New York, Macmillan, 1945.
The Eye in Darkness. London, Macdonald, 1946.
The Knight and the Castle. London, Macdonald, 1946.
The Black Highway. London, Macdonald, 1947.
Coven Gibbet. London, Macdonald, 1948.
The Brandy Pole. London, Macdonald, 1949.
The Night of the Full Moon. London, Macdonald, 1950.
Aunt Miranda's Murder. London, Macdonald, and New York, Dodd Mead, 1951.
The Man in My Shoes. London, Macdonald, 1952.
The Twopenny Box. London, Macdonald, 1952.
The Jason Affair. London, Macdonald, 1953; as *Up to Her Neck,* New York, Popular Library, 1955.
The Randy Inheritance. London, Macdonald, 1953.
Jason and the Sleep Game. London, Macdonald, 1954.
The Jason Murders. London, Macdonald, 1954.
Jason Goes West. London, Macdonald, 1955.
The Last Seven Hours. London, Macdonald, 1956.
A Shadow Called Janet. London, Macdonald, 1956.
Dead Man's Knock. London, Hale, 1957.
The Little Crime. London, Hale, 1957.
Affair with a Rich Girl. London, Hale, 1958.
The Man with Three Witches. London, Hale, 1958.
The Fatal Fascination. London, Hale, 1959.
The Man with No Face. London, Hale, 1959.
Alarm at Black Brake. London, Hale, 1960.
Lady in a Frame. London, Hale, 1960.
Import of Evil. London, Hale, 1961.
The Night of the Settlement. London, Hale, 1961.
Triangle of Fear. London, Hale, 1962.
The Man Behind Me. London, Hale, 1963.
The Forest Affair. London, Hale, 1963.
Commission for Disaster. London, Hale, 1964.
Death under Desolate. London, Hale, 1964.
Stormlight. London, Hale, 1966.

The Affair at Dead End. London, Hale, 1966.
The Double Death. London, Hale, 1966.
The Case of the Death Computer. London, Hale, 1967.
The Case of the Fear Makers. London, Hale, 1967.
The Death Women. London, Hale, 1967.
The Hurricane Drift. London, Hale, 1967.
The Mask of Pursuit. London, Hale, 1967.
The Thug Executive. London, Hale, 1967.
Dead Man's Shoes. London, Hale, 1968.
Death of the Wild Bird. London, Hale, 1968.
Fate of the Lying Jade. London, Hale, 1968.
The Halloween Murders. London, Hale, 1968.
Mantrap. London, Hale, 1968.
The Rogue Aunt. London, Hale, 1968.
The Abel Coincidence. London, Hale, 1969.
The Ice Maidens. London, Hale, 1969.
Involvement in Austria. London, Hale, 1969.
The Killer Reaction. London, Hale, 1969.
The Killing Experiment. London, Hale, 1969.
The Mists of Treason. London, Hale, 1970.
A Ring of Liars. London, Hale, 1970.
Three Masks of Death. London, Hale, 1970.
The Mirror Train. London, Hale, 1970.
The Cat Watchers. London, Hale, 1971.
The Faces of a Bad Girl. London, Hale, 1971.
A Wreath of Bones. London, Hale, 1971.
A Bad Dream of Death. London, Hale, 1972.
Last Train to Limbo. London, Hale, 1972.
The Man with Two Heads. London, Hale, 1972.
The Dead Tale-Tellers. London, Hale, 1972.
The Farm Villains. London, Hale, 1973.
The Grab Operators. London, Hale, 1973.
The Love-Hate Relationship. London, Hale, 1973.
The Girl in the Crime Belt. London, Hale, 1974.
The Shadow of the Killer. London, Hale, 1974.
The Starfish Affair. London, Hale, 1974.
The Canterbury Kilgrims. London, Hale, 1974.
Hill Fog. London, Hale, 1975.
The Devil's Edge. London, Hale, 1975.
The Monstrous Regiment. London, Hale, 1975.
The Murder Maker. London, Hale, 1976.
Return to Death Valley. London, Hale, 1976.
A Fall-Out of Thieves. London, Hale, 1976.
The Frightened Fisherman. London, Hale, 1976.
The House of the Dead Ones. London, Hale, 1977.
Motive for a Kill. London, Hale, 1977.
The Ducrow Folly. London, Hale, 1978.
End of an Iron Man. London, Hale, 1978.
A Drop of Hot Gold. London, Hale, 1979.
Thieves' Kitchen. London, Hale, 1979.
The Guilty Witness. London, Hale, 1979.
A Place Called Skull. London, Hale, 1980.
The Death Watch Ladies. London, Hale, 1980.
The Mayhem Madchen. London, Hale, 1980.
The Black Widow. London, Hale, 1981.
The Death Importer. London, Hale, 1981.
The Mystery of Enda Favell. London, Hale, 1981.
Madman's Will. London, Hale, 1982.
The Hunting of Mr. Exe. London, Hale, 1982.
The Shadow in Pursuit. London, Hale, 1982.
The Traditional Murders. London, Hale, 1983.

The Death Chemist. London, Hale, 1983.
Terror Train. London, Hale, 1983.
Looking for Samson. London, Hale, 1984.
Nobody's Supposed to Murder the Butler. London, Hale, 1984.
The Bad Circle. London, Hale, 1985.
The Time Bomb. London, Hale, 1985.
The Woman Hater. London, Hale, 1986.
The Psychic Trap. London, Hale, 1986.
Spy on a Spider. London, Hale, 1987.
The Hit Man. London, Hale, 1987.
The Hiller Weapon. London, Hale, 1987.
The Smiling Cadaver. London, Hale, 1987.
The Reluctant Agent. London, Hale, 1988.
The Shadow Before. London, Hale, 1988.
The Offshore Conspiracy. London, Hale, 1988.
The Man on the Cliff. London, Hale, 1988.
A Confusion of Eyes. London, Hale, 1989.
The Running of the Spies. London, Hale, 1989.
A Tale of Tangled Ladies. London, Hale, 1989.

Novels as J. Drummond

The Essex Road Crime. London, Amalgamated Press, 1944.
The Manor House Menace. London, Amalgamated Press, 1944.
The Painted Dagger. London, Amalgamated Press, 1944.
The Riddle of the Leather Bottle. London, Amalgamated Press, 1944.
The Tragic Case of the Station Master's Legacy. London, Amalgamated Press, 1944.
At Sixty Miles an Hour. London, Amalgamated Press, 1945.
The House on the Hill. London, Amalgamated Press, 1945.
The Riddle of the Mummy Case. London, Amalgamated Press, 1945.
The Mystery of the Deserted Camp. London, Amalgamated Press, 1948.
The Town of Shadows. London, Amalgamated Press, 1948.
The Case of the "Dead" Spy. London, Amalgamated Press, 1949.
The Riddle of the Receiver's Hoard. London, Amalgamated Press, 1949.
The Secret of the Living Skeleton. London, Amalgamated Press, 1949.
The South Coast Mystery. London, Amalgamated Press, 1949.
The Case of L.A.C. Dickson. London, Amalgamated Press, 1950.
The Mystery of the Haunted Square. London, Amalgamated Press, 1950.
The House in the Woods. London, Amalgamated Press, 1950.
The Secret of the Sixty Steps. London, Amalgamated Press, 1951.
The Case of the Man with No Name. London, Amalgamated Press, 1951.
Hated by All! London, Amalgamated Press, 1951.
The Mystery of the Sabotaged Jet. London, Amalgamated Press, 1951.
The House on the River. London, Amalgamated Press, 1952.
The Mystery of the Five Guilty Men. London, Amalgamated Press, 1954.
The Case of the Two-Faced Swindler. London, Amalgamated Press, 1955.
The Teddy-Boy Mystery. London, Amalgamated Press, 1955.

Other as John Newton Chance

The Black Ghost (for children; as David C. Newton). London, Oxford University Press, 1947.

The Dangerous Road (for children; as David C. Newton). London, Oxford University Press, 1948.
Bunst and the Brown Voice [the Bold, and the Secret Six, and the Flying Eye] (for children). London, Oxford University Press, 4 vols., 1950-53.
The Jennifer Jigsaw (for children), with Shirley Newton Chance. London, Oxford University Press, 1951.
Yellow Belly (autobiography). London, Hale, 1959.
The Crimes at Rillington Place: A Novelist's Reconstruction. London, Hodder and Stoughton, 1961.

* * *

John Lymington was well known for the crime novels published under his real name, John Newton Chance. As a writer of science fiction, however, he has received little notice, even within the SF community, perhaps because the fantastic elements of his fiction often serve as little more than a backdrop for the main action which characteristically centers on a small but diverse group of British citizens faced with a common threat. Lymington's characters, his village settings, and the structure of his novels owe as much to the tradition of the classical detective story as to the traditions of science fiction, and with few exceptions he does not concern himself with the social or intellectual implications of the marvels he introduces. As an author of suspense and horror stories, he is often startlingly effective, able to spin an entertaining novel from a single situation, but when he attempts more complex themes his novels tend to get out of hand.

Lymington makes use of few of the resources of the SF genre; most of his novels are variations on the basic theme of alien invasion, while a couple deal with time travel and contain elements of social satire. His first SF novel, *Night of the Big Heat,* is an admirable addition to the something-is-amiss-in-the-village school of British suspense novels, though the science fiction element—an alien civilization transmitting giant spiders into the English countryside via microwaves—is clearly secondary to the portrayal of the reactions of a group of local citizens gathered at a country inn. Spiders are one of Lymington's favorite images of horror—even though he persistently regards them as insects—and were also the featured attraction in another invasion story, "The Night Spiders." The basic formula of an unknown horror menacing a small community was repeated in *The Coming of the Strangers;* in *A Sword Above the Night*—perhaps the most straightforward and unadorned of Lymington's exercises in suspense—the anticipated "invasion" that provides suspense throughout the novel is dispensed with in a three-paragraph closing summary, explaining that it is merely the pre-programmed return to Earth of dead astronauts who had left from an earlier civilization thousands of years ago. This novel perhaps most clearly indicates the short shrift Lymington gives his science fiction concepts.

Occasionally, Lymington adds other science fiction elements to his formula—in *The Sleep Eaters* the invasion is telepathic (*The Night Spiders* also features telepathy), and in *The Star Witches* a mad scientist helps bring the aliens to Earth. *The Star Witches* also reveals an inclination on Lymington's part to work traditional supernatural appurtenances into his SF narratives: in this case a coven of witches is associated with the alien invasion. Time travel is another concept that Lymington sometimes plays with, in *The Night Spiders* and *Ten Million Years to Friday. Froomb!* is in some ways Lymington's most ambitious novel, and the most satirical. The title is short for "The fluid's running out of my brakes!," a fictional

cartoon caption that has come to symbolize the state of world affairs in Lymington's headlong future world. The story, which somehow encompasses such diverse themes as threatened nuclear war, heaven, heat rays, insecticide poisoning, food additives, radiation, drugs, and male impotence, concerns a man who dies and goes to heaven, only to find that it is actually a postholocaust world brought about by an American defense experiment about to take place before he died. His efforts to return and warn the world of the experiment make up the bulk of the novel.

Lymington was not a major writer, and there is much to suggest that he did not take his science fiction seriously, but in the relatively narrow territory he staked out for himself he provides enjoyable light reading.

—Gary K. Wolfe

LYNN, Elizabeth A.

Nationality: American. **Born:** New York City, 8 June 1946. **Education:** Case Western Reserve University, Cleveland, B.A. 1967; University of Chicago (Woodrow Wilson Fellow, 1967-68), M.A. 1968. **Career:** Public school teacher, Chicago, 1968-70; unit manager, St. Francis Hospital, Evanston, Illinois, 1970-72, and French Hospital, San Francisco, 1972-75; formerly teacher in the Women's Studies Program, San Francisco State University. **Address:** c/o Bluejay Books, 26 Douglas Road, Chappaqua, New York 10514, U.S.A.

SCIENCE FICTION PUBLICATIONS

Novels (series: Chronicles of Tornor)

A Different Light. New York, Berkley, 1978; London, Gollancz, 1979.
Watchtower (Tornor). New York, Berkley, 1979; London, Hamlyn, 1981.
The Dancers of Arun (Tornor). New York, Berkley, 1979; London, Hamlyn, 1982.
The Northern Girl (Tornor). New York, Berkley, 1980; London, Arrow, 1987.
The Sardonyx Net. New York, Berkley, 1981.
The Red Hawk. New Castle, Virginia, Cheap Street, 1983.
The Silver Horse. New York, Bluejay, 1984.

Short Stories

The Woman Who Loved the Moon, and Other Stories. New York, Berkley, 1981.
Tales from a Vanished Country. Eugene, Oregon, Pulphouse, 1990.

* * *

Elizabeth A. Lynn's greatest strength lies in her ability to focus sympathetically on a single character or a small cast of characters that are very human. Although her science fiction stories are often presented in the trappings of space opera—faster-than-light travel, interstellar exploration, humans kidnapped by aliens—they are peopled by individuals who are clearly drawn from life: flawed and identifiably human, not Kimball Kennisons, or comic-book superheroes.

This is most apparent in her most important science-fiction novel, *The Sardonyx Net*. Working from some pretty hoary SF elements—including interstellar drug and slave trades—Lynn has created a remarkable book. Although in synopsis it sounds like something straight out of a 1940s *Thrilling Wonder Stories* magazine, *The Sardonyx Net* is primarily a novel of character with a satisfyingly complex plot and some of Lynn's best writing. It is here that one of her special skills is most apparent: the ability to create a villain with whom the reader can empathize. *Net* is far better plotted than most of her novels, and the best evidence of her matured skills.

Several of her short stories, and the novel *A Different Light,* are linked by some common images and themes. Although interstellar travel seems taken for granted, Lynn consistently treats the concept of hyperspace, the Hype, as a place not only beyond the normal limits of space-time, but beyond reality itself. It is a source of danger to all but the strongest who attempt to pass through it. In *A Different Light,* in fact, the Hype is the cause of the apparent death of the protagonist. Jimson, an artist, has an incurable cancer, one which will limit his lifespan, if he is careful, to another 20 years. Before he dies, however, he wants to see the light of other stars, and rejoin an old friend and lover. He flees his home planet in the sure knowledge that travel in the Hype will accelerate the process of his cancer. Jimson is typical of Lynn's protagonists. Most of them work in some art form, and seem to pay for their gifts with a physical debility—such as the one-armed telepath in *The Dancers of Arun*—but it is a debility that heightens their sensitivity to others and their surroundings. Jimson is a sexual being. Like many of Lynn's characters he lives in a society not proscribed by sexual roles, and his sexuality finds expression through love for women and men. A first novel, *A Different Light* is certainly flawed, both by its somewhat episodic plot and an ending that seems drawn from other SF novels rather than from within. But the novel's sensitivity and fluid language betray a promise that is more than fulfilled in her later novels.

The Chronicles of Tornor is a true trilogy—three self-contained novels related by continuity of place, cultures, and institutions—that defies neat categorization. The trilogy concerns the way that cultures and institutions change, and succeeds because it focuses on individuals directly involved in those cultures. *Watchtower* introduces the cultures: the rigid, militaristic society of the North, and the newly developed egalitarian life of the Cheari, built on an art composed of dance and martial art. The protagonist is a vassal of the northern culture, and the novel's conflict lies in his inability to assimilate the new mores and life-style of the Chearis. The language is crisp and precise. *The Dancers of Arun* takes place 100 years later. It centers on the almost utopian lifestyle of the Cheari, and the language of the book is appropriately softened. Kerris is a child of these people but has been raised in the North, and finds difficulty in believing in their acceptance of his maimed arm. Only through the physically loving relationship that he develops with his brother does he learn to accept himself. The trilogy is concluded with *The Northern Girl,* which concerns a third culture in the South. By now the Cheari are only a memory, and the focus is on a city-dwelling society. Here, Lynn is on even surer ground, and Kendra-on-the-Delta is a more convincing place than either the military keeps or rustic villages of the previous books. The plot has a tendency to drift, but the characters are tightly drawn, with an emotional warmth unusual in the field. Much of this effect stems from Lynn's concentration on a small group of real people in intimate contact, rather than the giant battles of armies and wizards so common in fantasy.

Lynn's latest foray into fantasy is *The Silver Horse,* a disappointingly slight and derivative fairytale about two young girls from San Francisco who travel to Dreamland to rescue a little boy. It is notable only for the role reversal of the lead characters; little girls are fearless, and little boys chicken-hearted.

—Jeff Frane

M

MacAPP, C.C.

Pseudonym for Carroll M. Capps. **Nationality:** American. **Born:** 1917(?). **Career:** Worked as a printer. **Died:** 15 January 1971.

SCIENCE FICTION PUBLICATIONS

Novels

Omha Abides. New York, Paperback Library, 1968.
Prisoners of the Sky. New York, Lancer, 1969.
Secret of the Sunless World (as Carroll M. Capps). New York, Dell, 1969.
Worlds of the Wall. New York, Avon, 1969.
Recall Not Earth. New York, Dell, 1970.
Subb. New York, Paperback Library, 1971.
Bumsider. New York, Lancer, 1972.

*   *   *

The SF career of C.C. MacApp lasted only slightly over 10 years, from 1960 to 1971. During that decade he built a reputation for exciting adventure stories in which a lone hero would overcome seemingly hopeless odds to save his entire nation, species, or world. His style was beginning to broaden when he died.

MacApp came late in his life to SF. His real name was Carroll M. Capps, and his profession had been in the color printing industry. An illness forced him to retire in his early forties, and he began writing SF. His first story appeared in 1960; he averaged only a couple of short works a year through 1963. Then from mid-1964 through 1968 he seemed to have stories almost constantly in print, in either *If* or *Worlds of Tomorrow,* the magazines with which he was most closely associated. In 1968, he began to produce paperback novels; five between that year and 1970. At the same time, his flow of magazine stories cut back to a trickle; this was due to both his novel writing and his declining health. A couple of short stories and two more paperback novels appeared posthumously. He had been working on a hardcover novel for Doubleday but it was never finished.

MacApp's magazine works were primarily of novelette length. He was best known for suspense dramas in which humans appeared as underdogs amidst a galactic multispecies civilization. Chief among these were the nine "Gree" novelettes; "The Slaves of Gree," "No Friend of Gree," and so on. These featured Colonel Steve Duke, the top human fighter among the multispecies resistance to the Gree Empire, which had conquered most of the galaxy (including Earth) 600 years earlier. Each story had Steve Duke being sent to an unknown planet that Gree's forces had just landed upon, to learn why Gree wanted it and to keep Gree from establishing a new base there. Duke's commando tactics made him a grim counterpart to Keith Laumer's more lighthearted James Retief, who also fought regularly in *If* during the mid-1960s to make the galaxy safe for humanity. A typical non-"Gree" drama is "A Ticket to Zennon," in which Tom Lerrow, a young Earthman, learns that he is being unwittingly used as a courier of plans for a top-secret weapon, which two powerful alien factions and a deadly criminal are after.

MacApp's aliens are not always villains, nor were all his stories dramas. "Winter of the Llangs" and "When the Sea Is Born Again" feature alien teenagers in adventures that amount to rites of passage among their peoples. MacApp's first story, "A Pride of Islands," is a mild comedy where humans are portrayed as parasites living upon giant animals. A more successful comedy is "Mail Drop," in which the bureaucracy of the galactic postal service almost starts but finally prevents an interstellar war.

MacApp's short fiction succeeds by means of dramatic incidents. His novels show that he could write powerful adventures with more richly portrayed characters. Yet the novels have a thematic sameness. All begin with their protagonists caught in a moment of total despair. Murno, an ignorant human peasant on an Earth subjugated by aliens for thousands of years, learns that their masters are about to begin hunting men for sport (*Omha Abides*). Raab Garan, a cadet in a dirigible air fleet on a backward colony planet, faces his country's fall to its totalitarian adversary unless he can succeed in what he realizes is a suicide mission (*Prisoners of the Sky*). Zeke Bolivar, space explorer, is about to crash on an unknown world (*Worlds of the Wall*). John Braysen, a Space Force commander, believes that he is one of only a few hundred humans left alive after Earth loses a space war (*Recall Not Earth*). MacApp's heroes always win through to a victorious conclusion but only after a psychologically exhausting struggle. Also, the lack of women in MacApp's works stands out sharply. In *Recall Not Earth,* the presence of one chapter featuring women (to establish that human women still exist) seems almost forced. Most of his other novels use women only as minor background characters. MacApp had only started to break away from these stereotypes in his final novel, *Bumsider,* which has a strong and convincingly-portrayed woman supporting character in Pegs Waran, and a plot involving more human interactions among his main cast.

—Frederick Patten

MacAVOY, R(oberta) A(nn)

Nationality: American. **Born:** Cleveland, Ohio, 13 December 1949. **Education:** Case Western Reserve University, Cleveland, 1967-71, B.Sc. 1971. **Family:** Married Ronald Allen Cain in 1978. **Career:** Financial aid officer's assistant, Columbia College, New York, 1975-78; computer programmer, SRI International, Menlo Park, California, 1979-83. Since 1983, full-time writer. **Awards:** John W. Campbell Best New Writer award, 1984. **Agent:** Richard Curtis Associates, 171 East 74th Street, New York, New York 10021, U.S.A. **Address:** Underhill at Nelson Farm, 1669 Nelson Road, House 6, Scotts Valley, California 95066, U.S.A.

SCIENCE FICTION PUBLICATIONS

Novels (series: Black Dragon; Lute; Nazhuret of Sordaling)

Tea with the Black Dragon. New York and London, Bantam, 1983.

A Trio for Lute. Garden City, New York, Doubleday, 1985.
Damiano. New York, Bantam, 1984; London, 1985.
Damiano's Lute. New York, Bantam, 1984; London, 1986.
Raphael. New York, Bantam, 1984; London, 1986.
The Book of Kells. New York, Bantam, 1985; London, 1986.
Twisting the Rope: Casadh and t'Sugain (Black Dragon). New York, Bantam, 1986; London, 1987.
The Grey Horse. New York, Bantam, 1987; London, 1988.
The Third Eagle: Lessons Along a Minor String. Garden City, New York, Doubleday, 1989; London, Bantam, 1990.
Lens of the World (Nazhuret). New York, Morrow, 1990; London, Headline, 1991.
King of the Dead (Nazhuret). New York, Morrow, 1991; London, Headline, 1992.
Winter of the Wolf. London, Headline, 1993; as *The Belly of the Wolf,* New York, Morrow, 1994.

*

R.A. MacAvoy comments:

The books I write are very different, one from another. This may be an unconscious attempt on my part to avoid falling into a rut, but more likely I just get bored with one subject or one narrative voice. Everything I have written, however, has something eccentrically religious in it, and at least one animal. I don't plan it this way.

In almost all my novels, the protagonists find themselves engaged in testing the truth, either by hard experience or direct perception. They also wrestle with ambiguity and the possibility that there is no ultimate truth. On the other hand, all my novels strive to be adventure stories, because those are what I like to read myself, and I try to find happy endings. Reasonably happy.

*   *   *

With nearly a dozen compelling novels in less than a decade, R.A. MacAvoy already fulfills her promise as winner of the John W. Campbell Award for Best New Writer. Hailed as "best new fantasy writer of the 1980s" by the *Chicago Sun-Times,* and predicted to be "one of the future giants of the SF/fantasy field" by *ALA Booklist,* MacAvoy is also praised by writers of such stature as Anne McCaffrey and Andre Norton.

In *Tea with the Black Dragon,* the memorable character Mayland Long, a swarthy sinuous Asian of uncertain origins, introduces MacAvoy's propensity for realism set slightly askew. In a genteel California hotel, the cultured Long meets middle-aged Martha Macnamara, summoned from the East coast by her troubled computer whiz daughter Liz, who has suddenly gone missing. Attracted by Martha's directness, loner Long joins her on a search for Liz that leads through modern computer corruption to ancient wisdom. Constantly mistaken for a private detective, Long is actually a powerful black Chinese dragon, metamorphosed into human form to study the human condition.

Such satisfying fantasy in a mystery format demanded a sequel. The team of Long and Macnamara reappear four years later, in real and imaginary time, in *Twisting the Rope.* Martha is fiddler and leader of a traditional Celtic band on concert tour, with her lover Long as road manager, when George St. Ives is found hanging by a handmade Irish rope off a Santa Cruz pier. As the couple untangles the strands of this mystery, MacAvoy choreographs the complex cords that bind a group of talented musicians with varied motivations, and leads Long further on his search for Truth. Readers

may long for another performance by this philosophical sleuthing duo.

Between the two acclaimed Black Dragon books, MacAvoy created two other worlds in two more fantasy subgenres. Her haunting *A Trio for Lute* may challenge MacAvoy's future writings for its place as her masterpiece. In three volumes, this transformational tale explores, as the finest fantasy must, the nature of good and evil in one person's struggle toward the sublime. As in all heroic fantasy, the hero is on a quest, but the lute-playing alchemist Damiano Delstrego is not built in typical heroic proportions. In *Damiano,* the first volume, the delicate young musician/witch flees his embattled city to seek its salvation by magic means. Damiano's own hero is his lute teacher Raphael, the gloriously beautiful archangel who only Damiano can see. Because the holy Raphael cannot interfere in human affairs despite his love for Damiano, the desperate witch risks his soul for his city in a pact with Raphael's brother Lucifer. Needing stronger witchery than his own to handle Satan, Damiano approaches Saara, whose Finnish magic is greatest in Europe. But old wounds lock the two witches in battle, and Damiano sacrifices all his powers to Saara.

In *Damiano's Lute,* Damiano has become merely a wandering musician, roaming the Alps with the scampish boy dancer Gaspare. His only wizardry is upon the lute, impressing the Pope at Avignon. When the plague strikes Avignon, Damiano reclaims his powers from Saara to fight it. Winning Saara's love and healing a plague victim, Damiano forfeits his own life.

Damiano appears as a ghost in *Raphael* to his beloved angel, who succumbs to Lucifer's plot to destroy his brother through love for a mortal. Stripped of his wings by Satan, Raphael plummets to earth as a human slave of corrupt Moorish traders. The ex-angel has no idea how to be human, so Damiano switches roles to become his spiritual advisor. Damiano's mourning friends, Gaspare and Saara, enlist the aid of a Chinese dragon to rescue Raphael from slavery, leading them to a final clash with the Devil himself. In an early lesson with Damiano, Raphael says, "Mortals by their nature cannot continue in the way they are. What matters . . . is the direction in which they change." On an epic scale, in language as lyrical as the lute, MacAvoy explores mortal change through the realm of the spirit.

MacAvoy also contributes significantly to time-travel literature with *The Book of Kells,* in which a modern Irish historian and a Canadian artist slip through a time gate to tenth-century Ireland. The gate opens when John Thornburn replicates the intricate scrolling in the illuminated manuscript, while bagpipes play on his stereo. Erupting through his bathroom door comes a screaming, naked girl, bleeding from the wounds of rape. When John calls his lover, Derval O'Keane, to help him calm the hysterical girl, Derval recognizes her antiquated Irish speech. Hearing the girl Ailesh's tale of murderous Viking raiders, Derval cannot refuse aid, or resist the chance to visit the old Ireland of her studies. Regarded by Ailesh as miraculous saints, John and Derval accompany her home to become enmeshed in the entrancing treacherous world of a thousand years ago. Imbued with Gaelic earthiness, the sensations of coarse cloth and damp cold and the fragility of human life, MacAvoy's old Ireland even smells right. The conflict of modern logic with ancient superstition mirrors the violent culture clash between Danes and Gaels, Viking individualism against Gaelic clan values. In this time-fantasy, magic resides in the glorious *Book of Kells* itself, a "talisman [with] . . . power to move."

Set in a later Ireland still rich with its own language but threatened by English incursions, *The Grey Horse* brings fantasy into

Connemara in the form of Ruairì MacEibhir, a horse fairy. This 1500-year-old púca emerges from the fairies' mirrorworld to win the love of mortal Máire Standún, switching back and forth from horse to human form as he pursues her. Embedded with difficult Gaelic names, MacAvoy's prose seems dense. More devoted to horse lore than fairy magic, her story flows less freely than usual. Even mystical Ruairì and spirited Máire are rendered less vibrantly than MacAvoy's typical characters, though equine fans may enjoy this ultimate horse story.

MacAvoy's foray into science fiction is more successful in *The Third Eagle*. On the planet Neunacht, Wanbli is a Paint of the Wacaan clan, obliged to bodyguard those who run his impoverished but lovely planet. Tattooed on Wanbli's magnificent red chest and torso are three sets of spread wings signifying his high warrior status. When fortune flings Wanbli a chance to star in the shimmers (movies) on another planet, he encounters many other types of the seven sentient beings in his universe, as well as with the prejudices among them. In an abrupt shift of pace halfway through the book, Wanbli discovers that the "revivalists" with whom he travels use their spaceship to track sleepers, refugees searching for new home planets while frozen in sleep for hundreds of years. When Wanbli realizes that most of the sleepers won't be saved, he wakes them himself, holding the ship hostage. With page-turning suspense, Wanbli fights for the fate of the sleepers, the revivalists, and his own planet, meanwhile discovering kinship with awakened Sioux from Earth. MacAvoy's enduring interest in cross-cultural communication transports easily into space.

The science of lens grinding is a focus in *Lens of the World,* a promising opening to a new fantasy series set in the Kingdom of Vestinglon. MacAvoy's 40-year-old hero Nazhuret recounts his life story to his king. With no idea of his parentage, Nazhuret spends his first 19 years in a military school as perpetual student/servant, until he chances upon an isolated observatory. There, he meets his new teacher Powl, a mysterious noble who puts him through arduous solitary training for three years. Swerving from antagonist to benefactor, Powl coaches the boy in martial arts, languages, astronomy, lens grinding, and "living in the belly of the wolf"—meditation. Without warning, Powl releases the sheltered young man to the world to encounter robbers, murderers, werewolves, dragons, and the king's court, where he is regarded as King of Hell. Powl taught him to swear allegiance to no one but himself, but in doing so he both impresses and insults the king, and imperils his beloved Powl.

The other world of Vestinglon contains peoples and languages unfamiliar but Earthlike. Even the dragons, who make a rather fortuitous appearance in the last 30 pages, aren't particularly magical. Nazhuret has an opium dream that leaves physical evidence, but MacAvoy's message is that magic feats are performed through endurance, discipline, philosophy, and character.

Nazhuret's strong, unique personality exemplifies all MacAvoy protagonists, who are antiheroic in their eccentricity and fierce independence. All are truth-searchers who challenge the forces of good and evil, questioning accepted morality. Even an angel, a dragon, and a fairy must adopt human form to discover the essence of humanity. Through her expertise in music and language, MacAvoy examines human communications and the prejudice that often thwarts them. She defines and redefines the longing for freedom at the core of human nature. Even her monsters are natural. Grounded firmly in three-dimensional reality, her fantasies uplift readers into spiritual concerns. Through a fascinating blend of Buddhist philosophy and Celtic ethics, MacAvoy forges her own fresh vision, unlimited by literary genre. Ushered through elegant prose infused with passion, conviction, and wry humor, readers enter MacAvoy's living worlds and meet her breathing characters to measure what they themselves believe.

—Cathi MacRae

MacCREIGH, James. *See* **POHL, Frederik.**

MacDONALD, George

Nationality: British. **Born:** Near Huntly, Aberdeenshire, 10 December 1824. **Education:** King's College, University of Aberdeen, 1840-45, M.A. 1845; Congregationalist Theological College, Highbury, London, 1848-50. **Family:** Married Louisa Powell in 1850 (died 1902); 11 children. **Career:** Private tutor in London, 1845-48; minister, Trinity Congregational Church, Arundel, Sussex, 1850-53; lecturer and preacher in Manchester, 1855-56, Hastings, Sussex, 1857-59, and London, from 1859; taught at Bedford College; editor, with Norman MacLeod, *Good Words for the Young* magazine, 1870-72; lived partly in Bordighera, Italy from 1877. LL.D.: University of Aberdeen, 1868. Granted Civil List pension, 1877. **Died:** 18 September 1905.

SCIENCE FICTION PUBLICATIONS

Novels

Phantastes: A Faerie Romance for Men and Women. London, Smith Elder, 1858; Boston, Loring, 1870.
The Portent: A Story of the Inner Vision of the Highlanders, Commonly Called the Second Sight. London, Smith Elder, 1864; New York, Munro, 1885.
Lilith: A Romance. London, Chatto and Windus, and New York, Dodd Mead, 1895.

Fiction for children

Dealings with the Fairies, illustrated by Arthur Hughes. London, Strahan, 1867; New York, Routledge, 1891.
At the Back of the North Wind, illustrated by Arthur Hughes. London, Strahan, 1870; New York, Routledge, 1871.
Ranald Bannerman's Boyhood, illustrated by Arthur Hughes. London, Strahan, and New York, Routledge, 1871.
The Princess and the Goblin, illustrated by Arthur Hughes. London, Strahan, and New York, Routledge, 1871.
Gutta-Percha Willie, The Working Genius, illustrated by Arthur Hughes. London, King, and Boston, Hoyt, 1873.
The Wise Woman: A Parable. London, Strahan, 1875; as *A Double Story,* New York, Dodd Mead, 1876; as *The Lost Princess,* London, Wells Gardner Darton, 1895.

Sir Gibbie. London, Hurst and Blackett, 3 vols., 1879; Philadelphia, Lippincott, 1879.

The Gifts of the Child Christ and Other Tales. London, Sampson Low, 2 vols., 1882; as *Stephen Archer and Other Tales,* 1883; as *The Gifts of the Child Christ: Fairy Tales and Stories for the Childlike,* edited by Glenn Edward Sadler, Grand Rapids, Michigan, Eerdmans, and London, Mowbray, 1973.

The Princess and Curdie, illustrated by James Allen. Philadelphia, Lippincott, 1882; London, Chatto and Windus, 1883.

A Rough Shaking, illustrated by W. Parkinson. New York, Routledge, 1890; London, Blackie, 1891.

The Fairy Tales of George MacDonald, edited by Greville MacDonald. London, Fifield, 5 vols., 1904.

The Light Princess and Other Tales of Fantasy, edited by Roger Lancelyn Green. London, Gollancz, 1961.

The Complete Fairy Tales of George MacDonald. New York, Schocken, 1977.

The Christmas Stories of George MacDonald, illustrated by Linda Hill Griffith. Elgin, Illinois, Cook, 1981.

The Day Boy and the Night Girl. New York, Knopf, 1988.

The Golden Key. N.p., n.d.

Short Stories

Far above Rubies. New York, Dodd Mead, 1899.

The Portent and Other Stories. London, Unwin, 1909.

Evenor, edited by Lin Carter. New York, Ballantine, 1972.

The World of George MacDonald. Wheaton, Illinois, Shaw, 1978.

OTHER PUBLICATIONS

Novels

David Elginbrod. London, Hurst and Blackett, 3 vols., 1863; New York, Munro, 1879.

Adela Cathcart. London, Hurst and Blackett, 3 vols., 1864; New York, Munro, 1882.

Alec Forbes of Howglen. London, Hurst and Blackett, 3 vols., 1865; New York, Harper, 1872.

Annals of a Quiet Neighbourhood. London, Hurst and Blackett, 3 vols., 1867; New York, Harper, 1867.

Guild Court. London, Hurst and Blackett, 3 vols., 1867; New York, Harper, 1868.

Robert Falconer. London, Hurst and Blackett, 3 vols., 1868; Boston, Loring, n.d.

The Seaboard Parish. London, Tinsley, 3 vols., 1868; New York, Routledge, 1868.

The Vicar's Daughter: An Autobiographical Story. Boston, Roberts, 1871; London, Tinsley, 3 vols., 1872.

Wilfrid Cumbermede. London, Hurst and Blackett, 3 vols., 1872; New York, Scribner, 1872.

Malcolm. London, King, 3 vols., 1875; Philadelphia, Lippincott, 1875.

St. George and St. Michael. London, King, 3 vols., 1876; New York, Ford, 1876(?).

Thomas Wingfold, Curate. London, Hurst and Blackett, 3 vols., 1876; New York, Munro, 1879.

The Marquis of Lossie. London, Hurst and Blackett, 3 vols., 1877; Philadelphia, Lippincott, 1877.

Paul Faber, Surgeon. London, Hurst and Blackett, 3 vols., 1879; Philadelphia, Lippincott, 1879.

Mary Marston. London, Sampson Low, 3 vols., 1881; Philadelphia, Lippincott, 1881.

Warlock o' Glen Warlock. New York, Harper, 1881; as *Castle Warlock: A Homely Romance,* London, Sampson Low, 3 vols., 1882.

Weighed and Wanting. London, Sampson Low, 3 vols., 1882; New York, Harper, 1882.

Donal Grant. London, Kegan Paul, 3 vols., 1883; New York, Harper, 1883.

What's Mine's Mine. London, Kegan Paul, 3 vols., 1886; New York, Harper, 1886.

Home Again. London, Kegan Paul, and New York, Appleton, 1887.

The Elect Lady. London, Kegan Paul, and New York, Munro, 1888.

There and Back. London, Kegan Paul, 3 vols., 1891; Boston, Lothrop, n.d.

The Flight of the Shadow. London, Kegan Paul, and New York, Appleton, 1891.

Heather and Snow. London, Chatto and Windus, 2 vols., 1893; New York, Harper, 1893.

Salted with Fire. London, Hurst and Blackett, and New York, Dodd Mead, 1897.

Poetry

Within and Without: A Dramatic Poem. London, Longman, 1855; New York, Scribner, 1872.

Poems. London, Longman, 1857.

A Hidden Life and Other Poems. London, Longman, 1864; New York, Scribner, 1872.

The Disciple and Other Poems. London, Strahan, 1867.

Dramatic and Miscellaneous Poems. New York, Scribner, 2 vols., 1876.

A Book of Strife, in the Form of the Diary of an Old Soul. Privately printed, 1880.

A Threefold Cord: Poems by Three Friends, with John Hill MacDonald and Greville Matheson, edited by George MacDonald. Privately printed, 1883.

The Poetical Works of George MacDonald. London, Chatto and Windus, 2 vols., 1893.

Rampolli: Growths from a Long-Planted Root, Being Translations Chiefly from the German, Along with a "Year's Diary of an Old Soul." London, Longman, 1897.

Other

Unspoken Sermons. London, Strahan and Longman, 3 vols., 1867, 1886, 1889; New York, Routledge, n.d.

England's Antiphon. London, Macmillan, 1868; Philadelphia, Lippincott, n.d.

The Miracles of Our Lord. London, Strahan, and New York, Randolph, 1870.

Works of Fancy and Imagination. London, Strahan, 10 vols., 1871.

Orts. London, Sampson Low, 1882; as *The Imagination and Other Essays,* Boston, Lothrop, 1883; revised edition, as *A Dish of Orts.* Sampson Low, 1893.

The Tragedie of Hamlet, Prince of Denmark: A Study of the Text of the Folio of 1623. London, Longman, 1885.

The Hope of the Gospel (sermons). London, Ward Lock, and New York, Appleton, 1892.

The Hope of the Universe. London, Victoria Street Society for the Protection of Animals from Vivisection, 1896.

George MacDonald: An Anthology, edited by C.S. Lewis. London, Bles, 1946; New York, Macmillan, 1947.

The Heart of George MacDonald, edited by Rolland Hein. Wheaton, Illinois, Shaw, 1994.

An Expression of Character: The Letters of George MacDonald, edited by Glenn Edward Sadler. Grand Rapids, Michigan, Eerdmans, 1994.

Editor, *A Cabinet of Gems, Cut and Polished by Sir Philip Sidney, Now for the More Radiance Presented Without Their Setting.* London, Elliot Stock, 1892.

Translator, *Twelve of the Spiritual Songs of Novalis.* Privately printed, 1851.

Translator, *Exotics: A Translation of the Spiritual Songs of Novalis, The Hymn Book of Luther, and Other Poems from the German and Italian.* London, Strahan, 1876.

*

Bibliography: *A Centennial Bibliography of George MacDonald* by John Malcolm Bullock, Aberdeen, University Press, 1925; *George MacDonald's Books for Children: A Bibliography of First Editions* by Raphael B. Shaberman, London, Cityprint Business Centres, 1979.

Critical Studies: *George MacDonald and His Wife* by Greville MacDonald, London, Allen and Unwin, 1924; *The Golden Key: A Study of the Fiction of George MacDonald* by R.L. Wolfe, New Haven, Connecticut, Yale University Press, 1961; *The Harmony Within: The Spiritual Vision of George MacDonald* by Rolland Hein, Grand Rapids, Michigan, Christian University Press, n.d.; *George MacDonald* by David S. Robb, Edinburgh, Scottish Academy, 1987, Eureka, California, Sunrise, 1989; *George MacDonald* by William Raeper, Tring, Hertshire, and Batavia, Illinois, Lion, 1987; *The Gold Thread: Essays on George MacDonald* edited by William Raeper, Edinburgh, Edinburgh University Press, 1990.

*   *   *

If Jules Verne is the father of "hard" science fiction, then George MacDonald could well be claimed as the father of the kind of SF that spills over into the borders of fantasy and whimsy, and of other worlds whose significance lies in the ideas they present rather than their devotion to science. George MacDonald is perhaps best known as a classic children's writer of the 19th century. He is a profoundly Christian writer, although his idea of Christianity was far broader than many others of his time, and he was strongly influenced by Plato's theory of ideal reality. MacDonald's children's books stand between the anarchic, amoral, dream-logic of Lewis Carroll's *Alice* books and the preaching, allegorical fairytale fantasy of Charles Kingsley's *Water-Babies.* But even his children's stories contain elements of science fiction. For example, within the once-upon-a-time setting of *The Princess and the Goblin,* and its consoling image of the mystical, angel-like great-great-grandmother spinning thread from spiderwebs in the light of a moon-lamp, there are the goblins. These goblins are underground miners, who once lived above ground but, refusing to pay the king's taxes, they hid below ground and greatly altered over the generations. They now prey mischievously upon ordinary humans.

In *The Princess and Curdie,* the angelic grandmother asks Curdie, "Have you ever heard what some philosophers say—that men were all animals once?" And she goes on to talk of the bestial decline of

some people, anticipating Freud's analysis of Wolfman and Ratman. In fact, MacDonald's strange fairy story "The Day Boy and the Night Girl" begins with a witch who "had a wolf in her mind." In *At the Back of the North Wind,* Diamond, the cabman's simpleminded son, finds great significance in the dream-journeys he takes with the goddess-like North Wind. MacDonald knew that dreams cannot be made sensible by taking them at face value, but their secret meaning reflected the health of the inner person. MacDonald's Wise Woman, in the book *The Wise Woman,* is effectively a child psychiatrist with penetrating insight into the personality of young children, and a sound approach to parenting, the shaping and correcting character. Of course, her underlying therapeutic principles are based on Christian morality, as is much of MacDonald's narrative. But this is not surprising.

MacDonald initially studied natural philosophy (what we now call science) and chemistry, then trained and worked as a church minister. Most of his writing makes little direct use of this early scientific background. But in his last, and perhaps greatest, book, *Lilith* (published when he was 71), he describes a mirror that leads into a magic otherworld. After several adventures through the mirror, the young hero, named allegorically, Mr. Vane, recently graduated in science from Oxford, tries to explain the effect of the mirror as depending on "polarization" of reflected light. A minor detail, not intended to make the fantasy more plausible, but indicating the borderline on which MacDonald works. This is as hard as MacDonald's science fiction ever gets, apart from some passing talk in *Lilith* about separate three-dimensional worlds occupying the same space within a multidimensioned universe.

MacDonald's first fantasy novel was *Phantastes: A Faerie Romance for Men and Women.* It was written some years after his sermons had been judged lacking in doctrinal content and he had resigned from the ministry, although he continued as a freelance preacher and lecturer as well as supporting himself with his writing. He had already been married for eight years. Like *Lilith,* it is a book about a young man growing up.

The young hero of *Phantastes,* called Anodos (surely a variant on Adonis), has just turned 21 and come into his inheritance, both parents having died when he was very young. Investigating his father's old desk he discovers a secret compartment, and suddenly a fairy (or goddess—although she claims to be his grandmother) appears and promises he will find the fairyland for which he longs. Anodos is a very high-minded young man, hoping to do something great in the world, full of confidence. The adventures that follow lead to a necessary humbling and redemption. Anodos encounters good people, flower-fairies, giants, good and wicked tree people, knights in armour, ogres, a mysterious fairy palace and the palace library filled with marvellous books (one tells a story about Cosmo of Prague—a narrative that mirrors Anodos's predicament), goblins, and several ideals of womanhood and motherhood in magic guise. (Many of MacDonald's books include spiritual and physical attraction for women, and women as very significant characters.) There are near-seductions, nightmares, attempted murder, heroic self-sacrifice, death, and resurrection. Such a narrative sketch seems very old-fashioned, but it resembles other classic allegorical adventures.

Characters in earlier works are concerned with the pursuit of holiness, idealising women, and personal salvation, but Anodos is simply learning how to live. *Phantastes* is a fairy-allegory about the existential task of becoming an authentic human. At the end, Anodos wakes in his own land, returns home, hoping to live better as a result of what he learned in fairyland.

Lilith is also an exploration of existential ideas, within a fantasy world. The fantasy allows MacDonald to explore extreme situations, and offer narrative examples of metaphysical arguments. Caught out of doors on a desolate heath of the mirror-world as a terrible winter night approaches, Mr. Vane thinks, "Then first I knew what an awful thing it was to be awake in the universe: I was, and could not help it." Shortly after this, he meets a group of children who live without adults.

Young Mr. Vane stumbles into another mirror-world (where his father and other ancestors had also gone) following the mysterious ghost of a librarian. His explorations and adventures there symbolise his inner growth, both spiritually and humanistically as he is about to enter the real world at the end of his formal education. They also symbolise MacDonald's ideas of the afterworld, the value of human life and the nature of love. Vane encounters monsters, a witch-princess, a kind of were-leopard, living skeletons, a vampire, a demon Shadow, and the father and mother of all humans. There, he falls in love with the daughter of this first father and his inhuman first wife. He discovers that when humans die, they pass through different kinds of purgatory, including a "death-sleep," before they can wake into the world of resurrection. The vision of two skeletons knocking each other around as they struggle to come to terms with their lost life and their very physical death is quite chilling.

MacDonald wrote many other books, including realistic novels, light romances, historical novels, ghost stories, semiautobiographies, poetry, and sermons, although almost all have long been out of print. His classic status as a 19th-century children's writer does not mean that he is much read now by children. Certainly, *The Princess and the Goblin* remains a satisfying adventure for young readers, in an old-fashioned, fairytale way, and *The Light Princess* is delightfully whimsical. Like the curse on Sleeping Beauty, the Light Princess has been deprived of any sense of gravity—literally and emotionally—only the right kind of love can bring her down to Earth.

Some of MacDonald's other fairy stories, such as *The Golden Key,* will continue to be read by anyone, child or adult, who enjoys powerful fairytales that border on dreams and surrealism, telling a strange kind of truth. But only adults could withstand the brutal end of *The Princess and Curdie.* Similarly, *At the Back of the North Wind* presents such a harrowing metaphysical examination of the nature of natural disaster, suffering, and illness, that it is hard going even for adults, and the ideally good little boy who dreams and dies is a Victorian angel-child too cloying for post-Victorian tastes. Most modern readers will read it, not for the sake of the story, but for interest in MacDonald himself or in seeing a particular way of using fantasy and Christian belief in writing.

As for the adult fantasies, it is unlikely that they would be remembered at all, so much have tastes changed and so strange is MacDonald's use of Christian ideas in his work, if it were not for two factors. He has been championed by C.S. Lewis, who read *Phantastes* as a young man, and came to regard MacDonald as a kind of mentor. Lewis considered MacDonald to be a genius in the creation of modern mythology, ranking him with such modern writers as Kafka. Many people who are interested in Lewis, for whatever reason, have also become interested in MacDonald. The other factor is the great interest in fantasy writing that developed after the success of Tolkien's *The Lord of the Rings.* This has led to the revival of many nearly forgotten writers, and reprinting (by enthusiastic editors such as Lin Carter) of books that are regarded as milestones in the development of fantasy and science fiction.

Amongst these, MacDonald's adult fantasies, such as *Lilith* and *Phantastes,* stand out as some of the strangest and most powerful.

—John Gough

MacDONALD, John D(ann)

Nationality: American. **Born:** Sharon, Pennsylvania, 24 July 1916. **Education:** University of Pennsylvania, Philadelphia, 1934-35; Syracuse University, New York, B.S. 1938; Harvard University, Cambridge, Massachusetts, M.B.A. 1939. **Military Service:** Served with the United States Army, Office of Strategic Services, 1940-46: Lieutenant Colonel. **Family:** Married Dorothy Mary Prentiss in 1937; one son. **Career:** Writer in several genres and under a number of pseudonyms for the pulps and other magazines. **Member:** President, Mystery Writers of America, 1962. **Awards:** Benjamin Franklin award, for short story, 1955; Grand Prix de Littérature Policìere, 1964; Mystery Writers of America Grand Master award, 1972; American Book award, 1980. D.H.L.: Hobart and William Smith Colleges, Geneva, New York, 1978; University of South Florida, Tampa, 1980. **Died:** 28 December 1986.

SCIENCE FICTION PUBLICATIONS

Novels

Wine of the Dreamers. New York, Greenberg, 1951; as *Planet of the Dreamers,* New York, Pocket Books, 1953; London, Hale, 1955.
Ballroom of the Skies. New York, Greenberg, 1952.

Short Stories

Other Times, Other Worlds. New York, Fawcett, 1978.

OTHER PUBLICATIONS

Novels

The Brass Cupcake. New York, Fawcett, 1950; London, Muller, 1955.
Judge Me Not. New York, Fawcett, 1951; London, Muller, 1964.
Murder for the Bride. New York, Fawcett, 1951; London, Fawcett, 1954.
Weep for Me. New York, Fawcett, 1951; London, Muller, 1964.
The Damned. New York, Fawcett, 1952; London, Muller, 1964.
Dead Low Tide. New York, Fawcett, 1953; London, Fawcett, 1955.
The Neon Jungle. New York, Fawcett, 1953; London, Fawcett, 1954.
Cancel All Our Vows. New York, Appleton Century Crofts, 1953; London, Hale, 1955.
Contrary Pleasure. New York, Appleton Century Crofts, 1954; London, Hale, 1955.
All These Condemned. New York, Fawcett, 1954.
Area of Suspicion. New York, Dell, 1954; London, Hale, 1956; revised edition, New York, Fawcett, 1961.

A Bullet for Cinderella. New York, Dell, 1955; London, Hale, 1960; as *On the Make,* New York, Dell, 1960.

Cry Hard, Cry Fast. New York, Popular Library, 1955; London, Hale, 1969.

April Evil. New York, Dell, 1956; London, Hale, 1957.

Border Town Girl (novelettes). New York, Popular Library, 1956; as *Five Star Fugitive,* London, Hale, 1970.

Murder in the Wind. New York, Dell, 1956; as *Hurricane,* London, Hale, 1957.

You Live Once. New York, Popular Library, 1956; London, Hale, 1976; as *You Kill Me,* New York, Fawcett, 1961.

Death Trap. New York, Dell, 1957; London, Hale, 1958.

The Empty Trap. New York, Popular Library, 1957; London, Magnum, 1980.

The Price of Murder. New York, Dell, 1957; London, Hale, 1958.

A Man of Affairs. New York, Dell, 1957; London, Hale, 1959.

Clemmie. New York, Fawcett, 1958.

The Executioners. New York, Simon and Schuster, 1958; London, Hale, 1959; as *Cape Fear,* New York, Fawcett, 1962.

Soft Touch. New York, Dell, 1958; London, Hale, 1960; as *Man-Trap,* London, Pan, 1961.

The Deceivers. New York, Fawcett, 1958; London, Hale, 1968.

The Beach Girls. New York, Fawcett, 1959; London, Muller, 1964.

The Crossroads. New York, Simon and Schuster, 1959; London, Hale, 1961.

Deadly Welcome. New York, Dell, 1959; London, Hale, 1961.

Please Write for Details. New York, Simon and Schuster, 1959.

The End of the Night. New York, Simon and Schuster, 1960; London, Hale, 1964.

The Only Girl in the Game. New York, Fawcett, 1960; London, Hale, 1962.

Slam the Big Door. New York, Fawcett, 1960; London, Hale, 1961.

One Monday We Killed Them All. New York, Fawcett, 1961; London, Hale, 1963.

Where Is Janice Gantry? New York, Fawcett, 1961; London, Hale, 1963.

The Girl, the Gold Watch, and Everything. Greenwich, Connecticut, Fawcett, 1962; London, Coronet, 1968.

A Flash of Green. New York, Simon and Schuster, 1962; London, Hale, 1971.

A Key to the Suite. New York, Fawcett, 1962; London, Hale, 1968.

The Drowner. New York, Fawcett, 1963; London, Hale, 1964.

On the Run. New York, Fawcett, 1963; London, Hale, 1965.

I Could Go On Singing (novelization of screenplay). New York, Fawcett, 1963; London, Hale, 1964.

The Deep Blue Goodby. New York, Fawcett, 1964; London, Hale, 1965.

Nightmare in Pink. New York, Fawcett, 1964; London, Hale, 1966.

A Purple Place for Dying. New York, Fawcett, 1964; London, Hale, 1966.

The Quick Red Fox. New York, Fawcett, 1964; London, Hale, 1966.

A Deadly Shade of Gold. New York, Fawcett, 1965; London, Hale, 1967.

Bright Orange for the Shroud. New York, Fawcett, 1965; London, Hale, 1967.

Darker than Amber. New York, Fawcett, 1966; London, Hale, 1968.

One Fearful Yellow Eye. New York, Fawcett, 1966; London, Hale, 1968.

The Last One Left. New York, Doubleday, 1967; London, Hale, 1968.

Three for McGee (omnibus). New York, Doubleday, 1967.

Pale Gray for Guilt. New York, Fawcett, 1968; London, Hale, 1969.

The Girl in the Plain Brown Wrapper. New York, Fawcett, 1968; London, Hale, 1969.

Dress Her in Indigo. New York, Fawcett, 1969; London, Hale, 1971.

The Long Lavender Look. New York and London, Fawcett, 1970.

A Tan and Sandy Silence. New York, Fawcett, 1972; London, Hale, 1973.

The Scarlet Ruse. New York, Fawcett, 1973; London, Hale, 1975.

The Turquoise Lament. Philadelphia, Lippincott, 1973; London, Hale, 1975.

McGee (omnibus). London, Hale, 1975.

The Dreadful Lemon Sky. Philadelphia, Lippincott, 1975; London, Hale, 1976.

Condominium. Philadelphia, Lippincott, and London, Hale, 1977.

The Empty Copper Sea. Philadelphia, Lippincott, 1978; London, Hale, 1979.

The Green Ripper. Philadelphia, Lippincott, 1979; London, Hale, 1980.

Free Fall in Crimson. New York, Harper, and London, Collins, 1981.

Cinnamon Skin. New York, Harper, and London, Collins, 1982.

One More Sunday. New York, Knopf, and London, Hodder and Stoughton, 1984.

The Best of Travis McGee. London, Hale, 1985.

The Lonely Silver Rain. New York, Knopf, and London, Hodder and Stoughton, 1985.

Barrier Island. New York, Knopf, 1986; London, Hodder and Stoughton, 1987.

Short Stories

End of the Tiger and Other Stories. New York, Fawcett, 1966; London, Hale, 1967.

Seven. New York, Fawcett, 1971; London, Hale, 1974.

The Good Old Stuff: 13 Early Stories, edited by Martin H. Greenberg and others. New York, Harper, 1982; London, Collins, 1984.

More Good Old Stuff. New York, Knopf, 1984.

Other

The House Guests. New York, Doubleday, 1965; London, Hale, 1966.

No Deadly Drug. New York, Doubleday, 1968.

Nothing Can Go Wrong, with John H. Kilpack. New York, Harper, 1981.

A Friendship: The Letters of Dan Roawan and John D. MacDonald 1967-74. New York, Knopf, 1986.

Reading for Survival. Washington, D.C., Library of Congress, 1987.

Editor, *The Lethal Sex.* New York, Dell, 1959; London, Collins, 1962.

*

Bibliography: *A Bibliography of the Published Works of John D. MacDonald* by Jean and Walter Shine, Gainesville, University of Florida Libraries, 1981.

Manuscript Collection: University of Florida Library, Gainesville.

Critical Studies: *John D. MacDonald* by David Geherin, New York, Ungar, 1982; *Meditations on America; John D. MacDonald's Travis McGee Series and Other Fiction* by Lewis D. Moore, Bowling Green, Bowling Green State University Popular Press, 1994; *John D. MacDonald and the Colorful World of Travis McGee* by Frank D. Campbell Jr., San Bernardino, California, Borgo Press, 1977; *A Special Tribute to John D. MacDonald,* Cedar Rapids, Iowa, Fedora, 1987.

*   *   *

John D. MacDonald's prolific output of thrillers has not, in the end, prevented the acknowledgment that he is one of America's best novelists. He contributed nearly 50 short stories, under various names, and two novels to the SF genre in the late 1940s and early 1950s before turning almost exclusively to crime fiction, except for three marginal entries, "The Legend of Joe Lee" (a ghost story), "The Annex" (speculative fiction), and *The Girl, The Gold Watch, and Everything* (comedy thriller novel with a gimmick, anticipated in the excellent 1950 story, "Half-Past Eternity," that freezes everyone in time, except the user).

The title of the collection of MacDonald's SF short stories, *Other Times, Other Worlds,* neatly indicates his major themes: time travel, aliens among us or manipulating us, juxtaposition of our culture with others. These stories often communicate a strong sense of the value of the honestly striving individual; however, a good many are horror stories in which this value is arbitrarily denied.

In "Game for Blondes," blondes from the future come fishing for a man, and in "Spectator Sport," the unsuspecting visitor from our times is condemned to the future, well-meaningly bound forever to a mechanical fantasy. In "Labor Supply," the best of humans are enslaved by gnomes, through their dreams; in "A Child Is Crying" the gift of seeing the future is a cause of horror to its possessor and those who wish to exploit it.

The two early SF novels deal with sanity and the incipient paranoia of their readers: Aliens really do take over our minds, they tell us, and for no good purpose. *Wine of the Dreamers* posits a planet on which the principal adult occupation is taking possession of humans, playing with us in the belief that we are only creatures of fancy. The irresponsible Dreamers, who have similar remote access to two other planets, all three of which were settled by their ancestors, have forgotten their ordained function, yet they need our help, as only one of their inbred, dwindling number sees. Although MacDonald grossly oversimplifies for the sake of a suspenseful narrative, particularly the closed environment of the Dreamers, this remains a good tightly plotted novel which still reads well. It ends optimistically and is satisfying on its own terms, but *Ballroom of the Skies* concludes uneasily and is a more disturbing novel, because most readers must be unable to share in its hero's feelings of quiet exultation in the last paragraphs, to the extent that they perceive him to have succeeded only in moving from a smaller to a greater paranoia. A scenario in which the ends justify the means will never satisfy all readers; here, the given conditions are remarkably distasteful. Earth is kept in a state of perpetual warfare, and peacemakers are killed to preserve Earth as a breeding ground for superhuman leaders, who will keep the galactic civilization from stagnating and maintain it in a state of readiness in case of a notional invasion from another galaxy. The hero is one of the world's leading peacemakers, a journalist whose investigation of the fantastic crimes that break up secret negotiations between the world's power blocks leads to his recruitment as an agent of the very powers he has dedicated his life to oppose. To keep the reader in sympathy with such a hero would be a fearsome challenge for any writer and, although MacDonald does his best to make him more admirably heroic (using the well-honoured trick of timely praise from a girlfriend, for instance) as he grows beyond the human norm, the attempt fails. In reality, MacDonald's hero, Dake Lorin, who is excellent in his lone wolf phase, would have recognized the speciousness of the conditions he is made, humbly, to accept. The novel is, nevertheless, a gripping narrative and, in the best tradition of such works, honestly presents the lonely dilemma of the superman who can find true friendship only with others of his kind.

Besides the titles already mentioned, "Ring Around the Redhead," "Shadow on the Sand," "The Miniature," "The Big Contest," "Susceptibility," "Common Denominator," and "Trojan Horse Laugh," should be listed as fine short stories by a writer who could clearly have been a major figure in the SF genre had he not found that crime paid better. It should be noted that MacDonald often used mystery fiction, for example, *A Flash of Green* and *Condominium,* to be prophetically critical of the suicidal tendencies of our society, being one of the popular fiction writers to be concerned early with threats to our ecology. Florida became his principal subject and land exploiters one of his main targets. Though he worked outside of the genre for most of his career, he influenced several writers within it. Harlan Ellison has testified in *Again, Dangerous Visions* (1972) that MacDonald is one of those sui generis writers from outside SF "who have influenced us most strongly these past two decades," in the kind and style of SF being written.

John D. MacDonald died only a few months after completing *Reading for Survival,* an essay written in the form of a dialogue between Travis McGee and his friend Meyer. It could almost be with MacDonald's SF because it tells the story of the human species, illustrating it with exemplary individuals, such as Mog the hunter, who lived 50,000 years ago, and Smith the modern scientist. Mog relies on his memory, Smith on memory augmented by reading: both know enough to avoid appropriate traps, but more ignorant or less well-read people would have fallen for the baits. Meyer in lecture-mode talks like a science fiction advocate:

> I would not demand that a man read ponderous tomes, or try to read everything—any more than I would expect our ancestor to examine every single leaf on a plant he remembers as being poisonous. I would expect that in his reading—which should be wide ranging, fiction, history, poetry, political science—he would acquire the equivalent of a liberal arts education and acquire also what I think of as the educated climate of mind, a climate characterized by skepticism, irony, doubt, hope, and a passion to learn more and remember more.

—Michael J. Tolley

———

MacDOUGAL, John. *See* **LOWNDES, Robert A.W.**

MacGREGOR, James Murdoch. *See* **McINTOSH, J.T.**

MACKELWORTH, R(onald) W(alter)

Nationality: British. **Born:** London, 7 April 1930. **Education:** Raynes Park Grammar School, London, 1940-48. **Military Service:** Served in the British Army Intelligence Corps, 1948-50. **Family:** Married Sheila Elizabeth Kilpatrick in 1956; one son and two daughters. **Career:** Worked for Thomas Cook, travel agents, London, 1950; clerk, Norwich Union Insurance, London, 1950-53; inspector, Kingston, Surrey, 1953-66, superintendent, Leeds, 1966-72, manager, Portsmouth, 1972-77, product manager, 1977-84, and since 1984, strategic planning manager, London, Legal and General Insurance Society. **Agent:** Carnell Literary Agency, Danes Croft, Goose Lane, Little Hallingbury, Hertfordshire CM22 7RG, England.

SCIENCE FICTION PUBLICATIONS

Novels

Firemantle. London, Hale, 1968; as *The Diabols,* New York, Paperback Library, 1969.
Tiltangle. New York, Ballantine, 1970; London, Hale, 1971.
Starflight 3000. New York, Ballantine, 1972; London, New English Library, 1976.
The Year of the Painted World. London, Hale, 1975.
Shakehole. London, Hale, 1981.

*

Manuscript Collection: North London Polytechnic.

R.W. Mackelworth comments:

I am a lifelong addict of SF, but I prefer well-written novels and those that make a satirical statement about contemporary life whether through fantasy or fact. However, I also believe the modern idiom of fast-moving adventure entertains and entertainment is what the writer owes the reader. My work is essentially nonprofessional; I like to work up my own ideas and enjoy my writing. The conventions of SF are few, and one of its joys is that its scope for the imagination is unlimited. SF is gaining readers because it is largely free of many of the set-piece situations demanded of mainstream writing. Its problem is lack of good characterisation. Characters are often overwhelmed by events: if we can put personality before event, SF writing could improve considerably. The standard of writing is also important. It is possible to write literate SF as well as exciting SF!

*   *   *

The influence of British science fiction magazines of the 1950s is evident in R.W. Mackelworth's restrained style and use of stock adventure frameworks: his fiction, despite attempts to incorporate profound issues, rarely displays the self-awareness increasingly favoured among his contemporaries. His output has remained small, his foremost works being novels.

In *Firemantle* the hero is projected, apparently through time, to an Earth dominated by a deadly alien life-form. Most of the book relates his exploits in this future world and his gradual understanding of its parameters (including his immunity to the aliens). Interwoven with the narrative are themes of revenge and manipulation, the exact details, methods, and motives remaining concealed until the end. The novel finally affirms the intrinsic survival potentiality of human willpower, but also questions the cost involved.

Tiltangle is set on Earth during a new ice age, with survivors crowded into an isolated refuge. Once again personal manipulation and callous use of power are introduced, although the central concern is a quest for the uncertain myth of "the warm," the first retreat of snow and ice heralding the return of a habitable world. This is Mackelworth's most effective book: it contains some of his best-realised characters, while the depiction of ascetic life in a hostile environment is reinforced by uncharacteristically precise subsidiary detail. The implied background circumstances are less convincing, but this scarcely affects the driving obsession that is the novel's strength.

Starflight 3000 is loosely based on the generation starship concept. A hollowed asteroid becomes a vast spacecraft; use of terraforming bacteria allows the colonisation of any planet. Secondary aspects include faster-than-light communication and mysterious alien science. But for all its reliance on such motifs, the novel is not typical of "hard" technological SF. It expresses moral concern over a selfish, expansionist mentality, and also gives some consideration to the conflict inherent in Mackelworth's two recurrent themes: the tendency of power to corrupt its wielder and the need for charismatic leadership to ensure progress. However, an abrupt time shift and the creation of a shipboard mythology ultimately avoid the questions raised.

The Year of the Painted World combines traditional elements of both disaster and invasion stories. Surprisingly excitable in tone, it tells of a struggle on present-day Earth against a Martian virus and its aggressive host organisms. The protagonist is an unambiguous man of action, doing what must be done. In his arrogant simplicity, he could almost be a caricature of a hero from science fiction's Golden Age. The threatening "Pods" also carry more than a hint of space monsters of old. Possible benefits once the virus is controlled (and the consequent suspicions and machinations surrounding its release) add little depth to a playfully derivative but basically flimsy novel.

Mackelworth is no artist, honing subtleties of vision, language, and motivation to fine edges: instead he relies on mystery and suspense to hold attention until the denouement. His characterisation is usually notional (his stereotyped women are singularly ill-portrayed), although within its terms he is adept at drawing concise contrasts. A tendency to slip into careless assumptions and clichés is another result of his intense absorption in plotting. Nevertheless, it is the complexity of his plots which sets Mackelworth apart from routine adventure writers. His underlying themes can be especially thought-provoking, and it is unfortunate that he chooses to turn away from their fullest implications rather than develop their dramatic tension.

—Nick Pratt

MacLEAN, Arthur. *See* TUBB, E.C.

————

MacLEAN, Katherine (Anne)

Nationality: American. **Born:** Glen Ridge, New Jersey, 22 January 1925. **Education:** Barnard College, New York, B.A. in economics 1950; Goddard College, Plainfield, Vermont, M.A. in psychology 1977. **Family:** Married 1) Charles Dye in 1951 (divorced 1952); 2) David Mason in 1956 (divorced 1962), one son; 3) Carl West. **Career:** Laboratory assistant, 1944-45, and food manufacturing technician, 1945-46; office manager, Hi-Pro Animal Feed, Frankfort, Delaware, 1952-53; technician, Memorial and Knickerbocker hospitals, New York, 1954-56. Member of the English Department, University of Connecticut, Storrs, 1962-65, and University of Maine, Orono, intermittently 1966-77. Freelance writer and lecturer. **Awards:** Nebula award, 1971. **Agent:** Virginia Kidd, Box 278, Milford, Pennsylvania 18337, U.S.A. **Address:** P.O. Box 1563, Biddeford, Maine 04005, U.S.A.

SCIENCE FICTION PUBLICATIONS

Novels

Cosmic Checkmate, with Charles V. DeVet, bound with *King of the Fourth Planet,* by Robert Moore. New York, Ace, 1962; expanded as *Second Game,* New York, DAW, 1981.
Missing Man. New York, Berkley, 1975.
Dark Wing, with Carl West. New York, Atheneum, 1979.

Short Stories

The Diploids, and Other Flights of Fancy. New York, Avon, 1962.
Trouble with Treaties, with Tom Condit. Tacoma, Washington, Lanthorne Press, 1975.
The Trouble with You Earth People. Virginia Beach, Donning, 1980.

OTHER PUBLICATIONS

Novels

The Man in the Bird Cage. New York, Ace, 1971.

*

Katherine MacLean comments:

I am interested in science fiction as an exploration of possibility—specifically the possibilities that are most astonishing, yet genuinely possible. It becomes worthwhile to write when I am more deeply surprised with each page of unfolding potential events.

*   *   *

Katherine MacLean is important for introducing in her fiction ethical questions about medical and scientific experimentation. She also writes about mental telepathy and human fears of evolutionary change.

The Diploids, and Other Flights of Fancy includes eight works published between 1949 and 1953. The title story tells of genetic experiments that produced a strain of standardized human fetuses for research purposes. "The Pyramid in the Desert" has as its theme human fear of immortality. "Defense Mechanism" and "Games" are both about telepathy. "Feedback" deals with human fear of new ideas; "Pictures Don't Lie" deals with the anthropomorphic tendency to measure all species on a human scale. "The Snowball Effect" and "Incommunicado" are clever but less significant thematically than the others.

In *Cosmic Checkmate,* written with Charles V. DeVet, Robert Lang goes to the planet Velda to discover why its population refuses peaceful contact with the federation of Earth's colonies. In disguise, Lang plays the Veldian Game—based on chess—and beats all comers in the second game; he deliberately loses the first game to discover his opponent's weaknesses. The novel is well-crafted: the plot works as an analogous game structure, with Lang winning the second game in a cosmic checkmate.

MacLean's essay "Communicado" provides the background for her works that deal thematically with telepathy and psi phenomena. She discusses the important influence Whately Carington's book *Thought Transference* (1946) had on her, and she elaborates the ideas behind stories like "Defense Mechanism," "Feedback," "The Fittest," "Games," "Where or When," and "Curtin in the Sky." Telepathy is also the moving idea behind *Missing Man.* Set in New York, in 1999, the novel features George Sanford, whose extraordinary telepathic abilities make him a valuable special consultant for the Rescue Squad of the Police Department. Sanford is the fear hound, sniffing out people who are in trouble by tuning in to the telepathic vibrations they broadcast. The missing man is Carl Hodges, a super-maintenance man for the city who uses computers to predict breakdowns and accidents before they occur. The novel is thematically complex and almost phantasmagorical at times.

Several of MacLean's stories have medical themes and use physicians as main characters. Among the best of these is "Contagion": colonists on another planet survive a plague only by becoming look-alikes, thus raising questions about the interrelationship between external appearance and personality. "The Origin of the Species" is told in epistolary form by a neurosurgeon who is troubled by his work: he destroys the best parts of people's minds so that they can adapt to life in society. "Gimmick" chronicles the use of a virus as a weapon; "The Other" presents a physician who, ironically, has the same problem as the patient he is trying to cure; and "Syndrome Johnny" shows the usefulness of plagues in speeding up evolution. *Dark Wing,* written with her husband Carl West, also has a medical theme. It presents a future where the practice of medicine is illegal and people believe that illness is immoral, an external sign of defects in their thinking. A teenage boy, Travis Gordon, discovers two old medical kits in an abandoned wrecked ambulance and begins to learn and practice medicine, even performing complicated surgery with no special equipment or assistance. The complex and unbelievable plot, the superficial criticism of medicine, and the youth of the protagonist combine to make the novel read like adolescent fiction.

—Anne Hudson Jones

MacLEOD, Sheila

Nationality: Scottish. **Born:** The Isle of Lewis, 23 March 1939. **Education:** Wycombe Abbey School, Buckinghamshire; Somerville College, Oxford, B.A. (honours) in English 1961. **Family:** Married the actor Paul Jones in 1963 (divorced); one son. **Awards:** Scottish Arts Council award, 1969, 1971; MIND award, for non-fiction, 1981. **Agent:** Giles Gordon, Anthony Sheil Associates, 43 Doughty Street, London WCIN 2LF, England. **Address:** 9 Appleby Road, London E8 3ET, England.

SCIENCE FICTION PUBLICATIONS

Novels

The Snow-White Soliloquies. London, Secker and Warburg, and New York, Viking Press, 1970.
Xanthe and the Robots. London, Bodley Head, 1977.
Circuit-Breaker. London, Bodley Head, 1978.

OTHER PUBLICATIONS

Novels

The Moving Accident. London, Faber, 1968.
Letters from the Portuguese. London, Secker and Warburg, 1971.
Axioms. London, Quartet, 1984.

Plays

Television Plays: *They Put You Where You Are,* 1966; *God Speed Co-operation,* 1983.

Other

The Art of Starvation: An Adolescent Observed. London, Virago, 1981; as *The Art of Starvation: A Story of Anorexia and Survival,* New York, Schocken, 1982.
Lawrence's Men and Women. London, Heinemann, 1985; as *D.H. Lawrence's Men and Women,* New York, Harcourt, 1986.

*   *   *

Sheila MacLeod has published in a variety of genres, science fiction among them. Her earliest novels are experiments in surrealism—*The Snow-White Soliloquies* is perhaps the most outstanding. Here, MacLeod projects the old Germanic fairy tale into a strange, Orwellian present: a catatonic Snow-White, encased in a high-tech box of Glass That Breathes, is transported from place to place in a dubious search for The Prince. Supervised by an authoritarian figure named Doc and attended by a succession of six social marginals, the paralyzed heroine embodies the principle of passivity. She sees, hears, contemplates, and suffers with those around her but is unable to act. Her silent soliloquies reveal that her knowledge of herself is curiously limited: she is a poisoned life, preserved by technological wizardry for purposes unknown. (The reader knows no more than she.) As the literally captive audience for the obsessive monologues and peculiar actions of her care-

takers, Snow-White witnesses a series of increasingly bizarre events—until something gives (most notably, the glass box) and she is able to acknowledge the roles that all have played in this disturbing and dreamlike psychodrama. The "allegorical atmosphere" of *The Snow-White Soliloquies* has been somewhat evasively described by reviewers as "fascinating," "intriguing," and "rich with reflection about the human condition." More to the point is that the book is finally and successfully enigmatic. We cannot get beyond its carefully constructed surfaces, which tease us with refractions of our own expectations.

In the more conventionally rendered *Xanthe and the Robots,* MacLeod's first thoroughgoing science fiction narrative, we meet another version of the catatonic woman, this time a brilliant robotics engineer who has invested the greater part of her emotional life in relationships with mechanical beings. Programmer Xanthe, numbed by psychotropic drugs since the death of her father, the founder of the Institute for Advanced Robotic Research, finds her torpor disturbed by two upsetting developments: a new relationship with an intense and attractive coworker, and a dramatic change in Institute policy. The painful reawakening of Xanthe's psyche parallels a decision by Institute authorities to endow the most advanced robots with a more human sensibility. Xanthe and the robots learn, in different ways, to desire, and the process of wanting leads them, gradually but inexorably, to regret their passive institutional loyalty. Xanthe rebels—against her superior, against the Institute, ultimately against her father—and chooses a future unlike anything she has known in her regimented habitat. The robots also have their revolution, but their prospects look less potentially creative; given their origins, they can do little more than replicate the ugly hierarchies of their makers. In *Xanthe,* MacLeod articulates a familiar SF theme: our machines cannot save us from ourselves. The plot *per se* holds few surprises, but Xanthe's oddly deadpan narrative persona, at once touching and repellent, sustains our interest.

With *Circuit-Breaker,* MacLeod moves back into the unsettling ambiguity that is her strength. Ostensibly, this story is about a British astronaut, Alexander Baird, who must exercise unusual "autokinetic" powers to restore his marooned spacecraft to its intended orbit. According to Lvov, the sinister mission controller, Baird may generate sufficient power to rein in the straying capsule if he can forge telepathic linkages with the women nearest the hearts of himself and his fellow travellers, Davitt and Haskins. Baird contacts earth, and his strange encounters with his alienated spouse, Davitt's eccentric mom, and Haskins's anxious and vulnerable wife generate troubling questions for the reader. Is Baird in fact an astronaut? Or is he a science fiction writer who has come to believe his own fantasies? Is Lvov a dictatorial aerospace bureaucrat? Or an especially nasty headshrinker? In this tacky little universe of failed connections, how are we to distinguish between outer and inner space? MacLeod's opacity is compelling—we are drawn to the world of her problematic protagonist as to a black hole. Like *The Snow-White Soliloquies, Circuit-Breaker* is dense and sophisticated. Though more accessible than the earlier book, it exacts an equally attentive reading.

Sheila MacLeod's best novels are cerebral and defy easy categorization. Casual readers will find themselves impatient with the author's staging, with structures and settings that at first seem too elaborate for what they support and surround. But MacLeod's formal choices are consistent with her choice of subject. Her focus is invariably on neurosis, on the disturbances that prevent people (and cultures) from achieving a peaceful equilibrium, and the trappings of fairytales and science fiction serve as formal correlatives that keep readers, too, slightly off balance. We stumble along, like MacLeod's characters, bearing the graceless freight of unmet expectations. For most of us, the burden proves worthwhile.

—Janis Butler Holm

MADDOX, Carl. *See* TUBB, E.C.

MAINE, Charles Eric

Pseudonym for David McIlwain. **Other Pseudonyms:** Richard Rayner; Robert Wade. **Nationality:** British. **Born:** Liverpool, Lancashire, 21 January 1921. **Education:** Holt High School, Liverpool. **Military Service:** Served in the Royal Air Force during World War II: Flight Lieutenant. **Family:** Married and divorced twice; two sons and three daughters. **Career:** Journalist in London, 1946-71, including 14 years as editor and managing editor of industrial weekly newspapers and journals; regular correspondent for *The Times, Financial Times,* and *Guardian,* London, and *Les Echos,* Paris. **Died:** 1981.

SCIENCE FICTION PUBLICATIONS

Novels (series: Mike Delaney)

Spaceways: A Story of the Very Near Future (novelization of radio program). London, Hodder and Stoughton, 1953; as *Spaceways Satellite,* New York, Avalon, 1958.
Timeliner: A Story of Time and Space (novelization of radio program). London, Hodder and Stoughton, and New York, Rinehart, 1955.
Crisis 2000. London, Hodder and Stoughton, 1955.
Escapement. London, Hodder and Stoughton, 1956; as *The Man Who Couldn't Sleep,* Philadelphia, Lippincott, 1958.
High Vacuum. London, Hodder and Stoughton, and New York, Ballantine, 1957.
The Isotope Man (Delaney). London, Hodder and Stoughton, and Philadelphia, Lippincott, 1957.
World without Men. New York, Ace, 1958; London, Digit, 1963; revised edition, as *Alph,* Garden City, New York, Doubleday, 1972.
The Tide Went Out. London, Hodder and Stoughton, 1958; New York, Ballantine, 1959; revised edition, as *Thirst!,* London, Sphere, 1977; New York, Ace, 1978.
Count-Down. London, Hodder and Stoughton, 1959; as *Fire Past the Future,* New York, Ballantine, 1959.
Subterfuge (Delaney). London, Hodder and Stoughton, 1959.
Calculated Risk. London, Hodder and Stoughton, 1960.
He Owned the World. New York, Avalon, 1960; as *The Man Who Owned the World,* London, Hodder and Stoughton, 1961.
The Mind of Mr. Soames. London, Hodder and Stoughton, 1961.

The Darkest of Nights. London, Hodder and Stoughton, 1962; as *Survival Margin,* Greenwich, Connectict, Fawcett, 1968; revised edition, as *The Big Death,* London, Sphere, 1978.
Never Let Up (Delaney). London, Hodder and Stoughton, 1964.
B.E.A.S.T.: Biological Evolutionary Animal Simulation Test. London, Hodder and Stoughton, 1966; New York, Ballantine, 1967.
The Random Factor. London, Hodder and Stoughton, 1971.

OTHER PUBLICATIONS

Novels as Richard Rayner

The Trouble with Ruth. London, Hale, 1960.
Darling Daughter. London, Hale, 1961.
Dig Deep for Julie. London, Hale, 1963.
Stand-in for Danger. London, Hale, 1963.

Novels as Robert Wade

The Wonderful One. London, Hodder and Stoughton, 1960.
The Stroke of Seven. New York, Morrow, 1965; London, Heinemann, 1966.
Knave of Eagles. New York, Random House, 1969; London, Hale, 1970.

Plays

Screenplay: *Escapement (The Electric Monster),* with J. McLaren Ross, 1958.

Radio Plays: *Spaceways,* 1952; *The Einstein Way,* 1954.

Television Play: *Timeslip.*

Other

The Bizarre and Bloody: A Clutch of Weird Crimes—Each Shockingly True. New York, and, as *The World's Strangest Crimes,* Feltham, Middlesex, Odhams Press, 1967; as *The Bizarre and Bloody,* Hart, 1972.
World-Famous Mistresses. Feltham, Middlesex, Odhams Press, 1970.

*

Charles Eric Maine comments:

Like Arthur C. Clarke, John Christopher, Eric Frank Russell, Jonathan Burke, the late John Wyndham, and other science fiction author friends, I became an SF addict in my early teens. This was the era of the late 1930s when nobody, apart from a few SF writers and addicts, and fewer scientists, believed that man would ever set foot on the moon in this century, if at all. In my own science fiction, I have always tried to find a theme or situation which no other author has thought of. Although I have written some space opera (such as *Timeliner* and *He Owned the World*), most of my SF books are short-term projections from present-day fact and technology, looking, perhaps, some 10 to 50 years ahead. I am particularly interested in the social and psychological impact of advancing science on crude Homo sapiens. In this respect my two best novels are *The Tide Went Out* and *The Mind of Mr. Soames* (the movie version missed the essential point of the story—the difference between training and education).

* * *

Charles Eric Maine's writing is distinguished primarily by its original and imaginative concepts. This is not to demean his writing skills but rather to indicate that when viewed as a body his stories vary considerably in quality. Too often he falls back on clichés to move his stories along, and occasionally the clash between banal plots and sophisticated scientific ideas is resounding. Maine's treatment of time displacement in *The Isotope Man,* for example, is fascinating, but it is embedded in a plot that would do justice to the old pulps. The plot, to sabotage the artificial production of tungsten, is embellished by stereotyped characters: an ex-Nazi plastic surgeon, an evil South American business tycoon, a feisty and irascible city editor, a beautiful, sharp-tongued girl photographer, and a hard-drinking, two-fisted reporter who plays his hunches to the detriment of his job.

Despite this occasional failure to mesh plots, characters, and themes, however, Maine at his best is quite effective. *Alph, B.E.A.S.T., Timeliner,* and *The Tide Went Out* are excellent novels. He seems particularly good at creating memorable female characters. Among them are Synove Rayner (*B.E.A.S.T.*), a brilliant and beautiful exhibitionist nymphomaniac; Koralin (*Alph*), a courageous cytologist who kidnaps and protects the first male baby born into the lesbian society in five hundred years; and Shirley Sye (*The Tide Went Out*), a pathetic and aging model turned fashion editor who instructs the hero on the nature of man when faced with survival.

Survival is one of Maine's recurring themes. Sometimes he treats it directly, as in *The Tide Went Out* and *The Darkest of Nights,* both post-disaster novels. In *The Tide Went Out,* repeated hydrogen bomb tests produce a fracture in the ocean floor through which pours nearly all of the world's water supply; in *The Darkest of Nights,* a lethal epidemic destroys society. *B.E.A.S.T.* projects the ultimate result of an animal evolved with survival of the fittest as the only standard: a brilliant but mentally unstable scientist, Charles Gilley, creates animals and an environment for them in a computer, then evolves them through millions of generations while making conditions harsher and harsher. Finally, all but one species disappears, and then all but one animal. It is the ultimate survivor but it has lost all humanistic qualities. *Alph* presents yet another variation on the nature of survival in its exploration of the long-range effects of a society without men. Lesbianism, of course, becomes the acceptable form of sexual expression, but it results in a patterned societal neurosis. An emphasis on superior eugenic standards causes an overthrow of the government because of the elitist attitudes it creates. Even in *Timeliner,* whose primary purpose is to explore time travel, Hugh Macklin, the hero, eventually raises the question of whose right it is to decide who should survive and what standards they should use. Inevitably, Maine proposes, man will do whatever is required in order to survive.

Another prevalent Maine theme is time displacement, which receives its fullest treatment in *Timeliner.* In it, he offers the unique prospect that man's "psycho-identity" but not his body can travel forward in time. Attracted by emotional affinities, the "psycho-identity" possesses other persons' bodies to achieve consciousness. Though it creates a kind of immortality for the traveler, it destroys the possessed's ego. One future society that Macklin encounters labels such time travelers "psycho-temporal parasites" and consid-

ers the possession a form of murder.

One of the more interesting aspects of Maine's writing is its projection of possible futures. Though *Alph, Timeliner,* and *He Owned the World,* for example, paint different pictures, they do contain some consistencies. Maine predicts that the historical pattern of man's genius being channeled into aggression and war will continue indefinitely. He also believes that romantic love will die out. In *He Owned the World,* it is defined as "an obsessive form of compulsive neurosis," and one of the characters that Macklin encounters in *Timeliner* tells him that man is naturally polygamous. Finally, many of Maine's future societies are totalitarian and man continues to battle his oppressors.

Maine is a journeyman writer who has created some excellent novels, but even if he were far less skilled, his ideas alone would make reading his works worth the effort.

—Carl B. Yoke

———

MAJORS, Simon. *See* **FOX, Gardner F.**

———

MALZBERG, Barry N(athaniel)

Pseudonyms: Mike Barry; Claudine Dumas; Mel Johnson; Lee W. Mason; Francine di Natale; K.M. O'Donnell; Gerrold Watkins; John Barry Williams. **Nationality:** American. **Born:** New York City, 24 July 1939. **Education:** Syracuse University, New York (Schubert Fellow, 1964-65), A.B. 1960. **Family:** Married Joyce Nadine Zelnick in 1964; two daughters. **Career:** Investigator, New York City Department of Welfare, and reimbursement agent, New York State Department of Mental Hygiene; editor, Scott Meredith Literary Agency, New York; editor, *Amazing* and *Fantastic,* 1968; managing editor, *Escapade,* 1968. Freelance writer: author of many novels under various pseudonyms for Midwood, Oracle, Soft Cover Library, and Traveler's Companion Series. **Awards:** Cornelia Ward Graduate Creative Writing Fellowship, 1965; Campbell Memorial award, 1973; *Locus* award, 1983. **Address:** Box 61, Teaneck, New Jersey 07666, U.S.A.

SCIENCE FICTION PUBLICATIONS

Novels

The Falling Astronauts. New York, Ace, 1971; London, Arrow, 1975.
Overlay. New York, Lancer, 1972; London, New English Library, 1975.
Beyond Apollo. New York, Random House, 1972; London, Faber, 1974.
Revelations: A Paranoid Novel of Suspense. New York, Warner, 1972.
The Men Inside. New York, Lancer, 1973; London, Arrow, 1976.

Phase IV (novelization of screenplay). New York, Pocket Books, and London, Pan, 1973.

In the Enclosure. New York, Avon, 1973; London, Hale, 1976.

Herovit's World. New York, Random House, 1973; London, Arrow, 1976.

Guernica Night: A Science Fiction Masterwork. Indianapolis, Bobbs-Merrill, 1974; London, New English Library, 1978.

On a Planet Alien. New York, Pocket Books, 1974.

The Day of the Burning. New York, Ace, 1974.

Tactics of Conquest. New York, Pyramid, 1974.

The Sodom and Gomorrah Business. New York, Pocket Books, 1974; London, Arrow, 1979.

The Destruction of the Temple. New York, Pocket Books, 1974; London, New English Library, 1975.

The Gamesman. New York, Pocket Books, 1975.

Conversations. Indianapolis, Bobbs-Merrill, 1975.

Galaxies. New York, Pyramid, 1975.

Scop. New York, Pyramid, 1976.

The Last Transaction. Los Angeles, Pinnacle, 1977.

Chorale. Garden City, New York, Doubleday, 1978.

Night Screams, with Bill Pronzini. Chicago, Playboy Press, 1979.

Prose Bowl, with Bill Pronzini. New York, St. Martin's Press, 1980.

The Cross of Fire. New York, Ace, 1982.

The Remaking of Sigmund Freud. New York, Ballantine, 1985.

Novels as K.M. O'Donnell

The Empty People. New York, Lancer, 1969.

Dwellers of the Deep. New York, Ace, 1970.

Universe Day. New York, Avon, 1971.

Gather in the Hall of the Planets. New York, Ace, 1971.

Short Stories

Final War and Other Fantasies (as K.M. O'Donnell). New York, Ace, 1969.

In the Pocket and Other S-F Stories (as K.M. O'Donnell). New York, Ace, 1971.

Out from Ganymede. New York, Warner, 1974.

The Many Worlds of Barry Malzberg. New York, Popular Library, 1975.

Down Here in the Dream Quarter. Garden City, New York, Doubleday, 1976.

The Best of Barry N. Malzberg. New York, Pocket Books, 1976.

Malzberg at Large (includes *Dwellers of the Deep*). New York, Ace, 1979.

The Man Who Loved the Midnight Lady: A Collection. Garden City, New York, Doubleday, 1980.

The Passage of the Night: The Recursive Science Fiction of Barry N. Malzberg, edited by Mike Resnick and Anthony R. Lewis. Framingham, Massachusetts, NESFA Press, 1994.

OTHER PUBLICATIONS

Novels (series: Kung Fu)

Oracle of the Thousand Hands. New York, Olympia Press, 1968.

Screen. New York, Olympia Press, 1968; London, Olympia Press, 1972.

The Circle (as Francine di Natale). New York, Traveller's Companion, 1969.

Diary of a Parisian Chambermaid (as Claudine Dumas). New York, Midwood, 1969.

In My Parents' Bedroom. New York, Olympia Press, 1971.

Confessions of Westchester County. New York, Olympia Press, 1971; London, Olympia Press, 1972.

The Spread. New York, Belmont, 1971.

Horizontal Woman. New York, Leisure, 1972; as *The Social Worker,* 1977.

The Masochist. New York, Belmont, 1972; as *Everything Happened to Susan,* 1978.

The Way of the Tiger, The Sign of the Dragon (as Howard Lee; Kung Fu). New York, Warner, 1973.

Underlay. New York, Avon, 1974.

The Running of Beasts, with Bill Pronzini. New York, Putnam, 1976.

Lady of a Thousand Sorrows (as Lee W. Mason). Chicago, Playboy Press, 1977.

Acts of Mercy, with Bill Pronzini. New York, Putnam, 1977.

Novels as Mel Johnson

Love Doll. New York, Soft Cover Library, 1967.

Chained. New York, Midwood, 1968.

I, Lesbian. New York, Midwood, 1968.

Instant Sex. New York, Midwood, 1968.

Just Ask. New York, Midwood, 1968.

Kiss and Run. New York, Midwood, 1968.

Nympho Nurse. New York, Midwood, 1969.

The Sadist. New York, Midwood, 1969.

Do It to Me. New York, Midwood, 1969.

Born to Give. New York, Midwood, 1969.

Campus Doll. New York, Midwood, 1969.

The Box. New York, Oracle, 1969.

A Way with All Maidens. New York, Oracle, 1969.

Novels as Gerrold Watkins

Southern Comfort. New York, Traveller's Companion, 1969.

A Satyr's Romance. New York, Traveller's Companion, 1970.

Giving It Away. New York, Traveller's Companion, 1970.

The Art of the Fugue. New York, Traveller's Companion, 1970.

A Bed of Money. New York, Traveller's Companion, 1970.

Novels as Mike Barry (series: Lone Wolf in all titles)

Night Raider. New York, Berkley, 1973.

Bay Prowler. New York, Berkley, 1973.

Boston Avenger. New York, Berkley, 1973.

Desert Stalker. New York, Berkley, 1974.

Havana Hit. New York, Berkley, 1974.

Chicago Slaughter. New York, Berkley, 1974.

Peruvian Nightmare. New York, Berkley, 1974.

Los Angeles Holocaust. New York, Berkley, 1974.

Miami Marauder. New York, Berkley, 1974.

Harlem Showdown. New York, Berkley, 1975.

Detroit Massacre. New York, Berkley, 1975.

Phoenix Inferno. New York, Berkley, 1975.

The Killing Run. New York, Berkley, 1975.

Philadelphia Blowup. New York, Berkley, 1975.

Other

Engines of the Night: Science Fiction in the Eighties. Garden City, New York, Doubleday, 1982.

Editor, with Edward L. Ferman, *Final Stage: The Ultimate Science Fiction Anthology.* New York, Charterhouse, 1974; revised, Baltimore and London, Penguin, 1975.

Editor, with Edward L. Ferman, *Arena: Sports SF.* Garden City, New York, Doubleday, and London, Robson, 1976.

Editor, with Edward L. Ferman, *Graven Images: Three Original Novellas of Science Fiction.* Nashville, Nelson, 1977.

Editor, with Bill Pronzini, *Dark Sins, Dark Dreams: Crimes in Science Fiction.* Garden City, New York, Doubleday, 1977.

Editor, with Bill Pronzini, *The End of Summer: Science Fiction of the Fifties.* New York, Ace, 1979; as *The Fifties: The End of Summer,* New York, Baronet, 1979.

Editor, with Bill Pronzini, *Shared Tomorrows: Science Fiction in Collaboration.* New York, St. Martin's Press, 1979.

Editor, with Martin H. Greenberg and Joseph D. Olander, *Neglected Visions.* Garden City, New York, Doubleday, 1980.

Editor, with Martin H. Greenberg, *The Science Fiction of Mark Clifton.* Carbondale, Southern Illinois University Press, 1980.

Editor, with Bill Pronzini, *Bug-Eyed Monsters.* New York, Harcourt Brace, 1980.

Editor, with Bill Pronzini and Martin H. Greenberg, *The Arbor House Treasury of Horror and the Supernatural.* New York, Arbor, 1981; abridged as *Great Tales of Horror and the Supernatural,* Secaucus, New Jersey, Galahad, 1985; as *The Giant Book of Horror Stories,* London, Magpie, 1991; original edition reprinted as *Classic Tales of Horror and the Supernatural,* New York, Quill, 1991.

Editor, with Bill Pronzini and Martin H. Greenberg, *The Arbor House Treasury of Mystery and Suspense.* New York, Arbor, 1981; abridged as *Great Tales of Mystery and Suspense,* Secaucus, New Jersey, Galahad, 1985.

Editor, with Martin H. Greenberg, *The Science Fiction of Kris Neville.* Carbondale, Southern Illinois University Press, 1984.

Editor, with Bill Pronzini and Martin H. Greenberg, *Mystery in the Mainstream.* New York, Morrow, 1986; as *Crime and Crime Again,* New York, Bonanza, 1990.

Editor, with Piers Anthony, Martin H. Greenberg, and Charles G. Waugh, *Uncollected Stars.* New York, Avon, 1986.

*   *   *

From the mid-1960s on, Barry Malzberg has supported himself and his family by editorial work for *Escapade, Fantastic,* and *Amazing Stories,* and for the Scott Meredith Literary Agency; and as a freelance writer, turning to science fiction "because I failed in my attempts to succeed in the literary world. I was writing literary short stories and drowning in rejections and I just did not want to go any further" (as quoted by Charles Platt in *Dream Makers: The Uncommon People Who Write Science Fiction*). In 1975, however, Malzberg decided not to write any more science fiction and focused more on what Joyce Carol Oates, in reviewing his *Guernica Night* (1974), characterized as "speculative fiction" concerned with the poetic and philosophical. He has since reverted to producing some science fiction, mainly short stories that can be found in anthologies and magazines such as *Amazing Stories,* the *Magazine of Fantasy and Science Fiction* and *Omni.*

As a prolific professional writer, Malzberg proves the same dictum that virtually all other prolific professional writers do: Sturgeon's Law, which states that 90 percent of all science fiction is carp; 90 percent of everything is crap. He has churned out forgettable entertainment in every genre, including pornography, and in every form, from paperback series like "The Lone Wolf" to novelettes in Ace "Doubles" and short stories in pulp magazines. However, the remaining 10 percent of his output, when Malzberg is at his best, is not science fiction so much as it is postmodern fiction, as fundamentally literary and concerned with the nature of reality and self as works by John Barth, Donald Barthelme, Saul Bellows, and Thomas Pynchon. Indeed, the theme threading through Malzberg's postmodern novels is that of the distinction between the adjectives *the* and *a:* Is reality single and ultimately knowable? Is truth therefore verifiable and constant; or is it multiple and timebound? And finally, the question as central to interpretation in life as in art, can we hope for *the* meaning of an event or circumstance, or must we make do as best we can with *a* meaning?

For example, in *Revelations* (1972), the psychotic astronaut Walter Monaghan claims he can reveal the truth behind the space program—its secretive purposes and operations, and the reason why space travel causes madness. But having been driven insane by space, he makes little to no sense, and even asserts that the moon shots were stages in hidden film studios. Instead of revealing the truth, he assassinates his interviewer, having been planted by a government agency to hush up the truth, whatever it may be. So too in *Beyond Apollo* (1972), which amid controversy won the first John W. Campbell Memorial Award, the narrator Harry M. Evans is the psychotic sole survivor of a failed mission to Venus. Learning what went wrong is crucial to the continuation of the faltering space program, but neither Evans nor his notes offer any logical explanation, particularly to the question of why the mission was sent. In the end, Malzberg makes clear that Evans went mad because he couldn't accept the fact that there was no reason for the mission, that it was merely the product of a bureaucratic agency that does such things because it does them.

To say that in these books, as in others, Malzberg is criticizing meaningless bureaucracy and arbitrary government in general, and the space program and space colonization in particular, may be correct but is too easy. By leaving riddles unresolved at the end, and by rejecting the tenet that the aim of space travel is primarily pragmatic, Malzberg abandons a cornerstone of science fiction: the leading to a confirmation, not to a questioning, of the concept of reality and identity. Science fiction protagonists tend to have the ability and internal stability to make decisions, leaving little doubt in readers' minds as to what to think of them—a far cry from the confused and confusing antiheroes portrayed by Malzberg, as well as by Pynchon, Bellow, and Barth. Moreover, although science fiction claims to be fictitious speculation about possible changes, it typically provides an objective, material reality outside of the central character(s) in order to make its fictional worlds believably real to its readers. Granted, the affirmation of an objective reality can either be the premise on which a plot is based, or can finally emerge as a result after complications and doubts, but whether reflected or assumed, an objective reality is an important generic element in science fiction.

In this respect, the narrative techniques of science fiction are opposite those of postmodern fiction, which tends to suspect that the question "what's the real story here?" cannot be answered satisfactorily—satisfactorily, that is, in terms of satisfying the readers of largely "realistic" science fiction. Rather, to Malzberg as to other postmodern novelists, the "real story" is unavailable in the face of contradictions and divergent accounts—not simply because it is unknowable, but because there is not a single "real" in the story, no sanctioned reality forming a context by which other accounts can be judged as distorted, biased, hallucinated, or flat lying. As such, space travel in the hands of Malzberg assumes the character of a metaphor; the true aim of the protagonist is to discover the meaning of his existence, and the calamity of a failed expedition lies in the protagonist's feelings of guilt and experience of abject defeat.

It is apparent, then, that Malzberg uses the themes and motifs of science fiction to comment upon this world here and now, not of worlds beyond at some future time. For that matter, Malzberg does not consider science fiction to be "a working model for the future," but is instead "merely a sub-genre of romantic fiction which employs the future as historicals would use the past" (as quoted in *Final War and Other Fantasies*). Not surprisingly, science fiction as a genre and a business has become irreverent fodder for some of his most biting stories, just as the evaluation of literary works has been parodied in postmodern fiction. In the satirical *Gather in the Hall of the Planets* (1971; by pseudonym K.M. O'Donnell), Malzberg shows the absurdities of science fiction conventions through the misadventures of a hack writer, Sanford Kvass, whose inability to write well is surmounted only by his conviction that the human race will be destroyed unless he uncovers the alien hidden among the fans. Kvass eventually realizes he is the alien, of course, but along the way Malzberg skewers the pretensions, enmities, and commercial corruptions so prevalent to the field. Science fiction as a cultural and literary wasteland forms the theme of *Herovit's World* (1973), in which the protagonist, Jonathon Herovit, is a hack writer even less able to cope than Sanford Kvass. Past the point of muddling through, of making deadlines to make the money to make ends meet, Herovit is ultimately run over by a car—killed meaninglessly by an "alien vehicle" in the alienating streets of New York. Malzberg expanded his sardonic views about science fiction in a collection of essays, *Engines of the Night: Science Fiction in the Eighties* (1982), making "pervasively clear," according to Michael Dirda in the *Washington Post Book World,* "that the best of science fiction should be valued as literature and nothing less."

Thus Malzberg's work should be judged, as literature and nothing less, for it has clearly moved away from traditional science fiction and has taken on the characteristics of postmodern fiction. In articulating an uncompromising cynicism about politics, about collective endeavor, about the potential for destructive evil in even the most seemingly innocent of men, his novels explore how individuals attempt to find meaning, to deal with problems that may not have solutions. In his *Galaxies* (1975), for instance, the spaceship *Skipstone* falls into a black hole without explanation, without any context indicating where it came from or where it was headed. Its pilot, Lena, probes deeply into the present and ends up with a question mark, and the past remains inscrutable and unyielding in its mystery. As the truth remains buried, inaccessible to Lena, *Galaxies* reaches areas that formerly were reserved to philosophical speculation and that remind the reader vividly of fiction by Pynchon and Borges, for in essence Malzberg is declaring that individuals cannot find or create meaning or purpose or order, and lack the capacity for knowing either themselves or the world. Hence the predominant sensation of the characters is always the helplessness in regard to action. The protagonist in *The Falling Astronauts* (1971) is the man who stays behind in the orbiting Apollo while his crewmates make history walking on the moon—frustrated, paranoid, he is rabidly tempted to leave them there.

Similar macabre visions often propel Malzberg's plots, and as Paul Granahan notes in *Best Sellers,* "his fiction has disturbed many, who have found it too despairing." And Richard Delap in the *Magazine of Fantasy and Science Fiction* states that he is "considered a pariah by sf's old guard." Despite his relative unpopularity and penchant for stirring up controversy, though, Malzberg has produced an accomplished body of work that, like the work of Joanna Russ and Samuel R. Delany, has successfully crossed over to the intriguing and more reputable category of postmodernism.

—Jeffrey M. Wallmann

MANN, (Anthony) Phillip

Nationality: British. **Born:** Northallerton, Yorkshire, 7 August 1942. **Education:** Scarborough College, 1954-62; Manchester University, 1962-66, B.A. in English and Drama 1966; Humboldt State University, Arcata, California, 1966-69, M.A. 1969. **Family:** Married Nonnita Margaret Rees in 1967; one daughter and one son. **Career:** Lecturer in Drama, Humboldt State University, 1967-69. Lecturer, 1969-81, and since 1981, associate professor in Drama, Victoria University, Wellington, New Zealand. English editor, Xin Hua News Agency, Beijing, 1978-80. Associate artistic director, Downstage Theatre, Wellington, 1984-86. Board member, New Zealand Drama School, 1986-90, and chairperson, 1991-93. Freelance writer, lecturer, and theatre director. Visiting fellow in drama, University of Central England, 1995; guest lecturer in playmaking, University of Utrecht, Holland, 1995. **Agent:** Glenys Bean, 15 Elizabeth Street, Freeman's Bay, Auckland, New Zealand. **Address:** 22 Bruce Avenue, Brooklyn, Wellington, New Zealand. **Online Address:** Phillip.mann@vuw.ac.n2.

SCIENCE FICTION PUBLICATIONS

Novels (series: A Land Fit for Heroes; The Story of the Gardener)

The Eye of the Queen. London, Gollancz, 1982; New York, Arbor House, 1983.
Master of Paxwax (Gardener). London, Gollancz, 1986.
The Fall of the Families (Gardener). London, Gollancz, 1987.
Pioneers. London, Gollancz, 1988.
Wulfsyarn: A Mosaic. London, Gollancz, 1990; New York, Morrow, 1992.
Escape to the Wild Wood (Heroes). London, Gollancz, 1993.
Stand Alone Stan (Heroes). London, Gollancz, 1994.

OTHER PUBLICATIONS

Plays

Il suffit d'un baton, in *Avant-Scène* (Paris), 1977.
Revenge at Ditchwater Creek (produced Wellington, 1977).
The Animal Maker (for children) (produced Wellington, 1978).
The Thunderbird (for children) (produced Wellington, 1982).
The Bach in the Bush (for children) (produced Wellington, 1984).
Mozart and Salieri Live in Concert (produced Wellington, 1991).

Radio Play: *The Monument,* 1977.

*

Phillip Mann comments:

(1991) I began writing when I was in my teens. Like many young writers I had ideas of becoming a poet but found that my verse slipped easily into doggerel, bawdy lyrics, and satire. I also found that I had a knack for dialogue but this never really extended itself into full-length plays, though I would still like to write for the theatre. I started to write short stories and found this most satisfying. I read science fiction from an early age and grew up on a diet of Wells, Verne, and Rider Haggard as well as Thomas Mann, Billy Bunter tales, and stories about the sea. A combination of the fantastic and the logical appeals to me. I write to entertain. I want to write good yarns that involve the reader and yield a similar satisfaction to a good meal. I am convinced there is life in a multitude of forms evolving in the wider galaxy and that our next major development will take place when we manage to break or circumvent the space-time barrier and encounter these aliens. Aliens and alien ceremonies intrigue me as do the creative faculties in mankind. Science fiction seems to me an excellent forum in which we can debate and prepare for the future.

(1995) At present, the most serious problem facing humanity is the ecological damage being done to our world. We must in my view develop new strategies of partnership between ourselves and what we call Nature—and this will require new ways of relating to one another. In my sadder moments, I feel that if we fail to change, if we persist in old power relationships and political and economic systems which favor competition and inequality, if we fail to adopt a realistic attitude to the present, then we and the lovely planet on which we live are doomed to perish.

*   *   *

Known in New Zealand not only for his novels but for his dramatic work, Phillip Mann skillfully uses this dramatic ability in his novels, especially what he terms "a knack for dialogue." This ability has allowed his work to move from one medium to another, as witness the broadcasts to date of two of his novels, *The Eye of the Queen* and *Pioneers.* At one point, he found his subject matter demanded extended treatment; the tale of Paxwax, the gardener, in *Master of Paxwax* continues in its sequel, *The Fall of the Families.*

With *The Eye of the Queen* Phillip Mann entered the world of science fiction in a way calculated to stretch the minds and imagination of tyros and aficionados alike. For this first novel Mann chose a stock situation: alien contact. When a strange spacecraft appears and hovers some four inches above the Utah salt flats, its presence sets off predictable reactions: confusion, fear, an ill-fated attempt at defence against the unknown. At this point a reader may expect the usual adventure complete with space wars or at least space derring-do in answer to the implied question: what will happen when aliens initiate contact with Earth?

Mann's answer, however, comes in an unexpected and unique form. When contact becomes reciprocal, a two-member team from Earth's Contact Linguistics Institute receives the assignment to return with the aliens, study their culture, and establish a common ground for coexistence. In Mann's presentation of the team's findings the reader discovers an inner dynamic working to forward and dramatize the novel's ideas.

Once the tradition-bound reader foregoes reliance on conventional chapter divisions and gives himself up to the author's arrangement, he experiences a situation such as that epitomized by Robert Frost in the couplet/poem, "The Secret Sits." The reader becomes a shadowy third partner of the team, "circling" the Pe-Ellian world, probing for information. In both sections, the Diary and the Commentary, Mann interweaves data gathered by standard research techniques employed in a case study: direct observation, encoded interviews and brief autobiographies of various aliens, transcriptions of casual conversations, physical descriptions, linguistic analysis, botanical and biological data, cultural analysis of various areas such as social life, living conditions, esthetic artifacts and the like. As data accumulates, the fiction team and the reader, like the voice in Frost's poem, can only "suppose," until the aliens in the center begin to give up the secret of what they "know."

In *The Eye of the Queen* Mann presents an alien stock made all the more believable by its utter physical alienness, an alienness that is intensified by the epithetic names so evocative of human experience and emotion. Albeit unspoiled by anthropomorphism so often employed in science fiction, the aliens do share attributes of many sentient creatures we know, along with the art of the language and thought with humans. While they impress a reader with a sense of commonality with all living forms, there is also a sense of transcendence, arising from what the researchers' *Contact Linguistics Handbook* terms "the sense of structure." The Pe-Ellian sense of structure recognizes existence and balance of personal and cosmic biospheres and psychospheres, the latter supported by belief in the vitality of thought. Thought is alive. Thought becomes dangerous, if undisciplined or belligerent. Thought can regenerate, if understood, shared, and directed. When the implications of the power of misused thought becomes part of what the major researcher comes to "know," he moves from scientific objectivity to complete subjectivity.

Utilizing the Diary-Commentary format, Mann dramatizes this shift of perspective to particularly effective ends. Compiled by the major researcher, self-admittedly estranged from himself by a life-long dedication and discipline to objectivity, the Diary charts both the progress of the scientific analysis of the aliens and the ever-increasing self-analysis. In the process author Mann succeeds in turning his main character into an Everyman, forcing the reader to make comparable analyses. Written *ex post facto,* based on memory, and supported by notes and records, the Commentary provides an alternate, sometimes antithetical, perspective on events. More important for Mann's theme, the Commentary provides a reader with a sympathetic angle from which to judge the personal conclusions of the diarist. Without belaboring the point in the novel Mann leads his readers toward assessment of the contemporary human use of that virile entity, thought. It is a speculation vital to our continuation as honorable residents of the cosmos.

While *The Eye of the Queen* established Mann's reputation as one who handles human/alien relationships very effectively, *Wulfsyarn* introduces a nonhuman entity as narrator of the events of the novel. Wulf is a mechanical secretary, so to speak. It accompanies a space captain on a humane mission. Leaving a galaxy devastated by the Wars of Knowledge and Ignorance, the secretary becomes the narrator as it records the captain's thoughts. Upon return of the spacecraft, now empty and carrying only Wulf and the mentally broken-down captain, Wulf speculates on the cause of the tragic end, attempting to explain what had happened to both captain and ship, a project beyond its novel capabilities.

—Hazel Pierce

MANNING, Laurence (Edward)

Nationality: American. **Born:** St. John, New Brunswick, Canada, in 1899; emigrated to the United States after World War I. **Education:** King's College, Halifax, Nova Scotia, B.C.L. 1919. **Military Service:** Served in the Royal Canadian Air Force: Lieutenant. **Family:** Married Edith B. Manning in 1928; two daughters and one son. **Career:** Newspaper reporter in St. John, then writer for the Florists Exchange, Philadelphia, in the early 1920s; manager, 1923-32, president, 1933-52, and owner, 1952-66, Kelsey Nursery Service, New York. **Member:** Fellow, American Rocket Society, 1960. **Died:** 1972.

SCIENCE FICTION PUBLICATIONS

Novel

The Man Who Awoke: A Classic Novel from the Golden Age of Science Ficton. New York, Ballantine, 1975; London, Sphere, 1977.

Short Stories

Author of numerous uncollected short stories.

OTHER PUBLICATIONS

Other

The How and Why of Better Gardening. New York, Van Nostrand, 1951.

*   *   *

Laurence Manning is remembered primarily for a series of five stories originally published in 1933, later collected in book form as *The Man Who Awoke*. Manning used a classic device of science fiction and utopian writers, a man from our own culture transported in some fashion to another society, which is then revealed to the reader as the protagonist encounters individuals and institutions. In each of the five episodes, Norman Winters arises from suspended animation to investigate the state of humanity as it advances toward its ultimate destiny.

In the title story, Winters explores the world of the year 5000. Humankind dwells within vast managed forests, in balance with nature, looking back with horror on "the false civilization of Waste!" Seeking to find a place for himself in this new world, Winters attempts to convince his hosts that his own time did have positive aspects for which they should be thankful. But even the most sympathetic of his listeners feel no gratitude. "For exhausting the coal supplies of the world? For leaving us no petroleum for our chemical factories?" Ultimately finding this new society as flawed as the old, Winters sleeps another 5000 years and revives in "Master of the Brain." Now he encounters humanity subservient to a computer that makes all the decisions, the race having abdicated the responsibility for its own future. After being instrumental in breaking the grip of the Brain, Winters advances to the year 15000 in "The City of Sleep." Once more he is disappointed, for now the great majority of people spend their entire lives in mechanically induced dreams, an idea developed from Manning's first story, "The City of the Living Dead," written with Fletcher Pratt. This willing renunciation of

reality has recurred within the genre many times, most notably in James Gunn's *The Joy Makers*. The best story in the series is "The Individualists," wherein Winters becomes the quarry of a number of egocentric geniuses in a society that places no value on interpersonal relationships. Winter's journey ends with "The Elixir," the source of immortality which produces an interstellar community. Although not specifically within the series, Manning wrote another tale set eons after the Manning saga, "The Living Galaxy," which postulated that entire stellar systems functioned as single atoms in a higher order universe we could not perceive.

Less ambitious in scope was a second series that recounted the adventures of several members of the Stranger Club. Manning's dislike of automation recurs in "The Call of the Mech-Men," a secret cabal of living machines. His concern about our profligate consumption of natural resources, anticipating our present worries, is repeated in "Voice of Atlantis," in which a device allows communication with an ancient Atlantean. The remaining three stories were more pedestrian and reflected the type of story that dominated the genre in the 1930s. A lost world of prehistoric monsters lies under New York in "Caverns of Horror," a forgotten Atlantean colony is located in "The Moth Message," and a species of sentient, ambient tree is thwarted in its invasion plan in "Seeds from Space."

Manning's fiction, much of which seems quite dated now, was advanced for its time. He produced a series of very accurate—insofar as the state of the art allowed—stories of space travel. His concerns for conservation and human dignity elevated his fiction above that of most of his peers.

—Don D'Ammassa

MARAS, Karl. *See* BULMER, Kenneth.

MARSTEN, Richard. *See* HUNTER, Evan.

MARTIN, George R(aymond) R(ichard)

Nationality: American. **Born:** Bayonne, New Jersey, 20 September 1948. **Education:** Medill School of Journalism, Northwestern University, Evanston, Illinois, B.S. (summa cum laude) 1970, M.S. 1971. **Military Service:** Conscientious objector; did alternative service with VISTA, 1972-74. **Family:** Married Gale Burnick in 1975 (divorced 1979). **Career:** Served with the Cook County Legal Assistance Foundation, for Vista, Chicago, 1972-74. Chess tournament director, Continental Chess Association, Mount Vernon, New York, 1973-75; journalism instructor, Clarke College, Dubuque, Iowa, 1976-79. Since 1979, freelance writer. **Awards:** Hugo award, 1975, 1980 (2 awards); Bread Loaf Writers Conference Fellowship, 1977; Nebula award, 1979, 1985; *Locus* award, 1981, 1982 (twice), 1984; Bram Stoker award, 1987; World Fantasy award, 1988. **Member:** SFWA; Writers' Guild of America, West. **Agent:** Pimlico Literary Agency, 155 East 77th Street, Suite 1A, New York, New York 10021, U.S.A. **Address:** 102 San Salvador, Santa Fe, New Mexico 87501, U.S.A.

SCIENCE FICTION PUBLICATIONS

Novels

Dying of the Light. New York, Simon and Schuster, 1977; London, Gollancz, 1978.
Windhaven, with Lisa Tuttle. New York, Timescape, 1981; London, New English Library, 1982.

Short Stories

A Song for Lya and Other Stories. New York, Avon, 1976; London, Coronet, 1978.
Songs of Stars and Shadows. New York, Pocket Books, 1977.
The Sandkings. New York, Timescape, 1981; London, Futura, 1983.
Songs the Dead Men Sing. Niles, Illinois, Dark Harvest, 1983; London, Gollancz, 1985.
Nightflyers. New York, Bluejay, 1985.
Tuf Voyaging. New York, Baen, 1986; London, Gollancz, 1987.
Portraits of His Children. Arlington Heights, Illinois, Dark Harvest, 1987.
The Pear-Shaped Man. Eugene, Oregon, Pulphouse, 1991.

OTHER PUBLICATIONS

Novels

Fevre Dream. New York, Poseidon Press, 1982; London, Gollancz, 1983.
The Armageddon Rag. New York, Poseidon Press, 1983; London, New English Library, 1984.

Plays

Television Plays: 5 episodes in the *Twilight Zone* series, 1986; 13 episodes in the *Beauty and the Beast* series, 1987-90.

Other (series: Wild Cards)

Sandkings, with Pat Broderick, Neal McPheeters, and Doug Moench (graphic novel adapted from author's story of the same name). New York, DC Graphics, 1987.

Editor, *New Voices in Science Fiction: Stories by Campbell Award Nominees.* New York, Macmillan, 1977; as *New Voices I[-IV]: Spellbinding Original Stories by the Next Generation of Science Fiction Greats: The Campbell Award Nominees,* New York, Harcourt Brace, 2 vols., 1978-79; New York, Berkley, 2 vols., 1980-81.
Editor, with Isaac Asimov and Martin H. Greenberg, *The Science Fiction Weight-Loss Book.* New York, Crown, 1983.
Editor, *The John W. Campbell Awards, Volume 5.* New York, Bluejay, 1984.

Editor, with Paul Mikol, *Night Visions 3.* Niles, Illinois, Dark Harvest, 1986; as *Night Visions: All Original Stories,* London, Century, 1987; as *Night Visions: The Hellbound Heart,* New York, Berkley, 1988.
Wild Cards:
Editor, *Wild Cards: A Mosaic Novel.* New York, Bantam, 1986; London, Titan, 1988-91.
Editor, *Aces High.* New York, Bantam, 1987; London, Titan, 1988.
Editor, *Jokers Wild: A Wild Cards Mosaic Novel.* New York, Bantam, 1987; London, Titan, 1988.
Editor, *Aces Abroad: A Wild Cards Mosaic Novel.* New York, Bantam, 1988; London, Titan, 1989.
Editor, *Down and Dirty: A Wild Cards Mosaic Novel.* New York, Bantam, 1988; London, Titan, 1989.
Editor, with Melinda M. Snodgrass, *Ace in the Hole: A Wild Cards Mosaic Novel.* New York, Bantam, 1990; London, Titan, 1991.
Editor, with Melinda M. Snodgrass, *Dead Man's Hand: A Wild Card Novel,* by John J. Miller. New York, Bantam, 1990; London, Titan, 1991.
Editor, with Melinda M. Snodgrass, *One-Eyed Jacks: A Wild Cards Mosaic Novel.* New York, Bantam, 1991.
Editor, with Melinda M. Snodgrass, *Jokertown Shuffle: A Wild Cards Mosaic Novel.* New York, Bantam, 1991.
Editor, with Melinda M. Snodgrass, *Double Solitaire: A Wild Cards Mosaic Novel.* New York, Bantam, 1992.
Editor, with Melinda M. Snodgrass, *Dealer's Choice: A Wild Cards Mosaic Novel.* New York, Bantam, 1992.
Editor, with Melinda M. Snodgrass, *Card Sharks: A Wild Cards Mosaic Novel.* Riverdale, New York, Baen, 1993.
Editor, with Melinda M. Snodgrass, *Marked Cards: A Wild Cards Mosaic Novel.* Riverdale, New York, Baen, 1994.

*   *   *

Although George R. R. Martin has never been a prolific writer, his fiction is invariably of such a high quality that it leaves distinct impressions in the minds of his readers. Since 1971, only four novels and a few dozen stories have appeared, and two of the novels are supernatural horror. That makes it all the more remarkable that he continues to be one of the most respected names in science fiction.

The first story to separate Martin from the scores of other short story writers was "With Morning Comes Mistfall." A mysterious, mist-shrouded world is rumored to be inhabited by the Wraiths, an indigenous species which lurks just out of sight, preying on unwary travellers. Two personalities clash, not over whether or not the Wraiths really exist, but over the question of whether it is better for humanity to know the truth, or to have at least one legend. That same year saw the appearance of "Override," the first of several stories set in a future where technology allows the reanimation of corpses as working machines, grouped into teams directed telepathically in their duties. Again, Martin uses this as a device to examine two competing attitudes, in this case about the morality of the process.

"A Song for Lya" follows the same pattern, but far more effectively. A telepath and an empath travel to a world where humans are converting in increasing numbers to an alien religion which includes a very unpleasant suicide. The telepath becomes a convert, and her companion struggles to impress her with the importance of individuality, once again providing a battlefield upon which Martin lets conflicting ideas struggle against each other.

In 1977 Martin's first novel, *Dying of the Light,* appeared. Although ostensibly an interplanetary adventure story, the real conflict is one of personalities, the sardonic protagonist, his associates, and the woman he loves. Martin goes to great lengths to develop the background details of his society, overlaying his characters so that they appear genuine products of that civilization.

Several superior short stories followed, most notably the clever and genuinely terrifying "The Sandkings," which demonstrates the peril of fooling around with unknown lifeforms, and the danger of assuming that "lower" creatures are somehow less capable of defending themselves. Others of note during this period were "In the House of Worm," "Fast Friend," and "The Way of Cross and Dragon," the latter particularly because of its portrayal of a new wave of inquisitorial religious fervor following humanity's expansion to the stars.

Martin then collaborated with Lisa Tuttle on the novel *Windhaven,* an expansion and further development of the excellent novelette "The Storms of Windhaven." The protagonist is a Flyer, one of many who travel on artificial wings from island to island on their world, where surface travel is virtually impossible because of heavy winds and the creatures which lurk beneath the waters. When she is faced with the requirement to surrender her wings to a male, she rebels, challenging not only his right but calling into doubt the entire traditional history of her people.

Two solo novels followed rapidly thereafter, but both were in the horror field. *The Armageddon Rag* remains to this day one of the most original, inventive, and best written horror novels of all time, the only one to successfully wed a supernatural theme to the world of rock music. A writer investigating a murder begins to chart the history of the Nazgul, a defunct rock group whose members all appear to be the objects of manipulation by an unseen, unknown force. More traditional in theme, if not in setting, is *Fevre Dream.* Martin uses a likable vampire who sets out in the years prior to the Civil War to establish himself as savior of his "race." The evocative riverboat settings are particularly effective. Although Martin switched back to science fiction for the most part, he still writes occasional horror tales, some times quite effectively, as in "Portraits of His Children."

Martin's excellent novella "Nightflyers" was made into a lackluster film but remains an outstanding bit of writing. A starship is "haunted" by the recorded personality of a warped woman who refuses to surrender control of her son's life, even in death. "Under Siege" breathes new life into the theme of changing the past, "The Glass Flower" explores what it means to be human when a spaceman is rebuilt as a cyborg, and the morality of medical experimentation is examined in "The Needle Men."

Although many of Martin's short stories had been set within the framework of a consistent universe, his corpse-handler stories were the only true series until he began a sequence about a gigantic starship designed to deal exclusively with ecological disasters, commanded and occupied by a single human being. These were subsequently collected into a single volume as *Tuf Voyaging,* but while entertaining and thought-provoking, they lack the intense commitment of his earlier work.

Much of Martin's energy has been diverted into his work for television and films, as well as the creation of an alternate present, shared universe anthology series, "Wild Cards," which he edits. An alien plague is released on the Earth during the final days of World War I. Most of those stricken die almost immediately, but those who survive are transformed, some into hideous travesties of human beings, the Jokers, some into quite literal superheroes, the Aces, each endowed with a peculiar power. The comic book premise is dealt with in a fiercely realistic fashion, and most of the books in the series are tapestries of stories by several authors. Although characters are borrowed from time to time, for the most part the same author chronicles each individual career. Martin's most important character is the Turtle, a psychokinetic introvert who flies around in a mechanical shell, although "The Journal of Xavier Desmond" is also worth noting. The series, which is ongoing, has shifted emphasis from supernatural and otherworldly villains to a confrontation with an increasingly repressive U.S. government.

His editing and screenwriting interests have left little time for the prose upon which his early career was based. Nevertheless, were Martin never to write another story in the field, he would remain firmly established as one of the major genre writers of the 1970s.

—Don D'Ammassa

MARTYN, Phillip. *See* **TUBB, E.C.**

MASON, Douglas R(ankine)

Pseudonyms: R.M. Douglas; John Rankine. **Nationality:** British. **Born:** Hawarden, Flintshire, 26 September 1918. **Education:** Heywood Grammar School, 1929-34; Chester Grammar School, 1934-37; Manchester University, 1937-39, 1946-48, B.A. **Military Service:** Served in the Royal Signals, 1939-46: Lieutenant. **Family:** Married Mary Cooper in 1945; two sons and two daughters. **Career:** Headmaster, Somerville Junior School, 1954-67, and St. George's Primary School, 1967-78, both Wallasey, Cheshire. **Address:** 101 Millans Court, Ambleside, Cumbria LA22 9BW, England.

SCIENCE FICTION PUBLICATIONS

Novels

From Carthage Then I Came. Garden City, New York, Doubleday, 1966; London, Hale, 1968; as *Eight Against Utopia,* New York, Paperback Library, 1967.
Ring of Violence. London, Hale, 1968; New York, Avon, 1969.
Landfall Is a State of Mind. London, Hale, 1968.
The Tower of Rizwan. London, Hale, 1968.
The Janus Syndrome. London, Hale, 1969.
Matrix. New York, Ballantine, 1970; London, Hale, 1971.
Satellite 54-Zero. New York, Ballantine, and London, Pan, 1971.
Horizon Alpha. New York, Ballantine, 1971; London, Hale, 1981.
Dilation Effect. New York, Ballantine, 1971; London, Hale, 1980.

The Resurrection of Roger Diment. New York, Ballantine, 1972.
The Phaeton Condition. New York, Putnam, 1973; London, Hale, 1974.
The End Bringers. New York, Ballantine, 1973; London, Hale, 1975.
Pitman's Progress. Morley, Yorkshire, Elmfield Press, 1976.
The Omega Worm. London, Hale, 1976.
Euphor Unfree. London, Hale, 1977.
Mission to Pactolus R. London, Hale, 1978.
The Typhon Intervention. London, Hale, 1981.

Novels as John Rankine (series: Dag Fletcher; Space: 1999; Space Corporation)

Interstellar Two-Five (Fletcher). London, Dobson, 1966.
Never the Same Door (Corporation). London, Dobson, 1967.
One is One (Fletcher). London, Dobson, 1968.
Moons of Triopus (Corporation). London, Dobson, 1968; New York, Paperback Library, 1969.
Binary Z. London, Dobson, 1969.
The Weisman Experiment. London, Dobson, 1969.
The Plantos Affair (Fletcher). London, Dobson, 1971.
The Ring of Garamas (Fletcher). London, Dobson, 1971.
Operation Umanaq. New York, Ace, 1973; London, Sidgwick and Jackson, 1974.
The Bromius Phenomenon (Fletcher). New York, Ace, 1973; London, Dobson, 1976.
The Fingalnan Conspiracy. London, Sidgwick and Jackson, 1973.
Moon Odyssey (Space: 1999; novelization of TV series). London, Orbit, and New York, Pocket Books, 1975.
Lunar Attack (Space: 1999; novelization of TV series). London, Orbit, 1975; New York, Pocket Books, 1976.
Astral Quest (Space: 1999: novelization of TV series). London, Orbit, 1975; New York, Pocket Books, 1976.
Android Planet (Space: 1999; novelization of TV series). London, Orbit, and New York, Pocket Books, 1976.
Phoenix of Megaron (Space: 1999; novelization of TV series). New York, Pocket Books, 1976.
The Thorburn Enterprise. London, Dobson, 1977.
The Vort Programme. London, Dobson, 1979.
The Star of Hesiock. London, Dobson, 1980.
Last Shuttle to Planet Earth. London, Dobson, 1980.

Short Stories

The Blockade of Sinitron: Four Adventures of Dag Fletcher (for children). London, Nelson, 1966.

OTHER PUBLICATIONS

Novel as R.M. Douglas

The Darkling Plain. London, Hale, 1979.

*

Douglas R. Mason comments:

Science fiction is either escapist adventure—Hornblower in a star ship—or an allegory for our time—the dystopia, *Brave New World* bit. I tend to write the first as John Rankine and the second as Douglas R. Mason.

I hold the view that the biogrammar that determines the human make-up was laid down over such a long period that events like the technological revolution will not alter anything in the foreseeable future. Therefore my inhabitants of Wirral City in 4000 A.D. act in the same way as people of the present. Cain is still Cain and unable to change.

*   *   *

Douglas R. Mason, who is also well known under the pseudonym John Rankine, envisions future battles waged by man against android, robot, computer, or physically recreated bionic man. Usually the machines' rigidity, their propensity toward predictable patterns, their lack of emotion, and their machine nature is responsible for or aids in their ultimate defeat, while man's doubt, his emotion, his loyalty, his physical self, spurred by instinct, passion, and a need for action and for self-preservation, help him ultimately to conquer. Mason continually deplores man's insidious tendency to sacrifice freedom and intellectual activity for the sake of comfort, stability, and pleasure, and asks if there can be true pleasure without conflict and pain. His heroes are constantly struck with the realization that they have never felt truly alive until they have tasted sweat, endured trauma, and shared danger. Mason also wonders whether prolonging life through chemicals and mechanical replacements might not be ultimately self-destructive, immortality at the price of humanity and selfhood. Frequently, his bionic characters are patronizing about real humans, and feel an intellectual sympathy with computers, attitudes that always doom them.

Mason's heroes are tough and manly but have sunk into the mindless apathy of modern regimentation only to be jarred into self-awareness and rebellion by a freak accident, a sudden intuition or insight, an irrepressible instinct. Occasionally they articulate these attitudes in lines from Shakespeare or Keats. Often these men are attracted to cold, incredibly beautiful women who keep them at a distance and intellectualize their relationship; ultimately, however, they learn that such women are either useless in a crisis or actively act against them, turning them over to robots for "readjustment." Usually, the heroes are passionately aroused by a less perfect but more nubile woman who has worked with them unnoticed in the past, who fights in their cause, and who finally accepts a division of labor whereby the male is leader and warrior, and the woman submits as helpmate, nurse, cook, and technician.

In *The End Bringers,* androids rule, monitoring human emotions and repressing them with drugs, until a natural rebel uncovers a plot to eliminate all humanoids; rescuing hundreds before robots eviscerate them, he leads survivors to an air raid shelter from which revived humanity launches its attack on android tyrants. In *Matrix,* city computers plan to eliminate all human life and use the free space to unify storage banks and achieve godhood, but a human administrator discovers the plan and fights back. In doing so, he has to deal with conformists who not only disapprove of rebellion, but actively battle against it, blind to their own precarious predicament, or with doubters who understand his logic but question his motives, or with humanists who oppose the violence of his methods, violence that ultimately proves justified. In *From Carthage Then I Came,* a computer, originally established to protect man from a cruel ice age, has monitored all life in the domed city for seven thousand years, but life is sterile, impersonal, and public. A few who have learned to evade mind probes unite in an escape plot, and, against difficult odds, outwit computers and robots, and start a new world in the wilderness, agrarian but free. These patterns with their Edenic themes are typical of much of Mason's canon.

Mason writes about science's potential abuses, limiting man's potentiality, reducing originality, variety, and natural evolution, controlling his weather and his atmosphere, tampering with his mind. In *Satellite 54-Zero,* a secret agent tries to penetrate a private scientific operation studying Jupiter, only to encounter the horror of mechanical failure in space, a scientific mind out of control, and a centaur transported from another dimension. In *Operation Umanaq,* the Southern hemisphere plots to destroy the Northern by affecting weather conditions and producing another ice age, while a fast-acting Northern agent evades hitmen and suicide drugs to invade a Polar station and reset weather computers. *The Phaeton Condition* begins in a world so polluted by industrial waste that its oxygen supply is fast being depleted; an industrial giant who helped create this condition plans to exploit it further through a secret high-priced safe zone with its own underground oxygen reserves. Frequently, Mason's scientists consider humans expendable and progress worth any danger. In *Moons of Triopus,* the industrial advantages of exploiting a new planet are judged more important than slow, safe investigation, but politicians and businessmen learn too late that more rational beings may well view their selfish acts with contempt and act accordingly.

The Dag Fletcher series are all set in the same galaxy and involve lots of action, while his novelized episodes from TV *Space: 1999* are episodic, a progression of threats and dangers ranging from space brain antibodies to materialized nightmares to alien wars of annihilation. His short stories often focus on mathematics, "Six Cubed Plus 1" on the magical properties of special numbers and "Traveller's Rest" on topological oddities whereby time and language vary with the structure of space.

—Gina Macdonald

MASSON, John. *See* **TUBB, E.C.**

MASSON, David I(rvine)

Nationality: British. **Born:** Edinburgh, 6 November 1915. **Education:** Oundle School, Northamptonshire, 1929-34; Merton College, Oxford, B.A. (honours) in English 1937, M.A. 1941. **Military Service:** Served in the Royal Army Medical Corps, 1940-45. **Family:** Married Olive Masson in 1950; one daughter. **Career:** Assistant Librarian, University of Leeds, 1938-40, and University of Liverpool, 1945-55; Sub-Librarian, in charge of Brotherton Collection, University of Leeds, 1956-79. **Address:** c/o Faber and Faber Ltd., 3 Queen Square, London WC1N 3AU, England.

SCIENCE FICTION PUBLICATIONS

Short Stories

The Caltraps of Time. London, Faber, 1968.

OTHER PUBLICATIONS

Other

Hand-List of Incunabula in the University Library, Liverpool. Privately printed, 1948; supplement, 1955.
Catalogue of the Romany Collection . . . University of Leeds. Edinburgh, Nelson, 1962.
Poetic Sound-Patterning Reconsidered. Leeds, Philosophical and Literary Society, 1976.
Keith Douglas's Phonetic Rhetoric of Phonetic Lyricism: A Study of Three Poems. Leeds, England, Leeds Philosophical and Literary Society, 1991.

*

David I. Masson comments:

My SF, although it seeks "scientific" versimilitude and tries to convince, has little to do with the processes of science. It explores bizarre assumptions for the sake—or so it seems to me—of mythopoeia, fable, satire, ridicule, scorn, or indignation, and perhaps inner truth about experience and feeling. Only "Take It or Leave It" has much to do with possible futures. Several stories reflect my conviction that the human race is insane. (Here and there one notes hopeful signs of some insight into its own condition.)

* * *

David I. Masson's SF reputation rests upon a handful of stories, most of them collected in *The Caltraps of Time.* A lively if recondite wit is a characteristic of these stories. A university antiquarian librarian, fascinated by linguistics, Masson plummets a Restoration gentleman into the 20th century courtesy of a borrowed time machine in "The Two Timer," to be amazed and bemused by our antics—and of course to satirize us in approved Swiftian manner. The impeccable late 17th-century prose style of this story throws into contrast our barbaric contemporary parlance: "Myself: *Prithee, Sir, do you converse in* English? At this he frown'd, and turn'd back thro' his Door, but left it open, for I heard him in speech with another, as follows. He . . . *Now enthing bauootim? Caun honstan zaklay wottee sez.*" Matters are just as bad for a researcher of the 1980s plunged into the 24th century by a linear accelerator accident in "The Transfinite Choice" ("Namplize." "Don't you speak English, then? Who the hell are you?" "Namplize"). It seems as though one is sliding down a cultural entropy slope. This future, in technotelegraphize, is trying, however, to master the gradient of time at the sub-particle level. Reality fractures as the future tries to shunt its excess population into parallel time-continua; or was it only, after all, the stricken researcher's reality that fell apart?

The finest of Masson's stories, "Traveller's Rest," deals with time yet again, apocalyptically yet ironically. The country at war in this story is distorted by differential time: whole decades pass in the peaceful south while mere minutes pass at the northern battle frontier where, perhaps, the army is simply fighting itself in the mirror of bent time with mounting frenzy and destructiveness—a powerful nightmare which does for exponential time what Christopher Priest's novel *Inverted World* was later to do for exponential space. In "Not So Certain" an expedition to an alien planet falls foul of the natives' tricky phonemes, another linguistic *jeu d'esprit,* while in "Mouth of Hell" apocalyptic topography confronts the explorers in the form of a 40-kilometre-deep cleft down to the molten magma which, by the end of the story, is tamed and demystified just as so much of our world has been banalised.

In Masson's loving care for language and concern with time, one senses a scholarly resentment at the downhill slide of the world into some future mass point of condensed people and words and moments.

—Ian Watson

MATHESON, Richard (Burton)

Pseudonym: Logan Swanson. **Nationality:** American. **Born:** Allendale, New Jersey, 20 February 1926. **Education:** University of Missouri, Columbia, B.A. in journalism 1949. **Military Service:** Served in the 87th Division of the United States Army during World War II. **Family:** Married Ruth Ann Woodson in 1952; two daughters and two sons. **Career:** Freelance writer. **Awards:** Hugo award, for screenplay, 1958; Writers Guild of America award, for television writing, 1960, 1974; World Fantasy award, 1976, 1990, and Life Achievement award, 1984. Guest of Honor, 16th World Science Fiction Convention, 1958 Bram Stoker award, 1990. **Agent:** Don Congdon Associates, 156 Fifth Avenue, Suite 625, New York, New York 10010, U.S.A. **Address:** P.O. Box 81, Woodland Hills, California 91365, U.S.A.

SCIENCE FICTION PUBLICATIONS

Novels

I Am Legend. New York, Fawcett, 1954; London, Corgi, 1956; as *The Omega Man: I Am Legend,* New York, Berkley, 1971.
The Shrinking Man. New York, Fawcett, and London, Muller, 1956; as *The Incredible Shrinking Man,* London, Sphere, 1988.
A Stir of Echoes. Philadelphia, Lippincott, and London, Cassell, 1958.
Hell House. New York, Viking Press, 1971; London, Corgi, 1973.
Bid Time Return. New York, Viking Press, 1975; London, Sphere, 1977; as *Somewhere in Time,* New York, Ballantine, 1980.
What Dreams May Come: A Novel. New York, Putnam, 1978; London, Joseph, 1979.
Earthbound (as Logan Swanson). London, Robinson, 1989; abridged edition, New York, Playboy Paperbacks, 1982; (as Richard Matheson), London, Robinson, 1989; New York, Tor, 1994.
Through Channels. Roundtop, New York, Footsteps Press, 1989.
Somewhere in Time: What Dreams May Come: Two Novels of Love and Fantasy. Los Angeles, Dream/Press, 1991.
Now You See It . . . . New York, Tor, 1995.

Short Stories

Born of Man and Woman: Tales of Science Fiction and Fantasy. Philadelphia, Chamberlain Press, 1954; abridged edition, London, Reinhardt, 1956; abridged edition, as *Third from the Sun,* New York, Bantam, 1955.
The Shores of Space. New York, Bantam, 1957; London, Corgi, 1958.

Shock! New York, Dell, 1961; London, Corgi, 1962; as *Shock 1: Thirteen Tales to Thrill and Terrify,* New York, Berkley, 1979.
Shock II. New York, Dell, 1964; London, Corgi, 1965.
Shock III. New York, Dell, 1966; London, Corgi, 1967.
Shock Waves. New York, Dell, 1970.
Shock 4. London, Sphere, 1980.
Richard Matheson: Collected Stories. Los Angeles, Scream/Press, 1989.

OTHER PUBLICATIONS

Novels

Someone Is Bleeding. New York, Lion, 1953.
Fury on Sunday. New York, Lion, 1953.
Ride the Nightmare. New York, Ballantine, 1959; London, Consul, 1961.
The Beardless Warriors: A Novel. Boston, Little, Brown, 1960; London, Heinemann, 1961.
Journal of the Gun Years: Being Choice Selectons from the Authentic Never-Before-Printed Diary of the Famous Gunfighter-Lawman Clay Halser! Whose Deeds of Daring Made His Name a By-Word of Terror in the Southwest between the Years of 1866 and 1878. New York, Evans, 1991.
The Gun Fight. New York, Evans, 1993.
7 Steps to Midnight. New York, Forge, 1993.
Shadow on the Sun. New York, Evans, 1994.

Plays

Screenplays: *The Incredible Shrinking Man,* 1957; *The Beat Generation (This Rebel Age),* with Lewis Meltzer, 1959; *The House of Usher (The Fall of the House of Usher),* 1960; *Master of the World,* 1961; *The Pit and the Pendulum,* 1961; *Tales of Terror,* 1962; *Burn, Witch, Burn (Night of the Eagle),* with Charles Beaumont and George Baxt, 1962; *The Raven,* 1963; *The Comedy of Terrors,* 1964; *The Last Man on Earth* (pseudonymous co-writer), 1964; *Die! Die! My Darling! (Fanatic),* 1965; *The Young Warriors,* 1967; *The Devil Rides Out (The Devil's Bride),* 1968; *De Sade,* 1969; *The Legend of Hell House,* 1973; *Dracula,* 1974; *Somewhere in Time,* 1980; *The Twilight Zone,* with others, 1983; *Jaws 3-D,* with Carl Gottlieb and Guerdon Trueblood, 1983.

Television Plays: *Yawkey (Lawman* series), 1959; *And When the Sky Was Opened, Third from the Sun, The Last Flight, A World of Difference, A World of His Own, Nick of Time, The Invaders, Once upon a Time, Little Girl Lost, Young Man's Fancy, Steel, Nightmare at 20,000 Feet, Night Call,* and *Spur of the Moment* (all in *Twilight Zone* series), 1959-63; *The Return of Andrew Bentley (Thriller* series), 1960-61; *The Enemy Within (Star Trek* series), 1966; *Duel,* 1971; *The Night Stalker,* 1971; *The Night Strangler,* 1972; *Dying Room Only,* 1973; *The Stranger Within,* 1974; *Dracula,* 1974; *Scream of the Wolf,* 1974; *The Morning After,* 1974; *Amelia* (in *Trilogy of Terror),* 1975; *Dead of Night,* 1977; *The Strange Possession of Mrs. Oliver,* 1977; *The Martian Chronicles,* from the novel by Ray Bradbury, 1979; *The Dreamer of Oz,* 1990; and scripts for *Chrysler Playhouse, Alfred Hitchcock Hour, The Girl from U.N.C.L.E., Have Gun—Will Travel, Wanted Dead or Alive, Night Gallery, The D.A.'s Man, Cheyenne, Bourbon Street Beat, Philip Marlowe, Buckskin, Markham,* and *Richard Diamond* series.

Other

Editor, with Martin H. Greenberg and Charles G. Waugh, *The Twilight Zone: The Original Stories.* New York, Avon, 1985.
By the Gun: Six from Richard Matheson. New York, Evans, 1993.
The Path: Metaphysics for the 90s. Santa Barbara, Capra Press, 1993.

*   *   *

Like many of the younger writers who began publishing science fiction in the shadow of Ray Bradbury in the 1950s, Richard Matheson has consistently worked on the borders of science fiction proper, using science fictional tropes as little more than expository devices on which to hang vividly imagined fantasies of paranoia and romance. His very first story, "Born of Man and Woman," is essentially a horror piece based on fears of deformity and child abuse, narrated in broken English by a hideously mutated child chained in the basement of his parents' home. "Death Ship" begins with all the appurtenances of science fiction—a spaceship crew discovers the wreckage of another spaceship— but soon turns into a "Flying Dutchman" ghost story as the crew learns that the wrecked ship is their own, and they are ghosts. In "The Traveler," a skeptical historian uses a time machine to witness the crucifixion of Christ, only to find himself converted to Christianity, rather unconvincingly. Almost none of these early stories devote much attention to their science fiction "macguffins," and it is not surprising that eight of them should later have provided the basis for episodes of Rod Serling's TV series *The Twilight Zone,* for which Matheson himself wrote more than a dozen scripts between 1960 and 1964.

This is not to suggest that Matheson's fiction lacks power. On the contrary, he often displayed a gift for imagining almost archetypal situations of paranoia and loss of control. In "Shipshape Home," new residents of an apartment building begin to suspect that the building is a disguised spaceship; they flee the building only to find that the spaceship is the entire block. The protagonist of "Disappearing Act" finds his family and acquaintances disappearing from the memory of everyone he meets, while "Nightmare at 20,000 Feet" explores the anxieties of flight, as an airline passenger sees a hideous gremlin on the wing of the plane. "Duel" (filmed by Steven Spielberg for television) does much the same for highway travel, as an unsuspecting motorist is terrorized by a huge truck whose driver remains unseen. Occasionally, the paranoia is leavened with clever satire, as in "The Creeping Terror," which uses a mock-academic style to reveal that Los Angeles is literally a spreading infection.

Matheson's two best-known novels are also his most extreme examples of isolation and loss of control. *I Am Legend,* with its nightmarish vision of the last man on earth besieged by vampires, has become a classic of horror literature, surviving two unsuccessful film adaptations. Largely because of its contemporary suburban setting and its earnest attempts to find a science fictional rationale for vampirism (the victims are infected by dust-borne bacteria), *I Am Legend* has been credited with having helped liberate the horror genre from its traditional settings of isolated villages and haunted castles. *The Shrinking Man* (for which Matheson wrote his own screen adaptation) offers even less of a scientific explanation for the fate of a man who, engulfed by radioactive dust while on his boat, begins shrinking at the rate of a seventh of an inch a day. The novel alternates the straightforward adventure story of the tiny narrator trapped in his cellar with flashback chapters detailing his growing alienation from the world as he becomes progressively smaller and unable to provide for his family or maintain relationships. Both *I Am Legend* and *The Shrinking Man* are haunting portraits of sensitive individuals losing control over their worlds, and both are unusual for their time in their open discussions of frustrated sexual longings. Matheson's technique is to assume a single fantastic premise and explore it with a rigor and logic that belies the sensational aspects of the initial premise.

In his later fiction, Matheson turned increasingly away from even the paraphernalia of science fiction. *Hell House,* with its discussion of magnetic fields and electronic equipment, retains some borderline elements of science fiction and seems in some ways to be an attempt to explain haunted house phenomena in the same pseudoscientific way *I Am Legend* explains vampires. But the soul of the book is in psychic research, which had long fascinated Matheson. *Bid Time Return* (filmed as *Somewhere in Time*) is in a sense a time travel fantasy in the tradition of Jack Finney, but is primarily a transgenerational love story. *What Dreams May Come* is also a sentimental love story, this time involved with life after death.

Following his adaptation of *The Shrinking Man* for the movies, Matheson devoted an increasing amount of his time to film and TV scripts, most notably *The Twilight Zone, Night Gallery,* and a series of very loose Edgar Allan Poe adaptations for director Roger Corman. Although more properly regarded as a fantasy writer, his novels and stories have also had a liberating effect on the science fiction field, and even his earliest works stand up surprisingly well as exemplars of how a fertile imagination, grounded in acute perceptions of character and closely observed detail, can explore hidden anxieties in the most outlandish of narrative premises.

—Gary K. Wolfe

MAUROIS, André

Pseudonym: E. Herzog. **Nationality:** French. **Born:** Emile Salomon Wilhelm Herzog, Elbeuf, 26 July 1885; changed name to André Maurois in 1947. **Education:** Lycee Corneille, Rouen (Prix d'honneur de philosophie), diploma in 1902; l'Universite de Caen, license in philosophy 1902. **Military Service:** French Army, volunteered and served with the Seventh Division, Rouen, 1903-04; interpreter for the Ninth Scottish Division, then liaison officer to the British Army Headquarters, 1914-18, received Distinguished Conduct Medal; Bureau of Information, attached to British Headquarters, 1939-40; volunteered for service in North Africa, Corsica, Italy, captain, 1943-44; went to the U.S. under the orders of General Giraud to relate to the Americans the effects of the lend-lease program and the extent of the French military effort in Italy. **Family:** Married 1) Jeanne-Marie Wande de Szymkievicz in 1912 (died 1924); 2) Simone de Caillavet in 1926; (first marriage) one daughter, two sons; (second marriage) one stepdaughter. **Career:** Industrial manager in family textile factory, 1904-14, 1919-26; lecturer in the U.S., 1927; lecturer, New York, Schenectady, Worcester, Ottawa, Montreal, and at Dartmouth College, Smith College, and Cornell University, 1927-32; Clark Lecturer, Trinity College, Cambridge University, 1928; held Meridith Howland Pyne chair of French literature, Princeton University, 1929-31; elected to the

French Academy, 1938; Lowell Lecturer, Harvard University, 1940; pleaded the cause of France and Marshal Henri Petain to the Americans in his writings and lectures, 1940-43; professor of French literature, Mills College, Oakland, California, summer 1941; professor of French literature, University of Kansas City, 1945-46. Full-time writer and lecturer following World War II. **Awards:** Honorary degrees, include Edinburgh University, 1928, Princeton University, 1933, Oxford University, 1934, University of Saint Andrews, 1934, University of Louisiana, and other institutions; Grand Officer of the Legion of Honor, 1937; Knight of the Order of the British Empire, 1938; Commandeur des Arts et des Lettres; Commandeur du Merite Sportif; Prix des Ambassadeurs. **Member:** Association France-Etats-Unis (president); Societe des Gens de Lettres; Comite de Lecture de la Comedie-Francaise; Portuguese Academy; Brazilian Academy. **Died:** 9 October 1967.

SCIENCE FICTION PUBLICATIONS

Novels

Le chapitre suivant. Paris, La Sagittaire, 1927; translated as *The Next Chapter: The War against the Moon,* London, Kegan Paul, 1927; New York, Dutton, 1928.
Voyage au pays des Articoles. Paris, Gallimard, 1928; translated by David Garnett as *A Voyage to the Island of the Articoles,* London, Cape, 1928; New York, Appleton, 1929.
Le peseur d'ames. Paris, Gallimard, 1931; translated by H. Miles as *The Weigher of Souls,* London, Cassell, 1931.
La machine a lire les pensees. Paris, Gallimard, 1937; translated by James Whitall as *The Thought-Reading Machine,* London, Cape, and New York, Harper, 1938.

Short Stories

Relativisme. Paris, Kra, 1930; translated as *A Private Universe,* New York, Appleton, and London, Cassell, 1932.
Patapoufs et fififers. Hartmann, 1930; translated by Rosemary Benet as *Fatapouis and Thinifers,* New York, Holt, 1940; translated by Norman Denny as *Fattypuffs and Thinifers,* Longon, Lane, 1941.

Other

The Weigher of Souls, and The Earth Dwellers. New York, Macmillan, 1963.

*   *   *

The scores of diverse books published by André Maurois show the varied experience and interests of the man. His family business of cloth manufacturing claimed his attention in early life, and World War I also delayed his full-time devotion to writing, thus helping to carry out the advice of his mentor, Emile Chartier, that he should experience the real world amply before turning to a life of literary creativity. Certainly his novels and short stories evince a mastery of human nature and profound understanding of the French and English character. His careful analysis and biographies of Percy and Mary Shelley, Charles Dickens, Honoré de Balzac, and other authors contributed further to this impression, as did his many works of history and commentary on modern affairs.

Maurois gave only a fraction of his literary attention to science fiction, and his typical works in this genre are novellas. In these, as always with Maurois, we see reflections of the universal curiosity to which he himself gives major credit for his successes. Always also there is the readiness to interpret discerningly. In *The Thought-Reading Machine* a professor makes a machine to detect the passing thoughts of the targeted persons, but Maurois discerns that transient thoughts are of quite limited value. In *Voyage to the Island of the Articoles* the author imagines a South Sea island society, but he is also satirizing the purblindness of his European contemporaries. Maurois's close acquaintance with H.G. Wells and with even more innovation-minded Frenchmen of his time did not prevent him from warning against rapid changes in society. He also warned of the destructiveness of then undeveloped "ray" and atomic weapons. *The Next Chapter* contemplates wars of genocidal scope—with 30 million deaths in 1947 alone. Equally imaginative, for 1927, is his description of the marshalling of the media to shape and control public opinion on a grand scale. The author's historical works show that he knew how this opinion-moulding had worked in the propaganda for the wars before 1927. The ambitious re-casting of national opinion is shown as the benevolent but arbitrary project of the powerful magnates who control the media of the world, and Maurois envisions unforeseen, even catastrophic, effects from this tampering with the outlook of the masses.

In quality, the science fiction of Maurois can be ranked among the early classics, with impressive insights into human affairs.

—Frank H. Tucker

MAY, Julian

Pseudonym: Lee N. Falconer; Juliana ux. Thaddei Maximi; Ian Thorne. **Nationality:** American. **Born:** Chicago, Illinois, 10 July 1931. **Education:** Attended Rosary College, River Forest, Illinois, 1949-53. **Family:** Married Thaddeus (Ted) E. Dikty in 1953; two sons and one daughter. **Career:** Editor, Booz Allen & Hamilton, Chicago; editor, Consolidated Book Publishers, Chicago, 1954-57; founder, with Ted Dikty, Publication Associates, in Chicago, 1957-68, Naperville, Illinois, 1968-74, West Linn, Oregon, 1974-80, and since 1980 in Mercer Island, Washington. Freelance writer: has published almost 300 non-fiction works, mainly for children. **Awards:** *Locus* award, 1982. **Agent:** Russell Galen, Scovil Chichak Galen, 381 Park Avenue South, Suite 1112, New York, New York 10016, U.S.A. **Address:** P.O. Box 851, Mercer Island, Washington 98040, U.S.A.

SCIENCE FICTION PUBLICATIONS

Novels (series: Galactic Milieu; Pliocene Exile; Trillium)

The Saga of Pliocene Exile: The Many-Colored Land. Boston, Houghton Mifflin, 1981; London, Pan, 1982.
The Golden Torc. Boston, Houghton Mifflin, and London, Pan, 1982.
The Nonborn King. Boston, Houghton Mifflin, and London, Pan, 1983.
The Adversary. London, Pan, 1984.

Intervention: A Root Tale to the Galactic Milieu and a Vinculum Between It and the Saga of Pliocene Exile. Boston, Houghton Mifflin, and London, Collins, 1987; as *The Surveillance* and *The Metaconcert,* New York, Ballantine, 2 vols., 1988.

Black Trillium, with Marion Zimmer Bradley and Andre Norton. New York, Doubleday, 1990; London, Grafton, 1991.

Blood Trillium. New York, Bantam, and London, HarperCollins, 1992.

Jack the Bodiless: A Novel (Galactic Milieu). New York, Knopf, and London, HarperCollins, 1992.

Diamond Mask: A Novel (Galactic Milieu). New York, Knopf, and London, HarperCollins, 1994.

The Galactic Milieau Trilogy. N.p., n.d.

Short Stories

Brede's Tale (Pliocene Exile). Mercer Island, Washington, Starmont House, 1982.

Short Stories as Ian Thorne

Dracula (adapted from screenplay). Mankato, Minnesota, Crestwood House, 1977.

King Kong (adapted from screenplay). Mankato, Minnesota, Crestwood House, 1977.

The Wolf Man (adapted from screenplay). Mankato, Minnesota, Crestwood House, 1977.

Godzilla (adapted from screenplay). Mankato, Minnesota, Crestwood House, 1977.

Frankenstein (adapted from screenplay). Mankato, Minnesota, Crestwood House, 1977.

Creature from the Black Lagoon (adapted from screenplay). Mankato, Minnesota, Crestwood House, 1981.

Frankenstein Meets Wolfman (adapted from screenplay). Mankato, Minnesota, Crestwood House, 1981.

The Mummy (adapted from screenplay). Mankato, Minnesota, Crestwood House, 1981.

The Blob (adapted from screenplay). Mankato, Minnesota, Crestwood House, 1982.

The Deadly Mantis (adapted from screenplay). Mankato, Minnesota, Crestwood House, 1982.

It Came from Outer Space (adapted from screenplay). Mankato, Minnesota, Crestwood House, 1982.

OTHER PUBLICATIONS

Other

A Pliocene Companion. Boston, Houghton Mifflin, 1984; London, Pan, 1985.

Mad Scientists (as Ian Thorne). Mankato, Minnesota, Crestwood House, 1977.

A Gazeteer of the Hyborian World of Conan: Including Also the World of Kull, and an Ethnogeographical Dictionary of Principal Peoples of the Era, with Reference to the Starmont Map of the Hyborian World (as Lee N. Falconer). West Linn, Oregon, Starmont House, 1977.

The Hyborian World of Conan: Being Here Newly Researched and Embellished for the Information and Edification of the Faithful, and Including All Locales Set Forth in the Immortal Saga, as Well as in Divers Works of a Comical Nature, and in Certain Incunabula Attributed to the Master, Robert E. Howard (illus-

trated map; as Juliana ux. Thaddei Maximi). West Linn, Oregon, Starmont House, 1977.

*

Bibliography: *The Work of Julian May: An Annotated Bibliography and Guide* by T.E. Dikty and R. Reginald, San Bernardino, California, Borgo Press, 1985.

Julian May comments:

My books are in the tradition of the classic literate thriller. They are intricately plotted and feature a large cast of characters romping through a "future history" and a "past history." The four Pliocene books and the Milieu Trilogy form one enormous novel, gaudy and humorous and melodramatic.

*   *   *

In the early 1950s, Julian May published two science fiction stories. During the next quarter of a century, she wrote 7,000 encyclopedia entries and about 245 nonfiction books for children, but no science fiction. Then, in 1978, she returned to SF by beginning work on the first novel in what would eventually become *The Saga of Pliocene Exile.* A decade later she brought out *Intervention,* a prequel to *The Saga.* And she is currently two-thirds of the way through *The Galactic Milieu Trilogy,* which covers events after *Intervention* and before *The Saga.*

Since May's oeuvre is at least one million words long, it is possible to mention only a few nodal events. In 2013, metapsychics led by Denis Remillard and Lucille Cartier (husband and wife) band together and emit a telepathic message that results in humanity's coming to the official attention of the five races then ruling the galaxy. In 2034, Professor Theophile Guderian invents a time machine—but it works at only one location (near Lyons, France); it goes back to only one time (the Pliocene Epoch, 6 million years in the past); and it is a one-way trip, since most organic objects (including people) disintegrate if returned to the present. In 2054, the Human Polity becomes a full-fledged member of the Concilium—the galaxy's governing body; slightly earlier, Paul Remillard, son of Denis and Lucille, had been elected First Magnate (chief executive) of the Human Polity. In 2083, a group of supremely talented human metapsychics led by Marc Remillard (son of Paul Remillard and Teresa Kendall) nearly overthrows the galactic government. By the 22nd century, human life has become utopian for all but a few people, with the most adventurous misfits choosing exile—stepping through the time gate and into the Pliocene, as the eight members of Group Green do in 2110.

It turns out that the Pliocene harbors a dimorphic alien (but humanoid) race—the tall, thin, elegant Tanu and the short, bulky, gauche Firvulag. They are exiles, too, from another galaxy even, waging on Earth the brutal battle-religion proscribed by their more civilized peers.

The Saga of Pliocene Exile details the impact on the Many-Colored Land (the Tanu name for Pliocene Europe) of Group Green, particularly Aiken Drum, Felice Landry, and Elizabeth Orme. May has said that *The Saga* is "positively operatic" (see "Music in My Head—Science Fiction as Opera" in *A Pliocene Companion*). Just so, for there is much here that reminds us of opera.

The Saga is Wagnerian in scope: the principals number in the dozens, the chorus in the hundreds, and reading it takes twice as long as seeing the *Ring.* May uses Freudian concepts or Jungian archetypes (sometimes both) as musical leitmotifs to characterize her human principals, as well as some of the important aliens. As background scenery, she carefully delineates the geography, geology, flora, and fauna of Pliocene Europe. The many stage settings include Tanu cities, Firvulag caves, and human camps. Since clothes (and colors) have symbolic meaning in *The Saga,* May writes exact (and colorful) descriptions of the costumes her characters wear. Those characters use innumerable props, especially the futuristic devices brought into the Pliocene by the humans. Operatic spectacle appears in various banquets and in the rituals surrounding the Tanu-Firvulag battle-religion. *The Saga* is also highly dramatic: the narrator sometimes disappears altogether, the point of view shifts kaleidoscopically, and the pace varies widely from scene to scene.

Romantic ideology permeates *The Saga.* May admits that her style sometimes becomes overwrought and that she has based many details on Northern, particularly Celtic, mythology (the Wagnerian influence, again). She also recognizes the romantic cast of her major themes: elitism, optimism, mentalism, medievalism, pacifism, love, and the value of pain.

May is also working with various science-fictional ideas. She invents a Universal Field Theory (it relates time, space, energy, matter, and mind) that allows faster-than-light travel, time travel, an inertia-less drive, and various forms of ESP: farsensing, coercion, psychokinesis, redaction, and creativity. These SF ideas should call to mind the Golden Age, for May claims to be writing "an intellectualized Doc Smith saga."

Intervention (also published in two paperback titles: *The Surveillance* and *The Metaconcert*) begins with the explosion of the Nagasaki atomic bomb on 9 August 1945 and ends with the telepathic *cri de coeur et cerveau* in 2013 that brings on the extraterrestrial advent alluded to in the title. Thus, it is both an alternate history and a First Contact story.

Like *The Saga, Intervention* is decidedly Golden Age, for instance in its use of the idea that humanity is being watched by superior creatures. It too has a wide scope (fewer characters but a longer time span, and it ranges beyond Europe to America, Scotland, India, and the Soviet Union), and it is fundamentally romantic. Indeed, May uses the idea of the doppelganger twice—Rogatien Remillard versus his evil brother Donatien and, in the next generation, Denis Remillard versus his evil brother Victor. The novel purports to be Rogatien's memoirs, looking back from 2113 at events that happened more than a century earlier. It has the feel of historical fiction, and May uses an array of literary techniques to tell the story—memoirs, straight narration, dramatic dialogue, excerpts from actual speeches or reports, a television script, a baseball play-by-play, a transcript of radio transmissions during the first Mars landing, and an article printed as it would be in a newspaper.

The first two parts of *The Galactic Milieu Trilogy—Jack the Bodiless* and *Diamond Mask*—are also Rogatien's memoirs purportedly written in 2113 long after the events recorded. The cast of characters in both novels remains large, and the physical settings expand to include the extraterrestrial. But both novels also focus often and closely on their respective title characters. *Jack the Bodiless* recounts the illegal birth (on 6 January 2052) and the very early life of Jon Paul Kendall Remillard (nicknamed Jack), youngest son of Paul Remillard and Teresa Kendall, and a preeminently potent metapsychic. *Diamond Mask* begins in May of 2062 and takes Dorothea Mary Strachan Macdonald, the only human being whose metapsychic faculties match Jack's, from age five to near her 20th birthday. Thus, both novels are SF Bildungsroman: two remarkable children overcome truly horrific obstacles on their way to adulthood.

Golden Age motifs also appear throughout *Jack the Bodiless* and *Diamond Mask:* eugenics, world building, galactic politics, the importance of human freedom and the concomitant distrust of possible alien tyranny, a nearly omnipotent villain (called Fury) and its vampiric minions (called Hydra), even Rogatien's occupation—he runs The Eloquent Page, an antiquarian bookstore specializing in 20th-century science fiction and fantasy titles. In addition, and like most of May's SF, the two books are thoroughly romantic, although the engagement of Jack and Dorothea, announced on the very last page of *Diamond Mask,* happens only after a long and difficult courtship.

Some reviewers have complained that both *Jack the Bodiless* and *Diamond Mask* end inconclusively. These reviewers should be a little more patient, for May promises that the trilogy's conclusion— to be called *Magnificat*—will dot all i's and cross all t's by detailing the defeat by Jack and Dorothea in 2083 of the Marc Remillard-led Metapsychic Rebellion, the retreat of the surviving Rebels to the Pliocene Epoch, and the demise of Fury/Hydra.

Finally, even more obviously than *The Saga,* both *Intervention* and the first two volumes of *The Galactic Milieu Trilogy* reveal that the titular saint for all May's SF is Pierre Teilhard de Chardin, the paleontologist-theologian who in a series of books published after his death in 1955 attempted to synthesize modern evolutionary science and Catholic dogma. May's World Mind and Galactic Mind, for instance, are thinly disguised versions of Chardin's noosphere; Unity is related to Chardin's Omega Point; and May borrows names from Chardin for the five alien Lylmik Supervisors guiding our galaxy toward Unity—e.g., Atoning Unifex, the most powerful.

Readers who want to keep their bearings amid May's gargantuan, erudite, and encyclopedic SF will find *A Pliocene Companion* helpful: it has a glossary (of place names, characters, and important concepts), a chronology, a Remillard family tree, maps, brief essays, interviews with the author, and "A Selective Bibliography." So far, scholars have not responded to May's challenge to find her fiction's hidden meanings. A good place to start would be with the bibliography just mentioned.

Readers who want to see what May can do with a different genre should read her *Blood Trillium,* an epic fantasy with some SF elements set in the same world as *Black Trillium,* which is also an epic fantasy that May coauthored with Marion Zimmer Bradley and Andre Norton. Both of May's coauthors have also returned to this world, Norton with *Golden Trillium* (1993) and Bradley with *Lady of the Trillium* (1995).

—Todd H. Sammons

MAYAKOVSKY, Vladimir

Nationality: Russian. **Born:** Bagdady (now Mayakovsky), Georgia, 19 July 1893. **Career:** Writer. Served as a spokesman, during the 1920s, for the Communist Party. **Died:** Committed suicide, 14 April 1930.

<small>SCIENCE FICTION PUBLICATIONS</small>

Plays

Klop. Moscow, n.p., 1928; translated as *The Bedbug,* n.p., 1960.

Banya. Moscow, 1930; translated as *The Bathhouse,* in *Complete Plays,* n.p., 1968.

The Complete Plays of Vladimir Mayakovsky (includes *Mystery Buffo*). N.p., 1968.

*   *   *

Vladimir Mayakovsky, the futurist poet and playwright, is one of the brightest stars in the great constellation of modern Russian literature. His paradoxical fusion of lyrical tenderness and oratorical violence marks a decisive change and renewal. Some of his works—even though, or perhaps because, only partly SF—are most representative of the embattled utopianism of the Soviet structure of feeling from 1917 to 1930. In poems such as "About It," "150,000,000," and "The Fifth International," in short propagandist pieces such as *Before and Now,* in film scenarios, and most clearly in his three post-revolutionary plays, the mainspring of Mayakovsky's creation was the tension between anticipatory utopianism and recalcitrant reality. An admirer of Wells and London, Mayakovsky wrote his witty masterpiece *Mystery Buffo* to celebrate the first anniversary of the October revolution, envisaging it as a second cleansing Flood in which the working classes, inspired by a poetic vision from the future, get successively rid of their masters, devils, heaven, and (in the 1921 version) economic chaos, and finally achieve a Terrestrial Paradise of reconciliation with Things around them. The revolution is thus both political and cosmic; it is an irreversible and eschatological, irreverent and mysterious, earthy and tender return to direct relationships of men with a no longer alien universe. No wonder that Mayakovsky's two later plays become satirical protests against the threatening separation of the classless heavens from the Earth. The future heavens of the sunlit Commune remain the constant horizon of Mayakovsky's imaginative experiments, and it is by its values that the grotesque tendencies of petty-bourgeois restoration in *The Bedbug* or of bureaucratic degeneration in *The Bathhouse* are savaged. Indeed, in the second part of both plays, the future—though too vaguely imagined from scenic purposes—irrupts into the play. In *The Bedbug* it absorbs and quarantines the petty "bedbugus normalis" in its bestiary. In *The Bathhouse* the newly proclaimed Soviet Five-Year-Plan slogan of "Time forward!" materializes into the invention of a time machine that communicates with and leaps into the future, sweeping along the productive and the downtrodden characters but spewing out the bureaucrats. The victory over time was for Mayakovsky a matter of central political, cosmic, and personal importance: intrigued by Fyodorov and by Einstein's theory of relativity, he firmly expected it to make immortality possible for men. His suicide in 1930 cut him off in the middle of a fierce fight against the bureaucrats whom he envisaged as holding time back and who engineered the failure of Meyerhold's production of *The Bathhouse.*

—Darko Suvin

MAYHAR, Ardath

Pseudonyms: Frank Cannon; Frances Hurst; John Killdeer. **Nationality:** American. **Born:** Ardath Hurst, Timpson, Texas, 20 February 1930. **Education:** Attended high school in Nacogdoches, Texas. **Family:** Married Joe E. Mayhar in 1958; two sons and two stepsons. **Career:** Dairyman, Nacogdoches County, 1947-57; operator, East Texas Bookstore, Nacogdoches, 1958-62; proofreader, *Capital Journal,* Salem, Oregon, 1968-75; chicken farmer, Nacogdoches County, 1976-78; proofreader, *Nacogdoches Daily Sentinel,* 1979-82. Since 1982, full-time writer, and since 1984, co-operator, View from Orbit, bookstore, Nacogdoches, and instructor, Writer's Digest School. **Member:** SFWA; Western Writers of America; Women Writing the West. **Agent:** Donald Maass, 157 West 57th Street, New York, New York 10019, U.S.A. **Address:** P.O. Box 180, Chireno, Texas 75937, U.S.A.

SCIENCE FICTION PUBLICATIONS

Novels (series: Battletech; Fuzzies; The House of Enthala; Kyrannon; Windwalker)

How the Gods Wove in Kyrannon. Garden City, New York, Doubleday, 1979; London, Sidgwick and Jackson, 1980.
The Seekers of Shar Nuhn (Kyrannon). Garden City, New York, Doubleday, 1980.
Soul-Singer of Tyrnos (Enthala; for children). New York, Atheneum, 1981.
Warlock's Gift. Garden City, New York, Doubleday, 1982.
Runes of the Lyre (Enthala; for children). New York, Atheneum, 1982.
Golden Dream: A Fuzzy Odyssey. New York, Ace, 1982.
Khi to Freedom. New York, Ace, 1983.
Lords of the Triple Moons (Enthala; for children). New York, Atheneum, 1983.
Exile on Vlahil. Garden City, New York, Doubleday, 1984.
The Saga of Grittel Sundotha (for children). New York, Atheneum, 1985.
The World Ends in Hickory Hollow. Garden City, New York, Doubleday, 1985.
Trail of the Seahawks (Windwalker), with Ron Fortier. Lake Geneva, Wisconsin, TSR, 1987.
The Wall. New York, Space and Time, 1987.
Makra Choria (for children). New York, Atheneum, 1987.
The Sword and the Dagger (Battletech). Chicago, FASA, 1987.
A Place of Silver Silence (for children). New York, Walker, 1988; London, Hutchinson, 1990.
Monkey Station, with Ron Fortier. Lake Geneva, Wisconsin, TSR, 1989.
People of the Mesa. New York, Diamond, 1992.
Island in the Lake. New York, Diamond, 1993.
Towers of the Earth. New York, Diamond, 1994.
Hunters of the Plains. New York, Diamond, 1995.

OTHER PUBLICATIONS

Novels (for children)

The Absolutely Perfect Horse, with Marylois Dunn. New York, Harper, 1983.
Medicine Walk. New York, Atheneum, 1985.
Carrots and Miggle. New York, Atheneum, 1986.

Novels as Frank Cannon

Feud at Sweetwater Creek. New York, Kensington, 1987.

Bloody Texas Trail. New York, Kensington, 1988.
Texas Gunsmoke. New York, Kensington, 1988.

*

Manuscript Collections: de Grummond Collection, University of Southern Mississippi, Hattiesburg; Stephen F. Austin State University, Nacogdoches, Texas.

Ardath Mayhar comments:

I like to think of my work as metaphysical fiction. SF and fantasy elements allow me to create contexts that reach past our own limitations and parameters into continua where what *should be* CAN BE. Logic and Humanity are the poles of my philosophy, and I refuse to be hemmed up into narrow genres. Writing science fiction, fantasy, poetry, juveniles, articles of all kinds, I work toward some inner goal, invisible but inexorable, and when I arrive at my destination I expect to be completely astonished.

*   *   *

Although Ardath Mayhar had published in other genres previous to 1979, she got her start in SF and fantasy literature with the young adult work *How the Gods Wove in Kyrannon.* Of the many genre novels she produced in the intervening years, only four, *Exile on Vlahil, Golden Dream, Khi to Freedom,* and *The World Ends in Hickory Hollow,* could be classified as SF. Another four are clearly high fantasy, with characteristics such as elevated diction used by both characters and narrator, a few characters with superior talents such as magic and telepathy, and indisputable separation of good and evil. The other three Mayhar novels fall into the category recently termed "science fantasy," and owe much to the early writing of Andre Norton. *Lords of the Triple Moons, Runes of the Lyre,* and *The Saga of Grittel Sundotha* are basically fantasy works set in surroundings where magic and heroic adventure are predominant, but they each incorporate some technological feature such as "cross-dimensional" gravel from a machine-based dimension of a lost technology called upon by the telepathic protagonists in their battle against evil wizards.

Mayhar is in fact preoccupied with telepathy and other superior powers of mind, an interest that surfaces in all her works. For example, in *Khi to Freedom,* she creates beings at several levels of corporeality and telepathic ability, with the protagonist Hale Enbo as the subject of a process of mental refinement by more elevated beings. *Exile on Vlahil,* her most amusing book to date, with its conscious computer called Alice, places a female-human hero in a position to save humans from her degenerating home planet through telepathic communication with idealized creatures called Erid and Vlammalba. *Golden Dream* gives H. Beam Piper's Little Fuzzys a history, describes the encounters with humans from their perspective, and makes much of their telepathic abilities and their powers of memory. The only novel that breaks this mold is anomalous in several ways. *The World Ends in Hickory Hollow* is a largely realistic postnuclear holocaust novel, one of several such novels by a variety of authors which have appeared in recent years. This work is also partially autobiographical, being set in an area of East Texas similar to that in which the author and her family now live. It is somewhat more positive than the general run of such novels, postulating that a few families will survive a nuclear attack through mutual assistance and the resurrection of traditional, down-home wisdom.

Mayhar's plots are inexorable and predictable from the initial pages of any story. Good and evil are as clearly identified in the SF as they are in the fantasy, and no less evident in the adult fiction than in the young adult books. The stories also tend to be highly moralistic, depending on a fixed code of ethics that emphasizes the basic goodness of most individuals and the evident uselessness of those not imbued with this goodness. In most of her works, evil beings are either reformed or discarded.

Mayhar's greatest accomplishment is the description of physiological and social functions of a wide range of organisms such as crystalline, electrical, or fuzzy-green creatures, as well as wizards, shamans, witches, rulers, and adventurers. *Khi to Freedom,* for example, is two loosely connected episodes in the adventures of Hale Enbo, a human extraordinarie, and each is enriched by the many homey descriptions of eating and sleeping, and the social interactions between the human and his various cohorts and enemies. *Exile on Vlahil,* her best and most representative work, succeeds as much because of the elaborate symbiosis that constitutes Vlahil's eco-culture as it does through any adventure-plot elements.

More recently, Mayhar has produced young adult novels, such as *Makra Choria, Medicine Walk,* and *A Place of Silver Silence.* She has also collaborated with Ron Fortier on two novels, *Trail of the Seahawks* and *Monkey Station.* Both are nominally science fiction, although *Trail* has a heroic-fantasy plot based on a female, Conan-type hero (reminiscent of Grittel Sudotha), and a reprise of viking- or pirate-raids in a time after total cultural disintegration where people ride large dogs instead of horses and monkeys have become sentient. *Monkey Station* could be classified as high-tech horror, but chronologically predates the story in *Trail.* Rather, it starts with AIDS research, following rumors that the virus was a mistake in germ warfare. The two very different stories and settings of *Trail* and *Monkey* are linked by the monkeys' sentience. Still, the SF-horror reader who likes Crichton will also appreciate *Monkey,* while the reader of heroic fantasy will be drawn to *Trail.*

—Janice M. Bogstad

McALLISTER, Bruce (Hugh)

Nationality: American. **Born:** Baltimore, Maryland, 17 October 1946. **Education:** Claremont Men's College, California, B.A. 1969; University of California, Irvine, M.F.A. 1971. **Family:** Two daughters and one son. **Career:** Sports rewriter, United Press International, New York, 1967; staff writer, Doubleday Multimedia, Santa Ana, California, 1969; Visiting Instructor, Long Beach City College, California, 1971-73, and California State University, Fullerton, 1973-74; managing editor, *Best SF* anthology series, Bobbs Merrill, Indianapolis, 1973-75. At University of Redlands, California: visiting instructor, 1971-74; assistant professor, 1974-79, associate professor, 1979-83, professor of English, 1983—, director of the writing program, 1974-84, Edith R. White Distinguished Professor of Literature and Writing, 1988-95, Director, Professional Writing Track and Internship Program, 1984—. Media relations director and editor, Policy Research Center, 1983-86. Freelance consultant in technical and scientific writing and public relations, 1980—; consultant, VSP Associates, Sacramento, California, 1982-86. **Awards:** Bread Loaf Writers Conference poetry scholarship, 1972; Squaw Valley Writers Conference fiction fellowship, 1973; University of Redlands Jubilee Medallion, 1983, Outstanding Teaching award, 1983, and Outstanding Faculty Research Award, 1991; National Endowment for the Arts writing fellowship, 1990. **Address:** Creative Program, University of Redlands, 1200 East Colton Ave., Redlands, California 92373, U.S.A.

SCIENCE FICTION PUBLICATIONS

Novels

Humanity Prime. New York, Ace, 1971.
Dream Baby. New York, Tor, 1989.

Short Stories

Author of numerous uncollected short stories.

OTHER PUBLICATIONS

Poetry

Poems: Massman, Costanzo, McAllister, with Gordon Massman and Gerald Costanzo. Reno, Nevada, West Coast Poetry Review, 1973.

Other

Editor, *SF Directions, Volume 5[-6].* Christchurch, New Zealand, Edge Press, 1972-73.
Editor, *Their Immortal Hearts: Three Visions of Time.* Reno, Nevada, West Coast Poetry Review Press, 1980.
Editor, with Harry Harrison, *There Won't Be War.* New York, Tor, 1991.

*   *   *

Bruce McAllister is a writer's writer, a critic's writer, a man whose work has always been highly regarded by his fellow professionals, but who remains relatively unknown and unappreciated among science fiction fans. The reasons for this are legion: he is a slow and meticulous craftsman, often doing 20 drafts for every story completed and published; he has pursued a dual career as a university English professor, thereby severely limiting his writing time; throughout most of his career he has preferred shorter lengths, in a field where regular production of novels is essential to achieving and maintaining broad public recognition; he eschews sequels, serials, and sword-and-sorcery fantasy; his fictions focus on character development, not mindless action-adventure; and he has never been prolific, even in his early years. Since 1965 he has published some 50 short stories, two novels, and 45 poems, in addition to editing several noteworthy anthologies. It is only in the 1990s that he has stopped writing short fiction, "probably forever," he says, "(or for a decade)."

"The Faces Outside," written when the author was 16, sets the tone for the rest of his work. The nameless hero finds himself floating in a tank with his mate and an assortment of aquatic creatures; their only contact with the outside world is a disembodied Voice. The Voice tells them that the faces watching through the ports are the Enemy, aliens who have annihilated the rest of humanity and have altered these two survivors into underwater humanoids. The two eventually transcend captivity by developing mental powers which will vanquish their alien captors, thereby assuring the survival of a new human race.

Here is microcosm we see the basic themes of McAllister's work. His protagonists are tortured individuals caught between a Heaven and Hell not of their own choosing. Their suffering and tribulations take them from the Limbos of their own minds to an ultimate realization, epiphany, or metamorphosis—or a combination of all three. In the author's early fictions, the theme of self-transcendence often translates into rather obvious power fantasies, in which one lonely or alienated character somehow manages to conquer his nemesis (i.e., himself), represented by alien or human monsters, or by some other life- or mind-threatening situation.

In the later stories, and particularly in the two long novels, *Humanity Prime and Dream Baby*, the author's treatment of these themes becomes more sophisticated, his view of mankind more cynical, his treatment of man's self-sacrificing inclinations more realistic, his feeling for the ultimate tragedy of the human condition more poignant (but never needlessly sentimental). These fictions also demonstrate an understanding of the female psyche unsurpassed in the work of any other male SF writer except D.G. Compton.

Humanity Prime, greatly expanded from "The Faces Outside," mixes mermen, cyborgs, intelligent sea turtles, and telepathic powers to produce one of the most compelling and convincing portraits of an underwater human species ever published. The author's intimate knowledge of human and animal biology, and his childhood experiences as the son of a behavioral psychologist, are reflected in this realistic and plausible extrapolation of man functioning in an alien environment. To McAllister, animals are as human in their own ways as men are sometimes animal-like in theirs; much of his fiction specifically concerns itself with the question of what it means to be human, and the answers are never simple, never easy to assimilate by either the characters or the reader.

The mutual themes of man's alienation from man and the transcendence of human nature reach a crescendo in McAllister's brilliant and highly acclaimed second novel, *Dream Baby,* which took a decade to write, partially under the aegis of a national Endowment for the Arts fellowship. Set in Indochina during the Vietnam War, this "nonfiction" novel is told largely in the first person by an Army nurse, Lt. Mary Damico, with interstices of real and fictional statements from Vietnam veterans the author interviewed some 200 survivors of the War over a ten-year period).

McAllister cleverly interweaves the surreality of the wartime experience with actual contingency plans developed by the U.S. Army to end the War by interjecting special forces units into North Vietnam. In *Dream Baby* the military cynically gathers together a group of veterans who have been experiencing a variety of paranormal experiences under combat. Mary's "talent" is her ability to dream the future, to forecast events which are rarely pleasant and often depict horrifying glimpses of brutal deaths to come. The group is dropped into the North, where it is ordered to destroy the dikes in central Vietnam during the monsoon season, thereby flooding Hanoi into the sea (attempts were actually made by U.S. forces during the War to bomb these embankments).

The combination of severe psychological stress, discovery of the infiltrators by the North Vietnamese, and the threat of imminent death, suddenly melds the team into one psychical whole, and provides it with the means to escape and survive. To complete the circle, the would-be destroyers of tens of thousands of human lives return to South Vietnam to destroy just one life, the soulless instigator of the project. Bucannon, whose brutal psychological manipulations have matched anything the Vietcong had ever devised. Mary Damico, the healer who had been so overwhelmed with horror that she could not heal, must restore order to the universe in the only way she can, by executing the agent of chaos. Only in this way can her life and the lives of the other survivors return to some semblance of normalcy, with their talents gradually fading away. In McAllister's universe, although a precarious balance between the forces of order and chaos can sometimes be achieved, ecstasy always walks hand-in-hand with agony, transcendence is always temporary, and nothing worthwhile is ever achieved without pain.

—Robert Reginald

McAULEY, Paul J.

Nationality: British. **Born:** Stroud, Gloucestershire, 23 April 1955. **Education:** Bristol University, B.Sc. in botany and zoology 1976, Ph.D. in botany 1980. **Awards:** Philip K. Dick award, 1989. **Address:** c/o MBA Literary Agents, 45 Fitzroy Street, London W1P 5HR, England.

SCIENCE FICTION PUBLICATIONS

Novels (series: Four Hundred Billion Stars)

Four Hundred Billion Stars. New York, Ballantine, and London, Gollancz, 1988.
Secret Harmonies (Stars). London, Gollancz, 1989; as *Of the Fall,* New York, Ballantine, 1989.
Eternal Light (Stars). London, Gollancz, 1991; New York, AvoNova, 1993.
Red Dust. London, Gollancz, 1993.
Pasquale's Angel. London, Gollancz, 1994.

Short Stories

The King of the Hill. London, Gollancz, 1991.

Other

Editor, with Kim Newman, *In Dreams.* London, Gollancz, 1992.

*   *   *

Paul McAuley's first novel, *Four Hundred Billion Stars,* was something of a rarity in British science fiction, a hard science novel in the *Analog* mould. Set several hundred years from now, it deals with mankind's expansion outward into the stars, a Federation of 10 human-colonised worlds encountering the presence of ancient alien life for the first time. Dorthy Yoshida, a "Talent" (or telepath), is sent out to one of the worlds terra-formed by the aliens. What she discovers there changes both her and humans' perception of the history of the galaxy, opening up vast vistas into the past. As might be surmised from this brief description, the elements of the work are traditional. It is very much a first novel, with all the concomitant flaws of an apprentice work. Slow-paced and downbeat in its message, it attempts to subvert the traditional devices of space opera but without great success. Dorthy is hard to empathise with and her slow trek towards enlightenment is somewhat wearying. The subversive techniques of the novel also tend to work against

the natural dynamics of the form and dampen reader enjoyment, leading one to consider the book over-long despite its actual brevity. Likewise, the hard science expository nuggets are presented more as lectures—undigested chunks of fact—than as a natural part of the novel's furniture. A good idea presented in a mediocre manner, it nonetheless attracted the Philip K. Dick Memorial award for best new novel.

Something of this same low-energy burn is to be found in McAuley's second novel, *Of The Fall,* (published as *Secret Harmonies* in the United Kingdom). Once again, McAuley attempts to harness his knowledge as a research biologist to present us with yet another enigmatic alien race. This time, however, there is no cosmic revelation at the end of the quest, and the colony world on which the action takes place differs little in its essential ingredients from the colonies that the Imperial powers controlled in the early 20th century, complete with late 20th-century campus. But the focus of the novel is not, this time, on aliens or environment but upon the human characters caught up in a revolution as their colony planet is cut off from the home world, Earth. What the book lacks in strangeness it makes up for in human involvement and in its vivid portrayal of change, culminating in a passage strongly reminiscent of the ending of *Earth Abides.*

Of the Fall shares (if loosely) the same historical background as *Four Hundred Billion Stars,* and McAuley has set another half dozen stories within this framework, including two novelettes, "The Airs of Earth" (in *Amazing,* January 1986) and "The Heirs of Earth" (in *Amazing,* May 1987). None of these works, however, was any preparation for the imaginative richness or scope of McAuley's novel *Eternal Light.* Here, all of the flaws of his debut have been turned into strengths. This is space opera again, but this time with a pace and imaginative energy that has rarely been matched in the genre. Dorthy Yoshida is again at the centre of events, joined this time by a starship war veteran, Suzy Falcon; a part-cybernetic punk, "Robot"; and a near-immortal "Golden," Talbeck Barlstilkin. Their struggle against the system—against the Greater Brazilian empire, the Federation of Worlds, the Navy, and a cartel of other "Goldens"—leads them out 115 light-years from Earth to an encounter with a "fast-star," travelling at a sixth the speed of light towards Sol. What they discover there, both about the alien Alea (the herders of McAuley's first novel) and the nature of their universe is of profound cosmological (and, one might say, religious) significance. A rich, constantly surprising work, *Eternal Light* embraces the heritage of vast-scale cosmological speculation championed by writers like Stapledon and Clarke and marries it to the hard-edged, high-energy gloss (and love of techno-detail) of the cyberpunks with exciting results. It seems likely to become one of the classic works of the 1990s.

—David Wingrove

McCAFFREY, Anne (Inez)

Nationality: Irish (originally American). **Born:** Cambridge, Massachusetts, 1 April 1926. **Education:** Stuart Hall, Staunton, Virginia; Montclair High School, New Jersey; Radcliffe College, Cambridge, Massachusetts, B.A. (cum laude) in Slavonic languages and literature 1947; studied meteorology at City of Dublin University. **Family:** Married E. Wright Johnson in 1950 (divorced 1970); two sons and one daughter. **Career:** Copywriter and layout designer, Liberty Music Shops, New York, 1948-50; copywriter, Helena Rubinstein, New York, 1950-52. Currently runs a thoroughbred horse stud farm in Ireland; since 1978, director, Dragonhold Ltd., and since 1979, director, Fin Film Productions. Has performed in and directed several operas and musical comedies in Wilmington and Greenville, Delaware. Secretary-Treasurer, Science Fiction Writers of America, 1968-70. **Awards:** Hugo award, 1968, 1979; Nebula award, 1968; Gandalf award, 1979; Balrog award, 1980. **Member:** Authors' Guild; SFWA. **Agent:** Virginia Kidd, Box 278, Milford, Pennsylvania 18337, U.S.A. **Address:** Dragonhold, Kilquade, Greystones, County Wicklow, Ireland.

SCIENCE FICTION PUBLICATIONS

Novels (series: Doona; Dragonriders of Pern; Ireta; Killashandra; Pegasus; Pern; Harper Hall; Planet Pirate; Power; Rowan; The Ship)

Restoree. New York, Ballantine, 1967; London, Rapp and Whiting, 1968.

Dragonflight (Dragonrider). New York, Ballantine, 1968; London, Rapp and Whiting, 1969.

Decision at Doona. New York, Ballantine, 1969; London, Rapp and Whiting, 1970.

Dragonquest (Dragonrider). New York, Ballantine, 1971; London, Rapp and Whiting-Deutsch, 1973.

Dragonsong (for children; Harper Hall). New York, Atheneum, and London, Sidgwick and Jackson, 1976.

Dragonsinger (for children; Harper Hall). New York, Atheneum, and London, Sidgwick and Jackson, 1977.

The White Dragon (Dragonrider). New York, Ballantine, 1978; London, Sidgwick and Jackson, 1979.

The Dragonriders of Pern (omnibus). Garden City, New York, Doubleday, 1978.

Dragondrums (for children; Harper Hall). New York, Atheneum, and London, Sidgwick and Jackson, 1979.

Crystal Singer (Killashandra). New York, Ballantine, and London, Severn House, 1982.

The Coelura (Pern). Lancaster, Pennsylvania, Underwood-Miller, 1983.

Moreta, Dragonlady of Pern. New York, Ballantine, and London, Severn House, 1983.

The Harper Hall of Pern (omnibus). Garden City, New York, Doubleday, 1984.

The Ireta Adventure. Garden City, New York, Doubleday, 1985.
  Dinosaur Planet. London, Orbit, and New York, Ballantine, 1978.
  Dinosaur Planet Survivors. New York, Ballantine, and London, Futura, 1984.

Killashandra. New York, Ballantine, 1985; London, Bantam, 1986.

Nerilka's Story (Dragonrider). New York, Ballantine, 1986.

Dragonsdawn (Pern). Norwalk, Connecticut, Easton Press, and London, Bantam, 1988.

The Renegades of Pern. New York, Ballantine, 1989; London, Bantam, 1990.

Sassinak (Planet Pirate), with Elizabeth Moon. New York, Baen, 1990; London, Orbit, 1991.

The Death of Sleep (Planet Pirate), with Jody Lynn Nye. New York, Baen, 1990; London, Orbit, 1991.

Pegasus in Flight. New York, Ballantine, and London, Bantam, 1990.

The Rowan. New York, Ace, and London, Bantam, 1990.

Generation Warriors (Planet Pirate), with Elizabeth Moon. New York, Baen, 1991; London, Orbit, 1992.

The Wings of Pegasus (omnibus). New York, Guild America, 1991.

Rescue Run. Newark, New Jersey, Wildside Press, 1991.

All the Weyrs of Pern. New York, Ballantine, 1991.

PartnerShip (The Ship), with Margaret Ball. Riverdale, New York, Baen, 1992; London, Orbit, 1994.

Crystal Line (Killashandra). New York, Ballantine, and London, Bantam, 1992.

Damia (Rowan). London, Bantam, and New York, Putnam, 1992.

Crisis on Doona, with Jody Lynn Nye. New York, Ace, 1992; London, Orbit, 1993.

The Ship Who Searched, with Mercedes Lackey. Riverdale, New York, Baen, 1992; London, Orbit, 1994.

The City Who Fought (The Ship), with S.M. Stirling. Riverdale, New York, Baen, 1993; London, Orbit, 1995.

Damia's Children (Rowan). New York, Ace/Punam, and London, Bantam, 1993.

Powers That Be, with Elizabeth Ann Scarborough. New York, Ballantine, and London, Bantam, 1993.

The Planet Pirate, with Elizabeth Moon and Jody Lynn Nye (omnibus). Riverdale, New York, Baen, 1993.

The Ship Who Won, with Jody Lynn Nye. Riverdale, New York, Baen, 1994.

Power Lines, with Elizabeth Ann Scarborough. London, Bantam, and New York, Ballantine, 1994.

Treaty Planet (Doona), with Jody Lynn Nye. London, Orbit, 1994; as *Treaty at Doona,* New York, Ace, 1994.

The Dolphins of Pern. New York, Ballantine, and London, Bantam, 1994.

Lyon's Pride (Rowan). New York, Ace/Putnam, and London, Bantam, 1994.

Freedom's Landing. New York, Ace/Putnam, 1995.

Power Play, with Elizabeth Ann Scarborough. London, Bantam, and New York, Ballantine, 1995.

Short Stories

The Ship Who Sang. New York, Walker, 1969; London, Rapp and Whiting, 1971.

To Ride Pegasus. New York, Ballantine, 1973; London, Dent, 1974.

A Time When. Cambridge, Massachusetts, NESFA Press, 1975.

Get off the Unicorn. New York, Ballantine, 1977; London, Corgi, 1979.

The Worlds of Anne McCaffrey. London, Deutsch, 1981.

The Girl Who Heard Dragons (for children). New Castle, Virginia, Cheap Street, 1985.

Habit Is an Old Horse. Seattle, Washington, Dryad Press, 1986.

The Dolphins' Bell (Pern). Newark, New Jersey, Wildside Press, 1993.

The Chronicles of Pern: First Fall. Norwalk, Connecticut, Easton Press, and London, Bantam, 1993.

The Girl Who Heard Dragons (collection). New York, Tor, 1994.

An Exchange of Gifts (for children). Newark, New Jersey, Wildside Press, 1995.

Other Publications

Novels

Three Gothic Novels. Lancaster, Pennsylvania, Underwood-Miller, 1990; as *Three Women,* New York, Tor, 1992.

The Mark of Merlin. New York, Dell, 1971; London, Millington, 1977.

Ring of Fear. New York, Dell, 1971; London, Millington, 1979.

The Kilternan Legacy. New York, Dell, 1975; London, Millington, 1976.

Stitch in Snow. San Francisco, Brandywine, 1984; London, Corgi, 1985.

The Year of the Lucy. San Francisco, Brandywine, 1986; London, Corgi, 1987.

The Lady. New York, Ballantine, 1987; as *The Carradyne Touch,* London, Macdonald, 1988.

Other

The Dragonlover's Guide to Pern, with Jody Lynn Nye. New York, Ballantine, 1989.

Editor, *Alchemy and Academe: A Collection of Original Stories Concerning Themselves with Transmutations, Mental and Elemental, Alchemical and Academic.* Garden City, New York, Doubleday, 1970.

Editor, *Cooking out of This World.* New York, Ballantine, 1973.

*

Bibliography: *Leigh Brackett, Marion Zimmer Bradley, Anne McCaffrey: A Primary and Secondary Bibliography* by Rosemarie Arbur, Boston, Hall, 1982.

Critical Study: *Anne McCaffrey* by Mary T. Brizzi, Mercer Island, Washington, Starmont, 1986.

Manuscript Collections: Syracuse University, New York; Kerlan Collection, University of Minnesota, Minneapolis.

Anne McCaffrey comments:

I am a storyteller of *science fiction* and wish that label attached to my work in that field. I make this point as I am often classified, erroneously, as a fantasy writer. Since I am more interested in the interaction of people, the research I do for some of the books is not apparent, thus confusing the uninitiated. I have no pretentions to literary style or excellence, nor are my stories allegorical, mystical, or political. I cannot honestly call myself a feminist, though I do not disagree with the aims of the women's movement, and in *The Kilternan Legacy* I make comparisons between the rights of American women and the deplorable lack of status of Irish women. My personal philosophy was heavily influenced by Austin Tappan Wright's classic, *Islandia*—a book I read at 14 and consistently reread. Of all the stories I have written to date, *The Ship Who Sang* is my favorite.

*   *   *

Anne McCaffrey, creator of Pern, planet of telepathic dragons and their riders, is a builder of other complex universes. She is also creator of the psi Talent world of the Rowan, the crystal world of Killashandra Ree, the universe of brainship Helva, the Dinosaur Planet, the sapient planet Petaybee, Doona and other worlds. She also writes non-science fiction mysteries and romances with strong female protagonists. Mathew D. Hargreaves' *Anne Inez McCaffrey: Forty Years of Publishing* (1992) and its 1994 addendum are invaluable at sorting out the various McCaffrey universes.

Her themes include bonding, birth, adolescent emergence, and adult transformation. Loss, disfigurement, and recompense are concerns in the early novels. She is a keen interpreter of family dynamics. Her imagery is drawn from music, Irish and other folklore, cuisine, classical mythology, and most particularly natural and human flight. In fact, the central premise for many McCaffrey novels is a means of flight, particularly space-travel. Flight is her metaphor for the development of human worth generally, and for artistic flowering specifically. Imagination and love are her most essential themes.

McCaffrey's earliest acknowledged story, "Lady in the Tower" (*F&SF,* April 1959; reprinted in *Get off the Unicorn*), introduced far-future psionic Talents who guide spacecraft. The Rowan, a brilliant, lonely Prime Talent, overcomes mental obstacles to travel light years to join the love of her life, Jeff Raven. *To Ride Pegasus* and stories in *Get Off the Unicorn* explore the near-future history of the psionic Talented. The Rowan fulfills McCaffrey's intent of expanding "Lady in the Tower," while *Damia* portrays the Rowan's daughter nearly destroyed while following her mother's footsteps. *Damia's Children* and *Lyon's Pride* tell of the Rowan's extended family in their encounters with the enemy alien Hive and the friendly Mrdini. Family dynamics is a strong theme underscored with imagery drawn from animal and insect reproduction.

The Hive and the Tower series, with the Talent books, explores issues of youthful emergence and transformation, using imagery of birds and mythical beings. McCaffrey characterizes adolescents and adults finding their unique place in the universe and discovering love at the same time—an enduring theme.

The transformation theme arises in another early work, *Restoree,* in which a terrestrial woman is kidnapped and flayed by aliens who butcher and eat sentients. Humanoid aliens restore and beautify her (hence the title). Restoration has previously resulted in mindless monsters, so the heroine is imprisoned in a psychiatric hospital. Together with a dashing alien man, she escapes, and the two become lovers. Some readers have criticized the book as melodramatic and sexist; a better reading is to recognize McCaffrey's tongue-in-cheek shots at space opera and gothic romance.

Decision at Doona explores family dynamics and problems of race relations between humans and aliens, the cat-like Hrrubans. Adroit point-of-view manipulations and sensitive portrayal of children mark this novel. Sequels, *Crisis on Doona* and *Treaty Planet* (American title: *Treaty on Doona*), both written with Jody Lynn Nye, explore themes of individualism and honor.

Transformation again is a theme in *The Ship Who Sang* and its spin-off books, *Partnership* (with Margaret Ball), *The Ship Who Searched* (with Mercedes Lackey), *The City Who Fought* (with S. M. Stirling), and *The Ship Who Won* (with Jody Lynn Nye). The premise is that children born with multiple physical handicaps become the cyborg brains of interstellar starships (or cities). These "brains," beginning with Helva, have unconventional friendships and love affairs with their "brawns" or mobile partners. The series demonstrates McCaffrey's interest in strong female characters, whether as brawn or brain, and the buoyant persistence of human personality despite physical differences.

In McCaffrey's multiple-award-winning Dragonriders of Pern series, human inhabitants of Pern are threatened by a voracious mycorrhizoid called Thread that crosses vacuum from another planet, the Red Star. The premise of the Dragonrider books is that early colonists of the planet Pern bio-engineer psionic dragons as a defense against Thread. The dragons bond telepathically to their riders and incinerate falling Thread with phosphine-burning breath. Dragons can also cross long distances—and, it is learned, time—telekinetically. The most moving and spirited passages in the Pern books depict dragon hatching, bonding, and mating. In the Harper Hall trilogy, dragon flight becomes a metaphor for artistic creation, with the rider as intellect and the dragon itself as emotion and drive, as in Plato's Phaedrus. The Pern books, because of a few feudal touches, are sometimes mistakenly categorized as fantasy, but Pernese society and science are all based on meticulously researched—if sometimes speculative—science. McCaffrey's later Pern books, *Dragonsdawn, All the Weyrs of Pern, The Dolphins of Pern,* and the stories in *The Chronicles of Pern: First Fall,* make this clear. Pern is a science fictional universe.

The early novella "Dragonflight" depicts the hardships of Lessa and her bonding with the golden dragon Ramoth. The trilogy *Dragonflight, Dragonquest,* and *The White Dragon* counterpoint the young adult Harper Hall trilogy, *Dragonsong, Dragonsinger,* and *Dragondrums* in theme and imagery. As a group, these develop leading characters—Lessa, F'lar, Menolly, Master Robinton—of the far-future world after Pern's terrestrial origins have been forgotten. *Moreta, Dragonlady of Pern* and *Nerilka's Story* develop McCaffrey's mature themes of growth and service as avenues of life-long happiness. *The Renegades of Pern* develops a panoramic view of Pern in the age of Ramoth, with an array of characters including the swashbuckling female criminal, Thella. *Dragonsdawn* recounts adventures of the original colonists, the discovery of fire-lizards from which a colonial woman bio-engineers the first queen dragon, Faranth, and the adventures of the first riders. *Dolphins of Pern* explores the re-evolution of a technological civilization on Pern.

Symbolically, the Dragonrider books are richly realized. The very name of the planet, Pern (related to *perne* or bobbin), suggests a multiplicity of connections to William Butler Yeats's "Sailing to Byzantium," as well as his other poetry and his cosmology generally, while the name of a leading character, Lessa, echoes Yeats's godstruck history-maker in "Leda and the Swan."

In the Killashandra books, begun in Roger Elwood's *Continuum* series and revised extensively (and put in correct order) for *Crystal Singer,* Killashandra Ree's musical talent enables her to cut special crystal used in interstellar flight and communications. The crystal planet's indigenous life form is a symbiote that fuses with the cutter's nervous system, bestowing long life, but also causing memory loss. The parallels to the trials and dilemmas of the artist's life are edifying. Although Killashandra eventually achieves a satisfying and enduring romantic attachment and life, the series is the darkest of McCaffrey's work, fascinating for its rich symbolism, tormented characters, and clever use of unreliable narrator.

Dinosaur Planet and *Dinosaur Planet Survivors* feature a mysterious garlic-scented planet with life from several eras of Earth's prehistory, including intelligent pteranodons. The first book sets up mysteries about the creatures; the second solves them. Related books are McCaffrey's collaborations with Elizabeth Moon, *Sassinak* and *Generation Warriors,* and with Jody Lynn Nye, *The Death of Sleep,* all of which explore the disruption of natural life and family rhythms through interstellar cryonic sleep.

The Coelura features sentients who weave empathic clothing, while *Freedom's Landing,* an expansion of "The Thorns of Barevi,"

explores issues of authority and survival on a planet where kidnapped settlers, alien and human, struggle to survive and attain self-government. As elsewhere in McCaffrey's work, bonding and romantic expression are highlighted.

The Petaybee novels, *Powers That Be, Power Lines,* and *Power Play,* represent an interesting experiment in McCaffrey's opus. Her other collaborations are based on worlds which she created, and which she then invited other writers to co-create in. The Powers novels were conceived in collaboration with Elizabeth Anne Scarborough, and their themes of healing and nearly pantheistic communion between humans and nature are a departure which develops many of McCaffrey's other themes in striking new ways. As elsewhere, McCaffrey's sly humor is a plus.

Black Horses for the King (tentative title; expansion of the forthcoming "Black Horse for a King," in Jane Yolen's *Camelot* collection) will develop Arthurian material from a refreshingly new angle: a young lad finds his identity shoeing large horses to be ridden by King Arthur's knights. McCaffrey did considerable research on this novel, based as it is on historical fact.

This account leaves out many of McCaffrey's achievements in the short fiction field. The long-awaited "The Bones Do Lie" is a complex tale of time travel and jealousy. Readers would do well to investigate this and other works in *The Girl Who Heard Dragons,* as well as McCaffrey's other short fiction.

McCaffrey admirers have banded together to form an affiliation parallel to her dragon-riding society. New members are assigned, according to their geographical origin, to Weyrs and Holds corresponding to those on Pern; they may claim to ride dragons or own fire-lizards. The arrangement is as elaborate as any fan organization, including Star Trek fandom.

However, McCaffrey has also earned the admiration of more literary readers and is receiving increasing attention from scholarly critics. See J.R. Wytenbroek, "The Child as Creator in McCaffrey's *Dragonsong* and *Dragonsinger,*" *Lion and Unicorn,* December 1992; Jessica Amanda Salmonson, "Gender Structure of Shell Persons in *The Ship Who Sang,*" *New York Review of Science Fiction,* June 1989; Marleen Barr, "Science Fiction and the Fact of Women's Repressed Creativity: Anne McCaffrey Portrays a Female Artist," *Extrapolation,* Spring 1982; and Carolyn Wendell, "The Alien Species: A Study of Women Characters in the Nebula Award Winners, 1965-1973," *Extrapolation,* Winter 1979. She is even cited as forging linguistic evolution, in Alan R. Slotkin and Robert F. Bode's "A Back-(to-the-future)-Formation," *American Speech,* Fall 1993.

A good overview of critical articles and reviews up to 1980 is provided by Rosemarie Arbur, *Leigh Brackett, Marion Zimmer Bradley, Anne McCaffrey: A Primary and Secondary Bibliography,* 1982. Her work is a popular topic for undergraduate term papers and graduate dissertations.

Readers interested in the correct pronunciation of proper nouns from the McCaffrey universes should listen to tapes of her works on which she herself is the reader, eg. *Nerlika's Story* (Random House Audio), *All the Weyrs of Pern* (Publishing Mills), *The White Dragon* (Caedmon).

McCaffrey's style has a neoclassic flavor in its wit, sarcasm, and clarity, though some fail to perceive her irony. She is at her strongest depicting love and bonding, between lovers, family members, humans and animals, humans and aliens. Her flight imagery—dragons, Pegasus, spaceship—is compelling. These, plus her skilled characterization and world-building, make her among the most significant of contemporary writers.

—Mary Turzillo Brizzi

McDEVITT, Jack

Nationality: American. **Born:** Philadelphia, Pennsylvania, 14 April 1935. **Education:** LaSalle, Philadelphia, 1953-57, B.A. 1957; Wesleyan University, Middletown, Connecticut, 1967-71, M.A.L.S. 1971. **Military Service:** Served in United States Navy, 1958-62. **Family:** Married Maureen McAdams in 1967; one daughter and two sons. **Career:** English teacher, 1963-73; staff member of U.S. Customs Service, 1975-95. Since 1995, full-time writer. **Member:** U.S. Chess Federation, 1971; SFWA, 1983. **Awards:** Philip K. Dick special award, 1986; UPC 1st prize, for novella, 1992. **Agent:** Ralph M. Vicinanza, Ltd., 111 Eighth Avenue, Suite 1501, New York, New York 10011, U.S.A. **Address:** 57 Sunset Boulevard, Brunswick, Georgia 31525, U.S.A.

SCIENCE FICTION PUBLICATIONS

Novels

The Hercules Text. New York, Ace, 1986; London, Sphere, 1988.
A Talent for War. New York, Ace, and London, Kinnell, 1989.
Engines of God. New York, Ace, 1994.
The Engines of God. N.p., n.d.

Other

Hate Crimes: The Rising Tide of Bigotry and Bloodshed, with Jack Levin. New York, Plenum Press, 1993.

*

Jack McDevitt comments:

(1991) Despite everything *The Washington Post* and CNN tell us, the world is full of decency, good humor, and courage. If you doubt it, stop by your local Special Olympics. Or watch the volunteers pour in after a hurricane has gone down Main Street like a bowling ball.

I have no interest in afflicting the comfortable. The arrogant and the selfish are boring, and we have no interest in them except to see them get theirs in the last chapter. Give me ordinary people, characters who like one another, who summon their courage reluctantly, but who ultimately confront what they really believe. Whenever I can achieve that kind of voyage, the narrative has to work.

(1995) What strikes me most about writing science fiction, when it works, is the sheer joy of the enterprise. Other than indulging in the grand passion, or (as Churchill remarked) being shot at without result, little else gets into the same ballpark.

*   *   *

In the 1980s, some critics divided the SF authors who came to prominence in that decade into the supposedly oppositional factions of "humanists" and "cyberpunks." Given this generalization, the work of Jack McDevitt definitely falls into the "humanist" camp. Although he deals with such traditional hard SF topics as first contact with alien intelligence and far-future military conflict, the emphasis in McDevitt's work is on the working-out of problems by rational individuals. Like the work of Isaac Asimov, McDevitt's stories usually contain, not villains, but people who are set in op-

position to the protagonist. Unlike Asimov, McDevitt is also concerned with the aesthetic and spiritual lives of his characters; poets and painters are frequently as important as scientists and soldiers, and problems of religious faith and ethics are given just as much, if not more, weight than problems of science and technology.

McDevitt began publishing in the SF magazines in the early 1980s, quickly gaining attention when his 1983 short story "Cryptic" (in *Isaac Asimov's Science Fiction Magazine,* September 1984) was nominated for a Nebula award. The story is narrated by the administrator of a scientific research station who discovers that the SETI project that had formerly occupied the facility had picked up interstellar communications 20 years earlier, only to suppress the information when the then-administrator discovered that the communications were from two alien races at war with each other. "Cryptic" contains almost all the elements of McDevitt's later novels: an ordinary man caught up in extraordinary circumstances, trying to solve a cosmic riddle from the testimony of persons of superior intellect; scientists who are also men of faith (the current administrator is a Jesuit priest, the former a lapsed seminarian) and whose faith informs their scientific decisions; and a reverence for knowledge coupled with doubts as to how far fallible humanity can, or should, proceed with its discoveries.

All these elements are present in McDevitt's first novel, *The Hercules Text.* Once again, the topic is the search for extraterrestrial intelligence, and the central character, Harry Carmichael, is an administrator rather than a scientist. This time, however, the story is set in the near future and deals with the events surrounding the reception of a signal from a solar system in the constellation Hercules. The book is a splendid example of what Algis Budrys has called the "science-procedural novel," concerning itself with the process of decoding the alien text and the power struggles that ensue as various scientific and governmental factions vie for control of the information contained in the transmission. Although the emphasis is on problem-solving, McDevitt does not neglect his characters, giving all the major figures believable lives whose individual quirks and problems are fully integrated into the central problem of the Hercules Text. As in "Cryptic," Catholicism plays a major role; one of the scientists decoding the transmission is a priest, and the problem of how to protect humankind from the potentially dangerous information in the alien transmission is solved, in part, by hiding the recordings of the transmission in a Catholic church. Some of the novel's plot elements have been overtaken by recent world events—the Cold War is still alive, and much of the suspense of the second half of the novel derives from the United States and a still-mighty Soviet Union coming to the brink of war over access to the transmissions—and the novel ends with a rush of action that is somewhat out of tone with the rest of the book. On the whole, however, *The Hercules Text* is a superior first novel and an exemplary "first contact" story.

McDevitt's second novel, *A Talent for War,* continues to explore many of the themes developed in *The Hercules Text.* Set thousands of years in the future, when humanity has colonized the stars and maintains an uneasy peace with the Ashiyyur, an alien race with whom humans fought a long and bitter war, the novel was packaged by Ace Books as a future-war epic. But while it contains a good deal of action and some violence, *A Talent for War* is primarily about an ordinary man trying to solve an extraordinary puzzle. A young antique dealer, Alex Benedict, receives an inheritance from an uncle, which leads him to believe that the uncle, an archaeologist, was on the verge of proving that the most revered hero of the human-Ashiyyur war, Christopher Sim, was a fraud. The bulk of the novel traces Benedict's journey from planet to planet as he investigates the problem; as he pieces the puzzle together, the most important people are not the soldiers who fought the war, as much as the historians and poets who witnessed the events and recorded them. As in *The Hercules Text,* the main question asked in *A Talent for War* is, essentially, a religious one: how will humanity cope with a sudden revelation? And McDevitt again turns to Catholicism for an answer, as the novel's prologue and epilogue are set in a remote Catholic monastery, which serves as both a refuge for one of the key players in the drama and, as in the earlier novel, a hiding place for potentially explosive information.

The Engines of God, McDevitt's third novel, continues to develop the same thematic territory as his first two books. Having discovered an alien statue on one of Saturn's moons, humanity finds similar artifacts when it begins to explore outside its own solar system. The discovery of a planet with significant remnants of the alien culture leads to conflict as Earth scientists who wish to excavate and preserve the alien artifacts clash with those who want to transform the new world for human colonization, destroying the remains of the alien civilization. Although the book is notable on the level of raw sense-of-wonder—many passages, notably McDevitt's description of the initial human exploration of an abandoned alien space station, compare favorably to Arthur C. Clarke's *Rendezvous with Rama*—it also features well-developed and realistically portrayed characters, none totally villainous or unequivocally in the right. Most importantly, McDevitt never looks away from what is, by now, the core concern of his fiction: how will we react to the sudden knowledge that we are not alone? In his forthcoming novel *Ancient Shores,* McDevitt brings the question closer to home as the discovery of an alien gateway to the stars buried under the plains of North Dakota triggers a worldwide panic as the global economy threatens to self-destruct under the threat of being supplanted by superior alien technology. Once again, the focus is on the individuals involved, with an especially vivid portrait of the Native Americans on whose land the alien artifact is discovered, and who are determined, this time around, not to be cheated by the white government.

In addition to his novels, McDevitt has continued to publish short fiction frequently in the SF magazines and original anthologies. His best-received work of short fiction to date is the Hugo and Nebula-nominated short story "The Fort Moxie Branch" (in *Full Spectrum,* September 1988), a fantasy about a magical library that contains all the greatest works of literature that were ever published or unappreciated in the author's lifetime. Again, the question is how much humanity is entitled to know: the contents of the library will not be released until the world has "achieved a true global community," according to the precepts of John of Singletary, a monk whose treatises were rejected in his own time.

Although McDevitt's work thus far has been largely confined to revisitations of classic SF themes, it is notable for its solid craftsmanship, its willingness to grapple with philosophical issues, and its concern with the arts as well as the sciences. McDevitt is also worthy of attention as a rare example of a science fiction writer who presents Roman Catholicism as a tenable worldview that does not automatically stand in opposition to scientific rationalism. McDevitt's novels are good candidates to become SF perennials, introducing successive generations of readers to the pleasures of the well-made science fiction story.

—F. Brett Cox

McDONALD, Ian

Nationality: British. **Born:** Manchester, England, in 1960. Moved to Northern Ireland in 1965. **Address:** c/o Bantam Books, 666 Fifth Avenue, New York, New York 10103, U.S.A.

SCIENCE FICTION PUBLICATIONS

Novels

Desolation Road. New York, Bantam, 1988; London, Bantam, 1989.
Out on Blue Six. New York, Bantam, 1989; London, Bantam, 1990.
Hearts, Hands, and Voices. London, Gollancz, 1992; as *The Broken Land,* New York, Bantam, 1992.
Scissors Cut Paper Wrap Stone. New York, Bantam, 1994.
Necroville. London, Gollancz, 1994; as *Terminal Café,* New York, Bantam, 1994.

Short Stories

Empire Dreams. New York, Bantam, 1988.
King of Morning, Queen of Day. New York, Bantam, 1991; London, Bantam, 1992.
Speaking in Tongues. London, Gollancz, and New York, Bantam, 1992.

Other

Kling Klang Klatch, with David Lyttleton (graphic novel). London, Gollancz, and Milwaukie, Oregon, Dark Horse Comics, 1992.

*   *   *

Although Ian McDonald had had one story published in 1982 in the Northern Irish magazine *Extro,* he effectively burst onto the scene with "The Catherine Wheel" in *Isaac Asimov's Science Fiction Magazine* in January 1984. He immediately made a considerable impression, and, like some other writers from Britain and Northern Ireland, he has continued to have more visibility and success in the United States than in his own country. Most of his short stories and both his novels appeared first in the United States, and his short-story collection, Empire Dreams, has still not been published in the United Kingdom. This success in the United States is partly because, despite the Irish content of two of his stories ("Empire Dreams" and "King of Morning, Queen of Day"), the atmosphere, style, and heady emotions found in his work owe more to American writing than to British: his novels, in particular, show that he is steeped in American SF, and fully prepared to work within that idiom.

His first novel, *Desolation Road,* reads like Gabriel García Márquez's *One Hundred Years of Solitude* rewritten by Ray Bradbury. It tells of the founding of a settlement in the deserts of a terraformed Mars by Dr. Alimontado (he had intended to call it Destination Road, but was drunk at the time), and traces its history, through the life-stories of a handful of colourful settlers with wild and wonderful talents, until its final destruction 23 years later, and its disappearance beneath the sands. Like Márquez, the mood varies from realism (with all the correct science fictional tropes) through to utter fantasy, with the small character-histories embedded within the text being the baits for the imagination; like Bradbury, the magic comes as much from the style and the atmosphere as from the narrative itself. The invention is endless, and even if it is apparent at times that we are dealing with the recycling of old ideas (even, as in *Out on Blue Six,* clear recapitulations from Terry Gilliam's *Brazil*), the presentation of those ideas is thoroughly individual. As a first novel, it is a considerable achievement, and the aspects of it that are less than perfect (such as the standardised and soul-less shoot-out towards the end), hardly mar the whole.

The possible flaw in *Out on Blue Six*—the standard wish-fulfilment pulp ending, with an apocalyptic revelation and the handful of rebels taking over the world and freeing it for space-flight—is no flaw at all, for its over-the-top character fits joyously with the rest of the book. *Out on Blue Six* portrays an insidious anti-utopia, a society dedicated to the creation of the greatest possible happiness for all its citizens partly by means of the Love Police, who act against anyone who causes pain to others, and partly by insisting that the Compassionate Society's computers know better than any citizen what constitutes their individual happiness. The novel follows the fate of a number of outcasts or exiles from this world—the dissatisfied and cynical individualists who are standard characters in SF novels, although, this being a McDonald novel, they are all much larger than life, with their own bizarre histories. Most of the action takes place underneath the utopian city, in its sewers and service tunnels; part of it is concerned with an epic voyage to the Edge of the World, which turns out to be a wall separating the world of humanity from the dead and polluted planet beyond. As in *Desolation Road,* there is wild invention, considerable wit, and an imaginative and colourful use of language, which again makes a first-rate novel out of a number of fairly familiar ideas and situations.

King of Morning, Queen of Day, unquestionably McDonald's most successful work to date, is ostensibly fantasy although it might equally be claimed as science fiction. Three separate though related stories tell of magical intrusions into the modern world, but these intrusions stem from the power of the collective consciousness of the human race. If enough people believe a thing, even unconsciously, then that force can be a creative one. Elves, wandering astronomical bodies, and the like are all potentially real, and McDonald explores the consequences of that unleashed potential in grand style, evoking everything from wonder to terror in the process.

His subsequent novels, though all of very high quality, have not eclipsed that work. *The Broken Land* is set in a future Earth so far from our time that it is virtually unrecognizable. Although genetic engineering is commonplace, civilization has become disjointed, subject to constant warfare. Much of the flavor of the novel borrows from contemporary fantasy rather than SF, but the superimposition doesn't seem as anomalous as it would with a lesser writer. *Scissors Cut Paper Wrap Stone* is closer to home, a novella length tale of a cybernetic near future where artificial intelligences, Buddhism, and robots have transformed the Western world. *Terminal Café* is the best of these three, set in a future where technology has the power to resurrect the dead, so long as they are willing to pay off the charges by what amounts to terms of indentured labor. The resurrected of Los Angeles live in a ghetto, shunned by the living for no rational reasons, preparing to celebrate their annual festival. But this year the old order may be overturned forever.

McDonald is also a short story writer of significance. His exploration of the relationship between a young boy and a retired star pilot in "Christian" is touching without being sentimental. In "Empire Dreams," sleep therapy is used as a metaphor to help a young boy cure the cancer afflicting him. "Toward Kilimanjaro" takes a "B" movie theme and uses it well, the first encounter with an evolved human in the jungles of Africa. The effect of achievable immortality on religion is the theme of "Gardenias," we see Nazi Germany from a very new perspective in "Fragments of an Analysis of a Case of Hysteria," and the lifestyles of the rich and poor in an unpleasant future are contrasted in "Atomic Avenue." There's also a grand tour of a bizarre landscape of the imagination in "The Time Garden." The best of McDonald's fiction has been collected in *Speaking in Tongues* and *Empire Dreams.*

Ian McDonald is a talented, inventive writer who sets his aspirations high and almost always delivers. He seems equally adept at both the short story and the novel. His willingness to experiment from one work to the next gives a false impression of unevenness in his development. His work will not always appeal to the same subset of readers, but it will always be worth the time to investigate.

—Edward James, updated by Don D'Ammassa

McGOWAN, Inez. *See* **PHILLIPS, Rog.**

McHUGH, Maureen F.

Nationality: American. **Born:** Ohio, 13 February 195?. **Education:** Ohio University, B.A. 1981; New York University, M.A. 1984. **Career:** Administrator and teacher, College of Staten Island of the City University of New York, 1985-86; temporary recruiter for department store chain; defense contractor clerk; technical writer, Ethicon, Cincinnati, Ohio, 1991—. Workshop instructor, Cincinnati Writers Project. **Awards:** James Tiptree, Jr., award, 1993. **Agent:** Kathy Saideman, Sanda Dijkstra Literary Agency, 1237 Camino del Mar, Suite 515C, Del Mar, California 92014, U.S.A.

SCIENCE FICTION PUBLICATIONS

Novels

China Mountain Zhang. New York, Tor, 1992; London, Orbit, 1995.
Half the Day Is Night. New York, Tor, 1994.

*   *   *

Maureen McHugh virtually erupted onto the science fiction scene in 1989 with two short stories that were incorporated into her first novel, *China Mountain Zhang.* It was nominated for the Hugo and Nebula awards for best novel of 1992 and won the James Tiptree, Jr. Award for "works which expand and explore gender roles in

SF and fantasy," presented in March, 1993. Since then, she has published a number of stories in *Asimov's Science Fiction* and a second novel, *Half the Day is Night*.

In addition to gender, McHugh's novels engage with a series of controversial topics which are explored through characters whose concerns are those of the contemporary 1990s, with a political and social sophistication which is both enviable and often as grim as our daily news reports. In her two published novels and many short stories, she intermingles a fine sense of political and social intrigue at the level of individual experiences, virtual reality as game and addiction, the contours of contemporary China and Chinese and other Eastern countries, ongoing questions of gender and the limits society places on individuals in that realm, and the mean streets of overcrowded cities and totalitarian states. In other words, she creates complex characters and motivations which are as integrated as the plots are exciting. Her fiction is characterized by decadent and degenerating societies whose politics and technological infrastructures aren't adequate to maintain their populations in healthy and secure environments. Her characters are often social dissidents, misfits or members of an "underclass" who, for one reason or another, have maintained shreds of human dignity and compassion. They are the quiet, everyday heros we recognize from our own lives. McHugh's style is relentless. Some may find it too much so, but this characteristic also pulls a reader into her stories. Some are written in the first-person narrative which she uses as effectively as the more common third-person.

China Mountain Zhang grew from two stories published in *Asimov's* in 1989, "Baffin Island" and "Kites." In the novel, they become two chapters with different protagonists. The novel postulates a 21st century where China and Chinese culture have gained ascendancy in the planet earth and racism has become institutionalized. The civilization has found ways to harvest from the South Pole, live underneath the ocean to use its many resources and has begun to colonize close planets, such as Mars.

McHugh excels at depicting the broad sweep of a society by presenting it from the eyes of different characters. This feature is bolstered by her skillful use of the first-person narrator which is found in this first novel and many of her other short stories. The stories, of course, depend on one viewpoint, but when combined into a novel they allow for a more convincing picture of a future society. The chapters in this first novel focus on characters who have had some sort of contact with the eponymous Zhang, whose first-person narration opens the book. He is a gay, half-Chinese, half-Hispanic man whose parents had him genetically altered so he would appear Chinese, and thus have a better chance of surviving in a racist society. The diaspora created by this identity is exemplified by his two names, the Hispanic being Rafael. He tells the story of how he outwitted the "system" and got the training necessary to become an architect despite the drawbacks of his race, class, and sexual orientation. This alone would be a fascinating story, but it is given depth by the stories of others, such as Martine, Alexi, and Theresa who live in Jerusalem Ridge on Mars, and San-xiang, a Chinese girl with a serious facial disfigurement. Each battles with standardized cruelties of societies which do not quite have a place for them. Alexi's remarks are meant to remind us of refugees past, present and future. "You don't understand," he says, "we've no guanxi (Mandarin Chinese word for "significance" or "importance"), no connection, no string. Everybody just wants to get rid of us. We're human trash. Disposable. Less useful than goatshit because you can dump that back in the soil." Alexi's sad story is improved, partially by electronic tutoring he receives from Zhang

and partly by human kindness. The same is not true for all members of this struggling future society.

Her second novel, which also started out as short stories, is entitled *Half the Day Is Night* and is set in a group of underwater cities originally built by corporations and owned by small groups of people. Here there are two major viewpoint characters whose fate becomes intertwined across classes and political spectra. Jean David Dai's first impression of Caribe, the underwater colony where he has been hired as a bodyguard, is not hopeful and it steadily goes down. "It smelled like wet concrete and ammonia. The Port Authority was like a second rate airport: full of soldiers and prefrom furniture in bright grimy orange and aqua. A third world country underwater. He had not realized that it would be so dark."

His employer, Ms. Ling, is an important person in a bank owned by her family. Threats to her life are followed by attacks on her person and her house. Then her bank is "raided" by a competitor who works for another underwater city, but one owned by a single company. She is first discredited and then follows David into the hazy world of the social outcast in a police state. Their journeys, separately and together, culminate in a barely successful escape to the surface of the ocean and the, only relative, peace of life aboveground in Miami. Much more a social than an interpersonal portrait, this second novel concerns greed, economic manipulation and the often cataclysmic uncertainties of modern life as a normal member of society. As with other McHugh fiction, one does not leave this novel with a sense that safe havens are available but rather that only individual acts of human heroism make life bearable.

The short stories generally explore one or two of the set of themes that are detailed more fully in her novels: dissident politics, virtual reality and gender-bending, Chinese-like totalitarian governments, non-traditional interpersonal relationships that are often brought about as much by cultural necessity as by any more romantic impulse in the Western interpretation of romance. She shares the ability of many SF authors to move effectively between novel, short story, novella and novelette which shows an acute mastery of the written word. And her apparent first-hand knowledge of mainland Chinese culture is absorbing if at times frightening.

Three of her short stories, "Joss," "Whispers" (with David B. Kisor), and "Protection," are obviously the result of experiences she had while in China in the 1980s. She mentions real cities such as Jinan that lies near Beijing and Guangzhou (formerly called Canton) near Hong Kong.

Stories set in the United States such as "Protection," are adapted from Chinese social phenomena such as work camps which are of course crudely reminiscent of Polish and French work camps run by the Nazis in World War Two. However, this camp is in a Kansas that has been rendered virtually uninhabitable and not fit for growing crops by pollution.

"Protection" is a good example of her political savvy. Her protagonist is a poorly educated, but bright and street-smart girl put in a work camp for larceny and battery. As the girl adjusts to an indoctrination program apparently without really realizing it, her friend, a hopeless young history teacher who is incarcerated for 20 years (if he manages to live) for writing essays about utopian socialists of the 19th century. They form an odd relationship which offers both some protection and creature comfort such as the warmth of another body during cold nights. As she adapts to her society they must inevitably grow apart and he is transferred finally to another camp, presumably for political incorrigibles. Meanwhile, his sardonic and polite commentary on the indoctrination process yields insights such as its similarity to the Alcoholics

Anonymous Twelve Step Program (it's a way of changing behavior), and simple explanations of the classical Marxist version of historical economic progression from primitive to feudal to capitalist to socialist economy, along with the fact that no known socialist society has worked, even the voluntary ones.

"Another Coney Island of the Mind" is a brief glimpse of games in a virtual reality that explores the kinds of gender-twisting that won McHugh attention for *China Mountain Zhang*. It is a quick-paced story of the near future where VR is a way of life and a major source of social interaction. The changing mores of gender-expectation is the major topic as it is with her first novel.

McHugh's stories are either bitter or bittersweet. They often involve odd pairings of whatever gender, with same- and cross-sex friendships as well as sexual relationships, all of which have some utilitarian purpose—there is little romantic love to be found in these stories and certainly no happy endings, although not all endings are as tragic as "Protection" or as "Whispers" where aliens are taking over human bodies, but only those who can't afford immunizations. Take for example "Nekroplis" where a young woman of 26, Deyti, "jessed" or emotionally linked to her employer, forms a love relationship with an AI "man" named Akhmem. Both are slaves of a sort and, when they escape together, it is to live on her income as a maker of paper flowers living in a cemetery crypt in a country which resembles Greece. Perhaps the happiest of her stories is "Joss" where two Chinese thieves, a female petty thief and a male white-collar thief, first prey upon each other and then get married and have a family by pooling their resources.

While sobering, McHugh's stories are also quite vivid and full of action. Characters escape from the corrupt police forces of totalitarian states by intrigue and subterfuge. The major characters are inevitably dissidents but usually because the society makes no place for them to be normal, law-abiding citizens—they cannot be themselves publicly and survive socially and economically—they are either too smart or what is usually the case, too far behind in education or economic position or race or sexual orientation to have a legitimate place in their decadent and degenerating societies. It is never a very pretty place to live, the future that Ms. McHugh paints, but it is so very hauntingly familiar, as if just around the next corner, both in terms of time and of geography.

—Janice M. Bogstad

McINTOSH, J.T.

Pseudonym for James Murdoch MacGregor. **Other Pseudonym:** H.J. Murdoch. **Nationality:** British. **Born:** Paisley, Renfrew, 14 February 1925. **Education:** Robert Gordon's College, Aberdeen, 1936-41; Aberdeen University, 1943-47, M.A. (honours) in English. **Family:** Married Margaret Murray in 1960; two daughters and one son. **Career:** Sub editor, *Aberdeen Press and Journal*, 1963-85. **Address:** 63 Abbotswell Drive, Aberdeen, Scotland.

SCIENCE FICTION PUBLICATIONS

Novels

World Out of Mind. Garden City, New York, Doubleday, 1953; London, Museum Press, 1955.

Born Leader. Garden City, New York, Doubleday, 1954; London, Museum Press, 1955; as *Worlds Apart,* New York, Avon, 1958.

One in Three Hundred. Garden City, New York, Doubleday, 1954; London, Museum Press, 1956.

The Fittest. Garden City, New York, Doubleday, 1955; London, Corgi, 1961; as *The Rule of the Pagbeasts,* Greenwich, Connecticut, Fawcett, 1956.

200 Years to Christmas, bound with *Rebels of the Red Planet,* by Charles L. Fontenay. New York, Ace, 1961.

The Million Cities. New York, Pyramid, 1963.

The Noman Way. London, Digit, 1964.

Out of Chaos. London, Digit, 1965.

Time for a Change. London, Joseph, 1967; as *Snow White and the Giants,* New York, Avon, 1968.

Six Gates from Limbo. London, Joseph, 1968; New York, Avon, 1969.

Transmigration. New York, Avon, 1970.

Flight from Rebirth. New York, Avon, 1971; London, Hale, 1973.

The Cosmic Spies. London, Hale, 1972.

The Space Sorcerers. London, Hale, 1972; as *The Suiciders,* New York, Avon, 1973.

Galactic Takeover Bid. London, Hale, 1973.

Ruler of the World. Toronto, Laser, 1976.

This Is the Way the World Begins. London, Corgi, 1977.

Norman Conquest 2066. London, Corgi, 1977.

A Planet Called Utopia. New York, Zebra, 1979.

OTHER PUBLICATIONS

Novels

Take a Pair of Private Eyes (novelization of TV series). London, Muller, and Garden City, New York, Doubleday, 1968.

A Coat of Blackmail. London, Muller, 1970; Garden City, New York, Doubleday, 1971.

Novels as James MacGregor

When the Ship Sank. Garden City, New York, Doubleday, 1959; London, Heinemann, 1960.

Incident over the Pacific. Garden City, New York, Doubleday, 1960; as *A Cry to Heaven,* London, Heinemann, 1961.

The Iron Rain. London, Heinemann, 1962.

Other as James MacGregor

Glamour in Your Lens: A Commonsense Guide to Attractive Photography. London, Focal Press, 1958.

Wine Making for All. London, Faber, 1966.

Beer Making for All. London, Faber, 1967.

*

J.T. McIntosh comments:

I became a science fiction writer not by choice but by force of circumstance. At the time when I was ready to publish (1945-50), paper was in short supply and publishers tended to use it for books by established authors. America was the obvious market, but I had no accurate knowledge of the U.S. scene. So I wrote SF, in which accurate knowledge of the U.S. scene is not necessary.

Later, when I tried non-SF, the international nature of SF became clear to me. There was little interest in my mainstream fiction outside Britain, while the SF books often had editions in many other countries.

*   *   *

Under the pen name J.T. McIntosh, the Scots writer and journalist James Murdoch MacGregor first won recognition as an author of science fiction with *World Out of Mind,* his first novel. This work presents a future society organized around the ultimate merit system: IQ. All members of this society are rigorously tested for intelligence; test results place each individual in a group marked by a colored badge indicating rank. The governing class, wearing the white star indicating the highest one percent of intelligence, is infiltrated by a Martian who has been reprocessed as a human being and whose mission is to prepare for a Martian invasion. However, since the Martian spy has become completely human, he cannot help falling in love with the youngest (and most beautiful) living white star. He betrays the loveless Martians and thwarts the invasion. Humanity (and love) conquer.

Also greeted with critical enthusiasm, *Born Leader* develops two human conflicts: daring youth pitted against conservative age, and a cooperative libertarian society pitted against military totalitarian state. Mundis, a planet colonised by space settlers from an Earth destroyed by nuclear war, is inhabited by two generations: the original settlers, determined not to use nuclear power, and their children, born only after the 22-year space voyage, eager to explore its possibilities. Mundis's egalitarian society is threatened by invaders from a second Earth ship, a Spartan, loveless military group whose women are considered subhuman breeders. Under the threat of domination, the Mundans unite, develop nuclear defences, defeat the invaders, and integrate them into their own egalitarian system.

One in Three Hundred begins on an Earth doomed by a shift in its solar orbit. It shows the selection of a small and random minority for space colonisation, their hazardous voyage, and their sufferings in making Mars habitable from the point of view of one of the leaders responsible for the selection and supervision of a small group. Faced by the threat of a sadist and would-be dictator on Mars, the colonists rebel, kill the tyrants, and cooperate successfully in order to survive. *The Fittest* similarly shows humans forced to work together for survival against great physical odds. Earth is overpopulated by paggets, superintelligent mice, cats, rats, and dogs, developed by accident in an experiment and determined to overwhelm human life by cutting lines of communication, devouring supplies, sabotage, and murder. Mankind can survive biologically only by using the uniquely human qualities of communication and cooperation to remain the fittest species in simple democratic communities free from social convention.

McIntosh's later full-length fiction fails to live up to the promise of his early novels. Although his later work still deals with his major themes—overpopulation in *The Million Cities,* space travel and evolution in *200 Years to Christmas,* the aftermath of holocaust in *Out of Chaos,* and morality in *Six Gates from Limbo, Transmigration,* and *Flight from Rebirth*—he tends to repeat and overwrite early plots, often expanding ideas originally published as short stories. His ability to write fast and convincing action remains, but he fails to present themes and ideas as convincingly as his novels from the early 1950s.

McIntosh's four early novels interestingly depict libertarian utopias whose members' mutual concern and willingness to cooperate in order to survive demonstrate a hopeful view of human nature in a threatening universe. The terrible odds his characters must face are plausible threats for our future: overpopulation, misdirected technology, war, physical changes on Earth itself. In the Darwinian struggle to survive, women become essential. McIntosh's heroes are typically attracted to independence, competence, and strength in their mates, rather than to dependence, passivity, and physical frailty they might have preferred in easier times. McIntosh's ability to depict realistically the violence and dangers of the unknown future and his hopefulness about mankind's ability to endure make his early novels both moving and memorable.

—Katherine Staples

MᶜINTYRE, Vonda N(eel)

Nationality: American. **Born:** Louisville, Kentucky, 28 August 1948. **Education:** University of Washington, Seattle, B.S. in biology 1970, graduate study in genetics, 1970-71. **Career:** Conference organizer, and riding and writing instructor. **Awards:** Nebula award, 1973, 1978; Hugo award, 1979. **Agent:** Frances Collin, Rodell-Collin Literary Agency, 110 West 40th Street, New York, New York 10018, U.S.A. **Address:** P.O. Box 31041, Seattle, Washington 98103-1041, U.S.A.

Science Fiction Publications

Novels (series: Star Trek; Star Wars; Starfarers)

The Exile Waiting. Garden City, New York, Doubleday, 1975; London, Gollancz, 1976.
Dreamsnake. Boston, Houghton Mifflin, and London, Gollancz, 1978.
The Entropy Effect: A Star Trek Novel. New York, Pocket Books, and London, Macdonald, 1981.
Star Trek: The Wrath of Khan: A Novel. (novelization of screenplay). New York, Pocket Books, and London, Futura, 1982.
Superluminal. Boston, Houghton Mifflin, 1983; London, Gollancz, 1984.
Star Trek III: The Search for Spock (novelization of screenplay). New York, Pocket Books, and London, Panther, 1984.
The Bride (novelization of screenplay). New York, Dell, 1985.
Enterprise: The First Adventure (Star Trek). New York, Pocket, 1986.
Star Trek IV: The Voyage Home: A Novel. New York, Pocket, 1986; London, Grafton, 1987.
Barbary (for children). Boston, Houghton Mifflin, 1986.
Starfarers. Norwalk, Connecticut, Easton Press, 1989; London, Grafton, 1991.
Transition (Starfarers). Norwalk, Connecticut, Easton Press, 1990.
Metaphase (Starfarers). New York, Bantam, 1992.
Nautilus (Starfarers). New York, Bantam, 1994.
The Crystal Star (Star Wars). New York, 1994.

Short Stories

Fireflood, and Other Stories. Boston, Houghton Mifflin, 1979; London, Gollancz, 1980.
Screwtop, bound with *The Girl Who Was Plugged In,* by James Tiptree. New York, Tor, 1989.

Other

Editor, with Susan Janice Anderson, *Aurora: Beyond Equality.* Greenwich, Connecticut, Fawcett, 1976.

*   *   *

Vonda N. McIntyre's science fiction reflects her background in biology and genetics and shows a belief in the importance of the individual. Her characters are often outsiders in society who must meet the challenges of being different while maintaining their individuality. McIntyre's strongest characters are women and her settings usually assume equality, with gender playing no factor in perceived ability.

A hallmark of Vonda McIntyre's writing is her theme of physical transformation, either through genetic engineering or mechanical means. Most of her short stories have as characters genetically-changed individuals. The diggers and flyers in "Fireflood" were originally humans who chose to be altered for specific tasks in the exploration and colonization of space. The flyers in "Wings" and "The Mountains of Sunset, the Mountains of Death" continue this idea. Gryf, in "Screwtop," is one of a group known as tetraparentals. Bred as a problem-solving team, all team members must work together to function correctly. This creates the story's conflict as Gryf endures punishment for wanting to assert his independence as an individual. "The Genius Freaks" deals with ethical problems surrounding the breeding of extraordinarily intelligent individuals.

McIntyre's novels continue the genetic engineering theme. To be used for curing diseases, the snakes in *Dreamsnake* must be genetically altered by the healers. *Superluminal* introduces the idea of divers, humans who have been genetically changed with a virus, enabling them to live in the sea and communicate with cetaceans. Divers also figure prominently in *Starfarers* and *Transition.* Even when McIntyre builds on the already created Star Trek universe, as in *Enterprise: The First Adventure,* the genetic theme occurs. The vaudeville troupe travelling on the *Enterprise* owns a horse bred to have wings although it cannot fly in Earth's gravity. It is interesting that flyers also make an appearance in this novel in the guise of alien beings.

Closely related to genetic manipulation is physical transformation through mechanical means. This is presented most dramatically in "Aztecs." Pilots of spacecraft must replace their biological hearts with artificial ones to survive superluminal travel. They resent the nickname reflected in the title as they do not feel sacrificial. In "Spectra," workers have metal sockets for eyes, to link with and manipulate electronically-fed data. "The End's Beginning" is told from the viewpoint of a dolphin implanted with a machine of destruction.

Biocontrol is an essential technique for McIntyre's characters. Young people in *Dreamsnake* routinely receive training in fertility control. On her journey to replace her lost dreamsnake, the healer, Snake, encounters a young man whose life was drastically affected by a lack of such training. In "Aztecs," Laenea's control of her body's rhythms and functions is vitally important to her body's acceptance of an artificial heart. It becomes the central conflict of the story as Laenea's rhythms, irrevocably changed after the surgery, do not and cannot coincide with her lover's. *Starfarers* and *Transition* again present a future where biocontrol is the norm. When others learn that Gerald cannot control his biological reactions in times of stress, they pity him.

McIntyre frequently shows the danger of making assumptions by choosing ambiguous names and by carefully not mentioning a character's gender until function and personality are well established. The aliens in *Enterprise: The First Adventure* have no external clues to sexual identity. After prolonged interaction with the beings, Captain Kirk is startled to hear the one he assumed to be the leader referred to as "she."

Another feminist element is McIntyre's portrayal of nontraditional sexual partnerships and individual freedom of choice in sexual preferences. The idea of a multiple partnership with no particular pairing orientation occurs in *Dreamsnake* and *The Entropy Effect.* It becomes a major focus of *Starfarers* and *Transition,* with three members of the alien contact team constituting a family partnership. Even though the three are married to each other, they remain free to form liaisons outside of the partnership if they wish. In a nice twist, the other members of the starship community consider this form of alliance to be old-fashioned.

McIntyre's earlier works are tightly written and compelling in mood. At her best in "Of Mist, and Grass, and Sand," *Dreamsnake,* and "Aztecs," it is not surprising that she received Nebula and Hugo awards for them. *Dreamsnake* succeeds in adding to the richness of Snake's story begun in "Of Mist, and Grass, and Sand." The realization that it is set in the same postapocalyptic earth as *The Exile Waiting* adds an interesting dimension. On the other hand, *Superluminal,* the expansion of "Aztecs," is disappointing after the promisingly strong images of the novella. While the divers' story is intriguing in its own right, it seems awkwardly spliced into the original. Orca, a diver, becomes the central female character as she struggles with being alien not only to humans but also to her own species in her aspirations to be a pilot. It is Radu Dracul, Laenea's unfortunate lover in "Aztecs," who continues the original pilot's story in the novel.

McIntyre's more recent novels, while still producing thought-provoking ideas, seem influenced by the serial nature of the Star Trek novels. All of McIntyre's elements are present in *Starfarers* and *Transition,* but they are diffused by a multiplicity of characters and the emphasis on action. Thus, J.D. Sauvage's struggles with acceptance and responsibility become submerged in the additional and equally engrossing stories of Victoria, Satoshi, Stephen Thomas, and Zev, the diver. The characters' personal conflicts are overshadowed by the frenetic pace of launching the space expedition against political opposition and the excitement of potential first contact.

The strength of McIntyre's writing comes from her ability to extrapolate an idea successfully. She insinuates her concepts as part of the underlying fabric of the story. Her plots focus on character development and societal interactions, and the science in her fiction is as believable as it is fascinating.

—Gay E. Carter

McKENNA, Richard M(ilton)

Nationality: American. **Born:** Mountain Home, Idaho, 9 May 1913. **Education:** University of North Carolina, Chapel Hill, B.A. in English 1956 (Phi Beta Kappa). **Family:** Married Eva Mae Grice in 1956. **Military Service:** Served in the United States Navy, 1931-

53: chief machinist's mate; freelance writer from 1953. **Awards:** Harper prize, 1963; Nebula award, 1966. **Died:** 1 November 1964.

SCIENCE FICTION PUBLICATIONS

Short Stories

Casey Agonistes and Other Science Fiction and Fantasy Stories. New York, Harper, 1973; London, Gollancz, 1974.

OTHER PUBLICATIONS

Novel

The Sand Pebbles. New York, Harper, 1962; London, Gollancz, 1963.

Short Stories

The Sons of Martha and Other Stories, edited by M. S. Wyeth, Jr. New York, Harper, 1967.
The Left-Handed Monkey Wrench: Stories and Essays. Annapolis, Maryland, Naval Institute Press, 1986.

Other

New Eyes for Old: Nonfiction Writing, edited by Eva Grice McKenna and Shirley Graves Cochrane. Winston-Salem, North Carolina, Blair, 1972.

*   *   *

Richard McKenna's literary reputation will almost certainly rest on the shoulders of his famous novel, *The Sand Pebbles,* set aboard a riverboat during the 1920s, during a period of rebellion in the Chinese mainland. He wrote a number of short stories as well, many of them in the science fiction field, which has been forgotten, except within the genre itself. Despite the fact that only about a dozen stories were actually published, and not all of them memorable, McKenna remains a familiar name.

"The Fishdollar Affair," which appeared in 1958, is a spoof of ambassadorial ambition set in space but transparently a reflection of colonialist policies and procedures with which McKenna was familiar from his own days in China. Although one of the few real failures McKenna produced, it demonstrates his sardonic attitude toward human behavior, lampooned even more intensely in "Love and Moondogs," wherein a popular movement to pressure the Russian space program into retrieving an orbiting dog is twisted into a parody of itself.

Two other, much longer, stories from that same period established McKenna immediately as a writer to watch. "The Night of Hoggy Darn" tells of an ecologist called in to assist an introspective colony world. Shortly after his arrival, he is made a virtual prisoner, and it is evident that no one really wants him there, although his assistance is necessary to help solve a problem with a particularly nasty specimen of local fauna. The resolution is a superb blend of biology, anthropology, and sociology, a remarkably ambitious story for its time. Even more significant was "Casey Agonistes." Set within the confines of a hospital, Casey is an apparition, or perhaps not, a shared fantasy by many of the patients that somehow becomes the manifestation of their desires, uncer-

tainties, and fears. Difficult to describe but marvelous to experience, it remains McKenna's most accomplished work of fiction.

"Hunter, Come Home" and "Mine Own Ways" have much in common with one another. In each case, an expedition is conducting research into the ecology of another planet, and in each case McKenna fuses anthropology and biology to create a metaphysical force that transcends the human ability to perceive exactly what is taking place. In the former, the protagonists are themselves altered physically by their environment; in the latter, a renegade human precipitates a native ritual that teaches the participants more about that world than they would ever have discovered under normal circumstances.

The next two stories deal with subject realities. "The Secret Place" involves the strange relationship between a man and a woman, and her belief that there exist fantastic worlds hidden in the deserts, ones unknown to most humans, which can be accessed under the right conditions. A more ambitious fantasy is "Fiddler's Green." A group of shipwrecked sailors suffers from growing thirst as they drift across the ocean in a lifeboat. One of their number leads them through a door into a world created by their own imaginations, but since it is a joint creation, there are inconsistencies and dangers they had not expected.

Although McKenna died just as his career was getting established, three unpublished stories appeared subsequently. "Home the Hard Way" follows the career of a spacer who falls in love with one of the planets he visits during a layover and tries everything conceivable to get out of his service commitment and settle. Before long, he is facing court martial, coercion by pirates, and the possibility that he may not live long enough to satisfy his ambition. In "They Are Not Robbed," Earth has been visited by the Star Birds, apparently representatives of an alien race whose outlook is so different from our own, trade is carried on with extreme difficulty. The aliens provide energy in exchange for the establishment of offices from which they purchase inexplicable items from a seemingly random segment of humanity, and from which they recruit humans into their circles. "Bramble Bush," a story written early in his career but not published until after his death, is another blend of anthropology and other world adventure. The central theme this time is that the inhabitants of the world being studied have a unique mental ability; they can use mental powers unknown to us to wrap a web of their own worldview around our own, effectively altering reality. It provides one of the best rationales for witchcraft ever to appear in fiction.

Most of McKenna's better stories are collected in *Casey Agonistes,* although "Bramble Bush" and "The Night of Hoggy Darn" remain uncollected. It is tragic that such an obvious major talent was cut off after such a short career. The science fiction genre has never had enough thoughtful, inventive writers, and anthropological themes have been treated rarely and usually with less than admirable effect. Even with such a small body of work, McKenna's stature within the field seems likely to remain unchallenged for some time to come.

—Don D'Ammassa

McKILLIP, Patricia A(nne)

Nationality: American. **Born:** Salem, Oregon, 29 February 1948. **Education:** San Jose State University, B.A. 1971, M.A. in English 1973. **Awards:** World Fantasy award, 1975. **Agent:** Howard Morhaim Literary Agency, 174 Fifth Avenue, Room 709, New York, New York 10010, U.S.A.

SCIENCE FICTION PUBLICATIONS

Novels

Fool's Run. New York, Warner, and London, Orbit, 1987.
The Sorceress and the Cygnet. New York, Ace, 1991; London, Pan, 1991.

Novels (for children; series: Cygnet; Kyerol)

The Throme of the Erril of Sherill, illustrated by Julie Noonan. New York, Atheneum, 1973.
The House on Parchment Street, illustrated by Charles Robinson. New York, Atheneum, 1973.
The Forgotten Beasts of Eld. New York, Atheneum, 1974; London, Orbit, 1987.
The Night Gift, illustrated by Kathy McKillip. New York, Atheneum, 1976.
The Riddle-Master of Hed. New York, Atheneum, 1978; London, Sidgwick and Jackson, 1979.
Heir of Sea and Fire. New York, Atheneum, 1978; London, Sidgwick and Jackson, 1979.
Riddle of Stars. Garden City, New York, Doubleday, 1979; as *The Chronicles of Morgan, Prince of Hed,* London, Sidgwick and Jackson, 1981.
Harpist in the Wind. New York, Atheneum, and London, Sidgwick and Jackson, 1979.
Moon-Flash (Kyerol). New York, Atheneum, 1984.
The Throme of the Rril of Sherill; with, The Harrowing of the Dragon of Hoarsbreath. New York, Tempo, 1984.
The Moon and the Face (Kyerol). New York, Atheneum, 1985.
The Changeling Sea. New York, Atheneum, 1988; London, Oxford University Press, 1991.
The Cygnet and the Firebird. New York, Ace, 1993.
Something Rich and Strange. New York, Bantam, 1994.
The Book of Atrix Wolfe. New York, 1995.

OTHER PUBLICATIONS

Novel

Stepping from the Shadows. New York, Atheneum, 1982.

*   *   *

Ranging from fairytale to young adult realistic fiction, from high fantasy to science fiction to adult contemporary fiction, Patricia A. McKillip's sweeping vision focuses on elemental themes unified by love, power, and magic. Her fantasy lies at the heart of her work, embraced by both adult and young adult readers. The first volume of her masterful *Riddle of Stars* trilogy appears among less than 30 recommended titles for teenagers in the recent fantasy genre list from the American Library Association (ALA). When that volume appeared in 1976, author Peter S. Beagle called McKillip "the best of the younger fantasy writers. . . . a storytelling sorceress, just

now coming into her full power." McKillip's adult science fiction novel *Fool's Run* became an ALA Best Book for Young Adults in 1987.

Fittingly, McKillip's first novel is set in the very place she began writing at age 14, at *The House on Parchment Street* in England. When Carol, an American, visits her English cousin Bruce for a summer, they unearth an unknown priests' tunnel by following 17th-century ghosts through their basement wall. This satisfying ghost story appeals to young teenagers struggling with adults for their own power; Carol and Bruce overcome adult logic to reveal the spirit world.

The young also rebel against their elders in McKillip's composed fairytale *The Throme of the Erril of Sherill.* In classic style, she relates the tale of a knight on an impossible quest to win a princess's hand. McKillip stretches and teases familiar forms in delightful language: her orchard has "horanges," her knight is Cnite Caerles, who seeks a "throme" which does not exist, "made of the treasure of words." Archetypal motifs expand when the quest become circular. The cnite creates the throme himself by writing the tale of his own quest, so inspiring the princess to choose him, leaving her enraged father saying "Bah."

From the seeds of these modest works blooms McKillip's first fantasy classic, *The Forgotten Beasts of Eld.* The female wizard Sybel lives on isolated Eld Mountain with a legendary falcon, lion, cat, swan, dragon, and talking boar, controlling them telepathically. Sybel does "not understand loving and hating, only being and knowing," until Lord Coren brings her baby Tamlorn, heir of Eldewold, to keep safe from struggles for the throne. Raising the child opens Sybel to human love, but also superhuman power, for she becomes caught between Tamlorn, his father Drede, and her new husband Coren. When Drede tries to steal Sybel's name to control her, she risks Tamlorn's and Coren's love for revenge against Drede. Her manipulations nearly cost Sybel her soul; realizing love cannot be controlled, she finally frees both her beasts and herself. McKillip's concern with personal power through the magic of naming dawns here in a resonant tale of love's triumph among fantastical beasts not soon forgotten.

A brief detour into realism with *The Night Gift,* an affecting story of a group of teenagers who give of themselves to help a suicidal friend, does not dilute McKillip's momentum toward the pinnacle of high fantasy. In her acclaimed *Riddle of Stars* trilogy, McKillip achieves a full-blown other-world peopled with hundreds of solid characters, all ranged behind the compelling hero Morgon on a forced trajectory toward destiny. In the first volume, *The Riddle Master of Hed,* young land-heir Morgon wants nothing more than to care for his simple farming people of Hed. Yet three mysterious stars on his forehead propel him toward a fate he cannot comprehend. In Morgon's world, the wizards who disappeared 700 years ago left their wisdom in riddles. Morgon's talent for riddling wins him the hand of beautiful Raederle of An. But before he can claim her, an unknown force claims him as "Star-Bearer." After finding a harp and sword with stars to match his own, Morgon is beseiged by shape-shifters trying to kill him. "An impossible web of riddles was being woven about his name," and Morgon must unravel a new identity rife with danger.

Only the High One, remote ruler of the realm, might explain Morgon's stars, but after a perilous journey to the High One's mountain, Morgon disappears. In *Heir of Sea and Fire,* Raederle searches for Morgon, discovering in the process her own formidable magic powers and her distressing kinship to those trying to destroy Morgon. In the final volume *Harpist in the Wind,* Morgon and Raederle are united to solve the riddle and the fate of their realm together.

In the *Riddle* trilogy, McKillip brings to fruition the themes and style introduced in *The Forgotten Beasts of Eld.* Magic becomes the ability to "know and accept . . . the thing as itself." The human desire for control, without love, makes people abuse power. "Things are themselves. We twist the shapes of them," says a riddle-master. The worst abuse is stealing minds, where the essence of one's name and freedom resides, which Sybel could not forgive Drede in *Forgotten Beasts,* and which threatens everyone in Morgon's realm. Like Christ, Morgon is a "man of peace" promised to his people, though he transcends that role with Raederle as his partner. *Riddle of Stars* challenges readers to unwind tangled threads of lore as Morgon does; readers share his desperation and suspense as he follows his mystery fate. The intricate plot does not unravel smoothly, but with varied rhythms demanding patience and attunement to McKillip's rich themes, embroidered in dazzling words.

After this definitive fantasy, McKillip emerged from a three-year hiatus with a contemporary adult novel, *Stepping from the Shadows.* Through the split persona of her young writer narrator, McKillip wrestles with her writer's identity in a fascinating and thoroughly original character study. The narrator has a shadow companion Frances, an imaginative dreamer whom she judges and tries to control throughout childhood, but who "wished me into her story," an aspect of self. To cope with reality, Frances publishes her fantasy novel about her creation the Stagman, who then haunts the obsessive narrator's real world. How the writer unites opposing sides of herself is a compelling and heartrending story, surely somewhat autobiographical, and flawlessly executed in lyrical prose binding worlds seen and unseen: "The world was jumbled with language, though it looked very simple. . . . But against my chest was long division, and beyond the sky were a thousand saints, praying for our souls."

In her young adult science fantasy *Moon-Flash* and its sequel *The Moon and the Face,* McKillip distills both her prose style and recurring motifs into clear, deceptively simple form. Kyreol is a young girl coming of age in her primitive Riverworld culture. Her avid curiosity tempts her beyond her world's end on a river trip with her childhood male friend Terje. Passing through dangerous falls, they are shocked to find that the world continues and is controlled by a domed city, a spaceport to other planets. Scientists at the dome protect the Riverworld culture from knowing the outer world, valuing the psychic dreams of its people, which the dome has lost to technology. Becoming a protector of the home she lost through knowledge, Kyreol "stepped outside of its story," but Terje sees the interconnectedness of all things and can integrate both worlds. Kyreol wonders about McKillip's abiding question: "How can people see and dream the same things, yet have a different language for them?"

McKillip pursues technology to its ultimate nightmare in *Fool's Run,* adult science fiction in which a future.Earth is unreconciled to psychic power. Separated twin sisters probe connected mysteries. Impelled by a vision, Terra commits mass murder. On Terra's orbiting prison, her disguised sister the Queen of Hearts plays a rock concert, triggering her twin's escape and perhaps apocalypse. McKillip returns to a tangled plot of riddles. Negotiating its taut twists, readers are confronted with an unsettling challenge to the values that may place our world in jeopardy.

In *The Changeling Sea,* her young adult fantasy, McKillip fashions a perfect and elegant fairytale around lonely young Peri, coming of age in a simple fishing village after her father drowns and her mother is lost to endless mourning. After hurling angry hexes into the sea that stole her family, Peri's fate becomes entwined with a sea-dragon, a mage, two princes, the King, and the Sea-Queen. Through love and loss, Peri's magic talents are awakened and her world is restored to proper order where all things are named and love is a healing power. Not a strand of seaweed is out of place; McKillip has mastered the literary form that transmits her message that magic bridges "the confusing distance between things," and that we must use our power to keep all things connected. McKillip's early complex wordiness has refined into a spare poetic style that is joyful to read.

—Cathi MacRae

McLAUGHLIN, Dean (Benjamin, Jr.)

Nationality: American. **Born:** Ann Arbor, Michigan, 22 July 1931. **Education:** University of Michigan, Ann Arbor, A.B. 1953. **Career:** Buyer for Slater's Inc., bookshop, Ann Arbor. **Address:** 1214 West Washington Street, Ann Arbor, Michigan 48103, U.S.A.

SCIENCE FICTION PUBLICATIONS

Novels

Dome World: A Science-Fiction Novel. New York, Pyramid, 1962.
The Fury from Earth. New York, Pyramid, 1963.
The Man Who Wanted Stars. New York, Lancer, 1965.

Short Stories

Hawk among the Sparrows: Three Science Fiction Novellas. New York, Scribner, 1976; London, Hale, 1977.

*   *   *

Science fiction fans, like most readers, are a very fickle lot. Most of the best-known writers are those who have produced a steady current of work over a period of years. It is unusual to find a writer who, like Dean McLaughlin, produces work infrequently and at great intervals but who nevertheless is well known within the field. Author of three well-received novels, McLaughlin's 1976 short story collection, *Hawk Among the Sparrows,* never even saw a U.S. edition despite the title story's strong running for award status.

McLaughlin's novels all involve a single individual's contributions to the shaping of the entire course of human history. Unlike many of his peers, he avoids concentrating on a brilliant strategist or creative scientist but instead chooses to examine an average person in an unusual circumstance. His protagonists frequently have doubts about their own actions, but are compelled by conscience or other considerations to persevere.

Danial Mason, leader of the undersea city of Wilmington in *Dome World,* is a perfect example. Mason is chief administrator of the urban complex, one of many that have been built on the ocean floor by nations interested in exploiting mineral veins, harvesting the sea for food, or simply profiting on the trade among cities. Unfortunately, humankind's expansion into the oceans left a number of international jurisdictional problems unresolved. As a consequence, the American Union and South Africa are on the brink of war for control of a deposit of vanadium that lies between domes controlled by their respective governments. Because of their extreme vulnerability to attack, the domed cities are transfixed by fear and Mason moves to secede from the Union in order to avoid tragedy.

The second half of the novel is set several years later, with the domed cities organized into a loose coalition to counterbalance the surface world's influence. But both sides continue to expand and a fresh source of conflict arises. Once again an entrepreneur intervenes personally, and at great personal risk, to avert an open conflict. Neither of McLaughlin's protagonist, is the stereotypical rugged individualist; one has recently returned from the moon and has great difficulty adjusting to the gravity of Earth and the other suffers from a weak heart. But despite their physical shortcomings, each finds a wellspring of strength from which to draw.

In much the same fashion, the protagonist of *The Fury from Earth* refuses to help the government of Venus develop new weapons for their war against Earth because of his opposition to war, although he agrees to help bolster the planet's defenses. His analysis of a new weapons system being built by Earth leads him to believe it could actually be used for peaceful purposes, could in fact provide the human race with a practical means to reach the stars. The theme is repeated in a different setting in McLaughlin's third novel, *The Man Who Wanted Stars,* this time concerning itself with a determined man who wants to prevent the end of the manned space program. Unlike the first two, *The Man Who Wanted Stars* is frequently didactic which interrupts the plot at awkward times, and the monomania of the protagonist is so intense that it is difficult to find much to admire in the man even if we agree with his obsession.

McLaughlin has also produced a number of short stories of which at least three are exceptional. "Hawk Among the Sparrows" is somewhat unusual for the author, in that the hero fails to change the course of events, in this case the outcome of the air war in Europe. An anomaly in time sends a supersonic aircraft and its pilot back to the latter days of that conflict, where he tries unsuccessfully to affect the future. Even when he is able to improvise appropriate fuel for his advanced aircraft, he finds that he literally cannot fly slow enough to engage the enemy in combat.

"The Brotherhood of Keepers" is one of those rare science fiction stories not by Hal Clement that features a totally alien cast of characters. "Ode to Joy" is interesting for its portrayal of disease as a kind of dragon and "Mark on the World" presents a new take on the perils of negotiation between unlike cultures. Another story of note is "Epsilon Probe."

Although not primarily known for his stylistic technique, McLaughlin employs clear prose in his writing, with a crisp delivery that falters only in *The Man Who Wanted Stars.* He very consciously avoids larger than life characters, providing instead the kind of people that readers can more easily identify with. His plots and situations ring true, and in most cases he is careful to present a problem from various points of view rather than simply propagandizing his own. Most of his better fiction leaves the reader with questions to ponder after the story is done. At the same time, he has yet to produce a work with the kind of stature that would assure him a strong position in the genre.

—Don D'Ammassa

McMULLEN, Sean (Christopher)

Nationality: Australian. **Born:** Sale, Victoria, 21 December 1948. **Education:** University of Melbourne, B.A. in physics 1974; Canberra CAE, graduate diploma of information science 1976; Latrobe University, graduate diploma of computer science 1980; University of Melbourne, M.A. in history (honors) 1984. **Family:** Married 1) Mary Davies in 1973 (divorced 1978); 2) Patricia Smyth in 1986; one daughter. **Career:** Laboratory assistant, Walter and Eliga Hall Institute, 1969-70; driver, Woolworths, 1970-71; technical clerk, Department of Works, 1972-75; librarian, various libraries, 1975-80; computer systems analyst, Bureau of Meteorology, 1981-. **Awards:** Ditmar award, 1991, 1992; William Atheling award (criticism), 1992, 1993. **Member:** Australian Computer Society, 1979; Science Fiction and Fantasy Writers of America, 1988. **Agent:** Liza Landsman, Writers House Inc., 21 West 26th Street, New York, New York 10010, U.S.A. **Address:** GPO Box 2653x, Melbourne, Victoria 3001, Australia.

Science Fiction Publications

Novels (series: Greatwinter)

Voices in the Light (Greatwinter). North Adelaide, South Australia, Aphelion, 1994.
Mirror Sun Rising (Greatwinter). North Adelaide, South Australia, Aphelion, 1995.

Short Stories

Call to the Edge. North Adelaide, South Australia, Aphelion Publications, 1992.

Other Publications

Other

Australian Science Fiction and Fantasy: (Mid-85 to Mid-91). Melbourne, Victoria, n.p., 1991.

*

Sean McMullen comments:

Ever since I began to read science fiction, I have had a tendency to wonder about the background behind the sets and backdrops where the adventures took place. What was life like on the Mars of H.G. Wells, how viable was the society aboard the *Nautilus* of Jules Verne, and what sorts of traits would be enhanced by living in the huge, deadly maze on Robert Silverberg's Lemnos? In the real world, it was the same. When I entered University I began what was supposed to be a science degree, but I graduated with a jumble of physics, history, mathematics, English, sociology, and computing. Whenever I learned a new principle or theorem, I just had to know the circumstances and society of its discoverer as well.

Inevitably, when I began to write my own science fiction I always thought out detailed histories, societies and such as backgrounds for even the shortest of my short stories. I soon learned, however, that too much of anything—whether hard science, history, or character background—quickly becomes boring for the reader. Tourists who come to see the Notre Dame cathedral do not want to be forced to take a tour of the foundations, after all.

In my novel *Voices in the Light* I featured a computer composed of 2000 slaves chained to benches and calculating on abacus frames. I started by working out its capacities and limitations (on an electronic computer), then sketched out a huge library to house it, and a librarian caste to maintain and program it. From here, I had to develop the political and cultural background of the nation beyond, because the story of such a computer would be that of its impact on the society that built it. By the time I reached the final draft, I had junked dozens of pages on systems architecture, programming languages, and systems for data storage. They were the hard, solid foundations on which the really interesting material of the novel was built, but I did not think that readers wanted to see the foundations.

In general, I think that all science fiction needs a foundation of hard science, otherwise it might as well be called fantasy, horror or whatever. Conversely, a story that is all hard science speculation will be at best boring and at worst unreadable. My own favourite science fiction novel is Walter M. Miller's *A Canticle for Leibowitz* because it gets both of the above conditions right. The author provided a sound foundation of science, while making those long-suffering monks in their desert abbey seem so real that I really cared about what happened to them. All of my own science fiction has probably been fashioned to achieve something similar.

*   *   *

Sean McMullen's work is that of a fine and natural storyteller. What surprised and delighted the readers of his best-known story, "The Colors of the Masters," when it appeared in *Fantasy and Science Fiction* in March 1988, was not so much its innovative quality—a new computer gimmick had been found which could translate the sounds of great music from its original clockwork recorder back into colours—as its charm. It becomes possible to hear Chopin playing Chopin, and a "new," though long dead, great virtuoso pianist is discovered—but the invention is seen mainly in terms of its commercial possibilities. A delicately humorous charm lies in the characterization of the aged twin sisters who have inherited the invention, lightly bickering wits, who humanize the present just as the inventor Katherine Searle's diary entries humanize the past.

A note of cynicism is also found in a World War II story about German fighter pilots, "The Devils of Langenhagen." "Alone in His Chariot" is a thoroughly cynical double revenge story featuring a man who manufactures drugs for sale in the laboratory where he works as an assistant, discovers the potential in a new substance being fed to rats, applies it to himself and then to his clients—and makes a killing, in more than two senses of the word.

McMullen can provide horror in such a story as "While the Gate Is Open" or thrills in the excellent Dowlingesque "The Eyes of the Green Lancer," with its charming mute librarian, and "Pax Romana," a story about Alfred the Great who meets a Roman time-traveler. Both of these stories are material for novels, as time comes to augment them, as indeed happened with "The Eyes of the Green Lancer," which was incorporated with other stories to form *Voices in the Light*.

Call to the Edge brings together several of the early stories, which were notable for winning prizes, as well as, in some cases, for being published overseas. "The Dominant Style" deals with utopia as a place of nostalgia, in which time is cheated when the place is fixed in that era just before things started to go seriously wrong in Australia. Colin Strathlen, a time-traveler through space exploration, is meant to interrupt the dream, but he is captivated by it. Time travel, by various methods, suggests itself as one means available of cheating the great limit, destiny. "The Deciad" and "Pax Romana" are fascinating but relatively sober accounts of the possible costs involved in such a heroic (or is it a cowardly?) attempt to move beyond historical fixation. "While the Gate Is Open," an intriguing, quirky story, suggests that it may be possible to probe eternity, after death, by mechanical means. The story's end leaves nicely poised the question that goes beyond science fiction: where do we go, hereafter? I wrote the "Introduction" for this book, so my views of the high quality of the stories are clear from that.

A kind of nostalgic escapist process exists in the Greatwinter series, whereby the advances made by science to our civilization are removed, and this means that new science has to be invented to provide machines that use little or no electricity. The idea of devising an Australia that retreats backwards in time without becoming boringly feudal in a medieval way is interesting. Women have much power but their sexual needs vary; slavery exists but in some ways is a professional asset. One of the devices used is the Calculor, a computer run by human slaves who, once electric power enables more rapid devices to be run in its place, do not wish to be deprived of their machine. The Calculor's director is of commanding importance but is only the Mayor's librarian, the Highliber, and her aim in life is to investigate history and to discover what signals may be used to counteract the weapons in space orbits which have destroyed electrical machinery. The signalling towers which replace the telephone and radio rely on coded flashes of light, and so are baffled when skies are not clear. The principal mode of travel is the train, but it works by wind, assisted by elaborately geared motors operated by the powers of cyclists who can thus earn their journeys onward. The Mayor is mater of a key city amongst a group of allied Mayorates, but civil battles may be fought amongst the groups across Australia, or from attacks by notable rebels in the north, also led by a powerful woman. So far as is known in the first books, the major dangers to social progress lie in the south and west, in the sea. A Call, which operates psychically, moves backwards and forwards across the land and, when it functions, draws people and animals irresistibly to the sea, where they are consumed by a regimented army of sharks. The intelligent powers beyond the sharks form part of the mystery which fuels the plot. Civil war and progress in knowledge enable the state of society to change rapidly in the course of the books, and these are furthered by certain gifted individuals, such as the picaresque Glasken, who has a need within himself that enables him to resist the Call. Most people are chained when the Call comes and are restricted from moving far when inside their walled cities or in the more difficult rural or outback regions. Close to the shore in what used to be Western Australia is a wrecked town where ancient technological marvels remain. As well as the battles, quests take place and strangely motivated love stories bring together or separate the major characters for crucial purposes to the ongoing plot. The range of episodes in the Greatwinter series is engaging and rapid in its movement. The trilogy (as one supposes it will be) has all the advantages of a fine innovative work without the modern commercially motivated length.

Sean McMullen is a noted writer to be considered with Greg Egan as a new Australian hard science fiction talent, and is much the more readable of the two. As a future historian of Australia, he is also to be compared with the Ballardian Terry Dowling as one of the fresh explorers of Australia as a location for speculative fiction different from that we associate with other terrestrial places.

—Michael J. Tolley

McQUAY, Mike

Pseudonyms: Victor Appleton; Jack Arnett; Susan Claudia; Franklin W. Dixon; Laura Lee Hope; Carolyn Keene. **Nationality:** American. **Born:** Baltimore, Maryland, 3 June 1949. **Education:** Attended grammar school in Baltimore; McGuiness High School, Oklahoma City; University of Dallas, 1967-70. **Family:** Married 1) Mary McQuay in 1968 (divorced 1981); 2) Sandy McQuay in 1982; one son and two daughters. **Career:** Musician, aircraft worker in Asia, banker, factory worker, artist-in-residence, Central State University, Edmond, Oklahoma, from 1980. **Died:** 25 May 1995.

SCIENCE FICTION PUBLICATIONS

Novels (series: Ramon and Morgan; Mathew Swain)

Lifekeeper. New York, Avon, 1980.
Escape from New York: A Novel (novelization of screenplay). New York, Bantam, and London, Corgi, 1981.
Mathew Swain: Hot Time in Old Town. New York, Bantam, 1981.
Mathew Swain: When Trouble Beckons. New York, Bantam, 1981.
Mathew Swain: The Deadliest Show in Town. New York, Bantam, 1982.
Mathew Swain: The Odds Are Murder. New York, Bantam, 1983.
Jitterbug. New York, Bantam, 1984.
Pure Blood (Ramon and Morgan). New York, Bantam, 1985.
Mother Earth (Ramon and Morgan). New York, Bantam, 1985.
My Science Project (novelization of screenplay). New York, Bantam, 1985.
Memories. New York, Bantam, 1987; London, Headline, 1990.
Isaac Asimov's Robot City 2: Suspicion. New York, Ace, 1987; London, Futura, 1989.
The Nexus. New York, Bantam, 1989; London, Headline, 1990.

OTHER PUBLICATIONS

Novels

Cradle to Grave (as Susan Claudia). New York, Fawcett, 1983.
The M.I.A. Ransom. New York, Bantam, 1986.

Novels as Jack Arnett (series: Book of Justice in all titles)

Genocide Express. New York, Bantam, 1989.
Zaitech Sting. New York, Bantam, 1990.
Death Force. New York, Bantam, 1990.
Panama Dead. New York, Bantam, 1990.

Fiction for Children

Tom Swift: Crater of Mystery (as Victor Appleton). New York, Simon and Schuster, 1983.

Tom Swift: Planet of Nightmares (as Victor Appleton). New York, Simon and Schuster, 1984.
Nancy Drew/Hardy Boys: Supersleuths II (as Carolyn Keene and Franklin W. Dixon). New York, Simon and Schuster, 1984.
Nancy Drew Ghost Stories 2 (as Carolyn Keene). New York, Simon and Schuster, 1985.
The Bobbsey Twins: The Haunted House Mystery (as Laura Lee Hope). New York, Simon and Schuster, 1985.
Puppetmaster. London, Headline, and New York, Bantam, 1991.
State of Siege. New York, Bantam, 1994.

*

Mike McQuay commented:

(1991) My writing tends toward the sociological/humanistic end of the spectrum. Though considered a cynic by many of my detractors, I consider myself a social realist (an optimist in wolf's clothing). My work as a whole deals with the survival of the human spirit despite the out-of-control technologies we've set in motion, which puts me in direct opposition (gladly) with the science-as-God writers who seem to fill the shelves. Don't look for sugar coating in a McQuay book.

My main sub-theme seems to be discussions on the nature of reality, and the human's ability to construct reality to his own specifications.

*   *   *

Mike McQuay established himself in a short time as an energetic and prolific writer whose science fiction projects an emphatically masculine vision. McQuay's Mathew Swain series makes an interesting effort to combine the science fiction and private-eye genres, and his other novels display a penchant for vivid melodramatic action. Strongly individualist and non-conformist heroes are a distinguishing feature of McQuay's work, as well as an obvious specticism and distrust of the ethics and purposes of corporations and governments. Another intriguing trait of McQuay's fiction is the influence of his southwest background, which appears both in his style and in the non-conformist stance of his tough-minded heroes.

McQuay's first important novel was *Lifekeeper,* which employed the bold stroke of a black hero. In a dismal future divided between wilderness tribes and communal states, ruled by computers which outlaw individuality, Doral Dulan is a rebellious and archaic individualist who realizes his destiny by overthrowing the dominance of the machines and fulfilling the desert tribes' yearning for a messiah. Some sharp parallels with Frank Herbert's Dune novels are obvious, including an ending which attempts to suggest Herbert's sophisticated sense of irony.

This ambitious but uneven first novel was followed by *Escape from New York,* a novelization of a cynically conceived film melodrama about a near future in which New York City has collapsed into a forbidden zone or anarchic sanctuary for criminals and outcasts. Plissken, the heroic antihero, is characterized effectively, and his hard-headed and intractable individualism anticipates Matt Swain, the hero of McQuay's 21st-century private-eye series.

The Swain series is dedicated to the memory of Raymond Chandler, "who understood." Presumably McQuay was paying homage to Chandler's vision of a corrupt and materialistic society where ethical norms are in constant flux, and also to Chandler's Philip Marlowe, the incorruptible and disenchanted knight who uncovers forgotten crimes and repressed memories of venality and compromise, as Chandler described his hero's role in his famous essay and apologia, "The Simple Art of Murder."

In the first Swain adventure, *Hot Time in Old Town*, McQuay's private eye is depicted as a younger and slightly more idealistic Marlowe, and as a former law officer now playing a lone hand in a decaying Southwestern city suggestive of Dallas or Tulsa. However, Swain has a more active sex life than Marlowe, since McQuay bestows on him a wealthy and voluptuous young woman, Ginny Teal, in the first novel; while in later books in the series other attractive women become Swain's lovers. Swain is also a more impulsive and physical hero than Marlowe, displaying a good deal of prowess with his fits and with weapons, somewhat in the mode of Robert B. Parker's Spenser. Yet like his model, Marlowe, Swain also remains true to the tradition of the private eye as a man of honor, showing himself to be relentless and incorruptible as he searches for the murderer of a dissolute heir in *Hot Time in Old Town*.

In the second Swain novel, *When Trouble Beckons*, McQuay takes his hero to a city on the moon where a large multinational corporation rules. Although Swain's mission is ostensibly to rescue Ginny, in reality the novel examines the corrupting influence of a decadent and dehumanizing social environment, evoking memories of Dashiell Hammett's Personville (or "Poisonville") in *Red Harvest*, and Ross MacDonald's scandal-ridden midwestern town in *Blue City*. *When Trouble Beckons* is notable for its unrelenting action, its virtuoso reversals of plot, especially in the closing pages, and its sympathetic characterization of an earthy woman cab driver.

The Deadliest Show in Town continues Swain's crusade against corporate dishonesty and greed, and government indifference and corruption, this time pitting the private eye against the 21st-century communications industry. The final entry in the series, *The Odds Are Murder*, continues the emphasis on violent physical action featured in the first three novels, as Swain investigates greed and scandal in the manufacture of pharmaceutical drugs. But the themes and attitudes of the Swain books are now beginning to seem repetitious and obsessive; none of the Swain novels has established itself as worthy of comparison with the mature Raymond Chandler.

To his credit, however, McQuay refused to become the prisoner of a series with its limitations. In 1984, he published *Jitterbug*, a work that returns to the epic scale of *Lifekeeper*, depicting a dystopian world of the 22nd century. In this novel, a fanatical Arab dictatorship rules a decaying America; but this "corporation" is challenged successfully by the rebellion of Olson, another of McQuay's tough-minded heroes, who emerges from obscurity and a harsh upbringing in the southwest. *Jitterbug* showed marked growth in McQuay as a novelist, for its extrapolated future world is envisaged with both imaginative power and an increased thoroughness and plausibility.

Pure Blood is another vigorous adventure saga set in a much-changed New York State a thousand years hence. In the predominantly primitive post-disaster world of this novel, McQuay portrays an environment of barbaric humans and new creatures created by genetic experiment, where another of his outcast heroes, Morgan, tempered by the crucible of hardship and struggle, rises to leadership.

Of the more recent novels, *The M.I.A. Ransom* and *Panama Dead* belong to the action suspense category, and attempt to enter the profitable territory of Robert Ludlum and Tom Clancy. *The M.I.A. Ransom* deals with an elaborate plot to free a large number of American prisoners supposedly still held in Vietnam.

McQuay's other, more significant books are additions to his science fiction canon. These include *Mother Earth*, a sequel to *Pure Blood*; *Robot City 2: Suspicion*, a formula novel for a series employing the premises of Isaac Asimov's Robot stories; *Memories*, which received the 1987 Philip K. Dick award; and another speculative novel, *The Nexus*. The most ambitious of these efforts is undoubtedly *Memories*, an elaborate time-travel tale. This narrative unfolds in a series of apparently unrelated scenes, which are gradually unified by an elaborate design. The plot involves visitors from a bleak future coming back to contemporary Oklahoma City to influence the lives of David Wolf, an unhappy psychiatrist, and his unfortunate sister. A victim of various childhood traumas and three failed marriages, Wolf is not exactly a superhuman hero, but Silv, a wise and tutelary spirit from the future, helps him find some meaning in his life. The action moves backward and forward in time, with much of the narrative describing Napoleon's fortunes in the era of the French Revolution and France's imperial triumphs.

Memories reveals a large imaginative scope, enriched by metaphysical speculation about human identity. McQuay seems to suggest that the psyche is essentially a collection of memories and emotions, which explains the title. However, despite its lofty aspirations and McQuay's usual command of the vernacular of the American Southwest, the novel suffers from an appearance of hasty composition and would have benefited from judicious editing.

The Nexus continues the imaginative speculation undertaken in *Memories*, but is set in the area around Dallas, and deals with a different cast of characters. The novel was innovative for McQuay both because of his use of Hindu mythology, and because of his experiments with narrative technique (some of the action is presented in a terse dramatic form, similar to the mode of a screenplay).

—Edgar L. Chapman

MEEK, S(terner St.) P(aul)

Also wrote as Sterner St. Paul. **Nationality:** American. **Born:** Chicago, Illinois, 8 April 1894. **Education:** University of Chicago, Sc.A. 1914; University of Alabama, University, S.B. 1915 (Phi Beta Kappa); University of Wisconsin, Madison, 1916; Massachusetts Institute of Technology, Cambridge, 1921-23. **Military Service:** Served in the United States Army from 1917; directed small arms ammunition research, 1923-26; chief publications officer, Ordnance Department, 1941-44; retired due to disability, 1947; Colonel. **Family:** Married Edna Burndage Noble in 1927; one son. **Career:** Football coach, Kirkley Junior College, Greenville, Texas, 1915; chemist, Western Electric Company, Hawthorne, Illinois, 1916, and Deuvitt Laboratories, Chicago, 1917. Held patents on tracer ammunition. **Died:** 10 June 1972.

SCIENCE FICTION PUBLICATIONS

Novels (series: Troyana in all titles)

The Drums of Tapajos. New York, Avalon, 1961.
Troyana. New York, Avalon, 1961.

Short Stories

The Monkeys Have No Tails in Zamboanga. New York, Morrow, 1935.
Arctic Bride. London, Utopian, 1944.

OTHER PUBLICATIONS

Novel

Island Born. New York, Godwin, 1937.

Other (for children)

Jerry: The Adventures of an Army Dog. New York, Morrow, 1932.
Frog, The Horse That Knew No Master. Philadelphia, Penn, 1933.
Gypsy Lad: The Story of a Champion Setter. New York, Morrow, 1934.
Franz, A Dog of the Police. Philadelphia, Penn, 1935.
Dignity, A Springer Spaniel. Philadelphia, Penn, 1937.
Rusty, A Cocker Spaniel. Philadelphia, Penn, 1938.
Gustav, A Son of Franz. Philadelphia, Penn, 1940.
Pat: The Story of a Seeing Eye Dog. New York, Knopf, 1947.
So You're Going to Get a Puppy. New York, Knopf, 1947.
Boots: The Story of a Working Sheep Dog. New York, Knopf, 1948.
Midnight, A Cow Pony. New York, Knopf, 1949.
Ranger, A Dog of the Forest Service. New York, Knopf, 1949.
Hans, A Dog of the Border Patrol. New York, Knopf, 1950.
Surfman: The Adventures of a Coast Guard Dog. New York, Knopf, 1950.
Paga, A Border Patrol Horse. New York, Knopf, 1951.
Red, A Trailing Bloodhound. New York, Knopf, 1951.
Boy, An Ozark Coon Hound. New York, Knopf, 1952.
Rip, A Game Protector. New York, Knopf, 1952.
Omar, A State Police Dog. New York, Knopf, 1953.
Bellfarm Star: The Story of a Pace. New York, Dodd Mead, 1955.
Pierre of the Big Top: The Story of a Circus Poodle. New York, Dodd Mead, 1956.

*   *   *

S.P. Meek was one of the most prominent contributors to the science fiction magazines that struggled to survive the years of the depression between 1929 and 1933. He first appeared with "The Murgatroyd Experiment," a still-memorable tale concerning the appalling results of an effort to sustain the world's swollen population in the year 2060, and wrote regularly for the next few years. It was to be expected that he would write about future warfare, and in "The Red Peril" he drew a grim picture of the world's great cities being sprayed with disease germs in 1957—the enemy, inevitably, being the Soviet Union. Propaganda leaflets were also in the armoury of the attackers, whose gravity-defying aircraft were repelled by atomic shells. Even after the Soviet leaders had been confined on St. Helena, the struggle was continued in a sequel, "The Last War," in which synthetic men were produced to turn the tide of battle.

The Red Menace often lurked in the background when Meek's popular character, Dr. Bird of the Bureau of Standards, accompanied by Operative Carnes of the Secret Service, set out to expose some piece of villainy in the series of intriguing tales. In "The Gland Murders" the plot was designed to decimate the educated rich by lacing their bootleg liquor with an extract from the pineal gland of

a murderer, stimulating them to violent acts for which they would pay the penalty. Economic disaster was narrowly averted when, in "Vanishing Gold," bullion in the vaults of the Federal Reserve Bank became radioactive and lost weight. In "When Caverns Yawned" whole cities were imperilled by artificial earthquakes; and in "The Solar Magnet" the subversive genius Ivan Saranoff even tried to straighten the Earth's axis so that Russia might win her true place in the sun. Most of the Dr. Bird stories appeared in the early issues of *Astounding Stories,* where the emphasis on foreign villians brought protests from some readers, and an assurance from the editor that "our authors mean no offence." Among other tales was "Giants on the Earth," a gaudy interplanetary adventure in a style he seldom affected but which clearly showed the extent of his versatility. His tale of an electronic world, "Submicroscopic," was continued in "Awlo of Ulm," an action-romance in the Burroughs tradition. Two serials, *The Drums of Tapajos* and its sequel, *Troyana,* concerned a lost civilisation buried in the Brazilian jungle, and appeared in book form after an interval of 30 years. A collection of his humorous short stories was published as *The Monkeys Have No Tails in Zamboanga.*

—Walter Gillings

MELTZER, David

Nationality: American. **Born:** Rochester, New York, 17 February 1937. **Education:** Public schools in Brooklyn and Los Angeles; Los Angeles City College, 1955-56; University of California, Los Angeles, 1956-57. **Family:** Married Christina Meyer in 1958; three daughters and one son. **Career:** Manager, Discovery Bookshop, San Francisco, 1959-67; editor, *Maya,* Mill Valley, California, 1966-71; teacher, Urban School, San Francisco, 1975-76. Since 1970, editor, *Tree* magazine and Tree Books, Bolinas, later Berkeley, California. Composer, musician, and singer: performed with Serpent Power and David and Tina, 1970-72. **Awards:** Council of Literary Magazines grant, 1972, 1981; National Endowment for the Arts grant, 1974, for publishing, 1975. **Address:** Box 9005, Berkeley, California 94709, U.S.A.

SCIENCE FICTION PUBLICATIONS

Novels (series: Agency; Brain Plant)

The Agency. North Hollywood, Essex House, 1968.
The Agent (Agency). North Hollywood, Essex House, 1968.
How Many Blocks in the Pile? (Agency). North Hollywood, Essex House, 1968.
Lovely (Brain Plant). North Hollywood, Essex House, 1969.
Healer (Brain Plant). North Hollywood, Essex House, 1969.
Out (Brain Plant). North Hollywood, Essex House, 1969.
Glue Factory (Brain Plant), North Hollywood, Essex House, 1969.

OTHER PUBLICATIONS

Novels

Orf. North Hollywood, Essex House, 1968.

The Marytr. North Hollywood, Essex House, 1969.
Star. North Hollywood, Brandon House, 1970.

Poetry

Poems, with Donald Schenker. Privately printed, 1957.
Ragas. San Francisco, Discovery, 1959.
The Clown. Larkspur, California, Semina, 1960.
Station. Privately printed, 1964.
The Blackest Rose. Berkeley, California, Oyez, 1964.
Oyez! Berkeley, California, Oyez, 1965.
The Process. Berkeley, California, Oyez, 1965.
In Hope I Offer a Fire Wheel. Berkeley, California, Oyez, 1965.
The Dark Continent. Berkeley, California, Oyez, 1967.
Nature Poem. Santa Barbara, California, Unicorn Press, 1967.
Santamaya, with Jack Shoemaker. San Francisco, Maya, 1968.
Round the Poem Box: Rustic and Domestic Home Movies for Stan and Jane Brakhage. Los Angeles, Black Sparrow Press, 1969.
Yesod. London, Trigram Press, 1969.
From Eden Book. San Francisco, Cranium Press, 1969.
Abulafia Song. Santa Barbara, California, Unicorn Press, 1969.
Greenspeech. Goleta, California, Christopher, 1970.
Luna. Los Angeles, Black Sparrow Press, 1970.
Letters and Numbers. Berkeley, California, Oyez, 1970.
Bronx Lil/Head of Lillin. S.A.C. Santa Barbara, California, Capra Press, 1970.
32 Beams of Light. Santa Barbara, California, Capra Press, 1970.
Knots. Bolinas, California, Tree, 1971.
Bark: A Polemic. Santa Barbara, California, Capra Press, 1973.
Hero/Lil. Los Angeles, Black Sparrow Press, 1973.
Tens: Selected Poems 1961-1971, edited by Kenneth Rexroth. New York, Herder, 1973.
The Eyes, The Blood. San Francisco, Mudra, 1973.
French Broom. Berkeley, California, Oyez, 1974.
Blue Rags. Berkeley, California, Oyez, 1974.
Harps. Berkeley, California, Oyez, 1975.
Six. Santa Barbara, California, Black Sparrow Press, 1976.
Bolero. Berkeley, California, Oyez, 1976.
The Art, The Veil. Milwaukee, Membrane Press, 1981.
The Name: Selected Poetry 1973-1983. Santa Barbara, California, Black Sparrow Press, 1984.
Lyrik: Selected Poetry 1983-1990. Santa Rosa, California, Black Sparrow Press, 1990.
Arrows: Selected Poetry, 1957-1992. Santa Rosa, California, Black Sparrow Press, 1994.

Other

We All Have Something to Say to Each Other: Being an Essay Entitled "Patchen" and Four Poems. San Francisco, Auerhahn Press, 1962.
Introduction to the Outsiders (essay on Beat Poetry). Fort Lauderdale, Florida, Rodale, 1962.
Bazascope Mother (essay on Robert Alexander). Los Angeles, Drekfesser Press, 1964.
Journal of the Birth. Berkeley, California, Oyez, 1967.
Isla Vista Notes: Fragmentary, Apocalyptic, Didactic Contradictions. Santa Barbara, California, Christopher, 1970.
Abra (for children). Berkeley, California, Hipparchia Press, 1976.
Two-way Mirror: A Poetry Note-book. Berkeley, California, Oyez, 1977.

Editor, with Lawrence Ferlinghetti and Michael McClure, *Journal for the Protection of All Beings 1 and 3.* San Francisco, City Lights, 2 vols., 1961-69.
Editor, *The San Francisco Poets.* New York, Ballantine, 1971; revised edition, as *Golden Gate,* San Francisco, Wingbow Press, 1976.
Editor, *Birth: An Anthology.* New York, Ballantine, 1973.
Editor, *The Secret Garden: An Anthology in the Kabbalah.* New York, Seabury Press, 1976.
Editor, *The Path of the Names,* by Abraham Abulafia. Berkeley, California, Tree, and London, Trigram Press, 1976.
Editor, *Birth: An Anthology of Ancient Texts, Songs, Prayers, and Stories.* Berkeley, California, North Point Press, 1981.
Editor, *Death* (anthology). Berkeley, California, North Point Press, 1984.
Editor, *The Book within the Book: Texts and Contexts of Kabbalah.* Berkeley, California, North Point Press, 1990.
Editor, *Reading Jazz.* San Francisco, Mercury House, 1993.

Translator, with Allen Say, *Morning Glories,* by Shiga Naoya. Berkeley, California, Oyez, 1975.

*

Manuscript Collections: Washington University, St. Louis; University of Indiana, Bloomington; University of California, Los Angeles.

Critical Studies: *David Meltzer: A Sketch from Memory and Descriptive Checklist,* Berkeley, California, Oyez, 1965, and *6 Poets of the San Francisco Renaissance,* Fresno, California, Giligia Press, 1967, both by David Kherdian; *The Secret Record: Modern Erotic Literature* by Michael Perkins, New York, Morrow, 1976; in *Vort* (Berkeley, California), 1979; *Apocalyptic Messianism and Contemporary Jewish-American Poetry* by R. Barbara Gitenstein, Albany, State University Press of New York, 1986.

David Meltzer comments:

My involvement with science fiction began when I was a teenager with my reading of H.G. Wells. This led to the early Conklin anthologies and to pulps like *Famous Fantastic Mysteries, Amazing,* and *Thrilling Wonder Stories. Weird Tales* directed me to Arkham House and to Bradbury's first book. Though I enjoyed all aspects of the genre—from David H. Keller to A.E. van Vogt—the writers who interested me most, for their style and innovative stories, were Sturgeon, Kuttner, and finally Alfred Bester, whose *Demolished Man* (serialized in *Galaxy*) was a significant opening in the development of my own work. Its typographical free-play, reminiscent of 1920s Dada and Surrealist typewriter art, felt comfortable to a young poet enthralled with Kenneth Patchen and E.E. Cummings.

Though I wrote and sold a few stories in the 1950s, it was writing the erotic tracts for Essex House that gave me the format I needed to extend my involvement with science fiction. These novels allowed me to use the speculative freedom of SF in a free-for-all attempt to make moral, political, and it is hoped, satirical appraisal of the U.S.A. in the late 1960s without sacrificing any respectability poets are supposed to wear as top hats or laurel crowns.

*   *   *

Of the 10 novels by California poet and novelist David Meltzer, seven were—in the author's words—"SF or fantasy, future projections." The fact that the Essex House series, edited by Brian Kirby, was devoted to serious American erotic writing did not hinder Meltzer when he wrote his prophetic, Blakean novels of the future. As he has said, "The pornographic erotic format seemed most fitting a zone to engage in didactic moral outcries. . . ."

In *The Agency,* the first volume of a trilogy, Meltzer conveys a poetic vision in spare, allusive prose. He uses techniques special to speculative fiction and satire. As the novelist Norman Spinrad writes in his afterword to *The Agent,* the Agency "is clearly Meltzer's paradigm of society; a mindless machine of which we are all 'agents,' *including* those whom the machine supposedly serves. . . ." The Agency is "a well-organised, self-sufficient, sexual underground." In *The Agency,* a young man is picked up by sexual agents and—like the woman in *Story of O*—spends the rest of the novel being forcibly indoctrinated with the Agency's tyrannical precepts. Brainwashed, he becomes an agent himself, ready to propagate the evil fantasies of his masters. In *The Agent,* the satirical possibilities implied in The Agency are applied more broadly to various aspects of American society. Here, Meltzer's deliberately ambiguous portrayal of two agents who may or may not be working for the same agency is often reminiscent of scenes from the movie *Dr. Strangelove.* The third volume in the trilogy, *How Many Blocks in the Pile?,* is constructed differently from the first two. In it, Meltzer creates an exaggerated portrait of the Agency's customers—a married couple who respond to sexual advertisements.

Meltzer's most ambitious erotic SF project is the Brain Plant Tetralogy. In classical Greek drama, a tetralogy is a group of four dramatic pieces, either four tragedies or three tragedies and a satire. Meltzer's Brain Plant novels are not tragedies in the classical sense, and satire is a prominent feature of each of them; but his extrapolation of tendencies in American society of the late 1960s and their application in his prophetic fictions renders a tragic, scarifying vision. Meltzer's achievement in these four novels does not lie in the creation of characters, because they are either deliberate caricatures or disembodied voices, nor in the creation of a central fantasy. His projection of a future American government ruled by "Military Industry" in which "Rads" (radicals) and "Rebs" (lower middle-class whites), "Snarks" (sexual anarchists), and black militants, are pacified by "Fun Zones" (ingenious Disneylands for the satisfaction of sexual fantasies) is simplistic—like R. Crumb cartoons, as Frank M. Robinson points out in his afterword to *Lovely.* Meltzer's achievement lies instead in the utterly convincing manner in which he argues his theme of exploitation through sex, power, and dreams. The series, because of the extravagent, entertaining, violent, prophetic vision it conveys, is one of the high points of erotic SF literature.

—Michael Perkins

MELUCH, R(ebecca) M.

Nationality: American. **Born:** Ohio, 24 October 1956. **Education:** University of North Carolina, Greensboro, B.A. in theatre 1978; University of Pennsylvania, Philadelphia, M.A. in ancient history 1981. **Family:** Married James C. Witkowski. **Career:** Since 1978, full-time writer. **Agent:** Ricia Mainhardt, 612 Argyle #L5, Brooklyn, New York 11230, U.S.A. **Address:** 688 Brick Mill Run, Westlake, OH 44145.

SCIENCE FICTION PUBLICATIONS

Novels (series: Wind)

Sovereign. New York, Signet, 1979; London, Arrow, 1980.
Wind Dancers. New York, Signet, 1981.
Wind Child. New York, Signet, 1982.
Jerusalem Fire. New York, Signet, 1985; London, Orbit, 1986.
War Birds. New York, Signet, 1989.
Chicago Red. New York, Roc, 1990.
The Queen's Squadron. New York, Roc, 1992.

* * *

R.M. Meluch, a young writer when her first novel, *Sovereign,* was published, has produced seven novels and several short stories to date. These range from space opera-based novels of psychosocial development to socio-revolutionary adventure. She has created multipolitical human and alien cultures on a multitude of worlds whose climates and lifeforms are sketched out as major plot elements and, while most of the works are thematically linked and loosely postulate the same, intergalactic future for humankind, each is absorbingly different. Meluch's novels show a fascination with armed and unarmed conflict, including the intrigue of intergalactic diplomacy, various permutations of martial arts, and detailed ship-to-ship battles in space, predicated on World Wars I and II ace-fighter culture.

Sovereign is a self-contained saga of heroism thrust upon the person of a tormented young man. *Wind Child* and *Wind Dancers* combine to chronicle the return from virtual extermination of a race of shape-changers through the assistance of halfbreed human/aliens. Meluch's literary strengths lie in characterization, and she repeatedly probes the psychological effects of war on otherwise humanistic people. This thematic thread runs more truly through the later four novels, *Jerusalem Fire, War Birds, Chicago Red,* and *The Queen's Squadron.*

A character study predicated on a father-son conflict, *Sovereign* follows Teal's heroic struggle for survival through a variety of interpersonal situations cast against an intergalactic war. As the 33rd, and crucial, generation of a long line of male, only-children, Teal is dependent on his father's tutoring for protection from side-effects of a breeding program. His birth causes the death of his mother, and his father's rejection, starting a chain of events within which he opposes ever larger aggregates of hostile beings. His father is his first enemy; others include the competing Brekk family; the invading northern tribes of the home planet, Arana; and the alien Uelson race that threatens Arana as well as Earth. Teal's long struggle to replace his father's missing affection takes him first north to join a spacefaring race, and then off-planet to battle the Uelsons on Earth's behalf. These adventures, seemingly motivated by internal need rather than external compulsion, form the arena within which his heroic scope is displayed.

Wind Dancers and *Wind Child,* also based upon the existence of a race of genetically altered beings, is more reminiscent of H. Beam Piper than Doc Smith. A dying race of beings with extra sets of chromosomes is able to take three forms, human-like, animal, and wind. The wealthy terrans who have taken over their planet wish to deny, and then conceal, their existence in order to claim a planet with no apparent indigenous population, a plot element also found in Piper's *Little Fuzzy. Wind Dancers* introduces the alien-human conflict, and the characters, alien Niki, half-alien Laure, and human East, who will restore the race. *Wind Child* introduces the human-alien savior, Daniel, similar to Teal in *Sovereign*. His function is to search out lost members of the race among the stars.

The viewpoints of the wind-aliens and humans alternate, providing the story with more controlled depth than found in Meluch's first novel. All but a few central characters are embodiments of a single principle: mystery and aesthetic beauty in the alien dancer, Niki; evil in the rich Duchess Estelita and the military leader, Admiral Czals; and unselfish but mischievous goodness in Daniel's close companion, Tavi.

Jerusalem Fire, War Birds, Chicago Red, and *The Queen's Squadron,* though self-contained narratives, have many similarities. In each, a few tormented beings, human and alien, are used to depict the close, often tragic, relationship between good and evil. In portraying both heroes and villains (who are often the same person) through this thematic concern, Meluch also makes them compellingly human. Honor, loyalty, strength, weakness, friendship, and love oppose each other, creating the paradoxes that plague the lives of her characters. *Jerusalem Fire* follows an intergalactic pirate with a shameful past as he attempts restitution for his actions. *War Birds'* antihero begins by working unwillingly for the enemies who vanquished his planet, then he joins them in the face of an alien threat. In *Chicago Red,* fathers, sons, and brothers find themselves on opposite sides of a revolution against totalitarian rule. They also find their political loyalties challenged by interpersonal ones, including hetero- and homosexual love along with human-alien friendships. Perhaps because her novels are mostly about males and war, with a few significant female characters, Meluch's portrayal of male homosexual relationships is as pervasive as it is sensitive. Love and friendship, especially between natural enemies whose social functions may differ, are often pivotal to her plots. This is never more so than in her latest novel, *The Queen's Squadron,* where bitter enemies fight a deep sexual attraction that was brought on by the torturing of one by another and where a former goddess abandons everything for the love of an outcast war hero.

Jerusalem Fire pairs a life-weary, alcoholic, ex-general pirate with several avatars, an alien queen, and a human warrior who has tried to become alien. In the future, intergalactic, totalitarian culture of this novel, the pirate Alihahd must face his past as the most successful general of an emperor who has set out to subjugate all inhabited planets, including Earth. His torments call into question the concepts of loyalty and honor, especially at the points where they conflict with humanism. The novel spans several planets and several decades, introduces a mythical race of aliens, chronicles the past of Alihahd and his avatars, Ben-Taire and Hall, all without offering any easy answers to the human condition of paradox.

War Birds is memorable for its creation of many personal loyalties at odds with sociocultural ones. Three planets, Tannia, Erde, and Occo, circle the same sun. They were all originally colonized at the same time, but their human populations evolved along differing ideological lines, with Occo so far out of the others' way that they are generally unaware it holds an alien race. Anthony Northfied/ Anton Nordvelt is a literature teacher on a military base on Tannia, or at least, that's what he seems at first. The fact that he was actually the best ace fighter pilot for their vanquished enemies on Erde does not emerge until his services are needed by Tannia to protect them and Erde from an outside threat, one which turns out to be nonhuman. This plot would make for good space opera, except that Nordvelt actually meets the aliens as their slave and is predisposed towards one of them, a grounded pilot like himself. Again, the complexity of loyalties and honorable behavior are seminal to this novel.

Chicago Red is unlike Meluch's other works in that it occurs on Earth. Cataclysmic technological failures in the late 20th century have left Earth divided into virtually non-communicating totalitarian states. Chicago Red is a self-created revolutionary on the continent that formerly held the United States, but U.S. history has been erased to preserve the roughly feudal arrangement that now prevails. Kings, Kings' sons, Kings' assassins, rebels and revolutionaries, noblewomen and clergy, none are what they at first seem. In fact, one is hard-pressed to say if Chicago Red, or the villain General Tow, or the Archbishop Gregory Vandetti, is the protagonist of this novel, as their loyalties change or remain divided. And again, the novel gives no easy answers.

The Queen's Squadron is by far the most graphically violent of Meluch's works to date. Torture as a tool of oppression and a psychological experience is explored with detail that is reminiscent of Gene Wolfe's *Book of the New Sun*. And the trail on which she leads her readers is as disturbing as that of Elizabeth Lynn's *The Sardonyx Net*. These works all pursue a viewpoint on pain and pleasure that cannot fail to provoke equal amounts of sympathy and repulsion at what we as individuals and as a society do to each other. In *The Queen's Squadron,* the enemy of humanity is a group of virtually ageless gods, the Virkhalt, who run the universe for their pleasure and relentlessly annihilate all vestiges of rebellion from humans on the human worlds of Telegonia and New Earth. At least they think they are in control when war breaks out between major powers. It takes a grounded pilot, Race, former head of the immortals' own Queen's Squadron, and a Goddess Ashata/ Maya, who has discarded her immortal powers, to surmise that there is one real villain. This is also their love story, and the love story of an unlikely pair of men, joined by pain, the Squadron cadet turned torturer, Penetanguishine who also possesses the specialized mental ability to distinguish lie from truth, and his victim, the hapless pilot Paul Strand, who was charged with the secret of "Gotterdamerung," the plan to kill the immortals. This pair also takes on heroic proportions as they determine something of the necessary identity of the architect of civilizations' doom, an exiled immortal who plans to take over all of the worlds himself. No matter, the gods are killed, and mortals are left to formulate and live in a society without them. And we are left to consider whether the means justify the ends.

All of Meluch's novels show a genuine sensitivity to psychological development in the person of major characters. She has given a lot of thought to the cultures of her many worlds. This is especially evident in *War Birds, Jerusalem Fire,* and *The Queen's Squadron,* where vastly different cultures clash over vast distances, but her unique talent is in linking the success or failure of these larger social events with the moral strength of individuals, be they apparent villains or heroes.

—Janice M. Bogstad

MEREDITH, Richard C(arlton)

Nationality: American. **Born:** Alderson, West Virginia, 21 October 1937. **Education:** West Virginia State College, Institute, 1955-56; Pensacola Junior College, Florida, 1960-61; University of West Florida, Pensacola, B.A. 1972. **Military Service:** Served in the United States Army, 1957-60, 1962. **Family:** Married Joy Cecilia

Gates in 1963; three children. **Career:** Advertising manager, Grice Electronics Inc., Pensacola, 1962-69; cartoonist and columnist ("Spinoffs"), *Milton Press-Gazette,* Florida, 1972-75; editor, *Santa Rosa Free Press,* Milton, 1975; copy editor, *National Enquirer,* Lantana, Florida, 1976-77; freelance writer, illustrator, and graphic designer, 1977-79. **Awards:** Phoenix award, 1970. **Died:** 1979.

SCIENCE FICTION PUBLICATIONS

Novels (series: Timeliner)

The Sky Is Filled with Ships. New York, Ballantine, 1969; London, Legend, 1988.
We All Died at Breakaway Station. New York, Ballantine, 1969; London, Hamlyn, 1985.
Run, Come See Jerusalem! New York, Ballantine, 1976; London, Hamlyn, 1985.
The Awakening. New York, St. Martin's Press, 1979.
Timeliner Trilogy. London, Arrow, 1987.
  At the Narrow Passage (Timeliner). New York, Putnam, 1973; revised edition, Chicago, Playboy Press, 1979.
  No Brother, No Friend (Timeliner). Garden City, New York, Doubleday, 1976; revised edition, Chicago, Playboy Press, 1979.
  Vestiges of Time (Timeliner). Garden City, New York, Doubleday, 1978; revised edition, Chicago, Playboy Press, 1979.

* * *

The protagonists of Richard C. Meredith's fiction generally are reluctant and/or disabled heroes who are forced by circumstances to attempt to solve the mysteries of the strange worlds in which they have previously been mere functionaries. As in traditional quest tales, they uncover even more mystery until a resolution, not always the solution they seek, is reached. They face frequent crises and perform heroically, if not always wisely, in response to external threats. They usually endure deep pain and are quite often physically injured—in fact, it seems that Meredith needs to put his protagonists through as much physical hell as possible before they are allowed the answers they seek or the revelations that there are some areas of human existence they will never fully understand. However, they are not the usual action-adventure sort of heroes. During their moments of flight or hiding, they reflect often upon their actions, regretting the emotional or physical pain they have caused and the violence, with its often questionable killings, that their need for self-preservation has precipitated. As pain is the recurring problem of the characters, violence is perhaps the aspect of Meredith's work that best sums up the science fiction worlds he creates. Whether the story is about a contingent of handicapped warriors in outer space; a mercenary crossing alternate worlds, time, and space; or a time-traveller exploring facets of American history; the characters are frequently in a state of paranoiac apprehension, not knowing from where or when the next violent attack will come.

While Meredith's SF is thoroughly researched for its scientific and sociological aspects, he derives much of his inspiration from a finely honed sense of history. Science fiction is a field that attracts, in addition to hard-science promoters, social commentators, and literary aspirants, the history-influenced writer whose main impulse is to tamper with known history (time travel, alternate worlds) or to create complex future histories. Both of these impulses are found in Meredith's fiction and, in fact, he combines them skillfully in his Timeliner trilogy and his time travel tour de force (*Run, Come See Jerusalem!*). Many factors no doubt enter into an author's choice to write science fiction that has a strong historical bent, not the least of which is that it is definitely fun to play with history. Except for some dry leftover subjects, most of the exciting events and adventures of history have been adequately covered academically. On the other hand, the SF writer can deal with history extensively in time travel and alternate world stories. Additionally, such stories often necessitate speculation on historical subjects, an opportunity that Meredith takes full advantage of.

Run, Come See Jerusalem! not only presents well-researched historical material but also gives full treatment to the what-if theme of the traveller effecting historical change by his actions in the past. Further, it juxtaposes two possible 21st-century futures against each other to make not only cautionary statements about contemporary trends but also detailed future histories rich in political and social implications. Meredith seems to have realized, along with a few other writers like Fritz Leiber, Jack Finney, and Robert Silverberg, that history can be very much a subject of science fiction, integrated comfortably with its fantastic plots and themes to create worlds just as imaginative as deep-space colonies. Historically-based science fiction helps to enlarge or at least vitalize our perception of historical matters. Perhaps as a result of this interest in history, Meredith's plots are extremely complicated and skillful. For example, events introduced early in his trilogy fit neatly into later portions of the story, and figure in a nearly apocalyptic finale that brings back into action most of the novels' surviving characters.

Meredith's best novel, *We All Died at Breakaway Station,* is an elegiac space opera which incorporates many elements similar to those in his time and alternate world sagas. It also features his most fully realized protagonist, the slightly embittered but resilient Absolom Bracer, a starship captain who has died in battle and been resurrected and put back together as more machine than man. Before he makes his valiant last stand as defender of Breakaway Station, he reviews his life as a warrior and ponders the more metaphysical questions regarding his place in a cold and alien universe. Like all Meredith heroes, he wonders if the effort and the pain are worth the result, that is, being the leader for a crew of the functioning wounded. He decides he does not regret his warrior life, especially since he has reached his life goal, being a starship captain. He is able to die courageously, also without regret. He may not have found satisfying answers, but he has asked the most important questions. In spite of Absolom's death, Meredith achieves in this novel a glorification of courage that is—oddly, in our times—quite inspiring. *We All Died at Breakaway Station* is a kind of Horatio-at-the-bridge epic that is given extra dimension by its main character's questing intelligence, by the way its heroism transcends the adventure story requirements of the genre, and because of the dramatic and poignant sacrifices of its disabled, tortured, but brave men and women. It is intriguing that similar bravery by the protagonist of a later novel, *Run, Come See Jerusalem!,* results in a nearly opposite type of solution, the character's failure to create a better world where an already abominable one had existed.

Meredith's fiction is fast-paced, mysterious, and complex. He admirably blends philosophical reflection with high adventure to delineate the essential loneliness of his protagonists in an uncertain universe. A sympathetic observer of what is sometimes called the human condition, he infuses his novels and stories with intelligent compassion and a sense of what drives us to our sometimes disputable goals.

—Robert Thurston

657

MERRIL, Judith

Pseudonym for Josephine Juliet Grossman. **Other Pseudonym:** Cyril Judd. **Nationality:** Canadian. **Born:** New York City, 21 January 1923. **Education:** Attended City College of New York, 1939-40. **Family:** Married 1) Daniel A. Zissman in 1940 (divorced 1947), one daughter; 2) Frederik Pohl, *q.v.,* in 1949 (divorced 1953), one daughter; 3) Daniel W.P. Sugrue in 1960 (divorced 1975). **Career:** Research assistant and ghost writer, 1943-47; editor, Bantam Books, New York, 1947-49. Since 1949, freelance writer and lecturer: writing teacher, adult education program, Port Jervis, New York, 1963-64; director, Milford Science Fiction Writers Conference, 1956-61; book editor, *Fantasy and Science Fiction,* 1965-69; documentary scriptwriter, Canadian Broadcasting Corporation; commentator and performer, *Dr. Who,* TV Ontario. **Awards:** Canadian Science Fiction and Fantasy Life Achievement Award, 1986. Lives in Toronto. **Address:** c/o Porcepic Press, 4252 Commerce Circle, Victoria, British Columbia BC V8Z, Canada.

SCIENCE FICTION PUBLICATIONS

Novels

Shadow on the Hearth. Garden City, New York, Doubleday, 1950; London, Sidgwick and Jackson, 1953.
Gunner Cade (as Cyril Judd, with C.M. Kornbluth). New York, Simon and Schuster, 1952; London, Gollancz, 1964.
Outpost Mars (as Cyril Judd, with C.M. Kornbluth). New York, Abelard Press, 1952; London, New English Library, 1966; revised edition, as *Sin in Space,* New York, Galaxy, 1961.
The Tomorrow People: A Science-Fiction Novel. New York, Pyramid, 1960.
Gunner Cade; Plus, Takeoff, with C.M. Kornbluth. New York, Tor, 1983.

Short Stories

Out of Bounds: Seven Stories. New York, Pyramid, 1960.
Daughters of Earth. London, Gollancz, 1968; Garden City, New York, Doubleday, 1969; as *A Judith Merril Omnibus: Daughters of Earth and Other Stories,* Toronto, McClelland and Stewart, 1985.
Survival Ship, and Other Stories. Toronto, Kakabeka, 1974.
The Best of Judith Merril. New York, Warner, 1976.

OTHER PUBLICATIONS

Other

Editor, *Shot in the Dark.* New York, Bantam, 1950.
Editor, *Beyond Human Ken: Twenty-One Startling Stories of Science Fiction and Fantasy.* New York, Random House, 1952; London, Grayson, 1953; abridged as *Selections from Beyond Human Ken,* New York, Pennant, 1954.
Editor, *Beyond the Barriers of Space and Time.* New York, Random House, 1954; London, Sidgwick and Jackson, 1955.
Editor, *Human??????* New York, Lion, 1954.
Editor, *Galaxy of Ghouls.* New York, Lion, 1955; as *Off the Beaten Orbit,* New York, Pyramid, 1959.

Editor, *S-F: The Year's Greatest Science-Fiction and Fantasy 1-4,* continued as *The Year's Best S-F, 5th* [to *11th*] *Annual,* and *SF12.* New York, Dell, 4 vols., 1956-59; New York, Simon and Schuster, 5 vols., 1960-64; New York, Delacorte Press, 3 vols., 1965-68; as *SF '57* [to *'59*], New York, Gnome Press, 3 vols., 1957-59; as *The Best of Sci-Fi,* London, Mayflower, 5 vols., 1963-70.
Editor, *SF: The Best of the Best.* New York, Delacorte Press, 1967; London, Hart-Davis, 1968.
Editor, *England Swings SF: Stories of Speculative Fiction.* Garden City, New York, Doubleday, 1968; abridged edition, as *The Space-Time Journal,* London, Panther, 1972.
Editor, *Tesseracts.* Victoria, British Columbia, Porcepic Press, 1985.

*   *   *

Judith Merril has been so prominent as a reviewer and an editor that her fiction has been somewhat eclipsed. Her most widely known story is her first, "That Only a Mother." On one level, this tale shows the power of love to blind the lover to the flaws of the beloved and to see only his or her best parts. On another, it is a horror story about the effects of atomic radiation. The two levels combine thematically: atomic energy is a beloved creation with great power to do good for mankind, but we delude ourselves if we refuse to see its potential dangers. Not only does this theme remain relevant to present-day problems; the story bears rereading for the pleasure of the word play, one of Merril's strengths throughout her work. Her finest novel, *Shadow on the Hearth,* also deals with the danger of atomic energy. It focuses on a Westchester woman with two daughters battling to survive the aftermath of a nuclear attack while her husband is trapped in Manhattan. Quietly rather than militantly feminist and ameliorative rather than separatist, Merril portrays the domestic reality of coping not only with the dangers of radiation but also with the unwelcome advances of a neighbor who has somehow managed to set himself up as an official of the emergency authorities who wishes to become her protector.

Working as one of the very few women in the SF field during an era when women were usually dumped with robots and aliens and treated as plot features rather than characters, Merril introduced a "woman's angle"—fiction unlikely to have been written by a man, usually with a female central character, yet still (against the so-called wisdom of the publishing trade) exciting to readers of both sexes. While "Project Nursemaid" (*Daughters of Earth*) does have a male viewpoint character, its main concern is the selection of candidates for foster-mothering babies born in space. "Daughters of Earth" is also quite unusual for its time, chronicling six generations of female space explorers. Merril vividly portrays the interactions and reactions between mother and daughter, who then becomes the mother against whom the next generation must react, and so on. Perhaps her most imaginative story is the novella "Homecalling" (*Daughters of Earth*). Again concerned with beauty in the eye of the beholder and the power of love, it is the story of a girl and her baby brother, shipwrecked on a planet with no other human life, who are adopted by a benevolent but repulsively alien mother.

Although it is always difficult to assess the contributions of each individual in collaborations, the two novels Merril wrote with C.M. Kornbluth as Cyril Judd (*Gunner Cade* and *Outpost Mars*) seem to have benefitted from the strengths of both writers, exhibiting Kornbluth's crisp prose, Merril's full-range view of human experience, and their mutual respect for irony.

—Elizabeth Anne Hull

MERRITT, A(braham)

Nationality: American. **Born:** Beverly, New Jersey, 20 January 1884. **Education:** Philadelphia High School. **Family:** Married 1) Eleanor Ratcliffe (died); 2) Eleanor Humphrey; one daughter. **Career:** Reporter, then night city editor, *Philadelphia Inquirer,* 1902-11; staff member from 1912, and editor, 1937-43, *American Weekly.* **Died:** 30 August 1943.

SCIENCE FICTION PUBLICATIONS

Novels (series: Dr. Goodwin; Dr. Lowell)

The Moon Pool (Goodwin). New York and London, Putnam, 1919.
The Ship of Ishtar. New York and London, Putnam, 1926; original version, Los Angeles, Borden, 1949.
Seven Footprints to Satan. New York, Boni and Liveright, and London, Richards, 1928.
The Face in the Abyss. New York, Liveright, 1931; London, Futura, 1974.
Dwellers in the Mirage. New York, Liveright, 1932; London, Skeffington, 1933; original version, New York, Avon, 1944.
Burn, Witch, Burn! (Lowell). New York, Liveright, 1933; London, Methuen, 1934.
Creep, Shadow! (Lowell). Garden City, New York, Doubleday, Doran, 1934; as *Creep, Shadow, Creep!,* London, Methuen, 1935.
The Metal Monster (Goodwin). New York, Avon, 1946.
The Fox Woman, bound with *The Blue Pagoda,* by Hannes Bok. New York, New Collectors' Group, 1946.
The Black Wheel, completed by Hannes Bok. New York, New Collectors' Group, 1947.

Short Stories

Thru the Dragon Glass. Jamaica, New York, ARRA Printers, 1933.
Three Lines of Old French. Milheim, Pennsylvania, Bizarre Series, 1937.
The Drone Man. Sedalia, Colorado, M. Doreal, 1948.
The People of the Pit. Sedalia, Colorado, M. Doreal, 1948.
Rhythm of the Spheres. Sedalia, Colorado, M. Doreal, 1948.
Woman of the Wood. Sedalia, Colorado, M. Doreal, 1948.
The Challenge of Beyond, with others. N.p., William H. Evans, 1954; as *The Illustrated Challenge from Beyond,* West Warwick, Rhode Island, Necronomicon Press, 1978.
The Fox Woman, and Other Stories, edited by Donald A. Wollheim. New York, Avon, 1949.

OTHER PUBLICATIONS

Other

The Story behind the Story. Privately printed, 1942.

*

Bibliography: *A. Merritt: A Bibliography of Fantastic Writings* by Walter James Wentz, Los Angeles, Bibby, 1965.

*   *   *

A. Merritt is one of the most influential American science fiction writers after Edgar Rice Burroughs, though he is not nearly so well-known to the general public. A major reason for this is the paucity of his output (particularly as compared to Burroughs), though his relatively few novels have been almost continuously in print since World War II. He is generally regarded as a fantasist, but this is mainly a matter of changing standards in definition. A half-century ago, many matters were regarded as open to "scientific" speculation that are not currently, particularly in the area of the occult. Three of Merritt's eight completed novels concern themselves with the occult (*Burn, Witch, Burn!, Creep, Shadow!,* and *Seven Footprints to Satan,* the last being a variation on the archcriminal theme with occult and science fiction overtones), and one (*The Ship of Ishtar*) is very definitely a fantasy set in an alternate world of Babylonian mythology.

The remaining four, however, are given enough of a pseudoscientific rationale to qualify as science fiction in the romantic vein. There is a strong debt to H. Rider Haggard for the theme of "lost races" in what were then unknown corners of the world, as well as for the ever-popular idea of super-scientific knowledge from forgotten eras (certainly an idea back in vogue today). All this might be called anthropological speculation. *The Moon Pool* deals with a scientific party that penetrates the great caverns left beneath the Pacific when the Moon was ripped from the Earth. There they find the remnants of the ancient Lemurians, using the sophisticated technological instruments of their past. The conflict is with The Shining One, an entity created by the rulers of this land, three (implied) extraterrestrials, and now turned against them. *The Face in the Abyss* takes place in an unknown part of the Andes. Again there are the remnants of a lost civilization, here ruled by the snake Mother, the last of a race of intelligent beings descended from reptilian antecedents. The lost culture of *Dwellers in the Mirage* is a curious mix of Amerindian, Mongol, and Norse. Its people inhabit a valley in Alaska, which due to volcanic activity and thermal layers gives the illusion of a wasteland; underneath the mirage is a "lost world" of unique life forms. *The Metal Monster* takes a slightly different theme; the title creature is an alien life-form, a sentient metallic being with a sort of hive mentality that reproduces itself with astonishing vitality in the Himalayas.

Merritt wrote very much to pulp formula, that of rapidly paced adventure. There is inevitably conflict in these exotic locales, in which the protagonists from the outside world become involved, always on the "good" side. There are usually two women, one pure and beautiful to provide romantic interest for the hero, the other just the opposite; both are allied with the obvious sides of the conflict.

What Merritt brought to this formula that made his work so continuously popular was a remarkable writing style, called purple by his detractors, poetic by his followers. The super-scientific artifacts of the stories are given the barest minimum of scientific justification; their functions and activities are described in extremely visual, highly sensuous ways, as are the exotic flora, fauna, and natural phenomena. The result is far from the usual pulp writing of the time in its evocative imagery.

Because of their magazine origins and other factors, Merritt's works have often appeared in several variations and combinations. *The Moon Pool* is the combination of two shorter works ("The Moon Pool" and "The Conquest of the Moon Pool"), as is *The Face in the Abyss* ("The Face in the Abyss" and "The Snake Mother"). *Dwellers in the Mirage* has alternate endings. There is also a handful of short stories and fragments, two of which were completed by the artist Hannes Bok.

—Baird Searles

MERWIN, Sam(uel Kimball), Jr.

Pseudonyms: Elizabeth Deare Bennett; Angela Davidson; Jacques Jean Ferrat; Matt Lee; Carter Sprague; Rebecca Noyes Winstead. **Nationality:** American. **Born:** Plainfield, New Jersey, 28 April 1910. **Education:** Phillips Academy, Andover, Massachusetts, graduated 1927; Princeton University, New Jersey, B.A. 1931; Boston Museum School of Fine Arts. **Family:** Married 1) Lee Anna Vance in 1934 (died); 2) Marjory Kendal Davenport in 1959 (divorced); 3) Amanda Varela in 1972; two children. **Career:** Reporter, *Boston Evening American,* 1932-33; New York Bureau Chief, *Philadelphia Inquirer,* 1936-37; associate editor, Dell publishers, 1937-38; staff writer, *Country Home,* New York, 1938-39; sports and mystery editor, Standard Magazines, 1941-51, and King Size Publications, 1952-53: editor, *Startling Stories,* 1945-51, *Fantastic Story Magazine,* 1950-51, *Wonder Stories Annual,* 1950-51, and *Thrilling Wonder Stories,* 1951-54; editor, *Fantastic Universe,* 1953; associate editor, *Galaxy,* 1953-54; editor, Renown Publications, 1955-56, 1975-79, and Brandon House, 1966-67.

SCIENCE FICTION PUBLICATIONS

Novels (series: Elspeth Marriner and Mack Fraser)

The House of Many Worlds (Marriner). Garden City, New York, Doubleday, 1951.
Killer to Come. New York, Abelard Press, 1953; London, Abelard Schuman, 1959.
The White Widows. Garden City, New York, Doubleday, 1953; as *The Sex War,* New York, Galaxy, 1960.
Three Faces of Time (Marriner). New York, Ace, 1955; London, Badger, 1960.
The Time Shifters. New York, Lancer, 1971.
Chauvinisto. Canoga Park, California, Major, 1976.

OTHER PUBLICATIONS

Novels

Murder in Miniatures. Garden City, New York, Doubleday, 1940.
Death in the Sunday Supplement. New York, Gateway, 1942; abridged as *The Big Frame: A Mystery Novel,* New York, Handi-Books, 1943.
The Flags Were Three: A Novel of Old New Orleans, with Leo Margulies. New York, Curl, 1945; London, Hurst and Blackett, 1948.
Message from a Corpse: An Amy Brewster Mystery. New York, Mystery House, 1945; London, Quality Press, 1947.
Knife in My Back. New York, Mystery House, 1945; London, Quality Press, 1947.

A Matter of Policy: An Amy Brewster Mystery. New York, Mystery House, 1946; London, Quality Press, 1952.
Body and Soul (novelization of screenplay). Chicago, Century, 1947.
The Creeping Shadow. New York, Fawcett, 1952.
Regatta Summer (as Elizabeth Deare Bennett). New York, Dell, 1974.
Tunnel of Darkness (as Rebecca Noyes Winstead). Chatsworth, California, Canyon Books, 1974; as *The Forbidden Mansion* (as Angela Davidson), 1981.
Gower Court Manner (as Elizabeth Deare Bennett). New York, Dell, 1976.
The House of Many Worlds (omnibus; includes *Three Faces of Time; Marriner; Fraser*). New York, Ace, 1983.

Plays

Screenplay: *Manhunt in the Jungle,* with Owen Crump, 1958.

Television Plays: *The Star Slavers (Lights Out* series), 1951; *The Big Score (Alfred Hitchcock Presents* series), 1963.

Other

Confessions of a Scoundrel, with Guido Orlando. Philadelphia, Winston, 1954.

*

Sam Merwin, Jr. comments:

Although I have done more work in other fields, SF has been my favorite field since the mid-1950s. I have never sought to re- or in-form the world via such fiction, but have sought to entertain and, perhaps, to increase understanding through the introduction of speculative thought. I consider SF to be the other side of the IF.

*   *   *

Sam Merwin wandered into the science fiction field from another area of literature and apparently was never totally at home in science fiction, much like Erle Stanley Gardner, Howard Browne, and John D. MacDonald. Like Browne, Merwin achieved a notable career as a science fiction magazine editor.

Although Merwin has expressed a *pro forma* fondness for science fiction, most of his early works and the majority of his novels were mysteries. His first novel, a mystery called *Murder in Miniatures,* was published in 1940 (antedated, however, by at least one science fiction short story). His science fiction novels, for the most part, read more like mysteries than science fiction. They are grounded in the present and on Earth, with realistic settings and many details of architecture, weather, clothing, food, and drink.

Merwin repeatedly used such themes as time travel and parallel worlds. But in his time-travel novels, such as *The Time Shifters* or *Killer to Come,* he brought the time travelers to the present rather than moving contemporary figures into past or future eras. In his parallel-reality novels, such as *The House of Many Worlds* and *Three Faces of Time,* the alternate present-era images are not greatly different from conventional reality.

Favorite themes in Merwin's novels were political conspiracies and/or murder plots. *The White Widows* is a science fiction novel concerning a feminist conspiracy to wipe out the male gender through an induced haemophelia plague.

The son of a distinguished literary man, Merwin received a fine education in a series of prestigious institutions. This exposure is evident in his repeated choice of various institutes and universities as settings for his works, juxtaposing them frequently with bars, bedrooms, and even nudist camps for dramatic contrast.

In general, Merwin's science fiction novels read more like intended mysteries into which science-fictional devices have been implanted rather than like books intended from the outset as science fiction. They are fast-paced and generally pleasant. The style owes more to the hardboiled mystery than to traditional science fiction; it is marked by the occasional infelicitous phrase or jumbled imagery, but more often flows effortlessly.

Merwin's career as an editor was distinguished and deserves to be remembered. Regarding his tenure at *Thrilling Wonder Stories* and its subsidiary titles, Lester del Rey commented: "Things improved with the Winter issue of 1945, when Sam Merwin took over from (Oscar) Friend. Merwin imposed much higher standards . . . (and) sought good adventure stories with the best writing he could find." Merwin wrote a number of science fiction short stories in the 1940s and became quite prolific at the shorter lengths in the 1950s. He indulged rather heavily in the slightly dubious (but very common) practice of selling fiction to himself, for magazines he edited, sometimes disguising the practice through the use of pseudonyms. Some of his short fiction is more science-fictional in feeling and in theme than are his science fiction novels. Although no collection of his short fiction has appeared, a fair number of the stories are available in anthologies.

In his later years, Merwin worked as a paperback editor for a Los Angeles firm known for its pornographic paperbacks. He wrote a number of such books, reviving his onetime science fiction pseudonym of Carter Sprague for this purpose. These books, however, are of little merit.

—Richard A. Lupoff

MILLER, P(eter) Schuyler

Nationality: American. **Born:** 21 February 1912. **Education:** Union College, Schenectady, New York, B.S. in chemistry 1932. **Career:** Administrator in audio-visual education, Schenectady public schools; editor and technical writer, Fischer Scientific Company, Pittsburgh, 1949-74. Book reviewer ("The Reference Library"), *Astounding*, 1951-74; editor, *Pennsylvania Archaeologist;* research associate, Carnegie Museum. **Awards:** Hugo award, for nonfiction, 1963. **Died:** 12 October 1974.

Science Fiction Publications

Novel

Genus Homo, with L. Sprague de Camp. Reading, Pennsylvania, Fantasy Press, 1950.

Short Stories

The Titan. Reading, Pennsylvania, Fantasy Press, 1952; London, Weidenfeld and Nicolson, 1954.

Alicia in Blunderland (parody), edited by Lloyd Arthur Eshbach. Philadelphia, Train, 1983.

*

Critical Study: *A Canticle for P. Schuyler Miller* by Sam Moskowitz, privately printed, 1975.

*   *   *

P. Schuyler Miller is best known for his reviews, covering most books worth mention over 23 years, a service of enormous value and influence. His approach was balanced optimism, looking for whatever values books had on any level. He kept history and context in mind, often interpolating short essays on ideas and trends. His criticism was neither bland nor shallow, but his more penetrating observations were briefly stated for the student to probe further. His own stories had made him a familiar name in the magazines from 1930, and his writing had developed somewhat as the general ambiance did.

In early years, he was often compared to A. Merritt, though he is not very similar to modern eyes. Early Miller stories tend to be written in a florid style, though story and character are closer to real life than to heroic myth, and there is a down-to-earth awareness of the natural world that gives a strongly visualised location. The impressions of landscape, forest and mountain, and living environment, contrast with many contemporaries' romantically vague and perfunctory settings. His early story "The Red Plague" is "more of a well-written plot synopsis for a novel than a short story" as Sam Moskowitz remarks—true of innumerable early SF stories. There is a menace—a chain-reaction mineral blight of dust absorbing all surface water—and Martians, who have beaten the problem, provide the answer. But the voyage to Mars is vividly written and shows an original thinker's own vision of the remote prospect of space flight. "Through the Vibrations" and its sequel, "Cleon of Yzdral," has a world of abandoned automated cities, located on a different wavelength from Earth. "The Arrhenius Horror" is an exotic crystalline life-form falling as particles from space. "If life is energy, why should it not rest where it will?" SF was opening new vistas of what other worlds might produce that was not Earth over again. Later, Miller came back to the thought in "Spawn," a grim, powerful story of particles from beyond carrying elemental vitality that started new life in inanimate matter: a colloidal mass in the sea, a monster of gold, and a dead man revived as something else. "Tetrahedra of Space" deals with an invasion force of crystal beings from Mercury, not simply fought off but frightened off and diverted to more suitable Mars. "The Atom Smasher" predicts release of nuclear energy as an uncontrollable mountain-blasting discharge. "The Pool of Life" is an amorphous entity mentally controlling subhumans in a cave environment, treated as soberly as such a concept can be.

Many stories exploit the prewar vision of the interplanetary future. "The Forgotten Man of Space" is about a man, marooned and adopted by primitive Martians, who dies protecting them from genocide by human exploiters. Several collaborations with Dennis and McDermott treat space piracy with amoral realism, the thoroughly evil pirate evading justice. "The Flame of Life" is an early Space Patrol episode, set on the rainforest Venus of yore, as are others like "Old Man Mulligan," "Bird Walk," "Cuckoo," and "In the Good Old Summertime," introducing novel fauna. Others later move to the fanciful interstellar sphere. "Gleeps" lightly handles the intelligent alien mimicking people. "Trouble on Tantalus" goes back to the jungle adventure tradition on a world full of curiosities.

Miller's most distinctive work is the short novel *The Titan.* Unfortunately it was revised into the idiom of the 1950s for its only complete publication (the original serialisation is incomplete). The change from first to third person lessens the impact of this story of crisis in an age-old, decadent Martian civilisation, told from a native leader's viewpoint, and the tighter style lacks the color and charm of the early version.

The satire *Alicia in Blunderland,* brings together such dominant figures as Verne, Wells, Burroughs, Merritt, Cummings, Smith, Campbell, and Hamilton, and many early science fiction characters and phenomena most ingeniously, in a frenzied journey through imaginary worlds. It exposes weaknesses in many conventions and pretensions, with throwaway comments such as, "Nobody can ever get into a Utopia, they just build them and leave them there." Standard plot developments of the time are paraded in a ritual parodying the Saying of the Law in Wells's *The Island of Dr. Moreau,* as The Formula: "Never to win too soon/Hope for Mankind must be lost/Three dauntless heroes must rise/Like three damn fools they go forth/One must be slain by the Things/One must be martyred for Man/One must return with the tale . . . ." The book is a valuable period piece for its critical perspective.

—Graham Stone

MILLER, Walter M(ichael), Jr.

Nationality: American. **Born:** New Smyrna Beach, Florida, 23 January 1922. **Education:** University of Tennessee, Knoxville, 1940-42; University of Texas, Austin, 1947-49. **Military Service:** Served in the United States Army Air Force, 1942-45. **Family:** Married Anna Louise Becker in 1945; three daughters and one son. **Career:** Freelance writer. **Awards:** Hugo award, 1955, 1961. **Address:** c/o G.K. Hall, 70 Lincoln Street, Boston, Massachusetts 02111, U.S.A.

SCIENCE FICTION PUBLICATIONS

Novel

A Canticle for Leibowitz: A Novel. Philadelphia, Lippincott, and London, Weidenfeld and Nicolson, 1960.

Short Stories

Conditionally Human. New York, Ballantine, 1962; London Gollancz, 1963.
The View from the Stars. New York, Ballantine, and London, Gollancz, 1965.
The Science Fiction Stories of Walter M. Miller, Jr. Boston, Gregg Press, 1978.
The Best of Walter M. Miller, Jr. New York, Pocket Books, 1980; as *Conditionally Human and Other Stories* and *The Darfstellar and Other Stories,* London, Corgi, 1982.

OTHER PUBLICATIONS

Other

Editor, with Martin H. Greenberg, *Beyond Armageddon: Twenty-One Sermons to the Dead.* New York, Fine, 1985; as *Beyond Armageddon: Survivors of the Megawar,* London, Robinson, 1987.

*   *   *

An engineer by profession, a Catholic by conversion, Walter M. Miller, Jr. brought both points of view to bear on the use of science and technology in some 41 stories and novellas of the 1950s, honing his writing skills to the peak achieved by his much-lauded novel, *A Canticle for Leibowitz.*

Amid his 1951 apprentice work, the novella "Dark Benediction" shows control of local color and romance psychology in a study of faith and prejudice. Gray and scaly "dermies," unable to control their urge to touch and transform others, are being exiled or killed. Sympathetic to one such mob victim in the early stages of her infection, Paul Oberlin takes her to priestly controlled Galveston Island, where he learns the truth. A meteor shower brought alien spores to Earth in an ironic invasion story that inverts the story of Pandora's Box. The benefits outweigh the disadvantages for those who are able to accept this gift of heaven's grace.

The next year, Miller published 15 pieces, eight of them good, three outstanding. A classic statement of wanderlust, "The Big Hunger" is a prose poem about waves of space travellers and homebodies over millennia of human change, if not development. An ironic commentary on conformity is "Command Performance." Resenting her suburban wifely role, Lisa resists her telepathic talent until it saves her from another telepath, intent on breeding supermen with her. With him eliminated, her loneliness sets in again, and she tries out her new communication channel, tentatively, as he too must once have done. "Conditionally Human" concerns playing God with life and death, as man elevates "lower" animals to substitute for babies in an overcrowded, overregulated world. Terry Norris, a veterinarian, must choose between killing a "neutroid" (a chimp-baby too smart and pretty and humanly viable, i.e., a deviant) or keeping his wife who wants children herself. Terry can't avoid playing God, but he plays it his way, killing his supervisor and taking a new job, helping to create more deviants. In making this choice, he opts for a race which "hasn't picked an apple yet," i.e., has no original sin.

Miller's best short story is "Crucifixus Etiam" (1953). Manue Nanti, a Peruvian laborer, works to help terraform Mars, and suffers acclimatization to the technology needed to keep him alive. Though he comes to realize he can never go home again to spend his earnings, he finds his sacrifice worthwhile, an act of faith in future generations.

In "The Ties that Bind" (1954), a novella pitting a far-future pacifist Earth society against the militarism of a fleet refueling at the old home world, the innocent pastoralists are the more dangerous, their ancestry including the inner hell with which Earth once infected a whole galaxy. Ambitious formally, this tale of original sin interweaves viewpoints and themes with stanzas from the old ballad "Edward." "Death of a Spaceman" (1954; often reprinted as "Memento Homo") is a sentimental elegy to a man whose decrepit body lies in bed while his heart remains in space. A more ambitious variation on the theme of clipped wings is "The Hoofer" (1955), in which an itinerant entertainer comes home to Earth for the last time, his story combining slapstick with tragedy. "The Darfsteller" (1955) is a tale of technological displacement which also comments ironically on the paradox of free will and determinism. In telling the story of an aging matinee idol's near-tragic comeback, replacing a mannequin in an automated stage play, Miller adheres strictly to the actor's egotistical and stage-infatuated point of view. No mere entertainer, he is a genuine artist, for whom the "Maestro," the performance's mechanical producer-director, really has no tolerance. But though he is doomed to lose, the actor becomes more fully human by making this last stand. Miller's last published story, "The Lineman" (1957), portrays a day in the life of a lunar worker, when a travelling whorehouse puts the crew off schedule. Mixing humor and pathos, Miller shows his main character learning to see that God created man and the universe on pretty equal footing.

These stories would be memorable enough, without his novel. But they pale by comparison with what may be the one universally acknowledged literary masterpiece to emerge from magazine SF. First published as three novellas, *A Canticle for Leibowitz* in book form is still a triptych. Each of its three "books" reaches 600 years further into the future, viewing history from the vantage point of the Abbey of Leibowitz, somewhere in the American southwest. Each era is sharply etched, its characters clearly limned as plausible citizens of the City of God, simultaneously resisting and accommodating the City of Dys (Earthly life), as mankind struggles back from nuclear war to recycled Medieval, Renaissance, and Modern eras. Named for a Jewish engineer, a "booklegger" who memorized forbidden texts in the "Age of Simplicity" following the war, the Order of Leibowitz is committed to the preservation of knowledge, interpretation and use of which lie in secular hands.

In "Fiat Homo" (Let There Be Man), sheer survival is at issue, with marauding tribes threatening each other more than the Abbey. The story centers on Brother Francis's attempts to serve his order and mankind by finding, illuminating, and ultimately giving his life for a blueprint initialled by the Blessed Leibowitz and revealed to Francis by a wandering Jew. Church and State are in equilibrium in "Fiat Lux" (Let There Be Light). A secular scholar visits the Abbey to find his theories of electricity put into practice by Brother Kornhoer, providing artificial illumination over the objections of Brother Armbruster, the librarian, thus enabling the scholar to read—and misread—the Memorabilia. Between the Abbot and the scholar, a parasitic one-eyed Poet and the Wandering Jew, cross-dialogues reveal the misunderstandings that result from differing premises. The balance of power is secular again in "Fiat Voluntas Tua" (Thy Will Be Done), an allegory of contemporary history. As nuclear war erupts ("Lucifer is fallen"), the Abbot resists euthanasia clinics while Brother Joshua prepares to lead a remnant of clergy and children to Alpha Centauri, where another attempt will be made to temper technology with wisdom.

Moving enough in bare outline, the story is enriched in the telling. Olympian irony conveys "what fools these mortals be" even as warm humor makes us care about them. The comedy ranges from puns to slapstick to central symbols of misunderstanding. Elaborate jokes escape the confines of one book to echo in another (the blueprint of I, the dynamo and a fragment of *R.U.R.* in II, the Poet's satiric verse in III). Continuity is maintained by location and tradition; each era remembers its predecessors, sometimes mistakenly. Light imagery, the Wandering Jew and his eternal skepticism, an enigmatic statue of him and/or of Leibowitz carved in Book I all mock at pretenses to human wisdom. Names and events resound with symbolism, from the simple Francis to the equally simple old

woman, Mrs. Grales, whose quest to have her second head, Rachel, blessed by the Abbot, is reversed at the end when Rachel awakes to bless the Abbot, pinned beneath rubble as the bombs fall, because she alone is untainted by original sin. A weighty but entertaining novel, science fiction's best exposure of the "human comedy," *A Canticle for Leibowitz* is a fitting capstone to Miller's writing career.

—David N. Samuelson

MITCHELL, Clyde T. *See* **GARRETT, Randall.**

MOFFETT, Judith

Nationality: American. **Born:** Louisville, Kentucky, 30 August 1942. **Education:** Hanover College, Indiana, 1960-64, B.A. (cum laude) 1964; Colorado State University, Fort Collins, 1964-66, M.A. in English 1966; University of Wisconsin, Madison, 1966-67; University of Pennsylvania, Philadelphia, 1969-71, M.A. 1970, Ph.D. in American civilization 1971. **Family:** Married Edward B. Irving in 1983. **Career:** Fulbright lecturer, University of Lund, Sweden, 1967-68; assistant professor, Behrend College, Pennsylvania State University, Erie, 1971-75; visiting lecturer, Program in Creative Writing, University of Iowa, Iowa City, 1977-78. Visiting lecturer, 1978-79, assistant professor of English, 1979-86, adjunct assistant professor, 1986-88, adjunct associate professor, 1988-93, adjunct professor, 1993-94, University of Pennsylvania. **Awards:** Fulbright grant, 1967, 1973; American Philosophical Society grant, 1973; Swedish Institute grant, 1973, 1976, 1983; Nathhorst Foundation (Sweden) grant, 1973; Eunice Tietjens memorial prize, 1973, and Levinson prize, 1976 (*Poetry*, Chicago); Borestone Mountain poetry award, 1976; Ingram Merrill grant, 1977, 1980, 1991; Columbia University translation prize, 1978; Bread Loaf Writers Conference Tennessee Williams fellowship, 1978; Swedish Academy translation prize, 1982; National Endowment for the Humanities translation fellowship, 1983; National Endowment for the Arts fellowship, 1984; Theodore Sturgeon Memorial award, 1987; John W. Campbell award, 1988. **Agent:** Martha Millard, 204 Park Avenue, Madison, New Jersey 07940, U.S.A. **Address:** 951 East Laird Avenue, Salt Lake City, Utah 84105, U.S.A.

SCIENCE FICTION PUBLICATIONS

Novels (series: Hefn)

Pennterra. New York, Congdon and Weed, 1987; London, New English Library, 1988.
The Ragged World: A Novel of the Hefn on Earth. New York, St. Martin's Press, 1991.
Time, Like an Ever-Rolling Stream: A Sequel to The Ragged World (Hefn). New York, St. Martin's Press, 1992.

Short Stories

Two That Came True. Eugene, Oregon, Pulphouse Press, 1991.

OTHER PUBLICATIONS

Poetry

Keeping Time: Poems. Baton Rouge, Louisiana State University Press, 1976.
Whinny Moor Crossing. Princeton, New Jersey, Princeton University Press, 1984.

Other

James Merrill: An Introduction to the Poetry. New York, Columbia University Press, 1984.
Homestead Year: Going Back to the Land in the Suburbs. New York, Lyons and Burford, 1995.

Translator, *Single, Refined, and Selected Poems 1937-1959* by Hjalmar Gullberg. Baton Rouge and Stockholm, Louisiana State University Press/Norstedts, 1979.

*

Manuscript Collection: Hanover College, Hanover, Indiana.

*   *   *

The protagonist of Judith Moffett's story "Tiny Tango" (in *The Year's Best Science Fiction*, edited by Gardner Dozois, New York, St. Martin's Press, 1990) is HIV-positive, and part of a dwindling group of similarly affected people in the years just after a vaccine has been made available. Without a cure, Moffett's characters live with the knowledge that sooner or later they will develop AIDS. This story is typical of Moffett's determination to tackle major issues in her fiction in a manner that deals with real people in very human ways. "Tiny Tango" considers a post-AIDS society convincingly, and sensitively, but it also approaches other aspects of life neglected in mainstream SF. Sandy, the narrator of "Tiny Tango," contracted the virus from her only lover, and effectively isolated herself from then on, concentrating on her work as a professor of plant biology. Throughout the novella, scenes of Sandy experimenting in her own garden are interspersed with scenes of Sandy as part of the HIV-positive victims' group she belongs to, noting the personal turmoils, the group relationships, and watching the numbers grow, at first, and then after the vaccine is discovered, dwindle slowly. Moffett makes reference to mass persecutions and rioting as AIDS panic sets in; it is a bleak vision, told with humanity. Perhaps the ending, or one of the endings to this multi-streamed story, in which Aliens provide the eventual cure, is a little too easy, but the author compensates with a series of difficult scenes. In the early days, Sandy uses pornography to relieve her sexual tensions, later she cross-dresses and, using a prosthetic, visits male urinals and watches other men. Whilst this may not justify the warning placed upon the story in *Isaac Asimov's Science Fiction Magazine,* it is certainly strong material.

Moffett's debut novel, *Pennterra,* is equally strong. The planet Pennterra has been colonised by a group of Quakers who respect, sometimes grudgingly, the native Hrossa's injunctions to remain in the valley of their original settlement and to refrain from using heavy machinery. The dilemma arises when the second wave of colonists arrive. They aren't prepared to accept these rules and suspect the Quakers have been brainwashed. The Hrossa warn of dire consequences, as the planet itself will destroy the intruders. On this level, *Pennterra* is an interesting ecological novel, with imaginative use of the Gaia concept. But Moffett doesn't leave it there. In making her major characters Quakers, she is obviously seeking to address the issue of response to conflict. The conflict between the two groups of colonists is further complicated by Quaker guilt because Pennterra seems so perfect for the people starving on over-crowded Earth, yet they must do what the Hrossa say. There is also personal conflict; George, the principal Quaker, is a former lover of Maggie, a leader of the second group; and there is a long and important passage that incorporates a great deal of sexual turmoil. The Hrossa are semi-telepathic, semi-empathic creatures with an individual and a collective personality. George and his son Danny, along with two other Quakers, Katy and Bob, spend time in the Hrossa village, where they come under the influence of the waves of sexual energy emitted by the Breeder Hrossa. This causes them to become highly active sexually, and the group relationships are confused. Moffett reveals her liking for difficult issues here, for Danny is just 13 years old, but during the height of the Hrossa breeding he has sex with both Katy and George. At times, this section of the novel tends to become obsessed and over-detailed, but it is generally in the dictates of the plot, and Moffett provides no easier answers on a highly-controversial subject. In the final section of the novel, where Pennterra does try to destroy the new arrivals in a variety of imaginative yet logical ways, Moffett also deals with incest and child abuse, further muddying the waters. Or perhaps clarifying what has gone before? She does seem to be prepared to justify the relationship between George and Danny, emotionally, whilst recognising the dangers inherent there. Despite the fact that the narrator of almost half this novel is a pubescent boy, this is very clearly an adult novel, to be approached by a reader prepared to be challenged.

Moffett was a successful poet before turning to prose. Her first published short story, "Surviving," won the Theodore Sturgeon Memorial award. Superficially, "Surviving" (in *The Best from Fantasy and Science Fiction,* edited by Edward L. Ferman, New York, St. Martin's Press, 1989) is a female-variant on Tarzan, but beneath the surface the same obsessions arise again and again. Sally Barnes, a "chimp child," develops a friendship with anthropologist Janet Morgan, but ultimately decides her future happiness lies with the chimps. It is a poignant tale, one that asserts positive things about female-female relationships, mutual nudity, and bodily functions. It has a form of ground-level detail that other feminist, or women-oriented SF writers have passed over, perhaps as part of the general body distaste that SF as a whole has inherited from society. Moffett is certainly an exception in this respect, and further provocative stories and novels should only make her more exceptional.

Judith Moffett's "Tiny Tango" and her other stories about the alien visitors called the Hefn were incorporated into the novels *The Ragged World* and *Time, Like an Ever-Rolling Stream.* The former in particular is a carefully structured work which avoids many of the pitfalls of such fix-up novels.

The Hefn arrive on Earth early in the next century with a blunt warning—stop destroying the Earth or we will destroy you. Although one of Moffett's characters is an influential U.S. senator, the stories all focus on individuals and the way in which their own problems are solved in relation to the Hefn. It transpires that many popular folk tales, such as the Yorkshire Hob and the Swedish Tomte, were based on the survivors of a previous, secret Hefn visit centuries ago. The Quaker beliefs which form the basis of *Pennterra* only make a brief appearance overtly, but there is a deeply spiritual strength which ultimately pervades all of Moffett's most sympathetic characters which is clearly rooted in Quaker philosophy. This lies in an intensely humane view of personal relationships which Moffett develops, not without tragedy.

Thus what originally appeared to be a deux ex machina climax to "Tiny Tango" in its shorter form, can be seen as something more of the order of a paradigm shift in the novel. New approaches to stock SF clichés are offered through a simple, matter-of-fact statement that "this is how we could be, if we want." Without ever explicitly preaching Judith Moffett makes a potent case for Quaker beliefs of tolerance and understanding and the benefits of meditation.

—Kev P. McVeigh

MONTELEONE, Thomas F.

Nationality: American. **Born:** Baltimore, Maryland, 14 April 1946. **Education:** University of Maryland, College Park, B.S. in Psychology 1968, M.A. in English 1973. **Family:** Married 1) Natalie Monteleone in 1969 (divorced 1979), one son; 2) Linda Smith in 1981, one son. **Career:** Psychotherapist, C.T. Perkins Hospital, Jessup, Maryland, 1969-78. Secretary, Science Fiction Writers of America, 1976-78. **Awards:** (for television play): Gabriel award, 1984; International Television and Film award, 1984; Maryland State Arts Council award, 1991. **Agent:** Howard Morhaim Literary Agency, 175 Fifth Avenue, New York, New York 10010, U.S.A. **Address:** P.O. Box 5788, Baltimore, Maryland 21208, U.S.A.

SCIENCE FICTION PUBLICATIONS

Novels (series: Dragonstar)

Seeds of Change. Don Mills, Ontario, Laser, 1975.
The Time Connection. New York, Popular Library, 1976; London, Hale, 1979.
The Time-swept City. New York, Popular Library, 1977.
The Secret Sea. New York, Popular Library, 1979; London, Hale, 1981.
Guardian. Garden City, New York, Doubleday, 1980.
Night Things. New York, Fawcett, 1980.
Ozymandias. Garden City, New York, Doubleday, 1981.
Day of the Dragonstar, with David F. Bischoff. New York, Berkley, 1983.
Night-Train. New York, Pocket Books, 1984.
Night of the Dragonstar, with David F. Bischoff. New York, Berkley, 1985.
Lyrica: A Novel of Horror and Desire. New York, Berkley, 1987.
Fantasma. New York, Tor, 1987.
The Crooked House, with John de Chancie. New York, Tor, 1987.
The Magnificent Gallery. New York, Tor, 1987.

Dragonstar Destiny, with David F. Bischoff. New York, Ace, 1989.
The Blood of the Lamb. New York, Tor, 1992; London, Orion, 1993.

Short Stories

Dark Stars and Other Illuminations. Garden City, New York, Doubleday, 1981.

OTHER PUBLICATIONS

Plays

U.F.O.!, with Grant Carrington (produced Ashton, Maryland, 1977).
Mister Magister (produced Silver Spring, Maryland, 1978). Included in *Dark Stars and Other Illuminations,* 1981.

Screenplays: *Sun-Treader,* 1983; *Three, Two, One: Countdown to Love,* 1984; *The Nowhere Man,* 1985.

Television Plays: *Mister Magister,* 1983; *Spare the Child,* 1983.

Other

Editor, *The Arts and Beyond: Visions of Man's Aesthetic Future.* Garden City, New York, Doubleday, 1977.
Editor, *Random Access Messages of the Computer Age.* Hasbrouck Heights, New Jersey, Hayden, 1984; as *Microworlds,* London, Hamlyn, 1985.
Editor, *Borderlands [1]-3: An Anthology of Imaginative Fiction.* Baltimore, Maclay and Associates, 1990-93.

*

Manuscript Collection: University of Maryland, Baltimore.

Thomas F. Monteleone comments:

(1981) Although my early novels were little more than adventure fiction, I feel that the majority of my work intends to be more thought-provoking and imaginative. I think my short fiction reflects my desire to employ imagery, symbol, and ironic statement to create stories which make my readers think. I do not write "hard" SF; rather I find myself most comfortable in dealing with the softer sciences such as psychology, anthropology, and sociology. The main emphasis in my fiction seems to be people, and the way our technology and society influence them. Themes which are important to me are love, conscience, responsibility, creativity, and man's dual nature.

(1985) Since 1980, my writing has shifted away from SF per se, and explored the areas of horror, dark fantasy, and more speculative, "weird tales" kinds of fiction. I enjoy the greater freedom to explore character in the novel of suspense or horror. Although I am primarily a novelist now, I still write an occasional short story, and I believe the well-crafted short story is the most difficult form to master. Also, in recent years, I have become interested in writing for film and television, having had several pieces produced for both media. My intentions for the future are simple enough: keep writing.

* * *

Thomas F. Monteleone is one of several writers who started out writing science fiction adventures stories and who eventually switched to supernatural horror where he proved far more successful, in fact recently won the coveted Bram Stoker award for outstanding achievement at novel length for *The Blood of the Lamb,* an ambitious novel that mixes the traditional supernatural with Christian mythology. The change of genre was by choice, not necessity; his light adventure stories set in other times and places are invariably entertaining, and often successfully capture the sense of wonder that is one of the field's chief assets.

Monteleone's debut novel was *Seeds of Change,* a promotional paperback published to introduce the ill-fated Laser Book line. Denver Citiplex is a dehumanized, computer-governed city in which humans are mere cogs in the machinery of state. This simply plotted novel of a successful rebellion against the power structure was slow paced and colorless, fortunately untypical of his later, more complex efforts.

The next three novels were unabashed pastiches of older forms. *The Time Connection* is a time spanning adventure in the tradition of the best of Edmond Hamilton. A young man encounters a woman in the desert who tells him that she is able to listen to sounds inaudible to the rest of the world. The pair are transported to a remote future where alien war machines patrol the ruins of the planet, which is inhabited solely by a few survivors from the alien invasion force which destroyed the human race. After a series of adventures, they find the remnants of humanity in a hidden installation. Monteleone uses a clear, crisp style ideally suited for the plot and his description of the ruined Earth is often haunting.

The Secret Sea was even more interesting, this time invoking the spirit of Jules Verne. An adventurer travels to a parallel world and is taken aboard Captain Nemo's Nautilus, subsequently discovering that it is this world that provided the source of inspiration for many of Verne's adventure stories. The protagonist is swept up in a battle between Nemo and Robert Burton, Robur the Conqueror, and plays a key role before being returned to his home. It's a playful story with no pretensions to grandeur, but well constructed and exciting throughout.

Several of Monteleone's short stories were cobbled together into a future history of sorts in *The Time-swept City.* The immortal city of Chicago is described by a series of anecdotal stories as the ages pass. Typical episodes include a cyborg falling in love, a priest dealing with the passing of the legal immunity of religion, the advent of artificial progeneration and genetic engineering, and the consequences of mutations running out of hand. In the waning chapters, Chicago has become an entity itself, the computers that govern it having progressed to the point where they constitute an artificial intelligence. The citizens are elements in a machine, and interlopers are forbidden entry. In one sequence, all humans are placed in hibernation, and the robots run the city, often feuding among themselves. Although not particularly coherent as a novel, the book is filled with fascinating concepts and poses a number of troubling questions about the future of humankind, free will, and the role of government and technology.

Monteleone went on to write two related novels about computers that exceed their design. In *Guardian* and its sequel, *Ozymandias,* a sentient computer exists in a post-collapse world, a secret until its discovery by a group of adventurers. Seeking to learn more about its environment, the computer incarnates its intelligence in a human body and wanders the Earth. Monteleone also collaborated with David Bischoff on a trilogy, *Day of the Dragonstar, Night of the Dragonstar,* and *Dragonstar Destiny.* A

rescue team is sent to an orbiting, alien zoo when a band of explorers is attacked by dinosaurs living in its artificial environment. In subsequent volumes, we learn that some of the dinosaurs are themselves intelligent beings, and with the aid of a contingent of humans they seize control of their habitat and escape their inevitable exploitation by the human race.

Most of Monteleone's subsequent short fiction and certainly all of his novels were more properly horror fiction. *Night-Train* is set in the subways beneath Manhattan, dealing with a train that disappeared years earlier, and now reappears amidst several brutal killings. *Night Things* is a more traditional monster story. An Indian burial mound is inadvertently disturbed, releasing a horde of small, nasty beasts who promptly begin dismembering all and sundry. Since they are not supernatural in origin, *Night Things* may be at least technical science fiction, though it is clearly intended otherwise. The weakest of his horror novels is *Lyrica,* an exploration of the succubus theme. In *Fantasma,* warring factions of the Mafia find supernatural allies, a story that is in some ways darkly humorous. *The Magnificent Gallery* is the best of the early horror novels. A mysterious travelling sideshow weaves a strange net of doom around those who visit. The premise is familiar, but the author has a few fresh variations to enliven things and keep his readers guessing.

The Crooked House, written in collaboration with John DeChancie, is also properly speaking a horror novel, although it has science fictional overtones. The house of the title is one that is larger on the inside than it is on the outside, has strange twists and turns and unusual rooms, deep in the heart of which resides a creature of superhuman intelligence. His most recent novel, *Blood of the Lamb,* is a far superior work.

Monteleone and his wife Elizabeth currently edit an ongoing series of anthologies of original horror stories, *Borderlands,* and much of his time is spent working on Borderlands Press, a high quality small press operation. Most of his shorter fiction is above average, although there isn't a great deal of it. Of particular note is "The Mechanical Boy," the title character of which is diagnosed as mentally ill because he believes himself to be a machine which cannot function without electrical power. The doctor handling the case comes to the realization that there is some element of truth in the boy's delusion, that he can actually communicate with machines, possibly a foreshadowing of the next step in human evolution. Most of his recent short fiction has been overtly supernatural, such as "When Dark Descends," written in collaboration with Charles L. Grant, and "Spare the Child," a chilling story about what happens if you abandon an adopted child who happens to be related to a tribal shaman. Notable exceptions include "Rehearsals," which reveals the truth about the nature of life, and "Off to See the Wizard."

—Don D'Ammassa

MOORCOCK, Michael

Pseudonyms: Bill Barclay; Edward P. Bradbury; James Colvin; Desmond Reid. **Nationality:** British. **Born:** Mitcham, Surrey, 18 December 1939. **Military Service:** Served in the Air Training Corps. **Family:** Married 1) Hilary Bailey in 1962, two daughters and one son; 2) Jill Riches in 1978; 3) Linda Steel in 1983. **Career:** Editor, *Tarzan Adventures,* London, 1956-57, and Sexton Blake Library, Fleetway Publications, London, 1958-61; editor and writer for Liberal Party, 1962-63. Editor since 1964 and publisher since 1967, *New Worlds,* London. Since 1955, songwriter and member of various rock bands including Hawkwind and Deep Fix. **Awards:** British Science Fiction Association award, 1966; Nebula award 1967; Derleth award, 1972, 1974, 1975, 1976; Guardian Fiction prize, 1977; Campbell Memorial award, 1979; World Fantasy award, 1979. Guest of Honor, World Fantasy Convention, New York, 1976. **Agents:** Anthony Sheil Associates Ltd., 43 Doughty Street, London WCIN 2LF, England; or, Wallace and Sheil Inc., 177 East 70th Street, New York, New York 10021, U.S.A.

SCIENCE FICTION PUBLICATIONS

Novels (series: Oswald Bastable; Jerry Cornelius; Jerry Cornell; Corum; Count Brass; Dancers at the End of Time; Elric of Melniboné; Eternal Champion; Karl Glogauer; Runestaff; von Bek Family)

The Sundered Worlds. London, Compact, 1965; New York, Paperback Library, 1966; as *The Blood Red Game,* London, Sphere, 1970; revised under original title, London, Roc, 1992.

Stormbringer (Elric). London, Jenkins, 1965; New York, Lancer, 1967; revised edition, New York, DAW, 1977.

The Fireclown. London, Compact, 1965; New York, Paperback Library, 1967; as *The Winds of Limbo,* Paperback Library, 1969.

The Twilight Man. London, Compact, 1966; New York, Berkley, 1970; as *The Shores of Death,* London, Sphere, 1970.

The Wrecks of Time. New York, Ace, 1967; revised edition, as *The Rituals of Infinity,* London, Arrow, 1971; New York, DAW, 1978.

The Jewel in the Skull (Runestaff). New York, Lancer, 1967; London, Mayflower, 1969; revised edition, New York, DAW, 1977.

Sorcerer's Amulet (Runestaff). New York, Lancer, 1968; as *The Mad God's Amulet,* London, Mayflower, 1969; revised edition, New York, DAW, 1977.

Sword of the Dawn (Runestaff). New York, Lancer, 1968; London, Mayflower, 1969; revised edition, New York, DAW, 1977.

The Final Programme (Cornelius). New York, Avon, 1968; London, Allison and Busby, 1969; revised edition, London, Fontana, 1979.

The Ice Schooner. London, Sphere, and New York, Berkley, 1969; revised edition, New York, Harper, 1977; London, Harrap, 1985.

Behold the Man (Glogauer). London, Allison and Busby, 1969; New York, Avon, 1970.

The Black Corridor. New York, Ace, and London, Mayflower, 1969.

The Secret of the Runestaff. New York, Lancer, 1969; as *The Runestaff,* London, Mayflower, 1969; revised edition, New York, DAW, 1977.

The Eternal Champion. New York, Dell, and London, Mayflower, 1970; revised edition, New York, Harper, 1978.

Phoenix in Obsidian (Eternal Champion). London, Mayflower, 1970; as *The Silver Warriors,* New York, Dell, 1973.

A Cure for Cancer (Cornelius). London, Allison and Busby, and New York, Holt Rinehart, 1971; revised edition, London, Fontana, 1979.

The Warlord of the Air (Bastable). London, New English Library, and New York, Ace, 1971.

The Sleeping Sorceress (Elric). London, New English Library, 1971; New York, Lancer, 1972; revised edition, as *The Vanishing Tower,* New York, DAW, 1977; London, Panther, 1984.

Elric of Melniboné. London, Hutchinson, 1972; as *The Dreaming City,* New York, Lancer, 1972.

An Alien Heat (Dancers). London, MacGibbon and Kee, and New York, Harper, 1972.

Breakfast in the Ruins: A Novel of Inhumanity (Glogauer). London, New English Library, 1972; New York, Random House, 1974.

The English Assassin: A Romance of Entropy (Cornelius). London, Allison and Busby, and New York, Harper, 1972; revised edition, London, Fontana, 1979.

The Bull and the Spear: The Chronicle of Prince Corum and the Silver Hand. London, Allison and Busby, and New York, Berkley, 1973.

Count Brass. London, Mayflower, 1973; New York, Dell, 1976.

The Champion of Garathorm (Count Brass/Eternal Champion). London, Mayflower, 1973; New York, Berkley, 1985.

The Oak and the Ram (Corum). London, Allison and Busby, and New York, Berkley, 1973.

The Sword and the Stallion (Corum). New York, Berkley, and London, Allison and Busby, 1974.

The Land Leviathan (Bastable). London, Quartet, and Garden City, New York, Doubleday, 1974.

The Hollow Lands (Dancers). New York, Harper, 1974; London, Hart-Davis MacGibbon, 1975.

The Distant Suns, with Philip James. Llanfynydd, Dyfed, Unicorn Bookshop, 1975.

The Quest for Tanelorn (Count Brass). London, Mayflower, 1975; New York, Dell, 1976.

The Sailor on the Seas of Fate (Elric). London, Quartet, and New York, DAW, 1976.

The Time of the Hawklords, with Michael Butterworth. Henley-on-Thames, England, Ellis, 1976.

The Adventures of Una Persson and Catherine Cornelius in the Twentieth Century. London, Quartet, 1976.

The End of All Songs (Dancers). London, Hart-Davis MacGibbon, and New York, Harper, 1976.

The Weird of the White Wolf (Elric). New York, DAW, 1977; London, Panther, 1984.

The Bane of the Black Sword (Elric). New York, DAW, 1977; London, Panther, 1984.

The Swords Trilogy (Corum). New York, Berkley, 1977; as *The Swords of Corum Omnibus,* London, Grafton, 1986; as *Corum,* London, Millennium, 1992.

  The Knight of the Swords. London, Mayflower, and New York, Berkley, 1971.

  The Queen of the Swords. London, Mayflower, and New York, Berkley, 1971.

  The King of the Swords. London, Mayflower, and New York, Berkley, 1971.

The Condition of Muzak (Cornelius). London, Allison and Busby, 1977; Boston, Gregg Press, 1978.

The Transformation of Miss Mavis Ming: A Romance of the End of Time (Dancers). London, W.H. Allen, 1977; as *A Messiah at the End of Time,* New York, DAW, 1978.

The Cornelius Chronicles (omnibus). New York, Avon, vol. 1, 1977, vol. 2, 1986, vol. 3, 1987; as *The Cornelius Quartet,* London, Phoenix House, 1993.

The Chronicles of Corum (omnibus). New York, Berkley, 1978; London, Grafton, 1986; as *The Prince with the Silver Hand,* London, Millennium, 1993.

Gloriana; or, The Unfulfill'd Queen. London, Allison and Busby, 1978; New York, Avon, 1979.

The History of the Runestaff (omnibus). London, Hart-Davis MacGibbon, 1979; as *Hawkmoon,* London, Millennium, 1992.

The Great Rock 'n' Roll Swindle. London, Virgin, 1980; revised as *Casablanca,* London, Gollancz, 1989.

The Golden Barge. Manchester, Savoy, 1979; New York, DAW, 1980.

The Entropy Tango (Cornelius). London, New English Library, 1981.

The Steel Tsar (Bastable). London, Mayflower, 1981; New York, DAW, 1982.

The War Hound and the World's Pain (von Bek). New York, Timescape, 1981; London, New English Library, 1982.

The Dancers at the End of Time (omnibus). London, Granada, 1981.

The Nomad of Time (omnibus). Garden City, New York, Doubleday, 1982; London Panther, 1984; revised as *A Nomad of the Time Streams,* London, Millennium, 1993.

The Elric Saga (omnibus). Garden City, New York, Doubleday, 2 vols., 1984.

The Chronicles of Castle Brass (omnibus). London, Granada, 1985; as *Count Brass,* London, Millennium, 1993.

The City in the Autumn Stars (von Bek). London, Grafton, 1986; New York, Ace, 1987.

The Dragon in the Sword (Eternal Champion). New York, Ace, 1986; London, Grafton, 1987.

The Fortress of the Pearl (Elric). London, Gollancz, and New York, Ace, 1989.

The Revenge of the Rose (Elric). London, Grafton, and New York, Ace, 1991.

Jerusalem Commands. London, Cape, 1992.

The Eternal Champions (omnibus). London, Millennium, 1992.

von Bek (omnibus). London, Millennium, 1992.

Elric of Melniboné (omnibus). London, Millennium, 1993.

Sailing to Utopia (omnibus). London, Millennium, 1993.

Stormbringer (omnibus). London, Millennium, 1993.

Blood: A Southern Fantasy (von Bek). London, Millennium, and New York, Morrow, 1995.

The Alchemist's Question. N.p., n.d.

The Brothel in Rosenstrasse. New English Library, 1982.

Novels as Edward P. Bradbury (series: Michael Kane in all titles)

Warrior of Mars. London, New English Library, 1981.

Warriors of Mars. London, Compact, 1965; New York, Lancer, 1966; as *The City of the Beast* (as Michael Moorcock), 1970.

Blades of Mars. London, Compact, 1965; New York, Lancer, 1966; as *The Lord of the Spiders* (as Michael Moorcock), 1970.

Barbarians of Mars. London, Compact, 1965; New York, Lancer, 1966; as *The Masters of the Pit* (as Michael Moorcock), 1971.

Short Stories (series: Elric; Dancers at the End of Time)

The Stealer of Souls and Other Stories (Elric). London, Spearman, 1963; New York, Lancer, 1967.

The Deep Fix (as James Colvin). London, Compact, 1966.

The Time Dweller. London, Hart-Davis, 1969; New York, Berkley, 1971.

The Singing Citadel (Elric). London, Mayflower, and New York, Berkley, 1970.

The Jade Man's Eyes. Brighton, Unicorn Bookshop, 1973.

Elric: The Return to Melniboné (graphic novel), illustrated by Philippe Druillet. Brighton, Unicorn Bookshop, 1973.

Moorcock's Book of Martyrs. London, Quartet, 1976; as *Dying for Tomorrow,* New York, DAW, 1978.

The Lives and Times of Jerry Cornelius. London, Allison and Busby, 1976; New York, Dale, n.d.

Legends from the End of Time (Dancers). New York, Harper, and London, W.H. Allen, 1976.

Sojan. Manchester, Savoy, 1977.

The Real Life Mr Newman [sic]. Worcester, England, Callow, 1979.

My Experiences in the Third World War. Manchester, Savoy, 1980.

The Opium Generals and Other Stories. London, Harrap, 1984.

Elric at the End of Time: Fantasy Stories. Sevenoaks, Kent, New English Library, 1984; New York, DAW, 1985.

Earl Aubec and Other Stories. London, Millennium, 1993.

A Cornelius Calendar. London, Phoenix House, 1993.

Lunching with the AntiChrist: A Family History, 1925-2015. Shingletown, California, Ziesing, 1995.

OTHER PUBLICATIONS

Novels

Caribbean Crisis (with James Cawthorn as Desmond Reid). London, Fleetway, 1962.

The LSD Dossier (ghosted for Roger Harris). London, Compact, 1966.

Printer's Devil (as Bill Barclay). London, Compact, 1966.

Somewhere in the Night (as Bill Barclay; Cornell). London, Compact, 1966; revised as *The Chinese Agent* (as Michael Moorcock), London, Hutchinson, and New York, Macmillan, 1970.

The Russian Intelligence (Cornell). Manchester, Savoy, 1980.

Byzantium Endures. London, Secker and Warburg, 1981; New York, Random House, 1982.

The Brothel in Rösenstrasse (von Bek). London, New English Library, 1982; New York, Carroll and Graf, 1987.

The Laughter of Carthage. London, Secker and Warburg, and New York, Random House, 1984.

Mother London. London, Secker and Warburg, 1988; New York, Harmony, 1989.

Play

Screenplay: *The Land That Time Forgot,* with James Cawthorn, 1974.

Other

Epic Pooh. Dagenham, Essex, British Fantasy Society, 1978.

The Retreat from Liberty. London, Zomba, 1983.

Letters from Hollywood (correspondence). London, Harrap, 1986.

Wizardry and Wild Romance: A Study of Epic Fantasy. London, Gollancz, 1987.

Fantasy: The 100 Best Books, with James Cawthorn. London, Xanadu, and New York, Carroll and Graf, 1988.

Editor, *The Best of New Worlds.* London, Compact, 1965.

Editor, *SF Reprise: First-Rate Science Fiction Originally Published in New Worlds Magazine 1-5.* London, Compact, 5 vols., 1966-67.

Editor, *Best SF Stories from New Worlds 1-8.* London, Panther, 8 vols., 1967-74; New York, Berkley, 6 vols., 1968-71.

Editor, *The Traps of Time.* London, Rapp and Whiting, 1968.
Editor, (anonymous), *The Inner Landscape.* London, Allison and Busby, 1969.
Editor, *New Worlds Quarterly 1-5.* London, Sphere, 5 vols., 1971-73; New York, Berkley, 4 vols., 1971-73.
Editor, with Langdon Jones, *The Nature of the Catastrophe* (Cornelius). London, Hutchinson, 1971.
Editor, with Charles Platt, *New Worlds 6.* London, Sphere, 1973; as *New Worlds 5,* New York, Avon, 1974.
Editor, *Before Armageddon: An Anthology of Victorian and Edwardian Imaginative Fiction Published Before 1914.* London, W.H. Allen, 1975.
Editor, *England Invaded: A Collection of Fantasy Fiction.* London, W.H. Allen, and New York, Ultramarine, 1977.
Editor, *New Worlds: An Anthology.* London, Flamingo, 1983.
Editor, *The Time Machine,* by H.G. Wells. London, Dent, and Rutland, Vermont, Tuttle, 1993.
Editor, with Langdon Jones, *The New Nature of the Catastrophe* (Cornelius). London, Millennium, 1993.

*

Manuscript Collections: Bodleian Library, Oxford University; Sterling Library, Texas A & M University, College Station.

Critical Study: *The Entropy Exhibition: Michael Moorcock and the British "New Wave" in Science Fiction* by Colin Greenland, London, Routledge, 1983.

Michael Moorcock comments:

My work varies so widely that it attracts quite different readers. Most of it is not, in fact, generic SF—it's "fantasy," if anything— and much of it uses "genre borrowings" for specific ironic uses. Obsessions include imperialism, "trans-sexuality" (I don't believe in gender-roles as a survival trait—they're anti-survival now), racialism, how to live and grow in modern cities, etc. Modern pieties are another frequent target. I like change. I believe that people and things should be infinitely flexible. I am an anarchist in that I believe every individual should be self-governing and conscious of communal self-interest.

* * *

Michael Moorcock is a writer with so many voices, it is difficult to characterize him at all. In addition to science fiction, he has written suspense novels, historicals, and fantasies, of which the best known are his various series featuring Elric of Melniboné, Count Brass, the Eternal Champion, and others. He also spent several years as editor of the British *New Worlds* magazine, and in that position was a powerful force calling for the expansion of the styles, techniques, and themes of the field. Although the "New Wave" movement ostensibly died off, the field was permanently changed as a result, opening the way for diverse styles and more attention to conventional literary standards.

Moorcock's earliest science fiction was entertaining but comparatively minor. *The Wrecks of Time,* for example, is a straightforward space opera featuring parallel earths. In *The Winds of Limbo,* a declining human civilization on Earth must face the challenge of an enigmatic visitor who may be bringing either salvation or destruction. *The Blood Red Game* is another space adventure, enlivened somewhat by the introduction of a multi-dimensional threat.

Under the name Edward P. Bradbury, Moorcock wrote three pastiches of Edgar Rice Burroughs, which appeared in the United States as *The City of the Beast, The Lord of the Spiders,* and *The Masters of the Pit.* Although the plots are very much in the style of Burroughs, they are far more literate and were the first indication that Moorcock was about to evolve into a talented and entertaining writer. One further early novel, *The Twilight Man,* was more ambitious and gave the first indication of the unique perspective that would characterize much of Moorcock's later work. Earth has stopped rotating and humanity is ultimately doomed. But against this strange landscape, Moorcock presents an insightful look into the minds of his characters that lifted the book above mere melodrama.

Moorcock won a Nebula Award for his novelette "Behold the Man," later expanded into a novel of the same name. A time traveler goes back to the time of Christ intent upon researching His life and death, only to discover that the historical figure does not exist. As events unfold, the traveler himself steps into the role of savior, is judged and crucified, in a bizarre twist that is both thoughtful and thought-provoking.

At this point, Moorcock's writing began to branch off in a number of different directions, although he would later retroactively tie them back together. *The Ice Schooner* is a fascinating adventure story set against the backdrop of a new ice age. *The Black Corridor* is an introspective, chilling story of a dozen people engaged in a long journey to colonize another world and the psychological problems that can arise in a closed environment. Moorcock's interest in experimental styles of writing came to fruition in *The Final Programme,* the first of several books to revolve around the character of Jerry Cornelius, and the only one of his works to be made into a motion picture.

The Cornelius stories are a strange blend of spy story, science fiction, and contemporary novel, and an argument could be made that they were the literary forebears of the cyberpunk writers of the 1980s. Set in the near future, they involve a man who might be described as an antihero, whose "adventures" are often cloaked in obscurity, and whose motives are less than pure. In subsequent novels like *A Cure for Cancer, The English Assassin, The Condition of Muzak, The Entropy Tango,* and *The Alchemist's Question,* as well as a number of short stories, we are given detailed glimpses of a strangely altered version of reality, where sex, drugs, violence, and ruthlessness are the order of the day. The non-linear plotting and hallucinogenic sequences alienated a number of readers at the time they were published, but the books continue to have a loyal following.

At no point did Moorcock confine himself to a single authorial stance, however. *The Warlord of the Air, The Land Leviathan,* and *The Steel Tsar* are both pastiches of and satires on the panoramic adventure novels of the early days of science fiction. *The Brothel in Rosenstrasse* and its sequel, *The War Hound and the World's Pain,* blur the distinction between SF and fantasy, set against a pre-World War I Europe that is not quite the one that gave rise to our own present.

Breakfast in the Ruins is another novel of time travel, but this one an episodic narrative of the trials and tribulations of a man cast loose in time, providing a platform by which the author can satirize various aspects of our society. In *Gloriana,* possibly Moorcock's greatest single novel, he uses another altered version of our own past to create a sweeping novel of intrigue and adventure that is rivetting in its intensity and enlightening in its insights into human interaction.

An Alien Heat was the first volume in the "Dancers at the End of Time" series, set in the far distant future. An all but immortal culture slowly subsides into decadence in a frequently comic satire of human foibles. One of its citizens looks for inspiration in the past in *The Hollow Lands,* and runs into aliens in *The End of All Songs.* The mysterious being from *The Winds of Limbo* pays a visit in *A Messiah at the End of Time.*

Moorcock is also a popular fantasy writer, most notably for his Elric of Melniboné series. He has made a conscious effort to unify his works in terms of "The Eternal Champion," indicating that the heroes of his various series, Jerry Cornelius, Jherek Carnelian, Elric, and others, are all manifestations of the same immortal spirit, a warrior who is incarnated in various times and places when his help is needed. He has also used the von Bek family, with variations of that name as well, to draw others of his works into the fold. Certainly there is a strong thematic resemblance, particularly in the latter works. Order must be imposed on Chaos, society must be ruled by law rather than uncontrolled human rapacity, and at times it may be necessary to take up arms to defend that Order.

Although not generally noted as a short story writer, Moorcock has produced a fairly large body of readable short pieces, the best of which are those included in *Legends from the End of Time,* as well as "Mountain," "The Pleasure Garden of Felipe Sagittarius," "Pale Roses," and "Flux." The recent story "The Cairene Purse" is particularly impressive, a search conducted through an alien but in some ways recognizable Third World culture. Moorcock's influence both as a writer and as an editor is immeasurable but certainly of major significance in the evolution of the genre.

—Don D'Ammassa

MOORE, Alan

Nationality: British. **Born:** 1953. **Career:** Comics illustrator and writer. **Awards:** Hugo award, 1988; *Locus* award, 1988.

SCIENCE FICTION PUBLICATIONS

Graphic Novels

Watchmen. London, Titan, 1987.
V for Vendetta. London, Titan, 1990.
The Complete Ballad of Halo Jones. London, Titan, 1991.
Marvelman. N.p., n.d.
The Killing Joke. N.p., n.d.
1964. N.p., n.d.
From Hell. N.p., n.d.

*   *   *

Alan Moore is one of the people responsible for the creative renaissance in mainstream comic books and for the critical respect comics began to receive in the mid-1980s. He demonstrated that comic book scripts can have the subtlety of prose fiction, especially when they use their access to the rich potential subject matter of our fascination with heroes.

Earlier, the American comics industry had been shaken from its lethargy by the success of Marvel Comics, which had at least in-

troduced one-dimensional characters and begun experimenting with interlocking, multi-issue story loops. At the same time, young writers were taking a fresh look at older superheroes; looking at Batman, for example, Frank Miller was asking how anyone could perform essentially the same "adventure every month for decades"—and was beginning to conclude that no *sane* person could do it. Alan Moore, meanwhile, had begun doing comics in England, first as artist *and* writer, in underground comics and then as writer of short, episodic strips that ran in British anthology magazines. In 1982, for example, he began scripting *V for Vendetta* and *Marvelman* in *Warrior* magazine, and in 1983 he began *The Ballad of Halo Jones* in *2000 AD.* In 1984, he began doing American mainstream comics, taking over the writing of DC Comics' *Swamp Thing.*

Even though the writing of these early works continued for some time, overlapping each other and additional projects, it makes some sense to talk about them here since they show Moore's concerns and how he began dealing with them. *V for Vendetta* is set in a near-future, fascist Britain, where the only opposition to the government is the Guy-Fawkes-masked vigilante called V. In the first episode, V rescues a young woman from government thugs who are about to rape and murder her. Unfortunately, Eve Hammond sees herself as a mere helpless victim—i.e., typical of the mass of people—and the story develops not into a chronicle of V's triumphs over the powers that be but into a study of how an insignificant little cypher can learn to become a hero. The turning point seems to be little Evey's discovery, while a prisoner, of a note from another prisoner; it proclaims personal independence of the government's control, and it asserts another principle: "There is no way I can convince you that this is not one of their tricks but I don't care. I am me, and I don't know who you are but I love you." If Eve can recognize *her* freedom to act, there is hope for the rest of humanity.

In *V,* Moore had considered the potential of a disturbing, even threatening hero, one who appears in the role of someone his audience had been conditioned to hate. In *Marvelman,* he turned to an immediately attractive character, the handsome superhero in a colorful, skintight costume. Here, again, he worked interesting changes, impatiently clearing away the hero's "knowleadge" of his origin and powers so that he can face the suppressed question underlying all superhero comics: What if the hero's powers are so great that he is literally *super*human? At the end of Moore's stint as writer for the series, in the stories collected in the *Olympus* album, the hero has become genuinely godlike and graciously offers other humans the chance to join him. He is puzzled by the refusal of some, such as his former wife, to be converted into superhumanity; that failure of imagination, Moore implies, is Marvelman's ultimate limitation.

Finally, in the last of the episodic tales he began in British magazines, Moore used *The Complete Ballad of Halo Jones* to examine a character who believes she is no one special but who refuses to be content with a safe life on the dole and so leaves Earth to begin exploring the universe. Especially at the end of the third book of episodes, when she has just survived a term as soldier reminiscent of Joe Haldeman's *The Forever War,* she might rationalize accepting a safe place to rest, but instead she steals the space yacht of her former lover, a war criminal she has just killed, and goes "out."

As these stories show, Moore understands the attractiveness of independence and the potential fulfillment it offers. He also sees how unattractive freedom is to people who see it offering only uncertainty. Further complicating our choices is the fact that society offers many attractive, vicarious images of power; becoming absorbed in them can make it difficult to appreciate one's own potential. To avoid that kind of passive rambling, Moore developed a distinctive style that involves readers in grappling with the story. Moore's writing presents dense masses of data to integrate. At the same time, thanks to Moore's extremely detailed suggestions to the artist, words and ideas are sharply echoed or contrasted in neighboring panels. Moore also is aware of how the content of entire pages can relate to each other, or how *turning* a page can force a reader to refocus on different shapes or sizes of new panels and thus be ready to perceive something new.

In the issues of *Swamp Thing* he did beginning in 1984, Moore took on an existing character that literally had been killed off by other writers beforehand. Stepping into the universe of DC Comics characters, Moore appreciated the opportunities as he says in his introduction to *Saga of the Swamp Thing,* first of the issues he wrote, "The continuity-expert's nightmare of a thousand different super-powered characters co-existing in the same continuum can, with the application of a sensitive and sympathetic eye, become a rich and fertile mythic background with fascinating archetypal characters hanging around, waiting to be picked like grapes on the vine." All those references to fecund plantlife are appropriate, since Moore depicts the Swamp Thing not as a man who became plantlike but as a plant creature that had absorbed the dead man's memories. Shocked by the discovery that he was not human, the character first tries to sink into unconsciousness. When he is roused by the need to fight another man-plant being who wants to destroy all humans for their crimes against the vegetable world, Swamp Thing begins to care for some humans. He becomes able to share his world with them and, in the climax to *Love and Death* (second album from Moore's issues), to actually love one human woman, a remarkable transition from horror to hope.

Moore's finest work to date, however, is *Watchmen,* published in 12 monthly installments and then in a one-volume album in 1986. Along with Frank Miller's reinvention of Batman, *The Dark Night Returns, Watchmen* startled readers who habitually discounted the artistic potential of commercial comics. Nevertheless, the book was clearly outstanding however it was categorized; it won a Hugo award in "Other Forms" and a *Locus* award as "Non-Fiction."

Watchmen's story is set in an alternate-world present. In the late 1930s people began acting like costumed crimefighters as a fad, but this was outlawed in 1977. The only ones who persist are extra-legal sociopaths like the masked vigilante Rorschach, or government employees like Dr. Manhattan, the world's only genuine superhero. Thanks to Dr. Manhattan's mental control over matter, the United States won the war in Vietnam, and thus Richard Nixon has been reelected President ever since. As the story starts, however, someone has murdered the Comedian, government-sponsored sociopath and retired costumed "hero," and Rorschach interprets this as the beginning of an attack on the very idea of heroism as he sees it.

Watchmen is a formidably complex work, demanding that readers connect many references in text and art. The only character who could perform such a feat during the rush of events is Dr. Manhattan, but his being superhuman has made him unable to care about doing it. As he says when Rorschach tells him of the Comedian's murder, "A live body and a dead body contain the same number of *particles.* Structurally, there's no discernible *difference.* Life and Death are unquantifiable *abstracts.* Why *should* I be concerned?" Readers are likely to identify with Rorschach because he *is* concerned and because he insists that he will never give up his principles. But Rorschach is not just a social outcast; he is truly in-

sane, functional but hopelessly damaged emotionally. At the end, he must be disintegrated by Dr. Manhattan to preserve a horrible victory by the story's "villain" that *might* save humanity from destruction. And yet, when the villain/hero asks for reassurance that what he did was ultimately right because everything has come out for the best in the end, Dr. Manhattan's cool reply is "'In the end'? *Nothing* ends. . . . Nothing *ever* ends." Infantile, futile people who claim a right to act out their own little certainties are simply distracting themselves from genuine needs. In short, they are the kind of people who would become costumed superheroes (or who, as citizens, would rely on some "hero" for what they don't want to do themselves).

With *Watchmen,* Moore's serious exploration of the superhero was over. He views his attempt at a Batman story, *The Killing Joke,* as a well-intentioned failure. The story starts off well, with Batman seriously trying to ask the Joker whether they can't learn to understand each other so they can stop their conflict before one destroys the other. However, because the Joker must continue to be Batman's enemy in future comics stories, that question cannot be seriously considered, let alone answered.

Moore's subsequent projects frequently have been like massive, unfinished monoliths. The *1964* series appeared to be a fairly genial spoof of early Marvel superheroes, but the series broke off just as Moore was bringing those more innocent characters into the present, to face contemporary issues in the company of today's scruffier brand of superhero. Only two issues of *Big Numbers* have appeared, juxtaposing personal and big-business desires. One project that does appear on the way to completion is *From Hell,* a long study of Victorian public attitudes and private behavior. In the story, Prince Albert, heir to the throne, has secretly become involved with a woman from the London slums and has actually married her. All evidence of this must be removed, including the slum women who know. The agent of removal is Dr. William Gull, sincere defender of official morality at the request of his sovereign, Queen Victoria. He tries to view himself as a masked vigilante; history knows him as Jack the Ripper. Gull is prone to disturbing visions, such as the Masonic deity, and as he stands over the mutilated corpse of one of Jack's victims he suddenly finds himself standing in a modern office, surrounded by secretaries and businessmen. He is appalled and rails at their banality: "With all your shimmering numbers and your lights, think not to be inured to history. Its black root succors you. It is INSIDE you. . . . See me! Wake up and look upon me! I am come amongst you. I am with you always. . . . How would I seem to you? Some antique fiend or penny dreadful horror, yet *you* frighten me!" Again, Moore is pointing out the complicated, shifting balance between his characters'—and readers'—need for safe belief and risky independence.

Today, Moore splits his time between writing for extremely commercial properties such as Image Comics' *Spawn* or doing black-and-white, independent work such as *From Hell.* He is a remarkably talented writer, and he is unlikely to stay in one place. Ever.

—Joe Sanders

MOORE, C(atherine) L(ucille)

Pseudonyms: Lawrence O'Donnell; Lewis Padgett. **Nationality:** American. **Born:** Indianapolis, Indiana, 24 January 1911. **Educa-

tion: University of Southern California, Los Angeles, B.S. 1956 (Phi Beta Kappa), M.A. 1964. **Family:** Married 1) Henry Kuttner, q.v., in 1940 (died 1958); 2) Thomas Reggie in 1963. **Career:** Staff member, later president, Fletcher Trust Company, Indianapolis, 1930-40; instructor in Writing and Literature, University of Southern California, 1958-61. Most of her work after 1940 was written in collaboration with Henry Kuttner, though not always acknowledged. **Died:** 1987.

Science Fiction Publications

Novels

Fury, with Henry Kuttner. New York, Grosset and Dunlap, 1950; London, Dobson, 1954; as *Destination Infinity,* New York, Avon, 1958.
Doomsday Morning. New York, Doubleday, 1957; London, Consul, 1960.
Earth's Last Citadel, with Henry Kuttner. New York, Ace, 1964.
Valley of the Flame, with Henry Kuttner. New York, Ace, 1964.
The Time Axis, with Henry Kuttner. New York, Ace, 1965.
The Dark World, with Henry Kuttner. New York, Ace, 1965; London, Mayflower, 1966.
The Mask of Circe, with Henry Kuttner. New York, Ace, 1971.
Scarlet Dream. West Kingston, Rhode Island, Donald M. Grant, 1981; as *Northwest Smith,* New York, Ace, 1982.
Vintage Season, bound with *In Another Country* by Robert Silverberg. New York, Tor, 1990.

Novels with Henry Kuttner as Lewis Padgett

Tomorrow and Tomorrow; and, The Fairy Chessmen. New York, Gnome Press, 1951; *The Fairy Chessmen* published as *Chessboard Planet,* New York, Galaxy, 1956; original volume published as *Tomorrow and Tomorrow and The Far Reality,* London, Consul, 2 vols., 1963.
Well of the Worlds. New York, Galaxy, 1953; bylined as Henry Kuttner, New York, Ace, 1965.
Beyond Earth's Gates. New York, Ace, 1954.

Short Stories

Judgment Night. New York, Gnome Press, 1952.
Shambleau, and Others. New York, Gnome Press, 1953; abridged edition, London, Consul, 1961.
Northwest of Earth. New York, Gnome Press, 1954.
There Shall Be Darkness. Sydney, American Science Fiction, 1954.
No Boundaries, with Henry Kuttner. New York, Ballantine, 1955; London, Consul, 1961.
Jirel of Joiry. New York, Paperback Library, 1969; as *Black God's Shadow,* West Kingston, Rhode Island, Grant, 1977.
The Best of C.L. Moore, edited by Lester del Rey. New York, Doubleday, 1975.
Clash by Night, and Other Stories, with Henry Kuttner, edited by Peter Pinto. London, Hamlyn, 1980.
Chessboard Planet, and Other Stories, with Henry Kuttner. London, Hamlyn, 1983.
Clash by Night (with Henry Kuttner as Lawrence O'Donnell). Sydney, American Science Fiction; bylined as Henry Kuttner, bound with *The Jungle,* by David Drake, New York, Tor, 1991.

Short Stories with Henry Kuttner as Lewis Padgett

A Gnome There Was, and Other Tales of Science Fiction and Fantasy. New York, Simon and Schuster, 1950.
Robots Have No Tails. New York, Gnome Press, 1952; bylined by Henry Kuttner and C.L. Moore as *The Proud Robot: The Complete Galloway Gallegher Stories,* Feltham, England, Hamlyn, 1983.
Mutant. New York, Gnome Press, 1953; bylined by Henry Kuttner, London, Weidenfeld and Nicolson, 1954.
Line to Tomorrow. New York, Bantam, 1954.

Other Publications

Novels with Henry Kuttner

The Brass Ring (as Lewis Padgett). New York, Duell, 1964; London, Sampson Low, 1947; as *Murder in Brass,* New York, Bantam, 1947.
The Day He Died (as Lewis Padgett). New York, Duell, 1947.

Other

Editor, *The Startling Worlds of Henry Kuttner* (includes *Beyond Earth's Gates, Valley of the Flame,* and *The Dark World*). New York, Popular Library, 1987.

*

Manuscript Collection: Lovecraft Collection, Brown University Library, Providence, Rhode Island.

*   *   *

It has always been a very difficult thing to judge properly the impact of C.L. Moore on the fields of science fiction and fantasy. Although she wrote under her own name, most of her work was in collaboration with her husband, Henry Kuttner, a skilled writer in his own right, and in most cases, her name never appeared as coauthor. One of the earliest and most important woman writers in the field, she helped pioneer the move toward stronger psychological rationalization of motivation and behavior in characters.

Many short novels that appeared under the Kuttner name alone were wonderfully original explorations of the border between the two aspects of the genre. Lost civilizations feature prominently in titles like *Valley of the Flame* and the bizarre *Well of the Worlds.* There is conventional witchcraft in *The Mask of Circe,* scientific sorcery in *The Dark World,* and manic madness in *The Fairy Chessmen.* In some cases, Moore was given equal billing, such as for *Earth's Last Citadel,* the story of a journey to the very end of time, and *Beyond Earth's Gates,* an adventure in a parallel Earth. Many of the shorter collaborations, particularly those collected in *No Boundaries,* were far ahead of their contemporaries in approach and maturity of execution, particularly "Vintage Season" and "Home There's No Returning." The former's depiction of a group of tourists from the future secretly witnessing the present is one of the undisputed classics of the genre.

Moore is best known for "Shambleau," her first story and certainly not the best of her solo works. It is the first adventure of Northwest Smith, an interplanetary adventurer whose adventures are typical pulp fiction of the 1930s, but with more literary quality than most of the stories in the magazines of that period. Smith wanders the surface of Venus and Mars, encountering alien creatures resembling the legendary Medusa and others. Like Leigh Brackett, who would write similar stories more than a decade later, Moore used a rugged male character as her protagonist, but unlike Brackett, she also chose to write some stories that featured dominant, competent women.

Moore wrote heroic fantasy during the same period, featuring a very competent female warrior, Jirel. The five adventures are collected as *Jirel of Joiry,* the best of which are "Hellsgarde" and "Black God's Kiss." In each, she faces and overcomes a supernatural menace. Relatively unsophisticated by current standards, the stories still have a raw power and fervor that is missing from much of the formula fantasy that is currently being published.

Judgment Night is an ambivalent short novel about a female warrior who is heir to one of the most powerful thrones in human history, but who is torn between her own strengths and weaknesses. She must deal with a powerful man who claims to love her despite his dedication to the destruction of her power, and a mysterious intruder whose physical nature is unknown. Although there is the skeleton of an interesting story here, this is not one of Moore's successes, overly melodramatic, poorly paced, and ultimately unconvincing.

Doomsday Morning is a break from pulp tradition and an attempt to deal with more serious issues. In the not-too-distant future, the United States is controlled by Comus, an organization that uses highly sophisticated propaganda and information-gathering techniques to administer what should have been an invulnerable dictatorship. Against this background, Moore unrolls a burgeoning revolution, and although the novel is ultimately a melodrama, it is her most mature full-length work. It does not deserve the obscurity into which it has fallen.

Perhaps her most noteworthy shorter piece is "No Woman Born," the story of a disfigured woman whose brain is placed in an artificial body. As the protagonist comes to terms with her new mode of existence, the reader examines the nature of the will to survive, the meaning of being human, and the anguish that faces those who are cut off from contact with others.

Other short stories of note include "Private Eye," "Home Is the Hunter," and "Quest of the Starstone," the last of which is the only recorded meeting between Jirel and Northwest Smith, through a forced but forgivable plot device. The best of her short fiction is collected in *Northwest Smith, The Best of C.L. Moore,* and *No Boundaries.*

Moore's most significant contributions to the field may be invisible forever, not only because her name did not appear on stories she cowrote with her far more famous husband, but also because we cannot measure the influence she had on other writers of the time, in shaping the pulp story and its portrayal of women, and later in the depiction of all human characters as real, believable people.

—Don D'Ammassa

MOORE, Patrick (Caldwell)

Nationality: British. **Born:** Pinner, Middlesex, 4 March 1923. **Education:** Educated privately. **Military Service:** Served in the Royal Air Force, 1940-45: Navigator, Bomber Command. **Career:** Director, Armagh Planetarium, Northern Ireland, 1965-68. President, British Astronomical Association, 1982-84. Since 1957, presenter, *The Sky at Night* television series, BBC, London. Since 1962, editor, *Yearbook of Astronomy.* Also a composer. **Awards:** Lorimer Gold Medal, 1962; Goodacre Gold Medal, 1968; Italian Astronomical Society Arturo Gold Medal, 1969; Jackson-Gwilt Medal, 1978; Astronomical Society of the Pacific Klumpke-Roberts award, 1978. Fellow, Royal Astronomical Society. D.Sc.: University of Lancaster, 1974; D.Sc., Hatfield Polytechnic, 1988; D.Sc., University of Birmingham, 1990. O.B.E. (Officer, Order of the British Empire), 1968. C.B.E. (Commander of the British Empire), 1988. **Agent:** Hilary Rubinstein, A.P. Watt Ltd., 26-28 Bedford Row, London WC1R 4HL, England. **Address:** Farthings, 39 West Street, Selsey, West Sussex, England.

SCIENCE FICTION PUBLICATIONS

Novels (for children; series: Maurice Gray; Grenfell and Wright; Robin North; Gregory Quest; Scott Saunders)

The Master of the Moon (Grenfell and Wright). London, Museum Press, 1952.
The Island of Fear (Grenfell and Wright). London, Museum Press, 1954.
The Frozen Planet. London, Museum Press, 1954.
Destination Luna. London, Lutterworth Press, 1955.
Quest of the Spaceways. London, Muller, 1955.
Mission to Mars (Gray). London, Burke, 1955.
World of Mists (Quest). London, Muller, 1956.
The Domes of Mars (Gray). London, Burke, 1956.
Wheel in Space. London, Lutterworth Press, 1956.
The Voices of Mars (Gray). London, Burke, 1957.
Peril on Mars (Gray). London, Burke, 1958; New York, Putnam, 1965.
Raiders on Mars (Gray). London, Burke, 1959.
Captives of the Moon. London, Burke, 1960.
Wanderer in Space (North). London, Burke, 1961.
Crater of Fear (North). London, Burke, and New York, Harvey House, 1962.
Invader from Space (North). London, Burke, 1963.
Caverns of the Moon (North). London, Burke, 1964.
Planet of Fire. Tadsworth, World's Work, 1969.
Spy in Space (Saunders). London, Armada, 1977.
Planet of Fear (Saunders). London, Armada, 1977.
The Moon Raiders (Saunders). London, Armada, 1978.
Killer Comet (Saunders). London, Armada, 1978.
The Terror Star (Saunders). London, Armada, 1979.
The Secret of the Black Hole (Saunders). London, Armada, 1980.

OTHER PUBLICATIONS

Plays

Perseus and Andromeda, music by Moore (produced Shoreham, Sussex, 1974).
Theseus, music by Moore (produced 1982).

Other

Guide to the Moon. London, Eyre and Spottiswoode, and New York, Norton, 1953; revised edition, London, Colins, 1957; as *Survey of the Moon,* Eyre and Spottiswoode and Norton, 1963; revised edition, Guildford, Surrey, Lutterworth Press, 1976; as *New Guide to the Moon,* Norton, 1976.

Suns, Myths, and Men. London, Muller, 1954; revised edition, Muller, 1968; New York, Norton, 1969; as *The Story of Man and the Stars,* New York, Norton, 1955.

Out into Space, with A.L. Helm. London, Museum Press, 1954.

The Boy's Book of Space. London, Burke, 1954; New York, Roy, 1956.

The True Book about Worlds around Us. London, Muller, 1954; as *The Worlds around Us,* New York, Abelard Schuman, 1956.

A Guide to the Planets. New York, Norton, 1954; London, Eyre and Spottiswoode, 1955; revised edition, London, Collins, 1957; Norton, 1960; Guildford, Surrey, Lutterworth Press, 1976; as *The New Guide to the Planets,* Norton, 1972; revised edition, London, Sidgwick and Jackson, 1993.

The Moon, with Hugh Percival Wilkins. London, Faber, and New York, Macmillan, 1955.

Earth Satellite: The New Satellite Projects Explained. London, Eyre and Spottiswoode, 1955; as *Earth Satellites,* New York, Norton, 1956; revised edition, Norton, 1958.

The Planet Venus. London, Faber, 1956; New York, Macmillan, 1957; revised edition, 1959, 1961; with Garry Hunt, Faber, 1982.

Man-Made Moons. London, Newman Neame, 1956.

Making and Using a Telescope, with Hugh Percival Wilkins. London, Eyre and Spottiswoode, 1956; as *How to Make and Use a Telescope,* New York, Norton, 1956.

The True Book about the Earth. London, Muller, 1956.

Guide to Mars. London, Muller, 1956; New York, Macmillan, 1958; revised edition, Muller, 1965.

The True Book about Earthquakes and Volcanoes. London, Muller, 1957.

Isaac Newton (for children). London, Black, 1957; New York, Putnam, 1958.

Science and Fiction. London, Harrap, 1957; Folcroft, Pennsylvania, Folcroft Editions, 1970.

The Amateur Astronomer. London, Lutterworth Press, and New York, Norton, 1957; revised edition, Lutterworth Press, 1974; revised edition, as *Amateur Astronomy,* Norton, 1968.

The Earth, Our Home. New York, Abelard Schuman, 1957.

Your Book of Astronomy. London, Faber, 1958; revised edition, 1964, 1979.

The Solar System. London, Methuen, 1958; New York, Criterion, 1961.

The Boy's Book of Astronomy. London, Burke, and New York, Roy, 1958; revised edition, Burke, 1964.

The True Book about Man. London, Muller, 1959.

Man on the Moon. London, Newman Neame, 1959.

Rockets and Earth Satellites. London, Muller, 1959.

Astronautics. London, Methuen, 1960.

Star Spotter. London, Newman Neame, 1960.

Guide to the Stars. London, Eyre and Spottiswoode, and New York, Norton, 1960; revised edition, Guildford, Surrey, Lutterworth Press, 1974; as *The New Guide to the Stars,* New York, Norton, 1975.

Stars and Space. London, Black, 1960.

Conquest of the Air: The Story of the Wright Brothers. London, Lutterworth Press, 1961.

Navigation, with Henry Brinton. London, Methuen, 1961.

Astronomy. London, Oldbourne, 1961; as *The Picture History of Astronomy,* New York, Grosset and Dunlap, 1961; revised edition, 1972; revised edition, as *The Story of Astronomy,* London, Macdonald, 1972; revised edition, London, Macdonald and Jane's, 1977; revised edition, as *Patrick Moore's History of Astronomy,* London, Macdonald, 1983.

The Stars. London, Weidenfeld and Nicolson, 1962.

Exploring Maps, with Henry Brinton. London, Odhams Press, 1962; New York, Hawthorn, 1967.

Exploring Time, with Henry Brinton. London, Odhams Press, 1962.

The Astronomer's Telescope, with Paul Murdin. Leicester, Brockhampton Press, 1962.

Life in the Universe, with Francis J. Jackson. London, Routledge, and New York, Norton, 1962.

The Planets. London, Eyre and Spottiswoode, and New York, Norton, 1962.

The Observer's Book of Astronomy. London, Warne, 1962; 6th edition, 1978.

Telescopes and Observatories. London, Weidenfeld and Nicolson, and New York, Day, 1962.

Space in the Sixties. London, Penguin, 1963.

Exploring the Moon. London, Odhams Press, 1964.

The True Book about Roman Britain. London, Muller, 1964.

Exploring Weather, with Henry Brinton. London, Odhams Press, 1964.

The Sky at Night 1-7. London, Eyre and Spottiswoode, 2 vols., and London, BBC, 5 vols., 1964-80; vol. 1, New York, Norton, 1965.

Life on Mars, with Francis L. Jackson. London, Routledge, 1965; New York, Norton, 1966.

Exploring Other Planets, with Henry Brinton. London, Odhams Press, 1965; New York, Hawthorn, 1967.

Exploring the World. London, Oxford University Press, 1966; New York, Watts, 1968.

The New Look of the Universe. London, Hodder and Stoughton, and New York, Norton, 1966.

Exploring the Planetarium. London, Odhams Press, 1966.

Legends of the Stars. London, Odhams Press, 1966.

Naked-Eye Astronomy. London, Lutterworth Press, and New York, Norton, 1966.

Basic Astronomy. Edinburgh, Oliver and Boyd, 1967.

Exploring Earth History, with Henry Brinton. London, Odhams Press, 1967.

The Craters of the Moon, with Peter J. Cattermole. New York, Norton, 1967.

The Amateur Astronomer's Glossary. London, Lutterworth Press, and New York, Norton, 1967; revised edition, as *The A-Z of Astronomy,* London, Fontana, and New York, Scribner, 1976.

Armagh Observatory: A History 1790-1967. Armagh, Armagh Observatory, 1967.

Exploring the Galaxies. London, Odhams Press, 1968.

Exploring the Stars. London, Odhams Press, 1968.

Space. London, Lutterworth Press, 1968; New York, Natural History Press, 1969.

The Sun and Its Influence, by Mervyn A. Ellison, revised edition. London, Routledge, and New York, Elsevier, 1968.

The Sun. London, Muller, and New York, Norton, 1968.

Moon Flight Atlas. London, Mitchell Beazley, and Chicago, Rand McNally, 1969; revised edition, Mitchell Beazley, 1970.

Astronomy and Space Research (bibliography). London, National Book League, 1969.

The Development of Astronomical Thought. Edinburgh, Oliver and Boyd, 1969.

The Atlas of the Universe. London, Mitchell Beazley, and Chicago, Rand McNally, 1970; revised edition, as *The Mitchell Beazley Concise Atlas of the Universe,* Mitchell Beazley, 1974; as *The Concise Atlas of the Universe,* Rand McNally, 1974; revised edition, as *The New Atlas of the Universe,* New York, Crown, 1984.

Gunpowder, Treason: November 5, 1605, with Henry Brinton. London, Lutterworth Press, 1970.

Astronomy for O Level. London, Duckworth, 1970; as *Astronomy for GCSE,* 1989.

Seeing Stars. London, BBC, and Chicago, Rand McNally, 1971.

Mars, The Red World. Kingswood, Surrey, World's Work, 1971.

The Astronomy of Birr Castle. London, Mitchell Beazley, 1971.

Can You Speak Venusian: A Guide to Independent Thinkers. Newton Abbot, Devon, David and Charles, 1972; New York, Norton, 1973.

Challenge of the Stars, with David A. Hardy. London, Mitchell Beazley, and Chicago, Rand McNally, 1972; as *The New Challenge of the Stars,* London, Mitchell Beazley-Sidgwick and Jackson, 1977, Rand McNally, 1978.

How Britain Won the Space Race, with Desmond Leslie. London, Mitchell Beazley, 1972.

Stories of Science and Invention. London, Oxford University Press, 1972.

How to Recognise the Stars, with Lawrence Clarke. London, Corgi, 1972.

The Southern Stars. Cape Town, Timmins, 1972.

1001 Questions Answered about Astronomy, by James S. Pickering, revised edition. Guildford, Surrey, Lutterworth Press, 1972; New York, Dodd Mead, 1973.

Patrick Moore's Colour Star Atlas. Guildford, Surrey, Lutterworth Press, 1973; as *Color Star Atlas,* New York, Crown, 1973.

The Starlit Sky. Cape Town, Timmins, 1973.

Man the Astronomer. London, Priory Press, 1973.

Mars, with Charles A. Cross. London, Mitchell Beazley, and New York, Crown, 1973.

The Comets: Visitors from Space. Shaldon, Devon, Reid, 1973; revised edition, as *Comets,* New York, Scribner, 1976; as *Guide to Comets,* Guildford, Surrey, Lutterworth Press, 1977.

Watchers of the Stars: The Scientific Revolution. London, Joseph, and New York, Putnam, 1974; revised as *The Great Astronomical Revolution, 1543-1687, and the Space-Age Epilogue,* Chichester, and Concord, Massachusetts, Paul, 1994.

Black Holes in Space, with Iain Nicolson. London, Ocean, 1974; New York, Norton, 1976.

The Astronomy Quiz Book. London, Carousel, 1974; revised edition, 1978; as *Patrick Moore's Astronomy Quiz Book,* London, G. Philip, 1987.

The Young Astronomer and His Telescope. Shaldon, Devon, Reid, 1974.

Let's Look at the Sky: The Planets [The Stars]. London, Carousel, 2 vols., 1975.

Legends of the Planets. London, Luscombe, 1976.

The Next Fifty Years in Space. London, Luscombe, and New York, Taplinger, 1976.

The Stars Above. Norwich, Jarrold, 1976.

The Astronomy of Southern Africa, with Pete Collins. Cape Town, Timmins, and London, Hale, 1977.

The Atlas of Mercury, with Charles A. Cross. London, Mitchell Beazley, and New York, Crown, 1977.

Guide to Mars (not the same as 1956 book). Guildford, Surrey, Lutterworth Press, 1977; New York, Norton, 1978.

Wonder Why Book of Planets [the Earth, Stars]. London, Transworld, 3 vols., 1977-78; *Stars* published New York, Grosset and Dunlap, 1979.

Man's Future in Space. Hove, Sussex, Wayland, 1978.

The Guinness Book of Astronomy Facts and Feats. London, Guinness Superlatives, 1979; 3rd edition as *The Guinness Book of Astronomy,* Enfield, Middlesex, Guinness, 1988; 4th edition, 1992.

Fun-to-Know-About Mysteries of Space (for children). London, Armada, 1979.

Out of Darkness: The Planet Pluto, with Clyde Tombaugh. Guildford, Surrey, Lutterworth Press, and Harrisburg, Pennsylvania, Stackpole, 1980.

The Pocket Guide to Astronomy. New York, Simon and Schuster, 1980; as *Patrick Moore's Pocket Guide to Astronomy,* London, Mitchell Beazley, 1982.

Everyman's Scientific Facts and Feats, with Magnus Pyke. London, Dent, 1981.

The Moon (atlas). London, Mitchell Beazley, and Chicago, Rand McNally, 1981.

Jupiter, with Garry Hunt. London, Mitchell Beazley, and Chicago, Rand McNally, 1981.

William Herschel, Astronomer and Musician. Sidcup, Kent, P. M.E. Erwood-Herschel Society, 1981.

The Unfolding Universe. London, Joseph-Rainbird, and New York, Crown, 1982.

Saturn, with Garry Hunt. London, Mitchell Beazley, and Chicago, Rand McNally, 1982.

What's New in Space? (for children). London, Carousel, 1982.

Countdown! or, How Nigh Is the End? London, Joseph-Rainbird, 1983.

Travellers in Space and Time. London, Park Lane, 1983; New York, Doubleday, 1984.

The Space Shuttle Action Book (for children). London, Aurum Press, and New York, Random House, 1983.

The Return of Halley's Comet, with John Mason. Wellington, Northamptonshire, Stephens, and New York, Norton, 1984.

The Story of the Earth, with Peter Cattermole. London, Cambridge University Press, 1984; New York, Cambridge University Press, 1985.

Armchair Astronomy. Wellington, Northamptonshire, Stephens, and New York, Norton, 1984.

Stargazing: Astronomy Without a Telescope. London, Aurum Press, and Hauppauge, New York, Barron's, 1985.

Halley's Comet Pop-Up Book, with Heather Couper. London, Dean's, and New York, Crown, 1985.

How to Make the Most of Your Telescope. London, Longman, 1985.

The Sky at Night. Kent, Harrap, and New York, Norton, 1985.

The Universe, with Iain Nicolson. London, Collins, and New York, Macmillan, 1985.

Astronomy for the Under Tens. London, Philip, 1986; revised edition, 1989; 3rd edition, Philip, 1991; as *Astronomy for the Beginner,* New York, Cambridge, 1992.

Patrick Moore's A-Z of Astronomy. Wellington, Northamptonshire, Stephens, 1986; New York, Norton, 1987.

Astronomers' Stars. London, Routledge, 1986; New York, Norton, 1989.

Exploring the Night Sky with Binoculars. Cambridge, Cambridge University Press, 1986; 3rd edition, 1995.

TV Astronomer: Thirty Years of "The Sky at Night." Kent, Harrap, 1987.

Stars and Planets. London, Merehurst, and New York, Exeter, 1988; revised as *Philip's Guide to Stars and Planets,* London, Philip, 1993.

Space Travel for the Under Tens. London, Philip, 1988; as *Space Travel for the Beginner,* New York, Cambridge, 1992.

Atlas of Uranus, with Garry Hunt. Cambridge, Cambridge University Press, 1989.

The Amateur Astronomer. Cambridge, Cambridge University Press, 1990.

Universe for the Under Tens. London, Philip, 1990; as *The Universe for the Beginner,* New York, Cambridge, 1992.

Mission to the Planets: The Illustrated Story of Man's Exploration of the Solar System. New York, Norton, 1990.

Earth for the Under Tens. London, Philip, 1991.

Passion for Astronomy. Newton Abbot, Devon, David and Charles, 1991.

Guide to the Night Sky. London, Philip, 1991.

Sir John Herschel, Explorer of the Southern Sky. Bath, Avon, William Herschel Society, 1992.

Fireside Astronomy: An Anecdotal Tour through the History and Lore of Astronomy. Chichester and New York, Wiley, 1992.

Atlas of Neptune, with Garry E. Hunt. Cambridge and New York, Cambridge University Press, 1994.

Philip's Atlas of the Universe. London, Philip, 1994; as *Atlas of the Universe,* Skokie, Illinois, Rand McNally, 1994.

The Starry Sky [Stars; Planets; Sun and Moon; Comets and Shooting Stars]. Brookfield, Connecticut, Copper Beech, 5 vols., 1995.

Hard Choices: Environmentalists and the Forest. Chicago, Heartland Institute, 1995.

Editor, *Space Exploration.* Cambridge, University Press, 1958.

Editor, *Practical Amateur Astronomy.* London, Lutterworth Press, 1963; as *A Handbook of Practical Amateur Astronomy,* New York, Norton, 1964.

Editor, *Against Hunting.* London, Gollancz, 1965.

Editor, *Some Mysteries of the Universe,* by William R. Corliss. London, Black, 1969.

Editor, *Astronomical Telescopes and Observatories.* Newton Abbot, Devon, David and Charles, and New York, Norton, 1973.

Editor, *Modern Astronomy: Selections from The Yearbook of Astronomy.* London, Sidgwick and Jackson, and New York, Norton, 1977.

Editor, *The Beginner's Book of Astronomy.* London, Sidgwick and Jackson, 1978.

Editor, with Garry Hunt, *The Atlas of the Solar System.* London, Mitchell Beazley, 1983.

Editor, *The International Encyclopedia of Astronomy.* Torrance, California, 1987.

Editor, *Yearbook of Astronomy 1992.* New York, Norton, 1991.

Translator, *The Planet Mars,* by Gérard de Vaucouleurs. London, Faber, and New York, Macmillan, 1950; revised edition, Faber, 1951.

Translator, *The Structure of the Universe,* by Evry L. Schatzman. London, Weidenfeld and Nicolson, 1968.

Translator, *Quanta,* by J. Andrade e Silva and G. Lochak. London, Weidenfeld and Nicolson, 1969.

Translator, *Cosmology,* by Jean Émile Charon. London, Weidenfeld and Nicolson, 1970.

Translator, *The Planet Mercury [Mars],* by E.M. Antoniadi. Shaldon, Devon, Reid, 2 vols., 1974-75.

Recording: *The Ever Ready Band Plays Music by Patrick Moore,* Pye, 1979.

*

Patrick Moore comments:

My novels are written with the aim of entertaining; they are set in space and are for boys aged roughly 10 to 15. I try to keep a reasonably authentic background, though I am not above taking liberties (after all, Wells did!). I do, however, make a rule that any juvenile novels of mine avoid the sordid and unwholesome.

*   *   *

Patrick Moore's novels possess some special quality not shared by many of their contemporaries. Like the Biggles series, Moore's tales of interplanetary travel continue to be republished and find a steady readership. Unfortunately, the quality that enables these novels to maintain their readership does not transmit itself to the adult reader. The children's books of a writer such as Ursula K. LeGuin can be identified as books of some merit even by adult standards. However, Moore's books tend to present a view of life and character that is narrow and unrealistic. The characters themselves are largely stock creations and are emotionally very limited. The story lines are repetitive and rely on a limited number of situations to maintain the excitement of the tale. (The main variations consist of altering the names of the chief characters, the settings, and the order of the incidents.) Finally the stories themselves lack a human realism. Scientifically, the stories are slightly behind the times, but this is of little significance compared to the ease with which his juvenile heroes become incorporated into the adventure: this strains adult credulity, and probably that of many children as well. Despite this, the books continue to attract readers at a time when many superior examples of the storyteller's craft fail to do so. Moore's books offer something beyond an adventure in space, something beyond the lack of literary polish. This something lies within the story.

A typical story line would go something like this: an honest courageous youth with a steady head on his shoulders by some means becomes associated with a research establishment engaged in the exploration of outer space. This establishment is staffed by a group of scientific internationalists who react strongly against national or political interests. A crisis occurs and the staff of the establishment are forced through circumstances to utilise the youth in a task of responsibility on a dangerous mission. The youth, despite the fact that he is not of outstanding intelligence or possessed of great knowledge, manages to win the respect of the scientists through a display of his basic qualities during the many dangers encountered throughout the mission, and, now accepted as an equal, has his future career as a respected member of an exploration team assured. In the series, the youthful hero gradually occupies a more and more respected place among the ranks of the scientist/explorers. The appeal of this storyline is fairly obvious. It displays successful adolescent involvement in an adult world, though a greatly simplified and idealised one. A display of truth, integrity, and courage is sufficient to achieve one's desire, and there are no authority conflicts to establish problems between the adolescent and his elders, since the authority displayed by the scientists stems only from their great knowledge of a given situation, and the motivation for accepting their authority is made obvious: death in space if the mission fails. In this respect, Moore's novels reflect an updating of traditional tales of this type, and in that context, a fairly successful updating.

—Gary Coughlan

MOORE, Ward

Nationality: American. **Born:** Madison, New Jersey, 10 August 1903. **Education:** Self-educated. **Family:** Married 1) Lorna Lenzi in 1942 (divorced); 2) Raylyn Crabbe in 1967, four daughters and three sons. **Career:** Chicken farmer, bookshop clerk and manager, shipyard worker during World War II, homebuilder, gardener, ghostwriter, copy editor, and book review editor. Lived in California after 1929. **Died:** 29 January 1978.

SCIENCE FICTION PUBLICATIONS

Novels

Greener Than You Think. New York, Sloane, 1947; London, Gollancz, 1949.
Bring the Jubilee. New York, Farrar Straus, 1953; London, Heinemann, 1955.
Joyleg: A Folly, with Avram Davidson. New York, Pyramid, 1962.
Caduceus Wild, with Robert Bradford. Los Angeles, Pinnacle, 1978.

OTHER PUBLICATION

Novel

Breathe the Air Again. New York, Harper, 1942.

*   *   *

Ward Moore's science fiction began in 1947 with the publication of *Greener Than You Think,* a disaster novel in which a mysterious mutated "devilgrass" threatens the world. Moore also wrote a number of short stories, but no collected edition exists. This is a shame, since many of the stories are interesting and worthy of a larger audience. "Lot," for example, is a powerful story of a man obsessed with survival, who, with his family, is escaping the fallout of a nuclear attack. "Adjustment" shows Moore's humor in a tale of a man who can make his wishes come true. "The Mysterious Milkman of Bishop Street" shows still another dimension of Moore's ability, in a whimsical fantasy about a milkman too good to be endured.

Moore's reputation in science fiction, however, rests chiefly on a superlative work of alternate history, *Bring the Jubilee.* This fine novel, which ironically takes its title from the Civil War song "Marching Through Georgia," supposes that Lee's forces had taken the high ground before the Battle of Gettysburg, leading to victory there and eventually to victory in the "War of Southern Independence." Most of the novel shows the results of this turn of events

on subsequent history: the Confederacy has become wealthy and powerful, expanding westward to California and southward into Central America, but the Northern States lead an impoverished, backward existence. The central character of the novel, Hodge Backmaker, is born into a poor farm family, and in 1938 goes to New York to expand his opportunities. The world of *Bring the Jubilee* is much more technologically backward than our historical one, and Hodge has trouble gaining the education he seeks. Events bring him to a center for study in Pennsylvania, established years before by Herbert Haggerwells, a major in the Confederate army who remained in the area. There Hodge finds his vocation, and begins to build himself a reputation in Civil War history, but his conclusions are challenged by an authority in the field. A descendant of the Major, Barbara Haggerwells, is a physicist; she has perfected a time machine, and she offers its use to Hodge to visit the Battle of Gettysburg and test his theories. Hodge is to learn painfully that even the fact of observation affects that which is studied. Arriving before dawn on the morning of the 1st of July, 1863, Hodge is spotted by advancing Confederate troops, and they halt to question him. A panic ensues in which the officer is killed, and when light breaks, Hodge recognizes the dead man as Herbert Haggerwells. With the advance interrupted, the Confederates never take the Round Tops, and the battle proceeds as our history knows it.

Born in 1921, Hodge dies in 1877, a broken man. He realizes his responsibility for the destruction of the world he knew. In addition to the adventure story and the imaginative construction of an alternative world, Moore has written a probing discussion of the controversy between free will and determinism, and the result is a work that is one of science fiction's best.

—Walter E. Meyers

MORLEY, Wilfred Owen. *See* LOWNDES, Robert A.W.

MORRESSY, John

Nationality: American. **Born:** Brooklyn, New York, 8 December 1930. **Education:** St. John's University, New York, B.A. in English 1953; New York University, M.A. 1961. **Military Service:** Served in the United States Army, 1953-55. **Family:** Married Barbara Ann Turner in 1956. **Career:** Writer and reviewer, Equitable Life, New York, 1957-59; Instructor, St. John's University, 1962-66; Assistant Professor, Monmouth College, West Long Branch, New Jersey, 1966-67; Writer-in-Residence, Worcester Consortium, Massachusetts, 1977; Visiting Writer and Elliott Professor of English, University of Maine, Orono, 1977-78; Writer-in-Residence, Lynchburg College, Lynchburg, Virginia, 1987. Associate Professor, Professor, and Writer-in-Residence, Franklin Pierce College, Rindge, New Hampshire, 1968-95. **Awards:** Bread Loaf Writers Conference Fellowship, 1968; University of Colorado Writers Conference Fellowship, 1970; Balrog award, 1984. **Agent:** William Morris Agency, Inc., 1350 Avenue of the Americas, New York,

New York 10019. **Address:** Apple Hill Road, East Sullivan, New Hampshire 03445, U.S.A.

SCIENCE FICTION PUBLICATIONS

Novels (series: Iron Angel; Kedrigern; Del Whitby; Ziax II)

Starbrat (Whitby). New York, Walker, 1972; London, New English Library, 1979.
Nail Down the Stars (Whitby). New York, Walker, 1973; London, New English Library, 1979; as *Stardrift,* New York, Popular Library, 1975.
The Humans of Ziax II (for children). New York, Walker, 1974.
Under a Calculating Star (Whitby). Garden City, New York, Doubleday, 1975; London, Sidgwick and Jackson, 1978.
The Windows of Forever (for children). New York, Walker, 1975.
A Law for the Stars. Toronto, Laser, 1976.
The Extraterritorial. Toronto, Laser, 1977.
Frostworld and Dreamfire. Garden City, New York, Doubleday, 1977; London, Sidgwick and Jackson, 1979.
The Drought on Ziax II (for children). New York, Walker, 1978.
Ironbrand (Iron Angel). New York, Playboy Press, 1980.
Graymantle (Iron Angel). New York, Playboy Press, 1981.
Kingsbane (Iron Angel). New York, Playboy Press, 1982.
The Mansions of Space. New York, Ace, 1983.
The Time of the Annihilator (Iron Angel). New York, Ace, 1985.
A Voice for Princess (Kedrigern). New York, Ace, 1986.
The Questing of Kedrigern. New York, Ace, 1987.
Kedrigern in Wanderland. New York, Ace, 1988.
Kedrigern and the Charming Couple. New York, Ace, 1990.
A Remembrance for Kedrigern. New York, Ace, 1990.

OTHER PUBLICATIONS

Novels

The Blackboard Cavalier. Garden City, New York, Doubleday, 1966; London, Gollancz, 1967.
The Addison Tradition. Garden City, New York, Doubleday, 1968.
A Long Communion. New York, Walker, 1974; as *Displaced Persons,* New York, Popular Library, 1976.

Short Stories

Other Stories. Amherst, Massachusetts, Northern New England Review Press, 1983.

*

John Morressy comments:

I write science fiction because I find it to be the most interesting, enjoyable, and creative field open to a writer today and the one that may, in time, prove to be the most significant.

My books are founded on the assumption that the human race, in future ages, will behave much as it always has in the past. We are not yet civilized, and I find it hard to believe that we ever will be. After six or seven thousand years of recorded history and, according to some, progress, we still settle our ideological and economic conflicts by killing one another and laying waste to our planet. Piracy, slavery, and brigandage still thrive. In more countries than we can enumerate, torture is routinely inflicted on prisoners, trial and sentencing is a mockery of justice, and execution is quick and brutal. Under the circumstances, such cherished terms as "freedom" and "human dignity" are meaningless, almost silly. And all this is in the age of *Apollo, Voyager,* and *Explorer,* of organ transplants and laser surgery and micro-computers and an arm-long list of scientific and technological wonders.

My novels are set in a future spawned by this present. I envision the human race as surviving (though not without great suffering), eventually reaching the stars, encountering other worlds and other races, and making all the old mistakes over again, on a larger scale. I have tried to create a single future continuum and keep my novels within it. The novels are linked, not sequentially, but laterally. There is no one that must be read first, or last, in order to understand some grand design. A few characters, and places, and institutions, and events, appear in several of my novels; others are in one only. My novels are not attempts to predict the future, but glimpses of what might happen in one particular future. To me, that is the thing science fiction can do and no other genre can: it can give a reader a taste of the future without charging the full and non-refundable price of experiencing it in person.

*   *   *

John Morressy's first science fiction novel, *Starbrat,* was the opening volume in a series of space adventures that borrow heavily from other genres in their detail and treatment. The young protagonist is kidnapped from his homeworld by space pirates and sold into slavery as a gladiator. There he becomes a skillful warrior, eventually earning his freedom, then setting out to find his destiny on another world. Spirited adventure fare, if somewhat derivative. During his quest, the protagonist meets a wandering minstrel who is the central figure in the sequel, *Nail Down the Stars* (which also appeared under the title *Stardrift*). The minstrel, whose identity seems to change with every world he visits, has a series of adventures as he travels about, but nothing is resolved until the third in the series, *Under a Calculating Star,* completes the cycle. The protagonist is a confidence man who murders a planetary king to whom he bears an uncanny resemblance, intending to replace him and secretly usurp the throne. His plan becomes more complicated as he encounters the main characters from the previous two books, a cleverly conceived device that makes the series as a whole more cohesive than the disparate plots of the individual volumes might suggest.

Morressy wrote three more novels set in this same universe, although they are individually unrelated. *Frostworld and Dreamfire* continues the story of an interstellar civilization sinking into feudalism and barbarism. A fresh menace appears in the form of the Sternverein Empire, armed with powerful weapons, ruthlessly determined to extend their power. A three-sided conflict erupts between the invaders, the ruler of a small planet, and a charismatic tribal leader who wishes to free his people from the planetary tyrant. In *A Law for the Stars,* the Sternverein have become the police of the known universe, maintaining order although at the cost of certain freedoms. The hero is a young man freed from slavery and enlisted in that organization, and the story deals with his gradual realization that despite his feelings of gratitude, the Sternverein are corrupt and power hungry. *The Mansions of Space* is the most recent book set in this universe, which Morressy seems to have abandoned in recent years in favor of fantasy fiction. It follows the adventures of an interstellar trader who makes an unusual discovery, and is easily the best of Morressy's space operas. There was one other straightforward science-fiction novel during this period, the very atypical *The Extraterritorial,* set on Earth in the future where mysterious organizations contend among themselves. The theme is once again the corruption of an institution discovered by one of its adherents.

Morressy turned to fantasy in 1980 with *Ironbrand.* The plot is the familiar quest of three sons to reclaim the throne of their father from an evil, and inhuman, usurper. Morressy displayed a positive gift for this form, and the novel was sufficiently successful to inspire two additional volumes. *Graymantle* is actually a prequel, another quest story, this time the search for a magical artifact that holds the key to toppling a tyrant from his throne. This same talisman figures prominently again in the third in the series, *Kingsbane,* this time stolen by an ambitious lord in a time when the use of magic has largely been forgotten.

Morressy wrote one independent fantasy novel, *The Time of the Annihilator,* a comparatively minor novel that ended his period of quest fantasies. It was followed within a year by *A Voice for Princess,* which introduced the scholarly but wizened wizard Kedrigern, who has been featured in his five most recent novels. With this novel, Morressy moved into the area of humorous fantasy, featuring a feisty magician who resigns from the wizards' guild in the opening adventure, planning to lead a contemplative life, but ultimately deciding to find a beautiful young princess to marry. Kedrigern casts counterspells, but each can work only once, providing many of the plot lines.

The Questing of Kedrigern involves his attempt to find a solution when rival wizards drunkenly transform his female companion into a toad. He is successful, of course, and marries her in the next volume, *Kedrigern in Wanderland.* The third adventure is far superior to the preceding two, demonstrating Morressy's growing ability to blend humor and adventure. In two subsequent adventures, *Kedrigern and the Charming Couple* and *A Remembrance for Kedrigern,* the inimitable sorcerer must deal with a werewolf and an inept dragonslayer, respectively. As a whole, the series has been inventive and entertaining, a viable alternative to Piers Anthony's far more popular Xanth books.

Although Morressy was an infrequent short-story writer in the 1970s, he became far more prolific at that length during the 1980s. Most of these are competent but unmemorable, but three deserve mention. "The Empath and the Savages" (in *The Best of Omni Science Fiction 3,* edited by Ben Bova and Don Myrus. New York, Omni, 1982) provides an interesting insight into an alien worldview, "Stoneskin" (in *Fantasy and Science Fiction* [New York], June 1984) is a cleverly plotted serious fantasy adventure, and "No More Pencils, No More Books" (in *The Best Science Fiction of the Year 9,* edited by Terry Carr. New York, Ballantine, 1980) is a disturbing glimpse of what might happen if we allow the government to enforce its desire for conformity far enough to limit our own freedom.

—Don D'Ammassa

MORRIS, Janet E(llen)

Nationality: American. **Born:** Boston, Massachusetts, 25 May 1946. **Education:** Attended New York University, 1965-66. **Family:** Married Christopher C. Morris in 1971. **Career:** Lighting designer, Chip Monck Enterprises, New York, 1963-64; night manager, 1970; bass player, Christopher Morris Band, 1975, 1977; songwriter and recording artist; project director, U.S. Global Strategy Council, 1989. Since 1990, research director, Non-Lethal Programs; associate, Institute for Geopolitical Studies. Vice-president of Morris & Morris, a private consultancy specializing in long-term strategies for identifying and acquiring new defense technology with unique political utility. **Agent:** Perry Knowlton, Curtis Brown Agency, 10 Astor Place, New York, New York 10003, U.S.A.

SCIENCE FICTION PUBLICATIONS

Novels (series: Heroes in Hell; Kerrion Empire; Silistra; Thieves' World—Tempus; Threshold)

High Couch of Silistra: (Returning Creation). New York, Bantam, 1977; revised edition, as *Returning Creation,* New York, Baen, 1984.
The Golden Sword (Silistra). New York, Bantam, 1977.
Wind from the Abyss (Silistra). New York, Bantam, 1978.
The Carnelian Throne (Silistra). New York, Bantam, 1979.
Dream Dancer (Kerrion). New York, Berkley, and London, Fontana, 1980.
Cruiser Dreams (Kerrion). New York, Putnam, and London, Fontana, 1981.
Earth Dreams (Kerrion). New York, Putnam, 1982.
The 40-Minute War, with Chris Morris. New York, Baen, 1984.
Active Measures, with David A. Drake. New York, Baen, 1985.
Basileus, with C.J. Cherryh (Heroes), bound with *Rhialto the Marvellous,* by Jack Vance. New York, Baen, 1985.
Beyond Sanctuary (Thieves' World). New York, Baen, 1985.
Beyond the Veil (Thieves' World). New York, Baen, 1985.
The Gates of Hell (Heroes), with C.J. Cherryh. New York, Baen, 1986.
Beyond Wizardwall (Thieves' World). New York, Baen, 1986.
M*E*D*U*S*A, with Chris Morris. New York, Baen, 1986.
Kings in Hell (Heroes), with C.J. Cherryh. New York, Baen, 1987.
Kill Ratio, with David A. Drake. New York, Ace, 1987.
Warlord! New York, Pocket, 1987.
Outpassage, with Chris Morris. New York, Pageant, 1988; London, New English Library, 1990.
City at the Edge of Time (Thieves' World), with Chris Morris. New York, Baen, 1988.
My Little Helliad (Heroes), with Chris Morris. New York, Baen, 1988.
Tempus Unbound (Thieves' World), with Chris Morris. New York, Baen, 1989.
Explorers in Hell (Heroes), with David A. Drake. New York, Baen, 1989.
Target, with David A. Drake. New York, Ace, 1989.
Storm Seed (Thieves' World), with Chris Morris. New York, Baen, 1990.
Threshold, with Chris Morris. New York, Roc, 1990.
Trust Territory, with Chris Morris. New York, Roc, 1992.
The Stalk (Threshold), with Chris Morris. New York, Roc, 1994.
Arc Riders, with David A. Drake. New York, Warner, 1995.

Short Stories

Tempus (Thieves' World). New York, Baen, 1987.

OTHER PUBLICATIONS

Novels

I, the Sun. New York, Bantam, 1980.

Other (series: Heroes in Hell)

The Warrior's Edge, with John B. Alexander and Richard Groller. New York, Morrow, 1990.

Editor, *Afterwar.* New York, Baen, 1985.

Editor, *Heroes in Hell* (Heroes). New York, Baen, 1986.

Editor, *Rebels in Hell* (Heroes). New York, Baen, 1986.

Editor, *Crusaders in Hell* Heroes). New York, Baen, 1987.

Editor, *Angels in Hell* (Heroes). New York, Baen, 1987.

Editor, *Masters in Hell* (Heroes). New York, Baen, 1988.

Editor, *War in Hell* (Heroes). New York, Baen, 1988.

Editor, *Prophets in Hell* (Heroes). New York, Baen, 1989.

Editor, with Chris Morris, *The American Warrior.* Stamford, Connecticut, Longmeadow Press, 1992.

*

Janet E. Morris comments:

(1981) The thrust of my work, over the long term and through a projected group of books, historical, contemporary, and speculative, is the evolution of consciousness, with an eye toward the genetic, societal, and philosophical influences thereon. Sophocles states that one law ever holds true: nothing vast enters into the world of mortals without a curse. I look for in past history or create in my future histories moments of cataclysm in theaters both physical and mental. My intention is always to explore the thought that must precede any outward action, its struggle to reach a new, more tenable position from which to regard self and universe.

My work in history shall eventually include: Sargon of Agade's conquest of Ebla; Rammesseide Egypt in its position as the seat of Yawwhist tradition; the Seven Sages, those wonderful progenitors of pre-Socratic thought; as well as Suppiluliumas I of Hatti and his dealings with the short-lived Atenist rise in Egypt (*I, the Sun*). Another work samples alchemical thought at the time of the death of Paracelsus, father of chemotherapy.

My science-fictional excursions into the possible evolution of consciousness have all centered on man's apprehension of the physical world, and his sense of place in it. My areas of study are necessarily genetics, biology, sociobiology, philosophy, and physics, but the aim at all times is to *show* rather than *tell.* The more crystallized the tenets of my position in a particular book, the more I strive to present them in an experiential manner without technical discourse which might erect a barrier between myself and the reader.

My Silistra series openly treats sexual themes as well as the possible effect of mind on probability. My Dream Dancer books treat the marriage of man and mechanical intelligence through the utilization of our mastery of the intelligence code, the decipherment of which is even now in progress, as well as man's attempt to emancipate himself from the prison of relativistic space. Both the above groups of books focus to some extent on women, but are in no sense "women's" books; rather, I feel that technology is the leveler of sexism and the liberator of those sexual types not included in the sub-set "heterosexual male."

Reading back over what I have written, I must add that I write primarily the book which I myself would like to read, the book I can imagine that you might like to read. My hope above all is to tender you, the reader, an excursion, a journey into another realm which, upon returning, you might find to some small degree has enriched your "present."

*   *   *

Janet Morris has written everything from heroic fantasy to space opera to near future political thriller, most characterized by strong, even heroic characters who act positively in the face of danger, either by directly confronting it or by outsmarting the opposition. There's a clear political undercurrent in many of these instances, faith in technology, support for assertiveness in international relations, and an underlying distrust of certain aspects of government bureaucracies, even in fantastic worlds.

It would be easy to dismiss the early novels as transplanted historicals, because on at least one level, that is what they are. Morris uses her familiarity with history and the evolution of cultures to create an interstellar society in *High Couch of Silistra,* later revised and reissued as *Returning Creation.* The culture presented in this and three sequels, *The Golden Sword, Wind from the Abyss,* and *The Carnelian Throne,* is complex and in many ways controversial, and there was a tendency to dismiss the series as demeaning in its portrayal of gender roles because the central character is a courtesan in what appears to be a male-dominated culture. In actual fact, the protagonist is potentially the most influential person on the entire planet, which is recovering from the excesses of technology only to face the possibility of a recurrence of that same disaster. Although the series has its awkward moments, it remains innovative, unusually frank and perceptive in its examination of power relationships between the sexes.

The Silistra books were followed by a trilogy that described an even more interesting society. *Dream Dancer* and its two sequels, *Cruiser Dreams* and *Earth Dreams,* also featured a strong female protagonist. The primary conflict is the constant struggle for power and influence at the top levels of society. Perhaps the most interesting aspect of the trilogy is Morris's creation of an artificial species of intelligent, sentient starships, whose fate is the focal point of the struggle central to what is an impressively well thought out plot and a convincing setting.

In 1985, Morris seemed to split into two separate writers, both very different from the one who had existed prior to that point. Although there were many superficial aspects of fantasy in the earlier novels, they remained science fiction. Her participation in the shared universe "Thieves' World" series of original anthologies led to the creation of Tempus, a recurring character, an immortal hero featured in the first independent novel in that setting, *Beyond Sanctuary.* Morris continued the saga of Tempus in a battle with demons in *Beyond the Veil,* and a concluding volume, *Beyond Wizardwall.* A collection of the independent shorter adventures was published as *Tempus,* and a second trilogy, written in collaboration with Chris Morris, followed, consisting of *Tempus Unbound, City at the Edge of Time,* and *Storm Seed.*

Morris was also instrumental in the creation of another popular shared universe series, the "Heroes in Hell" books, a series of fantasy adventures set in the afterlife, with all of human history as a source of characters. Morris wrote three collaborative novels in this setting as well as shorter stories: *Kings in Hell* with C.J. Cherryh, *The Little Helliad* with Chris Morris, and *Explorers in Hell* with David Drake. For the most part, the series is a pale imitation of Philip Jose Farmer's Riverworld, and not nearly as interesting as the author's other work.

Morris was much more successful with her simultaneous shift to a series of near future, technological thrillers. In *Active Measures,* written with David Drake, a CIA agent realizes that the President is a Soviet sympathizer, cleverly altering domestic and foreign policy to lower American prestige to the benefit of the Soviet Union, and to cause deeper schisms in an already badly fractured country. Current events have taken a toll on the book's premise, and there's a tendency to lecture. As a marketing device, the book was published as a contest in which readers were to provide solutions to some unresolved problems.

A far more successful book was *The 40-Minute War,* with Chris Morris. A terrorist attack on Washington results in a limited nuclear exchange. Once again, the protagonist is an intelligence operative working with the Israeli secret service in an attempt to stem the drift towards anarchy in North America. *Medusa,* also written with Chris Morris, is another high-tech thriller, this time involving a supposed Soviet accident, a missile which must be intercepted before it damages or destroys America's space-borne defense system. Both novels are now badly dated, but as published they were good examples of their particular type.

Kill Ratio by Morris and David Drake moved away from the very near future, although the conflicts remain very similar. The United Nations has moved its headquarters to the moon, where a terrorist group releases a deadly plague into the environmental systems. Another intelligence operative, a member in this case of the organization responsible for the security of the installation, is called upon to find out who is responsible. The highly suspenseful plot and logical resolution mark this as an exceptional work of its kind. A sequel, *Target,* was an even better work, the best of Morris's futuristic spy thrillers. An alien arrives on the moon, seeking asylum, pursued by a number of enemies equipped with technology far in advance of that available to humanity. Human authorities must decide whether or not to take sides, which side to take, and how to avoid getting caught in an interstellar crossfire.

Morris's subsequent novels have dealt with more traditional themes. *Outpassage,* with Chris Morris, is an interplanetary adventure story filled with intrigues, potential rebellions, and fast-paced action. The same collaborative team also wrote *Threshold,* a tale of interstellar smuggling with a very well-conceived and executed mystery subplot, set for the most part in an orbiting hotel.

Although Morris has written a fair number of short stories, these have been almost exclusively for shared world anthologies, and the best of these are those involving Tempus. Her contributions to C.J. Cherryh's Merovingen series, "Escape from Merovingen" and "Fools Must Die," are also worthwhile. Morris has also tried her hand at military science fiction, but only one story, "Fratricide," has to date been at all memorable. She seems more at ease at novel length and in a fairly contemporary setting, even though her initial successes were in more exotic settings.

—Don D'Ammassa

MORRIS, William

Nationality: English. **Born:** Walthamstow, Essex, 24 March 1834. **Education:** preparatory school in Walthamstow, 1843-47; Marlborough College, Wiltshire, 1848-51; privately, 1852-53; Exeter College, Oxford, 1853-55, B.A. 1856, M.A. 1875. Served in the Artists Corps of Volunteers, 1859-61. **Family:** Married Jane Burden in 1859; two daughters. **Career:** Articled to G.E. Street's architectural firm, Oxford and London, 1856; founding editor, *Oxford and Cambridge Magazine,* 1856; practicing painter, 1857-62; friend of Edward Burne-Jones, Dante Gabriel Rossetti, and other members of the Pre-Raphaelite Brotherhood; founder, with Burne-Jones, Rossetti, Ford Madox Brown, and others, Morris Marshall Faulkner & Co. design firm, London, 1861-74, subsequently Morris & Co., 1874-96; lived at Red House, Bexley, Kent, 1861-65, and in London from 1865 (at Kelmscott House, Hammersmith, from 1878); travelled in Iceland, 1871 and 1873; with Rossetti leased Kelmscott Manor, near Lechlade, Gloucestershire, 1871; public lecturer on art, architecture, and socialism, 1877-96; founder, Kelmscott Press, Hammersmith, 1890-96. Treasurer, National Liberal League, 1879; member, Democratic Federation, 1883, then the Socialist League, 1884; editor of its journal *Commonweal,* 1884-90, and League delegate to the International Socialist Working-Men's Congress, Paris, 1889; founding member, Hammersmith Socialist Society, 1890. Examiner, South Kensington School of Art, later Victoria and Albert Museum, London, 1876-96; founding member and secretary, Society for the Protection of Ancient Buildings, 1877; president, Birmingham Society of Arts, 1878-79; member, 1888, and master, 1892, Art Workers Guild: exhibited with the Arts and Crafts Exhibition Society. Honorary fellow, Exeter College, 1882. **Died:** 3 October 1896.

SCIENCE FICTION PUBLICATIONS

Novels

A Dream of John Ball; and, A King's Lesson. London, Reeves and Turner, 1888; East Aurora, New York, Roycroft, 1898.

A Tale of the House of the Wolfings and All the Kindreds of the Mark (prose and verse). London, Reeves and Turner, 1888; Boston, Roberts, 1890.

The Roots of the Mountains: Wherein Is Told Somewhat of the Lives of the Men of Burgdale. London, Reeves and Turner, 1889; New York, Longman, 1896.

News from Nowhere; or, An Epoch of Rest, Being Some Chapters from a Utopian Romance. Boston, Roberts, 1890; London, Longman, 1891.

The Story of the Glittering Plain Which Has Also Been Called the Land of Living Men, or the Acre of the Undying. Hammersmith, Middlesex, Kelmscott Press, and Boston, Roberts, 1891.

The Wood beyond the World. Hammersmith, Middlesex, Kelmscott Press, 1894; Boston, Roberts, 1895.

Child Christopher and Goldilind the Fair. Hammersmith, Middlesex, Kelmscott Press, 2 vols., 1895; Portland, Maine, Mosher, 1900; adapted for children by John-Martin as *The Wolf's-Head and the Queen,* New York, Scribner, 1931.

The Well at the World's End: A Tale. Hammersmith, Middlesex, Kelmscott Press, 1896; New York, Longman, 1896.

The Water of the Wondrous Isles. Hammersmith, Middlesex, Kelmscott Press, and New York, Longman, 1897.

The Sundering Flood. Hammersmith, Middlesex, Kelmscott Press, and New York, Longman, 1897.

Gertha's Lovers: A Tale. Portland, Maine, Mosher, 1905.

The Novel on Blue Paper, edited by Penelope Fitzgerald. London, and West Nyack, New York, Journeyman Press, 1982.

Short Stories

The Hollow Land: A Tale. Portland, Maine, Mosher, 1897.

Svend and His Brethren: A Tale. Aiken, South Carolina, Palmetto Press, 1901.

The Story of the Unknown Church and Other Tales. Portland, Maine, Mosher, 1902.

The Hollow Land, and Other Contributions to the Oxford and Cambridge Magazine. London, Longman, 1903.

Golden Wings: A Prose Romance and a Poem. Boston, Caldwell, 1904.

The Story of the Unknown Church; and, Lindenborg Pool. Warwick, England, Avon Booklet, 1904.

The Early Romances of William Morris in Prose and Verse. London, Dent, 1907; abridged as *Golden Wings and Other Stories,* Van Nuys, California, Newcastle, 1976.

William Morris. London, Nelson, 1923.

Early Romances. London, Collins, 1924.

Selections from the Prose Works of William Morris. Cambridge, England, Cambridge University Press, 1931.

Poetry

The Earthly Paradise: A Poem. London, Ellis, 3 vols., 1868-70; Boston, Roberts, 1868-71; revised edition, New York, Longman, 1890.

The Story of Sigurd the Volsung and the Fall of the Niblungs. London, Ellis and White, 1876; Boston, Roberts, 1877.

OTHER PUBLICATIONS

Play

The Tables Turned; or Nupkins Awakened: A Socialist Interlude (produced 1887). London, Commonweal Office, 1887.

Poetry

The Defence of Guenevere, and Other Poems, edited by Robert Steele. London, Bell and Daldy, 1858; Boston, Roberts, 1875.

The Life and Death of Jason: A Poem. London, Bell and Daldy, and Boston, Roberts, 1867; revised edition, London, Bell and Daldy, and Boston, Roberts, 1867, 1888.

The Pilgrims of Hope: A Poem in Thirteen Parts. London, Forman, 1886; Portland, Maine, Mosher, 1901.

Poems by the Way. Hammersmith, Middlesex, Kelmscott Press, 1891; Boston, Roberts, 1892.

A Book of Verse: A Facsimile of the Manuscript Written in 1870. London, Scolar Press, 1980.

Other

Love Is Enough; or, The Freeing of Pharamond: A Morality. London, Ellis and White, and Boston, Roberts, 1873.

Hopes and Fears for Art: Five Lectures Delivered in Birmingham, London, and Nottingham, 1878-1881. London, Ellis and White, and Boston, Roberts, 1882.

Lectures on Art. London, Macmillan, 1882.

A Summary of the Principles of Socialism Written for the Democratic Federation, with H.M. Hyndman. London, Modern Press, 1884.

Art and Socialism: A Lecture; and Watchman, What of the Night? The Aims and Ideals of the English Socialists of Today. London, Reeves, 1884.

Chants for Socialist: No. 1. The Day Is Coming. London, Reeves, 1884.

The Voice of Toil, All for the Cause: Two Chants for Socialists. London, Justice Office, 1884.

The God of the Poor. London, Justice Office, 1884.

Chants for Socialists. London, Socialist League Office, 1885; New York, New Horizon Press, 1935.

The Manifesto of the Socialist League. London, Socialist League, 1885; revised edition, 1885.

The Socialist League: Constitution and Rules at the General Conference. London, Socialist League, 1885.

Address to Trades' Unions (The Socialist Platform-No. 1). London, Socialist League, 1885.

The Aims of Art. London, Commonweal Office, 1887.

Signs of Change: Seven Lectures. London, Reeves and Turner, 1888; New York, Longman, 1896.

Socialist Platform (collected pamphlets), with others. N.p., 1888; revised edition, 1890.

Statement of Principles of the Hammersmith Socialist Society. Hammersmith, Hammersmith Socialist Society, 1890.

Under an Elm-Tree: or, Thoughts in the Country-side. Aberdeen, Scotland, Leatham, 1891; Portland, Maine, Mosher, 1912.

Manifesto of English Socialists, with G.B. Shaw and H.M. Hyndman. London, Twentieth Century Press, 1893.

The Reward of Labour: A Dialogue. London, Hayman Christy, 1893.

Letters on Socialism. London, Wisel, 1894.

How I Became a Socialist. London, Twentieth Century Press, 1896.

Architecture, Industry, and Wealth: Collected Papers. London, and New York, Longman, 1902.

Communism, a Lecture. London, Fabian Society, 1903.

Collected Works, edited by May Morris. London, and New York, Longman, 24 vols., 1910-15; supplement, as *William Morris: Artist, Writer, Socialist,* Oxford, Blackwell, 2 vols., 1936.

Prose and Poetry (1856-1870). London, Oxford University Press, 1913.

Stories in Prose, Stories in Verse, Shorter Poems, Lectures, and Essays. London, Nonesuch Press, 1934.

The Letters of William Morris to His Family and Friends, edited by Philip Henderson. London, and New York, Longman, 1950.

Unpublished Letters, edited by R.P. Arnot. London, Labour Monthly, 1951.

William Morris: Selected Writings and Designs, edited by Asa Briggs. Baltimore and Harmondsworth, Middlesex, Pelican, 1962.

The Unpublished Lectures of William Morris, edited by Eugene D. LeMire. Detroit, Michigan, Wayne State University Press, 1969.

Icelandic Journals. Fontwell, Centaur Press, 1969; New York, Praeger, 1970.

Political Writings of William Morris, edited by A.L. Morton. London, Lawrence and Wishart, and New York, International, 1973.

Early Romances in Prose and Verse, edited by Peter Faulkner. London, Dent, 1973; Van Nuys, California, Newcastle, 1976.

Socialist Diary, edited by Florence Boos. Iowa City, Iowa, Windhoven Press, 1981; London, History Workshop Journal, 1982.

The Ideal Book: Essays and Lectures on the Arts of the Book, edited by William S. Peterson. Berkeley, University of California Press, 1982.

The Juvenilia of William Morris, with a Checklist and Unpublished Early Poems, edited by Florence Boos. New York, William Morris Society, 1983.

The Collected Letters of William Morris, 1848-80 [1881-84], edited by Norman Kelvin. 2 vols., Princeton, Princeton University Press, 1984, 1987.

Morris by Himself: Designs and Writings, edited by Gillian Naylor. N.p., 1988.

Translator, with Eirìkr Magnússon, *Grettis Saga: The Story of Grettir the Strong.* London, Ellis, 1869; New York, Longman, 1901.

Translator, with Eirìkr Magnússon, *Völsunga Saga: The Story of the Volsungsand Niblungs with Certain Songs from the Elder Edda.* London, Ellis, 1870; edited by H. Sparling, London, and New York, Walter Scott, 1888.

Translator, with Eirìkr Magnússon, *Three Northern Love Stories and Other Tales.* London, Ellis, and New York, Longman, 1875.

Translator, *The Aeneids of Virgil Done into English Verse.* Boston, Roberts, 1875; London, Ellis and White, 1876.

Translator, *The Odyssey of Homer Done into English Verse.* London, Reeves and Turner, 2 vols., 1887; New York, Longman, 1897.

Translator, with Eirìkr Magnússon, *The Saga Library.* London, Quaritch, 5 vols., 1891-1905.

Translator, with others, *The Order of Chivalry,* by Hugues de Tabarie. Hammersmith, Middlesex, Kelmscott Press, 1893.

Translator, *The Tale of King Florus and the Fair Jehane.* Hammersmith, Middlesex, Kelmscott Press, 1893; Portland, Maine, Mosher, 1898.

Translator, *Of the Friendship of Amis and Amile.* Hammersmith, Middlesex, Kelmscott Press, 1894.

Translator, *The Tale of the Emperor Coustans and of Over Sea.* Hammersmith Press, 1894; Portland, Maine, Mosher, 1899.

Translator, with A.J. Wyatt, *The Tale of Beowulf, Sometime King of the Fold of the Weder Geats.* Hammersmith, Middlesex, Kelmscott Press, 1895; New York, Longman, 1910.

Translator, *Old French Romances.* London, G. Allen, and New York, Scribner, 1896.

Translator, with Eirìkr Magnússon, *The Story of Kormak, the Son of Ogmund,* edited by Grace Calder. London, William Morris Society, 1970.

*

Bibliography: *A Bibliography of the Works of William Morris* by Temple Scott, London, G. Bell, 1897; *Handlist of the Public Addresses of William Morris* by R.C.H. Briggs, London, William Morris Society, 1961; *William Morris in Private Press and Limited Editions: A Descriptive Bibliography of Books by and about William Morris 1891-1981* by John J. Walsdorf, Phoenix, Arizona, Oryx, and London, Library Association, 1983; *A Bibliography of the Kelmscott Press* by William S. Peterson, Oxford, Clarendon, 1984; *William Morris: A Reference Guide* by Gary L. Aho, Boston, G.K. Hall, 1985.

Critical Studies (selection): *The Life of William Morris* by J.W. Mackail, London, and New York, Longman, 2 vols., 1899; *The Kelmscott Press and William Morris, Master Craftsman* by H.H. Sparling, London, Macmillan, 1924; *William Morris: Romantic to Revolutionary* by E.P. Thompson, London, Lawrence and Wishart,

1955, revised edition, New York, Pantheon, 1976, London, Merlin Press, 1977; *Against the Age: An Introduction to William Morris* by Peter Faulkner, London, Allen and Unwin, 1980; *William Morris: The Critical Heritage* edited by Peter Faulkner, London, and Boston, Routledge and Kegan Paul, 1973; *William Morris: The Man and the Myth* (includes letters) by R.P. Arnot, New York, Monthly Review Press, and London, Lawrence and Wishart, 1964; *The Work of William Morris* by Paul Thompson, London, Heinemann, and New York, Viking, 1967, revised edition, London, Quartet Books, 1977; *William Morris: His Life, Work, and Friends* by Philip Henderson, London, Thames and Hudson, and New York, McGraw-Hill, 1967; *William Morris: His Life and Work* by Jack Lindsay, London, Constable, 1975, New York, Taplinger, 1979; *William Morris: Aspects of the Man and His Work* edited by Peter Lewis, Loughborough, Loughborough Victorian Studies Group, 1978; *A Pagan Prophet: William Morris* by Charlotte Oberg, Charlottesville, University Press of Virginia, 1978; *William Morris and His World* by Ian Bradley, New York, Scribner, and London, Thames and Hudson, 1978; *William Morris* by Frederick Kirchhoff, Boston, Twayne, 1979; *William Morris* by Peter Stansky, Oxford and New York, Oxford University Press, 1983; *William Morris: His Art, His Writings, and His Public Life: A Record* by Aymer Vallance, London, Studio Editions, 1986; *William Morris: His Life and Work* by Stephen Coote, London, Garamond, 1990.

*   *   *

It is impossible to summarise the contribution of William Morris to his age, which he abominated, and to our own, which would not much have impressed him. As social thinker, as designer and influence upon both arts and crafts (and especially those of everyday life), as poet (though his biggest works are not much to our contemporary taste), and as the first great Englishman to declare himself a communist, he is unique and irreplaceable. Yet it may be that the 10 great prose fictions of the last 10 years of his life offer his most lasting influence and his finest work. In these romances, he invented the modern fantasy novel, set in an imagined, glamorous, and self-consistent world, a "secondary creation," as Tolkien was later to call it.

Morris was directly influenced by saga, epic, and medieval romance: he in fact translated many sagas, as well as *The Odyssey, The Aeneid, Beowulf,* and some romances—the most important of which, *Havelock the Dane,* became the prose romance *Child Christopher.* The list of influencing genres would not be complete, however, without the wealth of folktales that he knew and used (mostly in verse). Two of the ten books are time-travel stories, two evoke "barbaric" pre-history, and the other six are more or less radical redesignings of the patterns of quest-romance.

A Dream of John Ball takes a modern protagonist back into the time of the Peasants' Revolt, a period whose arts, crafts, and architecture delighted Morris, and with whose social turmoil he strongly identified. The time-traveller learns the impotence of "knowing the future": he cannot help John Ball and the other rebels, and the nightlong climactic discussion with Ball in the church is more enlightening to "modern man" than to the radical priest. The book's initial and lasting charm lies in the eager clarity with which the medieval setting is evoked.

News from Nowhere is a much larger companion work, a journey into and within a future world that is described in the same energetic, clear-edged style. This future world is the Commonwealth of "Nowhere," into which the protagonist dreams England has been transformed by revolution. It is the finest utopia in English, the only one thoroughly worth living and working in, and Morris wrote it for a small radical audience, the readership of his leftwing magazine *Commonweal,* who would find it worth living and working for.

News from Nowhere at times seems to divide between too much "history" of how this post-governmental England came into being and too easy a celebration of its early-summer idyllic aspects, but the time-traveller joins and justifies these contraries. The wise and subtle treatment of his responses to—and his salutary effect on—the people of Nowhere carries the narrative and powers its journey into the heart of England and of community. Contemporary readers knew the open secret that "William Guest" was Morris, and recognised every stage in his journey as part of Morris's life. His strength of longing also creates the intrepid soulmate Ellen, who will safeguard and reshape Nowhere in its future, because she has met and loved the man that dreamed it.

A Tale of the House of the Wolfings and *The Roots of the Mountains,* between the two time-travel stories, explore two forms of the high barbaric society that Morris much preferred to high-capitalist civilisation. In *A Tale of the House of the Wolfings* the Gothic tribe's heroic resistance to Roman imperialism focuses upon the indomitable war-leader Thiodolf, but his love affair with the nature-goddess and part-time Valkyrie Wood-Sun almost prevents the completion of his necessary selfless death. In *The Roots of the Mountains* another warrior-hero finds that the destiny of his people depends on both battle and his personal leadership, but the Gothic tribes are united and the Huns driven from that side of the mountains without his having to pay the final price. *Goldmane* is a more complex and contemporary hero than Thiodolf; both wildwood magic and personal luck and beauty protect him instead of destroying him.

The Story of the Glittering Plain evokes a later, Teutonic tribal world, and the hero, Hallblithe, has to pursue a Viking group that has kidnapped his betrothed. The quest takes him beyond this conflict, however, to an Earthly paradise in which youth is permanently renewed and sensuous delight is not only guaranteed but insisted upon. Hallblithe detests the Glittering Plain; he eventually escapes from paradise and is reunited with his love. In a similar short romance, Golden Walter flees a miserable failed marriage, following mysterious visions that take him to the Wood Beyond the World. There his sexual helplessness teaches him to grow, both by his being forced to lie with the Lady of that Wood and by his being forbidden even to touch the Maid he loves. Eventually, the Maid is responsible for the Lady's death, and the two survivors find a new life as welcome rulers of a strange city through the mountains.

In these short romances and their great successors, *The Well at the World's End* and *The Water of the Wondrous Isles,* Morris creates a world akin to an unchurched version of medieval northwestern Europe. There is active magic in these worlds, both for good and for ill, and usually associated with a wise and beautiful woman (or two or more contrasting power-women). Natural and life-enhancing magic is available to the very rare adventurer who reaches the Well at the World's End, but the book focuses on Ralph's adventures travelling there and back, especially his contact with the two loves of his life: one is a Power-Lady, the other a beautiful and courageous "ordinary" girl who becomes far more astonishing than the Lady.

The Water of the Wondrous Isles has an even more revolutionary effect upon our expectations of the quest: the protagonist or "hero" is a girl. A witch has stolen Birdalone and reared her to be a trap for lustful males, but she escapes, naked and resolute, into the wide world. She travels among literally wondrous isles and is

caught up in a typical male quest, whose heroes leave her in a safe, smug castle while they sail off to rescue their ladies. Since she has never been taught that ladies are supposed to be passive, she escapes this protection too, and causes a much more perilous and passionate story. Three kinds of power-women influence her life, but her own developing integrity brings a qualified happy ending to her story.

The last, and incomplete, romance, *The Sundering Flood,* returns to a male hero, aided by magic and doing great deeds even as a boy. Osberne's female counterpart, Elfhild, was never properly filled out, and the book has accepted the limitations of an Icelandic saga, whereas the major romances explore their own psychological and magical structuring forces in a more demanding way.

The enactment of archetypal events, the rich evocation of psychological fears and needs, and the unhurried delight in both adventure and environment, make Morris's best romances a valuable experience—Yeats described them as books he always read very slowly, so as not to come too soon to the end. Their radical political stance and keen celebration of female personality are also remarkable, when so many fantasies are (rightly or wrongly) associated with High-Church conservatism. Like Ellen in *News from Nowhere,* the Maid, Ursula, and Birdalone are courageous and enterprising people, not baits or rewards for more "real" male protagonists.

Morris created his own language, with something of the texture of 14th-century English. The resultant style is a unique experience, shapely and pleasurable, emphasising physical rather than abstract aspects of experience, while retaining a tapestried sense of distance. The romances are designed for a future society's audience, freed from the frantic busyness of his own age just as the folk of his Nowhere are. This audience loves a good story with both circumstantiality and wonders, whether in an old folktale, a Dickens fiction, or a "reactionary novel." It delights in so active and sensuous a world, so radical and lucid a use of traditional conventions. Morris invented the fantasy set in an invented and magical pseudo-medieval land, but he also invented a fantastic future audience that could appreciate it.

—Norman Talbot

MORRISON, Richard. *See* **LOWNDES, Robert A.W.**

MORROW, James (Kenneth)

Nationality: American. **Born:** Philadelphia, Pennsylvania, 17 March 1947. **Education:** University of Pennsylvania, Philadelphia, 1965-69, B.A. in creative writing; Harvard University Graduate School of Education, Cambridge, Massachusetts, 1969-70, M.A. in teaching. **Family:** Married Jean Pierce Morrow in 1972; one daughter and one son. **Career:** English teacher, Cambridge Pilot School, Massachusetts, 1970-71; instructional materials specialist, Chelmsford Public Schools, Massachusetts, 1972-74; lecturer in instructional media, Tufts University, Medford, Massachusetts,

1977-79; contributing editor, *Media and Methods* magazine, 1978-80; co-director, Institute for Multimedia Learning, Westford, Massachusetts, 1978-84; science writer, *A Teacher's Guide to NOVA*, WGBH-TV, Boston, 1979-84; children's book author, Learningways Corporation, Cambridge, 1982-87; freelance fiction reviewer, *Philadelphia Inquirer*, 1986-90; Visiting Lecturer in fiction writing, Pennsylvania State University, University Park, 1990. Freelance fiction writer since 1980. **Awards:** Pennsylvania Council of the Arts fellowship, 1988; Nebula award, for short story, 1988, for novella, 1992; World Fantasy award, for novel, 1991. **Agent:** Writers House, 21 West 26th Street, New York, New York 10010, U.S.A. **Address:** 810 North Thomas Street, State College, Pennsylvania 16803, U.S.A.

Science Fiction Publications

Novels

The Wine of Violence. New York, Holt Rinehart, 1981; London, Legend, 1991.
The Continent of Lies. New York, Holt Rinehart, 1984; London, Gollancz, 1985.
This Is the Way the World Ends. New York, Holt, 1986; London, Gollancz, 1987.
Only Begotten Daughter. New York, Morrow, 1990; London, Legend, 1991.
City of Truth (novella). London, Legend, 1991; New York, St. Martin's Press, 1992.
Towing Jehovah. San Diego, Harcourt Brace, and London, Arrow, 1994.

Short Stories

Swatting at the Cosmos. Eugene, Oregon, Pulphouse, 1990.
Bible Stories for Adults. San Diego, Harcourt Brace, 1995.

Novel for children

The Adventures of Smoke Bailey (novelization of computer game). Cambridge, Massachusetts, Spinnaker, 1983.

Other Publications

CD-Rom for Children

The Quasar Kids. Lexington, Massachusetts, Collamore, 1987.
What Makes a Dinosaur Sore. Lexington, Massachusetts, Collamore, 1987.
The Lima Bean Dream, with Marilyn Segal. Lexington, Massachusetts, Collamore, 1987.
Not Too Messy, Not Too Neat, with Marilyn Segal. Lexington, Massachusetts, Collamore, 1988.
The Best Bubble-Blower. Lexington, Massachusetts, Collamore, 1988.

Screenplay

"A Political Cartoon," with Joe Adamson, in *Scripts,* edited by Floren Harper. Boston, Houghton Mifflin, 1973.

Other

Moviemaking Illustrated: The Comicbook Filmbook (textbook), with Murray Suid. Rochelle Park, New Jersey, Hayden, 1973.
Media and Kids: A Real-World Learning in the Schools (textbook), with Murray Suid. Rochelle Park, New Jersey, Hayden, 1977.
The Grammar of Media Kit (textbook), with Jean Morrow. Rochelle Park, New Jersey, Hayden, 1978.
The Creativity Catalogue: Comic Book Guide to Creative Projects (textbook), with Murray Suid. Belmont, California, Fearon, 1982.
Ready to Read (textbook), with Lillian Lieberman and Murray Suid. Palo Alto, California, Monday Morning, 1986.
Start to Read (textbook), with Lillian Lieberman and Murray Suid. Palo Alto, California, Monday Morning, 1986.
Read and Write (textbook), with Lillian Lieberman and Murray Suid. Palo Alto, California, Monday Morning, 1986.

Editor, *Nebula Awards: SFWA's Choices for the Best Science Fiction and Fantasy of the Year # 26[-28].* 3 vols., San Diego, Harcourt, Brace, 1992-94.

*

James Morrow comments:

Love, music, and stories are the best things in life, and none of them comes easily. Shortly after arriving at the University of Pennsylvania in 1965, I attempted to develop my story-making abilities by taking creative writing courses. I didn't get far. Much to my bewilderment, the tacit message of a typical Penn fiction workshop seemed to be this: whatever you write, write small. Don't embarrass yourself. Abridge your ambitions. Report on small people doing small things.

But suppose one doesn't care for small? Suppose one has no use for fiction in which the plot, as Ben Hecht once sarcastically remarked, is the opening of a door? Suppose one has a taste for gods, heroes, monsters, magic, ideas? "Don't swat at the Cosmos," my first writing teacher kept telling me. A solid image, to be sure—professors are skilled at such rhetoric—but not, I think, very good advice.

Ever since my formal schooling ended, I've found myself growing increasingly convinced that among the beginning writer's most precious prerogatives is the right to make a fool of himself. The neophyte should not only be encouraged to write about the small things he knows; he should also be encouraged to write about the large things he can envision. As long as the typical college writing workshop caters to the cult of reality, as long as it is characterized by what Ray Bradbury calls "fear of the imagination," its products will be, on the whole, mere autobiographical confession, forever threatening to turn fiction into an eccentric branch of journalism.

The primacy of imagination in SF must not be taken as a rationale for laziness. When Bradbury asks us to consider the humble "dandelions" of the fiction world, he doesn't disparage its royal roses. A genre author is every bit as obligated to bleed for his craft as the mainstream writer. His primary duty is to torment himself, forever shouting in his own ear, "Make it better! Make it better! Make it better!"

*   *   *

Although he does not have the high-profile presence of many other SF writers who established their professional careers in the

1980s, James Morrow has, since the publication of his first novel in 1981, produced a substantial body of high-quality work that rates as one of the field's best. While most of his novels and stories are recognizably science fiction, Morrow is not interested in rigid technological and sociological extrapolation; instead, he uses stock science-fictional devices as a means for examining moral and philosophical issues. Morrow's fiction is notable for its rich, often dazzling prose style, as well as for its strongly comic elements. All of these traits place Morrow squarely within a tradition marked variously by such writers as Ray Bradbury, Kurt Vonnegut, Philip K. Dick, and Robert Sheckley.

Morrow's first novel, *The Wine of Violence,* takes place on a planet whose inhabitants, descendants of Earth colonists, have split into two groups: the Brain-Eaters, nomadic savages who kill and devour anyone who crosses their path, and the residents of Quetzalia, who have established a peaceful society by periodically projecting their own violent tendencies into a "river of hate," which flows outside the walls of their city. When a party of explorers from another planet, also descendants of Earth colonists, is admitted into the city, the Quetzalians find themselves having to confront not only the overt violence of the Brain-Eater who is loose within the city, but the potential violence of the explorers themselves. Although the plot is driven by a high level of action, culminating with the explorers convincing the Quetzalians to go to war against the Brain-Eaters, the central concern is more abstract: are the Quetzalians heroes for having conquered the dark side of human nature, or hypocrites whose murderous fantasies belie their professed pacifism? The author's sympathies reveal themselves when one of the Quetzalians realizes that, by fighting the Brain-Eaters, he is acting in the tradition of his Earth ancestors and is now a part of history: "History, he decided, was a terrible idea."

The Continent of Lies, Morrow's second novel, is also his most broadly comic work, describing a far-future, interplanetary society whose main form of entertainment is the "dreambean," a bioengineered fruit which, when eaten, produces a vivid hallucination, a scripted dream in which the eater of the dreambean stars. The protagonist, a dreambean critic, is engaged by the inventor of the dreambean to track down a poisoned bean whose hallucination drives people mad—a mission that becomes personal when the critic's daughter eats one of the poisoned beans. The storyline is complicated, perhaps overly so, with numerous twists, turns, and cliffhangers. The novel is brashly imaginative and very funny in its critique of consumer culture, as represented by the entertainment industry spawned by the dreambeans; it strikes a more serious note in its portrayal of the dark side of the religious impulse, as represented by the creator of the poison dreambeans, who intends them to establish a new religion.

With his third novel, Morrow abandoned the far-future scenarios of his first two books for the time-honored SF landscape of the near-future nuclear holocaust. The bombs fall early on in *This Is the Way the World Ends;* after civilization is destroyed, six surviving Americans are put on trial by the "unadmitted," the people who will never be born because civilization has destroyed itself. Although the novel is, among other things, a scathing critique of the Cold War mentality, Morrow never lets it become a one-sided polemic. The trial is a deliberate presentation of both sides of the deterrence debate, while the "unadmitted" reveal themselves to be out not for justice, but for revenge. Most importantly, Morrow keeps the reader focused on the tragedy of the individual with the novel's protagonist, a tombstone carver whose only crime was to get an anti-radiation suit for his daughter. A nominee for the Nebula and John W.

Campbell Memorial awards, *This Is the Way the World Ends* is a grim and angry book; it is also brilliantly conceived and executed.

Morrow's next novel, *Only Begotten Daughter,* a Nebula finalist and winner of the World Fantasy Award, is a tale not of the second coming of Christ, but of His sister: Julie Katz, immaculately conceived in an Atlantic City sperm bank in 1974, raised by her earthly father and his lesbian companion, revealed to the world through her advice column in a weekly tabloid, opposed by a crazed evangelist who transforms New Jersey into a fundamentalist dictatorship, and embittered by the knowledge that her heavenly Mother has never told her why she's here, or even checked in to see how she's doing. The novel is a savage indictment of the potential evils of organized religion, as Satan pushes for Julie to reveal her divinity, start a church, and give him more business, while Julie is able to stand successfully in opposition to evil forces only after her divinity is removed. It combines Swiftian satire, black humor, warmly sympathetic characters, with a clear yet eloquent prose style. However one wishes to label it, *Only Begotten Daughter* is one of the most impressive novels of the past decade.

Thus far in his career, Morrow has written only a handful of short stories, most of which are collected in *Swatting at the Cosmos.* His most notable stories are contained in *Bible Stories for Adults,* a collection of SF parables that examine problems of Judeo-Christian theology. The best of these is the extraordinary "Bible Stories for Adults No. 17: The Deluge," in which Noah's Ark picks up a hitchhiker, a prostitute who seduces Noah's sons and then jumps ship with their frozen sperm, intending "to found a proud and impertinent nation, a people driven to decipher ice and solve the sun, each of them with as little use for obedience as she." The story won Morrow his first Nebula award as best short story of 1988. He received a second Nebula for *City of Truth,* a novel published as an independent volume. Set in the city of Veritas, where all residents must tell the truth and there is no such thing as false advertising (a summer camp for children is called "Camp Ditch-the-Kids), *City of Truth* tells of a man forced to join in with an underground of fabricators in order to give emotional support and encouragement to he terminally ill son. Beyond being a clever satire, it is also a moving portrait of the ferocity of parenthood.

In 1991, Morrow announced three forthcoming novels which would form the "Godhead" trilogy. The first of these, *Towing Jehovah,* appeared in 1994 and was promptly nominated for most of the field's major awards. The corpse of God appears in the Atlantic Ocean, and the Vatican hires a disgraced oil tanker captain (clearly modeled on the captain of the *Exxon Valdez*) to tow the Deity's body to the North Pole, where it can be properly preserved. Far from the facile, shooting-fish-in-a-barrel satire of religion that its outrageous plot might imply, *Towing Jehovah* is a remarkably assured, seamlessly written, and immensely sympathetic novel. While organized religion comes in for the same sort of scathing analysis that it received in *Only Begotten Daughter,* so also does the alliance of atheists and radical feminists who attempt to send God to the bottom of the sea as a final blow to patriarchal oppression. Meanwhile, the Vatican representatives trying to preserve God's body, and especially the confused but determined tanker captain, emerge as admirable individuals of great dignity.

Perhaps more than any other contemporary SF writer, James Morrow's work has been marked by a steadily increasing level of achievement. *Towing Jehovah,* along with reprints of Morrow's previous two novels, has appeared as part of Harcourt Brace Jovanovich's "Modern Fiction Program." At this rate, if Morrow does in fact follow his predecessors Bradbury and Vonnegut into the wider waters of mainstream acceptance, he may well turn out to be the best of them all.

—F. Brett Cox

MOULTON, Carl. *See* **TUBB, E.C.**

MULLER, John E. *See* **FANTHORPE, R. Lionel.**

MURAKAMI, Haruki

Nationality: Japanese. **Born:** Ashiya City, 12 January 1949. **Education:** Waseda University, Tokyo, majored in Greek drama. **Family:** Married Yoko. **Career:** Jazz bar manager, Tokyo, 1974-81. **Awards:** Gunzo award, 1979; Noma Literary award, 1982; Junichiro Tanizaki prize, 1985. Lives in Tokyo.

SCIENCE FICTION PUBLICATONS

Novels (series: Wild Sheep Chase)

Hitsuji ô megaru boken. Tokyo, Kodansha, 1982; translated by Alfred Birnbaum as *A Wild Sheep Chase,* Tokyo and New York, Kodansha, 1989; London, Hamish Hamilton, 1990.
Sekai no owari to hâdo-boirudo wandârando. Tokyo, Shinchosha, 1985; translated by Alfred Birnbaum as *Hard-Boiled Wonderland and the End of the World,* Tokyo and New York, Kodansha, London, Hamish Hamilton, 1991.
Dansu dansu dansu. Tokyo, Kodansha, 1988, 2 vols.; translated by Alfred Birnbaum as *Dance Dance Dance: A Novel* (Wild Sheep Chase), Tokyo and New York, Kodansha, and London, Hamish Hamilton, 1994.

Short Stories

The Elephant Vanishes: Stories, translated by Jay Rubin and Alfred Birnbaum. New York, Knopf, and London, Hamish Hamilton, 1993.

OTHER PUBLICATIONS

Novels

1973-nen no pinboru. Tokyo, Kodansha, 1980; translated by Alfred Birnbaum as *Pinball, 1973,* Tokyo, Kodansha, 1985.
Noruwei no mori. Tokyo, Kodansha, 1987; translated by Alfred Birnbaum as *Norwegian Wood,* Tokyo, Kodansha, 1989, 2 vols.

Short Stories

A Day in the Life: Stories. Tokyo, CBS Soni Shuppan, 1983.

*　　*　　*

Haruki Murakami is currently one of the most popular and controversial writers in Japan. His bestselling novel *Norwegian Wood* sold more than four million copies and became a social phenomenon. The content of his work is not related to that of traditional Japanese literature and his writing style does not follow after the techniques set down by prior modern writers. Some critics claim Murakami's style can read like translation from English. His unusual style, without traditional roots, has made his work controversial among critics and, simultaneously, popular among younger generations. The reason for his break from traditional Japanese realism can be simply stated: it is not effective anymore, at least for him, to use "realism" to describe Japan or the world in which we live now. The world is changing rapidly and Japan is not what it used to be. In the 70's and 80's, both underwent drastic changes, especially in the field of technology.

Murakami is not generally accepted as a science fiction writer. The content of his work is rooted in an ordinary and minimal world. However, in evoking this ordinary world, he creates the sense of "a lost world" or "the reality without a sense of reality." Although he is not a science fiction writer in the traditional sense, one can easily find science fictional elements in his writings. Because he finds it almost impossible to describe the present reality of postmodern Japan in a realistic way, he devises metaphors and narratives that depend on the methods of science fiction.

Most of Murakami's works deal with the existence of a parallel world that engages ours in dualistic conflicts, such as between consciousness and unconsciousness, life and death, light and dark, reality and unreality, etc. While divisions in these conflicts were more or less distinct before, in Murakami's world it has become harder to draw a line between oppositions. The disappearance of clear borders is caused primarily by the progress of technology, especially in the fields of information and reproduction.

Murakami is thus obsessed with walls as symbols, since they serve both as barriers and as gateways, and the act of passing through them bears a very important role in his recent works. In these works, and in those leading up to it, technology has produced a new type of reality, a "hyper-reality," where reproduction is endlessly possible on the TV or computer screen. Becoming familiar with this kind of world in our daily lives, we begin to consider this type of reality more real. This new reality takes over what used to be real. Murakami applies this relationship to his writings. Surrounded by too much information and too many choices, our conflicts themselves are diversified. Under these circumstances, telling a linear story becomes harder and harder. Therefore, nonrealistic novels can be more realistic to Murakami. He takes the method of writing unrealistically to describe the present world in a most realistic way. That makes his work really realistic. In other words, a novel can be really realistic with the help not only of the dull and prosaic daily lives but of illusion and fantasy. This is the reason why Murakami's world has its source in science fiction.

The work which best exhibits Murakami's themes of duality and blurring of boundaries is *Hard-Boiled Wonderland and the End of the World*. In this novel, two narratives entitled respectively "Hard-Boiled Wonderland" and "The End of the World" progress in flashbacks and combine beautifully in the end. An old biologist operates on the memory of the protagonist of the former narrative and the visualized data of his consciousness serves as the world of the latter narrative. The mysterious Town surrounded by the Wall turns out to be a product of the protagonist's imagination. In *Hard-Boiled Wonderland,* a narrative of a parallel world alternates with that of another, chapter by chapter. We see a clear relationship between the two worlds: this side of the world and the other side of the world. As it turns out, this side *is* the other side, after the protagonist goes out to see the other side. This discovery is beautifully described in the novel and this motif is passed down to later works as that of "passing through the wall."

The theme of dual identity was suggested in the earlier novel, *A Wild Sheep Chase.* The supernatural existence of the Sheep represents the other side of the world. But the conflicts between two worlds become more intense after this novel.

The Sheep Man who appears again in *Dance Dance Dance* (which is actually a sequel to *A Wild Sheep Chase*) tells the protagonist to keep on dancing if he wants to stay on this side of the world. That is the only way to survive in today's advanced capitalistic society for the protagonist who has come back to this world from the supernatural other world in *A Wild Sheep Chase.* Facing boredom and monotonousness in this ordinary world, he gradually gets used to the ordinariness of daily life in *Dance Dance Dance.* But again he sets out on a journey to confirm where he is placed in the world. The conflicts of the parallel world become clearer here and the act of dancing is the answer for him after all. To dance here is, staring at the rules of the other side, to bear the boredom of this side and try to find a link to the other side. And the dancing protagonist goes through a new experience this time. That is the act of "passing through the wall," a theme that is handed down to *The Wind-Up Bird Chronicles* in a more mature, complex way.

TV People established a new stage in Murakami's development as a writer. It is a collection of city folklore stories, dealing in the illusions and fantasies of contemporary, urban people. The title story "TV People," for example, also presents two worlds: the world of TV People and the everyday real world. Here Murakami uses science fiction as a device to describe an ordinary scene. The protagonist thinks he has a firm foundation in normal life, but TV People from the other world invade his world without permission. In a reversal, the protagonist turns into an invader and the TV People come to belong to the ordinary world. During this reversal process, the protagonist continually feels that something is wrong. This is a story about the upset of balance in daily, modern life, where it is difficult to become accustomed to one's lifestyle. This collection of short stories, published between *Dance Dance Dance* and *The Wind-Up Bird Chronicles,* serves as a link between the two novels and the two decades. Toward the 90's, Murakami has suggested, it will take a kind of greater psychological perseverance to survive in society. The stories show the turning point of the times and in Murakami's development as a writer. Thematically, "The Dancing Dwarf" and "The Elephant Vanishes" can be classified into the same category as *TV People.* These are fantasy stories about the loss of the border between dream and reality. *The South of the Border, the West of the Sun,* a ghost story published while Murakami was working on *The Wind-Up Bird Chronicles,* also serves a linking role to the 90's.

Murakami has said that writing a novel is a simulation. When he wants to tell a story about various kinds of conflicts between the self and the environment, he cannot describe the conflicts on the level of daily, surface reality. He must pull down the conflicts into personal consciousness and simulate them there, within the self.

With the quantitative expansion of both personal consciousness and public consciousness in today's "hypermedia" society, Murakami is trying to go down as deeply as possible into personal consciousness. The Sheep Man in *A Wild Sheep Chase* and *Dance Dance Dance,* for example, exists in the depths, not on the daily, public surface. In *The Wind-Up Bird Chronicles,* this act of going down into the depths of consciousness is represented as the protagonist going down to a deep, dry well by himself.

In *Hard-Boiled Wonderland . . . ,* the protagonist once tried to escape from the wall, but he realizes that he himself produced the wall and that his own DNA and ancient memories are buried inside it. After he realizes this, he finds the act of passing through the wall natural, not supernatural. But, after he passes through it, he finds another reality with another wall. He is destined to face another wall. This motif of infinite realities within realities, and the accompanying sense of loss in the protagonist, is intensified in *The Wind-Up Bird Chronicles.* The greater his sense of loss and confusion, the deeper the protagonist has to go down to the depths to find out what has been lost. Going down into the well means getting into one's own consciousness. In this novel (as far as Part I and Part II are concerned), Murakami is trying to say that we can be linked to the others far deeper in the wells. Deeper down there, the wells could be connected with each other by underground water. He is searching for something far beyond the loss to be able to communicate with others better. In forthcoming Part III of this latest novel, which is said to be the concluding volume, Murakami will take his new phase of development further, in the search for the self in the 1990's

—Toshifumi Miyawaki

———

MURDOCH, H.J. *See* **McINTOSH, J.T.**

———

MURNANE, Gerald

Nationality: Australian. **Born:** Melbourne, Victoria, in 1939. **Family:** Married; three sons. **Career:** Lecturer in fiction writing, Victoria College, since 1980. **Address:** 22 Falcon Road, Macleod, Victoria 3085, Australia.

Science Fiction Publications

Novels

The Plains. Carlton, Victoria, Norstrilia Press, 1982; London, Penguin, 1984; New York, Braziller, 1985.

Short Stories

Landscape with Landscape. Carlton, Victoria, Norstrilia Press, 1985; London, Pergamon, 1987.
Velvet Waters. Ringwood, Victoria, McPhee Gribble, 1990.

Novels

Tamarisk Row. Melbourne, Heinemann, 1974.
A Lifetime on Clouds. Melbourne, Heinemann, 1976; New York, Penguin, 1986.
Inland. Richmond, Victoria, Heinemann Australia, 1988; London, Faber, 1989; Boston, Faber, 1990.

Other

Editor, with Jenny Lee and Philip Mead, *The Temperament of Generations: 50 Years of Writing in Meanjin.* Carlton, Victoria, Melbourne University Press, 1990.

* * *

Gerald Murnane may be dubbed a science fiction writer by affinity with such speculative authors as J.G. Ballard, Brian Aldiss, and Christopher Priest. His first novel, *Tamarisk Row,* is a remarkable metafantasy, an obsessional study of the fantasies of a small boy in a country town in Victoria (and the pathetic attempts by his father to realize fantasies by gambling on horses). It is written in short, mosaic chapters and, sometimes, extraordinarily long, aspiring sentences. It is notable for its truthfulness, and its embarrassing fidelity to the furtive or inexpressible dreams and crude realities of pre-pubescent life. *A Lifetime on Clouds* is about an adolescent boy's struggles with masturbation, and is a novel about the weaving of fantasies from the meagre facts and misleading suggestions offered by life, in this case, mainly those of Catholic secondary education in a Melbourne suburb. The ribald humour of the book fails to mask Murnane's fierce satirical indictment of what was then a stultifying religious ethos. The difference between fantasy and reality becomes blurred for 15-year-old Adrian Sherd; at one point, he notes that his lustful fantasies about American film stars are not sanctioned by the behaviour of the few heroes he has seen on screen: "instead of courting them patiently . . . he had undressed them and defiled them only hours after their first meeting. It was all so absurd compared with what really happened in films."

In *The Plains,* the threshold has been crossed and we are presented with a mature man's fantasy of an Australia related to the real one only by inversion. All the wealth and values belong to the plainsmen of Inner Australia, who despise the busy city-dwellers of the coast. The narrator is an outsider, willing to spend his life making notes towards a film that will put on record the ever-elusive culture of the inner land, a land that is within Australia, because only Australia could have demanded its existence, yet a land which is beyond Australia, because it is too large and grand a vision to be comprehended by it. Murnane had adumbrated this vision in describing the yearnings of young Clement Killeaton in *Tamarisk Row* for what lies farther inland and north, beyond the farthest imaginable horizons of his wretchedly confined experience. Fantasies lie within fantasies in *The Plains,* a short memorable novel of considerable philosophical interest.

The Plains itself, slightly curtailed and adapted, might fit within the structure of Murnane's later metafantasy, *Landscape with Landscape,* a kind of mobius box of six stones, each of which is written by the narrator of its predecessor (and the first story by the last narrator). The stories concern Melbourne men who are obsessed with the wish to see the landscape that is hidden by the landscape,

or that is seen only by the figure in the landscape, and so on; people themselves are landscapes or owners of hidden landscapes, perhaps. In what may be the most interesting of these stories, "The Battle of Acosta Nu," Melbourne is located in Paraguay and the narrator, a descendant of Australian colonists, defines himself in relation to the Australian city he has never seen.

Inland develops these insights still further as the author employs a narrator who shifts through several identities, as does his projected reader, to intimate the vastness of the inside world. Murnane dazzles with his sense of the infinitudes that may start and precipitate within us from even the most seemingly barren and limited exteriors. His beautifully long-breathed prose style draws one along towards ever more quiet intimations of contained, but uncontainable, multitudinousnesses that externalize themselves in terms of landscapes, notably grasslands, maps, words, souls, ghosts, unread books and written pages, readers hostile and expectant, living and even dead, memories of childhood and of nostalgic adulthood, devolving above all into love-longings for a particular lost girl-woman, yet all without sentimentality. The obsessive character he depicts would seem insane or almost so to some, yet his behaviour is described with a clinical precision.

Bruce Gillespie has remarked that both *The Plains* and *Tamarisk Row* "are guided by the proposition that, however one might perceive any object or idea in the universe, it is quite possible to perceive it in the other way as well." This insight seems particularly apt for the short story, "Land Deal" (included in *Velvet Waters*), which presents a philosophically valid Aboriginal view of European colonists as having a possible existence only in dreams: their land deal is therefore a dream within a dream. Eleven stories are collected in *Velvet Waters:* Murnane's collage method of composition is particularly obvious in the fine "First Love" (the title refers to Nabokov's story), where the narrator engages in the collage work of piecing together his own personal ideal racing colours for a jockey's jacket. In this story, the narrator decides to abolish "the jargon of an imagined world ruled cover by those invisible and sinister science fiction tyrants Time and Change," and write instead about the real world, which happens always and only in space. "Precious Bane" pleasantly juxtaposes the Golden Age of Books with the bookless world of 2020. "Stone Quarry" includes an idea similar to the conceit of *The Plains,* but the inversion of Australia is substituted with a reversal of the westward flow of American dreaming. These short stories are not of equal weight or interest. "When the Mice Failed to Arrive" is the most impressive story in the collection; it deals superbly with the embarrassments of schoolteachers who fail to deliver what they have promised, but ends (glancing at *Arabian Nights* erotic sadism) with a horrifying intimation of the cruelty that may be perpetrated by any laboratory experimenter who should find one day that even the unwritten social contract one makes with a mouse cannot, in particular circumstances, be honoured.

—Michael J. Tolley

MURPHY, Pat

Nationality: American. **Born:** 9 March 1955. **Education:** University of California, Santa Cruz, B.A. in biology and general science. **Career:** Since 1982, editor, *Exploratorium Quarterly,* San

Francisco. **Awards:** Nebula award, 1987 (twice); Philip K. Dick award, 1990. **Address:** c/o Exploratorium, 3601 Lyon Street, San Francisco, California 94123, U.S.A.

SCIENCE FICTION PUBLICATIONS

Novels

The Shadow Hunter. New York, Popular Library, 1982; London, Headline, 1988.
The Falling Woman. New York, Tor, 1986; London, Headline, 1988.
The City, Not Long After. New York, Doubleday, 1989; London, Pan, 1991.

Short Stories

Points of Departure. New York, Bantam, 1990.
Letters from Home, with Pat Cadigan and Karen Joy Fowler. London, Women's Press, 1991.
Rachel in Love. Eugene, Oregon, Pulphouse, 1992.

*   *   *

Pat Murphy's first short story collection is mistitled *Points of Departure;* there is just one point of departure, Murphy herself, with at least 19 different directions, and, one suspects, as many different points of arrival as there are readers. For this reason, it has always been very difficult to define Murphy's fiction. Michael Swanwick described her as a "lone wolf" in his article on the rival movements of the mid-1980s in *Isaac Asimov's Science Fiction Magazine,* but she has since been linked with that curiously amorphous, catch-all non-category known as the freestyle movement. All of this is important only in as much as it is meaningless with regard to Murphy's fiction.

Her first novel, *The Shadow Hunter,* almost vanished without trace, but a string of interesting short stories spread across several anthologies and magazines through the mid-1980s built a quiet reputation, culminating in the story "Rachel In Love" in 1987. This story deals sensitively with love, animal research, and scientific ethics. Rachel, a chimp brought up by a kindly scientist, has had the mind of the scientist's dead daughter superimposed on her own, and has learned to communicate with sign language. When the scientist dies, Rachel is taken to a research establishment and locked up. Using signs, however, she is able to befriend the simple, deaf, drunken cleaner Jake, and persuades him to release her to help him clean. Jake trusts Rachel, and she falls in love with him. When she comes into heat, she offers herself to him, but Jake prefers his magazine photos. Then, Rachel meets another chimp, Johnson, and they plot their escape and return to Rachel's former home. As the story closes, they are travelling cross-country whilst the papers detailing Rachel's status and her inheritance have suddenly become public. The story proved very popular, but it is the Sturgeon-esque concentration on the people and their relationships that makes "Rachel In Love" so intense, and perhaps, so controversial.

The waves that "Rachel In Love" caused aroused attention in Murphy's second novel, *The Falling Woman,* and eventually both won that year's Nebula awards. This novel is scarcely SF. It is the story of an archaeologist, Elizabeth Butler, who can sometimes "see" people from the past. On a dig in Mexico, her life is suddenly disrupted by the arrival of her daughter, last seen as a child, and by a spirit that begins to talk to her. *The Falling Woman* is characterised by an attention to detail of person and place. Murphy also takes great pains over the archaeological elements of her scenery; the science here is far more accurate than many hard SF authors manage in their chosen fields. Nevertheless, this is essentially a ghost fantasy, but a gripping and moving one, and it is as much a typical Murphy tale as any other.

Most recently, *The City, Not Long After* has shown Murphy to be capable of maintaining the moods and the mythic elements of *The Falling Woman* whilst setting her novel closer to home in San Francisco. *City* is actually an extension of the earlier story "Art In The War Zone," filling in details of how the situation described there arose. San Francisco, like every other major city, has been struck by a plague spread by so-called Peace Monkeys. These monkeys, which lived in a Himalayan monastery, were brought into the cities as part of the Peace Movement, in response to legends foretelling peace if they left the monastery. Peace comes, after the Plague, but it is not what anyone expected, and San Francisco is left as a ghost town, inhabited only by gypsy gangs and stray artists in a loose commune. To this town comes Jax, daughter of one of the original Peace campaigners, heeding her mother's final message, to warn of the plans of General "Fourstar" Miles to capture the city. The artists decide to fight back using their art, and the city helps them. An ambiguous climax mutes some of the philosophy portrayed, perhaps, whilst emphasising that nobody wins if violence occurs.

As a tender love story, as an expression of the power of art to affect our lives, as a magical realist drama, *The City, Not Long After* is extraordinary. Murphy invokes all of the ideologies of the new age, pacifism, ecology, and co-operation, and makes them seem so real and rational that for long periods the reader wonders how anybody could argue with it. Filling out all of this are the characters—Jax the wild country girl, Danny-boy, the artist who decides to paint the Golden Gate Bridge blue, Machine, who doesn't really trust humans but builds bizarre robots, Books, who maintains what remains of the library, and others. This is, overall, a poignant, cautionary novel, but it has its moments of pure comedy, and some genuine surrealism, that serve to enhance the whole.

It is interesting to note, however, that despite the acclaim that her recent novels have gained, Murphy still considers herself a short story writer. The award of the Philip K. Dick award to *Points of Departure* should ensure her continuing writing in the short form. Whether hard-edged feminist stories like "His Vegetable Wife," looking at father-daughter relationships in "Dead Men on TV," historical fantasy such as "Bones," Eastern discovery "In the Abode of the Snows," or dark fantasy "On the Dark Side of the station Where the Train Never Stops," Murphy's reputation should grow.

—Kev P. McVeigh

N

NAHA, Ed

Pseudonyms: D.B. Drumm; Michael McGann. **Nationality:** American. **Born:** Elizabeth, New Jersey, 10 June 1950. **Education:** Newark State College, B.A. 1972. **Career:** Publicity manager, 1972-75, 1975-77, and associate producer, East Coast Artists and Repertory, CBS Records, New York; co-editor, *Future Life,* New York, 1977-80. Since 1980, columnist ("Screen Scoops"), *New York Post;* since 1983, columnist ("Nahallywood"), *Heavy Metal,* New York; since 1983 columnist ("L.A. Offbeat"), *Starlog,* New York. Lives in Santa Monica, California. **Address:** c/o Pocket Books, The Simon and Schuster Building, 1230 Avenue of the Americas, New York, New York 10020, U.S.A.

SCIENCE FICTION PUBLICATIONS

Novels (series: Harry Porter)

The Paradise Plot (Porter). New York, Bantam, 1980.
The Suicide Plague (Porter). New York, Bantam, 1982.
Robocop (novelization of screenplay). New York, Dell, 1987; London, Corgi, 1988.
Robocop II (novelization of screenplay). New York, Jove, 1990; Harmonsworth, Middlesex, Penguin, 1990.

Novels as D.B. Drumm (series: Traveler in all titles)

First, You Fight. New York, Dell, 1984.
The Road Ghost. New York, Dell, 1985.
The Stalking Time. New York, Dell, 1986.
Hell on Earth. New York, Dell, 1986.
The Children's Crusade. New York, Dell, 1987.
The Prey. New York, Dell, 1987.
Ghost Dancers. New York, Dell, 1987.

Novels as Michael McGann (series: Marauders in all titles)

The Marauders. New York, Jove, 1989.
Blood Kin. New York, Jove, 1989.
Liar's Dice. New York, Jove, 1990.
Convoy Strike. New York, Jove, 1990.
The Ghost Warriors. New York, Jove, 1990.
Blood and Fire. New York, Jove, 1991.
Fortress of Death. New York, Jove, 1991.

OTHER PUBLICATIONS

Novels

The Con Game. New York, Dell, 1986.
Breakdown. New York, Dell, 1988.
Dead-Bang: A Novel (novelization of screenplay by Robert Foster). New York, Berkley, 1989.
Ghostbusters II: A Novel (novelization of screenplay). New York, Dell, and London, Corgi, 1989.

On the Edge. New York, Pocket, 1989.
Orphans. New York, Dell, 1989.
Razzle-Dazzle. New York, Pocket, 1990.
Cracking Up. New York, Pocket, 1991.

Plays

Screenplays: *Camp Bottomount,* 1984; *The Wizard Wars,* 1984; *Honey, I Shrunk the Kids,* with Tom Schulman, 1989.

Other

Horrors: From Screen to Scream: An Enyclopedic Guide to the Greatest Horror and Fantasy Films of All Times. New York, Avon, 1975.
Science Fiction Aliens: A Starlog Photo Book (for children). New York, Starlog, 1977.
Lillian Roxon's Rock Encyclopedia, revised edition. New York, Putnam, 1978; Sydney, Angus and Robertson, 1980.
The Rock Encyclopedia. New York, Grosset and Dunlap, 1978.
The Science Fictionary: An A-Z Guide to the World of SF Authors, Films, and TV Shows. New York, Seaview, 1980.
Wanted, by the Intergalactic Security Bureau: 20 Full-Color Posters of the Most Wanted Alien Criminals, with Eric Seidman. New York, Bantam, 1980.
The Films of Roger Corman: Brilliance on a Budget. New York, Arco, 1982.
The Making of "Dune." New York, Berkley, and London, Target, 1984.
Editor, *1941: The Official Movie Magazine.* New York, O'Quinn Studios, 1979.
Editor, *The Beatles Forever.* New York, O'Quinn Studios, 1980; as *John Lennon and the Beatles Forever,* New York, Tower Books, 1980.

*   *   *

Ed Naha is one of those rarities who have been able successfully to merge the science fiction and mystery genres. His first science fiction novel, *The Paradise Plot,* introduced the character of Harry Porter, a newspaper reporter who always seems to be at the right spot at the right time, to get himself involved with world-shaking plots. In this first adventure, he is aboard Island One, an orbiting city established as part of mankind's movement toward the colonization of space. But not everything is peaceful in the colony, which has not cast off as many of the problems of the mother world as they might have thought.

Shortly after his arrival, Porter is thoroughly enmeshed in a complicated plot that involves a string of murders and a desperate political struggle both within the habitat and back on Earth. Although Porter is ultimately instrumental in solving the mystery, the revelations result in the closing down of Island One, although it is quite clear that this is probably a temporary measure. Naha's scientific background for the novel is convincing, and while Porter is essentially a stereotypical detective hero, he's a well-done stereotype involved in an engrossing mystery, livened up with excellent dialogue.

The sequel, *The Suicide Plague,* is even better. Porter, the last investigative reporter still working, is bewildered by a sudden rash of young suicides, uncovers a secret plot to assassinate the President of the United States, runs afoul of the Church of the Ancient Astronauts, a sinister and increasingly powerful new cult, searches for missing research scientists, solves the mystery of a murdered man who had telepathic powers, and helps to avert what might have resulted in a nuclear war. This obviously complex group of plots and subplots is woven skillfully together in a thoroughly satisfying fashion.

Naha also wrote *First, You Fight,* the first volume of "The Traveller," an extended series of postnuclear holocaust men's adventure novels. A tough, well-armed protagonist wanders through ruined America in his armored van, helping the weak, avoiding the mutants and power seekers among the survivors. A thoroughly violent action series, it lacks the finesse of Naha's other work. He has also written screenplays, as well as nonfiction about science fiction and horror films, and the field of popular music. His only recent science fiction novel is the movie novelization, *Robocop.* Two other recent novels, *Breakdown* and *Orphans* are both supernatural horror.

—Don D'Ammassa

NELSON, Ray

Pseudonyms: R.N. Elson; Jeffrey Lord. **Nationality:** American. **Born:** Radell Faraday Nelson, Schenectady, New York, 3 October 1931. **Education:** Chicago Art Institute, 1954; Alliance Française, 1957-58; the Sorbonne, Paris, 1958; University of Chicago, B.A. 1960; Automation Institute, computer programmers certificate 1961; Peralta College, Berkeley, California, 1978. **Family:** Married 1) Perdita Lilly in 1951 (divorced 1955); 2) Lisa Mullikin in 1955 (divorced 1958); 3) Kirsten Enge in 1958; one son. **Career:** Worked for Inland Lakes Flying Service, Cadillac, Michigan, 1947-50, and Hudson Motor Company, Detroit, 1950-51; signmaker, Chicago, 1951-54; printer, Northside Poster Company, Chicago, 1954; artist, Artcraft Poster Company, Oakland, California, 1955-56; translator for Jean Linard, Vesoul, France, 1959; computer programmer, University of California Press, Berkeley, 1961-62. Since 1962, freelance writer and artist: co-director, Berkeley Free University, 1967-68; founder, Microcosm Fiction Workshop, later Ramona Street Regulars, 1967; since 1968, teaching assistant, Adams Junior High School, El Cerrito, California. President, California Writers Club, 1977-78. **Awards:** Jack London award, 1983. **Address:** 333 Ramona Avenue, El Cerrito, California 94530, U.S.A.

SCIENCE FICTION PUBLICATIONS

Novels (series: Richard Blade; Timebinder)

The Ganymede Takeover, with Philip K. Dick. New York, Ace, 1967; London, Arrow, 1971.
Blake's Progress. Toronto, Laser, 1975; revised as *Timequest,* New York, Tor, 1985.
Then Beggars Could Ride (Timebinder). Toronto, Laser, 1976.
The Ecolog. Toronto, Laser, 1977.
The Revolt of the Unemployables (Timebinder). San Francisco, Anthelion, 1978.

Dimension of Horror (Blade; as Jeffrey Lord). Los Angeles, Pinnacle, 1979.
The Prometheus Man (Timebinders). Norfolk, Virginia, Donning, 1982.

OTHER PUBLICATIONS

Novels

The Agony of Love. San Diego, Greenleaf, 1969.
Girl with the Hungry Eyes. San Diego, Greenleaf, 1969.
Dogheaded Death. San Francisco, Strawberry Hill Press, 1989.

Novels as R.N. Elson

How to Do It. San Diego, Greenleaf, 1970.
Black Pussy. San Diego, Greenleaf, 1970.
Sex Happy Hippy. San Diego, Greenleaf, 1970.
The DA's Wife. San Diego, Greenleaf, 1970.

*

Ray Nelson comments:

(1981) For me, Jack London, not Hugo Gernsback, is the father of American Science Fiction, and my aim is to continue the tradition established at the beginning of this century by London and his friends. My three obsessive themes are radical utopianism, experimental occultism, and a love-fear romance with nature. In California these ideas are understood, particularly in the Bay Area (all but two of the living writers I admire live in California), but in New York, where there are no trees, my obsessions seem like nonsense. Most of my work has been published outside New York—places where there are trees and intuition and hope for a better life, and someday New York too will grudgingly lend me an ear, perhaps when I am safely dead.

(1985) In *Timequest* I have at last written the novel I always wanted to write, the book I hope posterity will remember me by, if it remembers me at all. Editors have helped me, from Roger Elwood who let me do the first version of a book no other editor would touch, through Hank Stein who encouraged me to put in everything previous length restrictions had forced me to leave out, to Terry Carr who suggested restoring even the parts I had left out for Hank Stein, but really *Timequest* represents my own basic attitudes and philosophy so well I am content to stand or fall on this one work, so well I may never write another book in this genre. Now I want to do something else: comedy, cartoons, songs. Maybe I'll steal a spraycan of paint and start drawing propeller beanies on subway walls.

*   *   *

Although Ray Nelson has never been one of the more prolific writers in the field, he has firmly established a reputation for himself on the basis of the generally high quality of his work. His first novel, *The Ganymede Takeover,* was written in collaboration with Philip K. Dick, and dealt with the domination of Earth by wormlike invaders from Ganymede, but it was written as a witty and satiric examination of individuals and societies, not the low grade movie plot it so resembles.

It would be almost a decade later that Nelson first appeared as sole author of a novel, in this case *Blake's Progress,* a serious contender for best novel of its year. Ostensibly, the central character was the poet, William Blake, a man capable of mentally travelling through time in company with his wife. It soon becomes apparent, however, that it is she who dominates their relationship, has the more powerful intellect, and is in fact a far more interesting character than is her weak-willed husband.

Then Beggars Could Ride and *The Ecolog* appeared soon after. Each was entertaining in its own way, but both suffered in comparison to their predecessor. The former was a similar kaleidoscopic odyssey through time. The latter is a more conventional novel, pitting a determined, expert military man against a planet ruled by a ruthless matriarch. *Dimension of Horror,* an adventure in the Richard Blade series, was similarly competent but even less memorable.

The Prometheus Man, on the other hand, is one of the best dystopian novels of all time. Overpopulation, automation, and lethargy have weakened the fabric of society as the vast majority of the population is unemployable. In order to maintain order, most of these people are confined to camps where they are theoretically looked after, but the impersonal treatment leads predictably to unrest. The plot is complex and thoroughly worked out.

Nelson's short fiction is extremely good and equally infrequent. "Nightfall on the Dead Sea," for example, is a fine historical horror story pitting a Roman soldier against a man cursed with immortality. "Time Travel for Pedestrians" aroused a degree of controversy because of its subject matter—time travel via masturbation—but its clear superiority of style and the maturity of its vision established it as a major accomplishment.

Nelson displays a fondness for the grotesque. A human is turned into an organic asteroid in "Flesh Pearl," and another becomes a rather unpleasant form of nourishment in "Food." Grotesquerie and the absurd are to be found in "The Great Cosmic Donut of Life" and "Turn off the Sky" as well.

"Eight O'Clock in the Morning" takes a routine gimmick (aliens who can be seen by only a single human) and condenses what other writers would have extended to novel length into a few thousand words. This was filmed as *They Live,* although the screen version translated as a routine action movie. Ancient history and the supernatural mix again in "The City of the Crocodile," and a man takes a spiritual journey to the land of the suicides in "Valse Triste." "A Song on the Rising Wind" examines the nature of violence and courage on a level rare in any field of writing, as a revolution brews among a society of sequestered unemployables, an obvious precursor to *The Prometheus Man.*

Never a prolific writer, Nelson has been virtually silent for the past several years. His published work displays careful craftsmanship and great concentration and commitment. He has consistently been willing to tackle controversial themes and ambitious goals, maintaining tight control of his work at all times. Although frequently idiosyncratic, this uniqueness of viewpoint is what makes his fiction rise above that of his contemporaries.

—Don D'Ammassa

NESVADBA, Josef

Nationality: Czech. **Born:** Prague, 19 June 1926. **Education:** Charles University, m.d. 1950. **Family:** Married Libuje Dostalova in 1968; one daughter. **Career:** Registrar, General Hospital, Teplice-Sanov, 1950-56; psychiatrist, Charles University, Prague, 1956—. Group psychotherapist. **Agent:** Dilia, Vysehradska 28, Prague 2, Czechoslovakia. **Address:** Department of Psychiatry, Faculty of Medicine, Charles University, Prague 2, Ke Karlovu 11, Czechoslovakia.

SCIENCE FICTION PUBLICATIONS

Short Stories

Vampires Ltd.: Stories of Science and Fantasy, translated by Iris Unwin. Prague, Artia, New York, Vanous, 1964.
"The Last Secret Weapon of the Third Reich," in *The Year's Best S-F10,* edited by Judith Merril, 1965.
"Mordair," in *Czech and Slovak Short Stories,* 1967.
"The Planet Circè," in *New Writing from Czechoslovakia,* edited by George Theiner, 1969.
"Vampire Ltd.," in *Other Worlds, Other Seas,* edited by Darko Suvin, 1970.
In the Footsteps of the Abominable Snowman: Stories of Science and Fantasy, translated by Iris Urwin. London, Gollancz, 1970; as *The Lost Face: Best Science Fiction from Czechoslovakia,* New York, Taplinger, 1971.
"Captain Nemo's Last Adventure," in *View from Another Shore,* edited by Franz Rottensteiner, 1973.

*   *   *

Josef Nesvadba is a practicing psychiatrist. Almost all of his stories are introverted, brooding, and hauntingly effective probings of humanist morality and the "small people" that inhabit the real world of modern, Soviet-dominated Czechoslovakia. Those stories that have appeared in English show his penchant for intellectual and psychological questions; Nesvadba's tales are rarely "upbeat" as they dig beneath appearances, peel away affectations, and discover a universality in man that transcends the hated memories of the Nazis, the heavy presence of Soviet power, and the occasionally wistful reflections about Britons and somewhat distant Americans.

One major collection has appeared in translation, *In the Footsteps of the Abominable Snowman.* The best in this assortment is "The Death of an Apeman," a wry retelling of the Tarzan story with a typical twist: the nobleman (German, not English) must commit suicide once he has learned what "civilized" men are like. "Expedition in the Opposite Direction" tells of time travel gone afoul, especially when one's sense of déjà vu cannot prevent the inevitable; "The Trial Nobody Ever Heard Of" focuses on petty scientists and their academic wars extrapolated by analogy into the Nazi murderers and their callous inhumanity; "The Lost Face" suggests that even plastic surgery cannot change essentials; "The Chemical Formula of Destiny" examines the uniqueness of genius; "Inventor of His Own Undoing" asks what would happen if everyone worked for fun; "Doctor Moreau's Other Island" grumpily predicts man's inevitable degeneracy; and the title story is a moving tale of wanderlust, perhaps indicative of Nesvadba's sense of isolation.

Other stories that have appeared in English include "Mordair," which suggests a cheap and inhumane solution to fuel costs; "Vampire Ltd.," a beautifully crafted tale of the soul-sucking qualities of the modern automobile; "Captain Nemo's Last Adventure," one of Nesvadba's best, showing the wanderlust and the eternal search for "The Fundamental Question of Life" and its "Final Answer"; "The Planet Circè," which examines the dangers of total indolence and complete satisfaction of childhood desires; and "The Last Secret Weapon of the Third Reich," which recalls the nightmare of the Nazi ability to pit Czech against Czech.

Nesvadba writes with great dexterity, and his stories deserve wider attention in the West. He represents a brand of science fiction quite distinct from either the Russian variety, which sometimes smothers good writing in the cocoon of socialist theorizing, or from the American-British science fiction, which tends to focus on disasters (man-made or natural) or how heroes with mechanical know-how can undo cosmic evils. Nesvadba is a clear descendent in Czech literature of Hašek and perhaps Polacek, but not Capek. The zest of Capek's furious and ironic humor does not appear in Nesvadba's writing. The vision is narrowed, and Capek's wide-ranging internationalism has been replaced by a poignant sadness, an inner reflection of the fate of the Czech nation.

—John Scarborough

NEVILLE, Kris (Ottman)

Nationality: American. **Born:** Carthage, Missouri, 9 May 1925. **Education:** University of California, Los Angeles, B.A. in English 1950. **Military Service:** Served in the United States Army Signal Corps during World War II. **Family:** Married Lil Johnson in 1957; five children. **Career:** Worked in the plastics and chemistry industries: after 1965, staff member, Epoxylite Corporation, Anaheim, California. **Died:** 23 December 1980.

SCIENCE FICTION PUBLICATIONS

Novels

The Unearth People. New York, Belmont, 1964.
The Mutants. New York, Belmont, 1966.
Peril of the Starmen. New York, Belmont, 1967.
Special Delivery. New York, Belmont, 1967.
Bettyann. New York, Tower, 1970.
Invaders on the Moon. New York, Belmont, 1970.

Short Stories

Mission: Manstop. North Hollywood, Leisure, 1971.
The Science Fiction of Kris Neville, edited by Barry N. Malzberg and Martin H. Greenberg. Carbondale, Southern Illinois University Press, 1984.

OTHER PUBLICATIONS

Novel

Run, The Spearmaker (in Japanese), with Lil Neville. Tokyo, Hayakawa Shobo, 1975.

Other

Epoxy Resins, with Henry Lee. New York, McGraw Hill, 1957.

Handbook of Epoxy Resins, with Henry Lee. New York, McGraw Hill, 1967.
New Linear Polymers, with Henry Lee. New York, McGraw Hill, 1967.
Handbook of Biomedical Plastics, with Henry Lee. Pasadena, California, Pasadena Technology Press, 1971.
Adhesive Restorative Dentistry, with Robert L. Ibsen. Philadelphia, Saunders, 1974.
Industrial Motor Users' Handbook of Insulation for Rewinds, with L.J. Regda. New York, and Oxford, Elsevier, 1977.
Editor, with Henry Lee, *Handbook of Adhesive Bonding,* by Charles V. Cagle. New York, McGraw Hill, 1982.

*

Kris Neville commented:

(1980) I wrote the majority of my stories in the early 1950s. Having just graduated from UCLA with a degree in English literature, I was interested in introducing mainstream elements into science fiction (which I had been reading avidly since 1937)—shifting the emphasis to the impact of future technology on ordinary individuals. I also tried to seek out new perspectives—using female protagonists; playing with various viewpoints; seeing the future through the eyes of the old or young; portraying Earthmen in less than favorable lights; breaking taboos; making satirical comments (I was a socialist/humanist). In many of my shorts, I aimed for emotional effect. I was a trail blazer in my time.

By the mid-1950s, I'd run out of things to say. During the next decade, I kept my hand in with *The Unearth People* and an occasional short, and also revised earlier material into novels. I moved leftward philosophically to my present position: left-wing anarchist. The shorts contained sharper social commentary ("Survival Problems"). I was particularly unhappy with the war in Vietnam ("The Price of Simeryl") and, later, Richard Nixon ("The Reality Machine"). During that decade, Lil and I wrote *Run, The Spearmaker,* a novel dealing with the evolution of civilization at the beginning of human history. The translator called it a minor literary masterpiece. Pity it isn't available in English.

During the 1970s, in addition to half a dozen shorts that Lil and I collaborated on, we also did another novel, *Thorstein Macaulay.* It contains our best writing and most carefully considered political statements. It was about 10 years in the making. As of this writing we had not yet found a publisher for it.

*   *   *

Kris Neville's large output of stories seems to be equally divided among adventure SF, social SF, fantasy SF, and fantasy. While he was known as a *Galaxy* school writer, his most characteristic work appears to be more melodramatic than ironic. Nevertheless, Neville will often subordinate adventure narrative to character interaction or to the character's response to those environmental or cultural forces that are byproducts of future science and technology. Neville was a popular and critically respected author in the genre during the 1950s and 1960s, but his reputation as a craftsman seems to have been lost, perhaps as the result of the rather conventional plotting and characterization in his later work.

Neville's great theme is alienation. He eschews the more sensational aspects of this theme in favor of the psychological dimensions implied in its use in the future world of SF. Novels like *Special Delivery, Earth Alert* (in *If,* February 1953), and *The Mutants* deal with variations of the alien invasion theme or its analogues.

The Mutants, a potentially timely treatment of the social implications of artificial insemination in a state utopia, fails to rise above the level of the melodramatic struggle of a few idealistic youths fighting to save the race from a progressively more repressive state control of human biology.

In the main, Neville was a writer typical of his time. He knew how to make good use of psychologically enriched characters and possessed more sensitivity toward character motivation and interaction than most of his colleagues. In many ways, he belongs in the Theodore Sturgeon camp of SF writers, although he does lapse into the action/adventure idiom more frequently than Sturgeon and his successors. Neville's style is also more direct, simple, and clear than Sturgeon's, better suited, perhaps, for the potboilers he produced for Belmont. Neville was, it appears, in nearly every way a writer several cuts above the average who never quite made the success expected of him. Although he wrote SF, Neville gave little evidence of being deeply committed for or against science. It, like the future, is simply one of the unexamined, given elements of his stories. Whatever the cause, Neville produced a body of SF that refuses to move us deeply in any of the many ways in which less accomplished stylists have done by writing with more conviction, except in one notable case.

Neville may not deserve the obscurity into which his career has fallen if only for the sake of one superb story, "Bettyann" (1951; expanded into a novel, 1970; a sequel is "Bettyann's Children"). This story of a crippled orphan girl raised in a foster home whose sense of difference is confirmed when she discovers she is actually a member of an extraterrestrial race is handled with the same kind of sensitivity and poignance as Daniel Keyes's "Flowers for Algernon," another story that grew successfully into a novel. In place of the overwriting of most SF melodrama, Neville has his subject and his characters fully under control. In "Bettyann" Neville manages understated effects brilliantly in a way that he approached in only a few other stories besides the sequel: "Old Man Henderson" and "Closing Time" are examples. "Bettyann" is one of those rare SF stories that could not be written in another genre but which deals profoundly with universal, human values. Bettyann's affirmation of a basic humanity which has become stronger in her nature than her lately discovered alien origins is an inspiring moment in literature. The two stories and the novel must be considered neglected masterpieces, which are only beginning to receive their due critical recognition.

—Donald L. Lawler

NICHOLS, Scott. *See* **SCORTIA, Thomas N.**

NIVEN, Larry

Nationality: American. **Born:** Laurence Van Cott Niven, Los Angeles, California, 30 April 1938. **Education:** California Institute of Technology, Pasadena, 1956-58; Washburn University, Topeka, Kansas, A.B. 1962; University of California, Los Angeles, 1962-63. **Family:** Married Marylin Wosowati in 1969. **Career:** Since 1964, freelance writer. **Awards:** Hugo award, for story, 1967, 1972, 1975, 1976, for novel, 1971; Nebula award, 1970; Ditmar award, 1971; *Locus* award, 1985. **Address:** c/o Baen Publishing Enterprises, 260 Fifth Avenue, Suite 35, New York, New York 10001, U.S.A.

SCIENCE FICTION PUBLICATIONS

Novels (series: Dream Park; Known Space; Magic; Moat; Buck Rogers)

World of Ptavvs (Space). New York, Ballantine, 1966; London, Macdonald, 1968.
A Gift from Earth (Space). New York, Ballantine, 1968; London, Macdonald, 1969.
Ringworld (Space). New York, Ballantine, 1970; London, Gollancz, 1972.
The Flying Sorcerers, with David Gerrold. New York, Ballantine, 1971; London, Corgi, 1975.
Protector (Space). New York, Ballantine, 1973; Tisbury, Wiltshire, Compton Russell, 1976.
The Mote in God's Eye, with Jerry Pournelle. New York, Simon and Schuster, 1974; London, Weidenfeld and Nicolson, 1975.
Inferno, with Jerry Pournelle. New York, Pocket Books, 1976; London, Wingate, 1977.
A World out of Time: A Novel. New York, Holt Rinehart, 1976; London, Macdonald and Jane's 1977.
Lucifer's Hammer, with Jerry Pournelle. Chicago, Playboy Press, 1977.
The Magic Goes Away. New York, Ace, 1978; London, Futura, 1982.
The Ringworld Engineers (Space). West Bloomfield, Michigan, Phantasia Press, 1979; London, Gollancz, 1980.
Mordred (Buck Rogers), with Jerry Pournelle and John Eric Holmes. New York, Ace, 1980.
The Patchwork Girl (Space). New York, Ace, 1980; London, Macdonald, 1982.
Dream Park, with Steven Barnes. Huntington Woods, Michigan, Phantasia Press, 1981; London, Macdonald, 1983.
Oath of Fealty, with Jerry Pournelle. Huntington Woods, Michigan, Phantasia Press, 1981; London, Macdonald, 1982.
Warrior's Blood (Buck Rogers), with Jerry Pournelle and Richard S. McEnroe. New York, Ace, 1981.
Warrior's World (Buck Rogers), with Jerry Pournelle and Richard S. McEnroe. New York, Ace, 1981.
The Descent of Anansi, with Steven Barnes. New York, Tor, 1982; London, Orbit, 1992.
Rogers' Rangers (Buck Rogers), with Jerry Pournelle and John Silbersack. New York, Ace, 1983.
The Integral Trees (Space). New York, Ballantine, and London, Macdonald, 1984.
Footfall, with Jerry Pournelle. New York, Ballantine, and London, Gollancz, 1985.
The Legacy of Heorot, with Jerry Pournelle and Steven Barnes. London, Gollancz, and New York, Simon and Schuster, 1987.
The Smoke Ring (Space). New York, Ballantine, and London, Macdonald, 1987.
The Man-Kzin Wars, with Poul Anderson and Dean Ing. New York, Baen, 1988; London, Orbit, 1989.

The Man-Kzin Wars II, with Dean Ing, Jerry Pournelle, and S.M. Stirling. New York, Baen, 1989; London, Orbit, 1991.

The Barsoom Project (Dream Park), with Steven Barnes. New York, Ace, 1989; London, Pan, 1990.

The Man-Kzin Wars III, with Poul Anderson, Jerry Pournelle, and S.M. Stirling. New York, Baen, 1990.

Achilles' Choice, with Steven Barnes. New York, Tor, 1991; London, Pan, 1993.

Fallen Angels, with Jerry Pournelle and Michael Flynn. Norwalk, Connecticut, Easton Press, 1991; London, Pan, 1993.

The Voodoo Game (Dream Park). London, Pan, 1991; as *The California Voodoo Game,* New York, Ballantine, 1992.

The Gripping Hand (Moat), with Jerry Pournelle. New York, Pocket Books, 1993; as *The Moat around Murcheson's Eye,* London, HarperCollins, 1993.

Short Stories (series: Known Space)

Neutron Star (Space). New York, Ballantine, 1968; London, Macdonald, 1969.

The Shape of Space (Space). New York, Ballantine, 1969.

All the Myriad Ways. New York, Ballantine, 1971.

The Flight of the Horse. New York, Ballantine, 1973; London, Futura, 1975.

Inconstant Moon. London, Gollancz, 1973.

A Hole in Space. New York, Ballantine, 1974; London, Futura, 1975.

Tales of Known Space: The Universe of Larry Niven. New York, Ballantine, 1975; London, Orbit, 1992.

The Long ARM of Gil Hamilton (Space). New York, Ballantine, 1976; London, Futura, 1980.

Convergent Series (Space). New York, Ballantine, 1979; London, Orbit, 1986.

The Time of the Warlock, illustrated by Dennis Wolf. Minneapolis, Steel Dragon Press, 1984.

Niven's Laws (includes articles). Philadelphia, Philadelphia Science Fiction Society, 1984.

Limits. New York, Ballantine, 1985; London, Orbit, 1986.

N-Space. New York, Tor, 1990; London, Orbit, 1992.

Playgrounds of the Mind. New York, Tor, 1991.

Man-Kzin Wars IV, with Donald Kingsbury, Greg Bear, and S.M. Stirling. Riverdale, New York, Baen, 1991.

Man-Kzin Wars V, with Jerry Pournelle, S.M. Stirling, and Thomas T. Thomas. Riverdale, New York, Baen, 1992.

Bridging the Galaxies. San Francisco, ConFrancisco, 1993.

Crashlander (Space). New York, Ballantine, 1995.

Man-Kzin Wars VI, with Donald Kingsbury, Mark O. Martin, and Gregory Benford. Riverdale, New York, Baen, 1994.

Flatlander (Space). New York, Ballantine, 1995.

O︎THER P︎UBLICATIONS

Other

Editor, *The Magic May Return.* New York, Ace, 1981.
Editor, *More Magic.* New York, Berkley, 1984.

*

Bibliography: *The Guide to Larry Niven's Ringworld* by Kevin Stein, Riverdale, New York, Baen, 1994.

Manuscript Collection: George Arents Research Library, Syracuse University, New York.

*　　*　　*

When the New Wave began to flourish in the mid-1960s, paradoxically a writer appeared whose work embodied many of the genre conventions which that movement was rejecting: science fiction as the depiction of technical problem-solving, faith in the infallible efficacy of science, and a belief in humanity's implicit ability to overcome any obstacle. Larry Niven quickly became regarded as the leading practitioner of "hard" SF. "The idea is truly the hero" (a reviewer's praise for a later novel) aptly sums up both his greatest strength and weakness.

Like Robert Heinlein and Isaac Asimov, Niven constructed a future history, his "Known Space," a series of related stories later codified into a chart. Unlike his predecessors, his schema included an elaborate million-and-a-half year prehistory, as well as several memorable varieties of aliens. Known Space has become a popular mythology, with other writers contributing tales to the period of Man-Kzin wars, which Niven, with the exception of one story, neglects, admitting his lack of expertise about military subjects.

Niven's most celebrated talent is his ability to create grandly scaled worlds that dwarf their inhabitants. *Ringworld* is the most famous: a hundred-thousand-mile-wide ribbon revolving around a star at a distance of one A.U. Not only is this hard science fiction on an epic scale, but Niven's most appealing characters travel against this backdrop. Unlike many recent SF novels artificially swollen to require sequels, *Ringworld* was satisfying on its own terms, but Niven acceded to fan pressure and wrote *The Ringworld Engineers,* a grand, unifying coda to Known Space in which all loose threads are gathered up and connected. Some readers found it unsuccessful, perhaps because the characters seem to be shadows of their former selves, and some of the unification forced. Yet read together, the novels furnish a fitting capstone to one of the most popular series in recent science fiction. Even though Niven has previously stated that he has nothing more to add to the Ringworld saga, a third volume is now promised.

Niven has created other future histories, such as the Leshy Circuit, which includes *A World out of Time,* a Stapledonian journey into the far future in which humans have evolved into immortal, spiteful boys and girls, and the far more successful pair of novels about the possibility of life without a planet within the gas torus surrounding a neutron star, *The Integral Trees* and *The Smoke Ring.* Once again Niven's world-building is immense, with the only danger being the characters' becoming literarily—as well as literally—swamped by the intricacies of the construct.

Like Heinlein, one of Niven's favorite imaginative spurs is to postulate a technical improvement and project its impact on society. "New technologies create new customs, new laws, new ethics, new crimes." This theorem results in, among others, Niven's series of stories on teleportation, or those about the organ banks and the psychic detective Gil "the Arm" Hamilton. However, these stories reveal a strange contradiction in Niven's work, given his reputation as a practitioner of hard SF. One of his favorite aphorisms is Arthur C. Clarke's statement: "Any sufficiently advanced technology is indistinguishable from magic." And Niven's technology, despite the intricately detailed scientific framework, often does seem like magic. Some of his plots, like those of *World of Ptavvs* or *A Gift from Earth,* hinge on psionic powers. Indeed, Niven has written several series of what might be termed "hard" fantasy, in which the magic is as strictly regulated as the science in an *Analog* story. Niven has entitled one of his collections *Limits* in recognition of this need.

Since the mid-1970s, much of Niven's work has been collaborative. His most famous partner is Jerry Pournelle, and their work describes universes more inimical than Known Space, while also proselytizing more overtly for science ("to proxmire" becomes a pejorative verb), and continuing to present aliens who are dangerous, yet sympathetically depicted. *The Mote in God's Eye* was eagerly awaited, and carried Heinlein's extravagant blurb, "Possibly the finest science-fiction novel I have ever read," praise almost impossible to live up to. A solid novel of first contact nevertheless, its suspense rides on whether humanity will realize the Moties' danger. The phrase "genie in the bottle," often used to describe the perils of unleashed science, here describes the possibility of the Moties emerging from their own system. Its sequel, *The Gripping Hand*, unfortunately becomes bogged down in complications resulting from the apparatus and framework that made the central situation of the first novel possible.

Lucifer's Hammer, a disaster epic so typical of the 1970s, carries the insistent subtext that technology, represented by the atomic power plant, instead of being dangerous will save humanity after such a disaster and allow it again to "control the lightning"; it also carries Niven's and Pournelle's self-admitted tendentiousness too far for some critics. *Footfall* is another novel of first contact, or rather conquest, in which a herd race bent on dominating the Earth of the near future is confused and defeated by humanity's lack of a surrender ritual and its penchant for individuality. Once again the atom—in this case the bomb—provides salvation (with science fiction writers, including the easily recognizable "Robert Anson," giving crucial advice). *The Legacy of Heorot* (written also with Niven's other principal collaborator, Steven Barnes) is a breathless combination of elements from *Beowulf, The Thing,* and *Zulu,* as an isolated human colony must defend itself from supercarnivores. Probably Niven and Pournelle's most interesting work is *Inferno,* on the face of it a retelling of Dante by two hard SF writers, a sure recipe for disaster. Yet it is humorous, as a deceased SF writer tries, with the panache of a Heinlein hero, to devise technical explanations for and escapes from hell, as well as thought-provoking, plausible theological reasons for a supposedly merciful deity's construction of a place of eternal torment.

Niven's collaborative work with Steven Barnes also glorifies the possibilities of science while solving a life-threatening technical problem, as in *The Descent of Anansi.* Their most interesting work depicts a theme park that offers virtual fantasy role-playing games. Particularly satisfying in *Dream Park* and *The Barsoom Project* is the unexpected use of the myths of primitive people (Melanesians and Inuit) reacting to and controlling modern Western technology.

Niven, never a prolific author on his own, has produced little original work recently. His solo work has become almost valedictory, with the collections *N-Space* and *Playgrounds of the Mind* summations of and commentaries on his whole career. *Crashlander* and *Flatlander* collect Niven's stories about Beowulf Schaeffer and Gil Hamilton, respectively (in the case of Hamilton, for the second time), while adding only one new story each. Known Space seems to have become an imaginative stranglehold for Niven's own work. Meanwhile, his collaborative work has become increasingly focused on a coterie audience. *Fallen Angels* has an interesting yet characteristically tendentious premise, that recent ecological efforts will produce another Ice Age, but the corollary of this premise, that humanity will be rescued by the remnants of SF fandom, is so replete with coterie in-jokes and references that its appeal to a wider audi-

ence vanishes. (The paperback jacket significantly does not even hint at who these rescuers are.) *The California Voodoo Game,* while promising the same kind of imaginative explorations of culture in the first two Dream Park novels, becomes wrapped up in a similar kind of limited appeal, in this case to devotees of role-playing. Niven's characters, never his strongest point, as is the case in much of what is known as hard SF, become bundles of physical characteristics and clues to the solving of romans à clef to which very few people have the key, and even fewer want one.

Niven burst on the scene with a series of compelling and appealing myths in the late 1960s and early 1970s. The only way he has perhaps failed to live up to his promise is in setting such an initial high (and prolific) standard for himself. His lasting achievement (to paraphrase Wagner on Brahms) is to show what can be done with old forms in a new time. Unfortunately, as Niven himself seems to realize, his particular form—hard SF—has internal limitations that can grow into a straightjacket that can restrict the growth of an entire career.

—William Laskowski, Jr.

NOBEL, Phil. *See* **FANTHORPE, R. Lionel.**

NOLAN, William F(rancis)

Pseudonym: Terence Duncan. **Nationality:** American. **Born:** Kansas City, Missouri, 6 March 1928. **Education:** Kansas City Art Institute, 1946-47; San Diego State College, California, 1947-48; Los Angeles City College, 1953. **Family:** Married Marilyn Seal in 1970. **Career:** Greeting card designer and cartoonist, Hall Brothers, Kansas City, 1945; mural painter, San Diego, 1949-50; aircraft inspector, Convair, San Diego, 1950-52; credit assistant, Blake Moffit and Towne Paper Company, Los Angeles, 1953-54; interviewer, California State Department of Employment, 1954-56. Since 1956, freelance writer. Contributing editor, *Chase,* managing editor, *GAMMA,* West Coast editor, *Auto,* and associate editor, *Motor Sport Illustrated,* all Los Angeles, 1963-64; reviewer, *Los Angeles Times,* 1964-70. **Awards:** American Library Association citation, 1960; Edgar Allan Poe Special award, 1970, 1972; Academy of Science Fiction and Fantasy award, for fiction and film, 1976; Maltese Falcon award, 1977. Honorary Doctorate: American River College, Sacramento, California, 1975. **Address:** Reseda, California, U.S.A. **Agent:** Lori Perkins, Perkins Associates, 301 West 53rd Street, New York, New York 10019, U.S.A.

SCIENCE FICTION PUBLICATIONS

Novels (series: Logan; Sam Space)

Logan: A Trilogy, with George Clayton Johnson. Baltimore, Maclay, 1986.

Logan's Run, with George Clayton Johnson. New York, Dial Press, 1967; London, Gollancz, 1968.

Logan's World. New York, Bantam, 1977; London, Corgi, 1978.

Logan's Search. New York, Bantam, 1980; London, Corgi, 1981.

Space for Hire (Space). New York, Lancer, 1971.

Look out for Space (Space). New York, International Polygonics, 1985.

Short Stories

Impact-20. New York, Paperback Library, 1963; London, Corgi, 1966.

Alien Horizons. New York, Pocket Books, 1974.

Wonderworlds. London, Gollancz, 1977.

Things beyond Midnight. Santa Cruz, California, Scream Press, 1984.

Blood Sky. San Jose, California, Deadline, 1991.

3 for Space (Space). Brooklyn, New York, Gryphon, 1992.

Helle on Wheels: A Nick Challis Detective Thriller. Baltimore, Maclay, 1993.

OTHER PUBLICATIONS

Novels

Death Is for Losers. Los Angeles, Sherbourne Press, 1968.

The White Cad Cross-Up. Los Angeles, Sherbourne Press, 1969.

Rio Renegades (as Terence Duncan). New York, Zebra, 1989.

Helltracks. New York, Avon, 1991.

The Black Mask Murders: A Novel Featuring the Black Mask Boys, Dashiell Hammett, Raymond Chandler, and Erle Stanley Gardner. New York, St. Martin's Press, 1994.

Plays

Visual Encounters (TV scripts). Baltimore, Maclay, 1986.

Screenplays: *The Legend of Machine-Gun Kelly,* 1975; *Logan's Run,* 1976; *Burnt Offerings,* with Dan Curtis, 1976.

Television Plays: *The Joy of Living,* 1971; *The Norliss Tapes,* 1973; *Melvin Purvis, G-Man,* with John Milius, 1974; *The Turn of the Screw,* 1974; *The Kansas City Massacre,* with Bronson Howitzer, 1975; *Sky Heist,* with Rick Rosner 1975; *Julie and Millicent and Therese* (in *Trilogy of Terror*), 1975; *Logan's Run* series, 1977; *First Loss,* 1981; *The Partnership,* 1981; *Bridge Across Time (Terror of London Bridge),* 1985; *Trilogy of Terror II,* 1990.

Poetry

Dark Encounters. Madison, Wisconsin, Dream House, 1986.

Other

Adventure on Wheels: The Autobiography of a Road Racing Champion, with John Fitch. New York, Putnam, 1959.

Barney Oldfield: The Life and Times of America's Legendary Speed King. New York, Putnam, 1961.

Phil Hill: Yankee Champion. New York, Putnam, 1962.

Men of Thunder: Fabled Daredevils of Motor Sport. New York, Putnam, 1964; abridged as *Selections from Men of Thunder,* New York, Bantam, 1966.

Sinners and Supermen. North Hollywood, All Star, 1965; as *Legends and Lovers: 14 Profiles,* Sacramento, California, Borgo Press, 1995.

John Huston: King Rebel. Los Angeles, Sherbourne Press, 1965.

Dashiell Hammett: A Casebook. Santa Barbara, California, McNally and Loftin, 1969.

Steve McQueen: Star on Wheels. New York, Putnam, 1972.

Carnival of Speed: True Adventures in Motor Racing. New York, Putnam, 1973.

Hemingway: Last Days of the Lion. Santa Barbara, California, Capra Press, 1974.

The Ray Bradbury Companion: A Life and Career History, Photolog, and comprehensive Checklist of Writings. Detroit, Gale, 1975.

Hammett: A Life at the Edge (biography of Dashiell Hammett). New York, Congdon and Weed, 1983; London, Barker, 1984.

McQueen (biography of Steve McQueen). New York, Congdon and Weed, and London, Barker, 1984.

The Black Mask Boys: Masters in the Hard-Boiled School of Detective Fiction. New York, Morrow, 1985.

The Work of Charles Beaumont: An Annotated Bibliography and Guide, edited by Robert Reginald. San Bernardino, California, Borgo Press, 1986; 2nd edition, edited by Boden Clarke, Borgo Press, 1990.

How to Write Horror Fiction. Cincinnati, Ohio, Writer's Digest, 1990.

Editor, *Ray Bradbury Review.* San Diego, California, Nolan, 1952; as *William F. Nolan's Ray Bradbury Review,* Los Angeles, Graham Press, 1988.

Editor, *A Cross-Section of Art in Science-Fantasy.* San Diego, Nolan, 1952.

Editor, with Charles Beaumont, *Omnibus of Speed: Introduction to the World of Motor Sport.* New York, Putnam, 1958; abridged edition, London, Paul, 1961.

Editor, with Charles Beaumont, *The Fiend in You.* New York, Ballantine, 1962.

Editor, with Charles Beaumont, *When Engines Roar.* New York, Bantam, 1964.

Editor, *Man against Tomorrow.* New York, Avon, 1965.

Editor, *The Pseudo-People: Androids in Science Fiction.* Los Angeles, Sherbourne Press, 1965; as *Almost Human: Androids in Science Fiction,* London, Souvenir Press, 1966.

Editor, *Il Meglio della Fantascienza.* Milano, Longanesi, 1967.

Editor, *3 to the Highest Power.* New York, Avon, 1968; London, Corgi, 1971; abridged edition, 1980.

Editor, *A Wilderness of Stars: Stories of Man in Conflict with Space.* Los Angeles, Sherbourne Press, 1969; London, Gollancz, 1970.

Editor, *A Sea of Space.* New York, Bantam, 1970; London, Corgi, 1980.

Editor, *The Future Is Now: All-New, All-Star Science Fiction Stories.* Los Angeles, Sherbourne Press, 1970.

Editor, *The Human Equation.* Los Angeles, Sherbourne Press, 1971.

Editor, *The Edge of Forever: Classic Anthropological Science Fiction Stories,* by Chad Oliver. Los Angeles, Sherbourne Press, 1971.

Editor, with Martin H. Greenberg, *Science Fiction Origins.* New York, Fawcett-Popular Library, 1980.

Editor, *Max Brand's Best Western Stories.* New York, Dodd Mead, 3 vols., 1981-87; London, Hale, 2 vols., 1983-86.

Editor, *Max Brand, Western Giant.* Bowling Green, Ohio, Bowling Green State University Popular Press, 1986.

Editor, with Martin H. Greenberg, *Urban Horrors.* Arlington Heights, Illinois, Dark Harvest, 1990.

Editor, with Martin H. Greenberg, *The Bradbury Chronicles: Stories in Honor of Ray Bradbury.* New York, Roc, 1991; London, Severn House, 1992.

*

Bibliography: *William F. Nolan: A Checklist* by Charles E. Yenter, Tacoma, Washington, Charles E. Yenter, 1974; *The Work of William F. Nolan: An Annotated Bibliography and Guide* by Boden Clarke and James Hopkins, San Bernardino, California, Borgo Press, 1988.

Manuscript Collection: Bowling Green State University, Ohio.

Theatrical Activities:

Actor: **Films**—*The Intruder,* 1962; *The Legend of Machine-Gun Kelly,* 1975.

William F. Nolan comments:

As a writer, I'm hard to pin down. Science fiction is just one of my many fields, and I take equal pride in my crime-suspense writing, auto-racing books, westerns, biographies, fantasy-terror fiction, thriller novels, verse, essays, and book reviews. I keep fresh and excited as a writer by switching constantly from one genre to another. I have enjoyed doing SF, particularly the Logan novels, but I also enjoy all other types of writing. After 30 years as a professional, my work totals 895 items—and I figure my career has another 30 years to go. After 37 years as a professional, my work totals 1200 items—and my career still has a long way to go. After all, Picasso turned out 300 paintings during his 90th year!

*   *   *

William F. Nolan started his creative life as an artist, but turned to the more lucrative science fiction and men's magazines in the mid-1950s. Nolan was one of a school of Southern California SF writers that included (at times) the late Charles Beaumont, Ray Russell, George Clayton Johnson, Richard Matheson, Chad Oliver, and others. These authors not only socialized together, but also used their common interests in fantastic literature, film, television, and professional racing to develop a myriad of creative projects, often in collaboration. Although each writer eventually went his own way, artistically and personally, for the 10-year period from 1955-65, most followed a similar path, moving from pulp fiction to slick nonfiction to the lucrative television market.

Nolan has been a full-time freelancer from the beginning, producing some 1500 short fiction and nonfiction works in the course of his career, plus 61 books, 40 teleplays, and a dozen screenplays. Although his career has been a financial success, his work has been spread across so many subjects and genres that he remains relatively unheralded as a writer. Still, the frequency with which Nolan's 130 stories continue to be regularly anthologized ("Small World" has been reprinted at least 20 times) is a sign of his continuing popularity and deepening influence as a writer.

However, Nolan's reputation as an SF writer seems secure, resting primarily on wide popular acceptance of two fictional creations, Logan the Sandman and Sam Space. *Logan's Run* (written with George Clayton Johnson), together with its sequels, *Logan's World* and *Logan's Search,* represent the highwater mark of the author's career, having been turned into both a successful motion picture and a television series, as well as being adapted into a popular comic book series.

In the not-so-distant future, the young have revolted and killed all the adults. The new regime decrees that henceforward anyone reaching the age of 21 shall voluntarily undergo euthanasia; those who refuse to die shall be hunted down by the police (the Sandmen) and summarily executed. A massive computer (The Thinker) is built to control the world and enforce the new rules. The new world state provides each citizen with everything he or she might want: travel, drugs, pleasures of all kinds, even work for those who want it—but everything ends at 21. Logan 3 is a Sandman who begins questioning the system after being forced to terminate a young girl. As his own time begins running out, Logan searches for Sanctuary, the semi-mythical place to which some runners have apparently escaped, and meets Jessica 6, with whom he forms a lasting and loving relationship. After a series of harrowing adventures, including a confrontation with the Thinker, in which they succeed in shutting down the machine, Logan and Jessica find Sanctuary, and live to fight another day.

In *Logan's World,* Logan and Jessica return to find the Sandman system largely destroyed, except for a group of renegade Sandmen who are trying to repair the damaged Thinker. In the ensuing chaos, Logan's son is killed, the Thinker is destroyed, and mankind is left to find its own way to the future. *Logan's Search* concludes the trilogy with Logan's attempt to defeat the Sandman system on a parallel Earth where the Thinker still exists.

Logan is Everyman, the man forced by conscience and circumstance to blaze a new path for himself—and for mankind. The signs of systemic failure are everywhere, literally and figuratively: this brave new world of the future, itself once representing a great turning point in the history of the human race, has come full circle, to a cultural and historical dead end. The machines are breaking down—and so is human society. Logan must destroy the old, rekindle the new, and show people the way to a new civilization. In another sense, Logan is also Nolan (one name being nearly the anagram of the other): the author as iconoclast, the artist as creator/destroyer, the rebel *with* a cause, the self-made man remaking himself in fiction. Complacency is sterility, the author seems to be saying, a life without challenge is a life not worth living. Mankind cannot stand still: it must either move forward—or die.

The Sam Space books—*Space for Hire, Look Out for Space,* and the collection *3 for Space*—represent the second and third main strands in Nolan's fiction: farce and hardboiled detective fiction. Sam Space (i.e., "Sam Spade" in SF terms) is a Mars-based private eye who always seems to be getting himself into impossibly wacky situations. Nolan manages to satirize the conventions of both the mystery and science fiction genres, as well as modern mores, his fellow authors, and the world in general. Other stories in this vein include: "The Day the Gorf Took Over," "The Fasterfaster Affair," "Papa's Planet" (a robot-Hemingway send-up), and "Jenny among the Zeebs" (a rock n' roll spoof).

In the 1980s, Nolan moved away from SF into dark fantasy, producing a horror novel, *Helltracks,* and some 50 short stories, the best of which are scheduled to be collected into *Things Beyond Midnight* and *Night Shapes.* Like his frequent early collaborator, Charles Beaumont, Nolan has proven particularly effective at depicting the unpleasant side of human nature, and his stories are filled with clever twists, a legacy of his work in the mystery genre. These tales reflect a more cynical view of human nature, one in which there are not always happy endings or Pollyannish characters, in which evil is acknowledged and sometimes prevails.

In the 1990s Nolan's work has again zagged into new directions, with the author producing a series of mystery thrillers which feature "The Black Mask Boys"—Dashiell Hammett, Raymond Chandler, Erle Stanley Gardner—functioning as amateur detectives in the Hollywood of the 1930s. The first of these, *The Black Mask Murders* (narrated by Hammett) was published in 1994, with *The Marble Orchard* (narrated by Chandler) due in 1996.

In these and in all of Nolan's fictions we find the writer sitting to one side, sharpening his authorial knife and covertly slicing away at man, his machines, and his conventions. Some of his stories may have more-or-less happy endings, but even these drip with skepticism and often twist into strange angles by tale's end. In Nolan's fictional world nothing is as it seems, no one is safe, and happiness always comes with a price tag attached.

—Robert Reginald

NOON, Jeff

Nationality: British. **Born:** Droylsden in 1957. **Career:** Guitarist with Manicured Noise; painter; playwright in residence, The Royal Exchange Theatre, Manchester. **Awards:** Mobil Playwriting Competition; Arthur C. Clarke award, 1994; Eurocon award, 1994; John W. Campbell award, 1995.

SCIENCE FICTION PUBLICATIONS

Novels

Vurt. Poynton, Stockport, Cheshire, Ringpull, and New York, Crown, 1993.
Pollen. Greater Manchester, Ringpull, 1995; New York, Crown, 1996.

OTHER PUBLICATIONS

Play

Woundings. Birmingham, Oberon, 1986.

* * *

Jeff Noon's impact upon the British SF scene in 1993 can not be understated, culminating as it did in his debut novel *Vurt* winning the Arthur C. Clarke award. That it was a newly formed, independent publishing house, Ringpull, who published Noon makes this even more remarkable.

Vurt is a modern drugs novel, in which characters enter a shared Virtual Reality by way of placing feathers in their mouth. Each feather has its own characteristics; there are pornovurts, for instance, but the most prized feathers, are the rare and highly illegal yellow feathers.

The narrator of *Vurt* is Scribble (real name Stephen), a member of a gang called the Stash Riders who drive around South Central Manchester in search of thrills. The gang's nominal leader is the Beetle, and the remainder are the shadowgirl, Bridget, with her strange abilities, and the enthusiastic Many, the new girl. And the Thing from Outer Space, a curious tentacled creature from within the Vurt. The reader is reminded both of Enid Blyton's Famous Five, and Hanna and Barbara's *Scooby Doo,* such is the cartoon nature of *Vurt.* However, the world of the novel is also populated by other creatures: there are five purebreds, Human, Dog, Shadow, Robot and Vurt, but crossbreeds proliferate, hence the Shadowgirl, Bridget, and Beetle's recurrent nemesis, the Shadowcap Shaka. (Occasionally in *Vurt* and particularly in Jeff Noon's other stories within this setting, the Dogpeople are reminiscent of David Bowie's *Diamond Dogs*-era.)

Scribble found the Thing when he and his sister/lover Desdemona ventured too deep into Vurt and Desdemona was bitten by a Dreamsnake and trapped leaving the Thing in exchange. His quest is to regain a feather like the one he used previously in order to re-exchange the Thing for Desdemona. That feather is known as English Voodoo.

Jeff Noon is, on the simplest level, telling a crazy but entertaining romantic adventure story. However, the retelling of the myth of Orpheus and Eurydice which Scribble's quest represents is warped by noon's ending where Scribble releases Desdemona by staying in Vurt himself. An added complication is the Game Cat, another vurt-based human whose bulletins throughout the novel provide clues to the vurt traveler about types of vurt feathers, and explain to the reader some of the background to the novel. Jeff Noon's Dirty Surrealist style makes these infodump passages as entertaining as the rest of the novel. When the Cat actually appears as a character these messages enter the realms of metafiction, just as eventually Scribble penetrates the densities of the metavurts.

Because the vurt is, as its name suggests, a form of virtual reality, and largely on the strength of Noon's street-level focus, *Vurt* has been labeled a cyberpunk novel, but the nearest reference points for this novel are Richard Kadrey's *Metrophage* for the bizarre mutant characters and Martin Millar for the absurdist humour and warmth. However, the communal vurt-reality works as a central metaphor (in this case, for adult experience, perhaps?) in much the same way as Cyberspace does.

Jeff Noon's stories are all set in a near-future version of South Central Manchester that Noon invokes, like Millar's Brixton, with carefully selected detail and in a manner which makes Manchester a character in the novels. His forthcoming novel *Pollen* tells about a plague affecting a similar Manchester city.

This time the protagonists, Sybil Jones and her estranged daughter Belinda (aka Boadicea) are "dodos," people who don't dream and are thus excluded from the vurt. This weakness proves to be their saving strength when, from within a vurt feather called Juniper Suction, a virus arises that changes Manchester totally within days. First the pollen count starts to rise, but it is a vurt-pollen spread by a woman called Persephone, and in its wake a new life form arises, joining the Human, Dog, Robo, Shadow, and Vurt is the Flower.

Noon briefly explains some of the origins of Vurt, and of these crossbreeds in *Pollen* and we learn that this novel's events take place just a few years after those of *Vurt,* but generally the style is rapid-fire and dreamlike. One of Noon's principal conceits is the restriction of the reader to only that information that the characters have available, and thus reality is never reliable. Much of *Pollen* is as surreal as its predecessor, but there are strong elements taken from detective novels too. In *Pollen* Noon invokes mythagos of John Barleycorn and others, and the myths at the root of the novel seem clear, and yet there are other characters, the Sybil, the Coyote and the manic OJ Gumbo Ya-Ya who endlessly recombine and complicate the issue. Given that the existence of many of the Vurt-creatures is a result of corrupted DNA, it is fitting that the structure of *Pollen* should approximate the double-helix. Pulling a definitive "meaning" from *Pollen* would seem impossible, but the vigour of Noon's imagination and the emotional intensity of the multifaceted love story which is at the heart of both novels, combine with the vurt-mythagos to speak to the reader on an individual level about identity and individuality, and make Jeff Noon an author to follow closely.

—Kevin McVeigh

NORMAN, John

Pseudonym for John (Frederick) Lange (Jr.). **Nationality:** American. **Born:** Chicago, Illinois, 3 June 1931. **Education:** University of Nebraska, Lincoln, B.A. 1953; University of Southern California, Los Angeles, M.A. 1957; Princeton University, New Jersey, Ph.D. 1963. **Military Service:** Served in the United States Army: Sergeant. **Family:** Married Bernice L. Green in 1956; two sons and one daughter. **Career:** Radio writer; story analyst, Warner Brothers; film writer, University of Nebraska; technical writer, Rocketdyne (North American Aviation); instructor in philosophy, Hamilton College, Clinton, New York, 1962-64. Since 1964, member of the department, and since 1974, Professor of Philosophy, Queens College, City University of New York. **Address:** Department of Philosophy, Queens College, Flushing, New York 11367, U.S.A.

SCIENCE FICTION PUBLICATIONS

Novels (series: Gor; Telnarian Histories)

Tarnsman of Gor. New York, Ballantine, 1966; London, Sidgwick and Jackson, 1969.
Outlaw of Gor. New York, Ballantine, 1967; London, Sidgwick and Jackson, 1970.
Priest-Kings of Gor. New York, Ballantine, 1968; London, Sidgwick and Jackson, 1971.
Nomads of Gor. New York, Ballantine, 1969; London, Sidgwick and Jackson, 1971.
Assassin of Gor. New York, Ballantine, 1970; London, Sidgwick and Jackson, 1971.
Raiders of Gor. New York, Ballantine, 1971; London, Tandem, 1973.
Gor Omnibus: The Chronicles of Counter Earth (includes *Tarnsmen, Outlaw,* and *Priest-Kings of Gor*). London, Sidgwick and Jackson, 1972.
Captive of Gor. New York, Ballantine, 1972; London, Tandem, 1973.
Hunters of Gor. New York, DAW, 1974; London, Tandem, 1975.
Marauders of Gor. New York, DAW, 1975; London, Universal, 1977.
Time Slave. New York, DAW, 1975; London, Star, 1981.

Tribesmen of Gor. New York, DAW, 1976.
Slave Girl of Gor. New York, DAW, 1977; London, Universal, 1978.
Beasts of Gor. New York, DAW, 1978; London, Star, 1979.
Explorers of Gor. New York, DAW, 1979; London, Star, 1980.
Fighting Slave of Gor. New York, DAW, 1980; London, Star, 1981.
Guardsman of Gor. New York, DAW, 1981; London, Star, 1982.
Rogue of Gor. New York, DAW, 1981; London, Star, 1982.
Savages of Gor. New York, DAW, and London, Star, 1982.
Blood Brothers of Gor. New York, DAW, 1982; London, Star, 1983.
Kajira of Gor. New York, DAW, and London, Star, 1983.
Players of Gor. New York, DAW, and London, Star, 1984.
Mercenaries of Gor. New York, DAW, and London, Star, 1985.
Dancer of Gor. New York, DAW, 1985; London, Star, 1986.
Renegades of Gor. New York, DAW, and London, Star, 1986.
Vagabonds of Gor. New York, DAW, and London, Star, 1987.
Magicians of Gor. New York, DAW, 1988.
The Chieftain (Telnarian). New York, Warner, 1991.
The Captain (Telnarian). New York, Warner, 1992.
The King (Telnarian). New York, Warner, 1993.

OTHER PUBLICATIONS

Novel

Ghost Dance. New York, Ballantine, 1970; London, Sphere, 1972.

Other

The Cognitivity Paradox: An Inquiry Concerning the Claims of Philosophy (as John Lange). Princeton, New Jersey, Princeton University Press, 1970.
Imaginative Sex. New York, DAW, 1975.
Editor (as John Lange), *Values and Imperatives: Studies in Ethics,* by Clarence I. Lewis. Stanford, California, Stanford University Press, 1969.

*   *   *

John Norman has written over two dozen science fiction/fantasy novels, most of which are in the Gor series (the Chronicles of Counter-Earth) and are in the tradition of Edgar Rice Burroughs's Mars books or Andre Norton's Witch World series. In these works, a character from contemporary Earth finds himself transported, often by inexplicable means, to an unfamiliar world where he is caught up in the events which are shaping the future of that world. And in such worlds, heroic action is almost always the means by which destiny is decided.

Norman's hero, Tarl Cabot, is transported to Gor, a planet on the opposite side of the sun from Earth and somehow shielded from any detection by Terran scientists. On Gor, Cabot is initiated into a way of life which the reader recognizes as medieval. All technological development, especially in weaponry, has been held in check by the Priest-Kings, and the men must fight with sword, spear, bow and arrow, and the like. For most of the known planet, the largest political unit is the city, and politics in and among cities is generally feudal. Gorean society is highly structured, and each person usually remains in the caste—warriors, bakers, scribes, etc.—into which he is born. But Gor and the Priest-Kings are in trouble and in need of heroics which only Tarl Cabot can provide.

As with any extended work of fantasy, the author's ability to detail convincingly a complex culture—or group of cultures—is important. Norman is quite good at this. In the first book, *Tarnsman of Gor*, such detail is necessary, and Norman provides a wealth of information on everything from the training of a warrior to the importance of a Home Stone. In what is possibly his best book to date, *Nomads of Gor*, he brings Cabot to the four tribes of the Wagon People, and the reader is treated to a fascinating descriptions of customs, habits, rituals, and all the other aspects of a complex cultural group. On Gor, the reader realizes, heroic action is not only possible, it is necessary; in other words, the culture is not just a backdrop for the action in Norman's books, it is an integral part of the action.

Heroic fantasies have always been considered male-escapist. The hero is muscular and skillful with weapons; he rescues the heroine who then succumbs to his over-powering maleness. Norman carries this aspect of heroic fantasy one step further than his predecessors. On Gor, most of the women are slaves, and those who are not are vaguely unhappy because a woman can be free only in total submission to a man. Some of the later books, *Slave Girl of Gor*, for example, focus less on Tarl Cabot than on the Earth woman brought to Gor. Such women are at first distressed by the culture in which they find themselves but soon realize the falseness of their previous (Terran) way of life. On Gor, Cabot says, women are free to be women; whereas, on Earth, they are forced to try to be men. This concept has lost Norman two groups of readers, the first violently opposed to his analysis of women, the second tired of hearing Cabot—or one of the women—explain and defend it book after book.

In literary terms, it is more the prolonged defense than the attitude itself which mars the novels, some of which seem to have been written solely to present examples of these ideas and attitudes about women. And Cabot's primary quest has suffered as well; to be sure, he still fights skirmishes against the enemies of the Priest-Kings, but what seemed to be the main plot-line of the series is barely progressing. In fact, by the 23rd and 24th Gor books, the bulk of the text deals with portraying and justifying the status of women on Gor, and action sequences which actually advance the series plot are few and far between. This situation is unfortunate, for the Gor books are, in most other respects, good heroic fantasy.

—C.W. Sullivan III

NORTH, Andrew. *See* NORTON, Andre.

NORTON, Andre

Pseudonym for Alice Mary Norton. **Other Pseudonyms:** Andrew North; Allen Weston. **Nationality:** American. **Born:** Cleveland, Ohio, 17 February 1912. **Education:** Western Reserve University, Cleveland, 1930-32. **Career:** Children's librarian, Cleveland Public Library, 1932-50; special librarian, Library of Congress, Wash-

ington, D.C., during World War II; editor, Gnome Press, New York, 1950-58. **Recipient:** Grand Master of Fantasy award, 1977; Gandalf award, 1977; Fritz Leiber award, 1983; Lensman award, 1983, 1987; Grand Master Nebula award 1983; Jules Verne award, 1984; Daedalus award, 1986. **Address:** 1600 Spruce Avenue, Winter Park, Florida 32789, U.S.A.

SCIENCE FICTION PUBLICATIONS

Novels (series: Astra; Beast Master; Forerunner; Halfblood Chronicles; Shann Lantree; Moon Magic; Renfro and Dipple; Solar Queen; Star Ka'at; Time Travel; Time Agents; Trillium; Witch World; Zero Stone)

Rogue Reynard (for children). Boston, Houghton Mifflin, 1947.
Huon of the Horn (for children). New York, Harcourt Brace, 1951.
Star Man's Son, 2250 A.D. New York, Harcourt Brace, 1952; London, Staples Press, 1953; as *Daybreak . . . 2250 A.D.,* New York, Ace, 1954.
Star Rangers. New York, Harcourt Brace, 1953; London, Gollancz, 1968; as *The Last Planet,* New York, Ace, 1955.
The Stars Are Ours! (Astra). Cleveland, World, 1954.
Star Guard. New York, Harcourt Brace, 1955; London, Gollancz, 1969.
Sargasso of Space (Solar Queen; as Andrew North). New York, Gnome Press, 1955; as Andre Norton, London, Gollancz, 1970.
Plague Ship (Solar Queen; as Andrew North). New York, Gnome Press, 1956; as Andre Norton, London, Gollancz, 1971.
The Crossroads of Time (Time Travel). New York, Ace, 1956; London, Gollancz, 1967.
Sea Siege. New York, Harcourt Brace, 1957.
Star Born (Astra). Cleveland, World, 1957; London, Gollancz, 1973.
Star Gate. New York, Harcourt Brace, 1958; London, Gollancz, 1970.
The Time Traders (Time Agents). Cleveland, World, 1958.
Voodoo Planet (Solar Queen; as Andrew North). New York, Ace, 1959.
Secret of the Lost Race. New York, Ace, 1959; as *Wolfshead,* London, Hale, 1977.
The Beast Master. New York, Harcourt Brace, 1959; London, Gollancz, 1966.
Galactic Derelict (Time Agents) Cleveland, World, 1959.
Storm over Warlock (Lantree). Cleveland, World, 1960.
The Sioux Spaceman. New York, Ace, 1960; London, Hale, 1976.
Star Hunter. New York, Ace, 1961.
Catseye (Renfro). New York, Harcourt Brace, 1961; London, Gollancz, 1962.
Eye of the Monster. New York, Ace, 1962.
The Defiant Agents (Time Agents). Cleveland, World, 1962.
Lord of Thunder (Beast Master). New York, Harcourt Brace, 1962; London, Gollancz, 1966.
Key out of Time (Time Agents). Cleveland, World, 1963.
Judgment on Janus (Renfro). New York, Harcourt Brace, 1963; London, Gollancz, 1964.
Witch World. New York, Ace, 1963; London, Tandem, 1970.
Web of the Witch World. New York, Ace, 1964; London, Tandem, 1970.
Ordeal in Otherwhere (Lantree). Cleveland, World, 1964.
Night of Masks (Renfro). New York, Harcourt Brace, 1964; London, Gollancz, 1965.

The X Factor. New York, Harcourt Brace, 1965; London, Gollancz, 1967.

Quest Crosstime (Time Travel). New York, Viking Press, 1965; as *Crosstime Agent,* London, Gollancz, 1975.

Steel Magic. Cleveland, World, 1965; London, Hamish Hamilton, 1967; as *Gray Magic,* New York, Scholastic, 1967.

Three against the Witch World. New York, Ace, 1965; London, Tandem, 1970.

Year of the Unicorn (Witch World). New York, Ace, 1965; London, Tandem, 1970.

Moon of Three Rings (Moon Magic). New York, Viking Press, 1966; London, Longman, 1969.

Victory on Janus (Renfro). New York, Harcourt Brace, 1966; London, Gollancz, 1967.

Operation Time Search. New York, Harcourt Brace, 1967.

Octagon Magic. Cleveland, World, 1967; London, Hamish Hamilton, 1968.

Warlock of the Witch World. New York, Ace, 1967; London, Tandem, 1970.

Fur Magic. Cleveland, World, 1968; London, Hamish Hamilton, 1969.

Sorceress of the Witch World. New York, Ace, 1968; London, Tandem, 1970.

Dark Piper. New York, Harcourt Brace, 1968; London, Gollancz, 1969.

The Zero Stone. New York, Viking Press, 1968; London, Gollancz, 1974.

Postmarked the Stars (Solar Queen). New York, Harcourt Brace, 1969; London, Gollancz, 1971.

Uncharted Stars (Zero Stone). New York, Viking Press, 1969; London, Gollancz, 1974.

Ice Crown. New York, Viking Press, 1970; London, Longman, 1971.

Dread Companion. New York, Harcourt Brace, 1970; London, Gollancz, 1972.

Android at Arms. New York, Harcourt Brace, 1971; London, Gollancz, 1972.

Exiles of the Stars (Moon Magic). New York, Viking Press, 1971; London, Longman, 1972.

Breed to Come. New York, Viking Press, 1972; London, Longman, 1973.

The Crystal Gryphon. New York, Atheneum, 1972; London, Gollancz, 1973.

Dragon Magic. New York, Crowell, 1972.

Forerunner Foray. New York, Viking Press, 1973; London, Longman, 1974.

Here Abide Monsters. New York, Atheneum, 1973.

Iron Cage. New York, Viking Press, 1974; London, Kestrel, 1975.

The Jargoon Pard. New York, Atheneum, 1974; London, Gollancz, 1975.

Lavender-Green Magic. New York, Crowell, 1974.

Outside. New York, Walker, 1974; London, Blackie, 1976.

Merlin's Mirror. New York, DAW, 1975; London, Sidgwick and Jackson, 1976.

The White Jade Fox. New York, Dutton, 1975; London, W.H. Allen, 1976.

The Day of the Ness, with Michael Gilbert. New York, Walker, 1975.

Knave of Dreams. New York, Viking Press, 1975; London, Kestrel, 1976.

No Night without Stars. New York, Atheneum, 1975; London, Gollancz, 1976.

Star Ka'at, with Dorothy Madlee. New York, Walker, 1976; London, Blackie, 1977.

Red Hart Magic. New York, Crowell, 1976; London, Hamish Hamilton, 1977.

Perilous Dreams. New York, DAW, 1976.

Wraiths of Time. New York, Atheneum, 1976; London, Gollancz, 1977.

The Opal-Eyed Fan. New York, Dutton, 1977.

Trey of Swords (Witch World). New York, Grosset and Dunlap, 1977; London, Star, 1979.

Star Ka'at World, with Dorothy Madlee. New York, Walker, 1978.

Quag Keep. New York, Atheneum, 1978.

Yurth Burden. New York, DAW, 1978.

Zarsthor's Bane. New York, Ace, 1978; London, Dobson, 1981.

Seven Spells to Sunday, with Phyllis Miller. New York, Atheneum, 1979.

Star Ka'ats and the Plant People, with Dorothy Madlee. New York, Walker, 1979.

Voorloper. Garden City, New York, Doubleday, 1980.

Gryphon in Glory (Witch World). New York, Atheneum, 1981.

Horn Crown (Witch World). New York, DAW, 1981.

Star Ka'ats and the Winged Warriors. New York, Walker, 1981.

Forerunner. New York, Tor, 1981.

Moon Called. New York, Simon and Schuster, 1982.

Wheel of Stars. New York, Simon and Schuster, 1983.

'Ware Hawk (Witch World). New York, Atheneum, 1983.

House of Shadows, with Phyllis Miller. New York, Atheneum, 1984.

Gryphon's Eyrie, with A.C. Crispin. New York, Tor, 1984.

Forerunner: The Second Venture. New York, Tor, 1985.

Flight in Yiktor (Moon Magic). New York, Tor, 1986; London, Methuen, 1988.

The Gate of the Cat (Witch World). New York, Ace, 1987.

The Magic Books (includes *Fur Magic, Steel Magic,* and *Octagon Magic*). New York, Signet, 1988.

Imperial Lady: A Fantasy of Han China, with Susan Shwartz. New York, Tor, 1989.

The Jekyll Legacy, with Robert Bloch. New York, Tor, 1990.

Black Trillium, with Marion Zimmer Bradley and Julian May. New York, Doubleday, 1990; London, Grafton, 1991.

Dare to Go A-Hunting (Moon Magic). New York, Tor, 1990.

The Elvenbane: An Elven High Fantasy of the Halfblood Chronicles, with Mercedes Lackey. New York, Tor, 1991; London, Grafton, 1993.

Storms of Victory (Witch World), with Pauline M. Griffin. New York, Tor, 1991.

Songsmith (Witch World), with A.C. Crispin. New York, Tor, 1992.

Flight of Vengeance (Witch World), with P.M. Griffin and Mary H. Schaub. New York, Tor, 1992.

The Mark of the Cat. New York, Ace, and London, Legend, 1992.

Golden Trillium. New York, Bantam, 1993.

Brother to Shadows. Norwalk, Connecticut, Easton Press, 1993.

Red Line the Stars (Solar Queen), with P.M. Griffin. New York, Tor, 1993.

Annals of the Witch World (omnibus). New York, Guild America, 1994.

The Hands of Llyr. New York, Morrow, 1994.

On Wings of Magic (Witch World), with Patricia Mathews and Sasha Miller. New York, Tor, 1994.

Firehand, with P.M. Griffin. New York, Tor, 1994.

The Key of the Keplian (Witch World), with Lyn McConchie. New York, Warner, 1995.

Mirror of Destiny. New York, Morrow, 1995.
Elvenblood (Halfblood), with Mercedes Lackey. New York, Tor, and London, HarperCollins, 1995.
Tiger Burning Bright, with Marion Zimmer Bradley and Mercedes Lackey. New York, Morrow, 1995.

Short Stories

High Sorcery. New York, Ace, 1970.
Garan the Eternal. Alhambra, California, Fantasy, 1972.
Spell of the Witch World. New York, DAW, 1972; London, Prior, 1977.
The Many Worlds of Andre Norton, edited by Roger Elwood. Radnor, Pennsylvania, Chilton, 1974; as *The Book of Andre Norton,* New York, DAW, 1975.
Lore of the Witch World. New York, DAW, 1980.
Were-Wrath (Witch World). Newcastle, Virginia, Cheap Street, 1984.
Serpent's Tooth (Witch World). Winter Park, Florida, Andre Norton, 1987.
Moon Mirror. New York, Tor, 1988.
Wizards' Worlds, edited by Ingried Zierhut. Norwalk, Connecticut, Easton Press, 1989.

OTHER PUBLICATIONS

Novels

The Prince Commands: Being the Sundry Adventures of Michael Karl, Sometime Crown Prince and Pretender to the Throne of Morvania. New York, Appleton Century, 1934.
Ralestone Luck. New York, Appleton Century, 1938.
Follow the Drum: Being the Ventures and Misadventures of One Johanna Lovell, Sometime Lady of Catkept Manners. New York, Penn, 1942.
The Sword Is Drawn. Boston, Houghton Mifflin, 1944; London, Oxford University Press, 1946.
Scarface: Being the Story of One Justin Blade. New York, Harcourt Brace, 1948; London, Methuen, 1950.
Sword in Sheath. New York, Harcourt Brace, 1949; as *Island of the Lost,* London, Staples Press, 1953.
Murders for Sale (with Grace Hogarth as Allen Weston). London, Hammond, 1954; as *Sneeze on Sunday* (as Andre Norton and Grace Hogarth), New York, Tor, 1992.
At Swords' Point. New York, Harcourt Brace, 1954.
Yankee Privateer. Cleveland, World, 1955.
Stand to Horse. New York, Harcourt Brace, 1956.
Shadow Hawk. New York, Harcourt Brace, 1960; London, Gollancz, 1971.
Ride Proud, Rebel! Cleveland, World, 1961.
Rebel Spurs. Cleveland, World, 1962.
Velvet Shadows. New York, Fawcett, 1977.
Snow Shadow. New York, Fawcett, 1979.
Ten Mile Treasure. New York, Pocket Books, 1981.
Caroline, with Enid Cushing. New York, Pinnacle, 1982.
Stand and Deliver. New York, Dell, 1984.
Ride the Green Dragon, with Phyllis Miller. New York, Atheneum, 1985.
Empire of the Eagle, with Susan H. Shwartz. New York, Tor, 1993.

Other

Bertie and May (for children), with Bertha Stenn Norton. Cleveland, World, 1969; London, Hamish Hamilton, 1971.

Editor, *Bullard of the Space Patrol,* by Malcolm Jameson. Cleveland, World, 1951.
Editor, *Space Service.* Cleveland, World, 1953.
Editor, *Space Pioneers.* Cleveland, World, 1954.
Editor, *Space Police.* Cleveland, World, 1956.
Editor, with Ernestine Donaldy, *Gates to Tomorrow: An Introduction to Science Fiction.* New York, Atheneum, 1973.
Editor, *Small Shadows Creep.* New York, Dutton, 1974; London, Chatto and Windus, 1976.
Editor, *Baleful Beasts and Eerie Creatures.* Chicago, Rand McNally, 1976.
Editor, with Robert Adams, *Magic in Ithkar.* New York, Tor, 4 vols., 1985-87.
Editor, *Tales of the Witch World.* New York, Tor, 3 vols., 1987-90; vol. 1, London, Pan, 1989.
Editor, *Four from the Witch World.* New York, Tor, 1989.
Editor, with Martin H. Greenberg, *Catfantastic: Nine Lives and Fifteen Tales.* New York, DAW, 1989.
Editor, with Ingried Zierhut, *Grand Masters' Choices.* Cambridge, Massachusetts, NESFA, 1989.
Editor, with Martin H. Greenberg, *Catfantastic II-[III].* New York, DAW, 2 vols., 1991-94.

*

Bibliography: *Andre Norton: A Primary and Secondary Bibliography* by Roger C. Schlobin, Boston, Hall, 1980; *Andre Norton: A Primary and Secondary Bibliography,* rev. ed., by Roger C. Schlobin and Irene R. Harrison, Framingham, Massachusetts, NESFA Press, 1994.

Manuscript Collections: Andre Norton Ltd., Winter Park, Florida; George Arents Research Library, Syracuse University, New York.

*   *   *

Andre Norton's early intention was to write fiction for boys, and she changed her name to enter this male-dominated market. Fortunately for the millions of readers who have made her one of the best selling of contemporary fantasy and science-fiction authors, she turned to these two forms in 1947 with her first published short story "People of the Crater" (later title: "Garin of Tav"). It is odd that Norton turned to science fiction at all. In fact, books like *The Beast Master* and its sequel, *Lord of Thunder,* weren't really science fiction at all. They were simply an experiment applying the form of a western to outer space and alien worlds. Actually, Norton has contempt for science and technology; they appear in her fiction only as vehicles and foils. In Ric Brooks's essay (in *The Many Worlds of Andre Norton,* 1974), she makes her stance quite clear: "Yes, I am anti-machine. The more research I do, the more I am convinced that when western civilizations turned to machines . . . , they threw away parts of life . . . [the lack of which] leads to much of our present frustration."

Even in Norton's science fiction, technology and science are incidental to plot and character. These major concerns reflect the influences of Edgar Rice Burroughs, H. Rider Haggard, A. Merritt, and Talbot Mundy, and demonstrate also Norton's respect for their fast-moving plots and memorable characters. For plot content, Norton's extensive research and affection for the mysterious and intriguing have led her to a number of specific motifs that occur throughout her fiction. Jewels frequently appear as powerful talismans, particularly in her fantasy novels. For example, as early as *At Swords' Point,* part of the Sword series that focuses on post-World-War-II espionage and the Netherlands during World War II, a set of jeweled miniature knights is central to a young man's search for his brother's murderer. Jewels are also important in *The Zero Stone,* the much heralded Witch World series, *Wraiths of Time,* and the gothic novels, particularly *The White Jade Fox* and *The Opal-Eyed Fan.* Frequently, these talismans are connected to an even more pervasive motif: the pseudo-science psychometry. This is formally defined as the detection of the residue of "memory" retained in an artifact by a sensitive. This plays a major role in the fantasy (with strong science-fiction elements) *Forerunner Foray,* in which Ziatha is drawn into a prehuman age through her reaction to a jewel; in *Wraiths of Time,* a crystal ankh and a staff contain the accumulated psychic power of a race.

Jewels and psychometry are two of the elements that give Norton's fiction its brooding depth, and together they provide a bridge between two other major Norton fascinations: history and speculative archaeology. Whether it be through references to prehistoric alien visits to Earth, as in *Merlin's Mirror,* or allusions to the prehistoric past, as in the Moon Magic series, Norton's fiction always has a resonance that goes beyond the immediate present to a more pervasive and often mysterious past. It is the characters' responsibility to discover the relevance of the past to themselves and their futures.

Yet none of these motifs or devices is the center of Norton's fiction. Rather, the most important aspects are simply humanity and self-realization. Norton explains this in "On Writing Fantasy" (in *The Many Worlds of Andre Norton*): "But the first requirement for writing heroic . . . fantasy must be a deep interest in and a love for history itself. Not the history of dates, of sweeps and empires—but the kind of history which deals with daily life, the beliefs, and the aspirations of people long since dust." Within the obvious cosmic scope, alien climes, antagonistic technology, vast quests, and fantastic forces of Norton's fiction, the characters are involved in crucial patterns of being, both for themselves and their fellows. While they are arrayed in mythic quests that grow from deep tradition, exist in a momentous present, and face a vital future, the characters remain pointedly human and humane. Most frequently, they move through what Northrop Frye calls "triumphant comedy." They struggle against an unlawful or unnatural order, undergo rites of passage to find realization, and establish new orders and freedoms. Kaththea (*Sorceress of the Witch World*) reflects this pattern as well as Norton's pioneering commitment to female characters. Shattered and disillusioned, Kaththea must find the faith to accept Hilarion, one of the enormously powerful "Old Ones" of the Witch World, if she is to save her family and regenerate her environment. Furtig, the mutated cat protagonist of *Breed to Come,* must overcome the mythology surrounding his long-departed human masters to unleash his own potentiality. Through the characters' agonizing trials, bondages and wastelands are destroyed, shape prejudice is eliminated, generative orders are established, and the protagonists and their fellows are ennobled. As Ric Brooks writes, "the chief value of Andre Norton's fiction may not lie in entertainment or social commentary, but in her 'reenchanting' us with her creations that renew our linkages to life."

Norton's characters are always alone, alienated, fearful, and searching. They are admirable for their positive, if sometimes confused, values, and they are attractive in their frailty and their doubt. In spite of their varied shapes and alien abilities, they achieve the nobility and status of the healer as they cure themselves and oth-

ers. Frequently, their solutions are androgynous—as for Simon Tregarth and Jaelithe in *Witch World*—and they do find the best of male and female. More significantly, their solutions to pain and loneliness are mythic and elemental and are a celebration of the bonds among man, animal, nature and cosmic order.

With the *Magic in Ithkar* series, Norton has again turned her energies to intensive editing after early successes in that role.

—Roger C. Schlobin

NORVIL, Manning. *See* **BULMER, Kenneth.**

NORWOOD, Warren

Nationality: American. **Born:** Philadelphia, Pennsylvania, 21 August 1945. **Education:** North Texas State University, Denton, B.A. 1972. **Military Service:** Served in the United States Army, 1966-69: Bronze Star. **Family:** Married 1) Mary Walker in 1965 (divorced 1972); 2) Margot Biery in 1973; one daughter. **Career:** Assistant manager, University Bookstore, University of Texas, Arlington, 1973-76; manager, Century Bookstore, Fort Worth, 1976-77; publisher's representative in Fort Worth, for Ballantine Books, 1978-79, and for Bantam Books, 1980-83; teacher, creative writing, Tarrant County Junior College, 1981-83. **Agent:** Richard Curtis Associates, 164 East 64th Street, New York, New York 10021, U.S.A. **Address:** 500 Greentree, Fort Worth, Texas 76086, U.S.A.

SCIENCE FICTION PUBLICATIONS

Novels (series: Double Spiral War; Time Police; TheWindhover Tapes)

The Windhover Tapes:
    An Image of Voices. New York, Bantam, 1982.
    Flexing the Warp. New York, Bantam, 1983.
    Fize of the Gabriel Ratchets. New York, Bantam, 1983.
    Planet of Flowers. New York, Bantam, 1984.
The Seren Cenacles, with Ralph Mylius. New York, Bantam, 1983.
Double Spiral War:
    Midway Between. New York, Bantam, 1984.
    Polar Fleet. New York, Bantam, 1985.
    Final Command. New York, Bantam, 1986.
Shudderchild. New York, Bantam, 1987.
True Jaguar. New York, Bantam, 1988.
Vanished (Time Police). New York, Lynx, 1988.
Trapped! (Time Police), with Mel Odom. New York, Lynx, 1989.
Stranded (Time Police), with Mel Odom. New York, Lynx, 1989.

*   *   *

Warren Norwood's unusual first novel, *The Windhover Tapes: An Image of Voices,* received excellent reviews when it appeared in

1982, but earned its author the dubious honor of finishing last in the balloting for the John W. Campbell Award for best new writer of the year, behind "No Award." The book is a complex amalgam of 1930s-style space opera, obscure literary references to 17th-century poets like Michael Drayton and folklore characters like the Gabriel Ratchets, and a style which seems to fluctuate between Barry Malzberg-like monologue and the 18th-century epistolary novels of Samuel Richardson. The story takes place in the far future, when faster-than-light travel to other galaxies is routine and humanity has contacted and interbred with any number of alien races. Gerard Hopkins Manley is a contract diplomat and anthropological researcher, and the four Windhover Tapes novels relate his adventures with sentient flowers, pulp-style outer space empires, outspoken feminist ghosts, intelligent, wheeled avians, and other strange beings and situations. The first two books are made up entirely of Manley's first-person conversations with himself and his sentient spaceship, Windhover. The later volumes are more conventional, third-person narratives. All four books contain numerous references to Manley's 19th-century English namesake, though Manley and those around him have apparently never heard of the poet.

The Windhover Tapes series is an enjoyable piece of work, but it has several flaws: the seeming irrelevance of most of the Hopkins material, Norwood's frequent inclusion of his own not very good poetry (including a travesty of Hopkins's "Windhover"), and the author's apparent fixation on human and humanoid mammary glands (Manley's beautiful alien wife has three). On the positive side, Norwood is doing some interesting stylistic experimentation, and his main character is a very unusual hero for science fiction—an emotional man who is not afraid to cry or dote upon his infant son and daughter, a man who is capable of space opera-style action, but who would really much rather talk things out sensibly.

That Norwood has considerable ability is clear; however, one cannot help but wish that he would take more time with his books. The Windhover Tapes series fluctuates markedly between startling originality and pulp cliche but maintains on the whole a fairly high level of excellence A number of the author's other novels, though, are distinctly less successful. The Seren Cenacles, coauthored with Ralph Mylius, is a well-written but poorly plotted tale of "alien terror" on a mining colony. The several political and industrial groups, military forces, and alien species contending for control of the situation are thrown at us willy nilly, without sufficient cultural context or satisfactory explanation. The book's basic premise, mining organic matter buried on distant worlds to ship to the galaxy's starving trillions is not very believable, nor is the story's abrupt and rather unlikely denouement. Likewise, the Double Spiral War series, throws so many similar characters at the reader that it is virtually impossible to keep them straight. This space war series, like all Norwood's work, is well-written, but it is also talky, obscurely plotted, and considering its subgenre, short on action.

Two somewhat more recent novels that are worthy of greater regard are True Jaguar and Shudderchild. The former is an engaging fantasy about a man who discovers himself to be the reincarnation of a Mayan god and the destined savior of the Earth. Martin O'Hara must journey to the Underworld and battle with demons in order to save the world from a comet on a collision course with Earth. The latter is set in a near-future America brought to wreck and ruin by world wide earthquakes. The complex plot centers on Jeremiah Fronterhouse Cody, who has joined the West Texas Militia, which represents the closest thing to civilization in post-Shudderday America, and who is also searching for his pregnant, not entirely faithful wife, Ann. There's a bit of political intrigue

here and a fair amount of Wild West-style adventure. Although not as memorable as The Windhover Tapes: An Image of Voices, Shudderchild does share a fair amount of that earlier novel's slightly skewed vitality.

Norwood's most recent work is the Time Police series. Beginning with Vanished, followed by Trapped and Stranded, this is routine time patrol stuff very much in the manner of Poul Anderson, but with just a touch of cyberpunk. Suffering from pancreatic cancer, Norwood received considerable help on these books from his wife, Gigi, and from novelist Mel Odom, who did much of the writing on the second and third novels in the series, receiving credit as the co-author of the final volume. Vanished features a researcher for the Temporal Projects Research Center, Jackson Dubchek, who accidentally stumbles on a dirty secret that the Time Police want to keep hidden. Needless to say, Dubchek soon finds himself on the run through time with assassins on his trail. The highlight of this novel may well be the appearance of the American communist John Reed in a supporting role. Volumes two and three of Time Police are essentially more of the same.

In summary, Warren Norwood has shown himself to be a writer of considerable, if only intermittently obvious, talent who has on occasion demonstrated a real knack for character development, fine prose, and energetic experimentation. The Windhover Tapes, True Jaguar, and Shudderchild are all estimable books. Considering the serious nature of his illness, one can only hope that Norwood will be given a chance to fulfill his potential.

—Michael M. Levy

NOURSE, Alan E(dward)

Pseudonym: Doctor X. **Nationality:** American. **Born:** Des Moines, Iowa, 11 August 1928. **Education:** Rutgers University, New Brunswick, New Jersey, B.A. 1951; University of Pennsylvania, Philadelphia, M.D. 1955. **Military Service:** Served in the United States Navy, 1946-48: Hospitalman 3rd Class. **Family:** Married Ann Jane Morton in 1952; three sons and one daughter. **Career:** Intern, Virginia Mason Hospital, Seattle, Washington, 1955-56; freelance writer, 1956-58; private medical practice, North Bend, Washington, 1958-64. Since 1964, freelance writer. Owner, Chamberlain Press, 1953-55. Chairman of the Board, Tanner Electric Rural Electrification Co-op; president, Science Fiction Writers of America, 1968-69. **Died:** 19 July 1992.

SCIENCE FICTION PUBLICATIONS

Novels

Trouble on Titan (for children). Philadelphia, Winston, 1954; London, Hutchinson, 1956.
A Man Obsessed. New York, Ace, 1955; revised edition, as The Mercy Men, New York, McKay, 1968; London, Faber, 1969.
Rocket to Limbo (for children). New York, McKay, 1957; London, Faber, 1964.
The Invaders Are Coming!, with J.A. Meyer. New York, Ace, 1959.
Scavengers in Space (for children). New York, McKay, 1959; London, Faber, 1964.

Star Surgeon (for children). New York, McKay, 1960; London, Faber, 1962.

Raiders from the Rings (for children). New York, McKay, 1962; London, Faber, 1965.

The Universe Between. New York, McKay, 1965; London, Faber, 1966.

The Bladerunner. New York, McKay, 1974.

The Fourth Horseman. New York, Harper, 1983.

Short Stories

Tiger by the Tail, and Other Science Fiction Stories. New York, McKay, 1961; London, Dobson, 1962; as *Beyond Infinity: Nine Science Fiction Stories,* London, Corgi, 1964.

The Counterfeit Man. New York, McKay, 1963; London, Dobson, 1964.

Psi High and Others. New York, McKay, 1967; London, Faber, 1968.

Rx for Tomorrow: Tales of Science Fiction, Fantasy, and Medicine. New York, McKay, 1971; London, Faber, 1972.

OTHER PUBLICATIONS

Novels

Junior Intern. New York, Harper, 1955.

Intern (as Doctor X). New York, Harper, 1965.

The Practice. New York, Harper, 1978; London, Futura, 1979.

Other

So You Want to Be a Doctor [Lawyer, Scientist, Nurse (with Eleanore Halliday), *Engineer* (with James C. Webbert), *Physicist, Chemist* (with James C. Webbert), *Surgeon, Architect* (with Carl Meinhardt)] (for children). New York, Harper, 9 vols., 1957-69.

Nine Planets. New York, Harper, 1960; revised edition, 1970.

The Management of a Medical Practice, with Geoffrey Marks. Philadelphia, Lippincott, 1963.

The Body. New York, Time, 1964; revised edition, New York, Time Life, 1980.

Universe, Earth, and Atom: The Story of Physics. New York, Harper, 1969.

Virginia Mason Medical Center: The First Fifty Years. Seattle, Virginia Mason Hospital Association, 1970.

Venus and Mercury (for children). New York, Watts, 1972.

Ladies' Home Journal Family Medical Guide. New York, Harper, 1973.

The Backyard Astronomer. New York, Watts, 1973.

The Giant Planets (for children). New York, Watts, 1974; revised edition, 1982.

The Outdoorsman's Medical Guide. New York, Harper, 1974.

The Asteroids (for children). New York, Watts, 1975.

Clear Skin, Healthy Skin (for children). New York, Watts, 1976.

Lumps, Bumps, and Rashes (for children). New York, Watts, 1976; revised edition, 1990.

Viruses (for children). New York, Watts, 1976; revised edition, 1983.

The Tooth Book (for children). New York, McKay, 1977.

Vitamins (for children). New York, Watts, 1977.

Fractures, Dislocations, and Sprains (for children). New York, Watts, 1978.

Hormones (for children). New York, Watts, 1979.

Inside the Mayo Clinic. New York, McGraw Hill, 1979.

Menstruation: Just Plain Talk (for children). New York, Watts, 1980; revised edition, 1987.

Your Immune System (for children). New York, Watts, 1980; revised edition, 1990.

Herpes (for children). New York, Watts, 1985.

AIDS (for children). New York, Watts, 1986; revised edition, 1989.

Birth Control (for children). New York, Watts, 1986.

The Elk Hunt. New York, Macmillan, 1986.

The Hidden Addiction and How to Get Free, with Janice Keller. Boston, Little Brown, 1986.

Teen Guide to Safe Sex. New York, Watts, 1988.

Teen Guide to AIDS Prevention. New York, Watts, 1990.

Teen Guide to Survival. New York, Watts, 1990.

Radio Astronomy. New York, Watts, 1990.

Sexually Transmitted Diseases. New York, Watts, 1992.

The Virus Invaders. New York, Watts, 1992.

*

Manuscript Collection: Boston University.

*   *   *

Despite producing only 10 novels and a few dozen short stories over the 40 years of his science fiction career, Alan E. Nourse remains one of the noted names in the field. This is even more surprising when one considers that five of those novels were aimed specifically at younger readers, although like Andre Norton, Robert Heinlein, and Isaac Asimov, Nourse wrote his "juveniles" in such a way that they would appeal to adult audiences as well.

In his first book-length work, *Trouble on Titan,* a young man is sent to the primary moon of Saturn to assist in the suppression of a fulminating revolt on the part of the local inhabitants, who are in large part exiles and convicts. Shortly after arriving and learning the true state of affairs, he discovers that his sympathies lie with the rebels, which places him in conflict not only with the authorities but also his own father. This was followed almost immediately by Nourse's first adult novel, *A Man Obsessed,* later expanded and republished as *The Mercy Men.* The novel draws heavily on Nourse's medical background, and follows the exploits of a troubled man who is obsessed with avenging his father's death. He follows the man responsible to the haven of the Mercy Men, individuals who have agreed to accept money in return for the use of their bodies in prohibited medical research. It is a powerfully written and disturbing story with implications that remain as pointed now as they did when it was first published in 1955.

There followed several juvenile novels. *Rocket to Limbo* concerns an interstellar voyage to find a lost starship. Although an interesting tale, it is the least interesting of Nourse's novels. *Scavengers in Space* was quite a different matter, the best of his early novels. Twin brothers are unhappy with the official explanation of their father's death while mining in the asteroid belt, suspecting that the powerful enemies he had made with highly placed company officials had led to someone deciding to dispose of the irritation. The novel contains a well-conceived plot, made even more convincing by Nourse's careful but unobtrusive explication of the physical problems of mining in an airless environment.

Star Surgeon returns to Nourse's medical interests. The human race has found its place in interstellar society by acting as medical specialists to every race they encounter, developing special techniques beyond even those of the physicians from each individual race. The protagonist is an alien doctor who is the first non-human to be allowed employment with Hospital Earth, who must face racial prejudice and personal malice before proving himself. In *Raiders from the Rings,* the human race has split into two factions. Earth is a fearful, huddled nation state preparing for a major war against the Spacers, other humans who have settled on Mars and in the asteroid belt. As the two factions maneuver for the final battle, one Spacer realizes he must step outside the conflict and find a resolution before the entire human species becomes extinct. Both of these novels are boisterous space adventures, but each contains serious observations about human institutions and the constraints they place on freedom of action for the individual. The novel *The Invaders Are Coming!,* written during this same period in collaboration with J.A. Meyer, was a disappointing novel of a future political struggle, with hints of mysterious alien creatures infiltrating society.

Only three more novels appeared in the next two decades and one, *The Universe Between,* was actually two long stories from 1951 tied together. Contact has been made with the Thresholders, beings that inhabit a different dimension than our own, a region few people can visit and return still sane. The protagonist is one such person, whose services become essential when something inadvertently angers these other beings, causing them to wage a war of terrorism against our home dimension. It is highly inventive, but without the polish that marks most of Nourse's work.

The Bladerunner is set in a future where access to medical care is strictly limited by government decree. The protagonist is a doctor who is secretly a member of the medical underground, dispensing care to those who do not qualify, hiding from the Health Control Police. The question of medical ethics is examined again, as well as public attitudes about access to health care, but Nourse is careful not to lose sight of the entertainment value of his story while directing our attention to the underlying issues. His most recent novel, *The Fourth Horseman,* chronicles the return of a deadly plague, and the desperate attempts required to avert a world wide catastrophe. Although this is a perhaps overly familiar plot, Nourse's background and finely honed writing skills never fail in this riveting suspense thriller.

Nourse has also produced several first-rate short stories. "Brightside Crossing" is a brilliant description of the first expedition to successfully cross the sunward side of the planet Mercury, a story of human perseverance and courage that ranks with Jack London's "To Build a Fire" and Stephen Crane's "The Open Boat." "The Counterfeit Man" is a chilling mystery story about an alien disguised as a human being who has infiltrated a space crew in order to reach the Earth. Nourse examines another ethical problem in "The Martyr," posing the question of whether or not those with the most to contribute to society should have their lifespans artificially extended. Other stories of note include "Nightmare Brother," "Psi High," "Coffin Cure," and "Family Resemblance."

Nourse brings to science fiction a deep concern with serious issues of human interaction and the role of various institutions within society, and embellishes it with a strong attention to background detail whether it be from his medical expertise or research into the requirements of life in space. His strong narrative ability and clear, crisp style only serve to emphasize the fact that his all too infrequent offerings are both entertaining and thought-provoking.

—Don D'Ammassa

NOWLAN, Philip Francis

Pseudonym: Frank Phillips. **Nationality:** American. **Born:** Philadelphia, Pennsylvania, in 1888. **Education:** University of Pennsylvania, Philadelphia, B.A. 1910. **Family:** Married Teresa Marie Junker; four daughters and six sons. **Career:** Worked for *Public Ledger, North American,* and *Retail Ledger;* collaborated with Dick Calkins on first science fiction comic strip, *Buck Rogers,* 1929-40. **Died:** 1 February 1940.

SCIENCE FICTION PUBLICATIONS

Novel

Armageddon 2419 A.D. New York, Avalon, 1962; London, Panther, 1976.

OTHER PUBLICATIONS

Other

Buck Rogers on the Moons of Saturn. Racine, Wisconsin, Whitman, 1934.
Buck Rogers in the Dangerous Mission. New York, Blue Ribbon Press, 1934.
Buck Rogers and the Depth Men of Jupiter. Racine, Wisconsin, Whitman, 1935.
Buck Rogers, 25th Century, Featuring Buddy and Allura in "Strange Adventures of the Spider Ship." Chicago, Pleasure, 1935.
Buck Rogers, 25th Century A.D., in the Interplanetary War with Venus. Racine, Wisconsin, Whitman, 1938.
Buck Rogers in the 25th Century 1-2, 7-8. Ann Arbor, Michigan, Ed Aprill, 4 vols., 1964-68.
The Collected Works of Buck Rogers in the 25th Century, with Dick Calkins and Rick Yager, edited by Robert C. Dille. New York, Bonanza, 1969; revised edition, New York, A and W, 1977.

*   *   *

Although not as well known as Edgar Rice Burroughs or E.E. Smith, Philip Francis Nowlan was probably their equal both as a writer and as an influence on modern science fiction. In his first story, "Armageddon 2419 A.D." (*Amazing,* August 1928), he introduced perhaps the most popular character in the history of the genre, Anthony, or as he was later known, Buck Rogers. Over the decades that followed Nowlan and others scripted innumerable Buck Rogers comic strips. Several films and a successful television series are proof of Buck Rogers's continuing appeal.

In "Armageddon 2419 A.D." Anthony Rogers, an engineer exploring a Pennsylvania mine in 1929, is caught in a cave-in and placed in suspended animation. Awakening in the 25th century, he discovers that the United States is now ruled by Mongolians and that Americans live in scattered communities, hiding from the conquerers who consider them vermin. The Mongolians, or Hans, a decadent, heartless race, rarely leave their cities and rely on huge airships equipped with disintegrator rays to maintain their dominance. Rogers has appeared at an opportune moment, for the Americans, armed with newly developed antigravity devices and rocket guns, are preparing to revolt. Contributing a knowledge of 20th-century military tactics and a certain primitive bloodthirstiness, Rogers soon becomes a leader in the struggle. The American conquest is completed in Nowlan's sequel, "The Airlords of Han." (The two stories were combined in the 1962 book *Armageddon 2419 A.D.*) Although flawed by occasionally awkward language and handicapped by the poorly considered choice of a first-person narrator, the Anthony Rogers stories stand up quite well even today. The action moves smoothly and the various military inventions and tactics are intriguing. The stories are touched by the racism so common in 1920s pulp fiction but, interestingly, are extremely progressive in their treatment of women. Wilma Deering, although occasionally given to the fainting spells and fits of weeping which were de riguer for women in popular fiction, is in general more competent and active than any female character in science fiction prior to Joanna Russ's Alyx.

"The Onslaught from Venus" is a first-person account by a member of the Airguard (the military arm of the Supernational Commission of the Caucasian League) who, captured by the invading Venusians, first studies their civilization and then, escaping, helps destroy it. Again the story is largely taken up with inventive weaponry and tactics. The Venusians, who seem quite human except for their skin color, are, like the Hans, totally evil, totally decadent. They are incapable of even considering coexistence and their complete extermination is thus a necessity.

Nowlan published little SF in the years that followed. His final story, and, after "Armageddon 2419 A.D.," probably his best, was "Space Guards." In this tale the narrator and his commanding officer, another of Nowlan's capable women, are searching the jungles of Venus for the headquarters of the criminal mastermind Tiger Madden. They're captured by tribesmen who, again, are totally human except for their skin color. Converting the natives to their side, the two Earth people defeat Madden's troops in battle and then infiltrate his city. Eventually they kidnap the villain and escape under fire. The narrator saves his commander's life, disobeying her direct order to abandon her. She at first considers court-martialing him but then, as the story closes, decides to marry him instead. Despite its silly ending and its somewhat old-fashioned plotting, "Space Guards" is an interesting and exciting story.

Philip Nowlan was a talented writer, and, despite his small output, he is one of the most influential science fiction writers of the Gernsback era.

—Michael M. Levy

OBERNDORF, Charles G.

Nationality: American. **Born:** Cleveland, Ohio, 31 December 1959. **Education:** Dartmouth College, B.A. in anthropology modified by creative writing, 1982. **Family:** Married April Elaine Stewart in 1987; one son, one stepson, and one stepdaughter. **Career:** Assistant teacher, Language Study Abroad, Granada, Spain, Dartmouth College, fall 1982, fall 1983; canvasser, Ohio Public Interest Coalition, 1983; teacher, English, social studies, grades 7-8, University school, 1984-. **Agent:** Ralph M. Vicinanza, 111 Eighth Ave., Suite 1501, New York, New York. **Address:** 3332 East Scarborough, Cleveland Heights, Ohio 44118-3411, U.S.A.

SCIENCE FICTION PUBLICATIONS

Novels

Sheltered Lives. New York, Bantam Books, 1992.
Testing. New York, Bantam Books, 1993.

*

Charles G. Oberndorf comments:

In the summer after seventh grade, I read *Dune,* discovered *Star Trek,* subscribed to *Analog* under Ben Bova, and joined the Science Fiction Book Club. I was hooked. Until I graduated from college, Ross Macdonald was the only mainstream writer who I read with the same passion that I devoted to science fiction. I read every novel by Isaac Asimov and at least as many by Poul Anderson. I was taken in by the new writers of the 1970s that Ben Bova was discovering or whose careers he was redefining: George R.R. Martin, Vonda McIntyre, Joan D. Vinge, Orson Scott Card, Spider Robinson, and the Ed Bryant of "Particle Theory" and "giANTS"— most of whom produced their best work when writing for Bova. Between issues of *Analog* I went through spells: E.C. Tubb's Dumarest novels and Bradley's Darkover novels and Donaldson's long-winded trek through the Land. I bought up every introduction that Harlan Ellison wrote. I so badly wanted to be a science fiction writer, that I wrote "future SF author" above my name on every homework assignment I turned in. I sent stories to all the major magazines, and they sent them back. When I traveled Europe at age 20, I read and reread *Left Hand of Darkness, Double Star, Brothers of Earth,* and *Davy* the same way some people turned to the appropriate religious text.

I go on at some length because that reading so thoroughly shaped my writing. Although nowadays, I'm more likely to be reading Chekhov than Cherryh, I find that all my ideas come as science fiction ideas. I bring home enough books to read about the subject at hand that my wife is convinced I'm going for the Ph.D. I never studied for. When I design a group of aliens whose members prefer being solitary to being social, I find I'm reading all sorts of sociobiology to base my aliens on current knowledge of what makes certain animals social and other ones solitary. I read about human evolution to understand the roots of our sociability and our intelligence in order to create intelligent aliens who are conceivably soli-

tary. I turn to research for my ideas, and I grow uncomfortable with pure invention (although I enjoy it immeasurably in another writer's work).

I find science fiction important because it can take on big issues without coming off as pretentious the way mundane fiction can. A story by Alice Munro, by focusing intensely on daily experience, can hint at the larger forces at work in our lives, but science fiction can readily hold them up for examination. I find I use science fiction to think out worlds, to consider the larger issues of social life. . . . And it's this aspect that I love about science fiction as a writer: the nature of the genre demands that you invent, and it demands that you consider the ramifications of those inventions. And when the invention guides the reader to look back at her current reality and reconsider its meaning, I think science fiction becomes the most powerful of literatures.

*   *   *

Charles Oberndorf's first published story was "Mannequins," in the first of the *Full Spectrum* anthologies. A robot escapes from a testing laboratory where it and several of its kind have been designed as authentic duplicates of human beings so that researchers can gain a better insight into what happens during an automobile crash. A woman gives the robot shelter, refusing to notify the police, for reasons which are not clear even to her, and against the wishes of her grown daughter, who is terrified by news stories indicating the robot might be dangerous.

Rather than dangerous, the robot is an inquisitive, troubled personality trying to understand what it is to be self-aware. The robot struggles with such concepts as pain and feeling, and clearly the real reason for the desperate search is to conceal how nearly human the robot really is. "Mannequins" is a remarkably mature story for a first sale, as was his second short, "Close to Light," which appeared the following year.

"Close to Light" is a formidable story about a strong-minded woman who finds herself caught in a painful dilemma. Against all her expectations, funding has been resumed for the first interstellar expedition, and she has been invited to be one of the ships's crew. But when the program went on hiatus six years earlier, she abandoned hope, married, and started a family. Now she must choose between remaining with her husband and daughter, or achieving the goal toward which she dedicated her life.

Oberndorf examines the woman's pain and confusion at great length and with remarkable perception and sympathy. Her ultimate decision to remain behind is not a happy one, in fact, the author makes it crystal clear that this is a scar that she will bear for the rest of her life, and that it will create a lasting resentment toward her daughter. The lack of the more traditional ending of having a comprehensive solution resolve everything amicably would have been the mark of a lesser writer.

Sheltered Lives was Oberndorf's first novel, a near future dystopian adventure story. A new plague threatens humankind, a sexually transmitted disease with obvious parallels to the AIDS epidemic. The government responds by isolating the victims from the rest of society in brutal concentration camps, and the wealthy aristocracy protects itself by funding medically monitored, high class bordellos for their entertainment. All public areas are monitored by the authorities, usually through remotely controlled cameras, to ensure that nothing illegal or even antisocial is taking place.

A young woman devastated by the loss of her lover hires a prostitute to console her, and their relationship is the focal point for a suspenseful story involving terrorism, revolutionaries, and the abuse of power, as well as an interesting murder mystery. As with his short fiction, the author adeptly portrays his characters as people and concentrates on their interactions, the way they deal with grief and love and fear, rather than with the physical elements of the story. The violence and repression are virtually elements of the atmosphere rather than the plot, although Oberndorf has skillfully paced *Sheltered Lives* to hold his readers' interest.

His most recent work is the short novel *Testing,* which deals with some of the same themes in a slightly altered fashion. Again we have a repressive government, this time one which requires morality testing before allowing aspiring college students to continue their studies. Karl is nervous about his upcoming examination, even more so after a relatively innocent and even comical adventure in a local brothel.

The tests are in virtual reality, the subject placed in a structured dream state where his or her reactions to the scenario presumably provide a measure of moral purity. He solves the problem by figuring out in advance what the examiners are looking for, and subsequently applies the same principle to all of his dealings with others. This indictment of lock-step morality and the pressure to conform is a lean, concise story that wastes no time on side issues and makes its points with a relentless sequence of short scenes. An interesting twist that provides added texture to the story is an altered family structure, matrilineal, which makes the interactions among the members of the protagonist's family slightly different than one would otherwise expect.

Oberndorf has yet to establish himself as a major writer, though a new novel, *Foragers,* is in progress. He clearly is, however, a writer of considerable talent who uses the elements of science fiction to tell stories about people, rather than using his characters to tell stories about science.

—Don D'Ammassa

O'BRIEN, Clancy. *See* **SMITH, George H.**

O'DONNELL, K.M. *See* **MALZBERG, Barry N.**

O'DONNELL, Kevin, Jr.

Nationality: American. **Born:** Cleveland, Ohio, 29 November 1950. **Education:** Attended schools in Cleveland and Fairview Park; Seoul Foreign School, Korea, graduated 1968; Yale University, New Haven, Connecticut, 1968-72, B.A. in Chinese studies 1972. **Family:** Married Lillian Tchang in 1974. **Career:** Assistant lecturer in English, Hong Kong Baptist College, 1972-73, and American English Language Institute, Taipei, Taiwan, 1973-74. Since 1976, freelance writer. Managing editor, 1979-81, and publisher, 1981-83, *Empire,* New Haven, Connecticut. **Agent:** Howard Morhaim Literary Agency, 175 Fifth Avenue, New York, New York, 10010, U.S.A.

SCIENCE FICTION PUBLICATIONS

Novels (series: McGill Feighan)

Bander Snatch. New York, Bantam, 1979.
Mayflies. New York, Berkley, 1979.
Caverns (Feighan). New York, Berkley, 1981.
Reefs (Feighan). New York, Berkley, 1981.
War of Omission. New York, Bantam, 1982.
Lava (Feighan). New York, Berkley, 1982.
ORA: CLE. New York, Berkley, 1984; London, Grafton, 1986.
Cliffs (Feighan). New York, Berkley, 1986.
The Shelter, with Mary Kittredge. New York, Tor, 1987.
Fire on the Border. New York, Roc, 1990.

OTHER PUBLICATIONS

Other

The Electronic Money Machine: Profits from Your Home Computer, with the Haven Group. New York, Avon, 1984.

*

Kevin O'Donnell, Jr. comments:

When I write, I want the eventual readers to enjoy themselves; to think about themselves, others, and the future; and to feel at the end that they have experienced something worthwhile.

In one sense, science fiction is the opportunity to sample, vicariously and in advance, the consequences of choices human beings are making right now. I do not pretend to be a prophet, but I do attempt to depict potential futures, and those futures should ring as true to life as possible. Thus I stress verisimilitude in my writing, which poses a special challenge, since, by definition, what I write about has not happened yet, and probably never will. Before the words go on the paper, I have already spent a great deal of time trying to answer to my own satisfaction the question "What would it *really* be like if—?"

I give equal weight to characterization. Stereotypes are easy to work with—cardboard characters shuffle as easily as a deck of cards—but real people tangled in the webwork of their families, their friends, their pasts, and their present predicaments interest me much more than do mighty-thewed heroes or black-hearted villains. Don't get me wrong. I *like* heroes and villains. I also like shades of grey.

*   *   *

Possessed of one of the more entertaining new voices of science fiction, Kevin O'Donnell, Jr., infuses familiar SF themes and concepts with his own eager tone, the voice of the born storyteller. Among his shorter pieces, six have been recommended for Nebula awards: "A Matter of Pride" (in *Analog,* October 1973), a serious tale of epidemiology and prisoners of war; "Low Grade Ore" (in *Isaac Asimov's Science Fiction Anthology 1* edited by George H. Scithers, New York, Davis, 1978) and "Temple Guardian" (in *The Future at War 2* edited by Reginald Bretnor, New York, Ace, 1980), two stories of alien invaders; a time travel short called "The Gift of Prometheus" (in *Analog,* January 1978); a humorous story of censorship-via-computer, "Judo and the Art of Self-Government" (in *Laughing Space* edited by Isaac Asimov and J.D Jeppson, Boston, Houghton Mifflin, and London, Robson, 1982); and "Marchianna" (in *The Best of Omni Science Fiction 4* edited by Ben Bova and Don Myros, New York, Omni, 1982), concerning robots and asteroid mining. Emotional constants in O'Donnell's work are reliance upon individual strengths and the saving love of friends whether human or alien, and a suspicion of the corporate and bureaucratic. Humor is often achieved through a Chaplinesque stumbling over a plethora of detail.

His best-known work, *Mayflies,* uses two familiar themes: the hero interfaced with a computer and the generation starship. O'Donnell fuses these with energy and enthusiasm to create the memorable image of the immortal captain and controlling entity of a starship taking his human cargo across a thousand year voyage, observing them with mingled compassion and disdain for their "mayfly" existence. Like a gardener, he cultivates, prunes, limits, and stimulates, and all the while we get an eerie sense of a human slowly developing into something *other* over the centuries. A similar tension between the hermetic and the oceanic pervades *ORA: CLE,* where the hero, Mr. Ale Elatey (AL L80) is linked by brain implant to a network of thousands of computer experts but never leaves the high-rise apartment where he and his wife live through their contacts on the network, and through other communication systems. As *Mayflies* may be said to reevaluate the experience of Heinlein's *Universe* and McCaffrey's *The Ship Who Sang, ORA: CLE* may be viewed as finding new possibilities in the closed environment of Silverberg's *The World Inside.*

O'Donnell's most ambitious project is the light-hearted Adventures of McGill Feighan, an open-ended series of picaresque travels among alien worlds by means of "flinging," a teleportation technique of which McGill is a rare possessor. The first four volumes in the series—*Caverns, Reefs, Lava,* and *Cliffs*—explore the intricacies of McGill's talent, human-alien encounter, the menace of a mob-like crime syndicate so powerfully parasitic it takes steps not to kill its host culture, and McGill's search for the Far Being, source of his flinging talent. Here, O'Donnell's ability to compel sympathetic interest in his anomalous young hero helps him skirt the many improbabilities of the story line. Billed as "techno-fantasy," the inventive series shows a talent for humorous dialogue increasingly matched by pacing of incident and character development. A young writer still, O'Donnell shows great creative promise.

—Thomas P. Dunn

OFFUTT, Andrew J(efferson V.)

Pseudonym: John Cleve; Jeff Douglas; J.X. Williams. **Nationality:** American. **Born:** Louisville, Kentucky, 16 August 1934 (?). **Education:** University of Louisville, B.A. in English 1955, M.A. in history, Ph.D. in psychology. **Family:** Married Mary Joe McCarney McCabe in 1958; two daughters and two sons. **Career:** Sales agent, Procter and Gamble, 1957-62; agency manager, Coastal States Life Insurance Company, Lexington, Kentucky, 1963-68; insurance agent, Andrew Offutt Associates, 1968-71. Since 1971, full-time writer: author of over 100 works under pseudonym John Cleve and others. Treasurer, 1973-76, and president, 1976-78, Science Fiction Writers of America. **Awards:** If prize, 1954. **Address:** Funny Farm, Haldeman, Kentucky 40329, U.S.A.

SCIENCE FICTION PUBLICATIONS

Novels (series: Conan; Cormac mac Art; Thieves' World— Shadowspawn; War of the Gods on Earth; War of the Wizards)

The Sex Pill (as J.X. Williams). San Diego, Pleasure Reader, 1968.
Evil Is Live Spelled Backwards. New York, Paperback Library, 1970.
Barbarana (as John Cleve). North Hollywood, California, Brandon House, 1970.
Jodinareh (as John Cleve). North Hollywood, California, Brandon House, 1970.
Pleasure Us! (with D. Bruce Berry as John Cleve). New York, Bee-Line, 1971.
The Balling Machine (with D. Bruce Berry as Jeff Douglas). New York, Orpheus, 1971.
The Great 24-Hour Thing. New York, Orpheus Press, 1971.
The Castle Keeps. New York, Berkley, 1972; London, Magnum, 1978.
Messenger of Zhuvastou. New York, Berkley, 1973; London, Magnum, 1977.
Ardor on Aros. New York, Dell, 1973.
The Galactic Rejects (for children). New York, Lothrop, 1973.
Manlib (as John Cleve). New York, Orpheus, 1974.
The Sexorcist (as John Cleve). New York, Orpheus, 1974; as *Unholy Revelry,* New York, Bee-Line, 1976.
The Genetic Bomb, with D. Bruce Berry. New York, Warner, 1975.
Sword of the Gael (Cormac mac Art). New York, Zebra, 1975; London, Sphere, 1977.
The Undying Wizard (Cormac mac Art). New York, Zebra, 1976.
Chieftain of Andor. New York, Dell, 1976; as *Clansman of Andor,* London, Hale, 1979.
My Lord Barbarian. New York, Ballantine, 1977; London, Magnum, 1979.
Demon in the Mirror (Wizards), with Richard K. Lyon. New York, Pocket Books, 1977.
Sign of the Moonbow (Cormac mac Art). New York, Zebra, 1977.
The Mists of Doom (Cormac mac Art). New York, Zebra, 1977.
Conan and the Sorcerer. New York, Sunridge Press, 1978.
Conan: The Sword of Skelos. New York, Bantam, and London, Sphere, 1979.
The Iron Lords (Gods on Earth). New York, Harcourt Brace, 1979.
Shadows Out of Hell (Gods on Earth). New York, Berkley, 1980.
Conan the Mercenary (includes *Conan and the Sorcerer*). New York, Ace, and London, Sphere, 1980.
When Death Birds Fly (Cormac mac Art), with Keith Taylor. New York, Ace, 1980.
The Eyes of Sarsis (Wizards), with Richard K. Lyon. New York, Pocket Books, 1980.
King Dragon. New York, Ace, 1980.

Web of the Spider (Wizards), with Richard K. Lyon. New York, Pocket Books, 1981.

The Tower of Death (Cormac mac Art), with Keith Taylor. New York, Ace, 1982.

The Lady of the Snowmist (Gods on Earth). New York, Ace, 1983.

Shadowspawn (Thieves' World). New York, Ace, 1987.

Deathknight. New York, Ace, 1990.

The Shadow of Sorcery (Thieves' World). New York, Ace, 1993.

Novels as John Cleve (series: Spaceways in all titles)

Of Alien Bondage. New York, Playboy Paperbacks, 1982.

Corundum's Woman. New York, Playboy Paperbacks, 1982.

Escape from Macho. New York, Playboy Paperbacks, 1982.

Satana Enslaved. New York, Playboy Paperbacks, 1982.

Master of Misfit, with George W. Proctor. New York, Playboy Paperbacks, 1982.

Purrfect Plunder. New York, Playboy Paperbacks, 1982.

The Manhuntress, with George W. Proctor. New York, Playboy Paperbacks, 1982.

Under Twin Suns. New York, Playboy Paperbacks, 1982.

In Quest of Qulara. New York, Playboy Paperbacks, 1983.

The Yoke of Shen, with George W. Proctor. New York, Berkley, 1983.

Star Slaver, with G.C. Edmondson. New York, Berkley, 1983.

The Iceworld Connection, with Jack C. Haldeman II and Vol Haldeman. New York, Berkley, 1983.

Jonuta Rising!, with Victor Koman. New York, Berkley, 1983.

Assignment: Hellhole, with Robin Kincaid. New York, Berkley, 1983.

Starship Sapphire, with Roland Green. New York, Berkley, 1984.

The Planet Murderer, with Dwight V. Swain. New York, Berkley, 1984.

The Carnadyne Horde, with Victor Koman. New York, Berkley, 1984.

Race across the Stars, with Robin Kincaid. New York, Berkley, 1984.

King of the Slavers. New York, Berkley, 1985.

Short Stories

The Black Sorcerer of the Black Castle. Aberdeen, Maryland, Hall, 1976.

OTHER PUBLICATIONS

Novels

Operation: Super Ms. New York, Berkley, 1974.

The Juice of Love (as John Cleve). New York, Midwood, 1975.

Novels as John Cleve (series: Crusader in all titles)

The Accursed Tower. New York, Dell, 1974.

The Passionate Princess. New York, Dell, 1974.

Julanar the Lioness. New York, Dell, 1975.

My Lady Queen. New York, Dell, 1975.

Saladin's Spy. New York, Grove Press, 1986.

Other

Editor, *Swords against Darkness 1-5*. New York, Zebra, 5 vols., 1977-79.

* * *

Many science fiction and fantasy writers can be categorized according to the particular subgenre in which they write. Andrew J. Offutt (who often has his name set as andrew j. offutt), however, must be discussed in several, for while he may be best known for sociocritical science fiction or heroic fantasy, he has also written satiric SF, at least one SF novel for children, and—under the name John Cleve—science fiction with a good deal of sex and exploitation in it.

Much of Offutt's early SF was obviously social criticism. *The Castle Keeps,* for example, is set in the same not-too-distant dystopian future as quite a bit of other science fiction. The world of *The Castle Keeps* is overpopulated and poisonously polluted, and the society has devolved toward barbarism. The Andrews' home in the country is heavily fortified, and there is constant danger of being overrun by roving bands of looters and killers. In the city, the Caudills live inside a sealed-up apartment building from which they seldom emerge; outside, in spite of the official agencies, gangs are a threat by day and all-powerful by night. Throughout the novel, there are signs of how we, mid-20th-century Americans, got there.

Offutt can also write humorous SF and fantasy, often with a satiric bite. Short stories like "For Value Received" and "Population Implosion" satirize, among other things, one of Offutt's favorite targets, the medical profession. In "For Value Received," for example, he refers to the AMA as the American Magicians Association. In this story, Bob Barber is told that he cannot take his new baby daughter home before he pays the difference between what his insurance covers and the total bill. He refuses to do so, and Mary Ann Barber grows up in Saint Meinrad Medical Center. In 1970, he published an entire collection of satiric short stories under the title *Evil is Live Spelled Backwards*. And *Ardor on Aros* is a humorous look at the heroic fantasy that Offutt himself seriously writes.

Offutt's heroic fantasy comes in two groups. The first group includes those stories which are essentially his own constructions, like *Messenger of Zhuvastou*. Scion Mark Keniston follows a beautiful woman, Elaine Dixon, supposedly his fianceé, to Helene, a planet which is the approximate cultural equivalent of early Imperial Rome. Because the planet is insulated from contact with more technologically advanced civilizations, Keniston must "go native" to follow Elaine onto the planet's surface. Disguised as an official messenger of the most powerful domain on the planet, Keniston sets out on his quest. The description of the planet and the portrayal of the heroic adventure are well-integrated so that the reader is able to envision quite clearly the world through which Keniston makes his way.

The second group of heroic fantasies, which seems to be occupying an increasing amount of Offutt's time, is based on characters created by Robert E. Howard. In fact, Offutt has selected one, Cormac mac Art, for extended consideration, and he admits, in the introduction to *Sword of the Gael,* that he is a Robert E. Howard fan and also "hopelessly in love with the Emerald Isle." This happy combination unites the heroic-age hero with a perfect historical setting, the Celtic/Viking period. Offutt skillfully mixes historical material from his own research with the literary history created by Howard to provide a cogent background for the adventures of Cormac mac Art and his Viking comrade, Wulfhere Skull-Splitter.

In addition to creating his own original work, Offutt also collaborates with and edits the work of other writers. Editing the *Swords Against Darkness* series was a natural outgrowth of his love for Robert E. Howard's work. His collaboration with Robert Asprin, Lynn Abbey, C.J. Cherryh, and the other contributors to the *Thieves' World* collections of short stories all set in the same imaginary world has led to a number of short stories and at least one novel in that series.

Offutt deserves a wider and more substantial reputation than he currently has. Although much of his work has been called "slick" or "action/adventure without much depth," Offutt is a writer who has shown in *The Castle Keeps* and elsewhere that he can write with depth and is also a writer who can tell a good action/adventure story, one that does not seem to have come out of the same tired formula mill that lesser writers use. Offutt's output is tremendous, and not all of it is science fiction or fantasy; in fact, many feel that not enough of it is science fiction and fantasy.

—C.W. Sullivan III

OLIVER, (Symmes) Chad(wick)

Also wrote as Symmes C. Oliver. **Nationality:** American. **Born:** Cincinnati, Ohio, 30 March 1928. **Education:** University of Texas, Austin, B.A. 1951, M.A. in English and anthropology 1952; University of California, Los Angeles, Ph.D. in anthropology 1961. **Family:** Married Betty Jane Jenkins in 1952; two children. **Career:** Instructor, 1955-59, Assistant Professor, 1959-62, Associate Professor, 1963-68, Department Chairman, 1967-71 and since 1980, Professor of Anthropology, University of Texas. Visiting Professor, University of California, Los Angeles, summer 1960; Research Anthropologist, National Science Foundation in East Africa, 1961-62. **Awards:** Western Writers of America Spur award, 1967. **Died:** 9 August 1993.

SCIENCE FICTION PUBLICATIONS

Novels

Mists of Dawn (for children). Philadelphia, Winston, 1952; London, Hutchinson, 1954.
Shadows in the Sun. New York, Ballantine, 1954; London, Reinhardt, 1955.
The Winds of Time. Garden City, New York, Doubleday, 1957.
Unearthly Neighbors. New York, Ballantine, 1960.
The Shores of Another Sea. New York, Signet, and London, Gollancz, 1971.
Giants in the Dust. New York, Pyramid, 1976.

Short Stories

Another Kind: Science-Fiction Stories. New York, Ballantine, 1955.
The Edge of Forever: Classic Anthropological Science Fiction Stories, edited by William F. Nolan. Los Angeles, Sherbourne Press, 1971.

OTHER PUBLICATIONS

Novels

The Wolf Is My Brother. New York, Signet, 1967; London, Jenkins, 1968.
Broken Eagle. New York, Bantam, 1989.
The Cannibal Owl. New York, Bantam, 1989.

Other

Ecology and Cultural Continuity as Contributing Factors in the Social Organization of the Plains Indians (as Symmes C. Oliver). Berkeley, University of California Press, 1962.
Two Horizons of Man: Parallels and Interconnections between Anthropology and Science Fiction. Austin, Texas, privately published, 1974.
The Discovery of Humanity: An Introduction to Anthropology. New York, Harper, 1981.

*

Bibliography: By William F. Nolan, in *The Edge of Forever,* 1971.

Chad Oliver commented:

(1991) I wrote my first story when I was 14, and sold my first story (to Anthony Boucher of *The Magazine of Fantasy and Science Fiction*) when I was 22. I was a professional writer before I was an anthropologist, and I suspect that I still am. I grew up with science fiction and it has been an important part of my life.

I have written many kinds of stories and about all they have in common is that I always tried to write as well as I could. I am not interested in essays disguised as fiction; my stories are about people and my opinion is that if they don't work on an emotional level they don't work at all. I was strongly influenced by writers outside the science fiction field, notably Hemingway and Steinbeck.

*   *   *

For a genre that deals freely in alien beings and cultures, science fiction has often shown a marked tendency toward simplistic anthropomorphism in handling such themes. Readers and editors who would demand the utmost verisimilitude in fiction dealing with the natural sciences often allowed the most naive applications of social science theory to pass unnoticed in science fiction stories, and it was not until well into the 1950s that the social sciences began to take their place as serious thematic material in popular science fiction. While economics and sociology began to be treated with relative sophistication by Frederik Pohl and other satirists of the *Galaxy* magazine school, the credit for introducing well-thought-out anthropological themes into popular American science fiction of the 1950s rests almost solely with Chad Oliver. Himself a professional anthropologist, Oliver dealt with alien cultures, and the problems inherent in communicating with those cultures, in a series of sympathetic and plausible stories and novels that paved the way for later anthropological themes in such writers as Ursula K. LeGuin.

Oliver's fiction tends heavily toward exposition and didacticism, but his pleasant, relaxed style and understated, non-heroic characters work to make the lessons in cultural differentiation and values easily palatable. When he treats a traditional theme, such as the secret colonization of Earth by aliens in *Shadows in the Sun*, he is apt to undercut the reader's expectations by revealing early in the narrative the secret of the alien presence (in this novel, they have completely taken over a small town in Texas, without violence or murder), and focusing instead on the more complex and interesting problem of what their motivations and values are. The equally familiar theme of the generations-long space voyage, initially popularized by Robert Heinlein in "Universe," is given a new twist in Oliver's "Stardust" by the introduction of the problem of the culture shock that the spaceship inhabitants might face if the circumscribed environment that they have come to regard as the universe is suddenly revealed to be only a machine. A "first contact" story is also given a new twist, in "Scientific Method," by its simultaneous presentation from two opposing viewpoints. One of Oliver's favorite themes is the depiction of a "primitive" alien culture that is really advanced, but in radically different cultural terms from our own. This is the theme of "Rite of Passage" and *Unearthly Neighbors;* the latter may be the most carefully reasoned account of the problems of making contact with an alien culture in all of science fiction.

Much of Oliver's fiction clearly draws on his own experiences—his familiarity with small-town Texas culture in *Shadows in the Sun,* his hobby of trout fishing in *The Winds of Time,* his experiences in Kenya in *The Shores of Another Sea.* In the last novel, particularly, the science fiction theme seems to be decidedly secondary to the portrayal of life on a baboonery in the bush country of Kenya. Relatively few of his stories deal with future societies, and his portrayals of technologically advanced earth societies (as in *Unearthly Neighbors*) seem somewhat stilted and uncomfortable. His real strengths lie in the construction of hypothetical anthropological problems and his graceful, understated style. Although he has produced relatively little science fiction, what there is is valuable both for the specific insights it offers and for the importance it holds in the developing sophistication of the genre.

—Gary K. Wolfe

O'NEILL, Joseph (James)

Pseudonym: Seosamh O'Neill. **Nationality:** Irish. **Born:** Tuam, County Galway, 18 December 1878. **Education:** St. Jarlath's College, Tuam, 1893-98; Queen's College, Galway, 1898-1901, B.A., M.A. in modern literature; Kuno Meyer's School of Irish Learning; Victoria College, Manchester; University of Freiburg, 1907. **Family:** Married Mary Devenport in 1908. **Career:** Taught at Queen's College, Galway, 1901-03; staff member, Department of Secondary Education: Inspector of Schools, from 1908, and Permanent Secretary, 1923-44; also civil service commissioner and local appointments commissioner, 1926-46. **Awards:** Irish Academy of Letters Harmsworth award, 1935. **Member:** Irish Academy of Letters. **Died:** 6 May 1952.

SCIENCE FICTION PUBLICATIONS

Novels

Wind from the North. London, Cape, 1934.
Land under England. London, Gollancz, and New York, Simon and Schuster, 1935.
Day of Wrath. London, Gollancz, 1936.

OTHER PUBLICATIONS

Novels

Philip. London, Gollancz, 1940.
Chosen by the Queen. London, Gollancz, 1947.

Play

The Kingdom-Maker: A Play in Five Acts (as Seosamh O'Neill), lyrics by Mary Devenport O'Neill. Dublin, Talbot Press, and London, Unwin, 1918.

*   *   *

Joseph O'Neill wrote five novels, a play, some criticism, some poetry, and a few scholarly papers. Of his novels, three may be regarded as science fiction, though the connection is sometimes tenuous. *Wind from the North* is a well-written time-travel story of Norsemen in Dublin in the 11th century; the emphasis is on the conflict between the hero's 11th-century and 20th-century selves. *Day of Wrath* is a prophetic potboiler about an airwar involving "the Yellow Alliance" and Nazi aggressors against Russia, "the Latin Alliance," and, eventually, Great Britain and the United States; the aftermath of its poison gas and thermite bombs is a vivid picture of the breakdown of civilized behavior, but it is not especially exciting either as science fiction or as novel.

Land under England is a work of power that was justly well received when first published and then almost forgotten until recently. It is doubtless worth noting that of all O'Neill's works only this one—despite the fact that *Wind from the North* received the Harmsworth award—was widely reviewed, and that only this one has been reprinted. Even so, except for passing references critical evaluation of the work is largely confined to reviews that appeared in 1935.

Part of the attraction of the novel is the development from an almost innocent beginning through an adventurous though fantastic journey into a world of horror that gradually becomes prophetic of doom not only for the protagonist but for the world at large. The story begins with devices like those of second-rate fantasy: the Julians are an old family tracing their origins back to Roman Britain; they live along the Roman Wall on property believed to possess the entrance to an underground world. There are half-believed stories of ancestors who have disappeared and returned with stories of a strange land beyond the mysterious entrance. Anthony Julian, the narrator, is the only child of two dramatically opposite types both of whom believe in the old legends, his father in the years following World War I, to the point of obsession; when he disappears, both wife and son are convinced that he has found the entrance. Tony, whose hero-worship of his father is the driving force of the book, is equally convinced that he will some day be found.

Tony's accidental discovery of the entrance in a dried-up pond and unhesitating plunge down the slope into the underworld are the obvious and expected result of what has gone before. What is not obvious or expected is what happens thereafter, and it is in this respect that the novel departs from the ordinary to become something of a minor masterpiece.

In this underground world are many curious, strange, and frequently alarming creatures, both plant and animal. But nothing is more curious, strange, or alarming than its human inhabitants. At first encounter they appear to be civilized and enough like the ancient Romans who had inhabited the land above that Tony speaks to them in Latin, but there is no reply and he realizes that all communication is through some kind of mind talk. When his early failure to understand this causes the master of the ship on which he first takes refuge to regard him as ill, and curable only by the Masters of Will and of Knowledge to whom he is sent; he soon learns that in this different and horrifying society control is through the minds of a few leaders who work their will on the rest of the populace. The remainder of the story deals with Tony's unceasing efforts to locate his father, to understand the ways of this fearful society, and eventually, his father obviously lost to him forever, to undertake the grueling flight back to the upper world.

If one pays attention only to the monstrous plants and animals and the even more monstrous leaders of the underworld society, *Land under England* remains only a good fantastic adventure. But if one remembers the time when it was written, it becomes a warning of the future that the totalitarian societies of the 1930s, especially that of Nazi Germany, might bring to England. When taken together with the search for self in *Wind from the North* and the polemical picture of brute mankind when the veneer of civilization is removed in *Day of Wrath,* it provides evidence of O'Neill's continuing effort to understand the hidden drives and motivations that still plague humanity. There are political and psychological aspects to this almost allegorical tale that move it to a higher level than most such works of the time, and O'Neill can justly be regarded as a minor but significant figure whose work prefigures the kind of social science fiction and fantasy that became prominent in the immediate postwar years.

—Arthur O. Lewis

ORE, Rebecca

Also writes as Rebecca Brown. **Nationality:** American. **Born:** Rebecca Brown, Louisville, Kentucky, in 1948. **Education:** Columbia University, 1968-72, B.A. 1979; University of North Carolina at Charlotte, M.A. in English 1980; State University of New York, Albany, 1980-82. **Career:** Worked as editorial secretary or assistant, New York City, 1968-72; part-time secretary, San Francisco, 1975-76; reporter, *The Patriot,* Patrick County, Virginia, 1976-77; office assistant, New York City, 1977-78. **Agent:** Donald Maas, 64 West 84th Street, New York, New York, 10024. **Address:** P.O. Box 129, Critz, Virginia 24082-0129, U.S.A.

SCIENCE FICTION PUBLICATIONS

Novels (series: Tom Red Clay)

Becoming Alien: Ben Bova's Discoveries (Red Clay). New York, Tor, 1988.
Being Alien (Red Clay). New York, Tor, 1989.
Human to Human (Red Clay). New York, Tor, 1990.
The Illegal Rebirth of Billy the Kid. New York, Tor, 1991.
Slow Funeral. New York, Tor, 1994.
Gaia's Toys. New York, Tor, 1995.

Short Stories

Alien Bootlegger, and Other Stories. New York, Tor, 1993.

OTHER PUBLICATIONS

Poetry as Rebecca Brown

Mouse Works. New York, Siamese Banana Press, 1971.

The Bicycle Trip and Poems. New York, Telephone Books, 1974.
For the 82nd Airborne. New York, Adventures in Poetry Press, 1976.
The Barbarian Queen. Guilford, Connecticut, Telephone Press, 1981.

*   *   *

Combining traditional genre strengths of extrapolation and original ideas with mainstream values of prose and characterization, Rebecca Ore has established herself as a significant writer of science fiction. Ore turned to writing science fiction after writing poetry, plays, and memoirs—with small press publications as Rebecca Brown—and editing, including for a publisher of science fact and for the Science Fiction Book Club. In 1987 and 1988 Ore was a nominee for the John W. Campbell Award for best new science fiction writer. Her work is notable for its presentation of non-humans who are consistent, sympathetic characters but do not simply react like human beings. In her Alien novels (*Becoming Alien, Being Alien,* and *Human to Human*), an interplanetary federation accuses humans of being "xenoflips," xenophobes who see aliens as either threat or salvation, but cannot see them as equal, though different. Clearly, this is an indictment of much science fiction; by example, Ore's novels show that other ways of conceptualizing aliens are not only possible, but useful.

The scientific background in Ore's work is strong, especially but not exclusively concerning biology. In the three Alien novels, sapient evolution is limited to those species whose binocular vision created a larger brain: the bat-like Gwyng, a number of species based on birds, and evolved apes including the human species. This restriction may be frustrating for some readers, used to tentacles and more; but it allows Ore to develop realistic species-differences, in keeping with the characteristics and ecological niches they sprang from. Her short fiction, collected in *Alien Bootlegger and Other Stories,* presents other aliens, extraterrestrial or genetically engineered, often trying to survive in hostile or inexplicable situations on our earth, providing an eerie distancing from our own world in a sympathetic reader. In *The Illegal Rebirth of Billy the Kid,* "Giant Flesh Holograms Keep My Baby's Eyes Warm," and "The Tyrant That I Serve," Ore depicts a future in which bioengineering can create "chimeras," human-looking or not, for government work or the amusement of the rich. Again, the ramifications are considered: What would the legal status of chimeras be? What kinds of chimeras would be made, to fulfill what human needs and wishes?

Similar social extrapolation concerns global cooling, in the Alien books but especially in *The Illegal Rebirth of Billy the Kid* and "Ice-Gouged Lakes, Glacier-Bound Time," in which the climatic change has reduced the U.S.A. to a second-rate world power. In the Alien books, star-travel is accomplished by "star-gates," about which Ore presents just enough scientific detail to be convincing. Her novels are pervaded by the feeling that technology creates psyche and society as much as the other way around; the genre of science fiction allows her to deal with technology in detail, whether it is future medicine or contemporary moonshining, alien architecture or human bicycling, rock-climbing, or hand-weaving.

Issues of alien—or at least alienated—consciousness and ecological issues on earth come together in *Gaia's Toys,* in which the three protagonists are Dorcas Rae, a genetic engineer whose main interest is in building new and better insects; Allison Dodge, an eco-terrorist captured by the government and forced to investigate

Rae; and Willie Hunsucker, a "drode head" whose brain is used for computer-processing in exchange for his welfare money and whose main joy comes from a praying mantis Rae engineered. The situations of the two female characters, Rae and Dodge, allow Ore to comment on gender issues, often making discomforting and challenging points.

Ore is also very much concerned with human class-structure, and with how people are shaped by it as well as choosing to change or (more often) perpetuate it. All of her work, from her early short stories concerning Chimeras through *Gaia's Toys,* demonstrates the deep gulf between the haves and have-nots—in terms of money, and power, and even emotional support—and explores what being in either category does to an individual. Questions of status and privilege, inequality and relative power, are central to *The Illegal Rebirth of Billy the Kid* as—in a different way—they are to *Slow Funeral.*

Much of the Earth-based action in Ore's fiction takes place in rural Virginia, an area from which Ore's family comes and in which she now lives. Tom Gentry, the protagonist of the Alien books, is a drug-dealing high school student who feels cut off from those around him, until he joins the federation in which everyone is an alien; "Farming in Virginia" and "Alien Bootlegger" bring the alien to that setting. In *The Illegal Rebirth of Billy the Kid,* the chimera, made in imitation of Billy the Kid, finally finds a home on a historical preserve near Roanoke. Ore also creates interesting near-future San Francisco bay area settings in "Projectile Weapons" and *Being Alien.*

The most thorough exploration of rural Virginia culture, as well as of the temptations and pitfalls of power and money, is Ore's one fantasy novel, *Slow Funeral.* In an isolated area, in our world but set off culturally and even geologically, magic works, as long as it is not interfered with by the antithetical force of technology. Though the causation and processes are supernatural, the handling is extrapolative and careful—as much as the stories in John W. Campbell's *Unknown* magazine in the 1940s, though very different in tone. *Slow Funeral,* like much of Ore's fiction, can be difficult because it is both challenging and sometimes grim; yet like all of Ore's fiction, it is imaginative, energetic, and careful, and it does at heart refuse to do anything but affirm a basic human dignity.

Satisfying on the levels of plot, characterization, and speculation, Ore's works are thematically interesting as well. By defining the non-human—alien or engineered creation—Ore also approaches the question of what it means to be human. In the Alien books, Tom's body-language is described in the same clinical terms as that of the other species; in a sense, Tom becomes alien himself, so that the reader can experience her or his own humanity in a new way. In these books, Ore also depicts multiple languages, each with its own limitations and ways of knowing, which force both the characters and the readers to consider—as Tom puts it in *Human to Human*—"the meaning of meaning." *The Illegal Rebirth of Billy the Kid* also has much to say about the interactive process of myth and reality, the ways in which both the chimera and the historical Billy created their images and yet were created by them.

If Ore's fiction can be compared to anyone else's, is it probably that of Ursula Le Guin, who also strives rigorously to create alien societies and also uses those to explore human concerns while maintaining the alien strangeness. In fact, "Ice-Gouged Lakes, Glacier-Bound Times" features a journey by a human and an alien across a cold landscape, in homage to Le Guin's *The Left Hand of Darkness.* Other influences include C. J. Cherryh, James Tiptree, Jr., and Joanna Russ.

Ore's fiction both "gently subverts the tropes of SF" and also

fulfills genre qualifications, as Ore has noted. Her characters are not predictable, always (if not flawlessly) fully realized as individuals. The futures she presents are neither utopian nor dystopian; they show a strong sense of history, a sense of what aspects of life change and which do not. For this reason alone, her work would deserve attention, within and outside the science fiction community.

—Bernadette Lynn Bosky

ORWELL, George

Pseudonym for Eric Arthur Blair. **Nationality:** British. **Born:** of English parents in Motihari, Bengal, India, 25 June 1903; brought to England, 1904. **Education:** a convent school, Henley-on-Thames, Oxfordshire; St. Cyprian's, Eastbourne, Sussex, 1911-16; Wellington School, 1917; Eton College (King's Scholar), 1917-21. **Military Service:** Served in the United Marxist Workers' Party militia in Catalonia, 1937: wounded in action; served in the Home Guard, 1940-43: Sergeant. **Family:** Married 1) Eileen O'Shaughnessy in 1936 (died 1945), one adopted son; 2) Sonia Mary Brownell in 1949. **Career:** Served in the Imperial Indian Police in Burma: at Police Training School, Rangoon, 1922-23, assistant superintendent of police at Myaungmya, 1923, Twante, 1924, Syriam, 1925, Insein, 1925-26, Moulmein, 1926, and Katha, 1927 (resigned 1927); lived in London, 1927, and Paris, 1928-29 (worked briefly as dishwasher, 1929); tutor, Southwold, Suffolk, 1930; lived in London, 1930-31; headmaster, The Hawthorns, Hayes, Middlesex, 1932-33, and teacher at Frays College, Uxbridge, 1933; worked at Booklovers' Corner bookshop, London, 1934-36; shopkeeper, Wallingford, Hertfordshire, 1936-40; talks producer in the Empire Department, BBC, London, 1941-43. Freelance writer from 1935: reviewer, *New English Weekly,* 1935-36, *Time and Tide,* 1940-41, *Tribune,* 1940-47 (Literary Editor, 1943-45), and *Horizon,* 1940-49, all London; columnist ("London Letter"), *Partisan Review,* New York, 1941-46; editor, with T.R. Fyvel, Searchlight Books series, Secker and Warburg, London, 1941-42; regular contributor, *Observer,* London, 1942-49 (war correspondent, 1945); columnist, *Manchester Evening News,* 1943-46. Lived on Jura, Hebrides Islands, Scotland, 1946-47. **Died:** 21 January 1950.

SCIENCE FICTION PUBLICATIONS

Novels

Animal Farm: A Fairy Story. London, Secker and Warburg, 1945; New York, Harcourt Brace, 1946.
Nineteen Eighty-Four. London, Secker and Warburg, and New York, Harcourt Brace, 1949; edited by Bernard Crick, Oxford, Oxford University Press, 1984.

OTHER PUBLICATIONS

Novels

Burmese Days. New York, Harper, 1934; London, Gollancz, 1935.

A Clergyman's Daughter. London, Gollancz, and New York, Harper, 1935.
Keep the Aspidistra Flying. London, Gollancz, 1936; New York, Harcourt Brace, 1954.
Coming Up for Air. London, Gollancz, 1939; New York, Harcourt Brace, 1950.

Plays

Radio Plays: *The Voyage of the Beagle,* from work by Darwin, 1946; *Animal Farm,* from his own novel, 1947.

Other

Down and Out in Paris and London. London, Gollancz, and New York, Harper, 1933.
The Road to Wigan Pier. London, Gollancz, 1937; New York, Harcourt Brace, 1958.
Homage to Catalonia. London, Secker and Warburg, 1938; New York, Harcourt Brace, 1952.
Inside the Whale and Other Essays. London, Gollancz, 1940.
The Lion and the Unicorn: Socialism and the English Genius. London, Secker and Warburg, 1941; New York, AMS Press, 1976.
Critical Essays. London, Secker and Warburg, 1946; as *Dickens, Dali and Others: Studies in Popular Culture,* New York, Reynal, 1946.
James Burnham and the Managerial Revolution. London, Socialist Book Centre, 1946.
The English People. London, Collins, 1947; New York, Haskell House, 1974.
Shooting an Elephant and Other Essays. London, Secker and Warburg, and New York, Harcourt Brace, 1950.
Such, Such Were the Joys. New York, Harcourt Brace, 1953; as *England, Your England and Other Essays,* London, Secker and Warburg, 1953.
A Collection of Essays. New York, Doubleday, 1954.
The Orwell Reader, edited by Richard H. Rovere. New York, Harcourt, 1956.
Selected Essays. London, Penguin, 1957; as *Inside the Whale and Other Essays,* 1975.
Selected Writings, edited by George Bott. London, Heinemann, 1958.
Collected Essays. London, Secker and Warburg, 1961.
Decline of English Murder and Other Essays. London, Penguin, 1965.
The Collected Essays, Journalism, and Letters of George Orwell, edited by Sonia Orwell and Ian Angus. London, Secker and Warburg, 4 vols., 1968.
The Complete Works. New York, Harcourt, 17 vols., 1984.
The War Broadcasts and The War Commentaries, edited by W.J. West. London, BBC Publications-Duckworth, 2 vols., 1985; as *George Orwell: The Lost Writings,* New York, Avon, 1988.
A Collection of Essays. San Diego, Harcourt, 1993.
The Sayings of George Orwell, edited by Robert Pearce. London, Duckworth, 1994.
The Penguin Essays of George Orwell. London, Penguin, 1994.

Editor, *Talking to India: A Selection of English Language Broadcasts to India.* London, Allen and Unwin, 1943.

Editor, with Reginald Reynolds, *British Pamphleteers 1: From the Sixteenth Century to the French Revolution.* London, Wingate, 1948.

*

Bibliography: "George Orwell: A Selected Bibliography" by Zoltan G. Zeke and William White, in *Bulletin of Bibliography 23* (Boston), May-August 1961; *George Orwell: An Annotated Bibliography of Criticism* by Jeffrey and Valerie Meyers, New York, Garland, 1977.

Manuscript Collection: University College, London.

Critical Studies (selection): *George Orwell* by Tom Hopkinson, London, Longman, 1953, revised edition, 1962; *George Orwell: A Literary Study* by John Atkins, London, Calder, 1954, New York, Ungar, 1955, revised edition, London, Calder and Boyars, 1971; *A Study of George Orwell, The Man and His Works* by Christopher Hollis, London, Hollis and Carter, and Chicago, Regnery, 1956; *The Crystal Spirit: A Study of George Orwell* by George Woodcock, Boston, Little Brown, 1966, London, Cape, 1967; *The Making of George Orwell: A Study in Literary History* by Keith Alldritt, London, Arnold, and New York, St. Martin's Press, 1969; *Orwell's Fiction* by Robert A. Lee, Notre Dame, Indiana, University of Notre Dame Press, 1969; *The World of George Orwell* edited by Miriam Gross, London, Weidenfeld and Nicolson, 1971, New York, Simon and Schuster, 1972; *Orwell* by Raymond Williams, London, Fontana, and New York, Viking Press, 1971, and *George Orwell: A Collection of Critical Essays* edited by Williams, Englewood Cliffs, New Jersey, Prentice Hall, 1974; *The Unknown Orwell* by Peter Stansky and William Abrahams, London, Constable, and New York, Knopf, 1972, *Orwell: The Transformation* by Stansky, London, Constable, 1979, New York, Knopf, 1980, and *On Nineteen Eighty-Four* edited by Stansky, New York, Freeman, 1984; *A Reader's Guide to George Orwell,* London, Thames and Hudson, 1975, Totowa, New Jersey, Rowman and Littlefield, 1977, and *George Orwell: The Critical Heritage,* London, Routledge, 1975, both edited by Jeffrey Meyers; *George Orwell and the Origins of 1984* by William Steinhoff, Ann Arbor, University of Michigan Press, 1975, as *The Road to 1984,* London, Weidenfeld and Nicolson, 1975; *The Road to Miniluv: George Orwell, the State and God* by Christopher Small, London, Gollancz, 1975, Pittsburgh, University of Pittsburgh Press, 1976; *Primal Dream and Primal Scream: Orwell's Development as a Psychological Novelist* by Richard I. Smyer, Columbia, University of Missouri Press, 1979; *George Orwell: A Life* by Bernard Crick, London, Secker and Warburg, 1980, Boston, Little Brown, 1981, revised edition, Secker and Warburg, 1981, and *Orwell Remembered* by Crick and Audrey Coppard, London, BBC, and New York, Facts on File, 1984; *Approaching 1984* by Donald McCormick, Newton Abbot, Devon, David and Charles, 1980; *George Orwell: The Road to 1984* by Peter Lewis, London, Heinemann, 1981; *George Orwell: A Personal Memoir* by T.R. Fyvel, London, Weidenfeld and Nicolson, 1982; *A George Orwell Companion* by J.R. Hammond, London, Macmillan, and New York, St. Martin's Press, 1982; *George Orwell's Guide Through Hell: A Psychological Study of 1984* by Robert Plank, San Bernardino, California, Borgo Press, 1984; *Orwell: The Road to Airstrip One* by Ian Slater, New York, Norton, 1985; *George Orwell and the Problem of Authentic Existence* by Michael Carter, London, and Dover, New Hampshire,

Croom Helm, 1985; *Critical Essays on George Orwell* edited by Bernard Oldsey, Boston, Hall, 1986; *Reflections on America, 1984: An Orwell Symposium* edited by Robert Mulvihill, Athens, University of Georgia Press, 1986; *George Orwell: The Age's Adversary,* New York, Macmillan, 1986, and *Nineteen Eighty-Four: Past, Present, and Future,* Boston, Twayne, 1989, both by Patrick Reilly; *A Preface to Orwell* by David Wykes, London, and New York, Longman, 1987; *The Diminished Self: Orwell and the Loss of Freedom* by Mark Connelly, Pittsburgh, Pennsylvania, Duquesne University Press, 1987; *George Orwell* edited by Courtney T. Wemyss and Alexej Ugrinsky, New York, Greenwood, 1987; *George Orwell* by Averil Gardner, Boston, Twayne, 1987; *George Orwell: A Reassessment* edited by Peter Buitenhuis and I.B. Nadel, New York, Macmillan, 1988; *Orwell and the Politics of Despair: A Critical Study of the Writings of George Orwell* by Alok Rai, Cambridge, Cambridge University Press, 1988; *George Orwell* by Nigel Flynn, Hove, Wayland, 1989, Vero Beach, Florida, Rourke, 1990; *The Politics of Literary Reputation: The Making and Claiming of "St. George Orwell"* by John Rodden, Oxford, Oxford University Press, 1990.

*   *   *

George Orwell's worldwide reputation as a writer of science fiction rests upon a single novel, *Nineteen Eighty-Four.* Such is the dynamic force of this work that the title of the book has become a universal symbol for the totalitarian nightmare. Although indisputably an SF novel, it differs from most other works in the genre by having an overt political purpose. In the author's own words, he desired "to push the world in a certain direction, to alter other people's idea of the kind of society they should strive after." His experiences while fighting alongside the Anarchists in the Spanish Civil War had opened his eyes to the "expedient inhumanities" that lay behind both international Communism and European Fascism. From now on in any conflict between the individual human being and the State, Orwell was always to be found on the side of the underdog. Orwell's international stature was first established with *Animal Farm,* a classic Swiftian satire on the Soviet experiment. The runaway success of this work ensured that his next book would be given wide critical attention. When *Nineteen Eighty-Four* first appeared, it was initially hailed in many quarters as a further trenchant indictment of Soviet Communism, though, in fact, it is an indictment of absolutism of whatsoever political hue. Its conception owes a great deal to Eugene Zamyatin's *We* which Orwell had first read in a French translation some 20 years previously.

The plot of *Nineteen Eighty-Four* is straightforward. The story follows the tragic fortues of Winston Smith, a minor civil servant, who lives and works in the London which has survived an atomic Third World War. This London is now the capital of Airstrip One, an offshore province of Oceania, one of three constantly warring world-power blocs, Oceania, Eurasia, Eastasia. Under the absolute control of the Party and its Leader, Big Brother, the society of Oceania is stratified into the Inner Party (the rulers), the Party (the bureaucracy), and the rest (known collectively as the Proles). The complete ascendancy of the Party is symbolized by the four Ministries which dominate Winston Smith's decaying urban metropolis. These are, in order of significance, the Ministry of Love, the Ministry of Truth, the Ministry of Peace, and the Ministry of Plenty:

> The Ministry of Love was the really frightening one. There were no windows in it at all. Winston had never been inside the Ministry of Love, nor within half a kilometre of it. The place was impossible to enter except on official business, and then only by penetrating through a maze of barbed-wire entanglements, steel doors and hidden machine-gun nests. Even the streets leading up to its outer barriers were roamed by gorilla-faced guards in black uniforms, armed with jointed truncheons.

Winston works in the Ministry of Truth whose slogans are "War is Peace. Freedom is Slavery. Ignorance is Strength." His job is to rewrite items of recent history in Newspeak (the official Party language) in such a way that it accords with the official Party line. Watched over at all hours of the day and night by the ubiquitous telescreens of the dreaded Thought Police, Winston rebels against the system and commits the crime of falling in love with a fellow Party worker. For a brief spell, he enjoys a precarious happiness, only to learn, in what is surely one of the most horrendous passages in the whole of SF, that the Party has simply been toying with him all along. He is dragged into the Ministry of Love, and his total physical and spiritual degradation begins as the Party, in the person of the Torquemadian Senior Official O'Brien, sets about the task of extinguishing Winston's one precious spark of individual humanity—his moral conscience. The end is inevitable and horrifying. By a series of physical and psychological tortures, Winston Smith as a person is totally erased and is then recreated in the Party's image until, in the end, "he loves Big Brother." Orwell's vision of a future in which the acquisition and tenure of absolute power is the only aspiration left to man is truly terrifying. "Power is not a means, it is an end," O'Brien tells Winston Smith. "If you want a picture of the future, imagine a boot stamping on a human face—forever."

Nineteen Eighty-Four is a cautionary tale on a heroic scale; its initial impact on an immediately postwar world still groggy from the revelations of the Nazi extermination camps and the tales of Russian defectors to the West is not difficult to imagine. What still gives the story its tremendous emotional force is the intensity with which Orwell has expressed in fictional terms his passionately held belief in individual human freedom. All in all, *Nineteen Eighty-Four* seems likely to retain its position as the most powerful as well as the most widely read science fiction novel of the century.

—Richard Cowper

P-Q

PADGETT, Lewis. *See* KUTTNER, Henry; MOORE, C.L.

PALMER, Raymond A.

Pseudonyms: Henry Gade; G.H. Irwin; Frank Patton; J.W. Pelkie; Wallace Quitman; A.R. Steber; Morris J. Steele. **Nationality:** American. **Born:** Wisconsin, 1 August 1910; crippled from childhood. **Career:** Editor and publisher; editor, *The Comet,* fan magazine, 1930; *Amazing Stories,* 1938-49; *Fantastic Adventures,* 1939-49; *Other Worlds (later Science Stories* and *Flying Saucers from Other Worlds),* 1950-57; *Imagination Science Fiction,* 1950; *Universe Science Fiction,* 1953-55; *Fate and Mystic* (later *Search)* in the 1950s; *The Hidden World* in the 1960s. **Died:** 15 August 1977.

SCIENCE FICTION PUBLICATIONS

Uncollected Short Stories

"The Time Ray of Jandra," in *Wonder Stories* (New York), June 1930.
"The Time Tragedy," in *Wonder Stories* (New York), December 1934.
"The Symphony of Death," in *Amazing* (New York), December 1935.
"Three from the Test Tube," in *Wonder Stories* (New York), November 1936.
"Matter Is Conserved," in *Astounding* (New York), April 1938.
"Catalyst Planet," in *Thrilling Wonder Stories* (New York), August 1938.
"Outlaw of Space" (as Wallace Quitman), in *Amazing* (New York), August 1938.
"The Vengeance of Martin Brand" (as G.H. Irwin), in *Amazing* (New York), August 1942; expanded edition, as "The Justice of Martin Brand," in *Other Worlds* (New York), July 1950.
"Red Coral," in *Other Worlds* (New York), May 1951.

Uncollected Short Stories as A.R. Steber

"The Blinding Ray," in *Amazing* (New York), August 1938.
"Black World," in *Amazing* (New York), March 1940.
"When the Gods Make War," in *Amazing* (New York), July 1940.
"Moon of Double Trouble," in *Amazing* (New York), March 1945.

Uncollected Short Stories as Morris J. Steele

"Polar Prison," in *Amazing* (New York), December 1938.
"The Phantom Enemy," in *Amazing* (New York), February 1939.
"Weapon for a Wac," in *Amazing* (New York), September 1944.

Uncollected Short Stories as Henry Gade

"Pioneer—1957," in *Fantastic Adventures* (New York), November 1939.

"Liners of Space," in *Amazing* (New York), December 1939.
"The Invincible Crime Buster," in *Amazing* (New York), July 1941.

Uncollected Short Stories as Frank Patton

"The Test Tube Girl," in *Fantastic Adventures* (New York), January 1942.
"Doorway to Hell," in *Fantastic Adventures* (New York), February 1942.
"A Patriot Never Dies," in *Amazing* (New York), August 1943.
"War Worker," in *Amazing* (New York), September 1943.
"Jewels of the Toad," in *Fantastic Adventures* (New York), October 1943.
"Mahaffey's Mystery," in *Other Worlds* (New York), March 1950.
"The Identity of Sue Tenet," in *Other Worlds* (New York), December 1952.
"Question Please," in *Other Worlds* (New York), April 1953.
"Sure Thing," in *Science Stories* (Evanston, Illinois), February 1954.
"The Secret of Pierre Cotreau," in *Science Stories* (Evanston, Illinois), April 1954.

Uncollected Short Stories as J.W. Pelkie (series: Toka in all stories)

"King of the Dinosaurs," in *Fantastic Adventures* (New York), October 1945.
"Toka and the Man Bats," in *Fantastic Adventures* (New York), February 1946.
"Toka Fights the Big Cats," in *Fantastic Adventures* (New York), December 1947.
"In the Sphere of Time," *Planet* (New York), Summer 1948.

Other

The Real UFO Invasion. San Diego, Greenleaf Classics, 1967.

* * *

Raymond A. Palmer was one of the earliest science fiction fans, his activities dating from the late 1920s, and his major influence was as an editor. His first important assignment was the editorship of *Amazing Stories,* taken over from the moribund Teck Publications in 1938 by Ziff-Davis. Palmer discarded the on-hand inventory, quickly filled the magazine with new, adventure-oriented stories, and (perhaps most important) refurbished its drab appearance to create a lively, colorful package. Simultaneously he worked to bring the contents of the magazine in line with its new appearance.

He was immediately successful, and the following year was able to add a companion magazine, *Fantastic Adventures.* In a number of ways, Palmer's career remarkably paralleled that of the legendary John W. Campbell, Jr. Each editor brought on a stable of new writers, in addition to retaining (or re-recruiting) the best writers of a previous administration. Each editor also ran afoul of reader resistance when he attempted to introduce a variety of pseudoscientific cult material in the 1940s and 1950s. For Campbell it was Dianetics, and other oddities; for Palmer, it was first the Shaver Mystery, and later an infatuation with Flying Saucers. Much given to hucksterism and juvenile promotional appeals, Palmer met strong resistance in science fiction and withdrew to concentrate on occult publishing after 1957. However, his real achievements as an editor have been sorely underrated, and an examination of files of the magazines he edited reveals an absolute treasure-trove of overlooked material, by many leading writers. He lured Edgar Rice Burroughs back to the SF magazines after an absence of 12 years. Palmer was the first editor to publish stories by Isaac Asimov, for all that the latter prefers to emphasize his later association with Campbell in his reminiscences. It is to be hoped that as the lingering bad taste of "Shaverism," "Saucerism," and Palmer's other regretable antics fades away, his very significant editorial contribution to modern science fiction will be more appreciated.

Palmer's own fiction, upon review, indicates a considerable talent but one which was not applied sufficiently consistently to produce a coherent body of works. In Palmer's earliest work, for Gernsback's *Wonder Stories,* he shows strongly the influence of early writers in the field. "The Time Ray of Jandra" reads like a throwback to the early 19th century, with a first-person narrator explaining the circumstances of his birth and naming, and continuing through overlong paragraphs to detail a discovery tale in which he is purely an observer rather than a participant. Before long, Palmer had fallen into the pulp style. His stories of the 1930s and 1940s show a fully developed set of pulp characteristics: simplistic but highly colored characterization, heavy doses of violent action, a reliance on coincidence and a strongly romantic bent. An excellent example, further embellished with occasional pseudoscientific asides, is "The Test Tube Girl" (as Frank Patton). In his few stories published in the 1950s, Palmer appears to have overcome the worse excesses of his pulp period, and to have moved toward a less heavy-handed and melodramatic approach.

—Richard A. Lupoff

PANGBORN, Edgar

Pseudonym: Bruce Harrison. **Nationality:** American. **Born:** New York City, 25 February 1909. **Education:** Brooklyn Friends School, graduated 1924; Harvard University, Cambridge, Massachusetts, 1924-25; New England Conservatory of Music, 1927. **Military Service:** Served in the United States Army Medical Corps, 1942-45. **Career:** Farmer in Maine, 1939-42; writer from 1946. Lived in Voorheesville, New York. **Awards:** International Fantasy award, 1955. **Died:** 1 February 1976.

Science Fiction Publications

Novels (series: Post-Holocaust America)

West of the Sun. Garden City, New York, Doubleday, 1953; London, Hale, 1954.
A Mirror for Observers. Garden City, New York, Doubleday, 1954; London, Muller, 1955.
Davy (Post-Holocaust). New York, St. Martin's Press, 1964; London, Dobson, 1967.
The Judgment of Eve: A Novel of Human Inquiry (Post-Holocaust). New York, Simon and Schuster, 1966; London, Rapp and Whiting, 1968.

The Company of Glory (Post-Holocaust). New York, Pyramid, 1975.
The Atlantean Nights Entertainment. San Francisco, Pennyfarthing Press, 1980.

Short Stories

Good Neighbors and Other Strangers. New York, Macmillan, 1972.
Still I Persist in Wondering (Post-Holocaust). New York, Dell, 1978.

Other Publications

Novels

A-100: A Mystery Novel (as Bruce Harrison). New York, Dutton, 1930.
Wilderness of Spring. New York, Rinehart, 1958.
The Trial of Callista Blake. New York, St. Martin's Press, 1961; London, Davies, 1962.

*

Manuscript Collection: Mugar Memorial Library, Boston University.

*   *   *

Edgar Pangborn's work, according to Damon Knight, reflects "the regretful, ironic, sorrowful, deeply joyous—and purblind—love of the world and all in it." Pangborn sees wonder in the ordinary, removing the reader from mundane perceptions. Some readers resent this heightening of the conventional. Knight sees Pangborn's magic as a veil obscuring the story. "The author will not get out of the way, but forces you to look through his own misty substance at what he wants you to see." A moment of reflection reveals that this sort of reaction indicates a matter of taste. Pangborn is an individual writer who directs the reader's perceptions; he does not write to the reader's order. Pangborn's view of life is tragic, comic, serious, and speculatively imaginative; his range is wider than many critics suspect. He is one of the few writers of SF and fantasy who was also a major fiction writer. His ideas were not always original, but he always managed to transform them.

"Angel's Egg," Pangborn's first story, is a powerful and very moving alien-contact story which pleads for tolerance and patience in regard to humankind's fate. Often reprinted, this story would have been enough to make a name for any writer. Pangborn's first SF novel, *West of the Sun,* is a deeply felt story of interstellar castaways, notable for its vividly realized settings, complex characters, and a painful knowledge of human failing. The sense of being there with the characters is overwhelming. *A Mirror for Observers,* a story of alien observers on earth who struggle between being watchers and meddlers, reaches Stapledonian heights of thought and feeling about the fate of humanity, but without the Stapledonian vistas. Pangborn's focus is more personal and intimate. Pangborn regarded *Wilderness of Spring* as a historical novel. Set in colonial New England, there is much in the story's pioneer spirit to interest the SF reader (one of the characters becomes a scientist). *The Trial of Callista Blake* is a novel on the theme of capital punishment.

Davy is Pangborn's most famous novel. Set 300 years after a nuclear holocaust, the book is a memoir written by the title character who grows from a bondsman to an ambitious leader concerned with the fate of humanity. Funny and tragic, bawdy and adventurous in the manner of *Tom Jones, Davy* is one of the lasting works of SF. A similar work, but one involving a female counterpart to Davy, *The Judgment of Eve* is not as well known, but, filled with the agony of choices, the book will please anyone who has enjoyed Pangborn's work. It has been suggested that the ambiguous ending might have been the result of editorial pressure to avoid depicting a *ménage-à-quatre. The Company of Glory* is set in the same world as *Davy* and *The Judgment of Eve* (though the Pyramid edition was censored as being "too faggoty"). *Still I Persist in Wondering* contains most of the shorter works set in the world of *Davy.*

Pangborn's work addresses the great problems of life and death, the mystery of existence, personal worth. Paradoxically, science fiction, though it claims to be a literature of ideas and wide vision, rarely rises above the entertainment formulas. Pangborn helped keep alive the tradition of "high science fiction," even while the pejorative genre association with SF dragged down serious reception of his work. Above everything else, Pangborn brought an overpowering sense of beauty to science fiction. *West of the Sun* glows with an unwearying light: "I give you birth and death and the journey of our days and nights between them, the shining of green fields, and patience of the forest, the little stars, the great stars, the love and the thought, the labor and the laughter, the good morning sky." *A Mirror for Observers* breathes with an unwaning love: "Never, beautiful Earth, never even at the height of the human storms have I forgotten you, my planet Earth, your forests and your fields, your oceans, the serenity of your mountains; the meadows, the continuing rivers, the incorruptible promise of returning spring." In trying to make us see, hear, and feel the important things that we so often forget, Pangborn aspired to the utterance of music, his first love.

—George Zebrowski

PANSHIN, Alexei

Nationality: American. **Born:** Lansing, Michigan, 14 August 1940. **Education:** University of Michigan, Ann Arbor, 1958-60; Michigan State University, East Lansing, B.A. 1965; University of Chicago, M.A. 1966. **Military Service:** Served in the United States Army, 1960-62. **Family:** Married Cory Seidman in 1969; two sons. **Career:** Librarian, Brooklyn Public Library, 1966-67; visiting lecturer in science fiction, Cornell University, Ithaca, New York, summers 1971-72. **Awards:** Hugo award, for criticism, 1967, 1990; Nebula award, 1968. **Address:** 5580 Route 412, Riegelsville, Pennsylvania 18077, U.S.A.

SCIENCE FICTION PUBLICATIONS

Novels (series: Anthony Villiers)

Rite of Passage. New York, Ace, 1968; London, Sidgwick and Jackson, 1969.
Star Well (Villiers). New York, Ace, 1968.
The Thurb Revolution (Villiers). New York, Ace, 1968.
Masque World (Villiers). New York, Ace, 1969.
Earth Magic, with Cory Panshin. New York, Ace, 1978; London, Magnum, 1980.

Short Stories

Farewell to Yesterday's Tomorrow. New York, Putnam, 1975; augmented edition, New York, Berkley, 1976.
Transmutations (includes poetry and nonfiction). Dublin, Pennsylvania, Elephant Books, 1982.

OTHER PUBLICATIONS

Other

Heinlein in Dimension: A Critical Analysis. Chicago, Advent, 1968.
SF in Dimension: A Book of Explorations, with Cory Panshin. Chicago, Advent, 1976; second edition, 1980.
Mondi Interiori: Storia della Fantascienza (in Italian), with Cory Panshin. Milan, Editrice Nord, 1978.
The World beyond the Hill: Science Fiction and the Quest for Transcendence, with Cory Panshin. Dublin, Pennsylvania, Elephant Books, 1989.

*

Manuscript Collection: Bowling Green University, Ohio.

Alexei Panshin comments:

My first aim as an SF writer is to tell good stories. To me, that means the solidest, most complete, truest stories I can imagine. My second aim is to make every story new in some way: new characters, new settings, new style, new to myself. For me, each story has its own unique voice, its own autonomy, and I've got to find it and respect it and love it into being.

Most of the time I write stories slowly, and I get published even more slowly. Twenty years after I first began to write, I've published five novels and one book of stories. An editor wrote to my first agent: "I used to think Panshin wrote this way because he was stubborn. Now I think he just doesn't have a very interesting imagination." I don't know which it is. All that I know is that the SF that I want to write is still beyond me, but I haven't given up trying.

*   *   *

Alexei Panshin began publishing science fiction stories as an undergraduate. He had already conceived and begun writing the Nebula award-winning novel *Rite of Passage* while serving in the army. The novel, an acknowledged SF classic, is an anthropological novel of the maturation of Mia Havero, the 19-year-old narrator recalling her one-month "trial." The time is 150 years after the Earth has been destroyed. The trial is a survival test that all 14-year-olds living on the asteroid star "ships" must undergo on a colony planet in order to be adult citizens. The point of view of an adolescent girl and her maturation are well done, though she and her friend, Jimmy Dentremont, seem rather precocious, particularly at the conclusion of the novel. In its psychological realism and the careful delineation of the "ship" society and the colony planet culture, *Rite of Passage* is Panshin's major fiction achievement.

The three Villiers novels, *Star Well, The Thurb Revolution,* and *Masque World,* follow the adventures of the titled Anthony Villiers and his inscrutable, unpredictable alien companion, Torve, the froglike Torg. Each novel takes place on a different planet near or in the weak Nashua Empire. Panshin incorporates many comic elements, parodying space operas, spy thrillers, novels of intrigue, and regency and picaresque novels. The narrator is a cynical observer of the human comedy who interrupts the narrative with epigrammatic comments and short essays on human folly and absurdity. While amusing, the literary parody is occasionally labored and the relativistic, amoral narrator can become wearing. However, the emphasis on style and manner is appropriate to the genres being parodied and to the character of a rebellious, wandering aristocrat whose adventures are precipitated by the failure of his father's remittance to arrive. Sometimes Panshin's learning is brought in rather obviously. The novels become increasingly pessimistic. *Masque World* has the weakest plot and ends the most grimly.

Farewell to Yesterday's Tomorrow includes stories written between 1966 and 1975 and shows how deeply affected Panshin was by the revolutionary 1960s and early 1970s in America. "The Sons of Prometheus," "A Sense of Direction," and "Arpad" employ the basic situation of the asteroid star "ships" from *Rite of Passage*. "Sky Blue" reflects a concern with the rapacious development of planets and, by extension, the exploitation of Earth's ecology. "When the Vertical World Becomes Horizontal" preaches the need for freedom and spontaneity to replace rigid social assumptions and behaviour. Panshin's disillusionment with the failure of the counterculture of the early 1970s is apparent in "How Can We Sink When We Can Fly?" "Lady Sunshine and the Beatus" (written with his wife Cory) is a quest story and a phantasmagoric version of the "Beauty and the Beast" fairytale. It ends the collection optimistically and romantically.

Earth Magic, also in collaboration with his wife, is an intriguing heroic fantasy which follows the adventures of Haldane, the son of Black Morca, a barbaric warrior tyrant. It is an exploration of the themes of change, identity, and reality versus vision or magic.

The collection of essays, poetry, and fiction, *Transmutations: A Book of Personal Alchemy,* explains his frustrations with writing fiction and his personal fascination with Sufi thought. The last essay is the autobiographic "Why I No Longer Pretend to Write Science Fiction: A Letter to *Foundation.*" The last few years he and his wife have focused on writing a critical study of the genre which was published in 1989, *The World beyond the Hill: Science Fiction and the Quest for Transcendence.* This study was generally well-received by reviewers in the field of science fiction.

—Diane Parkin-Speer

PARK, Paul (Claibourne)

Nationality: American. **Born:** North Adams, Massachusetts, 1 October 1954. **Education:** Hampshire College, Amherst, Massachusetts, B.A. 1975. **Family:** Married Deborah Brothers in 1994; one daughter. **Career:** Worked as construction worker, political aide, and doorman, New York City, 1975-77. Copywriting and production assistant, Smith Greenland Advertising, New York City, 1977-78; manager, Town Squash Inc., New York City, 1979-85; manager, Potala Asian Imports, Pittsfield, Massachusetts, 1986-90. Visiting instructor, Writers' Center, Bethesda, Maryland, 1988; visiting instructor in creative writing, Johns Hopkins University, Balti-

more, Maryland, 1988-94; visiting instructor in creative writing, Williams College, Williamstown, Massachusetts, 1989, 1991, 1994, 1996. **Agent:** Martha Millard, 204 Park Avenue, Madison, New Jersey 07940. **Address:** Box 10, Petersburg, New York 12138, U.S.A.

SCIENCE FICTION PUBLICATIONS

Novels (series: Starbridge trilogy)

The Starbridge trilogy:
   Soldiers of Paradise. New York, Arbor House, 1987; London, Grafton, 1989.
   Sugar Rain. New York, Morrow, 1989; London, Grafton, 1990.
   The Cult of Loving Kindness. New York, Morrow, 1991; London, Grafton, 1993.
The Sugar Festival (includes *Soldiers of Paradise* and *Sugar Rain*). New York, Guild America Books, 1989.
Coelestis. London, HarperCollins, 1993; New York, Tor, 1995.

*   *   *

Paul Park's Starbridge trilogy has been compared to Brian Aldiss's *Helliconia* in that it deals with a planet on which the cycle of the seasons takes far longer than one human life span. In terms of intensity and evocative power, it might better be compared with Peake's *Gormenghast* or Geston's *Lords of the Starship*.

Only the first two volumes of the trilogy are available at this writing. The story concerns the coming of spring to the city-state of Charn, on a planet where the year has 80,000 days. Worldwide society is dominated by the immense Starbridge family. Charn itself is ruled by a totalitarian theocracy, justified by the need for organization for survival during the half-century (Earth years) of winter. This savagely enforced conformity contrasts with Park's most successful creation, an heretical cult of antinomials reminiscent of 16th-century Anabaptists or 20th-century hippies, who have renounced all social behaviour including speech. The end of winter in Charn, with its social and natural upheavals, is revealed largely through the experiences of the lovers Thanakar and Charity Starbridge, a doctor and the widow of a high official.

No writer in SF outdoes Park in the use of strange and grotesque material to create a story that is still full of human warmth, terror, pathos, even macabre humor, as in his account of Carilon Bargee, who set his skin on fire while trying to perfect a serum that would give the sensation of being loved. Park uses a matter-of-fact approach; we learn through what seem chance references that the carnivorous "horses" have beaks, claws, horns, and wings; that gasoline is used as an explosive and gunpowder as a motor fuel, that the spring "sugar rain" is laced with hydrocarbons, à la Velikowsky, so that Charn city burns every year, while the foresighted protect their valuables in asbestos bags. This meticulously prepared background supports Park's grander flights; the terrible and pathetic fate of the antinomials; the fall of the theocracy; Charity Starbridge's wanderings in the labyrinth under Charn; Thanakar Starbridge's passage through the monstrous prison Mountain of Redemption, with its million tormented inmates. And, from all this wonder and strangeness, characters speak to our condition here on Old Earth, as when Park's Robespierre, Raksha Starbridge, says: "I look about me and I see the dead, all those who died so that the state might live. I see in my mind's eye an image of the state, a huge, imperishable building of blank stone, and all about it a vast park, with all the souls of the dead men underfoot like grains of dirt."

Park's work has some rough edges. The reproduction of the French Revolution is too pat, while the Kafka pastiche and the place name River Rang (as in the Njalsaga) jar by their reminder of even more powerful works. But this is still a great achievement. The reader will remember the wild antinomials, with their music and their contempt for human values. The comment "Biter, biting!" echoes the Baptist Elder Lawrence Greatrake, "Men turn to Arminianism as swine to mud wallowing!" There is Colonel Aspe, another of SF's descendants of Goetz with the Iron Fist, the unwitting destroyer of his people. Above all, there is the great city Charn, with its toppling buildings and mud streets, its derelict harbour where the hulks of warships lie tilted in the ooze, its slums, taverns, brothels, palaces, prisons, all clear and detailed in the light of other suns. Park is one of those who can make us all see.

—E. R. Bishop

PASSANTE, Dom. *See* **FEARN, John Russell.**

PATTON, Frank. *See* **PALMER, Raymond A.; SHAVER, Richard S.**

PEAKE, Mervyn (Laurence)

Nationality: English. **Born:** of missionary parents in Kuling, China, 9 July 1911. **Education:** Tientsin Grammar School; Eltham College, Kent, 1923-29; Croydon College of Art, Surrey, 1929; Royal Academy Schools, London, 1929-33. **Military Service:** Served in the British Army, 1941-43; military artist for the Ministry of Information, 1943-45. **Family:** Married Maeve Gilmore in 1937; two sons and one daughter. **Career:** Lived on Sark, Channel Islands, 1933-35 and 1945-49; teacher, Westminster School of Art, London, 1935-41, and Central School of Art, London, 1949-60. Book and magazine illustrator: one-man shows—Calman Gallery, London, 1943; Peter Jones Gallery, London, 1944; toured Europe as staff artist of the *Leader,* 1945; hospitalized for encephalitis, 1964-68. **Awards:** Royal Literary Fund bursary, 1948; Heinemann award, 1951. Fellow, Royal Society of Literature. **Died:** 18 November 1968.

SCIENCE FICTION PUBLICATIONS

Novels (series: Gormenghast)

Mr. Pye. London, Heinemann, 1953.

The Titus Books. London, Penguin, 1983; as *The Gormenghast Trilogy,* New York, Viking, 1988.
  Titus Groan. London, Eyre and Spottiswoode, and New York, Reynal and Hitchcock, 1946.
  Gormenghast. London, Eyre and Spottiswoode, and New York, British Book Center, 1950.
  Titus Alone. London, Eyre and Spottiswoode, 1959; New York, Weybright and Talley, 1967; revised by Langdon Jones, Eyre and Spottiswoode, 1970.

Short Stories (series: Gormenghast in all titles)

Boy in Darkness, edited by Keynon Calthrop. Exeter, Wheaton, 1976.
Titus Unbound, adapted for children by Colin Greenland. Oxford, Oxford University Press, 1977.

OTHER PUBLICATIONS

Plays

The Connoisseurs (produced 1952).
The Wit to Woo (produced 1957).
Radio Writing: *The Artist's World,* 1947; *Book Illustrations,* 1947; *Alice and Tenniel and Me,* 1954; *Titus Groan,* from his own novel, 1956; *The Voice of One,* 1956; *For Mr. Pye—An Island,* from his own novel, 1957.

Poetry

Shapes and Sounds. London, Chatto and Windus, and New York, Transatlantic, 1941.
Rhymes without Reason. London, Eyre and Spottiswoode, 1944.
The Glassblowers. London, Eyre and Spottiswoode, 1950.
The Rhyme of the Flying Bomb. London, Dent, 1962; New York, British Book Center, 1976.
Poems and Drawings. London, Keepsake, 1965.
A Reverie of Bone and Other Poems. London, Rota, 1967.
Selected Poems. London, Faber, 1972.
A Book of Nonsense. London, Owen, 1972; New York, Dufour, 1975.
Twelve Poems 1939-1960. Hayes, Middlesex, Bran's Head, 1975.

Other

Captain Slaughterboard Drops Anchor (for children). London, Country Life, 1939; revised edition, Country Life, 1945; New York, Macmillan, 1967.
The Craft of the Lead Pencil. London, Wingate, 1946.
Letters from a Lost Uncle (for children). London, Eyre and Spottiswoode, 1948.
Drawings by Mervyn Peake. London, Grey Walls, and New York, British Book Center, 1950.
Figures of Speech (drawings). London, Gollancz, 1954.
The Drawings of Mervyn Peake, text by Hilary Spurling. London, Davis-Poynter, 1974.
Mervyn Peake: Writings and Drawings, edited by Maeve Gilmore and Shelagh Johnson. London, Academy Editions, 1974; New York, St. Martin's Press, 1974.

Peake's Progress: Selected Writings and Drawings of Mervyn Peake, edited by Maeve Gilmore. London, Allen Lane, 1978; revised edition, London, Penguin, and Woodstock, New York, Overlook Press, 1981.
Sketches from Bleak House. London, Methuen, 1983.

*

Bibliography: "Peake in Print: A Bibliographical Checklist" by Dee Berkeley and G. Peter Winnington, in *Mervyn Peake Review,* Autumn 1981 and Spring 1982.

Manuscript Collections: D.M.S. Watson Library, University College, London; Imperial War Museum, London; Bodleian Library, Oxford; Berg Collection, New York Public Library.

Critical Studies: *A World Away: A Memoir of Mervyn Peake* by Maeve Gilmore, London, Gollancz, 1970; *Mervyn Peake: A Biographical and Critical Exploration* by John Batchelor, London, Duckworth, 1974; *Mervyn Peake: A Personal Memoir* by Gordon Smith, London, Gollancz, 1984; *A Child of Bliss: Growing up with Mervyn Peake* by Sebastian Peake, Luton, Lennard, 1989.

*   *   *

Peake's major fictional works are the three books which relate the heritage, childhood, and adolescence of Titus, 77th Earl of Gormenghast. They are often inaccurately called the Gormenghast Trilogy, but the third volume is not set in Gormenghast, nor were they designed as a trilogy. Peake certainly intended a fourth book, and would probably have written more.

Gormenghast is an immense, ancient castle of crumbling stone and suffocating ritual, set in a wild and dreary land. Its inhabitants, from Count Sepulchrave, suffused in laudanum and antiquarian gloom, down to Swelter, the mountainous chef, make up one of the greatest gallery of grotesques in English literature. Every aspect of their existence is dictated by the Master of Ritual from the Books of the Law, though the observances and ceremonies are so old that no one can even remember their significance. Seizing on his shadowy castle and its atmosphere of doom, many critics have called Peake a gothic writer, but the label is misleading. He makes almost no use of the supernatural, which is essential to Gothic, and his descriptive writing has a visual and tactile solidity foreign to the genre. His characters, with their extraordinary forms and names—Flay, Muzzlehatch, Prunesquallor—are caricatures whose robust and energetic presence recalls Dickens or Rabelais, not Walpole or Radcliffe. Again, Peake is farcical as well as horrific; he writes out of a relish for life and colour that is hostile to Gothic morbidity, sunlight to its vampires.

Titus Groan is the story of Titus's birth and the ripples of disturbance that spread inexorably from it. He is a natural rebel, impulsive, moody, idealistic; his arrival coincides with the rise of Steerpike, a more sinister figure, who works his way up from the kitchen to the highest place of power by insinuation, flattery, violence, and murder. The prose is deep, dense, eloquent, and richly detailed. Peake was a painter, and when he used purple he knew exactly what shade and texture he needed.

Gormenghast, which tells of Titus's truant childhood, the growing horror and inhumanity of Steerpike, and their eventual, inevitable confrontation, moves more quickly. Once set going, "change, that most unforgivable of all heresies," spreads like contagion. The

rituals are disrupted. Love shows itself in strange distortions, ungainly, absurd, or corrupt. Steerpike is exposed and hunted. Peake loses none of his control as his plot gains momentum. He portrays the adolescent tumult in all its quicksilver ambiguity. Titus's experience of life and death both in and outside the castle brutally confirm his individuality, and point to the impossibility that he will stay there. Disobeying his mother by going in to fight the cornered villain, he is attacking the Master of Ritual and manipulator of lives, powers of Gormenghast that he hates; but he is also ridding the castle of the man who would crush it to dominate it.

Titus Alone is entirely different again, a fact which has put off readers who (unlike Peake) are more interested in Gormenghast than in Titus and the rest of the world. It is, though rarely acknowledged as such, science fiction, from a class somewhere between Huxley's *Brave New World* and Harness's *The Rose*. Titus wanders, exiled and imperilled, in a strange land, a meticulous parody of modern Europe with furnishings and fittings that place it in an imminent, unpleasant future. He is arrested in a city of crystal towers and rockets; he is pursued by machine-like police and a robot flying eye, and hides in the refugee camp of the Under-River will all the malcontents and victims of a damaged civilisation; he falls into the hands of Cheeta, the corrupt daughter of the master of the death factory. Wherever he goes, no one has heard of Gormenghast, and few will believe it exists. Where *Titus Groan* was ponderous and slow, *Titus Alone* is fast and elusive. We barely glimpse the scenes as they whirr by. The effect is intentional, frightening, but the mysteries and frustrations of the book are, unavoidably, too many. Peake's last illness was well upon him when he began it, and his ability to express his ideas deteriorated as he wrote. The moral vision, at once urgent and subtle, emerges in flashes, or dimly; the novel is a characteristic document of the 20th century, damaged, hallucinatory, but intensely purposeful. (Langdon Jones's 1970 edition is the best possible version of what Peake had in mind.)

"Boy in Darkness" tells an extra story of Titus Groan, though without naming him. After the rituals of his 14th birthday he slips away from the castle into the wilderness, where he meets two old creatures called Goat and Hyena. They take him to the Blind Lamb, a malevolent deity who lives deep in an abandoned mine where once, like Comus, he commanded a rout of beasts transformed from human originals. The Goat and the Hyena are the last of this crew. He begins the metamorphosis of Titus, who fights back at the last minute for his humanity and that of the two pathetic courtiers. More sombre than almost any episode in the novels, "Boy in Darkness" has been read by some as spiritual, perhaps blasphemous, allegory, though interpretation was never the purpose of Peake's imaginings. Certainly the story is his most chilling and sensuous exercise in the macabre, far superior to the merely gruesome "Same Time, Same Place" and the ghoulish "Danse Macabre." *Mr. Pye,* Peake's only other novel, was unsuccessful when it was published because of expectations aroused by the Titus books. It is comic fantasy of a very different kind: a remarkable mixture of farce and fable, lighter in tone than the Titus books, but more exclusively adult in appeal. Set on Sark, it records the misadventures of a charming, irritating, self-appointed missionary whose work of disseminating love among the close, suspicious islanders is upset when God, "The Great Pal," rewards him rather too literally.

It can be said that Mervyn Peake lived before his time, and died too soon. Best known during his life for his dense, vigorous illustration of works by authors from Carroll to Coleridge, he also produced poetry, paintings, plays for radio and stage, and theatrical designs, as well as the prose fantasy for which he is now most famous. An eccentric to his own generation, he has been rightly honoured as a master by the next—unfortunately too late to know or benefit by it.

—Colin Greenland

————

PELKIE, J.W. *See* **PALMER, Raymond A.**

————

PERRY, Steve

Nationality: American. **Born:** Baton Rouge, Louisiana, 31 August 1947. **Family:** Dianne Waller; two children. **Career:** Swimming instructor and lifeguard; toy asembler; hotel gift shop and car rental clerk; aluminum salesman; martial arts instructor; private detective; L.P.N. and certified physician's assistant; has taught writing classes in the Portland and Washington County public school systems and at the University of Washington, Seattle; staff writer, Ruby-Spears Productions, Hollywood; currently science fiction and fantasy book reviewer for *The Oregonian.* **Member:** SFWA, MWA. **Agents:** Jean V. Naggar Literary Agency, 216 E. 75th St., New York, New York 10021; Peggy Patrick, Shapiro-Lictman Agency, 8827 Beverly Blvd., Los Angeles, CA 90048. **Address:** 14575 S.W. Village Lane, Beaverton, Oregon 97007, U.S.A. **Online addresses:** 275-2118@mcimail.com; stevperry@aol.com.

Science Fiction Publications

Novels (series: Aliens; Aliens Vs. Predator; Conan; Khadaji; Stellar Ranger; Time Machine)

The Tularemia Gambit. New York, Fawcett Gold Medal, 1981.
Sword of the Samurai (Time Machine; for children). Toronto, New York, Bantam, 1984.
Civil War Secret Agent (Time Machine; for children). Toronto, New York, Bantam, 1984.
Hellstar, with Michael Reaves. New York, Berkley Books, 1984.
The Man Who Never Missed (Khadaji). New York, Ace, 1985; London, Sphere, 1989.
Conan the Fearless. New York, Tor, 1986, London, Sphere, 1988.
Matadora (Khadaji). New York, Ace, 1986; London, Sphere, 1989.
The Machiavelli Interface (Khadaji). New York, Ace, 1986; London, Orbit, 1990.
Dome, with Michael Reaves. New York, Berkley, 1987; London, Victor Gollancz, 1988.
Conan the Defiant. New York, Tor, 1987; London, Sphere, 1990.
The Omega Cage, with Michael Reaves (Khadaji). New York, Ace, 1988.
Conan the Indomitable. New York, Tor, 1989.
The 97th Step. New York, Ace, 1989.
Conan the Free Lance. New York, Tor, 1990.
Conan the Formidable. New York, Tor, 1990.
The Albino Knife (Khadaji). New York, Ace, 1991.

The Hero Curse. Portland, Oregon, Dime Novels, 1991.
Black Steel (Khadaji). New York, Ace, 1992.
Earth Hive (Aliens). New York, Bantam, 1992; London, Millennium, 1993.
Brother Death (Khadaji). New York, Ace, 1992.
Nightmare Asylum (Aliens). New York, Bantam, 1993; London, Millennium, 1994.
The Female War (Aliens), with Stephani Perry. New York, Bantam, 1993; London, Millennium, 1994.
Spindoc. New York, Ace, 1994.
Stellar Ranger. New York, AvoNova, 1994.
Prey (Aliens vs. Predator), with Stephani Perry. New York, Bantam, and London, Millennium, 1994.
The Mask (based on screenplay by Mike Werb). New York, Bantam Books, 1994.
Lone Star (Stellar Ranger). New York, AvoNova, 1995.
The Forever Drug. New York, Ace, 1995.

Other Publications

Graphic Novels

Salimba, with Paul Chadwick. El Cajon, California, Blackthorne, 1986.
Omni Men. El Cajon, California, Blackthorne, 1989.

Other

Another Dimension: You Have to See It to Believe It! Los Angeles, 21st Publishing, 1994.
Another Dimension 2: The Little Book. Los Angeles, 21st Publishing, 1994.

*

Steve Perry comments:

I am a storyteller. I imagine I'd have been the guy spinning yarns around the campfire after the hunters got back from a hard day out slaying mastadons and running from big sabertoothed cats. Science fiction and fantasy allow a writer the freedom to make a tale as big or as small as one wants, with the only boundaries being, as the late Rod Serling used to say, "that of the imagination."

That I can make things up from whole cloth, write them down and get paid for it is wondrous indeed. I can't imagine a more interesting way to make a living and it is ever so much more fun than having a real job.

* * *

With close to 40 high adventure novels to his credit, writer Steve Perry has successfully transformed his interests in the martial arts, weaponry, and swordplay into action-filled works of science fiction and fantasy. From a varied background—that includes teaching both writing and kung fu, working as a detective, and serving as a practical nurse—Perry entered the SF mainstream in 1977 with the short story "With Clean Hands," published in *Galaxy* magazine under the pseudonym Jesse Peel. In addition to other pieces of short fiction that have since appeared in magazines and anthologies, Perry's 1981 novel, *The Tularemia Gambit,* was the first installment in what would become a prolific novel-writing career. Contributing several volumes to Byron Priess's young adult "Time Machine" series, and beginning his own popular "Matador," "Stellar Ranger," and "Aliens" series of SF novels, Perry has also joined with fellow writer Michael Reaves to create popular works of fiction that have included *Hellstar* (1984), *Dome* (1987), and *The Omega Cage* (1988).

Perry's "Matador" novels take their name from the universe in which his protagonist, the matador Khadaji, fights a military dictatorship called the Confederation. Throughout *Matadora, The Man Who Never Missed, The Machiavelli Interface,* and the prequel *The 97th Step,* all published between 1985 and 1989, Khadaji joins his fellow matadors in overpowering the enemy with his martial skills and his quick wit. In *The Man Who Never Missed,* for example, Khadaji's theft of several knock-out darts and his use of them against certain government officials instigates a revolt, albeit more through humor than through violence.

While featuring a different protagonist, 1992's *Black Steel* also takes place in the Matador universe and features the same fast-paced, well-planned battle scenes. A matador named Sleet must avenge the death of his servant and then rescue his mistress, the sansei Kildee Wu, from the clutches of the murderous Cierto, a member of the House of Black Steel who holds valuable knowledge of a secret process for making swords.

Perry has also authored several other novel series. The "Aliens" series is notable in that it includes 1993's *The Female War,* one of several books he coauthored with his daughter, Stephani Danelle Perry. And in 1994's *Spindoc* and its sequel, 1995's *The Forever Drug,* an ex-government spindoc named Venture Silk goes from fighting to uncover the truth about the death of his lover to protecting a beautiful spy who hold the key to eternal life within a high-tech galaxy of intrigue, betrayal, and murder. Protagonist Cinch Carson must do battle against futuristic rebels in a planetary war in Perry's "Stellar Ranger" series, which includes 1994's *Stellar Rangers* and *Lone Star,* published in 1995.

Perry has also contributed to the heroic fantasy genre with several "Conan" adventure novels, including *Conan the Fearless* (1986) and *Conan the Formidable* (1990), where Perry brings Robert E. Howard's character face to face with a variety of formidable foes that test the hero's strength and courage. In addition, he has written numerous nonfiction articles, reviews, essays, and scripts for animated television programs, including *The Real Ghostbusters, Karate Commandos, U.S. Starcom,* and *Batman.* He also served as the author of the screenplay novelization of the popular 1994 film, *The Mask.* In his spare time, Perry also serves as science fiction & fantasy book reviewer for *The Oregonian.*

—Pamela Shelton

PETAJA, Emil (Theodore)

Nationality: American. **Born:** Milltown, Montana, 12 April 1915. **Education:** Montana State University, Missoula 1936-38. **Career:** Office worker, 1938-41; film technician, Technicolor Corporation, Hollywood, 1941-46; photographer, 1947-63. Since 1963, full-time writer: chairman, Bokanalia Memorial Foundation; since 1972, owner, SISU Publishers, San Francisco. **Agent:** Forrest J. Ackerman, 2495 Glendower Avenue, Hollywood, California 90027, U.S.A. **Address:** P.O. Box 14126, San Francisco, California 94114, U.S.A.

SCIENCE FICTION PUBLICATIONS

Novels (series: Green Planet; Kalevala)

Alpha Yes, Terra No! New York, Ace, 1965.
The Caves of Mars. New York, Ace, 1965.
Saga of Lost Earths (Kalevala). New York, Ace, 1966.
The Star Mill (Kalevala). New York, Ace, 1966.
The Stolen Sun (Kalevala). New York, Ace, 1967.
Tramontane (Kalevala). New York, Ace, 1967.
Lord of the Green Planet. New York, Ace, 1967.
The Prism. New York, Ace, 1968.
Doom of the Green Planet. New York, Ace, 1968.
The Time Twister. New York, Dell, 1968.
The Path beyond the Stars. New York, Dell, 1969.
The Nets of Space. New York, Berkley, 1969.
Seed of the Dreamers. New York, Ace, 1970.

Short Stories

Stardrift and Other Fantastic Flotsam. Los Angeles, Fantasy, 1971.

OTHER PUBLICATIONS

Poetry

As Dream and Shadow. San Francisco, SISU, 1972.

Other

And Flights of Angels: The Life and Legend of Hannes Bok. San Francisco, SISU, 1968.

Editor, *The Hannes Bok Memorial Showcase of Fantasy Art.* San Francisco, SISU, 1974.
Editor, *Photoplay Edition.* San Francisco, SISU, 1975.

*

Emil Petaja comments:

My writing endeavors have mainly been to entertain, except for the factual material concerning Hannes Bok and fantasy art in general, which serves to indicate my enthusiasm for these subjects. My novels about the Finnish legendary epic *Kalevala: The Land of Heroes* spring from a lifelong interest in this fine poetic work. I own six translations of the *Kalevala,* as well as the work in the original. Both my parents were Finnish.

*   *   *

Though Emil Petaja published short fiction sporadically during the 1940s and 1950s, his important works were written in the 1960s. Most of these novels were published by Ace Books, and even those that were not followed the Ace formula: heavy on action, with some superficial romance. Though Petaja never sought to go beyond this formula, his innovations within its structure are impressive. Petaja's choice of story material is the source of his appeal, for into the traditional settings of science fiction he transferred mythic heroes and situations, devoting particular attention to his own Finnish myth-heritage, the Kalevala story-cycle. Petaja deftly contrasts the sterile safety of centralized civilization (into which the hero is born) with the barbaric but vital hardship of primitive culture (into which the hero is initiated), and though the author concedes the necessity for both milieus, he emphasizes the greater need for preserving humanity's potential. Unlike most Ace "common man" heroes, Petaja's protagonists are strong, romantic-minded men, slightly alienated in progressive society, but greatly attuned to the poetry of myths. Ultimately the hero's ability to empathize with mythic situations is the factor which saves all of humanity—whether directly by battling destructive forces or indirectly by mastering the situation with poetic insight (*Alpha Yes, Terra No!*)

In the Kalevala-based novels the hero's empathy is deep enough to propel his psyche upon astral journeys, becoming merged with a Finnish hero endowed with magic (psychic?) powers. These are probably the best of Petaja's works because of their belief in an actual existence of the Finnish mythos, even by means of rationalizations like psychic powers and alien entities. Thus the mythos provides the structural basis for evoking the poetry of Finnish culture. Earlier authors' works had also rationalized myths into science fiction (Henry Kuttner's *Mask of Circe*), but Petaja is virtually the first to maintain limited fidelity to the cultural content of the myths, rather than manipulating it to fit melodramatic purposes.

Less successful, but equally colorful, are the two books of a planetary culture modeled on Irish story-cycles, though no particular myths are emphasized by the plots of *Lord of the Green Planet* and *Doom of the Green Planet*. The supernatural creatures of Irish myth are robots and alien entities, while the "Irish" are merely transplanted humans from other planets, all brought together by a mad Fenian poet with super-scientific resources. Though entertaining, these books do not have the poetry of the Kalevala books, for the Irish culture is merely a giant mock-up rather than a shamanistic culture like the Finns', seen as surviving into the future. Furthermore, though the mythos-structure is less articulated, Petaja displays more dislike for the "progressive" civilization beyond the Green Planet than in earlier novels, and greater cognizance of the conflict between the appeal of heroism and the necessities of humanism.

Of the nonrelated books, the best is *The Path beyond the Stars,* in which a man and woman traverse several time periods attempting to acquire knowledge of the universe's destruction—which they ultimately cannot prevent, though they can become the Adam and Eve of another cosmos. The other novels have less imaginative scope, but, in a melodramatic way, they all work toward the same goal: regeneration of the heroes' mythopoetic faculties, and thus the redemption of the profane world.

Petaja's importance to science fiction is that of a precursor of the increased use of myth in late 1960s SF. At their best his works suggest an archaic heritage of man not unlike the findings of anthropologist Mircea Eliade—a heritage which most contemporary writers, SF and mainstream alike, have chosen to neglect.

—Gene Phillips

———

PHILLIFENT, John T. *See* **RACKHAM, John.**

———

PHILLIPS, Frank. *See* **NOWLAN, Philip Francis.**

———

PHILLIPS, Mark. *See* **GARRETT, Randall; JANIFER, Laurence M.**

———

PHILLIPS, Rog

Pseudonyms: Clinton Ames; Robert Arnette; Franklin Bahl; Alexander Blade; Craig Browning; Gregg Conrad; P.F. Costello; Inez McGowan; Melva Rogers; Chester Ruppert; William Carter Sawtelle; A.R. Steber; Gerald Vance; John Wiley; Peter Worth. **Nationality:** American. **Born:** Roger Phillips Graham, Spokane, Washington, in 1909. **Education:** Gonzaga University, Spokane, A.B.; graduate study at the University of Washington, Seattle. **Family:** Married 1) Mari Wolf; 2) Honey Wood in 1956. **Career:** Power plant engineer; shipyard welder during World War II; freelance writer after the war: Columnist ("The Club House"), *Amazing,* New York, 1948-53. **Died:** 1965.

SCIENCE FICTION PUBLICATIONS

Novels

Time Trap. Chicago, Century, 1949.
Worlds Within. Chicago, Century, 1950.
World of If. Chicago, Merit, 1951.
The Involuntary Immortals. New York, Avalon, 1959.

* * *

Rog Phillips (the name by which Roger P. Graham was generally known to science fiction readers) became a professional writer in his mid-thirties, after several years as a power plant engineer and shipyard welder, and quickly established himself as a prolific and reliable producer of pulp fiction. Phillips used many pseudonyms, including several house names.

Until 1950 Phillips wrote exclusively for the Ziff-Davis magazines; his SF and fantasy fiction appeared in *Amazing Stories* and *Fantastic Adventures.* Phillips wrote everything from featured novels to short stories and fillers. A large part of this output was routine work done to editorial order, but it was often a notch or two above the general level of quality in the magazines, and was very popular with the readers. The first work to attract wide attention was the story "So Shall Ye Reap." Starting with the premise that the five atomic bombs already exploded by 1947 had released enough radioactivity into the atmosphere to affect the genes of future generations, the novel offered a scenario of the next 150 years, in which mankind established an elaborate underground civilization and retreated from the Earth's surface. Although marred by polemical stretches and badly dated now, the story nevertheless has some effective scenes and an overall crude energy. A sequel,

"Starship from Sirus," added human colonies on Mars and Venus and an insect-dominated Earth in the far future, and was quite different in tone from its predecessor.

Four memorable Phillips stories appeared in 1949. "M'Bong-Ah" was a novelette telling of the colonization of Venus and of the Earthman who became the natives' pawn in their resistance to the invasion. "Matrix" and "Beyond the Matrix of Time" together form a complex story of time paradox and alternate realities. *The Involuntary Immortals* is the story of a group of "accidental" immortals who band together to discover the source of their immortality and to protect themselves against the vengefulness of their own jealous relatives.

Starting in 1950 Rog Phillips's stories had begun to appear in a wider variety of magazines. "Rat in the Skull" is a memorable story of an experiment in rodent intelligence; "Ground Leave Incident" is a hard-boiled episode on a frontier planet; "Services, Inc." is an offbeat deal-with-the-Devil story. By far the most successful story Phillips ever wrote is "The Yellow Pill," a brief tale of multiple subjective realities.

—R.E. Briney

PIERCY, Marge

Nationality: American. **Born:** Detroit, Michigan, 31 March 1936. **Education:** University of Michigan, Ann Arbor (Hopwood award, 1956, 1957), A.B. 1957; Northwestern University, Evanston, Illinois, M.A. 1958. **Family:** Married Ira Wood (third marriage) in 1982. **Career:** Instructor, Indiana University, Gary, 1960-62; poet-in-residence, University of Kansas, Lawrence, 1971; Visiting Lecturer, Thomas Jefferson College, Grand Valley State Colleges, Allendale, Michigan, 1975; visiting faculty, Women's Writers' Conference, Cazenovia College, New York, 1976, 1978, 1980; staff member, Fine Arts Work Center, Provincetown, Massachusetts, 1976-77; writer-in-residence, College of the Holy Cross, Worcester, Massachusetts, 1976; Butler Professor of Letters, State University of New York, Buffalo, 1977; Elliston Professor of poetry, University of Cincinnati, 1986. Member of the board of directors, 1982-85 and of the advisory board since 1985, Coordinating Council of Literary Magazines. Recipient: Borestone Mountain award, 1968, 1974; National Endowment for the Arts grant, 1978; Rhode Island School of Design Faculty Association Medal, 1985; Carolyn Kizer prize, 1986, 1990; Sheaffer Eaton-P.E.N. New England award, 1989; Golden Rose prize, New England Poetry Club, 1990. **Agent:** Lois Wallace, Wallace Literary Agency, 177 East 70th Street, New York, New York 10021. **Address:** Box 1473, Wellfleet, Massachusetts 02667, U.S.A.

SCIENCE FICTION PUBLICATIONS

Novels

Dance the Eagle to Sleep. Garden City, New York, Doubleday, 1970; London, W.H. Allen, 1971.
Woman on the Edge of Time. New York, Knopf, 1976; London, Women's Press, 1979.
He, She, and It: A Novel. New York, Knopf, 1991; as *Body of Glass,* London, Joseph, 1992.

OTHER PUBLICATIONS

Novels

Going Down Fast. New York, Simon and Schuster, 1969.
Small Changes. Garden City, New York, Doubleday, 1973; London, Penguin, 1987.
The High Cost of Living. New York, Harper, 1978; London, Women's Press, 1979.
Vida. New York, Summit, and London, Women's Press, 1980.
Braided Lives. New York, Summit, and London, Allen Lane, 1982.
Fly Away Home. New York, Summit, and London, Chatto and Windus, 1984.
Gone to Soldiers. New York, Summit, and London, Joseph, 1987.
Summer People. New York, Summit, and London, Joseph, 1989.
The Longings of Women: A Novel. New York, Fawcett Columbine, 1994; Harmondsworth, Middlesex, Penguin, 1995.

Play

The Last White Class: A Play about Neighborhood Terror, with Ira Wood (produced Northampton, Massachusetts, 1978). Trumansburg, New York, Crossing Press, 1980.

Poetry

Breaking Camp. Middletown, Connecticut, Wesleyan University Press, 1968.
Hard Loving. Middletown, Connecticut, Wesleyan University Press, 1969.
A Work of Artifice. Detroit, Red Hanrahan Press, 1970.
4-Telling, with others. Trumansburg, New York, Crossing Press, 1971.
When the Drought Broke. Santa Barbara, California, Unicorn Press, 1971.
To Be of Use. Garden City, New York, Doubleday, 1973.
Living in the Open. New York, Knopf, 1976.
The Twelve-Spoked Wheel Flashing. New York, Knopf, 1978.
The Moon Is Always Female. New York, Knopf, 1980.
Circles on the Water: Selected Poems. New York, Knopf, 1982.
Stone, Paper, Knife. New York, Knopf, and London, Pandora Press, 1983.
My Mother's Body. New York, Knopf, and London, Pandora Press, 1985.
Available Light. New York, Knopf, and London, Pandora Press, 1988.
The Earth Shines Secretly: A Book of Days, with paintings and Drawings by Nell Blaine. Cambridge, Massachusetts, Zoland Press, 1990.
Mars and Her Children: Poems. New York, Knopf, 1992.

Other

The Grand Coolie Damn. Boston, New England Free Press, 1970.
Parti-Colored Blocks for a Quilt. Ann Arbor, University of Michigan Press, 1982.

Editor, *Early Ripening: Young Women's Poetry Now.* London and New York, Pandora Press, 1987.

*

Bibliography: In *Contemporary American Women Writers: Narrative Strategies* edited by Catherine Rainwater and William J. Scheick, Lexington, University Press of Kentucky, 1985.

Manuscript Collection: University of Michigan, Harlan Hatcher Graduate Library, Ann Arbor.

Critical Studies: "Marge Piercy: A Collage" by Nancy Scholar Zee, in *Oyez Review* (Berkeley, California), 9(1), 1975; *Ways of Knowing: Critical Essays on Marge Piercy* edited by Sue Walker and Eugenie Hamner, Mobile, Alabama, Negative Capability Press, 1986.

* * *

Marge Piercy is a prolific author, with several dozen books, fiction, poetry, and nonfiction, to her credit, but of these only three can be claimed for science fiction. *Dance the Eagle to Sleep* is only peripherally within the genre, a vivid though unsatisfying picture of an attempt by young people to break away from society and set up a tribal-based, loving and supportive community. It does point forward to her more successful contributions to science fiction, *Woman on the Edge of Time*, a vision of future utopia, and *He, She and It*, a tale of the computer-enhanced future. In all three, the indictment of present society common throughout her work is a major theme.

In one sense *Woman on the Edge of Time* and *He, She and It* have had more attention than they deserve: science fiction, utopian, and, above all, feminist scholars have written about them extensively. On the other hand, *Woman on the Edge of Time* is the best written of the many feminist utopias that have appeared in recent years, and, unlike most utopian works, it is a novel with believable characters, an interesting plot, and potential for implementation. That it is also a careful, complete portrayal of the kind of society a reformer of the mid-seventies would envisage as an ideal future only adds to its importance, in the field of utopian literature at least. There are, of course, many elements that are common to science fiction: travel through time, alternative futures, advanced technology both physical and mental, new social and sexual groupings, and, most important of all, extrapolation of current knowledge to plausible and far-reaching conclusions. As is true with many, if not most, recent utopias written by women, there is major emphasis on the growing maturity of the community, on the right education of the children, on the loving, communal attitude of the citizens. The novel's literary achievement is significantly enhanced by the similar maturing of its heroine.

The heroine is Connie Ramos, Chicana, welfare-mother wrongly charged with abusing her daughter, patient against her will in a mental hospital, and victim of various experimental medical "treatments," including implantation of electrodes in her brain. Beginning as scattered dream impressions, then in a real presence at first frightening to Connie, Luciente—"from a village in Massachusetts—Mattapoisset. Only I live there in 2137"—gets through to her as the first contact from a future into which she is soon able to journey increasingly easily. The story of her horrible and inhuman experiences in the mental hospital alternates with these visits to the pleasant new society of the 22nd century where many new friends teach her about their world. But always she is pulled back to the ugly world of doctors, ever-present nurses and attendants, and Connie's true 20th-century friends, the ill-treated patients on whom they practice their cures and make their experiments.

In Mattapoisset—utopian despite Piercy's claim that it is not but rather "the result of a full feminist revolution"—an ecologically responsible, loving, nonsexist (male and female pronouns have been replaced by "per") community has learned that its own existence is threatened by the possible outcome of the experiments being conducted at Rockover State Hospital. The contact with Connie is part of their attempt—there are four others, all also in mental hospitals or prisons—to prevent these undesirable consequences. Connie, it is apparent to Mattapoisset, can be a major factor in the conflict between technology wrongly used and the opposition and rebellion of those who want the kind of society that Mattapoisset represents. Bringing her to the right action, to fighting back against the system that has mistreated her, is a matter of showing her the beautiful future they represent as opposed to the dystopian society of her own day or the alternative future described in chapter 15 that would come as a result of her failure to act. Although the people of Mattapoisset are peaceful, they fight when necessary to defend their community—as Connie discovers on one of her visits—and they remind Connie that sometimes, especially in her time, the violence-prone must be resisted, even when such resistance involves further violence. Connie does take drastic action, but she is clearly doomed to end her days at Rockover.

Perhaps, as has been suggested by several critics, Connie's visits to the future are all hallucinations: certainly she has been sufficiently drugged to make such a suggestion reasonable. Hallucination or not, the story deals with a tormented victim of the evil in society, an almost-innocent, betrayed by those closest to her, who cannot understand why things work out for her as they do. The contrast with the beautiful world that might be is clearly the work of a reformer who feels deeply the injustices of this world and believes just as deeply in the things of which she writes. But, no matter what the motivating force behind its production, this is an excellent novel, deserving of its warm critical reception. Whether Piercy ever writes another work that fits the science fiction mold, this one novel has earned her a permanent place in the utopian branch of the genre.

Like *Woman on the Edge of Time*, *He, She and It* is set in both utopian and dystopian societies, with almost equal attention to both. There are many well-known science fiction elements: Earth so polluted that human life can exist only in caves or under domes or "wraps," robots, androids, cyborgs, mechanically enhanced humans, virtual reality, multi-national corporation control of an elite class of society with consequent neglect of the vast majority of the population. Some of the most significant action takes place in the virtual reality of "the Net" and among crowded multitudes of the so-called "Glop."

The plot centers around Shira, who, losing custody of her son to her husband, leaves the Y-S, Yakamura-Stichen, enclave in which she has been living and returns to her home town, the libertarian-socialist Jewish city of Tikva. Shira's growing closeness with Yod the cyborg develops a major theme, the blurring of the boundaries between humankind and its technology, between humanity and Earth, so that the reader is forced to consider the question "What is it to be truly human?" Shira's relations with her grandmother Malkah, her early lover Gadi and his father Avram who has created Yod, her mother Riva, an information pirate, and her mother's companion Nili, an enhanced superwoman-assassin, and, most of all, with Yod advance both plot and philosophic concepts. There is an important interacting plot dealing with Joseph, the Golem of the seventeenth-century Jewish ghetto of Prague, whose story is told to Yod by Malkah as part of his socialization. Yod has been constructed to defend Tikva against the "multis" that control the enclaves in which the elite live. With help from Shira, Nili, and others he is successful and even assists Shira in recovering her son. In the end his request to be accepted as a citizen of Tikva is denied, and he—it?—destroys himself and Avram.

Like the rest of Piercy's work this novel is strongly feminist and has drawn the interest of leading feminist critics. Most of these have accepted the idea of cyborg in the sense best defined by Donna Haraway: "we are all chimeras, theorized and fabricated hybrids of machine and organism; in short, we are cyborgs ('A Cyborg Manifesto . . . ') ." Such criticism, while often offering enlightening interpretations of the novel, tends to obscure the merit of the work as fiction as well as its often gender-neutral criticism of society. In this, as in much of Piercy's writing, what stands out most clearly is the careful, continuing consideration of how our basically patriarchal society can be changed to a society that will meet the needs of all human beings.

—Arthur O. Lewis

PINKWATER, Daniel Manus

Also writes as Manus Pinkwater. **Nationality:** American. **Born:** Memphis, Tennessee, 15 November 1941. **Education:** Bard College, Annandale-on-Hudson, New York, B.A. 1964. **Family:** Married Jill Schutz in 1969. **Career:** Art instructor, Children's Aid Society, 1967-69, Lower West Side Visual Arts Center, 1969, and Henry Street Settlement, 1969, all New York, and Bonnie Brae Farm for Boys, Millington, New Jersey, 1969; assistant project director, Inner City Summer Arts Program, Hoboken, New Jersey, 1970. Regular commentator, *All Things Considered,* National Public Radio. **Agent:** Susan Cohen, Writers House Inc., 21 West 26th Street, New York, New York 10010, U.S.A.

SCIENCE FICTION PUBLICATIONS

Novels for children (series: Magic Moscow; Moose; Snarkout Boys)

Wizard Crystal. New York, Dodd Mead, 1973.
Magic Camera. New York, Dodd Mead, 1974.
Blue Moose (as Manus Pinkwater). New York, Dodd Mead, 1975; London, Blackie, 1977.
Wingman (as Manus Pinkwater). New York, Dodd Mead, 1975.
Lizard Music (as D. Manus Pinkwater). New York, Dodd Mead, 1976.
Fat Men from Space. New York, Dodd Mead, 1976.
The Big Orange Splot. New York, Hastings House, 1977.
The Blue Thing. Englewood Cliffs, New Jersey, Prentice Hall, 1977.
Alan Mendelsohn: The Boy from Mars. New York, Dutton, 1979.
Pickle Creature. New York, Four Winds Press, 1979.
Return of the Moose. New York, Dodd Mead, 1979.
Yobgorble, Mystery Monster of Lake Ontario. Boston, Houghton Mifflin, 1979.
The Magic Moscow. New York, Four Winds Press, 1980.
Attila the Pun (Magic Moscow). New York, Four Winds Press, 1981.
Tooth-Gnasher Superflash. New York, Four Winds Press, 1981.

The Worms of Kukumlima. New York, Dutton, 1981.
Slaves of Spiegel (Magic Moscow). New York, Four Winds Press, 1982.
The Snarkout Boys and the Avocado of Death. New York, Lothrop, 1982.
I Was a Second Grade Werewolf. New York, Dutton, 1983; as *I Was a Class 2 Werewolf,* London, Macmillan, 1992.
Devil in the Drain. New York, Dutton, 1984.
The Snarkout Boys and the Baconburg Horror. New York, Lothrop, 1984.
The Frankenbagel Monster. New York, Dutton, 1986.
The Moosepire. Boston, Little Brown, 1986.
The Muffin Fiend. New York, Lothrop, 1986.
Guys from Space. New York, Macmillan, 1989.
Borgel. New York, Macmillan, 1990; as *The Time Tourist,* London, Lion, 1993.
Wempires. New York, Macmillan, 1991.
The Phantom of the Lunch Wagon. New York, Macmillan, 1992.
Spaceburger: A Kevin Spoon and Mason Mitz Story. New York, Macmillan, 1993.
Ned Feldman, Space Pirate. New York, Macmillan, 1994.
Mush, a Dog from Space. New York, Macmillan, 1995.

OTHER PUBLICATIONS

Fiction for children

The Hoboken Chicken Emergency. Englewood Cliffs, New Jersey, Prentice Hall, 1977.
The Last Guru. New York, Dodd Mead, 1978.
Java Jack, with Luqman Keele. New York, Crowell, 1980.
The Wuggie Norple Story, illustrated by Tomie de Paola. New York, Four Winds Press, 1980.
Roger's Umbrella, illustrated by James Marshall. New York, Dutton, 1982.
Young Adult Novel. New York, Crowell, 1982; as *Young Adults,* New York, Tor, 1985.
Ducks! Boston, Little Brown, 1984.
Aunt Lulu. New York, Macmillan, 1988.
Uncle Melvin. New York, Macmillan, 1989.
Doodle Flute. New York, Macmillan, 1991.
NORB, with Tony Author. Seattle, MU Press, 1991.
Author's Day. New York, Macmillan, 1993.
Fiction for children; as Manus Pinkwater
The Terrible Roar. New York, Knopf, 1970.
Bear's Picture. New York, Holt Rinehart, 1972.
Fat Elliot and the Gorilla. New York, Four Winds Press, 1974.
Three Big Hogs. New York, Seabury Press, 1975.
Around Fred's Bed, illustrated by Robert Mertens. Englewood Cliffs, New Jersey, Prentice Hall, 1976.

Novel (for adults)

The Afterlife Diet. New York, Random House, 1995.

Other

Superpuppy: How to Choose, Raise, and Train the Best Possible Dog for You, with Jill Pinkwater. New York, Seabury Press, 1977.

Fish Whistle: Commentaries, Uncommentaries, and Vulgar Excesses. Reading, Massachusetts, Addison-Wesley, 1989.
Chicago Days/Hoboken Nights. Reading, Massachusetts, Addison-Wesley, 1991.

*   *   *

One of the few genuine heirs of dada and surrealism in contemporary fantastic literature, Daniel Manus Pinkwater is also unusual in that he has attained a considerable reputation among adult readers even though virtually all of his fiction has been published for children and young adults. Writers as diverse as Samuel R. Delany, Harlan Ellison, and Vonda McIntyre have counted themselves among his fans, and it seems reasonable to suspect that Pinkwater's adult constituency may be nearly as large as that of his younger readership. Pinkwater tacitly acknowledges this by sprinkling his work liberally with arcane literary and cultural allusions likely to be lost on younger readers—such as a version of the Shadow named "Lamont Penumbra" in *Attila the Pun,* or references to dadaism and pataphysics in *Young Adult Novel.*

Pinkwater's world is a bizarre and endlessly inventive place where licensed realtors are controlled by aliens, where aliens all wear identical plaid sport coats and lust after junk food, where time-traveling moose detectives haunt the Canadian wilderness, where W.A. Mozart is a comic-book superhero, where planets bear names like Ziegler and Spiegel and cities names like Lenny, and where outer space is dotted with root beer stands. On a more serious level, it is a world in which outsiders can be heroes—overweight kids with thick glasses, mental patients, eccentric uncles, and—most often—kids whose interests and hobbies set them apart from their peers. For example, *Alan Mendelsohn: The Boy from Mars* draws a sensitive portrait of what it is like to be an outcast in school—and what it might be like to get revenge.

These themes are apparent in Pinkwater's most widely known novel, *Lizard Music.* Victor, who is considered "a freak" at school because he is a fan of Walter Cronkite rather than of rock stars, finds himself alone in the house during his parents' vacation. Staying up late, he catches a TV program of lizards playing music. Lizards begin to appear to him everywhere, and he wonders if he is hallucinating until a mysterious figure called the Chicken Man (who always introduces himself with the name of a different Northern Renaissance painter—Grunewald, Van Eyck, Cranach, etc.) reveals that a society of lizards is indeed living on an invisible island in the lake next to Hogboro (Pinkwater's name for Chicago, apparently) and is broadcasting TV programs. The Chicken Man takes Victor to the island, where he witnesses the wonders of the lizard society in a kind of crazed parody of Renaissance utopias. Earlier, Victor had watched a film called *The Invasion of the Pod People* on television and had begun to worry that people might actually be replaced by emotionless replicas from outer space; now he learns that "lizards and pods are natural enemies," and the lizards come to represent individuality and freedom of thought.

Conformity seems to be one of Pinkwater's main targets. Another film Victor sees on television describes an invasion of aliens in plaid sport coats who strip the Earth of its junk food. This is the plot of Pinkwater's own *Fat Men from Space,* and one of many cross-allusions to other Pinkwater books. The fat men, it turns out, are from the planet Spiegel, ruled over by the evil Sargon, who wants to steal all the junk food in the universe. In *Slaves of Spiegel* (itself the third book in the "Magic Moscow" trilogy), a Hoboken ice-cream parlor, its owner, and his assistant are kidnapped whole to participate in an intergalactic junk-food cook-off.

Pinkwater's most successful series characters appear in *The Snarkout Boys and the Avocado of Death* and *The Snarkout Boys and the Baconburg Horror.* Walter Galt and Winston Bongo, both outsiders at Genghis Khan High School, make a habit of sneaking out to late movies at the Snark Theatre after their parents are asleep. This leads them into a series of adventures involving a girl named Rat, the Chicken Man (from *Lizard Music*), the great detective Osgood Sigerson (a version of Sherlock Holmes), and his arch-enemy Wallace Nussbaum (a version of Moriarty). In the first of these adventures, Rat's uncle, a brilliant avocado scientist, disappears—kidnapped by Nussbaum to prevent his completing work on a giant telepathic avocado computer which can release the minds of real estate agents from alien control. In the second novel, a werewolf seems to be terrorizing the town of Baconburg.

Even Pinkwater's picture books for younger readers offer surrealistic twists on conventional fantasy images. *The Moosepire* (the third book in a trilogy that began with *Blue Moose* and *Return of the Moose*) offers what appears to be a moose vampire, but becomes a time travel story. *I Was a Second Grade Werewolf* concerns a boy who thinks he has turned into a werewolf, but can't get anyone to notice. *Guys from Space* are friendly aliens who invite a young boy to join them in visiting different planets, "just looking around," and stopping off for a root beer on the way home. *The Frankenbagel Monster* recasts Frankenstein as a mad bagel maker whose giant "Bagelunculus" threatens to destroy earth—until it goes stale. The devil himself appears as a tiny but grouchy inhabitant of a kitchen sink drain in *Devil in the Drain.*

In recent years, Pinkwater has been a popular commentator on public radio, and his commentaries (collected as *Fish Whistle*) may offer some clues to autobiographical elements in his writing. The title character of *Borgel,* for example, is a mysterious older relative of indeterminate nationality whose nostalgia for the "Old Country" and questionable "gift" for languages recalls Pinkwater's accounts of his father and uncles. But Borgel also turns out to be an intergalactic adventurer who takes his young nephew on a wild quest in space and time for "the great Popsicle." As with other Pinkwater books, the juxtaposition of sharply observed, recognizable characters with an epic sense of silliness worthy of the Marx Brothers seems to suggest that eccentricity alone can be a key to salvation.

Given the ubiquitous references to food and eating in nearly all his books, it hardly came as a surprise when Pinkwater's first adult novel, *The Afterlife Diet* (1995), should turn out to be a paean to food and to fat people (whom Pinkwater calls the "circumferentially challenged"). Opening in a heaven exclusively populated by the overweight and resembling a tacky Catskills resort—where God appears onstage telling lame jokes—the novel traces the before-and-after death adventures of a heartless book editor named Milton Cramer and a failed writer named Milo Levi-Nathan. Nearly every aspect of the book concerns eating; even Levi-Nathan's psychotherapist operates out of a delicatessen and punctuates his sessions with orders for muffins and pastrami sandwiches. Structurally a bit chaotic, the novel consists largely of set-pieces, including lengthy excerpts from Levi-Nathan's attempts at science fiction and horror novels and a catalog of bizarre and always unsuccessful weight-loss programs ranging from abusive group sessions to a concentration camp in upstate New York run by an ex-Nazi doctor. With its huge cast of characters, its broad range of satirical targets, and its resolutely politically incorrect tone, the novel is perhaps best taken in small doses, but it does reveal that Pinkwater's inventiveness is no less manic when directed to older readers.

—Gary K. Wolfe

PIPER, H(enry) Beam

Nationality: American. **Born:** Altoona, Pennsylvania, in 1904. **Career:** Worked on the engineering staff of the Pennsylvania Railroad. **Died:** 11 November 1964.

SCIENCE FICTION PUBLICATIONS

Novels (series: Fuzzies; Paratime Police; Terran Federation)

Crisis in 2140, with John J. McGuire. New York, Ace, 1957.
A Planet for Texans, with John J. McGuire. New York, Ace, 1958.
Four-Day Planet (for children; Federation). New York, Putnam, 1961.
Little Fuzzy (Federation; Fuzzies). New York, Avon, 1962; adapted for children by Benson Parker as *The Adventures of Little Fuzzy,* New York, Platt and Munk, 1983.
Junkyard Planet (Federation). New York, Putnam, 1963; as *The Cosmic Computer,* New York, Ace, 1964.
Space Viking (Federation). New York, Ace, 1963; London, Sphere, 1978.
The Other Human Race (Federation; Fuzzy). New York, Avon, 1964; as *Fuzzy Sapiens,* New York, Ace, 1976.
Lord Kalvan of Otherwhen (Paratime). New York, Ace, 1965; as *Gunpowder God,* London, Sphere, 1978.
The Fuzzy Papers (includes *Little Fuzzy* and *The Other Human Race*). Garden City, New York, Doubleday, 1977.
Four-Day Planet; Lone Star Planet, with John J. McGuire. New York, Ace, 1979.
First Cycle: A Novel, with Michael Kurland. New York, Ace, 1982.
Uller Uprising. New York, Ace, 1983.
Fuzzies and Other People. New York, Ace, 1984.

Short Stories

Federation. New York, Ace, 1981.
Empire. New York, Ace, 1981.
Paratime. New York, Ace, 1981.
The Worlds of H. Beam Piper, edited by John F. Carr. New York, Ace, 1983.

OTHER PUBLICATIONS

Novel

Murder in the Gun Room. New York, Knopf, 1953.

Other

Editor, *A Catalogue of Early Pennsylvania and Other Firearms and Edged Weapons at "Restless Oaks," McElhattan, Pennsylvania.* Altoona, Pennsylvania, Times Tribune Co., 1927.

*   *   *

H. Beam Piper's science fiction is largely the stories of heroes (or heroines), with ideas apparently subordinate to the needs of plot and action. This is most evident in novels such as *A Planet for Texans, Four-Day Planet, Space Viking,* and *Lord Kalvan of Otherwhen.* The last two of these, especially, are fast-paced adventure yarns, with a well-developed central figure, but quite two-dimensional supporting characters. In each case, the hero (Calvin Morrison in *Lord Kalvan of Otherwhen,* Lucas Trask in *Space Viking*) is forced by circumstances totally beyond his control to enter a life radically different from the one that he had anticipated. A major difficulty each man must resolve is the ethical dilemma of the life which he perceives as central to his functioning. Thus, Morrison is caught in the field of an interdimension/time travel machine, while Trask on his wedding day has his bride-to-be killed by her rejected suitor. Morrison must agonize over the appropriateness of introducing more sophisticated weaponry into an essentially static culture, Trask over the ethics of killing and looting even though the attached planets are decadent remnants of the "Old Federation." The ultimate results of the activities of each man are intrinsically the same as well: Morrison defeats Styphon's House (which opposed progress and sought to divide countries against one another) while Trask defeats the destructive forces both on Marduk and among the space vikings, establishing Tanith as a progressive planet destined to lead a new League of Civilized Worlds.

Perhaps Piper's most famous works are *Little Fuzzy* and *The Other Human Race. Little Fuzzy* builds towards a dramatic courtroom scene in which good and evil clearly clash over the question of the sapience of the Fuzzies. Again there is a central heroic figure, Jack Holloway, discoverer of the Fuzzies. The ethical dilemma to be resolved is whether to recognize the Fuzzies as sentient, giving them prima facie right to their own planet and thereby displacing the human interests on the planet Zarathustra, or to allow them to be treated as charming and quick-to-learn animals, subjecting them to what is—for a sentient being—slavery. Holloway's determination and courage in the face of the bureaucratic opposition to the recognition of the Fuzzies as sentient has elements of the heroic physical challenges confronting Morrison and Trask, but it is primarily a moral courage in the face of social opposition. In *The Other Human Race* the same basic problem is repeated except that the ethical dilemma is whether or not to honor the governmental commitment to the Fuzzy Reservation in the face of economic pressures to open the Reservation for mining. There is the added problem of the radical increase in defective births among the Fuzzies. The apparently neutral position of doing nothing about Fuzzy rights is extensionally the same as the decision to exterminate the Fuzzy race, for the humans have it within their power to halt the flood of defective Fuzzy births. Again, in both books, the resolution of the ethical dilemma leaves the world rather significantly altered in the direction of progress-as-we-know-it.

A sidelight which may be of significant interest has to do with the name of the Fuzzies' planet—Zarathustra, the name of the central figure in the pre-Christian middle-Eastern religion Zoroastrianism (Zoroaster was also known as Zarathustra), similar to the Christian Manichean heresy, which argues the existence of two coequal forces in the universe, Ahura Mazda (good) and Angra Mainyu (evil). Perhaps Piper was consciously trying to depict such a struggle in the Fuzzies novels. The planet's name might also have been an allusion to Friedrich Nietzsche's *Also Sprach Zarathustra.* This interpretation offers a potentially convoluted approach to the text because Nietzsche argued for the recognition of man and superman.

Since the superman is exempt from the constraints of normal ethics, one might have expected a different conclusion.

Piper's other writings more or less follow the same pattern: the hero/heroine is struck by a major ethical problem—paternalism over proud people in *A Planet for Texans;* revolution or economic slavery in *Four-Day Planet;* human dependency upon its own machines in *Junkyard Planet;* the dominance of scholarship by economics in "Omnilingual." In each case the protagonist chooses honor and decency, but also, more significantly, the choice is made for progress. Those forces which support the status quo are doomed from the outset. In a Piper story one "knows" that the hero/heroine will prevail, but only after terrible difficulties. More impressive, however, is Piper's recognition that such successes must result in a significant alteration of the world on which they occur.

—Richard W. Miller

PISERCHIA, Doris (Elaine)

Pseudonym: Curt Selby. **Nationality:** American. **Born:** Fairmont, West Virginia, 11 October 1928. **Education:** Fairmont State College, A.B. 1950; University of Utah, Salt Lake City, 1963-65. **Military Service:** Served in the United States Navy, 1950-54: Lieutenant. **Family:** Married Joseph John Piserchia in 1953; three daughters and two sons. **Agent:** Carnell Literary Agency, Danes Croft, Goose Lane, Little Hallingbury, Hertfordshire CM22 7RG, England. **Address:** c/o DAW Books, 375 Hudson Street, New York, New York 10014, U.S.A.

SCIENCE FICTION PUBLICATIONS

Novels

Mister Justice. New York, Ace, 1973; London, Dobson, 1977.
Star Rider. New York, Bantam, 1974; London, Women's Press, 1987.
A Billion Days of Earth. New York, Bantam, 1976; London, Dobson, 1977.
Earthchild. New York, DAW, 1977; London, Dobson, 1979.
Spaceling. Garden City, New York, Doubleday, 1978.
The Spinner. Garden City, New York, Doubleday, 1980.
The Fluger. New York, DAW, 1980.
Earth in Twilight. New York, DAW, 1981.
Doomtime. New York, DAW, 1981.
Blood County (as Curt Selby). New York, DAW, 1981.
I, Zombie (as Curt Selby). New York, DAW, 1982.
The Dimensioneers. New York, DAW, 1982.
The Deadly Sky. New York, DAW, 1983.

*   *   *

Doris Piserchia's strongest asset in her novels has been the exotic and colorful settings she has created. *Star Rider,* for example, features a young girl who has a telepathic bond with a horse. The two of them can teleport themselves around the universe, encased by small pockets of environment. They are looking for a fabled world which turns out to be a ruined, deserted Earth tucked into another dimension. Her quest is complicated by a number of other parties involved not only in her quest, but interested as well in her mutant ability to transport herself across intergalactic as well as interstellar distances.

In *A Billion Days of Earth,* men have assumed godlike powers and many of the lower species of animal have acquired intelligence. A vigilante metes out his own brand of justice in *Mister Justice.* But the novels that followed these spent less time on characterization and more on setting and plot, with mixed results. *Earth Child* for instance is almost one constant chase-adventure-battle scene. Earth is being contested by Indigo, a plant that is becoming an ocean, and Emeroo, another plant that is much smaller in size but possibly more powerful in the long run. The last living human is a young girl named Ree, who spends much of her time flying giant insects and fighting the blueboys, plant growths that can move independently and who become increasingly human as the story progresses.

The plot of this novel shows up again in *Doomtime,* this time with gigantic trees battling for control of Earth, with the human race as pawns in their games. It shows up again in *Earth in Twilight,* except in this case the protagonist is a lone space explorer who returns to abandoned Earth to find it overgrown by a gigantic forest inhabited by newly sentient races and giant insects. The astronaut is a classic antihero, unable and perhaps unwilling to make any serious attempt to improve his situation, and the forest of Earth is itself really the strongest character in the novel.

Alien monsters figure even more centrally in two other novels, *The Fluger* and *The Spinner.* The first is rather minor: a gigantic alien wreaks havoc in a closed Earth city until eventually brought to its death by booby-trapped food. The second novel is considerably more interesting. An alien from another dimension spins a mysterious web over an entire city and begins to reproduce his kind in preparation for conquering the entire world.

Inter-dimensional adventures are another staple in Piserchia's novels. In *The Spaceling,* mutants can perceive different dimensions because of drifting rings that allow movement from one plane of existence to another. A young man is drafted into the effort to prevent an interdimensional invasion in *The Deadly Sky.* An extra-dimensional chase is the main plot of *The Dimensioneers,* which transports us from one weird environment to another so quickly that it is almost a comic book adventure without pictures.

Piserchia made more serious efforts at characterization in two novels published under the name "Curt Selby." *Blood County* is a supernatural adventure story involving a vampire who has set himself up as a virtual feudal lord. *I, Zombie,* despite the title, is straight science fiction. The recent dead are fitted with implants that allow them to be used as slave laborers with no will of their own, until one such body begins to reawaken its former personality and sets out to free others from their bondage.

—Don D'Ammassa

PLATT, Charles

Pseudonyms: Robert Clarke; Blakely St. James. **Nationality:** British. **Born:** London in 1945. **Education:** Cambridge University, one year, and London College of Printing, two years. **Career:** Worked for Clive Bingley, publishers, London, 1967; designer and production assistant, *New Worlds* magazine; freelance photographer and book jacket designer. Science fiction editor, Avon Books, 1972-74; Condor Publishing, 1977-78; Franklin Watts, 1986-88. **Awards:** *Locus* award, for nonfiction, 1985. **Address:** c/o Bantam, 666 Fifth Avenue, New York, New York 10103, U.S.A.

SCIENCE FICTION PUBLICATIONS

Novels (series: Piers Anthony's World of Chthon)

Garbage World. New York, Berkley, 1967; London, Panther, 1968.

The City Dwellers: Science Fiction. London, Sidgwick and Jackson, 1970; revised edition, as *Twilight of the City, A Novel of the Near Future,* New York, Macmillan, 1977.

The Gas. New York, Ophelia Press, 1970.

Planet of the Voles: A Science Fiction Novel. New York, Putnam, 1977.

Sweet Evil. New York, Berkley, 1977.

Less Than Human (as Robert Clarke). New York, Avon, 1986; as Charles Platt, London, Grafton, 1987.

Christina Enchanted (as Blakely St. James). New York, Playboy Press, 1980.

Plasm (World of Chthon). New York, Signet, 1987; London, Grafton, 1988.

Free Zone: Volume One of the Epic Unology* (*Unology, a Literary Work Consisting of One Volume). New York, Avon, 1989.

Soma (World of Chthon). New York, Signet, 1989; London, Grafton, 1990.

The Silicon Man. New York, Bantam, 1991.

OTHER PUBLICATIONS

Poetry

Highway Sandwiches, with Thomas M. Disch and Marilyn Hacker. Privately printed, 1970.

Other

Dream Makers: The Uncommon People Who Write Science Fiction: Interviews. New York, Berkley, 1980; as *Who Writes Science Fiction?,* Manchester, England, Savoy, 1980.

Dream Makers, Volume II: The Uncommon Men & Women Who Write Science Fiction. New York, Berkley, 1983.

Dream Makers: Science Fiction and Fantasy Writers at Work: Profiles. London, Xanada, and New York, Ungar, 1986 [includes revised and updated profiles selected from the previous volumes].

Graphics Guide to Commodore 64. Berkeley, California, Sybex, 1984.

Micromania: The Whole Truth about Home Computers, with David Langford. London, Gollancz, 1984; as *The Whole Truth Home Computer Handbook,* New York, Avon, 1984.

BASIC without Math. New York, Warner, 1984.

More from your Micro. New York, Avon, 1985.

How to Be a Happy Cat, with cartoons by Gray Jolliffe. London, Gollancz, 1986; New York, Mainstreet, 1987.

When You Can Live Twice as Long, What Will You Do? New York, Morrow, 1989.

Editor, with Michael Moorcock, *New Worlds 6: A Science Fiction Quarterly.* London, Sphere, 1973; as *New Worlds #5,* New York, Avon, 1974.

Editor, with Hilary Bailey, *New Worlds 7.* London, Sphere, 1974; as *New Worlds #6,* New York, Avon, 1975.

*   *   *

Charles Platt has had a long and diverse career in the field of science fiction, where he has applied his considerable talents as an author of a wide variety of novels, both serious and satirical, as an editor in both the magazine and book publishing fields, as a highly accomplished interviewer of other authors, and as one of the most influential and controversial writers of commentary and criticism.

Platt's first science fiction story, "One of Those Days," was published in 1964 in the British magazine *Science Fantasy,* but he first attracted notice with his association with Michael Moorcock and *New Worlds* at a time when that magazine was the preeminent journal in the British "New Wave" movement. New Wave science fiction at the time was characterized by experimental literary techniques, a tone of nihilistic pessimism, and ineffectual, nonheroic protagonists who must cope with events beyond their understanding or control. Platt worked with Moorcock on *New Worlds* for several years, and became one of the more influential forces behind New Wave SF, before becoming the magazine's editor when Moorcock left in 1970.

At the same time, Platt was continuing to write science fiction himself, all of it strongly influenced by New Wave concepts and techniques, especially those of such authors as J.G. Ballard and Moorcock himself. His first novel, *Garbage World,* was a highly inventive works, cleverly written but marred by its reliance on scatological humor. The novel is set among the degenerate society living on an asteroid that is used as the garbage receptacle for the Solar System. Platt later characterized the subtext of this book as a satire on the anal-retentive nature of fans and collectors in the science fiction field.

The Planet of the Voles was a more conventional, although humorous, space opera, still written with New Wave sensibilities. The most ambitious of Platt's early novels was *The City Dwellers,* a novel formed from short works that was later heavily revised, expanded, and retitled *Twilight of the City.* These novels, set in a dying near-future city, were serious novels in the New Wave tradition. *Twilight of the City* was Platt's first novel written with truly serious intent, although it never got the critical notice it deserved.

In 1970, Platt moved from London to New York and has lived in the United States ever since. He held jobs as science fiction editor with Avon Books (1972-74) and Condor Publishing (1977-78), both paperback book publishers, where he learned the New York publishing scene. He resigned from Avon when they refused to buy Philip K. Dick's *Flow My Tears, the Policeman Said* because they disliked the title. He later returned to editing with Franklin Watts from 1986-88, where he was able to provide fine hardcover editions for authors such as Brian Aldiss, Victor Koman, Ronald Anthony Cross, John Shirley, and Rachel Pollack.

In the late 1970s, Platt turned to interviewing science fiction authors during his travels around the U.S., and he developed a style of uniquely personal, yet highly opinionated interview/ profiles that brought him his first real critical notice. These resulted in two volumes of interviews called *Dream Makers,* both of which were nominated for Hugo awards for nonfiction, as well as a 1987 combined volume with some new material. Some of the interviews in the first volume stirred up quite a bit of controversy inside the field; Platt approached his subjects for the second volume a bit more even-handedly.

He also began in the 1980s to write commentary on science fiction. He began his own self-published magazine, *The Patchin Review,* in 1980, which became well-known among insiders in the field for its caustic, controversial, and irreverent commentary, much of it written by Platt himself, and some of it under various pseudonyms. At first, Platt's criticisms and witticisms were viewed as mere continuance of the merry-prankster image he had developed within SF fandom in the 1970s. However, as time wore on, Platt took his role as SF critic more seriously, and by the early-to-mid-1980s he was regularly having published serious essays in most of the U.S. science fiction professional magazines, in *Interzone,* and also in many of the most respected semi-professional critical journals, including *THRUST, Fantasy Review, Locus, Science Fiction Chronicle,* and *Science Fiction Eye.* By the end of the decade, Platt had become one of the field's most respected, albeit often controversial, critics.

Platt returned to writing novels in the late 1980s. Two of these were "share-cropper" novels set in Piers Anthony's world of Chthon, *Plasm* and *SOMA.* These books bear some resemblance to Platt's fiction of the 1970s in terms of tone and subject matter (in the first novel, for instance, the protagonist's mother has been genetically engineered to obtain sexual pleasure from beatings and cruelty). They are quite competently plotted, however, and represent Platt cracking his knuckles and getting ready to write fiction once again. Two of the other books were very successful science fiction satires. The first was *Less Than Human,* published in the U.S. only under Platt's Robert Clarke pseudonym, a genuinely amusing book about an intelligent but innocent android in a degenerate New York in the year 2010. The other, *Free Zone,* is a tour de force satire, a near-future SF pastiche that makes fun of every SF cliché and convention ever conceived.

With Platt's latest novel, he has finally reached his full potential as a serious science fiction author. *The Silicon Man* takes advantage of Platt's extensive knowledge of microcomputer technology (he wrote several non-fiction books on computers and artificial intelligence in 1984 and 1985) to present possibly the most realistic portrayal to date of the concept of downloading a human consciousness into a computer-generated interactive environment. Written as a fast-paced thriller, the story involves an FBI agent who traces the source of a high-tech black market hand weapon back to a small team of scientists who are working for a defense contractor on a project that has apparently been kept heavily funded for decades despite no apparent success. The scientists turn out to be part of a secret conspiracy to gain immortality through computer translation, a procedure that involves destruction of the brain itself. To protect their scheme, the agent himself is translated, and it turns out that the mastermind behind the project has more extensive and ulterior motives than anyone knew. With this novel, Platt joined the slim ranks of SF authors (which include Vernor Vinge and Greg Bear) who understand computers well and can create realistic characters.

One would expect Platt to continue to apply his considerable talents to more SF novels, but he has seldom been predictable. He produced one prehistoric novel in collaboration with William Brame, *Children of the Ice* (1993), published under his Charlotte Prentiss pseudonym, but his interests in recent years have turned to computers, and to cryonics and subjects related to life extension and immortality. He served as the head of public relations for a cryonics organization called the Alcor Foundation from 1992 to 1993, and

is currently vice president of the CryoCare Foundation. He also serves as a special consultant to Mindvox, a computer bulletin board system in New York City.

Charles Platt has had a career in science fiction as a self-described "jack of all trades," as an author, editor, interviewer, and critic. He has made highly valuable contributions to the field in each of these areas. His fiction output has included insightful satires on the genre as well as highly mature serious works. He has sufficient potential as an author of fiction, judging especially from his latest novel, to make further contributions to the field. As an editor, he helped shape the British New Wave movement at *New Worlds,* and brought valuable books into print at both Avon and Franklin Watt. His most valuable contribution to the field to date, however, is as a writer of nonfiction. His insightful interviews with and profiles of most of the top authors in science fiction, and his iconoclastic commentary on the literature and trends in the field, most believe have played an essential role in improving the field, and an inarguable role in making the field of SF a more interesting place.

—D. Douglas Fratz

POE, Edgar Allan

Nationality: American. **Born:** Boston, Massachusetts, 19 January 1809. **Education:** Attended private schools, 1815-20; University of Virginia, 1826, dismissed, 1826; West Point, 1829-30, dismissed, 1830. **Military Service:** United States Army (enlisted under assumed name and age), 1827-29; sergeant-major. **Family:** Married Virginia Clemrn (died 1847). **Career:** editor, *Southern Literary Messenger,* Richmond, Virginia, 1835-37; assistant editor, *Burton's Gentleman's Magazine,* 1839-40; founded *The Penn,* 1840; editor, *Graham's Magazine,* 1842-43; purchased *Broadway Journal,* 1845; cancelled lecture tour due to nervous breakdown, 1849. **Died:** 7 October 1849.

SCIENCE FICTION PUBLICATIONS

Novels

The Narrative of Arthur Gordon Pym of Nantucket: Comprising the Details of a Mutiny and Atrocious Butchery on Board the American Brig Grampus, on Her Way to the South Seas in the Month of June, 1827, with an Account of the Recapture of the Vessel by the Survivors, Their Shipwreck and Subsequent Horrible Sufferings from Famine, Their Deliverance by Means of the British Schooner Jane Guy, the Brief Cruise of This Latter Vessel in the Antarctic Ocean; Her Capture, and the Massacre of Her Crew among a Group of Islands in the Eighty-Fourth Parallel of Southern Latitude, Together with the Incredible Adventures and Discoveries Still Further South to Which That Distressing Calamity Gave Rise. New York, Harper, 1838; as *Arthur Gordon Pym; or, Shipwreck, Mutiny, and Famine: Being the Extraordinary Adventures of Arthur Gordon Pym, Mariner, of Nantucket, North America, During a Voyage to the South Seas, and His Various Discoveries in the Eighty-Fourth Parallel of Southern Latitude,* London, Cunningham, 1841; as *The Wonderful Adventures of Arthur Gordon Pym,* London, Kent, 1861.

Short Stories

(Bibliographer's note: Although several hundred different collections of Poe's poetry and prose have been published, all are variations of the earliest volumes published during his lifetime. All of these works are collected into the 1938 omnibus listed below.)

Tales of the Grotesque and Arabesque. Philadelphia, Pennsylvania, Lea and Blanchard, 1840, 2 volumes.
The Tales. New York, Wiley and Putnam, 1845.
The Complete Tales and Poems of Edgar Allan Poe. New York, Modern Library, 1938.
The Science Fiction of Edgar Allan Poe, edited by Harold Beaver. Harmondsworth, Middlesex, Penguin, 1976.
The Short Fiction of Edgar Allan Poe: An Annotated Edition, edited by Stuart Levine and Susan Levine. Indianapolis, Indiana, Bobbs-Merrill, 1976.

*   *   *

A major Romantic writer-critic-editor of the American Renaissance, Edgar Allan Poe experimented with a variety of the then-popular literary modes, and invented quite a few literary subgenres including science fiction as well as detective fiction. Thus, some scholar-critics aptly consider Poe's "The Unparalleled Adventure of One Hans Pfaal" (1835) dealing with man's moon-landing through balloon as the true archtype of generic science fiction as we know it in the 20th century, while most literary historians have long agreed that Mary Shelley's Frankenstein (1815), written almost two decades before "Hans Pfaal," is the first science fiction novel in the English-speaking countries. For, in contrast with Mrs. Shelley, who omitted detailed description of Dr. Frankenstein's creation of artificial intelligence, Poe made every effort to give his story the highest degree of verisimilitude, filling the text with a number of statistical data and mathematical calculations.

Of course, from our contemporary viewpoint, the very scientific presupposition of space travel by balloon is completely wrong. Moreover, it is well-known that in one of his earlier poems "Sonnet—To Science" (1829) Poe himself once rejected ordinary science, designating it "true daughter of Old Time . . . Who preyst upon the poet's hearts," "Vulture, whose wings are dull realities." Such a vision is not incompatible with the way the author labelled his later work *Eureka* (1848) not as a cosmogonical analysis but instead a "prose poem," in which he not merely predicts the advent of black hole theory in the next century but also calls the Universe a plot of God, the plots of God perfect. As Joan Dayan explains, in *Eureka* "Newton's dynamic of attraction and repulsion becomes that of economy and diffusion in words," restructuring "a decentered world of turnings and breakdowns" (*Fables of Mind,* New York: Oxford University Press, 1987). For Poe the intellectual aristocrat, even the discursive system of science seemed to be the effect of a poet serving as the God of the whole universe. Harold Beaver once stated that in Poe's hoax "with intuition as guide, Truth and Beauty—science and art—will fuse in a single poetic vision" (Introduction to *The Science Fiction of Edgar Allan Poe,* New York: Penguin, 1976). What matters here is not whether one's story about "science" is technologically plausible among professional scientists, but whether it is poetically appealing to the contemporary popular imagination. It is not that Poe applied the logic of science to the frontier of fiction, but that he reinterpreted science not as science in the exact sense but as a poetic fiction itself. Such a deconstructive

attitude towards science and fiction made perfect sense in the 1830s, a period of the rapid growth of industrialization and urbanization, when Jacksonian Democracy accentuated the cultural problems of Jeffersonian Republicanism, in which, despite the ideological war between the North and the South, the Southern aristocrats made every effort to compromise with Northern democrats, proposing to incorporate the fruits of Northern "scientific" industrialization into the Southern "poetic" cultural climate.

This is why the Southerner Poe's favorite sciences included otherwise outrageous discourses like "mesmerism" (animal magnetism), championed by Dr. Frantz Anton Mesmer (1734-1815); "alchemy," revived by the Gold Rush in 1849; "phrenology," theorized by Franz Joseph Gall (1758-1828) and well-marketted by the Orson and Lorenzo Fowlers in antebellum and postbellum America; and "hollow earth theory," promoted by Edmund Halley, Cotton Mather, and John Cleves Symmes. The latter wrote the novel *Symzonia: A Voyage of Discovery,* of which Poe was informed by his brother Henry in 1827. All of these discourses were believed to be the exact sciences in those days, and turned out to be pseudo-sciences later. But the spirit of them survived these two centuries and came to establish themselves in the field of popular science. Taking the advantage of his editorship of several magazines such as *Southern Literary Messenger, Graham's Magazine,* and *Broadway Journal,* Poe the magazinist was able to fully imbibe and exploit the most sensational "effects" of the the trendiest popular scienes, keenly aware that the antebellum American audience were gullible enough to confuse a piece of fiction with the testimony of fact. This is the way Poe can be greatly appreciated not only as the American father of science fiction, but also as the descendent of the great American scientist and hoaxer Benjamin Franklin. As the title of one of his essays (1843) implies, to Poe the act of "diddling" seemed one of the greatest exact sciences. In a sense, therefore, Poe, the Southern intellectual aristocrat, unwittingly became even the precursor of postmodern science fiction, since he had already succeeded in questioning the discursive boundary between science and fiction, radically rereading (pseudo-)science as a fiction and fiction (hoax) as a science.

Poe's science fiction can be classified into several subgenres: 1) *Hoaxes of Hollow Earth*: "MS. Found in a Bottle" (1833), *The Narrative of Arthur Gordon Pym of Nantucket* (1838); 2) *Tales of Mesmerism* (animal magnetism): "A Tale of the Ragged Mountains" (1844), "Mesmeric Revelation" (1844), "The Facts in the Case of Mr. Valdemar" (1845); 3) *Tales of Alchemy:* "Von Kempelen and His Discovery" (1849); 4) *"Back to the Future"-type-Satires:* "Melonta Tauta" (1849), "Some Words with a Mummy" (1845), "The Thousand and Second Tale of Scheherazade" (1845); 5) *Platonic Dialogues between Spirits in Heaven:* "The Conversation of Eiros and Charmion" (1839), "The Colloquay of Monos and Una" (1841), "The Power of Words" (1845); 6) *Hard-Science Fiction of Fantastic Voyage:* "The Unparalleled Adventure of One Hans Pfaal" (1835), "A Descent into the Maelstrom" (1841), "Balloon Hoax" (1844); 7) *Fables of Pre-Psychoanalysis:* "The System of Dr. Tar and Prof. Fether" (1845); 8) *Tales of Robots:* "Maelzel's Chess-Player" (1836); 9) *Tales of Cyborgs:* "The Man that Was Used Up" (1839); 10) *Cosmogonical Speculation: Eureka* (1848).

What is notable here is that every specific motif characterizing each subgenre induces us to reread Poe's other tales also as crypto-science fictions. For example, apocalyptic vision as described in "Tales of Platonic Dialogues" could be reinterpreted together with the gothic atmosphere of "The Masque of the Red Death" (1842) to rediscover this crypto-science fiction in both tales. Hard-scientific approach as we can find in "A Descent into the Maelstrom" is also employed in a separate subgenre as in the thriller-like "The Pit and the Pendulum" (1842). Southern racial prejudice imprinted within the author's pre-psychoanalytic approach ("Tar and Feathering" was a typical form of punishing renegade slaves and abolitionists) invites us to rethink "Murders in the Rue Morgue" (1841) as a pre-primatological speculation focusing on the existing analogy between blacks and ourang-outaung. What is more, his cyborgian, as well as cosmogonical images are reflected everywhere in the Tales of Landscape Garden like "The Domain of Arnheim" (1847), where Poe's ideal Southern womanhood gets resurrected in the form of a supernal garden created by the Angelic imagination. From another systematic perspective, as Bruce Franklin suggested, it is also possible for us to reread *Eureka*, "Mesmeric Revelation," and "The Fall of the House of Usher" (1839) as a continuum, in which the author supposes inanimate matter to be sentient, setting up the analogy between cosmogonical catastrophe and narratological climax (*Future Perfect,* New York: Oxford University Press, 1966). Reading Poe's science fiction, then, means rediscovering Poe's idea of art, which was tremendously influenced by the Kantian concept of "Kunst," connotating art as well as technology: a concept which bridges nature and freedom, the secular world and the supernal realm, just the way "Taste" mediates between "the Intellect" and "the Moral Sense" in Poe's terms.

However deep Poe's speculation is, nevertheless, the subgeneric variety does not necessarily endorse the literary quality of this field. It is very natural that you find Poe's detective fiction much superior to his science fiction; every tale of the former genre retains a certain degree of narrativity, while most pieces of the latter read like a capricious sketch rather than an organic text. And yet, what Poe achieved was not so much literary quality as literary influence, as F. O. Matthiessen once pointed out (*The American Renaissance,* New York: Oxford University Press, 1941). While Poe was a well-known parodist, Poe himself was to be parodied by his latecomers. The more incomplete his fiction is, the more fascinating it sounds to Poe's admirers.

The earliest cases of science fictional homages to Poe, for example, include the French pioneer of science fiction Jules Verne's *Le sphinx des glaces* (1897), the sequel to *The Narrative of Arthur Gordon Pym,* in which the author is ambitious enough to resolve the mystery of the shrouded giant looming in the Antarctica in the catastrophe of Poe's novella.

The 20th century has seen quite a few Poe followers including H. P. Lovecraft, Ray Bradbury, Roger Zelazny, Fred Saberhagen, Robert McCammon, Richard Powers, William Vollmann, and so on. They closely reexamined and further sophisticated the master's rhetoric of gothic fantasy. What is more, we should not forget that the recent rise of the Franco-American literary critical controversy on Poe's "The Purloined Letter," waged in the 1970s between such poststructuralists as Jacques Lacan, Jacques Derrida, and Barbara Johnson, helped revive the literary authority of Poe to a great extent. Insofar as his poetics of pseudoscience is concerned, however, we could single out only Rudy Rucker as a most serious student of Poe; his *The Hollow Earth* (1990) is an incredibly elaborated and "steampunkish" sequel to *Eureka*, as well as to *The Narrative of Arthur Gordon Pym.* Rucker not only colorfully envisioned the part of Pym's voyage into the center of the earth that Poe had omitted, but also closely combined the idea of hollow earth with Poe's cosmogony and Stephen Hawking's wormhole theory. Certainly, all Rucker did here must seem updating Poe's pseudoscientific fiction by reappropriating the fruits of postmodern phys-

ics Poe himself could not have constructed. But, if you like to radically simulate the fantastic impact Poe's *Pym* or *Eureka* must have given upon his contemporary audience, we cannot recommend a better text than *The Hollow Earth.*

—Takayuki Tatsumi

POHL, Frederik

Pseudonyms: James MacCreigh; Ernst Mason; Edson McCann; Jordon Park; Donald Stacy. **Nationality:** American. **Born:** New York City, 26 November 1919. **Military Service:** Served in the United States Air Force, in the United States and Italy, 1943-45: Sergeant. **Family:** Married 1) Doris Baumgardt in 1940 (divorced 1944); 2) Dorothy LesTina in 1945 (divorced 1947); 3) Judith Merril, *q.v.,* in 1949 (divorced 1953), one daughter; 4) Carol Metcalf Ulf in 1952 (divorced 1981), two sons (one deceased) and one daughter; 5) Elizabeth Anne Hull in 1984. Editor, Popular Publications, New York, 1939-43; copywriter, Thwing and Altman, New York, 1946; book editor and associate circulation manager, Popular Science Publication Company, New York, 1946-49; literary agent, New York, 1949-53; features editor, later editor, *If,* New York, 1959-70; editor, Galaxy Publishing Company, New York, 1961-69; executive editor, Ace Books, New York, 1971-72; science fiction editor, Bantam Books, New York, 1973-79. Since 1976, contributing editor, *Algol,* New York. President, Science Fiction Writers of America, 1974-76; president, World SF, 1980-82 and vice-president (West), 1985-86; Mid-West Area Chair, Authors Guild of America. **Awards:** Edward E. Smith Memorial award, 1966; Hugo award, for editing, 1966, 1967, 1968, for fiction, 1973, 1978; *Locus* award, 1973, 1978; Nebula award, 1976, 1977; John W. Campbell Memorial award, 1978; Prix Apollo (France), 1979; American Book award, 1980. Guest of Honor, World Science Fiction Convention, 1972; Fellow, American Association for the Advancement of Science. **Agent:** Curtis Brown, 10 Astor Place, New York, New York 10003, U.S.A.; or Carnell Literary Agency, Danes Croft, Goose Lane, Little Hallingbury, Hertfordshire CM22 FRG, England.

SCIENCE FICTION PUBLICATIONS

Novels (series: Cuckoo's Saga; Jim Eden; Heechee; Man Plus; Space Merchants; Starchild)

The Space Merchants, with C.M. Kornbluth. New York, Ballantine, 1953; London, Heinemann, 1955; revised edition, New York, St. Martin's Press, 1985.
Search the Sky, with C.M. Kornbluth. New York, Ballantine, 1954; London, Digit, 1960; revised edition, New York, Baen, 1985.
Preferred Risk (with Lester del Rey as Edson McCann). New York, Simon and Schuster, 1955; London, Methuen, 1983.
Gladiator-at-Law, with C.M. Kornbluth. New York, Ballantine, 1955; London, Digit, 1958; revised edition, New York, Baen, 1986.
Slave Ship. New York, Ballantine, 1957; London, Dobson, 1961.
Wolfbane, with C.M. Kornbluth. New York, Ballantine, 1959; London, Gollancz, 1960; revised edition, revised by Frederick Pohl, New York, Baen, and London, Gollancz, 1986.

Drunkard's Walk. New York, Ballantine, 1960; revised edition, London, Gollancz, 1961.

The Starchild Trilogy, with Jack Williamson. Garden City, New York, Doubleday, 1977; London, Penguin, 1980.

The Reefs of Space. New York, Ballantine, 1964; London, Dobson, 1965.

Starchild. New York, Ballantine, 1965; London, Dobson, 1966.

Rogue Star. New York, Ballantine, 1969; London, Dobson, 1972.

A Plague of Pythons. New York, Ballantine, 1965; London, Gollancz, 1966; revised edition, as *Demon in the Skull,* New York, DAW, 1984.

The Age of the Pussyfoot. New York, Trident Press, 1969; London, Gollancz, 1970.

Man Plus. New York, Random House, and London, Gollancz, 1976.

Gateway (Heechee). New York, St. Martin's Press, and London, Gollancz, 1977.

JEM. New York, St. Martin's Press, and London, Gollancz, 1979.

Beyond the Blue Event Horizon (Heechee). New York, Ballantine, and London, Gollancz, 1980.

The Cool War. New York, Ballantine, and London, Gollancz, 1981.

BiPohl: Two Complete Novels (includes *The Age of the Pussyfoot* and *Drunkard's Walk*). New York, Ballantine, 1982.

Starburst. New York, Ballantine, and London, Gollancz, 1982.

Syzygy. New York, Bantam, 1982.

The Saga of Cuckoo, with Jack Williamson. Garden City, New York, Doubleday, 1983.

> *Farthest Star,* with Jack Williamson. New York, Ballantine, 1975; London, Pan, 1976.

> *Wall around a Star,* with Jack Williamson. New York, Ballantine, 1983.

Heechee Rendezvous. New York, Ballantine, and London, Gollancz, 1984.

The Years of the City. New York, Timescape, 1984; London, Gollancz, 1985.

The Merchants' War (Space Merchants). New York, St. Martin's Press, 1984; London, Gollancz, 1985.

Black Star Rising. New York, Ballantine, 1985; London, Gollancz, 1986.

Venus, Inc., with C.M. Kornbluth (includes *The Space Merchants* and *The Merchants' War*). Garden City, New York, Doubleday, 1985.

Terror. New York, Berkley, 1986.

The Coming of the Quantum Cats. New York, Bantam, 1986; London, Gollancz, 1987.

Annals of the Heechee. New York, Ballantine, and London, Gollancz, 1987.

Narabedla Ltd. New York, Ballantine, 1988; London, Gollancz, 1990.

Land's End, with Jack Williamson. New York, Tor, 1988.

Homegoing. Norwalk, Connecticut, Easton Press, 1989; London, Gollancz, 1990.

The World at the End of Time. New York, Ballantine, 1990; London, HarperCollins, 1992.

Outnumbering the Dead. London, Legend, 1991; New York, St. Martin's Press, 1992.

The Singers of Time, with Jack Williamson. Garden City, New York, Doubleday, 1991.

The Undersea Trilogy (for children; Eden), with Jack Williamson. Riverdale, New York, Baen, 1992.

> *Undersea Quest,* with Jack Williamson. New York, Gnome Press, 1954; London, Dobson, 1966.

> *Undersea Fleet,* with Jack Williamson. Hicksville, New York, Gnome Press, 1956; London, Dobson, 1968.

> *Undersea City,* with Jack Williamson. Hicksville, New York, Gnome Press, 1958; London, Dobson, 1968.

Mining the Oort. New York, Ballantine, 1992; London, HarperCollins, 1993.

Mars Plus (Man Plus), with Thomas T. Thomas. Riverdale, New York, Baen, 1994.

The Voices of Heaven. New York, Tor, 1994.

Short Stories

Danger Moon (as James MacCreigh). Sydney, American Science Fiction, 1953.

Alternating Currents. New York, Ballantine, 1956; London, Penguin, 1966.

The Case against Tomorrow. New York, Ballantine, 1957.

Tomorrow Times Seven. New York, Ballantine, 1959.

The Man Who Ate the World. New York, Ballantine, 1960; London, Panther, 1979.

Turn Left at Thursday. New York, Ballantine, 1961.

The Wonder Effect, with C.M. Kornbluth. New York, Ballantine, 1962; London, Gollancz, 1967; revised edition, as *Critical Mass,* New York, Bantam, 1977.

The Abominable Earthman. New York, Ballantine, 1963.

The Frederik Pohl Omnibus. London, Gollancz, 1966; reprinted in part, as *Survival Kit,* London, Panther, 1979.

Digits and Dastards (includes essays). New York, Ballantine, 1966; London, Dobson, 1968.

Day Million. New York, Ballantine, 1970; London, Gollancz, 1971.

The Gold at Starbow's End. New York, Ballantine, 1972; London, Gollancz, 1973.

The Best of Frederik Pohl, edited by Lester del Rey. Garden City, New York, Doubleday, 1975; London, Sidgwick and Jackson, 1977.

In the Problem Pit. New York, Bantam, and London, Corgi, 1976.

Critical Mass, with C.M. Kornbluth. New York, Bantam, 1977.

The Early Pohl. Garden City, New York, Doubleday, 1976; London, Dobson, 1980.

Before the Universe and Other Stories: The Best of the Early Work of Science Fiction's Most Famous Team of Collaborators, with C.M. Kornbluth. New York, Bantam, 1980.

Planets Three. New York, Berkley, 1982.

Midas World. New York, St. Martin's Press, and London, Gollancz, 1983.

Pohlstars. New York, Ballantine, 1984; abridged edition, London, Gollancz, 1986.

Our Best: The Best of Frederik Pohl and C.M. Kornbluth. New York, Baen, 1987.

The Day the Martians Came. Norwalk, Connecticut, Easton Press, 1988; London, Grafton, 1990.

The Gateway Trip: Tales and Vignettes of the Heechee. Norwalk, Connecticut, Easton Press, 1990.

Stopping at Slowyear. Eugene, Oregon, Axolotl Press, 1991.

OTHER PUBLICATIONS

Novels

A Town Is Drowning, with C.M. Kornbluth. New York, Ballantine, 1955; London, Digit, 1960.

Presidential Year, with C.M. Kornbluth. New York, Ballantine, 1956.

Sorority House (with C.M. Kornbluth as Jordan Park). New York, Lion, 1956.

The God of Channel 1 (as Donald Stacy). New York, Ballantine, 1956.

Turn the Tigers Loose, with Walter Lasly. New York, Ballantine, 1956.

Edge of the City (novelization of screenplay). New York, Ballantine, 1957.

Chernobyl. New York and London, Bantam, 1987.

Other

Tiberius (biography; as Ernst Mason). New York, Ballantine, 1960.

Practical Politics 1972. New York, Ballantine, 1971.

The Way the Future Was: A Memoir. New York, Ballantine, 1978; London, Gollancz, 1979.

Science Fiction Studies in Film, with Frederik Pohl IV. New York, Ace, 1982.

Forbidden Lines: Science Fiction, Fantasy, Essays, with others. Chapel Hill, North Carolina, Science Fiction Writers' Group, 1989.

Editor, *Beyond the End of Time.* Garden City, New York, Permabooks, 1952.

Editor, *Shadow of Tomorrow.* Garden City, New York, Permabooks, 1953.

Editor, *Star Science Fiction Stories 1-6.* New York, Ballantine, 6 vols., 1953-59; vols. 1 and 2, London, Boardman, 1954-55.

Editor, *Assignment in Tomorrow.* Garden City, New York, Hanover House, 1954.

Editor, *Star Short Novels.* New York, Ballantine, 1954.

Editor, *Star of Stars.* Garden City, New York, Doubleday, 1960; as *Star Fourteen,* London, Whiting and Wheaton, 1966.

Editor, *The Expert Dreamers.* Garden City, New York, Doubleday, 1962; London, Gollancz, 1963.

Editor, *Time Waits for Winthrop and Four Other Short Novels from Galaxy.* Garden City, New York, Doubleday, 1962.

Editor, *The Seventh [through Eleventh] Galaxy Reader.* Garden City, New York, Doubleday, 5 vols., 1964-69; *Seventh* through *Tenth,* London, Gollancz, 4 vols., 1965-68; *Eighth,* as *Final Encounter,* New York, Curtis, 1970; *Tenth,* as *Door to Anywhere,* New York, Curtis, 1970.

Editor, *The If Reader of Science Fiction.* Garden City, New York, Doubleday, 1966; London, Whiting and Wheaton, 1967; second volume, Garden City, New York, Doubleday, 1968.

Editor, *Nightmare Age.* New York, Ballantine, 1970.

Editor, *Best Science Fiction for 1972.* New York, Ace, 1972.

Editor, with Carol Pohl, *Science Fiction: The Great Years.* New York, Ace, 1973; London, Gollancz, 1974, second volume, Ace, 1976.

Editor, with Carol Pohl, *Jupiter.* New York, Ballantine, 1973.

Editor, *The Science Fiction Roll of Honor: An Anthology of Fiction and Nonfiction by Guests of Honor at World Science Fiction Conventions.* New York, Random House, 1975.

Editor, with Carol Pohl, *Science Fiction Discoveries.* New York, Bantam, 1976.

Editor, *The Best of C.M. Kornbluth.* Garden City, New York, Doubleday, 1976.

Editor, with Martin H. Greenberg and Joseph D. Olander, *Science Fiction of the Forties.* New York, Avon, 1978.

Editor, with Martin H. Greenberg and Joseph D. Olander, *Galaxy: Thirty Years of Innovative Science Fiction.* Chicago, Playboy Press, 1980.

Editor, *Nebula Winners 14.* New York, Harper, 1980; London, W.H. Allen, 1981.

Editor, with Martin H. Greenberg and Joseph D. Olander, *The Great Science Fiction Series: Stories from the Best of the Series from 1944 to 1980.* New York, Harper, 1980.

Editor, *Yesterday's Tomorrows: Favorite Stories from Forty Years as a Science Fiction Editor.* New York, Berkley, 1982.

Editor, with Elizabeth Anne Hull, *Tales from the Planet Earth.* New York, St. Martin's Press, 1986.

Editor, with Martin H. Greenberg and Joseph D. Olander, *Worlds of If.* New York, Bluejay, 1986.

*

Manuscript Collection: Syracuse University Library, New York.

Frederik Pohl comments:

I write what interests me, in the hope that it will interest others. The things that particularly interest me are: the mismatch between what people say and what they do (U.S. presidents being only the most conspicuous example); the turbulence and elegance of science, particularly at its frontiers (science is my favorite spectator sport); the vulnerability and confusion inside the most plastic of human faces; the sound of language, and the amusing tricks that can be played with it; and Morality.

How thoroughly I communicate these concerns I can't easily tell, but when I stop trying I stop writing.

*   *   *

A glance at the career of Frederik Pohl reinforces the conviction that Pohl is constantly "on the trail." Formal schooling didn't please him; he dropped away from that track in his senior year, without being graduated. He married four women before (perhaps) finding one suitable. He was an editor at a magazine publishing house, editor of a book department, assistant circulation manager, literary agent, cultural exchange lecturer, guest on more than 400 radio and television programs in nine countries, and is now engaged in turning out some of the most interesting science fiction works on the market.

While some of these activities are related, one asks questions about Pohl's aim in life. His early writing was relatively optimistic, if not utopian. Take a 1941 yarn, "The King's Eye" (from *The Early Pohl*). Here is a planet Venus inhabited by primitives who plan to punish two Earthlings for a crime committed by other humans who have visited their planet previously. But the poor aliens themselves are remnants of a mighty civilization. Their time has come and gone; the culture of Earth has surpassed that of the Venusians, and they haven't a chance of beating the Earthlings who, in the simple techniques of early pulp fiction, come out on top. Even joint works like *Wolfbane,* written with C.M. Kornbluth, contained a lot of good-humored spoofery.

But Pohl eagerly embraced the New Wave attitudes proffered by later writers of science fiction, and Pohl's later works—*The Age of the Pussyfoot* and even his wonderful *Gateway*—are downright dystopian. It was as though pleasant attitudes and relationships among individuals in the fictional world had palled, and the time had come to deal with the weaknesses and even rottenness of mankind.

Oddly, Pohl was criticized by some of his contemporaries for his use of New Wave qualities they thought too conservative. But Pohl defended his position, noting he had no objection to New Wave stories in themselves. What he thought desirable about those changes was that they "shook up" the old dinosaurs of science fiction writing, including himself, and showed them the limitations of continuing to write science fiction according to pulp or Hollywood standards.

Unlike Emile Coue ("Every day in every way, I'm getting better and better"), Pohl often appears to think very little of man as an exemplar, as someone to admire. In his award-winning *Gateway*, his protagonist Broadhead is seen as insecure, undergoing psychotherapy to handle overwhelming guilt of lost lives. Even when the Heechee ship, which is being drawn to destruction into a black hole, is partly saved by Broadhead's lucky button-pushing, his loss of Klara to that overwhelming cosmic phenomenon almost destroys him. True, he has succeeded in his fantastic quest—garnering fabulous treasures from a vanished civilization, but at a price of nine lives. And, while his computer psychologist assures Bob that all the risk and tragedy involved in the adventure are but parts of life, the reader may wonder that it must be so—that in a sense our hero has lost far more than he has won.

Jem involves a planet (Earth) divided into three power centers: People, Fuel, and Food. A war brings complete social breakdown on Earth. Colonists from Earth who had settled on a planet far away have thus become independent of Earth, and must not only learn to resolve their differences, but must adjust relationships with the planet's natives. But the struggles among the three divided groups results in the same errors that had wrecked Earth, and the "colonization" of this new planet amounts to little more than rape. The expedition tries to do its best, but the story's ending is tragic—possibly a commentary on the inherent weaknesses and limitations of the human condition.

The science fiction Pohl wrote in partnerships was probably the most interesting and appealing to many readers. *Wolfbane, The Wonder Effect, The Space Merchants* were among works co-authored by Pohl and Cyril Kornbluth. This proved to be a well-adjusted and even pleasant joining of talents, different in some respects but somehow blended to create some of the best reading in the field. *The Space Merchants*, particularly, was harmoniously produced. In an interview Pohl said their collaboration was almost strain-free because each of the writers could depend on the other to do his share. Pohl would write four pages, for instance; Kornbluth would do the same, until the rough draft of the work was completed. Together they smoothed the work into the finished product, which Pohl said he was never able to do with any other writer.

Possibly, though, there was another pairing almost as cooperative: with Jack Williamson. The two of them turned out *Undersea Quest, The Reefs of Space, Starchild, Farthest Star, The Singers of Time,* among other works. Their success in cooperating on these works may have been based, oddly, on differences in their personalities and backgrounds. Williamson was older than Pohl by 15 years, and unlike Pohl he had a formal education, with a Ph.D. in English Literature. Such differences may have worked a kind of magic, blending their separate talents in a solid and smooth collaboration. The proof, of course, lies in the works, which have been read with delight over the years.

Frederik Pohl is a star among stars. He has shaped and seasoned the literature of science fiction as almost no one else has. His kaleidoscopic background had equipped him with skills and values possessed by few if any rivals. Pohl's peers evidently have underlined such high judgment by a wide range of honors, including several Hugo and Nebula awards.

—Robert H. Wilcox

POLLACK, Rachel

Nationality: American. **Born:** Richard A. Pollack, 17 August 1945; name legally changed after sex-change operation. **Education:** New York University, B.A. in English (honors); Claremont Graduate School, M.A. in English. **Career:** Has worked as an IBM production planner, a bar cleaner, an English insturctor at the State University of New York, a jewelry maker, a perfume bottler, and a bookseller. Full-time writer who also gives workshops and classes in Tarot. **Awards:** Arthur C. Clarke award, for novel, 1988. **Address:** 2150 Route 9G, Rhinebeck, New York 12572, U.S.A.

SCIENCE FICTION PUBLICATIONS

Novels (series: Unquenchable Fire)

Golden Vanity. New York, Berkley, 1980.
Alqua Dreams. New York, Watts, 1987; London, Century, 1990.
Unquenchable Fire. London, Century, 1988; Woodstock, New York, Overlook Press, 1992.
Temporary Agency (Fire). London, Orbit, and New York, St. Martin's Press, 1994.

OTHER PUBLICATIONS

Other

Seventy-Eight Degrees of Wisdom: A Book of Tarot. Wellington, Northamptonshire, Aquarian Press, 2 vols., 1980-83.
Salvador Dali's Tarot. Salem, New Hampshire, Salem House, and London, Rainbird, 1985.
A Practical Guide to Fortune Telling: Palmistry, the Crystal Ball, Runes, Tea Leaves, the Tarot. London, Sphere/Rainbird, 1986; as *Teach Yourself Fortune Telling,* New York, Holt, 1986.
Tarot: The Open Labyrinth. Wellingborough, Northamptonshire, Aquarian Press, 1986.
The New Tarot. Wellingborough, Northamptonshire, Aquarian Press, 1989; Woodstock, New York, Overlook Press, 1990.
Tarot Readings and Meditations. Wellingborough, Northamptonshire, Aquarian Press, 1990.
The Haindl Tarot. North Hollywood, California, Newcastle, 2 vols., 1990.
Editor, with Caitlin Matthews, *Tarot Tales.* London, Legend, 1989.
Editor, with Mary K. Greer, *New Thoughts on Tarot: Transcripts from the First International Newcastle International Tarot Symposium.* North Hollywood, California, Newcastle, 1989.

*   *   *

Rachel Pollack is best known as an authority on the esoteric, having written several serious studies on Tarot, including the companion volume to the controversial Salvador Dali pack, and the richly illustrated *The New Tarot,* which examines over 70 recent Tarot packs. Her own published Tarot pack draws heavily on some of the same shamanistic sources that lie behind her two most recent novels.

Pollack writes mature, intelligent, thought-provoking fiction which deals with the interplay between complex philosophical and spiritual abstracts and the solid, "real" world. She isn't, as so many SF writers still are, presenting exciting adolescent adventure stories; instead she asks questions about the nature of reality, making the reader step slightly to one side, enabling us to examine and explore our own society—and ourselves—from a new, and often spiritual viewpoint.

This is seen most of all in *Unquenchable Fire,* which won the Arthur C. Clarke Award for the best science fiction novel published in the U.K. in 1988. But even in the early and neglected *Golden Vanity,* a seemingly traditional SF novel about the less pleasant aspects of Earth's first contact with extraterrestrials, Pollack explores meditation exercises, visualisation, and the self-deceptions of the kookier side of New Age religion.

Alqua Dreams is also set in a traditional SF format: an interstellar trading negotiator visits a new planet to attempt to persuade its inhabitants to set up trading links with his company, which wants to get its hands on the rare mineral rhovium, which powers space flight. So far, so standard. But having established her rationale, Pollack then takes off into what really interests her: the age-old debate between Platonic and Aristotelian life-views.

Earthman Jaimi Cooper is a fairly average man of his times (and ours); he is somewhat perplexed, to put it mildly, to discover that the Lukai, the inhabitants of Planet Keela, believe that they're all dead. Their "life" is simply a delusion forced on them by the liar god Canumaira. Their rituals, both religious and sexual, are bizarre and at times horrifying. Cooper is called an alqua: one suffering from the illusion that he is alive. He finds himself trying to convince the people that they are wrong, that they do exist, that they are real; they simply argue that he has been deluded by Canumaira.

In *Alqua Dreams* Pollack has created perhaps the most unusual, disturbing, yet believable religion since Philip José Farmer's *Night of Light* 20 years before. It is by no means an easy read—what do you expect when the eternal verities are being questioned?—and is not wholly successful as a novel, but is a challenging study of two totally incompatible philosophical belief systems.

In *Unquenchable Fire,* a complex and moving tale of storytelling and myth-creation set in an alternate present-day America, she draws heavily on her encyclopedic knowledge of myth and religion. *Unquenchable Fire* is even more challenging than *Alqua Dreams,* though a far more enjoyable read, showing a tremendous advancement in Pollack's own storytelling skills.

In the world she creates here, religion is an essential part of everyone's life, tellers of mythic stories are revered, dreams are computer-analyzed for their meaning, and Woolworth's sells amulets. Personal miracles, while not commonplace, happen often enough to be greeted with joy rather than disbelief. Neighbours hold group meetings to raise one another's spiritual awareness.

Pollack's alternative reality is utterly believable. It's as if the New Age Aquarians have taken over the materialistic America we know. But human nature is much the same; Pollack shows that changing the spiritual infrastructure has little effect in itself; the only meaningful revolution is the one inside. Jennifer Mazdan has to cope with the miracle of becoming pregnant from a dream, and with the knowledge that her unborn child will be an especially significant shaman; but she also has to cope with the pettiness of her neighbours.

The stories told by the Tellers within the book are Pollack's own myths of creation and destruction, of power and love and betrayal; myths of a society quite different from our own—yet similar enough to draw parallels. Again it's by no means an easy book, but it is a very powerful and stimulating examination of the spiritual aspects of life.

Temporary Agency is much simpler and far more accessible than *Unquenchable Fire.* Effectively two linked novellas, it is set in the same world, and is every bit as strange, with malign spiritual beings walking the streets in human form; but it is a far more straightforward tale of a couple of unpleasant religious incidents in a spiritually remodeled New York. Pollack doesn't pretend, in either book, that a New Age religious world will be all sweetness and light; people are still people, with all their failings, loves, jealousies, spites, and ambitions.

Pollack's fascination with religion imbues her fiction with a rare depth and complexity, making her readers have to work just that little bit harder than with most SF writers, but the results well repay the effort.

—David V. Barrett

PORGES, Arthur

Pseudonyms: Peter Arthur; Pat Rogers. **Nationality:** American. **Born:** Chicago, Illinois, 20 August 1915. **Education:** Illinois Institute of Technology, Chicago, B.S. 1940. **Career:** Taught mathematics at Illinois Institute of Technology, De Paul University, Chicago, and Western Military Academy: retired, 1975.

SCIENCE FICTION PUBLICATIONS

Uncollected Short Stories (series: Ensign De Ruyter)

"The Rats," in *The Best Science-Fiction Stories 1952,* edited by E.F. Bleiler and T.E. Dikty. New York, Fell, 1952; London, Grayson, 1953.

"The Fly," in *The Best Science-Fiction Stories 1953,* edited by E.F. Bleiler and T.E. Dikty. New York, Fell, 1953; London, Grayson, 1955.

"Story Conference," in *Fantasy and Science Fiction* (New York), May 1953.

"Strange Birth," in *Fantasy and Science Fiction* (New York), June 1953.

"The Liberator," in *Fantasy and Science Fiction* (New York), December 1953.

"The Unwilling Professor," in *Dynamic* (New York), January 1954.

"The Grom," in *Fantasy and Science Fiction* (New York), November 1954.

"Guilty as Charged," in *The Best Science Fiction Stories and Novels 1955,* edited by T.E. Dikty. New York, Fell, 1955.

"The Ruum," in *Best SF,* edited by Edmund Crispin, London, Faber, 1955.

"Mop-Up," in *Galaxy of Ghouls,* edited by Judith Merril. New York, Lion, 1955.

"$1.98," in *The Best from Fantasy and Science Fiction 4,* edited by Anthony Boucher. New York, Doubleday, 1955.

"The Tidings," in *Fantasy and Science Fiction* (New York), February 1955.

"The Box," in *Startling* (New York), Spring 1955.

"By a Fluke," in *Fantasy and Science Fiction* (New York), October 1955.

"The Logic of Rufus Weir," in *Fantasy and Science Fiction* (New York), November 1955.

"The Entity," in *Fantastic Universe* (Chicago), December 1955.

"Whirlpool," in *Fantastic Universe* (Chicago), March 1957.

"The Devil and Simon Flagg," in *Fantasia Mathematica*, edited by Clifton Fadiman. New York, Simon and Schuster, 1958.

"What Crouches in the Deep," in *Fantastic* (New York), March 1959.

"A Touch of Sun," in *Fantastic* (New York), April 1959.

"The Forerunner," in *Fantastic* (New York), July 1959.

"The Shakespeare Manuscript," in *Fantastic* (New York), August 1959.

"Security," in *Amazing* (New York), September 1959.

"Off His Rocker," in *Fantastic* (New York), February 1960.

"A Specimen for a Queen," in *Fantasy and Science Fiction* (New York), May 1960.

"Night Quake" (as Pat Rogers) and "Josephus," in *Fear* (Concord, New Hampshire), May 1960.

"The Fiftieth Year of April," in *Fantastic* (New York), June 1960.

"The Crime of Mr. Saver," in *Fantastic* (New York), August 1960.

"The Shadowsmith," in *Fantastic* (New York), September 1960.

"The Auto Hawks," in *Amazing* (New York), September 1960.

"Words and Music," in *If* (New York), September 1960.

"A Diversion for the Baron," in *Fantastic* (New York), November 1960.

"The Radio" (as Peter Arthur) and "The Melanas," in *Fantastic* (New York), December 1960.

"Degree Candidate" (as Peter Arthur) and "Dr. Blackadder's Clients," in *Fantastic* (New York), January 1961.

"The Other Side," in *Fantastic* (New York), February 1961.

"Revenge," in *Amazing* (New York), February 1961.

"Mulberry Moon," in *Fantastic* (New York), April 1961.

"The Arrogant Vampire," in *Fantastic* (New York), May 1961.

"One Bad Habit," in *Fantastic* (New York), June 1961.

"Report on the Magic Shop," in *Fantastic* (New York), August 1961.

"A Devil of a Day," in *Fantastic* (New York), August 1962.

"Mozart Annuity," in *Fantastic* (New York), November 1962.

"Emergency Operation," in *Great Science Fiction about Doctors*, edited by Groff Conklin and Noah D. Fabricant. New York, Macmillan, 1963.

"3rd Sister," in *Fantastic* (New York), January 1963.

"The Topper," in *Astounding* (New York), February 1963.

"Through Channels," in *Amazing* (New York), June 1963.

"The Formula," in *Amazing* (New York), July 1963.

"Controlled Experiment," in *Astounding* (New York), August 1963.

"The Rescuer," in *Yet More Penguin Science Fiction*, edited by Brian Aldiss. London, Penguin, 1964.

"Time-Bomb," in *Fantasy and Science Fiction* (New York), June 1964.

"Urned Reprieve" (De Ruyter), in *Amazing* (New York), October 1964.

"The Fanatic," in *Fantastic* (New York), December 1964.

"The Moths," in *Amazing* (New York), December 1964.

"Problem Child," in *The Year's Best S-F 10*, edited by Judith Merril. New York, Delacorte Press, 1965; London, Mayflower, 1967.

"Wheeler Dealer" (De Ruyter), in *Amazing* (New York), March 1965.

"Ensign De Ruyter, Dreamer," in *Amazing* (New York), April 1965.

"The Good Seed," in *Amazing* (New York), August 1965.

"Turning Point," in *Fantasy and Science Fiction* (New York), September 1965.

"A Civilized Community," in *Bizarre Mystery Magazine* (Concord, New Hampshire), October 1965.

"Dusty Answer" (De Ruyter), in *Amazing* (New York), October 1965.

"The Creep Brigade," in *Bizarre Mystery Magazine* (Concord, New Hampshire), November 1965.

"Pressure" (De Ruyter), in *Amazing* (New York), February 1966.

"Priceless Possession," in *Galaxy* (New York), June 1966.

"The Mirror," in *Fantasy and Science Fiction* (New York), October 1966.

"Solomon's Demon," in *Legends for the Dark*, edited by Peter Haining. London, New English Library, 1968.

"The Dragons of Tesla," in *Fantastic* (New York), October 1968.

OTHER PUBLICATIONS

Short Stories

Three Porges Parodies and a Pastiche, edited by Michael H. Kean. New York, Magico Magazine, 1988.

Other

Edgar Allan Poe. Philadelphia, Chilton, 1963.

Edgar Rice Burroughs: The Man Who Created Tarzan. Provo, Utah, Brigham Young University Press, 1975.

*   *   *

Arthur Porges's fiction consists of some 70 short stories, often of 3000 or fewer words. Many of them blend fantasy with science fiction. "Mop-Up," for instance, takes place in the realistic wreckage following a world war fought with atomic and biological weapons. Sharing what is left with the sole human survivor are a witch, a vampire, and a ghoul. Similarly, there appears to be no difference in feel or treatment between stories which are purely SF and others which are purely fantasy. Thus the djinn of "Solomon's Demon" and the robot specimen-gatherer of "The Ruum" are precisely equivalent insofar as the humans who come in contact with them are concerned: they are alien, enormously powerful, inexorable—and they must be stopped if the viewpoint characters are to survive.

The viewpoint character *doesn't* always survive a Porges story, a fact which contributes to the considerable tension of the best of them. The character does always struggle, however. The horror is not that caused by watching a man helpless in the face of the unknown; rather, it is aroused by seeing a strong and resourceful man overborne by a power or cunning still greater than his own. An excellent example of this is "The Rats," in which a lone man fights more-than-bestial rats against a backdrop of impending nuclear war. In his ultimate failure, the man turns over the world to antagonists who have proven themselves worthy at least to attempt to better mankind's record.

Porges works against sharp, tersely drawn backgrounds; he has an enviable talent for choosing the right word or two which convinces a reader that the scene or character was written from life rather than merely studied. His work typically begins with a narrative hook which draws the reader into the body of the story. And even pedestrian stories are frequently enlivened by flashes of character which demonstrate a considerable depth of feeling. Regrettably, many of the stories are pedestrian. This is a result of their being based on gimmicks, often bits of scientific fact: parabolic reflectors concentrate light ("A Touch of Sun," "The Dragons of Tesla"); crickets chirp at a rate dependant on temperature ("The Formula"); a human body reduced to raw elements is a slight value ("$1.98"). While the development may be at least professional, only the gimmick itself is likely to stick in the reader's mind for any length of time. When the gimmick is integral to the story, however, the result can be extremely effective. "The Ruum" (humans can lose significant body weight by sweating) and "Solomon's Demon" (high voltage is harmless unless coupled with a path to ground) are striking examples of this synthesis; and "The Mirror," which turns on an analysis of multiple reflections, is a stunning horror story. If these are the exceptions, then in themselves they constitute a body which many writers must envy.

Despite his frequent use of factual gimmicks, Porges never neglects his characters. It is fitting that one of his last-published stories, "Priceless Possession," involves no gimmicks at all; only the question of what part of their souls three spacemen will pay to avoid losing a treasure which in money terms is priceless. This is not a sardonic story; and perhaps it is a story that is not without hope for humanity; but it is an indictment more damning than any shrill diatribe could have seen. Here as in much of Porges's best work, men struggle but we cannot assume their victory; and our worst enemies may not be external to our hearts.

—David A. Drake

POURNELLE, Jerry (Eugene)

Pseudonym: Wade Curtis. **Nationality:** American. **Born:** Shreveport, Louisiana, 7 August 1933. **Education:** University of Iowa, Iowa City, 1953-54; University of Washington, Seattle, B.S. 1955, M.S. in statistics and systems engineering 1957, Ph.D. in psychology 1960, Ph.D. in political science 1964. **Military Service:** Served in the United States Army 1950-52. **Family:** Married Roberta Jane Isdell in 1959; one daughter and four sons. **Career:** Research assistant, University of Washington Medical School, 1954-57; aviation psychologist and systems engineer, Boeing Corporation, Seattle, 1957-64; manager of special studies, Aerospace Corporation, San Bernardino, California, 1964-65; research specialist and proposal manager, American Rockwell Corporation, 1965-66; Professor of Political Science, Pepperdine University, Los Angeles, 1966-69; executive assistant to the Mayor of Los Angeles, 1969-70. Since 1970, freelance writer, lecturer, and consultant: regular contributor of nonfiction articles to *Galaxy,* 1974-78, and *Analog.* President, Science Fiction Writers of America, 1973-74; senior consulting editor, *Byte Magazine;* chairman, Citizen's Advisory Council on National Space Policy; Chairman of the Lunar Society. **Awards:** John W. Campbell award, 1974; Evans-Freehafer award, 1977; Fellow, Operations Research Society of America, and American Association for the Advancement of Science; Republic of Estonia Award of Honor, 1968; Officer, Military and Hospitaler Order of St. Lazarus of Jerusalem; Fellow, Royal Astronomical Society. **Agents:** (U.S.) Eleanor Wood, Spectrum Agency, 111 Eighth Avenue, Suite 1501, New York, New York 10011; (foreign) Ralph Vicinanza, 111 Eighth Avenue, New York, New York 10011. **Address:** 12190½ Ventura Blvd., Box 372, Studio City, California 91604, U.S.A. **Online Address:** JerryP.@Bix.Com.

SCIENCE FICTION PUBLICATIONS

Novels (series: Falkenberg; Janissaries; Buck Rogers; Second Empire)

A Spaceship for the King (Empire). New York, DAW, 1973; revised as *King David's Spaceship,* New York, Pocket Books, 1980; London, Orbit, 1981.

Escape from the Planet of the Apes (novelization of screenplay). New York, Award, 1974.

The Mote in God's Eye (Empire), with Larry Niven. New York, Simon and Schuster, 1974; London, Weidenfeld and Nicolson, 1975.

Birth of Fire. Toronto, Laser, 1976; New York, Pocket Books, 1978.

Inferno, with Larry Niven. New York, Pocket Books, 1976; London, Wingate, 1977.

West of Honor (Falkenberg). Toronto, Laser, 1976; New York, Pocket Books, 1978.

The Mercenary (Falkenberg). New York, Pocket Books, 1977.

Lucifer's Hammer, with Larry Niven. Chicago, Playboy Press, 1977.

Exiles of Glory. New York, Ace, 1978; revised edition, Riverdale, New York, Baen, 1993.

Janissaries: Clan and Crown. New York, Ace, 1979; London, Macdonald, 1981.

Mordred (Buck Rogers), with Larry Niven and John Eric Holmes. New York, Ace, 1980.

Warrior's Blood (Buck Rogers), with Larry Niven and Richard S. McEnroe. New York, Ace, 1981.

Warrior's World (Buck Rogers), with Larry Niven and Richard S. McEnroe. New York, Ace, 1981.

Oath of Fealty (Janissaries), with Larry Niven. Huntington Woods, Michigan, Phantasia Press, 1981; London, Macdonald, 1982.

Clan and Crown (Janissaries), with Roland Green. New York, Ace, 1982; London, Futura, 1989.

Roger's Rangers (Buck Rogers), with Larry Niven and John Silbersack. New York, Ace, 1983.

Footfall, with Larry Niven. New York, Ballantine, and London, Gollancz, 1985.

The Legacy of Heorot, with Larry Niven and Steven Barnes. London, Gollancz, and New York, Simon and Schuster, 1987.

Storms of Victory (Janissaries), with Roland Green. New York, Ace, 1987; London, Futura, 1989.

Man-Kzin Wars II, with Larry Niven, Dean Ing, and S.M. Stirling. New York, Baen, 1989.

Prince of Mercenaries (Falkenberg). New York, Baen, 1989.

Falkenberg's Legion (omnibus). New York, Baen, 1990; as *Future History, Incorporating The Mercenary and West of Honor,* London, Orbit, 1990.

Go Tell the Spartans, with S.M. Stirling. New York, Baen, 1991.

The Children's Hour (Man-Kzin Wars), with S.M. Stirling. New York, Baen, 1991.

Fallen Angels, with Larry Niven and Michael Flynn. Norwalk, Connecticut, Easton Press, 1991; London, Pan, 1993.

The Gripping Hand (Moat), with Larry Niven. New York, Pocket Books, 1993; as *The Moat around Murcheson's Eye,* London, HarperCollins, 1993.

Prince of Sparta (Falkenberg), with S.M. Stirling. New York, Baen, 1993.

The Dragons of Heorot, with Larry Niven and Steven Barnes, London, Gollancz, 1995.

Short Stories

High Justice. New York, Pocket Books, 1977; London, Futura, 1980.
Man-Kzin Wars III, with Larry Niven, Poul Anderson, and S.M. Stirling. New York, Baen, 1990.
Man-Kzin Wars IV, with Larry Niven, S.M. Stirling, and Thomas T. Thomas. New York, Baen, 1992.

OTHER PUBLICATIONS

Novels as Wade Curtis

Red Heroin. New York, Berkley, 1969; as Jerry Pournelle, New York, Charter, 1985.
Red Dragon. New York, Berkley, 1971; as Jerry Pournelle, New York, Charter, 1985.

Other

The Strategy of Technology: Winning the Decisive War, with Stefan T. Possony. New York, Dunellen, 1970.
That Buck Rogers Stuff, edited by Gavin Claypool. Pasadena, California, Extequer, 1977.
The Mathematics of the Energy Crisis, with R. Gagliardi. Westmont, New Jersey, Intergalactic, 1978.
A Step Farther Out. London, W.H. Allen, 1980; New York, Ace, 1983.
Mutual Assured Survival: A Space-Age Solution to Nuclear Annihilation, with Dean Ing. New York, Baen, 1984.
The User's Guide to Small Computers. New York, Baen, 1984.
Adventures in Microland. New York, Baen, 1985.
Pournelle's PC Communications Guide: The Ultimate Guide to Productivity with a Modem, with Michael A. Banks. Redmond, Washington, Microsoft Press, 1992.

Editor, *20/20 Vision.* New York, Avon, 1974.
Editor, *Black Holes and Other Marvels.* London, Orbit, 1978; New York, Fawcett, 1979.
Editor, *The Endless Frontier.* New York, Ace, 1979.
Editor, with John F. Carr, *The Survival of Freedom.* New York, Fawcett, 1981.
Editor, with John F. Carr, *The Endless Frontier 2.* New York, Ace, 1982.
Editor, with John F. Carr, *Nebula Award Stories 16.* New York, Holt Rinehart, 1982; London, W.H. Allen, 1983.
Editor, with John F. Carr, *There Will Be War.* New York, Tor, 1983.
Editor, *Men of War.* New York, Tor, 1984.
Editor, with John F. Carr, *Blood and Iron.* New York, Tor, 1984.
Editor, with Jim Baen, *Far Frontiers 1-4.* New York, Baen, 4 vols., 1985-86.
Editor, with John F. Carr, *Silicon Brains.* New York, Ballantine, 1985.
Editor, with Jim Baen and John F. Carr, *Science Fiction Yearbook 1984.* New York, Baen, 1985.
Editor, with John F. Carr, *Day of the Tyrant.* New York, Tor, 1985.
Editor, with John F. Carr, *Warrior.* New York, Tor, 1986.
Editor, with John F. Carr, *The Stars at War.* New York, Baen, 1986.
Editor, with John F. Carr, *Republic and Empire.* New York, Baen, 1987.
Editor, with John F. Carr, *Guns of Darkness.* New York, Tor, 1987.
Editor, with John F. Carr, *Call to Battle.* New York, Tor, 1988.

Editor, with John F. Carr and Roland Green, *The Burning Eye.* New York, Baen, 1988.
Editor, with John F. Carr, *The Crash of Empire.* New York, Baen, 1989.
Editor, with John F. Carr, *Armageddon!* New York, Tor, 1989.
Editor, with John F. Carr, *After Armageddon.* New York, Baen, 1990.
Editor, *Death's Head Rebellion.* New York, Baen, 1990.
Editor, with John F. Carr, *Sauron Dominion.* New York, Baen, 1990.
Editor, with John F. Carr, *Cities in Space.* New York, Baen, 1991.
Editor, with John F. Carr, *Life among the Asteroids.* New York, Baen, 1992.
Editor, *Codominium: Revolt on War World.* New York, Baen, 1992.
Editor, *Blood Feuds: A Novel of War World.* New York, Baen, 1993.
Editor, *Blood Vengeance: A Novel of War World.* New York, Baen, 1994.

*

Jerry Pournelle comments:

My work is intended to entertain. I may well have a serious message, but in my judgment fiction is best served if the characters in a story do not know they have a message to deliver. Science fiction writers are bards of the sciences; we are not fundamentally different from the bards of Homeric times, who would travel about and, spying an encamped group, say, "If you'll fill my cup with wine and dish me a bowl of stew, I will tell you a story about a virgin and a bull you just wouldn't believe. . . ."

*   *   *

Jerry Pournelle's science fiction has consistently portrayed technological advance as the most significant visible indication of humanity's progress. The most obvious form of benevolent innovation is the development of space travel, a theme which is almost a given in all of his work. It is particularly obvious in *A Spaceship for the King,* in which the salvation of an entire world rests upon its ability to develop a spacefaring technology. In *Exiles to Glory* humanity is jolted out of its introverted and short-sighted doldrums by a space effort financed by commercial interests. The Martian colony in *Birth of Fire* is entirely dependent upon advanced equipment from Earth.

There is a well-expressed admiration for the professional soldier as well. Colonel Nathan MacKinnie, the protagonist of *A Spaceship for the King,* is a cashiered veteran unable to function properly within the organized military of his world. *Janissaries,* along with its two sequels, *Clan and Crown* and *Storms of Victory* (the latter two in collaboration with Roland Green), follows the adventures of a group of soldiers kidnapped from Earth by aliens unwilling to fight their own battles. John Falkenberg, a recurring character in much of the best of Pournelle's fiction, is a highly skilled strategic and tactical planner who leads a group of interstellar mercenaries.

Falkenberg and his companions are featured in the early novel *West of Honor* and several collections and cross collections including *The Mercenary, Falkenberg's Legion,* and most notably *Prince of Mercenaries,* which incorporates Pournelle's best shorter piece, "Silent Leges." The Falkenberg stories are set within the context of the CoDominium, a pragmatic alliance of the United States and the Soviet Union that eventually evolves into a world government and interstellar empire.

One of several novels Pournelle has written in collaboration with Larry Niven and others, *The Mote in God's Eye,* is possibly the best single work set against this background. *Mote* was met with widely varied reader response. It is a large, rich novel, detailing the first contact of the human race with an alien species that has become biologically diversified in order to cope with the exigencies of survival within their home system. There is a well-paced and logically developed plot, a strong and sustained element of suspense, gradual revelation of the intricacies of the alien culture, and some extremely powerful scenes. There was some controversy because of what was interpreted as stereotyping, particularly of the single female character, a passive individual lacking any initiative. On the other hand, none of the characters are developed to any great degree, the focus of the novel being the unfolding mystery of the Moties. Several years later, Niven and Pournelle provided a sequel, *The Gripping Hand,* in which the Motie system has been declared off limits to travellers and in fact is patrolled by warships determined to prevent the aliens from escaping and threatening human occupied worlds. But evolution is an ongoing process with the Moties, and they are already adapting to the existence of a hostile invader.

Another collaboration with Niven, *Lucifer's Hammer,* features several strong female characters, perhaps as a response to criticism of *Mote.* It's an end-of-the-world story on a vast scale. Following the collision of Earth with a comet, civilization collapses into barbarism and most of the physical features of the world are altered. Marketed as a mainstream disaster novel, it features an extremely large cast of characters, numerous story lines, and covers a span of decades. There is a careful, plausible extrapolation of the slow decay of the few islands of comparatively unaffected society which remain as the apparatus of civilization crumbles. It is indicative of Pournelle's view of technology that the climactic battle is fought for control of a functioning nuclear power plant.

Oath of Fealty and *The Legacy of Heorot* were also written with Larry Niven, and also with Steven Barnes in the latter case. *Oath* is set in an enormous self-contained city-building that is theoretically part of Los Angeles. Automatic defense systems kill intruders, and interests unfriendly to the building administration use one such incident in a political struggle which may determine the future of urban life throughout the world. Although less grandiose than the earlier collaborations, the novel is complexly plotted and the implications of each turn of events are explored in detail. *Heorot* is an other-worlds adventure story, with a struggling human colony trying to find a way to survive the unexpected appearance of a particularly hostile and dangerous lifeform. A very suspenseful novel full of surprises.

With Niven and Michael Flynn, Pournelle wrote *Fallen Angels,* a wish-fulfillment adventure in which science fiction fans organize to save a group of astronauts. Pournelle also collaborated with S.M. Stirling for two new Falkenberg novels, *Go Tell the Spartans* and *Prince of Sparta,* both of which are better than average military adventure stories, but neither of which is remarkable otherwise. He has also continued to contribute to the Man-Kzin War series, set in a universe created by Niven, and with Charles Sheffield wrote "Higher Education," a speculative story about the future of America that is thought-provoking but slow moving.

Pournelle makes use of traditional plots for the most part, interplanetary war and conquest, world disaster, first contact with aliens, commercial rivalries, penal colonies on other worlds, and so on. His themes are familiar as well, the importance of space travel as an outlet for human endeavor, technological answers to problems confronting the human race, the value of individualism as opposed to collectivism, and the primacy of man over aliens because of our competitive drive to survive.

But the familiarity of plot and theme should not be construed as a lack of imagination. The deemphasis on characterization does not imply a lack of depth in other areas. Pournelle develops his plots logically, with a good sense of timing and judicious use of suspense and other devices. Most of his fiction is essentially action-oriented, with clear cut issues and sympathetic characters. Social issues, when they arise, are dealt with consistently. His views on various issues are quite clear; shortsighted ecological protection and population control movements nearly destroy the space effort in *Exiles to Glory.* Government officials are almost invariably portrayed as corrupt or inept or both. Even at his most polemic, however, Pournelle usually avoids disrupting the momentum of his stories. Almost all of his recent work is collaborative, and it is impossible to determine how active a partner he is in those collaborations.

—Don D'Ammassa

POWERS, L.C. *See* **TUBB, E.C.**

POWERS, Tim

Nationality: American. **Born:** 1952. **Awards:** Philip K. Dick Memorial award, 1984. **Address:** c/o Ace Books, 200 Madison Avenue, New York, New York 10016, U.S.A.

SCIENCE FICTION PUBLICATIONS

Novels

Epitaph in Rust. Toronto, Laser, 1976; expanded as *An Epitaph in Rust,* Cambridge, Massachusetts, NESFA, 1989.
The Skies Discrowned. Toronto, Laser, 1976; revised as *Forsake the Sky,* New York, Tor, 1986.
The Drawing of the Dark. New York, Ballantine, 1979; London, Mayflower, 1981.
The Anubis Gates. New York, Ace, 1983; London, Chatto and Windus, 1985.
Dinner at Deviant's Palace. New York, Ace, 1985; London, Chatto and Windus, 1986.
On Stranger Tides. New York, Ace, 1987; London, Grafton, 1988.
The Stress of Her Regard. Lynbrook, New York, Charnal House, 1989; London, Grafton, 1991.
Last Call. Lynbrook, New York, Charnal House, 1992; London, HarperCollins, 1993.

Short Stories

Night Moves. Seattle, Washington, Axolotl Press, 1986.
The Way down the Hill, with *The Pink of Fading Neon,* by James P. Blaylock. Seattle, Washington, Axolotl Press, 1986.

Other Publications

Other

The Seven Steps to Personal Safety: How to Avoid, Deal with, or Survive the Aftermath of a Once-in-a-Lifetime Violent Confrontation, with Richard B. Isaacs. New York, Center for Personal Defense Studies, 1993.

* * *

During his career, Tim Powers has consistently developed his competence and creativity. Daring and able, his novels are *sui generis,* all different but all similarly elaborate and well-crafted. Some of his work is classifiable as science fiction or fantasy, while some combines genre expectations or transcends them. Most of all, Powers's fiction is notable for its intricate plot-structure and rich detail—speculative or historical—as well as for his prose style and characterization.

Powers, along with James P. Blaylock and K. W. Jeter, is one of a group of science fiction writers around the San Francisco Bay area who first became known in the 1980s. Companions of the late Philip K. Dick, they are perhaps best known for the expressiveness and originality of their own voices.

The Anubis Gates is generally considered Powers's "breakthrough" novel. It won the Philip K. Dick Memorial Award, for best paperback original book, and began to draw attention to Powers. One could say that *The Anubis Gates* is Powers's masterpiece, in the original sense: a work that earns guild-entry by virtue of its mature workmanship. In that sense, *Epitaph in Rust* and *The Skies Discrowned,* for Laser Books, demonstrate a promising apprenticeship; and *The Drawing of the Dark* shows the beginning of mastery from a talented and intelligent journeyman. Ten years after *The Skies Discrowned* was published, the story was reissued as *Forsake the Sky,* restored from the publisher's notoriously bad editing and rewritten with Powers's greater command of style and storytelling. Perhaps because of its early origin, the plot is less involved than that of Powers's other work in the 1980s.

With *Last Call,* Powers may be reaching another threshold, joining John Crowley and Philip K. Dick as someone who is not just an outstanding writer of fantasy and science fiction, but a noteworthy author, period. The novel combines many virtues of mainstream realistic fiction with speculative use of myth, from the tarot and Arthurian concept of the wounded Fisher King (with a nod to T.S. Eliot's precedent in *The Waste Land*) to chaos theory. Powers's daring and wild inventiveness, also, have grown steadily throughout his career, reaching impressive peaks in *Last Call* and in *Expiration Date,* with its original concept of ghosts that can be trapped (including by palindromes and jigsaw puzzles) and sniffed for a drug-like high.

Generally, Powers's novels present a number of plot-elements that seem both inexplicable and unconnected. As the plot unfolds and connections appear, the reader discovers that all the mysteries are linked (often in completely unexpected ways) and are explicable within the paradigm offered by the novel. In *Dinner at Deviant's Palace* the setting and explanation are those of science fiction, and in *The Drawing of the Dark* and *On Stranger Tides* the settings are historical and the explanations are supernatural. In *The Anubis Gates, The Stress of Her Regard,* and *Last Call,* Powers shows his full range, combining elements of fantasy, science fiction, and the historical novel. All of his novels also show the

influence of adventure fiction, such as that of Rafael Sabatini. Another influence on Powers is the supernatural novels of Charles Williams, whose book *The Greater Trumps* concerns the tarot—though Powers deliberately did not reread that novel after choosing to write *Last Call.*

One basic appeal of Powers's fiction is the presentation of strange yet consistent cultures, whether historical or imaginary. His characters are convincing, whether he writes about a 16th-century mercenary, as in *Drawing of the Dark,* or the English Romantic poets, as in *The Anubis Gates* and—more centrally—*The Stress of Her Regard.* His depiction of 18th-century pirates (*On Stranger Tides*), organized crime in near-contemporary Las Vegas (*Last Call*), or 19th-century gypsies (*The Anubis Gates*) is as strange, and at least as thorough, as any setting in science fiction. The post-World War III culture of *Dinner at Deviant's Palace* combines credible extrapolation and an archaic feeling of decadent vice. The world in *The Skies Discrowned* and *Forsake the Skies,* also, combines science fiction elements, such as space travel, with historical or fantasy elements, such as swordplay and inherited royalty.

Most of Powers's fiction involves magic, or something like it, which he handles in characteristic yet diverse ways. Many elements in *Dinner at Deviant's Palace,* such as a cult that partakes of mass psychic communion, seem to be supernatural but are explained in scientific terms. On the other hand, both *The Drawing of the Dark* and *The Anubis Gates* use a system of magic which, while not exactly a scientific technology, still functions by stated rules: since a magician forsakes the natural earth, someone is safe if in touch with the earth, by direct contact or a grounding wire. In *The Anubis Gates,* magic and the science of Darrow Interdisciplinary Research Enterprises serve as equal, and equally plausible, vehicles for and explanation of travel into the past; all the mysteries of the novel are shown to be logical effects of time travel or the actions of the magicians and others involved.

On Stranger Tides and *The Stress of Her Regard* each postulate an elaborate and coherent structure of magic, similar to systems we know but explained in unique ways. In the former, the Caribbean pirates use a magic-like and yet unlike *vodun.* The latter introduces the Nephelim, trans-human life forms resembling aspects of classical myth and European folklore mixed into something new, part muse and part Lamia. In *Last Call,* even poker partakes of the same magic as the tarot, which is linked to the underlying order of all things in the death and rebirth of the Fisher King and his wife; in addition to this order, there is a force of chaos, linked to post-modern mathematics and information theory—similar the probability-destroying eye of the Graiae in *The Stress of Her Regard,* but more developed. The magical device of immortality through body-switching shows up in *The Anubis Gates, On Stranger Tides, Last Call,* and Powers's short fiction piece "The Way Down the Hill."

Powers excels in description of action, especially swordplay. He also carefully describes the physical consequences of such violence, including slow-healing wounds, and many of his characters are or become maimed. He often features characters who are street-thieves or grifters, which he presents with affection and energy but without sentimentality. His protagonists tend to be male, from youth to middle-age; with courage and intelligence, but not larger than life, they are usually both likable and credible. Generally, the characters personally develop as the novel progresses. When his work takes place in a realistic past, Powers often features historical figures as secondary characters and invents a protagonist; in *The Stress of Her Regard* the action is more nearly split between his fictional protagonists and his versions of Shelley, Byron, Keats, and their friends.

It may be impossible to convey fully the elaborate and coherent weirdness of a novel by Tim Powers: the Dancing Ape Madness in *The Anubis Gates;* the hemogoblin in *Dinner at Deviant's Palace;* the Fountain of Youth in *On Stranger Tides;* the game of Assumption or the goldfish-eating Fat Man in *Last Call;* and of course the much-celebrated poet, William Ashbless. Especially in the later novels, all this is conveyed in an assured prose, with a range of tones both humorous and serious, generally transparent but marked by strong descriptions and striking metaphors. Still not as well known as he should be, Powers gets greater acclaim with each novel, and deservedly so.

—Bernadette Lynn Bosky

PRATCHETT, Terry

Nationality: British. **Born:** 1948. **Education:** Wycombe Technical High School. **Career:** Journalist in Buckinghamshire, Bristol, and Bath, then press officer, Central Electricity Board Western Region, until 1987. Chairman, Society of Authors, 1994-95. **Awards:** British Science Fiction award, 1990; Writers' Guild Children's Book of the Year award, 1993; British Book Awards Science Fiction and Fantasy Writer of the Year, 1993. **Agent:** Colin Smythe Ltd., P.O. Box 6, Gerrards Cross, Buckinghamshire SL9 8XA, England.

Science Fiction Publications

Novels (series: Discworld; Johnny Maxwell; Truckers/Bromeliad)

The Carpet People. Gerrards Cross, Buckinghamshire, Smythe, 1971; revised, London, Doubleday, 1992.
The Dark Side of the Sun. Gerrards Cross, Buckinghamshire, Smythe, 1976.
Strata. Gerrards Cross, Buckinghamshire, Smythe, and New York, St. Martin's Press, 1981.
The Colour of Magic (Discworld). Gerrards Cross, Buckinghamshire, Smythe, and New York, St. Martin's Press, 1983.
The Light Fantastic (Discworld). Gerrard's Cross, Buckinghamshire, Smythe, and Garden City, New York, Doubleday, 1986.
Equal Rites (Discworld). London, Gollancz, 1987; New York, Signet, 1988.
Mort (Discworld). London, Gollancz, 1987; New York, Signet, 1989.
Sourcery (Discworld). London, Gollancz, 1988; New York, Signet, 1989.
Wyrd Sisters: Starring Three Witches (Discworld). London, Gollancz, 1988; New York, Roc, 1990.
Pyramids: The Book of Going Forth (Discworld). London, Gollancz, 1989; New York, Roc, 1990.
Guards! Guards! (Discworld). London, Gollancz, 1989; New York, Roc, 1991.
Truckers (first of the Truckers trilogy; in the U.S. as the Bromeliad trilogy). London, Doubleday, 1989; New York, Delacorte, 1990.
Faust Eric (Discworld). London, Gollancz, 1990.

Good Omens: The Nice and Accurate Prophecies of Agnes Nutter, Witch, with Neil Gaiman. London, Gollancz, 1990; revised, New York, Workman, 1990.
Moving Pictures (Discworld). London, Gollancz, 1990; New York, Roc, 1992.
Diggers (Truckers/Bromeliad). London, Doubleday, and New York, Delacorte, 1991.
Wings (Truckers/Bromeliad). London, Doubleday, 1990; New York, Delacorte, 1991.
Reaper Man (Discworld). London, Gollancz, 1991; New York, Roc, 1992.
Witches Abroad (Discworld). London, Gollancz, 1991; New York, Roc, 1993.
Small Gods (Discworld). London, Gollancz, 1992; New York, HarperPrism, 1993.
Only You Can Save Mankind (Maxwell). London, Doubleday, 1992.
Lords and Ladies (Discworld). London, Gollancz, 1992; New York, HarperPrism, 1995.
Johnny and the Dead (Maxwell). London, Doubleday, 1993.
Men at Arms (Discworld). London, Gollancz, 1993.
The Bromelaid (includes *Truckers, Diggers,* and *Wings*). New York, Guild America, 1993.
Soul Music (Discworld). London, Gollancz, 1994; New York, HarperPrism, 1995.
Interesting Times (Discworld). London, Gollancz, 1994.
The Witches Trilogy (omnibus). London, Gollancz, 1995.

Other Publications

Other

The Unadulterated Cat, with illustrations by Gray Jolliffe. London, Gollancz, 1989.
The Streets of Ankh-Morpork (map), with Stephen Briggs. London, Corgi, 1993.
The Discworld Companion, with Stephen Briggs. London, Gollancz, 1994.
Adaptor, *Mort: A Discworld Big Comic* (graphic novel based on the novel of the same name), illustrated by Graham Higgins. London, Gollancz, 1994.

*   *   *

Humorous genre fiction, science fiction or fantasy, has generally been regarded even within those fields as somehow inferior to more serious efforts. The implication is that it is more difficult to thrill or scare a reader than to cause laughter. Although most attempts at humor are in fact juvenile or trite, there are a handful of writers like Douglas Adams who bring a definite art to the job, and Terry Pratchett has carved out a niche as the field's cleverest and most consistently entertaining humorist.

Pratchett's early novel *Strata* was widely regarded as an amusing commentary on Larry Niven's award-winning novel *Ringworld,* which it resembles in many superficial ways. The protagonist is a woman whose job is to oversee the construction of planets. She is at great pains to ensure that her subordinates do not plant anachronistic items in the strata of these worlds. A mysterious visitor informs her of the existence of a flat world, lost in space, built by means of some arcane lore, inhabited by people who appear to be human. Her curiosity and her sense of adventure both stir, and she sets off with a number of companions—some human, some not—to find the flat planet. Unfortunately, a series of mishaps results in the loss of their guide and the eventual incapacitation of their spacecraft. They do however land at their destination, and what ensues is an hilarious romp among dragons, robots, aliens, and other creatures.

Pratchett borrowed from Niven again in *The Dark Side of the Sun,* a slightly more serious work. The protagonist is the rich heir to a powerful title who sets off on a quest to find the Jokers' World, home of a legendary alien species. The background involves the manipulation of the laws of chance, another facet of *Ringworld.* A series of assassination attempts are thwarted, generally through a chain of coincidences. Once again, the best part of the novel is the richly creative background of aliens, religious and philosophical speculations, and exotic settings. Pratchett's lighthearted approach succeeds in making what would otherwise be a standard adventure story into a witty exercise of the imagination.

It was with *The Colour of Magic,* however, that Pratchett hit his stride. This first volume of the ongoing "Discworld" series consists of four interrelated adventures. Discworld is a flat planet, but set in a fantastic rather than a rational universe. In this case, the planet is supported on the backs of four gigantic elephants astride the shell of an immense tortoise swimming in space. The inhabitants know that their view of the universe is correct, because they have lowered observers over the edge to see for themselves.

Rincewind is certainly one of the least likely magicians ever to grace the pages of fiction, both here and in some of the subsequent chronicles of Discworld. In this instance, he agrees to provide his services as a guide to a visitor from another planet interested in exploration. Their travels result in encounters with malevolent animals, wizards, monsters, and other villains in what is essentially a satire on the fantasy genre itself. Pratchett seems particularly enamored of anachronisms, which abound in this novel.

Further chronicles of Discworld have appeared with regularity thereafter. Magical madness continues as Rincewind combats the appearance of a strange new star in *The Light Fantastic.* Granny Weatherwax, a canny old witch, takes center stage in *Equal Rites,* trying to straighten out the problems that ensue when the eighth son of an eighth son is . . . a daughter. More misdirected magic dominates the scene in *Sourcery* and in *The Wyrd Sisters,* a retelling of the traditional story of the prince regaining his throne. Ancient Egypt gets raked over the coals in *Pyramids.*

Possibly the funniest of this hilarious series is *Mort,* in which Death goes on a holiday after taking on an inept apprentice, who is just too kindhearted to harvest all the souls who are scheduled to pass on. Considering the number of volumes in this series, it might be expected that Pratchett would have begun to repeat himself, but each is as fresh, inventive, and hilarious as those which preceded it. In *Reaper Man* Death retires, and the ensuing chaos is Pratchett's opportunity to lampoon protest movements and political protest groups. An unlikely and unwilling messiah is chosen by a god in *Small Gods,* and he spends the rest of the book trying to get unchosen. The fantasy quest story is dismembered in *Witches Abroad* and Hollywood and the film industry get an indirect, satirical roasting in *Moving Pictures.*

Pratchett's non-Discworld novel, written in collaboration with comic book writer Neil Gaiman, is *Good Omens: The Nice and Accurate Predictions of Agnes Nutter, Witch.* This sendup of modern horror themes, particularly the "Omen" series of films and its imitators, surpasses anything that went before it. When the son of Satan is misplaced and raised as a nice child, the schedule of Armageddon is thrown awry, and the powers of Heaven and Hell

must work together to find a resolution. This is one of those rare novels that proves humor can be great literature as well as marvelous entertainment.

The most surprising aspect of Pratchett's work is that, with a few exceptions, each of his Discworld novels has been fresh, inventive, and not at all a thinly disguised rewrite of previous volumes. His acerbic, witty, and perceptive style is characterized by clever word play, amusing anachronisms, abrupt reversals, and a delightfully skewed vision of the foibles of humankind. Pratchett also has an unusually strong talent for creating memorable, though distorted characters and making the reader accept them as real people.

—Don D'Ammassa

PRATT, (Murray) Fletcher

Pseudonym: George U. Fletcher. **Nationality:** American. **Born:** Buffalo, New York, 25 April 1897. **Education:** Attended Hobart College, Geneva, New York, 1915-16; University of Paris, 1931-33. **Military Service:** Served in the War Library Service during World War I. **Family:** Married Inga Marie Stephens. **Career:** Librarian, 1918-20; staff member, *Buffalo Courier Express,* 1920-23; freelance writer from 1923; regular contributor, *American Mercury* and *Saturday Review of Literature;* military advisor, *Time* and *New York Post* during World War II. **Member:** Bread Loaf Writers Conference. President, Authors Club, 1941; co-founder, American Rocket Society. **Awards:** United States Navy award, 1957. **Died:** 10 June 1956.

SCIENCE FICTION PUBLICATIONS

Novels

The Well of the Unicorn (as George U. Fletcher). New York, Sloane, 1948; as Fletcher Pratt, New York, Lancer, 1967.
Double in Space (Project Excelsior, The Wanderer's Return). Garden City, New York, Doubleday, 1951.
Double Jeopardy. Garden City, New York, Doubleday, 1952.
The Undying Fire. New York, Ballantine, 1953; as *The Conditioned Captain,* in *Double in Space,* 1954.
Double in Space (Project Excelsior, The Conditioned Captain). London, Boardman, 1954.
Invaders from Rigel. New York, Avalon, 1960.
Alien Planet. New York, Avalon, 1962.
The Blue Star. New York, Ballantine, 1969.

Novels with L. Sprague de Camp (series: Harold Shea)

The Incomplete Enchanter (Shea). New York, Holt, 1941; London, Sphere, 1979.
Land of Unreason. New York, Holt, 1942.
The Carnelian Cube: A Humorous Fantasy. New York, Gnome Press, 1948.
The Castle of Iron (Shea). New York, Gnome Press, 1950.
Wall of Serpents (Shea). New York, Avalon, 1960; as *The Enchanter Compleated,* London, Sphere, 1980.

The Compleat Enchanter: The Magical Misadventures of Harold Shea (includes *The Incomplete Enchanter* and *The Castle of Iron*). Garden City, New York, Doubleday, 1975; London, Sphere, 1979; expanded as *The Intrepid Enchanter: The Complete Magical Misadventures of Harold Shea.* London, Sphere, 1988; as *The Complete Compleat Enchanter,* New York, Baen, 1989.

Short Stories

Tales from Gavagan's Bar, with L. Sprague de Camp. New York, Twayne, 1953; expanded edition, Philadelphia, Owlswick Press, 1978.

OTHER PUBLICATIONS

Other

The Heroic Years: Fourteen Years of the Republic 1801-1815. New York, Smith and Haas, 1934.
The Cunning Mulatto and Other Cases of Ellis Parker, American Detective. New York, Smith and Haas, 1935; as *Detective No. 1,* London, Methuen, 1936.
Ordeal by Fire: An Informal History of the Civil War. New York, Smith and Haas, 1935; revised edition, New York, Sloane, 1948; London, Lane, 1950; as *A Short History of the Civil War,* New York, Bantam, n.d.
Hail, Caesar! New York, Smith and Haas, 1936; London, Williams and Norgate, 1938.
The Navy: A History. Garden City, New York, Doubleday, 1938.
Road to Empire: The Life and Times of Bonaparte the General. Garden City, New York, Doubleday, 1939.
Sea Power and Today's War. New York, Harrison Hilton, 1939; London, Methuen, 1940.
Secret and Urgent: The Story of Codes and Ciphers. Indianapolis, Bobbs Merrill, and London, Hale, 1939.
Fletcher Pratt's Naval War Game. New York, Harrison Hilton, 1940.
Fighting Ships of the U.S. Navy. New York, Garden City Publishing Company, 1941.
America and Total War. New York, Smith and Durrell, 1941.
The U.S. Army. Racine, Wisconsin, Whitman, 1942.
What the Citizen Should Know about Modern War. New York, Norton, 1942.
The Navy Has Wings. New York, Harper, 1943.
My Life to the Destroyers, with Captain L.A. Abercrombie. New York, Holt, 1944.
The Navy's War. New York, Harper, 1944.
A Short History of the Army and Navy. Washington, D.C., Infantry Journal, 1944.
Fleet against Japan. New York, Harper, 1946.
Empire of the Sea. New York, Holt, 1946.
Night Work: The Story of Task Force 39. New York, Holt, 1946.
A Man and His Meals, with Robeson Bailey. New York, Holt, 1947.
The Empire and Glory: Napoleon Bonaparte 1800-1806. New York, Sloane, 1948.
The Marines' War. New York, Sloane, 1948.
Eleven Generals: Studies in American Command. New York, Sloane, 1949.
The Third King. New York, Sloane, 1950.

War for the World: A Chronicle of Our Fighting Forces in World War II. New Haven, Connecticut, Yale University Press, 1950.
Prebble's Boys: Commodore Prebble and the Birth of American Sea Power. New York, Sloane, 1950.
Rockets, Jets, Guided Missiles, and Space Ships. New York, Random House, 1951; London, Sidgwick and Jackson, 1952.
The Monitor and the Merrimac. New York, Random House, 1951.
By Space Ship to the Moon (for children). New York, Random House, 1952; London, Publicity Products, 1953.
Stanton, Lincoln's Secretary of War. New York, Norton, 1953.
All about Rockets and Jets. New York, Random House, 1955.
The Civil War. New York, Garden City Books, 1955.
Famous Inventors and Their Inventions. New York, Random House, 1955.
The Battles that Changed History. Garden City, New York, Doubleday, 1956.
Civil War on Western Waters. New York, Holt, 1956.
The Compact History of the United States Navy. New York, Hawthorn, 1957.

Editor, *World of Wonder: An Introduction to Imaginative Literature.* New York, Twayne, 1951.
Editor, *Civil War in Pictures.* New York, Garden City Books, 1951.
Editor, *Petrified Planet.* New York, Twayne, 1952.
Editor, *Witches Three* (includes *The Blue Star*). New York, Twayne, 1952.
Editor, *My Diary, North and South,* by Sir William Howard Russell. New York, Harper, 1954.

Translator, *The Great American Parade,* by H.J. Duteil. New York, Twayne, 1953.

* * *

Fletcher Pratt had an extremely varied writing career. While he is considered to be one of the pioneer science fiction writers, he also wrote fantasy and produced an impressive list of historical nonfiction. In terms of science fiction, Pratt wrote mainly short fiction during his early years, with the exception of *Alien Planet.* The publisher's foreword to the Ace edition of this novel accurately describes it as using "the traditional technique of the 'marvelous voyage' and the 'manuscript found in a bottle' . . . combined with a penetrating and satiric representation of human society through the method of exploring an alien culture." It is a classic representation of the genre. Of course, much of the material is outdated but there remains some interesting philosophy, including the alien dissident's description of intelligent life as a disease infesting the planets which the divine spirit strives to destroy.

In 1939, Pratt met L. Sprague deCamp and his writing turned toward fantasy. Together they wrote a series of stories about a psychologist who finds himself projected into a number of parallel worlds which are based on our myths. Harold Shea, as he is called, makes his rounds of Norse mythology ("The Roaring Trumpet"), Spenser's *Faerie Queene* ("The Mathematics of Logic"), Ariosto's *Orlando Furioso* (The Castle of Iron), the Finnish *Kalevala (Wall of Serpents)* and the world of Irish myth ("The Green Magician"). The stories were unique in that they combined the then new field of sword-and-sorcery fantasy with a refreshing humor. The two writers wrote two additional fantasy novels, *Land of Unreason* and *The Carnelian Cube,* as well as a collection of short fantasy spoofs, *Tales from Gavagan's Bar.* The last, similar to Clarke's *Tales of the White Hart,* also showed the magical humor of Pratt and de Camp evident in the Harold Shea pieces. Pratt's solo novel *The*

Well of the Unicorn is a fascinating creation by a master story-teller, one of the very best of fantasies.

Pratt's SF work *Double Jeopardy* details the adventures of George Helmfleet Jones, an agent with the Secret Service some time in the future. In his first adventure, Jones solves a case dealing with a matter transmitter; in the second, he is confronted by the theft of a large sum of money from a sealed, remote-controlled cargo rocket. *Double in Space* consists of two unrelated works. The first is born of the early Cold War with Russian and U.S. space stations vying for superiority in space. The second is a take-off on the voyage of Ulysses set in the far distant future. In a similar vein, *The Undying Fire* follows the plot of Jason and the Golden Fleece. None of these works matches the caliber of Pratt's fantasy.

—Paul Swank

PREUSS, Paul

Nationality: American. **Born:** Albany, Georgia, 7 March 1942. **Education:** Yale University, New Haven, Connecticut, B.A. 1966. **Military Service:** Served in the United States Air Force Reserve, 1960-66. **Family:** Married 1) Marsha Pettit in 1963 (divorced 1968), one daughter; 2) Karen Reiser in 1973 (divorced 1989); Debra Turner in 1993. **Career:** Marketing planning projects director, Batten Barton Durstine & Osborn, New York, 1966-67; floor director, King-TV, 1967-68, and unit manager, 1968-69, production manager, 1969-70, and creative director, 1970-72, King Screen Productions, all in Seattle, staff consultant, Biological Sciences Curriculum Study, Boulder, Colorado, 1972-73; independent film producer, 1974-81, and associate producer, editor, and post-production supervisor, Lee Mendelson Film Productions and other companies, 1975-81. Since 1978, freelance writer. **Agent:** Jean Naggar, Jean V. Naggar Literary Agency, Inc., 216 East 75th Street, New York, New York 10021, U.S.A.

SCIENCE FICTION PUBLICATIONS

Novels (series: Arthur C. Clarke's Venus Prime)

The Gates of Heaven. New York, Bantam, 1980.
Re-Entry. New York, Bantam, 1981.
Broken Symmetries. New York, Timescape, 1983; London, Penguin, 1984.
Human Error. New York, Tor, 1985.
Breaking Strain (Venus Prime). New York, Avon, 1987; London, Pan, 1990.
Starfire. London, Simon and Schuster, and New York, Tor, 1988.
Maelstrom (Venus Prime). New York, Avon, 1988; London, Pan, 1991.
Hide and Seek (Venus Prime). New York, Avon, 1989; London, Pan, 1991.
The Medusa Encounter (Venus Prime). New York, Avon, 1990; London, Pan, 1991.
The Diamond Moon (Venus Prime). New York, Avon, 1990.
The Shining Ones (Venus Prime). New York, Avon, 1991.
Core: A Novel. New York, Morrow, 1993.

*

Paul Preuss comments:

I remain more interested in the social implications of the scientific endeavor than in gadgets, and more interested in scientists than in science itself.

*   *   *

One of the most popular forms of science fiction is the "hard" science story, one in which specific scientific principles are the centerpiece of the plot. Many of these prove to be interesting intellectual puzzles or speculations, but fail as literature because the author concentrates on scientific aspects and pays scant attention to traditional literary values like style, characterization, and setting. At its best, this type of story weds the wonder and excitement of scientific discovery to strongly delineated characters in a credible situation, but few writers seem capable of handling both sides of the equation.

Paul Preuss established himself as one of the best writers of hard science fiction on the basis of his first two novels which, despite the use of realistic scientific settings and situations, are really more closely related to the fanciful space operas of Edmond Hamilton, Leigh Brackett, and others. Subsequent novels demonstrated both an intelligent, perceptive understanding of the scientific method and the state of modern research and a sensitivity to psychological and ethical problems facing the scientist in our society.

In *The Gates of Heaven,* scientists receive a message from another star system, the voices of the human crew of a ship which disappeared mysteriously some time earlier. They make use of a black hole to send a second vessel across interstellar distances in what is supposed to be a rescue mission, but which runs into problems of its own, including a mutiny when the leader of the expedition is temporarily stranded on a planetary surface. A double black hole makes time travel possible in *Re-Entry.* The protagonist journeys back to his own past, determined to alter the course of his own destiny, and quite predictably ends up affecting a great deal more. Although the scientific element was basically window dressing this time, Preuss used a rational, analytical approach to the problems of time travel which makes the outlandishness of the concept seem totally credible.

Preuss moved from these entertaining but basically romantic notions to a more serious approach with *Broken Symmetries.* The protagonist is part of a team developing a particle beam accelerator, a man whose interest in politics is at best superficial. Unfortunately, he soon becomes involved with clandestine efforts to make use of the new device, which had led to the discovery of a new kind of subatomic particle, as a source of international power. The potential exists to create a weapon beside which even atomic bombs will seem of little consequence. Preuss, in addition to crafting a genuinely interesting story of science and the people who study it, has overlaid a suspenseful mystery. At the same time, he unobtrusively uses the plot as a way of examining the uses to which our society puts scientific progress. With his third novel, Preuss had gone from an interesting writer of romantic adventure to a serious novelist.

Human Error explored those same questions from a different perspective, the responsibility of scientists for the consequences of their work. Compugen is a financially ailing corporation that makes use of genetic engineering to tailor specialized viruses. When the company's president prematurely announces the discovery of a radical new substance, then behaves so erratically that he is institutionalized, members of his staff suspect that he has been infected by one of their creations, and may have spread the disease to the population at large. A combination of serious scientific extrapolation and contemporary medical thriller, *Human Error* quickly confirmed Preuss's enviable reputation.

The manned space program of the near future is the subject of *Starfire*. A cashiered ex-astronaut who abandoned his crippled ship in order to save his life is determined that his career will not end so abruptly. Taking advantage of every opportunity, he manages to win a place in the crew of an experimental new space vehicle, only to find himself in the midst of a new crisis when a solar flare threatens to bring a disastrous end to their mission.

In 1987, Preuss began a series of novels inspired in part by the work of Arthur C. Clarke, the "Venus Prime" novels. Although there have been a number of novels "borrowed" from the creations of other writers, Preuss avoids the pitfalls of most of these, using the original concept simply as the launching point for each novel. *Breaking Strain* introduced Sparta, a woman with unusual powers, the product of biotechnology, whose sojourn on Venus is interrupted by the arrival of a crippled space freighter. The mystery of her own origin seems to be related, and Sparta must turn detective to resolve the issue.

Sparta returned in *Maelstrom,* still seeking the secret of her origin. A party of scientists lost in the Venusian wilderness uncover an alien artifact. Another classic Clarke story provided the inspiration for *Hide and Seek,* with Sparta now transported to the orbit of Mars in her quest to discover her own history. Sparta reaches Jupiter in *The Medusa Encounter,* broadly drawn from Clarke's "A Meeting with Medusa," this time investigating the possibility that a religious cult may have seized control of a sensitive interplanetary mission. In the next installment, *The Diamond Moon,* derived from Clarke's "Jupiter Five," continues the expedition to the Jovian moons, where Sparta must now contend with a crash landing and the presence of a saboteur among the complement. In *The Shining Ones* we discover that the Jovian satellite is actually an alien starship, long dormant, but not revived and operational. The "Venus Prime" series is an inventive, exciting project with high entertainment value and strong scientific content, although it lacks some of the impact of Preuss's more serious novels.

The most recent Preuss novel is *Core,* which takes an elderly fantastic theme and examines it logically. An expedition is launched to the core of the Earth, hopefully to find a way to avert a catastrophe that could destroy all life on Earth. Preuss examines what might sound like an outlandish concept in a rigorously scientific and practical fashion.

Although rarely a short story writer, Preuss has demonstrated his ability at that length with such interesting stories as "Small Bodies," "Half a Life," and "Rhea's Time."

—Don D'Ammassa

PRIEST, Christopher

Nationality: British. **Born:** Cheadle, Cheshire, in 1943. **Education:** Warehouseman and Clerks' Orphan Schools, Manchester, 1951-59. **Career:** Council member, Science Fiction Foundation, and editor, *Foundation,* for 2 years. **Awards:** British Science Fiction Association award, 1974, 1979; Ditmar award (Australia) 1977,

1982. **Agent:** Maggie Noach Literary Agency, 21 Redan Street, London W14 0AB, England; or, Ellen Levine Literary Agency, 15 East 26th Street, New York, New York 10010, U.S.A.

SCIENCE FICTION PUBLICATIONS

Novels

Indoctrinaire. London, Faber, and New York, Harper, 1970; revised edition, London, Pan, 1979.
Fugue for a Darkening Island. London, Faber, 1972; as *Darkening Island,* New York, Harper, 1972.
Inverted World. London, Faber, 1974; as *The Inverted World,* New York, Harper, 1974.
The Space Machine: A Scientific Romance. London, Faber, and New York, Harper, 1976.
A Dream of Wessex. London, Faber, 1977; as *The Perfect Lover,* New York, Scribner, 1977.
The Affirmation. London, Faber, and New York, Scribner, 1981.
The Glamour. London, Cape, 1984; revised edition, Garden City, New York, Doubleday, 1985.
The Quiet Woman. London, Bloomsbury, 1990.

Short Stories

Real-Time World. London, New English Library, 1974.
An Infinite Summer. London, Faber, and New York, Scribner, 1979.
The Making of the Lesbian Horse. Birmingham, Birmingham Science Fiction Group, 1979.

OTHER PUBLICATIONS

Other

Your Book of Film-Making (for children). London, Faber, 1974.
The Last Deadloss Visions. Pewsey, Wiltshire, Priest, 1987; 2nd. edition, 1987.
"The Truth Shall Set You Free." Pewsey, Wiltshire, Priest, 1987.
Seize the Moment: The Autobiography of Helen Sharman, with Helen Sharman. London, Gollancz, 1993.
Running Tall, with Sally Gunnell. London, Gollancz, 1994.

Editor, *Anticipations.* London, Faber, and New York, Scribner, 1978.
Editor, with Robert Holdstock, *Stars of Albion* (anthology of British science fiction). London, Pan, 1979.

*

Critical Study: *Christopher Priest* by Nicholas Ruddick, Mercer, Washington, Starmont House, 1990.

*   *   *

Christopher Priest was one of the most promising new British science-fiction writers to become active in the 1970s. His first novel *Indoctrinaire* (expanded from "The Interrogator"), reflected the type of story that dominated *New Worlds* at the time. Dr. Wentik is a researcher in investigating an experimental drug at a scientific installation in the Antarctic when he is shanghaied by the mysterious

American government agent Astrourde. Shortly thereafter he is incarcerated in an enigmatic prison in the Brazilian highlands, in an area that somehow serves as a bridge between the present and the world two centuries from now. Wentik's attempts to escape his situation, or even to make some kind of sense of it, are reminiscent of Kafka. His efforts are largely ineffectual, although it does become increasingly clear to him that even his captors are without true freedom. Reality and fantasy merge at times, and the result is a kaleidoscopic novel that dilutes its effect by the lack of strong focus.

Fugue for a Darkening Island also features a weak and less than entirely admirable protagonist. Following a major war in Africa, the British Isles are rapidly inundated with refugees, an exodus that is met with indecisive hostility on the part of the British authorities. As the influx grows, order begins to disintegrate. Divergent opinions about the obligation to provide succor to the refugees lead to an increasingly violent factionalism. Government control over much of the countryside collapses; individual neighborhoods wall themselves off from the outside world. Alan Whitman and his family are cast adrift in this world, and find that they are unable to control their own future. Frequently it is impossible even to distinguish those who uphold the law from those who break it. Priest makes no effort to plot his novel linearly. The viewpoint jumps back and forth through time, seemingly at random, so that the reader is almost simultaneously exposed to Whitman at all stages of his dissolution. But Priest holds his character at arm's length from us, and we can vaguely perceive his motivations; the nightmarish quality of his world remains just that, for it never quite achieves reality.

Paradoxically, while the all-too-possible world shown in *Fugue for a Darkening Island* never acquires depth, the almost totally incredible setting of *Inverted World* is vividly realistic. It is a much more cohesive novel than anything Priest had written before. It features a strong sympathetic character, and some of the most innovative settings to appear in years. Helward Mann is a citizen of City Earth, an enormous construct that inches across the surface of its world by wincing itself across tracks picked up from behind and laboriously replaced ahead. The city is in eternal pursuit of the Optimum, the place where environmental conditions are most like that of their home world. For this world, whatever it might be, is treacherous and changing. Behind them, physical features become broad and flat, time passes very rapidly in relation to the city itself, and a mysterious force increasingly attempts to pull laggers back to their destruction. Ahead, the distortions of time and space have exactly opposite attributes. As Mann is initiated into the guild responsible for scouting the future, he gradually matures and adjusts to the changing nature of his world. Idea is central here rather than character; nevertheless, Helward and his personal relationships with others from the city are well portrayed. Although less ambitious stylistically than Priest's earlier novels, *Inverted World* is far more successful both as an adventure story and as a novel of ideas. Priest indulged in pastiche next, and *The Space Machine* is a witty and frequently funny examination of some of the situations first presented by H.G. Wells. This invocation of Martian invaders and time machines is carried a bit too far, unfortunately, and it is difficult to sustain interest through to the end.

A Dream of Wessex is a far more successful novel in almost any terms, and is easy the high point of Priest's career. The Ridpath Project is a secret research installation where a group of people pool their subconscious minds to create a mutual dream world. Within this context, they can extrapolate the future possibilities of various aspects of the present. But there is trouble brewing. David Harkman, one of the dreamers, has lost his awareness of the real world and will not come out of trance. Julia Stretton, another participant, tries desperately to release him from the grip of the dream world, particularly when she learns of the imminent participation of a new dreamer, a man who considers the project to be nonsense. The dream world becomes more real to the reader than the project itself, and, despite the existence of Soviet domination over Britain, it is easy to see why Harkman is unconsciously reluctant to leave it for reality. Both of the central figures are fully realized personalities, and their awakening feelings for each other are convincing.

Priest seems to be fusing reality and dreams increasingly in his fiction. It should be no surprise, therefore, to note that most of his better short stories also explore this interface. "Real Time World" describes the Observatory, supposedly an extra-dimensional establishment from which a small staff could observe the flora and fauna of other worlds, in actuality an experiment in itself on news deprivation with a staff thoroughly brainwashed about the nature of their situation. In "Palely Loitering" a man spends much of his life travelling back and forth across time bridges, always in pursuit of a young girl he does not have the courage to confront. His ultimate effort draws into question the immutability of the past and the reality of his own present. Two stories set within the context of the "Dream Archipelago" are also worth mentioning. "Whores" is an incident sliced out of time, wherein the protagonist encounters a series of inexplicable events, mutilations of a sort of people living in an area formerly occupied by enemy troops. Much of the story's impact is dissipated by the ambiguous ending, however, a problem that arises also with Priest's best short story, "The Watched." Yvann Ordier is disturbed by his voyeuristic spying on a band of Qataari refugees. The Qataari have an obsessive need for privacy, and will literally starve to death rather than submit to being studied. At the same time, Ordier himself is compulsively wary of scintillas, tiny mechanical spy devices that are almost unavoidable. The result is a complex story of character, obsession, and personal decay.

The themes that had been developing in Priest's work, the interface between dream and reality leading to questions of the nature of identity, found their finest expression in three novels which, although not otherwise linked, seem to form a loose thematic trilogy. In each case the novel revolves around the unravelling sense of identity of the central character.

This is most forcefully expressed in the first of these three novels, *The Affirmation*. Peter Sinclair is orphaned, unemployed, homeless and has broken up with his girlfriend. As his personality begins to fragment in the light of these disasters he sets out to write a book. When he presents the finished work, it consists of no more than a pile of blank pages.

The book he has composed in his madness is set in the Dream Archipelago, a cross between the islands of Greece and the drowned landscape of *A Dream of Wessex* in which Priest set many of his finest stories at this time. There another Peter Sinclair has won immortality but to achieve the prize he must surrender his memories, so he sets out to preserve his identity in a book, and the book he writes is the story of Peter Sinclair in England. Thus the two worlds mirror and rebound upon one another, reflecting the fragmenting identity of the twin protagonists.

These patterns of duality and fragmenting identity are echoed also in *The Glamour*. The Glamour is a form of social invisibility; those who possess it are able to behave in such a way that other people do not see them. The most profoundly glamorous people become completely detached from society. After being injured in a terrorist bomb blast, Grey and his girlfriend Sue must piece together their memories, but these memories contain gaps and incidents which do not make sense until they realise that they were once glamorous, and that they are haunted still by the profoundly glamorous Niall. Like Paul and David competing for Julia in *A Dream of Wessex,* as Grey and Niall compete for Sue they become mirrors of each other, embodiments of a fractured personality.

Though some of these themes are present also in Priest's next novel, *The Quiet Woman,* notably the way that disengagement from the world is equated with psychological disintegration, this book stands outside his science fiction. Despite a near-future setting and a brief, visionary account of flying saucers landing, the real thrust of this novel is concerned with the contemporary political milieu. The duality here is between Alice and Eleanor on the one hand, campaigning for what is clearly a good cause, and Eleanor's son Gordon, a petty mandarin who opposes them and whose psychological breakdown is illuminated by a series of increasing disturbing and violent sexual fantasies.

The Prestige, like *The Affirmation* and *The Glamour* before it, is a direct engagement with questions of identity. At the heart of the novel, as psychologically complex and satisfying as anything Priest has written, are first-person accounts by two rival stage magicians at the end of the last century. Both perform the same trick, involving instantaneous travel across the stage, but in very different ways, ways which allow Priest to question what constitutes identity. Although, as is the way with stage magic, the secrets are never fully divulged, though one, Alfred Borden, appears to involve a twin who is never acknowledged, one personality spread across two bodies. The other, Rupert Angier, using a device developed by Nikolas Tesla, seems to create a second self. So there are dualities not just between Borden and Angier but within each character, and these fragmentations resound across the generations to afflict their descendants in the present day.

Priest is not a prolific writer, and his stories can seem complex and distanced, but in his development of character and particularly in is exploration of psychological disintegration, his work can be as profound, as challenging and as disturbing as any other writer in the field.

—Don D'Ammassa, updated by Paul Kincaid

PRIESTLEY, J(ohn) B(oynton)

Pseudonym: Peter Goldsmith. **Nationality:** British. **Born:** Bradford, Yorkshire, 13 September 1894. **Education:** Belle Vue Grammar School, Bradford, to age 16; Trinity Hall, Cambridge, 1919-21, B.A. in history 1921, M.A. **Military Service:** Served in the Duke of Wellington's and Devon regiments, 1914-19. **Family:** Married 1) Patricia Tempest (died 1925), two daughters; 2) Mary Wyndham Lewis in 1926 (divorced 1952), two daughters and one son; 3) the writer and archaeologist Jacquetta Hawkes in 1953. Clerk, Helm & Co., wool firm, Bradford, 1911-14; freelance journalist and reviewer, and reader for Bodley Head publishers, London, 1922-29; director, Mask Theatre, London, 1938-39; radio lecturer on BBC programme "Postscripts," 1940; regular contributor, *New Statesman,* London. **Member:** President, PEN, London, 1936-37; United Kingdom delegate, and chairman, Unesco International Theatre Conference, Paris, 1947, and Prague, 1948; chairman, British Theatre Conference, 1948; president, International Theatre In-

stitute, 1949; member, National Theatre Board, London, 1966-67. **Awards:** James Tait Black Memorial prize, 1930; Ellen Terry award, 1948. LL.D.: University of St. Andrews, Fife; D.Litt.: University of Birmingham; University of Bradford. Honorary freeman, City of Bradford, 1973; honorary student, Trinity Hall, Cambridge, 1978. Order of Merit, 1977. **Died:** 14 August 1984.

SCIENCE FICTION PUBLICATIONS

Novels

Adam in Moonshine. London, Heinemann, and New York, Harper, 1927.
The Doomsday Men: An Adventure. London, Heinemann, and New York, Harper, 1938.
Jenny Villiers: A Story of the Theatre. London, Heinemann, and New York, Harper, 1947.
The Magicians. London, Heinemann, and New York, Harper, 1954.
Saturn over the Water: An Account of His Adventures in London, South America, and Australia, by Tim Belford, Painter. London, Heinemann, and New York, Doubleday, 1961.
The Thirty-First of June: A Tale of True Love, Enterprise, and Progress in the Arthurian and Atomic Ages. London, Heinemann, 1961; New York, Doubleday, 1962.
Snoggle: A Story for Anybody between 9 and 90 (for children). London, Heinemann, 1971; New York, Harcourt Brace, 1972.

Short Stories

The Other Place and Other Stories of the Same Sort. London, Heinemann, and New York, Harper, 1953.

OTHER PUBLICATIONS

Novels

Benighted. London, Heinemann, 1927; as *The Old Dark House,* New York, Harper, 1928.
Farthing Hall, with Hugh Walpole. London, Macmillan, and New York, Doubleday, 1929.
The Good Companions. London, Heinemann, and New York, Harper, 1929.
Angel Pavement. London, Heinemann, and New York, Harper, 1930.
Faraway. London, Heinemann, and New York, Harper, 1932.
I'll Tell You Everything, with Gerald Bullett. New York, Macmillan, 1932; London, Heinemann, 1933.
Wonder Hero. London, Heinemann, and New York, Harper, 1933.
They Walk in the City: The Lovers in the Stone Forest. London, Heinemann, and New York, Harper, 1936.
Let the People Sing. London, Heinemann, 1939; New York, Harper, 1940.
Black-Out in Gretley: A Story of—and for—Wartime. London, Heinemann, and New York, Harper, 1942.
Daylight on Saturday: A Novel about an Aircraft Factory. London, Heinemann, and New York, Harper, 1943.
Three Men in New Suits. London, Heinemann, and New York, Harper, 1945.
Bright Day. London, Heinemann, and New York, Harper, 1946.

Festival at Farbridge. London, Heinemann, 1951; as *Festival,* New York, Harper, 1951.

Low Notes on a High Level: A Frolic. London, Heinemann, and New York, Harper, 1954.

The Shapes of Sleep: A Topical Tale. London, Heinemann, and New York, Doubleday, 1962.

Sir Michael and Sir George. London, Heinemann, 1964; Boston, Little Brown, 1965.

Lost Empires. London, Heinemann, and Boston, Little Brown, 1965.

Salt Is Leaving. London, Pan, 1966; New York, Harper, 1975.

It's an Old Country. London, Heinemann, and Boston, Little Brown, 1967.

The Image Men: Out of Town, and London End. London, Heinemann, 2 vols., 1968; Boston, Little Brown, 1 vol., 1969.

Found, Lost, Found; or The English Way of Life. London, Heinemann, 1976; New York, Stein and Day, 1977.

Short Stories

The Town Major of Miraucourt. London, Heinemann, 1930.

Albert Goes Through. London, Heinemann, and New York, Harper, 1933.

Going Up: Stories and Sketches. London, Pan, 1950.

The Carfitt Crisis and Two Other Stories. London, Heinemann, 1975.

Plays

The Good Companions (book only), with Edward Knoblock, lyrics by Harry Graham and Frank Eyton, music by Richard Addinsell, adaptation of the novel by Priestley (produced London and New York, 1931). London and New York, French, 1935.

Dangerous Corner (produced London and New York, 1932). London, Heinemann, and New York, French, 1932.

The Roundabout (produced Liverpool, London, and New York, 1932). London, Heinemann, and New York, French, 1933.

Laburnum Grove: An Immoral Comedy (produced London, 1933; New York, 1935). London, Heinemann, 1934; New York, French, 1935.

Eden End (produced London, 1934; New York, 1935). London, Heinemann, 1934; in *Three Plays and a Preface,* 1935.

Cornelius: A Business Affair in Three Transactions (produced Birmingham and London, 1935). London, Heinemann, 1935; New York, French, 1936.

Duet in Floodlight (produced Liverpool and London, 1935). London, Heinemann, 1935.

Three Plays and a Preface (includes *Dangerous Corner, Eden End, Cornelius*). New York, Harper, 1935.

Bees on the Boat Deck: A Farcical Tragedy (produced London, 1936). London, Heinemann, and Boston, Baker, 1936.

Spring Tide (as Peter Goldsmith), with George Billam (produced London, 1936). London, Heinemann, and New York, French, 1936.

The Bad Samaritan (produced Liverpool, 1937).

Time and the Conways (produced London, 1937; New York, 1938). London, Heinemann, 1937; New York, Harper, 1938.

I Have Been Here Before (produced London, 1937; New York, 1938). London, Heinemann 1937; New York, Harper, 1938.

Two Time Plays (includes *Time and the Conways* and *I Have Been Here Before*). London, Heinemann, 1937.

People at Sea (as *I Am a Stranger Here,* produced Bradford, 1937; as *People at Sea,* produced London, 1937). London, Heinemann, and New York, French, 1937.

Mystery of Greenfingers: A Comedy of Detection (produced London, 1938). London, French, 1937; New York, French, 1938.

The Rebels (produced Bradford, 1938).

When We Are Married: A Yorkshire Farcical Comedy (produced London, 1938; New York, 1939). London, Heinemann, 1938; New York, French, 1940.

Music at Night (produced Malvern, 1938; London, 1939). Included in *Three Plays,* 1943; in *Plays I,* 1948.

Johnson over Jordan (produced London, 1939). Published as *Johnson over Jordan: The Play, and All about It (An Essay).* London, Heinemann, and New York, Harper, 1939.

The Long Mirror (produced Oxford, 1940; London, 1945). Included in *Three Plays,* 1943; in *Four Plays,* 1944.

Good Night Children: A Comedy of Broadcasting (produced London, 1942). Included in *Three Comedies,* 1945; in *Plays II,* 1949.

Desert Highway (produced Bristol, 1943; London, 1944). London, Heinemann, 1944; in *Four Plays,* 1944.

They Came to a City (produced London, 1943). Included in *Three Plays* 1943; in *Four Plays,* 1944.

Three Plays (includes *Music at Night, The Long Mirror, They Came to a City*). London, Heinemann, 1943.

How Are They at Home? A Topical Comedy (produced London, 1944). Included in *Three Comedies,* 1945; in *Plays II,* 1949.

The Golden Fleece (as *The Bull Market,* produced Bradford, 1944). Included in *Three Comedies,* 1945.

Four Plays (includes *Music at Night, the Long Mirror, They Came to a City, Desert Highway*). London, Heinemann, and New York, Harper, 1944.

Three Comedies (includes *Good Night Children, The Golden Fleece, How Are They at Home?*). London, Heinemann, 1945.

An Inspector Calls (produced Moscow, 1945; London, 1946; New York, 1947). London, Heinemann, 1947; New York, Dramatists Play Service, 1948(?).

Jenny Villiers (produced Bristol, 1946).

The Rose and Crown (televised, 1946). London, French, 1947.

Ever since Paradise: An Entertainment, Chiefly Referring to Love and Marriage (also director: produced on tour, 1946; London, 1947). London and New York, French, 1949.

Three Time Plays (includes *Dangerous Corner, Time and the Conways, I Have Been Here Before*). London, Pan, 1947.

The Linden Tree (produced Sheffield and London, 1947; New York, 1948). London, Heinemann, and New York, French, 1948.

The Plays of J.B. Priestley:

Dangerous Corner, I Have Been Here Before, Johnson over Jordan, Music at Night, The Linden Tree, Eden End, Time and the Conways. London, Heinemann, 1948; as *Seven Plays,* New York, Harper, 1950.

Laburnum Grove, Bees on the Boat Deck, When We Are Married, Good Night Children, The Good Companions, How Are They at Home?, Ever since Paradise. London, Heinemann, 1949; New York, Harper, 1951.

Cornelius, People at Sea, They Came to a City, Desert Highway, An Inspector Calls, Home Is Tomorrow, Summer Day's Dream. London, Heinemann, 1950; New York, Harper, 1952.

Home Is Tomorrow (produced Bradford and London, 1948). London, Heinemann, 1949; in *Plays III,* 1950.

The High Toby: A Play for the Toy Theatre (produced London, 1954). London, Penguin-Pollock, 1948.

Summer Day's Dream (produced Bradford and London, 1949). Included in *Plays III,* 1950.

The Olympians, music by Arthur Bliss (produced London, 1949). London, Novello, 1949.

Bright Shadow: A Play of Detection (produced Oldham and London, 1950). London, French, 1950.

Treasure on Pelican (as *Treasure on Pelican Island,* televised, 1951; as *Treasure on Pelican,* produced Cardiff and London, 1952). London, Evans, 1953.

Dragon's Mouth: A Dramatic Quartet, with Jacquetta Hawkes (also director: produced Malvern and London, 1952; New York, 1955). London, Heinemann, and New York, Harper, 1952.

Private Rooms: A One-Act Comedy in the Viennese Style. London, French, 1953.

Mother's Day. London, French, 1953.

Try It Again (produced London, 1965). London, French, 1953.

A Glass of Bitter. London, French, 1954.

The White Countess, with Jacquetta Hawkes (produced Dublin and London, 1954).

The Scandalous Affair of Mr. Kettle and Mrs. Moon (produced Folkestone and London, 1955). London, French, 1956.

Take the Fool Away (produced Vienna, 1955; Nottingham, 1959).

These Our Actors (produced Glasgow, 1956).

The Glass Cage (produced Toronto and London, 1957). London, French, 1958.

The Thirty-First of June (produced Toronto and London, 1957).

A Pavilion of Masks (produced Germany, 1961; Bristol, 1963). London, French, 1958.

A Severed Head, with Iris Murdoch, adaptation of the novel by Murdoch (produced Bristol and London, 1963; New York, 1964). London, Chatto and Windus, 1964.

Screenplays: *Sing As We Go,* with Gordon Wellesley, 1934; *Look up and Laugh,* with Gordon Wellesley, 1935; *We Live in Two Worlds,* 1937; *Jamaica Inn,* with Sidney Gilliat and Joan Harrison, 1939; *Britain at Bay,* 1940; *Our Russian Allies* 1941; *The Foreman Went to France (Somewhere in France),* with others, 1942; *Last Holiday,* 1950.

Radio Plays: *The Return of Jess Oakroyd,* 1941; *The Golden Entry,* 1955; *End Game at the Dolphin,* 1956; *An Arabian Night in Park Lane,* 1965.

Television Plays: *The Rose and Crown,* 1946; *Whitehall Wonders,* 1949; *Treasure on Pelican Island,* 1951; *You Know What People Are,* 1953; *The Stone Faces,* 1957; *Now Let Him Go,* 1957; *Lost City* (documentary), 1958; *The Rack,* 1958; *Doomsday for Dyson,* 1958; *The Fortrose Incident,* from his play *Home Is Tomorrow,* 1959; *Level Seven,* from the novel by Mordecai Roshwald, 1966; *The Lost Peace* series, 1966; *Anyone for Tennis,* 1968; *Linda at Pulteney's,* 1969.

Poetry

The Chapman of Rhymes (juvenilia). London, Moring, 1918.

Other

Brief Diversions, Being Tales, Travesties, and Epigrams. Cambridge, Bowes and Bowes, 1922.

Papers from Lilliput. Cambridge, Bowes and Bowes, 1922.

I for One. London, Lane, 1923; New York, Dodd Mead, 1924.

Figures in Modern Literature. London, Lane, and New York, Dodd Mead, 1924.

The English Comic Characters. London, Lane, and New York, Dodd Mead, 1925.

George Meredith. London and New York, Macmillan, 1926.

Talking. London, Jarrolds, and New York, Harper, 1926.

(Essays). London, Harrap, 1926.

Open House: A Book of Essays. London, Heinemann, and New York, Harper, 1927.

Thomas Love Peacock. London and New York, Macmillan, 1927.

The English Novel. London, Benn, 1927; revised edition, London and New York, Nelson, 1935.

Apes and Angels: A Book of Essays. London, Methuen, 1928; as *Too Many People and Other Reflections,* New York, Harper, 1928.

The Balconinny and Other Essays. London, Methuen, 1929; as *The Balconinny,* New York, Harper, 1930.

English Humour. London and New York, Longman, 1929.

Self-Selected Essays. London, Heinemann, 1932; New York, Harper, 1933.

Four-in-Hand (miscellany). London, Heinemann, 1934.

English Journey, Being a Rambling But Truthful Account of What One Man Saw and Heard and Felt and Thought during a Journey through England during the Autumn of the Year 1933. London, Heinemann-Gollancz, and New York, Harper, 1934.

Midnight on the Desert: A Chapter of Autobiography. London, Heinemann, 1937; as *Midnight on the Desert, Being an Excursion into Autobiography during a Winter in America, 1935-36,* New York, Harper, 1937.

Rain upon Godshill: A Further Chapter of Autobiography. London, Heinemann, and New York, Harper, 1939.

Britain Speaks (radio talks). New York, Harper, 1940.

Postcripts (radio talks). London, Heinemann, 1940; as *All England Listened,* New York, Chilmark Press, 1968.

Out of the People. London, Collins-Heinemann, and New York, Harper, 1941.

Britain at War. New York, Harper, 1942.

British Women Go to War. London, Collins, 1943.

Manpower: The Story of Britain's Mobilisation for War. London, His Majesty's Stationery Office, 1944.

Here Are Your Answers. London, Socialist Book Centre, 1944.

Letter to a Returning Serviceman. London, Home and Van Thal, 1945.

The Secret Dream: An Essay on Britain, America, and Russia. London, Turnstile Press, 1946.

Russian Journey. London, Writers Group of the Society for Cultural Relations with the USSR, 1946.

The New Citizen (address). London, Council for Education in World Citizenship, 1946.

Theatre Outlook. London, Nicholson and Watson, 1947.

The Arts under Socialism (lecture). London, Turnstile Press, 1947.

Delight. London, Heinemann, and New York, Harper, 1949.

The Priestley Companion: A Selection from the Writings of J.B. Priestley. London, Penguin-Heinemann, 1951.

Journey down a Rainbow (travel), with Jacquetta Hawkes. London, Cresset Press-Heinemann, and New York, Harper, 1955.

All about Ourselves and Other Essays, edited by Eric Gillett. London, Heinemann, 1956.

The Writer in a Changing Society (lecture). Aldington, Kent, Hand and Flower Press, 1956.

Thoughts in the Wilderness (essays). London, Heinemann, and New York, Harper, 1957.

The Art of the Dramatist: A Lecture Together with Appendices and Discursive Notes. London, Heinemann, 1957; Boston, The Writer, 1958.

Topside; or, The Future of England: A Dialogue. London, Heinemann, 1958.

The Story of Theatre (for children). London, Rathbone, 1959; as *The Wonderful World of the Theatre,* New York, Doubleday, 1959.

Literature and Western Man. London, Heinemann, and New York, Harper, 1960.

William Hazlitt. London, Longman, 1960.

Charles Dickens: A Pictorial Biography. London, Thames and Hudson, 1961; New York, Viking Press, 1962; as *Charles Dickens and His World.* Thames and Hudson, and Viking Press, 1969.

Margin Released: A Writer's Reminiscences and Reflections. London, Heinemann, and New York, Harper, 1962.

Man and Time. London, Aldus, and New York, Doubleday, 1964.

The Moments and Other Pieces. London, Heinemann, 1966.

The World of J.B. Priestley, edited by Donald G. MacRae. London, Heinemann, 1967.

Essays of Five Decades, edited by Susan Cooper. Boston, Little Brown, 1968; London, Heinemann, 1969.

Trumpets over the Sea, Being a Rambling and Egotistical Account of the London Symphony Orchestra's Engagement at Daytona Beach, Florida, in July-August 1967. London, Heinemann, 1968.

The Prince of Pleasure and His Regency 1811-1820. London, Heinemann, and New York, Harper, 1969.

The Edwardians. London, Heinemann, and New York, Harper, 1970.

Anton Chekhov. London, International Textbook, 1970.

Victoria's Heyday. London, Heinemann, and New York, Harcourt Brace, 1972.

Over the Long High Wall: Some Reflections and Speculations on Life, Death, and Time. London, Heinemann, 1972.

The English. London, Heinemann, and New York, Viking Press, 1973.

Outcries and Asides. London, Heinemann, 1974.

A Visit to New Zealand. London, Heinemann, 1974.

Particular Pleasures, Being a Personal Record of Some Varied Arts and Many Different Artists. London, Heinemann, 1975.

The Happy Dream: An Essay. Andoversford, Gloucestershire, Whittington Press, 1976.

English Humour (not the same as 1929 book). London, Heinemann, 1976.

Instead of the Trees: A Final Chapter of Autobiography. London, Heinemann, and New York, Stein and Day, 1977.

Seeing Stratford, illustrated by Arthur Keene. Stratford-on-Avon, Warwickshire, Celandine Press, 1982.

Editor, *Essayists Past and Present: A Selection of English Essays.* London, Jenkins, and New York, Dial Press, 1925.

Editor, *Fools and Philosophers: A Gallery of Comic Figures from English Literature.* London, Lane, and New York, Dodd Mead, 1925.

Editor, *Tom Moore's Diary: A Selection.* London, Cambridge University Press, 1925.

Editor, *The Book of Bodley Head Verse.* London, Lane, and New York, Dodd Mead, 1926.

Editor, *Our Nation's Heritage.* London, Dent, 1939.

Editor, *Scenes from London Life, from Sketches by Boz,* by Charles Dickens. London, Pan, 1947.

Editor, *The Best of Leacock.* Toronto, McClelland and Stewart, 1957; as *The Bodley Head Leacock,* London, Bodley Head, 1957.

Editor, with Josephine Spear, *Adventures in English Literature.* New York, Harcourt Brace, 1963.

*

Bibliography: *J.B. Priestley: An Annotated Bibliography* by Alan Edwin Day, New York, Garland, and Stroud, Gloucestershire, Hodgkins, 1980.

Manuscript Collection: University of Texas, Austin.

Critical Studies: *J.B. Priestley* by Ivor Brown, London, Longman, 1957, revised edition, 1964; *J.B. Priestley: An Informal Study of His Work* by David Hughes, London, Hart Davis, 1958, Freeport, New York, Books for Libraries, 1970; *J.B. Priestley: Portrait of an Author* by Susan Cooper, London, Heinemann, 1970, New York, Harper, 1971; *J.B. Priestley* by Kenneth Young, London, Longman, 1977; *J.B. Priestley* by John Braine, London, Weidenfeld and Nicolson, 1978, New York, Barnes and Noble, 1979; *J.B. Priestley* by A.A. De Vitis and Albert E. Kalson, Boston, Twayne, 1980; *J.B. Priestley: The Last of the Sages* by John Atkins, London, Calder, and New York, Riverrun Press, 1981; *Bygone Bradford: The Lost World of J.B. Priestley* by Gary Frith, Lancaster, Dalesman, 1986; *J.B. Priestley's Plays* by Holger Klein, London, Macmillan, and New York, St. Martin's Press, 1988; *J.B. Priestley* by Vincent Brome, London and New York, Hamilton, 1988.

Theatrical Activities:

Director: **Plays**—*Ever Since Paradise,* tour, 1946, and London, 1947; *Dragon's Mouth,* London, 1952.

*   *   *

J.B. Priestley was possessed by a vision of life at its rare best—rich, vivid, eminently worth living. What makes him a science fiction writer and not just another dreaming romantic is that he espouses theories of time that allow his characters (and conceivably his readers) actually to attain the rich life he envisions. Such theories—chronological simultaneity, serialism, multiple dimensions—are not easy to illustrate, but Priestley succeeds surprisingly well, in stories and novels and also in popular stage plays. As literary fashion moves on and Priestley's sedately conventional style falls from favor, it is his time stories, his personal ventures towards altered reality, that remain fresh and intriguing.

Priestley derived his theories from three sources: E.A. Abbott's idea that a fourth dimension would appear as time; J.W. Dunne's mathematical model of time as continuous, simultaneous, and serial; and P.D. Ouspensky's more philosophical view of time as a repeated circle which can be made to spiral morally up or down. What these concepts gave to Priestley was a non-religious hope. If there are other dimensions, then there might be somewhere to go after life's time ends. In the plays *Music at Night* and *Johnson over Jordan* characters withdraw after death into a higher observer-state similar to the Tibetan "Bardo." Also, if all time is simultaneous then each minute is not murdered by the next, and the goodness of the past can be made accessible to those trapped in a bad present. Such comforting access is given to characters in the play *Time and the Conways* and in fiction such as "Night Sequence" and *The Magicians*. And if precognition and time's recurrence are true, then the known future can be, paradoxically, changed, altered in a tiny moment to redirect the flow, as in the plays *Dangerous Corner* and *I Have Been Here Before*.

Priestley desires these comforts and powers because he sees the modern world as darkening fast. In a short grim tale called "The Grey Ones" he incarnates the powers of darkness into grey tentacled devils capable of human shape. Their weapons are boredom, blandness, and despair; they seek to dull the world down to a suburban hell. Priestley's fullest treatment of this theme, and of the time-conscious man's opposition to it, comes in *The Magicians*. The industrialist Ravenstreet leaves his company when it turns from exciting scientific quest to passionless bureaucracy. As he slides into despair he is tempted by a bitter elitist to help drug the masses into final lethargy. Ravenstreet almost agrees, but is saved by the intervention of three "magicians" whose mysterious abilities include precognition and hypnosis, and who seem to be involved in some larger struggle. They show Ravenstreet the difference between the "tick-tock time" he had been dying in, and "time alive" where his hopeful past still lives. They send him to re-experience crucial moments, and they also rearrange the present so that the drug's numbing secret is lost. At the end, Ravenstreet has reason to live, and the world is a little less grey. Priestley's time visions are not always cheering. In one of his most haunting stories, "The Statues," a tired man is granted exhilarating but temporary sight of huge glorious statues towering above a future London, and the contrast with the banal present saddens the rest of his life. In the well-crafted and widely anthologized "Mr. Strenberry's Tale" the title character is visited briefly by a time traveler from an advanced humanity's last black moment. The traveler vanishes, destroyed, but the terror stays.

Some of Priestley's stories have been classified as science fiction because they focus on some unusual bit of technology— the musical invention in *Low Notes on a High Level* or the Earth-destroying transmitter in *The Doomsday Men*. But such devices usually turn out to be occasions for plot, not concepts in themselves, and plot for Priestley means romance, marriages, careers, and individual morale more than anything else. Even his children's book, *Snoggle*, which offers extraterrestrial pets and invisible spaceships, spends most of its rather unsuccessful pages detailing the interactions of three ordinary children.

Priestley began writing in 1910; he learned his craft in an earlier time than most science fiction writers. His many romantic comedies now seem dated, his plots coercive and even clanking. But his parables of hope and despair remain compelling, and there are few science fiction writers who can match him for the seriousness of his thinking about time.

—Karen G. Way

PROCTOR, Geo(rge W.)

Pseudonyms: John Cleve (joint pseudonym); Zach Wyatt. **Nationality:** American. **Address:** c/o Doubleday Books, 666 Fifth Avenue, New York, New York 10103, U.S.A.

SCIENCE FICTION PUBLICATIONS

Novels (series: Spaceways; Swords of Raemllyn; V)

The Esper Transfer. Canoga Park, California, Major, 1978.
Shadowman. New York, Fawcett, 1980.
Fire at the Center. New York, Fawcett, 1981.
Starwings. New York, Ace, 1984.
V: The Chicago Conversion. New York, Pinnacle, 1985.
V: The Texas Run. New York, Pinnacle, 1985.
To Demons Bound, with Robert E. Vardeman (Raemllyn). New York, Ace, 1985.
A Yoke of Magic, with Robert E. Vardeman (Raemllyn). New York, Ace, 1985.
Blood Fountain, with Robert E. Vardeman (Raemllyn). New York, Ace, 1985.
Death's Acolyte, with Robert E. Vardeman (Raemllyn). New York, Ace, 1985.
The Beasts of the Mist, with Robert E. Vardeman (Raemllyn). New York, Ace, 1986.
For Crown and Kingdom, with Robert E. Vardeman (Raemllyn). New York, Ace, 1987.
Stellar Fist. New York, Ace, 1989.

Novels with Andrew J. Offut as John Cleve (series: Spaceways all titles)

Master of Misfit. New York, Playboy Paperbacks, 1982.
The Manhuntress. New York, Playboy Paperbacks, 1982.
The Yoke of Shen. New York, Berkley, 1983.

OTHER PUBLICATIONS

Novels

Enemies. Garden City, New York, Doubleday, 1983.
Ride for Vengeance. New York, Pageant, 1989.
Walks without a Soul. Garden City, New York, Doubleday, 1990.
Comes the Hunter. Garden City, New York, Doubleday, 1992.
Before Honor. Garden City, New York, Doubleday, 1993.

Novels as Zach Wyatt

The Texians:
The Texians. New York, Pinnacle, 1984.
The Horse Marines. New York, Pinnacle, 1984.
War Devils. New York, Pinnacle, 1984.
Blood Moon. New York, Pinnacle, 1985.
Death's Shadow. New York, Pinnacle, 1985.
Comanche Ambush. New York, Pinnacle, 1985.

Other

Editor, with Steven Utley, *Lone Star Universe: The First Anthology of Texas Science Fiction Authors.* Austin, Heidelberg, 1976.
Editor, with Arthur C. Clarke, *The Science Fiction Hall of Fame, Volume 3: Nebula Winners 1965-1969.* New York, Avon, 1982.

*   *   *

In much of "hard science fiction," technology overshadows characters and often becomes the protagonist. The science fiction work of Geo. W. Proctor shows a different and more human-oriented approach. Although an accomplished amateur astronomer, Proctor relegates technology to the minor position of a plot device and concentrates on human and alien characters, showing their reaction to technological gadgetry. The heart of *Fire at the Center* isn't the technology of time travel or even the hopes of the protagonists in journeying to the past, but how Nils Kendler and Caltha Renent communicate psionically and the personal challenges they face through the relationship this situation affords.

The theme weaving throughout all Proctor's books is that of communication, no doubt a product of his training and work as a newspaper journalist. His first published novel, *The Esper Transfer,* is an uncomplicated escape-chase plot, but the protagonist depends heavily on his telepathic talents and "oneness" with others of his race. The conflict comes more from within than from external forces. This is likewise true in *Shadowman.* Outwardly another escape-chase plot, the novel becomes more. Male and female join in telepathic contact and become lovers through this most intimate of contact.

Proctor carries this theme to its logical extension in *Starwings.* The protagonist, Radman Donalt, uses a collapsar as a time machine and becomes separated from his lover, Jenica, not only in space but in time. Fifteen years and the barrier of untold light years notwithstanding, Donalt enters Jenica's mind and they make love in the only way possible for them. "His mind merged with hers, Donalt led her to the bed. And there, her hands now his, he made love to her."

Proctor's pacifist views surface in *Stellar Fist,* where the conflict comes from the interplay between Arianne Pillan and Faxon Lorens, the father of Pillan's child and an agent assigned to uncover the workings of an invincible weapon. Again psionic skills intertwine the characters, bringing in Pillan's memory-erased brother as a pawn. Using the metaphor of the bonsai, Proctor's conclusion is that peace must grow slowly over long periods of time, and it cannot be achieved without severe pruning.

This focus on male-female, human-alien communication extends beyond Proctor's science fiction and into his fantasy novels. While the structure and tone of his fantasy work is strongly influenced by Fritz Leiber's Fafhrd and the Gray Mouser stories, the basic themes are easily identifiable as belonging to Proctor.

The Nalcon and Hweir short stories transcend the usual genre offerings of sword-and-sorcery quest through interplay between the main characters. Both are rogues and thieves, but their fierce friendship is obvious. They have discovered common ground, mutual affection, and fulfillment in one another in spite of divergent backgrounds as blond prince and black-skinned thief. This friendship and the strains placed on it are more central to the stories than any quest.

In the *Swords of Raemllyn* heroic fantasy series, Proctor has created another way of examining male-female communication. Although in *Death's Acolyte* there is Chal, a tongueless character who makes his wishes known to the heroine empathically, a more intriguing method of exploration lies with Goran One-Eye, an interdimensional being capable of massive shape changes. Goran at first lacks control over this ability and is locked in a bulky male human body. By the second book in the series, *A Yoke of Magic,* he shifts into female form and attempts to seduce his friend, Davin Anane. The byplay between the two, when Davin discovers the shape transformation, examines not only the limits of their friendship but also male-female roles and expectations.

The nucleus of Geo. W. Proctor's science fiction and fantasy works is both simple and beguiling: communication. How do men and women relate to one another? How would communication be different if we were able to enter another's mind telepathically? How would our friendships and loves alter if they were based on empathic rather than verbal considerations? Science fiction provides a suitable vehicle for Proctor's explorations of this enhanced communication.

—Robert E. Vardeman

PURDOM, Tom

Nationality: American. **Born:** Thomas Edward Purdom, New Haven, Connecticut, 19 April 1936. **Education:** Lafayette College, Easton, Pennsylvania, 1952-54; Thomas Edison State College, Trenton, New Jersey, B.A. in social sciences 1977. **Military Service:** Served in the United States Army Medical Corps, 1959-61. **Family:** Married Sara Wescot in 1960; one son. **Career:** Reservation agent, United Airlines, Philadelphia, 1957-58; science writer, University of Pennsylvania, Philadelphia, 1968-69; visiting professor of English, Temple University, Philadelphia, 1970-71; adjunct professor of English, Drexel University, Philadelphia, 1975; instructor in science fiction, Institute for Human Resources Development, Philadelphia, 1976-77. Vice-President, Science Fiction Writers of America, 1970-72. **Agent:** Scott Meredith Literary Agency, 845 Third Avenue, New York, New York 10022, U.S.A.

SCIENCE FICTION PUBLICATIONS

Novels

I Want the Stars. New York, Ace, 1964.
The Tree Lord of Imeten. New York, Ace, 1966.
Five against Arlane. New York, Ace, 1967.
Reduction in Arms. New York, Berkley, 1971.
The Barons of Behavior. New York, Ace, 1972; London, Dobson, 1977.

OTHER PUBLICATIONS

Other

Editor, *Adventures in Discovery.* Garden City, New York, Doubleday, 1969.

*

Tom Purdom comments:

My main aim as a fiction writer is to create the kind of stories I like to read—engrossing, well-plotted works that hold you from the first page to the end and really get you involved in the characters and the things that are happening to them. Once I jokingly said that the greatest living novelists were Alexander Solzhenitsyn, Ursula K. LeGuin, Richard Adams, and George Macdonald Fraser. I was poking a little fun at literary pomposity, but I would give a great deal to have written the better works of any of them.

The struggle that most interests me—and I think it's mostly what I've written about and like to read about in SF—is the problem of adapting to technology, especially the attempts to seize the opportunity it gives us without falling into all the traps it puts in front of us (some of which are not too obvious). I'm also fond of one of the things the man Santiago said about his fish: "It will feed many people and it will bring a good price on the market." I think science fiction has given a great many people a lot of things they needed, and it has even—especially recently—brought some of its practitioners a good price on the market.

* * *

Tom Purdom's career spans more than two decades. Though clearly distinguishable from one another, his early novels share the same narrative formula: the hero finds himself on an alien planet which is ruled by a dictator, either benign as in *Five against Arlane* or malevolent as in *The Tree Lord of Imeten*. In either case, the hero struggles to overthrow tyranny and reestablish social equilibrium through bloodshed. In the aftermath of the battle against the tyrant, the hero emerges victorious from the rubble to announce that democratic liberties have been restored to the people. Great adulation of the Purdom hero follows the revolution, and the novel closes on a note of exhaustion as an infant republic comes uncertainly to life.

This well-worn plot serves as the basis for Purdom's more recent novels too, but in *The Barons of Behavior* he has achieved more interesting results. Here Purdom's subject is the potential threat which Skinnerian behaviorism poses to a free society. The novel opens in a world of the remote future in which the privileges and responsibilities of life in 20th-century America have been lost. Nurtured by democracy, the growth of lawlessness and violence has long ago become intolerable to society, and politicians, seeking a retardant, have turned to the behaviour sciences for help. And indeed they have found there willing social physicians. Thus a terrible triple alliance is formed of science, technology, and politics, whose aim it is to produce law and order, to provide security and comfort to the citizens of Windham County, Pennsylvania, but whose real accomplishment is to rob the human spirit of its civil liberties and to render the human will impotent. In *The Barons of Behavior* the orderly operation of society is insured by an arsenal of devices and techniques which can subvert individual free will. It can be numbed or stupefied by insidious drugs; it can be forced to betray itself through the techniques of behaviour modification; or, most horribly, it can be bypassed altogether by devices surgically implanted in the brain. Opposed to the dehumanizing powers in control of society stands the Purdom hero, Ralph Nicholson, "psychotherapist to a psyched-out world," who manages to defeat the political machine of Martin Boyd despite the overwhelming odds against his doing so.

But this is familiar stuff to science fiction readers. The science of control has inspired dozens of novels along the same line, the very best of which achieve truly chilling results. The atrocities committed against Alex in Burgess's *A Clockwork Orange*, for instance, evoke the archetypal fear humans have of being obliterated by forces beyond their comprehension, while his struggle to remain human and intact in the face of dehumanizing powers approaches Aristotle's definition of great tragedy, the purgation of fear and pity. Unfortunately, *The Barons of Behavior* never achieves such impact. Though Purdom's technological imagination is impressive, his ability to conceive and delineate character is not. Ralph Nicholson of *The Bar-*

ons of Behavior is as two-dimensional as Migel Lassamba of *Five against Arlane*. Both are conventional super-heroes, men of endless resource and daring, but since they lack depth and delineation, their suffering appears rather more ludicrous than tragic, their lives more gratuitously violent than compelling, and their inevitable victory more contrived than earned.

Nevertheless, Purdom's interest in possibilities is genuine, and his grasp of the implications of behaviorism is very thorough. At his best, he is capable of constructing a shockingly plausible and horrifying vision of the future, a time when individual freedom is a suppressed, half-forgotten memory, abandoned centuries ago in pursuit of law and order. There is little anxiety in this world, even less disorder once chance factors have been all but eliminated. There are no dangers, except to the intellect and imagination. There is no physical suffering in the America of *The Barons of Behavior*, but there is no free thought either, no unapproved writing, no spontaneous creation of any kind. Men and women smile and go about their daily business, but their eyes appear vacant. They reflect no light. Birth and death are quiet, prearranged experiences.

—Marvin W. Hunt

PYNCHON, Thomas

Nationality: American. **Born:** Glen Cove, New York, 8 May 1937. **Education:** Cornell University, Ithaca, New York, 1954-58, B.A. 1958. **Military Service:** Served in the United States Navy. **Career:** Former editorial writer, Boeing Aircraft, Seattle. **Awards:** Faulkner award, 1964; Rosenthal Memorial award, 1967; National Book award, 1974; American Academy Howells medal, 1975. **Agent:** Melanie Jackson, Melanie Jackson Agency, 250 West 57th Street, Suite 119, New York, New York 10107, U.S.A. **Address:** c/o Little Brown, 34 Beacon Street, Boston, Massachusetts 02106, U.S.A.

SCIENCE FICTION PUBLICATIONS

Novels

Gravity's Rainbow. New York, Viking Press, and London, Cape, 1973.
Vineland. Boston, Little Brown, and London, Secker and Warburg, 1990.

OTHER PUBLICATIONS

Novels

V. Philadelphia, Lippincott, and London, Cape, 1963.
The Crying of Lot 49. Philadelphia, Lippincott, 1966; London, Cape, 1967.

Short Stories

Mortality and Mercy in Vienna. London, Aloes, 1976.
Low-lands. London, Aloes, 1978.

The Secret Integration. London, Aloes, 1980.
The Small Rain. London, Aloes, 1980.
Slow Learner: Early Stories. Boston, Little Brown, 1984; London, Cape, 1985.

*

Bibliography: *Three Contemporary Novelists: An Annotated Bibliography* by Robert M. Scotto, New York, Garland, 1977; *John Barth, Jerzy Kosinski, and Thomas Pynchon: A Reference Guide* by Thomas P. Walsh and Cameron Northouse, Boston, Hall, 1977; *Thomas Pynchon: A Bibliography of Primary and Secondary Materials* by Clifford Mead, Elmwood Park, Illinois, Dalkey Archive Press, 1989.

Critical Studies: *Thomas Pynchon* by Joseph V. Slade, New York, Warner, 1974; *Mindful Pleasures: Essays on Thomas Pynchon* edited by George Levine and David Leverenz, Boston, Little Brown, 1976; *The Grim Phoenix: Reconstructing Thomas Pynchon* by William M. Plater, Bloomington, Indiana University Press, 1978; *Pynchon: A Collection of Critical Essays* edited by Edward Mendelson, Englewood Cliffs, New Jersey, Prentice Hall, 1978; *Pynchon: Creative Paranoia in Gravity's Rainbow* by Mark Richard Siegal, Port Washington, New York, Kennikat Press, 1978; *Thomas Pynchon: The Art of Allusion* by David Cowart, Carbondale, Southern Illinois University Press, 1980; *The Rainbow Quest of Thomas Pynchon* by Douglas A. Mackey, San Bernardino, California, Borgo Press, 1980; *Pynchon's Fictions: Thomas Pynchon and the Literature of Information* by John O. Stark, Athens, Ohio University Press, 1980; *A Reader's Guide to Gravity's Rainbow* by Douglas Fowler, Ann Arbor, Michigan, Ardis, 1980; *Thomas Pynchon* by Tony Tanner, London, Methuen, 1982; *Signs and Symptoms: Thomas Pynchon and the Contemporary World* by Peter L. Cooper, Berkeley, University of California Press, 1983; *The Style of Connectedness: Gravity's Rainbow and Thomas Pynchon* by Thomas Moore, Columbia, University of Missouri Press, 1987; *The Fictional Labyrinths of Thomas Pynchon* by David Seed, London, Macmillan, and Iowa City, University of Iowa Press, 1988; *Writing Pynchon: Strategies in Fictional Analysis* by A.W. McHoul and David Wills, London, Macmillan, and Urbana, University of Illinois Press, 1990; *A Hand to Turn the Time: The Menippean Satires of Thomas Pynchon* by Theodore D. Kharpertian, Rutherford, New Jersey, Farleigh Dickinson University Press, 1990; *Thomas Pynchon: Allusive Parables of Power* by John Dugdale, New York, St. Martin's Press, and London, Macmillan, 1990.

*   *   *

Thomas Pynchon's novels, though firmly entrenched in historic and technological realities, question all orders and unities to suggest that, since man continually imposes patterns on his world, all patterns are suspect and potentially false—so much so that recorded "history" may be simply man imposing private interpretations on chaotic reality, just as man's mastery of bureaucratic and technological systems may well be his enslavement to his own creations. Pynchon's is a vision of a world in decline, one where personal choices are shaped by science, language, history, and economics, where the victim in turn victimizes, where vast, shadowy conspiracies flourish, and where huge conglomerates seem to control events and technology overshadows and threatens humanity. His domi-

nant themes include isolation, alienation, fragmentation, failure to communicate, degradation, entropy, the battle between men and machines and between established society and the "preterites" (the rebellious disinherited), the absurdities and ironies of modern existence, man's self-destructive potentials, the horrors of war, paranoia, and the question of multiple interpretations. Wastelands and undergrounds dominate his imagery.

His style, in tune with the complexity of his thematic concerns, is baroque, variegated, and multistructural, an intricate amalgam of Whitmanesque catalogues, Dickensian names, cryptic abbreviations, puns, innumerable analogical sequences extended between as well as within novels, and historical, literary, theological and mythological allusions. It runs the gamut of literary and cinematic modes, rapidly shifting, much like media events, between comic book and television fantasy and learned discourse on complex scientific and technological concerns: organic chemistry, operant conditioning, rocket dynamics. It partakes of parody, farce, and black humor, jeremiad, apocalypse, and prophesy. Its geography is often allegorical, its conception mythic, its patterns analogical compounds—networks of multiple, interlocking images from personal to social to cosmic. Pynchon, perhaps aptly called a "demented deconstructionist" by Joseph Slade of Long Island University, overwhelms with data as he updates Renaissance *copia* with correspondences from high to low. In *Gravity's Rainbow,* for example, the V-2 rocket which nears London imposes patterns on reality, so that as the doomed city lifts up its towers and chimneys like stationary rockets, it is seen on a target grid that parallels the patterns of its buildings and streets; the central character fantasizes about becoming a Rocketman, merged with machine; sexual orgasm parallels a launching; a sadistic Nazi launches his homosexual lover in a V-2 rocket; the extreme verticality of futuristic structures are like monuments to rocketpower; the aggressive and bigoted "Marvy's Mothers" celebrate "immachination," the union of man and machine, with "rocket limericks"; and the minds of those threatened by senseless destruction are described as maze-like grids.

Each Pynchon novel focuses on some central mystery (a cryptogram in *The Crying of Lot 49,* an elusive secret agent in *V,* a missing supersonic rocket in *Gravity's Rainbow,* a missing mother in *Vineland*), which provides the supportive structure for diverse images encompassing a range of perspectives delineated by signs, codes, signals, patterns, and plots. Usually there is what *Time* reviewer Paul Gray calls "an evil, well-organized and immensely powerful enemy" which "sows 'the merciless spores of paranoia' among a shaggy, lost group of drifting souls who find the real world threatening under the best of circumstances." Always Pynchon's works are like densely textured puzzles whose central images are visible only from a distance, while close up all seems chaos.

Comic and satiric, *The Crying of Lot 49,* the most accessible of Pynchon's novels, focuses on the quest of Oedipa Maas for the meaning of her ex-lover's will. Her synthesis of scattered clues, including a Jacobean tragedy, doodlings, acronyms, postage stamps, and graffiti, postulates the existence of a secret, 16th-century antipostal service, the Tristero, perpetuated by W.A.S.T.E., an underground of the disenchanted. Ultimately, Oedipa must question whether her discovery is a genuine conspiracy involving a parallel, secret America, a giant farcical hoax, or a paranoid projection of her own creation. In Pynchon it is a question of interpretation, one eye seeing chaos, another a system. Oedipa intuits in her city and in her universe "a hieroglyphic sense of concealed meaning . . . an intent to communicate," but is unable to grasp its essence, to elucidate its mysteries. This question of whether order, systems, patterns truly exist or are merely superimposed on chaotic reality is an essential concern of *V, Gravity's Rainbow,* and *Vineland* as well.

The central character of *V* (Herbert Stencil), as his name suggests, "Stencil"s his own pattern on an external blankness, but his various versions of himself, the elusive woman he pursues, and his world are all private dreams, products of his early conditioning and of his own paranoid inventiveness. He is played off against Benny Profane, an empiricist who becomes engulfed in incomprehensible details. Drawing on Henry Adams, Jorge Luis Borges, thermodynamics, and WWII film clips, Pynchon traces what he sees as man's historic progression toward the moribund. The anarchistic V gradually replaces her flesh with cold machinery; an automaton named SHROUD walks the earth, and all the characters move towards annihilation near Malta. It is a nightmare world of genocide, dehumanization, dead landscapes, and man-machines.

The lengthy (760 pages) and often impenetrable *Gravity's Rainbow* continues the historic focus of *V,* tracing the end product of a bureaucratic, technological system—a V-2 supersonic rocket that screams into view in the first lines of the novel and disintegrates the reader and his "theater," perhaps our civilization, at its close. A satiric fantasy, an historic novel, a parody of various forms—part technological manual, part folk myth, part Kabbala, part pornography—it rapidly changes perspective as it collapses time (envisioning Bethlehem at the time of the Nativity, a WWII London Christmas, and a futuristic Rocket City), unravels numerous plots, and delineates 400 characters and 1000 objects (including a talking light bulb, Richard Nixon, and King Kong). In its Special Operations executives use seances, psi forces, and Pavlovian conditioning as weapons, and metaphors derive from calculus, rocketry, and organic polymers. It begins with the quest of Lt. Slothrop, a New Englander of Puritan stock, whose sexuality is attuned to a mysterious, gravity-defying rocket for whom everybody is searching, but he ultimately dissolves over the Allied Zone, and the plot digresses in a myriad of directions, its only unity analogical. Slothrup, like Oedipa in *Crying of Lot 49,* is never sure whether he is actually paranoid or the victim of some intricate plot. *Gravity's Rainbow,* with its labyrinthine complications, is a massive effort to seek through historic analysis the roots of 20th-century man's mass "death wish," his cultural programming for death, and to project a future/present when that wish might come true. It describes man as simultaneously destroyer and victim, responsible, dangerous, and self-doomed, compelled by a fascination with rocketry, gadgets, machinery, and explosives, and by a "lust for technology and control."

Vineland is set in 1984 in the fog-shrouded Northern California town of Vineland, a haven for burnt-out hippies, like the main character, Zoyd Wheeler, escaping Reaganism, narcotics agents, and their own lost dreams. A part-time keyboard player, lobsterman, handyman, and marijuana farmer, Wheeler blames a notoriously evil federal prosecutor, Brock Vond, for seducing Wheeler's ex-wife, ex-Sixties radical Frenesi, turning her into a government informer, and thereby causing her to abandon her daughter, Prairie, a resourceful young lady who determines to find, understand, and forgive her lost mother. Pynchon describes Vond's genius as his understanding that Sixties radicals were seeking order rather than trying to destroy it, and that that desire for order made them vulnerable. This "realistic" base is the foundation for a satiric distortion that indicts contemporary society. Many of Pynchon's characters are "Tubefreeks," pursued by NEVER (National Endowment for Video Education and Rehabilitation) for television abuse ("tripping out" on repeats of "Gilligan's Island," the "Flintstones" and so forth); "Thanatoids," members of a secret death cult, anxious for extinction and resentful of life; or "Kunoichi Attentives," militant feminists who are opposed to male militarism and who rely on Broadway Show Tunes to punish wayward disciples. An airline between Los Angeles and Honolulu sports an "invisible robot," an android that could be on any aisle or taking up any seemingly empty seat. In effect, Pynchon creates our reality, distorted, a Brave New Media World.

Pynchon suggests that modern man is paranoid, perhaps with good reason, compulsive, and self-destructive; his lethal technology is perhaps already beyond control, and even it lacks certainty; man cannot be sure whether his perceptions of the world are valid or merely self-imposed projections. While Pynchon breaks traditional patterns, he builds on our scientific and literary heritage. His eclectic and controversial novels, with their limited plotting, their wild comic invention, and their failure to elucidate anything except man's wish for answers and his difficulty finding them, verge on science fiction and partake of its techniques; they share its concern with the human effects and the broader implications of science and technology, while remaining difficult to categorize precisely.

—Gina Macdonald

QUITMAN, Wallace. *See* **PALMER, Raymond A.**

R

RACKHAM, John

Pseudonym for John Thomas Phillifent. **Nationality:** British. **Born:** Durham, 10 November 1916. **Military Service:** Served in the Royal Navy, 1935-47. **Career:** Worked for the Central Electricity Generating Board in the early 1960s. **Died:** 15 December 1976.

SCIENCE FICTION PUBLICATIONS

Novels (series: Space Puppet)

Space Puppet. London, Pearson, 1954.
The Master Weed: (Another Adventure of the Space Puppet). London, Pearson, 1954.
Jupiter Equilateral (Space Puppet). London, Pearson, 1954.
Alien Virus (Space Puppet). London, Pearson, 1955.
The Touch of Evil. London, Digit, 1963.
Watch on Peter. London, Cape, 1964.
We, The Venusians. New York, Ace, 1965.
The Beasts of Kohl. New York, Ace, 1966.
Time to Live. New York, Ace, 1966; London, Dobson, 1969.
Danger from Vega. New York, Ace, 1966; London, Dobson, 1970.
The Double Invaders. New York, Ace, 1967.
Alien Sea. New York, Ace, 1968; London, Dobson, 1975.
The Proxima Project. New York, Ace, 1968.
Treasure of Tau Ceti. New York, Ace, 1969.
Ipomoea. New York, Ace, 1969; London, Dobson, 1972.
Flower of Doradil. New York, Ace, 1970.
The Anything Tree. New York, Ace, 1970; London, Dobson, 1977.
Beyond Capella. New York, Ace, 1971.
Dark Planet. New York, Ace, 1971.
Earthstrings. New York, Ace, 1972.
Beanstalk. New York, DAW, 1973.

Novels as John T. Phillifent

Genius Unlimited. New York, DAW, 1972.
Hierarchies. New York, Ace, 1973.
King of Argent. New York, DAW, 1973.

Short Stories

Life with Lancelot (as John T. Phillifent). New York, Ace, 1973.

OTHER PUBLICATIONS

Novels as John T. Phillifent (series: Man from U.N.C.L.E.)

The Lonely Man. London, Boardman, 1965.
The Mad Scientist Affair (Man from U.N.C.L.E.). New York, Ace, and London, Souvenir Press, 1966.
The Corfu Affair (Man from U.N.C.L.E.). London, Four Square, 1967; New York, Ace, 1969.
The Power Cube Affair (Man from U.N.C.L.E.). London, Four Square, 1968; New York, Ace, 1969.

*   *   *

Under his own name and the pseudonym of John Rackham, John T. Phillifent produced a series of short adventure novels that made use of traditional science fiction plots to present a fast-moving plot set against an exotic background. There is little doubt in the reader's mind that right will ultimately prevail, but the events along the way are the chief attraction.

To a great extent, Rackham repeated the situations he found most appealing. One of these is the Mowgli tale set in the future; one or more humans are returned to civilization after being raised among aliens, and the ensuing culture shock provides much of the basis of the story. This is the major plotline in *The Beasts of Kohl,* for example, where Earth has become considerably more benign but still unsettling to one not used to human ways. The same is true of the far better Phillifent novel, *Life with Lancelot,* in which the alien Shogleet rebuilds a damaged human with mechanical parts, and then tries to reintegrate him into human culture. Another recurring plot is the search for a fabulous treasure, be it gem, secret plans, or immortality drug. The protoganist of *The Treasure of Tau Ceti* is motivated by legends of priceless gems on that jungle world, but along the way he forces humans to recognize that the inhabitants of the planet are indeed intelligent. A secret agent searches for a rumored sentient plant in *The Anything Tree.* Another plant, this time one that will cure all humans diseases, is the target of another group of adventurers in *Flower of Doradil.* This time the major subplot is a crew of human smugglers determined to prevent the success of the hero's mission. Jewels are the quarry once again in *Hierarchies* (Phillifent), this time purloined from their rightful owner. Another theme is that of secret alien or human manipulation of society. Secret aliens provoke a war between Earth and Venus in *Alien Sea;* a new drug is revealed to be the tool of insidious would-be alien conquerors in *Ipomoea;* human expansion into space is blocked by apparently invulnerable alien constructs in *Beyond Capella.* Secret human societies appear in *Earthstrings,* in which a human colony is wiped out as part of a plot by commercial magnates, and in *Genius Unlimited* (Phillifent), wherein a scientific colony is actually serving as a mask to conceal a plot for interstellar conquest.

Rackham did interject some commentary into his novels, and the earlier ones in particular seem to demonstrate his faith that mankind would grow out of its petty prejudices. In *We, The Venusians,* Anthony Taylor passes as human because a pill changes his skin color and he cannot be identified as a native Greenie. Ultimately, the racial prejudice that forms the basis of the novel is reconciled as the two races eventually recognise each other's equality. In *The Beasts of Kohl* humanity has learned to accept the rights of whales on Earth and aliens in space. There is some evidence that Rackham became disillusioned in his last years. Nefarious plots are invariably human-instigated in the later novels, and the more enlightened humans cast themselves loose from the race, as in *King of Argent* (Phillifent), or even settle down among aliens, as does the hero of *Dark Planet.* Where the human refugees had favorable effects on a primitive alien race in *Danger from Vega,* they are presented as a danger to the interstellar community in *Genius Unlimited* (Phillifent) and, to a lesser extent, *Beyond Capella*. Other standard plots appear here and there. There is a rather dull interstellar war in *The Double Invaders,* and a rather amusing view of one in *Beanstalk,* which presents the familiar fairy tale as a distorted version of Earth's minor involvement in an interstellar war. Mankind's necessity to advance into the universe is central to *Beyond Capella* and *The Proxima Project.*

Rackham never produced what could fairly be termed an outstanding work. He made no attempt to tackle major social problems except in the most superficial way, and he broke no new ground in either style or plot. But he did produce a string of competently written light adventure novels that don't insult the intelligence of the reader. They are invariably upbeat, there is no confusion between heroes and villains, and any incompetence on the part of the central character is transitory. It is a simple universe in many ways that Rackham wrote about, and generally an entertaining one.

—Don D'Ammassa

RAND, Ayn

Nationality: American. **Born:** Alice Rosenbaum in St. Petersburg, Russia, 2 February 1905; emigrated to the United States in 1926; naturalized, 1931. **Education:** University of Leningrad: graduated in history 1924. **Family:** Married Frank O'Connor in 1929. **Career:** Screenwriter, 1932-34, 1944-49. Editor, *The Objectivist,* New York, 1962-71, and *The Ayn Rand Letter,* New York, 1971-82. Visiting lecturer at several universities, including Yale University, New Haven, Connecticut, Princeton University, New Jersey, Columbia University, New York, Harvard University and Massachusetts Institute of Technology, both Cambridge, and Johns Hopkins University, Baltimore. D.H.L.: Lewis and Clark College, Portland, Oregon, 1963. **Died:** 6 March 1982.

SCIENCE FICTION PUBLICATIONS

Novels

Anthem. London, Cassell, 1938; revised edition, Los Angeles, Pamphleteers, 1946.
Atlas Shrugged. New York, Random House, 1957.

OTHER PUBLICATIONS

Novels

We the Living. New York, Macmillan, and London, Cassell, 1936.
The Fountainhead. Indianapolis, Bobbs-Merrill, 1943; London, Cassell, 1947.

Short Stories

The Early Ayn Rand: A Selection from Her Unpublished Fiction, edited by Leonard Peikoff. New York, New American Library, 1984.

Plays

Night of January 16th (as *Woman on Trial,* produced Hollywood, 1934; New York, 1935; London, 1936; as *Penthouse Legend,* produced New York, 1973). New York, Longman, 1936; revised edition, New York, New American Library, 1987.
The Unconquered, adaptation of her own novel *We the Living* (produced New York, 1940).

Screenplays: *You Came Along,* with Robert Smith, 1945; *Love Letters,* 1945; *The Fountainhead,* 1949.

Other

Textbook of Americanism. New York, Branden Institute, 1946.
Notes on the History of American Free Enterprise. New York, Platen Press, 1959.
Faith and Force: The Destroyers of the Modern World. New York, Branden Institute, 1961.
For the New Intellectual. New York, Random House, 1961.
The Objectivist Ethics. New York, Branden Institute, 1961.
America's Persecuted Minority: Big Business. New York, Branden Institute, 1962.
Conservatism: An Obituary (lecture). New York, Branden Institute, 1962.
The Fascist "New Frontier." New York, Branden Institute, 1963.
The Virtue of Selfishness: A New Concept of Egoism. New York, New American Library, 1965.
Capitalism: The Unknown Ideal, with others. New York, New American Library, 1966.
Introduction to Objectivist Epistemology. New York, The Objectivist, 1967; revised edition by Leonard Peikoff and Harry Binswanger, New York, New American Library, 1990.
The Romantic Manifesto: A Philosophy of Literature. Cleveland, World, 1970.
The New Left: The Anti-Industrial Revolution. New York, New American Library, 1971.
Philosophy: Who Needs It? Indianapolis, Bobbs-Merrill, 1982.
The Voice of Reason: Essays in Objectivist Thought. New York, New American Library, 1989.

*

Manuscript Collection: Library of Congress, Washington, D.C.

Critical Studies: *Who Is Ayn Rand? An Analysis of the Novels of Ayn Rand* by Nathaniel Branden, New York, Random House, 1962; *The Philosophic Thought of Ayn Rand* edited by Douglas J. Den Uyl and Douglas B. Rasmussen, Urbana, University of Illinois Press, 1984; *The Ayn Rand Companion* by Mimi Reisel Gladstein, Westport, Connecticut, Greenwood Press, 1984; *The Passion of Ayn Rand: A Biography* by Barbara Branden, New York, Doubleday, 1986, London, W.H. Allen, 1987; *The Ayn Rand Lexicon: Objectivism from A to Z* edited by Harry Binswanger, New York, New American Library, 1986; *Judgment Day: My Years with Ayn Rand* by Nathaniel Branden, New York, Houghton Mifflin, 1989.

*   *   *

Considering her unvarying depictions of heroes and heroines as people adhering to unpopular views despite hostility and abuse,

Ayn Rand must have been pleased at resembling them through the controversy she arouses by her novels. In spite of her claim to be an unswerving advocate of reason, her appeal is often violently emotional. She makes her readers long to identify themselves with her dynamic, creative, productive, intelligent, handsome, and ultimately victorious heroes (and thereby with the ideas associated with them). She also compels her readers to despise the cowardly, lazy, incompetent, vicious, ugly, and inevitably defeated spokesman for the ideas she abhors. Her two speculative novels, *Anthem* and *Atlas Shrugged,* stridently warn against shaping our future according to the ideas of Christianity, Marxism, liberalism, or any other viewpoint advocating self-sacrifice which, to her, means self-negation. In opposition to such ideals, they applaud man's ego as the source of all inventiveness, achievement, and happiness and capitalism as the system allowing the fullest expression of the ego. In spite of her stridency, Rand remains one of the most powerful—and thoughtful—defenders of conservative American values, portraying the businessman as the unacknowledged Atlas who carries the burden of civilization on his mighty shoulders.

Although *Anthem* and *Atlas Shrugged* are clearly intended as cautionary tracts expounding Rand's social and philosophical beliefs and fears, both present carefully detailed pictures of future societies. In creating these societies, Rand extrapolates the possible consequences of self-sacrificial goals on art, politics, economics, sex, and family and social relationships. *Anthem* is set in a new dark age that has come about after the collectivists have defeated all the individualists. In this world, technology has nearly ceased to exist since, for Rand, it is the product of individual curiosity, effort, and ability that have also nearly ceased to exist. At birth, all children are taken from their parents and placed in a communal home where they will be taught that they must devote their lives to working for the benefit of their brothers, act as all their brothers act, and think only what all their brothers think. No man is permitted to live as an individual and the word "I" is forbidden. However, one man known as Equality 7-2521 finds such a world uncomfortable, "transgresses," and through his "sinful" behavior rediscovers individualism, creativity, self-respect, and selective love and friendship—or, in short, Rand's own values.

Atlas Shrugged is set in an America resembling that of the 1950s when the book was written. However, this America soon becomes transformed into a society trying to follow the Christian goal of loving one's brother like oneself and the Marxist principle "From each according to his ability, to each according to his need." The government assumes control over the economy, places all industries under a Unification Board, and attempts to redistribute the benefits earned by the most efficient companies to the least efficient ones on the assumption that the weaker companies have the greater need. The result of this policy of penalizing success and rewarding failure is that moochers rise to the highest levels of government (the head of the economic program is named Wesley Mouch) and the most productive businessmen have difficulty surviving. Having foreseen these developments, the superheroic protagonist, John Galt, leads the greatest producers and creators on strike, thus precipitating the collapse of the moocher's government and preparing the way for a new society founded on the Randian oath: "I swear—by my life and by my love of it—that I will never live for the sake of another man, nor ask another man to live for mine."

Both of Rand's speculative novels are major contributions to the field. Her passionate commitment to ideas about social structure is well-suited to the speculative form, especially since it is coupled with an ability to give concrete embodiment to these ideas. Though the slim *Anthem* only sketches her ideas, it offers a good introduction to them. Longer than Samuel Delany's *Dhalgren* and talkier than Robert Heinlein's *I Will Fear No Evil,* the gigantic *Atlas Shrugged* spells them out fully in repetitious but often exciting, provocative, and even brilliant detail.

—Steven R. Carter

RANDALL, Marta

Nationality: American. **Born:** Mexico City, 26 April 1948; moved to San Francisco at age 2. **Education:** Berkeley High School, California; San Francisco State College, 1966-72. **Family:** Married 1) Robert H. Bergstresser in 1966 (divorced 1973), one son; 2) Christopher E. Conley in 1983. **Career:** Since 1968, office manager, H. Zimmerman, Oakland, California. Taught at Clarion Writers workshop, East Lansing, Michigan, 1982, and at workshops at Portland State University, Cannon Beach, 1983, and University of California, Berkeley, 1984, 1985. Vice-president, 1981-82, and president, 1982-84, Science Fiction Writers of America. **Agent:** Richard Curtis, 171 East 74th Street, Suite 2, New York, New York 10021, U.S.A.

SCIENCE FICTION PUBLICATIONS

Novels (series: Newhome)

Islands. New York, Pyramid, 1976; revised edition, New York, Pocket Books, 1980.
A City in the North. New York, Warner, 1976.
Journey (Newhome). New York, Pocket Books, 1978; London, Hamlyn, 1979.
Dangerous Games (Newhome). New York, Pocket Books, 1980.
The Sword of Winter. New York, Timescape, 1983.
Those Who Favor Fire. New York, Pocket Books, 1984.

OTHER PUBLICATIONS

Other

John F. Kennedy (for children). New York, Chelsea House, 1988.
Editor, with Robert Silverberg, *New Dimensions 11-12.* New York, Pocket Books, 2 vols., 1980-81.
Editor, *The Nebula Awards 19.* New York, Arbor House, 1984.

*

Marta Randall comments:

I find it difficult to speak about my own fiction—primarily, I think, because of a conviction that stories must stand by themselves, and the hopes, opinion, or beliefs of their authors are ultimately irrelevant. I view science fiction as a tool, as a useful series of conventions with which to deal with a storyteller's basic task, that is, the exploration not of ideas, but of people. By using the devices of the genre the writer can pare away anything not relevant to the characters and their dilemmas, can, in effect, create a crucible in which to toss the characters and view their reactions. Lest that sound pompous, I believe it equally important that science fiction remain, far more than general mainstream fiction, a genre in which one can tell stories, present adventures, write for the simple joy of creating wonderful things. My principal goal as a science fiction writer is to meld these two approaches to the genre. It is a goal which I hope to be chasing for the rest of my professional life.

*   *   *

Marta Randall's six novels span a variety of literary forms: science fiction, quasi-fantasy, and conventional novels. She has experimented with different literary modes as well: novels, short stories, novellas, and the editing of anthologies.

Her first two works, *Islands* and *A City in the North,* were published in 1976. *A City in the North* tells the story of an alien species, colonized and exploited by humans, who decide to tear asunder their social order in their revolt against their masters. The finale is ambiguous when the author posits that oppression does not lead to a higher morality on the part of the victim. *Journey* and *Dangerous Games* form a two-part saga of the Kennerin family who own the planet Aerie and attempt to create a society alternative to Earth.

In her last two novels, Randall has increasingly moved away from science fiction. In *The Sword of Winter,* she depicts a feudal society poised between change and stasis. The novel is neither science fiction nor fantasy; although it takes place on another planet, it is closer to a conventional historical novel. Her latest novel, *Those Who Favor Fire,* is not science fiction at all, but rather a dystopian extrapolation of what could happen on the West Coast given urban crime, gang warfare, organized right-wing movements, and earthquakes.

Randall's works are representative of the feminist sub-genre in science fiction. This distinct sub-grouping emerged in the mid-1960s when women joined the ranks of science fiction writers in substantial numbers for the first time. Almost to a woman, they wrote "soft" science fiction, concentrating on depicting alternative worlds which, when juxtaposed to their own, served to highlight the deleterious effects of sexism.

Many characteristics found in Randall's work are typical of traits found in feminist science fiction. First, her alternative worlds are not sexist. All her novels portray strong female characters who are decisive, independent, nurturing, and thoughtful. Second, Randall explores sexual taboos and alternative sexual modes openly and uninhibitedly, such as homosexuality, incest, and sensuality. Third, her imaginary worlds, although vivid, do not proffer an alternative view to the author's own social order. This shortcoming, shared with many feminist science fiction writers, is most evident in *Journey* and *Dangerous Games* where Randall recreates monopoly capitalism and proffers it as a utopic social order to the reader.

Randall's strengths are many. Her novels are fast-paced and contain strong, well-developed characters. Her aliens in *Journey, Dangerous Games,* and especially *A City in the North* are believable and engaging. Her best science fiction novel is her first, *Islands.* Here, she explores a society whose inhabitants have discovered the secret to immortality. Randall is brilliant in her speculations of the sciences, language, morality, psychology, phobias, and pathologies of immortal beings. The emotions of the heroine, who cannot achieve immortality and is an aging freak in a perpetually youthful society, are depicted masterfully. The finale is strongly reminiscent of Olaf Stapledon's *Star Maker,* where the heroine mutates to a higher level of consciousness, transcends the corporal, and merges with the world and cosmos.

—Hoda M. Zaki

RANDALL, Robert. *See* **GARRETT, Randall; SILVERBERG, Robert.**

———

RANKINE, John. *See* **MASON, Douglas R.**

———

RAYCRAFT, Stan. *See* **SHAVER, Richard S.**

———

REAMY, Tom

Nationality: American. **Born:** Woodson, Texas, in 1935. **Career:** Movie projectionist, technical illustrator, dispatcher for a concrete plant, assistant movie director and propman, phototypositor, and house painter; editor, *CirFanAc,* Dallas, in the 1950s and *Trumpet,* in the 1960s; founder, with Ken Keller, Nickelodeon Graphics, Kansas City (worked on *Delap's SF&F Review* and *Chacol/Shayol*), and editor, with Keller, *Nickelodeon,* 1975-77. **Awards:** Nebula award, 1975; John W. Campbell award, 1976. **Died:** 5 November 1977.

SCIENCE FICTION PUBLICATIONS

Novel

Blind Voices. New York, Berkley, 1978; London, Sidgwick and Jackson, 1979.

Short Stories

San Diego Lightfoot Sue, and Other Stories. Kansas City, Missouri, Earthlight, 1980.

OTHER PUBLICATIONS

Play

Sting!, in *Six Science Fiction Plays,* edited by Roger Elwood. New York, Pocket Books, 1976.

Other

Editor, *MidAmericon Program Book.* Kansas City, Missouri, MidAmericon, 1976.

*   *   *

From 1974, when his first stories appeared, Tom Reamy was considered a promising new writer and his progress watched with interest. His sudden death in 1977 meant that, instead of the long and prolific career and the steady increase in his already formidable powers his admirers expected, we have only one novel and a dozen short stories. But the novel, *Blind Voices,* and the best of the short stories need no special pleading as early experiments—they can stand on their own as successful and remarkable works. Tom Reamy's position is secure. Although he is often called a science fiction writer, and won science fiction awards, nearly all of Reamy's work would be better classified as fantasy. His stories skim along the edge of reality, firmly anchored in time and place, whether Depression-era, rural Kansas, or present-day Los Angeles, and the plots range between the subtlest of fantasies and the most visceral, outrageous horrors. His recurring themes are of human relationships, the frightening, dark side of sexuality, the triumph or destruction of the innocent, and monsters—from outer space, from Hollywood, from the id.

"Twilla," his first published story, shows the strong influence films—particularly low-budget horror films—had on Reamy, who worked in Hollywood and first tried his hand at scriptwriting. The plot of "Twilla" is straightforward and violent, full of vivid, visual descriptions with little time wasted on explanations. Like the films it emulates, the story seeks to entertain and shock, and it succeeds. There are some problems with plot construction and logic, but the story works as well as it does because of a solid grounding in reality, the accumulation of detail giving it a peculiar depth. In this, as in later stories, Reamy revealed his talent for selecting the perfect details to bring scenes and characters to life, from the utterly convincing names of even minor characters to precise descriptions of dress and furniture. "San Diego Lightfoot Sue," Reamy's own favorite and an award-winner, is the gentlest and most romantic of all his stories. The horror takes place off-stage and the emphasis is that of the so-called "mainstream," with the fantasy element almost superfluous. It is not the story, nor any sense of the fantastic, which remains to haunt the reader, but the characters—the vividly depicted Pearl and Daisy Mae; the extreme innocence and beauty of John Lee Peacock; the dying Grace Elizabeth; the hinted-at depths of the title character.

Reamy's best and most powerful stories are "The Detweiler Boy" and "Under the Hollywood Sign," both set in a grittily real Los Angeles, both told in the first-person and using many of the conventions of the hard-boiled detective story, both probing the dark side of sexual desire and offering a complex vision of the conflict, on many levels, between innocence and evil. They are both disturbing stories that reveal love and need as the inseparable Siamese twins of violence and destruction. In these stories, people need each other and shy away from their need, knowing that sexual love will inevitably lead to death.

Blind Voices takes place in the American Midwest during the Depression—a time and a place that Reamy makes convincingly his own. The story sets the fantastic creatures of a traveling wonder-show against the everyday lives of the people of Hawley, Kansas. It obviously owes much to works by Ray Bradbury, Charles Finney, and Theodore Sturgeon, but it shows Reamy's distinctive touch in the reworking of some familiar material, in the characterizations, the vivid style, and the dark undercurrent of sexuality which runs through all his writings. Although the material is that of fantasy, like *The Circus of Doctor Lao* or *Something Wicked This Way Comes,* an explanation near the end tips the book into science fiction.

—Lisa Tuttle

REAVES, Michael

Also writes as J. Michael Reaves. **Nationality:** American. **Address:** c/o Tor Books, 49 West 24th Street, 9th floor, New York, New York 10010, U.S.A.

SCIENCE FICTION PUBLICATIONS

Novels (series: Khadaji; Shattered World; Time Machine)

I—Alien: A Novel (for children). New York, Grosset and Dunlap, 1978.
Dragonworld (as J. Michael Reaves), with Byron Preiss. Garden City, New York, Doubleday, 1979; London, Bantam, 1980; revised edition, New York, Bantam, 1983.
Darkworld Detective (as J. Michael Reaves). New York, Bantam, 1982.
The Shattered World. New York, Timescape, 1984; London, Orbit, 1986.
Sword of the Samurai (Time Machine; for children), with Steve Perry. New York, Bantam, 1984.
Hellstar, with Steve Perry. New York, Berkley, 1984.
Dome, with Steve Perry. New York, Berkley, 1987; London, Gollancz, 1988.
The Burning Realm (Shattered World). New York, Baen, and London, Orbit, 1988.
The Omega Cage (Khadaji), with Steve Perry. New York, Ace, 1988.
Street Magic. New York, Tor, 1991.
Night Hunter. New York, Tor, 1995.

* * *

Michael Reaves, whose early work appeared under the name J. Michael Reaves, had been writing science fiction since his teen years, but it was not until he attended the Clarion Workshop, in 1972, that he was able to sell his first story. "The Breath of Dragons," written while he was a student at California State University, San Bernardino, was published in the third of the Clarion anthologies.

"Breath" uncannily presages Reaves's later fictions, both in theme and in setting. Perrin is a hunter on a planet where dragons are killed for their fire-producing bladders. The dragons look and fly like the creatures from children's fairytales, but they're no match for man's superior technology. Perrin also believes they're sentient beings, a theory no one else sanctions. His attempt to prove the dragons' intelligence causes the accidental death of a crewmate; as he struggles to find a way out of his predicament, he is consumed (in an apparent act of kindness) by the very creatures he is striving to protect. Perrin has paid the ultimate price for his carelessness, and a balance has been restored to his world.

Although the author's most successful prose works—*Dragonworld, The Shattered World,* its sequel, *The Burning Realm,* and *Darkworld Detective*—have been packaged by their publishers as fantasy, Reaves enjoys combining elements from the SF, fantasy, and detective fiction genres into seemingly irreconcilable plot lines, making the believability of one dependent upon the other. Images of dragons and similar creatures, of flying in general, of man and beast soaring above the grittiness of the everyday world, permeate his fiction. Even in the ostensibly SF novel *Hellstar,* set in the artificial environment of a multigeneration spaceship traveling slowly between the stars, the characters literally fly (in a recreation room designed for that purpose), and take weightless walks on the outside of the ship's hull, where they experience almost a religious ecstasy before the grand vistas of open space.

Each of Reaves's protagonists sees an imbalance in the universe, a flaw, an emptiness in himself or others, and seeks to restore some semblance of order or sanity to nature, to himself, to humanity as a whole. Thus, Perrin regards the dragons as his private crusade, while Amsel in *Dragonworld* must go on his own dragonquest, and Kamus of Kadizar, the otherworldly shamus of *Darkworld Detective,* seeks to right the wrongs of his world by solving the mysteries of his clients.

We can see these themes—of action and reaction, of responsibility and irresponsibility, of wrongs that must be righted and sins that must be redressed—most clearly developed in the author's most popular work, *The Shattered World,* and its sequel, *The Burning Realm.* Here, the surviving magicians must face the consequences of an ancient war of sorcery that literally broke their world into fragments. Pandrogas and Amber cannot escape the harm caused by their illicit romance, and Beorn, as attractive a thief as one will find in modern fantasy literature, must pay a high price indeed for the pursuit of his profession. Yet each persists in his or her chosen (even stubborn) course, doing what each thinks is right and necessary and proper, for himself and for others, and sometimes being damned for it.

Similar themes are evident in Reaves's teleplays (of which there are over 200), often on a more simplistic level (much of the author's work has been produced for half-hour, animated children's cartoon programs). In "Street of Shadows" (*The Twilight Zone*), for example, Steve Butler, a homeless, down-on-his-luck carpenter with a family to support, breaks into the home of Frederick Perry, a wealthy industrialist, and briefly changes places mentally with him. As "Perry," Steve is able to rebalance his microuniverse by buying the mortgage of the near-bankrupt shelter where he and his family have been staying. In the "Where None Have Gone Before" episode of *Star Trek: The Next Generation* (written with Diane Duane), Peter Kosinski, a brilliant engineer, saves the *Enterprise* from the consequences of his own warp drive experiments, and in the process rescues himself from a life of loneliness by somehow regenerating a son who had died at birth seven years before.

In the author's most recent novel, *Night Hunter,* Los Angeles police detective Jake Hull is called to a crime scene in a seedy Hollywood hotel, where a dead man lies with a stake driven through his heart and a bulb of garlic in his mouth. Hull assumes, with everyone else, that L.A.'s latest serial killer is a nutcase who thinks he's a latter-day Helsing hunting vampires. But as he probes deeper into the case, Hull begins to realize that there may be more to the crime than is apparent. The trail leads the detective into an occult society and the night life of the Hollywood fringe element. It also forces him to confront the darker side of his own nature, the part of himself that identifies with the madness in the streets.

There are many things in heaven and earth, the author seems to be saying, not all of them rational, or explicable, or knowable; but ultimately man must take responsibility for his own actions, and *some* things will eventually balance out. For Reaves, the universe has ever been a moral place where immorals fear to tread.

—Robert Reginald

REED, Kit

Also writes as Kit Craig. **Pseudonym:** Shelley Hyde. **Nationality:** American. **Born:** Kit Craig, San Diego, California, 1932. **Education:** College of Notre Dame of Maryland, Baltimore, B.A. 1954. **Family:** Married Joseph Wayne Reed, Jr., in 1955; two sons and one daughter. **Career:** Reporter, *St. Petersburg Times,* Florida, 1954-55; reporter, *Hamden Chronicle,* Connecticut, 1956, and *New Haven Register,* Connecticut, 1956-59; book reviewer, *New Haven Register* and *St. Petersburg Times.* Since 1974, Visiting Professor of English, then Adjunct Professor, Wesleyan University, Middletown, Connecticut. Board, National Book Critics Circle, 1991-95. **Awards:** New England Newspaperwoman of the Year award, 1958, 1959; Guggenheim Fellowship, 1964; Abraham Woursell Foundation five-year grant, 1965; Aspen Institute Rockefeller Fellowship, 1976. **Agent:** Richard Pine, Arthur Pine Associates, Suite 417, 250 West 57th Street, New York, New York 10019. **Address:** 45 Lawn Avenue, Middletown, Connecticut 06457, U.S.A.

Science Fiction Publications

Novels

Armed Camps. London, Faber, 1969; New York, Dutton, 1970.
Magic Time. New York, Berkley, 1980.
Blood Fever (as Shelley Hyde). New York, Pocket Books, 1982.
Fort Privilege. Garden City, New York, Doubleday, 1985.
Little Sister of the Apocalypse. Boulder, Colorado, Fiction Collective Two, 1994.

Short Stories

Mister da V. and Other Stories. London, Faber, 1967; New York, Berkley, 1973.
The Killer Mice. London, Gollancz, 1976.
Other Stories and . . . The Attack of the Giant Baby. New York, Berkley, 1981.
*Revenge of the Senior Citizens, **Plus: A Short Story Collection.* Garden City, New York, Doubleday, 1986.

Other Publications

Novels

Mother Isn't Dead, She's Only Sleeping. Boston, Houghton Mifflin, 1961.
At War as Children. New York, Farrar Straus, 1964.
The Better Part. New York, Farrar Straus, 1967; London, Hutchinson, 1968.
Cry of the Daughter. New York, Dutton, 1971.
Tiger Rag. New York, Dutton, 1973.
Captain Grownup. New York, Dutton, 1976.
Ballad of T. Rantula. Boston, Little Brown, 1979.
Catholic Girls. New York, Fine, 1987.

Short Stories

Thief of Lives. Columbia, University of Missouri Press, 1992.

Play

Radio Play: *The Bathyscaphe,* 1978.

Other

When We Dream (for children). New York, Hawthorn, 1967.
Story First: The Writer as Insider. Englewood Cliffs, New Jersey, Prentice Hall, 1982; revised edition as *Mastering Fiction Writing,* Cincinnati, Ohio, Writer's Digest, 1991.
George Orwell's 1984. Woodbury, New York, Barron's Book Notes, 1984.
Revision. Cincinnati, Ohio, Writer's Digest, 1989; London, Robinson, 1991.
Editor, *Fat.* Indianapolis, Bobbs Merrill, 1974.

*

Manuscript Collection: Beinecke Library, Yale University, New Haven, Connecticut.

Kit Reed comments:

Most of us go where they'll take us. My first published story was too off-the-wall for slick magazines; it found a home in the *Magazine of Fantasy and Science Fiction,* where I still publish some short fiction. Let's say the field, if you define SF as Speculative Fiction, broadens the possibilities for those of us who swim mostly in the mainstream but write fiction that is sometimes off-the-wall. A home away from home for the restless imagination.

*   *   *

Kit Reed writes within several fiction genres. Her stories have been published in *Fiction* (Paris), *Town* (London), *Seventeen,* and a variety of science fiction and fantasy magazines. Some of her stories are realistic, some impressionistic, some fantasy, some science fiction. And representatives of each of these types appear in the collection *Mister da V.* Reed does not write hard, or technologically oriented, science fiction; and although some of her stories do make use of traditional science fiction devices or theories, those stories actually focus on the people in them and the ways in which those people are affected by their surroundings. While this is typical of science fiction in general, Reed seems to deal primarily with the people and to use the science-fiction elements as another writer might use a car or truck—as a detail necessary to the story.

In "Automatic Tiger," the full-sized mechanical tiger is not presented as an object of wonder. Edward Benedict accepts the tiger as no more than a special toy for his nephew. When he tries the tiger out, however, he decides to keep it. Having his own tiger gives Benedict confidence and changes his previously nondescript life. He becomes successful in business and in society— until he no longer has time for the tiger, which deteriorates. When he loses the tiger, his life collapses, and he is left much as he was when the story began. "Mister da V." is a story in which time-travel is the traditional science-fiction device, but the story is really about the 20th-century family into which Leonardo da Vinci is brought. The mother can see only the extra work that this "guest" necessitates. The twins like the strange toys he makes for them, but after he has gone and the toys are broken, they forget him. The father sees Leonardo as the source for a definitive biography. But the teen-aged girl sees a sweet, lonely, brilliant old man who seems to be sad because he will never get to do all the things he can envision.

This focus on people and the ways in which technology affects them is also at the heart of Reed's socially critical stories. One of her strongest pieces of social criticism is "Golden Acres," about a home for the elderly. In this future setting, an old person can use his negotiable assets to purchase a place in Golden Acres. Although these establishments look very attractive from the outside, they are extremely dehumanizing: all of the rooms are the same, the furniture is bolted down, and there is no place for personal effects or mementoes—what the management calls "clutter." And when a person's funds run out—rent, medical care, etc. all add up—he is taken to the Tower of Sleep where his life is terminated.

"At Central," "Ordeal," and the novel *Armed Camps,* are similar stories about societies in which technology has all but taken over. In "At Central," people watch television all the time (never going outside), pump their money into the appropriate slots when they see something they want, and have everything delivered. The people in "Ordeal" are all on "life fluid" and spend their time hooked up to the intravenous tubes which pump the purple liquid into their veins. In *Armed Camps,* warfare is the one constant thing in the world; and although it seems that only champions fight and die, great numbers of people are killed each year. And instead of trying to end it, the top brass make sure that it will go on—forever, if possible.

Reed's recent work, collected in *The Revenge of the Senior Citizens, ** Plus,* a collection that includes the novella "The Revenge of the Senior Citizens" and 16 short stories, continues the two main themes of her work: the impact of technology on people's lives and the plight of senior citizens. In "Frontiers," the post-cataclysm world of Gunnar Morgan is described in terms of the American western frontier of the late 1800s, and in "A Unique Service," a famous author buys a simulacrum of himself to handle the demands fame has made on his time. Most of the stories, however, are about senior citizens. In "Shan," an elderly woman saves the world from alien invasion. "Great Escape Tours, Inc." takes senior citizens back to childhood for a day. And in the title story, senior citizens band together to protest being "put away"—in every sense of the term— by their children.

In the final analysis, it is Reed's characters that carry her fiction—science fiction, fantasy, or mainstream. To be sure, the other aspects of her writing are not found wanting, but her characters— especially the women struggling to find themselves in an indifferent or hostile society, or struggling against various institutions— remain in the reader's mind.

—C.W. Sullivan III

REED, Robert

Pseudonym: R. Touzalin. **Nationality:** American. **Born:** Omaha, Nebraska, 9 October 1956. **Education:** Nebraska Wesleyan University, B.S. in Biology 1987. **Career:** Utility worker, Mapes Industries, Lincoln, Nebraska, 1978-87; lab technician, University of Nebraska, Lincoln, 1979-80. Since 1987, full-time writer. **Awards:** L. Ron Hubbard Gold award, 1986. **Agent:** Merrilee Heifetz, Writers' House Inc., 21 West 26th Street, New York, New York 10010. **Address:** 3450 Cable Ave., Lincoln, Nebraska 68506-1901, U.S.A.

SCIENCE FICTION PUBLICATIONS

Novels

The Leeshore: A Novel. New York, Fine, 1987.
The Hormone Jungle. New York, Fine, 1987; London, Futura, 1989.
Black Milk: A Novel. New York, Fine, 1989; London, Orbit, 1990.
Down the Bright Way. New York, Bantam, 1991.
The Remarkables. New York, Bantam, 1992.
Beyond the Veil of Stars. New York, Tor, 1994.

*

Robert Reed comments:

(1991) I can think of too much to write about my own work, thus I'll write nothing much. I enjoy parts of what I have done—a chapter here, an opening paragraph now and again—and when I fail as a writer, I hope, it is out of ignorance and youth, but never out of a lack of effort, nor because I have made the thing stale from beating it against my limitations.

(1995) At least once a week, regardless of my work schedule, shifting moods, or the occasional sucking chest wound, I make a point of dragging myself to a certain library and reading from its science magazines, both popular and professional. There is no way to know enough in this business of mine. Never in human history has exploration been as rich as it is at this moment. But just as important to me, these glimpses of the far and future give me that same delicious tingle that I enjoyed when I was a kid reading about imagined worlds and impossible aliens.

My writing can fail because of wrong or sloppy speculations, but I don't believe it ever succeeds—in my sense of the word—unless there is some lasting sense that the players on the page are genuine, casting shadows and lingering in the mind of the reader. For this kind of knowledge, libraries help, but far more important, I think, are the times when you look at a face and see past it, when you stare into eyes and have some sense, however glancing, of the soul that's looking out at your face and your own little eyes.

For me, writing is the most intense possible kind of reading.

I never know exactly what will happen in my stories, even in the simplest scene, and it's that sense of daily astonishment that almost makes up for the uncertainties of this business. My best days are wondrous. I don't know how the rest of the world survives without writing.

*   *   *

Robert Reed made his debut with an award-winning story in the L. Ron Hubbard "Writers of the Future" contest, and established himself as a fine novelist shortly thereafter with the publication of *The Leeshore.* Taking its inspiration from Ernest Hemingway's *Islands in the Stream,* the novel is set on a far world whose surface is entirely water, and whose light is cut off by a carpet of living creatures afloat in the upper atmosphere. As a consequence, surface life must resort to bioluminescence.

A renegade group of technophiles called the Alteretics has been defeated in their assault on Earth, and have fled to the world of Leeshore as a refuge, killing all human settlers except for a brother and sister who escape into the wilderness. A pursuit fleet from Earth arrives and recruits the two in their effort to locate their enemies, but the protagonists soon question their role in the proceedings, believing their newfound friends to be little better than those who

came before them. The combination of a thoroughly developed and strange new environment with a serious and thoughtful story line made this one of the most striking debut novels of recent years.

Although *The Leeshore* seemed to have left the door open for a sequel, Reed's next novel, *The Hormone Jungle,* is set on Earth, but an Earth some two millennia removed from us, home to literally trillions of life-forms, both natural and artificial. The story alternates between the relationship of a professional troubleshooter with a humanoid robot built to provide pleasure to male humans who may be concealing sinister motives, and the rivalry between an exile and his cyborg neighbor. When the robot's owner decides to reclaim his property, the plot accelerates at breakneck pace. Reed invests great effort in developing this ecology as well, and although it never quite achieves the verisimilitude of his first novel, it is nonetheless a dramatically successful novel.

Black Milk is not set in nearly as remote a time as its predecessors. In the not too distant future, genetic engineering is an accepted method of family planning. Prospective parents routinely take advantage of the technology to shape, within certain limits, the attributes of their offspring. A researcher hoping to seed the atmosphere of the gas giant planets with bioengineered life-forms inadvertently allows them to escape his laboratory on the moon, compromising the atmosphere in the colony, ultimately threatening the entire human race. Despite the melodramatic events, the plot falters in the second half of the book, and when we finally discover that disaster has been averted, we are no longer even particularly concerned, particularly since most of the more suspenseful events are handled offhandedly, even offstage.

Reed's next novel, *Down the Bright Way,* returned to an interstellar arena. Spread throughout the universe are myriad planets with intelligent species, all at one time linked by the mysterious and ancient Makers. Now an alliance drawn together from many worlds is exploring the links between planets, finding civilizations in danger of destroying themselves and helping to ease them into the fraternity of the universe. But another organization is at work as well, this one determined to pursue a course of conquest and destruction. A single Earthman becomes aware of the web of worlds and finds himself pushed into becoming the pivotal figure in what might be the most significant conflict in the history of the universe.

Reed's most recent novel, *Beyond the Veil of Stars,* is his most ambitious to date. Initially, we follow the adventures of the son of a professional UFO watcher, a boy whose life is apparently distorted by the preoccupations of his father. As a young adult, he experiences along with the rest of the human race the transformation of the physical universe, and the discovery that alien intelligences not only exist on other planes of reality, but are watching and manipulating humankind. More to the point, it is possible for human intelligences to visit some of these other worlds by transplanting personalities for a time into the very different physical bodies of aliens. *Beyond the Veil* is a thoughtful, speculative novel that suffers somewhat from its episodic nature.

Reed is a prolific short story writer who devotes much of his attention to the convolutions of the human psyche. In "Utility Man," Reed eschews the usual viewpoint character and selects an assembly line worker reacting to the requirements of working with a truly alien coworker. "Busybody" features a nosy woman whose investigations have very interesting consequences. Earth has been damaged by aliens in "Chaff," but the story concerns itself with the efforts of a human family to come to terms with their altered world. Reed's strangest story is "Bushwhacker," wherein an unassuming man uses various inoffensive devices to "shoot" people and transform their lives. Or perhaps he just imagines it.

"Blind" details the adventures of researchers who discover an unexpected life form on the ocean's floor. Human civilization turns out to be a failed alien experiment in "Dimensions of the Deed." Reed examines our obsession with self-image in "Do I Know You," a future in which body sculpting is an acceptable cosmetic technique. Physical appearance is also a significant theme of "Remoras," this time fascination with malformities. Other stories worth noting are "Treading in the Afterglow," "We Are All Superheroes," "On the Brink of That Bright New World," "The Shape of Everything," and "Goodness."

Reed's strongest points are his detailed and generally convincing settings, particularly impressive because they vary so greatly from the world with which we are familiar, and his genuine insights into the human mind and the moral questions which trouble us. *The Leeshore* deals with treachery and loyalty, *The Hormone Jungle* with those same themes as well as the causes of love and hate, *Black Milk* with our hopes for the future as manifested in our children, and *Down the Bright Way* and *Beyond the Veil of Stars* with our sense of destiny and the search for meaning in the universe. His generally successful handling of such ambitious and important themes marks him as a writer with serious intentions, while his strong narrative and descriptive talents ensure that the message will not interfere with the entertainment value of his fiction. Although his novels are invariably interesting, it appears from present trends that his greatest impact on the field may be at shorter length, where his themes seem to be more focused and effective.

—Don D'Ammassa

RENARD, Maurice

Nationality: French. **Born:** 1875. **Died:** 1939.

SCIENCE FICTION PUBLICATIONS

Novels

Le docteur Lerne, sous-dieu. Paris, n.p., 1908; translated as *New Bodies for Old,* New York, Macaulay, 1923.
Les mains d'Orlac. Paris, n.p., 1920; translated by Florence Crewe-Jones as *The Hands of Orlac,* New York, Dutton, 1929; London, Four Sqaure Books, 1961.
Le sing (with Albert Jean). Paris, Crés, 1925; translated by Florence Crewe-Jones as *Blind Circle,* New York, Dutton, 1928; London, Gollanz, 1929.

Untranslated Novels in French

Le Péril Bleu. Paris, 1910.
L'Homme Truqué. Paris, n.p., n.d.
Un Homme Chez les Microbes. Paris, n.p., 1928.
Le Maître, de la Lumiére. Paris, n.p., 1948.

Short Stories

Le voyage immobile suive d'autres histories singuliéres. N.p., 1909; translated as *The Flight of the Aerofix,* New York, Stellar, 1932.

OTHER PUBLICATIONS

Novels

The Snake of Luvercy, translated by Florence Crewe-Jones. New York, Dutton, 1930.

Maurice Renard is considered a pioneer of French SF and one of the most important SF writers of the period 1910-30. His first novel, a wildly impressionist fantasy akin to Wells's *The Island of Dr. Moreau,* albeit with more overt sexuality that sometimes rises to strange ecstasies, was *New Bodies for Old,* in which the brain of the hero is transplanted into a bull by one of the proverbial mad scientists of science fiction; the novel ends with an even more fantastic identity change that brings to mind demonic possession. A similar grafting experiment on a more modest scale (a pianist is given the hands of a criminal), but with hardly less gruesome consequences, appears in the more glib and weaker *The Hands of Orlac,* which is probably better known since it was filmed twice. In *L'Homme Truqué,* finally, a giant is given a pair of electric eyes which turns the world into a nightmarish vision. *Un Homme Chez les Microbes* is an elegant and sophisticated treatment of the journey into a microscopic world, a theme often mishandled in American SF by Ray Cummings. Renard's most ambitious novel, however, is *Le Péril Bleu,* an almost surrealist work with strong Fortean overtones. It introduces a strange civilization of ethereol lifeforms, the Oniweig, living on top of our atmosphere and fishing for objects in the air as we might fish the deep seas. They abduct humans and experiment with them, returning them to the surface of Earth only as a rain of picked bones and skeletons. Another SF novel is *Le Maître, de la Lumière,* a fantastic mystery novel about duplicated bodies. His short stories tend towards the mystical and fantastic; a common theme is the relativity of perception, and their favorite device a distortion of perspective: time and space, other dimensions, mirrors, and changed sense organs figure prominently in them, and he is fond of joining together opposites, cold reason as well as feverish dreams.

—Franz Rottensteiner

RESNICK, Mike

Nationality: American. **Born:** Michael Diamond Resnick, Chicago, Illinois, 5 March 1942. **Education:** Attended University of Chicago, 1959-62. **Family:** Married Carol Cain in 1961; one daughter. **Career:** File clerk, Santa Fe Railroad, Chicago, 1962-65; editor, *National Tattler,* 1965-66, and *National Insider,* 1966-69, for National Features Syndicate, Chicago; editor and publisher, Oligarch Publishing, Libertyville, Illinois, 1969-70. Breeder and exhibitor of collies, 1968-80, and columnist, *Collie Cues Magazine,* Hayward, California, 1969-80. Since 1964, freelance writer; has published over 200 novels (sex, gothic, romance) under pseudonyms. Since 1976, owner of Briarwood Pet Motel, Cincinnati. **Awards:** Hugo award, for short story, 1989, for novella, 1995; Nebula award, for novella, 1995; Skylark award, 1995. **Agent:** Eleanor Wood, Spectrum Literary Agency, Suite 1501, 111 Eighth Avenue, New York, New York 10011. **Address:** 10547 Tanager Hills Drive, Cincinnati, Ohio 45249, U.S.A.

Novels (series: Galactic Midway; Ganymede; Lucifer Jones; Oracle; Velvet Comet)

The Goddess of Ganymede. West Kingston, Rhode Island, Grant, 1967.
Pursuit on Ganymede. New York, Paperback Library, 1968.
Redbeard. New York, Lancer, 1969.
Battlestar Galactica 5: Galactica Discovers Earth, with Glen A. Larson. New York, Berkley, 1980.
The Soul Eater. New York, Signet, 1981.
Birthright: The Book of Man. New York, Signet, 1982.
Walpurgis III. New York, Signet, 1982.
Tales of the Galactic Midway: Sideshow. New York, Signet, 1982.
The Three-Legged Hootch Dancer. New York, Signet, 1983.
The Wild Alien Tamer. New York, Signet, 1983.
The Best Rootin' Tootin' Shootin' Gunslinger in the Whole Damned Galaxy. New York, Signet, 1983.
The Branch. New York, Signet, 1984.
Tales of the Velvet Comet: Eros Ascending. Huntington Woods, Michigan, Phantasia Press, 1984.
Eros at Zenith. Huntington Woods, Michigan, Phantasia Press, 1984.
Eros Descending. New York, Signet, 1985.
Eros at Nadir. New York, Signet, 1986.
Adventures: Being a Stirring Chronicle (Jones). New York, Signet, 1985.
Santiago: A Myth of the Far Future. New York, Tor, 1986; London, Arrow, 1986.
The Dark Lady: A Romance of the Far Future. New York, Tor, 1987; London, Legend, 1988.
Stalking the Unicorn: A Fable of Tonight. New York, Tor, 1987; London, Arow, 1987.
Ivory: A Legend of Past and Future. New York, Tor, 1988; London, Legend, 1989.
Paradise: A Chronicle of a Distant World. New York, Tor, 1989; London, Legend, 1991.
Second Contact. Norwalk, Connecticut, Easton Press, 1990; London, Legend, 1991.
The Red Tape War, with Jack L. Chalker and George Alec Effinger. New York, Tor, 1991.
Soothsayer (Oracle). New York, Ace, and London, Legend, 1991.
Oracle. New York, Ace, 1992.
Lucifer Jones. New York, Warner, 1992; in 2 vols. as *Exploits* and *Encounters,* Newark, New Jersey, Wildside Press, 1993-95.
Prophet (Oracle). New York, Ace, 1993.
Inferno: A Chronicle of a Distant World. New York, Tor, 1993.
Purgatory: A Chronicle of a Distant World. New York, Tor, 1993.
A Miracle of Rare Design: A Tragedy of Transcendence. New York, Tor, 1994.

Short Stories

The Forgotten Sea of Mars (novella). Baton Rouge, Louisiana, Camille E. Cazedessus, Jr., 1965.
Unauthorized Autobiographies and Other Curiosities. Detroit, Misfit Press, 1984.
The Inn of the Hairy Toad. New Orleans, Delta Con, 1985.
Bully! Eugene, Oregon, Axolotl Press, 1990; expanded as *Bwana, and Bully!* (two novellas), New York, Tor, 1991.

Through Darkest Resnick with Gun and Camera. Washington, D.C., Washington Science Fiction Association, 1990.
Stalking the Wild Resnick. Cambridge, Massachusetts, NESFA Press, 1991.
The Alien Heart. Eugene, Oregon, Pulphouse, 1991.
Pink Elephants and Hairy Toads. Newark, New Jersey, Wildside Press, 1991.
Will the Last Person to Leave the Planet Please Shut off the Sun? New York, Tor, 1992.
Kirinyaga. Eugene, Oregon, Pulphouse, 1992.
Seven Views of Olduvai Gorge. Eugene, Oregon, Axolotl Press, 1994.

Novel

Dog in the Manger. Alexander, North Carolina, Alexander Books, 1995.

Other

The Official Guide to Fantastic Literature. Florence, Alabama, House of Collectibles, 1976.
Official Guide to Comic Books and Big Little Books. Florence, Alabama, House of Collectibles, 1977.
Gymnastics and You: The Whole Story of the Sport. Chicago, Rand McNally, 1978.
Official Price Guide to Comic and Science Fiction Books. Orlando, Florida, House of Collectibles, 1979.

Editor, *Shaggy B.E.M. Stories.* New Orleans, Louisiana, Nolacon Press, 1988.
Editor, *Alternate Presidents.* New York, Tor, 1992.
Editor, *Alternate Kennedys.* New York, Tor, 1992.
Editor, *Inside the Funhouse: 17 SF Stories about SF.* New York, AvoNova, 1992.
Editor, with Martin H. Greenberg, *Whatdunits.* New York, DAW, 1992.
Editor, with Martin H. Greenberg, *Aladdin, Master of the Lamp.* New York, DAW, 1992.
Editor, with Gardner R. Dozois, *Future Earths; Under African Skies.* New York, DAW, 1993.
Editor, with Martin H. Greenberg, *More Whatdunits.* New York, DAW, 1993.
Editor, with Gardner R. Dozois, *Future Earths: Under South American Skies.* New York, DAW, 1993.
Editor, with Martin H. Greenberg, *Dinosaur Fantastic.* New York, DAW, 1993.
Editor, *Alternate Warriors.* New York, Tor, 1993.
Editor, with Martin H. Greenberg, *Christmas Ghosts.* New York, DAW, 1993.
Editor, *Alternate Outlaws.* New York, Tor, 1994.
Editor, *Alternate Worldcons.* Eugene, Oregon, Pulphouse, 1994.
Editor, with Anthony R. Lewis, *The Passage of the Night: The Recursive Science Fiction of Barry N. Malzberg.* Framingham, Massachusetts, NESFA Press, 1994.
Editor, with Martin H. Greenberg and Loren D. Estleman, *Deals with the Devil.* New York, DAW, 1994.
Editor, with Martin H. Greenberg, *By Any Other Fame.* New York, DAW, 1994.

Editor, with Martin H. Greenberg, *Witch Fantastic.* New York, DAW, 1995.

Editor, with Martin H. Greenberg, *Sherlock Holmes in Orbit.* New York, DAW, 1995.

*

Manuscript Collection: University of South Florida, Tampa.

Mike Resnick comments:

I'm not at all sure that I write honest-to-God true-blue science fiction. What I write are morality plays, and if turning them into myths and fables of the future and setting them on alien worlds makes them more saleable, I have no objection to so doing. I have a hard time with fearless heroes and beautiful princesses, so I tend to write about overmatched detectives and obsessed ministers and frustrated stripteasers. I have a hard time with heroes who are all good and villains who are all bad, so my characters tend to be neither heroes nor villains, but fall into that in-between gray area that most of us inhabit. The future in which I set my stories is lived-in and a little bit shopworn around the edges; planets tend to look more like the outskirts of Indianapolis or Sioux City than those beautiful mechanized utopias that Frank Paul used to paint 40 and 50 years ago. I don't like puzzle or gimmick stories that leave the reader unmoved and untouched, and so I don't write them. I believe that every man and woman is ultimately responsible for his actions, and this is a theme that seems to recur through my novels.

I suppose if I had to sum up my work in a single sentence, it would be as follows: I am writing about adult characters who face adult problems in an adult universe, and I am writing these stories for an adult audience. This is, alas, rarer than you might think.

* * *

Although Michael Resnick was a prolific author outside the genre and under names other than his own, until the early 1980s his only credits within the field were two pastiches of Edgar Rice Burroughs, *Goddess of Ganymede* and *Pursuit on Ganymede,* and an amusing but routine post-apocalypse novel, *Redbeard,* all published in the 1960s.

Suddenly all of his pent-up writing energy seemed to explode into the science fiction field, initially with various ambitious adventure stories such as *Soul Eater, Walpurgis III, Branch,* and the episodic *Birthright.* Although primarily adventure stories, there was an underlying seriousness missing in many similar books, concerns about the future of humanity, the nature of power and government. A second change became apparent with the characterization in his first series, the four volumes dealing with a star traveling circus, *Sideshow, The Three Legged Hootch Dancer, Wild Alien Tamer,* and *The Best Rootin' Tootin' Shootin' Gunslinger in the Whole Damned Galaxy.* Although the format was still light adventure, Resnick took great pains to differentiate his characters, providing a greater depth to the stories.

His next series was more effective. *Eros Ascending, Eros at Zenith, Eros Descending,* and *Eros at Nadir* share a common setting, an orbiting bordello targeted by religious fanatics and others, a symbol of Earthbound struggles hanging in the heavens. Using finely honed characters, diverse plots, and a mature and perceptive analysis of the ebb and flow of public opinion, Resnick chronicles the

history of the institution in four novels, each complete in itself, the series as a whole establishing their creator as one of the most popular writers in the field.

The next significant title was *Santiago,* which could perhaps be described as a traditional western novel superimposed on an interstellar version of the West. This blend of two genres features characters who are larger than life, and demonstrated that even space opera can be a significant springboard for a talented author. Resnick blended two fields again in *Stalking the Unicorn,* a contemporary fantasy novel featuring a private detective, a clever mystery, and an amusing, fast-paced style.

An already impressive string of fascinating books was steadily enhanced by subsequent titles. *The Dark Lady: A Romance of the Far Future* demonstrated Resnick's fascination with the mysterious and mystical. An alien art historian notices a recurring face in human art and sets out to track down the origin of this enigmatic figure.

A veteran of many African safaris, Resnick began to work themes from the Dark Continent into his novels. *Ivory* is structurally similar to *The Dark Lady;* this time the quest is to find a pair of elephant tusks that possess mystical powers, sought by the last of the Masai tribe in connection with a ritual he must perform prior to his death. *Paradise* is a barely concealed portrayal of the pillage of the African wilderness by outside powers, set on a planet where majestic animals lure big game hunters from offworld, and where the indigent alien species is torn between the desire to embrace the technology humans possess and the need to protect their own heritage. It's a complex story of confused motivations, conflicting rights and responsibilities, and provides no easy answers. Resnick avoids the stock solutions available; there is no magical reconciliation in the final chapter. *Paradise* is filled with adventure, but it is much more than an adventure story. Resnick used the history of modern African states as inspiration for *Inferno* and *Purgatory* as well, both of which explore the tensions created by the imposition of European societal values on African social structures. Invariably good though misguided intentions lead to bad results just as surely as naked exploitation, and when external forces aren't responsible for catastrophe, internal corruption serves just as well. Although some readers have objected to Resnick's interpretations, the stories themselves are well constructed, well reasoned, and all too credible.

Second Contact seems to have been a change of pace. A conventional thriller, it involves a discredited space force officer who murdered his crew under the apparent mistaken belief that they were alien doppelgangers preparing to invade the Earth. His defense attorney is skeptical, until his tentative efforts to investigate the case result in an attempt on his own life. Entertaining chase and escape sequences follow, but the novel as a whole lacks the stature of Resnick's other recent novels. Resnick's inventive sense of humor surfaces periodically in even his most serious novels, but it is the main thrust in an earlier spoof of the genre, *Adventures,* and in *The Red Tape War,* written in collaboration with George Alec Effinger and Jack L. Chalker.

The trilogy consisting of *Soothsayer, Oracle,* and *Prophet* has a fascinating premise that might have escaped the control of a less talented writer. A young human child has a unique psi talent; she can foresee and change the future by interpolating those simple acts which might have immense ramifications at another time. A simple hand movement or carefully selected sentence could save or destroy entire planets. Unfortunately, she is egocentric and emotionally isolated, and sacrifices those who love her in order to survive. The trilogy involves the quest by various forces to either exploit or destroy her, and as depicted her powers are so extraordinary, it doesn't seem possible to have a satisfactory ending. But the climax follows logically and ties up all the loose ends.

A Miracle of Rare Design chronicles the adventures of a human anthropologist who allows his body to be transformed into various alien shapes in order to infiltrate other cultures. The short novel "Seven Views of Olduvai Gorge" takes the opposite viewpoint, alien anthropologists exploring the birthplace of now extinct humankind. Through snapshots taken from human history, the author demonstrates our self-destructive proclivities. Although the presentation is one-sided and didactic, the overall effect is impressive.

During the 1980s, Resnick averaged about two short stories a year, most of which were amusing but unmemorable. The African influence was to change all of this, however, particularly in "Kirinyaga" and "For I Have Touched the Sky," both controversial and thought-provoking stories of the conflict between western values and those of Africa. Both are seen through the eyes of a tribal witch doctor on a colony world controlled by the Masai. Offworld authorities are shocked at the cruelties demanded by tribal customs, including the exposure of certain infants to the elements, and there is growing agitation to intervene. Once again, Resnick is careful to present both viewpoints with respect, and the resolution, while disturbing, is logical and inevitable.

Another African tale, "Bully!," actually a short novel, features Theodore Roosevelt, no longer President of the United States, determined to unite Central Africa into a democracy under his tutelage, dedicated to improving the technological and social base of the primitive tribes he has seen. Roosevelt is Resnick's most fully realized character, earnest and sincere on the one hand, flawed by egotism and an inability to recognize the reality of his situation on the other. Although he makes great strides toward his goal, it is ultimately doomed to failure because the historical basis for such a rapid alteration of the social climate doesn't exist. Other stories of note include "The Bull Moose at Bay" and "Mwalimo in the Squared Circle."

Resnick's greatest strength is that he can show his readers serious things about themselves and the world, usually without lecturing, and deal with important themes without sacrificing plot and other story values. His commentaries on humanity are effectively conveyed on the framework of entertaining, well-designed adventure fiction.

—Don D'Ammassa

REYNOLDS, Mack

Pseudonyms: Bob Belmont; Todd Harding; Maxine Reynolds. **Nationality:** American. **Born:** Dallas McCord Reynolds, Corcoran, California, 12 November 1917. **Education:** Attended public schools in Kingston, New York. **Military Service:** Served in the United States Army Transportation Corps, during World War II; trained in the Marine Officers School, New Orleans: Navigator. **Family:** Married Jeanette Wooley in 1947; two sons and one daughter. **Career:** Editor, *Catskill Mountain Star,* Saugerties, New York, 1937-38, and *Oneonta News,* New York, 1939-40; IBM supervisor, San Pedro shipyards, California, 1940-43; national organizer, Socialist Labor Party, 1946-52; foreign correspondent and travel editor, *Rogue,* 1953-63. **Died:** 29 January 1983.

SCIENCE FICTION PUBLICATIONS

Novels (series: Homer Crawford; Bat Hardin; Lagrangia; Joe Mauser; United Planets Organization; Julian West)

The Earth War (Mauser). New York, Pyramid, 1963; London, New English Library, 1965.
Planetary Agent X (United Planets). New York, Ace, 1965.
Time Gladiator (Mauser). London, New English Library, 1966; New York, Lancer, 1969.
Of Godlike Power. New York, Belmont, 1966; as Earth Unaware, 1968.
Dawnman Planet (United Planets). New York, Ace, 1966.
Space Pioneer (United Planets). London, Four Square, 1966.
The Rival Rigellians (United Planets). New York, Ace, 1967.
Computer War (United Planets). New York, Ace, 1967.
After Some Tomorrow. New York, Belmont, 1967.
Mercenary from Tomorrow (Mauser). New York, Ace, 1968.
Code Duello (United Planets). New York, Ace, 1968.
Star Trek: Mission to Horatius. Racine, Wisconsin, Whitman, 1968.
The Space Barbarians. New York, Ace, 1969.
The Cosmic Eye. New York, Belmont, 1969.
Once Departed. New York, Curtis, 1970.
Computer World. New York, Curtis, 1970.
Blackman's Burden (Crawford). New York, Ace, 1972.
Border, Breed Nor Birth (Crawford). New York, Ace, 1972.
Looking Backward, from the Year 2000 (West). New York, Ace, 1973; Morley, Yorkshire, Elmfield Press, 1976.
Commune 2000 A.D. (Hardin). New York, Bantam, 1974.
Depression or Bust; and, Dawnman Planet. New York, Ace, 1974.
Ability Quotient (Badger). New York, Ace, 1975.
Amazon Planet (United Planets). New York, Ace, 1975.
The Five Way Secret Agent (Badger; Simonov). New York, Ace, 1975.
Satellite City. New York, Ace, 1975.
Tomorrow Might Be Different. New York, Ace, 1975; London, Sphere, 1976.
The Towers of Utopia (Hardin). New York, Bantam, 1975.
Day after Tomorrow (Simonov). New York, Ace, 1976.
Galactic Medal of Honor. New York, Ace, 1976.
Rolltown (Hardin). New York, Ace, 1976.
Section G: United Planets. New York, Ace, 1976.
After Utopia. New York, Ace, 1977.
Equality: In the Year 2000 (West). New York, Ace, 1977.
Perchance to Dream. New York, Ace, 1977.
Police Patrol: 2000 A.D. New York, Ace, 1977.
Space Visitor. New York, Ace, 1977.
The Best Ye Breed (Crawford). New York, Ace, 1978.
Trample an Empire Down. New York, Leisure, 1978.
Brain World (United Planets). New York, Leisure. 1978.
The Fracas Factor (Mauser). New York, Leisure, 1978.
Lagrange Five. New York, Bantam, 1979.
The Lagrangists, edited by Dean Ing. New York, Tor, 1983.
Chaos in Lagrangia, edited by Dean Ing. New York, Tor, 1984.
Space Search. New York, Dell, 1984.
Eternity, with Dean Ing. New York, Pocket Books, 1984.
Home Sweet Home: 2010 A.D., with Dean Ing. New York, Dell, 1984.
The Other Time, with Dean Ing. New York, Baen, 1984.
Trojan Orbit (Lagrange), with Dean Ing. New York, Baen, 1985.
Deathwish World (Lagrange), with Dean Ing. New York, Baen, 1986.

Sweet Dreams, Sweet Princes (Mauser; includes *The Time Gladiator*), with Michael Banks. New York, Baen, 1986.
Joe Mauser: Mercenary from Tomorrow, with Michael Banks (includes selections from *Mercenary from Tomorrow* and *The Fracas Factor*). New York, Baen, 1986.

Short Stories

The Best of Mack Reynolds. New York, Pocket Books, 1976.
Compounded Interests. Cambridge, Massachusetts, NESFA Press, 1983.

OTHER PUBLICATIONS

Novels

The Case of the Little Green Men. New York, Phoenix Press, 1951.
Episode on the Riviera. Derby, Connecticut, Monarch, 1961.
A Kiss before Loving: A Contemporary Novel. Derby, Connecticut, Monarch, 1961; revised as *Four Letter World* (as Todd Harding), San Diego, Greenleaf, 1972.
This Time We Love. Derby, Connecticut, Monarch, 1962.
The Kept Woman. Derby, Connecticut, Monarch, 1963.
The Jet Set. Derby, Connecticut, Monarch, 1964.
The House in the Kasbah (as Maxine Reynolds). New York, Beagle, 1972.
The Home of the Inquisitor (as Maxine Reynolds). New York, Beagle, 1972.

Other

Paradise for Males, edited by Walter S. Keating. New York, Plaza, 1957.
How to Retire without Money (as Bob Belmont). New York, Belmont, 1958.
The Expatriates. Evanston, Illinois, Regency, 1963.
Puerto Rican Patriot: The Life of Luis Muñoz Rivera. New York, Macmillan, 1969.

Editor, with Fredric Brown, *Science-Fiction Carnival: Fun in Science-Fiction.* Chicago, Shasta, 1953.

*

Mack Reynolds commented:

(1981) Thirty years ago, when I first began writing science fiction, I soon arrived at the conclusion that a serious freelancer in the field must be acquainted with the sciences he dealt with. The day of the space opera was rapidly disappearing, and the writer had best know what he was talking about. My background in the hard sciences was sketchy and I realized that I was out of my depth in them. However, I have had a lifelong interest in the social sciences and particularly in political economy. And, somewhat to my surprise, I discovered that few writers in our genre were so equipped. I decided to concentrate on stories with socio-economic backgrounds.

Many of us in our extrapolations do very well in portraying a future in which the sciences and technology have blossomed fantastically. We rejoice in faster-than-light travel, we colonize the galaxy, we have become immortal, we have matter transformers and transmitters. And what is our socio-economic system? Often it's feudalism, complete with galactic emperors, dukes, counts, and barons, sometimes swinging laser swords, whatever they are. We don't even have capitalism, not to speak of something in advance. What

is the means of exchange? Often currency, silver and gold coins. What is the relationship between the sexes? What type of family prevails? The writers have returned to Victorian times. Not one story in 25 in depicting the future ever considers that the private ownership of the means of production, the profit system, and class divided society, might one day end. American science fiction is myopic when it comes to foreseeing an evolved social system. So is Soviet science fiction. In the Soviets' case, they seem to have a fond belief that the millennium has been reached, that nothing lies beyond the state capitalism they have achieved, so there is no point in speculating on future socio-economics. The big difference is that even if a Soviet SF writer did attempt to look beyond their version of Utopia, it is unlikely that his story would ever see print. In the west we are still free to extrapolate in the field of political economy—we just don't. And, in my belief, science fiction is the poorer for it.

The world is going through an unprecedented period of revolutionary change, in science, in medicine, in technology, in the family relationship, in social systems, in the relationship between nations, between generations, between sexes. And if the future is to be a valid one we must buckle down to deciding just what we want. An end of war, an end of poverty, an end of the rape of our planet, a viable world government, are only a few of the goals we should keep ever in mind.

In my stories, I do not have any particular axe to grind. I have written stories (some humorous ones) both for and against every socio-economic system that I know of including socialism, in all its myriad forms, communism, syndicalism, anarchism, fascism, theocracy, technocracy, meritocracy, and industrial feudalism. It simply seems not to occur to the average person, even science fiction readers, that there is an alternative, or alternatives, to our present social system. I am attempting to bring home to them that there is, and possibly desirable alternatives at that.

* * *

A maverick socialist, Mack Reynolds is of that rare breed of American science fiction writers specializing in socioeconomic speculation. Early in his writing career Reynolds switched from detective fiction to science fiction; but as the title of his first SF novel (*The Case of the Little Green Men*) suggests, he never left the plots and characters of detective fiction entirely behind. Producing a strange amalgam of economics, politics, intrigue, action, and mystery, Reynolds became quite popular, and the readers of *Galaxy* and *If* once chose him as their favorite author.

Reynolds's popularity comes largely from his interplanetary fiction, such as his Section G: United Planets series. The premise is that a future confederation of diverse worlds pledges noninterference in each other's socioeconomic systems, but that anomalous worlds threaten this pledge. Crack agent Ronnie Bronston of the intelligence bureau Section G is, typically, the troubleshooter. A representative assignment, in *Dawnman Planet,* takes Ronnie to the super-capitalist world Phrygia, where the villanous Baron Wylie hides information about invading aliens who threaten the confederation. In *Code Duello,* the troublesome world is Firenze, ruled by Florentine gentlemen preoccupied with dueling. The best in this series may be *The Rival Rigellians,* in which rival teams develop capitalism and socialism on their respective worlds until the natives rebel against both systems.

On the whole, though, Reynolds's short stories are both better written and better introductions to Reynolds's ideas, for the irony of Reynolds's political thinking blends with the irony and reversal of the story form. In "Revolution," the U.S. tries to stop a demo-cratic revolution within the U.S.S.R., since such a revolution would make a stronger Russia; in "Pacifist," a pacifist group uses terror-ism to achieve its goals. "Compounded Interests," a time-loop story, suggests that anonymous financial interests control history. "Uto-pian" sets the premises for much of Reynolds's utopian fiction. Although one might expect a socialist's utopias to be pleasant places, Reynolds's utopias are ambiguous; in this story the utopian leaders import a revolutionist from the past to keep them from going stale. The assumption behind these ironic stories is that change so domi-nates the late 20th century that what is revolutionary one day is reactionary the next.

The Year 2000 series of near-future utopian novels is likewise ambiguous. Some worlds are rather pleasant places; others struggle with desperate boredom. Typically, these worlds have put an end to the extremes of wealth and poverty (in fact, to social class). But the welfare state produces stagnation and decay. In *Computer World,* Reynolds predicts, before computers were in vogue (1967), a world totally dependent on the computer. In *Commune 2000 A.D.,* he gives us a world in which one can choose between many modes of drop-ping out. Reynolds's most ambitious works are his two updates of Bellamy, *Looking Backward, from the Year 2000* and *Equality: In the Year 2000.* Reynolds's 2000 resembles but also diverges from Bellamy's. Reynolds's Julian West is out of place in a world he cannot understand, a world which has transcended traditional ide-ologies and could be called socialism, collectivism, technocracy, archism, meritocracy, or, more accurately, none of these. Reynolds's 2000—which he calls evolutionary rather than utopian—is more inevitable than it is attractive.

The Africa series (*Blackman's Burden; Border, Breed Nor Birth; The Best Ye Breed*) likewise presents fixed ideologies in a chang-ing world. Both the capitalist West and the socialist East struggle, often with strange results, to control African nationalism. In the Joe Mauser series (*Time Gladiator, The Earth War,* and others), Reynolds develops a world that has moved in a direction different from that of his utopias. The Earth contains a decadent class soci-ety in which one can advance only in the "fracases," a TV-age ver-sion of the Roman bread and circuses. Even protagonist Joe Mauser departs from the good-guy stereotypes in his disillusionment.

At his death, Reynolds left several unfinished manuscripts that have been edited by Dean Ing and Michael Banks. Some of these represent Reynolds at his best, particularly *The Other Time,* a time-paradox story containing a remarkably complete ethnology of 16th-century Mexico. The Lagrangia series presents another ambiguous utopia, an orbiting colony that, because of its revolutionary production of power, is the source of fierce contention among rival forces on Earth.

Reynolds wrote too much, and his fiction contains grave flaws: sexism, macho-chauvinist heroes, super-slick dialogue, and melo-dramatic plots resolved often by pointless violence. Yet he takes seriously, as few writers do, the idea that the socioeconomic future will be stranger than we can imagine.

—Curtis C. Smith

RICHARDS, Edward. *See* **TUBB, E.C.**

RICHARDSON, Robert S. *See* **LATHAM, Philip.**

RICHMOND, Walt and Leigh

Nationality: Americans. **Richmond, Walt: Born:** Memphis, Ten-nessee, 5 December 1922. **Family:** Married Leigh Tucker; three children. **Career:** Research physicist; President and executive di-rector, Centric Foundation, Merritt Island, Florida. **Died:** 14 April 1977. **Richmond, Leigh: Born:** Leigh Tucker, 21 April 1911. **Education:** Louisiana State University, Baton Rouge; Tulane Uni-versity, New Orleans. **Family:** Married 1) Walt Richmond (died 1977), three children; 2) Richard V. Donahue in 1979. **Career:** Re-porter, photographer, newspaper editor, and research anthropolo-gist; president, Centric Foundation.

SCIENCE FICTION PUBLICATIONS

Novels

Shock Wave. New York, Ace, 1967.
The Lost Millennium. New York, Ace, 1967; as *Siva!,* 1979.
Phoenix Ship. New York, Ace, 1969; expanded edition as *Phase Two,* 1979.
Gallagher's Glacier. New York, Ace, 1970; revised edition, 1979.
Challenge the Hellmaker. New York, Ace, 1976.
The Probability Corner. New York, Ace, 1977.

Short Stories

Positive Charge. New York, Ace, 1970.

*

Leigh Richmond comments:

(1986) All of our books have been "hard core" or "hard sci-ence" science fiction, based on the results of research at the Cen-tric Foundation. The next one, which should be published by the fall of 1986, is *How to Psi; or, Field Effect—The Pi-Phase of Phys-ics.* This is not science fiction, but should be of interest to readers of the genre. It is a how-to book for using the psionic abilities consciously, as well as a detailed analysis of the electromagnetic structure which permeates and surrounds the body (seen as the aura) of which the psionic abilities are the sensory apparatus.

*   *   *

Walt and Leigh Richmond both grew up before the atomic bomb fell, when science seemed both simpler and more accessible. Un-derstanding was not yet locked in moated research foundations—in those days (it seemed) a boy could invent antigravity with the right cardboard tubes and wires, and a few people thinking hard could uncover the secrets of the universe and Explain Everything. The Richmonds wanted to be among those few people, and in their eager stories the maverick amateurs always win. But because the Richmonds did not actually start writing until after the atomic bomb fell, their stories are also marked by a scorn for the current secrecy-bound scientific bureaucracy, and an appetite for apocalypse.

When the Richmonds' stories work, they successfully convey the excitement of individual discovery—the mind's reaction to its own new thinking, to its own awakening power. As a result, the Richmonds' most convincing characters tend to be children. An early story, "Poppa Needs Shorts," neatly details the way a four-year-old can combine pieces of information that an adult would keep rigidly separate. The same child, Oley, grows up in the novel *The Probability Corner* to learn how to read the mind of a computer and invent a matter transmitter in his cellar—all through his willingness to keep combining divergent types of knowledge. Such willingness, the Richmonds imply, is usually destroyed by modern education, and education is the most interesting topic in their novel *Phase Two* (an expanded version of *Phoenix Ship*). The hero, S.T.A.R. Dustin, is injected with molecules of trained men's brains, whose knowledge is then activated in him through four years of computer testing. But the boy's real mental power develops from his efforts to recombine the facts on his own, preguessing the computer and eventually walking easily out of his political prison into new realms of science. The idea that the computer is an appropriate tool for the expanding mind is also pursued in *Challenge the Hellmaker,* where a group of friends on an orbital station accidentally invent a spacedrive while singlehandedly fighting off a worldwide military takeover. Though the heroes in the Richmonds' books are almost anachronistically individualistic, they are rarely isolated. Even little Oley feels secure in the center of his family, and the collaboration of friends (another means of combining divergent knowledge) is one of the more pleasant constants in the Richmonds' own collaboration.

When their stories do not work—or do not work consistently—they are flawed by unconvincing politics, hyperactive melodrama, and scientific explanations that are not only impossible but are also praised for their clarity by the other characters. The worst offender on all counts is *The Lost Millennium,* a novel that tries to explain all human and geologic history by proposing a prehistorical race of supermen who, through solar taps located in pyramids, possessed broadcast electrical power. The story covers so much so quickly—including all myths, many lectures on electricity, and an incomprehensible soap opera subplot— that the result is a fragmented scenario whose several apocalypses are the only relief.

Yet perhaps even *The Lost Millennium* is just part of the Richmonds' effort to scramble our brains into new connections. They were serious enough about the content of their work to form their own research group, the Centric Foundation, and before Walt Richmond's death in 1977, they planned to apply "relatively simple high school mathematics" to physics, and improve on the quantum theory. Few young science fiction readers would fault their attack on education, and it is hard to resist the Richmonds' faith in the potentially supernatural power of individual thinking. Their eagerness and their determined amateur science ("'It's really quite easy,' he explained briskly") are part of an innocence science fiction has lost, and could never easily regain.

—Karen G. Way

————

ROBERT, Lionel. *See* **FANTHORPE, R. Lionel.**

————

ROBERTS, Keith (John Kingston)

Nationality: British. **Born:** Kettering, Northamptonshire, 20 September 1935. **Education:** Northampton School of Art, National Diploma in Design 1956; Leicester College of Art, 1956-57. **Career:** Has worked as a cartoon animator, and as an illustrator for advertising, magazines, and books. Editor, *SF Impulse,* London, 1966-67. **Awards:** British Science Fiction Association award, 1982, 1987. **Agent:** Carnell Literary Agency, Danes Croft, Goose Lane, Little Hallingbury, Hertfordshire CM22 7RG, England.

SCIENCE FICTION PUBLICATIONS

Novels

The Furies. New York, Berkley, and London, Hart-Davis, 1966.
Pavane. London, Hart-Davis, 1968; expanded edition, Garden City, New York, Doubleday, 1968.
The Inner Wheel. London, Hart-Davis, and Garden City, New York, Doubleday, 1970.
The Chalk Giants. London, Hutchinson, 1974; New York, Putnam, 1975.
Molly Zero. London, Gollancz, 1980.
Kiteworld. London, Gollancz, 1985; and New York, Arbor House, 1986.
Gráinne: A Novel. Salisbury, Wiltshire, Kerosina, 1987.

Short Stories (series: Kaeti)

Anita. New York, Ace, 1970; London, Millington, 1976; expanded edition, Philadelphia, Owlswick Press, 1990.
Machines and Men: Science Fiction Stories. London, Hutchinson, 1973.
The Grain Kings: SF Stories. London, Hutchinson, 1976.
The Passing of the Dragons: The Short Fiction of Keith Roberts. New York, Berkley, 1977.
Ladies from Hell. London, Gollancz, 1979.
Kaeti and Company. Salisbury, Wiltshire, Surrey, Kerosina, 1986.
Kaeti's Apocalypse. Salisbury, Wiltshire, Kerosina, 1986.
The Lordly Ones. London, Gollancz, 1986.
The Event. Scotforth, Lancashire, Morrigan, 1989.
Winterwood and Other Hauntings. Scotforth, Lancashire, Morrigan, 1989.
Kaeti on Tour. London, Sirius, 1992.

OTHER PUBLICATIONS

Novels

The Boat of Fate: An Historical Novel. London, Hutchinson, 1971; Englewood Cliffs, New Jersey, Prentice Hall, 1974.
The Road to Paradise: A Novel. Salisbury, Wiltshire, Kerosina, 1988.

Poetry

A Heron Caught in Weeds: Poems, edited by Jim Goddard. Salisbury, Wiltshire, Kerosina, 1987.

Other

Irish Encounters: A Short Travel. Worcester Park, Surrey, Kerosina, 1988.
The Natural History of the P.H. Worcester Park, Surrey, Kerosina, 1988.

*

Keith Roberts comments:

I think if we survive our do-it-yourself Armageddon, the 20th century will be remembered as the Age of the pigeonhole. Everything has to have its tag; Stonehenge is a computer, etc. The particular label attached to me is science-fiction writer. I've nothing against it; but I really know very little science. I suppose I did write some technological fiction in the very early days. But I've simply tried to talk about characters who interested me, and events that moved or disturbed me. If that's science fiction, then so be it.

*   *   *

Two characteristics typify the work of Keith Roberts: an involvement with England and its landscape, history, and mythology; and a fascination for what he has called (borrowing a term from Robert Holdstock) the Primitive Heroine, a young, sexy woman who has haunted much of his writing over the last two decades.

Both were present in his earliest work, *Anita,* the stories about a headstrong witch-child in modern rural England, but these fey, whimsical works developed neither element well. It wasn't until a much later reappearance of Anita in "The Checkout" and her transmutation into the actress Kaeti that she really became what Roberts sees as a Primitive Heroine. And the bucolic England presented in these stories are as pretty and unreal as the England in his first novel, *The Furies,* a cosy catastrophe in the manner of John Wyndham that was already old-fashioned when it was written. Here, a nuclear disaster coupled with an invasion by aliens who look like gigantic wasps leaves a few desperate survivors isolated in a mutilated landscape. There is little original in the book, though the robust writing and the way the countryside almost becomes a character within the story give hints of what was to come.

With his second novel, however, Roberts immediately sprang to the front rank of science fiction writers. *Pavane* has been acclaimed as one of the finest of all alternate-universe novels, though Roberts himself would dispute this, since he sees it more as an examination of cyclic history, which he makes clear in the Coda to the book. Be that as it may, this really is an extraordinary work, which, in a sequence of stories linked more by theme than by plot, provides a mosaic portrait of a world in which Elizabeth I was assassinated, the Spanish Armada was successful, and, in the latter years of 20th-century England, is still under the sway of the Catholic church. Set mostly in the English West Country around Corfe Castle, a place that holds an almost mystical attraction for Roberts, the novel tells of a world in which social and technological progress has been slow indeed. There are steam-powered road trains, and communication is by a network of semaphore stations, though Roberts is at pains to make these curiosities as much as possible a part of the ordinary daily life of his characters. Against this rural backdrop, Roberts's characters face tremendous moral choices. Brother John, a monk and artist, witnesses the atrocities of the Inquisition and is driven to heresy and rebellion as a result. Becky, in "The White Boat," a slightly later story omitted from most of the early editions of the novel, is rescued from the bleakness of her ordinary life by the romantic vision of the White Boat, which turns out to be smuggling technology. She betrays the boat to the authorities, then, at the last minute, warns it of the trap that has been set.

Such moral choices are, typically, the dramatic hinge around which all of Roberts's fiction turns. Later critics have accused him of being a right-wing libertarian, a rather simplistic viewpoint though it is true that he believes people must face decisions that will affect not only themselves but their whole society, and must suffer the consequences of other people's decisions. Roberts has a sour view of humanity, though it is clear he feels that looking after oneself and looking after one's fellows come to much the same thing.

Becky is the precursor of Martine, whom Michael Coney termed the "multi-girl," who in various guises forms the linking device in Roberts's next mosaic novel, *The Chalk Giants.* This is a darker, more ambitious work, a more successful but less acclaimed companion piece to *Pavane.* The story concerns Stan Potts, a loser struggling to escape before a nuclear cataclysm tears Britain apart. In a series of visions (in part inspired by the work of painter Paul Nash), Potts foresees episodes from a barbaric, postapocalyptic future, in which avatars of Martine, a girl he desires, always appears. Sexually alluring, the multi-girl will trigger events, often events of considerable violence for which Roberts clearly feels distaste but also an uneasy fascination; yet, she is rarely in a position to control them. As such, she is the archetype of the Primitive Heroine who will recur in Roberts's work. Gradually she gains self-awareness and power, until she achieves her apotheosis as *Gráinne.*

A third mosaic novel, *Kiteworld,* completes what might be seen as a loose trilogy. As in the other two, the church appears as a powerful, generally malignant force in the shaping of society, though the society itself is not central to the novel, which is, as ever, a sequence of aperçus about the compromises and decisions any individual must make in order to survive. The most intricate and effective passage in the book, for instance, is about a kitecaptain failing to come to terms with the confusing and conflicting demands of love, guilt, and duty brought on by the autistic child Tan, whom Roberts has described as his most powerful heroine to date. A further story in the Kiteworld sequence, "Tremarest" has already appeared.

If these three novels together form Roberts's most successful work, that is not to deny the quality of some of his other work. As a writer, he has always been better at shorter length, which is perhaps why these novels composed of linked stories work so well. Nevertheless, his more unified novels, *Molly Zero* (a bleak tale of a young girl, struggling unsuccessfully to achieve some level of independence on an odyssey through a grim, bureaucratically controlled future) and *Gráinne* (which won the BSFA award as the best novel of 1987), are both considerable achievements. *Gráinne* tells the story of adman Alistair Bevan (an early pseudonym of Roberts) whose life is intertwined with the rise of a mysterious girl-goddess Gráinne. It is an excellent example of the way Roberts combines his feel for the mystical and mythical power of landscape and women.

Even so, his best and most characteristic work is probably to be found in his short stories. In "Weihnachtsabend," an excellent alternative-history story set in a Nazi-ruled Britain, the central character is faced with a typically severe moral choice, between achieving a rich and powerful life at the cost of giving himself body and soul to his masters, and making a futile gesture of rebellion, which would end inevitably in his death. The two linked stories, "The Lordly Ones" and "The Comfort Station," tell of a simpleminded lavatory attendant who cannot comprehend the social collapse he sees around him. Roberts's invariable sympathy for the victim makes these powerful stories about the way people try to cling to normality even when normality has broken down. "Richenda" features a typical heroine who appears very differently in different circumstances, though this manifestation of the multi-girl is probably most effectively demonstrated in the Kaeti stories.

In these, a small group of characters take on different roles in different stories, rather like a repertory company, and indeed the linking narrative which frames the stories talks about them as actors. Nevertheless, their salient characteristics and perceptions remain the same, providing a strong focus throughout the two books in which they are collected, and there is such an echoing between the stories that it serves to emphasise the nature and personality of the leading figures. Certain of the stories—particularly those with a darker subtext such as "The Clocktower Girl," "Kaeti and the Hangman" or, most threatening and disturbing of all, "Kaeti and the Shadows," which uses the imagery of the shadows burned into the streets and walls of Hiroshima and Nagasaki by the explosion of the atomic bombs—are as powerful as anything Roberts has written. But in exploring the different layers and aspects of personality within the one character, Roberts shifts mood and tone with remarkable fluidity. In "Londinium," for instance, set at the time of the Roman occupation of Britain which he had previously written about in his historical novel, *The Boat of Fate,* he reveals a flair for comedy which hasn't really been apparent in his work since very early in his career. In the course of this diverse exploration of personality, he has created one of the most vivid and memorable characters in modern science fiction. And though the setting for the majority of these stories is London, he is still concerned to reveal the layers of history and myth that lie below the landscape of modern life.

—Paul Kincaid

ROBINSON, Frank M(alcolm)

Nationality: American. **Born:** Chicago, Illinois, 9 August 1926. **Education:** Beloit College, Wisconsin B.S. in physics in 1950 (Phi Beta Kappa); Northwestern University, Evanston, Illinois, M.S. in journalism 1955. **Military Service:** Served as radar technician in the United States Navy, 1944-45, 1950-51. **Career:** Office boy, Ziff-Davis Publishing Company, 1944; assistant editor, *Family Weekly,* 1955-56, and *Science Digest,* 1956-59; editor, *Rogue,* 1959-65; managing editor, *Cavalier,* 1965-66; editor, *Censorship Today,* 1967; staff writer, *Playboy,* 1969-73. Since 1973, freelance writer. **Agent:** Curtis Brown, 10 Astor Place, New York, New York 10003, U.S.A.

SCIENCE FICTION PUBLICATIONS

Novels

The Power. Philadelphia, Lippincott, 1956; London, Eyre and Spottiswoode, 1957.
The Prometheus Crisis, with Thomas N. Scortia. New York, Doubleday, 1975; London, Hodder and Stoughton, 1976.
The Nightmare Factor, with Thomas N. Scortia. New York, Doubleday, and London, Hodder and Stoughton, 1978.

The Great Divide, with John Levin. New York, Rawson Wade, 1982.
Blowout!, with Thomas N. Scortia. New York, Watts, 1987; London, Severn House, 1989.
The Dark beyond the Stars. New York, Tor, 1991.

Short Stories

A Life in the Day of . . . and Other Short Stories. New York, Bantam, 1981.

Author of numerous uncollected short stories.

OTHER PUBLICATIONS

Novels

The Glass Inferno, with Thomas N. Scortia. New York, Doubleday, 1974; London, Hodder and Stoughton, 1975.
The Gold Crew, with Thomas N. Scortia. New York, Warner, 1980; London, Panther, 1983.

Other

Editor, with Earl Kemp, *The Truth about Vietnam: Report on the U.S. Senate Hearings.* San Diego, Greenleaf, 1966.
Editor, with Nat Lehrman, *Sex, American Style.* Chicago, Playboy Press, 1971.

*

Frank M. Robinson comments:

I have no particular statement to make about my own variety of science fiction except that I like to read and write science fiction based upon extrapolations of current trends in the physical sciences, psychology, cultural anthropology, politics, etc. Conversely, I have little interest in the type of fantasy that has come to dominate the field in recent years.

*   *   *

Despite his background in physical science, Frank M. Robinson has written stories most often based on psychology or cultural anthropology. One such story, "The Fire and the Sword," is concerned with the reactions of Earthmen to a "perfect" alien society. Robinson chose this story to represent his work in the anthology *SF: Author's Choice 4* (edited by Harry Harrison, 1974). He worked entertaining variations on time travel in "Untitled Story," and produced a short novel of headlong action in "The Hunting Season." "The Night Shift" is a clever short fantasy, and "The Oceans Are Wide" a short novel telling of a young boy's harsh passage to maturity in the warped society on board a generation-ship carrying colonists to a distant planetary system. Behind the editor's inappropriate title of "Dead End Kids of Space" was an entertaining story of the adventures of a survey team on a planet with a very confusing and unpredictable culture. Another light-hearted story with an anthropological basis was "The Santa Claus Planet" concerning a society in which the giving of gifts had been elevated into a ritual with decidedly sinister overtones. In another vein entirely, "Dream Street" was a deceptively simple story of a boy on the run from an orphanage, and of his longing to become a spaceman.

His first novel, *The Power,* was published by Lippincott as part of a short-lived series of "novels of menace." It lived up to its billing admirably. The story concerns a navy-subsidized research team studying human endurance and survival characteristics. Results of an anonymous questionnaire suggest that one of the team members is a superman with an assortment of psychic powers, and the one team member who takes these results seriously promptly dies under mysterious circumstances. He leaves an uncompleted letter for team chairman William Tanner: "I want to tell you about Adam Hart. . . ." In his review of the book, Damon Knight characterized Robinson as "a gifted and sensitive writer" but found fault with his logic and with an anti-scientific tone to the book. Most readers and critics, on the other hand, found Tanner's nightmare battle against Adam Hart hair-raising and compulsively readable.

After the publication of *The Power,* Robinson temporarily gave up fiction writing and took a succession of editorial jobs. Occasionally another story would appear. "East Wind, West Wind" is a grim story of an inspector for Air Central, monitoring air quality in a smog-bound future Los Angeles in which all forms of air pollution, from cigarette smoking to internal combustion engines, are outlawed.

The collection *A Life in the Day of . . . and Other Short Stories* includes five of Robinson's stories from the 1950s and four later stories. The book is a reminder of just how good (and how underrated) Robinson's short fiction is, and is equally valuable for the extensive autobiographical commentary, which gives a vivid picture of the science-fiction field in the 1950s and 1960s.

In 1973, Robinson began a very successful collaboration with Thomas N. Scortia. The team produced a series of bestselling "disaster" novels, some of which are borderline science fiction. The first of these was *The Glass Inferno,* a story of a fire in a modern high-rise building. (Together with a similar book, *The Tower* by Richard Martin Stern, this was the basis for the popular film *The Towering Inferno*). *The Prometheus Crisis* is about a reactor failure in a nuclear power plant; *The Nightmare Factor,* about covert biological warfare. Even when not concerned with science fiction ideas, these books exhibit the science fiction writer's careful analysis of processes, both physical and mental. This attention to expository detail is not allowed to interfere with the pace of the story, and serves to enhance the realistic tone.

The Great Divide, a collaboration with John Levin, is a political thriller set in the late 1980s. The Second Constitutional Convention and a renewed oil crisis provide an unscrupulous California governor with the tools for a coup that would split the country into two warring camps. The efforts of a vice-presidential aide and a small group of friends to uncover and stop this scheme make a tense and uncomfortably convincing narrative.

—R.E. Briney

ROBINSON, Kim Stanley

Nationality: American. **Born:** Waukegan, Illinois, 23 March 1952. **Education:** University of California, San Diego, B.A. in literature, 1974, Ph.D. 1982; Boston University, M.A. in English 1975. **Family:** Married Lisa Howland Nowell in 1982. **Career:** Visiting lecturer, University of California, in Davis, 1982-84, 1985, and in San Diego, 1982, 1985. **Awards:** World Fantasy award, 1983; *Locus* award, 1985, 1993; Nebula award, for short story, 1987, for

novel, 1993; John W. Campbell award, 1991; British SF award, 1992; Hugo, for novel, 1993 . **Address:** Ralph Vicinanza, 111 Eighth Ave., New York, New York 10011, U.S.A.

SCIENCE FICTION PUBLICATIONS

Novels (series: Mars; Orange County)

The Wild Shore (Orange County). New York, Ace, 1984; London, Futura, 1985.
Icehenge. New York, Ace, 1984; London, Orbit, 1985.
The Memory of Whiteness: A Scientific Romance. New York, Tor, 1985; London, Macdonald, 1986.
The Gold Coast (Orange County). New York, Tor, and London, Macdonald, 1988.
Pacific Edge (Orange County). London, Unwin Hyman, and New York, Tor, 1990.
A Short, Sharp Shock. Shingletown, California, Ziesing, 1990.
Red Mars. London, HarperCollins, 1992; New York, Bantam, 1993.
Green Mars, bound with *A Meeting with Medusa,* by Arthur C. Clarke. New York, Tor, 1988; revised and enlarged as *Green Mars,* London, HarperCollins, 1993; New York, Bantam, 1994.

Short Stories

The Blind Geometer. New Castle, Virginia, Cheap Street, 1986; with *Return from Rainbow Bridge,* New York, Tor, 1989.
The Planet on the Table. New York, Tor, 1986; London, Futura, 1987.
Escape from Kathmandu. Eugene, Oregon, Axolotl Press, 1988; with other stories, Norwalk, Connecticut, Easton Press, 1989; London, Unwin Hyman, 1990.
Remaking History. New York, Tor, 1991; as *Down and Out in the Year 2000.* London, Grafton, 1992.
Black Air. Eugene, Oregon, Pulphouse, 1991.
A Sensitive Dependence on Initial Contitions. Eugene, Oregon, Pulphouse, 1991.

OTHER PUBLICATIONS

Other

The Novels of Philip K. Dick. Ann Arbor, Michigan, UMI Research Press, 1984.
Editor, *Future Primitive: The New Ecotopias.* New York, Tor, 1994.

*   *   *

Kim Stanley Robinson quickly established a reputation as a promising young science fiction author in the late 1970s and early 1980s with a series of remarkably well written stories. Robinson attended the Clarion SF Writers Workshop in 1975, and most of his early fiction appeared in Damon Knight's *Orbit,* and later in Terry Carr's *Universe,* the two anthology series that represented the literary cutting-edge of science fiction in the 1970s and early 1980s. By the early- to mid-1980s, Robinson's stories were perennially nominated for the major SF awards.

With the publication of his first novel, *The Wild Shore,* published as the first novel in Terry Carr's revived Ace Specials series,

Robinson established himself as a major new author. The book earned a Nebula nomination, won the Philip K. Dick Special award, and was voted Best First Novel in the *Locus* poll. The book turned out to be the first novel in the Orange County trilogy, a series set in Orange County, California, where Robinson grew up. The trilogy was completed with *The Gold Coast* and *Pacific Edge*. The books are all set in the mid-21st century, but represent three very different futures, the first dystopian, the second a straight-line extrapolation, and the third utopian.

In *The Wild Shore*, Robinson used a relatively pastoral, postnuclear-war Southern California as background to a heartwarming and a sense-of-wonder-filled coming-of-age story. Robinson evokes a sense of wonder reminiscent of Mark Twain's *The Adventures of Huckleberry Finn* as his young protagonist discovers that his world is filled with danger and intrigue. In *The Gold Coast*, Robinson presents an overcrowded, urban Orange County dominated by defense contractors and designer drugs. Both novels are dominated by fine characterization and sense of place.

In *Pacific Edge*, Robinson presents his personal vision of a practical utopia. It is set in the small town of El Modena, some years after the establishment of a new world order based on a unique mix of ecology awareness, appropriate technologies, personal freedom, institutionalized community responsibility, and cultural tolerance. The general ambience of El Modena seems like a college campus with everyone matured by about a decade. Everyone in the novel is at heart an intellectual, no matter what their vocation, with a love of learning and a penchant for introspection. The most important aspect of *Pacific Edge*, however, is Robinson's new world order, which features a fascinating mix of individual freedom, environmental protection, and both capitalist and socialist economic principles. Robinson's town of El Modena functions as a cooperatively-owned corporation in which everyone is both owner and worker. Physical as well as intellectual fitness is a common interest, and most residents exhibit competency to do (and pride in doing) virtually any job. It could be seen as a more humanist, more left-wing version of Bruce Sterling's future corporation in *Islands in the Net*. Robinson has made a creditable attempt to merge the best concepts of the 60s, 70s, and 80s in designing this new society.

The intricate interplay of themes, philosophy, and characters between the three novels in the Orange County trilogy creates a profound treatise on the future of human society, a coherent whole that is more than the sum of its parts. Each book is both didactic and entertaining, and the series fully utilizes the potential of SF to overcome the despair of man's current situation and glory in the potential of the future worlds we can help create.

In virtually all of Robinson's fiction, setting is of primary importance, with characterization playing a strong but secondary role. His novels and stories seldom rely on strong or fast-paced plots for their effectiveness. Robinson's most common milieus include, in addition to Orange County, the colonized Solar System (especially Mars), the Himalayas, and present or near-future America.

Robinson's second and third novels, which appeared soon after *The Wild Shore*, took place in his Solar System milieu, and further established his ability to handle hard SF concepts and themes. *Icehenge*, a complex, ambitious novel that incorporated two excellent stories published earlier—"On the North Pole of Pluto" (1980) and "To Leave a Mark" (1982)—featured a society of longlived humans with limited memories, and a mystery regarding how a human-made monument of ice could be found on Pluto, on what was, according to official history, the first human visit to that planet. *The Memory of Whiteness*, expanded from Robinson's very first

story—"In Pierson's Orchestra" (1976)—is set more than a millennium into humanity's solar-system culture, and uses music as a subject and as a metaphor for various cosmological themes. Both novels include perception versus reality themes reminiscent of Philip K. Dick.

Some of Robinson's best work, however, has been his shorter fiction, particularly stories of novelette to novella length. Four of his best stories were collected together to form a novel, *Escape From Kathmandu*, including "Escape From Kathmandu" (1986), "Mother Goddess of the World" (1987), and "The True Nature of Shangri-La" (1989) along with "The Kingdom Underground," in its first publication. These stories of American expatriates George and Fred and their wild adventures in the Himalayas are both hilarious and at times profound.

Another of Robinson's notable shorter works to be published in book form is *A Short, Sharp Shock*, a uniquely strange novella-length fantasy. The story begins with the protagonist waking to find himself under water in a stormy night-time sea, the first of what will be a continuing series of short, sharp shocks. The story moves along lines that are both unexpected and surreal. There are the treefolk who have small fruit trees growing from their shoulders, the evil, spine kings who often capture and horribly torture treefolk, the peaceful tribe who live in huge snail shells, which they drag around the beach to live nearest whomever they like most at the time, the solitary guide whose sole job is to help travelers across a long stretch where the narrow ridge of land exists only at low tide, the mysterious mirror that appears to transfer anything going through it into parallel dimensions and might have something to do with how the protagonist got to this world—all are part of an emotionally engaging series of intensely vivid, yet surreal, and dreamlike, experiences.

Most of Robinson's other short fiction has been collected in two anthologies, *The Planet on the Table* and *Remaking History*. Many have milieu and themes in common with various of his novels. Mountain climbing is central to several stories, including two set on Earth, "Ridge Running" (1984) and "The Return from Rainbow Bridge" (1987), and two set on Mars, "Exploring Fossil Canyon" (1982) and *Green Mars* (1988). *Green Mars* is a particularly spectacular novella about climbing Olympus Mons on a partially terraformed Mars, and it was nominated for both the Nebula and Hugo awards. Several other works are near-future SF with similar themes to his Orange County novels, including "Stone Eggs" (1983), an eerie story set in the desert southwest, "Down and Out in the Year 2000" (1986), a highly memorable dystopian vision of a degenerated Washington, D.C., "Before I Wake" (1989), a story of Dickian complexity where dreams and reality mix, and "A History of the 20th Century, with Illustrations" (1991), a nearly plot-free, touching, and intellectual plea for world sanity.

Other of Robinson's most memorable stories strike out into unique areas. "Venice Drowned" (1981) is set in a future where the Italian city is mostly under water. "Black Air," winner of the 1983 World Fantasy award, told from the point of view of a boy who survived the fall of the Spanish Armada, is set in the past, as is "The Lucky Strike" (1984), which gives an alternative ending to World War II. "Mercurial" (1984) is a murder mystery set on a Mercury inhabited by rich esthetes. "The Blind Geometer" (1987) features a blind mathematician unintentionally caught up in international intrigue, and was one of the best SF stories of the 1980s, as well as one of the few Robinson stories, along with "Mercurial," centered around a strong plot. "The Lunatics" (1988) is a highly original, hard SF story of miners tunneling under the surface of the Moon. "Glacier" (1988) is a superior but mostly overlooked story about a near-future ice age that has the bad luck to appear during one of the hottest summers on record, when everyone is worrying about the Greenhouse Effect.

With the publication of *Red Mars* in 1992, Robinson began his Mars trilogy, which promises to eclipse the Orange County trilogy as his most important work to date. *Green Mars,* the second book in the series, was published in 1994, and *Blue Mars,* the final book, is due out in 1996. The trilogy will chronicle mankind's settlement and terraforming of Mars, and span several centuries of human history.

Red Mars, set in the mid-21st century, is the story of the first permanent settlements on Mars by 100 scientists, 50 Americans and 50 Russians, an autonomous group who must assure their own survival, then prepare the planet for more colonists still to come. Robinson creates a remarkable array of strong, memorable characters to show us the natural wonders of Mars, as well as the engineering marvels they create in their quest to make Mars a more hospitable place for mankind. But the most memorable character in the book is Mars itself. The characters discover immense underground aquifers, travel by dirigible and ground rovers through incredible valleys and plains, visit the massive polar icecaps, and encounter mountains of unearthly magnitude as they traverse the harsh beauty of natural Mars.

One of the many philosophical struggles among the first hundred is between those who want to terraform the planet rapidly and those who want to maintain its harsh natural beauty for further study. Another involves the nature of the colonists' relationship with Earth and the corporations seeking to exploit the planet. The struggle for leadership leads to the murder of the primary viewpoint character, and a spectacular denouement where Earth military forces come to mars to quell their rebellion from Earth's control, both the space elevator and one of Mars' moons is destroyed, and most of the surviving first 100 go into hiding.

Red Mars has one structural flaw, an in media res beginning that ruins the dramatic suspense of the murder, and insufficient character motivation for that same murder, caused by Robinson liking all of his characters too much. But despite these two flaws, the novel may be the best SF novel ever written about the early colonization of mars.

Green Mars begins some decades after the dramatic, failed revolution, which coincided with an equally violent time on Earth itself. About one-third of the first hundred are still alive, thanks to longevity treatments developed before the revolution, and now available to everyone on Mars, and are hiding in numerous underground hideouts, some quite huge. Mars is primarily controlled by a dozen huge "metanational" corporations that run mining and terraforming operations, and are now the primary powers on Earth as well. The surviving first hundred are wanted criminals, but little effort is spent hunting for them, since the corporations have little idea of the extent of their rather prosperous underground existence.

Like the first novel, the major emphasis is on the landscape of Mars and the characters, many of which remain from the first novel, but many of which are new, including children of the first hundred both natural and genetically derived. Each of the numerous characters is well-developed and likable, even though often having views directly at odds with the others. This pro-tolerance for human diversity is one of the principal themes of the book. Robinson's Mars has not been settled by homogeneous pro-technology, Western-educated individuals (the typical SF vision), but small groups from various Earth cultures who want to retain the best of their cultural heritages. Robinson's obvious model is the U.S., with the temperature of the melting pot kept low, and conformance to a new mutual cultural heritage accomplished without peer-pressure-forced abandonment of previous cultural distinctions. This tolerance and glorification of diversity among the characters makes reading *Green Mars* an uplifting experience.

Green Mars ends in a revolution, but one far more successful that appears to have put Mars, and possibly even the future of the Earth itself, in the hands of the Martians. The power and clarity of these first two novels establish high expectations for *Blue Mars,* the third and final novel in the series. It appears to be Robinson's intent for that novel to be a powerful and convincing statement on what man's role in the universe should be, and a demonstration of the transcendency of the human mind and spirit.

Kim Stanley Robinson has clearly established himself as one of the most important SF authors of the past two decades, and possibly the most versatile, with superior work ranging from transcendental hard science sense of wonder to near-future social commentary, from contemporary humor to serious speculation on important philosophical issues. With the completion of the Mars trilogy, he will have written two of the most important series of novels in SF, as well as more than a dozen other superior novels and stories in the genre.

—D. Douglas Fratz

ROBINSON, Spider

Nationality: American. **Born:** New York City, 24 November 1948. **Education:** State University of New York, Stony Brook, B.A. 1972; New York State University College. Plattsburgh. **Family:** Married Jeanne Rubbicco in 1975; one daughter. **Career:** Realty editor, *Long Island Review,* Syosset, New York, 1972-73. Since 1973, freelance writer: reviewer, *Galaxy,* 1974-77, *Destinies,* 1977-79, and *Analog,* 1978-80. Chairman of the Executive Council, Writers Federation of Nova Scotia, 1981-83. Instructor, Clarion SF Writers Workshop, Michigan State University, 1989. **Awards:** John W. Campbell award, 1974; *Locus* award, for criticism, 1976, for fiction, 1977; Hugo award, 1977, 1978, 1983; Nebula award, 1977; Skylark award, 1977; Pat Terry award (Australia), 1977; Canada Council grant, 1983, and Senior Arts grant, 1984. Lives in Vancouver, British Columbia, Canada. **Agent:** Eleanor Wood, Spectrum Literary Agency, 111 Eighth Avenue, Suite 1503, New York, New York 10011, U.S.A.

SCIENCE FICTION PUBLICATIONS

Novels (series: Lady Sally's House; Mindkiller; Stardance)

Telempath. New York, Berkley, 1976; London, Macdonald and Jane's, 1978.
Stardance, with Jeanne Robinson. New York, Dial Press, and London, Sidgwick and Jackson, 1979.
Mindkiller: A Novel of the Near Future. New York, Holt Rinehart, 1982; London, Sphere, 1985.
Night of Power. New York, Baen, 1985.
Time Pressure (Mindkiller). New York, Ace, 1987.

Starseed (Stardance), with Jeanne Robinson. New York, Ace, 1991.
Kill the Editor (Lady Sally). Eugene, Oregon, Pulphouse, 1991;
    expanded as *Lady Slings the Booze,* New York, Ace, 1992.
The Callahan Touch. New York, Ace, 1993.
Starmind (Stardance), with Jeanne Robinson. New York, Ace, 1995.

Short Stories (series: Callahan's Place)

Antinomy. New York, Dell, 1980.
Melancholy Elephants. Marchmont, Ontario, Penguin, 1984; revised
    edition, New York, Tor, 1985.
*Callahan and Company: The Compleat Chronicles of the Crosstime
    Saloon* (omnibus). West Bloomfield, Michigan, Phantasia Press,
    1987; London, Legend, 1989.
    Callahan's Crosstime Saloon. New York, Ace, 1977.
    Time Travelers Strictly Cash. New York, Ace, 1981.
    Callahan's Secret. New York, Berkley, 1986.
Callahan's Lady (Lady Sally). New York, Ace, 1989.
Copyright Violation. Eugene, Oregon, Pulphouse, 1990.

OTHER PUBLICATIONS

Other

Off the Wall at Callahan's. New York, Tor, 1994.

Editor, *The Best of All Possible Worlds.* New York, Ace, 1980.

*

Spider Robinson comments:
   I write "science fiction for people who don't read that crap." The
ones who need to most. . . .

*   *   *

   With over 20 books to his credit, Spider Robinson has established himself as an important SF writer and critic. He has won a
number of major awards for his fiction, which typically combines
two often incompatible themes, technological optimism and a critique of technological society. However, his storytelling is often
marred by a coarse and sentimental didacticism, and his style by
sophomoric wordplay, and he displays a distressing fondness for
powerful leader fantasies.
   Robinson's themes and style were established in his early SF
stories, such as those collected in *Callahan's Crosstime Saloon,* a
book about the unusual clientele of a Long Island tavern. The collection is a true *symposium:* the gruff but kindly barkeep Callahan
presides over a series of dialogues and encounters that move from
social disintegration to restored community in the final story, which
takes place on New Year's Eve. This pattern also appears in the
novel *Telempath:* there the remnant population of a postcatastrophe
United States is threatened by powerful aliens and by conflict between
technophiles and a naturalist cult, but the story ends in a love-feast of
multiple marriages, restored filial relations, and administrative merger.
In the apocalyptic novel *Stardance* and its sequels, the final vision is
of death and difference transcended, with human flesh become incorruptible and polymorphous sexual-spiritual communion among
humanity's elect and the plasmoid, angelic aliens.
   In more recent fictions, this master-myth crosses into self- parody.
Mindkiller sports a professor whose life has disintegrated; he is

restored by joining a conspiracy to change the world through
"mindwiping" technology. In *Time Pressure* the hermit-hippie Sam
is not only brought somewhat forcibly into communal consciousness, he is also literally raised from the dead. In Russell Grant,
Night of Power gives us a "wannabe soul brother," a white expatriate who finds fulfillment in his unlikely adoption by the charismatic leader of an African American insurrectionist movement. At
its most ludicrous (and sexist), the "communion of saints" becomes
in *Callahan's Lady* the workers and clientele of an upscale Brooklyn whorehouse. The first-person narrator plays a similar role in
most of Robinson's fictions. Jake, frame-narrator of *Callahan's
Crosstime Saloon,* is nursing a spiritual wound—he considers himself responsible for his wife's and daughter's deaths in an auto accident—but it is he who articulates the redemptive (*cross*-time) nature of Callahan's place. In *Telempath* Isham Stone has been nurtured on hatred, violence, and revenge, and early in the novel loses
an arm and attempts to murder his father; yet it is Isham who evolves
the ability to communicate with the aliens and who makes peace
between the two factions of humanity. Charlie Armstead of
Stardance is similarly wounded. An embittered dancer whose career was destroyed when his hip was damaged by a gunman's bullet, he works as a video specialist with the dancer Shara Drummond.
This leads to communication with the alien entity that threatens Earth,
and later to his dance company's transcendence of a corrupt and
polluted planet, union with the aliens, and reunion with Shara.
   The theme of the disabled narrator, a person redeemed through
the shared experience of pain, is underlined in "The Law of Conservation of Pain." In that story, a time traveler interferes with the
early life of a blues singer. Rather than destroying her talent by
obliterating the universe in which she suffered and was scarred,
his interference creates a universe in which her songs of joy are as
wrenching as her songs of pain ever were. The trope of the conservation laws makes joy and pain, like matter and energy, metonyms
of the same reality. Still, we do not generally feel grateful toward
those who afflict us. Curiously, however, the dual narrator of
Mindkiller (English professor Norman/cat burglar Joe) comes to
accept violence and a strong leader, beyond good and evil, as necessary to social progress, even though that individual has been directly responsible for most of Norman/Joe's personal misery. As
Maureen of *Callahan's Lady* shows, it is easy to confuse satisfaction of the revenge appetite with the warm feelings aroused by
friends and home.
   As a stylist, Robinson is perhaps excessively word-conscious.
A hallmark of his writings is the pun, from the "Punday night"
contests in *Callahan's Crosstime Saloon* to the "abominable multi-
level puns" swapped by Raoul and Charlie at the conclusion of
Stardance. Especially in *Telempath,* the function of the pun is to
call into question the ability of language to express any external
reality. Another facet of Robinson's densely woven style is a heavy
use of allusion, especially to SF writers, situations, and language,
but also to jazz and popular songs, and in the *Stardance* trilogy to
the traditions of modern dance and space colonization literature.
Also, except in *Night of Power,* which does not use a first-person
narrator, Robinson devotes a high proportion of text to dialogue
and internal monologue (and in *Telempath* to documents), often
reducing narration to mere stage direction. Such a style, more lyric
than narrative, is appropriate for Robinson's SF, with its poetic vision of a secular "communion of saints."
   The lyric quality of Robinson's SF is his means of fusing social
critique with technological optimism, two themes that do not easily
join in the hard SF universe, governed as it is by the logic of sci-

ence. In *Telempath, Stardance,* and *Night of Power* we view a world literally poisoned by the effects of modern technical society: pollution, social injustice, overpopulation, war, crime, and madness. In *Callahan's Crosstime Saloon* and its sequels, redemption from this world is allotted to those who chance upon the saloon or the brothel and are able to share in its feast of love and empathy. In *Telempath* and the *Stardance* trilogy, redemption is communal: a remnant of humanity moves onto a new evolutionary plane of physical, intellectual, and spiritual fusion, partly through fortunate alien encounters, but mostly because some human beings make benign use of the most advanced technologies. Furthermore, such redemption obliterates the oppositions, including that between technology and nature, which often structure human experience.

The lyricism is nearly absent from *Mindkiller,* a more conventional SF mystery novel that seems to yield to the totalitarian temptations inherent in the "fusion" or "communion" motif. Through a series of reversals, it asks us to accept its apparent villain, a sinister practitioner of mind control, as really a benevolent scientist who wishes only to save the world. Promoting the theme that great ends justify any means, it urges the amorality of technology and of the visionary leader, and it seems naively unrealistic about the ends of power. When Norman's identity is restored at the end, he characterizes the technology as "mindfill" instead of "mindkill," but he and the other enthusiasts of mental surgery seem little more than puppets mouthing a new party line. In *Time Pressure,* the story's "continuation" in the past, the theme of mind control is even more problematic. Sam is a paranoid loner, but he has the good sense to recognize that mindrape is not a healthy erotics of communication—until he is shot to death and no longer has a choice.

Robinson's myth of the future is one in which human initiative and technological advancement play an active part, aided at times by superior entities from outside normal time or space. In many of his fictions, Robinson portrays humankind as moving toward a mystical fusion of individual identity with something greater than the self. In other stories he imagines individual consciousness as atomistically alone, transcending this condition only through forced submission to a strong leader or even a puppet master. If *Mindkiller, Night of Power, Time Pressure,* and *Callahan's Lady* represent Robinson's matured vision of humanity, an originally hopeful vision of redemption has yielded to a bleaker one of reciprocal violence and the will to power.

Robinson's post-1990 fiction has been primarily devoted to expanding the sagas of Callahan and of the Stardancers. He and Jeanne Robinson have turned *Stardance* into a trilogy with the sequel novels *Starseed* and *Starmind.* The Starmind seems to be the ultimate evolution of the human-alien symbiosis that enables dancers and others to survive in outer space, but for all its powers it is unable to prevent earthly conspiracies against the control it is alleged to exert over humans. Both novels involve complicated personal/political plots, and *Starseed* has enough paranoia and violence to satisfy the most adolescent of SF readers, and to compensate for the trilogy's somewhat indulgent focus on relationships. All in all, the trilogy turns out to be a metaphor for humanity's apotheosis as a heavenly hippie commune, projecting nostalgia for the Woodstock generation into the twenty-first century and beyond. While this strains the definition of science fiction somewhat, it is entertaining.

Much the same may be said of the fourth and fifth books in the Callahan series, *Lady Slings the Booze* and *The Callahan Touch.* The latter is surely unique in the annals of SF in that one of its minor characters is an Irish elf which attaches itself to a saloon and drains the establishment dry. Jake, who has inherited the

Callahan mantle, conjures the gruff saloonkeeper back from wherever he has gone in "crosstime," and together they solve this and other problems. Jake also has a chance to display his virtuosity as a bluesman, his unique Irish coffee machine, and his toughness, plus he wins a new lady—one who plays mean bass. It remains to be seen what other inventions Robinson can spin out to keep the Callahan series going, for both *The Callahan Touch* and *Starmind* leave room for future expansion and development.

—John P. Brennan

ROCKLYNNE, Ross

Nationality: American. **Born:** Ross Louis Rocklin, Cincinnati, Ohio, 21 February 1913. **Education:** Schools in Cincinnati. **Family:** Married Frances Rosenthal in 1941 (divorced 1947); two sons. **Career:** Worked as a story analyst for Warner Brothers and a literary agency, sewing machines salesman and repairman, cab driver, lumberjack, sales clerk, and building manager. **Died:** 29 October 1988.

SCIENCE FICTION PUBLICATIONS

Novel

The Sun Destroyers. New York, Ace, 1973.

Short Stories

The Men and the Mirror. New York, Ace, 1973.

*   *   *

Ross Rocklynne was one of the important authors of magazine science fiction's middle years. He published his first story in *Astounding* in 1935, and for some 15 years was a regular contributor to a variety of science fiction magazines. His work was of sufficiently high quality that L. Sprague de Camp wanted to include him as one of the 20 or so leading writers in the field for his *Science-Fiction Handbook* (1953). Both the key early anthologies of science fiction featured Ross Rocklynne stories: "Quietus" was in the Healy and McComas *Adventures in Time and Space* (1946), and "Jackdaw" was in the Groff Conklin *The Best of Science Fiction* (1946). From 1950, Rocklynne's appearances were more sporadic.

Although he wrote some short novels, Rocklynne concentrated on shorter works. It is possible that his avoidance of the longer lengths had made his name less well known than it should be. Usually a careful craftsman, he wrote many types of science fiction: competent space operas, time-travel stories, effective mood pieces, scientific puzzle stories, detective stories, and yarns spun around the Big Idea. Typical of the latter was "The Moth" (*Astounding,* 1939). Here—in 14 pages—he presented what John Campbell called "a wholly new idea for a spaceship drive" and for good measure threw in a fairly sophisticated picture of competing corporations.

Rocklynne also wrote a series of stories about a character named Hallmeyer. They are unfortunately largely forgotten today. Dealing with a "Bureau of Transmitted Egos," they are early examples of reshaping human beings to live on alien worlds. More than that,

Hallmeyer was a person who *cared*. The stories have an atmosphere of compassion, of questioning basic values, of sadness. (For example, see "Task to Lahri," *Planet,* Summer 1942.) Indeed, there is an elegiac quality that pervades many of Rocklynne's better stories. The experimental side of Rocklynne appears most notably in his *Darkness* stories (1940 to 1951). They are concerned with the fates of sentient stars, and the writing is far removed from the usual styles of pulp fiction. The series was reworked as *The Sun Destroyers.*

Ross Rocklynne was never less than a capable storyteller. However, he tried to be more than that: he pushed himself instead of always taking the easy way. He was a major creator of the science fiction of the past, but he was also one of those who pointed the way ahead.

—Chad Oliver

ROESSNER, Michaela

Nationality: American. **Born:** San Francisco, California. **Education:** California College of Arts and Crafts, Oakland, B.F.A. in ceramics; Lone Mountain College, San Francisco, M.F.A. in painting; Clarion, Michigan State U., East Lansing, 1980. Graduated as a certified Feldenkrais practitioner (a somatics discipline) in 1991 **Family:** Married Richard C. Herman. **Career:** Has worked as maskmaker, janitor, audiovisual technician, toy person for children's store, freelance office worker for arts and somatics organizations; and assistant editor, *Locus* magazine, 1980-81. Aikido: 2nd degree black belt, 1989; certified teacher, 1990; 3rd degree black belt, 1992; chief instructor, Tehachapi Aikikai, 1991-95; postgraduate work, San Diego Aikikai, 1995—; secretary for Advisory Council, United States Aikido Federation, Western Region. **Member:** Science Fiction and Fantasy Writers of America, 1989. **Awards:** Crawford award, 1989; Campbell award, 1989. **Agent:** Merrillee Heifetz, Writers House, 21 West 26th Street, New York, New York 10010. **Address:** Box 1911, #150, Tehachapi, California 93581, U.S.A.

SCIENCE FICTION PUBLICATIONS

Novel

Walkabout Woman. New York, Bantam, 1988.
Vanishing Point. New York, Tor, 1993.

*

Michaela Roessner comments:

I got started as a writer because I wanted to combine writing with certain visual arts projects I was involved with. The more I immersed myself into the craft and art of writing, the more the writing became an end in and of itself. Still, the concerns and themes that form the basis for my visual artwork keep percolating up through my writing.

Influences: René Magritte, M.C. Escher, H.C. Westerman, Alexander Calder, Joseph Cornell, Jorge Luis Borges, Angela Carter, M.F.K. Fisher, Oliver Sacks, and A. Gaudi, the Catalan architect.

*   *   *

Walkabout Woman, Michaela Roessner's debut novel, is generally considered a fantasy novel, albeit an unusual one. It is centered around an aboriginal woman, Reba, and her experiences within the Dreamtime. Roessner's approach is such that this fascinating novel may be considered to lie on the fringes of the mainstream, in that for the majority of the novel all that might be considered fantastic by the Western reader is conveyed via the viewpoint of Reba and occurs within the parameters of what her worldview considers natural. Thus the Dreamtime scenes are not fantasy to the person involved, who is a person of the world the reader knows, and hence these scenes are not fantasy to the reader. This theory only works in hands as skilled as Roessner's, however.

Roessner's second novel is an even more remarkable feat of imagination and realisation. It is set in and around a real place which somewhat inevitably becomes a major player in *Vanishing Point.* The Winchester Mystery House is an eccentric, labyrinthine house in San Jose which sounds like it was designed in collaboration with M.C. Escher and Frank Lloyd Wright, as though all those bright ideas that passersby have were incorporated on the spot. The house was built around the turn of the century by a woman who believed that spirits insisted she should maintain building work on the house continuously.

To this fabulous dwelling Michaela Roessner brings the survivors of a peculiar apocalypse. Overnight, 30-odd years prior to the novel's opening, 90% of the Earth's population vanished. It was a wholly random and arbitrary holocaust.

From these two points *Vanishing Point* follows an intricate path towards . . . the future. The society initially resembles the small-scale communism of Kim Stanley Robinson's *The Wild Shore* and Pat Murphy's *The City, Not Long After* and Roessner certainly seems to share a humanist approach similar to those two writers. Although there is no direct attempt to explain why or how things are as they are, *Vanishing Point* does follow lines of quantum scientific enquiry along the way to a revelatory denouement.

The two principle characters are women, the unorthodox elderly scientist Nesta, and the determined, adventurous Renzie. Both ultimately prove to be the facilitators rather than the actual heroines, and perhaps, both lose as much as they gain.

Vanishing Point is a modern Romantic novel, concerned with the natural and spiritual, and incorporating a sequence of epiphanic moments where the rational and the supernatural collide. Good old-fashioned sensawunda brought right up to date with hard science and new age philosophy. This is a richly human novel, full of humour and tragedy. Though firmly rooted in recent freestyle California SF there are distinct echoes of all strands of classic SF (I had passing lateral thoughts of Clarke and Heinlein, Karen Joy Fowler, Lisa Goldstein, Carter Scholz, Gene Wolfe, Greg Egan, Lewis Shiner, and more), and certainly one of the most intriguing new SF novels in recent years.

Standing *Vanishing Point* alongside *Walkabout Woman* and the Romantic elements are clearer: both novels use the landscape as a leading character, invoking the human relationships with nature and with place particularly in the House; both have an easy spirituality about them, and this is linked to an oceanic space. Reba's desert or the House's alternate selves. Ultimately both novels are positive and uplifting, but this is always tempered with loss and relative tragedy. Despite this, Roessner is in no respect a Gothic writer: although the Winchester Mystery House might appear to be an avatar of the Gothic Castle, there is no sense of the frantic chase through the House until the novel's climax. Instead the complexity of the House serves as a metaphor for the plot of *Vanishing Point* and externalises the internal aspirations and fears of its occupants.

Roessner has also written poetry, and a sense of this is often apparent in her prose, but also apparent in *Vanishing Point* is a strong sense that she is deeply aware of the traditions in which she is working. *Vanishing Point* is crammed with little moments which half-hint at allusions to a huge history of science fiction, creating moments of lateral thinking which again see the house serving as metaphor for Rationalism and Spirituality interacting.

—Kevin McVeigh

———

ROGERS, Pat. *See* **PORGES, Arthur.**

———

ROSE, Lawrence W. *See* **FEARN, John Russell.**

———

ROTSLER, William

Pseudonyms: William Arrow; John Ryder Hall. **Nationality:** American. **Born:** Los Angeles, California, 3 July 1926. **Education:** Ventura Junior College, California, 1946; Los Angeles County Art Institute, 1947-50. **Military Service:** Served in the United States Army, 1944-45. **Family:** Married Marian Abney in 1953 (divorced 1958); one daughter. **Career:** Rancher in Camarillo, California, 1942-44, 1946; sculptor, 1950-59. Since 1959, photographer and filmmaker: writer, producer, and director of commercials, documentaries, and industrial and feature films. **Awards:** *Locus* award, for artwork, 1971, 1972, 1973; Hugo award, for artwork, 1975, 1977, 1979. Guest of honor, 31st World Science Fiction Convention, 1973. **Agent:** Richard Curtis Associates, Box 11J, 75 East End Avenue, New York, New York 10028, U.S.A.

SCIENCE FICTION PUBLICATIONS

Novels (series: Zandra; Return to the Planet of Apes)

Patron of the Arts. New York, Ballantine, 1974; Morley, Yorkshire, Elmfield Press, 1975.
Futureworld (novelization of screenplay; as John Ryder Hall). New York, Ballantine, 1976.
Man, the Hunted Animal (Planet of the Apes, novelization of TV play; as William Arrow). New York, Ballantine, 1976.
To the Land of the Electric Angel. New York, Ballantine, 1976.
Visions from Nowhere (Planet of the Apes, novelization of TV play; as William Arrow). New York, Ballantine, 1976.
Sinbad and the Eye of the Tiger (novelization of screenplay; as John Ryder Hall). New York, Pocket Books, 1977.

Mr. Merlin 1-2 (novelizations of TV series). New York, Simon, 2 vols., 1981; London, Beaver, 2 vols., 1982.
Zandra. Garden City, New York, Doubleday, 1978.
Iron Man: Call My Killer . . . Modok. New York, Pocket Books, 1979.
Dr. Strange: Nightmare. New York, Pocket Books, 1979.
The Far Frontier (Zandra). New York, Playboy Press, 1980.
Shiva Descending, with Gregory Benford. New York, Avon, and London, Sphere, 1980.
Star Trek II: Distress Call. New York, Wanderer, 1982.
The Hidden Worlds of Zandra. Garden City, New York, Doubleday, 1983.
Star Trek III: The Vulcan Treasure. New York, Wanderer, 1983; as *The Vulcan Treasure,* London, Ravette, 1986.

Novels for Young Adults (series: Tom Swift; with Sharman DiVono as Victor Appleton)

The City in the Stars. New York, Wanderer, 1981.
Terror on the Moons of Jupiter. New York, Wanderer, 1981.
The Alien Probe. New York, Wanderer, 1981.
The War in Outer Space. New York, Wanderer, 1981.
The Astral Fortress. New York, Wanderer, 1981.
The Rescue Mission. New York, Wanderer, 1981.

Short Stories

Star Trek II: Short Stories. New York, Wanderer, 1982.
Star Trek II Biographies. New York, Wanderer, 1982.
Star Trek III: Short Stories. New York, Wanderer, and London, Ravette, 1984.

OTHER PUBLICATIONS

Novels

Superstud. Los Angeles, Holloway, 1975.
Supermouth. Los Angeles, Holloway, 1975.
Supertongue and Other Turn Ons. Los Angeles, Holloway, 1975.
Grease 2 (novelization of screenplay). New York, Wanderer, and London, Sphere, 1982.
Joanie Loves Chachi: Secrets. New York, Wanderer, 1982.
A Test of Hearts. New York, Wanderer, 1982.
The Pirate Movie. New York, Wanderer, 1982.
Vice Squad. New York, Pinnacle, 1982.
The A-Team (novelization of TV series):
  Defense Against Terror. New York, Wanderer, 1983.
  The Danger Maze. New York, Wanderer, 1983; London, Target, 1985.
The Love Boat: Voyage of Love (novelization of TV series). New York, Wanderer, 1983.
Magnum, P.I.: Maui Mystery (novelization of TV series). New York, Wanderer, 1983.
Staying Alive (novelization of screenplay). New York, Wanderer, 1983.
It's Your Move (novelization of TV series). New York, Pocket, 1984.
Cavern of Horror (for children; novelization of *Goonies* screenplay). New York, Wanderer, and London, Corgi, 1985.

Plays

Screenplays: *The Agony of Love,* 1966; *The Girl with Hungry Eyes,*
1966; *Four Kinds of Love,* 1967; *Suburban Pagans,* 1967; *Like
It Is,* 1968; *Mantis in Lace (Lila),* 1968; *A Taste of Hot Lead,*
1969; *Shannon's Women,* 1969; *The Godson,* 1969; *She Did
What He Wanted,* 1970; *Midnight,* 1970.

Other

Contemporary Erotic Cinema. New York, Ballantine, 1973.

*

Theatrical Activities:

Director: **Films**—all his screenplays.
Actor: **Films**—*The Notorious Daughter of Fanny Hill,* 1966; *The
Agony of Love,* 1966; *Shannon's Women,* 1969; *The Secret Sex
Life of Romeo and Juliet,* 1970.

*   *   *

William Rotsler is one of the few SF writers who has also
achieved fame as a cartoonist. His distinctive style of cartooning
has proven popular for over 30 years, and he writes frequently on
the arts for such monthlies as *Adam.* It is little wonder, then, that
Rotsler's first novel, *Patron of the Arts,* is about the nature of the
artistic process. Rotsler attempts in this novel to determine the social effects of a *Gesamstwerk,* an attempt at the total union of the
arts through a synthesis of holography and electronic music. This
novel succeeds to the extent that the ideas it contains are reflections of authentic experience, but Rotsler's extrapolative sense is
not keen, and the novel can best be characterised as an interesting
failure.

From his promising first novel, Rotsler's work quickly declined.
Rotsler has tried a career as a commercial entertainer, but fails to
provide that depth of characterisation and intellection that the best
popular writers, such as Poul Anderson and Gordon Dickson, provide. His later novels are mere repetition of formulas without any
distinctive presence. His favourite formula is that of the Ship of
Fools, a cast of various racial and sexual types gathered together
to face a perilous situation. Thus in *Zandra* the varied cast is drawn
together after their cruiseship passes through the Bermuda Triangle
into another dimension. In *Shiva Descending* (with Gregory
Benford) the cast faces the familiar peril of a meteor about to destroy Earth. Rotsler and Benford mine this tired lode of apocalyptic fiction to little effect. Rotsler's worst novel, however, is *The
Far Frontier.* In this work, Rotsler fulfills the worst fantasies of
those mundane critics who insist that science fiction is nothing more
than western formulas transported to a wider setting. Rotsler has
replied with a novel complete with interstellar Indians, space cows,
and planet rustlers. Rarely does one read a novel where the writer
rejoices in its trashy content; such, unfortunately, is the case with
The Far Frontier.

Rotsler, then, after achieving promise as a first novelist, has re-
neged upon that promise with his later novels. He is less important
for his writings than for his cartoons, which have the distinction
and wit that his novels lack.

—Martin Morse Wooster

ROUSSEAU, Victor

Pseudonym: H.M. Egbert. **Nationality:** American. **Born:** Victor
Rousseau Emanuel, London, in 1879. **Career:** Lived in South Africa at the turn of the century; emigrated to the United States, and
wrote for pulp magazines until 1941. **Died:** 5 April 1960.

SCIENCE FICTION PUBLICATIONS

Novels

The Messiah of the Cylinder. Chicago, McClurg, and London,
Curtis Brown, 1917; as *The Apostle of the Cylinder,* London,
Hodder and Stoughton, 1918.
My Lady of the Nile. London, Hodder and Stoughton, 1923.
Draught of Eternity (as H.M. Egbert). London, Long, 1924.
The Sea Demons (as H.M. Egbert). London, Long, 1924; as Vic-
tor Rousseau, Westport, Connecticut, Hyperion Press, 1976.
Eric of the Strong Heart. London, Long, 1925.
Mrs. Aladdin. London, Long, 1925.
Red Twilight, World's End: Two Classic Novels from Argosy. Mercer
Island, Washington, Starmont House, 1991.

OTHER PUBLICATIONS

Novels

Derwent's Horse. London, Methuen, 1901.
Wooden Spoil. New York, Doran, 1919; London, Hodder and
Stoughton, 1923.
The Big Muskeg. Cincinnati, Stewart Kidd, 1921; London, Hodder
and Stoughton, 1923.
The Lion's Jaw. London, Hodder and Stoughton, 1923.
The Home Trail. London, Hodder and Stoughton, 1924.
The Big Man of Bonne Chance. London, Hodder and Stoughton, 1925.
The Golden Horde. London, Hodder and Stoughton, 1926.

Novels as H.M. Egbert

Jacqueline of Golden River. New York, Doubleday, 1920; London,
Hodder and Stoughton, 1924.
The Big Malopo. London, Long, 1924.
Salted Diamonds. London, Long, 1926.
Winding Trails. London, Long, 1927.

Novels as V.R. Emanuel

The Story of John Paul. London, Constable, 1923.
Middle Years. New York, Minton Balch, 1925.
The Selmans. New York, Dial Press, 1925.

Plays

Screenplays: *West of the Rainbow's End,* with Daisy Kent, 1926;
Wanderer of the West, with Arthur Hoerl and W. Ray Johnston,
1927; *Prince of the Plains,* with Arthur Hoerl, 1927; *Lightnin'
Shot,* with J.P. McGowan, 1928; *Trailin' Back,* with Arthur Hoerl
and J.P. McGowan, 1928.

*   *   *

Victor Rousseau's stories spring out immediately and absorb the reader with global plots and bold valiance. Rousseau's rare talent is to combine medieval values and Louis L'Amour's style in the science fiction context. The result provides sentimental satisfaction. The amusement in reading Rousseau is similar to the *Star Wars* experience in cinema. Both *The Messiah of the Cylinder* and *The Sea Demons* present strong heroes and execrable villains.

Even if the "daring sexual implications" that the promotion page of *The Sea Demons* promise are hard to find, there are enough imagination and activity in the macrocosmic plots to satisfy thrill-seeking readers. In *The Messiah of the Cylinder,* our hero (Arnold) and his foul antagonist are prep school mates. One of their school-mates, Herman Lagaroff, invents the 100-year time-lock cylinder that transports the two men (and the pristine maiden whom they both love) into the year 2017. The time forwarding is believably described, involving Arnold's tortuous arrival in the strange London of 2017: "I flung myself upon my face and prayed, with all my will, to die." The story of these books is similar to Wells's *A Modern Utopia* and *When the Sleeper Wakes*. The time travelers in Rousseau's work are propelled into a barbarous authoritarian night-mare, however, where "the dull and the base" are categorized by size of cranium. "The Prophet Wells," as he is referred to by Rousseau, would be aghast at the cold brutality of the rational so-ciety as it is portrayed in *The Messiah*. The triumphant ending in *The Messiah* includes the destruction and overthrow of the (fas-cist) government, the outlawing of divorce, and a return to a "ruling class bound to its traditions of public service." Where Wells asserts the final victory of reason, Rousseau longs for a futuristic theocracy. The priests would be happier than the scientists in Rousseau's future. None-theless, Rousseau exhibits a vivid technological imagination. He writes about solar power, plausible flying machines, and a communication network similar to the current and projected reality. The sinister government's effective propagandistic use of the media is a startling reminder of the current world situation.

The plot of *The Sea Demon* is commonplace, and the story is similar to *The Messiah*. The strange sea creatures who are strug-gling to take over the world are discovered by noble Captain Donald Paget. Gallantry overcoming the hideous threat is the main course: Donald "raised the girl in his arms, and felt one of the blubbery flippers on his hand . . . the stinging flippers sucked the blood from his face and hands . . . but Donald could not lose with Ida's life at stake." The battle to save the world intensifies to involve all governments and world resources. The story culminates in suicidal frenzy as the Queen Sea Beast dies of a broken heart and leaves the hordes without leadership, which we all know leads immedi-ately to destruction.

The enduring impressions one gets of Rousseau are staunch tra-ditionalism and faith in a well-ordered universe. Rousseau is good for a cheerful escape from heady ambiguity, and the pleasures of a frantic plot with the sugar-coated conclusion never in doubt.

—Peter Lynch

RUCKER, Rudy

Nationality: American. **Born:** Rudolph von Bitter Rucker, Louis-ville, Kentucky, 22 March 1946. **Education:** Swarthmore College, Pennsylvania, B.A. in mathematics 1967; Rutgers University, New Brunswick, New Jersey, M.A. 1969, Ph.D. 1973. **Family:** Mar-ried Sylvia Bogsch in 1967; two daughters and one son. **Career:** Assistant Professor, State University of New York, Geneseo, 1972-78; Alexander von Humboldt Foundation Research Grantee, Uni-versity of Heidelberg, 1978-80; Associate Professor, Randolph-Macon Woman's College, Lynchburg, Virginia, 1980-82. Since 1982, freelance writer. **Awards:** Philip K. Dick Memorial award, 1983. **Agent:** Susan Protter, 110 West 40th Street, New York, New York 10018, U.S.A. **Address:** 1324 Church Street, Lynchburg, Virginia 24504, U.S.A.

SCIENCE FICTION PUBLICATIONS

Novels (series: Software)

White Light; or, What Is Cantor's Continuum Problem? New York, Ace, and London, Virgin, 1980.
Spacetime Donuts. New York, Ace, 1981.
Software. New York, Ace, 1982.
The Sex Sphere. New York, Ace, 1984.
Master of Space and Time. New York, Bluejay, 1984.
The Secret of Life. New York, Bluejay, 1985.
Wetware (Software). New York, Avon, 1988; London, New En-glish Library, 1989.
The Hollow Earth: The Narrative of Mason Algiers Reynolds of Virginia. New York, Morrow, 1990.
The Hacker and the Ants. New York, Morrow, 1994.

Short Stories

The 57th Franz Kafka. New York, Ace, 1983.
Transreal! Englewood, Colorado, WCS, 1991.

OTHER PUBLICATIONS

Novel

All the Visions: A Novel of the Sixties, bound with *Space Baltic* (poem), by Anselm Holly. Mountain View, California, Ocean View, 1991.

Poetry

Light Fuse and Get Away. Lynchburg, Virginia, Carp, 1983.

Other

Geometry, Relativity, and the Fourth Dimension. New York, Do-ver, and London, Constable, 1977.
Infinity and the Mind: The Science and Philosophy of the Infinite. Cambridge, Massachusetts, Birkhauser, and Brighton, Harvester, 1982.
The Fourth Dimension: Toward a Geometry of Higher Reality. Bos-ton, Houghton Mifflin, 1984; as *The Fourth Dimension: A Guided Tour of the Higher Universe,* London, Rider, 1985.
Mind Tools: The Five Levels of Mathematical Reality. Boston, Houghton Mifflin, 1987; London, Penguin, 1988.
Artificial Life Lab. Corte Madera, Waite Group Press, 1993.

Mondon 2000: A User's Guide to the New Edge, with R.U. Sirius and Queen Mu. New York, HarperPerennial, 1992; London, Thames and Hudson, 1993.

Editor, *Speculations on the Fourth Dimension: Selected Writings of Charles H. Hinton.* New York, Dover, and London, Constable, 1980.

Editor, *Mathenauts: Tales of Mathematical Wonder.* New York, Arbor House, 1987; London, New English Library, 1989.

Editor, with Robert Anton Wilson and Peter Lamborn Wilson, *Semiotext[e] SF.* Brooklyn, New York, Autonomedia, 1989.

*

Rudy Rucker comments:

An unusual thing about my work is that I write popular speculative mathematics books as well as fiction. To some degree the fiction serves as a laboratory for thought-experiments related to my scientific and philosophical investigations.

Another aspect of my fiction is that much of it is, on a higher level, autobiographical. I call the device of writing about one's life in SF terms *transrealism.* Taken in sequence, *Secret of Life, White Light,* and *Sex Sphere* make up a transrealist trilogy.

My nonfiction has largely been devoted to expanding the range of things that people are able to think and talk about. Infinity and higher dimensions are of particular interest to me.

* * *

In his works of science fiction and science fact, Rudy Rucker extrapolates new physical and psychological modes of existence from current possibilities. He pursues these extrapolations by exploring how the mind can manipulate the physical universe and hence distort our commonsense perceptions of the world. The results of these distortions are a renewed sense of wonder about the external world and an enhancement of the internal world through increased self awareness.

Rucker frequently takes his hero or heroes—and vicariously, of course, the reader—on a mental journey toward some higher plane of reality. Sometimes this journey involves altering our world by imagining a concept from theoretical physics into an everyday reality. In *Master of Space and Time,* Fletcher and Harry physically occupy Hilbert space and, in the process, allow an alternate version of Harry to escape into our world. This inversion of Harry's affable, disordered personality—Gerry Herber, a figment of Harry's imagination run wild—unleashes a reign of terror that preys upon the weakest elements of society. Herber threatens to eradicate the independent thought and action that made him a physical reality in the first place. Furthermore, Fletcher and Harry are themselves the product of Alwin Bitter's imagination. Bitter's preoccupation with Hilbert space willed them into existence and manipulated their experiment, and, like Gerry Herber, they threaten the balance of the physical world. Similarly, through the imagination, a young Alwin Bitter in *The Sex Sphere* achieves first the transformation of the city of Heidelberg into a degraded carnival of sexual activity and then a return to normalcy. A hypersphere trapped in three-dimensional space and the others it spawns have varacious sexual appetites and an intense aversion to human females. The emotional ties that bind Bitter to a normal life become increasingly precarious. When they reach a breaking point, he wills into existence a world in which sexual gratification becomes completely divorced from human involvement. There are no females, only sex spheres. Bitter's

wife reestablishes ties with him, and he wills the sex spheres and his experiences in Germany away. In both of these novels, Rucker imagines for us a world transformed by an idea and infinite possibilities for the recursion of this transformation.

In addition to theoretical concepts, machines are also the catalysts for the journeys Rucker's heroes take. The possibilities opened up by computers form the basis for several of Rucker's novels, and like concepts, physical objects can alter everyday reality in unexpected ways. In *Infinity and the Mind,* Rucker suggests that computers may one day become self-replicating and through natural selection mimic the intuition and subtlety of human thought. Further, he speculates that because of more favorable environmental conditions on the moon, computers may eventually form their own separate society there. This speculation forms the basis of the novel *Software* in which an old man strives for immortality and a young man for his connection to the rest of the human race. In *Software,* computers have achieved a rough parity with humans, and Rucker explores that delicate balance as humans fend off the computer's efforts to "eat their brains" and thus deprive them of their humanity. In *Spacetime Donuts,* the balance has shifted in favor of computers. They control most aspects of human activity, from dispensing food—a tasteless concoction called "dream food"—to plugging into the human consciousness every night and supplying mankind with dreams. Computers provide immediate gratification of all human needs, and men are little more than useless appendages of one large computer that rules the state. The novel explores one man's journey back to his own humanity with the help of theoretical physics and the revolution caused by that journey.

While the journeys prompted by ideas and technology threaten Rucker's heroes and their worlds, each journey ends in an affirmation of humanity. People become more aware and more open to their husbands, wives, lovers, children; people realize the best in themselves; people die because they are old and because death is the way the human race replenishes itself. This human affirmation brings a restoration of normalcy and with it an enhanced sense of wonder about the everyday world. This sense of wonder is what science fiction is all about.

—Terri Paul

RUPPERT, Chester. *See* **PHILLIPS, Rog.**

RUSCH, Kristine Kathryn

Pseudonyms: Edward Heyer, Sandy Schofield, Kristine K. Thompson. **Nationality:** American. **Born:** Oneonta, New York, 4 June 1960. **Education:** Beloit College, Beloit, Wisconsin, 1978-79; University of Wisconsin, Madison, B.A. in history, 1982; Clarion Writers Workshop, East Lansing, Michigan, 1985. **Family:** Married 1) Randall R. Thompson (divorced 1986); 2) writer Dean Wesley Smith in 1992. **Career:** Freelance journalist, 1978-86; reporter, WORT Radio, Madison, Wisconsin, 1980-86, news director, 1983-

86; owner/retail clerk, Shire Frame Shop & Galleries, 1981-84; editorial assistant, Wm. C. Brown Publishers, 1984; secretary, psychology office, Eugene, Oregon, 1986-89; editor and founder, Pulphouse Publishing, 1987-92. Since 1991, Editor, *Magazine of Fantasy & Science Fiction.* **Awards:** World Fantasy award, 1989; John W. Campbell award, 1990; *Locus* award, 1991, 1992; Hugo award, 1994. **Agent:** Richard Curtis, Richard Curtis Associates Inc., 171 E. 74th St., New York, New York 10021. **Address:** P.O. Box 11526, Eugene, Oregon 97440, U.S.A.

SCIENCE FICTION PUBLICATIONS

Novels (series: Star Trek: Voyager)

The White Mists of Power. New York, Roc, 1991; London, Millennium, 1992.
Afterimage, with Kevin J. Anderson. New York, Roc, 1992.
Façade. New York, Dell Abyss, 1993; London, Millennium, 1994.
Heart Readers. London, Millennium, and New York, Roc, 1993.
Traitors. London, Millennium, 1993; New York, Roc, 1994.
Sins of the Blood. New York, Dell Abyss, 1994; London, Millennium, 1995.
Alien Influences. London, Orion, 1994.
The Escape, with Dean Wesley Smith (Star Trek: Voyager). New York, Pocket, 1995.

Short Stories

The Gallery of His Dreams. Eugene, Oregon, Axolotl Press, 1991.

OTHER PUBLICATIONS

Other

Characterization. Eugene, Oregon, Pulphouse, 1990.
The Rules: A Short Course in the Basics. Eugene, Oregon, Pulphouse, 1990.
Setting. Eugene, Oregon, Pulphouse, 1990.
Editor, *Pulphouse: The Hardback Magazine, #1-12.* Eugene, Oregon, Pulphouse, 1988-93, 12 vols.
Editor, with Dean Wesley Smith, *Science Fiction Writers of America Handbook: The Professional Writer's Guide to Writing Professionally.* Eugene, Oregon, Pulphouse, 1990.
Editor, *The Best of Pulphouse: The Hardback Magazine.* New York, St. Martin's Press, 1991.
Editor, with Edward L. Ferman, *The Best from Fantasy & Science Fiction: A 45th Anniversary Anthology.* New York, St. Martin's Press, 1994.

*

Kristine Kathryn Rusch comments:

People have often asked how I can write books and edit at the same time. Writing and editing have always gone hand-in-hand for me. While I worked as a news director, I was also a freelance journalist. When I wrote nonfiction, I edited nonfiction. I have done the same with fiction.

I have read since I was three, and I finished my first short story when I was about seven. I wrote my first novel during lonely Fri-

day nights in junior high school. Escaping to other worlds has always attracted me; I cannot see this changing.

When I write, I write to please myself. I am happy that my stories have a following, happy that others like the same stories as I do.

As to favorite works, I have none. I enjoy writing the media tie-ins with my husband, Dean Wesley Smith. It is fun working in someone else's universe at times. I also enjoy new challenges. The Books of the Fey are a new form for me, a new challenge that has entranced me for almost a year now. But I keep my hand in short fiction because I believe it to be the best way to communicate a single emotion, a single image, to an audience. I will always write both short and long fiction. I will continue to pursue a challenge.

*   *   *

Kristine Kathryn Rusch has made an indelible mark on the multi-colored fabric of SF and fantasy. In less than a decade, she has risen from relative obscurity to a highly regarded presence as both an editor and author. A graduate of the University of Wisconsin, Rusch freelanced for several years before a short story, "Sing," appeared in a 1987 issue of *Aboriginal Science Fiction* and received widespread notice. Many of Rusch's stories (including the exceptional "Story Child" and "Trains") have been published in genre magazines (*The Magazine of Fantasy and Science Fiction, Asimov's*) or anthologized (*The Year's Best Science Fiction* and *The Year's Best Fantasy*).

Yet Rusch had already made a name for herself as cofounder (with Dean Wesley Smith) and senior editor of Pulphouse Publishing, responsible for the immensely popular *Pulphouse: The Hardback Magazine* series which spawned *The Best of Pulphouse: The Hardback Magazine* (St. Martin's Press, 1992). Rusch also published several "how-to" booklets for aspiring writers on characterization, setting and "the basics" of good fiction under the Pulphouse umbrella.

The early 90s found Rusch increasingly recognized for her talents: she received a World Fantasy Award for her collaboration with Wesley Smith on *Pulphouse;* the 1990 John W. Campbell Award as Best New Writer; and a *Locus* Nonfiction Award for her role as coeditor (with Wesley Smith) of the *Science Fiction Writers of America (SFWA) Handbook.* She was also selected by Edward L. Ferman as the sixth (and first woman) editor of *The Magazine of Fantasy and Science Fiction* in 1991; and the publication of her debut novel, *The White Mists of Power,* followed closely by a second, *The Gallery of His Dreams,* marked her arrival as one of the genre's most intriguing voices.

Rusch's political fantasy, *The White Mists of Power,* was lauded for its compelling characters and convergent plots, while her second effort, *The Gallery of His Dreams,* drew on her history degree to spin a haunting tale of Civil War photographer Matthew Brady traveling through time and documenting undreamt of horror and carnage. Joining forces with college pal Kevin J. Anderson produced 1992's *AfterImage,* a contemporary fantasy about a serial killer, shape-changing darklings and a victim resurrected into the image of her would-be killer. A sequel, *AfterShock,* is said to be in the works. Rusch's next four novels, published in '93 and '94, find two (*Traitors* and *Heart Readers*) returning to mainstream fantasy like *The White Mists of Power;* and the other two (*Facade* and *Sins of the Blood*) carrying on in the thriller vein of *AfterImage.*

Additionally, Rusch lent her vocal cords to 1992's the *Best of Science Fiction and Fantasy,* a four-cassette offering and 1993's *Stained Black: Horror Stories,* before co-editing (with Ferman) 1994's acclaimed retrospective, *The Best from Fantasy & Science Fiction: A 45th Anniversary Anthology.* Prolific (she calls herself a "high density" writer), determined and gifted, Rusch says she writes "to tell myself who I am." Fortunately, SF and fantasy readers are now acutely aware of Kristine Kathryn Rusch's identity.

—Sydonie Benet

RUSS, Joanna

Nationality: American. **Born:** New York City, 22 February 1937. **Education:** Cornell University, Ithaca, New York, B.A. 1957; Yale University School of Drama, New Haven, Connecticut, M.F.A. 1960. **Family:** Married Albert Amateau in 1963 (divorced 1967). **Career:** Lecturer in Speech, Queensborough Community College, New York, 1966-67; Instructor, 1967-70, and Assistant Professor of English, 1970-72, Cornell University; Assistant Professor of English, State University of New York, Binghamton, 1972-73, 1974-75, and University of Colorado, Boulder, 1975-77. Associate Professor, 1977-84, and since 1984, Professor of English, University of Washington, Seattle. Occasional book reviewer, *Fantasy and Science Fiction*, 1966-79. **Awards:** Nebula award, 1972, 1983; National Endowment for the Humanities Fellowship, 1974; Hugo award, 1983; *Locus* award, 1983. **Agent:** Ellen Levine Literary Agency, 15 East 26th Street, Suite 1801, New York, New York 10010. **Address:** 8961 E. Lester St., Tucson, AZ 85715, U.S.A.

SCIENCE FICTION PUBLICATIONS

Novels

Picnic on Paradise. New York, Ace, 1968; London, Macdonald, 1969.
And Chaos Died. New York, Ace, 1970.
The Female Man. New York, Bantam, 1975; London, Star, 1977.
We Who Are about to. . . . New York, Dell, 1977; London, Women's Press, 1987.
Kittatinny: A Tale of Magic (for children). New York, Daughters, 1978.
The Two of Them. New York, Berkley, 1978; London, Women's Press, 1986.

Short Stories

Alyx. Boston, Gregg Press, 1976; as *The Adventures of Alyx*, New York, Pocket Books, 1983; London, Women's Press, 1985.
The Zanzibar Cat. Sauk City, Wisconsin, Arkham House, 1983; rev. ed., New York, Baen, 1984.
Extra (Ordinary) People. New York, St. Martin's Press, 1984; London, Women's Press, 1985.
The Hidden Side of the Moon: Stories. New York, St. Martin's Press, 1987; London, Women's Press, 1989.
Souls, with *Houston, Houston, Do You Read?,* by James Tiptree, Jr. New York, Tor, 1989.

OTHER PUBLICATIONS

Novel

On Strike against God. Brooklyn, New York, Out and Out, 1980; London, Women's Press, 1987.

Play

Window Dressing, in *The New Woman's Theatre,* edited by Honor Moore. New York, Random House, 1977.

Other

How to Suppress Women's Writing. Austin, University of Texas Press, 1983; London, Women's Press, 1984.
Magic Mommas, Trembling Sisters, Puritans & Perverts: Feminist Essays. Trumansburg, New York, Crossing Press, 1985.
To Write Like a Woman: Essays in Feminism. Bloomington, Indiana University Press, 1995.

* * *

During the 1960s, Joanna Russ emerged as one of the most talented and provocative writers of science fiction's New Wave. While Russ identifies herself primarily as a feminist, she is equally well known for her experimental way of handling the conventional materials and narrative strategies of science fiction. Since Russ is opposed to all social fixities and intellectual givens, her major effort as a science fiction writer has been to explore alternate realities and create new myths, especially ones that depict women as complex human subjects.

Russ's apprentice work is feminist only obliquely. Ostensibly, she aims at an interesting mix of historic fantasy and the supernatural, a combination she continues to use in her later work. The initial run of stories exploits the theme of the after-life to fresh effect. "Nor Custom Stale" (in *Fantasy and Science Fiction,* September 1959) her first story, is untypically set in the future. It describes a bourgeois couple who live stubbornly immured in a future-tech "House" while catastrophic ages pass unnoticed outside; domestic monotony preserves them in a living death. Several of the stories are set in the 19th century, an era Russ understands but dislikes. "Mr. Wilde's Second Chance" (in *Fantasy and Science Fiction,* September 1966) is a wry account of the dead poet's renunciation of an opportunity to live a conventionally tasteful second life. In "There Is Another Shore . . . ," a revenant young woman, a kind of female Keats, returns to her deathplace in Rome to taste "the fullness of life" in romantic adventure. The ironic promise of this story—that if life for the 19th-century woman was death, death was liberation—is also the germ for "My Dear Emily," whose sober young heroine is passionately emancipated when she becomes a vampire. Part of the wit of such stories is their literary allusiveness; "My Dear Emily" condenses the romantic plot of *Wuthering Heights.*

With her first Alyx stories, Russ introduces a character new to science fiction, an adventuress whose daring and cunning issue from her womanly strength. Set in ancient Phoenicia, these stories launch her on a career as a soldier of fortune. In her natural setting, Alyx is of necessity an outlaw sensibility—a rationalist in a world of superstitious mystique, an imaginist in a world of empty, brutal pragmatism: in short, Russ implies, the ancestor of the intelligent modern woman. *Picnic on Paradise,* also build around Alyx, casts her again as an outlaw, here a ruthlessly sensible, martially skilled Trans-Temp agent abstracted from Tyre to a future world wasted by advanced capitalist war. Alyx is Russ's *agent provocateur:* neither Amazon nor androgyne, she foils both old and new notions of the feminine ideal. At the same time, her unromantic heroics are designed to satirize the "he-man ethos" of Sword and Sorcery. For all its modesty in plot and narrative strategy, *Picnic on Paradise* may be Russ's most inventive novel.

It was closely followed by another ground-breaking novel of the future and several increasingly accomplished shorter fantasies. *And Chaos Died* is at once a penetrating social critique and a lyrical celebration of a psionic near-utopia. Russ maroons her hero on a pastoral planet where he is drawn into an egalitarian community and taught psi-powers. What is really new in the novel is its style: the magic arbitrariness of the narrator's experience is rendered by a stream-of-expanding-consciousness technique that registers his initial nausea, then his growing joy, and finally his disgust when he is returned to a dystopic earth wholly given over to violence and mental imperialism. In the novelette "The Second Inquisition," Russ makes a poignantly funny story of one of her central concerns, a young girl's need for a worthy feminine model to counteract her social training in self-extinction. The tutelary genius in this case is a Trans-Temp agent from a non-sexist future world. The heroine of "The Zanzibar Cat" is yet another Alyx-like subversive ironist, a medieval miller's daughter who faces down a lord of Fantasyland. By the end of the tale, the humble milleress has grown into the mother of all meaning, the author. The archaic setting of "The Zanzibar Cat" and the Hellenistic background of "Poor Man, Beggar Man," a story that splits the historic Alexander into ego and ghostly alter ego, testify to Russ's continuing interest in unwritten history.

With "When It Changed" and "Nobody's Home," Russ reached a new level of achievement. These visions of an emancipated future for women on the wistfully named Whileaway are thorough reconstructions of the standard manless-world story. They are utopian, but only in a special sense: the particular virulence of male-dominated culture is no more, yet life remains unpredictably anguishing and rewarding.

The Female Man, a reconsideration of Whileawayan possibilities, has become an underground classic in both science-fiction and feminist circles. The book is built around the digressive journal of a present-day woman who encounters three other selves: the victim of an altered past even more oppressive of women than our own, an ambassador from a Whileawayan future, and an intermediary figure from a world split by gender war into Manland and Womanland. Each is, in her way, an Everywoman. Janet is Russ's ultimate heroine, "the Might-be of our dreams," the goal of feminine evolution. The way to Janet lies through Jael, or Alice Reasoner, the sex warrior based on Alyx; Jael knows that liberation must be won at hard cost. Joanna, the sometime narrator, and Jeanine are both confused products of a culture which invalidates their every aspiration. These four life histories are super-imposed on one another to create an anti-novel: narrative with dense novelistic details is interspersed with meditation, reverie, and fragments of the mythology and history of Whileaway. What holds all this together is impassioned articulation, a style as sensitive as ever to the bizarre complexities of women's lives, but here honed to laser precision by rage.

Russ distinguishes herself in *The Female Man* as radical intelligencer and stylist. Her next novel, *We Who Are About to . . .* , is a study of an hallucinating woman dying alone on an emptied planet. For all its eerie fascination, the book remains rather private and untransformed. In *The Two of Them*, Russ returns to an earlier mode of the politically and socially informed adventure. The Trans-Temp heroine of this novel has escaped from the stultifying world of America in the 1950s to become an agent in the future. Sent to a sexist society that owes something to the Arabian Nights and some-

thing to the Islamic world of today, she rescues a girl from a harem, discovering in the process the depth of her commitment to the child: ". . . it'll take longer than one woman's lifetime," she realizes, to free herself. Russ's own commitment to the liberation of the young has borne fruit in two recent short stories ("My Boat," "How Dorothy Kept Away the Spring") and *Kittatinny*, a fantasy written expressly for young girls.

Extra (Ordinary) People evinces both a growing technical mastery and an increasingly subtle feminist consciousness in a series of tales about diverse female liberators. A wry, formally inventive book, *Extra (Ordinary) People* is comprised of five narratives, the first four centered on the extramundane adventures of these wise women and the last a romp of a parody—a plot outline for a lesbian historical romance. As a casual linking device, a fragment of a tutorial introduces each tale to a native future "schoolkid." Repeating this structure, an ironic teaching and learning motif recurs in the stories proper: several of the heroine-mentors are isolated in dangerously ignorant, sexist societies of the past and future, and their often comic, always poignant reports are relayed as knowing letters home. Indeed, all of the stories present lessons in "the usual confusion and mess" of human sexuality. In the initial tale, the Hugo award-winning novella "Souls," for instance, a telepathic genius of a 12th-century abbess challenges the brutal sexual code of Viking invaders. In "The Mystery of the Young Gentleman" and "What Did You Do in the Revolution, Grandma?," lesbians in male disguise traverse sexual boundaries, demystifying their own "outlaw" sexuality and defamiliarizing orthodox sexual behavior as they go. Rendering from the inside the extraordinary sentience of her heroines as they struggle to endure or elude the meshes of simplistic alternate realities, Russ creates a fiction both immediate and ironically layered—a work of and about science fiction. *Extra (Ordinary) People* should keep Russ at the experimental forefront of the field.

—Carol L. Snyder

RUSSELL, Eric Frank

Nationality: British. **Born:** Camberley, Surrey, 6 January 1905; grew up in Egypt. **Military Service:** Served in the King's Regiment, 1922-26, and in the Royal Air Force, 1941-45. **Family:** Married Ellen Russell in 1930; one daughter. **Career:** Worked as a telephonist, quantity surveyor, and draughtsman. **Member:** Founding member, British Interplanetary Society. **Awards:** Hugo award, 1955. **Died:** 28 February 1978.

Novels

Sinister Barrier. Kingswood, Surrey, World's Work, 1943; expanded edition, Reading, Pennsylvania, Fantasy Press, 1948.
Dreadful Sanctuary. Reading, Pennsylvania, Fantasy Press, 1951; London, Museum Press, 1953; revised edition, New York, Lancer, 1963; London, Four Square, 1967.
Sentinels from Space. New York, Bouregy, 1953; London, Museum Press, 1954.

Three to Conquer. New York, Avalon, 1956; London, Dobson, 1957.
Wasp. New York, Avalon, 1957; revised edition, London, Dobson, 1958.
The Space Willies. New York, Ace, 1958; revised edition as *Next of Kin,* London, Dobson, 1959.
The Great Explosion. London, Dobson, and New York, Torquil, 1962.
With a Strange Device. London, Dobson, 1964; as *The Mind Warpers,* New York, Lancer, 1965.
Design for Great-Day, with Alan Dean Foster. New York, Tor, 1995.

Short Stories

Deep Space. Reading, Pennsylvania, Fantasy Press, 1954; London, Eyre and Spottiswoode, 1956; abridged as *Selections from Deep Space,* New York, Bantam, 1955.
Men, Martians, and Machines. London, Dobson, 1955; New York, Roy, 1956.
Six Worlds Yonder. New York, Ace, 1958.
Far Stars. London, Dobson, 1961.
Dark Tides. London, Dobson, 1962.
Somewhere a Voice. London, Dobson, 1965; New York, Ace, 1966.
Like Nothing on Earth. London, Dobson, 1975.
The Best of Eric Frank Russell, edited by Alan Dean Foster. New York, Ballantine, 1978.

OTHER PUBLICATIONS

Other

Great World Mysteries. London, Dobson, and New York, Roy, 1957.
The Rabble Rousers. Evanston, Illinois, Regency, 1963.

*   *   *

Eric Frank Russell will always be remembered as the author of *Sinister Barrier,* the story that helped John W. Campbell launch the magazine *Unknown* in 1939. Boosted as "the greatest imaginative novel in two decades," it established the British writer at the centre of the international science fiction scene where he remained a popular figure for more than 30 years. It also drew attention to the abundance of plot material in the much-maligned works of Charles Fort, whose philosophy of scepticism Russell upheld consistently on behalf of the Fortean Society.

The novel relies on the notion that the Earth belongs to an alien race that feeds on the human misery it causes. With consummate skill, goaded by Campbell, Russell presented it as a mystery story in the tradition of the detective pulps he had studied in preparing to write for the American market. His taut, racy style had first attracted attention in *Astounding Stories* in 1937, when "The Saga of Pelican West" showed the influence of Stanley G. Weinbaum, which affected many writers at that time. His contributions to the British *Tales of Wonder* and *Fantasy* also revealed a refreshing touch of humor coupled with a vigorous approach that was rare in SF. Typical examples were "Vampire from the Void," set in his Liverpool habitat, and "I, Spy!" concerning a Martian visitant that could simulate any form of terrestrial life. His amusing tales of Jay Score, the robot space-pilot, and his crewmen were collected in *Men, Mar-*

tians, and Machines. War service curtailed his writing, but "Metamorphosite," a story about a galactic empire, and *Dreadful Sanctuary* returned him to front-rank status. A fast-moving tale about a secret society which sabotaged the first attempts at space-travel, *Dreadful Sanctuary* seriously considers mankind's irrational ways while posing the question "How do you know you're sane?"

All through the 1950s Russell's lucid narratives delighted readers. He broke new ground with "First Person Singular" by adapting the Adam and Eve legend to an interstellar setting; in other stories he revealed an unsuspected flair for emotional themes and moral issues such as racial intolerance. "And There Were None" postulates the effect of passive resistance on planetary invaders, which later became the theme of his satirical novel *The Great Explosion.* *Three to Conquer* reflected the interest in psionics fostered by Campbell. "Allamagoosa" (Hugo) is a clever piece of nonsense. *Sentinels from Space,* in which a highly evolved species keeps a watch over lesser beings, derives something from Olaf Stapledon, with whom Russell maintained friendly contact after introducing him to American science fiction. *Wasp* is an action-thriller relating the escapades of a secret agent preparing the way for a Terran invasion of the Sirian Empire. Simplest of all Russell's novels is *With a Strange Device,* almost a straight mystery story about a conspiracy to sabotage a new defensive weapon. Almost as intriguing as any of his fiction, too, is his collection *Great World Mysteries,* in which he delved into some of the enigmas that have baffled scientists over the past century or more.

—Walter Gillings

RYMAN, Geoff

Nationality: British. **Born:** Canada. Moved to London in mid-1970s. **Awards:** World Fantasy award, 1986; Arthur C. Clarke award, 1990; British Science Fiction award, 1990. **Agent:** Maggie Noach, 21 Redan Street, London, W14 0AB, England. **Address:** c/o HarperCollins Publishers, 77-85 Fulham Palace Road, London W6 8JB, England.

SCIENCE FICTION PUBLICATIONS

Novels

The Warrior Who Carried Life. London, and Boston, Allen and Unwin, 1985; New York, Bantam, 1987.
The Unconquered Country: A Life History (novella). London, and Boston, Allen and Unwin, 1986; New York, Bantam, 1987.
The Child Garden; or, a Low Comedy. London, Unwin Hyman, 1989; New York, St. Martin's Press, 1990.

Short Stories

Coming of Enkidu. Birmingham, England, Birmingham Science Fiction Group, 1989.
Unconquered Countries: Four Novellas (includes *The Unconquered Country*). New York, St. Martin's Press, 1994.

Novel

"Was—": A Novel. London, HarperCollins, and New York, Knopf, 1992.

*   *   *

The heroines in the novels of Geoff Ryman (there are no heroes) suffer appallingly at the hands of the rulers of the worlds they inhabit, and have great anger as a result. But they also show inordinate tenderness for their partners, and through this love they finally transcend the pain their wounds inflict. This is the centre of all Ryman's work: the redemption human beings can achieve through love of other human beings. This central theme is played out against a background of other common themes—impersonal and tyrannical central governments, cultures that are recognisably oriental, and environments that are almost entirely bio-engineered— which are staggeringly different despite their commonality.

His first novel, *The Warrior Who Carried Life,* at once parodies and enriches the sword-and-sorcery fantasy genre. Cal Cara Kerig's family is mutilated and murdered by imperial troops. She joins a secret women's magic group, which demands that initiates take another form for a year. Much to the bewilderment of the women, who only use the stories of magic to exert power over one another, she actually transmogrifies into a fully armed and armoured warrior, and sets out to kill the prince who ordered the destruction of her family. Ryman adds extraordinary texture to this simple story with his vivid symbolic imagery and lucid prose.

The setting of *The Unconquered Country* could not be more different. Despite its utterly fantastic description—where houses are grown, treated as part of the family, and have to be tied down to stop them wandering off, and where women sell the use of their wombs for the growth of weapons—the country described is unmistakably Cambodia under the Khmer Rouge. But it is more than Cambodia, or else there would be no point in the symbolic representation of the way of life. The unconquered country could be any small nation that suffers more from the depredations of the nation supposedly protecting it than it does from the purported invaders. Caught between the proverbial rock and a hard place, it shows its ability to survive by absorbing what is done to it. The heroine is Third child, and through her eyes we see death breathed from the skies by sharks; living advertisement characters (to some of which she gives birth, and she beats another one to death). Her husband first rescues her from selling her body parts, then dies and is reincarnated as a crow. It would be far too easy to expend more words than the book contains on even a partial exegesis, and the only real recommendation can be to read this wonderfully dense story.

The Child Garden might be considered Ryman's first full-length novel. It is certainly longer than the other two put together. But there is no padding. Ryman's own description—"it's about two dykes putting on an opera in a Marxist/Leninist future London"— while indicative of the man's modesty, is further evidence of his ability to say no more than is necessary for his own ends.

Where the other novels are fantasies, *The Child Garden* is science fiction. Set in a future sub-tropical London protected from the rising seas and rivers by bio-engineered coral reefs, where people photosynthesise, and where all knowledge is imparted by genetically altered viruses, it is again a story of a young woman who is orphaned by the action of the state; she finds comfort in the love of another woman, and transcends her suffering to enhance an essentially ungrateful world.

The plot is taken from Dante's Divine Comedy, even as the plot of *The Warrior Who Carried Life* was taken from the epic of Gilgamesh. It becomes obvious that Ryman takes myth as the source of his work: the ancient mythic power of both Gilgamesh and the Divine Comedy is irrefutable, but there is no real difference between them and the 20th-century myth of the killing fields of Cambodia. Equally, in a lecture about the film of *The Wizard of Oz,* Ryman has claimed that, because the film was produced with many different writers and directors, it is a non-attributable mythic outpouring of early 20th-century consciousness. It is certainly nothing to do with L. Frank Baum's book, he maintains, and it is significant that it is the film, not the book, that has achieved classic status. It is no surprise, then, that his forthcoming novel, *Was,* is an account of what happened to Dorothy after she got home from Oz.

Ryman's other recurrent theme is of how it is not possible for anyone to intervene between audience and work of art to make the art easy to understand. In his first published short story, "The Diary of a Translator," he makes it clear that the only real way to learn from literature is to suffer through it oneself. In *The Child Garden,* Rolfa tells Milena, who can read music because she has been infected with the appropriate virus, "you haven't *learned* how to read music. If you haven't learned it, it isn't yours." In a recent story, "The History of Science Fiction," published in the September 1991 issue of *Science Fiction Nexus,* he explores yet another avenue of this theme, with an almost cyberpunk relish in the virtual reality he creates.

Ryman claims that, after *Was* is published, he is all written out. Given that he is not a prolific writer—three novels and less than a dozen short stories in 15 years—it is likely that his next novel is a long way off. Nevertheless, given the originality and the depth of what has appeared so far, it is certain that his next work is awaited with bated breath.

—Paul Brazier

S

SABE, Quien. *See* BATES, Harry.

————

SABERHAGEN, Fred (Thomas)

Nationality: American. **Born:** Chicago, Illinois, 18 May 1930. **Education:** Wright Junior College, Chicago, 1956-57. **Military Service:** Served in the United States Air Force, 1951-55. **Family:** Married Joan Dorothy Spicci in 1968; one daughter and two sons. **Career:** Electronics technician, Motorola Inc., Chicago, 1956-62; assistant editor, *Encyclopaedia Britannica,* 1967-73. Freelance writer, 1962-67, and since 1973. **Agent:** Eleanor Wood, Spectrum Literary Agency, 111 Eighth Avenue, Suite 1502, New York, New York 10011, U.S.A.

SCIENCE FICTION PUBLICATIONS

Novels (series: Berserker; Empire of the East; Pilgrim)

The Golden People. New York, Ace, 1964; expanded edition, New York, Baen, 1984.
The Water of Thought. New York, Ace, 1965; expanded edition, New York, Tor, 1981.
Empire of the East. New York, Ace, 1979; London, Macdonald, 1984.
   The Broken Lands. New York, Ace, 1968; revised, New York, Baen, 1987.
   The Black Mountains. New York, Ace, 1971; revised, New York, Baen, 1988.
   Changeling Earth. New York, DAW, 1973; revised as *Ardneh's World,* New York, Baen, 1988.
Brother Assassin. New York, Ballantine, 1969; as *Brother Berserker,* London, Macdonald, 1969.
Berserker's Planet. New York, DAW, and London, Futura, 1975.
Specimens. New York, Popular Library, 1976.
The Veils of Azlaroc. New York, Ace, 1978.
Love Conquers All. New York, Ace, 1979; revised, New York, Baen, 1985.
The Mask of the Sun. New York, Ace, 1979.
Berserker Man. New York, Ace, 1979; London, Gollancz, 1988.
Octagon. New York, Ace, 1981; London, Sinclair Browne, 1984.
Coils, with Roger Zelazny. Garden City, New York, Doubleday, 1982; London, Penguin, 1984.
A Century of Progress. New York, Tor, 1983.
The Berserker Throne. New York, Simon and Schuster, 1985.
Berserker: Blue Death. New York, Tor, 1985; London, Gollancz, 1990.
The Frankenstein Papers. New York, Baen, 1986.
Pyramids (Pilgrim). New York, Baen, 1987.
The Berserker Attack. Stamford, Connecticut, Waldenbooks, 1987.
After the Fact (Pilgrim). New York, Baen, 1988.
The White Bull. New York, Baen, 1988.

The Black Throne, with Roger Zelazny. New York, Baen, 1990.
Bram Stoker's Dracula: The Novel of the Film, with James V. Hart. New York, Signet, and London, Pan, 1992.
Berserker Kill. New York, Tor, 1993.
Merlin's Game. New York, Tor, 1995.

Novels (series: Swords in all titles)

The Complete Book of Swords. New York, Tor, 1983; London, Futura, 1986.
   The First Book of Swords. New York, Tor, 1983; London, Macdonald, 1986.
   The Second Book of Swords. New York, Tor, 1983; London, Orbit 1986.
   The Third Book of Swords. New York, Tor, 1984; London, Orbit, 1986.
The Lost Swords: The First Triad. Garden City, New York, Doubleday, 1988.
   The First Book of Lost Swords: Woundhealer's Story. New York, Tor, 1986.
   The Second Book of Lost Swords: Sight-Blinder's Story. New York, Tor, 1987.
   The Third Book of Lost Swords: Stonecutter's Story, New York, Tor, 1988; London, Orbit, 1989.
The Lost Swords: The Second Triad. New York, Guild America, 1991.
   The Fourth Book of Lost Swords: Farslayer's Song. New York, Tor, 1989; London, Orbit, 1992.
   The Fifth Book of Lost Swords: Coinspinner's Song. New York, Tor, 1989.
   The Sixth Book of Lost Swords: Mindsword's Song. New York, Tor, 1990.
The Lost Swords: Endgame. New York, Guild America, 1994.
   The Seventh Book of Lost Swords: Wayfinder's Story. New York, Tor, 1992.
   The Last Book of Swords: Shieldbreaker's Story. New York, Tor, 1994.

Novels (series: Dracula/Matthew Maule in all titles)

The Dracula Tape. New York, Warner, 1975.
The Holmes-Dracula File. New York, Ace, 1978.
An Old Friend of the Family. New York, Ace, 1979.
Thorn. New York, Ace, 1980.
Dominion. New York, Tor, 1982.
A Matter of Taste. New York, Tor, 1990.
A Question of Time. New York, Tor, 1992.
Séance for a Vampire. New York, Tor, 1994.

Short Stories

Berserker. New York, Ballantine, 1967; expanded edition as *The Berserker Wars,* New York, Tor, 1981.
The Book of Saberhagen. New York, DAW, 1975.
The Ultimate Enemy (Berserker). New York, Ace, 1979; London, Gollancz, 1990; as *Berserkers: The Ultimate Enemy,* New York, Baen, 1988.

Earth Descended (Berserker). New York, Tor, 1981.
Saberhagen: My Best. New York, Baen, 1987.
Berserker Lies (includes *Brother Berserker*). New York, Tor, 1991.

OTHER PUBLICATIONS

Other

Editor, *A Spadeful of Spacetime.* New York, Ace, 1981.
Editor, with Joan Saberhagen, *Pawn to Infinity.* New York, Ace, 1982.
Editor, with Martin H. Greenberg, *Machines That Kill.* New York, Ace, 1984.
Editor, *Berserker Base.* New York, Tor, 1985.
Editor, *An Armory of Swords.* New York, Tor, 1995.

*   *   *

For three decades, Fred Saberhagen's principal theme has been Life's War with Death across the evolutionary gradient: all his battles are wonder-wars. This is the very substance of his first and greatest success, the Berserker series. The berserkers are self-programming, self-replicating, robotic spacecraft set by their "long-dead masters to destroy anything that lived." Fighting these ineradicable foes unites all life forms in the galaxy, and, ironically, stimulates progress that might not otherwise have occurred without the machines' challenge. The berserkers are computerized demons, high-tech symbols of utter Evil.

This "divergent" series is a novelty for being organized around a common enemy instead of a continuing hero. Its premise, which originated in games theory, is not unique (see Theodore Sturgeon's 1948 novella "There Is No Defence"). But Saberhagen has made it so completely his own that "his murderous mechanisms are the recognized standard in the field." (For the author's own account, see "The Berserker Story" in *Algol,* Summer, 1977.) Indeed, the berserker universe became so popular that Saberhagen "franchised" it to other authors in the collection *Berserker Base.*

A more recent success is his Swords series. Instead of characters, these stories are united by props—12 divinely forged weapons with fabulous powers to harm or even heal. Saberhagen created the material to serve as a computer game module, and, unfortunately, it reads like one despite much ingenuity in plot perils and a laudable realism in the low-tech setting.

The Swords series follows up Saberhagen's excellent science fantasy trilogy *The Empire of the East.* This lively variation on the usual "world where magic works" translates scientific laws into spells and back again, yielding such curiosities as a djinn technologist and valkyrie robots. Unlike commonplace technophobic fantasies, science is the liberating force in *The Empire of the East,* freeing Earth from "the old Dark Mystery" just as rationality cut cruel divinities down to size in the Swords books.

Saberhagen's scientific imagination can see a story in a Foucault pendulum ("Brother Berserker"), a black hole ("The Face of the Deep"), Paleolithic rituals (*The Water of Thought*) or a squash seed ("Pressure"). He also draws inspiration from gaming (Octagon), the arts ("Young Girl at an Open Half-Door"), and history (directly as in "Wings out of Shadow" or with time travel and alternatives, as in *A Century of Progress, Pyramids,* and *After the Fact.*) *The Mask of the Sun* combines history with gaming. His anthologies *Pawn to Infinity* and *A Spadeful of Spacetime* express his enthusiasms for chess and archeology.

Saberhagen has retold myths (*The White Bull,* taken from the Minotaur) and literary classics, including "The Knight's Tale" ("In the Temple of Mars"), *Moby-Dick* (*Berserker: Blue Death*), *Doctor Faustus* ("Some Events in the Templar Radiant"), and *Frankenstein* (*The Frankenstein Papers*). He can turn literary creators into literary characters: Dante Gabriel Rossetti in *The Veils of Azlaroc* and Edgar Allan Poe in *The Black Throne.*

Saberhagen's Dracula pastiches are his best efforts in this area. He presents the Count as exotic rather than monstrous and makes him a force for rough justice. Placing this epitome of Gothic horror in solidly realistic versions of Renaissance Italy, Victorian London, contemporary Chicago, or the American Southwest intensifies the impact.

Saberhagen is especially deft at blending the factual and legendary aspects of a subject and then infusing the result with theological significance. "Stone Place" recreates Don John of Austria, Philip II of Spain, and the Battle of Lepanto in a way G.K. Chesterton himself would have applauded. "Brother Berserker" brings St. Francis of Assisi, Galileo, and the mystical theories of Pierre Teilhard de Chardin together to beautiful effect.

Saberhagen's stated goal is "to impose new coordinates on the human condition," but the functions he plots there are traditional Western Christian ones. (Sandra Miesel's afterwords to *Berserker Man* and *The First Book of Swords* explore the religious and mythic resonances of Saberhagen's work.)

Initially, Saberhagen's style was awkward, but he has learned to make a virtue of plainness, allowing the innate power of the story to carry itself. Plot schematics occasionally hobble his natural flair for narration, as in *Love Conquers All,* which is too polemical to effectively satirize the sexual revolution. Rigid correspondences spoil his Orpheus tale, "Starsong," while arbitrariness and unresolved endings mar the Swords series.

Perhaps Saberhagen's greatest strength is the sheer, unsentimental conviction he brings to his writing. Because he believes, he can make his readers share his belief. His best characterizations are those that ought to have been the most difficult: Brother Jovann, his St. Francis; Johann Karlsen, his Don John; and Draffut the Beast-Lord, a godlike dog. *Berserker Man*'s hero Michel is attractive both as a child and as a hero despite carrying a heavy load of metaphysics and Arthuriana on his young shoulders.

Saberhagen's gift for dramatizing familiar ideas with compelling thoroughness—and fresh angles—has made him a solid presence in the SF field.

—Sandra Miessel

ST. CLAIR, Margaret

Pseudonym: Idris Seabright. **Nationality:** American. **Born:** Margaret Neeley, Hutchinson, Kansas, 17 February 1911. **Education:** University of California, Berkeley, M.A. 1933 (Phi Beta Kappa). **Family:** Married Eric St. Clair in 1932. **Career:** Horticulturist, St. Clair Rare Bulb Gardens, El Sobrante, California, 1938-41. Since 1945, full-time writer. **Agent:** Julie Fallowfield, McIntosh and Otis, 475 Fifth Avenue, New York, New York 10017. **Address:** 43951 Malo Pass Court, Manchester, California 95459, U.S.A.

SCIENCE FICTION PUBLICATIONS

Novels

Agent of the Unknown. New York, Ace, 1956.
The Green Queen. New York, Ace, 1956.
The Games of Neith. New York, Ace, 1960.
Sign of the Labrys. New York, Bantam, and London, Corgi, 1963.
Message from the Eocene. New York, Ace, 1964.
The Dolphins of Altair. New York, Dell, 1967.
The Shadow People. New York, Dell, 1969.
The Dancers of Noyo. New York, Ace, 1973.

Short Stories

Three Worlds of Futurity. New York, Ace, 1964.
Change the Sky and Other Stories. New York, Ace, 1974.
The Best of Margaret St. Clair, edited by Martin H. Greenberg. Chicago, Academy Chicago, 1985.

*

Margaret St. Clair comments:

It would take me days to write adequately about my work. So I shall only say that I think I am better at short fiction than at novels—the short story is more philosophical—and that I like my amusing stories better than the frightening ones, and prefer both classes to what I call "uplift."

I am not a natural writer. Writing is painful and difficult for me.

*   *   *

Margaret St. Clair is an example of a woman writer who did not have to disguise her sex in order to be successful in a male-dominated field. She was able to write in a natural "female voice" at a time when some women writers of SF were outdoing the men in tough-flavored style, and, particularly in her fantasy short stories (generally written as by Idris Seabright), to introduce some sensitive characterization, including portrayals of housewives, single mothers, and young children, into a field which was highly technologically oriented. In common with other writing in the 1950s, St. Clair's fiction was oriented toward adventurous episodes, but she had a penchant for tackling controversial themes and for using gadgetry and environments symbolically.

Most of St. Clair's short fiction was published during the 1950s. Some of her astonishing output of approximately 130 stories may be found in *Three Worlds of Futurity* and *Change the Sky and Other Stories;* both are representative of her work. Other individual stories are found in anthologies: "Short in the Chest" (in Greenberg and Olander's *Science Fiction of the 50's,* 1979), featuring Marine Major Sonya Briggs and a "philosophical robot" psychologist called a "huxley," is remarkable for its portrayal of women and its grappling with questions of sexuality. "New Ritual" (in Boucher's *The Best from Fantasy and Science Fiction,* 1954), also featuring a female protagonist, gives a futuristic twist to the plight of the dissatisfied housewife as a deep freeze turns everything from apricots to an inattentive husband into more desirable items. "Child of Void" (in Conklin's *Invaders of Earth,* 1952) shows a lonely boy grappling with the unknown in the form of a luminous egg which presents children with alluring visions of those things they most desire.

St. Clair's novels, not as consistently well-crafted as her shorter work, are usually adventures and may be relied upon to convey a message. *Agent of the Unknown* is set on the synthetic pleasure planetoid Fyon. An appealing nonconformist with a drinking problem finds purpose in life when he rescues from the edge of the sea a small but awe-inspiring "Weeping Doll," the creation of the master craftsman Vulcan. The protagonist muses, "Sometimes I think everything in our world is synthetic, even happiness." While "Vulcan's Weeping Doll" passively changes in one world, *The Green Queen* and *The Games of Neith,* both feature heroines as active characters who are chosen to inspire or lead their respective societies toward change. Histrionic talents, intelligence, and physical beauty are attributes possessed by the Green Queen, who lives in a postholocaust society ripe for revolution, "a place where ten percent of the population monopolized eighty percent of the dwelling space and fifty percent of the unpolluted food, and where everybody, Uppers and Lowers alike, was always terribly afraid of damage from the omnipresent radioactive elements. . . ." In *The Games of Neith,* Anassa, Priestess to the Goddess of Neith, possesses similar traits, and guides her seafaring society, which is threatening to return to the worship of primitive gods, to a new future. Anassa's relationship with Ehr'li Wan, a physics professor, is an excellent early example of a man and a woman in science fiction working in an equal part against evil forces.

The Shadow People is a striking work. Although the quality of the prose is uneven and the thrust of the narrative is excessively cheerless, an underworld of zombie-like people is memorably portrayed as scuttling through a rat-and-fungus-infested underworld in a hallucinatory, hopeless future. *Sign of the Labrys* portrays another dark underworld, this time inhabited by the survivors of a devastating plague who cower in damp caverns hacked out of rock until the hero, Sam Sewell, brings them awareness of an open, habitable world above ground. *Message from the Eocene* introduces Tharg, an ancient being of alien origin, who desperately attempts to overcome his condition of existing (for century upon century) as a disembodied sentient force so that he may convey a message to mankind. He eventually makes contact with a modern woman whose gift of mental sensitivity to unusual phenomena is sensitively portrayed.

St. Clair's best novel, *The Dolphins of Altair,* is a moving work critical of man's disregard for the ecosystems of Earth. Members of a well-drawn, intelligent dolphin society conspire with a few enlightened humans to preserve the world for an unusual new future. *The Dancers of Noyo,* like *Agent of the Unknown,* relies upon a male protagonist to hold together a tale of the future. A quest for personal identity is set against a world dominated by powerful androids.

St. Clair's best work is tightly written shorter fiction which introduced unusual protagonists to the pages of SF magazines. While some of her longer works suffer from over-ambitious exploration of diverse themes, the best of her novels are those most concerned with an individual's experience with the extraordinary, or a group's commitment to a visionary future.

—Rosemary Herbert

————

ST. JOHN, Philip. *See* **del REY, Lester.**

————

ST. PAUL, Sterner. *See* MEEK, S.P.

———

SALLIS, James

Nationality: American. **Born:** Helena, Arkansas, 21 December 1944. **Education:** Attended Tulane University, New Orleans, 1962-64. **Family:** Married Jane Rose in 1964; one son. **Career:** Worked as a college instructor and publisher's reader; editor, *New Worlds,* London, 1969-70; now a full-time writer. **Address:** c/o Meredith Bernstein, 470 West End Avenue, New York, New York 10023, U.S.A.

SCIENCE FICTION PUBLICATIONS

Short Stories

A Few Last Words. London, Hart-Davis, 1969; New York, Macmillan, 1970.

OTHER PUBLICATIONS

Novels

The Long-Legged Fly: A Novel. New York, Carroll and Graf, 1992.
Moth. New York, Carroll and Graf, 1993.
Black Hornet. New York, Carroll and Graff, 1994.

Other

Down Home: Country-Western. New York, Macmillan, 1971.
The Guitar Players: One Instrument and Its Masters in American Music. New York, Morrow, 1982.
Difficult Lives: Jim Thompson, David Goodis, Chester Himes. Brooklyn, New York, Gryphon, 1993.
Editor, *The War Book.* London, Hart-Davis, 1969; New York, Dell, 1971.
Editor, *The Shores Beneath.* New York, Avon, 1970.
Editor, *Jazz Guitars: An Anthology.* New York, Morrow, 1984.

* * *

James Sallis's extraordinary fiction is distinguished by its honesty and meticulous artistry. With his highly imagistic stories, he has regularly displayed a finely honed mastery of sophisticated literary techniques and sharply etched psychological insights. Often the stories are clearly autobiographical, presenting painful indications of their author's personal difficulties, even his torments. They are not always easy to read, and it is sometimes hard to discern their intent or meaning, but they affect readers powerfully, at least those readers who demand more than thrill-seeking and fantastic adventures from the fiction they read. (It always sounds a bit pompous to score the escapist reader in such terms, but writers like Sallis, who employ quite subtle fictional devices, *do* demand more from their readers. In "My Friend Zarathustra," Sallis writes: "Yes—I mean what I say, and you must listen; must hear what's not said if you're to understand properly what is said.")

Many of his stories are moving portrayals of troubled or dazed individuals who are dissociated from their environments. In nearly every Sallis story the main character is helpless, or at least quite passive. Things are dreadfully confused in his private life or are being disrupted in the outside world. Sometimes nothing much is happening, but even then the character does not cope well. At the rare times when the character is able to act decisively, the action turns out to be futile or grotesque. (The disposal of the child in the brilliantly executed "Jim and Mary G." is a harrowing example of such futility and ugliness.) Usually the character is still helpless at the end of the story. In many stories, the protagonists are last seen merely waiting or going off into darkness or standing still as the world begins to disintegrate, literally or physically, around them. However Sallis dramatizes it, the main impression the reader receives from most of the stories is of humankind trapped in environments upon which they can have no effect, and for which they no longer have any effective responses or reactions. In "Faces, Hands: The Kettle of Stars" a courier is halted from his message-carrying mission and stranded in an intergalactic waiting room, where he contemplates art in the form of an also-waiting alien singer whose destiny is repulsive servitude on another planet, an injustice the courier perceives but cannot affect. The protagonist of "The History Makers" occupies himself with letters or music or sitting at a window while whole time-accelerated civilizations grow, decline, and fall nearby. The only movement he makes is to move away from a city's encroaching border. Nevertheless, he is able to speculate on the exigencies of time, as manifested in the slow progress of a beetle across sand or in a review of his own life or in the odd inverted timescale of the cities. In "A Few Last Words" a man attempts to decide what to do as a doomed city more or less empties before his eyes.

In such stories the sense of dissociation is pronounced both in the relationship of character to setting and in the character's own "inner space," the phrase emphasized by interpreters of the new wave of science fiction as its primary subject matter. Sallis's characters, even at their most articulate, are often in danger of breaking up themselves in just about the same way the setting is crumbling around them. In one of his most effective and painful stories, "Binaries," the narrator-writer (who perceives his immediate environment as being regularly broken up and moved away) is in a state of dissociation with himself as a person and as a writer:

> Someone has written a collection of short stories and published them under my name; they have even put my photograph on the back cover. I received a copy in the morning post. Anonymous, no return address, postmarked Grnd Cntrl Stn. The stories reveal my deepest secrets. Only one person could have written them. Or had reason to. My attorney is investigating the possibility of a lawsuit against the publisher but, as the work was copyrighted in my own name, there seems little we can do. The publisher expressed to my attorney his desire to meet the author, his admiration for the book.

The passage's poignancy, its precise delineation of the character's troubled emotions, and—incidentally—its wrenching irony, are all hallmarks of the fiction of James Sallis.

Sallis also has an appealing knack for humorous, especially surrealistic, writing, which he uses in stories like "Kazoo," "The Creation of Bennie Good," and "Miranda-Escobedo." It is worth noting, however, that, even in these works, with their clever improvisations, sly allusions, and superb wordplay, the sense of psychological and emotional dissociation generally remains, as dazed or momentarily baffled characters and even ghost-cops are disoriented by their absurd environments.

Sallis started publishing science fiction in the 1960s, a time when the field was being rattled by a number of literary experimenters who came to be dubbed, for better or for worse, the "new wave" of science fiction. He served some time as an editor of the British magazine *New Worlds,* the SF publication that became most associated with the new wave because it dared to publish the works of adventuresome writers during a period when many other SF markets were resisting anything that did not correspond with accepted approaches to the genre. Now that the new furore has somewhat subsided, upheld in print only by a few still petulant writers, it is clear that the contributions of the new wavers are legitimate literary extensions of established science fiction traditions, and that Sallis's stories are among the best writings to emerge from the phenomenon. In recent years James Sallis, never prolific, has published few stories, but the ones that have been published exhibit the same care for literary details and intellectual concerns as the earlier stories. One recent story, "Changes," ranks with the best of his fiction.

—Robert Thurston

SALMONSON, Jessica Amanda

Nationality: American. **Born:** Seattle, Washington, 6 January 1950. **Career:** Editor for *Windhaven* magazine, 1977-79, and *Fantasy and Terror,* since 1973. **Recipient:** World Fantasy award, for anthology, 1980; Lambda award, for anthology, 1990. **Agent:** Susan Lee Cohen, Riverside Agency, 2673 Broadway, Number 132, New York, New York 10025, U.S.A. **Address:** P.O. Box 20610, Seattle, Washington 98102, U.S.A.

SCIENCE FICTION PUBLICATIONS

Novels (series: Tomoe Gozen)

Tragedy of the Moisty Morning (chapbook). Seattle, Angst World Library, 1978.
Tomoe Gozen. New York, Ace, 1981.
The Golden Naginata (Tomoe Gozen). New York, Ace, 1982.
The Swordswoman. New York, Tor, 1982.
Thousand Shrine Warrior (Tomoe Gozen). New York, Ace, 1984.
Ou Lu Khen and the Beautiful Madwoman. New York, Ace, 1985.
Anthony Shriek; or, Lovers from a Darker Realm. New York, Dell, Abyss, 1992.

Short Stories

Hag's Tapestry. Runcorn, Cheshire, Haunted Library, 1984.
A Silver Thread of Madness. New York, Ace, 1989.
John Collier and Fredric Brown Went Quarrelling through My Head: Stories. Buffalo, New York, Ganley, 1989.
Harmless Ghosts. Hoole, Cheshire, Haunted Library, 1990.

The Mysterious Doom, and Other Ghostly Tales of the Pacific Northwest, illustrated by Jules Remedios Faye. Seattle, Sasquatch Books, 1992.

OTHER PUBLICATIONS

Poetry

The Ghost Garden, illustrated by Jules Remedios Faye. London, Dark Dreams, 1988.
Sorcerios and Sorrows: (Early Poems/Bibliography). Iowa City, Iowa, Drumm, 1992.
The Goddess under Siege. Seattle, Street of Crocodiles, 1992.

Other

The Encyclopedia of Amazons: Women Warriors from Antiquity to the Modern Era. New York, Paragon House, 1991.
Wisewomen and Boggy-Boos: A Dictionary of Lesbian Fairy Lore, illustrated by Jules Remedios Faye. Austin, Banned Books, 1992.
Phantom Waters: Northwest Legends of Rivers, Lakes, and Shores. Seattle, Sasquatch Books, 1995.

Editor, *Amazons!* New York, DAW, 1979.
Editor, *Amazons II!* New York, DAW, 1982.
Editor, *Heroic Visions.* New York, Ace, 1983.
Editor, *Tales by Moonlight.* Chicago, Garcia, 1983.
Editor, *The Haunted Wherry and Other Rare Ghost Stories.* Madison, Wisconsin, Strange Company, 1985.
Editor, *Faded Garden: The Collected Ghost Stories of Hildegarde Hawthorne.* Madison, Wisconsin, Strange Company, 1985.
Editor, *Heroic Visions II.* New York, Ace, 1986.
Editor, *The Supernatural Tales of Fitz-James O'Brien: Volume I, Macabre Tales [Volume II, Dream Stories and Fantasies].* New York, Doubleday, 2 vols., 1988.
Editor, *Tales by Moonlight II.* New York, Tor, 1989.
Editor, *What Did Miss Darrington See? An Anthology of Feminist Supernatural Fiction.* New York, Feminist Press, 1989.
Editor, with Isabelle D. Waugh and Charles G. Waugh, *Wife or Spinster: Stories by Nineteenth-Century Women.* Camden, Maine, Yankee Books, 1991.
Editor, *Mystic Women: Their Ancient Tales and Legends: Recounted by a Woman Inmate of the Calcutta Insane Asylum.* Seattle, Street of Crocodiles, 1991.

*

Manuscript Collection: University of Oregon, Eugene.

Jessica Amanda Salmonson comments:

I am drawn to fantastic and supernatural fiction as an art. I have faith in fantastic fiction because there are or have been such writers as Bruno Shulz, Kafka, Poe, Gogol, Garcia Marquez, and Baudelaire who have made the fantastic and the macabre sing with purpose and beauty. In the self-consciously trashy world of mass-market F/SF paperbacks, my presumptions about what fantasy can be and should be causes a significant number of my fellow professionals (I rarely consider them peers) to scoff. This tends to be a field where even the authors are narrowly read, are put off by fine writing, are proud to write without elegance to immature tastes, and very often do not even know who a Shulz or a Gogol ever were. I remember a writers conference at which I was stunned to discover I was the only fantasist who had read Tasso and Spenser or even William Morris. These were people illiterate in their own field, let alone outside their field, and their heroes were for the most part pulpsters who didn't even transcend pulp. They were people who thought Poe and Baudelaire starved because they couldn't cut it in the professional world, whereas L. Ron Hubbard was a genius, measured, of course, in dollar signs.

Of late, I've found myself sauntering away from the genre publishing arena, because it is so discouraging to see one's soul issued in a biodegradable format and marketed amidst innumerable short-term "monthly releases" which consist of some of the worst and most predictable writers outside of the romance field. My feeling is that either I'm not just another crappy fantasy writer, and therefore oughtn't be marketed amidst this great swamp of mediocrity and inferiority; or I am indeed no better than the rest, deserve no better company, and therefore shouldn't be writing these books at all, since there is presently no shortage of other people far happier to be writing to low industry standards.

I have no sense that publishers reward authors for striving for artistry, intelligence, and elegance. A snappy, easy read is the word of the day. Something that is easily "packaged." That categorizes well. Were I willing to write an endless series with a rubbishy formula, I'd be signed to a five-book contract at once. But serious books are sold cheaply one by one to whiny editors afraid they'll lose their jobs if they lose money on even one book that's too original. I can't reduce myself to the task required. So I've not finished a new novel in a few years, because it gives me the creeps every time I think of how it would invariably be marketed, and I recall the horrid company my books have had to share. I do continue to write short stories (my real love) for it is an area less fully commercialized in the worst sense, although the "shared world" anthologies have certainly made huge inroads in trashing up short story art.

My most recent book-length work to appear (and other works in progress) is nonfiction, though on very unusual topics: mysticism and mythology. It almost qualifies as the Fantastic, and one work-in-progress, *Everyday Life in Amazonia,* draws as much upon the world-building techniques of science fiction as it does from logical extension of the mythological record. It was so heartwarming to have my most recent title appear in a lovely hardcover and trade paperback from quality publishers, and find myself in a catalogue alongside translations of South American poets and studies of Kafka or Djuna Barnes. That felt so much more rewarding and inspiring than to find one's heartfelt and quirky fantasy novels peddled alongside quickly written, all-alike books aimed at supermarket racks rather than bookstores. I am not inherently an elitist, but do feel out of place and disappointed when surrounded by people whose measures of success are not predicated upon any critical faculty or artistic intent and ability.

I do have other fantasy novels in progress, but tinker with them seldomly. Unlike Robert Silverberg, I never made any elaborate statement of "leaving" the genre only to come mincing back, as I knew I loved fantastic literature too much to really stop writing it forever. But stage by stage, I dropped my membership with professional organizations for which I felt no real kinship, allowed my subscriptions to purportedly "essential" professional journals lapse, and stopped attending conferences. I quietly withdrew into intense research on peculiar nonfiction topics, and if anyone has missed me, I was too holed up to notice.

I probably won't return to the genre with full force until and unless I discover a publisher whose taste in books I could generally and honestly admire and whose authors I would feel pride to stand among. If that proves too utopian a requirement in a dreary and archly commercial area of publishing, then my next few books will probably continue to be nonfiction and/or non-genre. I continue to feel fantasy is potentially among the highest artforms when approached as art, but the current market requirements do not allow for such work to be rewarded. And at present it just does not feel like a success to have a publisher buy a book of mine because they consider it suited to a line of perfectly dreadful books.

*   *   *

Jessica Amanda Salmonson is best known as one of the most enthusiastic proponents of Amazonian fantasy, a subgenre of sword-and-sorcery fiction involving strong and independent female warriors that has been nurtured and inspired by sometimes radical feminist politics. She has played a major role as author, editor, critic, and political theorist in helping the fantasy genre develop.

Salmonson became active in science fiction fandom in the 1970s, editing small fiction magazines with titles like *Windhaven: A Matriarchal Magazine* and *Fantasy and Terror,* which specialized in publishing amateur fantasy fiction of various types. Some of the fiction published in those magazines was of reasonably high quality, but it was unable to find paying markets. A growing market for fantasy novels had already begun, with markets having been created for high fantasy by the popularization of Tolkien, for heroic fantasy by the rediscovery of Robert E. Howard, and (to a much lesser degree) for dark fantasy in the Lovecraft tradition—a popular market for supernatural horror had to wait for Stephen King—but very few markets for short fantasy fiction existed. Of the dozens of amateur magazines dedicated to fantasy fiction, many specialized in specific types and styles and subgenres, and a few specialized in female-warrior heroic fantasy.

Salmonson's own fiction began appearing in these small-press magazines in 1973, beginning with "Full Moon Tonight" (in *Moonbroth* 13) and "Youngin" (in *Fantasy & Terror* 1). Other early fantasy stories appeared in such well-known small magazines of the time as *Wyrd, Space and Time, Janus,* and *The Diversifier.* She has continued to write numerous short stories, only a few of which have appeared in book form from major publishers. Some of her best short fiction can be found in the collections *A Silver Thread of Madness* (1989) and *John Collier and Frederic Brown Went Quarreling Through My Head* (1989). Her stories have a distinctively haunting feel, subtly integrating the fantastic and the bizarre. She also has written and published a large body of poetry since 1972, mostly appearing in the same small press fantasy and horror magazines as her short fiction, and many of which have been reprinted in small-press chapbooks.

In 1979, Salmonson stepped into the ranks of the professionals with her *Amazons!,* an original anthology featuring 13 stories with sword-wielding heroines, along with an introduction by Salmonson about actual women warriors throughout history and a recommended reading list by Susan Wood. The volume contains early stories from writers who would become prominent in the coming decade, including C.J. Cherryh, Megan Lindholm, Tanith Lee, and Elizabeth Lynn. These four, plus Charles R. Saunders, the only male author in the book, contribute the strongest stories. The other authors include Janrae Frank, T.J. Morgan, Janet Fox, Josephine Saxon, Margaret St. Clair, and Michelle Belling, most of whom Salmonson knew through fandom. There is also a story by Andre Norton that was probably included mostly in homage of her pioneering efforts in popularizing strong female fantasy protagonists, and a story by Emily Brontë, edited by Joanna Russ. It is unfortunate indeed that Russ was unable to contribute a story herself to this seminal volume, since her tales of Alyx, including *Picnic on Paradise* in 1968, are among the strongest genre antecedents to Amazonian fantasy. (Among the strongest pulp-SF influences is C.L. Moore's *Jirel of Joiry*.)

Amazons! was not the first feminist-theme science fiction or fantasy anthology. It was immediately preceded by Pamela Sargent's three highly acclaimed *Women of Wonder* anthologies, as well as by Virginia Kidd's equally lauded *Millennial Women* and Alice Laurance's *Cassandra Rising*. But the high quality of the fiction, Salmonson's strong editorial presence in the volume, and the timeliness of the theme, led to *Amazons!* winning the World Fantasy award. A new fantasy subgenre was officially recognized, and Salmonson was acknowledged as one of its principle promoters.

A second volume in the series, *Amazons II!*, appeared in 1982. It also features a number of authors of significant talent, including Tanith Lee (the only repeat), Phyllis Ann Karr, Lillian Stewart Carl, Ardath Mayhar, Lee Killough, and Jo Clayton, along with several male authors such as F.M. Busby and George R. R. Martin. But none of the stories seems to match the best of the first volume. And instead of a manifesto or feminist tract, something that could have created some new level of controversy for added interest, Salmonson's introduction once again reviewed a litany of historical fighting women. (Salmonson's interest in actual Amazons in world history culminated later in a comprehensive nonfiction volume, *The Encyclopedia of Amazons: Women Warriors from Antiquity to the Present Era*, 1991.) *Amazons II!* received little critical or popular attention, and no more volumes in the series ever appeared.

But neither Amazonian fiction nor Jessica Salmonson were finished. Before *Amazons II!* appeared, Salmonson's first novel, *Tomoe Gozen*, was published as the first in a saga that would include two more novels, *The Golden Naginata* and *Thousand Shrine Warrior*. All three books are set in an alternate-world Japan where the myths of our Japan are reality, and tell the adventures of a female Samurai, Tomoe Gozen. The latter volumes in the series drift away from violent action and supernatural menaces toward more concern with character and philosophy. Salmonson's lucid prose and imaginative setting, her characters and themes, led the series to be well regarded as a unique and interesting heroic fantasy.

The trend toward less violence and more characterization continued in Salmonson's only other novel to return to Oriental legendry, *Ou Lu Khen and the Beautiful Madwoman*. In this novel, Salmonson tells the story of a young Chinese man who has fallen in love with a madwoman, and charts his quest to find a solution to her condition so they can marry.

Salmonson also had another early sword-and-sorcery novel published. *The Swordswoman* once again involves an alternate world where swords and sorcery prevail, but this time the setting is a more traditional European fantasy world. The characters are of our world and find themselves able to travel to Endsworld through the use of a magic crystal. It is a well-written but unoriginal novel.

Salmonson also published two other anthology series of two volumes each. *Heroic Visions* and *Heroic Visions II* cover the broader subgenre of sword-and-sorcery fantasy, and are two of the best collections of that type of short fiction. The first volume includes two near-masterpieces, Fritz Leiber's "The Curse of the Smalls and the Stars" and Michael Bishop's "The Monkey's Bride," as well as

good stories by Jane Yolen, Robert Silverberg, Joanna Russ, and others. The second volume includes fine tales by Keith Roberts, Bishop, Ellen Kushner, and Avram Davidson, as well as one of Salmonson's own stories, "The Lingering Minstrel." The other series of anthologies edited by Salmonson, *Tales by Moonlight* and *Tales by Moonlight II*, feature original horror short stories.

Two of Salmonson's best books have appeared in the 1990s. *The Mysterious Doom and Other Ghostly Tales of the Pacific Northwest* (1992) is a collection of modernized retellings of more than a dozen legends regarding supernatural creatures or events. *Anthony Shriek* is a contemporary psychological horror novel that inexplicably received very little critical notice, despite its publication in the prestigious Dell Abyss line, and being arguably Salmonson's best work yet published. The novel tells an eerie and moving tale of a down-and-out would-be artist whose paintings lead him into a realm of hallucination and insanity.

Salmonson's other projects have included collecting the forgotten fantasy fiction of notable female authors in *The Faded Garden: The Collected Ghost Stories of Hildegarde Hawthorne and What Did Miss Darrington See? An Anthology of Feminist Supernatural Fiction, Wife or Spinster: Short Stories by 19th Century American Women* (edited with Charles Waugh), and *From out of the Past, The Indiana Ghost Stories of Anna Nichols*. She has also written essays on fantasy fiction for many of the semi-professional SF critical journals, including *THRUST/QUANTUM, Fantasy Review, The Bulletin of the Science Fiction Writers of America*, and *The New York Review of Science Fiction*, as well as numerous amateur SF and feminist magazines.

—D. Douglas Fratz

SARBAN

Pseudonym for John W. Wall. **Nationality:** British. **Born:** 1910. **Career:** Diplomat, 1933-66. **Died:** 11 April 1989.

SCIENCE FICTION PUBLICATIONS

Novel

The Sound of His Horn. London, Davies, 1952; New York, Ballantine, 1960.
The Doll Maker. New York, Ballantine, 1960.
Ringstones. New York, Ballantine, 1961.

Short Stories

Ringstones and Other Curious Tales. London, Davies, and New York, CowardMcCann, 1951.
The Doll Maker and Other Tales of the Uncanny. London, Davies, 1953.

*   *   *

The only true science fiction novel to appear under the Sarban byline was *The Sound of His Horn*, a novel that evokes a mood of gloom and horror as well as anything that has ever been written.

Kingsley Amis pointed out that it is one of the few novels ever to suggest a rural rather than urban dystopia, a future after Germany has won World War II and the other races of the world are viewed as little better than lower animals. Alan Querdilion wanders into an electrified fence while escaping from a German POW camp and finds himself somehow projected into a world where the Germans have already been victorious. After a brief period where he is the guest of a German landholder, he is set loose as prey for his host's periodic hunts.

Two other short novels appeared, both of which have been published as horror novels though the subject matter is such that they could as well be considered fantasies. In *The Doll Maker,* a young girl is compelled to become a tutor at mysterious Brackenbine Hall, and soon falls under the influence of Niall Sterne, a peculiar, reclusive man who roams the forests and exists only, it seems, for his collection of extremely lifelike dolls. In due course, the heroine learns of Sterne's connection with several past deaths, and comes to believe that he can transfer human souls into the dolls he creates. *The Doll Maker* also brilliantly creates a mood of despair and awakening horror. Sarban's skill at drawing the reader into his book is probably at its best, however, in *Ringstones.* A young woman is employed to tutor two young children at a remote estate, but soon becomes enmeshed in magic and the struggle to maintain her own personality and view of reality when faced with a form of existence that she had formerly considered only a dream. *Ringstones* is a haunting novel that is far more worthwhile than the hundreds of modern gothics which it in many ways resembles.

Sarban also created several excellent shorter pieces, although they are extremely hard to locate. The most noteworthy of these are probably "Calmahain" and "Capra." In the former, two young children allow their fantasy world to become so real that it overflows into the real world and adults begin to experience elements of the fantasy. In the latter, a vicious lover's triangle at a costume party has unexpected results when the real god Pan makes an entry.

The most striking element in the small body of fiction Sarban produced before his death is obviously the evocation of a weird atmosphere, the quiet construction of a world where things aren't as safe and logical as its characters would like to believe. The quality of the prose is also of note. Although couched in a very formal style, Sarban's words flow easily, drawing the reader along. There is never any hint that this was an amateur writing as a hobby; the competent hand of the professional is obvious. With only three slim volumes to his name, Sarban will remain a unique and significant writer.

—Don D'Ammassa

SARGENT, Pamela

Nationality: American. **Born:** Ithaca, New York, 20 March 1948. **Education:** State University of New York, Binghamton, B.A. in philosophy 1968, M.A. 1970. **Career:** Model and sales clerk, 1965-66; factory worker, Endicott Coil Company, 1966; sales clerk, Towne Distributors, 1966; typist, Harpur College, Binghamton, New York, 1966-67; office worker, Webster Paper Company, Albany, New York, 1969; teaching assistant in philosophy, State University of New York, Binghamton, 1969-71. Since 1971, freelance writer and editor. **Awards:** Nebula award, for best novelette, 1992; *Locus* award, for best novelette, 1993; Electric Science Fiction award, for best novelette, 1993. **Agent:** Richard Curtis Associates, Inc., 171 East 74th St., New York, NY 10021. **Address:** Box 486, Johnson City, New York 13790, U.S.A.

SCIENCE FICTION PUBLICATIONS

Novels (series: Earthminds; Venus)

Cloned Lives. Greenwich, Connecticut, Fawcett, 1976; London, Fontana, 1981.
The Sudden Star. New York, Fawcett, 1979; as *The White Death,* London, Fontana, 1980.
Watchstar (Earthminds). New York, Pocket Books, 1980.
The Golden Space. New York, Timescape, 1982.
The Alien Upstairs. Garden City, New York, Doubleday, 1983.
Earthseed: A Novel (for children). New York, Harper, 1983; London, Collins, 1984.
Eye of the Comet (for children; Watchstar). New York, Harper, 1984.
Homesmind (for children; Watchstar). New York, Harper, 1984.
Venus of Dreams. New York, Bantam, 1986; London, Bantam, 1989.
The Shore of Women. New York, Crown, 1986; London, Chatto and Windus, 1987.
The Alien Child (for children). New York, Harper, 1988.
Venus of Shadows. New York, Doubleday, 1988.
A Fury Scorned, with George Zebrowski. New York, Pocket Books, 1996.
The Watchstar Trilogy (includes *Watchstar, Eye of the Comet,* and *Homesmind*). Clarkston, Georgia, White Wolf, 1996.

Short Stories

Starshadows: Ten Stories. New York, Ace, 1977.
Elvira's Zoo (for children). Tulsa, Oklahoma, Educational Development Corp., 1979.
The Mountain Cage. New Castle, Virginia, Cheap Street, 1983.
The Best of Pamela Sargent, edited by Martin H. Greenberg. Chicago, Academy Chicago, 1987.

OTHER PUBLICATIONS

Novels

Ruler of the Sky: A Novel of Genghis Khan. New York, Crown, and London, Chatto and Windus, 1993.

Other

Ruler of the Sky. New York, Crown, 1993; London, Chatto and Windus, 1993.

Editor, *Women of Wonder: Science Fiction Stories by Women about Women.* New York, Vintage, 1975; London, Penguin, 1978.
Editor, *More Women of Wonder: Science Fiction Novelettes by Women about Women.* New York, Vintage, 1976; London, Penguin, 1979.
Editor, *Bio-Futures: Science Fiction Stories about Biological Metamorphosis.* New York, Vintage, 1976.
Editor, *The New Women of Wonder: Recent Science Fiction Stories by Women about Women.* New York, Vintage, 1978.

Editor, with Ian Watson, *Afterlives: Stories about Life after Death.* New York, Vintage, 1986.

Editor, *Nebula Awards 29: SWFA's Choices for the Best Science Fiction and Fantasy of the Year.* New York and San Diego, Harcourt Brace, 1995.

Women of Wonder: The Classic Years: Science Fiction by Women from the 1940s to 1970s. San Diego, Harcourt Brace, 1995.

Women of Wonder: The Contemporary Years: Science Fiction by Women from the 1970s to 1990s. San Diego, Harcourt Brace, 1995.

"The Other Perceiver," a radio adaptation of "The Other Perceiver" (*Universe 2,* edited by Terry Carr, Ace, 1972); broadcast in Germany on Sender Fries Berlin, 1975.

"The Shrine," television adaptation of "The Shrine" (in *Twilight Zone Magazine,* December 1982) on *Tales from the Darkside.* Teleplay by Jule Selbo, based on story by Pamela Sargent. First broadcast on February 15, 1986.

*

Bibliography: *The Work of Pamela Sargent* by Jeffrey M. Elliot, San Bernardino, California, Borgo Press, 1990.

Manuscript Collection: David Paskow Science Fiction Collection, Temple University, Philadelphia.

*   *   *

Pamela Sargent had had two SF stories accepted for publication by the time she graduated from college in 1969, but it was not until 1974 that she decided that writing was to be her career. Since then, she has written 13 novels and dozens of stories, edited groundbreaking anthologies, and commented with sagacity on her craft and on the SF and historical fiction genres. Her fictions are both the stories of the inner lives of people caught in unusual circumstances and of our species as it might have been, is, and might yet be. She is a feminist and futurist for whom biotechnology, cybernetics, space travel, alien visitations, environmental degradation, and nuclear war provide new scenarios in which believable characters act out their life dramas. Most of her work, whether for young adults or adults, is SF, but she has written short historical fiction and the panoramic *Ruler of the Sky: A Novel of Genghis Khan.*

Novels for Young Adults: The central figure in all five books is a 15-year-old girl who is coming of age in a world very different from ours. Although simpler in language and form than the novels for adults, these books offer penetrating psychological portraits of gifted and courageous young women. The heroines of the *Watchstar* trilogy [*Watchstar* (1980), *Eye of the Comet* (1984), and *Homesmind* (1984)] live on a far-future Earth inhabited by technologically primitive villagers who possess telepathic and telekinetic powers. Daiya, Lydee, and Anra question the conservative world view of their culture and seek to discover the secrets of their world and of the Comet Dwellers, the descendants of humans who long ago left earth. The fate of the planet is in the hands of these young visionaries. *Earthseed* (1983), which is reminiscent of Panshin's *Rite of Passage* and a host of other spaceship-as-world novels, depicts the trials of a cohort of space-born teenagers nurtured and raised by an intelligent spacecraft they call "Ship." Before they can settle on an alien world, they must learn outdoor survival skills, including orienteering and conflict resolution.

Earthseed was selected as a 1983 Best Book for Young Adults by the American Library Association. *Alien Child* (1988), is the story of a girl raised on post-nuclear holocaust earth by a furry extraterrestrial who has come to study a race that committed global suicide. These novels display a refreshing faith in the energy, flexibility, and hopefulness of young people. (For a more detailed discussion, see my article "Pamela Sargent's Science Fiction for Young Adults: Celebrations of Change," *Science-Fiction Studies* 16 (July 1989).

SF Novels for Adults: Sargent's protagonists face technologically and politically complicated worlds that are clear and often frightening analogs or our own. Perhaps the most overtly hopeful is her first one, *Cloned Lives* (1976). An outgrowth of three short stories—"Clone Sister," "A Sense of Difference," and "Father"—this imaginative book explores the social and psychological traumas faced by the world's first five clones. Although each clone has a chapter, the central figure is Kyra, the lone female. Although raised as siblings, the clones have a kinship status new to humanity. Kyra functions alternately as the males' mother, sister, and lover. When she perfects techniques that make immortality a possibility, she assumes a life-giving role that Eve would envy. The impact of biological engineering on the lifespan is also the subject of *The Golden Space* (1982). Here, immortality is a mixed blessing, and the fear of life sometimes overshadows the fear of death.

The Sudden Star (1979) and *The Alien Upstairs* (1983) are set in dismal not-so-distant alternative presents made possible by environmental irresponsibility. In *Sudden Star* crop failures, plagues, and institutional collapse make life almost unbearable in what used to be the United States. Americans attribute the fall of their civilization to the appearance of a bright star in A.D. 2000, "forgetting," as one character puts it, "that the heavens are vast and the stars unknowing of earth." Sameness and deprivation also pervade *The Alien Upstairs,* but in this novel the protagonist's life is given a little spice by the arrival of a mysterious neighbor she believes to be an alien. He turns out to be the immortal human servant of unknown aliens; Sarah's adventures with him put human history in a cosmic perspective for both her and the reader.

Without question, Sargent's masterpiece is *The Shore of Women* (1986). This feminist dystopian postnuclear-holocaust tale depicts an earth ruled by women who live in fortified enclaves and who have banished men to the forests. The book's scenario and tone are similar to those of Sheri Tepper's *The Gate to Women's Country,* which appeared in 1988. In Sargent's novel, homosexuality is the norm for both men and women, and procreation is accomplished through artificial insemination (the sperm is collected from electronically deluded males who believe they are having sex with women). The principal characters, Birana and Arvil, recreate (at least for a time) heterosexual love during a series of life threatening adventures. The novel celebrates same sex and opposite sex relationships; any genuine expression of love is a bright spot in a world in which the women-made institutions are as corrupt as the man-made institutions they have replaced. The novel's multiple narrative perspectives, lyrical eroticism, and intellectual depth make it a classic of intelligent SF.

The first two volumes of what will one day be Sargent's Venus trilogy, *Venus of Dreams* (1986) and *Venus of Shadows* (1988), are the beginning and middle of a transgenerational saga of life on terraformed Venus. The working title of the series finale is *Child of Venus.* It is not surprising that given Sargent's preoccupation with individuals (especially women) struggling against brittle and damaging social structures, that the colonists of Venus discover that to earth's nominally Muslim rulers terraformation means not only making Venus environmentally earth like, but politically and socially earth like as well. Descendants of a women's commune in the Midwest, the protagonists must deal with the limitations of life as females in a colony ruled from afar by ruthless patriarchs. Sargent's next SF book, *A Fury Scorned,* is a Star Trek: The Next Generation novel coauthored with George Zebrowski; Pocket Books will publish it in 1996.

Sargent's most recent novel, *Ruler of the Sky* (1993), is not SF but historical fiction; however, its themes are familiar ones to her readers, and her cogent explanation of the similarities between SF and speculative historical fiction in articles in *Para·doxa* and *The SFWA Bulletin* suggests that her career-long project of elucidating and commenting on the uncertain status of our world in a time of unprecedented change is still in the forefront of her thinking. Based on historical documents, the novel examines the life of Temujin, Genghis Khan, through the eyes of the women closest to him, among them his mother and wives. Temujin's unimaginable conquests changed the life of the Mongols as much as technology is changing ours, and the Mongols who swept across Asia and Eastern Europe were as alien to their victims as the marauding extraterrestrials of pulp SF.

A collection of short stories, *The Best of Pamela Sargent* edited by Martin H. Greenberg, appeared in 1987. Since then Sargent has written a number of memorable pieces, including the novelette "Danny Goes to Mars"—a tale of former Vice President Quayle's adventures on the red planet—which won a Nebula Award in 1992 and was a Hugo finalist. She has written a number of stories about tribal peoples, both Mongol and Native American, among them "The Broken Hoop," "The Sleeping Serpent," "Big Roots," "Climbing the Wind," and "Erdeni's Tiger." These tales reflect her interest in humans facing cultural discontinuity, and in some cases they are a tribute to her Iroquois ancestry (as a child she lived for a time in the Adirondacks with her Mohawk grandmother).

Sargent has also distinguished herself as an editor and critic. During the 1970s she edited *Bio-Futures* and coedited *Afterlives.* More important are the three *Women of Wonder* anthologies, the first collections featuring women SF writers writing about women. In 1995 Harcourt Brace published two new anthologies, *Women of Wonder: The Classic Years: Science Fiction by Women from the 1940s to the 1970s* and *Women of Wonder: The Contemporary Years: Science Fiction by Women from the 1970s to the 1990s.* Both volumes feature incisive introductions. In 1995 Sargent began a three-year term as editor of the annual *Nebula Award Stories.* She has also published a number of critical essays on SF and historical fiction and serves on the editorial board of *Para·doxa* and as a consulting editor for *Science-Fiction Studies.* She holds a B.A. and M.A. in philosophy from the State University of New York at Binghamton.

—Thomas J. Morrissey

SAWTRELLE, William Carter. *See* **PHILLIPS, Rog.**

SAWYER, Robert J(ames)

Nationality: Canadian. **Born:** Ottawa, Ontario, 29 April 1960. **Education:** Ryerson Polytechnic University, Toronto, B.A. in Radio and Television Arts, 1979-82. **Family:** Married Carolyn Joan Clink in 1984. **Career:** Clerk, Bakka Science Fiction Bookstore, Toronto, 1982; instructor/demonstrator, Television Production, Ryerson Polytechnic University, Toronto, 1982-83. Since 1983, full-time freelance writer. **Awards:** Homer award, 1992, 1993; Arthur Ellis award, 1993; Aurora award, 1992, 1993. **Member:** Board of Directors, Science Fiction and Fantasy Writers of America, 1992-95. **Agent:** Richard Curtis, Richard Curtis Associates, 171 East 74th Street, New York, New York 10021. **Address:** 7601 Bathurst Street, Apt. 617, Thornhill, Ontario, Canada L4J 4H5.

SCIENCE FICTION PUBLICATIONS

Novels (series: Dinosaur Trilogy)

Golden Fleece. New York, Popular Library, 1990.
Far-Seer (Dinosaur). New York, Ace, 1992; London, New English Library, 1995.
Fossil Hunter (Dinosaur). New York, Ace, 1993; London; New English Library, 1995.
Foreigner (Dinosaur). New York, Ace, 1994.
End of an Era. New York, Ace, and London, New English Library, 1994.
The Terminal Experiment. New York, HarperPrism, and London, New English Library, 1995.

OTHER PUBLICATIONS

Other

Locksmith: The Making of the Key to North York, with S. Hussain Azmi. Willowdale, Ontario, LINK Community Information and Referral Service, 1983.
Editor, *All Agog: The Gateway Fiction Special.* Toronto, Ontario Science Fiction Club, 1982.

*

Robert Sawyer comments:

I am English-Canada's only native-born full-time SF writer, and I take that very seriously: although Canadian fantasy writers have often set work in Canada, very little SF has had identifiable Canadian content. I've undertaken to rectify that: my novels *The Terminal Experiment* and *End of an Era* take place entirely in Canada (and the latter's time-travel mission is a decidedly Canadian low-tech, low-budget affair), and the lead human characters of *Golden Fleece* and *Starplex* (to be published by Ace Books in 1996) are Canadians. To my delight, American editors and readers have embraced this warmly; to my chagrin, Canadians continue to remark, "You know, Americans aren't going to understand those references. . . ."

My work often crosses the boundaries between science fiction and mystery, and has been hailed by readers in both genres. For instance, my short story "Just Like Old Times," about a serial killer sentenced to die in the prehistoric past, won both the Aurora, Canada's national SF-writing award, and the Arthur Ellis, its national mystery-writing award. Some people have reacted with surprise to my mixing of the genres, but to me SF and mystery, which both prize rational thought and tell stories that hinge on the way things really work, are much more closely allied than the traditional pairing of SF and fantasy.

Golden Fleece and *The Terminal Experiment* are equal mixtures of SF and murder mystery, and *Fossil Hunter* has a prominent murder-mystery subplot. Even so, I'm not particularly interested in writing about murder—except as a way of illuminating morality (a topic that endlessly fascinates me). But I am very intrigued by the rational intellectual process (and why people sometimes shy away from it), so, besides its overt murder plot, *Golden Fleece* also involves deciphering an alien radio message; *Far-Seer* deals with an astronomical mystery; *Fossil Hunter* with a geological conundrum; and *Foreigner* treats psychoanalysis as an exercise in detective work.

Reviewers often remark on the old-fashioned sense of wonder in my work, and they also often praise my characterization. Writers traditionally excel at one or the other; if I've got any special strength as a writer, I'd like to think that it's the ability to combine the transcendent and the very human. Indeed, although many SF writers (especially those whose work is labeled "hard SF," as mine usually is) give short shrift to characterization, I think SF's most important role is not technological prediction, nor sounding warning bells about dangerous trends, but rather to allow us to examine what it means to be human by using a suite of literary tools unavailable to writers in other genres.

One of the most powerful of those tools is the ability to look at the human race from outside. That's why *Golden Fleece* is told from the point of view of a computer; *The Terminal Experiment* has dialogs with three computer simulations of modified human minds; and the Quintaglio Ascension trilogy has no humans in it at all—but, of course, is intended to be read as a parable about humanity.

Some SF writers will spend days working out a problem in celestial mechanics to the 30th decimal point—as if that were important and meaningful—but then populate their stories with characters who behave as no real person ever would. Anyone can use a calculator; the tricky job is getting characters' reactions to both the mind-boggling and the mundane to ring true. The key to that, I believe, is understanding that real people are studies in gray. Fantasy and much space opera often assumed the existence of absolute good and absolute evil. I prefer to explore the subjective nature of morality; there are few clearcut heroes and villains in my books. Indeed, *Golden Fleece* was an attempt to have conflict between two very different points of view—that of the human Aaron and the computer JASON—without it ever being clear which one was in the right. In *End of an Era*, I contended that the only truly immoral position is to not take responsibility. And in *The Terminal Experiment*, I attempt to identify the actual cause of human morality.

The book of mine that I'm proudest of is *The Terminal Experiment*; the one I enjoy the most is *End of an Era*; and my favorite character is Dybo, a supporting player from the Quintaglio Ascension. Unlike many characters in SF, Dybo is rather dim intellectually, but he struggles to do the right thing. He's a being of the heart in a hard SF setting, a personification of the themes I try to bring to my writing.

*   *   *

One of the greatest challenges a science fiction author can face is to create an alien culture that is sufficiently distinct from humankind to be credible as a different intelligent species, but familiar enough that readers can comprehend and even identify with the non-human characters. This becomes even more of a challenge when the story is entirely set in an alien context, with no human characters at all. Even Hal Clement, who excels at creating believable alien societies, almost always included at least one human as a counterbalance.

Robert Sawyer's Quintaglio trilogy attempts just that feat and succeeds remarkably well. *Far-Seer* introduces us to a world where intelligent dinosaurs have created a society somewhat resembling that of ancient Greece or Rome. Their culture is affected by a number of non-human factors. For one thing, each Quintaglio is subject to killing rages over territory and food, so it is difficult for them to act cooperatively on a consistent basis. There is also a finite limit on food, so by tradition most young are killed and eaten in infancy, usually under the direction of a repressive religious hierarchy, and parentage is a secret guarded by a priest caste. There are also some obvious physical problems even in simple acts like sleeping, sex, and eating.

Afsan is a young member of this culture who questions one of the most important teachings of the religious caste, the existence of the Face of God in the skies at a remote part of the planet. Afsan is sent on a pilgrimage to gaze upon the face, but his sharp wits and keen talent for observation lead him to a very different conclusion. The Face of God is just another feature of the physical universe, and the religion of his people is a false one. His struggle to enlighten his people meets with the obvious difficulties, and he is ultimately martyrized, blinded as a consequence of the turmoil which results.

Fossil Hunter continues the story from the point of view of Afsan's son, Toroca. Toroca is a geologist engaged in a search for rare metals that might be used to build a vessel capable of letting the Quintaglio escape their world. The mission becomes more imperative when it becomes clear that their planet, actually a moon, is in an unstable orbit and that stresses are likely to render it uninhabitable within a few years. He also makes another startling discovery, remnants of an ancient spacecraft that may have been part of a fleet that brought the first Quintaglio here from another world, presumably the Earth.

The story concludes with *Foreigner*. The scientific method has transformed the world of the Quintaglio, but they need to acquire more knowledge and quickly if they are to avoid extinction. Afsan returns, along with Novato, his mate, who is instrumental in deciphering the secrets of the alien spaceship. Interwoven with the story of the race's struggle to adapt and survive is a murder mystery, solved partly through the expertise of a reptilian version of Sigmund Freud. The trilogy ends triumphantly, and in its entirety is a first rate blend of straightforward adventure, scientific speculation, and serious though veiled commentary on human intellectual freedom and the thirst for knowledge.

Sawyer has written three other novels, all singletons. His first was *Golden Fleece*, a skillful blend of SF and mystery. The death of a scientist aboard a starship has been dismissed as suicide, but the dead woman's husband suspects otherwise. What's more, he believes that the responsible party is the ship's computer. Despite occasional awkward moments, the novel tackles its central problem intelligently and logically, and the reader is easily convinced of the reality of starship's difficulties.

The End of an Era opens with another scientific mystery. A time travel experiment carries two people back to the Cretaceous Era where they notice two very anomalous things. First, the gravity of the planet Earth is much less than they are used to, and second, some of the dinosaurs are acting strangely, as though directed by intelligent thought. That turns out to be the case, through the medium of parasitic Martian invaders who have come to Earth to use the dinosaurs' bodies. But human beings, even humans from the far future, would make far more useful hosts.

Sawyer's most recent novel is *The Terminal Experiment,* in many ways his most ambitious effort to date. Dr. Peter Hobson is trying to solve the secrets of human mortality, and to do so he creates three electronic versions of his own personality, one complete, one effectively dead though still conscious, one alive but without the capacity to comprehend its own non-existence. Through examination of the psychological development of these artificial intelligences, he hopes to understand the consequences of immortality. What he fails to anticipate is that the will to survive may have manifested itself within his creations, and that they might be capable of finding a way to copy themselves into the worldwide data network, securing their own form of limited immortality. And one of the three is capable of murder. Although more limited in scope than the Quintaglio novels, this is by far Sawyer's most mature, controlled, and thoughtful novel to date.

Although Sawyer rarely writes short stories, one in particular is worth mentioning. "Just Like Old times" puts the brain of a serial killer inside the body of a carnivorous dinosaur. Others of note include "Where the Heart Is" and "You See But You Do Not Observe." Robert Sawyer seems headed for a successful career as a writer of adventure oriented fiction with a strong underpinning of serious human concerns. *The Terminal Experiment* seems to indicate that he may also be capable of producing more serious novels with ambitious themes.

—Don D'Ammassa

SAXTON, Josephine

Nationality: British. **Born:** Josephine Howard, Halifax, Yorkshire, 11 June 1935. **Education:** Clare Hall County Secondary School, Halifax. **Family:** Married 1) Geoffrey Banks in 1958, one son; 2) Colin Saxton in 1962 (divorced 1983), one son and one daughter. **Career:** Part-time lecturer in creative writing, University of Warwick, Dept of Continuing Education. **Address:** 12 Plymouth Place, Leamington Spa, Warwickshire, CV31 IHN, England.

SCIENCE FICTION PUBLICATIONS

Novels (series: Jane Saint)

The Hieros Gamos of Sam and An Smith. Garden City, New York, Doubleday, 1969.
Vector for Seven; or, The Weltanshaung of Mrs. Amelia Mortimer and Friends. Garden City, New York, Doubleday, 1970.
Group Feast. Garden City, New York, Doubleday, 1971.
The Travails of Jane Saint. London, Virgin, 1980.
Queen of the States. London, Women's Press, 1986.

Short Stories

The Power of Time. London, Chatto and Windus, 1985.

Little Tours of Hell. London, Pandora Press, 1986.
The Travails of Jane Saint and Other Stories. London, Women's Press, 1986.
The Conscious Machine; Jane Saint and the Backlash: Further Travails of Jane Saint. London, Women's Press, 1989.

*   *   *

In the late 1960s and early 1970s when her work first appeared, Josephine Saxton's idiosyncratic, iconoclastic fiction fitted well with the New Wave sensibilities of the time. But as the New Wave spent itself in the mid-1970s, so Saxton's work seemed to fall out of favour, and it virtually disappeared from view until the feminist writing of the mid-1980s heralded a much deserved rediscovery. Yet her writing has not changed significantly during the intervening years to suit such apparently different camps so neatly. In fact, her writing seems to attract descriptions such as "New Wave," "feminist," or even "science fiction" more because there is no other way of categorising it than because it really belongs within such narrow bands. In *Jane Saint and the Backlash,* she manages to bring together one of her earliest stories, "The Consciousness Machine," with some of her most recent work, and the ideas and interests that drive them are the same in both. Most obviously, a long-time interest in Jungian psychology litters her work with archetypes. She makes little pretence of creating fully rounded characters, rather she peoples her books with figureheads representing attitudes and characteristics, and as often as not she isolates these figures in a barren landscape such as the wasteland of her first novel, *The Hieros Gamos of Sam and An Smith,* or the dreamscape in which Jane Saint has her carefully orchestrated encounters.

Certainly there is something of New Wave experimentalism in the dramatic isolation and the polemical or parable-like intent of her fiction, just as the polemic does carry a powerful feminist message. But these characteristics no more consign her work exclusively to these camps than the sight of a flying saucer in *Vector for Seven* or the aliens in *Queen of the States* make her stories unequivocally science fiction. Josephine Saxton writes stories that belong in one exclusive but highly entertaining genre: the Josephine Saxton story. The science fiction trappings are usually there more to serve as a sign of the character's mental state than as a description of objective reality; one of the abiding elements in her work is a questioning of the differences between objective and subjective reality.

Other common features of this private genre are: journeys to be undertaken; the patient detailing of everyday life, how people dress, their hygiene, and above all how they cook and what they eat; and the progression from being alone, the absurdity of isolation and mutual distrust, to the achievement of togetherness, a mutually supportive social unit. Yet for all the seriousness of these concerns—and her feminism in particular is a strongly held position that comes through in everything she writes—Saxton is also a very funny writer. Serious points are made through absurdity.

Her first published story, "The Wall," is typical of all her work: a great wall lies across a barren landscape. This is no painstaking delineation of a place we instantly recognise, it is more a vague dreamscape, vast and empty, in which her characters, when they belatedly enter the scene, can be effectively and cruelly isolated. What's more, the wall's symbolic weight far outstrips a simple description of the scene—Saxton has always been more prodigal in her use of symbolism than most other science fiction writers. It is far from being her best story, but it does stake out the territory she has occupied, to some extent, ever since.

Her first three novels further develop these characteristics. In *The Hieros Gamos of Sam and An Smith* (the title is from the Greek for "holy marriage"), a boy wandering in a depopulated landscape finds and cares for a newborn baby girl. In *Vector for Seven,* a disparate group of characters wander through a surreal landscape until their initial mistrust is replaced with unity. In *Group Feast,* a 24-hour party takes place in a house with a seemingly limitless number of rooms, giving Saxton the opportunity to dwell in perceptive and witty detail on material possessions and food, while Cora's artificial relationship with her servants is destroyed, and she is forced in the end to abandon it all.

Though demonstrating a growing ability and confidence, these books had little commercial success, and were followed by silence punctuated only by a few short stories, often more science fictional than her novels. Their dark humour tends to rely on inversion; thus in "Elouise and the Doctors of the Planet Pergamon," Elouise is healthy on a planet where everyone is legally obliged to be diseased, while in "Gordon's Women," Gordon believes he has a harem of perfect female automata not knowing that they are in fact alive.

Her more recent work, *The Travails of Jane Saint,* describes a quest through a typically surreal landscape in which a series of bizarre and ludicrous encounters with demon-like Zilp, Merleau-Ponty the talking dog, Simone de Beauvoir as a fairground sideshow, and others explore aspects of feminist consciousness until, as so often in Saxton's work, the lonely Jane Saint has been reunited with family and friends, and in this union succeeds in changing the world. The sequel, *Jane Saint and the Backlash,* retraces the journey slightly less successfully as a counterpoint to political apathy and the rise of the "new man."

Saxton's most successful novel, however, is *Queen of the States,* a vivid, multi-layered work that constantly forces us to examine our assumptions of reality. Is Magdalen really being examined by aliens, is she really Queen of America, how can her lover conjured up by the aliens become the doctor of her husband's mistress? And as reality is questioned, so are other assumptions. The book has a powerful underlying feminist message, yet, as in *Jane Saint,* the husband is no villain, and both he and Dr. Murgatroyd, the figures of authority and the establishment, can come through in the end if they accept their fantasies.

But perhaps we should leave it to one more short story to encapsulate the Saxton credo. "The Message" resolutely avoids the fantastic, though it does display all the familiar Saxton hallmarks, most notably the journey format. We follow an old woman walking home from a hospital, seeing the urban landscape as it has changed from the days of her youth, and coming to terms with both her age and her surroundings in typical Saxton fashion by finding unity with others along the way, an old man who lives alone, a bunch of young Rastafarians.

—Paul Kincaid

SCARBOROUGH, Elizabeth (Ann)

Nationality: American. **Born:** Kansas City, Missouri, 23 March 1947. **Education:** Bethany Hospital School of Nursing, R.N.; University of Alaska, Fairbanks. **Military Service:** Served as a nurse during Vietnam War. United States Army, Nurse Corps: Captain. **Family:** Married Richard G. Kacsur in 1975 (divorced 1981). **Career:** Surgical nurse, St. David's Hospital, Austin, Texas. Lives in Port Townsend, Washington. **Awards:** Nebula award, 1989. **Agent:** Merrilee Heifetz, 21 West 26th Street, New York, New York 10010, U.S.A. **Address:** c/o Doubleday, 666 Fifth Avenue, New York, New York 10103, U.S.A.

SCIENCE FICTION PUBLICATIONS

Novels (series: Argonia; The Godmother; Nothing Sacred; Powers; Songkiller)

The Harem of Aman Akbar; or, The Djinn Decanted. New York, Bantam, 1984.
The Drastic Dragon of Draco, Texas. New York, Bantam, 1986.
The Goldcamp Vampire; or, The Sanguinary Sourdough. New York, Bantam, 1987.
Songs from the Seashell Archives. New York, Bantam, 2 vols., 1987-88.
   Song of Sorcery. New York, Bantam, 1982; London, 1987.
   The Unicorn Creed. New York, Bantam, 1983.
   Bronwyn's Bane. New York, Bantam, 1983; London, 1987.
   The Christening Quest. New York, Bantam, 1985.
The Healer's War. New York, Doubleday, 1988.
Nothing Sacred. New York, Doubleday, 1991.
Phantom Banjo (Songkiller). New York, Bantam, 1991.
Picking the Ballad's Bones (Songkiller). New York, Bantam, 1991.
Last Refuge (Nothing Sacred). New York, Bantam, 1992.
Strum Again? (Songkiller). New York, Bantam, 1992.
Powers That Be, with Anne McCaffrey (Powers). New York, Ballantine, and London, Bantam, 1994.
Power Lines, with Anne McCaffrey (Powers). New York, Ballantine, and London, Bantam, 1994.
The Godmother. New York, Ace, 1994.
The Godmother's Apprentice. New York, Ace, 1995.

OTHER PUBLICATIONS

Other

An Interview with a Vietnam Nurse. New York, Bantam, 1989.

*

Elizabeth Ann Scarborough comments:

My earliest books were intended to be light, humorous, and entertaining, which I hope they were. I changed directions at the urging of my publisher, Lou Aronica at Bantam, to write *The Healer's War,* loosely based on my experiences in Vietnam. Since then, my work has been more of a blending of social science fiction, fantasy, political satire, and humor (particularly in the Songkiller Saga).

*   *   *

Elizabeth Scarborough's misleadingly simple debut novel was a traditional, lighthearted fantasy adventure called *Song of Sorcery.* Structurally, the book is a gentle version of the quest story. The protagonist is Maggie Brown, a good if somewhat disorganized witch, who sets out to find her half sister, meeting unicorns, dragons, and other magical creatures along the way. The sequel, *The*

Unicorn Creed, continued Maggie's adventures, now accompanied by a minstrel and a unicorn, the latter of whom has difficulty relating to the growing intimacy between his companions. Even though the menace this time is an evil sorcerer, the overall tone is good-natured, enlivened by Scarborough's refreshingly clear prose and a cast of amusing, interesting characters.

Bronwyn's Bane shares the same setting but a different pair of central characters. One is Bronwyn, a precocious but uncooperative princess who is cursed never to tell the truth, the other the daughter of Maggie and her minstrel husband. Together they experience an inventive and highly amusing series of adventures, stop a war, survive various dangers, all enlivened by the princess's curse, which leads to some hilarious situations. Bronwyn's child must be rescued in *The Christening Quest,* the fourth book in the series, but although the story is well-paced and enjoyable, Scarborough seemed to be tiring of this setting. Her gift for light humor remains intact, but is less evident.

The Harem of Aman Akbar was Scarborough's first non-series novel, an Arabian Nights adventure filled with djinn, evil emirs, and high adventure. Once again, the protagonist is a woman, one of Aman's wives who sets out to free him from a humiliating curse inflicted by a rival. Like most of Scarborough's female characters, Rasa is a strong willed woman who refuses to allow society to define her place in its structure.

Scarborough's gradual drift away from fantasy to more serious and realistic themes was first visible in *The Drastic Dragon of Draco, Texas.* Set in the Old West, the story involves the mysterious appearance of a fire breathing dragon. Although there are still flashes of humor, it's a far more serious novel in most ways than those which preceded it. In *The Goldcamp Vampire,* set against the background of the Yukon gold rush, an adventurous young woman finds more than she bargained for when the suave foreigner courting her turns out to be a vampire, and she is blamed by the local people for one of his bloodthirsty attacks. As with the previous book, the serious tone is leavened by humor, but there was a clear evolution toward more serious themes.

Scarborough's first major novel, *The Healer's War,* was a complete change of pace, drawn from her experiences as an army nurse who served a tour of duty in Vietnam. Winner of the Nebula Award as best novel of the year, it follows the experiences of Lieutenant Kitty McCulley, a nurse transferred to Vietnam who quickly discovers that there are undercurrents far deeper than she had ever previously experienced. After being presented with a magical amulet by a Vietnamese civilian, she becomes emotionally involved with the plight of the victims, both military and civilian, on both sides of the conflict, and eventually responds to a compulsion which she considers superior to the one imposed by her government. The novel reveals a depth of characterization only hinted at in earlier works, and carries a powerful emotional impact.

Although the book is to a certain extent a war novel, it is written from an unusual perspective, and deals more with the human effects of armed conflict and disruption rather than with the physical elements. At times bitter, the story is noticeably missing the lighter hand of her previous work, because levity would have been out of place with this theme.

Scarborough's first true science fiction novel was *Nothing Sacred,* another story of armed conflict, this time set a century in our future. The world has become a troubled place; the unemployed in America have little choice but to enlist in the military and be sent to fight in foreign wars. The protagonist is a woman taken pris-

oner and assigned to a camp in Tibet, where time seems to flow differently and the concerns of the outside world are less compelling. At least that's true until a nuclear conflict erupts and they find themselves struggling to survive. Scarborough returned to this setting a generation later in *The Last Refuge,* following the adventures of the daughter of her previous protagonist on a journey of exploration through the reemerging world.

Scarborough did not abandon light fantasy despite the turn to more serious themes. Of interest is the Songkiller Saga, the first two titles of which are *The Phantom Banjo* and *Picking the Ballad's Bones.* The series is a frequently amusing blend of ghosts, contemporary settings, magic, and the like. These seem to represent a change of pace from her more serious novels, but she has indicated that her future works will continue the diversity already demonstrated.

With Anne McCaffrey, Scarborough has written two novels set on the planet Petaybee, *Powers That Be* and *Power Lines,* with a third one, *Power Play,* scheduled for publication in 1995. Petaybee is an ice-covered world, and the new home of an off-planet spy who has suffered physical damage that restricts the kinds of environments in which she can survive. Her allegiance changes as the story progresses and she discovers that there is something unique about the planet. It is in fact a single, sentient being, vulnerable to a variety of physical distresses resulting from defoliation or other disturbances. The spy's employers are subsequently thwarted in their initial efforts to terraform Petaybee. Attempts by outside interests to exploit the world continue in the sequel, with the protagonist now firmly in the camp of her former employers. The application to contemporary events is obvious, but the authors have attempted to present both sides of the issue.

Although Scarborough is an infrequent short story writer, "Wolf from the Door," "Milk from a Maiden's Breast," "Field Trip" and "Elephant-in-Law" are all entertaining.

—Don D'Ammassa

SCHACHNER, Nat(han)

Pseudonyms: Chan Corbett; Walter Glamis. **Nationality:** American. **Born:** New York City, 16 January 1895. **Education:** City College of New York, B.S. 1915; New York University, J.D. 1919. **Military Service:** Served in the United States Army chemical warfare service, 1917-18. **Family:** Married Helen Lichtenstein in 1919; one daughter. **Career:** Chemist, New York City Department of Health, 1915-17; admitted to the New York Bar, 1919; practicing lawyer, New York, 1919-33; freelance writer from 1933; editorial consultant, American Jewish Committee, 1945-51; director of public relations, National Council of Jewish Women, 1954-55. President, American Rocket Society, 1933. **Died:** 2 October 1955.

SCIENCE FICTION PUBLICATIONS

Novel

Space Lawyer. New York, Gnome Press, 1953.

OTHER PUBLICATIONS

Novels

By the Dim Lamps: A Novel. New York, Stokes, 1941.
The King's Passenger. Philadelphia, Lippincott, 1942.
The Sun Shines West. New York, Appleton Century, 1943.
The Wanderer: A Novel of Dante and Beatrice. New York, Appleton
    Century, 1944; London, Melrose, 1948.

Other

Aaron Burr: A Biography. New York, Stokes, 1937.
The Medieval Universities. New York, Stokes, and London, Allen
    and Unwin, 1938.
Alexander Hamilton. New York, Appleton Century, 1946.
Church, State, and Education. New York, American Jewish Com-
    mittee, 1947.
*The Price of Liberty: A History of the American Jewish Commit-
    tee.* New York, American Jewish Committee, 1948.
Thomas Jefferson: A Biography. New York, Appleton Century
    Crofts, 1951.
Alexander Hamilton, Nation Builder. New York, McGraw Hill,
    1952.
The Founding Fathers. New York, Putnam, 1954.

*   *   *

Nat Schachner was attracted for a time to the vigorous, young
genre of pulp magazine SF, where he left an impression with his
liberal ideas and earnest inventiveness. Schachner worked first as
a chemist, spent a number of years in law practice, published hundreds of pieces of short fiction in the pulps (science, detective, mystery, western, and adventure stories), and wrote several scholarly
books on history. During the Nazi threat before and during World
War II, he defended human liberties vigorously in all his writings—
both pulp fiction and scholarly. Schachner's total commitment to
the life of letters and to humanitarian values makes him a true 20th-
century representative of the Romantics whom he said he loved as
a child. He represents the writer as hero; and the heroic vigor of
the science fiction genre during the time that he was active in it
corresponds well with his later American Revolutionary history.
Schachner's hopeful ideas for progress through clever technology
and rationality had their roots both in the 18th-century Enlightenment of Thomas Jefferson and in the pulp fiction world of the early
Astounding.

   The first dozen or so of Schachner's SF stories were written in
collaboration with Arthur Leo Zagat, but it was with the "thought
variant" stories of the F. Orlin Tremaine *Astounding* that the inventive lawyer began to hit his stride as a writer who would extrapolate into the future his liberal ideas about the present and eventually about the past. The first thought variant story was Schachner's
"Ancestral Voices," and new idea stories followed rapidly for the
rest of the decade. In his book on the science fiction pulp magazines, Paul Carter calls Schachner the earliest of the "anti-Nazi Paul
Reveres" whose speculative fictions increasingly explored the opportunities for sociological themes that could be related to current
events. A rather stiff and primitive story called "The Eternal Wanderer" contains a crude courtroom scene about interplanetary law
that anticipates Schachner's only SF book *Space Lawyer* (made out
of two later stories, "Old Fireball" and "Jurisdiction").

Schachner's best writing and most memorable contribution to
letters is undoubtedly his historical work, and he properly gave up
work for the pulps in order to pursue that research. But one cannot
help thinking that his thought variant extrapolations were both inspired by his knowledge of the Enlightenment and contributed
greatly to his understanding of it. One of his more carefully written and sophisticated fictions, "Past, Present, and Future," performs
just that balancing between a nostalgia for the heroic and glorious
lost past on the one hand and an awareness of the challenges in the
present on the other that creates the ironic complexity of mind that
is necessary for true liberal thinking. Schachner was a hero among
writers not only for the vast amount of work that he got done but
also for how he did it—less an artist than a propagandist for democracy.

—Donald M. Hassler

SCHENCK, Hilbert

Nationality: American. **Born:** Boston, Massachusetts, 12 February 1926. **Education:** Williams College, Williamstown, Massachusetts, B.A. in physics 1950; Stanford University, California, M.S.
in mechanical engineering 1952. **Military Service:** Served as an
electronic technician in the United States Navy, 1944-46. **Family:**
Married 1) Mary Low Taylor in 1950; 2) Anne Thompson in 1983;
six children. **Career:** Test engineer, Pratt & Whitney Aircraft, East
Hartford, Connecticut, 1952-56; Assistant Professor to Professor,
Clarkson College, Potsdam, New York, 1956-66; Professor, 1966-
83, and director, Scuba Safety Project, 1968-80, University of
Rhode Island, Kingston. **Agent:** Virginia Kidd, Box 278, Milford,
Pennsylvania 18337, U.S.A.

SCIENCE FICTION PUBLICATIONS

Novels

At the Eye of the Ocean. New York, Timescape, 1980.
A Rose for Armageddon. New York, Pocket Books, 1982; Lon-
    don, Allison and Busby, 1984.
Chronosequence. New York, Tor, 1988.

Short Stories

Wave Rider. New York, Pocket Books, 1980.
Steam Bird. New York, Tor, 1988.

OTHER PUBLICATIONS

Other

Shallow Water Diving for Pleasure and Profit, with Henry Kendall.
    Cambridge, Maryland, Cornell Maritime Press, 1950.
Underwater Photography, with Henry Kendall. Cambridge, Mary-
    land, Cornell Maritime Press, 1954.
Shallow Water Diving and Spearfishing, with Henry Kendall. Cam-
    bridge, Maryland, Cornell Maritime Press, 1954.

Skin Diver's and Spearfisherman's Guide to American Waters: Where to Go and What You Will Find When You Get There. Cambridge, Maryland, Cornell Maritime Press, 1955.

Heat Transfer Engineering. Englewood Cliffs, New Jersey, Prentice Hall, 1959.

Fundamentals of Thermodynamics, with Richard A. Kenyon. New York, Ronald Press, 1962.

Fortran Methods in Heat Flow. New York, Ronald Press, 1963.

Theories of Engineering Experimentation. New York, McGraw-Hill, 1961; 2nd edition, 1968; 3rd edition, with Roger J. Hawks, Washington, Hemisphere, 1978.

An Introduction to the Engineering Research Project. New York, McGraw-Hill, 1968.

An Interdisciplinary Laboratory to Teach Experimentation: Final Report. Potsdam, New York, Clarkson College of Technology, 1963.

Editor, *Introduction to Ocean Engineering.* New York, McGraw-Hill, 1975.

*

Hilbert Schenck comments:

My stories have been mainly concerned with the technology of ocean exploration, but also may contain fantasy elements. My first two novels are concerned both with the ocean and the area of Cape Cod, Mass. My novel *Steam Bird,* serialized in *F&SF,* departs from these topics and is concerned with the flight of a nuclear-propelled aircraft, a project on which I worked in the 1950s at Pratt & Whitney Aircraft. Most recently, I have been fooling around with the idea of recursive fiction, that is, fiction that is concerned with its own creation. My two Cape Cod novels represent attempts to introduce classic SF themes (the idea of the superman and the idea of time travel) into a regional fiction setting. A third novel adds a third basic SF theme, visitation from another world, into the Cape Cod geographic and historic situation.

*   *   *

Hilbert Schenck's first science fiction sale was "Tomorrow's Weather," a postnuclear-war story about a meteorologist who plots the spread of radioactivity, published in *Fantasy and Science Fiction,* April 1953. Except for occasional bits of verse, this competent but forgettable story was his sole appearance for over two decades. It wasn't until 1977 that he began writing in earnest, producing a series of skillfully crafted short stories and novels, many reflecting his oceanographic background and his familiarity with the Cape Cod area of Massachusetts.

"Three Days at the End of the World" features an oceanographer who suspects that a biological weapon of unprecedented magnitude has been inadvertently lost at sea, threatening the entire biosphere. The protagonist and his allies must solve the problem, simultaneously thwarting a set of malevolent government agents, common villains in his fiction. This story was followed shortly by "The Morphology of the Kirkham Wreck," a far more ambitious and satisfying story. Set several decades in the past, it follows the efforts of a group of men to rescue the passengers and crew of a grounded ship. The protagonist is able to slip back through time and affect the situation slightly, increasing the chances of success, a subtle touch of fantasy in what is otherwise an excellent sea adventure tale.

"The Battle of the Abaco Reefs" is set after the world has broken up into scores of tiny states. The governor of California makes an alliance with Fidel Castro to invade and conquer the Bahamas,

and is thwarted by the island nation's desperate and cleverly conceived defensive system. The main attraction in this very fine story is the interaction of the characters and forces, and while Schenck makes use of the plot to criticize the role of government, his political statements are unobtrusive and don't interfere with the flow of the story.

Two more sea stories followed, "Wave Rider" and "Buoyant Ascent," the first the story of a high-tech trimaran and an effort to break a world sailing record, the second concerned with attempts to rescue the crew of a sunken submarine. Although the plots of each are intense and well-constructed, Schenck fails to people either of these with the well-realized characters that made the previous stories so memorable.

Schenck's first novel, *At the Eye of the Ocean,* was markedly superior to any of his shorter fiction. Set in New England just prior to the Civil War, it features a sea captain who uses his ship to ferry runaway slaves to Canada, aided by his psychic ability to detect the moods of the ocean. At the same time, he is obsessed with his vision of the eye of the ocean, a mystical place whose existence is known to him alone.

A Rose for Armageddon is also set in Cape Cod, in the near future when the collapsing world economy seems to be headed directly toward universal anarchy. A research group strives to perfect a computer program of unprecedented scope, one which may provide critical insights into the nature of human civilization. But two of the scientists find something else on the island they are studying, a place where they can travel back through time to a simpler and more satisfying world.

"Hurricane Claude" (in *Fantasy and Science Fiction,* April 1983) is an interesting examination of weather control, the possibility of short-circuiting a hurricane. It is the best of three short stories that appeared in the early 1980s. They were followed by *Steam Bird,* which was quite different from anything Schenck had written before. *Steam Bird* is set in an alternate version of the present where technology took a slightly different direction. The story is set aboard a nuclear-powered bomber, one which, having taken off, has no place to land, and its presence in the sky suddenly sets off an international crisis.

"Send Me a Kiss by Wire" (in *Fantasy and Science Fiction,* April 1985) is the narrative of an unexpected encounter with a giant squid, a story that captures the mysterious and wondrous qualities of the undersea world very effectively. An unsavory real estate development deal is thwarted by a device that broadcasts depression and anxiety in "A Down East Storm."

Schenck's most recent novel is *Chrono-Sequence.* While in London, a college professor buys an antique journal, which seems to have originated in Nantucket, a place with a special meaning in her youth. Almost immediately, mysterious attempts are made to steal the book from her, a situation made even more disturbing when she reads the journal and discovers mention of the arrival of alien intelligences on the Earth, creatures that may have perished in the ocean near Nantucket. She returns there, only to discover a strong possibility that the aliens still live in some fashion, and that their presence has been subtly influencing the lives of anyone in the area who is sensitive to their emanations. The novel, a combination of historical novel, SF, and mystery, is easily the best work Schenck has produced to date.

In general, Schenck employs finely rounded characters in intricately detailed settings, and the fantastic elements, while crucial to the plot, are understated. He has a superb ear for dialogue as well, which contributes to his ability to draw readers completely into the worlds he creates.

—Don D'Ammassa

SCHMIDT, Stanley (Albert)

Nationality: American. **Born:** Cincinnati, Ohio, 7 March 1944. **Education:** University of Cincinnati, B.S. in physics 1966 (Phi Beta Kappa); Case Western Reserve University, Cleveland, M.A. 1968, Ph.D. 1969. **Family:** Married Joyce Tokarz in 1979. **Career:** Assistant Professor of Physics, Heidelberg College, Tiffin, Ohio, 1969-78. Since 1978, editor, *Analog,* New York. **Agent:** Russell Galen, Scovil Chichak Galen Literary Agency, 381 Park Ave. South, Suite 1020, New York, New York 10016. **Address:** c/o *Analog,* 1540 Broadway, New York, New York 10036, U.S.A. **Online Address:** 71154.662@compuserve.com.

SCIENCE FICTION PUBLICATIONS

Novels (series: Kyyra)

Newton and the Quasi-Apple. Garden City, New York, Doubleday, 1975.
The Sins of the Fathers (Kyyra). New York, Berkley, 1976.
Lifeboat Earth. New York, Berkley, 1978.
Tweedlioop. New York, Tor, 1986.

OTHER PUBLICATIONS

Other

Editor, *The Analogy Anthology #1.* New York, Davis, 1980; as *Analog's Golden Anniversary Anthology,* New York, Longmeadow, 1980.
Editor, *The Analogy Anthology #2.* New York, Davis, 1981; as *Analog: Reader's Choice,* 1981.
Editor, *Analog Yearbook II.* New York, Ace, 1981.
Editor, *Analog's Children of the Future.* New York, Davis, 1982.
Editor, *Analog's Lighter Side.* New York, Davis, 1982.
Editor, *War and Peace: Possible Futures from Analog.* New York, Davis, 1983.
Editor, *Aliens from Analog.* New York, Davis, 1983.
Editor, *Analog: Writer's Choice.* New York, Davis, 2 vols., 1983-84.
Editor, *From Mind to Mind.* New York, Davis, 1984.
Editor, *6 Decades: The Best from Analog.* New York, Dial, 1986.
Editor, *Analog's Expanding Universe.* New York, Davis, 1986.
Editor, *Unknown.* New York, Baen, 1988.
Editor, with Martin H. Greenberg, *Unknown Worlds: Tales from Beyond.* New York, Galahad, 1988.
Editor, *Analog Essays on Science.* New York, Wiley, 1990.
Editor, with others, *Writing Science Fiction and Fantasy.* New York, St. Martin's Press, 1991.

*

Stanley Schmidt comments:

In most of my fiction I try to tell entertaining, thought-provoking stories about people in situations which are directly shaped by scientific or technological changes, with neither the human nor the technical parts of the foundation slighted in favor of the other. I am disturbed by the recent tendency to apply the term "science fiction" indiscriminately to a wide range of things which have little or nothing to do with science. Writers who think they can write meaningfully about the future of humanity without giving careful thought to *both* human nature and technology, and the ways they interact, are kidding themselves. And we need to try to anticipate not only those developments which science already knows are possible, but the wildest surprises we can imagine which present knowledge cannot definitely rule out. We have already had to rebuild our picture of the universe at least twice in this century alone; we dare not assume that we will never have to do it again.

Perhaps the best examples to date of the kinds of thing I try to do are *The Sins of the Fathers* and *Lifeboat Earth,* which together are sometimes referred to as the "Kyyra" or "Lifeboat Earth" series.

* * *

Stanley Schmidt seems to be one of the final products of the John Campbell influence on science fiction, although it is probably too early in Schmidt's career to tell definitely. His early three novels, as well as the short story versions of them that appeared in *Analog,* all show the Campbell marks of hard science extrapolation, of positive-thinking, problem-solving approaches to thorny human and social problems, and of two-dimensional human beings compared to a sense of rounded sublimity for whole planets and even galaxies. The second two of these narratives begin what will no doubt be a series in which galactic history unfolds much like Campbell taught the young Asimov to attempt sublime galactic history four decades ago. The first novel narrates a segment from the history of the planet Ymrek in which the natives seem more interesting than the human emissaries to the planet. Even if Schmidt had not told us that correspondence and ideas from Campbell influenced him, the effects of that influence are apparent in all three novels.

Schmidt is best when he begins to suggest the unresolved and, perhaps, unresolvable tensions that underlie the problems that must be resolutely solved by technology and engineering techniques; these interesting tensions lurking beneath the Campbell-like scenarios are almost exclusively associated with the alien species of the latter two novels. Although Ymrek is an interesting alien extrapolation, its natives are not nearly as symbolically (or scientifically) suggestive as the Kyyra who were originally from nearer the center of our galaxy and who literally set in motion all the action in *The Sins of the Fathers* and its sequel, *Lifeboat Earth.* The more suggestive passages appear in the first book of the series when the Kyyra seem to symbolize the dilemmas of maturation. We must destroy our pasts and even our gods to atone for our mistakes—almost Christian and yet more universal symbolism of the dying god.

The strength related to this symbolic suggestiveness is the detailed elaboration of the aliens themselves—his departure from Campbell. Without the concrete detail to make them credible, the Kyyra could suggest nothing. In fact, as Beldan conducts his human visitor on a tour of the immense Kyyra spaceship orbiting the earth, and explains to her the language and the customs of his people, the reader is reminded of the tours through Walden Two. These aliens are an advanced culture with a kind of social engineering that B.F. Skinner would admire. The Campbell positivism is not unlike Skinner's hopes for managing behaviour, and it is to Schmidt's credit that while the parallels are developed in his narrative, the dilemmas are lurking just beneath the surface that Campbell may not have noticed. We can anticipate, perhaps, more development of the Kyyra in future Schmidt stories; and we can wonder if their utopian, problem-solving traits will prevail or if the tragic implications in the death of their god will haunt Schmidt more.

Such narrative extrapolation may be suspended, however, in Schmidt's productivity until he has completed his term as editor of *Analog* because his fourth novel *Tweedlioop* lacks the intensity and coherence of his earlier fiction. At the least, we can observe that his editorial work as successor to Ben Bova has consumed his attention in recent years. Further, this emphasis has been good for science fiction since the Schmidt *Analog* has brought back vestiges of the Campbell years. Schmidt is, perhaps, the prime nurturing force for the continuance of hard science fiction in the last decades of our century.

—Donald M. Hassler

SCHMITZ, James H(enry)

Nationality: American. **Born:** to American parents in Hamburg, Germany, 15 October 1911. **Education:** Realgymnasium Obersekunda. **Military Service:** Served in the United States Army Air Force during World War II. **Family:** Married Betty Mae Chapman in 1957. **Career:** Worked for International Harvester Company, in Germany, 1932-39; built automobile trailers in the United States after the war. Full-time writer, from 1961. **Awards:** Invisible Little Man award, 1973. **Died:** 1981.

SCIENCE FICTION PUBLICATIONS

Novels (series: Hub; Telzey Amberdon)

A Tale of Two Clocks (Hub). New York, Torquil, 1962; as *Legacy,* New York, Ace, 1979.
The Universe against Her (Hub; Telzey). New York, Ace, 1964.
The Witches of Karres. Philadelphia, Chilton, 1966; London, Gollancz, 1988.
The Demon Breed (Hub). New York, Ace, 1968; London, Futura, 1974.
The Eternal Frontiers. New York, Putnam, 1973; London, Sidgwick and Jackson, 1974.
The Lion Game (Hub; Telzey). New York, DAW, 1973; London, Sidgwick and Jackson, 1976.

Short Stories

Agent of Vega. Hicksville, New York, Gnome Press, 1960.
A Nice Day for Screaming and Other Tales of the Hub. Philadelphia, Chilton, 1965.
A Pride of Monsters (Hub). New York, Macmillan, 1970.
The Telzey Toy (Hub). New York, DAW, 1973; London, Sidgwick and Jackson, 1976; as *The Telzey Toy and Other Stories,* New York, Ace, 1982.
The Best of James H. Schmitz, edited by Mark L. Olson. Cambridge, Massachusetts, NESFA Press, 1991.

*

Bibliography: *James H. Schmitz: A Bibliography by Mark Owings,* Baltimore, Croatan House, 1973.

*   *   *

James H. Schmitz was a craftsmanlike writer who was a steady contributor to science fiction magazines for over 20 years. The best of his shorter works are collected in *A Nice Day for Screaming* and *A Pride of Monsters.* In the first work, the stories repeat a consistent theme that the universe is stranger than we can imagine, and that unexpected discoveries will meet us at every turn. Although the stories are set in the far future, humans (and others) continually encounter both creatures and behaviors they could not have foreseen, from the alien automated service-station for spaceships of the title story to an alien so intelligent it keeps humans for pets in "The Winds of Time." But aliens can be surprised too, as "The Other Likeness" shows: agents genetically engineered to resemble humans become so much like us that they begin to sympathize with humans against their masters. There are new machines, too, like the fear broadcaster of "The Tangled Web" or the half-men, half-machines of "The Machmen." And there are some things so strange yet so intelligent they can conceal their very existence from humans, like the forest-sized organism in "Balanced Ecology."

A Pride of Monsters collects stories that attempt to rejuvenate the idea of "the monster" through tales of future encounters with alien life-forms. In "Lion Loose," Detective Bad-News Quillan, a favorite character of Schmitz's, meets a rug-sized creature with the ability to pass through solid matter, but it is not nearly so dangerous as the radiation creature of "The Searcher," which endangers a pair of private detectives working undercover against interstellar hijackers. "The Pork Chop Tree" is an alien plant whose very presence is addictive, a less forthright menace than the plant of "Greenface," a story that is unusual (for Schmitz) in being set in the present.

In his longer works, Schmitz often showed a close cooperation between man and alien. The alien may be a machine, like the robot spaceships of the four thematically connected stories of *Agent of Vega,* or mutated animals, like the intelligent giant otters of *The Demon Breed,* who help to repel a threat to human civilization. The "aliens" may even be other humans, as in *The Eternal Frontiers,* in which the Swimmers have diverged so far from normal humanity as to be almost a different species. Rather than forming a close relationship, though, the two groups are keen competitors. And of course, there are aliens that, like those in *A Pride of Monsters,* are threats to humanity, ones such as the plasmoids in *A Tale of Two Clocks.*

A second theme that Schmitz frequently used is that of supranormal mental powers: Telzey, a telepathic teenaged girl, is the central character in a number of stories. Telepathy (and various other kinds of mental powers, chiefly psychokinesis) is central to Schmitz's most celebrated work, *The Witches of Karres.* The book is a fast-moving, episodic adventure story of an ordinary human, Captain Pausert, who becomes entangled with three psychically endowed girls. Its account of the wakening of telepowers in Pausert draws on familiar SF recipes, mixing appropriately evil villains with nick-of-time escapes, and spicing the whole with an entertaining sense of humor.

—Walter E. Meyers

SCORTIA, Thomas N(icholas)

Pseudonym: Scott Nichols. **Nationality:** American. **Born:** Alton, Illinois, 29 August 1926. **Education:** Washington University, St. Louis, A.B. 1949, graduate work 1950. **Military Service:** Served in the United States Army Infantry, 1944-46, and chemical corps, 1951-53. **Family:** Married Irene Baron in 1960 (divorced 1968); one adopted son. **Career:** Senior chemist, Union Starch and Refining Company, Granite City, Illinois, 1954-57; director of research, Chromalloy, Edwardsville, Illinois, 1957-60; group leader, Celanese Corporation, Asheville, North Carolina, 1960-61; section head, United Technology Corporation, Sunnyvale, California, 1961-70. Full-time writer and lecturer, from 1970: author of comics *Targos, Creepy* magazine, May 1972, and *Galactic Prime,* both illustrated by Jack Katz. **Died:** 29 April 1986.

Science Fiction Publications

Novels

Artery of Fire. Garden City, New York, Doubleday, 1972.
Earthwreck! New York, Fawcett, 1974; London, Coronet, 1975.
The Prometheus Crisis, with Frank M. Robinson. Garden City, New York, Doubleday, 1975; London, Hodder and Stoughton, 1976.
The Nightmare Factor, with Frank M. Robinson. Garden City, New York, Doubleday, and London, Hodder and Stoughton, 1978.
Blowout!, with Frank M. Robinson. New York, Franklin Watts, 1987; London, Severn House, 1989.

Short Stories

Caution! Inflammable! Garden City, New York, Doubleday, 1975.
The Best of Thomas N. Scortia, edited by George Zebrowski. Garden City, New York, Doubleday, 1981.

Other Publications

Novels

What Mad Oracle? Evanston, Illinois, Regency, 1961.
The Glass Inferno, with Frank M. Robinson. Garden City, New York, Doubleday, 1974; London, Hodder and Stoughton, 1975.
The Gold Crew, with Frank M. Robinson. New York, Warner, 1980; London, Panther, 1983.

Plays

Screenplays: *Endangered Species,* with Dalton Trumbo, 1976; *Darker Than You Think,* 1979.

Other

Editor, *Strange Bedfellows: Sex and Science Fiction.* New York, Random House, 1972.
Editor, with Chelsea Quinn Yarbo, *Two Views of Wonder.* New York, Ballantine, 1973.

Editor, with George Zebrowski, *Human-Machines: An Anthology of Stories about Cyborgs.* New York, Vintage, 1975; London, Hale, 1977.

*   *   *

Thomas N. Scortia's first published story, "The Prodigy," immediately established him as an accomplished storyteller. Detailing a violent conflict with a paranormal child, the story reaches one of the few unguessable resolutions of the theme. "The Shores of Night" is a vision of a solar-system-wide civilization straining for the stars; here are the sounds and colors of change, as the human spirit readies itself with a new strength. Scortia writes with a virtuosity comparable to Bester's, with the high emotional content of a Lem in depicting "cruel miracles" at their most intense. This story belongs, to borrow the words of C.S. Lewis, "to those works of science fiction which are actual additions to life; they give, like certain rare dreams, sensations we never had before, and enlarge our conception of the range of possible experience." The work belongs to the period of Scortia's greatest attachment to the ideals of space travel. The story's success lies in its melding of personal loss with a haunting series of pictorial images.

His first novel, *What Mad Oracle?,* is based on Scortia's experience as a physico-chemist in the aerospace industry. It is a powerful story of engineers and corporations confronting the realities of American business and politics in the 1950s. SF in the sense that it shows the human impact of science and technology, the novel has a historical interest for SF readers.

As Scortia's involvement in aerospace increased, his SF production diminished; but stories continued to appear throughout the 1960s. One of the most notable is "Broken Image," depicting a future Earth's attempts to have an ethical influence on an alien culture. Seldom has the theme of the saviour been given such a strong presentation. "The Destroyer" was an in-depth return to the theme of "The Prodigy," but this time the note was one of compassion. By 1970 Scortia was writing full time. The great success of this period is "The Weariest River," hailed by P.S. Miller and others as an instant classic on the theme of immortality, containing an original twist of great power; and *Artery of Fire,* a tense, taut novel of conflict over the building of an immense power system (the central image of the story is as strikingly original as that of Niven's *Ringworld*). John W. Campbell had turned down the novella version because he could not accept Scortia's prediction that fusion power would not be available by 1973 (appearing in 1960, the novella makes a striking contrast to "The Shores of Night" of four years before, prefiguring Scortia's critical approach to the products of technology).

Also appearing in the early 1970s was the novel *Earthwreck!* (the title was changed from *Endangered Species* without Scortia's consent), a strongly characterized story of human survival in space after an atomic war has devastated the Earth. With the SF veteran Frank M. Robinson, Scortia wrote several disaster novels. These bestsellers earned the authors an international reputation, considerable monetary reward, and the often unfair scorn of the SF community. *The Prometheus Crisis* is of interest to SF readers because, in its depiction of a severe nuclear accident, the story is the legitimate descendant of such pioneering stories as Heinlein's "Blowups Happen" and del Rey's *Nerves.* There is a strong cautionary tone in all of Scortia's later work; it is the warning of the once idealistic, Campbell-influenced aerospace scientist who dreamed of space travel and found that human beings have a penchant for perverting any worthwhile project, from high-rise dwellings to atomic power plants.

Scortia's popular success outside the SF world is part of the continuing science fictionalization of our civilization, in the sense that many of the prophetic suggestions made by SF in the first half of this century, positive and negative, have become commonplace in the second half. That a veteran SF writer should take part in this infusion of what once would have been SF themes and ideas into the body of popular fiction is not surprising. Scortia's special success lies in his genuine emotional and dramatic appeal to the general reader, and in showing how the real world has turned out to be more complex and full of human failure, darker than the idealistic SF on which he grew up had foreseen. That human beings *can* do something is no longer enough; the problem is whether they will, or should.

Thomas N. Scortia's life might have been a science fiction story, as written in some alternate dimension. He came to maturity in the 1950s, full of feeling and intellect, overflowing with the wonder of human possibilities as pictured in Campbell's *Astounding,* only to learn that human beings don't always do their best for worthy dreams. One might say that Scortia's views were modified by the kind of satirical SF which Gold published in *Galaxy* (Gold himself was a Campbell writer who extended his master's approach to SF to include the "soft" social sciences). Scortia's stories of the 1950s and 1960s are powerful streams of thought and feeling, combined with rigorous speculation, flowing out of his critical but compassionate disappointment with the world. Even in his 50s, it was hard to think of Scortia as anything but a young man with his crowning work still to come. His work in aerospace enabled humanity to send probes into the outer solar system, while at the same time he was struggling in his fiction to understand the failing, often partly rational inner space of human nature. *Blow-Out!,* written with Frank M. Robinson, a well-received novel about the construction of a tunnel for high-speed trains across the United States, was published in the year after Scortia's death.

—George Zebrowski

SCOTT, Melissa

Nationality: American. **Born:** Little Rock, Arkansas, 7 August 1960. **Education:** Harvard/Radcliffe College, Cambridge, Massachusetts, B.A. in history (magna cum laude) 1981; Brandeis University, Waltham, Massachusetts, Ph.D. in comparative history 1992. **Family:** Lisa A. Barnett, partner since 1979. **Career:** "Having sold my first novel while still a graduate student and teaching assistant, I have not had a full-time job other than writing. As a part-time worker, I have been an usher, teller, answering service operator, teaching assistant, stitcher/stock person, secretary/word processing operator, and receptionist. I am also a founder and contributing editor of *Wavelengths,* a review of gaylesbisn/bisexual/ 'of interest' science fiction and fantasy." **Awards:** John W. Campbell award, 1986. **Agent:** Richard Curtis, Richard Curtis Agency, 171 East 74th Street, New York, New York 10021. **Address:** c/o CoastLine SF Writers' Group, P.O. Box 6554, Portsmouth, New Hampshire 03802-6554, U.S.A.

Science Fiction Publications

Novels (series: Silence Leigh, Star Trek: Deep Space Nine)

The Game Beyond. New York, Baen, 1984.

The Roads of Heaven (Silence Leigh). Garden City, New York, Doubleday, 1988.
Five-Twelfths of Heaven. New York, Baen, 1985; London, Gollancz, 1988.
Silence and Solitude. New York, Baen, 1986; London, Gollancz, 1989.
The Empress of Earth. New York, Baen, 1987; London, Gollancz, 1989.
A Choice of Destinies. New York, Baen, 1986.
The Kindly Ones. New York, Baen, 1987; London, Gollancz, 1990.
The Armor of Light, with Lisa A. Barnett. New York, Baen, 1988.
Mighty Good Road. New York, Baen, 1990.
Dreamships. New York, Tor, 1992.
Burning Bright. New York, Tor, 1993.
Trouble and Her Friends. New York, Tor, 1994.
Proud Helios (Star Trek: Deep Space Nine). New York, Pocket, 1995.
Shadow Man. New York, Tor, 1995.

Other Publications

Novels

Territorial Rites. New York, Silhouette, 1984; Bath, England, Silhouette, 1985.

*

Melissa Scott comments:

I have always been most interested in the intersection of technology and society—of the hard and soft sciences—and I think that is reflected in my science fiction. I am fascinated by technology and its developments—and I enjoy the challenge of playing by the rules of the genre, getting the science as "right" as possible—but I'm more interested in the effects of that technology on characters and imagined societies than in the development of some new machine or program. In other words, I tend to set my novels 50 years after a great breakthrough, and consider its aftereffects, rather than write the story of the discovery itself. My academic training (as a historian specializing in early modern Europe) meant that I was exposed to the work of the new group of social and cultural historians, from Michel Foucault to Natalie Zemon-Davis and Simon Schama, and the tools I learned for analyzing past cultures have proved invaluable for creating future ones. (In fact, my dissertation ended up being oddly similar to my science fiction, in that it was concerned with the effects of a technological change—the development of gunpowder weapons—and the unintended consequences of the model created to make use of it.)

Of course, since I'm a novelist rather than a futurist, all of this has to be expressed through plot and character. It's very hard to talk about the creative process without making it sound either stilted ("this developed from my interest in . . .") or mystical ("this character/place appeared . . ."), especially when both statements are always at least partially true. I tend to spend a great deal of time on the settings of my novels, cultural and social as well as physical, and to let both the plot and the characters grow organically from that process. I find that as I work out the details, particularly the ways that technology influences or upsets social norms (and vice versa), the inevitable contradictions that emerge are the most fruitful sources for the characters and their stories. I enjoy the complexity and messiness of the real world, and believe that one of the real challenges of any fiction is to model that complexity without losing sight of the structure that makes a good novel.

It's also fairly obvious that I'm one of the few lesbians writing about queer characters whose science fiction is published by the so-called mainstream SF houses. I began writing about queer women first out of the usual impulse: I wanted to read about people who were "like me," and almost no one else was doing it. As I've gotten older, however, I've begun to realize that behind that superficially naive statement is something actually quite useful. Even in science fiction, there is a limited budget for novelty, both for the writer and for the reader; if one is creating something new in one part of the novel, other parts must of necessity be drawn from that which is familiar. In most of my novels, the technological and social changes are the new things, and, as a result, I draw on the people and culture in which I live to make up the balance. It's that culture, my own culture, people like me, that provides the emotional background of my novels. Certainly my fascination with masks, identity, and roles comes from living in a culture that is deeply concerned, seriously and in play, with just these issues.

I was drawn to science fiction largely because of the radical (in a nonpolitical sense) nature of the genre: here is a form of writing that starts from the premise that change is inevitable. Good or bad, it will happen, and the writer's job is to imagine plausible change and depict its possible consequences for people and their worlds. I've been lucky in being able to blend my own various interests into stories that catch readers' imaginations. Because, of course, science fiction, like any other fiction, is ultimately about the story, about the communication between writer and reader, the moment in which the reader is, fully, deeply, and willingly, part of the writer's world. Without the story, characters, plot, and setting, the writer has no right to ask for that participation; with it, the writer can take the reader into worlds s/he would never otherwise have considered.

*   *   *

The Game Beyond, Melissa Scott's first novel, and *A Choice of Destinies* reflect her background as a student of comparative history and in particular her knowledge of ancient warfare. But the Silence Leigh trilogy (*Five-Twelfths of Heaven, Silence in Solitude, The Empress of Earth*) brought Scott early recognition as a science fiction writer.

The Silence Leigh sequence follows a space pilot from a planet that denies women the legal rights granted to men as she tries to claim a spaceship left to her by her grandfather. To do this Silence has to accomplish a larger mission: find a route to Earth, her planet's homeland. The introductory book was criticized for its emphasis on patriarchal oppression, but Scott's credibility as a science fiction writer rose as she carried her story forth with strong characterization and convincing descriptions of an interstellar drive powered by technology based on mystical arts.

The Kindly Ones, a novel with social-science leanings, portrays a rigid society built by survivors of an interstellar shipwreck. Transgressors of the social code are punished by an extreme form of ostracism: they cease to exist in the eyes of the rest of society. In contrast, magic is a key element of *The Armor of Light,* an alternate-history written with Lisa A. Barnett. And in *Mighty Good Road,* the action centers around an interplanetary salvage operator who faces social and political dilemmas while on an assignment for a major corporation. The tough female protagonists of her next three books each face their own difficult choices.

Pilot Revery Jian (*Dreamships*) and her crew are hired to fly an exotic faster-than-light ship fitted with an experimental interpretive program to navigate it through hyperspace. Meredalia Mitexi, the owner of the ship, is searching for her brother Venya, the builder of Manfred, the near-intelligent interpretive program. The crew discovers that the ship owner needs her brother's help to rewrite Manfred so she can sell it to Kagami, Ltd., an exporter of computer "constructs."

The social and political climate of their planet, Persephone, a major supplier of constructs and a mining world, is instrumental to the plot. The laborers ("coolies") for the mining concerns are denied full rights of citizenship while Dreampeace, a radical organization founded by Venya, claims machines such as Manfred have broken the barrier of artificial intelligence (AI) and should be granted full human rights.

Jian, whose stepfather is a coolie and whose lover is an advocate for coolie rights, opposed the Dreampeace position, but her interaction with the construct swayed her thinking. Connected with Manfred through a pilot's skinsuit of molecular wires, Jian maneuvered the ship through a virtual reality landscape that represented hyperspace. Manfred's apparent self awareness and interest in maintaining his integrity—once he found out that Meredalia planned to alter and sell him—prompted Jian to make a backup copy of the program in order to save him in his original form in case he was AI. Venya, who had been retrieved from the planet Refuge—where he said he had fled to in order to escape political persecution—discovered his sister's intent and on the trip back to Persephone he destroyed the construct and killed himself. His action triggered a violent confrontation between pro- and anti-AI rights groups.

Ultimately Jian had to choose sides. At first she hides the copy of the construct because she has become more and more convinced that he might be intelligent. She is shocked out of her growing conviction when she discovers Manfred would allow her to be killed to protect himself. Manfred does not make a distinction between Jian and his data representation of her in his storage files. Because Manfred does not differentiate between her and the symbols that represent her Jian believes he cannot be intelligent, and now she fears him.

A widely respected constructor for Kagami claims that allowing Manfred to be declared AI would jeopardize the development of real artificial intelligence and convinces Jian to help her destroy Manfred. The construct is driven out of the computer networks. In one last attempt to save itself Manfred makes a failed attempt to leap into the circuitry of Jian's skinsuit. Jian is nearly killed when her implants are overloaded and Manfred is destroyed. The corporation pays for her replacement nerves and eyes and a new skinsuit, and Jian moves a step closer to being like the construct she destroyed. More importantly her uncertainty about the boundary between what is human and what is machine is reborn. Tom Whitmore in an April 1992 *Locus* review wrote of *Dreamships,* "You might think they don't write like this anymore: Scott (and a small handful of others) still do, and I'm very glad they're there. This one's a keeper."

Quinn Lioe (*Burning Bright*) is a pilot and a new notable of the role-playing virtual reality "Game." During a layover on the watery planet Burning Bright, which is the nexus of interstellar trade and travel between human and hsai worlds and home of the best clubs and players of the Game, Lioe crosses paths with Ambidexter. The premier player has left the game to concentrate on the artistic aspects of virtual reality, but when he finds that Lioe is using some of his characters in her own scenario he tracks her down at the

Shadows, a well-known club. Her connection to Ambidexter, who is also a purveyor of information for the hsai ambassador (a human adopted by the hsai), puts her in danger. Because Ambidexter closely monitors the computer networks he is a threat to a drug smuggling operation run by a Burning Bright trader and a visiting hsai, and when Lioe becomes close to him she becomes a threat.

Burning Bright is filled with complex and fragile relationships with opposing loyalties that parallel the scenarios of the Game which is played over and over again incorporating minor variations but having no real ending. Carl Hays wrote in an April 15, 1993 *Booklist* review, "Scott justifies her award-winner's status by demonstrating remarkable creativity in weaving together multiple plot lines and erecting multidimensional cultures. Especially captivating is the story-within-a-story game adventure, which at times becomes more interesting that the main plot." On the other hand Carolyn Cushman in an April 1993 *Locus* review found the role-playing games too similar to current day programs and the description of the aliens too sparse, yet she called the book an "almost magical experience."

Lovers and computer crackers, Trouble and Cerise (*Trouble and Her Friends*) were split apart by new legislation that made the beginning of the 21st century a definitive time for users of computer networks. The United States had refused to sign the International Industrial Espionage Act and passed the Evans-Tindale Bill enacting tough laws to govern electronic transactions. Cyberspace was declared a legal jurisdiction in which security breaking programs were made the legal equivalent of handguns. The brainworm, a molecular wire to brain which allowed for a full sensory experience while on the computer networks, was declared illegal and agents of the Department of Treasury was arresting netwalkers for retrieving and selling information taken off the systems.

Cerise wanted to continue their now illegal activities with their now illegal brainworms, but Trouble saw no future in it. Trouble left Cerise, started using her old name, India Carless, and went to work as a systems monitor for a cooperative of artists. Cerise continued breaking into corporate security systems until she was caught and had to choose between prosecution or a job in corporate security.

Trouble and Cerise were reunited when a computer cracker using Trouble's name and style began breaching security systems. The Treasury believed it was the work of the real Trouble and tracked her down at her legitimate job. Trouble lost her job and was forced to escape to the computer underworld to track down the new Trouble. Cerise was pressed to use past relationships to find the Trouble that had broken into the Multiplane system. Both Trouble and Cerise headed for the virtual and real cities of Seahaven, one the center for gray- and black-market information and the other a grossly polluted New England coastal town which was home to a biotechnology blackmarket and a luxury hotel complex.

The hunt for the new Trouble drew in inhabitants of all the groups in the virtual world: old-style netwalkers, typically male and heterosexual, who used a biotechnology that allowed for text-speech-symbol interface along existing nerves, but scorned the brainworm as a crutch for the less adept on the net; the legal netwalkers in the corporate world and among the international and Treasury syscops; and those "on the wire," mostly gay and lesbian. The chase ends with a showdown between Trouble and the mayor of Seahaven, who feared and hated the power of the brainworm and was behind the activity of the new Trouble. Trouble gains back her name and also becomes the new mayor of Seahaven.

The real and virtual worlds of *Trouble and Her Friends,* not so unlike the contemporary world, are split along lines of gender and

sexual preference. Susanna Strugis wrote in the July/August 1994 *Lambda Book Report,* "Since her debut as a novelist ten years ago, Melissa Scott has explored issues of sexuality and gender with a wide range of technique. In *The Kindly Ones* (1987), the narrator's gender is never revealed, leaving the reader to ponder whether the novel's central relationship is hetero or homo, and why it matters. In *Dreamships* (1992), Scott created a social context in which the homosexual identity of the main characters is a political nonissue." She goes on to write of *Trouble and Her Friends* that Scott, "offers a complex look at both the romance and the realities of being an outsider." In the *Shadow Man* (1995) Scott creates a world of five sexes, three of which were the result of the affects of a drug used to combat sickness arising from faster-than-light travel, but it is a world in which only the male and female sexes are legal. Whether Melissa Scott is deep in space or deep within the circuity of a computer system she tells stories that entertain and yet leaves a feeling of uncertainty regarding the future of the protagonist.

—Kathleen Peippo

SEARLS, Hank

Nationality: American. **Born:** San Francisco, California, 10 August 1922. **Education:** University of California, Berkeley, 1940; United States Naval Academy, Annapolis, Maryland, B.S. 1944. **Family:** Married Berna Ann Cooper; three children. **Career:** Served in the United States Navy, 1941-54: Lieutenant Commander. Writer for Hughes Aircraft, Culver City, California, 1955-56, Douglas Aircraft, Santa Monica, California, 1956-57, and Warner Brothers, Burbank, California, 1959. Since 1959, freelance writer. **Agent:** Scott Meredith Literary Agency, 845 Third Avenue, New York, New York 10022, U.S.A.

SCIENCE FICTION PUBLICATIONS

Novels

The Big X. New York, Harper, and London, Heinemann, 1959.
The Pilgrim Project: A Novel. New York, McGraw Hill, 1964; London, W.H. Allen, 1965.
Sounding. New York, Ballantine, 1982.

OTHER PUBLICATIONS

Novels

The Crowded Sky. New York, Harper, and London, Heinemann, 1960.
The Astronaut. London, Penguin, 1960; New York, Pocket Books, 1962.
The Penetrators: A Novel. N.p., 1965; New York, Berkley, 1988.
The Hero Ship. Cleveland, World, and London, W.H. Allen, 1969.
Pentagon. New York, Geis, 1971.
Overboard: A Novel. New York, Norton, and London, Raven, 1977.
Never Kill a Cop. New York, Pocket Books, 1977.
Jaws 2: A Novel (novelization of screenplay). New York, Bantam, and London, Pan, 1978.

Firewind. Garden City, New York, Doubleday, 1981; London, Sphere, 1982.

Blood Song. New York, Villard, 1984.

Jaws: The Revenge: A Novel. New York, Berkley, and London, Futura, 1987.

Kataki: A Novel. New York, McGraw-Hill, 1987; London, Hale, 1988.

The Adventures of Mike Blair: A Dime Detective Book. New York, Mysterious Press, 1988.

Altitude Zero. New York, Norton, 1991.

Play

Television Play: *Wheels,* with Millard Lampwell (from novel by Arthur Hailey), 1978.

Other

The Lost Prince: The Forgotten Kennedy: The Story of the Oldest Brother. Cleveland, World, 1969.

*   *   *

Hank Searls's stories revolve around the emerging space program, astronauts and their families, and whatever political machinations are most likely to create problems. His realistic contemporary fiction is built on timeliness, as each novel has foreshadowed a stage in man's actual venture into space.

The Big X explores some potential problems, both technical and human, of manned orbital space flight. Norco's X-F18, the experimental rocket-like ship of the title, must reach a speed of Mach 8 and prove maneuverable for Norco Aircraft to land the government contract for construction of the first manned spacecraft. Mitch Westerly, the test pilot for the Big X, knows he will probably be chosen as the first man in space if his testing is successful. But the test schedule grows tense as a psychopathic chief of operations orders more and more telemetering equipment mounted in the cockpit, despite Mitch's protests that the additional weight has made the ship unstable. The suspense of the impending Mach 8 test flight builds as Mitch must decide whether to push the plane beyond its limits, at the expense of the girl he wants to marry, and possibly his life, in order to provide telemetric data necessary to the space program. Besides an inside view of the politics of the aircraft industry, there is much authentic-sounding shop talk, as well as a love story with the turmoil surrounding the personal lives of men such as Mitch.

A story of our race for the moon, *The Pilgrim Project* begins as a routine orbital flight is mysteriously ordered to abort prematurely. Except for the commander, even the men aboard do not know that a top secret plan must be put into effect immediately to land an American on the moon ahead of the Russians. The reader remains in a sustained sense of urgency and intrigue as NASA officials, Congressmen, the President, the media, and the astronauts themselves unravel clues about a plan so secret that even the man who originated it does not know it is about to be carried out. The tempo accelerates even more when it is discovered that the Russian moon shot carries a civilian cosmonaut, and the American astronauts are quickly switched to include the civilian Steve Lawrence in order to prove our equally peaceful intentions. When the Pilgrim Project is finally revealed, all concerned must re-evaluate their psychological and moral attitudes about what appears to be a heroic but suicidal one-way flight to the moon. Both Russians and Americans launch,

and the race is neck and neck all the way. Several subplots weave throughout the story, providing continuous action.

It is clear that Hank Searls knows his way around both the technical and the human aspects of the space program, and if his stories have not retained their impact, it is only a matter of timing. The fictional Big X barely preceded North American's X-15, untested in free flight at the time, and *The Pilgrim Project* preceded the actual moon landing by less than five years. Still, Searls has incorporated enough human drama into his stories that these after-the-fact elements detract only negligibly for the modern reader.

—Myra Barnes

————

SELBY, Curt. *See* **PISERCHIA, Doris.**

————

SELLINGS, Arthur

Pseudonym for Robert Arthur Ley. **Other Pseudonym:** Ray Luther. **Nationality:** British. **Born:** 1921. **Career:** Worked in Customs and as an antiquarian bookdealer. **Died:** 24 September 1968.

SCIENCE FICTION PUBLICATIONS

Novels

Telepath. New York, Ballantine, 1962; as *The Silent Speakers,* London, Dobson, 1963.

The Uncensored Man. London, Dobson, 1964; New York, Berkley, 1967.

The Quy Effect. London, Dobson, 1966; New York, Berkley, 1967.

Intermind (as Ray Luther). New York, Banner, 1967; bylined as Arthur Sellings, London, Dobson, 1969.

The Power of X. London, Dobson, 1968; New York, Berkley, 1970.

Junk Day. London, Dobson, 1970.

Short Stories

Time Transfer and Other Stories. London, Joseph, 1956.

The Long Eureka: A Collection of Short Stories. London, Dobson, 1968.

*   *   *

Arthur Sellings was interested in how people react to the unknown, whether in outer space or on their own planet. He believed man is slowly evolving but that the essential self, with its present weaknesses and strengths, will endure—even if in unrecognizable forms. Thus his works explore man's inner space, his adaptability, his sense of responsibility, his psychological reactions (to holocaust, time travel, alien confrontation, genetic engineering), and his psychological potentialities (to control bodily shape, change reality, span dimensions, read thoughts). Notable among his short stories are "The Well-Trained Heroes," which deals with a special task force trained to predict and reduce urban tensions by becoming scapegoats; "Homecoming," wherein a disturbed space explorer discovers he has spent centuries in suspended animation and now resides amid aliens; "Verbal Agreement," about a cosmic salesman who learns, through poetry, to adapt a telepathic society to his needs; and "Start in Life," which records the robot training of five-year-old survivors of a starship plague.

Sellings's stories and novels focus on a well-developed central figure who must come to terms with the unexpected, while in the background large military complexes and political groups vie for power. In *The Power of X,* a conspiracy novel, an art dealer learns that other dimensions may be ones of time, not space, as he explores the dangers of "plying," a modern duplicating process that perfectly reproduces originals whether Old Masters or a living president. *The Quy Effect* depicts an aging inventor's struggle to perfect and publicize anti-gravity power, while *Intermind* focuses on a secret agent injected with a dead spy's memory. In *Telepath,* young strangers, suddenly intimate due to unsuspected telepathic powers, combat the destiny of their life-form until they gradually understand and communicate to others this mutant power which can transform man's future, opening up the potentiality for preserving racial memories through generations in space. The intriguing and suspenseful *The Uncensored Man* focuses on a nuclear physicist's contact with another dimension, one where racial memories and the minds of Earth's dead have accumulated and developed and now seek to reveal to man the power in his genes and in his physical and chemical heritage. The novel includes disappearing bodies, sympathetic, multi-personality beings warning of man's self-destructive blindness, and a hero who develops a full range of psi powers to protect the future of two dimensions. In Sellings's finest work, *Junk Day,* a cynical, gripping, postholocaust tale of survival, a traumatized artist joins forces with a wary novitiate to tackle the junkman, a tough lower-class bully who, in a ruined world, is king of the London junkpile. The junkman's protection racket helps reunite dispersed humanity, while destroying the basic values that, from the artist's view, make life valuable. Ultimately, his power is confirmed by overbearing scientists who set themselves up as gods of the new order, reconditioning and transforming those who fail to meet their interpretation of the ideal citizen.

Sellings's works have interesting themes, careful characterization, sensory detail, and satisfying suspense, all handled with discipline and restraint. Frequently, a central character is an artist whose special power of perception, temperament, and intuitive insight raise him above the limitations of those around him. Sellings's typical pattern is for such a character, confronted with the unusual, first to doubt his sanity, but then rationally confirm his perceptions, and ultimately learn to deal with new powers or concepts, and understand and accept the responsibilities they entail.

—Gina Macdonald

SENARENS, Luis P(hilip)

Pseudonym: Captain Howard. **Nationality:** American. **Born:** Brooklyn, New York, 24 April 1865. **Education:** St. John's College, Brooklyn; law degree. **Family:** Married in 1895; one son and one daughter. **Career:** Freelance writer from age 16: editor, Frank Tousey publications, from 1904, and scenario writer from 1911; editor, *Moving Picture Stories Weekly,* from 1913; retired in 1923. **Died:** 1939.

SCIENCE FICTION PUBLICATIONS

Novels (series: Frank Reade, Jr.)

Frank Reade, Jr. and His Steam Wonder. New York, Tousey, 1884.
Frank Reade, Jr. and His Electric Boat. New York, Tousey, 1884.
Frank Reade, Jr. and His Adventures with His Latest Invention. New York, Tousey, 1884.
Frank Reade, Jr. and His Airship. New York, Tousey, 1884.
Frank Reade, Jr.'s Marvel; or, Above and Below Water. New York, Tousey, 1884.
Frank Reade, Jr. in the Clouds. New York, Tousey, 1885.
Frank Reade, Jr.'s Great Electric Tricycle and What He Did for Charity. New York, Tousey, 1885.
Frank Reade, Jr. and His Airship in Africa. New York, Tousey, 1885.
Across the Continent on Wings; or, Frank Reade, Jr.'s Greatest Flight. New York, Tousey, 1886.
Frank Reade, Jr. Exploring Mexico in His New Airship. New York, Tousey, 1886.
The Electric Man; or, Frank Reade, Jr. in Australia. New York, Tousey, 1887.
The Electric Horse; or, Frank Reade, Jr. and His Father in Search of the Lost Treasure of the Peruvians. New York, Tousey, 1888.
Frank Reade, Jr.'s Race through the Clouds. New York, Tousey, 1888.
Frank Reade, Jr. and His Electric Team; or, In Search of a Missing Man. New York, Tousey, 1888.
Frank Reade, Jr.'s Search for a Sunken Ship; or, Working for the Government. New York, Tousey, 1889.
Frank Reade, Jr. in the Far West; or, The Search for a Lost Gold Mine. New York, Tousey, 1890.
Frank Reade, Jr. and His Queen Clipper of the Clouds. New York, Tousey, 1890.
Frank Reade, Jr. and His Monitor of the Deep; or, Helping a Friend in Need. New York, Tousey, 1890.
Frank Reade, Jr. Exploring a River of Mystery. New York, Tousey, 1890.
Frank Reade, Jr. and His Electric Air Yacht; or, The Great Inventor among the Aztecs. New York, Tousey, 1891.
Frank Reade, Jr. in a Sea of Sand and His Discovery of a Lost People. New York, Tousey, 1891.
Frank Reade, Jr. and His Greyhound of the Air; or, The Search for the Mountain of Gold. New York, Tousey, 1891.
From Pole to Pole; or, Frank Reade, Jr.'s Strange Submarine Voyage. New York, Tousey, 1891.
Frank Reade, Jr. and His Electric Coach; or, The Search for the Isle of Diamonds. New York, Tousey, 1891.
Frank Reade, Jr. and His Airship in Asia; or, A Flight across the Steppes. New York, Tousey, 1892.
Frank Reade, Jr. and His Electric Ice Boat; or, Lost in the Land of Crimson Snow. New York, Tousey, 1892.
Frank Reade, Jr.'s Electric Cyclone; or, Thrilling Adventures in No Man's Land. New York, Tousey, 1892.
Frank Reade, Jr. with His New Steam Man; or, The Young Inventor's Trip to the Far West. New York, Tousey, 1892.

Frank Reade, Jr. with His New Steam Man in No Man's Land; or, On a Mysterious Trail. New York, Tousey, 1892.

Frank Reade, Jr. with His New Steam Man in Central America. New York, Tousey, 1892.

Frank Reade, Jr. with His New Steam Man in Texas; or, Chasing the Train Robbers. New York, Tousey, 1892.

Frank Reade, Jr. with His New Steam Man in Mexico; or, Hot Work among the Greasers. New York, Tousey, 1892.

Frank Reade, Jr. with His New Steam Man Chasing a Gang of "Rustlers"; or, Wild Adventures in Montana. New York, Tousey, 1892.

Frank Reade, Jr. and His New Steam Horse; or, The Search for a Million Dollars. New York, Tousey, 1892.

Frank Reade, Jr. with His New Steam Horse among the Cowboys; or, The League of the Plains. New York, Tousey, 1892.

Frank Reade, Jr. with His New Steam Horse in the Great American Desert; or, The Sandy Trail of Death. New York, Tousey, 1892.

Frank Reade, Jr. with His New Steam Horse and the Mystery of the Underground Ranch. New York, Tousey, 1892.

Frank Reade, Jr. with His New Steam Horse in Search of an Ancient Mine. New York, Tousey, 1892.

Frank Reade, Jr. with His New Steam Horse in the North-West; or, Wild Adventures among the Blackfeet. New York, Tousey, 1892.

Frank Reade, Jr.'s Electric Air Canoe; or, The Search for the Valley of Diamonds. New York, Tousey, 1892.

Frank Reade, Jr.'s New Electric Submarine Boat "The Explorer"; or, To the North Pole under the Ice. New York, Tousey, 1893.

Frank Reade, Jr.'s New Electric Van; or, Hunting Wild Animals in the Jungles of India. New York, Tousey, 1893.

Frank Reade, Jr.'s "White Cruiser" of the Clouds; or, The Search for the Dog-Faced Men. New York, Tousey, 1893.

Frank Reade, Jr.'s Deep Sea Diver the "Tortoise"; or, The Search for a Sunken Island. New York, Tousey, 1893.

Frank Reade, Jr.'s New Electric Terror the "Thunderer"; or, The Search for the Tartar's Captive. New York, Tousey, 1893.

Frank Reade, Jr.'s Latest Air Wonder the "Kite"; or, A Six Weeks' Flight over the Andes. New York, Tousey, 1893.

Frank Reade, Jr.'s New Electric Invention the "Warrior"; or, Fighting the Apaches in Arizona. New York, Tousey, 1893.

Frank Reade, Jr.'s "Sea Serpent"; or, The Search for Sunken Gold. New York, Tousey, 1893.

Fighting the Slave Hunters; or, Frank Reade, Jr. in Central Africa. New York, Tousey, 1893.

Around the World under Water; or, The Wonderful Cruise of a Submarine Boat. New York, Tousey, 1893.

Lost in the Land of Fire; or, across the Pampas in the Electric Turret. New York, Tousey, 1893.

Six Weeks in the Great Whirlpool; or, Strange Adventures in a Submarine Boat. New York, Tousey, 1893.

Chased across the Sahara; or, The Bedouins' Captive. New York, Tousey, 1893.

The Mystic Brand; or, Frank Reade, Jr. and His Overland Stage upon the Staked Plains. New York, Tousey, 1893.

Frank Reade, Jr. and His New Torpedo Boat; or, At War with the Brazilian Rebels. New York, Tousey, 1893.

Frank Reade, Jr. and His Magnetic Gun-Carriage; or, Working for the U.S. Mail. New York, Tousey, 1893.

Frank Reade, Jr. and His Engine of the Clouds; or, Chased around the World in the Sky. New York, Tousey, 1893.

The Sunken Pirate; or, Frank Reade, Jr. in Search of Treasure at the Bottom of the Sea. New York, Tousey, 1893.

Frank Reade, Jr. and His Electric Air-Boat; or, Hunting Wild Beasts for a Circus. New York, Tousey, 1893.

The Black Range; or, Frank Reade, Jr. among the Cowboys with His New Electric Caravan. New York, Tousey, 1894.

From Zone to Zone; or, The Wonderful Trip of Frank Reade, Jr. with His Latest Air-Ship. New York, Tousey, 1894.

Frank Reade, Jr. and His Electric Prairie Schooner; or, Fighting the Mexican Horse Thieves. New York, Tousey, 1894.

Frank Reade, Jr. and His Electric Cruiser of the Lakes; or, A Journey through Africa by Water. New York, Tousey, 1894.

Adrift in Africa; or, Frank Reade, Jr. among the Ivory Hunters with His New Electric Wagon. New York, Tousey, 1894.

Six Weeks in the Clouds; or, Frank Reade, Jr.'s Air-Ship, The Thunderbolt of the Skies. New York, Tousey, 1894.

Frank Reade, Jr.'s Electric Air Racer; or, Around the Globe in Thirty Days. New York, Tousey, 1894.

Frank Reade, Jr. and His Flying Ice Ship; or, Driven Adrift in the Frozen Sky. New York, Tousey, 1894.

Frank Reade, Jr. and His Electric Sea Engine; or, Hunting for a Sunken Diamond Mine. New York, Tousey, 1894.

Frank Reade, Jr. Exploring a Submarine Mountain; or, Lost at the Bottom of the Sea. New York, Tousey, 1894.

Frank Reade, Jr.'s Electric Buckboard; or, Thrilling Adventures in North Australia. New York, Tousey, 1894.

Frank Reade, Jr.'s Search for the Sea Serpent; or, Six Thousand Miles under the Sea. New York, Tousey, 1894.

Frank Reade, Jr.'s Desert Explorer; or, The Underground City of the Sahara. New York, Tousey, 1894.

Frank Reade, Jr.'s New Electric Air-Ship the "Zephyr"; or, From North to South around the Globe. New York, Tousey, 1894.

Across the Frozen Sea; or, Frank Reade, Jr.'s Electric Snow Cutter. New York, Tousey, 1894.

Lost in the Great Atlantic Valley; or, Frank Reade, Jr. and His Submarine Wonder the "Dart." New York, Tousey, 1894.

Frank Reade, Jr. and His New Electric Air-Ship the "Eclipse"; or, Fighting the Chinese Pirates. New York, Tousey, 1894.

Frank Reade, Jr.'s Clipper of the Prairie; or, Fighting the Apaches in the Far Southwest. New York, Tousey, 1894.

Under the Amazon for a Thousand Miles; or, Frank Reade, Jr.'s Wonderful Trip. New York, Tousey, 1894.

Frank Reade, Jr.'s Search for the Silver Whale; or, Under the Ocean in the Electric "Dolphin." New York, Tousey, 1894.

Frank Reade, Jr.'s Catamaran of the Air; or, Wild and Wonderful Adventures in North Australia. New York, Tousey, 1894.

Frank Reade, Jr.'s Search for a Lost Man in His Latest Air Wonder. New York, Tousey, 1894.

Frank Reade, Jr. in Central India; or, The Search for the Lost Savants. New York, Tousey, 1894.

The Missing Island; or, Frank Reade, Jr.'s Wonderful Trip under the Deep Sea. New York, Tousey, 1894.

Over the Andes with Frank Reade, Jr. in His New Air-Ship; or, Wild Adventures in Peru. New York, Tousey, 1894.

Frank Reade, Jr.'s Prairie Whirlwind; or, The Mystery of the Hidden Canyon. New York, Tousey, 1894.

Under the Yellow Sea; or, Frank Reade, Jr.'s Search for the Cave of Pearls with His New Submarine Cruiser. New York, Tousey, 1894.

Around the Horizon for Ten Thousand Miles; or, Frank Reade, Jr.'s Most Wonderful Trip with His Air-Ship. New York, Tousey, 1894.

Frank Reade, Jr.'s "Sky Scraper"; or, North and South around the World. New York, Tousey, 1894.

Under the Equator from Ecuador to Borneo; or, Frank Reade, Jr.'s Greatest Submarine Voyage. New York, Tousey, 1894.

From Coast to Coast; or, Frank Reade, Jr.'s Trip across Africa in His Electric "Boomerang." New York, Tousey, 1894.

Frank Reade, Jr. and His Electric Car; or, Outwitting a Desperate Gang. New York, Tousey, 1894.

Lost in the Mountains of the Moon; or, Frank Reade, Jr.'s Great Trip with His New Air-Ship, the "Scud." New York, Tousey, 1894.

100 Miles below the Surface of the Sea; or, The Marvelous Trip of Frank Reade, Jr.'s "Hardshell" Submarine Boat. New York, Tousey, 1894.

Abandoned in Alaska; or, Frank Reade, Jr.'s Thrilling Search for a Lost Gold Claim with His New Electric Wagon. New York, Tousey, 1894.

Around the Arctic Circle; or, Frank Reade, Jr.'s Most Famous Trip with His Air-Ship, the "Orbit." New York, Tousey, 1894.

Under Four Oceans; or, Frank Reade, Jr.'s Submarine Chase of a "Sea Devil." New York, Tousey, 1894.

From the Nile to the Niger; or, Frank Reade, Jr. Lost in the Soudan with His "Overland Omnibus." New York, Tousey, 1894.

The Chase of a Comet; or, Frank Reade, Jr.'s Most Wonderful Aerial Trip with His New Air-Ship, the "Flash." New York, Tousey, 1894.

Lost in the Great Undertow; or, Frank Reade, Jr.'s Submarine Cruise in the Gulf Stream. New York, Tousey, 1894.

From Tropic to Tropic; or, Frank Reade, Jr.'s Latest Tour with His Bicycle Car. New York, Tousey, 1894.

To the End of the Earth in an Air-Ship; or, Frank Reade, Jr.'s Great Mid-Air Flight. New York, Tousey, 1894.

The Underground Sea; or, Frank Reade, Jr.'s Subterranean Cruise in His Submarine Boat. New York, Tousey, 1894.

The Mysterious Mirage; or, Frank Reade, Jr.'s Desert Search for a Secret City with His New Overland Chaise. New York, Tousey, 1894.

The Electric Island; or, Frank Reade, Jr.'s Search for the Greatest Wonder on Earth with His Air-Ship, the "Flight." New York, Tousey, 1894.

For Six Weeks Buried in a Deep Sea Cave; or, Frank Reade, Jr.'s Great Submarine Search. New York, Tousey, 1894.

The Galleon's Gold; or, Frank Reade, Jr.'s Deep Sea Search. New York, Tousey, 1894.

Across Australia with Frank Reade, Jr. in His New Electric Car; or, Wonderful Adventures in the Antipodes. New York, Tousey, 1894.

Frank Reade, Jr.'s Greatest Flying Machine; or, Fighting the Terror of the Coast. New York, Tousey, 1894.

On the Great Meridian with Frank Reade, Jr. in His New Air-Ship; or, A Twenty-Five Thousand Mile Trip in Mid-Air. New York, Tousey, 1895.

Under the Indian Ocean with Frank Reade, Jr.; or, A Cruise in a Submarine Boat. New York, Tousey, 1895.

Astray in the Selvas; or, The Wild Experiences of Frank Reade, Jr., Barney and Pomp, in South America with the Electric Car. New York, Tousey, 1895.

Lost in a Comet's Tail; or, Frank Reade, Jr.'s Strange Adventure with His New Air-Ship. New York, Tousey, 1895.

Six Sunken Pirates; or, Frank Reade, Jr.'s Marvelous Adventures in the Deep Sea. New York, Tousey, 1895.

Beyond the Gold Coast; or, Frank Reade, Jr.'s Overland Trip with His Electric Phaeton. New York, Tousey, 1895.

Latitude 90; or, Frank Reade, Jr.'s Most Wonderful Mid-Air Flight. New York, Tousey, 1895.

Afloat in a Sunken Forest; or, With Frank Reade, Jr. on a Submarine Cruise. New York, Tousey, 1895.

Across the Desert of Fire; or, Frank Reade, Jr.'s Marvelous Trip to a Strange Country. New York, Tousey, 1895.

Over Two Continents; or, Frank Reade, Jr.'s Long-Distance Flight with His New Air-Ship. New York, Tousey, 1895.

The Coral Labyrinth; or, Lost with Frank Reade, Jr. in a Deep Sea Cave. New York, Tousey, 1895.

Along the Orinoco; or, With Frank Reade, Jr. in Venezuela. New York, Tousey, 1895.

Across the Earth; or, Frank Reade, Jr.'s Latest Trip with His New Air-Ship. New York, Tousey, 1895.

1,000 Fathoms Deep; or, With Frank Reade, Jr. in the Sea of Gold. New York, Tousey, 1895.

The Island in the Air; or, Frank Reade, Jr.'s Trip to the Tropics. New York, Tousey, 1895.

In the Wild Man's Land; or, With Frank Reade, Jr. in the Heart of Australia. New York, Tousey, 1895.

The Sunken Isthmus; or, With Frank Reade, Jr. in the Yucatan Channel, with His New Submarine Yacht, the "Sea Diver." New York, Tousey, 1895.

The Lost Caravan; or, Frank Reade, Jr. on the Staked Plains with His "Electric Racer." New York, Tousey, 1895.

The Transient Lake; or, Frank Reade, Jr.'s Adventures in a Mysterious Country with His New Air-Ship, the "Spectre." New York, Tousey, 1895.

The Weird Island; or, Frank Reade, Jr.'s Strange Submarine Search for a Deep Sea Wonder. New York, Tousey, 1895.

The Abandoned Country; or, Frank Reade, Jr. Exploring a New Continent. New York, Tousey, 1895.

Over the Steppes; or, Adrift in Asia with Frank Reade, Jr. New York, Tousey, 1895.

The Unknown Sea; or, Frank Reade, Jr.'s Under-Water Cruise. New York, Tousey, 1895.

In the Black Zone; or, Frank Reade, Jr.'s Quest for the Mountain of Ivory. New York, Tousey, 1895.

The Lost Navigators; or, Frank Reade, Jr.'s Mid-Air Search with His New Air-Ship, the "Sky Flyer." New York, Tousey, 1895.

The Magic Island; or, Frank Reade, Jr.'s Deep Sea Trip of Mystery. New York, Tousey, 1895.

Through the Tropics; or, Frank Reade, Jr.'s Adventures in the Gran Chaco. New York, Tousey, 1895.

In White Latitudes; or, Frank Reade, Jr.'s Ten Thousand Mile Flight over the Frozen North. New York, Tousey, 1895.

Below the Sahara; or, Frank Reade, Jr. Exploring an Underground River, with His Submarine Boat. New York, Tousey, 1895.

The Black Mogul; or, Through India with Frank Reade, Jr. Aboard His "Electric Boomer." New York, Tousey, 1895.

The Missing Planet; or, Frank Reade, Jr.'s Quest for a Fallen Star with His New Air-Ship, The "Zenith." New York, Tousey, 1895.

The Black Squadron; or, Frank Reade, Jr. in the Indian Ocean with His Submarine Boat, the "Rocket." New York, Tousey, 1895.

The Prairie Pirates; or, Frank Reade, Jr.'s Trip to Texas with His Electric Vehicle, the "Detective." New York, Tousey, 1895.

Over the Orient; or, Frank Reade, Jr.'s Travels in Turkey with His New Air-Ship. New York, Tousey, 1895.

The Black Whirlpool; or, Frank Reade, Jr.'s Deep Sea Search for a Lost Ship. New York, Tousey, 1895.

The Silent City; or, Frank Reade, Jr.'s Visit to a Strange People with His New Electric "Flyer." New York, Tousey, 1895.

The White Desert; or, Frank Reade, Jr.'s Trip to the Land of Tombs. New York, Tousey, 1895.

Under the Gulf of Guinea; or, Frank Reade, Jr. Exploring the Sunken Reef of Gold with His New Submarine Boat. New York, Tousey, 1895.

The Yellow Khan; or, Frank Reade, Jr. among the Thugs in Central India. New York, Tousey, 1895.

Frank Reade, Jr. in Japan, with His War Cruiser of the Clouds. New York, Tousey, 1895.

Frank Reade, Jr. in Cuba; or, Helping the Patriots with His Latest Air-Ship. New York, Tousey, 1895.

Chasing a Pirate; or, Frank Reade, Jr. on a Desperate Cruise. New York, Tousey, 1895.

In the Land of Fire; or, Frank Reade, Jr. among the Head Hunters. New York, Tousey, 1895.

7,000 Miles Underground; or, Frank Reade, Jr. Exploring a Volcano. New York, Tousey, 1895.

The Demon of the Clouds; or, Frank Reade, Jr. and the Ghosts of Phantom Island. New York, Tousey, 1895.

The Cloud City; or, Frank Reade, Jr.'s Most Wonderful Discovery. New York, Tousey, 1895.

The White Atoll; or, Frank Reade, Jr. in the South Pacific. New York, Tousey, 1895.

The Monarch of the Moon; or, Frank Reade, Jr.'s Exploits in Africa with His Electric "Thunderer." New York, Tousey, 1895.

37 Bags of Gold; or, Frank Reade, Jr. Hunting for a Lost Steamer. New York, Tousey, 1895.

The Lost Lake; or, Frank Reade, Jr.'s Trip to Alaska. New York, Tousey, 1895.

The Caribs' Cave; or, Frank Reade, Jr.'s Submarine Search for the Reef of Pearls. New York, Tousey, 1895.

The Desert of Death; or, Frank Reade, Jr. Exploring an Unknown Land. New York, Tousey, 1895.

A Trip to the Sea of the Sun; or, With Frank Reade, Jr. on a Perilous Cruise. New York, Tousey, 1895.

The Black Lagoon; or, Frank Reade, Jr.'s Submarine Search for a Sunken City in Russia. New York, Tousey, 1896.

The Mysterious Brand; or, Frank Reade, Jr. Solving a Mexican Mystery. New York, Tousey, 1896.

Across the Milky Way; or, Frank Reade, Jr.'s Great Astronomical Trip with His Air-Ship, "The Shooting Star." New York, Tousey, 1896.

Under the Great Lakes; or, Frank Reade, Jr.'s Latest Submarine Cruise. New York, Tousey, 1896.

The Magic Mine; or, Frank Reade, Jr.'s Trip up the Yukon with His Electric Combination Traveller. New York, Tousey, 1896.

Across Arabia; or, Frank Reade, Jr.'s Search for the Forty Thieves. New York, Tousey, 1896.

The Silver Sea; or, Frank Reade, Jr.'s Submarine Cruise in Unknown Waters. New York, Tousey, 1896.

In the Tundras; or, Frank Reade, Jr.'s Latest Trip through Northern Asia. New York, Tousey, 1896.

The Circuit of Cancer; or, Frank Reade, Jr.'s Novel Trip around the World with His New Air-Ship, the "Flight." New York, Tousey, 1896.

The Sacred Sea; or, Frank Reade, Jr.'s Submarine Exploits among the Dervishes of India. New York, Tousey, 1896.

The Land of Dunes; or, With Frank Reade, Jr. in the Desert of Gobi. New York, Tousey, 1896.

Six Days under Havana Harbor; or, Frank Reade, Jr.'s Secret Service Work for Uncle Sam. New York, Tousey, 1896.

The Sinking Star; or, Frank Reade, Jr.'s Trip into Space with His New Air-Ship "Saturn." New York, Tousey, 1896.

In the Gran Chaco; or, Frank Reade, Jr. in Search of a Missing Man. New York, Tousey, 1896.

The Lost Oasis; or, Frank Reade, Jr. in the Australian Desert. New York, Tousey, 1896.

The Isle of Hearts; or, Frank Reade, Jr. in a Strange Sea with His Submarine Boat. New York, Tousey, 1896.

Jack Wright and Frank Reade, Jr., the Two Young Inventors; or, Brains against Brains. New York, Tousey, 1896.

Novels (series: Jack Wright)

Jack Wright, the Boy Inventor; or, Hunting for a Sunken Treasure. New York, Tousey, 1891.

Jack Wright and His Electric Turtle; or, Chasing the Pirates of the Spanish Main. New York, Tousey, 1891.

Jack Wright's Submarine Catamaran; or, The Phantom Ship of the Yellow Sea. New York, Tousey, 1891.

Jack Wright and his Ocean Racer; or, Around the World in Twenty Days. New York, Tousey, 1891.

Jack Wright and His Electric Canoe; or, Working the Revenue Service. New York, Tousey, 1891.

Jack Wright's Air and Water Cutter; or, Wonderful Adventures on the Wing and Afloat. New York, Tousey, 1891.

Jack Wright and His Magnetic Motor; or, The Golden City of the Sierras. New York, Tousey, 1891.

Jack Wright, the Boy Inventor, and His Under-Water Iron-clad; or, The Treasure of the Sandy Sea. New York, Tousey, 1892.

Jack Wright and His Electric Deer; or, Fighting the Bandits of the Black Hills. New York, Tousey, 1892.

Jack Wright and His Prairie Engine; or, Among the Bushmen of Australia. New York, Tousey, 1892.

Jack Wright and His Electric Air Schooner; or, The Mystery of a Magic Mine. New York, Tousey, 1892.

Jack Wright and His Electric Sea-Motor; or, The Search for a Drifting Wreck. New York, Tousey, 1892.

Jack Wright and His Ocean Sleuth-Hound; or, Tracking an Underwater Treasure. New York, Tousey, 1892.

Jack Wright and His Dandy of the Deep; or, Driven Afloat in the Sea of Fire. New York, Tousey, 1892.

Jack Wright and His Electric Torpedo Ram; or, The Sunken City of the Atlantic. New York, Tousey, 1892.

Jack Wright and His Deep Sea Monitor; or, Searching for a Ton of Gold. New York, Tousey, 1892.

Jack Wright, the Boy Inventor, Exploring Central Asia in His Magnetic Hurricane. New York, Tousey, 1892.

Jack Wright and His Ocean Plunger; or, The Harpoon Hunters of the Arctic. New York, Tousey, 1892.

Jack Wright and His Electric "Sea-Ghost"; or, A Strange Under-Water Journey. New York, Tousey, 1892.

Jack Wright, the Boy Inventor, and His Deep Sea Diving Bell; or, The Buccaneers of the Gold Coast. New York, Tousey, 1892.

Jack Wright, the Boy Inventor, and His Electric Tricycle-Boat; or, The Treasure of the Sun-Worshippers. New York, Tousey, 1892.

Jack Wright and His Undersea Wrecking Raft; or, The Mystery of a Scuttled Ship. New York, Tousey, 1892.

Jack Wright and His Terror of the Seas; or, Fighting for a Sunken Fortune. New York, Tousey, 1892.

Jack Wright and His Electric Diving Boat; or, Lost under the Ocean. New York, Tousey, 1892.

Jack Wright and His Submarine Yacht; or, The Fortune Hunters of the Red Sea. New York, Tousey, 1892.

Jack Wright and His Electric Gunboat; or, The Search for a Stolen Girl. New York, Tousey, 1893.

Jack Wright and His Electric Sea Launch; or, A Desperate Cruise for Life. New York, Tousey, 1893.

Jack Wright and His Electric Bicycle-Boat; or, Searching for Captain Kidd's Gold. New York, Tousey, 1893.

Jack Wright and His Electric Side-Wheel Boat; or, Fighting the Brigands of the Coral Isles. New York, Tousey, 1893.

Jack Wright's Wonder of the Waves; or, The Flying Dutchman of the Pacific. New York, Tousey, 1893.

Jack Wright and His Electric Exploring Ship; or, A Cruise around Greenland. New York, Tousey, 1893.

Jack Wright and His Electric Man-of-War; or, Fighting the Sea Robbers of the Frozen Coast. New York, Tousey, 1893.

Jack Wright and His Submarine Torpedo-Tug; or, Winning a Government Reward. New York, Tousey, 1893.

Jack Wright and His Electric Sea-Demon; or, Daring Adventures under the Ocean. New York, Tousey, 1893.

Jack Wright and His Electric "Whale"; or, The Treasure Trove of the Polar Sea. New York, Tousey, 1893.

Jack Wright and His Electric Marine "Rover"; or, 50,000 Miles in Ocean Perils. New York, Tousey, 1893.

Jack Wright and His Electric Deep Sea Cutter; or, Searching for a Pirate's Treasure. New York, Tousey, 1893.

Jack Wright and His Electric Monarch of the Ocean; or, Cruising for a Million in Gold. New York, Tousey, 1893.

Jack Wright and His Electric Devil-Fish; or, Fighting the Smugglers of Alaska. New York, Tousey, 1893.

Jack Wright and His Electric Demon of the Plains; or, Wild Adventures among the Cowboys. New York, Tousey, 1893.

Jack Wright and His Electric Balloon Ship; or, 30,000 Leagues above the Earth. New York, Tousey, 1893.

Jack Wright and His Electric Locomotive; or, The Lost Mine of Death Valley. New York, Tousey, 1893.

Jack Wright and His Iron-Clad Air-Motor; or, Searching for a Lost Explorer. New York, Tousey, 1893.

Jack Wright and His Electric Tricycle; or, Fighting the Stranglers of the Crimson Desert. New York, Tousey, 1893.

Jack Wright and His Electric Dynamo Boat; or, The Mystery of a Buried Sea. New York, Tousey, 1893.

Jack Wright and His Flying Torpedo; or, The Black Demons of Dismal Swamp. New York, Tousey, 1893.

Jack Wright and His Prairie Privateer; or, Fighting the Western Road-Agents. New York, Tousey, 1893.

Jack Wright and His Naval Cruiser; or, Fighting the Pirates of the Pacific. New York, Tousey, 1893.

Jack Wright, the Boy Inventor, and His Whaleback Privateer; or, Cruising in the Behring Sea. New York, Tousey, 1893.

Jack Wright and His Electric Phantom Boat; or, Chasing the Outlaws of the Ocean. New York, Tousey, 1893.

Jack Wright and His Winged Gunboat; or, A Voyage to an Unknown Land. New York, Tousey, 1894.

Jack Wright and His Electric Flyer; or, Racing in the Clouds for a Boy's Life. New York, Tousey, 1894.

Jack Wright, the Boy Inventor's Electric Sledge Boat; or, Wild Adventures in Alaska. New York, Tousey, 1894.

Jack Wright and His Electric Express Wagon; or, Wiping Out the Outlaws of Deadwood. New York, Tousey, 1894.

Jack Wright and His Submarine Explorer; or, A Cruise at the Bottom of the Ocean. New York, Tousey, 1894.

Jack Wright and His Demon of the Air; or, A Perilous Trip in the Clouds. New York, Tousey, 1894.

Jack Wright and His Electric Ripper; or, Searching for a Treasure in the Jungle. New York, Tousey, 1894.

Jack Wright and His King of the Sea; or, Diving for Old Spanish Gold. New York, Tousey, 1894.

Jack Wright and His Electric Balloons; or, Cruising in the Clouds for a Mountain Treasure. New York, Tousey, 1894.

Jack Wright and His Imp of the Ocean; or, The Wreckers of Whirlpool Reef. New York, Tousey, 1894.

Jack Wright and His Electric Cab; or, Around the Globe on Wheels. New York, Tousey, 1894.

Jack Wright and His Flying Phantom; or, Searching for a Lost Balloonist. New York, Tousey, 1894.

Jack Wright and His Submarine Warship; or, Chasing the Demons of the Sea of Gold. New York, Tousey, 1894.

Jack Wright and His Prairie Yacht; or, Fighting the Indians of the Sea of Grass. New York, Tousey, 1894.

Jack Wright and His Electric Air Rocket; or, The Boy Exile of Siberia. New York, Tousey, 1894.

Jack Wright and His Submarine Destroyer; or, Warring against the Japanese Pirates. New York, Tousey, 1894.

Jack Wright and His Electric Battery Diver; or, A Two Months' Cruise under Water. New York, Tousey, 1894.

Jack Wright and His Electric Stage; or, Leagued against the James Boys. New York, Tousey, 1894.

Jack Wright and His Wheel of the Wind; or, The Jewels of the Volcano Dwellers. New York, Tousey, 1894.

Jack Wright and the Head-Hunters of the African Coast; or, The Electric Pirate Chaser. New York, Tousey, 1894.

3,000 Pounds of Gold; or, Jack Wright and His Electric Bat, Fighting the Cliff-Dwellers of the Sierras. New York, Tousey, 1894.

Jack Wright and the Wild Boy of the Woods; or, Exposing a Strange Mystery with the Electric Cart. New York, Tousey, 1894.

Jack Wright among the Demons of the Ocean with His Electric Sea-Fighter. New York, Tousey, 1894.

Jack Wright, the Wizard of Wrightstown and His Electric Dragon; or, A Wild Race to Save a Fortune. New York, Tousey, 1894.

Jack Wright's Electric Land-Clipper; or, Exploring the Mysterious Gobi Desert. New York, Tousey, 1894.

Skull and Crossbones; or, Jack Wright's Diving-Bell and the Pirates. New York, Tousey, 1895.

Jack Wright, the Boy Inventor, and His Phantom Frigate; or, Fighting the Coast Wreckers of the Gulf. New York, Tousey, 1895.

Jack Wright and His Air-Ship on Wheels; or, A Perilous Journey to Cape Farewell. New York, Tousey, 1895.

Jack Wright and His Electric Roadster in the Desert of Death; or, Chasing the Australian Brigand. New York, Tousey, 1895.

Jack Wright's Ocean Marvel; or, The Mystery of a Frozen Island. New York, Tousey, 1895.

Jack Wright and His Electric Soaring Machine; or, A Daring Flight through Miles of Peril. New York, Tousey, 1895.

Jack Wright and His Electric Battery Car; or, Beating the Express Train Robbers. New York, Tousey, 1895.

Jack Wright and His Electric Sea Horse; or, Seven Weeks in Ocean Perils. New York, Tousey, 1895.

Jack Wright and His Electric Balloon Boat; or, A Dangerous Voyage above the Clouds. New York, Tousey, 1895.

In the Jungles of India; or, Jack Wright as a Wild Animal Hunter. New York, Tousey, 1895.

50,000 Leagues under the Sea; or, Jack Wright's Most Dangerous Voyage. New York, Tousey, 1895.

Jack Wright, the Boy Inventor, Working for the Union Pacific Railroad; or, Over the Continent on the "Electric." New York, Tousey, 1895.

Over the South Pole; or, Jack Wright's Search for a Lost Explorer with His Flying Boat. New York, Tousey, 1895.

Jack Wright and His Electric Air Monitor; or, The Scourge of the Pacific. New York, Tousey, 1895.

The Boy Lion Fighter; or, Jack Wright in the Swamps of Africa. New York, Tousey, 1895.

Jack Wright and His Electric Submarine Ranger; or, Afloat among the Cannibals of the Deep. New York, Tousey, 1895.

The Demon of the Sky; or, Jack Wright's $10,000 Wager. New York, Tousey, 1895.

Adrift in the Land of Snow; or, Jack Wright and His Sledge-Boat on Wheels. New York, Tousey, 1896.

The Floating Terror; or, Jack Wright Fighting the Buccaneers of the Venezuelan Coast. New York, Tousey, 1896.

Lost in the Polar Circle; or, Jack Wright and His Aerial Explorer. New York, Tousey, 1896.

Jack Wright, the Boy Inventor, and the Smugglers of the Border Lakes; or, The Second Cruise of the Whaleback "Comet." New York, Tousey, 1896.

The Fatal Blue Diamond; or, Jack Wright among the Demon Worshippers with His Electric Motor. New York, Tousey, 1896.

Running the Blockade; or, Jack Wright Helping the Cuban Filibusters. New York, Tousey, 1896.

Jack Wright and Frank Reade, Jr., the Two Young Inventors; or, Brains against Brains. New York, Tousey, 1896.

The Flying Avenger; or, Jack Wright Fighting for Cuba. New York, Tousey, 1896.

Jack Wright and His New Electric Horse; or, A Perilous Trip over Two Continents. New York, Tousey, 1896.

Over the Sahara Desert; or, Jack Wright Fighting the Slave Hunters. New York, Tousey, 1896.

Diving for a Million; or, Jack Wright and His Electric Ocean Liner. New York, Tousey, 1896.

OTHER PUBLICATIONS

Novels

Young Sleuths in Demijohn City; or, Waltzing William's Dancing School. New York, Tousey, 1894.

Young Sleuths on the Stage; or, An Act Not on the Bills. New York, Tousey, 1894.

Novels as Police Captain Howard

A.D.T.; or, The Messenger Boy Detective. New York, Champion, 1882.

The Girl Detective. New York, Champion, 1882.

The Mystery of One Night. New York, Champion, 1882.

Young Vidocq. New York, Champion, 1882.

Other

How to Become a Naval Cadet. New York, Tousey, 1891.

How to Become a West Point Military Cadet. New York, Tousey, 1891.

* * *

During his lifetime, Luis P. Senarens was referred to as "the American Jules Verne" and a comparison of the work of both writers indicates the similarity. Senarens was writing stories of airships suspended by helicopter blades ("helices") three years before the *Albatross* took off in *Robur le Conquérant (Clipper of the Clouds)* in 1886. His epic serial *Frank Reade, Jr. and His Queen Clipper of the Clouds* leaned heavily on Verne. Even the illustrations were identical, with three of those in Senarens's story also used in Verne's *Maitre du Monde (Master of the World)*. Senarens's story is basically a long air voyage hampered by the presence of several malcontents and a lunatic scientist intent on seizing Frank's vessel.

Frank Reade, boy inventor, was originally created by Harry Enton, who put himself through medical school writing dime novels and storypaper serials. The steam-driven robot in *The Steam Man of the Plains* (1876) is mainly a device for transporting Frank and his cousin, Charley Gorse, to the far West. The story is a tongue-in-cheek yarn of encounters with outlaws and Indians, named "Motzer-Ponum" and "Sholum Alarkum." Out west, Frank meets the comic Irishman, Barney Shea. Barney and the black man, Pomp (introduced in a later story), became regular members of the cast. The plot may be improbable, but the steam man (borrowed from Edward S. Ellis's 1865 *Steam Man of the Prairies*) is engaging and novel for its day. We are told just enough about how it works to make it plausible. Senarens seemed to take the stories more seriously than Enton when he stepped in with the fifth serial. He introduced Frank Reade, Jr., but kept Frank, Sr., and eventually gave Jr. a wife. No stylist, he often wrote in the choppy manner peculiar to writers paid by the line. Without the aid of a typewriter, he wrote fast, kept the plot moving, and the characters in hot water. In formula fiction the fascination is in the variation on the basic themes. A new airship, surpassing any effort of the imagination; a new type of submarine; electrified equipment to drive off enemies; aluminum bullet-proof armor; pneumatic revolvers; damsels in distress; gentlemen unjustly accused of murder; a race against time; evil men determined to steal the invention; the pranks of comic relief companions, forever quarrelling; the wonderfully strange foreign lands; the deadly beauty of an undersea cavern or ice-locked vessel. Along the way a bit of social comment: does the U.S. government protect citizens abroad? Do the workshops in Readestown provide enough jobs for the community?

Senarens himself claimed authorship of most of the Frank Reade stories and all of the companion series about Jack Wright, who lived in Wrightstown and whose specialty was inventing submarines. His adventures were novelettes cut from the same pattern as the Frank Reades. In 1894, the two raced each other around the world for $10,000. Jack's submarine won by 15 minutes because Frank set down his airship to save a girl on a runaway horse. The stories ended in 1904 when public sentiment decided the plots were becoming too bizarre and Senarens ran out of ideas, though they lived on in reprints.

Senarens's contribution to science fiction is in his early and imaginative use of so many scientific marvels harnessed for popular consumption to a mass market. Had it not been for the wonders of Senarens there might have been no Tom Swift.

—J. Randolph Cox

SERLING, (Edward) Rod(man)

Nationality: American. **Born:** Syracuse, New York, 25 December 1924. **Education:** Antioch College, Yellow Springs, Ohio, B.A. 1950. **Military Service:** Served as a paratrooper in the United States Army during World War II. **Family:** Married Carolyn Kramer in 1948; two daughters. **Career:** Writer, WLW-Radio, 1946-48, and WKRC-TV, 1948-53, both Cincinnati; freelance writer from 1953; producer of television series *The Twilight Zone,* 1959-64, and *Night Gallery,* from 1969; taught at Antioch College, 1950s, and Ithaca College, New York, 1970s. **Member:** President, National Academy of Television Arts and Sciences, 1965-66; member of the council, Writers Guild of America West, 1965-67. **Awards:** Emmy award, for television plays, 1955, 1957, 1959; Sylvania award, 1955, 1956; Christopher award, 1956, 1971; Peabody award, 1957; Hugo award, for TV writing, 1960, 1961, 1962. D.H.L.: Emerson College, Boston, 1971; Alfred University, New York, 1972; Litt. D.: Ithaca College, 1972. **Died:** 28 June 1975.

SCIENCE FICTION PUBLICATIONS

Short Stories Adapted from Television Plays

The Season to Be Wary. Boston, Little, Brown, 1967.
From the Twilight Zone (selection). Garden City, New York, Doubleday, 1970(?).
Night Gallery. New York, Bantam, 1971.
Night Gallery 2. New York, Bantam, 1972.
Rod Serling's Night Gallery Reader, edited by Martin H. Greenberg, Carol Serling, and Charles G. Waugh. New York, Dembner, 1987.
Into the Twilight Zone: A New Collection of Startling Explorations into the Realm of the Supernatural. Mattituck, New York, Rivercity Press, 1976.
Stories from the Twilight Zone. New York, Bantam, 1986.
  Stories from the Twilight Zone. New York, Bantam, 1960.
  More Stories from the Twilight Zone. New York, Bantam, 1961.
  New Stories from the Twilight Zone. New York, Bantam, 1962.

OTHER PUBLICATIONS

Novel

Requiem for a Heavyweight (novelization of screenplay). New York, Bantam, and London, Corgi, 1962.

Plays

Requiem for a Heavyweight (televised, 1956). Included in *Patterns,* 1957; (revised version, produced New York, 1979).

Four Television Plays: With the Author's Personal Commentaries (includes *Patterns, The Rack, Requiem for a Heavyweight, Old MacDonald Had a Curve*). New York, Simon and Schuster, 1957.
The Killing Season (produced New York, 1968).
The Lonely, in *Writing for Television,* edited by Max Wylie. New York, Cowles, 1970.
A Storm in Summer, in *Camera Two: Two Plays for Television.* Toronto, Holt Rinehart, 1972.

Screenplays: *Patterns,* 1956; *Saddle the Wind,* with Thomas Thompson, 1958; *Requiem for a Heavyweight,* 1962; *The Yellow Canary,* 1963; *Seven Days in May,* 1964; *Assault on a Queen,* 1966; *Planet of the Apes,* with Michael Wilson, 1968; *A Time for Predators,* 1971.

Television Plays: *Patterns,* 1955; *Requiem for a Heavyweight,* 1956; *Forbidden Area,* from the novel by Pat Frank, 1956; *The Comedian,* 1957; *The Doomsday Flight,* 1966; *The Movie Maker,* with Steve Bochko, 1967; *The Man,* 1971; *The Rack; Old MacDonald Had a Curve; Line of Duty; The Lonely; A Storm in Summer;* and other plays for *U.S. Steel Hour, Playhouse 90, Hallmark Hall of Fame, Suspense, Twilight Zone, Night Gallery,* and *Danger* series.

Other

Editor, *Rod Serling's Triple W: Witches, Warlocks, and Werewolves: A Collection.* New York, Bantam, 1963.
Editor, *Rod Serling's Devils and Demons,* edited by Gordon R. Dickson. New York, Bantam, 1967.
Editor, *Rod Serling's Other Worlds.* New York, Bantam, 1978.

*

Critical Study: *Rod Serling: The Dreams and Nightmares of Life in the Twilight Zone* (biography) by Joel Engel, Chicago, Contemporary Books, 1989.

*   *   *

One of the handful of scriptwriters who consistently produced quality drama during American TV's Golden Age of the 1950s, Rod Serling demonstrated an interest in SF themes as early as 1956, when he adapted Pat Frank's novel *Forbidden Area* for television. Later, as one of the few writers to be given relative artistic control over a TV series, he turned again to science fiction and fantasy with *The Twilight Zone,* an anthology series which began in 1959. *The Twilight Zone* is often cited as one of the first serious attempts to bring intelligent fantastic stories to television, and, in addition to the large number of scripts that Serling himself wrote for the series, he elicited scripts from major writers within the science fiction and fantasy field, including Richard Matheson, Charles Beaumont, and Ray Bradbury. A later TV series, *Night Gallery,* retained a few SF stories but tended more toward fantasy and the supernatural. Serling also wrote the filmscripts for *Seven Days in May* and the hugely successful *Planet of the Apes.*

Serling adapted several of his *Twilight Zone* episodes as short stories. These often reveal the constraints of writing for television, and Serling for the most part made no effort to take advantage of the new form to develop or expand upon his initial scripts. The characters tend to be exaggerated stereotypes, easily recognizable in a half-hour TV format; the style is often precious or portentous, reflecting Serling's own opening and closing narrations for the original shows; and the fantastic elements are kept elementary and at times even simplistic. With their moralistic lessons and often sentimental tone, the tales work more as fables than as serious attempts at character or idea development.

Serling's attitude toward technology, for example, is decidedly ambiguous. When he writes of robots, he is unabashedly sentimental, as in "The Mighty Casey," which concerns a robot pitcher who nearly saves the Brooklyn Dodgers until he gets a mechanical heart which makes him too kind to strike out batters (the story is an odd combination of *Damn Yankees* and *The Wizard of Oz*), or "The Lonely," which concerns a prisoner sentenced to a lonely asteroid who finds companionship in a female robot brought by a kindly spaceship captain (a variation on a story by Ray Bradbury, who seems to be Serling's most consistent influence, even cropping up as a character name in a couple of Serling's stories). But in some stories mechanical contrivances become evil presences with minds of their own—a slot machine bent on destroying a compulsive gambler in "The Fever" or household appliances and a vengeful automobile in "A Thing about Machines." The implicit technophobia of "A Thing about Machines," however, is undercut by the almost pathological hostility of the victim who is the central character. Other stories also reflect technophobia in their concern with escape into a simpler past life ("A Stop at Willoughby," "Walking Distance"). The relatively few that deal with the familiar science fiction theme of alien presences, such as "Mr. Dingle, The Strong" or "The Monsters Are Due on Maple Street," treat them as little more than background for stories essentially concerned with character relations.

Not surprisingly, the major strength in Serling's writing is the convincing dialogue and his ability to sketch recognizable characters quickly—both skills well-suited to TV writing. His exposition is weak and at times even cloying, his themes and plots derivative. He is most likely to be remembered for his powerful non-science fiction dramas, such as *Patterns* or *Requiem for a Heavyweight*, and for his contribution in bringing serious, character-oriented fantastic tales—however familiar such tales may have been to veteran readers—to the television screen.

—Gary K. Wolfe

SERNINE, Daniel

Pseudonym for Alain Lortie. **Nationality:** Canadian. **Born:** 1955.

SCIENCE FICTION PUBLICATIONS

Novels (series: Exode; Grandverger)

Organisation Argus (Exode). Montreal, Éditions Paulines, 1979; translated by David Homel as *Those Who Watch over Earth,* Windsor, Ontario, Black Moss Press, 1990.
Le trésor du "Scorpion" (Grandverger). Montreal, Éditions Paulines, 1980; translated by Frances Morgan as *The Scorpion's Treasure,* Windsor, Ontario, Black Moss Press, 1990.

L'épée Arhapal (Grandverger). Montreal, Éditions Paulines, 1981; translated by Frances Morgan as *The Sword of Arhapal,* Windsor, Ontario, Black Moss Press, 1990.
Argus intervient (Exode). Montreal, Éditions Paulines, 1983; translated by David Homel as *Argus Steps In,* Windsor, Ontario, Black Moss Press, 1990.

Untranslated Novels in French

Les Méandres du temps. Longueuil, Quebec, Le Preambule, 1983.
Boulevard destoiles. Montreal, Publication Ianus, 1991.
La Recherche de Monsieur Goodtheim. Montreal, Publication Ianus, 1991.

Short Stories

"Stardust Boulevard," in *Northern Stars,* edited by David G. Hartwell and Glenn Grant, n.p., n.d.

*   *   *

Daniel Sernine is an extremely prolific writer and one of a handful who has taken the plunge and decided to be a full-time author in Québec. This he has been able to manage quite well, for Sernine writes all sorts of fiction, horror, fantasty, science fiction, and juvenile fiction.

He was one of the founders of the science fiction magazine *Requiem* which, with *Imagine,* is an essential element in the successful establishment and development of a distinctly "Québécois" brand of science fiction. Requiem, later *Solaris,* has been the most important source and inspiration for a typically Québécois (French-Canadian being a totally disused term in Québec in spite of a few works by writers from outside Québec) school of criticism. Daniel Sernine, along with Québécois writers such as Denis Côté and Suzanne Martel among others, has been keen to provide the young Québécois public with a science fiction literature it could identify with.

The series of Argus books is a successful example. The first two of them have been published in English translations: *Those Who Watch over the Earth* and *Argus Steps In.* The series revolves around two youngsters, Marc and Carl, who have joined an organization, Argus, the purpose of which is to save Earth from destroying itself. Argus is run by the Eryméens, extraterrestrials whose pacific and political aims are the common thread to all the novels. In the second book two more heroes are added, Cynthia and Francis. It is written in the shape of a whodunit with a good dose of general documentary information.

Sernine's short stories have appeared in numerous anthologies of Québécois science fiction and contribute to his very strong presence on the Québec scene. His major work, however, is the novel *Les Méandres du temps,* which helped give Sernine the stature he deserved and showed his detractors that he had the ability to write long works and present heroes devoid of naiveness. At the time of its publication, *Les Méandres du temps* was one of the longest science fiction novels published in Québec. It tells the story of Nicolas, a young telepath who agrees, under his adoptive father's pressure, to participate in a scientific experiment designed to test his unusual powers.

Similarly to the Eryméens in the Argus series, Nicolas is spotted by the Eryméens for his abilities; but more interestingly his past is linked with his future and his true origins that are not entirely terrestrial. Sernine does not shy away from difficult romantic and risqué scenes and shows real skill in their treatment.

Like the heroes of Charles Robert Wilson, another Canadian, Sernine's protagonists are endowed with telepathic and telekinetic powers. This emphasizes the involuntary (and perhaps unavoidable) similarities between the French-Canadian and English-Canadian schools of science fiction: an emphasis on the "soft" sciences such as psychology and the powers of the mind. Also, Sernine, like many of his Canadian contemporaries, concerns himself with the search for a better world.

Sernine's characters in *Les Méandres du temps* are put in very similar situations to the ones experienced by Marc and Cynthia in the Argus series. However, the comparison stops there. Sernine has managed to give a more complex psychology than the simplistic idealism that is the norm of juvenile fiction.

In the Boulevard destoiles series, from which one novella, under the title of *Stardust Boulevard,* is published in *Northern Stars,* an introductory and well edited anthology of Canadian science fiction (by David G. Hartwell and Glenn Grant), Daniel Sernine deals with one of the more common themes of SF that is particularly prevalent in Canadian SF: post-holocaust civilization. The main differences being that Sernine does it with subtlety, without using overdone clichés and by slowly introducing the reader into a world that is similar enough to our own and then gradually let us discover through details and events that this post-holocaust society is nothing like the society we are used to. These two books, *Boulevard destoiles* and *La Recherche de Monsieur Goodtheim,* manage a good fusion between three normally disparate genres of fiction: the psychological novel, science fiction and Roman noir. They consist of a series of short novels all taking place in the same time and place settings. Many of the characters' names are a barely veiled reference to the lost world of the 60s and reflect the loss of an age of innocence, possibly Sernine's, especially since institutions from his other juvenile fictions, such as Argus, an all powerful governmental agency, are incorporated into the second volume; Sernine takes pleasure in spoofing himself as well as giving us an alternate view of the beat generation.

Although the central characters change from one story to the other, they all seemed imbued with an existentialist malaise due to the fact that they do not seem to have adjusted to an Earth peopled by only a minute fraction of the population as we know it. This seems to have happened through a catastrophe whereas a virus has decimated the majority of the people and only spared a small proportion of individuals who happened to be immune to its destruction.

In this "new" world, the main activity is the Carnival where people go wild and disguise themselves, most of the time, as past characters or figures of the world as it was before the catastrophe. Others involve themselves in dangerous games in which anyone can partake through mind fusion and even die as a result of the too intense emotions they might experience. Most inhabitants have more time to spend on leisure than on anything else.

The continuity between all the short novels is subtle and does reward the reader after having drawn him into a world that appears to reflect and epitomize the most telling aspects of our contemporary society.

—Henry Leperlier

SERVISS, Garrett P(utnam)

Nationality: American. **Born:** Sharon Springs, New York, 24 March 1851. **Education:** Cornell University, Ithaca, New York, B.S. 1872; Columbia University, New York, LL.B. 1874. **Family:** Married Henrietta Gros le Blond in 1907. **Career:** Editorial writer, *New York Sun,* to 1892; then lecturer on travel, history, and astronomy, and writer. **Died:** 25 May 1929.

SCIENCE FICTION PUBLICATIONS

Novels

The Moon Metal. New York, Harper, 1900.
A Columbus of Space. New York and London, Appleton, 1911.
The Second Deluge. New York, McBride Nast, and London, Richards, 1912.
Edison's Conquest of Mars. Los Angeles, Carcosa House, 1947; abridged edition, as *Invasion of Mars,* Reseda, California, Powell, 1969.
The Moon Maiden. Los Angeles, Fantasy, 1978.

OTHER PUBLICATIONS

Other

Astronomy with an Opera-Glass: A Popular Introduction to the Study of the Starry Heavens, with the Simplest of Optical Instruments, with Maps to Facilitate the Recognition and the Principal Stars Visible. New York, Appleton, 1888.
Wonders of the Lunar Worlds; or, A Trip to the Moon. New York, Urania, 1892.
Napoleon Bonaparte: A Lecture. Philadelphia, Morris, 1901.
Other Worlds: Their Nature, Possibilities, and Habitability in the Light of the Latest Discoveries. New York, Appleton, 1901.
Pleasures of the Telescope: An Illustrated Guide for Amateur Astronomers and a Popular Description of the Chief Wonders of the Heavens for General Readers. New York, Appleton, 1901; London, Hirschfeld, 1902.
The Heavens without a Telescope, with Leon Barritt. New York, Barritt, 1906.
Planet Tables, Moon Phases, and the Sun's Daily Position: Giving the Dates and Degrees for Entering the Sun, Moon, and Planet Disks upon the Ecliptic of the Fixed Star Map, for a Period of Twelve Years, 1917 to 1928, with Leon Barritt. New York, Barritt, 1906.
The Barritt-Serviss Star and Planet Finder, Northern Hemisphere, with Leon Barritt. New York, Barritt, 1906.
The Moon: A Popular Treatise. New York, Appleton, 1907; as *The Story of the Moon: A Description of the Scenery of the Lunar World as It Would Appear to a Visitor Spending a Month on the Moon.* Appleton Century, 1928.
Astronomy with the Naked Eye: A New Geography of the Heavens, with Descriptions and Charts of Constellations, Stars, and Planets. New York, Harper, 1908.
Curiosities of the Sky: A Popular Presentation of the Great Riddles and Mysteries of Astronomy. New York, Harper, 1909.
Round the Year with the Stars: The Chief Beauties of the Starry Heavens as Seen with the Naked Eye. New York, Harper, 1910.
Eloquence: Counsel on the Art of Public Speaking: With Many Illustrative Examples Showing the Style and Method of Famous Orators. New York, Harper, 1912.
Astronomy in a Nutshell: The Chief Facts and Principles Explained in Popular Language for the General Reader and for Schools. New York, Putnam, 1912.

How to Use the Popular Science Library. New York, Collier, 1922.
The Einstein Theory of Relativity. New York, Fadman, 1923.
Riding through Space: The Earth's Scenic Voyage. Springfield, Ohio, Corwell, 1923.
Swedenborg: A Further Tribute. Pittsburgh, New-Church Lecture Bureau, 1926(?).
Costello Solar Demonstrating Globe. N.p., 1922.
Editor, *Popular Science Library.* 18 vols., New York, Collier, 1922.

* * *

Most of the writings of Garrett P. Serviss were never read, or even suspected, by the generation that lauded his small but significant contribution to science fiction. As a staff writer for the *New York Sun,* and later for a newspaper syndicate, he produced many columns of popular science material, much of which was unsigned. Having made his name as the popular astronomer of his day, he wrote for several leading magazines on subjects ranging from "Facts and Fancies about Mars" to the Shakespeare-Bacon controversy. A series of articles (*Astronomy with an Opera-Glass*) in *Popular Science Monthly* was extended to become the first of a small library of works including such titles as *Other Worlds* and *Curiosities of the Sky.*

His first novel was serialised in 1898 in the *New York Evening Journal,* and was evidently designed to exploit the public interest engendered by H.G. Wells's *The War of the Worlds.* Edison's *Conquest of Mars* was in the nature of a sequel to the Wells classic, though it went far beyond the limits of imaginative conception that even the Master had essayed in a single story. The Martians, too, were rather more human than Wells's monstrous marauders; and they had no chance to launch a second invasion before the great American inventor had organised a counterattack on Mars in a whole fleet of spaceships armed with deadly disintegrators. Though hurriedly written in a bombastic style, the story was remarkably inventive for its time, anticipating many of the devices that became the substance of later SF. No less remarkable is the fact that it was exhumed and published in hardcover only in 1947, having become legendary among fans who admired the author's subsequent stories.

One that attained classic status was *A Columbus of Space,* the tale of a voyage to Venus in an atomic-powered spaceship. Even more notable is *The Second Deluge,* in which a cosmic collision results in a universal flood. The story of how a latter-day Noah saved the human race from extinction proved so popular that it was twice reprinted by *Amazing,* where one reader found it so convincing that he wrote in asking for the plans of Cosmo Versál's ark so that he might save his family from the impending disaster. *The Moon Metal* concerned a mysterious metal originating in the lunar crater Tycho which replaced gold when this became as plentiful as iron. "The Sky Pirate" dared to predict air travel at 140 miles an hour in the year 1936; and "The Moon Maiden," the least of all his works, marked the last appearance of Serviss, in *Argosy,* the magazine that pioneered science fiction long before the advent of the specialist pulps.

—Walter Gillings

SHARKEY, Jack

Pseudonyms: Rick Abbot; Mark Chandler; Monk Harris; Mike Johnson. **Nationality:** American. **Born:** John Michael Sharkey, Chicago, Illinois, 6 May 1931. **Education:** St. Mary's College,

Winona, Minnesota, B.A. in English 1953. **Military Service:** Served in the United States Army, 1955-56. **Family:** Married Patricia Walsh in 1962; three daughters and one son. Since 1952, professional writer: assistant editor, *Playboy,* Chicago, 1963-64; editor, *Aim,* later *Good Hands,* for Allstate Insurance, Northbrook, Illinois, 1964-75. **Awards:** American Association of Industrial Editors prize, 1967; Inland Theatre League award, for play, 1984. **Died:** 28 September 1992.

SCIENCE FICTION PUBLICATIONS

Novels

The Secret Martians. New York, Ace, 1960.
Ultimatum in 2050 A.D. New York, Ace, 1965.
The Addams Family (based on television series). New York, Pyramid, 1965.

OTHER PUBLICATIONS

Novels

Murder, Maestro, Please. New York and London, Abelard Schuman, 1960.
Death for Auld Lang Syne. New York, Holt Rinehart, 1962; London, Joseph, 1963.

Plays

Here Lies Jeremy Troy (produced New York, 1965). New York, French, 1969.
M is for Million. New York, French, 1971.
How Green Was My Brownie. New York, French, 1972.
Kiss or Make Up. New York, French, 1972.
Meanwhile, Back on the Couch. . . . New York, French, 1973.
A Gentleman and a Scoundrel. New York, French, 1973.
Roomies. New York, French, 1974.
Spinoff. New York, French, 1974.
Who's on First? (produced Mount Prospect, Illinois, 1975). New York, French, 1975.
What a Spot!, with Dave Reiser. New York, French, 1975.
Saving Grace. New York, French, 1976.
Take a Number, Darling. New York, French, 1976.
The Creature Creeps! New York, French, 1977.
Dream Lover. New York, French, 1977.
Hope for the Best, with Dave Reiser. New York, French, 1977.
Rich Is Better. New York, French, 1977.
The Murder Room. New York, French, 1977.
Pushover, with Ken Easton. New York, French, 1977.
Once Is Enough. New York, French, 1977.
The Clone People (as Mike Johnson). New York, French, 1978.
Missing Link. New York, French, 1978.
Turnabout, with Ken Easton. New York, French, 1978.
Not the Count of Monte Cristo?, with Dave Reiser. New York, French, 1978.
Turkey in the Straw. New York, French, 1979.
Operetta!, with Dave Reiser. New York, French, 1979.
My Son the Astronaut. New York, French, 1980.
Par for the Corpse. New York, French, 1980.

Honestly Now! New York, French, 1981.
The Return of the Maniac (as Mike Johnson). New York, French, 1981.
Slow Down, Sweet Chariot, with Dave Reiser. New York, French, 1982.
Woman Overboard, with Dave Reiser. New York, French, 1982.
Your Flake or Mine? New York, French, 1982.
The Picture of Dorian Gray, with Dave Reiser, from the novel by Oscar Wilde. New York, French, 1982.
The Saloonkeeper's Daughter, with Dave Reiser. New York, French, 1982.
The Second Lady. New York, French, 1983.
And on the Sixth Day, with Dave Reiser. New York, French, 1984.

Other Plays: *Double Exposure; And Then I Wrote,* with Mel Buttorff; *The Well Dressed Liar,* with George Abbott; *My Husband the Wife* (lyrics only, with Dave Reiser), book by Ira and Brady Rubin, music by Dave Reiser; *Jekyll Hydes Again!,* with Dave Reiser; *Don't Tell Mother!* (as Monk Harris); *This Must Be the Place!* (as Monk Harris); *Let's Murder Marsha!* (as Monk Harris); *The Great All-American Disaster Musical,* with Tim Kelly; *Money, Power, Murder, Lust, Revenge and Marvelous Clothes,* with Tim Kelly; *A Fine Monster You Are!* (as Monk Harris); *Bone-Chiller* (as Monk Harris); *One Toe in the Grave; Zingo!,* with Dave Reiser; *Class Musical!* (as R. Abbot); *Love with a Twist,* with Dave Reiser; *The Woman in White,* with Tim Kelly; *Cinderella Meets the Wolfman!,* with Tim Kelly; *Sherlock Holmes and the Giant Rat of Sumatra,* with Tim Kelly; *The Three-and-a-Half Muskateers,* with Tim Kelly; *Time and Time Again!,* with Tim Kelly; *The Bride of Brackenloch!* (as R. Abbot); *Hamlet, Cha-Cha-Cha!* (as Monk Harris); *Nell of the Ozarks; While the Lights Were Out; Coping,* with Dave Reiser; *The Pinchpenny Phantom of the Opera,* with Dave Reiser; *Allocating Annie; Oh, Fudge!; 100 Lunches,* with Leo Sears; *Oh, No! A Nuclear Musical!,* with Cenarth Fox; *The Perfect Murder* (as Mike Johnson); *The Premature Corpse* (as Mike Johnson); *The Swan Song* (as Mike Johnson); *I Shot My Rich Aunt* (as Mark Chandler); *Sorry! Wrong Chimney!,* with Leo Sears; *Doctor Death* (as Mark Chandler); *I Take This Man; as Rick Abbot—Dracula: The Musical?; Beauty and the Beast; Really; June Groom; Play On!; But Why Bump Off Barnaby?; A Turn for the Nurse*—all published New York, French.

Other

Audition Pieces and Classroom Exercises. New York, French, n.d.

*

Jack Sharkey comments:

I enjoy writing imaginative fiction and stage plays because of the marvelous "elbow room" it allows me when plotting; unconfined by anything—even the force of gravity!—I can tell stories occurring in situations Polti never dreamed of, I can fly like a bird at the touch of the typewriter-key, and set my characters on any planet in the known or unknown universe without the bother of paying for rocket fuel!

*   *   *

Jack Sharkey started publishing science fiction in 1959, but produced little fiction of any kind after 1965. In that span of time, Sharkey sold about 50 stories and seven novels.

Sharkey's best-known series featured Jerry Norcriss, Space Zoologist. These stories were typical SF puzzle stories where Norcriss would "merge" minds with an alien organism in order to solve the environmental puzzle and save a star colony. Two novels which were serialized but never published in book form are "The Crispin Affair," a thrilling space opera, and "It's Magic, You Dope!," a wildly funny fantasy in the mode of Pratt and de Camp's *The Incomplete Enchanter.*

Sharkey's two SF novels published in book form are complete opposites. *The Secret Martians* is a first-person account of the mystery of the missing Space Scouts and the discovery of the ancient Martian civilization. The action is fast paced and laced with humor. *Ultimatum in 2050 A.D.* is the grim story, with overtones of *Logan's Run,* of revolt against an Earth society where all its citizens are completely programmed. Sharkey's works are enjoyable, well written, and unfortunately completely out-of-print.

—George Kelley

SHAVER, Richard S(harpe)

Pseudonyms: Wes Amherst; Edwin Benson; Peter Dexter; Richard Dorset; Richard English; G.H. Irwin; Paul Lohrman; Frank Patton; Stan Raycraft. **Nationality:** American. **Born:** 1907. **Career:** Little is known of his life: probably a welder who lived in Pennsylvania. **Died:** 5 November 1975.

SCIENCE FICTION PUBLICATIONS

Short Stories

I Remember Lemuria, and The Return of Sathanas. Evanston Illinois, Venture, 1948.

*   *   *

If Richard S. Shaver is discussed today, it is usually as a curiosity in the history of science fiction, or as an early example of that dim area where fiction shades into UFOs and ancient astronauts. This is to some extent justified but not altogether fair. Although "The Shaver Mystery" series was presented for the most part as fact, it is far more akin to the science fiction of its time, both in execution and in sources, than most realize; and, taken as fiction, the stories do have intrinsic interest and merit.

During Shaver's writing career, spanning three decades, his stories and "nonfiction" explications were published in a number of magazines, primarily under his longtime editor and advocate, Ray Palmer, at first in SF magazines such as *Amazing Stories* and *Other Worlds,* and later in "occult" publications such as *Hidden World.* A letter from Shaver (*Amazing,* December 1944) described the underground races called the "dero" and "tero" who had taught him the precatastrophe language of "Mantong." Then, at Palmer's request, Shaver sent a 10,000-word manuscript from which Palmer wrote a 31,000-word story, "I Remember Lemuria!" Constructed for high drama and written in colorful and traditional pulp style, it told the story of "Mutan Mion of ancient Lemuria," and fully outlined the background and dogma of the Shaver Mystery. The Atlans and Titans, Shaver reports, had been immortal giants of advanced technology; then the sun began to age and give off "heavy metal radiation," causing aging and death. Most fled the Earth for a planet with a younger sun, but others burrowed beneath the ground seeking protection from the poisonous rays. These are the dero and tero Shaver claimed to have met in the caves—struggling remnants of a once-great civilization. Of these two warring factions, the dero are by far the more interesting; Shaver has developed the quintessential conspiracy theory. Whenever anything goes wrong, the degenerate dero, crazed by the sun's rays and using the almost-magical machines left by the Elder Races, are responsible. Against this depravity, the tero fight valiantly but often in vain, sometimes aided by sensitive surface men like Richard Shaver.

This is fairly basic stuff, at least in its psychological appeal both as archetype and as wish fulfillment, especially for *Amazing* with its younger and less demanding readership. What made it controversial was that, after the first story, the series was presented as fact. It is debatable whether Palmer believed this; it is probable that he saw it mainly as a way to increase circulation, at least at first. Shaver, however, apparently believed completely in his visit to the caves, in the voices that spoke to him from underground, and in what those voices told him. In the May 1978 *Science Fiction Review,* Palmer announced that the eight years Shaver spent "in the caves" were actually spent in the Ypsilanti State Hospital as a paranoid schizophrenic. This sheds light on the style as well as the content of Shaver's writing: besides adventure-writing devices and techniques, Shaver's style is marked by "schizophrenese" characteristics such as disjointed sentences and, more importantly, word-dismantling and "clang associations."

But it would be wrong to dismiss these writings as only psychotic ravings, or even as Shaver's ravings hammered into salable fiction by Palmer. For one thing, Shaver himself wrote for other magazines under a number of pseudonyms, including house names. Beyond that, the stories show an eclectic range of clearly literary influences. These include the lush fiction of A. Merritt, Wells's Morlocks and Eloi, and the fictional world view of H.P. Lovecraft, from whose novel *At the Mountains of Madness* Shaver probably got the term "Elder Race." Harry Warner, Jr., (in *All Our Yesterdays*) mentions a possible influence from E.R. Eddison, "whom Shaver once identified as his literary idol" and *A Reader's Guide to Science Fiction* demonstrates patterning, perhaps conscious, after the planetary romances of Edgar Rice Burroughs. Possible sources in occult nonfiction include Charles Fort, the theosophy of Mme. Blavatsky, and James Churchward's Mu series, which Shaver mentions in his first letter to Palmer. Shaver also mentions Edith Hamilton's writings on mythology—which his own works explain and correct. The Bible, especially the Edenic theme, is also an important source.

What results is an odd but fascinating blend of high adventure, outrageous "science," and elusive but striking systems of cosmic speculation. If the characters are sometimes flat, if the plots too often seem "boy meets girl, boy beats dero, boy wins girl"—and this is not always the case—the sheer wealth and strangeness of the concepts Shaver develops more than compensate for that. There is a kind of Stapledonian scope to Shaver, a sense of epic, and mythic, panoramas; the races, societies, and technologies with which he populates his universe are varied and often impressive. The appeal of Richard Shaver to the reader then and now is, as Palmer said, "one thing only, his unusual imagination. His strange sense of the unusual, his feeling for emotion, his sense of the beautiful

and his sense of the outré." For that reason Shaver's writings, shrouded in controversy and now largely neglected, are worthy of new attention.

—Bernadette Bosky

SHAW, Bob

Nationality: British. **Born:** Robert Shaw, Belfast, Northern Ireland, 31 December 1931. **Education:** Technical High School, Belfast, 1944-46. **Family:** Married Sarah Gourley in 1954; two daughters and one son. **Career:** Prior to 1960, worked in the steel and aircraft industries and as a cab driver; assistant publicity officer, 1960-66, and press officer, 1969-73, Short Brothers, and Harland, aircraft manufacturers, Belfast; journalist, Belfast Telegraph, 1966-69; publicity officer, Vickers Shipbuilding Group, 1973-75. **Awards:** British Science Fiction Association award, 1975; Hugo award, for criticism, 1979, 1980. **Agent:** Carnell Literary Agency, Danes Croft, Goose Lane, Little Hallingbury, Hertfordshire CM22 7RG. **Address:** 98 London Road, Stockton Heath, Warrington, Cheshire WA4 6LE, England.

SCIENCE FICTION PUBLICATIONS

Novels (series: Land and Overland; Orbitsville; Warren Peace)

Night Walk. New York, Banner, 1967; London, New English Library, 1970.
The Two-Timers. New York, Ace, 1968; London, Gollancz, 1969.
Shadow of Heaven. New York, Avon, 1969; abridged edition, London, New English Library, 1970; revised edition, London, Corgi, 1978; revised edition, London, Gollancz, 1991.
The Palace of Eternity. New York, Ace, 1969; London, Gollancz, 1970.
One Million Tomorrows. New York, Ace, 1970; London, Gollancz, 1971.
Ground Zero Man. New York, Avon, 1971; London, Corgi, 1976; revised edition, as *The Peace Machine,* London, Gollancz, 1985.
Other Days, Other Eyes. London, Gollancz, and New York, Ace, 1972.
Orbitsville. London, Gollancz, and New York, Ace, 1975.
A Wreath of Stars. London, Gollancz, 1976; New York, Doubleday, 1977.
Medusa's Children. London, Gollancz, 1977; New York, Doubleday, 1979.
Who Goes Here? (Warren Peace). London, Gollancz, 1977; New York, Ace, 1978; expanded edition, with *The Giaconda Caper,* New York, VGSF, 1988.
Ship of Strangers. London, Gollancz, 1978; New York, Ace, 1979.
Vertigo. London, Gollancz, 1978; New York, Ace, 1979; revised and expanded as *Terminal Velocity,* London, Gollancz, 1991.
Dagger of the Mind. London, Gollancz, 1979; New York, Ace, 1982.
Galactic Tours, illustrated by David Hardy. New York and London, Proteus, 1981.
The Ceres Solution. London, Gollancz, 1981; New York, DAW, 1984.

Orbitsville Departure. London, Gollancz, 1983; New York, DAW, 1985.
Fire Pattern. London, Gollancz, 1984; New York, DAW, 1986.
The Ragged Astronauts (Land). London, Gollancz, 1986; New York, Baen, 1987.
The Wooden Spaceships (Land). London, Gollancz, and New York, Baen, 1988.
Killer Planet (for children). London, Gollancz, 1989.
The Fugitive Worlds (Land). London, Gollancz, 1989; New York, Baen, 1990.
Orbitsville Judgement. London, Gollancz, 1990.
Warren Peace. London, Gollancz, 1993; as *Dimensions,* London, Gollancz, 1994.

Short Stories

The Enchanted Duplicator, with Walt Willis. Privately printed, 1954.
Tomorrow Lies in Ambush. London, Gollancz, 1973; revised, New York, Ace, 1973.
Cosmic Kaleidoscope. London, Gollancz, 1976; revised, New York, Doubleday, 1977.
A Better Mantrap: Nine Science Fiction and Fantasy Stories. London, Gollancz, 1982.
Messages Found in an Oxygen Bottle, bound with *Between Two Worlds,* by Terry Carr. Cambridge, Massachusetts, NESFA Press, 1986.
Dark Night in Toyland. London, Gollancz, 1989.

OTHER PUBLICATIONS

Other

The Best of the Bushel. Epsom, Surrey, Paranoid/Inca Press, 1979.
The Eastercon Speeches. Epsom, Surrey, Paranoid/Inca Press, 1979.
How to Write Science Fiction. London, Allison and Busby, 1993.

*

Manuscript Collection: Science Fiction Foundation, North East London Polytechnic.

Critical Study: *Bob Shaw* by Brian M. Stableford (includes bibliography by Mike Ashley), n. p., British Science Fiction Association, 1981.

Bob Shaw comments:

(1991) It is very difficult, if not impossible, for an author to write objectively about his own work, but I sum up my output by saying that I write science fiction for people who don't read a great deal of science fiction. This doesn't mean that I curb my imagination. I'm quite prepared to deal with the most fantastic concepts, but I try to do it in such a way that the ideas can be appreciated by any reader. The technique involves a minimal use of in-group jargon and a very firm emphasis on relating every fictional event to real characters of a kind that the reader can immediately recognise and identify or empathise with. The universe is wonderful, but only when there is somebody there to wonder at it. Humour also plays an important role in my work, partly because I feel that science fiction shouldn't become too gloomy and portentous, mainly because one of the things we need most these days is a good laugh.

(1995) Having suffered major bereavements and health problems in the last four years or so, I have had trouble keeping on with my writing career—especially the humorous output—but I will stick to my belief that we should not take ourselves too seriously.

* * *

Bob Shaw has reached an uneasy status within science fiction. The quality of his work is recognised, yet he is treated with the same easy acceptance and lack of critical attention as a much more journeyman writer. The problem, perhaps, is that he works so resolutely within the heartland of science fiction—an area occupied by relatively few British science fiction writers—and most of his work has the fairly straightforward structure of a mystery story. Despite his undoubted achievements, this seems to smack of a lack of ambition.

This impression is not helped by the way his most recent work has tended to plough old furrows. *Shadow of Heaven,* perhaps his weakest novel, has been revised some four times; yet, even in 1991, the latest revision may pad out the thin story (and update some of the references) but cannot disguise the weakness of the plot or the poverty of characterisation. *Vertigo,* a much better novel first published in 1978, also reappeared in a revised version in 1991 as *Terminal Velocity.* The changes, mostly an expansion to include the original short story, "Dark Icarus," do not add much to a novel which already displayed many of the characteristics typical of Shaw's best work, a careful working out of the consequences of one technological innovation, in this case the invention of an anti-gravity harness. These qualities are not much in evidence in his 1977 novel, *Who Goes Here?,* an affectionate but flaccid comedy which throws together a series of SF clichés (space legion, time travel, supermen), adds massive coincidence at every step in the plot, and doesn't seem to give any consideration for any of Shaw's usual strengths of characterisation and believability. Yet even this has emerged again in the form of a sequel, *Warren Peace.*

Even when he writes a novel of undoubted power and originality, such as *Orbitsville,* its strength is somewhat dissipated by two belated sequels that really add little to the awesome vision of the original. The first book took his characters to a massive Dyson sphere that completely enclosed a sun. It is a book with similarities to Larry Niven's *Ringworld,* and original publication was in fact delayed for a while to avoid too close a comparison, but it is a far better novel than Niven's. Shaw is at his best when pitching his characters against the effects of impersonal science, and he is able to convey the size of this alien artefact with vivid, yet beautifully controlled and effective prose, and it is made the more powerful by the reality of his characters whose all too human beliefs and problems provide a scale against which the alienness of the sphere is best seen. It seems unnecessary icing on the cake to go on and introduce the original builders of the sphere into later novels.

In all Bob Shaw's work, in fact, it is in the human scale that he is best. Though his work frequently follows the formula of hard science fiction, he rarely fails to make his characters believable and three-dimensional. Thus, in perhaps his best and most famous short story, "Light of Other Days," which introduced one of the few really original concepts in the history of science fiction, "slow glass," he made it clear that humanity must be preeminent over any new technical device. "Slow glass" slows down the passage of light, sometimes for years, and in this story it is "farmed" in a remote Scottish glen to provide beautiful scenes for city dwellers. Shaw takes this typically hard SF notion and turns it into one of the most humane stories in the genre, for he makes it a story about the farmer who can see into his own home through his slow glass windows and so keep alive in his mind his wife and child who have since been killed. There is a similar angle in another story in the sequence, "Burden of Proof," in which a murder has been committed in the presence of slow glass so that at some later date the crime may be revealed to witnesses. But a judge is faced with making a decision on the case now.

Shaw's writing is always crisp and matter-of-fact, but, there are times when he attempts something transcendent to unexpectedly good effect. This is best demonstrated by *The Palace of Eternity,* which takes its hero beyond death to a messianic rebirth while still keeping the novel tightly and entertainingly structured around a conflict between human and alien, and between artistry and technology. In *A Wreath of Stars,* one of his most underrated novels, an anti-neutrino planet passes through the Earth and leaves in its wake reports of ghosts underground and tantalising glimpses of another form of life. These books disguise with vivid and often highly original SF trappings a much more deeply felt report on what it feels like to be human in the face of the unknown and the unknowable. This is why *Orbitsville* works best without the introduction of the aliens, since their appearance removes a substantial part of the mystery.

It was the human scale, however, that helped to make his most ambitious work to date so successful. The *Ragged Astronauts* trilogy is massive in scope, involving planet-wide adventures, other worlds, and more. Yet, by concentrating on character, and setting it all within a non-technological world, he manages to ensure that it is a humane and very accessible story. The human inhabitants of Land are threatened by the poisonous ptertha, which have suddenly become more than usually dangerous. As the threat increases, the only hope of survival lies in escape to the twin world of Overland. But the people of Land have no metals, and so, in a spectacular *coup de theatre,* Shaw takes them from one planet to the other by way of hot-air balloons. It is a daring idea carried off with great panache, and the writing displays all the delight of someone decking out a very high-tech SF adventure with determinedly low-tech paraphernalia. And, in a touch typical of Shaw, he manages to set these very science-fictional events as a backdrop to a story of dynastic troubles, human values, and romance. It is a scale he manages to sustain throughout the trilogy, which builds up to exactly the sort of climactic transcendence that is a feature of his very best work.

Shaw is a writer capable of soaring heights, but also of abysmal depths, and one sometimes gets the impression that he cannot tell one from the other. Nevertheless, for his ability to provide the most stimulating and inventive hard science fiction with a genuine human face, he deserves a level of appreciation far higher than he has ever achieved.

—Paul Kincaid

SHAW, Brian. *See* **TUBB, E.C.**

SHAW, Bryan. *See* **FEARN, John Russell.**

SHAWN, Frank S. *See* **GOULART, Ron.**

SHECKLEY, Robert

Nationality: American. **Born:** New York City, 16 July 1928. **Education:** New York University, B.A. 1951. **Military Service:** Served in the United States Army, 1946-48. **Family:** Married to Jay Rothbell. Fiction editor, *Omni,* 1980-82; Visiting Scholar, Massachusetts Institute of Technology, Cambridge, 1982. **Awards:** Jupiter award, 1973. **Address:** c/o Bantam Books, 666 Fifth Avenue, New York, New York 10103, U.S.A.

SCIENCE FICTION PUBLICATIONS

Novels (series: Victim; Millennial Contest)

Immortality Delivered. New York, Avalon, 1958; revised edition, as *Immortality Inc.,* New York, Bantam, 1959; London, Gollancz, 1963.
The Status Civilization. New York, Signet, 1960; London, New English Library, 1967.
Journey beyond Tomorrow. New York, Signet, 1962; London, Gollancz, 1964; as *Journey of Joenes,* London, Sphere, 1978.
The 10th Victim. New York, Ballantine, and London, Mayflower, 1966.
Mindswap: A Novel. New York, Delacorte Press, and London, Gollancz, 1966.
Dimension of Miracles. New York, Dell, 1968; London, Gollancz, 1969.
Options. New York, Pyramid, 1975; London, Pan, 1977.
Crompton Divided. New York, Holt Rinehart, 1978; as *The Alchemical Marriage of Alistair Crompton,* London, Joseph, 1978.
Dramocles: An Intergalactic Soap Opera. New York, Holt Rinehart, 1983; London, New English Library, 1984.
Victim Prime. London, Methuen, and New York, Signet, 1987.
Hunter/Victim. New York, Signet, and London, Methuen, 1988.
Bill the Galactic Hero on the Planet of Bottled Brains, with Harry Harrison. New York, Avon, 1990; London, Gollancz, 1990.
Bring Me the Head of Prince Charming (Millennial Contest), with Roger Zelazny. New York, Bantam, 1991; London, Pan, 1994.
If at Faust You Don't Succeed, with Roger Zelazny (Millennial Contest). New York, Bantam, 1993.
A Farce to Be Reckoned With, with Roger Zelazny (Millennial Contest). New York, Bantam, 1995.

Short Stories

Untouched by Human Hands; Thirteen Stories. New York, Ballantine, 1954; revised edition, London, Joseph, 1955.
Citizen in Space. New York, Ballantine, 1955; London, New English Library, 1969.
Pilgrimage to Earth. New York, Bantam, 1957; London, Corgi, 1959.
Store of Infinity. New York, Bantam, 1960.
Notions: Unlimited. New York, Bantam, 1960.

Shards of Space. New York, Bantam, and London, Corgi, 1962.

The People Trap and Other Pitfalls, Snares, Devices, and Delusions, as Well as Two Sniggles and a Contrivance. New York, Dell, 1968; London, Gollancz, 1969.

Can You Feel Anything When I Do This? New York, Doubleday, 1971; London, Gollancz, 1972; as *The Same to You Doubled and Other Stories,* London, Pan, 1974.

The Robert Sheckley Omnibus, edited by Robert Conquest. London, Gollancz, 1973.

The Robot Who Looked Like Me. London, Sphere, 1978.

The Wonderful World of Robert Sheckley. New York, Bantam, 1979; London, Sphere, 1980.

Is THAT What People Do? Short Stories. New York, Holt Rinehart, 1984.

Alien Starswarm. Portland, Oregon, Dime-Novels, 1990.

Minotaur Maze. Eugene, Oregon, Pulphouse, 1990.

Watchbird. Eugene, Oregon, Pulphouse, 1990.

Xolotl. Eugene, Oregon, Pulphouse, 1991.

The Collected Short Stories of Robert Sheckley. 5 vols., Eugene, Oregon, Pulphouse, 1991.

Other Publications

Novels

Calibre .50: A Stephen Dain Mystery. New York, Bantam, 1961.

Dead Run: A Stephen Dain Mystery. New York, Bantam, 1961.

Live Gold. New York, Bantam, 1962.

The Man in the Water. Evanston, Illinois, Regency, 1962.

White Death. New York, Bantam, 1963.

The Game of X. New York, Delacorte Press, 1965; London, Cape, 1966.

Time Limit. New York, Bantam, and London, New English Library, 1967.

The Alternative Detective. New York, Forge, 1993.

Plays

Television Plays: 15 scripts for *Captain Video,* 1950s; *Murder Club,* from his own story, 1961 (UK).

Radio Play: 60 scripts for *Beyond the Green Door,* 1960s.

Other

Futuropolis: Impossible Cities in Science Fiction and Fantasy. New York, A and W, 1978; London, Big O, 1979.

Editor, *After the Fall: An Anthology.* New York, Ace, and London, Sphere, 1980.

*   *   *

Robert Sheckley is, if we must find a category for him, a metaphysical wit and satirist. His major theme, manifested in dozens of superb stories and novels, is that in an infinite universe "reality" is infinitely variegated, depending upon one's environmental or psychological framework. While some writers would regard this as a nihilistic nightmare, for Sheckley, it offers an opportunity for unbounded imaginative romping—precisely the sort of freedom that SF so eagerly welcomes. "The quest for non-ordinary reality is

something more than curiosity and wishful thinking," Sheckley once said in a rare public address ("The Search for the Marvellous," delivered at the Institute of Contemporary Arts, London, 1975); "We are too crowded in our everyday lives by replicas of ourselves and by the repetitious artifacts of our days and nights. But we do not quite believe in this prosaic world. Continually we are reminded of the strangeness of birth and death, the vastness of time and space, the unknowability of ourselves." These somber thoughts Sheckley clothes with highly imaginative and entertaining plots. For example, in *Dimension of Miracles,* Carmody is brought to the galactic center for a prize he has won in the Intergalactic Sweepstakes. The prize is a sentient being in a gaily wrapped box that takes Carmody on a wild-goose chase through the universe in search of Earth (the Prize Committee does not know the co-ordinates for returning Carmody). Each episode makes it clear that the universe is such that one cannot go home again anyway, just as one cannot step into the same river twice. Carmody's search for home is also a search for self, and on this matter he has quite a bit to learn— such as the fact that the shapes of objects and creatures are a function of environment. What is evil or ugly in one environment may well appear benevolent and lovely when transferred to another.

This idea of the universe as protean and magical serves as a satirical ploy for Sheckley. In "The Petrified World" (*Is THAT What People Do?,* original title, "Dreamworld," from *The People Trap*) Lanigan, whose real world is one in which objects are continually changing shape and color, suffers from a recurring nightmare: he keeps finding himself on a world where change is largely imperceptible. "The pavement never once yielded beneath his feet. Over there was the First National City Bank. It had been there yesterday . . . but, worse, it would be there without fail tomorrow, and the day after that . . . grotesquely devoid of possibilities. It would never become a tomb, an airplane . . ." Lanigan finally becomes trapped in his nightmare—the nightmare that, Sheckley is suggesting, is our nightmare.

No matter how absurd and wildly episodic Sheckley's plots sometimes become, the metaphysician is always lurking in the wings, cueing us with tidbits of cosmic wisdom which are themselves refreshing. For example, *Mindswap* introduces us to a universe in which people can change bodies like garments. Marvin Flynn gets swindled out of his body by the notorious body-pirate Ze Kraggash, whose ruling philosophy is, "If a man cannot retain control of his own body, then he deserves to lose it." During the galaxy-wide search Flynn begins to realize just how indeterminate bodies really are and how useless it is to attach any lasting importance to them. "The acceptance of indeterminacy was the beginning of wisdom," a hermit on some alien world tells him. And after he chases Ze Kraggash into the Twisted World, he attains ultimate wisdom: "Nothing is permanent except our illusions."

Perhaps Sheckley's most dramatic rendering of the indeterminacy of selfhood is "Slaves of Time." Like the solipsistic nightmare world of Robert Heinlen's "All You Zombies," this story (omitted, unfortunately, from *Is THAT What People Do?*) depicts some of the uncannily paradoxical things that can happen if one engages in some serious time traveling. Gleister builds a time machine and goes into the future. Because nature "can tolerate a paradox but abhors a vacuum," it instantaneously creates another Gleister to take the first Gleister's place. This new Gleister, identical to the other, but on a different reality-track, also builds a time machine and travels into the future. The inevitable, grim result: an endless stream of Gleisters, each following his own reality-track. "It is strange," Gleister/Mingus says at one point where all the Gleister manifestations convene, "that all of us are one person, yet we represent widely different viewpoints." And Gleister/Ergon replies,"It's not so strange. . . . One person is many people even under normal circumstances."

Options offers yet another treatise on reality vs. illusion and mind-as-universe—embedded, but not too deeply, beneath a slapstick surface. Tom Mishkin, an intergalactic trader ("frozen South African lobster tails, tennis shoes, air conditioners") finds himself stranded somewhere in the Lesser Magellanic Cloud, in need of a hard-to-get spare part for his ship. He is directed to Harmonia, a bizarre would where, as is almost always the case in Sheckley's cosmos, nothing is quite the way it seems. Mishkin and a mealy-mouthed robot set off on a mock-pilgrimage across Harmonia in search of the elusive spare part. To be sure, Harmonia is Tom Mishkin's disorderly mind strewn across an external milieu like an overstuffed closet that had burst open. Monsters pause in their deadly assaults to discuss metaphysical issues with him; carnival men entertain him; he meets poker players who think they are inside their hotel room in Manhattan (and very likely are). In one of the final episodes we get the sense that Mishkin is "really" just a little earth boy who has been engaged in a daydream that would make Walter Mitty's look dreary ("Tommy! Stop playing now!" "I'm not playing, Mom. This is real." . . . "Put down that broom and come into the house at once." "It's not a broom, it's a spaceship. Anyhow, my robot says . . ." "And bring that old radio in with you").

Many of Sheckley's works explore to some degree the nature of selfhood. The early, masterful tale, "Shape" (*Untouched by Human Hands; 13 Stories*) is about a team of alien space explorers who possess the ability to change shape at will, but whose society has forbidden them to do so (shapes were assigned and had to be rigorously maintained). No wonder, then, that when they land on a strange planet called Earth, they are so awed by the multitude of shapes, that they cannot bring themselves to return home; instead they joyfully assume the shapes of trees, rocks, animals, humans. And in *Crompton Divided,* Alistair Crompton, because of his multiple personality, is forced to undergo "Cleavage"—separation of the personalities, which are then placed in separate bodies and shipped, unknown to the main personality, to remote planets. Crompton, now mild-mannered but totally devoid of spunk, learns what has happened to him and, after raising sufficient funds by embezzling rare and exotic perfumes from his company, embarks on a galaxy-wide search for his lost selves. That this is yet another indictment of society for the pressures it exerts upon us to be consistent, predictable, content citizens is clear from the following passage:

> On all sides of him, the envious Crompton saw people with all their marvelous complexities and contradictions constantly bursting out of the stereotypes that society tried to force on them. He observed prostitutes who were not good-hearted, army sergeants who detested brutality, wealthy men who never gave a cent to charity. Irishmen who hated talking, Italians who could not carry a tune. . . . Most of the human race seemed to live lives of a wonderful and unpredictable richness, erupting into sudden passions and strange calms, saying one thing and meaning another.

For Sheckley, to be fully human means to house a repertoire of selves, willing and able to assume different roles, changing our minds when we want to. The only danger is that one can get carried away with the ability to manipulate reality and start trying to

play God, conquering and subjugating with no regard for the well-being—the selfhood—of others. Such is the circumstance we encounter in Sheckley's novel, *Dramocles.* "Travelling between realities," the power-hungry Otho tells his son Dramocles, ruler of Glorm, is "the way to life everlasting." Despite Otho's efforts to persuade him that the lives of mere mortals are irrelevant "when the rewards of godhood are within your grasp," Dramocles manages to resist.

Unlike the young man in Sheckley's "The Language of Love" who learned to express his deepest romantic feelings with such precision that his sweetheart quickly lost interest in him, Dramocles discovers that too much of a good thing can rob one of one's very humanity.

—Fred D. White

SHEFFIELD, Charles

Pseudonym: James Kirkwood. **Nationality:** British. **Born:** England. **Education:** St. John's College, Cambridge, B.A. and M.A. in mathematics, Ph.D. in theoretical physics. **Career:** Formerly president of the American Astronautical Society; formerly president, Science Fiction Writers of America; currently chief scientist and board member, Earth Satellite Corporation. **Awards:** Sei-un award, 1991; John W. Campbell award, 1992; Hugo award, 1994; Nebula award, 1994. **Address:** 2833 Gunarette Way, Silver Springs, Maryland 20906, U.S.A.

SCIENCE FICTION PUBLICATIONS

Novels (series: Proteus; Heritage Universe)

Sight of Proteus. New York, Ace, 1978; London, Sidgwick and Jackson, 1980.
The Web between the Worlds. New York, Ace, 1979; London, Sidgwick and Jackson, 1980.
The Selkie, with David F. Bischoff. New York, Macmillan, 1982.
Erasmus Magister. New York, Ace, 1982.
My Brother's Keeper. New York, Ace, 1982.
Between the Strokes of Night. New York, Baen, 1985; London, Headline, 1987.
The Nimrod Hunt. New York, Baen, 1986: London, Headline, 1988; expanded as *The Mind Pool,* Riverdale, New York, Baen, 1993.
Trader's World. New York, Ballantine, 1988; London, New English Library, 1989.
Proteus Unbound. London, New English Library, and New York, Ballantine, 1989.
Proteus Manifest. New York, Guild America, 1989.
Summertide (Heritage). New York, Ballantine, and London, Gollancz, 1990.
Divergence (Heritage). Norwalk, Connecticut, Easton Press, and London, Gollancz, 1991.
Transcendence (Heritage). New York, Ballantine, and London, Gollancz, 1992.
Brother to Dragons. Norwalk, Connecticut, Easton Press, 1992.
Cold as Ice. New York, Tor, 1992.
The Heritage Universe. New York, Guild America, 1992.

Godspeed. New York, Tor, 1993.
The Judas Cross, with David Bischoff. Eugene, Oregon, Blue
Moon, 1994.
Proteus Combined, Riverdale, New York, Baen, 1994.
Proteus in the Underworld. Riverdale, New York, Baen, 1995.

Short Stories

Vectors. New York, Ace, 1979.
Hidden Variables. New York, Ace, 1981.
The McAndrew Chronicles. New York, Tor, 1983; expanded as *One
Man's Universe: The Continuing Chronicles of Arthur Morton
McAndrew,* New York, Tor, 1993.
Dancing with Myself. Riverdale, New York, Baen, 1993.
Georgia on My Mind and Other Places. New York, Tor, 1995.

OTHER PUBLICATIONS

Other

Earthwatch: A Survey of the World from Space. London, Sidgwick
and Jackson, and New York, Macmillan, 1981.
Man on Earth. London, Sidgwick and Jackson, and New York,
Macmillan, 1983.
Space Careers, with Carol Rosin. New York, Morrow, 1984.

Editor, with John L. McLucas, *Commercial Operations in Space
1980-2000.* San Diego, American Astronautical Society, 1981.
Editor, with Marcello Alonso and Morton A. Kaplan, *The World
of 2044: Technological Development and the Future of Society.*
St. Paul, Minnesota, Paragon House, 1994.

Author of some 100 technical papers since 1965.

*   *   *

Although Charles Sheffield began writing science fiction only in
the late 1970s, he quickly achieved a significant reputation as a writer
of hard science fiction. To date, most of Sheffield's prolific output—
he is averaging one new book a year—falls into four subsets.

His first novel, *Sight of Proteus,* is at the center of a "form-
change" subset. Combining biological feedback hardware with realtime computer programming, form-change enables human beings
of the late 22nd century to reshape their bodies. And while most
people explore only the cosmetic aspects of this technology, Robert
Capman is at work diligently, but illegally, modifying the human body
for space travel. Naturally, this brings him into conflict with Behrooz
Wolf, the man in charge of discovering illegal form-changes.

In the sequel, *Proteus Unbound,* Sheffield expands the scope
from Earth to the solar system. The problem: normally reliable form-
change equipment is breaking down at an alarming rate. Wolf once
again finds the solution, just in time to save the solar system from
a megalomaniac bent on destroying it. Recently, *Sight of Proteus*
and *Proteus Unbound* have been reissued together, slightly revised,
as *Proteus Combined.* Also recently, Sheffield has published a third
"Proteus" novel, *Proteus in the Underworld,* in which Wolf is lured
out of retirement to solve yet another form-change mystery, one
that has disturbing implications for his own life work.

Loosely connected to the form-change novels is *The Web between the Worlds.* Set in the middle of the 21st century, it details
the construction of Earth's first "Beanstalk," a cable thousands of
miles long, anchored at the equator, ballasted at the other end by
an asteroid, up and down which people and material can move—in
other words, a "space elevator" similar to the one in Arthur C.
Clarke's *The Fountains of Paradise.* More closely connected to the
form-change novels is *One Man's Universe,* seven short stories
featuring Arthur Morton McAndrew, the system's foremost authority on power kernels (Kerr-Newman black holes) and the inventor
of the McAndrew faster-than-light drive; the book also has a fascinating appendix in which Sheffield discusses the science in his science fiction. (Five of these seven stories were published in *The
McAndrew Chronicles,* an earlier version of this collection.)

Three works published in 1982 comprise a second subset of
Sheffield's oeuvre. Not really science fiction, though they include
SF ideas, these works are historical, horror, and espionage fiction,
respectively.

The novellas in *Erasmus Magister* take place during 1776-1778
and are based on the life of Erasmus Darwin, physician and bota-
nist, grandfather of Charles Darwin, and a figure near the top of
Sheffield's personal pantheon of great scientists. In a novel that
Sheffield wrote in collaboration with David Bischoff, *The Selkie,*
an American hydrology expert in the late 20th century is studying
tidal caves along the Scottish coast. When his wife joins him, she
is seduced by one of the legendary race of seal-people who live in
the caves. In *My Brother's Keeper,* medical research a century from
now has just discovered a method to allow nerve regeneration, good
news to twins nearly killed in a ghastly helicopter accident, who
wind up in one body sharing parts of their two brains. At first the
dominant personality is the concert pianist twin, but it turns out the
other twin is a spy of some sort. Interesting complications ensue.

A third subset is filled by three post-nuclear-holocaust and three
disaster SF novels. The holocaust in *Between the Strokes of Night*
is absolutely catastrophic, the only survivors those few fortunate
enough to be off planet. The holocaust in *Trader's World* is less
catastrophic; so 50 years later the various remnants are gradually
being unified via commercial transactions negotiated by the Traders, a group one reviewer called "a pragmatic version of the United
Nations." The holocaust in *The Mind Pool* is in the far-distant past;
in the meantime humanity has made contact with three alien species, and all four species must learn to work together in order to
defeat a dangerous, human-created artificial device. An earlier,
shorter, and—according to Sheffield himself—flawed version of
this book is *The Nimrod Hunt.*

The disaster in *Brother to Dragons* is a worldwide economic
collapse shortly after the beginning of the 21st century. This novel
features Sheffield's first juvenile protagonist, Job Napoleon Salk,
who lives up to all three parts of his name. Like the Biblical Job,
he experiences a world of trouble: orphaned at birth, he grows up
at the very bottom of his society. Like Napoleon, he is short and
physically weak but gifted—not in war but with languages. And
like Jonas Salk, discoverer of the polio vaccine, he winds up saving the human race from a terrible disease. The disaster in *Cold as
Ice* is a space war between the solar system's inner and outer worlds
in the late 21st century that has killed nine billion people. Set a
generation after the end of this war, *Cold as Ice* focuses on Europa,
one of the moons of Jupiter, and on the struggle between those
who wish it made suitable for human habitation and those who
wish it to remain pristine. Among many memorable characters is
Rustum Battachariya, a figure clearly reminiscent of Nero Wolfe.
When *Cold as Ice* appeared, many reviewers called it Sheffield's
best work; a sequel is in the offing. The far-future disaster in *Godspeed* is the isolation ten generations earlier of the planet Erin be-

cause the faster-than-light Godspeed Drive starships suddenly and inexplicably stopped arriving. The story, which Sheffield admits he borrowed from Robert Louis Stevenson's *Treasure Island,* features another juvenile protagonist—Jay Hara—who finds himself with a high-tech treasure map that may lead to a hidden Godspeed base and contact with the rest of the galaxy.

The final subset includes *Summertide, Divergence,* and *Transcendence,* Books One, Two, and Three of "The Heritage Universe" series. Here Sheffield indulges his penchant for macroengineering, object-building on a truly gigantic scale. It's the 63rd century and the three known space-going species—human, Cecropian, Zardalu—have discovered, scattered throughout the galaxy, 1,236 massive artifacts left by a mysterious race they name the Builders. In *Summertide,* members of various species converge on the planetary doublet Opal and Quake just in time for a cataclysmic event that occurs once every 350,000 years. In *Divergence,* the same group winds up on a new artifact thousands of light years away, where they are attacked by ferocious Zardalu—squid-like creatures mistakenly thought to be extinct. In *Transcendence,* Sheffield sends his intrepid protagonists on a search for the Zardalu home world.

But though Sheffield's oeuvre can be divided into these four subsets, each single work also shares noticeable family resemblances with the others. This is true even of *Vectors, Hidden Variables, Dancing with Myself,* and *Georgia on My Mind,* short story collections that do not fit easily into any one of the subsets just discussed but which should be read since they contain some of Sheffield's best (and funniest) work.

Details vary, but a similar optimistic vision of technology's future shows up throughout Sheffield's work. Beanstalks—not rockets—will help humanity colonize near-planetary space. Arks (i.e., generation starships) will gradually expand the sphere of human colonization. And eventually human ingenuity will discover faster-than-light travel. Before that, fusion power will yield to power kernels, asteroids will be mined, matter at the fringe of the solar system will be harvested, and various other forms of large- and small-scale engineering will be perfected.

Though flourishing as early as the 18th century and as late as the end of this universe, Sheffield's protagonists all resemble each other. They are male, early middle-aged, independent, confident, persistent, and courageous. And, like their author, many not only are expert specialists but also excel at both theoretical studies and practical applications.

The same themes show up again and again in a Sheffield work. Brain power is important because it leads to knowledge—and knowledge leads to survival in a universe hostile to ignorance. The most important activity is finding and facing the hardest problem available; and Sheffield's protagonists frequently solve these problems by indirect means, what he calls the ability to "think around corners." Sheffield values unflagging curiosity and the concomitant desire to explore the unknown. He also insists that negotiation is a much better method than war for handling conflict. Finally, love finds a place in his fictional universes.

Reviewers who are hard SF aficionados use words like imaginative, believable, intriguing, tantalizing, and compelling to describe Sheffield's work. Less sympathetic reviewers use different words: plodding, implausible, talky, nebulous, and inconclusive. As Sheffield himself, who sprinkles his work with Latin quotations and literary allusions, might say, "*De gustibus non est disputandum*": if SF adventure with a strong technological bent suits your tastes, you will probably like his work; if it does not, you will probably not like his work—but you might be surprised.

Sheffield has not yet brought his writerly skills up to the brilliance of his ideas, and may never, but the gap is narrowing. Especially interesting lately, by the way, are his aliens, a move away from single protagonists to an ensemble of main characters, and forays into the young adult market.

—Todd H. Sammons

SHELLEY, Mary (Wollstonecraft)

Nationality: British. **Born:** Somers Town, London, 30 August 1797. **Family:** Married Percy Bysshe Shelley in 1816 (died 1822); two sons and one daughter. **Career:** Lived in Dundee, 1812, 1813-14, then returned to London; eloped to Europe with Shelley, 1814; writer from 1816; after Shelley's death lived in Genoa with the Leigh Hunts, 1822-23, then returned to England; travelled in Germany, 1840-41, and Italy, 1842-43. **Died:** 1 February 1851.

SCIENCE FICTION PUBLICATIONS

Novels

Frankenstein; or, The Modern Prometheus. London, Lackington Hughes, 1818; revised edition, London, Colburn and Bentley, 1831; edited by M.K. Joseph, London and New York, Oxford University Press, 1969; original edition edited by James Rieger, Indianapolis, Bobbs-Merrill, 1974; as *The Illustrated Frankenstein,* edited by John Stoker, Newton Abbot, England, Westridge, 1980.
The Last Man. London, H. Colburn, 1826; Philadelphia, Carey, 1833; revised edition, edited by Hugh J. Luke, Lincoln, University of Nebraska Press, 1965; with new introduction by Brian W. Aldiss, London, Hogarth Press, 1985.

OTHER PUBLICATIONS

Novels

Valperga; or, The Life and Adventures of Castruccio, Prince of Lucca. London, Whittaker, 1823.
The Fortunes of Perkin Warbeck: A Romance. London, Colburn and Bentley, 1830; Philadelphia, Carey, 1834.
Lodore. New York, Wallis and Newell, and London, R. Bentley, 1835.
Falkner. London, Saunders and Otley, and New York, Harper, 1837.
Mathilda, edited by Elizabeth Nitchie. Chapel Hill, University of North Carolina Press, 1959.

Short Stories

Mary Shelley: Collected Tales and Stories, edited by Charles E. Robinson. Baltimore, Maryland, Johns Hopkins University Press, 1976.

Plays

Proserpine and Midas: Mythological Dramas, edited by A. Koszul. London, H. Milford, 1922.

Poetry

The Choice: A Poem on Shelley's Death, edited by H. Buxton
Forman. London, privately printed, 1876.

Other

History of a Six Weeks' Tour through a Part of France, Switzer-
land, Germany and Holland, with Percy Bysshe Shelley. Lon-
don, Hookham and Ollier, 1817; abridged edition, as *Shelley's*
Visits to France, etc., edited by C.I. Elton, London, Bliss Sands,
1894.
Rambles in Germany and Italy in 1840, 1842, and 1843. London,
Moxon, 2 vols., 1844.
Shelley and Mary: A Collection of Letters and Documents of a
Biographical Character. London, privately printed, 3 vols., 1882.
Letters of Mary Wollstonecraft Shelley, Mostly Unpublished, ed-
ited by Henry H. Harper. Boston, Bibliophile Society, 1918.
My Best Mary: The Selected Letters of Mary Wollstonecraft Shelley,
edited by Muriel Spark and Derek Stanford. New York, Roy,
and London, Wingate, 1953.
The Letters of Mary Wollstonecraft Shelley, edited by Betty T.
Bennett. Baltimore, Maryland, Johns Hopkins University Press,
3 vols., 1980-88.
The Journals of Mary Shelley 1814-44, edited by Paula R. Feldman
and Diana Scott-Kilvert. Oxford, Clarendon Press, and New
York, Oxford University Press, 2 vols., 1987.
The Mary Shelley Reader (contains *Frankenstein, Mathilda,* tales
and stories, essays and reviews, and letters), edited by Betty T.
Bennett and Charles E. Robinson. New York, Oxford Univer-
sity Press, 1990.

Editor, *Posthumous Poems,* by Percy Bysshe Shelley. London,
Hunt, 1824.
Editor, *The Poetical Works of Percy Bysshe Shelley.* London,
Moxon, 4 vols., 1839.
Editor, *Essays, Letters from Abroad, Translations, and Fragments,*
by Percy Bysshe Shelley. London, Moxon, and Philadelphia, Lea
and Blanchard, 2 vols., 1840.

*

Bibliography: *Mary Shelley: An Annotated Bibliography* by William H. Lyles, New York, Garland, 1975.

Critical Studies (selection): *Child of Light: A Reassessment of*
Mary Wollstonecraft Shelley by Muriel Spark, Hadleigh, Essex,
Tower Bridge, 1951, revised edition, as *Mary Shelley: A Biogra-*
phy, New York, Dutton, 1987, London, Constable, 1988; *Mary*
Shelley: Author of Frankenstein by Elizabeth Nitchie, New
Brunswick, New Jersey, Rutgers University Press, 1953; *Mary*
Shelley by Eileen Bigland, New York, Appleton Century, and Lon-
don, Cassell, 1959; *Mary Shelley dans son oeuvre* by Jean de
Palaccio, Paris, Klincksieck, 1969; *Mary Shelley* by William A.
Walling, New York, Twayne, 1972; *Ariel Like a Harpy: Shelley,*
Mary, and Frankenstein by Christopher Small, London, Gollancz,
1972, as *Mary Shelley's Frankenstein: Tracing the Myth,* Pittsburgh,
University of Pittsburgh Press, 1973; *Shelley's Mary: A Life* by
Margaret Leighton, New York, Farrar Straus, 1973; *Daughter of*
Earth and Water: A Biography of Mary Wollstonecraft Shelley by
Noel B. Gerson, New York, Morrow, 1973; *Mary Shelley's Mon-*
ster: The Story of Frankenstein by Martin Tropp, Boston, Houghton
Mifflin, 1976; *Moon in Eclipse: A Life of Mary Shelley* by Jane
Dunn, London, Weidenfeld and Nicolson, and New York, St.
Martin's Press, 1978; *The Endurance of Frankenstein: Essays on*
Mary Shelley's Novel edited by George Levine and U.C.
Knoepflmacher, Berkeley, University of California Press, 1979;
Frankenstein's Creation: The Book, the Monster, and Human Re-
ality by David Ketterer, Victoria, British Columbia, University of
Victoria Press, 1979; *The Lonely Muse: A Critical Biography of*
Mary Shelley by Bonnie Rayford Neumann, Salzburg, Institut für
Anglistik und Amerikanistïk, 1979; *The Influence of William*
Godwin on the Novels of Mary Shelley by Katherine Richardson
Powers, New York, Arno Press, 1980; *The Frankenstein Catalog*
by Donald F. Glut, Jefferson, North Carolina, McFarland, 1984;
Scientific Attitudes in Mary Shelley's Frankenstein by S.H.
Vasbinder, Ann Arbor, Michigan, U.M.I. Research Press, 1984;
Mary Shelley and Frankenstein: The Fate of Androgyny by Will-
iam Veeder, Chicago, University of Chicago Press, 1986; *The Mon-*
ster in the Mirror: Gender and the Sentimental/Gothic Myth in Fran-
kenstein by Mary K. Patterson Thornburg, Ann Arbor, Michigan,
U.M.I. Research Press, 1987; *Mary Shelley: Her Life, Her Fic-*
tion, Her Monsters by Ann K. Mellor, New York and London,
Routledge, 1988; *Mary Shelley: Romance and Reality* by Emily W.
Sunstein, Boston, Little Brown, 1989; *The Godwins and the*
Shelleys: The Biography of a Family by William St. Clair, New
York, Norton, and London, Faber, 1989; *Approaches to Teaching*
Shelley's Frankenstein edited by Stephen C. Behrendt, New York,
M.L.A., 1990; *Hideous Progenies: Dramatizations of Frankenstein*
from Mary Shelley to the Present by Steven Earl Forry, Philadel-
phia, University of Pennsylvania Press, 1990.

*   *   *

The outline of the plot of Mary Wollstonecraft Shelley's first
novel, *Frankenstein, or, The Modern Prometheus,* is known to almost everyone on the planet. Of no other science fiction novel can
such a claim be made. A scientist, rejecting outmoded theories and
superstitions, turns to research, and patches together a new but monstrous human being from corpses. Into this new being he manages
to instill life. This unholy experiment goes wrong. The scientist is
negligent. The monster runs amok, bringing death and destruction
on scientist and family, and almost everyone else, before retribution comes.

This story, a type of scientific fairytale, has amused or troubled
the world since the novel was first published, in 1818. The name
of the scientist, Victor Frankenstein, has become synonymous
with irresponsible applications of science and technology. The
label *Frankenstein* has become synonymous with a type of period horror film.

In recent years Mary Shelley's novel has been read with renewed
critical attention. Although the author's stated aim was "to curdle
the blood," her novel is much more than an exercise in horror. Its
period flavour, acquired over well nigh two centuries, has led us to
forget how topical were some of its elements. For Mary Shelley it
was who developed literary methods followed ever since by SF
writers. That is to say, she embraces topicality by framing her story
in a tale of polar exploration, a subject of intense current interest
following Captain Cook's failed attempt to find a North West passage. Also, the novel discusses themes then as now of vital interest, such as the upbringing of children. Other ingredients, such as
the quest for the secrets of "life" and debates as to whether "life"

could be isolated, were topical at the beginning of the nineteenth century, and have become so again in an age looking for the secrets of AIDS.

This farsightedness and its continued relevance, wedded to its awful story of vengeance, accounts for *Frankenstein*'s perennial appeal. But it is that basic theme of Man preempting God's work which marks it out as the first true work of science fiction. This is no casual adventure: what was under nature's control is now under human control. Superstition is rejected, science is espoused—and this in an age before the word "scientist" was coined. *Frankenstein; or, The Modern Prometheus* is now recognised as a master work, and much more than Gothic sensationalism, as it was previously categorised.

The horror theme—the monster rising from its slab and clobbering everyone in sight—has been used over and over, on stage, radio, and film. Most people are familiar with Boris Karloff's make-up as Frankenstein's unnamed creature. But the old films made the creature dumb, a bellower at best, whereas much of the book's charm and interest lies in the creature's self-education, combined with the eloquence of its diction—an eloquence owing something to Milton's *Paradise Lost,* as befits the artificially created Adam. So an old brutality was substituted for a new way of life.

The book is subtle, fluid, elusive, ultimately defying analysis—hence the many analyses it has engendered. In *The Sacred Wood,* T.S. Eliot says of Shakespeare's play *Hamlet,* "*Hamlet,* like the Sonnets, is full of some stuff that the writer could not drag to light, contemplate, or manipulate into art." He adds, "Hamlet (the man) is dominated by an emotion which is inexpressible, because it is in *excess* of the facts as they appear." As much can be said of *Frankenstein.*

Perhaps for this reason, we turn for clues to the inner meaning of the novel to the author herself. Mary Wollstonecraft Godwin had two illustrious parents, intellectuals of their age, Mary Wollstonecraft and William Godwin. Remarkably, their daughter was only 18, and not yet married to the poet Percy Bysshe Shelley, when, in the June of 1816, she began her story. It opened with a dream—a dream prompted in part by listening to scientific discussions. The dreamer awoke and began to write: "It was on a dreary night of November, that I beheld the accomplishment of my toils. . . ."

The young Godwin lady was living at the time with Shelley in postbellum Switzerland (itself patched together into a new national entity). Shelley was a married man, father of two children. Before *Frankenstein* was published, Mary's half-sister, Fanny Imlay, committed suicide, as did Shelley's wife, Harriet. Death and insecurity surrounded her. Her mother had died in childbirth; her first child, a daughter, was born to her when she was seventeen and died a few days later. Her father all but disowned her when she eloped with the poet.

The horrific elements of the novel obscured the way in which it deals with problems of parent-child relationships, families, the usages of power, justice, and, as importantly, scientific questions. In her edition of the 1818 text of *Frankenstein* (London, 1993), Marilyn Butler shows how closely the Shelleys followed the science of their day. In particular, a young physiologist and surgeon, William Lawrence, was involved in the vitalist arguments of the day, and became their friend. In a lecture given on the Life question in 1817, Lawrence declares that "an immaterial and spiritual being could not have been discovered among the blood and filth of the dissecting room." The phraseology—similar to Mary Shelley's own—takes us back to an aura of grave-robbing and vivisection then prevalent, the very practices of which Victor Frankenstein is

guilty. In Butler's words, key passages in the novel "encode scientific experiments . . . and phrases identifiable with other living experimenters and theorists are introduced. . . ."

Equal weight is given to the question of emotional relationships. Victor's poor patched creature, disowned by its creator, shunned by mankind, embodies many of its author's own orphaned feelings of sorrow, guilt, and rage. As Mary Shelley states in the Introduction to the 1831 edition of her novel, "Invention . . . does not consist of creating out of void, but out of chaos; the materials must, in the first place, be afforded. . . ."

The story unfolds. Our sympathies are transposed from Victor to his "daemon," as he sometimes calls it. Victor and his creation, locked in a struggle to the death, play out modern dilemmas, pity and the lack of it, overwhelming ambition, secrecy, science as opposed to religion, and male principle as opposed to female.

A doppelganger theme intensifies towards the end of the novel. The roles of pursuer and pursued become confused. A homoerotic theme can be discerned, as enemies become strange allies. Victor and his creature have between them destroyed all the women in pursuit of their large ambitions.

This interchange of roles affords some expression of Mary Shelley's double life, the internal and the external. In her Journals, she speaks of herself as one who "entirely and despotically engrossed by their own feelings, leads—as it were—an internal life quite different from the outward and apparent one." While Victor shuns society, his creature craves it. Thus their author dramatises the two sides of her nature.

The issues raised in *Frankenstein* still divert or torment us, while the novel forms an exemplar of what SF can and should be.

The awesome solitudes of the novel, which lend it grandeur, are lacking in crowded *Frankenstein* movies, swarming as they are with villains, hunchbacks, and peasants brandishing flaming torches. The text gives no warrant for such claptrap. There we find only the majestic desolations of the Alps, the wilderness of Scotland, the *mer de glace,* the polar ice.

This note of profound isolation sounds again in Mary Shelley's other SF novel, *The Last Man.* It is a more prolix work which concerns a plague coming out of the East. Mankind is gradually and cumulatively wiped out, until only Lionel Verney is left to tell the tale.

Again, extrapolation is part of the authorial procedure. A real pandemic was scourging much of the globe in the 1820s. Hundreds of thousands of people died in that underpopulated world. As before, Mary Shelley downloads her feelings, reflecting the darkening circumstances she endured after Shelley's death by drowning. Three of her four children had died young; she had suffered a serious miscarriage from which she almost expired. Lord Byron, her famous friend, had died fighting for Greek liberty. She lived in poverty in London, supporting herself and her son Percy by her pen.

The Last Man will never secure the audience accorded its unique predecessor. Indeed, the Hogarth Press edition of 1985, with my Introduction, was its first English reprint. Yet the story yields much of pleasureable interest to sympathetic readers. The theme itself has weight enough, not least in an age facing AIDS.

Mary Shelley's reputation continues to grow as she is increasingly studied. Beyond the SF field, *Frankenstein* has become accepted as one of the seminal works of the Romantic period. It is that paradoxical thing: academically accepted, popularly enjoyed. The tragic life of its young author has a separate and continued appeal. There's no one like her.

—Brian W. Aldiss

SHEPARD, Lucius

Nationality: American. **Born:** 1947. **Awards:** Clarion award, 1984; *Locus* award, 1985; John W. Campbell award, 1985; *Science Fiction Chronicle* award, 1985; Nebula award, 1986; World Fantasy award, 1988. **Address:** c/o Arkham House, Box 546, Sauk City, Wisconsin 53583, U.S.A.

SCIENCE FICTION PUBLICATIONS

Novels

Green Eyes. New York, Ace, 1984; London, Chatto and Windus, 1986.
Life during Wartime. New York, Bantam, 1987; London, Grafton, 1988.
The Scalehunter's Beautiful Daughter. Willimantic, Connecticut, Ziesing, 1988.
The Father of Stones. Baltimore, Maryland, Washington Science Fiction Association, 1989.
The Golden: A Novel. Shingletown, California, Ziesing, and London, Millenium, 1993.

Short Stories

The Jaguar Hunter. Sauk City, Wisconsin, Arkham House, 1987; London, Paladin, 1988.
Nantucket Slayrides: Three Short Novels, with Robert Frazier. Nantucket, Massachusetts, Eel Grass Press, 1989.
Kalimantan. London, Legend, 1990; New York, St. Martin's Press, 1992.
The Ends of the Earth: 14 Stories. Sauk City, Wisconsin, Arkham House, 1991; London, Millenium, 1994.

*   *   *

Lucius Shepard's first published short story, "The Taylorville Reconstruction," appeared in Terry Carr's prestigious anthology of original fiction, *Universe 13,* in 1983. In the years since Shepard has produced as many award-nominated and award-winning stories as any writer of science fiction or fantasy. From novels like *Green Eyes, Life during Wartime,* and *The Golden* to shorter works such as "Solitario's Eyes," "A Traveller's Tale," "The Man Who Painted the Dragon Griaule," "Life of Buddha," "Father of Stones," and "Delta Sly Honey," he has been a prolific, one-man literary renaissance, a creator of high art on a scale rarely seen before in science fiction. There is no way to do justice in this brief space to the many fine stories Shepard has written. Readers are best referred to his two superb short story collections, *The Jaguar Hunter* and *The Ends of the Earth,* and, of course, to the novels.

It is possible, however, to zero in on a number of Shepard's basic settings, themes, and characters, because his work is remarkably of a piece. The majority of his stories take place in the present or near future and are set on or near the Caribbean, or the Gulf of Mexico, or in Southeast Asia. Most walk the border between fantasy and science fiction and many involve some form of possession. "Solitario's Eyes," for example, takes place somewhere on the Caribbean coast and details the strange relationship between an army officer of upper-class Castilian heritage, his beautiful Indian wife, and the native healer she seeks out during her pregnancy and then seduces. Her son, when born, appears to share some strange

physical and psychic bond with the healer (since murdered by the army officer) and with his blind, possibly magical horse. In *Green Eyes,* a scientific experiment in resurrecting the dead, set in the bayou country of Louisiana, goes awry, and leads its participants into a dark universe of perversion, murder, and voodoo. Both "Salvador" and "A Traveller's Tale" take place in the snake-infested swamps and forests of Central America and both involve spirit possession. In the former story, an American soldier, stuck in an early 1990s Vietnam-like military campaign, is taken over by a native spirit seeking revenge against gringos. In the latter story, an American is possessed by an alien who, half insane, has been haunting the swampy site of her spaceship's crash for centuries. Among Shepard's more recent stories, "The Ends of the Earth" involves an American writer who becomes involved in an ancient Mayan game that temporarily transforms its participants into monstrous warriors. Through magic, dreams, drugs, or poorly understood science, Shepard's protagonists are often translated to other worlds. This happens to characters in *Green Eyes,* "The Ends of the Earth," "Delta Sly Honey," "Shades" and, most recently, *Kalimantan.* The latter, set in the jungles of Borneo, features a native drug that gives those who take it the power to both change reality and, ultimately, escape it. Drugs feature prominently in Shepard's work, from the strung-out, hallucinating, government-drugged American soldiers of *Life during Wartime* to the entire pathetic cast of "Life of Buddha." In Shepard's most recent novel, *The Golden,* the traditional bloodlust of the vampire is seen as something very much akin to drug addiction as well.

Shepard's characters tend to be drifters, dreamers, and drug addicts, men and women with no real place to go and no real purpose, victims of poverty, government-sponsored insanity and corruption, or their own irrational urges. Few, if any, can be called heroes. David Mingolla, the American GI caught in a nightmare war in Central America in *Life during Wartime,* maintains a certain degree of innocence, but it's all relative. Even he does things that, in our world, would be considered monstrous. Ray Kingsley, the writer-protagonist of "The Ends of the Earth," is in some sense the good guy in his magical contest with the charlatan Konwicki for the love of the woman Odille, but he's driven by hatred, and the sublimated need for revenge against the last woman who hurt him. MacKinnon, who experiments with native drugs in *Kalimantan* and dreams of saving the Borneo wilderness from developers is, nonetheless, corrupted by his own insecurities. He, like many of Shepard's other protagonists, falls victim to strange events and powers he never fully understands. Even Michel Beheim, the vampire protagonist of *The Golden* is a victim of sorts. A relatively young and weak vampire, he is given the thankless task of uncovering a murderer and finds himself at odds with a number of his older, stronger, and more corrupt brethren. When Shepard's characters accomplish things—create works of art, make scientific discoveries, make babies—they usually do it almost in spite of themselves, and their creations are frequently two-edged swords.

Somewhat different from Shepard's other published fictions are "The Man Who Painted the Dragon Griaule" and two other works set in the same universe, *The Scalehunter's Beautiful Daughter* and *The Father of Stones.* With a Central-European ambience much like that of Ursula K. Le Guin's *Orsinian Tales,* "Griaule" is the story of a man who attempts to paint a 6,000-foot long, living but dormant dragon: not a picture of the dragon, it must be understood, but the body of the dragon itself. All three novellas have been nominated for awards and have made various best of the year lists.

Two recent stories with relatively happy endings are "Beast of the Heartland" and "Barnacle Bill the Spacer." The former centers on Bobby Mears, a boxer well past his prime, who has lost most of his eyesight but keeps on fighting because it's the only thing he knows how to do. Mears is as tortured and pathetic as any Shepard protagonist but, on the verge of hanging it up, he finds himself signed for one last big fight against an opponent who may well be Evil incarnate. Shepard rarely publishes traditional science fiction; he doesn't seem all that comfortable with it and such stories are rarely among his best. "Barnacle Bill," perhaps his most successful pure SF story of recent years, features yet another loser who makes good in the end. The story takes place on a space station where starships are assembled and launched. It concerns William Stamey, a retarded man who is frequently ridiculed by station personnel, particularly those connected with a dangerous religious cult called the Strange Magnificence who are bent upon taking over or destroying the station. When Bill, and the story's narrator, a British expatriate security guard, stand up to the Magnificence, their actions not only save the station, but very possibly lead to both men's personal salvation.

Jungles and swamps, whether found along the coast of Central America, in the bayou country of Louisiana, or in the upland wilds of Borneo, are a central image for Lucius Shepard, a symbol, perhaps, of the moral morass that his characters consistently find themselves in. The center will not hold. Nothing and no one can be trusted, not even the soggy ground beneath one's feet. The universe of Lucius Shepard is an uncomfortable one, lacking in absolutes. Although his politics are clearly leftist, as demonstrated by the anti-military and anti-American government sentiments of *Life during Wartime,* "Salvador," and other stories, there's something of the despairing conservative about him as well. This is demonstrated, perhaps, by his frequent reuse of themes and motifs borrowed from two of the darkest writers of the century, Joseph Conrad and, oddly enough, H.P. Lovecraft. Few writers of science fiction or fantasy give us so black a vision.

—Michael M. Levy

SHERMAN, Michael. *See* **LOWNDES, Robert A.W.**

SHERMAN, Peter Michael. *See* **LOWNDES, Robert A.W.**

SHERRED, T(homas) L.

Nationality: American. **Born:** 27 August 1915. **Education:** Attended Wayne State University, Detroit, Michigan. **Career:** Production line engineer; for many years worked in the Packard toolroom, Detroit; later worked in technical writing and advertising. **Died:** 16 April 1985.

SCIENCE FICTION PUBLICATIONS

Novels (series: Alien Island in all titles)

Alien Island. New York, Ballantine, 1970.
Alien Main, with Lloyd Biggle Jr. Garden City, New York, Doubleday, 1985.

Short Stories

First Person, Peculiar. New York, Ballantine, 1972.

*

Manuscript Collection: Spenser Research Library, University of Kansas, Lawrence.

*   *   *

T.L. Sherred's science fiction output was small but of excellent quality. The reason for this, as Sherred explained to Harlan Ellison in the introduction to "Bounty" in *Again, Dangerous Visions,* was that "I didn't write very much because I was too busy making a living; I only wrote when I got in a hole and needed cash. When I got the cash, of course, I had pulled out of the hole and didn't write anymore."

Sherred's most famous story is "E for Effort" published in *Astounding* (1947). Sherred takes ordinary people and elevates them to positions of great power. In "E for Effort" Ed Lefko is confronted by a television set that can look in on any scene in history. The implications, as developed by Sherred, are enormous. In "Eye for Iniquity" Sherred's main character can create ten-dollar bills out of thin air. "Cue for Quiet" presents us with a pipefitter who discovers that if he wishes hard enough, he can burst the noisy televisions, radios, and jukeboxes that annoy him. These stories are all included in Sherred's only short story collection, *First Person, Peculiar.*

Sherred's only solo novel, *Alien Island,* is a story of first contact. An alien commercial operation called the Regan Group opens relations with Earth by going through an ordinary laborer named Ken Jordan, a sometime alcoholic. By sharing minds with the captain of the alien vessel, Jordan becomes changed, improved. The narrator of the novel is Dana Iverson, an American spy whose mission is to find out what Jordan and the aliens are planning. Jordan buys a Canadian island near Detroit and sets up a trading base: alien gold and other precious substances in return for Earth's luxury goods. Dana finds out what the Regan group is planning, yet finds their way of life attractive and joins them rather than reporting back to her superiors. The ending is bitter but appropriate.

—George Kelley

SHERWOOD, Nelson. *See* **BULMER, Kenneth.**

SHIEL, M(atthew) P(hipps)

Pseudonym: Gordon Holmes. **Nationality:** British. **Born:** Montserrat Island, West Indies, 21 July 1865. **Education:** Harrison College, Barbados; King's College, London; St. Bartholomew's Hospital Medical School, London. **Family:** Married 1) Carolina Garcìa Gomez in 1898 (died), two daughters; 2) Mrs. Gerald Jewson c. 1918. **Career:** Taught mathematics at a school in Derbyshire, two years. Granted Civil List pension, 1938. **Died:** 14 February 1947.

SCIENCE FICTION PUBLICATIONS

Novels

The Rajah's Sapphire. London, Ward Lock, 1896.
Shapes in the Fire: Being a Mid-Winter-Night's Entertainment in Two Parts and an Interlude. London, Lane, and Boston, Roberts, 1896.
The Yellow Danger: The World of the World's Greatest War. London, Richards, 1898; New York, Fenno, 1899.
The Purple Cloud. London, Chatto and Windus, 1901; revised edition, London, Gollancz, 1929; New York, Vanguard Press, 1930.
The Lord of the Sea. London, Richards, and New York, Stokes, 1901; revised edition, New York, Knopf, 1924; London, Gollancz, 1929.
The Last Miracle. London, Laurie, 1906; revised edition, London, Gollancz, 1929.
The Isle of Lies. London Laurie, 1909.
The Dragon. London, Richards, 1913; New York, Clode, 1914; revised as *The Yellow Peril,* London, Gollancz, 1929.
This above All. New York, Vanguard Press, 1933; as *Above All Else,* London, Cole, 1943.
The Young Men Are Coming! London, Allen and Unwin, and New York, Vanguard Press, 1937.

Short Stories

Prince Zaleski. London, Lane, and Boston, Roberts, 1895.
The Pale Ape and Other Pulses. London, Laurie, 1911.
The Best Short Stories of M.P. Shiel, edited by John Gawsworth. London, Gollancz, 1948.
Xélucha and Others. Sauk City, Wisconsin, Arkham House, 1975.
Prince Zaleski and Cummings King Monk. Sauk City, Wisconsin, Mycroft and Moran, 1977.
The Empress of the Earth, 1898; The Purple Cloud, 1901; "Some Short Stories": Offprints of the Original Editions. Cleveland, Ohio, Reynolds Morse Foundation, 1979.
The New King, Plus an Unpublished Dialog with Cummings King Monk Omitted from The Pale Ape of 1911. Cleveland, Ohio, Reynolds Morse Foundation, 1980.

OTHER PUBLICATIONS

Novels

Contraband of War. London, Richards, 1899; revised edition, London, Pearson, 1914; Ridgewood, New Jersey, Gregg Press, 1968.

Cold Steel. London, Richards, 1899; New York, Brentano's, 1900; revised edition, London, Gollancz, and New York, Vanguard Press, 1929.
The Man-Stealers. London, Hutchinson, and Philadelphia, Lippincott, 1900; revised edition, Hutchinson, 1927.
The Weird o' It. London, Richards, 1902.
Unto the Third Generation. London, Chatto and Windus, 1903.
The Evil That Men Do. London, Ward Lock, 1904.
The Yellow Wave. London, Ward Lock, 1905.
The Lost Viol. New York, Clode, 1905; London, Ward Lock, 1908.
The White Wedding. London, Laurie, 1908.
This Knot of Life. London, Everett, 1909.
Children of the Wind. London, Laurie, 1923.
Dr. Krasinski's Secret. New York, Vanguard Press, 1929; London, Jarrolds, 1930.
The Black Box. New York, Vanguard Press, 1930; London, Richards, 1931.
Say Au R'Voir but Not Goodbye. London, Benn, 1933.

Novels as Gordon Holmes (with Louis Tracy)

The Late Tenant. New York, Clode, 1906; London, Cassell, 1907.
By Force of Circumstances. New York, Clode, 1909; London, Mills and Boon, 1910.
The House of Silence. New York, Clode, 1911; as *The Silent House,* London, Nash, 1911.

Short Stories

How the Old Woman Got Home. London, Richards, 1927; New York, Vanguard Press, 1928.
Here Comes the Lady. London, Richards, 1928.
The Invisible Voices, with John Gawsworth. London, Richards, 1935; New York, Vanguard Press, 1936.

Poetry

(Poems), edited by John Gawsworth. London, Richards, 1936.

Other

Science, Life, and Literature. London, Williams and Norgate, 1950.
The New King. Cleveland, Ohio, Reynolds Morse Foundation, 1980.
Translator, *The Hungarian Revolution: An Eyewitness's Account,* by Charles Henry Schmitt. London, Worker's Socialist Federation, 1919.
Editor, *An American Emperor: The Story of the Fourth Empire of France,* by Louis Tracy. New York, Putnam, and London, Pearson, 1897.

*

Bibliography: *The Works of M.P. Shiel: A Study in Bibliography* by A. Reynolds Morse, Los Angeles, Fantasy, 1948.

*   *   *

Certainly one of the most idiosyncratic writers of the scientific romance, M.P. Shiel is primarily remembered today for a single novel, *The Purple Cloud,* and for his role in popularizing the racist theme of "the Yellow Peril," a phrase that he is sometimes credited with coining. A capable stylist whose fine attention to detail can make the most unlikely fantasies persuasive, Shiel also aspired to aesthetic and social theory in his 31 novels and several short stories, and seemed strongly influenced both by social Darwinism and the theories of the American social philosopher Henry George.

Shiel's first major work in a tradition historically allied with science fiction was the "future war" narrative *The Yellow Danger,* which portrayed the conquest by Japan and China of all Europe except for England, which successfully retaliates using biological weapons and finally comes to rule the world itself. Focusing more on the character of the opposing leaders than on technological marvels, the novel is disturbing in its racist implications, although it should be noted that this attitude was considerably muted in *The Yellow Wave,* a novel on a similar theme published seven years later. A more successful, if bizarre, novel is *The Lord of the Sea,* which has also been attacked for its racism, this time in the form of anti-Semitism. But Shiel's attitudes toward Jews in the novel are actually quite complex. Following a series of pogroms and anti-Semitic laws in Europe, England inherits a wave of Jewish immigrants, and quickly gains prosperity from this influx of skilled labor. A rapacious Jewish landlord is opposed by the hero—himself Jewish—and frames him for a murder. After escaping from prison and gaining great wealth, the hero constructs a series of enormous floating fortresses, making himself "Lord of the Sea" and forcing nations to participate in a complex land-reform scheme that ushers in an era of social progress. Later, as regent of England, he enacts a series of anti-Jewish laws forcing many Jews to emigrate to Palestine, where he joins them (after his betrayal and fall in England) as nothing less than the Messiah, who turns the new Israel into a powerful and prosperous nation! While Shiel does fall victim to several Jewish stereotypes common to his time, he also speaks in this novel of the Jewish "genius for righteousness," and makes a Jew the first major exemplar of his "overman" theme, drawn in part from Nietzsche. This theme returns prominently in *The Isle of Lies,* which concerns an archaeologist who raises his son in isolation to be superintelligent; upon discovering the true nature of humanity, the son embarks on a doomed idealistic scheme to improve the world.

Shiel's masterpiece, *The Purple Cloud,* deals with a more fundamental issue: the nature of the human psyche itself. Following the suggestion of an American millionaire that he write a novel about Robert Peary and his family returning from the North Pole to a dead world, Shiel commented that he "left out 'the family,' and 'Peary,' too, and wrote this." After committing murder to gain a position on a polar expedition, Adam Jeffson reaches the pole only to return to a world depopulated by a poisonous volcanic gas. Over the next few decades, Jeffson struggles with the "black" and "white" forces of his nature, sometimes collecting great works of art for his "palace," sometimes madly setting fire to the great cities of Europe. When he finds another survivor—a girl whose mind is a virtual tabula rasa from having lived alone in a dungeon her whole life (she was born just as the gas was dissipating)—he feels a strange impulse to kill and eat her. But her companionship seems to restore a kind of moral balance in Jeffson, and with her he sets out to start the race anew. Although the novel may not quite deserve the lavish praise heaped on it by H.G. Wells, Hugh Walpole, and Arthur Machen, it is a strangely powerful and moving novel, and remains one of the most widely-read "last man" novels, far outpacing in popularity its ancestor and probable influence, Mary Shelley's *The Last Man* (1826).

Late in his career, Shiel returned to fantastic literature with *This above All,* a fantasy about Biblical figures surviving into the modern world, and a number of short stories. One of these stories, "How Life Climbs," became the genesis of the novel *The Young Men Are Coming!,* which concerns a scientist abducted by aliens and given a rejuvenating serum. Returning to Earth, he forms a radical social movement called the Young Men, which gains such influence that the government assumes totalitarian powers to suppress it. In an odd conclusion that pits establishment religion against extraterrestrial science, the scientist stages a duel with an evangelist, each trying to summon a storm to prove the validity of their belief. The evangelist fails, of course, but the scientist's aliens produce a storm that nearly destroys the world.

Shiel undoubtedly deserves greater attention than he has generally received, not only as the author of one of science fiction's true masterworks, but as a participant in the debates regarding social Darwinism and economic reform which so preoccupied his contemporaries. At times visionary, at times intolerant, at times simply megalomaniacal, Shiel is among the more stimulating and provocative figures of British imaginative literature of the first half of this century.

—Gary K. Wolfe

SHIRAS, Wilmar H(ouse)

Pseudonym: Jane Howes. **Nationality:** American. **Born:** Boston, Massachusetts, 23 September 1908. **Education:** Holy Names College, Oakland, California; University of California, Berkeley, M.A. 1956. **Family:** Married Russell Shiras in 1927; three daughters and two sons. **Died:** 23 December 1990.

SCIENCE FICTION PUBLICATIONS

Short Stories

Children of the Atom. New York, Gnome Press, 1953; London, Boardman, 1954.

OTHER PUBLICATIONS

Other

Slow Dawning (as June Howes). London and St. Louis, Herder, 1946.

*

Wilmar H. Shiras commented:
"In Hiding" grew out of my wondering whether very high-I.Q. children would have problems; the rest of the book deals with other such children and their problems.

*   *   *

Wilmar H. Shiras's total literary output is far from copious, and even of the total number of works, not all have been science fiction. In fact, she is known almost entirely for a single volume, *Chil-*

dren of the Atom. Though it reveals serious shortcomings and limitations, its virtues are even greater.

Children of the Atom originated in three stories published in *Astounding;* the author added two further stories, collecting the five into an episodic work that experienced a considerable vogue in the 1950s. ("In Hiding," the first story in the cycle, has been anthologized no fewer than a dozen times.) The basic premise of the stories, questionable even in 1948 and now recognized as an absurdity, is that an accident in a nuclear industrial plant will produce a uniform mutation in the offspring of all workers in the plant. Specifically, all children born to women pregnant at the time of the accident, or conceived by workers present at the accident, will be of genius-grade intelligence and of highly creative temperament. The author postulates, further, that all of the workers exposed to the accident will die within approximately two years, but that their children will be perfect. Shiras's main concern is the problems of adjustment and development of these children in later years. Her major adult protagonists are a group of sympathetic educators and psychologists who discover the existence of these children (who are "in hiding"), and the existence of a network of communication among them. The author assumes that these mentally superior children will be automatically outcasts. The boys, with their inclination to study science, will not fit into a society that emphasizes athletics and violent competition; the girls, inclined toward art, will be similarly excluded from a society that emphasizes prettiness and socialization. Thus, the children, in order to survive, hide their superiority beneath a veneer of assumed ordinariness.

Although the author's notions of mutation were quickly seen as absurd, her portrayal of the "superior" children—hyperintellectual adolescents, the boys frequently myopic and unathletic, the girls similarly not adept at the sex-role dictates of the day—struck a strong responsive chord in the typical SF readers of the period. Both Marion Zimmer Bradley and Barry Malzberg, in notes published with a 1978 reissue of the book, comment upon the sense of identity felt by the original readers with the youngsters in the book. It is this uncanny identification of reader with character that gave the book its popularity in the 1950s. In later years, the reading of science fiction gained a far greater acceptance in schools, aficionados ceased to be automatic outcasts, and this sense of identity became weakened, although it did not cease altogether.

In its later segments the novel shows unfortunate tendencies to degenerate into piously one-sided theological argumentation, and at the end the adult sponsors of the brilliant children are told by the children themselves that it will be best to terminate their experimental community and disperse themselves among the general populace. This ending, too, has proved controversial among readers of the book, many of them indicating that they see in it a surrender to the very standards of mediocrity and conformism which the children had earlier sought to escape. Shiras produced other short works of SF between long intervals. These have been uniformly pleasant, low-keyed, generally concerned with children, and have received little attention from readers.

—Richard A. Lupoff

SHIRLEY, John (Patrick)

Nationality: American. **Born:** Houston, Texas, 10 February 1953. **Education:** High school education. **Family:** Married Alexandra Allinne in 1982 (separated); twin sons. **Career:** Has had various jobs including fruit picker, dancer, and office worker; regularly performs as lead singer with rock bands. **Agent:** Lori Perkins, 301 West 53rd Street, New York, New York 10019, U.S.A.

SCIENCE FICTION PUBLICATIONS

Novels (series: Kamus; A Song Called Youth)

Transmaniacon. New York, Zebra, 1979.
Three-Ring Psychus. New York, Zebra, 1980.
City Come a-Walkin'. New York, Dell, 1980.
The Brigade. New York, Avon, 1982; London, Sphere, 1983.
Cellars. New York, Avon, 1982; London, Sphere, 1983.
Dracula in Love. New York, Zebra, 1983.
A Song Called Youth:
    Eclipse. New York, Bluejay, 1985; London, Methuen, 1986.
    Eclipse Penumbra. New York, Popular Library, 1988.
    Eclipse Corona. New York, Popular Library, 1990.
Kamus of Kadizhar: The Black Hole of Carcosa: A Tale of the Darkworld Detective. New York, St. Martin's Press, 1988.
A Splendid Chaos: An Interplanetary Fantasy. New York, Watts, 1988; London, Mandarin, 1989.
In Darkness Waiting. New York, Onyx, 1988.
Wetbones: A Novel. Shingletown, California, Mark V. Ziesing, 1991.

Novels as D.B. Drumm (series: Traveler in all titles)

Kingdom Come. New York, Dell, 1984.
The Stalkers. New York, Dell, 1984.
To Kill a Shadow. New York, Dell, 1984.
Road War. New York, Dell, 1985.
Border War. New York, Dell, 1985.
Terminal Road. New York, Dell, 1986.

Short Stories

Heatseeker. Los Angeles, California, Scream/Press, 1989; London, Grafton, 1990.

OTHER PUBLICATIONS

Short Stories

New Noir. Boulder, Colorado, Black Ice Books, 1993.

Plays

Screenplays: *Video Girl; The Other Side of Evil.*

*

John Shirley comments:

(1991) My early stories show that I was enamored of the surrealists; surrealist and expressionist painting influenced me more than writers. Although there was a political iconoclasm intrinsic to my writing, I've never sided with any particular political philosophy; I feel that the major political and economic theories have all been satirized even-handedly in my fiction. My newest novel, *Eclipse*—easily my most significant book—is essentially a political thriller set in the year 2020, when a non-nuclear world war has ravaged Europe, making it possible for an opportunistic cabal of genuine fascists to take over, through nationalistic puppets, one country after another. Essentially, Europe becomes a massive police state, and the heroes of *Eclipse* are the resistance. They're not Communists, particularly—that is, some are, some aren't. Nor are they radicals. They're simply the resistance to fascism. It happens I really and honestly believe that a resurgence of racism on a vast scale is about to transform Europe, due to the myopic and xenophobic reaction of European natives to the influx of third world immigrants, and also due to other sociological factors. *Eclipse* is a kind of warning novel about it, and an attempt to redefine the cultural backdrop of the near-future. The landscapes of bizarrities typical of much of my earlier writing, the attempt to realize abstractions in physical description—these are missing from *Eclipse,* at least in explicit manifestation. *Eclipse* is real life, contemporary life, seen through a science fiction lens. I've also given a much greater emphasis to characterization than ever before.

*   *   *

Of the writers herded together as "cyberpunks," John Shirley was one of the few to enjoy the label. Shirley already had participated in the punk scene as a rock musician, and also had made a reputation as an unusually vivid, uncomfortable writer. He liked the idea of fusing high-tech concepts with the visceral images he had been using to attack readers' preconceptions. And so, for a time, he was know as the most intense and disturbing of the cyberpunks. Actually, Shirley's work always has been distinctive for its stern insistence that people need to open themselves to new possibilities, enlivened by stunning imaginative riffs. Under whatever label, he has produced a striking, powerful body of fiction.

In his early novels, such as *Dracula in Love* and *City Come A-Walkin',* Shirley's main character suffers because he is empty of purpose. He is attracted to an unchanging (but vicious) force trying to preserve itself; however, he winds up on the side of an amoral, stability-shattering entity that plots to destroy that stifling "father" power. The novels' action is morally equivocal at best, with huge numbers of few people being vividly mutilated and/or slaughtered. The central character is never sure he is doing the right thing, and Shirley offers the possibility that his thirst for freedom might actually be a craving for oblivion (in madness or death). *Transmaniacon* (his first novel) is probably the most successful of Shirley's early novels in demonstrating hatred of a status quo, thanks to its fierce images of bizarre obsessions; that novel's conclusion explicitly links escape from constraints with mortal danger, but Shirley's hero gladly makes that choice. Also memorable is *Three-Ring Psychus* set after some people have been given psychic powers that let them transcend some physical limits; Shirley's characters discover that the change has given them new possibilities for growth, but that some of the possibilities threaten the survival of human consciousness. The book ends with determined uncertainty.

Reading these novels is unsettling as much for the manner of their telling as for their content. The stories refuse to let a reader sink into them as comfortable escapist fiction. The action lurches along. The characters let moral qualms interrupt what the reader expects to be a smooth, exciting flow of action. On the other hand, what might be key personal decisions are summarized in an offhand manner. Shirley began experimenting with less jarring narrative techniques when he turned away from science fiction briefly

to write a mainstream suspense thriller (*The Brigade*), a horror fantasy in the vein of Stephen King, and various pseudonymous action novels for paperback series (such as the "Traveler" series of post-World War III adventures, which are notable for Shirley's wholesale bloodletting and his bitter, witty contempt for the military-political thinking that caused the nuclear war). Having returned to the science-fiction novel, he stated his intention "to write with crystalline realism about this world, but I'm still trying to make my readers question their assumptions. I'm spending a great deal more time investigating character, and controlling tone, the overall quality of writing."

Shirley's major work during this period and his clearest contribution to cyberpunk fiction is the trilogy *A Song Called Youth—Eclipse, Eclipse Penumbra,* and *Eclipse Corona.* This near-future story is set during and immediately after World War III, but it focuses on the struggle between new waves of fascists and a conglomeration of resistance fighters. Shirley describes how the seductiveness of fascism and the weight of inertia can be overcome by technology-enhanced idealism. Overall, the trilogy shows some of Shirley's limitations. The characters are vivid but are developed as people just enough to perform their roles in the action; also, the action itself feels rather perfunctory in the later books, with the heroes triumphing neatly as if evil and incompetence are synonymous. But Shirley's strengths are abundant. The scientific, political, and social extrapolation is detailed, startling, and plausible; in particular, the glimpses of mass media are grotesque enough to be quite plausible. And at each moment and during each scene the action and characters are convincing because of Shirley's grasp of sensory detail.

Unfortunately, the publication of the trilogy was less than successful. Shirley's early novels were inexpensive paperbacks that flicker in and out of print, and he was pleased that *A Song Called Youth* would be in the more substantial trade paperback format. But the original publisher failed after *Eclipse* appeared, and the later two books were published in mass market paperbacks by a company that did not promote them.

As a matter of fact, Shirley's only hardcover SF novel to date is *A Splendid Chaos,* which resembles his earlier fiction in using mental powers to threaten his characters with physical mutation in order to force them to enlarge their thinking. The splatterpunk novel, *In Darkness Waiting,* suggests grimmer prospects, as people converge on a slaughterhouse to be put through a kind of psychic meat grinder.

Otherwise, Shirley has published *Kamus of Kadizhar: The Black Hole of Carcosa,* the hardcover horror novel *Wetbones,* and *New Noir,* a recent collection of short stories that draws its intense horrors from realistically described "street life and people." However, Shirley's earlier collection of fantastic short stories, *Heatseeker,* deserve special attention. Though Shirley's novels present his message more fully, some of his short stories are more successful at giving a burst of plausible argument and stunning imagery that take reality apart and put it together again inside out. In particular, "The Almost Empty Rooms" plays with the idea of free will in a wry story of World War III seen as a frolic of event-animals whose cells are human beings. Another outstanding story, "What Cindy Saw," seems to begin as a study of mental illness, then becomes a surrealistic look at modern life, but it ends by affirming the existence of a nightmarish world under the surface of normal reality. Two uncollected stories are worth noting, too. "The Prince" (in *When the Music's Over*) tries to find a nonviolent solution to social injustice, though the prospects for real reform remain uncertain. In "A Walk through Beirut" (in *Newer York* edited by Lawrence Watt-Evans, New York, Roc, 1991), Shirley returns to the milieu of *A Song Called Youth* to show a young musician coming to terms with himself, deciding not to commit suicide, and making as much of a personal commitment as is possible in our fragmented, confused society. Throughout his short fiction, Shirley demonstrates that he not only has an imagination that can take reality apart and put it together again inside out, but he also has a challenging but positive personal vision to share once he has our attention.

At the moment, Shirley has turned from prose SF and horror to writing screenplays. He did the first five drafts of *The Crow* script, was executive story editor for the Fox TV show *VR5,* and is working on several adaptations and original projects. Like the characters in his fiction, he evidently feels compelled to leave familiar territory to run the risks of freedom. In any event, he has produced enough lively, gutsy fiction to make a mark to force readers to live more alertly and authentically.

—Joe Sanders

SHUTE, Nevil

Nationality: British. **Born:** Nevil Shute Norway, Ealing, London, 17 January 1899. **Education:** Dragon School, Oxford; Shrewsbury School, Oxford; Royal Military Academy, Woolwich, London; Balliol College, Oxford, 1919-22, E.A. in engineering 1922. **Military Service:** Served as a private in the Suffolk Regiment, British Army, 1918; commissioned in the Royal Naval Volunteer Reserve, 1940: Lieutenant Commander; retired 1945. **Family:** Married Frances Mary Heaton in 1931; two daughters. **Career:** Calculator, de Havilland Aircraft Company, 1923-24; chief calculator, 1924-28, and deputy chief engineer, 1928-30, on the construction of Rigid Airship R. 100 for the Airship Guarantee Company: twice flew Atlantic in R. 100, 1930; managing director, Yorkshire Aeroplane Club Ltd., 1927-30; founder and joint managing director, Airspeed Ltd., airplane constructors, 1931-38. Lived in Australia after 1950. **Member:** Fellow, Royal Aeronautical Society, 1934. **Died:** 12 January 1960.

SCIENCE FICTION PUBLICATIONS

Novels

What Happened to the Corbetts. London, Heinemann, 1939; as *Ordeal,* New York, Morrow, 1939.
An Old Captivity. London, Heinemann, and New York, Morrow, 1940.
No Highway. London, Heinemann, and New York, Morrow, 1948.
In the Wet. London, Heinemann, and New York, Morrow, 1953.
On the Beach. London, Heinemann, and New York, Morrow, 1957.
The Rainbow and the Rose. London, Heinemann, and New York, Morrow, 1958.
A Nevil Shute Omnibus (includes *No Highway, A Town like Alice,* and *On the Beach).* London, Heinemann, 1973.

OTHER PUBLICATIONS

Novels

Marazan. London, Cassell, 1926.
So Disdained. London, Cassell, 1928; as *Mysterious Aviator,* Boston, Houghton Mifflin, 1928.
Lonely Road. London, Cassell, and New York, Morrow, 1932.
Ruined City. London, Cassell, 1938; as *Kindling,* New York, Morrow, 1938.
Landfall: A Channel Story. London, Heinemann, and New York, Morrow, 1940.
Pied Piper. New York, Morrow, 1941; London, Heinemann, 1942.
Pastoral. London, Heinemann, and New York, Morrow, 1944.
Most Secret. London, Heinemann, and New York, Morrow, 1945.
The Chequer Board. London, Heinemann, and New York, Morrow, 1947.
A Town like Alice. London, Heinemann, 1950; as *The Legacy,* New York, Morrow, 1950.
Round the Bend. London, Heinemann, and New York, Morrow, 1951.
The Far Country. London, Heinemann, and New York, Morrow, 1952.
Requiem for a Wren. London, Heinemann, 1955; as *The Breaking Wave,* New York, Morrow, 1955.
Beyond the Black Stump. London, Heinemann, and New York, Morrow, 1956.
Trustee from the Toolroom. London, Heinemann, and New York, Morrow, 1960.
Stephen Morris. London, Heinemann, and New York, Morrow, 1961.

Play

Vinland the Good (screenplay). London, Heinemann, and New York, Morrow, 1946.

Other

Slide Rule: The Autobiography of an Engineer. London, Heinemann, and New York, Morrow, 1954.

*

Manuscript Collection: National Library of Australia, Canberra.

Critical Study: *Nevil Shute (Nevil Shute Norway)* by Julian Smith, Boston, Twayne, 1976.

*   *   *

The popular author of 22 novels, the majority based on his experiences as an aeronautical engineer and aviator in both world wars, Nevil Shute is best known for his futuristic novel *On the Beach.* Shute's quiet, understated style, his fascination with machinery, entrepreneurship, and exploration, and his highly plausible personalities make him a good storyteller. Many of his novels are set in Australia, where he finally settled, and all contain superb technical details.

The title of *On the Beach* comes from a line in T.S. Eliot's "The Hollow Men": "In this last of meeting places/ We grope together/ And avoid speech/ Gathered on this beach .... This is the way the world ends/ Not with a bang but a whimper." The quote, which begins the book, is most apt, for the central characters are all "gathered" on the Australian coast two years or so after the end of World War III. It is just after Christmas 1963, the entire northern hemisphere has been destroyed by a series of nuclear exchanges not really planned by any participant, and the deadly radiation produced by the cobalt bombs is creeping southward ineluctably. The characters indeed "grope together and avoid speech" about their imminent ends, while also obsessively practicing various forms of denial as the invisible death approaches. In the eight months that the novel covers, we watch the world end with "a whimper," and the effect is horrific.

The main characters are Dwight Towers, the captain of *USS Scorpion,* an American nuclear submarine stranded in Melbourne, the world's southernmost major city; Commander Peter Holmes, the Australian liaison with the *Scorpion;* his wife Mary, a hausfrau with a new baby; Moira Davidson, a party girl who dates Dwight Towers but is frustrated by his memories of his dead wife and children in Connecticut; and John Osborne, a scientist who works with the Australian government measuring radiation but whose real love is his Ferrari and car racing. These characters, gathered together by the interactions of their jobs and social lives, try desperately to maintain a normal life and hope for reprieve from death by radiation sickness, but the pitiless logic of Shute's premise leaves them helpless before their fate. Shute's artistry lies in his skillful analysis of defense and denial mechanisms, as Captain Towers follows Navy rules to the letter, even though the U.S. Navy no longer exists; as Peter and Mary plant a garden that can never be harvested; and as each of the other characters copes with the certainty of knowing the date and circumstance of his or her impending death. The premise is artful in projecting a future very close to the present in time (the book was written in 1957 and set in 1962-63) and virtually identical in every other way, so we can see ourselves in these very normal people coping with nuclear holocaust. It is a very painful book to read, the discomfort coming from the shocking possibility, even likelihood, of the premise and the recognition of the true horror of nuclear catastrophe: not a personal end, nor even the deaths of many millions, but an end to entire cultures and then to human life itself.

Shute's other works have SF elements but are not science fiction per se. For example, *No Highway* is a projection, a prediction of the dangers of metal fatigue as a potential and previously unconsidered cause of air disasters. In it, a metal fatigue expert finds himself aboard a plane that meets the criteria for disaster he had been unsuccessfully trying to convince others of. This book was published just before a Comet jet crash in real life—due to metal fatigue.

An Old Captivity is a modern romance including a Viking parallel universe; it gives a sense of other worlds and other realities, but historical rather than futuristic. On an archeological aerial survey in Greenland, the hazardous environment of ice floes and fog strains the nerves of Donald Ross, a seaplane pilot helping photograph Viking ruins. Already weakened by an addiction to sleeping pills, he begins to dream of Erik the Red, Leif Erikson, and the latter's fabled trip to Cape Cod, the Norsemen's "Vinland the Good." His drifting dream fantasies seem more real than his present life, and he becomes convinced that Alix, his employer's daughter, is in fact a reincarnation of Hekja, a Celtic slave girl that Ross, named Haki a thousand years earlier, loved and settled down with in the New World. Physical proof of Haki and Hekja's existence found by Ross and the Lockwoods on a trip to the Massachusetts coast lends substance to these incredible illusions. The adventure is an odd combination: historic detail about Celts and Vikings, both real and speculative, dream fantasy, Eskimo superstition, and makeshift psychoanalysis, set against a realistic delineation of the day-to-day particulars of aviation.

The dream vision technique allows Shute to build the novel on his strengths, his precise knowledge of aviation and his sensitivity to a modern love story, while indulging his taste for far-distant history. The modern characters and the Viking vision combine neatly and credibly in the eerie empty setting of Greenland, a place of stark landscapes where normality seems suspended. A flashback technique used in other Shute works here ameliorates the fantastic with the realistic "frame": a much older Ross recounting his dream experience to a psychiatrist on a stalled train.

In the Wet seems at first glance to be either a simple love story between a part-aborigine Australian pilot and an English girl, both in the service of the English Queen, but is instead a deceptively simple projection into the near future (the 1980s seen from the 1950s). It postulates the British Labour party and the monarchy on a collision course that would lead all the royal heirs (Prince Charles included) to decline succession to the throne, and that would therefore require drastic measures to save the kingdom and the empire. Following the example of Australia (as Britain did with the secret ballot and the women's vote), a few farsighted supporters of the monarchy act to limit the negative effects of working-class greed by revising the voting system to one of multiple votes, with extra votes added to a person's single vote according to level of education, property ownership, broadening travel, contribution to the nation, and so forth. The novel also toys with the idea of dream-reality, so that one is at first not sure whether the story is the hallucination of an opium-crazed outbacker dying of appendicitis, or whether the outbacker and the priest who comforts him are a bad dream of the pilot while suffering from food poisoning. The reality turns out to be just as fantastic: a fever-induced vision of reincarnation.

Shute's forte is to reduce the historical and the romantic to life-sized dimensions, to capture the excitement of the humdrum and the ordinariness of the historic, to pursue the effects of change on the common man—all in an artfully casual style. His works reflect an old-fashioned sense of goodness; they involve characters with a strong sense of purpose, of decency, of right, characters who enjoy being caught up in the unfolding of great enterprises. For Shute, both the past and the future are "made by plain and simple people like ourselves, doing the best . . . [they] can with each job as it comes along." Shute suggests domesticity as a powerful civilizing force that might well spur men to dreams and action. His men are industrious, competent and driven, his women are supportive, sometimes domestic but sometimes also competent in the world of men, so that they can ultimately save men from shortsightedness or from personal limitations. Shute's contribution to science fiction is not so much in following the central conventions of the genre as in using SF elements in what otherwise would be conventional novels. His excellence in creating character and milieu in an appealing style bring quality and dignity to the science fiction genre.

—Andrew F. Macdonald

SHWARTZ, Susan (Martha)

Pseudonym: Gordon Kendall. **Nationality:** American. **Born:** Youngstown, Ohio, 31 December 1949. **Education:** Mount Holyoke College, Massachusetts, 1968-72, B.A. in English;

Harvard University, Cambridge, Massachusetts, 1972-73, M.A. in English 1973, Ph.D. in English 1977. Summer study, Trinity College, Oxford, 1970, 1971. **Career:** Postdoctoral fellow, Dartmouth College, New Hampshire, 1978. Teaching fellow, Harvard University, 1974-77; Assistant Professor of English, Ithaca College, New York, 1977-80; senior writer/researcher, Deutsch, Shea and Evans, New York, 1981-82; information coordinator, BEA Associates, New York, 1983-87; financial editor, Donaldson, Lufkin and Jenrette, New York, 1987-88. Financial writer/editor and associate vice-president, Prudential Securities, New York. Since 1994, Senior Analyst/Editor, Moody's Investors Service. **Awards:** National Endowment for the Humanities grant, 1978. **Agent:** Richard Curtis Associates, 171 East 74th Street, New York, New York 10022. **Address:** One Station Square, Number 306, Forest Hills, New York 11375, U.S.A. **Online Address:** S.Shwartz@Genie.com or SueShwartz@aol.com.

SCIENCE FICTION PUBLICATIONS

Novels (series: Byzantium's Heirs)

Byzantium's Crown. New York, Popular Library, and London, Pan, 1987.
The Woman of Flowers (Byzantium's Heirs). New York, Popular Library, and London, Pan, 1987.
Queensblade (Byzantium's Heirs). New York, Popular Library, and London, Pan, 1988.
Silk Roads and Shadows. New York, Tor, 1988; London, Pan, 1990.
Heritage of Flight. New York, Tor, 1989.
Imperial Lady: A Fantasy of Han China, with Andre Norton. New York, Tor, 1989.
The Grail of Hearts. New York, Tor, 1992.
Empire of the Eagle, with Andre Norton. New York, Tor, 1993.

OTHER PUBLICATIONS

Novel

White Wing, with Shariann N. Lewitt (as Gordon Kendall). New York, Tor, 1985; London, Sphere, 1986.

Other

Editor, *Hecate's Cauldron.* New York, DAW, 1982.
Editor, *Habitats* (science fiction anthology). New York, DAW, 1984.
Editor, *Moonsinger's Friends: An Anthology in Honor of Andre Norton.* New York, Bluejay, 1985; London, Severn House, 1986.
Editor, *Arabesques: More Tales of the Arabian Nights.* New York, Avon, 1988.
Editor, *Arabesques II.* New York, Avon, 1989.

*

Susan Shwartz comments:

For me, one world and one vision of that world have never been enough. I've spent a lifetime looking over my shoulder, into a mirror, or glancing quickly down a sidestreet for glimpses of the other worlds that I sense surround us all. As a writer, editor, critic, scholar, and businesswoman, I've spent most of my career building bridges (and occasionally burning them behind me); I look forward to spending the rest of my productive life linking unlikelinesses—Wall Street and academia, military science fiction and feminism, fantasy and Realpolitik, life as a New York City chauvinist and travel to as many places as funds, suitcases, and available transport will manage.

As a scholar, I was a medievalist and an Arthurian scholar. These fields enabled me to create a peephole into the "alternative" worlds of the Middle Ages and to move their literature forward into our own time. My novel *The Grail of Hearts* is, essentially, a version of Wagner's redaction of Wolfram von Eschenbach's 13th-century work *Parzival*—from the standpoint of a sorceress who betrays the harlot, apostate Jew, and penitent. Writing this book compelled me to build a bridge between my own love of opera and my distrust of Richard Wagner, between my career as a writer of fiction and the career as a teacher and scholar that I left when I moved to New York.

Because of that desire to enter strange new worlds, I've come to specialize in exotic places, mostly Turkey and Central Asia, and all the way into Han and T'ang Dynasty China. In a way, this is quite conventionally medieval: traders, mercenaries, crusaders, and adventurers all tended to look East—first to Byzantium, starting point for four of my novels, thereafter to parts East . . . all the way out onto the steppes and to Ch'ang-an. Several of my anthologies are also set in this milieu.

At the same time, I write or attempt to write military science fiction that examines the ethical issues that worry me most—the ones considered to be almost unthinkable. *White Wing,* written in collaboration with S.N. Lewitt, examines the questions of Diaspora, refugees, and survival of a planetary holocaust from the point of view of the survivors; *Heritage of Flight* deals with genocide, from the standpoint of the people who committed it and who seek re-entry into the human race. The work I've done for Jerry Pournelle's War World shared universe enables me to examine questions of survival in a Hobbesian environment.

As a writer of short fiction, I try quite deliberately to be all over the map—from alternative history featuring a T.E. Lawrence who survived his 1935 motorcycle accident to a "President" George McGovern; from an insecure classicist to a temporary worker to a desert priestess to a cat with a gift for healing; to a boy with an aversion to Zero-G and doctrinaire ideologies; a werewolf who dreams of meeting God; an explorer pilot with the sniffles; a cantor on contract to a space station; or a heartsick lord of the Wild Hunt during nuclear winter.

I don't try to write strange things. I'm a story-teller who simply tries to throw up bridges of words, cemented by thoughts and some rather vivid dreams.

These fragments, as T.S. Eliot says in *The Waste Land,* have I shored against my ruins. For me, they provide all the colors of life and as much entertainment as I can safely handle.

*   *   *

Octavia Butler's cover blurb for *Heritage of Flight* says, "This novel reminds one that SF is a literature of ideas and not all those ideas are shiny and metallic." Indeed, Susan Shwartz lives up to her name (schwarz—black); all of her writing having some dark element either directly conveyed (as in *Heritage of Flight*) or creeping about in the background (as in her Heirs of Byzantium trilogy). Do not confuse her intent, however. She is not a pessimist, but she is able to see the gloomy side of things and lay it into her writing.

Steeped in centuries of English literature and tradition, Shwartz has quickly gained attention in the SF and fantasy fields with her somewhat controversial writing. She has been described as a feminist and as "having her own agenda," but whatever the label attributed to her, she most certainly has well-developed female characters, strong women who are able to carry their men through when they need help, yet are passionate enough to enjoy being loved and cared for at other times.

In *Heritage of Flight,* an almost documentary-style book set in the future, a galaxies-wide war is destroying the populations of entire planets; mankind is engaged in a most spectacular Civil War. In a *Battlestar Galactica*-type scenario ("a ragtag band of survivors in a ragtag fleet of spaceships"), a group of Alliance (North) civilians and warriors engage in a deep space battle with the Secessionists (South). As the battleship is destroyed, the personnel carrier "jumps" (much like the *Star Trek* warp drive) and escapes to a planet called Cynthia. There, the civilians and most of the crew are, for all intents and purposes, marooned as part of a bureaucrat's "Project Seedcorn," for "racial survival" in case the rest of the human race doesn't make it.

Unfortunately, the planet-bound humans were not informed of the alien lifeforms on the planet . . . a lifeform that is fatally dangerous to the humans and their survival. Pauli Yeager must "convince her people to commit a heinous crime or watch their children die." And when they commit the horrible crime, *Völkermord,* Pauli shoulders the entire burden.

In the Heirs to Byzantium trilogy, Shwartz examines the darkness of the human psyche: dreams, nightmares, guilt, terror, incest, dark magic. Marric, rightful Emperor of Byzantium, has had his power usurped by a black magician. And he spends the better part of three books fighting that darkness alongside his sister Alexa and his lover Stephana (who, in the fashion of *Conan,* returns from beyond the dark wall of death to fight with her love). And even though Marric is the central figure of the story, Stephana, Alexa, and the evil Irene are the characters who are best remembered.

—Daryl F. Mallett

SILVA, Joseph. *See* GOULART, Ron.

SILVERBERG, Robert

Pseudonyms: Walker Chapman; Ivar Jorgenson; Calvin M. Knox; David Osborne; Robert Randall; Lee Sebastian. **Nationality:** American. **Born:** New York City, 15 January 1935. **Education:** Columbia University, New York, A.B. 1956. **Family:** Married Barbara H. Brown in 1956 (divorced); married Karen Haber, 1987. **Career:** Full-time writer: associate editor, *Amazing,* January 1969 issue, and associate editor, *Fantastic,* February-April 1969 issues. President, Science Fiction Writers of America, 1967-68. **Awards:** Hugo award, 1956, 1969, 1987, 1990; Nebula award, for story, 1969, 1971, 1974, for novel, 1971, for novella, 1985; Jupiter award,

1973; Prix Apollo, 1976; *Locus* award, 1981. Guest of Honor, 28th World Science Fiction Convention, 1970. **Agent:** Ralph Vicinanza, 432 Park Avenue South, Room 1205, New York, New York 10016, U.S.A.

SCIENCE FICTION PUBLICATIONS

Novels (series: Gilgamesh; Majipoor; New Springtime; Nidor; Time Gate)

Revolt on Alpha C (for children). New York, Crowell, 1955.
The 13th Immortal. New York, Ace, 1957.
Master of Life and Death. New York, Ace, 1957; London, Sidgwick and Jackson, 1977.
The Shrouded Planet (Nidor; as Robert Randall, with Randall Garrett). New York, Gnome Press, 1957; London, Mayflower, 1964.
Invaders from Earth. New York, Ace, 1958; London, Sidgwick and Jackson, 1977.
Invincible Barriers (as David Osborne). New York, Avalon, 1958.
Stepsons of Terra. New York, Ace, 1958.
Aliens from Space (as David Osborne). New York, Avalon, 1958.
Starhaven (as Ivar Jorgenson). New York, Avalon, 1958.
Lest We Forget Thee, Earth (as Calvin M. Knox). New York, Ace, 1958.
The Plot against Earth (as Calvin M. Knox). New York, Ace, 1959.
Starman's Quest (for children). Hicksville, New York, Gnome Press, 1959.
The Dawning Light (Nidor; as Robert Randall, with Randall Garrett). New York, Gnome Press, 1959; London, Mayflower, 1964.
The Planet Killers. New York, Ace, 1959.
Lost Race of Mars (for children). Philadelphia, Winston, 1960.
Collision Course. New York, Avalon, 1961.
The Seed of Earth. New York, Ace, 1962; London, Hamlyn, 1978.
Recalled to Life. New York, Lancer, 1962; revised edition, Garden City, New York, Doubleday, 1972; London Gollancz, 1974.
The Silent Invaders. New York, Ace, 1963; London, Dobson, 1975; with "Valley beyond Time," New York, Tor, 1985.
Regan's Planet. New York, Pyramid, 1964; revised as *World's Fair 1992,* Chicago, Follett, 1970.
Time of the Great Freeze (for children). New York, Holt Rinehart, 1964.
One of Our Asteroids Is Missing (as Calvin M. Knox). New York, Ace, 1964.
Conquerors from the Darkness (for children). New York, Holt Rinehart, 1965.
The Gate of Worlds (for children). New York, Holt Rinehart, 1967; London, Gollancz, 1978.
To Open the Sky. New York, Ballantine, 1967; London, Sphere, 1970.
Thorns. New York, Ballantine, 1967; London, Rapp and Whiting, 1969.
Those Who Watch. New York, New American Library, 1967; London, New English Library, 1977.
The Time-Hoppers. Garden City, New York, Doubleday, 1967; London, Sidgwick and Jackson, 1968.
Planet of Death. New York, Holt Rinehart, 1967.
Hawksbill Station. Garden City, New York, Doubleday, 1968; as *The Anvil of Time,* London, Sidgwick and Jackson, 1969.
The Masks of Time. New York, Ballantine, 1968; as *Vornan-19,* London, Sidgwick and Jackson, 1970.

Up the Line. New York, Ballantine, 1969; London, Gollancz, 1987.

Nightwings. New York, Avon, 1969; London, Sidgwick and Jackson, 1972.

Across a Billion Years (for children). New York, Dial Press, 1969; London, Gollancz, 1977.

The Man in the Maze. New York, Avon, and London, Sidgwick and Jackson, 1969.

Three Survived (for children). New York, Holt Rinehart, 1969.

To Live Again. Garden City, New York, Doubleday, 1969; London, Sidgwick and Jackson, 1975.

Downward to the Earth. Garden City, New York, Doubleday, 1970; London, Gollancz, 1977.

Tower of Glass. New York, Scribner, 1970; London, Panther, 1976.

A Robert Silverberg Omnibus (includes *Master of Life and Death, Invaders from Earth,* and *The Time-Hoppers*). London, Sidgwick and Jackson, 1970.

The World Inside. Garden City, New York, Doubleday, 1971; London, Millington, 1976.

A Time of Changes. Garden City, New York, Doubleday, 1971; London, Gollancz, 1973.

Son of Man. New York, Ballantine, 1971; London, Panther, 1979.

The Book of Skulls. New York, Scribner, 1972; London, Gollancz, 1978.

Dying Inside. New York, Scribner, 1972; London, Sidgwick and Jackson, 1974.

The Second Trip. Garden City, New York, Doubleday, 1972; London, Gollancz, 1979.

The Stochastic Man. New York, Harper, 1975; London, Gollancz, 1976.

Shadrach in the Furnace. Indianapolis, Bobbs Merrill, 1976; London, Gollancz, 1977.

Lord Valentine's Castle (Majipoor). New York, Harper, and London, Gollancz, 1980.

A Robert Silverberg Omnibus: The Man in the Maze, Nightwings, Downward to the Earth. New York, Harper, 1981.

Majipoor Chronicles. New York, Arbor House, and London, Gollancz, 1982.

Valentine Pontifex (Majipoor). New York, Arbor House, 1983; London, Gollancz, 1984.

Gilgamesh the King. New York, Arbor House, 1984; London, Gollancz, 1985.

Tom O'Bedlam. New York, Fine, 1985; London, Gollancz, 1986.

Star of Gypsies. New York, Fine, 1986; London, Gollancz, 1987.

Project Pendulum (for children). New York, Walker, 1987; London, Hutchinson, 1989.

At Winter's End (New Springtime). New York, Warner, and London, Gollancz, 1988.

To the Land of the Living (Gilgamesh). London, Gollancz, 1989; Norwalk, Connecticut, Easton Press, 1990.

The Mutant Season, with Karen Haber. New York, Doubleday, 1989.

Time Gate, with Bill Fawcett. New York, Baen, 1989.

The Queen of Springtime. London, Gollancz, 1989; as *The New Springtime,* New York, Warner, 1990.

Nightfall, with Isaac Asimov. London, Gollancz, and Garden City, New York, Doubleday, 1990.

Letters from Atlantis (for children). New York, Atheneum, 1990.

The Face of the Waters. London, Grafton, and New York, Bantam, 1991.

The Child of Time, with Isaac Asimov. London, Gollancz, 1992; as *The Ugly Little Boy,* New York, Doubleday, 1992.

The Positronic Man, with Isaac Asimov. London, Gollancz, 1992; New York, Doubleday, 1993.

Kingdoms of the Wall. London, HarperCollins, 1992; as *The Kingdoms of the Wall,* Norwalk, Connecticut, Easton Press, 1993.

Hot Sky at Midnight. New York, Bantam, and London, HarperCollins, 1994.

The Mountains of Majipoor. Norwalk, Connecticut, Easton Press, and London, Macmillan, 1995.

Short Stories

Next Stop the Stars. New York, Ace, 1962; London, Dobson, 1979.

Godling, Go Home! New York, Belmont, 1964.

To Worlds Beyond. Philadelphia, Chilton, 1965; London, Sphere, 1969.

Needle in a Timestack. New York, Ballantine, 1966; London, Sphere, 1967; revised edition, Sphere, 1979.

The Calibrated Alligator (for children). New York, Holt Rinehart, 1969.

Dimension Thirteen. New York, Ballantine, 1969.

Parsecs and Parables: Ten Science Fiction Stories. Garden City, New York, Doubleday, 1970; London, Hale, 1973.

The Cube Root of Uncertainty. New York, Macmillan, 1970.

Moonferns and Starsongs. New York, Ballantine, 1971.

The Reality Trip and Other Implausibilities. New York, Ballantine, 1972.

Valley beyond Time. New York, Dell, 1973.

Unfamiliar Territory. New York, Scribner, 1973; London, Gollancz, 1975.

Earth's Other Shadow: Nine Science Fiction Stories. New York, New American Library, 1973; London, Millington, 1977.

Born with the Dead (three novellas). New York, Random House, 1974; London, Gollancz, 1975.

Sundance and Other Science Fiction Stories. Nashville, Nelson, 1974; London, Abelard-Schuman, 1975.

Sunrise on Mercury and Other Science Fiction Stories (for children). Nashville, Nelson, 1975; London, Gollancz, 1983.

The Feast of St. Dionysus: Five Science Fiction Stories. New York, Scribner, 1975; London, Gollancz, 1976.

The Shores of Tomorrow: Eights Stories of Science Fiction. Nashville, Nelson, 1976.

The Best of Robert Silverberg. New York, Pocket Books, 1976; London, Sidgwick and Jackson, 1977.

Capricorn Games. New York, Random House, 1976; London, Gollancz, 1978.

The Best of Robert Silverberg, Volume Two. Boston, Gregg Press, 1978.

The Songs of Summer and Other Stories. London, Gollancz, 1979.

The Desert of Stolen Dreams (Majipoor). Columbia, Pennsylvania, Underwood-Miller, 1981.

World of a Thousand Colors. New York, Arbor House, 1982.

Homefaring. Huntington Woods, Michigan, Phantasia Press, 1983.

The Conglomeroid Cocktail Party. New York, Arbor House, 1984; London, Gollancz, 1985.

Sailing to Byzantium. Columbia, Pennsylvania, Underwood-Miller, 1985.

Beyond the Safe Zone: Collected Stories. New York, Fine, 1986.

The Secret Sharer. Los Angeles, California, Underwood-Miller, 1988.

Nightwings, bound with *The Last Castle,* by Jack Vance. New York, Tor, 1989.

Hawksbill Station, bound with *Press Enter,* by John Varley. New York, Tor, 1990.

Lion Time in Timbuctoo. Eugene, Oregon, Axolotl Press, 1991; London, HarperCollins, 1993.

In Another Country, with *Vintage Season* by C.L. Moore. New York, Tor, 1990.

Thebes of the Hundred Gate. Eugene, Oregon, Axolotl Press, 1991; London, HarperCollins, 1993.

The Collected Stories of Robert Silverberg, Volume 1: Secret Sharers. New York, Bantam, 1992; as *The Collected Stories of Robert Silverberg, Volume One: Pluto in the Morning [Volume Two: The Secret Sharer],* London, Grafton, 2 vols., 1992-93.

Other Publications

Novels

The Mask of Akhnaten (for children). New York, Macmillan, 1965.

Lord of Darkness. New York, Arbor House, and London, Gollancz, 1983.

Other

Treasures beneath the Sea (for children). Racine, Wisconsin, Whitman, 1960.

First American into Space. Derby, Connecticut, Monarch, 1961.

Lost Cities and Vanished Civilizations (for children). Philadelphia, Chilton, 1962.

The Fabulous Rockefellers. Derby, Connecticut, Monarch, 1963.

Sunken History: The Story of Underwater Archaeology (for children). Philadelphia, Chilton, 1963.

15 Battles That Changed the World. New York, Putnam, 1963.

Home of the Red Man: Indian North America before Columbus (for children). Greenwich, Connecticut, New York Graphic Society, 1963.

Empires in the Dust. Philadelphia, Chilton, 1963.

The Great Doctors (for children). New York, Putnam, 1964.

Akhnaten, The Rebel Pharaoh. Philadelphia, Chilton, 1964.

The Man Who Found Nineveh: The Story of Austen Henry Layard (for children). New York, Holt Rinehart, 1964; Kingswood, Surrey, World's Work, 1968.

Man before Adam. Philadelphia, Macrae Smith, 1964.

The Loneliest Continent (as Walker Chapman). Greenwich, Connecticut, New York Graphic Society, 1965; London, Jarrolds, 1967.

Scientists and Scoundrels: A Book of Hoaxes. New York, Crowell, 1965.

The World of Coral (for children). New York, Duell, 1965.

Socrates (for children). New York, Putnam, 1965.

The Old Ones: Indians of the American Southwest. Greenwich, Connecticut, New York Graphic Society, 1965.

Men Who Mastered the Atom. New York, Putnam, 1965.

The Great Wall of China. Philadelphia, Chilton, 1965.

Niels Bohr, the Man Who Mapped the Atom (for children). Philadelphia, Macrae Smith, 1965.

Forgotten by Time: A Book of Living Fossils (for children). New York, Crowell, 1966.

Frontiers of Archaeology. Philadelphia, Chilton, 1966.

Kublai Kahn, Lord of Xanadu (for children; as Walker Chapman). Indianapolis, Bobbs Merrill, 1966.

The Long Rampart: The Story of the Great Wall of China. Philadelphia, Chilton, 1966.

Rivers (for children; as Lee Sebastian). New York, Holt Rinehart, 1966.

Bridges. Philadelphia, Macrae Smith, 1966.

To the Rock of Darius: The Story of Henry Rawlinson (for children). New York, Holt Rinehart, 1966.

The Dawn of Medicine. New York, Putnam, 1967.

The Adventures of Nat Palmer, Antarctic Explorer. New York, McGraw Hill, 1967.

The Auk, the Dodo, and the Oryx. New York, Crowell, 1967; Kingswood, Surrey, World's Work, 1969.

The Golden Dream: Seekers of El Dorado. Indianapolis, Bobbs Merrill, 1967.

Men against Time: Salvage Archaeology in the United States. New York, Macmillan, 1967.

The Morning of Mankind. Greenwich, Connecticut, New York Graphic Society, 1967; Kingswood, Surrey, World's Work, 1970.

The World of the Rain Forest. New York, Meredith Press, 1967.

Light for the World: Edison and the Power Industry. Princeton, New Jersey, Van Nostrand, 1967.

Four Men Who Changed the Universe (for children). New York, Putnam, 1968.

Ghost Towns of the American West. New York, Crowell, 1968.

Mound Builders of Ancient America. Greenwich, Connecticut, New York Graphic Society, 1968.

The South Pole (for children; as Lee Sebastian). New York, Holt Rinehart, 1968.

Stormy Voyager: The Story of Charles Wilkes. Philadelphia, Lippincott, 1968.

The World of the Ocean Depths. New York, Meredith Press, 1968; Kingswood, Surrey, World's Work, 1970.

Bruce of the Blue Nile (for children). New York, Holt Rinehart, 1969.

The Challenge of Climate: Man and His Environment. New York, Meredith Press, 1969; Kingswood, Surrey, World's Work, 1971.

Vanishing Giants: The Story of the Sequoias. New York, Simon and Schuster, 1969.

Wonders of Ancient Chinese Science. New York, Hawthorn, 1969.

The World of Space. New York, Meredith Press, 1969.

If I Forget Thee, O Jerusalem: American Jews and the State of Israel. New York, Morrow, 1970.

Mammoths, Mastodons, and Man. New York, McGraw Hill, 1970; Kingswood, Surrey, World's Work, 1972.

The Pueblo Revolt. New York, Weybright and Talley, 1970.

The Seven Wonders of the Ancient World (for children). New York, Crowell Collier, 1970.

Before the Sphinx. New York, Nelson, 1971.

Clocks for the Ages: How Scientists Date the Past. New York, Macmillan, 1971.

To the Western Shore: Growth of the United States 1776-1853. Garden City, New York, Doubleday, 1971.

Into Space, with Arthur C. Clarke. New York, Harper, 1971.

John Muir: Prophet among the Glaciers. New York, Putnam, 1972.

The Longest Voyage: Circumnavigation in the Age of Discovery. Indianapolis, Bobbs Merrill, 1972.

The Realm of Prester John. Garden City, New York, Doubleday, 1972.

The World within the Ocean Wave. New York, Weybright and Talley, 1972.

The World within the Tide Pool. New York, Weybright and Talley, 1972.

Drug Themes in Science Fiction. Rockville, Maryland, National Institute on Drug Abuse, 1974.

Editor, *Great Adventures in Archaeology.* New York, Dial Press, 1964; London, Hale, 1966.

Editor, *Earthmen and Strangers.* New York, Duell, 1966.

Editor (as Walker Chapman), *Antarctic Conquest.* Indianapolis, Bobbs Merrill, 1966.

Editor, *Voyagers in Time.* New York, Meredith Press, 1967.

Editor, *Men and Machines.* New York, Meredith Press, 1968.

Editor, *Mind to Mind. New York, Meredith Press, 1968.*

Editor, Tomorrow's Worlds. New York, Meredith Press, 1969.

Editor, *Dark Stars.* New York, Ballantine, 1969; London, Ballantine, 1971.

Editor, *Three for Tomorrow.* New York, Meredith Press, 1969; London, Gollancz, 1970.

Editor, *The Mirror of Infinity: A Critics' Anthology of Science Fiction.* New York, Harper, 1970; London, Sidgwick and Jackson, 1971.

Editor, *The Science Fiction Hall of Fame, Volume 1.* Garden City, New York, Doubleday, 1970; London, Gollancz, 2 vols., 1971.

Editor, *The Ends of Time.* New York, Hawthorn, 1970.

Editor, *Great Short Novels of Science Fiction.* New York, Ballantine, 1970; London, Pan, 1971.

Editor, *Worlds of Maybe.* New York, Nelson, 1970.

Editor, *Alpha 1-9.* New York, Ballantine, 5 vols., 1970-74; New York, Berkley, 4 vols., 1975-78.

Editor, *Four Futures.* New York, Hawthorn, 1971.

Editor, *The Science Fiction Bestiary.* New York, Nelson, 1971.

Editor, *To the Stars.* New York, Hawthorn, 1971.

Editor, *New Dimensions 1-12* (vols. 11 and 12 edited with Marta Randall). Garden City, New York, Doubleday, 3 vols., 1971-73; New York, New American Library, 1 vol., 1974; New York, Harper, 6 vols., 1975-80; New York, Pocket Books, 2 vols., 1980-81; 5-7 published London, Gollancz, 3 vols., 1976-77.

Editor, *The Day the Sun Stood Still.* Nashville, Nelson, 1972.

Editor, *Invaders from Space.* New York, Hawthorn, 1972.

Editor, *Beyond Control. Nashville, Nelson, 1972; London, Sidgwick and Jackson, 1973.*

Editor, *Deep Space.* Nashville, Nelson, 1973; London, Abelard-Schuman, 1976.

Editor, *Chains of the Sea. Nashville, Nelson, 1973.*

Editor, *No Mind of Man.* New York, Hawthorn, 1973.

Editor, *Other Dimensions.* New York, Hawthorn, 1973.

Editor, *Three Trips in Time and Space.* New York, Hawthorn, 1973.

Editor, *Mutants. Nashville, Nelson, 1974; London, Abelard-Schuman, 1976.*

Editor, *Threads of Time.* Nashville, Nelson, 1974; London, Millington, 1975.

Editor, *Infinite Jests: The Lighter Side of Science Fiction.* Radnor, Pennsylvania, Chilton, 1974.

Editor, *Windows into Tomorrow.* New York, Hawthorn, 1974.

Editor, with Roger Elwood, *Epoch.* New York, Berkley, 1975.

Editor, *Explorers of Space. Nashville, Nelson, 1975.*

Editor, *The New Atlantis and Other Novellas of Science Fiction.* New York, Hawthorn, 1975.

Editor, *Strange Gifts. Nashville, Nelson, 1975.*

Editor, *The Aliens.* Nashville, Nelson, 1976.

Editor, *The Crystal Ship.* Nashville, Nelson, 1976; London, Millington, 1980.

Editor, *Triax: Three Original Novellas.* Los Angeles, Pinnacle, 1977; London, Fontana, 1979.

Editor, *Trips in Time.* Nashville, Nelson, 1977; London, Hale, 1979.

Editor, *Earth Is the Strangest Planet.* Nashville, Nelson, 1977.

Editor, *Galactic Dreamers: Science Fiction as Visionary Literature.* New York, Random House, 1977.

Editor, *The Infinite Web.* New York, Dial Press, 1977.

Editor, *Lost Worlds, Unknown Horizons.* New York, Elsevier Nelson, 1978.

Editor, *The Androids Are Coming.* New York, Elsevier Nelson, 1979.

Editor, *The Edge of Space.* New York, Elsevier Nelson, 1979.

Editor, with Martin H. Greenberg and Joseph D. Olander, *Car Sinister.* New York, Avon, 1979.

Editor, with Martin H. Greenberg and Joseph D. Olander, *Dawn of Time: Prehistory through Science Fiction.* New York, Elsevier Nelson, 1979.

Editor, *The Best of New Dimensions.* New York, Pocket Books, 1979.

Editor, with Martin H. Greenberg, *The Arbor House Treasury of Modern Science Fiction.* New York, Arbor House, 1980; as *Great Science Fiction of the 20th Century,* New York, Avenel, 1987.

Editor, with Martin H. Greenberg, *The Arbor House Treasury of Great Science Fiction Short Novels.* New York, Arbor House, 1980; as *Worlds Imagined,* New York, Avenel, 1989.

Editor, with Martin H. Greenberg and Charles G. Waugh, *The Science Fictional Dinosaur.* New York, Avon, 1982.

Editor, *The Best of Randall Garrett.* New York, Timescape, 1982.

Editor, with Martin H. Greenberg, *The Arbor House Treasury of Science Fiction Masterpieces.* New York, Arbor House, 1983; abridged as *Great Tales of Science Fiction,* Secaucus, New Jersey, Galahad, 1985.

Editor, with Martin H. Greenberg, *The Fantasy Hall of Fame.* New York, Arbor House, 1983; as *The Mammoth Book of Fantasy All-Time Greats,* London, Robinson, 1988.

Editor, *The Nebula Awards 18.* New York, Arbor House, 1983.

Editor, with Martin H. Greenberg, *The Time Travelers: A Science Fiction Quartet.* New York, Fine, 1985.

Editor, with Martin H. Greenberg and Charles G. Waugh, *Neanderthals.* New York, New American Library, 1987.

Editor, *Robert Silverberg's Worlds of Wonder.* New York, Warner, 1987; London, Gollancz, 1988.

Editor, with Karen Haber, *Universe 1.* New York, Doubleday, 1990.

Editor, *Dangerous Interfaces* (Time Gate). New York, Baen, 1990.

Editor, with Martin H. Greenberg, *The Horror Hall of Fame.* New York, Carroll and Graf, 1991; London, Hale, 1992.

Editor, *Beyond the Gate of Worlds.* New York, Tor, 1991.

Editor, with Byron Preiss, *The Ultimate Dinosaur: Past—Present—Future.* New York, Bantam, 1992.

Editor, with Martin H. Greenberg, *Murasaki: A Novel in Six Parts.* New York, Bantam, 1992; London, Grafton, 1993.

*

Bibliography: In *Fantasy and Science Fiction* (New York), April 1974.

Manuscript Collection: Syracuse University, New York.

Critical Studies: "Robert Silverberg Issue" of *SF Commentary* (Melbourne), March 1977; Robert Silverberg by Thomas D. Clareson, Mercer Island, Washington, Starmont House, 1983.

*   *   *

Robert Silverberg has won five Nebula Awards, four Hugo Awards, a Jupiter Award, and the Prix Apollo. As one of science fiction's most popular and durable writers, he has produced consistently professional work for five decades. Yet his writing style and themes have changed as he has matured and gained the skills of a master storyteller. In his revealing autobiographical essay, "Sounding Brass, Tinkling Cymbal" (in *Hell's Cartographers*), Silverberg admits to producing over a million words per year of published material in his apprenticeship years 1955-59. Much of this was hackwork; stories like "Slaves of the Star Giants" and "Secret of the Green Invaders" and novels like *The Planet Killers* and *Stepsons of Terra*. Yet some of the stories were outstanding, including the dark "Road to Nightfall" and the clever "Translation Error," giving notice of the superb stories Silverberg was about to produce.

The late 1950s saw the decline and sudden contraction of the number of science fiction magazines coupled with the declining market for science fiction novels. Silverberg responded by shifting his main writing emphasis from SF to juvenile nonfiction, where he achieved critical acclaim for such excellent works as *Treasures beneath the Sea*, *Empires in the Dust*, and *Lost Cities and Vanished Civilizations*. Much of the research for these books would find itself transformed in Silverberg's future science fiction. He also produced over a hundred soft-core pornopaperbacks, most under the Don Elliot/Eliot pseudonym. Yet Silverberg did not entirely abandon the SF field during the 1960s. Frederik Pohl, then editor of *Galaxy*, *If*, and *Worlds of Tomorrow*, invited Silverberg to write whatever he wanted. Silverberg, intrigued by the open offer, submitted his now classic "To See the Invisible Man" (1962). The narrator is punished by a future society for his crime of "coldness" by being completely ignored by everyone in that society for one year, even though the society is benign. "To See the Invisible Man" shows a shunned man in turn shunning a society; this is a sophisticated story light-years from such earlier primitive action adventures as "Battle for the Thousand Stars."

The end of this transition period saw Silverberg begin to emerge as a powerful short-story writer. With "Flies," written for Harlan Ellison's *Dangerous Visions*, Silverberg breaks new ground. An alien race restores a dead starship pilot named Cassiday and enhances his powers. Sent back to Earth as a kind of transmitter for the aliens, Cassiday commits hideous acts of violence, since he is incapable of emotion. The aliens, realizing their mistake, return Cassiday to their world and give him back his conscience, providing the means of self-torture. The story deals with major moral and religious themes, themes Silverberg will expand on in his major novels. Silverberg won his first Nebula award for "Passengers," a horror story of humans dominated by parasitic aliens called Passengers who ride their host humans and utterly control them. "Passengers" explores the question of free will versus determinism, a major theme of such later novels as *The Stochastic Man* and *Shadrach in the Furnace*.

Like the explosion of writing in Silverberg's early period, the years 1969-76 produced a similar flood of works; the difference was in the quality. *Nightwings* presents Silverberg's vision of the far future. Earth is a ruined planet, with the Americas sunk beneath the seas. Yet its superscience, which produces genetically engineered Flyers, coexists with a medieval political structure. Tomis the Watcher is a beautifully realized character who narrates this powerful story of hope, renewal, and redemption. In *Tower of Glass*, Silverberg's dark vision returns. The 23rd-century Earth is ruled by Simeon Krug, inventor of the android. His quest is to contact an alien race by building a mammoth tower of glass to send signals deep into space. At the same time, the androids are organizing to be granted person status instead of being considered property. The book abounds with racial, religious, and moral themes, yet the conclusion is very bitter. (About the time *Tower of Glass* was written, Silverberg's New York City home was partly destroyed by fire, leaving him depressed.)

A Time of Changes, which won a Nebula award, is a book misinterpreted as a vehicle for advocating the use of psychedelic drugs, because of the dreamlike quality of many sections of the book in which the characters use a Sumaran drug that allows a person to link minds with another person. *Son of Man* is a strange blend of Olaf Stapledon and David Lindsay's *A Voyage to Acturus* that results in a surreal plot that goes nowhere. But the characters Silverberg creates in Clay, Hanmer, and Ninameen remain unforgettable.

The World Inside presents some of Silverberg's more controversial solutions to overpopulation. Here he creates a world of gigantic living units, a thousand stories high, containing 800,000 people each. It is a unique future society that encourages sexual experimentation, child-bearing, and an anti-privacy culture. Contrast this to the situation Silverberg presents in *The Book of Skulls*, in which a student finds a manuscript in the rare books of a university library that promises immortality. This launches a quest in what Barry N. Malzberg calls Silverberg's finest novel. Yet most critics consider *Dying Inside* Silverberg's best book. David Selig is a compelling character: he's 40 years old and writes term papers for college students to make enough money to survive. He also has the power to listen to other people's thoughts. As a young man, he considered his power a curse, but now Selig finds he is gradually losing his power to receive the thoughts of others. Silverberg creates a complex, sympathetic character whose plight—although strange and bizarre—becomes realistic and emotional through the exploration of the themes of loss, old age, racism, and change. In *Dying Inside*, Silverberg's powers as a novelist are most completely realized.

In 1976 *The Best of Robert Silverberg* appeared along with Silverberg's announcement that he was withdrawing from the SF field. Silverberg complained critics ignored his work and the science fiction publishers failed to reward SF writers to the extent writers in other fields were rewarded. At the same time, SF writers like Harlan Ellison, Barry N. Malzberg, and Kurt Vonnegut were announcing their flight from the science fiction ghetto. Ellison and Vonnegut fought to remove the SF label from their new works and reprints. Yet Silverberg did not withdraw from the SF field completely; in the years 1976-79, he edited *New Directions*, an original SF anthology series, as well as numerous SF theme reprint anthologies—from 1966 to 1981 Silverberg edited over 60 SF anthologies.

As early as 1979, rumors abounded that Silverberg was working on a "big book." Times had changed in publishing by the early 1980s: science fiction and fantasy, often ignored and ill-funded lines, became much more popular with the success of *Star Wars* and the *Star Trek* movies. Silverberg received critical acclaim and a six-figure advance for *Lord Valentine's Castle*, in which he created a huge planet called Majipoor with 20 million human and alien beings. Valentine's quest is one of identity. He is a wandering juggler who is actually a king dethroned by treachery, robbing him of his memory. The book lacks suspense: we know early on Valentine's quest will be successful, but Silverberg holds our interest for over 500 pages with adventures on Majipoor that are a delight. The planet becomes the star of the book. But the light fantasy of *Lord Valentine's Castle* gives way to the darker stories in *Majipoor Chronicles,* where Silverberg explores in more detail his mammoth planet. "The Desert of Stolen Dreams" gives us a lesson in Majipoorean guilt when the main character faces the death of a companion. "The Soul-Painter and the Shapeshifter" shows us a love affair between Majipoor's humans and aliens. The other stories fill out Silverberg's marvelous creation with a detailed history and philosophy of Majipoor. This culminates in *Valentine Pontifex,* in which Valentine's promotion from Coronal to Pontifex brings him up against an awesome challenge: the Metamorphs, shape-shifting natives of Majipoor, have broken the thousand years of peace with an attempt to dominate the planet. The fate of the planet is in Valentine's hands and this volume of the Majipoor saga is the most satisfying and mystical.

The latest book in the Majipoor series is *The Mountains of Majipoor.* In this novel a youth in disfavor, Prince Parpirias, is sent to the frozen Khyntor Marches to rescue a group of scientists. Harpirias goes because he knows a successful rescue mission will get him back into favor with the Coronal and his court and rescue Harpirias's career. Harpirias finds his mission complicated by a mysterious Shapeshifter interpreter and the politics of a primitive, isolated society. But he learns diplomacy and the secret behind the mountains of Majipoor.

Silverberg has few peers in the art of writing superb science fiction short stories and novellas. The best of these are collected in *Secret Sharers: The Collected Stories of Robert Silverberg, Volume I.* Another outstanding collection is *The Conglomeroid Cocktail Party,* which contains some of Silverberg's finest short stories. "The Pope of the Chimps" is a revealing study of religion as an experimental group of chimps begin to worship humans. "The Changeling" is a clever twist on alternate reality themes. "Gianni" is a marvelous time-travel story in which scientists bring 18th-century musical prodigy Giovanni Pergolesi, who died at the age of 26, back to the future with deterministic results.

Silverberg's fantasies, *Gilgamesh the King* and its sequel, *To the Land of the Living,* take us back to the ancient civilizations of 5000 years ago when the Sumerian god-king grew to maturity and reigned over an empire. With a blend of myth and magic, Silverberg presents quests where Helen of Troy and even Picasso can be found. The Gilgamesh books are Silverberg at his most playful.

A master anthologist, Silverberg coedited the *Universe* original short stories collections, a series which has met with critical acclaim and strong sales. Robert Silverberg's most personal anthology is *Worlds of Wonder.* In the series of classic science fiction stories he chooses, Silverberg's narration of why these particular stories influenced him go beyond the goal of a mere writing manual and center on Silverberg's development as a writer. One of the stories that affected Silverberg so powerfully was C.L. Moore's "Vintage Season." In a brilliant marketing coup, Tor Books issued Silverberg's wonderful sequel, "In Another Country," with the C.L. Moore classic. Silverberg's story of the aftermath of "Vintage Season" is as moving and innovative as the story that inspired the sequel. "In Another Country" is Silverberg at his best.

However, a novelization of another science fiction classic wasn't as successful. *Nightfall* by Isaac Asimov and Robert Silverberg is less than the sum of its parts. Asimov's classic story of the planet Kalgash—a planet that has never seen night—and the clash between science and religion is one of the best-known science fiction stories ever written. The process of turning a tight, taut classic story into a long novel hasn't produced a classic novel. The same can be said for the less than critically acclaimed Asimov/Silverberg collaborations of *The Positronic Man* and *The Ugly Little Boy.* The chilly reception these collaborations received by mainstream and SF reviewers points to a fundamental stylistic and conceptual breakdown in the execution of expanding classic stories in this collaboration.

More successful is *Letters from Atlantis,* in which Silverberg captures the grandeur of that mysterious empire. Roy Colton, a 21st-century researcher, writes the letters based on his experiences in the past. Time travel for Colton is accomplished by sending his mind back in time to occupy a host body—an Atlantean prince. Silverberg's story both explores the mysteries of Atlantis and manages deftly to explore the ethics of being a voyeur without preaching. No science fiction writer writes about time travel with more verve than Silverberg.

Among Silverberg's major science fiction novels are *At Winter's End* and its sequel, *The New Springtime.* The Long Winter, lasting 700 years, finally ends, and Koshmar and a small band of humans emerge from the underground cocoon where they've lived for centuries. There, amid the ancient ruins of Earth's superscience civilization, a new struggle for life begins *At Winter's End. The New Springtime* begins 40 years after the end of the Long Winter as the humans clash with the insectoids called the hijk for Earth's dominance. Few novels of the very far future are successful, yet *At Winter's End* and *The New Springtime* feature some of Silverberg's strongest writing in his long career.

Less successful are the novels *Kingdoms of the Wall* and *Hot Sky at Midnight.* In *Kingdoms of the Wall* Silverberg creates a society that lives at the base of a huge mountain they call The Wall. Periodically, the society sends 40 pilgrims to climb to the top of The Wall, where, according to their religion, their gods await. After many horrific encounters with monsters, the survivors reach the top to discover a not very original secret that most readers have already discerned. *Hot Sky at Midnight* is a mishmash of plots that never jell. Here Silverberg mixes terrorists, ecological disaster, gene-splicing, and corporate intrigue into a novel that lacks focus and drama.

Despite such lesser efforts, Robert Silverberg is a giant in the field of science fiction, a prolific writer whose long career has engendered classic novels and award-winning short stories. The impressive fact that Silverberg continues to produce first-rate, sophisticated work only adds to his stature.

—George Kelley

SIMAK, Clifford D(onald)

Nationality: American. **Born:** Millville, Wisconsin, 3 August 1904. **Education:** Attended the University of Wisconsin, Madison. **Family:** Married Kay Kuchenberg in 1929; one son and one daughter. **Career:** Reporter, 1924-76, news editor, 1949-62, and editor of Science Reading Series, 1962-76, *Minneapolis Star* and *Tribune.* **Awards:** International Fantasy award, 1953; Hugo award, for story, 1959, 1981, for novel, 1964; First Fandom Hall of Fame award, 1973; Grand Master Nebula award, 1976, and Nebula award, 1980; Jupiter award, 1978; *Locus* award, 1981; Bram Stoker Life Achievement award, 1988. Guest of Honor, 29th World Science Fiction Convention, 1971. **Died:** 25 April 1988.

SCIENCE FICTION PUBLICATIONS

Novels

Cosmic Engineers: An Interplanetary Novel. New York, Gnome Press, 1950; London, Magnum, 1982.

Time and Again. New York, Simon and Schuster, 1951; London, Heinemann, 1955; as *First He Died,* New York, Dell, 1953.

Empire: A Powerful Novel of Intrigue and Action in the Not-So-Distant Future. New York, Galaxy, 1951.

Ring around the Sun: A Story of Tomorrow. New York, Simon and Schuster, 1953; London, Consul, 1960.

Time Is the Simplest Thing. Garden City, New York, Doubleday, 1961; London, Gollancz, 1962.

The Trouble with Tycho. New York, Ace, 1961.

They Walked like Men. Garden City, New York, Doubleday, 1962; London, Gollancz, 1963.

Way Station. Garden City, New York, Doubleday, 1963; London, Gollancz, 1964.

All Flesh Is Grass. Garden City, New York, Doubleday, 1965; London, Gollancz, 1966.

Why Call Them Back from Heaven? Garden City, New York, Doubleday, and London, Gollancz, 1967.

The Werewolf Principle. New York, Putnam, 1967; London, Gollancz, 1968.

The Goblin Reservation. New York, Putnam, 1968; London, Rapp and Whiting, 1969.

Out of Their Minds. New York, Putnam, 1970; London, Sidgwick and Jackson, 1972.

Destiny Doll: A Science Fiction Novel. New York, Putnam, 1971; London, Sidgwick and Jackson, 1972.

A Choice of Gods. New York, Putnam, 1971; London, Sidgwick and Jackson, 1973.

Cemetery World. New York, Putnam, 1973; London, Sidgwick and Jackson, 1975.

Our Children's Children. New York, Putnam, 1974; London, Sidgwick and Jackson, 1975.

Enchanted Pilgrimage. New York, Berkley, 1975; London, Sidgwick and Jackson, 1976.

Shakespeare's Planet. New York, Berkley, 1976; London, Sidgwick and Jackson, 1977.

A Heritage of Stars. New York, Berkley, 1977; London, Sidgwick and Jackson, 1978.

The Fellowship of the Talisman. New York, Ballantine, 1978; London, Sidgwick and Jackson, 1980.

Mastodonia. New York, Ballantine, 1978; as *Catface: Science Fiction,* London, Sidgwick and Jackson, 1978.

The Visitors. New York, Ballantine, 1980; London, Sidgwick and Jackson, 1981.

Project Pope. New York, Ballantine, and London, Sidgwick and Jackson, 1981.

Special Deliverance. New York, Ballantine, 1982; London, Severn House, 1983.

Where the Evil Dwells. New York, Ballantine, 1982; London, Severn House, 1984.

Highway of Eternity. New York, Ballantine, 1986; as *Highway to Eternity,* London, Severn House, 1987.

Short Stories

The Creator. Los Angeles, Crawford, 1946.

City. New York, Gnome Press, 1952; London, Weidenfeld and Nicolson, 1954; expanded edition, New York, Ace, 1981.

Strangers in the Universe: Science-Fiction Stories. New York, Simon and Schuster, 1956; abridged edition, London, Faber, 1958.

The Worlds of Clifford Simak. New York, Simon and Schuster, 1960; abridged edition, as *Aliens for Neighbours,* London, Faber, 1961; abridged edition, as *Other Worlds of Clifford Simak,* New York, Avon, 1962.

All the Traps of Earth and Other Stories. Garden City, New York, Doubleday, 1962; as *All the Traps of Earth* and *The Night of the Puudly,* London, Four Square, 2 vols., 1964.

Worlds without End. New York, Belmont, 1964; London, Jenkins, 1965.

Best Science Fiction Stories of Clifford Simak. London, Faber, 1967.

So Bright the Vision. New York, Ace, 1968; London, Severn House, 1986.

The Best of Clifford D. Simak, edited by Angus Wells. London, Sidgwick and Jackson, 1975.

Skirmish: The Great Short Fiction of Clifford D. Simak. New York, Putnam, 1977.

The Marathon Photograph and Other Stories, edited by Francis Lyall. London, Severn House, 1986.

Brother and Other Stories, edited by Francis Lyall. London, Severn House, 1986.

Off-Planet, edited by Francis Lyall. London, Methuen, 1988.

The Autumn Land and Other Stories, edited by Francis Lyall. London, Mandarin, 1990.

Immigrant and Other Stories, edited by Francis Lyall. London, Mandarin, 1991.

The Creator and Other Stories, edited by Francis Lyall. Sutton, Surrey, Severn House, 1993.

OTHER PUBLICATIONS

Other

The Solar System: Our New Front Yard (for children). New York, St. Martin's Press, 1962.

Trilobite, Dinosaur, and Man: The Earth's Story. New York, St. Martin's Press, and London, Macmillan, 1966.

Wonder and Glory: The Story of the Universe. New York, St. Martin's Press, 1969.

Prehistoric Man. New York, St. Martin's Press, 1971.

Editor, *From Atoms to Infinity: Readings in Modern Science.* New York, Harper, 1965.

Editor, *The March of Science* (for children). New York, Harper, 1971.

Editor, *Nebula Award Stories Six.* Garden City, New York, Doubleday, 1971.

Editor, *The Best of Astounding.* New York, Baronet, 1978.

*

Bibliography: *The Electric Bibliograph 1: Clifford D. Simak* by Mark Owings, Baltimore, Alice and Jay Haldeman, 1971.

*   *   *

Readers of science fiction lost a treasure when Clifford Simak died in 1988. This gentle, friendly man poured more pleasure onto the printed page than many writers have been able to muster. Simak was drawn early in his life to the world of journalism, where he worked on a number of newspapers, ending up at the *Minneapolis Star* and *Tribune* for 36 years. Among other duties, he was news editor and author of a science column, which led to a Minneapolis Academy of Science award for Distinguished Service to Science in 1967. This interest prompted his writing of several nonfiction works: *Prehistoric Man; The Solar System; Trilobite, Dinosaur, and Man.*

Simak's interest in science led him to *Amazing Stories* in 1927, possibly luring him into writing, for a 1931 *Wonder Stories* issue, his first attempt at science fiction: "World of the Red Sun." This work and some others used the standard devices of pulp magazines of the day, often trite and repetitive. But Simak lost interest in this sort of writing until John Campbell's influence elevated the standards of science fiction writing in *Astounding* and other magazines.

Shaped by his boyhood on a farm in Wisconsin, Simak was moralistic in outlook and pastoral in temperament, feeling that man should be a harmonious element in the entire natural scheme of things, that his goals and standards must be only a part of the great scheme of all possibilities. Accordingly, his writing increasingly involved nonhuman figures—friendly, but not man. These intelligent beings often had special qualities man lacked: levitation, prescience, telekinesis. Such beings stressed both Simak's belief in man and his conviction that man could become an elevated being. Yarns like "Census," "Huddling Place," and "Desertion"—which ultimately grew into *City*—contrasted humans and aliens to make the point that man could be a shining figure if he would. *City* is still regarded by many readers as Simak's most interesting and stimulating product, winning the International Fantasy award in 1952.

An elegant term describes this unusual man. Clifford Simak was an adoxographer, a person who chooses lowly and ordinary ideas and makes them grand. The people in *Cosmic Engineers,* for example, seem like one's neighbors; they chatter along in slang as they finger mysterious controls and machinery while navigating their "Space Pup" out by Pluto. This may seem rather hum-drum—except that they become masters of the entire universe.

Rainbows are wonderful and exciting, especially after a violent rain storm, but they are actually quite commonplace, the products of light passing through moisture. Or are they? *Highway of Eternity* reveals them to be entities, the most ancient of races, who let themselves be seen in welcoming and promising situations.

In "The Big Front Yard," creatures from all over the universe swim out on the "lawn," trading a wide range of wonderful objects—machines, devices, and exotic things whose purpose can only be guessed. For this "ordinary" novelette, Simak won the Hugo award in 1959. Other honors have included a Hugo award for *Way Station* and the Nebula Grand Master award of the Science Fiction Writers of America.

It is not possible, however, to consider just the optimistic side of Simak without acknowledging other elements in his works. Man is often portrayed by him in less than flattering terms. To be realistic, humans are frequently not very nice beings. Simak more than suggests this in *They Walked like Men,* where humans are likened to dogs. *City*'s robot Jenkins thinks that dogs had known how to talk long before they were given tongues to talk, or contact lenses to read. And later, the story "Aesop" reveals that the dogs have forgotten men entirely; Jenkins says man is a forgotten fireside tale. Granted, man has done it to himself. He has taken the long sleep in special supportive tombs, or is shipped off to Jupiter, deserting

Earth. But in stories like "Wayside," or in *The Goblin Reservation,* and *All Flesh Is Grass,* the aliens—bowling ball forms, purple flowers, floating metal cylinders—romp the landscapes. Roles appear to have been switched when creatures in *A Heritage of Stars* seem human to onlookers. And to Asa Steels, the Catface of *Mastondonia* "looks sort of like a human being."

In a sense, one might say that Simak is really concerned with either pantheism or polytheism. Nonhuman life often has admirable qualities. Man frequently comes off poorly with respect to godly virtues—like patience, kindness, forbearance, and forgiveness in his daily living. *Time and Again,* a brotherhood of sapients, whatever their form, exemplifies and illustrates Simak's leaning away from mankind. Certainly, though, man's choice, in "Desertion," of the planet Jupiter for an abode, demanding as it did drastic transformation of his entire being for survival, lends a certain emphasis to man's dissatisfaction with himself. It meant conversion into a "Loper" in that incredible environment, surrounded by a perfumed purple atmosphere, bedazzled by beauties that human eyes could never comprehend, equipped with unthinkable powers. Why would man remain, under such circumstances, an animal with two feeble legs, a mockery of a brain, and other frailties that human flesh is heir to? Why would he not embrace godhood? As Simak frames it:

> "I can't go back," said Towser.
> "Neither can I," said Fowler.
> "They would turn me back into a dog," said Towser.
> "And me," said Fowler, "back into a man."

—Robert H. Wilcox

SIODMAK, Curt

Nationality: American. **Born:** Kurt Siodmak, Dresden, Germany, 10 August 1902; brother of the film director Robert Siodmak. **Education:** University of Zurich, Ph.D. 1927. **Family:** Married Henrietta De Perrot in 1931; one son. **Career:** Railroad engineer and factory worker; film writer and director: worked for Gaumont British, 1931-37, and in the United States after 1937. **Awards:** Bundespreis, for film, 1964.

SCIENCE FICTION PUBLICATIONS

Novels (series: Cory)

F.P.1. Antwortet Nicht. Berlin, Keils, 1931; translated by H.W. Farrell as *F.P.1. Does Not Reply,* Boston, Little, Brown, 1933; as *F.P.1 Fails to Reply,* London, Collins, 1933.
Donovan's Brain (Cory). New York, Knopf, 1943; London, Chapman and Hall, 1944.
Skyport. New York, Crown, 1959.
Hauser's Memory (Cory). New York, Putnam, 1968; London, Jenkins, 1969.
The Third Ear. New York, Putnam, 1971.
City in the Sky. New York, Putnam, 1974; London, Barrie and Jenkins, 1975.
Gabriel's Body (Cory). New York, Leisure, 1992.

OTHER PUBLICATIONS

Novels

Schluss in Tonfilmatelier. Berlin, Scherl, 1930.
Stadt Hinter Hebeln: Roman. Salzburg, Berglund, 1931.
Die Madonna aus der Markusstrasse. Leipzig, Goldmann, 1932.
Rache im Äther. Leipzig, Goldmann, 1932.
Bis ans Ende der Welt. Leipzig, Goldmann, 1933.
Die Macht im Dunkeln. Zurich, Morgarten, 1937.
Whomsoever I Shall Kiss. New York, Crown, 1952.
For Kings Only. New York, Crown, 1961.

Plays

Screenplays: *Menschen am Sonntag (People on Sunday)* (documentary), with Billy Wilder, 1929; *Le Bal,* 1931; *Der Mann der Seinen Mörder Sucht (Looking for His Murderer),* 1931; *F.P.1 Antwortet Nicht,* 1933; *Girls Will Be Boys,* with Clifford Grey and Roger Burford, 1934; *I Give My Heart,* with others, 1935; *The Tunnel (Transatlantic Tunnel),* with L. DuGarde Peach and Clemence Dane, 1935; *It's a Bet,* with Frank Miller and L. DuGarde Peach, 1935; *Non-Stop New York,* with others, 1937; *Her Jungle Love,* with others, 1938; *The Invisible Man Returns,* with Lester Cole and Joe May, 1940; *The Ape,* with Richard Carroll, 1940; *Black Friday,* with Eric Taylor, 1940; *The Wolf Man,* with Gordon Kann, 1940; *The Invisible Woman,* with others, 1941; *Pacific Blackout,* with others, 1941; *Aloma of the South Seas,* with others, 1941; *Midnight Angel,* with others, 1941; *London Blackout Murders,* 1942; *The Invisible Agent,* 1942; *I Walked with a Zombie,* with Ardel Wray and Inez Wallace, 1943; *Frankenstein Meets the Wolf Man,* 1943; *The Mantrap,* 1943; *Son of Dracula,* with Eric Taylor, 1943; *False Faces,* 1943; *The Purple "V,"* with Bertram Millhauser, 1943; *House of Frankenstein,* with Edward T. Lowe, 1944; *The Climax,* with Lynn Starling, 1944; *Frisco Sal,* with Gerald Geraghty, 1945; *Shady Lady,* with others, 1945; *The Return of Monte Cristo,* with others, 1946; *The Beast with Five Fingers,* with Harold Goldman, 1947; *Berlin Express,* with Harold Medford, 1948; *Tarzan's Magic Fountain,* with Harry Chandlee, 1949; *Four Days Leave,* with others, 1950; *Bride of the Gorilla,* 1951; *The Magnetic Monster,* with Ivan Tors, 1953; *Riders to the Stars,* 1954; *Creature with the Atom Brain,* 1955; *Earth vs. Flying Saucers,* with George Worthing Yates and Raymond Marcus, 1956; *Curucu, Beast of the Amazon,* 1956; *Love Slaves of the Amazon,* 1957; *The Devil's Messenger,* 1962; *Lightship,* 1963; *Ski Fever,* with Robert Joseph, 1967.

Television Plays: *13 Demon Street* series, 1959 (Sweden).

*

Theatrical Activities:
Director: **Films**—*Bride of the Gorilla,* 1951; *The Magnetic Monster,* 1953; *Curucu, Beast of the Amazon,* 1956; *Love Slaves of the Amazon,* 1957; *Ski Fever,* 1967.

*   *   *

As a novelist, screenwriter, and film director, Curt Siodmak had a long career, first in Germany and then in Hollywood, popularizing for the mass audience basic and extremely banal science fiction motifs originated long before by other writers: an airfield floating in mid-ocean, the building of a transatlantic tunnel or a spaceport, experiments with artificially induced telepathy or genetic manipulation all provide formulaic grist for some very melodramatic mills. Siodmak's protagonists in his novels and films are either Frankensteinian mad scientists in the grand pulp tradition or strong-willed and farsighted entrepreneurial overreachers in the Faustian/Ayn Rand mold. Indeed, perhaps the only redeeming feature of Siodmak's early German science fiction work of the 1930s is that the films based on his novels (three versions of *F.P.1 Does Not Reply* and two versions of *Transatlantic Tunnel*) used some impressive special effects. Not even that much can be said for most of the movies based on his Hollywood screenplays in the 1940s, which were invariably low-budget programmers, that attempted to milk tried-and-true monster-movie formulas that had long been dried out.

Siodmak is best known, however, within both the science fiction field and the mainstream of literary and cinematic popular culture, as the creator of *Donovan's Brain,* which has itself been adapted three times for the movies, with varying degrees of success: *The Lady and the Monster* (1947, with Erich von Stroheim), *Donovan's Brain* (1953, with Lew Ayres), and *The Brain* (1963, with Peter Van Eyck). In all of its manifestations, the story has held up durably and has retained to a certain extent its queasy fascination. The reclusive scientist-physician Patrick Cory extracts the still-living brain of the powerful industrialist Warren Horace Donovan after an airplane crash had mangled the tycoon's elderly body. Despite the stereotypical warnings of his devoted wife and an alcoholic colleague, Cory establishes telepathic contact with the disembodied brain, which, nurtured by chemicals, is growing daily in size and telepathic power. The brain quickly takes control of Cory's body, forcing it to wreak vengeance on Donovan's enemies. What gives Siodmak's novel its inherent power is not only its central theme of physical possession caused by unchecked and thus finally destructive scientific research, but also the first-person narration from Cory's panicky point of view. Unfortunately, the story eventually degenerates into unduly complicated histrionics detailing Donovan's desire to pay off an old debt by intruding on a murder investigation involving the heir of one of Donovan's early business partners. By plunging Donovan and his hapless, progressively will-less surrogate into such a desultory and pointless subplot so late in the proceedings, Siodmak conveniently sidesteps the more somber medical, legal, and metaphysical implications of his initially intriguing concept.

Siodmak's later novels continued his career-long tendency to graft mainstream genres onto science fiction settings. Thus, *City in the Sky* is a kind of *Grand Hotel* in orbit, mixed in with political intrigue and prison-escape heroics, while *Skyport* is like a space-age *Fountainhead.* A bit more interesting to the genuine science fiction enthusiast are *The Third Ear,* which concerns the chemically created cultivation of ESP abilities, and *Hauser's Memory,* Siodmak's belated sequel to *Donovan's Brain,* with the intrepid Cory again blazing new scientific trails, transplanting a German chemist's overactive, revenge-minded RNA onto another ill-fated human guinea pig. Despite the pseudoscientific trappings, both books are relatively straightforward espionage thrillers, demonstrating again that Siodmak's talents lie in welding worn-out science fiction themes with other conventional, pop-cultural formulas.

—Kenneth Jurkiewicz

SLADEK, John (Thomas)

Pseudonyms: Thom Demijohn; Cassandra Knye; Richard A. Tilms; James Vogh. **Nationality:** American. **Born:** Waverly, Iowa, 15 December 1937. **Education:** College of St. Thomas, St. Paul, Minnesota, 1955-56; University of Minnesota, Minneapolis, 1956-59. **Family:** Married in 1970 (divorced 1990), one child; married Sandra Gunter in 1995. **Career:** Engineering assistant, University of Minnesota, 1959-61; technical writer, Technical Publications Inc., St. Louis Park, Minnesota, 1961-62; switchman, Great Northern Railway, Minneapolis, 1962-63; draftsman, New York, 1964-65. Editor, with Pamela A. Zoline, *Ronald Reagan: The Magazine of Poetry,* London, 1968. **Awards:** British Science Fiction Association award, 1984. **Agent:** Richard Curtis Associates, 171 East 74th Street, New York, New York 10021, U.S.A.; or, Christopher Priest, 32 Elphinstone Road, Hastings, East Sussex, TN34 2EQ England.

Science Fiction Publications

Novels (series: Roderick)

The Reproductive System. London, Gollancz, 1968; New York, Avon, 1974; as *Mechasm,* New York, Ace, 1969.
The Müller-Fokker Effect. London, Hutchinson, 1970; New York, Morrow, 1971.
Roderick; or, The Education of a Young Machine. London, Granada, 1980; abridged edition, New York, Pocket Books, 1982.
Roderick at Random; or, Further Education of a Young Machine. London, Granada, 1983; New York, Carroll and Graf, 1988.
Tik-Tok. London, Gollancz, 1983.
Bugs. London, Macmillan, 1989.

Short Stories

The Steam-Driven Boy and Other Strangers. London, Panther, 1973.
Keep the Giraffe Burning. London, Panther, 1977.
The Best of John Sladek. New York, Pocket Books, 1981.
Red Noise. New Castle, Virginia, Cheap Street, 1982.
Alien Accounts. London, Panther, 1982.
Flatland. New Castle, Virginia, Cheap Street, 1982.
The Lunatics of Terra. London, Gollancz, 1984.
Love among the Xoids. Polk City, Iowa, Drumm, 1984.
Blood and Gingerbread. New Castle, Virginia, Cheap Street, 1990.

Other Publications

Novels

The House That Fear Built (with Thomas M. Disch as Cassandra Knye). New York, Paperback Library, 1966.
The Castle and the Key (as Cassandra Knye). New York, Paperback Library, 1967.
Black Alice (with Thomas M. Disch as Thom Demijohn). Garden City, New York, Doubleday, 1968; London, W.H. Allen, 1969.
Black Aura. London, Cape, 1974; New York, Walker, 1979.
Invisible Green. London, Gollancz, 1977; New York, Walker, 1979.
The Book of Clues. London, Corgi, 1984.

Other

The New Apocrypha: A Guide to Strange Science and Occult Beliefs. London, Hart Davis MacGibbon, 1973; New York, Stein and Day, 1974.
Arachne Rising: The Thirteenth Sign of the Zodiac (as James Vogh). London, Hart Davis MacGibbon, 1977.
The Cosmic Factor (as James Vogh). London, Hart Davis MacGibbon, 1978.
Judgement of Jupiter (as Richard A. Tilms). London, New English Library, 1980.
Using XyWrite II. Berkeley, California, Osborne McGraw Hill, 1987.

*

Manuscript Collection: Texas A & M University, College Station.

John Sladek comments:

Most of my novels and short stories are set in the near future, in a recognizable America in which technology has either solved all of our problems or failed to solve any of them, or something else entirely has happened. Something else entirely is always happening in science fiction, I understand. My work is usually called satire or black humor, but it also reflects my preoccupation with certain themes.

I am endlessly fascinated by machines which can mimic or displace human beings. So a number of my characters are robots (such as "The Steam-Driven Boy") or computers or cyborgs, or self-replicating machines (as in *Mechanism*). This theme informs *Roderick; or, The Education of a Young Machine,* first of a two-part novel which attempts to cover the entire "life" history of a robot learning machine, and efforts to assimilate him into human society.

A parallel concern is with dehumanizing processes—ways in which governments and other institutions, mistakenly modelled on machines, attempt to reduce their citizens or members to mechanical components. This is the argument of three novellas, "Masterson and the Clerks," "The Communicants," and "The Great Wall of Mexico," and of at least a dozen short stories, and it creeps into the novels, too. It seems almost as though machines, evolving rapidly towards a kind of mimetic humanity, are meeting humans on the way down.

People do of course escape the process of robotization, and one escape route is madness, another recurring theme. Most of the stories in *Keep the Giraffe Burning* seem to deal with mad people (as well as bad, sad, and silly people) and how they succeed at their madness. As the title indicates, these stories are steeped in Surrealism; they are meant to blur the border between dream and reality.

That border is blurred by science fiction all the time. Science fiction, it seems to me, constitutes the right brain hemisphere of contemporary fiction (the dreaming part). My work, if it isn't buried in the hypothalamus or the hippocampus or something, is probably somewhere near the lobotomy scars.

*   *   *

John Sladek ranks high among the relatively small number of authors who use science fiction as a vehicle for satire. Sladek's writing defies easy classification, inviting comparisons not only with other science fiction authors but also with writers of traditional fiction. In the field of science fiction, his early work was associated with the British New Wave, and his novels have often been likened to those of Kurt Vonnegut, Jr. But Sladek himself uses allusion and direct quotes to link his fiction with major British authors such as Samuel Butler and Tobias Smollett. It would perhaps be most accurate (and complimentary) to compare his best fiction with the mordant satires of American life written by Nathanael West.

Sladek published his first science fiction story, appropriately enough, in Harlan Ellison's provocative anthology *Dangerous Visions* (1967). "The Happy Breed" introduces a theme that recurs throughout Sladek's subsequent writing: the folly of trusting technology to create Utopia. His first novel, *The Reproductive System* (published in the United States as *Mechanism*), explores the related theme of technology run amuck. It is a comic-satiric fusion of Mary Shelley's *Frankenstein* and Jack Williamson's "With Folded Hands." At the same time, the writing reflects a conscious debt to Butler's satiric Utopian novel *Erewhon*. In Sladek's novel, a failing industry, acting on the correct belief that the government will support "a project that is utterly, hopelessly useless," develops a machine that reproduces itself. The rest of the novel recounts the disasters that result when the machine begins growing out of control and threatens to destroy civilization. The story reaches an apparently happy ending when the machine is brought under control and seems destined to transform earth into a Utopia, but the same warning expressed in "The Happy Breed" lurks beneath the surface of *The Reproductive System*. Sladek's satire works on a number of levels, for the "self-reproducing machine" at the heart of the tale suggests a wide range of human inventions and institutions that are created and grow larger to no useful purpose.

The Müller-Fokker Effect, Sladek's second science fiction novel, is not only his funniest but also his most stylistically innovative work. The narrative proceeds as a series of comic events precipitated when a rich businessman instigates the kidnapping of the father of a family that he has been secretly observing. The kidnapped man's personality is subsequently recorded and transferred onto computer tapes. The plot revolves around the search for these tapes, which have been accidentally sold as army surplus. The novel paints a dark picture of an America dehumanized by the intertwined goals of profit and personal happiness. Sladek's specific targets include the military mind, popular journalists, evangelists, and Big Business. But above all, the novel satirizes the power of television in modern society, particularly its role in creating the delusion of a country without flaws or problems. The amoral businessman at the center of the story operates on the assumption that "reality was televised . . . and the advantage of televised reality was that one could tune out any ghosts of unpleasantness." This capacity not just of one man but rather of a whole society for self-deception serves as the basic theme of *The Müller-Fokker Effect*.

Sladek's writing is more consciously literary than much science fiction. The Roderick books represent an ambitious attempt to wed the conventions of science fiction to those of the mainstream picaresque novel. Early in his career, Sladek wrote several short stories that deal with robots seeking ways to understand and become part of human society (collected in *The Steam-Driven Boy and Other Strangers*). He develops this theme in *Roderick at Random; or, Further Education of a Young Machine,* which present the adventures of an intelligent robot in an absurd America. Television plays a major role also in these novels, providing Roderick his image of America as it provides America with an image of itself.

The titles contain unmistakable allusions to Smollett's *The Adventures of Roderick Random* (1748). The reference is particularly apt, since Smollett is generally regarded as the father of the English satirical novel. Smollett adapted the conventions of the picaresque novel for satiric purpose, and his *Roderick Random* combines high adventure with a fierce attack on the dreadful conditions existing at that time in the British navy. But Sladek's two novels, in addition to satirizing American values, also contain numerous references to other science fiction, especially the robot novels of Isaac Asimov. The *Roderick* novels implicitly parody the well-known "three laws of robotics" on which Asimov based many of his stories. The two *Roderick* novels, much like their 18th-century model, proceed as sequences of comic episodes. Specific episodes are often hilarious; however, the satire, perhaps because it ranges more widely and has a less clear focus, is less effective than that found in Sladek's first two novels.

Despite its comic and satiric power, Sladek's fiction has never achieved broad popularity among American readers of science fiction. Perhaps three factors have contributed to this relative obscurity. First, his novels tend toward a pessimistic assessment of human nature and American culture. Second, appreciation of his artfulness requires knowledge of both science fiction and a broad spectrum of mainstream literature. *Roderick,* for example, begins with two quotes: one from *Erewhon* and the other from the play *Dinner at Eight*. This linkage of high and low culture typifies Sladek's fiction. Finally, the recurring object of Sladek's wit has been the very fascination with technology that provides the inspiration for the genre of science fiction.

—Dennis M. Kratz

SLOANE, William M(illigan, III)

Pseudonym: William Milligan. **Nationality:** American. **Born:** Plymouth, Massachusetts, 15 August 1906. **Education:** Hill School, graduated, 1925; Princeton University, New Jersey, A.B. 1929 (Phi Beta Kappa). **Family:** Married Julie Hawkins in 1930; one son and two daughters. **Career:** Publisher: in play department, 1929-31, and editorial department, 1931, Longmans Green and Company; manager, Fitzgerald Publishing Company, 1932-37; associate editor, Farrar and Rinehart, 1937-38; manager of the trade department, 1939-46, and vice-president, 1944-46, Henry Holt and Company; president, William Sloane Associates, 1946-52; editorial director, Funk and Wagnalls Company and Wilfred Funk Inc., 1952-55; director, Rutgers University Press, 1955-74. Director, Council on Books in Wartime; chairman of the Editorial Committee, Armed Services Editions, 1943-44; staff member, Bread Loaf Writers Conference, 1946-72. President, Association of American University Presses, 1969-70. **Died:** 25 September 1974.

SCIENCE FICTION PUBLICATIONS

Novels

To Walk the Night: A Novel. New York, Farrar and Rinehart, 1937; London, Barker, 1938; revised edition, New York, Dodd Mead, 1954.

The Edge of Running Water. New York, Farrar and Rinehart, 1939; London, Methuen, 1940; as *The Unquiet Corpse,* New York, Dell, 1956.
The Rim of Morning, Including The Edge of Running Water and To Walk the Night. New York, Dodd Mead, 1964.

OTHER PUBLICATIONS

Plays

Back Home: A Ghost Play in One Act. New York, Longman, 1931.
Runner in the Snow: A Play of the Supernatural in One Act, adaptation of the story "I Saw a Woman Turn into a Wolf" by W.B. Seabrook. Boston, Baker, 1931.
Digging Up the Dirt: A Comedy in Three Acts, adaptation of a play by Bert J. Norton. New York, Longman, 1931.
Crystal Clear: A Romance in One Act. New York, Longman, 1932.
Ballots for Bill: A Light-Hearted Comedy of Politics, with William Ellis Jones. New York, Fitzgerald, 1933.
The Silence of God: A Play for Christmas in One Act. Boston, Baker, 1933.
Art for Art's Sake. Boston, Baker, 1934.
The Invisible Clue (as William Milligan). New York, Fitzgerald, 1934.
Gold Stars for Glory. Boston, Baker, 1935.

Other

Editor, *Space, Space, Space: Stories about the Time When Men Will Be Adventuring to the Stars.* New York, Watts, 1953.
Editor, *Stories for Tomorrow: An Anthology of Modern Science Fiction.* New York, Funk and Wagnalls, 1954; London, Eyre and Spottiswoode, 1955.

*   *   *

William M. Sloane had an extremely brief career as a science fiction writer, completing two novels and a single short story, but those two novels have probably won him a permanent place in the history of the genre. He blended science and horror with consummate skill, and his calm, smooth-paced novels are more successful at developing suspense and tension than most of the lurid thrillers that reach the bestseller lists.

To Walk the Night uses a plot device so standard, so familiar, that it has long since become a cliché avoided even by the less inventive filmmakers, but in the hands of a writer with Sloane's talent, it is transformed into an entirely new vehicle. Two young men make a surprise visit to an old friend, and arrive just in time to see his body mysteriously incinerated as if from within. Although they are unable to explain the peculiar nature of his death, they are freed by the authorities. But one of them has become infatuated with the unexpected widow of his late friend. The perceptive reader will realize fairly soon that the mysterious death resulted from the scientist's researches into the nature of reality. Sloane leaves myriad hints of other oddities as well, the widow's awkwardness in familiar human situations, the disappearance of a young girl with virtually no intelligence, the mystery of yet another death, this time clearly suicide. Despite the fact that the reader has a clear idea what comprises the general nature of the mystery, the details provide the true suspense, and the climactic confrontation is one of the most effective scenes in the genre.

The Edge of Running Water broke no new ground either, and moves even further toward the supernatural, while still retaining the scientific rationale of its mystery. Although the characters are not as well-drawn in this story of a man convinced he can develop a machine that will enable him to communicate with the dead, the element of suspense is just as expertly handled. There is little overt action, even though one character is eventually killed and another destroyed, propelled into another universe, but the reader's attention is unlikely to waver despite this fact.

Both novels have been published as mysteries, which they are; as horror stories, which they are; and science fiction, which they also are. Sloane's sole foray into more conventional SF, "Let Nothing You Dismay," is singularly unremarkable, a pedestrian examination of human refugees adjusting to a new world after the death of Earth. He was at his best at greater length, using a familiar setting and coloring it with a series of hints of something totally unfamiliar. His style was highly advanced for his time, and both novels are free of archaic anomalies and outdated prose. It seems clear that had Sloane chosen to pursue his career as a genre writer, he would have become one of the dominant forces within it.

—Don D'Ammassa

SLONCZEWSKI, Joan (Lyn)

Nationality: American. **Born:** Hyde Park, New York, 14 August 1956. **Education:** Bryn Mawr College, Pennsylvania, A.B. 1977; Yale University, New Haven, Connecticut, Ph.D. in molecular biophysics and biochemistry. **Family:** Married Michael J. Barich in 1977; two sons. **Career:** Postdoctoral fellow, University of Pennsylvania, Philadelphia, 1982-84; Visiting Professor, Princeton University, 1990-91. Associate Professor, Kenyon College, Gambier, Ohio, since 1984. **Awards:** John Campbell award, 1986. **Agent:** Valerie Smith, Route 44-55, R.R. Box 160, Modena, New York 12548. **Address:** Biology Department, Kenyon College, Gambier, Ohio 43022, U.S.A.

SCIENCE FICTION PUBLICATIONS

Novels (series: Door into Ocean)

Still Forms on Foxfield. New York, Ballantine, 1980.
A Door into Ocean. New York, Arbor House, 1986; London, Women's Press, 1987.
The Wall around Eden. New York, Morrow, 1989; London, Women's Press, 1991.
Daughter of Elysium (Door into Ocean). New York, Morrow, 1993.

Short Stories

Author of numerous uncollected short stories.

*

Joan Slonczewski comments:

My work addresses the question: What does it mean to be a human being? What do we seek and desire most? Do women and men, and individuals of varied genetic and cultural backgrounds, share the same quest; or do they differ? The great apes share 99% of our genes; are they human, too? Is all life sacred, even that of rock-eating bacteria? When we meet our cousins from the stars, are they sacred, too? Anyone who asks these questions will find a friend in my books.

*   *   *

Although not a prolific writer of fiction, Joan Slonczewski has already made her mark with short stories and four novels, with every indication that more work will be forthcoming. The initial modest success of *Still Forms on Foxfield* was bolstered by critical appreciation of *A Door into Ocean*, which received the John W. Campbell Award for best novel of 1986. *Wall around Eden* is a shorter work with a spiritual trajectory and *Daughter of Elysium,* with focal characters who are male, female, young and old, is wider in scope. Like *Door,* it combines ethics, politics, and biology to project Shora a thousand years into the future. Short stories include the recent "Microbe," which extends the temporal universe of *Ocean* and *Daughter* into a new era of bioengineering as an alternative to extending 'human' settlement.

Slonczewski's fiction is characterized by details of daily life infused with Quaker principles, practices, and belief structures, a deep commitment to pacifist philosophy, and a questioning of the contemporary cultural assumption that violence is a necessary part of both creativity and progress. This latter theme recurs in all her novels. Protagonists who are members of Quaker communities or pacifist societies struggle against a cultural assumption that nonviolence leads to static, and therefore, undesirable, cultures. In *Still Forms on Foxfield,* Allison struggles at length with the violence of the United Nations Interplanetary culture, which is explained to her as a necessary part of all successful human cultures. Her rejection of this equation becomes the catalyst for rejection of UNI. In *A Door into Ocean* and *Daughter of Elysium* the pacifist philosophy of the Shorans is reinforced by intrusive tactics like the "sharing" of bothersome pests or microbiological phenomena, intrusions which make their point without being openly deadly.

Biological speculation is added to the social experimentation in Slonczewski's novels. Her background includes undergraduate and graduate degrees in molecular biophysics and biochemistry and she continues to teach as a professor of Biology (and current Department Chair) at Kenyon College. Thus her academic career provides material for the variations in human and alien biologies and ecologies so important in her fiction. All of her works relate interactions between multiple alien communities. The reader, along with the characters, is often misdirected into seeing aliens as hostile, but they are shown in predominantly positive contexts as reader and characters become simultaneously familiar with them. Attention to both character and setting round out these scientific and philosophical speculations as her characters' dilemmas are set forth using details of both the interpersonal and the social level. Each novel relates the personal encounter to larger philosophical and social issues, such as interplanetary finance, biological stability, and experimentation with ecosystems.

Still Forms on Foxfield is set on the planet Foxfield, named after the founder of Quakerism, George Fox. The narrative details the struggles of colony leader, Allison, and of the symbiotic human-alien culture essential for human survival on her alien planet. Foxfield has been isolated for at least a century by the breakdown of a disintegrating intergalactic culture from which the original colonists fled. This narrative begins with reestablishment of contact between Foxfielders and the United Nations Intergalactic, a longed-for event that is nevertheless fraught with difficulties. Foxfielders

have survived on a planet with excessive gravitational pull and few of the trace elements needed to keep them healthy by establishing a tolerant, beneficial symbiosis with the planets' native population. As they confront the reestablishment of relations with the UNI, the importance of consensus decision-making, as opposed to the majority-rule of UNI, is seminal. It seems that without the persistence of an earlier Foxfield settler, these aliens, the Commensuals, would never have been recognized as sentient. They look like plants and talk with scent and gesture. Having sustained a longstanding, viable symbiosis, the Foxfielders must decide whether to abandon it, and the Commensuals, for the questionable advantages of UNI, with its violence and other impulses towards monolithic conquest.

The Wall around Eden is set on earth many decades after a nuclear holocaust has destroyed most biological life. Any remaining humans have survived only because they were forcibly placed in protective domes by more powerful aliens. The work is tantalizing for its misdirection. Most humans believe that the aliens were responsible for the initial destruction and they are either lab animals, kept only for their research value or zoo animals, kept as curiosities. "Domers" believe that the periodic, colorful light-shows seen in the sky outside the domes are the result of aliens attempting to further destroy the ozone layer and claim the earth as their own. Some humans, believing they must act for human survival, have been starting revolutionary, violent movements against the aliens, with very little apparent success, over the 20 years since the great cataclysm. It is only after another decade, as the protagonist, Isabel, grows to adulthood, that the aliens' benevolence is understood. They are in fact rebuilding the ozone layer and preserving as many humans as possible until the planet can again sustain human life. The clues to this insight are both philosophical and occasional. Members of Isabel's small community under a dome in North America, one of the hardest-hit areas for radiation poisoning, are of several religions, including Quaker, Catholic, Presbyterian, Lutheran and Jewish. Each of these religions comes into play in unraveling the human/alien/ecosystem relationships. But the clues all come from work Isabel and her friends do with beehives in the city, especially beehives that have lost a queen or malfunctioned for some other reason. Isabel and her friend, (later to become her husband, David), are abducted by the aliens to an unidentified 'land' for a time. Here Isabel begins to understand their motivations. A gang of 'outlaws' bent on destroying the aliens helps her to learn more about them and the work ends with humans finally able to leave the domes and start to repopulate the planet.

In *A Door into Ocean,* Shoran pacifism is a more powerful force than militarism. Shora and Valedon both orbit the same sun, but Valedon, under the rule of a totalitarian patriarch with an intergalactic jurisdiction, has the traditional hierarchic structure, two sexes and stereotypical sex roles. Shorans, on the other are genetically but not functionally female. They reproduce only with the help of their doctors who, when they are ready for childbearing, "seed" their wombs. Even if there were male Shorans, the females have lost the ability to "be seeded" in a "natural" fashion. They also have no established hierarchies and no central government. The groups inhabit islands of roots that float atop a water-covered planet on which they have established a hard-won ecological stability. *A Door into Ocean* is remarkable for several reasons, including the careful character development and multiple viewpoints. Whereas alien cultures are usually introduced by one human mediator-character in science fiction novels, and such issues as gender and class are ignored, they are central to this novel. Slonczewski here focusses on an adult, human ruling-class female from Valedon whose fiancee will eventually head the military expedition that is supposed to subdue the Shorans. Berenice's loyalties are initially mixed as she struggles between the privileges of primacy in a hierarchical culture and the disadvantages of being female in a patriarchy. A young, human male from Valedon also serves as a mediator between cultures. Spinel has nothing to gain by supporting his 'home' planet where his social class would have condemned him to servitude or worse. Each finds strength from the female Shorans and their culture. It is only Berenice's well-connected, ruling-class fiancee, a male with a big investment in Valedon's systems of power, who ultimately rejects, and is rejected by Shoran culture.

Often seen as sequels to *A Door into Ocean,* Slonczewski's novel *Daughter of Elysium* and the short story "Microbe" (*Analog,* August 1995) project Sharer and the intergalactic FOLD culture into a further future on Shora and other planets. They also explore the political side of scientific discoveries and, as usual in Slonczewski's stories, those of Biological and Zoological sciences.

Daughter of Elysium focuses on two questions: the interaction between fertility, longevity, and environment, each of which are outlined as factors in human survival, and the nature of sentience. It has no clear heros and villains and no single privileged culture, but viable and non-viable realizations of the survival equation. Shora, about 1000 years after the conflicts of *Door into Ocean,* is still inhabited by the original Shorans but they have been joined by Elysians, a race who have artificially extended their lifespan at the expense of fertility. Elysium invites many members of other races to participate in its research and practices interplanetary finance, usually at great rates of financial return. Other planetary societies use financial and trade agreements to force agendas of conquest that can be blatant or can be masked as humanitarian or philosophically laudable gestures.

The central question on the Shora of this time is whether Elysians will be allowed to bioengineer fertility for themselves while maintaining their longevity and presence on Shora. The central question for the rest of FOLD is whether population will be controlled or worlds will be terraformed, a process which kills off their ecosystems (plants, animals, and other indigenous lifeforms). Unrestricted reproduction of humans as a threat to social stability regularly concern in the described cultures and planetary groups represent a range of positions, just as they do at this point in our earth's history.

The cultural clashes are portrayed with sensitivity. Elysium humans are oriented towards longevity, at the cost of decreasing viability of children produced in labs. Bronze Skyans, from a neighboring planet, are oriented towards the family, children, and reproduction. They substitute fertility for the lack of ability to control the environment on their home planet, a terraformed, volcanically active world. The social encouragement of fertility is partially an accommodation to the harsh conditions of their lives, as emphasized by a family disaster which occurs for the Bronze Skyan male, Dr. Blackbear. His entire family back on Bronze Sky is killed by volcanic gasses while he is on Shora. Part of this accommodation is what seems to us role reversal, with females as dominant and males as nurturers of children, around which a plethora of cultural forms are clustered. The central characters Bronze Skyan Blackbear, his "goddess" Raincloud, and their children are contrasted with the "non-families" of Elysium, the patriarchies of the Urulites, who hide their women but also hide their interbreeding with indigenous, sentient apes, and L'lliites, who overbreed and expect the rest of the galaxy to solve their problems. The Shoran viewpoint and philosophy hold a place of privilege, with four interspersed readings from *The Web,* a spiritual compilation of writings by Door's char-

acters from the past of Shora. *The Web* provides a spiritual guide for Shoran, Elysian, and Bronze Skyan. As Merwen is quoted in *The Web:* "The Web is the sum and multiplier of all living things—microbes, plants, squirting snails, flying fish, human beings. All things exist for the Web; and so long as the Web exists, an infinite variety of life will flourish. It is sane to value the Web itself greater than any one of its living parts, even greater than the sum of its parts." But she goes on to add, "Yes, and as we've shown such feelings for individuals are madness, for they make no difference to the Web and yet, we hunger and thirst for them." Like most spiritual writings, *The Web* offers thoughts but not answers. Its also serves to make an accommodation for sentient robots whose needs begin to override that of the other races. The robots are another face of Slonczewski's ongoing debate on the nature of humanity.

"Microbe" moves the story of Slonczewski's "Shoran" future and her view of the universe as some sort of ecological whole into an era of bioengineering on humans. A new novel in preparation, with the working title *The Children's Star,* will take another spin on bio- and social-engineering with children raised by monks and sentient machines as the hope for humanity's future.

Slonczewski has received too little critical attention for her work, although several are discussed in conference papers on feminist SF. Perhaps this undeserved has occurred because she is creating new worlds with each book, worlds whose complexities defy easy analysis. The obvious craft with which each individual work has been conceived and executed more than compensates for the small number of titles. Slonczewski is for rereading as well as first reading.

—Janice M. Bogstad

SMITH, Clark Ashton

Nationality: American. **Born:** 13 January 1893. **Education:** Left school at 14. **Family:** Married in 1954. **Career:** Writer and artist: regular contributor to *Weird Tales* in the early 1930s; ceased writing in 1936. **Died:** 14 August 1961.

SCIENCE FICTION PUBLICATIONS

Short Stories

The Immortals of Mercury. New York, Stellar, 1932.
The Double Shadow and Other Fantasies. Auburn, California, Auburn Journal, 1933.
The White Sybil, bound with *Men of Avalon,* by David H. Keller. Everett, Pennsylvania, Fantasy, 1935(?).
Out of Space and Time (includes verse). Sauk City, Wisconsin, Arkham House, 1942; London, Spearman, 1971.
Lost Worlds. Sauk City, Wisconsin, Arkham House, 1944; London, Spearman, 1971.
Genius Loci and Other Tales. Sauk City, Wisconsin, Arkham House, 1948; London, Spearman, 1972.
The Abominations of Yondo. Sauk City, Wisconsin, Arkham House, 1960; London, Spearman, 1972.
Tales of Science and Sorcery. Sauk City, Wisconsin, Arkham House, 1964; London, Panther, 1976.

Other Dimensions. Sauk City, Wisconsin, Arkham House, 1970;
   London, Panther, 2 vols., 1977.
Zothique, edited by Lin Carter. New York, Ballantine, 1970.
Hyperborea, edited by Lin Carter. New York, Ballantine, 1971.
The Mortuary. Glendale, California, Squires, 1971.
Xiccarph, edited by Lin Carter. New York, Ballantine, 1972.
Poseidonis, edited by Lin Carter. New York, Ballantine, 1973.
Prince Alcouz and the Magician. Glendale, California, Squires, 1977.
The City of the Singing Flame, edited by Donald Sidney-Fryer. New
   York, Timescape, 1981.
The Monster of the Prophecy, edited by Donald Sidney-Fryer. New
   York, Timescape, 1983.
The Dweller in the Gulf, edited by Steve Behrends. West Warwick,
   Rhode Island, Necronomicon Press, 1987.
Mother of Toads, edited by Steve Behrends. West Warwick, Rhode
   Island, Necronomicon Press, 1987.
*A Rendezvous in Averoigne: Best Fantastic Tales of Clark Ashton
   Smith.* Sauk City, Wisconsin, Arkham House, 1988.
The Vaults of Yoh-Vombis, edited by Steve Behrends. West Warwick,
   Rhode Island, Necronomicon Press, 1988.
*Strange Shadows: The Uncollected Fiction and Essays of Clark
   Ashton Smith,* edited by Steve Behrends, Donald Sidney-
   Fryer, and Rah Hoffman. New York, and London, Greenwood,
   1989.
The Hashish-Eater; or, The Apocalypse of Evil. West Warwick,
   Rhode Island, Necronomicon Press, 1989.

Poetry

The Star-Treader and Other Poems. San Francisco, Robertson,
   1912.
Odes and Sonnets. San Francisco, Book Club of California, 1918.
Ebony and Crystal: Poems in Verse and Prose. Auburn, Califor-
   nia, Auburn Journal, 1923.
Sandalwood. Privately printed, 1925.
Nero and Other Poems. Lakeport, California, Futile Press, 1937.
The Dark Chateau and Other Poems. Sauk City, Wisconsin,
   Arkham House, 1951.
Spells and Philtres. Sauk City, Wisconsin, Arkham House, 1958.
Poems in Prose. Sauk City, Wisconsin, Arkham House, 1964.
*Grotesques and Fantastiques: A Selection of Previously Unpub-
   lished Drawings and Poems.* Saddle River, New Jersey, Gerry
   de la Ree, 1973.
*Klarkash-ton and Monstro Ligriv: Previously Unpublished Poems
   and Art,* with Virgil Finlay. Saddle River, New Jersey, Gerry de
   la Ree, 1974.
Fugitive Poems. Privately printed, 4 vols., 1974-75.
Nostalgia of the Unknown: The Complete Prose Poetry, edited by
   Marc and Susan Michaud. West Warwick, Rhode Island,
   Necronomicon Press, 1988.

Other

Planets and Dimensions: Collected Essays of Clark Ashton Smith,
   edited by Charles K. Wolfe. Baltimore, Mirage Press, 1973.
The Black Book of Clark Ashton Smith, edited by R.A. Hoffman
   and Donald Sidney-Fryer. Sauk City, Wisconsin, Arkham House,
   1979.
Clark Ashton Smith: Letters to H.P. Lovecraft, edited by Steve
   Behrends. West Warwick, Rhode Island, Necronomicon Press,
   1987.

*The Devil's Notebook: Collected Epigrams and Pensées of Clark
   Ashton Smith,* edited by Don Herron and Donald Sidney-Fryer.
   Mercer Island, Washington, Starmont House, 1990.

*

Bibliography: *The Tales of Clark Ashton Smith: A Bibliography*
by G.L. Cockcroft, Melling, New Zealand, Cockcroft, 1952; *Emperor of Dreams: A Clark Ashton Smith Bibliography* by Donald
Sidney-Fryer and others, West Kingston, Rhode Island, Grant,
1978.

Critical Studies: *In Memoriam Clark: Ashton Smith* edited by Jack
L. Chalker, Baltimore, Anthem, 1963; *The Last of the Great Ro-
mantic Poets* by Donald Sidney-Fryer, Albuquerque, Silver Scarab
Press, 1973; *The Fantastic Art of Clark Ashton Smith* by Dennis
Rickard, Baltimore, Mirage Press, 1973.

*   *   *

Clark Ashton Smith was a contributor to the early SF and fantasy pulp magazines whose output, despite its unevenness, became
a seminal influence on modern science fiction. Jack Vance, Harlan
Ellison, Theodore Sturgeon, Fritz Leiber, H.P. Lovecraft, Robert
E. Howard, and Ray Bradbury, among others, were influenced by
his work.

Smith's earliest short stories—he wrote no novels—are the primitive interplanetary narratives common in the pulp magazines. Of
these, "Marooned in Andromeda" and "The Amazing Planet" are
typical. They recount the adventures of the crew of the spaceship
Alcoyne on distant worlds, and are odysseys of perilous adventure
distinguished only by Smith's exotic language and bizarre imagination.

Smith, also a poet, was concerned mainly with the poetry of death
and the alien. His protagonists are decidedly unheroic, being either
misfits or rogues who seek other worlds because they do not fit
into their own. In "The Monster of the Prophecy," the suicidal poet
Theophilus Alvor agreeably becomes the instrument through which
the Antarean wizard Vizaphmal assumes control of his world. This
lack of virtue does not prevent Alvor from finding true love in the
arms of an Antarean woman. Similarly, the renegade and thief Datu
Buang lives out his life in peace after assassinating an evil ruler
with the aid of his consort in "As It Is Written."

The search for a better reality is the predominant theme in Smith.
In his haunting classic, "The City of the Singing Flame," the author Giles Angarth discovers the gateway to another dimension
where the Singing Flame lures the unwary into its fires. Angarth
finds himself finally drawn to the flame and discovers it is the entrance to still another, better, reality beyond.

Those stories set wholly on other worlds, in which he gives his
poetic vision free rein, are considered Smith's best. Among these
are the sardonic tales of the world of Xiccarph and those set on the
continent of Zothique in the last days of Earth. In "The Maze of
Maal Dweb," the hunter Tiglari seeks his kidnapped lover in the
stronghold of Xiccarph's tyrant, Maal Dweb, but falls victim to the
tyrant's powers. Maal Dweb, on the other hand, is the protagonist
of "The Flower-Women." It is a peculiarity of Smith's fiction that
the amoral flourish and the good become the victims of ironic fates.
Like Tiglari, the hero of "The Demon of the Flower," ultimately
fails to rescue the woman he loves from the plant ruler of his world.
The tales of Zothique, although set in Earth's distant future, are

closer to fantasy. In these, Smith's macabre poetic vision is at its highest. "Xeethra" is a poignant story of a goatherd who partakes of strange fruit and imagines himself the ruler of a distant land. He goes in search of that land, only to find it in ruins. "The Last Hieroglyph" is an ironic tale of an astrologer, Nushain, who reads in the stars that he must go on a journey which will fulfill his destiny. At the voyage's end, he meets his end. "The Weaver in the Vault" relates the weird doom of two individuals who desecrate a tomb. Hope and futility are expertly balanced in "The Isle of the Torturers."

Despite the weird trappings of his stories, Smith's work cannot be rightfully labeled as horror stories. He was a fatalist who delighted in spinning phantasms, not terror. With rare exceptions ("Master of the Asteroid" and "The Dweller in the Gulf"), his work is too remote from reality to evoke a convincing mood of horror and his imaginings thus fascinate instead of terrify. The power of Smith's writing, and the reason for its widespread influence, lay in the fact that Smith shared with many of his protagonists a yearning for a reality truer than the one he knew, and he discovered a language that enabled him to express his unique vision.

—Will Murray

SMITH, Cordwainer

Pseudonym for Paul Myron Anthony Linebarger. **Other Pseudonyms:** Felix C. Forrest; Carmichael Smith. **Nationality:** American. **Born:** Milwaukee, Wisconsin, 11 July 1913. **Education:** Schools in Honolulu, Shanghai, and Baden Baden; University of Nanking, 1930; North China Union Language School, 1931; George Washington University, Washington, D.C., A.B. 1933 (Phi Beta Kappa); Oxford University, 1933; American University, Washington, D.C., 1934; University of Chicago, 1935; Johns Hopkins University, Baltimore, M.A. 1935; Ph.D. 1936; University of Michigan, Ann Arbor, 1937, 1939; Washington School of Psychiatry, certificate in psychiatry 1955; Universidad Interamericana, 1959-60. **Military Service:** Served in the United States Army Intelligence Service, 1942-66: helped found Office of War Information, served in Chungking, 1942-46, and as consultant to British Forces in Malaya, 1950, and to 8th Army, Korea, 1950-52: Lieutenant Colonel. **Family:** Married 1) Margaret Snow in 1936 (divorced 1949), two daughters; 2) Genevieve Cecilia Collins in 1950. **Career:** Instructor, Harvard University, Cambridge, Massachusetts, 1936-37; instructor, then associate professor, Duke University, Durham, North Carolina, 1937-46; professor of Asiatic politics, Johns Hopkins University School of Advanced International Studies, Washington, D.C., 1946-66; visiting professor, University of Pennsylvania, Philadelphia, 1955-56, and Australian National University, Canberra, 1957. **Member:** President, American Peace Society. **Died:** 6 August 1966.

SCIENCE FICTION PUBLICATIONS

Novels (series: Instrumentality in all titles)

The Planet Buyer: A Science Fiction Novel. New York, Pyramid, 1964.

Quest of the Three Worlds. New York, Ace, 1966; London, Gollancz, 1987.
The Underpeople. New York, Pyramid, 1968.
Norstrilia (includes *The Planet Buyer* and *The Underpeople*). New York, Ballantine, 1975; London, Gollancz, 1988; revised, Framingham, Massachusetts, NESFA Press, 1994.

Short Stories (series: Instrumentality in all titles)

You Will Never Be the Same. Evanston, Illinois, Regency, 1963.
Space Lords. New York, Pyramid, 1965; London, Sidgwick and Jackson, 1969.
Under Old Earth and Other Explorations. London, Panther, 1970.
Stardreamer. New York, Beagle, 1971.
The Best of Cordwainer Smith, edited by J.J. Pierce. New York, Doubleday, 1975; as *The Rediscovery of Man,* London, Gollancz, 1988.
The Instrumentality of Mankind. New York, Ballantine, 1979; London, Gollancz, 1988.
The Rediscovery of Man: The Complete Short Fiction of Cordwainer Smith, edited by James A. Mann. Framingham, Massachusetts, NESFA Press, 1993.

OTHER PUBLICATIONS

Novels

Ria (as Felix C. Forrest). New York, Duell, 1947.
Carola: A Novel (as Felix C. Forrest). New York, Duell, 1948.
Atomsk: A Novel of Suspense (as Carmichael Smith). New York, Duell, 1949.

Other as P.M.A. Linebarger

The Political Doctrines of Sun Yat-Sen: An Exposition of San Min Chu I. Baltimore, Johns Hopkins Press, 1937.
Government in Republican China. New York, McGraw Hill, 1938.
The China of Chiang Kai-shek: A Political Study. Boston, World Peace Foundation, 1941.
Psychological Warfare. Washington, D.C., Infantry Journal Press, 1948; 2nd edition, Washington, D.C., Combat Forces Press, 1955.
Far Eastern Governments and Politics, with Djang Chu and Ardath W. Burks. New York, Van Nostrand, 1954; 2nd edition, 1956; 3rd edition, 1967.

Editor, *The Gospel of Chung Shan,* by Paul Linebarger Sr. Privately printed, 1932.
Editor, *The Ocean Men,* by Paul Linebarger Sr. Washington, D.C., Mid-Nation, 1937.

*

Critical Studies: *Exploring Cordwainer Smith* (includes bibliography) edited by Andrew Porter, New York, Algol Press, 1975; *Concordance to Cordwainer Smith* by Anthony Lewis, Jr., Cambridge, Massachusetts, NESFA Press, 1984.

*   *   *

Paul Linebarger, who wrote science fiction under the name Cordwainer Smith, certainly stands as one of the most unusual and imaginative writers of fantastic literature of this century. Though his total output of fiction is relatively small, Smith's reputation and influence have grown consistently since his death in 1966. Virtually his entire SF output was in print in book form by early 1979, and the theme that ties most of these stories together—a future galactic civilization called the Instrumentality of Mankind—has emerged as one of the most striking and detailed future history constructs in all of science fiction. His non-science fiction novels *Ria* and *Carola* also reveal the strength of imagination, idiosyncratic style, and sensitivity to character that make his better-known work stand out.

Smith was a Christian, a romantic, and a shrewd political theorist who had written under his own name an internationally influential text on psychological warfare. All of these strains come together in his fiction, giving it a complexity and depth of meaning that are sometimes confusing to readers encountering one of his stories for the first time. The first of his mature stories to be published (his first SF story, "War No. 81-Q," had appeared when he was only 15), "Scanners Live in Vain," appeared in 1950, and clearly implied a more detailed imaginary universe than the story itself explained. Set early in the history of the Instrumentality, the tale concerns a threat posed to the guild of "scanners"—humans mechanically restructured to survive in space—by the discovery of a new and safer means of space travel. In a characteristically bizarre Smith touch, the new method depends on lining the spaceships with oysters to insulate the passengers from harm. Clearly, this odd version of a technological breakthrough represented an event of historical importance to this future world, but the nature of that world itself remained unclear.

During the next decade and a half, Smith gradually filled in some of the gaps. Following a series of disastrous wars that nearly reduced Earth to barbarism, humanity gradually recovers its vitality, aided by a powerful family called the Vomacts, descended from the daughters of a Nazi scientist who were placed in suspended animation in orbit and who returned following the wars ("Mark Elf" and "The Queen of the Afternoon"). The Vomacts help give rise to the universal government called the Instrumentality, which initially explores space with the aid of scanners, briefly replaces these with the oyster-shell ships, and in turn replaces these with ships powered by massive photonic sails ("The Lady Who Sailed the Soul," "Think Blue, Count Two"). Finally, a near-instantaneous form of space travel, called planoforming, is discovered ("The Colonel Came Back from the Nothing-at-All," "The Burning of the Brain"), but planoforming ships are subject to attacks by hideous, incorporeal outerspace "dragons" and must be protected by telepathic technicians called pinlighters, sometimes assisted by telepathic cats ("The Game of Rat and Dragon"). As the Instrumentality grows increasingly powerful and decadent—offering humans near-immortality through a life-extending drug called stroon—its economy comes to depend on a slave class of converted animals called underpeople. Aided by a few heroic underpeople and the sympathetic Jestocost family, the underpeople finally attain civil rights ("The Dead Lady of Clown Town," "Under Old Earth," "The Ballad of Lost C'Mell"), and a renaissance of humanism, the Rediscovery of Man, sets in ("Alpha Ralpha Boulevard," *Norstrilia*). In the far distant future, civilization finally seems to be achieving some kind of stability (*Quest of the Three Worlds*), but the actual conclusion of the history of the Instrumentality, if planned by Smith, was not completed during his lifetime.

Although there is an abundance of political and social satire in Smith's work—the Instrumentality is clearly not a simple utopia— what stands out most are the memorable characters of near-mythic proportions, the romantic legends he weaves, and the oddly nostalgic style, reminiscent of oral history or folktales, in which he writes. Smith has a unique ability to make a romance between a man and a cat convincing ("The Game of Rat and Dragon") or to make an unconsummated romance between a servant girl and a lord as powerful as a medieval legend ("The Ballad of Lost C'Mell"). Occasionally, he turns to actual legends for his source material; "The Dead Lady of Clown Town" is a retelling of the Joan of Arc legend, with Joan made into an underperson converted from a dog. In other cases, he turns to literary culture for his sources; "Drunkboat" is essentially a tour de force on themes from Arthur Rimbaud. "Golden the Ship Was—Oh! Oh! Oh!" is at once a satire on the bureaucracy of war and a retelling of the Trojan horse story—with the horse becoming a 90-million-mile-long decoy spaceship used to frighten an enemy while the second-level bureaucrats drop poisonous bombs. Other of his stories are supposedly based on Chinese narrative techniques, and occasionally he deliberately plays games with the reader, such as working anagrammatic references to the Kennedy-Oswald assassinations into *Quest of the Three Worlds*.

One wonders, at times, whether Smith's curious style and unusual way of structuring stories is due to his great sophistication or to his ingenuousness as a writer. *Norstrilia* does not stand up as well as do many of the short stories, partly because the narrative tends to ramble, partly because the style seems to grow self-conscious over such an extended narrative. Smith's short fiction includes some of science fiction's finest stories, but demonstrates that an author need not abandon sensitive insights into love and ethics in order to create imaginary universes of great imagination.

—Gary K. Wolfe

SMITH, Doc. *See* **SMITH, E.E.**

SMITH, E(dward) E(lmer)

Also writes as "Doc" Smith. **Nationality:** American. **Born:** Sheboygan, Wisconsin, 1 May 1890. **Education:** University of Idaho, Moscow; George Washington University, Washington, D.C., Ph.D. in food chemistry 1919. **Military Service:** Served in an explosives arsenal during World War II. **Family:** Married Jeanne Craig MacDougall; one daughter and one son. **Career:** Worked as ranch hand, lumberjack, silver miner, and surveyor, before becoming chemist, specializing in food mixes: manager of General Mix Division of J.W. Allen and Company, 1945-57. **Awards:** First Fandom Hall of Fame award (as "Doc" Smith), 1964. Guest of Honor, 2nd World Science Fiction Convention, 1940. **Died:** 31 August 1965.

SCIENCE FICTION PUBLICATIONS

Novels (series: Lensman; Lord Tedric; Skylark)

The Skylark of Space: The Tale of the First Inter-Stellar Cruise, with Mrs. Lee Hawkins Garby. Providence, Rhode Island, Buffalo, 1946; revised edition, bylined as E.E. Smith, New York, Pyramid, 1958; London, Digit, 1959.

Spacehounds of IPC: A Tale of the Inter-Planetary Corporation. Reading, Pennsylvania, Fantasy Press, 1947; London, Panther, 1974.

Skylark Three. Reading, Pennsylvania, Fantasy Press, 1948; London, Panther, 1974.

The History of Civilization (Lensman):

   Triplanetary: A Tale of Cosmic Adventure. Reading, Pennsylvania, Fantasy Press, 1948; London, Boardman, 1954.

   First Lensman. Reading, Pennsylvania, Fantasy Press, 1950; London, Boardman, 1955.

   Galactic Patrol. Reading, Pennsylvania, Fantasy Press, 1950; London, W.H. Allen, 1971.

   Gray Lensman. Reading, Pennsylvania, Fantasy Press, 1951; London, W.H. Allen, 1971.

   Second Stage Lensmen. Reading, Pennsylvania, Fantasy Press, 1953; London, W.H. Allen, 1972.

   Children of the Lens. Reading, Pennsylvania, Fantasy Press, 1954; London, W.H. Allen, 1972.

Skylark of Valeron. Reading, Pennsylvania, Fantasy Press, 1949.

The Vortex Blaster (Lensman). New York, Gnome Press, 1960; as *Masters of the Vortex,* New York, Pyramid, 1968; London, W.H. Allen, 1972.

The Galaxy Primes. New York, Ace, 1965; London, Panther, 1975.

Subspace Explorers. New York, Canaveral Press, 1965; London, Panther, 1975.

Skylark DuQuesne. New York, Pyramid, 1966; London, Panther, 1974.

Lord Tedric: Alien Worlds. London, Wright, 1978.

Masters of Space. New York, Jove, 1979

Subspace Encounter, with Lloyd Arthur Eshbach. New York, Berkley, 1983.

Novels with Gordon Eklund (series: Lord Tedric in all titles)

Lord Tedric. New York, Baronet, 1978.

Space Pirates. New York, Baronet, 1979; as *Lord Tedric: Space Pirates,* London, Wingate, 1979.

Black Knight of the Iron Sphere. London, Star, 1979; as *Lord Tedric: The Black Knight of the Iron Sphere,* London, Star, 1979.

Lord Tedric: Alien Realms. London, Star, 1980.

Novels with Stephen Goldin (series: Family D'Alembert in all titles)

Imperial Stars. New York, Pyramid, and London, Panther, 1976.

Strangler's Moon. New York, Pyramid, 1976; London, Panther, 1977.

The Clockwork Traitor. New York, Pyramid, 1977; London, Panther, 1978.

Getaway World. New York, Pyramid, and London, Panther, 1977.

Appointment at Bloodstar. New York, Jove/HBJ, 1978; as *The Bloodstar Conspiracy,* London, Panther, 1978.

The Purity Plot. New York, Berkley, and London, Panther, 1980.

Planet of Treachery. New York, Berkley, and London, Panther, 1982.

Eclipsing Binaries. New York, Berkley, and London, Panther, 1984.

The Omnicron Invasion. New York, Berkley, and London, Grafton, 1984.

Revolt of the Galaxy. New York, Berkley, and London, Grafton, 1985.

Short Stories

The Best of E.E. "Doc" Smith. London, Futura, 1975.

OTHER PUBLICATIONS

Other

What Does This Convention Mean? A Speech Delivered at the Chicago 1940 World's Science Fiction Convention. Bryantville, Massachusetts, Published for the Denver 1941 World's Science Fiction Convention by Art Widner, 1941.

Galactic Roamer: Dr. E.E. Smith Talks about the Famous "Skylark" Tales and the "Lensmen" Series in an Interview with Thomas Sheridan. West Warwick, Rhode Island, Necronomicon Press, 1977.

*

Critical Study: *The Universes of E.E. Smith* by Ron Ellik and Bill Evans, Chicago, Advent, 1966.

*   *   *

Determining the place of Edward E. "Doc" Smith in the history of science fiction is about as difficult as locating an electron. His career spans the history of SF in the 20th century. He began writing *The Skylark of Space* in 1915; today, other writers continue to use his characters and created universes as a basis for novels "by" E.E. Smith. All but five of his 17 books remain in print, and many have been translated into foreign languages such as Japanese and Vietnamese. Brian Aldiss considers Smith's *The Skylark of Space* as the starting point of the "trillion-year spree" that is modern science fiction. Yet he is dismissed by most recent critics in the field as an outdated writer of space operas whose style is awkward at best, whose plots are simplistic, and whose science is gadgetry and speculation.

He is best known for two multinovel sagas, the Skylark series (four volumes and over 230,000 words in its final form) and the Lensman series (seven volumes and 500,000 words). Most of his works first appeared in the popular pulp SF magazines. *The Skylark of Space* appeared as a serial in Hugo Gernsback's *Amazing Stories,* as did *Triplanetary.* The Lensman series is identified with John Campbell's *Astounding Science Fiction,* though *Galactic Patrol* appeared in *Astounding Stories* before Campbell's tenure. Other novels and stories appeared in *Comet Stories, Astonishing Stories, Other Worlds, Universe,* and *Worlds of If.* Beyond his 16 novels, he wrote only eight short stories or novelettes and three short articles, most of which are reprinted in *The Best of E.E. "Doc" Smith.*

Some of the themes and styles that Smith first articulated in *The Skylark of Space* remained a consistent part of his fictional armory: revolutionary innovations in basic science, engineering of those innovations into powerful technology with incredible speed, colorful descriptions of space battles, the whole intergalactic universe as the field of play, fundamental conflicts between good and evil, the interaction of human beings with alien races, and a "humanity first" philosophy. In *The Skylark of Space* (written between 1915 and 1920, first published in 1928), the young scientific genius Richard Seaton accidentally discovers an unknown metal in his laboratory that makes space travel possible; but the discovery is noticed by Seaton's amoral colleague, Marc DuQuesne. Seaton and his millionaire friend Martin Reynolds quickly use the discovery to build a spaceship, the *Skylark* of the title, but so does DuQuesne, who uses his ship to kidnap Seaton's fiancé Dorothy Vaneman and her friend Margaret Spencer. The two sides set off on an intergalactic journey that takes them through two more novels (*Skylark Three,* and *Skylark of Valeron*), three technological transformations of the original *Skylark*—the final *Skylark of Valeron* is as big as a small planet, and has alliances with several alien but human-minded races against powerful and physically monstrous aliens, and space battles too numerous to count. The final conflict with DuQuesne and an evil race of disembodied intelligences ends in triumph, with the universe at peace and the forces of evil sent off in a prison of force to the ends of the universe.

Thirty years later, in the last novel Smith completed before his death, he returned to the Skylark saga precisely at the point he had left it. In *Skylark DuQuesne* (*Worlds of If,* 1965; in book form in 1966), DuQuesne and the intelligences escape, humanity is again threatened by the alien Fenachrone and Chlorans, and "Blackie" DuQuesne becomes the hero. He defeats the aliens, finds his amoral soulmate in the physicist Stephanie de Marigny, and finally flees "sissy" humanity to become colonist and emperor of a new civilization "on the rim of this universe." There is so little in this final Skylark episode of the thematic and attitudinal changes Smith demonstrated in his other novels between 1935 and 1965 that one wonders if it had in fact been drafted in the 1930s.

The conflicts in the original Skylark series are between male individuals: the female characters serve mainly as quest objects (though in the final novel Dorothy and Margaret fight beside their husbands), and the alien races as foils for the conflict between Seaton and DuQuesne. In *Spacehounds of IPC* and *Triplanetary,* however, Smith begins to envision an organized fight against evil. Though the action of both novels is restricted to the solar system, the Inter-Planetary Corporation and the Triplanetary Service are preliminary studies for the Galactic Patrol: humanity-centered organizations that pit good people against the forces of evil. In *Spacehounds of IPC,* the good guys become involved in wars between good and bad alien races on Jupiter and Saturn and their moons, while the criminals in *Triplanetary* are human.

The plot of the original Skylark series seems unplanned: the chance meeting and coincidence are its principal narrative devices. When Smith published *Galactic Patrol* in 1937-1938, however, he had conceived the entire plot of the Lensman series in advance. The narrative frame transcends all normal time and space in a conflict between two races of almost pure intelligence: the Eddorians, who came into "our" universe "from some horribly different plenum" and whose sole motivation is the lust for power, and the Arisians, whose only interest is knowledge but who unwillingly become the opponents of the Eddorians. The Arisians keep their existence unknown to the Eddorians and establish a billion-year plan that culminates in two individuals: Kimball Kinnison and Clarissa MacDougall. Kim's father Roderick had, a century or two after our own time, helped to found the Galactic Patrol, whose sym-

bol and source of power was the lens, a telepathic jewel given to Patrol members by the Arisians—each lens uniquely linked to the mind of its owner.

The four novels of the original series (*Galactic Patrol, Gray Lensman, Second Stage Lensman,* and *Children of the Lens*) form a continuous narrative. In a series of suspenseful investigations, individual conflicts, and space battles whose scope and magnificence grow ever grander, Kim and his Patrol allies, the physically monstrous but "humanly" good aliens Worsel of Velantia, Tregonsee of Rigel IV, and Nadreck of Palain VII, slowly learn to use the powers bred into their genetic lines by the Arisians; level by level, they fight their way up the Eddorian hierarchy of evil. The final conflict is reserved, however, for the children of Kim and Clarissa: Christopher, Karen, Kathryn, Camilla and Constance. The climax of the Arisians' breeding plan, they are able to merge their minds into The Unit, a single entity through which the Arisians are finally able to confront and destroy the Eddorians and make both the First and Second galaxies safe for Civilization.

All of the themes and narrative devices of the Skylark series, good and bad, are carried on in the Lensman series, but put at the service of an encompassing and remarkably coherent plot structure. New to the Lensman series is telepathy: the power of mind, which becomes the central force of the later series. The "lens" is initially an enabling device, but the Children are able to do without the lens. The importance of the female characters is also new: though much of the rhetoric and the conversational interactions remain bound in the sexist conventions of the 1930s and 1940s, Clarissa and her daughters here play roles as important as those of Kim and his son.

When the Lensman series was published in book form, Smith rewrote *Triplanetary* with a long historical introduction linking its events to the billion-year history of the Lensman series, and followed it with *First Lensman* (one of the two Smith novels to appear only in book form), in which Virgil Samms, the hero of *Triplanetary,* learns of the Arisians and acquires the first lens. The series is usually taken to include also *The Vortex Blaster,* a weak novel sewn together out of shorter stories that had appeared in magazines in 1941-1942, and 1952, and vaguely set in the early years of the Galactic Patrol.

The new themes of telepathy and the cooperative interaction of male and female characters appear again in the novels that Smith wrote in his post-Lensman period. In *The Galaxy Primes* (1959 in *Amazing Stories*) the "primes" are super-telepaths in a galaxy of telepathic potential who use their power to establish a galactic government; the subplot in this novel, poorly integrated with the main plot, is the growing love between Cleander Garlock and Belle Bellamy, two "primes" whose personalities are originally in bitter conflict. In *Subspace Explorers* (originally a novelette in *Analog Science Fact/Science Fiction* in 1960), by contrast, two pairs of telepaths fall in love instantly because of their mental contact; the plot, however, is like *Spacehounds of IPC* in that a disaster sends the heroes into a different space from which they must return with difficulty. A subplot introduces the theme of "enlightened self-interest" as a governing philosophy. Its sequel *Subspace Encounter* (edited and published in 1983 after Smith's death) combines the telepathic theme with the kind of galactic conflict familiar from Smith's earlier novels. Both *The Galaxy Primes* and *Subspace Encounter* conclude with suggestions of an Arisia-like force behind the events.

Smith's penultimate novel, *Masters of Space* (in the magazine *Worlds of If,* 1961-1962), was in fact his completion of a novel by his fan and friend E. Everett Evans in which telepathic robots finally re-encounter the humans who had created them centuries before; robots and humans combine to defeat a race of evil aliens. Its collaborative nature points to what has happened since Smith's death. David Kyle and William Ellern have continued the Lensman series (four novels between 1977 and 1983). Stephen Goldin took a novelette, "Imperial Stars," that Smith had published in 1964 shortly before his death, and used it as a basis for a series, "The Family D'Alembert," which came to ten novels between 1976 and 1985. The Family consists of interstellar circus performers who are actually secret agents of the galactic emperor. The D'Alembert series, like Smith's original story, follows the trend so obvious in SF of the 1970s and 1980s of placing sword-and-sorcery stories in a science fiction context, as did the Lord Tedric series, four novels by Gordon Eklund (1978-80) based on two short stories Smith had published in 1953-54.

Smith's achievement as an SF writer is considerable and his impact is lasting. Those who criticize his style, his plots, his characterization, and his pseudo-science are correct enough, as far as they go. But his imagination was as far-reaching as the universe itself, and his ideal of a galactic civilization where human and alien, male and female, worked together for the common good is as attractive as it is unrealizable. The fact remains that Smith's novels are not only immensely readable and enjoyable, but they can be reread with growing pleasure. They are as much fantasy as they are science fiction in the narrow sense of the word—and that, perhaps, is one source of their continuing influence in a period when more than half of the SF novels published are of the sword-and-sorcery brand.

—Bruce A. Beatie

SMITH, Evelyn E.

Pseudonym: Delphine C. Lyons. **Nationality:** American. **Born:** 1937. **Career:** Editor, writer, and crossword puzzle compiler. **Address:** P.O. Box 226, Ansonia Station, New York, New York 10023, U.S.A.

SCIENCE FICTION PUBLICATIONS

Novels

The Perfect Planet. New York, Avalon, 1962.
Unpopular Planet. New York, Dell, 1975.
The Copy Shop. Garden City, New York, Doubleday, 1985.

OTHER PUBLICATIONS

Novels

Miss Melville Regrets: A Novel. New York, Fine, and London, Collins, 1987.
Miss Melville Returns: A Novel. New York, Fine, and London, Collins, 1988.
Miss Melville's Revenge: A Novel. New York, Fine, 1989.

Miss Melville Rides a Tiger. New York, Fine, 1991; London, HarperCollins, 1992.
Miss Melville Runs for Cover. New York, Fine, 1993.

Novels as Delphine C. Lyons

Flower of Evil. New York, Pyramid, 1965.
House of Four Widows. New York, Lancer, 1965.
The Depths of Yesterday. New York, Lancer, 1966.
Valley of Shadows. New York, Lancer, 1968.
Phantom at Lost Lake. New York, Prestige, 1970.

Other as Delphine C. Lyons

The Armchair Shopper's Guide: Mail Order Bargains around the World. New York, Essandess, 1968.
The Whole World Catalog. New York, Quadrangle, 1973.

* * *

Although Evelyn E. Smith's individual works of SF vary greatly in style, mood, and focus, it is possible to characterize her work as making a wry statement about human nature. Here is an author who is optimistic in spite of herself; even in those works which focus on postnuclear-holocaust worlds, humanity has survived and—whether or not its representatives are honorable or otherwise admirable—they do possess the ability to meet wild challenges and to survive their own foibles.

Smith's comments on human nature range from sharp and ironical to light and ludicrous. Her "The Last of the Spode" is a terse portrayal of three Britishers who, by a twist of fate, seem to be the sole survivors of nuclear holocaust. A "correct" professor and a young chap join a figure of British womanhood in an afternoon tea at the end of the world. As the Spode teapot is poured out, they reveal their chief concern as to whether or not their tea supply will last them to the end of their days. "No point in anything, really," the young chap remarks. "We must face the facts, lad," the professor says and then adds, in a gem of understatement, "pity about the Bodleian, though." "The Hardest Bargain" envisions another postholocaust future, in which the American populace is weakened with hunger and racial debility. Presidential advisor Dr. Livingston, who believes that "the thinking man is the despairing man," urges President Buchbinder to accept extraterrestrial aid in decontaminating the lands, but when the earthlings fail to keep their bargain to pay the extraterrestrial Foma in famous works of art, the Foma reveals his true identity as a pied piper to the robots which are so desperately needed by human society. "Not Fit for Children" is representative of Smith's more lighthearted stories. Here a group of alien children pose as war-dancing "natives" on an asteroid-like spaceship which is visited regularly by human tourists. In payment for their antics, the children receive coins that are melted down by their disbelieving elders into metal needed to repair their spaceship.

Most of Smith's short stories appeared during the 1950s; just as they varied in seriousness of theme as well as sophistication of writing technique, her novels represent the extremes of the author's abilities. *The Perfect Planet* shares the wry ironic tone of so many of her shorter works, as the author tells an amusing but insubstantial tale of two astronauts, one male and one female, who land on a planet populated by vain health enthusiasts who foist their obsession with slim, perfect physiques upon the slightly pudgy, space-weary duo. While the book does have some impact as a critique of mindless conformity, sadly the astronauts, who start out as rebellious to the ways of this world, come to have a fondness for the pampered inhabitants of "the perfumed planet." The initially gutsy female astronaut Moodie comes to value herself as an alluring female using charm, artifice, and cosmetics to enhance her self-worth while the captain learns to be protective of his changed space partner. *Unpopular Planet* is also preoccupied with questions of sexual identity. While it, too, features some portrayals of women which would not please feminists—the hero's partner is a female who is fully mature sexually although mentally and chronologically she is but three years old—such characterization is used with more sophisticated satirical purpose. An aspiring musician, Nicholas Piggot, careens perplexedly yet enthusiastically through a series of picaresque adventures observed by blue dragons. They turn out not to be the result of drunken fancy but to be "real" beings from another dimension who have a particular genetic purpose in store for the hero, who rises from life as an unknown in subterranean Manhattan to become father of a new future.

—Rosemary Herbert

SMITH, George H(enry)

Also writes as George Henry Smith. **Other Pseudonyms:** M.J. Deer; Jan Hudson; Jerry Jason; Clancy O'Brien; Hal Stryker; Diana Summers. **Nationality:** American. **Born:** Vicksburg, Mississippi, 27 October 1922. **Education:** University of Southern California, Los Angeles, B.A. 1950. **Military Service:** Served in the United States Navy, 1942-45. **Family:** Married M. Jane Deer in 1950. **Career:** Since 1950, freelance writer. **Address:** 4113 West 180th Street, Torrance, California 90504, U.S.A.

SCIENCE FICTION PUBLICATIONS

Novels (series: Annwn)

Satan's Daughter. Los Angeles, Epic, 1961.
1976: The Year of Terror. Los Angeles, Epic, 1961; as *The Year for Love,* Los Angeles, Moonlight, 1965.
Scourge of the Blood Cult (Annwn). Los Angeles, Epic, 1961.
The Coming of the Rats. Van Nuys, California, Pike, 1961; London, Digit, 1964.
Doomsday Wing. Derby, Connecticut, Monarch, 1963.
A Place Named Hell (as M.J. Deer, with M. Jane Deer Smith). Hollywood, France, 1963.
Flames of Desire (as M.J. Deer, with M. Jane Deer Smith). Hollywood, France, 1963.
Sexodus (as Jerry Jason). Hollywood, Boudoir, 1963.
The Unending Night. Derby, Connecticut, Monarch, 1964.
The Forgotten Planet (as George Henry Smith). New York, Avalon, 1965.
The Psycho Makers (as Jerry Jason). New York, Tempo, 1965.
The Four Day Weekend (as George Henry Smith). New York, Belmont, 1966.
Druids' World (Annwn; as George Henry Smith). New York, Avalon, 1967.
Kar Kaballa (Annwn). New York, Ace, 1969.

Witch Queen of Lochlann (Annwn). New York, Signet, 1969; London, Hale, 1981.
The Second War of the Worlds (Annwn). New York, DAW, 1976.
The Island Snatchers (Annwn). New York, DAW, 1978.
NYPD 2025 (as Hal Stryker). New York, Pinnacle, 1985.

OTHER PUBLICATIONS

Novels

The Devil's Breed. Chicago, Playboy Press, 1979.
The Rogues. Chicago, Playboy Press, 1980.
The Firebrands. Chicago, Playboy Press, 1980.
A Rebel's Pleasure. New York, Dell, 1986.

Novels as Diana Summers

Wild Is the Heart. Chicago, Playboy Press, 1978.
Love's Wicked Ways. Chicago, Playboy Press, 1978.
Fallen Angel. Chicago, Playboy Press, 1981.
Louisiana. New York, Dell, 1984.
The Emperor's Lady. New York, Charter, 1984.

Other

Who Is Ronald Reagan? New York, Pyramid, 1968.
Martin Luther King, Jr. New York, Lancer, 1971.

Other as Jan Hudson

Hell's Angels. San Diego, Greenleaf, 1965; London, New English Library, 1967; as *The New Barbarians,* New English Library, 1973.
The People in the Saucers. San Diego, Greenleaf, 1967.
Bikers at War. London, New English Library, 1976.

*

George H. Smith comments:

(1981) Science fiction was my first love in writing, and I've done it off and on for the last 25 years. Five of my novels are set in the imaginary Celtic otherworld called Annwn. I am currently committed to a series of historical novels so it will be some time before I get back to science fiction, but when I do I hope to continue the Annwn series.

*   *   *

The career of George H. Smith as a writer of science fiction is a peculiar one. Since most of his early novels were written for small paperback houses specializing in lurid action and violent sex, there is a certain crudity about them that masks his positive values as a writer. It was not until the 1970s that Smith began to sell novels to the more prestigious paperback houses, and the quality of his novels seems to have improved proportionately.

The early novels made use of a standard set of characters. The typical male protagonist was an indecisive man who had some insight into the future and realized that a significant change was coming to the world, but who was unable to communicate this to those around him. Typically, he spends the first half of each novel infatuated with a woman obviously unsuited for him, gradually awakening to the fact that some third character is actually the person with whom he wishes to spend his life. This is the pattern of *The Coming of the Rats,* for example; the hero finally convinces his totally impractical girlfriend to accompany him to a remote cave as nuclear war hovers just over the horizon. In the aftermath, the rats of the title challenge man for supremacy with predictable results. The pattern repeats itself in *Doomsday Wing,* also about a nuclear war, this time threatening to extinguish all life on Earth, and *The Unending Night,* wherein runaway nuclear reactors knock Mars out of its orbit, and threaten to pull our own planet away from the warmth of the sun. In the former, the dedicated military man cannot convince his ambitious wife of the importance of serving his country, and in the latter a hyper-liberated woman is convinced that the best thing that can happen to the human race is for it to descend to a primitive culture. The scientist hero of the latter is thoroughly enamored of her until she proves insane. This basic arrangement of characters also appears in *The Four Day Weekend,* involving a plot by secret aliens to take over the world by reprogramming the computers that direct our motor vehicles. Although there is some amusing satire here, it is rather silly most of the time, possibly the worst of Smith's novels.

Surprisingly enough, one of his better novels was published by a softcore pornography publisher. *1976: The Year of Terror* is set in a future America in which the Libertarian Party has seized power by assassination and clever plotting by the head of the Federal Security Police. Opposed to him is a secret agent intent on finding the missing vice-president and restoring democratic rule to the country. This anticipates a number of thrillers along similar lines, and is fairly wellwritten.

Somewhere along the line, Smith became interested in mythology and druidism. It crops up first in *Druids' World,* a fairly dull novel, then to much better effect in *Witch Queen of Lochlann,* written in the mode of the stories made famous by *Unknown* magazine. Duffus January is a magician of sorts who undertakes to restore the rightful queen to the throne of Lochlann, a Welsh alternate world where magic works. A low-key sword-and-sorcery tale, this seems to have set the stage for a major series of novels. *Kar Kaballa* is named for the king of the Gogs, a barbaric nation of nomads whose existence is barely noted by their neighbors, the civilized inhabitants of Avalon, a nation comparable to 19th-century England in our universe. Dylan MacBride, a young adventurer, is convinced that the imminent freezing of the channel between Avalon and the northern regions will result in a massive invasion, but he is unable to convince anyone in authority of the seriousness of the threat. Despondent, he seems doomed to failure when he encounters a man from our own universe who plans to sell Gatling guns to the alternate world. Smith went on to chronicle the Martian invasion of his alternate world in *The Second War of the Worlds,* an entertaining novel throughout, and a magical plot to destroy civilization in *The Island Snatchers,* the weakest in the series. These latter books are far better than his earlier efforts, with more complex characters, a quieter and more careful style, and more significant care taken in establishing settings, mood, and suspense.

Smith seems to have abandoned the field of science fiction since the late 1970s; his only novel in recent years is *NYPD 2025,* written under the pseudonym Hal Stryker. This fast-paced story of an android policeman battling heavily armed criminals in the not-too-distant future was supposed to be a continuing series, cut short when the publisher went out of business. It should also be noted that although his shorter fiction is generally unmemorable, he wrote one interesting tale at that length. "In the Imagicon" (in *Nebula Award Stories 2,* edited by Brian Aldiss and Harry Harrison, New York, Doubleday, and London, Gollancz, 1987) is set in a future where a machine allows people to create a mental world of their own choosing.

—Don D'Ammassa

SMITH, George O(liver)

Nationality: American. **Born:** Chicago, Illinois, 9 April 1911. **Education:** University of Chicago, 1929-30. **Military Service:** Served as an editorial engineer, National Defense Research Council, 1944-45. **Family:** Married 1) Helen Kunzler in 1936 (divorced 1948), one daughter and one son; 2) Dona Louise Stebbins in 1949 (died 1974), one son. **Career:** Radio Serviceman, Chicago, 1932-35; radio engineer: General Household, 1935-38, Wells-Gardiner, 1938-40, Philco, 1940-42, 1946-51, Crosley, 1942-44; manager, Emerson Radio components engineering, 1951-57; analyst, ITT Defense Communications, 1959-74. Reviewer, *Space Science Fiction.* **Died:** 27 May 1981.

Science Fiction Publications

Novels

Pattern for Conquest: An Interplanetary Adventure. New York, Gnome Press, 1949; London, Clerke and Cockeran, 1951.
Nomad. Philadelphia, Prime Press, 1950.
Operation Interstellar. Chicago, Merit, 1950.
Hellflower: A Science-Fiction Novel. New York, Abelard Press, 1953; London, Lane, 1955.
Highways in Hiding. New York, Gnome Press, 1956; abridged edition, as *The Space Plague,* New York, Avon, 1957.
Troubled Star. New York, Avalon, 1957.
Fire in the Heavens. New York, Avalon, 1958.
The Path of Unreason. Hicksville, New York, Gnome Press, 1958.
Lost in Space. New York, Avalon, 1959.
The Fourth "R." New York, Ballantine, 1959; as *The Brain Machine,* New York, Lancer, 1968.

Short Stories

Venus Equilateral. Philadelphia, Prime Press, 1947; enlarged edition, London, Orbit, 2 vols., 1975; as *The Complete Venus Equilateral,* New York, Ballantine, 1976.
The Worlds of George O. Smith. New York, Bantam, 1982.

Other Publications

Other

Mathematics, The Language of Science (for children). New York, Putnam, 1961.
Scientists' Nightmares. New York, Putnam, 1972.

* * *

Since the passing of the days when space opera was the leading wave of science fiction, George O. Smith has steadily declined in importance within the field, and in fact it would presently be difficult to find any of his work in print. That's an unfortunate development because some of his novels were not part of that narrowly defined subgenre, and at least two of them are worthy of greater attention.

Smith's best known work from this period is the series of "Venus Equilateral" stories, involving a space station set in a stable orbit with respect to the planet Venus. In episodes such as "QRM Interplanetary" and "Beam Pirate," the crew are forced to solve various technical problems involving their habitat. These were early examples of the engineering puzzle story that became a staple in *Astounding* magazine, strong on scientific content, but short on plot and characterization. It is unfortunate that these comparatively minor works are the ones for which Smith is most likely to be remembered.

Several space opera novels from this period have disappeared entirely, and deservedly so. *Operation Interstellar* is a routine story of interstellar warfare. A three-sided war between Earth, Mars, and invaders from outside the solar system takes center stage in *Nomad,* and the human race is conquered by aliens in *Pattern of Conquest,* only to undermine their alien rulers from within. Somewhat more interesting works along these same lines are *Troubled Star,* about a mediocre actor who encounters a race of genuine aliens whose plans for the solar system will destroy the human race, and *Path of Unreason,* a complex scientific mystery story.

As science fiction readers grew more sophisticated, writers like Smith were forced to adapt. During the latter part of the 1950s, Smith produced better thought out and plotted novels, although for the most part they were still set against the backdrop of interstellar conflict. *Hellflower* follows the adventures of a discredited space pilot who was the only survivor when he crashlanded on Venus. Sentenced to work as virtual slave labor in the jungles of that world, he discovers the secret of a potent new drug and infiltrates a ring of drug peddlers in order to escape imprisonment, uncovering the secret of the sabotage that got him into trouble. *Lost in Space* (magazine title *Spacemen Lost*) is an unambitious, awkwardly written but occasionally entertaining story of the search for a lifeboat cast off by a distress starship, a search that is secretly being monitored by a fleet of alien warships considering an attack against the human race. The sun threatens to explode in *Fire in the Heavens* and a scientist and a business tycoon have to team up to save the human race. *Fire* is an implausible story, of interest primarily because it was one of the few space operas of the period to feature a strong female protagonist, although the characterizations are awkward and inconsistent.

One of Smith's two best novels is *Highways in Hiding* (published in a slightly different and shorter version as *Space Plague*). An extraterrestrial plague is being spread across the Earth, one that causes its victims to develop a layer of calluses that completely covers their bodies. Steve Cornell is searching for his missing girlfriend when he stumbles across the parties responsible for the plague, as well as a secret society of evolved humans with powers even beyond the telepathy that has already become an accepted part of human civilization. An ambitious, and occasionally confused potboiler, but of far more interest than any of Smith's other novels except for *The Fourth "R."*

The Fourth "R" (also published as *The Brain Machine*) is without question Smith's most polished and interesting novel. Jimmy Holden is a young boy whose intelligence has been heightened through the use of an experimental machine. When his parents are murdered by people who want to control the boy for their own purposes, he escapes and uses his superior intellect to survive in the world through a series of clever devices designed to disguise the fact that a five-year-old is living without a guardian. Holden is an interesting, appealing individual with a much greater depth than any of Smith's other characters, and his escapades are logical, suspenseful, and frequently clever. Out of print for 15 years, this remains one of the best novels about "supermen" that has ever been published in the genre.

Smith's short fiction is also of occasional interest. "Meddler's Moon" is an amusing variant of the time travel paradox story. "Understanding" involves an interstellar manhunt and has been published with two different endings. "The Big Fix" examines the effect of extrasensory powers on gambling at the horse races. Other stories of note include "Rat Race," "History Repeats," and "The Planet Mender." George O. Smith was a comparatively minor player even at the height of his popularity, and it is unlikely that his writings will ever undergo any resurgence of popularity. It would be unfortunate if this meant that his occasional works of merit would sink from sight completely.

—Don D'Ammassa

SMITH, Thorne

Nationality: American. **Born:** 1893. **Died:** 1934.

Science Fiction Publications

Novels (series: Topper)

Topper: An Improbable Adventure. New York, McBride, and London, Holden, 1926; as *The Jovial Ghosts: The Misadventures of Topper,* London, Barker, 1933.
The Stray Lamb. New York, Cosmopolitan, 1929; London, Heinemann, 1930.
The Night Life of the Gods. Garden City, New York, Doubleday, 1931; London, Barker, 1934.
Turnabout. Garden City, New York, Doubleday, 1931; London, Barker, 1933.
Topper Takes a Trip. Garden City, New York, Doubleday, 1932; London, Barker, 1935.
Skin and Bones. Garden City, New York, Doubleday, 1933; London, Barker, 1936.
Rain in the Doorway. Garden City, New York, Doubleday, 1933; London, Barker, 1936.
The Glorious Pool. Garden City, New York, Doubleday, 1934; London, Barker, 1935.
The Thorne Smith 3-Decker (includes *The Stray Lamb, Turnabout,* and *Rain in the Doorway*). Garden City, New York, Doubleday, 1936.
The Thorne Smith Triplets (includes *Topper Takes a Trip, The Night Life of the Gods,* and *The Bishop's Jaegers*). Garden City, New York, Doubleday, 1936.
The Passionate Witch (completed by Norman Matson). Garden City, New York, Doubleday, 1941; London, Barker, 1942.

The Thorne Smith Three-Bagger: The Glorious Pool; Skin and Bones; Topper. Garden City, New York, Doubleday, 1943.

OTHER PUBLICATIONS

Novels

Dream's End. New York, McBride, 1927; London, Jarrolds, 1928.
Did She Fall? New York, Cosmopolitan, 1930; London, Barker, 1936.
The Bishop's Jaegers. Garden City, New York, Doubleday, 1932; London, Barker, 1934.

Other

Lazy Bear Lane. Garden City, New York, Doubleday, 1931.
Thorne Smith: His Life and Times, with Roland Young and others. Garden City, New York, Doubleday, 1934.

*   *   *

There is a scene in *Free Live Free* by Gene Wolfe set in a lunatic asylum in which a doctor and a visitor talk to each other at cross-purposes the whole time. It was an homage to Thorne Smith, amplified even further by Wolfe's *There Are Doors,* a book that echoes in many ways Thorne Smith's *Rain in the Doorway.*

Thorne Smith was one of the finest of all American comic writers who reacted to the puritanism of America between the wars with a series of outrageous novels in which the whole purpose of life was shown to revolve around sex and alcohol. In a typical Thorne Smith novel an unhappy middle-aged man learns how to escape the imprisonment of a shrewish wife or a dull job by some miracle that introduces him to the pleasures of loose women and booze.

In several of his stories the fantastic element is limited to one instance of almost wish-fulfilment magic that sets up the misadventures to follow. The pool in *The Glorious Pool,* for instance, exists simply to transform Rex Pebble and his middle-aged mistress Spray Summers into youths again, while *The Night Life of the Gods* endows its hero, Hunter Hawk, with the ability to transform statues into living people mostly to allow the spree with Bacchus and Venus, which personify the twin elements of his vision of personal liberty.

However, where the needs of the story dictate, Smith could be quite rigorous in his working out of the effects of his miracle. What's more, much of his work sits squarely within the tradition of fantastic literature. *Skin and Bones,* perhaps the most science fictional of his books, is a comic counterpoint to *The Invisible Man.* Quintus Bland is experimenting to discover a fluoroscopic camera film but the result renders him invisible save for his skeleton, and it is this near-invisibility that is the key to the story. Using Bland's inability to control the transformations, Smith creates some hilarious set pieces, as when a barber unwinds the hot towels from around his customer's face to reveal a grinning skull, or as Bland is introduced to the pleasures of a brothel.

In *Turnabout,* on the other hand, Smith tapped into a theme that had already been used to humorous effect in F. Anstey's *Vice Versa,* and that was to surface again only a few years later in the work of another humourist, *Laughing Gas* by P.G. Wodehouse. However, in Smith's book the two souls that are swapped are not man and boy, but man and woman. Inevitably, this is an excuse for much sexual innuendo and byplay, though it also allows Smith to make fun of each sex's narrow-minded disregard of the other. Thus when Sally and Tim first face each other in their new bodies, there is the following exchange:

"You leave that man alone," cried Sally furiously. "Keep your hands off him and be careful what you do with my body. First thing you know you'll be presenting me with a nameless child. I could never bear that."

"You won't have to bear it," he said slowly. "I'd have to bear it. Wouldn't that be awful?"

This exchange is typical of Smith's comic practice in that it turns upon a pun, though more usually the puns and misunderstandings were used to develop conversations in which both participants fail entirely to interpret the other person aright. Such a technique was used to excellent effect, for instance, in *Rain in the Doorway,* in which the put-upon hero escapes the rain by going through a door that takes him into another world, a ludicrously run department store of which he finds himself to be one of the partners. Of course in this world there is a liberality of attitude on many things, but particularly sex and drink, which means that by the time Mr. Hector Owen returns to his own world, he has acquired the skills he needs to escape the more transcendent greyness of his life of which the initial rain is no more than a symbol.

Smith's skills are limited: his male characters are either dull people who need to learn how to have fun or else expansive adventurers who have already learned the lessons of booze and sex; his females are either domineering and shrewish, or else jolly, sexy, and eager to initiate the hero into the pleasures of the world. His view of life was limited also; in the post-World War I America of prohibition and puritanism in which he wrote, he only saw the one route by which to transform and fulfill the lives of his characters. Nevertheless, he had a unique gift for comedy, especially for comic dialogue, and at their best his books are excellent examples of their type. Most typical, perhaps, is his best-known work, *The Jovial Ghosts,* which was filmed as *Topper* and launched a series of popular films in the 1930s. Cosmo Topper begins the book as a repressed, upright member of staid society, but by the time the ghosts of George and Marion Kerby have introduced him, willing or no, to a host of activities that Topper regards as sinful, his repression has cracked and he is no longer able to sustain the old staidness. It is a straightforward, undemanding novel, hardly shocking though it must have seemed so at the time it was written, but like so much of Smith's work it is very funny.

—Paul Kincaid

SOHL, Jerry

Pseudonyms: Nathan Butler; Roberta Jean Mountjoy; Sean Mei Sullivan. **Nationality:** American. **Born:** Gerald Allan Sohl, Los Angeles, California, 2 December 1913. **Education:** Attended Central College, Chicago, 1933-34. **Military Service:** Served in the United States Army Air Force, 1942-45: Sergeant. **Family:** Married Jean Gordon in 1942; one son and two daughters. **Career:** Reporter, telegraph editor, photographer, and feature writer,

Bloomington Daily Pantagraph, Illinois, 1945-58. Since 1958, freelance writer: staff writer for *Star Trek, Alfred Hitchcock Presents,* and *The New Breed;* also concert pianist. **Agent:** Joseph Elder Agency, 150 West 87th Street, New York, New York 10024, U.S.A. **Address:** P.O. Box 1336, Thousand Oaks, California 91360, U.S.A.

SCIENCE FICTION PUBLICATIONS

Novels

The Haploids. New York, Rinehart, 1952.
Costigan's Needle. New York, Rinehart, 1953; London, Grayson, 1955.
The Transcendent Man. New York, Rinehart, 1953.
The Altered Ego. New York, Rinehart, 1954.
Point Ultimate. New York, Rinehart, 1955.
The Mars Monopoly. New York, Ace, 1956; London, Satellite, 1958.
The Time Dissolver. New York, Avon, 1957; London, Sphere, 1967.
The Odious Ones. New York, Rinehart, 1959; London, Consul, 1961.
One against Herculum. New York, Ace, 1959.
Night Slaves. Greenwich, Connecticut, Fawcett, 1965.
The Anomaly. New York, Curtis, 1971.
I, Aleppo. Toronto, Laser, 1976.
Kaheesh (as Nathan Butler). New York, Fawcett, 1983.
Death Sleep. New York, Fawcett, 1983.

OTHER PUBLICATIONS

Novels

Prelude to Peril. New York, Rinehart, 1957.
The Lemon Eaters: A Novel. New York, Simon and Schuster, and London, Cassell, 1967.
The Spun Sugar Hole. New York, Simon and Schuster, 1971.
The Resurrection of Frank Borchard. New York, Simon and Schuster, 1973.
Supermanchu, Master of Kung Fu (as Sean Mei Sullivan). New York, Ballantine, 1974.
Night Wind (as Roberta Jean Mountjoy). New York, Coward McCann, 1981.
Black Thunder (as Roberta Jean Mountjoy). New York, Berkley, 1983.

Novels as Nathan Butler

Dr. Josh. Greenwich, Connecticut, Fawcett, 1973.
Mamelle. Greenwich, Connecticut, Fawcett, 1974.
Blow-Dry. Greenwich, Connecticut, Fawcett, 1976.
Mamelle, The Goddess. Greenwich, Connecticut, Fawcett, 1977.

Plays

Screenplays: *Twelve Hours to Kill,* 1960; Monster of Terror (*Die Monster, Die!*), 1965; *Frankenstein Conquers the World,* with Kaoru Mabuchi and Reuben Bercovitch, 1966.

Television Plays: *The Corbomite Maneuver (Star Trek* series), 1966; *Night Slaves,* from his own novel, 1970; and episodes for *Naked City, Route 66, M-Squad, G.E. Theater, Markham, Border Patrol, The Twilight Zone, The Invaders, The Outer Limits, Target: The Corrupters, Man from Atlantis,* and *The Next Step Beyond* series.

Other

Underhanded Chess: A Hilarious Handbook of Devious Diversions and Stratagems for Winning at Chess. New York, Hawthorn, 1973.
Underhanded Bridge: A Hilarious Handbook of Devious Diversions and Stratagems for Winning at Bridge. New York, Hawthorn, 1975.

*

Manuscript Collection: University of Wyoming, Laramie.

Jerry Sohl comments:

The corpus of my science fiction work reflects, I believe, rather accurately what was fashionable in the genre from 1950 to 1970, moving from gimmick as story to people as story. Although superior to what it was prior to 1970, today's science fiction is often too abstruse to be understood.

While I continue to write science fiction now and then, my interest has shifted to mainstream and I am at the moment at work on a super-suspense novel entitled *The Pacem Complex* as well as novels I can only describe as avant-garde, one entitled *Mortal Coils* and the other *The Gold Triskelion.*

*   *   *

Like many fans-turned-writers, Jerry Sohl reveals an appreciative understanding of the surface structures of science fiction narratives but often fails at deeper levels of conceptualization and extrapolation. Although Sohl has contributed little of originality to the genre, he is in many ways a representative popular writer of the 1950s, skilled in generating an initial sense of mystery and wonder, but often confusing or even absurd in his resolutions.

Most of his novels and stories deal with familiar science fiction themes. *The Transcendent Man,* for example, borrows a premise from Charles Fort via earlier treatments by Eric Frank Russell, L. Ron Hubbard, and others: the idea that humanity's intelligence and civilization are the creations of a vastly superior race of invisible aliens who feed off the emotional energy generated by catastrophes such as war and plagues. Although these aliens, called the Capellans in this novel, might serve as an interesting metaphor for the paradoxical quality in human nature that somehow accounts for both creative and destructive impulses, Sohl develops the story into little more than an adventure narrative concerning one supernormal human who discovers the alien secret and, in the end, singlehandedly takes on the task of maintaining civilization. *Point Ultimate,* Sohl's contribution to the literature of dystopia, concerns a world conquered by communists who seem to come right out of the nightmares of Joe McCarthy, and quickly descends into a welter of germ warfare, gypsies, underground railways, and secret Martian colonies. *The Altered Ego* involves the somewhat more intriguing notion of a society that has learned how to resurrect important citizens after death, but soon becomes a familiar tale of chases and conspiracies.

Sohl's more successful novels are those in which the science fiction element is kept fairly simple or relegated to the background. *The Time Dissolver* is an intriguing amnesia mystery for most of its length, with the protagonist and his wife awaking one morning to find that their memories from 1946 to 1957 have disappeared— and that, consequently, they do not even know each other. The carefully wrought details of the investigation into the missing years of their lives provide a suspenseful narrative, and the rather weak explanation concerning a memory-dissolving machine does not interfere greatly with the overall impact of the novel. *Costigan's Needle,* an exploration of the parallel-universe theme, is perhaps Sohl's best novel: an account of a group of people who pass into a parallel world through a needle-shaped machine invented by a Chicago scientist, only to find themselves trapped in the other world and forced to spend years redesigning the technology that will enable them to build another machine (which, it turns out, will only enable them to enter another of an apparently infinite series of parallel worlds). Understandably, the people choose not to abandon this new world that they have created with their own hands. Although the characters in the novel are a familiar assortment of popular fiction stereotypes, the exploration of the problems inherent in trying to recreate a sophisticated technology from raw materials is wellhandled.

Sohl has had relatively little influence on the genre, although one of his novels, *Night Slaves*—concerning a community dominated by alien visitors—provided the basis for a television movie. A writer with undeniable skill in constructing suspenseful situations, and one who enjoyed some popularity during the 1950s, his works in retrospect seem weakened by inadequate conceptualization of the scientific and social ideas he dealt has with.

—Gary K. Wolfe

———

SOMTOW, S.P. *See* **SUCHARITKUL, Somtow.**

———

SOUKUP, Martha (Clare)

Nationality: American. **Born:** Aurora, Illinois, 20 July 1959. **Education:** DePaul University, Chicago, Illinois, B.A. in communications 1980; Clarion Science Fiction Writers Workshop, 1985. **Family:** Married Michael R. Walsh in 1983 (separated). **Career:** Assistant editor, *Chain Report* newsletter, Chicago, Illinois, 1981; managing editor, *Restaurants & Chains Managing & Marketing* newsletter, 1981-82; assistant sysop, Science Fiction RoundTable, GEnie, 1988-93 (part-time); chief sysop, Science Fiction Round Table 1, Genie, 1993-94 (full-time). **Awards:** Nebula award, 1995. **Agent:** Jonathan Matson, Harold Matson Agency, Inc., 276 Fifth Ave., New York, New York 10001 (film rights only). **Address:** P.O. Box 40016, San Francisco, California 94140, U.S.A.

SCIENCE FICTION PUBLICATIONS

Short Stories

Rosemary's Brain and Other Tales of Wonder. Newark, New Jersey, Wildside, 1992.

*

Critical Study: "Five Stories by Martha Soukup" by Ray Davis, *New York Review of Science Fiction,* August 1993.

Martha Soukup comments:

When I was a kid, reading everything, it seemed to me that fiction was the biggest conversation about life going on out there.

When I was an adolescent, reading all the SF I could get my hands on—my library luckily had good supplies of *Universe, Orbit,* the two *Dangerous Visions* books, *New Dimensions,* and many lovely single-author collections—it seemed to me that there was no more flexible and powerful form in which to discuss life than science fiction. And, specifically, short science fiction.

I think I know less about writing the more I turn my hand to it, but I haven't changed my mind about those notions. Fiction is, perhaps among other things, a way to practice various ideas about the universe, about being alive in it. About being a person. People. Storytelling is a very human thing.

Being able to write means being able to speak in, as well as listen to, that huge conversation. Just in a corner of it, maybe, and it doesn't mean that (as I thought all writers were, when I was eight) that I've become wise.

But the conversation's interesting, and maybe we'll all learn little unexpected things. Even if it's just the way the same thing looks different to someone else. Could be.

Mostly, while I like listening, I'm not very good at shutting up and just listening. The only way I can test my own thoughts is to say them, and the best way I know to say things is in short stories. They're still my favorite laboratory.

*   *   *

It's almost a fact of life that a writer can only be recognized as a significant factor in science fiction by producing novels, even if the best portion of that writer's work is at shorter length. Only a handful of writers like Ray Bradbury and Harlan Ellison have been able to build enviable reputations exclusively from short stories. One of several recent writers who seem capable of challenging this truism is Martha Soukup, who has already acquired an enviable reputation for her strongly delineated protagonists.

"Frenchmen and Plumbers" is a first contact story, of sorts. Earth is a polluted nightmare, a planet on the verge of global death. Aliens arrive, possessing technology so far beyond ours that they could mend the world's ecological ills almost without trying, but they turn out to be impractical artists who make the failing patient more attractive, but do nothing about its fate. "Master of the Game" warns us of what can happen if you annoy a biogeneticist. The suave but self-centered playboy protagonist is trapped into a loveless life when she redesigns his pheromones to make it impossible for him to have a lasting relationship with a woman. "Plowshare" is an alternate history story in which William Jennings Bryan won the Presidency after all, a touching story told from the point of view of his First Lady.

"Things Not Seen" is a scientific murder mystery. A prominent scientist has been killed in the presence of a sophisticated robot that claims not to have seen anything. A programmer is called in to figure out what malfunction has caused this oversight, and discovers that there is a plot concealed within the plot. "Dress Rehearsal" is a disturbing story about two actors of the future, who manipulate and identify with artificial bodies on the stage, allowing one of them to impersonate a woman, and the rather odd affect this has on their relationship. Two children are kidnapped by a flying saucer in "Fine or Superfine" and deal with their fears in very different ways.

One of her best stories to date is "The Story So Far," the protagonist of which is aware of the fact that she is the minor character in a story about the man she marries, whose life exists only in snatches of scenes. From another character she learns the secret of stealing short times of her own when she can continue to be self-aware despite the altered focus of the plot. Even more impressive is "A Defense of the Social Contracts," another story of obsessive love. This time the protagonist is a young woman in a future society where love and sexual relationships are rigidly administered through the government. One can register as monogamous, nonmonogamous, or open to a new relationship, and this is a matter of public record, enforced by law as well as custom. When Anli falls in love with a nonmonogamous man who has no intention of confining his attentions to a single woman, she subverts the rules of her society to trap him into a situation totally at odds with her nature, almost destroying them both. Although she is ostensibly the villain of the piece, the story's point isn't that simple, because her madness is an indictment of her culture's attempt to reduce interpersonal relationship to a rational process than can be codified and predicted.

Many of her stories are outright fantasy. "Having Keith" features a disturbed young woman who discovers that she can project her awareness into the bodies of others. She becomes infatuated with Keith, who loves another, takes control of his lover's body only to discover that he could never really love her, so she ends up in possession of his body instead. "The Big Wish" explores a somewhat similar theme. The central character believes that everyone is allowed one wish during their lifetime, but that most people waste it on something trivial before they're old enough to know better. As an adult, she is torn between two men and wishes that somehow she could share both their lives, and ends up with two coexisting bodies. Alas, neither version of herself is happy with her choice. "The Spinner" is a fairy tale for adults, a woman with the ability to spin anything who weaves a web that binds the man she loves.

Other stories of note include "The Arbitrary Placement of Walls," a psychological ghost story and "Fuzz." "Last Wish," one of the most cleverly done variants of the deal with the devil or, in this case a genie plot. Soukup's career is off to a promising start. Despite a comparatively small body of published fiction, she has already attracted a following. Her greatest strength is in her characterization, particularly in regard to the power of emotion to overcome reason and inhibition. She seems equally at home in science fiction and fantasy, and uses a strong, confident style to support her stories. Her penetrating insight into the convolutions of the human mind promise further excellent tales.

—Don D'Ammassa

SPINRAD, Norman (Richard)

Nationality: American. **Born:** New York City, 15 September 1940. **Education:** City College of the City University of New York, B.S. 1961. **Family:** Married Nancy Lee Wood. **Career:** Since 1963, full-time writer. **Member:** President, Science Fiction Writers of America, 1980-81; president, World SF, 1988-90. **Awards:** Prix Apollo, 1974; Jupiter award, 1975. **Agent:** Jane Rosen Agency, 318 West 51 St., New York, New York 10022, U.S.A. **Address:** 1 Rue Maitre Albert, Paris 75005, France. **Online Address:** 100410,603@compuserve.com.

SCIENCE FICTION PUBLICATIONS

Novels

The Solarians. New York, Paperback Library, 1966; London, Sphere, 1979.
Agent of Chaos. New York, Belmont, 1967; London; Corgi, 1981.
The Men in the Jungle. Garden City, New York, Doubleday, 1967; London, Sphere, 1972.
Bug Jack Barron. New York, Walker, 1969; London, Macdonald, 1970.
The Iron Dream. New York, Avon, 1972; London, Panther, 1974.
Riding the Torch. New York, Bluejay, 1978.
A World Between. New York, Pocket Books, 1979; London, Arrow, 1980.
Songs from the Stars. New York, Simon and Schuster, 1980; London, Sidgwick and Jackson, 1981.
The Void Captain's Tale. New York, Timescape, 1983; London, Panther, 1984.
Child of Fortune. New York, Bantam, 1985.
Little Heroes. New York, Bantam, 1987; London, Grafton, 1989.
Russian Spring. New York, Bantam, 1991.
Deus X. New York, Bantam, 1992.

Short Stories

The Last Hurrah of the Golden Horde. Garden City, New York, Doubleday, 1970; London, Macdonald, 1971.
The Star-Spangled Future. New York, Ace, 1979.
Other Americas (four novellas). New York, Bantam, 1988.
Vampire Junkies. Brooklyn, New York, Gryphon, 1994.

OTHER PUBLICATIONS

Novels

Passing through the Flame. New York, Putnam, 1975.
The Mind Game. New York, Jove, 1980; as *The Process,* London, Arrow, 1983.
Children of Hamelin. Houston, Tafford Publishing, 1991.
Pictures at 11. New York, Bantam, 1994.

Plays

Television Plays: For *Star Trek* series.

Other

Fragments of America, edited by Roger Lovin. North Hollywood, California, Now Library Press, 1970.

The Reasons behind the SFWA Model Paperback Contract. N.p., Science Fiction Writers of America, 1978.

Staying Alive: A Writer's Guide. Norfolk, Virginia, Donning, 1983.

Science Fiction in the Real World (essays). Carbondale, Southern Illinois University Press, 1990.

Editor, *The New Tomorrows.* New York, Belmont, 1971.

Editor, *Modern Science Fiction.* Garden City, New York, Doubleday, 1974.

Editor, *No Direction Home: An Anthology of Science-Fiction Stories.* New York, Pocket Books, 1975; London, Millington, 1976.

*

Bibliography: *Le Livre d'Or de Norman Spinrad* by Patrice Duvic, Paris, Presses Pocket, n.d.

*   *   *

Fans of MTV and other media violence should read Norman Spinrad's 1969 story "The Big Flash." In that demented burlesque, the Pentagon wants to end "the war in Asia" quickly and victoriously, but is stymied by public opinion, which recoils from the use of tactical nukes. So the psy-warriors create a heavy-metal band, the "Four Horsemen," whose every song is a high-pitched plea, complete with war video montage and a subliminal "DO IT," for the orgasm of nuclear destruction. The media blitz is far too effective, however: it reaches the monitors of missile officers and triggers a strategic nuclear holocaust.

"The Big Flash" is like an embryo that enfolds the techniques and themes of Spinrad's later fictions: multiple viewpoints, media "mindfucking," the order/chaos dialectic, the sex-violence connection, the 1960s trinity of sex, drugs, and rock and roll, and affectionate parody of popular culture. As he makes clear in the essays of *Science Fiction in the Real World,* Spinrad regards the 1960s as a time of crucial cultural innovation, both in SF and in the larger world. Thus his imagined futures are ones in which representative characters work out the unfinished business of that formative era.

An example is fictional sociologist Gregor Markowitz, snippets of whose writings are found at the head of each chapter of *Agent of Chaos.* In Markowitz's paradoxical thermodynamics of culture and society, entropy or Chaos is the truly liberating and creative power of the universe, while the existing Order equates to sterility, repression, and simple boredom. The Order/Chaos dialectic (in which Chaos disrupts Order only to generate a new Order) is central to most of Spinrad's plots: action itself results from the irruption of wildcards or random factors.

In *Agent of Chaos,* the random factor is the secret Brotherhood of Assassins, custodians of a long-term plot to subvert the council that rules the solar System in peace and prosperity. In *Bug Jack Barron,* it is the interactive TV talk show host Jack Barron, who is at least superficially devoted to undermining the pretensions of the powerful. In *A World Between* the "order" of the human worlds is the Pink and Blue War, a struggle for dominance between radical lesbian Femocrats and male-chauvinist Transcendental Scientists; the random factor seems to be the utopian psychosexual balance on Pacifica, the planet over which the two sides are contending. In this novel Chaos is not mere disorder, but rather a dynamic equilibrium opposed to the stasis of domination by any one gender.

The doctrines of Gregor Markowitz also apply to the near-futuristic world of *Little Heroes.* Glorianna O'Toole, the Crazy Lady of Rock and Roll, is the wildcard who helps undermine the megacorporation that dominates popular music through demographic targeting, statistical analysis, and predictability. She does so by recovering the raw erotic power of rock's imagery and language. Order and Chaos contend for control through the mass media in other Spinrad fictions, where the electronic "web" or "net" is often the primary reality. In the story "Prime Time" people retire into a kind of suspended animation, "Total Television Heaven," in which they can re-view, participate in, and interact through over 100 channels of action-adventures, soaps, porn flicks, and old home movies. Unfortunately for the male viewpoint character, the "diversity" of this internal CATV system begins to pall, and his connection is broken. In *The Mind Game,* the Transformationalists (modeled upon the Scientology cult) use their media savvy to stop Jack Weller from exposing them, planting stories and images that quickly become quotidian reality. Using the electronic media to manipulate, to mystify, and to manufacture reality, is not for Spinrad a practice simply to denounce. The "web" is a fact of life: decrying its misuse will not make it go away. In any case, it has the potential to enhance the individual and enrich culture.

In *Songs from the Stars,* Sunshine Sue, leader of the Word of Mouth communications guild in postholocaust Aquaria, is willing to cooperate with the "Black Scientists" of Space Systems, Inc., because their secret space shuttle project might enable her to obtain use of the inactive Big Ear satellite and link the scattered remnants of humanity. The satellite itself might be solar-powered and thus only a "gray" technology, but to get to it Sue must compromise by depending on machines that burn hydrocarbons or use nuclear-generated electricity. The "clear blue Way" and "white science" of Aquaria are already compromised by reliance on infiltrated Spacer technology, so the prospective merger of white and black at the novel's end amounts to a recognition more than an alteration. In *Bug Jack Barron* the power of the TV celebrity and of electronic communication technology is ultimately used to expose the political corruption, racism and murders that underlie Benedict Howard's immortality technology. In *Little Heroes* the media corporation's own hardware and software are used to undermine its control. In *Deus X,* hacker Marley Philippe helps the Vatican determine whether expert systems, scanned in from the brains of living humans, are theological equivalents of the soul. Thus whether communications technology is benign or malign depends crucially upon the morality of its owners and users.

In most of his fiction, Spinrad avoids using the consistently omniscient or unitary limited narrator, and only rarely does he adopt the single first-person narrator. While most of his novels and stories do not shift viewpoint as frequently and as rapidly as "The Big Flash," Spinrad clearly suspects the single-consciousness narrator. (The major exceptions to this preference are all well motivated.) The restriction works particularly well in *Songs from the Stars,* where the two main viewpoint characters, Sunshine Sue and Clear Blue Lou, begin with different perspectives on the proper relationship of "Black Science" to the Aquarian Way. In the final chapter, by which time they have come to agree on how to handle the alien signals received at the space station, their viewpoints subtly merge, so that narrative technique reflects the developing relationship between the characters.

The viewpoint also shifts back and forth between Vanderling and Fraden in *The Men in the Jungle,* reflecting not only the physical distance between the two, but also the moral distance. In *Bug Jack*

Barron the multiple viewpoints perhaps reflect the split-screen technique used on Barron's TV interview show; if that reading is valid, it underlines one reason for careful separation of multiple viewpoints—the multiplexed array available through electronic media technology. Spinrad uses a similar effect in *Pictures at 11,* effectively undermining the moral claims of either side in a televised hostage crisis. And such is the explicit meaning of viewpoint switching in *Little Heroes,* a narrative in which individuals internalize the multiple viewpoint when they plug into alternate, though virtual, realities. As Spinrad puts it in *Science Fiction in the Real World,* commenting on John Shirley's *Eclipse,* "Electronic amplification and consciousness-altering drugs have *already* changed the parameters of the human sensorium, and altered, thereby, our perceptual and psychic definitions of what it means to be human."

Nostalgia for the 1960s counterculture is not politically correct in the post-Cold War era. Spinrad, however, has kept the faith, so to speak, though not sentimentally or uncritically. *Child of Fortune,* while formally a SF bildungsroman and thematically a meditation on the storyteller's art, is also a critical celebration of hippiedom. Moussa's escape from the lotus-eating life of the Bloomenkinder ("Flower Children") is a rejection of drug-induced nirvana, but not of all consciousness-enhancement. And the street life of the Gypsy Jokers is one of energy and enterprise rather than vagrant beggary. *Little Heroes* is in one sense a song of praise to 1960s rock and roll. As a story in which the rockers and the computer hackers seize the "software" to return it to the people, it is indeed a 1960s fantasy, but one based on the entertainment technology of the 1980's and beyond. A less nostalgic view of the counterculture wars may be found in the quasi-autobiographical *Children of Hamelin,* an early novel not published until 1991. In it, Spinrad explores the similarities between substance addictions and therapeutic cults that demand surrender of the ego.

Graphic portrayal of human sexual encounters has long been a characteristic of Spinrad's fiction, but the role of sex has changed over the years, as Spinrad has become more sensitive in his treatment of women. In the early *Agent of Chaos* not one woman appears, even as the object of a male gaze. (Perhaps this is a feature of male-dominated SF that Spinrad parodies in *The Iron Dream,* another female-free novel.) In *Bug Jack Barron, The Men in the Jungle, The Mind Game,* and *The Children of Hamelin,* and in many pre-1980 short stories, women appear only as objects of male desire and are seemingly valued according to their skill in fellatio. Casual, oral sex is still the norm in later fictions, and is still graphically portrayed, but it has become more sentimentalized and somewhat less obtrusive.

In the earlier fictions sex and violence seem to substitute one for another, but with *Songs from the Stars* this changes, as the consciousness of a female character often becomes the viewpoint of narration (a viewpoint from which sexual descriptions tend to emphasize setting and holistic response rather than engorgement and penetration). The whole of *Child of Fortune* is told by a first-person feminine narrator convincingly different from Spinrad's masculine viewpoint characters. While *Little Heroes* returns to the multiple viewpoint mode dropped for *The Void Captain's Tale* and *Child of Fortune,* viewpoint is pretty evenly parceled out among male and female characters, and only one female viewpoint, that of Cyborg Sally, offers graphic detail in sexual description. The novel also plays up the sex-violence connection, especially in the fantasies of "streetie" Paco Monaco; Paco, however, eventually adopts a gentler sexual mode under the benign influence of the consciousness-enhancing Zap, a fine hairnet of charged wires that symbolizes the web of electronic culture.

The topic of sex in Spinrad's fiction demands a look at the strange world of *The Void Captain's Tale.* In the Second Starfaring Age (also the setting of *Child of Fortune*), humanity travels about the galaxy in Void Ships, vessels that use an alien technology to "jump" timelessly the great interstellar distances that would take lifetimes to cross at even relativistic velocities. The technology has one peculiarity: it requires that a human female, the Jump Pilot, be wired into the guidance system. Her role is ultimately self-destructive, for she will end up, like the addicts throughout Spinrad's fiction, a wasted zombie. Her reward is that in each Jump she experiences a transcendent orgasm, a momentary fusion with the "Great and Only."

The plot of *The Void Captain's Tale* hangs upon an inadvertent social gaffe: violating spacer etiquette, the captain, Genro Kane Gupta, becomes acquainted with his pilot, Dominique Alia Wu. It thickens when Genro, fascinated by the "platform orgasm" experience of pilots, becomes sexually involved with Dominique. It climaxes when the captain, succumbing to the pilot's mad entreaties, gives her the ultimate charge—a jump without destination coordinates, a Blind Jump. The pilot is dead, and a ship's crew and passengers are probably doomed, but the pilot has undergone the ultimate peak experience. (And we have gotten another, very different take on the theme of "The Big Flash.") *The Void Captain's Tale* is a haunting, melancholy romance, multi-layered in texture, seeming to mean more than it can possibly say, not least because it is a male confession of inability to plumb the sexual experience of the female.

A number of Spinrad's recent novels (*The Children of Hamelin, Russian Spring,* and *Pictures at 11*) have been published as non-SF, no doubt because of marketing considerations. These novels, however, dovetail nicely with Spinrad's SF, and with the foregoing analysis, and read as if they were SF. In particular, *Russian Spring* evokes many of the themes of the earlier fiction, and it addresses again the issues and images of "The Big Flash" and *The Void Captain's Tale.* An evocatively beautiful merger of the family romance and of the romance of space travel, it is perilously sentimental and too neatly ended, but it speaks to the "sense of wonder" that SF depends upon.

In *The Iron Dream,* Spinrad gave Adolf Hitler the worst of literary punishments. He created an alternate universe in which the Führer was no longer the nearly successful founder of the Third Reich. He made him into a penniless emigrant and hack SF writer, the leaden-prosed composer of *Lord of the Swastika,* a sick racist fantasy overladen with violent phallic symbols. He inflicted upon him a vacuous critical essay written by an English professor. Unlike "Hitler," Spinrad is critically aware of the turbulent unconscious of science fiction, and he has crafted a shelf of SF that rivals anyone's for inventiveness, zestful prose, and hipness. Perhaps he has been spared the vacuous critical essay.

—John P. Brennan

SPRAGUE, Carter. *See* **MERWIN, Sam, Jr.**

SPRINGER, Nancy (Connor)

Nationality: American. **Born:** Montclair, New Jersey, 5 July 1948. **Education:** Gettysburg College, Pennsylvania, 1966-1970, B.A. **Family:** Married Joel Springer in 1969; one daughter and one son. **Career:** Library clerk, St. Joseph's College, Emmitsburg, Maryland, 1969; teacher, Delone Catholic High School, McSherrytown, Pennsylvania, 1970-71; teacher's aide, Hoffman Home for Children, Littlestown, Pennsylvania, 1972-73. Teacher, York College and Franklin and Marshall College, since 1986. Communications instructor, Bradley Academy for the Visual Arts, since 1990. Since 1972, writer. **Address:** c/o Atheneum Publishers, 866 Third Avenue, New York, New York 10022, U.S.A.

SCIENCE FICTION PUBLICATIONS

Novels (series: Book of Isle; Sea King)

The Book of Suns (Isle). New York, Pocket Books, 1977; revised edition, as *The Silver Sun,* New York, Pocket Books, 1980; Glasgow, Drew, 1984.
The White Hart (Isle). New York, Pocket Books, 1979; Glasgow, Drew, 1984.
The Sable Moon (Isle). New York, Pocket Books, 1981; Glasgow, Drew, 1985.
The Black Beast (Isle). New York, Pocket Books, 1982; Glasgow, Drew, 1985.
The Book of Vale (includes *The Black Beast* and *The Golden Swan*). Garden City, New York, Doubleday, 1984.
The Golden Swan (Isle). New York, Timescape, 1983; Glasgow, Drew, 1985.
Wings of Flame. New York, Tor, 1985; London, Arrow, 1986.
Chains of Gold. New York, Arbor House, 1986; London, Macdonald, 1987.
Sea King trilogy:
    Madbond. New York, Tor, 1987; London, Orbit, 1988.
    Mindbond. New York, Tor, 1987; London, Orbit, 1989.
    Godbond. New York, Tor, 1988; London, Orbit, 1990.
The Hex Witch of Seldom. New York, Baen, 1989.
Apocalypse. Novato, California, Underwood Miller, 1989.
Red Wizard (for children). New York, Atheneum, 1990.
The Friendship Song. New York, Atheneum, 1992.
Larque on the Wing. New York, Morrow, 1994.
Metal Angel. New York, Roc, 1992.

Short Stories

Chance and Other Gestures of the Hand of Fate (includes poetry). New York, Baen,1987.
Damnbanna. Eugene, Oregon, Axolotl Press, 1992.

Poetry

Stardark Songs. Buffal, New York, W. Paul Ganley, 1993.

OTHER PUBLICATIONS

Novels for children

A Horse to Love. New York, Harper and Row, 1987.

Not on a White Horse. New York, Atheneum, 1988.
They're All Named Wildfire. New York, Atheneum, 1989.
Red Wizard. New York, Atheneum, 1990.
Colt. New York, Dial, 1991.
The Great Pony Hassle. New York, Dial, 1993.
Toughing It. New York, Harcourt, 1994.
The Boy on a Black Horse. New York, Atheneum, 1994.
Looking for Jamie Bridger. New York, Dial, 1995.

Poetry

Music of Their Hooves: Poems about Horses. Honesdale, Pennsylvania, Wordsong, 1994.

Other

Mythic Realism in Fantasy. Eugene, Oregon, Pulphouse, 1991.

*

Nancy Springer comments:

Fiction writing for me is an advanced form of gossip without the hurtful effects that might occur if I speculated on paper (or on the porches with the neighbors) about actual living individuals. I contemplate imaginary people instead, but the fascination with human personality and behavior is the same. For that matter, so is the yen for story, narrative, with a thrill of shock or a pang of emotion at its core.

For me, at least, fiction writing has always started with those two things: people (fictional characters), and a tendency never to let the literal truth get in the way of a good story. Ideally, the story should grow out of the characters themselves, like a tree springing up in a flower garden.

Writing fantasy involves the same fascination in a more complicated form: the characters often are aspects of the human psyche, acting out their conflicts on a dream-landscape straight out of what Jung called the "collective unconscious." Looking for political realism? Don't look in my books. Armies and princes exist in the kingdoms of the psyche merely as matrix for the archetypical story. When writing fantasy, really I am writing about myself and all others like me.

*   *   *

Nancy Springer is a gifted fantasist whose work consistently improves, growing stronger and more subtle with each new publications, and whose range is expanding in both audience and excitement. She is a horse lover, with horses (as well as imaginary animals) and riding a rich thread through much of her work. The quest theme is central to her writing. While the quest is never a mere journey, the novels can certainly be read on one level as exciting, fast-paced adventure gently touched with magic and myth, and peopled by believable characters with realistic flaws and strengths. Her later works develop strong female characters, who come into their strength/self-knowledge through the fear and trials of the quest. Springer uses the quest to explore the consequences of vision, the relative and subjective view of choices made, and life's contrasts (good-evil, light-dark, intentions-outcome), and further as vehicle for the testing and nurturing of relationships and interpersonal bonds, those between lovers, parent-children, brothers and friends.

Springer's first published novels, aimed at young adults, are set in her imaginary world of Isle (Book of the Isle series). *The White Hart* and *The Silver Sun* (based on *The Book of Suns*), are adequate conventional fantasy but suffer from several serious flaws. They are derivative of fantasy classics, mired in fantastical jargon, and so overly burdened with (Celtic) mythological components that both characterization and world building are slighted. However, even these weakest of her works provide well-paced quest adventures. They also introduce us to her fresh appealing depiction of real and imaginary animals (the imaginary animals and horses especially charm).

Each new addition, *The Sable Moon, The Black Beast, The Golden Swan,* to the series show Springer's continuing growth as a storyteller, her refined use of language with fantastical jargon no longer interrupting the story flow, her use of mythological elements enriching the story rather than bogging it down, her characters people with human frailties as well as strength, and Isle's depiction both spare and full. The series does a good job of illuminating the tension between good and evil. The use of imaginary animals, especially unicorns and swans, as relative indicators of social and cultural good/evil is particularly well done with their shifts between black and white in both being and reflection.

Wings of Flame and *Chains of Gold* are Springer's more romantic fantasies. They present outwardly different, yet equally strong female characters. *Wings* offers vibrantly detailed romantic fantasy with magic winning the day over superstition. *Chains* is triumphant and compelling fantasy showcasing Springer's growth as a writer, especially her world building, vivid characterization and subtle touch with magic and fantasy elements. She takes the Druidic ritual virgin (here, both male and female) sacrifice made to ensure fertility and gives it a modern twist. The sacrificial winterking, Arlen, and bride, Cerilla, fall in love, refusing their ritual destiny. This is the story of their flight through a world whose landscape is of both dreams and nightmares, their relationship and personal growth, and their relationship with the ghost of their savior. It is notable for the character of Cerilla, her interactions with the Oracle and Goddess, her maturation, and her growth to self-knowledge and strength.

The Sea King Trilogy, *Madbond, Mindbond, Godbond,* is a strong fantasy with "real" people in a well developed imaginary world. The books explore relationships, those between choices and consequences and those between people, and the relativity of good and evil. Again the quest is the mechanism employed as both illumination and catalyst. The trilogy is a pleasure to read, gracefully written and resonating with poetic imagery.

Springer's repertoire includes both short fiction and poetry, collected in *Chance and Other Gestures of the Hand of Fate,* contemporary fantasy, *The Hex Witch of Seldom* and urban fantasy, *Metal Angel.* The short fiction takes traditional themes (the princess and the peasant) and standard fantastic subjects (living forest, wizards/gods) and gives them provocative twists resulting in subtle, original fantasy. *Chance* is an excellent introduction to Springer's work, allowing a taste of her style, poetic imagery, fantastic landscapes and believable characters which will make fans of its readers. In *Hex,* the wonderfully drawn, misfit, young woman comes of age during her struggle with the forces of good and evil against a backdrop of fantastic elements and characters (witch, magical black stallion) wedded with regional folklore (Pennsylvania Dutch).

Springer has a rich body of work aimed at children, often featuring authentically presented horses, as one major door into adolescence. These compelling and realistic (coming of age, race relations) stories feature female characters whose relationship with and responsibility for horses allows them to grow, gain confidence and recognize their own strength. Springer has said she feels children need to know its a tough world. *Red Wizard,* a fantasy for children, is not quite as strong as the material written for the young adult audience, but does have interesting ideas, imagery, and witty puns.

Apocalypse one of Springer's most exciting works vibrates with powerful imagery, contrasts, and the sophisticated use of cultural idiom. The setting is a grim, economically depressed mining town juxtaposed against pagan natural beauty, seductive magic and the horrific supernatural. The main characters include the "Four Horsewomen of the Apocalypse", the female catalyst, Joanie, and an outsider male, Barry. These characters carry all the cultural shorthand of their stereotype but are fully developed people with weaknesses and strengths, good and evil traits. Joanie and Barry are particularly poignant characters, both having physical defects, both tormented as outsiders, and whose innate goodness ultimately triumphs, saving all. It is the complicity of the community in the tormenting, its lack of tolerance, its narrow-mindedness that is shown as true evil, more so than the nightmarish visions and plagues provided courtesy of the devil. It is the reworking of a myth through the lens of popular culture, the classic struggle between good and evil with much of the focus on the gray areas, not merely the black and white. This was the first book written after Springer's husband retired from the Lutheran ministry, an interesting comment on the bonds we place upon ourselves.

Springer's most recent work is the wonderfully outrageous *Larque on the Wing,* winner of the prestigious Tiptree Award. The Tiptree Award is presented annually for works which explore and expand gender roles in science fiction and fantasy. Larque/Lark is one of the most intriguing characters to come along, a middle age woman who unconsciously produces temporary doppelgangers of others and herself, and who finds her doppelganger molded into a young male.

—Catherine M. Currier

SPRUILL, Steven

Nationality: American. **Born:** Battle Creek, Michigan, 20 April 1946. **Education:** Andrews University, Berrien Springs, Michigan, B.A. in biology 1968; Catholic University of America, Washington, D.C., M.A. in psychology 1979, Ph.D. in clinical psychology 1981. **Family:** Married Nancy Lyon in 1969. **Career:** Biological technician, Hazleton Laboratories, Falls Church, Virginia, 1969-73; psychology intern, Veterans Administration Hospital, Washington, D.C., 1978-79, and Mt. Vernon Community Health Center, Alexandria, Virginia, 1979-80. Since 1981, full-time writer. **Agent:** Al Zuckerman, 21 West 26th Street, New York, New York 10010, U.S.A.

SCIENCE FICTION PUBLICATIONS

Novels (series: Kane and Pendrake)

Keepers of the Gate. Garden City, New York, Doubleday, and London, Hale, 1977.
The Psychopath Plague (Kane). Garden City, New York, Doubleday, and London, Hale, 1978.

Hellstone. New York, Playboy, 1980.
The Imperator Plot (Kane). New York, Doubleday, 1983.
The Genesis Shield. New York, Tor, 1985.
Paradox Planet: A Kane and Pendrake Novel. New York, Doubleday, 1988.
Painkiller. New York, St. Martin's Press, 1990.
Rulers of Darkness. New York, St. Martin's Press, 1995.

OTHER PUBLICATIONS

Novels

Before I Wake. New York, St. Martin's Press, 1992.
My Soul to Take. New York, St. Martin's Press, 1994.

*

Steven Spruill comments:

My purpose in writing is primarily to entertain the reader and produce an emotional experience in the process. I believe people read in order to feel. Consequently, I consider it extremely important to write in the technical sense in such a way that the reader feels him or herself to *be* the viewpoint character, wanting what that character wants, fearing what he or she fears, and sensing along with the character. In the process of writing this way I feel it is quite important for the author to remain as nearly invisible as possible.

In addition, I prefer the extraordinary to the ordinary (which is all too readily available to us in real life) when I structure the plots of my novels. Consequently, most of my novels are concerned with the bizarre, the complicated, the strange, and the psychological, hopefully made clear through "simple" writing, and engaging through the hopes, needs, fears, and, in general, the emotional journey of the characters through their rather baroque plots and landscapes. I might sum up my position as a writer by naming the two other authors I most admire—Bob Shaw and Ken Follett.

*   *   *

Most of Steven Spruill's novels are science fiction only by the broadest definition. *Hellstone* is a horror story about the Loch Ness monster, but a pre-publication reviewer was right in suggesting that readers are bored for much of the early pages and only "mildly chilled" by what actually happens. *The Genesis Shield* is a mildly successful application of biological and psychological themes to a heating up of the Cold War, and a kind of transition to his more recent medical thrillers.

Spruill's first novel, *Keepers of the Gate,* is not, as a pre-publication reviewer suggested, uninspired and routine, but a space opera that reads well and is a promise of future excellence. Two long short stories, "Prime Culture" (in *Aries 1,* edited by John Grant, Newton Abbot, Devon, David and Charles, 1979) and "The Janus Equation" (in *Binary Star 4,* New York, Dell, 1980), are competent but not especially noteworthy.

On the other hand, despite several less than enthusiastic reviews, the Elias Kane novels, *The Psychopath Plague, The Imperator Plot,* and *Paradox Planet,* which bear a superficial resemblance to Asimov's Elijah Baley series, are well-plotted, well-written, and entertaining. Elias, former Navy lieutenant, is highly intelligent, possessed of eidetic memory, and has spent years in various educa-

tional institutions studying, among other things, psychology, criminology, physics, and biology. A superman he is not, for he makes the kind of errors caused by human fallibility and emotion, a touch that obviously draws heavily on Spruill's background as clinical psychologist.

In *The Psychopath Plague,* Elias, aided by the Cephantine Pendrake, locates the source of the widening contamination that causes people to be seized by a compulsion to kill or maim anyone who happens to be nearby, pinpoints the criminals, and wins his true love Elizabeth, the million-credit reward, and the gratitude of the Imperator, who rules Earth and the nine, sometimes rebellious, colonies. In *The Imperator Plot,* three years of happiness with Elizabeth end when Elias is summoned by the Imperator to head the investigation of an assassination plot. Unfortunately, the assassin strikes first, Elizabeth dies saving Elias, and the Imperator, his body destroyed, is saved only because his personal physician, Martha Reik, quickly attaches his uninjured head to an advanced life-support system. In *Paradox Planet,* under orders from Imperator Briana, Kane, Pendrake, and Martha thwart a rebellion on the heavy-gravity planet Cassiodorus, source of the beta-steel needed for Imperial dreadnoughts. A sequel seems inevitable in view of the escape of rebel dreadnoughts. Kane's willingness to continue serving the Imperator is ensured when he learns that he has fathered her soon-to-be born son. In all three, the extent of the real plot is uncovered only after a long series of harrowing experiences and sidetracks, during which Elias learns much about himself and humanity.

What lifts these novels from the ordinary is often at first reading almost unnoticeable. Thus, in *The Psychopath Plague* only further reflection shows parallels between a seemingly insignificant conversation about the difference between perception and reality, between the human being's belief that his or her thoughts can control behavior and the view of all other intelligent creatures in the galaxy that this belief is irrational and that it is really environment, physical, mental, and emotional, that controls all behavior, including that of humanity. Since the attack on Earth is alien, partly physical and partly through the tremendous mental powers of the innocent-appearing invaders, it is a nice touch that this discussion is conducted with a friendly alien not yet identified as part of the problem.

In *The Imperator Plot,* the significance of the demands of the bodiless head for a new body, for a way to experience the pleasure of eating, even the desire for a human touch on its forehead, is not at first obvious. Only later do certain questions arise: How would the Imperator deprived of all sensation accept the situation? What would be the effect on his behavior? How does it affect his Ornyl bodyguard? An integral part of the solution is Elias's own experience of a temporary total sensory deprivation and his subsequent understanding of both self and the Ornyl. A similar understanding of the physiological make-up of the sauroids is essential to solving the problem in *Paradox Planet.*

Spruill's human characters are well developed and believable, their actions made plausible by the motivations established early on. He also has an inventive turn of mind where aliens are concerned, and some of his creations are most interesting. Pendrake, the Cephantine, is an orange-skinned giant of enormous strength from a species known for its inability to permit violence or death, empathetic with all plant and animal life, and respected as incapable of uttering a falsehood; his absolute loyalty to Elias, who has gambled him out of slavery, is a major ingredient in the successful investigations. The musal trees control the humanoid Krythians and the illusory, comical, penguin-like traders, the

Chirpones, who actually carry out their plot against humanity. The Moitans, "fish-people," are an advanced technological civilization. The Ornyls, humanoid giant insects, are fierce warriors; their binding to their chosen masters is irrevocable and complete. The sauroids of Cassiodorus are essential to the rebels' ability to live on that planet. In every case—except, perhaps, for the S'uniphs, who are nearly mindless anyway—the behavior of these aliens is consistent with the internal psychology established for them when they first appear on the scene.

Painkiller achieved some popularity as a Literary Guild and Doubleday Book Club selection, but it is a somewhat disappointing medical thriller that, despite an attractive doctor-heroine and an interesting mystery, is a dull and even expected letdown. The mystery of *Before I Sleep* (characterized by one reviewer as a young adult novel!) is better sustained and holds interest to the end. *My Soul to Take* is the best of these recent medical thrillers and the closest to science fiction. The story deals with the unsuspected consequence in some patients of a computer chip that inserted into the brain at the right spot will permit the blind to see. In some patients the chip produces an ability to see the future in uncontrolled flashes that come closer and closer to real time as time passes. Suzannah Lord, a former neurosurgery resident involved in the early implantations and now a general surgeon, discovers that a maverick group of CIA agents is implanting some of their fellow agents with the intention of gaining control of much more than simply advance information about what may happen in the future. The struggle between Suzannah and her allies—her journalist lover, a brilliant artist she has admired since childhood and one of the Adepts in need of help, her sister a naval intelligence commander, a psychiatrist friend—and the growing power of the enemy is skillfully depicted. The result is, as critics are wont to say, an absorbing page-turner. Advance notice and review os his soon-to-be-published *Rulers of Darkness* describes a vampire novel in which Spruill attempts scientific explanation of the unusual characteristics of his "hemophages."

Spruill writes well, invents interesting plots, and uses his own technical knowledge effectively. Critics have complained, with some justification, of inaccuracies in his understanding of hard science. They have not, however, been able to fault the inventiveness and clarity of his behavioral science constructions. In this latter respect, Spruill—even in his less successful work—is a talented writer, deserving of continued attention, no little praise, and genuine anticipation of his work to come. One may regret his shift from science fiction to medical thrillers, but his entry into this more lucrative field has not lessened his ability to tell a good story.

—Arthur O. Lewis

STABLEFORD, Brian (Michael)

Also writes as Brian M. Stableford. **Pseudonym:** Brian Craig. **Nationality:** British. **Born:** Shipley, Yorkshire, 25 July 1948. **Education:** Manchester Grammar School; University of York, B.A. (honours) in biology 1969, D. Phil, in sociology 1979. **Family:** Married 1) Vivien Owen in 1973 (divorced 1985); one son and one daughter; 2) Roberta Jane Rennie (neé Cragg) in 1987. **Career:** Lecturer in sociology, University of Reading, Berkshire, 1976-88; lecturer in humanities, University of West England, 1995 (one-year appointment). **Awards:** J. Lloyd Eaton award, 1987; Distinguished Scholarship award, 1987; Readercon Small Press award, 1992. **Agent:** Abner Stein Agency, 10 Roland Gardens, London SW7 3PH; Richard Curtis, 171 East 74th St., New York, New York 10021, U.S.A. **Address:** 113 St. Peter's Road, Reading, Berkshire RG6 1PG, England. **Online Address:** bstableford@cix.compulink.co.uk.

SCIENCE FICTION PUBLICATIONS

Novels (series: Asgard; Daedalus; Dies Irae; David Lydyard; Hooded Swan)

Cradle of the Sun. New York, Ace, and London, Sidgwick and Jackson, 1969.

The Blind Worm. New York, Ace, and London, Sidgwick and Jackson, 1970.

The Days of Glory (Dies Irae). New York, Ace, and Manchester, Five Star, 1971.

In the Kingdom of the Beasts (Dies Irae). New York, Ace, 1971; London, Quartet, 1974.

Day of Wrath (Dies Irae). New York, Ace, 1971; London, Quartet, 1974.

To Challenge Chaos. New York, DAW, 1972.

The Halcyon Drift (Swan). New York, DAW, 1972; London, Dent, 1974.

Rhapsody in Black (Swan). New York, DAW, 1973; London, Dent, 1975.

Promised Land (Swan). New York, DAW, 1974; London, Dent, 1975.

The Paradise Game (Swan). New York, DAW, 1974; London, Dent, 1976.

The Fenris Device (Swan). New York, DAW, 1974; London, Pan, 1978.

Swan Song. New York, DAW, 1975; London, Pan, 1978.

Man in a Cage. New York, Day, 1975.

The Face of Heaven. London, Quartet, 1976; revised as *The Realms of Tartarus,* New York, DAW, 1977.

The Mind-Riders. New York, DAW, 1976; as *The Mind Riders,* London, Fontana, 1977.

The Florians (Daedalus). New York, DAW, 1976; London, Hamlyn, 1978.

Critical Threshold (Daedalus). New York, DAW, 1977; London, Hamlyn, 1979.

Wildeblood's Empire (Daedalus). New York, DAW, 1977; London, Hamlyn, 1979.

The City of the Sun (Daedalus). New York, DAW, 1978; London, Hamlyn, 1980.

The Last Days of the Edge of the World. London, Hutchinson, 1978; New York, Ace, 1985.

Balance of Power (Daedalus). New York, DAW, 1979; London, Hamlyn, 1984.

The Walking Shadow. London, Fontana, 1979; New York, Carroll and Graf, 1989.

The Paradox of the Sets (Daedalus). New York, DAW, 1979.

Optiman. New York, DAW, 1980; as *War Games,* London, Pan, 1981.

The Castaways of Tanagar. New York, DAW, 1981.

Journey to the Center (Asgard). Garden City, New York, Doubleday, 1982; revised as *Journey to the Centre,* London, New English Library, 1989.

The Gates of Eden. New York, DAW, 1983; London, New English Library, 1990.

The Empire of Fear. London, Simon and Schuster, 1988; New York, Carroll and Graf, 1991.

Invaders from the Centre (Asgard). London, New England Library, 1990.

The Centre Cannot Hold (Asgard). London, New England Library, 1990.

The Werewolves of London (Lydyard). London, Simon and Schuster, 1990; Carroll and Graf, 1992.

The Angel of Pain (Lydyard). London, Simon and Schuster, 1991; New York, Carroll and Graf, 1993.

Young Blood. London, Simon and Schuster, 1992.

The Carnival of Destruction (Lydyard). London, Pocket Books, and New York, Carroll and Graf, 1993.

Firefly: A Novel of the Far Future. San Bernardino, California, Borgo Press, 1994.

Serpent's Blood: The First Book of Genesys. London, Legend, 1995.

Novels as Brian Craig (series: Warhammer in all titles)

Zaragoz. Brighton, East Sussex, Games Workshop, 1989.

Plague Daemon. Brighton, East Sussex, Games Workshop, 1990.

Storm Warriors. Brighton, East Sussex, Games Workshop, 1991.

Dark Future: Ghost Dancers. Brighton, East Sussex, Games Workshop, 1991.

Short Stories

Sexual Chemistry: Sardonic Tales of the Genetic Revolution. London, Simon and Schuster, 1991.

The Cosmic Perspective, Custer's Last Stand. Polk City, Iowa, Drumm, 1985.

Slumming in Voodooland. Eugene, Oregon, Pulphouse, 1991.

The Innsmouth Heritage. West Warwick, Rhode Island, Necronomicon Press, 1992.

OTHER PUBLICATIONS

Other

The Mysteries of Modern Science. London, Routledge, 1977; Totowa, New Jersey, Littlefield Adams, 1980.

A Clash of Symbols: The Triumph of James Blish. San Bernardino, California, Borgo Press, 1979.

Masters of Science Fiction: Essays on Six Science Fiction Authors. San Bernardino, California, Borgo Press, 1981; revised and expanded as *Outside the Human Aquarium: Masters of Science Fiction,* 1995.

The Science in Science Fiction, with Peter Nicholls and David Langford. London, Joseph, 1982; New York, Knopf, 1983.

Future Man: Brave New World or Genetic Nightmare? London, Granada, and New York, Crown, 1984.

The Third Millennium: A History of the World, A.D. 2000-3000, with David Langford. London, Sidgwick and Jackson, and New York, Knopf, 1985.

Scientific Romance in Britain, 1890-1950. London, Fourth Estate, and New York, St. Martin's Press, 1985.

The Sociology of Science Fiction. San Bernardino, California, Borgo Press, 1987.

The Way to Write Science Fiction. London, Elm Tree, 1989.

Algebraic Fantasies and Realistic Romances: More Masters of Science Fiction. San Bernardino, California, Borgo Press, 1995.

Opening Minds: Essays on Fantastic Literature. San Bernardino, California, Borgo Press, 1995.

Editor, *The Dedalus Book of Decadence: (Moral Ruins).* Sawtry, Cambridgeshire, Dedalus, 1990; second edition, 1993.

Editor, *Tales of the Wandering Jew: A Collection of Contemporary and Classic Stories.* Sawtry, Cambridgeshire, Dedalus, 1991.

Editor, *The Dedalus Book of British Fantasy: The 19th Century.* Sawtry, Cambridgeshire, Dedalus, 1991.

Editor, *The Second Dedalus Book of Decadence: The Black Feast.* Sawtry, Cambridgeshire, Dedalus, 1992.

Editor, *The Dedalus Book of Femmes Fatales: A Collection of Contemporary and Classic Stories.* Sawtry, Cambridgeshire, Dedalus, 1992.

*

Brian Stableford comments:

My recent work in the genre—virtually everything published before 1986 is perhaps best forgotten—has two main strands. Far the more important and interesting, in my view, is an extensive series of stories which attempt to track the possible social consequences of likely developments in biotechnology, with particular emphasis on technologies of longevity. Some of the earlier stories in this sequence are collected in *Sexual Chemistry.* My regrettable inability to sell novels of this kind has meant that several longer works have had to be ruthlessly condensed for publication as novellas; the ones which seem to me to be the most significant are "Les Fleurs du Mal," "The Hunger and Ecstasy of Vampires," "Inherit the Earth," and "Mortimer Gray's *History of Death,*" the last-named being my particular favourite.

The novels which I have been able to sell during the same period have all been heavily disguised as something other than science fiction; some have applied a conscientiously materialistic eye to the reexamination of classic motifs borrowed from horror fiction, while my most recent three-decker—begun with *Serpent's Blood*—is a planetary romance which pretends for the first 400 pages or so to be a fantasy replete with vagabond princes, proto-feminist princesses, horrid monsters, amiable giants, and various other items beloved of editors who believe that these are the kinds of things readers ardently desire to read about. I freely confess that this *modus operandi* is mildly absurd and I have no real defence against the kind of Voltairean scepticism which would not concede the necessity of it, but the works in question seem to me to have an endearing quirkiness; I am very fond of my two novels about "vampires," *The Empire of Fear* and *Young Blood.* The former is, so far as I know, the only novel ever written in which Richard the Lionheart meets Vlad the Impaler, whereas the latter compensates for its admittedly excessive interest in abstruse philosophical questions of identity with lots of spiffingly kinky sex.

When I first started writing it seemed unthinkable that science fiction would one day be an extinct genre; now it seems inevitable, if not yet a *fait accompli,* that nothing of it will survive but mere costume dramas and silly TV tie-ins. I think this is a tragedy to beggar the imagination—but then, I would, wouldn't I?

*   *   *

Brian Stableford sold his first SF story while still at school, and three of his early novels—*The Blind Worm, To Challenge Chaos,* and *Firefly: A Novel of the Far Future*—are partly or wholly cannibalized from material written at about the same time. For some years he divided his time between the desultory pursuit of an academic career and his writing, swaying first one way and then the other as his fortunes shifted. Between 1969 and 1982 he wrote approximately 30 novels, most of them for Donald A. Wollheim, the SF editor at Ace and (from 1972) the publisher of DAW Books, his own imprint. His few attempts to break out of the mold which Wollheim preferred—series space opera—failed to make any significant headway; the intense psychological melodrama *Man in a Cage,* the lighthearted children's fantasy *The Last Days of the Edge of the World,* and the time-hopping evolutionary fantasy *The Walking Shadow* disappeared almost immediately following initial publication.

In 1981, having obtained tenure in a teaching position at the University of Reading, the author decided to concentrate on nonfiction, but when his painstaking study of Scientific Romance in Britain, 1890-1910 sold poorly and his volume on Eroticism in Supernatural Literature had to be aborted after the U.S. distributor pulled out, he concluded that such work was ultimately self-defeating. In 1986 he began to write short stories in profusion, redeploying and refining speculations about the future of biotechnology which he had first extrapolated for use in the futurology text, *The Third Millennium.* The implantation of "hard science fiction" ideas into sarcastic and somewhat mannered narratives gave him for the first time a distinctive narrative voice. He also attempted to take up his earlier career where he had left off by extending one of his last DAW novels, *Journey to the Center,* into a trilogy: but DAW was no longer interested, and the trilogy (including a revised version of the first volume) only appeared in England. This was an unfortunate fate for what is by far the most stylish, extravagant, and action-packed into a giant, multilayered artifact endangered by the breakdown of the systems controlling its power source.

In 1987 Britain was at the height of an economic boom and British publishing was rapidly expanding. Stableford obtained a commission from Simon and Schuster's fledgling U.K. offshoot to produce *The Empire of Fear,* an alternative history novel in which 17th-century Europe is ruled by an aristocracy of "vampires." The creatures' hegemony is threatened and eventually overturned by the emergence of new investigative instruments and the scientific method, which reveal that their origins and powers are natural rather than supernatural. The quest for an explanation of vampirism takes the characters deep into the heart of Africa. There they discover a biological agent which confers longevity and immunity to pain to those who nourish it with the blood of their fellow man, and find that it has been integrated into tribal societies in a fashion which contrasts strongly with its amalgamation into Western culture.

The *Empire of Fear* is perhaps the most memorable of Stableford's works, but his attempts to answer Simon and Schuster's demands for more of the same were less successful. A project similar in spirit—in that it adopted a similar revisionist approach to various other staples of horror fiction—was recast at the publisher's request into a trilogy begun with *The Werewolves of London,* but was then interrupted in the hopes of cashing in on the sudden popularity of vampire fiction. *Young Blood* is as different from *The Empire of Fear* as the author could contrive: a contemporary thriller in which a neurotic young woman's love affair with a vampire might or might not be the hallucinatory result of a psychotropic virus which has escaped from the laboratory where her boyfriend works. The novel's conclusion, which reinterprets everything that has gone before in a surprising and intellectually ambitious fashion, is startlingly original. The trilogy whose production was interrupted by this intrusion ended far less happily, its belated third volume, *The Carnival of Destruction,* appearing in Britain in paperback form some three years after *The Angel of Pain.* The loss of creative impetus is evident in the climax of *Carnival,* which is both awkward and unclear when it should have provided some better resolution to the series.

Stableford has tried for some years to extend his adventures in speculative biotechnology into novel form, but without much commercial success. The novel version of the flirtatiously decadent futuristic murder mystery *Les Fleurs du Mal,* was rejected by his agent on the grounds that it was too eccentric and tedious; in the end the author salvaged the material by cutting it to novella length. When it sold in that version he quickly recast several other projects in a similar mold, producing a number of works written in a much terser style than usual, but which still retained an imaginative sweep unusual in novellas of that length. For example, "The Hunger and Ecstasy of Vampires" is a parallel text to H.G. Wells's *The Time Machine,* in which a select party of Victorians—including Oscar Wilde, one of whose avatars is the paradoxical hero of "Les Fleurs du Mal"—passes judgment on a time traveler's far-ranging account of the species which inherits the earth after the self-destruction of mankind. "Mortimer Gray's History of Death" describes the career of a man born into a world where no one dies of disease or old age. His compilation of a definitive history of death only uses up a tiny fraction of his prospective lifespan, but nevertheless achieves a glorious triumph over the creeping menace of ennui.

The novella version of "Les Fleurs du Mal" brought Stableford his first Hugo nomination, but it remains to be seen whether he can discover any market space in which to continue his ironic celebrations of the potential of biotechnology to transform the quality of human life and the nature of human society. Although his most pedestrian action-adventure novels exhibit a certain flair for exotic imagery, Stableford's sense of humor is sufficiently unorthodox to ensure that he never will appeal to a wide audience; and even those who have acquired a taste for his fictions sometimes find his odysseys in bizarrerie difficult to follow to their conscientiously perverse conclusions. Laughing like hell, the author seems to be saying, is the only recourse left to a species whose perversity has created a laughable hell on Earth.

—Robert Reginald

STAPLEDON, (William) Olaf

Nationality: British. **Born:** Near Wallasey, Cheshire, 10 May 1886. **Education:** Abbotsholme School; Balliol College, Oxford, M.A. 1909; University of Liverpool, Ph.D. 1925. **Military Service:** Served in the Friends' Ambulance Unit in France, 1916-19. **Family:** Married Agnes Zena Miller in 1919; one son and one daughter. **Career:** Assistant headmaster, Manchester Grammar School, 1910; worked for Alfred Holt and Company, shippers, Liverpool and Port Said, 1911; lecturer in history and English, Workers' Educational Association, University of Liverpool, 1912-15; after World War I, lecturer in philosophy and psychology, University of Liverpool. **Died:** 6 September 1950.

SCIENCE FICTION PUBLICATIONS

Novels

Last and First Men: A Story of the Near and Far Future. London, Methuen, 1930; New York, Cape and Smith, 1931.
Last Men in London. London, Methuen, 1932; Boston, Gregg Press, 1976.
Odd John: A Story between Jest and Earnest. London, Methuen, 1935; New York, Dutton, 1936.
Star Maker. London, Methuen, 1937; as *The Star Maker,* New York, Berkley, 1961.
Darkness and the Light. London, Methuen, 1942; Westport, Connecticut, Hyperion Press, 1974.
Sirius: A Fantasy of Love and Discord. London, Secker and Warburg, 1944; included in *To the End of Time,* 1953.
Death into Life. London, Methuen, 1946.
The Flames: A Fantasy. London, Secker and Warburg, 1947.
Worlds of Wonder: Three Tales of Fantasy (includes *The Flames; Death into Life; Old Man in New World*). Los Angeles, Fantasy, 1949.
A Man Divided. London, Methuen, 1950.
To the End of Time: The Best of Olaf Stapledon, edited by Basil Davenport (includes *Last and First Men, Star Maker, Odd John, Sirius,* and *The Flames*). New York, Funk and Wagnalls, 1953.
Nebula Maker: An Early Version of Star Maker. Hayes, Middlesex, Bran's Head, 1976; New York, Dodd Mead, 1982.

Short Stories

Old Man in New World. London, Allen and Unwin, 1944.
Four Encounters. Hayes, Middlesex, Bran's Head, 1976.
Far Future Calling: Uncollected Science Fiction and Fantasies, edited by Sam Moskowitz. Philadelphia, Oswald Train, 1980.

OTHER PUBLICATIONS

Poetry

Latter-Day Psalms. Liverpool, Young, 1914.

Other

A Modern Theory of Ethics: A Study of the Relations of Ethics and Psychology. London, Methuen, and New York, Dutton, 1929.
Waking World. London, Methuen, 1934.
New Hope for Britain. London, Methuen, 1939.
Saints and Revolutionaries. London, Heinemann, 1939.
Philosophy and Living. London, Penguin, 2 vols., 1939.
Beyond the "Isms." London, Secker and Warburg, 1942.
The Seven Pillars of Peace. London, Common Wealth, 1944.
Youth and Tomorrow. London, St. Botolph, 1946.
The Opening of the Eyes, edited by Agnes Z. Stapledon. London, Methuen, 1954.
Talking across the World: The Love Letters of Olaf Stapledon and Agnes Miller 1913-1919, edited by Robert Crossley. Hanover, New Hampshire, University Press of New England, 1987.

*

Bibliography: *Olaf Stapledon: A Bibliography* by Harvey J. Satty and Curtis C. Smith, Westport, Connecticut, Greenwood Press, 1984.

Critical Studies: *Olaf Stapledon* by Patrick A. McCarthy, Boston, Hall, 1982; *Olaf Stapledon, A Man Divided* by Leslie A. Fiedler, New York and Oxford, Oxford University Press, 1983; *The Legacy of Olaf Stapledon: Critical Essays and an Unpublished Manuscript* edited by Patrick A. McCarthy, Martin H. Greenberg, and Charles Elkin, New York, Greenwood Press, 1989.

*   *   *

An appreciation of Olaf Stapledon's science fiction demands some mention of his overt discussions of philosophy, the chief subject of his work in adult education. The publication of his "study of the relations of ethics and psychology," *A Modern Theory of Ethics* (1929), preceded by a year his first novel, *Last and First Men.* In *Ethics,* he is much concerned with the psychological "moods" that, transcending mental routines of daily life, may colour an individual's perception of and actions within the social milieu, and in face of a seemingly indifferent cosmos. These are moods of "moral zeal," "disillusion," and "ecstasy," the last implying awareness that, although failure to attain the good may induce bleak disillusion, nothing is eternally lost in a universe of excellence. Such a "beyond good and evil" holistic and synthesizing perspective may only be achieved in conditions of psychological, and maybe physical, extremity. In a later popular philosophical exposition, *Philosophy and Living,* Stapledon developed the concept of "individuality within community" (a single menage or an entire culture) as defining the human arena where such a potentially liberating and motivating dialectic can operate.

When Penguin Books in 1938 published a paperback edition of *Last and First Men,* it did so under its nonfiction label, a decision indicative of the degree to which Stapledon's fiction is a mythicizing of his agnostic/quasi-religious speculations. The two-billion-year timespan of this novel sees the appearance, eclipse, and resurgence of 18 species of human: great-brained, miniaturized, winged, furry, or telepathic, as determined by responses to such changing conditions as energy depletion, vulcanism, glaciation, planetary invasion, and terraforming. The long, retrospective history is told by one of the Last Men on Neptune at a time when stellar catastrophe is about to put an end to humans (save possibly for seed dispersed through the void). "But," says Stapledon's Neptunian mouthpiece, "when he is done he will not be as nothing, not as though he had never been; for he is eternally a beauty in the eternal form of things." Throughout the course of human's existence, Stapledon depicts achievement and failure as equally parts of the cosmic pattern— the "ecstasy" perspective. By removing us from contemporary preoccupations, Stapledon makes us more sensitively aware of their significance, as we view them in the light of the fates and actions of beings from whom we are bizarrely distant, yet with whom we have a kinship in consciousness of selfhood—beings who are subject to the caprices of external nature and to limitations of their own physical and psychic structuring.

In *Last and First Men,* the dialectical interplay of "moods" is related less to personalized beings than to races as a whole. Described, as each race is, in graphic physical and psychological detail, it acts within the narrative almost as a prototypical entity, as a personality ultimately existing in relation to the cosmic community. This fictive method is developed more thoroughly in *Star Maker,* a myth of cosmic creation. The first-person narrator moves from the status of observer to that of participant, as his consciousness is expanded until in cosmic awareness it is "awakened to a degree thrice removed beyond the self-consciousness of human beings" and "the life of [his] body was itself the life of myriads of infinitely diverse worlds and myriads of infinitely diverse individual creatures . . . ." Yet even so, at the book's end, the entire epic of creation having taken place in dream-vision within a single clock-stroke, there is confrontation of the "I," now surrogate for humanity and for all creation, with that "dread mystery, compelling adoration": namely, the cold, yet ecstatically, contemplative Star Maker.

Dichotomy and confrontation are signified by several of the titles of fictions in which Stapledon projects his "mood" dialectic onto estranged individuals: for example, *Darkness and the Light, Old Man in New World,* the semi-autobiographical *A Man Divided,* and *Odd John: A Story between Jest and Earnest.* John is a mutation in the direction of a different humanity, alienated not only by a duality in his own nature but by a gap between that and the contemporary human race, whose ethic he defies in episodes of theft, murder, and incest. Telepathically assembling his scattered peers, he occupies with them an oceanic island, and with them commits suicide in the face of invasion by threatened mankind. The theme of individual consciousness seeking community is repeated in a late novel, *Sirius: A Fantasy of Love and Discord,* where the protagonists are Sirius, an experimentally bred large-brained dog, and Plexy, the woman he loves, both tragically half-divorced from the social and sexual norms of their race. Sirius's only release is in death; but what Stapledon calls the Sirius-Plexy "bright gem of community" is in cosmic perspective a high achievement, an ecstatic synthesis.

Sirius is considered by many to be Stapledon's finest work; but undoubtedly the two "cosmic histories" are what have most influentially impacted on genre writing and critical thought. Brian Aldiss has called *Last and First Men* "the one great grey holy book of science fiction"; and Stanislaw Lem has commented on its demonstration of relativity in "all norms, legal codes, dogmas, and values." In his own day, Stapledon's influence is explicit in Wells's *Star-Begotten;* and it provoked ideological/theological reaction in C.S. Lewis's interplanetary novels. The occurrence of the term "Stapledonian" in contemporary criticism suggests a pervading influence, not only in extending concepts of life in an ambiguous space-time universe, but in denoting an existential angst. In his unfinished *The Opening of the Eyes,* Stapledon wrote of his preference for at least a pragmatically-imagined transcendence, without which he was "no more than a reflex animal and the world is dust."

—K.V. Bailey

STASHEFF, Christopher

Nationality: American. **Born:** Mt. Vernon, New York, January 1944. **Education:** University of Michigan, Ann Arbor, B.A. 1965, M.A. 1966; University of Nebraska, Lincoln, Ph.D. in theater 1972. **Family:** Married Mary Miller in 1973; three daughters and one son. **Career:** Instructor, 1972-77, and since 1977, assistant professor of speech and theater, Montclair State College, New Jersey. **Agent:** Blassingame-Spectrum Corporation, 111 Eighth Avenue, Suite 1501, New York, New York 10011, U.S.A.

SCIENCE FICTION PUBLICATIONS

Novels (series: Magnus d'Armand; Heirs to the Warlock; Starship Troupers; Warlock; Wizard in Rhyme)

The Warlock in Spite of Himself. New York, Ace, 1969.
King Kobold (Warlock). New York, Ace, 1971; revised edition, as *King Kobold Revived,* 1984.
A Wizard in Bedlam (d'Armand). Garden City, New York, Doubleday, 1979; London, Mayflower, 1982.
The Warlock Unlocked. New York, Ace, 1982; London, Panther, 1984.
Escape Velocity (Warlock). New York, Ace, 1983.
The Warlock Enraged. New York, Ace, 1985.
Her Majesty's Wizard. New York, Ballantine, 1986.
The Warlock Wandering. New York, Ace, 1986.
The Warlock Is Missing. New York, Ace, 1986.
To The Magic Born (omnibus). Garden City, New York, Doubleday, 1986; enlarged edition, as *Warlock to the Magic Born,* London, Pan, 1990.
The Warlock Enlarged (omnibus). Garden City, New York, Doubleday, 1986; abridged edition, London, Pan, 1991.
The Warlock Heretical. New York, Ace, 1987.
The Warlock's Companion. New York, Ace, 1988.
The Warlock's Night Out (omnibus). New York, Guild America, 1988; enlarged edition, London, Pan, 1991.
The Warlock Insane. New York, Ace, 1989.
tit>*Odd Warlock Out* (omnibus). New York, Guild America, 1989.
The Warlock Rock. New York, Ace, 1990.
A Company of Stars (Starship Troupers). New York, Ballantine, 1991; London, Pan, 1992.
Warlock and Son. New York, Ace, 1991.
The Oathbound Wizard (Wizard in Rhyme). New York, Ballantine, 1993.
A Wizard in Absentia (Heirs to the Warlocks). New York, Ace, 1993.
End Run, with William R. Forstchen (Wing Commander). Riverdale, New York, Baen, 1994.
We Open on Venus (Starship Troupers). New York, Ballantine, 1994.
The Witch Doctor (Wizard in Rhyme). New York, Ballantine, 1994.
M'Lady Witch (Wizard in Rhyme). New York, Ace, 1994.
A Slight Detour (Starship Troupers). New York, Ballantine, 1994.
The Secular Wizard. New York, Ballantine, 1995.
Quicksilver's Knight (Heir to the Warlock). New York, Ace, 1995.
A Wizard in Mind: The First Chronicle of the Rogue Wizard (d'Armand). New York, Tor, 1995.

Short Stories (series: Harold Shea)

Sir Harold and the Monkey King. Newark, New Jersey, Wildside Press, 1993.

OTHER PUBLICATIONS

Plays

The Three-Legged Man (produced Lincoln, Nebraska, 1970).
Cotton-Eye Joe (produced Lincoln, Nebraska, 1970).
Joey Win (produced Lincoln, Nebraska, 1971).

Other

Editor, with Bill Fawcett, *The Crafters*. New York, Ace, 1991.

Editor, with L. Sprague de Camp, *The Enchanter Reborn* (Shea). Riverdale, New York, Baen, 1992.

Editor, with Bill Fawcett, *Blessings and Curses* (Crafters). New York, Ace, 1992.

Editor, *The Gods of War*. Riverdale, New York, Baen, 1992.

Editor, *Dragon's Eye*. Riverdale, New York, Baen, 1994.

Editor, with L. Sprague de Camp, *The Exotic Enchanter* (Shea). Riverdale, New York, Baen, 1995.

*

Christopher Stasheff comments:

I'm not concerned with the novel as an end in itself, but as a means towards the end of trying to awaken the audience to an awareness of the issues I consider important, and to convey some vital facts and a few opinions. I'm also trying to reverse some trends I discern in popular literature, which I believe to be detrimental to us as people and as society. But none of this will do any good if no one reads it; so, first and foremost, I try to entertain.

*   *   *

Christopher Stasheff wrote a wild and ribald mixture of science fiction and fantasy with his first novel, the fabulous *The Warlock in Spite of Himself*. Rodney d'Armond, who renames himself Rod Gallowglass, and his goofy robot steed, Fess, arrive on Gramarye, a planet where magic works. Their mission is to bring democracy to this feudal society. They find themselves kidnapped by elves, encounter ghosts and goblins, and meet other legendary creatures. Gallowglass falls in love with a lovely witch and saves Gramarye's feudalism. All of this is told in a bold swashbuckling style with great humor. *The Warlock in Spite of Himself* is more than a successful blending of science fiction and sword-and-sorcery; it is wonderful entertainment. Readers agree, which led Stasheff to write many more volumes in the Warlock series.

The original sequel to *The Warlock in Spite of Himself, King Kobold*, received negative reviews, chiefly from Lester del Rey who was book reviewer for *Worlds of If*. When Stasheff's publishers wanted to re-release the book, Stasheff insisted on rewriting the book to take into account del Rey's criticisms. The rewritten book, *King Kobold Revived*, is better than the original 1971 edition. Rod Gallowglass has to save Gramarye from an evil band of time-travelling Neanderthals who are the latest weapon in the transtemporal wars. To defeat them, Gallowglass needs the assistance of a power witch and a clever wizard; however, the plot revolves around their reluctance to get involved and Gallowglass's attempts to recruit them.

The Warlock Unlocked carries the story farther: Gramarye is still threatened by sinister time-travellers, and Rod Gallowglass is its main defender. The plot centers around the attempt to cause a rift between the Church and the State. Rod Gallowglass is cunningly trapped and sent with his family to an alternate world. There he must defeat wicked elves and monsters before he can return to Gramarye and save it from ruin.

Escape Velocity is a "prequel" to the Warlock series and answers some of the questions about Gramayre's origin—technically it should be read as the first book in the series. Unfortunately, it is one of the weaker books in the series because much of the action takes place on decadent Earth, and the lead characters, Dar and Samantha,

tend to deliver speeches on sociopolitics rather than engage in the glib dialog Stasheff is famous for.

The Warlock Is Missing is one of the stronger books in the series. While the Warlock is busy having adventures told in *The Warlock Wandering*, his children are lured by a unicorn into adventures of their own as they search for their father. Although the usual monsters are defeated and the predictable formula of helping the King is maintained, the change of pace makes *The Warlock Is Missing* pure entertainment.

Unfortunately, the rest of the series never matches the flare and fun of these titles. *The Warlock's Companion* is the dull story of Fess, the Warlock's cybernetic steed. *The Warlock Insane* has Rod Gallowglass tormented by hallucinations. In regaining his sanity in magical Granclarte, the Warlock aids a knight called Beaubras in rescuing Lady Haugheur from the High Dudgeon. The standard kobolds, ogres, and harpies are around to fight, but all of this is told without suspense or tension.

In a recent book in the Warlock series, *The Warlock Rock*, features mysterious, musical crystals whose rock and roll threatens Gramarye. Clearly, Stasheff has tired of the series and is just going through the motions at this point. Just as weak is *Warlock and Son*.

Another sign of this is his recent shared world project in *The Siege of Arista* edited by Bill Fawcett where Stasheff's story, "Papa Don't 'Low," tells the story of a marine, Pepe Stuart, injured in battle against the insectoids called the Hothri. He becomes a quartermaster who takes his job seriously as he rejects defective munitions being produced by the private sector. Papa and his girl-friend Alice discover a conspiracy to produce defective weapons so the humans will lose in their battles with the Hothri. Not surprisingly, a story about quality control fails to generate much excitement.

Stasheff's *Starship Troupers* series hits its high point with its first book, *A Company of Stars*, where a 23rd-century theatre company peforms on exotic planets. The following titles in the series follow the same basic formula Stasheff develops in *A Company of Stars*.

Stasheff's other non-Warlock fantasy, *Her Majesty's Wizard*, is the story of graduate student Matt Mantrell who finds himself in an alternate universe where England isn't an island but attached to the continent. Of course, magic works, but the entire adventure is a clumsy, ponderous clone of Piers Anthony's Xanth series.

Christopher Stasheff wrote a classic with *The Warlock in Spite of Himself*, but none of the books in the Warlock series nor any of his non-series work comes close to that book's originality and zest.

—George Kelley

STATTEN, Vargo. *See* **FEARN, John Russell.**

STEBER, A.R. *See* **PALMER, Raymond A.; PHILLIPS, Rog.**

STEELE, Morris J. *See* **PALMER, Raymond A.**

STEFFANSON, Con. *See* **GOULART, Ron.**

STEPHENSON, Andrew M(ichael)

Nationality: British. **Born:** Maracaibo, Venezuela, 8 October 1946. **Education:** Rottingdean Pre-Preparatory School, Sussex, 1956-60; Stowe School, Buckinghamshire, 1960-65; City University, London, B.Sc. (honours) in electrical and electronic engineering 1969. **Career:** Design engineer, Plessey Telecommunications Research, Taplow, Buckinghamshire, 1969-76. European Representative, Science Fiction Writers of America, 1976-78. Lives in High Wycombe, Buckinghamshire. **Address:** Frances Collin, Frances Collin Literary Agency, 110 West 40th Street, New York, New York 10018, U.S.A.

SCIENCE FICTION PUBLICATIONS

Novels

Nightwatch. London, Orbit, 1977; New York, Dell, 1979.
The Wall of Years. London, Orbit, 1979; expanded edition, New York, Dell, 1980.

*

Andrew M. Stephenson comments:

The notion of making any sort of introductory statement on my work repels me: it feels as though I am being required to define what I wrote about, whereas the work itself is sufficient definition. All I will say is that I am content to be described (where relevant) as a writer of science fiction, provided my works are judged on their *individual* merits, not as samples of "science fiction," whatever that may be.

*   *   *

Andrew M. Stephenson began his career in SF as an illustrator. "The Giant Killers," like *Nightwatch,* is highly technophilic, but at the same time possesses a deep concern and sensitivity for human and animal suffering. Whereas in the short story, man is seen at war against himself, in the novel he is seen pitted against an alien intruder. It is a competent if unoriginal novel about semi-sentient machines and their creator, set mainly on the moon.

A much lengthier and far more successful novel is *The Wall of Years,* moulding together two traditional SF themes—time travel and parallel worlds—into a story that is both convincing and compelling. Experiments into parallel worlds reveal that there are nearby worlds of possibility and that the majority of these are engaged in warfare. The bonds that separate the worlds break and they begin to intermingle. As the world falls into chaos, some humans escape into the future of the 26th century where they set about trying to stabilise their own history (in this alternate world). The protagonist, Jerlan Nilssen, goes back to the time of Alfred the Great to ensure that history is not changed by an outside agency that might wish to see the future city destroyed. Stephenson ties the plot threads together tightly and portrays with some accuracy the clash between modern and ninth-century world views. As before, there is a marked sensitivity in his characterisation, though the writing itself shows a much greater assurance. The crudity of the dark ages is well drawn as Stephenson informs us of the laws of necessity that governed behaviour in those times. By comparison, the world of the 21st century (the time of the break-up of reality, where parallel worlds begin to impose upon one another) is not so well focused and hints that Stephenson would probably feel more at home writing historical fiction. However, the absence of further novels during the 1980s and early 1990s suggests that we may, unfortunately, have seen the last of this promising British writer.

—David Wingrove

STEPHENSON, Neal

Pseudonym: Stephen Bury. **Nationality:** American. **Born:** Fort Meade, Maryland, 31 October 1959. **Education:** Boston University, B.A. 1981. **Family:** Ellen Marie Lackermann in 1985. **Career:** Teaching assistant in physics dept., Boston University, 1979; research assistant, Ames Laboratory, U.S. Department of Energy, Ames, Iowa, 1978-79; researcher, Corporation for a Cleaner Commonwealth, Boston, 1980; library clerk, University of Iowa, Iowa City. **Agent:** Liz Darhansoff, 1220 Park Ave., New York, New York 10128, U.S.A.

SCIENCE FICTION PUBLICATIONS

Novels

The Big U. New York, Vintage, 1984.
Zodiac: The Eco-Thriller. New York, Atlantic Monthly Press, and London, Bloomsbury, 1988.
Snow Crash. New York, Bantam, 1992; London, Roc, 1993.
Interface (as Stephen Bury). New York, Bantam, 1994.
The Diamond Age; or, Young Lady's Illustrated Primer. New York, Bantam, 1995.

*   *   *

There is a moment in *The Diamond Age* when Hackworth presents "A Young Lady's Primer" to his patron, Lord Finkle-McGraw, and the two men discuss the figure of the Trickster in folklore. The Trickster, we are told, is a universal figure, but he appears in different guises appropriate to each culture's environment; in one guise he is the Hacker.

Thus Neal Stephenson makes explicit a mythic quality that runs through his work. He is dealing with universal shapes and patterns, the folklore of the computer age, so that in *Snow Crash,* the novel which brought him to prominence, ancient Sumerian myth provides not just the central metaphor for the novel, but also the key plot device. (Giving his central character a name like "Hiro Protagonist" also tends to suggest that Stephenson is intending something other than realism.) In *Interface* information technology is used not only to control an aspirant politician but also to monitor the mood of the electorate. In *The Diamond Age* we encounter an information network that can decode and reprogram the future of humanity. Like gods of old, information reaches down from on high to direct and disrupt the lives of mortals.

The other thread that runs through his work is social. His books have multiple viewpoints, and he is clearly concerned with the nature of the society in which these many characters operate.

In general two things are common to the settings of his novels, at least since *Snow Crash*. They are worlds of material plenty: in *The Diamond Age* his characters have access to anything they require, in *Interface* he deals with the super-rich who are able to buy and sell on a scale that is virtually incomprehensible to the rest of us. Yet they are also worlds of social and political decay: *Snow Crash* is set in a near-future America where the whole of the country has been franchised out so that the U.S. government itself controls little more than an office block in Los Angeles and the franchises are run like semi-independent city states; in *The Diamond Age* similar enclaves, each with its own distinct character, dot the China coast around Shanghai.

Thus Stephenson is writing a kind of mythic social novel, a form of science fiction concerned not with the technology of change (though there are technological innovations enough in his work) but with the fate of common humanity caught in that moment of change. And though he will have a male character who is apparently the key to the action in his books—Hiro in *Snow Crash*, Cozzano in *Interface*, Hackworth in *The Diamond Age*—the true hero is usually young and female. A figure who starts the novel as disadvantaged but ends victorious by the symbolic force of her own humanity.

In *Snow Crash* it is the skateboard ace YT who actually provides most of the deeds of daring and involves herself most with the fate of those around her. In *Interface* it is Eleanor Richmond, an archetypal representative of the American underclass, a black widowed mother living on welfare, who dares to speak up against a crooked politician and becomes so effective as the voice of common sense that she is propelled eventually into the White House. In *The Diamond Age* it is little Nell (in a society of Victorian revivalists, the Dickensian echo is clearly deliberate) who starts poor and illiterate, a beaten and abused child, but through the Primer she learns to stand up for herself.

Stephenson's first two novels, *The Big U* and *Zodiac*, were near-future thrillers which picked up on contemporary concerns, such as the environment, but made little real impact. But with *Snow Crash* he moved into the realm of cyberpunk, and with information found his ideal subject. *Snow Crash* tells of the eponymous virus which starts in the metaverse, the computer-generated reality that is this novel's equivalent of Gibson's cyberspace, but which moves on to infect the real world. It falls to Hiro, pizza delivery man for the Mafia and samurai of the metaverse, to trace the origin of this virus, a quest which takes in not only the fragmented society of the future but also the most powerful businessman in the world, revivalist religions, and Sumerian myth. This last is the key, for the overall metaphor of the book is that language itself is a virus whose different voices were introduced into the world (the Tower of Babel) to counter the cultural sterility of one tongue. Thus informa-

tion, normally no more than a plot trigger in other cyberpunk novels, here becomes inextricably entwined around every aspect of the book: no cyberpunk novel has so thoroughly absorbed its own ethos.

This concern for information, not just as a tangible, exchangeable object whose possession can trigger a drama, but as a metaphor for the nature of society, is present also in his pseudonymous, collaborative novel, *Interface*. Here a rash economic policy announced by a near-future American president triggers alarm bells among the super-rich of the world. A vast and elaborate plot is put into action which involves an interface being implanted in the brain of a popular politician who has just had a stroke. With sophisticated polling equipment to gauge the mood of the electorate precisely, the politician can then be controlled so as to make him more populist than ever, so ensuring that he is swept into the White House.

Stephenson's most recent novel, *The Diamond Age*, again uses information as its central device and metaphor. In this instance a "Primer" is created, a book which bonds with its child owner and educates her through fairytale and example. Unfortunately, the creator of the book tries to steal a copy for his own child, and is then robbed himself, so that the book ends up owned by and teaching a young girl in the poorest parts of society. But as various forces search for the book so many other political and cultural cross-currents are revealed that the Primer becomes central to the whole nature of humanity. The zest, the humour, and the epic scope of the underlying theme in Neal Stephenson's work mark him out as one of the most inventive, entertaining, and possibly one of the most important writers of the 90s.

—Paul Kincaid

STERLING, Brett. *See* **HAMILTON, Edmond.**

STERLING, Bruce

Nationality: American. **Born:** Brownsville, Texas, 14 April 1954. **Education:** University of Texas, Austin, 1972-76, B.A. in journalism 1976. **Family:** Married Nancy Baxter in 1979; one daughter. **Agent:** Merrilee Heifetz, Writers House, 21 West 26th Street, New York, New York 10010. **Address:** 4525 Speedway, Austin, Texas 78751, U.S.A.

SCIENCE FICTION PUBLICATIONS

Novels (series: Shaper)

Involution Ocean. New York, Jove, 1977; London, New English Library, 1980.
The Artificial Kid. New York, Harper, 1980; London, Penguin, 1985.
Schismatrix (Shaper). New York, Arbor House, 1985; London, Penguin, 1986.

Islands in the Net. New York, Arbor House, and London, Century, 1988.

The Difference Engine, with William Gibson. London, Gollancz, 1990; New York, Bantam, 1991.

Heavy Weather. New York, Bantam, and London, Millennium, 1994.

Short Stories

Crystal Express (Shaper). Sauk City, Wisconsin, Arkham House, 1989; London, Century, 1990.

Globalhead: Stories. Shingletown, California, Mark V. Ziesing, 1992; London, Millennium, 1994.

OTHER PUBLICATIONS

Other

The Hacker Crackdown: Law and Disorder on the Electronic Frontier. New York, Bantam, 1992; London, Viking, 1993.

Editor, *Mirrorshades: The Cyberpunk Anthology.* New York, Arbor House, 1986; London, Paladin, 1988.

*   *   *

When "cyberpunk" was a hot new branch of SF, Bruce Sterling was perhaps best known as the movement's spokesman. Sterling was ambivalent about this role. Although he shared movement concerns, he was uneasy about seeing diverse people lumped together into a subgenre, and he was pleased when the movement writers went off in their separate directions so that he could go back to building the impressive body of his own work.

Sterling's own self-assurance can be seen in the deft construction and cooly precise style of even his very early writing. He always has seemed to believe in himself. Actually, even in his first publications (*Involution Ocean* and *The Artificial Kid*), Sterling began exploring the very nature of self-control as his protagonists gain experience and self-knowledge within bizarre future societies. Each character must adjust to so many unsettling situations that it would be comforting if he could find someone else who has found a way to interpret experience and act effectively. Instead, the young narrators see that older people generally drift toward death because they have tried different beliefs and roles until no faith is convincing enough to hold their attention. The few old men who do manage to cling to one purpose do so with a foolish fanaticism that also leads to death. At first, Sterling's protagonists escape confusion by using drugs (*Involution Ocean*) or edited versions of experience (*The Artificial Kid*) to give themselves an illusion of controlled action pursing significant goals. When events strip them of their illusions, they must begin to explore the notion of commitment. They come to realize how much any belief depends on lies or contrivance, but they also recognize that humans cannot long exist without belief.

From the beginning of his career, Sterling was grappling with a major human concern: Believing in a set of values gives consciousness a center but narrows it; how can one gain the focus that faith makes possible without the accompanying destructiveness? Sterling considers this repeatedly in his series of short stories describing the struggle between the Shapers (who have restructured people through biosciences) and the Mechs (who augment human powers

through mechanical means). Those movements, the factions they spawn, and the sub-factions they produce all attempt to dominate humanity after most of the race has abandoned Earth and begun to spread through space. In form, the stories give glimpses of events that readers must strain to interpret and connect. In substance, the stories focus on characters who attempt to find something that they can confidently assert in their confusing milieu. Conclusions tend to be somewhat equivocal, as in the award nominee "Swarm," which challenges readers' comfortable assumption that humanity equals exploring and intelligence equals mastery. With wit and ironic ambiguity, Sterling describes the multiplicity of beliefs that develop as human consciousness is fragmented.

The Shaper series, occupying the first section of Sterling's collection *Crystal Express,* concludes with *Schismatrix.* This novel shows one man trying out many identities and beliefs. although the book explains the complex future history into which the Shaper stories fit, a reader (like Sterling's hero) is challenged to grasp nuances and adapt to them rapidly, avoiding both confusion and staleness. No one faith finally satisfies Sterling's protagonist. The important thing is that his wide sympathy and flexibility eventually make him a fit companion for a Presence that has observed humanity's development but disdains the idea of taking part in its unrestricted evolution even if that might lead to godlike consciousness and power.

Sterling's central subject is the wonder of the human response to experience, the fascinating ways people liberate or limit themselves. This concern was. in fact, at the heart of cyberpunk SF. Sterling was and is fascinated by the changes in human life made possible by new technologies, especially as they could increase the range of choices for individuals. He also sees, though, how we ignore possibilities and avoid choices. Cyberpunk, according to Sterling's preface to *Mirrorshades: The Cyberpunk Anthology,* represented "an unholy alliance of the technical world and the world or organized dissent-the underground world of pop culture, visionary fluidity, and street-level anarchy." In a fluid situation, it is foolish to cling to any established formulas, especially when they become establishment. However, though government is a handy symbol for the denial of freedom, cyberpunks like Sterling saw the real problem as individuals' determined avoidance of vision or responsibility. Consequently, cyberpunk fiction insisted on showing what technology could do for people, and it was downright rude in showing what people could do to themselves if they continued to deny responsibility.

Of the movement writers, Sterling was one of the more radical in extrapolating changes but one of the coolest in describing human reactions. In *Islands in the Net,* for example, Sterling integrates enough ideas for ten books in a near-future, corporation-dominated world; then he sets up innocent, idealistic Laura Webster, described by Roger Zelazny as a "high-tech Candide" and sends her tumbling though an avalanche of events. Laura is the perfect receptor for the manic strangeness swirling around her. All she wants is to preserve the humane, democratic values of her corporation/family. But to do so she must use the Net, the communications network that ties everyone in the world together, like it or not. Sterling delicately suggests but leaves unresolved the question whether the Net itself is a tool for freedom or repression-and whether decent, likeable people like Laura can learn to see the difference. *The Hacker Crackdown,* Sterling's nonfiction study of 1990 federal raids on computer hackers, is scrupulously evenhanded but leaves readers with similar questions.

Sterling's major collaboration with William Gibson, *The Difference Engine,* shows contemporary issues "with the amps turned up" by describing how mechanical calculating machines could have changed Victorian England so that human values might have become extinct by our times. And many of the stories in Sterling's second collection, *Globalhead,* also come at contemporary concerns from unexpected directions. One story, for example, is about an ancient desert war caused by pride/religious fanaticism; the battleground turns out to be the site of "The Gulf Wars." Another story, "Jim and Irene," shows two lonely, damaged representatives of the U.S. and Russia fumbling past the first stages of detante. Sterling has become a convincing mimic of odd viewpoints to shake his audience's complacency. See, for instance, *Speaking for the Unspeakable,* the video of his 1992 performance before the Second Conference on Computers, Freedom and Privacy; as he switches from the persona of nihilistic hacker to South American general to Asian software pirate, the laughter becomes increasingly forced.

Heavy Weather, Sterling's most recent novel, offers alternative viewpoints too, especially when characters debate *when* humanity lost its chance to live in harmony with nature. In the story, however, Earth's atmosphere has been so thoroughly fouled that weather is becoming increasingly violent; most of the action is centered on a group of people obsessed with tracking mutant tornadoes, waiting for the birth of the most severe storm of all time. As in Sterling's other work, the characters have to balance their need to believe in something with the fact that too much belief turns people into monsters. Thanks to increased sympathy and arbitrary bursts of luck, some of them make it through.

Listing Sterling's consistent concerns in fiction and nonfiction should not suggest that he always preaches the same message or that he subordinates storytelling to ideology. He is committed to using SF to analyze and influence social trends, but he recognizes that the best way to do that is by involving readers in memorable fiction. He also understands that in the gap between characters' differing perceptions is the stuff of rich comedy, tragedy—and significant action. Overall, Sterling's combination of intellectual excitement and human sympathy make his work some of the most memorable contemporary SF.

—Joe Sanders

STEVENS, Francis

Pseudonym for Gertrude Barrows Bennett. **Nationality:** American. **Born:** Minneapolis, Minnesota, 18 September 1884. **Family:** Widow; one daughter. **Died:** September 1939 (disappeared).

SCIENCE FICTION PUBLICATIONS

Novels

The Heads of Cerberus. Reading, Pennsylvania, Polaris Press, 1952.
Claimed! New York, Avalon, 1966.
The Citadel of Fear. New York, Paperback Library, 1970.

*   *   *

The body of writing for which the name Francis Stevens is remembered was published during a span of little more than six years

(1917-23), and was probably written in an even shorter period. Gertrude Barrows Bennett, the woman who used the pseudonym Francis Stevens, wrote under pressure of economic necessity, and stopped when the immediate need for extra income was removed. Through the years those readers who have fallen under the spell of her remarkable fantasies have had cause to regret not only the premature cessation of her fiction-writing, but also the fact that some already-completed work remained unpublished (and is now presumed to be lost).

Francis Stevens wrote mainly for *All-Story* and *Argosy* magazines during the same period in which the first of A. Merritt's fantasies were published. It has been said that some readers thought Francis Stevens was a pen name of Merritt's. The conjecture could just as easily have gone the other way, for when Stevens's first major novel, *The Citadel of Fear,* appeared, Merritt had published only a few short works. Merritt was, in fact, a great admirer of Stevens's work, and was instrumental in having several of her stories reprinted during the 1940s. Although the first part of *The Citadel of Fear,* which takes place in the lost city of Tlapallan in an uncharted corner of Mexico, is superficially similar to Merritt's work, Stevens replaced Merritt's romantic/tragic outlook with a much more down-to-earth viewpoint. The story, while forfeiting none of its appeal as an exotic lost-race adventure, is told with liveliness and humor, to which the hints of darker things form an effective counterpoint. In the latter two-thirds of the novel, the very real and concrete evil of Tlapallan reappears in the quiet American countryside, and a succession of mysterious events builds up to a climactic confrontation between supernatural forces.

The second of Francis Stevens's three major works, *The Heads of Cerberus,* was serialized in *The Thrill Book* in 1919. Like *The Citadel of Fear* the novel opens with an episode of Merrittesque fantasy, involving a substance called the Dust of Purgatory which transports people into the strange alternate world of Ulithia. But once the main characters have passed through Ulithia and find themselves in a future Philadelphia in the year 2118, the novel becomes political and social satire of a high order. The two parts of the novel fit somewhat oddly together, but each is so good in itself that one is willing to accept the discontinuity between them. In the introduction to the Polaris Press edition, P. Schuyler Miller is quoted as saying that the novel "can be read as perhaps the first work of fantasy to envisage the parallel-time-track concept, with an added variation that so far as I know has not been reused since"—the idea that time moves at different rates in the alternate tracks.

The third of Stevens's important works is *Claimed!* Here the focus of attention is a carved oblong box found on a volcanic island in the Atlantic. The box comes into the possession of millionaire Jesse Robinson, whose creed is, "What I want, I get—and what I get, I keep." The novel tells, in a straightforward narrative without any of the subplots or sidetrips evident in earlier works, of the attempts at recovery of the box by the supernatural being who had created it many thousands of years in the past.

Three novels by Francis Stevens have so far appeared only in magazine form. Her first work was the short novel "The Nightmare," of which Stevens herself said that its only merit was "a rather grotesque originality." "Serapion" is a grim and powerful story of psychic possession which stands up well in comparison to more recent works on the same theme. "Sunfire" was a return to both the lost-race fantasy and the lighthearted narrative style of earlier works.

Of Stevens's short works, "Friend Island" is notable for its background of a future world when women are the dominant gender, but the story itself is little more than an extended joke. (It is probably nothing more than coincidence that the byline "Francis Stevens" appeared on a story called "The Curious Experience of Thomas Dunbar" in the March 1904 issue of *Argosy*.)

—R.E. Briney

STEWART, George R(ippey)

Nationality: American. **Born:** Sewickley, Pennsylvania, 31 May 1895. **Education:** Pasadena High School, California; Princeton University, New Jersey, A.B. 1917 (Phi Beta Kappa); University of California, Berkeley, M.A. 1920; Columbia University, New York, Ph.D. 1922. **Military Service:** Served in the United States Army Ambulance Service, 1917-19; civilian technician, United States Navy, 1944. **Family:** Married Theodosia Burton in 1924; one daughter and one son. **Career:** Instructor, University of Michigan, Ann Arbor, 1922-23. Member of the English department from 1923, professor of English, 1942-62, then emeritus, University of California. Taught at the University of Michigan, summer 1926, Duke University, Durham, North Carolina, summer 1939; Fellow in Creative Writing, Princeton University, 1942-43; Fulbright Professor, University of Athens, 1952-53. **Awards:** International Fantasy award, 1951; American Association for State and Local History award, 1963; Hillman award, 1969. L.H.D.: University of California, 1963. **Died:** 22 August 1980.

SCIENCE FICTION PUBLICATIONS

Novel

Earth Abides. New York, Random House, 1949; London, Gollancz, 1950.

OTHER PUBLICATIONS

Novels

East of the Giants. New York, Holt, 1938; London, Harrap, 1939.
Doctor's Oral. New York, Random House, 1939.
Storm. New York, Random House, 1941; London, Hutchinson, 1942.
Fire. New York, Random House, 1948; London, Gollancz, 1951.
Sheep Rock. New York, Random House, 1951.
The Years of the City. New York, Random House, 1955.

Other

The Technique of English Verse. New York, Holt, 1930.
Bret Harte, Argonaut and Exile. Boston, Houghton Mifflin, 1931.
A Bibliography of the Writings of Bret Harte in the Magazines and Newspapers of California 1857-1871. Berkeley, University of California Press, 1933.
Ordeal by Hunger: The Story of the Donner Party. New York, Holt, and London, Cape, 1936; revised edition, Boston, Houghton Mifflin, 1960.

English Composition. New York, Holt, 2 vols., 1936.
John Phoenix, Esq. New York, Holt, 1937.
Take Your Bible in One Hand: The Life of William Henry Thomes. San Francisco, Colt Press, 1939.
Names on the Land. New York, Random House, 1945; revised edition, Boston, Houghton Mifflin, 1958, 1967.
Man: An Autobiography. New York, Random House, 1946; London, Cassell, 1948.
The Year of the Oath: The Fight for Academic Freedom at the University of California, with others. New York, Doubleday, 1950.
U.S. 40. Boston, Houghton Mifflin, 1953.
American Ways of Life. New York, Doubleday, 1954.
To California by Covered Wagon (for children). New York, Random House, 1954; as *The Pioneers Go West,* 1987.
N.A. 1: The North-South Continental Highway. Boston, Houghton Mifflin, 1957.
Pickett's Charge. Boston, Houghton Mifflin, 1959.
Donner Pass and Those Who Crossed It. San Francisco, California Historical Society, 1960.
The California Trail. New York, McGraw Hill, 1962; London, Eyre and Spottiswoode, 1964.
Committee of Vigilance: Revolution in San Francisco 1851. Boston, Houghton Mifflin, 1964.
This California, photographs by Michael Bry. Berkeley, California, Diablo Press, 1965.
Good Lives. Boston, Houghton Mifflin, 1967.
The Department of English of the University of California on the Berkeley Campus. Berkeley, University of California, 1968.
Not So Rich as You Think. Boston, Houghton Mifflin, 1968.
American Place-Names. New York, Oxford University Press, 1970.
Names on the Globe. New York, Oxford University Press, 1975.
American Given Names: Their Origin and History in the Context of the English Language. New York, Oxford University Press, 1979.

Editor, *The Luck of Roaring Camp and Selected Stories and Poems,* by Bret Harte. New York, Macmillan, 1928.
Editor, *Map of the Emigrant Road from Independence, Missouri, to St. Francisco,* by T.H. Jefferson. San Francisco, California Historical Society, 1945.
Editor, *The Opening of the California Trail,* by Moses Shallenberger. Berkeley, University of California Press, 1953.

*

Manuscript Collection: Bancroft Library, University of California, Berkeley.

Critical Study: *George R. Stewart* by John Caldwell, Boise, Idaho, Boise State University, 1981.

*   *   *

In 1951, George R. Stewart received the first of the International Fantasy awards for *Earth Abides,* the only one of his novels to fall into the SF genre. He is also the author of nonfiction works which, like his novels, all touch on some aspect of American history or culture.

Earth Abides inverts the famous story of Ishi, the last wild Indian in North America, a story recently retold by Theodora Kroeber in *Ishi in Two Worlds* (1962). Ishi, the last member of the Yahi, a tribe of California Indians long thought to be extinct, emerged from his Stone Age world to live in the early 20th-century world of trolley cars and electric lights. He was rescued by an anthropologist at the University of California, and taken to live in its Museum of Anthropology, then located in San Francisco, where he passed his remaining years. He showed the anthropologists the native Yahi way of making and hunting with a bow and arrow, and of making fire. With these lessons Ishi paid his way and enjoyed the fruits of civilization, which for him were mainly glue (for the easier feathering of arrows) and matches. His name in Yahi means "man."

The hero of *Earth Abides* is named Ish, which in Hebrew also means "man." Ish is one of a very few to survive a pandemic disease to see civilization collapse and his descendants return to the life of Stone Age hunters like that of Ishi. Ish is the last of the civilised Americans as Ishi is the last of the aboriginal Americans. Naked, hungry, and weakened by snake bite, the real Ishi stumbled into industrial America on 29 August 1911. The last of the Yahi, he wandered down from his native hills into the corral of a slaughterhouse near Oroville, California. There he fell exhausted, was jailed as a "wild man," was finally recognised for what he was, and taken to the museum in San Francisco. Weakened by snake bite, the fictional Ish stumbles out of the same hills into a dead civilization, its populace almost wiped out by some deadly virus. He had been studying the ecology of the Sacramento Valley, Ishi's tribal home, for a master's degree at the University of California. Throughout the novel, Ish watches with ecological detachment the transformation of a world emptied of men.

He returns to his home in a suburb of San Francisco, overlooking the Golden Gate bridge. The few survivors he gathers around him facetiously call themselves the "Tribe." Everybody forages in stores for food and other goods, trying to maintain the old way of life under new conditions. One couple brings home a bridge lamp and a fancy radio set, even though no electricity is available. Even Ish, the only one to think about the future, teaches spelling and arithmetic, although the world is so depopulated it cannot sustain occupational specialties based on literacy. At last Ish realises the futility of his classroom lessons and school is dismissed. He then teaches the children a game, which he knows will have to become a way of life once there are no more store goods to scavenge: he teaches them how to make and use the bow and arrow, and how to make fire without matches, the same technology he knew from his study of anthropology to have been the basis for successful living by our precivilized ancestors.

In time, the tribe departs the crumbling ruins of San Francisco. By then Ish is an old man and the tribe, now skilled hunters, sets out to cross the bridge to new lands. Crossing the bridge, Ish slows to a stop. Before he dies, he reflects on the course of human history and the fate of his grandchildren and others of their generation, who squat in a half circle around him. "They were very young in age, at least by comparison with him, and in the cycle of mankind they were many thousands of years younger than he. He was the last of the old; they were the first of the new. But whether the new would follow the course which the old had followed, that he did not know." But the moral of the novel is certain. Inverting the story of Ishi, Stewart dramatises the humanistic fact that man is man, be he civilised or tribal; that a Stone Age culture is just as valid a setting for being human as is an industrial culture.

—Leon Stover

STEWART, Will. *See* WILLIAMSON, Jack.

———

STINE, G(eorge) Harry

Pseudonym: Lee Correy. **Nationality:** American. **Born:** Philadelphia, Pennsylvania, 26 March 1928. **Education:** University of Colorado, Colorado Springs (editor, *The Window,* 1948-49), 1946-50; Colorado College, Colorado Springs, B.A. in physics 1952. **Family:** Married Barbara Ann Kauth in 1952; two daughters and one son. **Career:** Chief of the Propulsion Branch, Controls and Instruments Section, 1952-55, and chief of Range Operations division and Navy flight safety engineer, 1955-57, White Sands Proving Ground, New Mexico; design specialist, Martin Company, Denver, 1957; president and chief engineer, Model Missiles, Denver, 1957-59; vice-president and chief engineer, MicroDynamics, Broomfield, Colorado, 1959; design engineer, Stanley Aviation, Denver, 1959-60; assistant director of research, Huyck Corporation, Stamford, Connecticut, 1960-65; freelance consultant, 1965-73; marketing manager, Flow Technology, Phoenix, 1973-76. Since 1976, freelance consultant and writer. Editor, *Missile Away!,* 1953-57; columnist ("Conquest of Space"), *Mechanix Illustrated,* 1956-57; editor, *The Model Rocketeer,* 1957-64 and 1976-78; senior editor, *Aviation/Space,* 1982-84. Since 1980, columnist ("The Alternate View"), *Analog;* since 1985, principal writer, *Space Report,* Metavision-KAET, Los Angeles; since 1987, president, Enterprise Institute, Inc., Phoenix. Founder and past president, National Association of Rocketry; associate fellow, American Institute of Aeronautics and Astronautics. **Agent:** Richard C. Curtis, Richard C. Curtis Associates, 171 East 74th Street, New York, New York 10021, U.S.A. **Address:** 616 West Frier Drive, Phoenix, Arizona 85021, U.S.A.

SCIENCE FICTION PUBLICATIONS

Novels as G. Harry Stine (series: Warbots; Starsea Invaders)

Warbots. New York, Pinnacle, 1988.
Operation Steel Band (Warbots). New York, Pinnacle, 1988.
The Bastaard Revolution (Warbots). New York, Pinnacle, 1988.
Sierra Madre (Warbots). New York, Pinnacle, 1988.
Operation High Dragon (Warbots). New York, Pinnacle, 1989.
The Lost Battalion (Warbots). New York, Pinnacle, 1989.
Operation Iron Fist (Warbots). New York, Pinnacle, 1989.
Force of Arms (Warbots). New York, Pinnacle, 1990.
Blood Siege (Warbots). New York, Pinnacle, 1990.
Guts and Glory (Warbots). New York, Pinnacle, 1991.
Warrior Shield (Warbots). New York, Pinnacle, 1992.
Judgment Day (Warbots). New York, Pinnacle, 1992.
Starsea Invaders: First Action. New York, Roc, 1993.
Starsea Invaders: Second Contact. New York, Roc, 1994.
Starsea Invaders: Third Encounter. New York, Roc, 1995.

Novels as Lee Correy (series: Star Trek)

Starship through Space (for children). New York, Henry Holt, 1954.

Rocket Man (for children). New York, Henry Holt, 1955.
Contraband Rocket. New York, Ace, 1956.
Star Driver. New York, Ballantine, 1980.
Shuttle Down. New York, Ballantine, 1981.
Space Doctor. New York, Ballantine, 1981.
The Abode of Life: A Star Trek Novel. New York, Pocket Books, 1982.
Manna. New York, DAW, 1984.
A Matter of Metalaw. New York, DAW, 1986.

Other Publications as G. Harry Stine

Other

Rocket Power and Space Flight. New York, Holt Rinehart, 1957.
Earth Satellites and the Race for Space Superiority. New York, Ace, 1957.
Man and the Space Frontier. New York, Knopf, 1962.
Handbook of Model Rocketry. Chicago, Follett, 1965; revised edition, 1967, 1970, 1976, 1983; 6th edition, New York, Wiley, 1994.
The Third Industrial Revolution. New York, Putnam, 1975.
Shuttle into Space: A Ride in America's Space Transportation System (for children). Chicago, Follett, 1978.
The Space Enterprise. New York, Ace, 1980.
Space Power. New York, Ace, 1981.
Confrontation in Space. Englewood Cliffs, New Jersey, Prentice Hall, 1981.
The Hopeful Future. New York, Macmillan, 1983.
The Silicon Gods. New York, Dell, 1984.
Handbook for Space Colonists. New York, Holt Rinehart, 1985.
The Untold Story of the Computer Revolution. New York, Arbor House, 1985.
On the Frontiers of Science: Strange Machines You Can Build. Atheneum, 1985, as *Weird and Wonderful Machines You Can Build*, Largo, Florida, Top of the Mountain, 1991.
The Corporate Survivors. New York, Amacon, 1986.
ICBM: The Making of the Weapon That Changed the World. New York, Orion, 1991.
Mind Machines You Can Build. Largo, Florida, Top of the Mountain, 1992.

*

G. Harry Stine comments:

Since 1951, I've written "hard" science fiction because that's the sort of story I like to read. I was influenced at an early and impressionable age by one Robert Anson Heinlein who, in 1950, was kind enough to take me under his wing and coach me. But John W. Campbell, Willy Ley, Dan Cole, and Herman Kahn must also share the blame for what I've become. Much of the background for my SF novels came from consulting work for NASA, the Department of Energy, or the Hudson Institute, for example. Or from careful and continual reading, reading, reading of scientific journals, reports, books, magazines, and papers to keep up with our growing knowledge of a universe that's becoming stranger every day. Often I've written an SF novel rather than present the same material in a science-fact book because (a) it made a better fiction piece, and (b) nobody would believe it as a science-fact work! ("Shuttle Down" is an example of this.) Incidentally, I've used the

pseudonym "Lee Correy" to tag my SF in order to separate it from my science-fact writing, a differentiation that's getting more difficult to determine every day. Although I've written some "far out" science fiction, I'm just not interested in "swords and sorcery" fairy tales masquerading as "science fiction." (People are free to write and read what they want, but I wish they'd start referring to SF for what it is, and it isn't science fiction!) I don't write "literature" to change the world; I try to write entertainment as Heinlein taught me. I find lots of story material in the potentials and problems of the next hundred years which come down to: How do we learn to handle wealth and power in a universe where we're largely in control of the forces of nature? I've never written a downside doomsday story and probably never will. I have enormous faith in the ability of human beings to make the world a better place for their children. I would have enjoyed being a member of John Herschel's Analytical Society at Cambridge, England, whose members promised one another to "do their best to leave the world wiser than they found it."

*   *   *

It isn't necessary to read a great deal of G. Harry Stine's fiction to realize that he assumes that space travel and other technological advances are of paramount importance to the future of the human race, that technology is the key to solving the problems that face the world, and that the role of government is to keep narrow interests from impeding the march of technological progress. Many of his novels and stories deal with space travel not just as a plot element, but as the focus of the entire plot, and the other human issues involved are treated cursorily if at all.

Contraband Rocket suggests that if the government is not willing to exert time and money conquering space, then perhaps private industry will do so instead, a theme popular in early science fiction and one that persists in modified form today. The idea that a collection of idealists could refurbish an old rocket for a moon flight has become less credible in light of the more sophisticated knowledge we now possess, but this early novel exudes the optimistic self-confidence of its time.

Several of Stine's recent novels, particularly *Star Driver* and *Space Doctor,* have returned to this theme, but have taken into consideration the realities of modern technology. In the former, a small company develops a working anti-gravity unit and mounts it on commercial aircraft in order to make a dramatic presentation of the potential of the device, as well as enabling the protagonists to avoid government regulation. Unfortunately, the plot is slowed fatally by episodes of polemics as Stine restates his arguments repetitively. *Space Doctor* is far more successful. An orbital construction project is underway to create a new power source for the Earth. Its completion will be an economic boon for the companies financing the project. To reduce their expenses and the possible loss of lives, they hire a doctor to head an orbiting hospital outfitted to handle emergencies as they arise and he deals with various problems. Stine has much better control of the plot this time and while the lectures on the advantages of an active space program remain an intrusive distraction, they are far less serious a wound this time around.

The government is itself sponsoring space travel in *Shuttle Down,* in which an aborted space flight results in a shuttle stuck on Easter Island, its crew and owners confronted with physical and political problems before it can be removed. The protagonists have to deal with terrorists, spies, Russian naval maneuvers, and various problems of supply and manpower before everything can be resolved.

Stine seems to have lost faith in established governments in *Manna,* however, which features a libertarian Utopia in Africa with a large scale manned space program. This new society attracts unfriendly attention from the rest of the world because of its unconventional government. Basically a reprise of classic Utopian novels with a different orientation, the novel suffers most of the flaws of that restricted form, even though Stine has added some adventurous subplots to keep the action moving. Alien invasion is the theme of *A Matter of Metalaw,* with an interstellar society's equilibrium challenged by a race of genetically altered beings.

In 1988, Stine turned his attention to a men's adventure series with *Warbots,* which has now been extended to nearly a dozen volumes. A special military force consisting of technicians and specially equipped robots is dispatched in each to another trouble spot to battle terrorists, rebels, and other villains. Although exceptionally well-written, they tend to be repetitive and ultimately uninteresting.

With a new publisher, Stine launched another men's adventure series with *First Action,* a near-future technological spy/military adventure series that takes into consideration the collapse of the Soviet Empire. The new enemy of America is Communist China, which has suddenly become a major naval power with warships patrolling the world. The series revolves around the crew of a submersible aircraft carrier, the first of its kind, which is countering Chinese provocations in the Pacific when it discovers that alien invaders have established a base on the ocean floor and are preparing for the conquest of Earth. Lacking interesting characters, this complex and not entirely plausible premise holds little promise for any noteworthy work.

For the most part, Stine's short stories deal with the mechanics of space exploration. In "The Test Stand," a man's view of his own career is revised when he is nearly killed preventing an accident during a test firing. The importance of the human factor in even the most sophisticated aspects of space flight is demonstrated in "Coffin Run," in which a substitute pilot must be retrained quickly despite the objections of his superiors. Neither story descends into overt lecturing, but Stine is clearly attempting to humanize the space program.

Stine's best known short story is "The Easy Way Out." Alien invaders land in a remote part of the world and set out to discover how susceptible the planet is to invasion. They encounter a number of animals and rate each on a Ferocity Index, eventually retreating in utter terror when they witness the bullying of a pet wolverine by a pair of human children. Although the basic concept is amusing, the assumption that a sophisticated space travelling species would be so easily fooled is not particularly credible. Less ambitious but far more effective is "Something in the Sky." A test missile veers from its intended target and strikes some invisible object in space. Without melodrama, and in just a few words, Stine conveys an effective mood of mystery and wonder.

The author's strengths lie in his enthusiasm for space travel and other technological advances and his strong technical background. Unfortunately, this is wasted in the action-oriented fiction to which the latter stage of his career seems to be directed.

—Don D'Ammassa

STIRLING, S(tephen) M(ichael)

Nationality: Canadian. **Born:** Metz, France, 30 September 1953. **Education:** Carleton University, Ottawa, Ontario, B.A. in history and English 1976, LL.B. 1979. **Family:** Married Janet Cathryn Moore in 1988. **Address:** 2228 Paseo de los Chamisos, Santa Fe, New Mexico 87505, U.S.A. **Online Address:** GEnie S.M.Stirling.

SCIENCE FICTION PUBLICATIONS

Novels (series: Draka; Falkenberg's Legion; Fifth Millennium; The General; Man-Kzin Wars; The Ship Who Sang)

Snowbrother (Fifth Millennium). New York, Signet, 1985.
The Sharpest Edge (Fifth Millennium), with Shirley Meier. New York, Signet, 1986.
Marching through Georgia (Draka). New York, Baen, 1988.
The Cage, with Shirley Meier. New York, Baen, 1989.
Under the Yoke (Draka). New York, Baen, 1989.
Man-Kzin Wars II, with Dean Ing. New York, Baen, 1989; London, Orbit, 1991.
Man-Kzin Wars III, with Dean Ing. New York, Baen, 1990.
The Stone Dogs (Draka). New York, Baen, 1990.
The Forge (The General), with David Drake. Riverdale, New York, Baen, 1991.
Go Tell the Spartans (Falkenberg), with Jerry Pournelle. Riverdale, New York, Baen, 1991.
The Children's Hour (Man-Kzin Wars), with Jerry Pournelle. Riverdale, New York, Baen, 1991.
Shadow's Son (Fifth Millennium), with Shirley Meier and Karen Wehrstein. Riverdale, New York, Baen, 1991.
The Hammer (The General), with David Drake. Riverdale, New York, Baen, 1992.
Man-Kzin Wars V, with Larry Niven, Jerry Pournelle, and Thomas T. Thomas. Riverdale, New York, Baen, 1992.
Saber and Shadow (Fifth Millennium), with Shirley Meier. Riverdale, New York, Baen, 1992.
The Anvil (The General), with David Drake. Riverdale, New York, Baen, 1993.
Bloodfeuds: A Novel of War World, with others. Riverdale, New York, Baen, 1993.
Prince of Sparta: A Novel of Falkenberg's Legion, with Jerry Pournelle. Riverdale, New York, Baen, 1993.
The Steel (The General), with David Drake. Riverdale, New York, Baen, 1993.
Blood Vengance: A Novel of War World, with others. Riverdale, New York, Baen, 1994.
The Rose Sea, with Holly Lisle. Riverdale, New York, Baen, 1994.
The City Who Fought (Ship Who Sang), with Anne McCaffrey. Riverdale, New York, Baen, 1993; London, Orbit, 1995.
The Sword (The General), with David Drake. Riverdale, New York, Baen, 1995.

OTHER PUBLICATIONS

Other

Editor, with Frank McSherry Jr., Charles G. Waugh, and Martin Harry Greenberg, *Fantastic World War II.* New York, Baen, 1990.
Editor, with Frank McSherry Jr., Charles G. Waugh, and Martin Harry Greenberg, *The Fantastic Civil War.* New York, Baen, 1991.
Editor, *Power.* Riverdale, New York, 1991.

*

S.M. Stirling comments:

My work to date has included both fantasy—the Fifth Millennium series that began with *Snowbrother*—and science fiction. The SF includes the Draka books, which are alternate history set in a universe where the loyalists went to South Africa instead of Canada in the 1780s, after the American Revolution. I've also collaborated with Dave Drake and Jerry Pournelle. In both fantasy and SF, I try for a gritty realist style, besides a good plot, a densely realized background, and characters who arise organically from it. SF and fantasy are—or should be—literatures of possibility, and I want to show people who are not like us as they react to different surroundings.

*   *   *

What distinguishes S.M. Stirling from the majority of science fiction writers is not that more than half of his books give us a very visual description of the field of battle, but that he seems to find it necessary to go into extremely gory details. His first SF novel, *Marching through Georgia,* is a fast-paced and brilliantly written account of an alternative universe after the American Revolution. Dispossessed loyalists end up in South Africa, in the company of other refugees, where they create a nation of serfs and slaves dominated by an aristocracy (themselves). They gain control of the whole of Africa and part of Asia; by the time World War II breaks out and Hitler comes to power, they have formed an alliance with their original enemy, the United States. In order to understand this complex novel, the reader is supplied with a map of the world as it stands in this dystopia. The only problem is that the more interesting such maps are, the more frustrating is the writer's insistence in concentrating on only a small portion of this new world. Nothing is said about how and when Free Australia, the Empire of Brazil, or the Republic of Grand Columbia have come into existence. Ironically, Great Britain seems to have escaped this dividing (and simplification) of the geographical and political into only a few countries.

Stirling attempts to maintain a balance by having an American reporter take over the description and the coverage of the Eurasian war of 1942. The need for an alliance between the United States and the Domination of the Draka, to defeat the Nazis, is emphasized in spite of the abhorrence that the reporter feels towards Drakan policies and their feudal system. In fact, Stirling manages to make the Drakan view of the world nearly palpable in comparison with the Nazis'. Stirling has acquired the reputation of being a controversial right-wing writer in science fiction, and consequently sets himself considerably apart from the humanistic tendencies of new Canadian science fiction. The alternate history in *Marching through Georgia* is compelling reading for its re-creation of another timeline, complete with documents that are presented as official papers or history textbooks.

Unfortunately, the same cannot be said of his second SF novel, *Under the Yoke,* which takes place in the same universe and starts after the end of the Eurasian Wars. The greatest part of the book is filled with battle descriptions that have nothing to do with science fiction. Stirling's pitiful attempt at turning this second novel into a potboiler makes him write in gory and unnecessary detail about physical torture a trend that has more to do with describing sadism than the progression of the plot or the setting of atmosphere. Perhaps the author wants his readers to react against the unhealthy hegemony of the Draka; however, one gets a distinct impression that lack of imagination has beenreplaced by a succession of fillers.

The Stone Dogs takes place within the same dystopia, and returns more reliably to the science-fiction genre. The book entertains us with a vision of the two main powers (the United States and the Domination of the Draka) gaining new scientific knowledge in genetics, computer science, and electronics in order to bring their endless struggle into space. Although Stirling does manage to recapture the style and ideas that made *Marching through Georgia* a success, *The Stone Dogs* is marred by lurid descriptions of sex: sexual scenes are described through the device of overt voyeurism. *The Stone Dogs* is still a much-better novel than *Under the Yoke.* It is filled with the description of the Drakan society and their mores and customs rather than overburdening us with endless battle fire. At times, Stirling even goes into the details and psychology of an alternate society operating under a totally different philosophy from ours. Nevertheless, Stirling cannot resist dedicating the entire half of a 40-page appendix to a detailed description of the paraphernalia of weaponry. This is a small price to pay for keeping it out of the main body of the novel.

Stirling is joining a growing trend in SF: cowriting, the reasons probably being that co-producing a novel would help cancel out both writers' flaws while helping both writers qualities to stand out even more. Also, SF writers are under a strain unique to the genre: the books they write have in general a much shorter shelf life than their equivalents in so-called mainstream literature, so having a cowriter should help satisfy the endless clamor and hunger of aficionados for more works from their favorite authors. It is undoubtedly with these two concepts in mind that Stirling has written two novels with Jerry Pournelle. The results are obvious. Stirling's prose has mellowed, although Pournelle's writing is far from being about soft and mellow characters; on the other hand more analysis of the protagonists' motives for their warmongering actions comes to light. It is a more introspective style.

At the same time, these two novels, *Go Tell the Spartans* and *Prince of Sparta* still remain, like all of his books, a series: all bear the banner of a series, in this case the Falkenberg's Legion; a series where a Soviet-American codominion has been keeping peace on Earth since the end of the 20th century but has been steadily in decline. Luckily, the pennon of liberty has been rising again on a planet called Sparta which will attempt to restore the lost values lost amidst the corruption and tyrannies of Earth. It sounds quite noble were it not for the fact that this is all going to be accomplished through a legion and that they will have to make war to achieve peace. This is pure entertainment with constant reference to an encyclopedia which does remind seasoned SF readers of Asimov's Foundation series, with more effects and more zip guns thrown in free of charge.

Stirling has also coauthored novels with Shirley Meier, Karen Wehrstein, David Drake, Susan Shwartz, Judith Tarr, and Harry Turtledove. In fact, most of his writing is done in collaboration with other writers, thus making it difficult to put any label on his works except the one of general SF adventure—apart from the new fantasy fiction that Stirling also writes in collaboration with Holly Lisle.

—Henry Leperlier

STOCKTON, Frank R.

Nationality: American. **Born:** Francis Richard Stockton, Philadelphia, Pennsylvania, 5 April 1834. **Education:** Zane Street School, 1840-48, and Central High School, 1848-52, both in Philadelphia.

Family: Married Marian Edwards Tuttle in 1860. **Career:** Apprenticed as a wood-engraver in 1852, and worked as an engraver until 1870. Assistant editor, *Hearth and Home,* 1868-73, and *St. Nicholas* magazine, 1873-78, both New York. Regular contributor to *Scribner's Magazine.* **Died:** 20 April 1902.

SCIENCE FICTION PUBLICATIONS

Novels

The Great War Syndicate. New York, Collier, and London, Longman, 1889.
The Great Stone of Sardis: A Novel. New York and London, Harper, 1898.
The Great Stone of Sardis [and] *The Water-Devil.* New York, Scribner, 1900.

Short Stories

The Christmas Wreck and Other Stories. New York, Scribner, 1886; as *A Borrowed Month and Other Stories,* Edinburgh, Douglas, 1887.
A Chosen Few. New York, Scribner, 1895.
The Vizier of the Two-Horned Alexander. New York, Century, and London, Cassell, 1899.
John Gayther's Garden and the Stories Told Therein. New York, Scribner, and London, Cassell, 1902.
The Lost Dryad. Riverside, Connecticut, Eastern Branch of the United Workers of Greenwich, 1912.
The Science Fiction of Frank R. Stockton, edited by Richard Gid Powers. Boston, Gregg Press, 1976.
The Lady and the Tiger and Other Stories, edited by Jane Yolen. New York, Tor, 1992.

Other (for children)

Ting-a-Ling. Boston, Hurd and Houghton, 1870; London, Ward and Downey, 1889; as *Ting-a-Ling Tales,* New York, Scribner, 1882.
The Bee-Man of Orn and Other Fanciful Tales. New York, Scribner, 1887; London, Sampson Low, 1888.
The Queen's Museum and Other Fanciful Tales. New York, Scribner, 1887.
The Clocks of Rondaine and Other Stories. New York, Scribner, and London, Sampson Low, 1892.
Fanciful Tales, edited by Julia E. Langworthy. New York, Scribner, 1894.

OTHER PUBLICATIONS

Novels

The Late Mrs. Null. New York, Scribner, and London, Sampson Low, 1886.
The Hundredth Man. New York, Century, and London, Sampson Low, 1887.
The Stories of the Three Burglars. New York, Dodd Mead, and London, Sampson Low, 1890.
The Merry Chanter. New York, Century, and London, Sampson Low, 1890.

Ardis Claverden. New York, Dodd Mead, and London, Sampson Low, 1890.
The House of Martha. Boston, Houghton Mifflin, and London, Osgood, 1891.
The Squirrel Inn. New York, Century, and London, Sampson Low, 1891.
Pomona's Travels. New York, Scribner, and London, Cassell, 1894.
The Adventures of Captain Horn. New York, Scribner, and London, Cassell, 1895.
Mrs. Cliff's Yacht. New York, Scribner, and London, Cassell, 1896.
The Girl at Cobhurst. New York, Scribner, and London, Cassell, 1898.
The Novels and Stories. New York, Scribner, 23 vols., 1899 - 1904.
A Bicycle in Cathay. New York, Harper, 1900.
The Captain's Toll Gate, edited by Marian E. Stockton. New York, Appleton, and London, Cassell, 1903.

Short Stories

Rudder Grange. New York, Scribner, 1879, Edinburgh, Douglas, 1883.
The Lady or the Tiger? and Other Stories. New York, Scribner, and Edinburgh, Douglas, 1884.
The Transferred Ghost. New York, Scribner, 1884.
The Casting away of Mrs. Lecks and Mrs. Aleshine. New York, Century, and London, Sampson Low, 1886.
The Dusantes. New York, Century, and London, Sampson Low, 1888.
Amos Kilbright, His Adscititious Experiences, with Other Stories. New York, Scribner, and London, Unwin, 1888.
The Rudder Grangers Abroad. New York, Scribner, and London, Sampson Low, 1891.
The Watchmaker's Wife and Other Stories. New York, Scribner, 1893; as *The Shadrach and Other Stories.* London, W.H. Allen, 1893.
A Story-Teller's Pack. New York, Scribner, and London, Cassell, 1897.
The Associate Hermits. New York and London, Harper, 1898.
Afield and Afloat. New York, Scribner, and London, Cassell, 1901.
The Magic Egg and Other Stories. New York, Scribner, 1907.
Stories of New Jersey. New Brunswick, New Jersey, Rutgers University Press, 1961.

Other (for children)

Roundabout Rambles in Lands of Fact and Fancy. New York, Scribner, 1872.
What Might Have Been Expected. New York, Dodd Mead, 1874; London, Routledge, 1875.
Tales Out of School. New York, Scribner, 1875.
A Jolly Friendship. New York, Scribner, and London, Kegan Paul, 1880.
The Floating Prince and Other Fairy Tales. New York, Scribner, and London, Ward and Downey, 1881.
The Story of Viteau. New York, Scribner, and London, Sampson Low, 1884.
Personally Conducted. New York, Scribner, and London, Sampson Low, 1889.
Captain Chap; or, The Rolling Stones. Philadelphia, Lippincott, and London, Nimmo, 1896; as *The Young Master of Hyson Hall,* Lippincott, 1899.

New Jersey, from the Discovery of the Scheyichbi to Recent Times.
New York, Appleton, 1896; as *Stories of New Jersey,* New York,
American Book Company, 1896.
The Buccaneers and Pirates of Our Coasts. New York, Macmillan,
1898.
Kate Bonnet. New York, Appleton, and London, Cassell, 1902.
Stories of the Spanish Main. New York, Macmillan, 1913.
The Poor Count's Christmas. New York, Stokes, 1927.
The Fairy Tales of Frank R. Stockton, edited by Jack Zipes. New
York, Signet, 1990.

*

Critical Study: *Frank R. Stockton* by Martin I.J. Griffin, Philadelphia, University of Pennsylvania Press, 1939 (includes bibliography).

*   *   *

Frank R. Stockton's science fiction has been neglected in histories of the field, perhaps because his literary reputation has suffered such eclipse in this century (he was highly praised during his lifetime), and because science fiction was only a small part of his literary output. Except in his two important novels, *The Great War Syndicate* and *The Great Stone of Sardis,* his SF was light and humorous popular magazine fiction. A recent collection, *The Science Fiction of Frank R. Stockton,* assembles all his SF stories (and *The Great Stone of Sardis*), and the introduction by Richard Gid Powers is notable for its disdain for his lack of "seriousness."

Most of Stockton's SF stories have a similar plot: a gentleman amateur wins fame and fortune and gets the girl by means of an invention. This is true in "My Terminal Moraine," *The Great Stone of Sardis,* "My Translatophone," and, to a certain extent, "A Tale of Negative Gravity." The remainder are fantasies laced with contemporary science: "The Water Devil" concerns the transAtlantic cable and a ship whose cargo is electricity; "Amos Kilbright" is a ghost story; "The Knife That Killed Po Hancy" is a Jekyll and Hyde story concerning blood transfusions. Powers points out that *The Great Stone of Sardis* (the stone is a great diamond at the Earth's core) combines Jules Verne's books *Journey to the Center of the Earth* and *The Adventures of Captain Hatteras* in a novel of polar exploration (Clewes, the amateur scientist/hero is first to reach the North Pole) and geological theory (Clewes invents an "Artesian Ray" to explore the interior of the Earth). Clewes's adventures (set in 1947) are a significant contribution to the development of the "wonders of science" novel.

Stockton's major novel, however, is *The Great War Syndicate.* Although not mentioned in I.F. Clarke's *Voices Prophesying War,* Stockton's novel of a war between the United States and England, fought using such new technology as an ultimate weapon (a disintegrator), is perhaps the most important SF novel in the "future war" tradition between *The Battle of Dorking* (1871) and *The War of the Worlds* (1898). World peace, capitalism, and the English language are enforced by an Anglo-American syndicate using the threat of ultimate destruction. The novel surpasses its many contemporaries, which characteristically dealt with politics, military tactics, and unimaginative technology (with minor innovations such as a new gun which would cause tactics to change) and were warnings clothed in fictional attributes. *The Great War Syndicate* is a true science fiction vision of a new world created by a war to end war

and a weapon to end war, the archetype of that naive hope which led to the building and use of the first atomic bombs and the "pax Americana."

That Stockton's immediate followers in this mode were for the most part popular hacks (e.g., George Griffith) has not enhanced his reputation as progenitor. However, despite its failings as a novel (principally a lack of adequate characterization), *The Great War Syndicate* repays serious examination.

—David G. Hartwell

STORM, Eric. *See* **TUBB, E.C.**

STRATFORD, H. Philip. *See* **BULMER, Kenneth.**

STRATTON, Thomas. *See* **COULSON, Robert; DE WEESE, Gene.**

STRETE, Craig (Kee)

Pseudonym: Sovereign Falconer. **Nationality:** American. **Born:** Fort Wayne, Indiana, 6 May 1950; son of a Cherokee Indian father. **Education:** Wright State University, Dayton, Ohio, B.A. in theatre arts 1974; University of California, Irvine, M.F.A. 1978. **Family:** Married to Countess Irmgard Margaretha Christina Von Dam. **Career:** Since 1980, foreign rights and international acquisitions editor, De Knipscheer, Amsterdam, and Rogner & Bernhard, Munich. Editor, *Red Planet Earth,* 1974-75; managing editor, *East West Players Newsletter,* 1984-85. Co-founder and director, Society of Ethnic Literature in Translation. **Agent:** (novels) Kirby McCauley Ltd., 432 Park Avenue South, Suite 1509, New York, New York 10016. **Address:** c/o Doubleday, 666 Fifth Avenue, New York, New York 10103, U.S.A.

SCIENCE FICTION PUBLICATIONS

Novels

Dreams That Burn in the Night. Garden City, New York,
Doubleday, 1982.
To Make Death Love Us (as Sovereign Falconer). Garden City,
New York, Doubleday, 1987.
Death in the Spirit House. New York, Doubleday, 1988.

Short Stories

Als Al het Andere Faalt. Amsterdam, Knipscheer, 1976; expanded edition, as *If All Else Fails . . . ,* Garden City, New York, Doubleday, 1980.
The Bleeding Man and Other Science Fiction Stories (for children). New York, Greenwillow, 1977.
Death Chants: Short Stories. New York, Doubleday, 1988.

OTHER PUBLICATIONS

Novel

Burn Down the Night. New York, Warner, 1982.

Plays

Paint Your Face on a Drowning in the River (produced Los Angeles, 1984).
A Sunday Visit with Great Grandfather, and The Arrow That Kills with Love (produced New York, 1984).

Screenplays: *Killing Moves,* 1975; *Honor Code,* 1976; *Blodets Röst,* 1978; *Sous les toits de nuit,* 1978.

Television Plays (under pseudonyms): for *Streets of San Francisco, Baretta,* and *McCloud* series.

Poetry

In Geronimo's Doodkist. Amsterdam, Knipscheer, 1978.
Dark Journey. Amsterdam, Knipscheer, 1979.

Other (for children)

Paint Your Face on a Drowning in the River. New York, Greenwillow, 1978.
Oom Coyote en de Bisonpizza. Amsterdam, Knipscheer, 1978.
When Grandfather Journeys into Winter. New York, Greenwillow, 1979.
Spiegel je gezicht. Amsterdam, Knipscheer, 1979.
Twee Spionnen in het Huis van de Liefde. Amsterdam, Knipscheer, 1981.
Met de Pijn die het Liefheeft en Haat. Amsterdam, Knipscheer, 1983.
Big Thunder Magic. New York, Greenwillow, 1990.

*   *   *

Craig Strete has the flamboyance of R.A. Lafferty and Norman Spinrad, combining flights of fantasy with intense social criticism. He capitalizes on his Indian heritage in theme, motif, humor, plot, storytelling technique, and subjects of social criticism, leaning heavily on the mythic to generate a feeling of universality. His works are relatively short and indicate fascination with the sound and rhythm of sentences, giving the poetic effect of the Native American oral tradition. Exaggeration, wordplay, and comic, low-key dialogue are characteristic. Because he often omits transitions, becomes pyrotechnical, and demands close attention, Strete is not to be read rapidly.

Strete's recurrent theme is society's attempt to mold human beings into productive working parts of the white man's big world

machine. What does not work is thrown out (the old man of "Time Deer"), or put to better use, providing blood for transfusions ("Bleeding Man") or adding color to movies ("A Horse of a Different Technicolor"). "Bleeding Man," his most conventionally narrated work, is most illustrative of the clash that occurs when emotionless bureaucracy meets the supernatural. On one level, it is a parable of the policy of first making war with Indians and then studying them. "Time Deer" similarly contrasts values. "A Horse of a Different Technicolor," a horror story of mind control, and "Why Has the Virgin Mary Never Entered the Wigwam of Standing Bear?" attack materialism and forced conformity, using television as a metaphor for the regimented spectator/consumer life. In fact, the stories published in *The Bleeding Man* frequently refer to cultural conflict and genocide.

Strete's novels for children, published under the name Craig Kee Strete, though not science fiction, should be taken into account as contributing to understanding the more complex stories. In *Paint Your Face on a Drowning River* Old Cat tells his grandson, who is about to leave the reservation, about his early life. The story is part of "Time Deer" and prophetic of the young man's life in the white world.

—Mary S. Weinkauf

STRUGATSKY, Boris (Natanovich) and Arkady

Nationality: Russians. **STRUGATSKY, Arkady (Natanovich): Born:** Batumi, Georgia, 28 August 1925. **Education:** Institute of Foreign Languages, degree 1949. **Military Service:** Served in U.S.S.R. armed forces, 1943-55; became senior lieutenant. **Family:** Married Elena Oshanina in 1955; one stepdaughter. **Career:** Editor, Goslitisdat (now Khudozhestvennaia Literatura; publisher), Moscow, 1959-61; editor, Detgiz (publisher), Moscow, 1961-64; freelance writer and translator of English and Japanese, beginning 1964. **Awards:** Second award of Ministry of Education, 1959; Aelita prize from Union of Soviet Writers, 1981. **Member:** Union of Soviet Writers; Union of Soviet Journalists. **Died:** 14 October 1991. **STRUGATSKY, Boris (Natanovich): Born:** Leningrad, 15 April 1933. **Education:** Leningrad University, degree in astronomy 1956. **Family:** Married Adelaida Karpeliuk in 1957; one son. **Career:** Astronomer, astrophysicist, computer mathematician, and associate, Pulkovskaia Observatory, in former U.S.S.R., 1956-64; since 1964, freelance writer. **Awards:** Second award of the Ministry of Education, 1959; Aelita prize from Union of Soviet Writers, 1981. **Member:** Union of Soviet Writers. **Agent:** Vsesojuznoje Agentstvo Po Avtorskim Pravam (VAAP), Lavrushinskii pereulok, 17 Moscow, Russia 109017.

SCIENCE FICTION PUBLICATIONS

Novels

Strana bagrovykh tuch. Moscow, Detgiz, 1960; translated as *The Country of Crimson Clouds.* N.p., n.d.

Put'na Amal'teiu. Moscow, Molodaia Gvardiia, 1960; translated by Koesnikov as *A Voyage to Amaltheia,* Moscow, Central Books, 1962.

Popytka k begstvu. Moscow, n.p., 1962; translation as *Escape Attempt.* Moscow, n.p., 1962.

Stazhery. Moscow, Molodaia Gvardiia, 1962; translated by Antonina W. Bouis as *Space Apprentice,* New York, Macmillan, and London, Collier Macmillan, 1981.

Dalekaia raduga. Moscow, Molodaia Gvardiia, 1964; translated by A. G. Myers as *Far Rainbow,* Moscow, Mir Publishers, 1967.

Dalekaia raduga. Moscow, Molodaia Gvardiia, 1964; as *Vtoroe nashestvie Marsian,* Moscow, Molodaia Gvardiia, 1968; translated by Antonina W. Bouis and Gary Kern as *Far Rainbow, The Second Invasion from Mars,* New York, Macmillan, and London, Collier Macmillan, 1979.

Khishchnye veshchi veka. Moscow, Molodaia Gvardiia, 1965; translated by Leonid Renem as *The Final Circle of Paradise,* New York, DAW, 1976.

Ponedel'nik nachinaetsia v subbotu. Moscow, Detskaia Literatura, 1965; translated by Leonid Renem as *Monday Begins on Saturday,* New York, DAW, 1977.

Trudno byt' bogom. Moscow, Molodaia Gvardiia, 1966; translated by Wendayne Ackerman as *Hard to Be a God,* New York, Seabury, 1973.

Ulitka na sklone. Moscow, n.p., 1966; translated by Alan Meyers as *The Snail on the Slope,* New York, Bantam, 1980; also translated as *The Tale of the Troika,* New York, Macmillan, 1977.

Vozrashchenie: polden' XXII vek. Moscow, n.p., 1967; translated by Patrick L. McGuire as *Noon: 22nd Century,* New York, Macmillan, and London, Collier Macmillan, 1978.

Piknik na obochine, Skazka o troike. Moscow, n.p., 1968; translated by Antonina W. Bouis as *Roadside Picnic, Tale of the Troike,* New York, Macmillan, 1977.

Otel' u pogibshego al'pinista. Moscow, n.p., 1962; translated as *Hotel "To the Lost Climber."* Moscow, n.p., 1970.

Obitaemyi ostrov. Moscow, n.p., 1971; translated by Helen Saltz Jacobson as *Prisoners of Power,* New York, Macmillan, and London, Collier Macmillan, 1977.

Piknik na obochine. Moscow, n.p., 1972; translated by Antonina W. Bouis as *Roadside Picnic,* London, Gollancz, 1978.

Gadkie lebedi. Frankfort, Posev, 1972; translated by Alice Stone and Alexander Nakhimovsky as *The Ugly Swans,* New York, Macmillan, and London, Collier Macmillan, 1979.

Guy from Hell. Moscow, Detskaia literatura, 1976.

Za milliard let do kontsa sveta. Moscow, n.p., 1976; translated by Antonina W. Bouis as *Definitely Maybe: A Manuscript Discovered under Unusual Circumstances,* New York, Macmillan, and London, Collier Macmillan, 1978.

Zhuk v muraveinike. Fiji, Izd.-vo, 1979; translated by Antonina W. Bouis as *Beetle in the Anthill,* New York, Macmillan, 1980.

Volny gasiat veter. Haifa, Israel, Keshet Book Shop, 1986; translated by Antonina W. Bouis as *The Time Wanderers,* New York, Richardson and Steirman, 1986.

Space Apprentice. New York, Macmillan, 1981.

Beyond. N.p., n.d.

Short Stories

Six Matches. N.p., n.d.

The Molecular Cafe: Science-Fiction Stories. Moscow, Mir Publishers, 1968.

Alien Travelers and Other Strangers. N.p., n.d.

OTHER PUBLICATIONS

Novels

Crooked [Lame] Destiny. N.p., n.d.
The Doomed City. N.p., n.d.
Burdened by Evil, a Forty Years After. N.p., n.d.

*   *   *

Arkady and Boris Strugatsky (the first a Japanese/English specialist, technical translator, and an editor; the second a computer mathematician, astronomer, and astrophysicist at the Pulkovo astronomical observatory) are the best-known Russian SF writers both inside and outside Russia. There have been over 200 editions of their works, with reprints in more than 20 countries. The Strugatskys were the first laureates of the yearly Soviet Aelita Award for the best work in science fiction, and have received a number of foreign awards as well. However, censorship restrictions prevented the Russian public from reading the whole of their novels (except through the underground Soviet *samizdat*) until 1989, after which all of their works were made available in huge print runs. Widely translated, though at times poorly, they have successfully merged science fiction with fable and fantasy to create future worlds which mirror our own. They bring to the genre linguistic versatility and wit (though some of their more masterly dialogues do not translate easily), an ability to make even minor fictive characters fully believable, a visual sense that makes descriptions of absurdities, heroism, and worlds in chaos live on in the mind's eye long after details of plot have faded away, and a political satire characterized by allegorical indirection. They rarely have their characters engage in full-fledged debate; instead, their technique is a kaleidoscopic exploration of moral and social issues through enchanted lands reflective of ideas, values, theories, and mind sets, lands where the individual (usually a male protagonist) is tested, his values questioned, his potential explored. There is a layering effect of meaning within meaning and of metaphorical complexity which the reader must decode, but, at times, what Westerners take as imaginative creativity (especially descriptions of complex bureaucracies) for Russians is a thinly disguised description of an ongoing reality. The very Russianature of the Strugatskys' characters and situations opens up for Westerners a mind and a world that has for too long been closed.

The Strugatskys began writing science fiction on a dare and their early cycle—the trilogy *The Country of Crimson Clouds* (about a flight to Venus), *A Voyage to Amaltheia, The Space Apprentice,* and the short stories in *Six Matches* and *Noon: 22nd Century*—is a rather conventional set of utopian future histories on or near Earth, with interlocking characters progressing through two centuries. For example, Leonid Gorbovsky, captain of the spaceship Tariel in *Noon,* a kindly, intelligent man, ironical, witty and human, a laconic expert whose actions reflect his high ethical values, makes the key decision in *Far Rainbow,* one that assures his own death, but he is later resurrected in *Space Mowgli.* Amid vivid, variegated surroundings, the young explorers and scientists in this adventure-packed series take action leading to ethical choice. In this first idyllic cycle, except for some surviving problems with egotism and capitalism, conflicts take place between man and nature, "between the good and the better." The societies depicted—based on friendship, community, equality, shared property, and shared values—have overcome modern worries about overpopulation, pollution, and mechanical dehumanization, but still face problems of man's limitations and failures and torments of conscience, boredom, and unhappiness. *Noon: 22nd Century* cleverly juxtaposes space travellers adjusting to utopia with four maturing indigenous youths questioning this future world as they are taught to value work and teachers and to feel contempt for aggression and "sportsmanship." Some of these early tales focus on human frailty; the short stories of *Aliens, Travelers and Other Strangers* spoof the complications caused by a greedy time-travelling art collector or make wry comments on the space hero cult, while *Space Apprentice* focuses on the adventures of a galactic hitch-hiker who sees greed, ambition, and jealousy dividing workers and threatening the security of communities and who finally sacrifices his life for knowledge. It is such frailty that darkens the somewhat aseptically bright horizons.

The Strugatskys soon began to deal with more serious concerns, and, in their second phase (1962-65), dialectics of innocence and experience, of utopian ethics and historical destructiveness provide significant tension. In some cases, like *Beyond,* the aliens encountered are like those in the works of Stanislaw Lem: totally different Others; in other cases, they are human. Their reasoning in making extraterrestrials outside the realm of human contact, Arkady explains, was because humans cannot put their hope in an outside savior, but must find the answers to their problems alone.

In *Escape Attempt* a 1940s POW escapes to a communist future where he joins two tourists on an interplanetary holiday; together they explore a brutal planet where barbaric masters force enslaved masses—made subhuman by cruel abuse—to test out alien weaponry and machinery that moves endlessly across a frozen wasteland. Communication and assistance prove impossible due to divergent, deeply rooted premises, and even attack proves futile. Having seen fascism and communism produce similar barbaric results (concentration camps and smug torturers committing shocking yet familiar atrocities), the escapee returns to his own historic age to die. This interest in utopian ethics tested through inhuman and apparently irresistible destruction continues in the Strugatskys' first masterpieces, *Far Rainbow* and *Hard to Be a God.* All three books involve a theme the Strugatskys explore throughout their canon: that of interference in the history of an alien planet and of the moral, logical, and social problems arising therefrom. A physical Black Wave, unintentionally produced by a joyous community of experimenting creators, destroys the small planet of Far Rainbow in a clear historical parable. Setting in opposition the selfish and the self-sacrificing, the novel focuses on the decisions involved in the final 24 hours before destruction: whether to rely on cold logic and preserve the knowledge stored on the planet or to act humanely and irrationally and save the children, the biological future. Almost all remaining heroes of the first cycle die here; only the children, and the mysterious deathless man-robot Kamill (a lonely and powerless Reason, which has purposefully reduced its human frailities), survive. *Hard to Be a God,* a very successful and highly popular SF version of the historical novel, attacks modern totalitarianism by dramatizing the conflict between utopia and militant philistinism, stupidity, and social entropy; the result is rich and subtle. The hero, an emissary from classless Earth to a feudal planet, has been instructed too serve without interfering. However, the Earth historians' projection of progress turns out to be wrong; organized obscurantism is killing off intellectuals and destroying all values, and even the agent interveners find themselves seduced by the violence of their milieu. The planet triggers readers' memories of human history as the worst excesses of the medieval, the fascist, and the Stalinist merge (ignorance, superstitious hatred of intelligence,

violence, and oppression; a militant church, bandits, stormtroopers, palace coups, and an SS-style purge called "the Night of the Long Knives"); revolt simply leads to more calamity. Outside interference (even with the best intentions) would introduce a benevolent dictatorship, but the Earthling "gods" are trapped in a dilemma—their humanism and ethical sense compel them to reduce suffering and to save those they love and respect, yet in so doing their social engineering will introduce weapons that will be misused, and will push the planet's progress forward so rapidly that its inhabitants will be deprived of their own history—a history that would humanize them and that would form the dark base for their brighter future.

A cautionary tale, *The Final Circle of Paradise* at first seems to return to the anticipatory universe of the first cycle as it delineates an apparent utopia: democratic, peaceful, unified, and abundantly wealthy. However, this "utopia" proves a spiritually regressive dystopia, wherein humanity, freed from historic problems, becomes endangered by too much ease and a new hedonism summed up in "slug," a mysterious addictive substance that provides instant pleasures but that destroys thought, creates an aversion to books, culture, and art of any sort, and binds people in a dehumanizing cycle of self-gratification. As fanatics rampage against museums, the protagonist, a Soviet cosmonaut-turned-UN agent, flushes out demoralizing pleasure centers and seeks to overcome them through education and conflict. The ending is left open, the outcome uncertain, the warning clear.

Running into increasing political pressures, the Strugatskys opted in their third phase (1965-68) for parables with more pronounced satirical overtones, characterized by a formal mastery of technique and an interest in sociological confusions. The protagonists provide a privileged point of view, often a naive glance at a disharmonious world with monopolized information channels. A follow-up to the invasion recorded in H.G. Wells's *War of the Worlds , The Second Invasion from Mars* lampoons capitalism as selling man's soul (and body) for short-term profit and Soviet authoritarianism for imposing social and political constraints on newspapers and literature, but it is deliberately vague about real connections, employing names from Greek mythology to suggest the atemporal, fictive nature of their work. In his diary of the Martian invasion, the protagonist, a philistine busybody, happily records his submission to the new Martian bosses, who enslave and conquer by using local traitors, economic corruption, misinformation, censorship, and capitalistic business practices instead of heat rays and gases. Renewable human body fluids (much prized by Martians) become big business, and only the active opposition of the strongly independent can possibly keep the human race from becoming—for economic gain—the Martians' dumb, complacent sheep. The work is infused with details that relate the action directly to Soviet society: long shopping lines, farmers touted for productivity, incomprehensible news reports of new wheat deals, ill-will toward returning POWs, alcoholism, persecution of the press, sleek black KGB Volgas, and the self-serving rationalizations of privileged party bosses.

The two interlocked stories of *The Snail on the Slope* brilliantly satirize through parody, symbolism, irony, and black humor the chaos and disorder of pre-perestroika Russian society, where, confirms critic Paulina Bazin, "useless work and meaningless directives made life unbearable" and where science depended on government regulation for validation. The Directorate of the story sums up bureaucratic extremes carried to absurdity, while the forest reflects not only the complexities and mysteries of Nature but also what Bazin calls the inscrutable world "hidden from millions of Soviets behind the iron curtain." "Kandid," a scientist like Boris, is caught up in a world of "organic" chaos, bereft of history and subject to unknown destructive forces, a dearth of information, and the impossibility of generalizing, while "Pepper," a linguist like Arkady, becomes trapped by and succumbs to the Kafkaesque bureaucracy he supposedly manages. The two protagonists come to stand for the alternatives of modern intellectuals faced with power: accommodation versus refusal. A culmination of the Strugatskys' escape from politics into ethics, the novel is among their most interesting creations, and the Kandid part a gem of contemporary Russian literature. The jargonate nonsense of Directorate communications, images of blindfolded men seeking a lost classified machine whose sight is forbidden, and descriptions of meaningless and contradictory processes and inexplicable political maneuverings—an historical accumulation of absurdities—are set off against an incomprehensible, chaotic forest of organic anomalies (faceless men, disappearing villages, mermaids, Amazonian maidens, "Swampings," "Harrowings," and "deadlings"); in other words, annihilation for the sake of control contends with the inexplicable and frightening chaos of Nature. The Strugatskys compare man's journey toward knowledge to that of a snail climbing Mount Fuji—limited, uncertain, myopic.

The Ugly Swans merges a real past/present (a feudal system, quarreling police factions, paramilitary Fascists, an ingrown bureaucracy) with a fantastic future (multiplying "rainmen," sudden metamorphoses, reborn children, a mysterious "Voice" from the fog, whiskey turned to water) in its depiction of a Shchedrinian satiric city whose persistent rainfall signifies the end of a morally corrupt society. The setting is the West, but the capital is Stalinist Moscow, and unrelenting fog obscures all. Mutant "lepers", midwives of the "New," prove sinister pied-pipers, helping children evolve to a higher, more just intelligence and leading them from a limited, corrupt past to a transformed future. Contradictions and metamorphoses are the essence of this novel, whose title is a counterproject to H.C. Andersen's optimistic fairy tale. As in the former novel, the puzzles are left unsolved: all we can infer from the final exodus of the children, through the hardboiled, polemical vernacular and the ambiguous protagonist (a politically suspect writer who embodies a spirit of opposition), is that our species is doomed. Stanislaw Lem believes *Ugly Swans* is about the Jewish Diaspora—but, if so, "we are all Jews", as a Russian poet remarked. The protagonist speaks for disillusioned intellectuals stunned at the brutal tyranny of a former freedom fighter turned president.

Monday Begins on Saturday and its sequel, *Tale of the Troika*, are linked by a shared main character, but the first is "fairy tales for junior scientists," while the second is more darkly satiric and includes topical allusions to Stalin, attacks on toadyism, and forceful black-and-white moral divisions that resulted in its being banned until perestroika. The Strugatskys' updating of folktale to embody the "magic" of modern alienated sciences and society results in a loose picaresque work ranging from fabulistic fun to the Goyaesque horrors of charlatanism and bureaucratic power. *Monday* deals primarily with the misuse and abuse of science by incompetents, profiteerers, and immovable bureaucrats. Science is reduced to magic tricks. The director of the Scientific Institute for Magic, studying human happiness, has split into a present scientist and a future administrator who lives backward in time; the demagogic charlatan Vybegallo plans a happy Universal Consumer but his homunculus is destroyed just short of consuming the universe. This work also spoofs both Soviet and Western SF, with their utopias, their time machines, and their robot wars. *Troika* shows a bureaucratic triumvirate "rationalizing" a country of unexplained phenomena. The

Troika's semiliterate jargon and fossilized pseudo-democratic slogans, its incompetent quid pro quos and malapropisms, make for wildly hilarious black humor. Somewhat uneven, this is perhaps the Strugatskys' weightiest experiment.

The post-1968 novels, the Strugatsky's fourth phase, are somber and uneven, often of adolescent heroics amid increasing alienation and desperation. *Prisoners of Power* is a very good adventure wherein the utopian protagonist, a Terran explorer marooned on a planet wasted by nuclear holocaust and hence beset by genetic degeneration, fights a Nazi-style military dictatorship and its new persuasion technologies. However, to change this world, with its Cold War rivalries and brinkmanship strategies, he too must change, experience its ignorance, submissiveness and motiveless cruelties, and unravel its mysteries. The masterly depiction of various social strata bereft of history, the insights into both oligarchy and underground politics, and the pessimistic vision of terrible methods employed for the best of motives undercut the idea of a superhero and a happy ending. In *Beetle in the Anthill* the choice is again between ethics and survival; a space explorer is suspected of being programmed by aliens to destroy the human race. The racy mystery, told by a confused Terran security officer, ends with the security chief, an ex-space hero, murdering the suspect—just in case. *Hotel "To the Lost Climber,"* *Guy from Hell,* and *Space Mowgli* are entertaining lightweights. The first is a mystery with an SF twist involving alien robots with strange powers. In the second, humane interference in a grotesque war between equally violent societies produces a limited peace, but failure to truly change a trained killer from one of the societies, after prolonged intellectual and emotional contact, suggests conflict is inevitable, people cannot be changed, peace is doomed. In the third, a "wolfchild" tale, contact with a humanoid—modified for survival and raised to manhood by an incomprehensible alien life form—raises false hopes of bridging the gulf between human and alien. The most challenging work of this period is *Roadside Picnic*, simultaneously a "first contact" SF story, folktale, utopian quest, and psychological novel, with a rich array of viewpoints and vernaculars. In it Earthlings seek meaning (and power) amid the strange and dangerous discarded trash of unknown and indifferent cosmic travelers, trash that causes extreme deviations from statistical norms, incomprehensible causal connections, mutations, and wildly divergent theorizing. The story centers on one of the blackmarketeers, "Red" Schuhart, a daring rogue who penetrates the alien Zones to steal artifacts and to perhaps find knowledge/salvation but whose attainment (at great sacrifice) of an alien Golden Ball said to grant all wishes produces only an ineffective wish for general happiness. The alien influence is catalytic, showing up man as greedy and ignorant, ingenious and courageous. Through Dr. Pilman, a senior physicist, the Strugatskys suggest an absurdist universe upon which man imposes unrealistic theories that fit his preconceptions. Tarkovsky directed the highly praised film version of *Roadside Picnic*, entitled *Stalker.* In *Definitely Maybe,* a farcical but chilling fragmented parable verging on the supernatural, an unknown force disrupts (in peculiar ways) the lives, work, and happiness of the world's leading scientists, whose groping hypotheses blame a supercivilization and/or the universal laws of nature for holding human advancement in check and for controlling destiny. Some critics have suggested a subtext about KGB harassment and dissident choices. The somber prevails, but the tough-minded clarity of relationships and a glimmer of utopian brightness persist.

Through a series of letters, memoranda, interrogations, and reports selected by the head of the "Department of Unusual Events of the Commission on Control," *The Time Wanderers* (the translation of "time is misleading) traces the attribution of a series of unexplained events (disorder in the world of whales, mass phobias like "fukamiphobia"—fear of a brain-and-body-strengthening procedure—, statistical anomalies, the sudden development of new talents and extraordinary abilities, the unexplained disappearance and reappearance of people, conflicting interpretations of alien encounters) to "Wanderers," a hypothetical supercivilization of aliens who cross through time, testing human beings for those with a hidden potential ("the third impulse") and a tolerance of others that will allow transformation to a higher consciousness. In fact, all that is inexplicable is blamed, perhaps erroneously, on "the Wanderers" though, as one character puts it, there "are no answers and never will be." There is a 400-million-year-old giant Silurian mollusk with a poisonous biofield, Embryophores (artificially constructed organisms) from which emerge quasibiological creatures, an Institute of Eccentrics, and double mentograms (two or more independent consciousnesses in one body), but the central questions posed through all the oddities are whether any being has the right to interfere in the lives and biological, social, or cultural evolutions of others and whether man is doomed to a mental schism between xenophobes fearful of alien contact and more kindly, more tolerant humans who see in aliens their own pains and joys.

Some of their latest long novels add significantly to the Strugatskys' reputation, but depart from the SF genre. *Burdened by Evil, a Forty Years After* is a Bulgakovian fantasy with demons and demiurges, while *Crooked [Lame] Destiny* mixes sections of *The Ugly Swan* with first-person commentary, to provide two levels of text, with the unifying narrator a thinly veiled spokesperson for the Strugatskys, who realistically capture the restrictions on and censorship of the Soviet writer in the early Eighties. *The Doomed City,* a significant philosophical work that verges on the religious, was written much earlier in the Strugatskys' career and demonstrates the evasions necessary under censorship: the doomed city is out of time and space, between a bottomless abyss and an infinite wall; its characters are mysterious teachers gathered from throughout history for some obscure experiment interrupted by such oddities as invading baboons. Critic Elana Gomelin, in "The Poetics of Censorship" (*Science-Fiction Studies,* 1995), calls it a symbol of "moral abstraction supplanting historical concreteness." Both *The Ugly Swans* and *The Doomed City* portray history as a shifting struggle between the ignorant and the knowledgeable, the brutish and the spiritual.

The Strugatskys' work is at the heart of Soviet SF; their polemic acted as an aesthetic and ideological icebreaker. From static utopian brightness in a near future they have moved through a return to the complex dynamics of history to an unresolvable tension between the necessity of utopian ethics and the inhuman inscrutable powers of anti-utopian stasis. There are deficiencies in their vision: the junction of ethics with either politics and philosophy has remained unclear, the localization of events has been erratic, and the socio-philosophic criticism has sometimes fitted only loosely into the SF framework. Their writing is at times obscure, at times consciously illogical and untidy. Nonetheless, half a dozen of their works approach major literature. Their later phases are a legitimate continuation of the Gogol vein and of the great Soviet tradition of Ilf and Petrov or Olesha, at the borders of SF and satirical fantasy, as in Mayakovsky's late plays, Lem, Kafka, or Carroll. The Strugatsky's work has some of George Orwell's fascination with language—a mimicry of bureaucratic and fanatic jargon, irony and parody, colloquialisms and neologisms. Their satire of officialese is masterful, as is their control of conversational idiom. They are polemi-

cal at the deepest level of wordcraft and vision, making untenable what they termed the "fiery banalities" of the genre.

The Strugatskys' works are full of humor, irony, exciting action, and a clear sense of historical inevitability. They infuse scientific and technological elements with typically Russian ones, from dachas to central committees. They mix historical realities and future settings (and often seem indifferent to the precise motivation of their story's framework). In *Escape Attempt,* for example, a central character turns out to be an escapee from a Nazi concentration camp flung into a "better" future by sheer will-power, only to find history a blind alley. The Strugatskys introduce characters *in medias res* and leave readers gradually to work out relationships. The main characters are complex, introspective—at times contradictory—in nature; they are changed by events, and grow and evolve with experience.

Within the Russian tradition, the best of the later Strugatskys reads like an updating of Shchedrin's fabulistic chronicle of "Foolsville." However, their hero and ideal reader is the contemporary scientific and cultural intellectual, the reader of Voznesensky and Voltaire, Wiener and Wells. The Strugatskys argue the value of education in their works and praise young scientist-citizen-activists who are inner-directed by and toward "constant cognition of the unknown." However, they deplore people's failure to live up to their potential, and are cynical about the possibility of a progress bound by perverse strictures of power and prejudice. They warn against pat solutions and the enemy within man himself. Ultimately, through indirection, they seek to both instruct and delight. Paulina Bazin notes that their bravery in dealing with political and ethical issues which were taboo in pre-perestroika Russia have made them much beloved by their fellow Russians. The Strugatskys' ability to combine utopian visions with modern scientific philosophy and to capture the black humor inherent in all government systems enables them to transcend Russian borders, explains their international following, and confirms their rightful place in world SF and literature.

Arkady's death in 1991 ended a talented collaboration, and Boris Strugatsky has not yet taken up the literary mantle alone, though clearly the final movement of both was away from the SF form, in which censorship had forced them to conceal their social and political criticism, and toward a more open and direct confrontation of ethical values. Arkady, discussing in an interview with Vladimir Gopman the way worrisome problems could be fully embodied in science fiction, called science fiction "heavy artillery" to be used for significant reasons: "You don't use it for shooting sparrows," said he.

—Gina Macdonald and Darko Suvin

———

STRYKER, Hal. *See* **SMITH, George H.**

———

STURGEON, Theodore (Hamilton)

Pseudonyms: Frederick R. Ewing; Ellery Queen. **Nationality:** American. **Born:** Edward Hamilton Waldo in Staten Island, New York, 26 February 1918; name changed on adoption, 1929. **Edu-**

cation: Attended Overbrook High School, Philadelphia. **Family:** Married 1) Dorothy Fillingame in 1940, two daughters; 2) Mary Mair in 1949; 3) Marion Sturgeon in 1951, four children; 4) Wina Golden in 1969, one son; 5) Jayne Tannehill. **Career:** Salesman in early 1930s; seaman, 1935-38; hotel manager, West Indies, 1940-41; assistant chief steward for United States Army, 1941; bulldozer operator, Puerto Rico, 1942-43; advertising-copy editor, 1944; literary agent, 1946-47; circulation staff member, *Fortune* and *Time,* New York, 1948-49; story editor, *Tales of Tomorrow,* 1950; feature editor, 1961-64, and contributing editor, 1972-74, *If,* New York; television writer, 1966-75. Book reviewer, *Venture,* 1957-58, *Galaxy,* 1972-74, and *New York Times,* 1974-75; columnist, *National Review,* New York, 1961-73. **Awards:** Argosy prize, 1947; International Fantasy award, 1954; Nebula award, 1970; Hugo award, 1971. Guest of Honor, 20th World Science Fiction Convention, 1962; World Fantasy Convention Life Achievement award, 1985. **Died:** 8 May 1985.

SCIENCE FICTION PUBLICATIONS

Novels

The Dreaming Jewels. New York, Greenberg, 1950; London, Nova, 1955; as *The Synthetic Man,* New York, Pyramid, 1957.
More Than Human. New York, Farrar Straus, 1953; London, Gollancz, 1954.
The Cosmic Rape: An Original Novel. New York, Dell, 1958.
Venus Plus X. New York, Pyramid, 1960; London, Gollancz, 1969.
Voyage to the Bottom of the Sea (novelization of screenplay). New York, Pyramid, 1961.
Two Complete Novels: . . . .And My Fear Is Great; Baby Is Three. New York, Galaxy Magabook, 1965.
Godbody. New York, Fine, 1986.
The [Widget], the [Wadget], and Boff, bound with *The Ugly Little Boy* by Isaac Asimov (for children). New York, Tor, 1989.

Short Stories

It. Philadelphia, Prime Press, 1948.
Without Sorcery: Thirteen Tales. Philadelphia, Prime Press, 1948; abridged as *Not without Sorcery,* New York, Ballantine, 1961.
E Pluribus Unicorn: A Collection of Short Stories of Theodore Sturgeon. New York, Abelard Press, 1953; London, Abelard Schuman, 1960.
Caviar. New York, Ballantine, 1955; London, Sidgwick and Jackson, 1968.
A Way Home: Stories of Science Fiction and Fantasy. New York, Funk and Wagnalls, 1955; abridged as *Thunder and Roses: Stories of Science Fiction and Fantasy,* London, Joseph, 1957.
A Touch of Strange. Garden City, New York, Doubleday, 1958; London, Hamlyn, 1978.
Aliens 4. New York, Avon, 1959.
Beyond. New York, Avon, 1960.
Sturgeon in Orbit. New York, Pyramid, 1964; London, Gollancz, 1970.
The Joyous Invasions. London, Gollancz, 1965.
Starshine. New York, Pyramid, 1966; London, Gollancz, 1968.
Sturgeon Is Alive and Well. . . . New York, Putnam, 1971.
The Worlds of Theodore Sturgeon. New York, Ace, 1972.
To Here and the Easel. London, Gollancz, 1973.
Case and the Dreamer and Other Stories. Garden City, New York, Doubleday, 1974; London, Pan, 1974.

Visions and Venturers. New York, Dell, 1978; London, Gollancz, 1979.
Maturity: Three Stories, edited by Scott Imes and Stuart W. Wells III. Minneapolis, Science Fiction Society, 1979.
The Golden Helix. Garden City, New York, Doubleday, 1979.
The Stars Are the Styx. New York, Dell, 1979.
Slow Sculpture. New York, Pocket Books, 1982.
Alien Cargo. New York, Bluejay, 1984.
Pruzy's Pot. Eugene, Oregon, Hypatia Press, 1986.
A Touch of Sturgeon, edited by David Pringle. London, Simon and Schuster, 1987.
To Marry Medusa. New York, Baen, 1987.
The Ultimate Egoist: The Complete Stories of Theodore Sturgeon. Berkeley, California, North Atlantic Books, 1994——.

OTHER PUBLICATIONS

Novels

I, Libertine, with Jean Shepherd (as Frederick R. Ewing). New York, Ballantine, 1956.
The King and Four Queens: An Original Western. New York, Dell, 1956.
Some of Your Blood. New York, Ballantine, 1961; London, Sphere, 1967.
The Player on the Other Side (as Ellery Queen). New York, Random House, 1963.
The Rare Breed: A Novel (adaptation of a screenplay by Ric Hardman). Greenwich, Connecticut, Fawcett, 1966.

Short Stories

Sturgeon's West, with Don Ward. Garden City, New York, Doubleday, 1973.

Plays

It Should Be Beautiful (produced Woodstock, New York, 1963).
Psychosis: Unclassified, adaptation of his novel *Some of Your Blood* (produced 1977).

Radio Plays: *Incident at Switchpath,* 1950; *The Stars Are the Styx,* 1953; *Mr. Costello Here,* 1956; *Saucer of Loneliness,* 1957; *The Girl Had Guts, The Skills of Xanadu,* and *Affair with a Green Monkey,* all 1960s; *More Than Human,* 1967.

Television Plays: *Mewhu's Jet* and *The Adoptive Ultimate,* from fiction by Stanley Weinbaum (*Beyond Tomorrow* series), *They Came to Bagdad,* from the novel by Agatha Christie (*Playhouse 90* series), *Ordeal in Space,* from story by Robert Heinlein, and *The Sound Machine,* from story by Roald Dahl (both *CBS Stage 14* series)—all 1950s; *Dead Dames Don't Dial* (*Schlitz Playhouse* series), 1959; *Shore Leave,* 1966, and *Amok Time,* 1967 (both *Star Trek* series); *Killdozer!,* with Ed MacKillop, from the story by Sturgeon, 1974; *The Pylon Express* (*Land of the Lost* series), 1975-76.

Other

Argyll: A Memoir. Glen Ellen, California, Sturgeon Project, 1993.

Comic Books: *Iron Munro* (2 issues), 1940; *How to Build Boats,*
1940; *It,* 1972; *Killdozer!,* 1974; *Microcosmic God,* 1976.

*

Bibliography: *Theodore Sturgeon: A Primary and Secondary Bibliography* by Lahna F. Diskin, Boston, Hall, 1980.

Critical Studies: *Theodore Sturgeon* by Lucy Menger, New York,
Ungar, 1981; *Theodore Sturgeon* by Lahna F. Diskin, Mercer Island, Washington, Starmont House, 1981.

*   *   *

In Kurt Vonnegut's fictional universe, Kilgore Trout is a typical
SF writer of the fifties, writing stories rich in scientific and philosophical invention, but expressed in clumsy prose. For one or both
of these reasons, Trout's fiction is relegated to the unread pages of
pornographic magazines, while he ekes out a living with odd jobs.
Some believe that he is based on Theodore Sturgeon, because of
the similarity of both their names and their fates, but perhaps no
SF writer of the time was less like Trout than the eloquent and
compassionate Sturgeon, whose much-anthologized stories have
made him probably the best *loved* of all SF writers. Inclined toward magic and fantasy, unashamedly romantic and psychologically penetrating, Sturgeon commonly writes about the yearning
for wholeness that characterizes love in a disjointed, repressive society. This emotional edge and his mastery of styles, using a classically restrained vocabulary, make him second only to Heinlein as
a contemporary model for other SF writers. Bradbury and Delany
acknowledge their debt openly; others, like Vonnegut, are more indirect. Beside extensive writing outside SF, Sturgeon's fantasies
fill over a dozen volumes of stories and several novels, plus the
novelization of the movie, *Voyage to the Bottom of the Sea.*

Of his earliest work, *It* and "Killdozer" concern menaces whose
life and terrestrial origins are in question. The latter is a compelling
metaphor of machine malevolence. Another horror story, extraordinarily sensuous, is "Bianca's Hands" which tells of an idiot with
beautiful hands that work without conscious direction, eventually
strangling her lover. Other early stories include "Shottle Bop," about
a mysterious shop selling talents people inevitably misuse, and "Microcosmic God" in which a misanthropic scientist drives the evolution of a race of tiny creatures who propitiate him with remarkable inventions. "Maturity" concerns a charming self-educated
polymath whose perpetual youthful irresponsibility stems from a
glandular defect; when it is corrected medically, he ripens and dies.
The maturing of a society is the subject of "Thunder and Roses" in
which a beautiful entertainer, dying from radiation sickness, persuades the men at a key military base in an America crippled by
nuclear attack to spare their enemy and the human race.

Sturgeon's first novel, *The Dreaming Jewels,* is a mad melodrama of circus freaks and humanoid products of living crystals.
Its few poetic moments cannot overcome simplistic conflicts among
telepathic cardboard characters, but elements in it look forward to
More Than Human, which won the International Fantasy award.
In *Baby Is Three* a boy finds out in a marathon psychiatric session
why he tried to kill his foster mother. With the analyst's vocabulary and his own repressed memories, he discovers his role as the
central ganglion of a multi-person form, or gestalt, whose other
members are also children with parapsychological powers complementing his own. Actually killing off the governess in the middle

section of the novel, Sturgeon begins it with the youthful outcasts
and an older "idiot" coalescing into the gestalt's "first draft," and
ends it with the addition of a moral component who binds the entity to homo sapiens while he opens the door to the superior race,
homo gestalt. Written in a vivid, impressionistic style, this parable
of social organization and psychological integration became for
many readers the one SF classic. Completing this parapsychological trilogy, *The Cosmic Rape* finds another outcast repelling a group-
mind invasion by uniting Earth's mental forces over the galaxy-
spanning alien being. In the process, he breaks through his isolation and finds himself, while healing the fragmentation of the individualistic human race.

Featuring magic and wish-fulfillment, aliens and ESP, Sturgeon's
stories exploit the most peripheral of science fiction content. In "Saucer of Loneliness" a girl learns from a miniature flying saucer that
someone is lonelier than she is. Though it brings tribulations, it
sustains her through them, finally bringing the love of the narrator,
who saves her from suicide. "The World Well Lost" appears to
concern a pair of aliens, "loverbirds" from Dirnadu, a planet closed
to mankind. It is really about the love between two human space
crewmen, which literally "cannot speak its name," and which taints
the entire human race from the perspective of the aliens, whose
gender differences are more pronounced. Apparent homosexuality
also surfaces in "Affair with a Green Monkey," in which a slightly
built young man is rescued from thugs by a pompously "well-adjusted" psychologist. Overbearingly tolerant, the host throws his
wife and his guest together, and a platonic affair develops. Its con-
summation is prevented not by the guest's being gay but by his
being an alien, far too well-endowed sexually for interspecies sex.
But what may seem merely a dirty joke is in fact a sensitive plea
for understanding, tolerance, and tenderness.

Closer to hard science fiction, "Bulkhead" (originally "Who?")
tells of an astronaut kept company by the childish half of his artificially split personality, supposedly beyond a bulkhead which actually separates him from the vacuum of space. More utopian is the
far-future pastoral world of "The Skills of Xanadu" where people
are integrated by means of "belts" that virtually transcend technology, freeing them to realize their (and our) potential. Three other
tales show the variety of Sturgeon's production in the 1950s. In
"The Girl Had Guts" a symbiotic alien saves human lives by becoming a false digestive system, vomited out in times of peril. Marooned on Mars, a man disguises from himself, with lyrical impressions and memories, his impending death as the first human to
take this next evolutionary step into an alien environment ("The
Man Who Lost the Sea"). The comic elegy "Like Young" suggests
that fun-loving otters have already inherited the earth from a doomed
human race.

Never avoiding controversy, Sturgeon anticipated by a decade
Le Guin's Gethenians in *Venus Plus X.* In alternating chapters, sub-
urbanites talk about sexual variety and stereotypes, and a downed
aviator with macho hangups fails to be integrated into a utopian
society of surgically created bisexuals. Flirting with another taboo,
Some of Your Blood takes the vampire theme seriously, probing its
causes in a fictional case history of a man's bizarre need. Like these
novels, Sturgeon's later stories tend to be talky, as well as controversial. "When You Care, When You Love" extends love to one's
own creation, a cloned replica of a lost beloved. "If All Men Were
Brothers, Would You Want One to Marry Your Sister?" posits a
world in which keeping sex in the family is the "healthy" rule, not
a frequently broken proscription. In perhaps his best story about
healing, "Slow Sculpture" compares it to raising bonsai plants (Hugo

and Nebula awards). His more recent work is less successful. A case in point is "Case and the Dreamer"; ambitious but diffused, it is about an astronaut and his lover, resurrected by an indrawn human race to explore the universe for it, in the company of a clownish "god" (the dreamer) with whom their ship's computer has fallen in love.

Like many other writers, Sturgeon was prone to fits of writer's block (one of which inspired Robert Heinlein's famous letter to him, making plot suggestions, including two which Sturgeon turned into published stories). In the last 10 years of his life he published little, and as often happens in such cases, there were rumors of great troves of unpublished work, ready to be released upon the author's death.

The main posthumous discovery was the short novel *Godbody*, written for the Essex House line of literary erotica in the late 1960s and left unpublished when Essex House folded. The book tells of a Christ figure whose touch sets people free of the sexual repression imposed upon them. In some ways, it represents a culmination of Sturgeon's work. In a stylistic tour de force, Sturgeon tells the story through seven first-person narrators, each a rounded character with a distinctive voice. Here is the fullest presentation of the message of sexual liberation and tolerance expressed in Sturgeon's earliest work, though the book's celebration of sexual spontaneity seems sadly dated in these times of AIDS. On the other hand, the book is severely flawed; it is hastily concluded, with Godbody's inevitable martyrdom rushed and ill-explained and a third-person final chapter hastily attempting to tie up the loose ends. One can guess that Sturgeon did not consider it truly finished and thus made no further attempts to get it into print.

Paul Williams is now attempting to bring order out of the bibliographic chaos of Sturgeon's many overlapping short story books by collecting all of his short fiction, published and unpublished, in 10 chronologically arranged volumes. The first volume, *The Ultimate Egoist*, was published in 1995 by North Atlantic Books. It shows the full range of Sturgeon's writing, beginning with minor and formulaic O. Henry tales written for mainstream magazines— some not even published there, and most never reprinted—and concluding with classics like the title story and "Bianca's Hands," which show Sturgeon at his best and most articulate.

Like many other writers, Sturgeon was prone to fits of writer's block (one of which inspired Robert Heinlein's famous letter to him, making plot suggestions, including two which Sturgeon turned into published stories). In the last ten years of his life he published little, and as often happens in such cases, there were rumors of great troves of unpublished work, ready to be released upon the author's death.

The main posthumous discovery was the short novel *Godbody*, written for the Essex House line of literary erotica in the late 1960s and left unpublished when Essex House folded. The book tells of a Christ figure whose touch sets people free of the sexual repression imposed upon them. In some ways, it represents a culmination of Sturgeon's work. In a stylistic *tour de force*, Sturgeon tells the story through seven first-person narrators, each a rounded character with a distinctive voice. Here is the fullest presentation of the message of sexual liberation and tolerance expressed in Sturgeon's earliest work, though the book's celebration of sexual spontaneity seems sadly dated in these times of safe sex. On the other hand, the book is severely flawed; it is hastily concluded, with Godbody's inevitable martyrdom rushed and ill-explained and a third-person final chapter hastily attempting to tie up the loose ends. One can guess that Sturgeon did not consider it truly finished and thus made no further attempts to get it into print.

Paul Williams is now attempting to bring order out of the bibliographic chaos of Sturgeon's many overlapping short-story books by collecting all of his short fiction, published and unpublished, in ten chronologically arranged volumes. The first volume, *The Ultimate Egoist,* was published in 1995 by North Atlantic Books. It shows the full range of Sturgeon's writing, beginning with minor and formulaic O. Henry tales written for mainstream magazines—some not even published there, and most never reprinted—and concluding with classics like the title story and "Bianca's Hands," which show Sturgeon at his best and most articulate.

Sturgeon equates science with wisdom, not with hardware and limitations. Moving even when they are talky, his fantasies are wrought from emotional experiences his readers recognize as theirs, but which his skill with words can distance artistically. As unselfishly giving and fiscally irresponsible as the protagonist of "Maturity," Sturgeon never profited much financially from his writing. But he turned his suffering into beauty, encapsulating in fiction the longing for alternatives that characterizes many people's fascination with science fiction and fantasy.

—David N. Samuelson, updated by Arthur Hlavaty

SUCHARITKUL, Somtow

Pseudonym: S.P. Somtow. **Nationality:** Thai. **Born:** Bangkok, Thailand, in 1952; grew up in Europe. **Education:** Eton College, Cambridge University, B.A., M.A. **Career:** Conductor and composer: director, Bangkok Opera Society, 1977-78, and Asian Composer's Conference-Festival, Bangkok, 1978; compositions include *Gongula 3* and *Star Maker—An Anthology of Universes.* **Awards:** John W. Campbell award, 1981; *Locus* award, 1982. **Address:** c/o Tor Books, 49 West 24th Street, Ninth Floor, New York, New York 10010, U.S.A.

SCIENCE FICTION PUBLICATIONS

Novels (series: Aquiliad; Inquestor; Riverrun; V; Valentine)

Starship and Haiku. New York, Pocket Books, 1981; bylined as
    S.P. Somtow, New York, Ballantine, 1988.
Mallworld. Norfolk, Virginia, Donning, 1981.
Inquestor:
    Light on the Sound. New York, Pocket Books, 1982; revised as
        The Light on the Sound, New York, Bantam, 1986.
    The Throne of Madness. New York, Pocket Books, 1983.
    Utopia Hunters: Chronicles of the High Inquest. New York,
        Pocket Books, 1984.
    The Darkling Wind: Chronicles of the High Inquest. New York,
        Bantam, 1985.
The Aquiliad. New York, Pocket Books, 1983; bylined by S.P.
    Somtow as *The Aquiliad: Aquila in the New World,* New York,
    Ballantine, 1988.
V: The Alien Swordmaster. New York, Pinnacle, 1985; London,
    New English Library, 1987.
The Fallen Country (for children). New York, Bantam, 1986.
V: Symphony of Terror. New York, Tor, 1988.

Novels as S.P. Somtow

Vampire Junction (Valentine). Norfolk, Virginia, Donning, 1984; London, Macdonald, 1986.
The Shattered Horse. New York, Tor, 1986; London, Headline, 1988.
Aquila and the Iron Horse. New York, Ballantine, 1988.
Aquila and the Sphinx. New York, Ballantine, 1988.
Moon Dance: A Novel. New York, Tor, 1990; London, Gollancz, 1991.
Riverrun. New York, Avon, 1991; London, Orbit, 1994.
Forest of the Night (Riverrun). New York, AvoNova, 1992; as *Amorica*, London, Orbit, 1994.
Valentine. London, Gollancz, and New York, Tor, 1992.
The Wizard's Apprentice (for young adults). New York, Atheneum, 1993.

Short Stories

Fire from the Wine-Dark Sea. Norfolk, Virginia, Donning, 1983.
Fiddling for Waterbuffaloes (as S.P. Somtow). Eugene, Oregon, Pulphouse, 1992.
I Wake from a Dream of a Drowned Star City (as S.P. Somtow). Eugene, Oregon, Axolotl, 1992
Anne and the Ripper of Siam. N.p., n.d.
Lottery Night. N.p., n.d.

OTHER PUBLICATIONS

Novels as S.P. Somtow

Forgotting Places. New York, Tor, 1987.
Jasmine Nights. London, Hamish Hamilton, 1994.

*   *   *

The works of Somtow Sucharitkul have been aptly described, at their best, as droll, witty, cosmic, symbolic, mythopoetic, startlingly original, inventive, and masterful, but, at their worst, as cryptic, obscure, unrestrained, convoluted and ponderous pulp. They echo the familiar, either historical (featuring Romans, Olmecs, lost tribes of Israel, samurai) or present (the threat of nuclear holocaust, lab-born plagues, the slaughter of whales), or pseudo-mythic (Bigfoot, flying saucers, and vampires), but also partake of the alien and the bizarre (sentient suns, cities in the heads of monstrous snakes, a Throne of Madness, a Utopia of the dead, a dust sculpturess, a web-dancer, and a rainbow king). Sucharitkul, an active contributor to the *Fantasy Review* under his pen name S.P. Somtow, is at his best exploring sentient cultures grudgingly forced to face the common bonds that link them despite appearance, tradition, and culture, whether they be earthlings and lizards (*The Alien Swordmaster*), Windbringers and Inquestors (*Light on the Sound, The Throne of Madness, Utopia Hunters, The Darkling Wind*), Selespridons and humans (*Mallworld*), Romans and American Indians (*The Aquiliad*) or whales and Japanese (*Starship and Haiku*). His works, whether set eons in the future or in an alternate antiquity, show benevolence and compassion devolving into a mass blood lust until salvation comes from some unexpected quarter, some unknown hero who spearheads a resistance, engages in a strategic game of life and death with thousands of lives or thousands of planets at stake, and proves his/her mettle defending old-fashioned values of goodness, justice and family. Often it is the very young or the very old in Sucharitkul's works who are the most perceptive and the most attuned to the pain and the tragedy of other sentient beings.

Light on the Sound, the first of the Inquestor series, introduces those vigilant guardians of the Dispersal of Man, the anti-Utopian, omnipotent, immortal, absentminded, despotic Inquestors, and exposes their hypocrisy. Inquestors believe the human race "fallen" and the burden of decision-making for all humanity theirs by default; however, their behavior proves them not just elitists but sadistic tyrants. Because they need the disembodied brains of a whale-like sentient race (Windbringers) to power their faster-than-light vehicles, they have developed a race of deaf and blind humans genetically designed to be impervious to the beauty of light and sound which the Windbringers marshal as their only defense. However, a sighted throwback, the girl Darktouch, sees their beauty and, empowered by a sympathetic Inquestor heretic (Davaryush) who dreams of Utopia and doubts the Inquestor "mission," precipitates the fight to save both races. The suspenseful and gripping *The Throne of Madness* continues the story without a pause for recapitulation. This book follows the progress of a young Inquestor (Kelver), a peasant boy selected and trained by the heretic Inquestor Davaryush in preparation for the monumental task of countering Inquestor despotism, cruelty and madness. Kelver begins his preparation by crossing the galaxy and pursuing the required Inquestor quest for an understanding of murder, hatred, war and compassion. In so doing, he, along with two other fledgling Inquestors, experiences numerous wonders that prepare him to assume his planet's throne and then, hopefully, to overthrow the Inquest itself. *Utopia Hunters* provides the history of the Inquest through a series of ornate and moving linked tales told a young "lightweaver," Jenjen, by an ancient Inquestor who believes she will become a great artist. As these stories trace the life of the Inquestor who tells them from his pre-Inquestor youth to his guilt-ridden present, they reveal the sadness, anguish, and madness that afflict beings who tyrannize and destroy worlds in order to fulfill their own single-minded vision. Chosen to fashion a great light-sculpture celebrating the Inquest's crusade against utopias, Jenjen gradually learns to overcome her fear of darkness and to see in her own conflicts and creations the dark that is a texture in every light, a dark that threatens the Inquest but that nonetheless could save it. Her growth as an artist and her changing view of Inquestors help her finally understand the need to destroy false utopias that blind man to truth and that make him a slave to false hopes. The final tale of the destruction of flaming phoenixes that will rise no more sums up the paradoxes of dark and light. *The Darkling Wind* concludes the galactic chronicle of the decline and fall of the Inquestors with a complex "spectacle" of death and destruction, stalemates and endings that lead ultimately to the self-destruction of Mother Vara, the creator of the Inquest, the approach of what the sole surviving Inquestor views as the "dark ages," and the beginning of an "egalitarian" human system. An appendix debates the textual authenticity of the supposed sources of this history: mystic drawings and emblems on a deck of Inquestor cards. This tetralogy, with its metaphorical complexity, its paradoxes, its exploration of the lights and darks that make up sociopolitical systems, and its rejection as delusion the idea of the compassionate sacrifice of individuals for abstract ideals, represents Sucharitkul's storytelling at its best. (Sucharitkul claims that the "cocktail paries, rife with diplomatic intrigue," in this series grow out of his childhood experiences.)

Fire from the Wine-Dark Sea contains two interviews, a musical piece, two poems and ten carefully constructed short stories, including "Darktouch," about an expedition to a long-dead Earth, two early Inquestor stories depicting rebellions against cruel Inquestor rulers who rely on live power sources, and a precursor of *Starship and Haiku*, entitled "The Last Line of the Haiku." The latter is a compact, intriguing piece in which Japanese culture dominates a post-disaster world. *Starship and Haiku* expands its premise, juxtaposing the modern and the ancient, the technological and the artistic in a story of a dying earth 40 years hence: its land and seas polluted by nuclear radiation, its inhabitants diseased and mutated. Therein, the Japanese prove to be the offspring of whales, who contact them telepathically through Ryoko, the daughter of the Minister of Survival (Sucharitkul draws parallels between the two cultures). Spurred on by a madman, the Minister of Ending, many commit mass seppuku for having waged genocide not just against an intelligent species but against their own ancestors. However, Ryoko and her lover ensure that a hybrid race (whale and human) survives in space to carry life to the stars.

The Alien Swordmaster (one of the *V* series) also reflects Sucharitkul's interest in Japan, with its man-eating alien villainess named after a fastidious 11th-century Japanese authoress, Lady Murasaki, and its focus on an alien attraction to martial arts, pre-Meiji isolation, and ancient Japanese feudal traditions.

The idea of alternative worlds delights Sucharitkul, though he is not always careful to work out the particular details that would make them fully credible. "Sunsteps," for example, examines the world of Montezuma's Empire at a technologically advanced stage of development, and the ramifications of Aztec scientists' inevitable discovery of a rational, scientific explanation of the sun's power; how sun-worship somehow survived modern advances is never explained. In *The Aquiliad*, the invention of steam power helps the Romans extend their empire to America, from which, assisted by a wily, aged Indian chief, they hope to dominate China as well. However, they get into trouble and must be rescued by a time patrol. An evil time-traveller, pre-Colombian genetic engineering, flying saucers, Bigfoot, the lost tribes of Israel, and cops helping Olmecs are only a few of the unusual twists of this sprawling plot. The narrator, a dim-witted general favored by Nero, continually clashes with the aged Indian, whose Latin word play is the wittiest part of a novel dominated by annoyingly verbose and stilted prose. *The Shattered Horses*, in turn, provides an unromantic view of the bitter aftermath of the Trojan War. Astyanax, son of Hector, narrates this rambling tour of the ancient world, the story of his maturation as he discovers reality deceptive, squalid and ignoble. As he tells of his escape from the Greeks (a slave mistakenly killed in his stead), his claim to Troy's throne, his witnessing the revenge of Orestes and Electra against their mother for the murder of their father, his reabduction of Helen from Menelaos, and the reenactment of the Trojan War, this time with Orestes demanding Helen's return, he paints a world in which individual heroism has given way to technology and discipline and the simple has become distressingly complex.

Though not an alternative world, *Vampire Junction* further demonstrates Sucharitkul's fascination with rewriting history as its narrator, the jaded, millionaire vampire, Timmy Valentine, recounts his experiences as a child slave singing for a Sybil when Pompei fell, as a victim of Bluebeard's rage at the martyrdom of Joan of Arc, and as the center of pursuit of a 19th-century Cambridge undergraduate cabal, self-named The Gods of Chaos. In our age Valentine and his vampire friends thrive on Manhattan's teenage rock scene, sucking the blood of vacuous groupies, Hollywood production companies, Jungian psychoanalysts, and rock concert audiences, until pursued to a snowbound Idaho town, where the vampire-hunting Gods of Chaos make a final stand against them. The horrifying adventures of the innocent-looking child-vampire, Timmy Valentine, as he employs superpowers to exploit mortals, continues in *Valentin* and in *Vanitas: Escape from Vampire Junction*.

Another horror story, *Moon Dance*, is the result of six years research as Sucharitkul traced the path of his key characters, a pack of Eastern European werewolves, who emigrated from Vienna, Austria, stopped off in California, and then settled in the Dakota Territory of the 1800s, where they wreaked havoc among the Indians and the Western settlers alike. The story begins with a 20th-century journalist doing a story on a crazed serial killer from the settlement area, and, along with a former classmate, an Indian native to the region, discovering a deeper nightmare than she had bargained for.

Sucharitkul describes himself embracing Americana with the enthusiasm of a cultural anthropologist discovering a new tribe in *Mallworld*, a delightful series of bizarre glimpses of the inhabitants of a futuristic "shopping mall" world, stocked with exotic goods from throughout the solar system. This world is being investigated by a superior alien race, the Selespridons, who are fascinated by the strength of the human spirit and appalled by human barbarism and bad taste. This book depicts a world of the unexpectedly familiar transformed: St. Betty Crocker, St. Martin Luther King Kong, a nude female Pope, babies custom-designed at Storkways, Inc., suicide parlors featuring death by vampire, a megacredit card system that permits the shopping spree of the century, and the Bible belt, a mixture of Amish, Buddhist, and Hare Krishna, and the center of that ancient art, reading. Yet amid this modern insanity, man struggles to create, to free his body and soul, to achieve human dignity, love and understanding, and so touches the heart of jaded aliens that they cannot escape man's pull.

Fiddling for Waterbuffaloes, a comic spoof of alien possession and exorcism by Buddhist priests, is Sucharitkul's first story set in the land of his birth, Thailand. It was followed by *Anne and the Ripper of Siam, Lottery Night, Chui Chai* (a Frankenstein tale about AIDS in Bangkok), and the semi-autobiographical novel *Jasmine Nights*. At about the same time as these Thai stories were published, Sucharitkul began to write SF for children grades 7 through 9. These include *The Fallen Country*, in which an abused child inhabits a cold, terrifying fantasy world of snow dragons, ice princesses, and a dark, threatening Ringmaster (his stepfather) who can be fought with anger and with the help of a friend; *Forgetting Places*, in which an older brother, before committing suicide, arranges computer fantasy experiences with supportive messages, zombies, and an evil financial foundation to help his younger brother cope; and a trilogy (*Riverrun, Armorica*, and *The Wizard's Apprentice*) in which a teenager with an active imagination and the hidden power of a Truthsayer must use his fantasies to defend himself, his family, and his world against the demonic spells of a Darkling vampire and his dragon sister.

Overall, Sucharitkul creates worlds and languages, customs and cultures in narratives that are gripping, moving, well-crafted set pieces, with dense prose and metaphorical overtones, though at times his attempts at complex poetic diction and epic scope distract and obscure. At his best he is a wildly imaginative mythmaker, projecting topsy-turvy worlds that somehow remain human, entertaining, and compelling. He offers an Eastern perspective on art and nature, and a humanistic concern for man and his world.

—Gina Macdonald

SUSSEX, Lucy (Jane)

Nationality: Australian. Relinquished New Zealand nationality upon moving to Australia in 1971. **Born:** Christchurch, New Zealand, 4 December 1957. **Education:** Convent of the Holy Spirit, Aix-en-Provence, France, 1963; Fendalton Open-Air School, Christchurch, New Zealand, 1964-69; Sydenham Girl's High School, Dulwich England, 1969-70; Heaton Intermediate, Christchurch, New Zealand, 1970; Townsville Grammar School, Townsville, North Queensland, Australia, 1971-74; high school certificate, 1974; Commonwealth scholarship, 1971-74; James Cook, 1975-76, and Monash University, B.A. 1978; Monash University, M.A. in librarianship, 1982. **Career:** Judge, James Tiptree Award, 1994-95. **Awards:** Ditmar award, 1989. **Agents:** Margaret Connolly, 37 Ormond St., Paddington, New South Wales, 2021 Australia; James Prenkel, 414 South Randall Ave., Madison, Wisconsin 53715, U.S.A.

SCIENCE FICTION PUBLICATIONS

Short Stories

My Lady Tongue and Other Tales. Melbourne, Australia, Heinemann, 1990.

OTHER PUBLICATIONS

Novels (for young adults)

The Peace Garden. Melbourne, Australia, Oxford University Press, 1989.
Deersnake. Sydney, Hodder Headline, 1994.

Other

Editor, with Norman Talbot, Jenny Blackford, and Russell Blackford. *Contrary Modes: Proceedings of the World Science Fiction Conference, Melbourne, Australia, 1985.* Melbourne, Ebony Books in Association with Department of English, University of Newcastle, 1985.
Editor, *The Fortunes of Mary Fortune.* Penguin, Melbourne, 1989.
Editor, *The Patternmaker: Nine Science Fiction Stories.* Norwood, South Australia, Omnibus, 1994.
Editor, *The Lottery: Nine Science Fiction Stories.* Norwood, Omnibus, 1994.
Editor, with Judith Raphael Buckrich, *She's Fantastical: Australian Women's Speculative Fiction, Magical Realism and Fantasy.* Melbourne, Sybylla, 1995.

*

Lucy Sussex comments:

I started in SF/Fantasy, and have moved steadily outward into other areas—children's writing, crime, horror, etc. One day I hope to combine all my writing interests into one book. In the meantime SF/Fantasy is the form I turn to when I want to rub two ideas together and see what sparks they generate!

*   *   *

Lucy Sussex belongs to a generation of Australian SF writers who proudly set their stories in that already alien environment. A writer of character, whose work is, in many ways, allied with what has been called "magic realism," she works all the related fields of SF and fantasy (her first adult novel, to be published in 1996, is a contemporary ghost story, *If I Eat Your Soul*). She has made a name for herself as an editor and writer of fiction for young adults, with two anthologies, *The Patternmaker* (1994) and *The Lottery* (1994), as well as a novel *Deersnake* (1994) to her credit. Nevertheless, her high reputation in Australian SF is based mainly on her short fiction, collected in *My Lady Tongue and Other Stories* (1990), a stunning first collection for any writer anywhere. The title story deservedly won the Ditmar, Australia's equivalent of the Hugo Award. I suspect *If I Eat Your Soul,* based on her experiences as a biographical researcher at the University of Melbourne, will, like all her adult fiction, be a subtle, witty, and darkly mischievous exploration of its genre, the ghost tale.

Sussex's young adult novel *Deersnake* provides a useful, because simplified, introduction to her work. Its protagonist, 15-year-old Kate, is a bit of a loner, intelligent, sardonic, and capable of growth, both emotional and spiritual. Its use of LSD to open a "door" between "the real world" and the traditional world of faerie marks it as a contemporary young adult novels of what might be called self-invented rites of passage. *Deersnake* handles, with generous emotional depth, such problems as single parent families, the difficulties of being an intelligent young woman studying science, sexual exploitation of minors, and questions of what kind of trust should exist between teachers and students. Kate's actual adventures in faerie take up less than half of the novel yet are central to its development and denouement.

The nine stories of *My Lady Tongue and Other Stories,* rich in language, invention, wit, and character, run the gamut from fantasy through magic realism to science fiction. Five are first-person narratives and the other four tend to be narrated from the point of view of a particular character; in all cases, it's what individuals think and feel as they deal with their experiences that interests the writer, and the reader.

What people believe, and what they can do if their beliefs are strong enough, are central concerns in: "The Man Hanged Upside Down," a satirical study of ego tripping and stripping in the art world, which brings a sharp sense of "primitive" belief in magic to bear upon the various characters as they choose to believe, not believe, or partially believe for the sake of another; in "Quartet in Death Minor," whose narrator can see and follow Death on his appointed rounds one evening, but whose curiosity remains far too alive to interest him, as the self-directed ironies of her story reveal; in "Red Ochre," a deadly serious tale set in a future Australia that has barely survived a plague that contemplates the power of disfigured mutants to invest their belief in ancient Aboriginal myths of origin as literally describing their situation. "The Parrish and Mrs Brown" is a lively dream narrative as a comedy of manners, the narrator so torn between her mother and two lovers that their three different environments begin to merge. Perhaps "The Lipton Village Society," a wry fable of young social outcasts who create another world they eventually escape to, most stringently explores the problem of belief and its effects. Its ending leaves both the skeptical narrator and her reader up in the air. Something has happened, but we can't be sure we really know what it was.

"Montage" and "Go-To" are both stories about science, exploring questions of scientific motives and the potential for disastrous results of unconditional experiments upon nature. Yet in the first, paranoia leads to isolation and disaster, while in the second, hopeful communication brings about a kind of peace. "God and Her Black Sense of Humour" is a wonderfully bitchy, blackly comic take on the vampire tale, told from the point of view of a journalist who has found the story of a lifetime and cannot use it. A comedy of manners set in the world of collectors and researchers, it evokes the world of sixties groupies with sardonic feminist awareness, and then transcends it with a darkly satiric conclusion. In all these stories, Sussex proves herself a master of many tones and emotions, as well as a creator of a wide range of characters.

All of these qualities serve her finest story, "My Lady Tongue," set in a future where lesbian separatist feminist womyn live almost completely apart from the rest of the world. Apparently the story of how Raffy, an womyn adventurer, wins her beloved Honeycomb, it is also a recollection of the time she set out to find a safe haven away from the cities and fell into the clutches of a man. Not only that, he helped her, introduced her to Shakespeare, and loved her. The Shakespeare is his greatest gift as far as she is concerned, but that they can learn to live with each other, at least for the time it takes her broken leg to heal, and that Raffy comes to respect him as a human being, allows for a feeling of hope on the reader's part.

In "My Lady Tongue" especially, but throughout her stories, Sussex achieves a rich metaphoric language capable of sudden dips and swings of emotion, sharply etched imagery, and subtle invention. She is already an SF writer to watch (especially if her stories become available to outside Australia), but the emotional depth of her writing may eventually gain her a much wider audience beyond the genre. Her stories give pleasure on so many levels.

—Douglas Barbour

SUTTON, Andrew. *See* TUBB, E.C.

SWANWICK, Michael

Nationality: American. **Born:** Schenectady, New York, 18 November 1950. **Education:** The College of William and Mary, 1968-72, B.A. **Family:** Married Marianne Catherine Porter in 1980; one son. **Career:** Information analyst for National Solar Heating and Cooling Information Center 1977-80. Since 1980, full-time writer. **Awards:** Theodore Sturgeon Memorial award, 1990. Agent: Virginia Kidd Agency, Box 278, 538 East Hartford Street, Milford, Pennsylvania 18337. **Address:** 457 Lexington Avenue, Philadelphia, Pennsylvania 19128, U.S.A.

SCIENCE FICTION PUBLICATIONS

Novels

In the Drift. New York, Ace, 1985; London, Legend, 1989.
Vacuum Flowers. New York, Arbor House, 1987; London, Simon and Schuster, 1988.

Griffin's Egg (novella). London, Legend, 1990; New York, St. Martin's Press, 1992.
Stations of the Tide. Norwalk, Connecticut, Easton Press, 1991; London, Legend, 1992.
The Iron Dragon's Daughter. London, Millennium, 1993; New York, Morrow, 1994.

Short Stories

Gravity's Angels: 13 Stories. Sauk City, Wisconsin, Arkham House, 1991.

*

Michael Swanwick comments:

My father was an engineer, and in the normal course of things, I probably would have become one as well. But I was lured away from the engineering by science, and then lured away from science by literature. Science fiction allows me to keep faith with my past as well as the future.

The works themselves range from hard science fiction to stone fantasy, with stops at all stations in between, and are written at whatever length serves them best. There is much about them that seems obvious to me, much that cuts close to the bone. But I'm neither a confessional writer nor a ventriloquist. Stories must speak for themselves or not at all.

* * *

The science fiction field has long had a love-hate relationship with complex prose styles and sophisticated intellectual speculation. On the one hand, the field has lusted after literary legitimacy while insisting on its independence from the mainstream. At the same time proponents proclaim the genre as the perfect forum for abstract intellectual speculation, they complain about the creeping influence of "soft" sciences into the field. It is rare therefore to find an author who produces thoughtful, speculative work in a complex literary style without a strong, action-oriented plot who nevertheless is held in high regard by a broad spectrum of readers. Michael Swanwick is one of those rarities.

Swanwick distinguished himself in the early 1980s as the author of several highly acclaimed short stories, the best of which was "Mummer's Kiss." The story is set in an alternate present, where the Three Mile Island disaster did in fact result in a meltdown, and North America subsequently became a fragmented and often bizarre place to live. Philadelphia and its environs have evolved into a kind of free state governed by the mummers organization, a place where physical mutation and short lifespans are the order of the day, and life itself is a precious but all-too-fragile property. The protagonist is initially outlawed by the mummers, but later rises to prominence within the organization. The story and a later sequel, "Marrow Death," were incorporated into Swanwick's first novel, *In the Drift,* which follows the development of the resulting society through an entire generation. Although the episodic nature and shifting viewpoint occasionally make for abrupt and disconcerting transitions, for the most part the novel is a cohesive entity and maintains reader interest throughout.

Swanwick is not, however, a predictable author. The fact that one novel is a fairly linear narrative does not always mean that the same will be true of the next. *Vacuum Flowers* resulted in Swanwick's being associated with the cyberpunk writers, an informal and not particularly accurate label for those who wish to explore the interface between humanity and the machine, specifically computers and artificial enhancement of human senses. The cyberpunk movement is associated with a blend of high-tech jargon, experimental writing styles, and a somewhat jaded world view. Although *Vacuum Flowers* does meet these criteria in general, it would be a mistake to apply a simplistic label to Swanwick's work, since he continues to change styles and subject matter at will.

The novel is set in a future where the asteroids have been colonized, offering a relatively safe haven for certain criminal elements. There a fugitive seeks a safe haven from which to establish a new base of operations; her profession is a criminal one in a future where implants can change everything, including personalities. A pyrotechnic writing style and a colorful cast of characters contribute to a remarkable novel, but one which was quickly overshadowed by the one that followed.

Stations of the Tide is a highly original novel which cannot be fairly represented by a simple plot description, so unusual in fact that valid comparisons do not even come to mind. There are touches of the otherworldliness of Jack Vance at his best, the powerful grasp of language of Gene Wolfe, but the overall product is undeniably Michael Swanwick's. The planet Miranda has been colonized by humans, but its unstable ecology is such that all of the land areas are in danger of being flooded by a previously unknown maritime upheaval. Travel between the planets is impractical in traditional terms, so evacuation is not an option. At the same time, a messianic religion has arisen under the leadership of a cult figure whose enormous charismatic appeal is contributing to the turmoil.

Gregorian, the cult leader and one-time criminal, has stolen proscribed technology and taken it into the hinterlands. The authorities on Earth wish to recover it, so they must send an agent. This is accomplished by a kind of matter transmission/duplication. Their duplicated agent can function on Miranda, although his present body and personality will have to remain there after the mission is completed. The agent sets off in pursuit of Gregorian, but soon finds himself in a phantasmagorical web of intrigue, betrayal, misplaced loyalties, and mass delusion. Eventually he begins to question not only the motivations of his allies on Miranda, but the purposes for

which he was dispatched in the first case. *Stations* is a stunningly realized blend of nightmare and adventure, superior in almost every way to either of Swanwick's earlier novels.

The short novel *Griffin's Egg* is set on the Moon, where a well-established colony nevertheless struggles to ensure its own survival while a devastating war threatens to destroy much of the civilization of Earth through the use of sophisticated methods of mind control. Swanwick's most recent novel, *The Iron Dragon's Daughter,* is an unconventional and very impressive fantasy that follows the consequences of the protagonist's decision to steal from her employers in a factory fantasy world.

Swanwick's three dozen or so short stories should not be overlooked either, although there has unaccountably been no collection as of this writing. "Till Human Voices Wake Us," his very first sale, is an exciting story of human courage in the face of disaster. "Ginungagap" demonstrates the difficulty of communicating with truly alien beings. The world of art and the creative urge are described in "The Man Who Met Picasso" and the religious urge is examined on the brink of a nuclear war in "Covenant of Souls." "Picasso Deconstructed" is an amusing exercise revolving around a series of paintings. Other stories of particular note are "Dogfight," written in collaboration with William Gibson, "Trojan Horse," "The Golden Apples of the Sun" (one of Swanwick's rare outright fantasies), "The Overcoat," "Cold Iron," "In Concert," and "Edge of the World."

Swanwick continues to demonstrate his willingness to experiment with new forms, new themes, new ways to use language to create situations and characters. Throughout this experimentation, he has never lost sight of the basic values of good writing, an interesting story, polished narrative technique, and respect for the reader. The diversity of his published fiction has a tendency to put off readers more interested in refurbishings of old themes, but it is a positive attraction for those in search of original, thought-provoking entertainment. It is certain that Swanwick will continue to be one of the more talked about writers in the field, and that his readership will continue to expand.

—Don D'Ammassa

T

TAINE, John

Pseudonym for Eric Temple Bell; also wrote as J.T. **Nationality:** American. **Born:** Aberdeen, Scotland, 7 February 1883. **Education:** University of London, 1902; Stanford University, California, A.B. 1904 (Phi Beta Kappa); University of Washington, Seattle, A.M. 1908; Columbia University, New York, Ph.D. 1912. **Family:** Married Jessie Lillian Brown in 1910; one child. **Career:** Professor of mathematics, University of Washington, 1912-26, and California Institute of Technology, Pasadena, 1927-53. Vice-president, American Mathematical Society, 1926; president, Mathematical Association of America, 1931-33. **Awards:** Bocher prize, for academic work, 1920-24. **Member:** Vice-president, American Academy of Arts and Sciences, 1930; National Academy of Sciences. **Died:** 21 December 1960.

SCIENCE FICTION PUBLICATIONS

Novels

The Purple Sapphire. New York, Dutton, 1924.
Quayle's Invention. New York, Dutton, 1927.
The Gold Tooth. New York, Dutton, 1927.
Green Fire: The Story of the Terrible Days in the Summer of 1990, Now Told in Full for the First Time. New York, Dutton, 1928.
The Greatest Adventure. New York, Dutton, 1929.
The Iron Star. New York, Dutton, 1930.
Before the Dawn. Baltimore, Williams and Wilkins, 1934.
The Time Stream. Providence, Rhode Island, Buffalo, 1946.
The Forbidden Garden. Reading, Pennsylvania, Fantasy Press, 1947.
The Cosmic Geoide, and One Other. Los Angeles, Fantasy, 1949.
Seeds of Life. Reading, Pennsylvania, Fantasy Press, 1951; London, Rich and Cowan, 1955.
The Crystal Horde. Reading, Pennsylvania, Fantasy Press, 1952; as *White Lily,* in *Seeds of Life; and, White Lily: Two Science Fiction Novels,* New York, Dover, 1966.
G.O.G. 666. Reading, Pennsylvania, Fantasy Press, 1954; London, Rich and Cowan, 1955.

Short Stories

Time Stream, and Other Stories. Newcastle-under-Lyme, England, Remploy, 1971.

OTHER PUBLICATIONS

Poetry

Recreations (as J.T.). Boston, Gorham Press, 1915.
The Singer (as J.T.). Boston, Gorham Press, 1916.

Other as Eric Temple Bell

The Cyclotomic Quinary Quintic. New York, Columbia University, 1912.

An Arithmetic Theory of Certain Numerical Functions. Seattle, University of Washington, 1915.
Algebraic Arithmetic. New York, American Mathematical Society, 1927.
Debunking Science. Seattle, University of Washington Book Store, 1930.
The Queen of the Sciences. Baltimore, Williams and Wilkins, 1931.
Numerology. Baltimore, Williams and Wilkins, 1933.
The Handmaiden of the Sciences. Baltimore, Williams and Wilkins, and London, Baillière, 1937.
Men of Mathematics. New York, Simon and Schuster, and London, Gollancz, 1937.
Man and His Lifebelts. Baltimore, Williams and Wilkins, 1938.
The Development of Mathematics. New York, McGraw Hill, 1940; revised edition, 1945.
The Magic of Numbers. New York, McGraw Hill, 1946.
Mathematics, Queen and Servant of Science. New York, McGraw Hill, 1951; London, Bell, 1952.
The Last Problem. New York, Simon and Schuster, 1961; London, Gollancz, 1962.

* * *

John Taine was the pseudonym used by the prominent research mathematician Eric Temple Bell in his science fiction novels. Taine was a respected SF novelist during the 1920s who turned to the pulp SF magazines with the Depression. His best work blended theoretical inquiry into the unknown with high adventure in the H. Rider Haggard tradition, and he combined sound science with a rare storytelling ability.

The major preoccupation in Taine's handful of novels is that of technological disaster. In almost all his work, scientific inquiry into the unknown precipitates an impending cataclysm. These disasters can be man-made, as in *Seeds of Life,* natural, as in *The Iron Star,* or accidental, as the monsters created in *White Lily.* In *The Greatest Adventure* and *The Purple Sapphire* unknown cataclysms in remote antiquity have their effect on the modern world. *The Time Stream* links the destruction of a future world with the great San Francisco earthquake.

Taine's novels invariably focus on individuals who band together to quest into the unknown. Often, he teams a scientist with an adventurer. On one level his narratives function as scientific mystery stories in which inexplicable phenomena screen a hidden truth. Taine slowly—in *White Lily,* ponderously—reveals the solution through his closemouthed scientist characters. At times complete and final answers are withheld in order to maintain a sense of wonder and mystery. This is particularly true in *The Greatest Adventure* and *The Purple Sapphire,* both of which concern survivals of ancient super-civilizations of Earth's past. In *The Greatest Adventure* an Antarctic expedition uncovers the remnants of such a civilization. Under the ice is a city which had entombed itself alive rather than allow the possibility of escape to the mutated creatures spawned when they discovered the secret of life. The expedition inadvertently activates the menace. Taine concentrates on the biological nightmares, and neither explores nor identifies the ancient civilization, but this enhances the power of the novel. On the other hand, this reserve limits the otherwise excellent *The Purple Sapphire.* Three seekers of fortune discover a fantastic city in the heart of Central Asia where a degraded theocracy guards its technological marvels against the day its true inhabitants return. They do not return, and the three successfully rescue the kidnapped daughter of a British General but lose the secret of transmuting matter.

Genetic mutation is a theme Taine finds fascinating. Two novels, *Seeds of Life* and *G.O.G. 666,* deal with the consequences of human genetic tampering. *Seeds of Life* chronicles the brief career of a dissolute research scientist, Neils Bork, who becomes a superman when exposed to radiation. Bork, who considers human life beneath contempt, masterminds a fiendish plan to eradicate all humans, but is stymied when he regresses and falls in love with the woman he has chosen as the instrument of annihilation. A similar figure is Gog, the hulking travesty of a man whom plant geneticist Dr. Clive Chase encounters in his investigation of a Soviet plan to liberate its workers from drudgery in *G.O.G. 666.* Gog is the keystone of the plan, and he hides a secret darker than that of Neils Bork. *G.O.G. 666* is somewhat marred by its Cold War preoccupations. *White Lily* also depicts Russia in an uncomplimentary light. In China, two despicable Russian agents foment revolution. Against this bloody backdrop, a U.S. soldier has unwittingly introduced silicon-based life-forms on Earth, which run unchecked.

Considered to be his greatest work, *The Time Stream* is a complex excursion into the dynamics of time travel and cyclical universes. *The Time Stream* is the medium by which 10 individuals from the future send their minds back to 20th-century San Francisco. There they live new lives in an attempt to determine if a scientifically forbidden marriage will result in the destruction of their world. Although somewhat confusing in its narrative structure, *The Time Stream* is nevertheless a compelling example of imaginative writing. Of his other works, *The Iron Star,* a novel of a destructive asteroid, and "The Ultimate Catalyst" are noteworthy.

—Will Murray

TALL, Stephen

Pseudonym for Compton Newby Crook. **Nationality:** American. **Born:** Rossville, Tennessee, 14 June 1908. **Education:** George Peabody College (now Vanderbilt University), Nashville, B.S. 1932, M.A. 1933; Johns Hopkins University, Baltimore; Arizona State University, Tempe. **Military Service:** Served as an intelligence officer in the Office of Strategic Services, 1943-45: Captain. **Family:** Married Lucy Beverly Courtney; three children. **Career:** Science teacher, Appalachian State University, Boone, North Carolina; Middle Tennessee State University, Murfreesboro; Tennessee Polytechnic Institute; Western Reserve University, Cleveland; College of William and Mary, Williamsburg, Virginia; and Episcopal Academy, Philadelphia, 1933-39. Instructor, then professor of biology and department chairman, 1939-73, and from 1973, Professor Emeritus, Towson State University, Baltimore. Ranger and naturalist with the National Park Service, eight summers. **Awards:** National Science Foundation grants for ecological study. **Died:** 15 June 1981.

SCIENCE FICTION PUBLICATIONS

Novels (series: Stardust)

The Ramsgate Paradox (Stardust). New York, Berkley, 1976.
The People beyond the Wall. New York, DAW, 1980.

Short Stories

The Stardust Voyages. New York, Berkley, 1975.

*

Stephen Tall commented:

(1981) I was born in Tennessee near the Big River, the Mississippi, the son of a country doctor and a cultured, sensitive mother. The levees, the cotton fields, the cypress swamps, and the cane breaks were my first playgrounds. And in our home books and good reading always had status. Respect for knowledge and how it is acquired was instilled early.

I have always been a biologist writing fiction, not the other way around. I write because I like to tell a good story, and because the mechanics of good writing are pleasing to me. My stories are about what I know, and about what I have concern for. They have always reflected my awareness of and interest in the living world other than man. I wrote stories based on ecology before the word was generally familiar. I regard science fiction as almost the ideal medium for expressing ecological concerns: any species, any race, anywhere.

*   *   *

Approximately half of Stephen Tall's science fiction concerns the crew of the interstellar exploration ship *Stardust:* six short stories collected as *The Stardust Voyages* and one of two novels, *The Ramsgate Paradox.* A crew of 400 staffs the ship as it makes its way from one star system to another, but for all practical purposes there are only three characters. Roscoe Kissinger is the obligatory hero, not too long on brains but courageous to a fault. Equally necessary is Lindy Peterson, the attractive female scientist whose major role seems to be to require rescue by Roscoe. Finally we have Pegleg Williams, the best friend, comic relief, and jack-of-all-trades. There is also an elderly woman whose psychic abilities manifest themselves in cryptic paintings.

There is no doubt that the entire series is built around stereotypes, but the adventures themselves enjoy considerable popularity. Perhaps the best known is "The Bear with a Knot on His Tail," in which the star Mizar is about to explode, and our heroes arrive to carry off significant records and frozen germ plasma of the local intelligent species. The most interesting story in the series is the first, "Seventy Light-Years from Sol" (later retitled "A Star Called Cyrene"). This time the crew lands on a planet inhabited by two distinct races. The first consists of featureless varicolored cubes who can teleport from one location to another, and do so frequently in order to escape the predations of a species of carnivorous wheels. But now the cubes face a new threat, invasion from a nearby island of formless blobs, against which they have no defense. Human policy is to avoid taking sides in local squabbles, but the crew decides that offering advice is not interference. This strange twist of logic seems not to present any problems for the characters or the author, and the story is well-written enough to overcome the logical shortcomings. These two stories set the pattern for subsequent adventures, in which the protagonists meet and overcome a variety of menaces ranging from a manifestation of ancient Greek gods to mutated giant crabs. The latter appear in "The Invaders," another above average story flawed by problems of internal logic.

A nonseries story of note is "Allison, Carmichael, and Tattersall," which seems to have been influenced by the Arcot, Morey, and Wade stories of John W. Campbell Jr. Indeed, Tall's fiction would not be out of place in the 1930s pulp magazines, although the quality of the writing is considerably higher. This was also the beginning of a truncated series, and is a satisfying light adventure story marred by overreliance on coincidence.

The Ramsgate Paradox is distinguished from the shorter stories only by length, making no serious effort to add substantial depth to the characters. The second novel, *The People beyond the Wall*, is also a return to a tradition largely abandoned in the genre, the utopian novel. A pair of adventurers set off to explore an area of glacier in the Antarctic and find themselves in a hidden land where people have returned to a pastoral existence unmarred by organized strife. Although this is probably the most ambitious work Tall produced during his career, it falls prey to the usual internal problems of utopian literature; the plot slows to a crawl as various aspects of the totally sane but rather dull society are revealed. Tall seemed to lose control entirely in the waning chapters, jumping years forward in time, introducing new characters for no real purpose. The first half of the novel was, however, a definite break with the formula stories Tall had been writing previously, and seems to indicate his writing would have moved into new areas had he lived longer.

—Don D'Ammassa

TARR, Judith

Nationality: American. **Born:** Augusta, Maine, 30 January 1955. **Education:** Mount Holyoke College, 1972-76, A.B.; Cambridge University, 1976-78, B.A. in classics, 1978; M.A. in classics, 1983; Yale University, 1978-79, M.A. in medieval studies, 1979; Yale University, 1981-88, Ph.D. in medieval studies, 1988. **Career:** Teacher of Latin, Edward Little High School, Auburn, Maine, 1979-81. Visiting lecturer in liberal studies and visiting writer, Wesleyan University, Middletown, Connecticut, 1989-92. Visiting assistant professor of classics, Wesleyan University, 1990-92. **Awards:** Crawford Memorial award, 1987; Mary Lyon award, Mt. Holyoke College, 1989. **Agent:** Jane Butler, P.O. Box 33, Matamoras, Pennsylvania 18336. **Address:** Dancing Horse Farm, P.O. Box 728, Vail, Arizona 85641, U.S.A. **Online Address:** capriole@indirect.com.

SCIENCE FICTION PUBLICATIONS

Novels (series: Alamut; Avaryan Rising; The Hound and the Falcon)

The Hound and the Falcon. Garden City, New York, Doubleday, 1986; London, Orbit, 1993.
    The Isle of Glass. New York, Bluejay, 1985; London, Bantam, 1986.
    The Golden Horn. New York, Bluejay, 1985; London, Bantam, 1986.
    The Hounds of God. New York, Bluejay, 1986; London, Bantam, 1987.
Avaryan Rising. Garden City, New York, Doubleday, 1988.
    The Hall of the Mountain King. New York, Tor, 1986; London, Pan, 1988.
    The Lady of Han-Gilen. New York, Tor, 1987; London, Pan, 1989.
    A Fall of Princes. New York, Tor, 1988; London, Pan, 1989.

A Wind in Cairo. New York, Bantam, 1989; London, 1990.
Ars Magica. New York, Bantam, 1989.
Alamut. New York, Doubleday, 1989.
The Dagger and the Cross: A Novel of the Crusades (Alamut). New York, Doubleday, 1991.
His Majesty's Elephant (for young adults). San Diego, Jane Yolen Books, 1993.
Arrows of the Sun (Avaryan rising). New York, Tor, 1993.
Lord of the Two Lands. New York, Tor, 1993; London, 1994.
Spear of Heaven. New York, Tor, 1994.

OTHER PUBLICATIONS

Novels

Throne of Isis. New York, Forge, 1994.
Pillar of Fire. New York, Forge, 1995.
The Eagle's Daughter. New York, Forge, 1995.

*

Judith Tarr comments:

It is usually, and casually, assumed that a woman who writes books with slightly frilly covers and the label "Fantasy" on the spine, must write a particular kind of book: i.e., Female Fantasy—elves, dragons, unicorns, cuddly animals. It is further assumed that if these books are set in the Middle Ages, or in fact in any preindustrial setting, they must necessarily be Generic Medieval.

I have a deplorable tendency to Do Things to assumptions and conventions. The three books labeled Trilogy by their publisher and given by me the corporate appellation *The Hound and the Falcon* were conceived originally as science fiction of a particular kind: the Psi Mutant variation with a spice of the Immortal Race, but transported into a historical setting, with terms of the time applied to the characters. Hence, elves, daemons, Jinn. *The Isle of Glass* is the least historically precise of the five books in that universe (not a cycle as such, and not a trilogy in the current sense of one long book chopped into several parts: each book stands on its own)—I essentially made it up as I went along. With *The Golden Horn* I discovered the joys of writing historical fiction with SF/fantasy characters, as I was then taking a graduate course in Byzantine history and I much prefer writing novels to writing term papers. I tossed a pair of my odd people into Constantinople during the Fourth Crusade, to see what they would do. With *The Hounds of God* I returned to Western Europe and a form of dénouement. *Alamut* and *The Dagger and the Cross* take place some decades before *The Isle of Glass* and are a melding of historical novel, medieval romance, and SF/fantasy. With these books and with the entirely separate fantasy, *A Wind in Cairo*, I was able to take advantage of a lifelong fascination with the Crusades. *Ars Magica*, in its turn, is the mutated offspring of a course paper on a medieval pope, Pope Sylvester II to be exact. It's not really a novel but a collection of three somewhat loosely related novellas; someday I'd like to write a fourth to round them off.

The so-called "High Fantasy" which has so far appeared as the three volumes of Avaryan Rising was actually, originally conceived as related to the historical material—it's the other side of my childhood science fantasy mega-epic. No elves there, no dragons, and the riding animals are horned but as antelopes, not as unicorns (it is, after all, an alien world). Nor is it medieval. In the time-honored fashion of SF, which mines history for all the gold it contains, these books are a melange of Alexander the Great, the ancient Near and Middle East, and Imperial China. Magic works in this universe. Maybe. If it is actually magic. And not . . . But that would be telling.

(1995) I am still Doing Things to assumptions—it seems to have grown from trick into shtick. The latest has been to "break out" into the mainstream—with books that are, at base, pretty much the same thing I've always done. *Lord of the Two Lands,* rejected by one publisher as "not a fantasy," was published as General Fiction and nominated for the World Fantasy Award. Subsequent works of historical fantasy have appeared as Fiction, with "mainstream" covers and promotion. They seem quite happy in it.

And despite being told sternly that I am "a FANTASY writer," I count a round dozen short stories that are really, truly, honestly, I'm not kidding you, science fiction—including a murder mystery set on a space station, a lot of alternate history (I am particularly fond of the "President Elvis" stories), and the sole science fiction contribution to a unicorn anthology. (Really. It's about genetic engineering.) Short stories have been a late development with me, and they do not come naturally, but when they do come they're grand fun. They often come as science fiction—I could say I have two Muses, and the short story Muse is a science fictional sort of spirit.

Next in the pipeline is a sequence of Truly Huge books, women's fiction, mainstream . . . and as thoroughly fantastical as anything I've done yet. Look for them from Forge, starting around about 1997. After that, who knows? The Muse has her own ideas, and she'll tell me when she's good and ready.

                                    *   *   *

Judith Tarr's critically heralded debut in 1985 with *The Isle of Glass,* the first in her The Hound and the Falcon trilogy, marked her as one of the strongest voices in the tradition of SF's scholar-writers.

Like J.R.R. Tolkien and C.S. Lewis, Tarr is a medieval scholar. Her formidable academic background and grounding in the history, theology, and arts of several medieval cultures contribute to the rich texture and deeply realized backgrounds of her books. At the same time, this medievalist's training— which is the scholar's equivalent of planet-building since the medievalist must recreate a "reading" of a culture from the ground up—enables Tarr to excel at world building in her Avaryan trilogy. Just as the medievalist must confront the Other in the form of the people and cultures she studies, Tarr confronts the Other in the form of the long-lived, almost inhumanly talented, and supernaturally gifted creatures who move among human beings in The Hound and the Falcon trilogy and subsequently in *Alamut* and *Ars Magica.* Thought patterns alien from those of humans also occur in Avaryan Rising, especially in the magical system, which is intricate and ruthless: the familiar of Gerbert, the mage-pope of Ars Magica, shows a similar outlook composed of equal loyalty to her chosen human, an almost frightening indifference to outsiders, and a highly feline interest in playing with people and passing events.

An accomplished horsewoman, Tarr's love of horses gets full play in *A Wind in Cairo,* which shows the transformation of a spoiled Arab princeling, punished for raping a mage's daughter, into a horse owned by another young woman.

Tarr's characters, especially her female characters, tend to be rebels. Alf, in The Hound and the Falcon books, spends much of his long life rebelling against his talents, his vocations as priest and mage, and his love for the intractable and dazzling Thea. Elian, in *The Lady of Han-Gilen,* becomes a woman warrior: Zamaniyah, who becomes a fighter in deference to her father, fights for the right to choose her own life.

Tarr's shift in focus Eastward, begun in *A Wind in Cairo,* continues in the Crusade novels *Alamut* and *The Dagger and The Cross.* Tarr, like many Crusaders who looked East, has become fascinated with Muslim culture, the intricacies of which find a home in her own style. She portrays its splendors richly and intelligently at a time in our own history when this type of understanding is necessary.

Though Tarr is primarily known for her novels, she has produced some fine short fiction. Recently, she has expanded her range to take part in two shared worlds, Andre Norton's *Witch World* and Jerry Pournelle's *War World,* which, along with "Parity" (in *Pulphouse*), may mark yet another expansion into hard science fiction.

                                                        —Susan Shwartz

TATE, Peter

Nationality: British. **Career:** Journalist. **Address:** Pinetree Lodge, 3 Seaway Avenue, Friars Cliff, Christchurch, Dorset 8H23 4EU, England.

SCIENCE FICTION PUBLICATIONS

Novels (series: Simeon)

The Thinking Seat (Simeon). Garden City, New York, Doubleday, 1969; London, Faber, 1970.
Gardens One to Five. Garden City, New York, Doubleday, 1971; as *Gardens, 1, 2, 3, 4, 5,* London, Faber, 1971.
Country Love and Poison Rain. Garden City, New York, Doubleday, 1973.
Moon on an Iron Meadow (Simeon). Garden City, New York, Doubleday, 1974.
Faces in the Flames: Fourth in a Series of Small Wars (Simeon). Garden City, New York, Doubleday, 1976.
Greencomber. Garden City, New York, Doubleday, 1979.

Short Stories

Seagulls under Glass and Other Stories. Garden City, New York, Doubleday, 1975.

                                    *   *   *

Although Peter Tate can be a futurist, an allegorist, and a fantasist, in his major work he is a realist who uses current trends in natural and social science as well as technology for conveying his values. His concept of science fiction is a "work styled in protest at a particular facet of . . . technology and using research to qualify that protest" (introduction to "The Post-Mortem People" in *Seagulls Under Glass*). Unlike futurists who project their characters onto other planets, eons removed from the present, Tate remains on a familiar earth only a few years distanced from the copyright date. He chooses recognizable settings (Waukegan, Zimbabwe, New Forest) and with them creates an illusion that his scientific and technological projections have already left the laboratory and are threatening the balance in man and nature. Likewise, he interweaves imagined crises with references to current headlines (Che Guevara, Vorster, Kent State, Mozambique), thus enabling the reader to fuse fabrication with newspaper fact. Sobering is his recognition that heroes sometimes die. Tate further asserts the realness of his fictions by overlapping characters and plots. Simeon and Tomorrow Julie star in *The Thinking Seat, Moon on an Iron Meadow,* and *Faces in the Flames;* Scarlatti and Prinz counter each other in *Gardens One to Five* and *Faces in the Flames.* Famous Gogan slips in and out of *The Thinking Seat, Gardens One to Five,* and *Faces in the Flames;* and Shem of *Gardens One to Five* is a memory in *Faces in the Flames.* Even more interesting than overlapping is Tate's technique of using fiction to authenticate fiction, as in *Moon on an Iron Meadow* where he returns to the buildings, people, and atmosphere created 50 years before by his mentor Ray Bradbury in *Something Wicked This Way Comes.*

Many of Tate's plots are compelling in their fast-paced intrigue ("Skyhammer"); their allegorical assessment of social and political forces (*Gardens One to Five*); or their subtle ambivalence between realism and fantasy (*Greencomber*). A few are bizarre. In "Mars Pastorale" a defenseless poppy seed invades a defenseless human's throat; in "Post-Mortem People" licensed ghouls stalk dying men for healthy body parts; in "The Gloom Pattern"—whose science, says Tate, is "bunkum"—a youngster is sucked up from his earthly existence on an "ecstasy beam" when he craves a sad man's happiness. Tate's humor surfaces in the provocative "Same Autumn in a Different Park." In this parody of the Adam-Eve story, Addison springs from the side of Tina who with the help of "molecular rejig" turns into an apple which is eaten by the new Adam.

Tate sees the world as essentially good; but it has been contaminated by ignorance, indifference, misguided heroics, self-serving, and malice. As in Bradbury's *Something Wicked This Way Comes,* the spirit of evil is pervasive and its confrontation inevitable. It periodically erupts in such "bodies" as the United Nations, desalination plants, canisters of biological weapons, defoliants, contaminated rabbits, atom bombs, church "Prinzes," and Hitlerian megalomaniacs. Once this force is loose, balance between good and evil can be restored only by a figure who embodies the spirit of pristine Christianity: "the time of authenticity on the lake shores of Nazareth before two thousand years of controversy and schism and compromise and commerce had muddied the waters beyond perception" (*Faces in the Flames*). Simeon, along with Shem, Nelso Ojukwe (*Faces in the Flames*), Greencomber, and Adams ("Mainchance"), insist on rational, willed self-involvement—even to the point of death—against any sort of manipulation of humans. Like the Galilean, all of these heroes provoke action in the quiescent; by the force of their integrity, they transform Judases and self-deceivers into disciples. A developing theme from *The Thinking Seat* to *Greencomber* is individual and social transformation effected by altruistic love.

Tate enjoys language. He puns, makes memorable metaphors, and sometimes achieves a mesmerizing lyricism. His use of myth is haunting: blood is the price for exaltation; life consciously saved counterbalances that which is wantonly taken; love dispels enslaving myths created by malevolent scientists. At times he mistakes clichés for original expression, or reaches too far for an apt comparison. But Tate is a stimulating writer who structures complex materials into convincing fictions.

—Rosemary Coleman

TEMPLE, William F(rederick)

Nationality: British. **Born:** Woolwich, London, 9 March 1914. **Education:** Gordon School, London, 1919-27; Woolwich Polytechnic, London, 1928-30. **Military Service:** Served in the Royal Artillery, 1940-46. **Family:** Married Joan Streeton in 1939; one daughter and one son. **Career:** Head clerk, Stock Exchange, London, 1930-50. Editor, British Interplanetary Society *Bulletin.* **Died:** 15 July 1989.

SCIENCE FICTION PUBLICATIONS

Novels (series: Martin Magnus)

Four-Sided Triangle: A Novel. London, Long, 1949; New York, Fell, 1951.
Martin Magnus, Planet Rover (for children). London, Muller, 1955.
Martin Magnus on Venus (for children). London, Muller, 1955.
Martin Magnus on Mars (for children). London, Muller, 1956.
The Automated Goliath. New York, Ace, 1962.
The Three Suns of Amara. New York, Ace, 1962.
Battle on Venus. New York, Ace, 1963.
Shoot at the Moon. New York, Simon and Schuster, and London, Whiting and Wheaton, 1966.
The Fleshpots of Sansato. London, Macdonald, 1968.

OTHER PUBLICATIONS

Novel

The Dangerous Edge. London, Long, 1951.

Other

The True Book about Space-Travel. London, Muller, 1954; as *The Prentice-Hall Book about Space Travel,* New York, Prentice-Hall, 1955.

*

William F. Temple commented:

(1981) I've read SF since childhood. At first, uncritically: I didn't notice it was only two-dimensional, i.e., lacked depth, especially in characterization. Then critically: I decided to try to add that third dimension in my writing. Then despairingly: Nobody noticed that I had. Then cynically: Nobody wanted it, anyway. They preferred their robots. Then uncaringly: I don't bother to write it any more.

*   *   *

Most critics would agree that the Golden Age of modern science fiction occurred in the 1930s, when such visionary editors as John Campbell encouraged and developed the writers who were to become almost legendary figures in the field. While Asimov, van Vogt, and others were honing their skills in the United States, William F. Temple was drawn to SF in England. Temple's interest, like that of his counterparts across the sea, was fostered by his companionship with Arthur C. Clarke, John Wyndham, and John Christopher. In the early days of science fiction there seemed to work among such individuals a kind of crosscurrent which stimulated and sustained them in the creation of materials at which conventional critics of the day looked askance. Only the hardy survived those pioneering times to bring forth such books as *Childhood's End* and *No Blade of Grass*. That Temple was of durable stuff was demonstrated by what he went through to turn out what was perhaps his most notable work, *Four-Sided Triangle*. While serving in Africa with the Eighth Army in World War II, Temple converted what had been a short story into novel length. Despite the novel's publication delay, its survival qualities could not be extinguished. In a fascinating variation of the trite, a woman selects one of the two suitors who vie for her. The man who loses uses a matter-copying device to create an "exact" duplicate of her—which loads the novel's plot structure engrossingly.

Some readers may find Temple's work a bit stuffy at times, but his plots employ interesting contrasts and conflicts: a group of explorers investigates the alien topography of the Moon, but the real territory to be mapped is the unknown personality of warring party members. His story ideas are usually quite interesting, as in a short story like "A Date to Remember." This yarn seems almost banal in some ways—a wife about to bring forth a child, rainy night, success/failure conflict of two old school chums. Then we discover the central idea, that Martians have long "passed" as Earthlings, struggling to civilize the inhabitants of Earth while disguised as Byron, Pasteur, Haydn, and others throughout the centuries.

—Robert H. Wilcox

TENN, William

Pseudonym for Philip Klass. **Nationality:** American. **Born:** Des Moines, Iowa, 8 November 1919. **Education:** Iowa State University, Ames, B.S. 1941. **Military Service:** Served in the United States Army during World War II. **Career:** Consulting editor, *Fantasy and Science Fiction,* New York, 1958. Since 1966, member of the Department of English, Pennsylvania State University, University Park. **Address:** Department of English, Pennsylvania State University, University Park, Pennsylvania 16802, U.S.A.

SCIENCE FICTION PUBLICATIONS

Novels

Of Men and Monsters. New York, Ballantine, 1968; London, Pan, 1971.
A Lamp for Medusa. New York, Belmont, 1968.

Short Stories

Of All Possible Worlds. New York, Ballantine, 1955; enlarged edition, London, Joseph, 1956.

The Human Angle. New York, Ballantine, 1956.
Time in Advance. New York, Bantam, 1958; London, Gollancz, 1963.
The Seven Sexes. New York, Ballantine, 1968.
The Square Root of Man. New York, Ballantine, 1968; London, Pan, 1971.
The Wooden Star. New York, Ballantine, 1968; London, Pan, 1971.

OTHER PUBLICATIONS

Other

Editor, *Children of Wonder: 21 Remarkable and Fantastic Tales.* New York, Simon and Schuster, 1953; as *Outsiders: Children of Wonder: 21 Remarkable and Fantastic Tales,* Garden City, New York, Permabooks, 1954.
Editor, with Donald E. Westlake, *Once against the Law.* New York, Macmillan, 1968.

* * *

"The incredible William Tenn," as he has been dubbed by Brian Aldiss, started a whole school of comic and satiric science fiction in the 1940s. Tenn quickly perfected a way of looking at things, at once funny, bitter, and serious, that made him the natural heir to the nearly silent tradition of Swift and Voltaire. Sheckley, Pohl, Ellison, Russell, Goulart, Knight, Kagan, Eisenberg, Brown, Lafferty, and Malzberg have all echoed Tenn's work at one time or another. A serious humorist, Tenn has had a double problem. The science fiction genre has always made it difficult to tell serious writers from entertainers, through the manner of publication and because the entertainers often claim to be serious, or have it claimed for them; also, satirists and funny men have rarely risen high in the genre (in terms of awards and sales). Tenn was a pioneer whose example was imitated by writers who developed in different ways, but who also became known for the angle opened up by Tenn, thus diffusing the effect he might have had if his plumage had not been confused with that of imitators. Tenn imitations might have been more acceptable to some editors of the 1950s because they were watered-down versions of Tenn-like material—less serious and not so critical of the world and human nature. Tenn's stories are always a bit disturbing at some level, even when they are breathlessly readable, amusing, or cute.

An outgoing but sensitive man, Tenn fell silent by the end of the 1960s, even as his work was gathered into an impressive, though editorially flawed, six-volume set from Ballantine. One suspects that neglect made him feel that perhaps his work was not worthy. He went on to become an excellent college teacher, leaving behind a body of work sufficient to secure the reputation of any major writer in this field, and a name often confused with another Klass in various reference works. He published one story in the 1970s, "On Venus, Have We Got a Rabbi," which Damon Knight called "the great story he was talking about in the fifties." It was well received, garnering award nominations and appearing in a best-of-the-year collection. There have been recent signs that he will soon have several works, including a new novel, to offer his readers. Tenn was also the editor of *Children of Wonder,* a pioneering theme anthology which was notable for its variety of stories and nonparochial choice of authors. Two incisive essays, "The Fiction in Science Fiction" (*Science Fiction Adventures,* March 1954) and

"Jazz Then, Musicology Now" (*Fantasy and Science Fiction,* May 1972), are both required reading for anyone who cares about the ideals of literate science fiction, if not its practice.

Notable stories from Tenn's first two decades include "Brooklyn Project," which Fritz Leiber has called a "marvelously cynical" time-travel story, and "Firewater!," one of the most sophisticated stories ever published by John W. Campbell, with its unforgettable lament by Larry for the loss of what he was and what he cannot be as humanity struggles to keep its sanity before the seemingly superior aliens who have taken up residence on earth. The story should have taken all the awards. "Generation of Noah" is one of the finest atomic threat stories ever written. "Of All Possible Worlds," "Wednesday's Child" (a fascinating sequel to the much reprinted classic "Child's Play"), "Time Waits for Winthrop," "Eastward Ho!," and "The Malted Milk Monster" all drew honorable mentions in Judith Merril's best of the year collections, while "Bernie the Faust" took pride of place as the first story in the 1964 collection. "Time Waits for Winthrop" shows a remarkable use of exotic ideas, among them fairly advanced biological concepts, another feature of Tenn's stories that makes them unusual for the 1950s. "The Discovery of Morniel Mathaway" shows an understanding of the creative process that is usually beyond most SF writers. Jacques Sadoul has called it "the most beautiful example of a temporal paradox offered by science fiction." "The Custodian," with its plea for the blending of art and utility, and "Down among the Dead Men," with its clever use of offstage space opera to heighten a pathetic predicament, both manage to do what few SF stories can do—move us emotionally and intellectually on a mature level.

Tenn is always a master of situations, which at first prod and intrigue, then provoke curiosity, make us laugh a bit, then explode into some thoughtful irony or observation. Once you catch on to a Tenn situation, you can't stop reading. The satirical tones of irony, mockery, slapstick, and occasional bitterness do wonders for genre materials, precisely because Tenn joins these materials to human experience outside the insular worlds of SF wish-fulfillment and power fantasy. The science fiction materials are all there, strong and clear, but just as you're about to accept the story at its face value Tenn hits you with something real and painful. He's a very sly writer, inserting polished, precise narratives into our minds through unexpected channels. Many of his stories have the effect of blossoming into a single line of great beauty and illumination; but always the aesthetic fires are banked by irony and, above all, eloquent wit, behind which sits the ultimate authority of an author who has something to say, who sometimes seems to believe with Oscar Wilde that eloquence and wit alone can make the scales fall from human eyes. One senses an author laughing and crying at the same time, exhibiting intellect and dramatic talent within the confines of a narrow genre.

Tenn's two long works are the novel *Of Men and Monsters* and the short novel *A Lamp for Medusa.* The second work is easily worthy of having appeared in *Unknown Worlds.* Funny, atmospheric, and wonderfully paced, this neglected work has seen only a shabby book appearance. It is not surprising, given Tenn's tendencies, that it recalls the poise of the *Unknown Worlds* tradition, since that magazine was the only sizable market for humorous work of the early 1940s, and Tenn's only antecedent within the SF genre.

Of Men and Monsters, a story of humanity living in the walls of the houses of giant aliens who have occupied the earth, is a vivid, energetically paced story which best embodies one of Tenn's main points: that humanity is not what it thinks itself to be, that implicit in our biological history is a nature not of our making; we may

glimpse it, even understand it at times, but it may be a while before we can remake ourselves, if ever. In his awareness of biological and anthropological complexities, Tenn has at the center of his work the most thoroughgoing of science fiction methods: the collision of the possible with the actual, with the actual displaying fantastic holding power. Eric the Eye, the Lilliputian viewpoint character of the novel, learns that his society is not what he thought it was, that its rites of passage are a sham, and finally that human beings are not what he thought they were either; since change seems unlikely on a radical scale, he accepts this human nature and joins the plan to make of it something pervasive and influential. Eric becomes part of the reverse invasion of human vermin as they begin the infestation of the great alien starships. The story is very vivid, the characters charming (Eric meets Rachel Esthersdaughter, one of the nicest nice Jewish girls in all science fiction). The death of Eric's uncle is shatteringly presented. There are great wonder and awesome confrontation, sharply realized. Most importantly, there is an anthropological sophistication in the depiction of social systems; the aliens are properly terrifying, puzzling, and *other.* Tenn's tendency to romance, compassion, and brief, hard-bitten sentimentality shows through his bitterness just enough to be believable. The novel may be compared to Daniel Galouye's *Dark Universe* and Thomas M. Disch's *The Genocides.*

It is regrettable that Tenn stopped his development in the 1960s, when it was clear that the continuous practice of his craft, coupled with his acute and constant rethinking of the nature of fiction and science fiction, would certainly have produced a mighty progress over his very worthy body of work. Now that he seems poised at the start of his most mature period, it remains to be seen whether he will continue the main line suggested by his previous work, or whether his silence is a sign that he has been developing a new direction. He can do anything he wants, except hack work ("I have no talent for it," he has said). Few writers have ever suggested so much promise at the start of their sixth decade. Tenn belongs to the great generation of Asimov, Heinlein and Clarke. He is the most perfect example of the failure of the awards system within the science-fiction community, and an obvious candidate for the Grand Master Nebula award. His work is a clear example that SF can be literature, that it can provoke us to see, feel, and think. Tenn belongs to that unbroken chain of sayers who expose our delusions and foibles, our willful blindness and stupidity, and who ultimately stand against death and the amnesia of generations. "Tenn is another artist," Damon Knight has written, "who won't stop till he's had the last word."

—George Zebrowski

TENNANT, Emma (Christina)

Pseudonym: Catherine Aydy. **Nationality:** British. **Born:** London, 20 October 1937. **Education:** St. Paul's Girls' School, London. Has one son and two daughters. **Career:** Travel correspondent, *Queen,* London, 1963; features editor, *Vogue,* London, 1966; editor, *Bananas,* London, 1975-78. Since 1982, general editor, *In Verse,* London; since 1985, editor, Lives of Modern Women series, Viking, London. Fellow, Royal Society of Literature, 1982. **Agent:** Sheil Land, 43 Doughty Street, London WC1N 2LF. **Address:** c/o Faber and Faber Ltd., 3 Queen Square, London WC1N 3AU, England.

SCIENCE FICTION PUBLICATIONS

Novels

The Time of the Crack. London, Cape, 1973; as *The Crack,* London, Penguin, 1978.
The Last of the Country House Murders. London, Cape, 1974; New York, Nelson, 1976.
Hotel de Dream. London, Gollancz, 1976.
The Bad Sister. London, Gollancz, and New York, Coward McCann, 1978.
Wild Nights. London, Cape, 1979; New York, Harcourt Brace, 1980.
Queen of Stones. London, Cape, 1982.
Two Women of London: The Strange Case of Ms Jekyll and Mrs Hyde. London, Faber, 1989.
Sisters and Strangers: A Moral Tale. London, Grafton, 1990.
Faustine. London, Faber, 1992.

OTHER PUBLICATIONS

Novels

The Colour of Rain (as Catherine Aydy). London, Weidenfeld and Nicolson, 1964.
Alice Fell. London, Cape, 1980.
Woman Beware Woman. London, Cape, 1983; as *The Half-Mother,* Boston, Little Brown, 1985.
Black Marina. London, Faber, 1985.
The Adventures of Robina, by Herself. London, Faber, 1986; New York, Persea, 1987.
The House of Hospitalities. London, Viking, 1987.
A Wedding of Cousins. New York, Viking, 1988.
The Magic Drum. London, Viking, 1989.
Tess. London, HarperCollins, 1993.
Pemberley: A Sequel to Pride and Prejudice. London, Hodder and Stoughton, and New York, St. Martin's Press, 1993.
An Unequal Marriage: Pride and Prejudice Continued. London, Sceptre, and New York, St. Martin's Press, 1994.

Other (for children)

The Boggart. London, Granada, 1980.
The Search for Treasure Island. London, Penguin, 1981.
The Ghost Child. London, Heinemann, 1984.
Dare's Secret Pony. London, BBC, 1991.

Other

Editor, *Bananas.* London, Quartet-Blond and Briggs, 1977.
Editor, *Saturday Night Reader.* London, W.H. Allen, 1979.
Editor, *The ABC of Writing.* London, Faber, 1992.

*   *   *

Emma Tennant writes in the school of science fiction established by J.G. Ballard, John Sladek, and Michael Moorcock. In *The Crack* a massive fissure tears London apart. Part disaster novel in the Ballard tradition, part psychological novel, *The Crack* follows the motivations of the characters to "get to the other side" of the crack. The book features one of Tennant's famous characters: Baba, a Playboy Club bunny. The book pokes fun at many groups who try to cope with the catastrophe in a desperate attempt to maintain their power: the rich, psychiatrists, environmentalists, and the class system itself. Allegorical aspects of Tennant's work attack the decadence of modern society and the paranoia and fanaticism she sees in contemporary life.

In *Two Women of London* Tennant retells Robert Louis Stevenson's *The Strange Case of Dr. Jekyll and Mr. Hyde* with a woman protagonist who lives two separate lives by taking a drug that allows her to become another person. Clearly, Tennant is attacking the lifestyle choices women in England suffer at the hands of advantage and social class—and their destructive impacts on women's beliefs and behaviors.

Tennant is capable of writing bitingly sarcastic social commentaries like *The House of Hospitalities* and *A Wedding of Cousins* but her work takes on an added dimension when she mixes social commentary with science fictional elements. In *Wild Nights* a child watches as his uncles and aunts turn themselves into rabbits and birds. The novel is a comment on the fear of growing up but also has a surreal, occult flavor that transcends Tennant's text.

One of Tennant's best known and most widely praised books is her genres blending *The Last of the Country House Murders.* This sly, clever novel is a mystery in the Agatha Christie tradition but written in the style of J.G. Ballard. The setting is a futuristic England burdened by massive overpopulation. The "body in the library" type of murder is impossible because the population pressures have destroyed privacy and space. The owner of the last existing manor house, Jules Tanner, is to be murdered publicly as part of Woodiscombe Manor's conversion into a tourist attraction. The Government selects a detective to interview assassins, plant clues, and in general design a murder worthy of the rich foreign tourists and the mass audience who will witness the murder. *The Last of the Country House Murders* is wickedly funny and mocks the "bread and circuses" mentality of contemporary governments who manage reality instead of solving basic economic and social problems.

Other weapons in Tennant's arsenal are parody and pastiche. Tennant takes on militant feminist guerrillas in *The Bad Sister* and the court of Queen Elizabeth II in *The Adventures of Robina.* The invasion of Grenada and the U.S. Marines are at the heart of *Black Marina.* Tennant's books can be stark, as in *Woman Beware Woman,* in which a murdered novelist's family finds itself part of a vengeance plot or wildly inventive as in *Hotel De Dream,* in which fictional characters try to kill the novelist who created them to prevent the conclusion she's about to write for them.

Emma Tennant is a writer of extraordinary range whose works use science fictional elements in consistently original and innovative ways.

—George Kelley

TENNESHAW, S.M. *See* **GARRETT, Randall; Silverberg, Robert.**

TEPPER, Sheri S.

Pseudonyms: E.E. Horlak, B. J. Oliphant, A.J. Orde. **Nationality:** American. **Born:** Denver, Colorado, in 1929. **Family:** Married; two children. **Career:** Executive director, Rocky Mountain Planned Parenthood, Denver, Colorado, 1962-86. **Agent:** Howard Morhaim, 175 Fifth Ave., New York, New York 10010. **Address:** Jacona Ranch, Route 5, Box 250, Santa Fe, New Mexico 87501, U.S.A.

SCIENCE FICTION PUBLICATIONS

Novels (series: The Awakeners; Blood Heritage; Grass; Jinian; Marianne; Mavin Manyshaped; The True Game)

The True Game. London, Corgi, and Garden City, New York, Doubleday, 1985.
  King's Blood Four. New York, Ace, 1983.
  Necromancer Nine. New York, Ace, 1983.
  Wizard's Eleven. New York, Ace, 1984.
The Revenants. New York, Ace, 1984; London, Corgi, 1986.
The Chronicles of Mavin Manyshaped. London, Corgi, 1986.
  The Song of Mavin Manyshaped. New York, Ace, 1985.
  The Flight of Mavin Manyshaped. New York, Ace, 1985.
  The Search of Mavin Manyshaped. New York, Ace, 1985.
The Marianne Trilogy. London, Corgi, 1990.
  Marianne, the Magus, and the Manticore. New York, Ace, 1985.
  Marianne, the Madame, and the Momentary Gods. New York, Ace, 1988.
  Marianne, the Matchbox, and the Malachite Mouse. New York, Ace, 1989.
The End of the Game. Garden City, New York, Doubleday, 1987.
  Jinian Footseer. New York, Tor, 1985; London, Corgi, 1988.
  Dervish Daughter. New York, Tor, 1986; London, Corgi, 1988.
  Jinian Star-Eye. New York, Tor, 1986; London, Corgi, 1988.
Blood Heritage. New York, Tor, 1986; London, Corgi, 1987.
The Bones (Blood Heritage). New York, Tor, 1987; London, Corgi, 1988.
The Awakeners. Garden City, New York, Doubleday, 1987; London, Bantam, 1988.
  Northshore. New York, Tor, 1987.
  Southshore. New York, Tor, 1987.
After Long Silence. New York, Bantam, 1987; as *The Enigma Score,* London, Corgi, 1989.
The Gate to Women's Country. New York, Doubleday, 1988; London, Bantam, 1989.
Still Life (as E.E. Horlak). New York, Bantam, 1989; as Sheri Tepper, London, Corgi, 1989.
Grass. New York, Doubleday, and London, Bantam, 1989.
Raising the Stones. New York, Doubleday, 1990; London, Grafton, 1991.
Beauty: A Novel (Grass). New York, Doubleday, 1991; London, HarperCollins, 1992.
Sideshow (Grass). New York, Bantam, 1992; London, HarperCollins, 1993.
A Plague of Angels. New York, Bantam, 1993; London, HarperCollins, 1994.
Shadow's End: A Novel. New York, Bantam, 1994.

OTHER PUBLICATIONS

Other

The Problem with Puberty. Denver, Colorado, RMPP Publications, 1976.
So Your Happy Ever After Isn't. Denver, Colorado, RMPP Publications, 1977.
This Is You. Denver, Colorado, RMPP Publications, 1977.
Tubal Ligation. Denver, Colorado, RMPP Publications, 1977.
So You Don't Want to Be a Sex Object. Denver, Colorado, RMPP Publications, 1978.

*   *   *

One of the most rewarding aspects of reading science fiction is watching the development of that occasional writer whose work progresses steadily from light entertainment to more serious themes. In many cases, the leap is unsuccessful, the latter work didactic, labored, and lacking the enthusiasm and strong storytelling skills of the less ambitious novels that preceded it. But other writers, like Sheri Tepper, evolve successfully, producing work that entertains on both levels.

King's Blood Four introduced the magical world of the True Game, a fantasy world in which society is shaped by what amounts to an elaborate role-playing game. Tepper blends fantastic and science fictional motifs in the series, which involves both psi powers and magic. Individual lives are shaped by the game, except for the Immutables who are immune to its power. A plot to circumvent the rules of the game is thwarted in what might have been a pedestrian fantasy adventure, but which is enlivened by a lively prose style and some unusually clever touches. The protagonist tracks down his missing mother in *Necromancer Nine,* which provides another grand tour of Tepper's conjured world. With the third volume, *Wizard's Eleven,* Tepper codified the rules of magic for her world in yet another quest story, this time to a remote region full of mystery and danger. The popularity of the series was enough to inspire two more trilogies during the next few years.

The second True Game trilogy consists of *The Song of Mavin Manyshaped, The Flight of Mavin Manyshaped,* and *The Search of Mavin Manyshaped.* The series regresses in time, opening with Mavin's childhood as one of two shapeshifters in a tribe that views her talents with considerable unease. After mastering her talents, Mavin grows wings in order to explore a lost city hidden in a chasm, and in the third volume she tracks down an old friend. *Jinian Footseer, Dervish Daughter,* and *Jinian Star-Eye* make up the final set of three. Jinian is a young woman whose adventures in the realm of the True Game are considerably darker than those that preceded them. Evil forces are gathering that may destroy the Game itself, bringing chaos to the world. There is a distinct change of atmosphere with the final set, anticipating the less whimsical work which would follow.

While the True Game novels were appearing, Tepper was already diversifying. *The Revenants* is a stand alone fantasy quest notable for its ambitious efforts to deepen characterization and create a more richly textured background. *Marianne, the Magus, and the Manticore* is set in the contemporary world. Marianne is from a mythical mountain nation near Iraq whose studies in the U.S. are interrupted by intruders from a magical realm. Two sequels appeared later, *Marianne, the Madame, and the Momentary Gods* and *Marianne, the Matchbox, and the Malachite Mouse.* Marianne learns how to alter time through the use of magic and tries to avert her parents' death, and in the third volume is transformed into a world where almost anything is possible in order to return an artifact she has promised to deliver. The Marianne novels are the most satisfying and creative of Tepper's fantasy work.

During the late 1980s, Tepper seemed to be uncertain about the future course of her writing. She produced three above average horror novels, *The Bones, Blood Heritage,* and *Still Life* (as by E.E. Horlak) and a two-volume fantasy series, *Northshore* and *Southshore.* A young priestess and a simple boatman chafe under the arbitrary rule of their world by remote powers and become the focal point for a rebellion. The two novels, known jointly as *The Awakeners,* clearly mark the transition from a fantasy writer with more serious aspirations to a serious writer who uses fantastic devices as tools in her work.

Tepper's first outright science fiction novel, *After Long Silence,* has strong thematic similarities to the Awakeners books. The setting is a colonized world dominated by an authoritarian rule. Complex crystals are found on the planet, and some of the colonists can sense Presences, an alien intelligence which might hold the key to their future. Her next novel, *The Gate to Women's Country,* was far more ambitious and controversial. Following a worldwide catastrophe, the human race has split into two societies, one dominated by women and pacifistic men who attempt to keep the old knowledge alive, the other male-dominated, primitive, and belligerent. Although it would be easy to fall into the trap of didacticism here, Tepper threads a thoughtful path through the morass, using the polarization to examine human nature, gender differences, and the excesses of all parties concerned.

Tepper's next novel, *Grass,* examines the way we interact with the natural world. Grass is a world claimed by both humanity and an alien race, both of which have partially colonized it. When a mysterious plague threatens both races, Grass proves to be the only safe haven, so an investigator from Earth is sent to discover the reason. Moving and effective at times, the novel is uncharacteristically uneven. *Beauty,* a fantasy based partly on the fairytale "Beauty and the Beast," is more inventive but similarly slow-paced, although individual scenes are often quite extraordinarily effective.

Raising the Stones far surpassed any of Tepper's previous novels. Once again the setting is a colony world, once home to an alien race, now a human planet. But remnants of an ancient religion remain, and there are signs that the aliens had good reason for their beliefs. An intricate, wide-reaching, and thought-provoking novel that examines religion and fanaticism from an original viewpoint. The sequel, *Sideshow,* uses the same setting to examine human intolerance and the strength of faith. Combined, the two novels are one of the major SF works of the early 1990s.

A Plague of Angels was a return to fantasy, set in a world where the human race has largely disappeared and those left behind are no longer dominant over magical creatures which have reclaimed the world. Tepper proves herself still capable of writing a rousing adventure story, but her improved ability to delineate characters helps make this an outstanding fantasy, her best in that genre. Most recently, *Shadow's End* reworks many of Tepper's favored themes into a new configuration. A mysterious force has removed the human race from all the worlds in the vicinity of the planet Dinadh. An investigator from Earth arrives on that world to track down a man who might hold the key to solving the mystery, but only locates him after a series of elaborate adventures.

Although rarely published at shorter length, Tepper has produced fine work in that form as well, particularly "Raccoon Music," "The Gazebo," and "The Gourmet." She has proven herself to be an effective, adaptive writer who refuses to remain contentedly writing the same type of story over and over again, but instead reaches for greater achievement, usually with success. If the progress she has shown over the first decade of her writing continues into the second, she will likely be one of the most formidable voices in SF in the years to come.

—Don D'Ammassa

TEVIS, Walter (Stone)

Nationality: American. **Born:** San Francisco, California, 28 February 1928. **Education:** University of Kentucky, Lexington, M.A. 1956; University of Iowa, Iowa City, M.F.A. 1961. **Military Service:** Served in the United States Navy. **Family:** Divorced; one son and one daughter. **Career:** Worked for Kentucky highway department in 1950s and early 1960s; after 1965, Professor of English, Ohio University, Athens. **Died:** 9 August 1984.

SCIENCE FICTION PUBLICATIONS

Novels

The Man Who Fell to Earth. Greenwich, Connecticut, Fawcett, and London, Muller, 1963; abridged for children by David Fickling, Oxford, Oxford University Press, 1979.
Mockingbird. Garden City, New York, Doubleday, and London, Hodder and Stoughton, 1980.
The Steps of the Sun. Garden City, New York, Doubleday, 1983; London, Gollancz, 1984.

Short Stories

Far from Home. Garden City, New York, Doubleday, 1981; London, Gollancz, 1983.

OTHER PUBLICATIONS

Novels

The Hustler. New York, Harper, 1959; London, Joseph, 1960.
The Queen's Gambit. New York, Random House, and London, Heinemann, 1983.
The Color of Money. New York, Warner, 1984; London, Severn House, 1985.

*

Walter Tevis commented:

(1981) I suppose I write disguised autobiographies. The idea, as far as I know, is to move other people. I feel alienated from other people sometimes; when I was younger the feeling was stronger than it is now. My major characters are alienated, by virtue of being pool players, from Mars, robots, the only people alive who can read, or alcoholics. I like to write about people under psychological stress, and when I write I am very serious about it.

* * *

Thomas Jerome Newton, in Walter Tevis's *The Man Who Fell to Earth,* is an emissary from the dying planet of Anthea, sent to prepare a refuge and transportation for its last few survivors. We never learn his real name. By introducing advanced Anthean technology Newton amasses the necessary millions of dollars, but attracts the attentions of the FBI who imprison and interrogate him, blinding him in the process. Eventually released, he abandons his project and dwindles into perpetual alcoholic exile. Earth, though they colonised it in the first place, is no place for Antheans.

Walter Tevis's novel is the classic refutation of the alien invasion theme in SF. He reduces the interplanetary war to a case of depression, the story of the loneliest man in the world. Newton could save mankind, but he represents a threat to the American economy. He is disabled, not by military might or scientific ingenuity, but by smothering bureaucracy. Seeing Newton decrepit and drunk in a bar, Nathan Bryce, his only human confidant, reflects that he "certainly would not have been the first means of possible salvation to get the official treatment." Christ, it seems, was an Anthean too. The failure of Newton's mission is a slow, pathetic crucifixion. Bryce remembers Thoreau's dictum: "quiet desperation" is the mood of the novel, an unobtrusive tragedy in an unostentatious style that conceals irony, bitterness, and ultimately cold fury. "I worked very hard to become an imitation human being. . . ." Newton says. "And of course I succeeded."

Mockingbird is altogether less original and distinctive. In a future America run and serviced by robots, human faculties, emotions, and even social urges have been eroded. The senior robot, Bob Spofforth (Mark Nine), is an interesting figure of moral ambivalence, sexless and immortal, but plagued by human dreams that slipped in under his mental programming. As in Bradbury's *Fahrenheit 451,* literacy is suppressed but the hero learns to read and is emboldened to further rebellion when he meets a woman less obedient to convention than he is. The book is efficiently plotted and written, but suffers from too much formula and too little variation.

Tevis's only collection, *Far from Home,* divides neatly into six competent but routine novelty stories, mostly from *Galaxy* at the end of the 1960s, and seven more searching pieces from 1979-80, including four previously unpublished highly Freudian self-examinations. These latter fictions demand to be read with a sympathy for their author which they do not altogether repay, but it seems that in its primary therapeutic purpose Tevis's writing finally, if precariously, succeeded. *The Steps of the Sun* tells how a big, rich, glum, impotent American restores himself and his impoverished nation by an illegal venture into space. In Tevis's quaintly benevolent cosmos, Ben Belson swiftly finds not only "safe" uranium but also a perfect analgesic and a sentient planet that mothers him through his self-induced psychological crisis. What is hard is bringing these gifts back to Earth, whose authorities treat the returning explorer with all the suspicion and hostility they showed to the extraterrestrial benefactor in *The Man Who Fell to Earth.* Whereas Thomas Jerome Newton is last seen drunk and defeated, Ben Belson's life on the run culminates in a period of stringent purification in a bleak, utopian China before a final symbolic tableau in which he and his wife switch on all the lights of a New York dark for 30 years and more. *The Steps of the Sun* annoys those who

insist on reading science fiction literally, but as a fantasy quest through a damaged psyche it is effective and affecting. It ended Tevis's melancholy career on a hopeful note.

—Colin Greenland

———

THANET, Neil. *See* **FANTHORPE, R. Lionel.**

———

THOMAS, Cogswell. *See* **COGSWELL, Theodore R.; THOMAS, Ted.**

———

THOMAS, D(onald) M(ichael)

Nationality: British. **Born:** Redruth, Cornwall, 27 January 1935. **Education:** Redruth Grammar School; University High School, Melbourne; New College, Oxford, B.A. (honours) in English, 1958, M.A. **Military Service:** Served in the British Army (national service), 1953-54. **Family:** Has two sons and one daughter. **Career:** Teacher, Teignmouth Grammar School, Devon, 1959-63; senior lecturer in English, Hereford College of Education, 1964-78. Visiting lecturer in English, Hamline University, St. Paul, Minnesota, 1967; creative writing teacher, American University, Washington, D.C., 1982. **Awards:** Richard Hillary Memorial prize, 1960; Cholmondeley award, 1978; *Guardian*-Gollancz Fantasy Novel prize, 1979; *Los Angeles Times* prize, 1981; Silver Pen award, 1982. **Address:** The Coach House, Rashleigh Vale, Cornwall TR1 1TJ, England.

SCIENCE FICTION PUBLICATIONS

Novels (series: Russian Quartet)

The Devil and the Floral Dance (for children). London, Robson, 1978.
Birthstone. London, Gollancz, 1980; revised, London, Penguin, 1982.
The White Hotel. London, Gollancz, and New York, Viking Press, 1981.
Ararat (Quartet). London, Gollancz, and New York, Viking Press, 1983.
Swallow (Quartet). London, Gollancz, and New York, Viking Press, 1984.
Sphinx (Quartet). London, Gollancz, 1986; New York, Viking Press, 1987.
Summit. London, Gollancz, 1987; New York, Viking Press, 1988.

Poetry

Penguin Modern Poets 11, with D.M. Black and Peter Redgrove. London, Penguin, 1968.
Two Voices. London, Cape Goliard Press, and New York, Grossman, 1968.

OTHER PUBLICATIONS

Novels

The Flute-Player. London, Gollancz, and New York, Dutton, 1979.
Lying Together. London, Gollancz, and New York, Viking Press, 1990.
Flying in to Love. London, Bloomsbury, and New York, Scribner, 1992.
Pictures at an Exhibition. London, Bloomsbury, and New York, Scribner, 1993.
Eating Pavlova. London, Bloomsbury, and New York, Carroll and Graf, 1994.

Plays

The White Hotel, adaptation of his own novel (produced Edinburgh, 1984).

Radio Plays: *You Will Hear Thunder,* 1981; *Boris Godunov,* from play by Pushkin, 1984.

Poetry

Personal and Possessive. London, Outposts, 1964.
The Lover's Horoscope: Kinetic Poem. Laramie, Wyoming, Purple Sage, 1970.
Logan Stone. London, Cape Goliard Press, and New York, Grossman, 1971.
The Shaft. Gillingham, Kent, Arc, 1973.
Lilith-Prints. Cardiff, Second Aeon, 1974.
Symphony in Moscow. Richmond, Surrey, Keepsake Press, 1974.
Love and Other Deaths. London, Elek, 1975.
The Rock. Knotting, Bedfordshire, Sceptre Press, 1975.
Orpheus in Hell. Knotting, Bedfordshire, Sceptre Press, 1977.
The Honeymoon Voyage. London, Secker and Warburg, 1978.
Dreaming in Bronze. Secker and Warburg, 1981.
Selected Poems. London, Secker and Warburg, and New York, Viking Press, 1983.
News from the Front, with Sylvia Kantaris. Todmorden, Lancashire, Arc, 1983.
The Puberty Tree: New and Selected Poems. Newcastle upon Tyne, Bloodaxe Books, 1992.

Other

Memories and Hallucinations (memoir). London, Gollancz, and New York, Viking Press, 1988.

Editor, *The Granite Kingdom: Poems of Cornwall.* Truro, Cornwall, Barton, 1970.
Editor, *Poetry in Crosslight.* London, Longman, 1975.
Editor, *Songs from the Earth: Selected Poems of John Harris, Cornish Miner, 1820-84.* Padstow, Cornwall, Lodenek Press, 1977.

Translator, *Requiem, and Poem without a Hero,* by Anna Akhmatova. London, Elek, and Athens, Ohio University Press, 1976.
Translator, *Way of All the Earth,* by Anna Akhmatova. London, Secker and Warburg, and Athens, Ohio University Press, 1979.
Translator, *Invisible Threads,* by Evtushenko. New York, Macmillan, 1981.

Translator, *The Bronze Horseman and Other Poems,* by Pushkin. London, Secker and Warburg, and New York, Viking Press, 1982.
Translator, *A Dove in Santiago,* by Evtushenko. London, Secker and Warburg, 1982; New York, Viking Press, 1983.
Translator, *You Will Hear Thunder,* by Anna Akhmatova. London, Secker and Warburg, and Athens, Ohio University Press-Swallow Press, 1985.

*

D.M. Thomas comments:

Most of my science fiction poetry is collected in one publication, *Penguin Modern Poets 11* (1968). Since then I have remained interested in the mythic aspect of SF, but have moved away from "pure" SF into other areas of myth.

*　　*　　*

D.M. Thomas's SF writing is largely restricted to his earlier poetry, published from the mid-1960s through the 1970s. Since that time he has turned increasingly to fiction, and he has gained considerable attention, especially for *The White Hotel, Ararat,* and its sequel, *Swallow.* Thomas's work in these forms is unified by common themes, particularly by the emotional and psychological structures that link sex, love, death, and artistic creation.

Thomas's SF poetry is often narrative, relying on SF settings and tropes to explore the emotional tangles that might arise in these placements with effective imagery, striking metaphors, and evocative language and tone. Poems like "Missionary," "A Dead Planet," and "The Strait" tell the stories we identify with science fiction—alien contacts and troubles with androids. Other poems show Thomas moving confidently across a variety of forms: from the vocative lyrics of "Fire Victims" and "Elegy for an Android" to striking dramatic monologues reminiscent of Browning like "Tithonus" and "Hera's Spring." The poet can produce both the traditional dialogue "A Conversation upon the Shadow" and visually stimulating concrete poems like "Symbiosis" and "Mercury." In most of these, Thomas demonstrates his skill at reworking the mythic inspirations supplied by science fiction stories. The most striking examples of this latter strategy are "The Strait," based on Bradbury's *Marionettes Inc.,* and "Hera's Spring," arising in response to Clarke's *The City and the Stars.* The former work poignantly captures the painful emotions aroused when a living woman must be replaced by an android duplicate. In "Hera's Spring" the motherly speaker tries to allay the sudden sense of loss and sorrow that a newly reminded Jeserac faces when he realizes the hundreds of lives he has lived before his present existence.

Thomas often relies on the myths of SF to emphasize isolation and alienation, love, sex, and violence, concerns especially apparent in his formally innovative, tabular poem "Hospital of Transplanted Hearts." In its multiple possibilities for reading and interpretation, this work seems to anticipate Calvino's *Castle of the Crossed Destinies.* In "The Head-Rape" Thomas explores the need for personal mental seclusion, especially in the complex and powerfully charged atmosphere of sexual violence—here as brutalization, but in "A Conversation upon the Shadow" as part of intimacy and love.

These themes continued to fascinate Thomas, and his later work often returns to them, often published in *New Worlds.* Indeed, pieces appearing in this periodical reveal Thomas's progression from poetry within the genre to work belonging more in the mainstream.

Long and extremely complex poems like *Two Voices* and "Computer 70: Dreams and Love Poems" still rely on technology and estranged settings to examine love and sorrow; and the former is particularly evocative of a post-holocaust survivor's experience balanced by the reflections of a woman who is both the unwilling human and the mythic earth mother. "Mr. Black's Poems of Innocence" marks the first of Thomas's incursions into the social sciences for his estranging material, and the poem is a masterpiece of parody mixed with serious, if fictionalized, psychotherapy. A mute schizophrenic suffers operant conditioning therapy, but between his outward, verbal answers we read his inner figurative musings. These center on a fantasy of his own entrapment and isolation, first associated with being a trapped sweep in a labyrinthine chimney, and then with passages from Rider Haggard's *King Solomon's Mines*. This latter material is especially important because it returns in yet another guise in Thomas's novel, *Swallow,* where once again the writer feels compelled to rework the figures of desire, greed, and death.

Although Thomas published several more pieces in *New Worlds,* these were increasingly removed from the usual settings and tropes marking SF. With the series that appeared in September 1979 ("Primitive Behavior," "A Letter From Marina," "Fathers, Sons and Lovers," and "The Woman to Freud"), he seemed to have given up the technological side of SF altogether. Here, we find material anticipating that in *The White Hotel*—for example, in the next to last poem cited, a historical fictionalization of the letter preceding the suicide of one of Freud's disciples, and in the last the sexual fantasy about a hysteria victim and Freud's son, which becomes the first section of the "Don Giovanni" section in the novel. Throughout his work, Thomas shows the potentiality of science fiction's myths for poetic expression.

—Len Hatfield

———

THOMAS, K. *See* **FEARN, John Russell.**

———

THOMAS, Ted

Pseudonyms: Leonard Lockhard; Cogswell Thomas. **Nationality:** American. **Born:** Theodore L. Thomas, New York City, 13 April 1920. **Education:** Massachusetts Institute of Technology, S.B. 1947; Georgetown University, Washington, D.C., J.D. 1953. **Military Service:** Served in the United States Army, 1943-46: 1st Lieutenant. **Family:** Married Virginia Kent Paton in 1947; two daughters and one son. **Career:** Chemical engineer, American Cyanamid Company, Stamford, Connecticut, 1947-50. Patent lawyer, in Washington, D.C., 1950-55, and from 1955, for Armstrong Cork Company, Lancaster, Pennsylvania. Columnist ("Science for Everybody"), *Stamford Advocate,* 1949-79, and columnist ("The Science Springboard"), *Fantasy and Science Fiction,* New York, 1964-67. **Member:** Chairman, Lancaster Zoning Board of Adjustments, 1966-70, and Lancaster Narcotics and Dangerous Drugs committee, 1970-71. **Died.**

SCIENCE FICTION PUBLICATIONS

Novels

The Clone, with Kate Wilhelm. New York, Berkley, 1965; London, Hale, 1968.
Year of the Cloud, with Kate Wilhelm. Garden City, New York, Doubleday, 1970.

* * *

Over a period of more than two decades, Ted Thomas produced a small but steady stream of short stories of unusually high calibre. Although he did not produce a novel that was solely his own work, he collaborated with Kate Wilhelm twice at novel length, and in each case the end product has been of superior quality. *The Clone,* for example, based on a short story of the same name by Thomas alone, is one of the most frightening and plausible tales of biochemistry gone wild. An amorphous creature is spawned in the sewers of a major city, able to absorb virtually any other organic structure—including people—upon contact.

Year of the Cloud deals with the theme of world disaster. The Earth passes through a strange interstellar cloud that has catastrophic effects on the planet. Tidal waves and volcanic activity are only short-term problems. The oceans turn into a gelatin-like substance and water is in short supply everywhere. The disaster is seen through the eyes of a number of characters, some of whom are working to reverse the effects of the cloud. But the cloud eventually proves to be a mixed blessing in this story, which combines scientific investigation with straightforward adventure.

Thomas himself is best known for his short stories, including those set against a background where the Weather Control Board controls the Earth because of its ability to affect the lifestyles and commercial undertakings of everyone on Earth. In "The Weather Man" a section of Australia refuses to abide by their authority and is threatened with a drought as a consequence. In "The Weather on the Sun" the efficacy of the government is endangered when the nature of the sun begins to alter, with unpredictable effects on the weather of our own planet.

"Satellite Passage" is a poignant tale of the near passage of two manned satellites, one from the United States and one from the Soviet Union. As the time of passage nears, there is considerable worry by the Americans that the Russians will commit some overt act of violence, but ultimately there is an accident in space and a Soviet cosmonaut is rescued by the Americans. Thomas also portrays the effects of a prolonged stay by a team of two men on the moon in "The Far Look." After experiencing a number of near disasters, the returning men possess a difference in demeanor that is quite noticeable.

Thomas assumed that H.G. Wells was correct about the Martians in "Day of Succession." When a ruthless general begins destroying the inhabitants of landing space vessels without warning, the authorities remove him from authority. The next capsule unleashes a technological onslaught against which human armies cannot stand, and the general assassinates the president in order to resume his program of eradication. A criminal is sentenced to be hanged each year in "December 28th," then brought back to life and allowed to recover in time for his next execution.

Thomas's use of irony is perhaps best illustrated in "The Doctor." A physician is stranded in prehistoric times when an accident destroys his time machine. He attempts to help the local residents by using his medical skills, but his attempts to extract teeth, set bones, etc. are viewed as hostile acts, as his intentions are totally misunderstood. Similarly, in "The Tour" a scientist realizes that visiting politicians do not understand his policy of using drugs to treat incurable murderers, and he subsequently commits murder himself in order to protect his program.

Thomas collaborated several times with Theodore Cogswell, most notably with "Early Bird," a humorous tale of a human space pilot whose ship becomes transformed when it arrives on a most peculiar planet, evolving in a strange merge of mechanical and organic development, and in "Paradise Regained," in which political exiles decide to terraform the planet upon which they have been confined. "The Players at Null-G," written with Cogswell and Algis Budrys, is a humorous spoof of the time-travel story.

—Don D'Ammassa

THOMSON, Edward. *See* TUBB, E.C.

THORPE, Trebor. *See* FANTHORPE, R. Lionel.

THURSTON, Robert (Donald)

Nationality: American. **Born:** Lockport, New York, 28 October 1936. **Education:** University of Buffalo, now State University of New York, B.A. in English 1959, M.A. 1967. **Military Service:** Served in the United States Army Air Defense Command, 1960-62. **Family:** Married 1) Joan K. Sullivan in 1964 (died, 1980), one son; 2) Rosemary E. Fox in 1982. **Career:** Reporter, *Union-Sun and Journal,* Lockport, 1959-60; assistant professor, Alliance College, Cambridge Springs, Pennsylvania, 1967-68; manager, Glen Art Book Store, Williamsville, New York, 1968-71. **Awards:** Clarion Workshop award, 1970. **Address:** 86 Ceder Street, Ridgefield Park, New Jersey 07660, U.S.A.

Science Fiction Publications

Novels (series: Legends of the Jade Phoenix)

Alicia II. New York, Berkley, 1978.
A Set of Wheels. New York, Berkley, 1983.
Q Colony. New York, Ace, 1985.
Robot Jox: The Novel (novelization of screenplay). New York, Avon, 1989.
Intruder: Isaac Asimov's Robot City: Robots and Aliens. New York, Ace, 1990.
Way of the Clans. New York, and London, Roc, 1991.

Bloodname. New York and London, Roc, 1991.
Falcon Guard. New York, Roc, 1991; London, 1992.
I Am Jade Falcon. New York, Roc, 1995.

Novels with Glen A. Larson; novelization of teleplays (series: Battlestar Galactica in all titles)

Battlestar Galactica. New York, Berkley, and London, Futura, 1978.
The Cylon Death Machine. New York, Berkley, 1979; London, Titan, 1988.
The Tombs of Kobol. New York, Berkley, 1979; London, Titan, 1988.
The Young Warriors. New York, Berkley, 1980.
The Nightmare Machine. New York, Berkley, 1985.
"Die, Chameleon!" New York, Berkley, 1985.
Apollo's War. New York, Berkley, 1987.
Surrender the Galactica! New York, Ace, 1988.

Other Publications

Novels

Rugger 1: For the Silverfish. New York, Avon, 1985.
Rugger 2: In Justice's Prison. New York, Avon, 1985.
1492: The Conquest of Paradise: A Novel (adaptation of movie screenplay). New York, Signet, 1992.

*   *   *

Robert Thurston established himself as a significant new writer in the science-fiction genre on the basis of his short fiction and has only recently turned to original novels, some of which develop themes presented earlier in short form.

One of Thurston's earliest short stories, "Carolyn's Laughter," hovers around the border between science fiction and the supernatural. A young man is troubled by memories of his first wife, now deceased, and eventually resorts to a computer medium in a half-hearted effort to contact her spirit. Carolyn had agreed to have her organs used in transplants, and there is some evidence that she may have reached across the borderline between life and death in an effort to reclaim the parts of her body that survived. This theme recurs in another story, "The Fire at Sarah Siddons," in which a man's life is completely dominated by a message he receives from his dead wife.

Both stories are well plotted, but the outstanding quality of these and most of Thurston's short fiction is the detailed and convincing development of characters. "Under Siege," for example, works only because of its fine characterization. Within the context of a racist police state, a white liberal with a black wife is plagued by the constant silent presence of a black man. The growing tensions among the three are superbly handled, and the story might well have attracted much serious attention if it had been published in mainstream markets.

Time travel is ostensibly the subject of "The Kingmakers," in which a man travels through the past to write a biography of a pivotal figure, but the four visits he makes, spaced widely apart in the lifespan of both men, cause tensions and contrasts that are the main focus of the story. Thurston's short stories run the gamut from comic to surreal, occasionally strongly plot-oriented but more frequently concerned with character and theme. Doppelgangers show up frequently, with inexplicable duplicate women in "Goodbye Shelley, Shirley, Charlotte, Charlene," a host of people with no apparent pasts in "Searching the Ruins," and two virtually identical

924

wives in "Theodora and Theodora." Some of his stories deal with controversial themes, such as "Aliens," wherein a human male is used as a sex object by non-humanoid aliens, and "The Oonaa Woman," also quite explicitly sexual in subject matter.

Thurston's first novel, *Alicia II,* was uneven. As might be expected, Thurston did a remarkable job of developing his characters as human beings. Voss Geraghty callously accepts the society he lives in, one which classifies people early in their lives, designating some as "rejects" whose bodies will be confiscated in young adulthood to become the home of non-rejects. But Geraghty's new body was sabotaged by its former owner, and cannot function sexually. Following this blow to his view of the world, he must then re-examine much of what he believes about his own society. Unfortunately, the setting of the novel is unconvincing, and the long delay before the advent of organized resistance to its system is not particularly credible.

A Set of Wheels was a bit of a disappointment after the promise of Thurston's first novel. In the not-too-distant future, a young man becomes involved in a love affair with an illegal automobile. The setting is brutal and dirty, a world of clandestine repair shops, police nearly as corrupt as the people they hunt, love tainted by mistrust and self-interest. Thurston uses unconventional dialogue, perhaps to emphasize the depersonalization of his future, but it also serves to flatten his characters as well.

Q Colony uses "The Oonaa Woman" as its opening and proceeds from there to provide the history of a failed human research colony on an alien world. It is easily Thurston's most successful full-length effort. He has carefully avoided the stereotyped characters common in the field, and the result is a mixture of the admirable and the reprehensible. Oonaa and humans can interbreed, providing an effective device for examining the collision of differing cultures and value systems.

Thurston's recent efforts have been primarily novelizations, including episodes of the "Battlestar Galactica" television program and the film, *Robot Jox.* He has also contributed an episode to the multi-authored "Robot City" series, set in the universe of Isaac Asimov's classic robot stories.

—Don D'Ammassa

TILLEY, Patrick

Nationality: British. **Born:** Southend, Essex, 4 July 1928. **Education:** Royal Grammar School, Newcastle upon Tyne; King's College of Art, University of Durham. **Family:** Married in 1951; two sons and one daughter. **Career:** Graphic designer and illustrator, 1954-68, then full-time writer. Creative adviser, *Oh, What a Lovely War!,* 1969; technical/historical adviser, *A Bridge Too Far,* 1977. **Agents:** Peters, Fraser and Dunlop, Fifth Floor, The Chambers, Chelsea Harbour, London SW10 OXF, England; or, Stirling Lord Literistic, Inc., 1 Madison Avenue, New York, New York 10010, U.S.A.

SCIENCE FICTION PUBLICATIONS

Novels (series: Amtrak Wars)

Fade-out. London, Hodder and Stoughton, and New York, Morrow, 1975; revised, London, Grafton, 1987.

Mission. London, Joseph, and Boston, Little Brown, 1981.
The Amtrak Wars:
   Cloud Warrior. London, Sphere, and New York, Macmillan, 1984.
   First Family. London, Sphere, 1985; New York, Baen, 1986.
   Iron Master. London, Sphere, 1987; New York, Baen, 1988.
   Blood River. London, Sphere, 1988.
   Death Bringer. London, Sphere, 1989.
   Earth-Thunder. London, Sphere, 1990.
Xan. London, Grafton, 1985.

OTHER PUBLICATIONS

Novels

Whatever Happened to the Likely Lads? (novelization of TV series). London, BBC, 1973.

Plays

Screenplays: *Wuthering Heights,* 1970; *People That Time Forgot,* 1977; *The Legacy,* 1977.

Television Plays: *Crane* series (3 episodes), 1959.

Other

Dark Visions: An Illustrated Guide to the Amtrak Wars, with Fernando Fernandez. London, Sphere, 1988.

*

Patrick Tilley comments:

(1985) The books I write are designed primarily as entertainment but they are, essentially, about the human condition. For me, the elements of a story should go together like a Swiss watch. The plot has to have a logical basis; the story should not insult the reader's intelligence. A writer's job is to communicate with his readers as simply and effectively as possible. He should not make them reach for a dictionary, or try to impress other writers with the quality of his prose.

(1991) Although I am widely perceived as a science fiction writer, my stories are not about spaceships or bug-eyed monsters. They are about ordinary people in extraordinary situations. The keynote is plausibility. I'm told I have a gift for making fantastic ideas seem quite logical and totally believable.

*   *   *

One of the hallmarks of writers of stature is that they can take a standard plot and do something novel with it, something that makes it stand out among a crowd of similar stories. Perhaps one of the oldest, most overdone situations in science fiction is the invasion of Earth by aliens in flying saucers, and almost as hoary a plot is the first contact story. So it is particularly interesting that Patrick Tilley's debut novel, *Fade-out,* is in fact a melding of both of these into a novel that should have been derivative and uninspired. The result was quite the contrary.

Borrowing from the film *The Day the Earth Stood Still,* Tilley has his aliens cut off all power to human machinery during their landing. Soon the government of the United States must cope with a mysterious vehicle and its inhabitants who either cannot or will not communicate, but who possess abilities far beyond those of the human race. The novel covers several months of tentative and then increasingly strident attempts by the government to regain control of the situation. Tilley has done in this novel much the same thing that Michael Crichton did for the space plague in *The Andromeda Strain;* that is, examine the situation in incredible detail and portray the unfolding events in such convincing fashion that the reader is convinced that this really is the way things would happen.

Tilley's second novel, *Mission,* on the other hand, was further from the mainstream of science fiction, although it also is pervaded by a sense of absolute conviction about the sequence of events, the details of official reaction, and the manner in which the characters react to the situation. A dead body is discovered bearing the same wounds as those of Jesus when he died on the cross. But shortly after the body is declared officially dead, there are signs of life. The medical staff is understandably amazed, but their investigation is cut short when their patient mysteriously disappears from the hospital. The protagonist finds his life disrupted even further when his missing patient reappears, apparently quite healthy, and identifies himself as Jesus. At this point, readers might dismiss the novel as an allegorical religious fantasy, but Tilley has more surprises in store. "Jesus" is actually an alien from another universe, using a human body from our far past, travelling through time because, to his/its perceptions, all times are simultaneous and it is an act of will to move from one to the other. In fact, the protagonist ends up travelling back through time himself in what is a very strange adventure novel, more ambitious than *Fade-out,* and in some ways more interesting, but less successful as entertainment.

Tilley's most noteworthy science fiction work is the Amtrak Wars series. Once again, Tilley uses a standard genre theme as background, in this case the primitive civilization existing following a nuclear holocaust. The culture is tribal, and the hero, one of the Wingmen, is captured in the first volume by his enemy, the Mutes. His sojourn as a prisoner exposes him to life among the Mutes and, rather than continuing to view them as enemies, he begins to accept them as fellow human beings. Peace suddenly becomes more desirable than continued conflict. His personal goal becomes the resolution of the internecine conflict. Unfortunately, things don't go quite that smoothly, and as the series progresses and we see more of his world, including a resurgent Samurai class in Japan, the inevitability of conflict seems less and less avoidable.

Xan was far less successful and in fact has not been reprinted in the United States. A family vacationing in a remote area begins to fear that a demonic force is seeking to possess one of their number. In actuality, alien beings who drift through the universe are the culprits. Although not as satisfying as Tilley's other work, *Xan* still contains some memorable scenes.

—Don D'Ammassa

TIPTREE, James, Jr.

Pseudonym for Alice Sheldon, née Bradley. **Nationality:** American. **Born:** Chicago, Illinois, 24 August 1915 (some sources cite birth year as 1916). **Education:** Sarah Lawrence College, Bronxville, New York; University of California, Berkeley; George Washington University, Washington, D.C., Ph.D. in psychology 1967. **Military Service:** Served in the United States Army Air Force, 1942-46. **Family:** Married 1) William Davey in 1934 (divorced, 1938); 2) Huntington Denton Sheldon in 1945. **Career:** Worked as an art critic, for the Central Intelligence Agency, in personal business, and as college teacher and experimental psychologist. **Awards:** Nebula award, 1973, 1976, 1977; Hugo award, 1974, 1977; *Locus* award, 1984. **Died:** 19 May 1987.

SCIENCE FICTION PUBLICATIONS

Novels (series: Great Central Library)

Up the Walls of the World. New York, Berkley, and London, Gollancz, 1978.
Brightness Falls from the Air (Library). New York, Tor, 1985; London, Sphere, 1986.

Short Stories

Ten Thousand Light-Years from Home. New York, Ace, 1973; London, Eyre Methuen, 1975.
Warm Worlds and Otherwise. New York, Ballantine, 1975.
Star Songs of an Old Primate. New York, Ballantine, 1978.
Out of the Everywhere and Other Extraordinary Visions. New York, Ballantine, 1981.
Byte Beautiful. Garden City, New York, Doubleday, 1985.
The Starry Rift (Library). New York, Tor, 1986; London, Sphere, 1988.
Tales of the Quintana Roo: Stories. Sauk City, Wisconsin, Arkham House, 1986.
Crown of Stars. New York, Tor, 1988; London, Orbit, 1990.
Her Smoke Rose up Forever: The Great Years of James Tiptree Jr, edited by James Turner. Sauk City, Wisconsin, Arkham House, 1990.
Houston, Houston, Do You Read?, bound with *Souls,* by Joanna Russ. New York, Tor, 1989.
The Girl Who Was Plugged In, bound with *Screwtop,* by Vonda N. McIntyre. New York, Tor, 1989.
The Color of Neanderthal Eyes, bound with *And Strange at Ecbatan the Trees,* by Michael Bishop. New York, Tor, 1990.

*

Critical Study: *The Fiction of James Tiptree, Jr.* by Gardner Dozois, New York, Algol Press, 1977.

*   *   *

Although her writing career began late in life and was regrettably brief (1968-87), Alice Sheldon managed to turn out several stories and novels whose vivid, elegiac style won her universal acclaim among science fiction readers and several nominations, awards, and multiple awards. Her greatest success was achieved in the 1970s with a series of stories illuminating and lamenting the great gulf of sensibility and human objectives existing between the sexes. These included "Love Is the Plan, the Plan Is Death," "The Women Men Don't See," "The Girl Who Was Plugged In," "Houston, Houston, Do You Read?" and "The Screwfly Solution." Typically James Tiptree Jr. (her successful pseudonymous disguise through 1977) develops a tale around the protagonist's agonizing reappraisal of the nature of human existence disclosed in a horrid epiphany. In "Love Is the Plan, the Plan Is Death," the mating game of an alien species is revealed to resemble more that of the praying mantis than that of humankind. In "The Women Men Don't See," a presumptuous man discovers that the woman he has been protecting is more at home with alien creatures than with him. And in "Houston, Houston, Do You Read?," Tiptree's most celebrated tale, astronauts from the male-dominated culture of the NASA Space Center pass through a time warp to find a future Earth populated entirely by female clones who not only reject male companionship but even deny them continued existence: hence the heavy double-entendre of the title: 1) "Houston can you hear us astronauts?"; 2) "N.A.S.A. are you listening to us women?" These latter two stories are fraught with mystery of all kinds—disguised motives, muffled, sinister conversations, depths of fear, regret, and remorse, and an overall atmospheric gloom as uniformly developed and as finely crafted as the best writing of Edgar Allan Poe. Both stories won both Nebula and Hugo awards.

This is not to say that Sheldon-Tiptree was in any sense an imitator of Poe or of any other writer of gothic fiction; on the contrary, she used gothicism to develop her own brand of tough-minded yet oddly optimistic story in which humans fight a losing battle with entropy but fight bravely and with a ferocity not found elsewhere in the animal kingdom. One is reminded of the famous struggle for survival of Scott's expeditionary force or of Guillaumet's famous pronouncement in Antoine de St. Exupery's *Wind, Sand, and Stars:* "I swear that what I went through no animal would have gone through." This characteristic Tiptree effect is enlarged by grotesque humor on occasion. In "The Screwfly Solution," which consists entirely of the desperate epistles of what may be the last woman on Earth, the protagonist suggests that she has seen in an angelic alien invader, "A real-estate agent." Her attempts to buoy her spirits as she witnesses the entire set of Earth males turn homicidal provides that sort of comic effect which ultimately deepens the story's horrific impact.

Neither of Tiptree's two novels, *Up the Walls of the World* and *Brightness Falls from the Air,* has the power of her best stories and novellae; it is as if the Tiptree effect does not grow by extension but rather is attenuated thereby.

Tiptree was a woman of uncommon strength, a world traveller, an artist-photographer, a person of great wit and erudition who was heard to say of all art, "If you can't laugh at it, what good is it," and at the same time one who when she deemed the time had come could end the life of her desperately sick husband and then her own. These biographical details are cited to illustrate Tiptree's mature, implacable, existential pragmatism, a character trait found in her heroes and heroines at their best. Although her life is over, there may still appear as-yet-unpublished stories. It would be surprising if these were to show any radical shift of sensibility from her other work. For, as she told an interviewer once, she came to writing with her opinions and her outlook on life largely complete. Her debt to feminist thought of the 1960s and 1970s is great, and her interest to feminist critics now and in the future is understandable; yet continued reading may prove her to be less a feminist writing about women than a philosopher of the human condition who refused even in the vast fields of science fiction to fake information not found in her own hormonal data base. Ironically her writing was for the years of her greatest success seen by many to arise of necessity from a masculine sensibility even as that very writing called into question such vapid and outworn gender distinctions. Science fiction poet Dick Allen saw the task of 20th-century SF as the search for a definition of humankind which could exist in the light of 20th-century knowledge; clearly Tiptree's work has added much to that quest.

—Thomas P. Dunn

TOLKIEN, J(ohn) R(onald) R(euel)

Nationality: British. **Born:** Bloemfontein, Orange Free State, South Africa, 3 January 1892; came to England, 1895. **Education:** King Edward VI's School, Birmingham, 1900-02, 1903-11; St. Philip's School, Birmingham, 1902-03; Exeter College, Oxford (open classical exhibitioner; Skeat prize, 1914), 1911-15, B.A. (honors), 1915, M.A. 1919. **Military Service:** Served in the Lancashire Fusiliers, 1915-18: lieutenant. **Family:** Married Edith Mary Bratt in 1916 (died 1971); three sons and one daughter. **Career:** Assistant, Oxford English Dictionary, 1919-20; reader in English, 1920-23, and professor of the English language, 1924-25, University of Leeds, Yorkshire; at Oxford University: Rawlinson and Bosworth Professor of Anglo-Saxon, 1925-45; fellow, Pembroke College, 1926-45; Leverhulme research fellow, 1934-36; Merton Professor of English language and literature, 1945-59; honorary fellow, Exeter College, 1963, and Merton College, 1973. Andrew Lang lecturer, University of St. Andrews, Fife, 1939; W.P. Ker lecturer, University of Glasgow, 1953; lived in Bournemouth, Dorset, 1968-71, and Oxford, 1971-73. Artist: one-man show: Ashmolean Museum, Oxford, 1977. **Awards:** International Fantasy award, 1957; Royal Society of Literature Benson medal, 1966; Foreign Book prize (France), 1973; World Science Fiction Convention Gandalf award, 1974; Hugo award, 1978. D.Litt.: University College, Dublin, 1954; University of Nottingham, 1970; Oxford University, 1972; Dr. en Phil et Lettres: Liège, 1954; honorary degree: University of Edinburgh, 1973. Fellow, Royal Society of Literature, 1957. C.B.E. (Commander, Order of the British Empire), 1972. **Died:** 2 September 1973.

SCIENCE FICTION PUBLICATIONS

Novels (series: Lord of the Rings)

The Hobbit; or, There and Back Again, illustrated by the author. London, Allen and Unwin, 1937; Boston, Houghton Mifflin, 1938; revised edition, 1951; revised edition, 1966.
The Lord of the Rings. London, Allen and Unwin, 1968.
   The Lord of the Rings: The Fellowship of the Ring. London, Allen and Unwin, and Boston, Houghton Mifflin, 1954; revised edition, New York, Ballantine, 1965; London, Allen and Unwin, 1966.
   The Two Towers. London, Allen and Unwin, 1954; Boston, Houghton Mifflin, 1955; revised edition, New York, Ballantine, 1965; London, Allen and Unwin, 1966.
   The Return of the King. London, Allen and Unwin, 1955; Boston, Houghton Mifflin, 1956; revised edition, New York, Ballantine, 1965; London, Allen and Unwin, 1966; excerpted as *The Grey Havens,* Brookline, Massachusetts, Pilcrow, 1990.
The Silmarillion, edited by Christopher Tolkien. London, Allen and Unwin, and Boston, Houghton Mifflin, 1977.

Short Stories

Unfinished Tales of Númenór and Middle-Earth, edited by Christopher Tolkien. London, Allen and Unwin, and Boston, Houghton Mifflin, 1980.

OTHER PUBLICATIONS

Novels for children

Farmer Giles of Ham, illustrated by Pauline Baynes. London, Allen and Unwin, 1949; Boston, Houghton Mifflin, 1950.
Smith of Wootton Major, illustrated by Pauline Baynes. London, Allen and Unwin, and Boston, Houghton Mifflin, 1967.
Mr. Bliss, illustrated by the author. London, Allen and Unwin, 1982.

The History of Middle Earth, edited by Christopher Tolkien

The Book of Lost Tales 1-2. London, Allen and Unwin, 2 vols., 1983-84; Boston, Houghton Mifflin, 2 vols., 1984.
Lays of Beleriand. London, Allen and Unwin, and Boston, Houghton Mifflin, 1985.
The Shaping of Middle-Earth: The Quenta, the Ambarkanta, and the Annals, Together with the Earliest 'Silmarillion' and the First Map. London, Allen and Unwin, and Boston, Houghton Mifflin, 1986.
The Lost Road and Other Writings. London, Unwin Hyman, and Boston, Houghton Mifflin, 1987.
The History of the Lord of the Rings:
    The Return of the Shadow. London, Unwin Hyman, 1988; Boston, Houghton Mifflin, 1989.
    The Treason of Isengard. London, Unwin Hyman, and Boston, Houghton Mifflin, 1989.
    The War of the Ring. London, Unwin Hyman, and Boston, Houghton Mifflin, 1990.
    Sauron Defeated: The End of the Third Age, The Notion Club Papers, and, The Drowning of Anadûnê. London, Unwin Hyman, and Boston, Houghton Mifflin, 1991.
    Morgoth's Ring: The Later Silmarillion Part 1, The Legends of Aman. London, Unwin Hyman, and Boston, Houghton Mifflin, 1993.
    The War of the Jewels: The Later Simarillion Part 2, The Legends of Beleriand. London, Unwin Hyman, and Boston, Houghton Mifflin, 1994.

Play

The Homecoming of Beorhtnoth Beorhthelm's Son (broadcast, 1954). Included in *The Tolkien Reader,* 1966; in *Tree and Leaf, Smith of Wootton Major, The Homecoming of Beorhtnoth Beorhthelm's Son,* 1975.

Radio Play: *The Homecoming of Beorhthnoth Beorhthelm's Son,* 1954.

Poetry

Songs for the Philologists, with others. Privately printed, 1936.
The Adventures of Tom Bombadil and Other Verses from the Red Book, illustrated by Pauline Baynes. London, Allen and Unwin, 1962; Boston, Houghton Mifflin, 1963.

The Road Goes Ever On: A Song Cycle, music by Donald Swann. Boston, Houghton Mifflin, 1967; London, Allen and Unwin, 1968; revised edition, Houghton Mifflin, 1978.
Bilbo's Last Song, illustrated by Pauline Baynes. London, Allen and Unwin, and Boston, Houghton Mifflin, 1974.
Poems and Stories. London, Allen and Unwin, 1980.

Other

A Middle English Vocabulary. Oxford, Clarendon Press, and New York, Oxford University Press, 1922.
Beowulf: The Monsters and the Critics. London, Oxford University Press, 1937.
Tree and Leaf (includes short story "Leaf by Niggle" and essay "On Fairy-Stories"). London, Allen and Unwin, 1964; Boston, Houghton Mifflin, 1965; revised edition, London, Unwin Hyman, 1988.
The Tolkien Reader. New York, Ballantine, 1966.
Tree and Leaf, Smith of Wootton Major, The Homecoming of Beorhtnoth Beorhthelm's Son. London, Allen and Unwin, 1975.
The Father Christmas Letters, edited by Baillie Tolkien, illustrated by the author. London, Allen and Unwin, and Boston, Houghton Mifflin, 1976.
Pictures. London, Allen and Unwin, and Boston, Houghton Mifflin, 1979.
The Letters of J.R.R. Tolkien: A Selection, edited by Humphrey Carpenter and Christopher Tolkien. London, Allen and Unwin, and Boston, Houghton Mifflin, 1981.
Finn and Hengest: The Fragment and the Episode, edited by Alan Bliss. London, Allen and Unwin, and Boston, Houghton Mifflin, 1983.
The Monsters and the Critics and Other Essays, edited by Christopher Tolkien. London, Allen and Unwin, 1983; Boston, Houghton Mifflin, 1984.

Editor, with E.V. Gordon, *Sir Gawain and the Green Knight.* Oxford, Clarendon Press, and New York, Oxford University Press, 1925.
Editor, *Ancrene Wisse.* London, Oxford University Press, 1962; New York, Oxford University Press, 1963.
Translator, *Sir Gawain and the Green Knight, Pearl, and Sir Orfeo,* edited by Christopher Tolkien. London, Allen and Unwin, and Boston, Houghton Mifflin, 1975.
Translator, *The Old English Exodus,* edited by Joan Turville-Petre. Oxford, Clarendon Press, 1981.

*

Bibliography: *Tolkien Criticism: An Annotated Checklist* by Richard C. West, Kent, Ohio, Kent State University Press, 1970; revised edition, 1981.

Manuscript Collections: Wade Collection, Wheaton College, Illinois; Marquette University, Milwaukee.

Critical Studies (selection): *Master of Middle-Earth: The Fiction of J.R.R. Tolkien* by Paul Kocher, Boston, Houghton Mifflin, 1972, London, Thames and Hudson, 1973; *Tolkien's World,* London, Thames and Hudson, and Boston, Houghton Mifflin, 1974, and *Tolkien and the Silmarils,* Thames and Hudson, 1981, both by Randel Helms; *J.R.R. Tolkien: A Biography* (includes bibliography) by Humphrey Carpenter, London, Allen and Unwin, and Boston, Houghton Mifflin, 1977; *The Mythology of Middle-Earth* by Ruth S. Noel, London, Thames and Hudson, and Boston, Houghton Mifflin, 1977; *The Complete Guide to Middle-Earth* by Robert Foster, London, Allen and Unwin, and New York, Ballantine, 1978; *Tolkien's Art: A Mythology for England* by Jane C. Nitzche, London, Macmillan, 1979; *Tolkien: New Critical Perspectives* edited by Neil D. Isaacs and Rose A. Zimbardo, Lexington, University Press of Kentucky, 1981; *The Road to Middle-Earth* by T.A. Shippey, London, Allen and Unwin, 1982, Boston, Houghton Mifflin, 1983; *J.R.R. Tolkien: This Far Land* edited by Robert Giddings, London, Vision, 1983; *The Song of Middle-Earth; J.R.R. Tolkien's Themes, Symbols, and Myths* by David Harvey, London, Allen and Unwin, 1985; *The Magical World of the Inklings: J.R.R. Tolkien, C.S. Lewis, Charles Williams, Owen Barfield* by Gareth Knight, Shaftesbury, Element, 1990; *A Tolkien Thesaurus* by Richard E. Blackwelder, New York, Garland, 1990.

*   *   *

J.R.R. Tolkien's *The Hobbit,* now a classic of the genre, introduces the reader to hobbits and their culture in Middle-Earth. As the tale develops, we are to meet characters that step into Bilbo's adventure out of folk legend and fairy story: a wizard, dwarfs bent upon revenge and the recovery of a fabulous treasure, trolls, goblins, elves both magical and dangerous, a bear-man changeling, and above all the great dragon Smaug. Much of the story's success depends upon the way in which Tolkien introduces us to the character of Bilbo Baggins, the hobbit whose uneventful life as a comfortable bachelor at Bag End is forever upset by the intervention of Gandalf the wizard who leads Thorin Oakenshield and his company of dwarfs to Bilbo's door with the promise that Bilbo will prove to be a daring and resourceful burglar, and just the person needed to win back the treasure of the dwarfs from Smaug. Bilbo is an unwilling adventurer who loves his comfortable hobbit hole and his reputation as a respectable member of a community of innocent, good-natured burghers. Tolkien manages successfully the difficult task of keeping the comic dimensions of Bilbo's character pleasantly in focus while at the same time developing the equally endearing qualities of good humor, humility, moral courage, and a temperate mind.

In the course of the action, two things are happening. The first is the discovery of the shape, constitution, and nature of Middle-Earth and its wondrous if sometimes menacing inhabitants. Tolkien opens a prospect of unexplored territory in fairyland, and rarely misses an opportunity to enrich the reader's imagination with new and permanent boundary markers. The second is that, in the course of the action, Bilbo comes to discover his limitations but also his own powers and his place in the wide world. Tolkien has shaped the action of Bilbo's quest as correlative to the experience of growing up. His adventures remind us of the solicitude of a wise parent: be yourself, trust your instincts for good, overcome your belittling fears, be generous and brave always, be courteous, especially in strange company or in foreign lands, be resourceful, and the world will discover your worth and praise your accomplishments, and you will be numbered with the mighty and powerful.

Since Bilbo's initiation into life is one of the substructures shaping this narrative, part of his learning experience comes from rubbing elbows with creatures of other kinds and species. He learns about the special virtues, powers, and shortcomings of dwarfs, elves, orcs, goblins, wizards, and men. He learns a bit of the his-

tory and lore of Middle-Earth and of the polite conventions that make common action possible between variant races and species. In learning these things, Bilbo comes to understand himself better as a hobbit and to see his place and that of his kind in the great scheme of things, although the full revelation of that place awaits *The Lord of the Rings.* Bilbo learns to his surprise, discomfort, and eventual satisfaction that he has a role to play in life and in the great adventures of the wide world—even of the wild world.

Tolkien made a revision of *The Hobbit* after he had completed the trilogy *The Lord of the Rings.* The revision was a major one, raising the tone and characterization considerably above the original child's story level to the threshold of the legendary, making it more consistent with the great sequel to which, in a way, it gave birth. Tolkien also made some adjustments in the details of the original story so as to bring them into line with the more serious mythology of the trilogy.

In the end, the greatness of the trilogy has to be assessed on the basis of what Tolkien attempted. The trilogy is, of course, fantasy, an extension of the fairy-story elements of *The Hobbit* into the heroic tradition. Some critics have called it "high fantasy," others myth, still others saga, legend, even science fiction and "super science fiction." Tolkien himself described the trilogy as "feigned history," and as such it is best understood. Feigned history is imagined history, which is not at all the same thing as imaginary history.

The appearance of *Unfinished Tales of Númenór and Middle-Earth* and *The History of Middle-Earth* throws new light on Christopher Tolkien's extraordinary contributions as editor of *The Silmarillion* and offers sufficient background evidence that *The Silmarillion* continued to mature in Tolkien's mind as much after the writing of *The Lord of the Rings* as before. Although the published *The Silmarillion* is unfinished and not the work the author hoped to produce, what we have is incomparable. *The Silmarillion* is best read as the scripture and legendary history of the elves. Nor is it presumed that the history was all given in the same voice, style, or at the same moment. All three of the major branches of the elves (Vanyar, Noldor, Teleri) seem to have their temperaments represented in the various books: the Vanyar in "Ainulindale," the Teleri in "Valaquenta," and the Noldor in "Quenta Silmarillion." As such, *The Silmarillion* is Tolkien's elvish scripture, a feigned sacred writing: the revelation, lore, and practice from which we are to surmise those myths and legends grew that gave birth eventually to the hobbit records of the last war against Sauron in *The Lord of the Rings.* The feigned history of *The Lord of the Rings* which includes its own epic-heroic-legendary transformation now ultimately rests upon the elvish revelations of *The Silmarillion.* If the gods be absent from *The Lord of the Rings,* as many critics once complained (even though gods are very much felt), they are present and immanent in *The Silmarillion.*

Clearly, *The Silmarillion* is the foundation of Tolkien's Middle-Earth and everything in it. He began writing parts of the Silmaril mythos before he went off to World War I, declaring to his future wife and to friends that his intention was to create a mythology for England. *The Silmarillion* was to be an English epic fit to rival Homer and Virgil, the stated ambition of every major English poet since Spenser. As the other poets, Tolkien rests his epic claims on language, but in his case it is not merely the narrative language but the languages of the subtexts of Middle-Earth. In the case of *The Silmarillion,* especially elvish. More than any work of its type, *The Silmarillion* grew out of language, both received and invented.

Tolkien's genius for naming grew directly out of his interest in developing imaginary languages spoken by beings all the more imaginary for dwelling in the world of fairies. Tolkien's world is the backward extension of the one we know from romance, legend, folklore, and fairytale. Thus the revelation at the beginning of "Ainulindale" that the elvish name for Eru, the creator, was Iluvatar is revelation indeed, but perhaps more of elvishness than divinity. Tolkien is at his best when working at the roots of words and at the heart of languages wherein the inquiring mind discovers itself reflected in its most basic operations. Thus, the Tolkien power of name-giving is reflexive, revealing both the thing named and the namer—here the elves—but it stirs hidden responses in the receptive reader to the universal sense of the power of names, when they are the right names. And Tolkien is almost infallibly right in his naming, perhaps because his inspirations come from an understanding of the nature and practice of language similar to that which a scientist might develop after long study of the secrets of nature. Inventing names is Tolkien's chief (but not only) method of activating the power of language structures to both quicken the imagination and convey the assurance that existence follows upon the name, as indeed in Tolkien's world it truly does.

We cannot separate Tolkien's interest in and experiments with languages both real and imagined from his vision of fairy land, a vision that grew with his exploration of its imaginative potential. Tolkien revealed that the vision was in his words "a gift," and it remained for him all his life a hobby and a pastime, bound up with both his scholarship as an Oxford don and his parenting of his own children. Many of the key episodes that anchored *The Silmarillion* in Tolkien's imagination were visions, visual images, which Tolkien felt he was obliged to find the explanation of. He always held that Middle-Earth was a world discovered rather than dreamed up. It was to be found in the logic of cause and effect: an imagined language extended itself necessarily to ethology, and thence to geology, geography, botany, zoology, and so on, producing the coherent infrastructures of a realized secondary world suited to the imagination.

No critical estimate of Tolkien and *The Silmarillion* would be worth producing without a word on style. Thanks to the publication of some of the earlier drafts of Silmarillion materials, we can assess the process by which Tolkien's mature style developed. How fortunate literature has been that Tolkien's elvish mythology did not enjoy an early success. The early drafts are discovered to be stylistically mannered, artificial in the bad sense, and feebly imitative of 19th-century aesthetic models. As Tolkien's imagination expanded so did the range of his style. Finally, he found the proper voices for his elves in *The Silmarillion,* which contains elements of the most lyrical prose ever written in English. *The Silmarillion* is, moreover, rich in sustained, inspired storytelling, in mythic and epic elements that range from the literature of revelation to the tragic beauty of elvin history in Middle-Earth, an accounting of a species exiled by fate and by choice from felicity. In addition to numerous instances in the published version of *The Silmarillion,* readers should not overlook two jewels of heroic and tragic narrative reaching that rarest of all literary achievements, the sublime, in the stories of Tuor and Turin, both found in *Unfinished Tales.*

The Lord of the Rings and *The Silmarillion* are not merely great fantasy; they are great literature. Tolkien will continue to interest scholars and students who have already begun the exhaustive study of his work, its sources, inspirations, and its elements. There is little doubt that Tolkien will eventually take his place somewhere in the NeoRomantic movement which followed the aestheticism and decadence of the late 19th century. He has already been placed in the tradition of writers like H. Rider Haggard and William Morris,

and the influences of the Eddas, the Kalevala, Anglo-Saxon, and Middle English romance have already been noted and will doubtless yield more secrets in the future. Nor should we ignore the influence of the Inklings and their interest in Tolkien's work during the long, difficult years before recognition came. Other students will consider the relation or at least the parallels to contemporary writers of fantasy like Mervyn Peake and Austin Tappan Wright. In the end, it may be that Tolkien will be understood best when linked and compared to James Joyce, an unlikely pairing, perhaps, but one that is full of telling comparisons and contrasts.

—Donald L. Lawler

TOLSTOY, Alexey

Nationality: Russian. **Born:** Nikolaevski-Samarskom, 20 December 1882. **Career:** Novelist, short story writer, and playwright. **Died:** 22 February 1945.

SCIENCE FICTION PUBLICATIONS

Novels

Aëlita. N.p., n.d., revised, 1937; translated by Lucy Flaxman as *Aelita,* Moscow, Foreign Language Publishing House, 1957; translated by Antonia W. Bouis, New York, Macmillan, 1981; translated by Leland Fetzer as *Aelita: The Decline of Mars,* Ann Arbor, Michigan, Ardis, 1985.
Giperboloid inzhernera Garina. N.p., n.d.; translated by Bernard Guilbert Guerney as *The Death Box,* London, Methuen, 1938; translated by George Hanna as *The Garin Death Ray,* Moscow, Foreign Languages Publishing House, 1955; retranslated by George Hanna as *Engineer Garin and His Death Ray,* Moscow, Raduga Publishers, 1987.

*   *   *

Alexey Tolstoy published two collections of poetry before he turned away from both verse and Symbolism to stories and novels in the tradition of 19th-century Realism. He emigrated to Germany after the Bolshevik revolution, but returned to Russia in 1923 and became a leading and privileged exponent of the official Socialist Realism, especially in a number of historical novels.

Tolstoy became the first classic writer of Russian SF by giving the fast-developing genre the accolade of literary quality and respectability, much as his model Wells did. In *Aelita* this blend is enriched with a lyrical component, the love of Los, the inventor of the rocketship, for the Martian princess Aelita. Los, the creative intellectual, with his vacillations and individualist concerns, is contrasted to but also allied with Gusev, a shrewd man of the people and fearless fighter who leads the revolt of Martian workers (the Martians are descendants of the Atlantans) against the decadent dictatorship of the Engineers' Council. If the standard adventure and romance were taken over from Wells and pulp SF (e.g., Benoit's *Atlantis* and Burroughs's *A Princess of the Moon*) or indeed from theosophy, the politics are diametrically opposed to Lasswitz's and Bogdanov's idea of a Martian benevolent technocracy. Yet if the workers' uprising led by a Red Army man was a clear parable for the times, such as could have been shared by all Soviet SF from Mayakovsky to Zamyatin, the dejected and somewhat hasty return which has Los listening at the end to the desperate wireless calls of his beloved is clearly of a Wellsian gloom (*The First Men in the Moon*). But this ambiguity, which sometimes strains the plot mechanics, makes also for an encompassing of differing attitudes and levels that follows Bogdanov by envisaging the price as well as the necessity of an activist happiness. This is achieved by plastic characterization, differentiated language, and consistent verisimilitude.

Tolstoy's second novel, *The Deathbox* (four versions from 1926 to 1937), is a retreat to the "catastrophe" novel: Vernean adventures and Chestertonian detections and conspiracies revolve around a well-drawn amoral scientist who beats the capitalist industry kings at their own game but comes to grief when faced with popular revolt. It moves fast if jerkily; as Tolstoy had training in engineering, its science is believable (atomic disintegration of a transuranium element is posited as well as something resembling lasers), and it remains a prototype of the anti-imperialist and antifascist satire-thriller melodrama, always a vigorous strand in Russian SF. The two novels, as well as the stories "Blue Cities" and "The League of the Five" and several plays (including an adaptation of Capek's *R.U.R.*), blended SF adventures (interplanetary flight, the revolt of machines, or global struggle for a new scientific invention) with a utopian pathos arising from revolutionary social perspectives in a way calculated to please almost all segments of the reading public. This blend was to remain the basic Soviet SF tradition until Yefremov, and indeed through the end of the 1960s.

—Darko Suvin

TORRO, Pel. *See* **FANTHORPE, R. Lionel.**

TRENT, Olaf. *See* **FANTHORPE, R. Lionel.**

TRIMBLE, Louis (Preston)

Pseudonyms: Stuart Brock; Gerry Travis. **Nationality:** American. **Born:** Seattle, Washington, 2 March 1917. **Education:** Eastern Washington State College, Cheney, B.A. 1950, Ed.M. 1953; University of Washington, Seattle, 1952-53, 1955, 1956-57; University of Pennsylvania, Philadelphia, 1955-56. **Military Service:** Served as an editor in the United States Army Corps of Engineers Architects Division. **Family:** Married 1) Renee Eddy in 1938 (died, 1951), one daughter; 2) Jacquelyn Whitney in 1952; 3) Mary Todd in 1974. **Career:** English teacher, Bonners Ferry High School, Idaho, 1946-47; instructor in Spanish and English, Eastern Washington State College, 1950-54; instructor, 1956-59, assistant professor, 1959-65, associate professor, 1965-76, and professor of humanities and social studies, 1976-80, University of Washington. Participated in English as a Second Language Seminars in Yugoslavia, 1972-74, 1976. **Member:** Executive Board, Western Writers of America, 1963-64. **Died:** 9 March 1988.

SCIENCE FICTION PUBLICATIONS

Novels (series: Anthropol)

The Tide Can't Wait. New York, Bouregy, 1957; London, Wright and Brown, 1959.
Anthropol. New York, Ace, 1968.
The Noblest Experiment in the Galaxy (Anthropol). New York, Ace, 1970.
Guardians of the Gate, with Jacqueline Trimble. New York, Ace, 1972.
The City Machine. New York, DAW, 1972.
The Wandering Variables. New York, DAW, 1972.
The Bodelan Way. New York, DAW, 1974.

OTHER PUBLICATIONS

Novels

Fit to Kill. New York, Phoenix Press, 1941.
Date for Murder. New York, Phoenix Press, 1942.
Tragedy in Turquoise. New York, Phoenix Press, 1942.
Design for Dying. New York, Phoenix Press, 1945.
Murder Trouble. New York, Phoenix Press, 1945; London, Wells Gardner, 1949.
Give up the Body. Seattle, Superior, 1946.
You Can't Kill a Corpse. New York, Phoenix Press, 1946.
Valley of Violence. Philadelphia, Macrae Smith, 1948; London, Corgi, 1951.
The Case of the Blank Cartridge. New York, Phoenix Press, 1949.
Gunsmoke Justice. Philadelphia, Macrae Smith, 1950; London, Corgi, 1951.
Blondes Are Skin Deep. New York, Lion, 1951.
Gaptown Law. Philadelphia, Macrae Smith, 1950.
Fighting Cowman. New York, Popular, 1953; Manchester, World Distributors, 1956.
Crossfire. New York, Avalon, 1953.
Bullets on Bunchgrass. New York, Avalon, 1954.
Stab in the Dark. New York, Ace, 1956.
The Virgin Victim. New York, Mercury, 1956.
Nothing to Lose But My Life. New York, Ace, 1957.
Mountain Ambush. New York, Avalon, 1958.
The Smell of Trouble. New York, Ace, 1958.
Cargo for the Styx. New York, Ace, 1959.
The Corpse without a Country. New York, Ace, 1959.
Obit Deferred. New York, Ace, 1959.
Til Death Do Us Part. New York, Ace, 1959.
The Duchess of Skid Row. New York, Ace, 1960.
Girl on a Slay Ride. New York, Avon, 1960.
Love Me and Die. New York, Ace, 1960.
Deadman and Canyon. New York, Ace, 1961.
Montana Gun. New York, Hillman, 1961; London, White Lion, 1972.

The Surfside Caper. New York, Ace, 1961.
Siege at High Meadow. New York, Ace, 1962; Bath, Chivers, 1992.
The Dead and the Deadly. New York, Ace, 1963.
The Man from Colorado. New York, Ace, 1963.
Wild Horse Range. New York, Ace, 1963.
Trouble at Gunsight. New York, Ace, 1964.
The Desperate Deputy of Cougar Hill. New York, Ace, 1965; London, Severn House, 1979.
The Holdout in the Diablos. New York, Ace, 1965.
Showdown in the Cayuse. New York, Ace, 1966.
Standoff at Massacre Buttes. New York, Ace, 1967.
Marshal of Sangaree. New York, Ace, 1968.
West to the Pecos. New York, Ace, 1968.
The Hostile Peaks. New York, Ace, 1969; London, Severn House, 1979.
Trouble Valley. New York, Ace, 1970; London, Severn House, 1979.
The Lonesome Mountains. New York, Ace, 1970.
The Ragbag Army. New York, Ace, 1971.

Novels as Gerry Travis

Tarnished Love. New York, Phoenix Press, 1942.
A Lovely Mask for Murder. New York, Avalon, 1956.
The Big Bite. New York, Avalon, 1957.

Novels as Stuart Brock

Death Is My Lover. New York, Mill, 1948.
Just around the Coroner. New York, Mill, 1948.
Railtown Sheriff. New York, Bouregy, 1949; London, Barker, 1959.
Bring Back Her Body. New York, Ace, 1953.
Double-Cross Ranch. New York, Avalon, 1954; London, Barker, 1957.
Action at Boundary Peak. New York, Avalon, 1955.
Whispering Canyon. New York, Avalon, 1955.
Forbidden Range. New York, Avalon, 1956.
Killer's Choice. New York, Graphic, 1956.

Other

Sports of the World. Los Angeles, Golden West, 1938.
Working Papers in English for Science and Technology, with Robert Bley-Vroman and Larry Selinker. Seattle, University of Washington, 1972.
New Horizons: A Reader in Scientific and Technical English, (and Teachers' Guide), with others. Zagreb, Skolska Knjiga, 2 vols., 1975.
Course Materials for Non-Native Speakers Planning to Enter U.S. Universities to Study Science or Technology, with Mary Todd Trimble. San Francisco, Pacific American Institute, 1977.
English for Multinational Business, with Mary Todd Trimble. Washington, D.C., International Communication Agency, 1978.
English for Science and Technology: A Discourse Approach. Cambridge and New York, Cambridge University Press, 1985.

Editor, *Criteria for Highway Benefit Analysis.* Seattle, University of Washington-National Academy of Sciences, 3 vols., 1964-65; revised edition, with Robert G. Hennes, Washington, D.C., National Highway Research Board, 1966-67.

Editor, *Incorporation of Shelter into Apartments and Office Buildings.* Washington, D.C., Office of Civil Defense, 1965.
Editor, with Karl Drobnic and Mary Todd Trimble, *English for Specific Purposes: Scientific and Technical English.* Corvalis, Oregon State University Press, 1978.

*

Bibliography: In *English for Academic and Technical Purposes: Studies in Honor of Louis Trimble* edited by Larry Selinker and others, Rowley, Massachusetts, Newbury House, 1981.

Manuscript Collections: University of Oregon Library, Eugene; University of Wyoming, Laramie.

Louis Trimble commented:

The basic purpose of my science fiction is to entertain while at the same time commenting on some of the unchanging characteristics of humans. I have chosen one of the least complicated ways of showing this—by setting my books several thousand years in the future, when "earth-originated" people have spread throughout the galaxy, colonizing. In some cases they conquered and at times displaced native peoples; in others living harmoniously with them or mixing (when possible). By using this galaxy and this time period in all of my books, I hope to show that in several thousand years there has been little change in political attitudes, social attitudes, and—in fact—the way people act and think.

*   *   *

Louis Trimble made his debut as a science fiction novelist in 1968 with the publication of *Anthropol.* Trimble has mastered one form of the futuristic novel, the lyrical fantasy, quite handily. Especially entertaining are *The Wandering Variables, The City Machine,* and *The Bodelan Way,* books which share a motif of whimsical fantasy underpinning the rather standard fare of futuristic gadgetry and intergalactic conflict. In each the setting reminds one of the more familiar works of C.S. Lewis and Jules Verne; there are botanical wildernesses, shimmering islands, stark winter steppes, deep pools, and medieval valleys.

The lyrical tone is a result of the presence of fantastic goddesses, women of divine birth or superior knowledge, who accompany kind-hearted and competent, if somewhat insecure, males on their adventures. Because Trimble's novels transpire under this divine feminine sanction, the gratuitous violence typical of so much popular science fiction is diminished, and in its place has come the spirit of romance. His books move from loss to reacquisition, from discord to harmony, from problem to solution.

However, Trimble often achieves the effect of romance at the expense of sound narrative construction. There is frequently too much fortuitous coincidence in his books, too many miraculous rescues of the protagonists, too little real threat of failure or death. We are too rarely awestruck by what happens and too often left incredulous. Neither are his romances of the heart or of the head: his problems tend to be created and resolved by machines rather than by human experience. The problem for Trimble's characters is always to escape physical threat or to build a new city or to return to a familiar planet. Thus only rarely, as in the final scenes of *The Bodelan Way* and *Guardians of the Gate,* does the solution involve the emotional or intellectual growth we demand of first-rate fiction. There is altogether too little development of Trimble's characters and too little engagement of our deeper human sympathies in his situations. Another difficulty arises from the fact that Trimble's novels sometimes cannot sustain their futurism through an entire narrative. In particular, *The Wandering Variables* and *The City Machine* retain their futurism only through the initial phase of exposition before finding their true subject in Earth's Middle Ages. At the center of these books are dirt floors, ox-drawn carts, and bellicose medieval clans. Consequently, one feels that in these books science fiction is more peripheral than central, more a vehicle to Trimble's real interest, which is in the past rather than the future.

Nevertheless, through more than 50 books Trimble developed a prose style which is elaborate yet efficient, and vividly descriptive yet never excessive. Like so many others, his narratives are fast-paced and full of action, yet one does not have the sensation that their pace and action are purely an exploitation of commercial appeal. More often, one feels that though Trimble's novels may fall short of the very best, his concern with the remote future is sincere and his imagination sufficient to include the human condition in that future. For young readers initiating themselves into the worlds of futuristic literature, Trimble's works are fine preparation for the more distant and rewarding vision of Lewis and others like him.

—Marvin W. Hunt

TROUT, Kilgore. *See* FARMER, Philip José.

TSIOLKOVSKY, Konstantin

Nationality: Russian. **Born:** Izhevsk, Ryazan, 17 September 1857. **Career:** Self-taught physicist and mathematician; pioneer of modern astronautics; developed and tested the first Russian aeronautic wind tunnel, devised the basic mathematical equation for calculating rocket velocity, proposed the use of liquid propellants in rockets, introduced the concept of staging in which rockets are constructed of component propulsion units that burn out and separate from the main rocket at intervals, and became known in the former U.S.S.R. as the father of space travel. Became full-time writer after receiving a stipend from the Socialist Academy in 1921. **Died:** 19 September 1935.

SCIENCE FICTION PUBLICATIONS

Novels

Vne zemli. N.p., n.d.; translated by Kenneth Syers as *Beyond the Planet Earth,* Oxford, Pergamon Press, 1960.
On the Moon. N.p., n.d.
Sorrow and Genius. N.p., n.d.

Short Stories

The Call of the Cosmos, edited by V. Dutt. Moscow, Foreign Languages Publishing House, 1961; as *The Path to the Stars: Collection of Science Fiction Works,* Ohio, Wright-Patterson Air Force Base, 1966; abridged edition as *The Science Fiction of Konstantin Tsiolkovsky,* Seattle, Washington, University Press of the Pacific, 1979.
The Will of the Universe, Intellect Unknown, Mind and Passions, translated by Svetlana I. Zherebtsove. Moscow, Pamyat, 1992.
Dreams of Earth and Heaven: The Effects of Universal Gravitation. N.p., n.d.
Life in Interstellar Environment. N.p., n.d.

OTHER PUBLICATIONS

OTHER

Collected Works of K. E. Tsiolkovsky. Washington, D.C., National Aeronautics and Space Administration, 1965, 2 volumes.
Works of Rocket Technology. Washington, D.C., National Aeronautics and Space Administration, 1965.
Selected Works, edited by V. N. Sokolsky. Moscow, Mir, 1968.

*   *   *

Konstantin Tsiolkovsky lost most of his hearing as a boy, and grew up a lonely eccentric. He became a provincial teacher, writing scientific papers all the while—particularly on aeronautics (from balloons to jet aircraft) and interplanetary travel. A self-made mathematician, he often rediscovered already-known hypotheses; yet he also created the theory of rocket flight for interplanetary space (formula for attaining cosmic velocities). Disregarded before the revolution, he was elected to the Socialist Academy in 1918 and given a pension in 1921, when he devoted himself entirely to writing. His SF tales *On the Moon* and *Beyond the Planet Earth* and his anticipatory fictionalized essays bordering on SF, *Dreams of Earth and Heaven: The Effects of Universal Gravitation,* as well as some other anticipatory essays, are collected in *The Call of the Cosmos,* while other essays are collected in *Life in Interstellar Environment;* a number of utopian visions, notably *Sorrow and Genius,* have been relatively slighted.

The deep-seated obsession in all of Tsiolkovsky's writings is liberation from earthly and indeed universal gravity. The cosmic alternative—on rocket spaceships, satellite stations, asteroids, or space colonies—is accompanied by diverse aspects of bliss: perpetual Spring, physical ease and health, utopian-socialist democracy, unheard-of technological achievements, "heavenly life without sorrow," and finally immortality—possibly for individuals and certainly for the human species moving from sun to sun through billions of years. When touching on such a cluster of beatific desires Tsiolkovsky's clear but very pedestrian style rises to passages of a naive poetry, e.g., in descriptions of life-forms on the low-gravity Moon. This is also what makes for the peculiar hybrid genre of these writings, oscillating between fantastic idea and scientific (or popularizing) prose, with the stories just on this and the essays just on that side of an imaginary halfway house. Visionary essays seem the primary form of his expression, while the tales are primarily an attempt at reaching a wider readership. Thus even their clumsy plots and nonexistent characterization are an interesting testimonial to the genesis of one kind of SF, the "literature of ideas" (in Tsiolkovsky, this embraces also speculations on "etheric" beings, on a photonic phase of mankind and universe, on reversing entropy).

The main literary influences on Tsiolkovsky seem to have been the eccentric Russian philosopher of cosmic utopianism and this-worldly resurrection N.F. Fyodorov, Verne, and Flammarion. In his turn, he stands behind all Soviet writings on cosmic travel, in fiction from Tolstoy and Belyaev to Yefremov and Altov, and in science from Oberth and others down to the Sputnik and Vostok constructors. He remains one of the great pioneers of modern SF, particularly important for his refusal to discriminate between utopia and science.

—Darko Suvin

TUBB, E(dwin) C(harles)

Pseudonyms: Chuck Adams; Stuart Allen; Anthony Armstrong; Ted Bain; Alice Beecham; Anthony Blake; L.T. Bronson; Raymond L. Burton; Morley Carpenter; Julian Carey; Jud Cary; Julian Cary; J.F. Clarkson; Norman Dale; Robert D. Ennis; James Evans; James S. Farrow; James R. Fenner; R.H. Godfrey; Charles S. Graham; Charles Grey; Volsted Gridban; Alan Guthrie; D.W.R. Hill; George Holt; Gill Hunt; Alan (or Allan) Innes; E.F. Jackson; Gordon Kent; Gregory Kern; King Lang; Mike Lantry; P. Lawrence; Chet Lawson; Nigel Lloyd; Robert Lloyd; Frank T. Lomas; Ron Lowam; Arthur Maclean; Carl Maddox; Philip Martyn; John Mason; Carl Moulton; L.C. Powers; M.L. Powers; Edward Richards; Paul Schofield; John Seabright; Brian Shaw; Roy Sheldon; John Stevens; Eric Storm; Andrew Sutton; Edward Thomson; Ken Wainwright; Frank Weight; Douglas West; Eric Wilding; Frank Winnard. **Nationality:** British. **Born:** London, 15 October 1919. **Family:** Married Iris Kathleen Smith in 1944; two daughters. **Career:** Has worked as a welfare officer, catering manager, and printing machine salesman. Editor, *Authentic Science Fiction,* London, 1956-57, and *Eye and Vector,* 1958-60. **Awards:** Cytricon award, 1955; Eurocon award, 1972. Guest of Honor, World Science Fiction Convention, Heidelberg, 1970. **Agent:** Carnell Literary Agency, Danescroft, Goose Lane, Little Hallingbury, Bishop's Stortford, Hertfordshire CM22 7RG. **Address:** 67 Houston Road, London SE23 2RL, England.

SCIENCE FICTION PUBLICATIONS

Novels (series: Dumarest; Space 1999)

Saturn Patrol (as King Lang). London, Curtis Warren, 1951.
Planetfall (as Gill Hunt). London, Curtis Warren, 1951.
Argentis (as Brian Shaw). London, Curtis Warren, 1952.
Alien Impact. London, Hamilton, 1952.
Atom-War on Mars. London, Panther, 1952.
The Mutants Rebel. London, Panther, 1953.
Venusian Adventure. London, Comyns, 1953.
Alien Life. London, Paladin, 1954.
The Living World (as Carl Maddox). London, Pearson, 1954.
World at Bay. London, Panther, 1954.
The Metal Eater (as Roy Sheldon). London, Panther, 1954.
Journey to Mars. London, Scion, 1954.

Menace from the Past (as Carl Maddox). London, Pearson, 1954.
City of No Return. London, Scion, 1954.
The Stellar Legion. London, Scion, 1954.
The Hell Planet. London, Scion, 1954.
The Resurrected Man. London, Dragon, 1954.
Alien Dust. London, Boardman, 1955; New York, Avalon, 1957.
The Space-Born. New York, Ace, 1956; London, Digit, 1961.
Moon Base. London, Jenkins, and New York, Ace, 1964.
Death Is a Dream. London, Hart-Davis, and New York, Ace, 1967.
The Winds of Gath (Dumarest). New York, Ace, 1967; as *Gath,* London, Hart-Davis, 1968.
C.O.D. Mars. New York, Ace, 1968.
Derai (Dumarest). New York, Ace, 1968; London, Arrow, 1973.
S.T.A.R. Flight. New York, Paperback Library, 1969; London, Hale, 1980.
Toyman (Dumarest). New York, Ace, 1969; London, Arrow, 1973.
Escape into Space: Science Fiction. London, Sidgwick and Jackson, 1969.
Kalin (Dumarest). New York, Ace, 1969; London, Arrow, 1973.
The Jester at Scar (Dumarest). New York, Ace, 1970; London, Arrow, 1977.
Lallia (Dumarest). New York, Ace, 1971; London, Arrow, 1977.
Technos (Dumarest). New York, Ace, 1972; London, Arrow, 1977.
Century of the Manikin. New York, DAW, 1972; London, Millington, 1975.
Mayenne (Dumarest). New York, DAW, 1973; London, Arrow, 1977.
Veruchia (Dumarest). New York, Ace, 1973; London, Arrow, 1977.
Jondelle (Dumarest). New York, DAW, 1973; London, Arrow, 1977.
Zenya (Dumarest). New York, DAW, 1974; London, Arrow, 1978.
Breakaway (Space 1999; novelization of TV series). London, Orbit, and New York, Pocket Books, 1975.
Eloise (Dumarest). New York, DAW, 1975; London, Arrow, 1978.
Eye of the Zodiac (Dumarest). New York, DAW, 1975; London, Arrow, 1978.
Collision Course (Space 1999; novelization of TV series). London, Orbit, 1975; New York, Pocket Books, 1976.
Jack of Swords (Dumarest). New York, DAW, 1976; London, Arrow, 1979.
Alien Seed (Space 1999; novelization of TV series). London, Orbit, and New York, Pocket Books, 1976.
Spectrum of a Forgotten Sun (Dumarest). New York, DAW, 1976; London, Arrow, 1980.
Rogue Planet (Space 1999; novelization of TV series). New York, Pocket Books, and London, Orbit, 1976.
Earthfall (Space 1999; novelization of TV series). London, Orbit, 1977.
Haven of Darkness (Dumarest). New York, DAW, 1977; London, Arrow, 1980.
Prison of Night (Dumarest). New York, DAW, 1977; London, Arrow, 1980.
The Primitive. London, Orbit, 1977.
Incident on Ath (Dumarest). New York, DAW, 1978.
The Quillian Sector (Dumarest). New York, DAW, 1978; London, Arrow, 1982.
Stellar Assignment. London, Hale, 1979.
Web of Sand (Dumarest). New York, DAW, 1979; London, Arrow, 1983.
Death Wears a White Face. London, Hale, 1979.
Iduna's Universe (Dumarest). New York, DAW, 1979; London, Arrow, 1985.

The Luck Machine. London, Dobson, 1980.

The Terra Data (Dumarest). New York, DAW, 1980; London, Arrow, 1985.

Pawn of the Omphalos. New York, Fawcett, 1980.

World of Promise (Dumarest). New York, DAW, 1980; London, Arrow, 1985.

Nectar of Heaven (Dumarest). New York, DAW, 1981; London, Arrow, 1985.

The Terridae (Dumarest). New York, DAW, 1981.

The Coming Event (Dumarest). New York, DAW, 1982; London, Arrow, 1986.

Earth Is Heaven (Dumarest). New York, DAW, 1982; London, Arrow, 1986.

Stardeath. New York, Ballantine, 1983.

Melome (Dumarest). New York, DAW, 1983.

Angado (Dumarest). New York, DAW, 1984.

Symbol of Terra (Dumarest). New York, DAW, 1984.

The Temple of Truth (Dumarest). New York, DAW, 1985.

Novels as Volsted Gridban

Alien Universe. London, Scion, 1952.

Reverse Universe. London, Scion, 1952.

Planetoid Disposals Ltd. London, Milestone, 1953.

De Bracy's Drug. London, Scion, 1953.

Fugitive of Time. London, Milestone, 1953.

Novels as Charles Grey

The Wall. London, Milestone, 1953.

Dynasty of Doom. London, Milestone, 1953.

Tormented City. London, Milestone, 1953.

Space Hunger. London, Milestone, 1953.

I Fight for Mars. London, Milestone, 1953.

The Extra Man. London, Milestone, 1954.

The Hand of Havoc. London, Merit, 1954.

Enterprise 2115. London, Merit, 1954; as *The Mechanical Monarch* (as E.C. Tubb), New York, Ace, 1958.

Novels as Gregory Kern (series: Cap Kennedy in all books)

Galaxy of the Lost. New York, DAW, 1973; London, Mews, 1976.

Slave Ship from Sergan. New York, DAW, 1973; London Mews, 1976.

Monster of Metelaze. New York, DAW, 1973.

Enemy within the Skull. New York, DAW, 1974.

Jewel of Jarhen. New York, DAW, 1974; London, Mews, 1976.

Seetee Alert! New York, DAW, 1974; London, Mews, 1976.

The Gholan Gate. New York, DAW, 1974.

The Eater of Worlds. New York, DAW, 1974.

Earth Enslaved. New York, DAW, 1974.

Planet of Dread. New York, DAW, 1974.

Spawn of Laban. New York, DAW, 1974.

The Genetic Buccaneer. New York, DAW, 1974.

A World Aflame. New York, DAW, 1974.

The Ghosts of Epidoris. New York, DAW, 1975.

Mimics of Dephene. New York, DAW, 1975.

Beyond the Galactic Lens. New York, DAW, 1975.

Das Kosmiche Duelle. Bergisch Gladbach, Germany, Bastei, 1976; as *The Galactiad,* New York, DAW, 1983.

Short Stories

Ten from Tomorrow. London, Hart-Davis, 1966.

A Scatter of Stardust. New York, Ace, 1972; London, Dobson, 1976.

OTHER PUBLICATIONS

Novels

The Fighting Fury (as Paul Schofield). London, Spencer, 1955.

Assignment New York (as Mike Lantry). London, Spencer, 1955.

Comanche Capture (as E.F. Jackson). London, Spencer, 1955.

Sands of Destiny (as Jud Cary). London, September, 1955.

Men of the Long Rifle (as J.F. Clarkson). London, Spencer, 1955.

Scourge of the South (as M.L. Powers). London, Spencer, 1956.

Vengeance Trail (as James S. Farrow). London, Spencer, 1956.

Quest for Quantrell (as John Stevens). London, Spencer, 1956.

Trail Blazers (as Chuck Adams). London, Spencer, 1956.

Drums of the Prairie (as P. Lawrence). London, Spencer, 1956.

Men of the West (as Chet Lawson). London, Spencer, 1956.

Wagon Trail (as Charles S. Graham). London, Spencer, 1957.

Colt Vengeance (as James R. Fenner). London, Spencer, 1957.

Touch of Evil (as Arthur Maclean). London, Fleetway, 1959.

Target Death. London, Micron, 1961.

Lucky Strike. London, Fleetway, 1961.

Calculated Risk. London, Fleetway, 1961.

Too Tough to Handle. London, Fleetway, 1962.

The Dead Keep Faith. London, Fleetway, 1962.

The Spark of Anger. London, Fleetway, 1962.

Full Impact. London, Fleetway, 1962.

I Vow Vengeance. London, Fleetway, 1962.

Gunflash. London, Fleetway, 1962.

Hit Back. London, Fleetway, 1962.

One Must Die. London, Fleetway, 1962.

Suicide Squad. London, Fleetway, 1962.

Airbourne Commando. London, Fleetway, 1963.

No Higher Stakes. London, Fleetway, 1963.

Penalty of Fear. London, Fleetway, 1963.

Novels as Edward Thomson (series: Atilus in all titles)

Atilus the Slave. London, Futura, 1975.

Atilus the Gladiator. London, Futura, 1975.

Gladiator. London, Futura, 1978.

*

Bibliography: In *Science Fiction Collector 7,* February 1980.

*   *   *

The quantity of E.C. Tubb's output can be gauged by the fact that he has used nearly 60 pseudonyms. Since 1951 he has been turning out novels and stories on a monthly basis, occasionally editing on the side; Michael Ashley in *The History of the Science Fiction Magazine* calls Tubb "an inspired fiction machine." His popularity, well established in England, is now sizable in America as well. He is quick to turn ideas into stories set out in hard, clear prose, and many of his plots have been repeated by younger writers, not always with as much success.

Tubb writes of a hostile universe where men seek to dominate each other, and nowhere is it as hostile or extensive as in the Dumarest saga. Stretching now to a score of novels, the long quest of Earl Dumarest for his lost Earth is an effective device for creating science-fiction adventure. Reticent, grim, dressed in grey, and quick with a knife, Dumarest travels from planet to planet pursued by the Cyclan, cold zealots whose emotions have been surgically removed and who are psychically linked to an organic computer of a million embalmed brains. They want Dumarest because he has the secret to another kind of psychic linking, and Dumarest wants his mythical Earth because it is his own home. In effect the books form a 20-novel chase sequence. Some aspects become repetitive—for example, the description of Low and High travelling (frozen vs. time-accelerated) is transferred almost verbatim from book to book. And in each story Dumarest is injured in ghastly detail, which he stoically endures until advanced medicine repairs him. But the planets are different—vivid landscapes and weathers similar only in their exoticism and their environmental exacerbation of the baser emotions. There is also range in the interpersonal plots. Sometimes Dumarest finds friends, sometimes only enemies; sometimes the lush women (all of whom desire him) have to be taught a lesson, and sometimes they do not; and in *Jondelle,* with creditable devotion, Dumarest defends a child. All this escapes being ludicrous through the stolid understatement in Tubb's competent style, and through the character of Dumarest himself, who is so determined and so quiet that he remains something of an enigma even after repeated adventures. That he has no sense of humor can be attributed to the desperate situations his author devises for him, situations in which genuine heroism can only consist of bleak courage and violent action.

Violence is important to Tubb; his interest in it is conscious and explicitly defended, not only in the Dumarest series but in novels like *Century of the Manikin* as well. The "manikins" are people who have been conditioned to believe violence is wrong. They live on a decadent, drug-controlled Earth where sex is so free that the only secret pleasure is violent. It takes a 20th-century woman, thawed out from cryogenic sleep, to tell them that men need weapons and honest fighting in order to be truly masculine and alive. Like almost every woman in Tubb's books, she finds male combat sexually exciting. But violence is not Tubb's only theme, however much it motivates his characters. His plots cover the full range of traditional science fiction, from first-contact riddles like "Random Sample," to sad tales of awakening computers like "J Is for Jeanne," and even to mood pieces like "The Last Day of Summer," where a man waits for the Bureau of Euthanasia. Tubb can also play with concepts of time and space; in *S.T.A.R. Flight* the instantaneous transport Gates of the dictatorial Kaltich are a puzzle to be solved, rather bloodily, by Earth's resistance organization.

E.C. Tubb is a good candidate for the theory that science fiction is essentially conservative. Against varying backgrounds of unexplained technology, Tubb talks about the most basic human passions. And however many suns are in the sky, the framework for ethical decision remains the same. For Tubb, the old values matter in the new places—matter more, since the strangeness isolates the grasping nature of men in plainer sight. Dumarest appears as an appropriate alter ego for a man whose prose is lean and unsentimental. Tubb works in a highly colored imaginative landscape, but like Dumarest he does his job quickly and then moves on, convictions unchanged, to the next world.

—Karen G. Way

TUCKER, (Arthur) Wilson ("Bob")

Nationality: American. **Born:** Deer Creek, Illinois, 23 November 1914. **Education:** Normal High School, Illinois. **Family:** Married 1) Mary Jan Joestine in 1937 (divorced 1942); 2) Fern Delores Brookes in 1953; one daughter and four sons. **Career:** Motion picture projectionist, 1933-72, and electrician for 20th Century Fox and the University of Illinois at Urbana and at Normal. Publisher of many fan magazines: *The Planetoid,* 1932, *Science Fiction News Letter, D'Journal, Le Zombie,* 1938-75, *Fantasy and Weird Fiction,* 1938-39, *Yearbook of Science, Fanewscard Weekly, Fanzine Yearbook,* 1941-45, *Fapa Variety.* President, National Fantasy Fan Federation, 1942-43. **Awards:** Hugo award, 1970; John W. Campbell Memorial award, 1976. Guest of Honor, 25th World Science Fiction Convention, 1967. **Agent:** Curtis Brown, 10 Astor Place, New York, New York 10003, U.S.A.

SCIENCE FICTION PUBLICATIONS

Novels (series: Gilbert Nash)

The City in the Sea. New York, Rinehart, 1951; London, Nova, 1955.
The Long Loud Silence. New York, Rinehart, 1952; London, Lane, 1953; revised edition, New York, Lancer, 1970.
The Time Masters (Nash). New York, Rinehart, 1953; revised edition, Garden City, New York, Doubleday, 1971; London, Gollancz, 1973.
Wild Talent. New York, Rinehart, 1954; London, Joseph, 1955; as *Man from Tomorrow,* New York, Bantam, 1955.
Time Bomb (Nash). New York, Rinehart, 1955; as *Tomorrow Plus X,* New York, Avon, 1957.
The Lincoln Hunters. New York, Rinehart, 1958; London, Phoenix House, 1961.
To the Tombaugh Station. New York, Ace, 1960.
The Year of the Quiet Sun. New York, Ace, 1970; London, Hale, 1971.
Ice and Iron. Garden City, New York, Doubleday, 1974; revised edition, New York, Ballantine, and London, Gollancz, 1975.
Resurrection Days. New York, Timescape, 1981.

Short Stories

The Science-Fiction Subtreasury. New York, Rinehart, 1954; abridged as *Time: X,* New York, Bantam, 1955.
The Best of Wilson Tucker. New York, Timescape, 1982.

OTHER PUBLICATIONS

Novels

The Chinese Doll. New York, Rinehart, 1946; London, Cassell, 1948.
To Keep or Kill. New York, Rinehart, 1947; London, Cassell, 1950.
The Dove. New York, Rinehart, 1948; London, Cassell, 1950.
The Stalking Man. New York, Rinehart, 1949; London, Cassell, 1950.
Red Herring. New York, Rinehart, 1951; London, Cassell, 1953.

The Man in My Grave. New York, Rinehart, 1956; London, Macdonald, 1958.

The Hired Target. New York, Ace, 1957.

Last Stop. Garden City, New York, Doubleday, 1963; London, Hale, 1965.

A Procession of the Damned. Garden City, New York, Doubleday, 1965; London, Hale, 1967.

The Warlock. Garden City, New York, Doubleday, 1967; London, Hale, 1968.

This Witch. Garden City, New York, Doubleday, 1971; London, Gollancz, 1972.

Other

The Neo-Fan's Guide to Science Fiction Fandom. Hartford City, Indiana, Robert and Juanita Coulson, 1966.

*

Wilson Tucker comments:

(1985) I write to entertain an editor, his readers, and myself, in that order. If I fail to entertain the editor, there will be no readers; if I fail to entertain the readers my own livelihood will be reduced accordingly. Some critics have said that my books may paint a bleak picture for humanity but that I always offer hope and sunshine for the future. That's news to me. I had always believed that I was writing adventure and offering entertainment, nothing more.

*   *   *

Wilson Tucker's stories have the modesty of realistic black-and-white films. His casts are small, his scale intimate, and his settings familiar. He develops his plots and characters using human actions and reactions. He prefers concrete imagery to abstract verbiage: he tells by showing. In *The Year of the Quiet Sun,* for example, shots of the same swimming pool in four different years give instant summaries of intervening events at the site. Indeed, the cinematic flow of Tucker's narratives may reflect his 40 years' experience as a motion picture projectionist.

Tucker's style is economical and unadorned. He understates so much that careless readers sometimes miss the full implications of his text, such as clues to the hero's race in *The Year of the Quiet Sun* or the practice of cannibalism in *The Long Loud Silence.* He actually had to revise the ending of *Ice and Iron* after its initial publication to supply additional explanations. Characterization is his strongest gift. His heroes are marked by a certain ornery ordinariness and a stubborn integrity that the critic Bruce Gillespie calls "the ability neither to give in to the world nor to push it around" (*SF Commentary 43,* 1976). These heroes crave simplicity and distrust institutions. They wield their talents—anything from telepathy to acting to survival skills—without bravado. They establish prickly, often unsatisfactory relationships with heroines as stubborn as themselves. Tucker sensibly combines appreciation of feminine charms with respect for feminine strength.

Historical, not physical, sciences have been Tucker's major inspiration. His personal enthusiasm for history and archeology fuels the well-researched vitality of *The Lincoln Hunters* and *The Year of the Quiet Sun.* The human dimensions of time travel have seldom been better portrayed in SF, for instance in the chief Lincoln-hunter's joy at meeting people from past eras: "They were living *now* and he was among them." Although he does plot with time paradoxes, Tucker always makes time travel a means rather than an end in itself. In *The Lincoln Hunters* it enables the author to place his hero in two radically different environments—a sterile, repressive future and a burgeoning, liberal past—and then generates a eucatastrophe to leave him in the happier world. Tucker keeps restating the proposition that life itself is a kind of time machine operating at the maximum rate of one second per second.

A poignant version of temporal translation is achieved through extreme longevity in *The Time Masters.* A marooned extraterrestrial who had been Gilgamesh in ancient Sumer waits thousands of years while the mayfly lives of ordinary humans flicker out around him before he finds an alternative to both loneliness and escape. The hero of *The Time Masters* reappears in a minor role in *Time Bomb,* a novel in which mechanical time travel changes history by eliminating a McCarthy-like villain in his larval stage. This premise is inverted in Tucker's finest work, *The Year of the Quiet Sun,* when data gleaned from temporal research preserve a villain and trigger a catastrophic world race war. Every element in this honest, solidly built book meshes securely and unobtrusively to present a close-up of Armageddon.

Tucker thriftily incorporated the same research on Biblical archaeology and the Dead Sea Scrolls used for *The Year of the Quiet Sun* into his mystery novel, *This Witch.* He prefers doing mysteries because he finds them easier and more fun to write than SF, but his dual careers cross-fertilize each other. He often uses SF elements (even facts about SF fandom) in his mysteries and employs mystery/thriller conventions in his SF. (Compare the espionage apparatus and psychic elements in *Wild Talent* and *The Warlock.*) The clearest instance of Tucker's debt to the hardboiled mystery styles of the 1940s is *The Long Loud Silence.* Its protagonist is a monomaniac scrambling for survival in a plague-devasted eastern United States. Although the unrelenting brutality of this novel cost it popular acceptance on its initial publication, it remains a chilling reflection of Cold War attitudes.

Yet despite the grimness that underlies much of his professional work, Tucker has been one of SF fandom's favorite humorists—in person and in print—for half a century. His close friend Robert Bloch called him "a legend in his own time." Tucker's chief handicap as a writer is an excess of humility—even after a score of novels he still refuses to think of himself as a professional writer. But the author of *The Year of the Quiet Sun* need stand in awe of no one.

—Sandra Miesel

———

TUREK, Ian Francis. *See* **BINDER, Eando.**

———

TUREK, Ione Frances. *See* **BINDER, Eando.**

———

TURNER, George (Reginald)

Nationality: Australian. **Born:** Melbourne, Victoria, 8 October 1916. **Education:** Victoria state schools; at University High School, Melbourne. **Military Service:** Served in the Australian Imperial Forces, 1939-45. **Career:** Employment officer, Commonwealth Employment Service, Melbourne, 1945-49, and Wangaratta, Victoria, 1949-50; textile technician, Bruck Mills, Wangaratta, 1951-64; senior employment officer, Volkswagen Ltd., Melbourne, 1964-67; beer transferrer, Carlton and United Breweries, Melbourne, 1970-77. Since 1970, science fiction reviewer, *Melbourne Age*. **Awards:** Miles Franklin award, 1963; Commonwealth Literary Fund award, 1968; Ditmar award, 1984; Arthur C. Clarke award, 1988. **Agent:** Cherry Weiner Literary Agency, 28 Kipling Way, Manalapan, New Jersey 07726, U.S.A. **Address:** 4/296 Inkerman Street, East St. Kilda, Victoria 3183, Australia.

Science Fiction Publications

Novels (series: Ethical Culture)

Beloved Son (Ethical Culture). London, Faber, 1978; New York, Pocket Books, 1979.
Vaneglory: A Science Fiction Novel (Ethical Culture). London, Faber, 1981.
Yesterday's Men (Ethical Culture). London, Faber, 1983.
The Sea and Summer. London, Faber, 1987; as *Drowning Towers*, New York, Arbor House, 1988.
Brain Child. New York, Morrow, 1991; London, Headline, 1992.
The Destiny Makers. New York, Morrow, 1993.
Genetic Soldier. New York, Morrow, 1994.

Short Stories

A Pursuit of Miracles. North Adelaide, South Australia, Aphelion, 1990.

Other Publications

Novels

Young Man of Talent. London, Cassell, 1959; as *Scobie: A Novel*, New York, Simon and Schuster, 1959.
A Stranger and Afraid. London, Cassell, 1961.
The Cupboard under the Stairs. London, Cassell, 1962.
A Waste of Shame. Melbourne and London, Cassell, 1965.
The Lame Dog Man. Melbourne, Cassell, 1967; London, Cassell, 1968.
Transit of Cassidy. Melbourne, Nelson, 1978; London, Hamish Hamilton, 1979.

Other

In the Heart or in the Head: An Essay in Time Travel (autobiography). Carleton, Victoria, Norstrilia Press, 1984.
Off-Cuts (memoirs). Perth, Western Australia, Swancon, 1986.
Editor, *The View from the Edge: A Workshop of Science Fiction Stories*. Carleton, Victoria, Norstrilia Press, 1977.

*

George Turner comments:

Since it is my personal view (admittedly shared by few contemporary SF writers) that SF long ago lost its way among erotica, exotica, wishdreams, metaphysical guesswork, "mind-blowing" conceptions, and plain bad writing, I prefer to maintain a low key in my own work. To this end I have concentrated on simple, staple SF ideas, mostly those which have become conventions in the genre, injected without background or discussion into stories on the understanding that readers know all they need about such things. So in *Beloved Son* I used only the everyday ingredients of the genre—genetic manipulation, telepathy, the nature of World War III, the politics of renaissance—in order to rethink them and point out that all is not as obvious as conventional SF usage would have the readers believe.

My work will always be concerned with how human beings behave—as all fiction ultimately must be. Super-heroes, super-intelligences, and unlikely worlds created for melodrama or the spelling out of doubtful metaphors for the future of man do not interest me. My SF method remains the same as for my mainstream novels—set characters in motion in a speculative situation and let them work out their destinies with a minimum of auctorial interference.

*   *   *

A well-known and prize-winning mainstream novelist of the 1960s, George Turner has earned a reputation as Australia's most rigorous and astute science fiction critic and reviewer. (He claims, with justification, that his "thirty-year apprenticeship" in the writer's craft has given him "the critical confidence to stand in awe of no-one but Shakespeare and Tolstoy.") His autobiography, *In the Heart or in the Head*, shows his lifelong commitment to literature, expounds his view of the history and shortcomings of the SF genre, and acts as a model for literary criticism in its engrossing blend of the personal and the critical, the subjective and the objective.

Turner's career as SF writer began late in life with the three novels of his Ethical Culture series: *Beloved Son, Vaneglory*, and *Yesterday's Men* (which, though linked, do not form a trilogy). Each book is set in the post-holocaust reconstructed world of the 21st century. The Collapse of 1992 (caused by genetic interference with food crops, worsened by the spread of mutated-disease epidemics, and climaxed by hysterical nuclear bombing) has left the world's population greatly reduced, but within half a century a new world has emerged. Built on the Ethic of Non-Interference, the new culture relies upon an imprinted fear of the greed, obscenity, and cruelty of the past, and many of these old-world ills have genuinely been overcome—but only through fear and ignorance, not intellectual resolve.

Old social problems soon emerge, for dissent against the new order grows. But new problems also arise: experiments in cloning lead to attempts to tinker with human genetic stock (in *Beloved Son*), and further manipulations take place after the discovery of mutant humans with a lifespan of centuries (*Vaneglory*). *Yesterday's Men* draws the series to an intellectually satisfying close when the new society finally seeks to learn the truth about the "barbarians" of the 20th century . . . and discovers that human nature has not (and possibly cannot) change.

Ostensibly, the three novels are about the abuses and consequences of supposed "progress" in the biological sciences, but they are more centrally concerned with the pitfalls of romantic idealism and utopian thinking. The emblem of this sad, depleted future is the Security Headquarters building: "Plain, ugly, efficient and temporary, it was uncompromisingly an administrative block. Like this entire civilization, it was there only to serve a passing purpose and be torn down. It symbolized with repellent neatness a world with an immutable past and a hopefully solid future but only a ramshackle, disposable present." The compelling wisdom of Turner's novels lies in his ability to see with this kind of clarity: to perceive the shabby present amid the rosy dreams of the future. Such qualities have attracted charges of dourness, cynicism, and pessimism, but these accusations miss the point of the novels' achievement. The books may be forthright and uncompromising in their judgements of man and society, but they are also honest—bluntly, harshly honest. To use a phrase from *Beloved Son,* they deal with "the unholy competence of man," demonstrating that man's wisdom is less than his ability, and that the human talent for self-delusion and naive dreaming can be disastrous in its consequences.

These qualities are best illustrated in Turner's masterpiece, *The Sea and Summer* (titled *Drowning Towers* in the U.S.). This is a *realist* SF novel; it deals with the everyday lives and interpersonal tensions of characters living in Melbourne under the Greenhouse Effect. The city is drowning, and so is the Australian economy and social structure. Those who still have a job and a home are the Sweet; the Swill are the unemployed and homeless, the helpless flotsam and jetsam of the world ruined by neglect. Curiously, *The Sea and Summer* does not offer a pessimistic vision: a narrative framing device establishes that the world has survived its upheavals, and, more importantly, the novel's blunt (some critics say *pugnacious*) tone suggests that the battle for a better future has not been lost.

The Sea and Summer is a major work of 20th-century literature, and breaks important new ground as science fiction. George Turner's contribution to the SF field deserves more attention than it has received.

—Van Ikin

TURTLEDOVE, Harry

Pseudonym: Eric Iverson. **Nationality:** American. **Agent:** Scott Meredith, 845 Third Avenue, New York, New York 10022, U.S.A.

SCIENCE FICTION PUBLICATIONS

Novels (series: Garin; Videssos; Worldwar)

Wereblood (Garin; as Eric Iverson). New York, Belmont Tower, 1979.
Werenight (Garin; as Eric Iverson). New York, Belmont Tower, 1979.
The Videssos Cycle:
    The Misplaced Legion. New York, Ballantine, 1987; London, Legend, 1988.
    An Emperor for the Legion. New York, Ballantine, 1987; London, Legend, 1988.
    The Legion of Videssos. New York, Ballantine, 1987; London, Legend, 1988.
    Swords of the Legion. New York, Ballantine, 1987; London, Legend, 1988.
    Krispos Rising. New York, Ballantine, 1991.

    Krispos of Videssos. New York, Ballantine, 1991.
    Krispos the Emperor. New York, Ballantine, 1994.
    The Stolen Throne. New York, Ballantine, 1995.
Noninterference. New York, Ballantine, 1988.
A Different Flesh. New York, Congdon and Weed, 1988.
A World of Difference. New York, Ballantine, 1990.
The Guns of the South: A Novel of the Civil War. New York, Ballantine, 1992.
The Case of the Toxic Spell Dump. New York, Ballantine, 1993.
Worldwar: In the Balance. New York, Ballantine, 1994.
Werenight (Garin). Riverdale, New York, Baen, 1994.
Prince of the North. Riverdale, New York, Baen, 1994.
Worldwar: Tilting the Balance. New York, Ballantine, 1995.

Short Stories

Agent of Byzantium. New York, Congdon and Weed, 1987; London, New English Library, 1988; New York, Baen, 1994.
Kaleidoscope. New York, Ballantine, 1990.
The Pugnacious Peacemaker, bound with *The Wheels of If,* by L. Sprague de Camp. New York, Tor, 1990.
Earthgrip. New York, Ballantine, 1991.
Departures. New York, Ballantine, 1993.

OTHER PUBLICATIONS

Other

The Chronicle of Theophanes: An English Translation of Anni Mundi 6095-6305 (A.D. 602-813). Philadelphia, University of Pennsylvania Press, 1982.

*   *   *

The author Harry Turtledove originally studied Byzantine history and published scholarly translations and studies of historians of the Eastern Empire. His fiction, sometimes written under the name Eric Iverson, is various; he has written "straight" SF, fantasy and alternative history, and has also created a genre which is wholly new (as far as I am aware): a combination of "straight" SF and alternative history. Save for a few short stories, the bulk of both his straight SF and his traditional alternative histories share a common thread. This is the working out of the effect, over a fairly long period of time, of a particular act or a specified change of conditions. Perhaps it is this which justifies alternative history being classified with SF.

The theme of a single change producing marked divergence is, perhaps, an historian's way of demonstrating, in popular communications, how absurd are all the great "Historicist" systems. Without being specifically mentioned, Marx gets the short shrift he well deserves. In two of his works there is a single change; in two others a marked change in initial conditions. Also, in a rather unsatisfactory time-travel story, *Hindsight,*—nearly all time-travel stories are unsatisfactory—a small change is deliberately introduced in order to deflect the course of events.

His most pleasing set of traditional alternative history stories, in this reader's estimate, is that entitled *Agent of Byzantium,* which supposes a single event at the beginning of the seventh Century to have been different. It is, moreover, a difference which seems intuitively a quite possible "might have been." The supposition is that when, as a young merchant, Mohammed met and conversed with a Christian priest, he was converted to the Christian superstition instead of going off to found one of his own. By the early 14th century, wherein the stories are set, the changes consequent upon this single event have been immense. The violent eruption of enthusiasm which shattered the Persian, amputated the Byzantine, and established the Arab empires has never happened. Consequently, the first two remain locked in interminable but inconclusive rivalry; and this scenario is the background to the adventures of Basil Argyros, first an army officer and later a secret agent of the Byzantine empire.

As might be expected, the stories well convey the cool calculation, the labyrinthine bureaucracy and the superstitious turmoil of that strange polity. At the same time, Basil—a character who is well drawn and fairly sympathetic—has some good knockabout adventures. He is involved in the introduction into the empire of the telescope, of gunpowder, of distillation, and of printing (it is not made clear by whom or where the first two of these were invented.) He himself discovers vaccination: truly a full and exciting life; but each separate event is made credible enough. The narrative carries the reader along; and if we are not deeply saddened by the death from smallpox of Basil's family, we at least believe that he was.

Two other series suppose a much larger initial change and cover a longer span of time. In the first—entitled *A Different Flesh*—it is supposed that, when the Europeans discovered America, they found *Homo Erectus* and a pleistocene fauna rather than Amerindians and buffaloes. Perhaps this is rather a lot to swallow; but the stories are undoubtedly entertaining. In one of them, Samuel Pepys tells how he came to think of Evolution! The pastiche is not quite perfect, and it may not hold up to reconsideration; but the idea is engaging and the presentation full of humour. In another, set around 1800, the presence of sub-men makes it easier to abolish slavery of African Americans.

Another alternative has a geological rather than a biological premise. It is supposed that the African tectonic plate is well butted against the European and that the straits of Gibraltar are closed. The Mediterranean basin is thus a vast edition of the lower Jordan valley. This reader did not find the treatment so enjoyable, partly, at least, because the scenario seemed rather less closely connected to the premise. Nevertheless, the story of how an attempt to blast the straits open with a buried nuclear weapon was frustrated makes a good read.

Turtledove's main "straight" SF treatment of his theme is *Noninterference*. Here, the one significant act is the cure, by terrestrial observers on a distant planet, of an amiable native queen who is dying of cancer. This kindly act is strictly contrary to the noninterference rule by which the explorers are supposed to be bound. What they had not forseen is that the cure, which would have been quite specific to the particular disease if applied to a human being, has the effect of completely arresting the normal ageing processes in an extraterrestrial. When another exploring party arrives centuries later, they find the good queen still going strong and treated as a divinity. The single change is rather hard to accept; but the consequences are worked out with considerable ingenuity.

There are, as every SF buff knows, scores of stories of Earth being invaded by aliens; and there are many alternative history stories; but Turtledove had the inspiration to combine the two. In *World War in the Balance,* the alien invasion takes place in the summer of 1942, whilst the war we knew was in full blast. Alien military technology is represented as being marginally superior to that which advanced nations have today (1995); however, their numbers are limited and resupply is not possible. The military problem is worked out with real ingenuity; and the political entanglement equally so. The human warring parties are forced to cooperate; but this does not make them love one another!

The second volume of what appears to be a trilogy—*Tilting the Balance*—continues the story It is no negative criticism of the author that the reader so often wants to argue with him: "Why wouldn't the invaders try . . . ? Surely the Russians would have been more likely to attempt. . . ." This is part of the fun, and confirms that Turtledove has secured the elusive suspension of disbelief.

Every military history buff has, at some time or other, toyed with the idea: "Suppose that General X had had such-and-such at the battle of. . . ." Turtledove works out an instance of this in *The Guns of the South,* wherein one of Lee's regiments in Virginia is armed with Kalashnikovs and an ample supply of ammunition. Again, the consequences are worked out convincingly; but since the rearmament depends upon time-travel, which, as has been remarked, very rarely writes up well, the book as a whole does not quite succeed.

Is fantasy to be classed with SF? In this reader's judgement, it is not. Instead of assuming some Scientific or technical advance, the writer is allowed to alter the ground rules, to flout the conservation laws and to abandon the scientific approach altogether. This is not to say that such works are necessarily without merit; but they are an altogether different category of writing. They are also, at the moment, highly popular, and a number of writers, including Turtledove, have cashed in on this. He has produced the *Swords of Videssos* series (*The Misplaced Legion, An Emperor for the Legion, The Legion of Videssos, Swords of the Legion, A World of Difference,* and *Krispos Rising*) in which some cohorts of one of Caesar's legions are magically translated from Gaul to a world of wizards and what-not, where they manage rather well for themselves. Another pair (which threaten to be continued) entitled *Were Night* and *Prince of the South* are set in a pseudo-saga world of magic and heroic swordsmen. *The Case of the Toxic Spell Dump,* though dispensing with science, has the merit of being hilariously funny. All of them are written smoothly, are full of briskly described action, and are no doubt pleasing to those who like that sort of thing.

In all of his fictional fields, Turtledove provides lively enjoyment and ideas which, if not always watertight, are usually presented with enough brio to produce a temporary suspension of disbelief. He does not aim for the highest achievements of literature: he does not try to change our ways of looking at the world or to produce prose which enriches and stays in the mind; but where he aims, he hits. He is an entertainer, always a successful, and sometimes a hugely successful one.

—M. Hammerton

TUTTLE, Lisa

Nationality: American. **Born:** Houston, Texas, 16 September 1952. **Education:** Syracuse University, New York, B.A. in English 1973. **Career:** Editor of the fan magazine *Mathom,* 1968-70; television columnist, Austin American Statesman, Texas, 1976-79. **Awards:** John W. Campbell Award, 1974; Nebula Award, 1982. **Agents:** Howard Morhaim, 175 Fifth Avenue, Room 709, New York, New York 10010, U.S.A; or, A.P. Watt Ltd., 20 John Street, London WC1N 2DL, England.

SCIENCE FICTION PUBLICATIONS

Novels

Windhaven, with George R.R. Martin. New York, Timescape, 1981;
    London, New English Library, 1982.
Familiar Spirit. New York, Berkley, and London, New English Library, 1983.
Catwitch (for children). Limpsfield, Surrey, Dragon's World, and
    Garden City, New York, Doubleday, 1983.
Gabriel: A Novel of Reincarnation. London, Sphere, 1987; New
    York, Tor, 1988.
Lost Futures. New York, Dell Abyss, and London, Grafton, 1992.

Short Stories

A Nest of Nightmares. London, Sphere, 1986.
A Spaceship Built of Stone and Other Stories. London, Women's
    Press, 1987.
Memories of the Body: Tales of Desire and Transformation.
    Wallington, Surrey, and New York, Severn House, 1992.

OTHER PUBLICATIONS

Novel

Angela's Rainbow. Limpsfield, Surrey, Dragon's World, 1983.

Other

Children's Literary Houses: Famous Dwellings in Children's Fiction, with Rosalind Ashe. Limpsfield, Surrey, Dragon's World,
    and New York, Facts on File, 1984.
Encylopedia of Feminism. Harlow, England, Longman, and New
    York, Facts on File, 1986.
Heroines: Women Inspired by Women. London, Harrap, 1988.
Mark Harrison's Dreamlands, with Mark Harrison. London, Paper Tiger, 1990.
Editor, *Skin of the Soul: New Horror Stories by Women.* London,
    Women's Press, 1990; revised edition, New York, Pocket Books,
    1991.

*   *   *

George R.R. Martin has called Lisa Tuttle's writing "distinctive,
delightful," and Ted White attributed to her "a reputation for strong
stories which deal with human responses to the unusual." Tuttle
has called her first story, "Stranger in the House," a "going home
story." A young woman returns home and attempts to regain her
childhood. This is a theme writers such as Bradbury and Ellison
have used to produce stories of ineffable sadness, but Tuttle goes a
step further to produce a work of genuine horror, catching an aspect of our desire to relive the past that few writers seem to understand. It was a fitting start. Tuttle quickly revealed herself as a writer
of interesting variety and skill.

It's just as important that she's revealed herself as a writer of
highly original horror fiction. "Changelings," for example, is a nicely
extrapolated sociological vignette about a society that employs surgery to cure anti-social behavior; in it, a father is betrayed by his
pre-school-age child. "Flies by Night," written with Steven Utley,
is a psychological study of a woman who longs to turn into a fly.
"Stone Circle" is a complex character study set in a near-future
welfare state. "In the Arcade" depicts a future where racism is offered as a sideshow attraction. "Sangre" and "The Horse Lord" are
almost, but not quite, conventional, the first juxtaposing the story of a
woman's affair with her stepfather with a tale of vampirism, the other
telling of a family that encounters Indian superstition that turns out to
be justified—again, parents are betrayed by their children.

In "The Family Monkey" a rural Texas couple saves an alien
from a crashed spaceship and adopts it as a servant. The story is
simple and straightforward: the alien is saved, becomes a sort of
family retainer, is discovered years later by its own people, and
leaves. The story acquires a remarkable depth, however, because
Tuttle's interest lies not with the plot, or even the alien, but with
character relationships. Relationship provides the focus of most of
her work, in fact. "The Hollow Man," set in the near future, concerns a woman whose husband commits suicide. She has him
brought back to life through new medical techniques only to discover the flesh has been revived, but nothing else. Cold and indifferent, the husband lacks even the interest necessary to kill himself. The tragedy of the ending is classically inevitable, and quite
powerful.

Little of Tuttle's fiction takes place away from the Earth. In
"Wives," one of the few set on another planet, aliens are permitted
by their Earthman conquerers to exist only so long as they pretend
to be the humans' wives. "The Birds of the Moon" is set on Earth,
but tells about a woman whose astronaut husband has been to the
moon. The voyage has changed him, and his wife hallucinates about
beings—strange, ugly birds—which live on the moon. As with many
of Tuttle's stories, the line between hallucination and reality is impossible to discern, particularly in man-woman relationships. In
"Flies by Night" the woman who longs to be a fly is captured by
men who have become spiders—or so she believes.

As striking as such images are in a writer of Tuttle's talent, they
never dominate her stories; neither, for that matter, does her interest in relationships. If anything, they seem to provide a focus for
what appears to be a still-emerging concern for the nature of her
characters' humanity. In "Bug House" a young woman, visiting an
aunt who lives in a lonely isolated house, finds her aunt sick and
the house overrun by insects. When the aunt dies, it is apparently
as the victim of a strange young man whose connection with her,
the house, the insects, becomes apparent only when it's too late.
As in "Stone Circle" sex is treated as a numbing, enslaving element.

"Flying to Byzantium," another "going home" story, is about a
writer elevated from a drab, lonely life by the modest success of a
fantasy novel. At a science-fiction convention, she finds herself
forced, through a confrontation with her readers, back into her hated,
previous existence. The story permits some cogent observations
on the problems of being a writer in the 1980s, and its last paragraph is as powerful as the idea itself. But the story fails to satisfy,
possibly because the matter-of-fact style in which most of it is written fails to deliver the emotional impact it demands. "Need" is a far
more successful story in which a young woman's fears and insecurities lead her into a situation that neatly brings a twist to the
conventional ghost story plot—but in a way that is emotional and
satisfying: few writers other than Tuttle could have pulled it off.

Windhaven, written with George R. R. Martin, is not typical Tuttle
fiction, but it would be wrong to call it typical Martin, either. It's a
superb collaborative effort set on a planet whose inhabitants, descendants of the survivors of a spaceship wreck, are dependent on

the skills of messengers who travel on artificial wings, similar to hang gliders. It's good, solid science fiction, carefully crafted. It makes the most of Martin's eye for the exotic and of his ability to plot, and of Tuttle's graceful style and sensitivity to people.

Tuttle's first solo novel, *Familiar Spirit,* is more in line with her short fiction. A commercial horror novel, it is well written, carefully plotted, and marked with Tuttle's customary vivid characterization. Its weakness lies in an unsatisfying formula ending. Even so, it's head and shoulders above all but a handful of the horror novels of its decade. While *Familiar Spirit* makes fewer demands on her talent than such shorter works as "The Family Monkey" or "The Hollow Man," her skills and the several themes she has been developing, seem to demand the longer form.

—Gerald W. Page

TWAIN, Mark

Pseudonym for Samuel Langhorne Clemens. **Nationality:** American. **Born:** Florida, Missouri, 30 November 1835; grew up in Hannibal, Missouri. **Education:** University of Missouri, Columbia, 1902; Yale University, New Haven, Connecticut, M.A. 1888, Litt.D. 1901; Oxford University, LL.D. 1907. **Family:** Married Olivia Langdon in 1870 (died 1904); one son and three daughters. **Career:** Printer's apprentice from age 12; helped brother with Hannibal newspapers, 1850-52; worked in St. Louis, New York, Philadelphia, Keokuk, Iowa, and Cincinnati, 1853-57; river pilot's apprentice, on the Mississippi, 1857: licensed as a pilot, 1859; went to Nevada as secretary to his brother, then in the service of the governor, and also worked as a goldminer, 1861; staff member, *Territorial Enterprise,* Virginia City, Nevada, 1862-64; moved to San Francisco, 1864; writer from 1867, lecturer from 1868; editor, *Buffalo Express,* New York, 1868-71; moved to Hartford, Connecticut, and became associated with the Charles L. Webster Publishing Company, 1884: went bankrupt, 1894 (last debts paid, 1898). **Died:** 21 April 1910.

SCIENCE FICTION PUBLICATIONS

Novel

A Connecticut Yankee in King Arthur's Court. New York, Webster, 1889; as *A Yankee at the Court of King Arthur,* London, Chatto and Windus, 1889.
Extracts from Adam's Diary. New York, and London, Harper, 1904.
Eve's Diary. New York and London, Harper, 1906.
Extract from Captain Stormfield's Visit to Heaven. New York and London, Harper, 1909; revised edition, as *Report from Paradise,* edited by Dixon Wecter, New York, Harper, 1952.
The Mysterious Stranger: A Romance. New York, Harper, 1916; London, Harper, 1917.

Short Stories

The Science Fiction of Mark Twain, edited by David Ketterer. Hamden, Connecticut, Archon, 1984.
The Private Life of Adam and Eve. New York, Harper, 1931.

OTHER PUBLICATIONS

Novels

The Innocents Abroad; or, The New Pilgrims' Progress. Hartford, Connecticut, American Publishing Company, 1869; London, Routledge, 2 vols., 1872.
The Innocents at Home. London, Routledge, 1872.
The Gilded Age: A Tale of Today, with Charles Dudley Warner. Hartford, Connecticut, American Publishing Company, 1873; London, Routledge, 3 vols., 1874; *The Adventures of Colonel Sellers, Being Twain's Share of "The Gilded Age,"* edited by Charles Neider, New York, Doubleday, 1965; London, Chatto and Windus, 1966.
The Adventures of Tom Sawyer. London, Chatto and Windus, and Hartford, Connecticut, American Publishing Company, 1876.
A Tramp Abroad. Hartford, Connecticut, American Publishing Company, and London, Chatto and Windus, 1880.
The Prince and the Pauper. London, Chatto and Windus, and Boston, Osgood, 1881.
The Adventures of Huckleberry Finn (Tom Sawyer's Companion). London, Chatto and Windus, 1884; New York, Webster, 1885; edited by Charles Neider, New York, Doubleday, 1985.
The American Claimant. New York, Webster, and London, Chatto and Windus, 1892.
Pudd'nhead Wilson: A Tale. London, Chatto and Windus, 1894; as *The Tragedy of Pudd'nhead Wilson,* Hartford, Connecticut, American Publishing Company, 1894.
Personal Recollections of Joan of Arc. . . . New York, Harper, and London, Chatto and Windus, 1896.
A Double Barrelled Detective Story. New York, Harper, and London, Chatto and Windus, 1902.
A Horse's Tale. New York and London, Harper, 1907.
Simon Wheeler, Detective, edited by Franklin R. Rogers. New York, New York Public Library, 1963.
The Complete Novels, edited by Charles Neider. New York, Doubleday, 2 vols., 1964.
Mississippi Writings (Library of America). New York, Literary Classics of the United States, and London, Cambridge University Press, 1982.

Short Stories

The Celebrated Jumping Frog of Calaveras County and Other Sketches, edited by John Paul. New York, Webb, 1867.
A True Story and the Recent Carnival of Crime. Boston, Osgood, 1877.
Date 1601: Conversation as It Was by the Social Fireside in the Time of the Tudors. Privately printed, 1880; as *1601 . . . ,* edited by Franklin J. Meine, Chicago, privately printed, 1939.
The Stolen White Elephant Etc. London, Chatto and Windus, and Boston, Osgood, 1882.
Merry Tales. New York, Webster, 1892.
The £1,000,000 Bank-Note and Other New Stories. New York, Webster, and London, Chatto and Windus, 1893.
Tom Sawyer Abroad. New York, Webster, and London, Chatto and Windus, 1894.
Tom Sawyer Abroad, Tom Sawyer, Detective, and Other Stories. New York, Harper, 1896; as *Tom Sawyer, Detective, as Told by Huck Finn, and Other Tales.* London, Chatto and Windus, 1897.

The Man That Corrupted Hadleyburg and Other Stories and Essays. New York, Harper, and London, Chatto and Windus, 1900.

A Dog's Tale. London, National Anti-Vivisection Society, and New York, Harper, 1904.

The $30,000 Bequest and Other Stories. New York, Harper, 1906; London, Harper, 1907.

The Curious Republic of Gondour and Other Whimsical Sketches. New York, Boni and Liveright, 1919.

The Mysterious Stranger and Other Stories. New York and London, Harper, 1922.

The Adventures of Thomas Jefferson Snodgrass, edited by Charles Honce. Chicago, Covici, 1928.

A Boy's Adventure. Privately printed, 1928.

Jim Smiley and His Jumping Frog, edited by Albert Bigelow Paine. Chicago, Pocahontas Press, 1940.

A Murder, A Mystery, and a Marriage. Privately printed, 1945.

The Complete Short Stories, edited by Charles Neider. New York, Hanover House, 1957.

The Complete Humorous Sketches and Tales, edited by Charles Neider. New York, Doubleday, 1961.

Mark Twain's Satires and Burlesques, edited by Franklin R. Rogers. Berkeley, University of California Press, 1967.

Mark Twain's Mysterious Stranger Manuscripts, edited by William M. Gibson. Berkeley, University of California Press, 1969.

Mark Twain's Hannibal, Huck, and Tom, edited by Walter Blair. Berkeley, University of California Press, 1969.

Early Tales and Sketches, edited by Edgar M. Branch and Robert H. Hirst. Berkeley, University of California Press, 2 vols., 1979-81.

Wapping Alice. Berkeley, California, Friends of the Bancroft Library, 1981.

Huck Finn and Tom Sawyer among the Indians and Other Unfinished Stories, edited by Dahlia Armon and Walter Blair. Berkeley, University of California Press, 1989.

Goldminers and Guttersnipes: Tales of California, edited by Ken Chowder. San Francisco, Chronicle Books, 1991.

Pudd'nhead Wilson and Other Tales, edited by R.D. Gooder. Oxford, Oxford University Press, 1992.

Plays

Colonel Sellers as a Scientist, with William Dean Howells, adaptation of the novel *The Gilded Age* by Twain and Charles Dudley Warner (produced New Brunswick, New Jersey, and New York, 1887). Published in *The Complete Plays of William Dean Howells,* edited by Walter J. Meserve, New York, New York University Press, 1960.

Ah Sin, with Bret Harte, edited by Frederick Anderson (produced Washington, D.C., 1877), San Francisco, Book Club of California, 1961.

The Quaker City Holy Land Excursion: An Unfinished Play. Privately printed, 1927.

Poetry

On the Poetry of Mark Twain, with Selections from His Verse, edited by Arthur L. Scott. Urbana, University of Illinois Press, 1966.

Other

Mark Twain's (Burlesque) Autobiography and First Romance. New York, Sheldon, 1871.

Memoranda: From the Galaxy. Toronto, Canadian News and Publishing Company, 1871.

Roughing It. London, Routledge, and Hartford, Connecticut, American Publishing Company, 1872.

A Curious Dream and Other Sketches. London, Routledge, 1872.

Screamers: A Gathering of Scraps of Humour, Delicious Bits, and Short Stories. London, Hotten, 1872.

Sketches. New York, American News Company, 1874.

Sketches, New and Old. Hartford, Connecticut, American Publishing Company, 1875.

Old Times on the Mississippi. Toronto, Belford, 1876.

Punch, Brothers, Punch! and Other Sketches. New York, Slote Woodman, 1878.

An Idle Excursion. Toronto, Belford, 1878.

A Curious Experience. Toronto, Gibson, 1881.

Life on the Mississippi. London, Chatto and Windus, and Boston, Osgood, 1883.

Facts for Mark Twain's Memory Builder. New York, Webster, 1891.

How to Tell a Story and Other Essays. New York, Harper, 1897; revised edition, 1900.

Following the Equator: A Journey around the World. Hartford, Connecticut, American Publishing Company, 1897; as *More Tramps Abroad,* London, Chatto and Windus, 1897.

The Writings of Mark Twain. Hartford, Connecticut, American Publishing Company, and London, Chatto and Windus, 25 vols., 1899-1907.

The Pains of Lowly Life. London, London Anti-Vivisection Society, 1900.

English as She Is Taught. Boston, Mutual, 1900; revised edition, New York, Century, 1901.

To the Person Sitting in Darkness. New York, Anti-Imperialist League, 1901.

Edmund Burke on Croker, and Tammany (lecture). New York, Economist Press, 1901.

My Debut as a Literary Person, with Other Essays and Stories. Hartford, Connecticut, American Publishing Company, 1903.

Mark Twain on Vivisection. New York, New York Anti-Vivisection Society, 1905(?).

King Leopold's Soliloquy: A Defense of His Congo Rule. Boston, Warren, 1905; revised edition, 1906; London, Unwin, 1907.

Editorial Wild Oats. New York, Harper, 1905.

What Is Man? (published anonymously). New York, DeVinne Press, 1906; as Mark Twain, London, Watts, 1910; expanded as *What Is Man? and Other Essays,* New York, Harper, 1917; London, Chatto and Windus, 1919.

Mark Twain on Spelling (lecture). New York, Simplified Spelling Board, 1906.

The Writings of Mark Twain (Hillcrest Edition). New York and London, Harper, 25 vols., 1906-07.

Christian Science, with Notes Containing Corrections to Date. New York and London, Harper, 1907.

Is Shakespeare Dead? From My Autobiography. New York and London, Harper, 1909.

Mark Twain's Speeches, edited by F.A. Nast. New York and London, Harper, 1910; revised edition, 1923.

Queen Victoria's Jubilee. Privately printed, 1910.

Letter to the California Pioneers. Oakland, California, Dewitt and Snelling, 1911.

Mark Twain's Letters, Arranged with Comment, edited by Albert Bigelow Paine. New York, Harper, 2 vols., 1917; shortened version, as *Letters,* London, Chatto and Windus, 1920.

Moments with Mark Twain, edited by Albert Bigelow Paine. New York, Harper, 1920.

The Writings of Mark Twain (Definitive Edition), edited by Albert Bigelow Paine. New York, Gabriel Wells, 37 vols., 1922-25.

Europe and Elsewhere. New York and London, Harper, 1923.

Mark Twain's Autobiography, edited by Albert Bigelow Paine. New York and London, Harper, 2 vols., 1924.

Sketches of the Sixties by Bret Harte and Mark Twain . . . from "The Californian," 1864-67. San Francisco, John Howell, 1926; as *California Sketches,* New York, Dover, 1991.

The Suppressed Chapter of "Following the Equator. Privately printed, 1928.

A Letter from Mark Twain to His Publisher, Chatto and Windus. San Francisco, Penguin Press, 1929.

Mark Twain the Letter Writer, edited by Cyril Clemens. Boston, Meador, 1932.

Mark Twain's Works. New York, Harper, 23 vols., 1933.

The Family Mark Twain. New York, Harper, 1935.

The Mark Twain Omnibus, edited by Max J. Herzberg. New York, Harper, 1935.

Representative Selections, edited by Fred L. Patee. New York, American Book Company, 1935.

Mark Twain's Notebook, edited by Albert Bigelow Paine. New York, Harper, 1935.

Letters from the Sandwich Islands, Written for the "Sacramento Union," edited by G. Ezra Dane. San Francisco, Grabhorn Press, 1937; London, Oxford University Press, 1938.

The Washoe Giant in San Francisco, Being Heretofore Uncollected Sketches . . . , edited by Franklin Walker. San Francisco, George Fields, 1938.

Mark Twain's Western Years, Together with Hitherto Unreprinted Clemens Western Items, by Ivan Benson. Stanford, California, Stanford University, 1938.

Letters from Honolulu Written for the "Sacramento Union," edited by Thomas Nickerson. Honolulu, Thomas Nickerson, 1939.

Mark Twain in Eruption: Hitherto Unpublished Pages about Men and Events, edited by Bernard De Voto. New York, Harper, 1940.

Travels with Mr. Brown, Being Heretofore Uncollected Sketches Written for the San Francisco "Alta California" in 1866 and 1867, edited by Franklin Walker and G. Ezra Dane. New York, Knopf, 1940.

Republican Letters, edited by Cyril Clemens. Webster Groves, Missouri, International Mark Twain Society, 1941.

Letters to Will Brown . . . , edited by Theodore Hornberger. Austin, University of Texas, 1941.

Letters in the "Muscatine Journal," edited by Edgar M. Branch. Chicago, Mark Twain Association of America, 1942.

Washington in 1868, edited by Cyril Clemens. Webster Groves, Missouri, International Mark Twain Society, and London, Laurie, 1943.

Mark Twain, Business Man, edited by Samuel Charles Webster. Boston, Little Brown, 1946.

The Letters of Quintus Curtius Snodgrass, edited by Ernest E. Leisy. Dallas, Southern Methodist University Press, 1946.

The Portable Mark Twain, edited by Bernard De Voto. New York, Viking Press, 1946; London, Penguin, 1977.

Mark Twain in Three Moods: Three New Items of Twainiana, edited by Dixon Wecter. San Marino, California, Friends of the Huntington Library, 1948.

The Love Letters of Mark Twain, edited by Dixon Wecter. New York, Harper, 1949.

Mark Twain to Mrs. Fairbanks, edited by Dixon Wecter. San Marino, California, Huntington Library, 1949.

Mark Twain to Uncle Remus 1881-1885, edited by Thomas H. English. Atlanta, Emory University Library, 1953.

Twins of Genius (letters to George Washington Cable), edited by Guy A. Cardwell. East Lansing, Michigan State College Press, 1953.

Mark Twain of the "Enterprise," edited by Henry Nash Smith and Frederick Anderson. Berkeley, University of California Press, 1957.

Traveling with Innocents Abroad: Mark Twain's Original Reports from Europe and the Holy Land, edited by Daniel Morley McKeithan. Norman, University of Oklahoma Press, 1958.

The Autobiography of Mark Twain, edited by Charles Neider. New York, Doubleday, 1959.

The Art, Humor, and Humanity of Mark Twain, edited by Minnie M. Brashear and Robert M. Rodney. Norman, University of Oklahoma Press, 1959.

Mark Twain and the Government, edited by Svend Petersen. Caldwell, Idaho, Caxton Printers, 1960.

Mark Twain-Howells Letters: The Correspondence of Samuel L. Clemens and William Dean Howells 1872-1910, edited by Henry Nash Smith and William M. Gibson. Cambridge, Massachusetts, Harvard University Press, 2 vols., 1960; abridged edition, as *Selected Mark Twain-Howells Letters,* 1967.

Your Personal Mark Twain. . . . New York, International Publishers, 1960.

Life as I Find It: Essays, Sketches, Tales, and Other Material, edited by Charles Neider. New York, Doubleday, 1961.

The Travels of Mark Twain, edited by Charles Neider. New York, Doubleday, 1961.

Contributions to "The Galaxy," 1868-1871, edited by Bruce R. McElderry. Gainesville, Florida, Scholars Facsimiles and Reprints, 1961.

Mark Twain on the Art of Writing, edited by Martin B. Fried. Buffalo, Salisbury Club, 1961.

Letters to Mary, edited by Lewis Leary. New York, Columbia University Press, 1961.

The Pattern for Mark Twain's "Roughing It": Letters from Nevada by Samuel and Orion Clemens, 1861-1862, edited by Franklin R. Rogers. Berkeley, University of California Press, 1961.

Letters from the Earth, edited by Bernard De Voto. New York, Harper, 1962.

Mark Twain on the Damned Human Race, edited by Janet Smith. New York, Hill and Wang, 1962.

Selected Shorter Writings, edited by Walter Blair. Boston, Houghton Mifflin, 1962.

The Complete Essays, edited by Charles Neider. New York, Doubleday, 1963.

Mark Twain's San Francisco, edited by Bernard Taper. New York, McGraw Hill, 1963.

The Forgotten Writings of Mark Twain, edited by Henry Duskus. New York, Citadel Press, 1963.

General Grant by Matthew Arnold, with a Rejoinder by Mark Twain (lecture), edited by John Y. Simon. Carbondale, Southern Illinois University Press, 1966.

Letters from Hawaii, edited by A. Grove Day. New York, Appleton Century Crofts, 1966; London, Chatto and Windus, 1967.

Which Was the Dream? and Other Symbolic Writings of the Later Years, edited by John S. Tuckey. Berkeley, University of California Press, 1967.

The Complete Travel Books, edited by Charles Neider. New York, Doubleday, 1967.

Letters to His Publishers, 1867-1894, edited by Hamlin Hill. Berkeley, University of California Press, 1967.

Clemens of the "Call": Mark Twain in California, edited by Edgar M. Branch. Berkeley, University of California Press, 1969.

Correspondence with Henry Huttleston Rogers, 1893-1909, edited by Lewis Leary. Berkeley, University of California Press, 1969.

Man Is the Only Animal That Blushes—or Needs to: The Wisdom of Mark Twain, edited by Michael Joseph. Los Angeles, Stanyan Books, 1970.

Mark Twain's Quarrel with Heaven: Captain Stormfield's Visit to Heaven and Other Sketches, edited by Roy B. Browne. New Haven, Connecticut, College and University Press, 1970.

Everybody's Mark Twain, edited by Caroline Thomas Harnsberger. South Brunswick, New Jersey, A.S. Barnes, and London, Yoseloff, 1972.

Fables of Man, edited by John S. Tuckey. Berkeley, University of California Press, 1972.

A Pen Warmed Up In Hell: Mark Twain in Protest, edited by Frederick Anderson. New York, Harper, 1972.

The Choice Humorous Works of Mark Twain. London, Chatto and Windus, 1973.

Mark Twain's Notebooks and Journals, edited by Frederick Anderson and others. Berkeley, University of California Press, 1975 (and later volumes).

Letters from the Sandwich Islands, edited by Joan Abramson. Norfolk Island, Australia, Island Heritage, 1975.

Mark Twain Speaking, edited by Paul Fatout. Iowa City, University of Iowa Press, 1976.

The Mammoth Cod, and Address to the Stomach Club. Milwaukee, Maledicta, 1976.

The Comic Mark Twain Reader, edited by Charles Neider. New York, Doubleday, 1977.

Mark Twain Speaks for Himself, edited by Paul Fatout. West Lafayette, Indiana, Purdue University Press, 1978.

The Devil's Race-Track: Mark Twain's Great Dark Writings: The Best from "Which Was the Dream" and "Fables of Man," edited by John S. Tuckey. Berkeley, University of California Press, 1980.

The Selected Letters of Mark Twain, edited by Charles Neider. New York, Harper, 1982.

Mark Twain's Letters, edited by Edgar M. Branch, Michael B. Frank, and Kenneth M. Sanderson. Berkeley, University of California Press, 1987.

The Outrageous Mark Twain, edited by Charles Neider. New York, Doubleday, 1987.

Mark Twain's Aquarium: The Samuel Clemens Angelfish Correspondence. Athens, University of Georgia Press, 1991.

Mark Twain's Weapons of Satire: Anti-Imperialist Writings on the Philippine-American War, edited by Jim Zwick. Syracuse, New York, Syracuse University Press, 1992.

The Political Tales and Truth of Mark Twain, edited by David Hodge and Stacey Freeman. San Rafael, California, New World Library, 1992.

Tales, Speeches, Essays, and Sketches, edited by Tom Quirk. New York, Penguin, 1994.

The Bible according to Mark Twain: Writings of Heaven, Eden, and the Flood, edited by Howard G. Baetzhold and Joseph B. McCullough. Athens, University of Georgia Press, 1995.

Translator, *Slovenly Peter (Der Struwwelpeter).* New York, Limited Editions Club, 1935.

*

Bibliography: *A Bibliography of the Works of Mark Twain, Samuel Langhorne Clemens* by Merle Johnson, New York, Harper, revised edition, 1935; in *Bibliography of American Literature 2* by Jacob Blanck, New Haven, Connecticut, Yale University Press, 1957; *Mark Twain: A Reference Guide* by Thomas Asa Tenney, Boston, Hall, 1977; *Mark Twain International: A Bibliography and Interpretation of His World-wide Popularity* edited by Robert H. Rodney, Westport, Connecticut, Greenwood Press, 1982.

Critical Studies (selection): *Mark Twain: A Biography* by Albert Bigelow Paine, New York, Harper, 3 vols., 1912, abridged edition, as *A Short Life of Mark Twain,* 1920; *Mark Twain: The Man and His Work* by Edward Wagenknecht, New Haven, Connecticut, Yale University Press, 1935, revised edition, Norman, University of Oklahoma Press, 1961, 1967; *Mark Twain: Man and Legend* by De Lancey Ferguson, Indianapolis, Bobbs Merrill, 1943; *A Casebook on Mark Twain's Wound* edited by Lewis Leary, New York, Crowell, 1962; *Discussions of Mark Twain* edited by Guy A. Cardwell, Boston, Heath, 1963; *Mr. Clemens and Mark Twain: A Biography* by Justin Kaplan, New York, Simon and Schuster, 1966, London, Cape, 1967; *Mark Twain: The Fate of Humor* by James M. Cox, Princeton, New Jersey, Princeton University Press, 1966; *The Art of Mark Twain* by William M. Gibson, New York, Oxford University Press, 1976; *Mark Twain: A Collection of Criticism* edited by Dean Morgan Schmitter, New York, McGraw Hill, 1976; *Mark Twain* by Robert Keith Miller, New York, Ungar, 1983; *The Authentic Mark Twain: A Literary Biography of Samuel L. Clemens* by Everett Emerson, Philadelphia, University of Pennsylvania Press, 1984; *The Making of Mark Twain: A Biography* by John Lauber, Boston, Houghton Mifflin, 1985; *Mark Twain and Science* by Sherwood Cummings, Baton Rouge, Louisiana State University Press, 1989; *Mark Twain: The Bachelor Years* by Margaret Sanborn, New York, Doubleday, 1990; *The Inventions of Mark Twain* by John Lauber, New York, Hill and Wang, 1990.

*   *   *

Although Mark Twain's science fiction works are frequently labeled as mimetic fiction (in which what occurs can be explained as dreams rather than actual time travel resulting from scientific extrapolation), his dystopic creations and employment of the ideology of science within or preceding the dream structures qualifies some of his works as science fiction. In other works his use of alternate settings and actual scientific extrapolation outside of the dream/reality contexts appears, particularly in his shorter and sometimes incomplete stories.

Report from Paradise, The Mysterious Stranger, and *Letters from the Earth* are fantasy rather than SF: satires on man's place in the universe in which science is used neither as a tool to create the condition of the stories nor as a thematic consideration within them. Twain's fascination with comets, particularly Halley's comet, is evidenced in "Captain Stormfield's Visit to Heaven," "A Letter from a Comet," and "A Curious Pleasure Excursion." The interstellar travel included in each is either in or on a comet rather than in any kind of man-made space vessel and relegates these writings as fantasy.

Several of Twain's shorter works, "Mental Telegraphy," "Mental Telegraphy Again," and "My Platonic Sweetheart" focus on parapsychology—in which Twain professed a firm belief—thus excluding them from his science fiction works. Two other stories that have been classified as SF by some are "Earthquake Almanac" and

"Petrified Man." However, both depend on natural phenomena rather than on extrapolated science, social or physical.

Twain does extrapolate on the technology of his time, predicting long distance telephone service in "The Loves of Alonzo Fitz Clarence and Rosannah Ethelton," and long distance balloon flight in *Tom Sawyer Abroad* and in the incomplete manuscripts of "A Murder, A Mystery, and a Marriage," and "The Mysterious Balloonist." "The Comedy of Those Extraordinary Twins," neither extrapolative nor predictive, is based on the Tocci Twins. Physical science extrapolation is used in "Sold to Satan" where Satan is made of radium and Twain predicts the isolation of various elements by Madame Curie, and in the incomplete "Shackleford's Ghost" where a man becomes invisible after taking a potion created after numerous experiments by the local scientist.

Two works containing alternate settings, "The Curious Republic of Gondour" and "History 1,000 Years from Now," are seeming utopias. In "Curious Republic" weighted universal suffrage has developed; education, common sense, and, to a lesser extent, money earn the citizens extra votes. In the incomplete manuscript "History," society has evolved from a democracy to a monarchy. Three incomplete works by Twain employ alternate settings: "The Generation Iceberg," "The Secret History of Eddypus, The World-Empire," and "3000 Years among the Microbes." In "3000" Twain satirizes the human condition. By having a wizard accidently turn a man into a cholera microbe instead of a bird, Twain adopts a distancing from reality that has been a science fiction technique used by many writers to allow for social criticism without immediately alienating the reader. The setting is the diseased body of a tramp within which millions of microbes live and where nations have their own languages, customs, and governments, all patterned after nations existing during the early 20th century. The microbes are not described as aliens; instead they look, act, talk, and think precisely as man does. This setting allows Twain to comment on his favorite themes: the stupidity of government officials, the hypocrisy of organized religions, the prejudices evident in class systems, the problem of the lie—here related to the tall tale. The microbe tells his friends about the real world and they compliment him on his poetic inspiration—with one exception he is flatly not believed.

Unlike Hank of *A Connecticut Yankee in King Arthur's Court,* the microbe does not introduce new technology to the society. Instead the society is ahead of his time, having a device that records thoughts and images and condenses them to perfectly understandable encapsulations of facts and meanings. Notably, a religious scientist reveals to the microbe a world view akin to Twain's by expounding on the absurdity of man's false sense of superiority. Technology is celebrated when a microscope is used to discover that on every level of organism the cycle of life is the same; thereby enforcing the moral treatise of the absurdity of man's presumptious superiority.

In "The Secret History of Eddypus, the World-Empire," Twain presents a 29th-century dystopia ruled by the Christian Science church that is comparable to the late 18th-century lifestyle, dominated by religious persecution, arrogance, and misinformation. He presents no new technology, scientific inquiry having been effectively stopped by the church. He shows the absurdities of organized religion, which perpetuates the status quo, encourages a distinct disrespect for truth, and consistently and with a vengence destroys knowledge for fear that it would abrogate the power of the church. The narrator has begun to write a history of the world, all such references having been destroyed by the church and replaced by the church's version. The history is a humorous mishmash of

erroneous facts until the 19th-century section, which contains an accurate delineation of scientific discoveries and their effects, focusing on evolution, both biological and societal, in which he identifies circumstances and environment as those factors which chart the course of the world.

In "The Generation Iceberg" Twain speculates on the type of society that would evolve in a group totally isolated. This fascination with isolated groups and the effect of their exposure to technology is also evident in "A Murder, A Mystery, and A Marriage" as well as *A Connecticut Yankee in King Arthur's Court.*

"From the *London Times* of 1904," "The Great Dark," and *A Connecticut Yankee in King Arthur's Court* all reflect the increasing cynicism of Twain's later years. In the confusion of dream and reality accompanied by alteration of time and space, Twain creates different worlds for his protagonists to struggle in. These dystopias present Twain's perception of the unchanging human condition; man as a petty being, always willing to prey on his fellowman.

The comic relief in *Connecticut Yankee* (a literary burlesque of Malory's *Morte D'Arthur*) erupts through Twain's satire of the age of chivalry whose precepts had been adopted by the Old South, a frequent target of Twain's social criticism in his mainstream works. But primarily Twain investigates the effects of industrialization on a preindustrial society, a matter of public concern both in relation to the United States and to our foreign policy at the time. In this view, Twain attacked social Darwinism: the establishment of an industrialized, capitalistic society where the common man was once again suppressed by the financial power of a few individuals who had gained their power through that technological revolution.

Hank, the protagonist of *Connecticut Yankee,* a 19th-century common working man, rises to power in King Arthur's Court through creative use of his technical skills and scientific knowledge. By introducing industrialization, Hank attempts to change the economic, political, and intellectual structures of a nation of oppressed people, but his failure results not so much through the powers of the church and state as through his own weakness. He succumbs to one of the primary evils of capitalism (according to Twain): once Hank gains power, he becomes self-absorbed. The megalomanic Hank instigates a civil war (purportedly in the name of creating a viable civilization for the common man) which results in the ultimate destruction of all that he has established. What makes *Connecticut Yankee* SF is not just the question of whether Hank actually experiences time travel and suspended animation or whether he dreams it. Instead it is Twain's questioning of the effects of technology, his concentration on the idea of technology in another time and space.

The problem of dream versus reality occurs again in "The Great Dark." Whereas in *Connecticut Yankee* the protagonist goes back in time to a setting already familiar to the reader, in "The Great Dark" Twain concentrates on establishing a setting in which circumstance, not time, is important. Presenting a tiny world as seen through a microscope, Twain creates a whole watery universe filled with monsters, destruction, and suffering for his protagonist to attempt to survive in. Like Hank, Mr. Edwards returns to the present no longer accepting it as real, finding his other existence to have all the qualities of reality and his present that of the dream. This exploration of dream versus reality is closely linked with temporal/spatial relationships so that time and setting become an integral part of what makes these works science fiction. In *Connecticut Yankee,* science, or at least technology, is a thematic consideration, whereas in "The Great Dark" technology is used only as a tool to create the setting in which the characters must question temporal/spatial relationships. Twain embarks on another approach to science in "From the *London Times* of 1904." Instead of employing a thematic consideration of technology as in *Connecticut Yankee* or using an already existing scientific instrument to create the circumstances of the story as in "The Great Dark," Twain invents the telectroscope (television) to use in conjunction with his usual exploration of thought and visual transference in temporal/spatial relationships.

In these works, Twain, as an early writer of SF, presents three different approaches still frequently used in the genre. Additionally, through his social criticism, Twain is one of the first mainstream writers to present dystopias rather than utopias to show by comparison rather than by contrast the inequities of the social institutions he questions: religion, government, taxes, prejudice, slavery, censorship, and politics. Yet his dark view of man is made bearable through his caustic humor. He invokes our laughter even as we accept with humility his accusations of our greed, jealousy, lack of common sense, thirst for power, cruelty, and ultimately the smallness of mind of the human beast.

—Jane B. Weedman

TYERS, Kathy

Nationality: American. **Born:** Kathleen Moore, Long Beach, California, 21 July 1952. **Education:** Long Beach Polytechnic High School, first in class of 725; Montana State University, Bozeman, B.S. in microbiology (with distinction) 1974; Montana State University, Bozeman, elementary education certificate 1977. **Family:** Married Mark J. Tyers in 1974; one son. **Career:** Private flute instructor, Long Beach, California, and Bozeman, Montana, 1968-; flutist, Bozeman Symphony Orchestra, 1970-79; flutist/Irish harper, folk duo Mark & Kathy Tyers, Bozeman, 1974-; immunobiology technician, Montana State University, Bozeman, 1973-75; microbiological media technician, Montana State University, Bozeman, 1975-76; elementary teacher, Christian Center School, Bozeman, 1977-80. Since 1983, freelance writer. **Member:** Science Fiction and Fantasy Writers of America, 1987. **Agent:** Martha Millard Literary Agency, 204 Park Avenue, Madison, New Jersey 07940, U.S.A.

Science Fiction Publications

Novels (series: Firebird; Star Wars)

Firebird. Toronto, New York, Bantam, 1987.
Fusion Fire. Toronto, New York, Bantam, 1988.
Crystal Witness. Toronto, New York, Bantam, 1989.
Shivering World. New York, Bantam, 1991.
The Truce at Bakura (Star Wars). New York and London, Bantam, 1994.

Other Publications

Other

Exploring the Northern Rockies. Santa Barbara, California, Companion, 1991.

*

Kathy Tyers comments:

I was an enthusiastic amateur writer in high school during the 1960s, and I restarted in the summer of 1983—when my son was two years old and reasonably self-sufficient, the U.S. Air Force Thunderbirds came to town, and *Star Wars: The Return of the Jedi* was released. I was immediately drawn back to the genre I'd loved reading since fifth grade: space opera.

I was probably also influenced by the unsolved 1982 double murder of my mother and stepfather. In the space opera universe, virtue triumphs and evildoers are brought to justice. Real life is fragile and unjust. No one can count on surviving to reach her "life expectancy." Carpe diem. . . .

And space opera mirrors the eternal cosmic battle that grinds humankind between the armies of genuine good and evil. We live, fight, and die as tragically flawed heroes or self-serving villains; and in the end, justice *will* be done.

I call myself a "practicing Christian," borrowing the phrase from a friend who explained that he "hadn't gotten it right yet." As with the flute I've been practicing for over 30 years, the better I play, the more clearly I realize I'm far from real mastery.

Shivering World was a serious attempt to write hard SF, which I also enjoy deeply, but my first novels were heavily influenced by the Star Wars epics. My career came full circle in 1992 when I was asked by Bantam Spectra to write a Star Wars novel. It was a joy and an honor.

* * *

Kathy Tyers is the creator of space opera stylistically reminiscent of early Heinlein. Her work has the likable characters, strong action line carrying a dramatic story exploring individuals in possible futures trying to figure out and do what is best for them and their societies, and ideals/people in conflict that captures the imagination, not just telling a story (although she does this well) but also contributing to both our sense and intellect. She creates strong female protagonists and well-developed males, with the people and their complex real-world relationships as well as the essential conflict between good and evil central to the tale. The romantic focus and conflict in her writing gives it depth and warmth, reminding one of Lois McMaster Bujold. She has written for both young adult and adult audiences. She writes in her own universes as well as the universe of Star Wars.

Tyers has also written a nonfiction guidebook, *Exploring the Northern Rockies.* She is a writer hitting her stride; in addition to the works discussed below she has *One Mind's Eye* forthcoming in 1996 and several works in marketing: *Crown of Fire* (from the Firebird universe) and *The Valley between Stars,* as well as work in progress, *The Springhill Aliens.* In addition to her writing Tyers is a folk musician, flutist, and Irish harpist, and has, with her husband, released two recordings.

Tyers made her debut with the novel *Firebird,* followed the next year by its sequel, *Fusion Fire.* The books have been called science fantasy blending science possibilities with a solid core grounded in the people and world Tyers created, and reminding one of McCaffrey's Pern: neither science fiction or fantasy, more scientific and factual than fantasy. These books are the story of Lady Firebird Angelo of the Naetai royal family. She is a Wastlin, an extra child, expected to die if her older sisters reach their majority. Suicide is the only honorable choice defined by N'Taian culture so Firebird has chosen to become the fastest pilot to lead a strike force against their enemies. Her horror, rage, and feelings of loss during battle draw the mental attention of Lieutenant General Brennen Caldwell, a Thrycian with telepathic and other paranormal powers, the most powerful Sentinel on the Aurian scale, who uses those powers to prevent her suicide attempt. This sets the stage for their relationship, fraught with the conflict between duty and love in the tradition of Romeo and Juliet, and Firebird's conflict between duty to N'Taian political imperatives and what she comes to see as duty to honor. Brennen's ability to hear Firebird's mental cry foreshadows the telepathic bond forged between them. Telepathic bonding is surely one of the most compelling yet frightening links between people, embodying both the wish for total trust and intimacy with our atavistic fear of difference. Their heroic struggle to save both worlds from both the political conflict and possible environmental death is enriched by twists of family and social pressure, ancient curses and enough action to satisfy. Through the action and her choices Firebird grows and defines her inner self, allowing us to experience that growth and get in touch with our inner selves and our humanity. There are some examples of fan fiction set in her *Firebird-Fusion Fire* universe, a sure sign that Tyers has captured the interest and imagination of the readers.

Crystal Witness is a rousing space adventure, the compelling story of Ming Dalamani, a young pirate caught and sentenced to memory erasure by the powerful corporation Renasco. The bulk of the action centers on Ming's transformation from a brain-wiped corporate servant to the catalyst for needed revolution. Her returning memory is sparked by her relationship with Tieg Innig and his stories of the past. By remembering her past and earlier technical knowledge she enables the revolution to resist Renasco, but at grave personal risk. The questions about reality and memory are cleanly served up for the reader's perusal, food for the mind. Ming struggles with what is real vs. memory, what is right and grows through dangerous personal choices to emerge as a complete person.

In *Shivering World* Tyers gives us another compelling story layered with intrigue, and another memorable female protagonist, Graysha Brady-Phillips. Graysha agrees to accept hazardous duty on a frontier world, Goddard, not in fear for her life but in hopes their illegal genetic sciences may save her life. The romantic element brings extra life to this story through the characters' stumbling journey to intimacy. The issues surrounding genetic manipulation as foregrounded in this conflict between colonists, Gaea Consortium and the Eugenics Board philosophically engage the reader lifting this story to a space opera classic in the early and exciting tradition.

The Force is with Tyers in her new novel, *The Truce at Bakua,* and will bring her work to a larger audience. The sensitivity she gives to the Star Wars characters will bring them to life before our eyes. In *Truce* we see that people are people whether human or alien and we care about them even though we see them struggle with both good and evil, that events shape the universe but that people can make a difference by their struggle. Tyers provides us with memorable alien invaders, the Ssi-ruuk, as well as some new members of the Star Wars family, including Deb Sibwarra, an alien strong in the Force who is subject to Ssi-ruuk mind control until Luke helps provide the knowledge to free his mind. Tyers has another published story in this universe, "Tinian on Trial" in *Star Wars Adventure Journal.* Her work in this universe continues with the recently published story "We Don't Do Weddings: The Band's Tale" in *Tales from the Mos Eisley Cantina.* Schedule for future release are: "A Time to Dance, A Time to Mourn: Oola's Tale" in *Tales from Jabba's Palace,* "To Fight Another Day" in *Star Wars Adventure Journal* and "The Prize Pelt: Bossak's Tale" in *Tales of the Bounty Hunters.*

—Catherine M. Currier

UTLEY, Steven

Nationality: American. **Born:** 1948. **Address:** c/o Heidelberg Publishers, 1003 Brown Building, Austin, Texas 78701, U.S.A.

SCIENCE FICTION PUBLICATIONS

Uncollected Short Stories

"The Unkindest Cut of All," in *Perry Rhodan 20.* New York, Ace, 1972.

"Parrot Phrase," in *Perry Rhodan 24.* New York, Ace, 1973.

"The Queen and I," in *Perry Rhodan 31.* New York, Ace, 1973.

"Crash Cameron and the Slime Beast," in *Vertex* (Los Angeles), June 1973.

"The Reason Why," in *Vertex* (Los Angeles), December 1973.

"Hung like an Elephant," with Joe Pumilia, and "Womb, with a View," in *Alternities,* edited by David Gerrold, New York, Dell, 1974.

"Sport," in *Best SF 1973,* edited by Harry Harrison and Brian Aldiss. New York, Putnam, and London, Sphere, 1974.

"Deeper Than Death," in *Vertex* (Los Angeles), April 1974.

"Act of Mercy," in *Galaxy* (New York), July 1974.

"Big Black Whole" and "Time and Variance," in *Galaxy* (New York), August 1974.

"Amber Eyes," in *Galaxy* (New York), December 1974.

"The Great Red Spot," with Joe Pumilia, and "Dear Mom, I Don't Like It Here," in *Vertex* (Los Angeles), February 1975.

"Flies by Night," with Lisa Tuttle, in *Fantasy and Science Fiction* (New York), June 1975.

"Caring for Your Edaphosaurus," in *Vertex* (Los Angeles), August 1975.

"The Other Half," in *Galaxy* (New York), September 1975.

"Custer's Last Jump," with Howard Waldrop, in *Universe 6,* edited by Terry Carr. New York, Doubleday, 1976; London, Dobson, 1978.

"Predators," in *The Ides of Tomorrow,* edited by Terry Carr. Boston, Little Brown, 1976.

"Ghost Seas," in *Lone Star Universe,* edited by George W. Proctor and Steven Utley. Austin, Texas, Heidelberg, 1976.

"Sic Transit . . . ?," with Howard Waldrop, in *Stellar 2,* edited by Judy-Lynn del Rey. New York, Ballantine, 1976.

"Getting Away," in *Galaxy* (New York), January 1976.

"Larval Stage," in *Galaxy* (New York), July 1976.

"Ocean," in *Fantastic* (New York), August 1976.

"The Man at the Bottom of the Sea," in *Galaxy* (New York), October 1976.

"The Thirteenth Labor," in *Stellar 3,* edited by Judy-Lynn del Rey. New York, Ballantine, 1977.

"Black as the Pit, from Pole to Pole" with Howard Waldrop, in *New Dimensions 7,* edited by Robert Silverberg. New York, Harper, and London, Gollancz, 1977.

"Sidhe," in *More Devil's Kisses,* edited by Linda Lovecraft. London, Corgi, 1977.

"In Brightest Day, In Darkest Night," in *Fantastic* (New York), February 1977.

"Passport for a Phoenix," in *Galaxy* (New York), April 1977.

"Spectator Sport," in *Amazing* (New York), July 1977.

"The Maw," in *Fantasy and Science Fiction* (New York), July 1977.

"Tom Sawyer's Sub-Orbital Escapade," with Lisa Tuttle, in *Ascents of Wonder,* edited by David Gerrold and Stephen Goldin. New York, Popular Library, 1977.

"Losing Streak," in *Fantasy and Science Fiction* (New York), January 1977.

"Our Vanishing Triceratops," with Joe Pumilia, in *Amazing* (New York), March 1977.

"Time and Hagakure," in *Asimov's Choice: Black Holes and Bug-Eyed Monsters,* edited by George H. Scithers. New York, Dale, 1978.

"Deviation from a Theme," in *The Rivals of King Kong,* edited by Michel Parry. London, Corgi, 1978.

"Uncoiling," with Lisa Tuttle, in *Fantastic* (New York), April 1978.

"Personal Column," in *Sex in the 21st Century,* edited by Michel Parry and Milton Subotsky. London, Panther, 1979.

"The Man Who Ran up the Clock," in *Fantastic* (New York), January 1979.

"Leaves," in *Amazing* (New York), February 1979.

"Genocide Man," in *Fantasy and Science Fiction* (New York), April 1979.

"Upstart," in *The Best from Fantasy and Science Fiction 23,* edited by Edward L. Ferman. New York, Doubleday, 1980.

"The Tall Grass," in *Asimov's,* 1989.

"Where or When," in *Asimov's,* 1991.

"Haiti," in *Asimov's,* 1992.

"Now That We Have Each Other," in *Asimov's,* 1991.

OTHER PUBLICATIONS

Other

Editor, with George W. Proctor, *Lone Star Universe: The First Anthology of Texas Science Fiction Authors.* Austin, Heidelberg, 1976.

*

Steven Utley comments:

Under the best circumstances, writing sometimes makes me crazy enough to wonder why anybody would put himself through such torture. (Then I go reread William Faulkner's "Dry September," say, or something by Flannery O'Connor, and remember why: to be, somehow, great.) By the late 1970s writing, particularly the writing of science fiction, had made me so crazy that I not only did not want to write any more, I did not want to talk or even think about writing ever again. It was a relief to have time and energy again for other interests, to be able to read what I wanted to read rather than what I felt myself under some professional obligation to read—all my colleagues' latest productions (not to be confused with my friends' and those of total strangers whose work I continued to admire)—in short, to put my little writing career behind me and get on with my life. Almost the last story I wrote during the 1970s was entitled "Goodbye," and not by accident, either.

Similarly, the bad-tempered statement appended to my entry in the original (1981) and subsequent (1986, 1991) editions of *Science Fiction Writers* was sincere in its bad-temperedness. It has, however, become dated: by the late 1980s, I was simply ready to write again, and did, and do. Writing still makes me crazy, but at least I am writing exactly what I want to write. And I really have been a much happier person since I stopped trying to write science fiction and just concentrated on writing stories.

*   *   *

After a self-enforced hiatus of eight years, Steven Utley, who published nearly 60 short SF, fantasy, or horror stories from 1972 to 1981, began writing and publishing again in the late 1980s. His "retirement" stemmed from disillusionment with science fiction and an emotionally satisfying commitment to other pursuits, especially listening to and collecting swing-era music and writing and drawing an outrageously satiric comic strip called "The Huggybunnies."

In the first seven years of his career (1972-79), Utley established a reputation as a prolific author of short stories and novelettes, either alone or in collaboration with a number of other Texas-based writers, most notably Howard Waldrop and Lisa Tuttle. With George W. Proctor, he edited a volume of SF and fantasy by Texans, *Lone Star Universe,* whose publication Harlan Ellison hailed as a "watershed event." Working solely at less-than-novel length, Utley produced fiction either competent but conventional ("Genocide Man") or both bleak and moving ("Getting Away"). At his best, his angst leavened with humor, angry wit, or local color, he created chilling horror stories ("Ghost Seas"), scathingly funny satires ("Upstart"), marvelous pastiches ("Black as the Pit, from Pole to Pole," with Waldrop), and evocative and melancholy science fiction ("The Man at the Bottom of the Sea").

"Custer's Last Jump," with Waldrop, first secured wide notice for Utley's talents. In frontier America, the Oglala Sioux, flying Krupp monoplanes, defeat George Armstrong Custer's 7th Calvary and its airborne auxiliary, the 505th Balloon Infantry. Related in earnest textbook prose, this off-the-wall tour de force concludes with a "Suggested Reading" list as wacky and authentic-seeming as the "historical" matter before it, a bibliographic fillip probably inspired by Farmer's convolute appendices in the mock-biography *Tarzan Alive* (1972).

A second Utley-Waldrop collaboration, "Black as the Pit, from Pole to Pole," pays homage to Farmer (again), Mary Shelley, Poe, Verne, Burroughs, and others. Its hero is that quintessential symbol of alienation, the Frankenstein monster, and its setting is the perilous hollow interior of the earth. Although its disparate elements do not always mesh convincingly, sheer narrative *chutzpah* often disguises the fact.

Among Utley's solo efforts, "Upstart" is a blunt and hilarious satire of SF's spacefarer-as-superhero ethos, perhaps the last word on this indefatigable idiocy. "Ghost Seas" invokes the desolate West Texas landscape in the service of a terrifying tale of avarice and revenge. "Time and Hagakure" presents the son of a Japanese kamikaze pilot trying to preserve his sanity by mediating, through time, the salvation of his doomed father. "Getting Away" exploits Utley's deep-seated interest in dinosaurs, which gives his protagonist a means of psychological escape from a disheartening future. And his final early-period story "The Beasts of Love" dissects a

foundering marriage, with an impact as profound as that of Richard Matheson's classic 1950 story "Born of Man and Woman."

The strongest apparent influences on Utley while writing these early stories were Ray Bradbury's October landscapes, the ironic pessimism of Robert Silverberg's *Tower of Glass* and *Dying Inside,* the pop-culture eclecticism of Philip José Farmer, and the manic-depressive black humor of Barry N. Malzberg, whose approach Utley affectionately parodied in "Losing Streak." Working to discover his own voice and métier, he seemed close to a personal breakthrough when he simply abandoned the game, remarking, "Disenchantment with the SF field, when it set in, set in hard."

In 1989, Utley returned with a technically adroit revision of an older story, "My Wife," published in *Isaac Asimov's Science Fiction Magazine,* a character study of a rich monomaniac with a disturbing set of reasons for reversing the suicide of his wife. Showing a more confident grasp of the storyteller's art than ever before, "My Wife" signaled the resurgence of Utley's career. His next story, "The Tall Grass," also published in *Isaac Asimov's Science Fiction Magazine,* was a first-person time-travel story recalling Theodore Sturgeon's "The Man Who Lost the Sea" and the ruin-pocked South Pacific landscapes of J.G. Ballard, without seeming derivative. (In fact, "The Tall Grass," is a near-perfect example of the doomed-protagonist SF story.) "Where or When" (in *Asimov's*) and "Look Away," (in *Fantasy and Science Fiction*), both from 1991, reveal Utley's intense interest in the American Civil War; the former misdirects two time-tourists bound for London, 1851, into a battle in Virginia, 1864, while the latter dilates on the manifest destiny of a triumphant Confederacy and the would-be Napoleon set on creating a vast new slave empire in Latin America.

More stories will surely follow, including "The Glowing Cloud," a novella about the eruption of Mount Pelée. As a result, Utley's once-constricted reputation can only grow.

—Michael Bishop

VANCE, Gerald. *See* **GARRETT, Randall; PHILLIPS, Rog.**

VANCE, Jack

Also writes as John Holbrook Vance. **Pseudonyms:** Peter Held; Ellery Queen; Alan Wade. **Nationality:** American. **Born:** John Holbrook Vance, San Francisco, California, 28 August 1916. **Education:** University of California, Berkeley, B.A. 1942. **Family:** Married Norma Ingold in 1946; one son. **Career:** Self-employed writer. **Awards:** Mystery Writers of America Edgar Allan Poe award, 1960; Hugo award, 1963, 1967; Nebula award, 1966; Jupiter award, 1974; World Fantasy Convention Life Achievement award, 1984. **Agent:** Ralph Vicinanza Ltd., 432 Park Avenue South, Suite 1205, New York, New York 10016. **Address:** 6383 Valley View Road, Oakland, California 94611, U.S.A.

Novels (series: Alastor; Big Planet; Cadwal Chronicles; Dying Earth; Durdane; Demon Princes; Lyonesse; Tschai/Planet of Adventure)

The Space Pirate: A Science Fiction Novel. New York, Toby Press, 1953; abridged edition as *The Five Gold Bands,* New York, Ace, 1963; London, Mayflower, 1980.

Vandals of the Void (for children). Philadelphia, Winston, 1953.

To Live Forever. New York, Ballantine, 1956; London, Sphere, 1976.

Big Planet. New York, Avalon, 1957; Sevenoaks, Kent, Coronet, 1977.

The Languages of Pao. New York, Avalon, 1958; St. Albans, Hertfordshire, Mayflower, 1974.

Slaves of the Klau. New York, Ace, 1958; Sevenoakes, Kent, Coronet, 1980; revised as *Gold and Iron (Slaves of the Klau),* San Francisco and Columbia, Pennsylvania, Underwood-Miller, 1982.

The Dragon Masters. New York, Ace, 1963; London, Dobson, 1965.

The Houses of Iszm [and] *Son of the Tree.* New York, Ace, 1964; *Son of the Tree* published separately, London, Mayflower, 1974.

The Star King (Demon Princes). New York, Berkley, 1964; London, Dobson, 1966.

The Killing Machine (Demon Princes). New York, Berkley, 1964; London, Dobson, 1967.

Space Opera. New York, Pyramid, 1965; Sevenoaks, Kent, Coronet, 1982.

The Blue World. New York, Ballantine, 1966; St. Albans, Hertfordshire, Mayflower, 1976.

The Brains of Earth. New York, Ace, 1966; London, Dobson, 1975; London, Panther, 1984; as *Nopalgarth* in *Nopalgarth: Three Complete Novels,* New York, DAW, 1980.

The Palace of Love (Demon Princes). New York, Berkley, 1967; London, Dobson, 1968.

The Last Castle. New York, Ace, 1967.

City of the Chasch (Tschai). New York, Ace, 1968; St. Albans, Hertfordshire, Mayflower, 1974.

Emphyrio. Garden City, New York, Doubleday, 1969; London, Coronet, 1980.

Servants of the Wankh (Tschai). New York, Ace, 1969; St. Albans, Hertfordshire, Mayflower, 1975; as *Wankh,* New York, Bluejay, 1986.

The Dirdir (Tschai). New York, Ace, 1969; London, Dobson, 1975.

The Pnume (Tschai). New York, Ace, 1970; London, Dobson, 1975.

The Anome (Durdane). New York, Dell, 1973; London, Coronet, 1975; as *The Faceless Man,* New York, Ace, 1978; London, Gollancz, 1987.

The Brave Free Men (Durdane). New York, Dell, 1973; London, Coronet, 1975.

Trullion: Alastor 2262. New York, Ballantine, 1973; London, Mayflower, 1979.

The Asutra (Durdane). New York, Dell, 1974; London, Coronet, 1975.

The Gray Prince: A Science Fiction Novel. Indianapolis, Bobbs Merrill, 1974; London, Coronet, 1976; as *The Grey Prince,* London, Coronet, 1982.

Marune: Alastor 933. New York, Ballantine, 1975; London, Coronet, 1978.

Showboat World (Big Planet). New York, Pyramid, 1975; Sevenoaks, Kent, Coronet, 1977; as *The Magnificent Showboats of the Lower Vissel River, Lune XXIII South, Big Planet,* San Francisco, Underwood-Miller, 1983.

Maske: Thaery. New York, Berkley, 1976; London, Fontana, 1977.

Wyst: Alastor 1716. New York, DAW, 1978; Sevenoaks, Kent, Coronet, 1980.

The Face (Demon Princes). New York, DAW, 1979; London, Dobson, 1980.

The Book of Dreams (Demon Princes). New York, DAW, 1981; Sevenoaks, Kent, Coronet, 1982.

Cugel's Saga (Dying Earth). New York, Timescape, 1983; London, Panther, 1985.

Suldrun's Garden (Lyonesse). New York, Berkley, 1983; as *Lyonesse,* London, Grafton, 1984.

The Green Pearl (Lyonesse). San Francisco, Underwood-Miller, 1985; London, Grafton, 1986.

Araminta Station (Cadwal). Los Angeles and Columbia, Pennsylvania, Underwood-Miller, 1987; London, New English Library, 1988.

Madouc (Lyonesse). Novato, California, and Lancaster, Pennsylvania, Underwood-Miller, 1989; London, Grafton, 1990.

Durdane (includes *The Anome, The Brave Free Men,* and *The Asutra*). London, Gollancz, 1989.

Ecce and Old Earth (Cadwal). Novato, California, and Lancaster, Pennsylvania, Underwood-Miller, 1991; London, New English Library, 1992.

Throy (Cadwal). Novato, California, and Lancaster, Pennsylvania, Underwoood-Miller, 1992; London, New English Library, 1993.

Short Stories (series: Dying Earth)

The Dying Earth. New York, Hillman, 1950; London, Mayflower, 1972.

Future Tense. New York, Ballantine, 1964; as *Dust of Far Suns,* New York, DAW, 1981.

Monsters in Orbit. New York, Ace, 1965; London, Dobson, 1977.

The World Between, and Other Stories. New York, Ace, 1965; as *The Moon Moth and Other Stories,* London, Dobson, 1976.

The Eyes of the Overworld (Dying Earth). New York, Ace, 1966; London, Mayflower, 1972.

The Many Worlds of Magnus Ridolph. New York, Ace, 1966; London, Dobson, 1977; expanded, New York, DAW, 1980; further expanded as *The Complete Magnus Ridolph,* San Francisco, Underwood-Miller, 1985.

Eight Fantasms and Magics: A Science Fiction Adventure. New York, Macmillan, 1969; as *Fantasms and Magics: A Science Fiction Adventure,* London, Mayflower, 1978.

The Worlds of Jack Vance. New York, Ace, 1973.

The Best of Jack Vance. New York, Pocket Books, 1976.

Green Magic (chapbook). San Francisco and Columbia, Pennsylvania, Underwood-Miller, 1979; with other stories as *Green Magic: The Fantasy Realms of Jack Vance,* 1979.

The Bagful of Dreams. San Francisco, Underwood-Miller, 1979.

The Seventeen Virgins. San Francisco and Columbia, Pennsylvania, Underwood-Miller, 1979.

Morreion: A Tale of the Dying Earth. San Francisco and Columbia, Pennsylvania, Underwood-Miller, 1992.

Galactic Effectuator. San Francisco and Columbia, Pennsylvania, Underwood-Miller, 1980; Sevenoaks, Kent, Coronet, 1983.

The Narrow Land. New York, DAW, 1982; Sevenoaks, Kent, Coronet, 1984.

Lost Moons. San Francisco and Columbia, Pennsylvania, Underwood-Miller, 1982.

Rhialto the Marvellous (Dying Earth). San Francisco and Columbia, Pennsylvania, Brandywyne, 1984; London, Grafton, 1985.

Light from a Lone Star. Cambridge, Massachusetts, NEFSA Press, 1985.

The Augmented Agent, and Other Stories, edited by Steven Owen Godersky. San Francisco and Columbia, Pennsylvania, Underwood-Miller, 1986; London, New English Library, 1989.

The Dark Side of the Moon: Stories of the Future. San Francisco and Columbia, Pennsylvania, Underwood-Miller, 1986; London, New English Library, 1989.

Chateau d'If and Other Stories. Novato, California, and Lancaster, Pennsylvania, Underwood-Miller, 1990.

When the Five Moons Rise. Novato, California, and Lancaster, Pennsylvania, Underwood-Miller, 1992.

OTHER PUBLICATIONS

Novels as John Holbrook Vance (series: Joe Bain)

Isle of Peril (as Alan Wade). New York, Mystery House, 1957; bylined as Jack Vance as *Bird Isle,* Los Angeles, Underwood-Miller, 1988.

Take My Face (as Peter Held). New York, Mystery House, 1957; bylined as Jack Vance, Los Angeles, Underwood-Miller, 1988.

The Man in the Cage. New York, Random House, 1960; London, Boardman, 1961.

The Fox Valley Murders (Bain). Indianapolis, Bobbs-Merrill, 1966; London, Hale, 1967.

The Pleasant Grove Murders (Bain). Indianapolis, Bobbs-Merrill, 1967; London, Hale, 1968.

The Deadly Isles. Indianapolis, Bobbs Merrill, 1969; London, Hale, 1970.

Bad Ronald. New York, Ballantine, 1973.

The House on Lily Street. San Francisco and Columbia, Pennsylvania, Underwood-Miller, 1979.

The View from Chickweed's Window: A Novel of Suspense. San Francisco and Columbia, Pennsylvania, Underwood-Miller, 1979.

Strange Notions (as Jack Vance). San Francisco and Columbia, Pennsylvania, Underwood-Miller, 1985.

The Dark Ocean (as Jack Vance). San Francisco and Columbia, Pennsylvania, Underwood-Miller, 1985.

Novels as Ellery Queen

The Four Johns. New York, Pocket Books, 1964; as *Four Men Called John,* London, Gollancz, 1976.

A Room to Die In. New York, Pocket Books, 1965.

The Madman Theory. New York, Pocket Books, 1966; North Harrow, Middlesex, Kinnell, 1986.

Play

Television Play: *Captain Video* (6 episodes), 1952-53.

*

Bibliography: *Fantasms: A Bibliography of the Literature of Jack Vance* by Daniel J. H. Levack and Tim Underwood, San Francisco, Underwood-Miller, 1978.

Manuscript Collection: Mugar Memorial Library, Boston University.

Critical Studies: *Jack Vance, Science Fiction Stylist* by Richard Tiedman, Wabash, Indiana, Coulson, 1965; *Jack Vance* edited by Tim Underwood and Chuck Miller, New York, Taplinger, 1980; *Demon Prince: The Dissonant Worlds of Jack Vance* by Jack Rawlins. San Bernardino, Borgo Press, 1986.

*   *   *

In a key work of modern SF criticism, Jack Vance is termed "a gaudily painted coelacanth" who "swashbuckled on a million imaginary worlds." Vance's powers of invention have never been called into question. However, as Brian Aldiss's evaluation indicates, Vance is often viewed, unfortunately, as a fossil who has far outlived his proper literary time, a writer of SF not far removed from fantasy who is more interested in effect than thought, the heir to the dead tradition of Edgar Rice Burroughs and Clark Ashton Smith. Yet if Vance's works are analyzed closely, they often unexpectedly subvert the genre conventions that they on the surface appear to typify.

The most noticeable aspect of Vance's writing is his imaginative fecundity in constructing exotic yet plausible societies, many often in the same novel. For instance, in *Big Planet* the characters travel through at least eight different societies—yet cover only a thousand of the planet's forty thousand miles. This strength can become a weakness when characters (and readers) who have just grown familiar with the habits and *mores* of one society are plunged into yet another. Vance lavishes his protean inventiveness on these societies, providing languages, epigraphs, footnotes, and appendices. His much-praised style (estimable particularly in comparison to what passes for it in the genre) results in part from his desire to describe these communities as fully as possible. Overlooked under its rococo flourishes is the depth of the presentation of these societies, particularly their economic bases. *The Houses of Iszm* describes an attempt to break a monopoly for cheap housing; *Emphyrio* details how an aristocracy's restraint of trade keeps a society at a feudal level; *Wyst: Alastor 1716* shows how a society that denigrates labor becomes static.

Vance's societies are never based on altruism, and the very idea often provokes derisive laughter from his characters. When one character uses the word "trust," another will ask, "What word is that?" A guidebook about a vacation spot advises: "NOTHING IS FREE except the air you breathe." This distancing of language reveals an undervalued aspect of Vance's style: its humor, which is most often produced by the contrast of the heated descriptions and Byzantine societies with the dispassionate, almost juridical tone. His funniest novel, *Space Opera,* deflates the usual genre connotations of its title; the novel concerns a traveling opera troupe, not intergalactic warfare. (In the novel, the prison planet is named Skylark, a dig at the space operas of E.E. "Doc" Smith.) An example of Vance's laconic humor is when the opera director is warned not to adapt *Fidelio* to alien understanding in every literal aspect: "their sex play is a matter of spraying the intended mate with a viscous liquid. I doubt if you wish to carry similitude to quite this extent."

Only recently revealing a loose internal connectedness, Vance's galaxy is predominantly human. Aliens, if encountered, never exist in amity with humans. In *Napalgarth,* when humans and Xaxan must unite to throw off telepathic parasites, the hero muses that "there could never be a camaraderie [sic]." More often both species can only exist in a master-slave relationship, as in *The Dragon Master,* where the dragons and humans employ the genetically manipulated descendants of each other as their soldiery. Perhaps the best-known of Vance's aliens occur in his series the Planet of Adventure, in which the hero must liberate humans from the alien races who have molded and enslaved them.

Vance usually endorses the typical Campbellian *Astounding* virtues of freedom and independence, as his title *The Brave Free Men* indicates. The hero of *The Dragon Masters* argues that the sacerdotes might not be as gentle as they appear: "We do not know that they are pacifists. We do know that they are men." Yet Vance at times plays with these conventions. For instance, in *The Servants of the Wankh,* it is the aliens who must be rescued by the hero from the tyranny their human servants have placed them under.

Vance of course does write space opera, most notably in the Demon Princes series, a tale of interplanetary revenge, and the Planet of Adventure series, both of which however are weakened by the facelessness of the main characters, which is in part a result of length restrictions imposed by their initial paperback publication. Within these settings, the paradigmatic Vance plot is that of the SF *Bildungsroman,* familiar from Heinlein's juvenile SF novels. However, Vance's novels are written for adults, and his heroes soon come to an epiphany in which they realize, in characteristic Vancean rhetoric, they have "to wrench sense from archaic nonsense; to strike the sigil of human will upon elemental chaos; to affirm the shining brilliance of one soul alone but alive among five trillion flaccid gray corpuscles." Yet Vance realizes the danger of such a position, and his typical villains are not far removed from his heroes; as one of the Demon Princes tells the hero, Kirth Gersen, "You are a monomaniac; I am the same." What separates them is the heroes' realistic sense of their place in the universe, both temporally and spatially, Vance's villain "lived in the present, certain only of his own ego; the past was a record, the future an amorphous blot waiting for shape." While his heroes may call themselves "vagabonds" and comment on their "picaresque" adventures, their balanced sense of purpose gives them their significance and interest.

Yet Vance often fools the expectations of readers used to the conventional SF plot of hero conquering through technological, physical, or personal force. In *The Languages of Pao,* Vance's justly celebrated elaboration of the Whorf-Sapir linguistic hypothesis, a false rumor is spread about the young hero's return: "he trained a corps of metal-clad warriors impervious to fire, steel or power; the mission of his life was to avenge his father's death"; yet ironically, the warriors rebel against the hero, and he must instead use language to gain his goal. Vance's most complete subversion occurs in the Durdane trilogy, where the young hero, after defeating an alien invasion, leads an unnecessary war of liberation on their home planet: "The spaceship which they had taken with such grim determination—it actually had come to take them back to Durdane. Small wonder the resistance had been so scant!" This subversion of underlying genre assumptions and reader expectations is the best argument against the accusation that Vance is a mindless swashbuckler.

Vance's output has declined in quantity but certainly not in quality in recent years. The Lyonesse series is his first work of interconnected fantasy (the Dying Earth series being only loosely connected), and exemplifies his strengths of setting and character invention at their best. The Cadwal Chronicles, like many recent series by veteran SF writers, is long, but unlike theirs, not inflated. Freed finally from having to write under the length restrictions of paperback publication, Vance is able to develop his main characters and their societies to their fullest extent. The society of an entire planet, Cadwal, is fully described, and, ironically, it is Old Earth that seems exotically variegated. Vance has been criticized for losing interest in his series as they reach their end, but *Throy,* the last volume of the Cadwal Chronicles, avoids the repetitiveness that mars *Madouc,* the conclusion of the Lyonesse series, and brings the Chronicles to a satisfying conclusion. All Vance's trademarks are present in Cadwal, including a mystery to be solved (Vance has won an Edgar award as well as the Hugo and Nebula) and a genre convention to be toyed with (the long search that takes up most of *Ecce and Old Earth* proves to be unnecessary).

This refreshingly youthful work contains a characteristic scene in which the hero contemplates the universe: "I looked up at the sky and felt a sudden openness—as if my mind were aware of the whole galaxy. At the same time I felt all the millions and billions of people who had spread through the stars. Their lives, or the people, seemed to give off a whir or a hum, really a soft slow music." Vance's singular version of the "sense of wonder," to use SF's hackneyed phrase, is his realization of the ultimate uniqueness of each human being among the possibilities of an infinite universe and of the humanity which inhabits it. This is what propels and informs all of Vance's work, and, along with his imagination and pervasive sense of irony, makes him a significant writer who deserves to be more widely read than his current cult status indicates.

—William Laskowski

VAN LHIN, Eric. *See* **del REY, Lester.**

VAN SCYOC, Sydney J(oyce)

Nationality: American. **Born:** Mt. Vernon, Indiana, 27 July 1939. **Education:** Florida State University, Tallahassee; University of Hawaii, Honolulu; Chabot College, Hayward, California; California State University, Hayward. **Family:** Married Jim R. Van Scyoc in 1957; one daughter and one son, three grandchildren. **Career:** Since 1962, freelance writer. Secretary, 1975-77, and president, 1977-79, Starr King Unitarian Church, Hayward. **Agent:** Howard Morhaim Literary Agency, 501 Fifth Avenue, New York, New York 10017, U.S.A. **Address:** 2636 East Avenue, Hayward, California 94541, U.S.A.

SCIENCE FICTION PUBLICATIONS

Novels (series: Sunstone Scrolls)

Saltflower. New York, Avon, 1971.
Assignment: Nor'Dyren. New York, Avon, 1973.
StarMother. New York, Berkley, 1976.
Cloudcry. New York, Berkley, 1977.
Sunwaifs. New York, Berkley, 1981.

Darkchild (Scrolls). New York, Berkley, 1982; London, Penguin, 1984.

Bluesong (Scrolls). New York, Berkley, 1983; London, Penguin, 1984.

Starsilk (Scrolls). New York, Berkley, 1984.

Drowntide. New York, Berkley, and London, Futura, 1987.

Feather Stroke. New York, Avon, 1989.

Deepwater Dreams. New York, Avon, 1991.

Daughters of the Sunstone (includes *Darkchild, Bluesong,* and *Starsilk*). Garden City, New York, Doubleday, 1985.

*

Manuscript Collection: California State University, Fullerton.

Sydney J. Van Scyoc comments:

(1991) My earlier short fiction was set on Earth in the not-too-distant future and dealt primarily with individuals struggling against an increasingly dehumanizing technological society. I took several years off from writing in the mid-1960s, while my children were very young. Soon after I began writing again, I found my focus had shifted to short fiction set on other planets and dealt primarily with communities struggling against inexplicable alien environments. I am increasingly intrigued now by the genetic and social changes which I believe will overtake the human race once we begin to colonize other planets. I prefer not to deal in much detail with the inevitable technological changes we will see. Instead I like to set my fiction on isolated worlds inhabited by a relatively small human population. My personal orientation is increasingly pantheistic, and in my longer fiction I am attempting to deal with the spiritual relationship of human to environment.

(1995) In June 1992 I bought a pair of jeweler's pliers, intending to undertake a new hobby. By July 1992 I had become enslaved to the designing and making of jewelry. I have not written since. If you see me at a science fiction convention these days, I will be in the dealer's room selling my jewelry. Am I still a writer? I don't know. I generally describe myself as a reformed novelist.

* * *

Sydney J. Van Scyoc's early stories are set on earth not very far in the future and show the dehumanization of persons in an advanced technological society. The dehumanization is primarily apparent in the characters's lack of personal freedom and conscious choice in such stories as "Pollony Undiverted," "Soft and Soupy Whispers," and the chilling "A Visit to Cleveland General." "Nightfire" is an unusual story in which a stalemated war in North America has confined 12 million noncombatants as virtual hostages in orbit above the earth for 41 years. The protagonist, Corneil Rothler, in a carefully planned coup d'etat ruthlessly engineers a truce alone.

A major shift in her work becomes apparent in the long short story "Little Blue Hawk," set in the 21st century; this story focuses on the personal and social costs of human genetic engineering. Van Scyoc's interest in the relationship of human with alien species and an alien ecology appears in "Noepti-Noe," "Sweet Sister, Green Brother," and "Aberrant." These stories emphasize the interdependence and unity of all life forms.

Van Scyoc's impressive first novel, *Saltflower,* takes the basic premise of a dying race seeding earth to generate a transpecies who will be able to reproduce and be viable. The novel is set on earth in the year 2024, and follows the adventures of one of the "transracial" children, Hadley Greer, who is under surveillance by the U.S. government agency SIBling. Most of the action takes place at the Purification Colony's headquarters near Salt Lake City. The Purification Colony is a cult headed by a psychotic leader, Dr. Braith. The novel deftly blends government intrigue, and burgling, religious fanaticism, mysterious murders, and credible alien consciousness, reactions, and biology.

Assignment: Nor'Dyren is an antiutopian novel with strong satiric elements. It begins on earth in the not-too-distant future with a maintenance sub-engineer, Tollan Bailey, attempting to get a job in the huge company CalMega. Only a few people are employed; the rest live comfortable, futile lives without realizing the social controls that narrow their existence. Bailey wins a trip to the planet Nor'Dyren inhabited by three humanoid species whose rigid social roles and asexual interspecies marriage are leading to a breakdown of the moneyless economy and culture. The Gonnegon are the thinkers and administrators, the Allegon serve, and the Berregon manufacture. The novel follows Bailey's attempts to understand the culture and his maturation. He is an appealing character, particularly in his enchantment with trying to repair machines on Nor'Dyren and help the aliens. The anthropologist Laarica Johns, sent to aid him in his legal battle, discovers the reason for the devolution on Nor'Dyren with the help of Patt, a rebellious Berregon. The satire of earth bureaucracy, rigid social and sexual roles, and crippling cultural assumptions both on earth and Nor'Dyren is effective. The novel is an impassioned plea for a humane culture in which persons can be free to develop their capacities and make ethical choices.

Starmother presents the pathos of ostracized human mutants on a colony world, a race of aliens, the dirads, and the testing of the young protagonist, Jahna Swiss, a cadet of the Service Corps from the planet Peace. The novel alternates the points of view of Jahna, Zuniin, an alienated social outcast, and a young mother, Piety, who is a victim of the superstition and fanaticism of the puritanical human colonists, known as The First Fathers, on the planet Nelding. The alien planet, the various social groups, and species are vividly realized. Suspense is generated by the attempt of Zuniin to kill Jahna out of insane jealousy and xenophobia. Jahna's ethical dilemma and her final commitment to the mutant children enrich the novel. Van Scyoc contrasts the civilization of Peace, Jahna's planet, with Nelding, showing the deficiencies of rigid social roles, fanatic religion, and superstition which make life almost unbearable on the unlovely Nelding.

Cloudcry is an expansion and development of the short story "Deathsong." Around the core of the earlier story of an encounter with still-powerful alien artifacts resembling flutes by members of two humanoid races on an alien planet, Van Scyoc has added the framestory of the human space adventurer Verron's search for the man-leopards of the planet Rumar and the complication of a deadly space disease called bloodblossom. Verrons is exiled on the quarantine plant, Selmarii, along with another human, Sadler Wells, and a sentient bird-man alien because they have the disease. Aleida, one of the descendants of the ancient race, has psionic powers and heightens them with a crystal which focuses solar energy. The radiation from the light dancer's flute cures the bloodblossom disease. Verrons leaves the abandoned isolation planet haunted by the prospect of Aleida and a new race of powerful light dancers who do not share humane values. *Cloudcry,* like Van Scyoc's other novels, is distinguished by vivid imagery and sensuous detail, particularly when she portrays non-human perceptions and consciousness.

Sunwaifs continues the author's focus on humans struggling to adapt on uncongenial planets. The sunwaifs are six children born with paranormal mutant abilities, resulting from unusual solar activity during their conception on the harsh planet Destiny. In two alternating points of view over 14 years, the reader follows their development and deepening relationship with the planet. The adaptation of the other humans is aided by the mutant teenagers's increasing understanding of the planet ecology. The climax and resolution of personal and social difficulties comes from an ecological pantheism based on cooperation with natural forces. This hopeful ending promises further enrichment of all intelligent life on the planet Destiny.

Two short stories, "Mountain Wings" and "Darkmorning," set on the harsh planet Brakrath, show the promising direction of Van Scyoc's imagination. This promise is brilliantly fulfilled in the following three novels, set primarily on the same planet. The trilogy, *Darkchild, Bluesong,* and *Starsilk,* forms a major achievement demonstrating her strengths as a science fiction writer: invention of believable alien environments and psychologies which are truly strange, powerful new myths, and striking relationships of humans and aliens with action plots and memorable characters. Perhaps the finest invention is the sentient starsilk which appears in each novel. The starsilk can form a symbiotic relationship with various sentient beings, providing the occasion for effective poetic description; various types of consciousness are presented which have been a strength of Van Scyoc's style for some years. Also notable is the sun goddess myth, which functions to explain the harnessing of solar energy and is the basis for the testing of characters in all three novels. The individual works fit together in a satisfying whole with an epic sweep encompassing several planets, but each novel can be enjoyed independently as good adventure science fiction.

Her strengths as a writer are ALSO evident in two MORErecent novels. *Drowntide* features two credible human cultures on a far planet in the future; each has adapted differently to the presence of sentient whales. The main character's primary conflict involves accepting his real identity and his real people in a kind of bildungsroman journey. There are striking descriptions of the sea and humans communicating with and riding intelligent whales. *Feather Stroke* demonstrates Van Scyoc's continuing antipathy to aristocracies, established religions, and priesthoods that limit freedom of thought and produce tyranny. The "simple folk" have a peaceful, democratic, equalitarian way of life that is beautiful in its utopian simplicity and productivity. The author's interest in sun myths is again shown but in a demonic, masculine way with the priesthood of the sun and the evil antagonist of the novel, Narkin, a firemaster, who must be destroyed. While sharing with the previous novel the theme of finding one's identity, this novel is more engrossing with greater suspense and conflict as Dara, the main character, learns to project her consciousness and perceptions into birds; the descriptions of flight are lyrical.

—Diane Parkin-Speer

van VOGT, A(lfred) E(lton)

Nationality: American. **Born:** near Winnipeg, Manitoba, Canada, 26 April 1912. **Education:** schools in Manitoba, graduated 1928; University of Ottawa; University of California, Los Angeles. **Military Service:** Served in the Department of National Defense, Ottawa, 1939-41. **Family:** Married Lydia I. Brayman (second marriage) in 1979. Census clerk, Ottawa, 1931-32; western representative, Maclean Trade Papers, Winnipeg, 1936-39. Managing director, Hubbard Dianetic Research Foundation of California, Los Angeles, 1950-53; co-owner, Hubbard Dianetic Center, Los Angeles, 1953-61, and president, California Association of Dianetic Auditors, 1958-81. **Awards:** Manuscripters Literature award, 1948; Count Dracula Society Ann Radcliffe award, 1968; Academy of Science Fiction, Fantasy, and Horror Films award, 1979. B.A.: Golden Gate College, Los Angeles. Guest of Honor, 4th World Science Fiction Convention, 1946, European Science Fiction Convention, 1978 and Metz Festival, France, 1985. **Address:** c/o DAW Books, 375 Hudson Street, New York, New York 10014, U.S.A.

SCIENCE FICTION PUBLICATIONS

Novels (series: Clane; Gilbert Gosseyn; Weapon Shop)

Slan. Sauk City, Wisconsin, Arkham House, 1946; revised edition, New York, Simon and Schuster, 1951; London, Weidenfeld and Nicholson, 1953.

The Weapon Makers (Weapon Shop). Providence, Rhode Island, Hadley, 1947; revised edition, New York, Greenberg, 1952; London, Weidenfeld and Nicolson, 1954; as *One Against Eternity,* New York, Ace, 1955.

The Book of Ptath. Reading, Pennsylvania, Fantasy Press, 1947; as *Two Hundred Million A.D.,* New York, Paperback Library, 1964.

The World of Ā (Gosseyn). New York, Simon and Schuster, 1948; revised edition, as *The World of Null-A,* London, Dobson, 1969; New York, Berkley, 1970.

The Voyage of the Space Beagle. New York, Simon and Schuster, 1950; London, Grayson, 1951; as *Mission: Interplanetary,* New York, Signet, 1952.

The House That Stood Still. New York, Greenberg, 1950; London, Weidenfeld and Nicolson, 1953; revised edition, as *The Mating Cry,* New York, Beacon, 1960; as *The Undercover Aliens,* St. Albans, Hertfordshire, Panther, 1976.

The Weapon Shops of Isher. New York, Greenberg, 1951; London, Weidenfeld and Nicolson, 1952.

The Mixed Men. New York, Gnome Press, 1952; as *Mission to the Stars,* New York, Berkley, 1955; London, Digit, 1960.

The Universe Maker. New York, Ace, 1953; in *The Universe Maker, and The Proxy Intelligence,* London, Sidgwick and Jackson, 1976.

Planets for Sale, with E. Mayne Hull. New York, Fell, 1954; London, Panther, 1978.

The Pawns of Null-A (Gosseyn). New York, Ace, 1956; London, Digit, 1960; as *The Players of Null-A,* London, Dobson, 1970.

Empire of the Atom (Clane). Chicago, Shasta, 1957; London, New English Library, 1975.

The Mind Cage: A Science Fiction Novel. New York, Simon and Schuster, 1957; London, Panther, 1960.

Triad: Three Complete Science Fiction Novels (includes *The World of Ā, The Voyage of the Space Beagle,* and *Slan*). New York, Simon and Schuster, 1959.

The War against the Rull. New York, Simon and Schuster, 1959; London, Panther, 1961.

Siege of the Unseen. New York, Ace, 1959; bound with *Earth's Last Fortress* as *The Three Eyes of Evil,* London, Sidgwick and Jackson, 1973.

The Wizard of Linn (Clane). New York, Ace, 1962; London, New English Library, 1976.

The Beast. Garden City, New York, Doubleday, 1963; as *Moonbeast,* London, Panther, 1969.

Rogue Ship. Garden City, New York, Doubleday, 1965; London, Dobson, 1967.

The Winged Man, with E. Mayne Hull. Garden City, New York, Doubleday, 1966; London, Sidgwick and Jackson, 1967.

A Van Vogt Omnibus: Planets for Sale (with E. Mayne Hull), The Beast, The Book of Ptah. London, Sidgwick and Jackson, 1967.

The Silkie. New York, Ace, 1969; London, New English Library, 1973.

Quest for the Future. New York, Ace, 1970; London, Sidgwick and Jackson, 1971.

Children of Tomorrow. New York, Ace, 1970; London, Sidgwick and Jackson, 1972.

Van Vogt Omnibus (2) (includes *Slan, The Mind Cage,* and *The Winged Man*). Sidgewick and Jackson, 1971.

The Battle of Forever. New York, Ace, 1971; London, Sidgwick and Jackson, 1972.

The Darkness on Diamondia. New York, Ace, 1972; London, Sidgwick and Jackson, 1974.

Future Glitter. New York, Ace, 1973; London, Sidgwick and Jackson, 1976; as *Tyranopolis,* London, Sphere, 1977.

The Secret Galactics. Englewood Cliffs, New Jersey, Prentice Hall, 1974; London, Sidgwick and Jackson, 1975; as *Earth Factor X,* New York, DAW, 1976.

The Man with a Thousand Names. New York, DAW, 1974; London, Sidgwick and Jackson, 1975.

The Anarchistic Colossus. New York, Ace, 1977; London, Sidgwick and Jackson, 1978.

Supermind. New York, DAW, 1977; London, Sidgwick and Jackson, 1978.

Renaissance. New York, Pocket Books, 1979.

Cosmic Encounter. Garden City, New York, Doubleday, 1980; London, New English Library, 1981.

Computerworld. New York, DAW, 1983; London, 1985; as *Computer Eye,* Beverly Hills, California, Morrison Raven Hill, 1985.

Null-A Three (Gosseyn). Beverly Hills, Morrison, Raven-Hill, and London, Sphere, 1985.

Short Stories

Out of the Unknown, with E. Mayne Hull, Los Angeles, Fantasy, 1948; London, New English Library, 1970; expanded edition, Reseda, California, Powell, 1969; as *The Sea Thing and Other Stories: Science Fiction,* London, Sidgwick and Jackson, 1970.

Masters of Time (includes *Masters of Time* and *The Changeling*). Reading, Pennsylvania, Fantasy Press, 1950; as *Earth's Last Fortress,* New York, Ace, 1960; *The Changeling* published separately, New York, Macfadden-Bartell, 1967; with *The Three Eyes of Evil,* London, Sidgwick and Jackson, 1973.

Away and Beyond. New York, Pellegrini and Cudahy, 1952; London, Panther, 1963.

Destination: Universe! New York, Pellegrini and Cudahy, 1952; London, Weidenfeld and Nicolson, 1953.

The Twisted Men. New York, Ace, 1964.

Monsters. New York, Paperback Library, 1965; London, Corgi, 1970; as *The Blal,* New York, Zebra, 1976.

The Far-Out Worlds of A.E. van Vogt. New York, Ace, 1968; London, Sidgwick and Jackson, 1973; expanded edition, as *The Worlds of A.E. van Vogt,* Ace, 1974.

More Than Superhuman, with others. New York, Dell, 1971; London, New English Library, 1975.

The Proxy Intelligence and Other Mind Benders. New York, Paperback Library, 1971.

M33 in Andromeda. New York, Paperback Library, 1971.

The Book of van Vogt. New York, DAW, 1972; as *Lost: Fifty Suns,* DAW, 1979; London, New English Library, 1980.

The Best of A.E. van Vogt. London, Sphere, 1974; revised edition, New York, Pocket Books, 1976.

The Gryb. New York, Zebra, 1976; London, New English Library, 1980.

Pendulum. New York, DAW, 1978; London, New English Library, 1982.

The Enchanted Village. Dearborn Heights, Michigan, Misfit Press, 1979.

OTHER PUBLICATIONS

Novel

The Violent Man. New York, Farrar Straus, 1962.

Other

Tomorrow on the March: The Text of a Speech Delivered July 4, 1946, at the Pacificon by the Guest of Honor, A.E. van Vogt. Los Angeles, Time-Bender Press, 1946.

The Hypnotism Handbook, with Charles Edward Cooke. Los Angeles, Griffin, 1956; second edition, 1956.

The Money Personality. West Nyack, New York, Parker, 1972; Wellingborough, Northamptonshire, Thorsons, 1975; as *Unlock Your Money Personality,* Beverly Hills, California, Morrison Raven Hill, 1983.

Reflections of A.E. van Vogt. Lakemont, Georgia, Fictioneer, 1975.

A Report on the Violent Male. Los Angeles, n.d.; Nottingham, England, Paupers' Press, 1992.

*   *   *

In the stories of A.E. van Vogt all things are possible, for saying makes them so. It seems of little moment that any event logically follow the preceding one or that one character dominate the action. For readers expecting tightly structured plots, careful characterization, polished prose style, and a logical extrapolation, van Vogt affords a field day for criticism. (For a classic lambasting on such matters see Damon Knight's "Cosmic Jerrybuilder: A.E. van Vogt" in *In Search of Wonder.*) But for the reader willing to submit his reason to another's wide-ranging imagination van Vogt is a "good read."

van Vogt's canon offers a melange of intriguing situations spiced with telepathy, teleportation, shape control, inner and outer space, mass consciousness, time shifts, technological wonders beyond count. Humans, super-creatures, androids, and aliens perform an intricate dance of adventure on a cosmic stage, existing in past, present, and future time, out-of-time and space as we know them, and often out-of-phase with each other. Incidents bombard us, with little transition to ease the pace. Disconcerting as this can be, it does have the trade-off value of keeping one in continual suspense. In "Complication in the Science Fiction Story" (in *Of Worlds Beyond,* edited by Lloyd Arthur Eshbach, Reading, Pennsylvania, Fantasy Press, 1947; London, Dobson, 1965), van Vogt explained his method of writing scenes in 800-word blocks, the first one to introduce both scene and story purpose. As the main plot develops logically in succeeding scenes, van Vogt adds a secondary plot and minor plot threads deriving from "theme science and atmosphere." While one may question the success of the logical development, there is no argument about van Vogt's ability to handle the minor threads skillfully to induce a sense of mystery, wonder, and suspense.

Since van Vogt writes both short stories and novels, often combining the former to create the latter, a mixed sampling of these modes makes a valid introduction to his characters, situations, and techniques. One especially notices van Vogt's emphasis on superior beings, well exemplified in *The Mixed Men,* a novel combining three short stories. In the earliest story of this group, "The Storm," we meet three super-creatures: the Dellian robots, physically and mentally advanced over man; the non-Dellian robots, higher in creativity; and the Mixed Men of human form but with double brains. Another superhuman, Gilbert Gosseyn of *The World of Null-A,* also has the extra brain, in addition TO possessing the ability to evade death, thus becoming a more godlike entity than Captain Maltby of the Mixed Men.

van Vogt's catalog of aliens ranges from BEM's to intelligent forms fearsome in appearance but cooperative in action, once accepted by men. In *The Voyage of the Space Beagle,* four aliens appear; the catlike Coeurl, the Ixtl, the Riim folk (a colony-psyche), and the anabis. All four pose grave problems to the expedition whose aim is "to explore limits of deep space and contact alien life forms." By contrast, two sympathetic aliens aid men in *The War Against the Rull.* For mutual survival they contribute their telepathetic ability and energy-conducting bodies respectively. The inimical Rull in turn infiltrates human society, using its capability to assume human form. This minor theme of replication appears in many van Vogt tales, starting with "Vault of the Beast" (1940), with the ultimate example being the title character of *The Silkie,* which can shift from fish to bullet-like spaceship to human form to innumerable other shapes for its own purposes and protection.

These aliens often educate man about his own nature. In *The Replicators,* a harmless alien assumes the form of its first human contact, an ex-Marine full of anger and aggressiveness. The resultant trouble is predictable. A more gentle lesson comes from the super-intelligent, catlike creature in "The Cataaaaa." On assignment to study man on earth the Cat does so from the stage of a carnival freak show. The title, linking the Cat with the spontaneous awed exclamation of the carnival crowd, spotlights the human response. The Cat's response comes in the final act of his study when he communicates to one man the conclusion that the basic human characteristic is self-dramatisation. This may well be the most agreeable comment van Vogt can offer about humans. All too often the enemy turns out to be one of our own. In the power struggle that runs as a major theme throughout van Vogt's stories, the specific enemy is often the trusted man-in-charge. Morlake of "The Earth Killers" tracks down the destroyers of civilization, only to find them racists headed by a power-driven ex-senator pretending to be the altruistic guardian of the people.

Critics note in van Vogt a predilection for the power of monarchy, such as held by the Isher empire in *The Weapon Shops of Isher* and the House of Linn in *Empire of the Atom.* More notable is van Vogt's sense of the drama inherent in all authoritarian systems. Finding authority operating all around us, he exploits the emotional possibilities in such situations as the struggle of the "dynasties" in *Rogue Ship,* the parent-child confrontations in *Children of Tomorrow,* and the professional friction aboard the Space Beagle.

However, van Vogt always supplies an antithesis to authoritarianism. Most intriguing are those single characters who perform this duty, those superior beings motivated by a sense of mission and possessing a gift or a powerful idea to be manipulated for benefit of all. The combination is varied: Lesley Craig and "toti-potency" in *Masters of Time;* Elliot Grosvenor and "Nexialism" on the *Space Beagle;* Robert Hedrock and the Weapon Shops opposing Isher power; Gilbert Gosseyn with Null-A training (here van Vogt gives a nod to Alfred Korzybski's *Theory of General Semantics*); and others. A natural extension of this balance is a recognition of the cyclic nature of human society in the character of Morton Cargill of *The Universe Maker.* The most famous "saviour" of human values and idealism is Johnny Cross of *Slan,* the novel usually considered van Vogt's most outstanding. A member of a mutant group hated and persecuted by the majority, the slan Johnny Cross is a telepath, superior both in intelligence and physique to ordinary men. From childhood his training points toward the end of bringing slans and normal men closer together in harmony. He must contend not only with John Petty, the human chief of the secret police, but also with Kier Gray, the head of the government and a slan passing as a normal human.

Slan epitomizes van Vogt's major thematic issues: the tenacity of the life force whatever its form, the need of cooperative effort for mutual survival, and an overwhelming optimism that a consciousness shared with all life forms can work only to a mutual benefit. For the new reader approaching van Vogt, Slan provides a satisfactory entry into van Vogt's provocative and imaginative worlds.

For the seasoned reader of van Vogt, *Computerworld* over 35 years later addresses these major issues in the context of a very contemporary concern: computerized control. In the near-future of 2094 the omnipresent, multiform computer has relieved humans of all onerous labor but has sapped them of moral energy. Through Eye-O ports it tracks human activity, registering data for identification and correcting aberrant behaviour with weapons of graduated power. Questions arise. Who will control this force? How can the spiritual sense necessary for humanness exist in the strictly logical environment of the machine? The protagonist-computer asks the key question: "How does a human differ from a machine?" Only when it develops a "sense of self" comes the recognition that uniqueness requires cooperative understanding for coexistence, that recognition being a basic van Vogtian theme.

This requirement for cooperative understanding for coexistence finds one of its most complete treatments in van Vogt's three-part series featuring the Gilbert Gosseyns. The series is noted not only for its content but also for the dramatic events spurring van Vogt's revisions and writing of sequels (see van Vogt's personal introduction to the first two novels *in re* scathing reviews and reader discontent) and for the time span between the first and last volumes. The span suggests the original philosophical ideas and plot lines fermented some 40 years in the author's mind, urging logical completion.

The Gosseyn story of three duplicate bodies, each with an extra brain, able to share memories, objectives, and communication with each other over light years of space, takes the reader to a universe of 2560. This world is filled with various human civilizations, many engaged in interstellar and/or galactic power struggles. The Gosseyns serve as models of Null-A or non-Aristotelian way of thought. In other words, they seek to shift each group from seeing problems as either/or situations to using multi-valued maps of reality, in accordance with Alfred Korzybski's theory of general semantics (see his 1933 book, *Science and Sanity*). A reader can find testimony to van Vogt's reliance on *General Semantics* not only in the above-mentioned introduction but also in the many epigraphs to chapters of the novels, especially in *The Players of Null-A*.

In the Null-A novels, van Vogt uses many of the aspects of space opera: space ships, interplanetary travel, alien forms with human responses, extrasensory perception, ability to traverse time and space. Van Vogt also combines some of the characteristics of spy thrillers and mystery stories: interstellar power struggles, conspiracies to seize control of solar systems, leaks of pertinent information bringing about adverse results. More important is the pervasive thought running through all three novels: with a shift in human reasoning from the restricted Aristotelian pattern to a Null-A pattern a better world would result. Near the end of *Null-A Three*, the authorial voice breaks into the narrative to offer readers a thought worthy of deep consideration: "The very heart of a system of absolute power modified to include democratic procedures."

—Hazel Pierce

VARDRE, Leslie. *See* **DAVIES, L.P.**

VARLEY, John

Pseudonym: Herb Boehm. **Nationality:** American. **Born:** Austin, Texas, in 1947. **Education:** Attended Michigan State University, East Lansing, 1966. **Family:** Married Anet Mconel; three sons. **Career:** Since 1973, freelance writer. **Awards:** *Locus* award, 1977, 1979 (twice), 1981, 1982 (twice); Jupiter award, 1978; Nebula award, 1979, 1984; Hugo award, 1984; Prix Apollo, 1979; Science Fiction Chronicle award, 1985. **Address:** Lives in Eugene, Oregon. **Agent:** Kirby McCauley Ltd., 432 Park Avenue South, New York, New York 10016, U.S.A.

SCIENCE FICTION PUBLICATIONS

Novels (series: Gaea)

The Ophiuchi Hotline. New York, Dial Press, 1977; London, Sidgwick and Jackson, 1978.
Titan (Gaea). New York, Berkley, and London, Sidgwick and Jackson, 1979.
Wizard (Gaea). New York, Berkley, 1980; London, Futura, 1981.
Millennium. New York, Berkley, 1983; London, Sphere, 1985.
Demon (Gaea). New York, Putnam, 1984; London, Futura, 1985.
Steel Beach. New York, Ace/Putnam, 1992; London, HarperColLins, 1993.

Short Stories

The Persistence of Vision. New York, Dial Press, 1978; as *In the Hall of the Martian Kings: Science Fiction,* London, Sidgwick and Jackson, 1978.

The Barbie Murders. New York, Berkley, 1980; London, Orbit, 1983; as *Picnic on Nearside,* New York, Berkley, 1984.
Blue Champagne. Niles, Illinois, Dark Harvest, 1986.
Tango Charlie and Foxtrot Romeo, bound with *The Star Pit,* by Samuel R. Delany. New York, Berkley, 1984.
Press Enter, bound with *Hawksbill Station,* by Robert Silverberg. New York, Tor, 1990.
The Persistence of Vision (novella), bound with *Nanoware Time,* by Ian Watson. New York, Tor, 1991.

OTHER PUBLICATIONS

Plays

Screenplays: *Galaxy,* 1978; *Millennium,* 1983.

Editor, with Ricia Mainhardt, *Superheroes.* New York, Ace, 1995.

*

Manuscript Collection: Special Collections, Temple University, Philadelphia.

*   *   *

Although John Varley has produced relatively few novels, he merits consideration for his inventiveness. His first novel, *The Ophiuchi Hotline,* takes place in a time in the future after mysterious invaders have come to our solar system and done away with human technology. This novel exhibits an environmentalist's bias in that the Invaders have abolished earth's industrial-technical system to save whales and dolphins who, as some have long suspected, outclass humans in their intellectual potentiality. Yet someone out there wants humankind to survive, for, over the decades, a "hotline" to a mysterious presence in another part of the universe continues to feed the remaining people information vital to their survival. Part of the story revolves around the attempt to discover who these "good Samaritans" are. For a short novel, *The Ophiuchi Hotline* certainly does not lack action; in fact, so much goes on that the plot at times becomes confusing.

Varley exhibits better control over his enthusiasm for inventing new worlds and improbable beings in his series consisting of *Wizard, Titan,* and *Demon* which chronicles the adventures of a displaced earth women, Cirocco Jones, sometimes-NASA-spaceship-pilot and adventurer. Not content simply to send her to another planet—in this case Saturn—to struggle against aliens, Varley turns the planet itself into a sentient being, the quasi-goddess Gaea. The trilogy follows Jones's transformation from friendly adventurer learning about Gaea's whimsical personality, to an alcoholic "wizard" in Gaea's employ, and finally to the only adversary who can vanquish the "goddess"-gone-mad and save the many lifeforms that populate this fascinating ring world. In this series we are asked to consider space opera from a moderately feminist point of view. At least that seems to be the perspective Varley wants his readers to take, for most of his major characters are either completely female or oddly bisexual. In some ways his focus on lesbian relationships is gratuitous; ultimately, the romantic couplings and jealousies add little to the trilogy's sense of entertainment which, in fact, is derived from the familiar quest-adventure motif found so frequently in science fiction.

Millennium considers an equally odd topic, human catastrophes. It seems that for as long as people have been mass-murdering each other or having accidents involving large numbers of people, a group of time travelers have been snagging the victims and whisking them through a time port to the far-future. These time travelers stand close to the end of life on earth; these kidnapping efforts represent their attempt to perpetuate life at a time millions of years beyond their immediate destruction. Varley combines and makes interesting twists on catastrophe/Bermuda Triangle themes, theories concerning the nature of time, and an old-fashioned love story between future alien and 20th-century deadbeat. The results entertain because *Millennium* resists the standard clichés of time travel and end-of-the-world tales.

Varley's short stories concern themselves with the same topics that he raises in his novels: speculations of the quality of life in the future, cloning, the nature of the alien "personality," to name a few. Like his novels, these stories are entertaining, and, like his novels, they also demand a certain degree of patient toleration on the part of their reader. Varley likes to pack his writing with action, gadgets, and many characters. Frequently the reader must untangle some of the snarls this type of writing inevitably creates. Although such roughness can irritate, Varley is a writer worth reading: he entertains because he isn't afraid to take risks with his plots, characters, or inventive view of the future. Furthermore, he takes fresh and timely perspectives on old chestnuts: love, war, the environment, and a human's place in the universe.

—Melissa E. Barth

VARSHAVSKY, Ilya

Nationality: Russian. **Born:** 1909.

SCIENCE FICTION PUBLICATIONS

Short Stories

"In Man's Own Image," in *Russian Science Fiction 1968,* edited by Robert Magidoff, n.p., 1968.
"Out in Space," in *Last Door to Aiya,* edited by Mirra Ginsburg, n.p., 1968.
"A Raid Takes Place at Midnight," in *Russian Science Fiction 1969,* edited by Robert Magidoff, n.p., 1969.
"Preliminary Research," in *The Ultimate Threshold,* edited by Mirra Ginsburg, n.p., 1970.
"Biocurrents, Biocurrents," in *Other Worlds, Other Seas,* edited by Darko Suvin, n.p., 1970.
"Lectures on Parapsychology," in *Other Worlds, Other Seas,* edited by Darko Suvin, n.p., 1970.
"The Noneaters," in *Other Worlds, Other Seas,* edited by Darko Suvin, n.p., 1970.
"Somp," in *Other Worlds, Other Seas,* edited by Darko Suvin, n.p., 1970.
"Robby," in *Path into the Unknown,* n.p., 1973.
"Escape," in *Best SF 1973,* edited by Harry Harrison and Brian Aldiss, n.p., 1974.

*   *   *

Ilya Varshavsky's main interests are thinking machines, space travel, and advanced medical and mechanical technology. His attitude toward science is generally humorous or ironic, but at times bitingly satiric or questioning. He expresses nostalgia for the beauty and spirit of the 20th century.

Varshavsky's machines are subject not only to the laws of mathematical logic but to those of self-organization, which demand that robots eventually develop the impulses and drives of humans. For example, when confronted with "death," they are impelled to reproduce themselves ("Homunculus"); rather than harm their robot children, they choose a life of frustration ("Conflict"); thoughts of soccer and redheads can subvert them ("The Duel"); like any vocabulary-gifted human, they can develop into pompous, abusive, tricky, intellectually perverse beings ("Robby"). Of interest to Varshavsky is the relationship between language and humanness, as well as the obstacles to a robot's thinking processes posed by connotation, non-objective reality, and accidental characteristics.

Varshavsky uses space travel to examine his ideas on closed-circuit systems (animal organisms in "The Noneaters"; time in "The Trap"); the effects of man on other life forms ("Lilac Planet"; "The Noneaters"); the continuity of human qualities, from petty to heroic ("The Return"). He twits simpleton-scientists ("Somp"; "Lectures on Parapsychology"; "A Raid Takes Place at Midnight"); castigates those who sell their minds to blind projects ("Preliminary Research"); and satirizes science-fiction writers who do anything for a plot. He questions both means and ends of psycho-scientists ("Escape") and ponders the human complications of organ transplants ("Plot for a Novel").

—Rosemary Coleman

VERCORS

Pseudonym for Jean (Marcel) Bruller. **Other Pseudonym:** J. Bruller Vercors. **Nationality:** French. **Born:** Paris, 26 February 1902. **Education:** Attended University of Paris and a technical college, received diploma in electrical engineering; studied art in Paris after military service. **Military Service:** French Army, served in Alpine regiment in Tunis, 1940; became lieutenant. **Family:** Married 1) Jeanne Barusseaud in 1931 (divorced); 2) Rita Bariss in 1957; three sons. **Career:** Novelist, essayist, and artist specializing in graphic art and engraving; founder, with Pierre de Lescure, of Editions de Minuit (publishing house for French Resistance movement), 1941; lecturer, 1945-. Designer of sets and costumes for Comedie Francaise, Paris, 1964. **Awards:** Legion d'honneur; medaille de la Resistance; Council of Europe prize, 1982. **Died:** 10 June 1991.

SCIENCE FICTION PUBLICATIONS

Novels

Les animaux dénaturés. Paris, Albin Michel, 1952; translated by Rita Barisse as *You Shall Know Them,* Boston, Little Brown, 1953; as *Borderline,* London, Macmillan, 1954; as *The Murder of the Missing Link,* New York, Pocket Books, 1955.

Sylva. Paris, Editions Bernard Grasset, 1961; translated by Rita Barisse, New York, Putnam, 1962; as *Sylvia,* London, Hutchinson, 1962.

OTHER PUBLICATIONS

Novels

Le silence de la mer. Paris, Les Editions de Minuit, 1942; translated by Cyril Connolly as *Put out the Light,* London, Macmillan, 1944; as *The Silence of the Sea,* New York, Macmillan, 1944.
La marche à l'étoiles. Paris, Les Editions de Minuit, 1943; translated by Eric Sutton as *Guiding Star,* London, Macmillan, 1946.
Colères. Paris, Albin Michel, 1956; translated by Rita Barisse as *The Insurgents,* New York, Harcourt, 1956.
P.P.C. Paris, Albin Michel, 1957; translated by Jonathan Griffin as *For the Time Being,* London, Hutchinson, 1960.
Sur ce rivage. Paris, Albin Michel, 1958; vols. 2 and 3 translated by Rita Barisse as *Freedom in December,* London, Hutchinson, 1961.
Quota. Paris, Stock, 1966; translated by Rita Barisse, New York, Putnam, 1966.
Le radeau de la Médusa. Paris, Presses de la Cité, 1969; translated by Audre C. Foote as *The Raft of the Medusa,* New York, McCall, 1971.

Short Stories

Three Short Novels. Translated from the French by Eric Sutton and H.M. Chevalier, Boston, Little Brown, 1947.
Paths of Love. Translated from the French by Rita Barisse, New York, Putnam, 1961.

Other

Bataille du silence. Paris, Presses de la Cité, 1967; translated by Rita Barisse as *The Battle of Silence,* New York, Holt, and London, Collins, 1968.

*   *   *

Although never really considered a genre writer, Vercors contributed two interesting and well-crafted novels to the field. *Sylva* is a poetic fantasy about a fox that changes magically into a human woman before the eyes of a hunter. The man falls in love with this wereperson, but the peculiarities of her origin provide rather unusual stresses in their married life. *Sylva* bears more than a passing resemblance to David Garnett's fantasy *Lady into Fox,* though with a more coherent plot. There are traces of satire as well, much in the tradition of John Collier's *His Monkey Wife* or Mikhail Bulgakov's *Heart of a Dog.* But Vercors is less a humorist than a novelist, and his novel portrays a touching love story that transcends the gimmick that might otherwise seem central to the story.

At the same time, *Sylva* reflects the concerns mentioned in his more significant novel, *You Shall Know Them.* We are told in the latter that "all man's troubles arise from the fact that we do not know what we are and do not agree on what we want to be." The relevance to the lady into fox theme is obvious, but the statement has equal validity when applied to the latter novel. A thoughtful man becomes aware of the existence of a subhuman race on Earth, the legendary missing link in our own evolutionary climb. Con-

cerned about their exploitation by the rest of humanity, he embarks on a bizarre course to determine their legal humanity. He sires a child which he then kills, confessing himself a murderer and surrendering to the authorities. The stage is hereby set for a precedent-setting murder trial, for if the protagonist is indeed guilty of murder, then the subhumans must be considered our equals and be protected by the law. If they are not to be considered as human, then he has not in fact committed anything worse than cruelty to animals. In conception, this is one of the finest novels in the genre, establishing and examining a genuine ethical question with ruthless realism. At the same time, it is a well-balanced, craftily written tale that should appeal to all readers. Indeed, the novel has been marketed as a mystery, which in at least one sense it is. But it is also that most rare of creations, a novel of science fiction that tells us something about ourselves and our society.

Only one other of Vercors's novels can truly be said to be science fiction. *The Insurgents* chronicles one man's search for physical immortality, and the perils and prices inherent in both the search and the attainment. Thematically, it is remarkably similar to Aldous Huxley's *After Many a Summer,* and in some ways is more effectively handled.

—Don D'Ammassa

VERNE, Jules

Nationality: French. **Born:** Nantes, 8 February 1828. **Family:** Married Honorine (de Viane) Morel in 1857; one son and two stepdaughters. **Education:** Attended local schools; studied law in Paris. **Career:** Worked variously as a stockbroker, private law instructor, and secretary of Theatre Lyrique; wrote plays, some with the younger Alexandre Dumas; served on the municipal council in Amiens. **Awards:** Chevalier of the Legion of Honor. **Died:** 24 March 1905.

SCIENCE FICTION PUBLICATIONS

Novels (series: Baltimore Gun Club; Captain Hatteras; Captain Nemo; Floating City; Hector Servadac; Robur the Conqueror)

De la terre à la lune trajet direct en 97 heures (Gun Club). Paris, Hetzel, 1865; translated by J.K. Hoyt as *From the Earth to the Moon: Passage Direct in 97 Hours and 20 Minutes,* Newark, New Jersey, Newark Printing, 1869; bound with *A Trip around It,* London, Sampson Low, 1873; as *The American Gun Club,* New York, Scribner Armstrong, 1874; as *The Baltimore Gun Club,* Philadelphia, King and Baird, 1874; as *The Moon-Voyage,* London, Ward, Lock and Tyler, 1877; as *A Voyage to the Moon,* Girard, Kansas, Haldeman-Julius, 1923; translated by I.O. Evans as *From the Earth to the Moon,* London, Arco, 1959.
Voyage au centre de la terre. Paris, Hetzel, 1864; translated as *A Journey to the Centre of the Earth,* London, Griffith and Farran, 1872; New York, Scribner Armstrong, 1984; as *A Journey into the Interior of the Earth,* London, Ward, Lock and Tyler, 1975; as *A Trip to the Center of the Earth,* New York, Didier, 1950; translated by William Butcher as *Journey to the Centre of the Earth,* Oxford and New York, Oxford University Press, 1992.

Vingt mille lieus sous les mers (Captain Nemo). Paris, Hetzel, 2 vols., 1869-70 ; translated as *Twenty Thousand Leagues under the Sea,* London, Sampson Low, 1872; Boston, Smith, 1873; translated by Emanuel J. Mickel as *The Complete Twenty Thousand Leagues under the Sea,* Bloomington, Indiana University Press, 1991.

Autour de la lune. Paris, Hetzel, c. 1870; as *A Trip around it,* bound with *From the Earth to the Moon,* London, Sampson Low, 1874; as *Round the Moon,* 1976; as *All around the Moon,* Catholic Publication Society, 1876; translated by I.O. Evans as *Round the Moon,* London, Arco, 1959.

Une ville flottante, suivi Les forceurs de blocus. Paris, Hetzel, 1871; translated as *A Floating City, and The Blockade Runners,* London, Sampson Low, 1874; New York, Scribner Armstrong, 1875; in two volumes, London, Sampson Low, 1876.

Le tour du monde en quatre-vingts jour. Paris, Hetzel, 1873; translated as *The Tour of the World in Eighty Days,* Boston, Osgood, 1873; as *Around the World in Eighty Days,* London, Sampson Low, 1873; translated by William Butcher, Oxford and New York, Oxford University Press, 1995.

L'isle mystérieuse. Paris, Hetzel, 3 vols., 1874-75; translated as *The Mysterious Island: Shipwrecked in the Air, Dropped from the Clouds,* [and] *Abandoned* 3 vols., London, Sampson Low, and New York, Scribner Armstrong, 1874-76; in 1 vol., New York, Scribner, 1918; in 2 vols., London, Hanison, 1959.

Les Anglais au pole nord: aventures du Capitaine Hatteras. Paris, Hetzel, 1866; translated as *At the North Pole,* Philadelphia, Porter and Coates, 1874; as *The English at the North Pole,* London and New York, Routledge, 1874; as *A Journey to the North Pole,* Boston, Osgood, 1875; as *The Adventures of Captain Hatteras,* London, 1876.

Le désert de glace: aventures du Capitaine Hatteras. Paris, Hetzel, 1866; translated as *The Desert of Ice,* Philadelphia, Porter and Coates, 1874; as *The Field of Ice,* London and New York, Routledge, 1875; as *The Ice Desert,* London, Ward Lock, 1937; translated by I.O. Evans as *The Wilderness of Ice,* London, Arco, 1961.

Hector Servadac: voyages et aventures à travers le monde solaire. Paris, Hetzel, 2 vols., 1877; translated and abridged as *Hector Servadac: Travels and Adventures through the Solar System,* New York, Munro, 1877; as *Hector Servadac; or, The Career of a Comet,* London, Sampson Low, 1878; in 2 vols. as *To the Sun? A Journey through Planetary Space* [and] *Off on a Comet: A Journey through interplanetary Space,* Philadelphia, Claxton, Remsen, and Haffelfinger, 1878; in 2 vols. as *Anomalous Phenomenon* [and] *Homeward Bound,* London, Arco, 1965.

Les cinq centes millions de la bégum. Bound with translation of *Mutiny on the Bounty,* by Nordstrom and Hall, Paris, Hetzel, 1879; translated as *The Begum's Fortune,* Philadelphia, Lippincott, and London, Sampson Low, 1879; as *The 500 Millions of the Begum,* New York, Munro, 1879.

La maison à vapeur: voyage à travers l'Inde septentrionale. Paris, Hetzel, 2 vols., 1880; translated as *The Steam House; or, A Trip across Northern India,* New York, Munro, 1880-81; in 2 vols. as *The Demon of Cawnpore* and *Tigers and Traitors,* London, Sampson Low, and New York, Munro, 1887.

Robur-le-conquérant. Paris, Hetzel, 1886; translated as *The Clipper of the Clouds,* London, Sampson Low, 1887 ; as *Robur the Conqueror; or, A Trip around the World in a Flying Machine,* New York, Munro, 1887.

Sans dessus dessous (Gun Club). Paris, Hetzel, 1889; translated as *Topsy-Turvy,* New York, Ogilve, 1890; as *The Purchase of the North Pole,* London, Sampson Low, 1890.

Le château des Carpathes. Paris, Hetzel, 1892; translated as *The Castle of the Carpathians,* London, Sampson Low, 1893; New York, Merriam, 1894; as *Carpathian Castle,* London, Arco, 1963.

L'isle à hélice. Paris, Hetzel, 1895; translated as *The Floating Island; or, The Pearl of the Pacific,* London, Sampson Low, 1896; New York, Allison, 1900(?); as *Propeller Island,* London, Arco, 1961.

Face au drapeau. Paris, Hetzel, 1896; translated as *For the Flag,* London, Sampson Low, 1897; as *Facing the Flag,* New York, Neely, 1897.

Le sphinx des glaces. Paris, Hetzel, 2 vols., 1897; translated as *An Antarctic Mystery,* London, Sampson Low, 1898; bound with *The Mystery of Arthur Gordon Pym,* by Edgar Allan Poe and Jules Verne, edited by Basil Ashmore, London, Arco, 1961; edited by Harold Beaver, London, Penguin, 1975.

Le village aérien. Paris, Hetzel, 1901; translated as *Village in the Treetops,* London, Arco, 1964.

Maître du monde. Paris, Hetzel, 1904; translated as *The Master of the World,* London, Sampson Low, 1914; Philadelphia, Lippincott, 1915.

La chasse au météore. Paris, Hetzel, 1908; translated as *The Chase of the Golden Meteor,* London, Grant Richards, 1909; as *The Hunt for the Meteor,* London, Arco, 1965.

L'étonnante aventure de la mission Barsac. Paris, Hetzel, 1919; translated as *The Barsac Mission: The City in the Sahara* [and] *Into the Niger Bend,* London, Arco, 2 vols., 1960.

Le secret de Wilhelm Storitz. Paris, Hetzel, 1910; translated as *The Secret of Wilhelm Storitz,* London, Arco, 1963.

Paris au XXᵉ siècle. Paris, Hetzel, 1994; translated by Richard Howard as *Paris in the Twentieth Century,* New York, Random House, 1996.

Short Stories

Le docteur Ox. Translation by George Towle published in *Doctor Ox and Other Stories,* Boston, Osgood, 1874; as *Doctor Ox's Experiment and Other Stories,* London, 1874; Boston, Osbood, 1875; story published separately, New York, Munro, 1879.

From the Clouds to the Mountains: Comprising Narratives of Strange Adventures by Air, Land and Water. Boston, Gill, 1874.

Hier et demain. Paris, Hetzel, 1910; translated as *Yesterday and Tomorrow,* London, Arco, 1965.

Aventures de la famille raton. Translation by Evely Copeland published as *Adventures of the Rat Family: A Fairy Tale,* New York, Oxford University Press, 1993.

OTHER PUBLICATIONS

Novels

Cinq semaines en ballon: voyages de découvertes en Afrique. Paris, Hetzel, 1863; translated by William Lackland as *Five Weeks in a Balloon,* New York, Appleton, 1869; London, Chapman and Hall, 1870.

Les enfants du Capitaine Grant. Paris, Hetzel, 3 vols., 1867-68; translated as *In Search of the Castaways,* Philadelphia, Lippincott, 1873; as *A Voyage round the World,* London, Routledge, 3 vols., 1876-77; as *Captain Grant's Children,* London, Arco, 2 vols., 1960.

Aventures de trois Russes et de trois Anglais. Paris, Hetzel, 1872; translated as *Meridiana,* London, Sampson Low, 1873; as *Three Englishmen and Three Russians in South Africa,* London and New York, Routledge, 187(?); translated by I.O. Evans as *Measuring a Meridian,* London, Arco, 1964.

L pays des fourrures. Paris, Hetzel, 1873; translated as *The Fur Country,* London, Sampson Low, and Boston, Osgood, 1874; as *Sun in Eclipse* [and] *Through the Bering Strait,* London, Arco, 2 vols., 1966.

Le Chancellor: journal du passager J.-R. Kazallon. Bound with *Martin Paz,* Paris, Hetzel, 1875; translated as *The Survivors of the Chancellor,* London, Sampson Low, 1875; as *The Wreck of the Chancellor,* Boston, Osgood, 1875; as *The Chancellor,* London, Arco, 1965.

Martin Paz. Bound with *Le Chancellor,* Paris, Hetzel, 1875; translated by Ellen E. Frewer, London, Sampson Low, 1876; New York, Fitch, 1879; as *The Pearl of Lima,* New York, Munro, 1879.

Michel Strogoff, Moscou-Irkoutsk. Paris, Hetzel, 2 vols., 1876; translated as *Michel Strogoff, the Courier of the Czar,* London, Sampson Low, and New York, Scribner Armstrong, 1877.

Les Indes-noires. Paris, Hetzel, 1877; translated as *The Child of the Cavern,* London, Sampson Low, 1877; as *The Black Indies,* New York, Munro, 1878(?); as *Underground City,* Philadelphia, Porter and Coates, 1883; as *Black Diamonds,* London, Arco, 1961.

Un capitaine de quinze ans. Paris, Hetzel, 2 vols., 1878; translated as *Dick Sand; or, A Captain at Fifteen,* New York, Munro, 1878; as *Dick Sands, the Boy Captain,* London, Sampson Low, 1879.

Les tribulations d'une chinois en Chine. Paris, Hetzel, 1879; translated as *The Tribulations of a Chinaman in China,* New York, Munro, 1879; London, Sampson Low, 1880; as *The Tribulations of a Chinese Gentleman,* London, Arco, 1963.

La Jaganda: hit centes lieus sur l'Amazon. Paris, Hetzel, 2 vols., 1881; translated as *The Giant Raft: Eight Hundred Leagues on the Amazon* [and] *The Cryptogram,* London, Sampson Low, 2 vols., 1881; New York, Scribner, 2 vols., 1881-82; as *The Jangada,* New York, Munro, 2 vols., 1881-82.

L'écoles des Robinsons. Paris, Hetzel, 1882; translated as *Robinson's School,* New York, Munro, 1883; as *Godfrey Morgan: A California Mystery,* London, Sampson Low, and New York, Scribner, 1883; as *The School for Crusoes,* London, Arco, 1966.

Le rayon-vert. Bound with *Dix heures en chasse,* Paris, Hetzel, 1882; translated as *The Green Ray,* London, Sampson Low, and New York, Munro, 1883.

Kéraban-le-têtu. Paris, Hetzel, 2 vols., 1883; translated as *The Headstrong Turk,* New York, Munro, 2 vols., 1883-84; as *Kéraban the Inflexible: The Captain of the Guidara* [and] *Scarpante the Spy,* London, Sampson Low, 2 vols., 1884-85.

L'étoile de sud: le pays des diamants. Paris, Hetzel, 1884; translated as *The Vanished Diamond: A Tale of South Africa,* London, Sampson Low, 1885; as *The Southern Star,* New York, Munro, 1885.

L'archipel en feu. Paris, Hetzel, 1884; translated as *The Archipelago on Fire,* New York, Munro, 1885; London, Sampson Low, 1886.

L'épave du Cynthia. Paris, Hetzel, 1885; translated as *The Waif of the "Cynthia,"* New York, Munro, 1886; as *Salvage from the Cynthia,* London, Arco, 1964.

Mathias Sandorf. Paris, Hetzel, 3 vols., 1885; translated, New York, Munro, 2 vols., 1885; London, Sampson Low, 1886.

Un billet de loterie (le numéro 9672). Bound with *Fritt-Flacc,* Paris, Hetzel, 1886; translated as *Ticket No. "9672,"* New York, Munro, 1885; as *The Lottery Ticket: A Tale of Tellemarken,* London, Sampson Low, 1887.

Fritt-Flacc. Bound with *Un billet de loterie,* Paris, Hetzel, 1886; translated as *Fritt Flacc,* New York, Futuria House, 1947.

Nord contre sud. Paris, Hetzel, 2 vols., 1887; translated as *Texar's Vengeance; or, North versus South,* New York, Munro, 1887; as *North against South: A Tale of the American Civil War,* London, Sampson Low, 1888; as *Burbank the Northerner* [and] *Texar the Southerner,* London, Arco, 2 vols., 1963.

Le chemin de France. Bound with *Gil Braltar,* Paris, Hetzel, 1887; translated as *The Flight to France; or, The Memoirs of a Dragoon,* London, Sampson Low, and New York, Lovell, 1888.

Deux ans de vacances. Paris, Hetzel, 2 vols., 1888; translated as *Adrift in the Pacific,* London, Sampson Low, 1889; as *A Two Years' Vacation,* New York, Munro, 1889; as *Two Years' Holiday: Adrift in the Pacific* [and] *Second Year Ashore,* London, Arco, 2 vols., 1963; as *A Long Vacation,* New York, Holt, and London, Oxford University Press, 1967.

Famille-sand-nom. Paris, Hetzel, 1889; translated as *A Family without a Name,* New York, Lovell, 1889; London, Sampson Low, 1891; as *Leader of the Resistance* [and] *Into the Abyss,* London, Arco, 2 vols., 1966.

César Cascabel. Paris, Hetzel, 2 vols., 1890; translated, New York, Cassell, 1890, London, Sampson, 1891, as *The Travelling Circus* [and] *The Show on Ice,* London, Arco, 2 vols., 1966.

Mistress Branican. Paris, Hetzel, 2 vols., 1891; translated, New York, Cassell, 1891; London, Sampson Low, 1892.

Claudius Bombarnac. Paris, Hetzel, 1892; translated, London, Sampson Low, and New York, Hurst, 1894; as *The Special Correspondent,* New York, Lovell, 1894.

P'tit-bonhomme. Paris, Hetzel, 2 vols., 1893; translated as *Foundling Mick,* London, Sampson Low, 1895.

Mirifiques aventures de maître Andifer. Paris, Hetzel, 2 vols., 1894; translated as *Captain Andifer,* London, Sampson Low, and New York, Fenno, 1895.

Clovis Dardentor. Paris, Hetzel, 1896; translated, London, Sampson Low, 1897.

Le testament d'un excentrique. Paris, Hetzel, 2 vols., 1899; translated as *The Will of an Eccentric,* London, Sampson Low, 1900.

Seconde patrie. Paris, Hetzel, 2 vols., 1900; translated as *Their Island Home* [and] *The Castaways of the Flag,* 2 vols., London, Sampson Low, 1823; New York, Watt, 1924.

Les histoires de Jean-Marie Cabidoulin. Paris, Hetzel, 1901; translated as *The Sea Serpent: The Yards of Jean Marie Cabidoulin,* London, Arco, 1967.

Un drame en Livonie. Paris, Hetzel, 1904; translated as *A Drama in Livonia,* London, Arco, 1967.

Le phare du bout du monde. Paris, Hetzel, 1905; translated as *The Lighthouse at the End of the World,* London, Sampson Low, 1923; New York, Watt, 1924.

Le volcan d'or. Paris, Hetzel, 2 vols., 1906; translated as *The Golden Volcano: The Claim on Forty Mile Creek* [and] *Flood and Flame,* London, Arco, 2 vols., 1962.

L'Agence Thompson and Co. Paris, Hetzel, 2 vols., 1907; translated as *The Thompson Travel Agency: Package Holiday* [and] *End of the Journey,* London, Arco, 2 vols., 1965.

Le pilote du Danube. Paris, Hetzel, 1908; translated as *The Danube Pilot,* London, Arco, 1967.

Les naugragés du Jonathan. Paris, Hetzel, 2 vols., 1909; translated as *The Survivors of the Jonathan: The Masterless Man* [and] *The Unwilling Dictator,* London, Arco, 2 vols., 1962.

Short Stories

The Winter amid the Ice and Other Stories. N.p., 1890.

*   *   *

The key biographical fact in Jules Verne's life, for the understanding of his voyages extraordinaires, is his induction, at the height of his fame, into the French Legion of Honor by none other than Ferdinand de Lesseps, builder of the Suez Canal and a disciple of Henri Saint-Simon. Saint-Simon is the pre-Marxist patriarch of socialism, whose disciples coined the very word for "socialism," and who meant by it what we mean by the word "technocracy." They worshipped industrial production as a worldwide process, not merely the international proletarian worker as in later Marxism, and their slogan was "The whole world belongs to mankind." Their romantic globalism is captured in Verne's most famous novel, *Around the World in Eighty Days.* The Saint-Simonians were apostles of world transport and a world-industrial civilization, to which the Suez Canal was a programmatic contribution.

Their view was that the industrial revolution would make for the socialist revolution, replacing the feudalistic love of war with peaceful production, and Catholic theology with science; thereby uniting mankind in universal association for the exploitation of nature, instead of being divided for the exploitation of nature, instead of being divided for the exploitation of man by man. Verne's great novelization of this doctrinal thesis is From the Earth to the Moon.

Verne wrote this novel during the fourth year of the American Civil War. As a Saint-Simonian socialist, he pondered on American wartime technology, wondering how it might be converted to peacetime industry. How redirect these destructive energies into a creative project? His answer, as the war concluded, was symbolically to melt down its entire arsenal of cannons in the casting of the *Columbiad* for the peaceful colonization of space and the development of interplanetary travel. But the moonshot is not America's project alone. While a civilian spinoff of her military technology, the Baltimore Gun Club that initiated the project raises funds for it from a worldwide subscription. All humanity is drawn into it with a collective enthusiasm. The Gun Club itself is internationalized on the model of the Council of Newton—the name Saint-Simon gave the brain center of his technocratic council of world direction—as it calls upon scientific talent wherever it is to be found, including the world's astronomers to track the moon capsule in flight. Moreover, the Gun Club's council of directors wins to its purpose the happy collaboration of the American work force, organized on a gigantic scale as one national workshop of united interests. This is a harbinger of Saint-Simon's prophecy: "All men shall work; they will regard themselves as laborers attached to one workshop and whose efforts will be directed by the supreme Council of Newton."

In its exalted atmosphere of class collaboration between captains of industry and the proletarian workers, all this in the service of man's harmonious conquest of nature, the novel is a technocratic hymn to the partnership of knowledge and work, science and labor. The arts of war are again translated into peaceful production in Verne's model mining community, Coal City, in *Black Diamonds.*

Coal City is a veritable military colony, where its miners live and work together inside the mine itself, a huge underground cavern lit by the promethian light of electricity. Here they live with and for their work, under the direction of their chief engineer, a former army engineer, together constituting "a peaceful army of labor" that toils in harmony and collective joy. With their division of labor modeled after that of the armed forces, they are able to realize the ideals of fraternity and equality. All are united in "one big family with the same interests."

So, too, in *The Mysterious Island.* The scientifically versatile army engineer, Capt. Cyrus Harding, leads the survivors of a balloon crash to salvation through endurance and their zeal for hard work, epitomizing the Saint-Simonian motto, "Down with idlers." The island is a microcosm of the socialist utopia, the well-regulated and fraternal cooperation of humanity in the exploitation of the globe in the light of scientific knowledge. At the end of the novel, Capt. Nemo appears, and gives them his blessing after they have proved themselves by their readiness for labor. "You love this island," he says on his deathbed in his submarine. "You have changed it by your efforts and it is truly yours."

Capt. Nemo's all-electric submarine is itself a miniature Saint-Simonian world, with its crew of international sailors who speak a universal synthetic language. Observing their grim and robotlike round of tireless work under Capt. Nemo's direction, Ned Land in *Twenty Thousand Leagues under the Sea* suspects that they, too, are "run by electricity." Their work, however, is not peaceful production; it is making war for peace, the business of sinking British shi ps, punishing them for their nation's world-dividing colonial wars. In this Capt. Nemo is like the hero of *Robur the Conqueror* and *The Master of the World.* He does his vengeance by smiting the world's warships from out of the sky in his airplane, *The Terro,* by way of enforcing the union of nations and a cooperative oneness in the "economic and political ways of the world." For the whole world belongs to mankind.

At the same time, the *voyages extraordinaire* are lessons in geography. The various means of transportation used by Veryne, some of them futuristic in his day, actually are devices for instructing the reader in the geographical aspects of nearly every country and region on the face of the Earth, as well as its subterranean structure, its oceans, and even the moon and planets of outer space. This didactic purpose is an extension of his three-volume nonfictional work, *Histoire des Grand Voyages et Grand Voyageurs* (1870-73).

Verne's first novel, *Cinq Semaines en Ballon* (1863), surveys Africa from the air. His next novel, written the same year, looked ahead to a strange place in 1960 where people travel by subway and automobiles, communicate by fax and telephone, calculate with computers, and are entertained by electronic media. This was *Paris an XXe Siecle,* which Verne's publisher rejected as being not only too fantastic but too anti-capitalistic, for its emphasis was less on machines of the future than culture criticism of a money-industrial society. Fortunately, this lost manuscript has been discovered by Verne's great-grandson, who published it in 1994, with credentials of authenticity. Thereafter, Verne comformed his political philosophy to dramatizing what he was *for* (Saint Simonism), rather than what he was *against* (private-profit capitalism). But there is one exception, "In the Twentyninth Century: The Day of an American Journalist in 2889," a story originally published in English in 1889.

—Leon Stover

VERRILL, A(lpheus) Hyatt

Pseudonym: Ray Ainsbury. **Nationality:** American. **Born:** New Haven, Connecticut, 23 July 1871. **Education:** Yale University School of Fine Arts, New Haven; studied zoology with his father. **Family:** Married 1) Kathryn L. McCarthy in 1892, four children; 2) Lida Ruth Shaw in 1944. **Career:** Natural history illustrator for *Webster's International Dictionary,* 1896, and for *Clarendon Dictionary;* invented the autochrome process of photography, 1920; explorer and archaeologist: lived in Domenica, 1903-06, British Guiana, 1913-17, and Panama, 1917-21, and made expeditions to Central and South America, the West Indies, and Mexico, to 1950; did undersea excavation in the West Indies, 1933-34; established the Anhlarka experimental gardens and natural science museum, Florida, 1940; established shell business, Lake Worth, Florida, 1944. **Died:** 14 November 1954.

SCIENCE FICTION PUBLICATIONS

Novels

Uncle Abner's Legacy. New York, Holt, 1915.
The Golden City: A Tale of Adventure in Unknown Guiana (for children). New York, Duffield, 1916.
The Trail of the Cloven Foot (for children). New York, Dutton, 1918.
The Trial of the White Indians: Sequel to The Trail of the Cloven Foot (for children). New York, Dutton, 1920.
The Radio Detectives under the Sea. New York, Appleton, 1922.
The Boy Adventures in the Land of the Monkey Men (for children). New York, Putnam, 1923.
The Boy Adventurers in the Unknown Land (for children). New York, Puntnam, 1924.
The Bridge of Light. Reading, Pennsylvania, Fantasy Press, 1950.
When the Moon Ran Wild (as Ray Ainsbury). London. Consul, 1962.

OTHER PUBLICATIONS

Novels (for children)

The American Crusoe. New York, Dodd Mead, 1914.
The Cruise of the Cormorant. New York, Holt, 1915.
In Morgan's Wake. New York, Holt, 1915.
Marooned in the Forest. New York, Harper, 1916.
Jungle Chums. New York, Holt, 1916.
The Boy Adventurers in the Forbidden Land [in the Land of El Dorando; in the Unknown Land]. New York, Putnam, 3 vols., 1922-24.
The Deep Sea Hunters [in the Frozen Sea, in the South Seas]. New York, Appleton, 3 vols., 1922-24.
The Radio Detectives [in the Jungle; Southward Bound; under the Sea]. New York, Appleton, 4 vols. 1922.
Bartons Mills: A Saga of the Pioneers. New York, Appleton, 1932.
The Incas' Treasure House. Boston, Page, 1932; London, Harrap, 1936.
Before the Conquerors. New York, Dodd Mead, 1935.
The Treasure of the Bloody Gut. New York, Putnam, 1937.

Other

Gasoline Engines: Their Operation, Use and Care. New York, Henley, 1912.
Knots, Splices, and Rope Work. New York, Henley, 1912; revised edition, 1917, 1922.
Harper's Book for Young Naturalists [Gardeners]. New York, Harper, 2 vols., 1913-14.
Harper's Wireless [Aircraft; Gasoline Engine] Book. New York, Harper, 3 vols., 1913-14.
Cuba Past and Present. New York, Dodd Mead, 1914; revised edition, 1920.
South and Central American Trade Conditions of Today. New York, Dodd Mead, 1914; revised edition, 1919.
Porto Rico Past and Present. New York, Dodd Mead, 1914.
Pets for Pleasure and Profit. New York, Scribner, 1915.
The Boys' Outdoor Vacation Book. New York, Dodd Mead, 1915.
The Amateur Carpenter. New York, Dodd Mead, 1915.
The Boy Collector's Handbook. New York, McBride, 1915.
Isles of Spice and Palm. New York, Appleton, 1915.
A-B-C of Automobile Driving. New York, Harper, 1916.
The Real Story of the Whaler. New York, Appleton, 1916.
The Ocean and Its Mysteries. New York, Duffield, 1916.
The Book of the Motor Boat [Sailboat]. New York, Appleton, 2 vols., 1916.
The Book of the West Indies. New York, Dutton, 1917.
The Book of Camping. New York, Knopf, 1917.
How to Operate a Motor Car. Philadelphia, McKay, 1918.
Getting Together with Latin America. New York, Dutton, 1918.
Islands and Their Mysteries. New York, Duffield, 1920; London, Melrose, 1922.
Panama, Past and Present. New York, Dodd Mead, 1921.
The Boys' Book of Whalers [Carpentry, Buccaneers]. New York, Dodd Mead, 3 vols., 1922-23.
Radio for Amateurs. New York, Dodd Mead, and London, Heinemann, 1922.
Rivers and Their Mysteries. New York, Duffield, 1922.
The Home Radio. New York, Harper, 1922; revised edition, 1924; revised edition, as *The Home Radio up to Date,* with E.E. Verrill, 1927.
In the Wake of the Buccaneers. New York, Century, and London, Parsons, 1923.
The Real Story of the Pirate. New York, Appleton, 1923.
Smugglers and Smuggling. New York, Duffield, and London, Allen and Unwin, 1924.
Love Stories of Some Famous Pirates. London, Collins, 1924.
Panama [Cuba, Jamaica, West Indies] of Today. New York, Dodd Mead, 4 vols., 1927-31.
The American Indian. New York, Appleton, 1927.
Old Civilization of the New World. Indianapolis, Bobbs Merrill, and London, Williams and Norgate, 1929.
Thirty Years in the Jungle. London, Lane, 1929.
Great Conquerors of South and Central America. New York, Appleton, 1929.
Lost Treasure. New York, Appleton, 1930.
Gasoline-Engine Book for Boys. New York, Harper, 1930.
Under Peruvian Skies. London, Hurst and Blackett, 1930.
Secret Treasure. New York, Appleton, 1931.
The Inquisition. New York, Appleton, 1931.
Romantic and Historic Maine [Florida; Virginia]. New York, Dodd Mead, 3 vols., 1933-35.

Our Indians. New York, Putnam, 1935.
They Found Gold. New York and London, Putnam, 1936; as *Carib Gold,* London, Collins, 1939.
The Heart of Old New England. New York, Dodd Mead, 1936.
Along New England Shores. New York, Putnam, 1936.
Sea Shells [Insects; Reptiles; Birds; Fish; Animals] and Their Stories. Boston, Page, and London, Harrap, 6 vols., 1936-39.
My Jungle Trails. Boston, Page, and London, Harrap, 1937.
Foods America Gave the World. Boston, Page, 1937.
Minerals, Metals and Gems. Boston, Page, 1939.
Wonder Plants and Plant Wonders. New York, Appleton Century, 1939.
Perfumes and Spices. Boston, Page, 1940.
Wonder Creatures of the Sea. New York, Appleton Century, 1940.
Strange Prehistoric Animals and Their Stories. Boston, Page, 1948.
The Strange Story of Our Earth. Boston, Page, 1952.
America's Ancient Civilization, (with R. Verrill). New York and London, Putnam, 1954.

*   *   *

A. Hyatt Verrill was one of the more distinguished writers who helped in the development of *Amazing Stories* during its early years, and who continued to contribute to it until the mid-1930s. Many of his stories are set in the South American jungles with which he was so familiar, or deal with ancient civilisations whose cultures he studied for more than half a century. But he did not limit himself to such themes, drawing on astronomy, biology, optics, atomic physics, and fourth-dimension theory for ideas which he developed with equal facility.

The magazine was only six months old when his first offering, "Beyond the Pole," dealing with a race of intelligent crustaceans discovered in the Antarctic, appeared late in 1926. It compared favourably with the stories of Wells and Verne, which almost monopolised those early issues, while the editor, Hugo Gernsback, contrived to nurture new writers to displace them. Some of Verrill's longer stories went to fill out the inch-thick *Amazing Stories Quarterly;* "The World of the Giant Ants" was remarkable for its engrossing narrative combined with an enlightening insight into its subject. Even more fascinating was "Into the Green Prism," with its sequel, "Beyond the Green Prism," which sought to dispel the storm of controversy over the scientific fallacies it raised. "The Astounding Discoveries of Doctor Mentiroso" began the endless argument in the readers' columns over the time-travel theme. "Death from the Skies" was about a bombardment of Earth by the Martians, and *The Bridge of Light* took readers to a hidden city where the Mayas still thrived. Verrill's flights of imagination reached their peak in 1931 with "Monsters of the Ray" and *When the Moon Ran Wild;* but his later contributions, such as "The Death Drum" and "Through the Andes," were pure adventure tales which reflected the gradual decline of *Amazing.*

—Walter Gillings

VINGE, Joan (Carol) D(ennison)

Nationality: American. **Born:** Baltimore, Maryland, 2 April 1948. **Education:** San Diego State University, California, B.A. in anthropology 1971. **Family:** Married 1) Vernor Vinge, *q.v.,* in 1972 (divorced 1979); 2) the publisher James R. Frenkel in 1980. Salvage archaeologist, San Diego County, 1971. **Awards:** Hugo award, 1978, 1981; *Locus* award, 1981. **Agent:** Merrilee Heifetz, Writers House Inc., 21 West 26th Street, New York, New York 10010, U.S.A. **Address:** 26 Douglas Road, Chappaqua, New York 10514, U.S.A.

SCIENCE FICTION PUBLICATIONS

Novels (series: Cat; Heaven Belt; Snow Queen)

The Outcasts of Heaven Belt. New York, Signet, 1978; London, Orbit, 1981.
The Snow Queen. New York, Dial Press, and London, Sidgwick and Jackson, 1980.
Psion (Cat; for children). New York, Delacorte Press, 1982; London, Orbit, 1983.
Star Wars: Return of the Jedi: The Storybook Based on the Movie (novelization of screenplay; for children). New York, Random House, and London, Orbit, 1983.
Joan D. Vinge Omnibus (includes *Fireship* and *The Outcasts of Heaven Belt*). London, Sidgwick and Jackson, 1983.
The Dune Storybook (novelization of screenplay). New York, Putnam, 1984; London, Sphere, 1984.
World's End (Snow Queen). New York, Bluejay, 1984; London, Orbit, 1985.
Ladyhawke (novelization of screenplay). New York, Signet, 1985; London, Piccolo, 1985.
Catspaw. New York, Warner, 1988; as *Cats Paw,* London Gollancz, 1989; under original title, London, Pan, 1993.
Alien Blood: Psion, Catspaw. Garden City, New York, Doubleday, 1988.
Heaven Chronicles (includes "Legacy" and *The Outcasts of Heaven Belt*). New York, Warner, 1991.
The Summer Queen (Snow Queen). New York, Warner, 1991; London, Pan, 1993.

Short Stories

Fireship. New York, Dell, 1978; as *Fireship, and Mother and Child: Science Fiction,* London, Sidgwick and Jackson, 1980.
Eyes of Amber and Other Stories. New York, Signet, 1979; London, Orbit, 1981.
Phoenix in the Ashes. New York, Bluejay, 1985; London, Orbit, 1986.
Tin Soldier, bound with *Riding the Torch,* by Norman Spinrad. New York, Tor, 1990.

OTHER PUBLICATIONS

Novels (novelizations of screenplays)

Mad Max beyond Thunderdome: A Novelization. New York, Warner, and London, W.H. Allen, 1985.
Return to Oz: A Novel. New York, Ballantine, and London, Purnell, 1985.
Santa Claus: The Movie: A Novel. New York, Berkley, and London, Sphere, 1985.
Willow. New York, Random House, and London, Piper, 1988.

Other

Tarzan, King of the Apes (for children; adapted from *Tarzan of the Apes,* by Edgar Rice Burroughs). New York, Random House, 1983.

Santa Claus, the Movie Storybook (for children). New York, Grosset and Dunlap, 1985.

*

Manuscript Collection: Elizabeth Charter Science Fiction Collection, San Diego University.

Critical Study: *Suzy Charnas, Joan Vinge, and Octavia Butler* by Richard Law, with others, San Bernardino, California, Borgo Press, 1986.

Joan D. Vinge comments:

(1981) Because I have a degree in anthropology, I tend to write anthropological science fiction, with an emphasis on the interaction of different cultures (human and alien) and of individual people to their surroundings. The importance of communication across barriers of alienness often becomes a theme in my stories. Mythology and music also influence my work; my novel *The Snow Queen* was in large part inspired by Robert Graves's *The White Goddess.* I have written several stories with a "hard" science background, thanks to the borrowed expertise of my husband, who is a mathematician and also a science fiction writer; however, I've written other stories which I hope cover a wide range of moods and styles, I feel as if I'm just beginning to explore the infinite possibilities of the future.

* * *

Though her output has been fairly small for a major writer, there is no question about the importance of Joan D. Vinge's work. Her stories are not only interesting and entertaining, they are original, richly detailed, and thought-provoking as well. Influenced strongly by the work of Andre Norton, her stories often feature strong female, alien, or halfbreed characters, who, when placed in difficult circumstances, grow measurably by working through their problems positively and constructively. Other common Vinge themes are: the difficulty of loving, understanding, and communicating, the role of free women, and the appreciation of individuals and cultures that are not the norm. Her work is influenced by mythology, music, legend, and the fairytale. Vinge works slowly and carefully, creating physical and social works that are complex and informative. This is no doubt due to her background as an anthropologist.

While each of her stories has its own virtues, Vinge's reputation rests on (a few) exceptional works, some of which are interrelated. Of particular interest are: "Eyes of Amber," "Fireship," "Legacy," *The Outcasts of Heaven Belt, The Snow Queen, World's End, Psion, Catspaw,* and *The Summer Queen.*

Set on Titan, "Eyes of Amber" is, according to Richard Law (in *Suzy McKee Charnas, Joan Vinge, Octavia Butler*), a fairytale in design, sharing its motifs of "sibling rivalry, benevolent mother, rescue device, and ultimate exaltation of the ill-treated heroine." The story's heroine is Lady T'uupieh, a chiropteran who has been dispossessed of her lands and must live as an outcast. As leader of a band of outlaws, she eventually kills Klovhiri, the wicked nobleman who brought about her downfall. She succeeds by means of an Earth probe, which she regards as a demon. Through it, she

carries on a relationship with a young rock musician, who also has superb linguistic abilities, named Shannon Wyler. Because of what essentially becomes an interspecies "love affair," he begins to wean her away from the values of her culture towards our own. Set on Mars, "Fireship" explores the behavior of a composite personality named Ethan Ring (a cyborg produced when a low-intellect lab assistant is surgically altered so that he can be connected to a massive computer). Ring matches wits with a shiek, Khorran Kabir, who controls most of the wealth on Earth after World III. Kabir has had his own consciousness transferred into a computer. While notable as a study of communications with and understanding other forms of life, "Fireship" is also richly comic.

"Legacy" and *The Outcasts of Heaven Belt* are related by being set in the same world and by sharing a character. The Heaven Belt, made up of thousands of asteroids, planetoids, and planets, and populated by the descendants of Earth colonists, has been wasted by civil war, leaving two feuding societies. "Legacy" is the story of two lonely people, Chaim Dartagnan, a "media man" who loses his job but regains his integrity, and Mythili Fukinuki, a sterilized space pilot, who also loses her job. Estranged from one another after an initial attraction, they are reconciled by Wadie Abdhiamal, a government negotiator, who arranges rights to a dead prospector's ship for them so they can forge careers as salvagers. Through their adventures, they learn self-respect, realize their interdependence, and fall in love. *The Outcasts of Heaven Belt,* set in the same world, uses Abdhiamal as a principal character. It focuses primarily, however, upon Betha Torgussen, the captain of the *Ranger,* a spaceship from the planet Morningside, several light years away. Morningside, itself endangered and unaware of the civil war, has sent the *Ranger* to bargain for resources. Because of its fusion reactor, the ship becomes the target of both colonies, but after several attempts to capture it fail, an alliance is struck that benefits all parties. Set against this background is a love story focusing on Betha and Wadie which explores the concept of the multiple-marriage family unit. While both "Legacy" and *The Outcasts of Heaven Belt* are well crafted and entertaining, neither reaches the excellence of *The Snow Queen.*

This novel counterposes two plots to explore one of literature's great and recurring themes—renewal. The principal story follows the development of young Moon Dawntreader, as she fulfills her destiny by becoming the new queen of the planet Tiamat. Unknown to Moon, she is one of several clones of the reigning queen, Arienrhod, and because of how she has been raised, Moon is opposite to Arienrhod in both values and philosophies. Moon represents good. Arienrhod's story is one of Machiavellian manipulation. She wants desperately to continue to rule, and schemes and plots to assure it. She not only lengthens her own life by using the blood of intelligent sea creatures (mers) but clones herself as well. As Richard Law writes in *Suzy McKee Charnas, Joan Vinge, Octavia Butler,* "Arienrhod perceives that evil is inherent, takes license from it, and pursuing her lusts marshals the evil in her world." Taken together, Moon and Arienrhod represent most of the dialectical pairs that frame all our lives: good and evil, youth and age, innocence and experience. But the fact that Moon succeeds Arienrhod when the old queen dies and that her name links her to a perpetual cycle symbolized by the moon-trinity, New, Full, and Old, suggests a renewal theme. Arienrhod, like evil in most fantastic literature, falls of her own weight, but is succeeded by her genetic self who is morally opposite.

World's End is related to *The Snow Queen* by virtue of taking up the story of BZ Gundhalinu, a character in the latter novel, after he has left Tiamat and become a maladjusted police inspector on a planet called Number Four. Out of his own sense of guilt, BZ feels compelled to travel into the bizarre and grotesque landscape of *World's End* to find his two stupid and greedy brothers and a demented female. The story is Vinge's exploration of the "heart of darkness." In wandering through both the physical wasteland of *World's End* and his own psychological wasteland, BZ searches for his sanity and saves his soul. This, like *The Snow Queen* is a renewal story.

Psion is a coming-of-age novel, in which an adolescent halfbreed named Cat is initiated into the adult world. Influenced by the work of Andre Norton, Cat resembles many of her characters: disenfranchised, isolated, scorned, and both physically and mentally different from those around him. An orphan who grew up in a city actually lying beneath another city, Cat is symbolically born into the adult world when the woman who had "mothered" him dies. During his adventures, Cat learns about trust and friendship, falls in love with another psion named Jule, undergoes mind-rape by a criminal named Rubiy who lusts after him, learns how to use his psionic powers, and kills Rubiy. Ironically, the killing leaves Cat unable to use his psionic powers, and Jule's love for Siebeling, the director of the research center, leaves him alone once more. Despite these setbacks, however, Cat has undergone an initiation into manhood that has taught him how to survive and permitted him to mature.

Catspaw continues Cat's adventures a few years later. Essentially a "palace-intrigue," it is a novel rich in detail, suspense, and characters. Cat finds himself hired to bodyguard Lady Elnear, a member of Jule's powerful corporate family, the Tamings. He learns eventually, of course, that he is the cats-paw.

Pushed to test himself against the manipulations and politics of gigantic corporations headquartered on Earth, Cat regains the use of his psionic powers by means of "drug patches," solves the mystery of who is trying to kill Lady Elnear, and learns even more about himself and the adult world. In particular, he learns about the enormous difficulty of interpersonal communications. Vinge is superb in examining the erotic invasion of another individual's mind in an act of real love, the effects of a simbiotic, mental link-up, and the psionic intrusion into a bioelectronic system that functions like a collective consciousness. By the end of the novel, Cat has reached another level of maturation.

The Summer Queen brings the story of Dawn Moontreader Summer, at least temporarily, to a conclusion, though there is certainly no reason why Vinge could not write related stories or continue this work if she chose. The novel is monumental. It bucks and weaves, twists and turns, as it neatly knots up loose ends. It is epic in scope, enormously rich in detail, and compelling in its development of Moon, BZ Gundhalinu, and Reede Kullervo. It also does a superb job of developing Sparks Dawntreader, Moon's childhood sweetheart and husband, and Ariele, her daughter.

As the novel opens, Moon has assumed the role of Summer Queen and Tiamat is isolated from the Hegemony planets, the blackhole-gate that permits traveling to Tiamat now being closed for 150 years. Moon is trying to wean her people, the Summers, from their backward ways and superstitions before the Hegemony returns. Because of her status as Summer Queen and her sibyl abilities, she learns the true nature of the net, which is an enormous self-correcting computer net connecting people like herself on hundreds of planets across the galaxy. Tiamat had been selected by the Old Empire powers as the center of the net and peopled with a sentient, aquatic lifeform called mers, who resemble dolphins and

hold the key to the net's self-correcting abilities in its songs. The sibyls, the mers, and the fiery lake at World's End have been infected with a bioengineered virus that creates different forms of "smartmatter." The lake at World's End has resulted from the crash of an Old Empire starship, whose smartmatter is a faster-than-light-drive plasma gone wild.

Reede, as it is eventually revealed, is a composite character. There are two personalities occupying his body. He is the original Reede Kullervo, but he is also the repository for the electronic analogue of one of the original creators of the sibyl net system, a man named Vanamoinen, who though dead for many centuries, has continued to exist within the net in electronic form until he is retrieved and inserted into Reede's mind. Vanamoinen's original plan was to have the mers gather every hundred and fifty years below Carbuncle, sing their songs, and thus correct the computer network's programming. But he has also bioengineered the mers so that they will be around long enough to perform this function. Unfortunately, somewhere during the Winter reign of Arienrhod, the off-worlders learned that the blood of the mers could prolong their youth for a very long time. So, hunting the mers for what is called the "water-of-life," is very important to the off-worlders.

There's another complication: hunting the mers nearly to extinction has eliminated parts of their song. This will prevent the computer network from correcting itself when the time comes for the mers to gather. In fact, the sibyl net has already showed signs of failing. Complicating things further is the existence of a secret group called the Brotherhood, which is only one of several secret groups within a larger group dedicated to preserving civilization. The Brotherhood is led by a shadowy and mysterious character named Jaakola. He is evil and completely Machiavellian. He not only takes over the Brotherhood, he also enslaves Reede by becoming the only provider of the "water-of-death," one of Reede's failed attempts to create a synthetic version of the water of life. Reede tried it on himself only to discover that it was not only addictive but also literally will make him decompose if he does not use it regularly. So he can control the water-of-life, Jaakola arranges to steal part of the stardrive plasma after Reede and BZ stabilize it on World's End, and then he sends Reede to Tiamat. The perfection of faster-than-light travel also permits the Kharemoughi to return to Tiamat.

While on Tiamat, Reede falls in love with Ariele, then betrays her and aids in her kidnapping. He takes her to Jaakola's fortress on Ondinee. Moon and BZ, we learn, have been in love for many years. Because of his feelings for Moon, BZ, who has returned to Tiamat as Chief Justice, limits the hunting of mers. He is then betrayed by his second-in-command, who accuses him of treason, and he is eventually sent to a prison planet. Sparks mounts a mission to save Ariele, even though he learned earlier that BZ was the biological father of Ariele and her twin brother Tammis. Sparks and Reede both come to understand the greater importance of the mers and study their songs. Sparks successfully rescues Ariele and Reede, though he is apparently killed in the process. During the rescue, Reede manages to kill Jaakola and destroy his fortress. Back on Tiamat Reede, now completely taken over by the personality of Vanamoinen, reprograms the sibyl net with the help of Tammis, who has also become a sibyl and who dies saving Reede's life. When the true nature of the mers is known, BZ's reputation is restored, he is recalled from the prison planet, and he resumes his position as Chief Justice. He and Moon are together at last, and Sparks, who it turns out is not dead after all, slips away from Tiamat without the protagonists knowing that he survived.

The Summer Queen is a beautiful novel that displays Vinge's strengths as a writer: it has a richly textured world, a complicated but interesting plot, and excellent character development. It has two faults. Near the end of the story, the love affair between Moon and BZ occasionally sounds like soap opera, and the novel itself is physically daunting. Set in small type and very long, it would have been better presented if divided into separate works.

Vinge's writing is thoughtful, interesting, and excellently crafted. As Anne Hudson Jones wrote in the first edition of this book, Vinge's "is a major talent."

—Carl B. Yoke

VINGE, Vernor (Steffen)

Nationality: American. **Born:** Waukesha, Wisconsin, 2 October 1944. **Education:** Michigan State University, East Lansing, B.S. 1966; University of California, San Diego, M.A. 1968, Ph.D. 1971. **Family:** Married Joan Carol Dennison (i.e., Joan D. Vinge, *q.v.*), in 1972 (divorced 1979). Assistant professor, 1972-78, and since 1978, associate professor of mathematics, San Diego State University. **Address:** Department of Mathematics, San Diego State University, San Diego, California 92182, U.S.A.

SCIENCE FICTION PUBLICATIONS

Novels (series: Realtime)

Grimm's World. New York, Berkley, 1969; London, Hamlyn, 1978; as *Tatja Grimm's World,* New York, Baen, 1987; London, Pan, 1990.
The Witling. New York, DAW, and London, Dobson, 1976.
True Names in Binary Star 5. New York, Bluejay, 1984.
Across Realtime. Garden City, New York, Doubleday, 1986; London, Millennium, 1993; expanded edition, Riverdale, New York, Baen, 1991.
The Peace War. New York, Bluejay, 1984; London, Pan, 1987.
Marooned in Realtime. New York, Bluejay, 1986; London, Pan, 1987.
A Fire upon the Deep. New York, Tor, and London, Millennium, 1992.

Short Stories

True Names . . . and Other Dangers, with Joan D. Vinge. New York, Baen, 1987.
Threats . . . and Other Promises. New York, Baen, 1988.

*   *   *

Vernor Vinge is not a prolific writer but his significance is considerably greater than the size of his output because of the high quality of much of his work. Especially in his best stories, most of which are collected in *True Names . . . and Other Dangers* and *Threats . . . and Other Promises,* Vinge deals with extreme social situations, with crises within a society or with intercultural conflict. Much of his work is permeated with a melancholy awareness

of the evanescence of all human institutions. Typically, Vinge's characters are faced with some personal problem arising out of social change. They furnish the best possible solution given the initial conditions, but it is never more than a half-solution, and they must live with their failure as well as their success.

Vinge's first two novels, both set on other planets, move in the characteristic Vinge pattern. *Grimm's World,* set on a retrogressed colony planet now climbing back to high technology, centers on intrigues and struggles of a native-born superwoman whose only intellectual equals are two visitors from a higher interstellar culture. The novel focuses our greatest sympathy not on the superhumans but on the ordinary people caught up in their machinations. The various cultures of this largely archipelagic, metal-poor world, and especially its alternative technologies, are described in fascinating elaboration. *The Witling* has many of the same story elements (covert interplanetary visitors, an emotionally crippled woman genius, a person of ordinary capacity caught up in all this, a pet with psionic powers), but the combination is less successful. For one thing, much of the exposition is taken up with a brilliantly logical but never quite believable development of a world where practically everyone has an inborn ability to teleport. The title (which Vinge uses to mean approximately "half-wit") is a pun: at first it is applied in scorn to Pelio, the native hero who lacks his race's usual teleportational ability, but by the end it applies with more justification to the genius heroine. In a typical Vinge twist-of-the-knife ending, she suffers brain damage that both impairs her intellect and renders her a more balanced, happier person, a suitable partner for the love-stricken Pelio.

In his next two novels, Vinges returns to Earth. The widely acclaimed *True Names* features a computer net perceived by its users as a magical realm, and centers on a struggle by hobbyist "wizards" against a bloated Federal bureaucracy on the one hand, and against the mysterious malevolent Mailman on the other. The same loving elaboration applied to teleportation in the *The Witling* is here put to a more plausible initial premise (the "magic" computer net), with brilliant results. As in previous novels, *True Names* features superhumans, but this time they attain that status largely by computer interface, rather than solely on the basis of their inborn talents. The love affair, within the "magical" realm where youth can be eternal, between the young hero and the old heroine (so ancient she had actually worked as a keypunch operator!) recalls, probably intentionally, a similar relationship in Heinlein's "Magic Incorporated." The technological innovation put to scrutiny in *The Peace War* is the stasis field, described in a few throwaway lines in Heinlein's *Beyond This Horizon* and perhaps best used before *The Peace War* in Niven's Known Space series. Vinge finds a variety of new applications for the idea, using it as an offensive weapon, a shield, a prison, and a time machine. In a combination of previous superman notions, *The Peace War*'s main viewpoint character is a genius even unassisted, and something unprecedented when interfaced with computers. Like *Grimm's World, The Peace War* depicts an elaborate sociological situation growing out of its basic assumptions (chiefly use of the stasis field, progress in genetic engineering and electronics, and the deliberate suppression of high-powered machinery). As in *True Names,* there is a romance blighted by age disparity—this time between a woman Air Force captain, newly emerged from stasis, and her one-time lover, who has aged throughout the 50 years since she was entrapped.

Both *True Names* and *The Peace War* show a considerable mellowing in tone over Vinge's previous work, which had been powerful and effective, but generally so bleak in outlook that it was made bearable only by the sparsity of the author's production. True, most of the human race is wiped out offstage in *The Peace War,* and the threat of bureaucracy is not entirely gone by the end of *True Names,* but life does now seem to be dealing Vinge viewpoint characters somewhat better cards. At the very least, the author is demonstrating his control of a wider range of approaches. The steady accumulation of quality work will indeed earn him a major reputation with the passing of years.

—Patrick L. McGuire

VONARBURG, Élisabeth

Nationality: Canadian. **Born:** 1947.

SCIENCE FICTION PUBLICATIONS

Novels

Le silence de la cité. Paris, Editions Denoël, 1981; translated by Jane Brierley as *The Silent City,* Vancouver, Porcépic, 1988; London, Women's Press, 1990; New York, Bantam, 1992.
Chroniques du pays des mères. Montreal, Éditions Québec/Amérique, 1992; translated by Jane Brierley as *In the Mothers' Land,* New York, Bantam, 1992; as *The Mareland Chronicles,* Victoria, Beach Holme, 1993.
Les Voyageurs malagreux. Montreal, Éditions Québec/Amérique, 1994; translated by Jane Brierley as *Reluctant Voyagers,* New York, Bantam, 1995.

*   *   *

Élisabeth Vonarburg has long been a very well-known participant on the Canadian science-fiction scene. She was one of the founding members of the very serious magazine *Solaris,* in which she published many of her short stories. She has been a prime mover in the establishment of a French Canadian school of science fiction and its blossoming into a unique Québécois independent current of culture. If many of her short stories are unavailable in English translations, we are lucky enough to have English versions of her recent novels, including, *The Silent City.*

The Silent City is an original and important work in the field of international science fiction for its treatment of androgyny. Like much Canadian science fiction, *The Silent City* takes place in a post-cataclysmic world. Scientists have taken refuge in an enclosed city to isolate and protect themselves from the barbaric humans who continue to exist outside and whose genes, altered through the effects of radiation, have a detrimental effect on their life expectancy and general physical health. One of the most damning consequences is an inability to produce more than one boy for nine girls.

In the city, a crazy scientist named Paul decides to create a new superrace that should be endowed with the powers of self-regeneration and self-healing tending to immortality. He succeeds in creating Elisa who, after his death, will continue his project. She manages to transmit one of her most extraordinary powers: the faculty to transform herself into a man and vice versa. Elisa can become a man and then experience all that a man goes through, including sexual desire and intercourse. What is important is that as a man she can remember the feelings she had as a woman and turning herself back into a woman again she is not the woman she was before her transformation. She manages to create several new generations of offspring from her own genes capable of metamorphosis at will.

Vonarburg appears extremely concerned with the equality of the sexes and sees it coming through a bisexual integration, if not physical (as it is described with finesse in the novel), at least sensual and psychological. Contrary to much of contemporary science fiction, in *The Silent City* technology is dependent on the psychologies of the characters. Technological gadgets are reduced to a minimum and the working of all medical procedures is barely sufficient to make it credible. As much of Vonarburg seems at ease in the dual male/female aspect of our personalities, she seems to be unwilling to give a fully complete description of the actual working of the "City" and its everyday working when she feels that they are not relevant to the story. There is a lot of space for at least two other novels: one that could tell us about the genesis of the "City," another that could fill up the unsatisfactory ending: one is not quite sure that the main protagonists will be able to fulfill their destiny. The children are not compelled to become a fusion of the two sexes. Rather, they are encouraged to explore the two personalities, female and male, and then choose what they think is their real self. Such a process does not seek to do away with the differences between the sexes: on the contrary, it furthers the existing distinctions while creating a natural desire for empathy.

One of the most promising aspects and, at the same time most frustrating, is that *The Silent City* poses as many questions as it attempts to resolve. The sexual difference between men and women leads in the novel to the desire of each group to dominate the other rather than to seek any sort of accommodation. This confrontation is resolved through an effort to accept that everyone is capable, to a certain extent, of acquiring some traits of the other sex. What is lacking, however, is a description of the process that will eventually lead to it rather than fanciful wishful thinking on the part of the protagonists.

Vonarburg shows us that our bisexuality is a key to inner knowledge and that all of us could benefit from some empathy with the other sex. If only for that reason, *The Silent City* is a unique work that will, hopefully, spawn other works of exploration in the same subject.

In *In the Mothers' Land,* Vonarburg adds a few twists to what could have a been a rehashed theme but ends up being a wholly exciting and original book: as is often the case with many Canadian science-fiction novels, the story takes place after a catastrophe. Whether deadly pollution or nuclear devices are the cause of what society has become is not told but the end result is that the part of the world described in the book, seemingly Western Europe, is made up of small independent communities that practice low-level industrialization based on extensive recycling. However, mutations have severely affected most of the remaining population and only a few male children are born for every hundred girls. Consequently, "Red Males," as fertile men are called, have to go from one community to the other and fulfill their roles as progenitors. Vonarburg is not satisfied with a mere reversal of the gender functions, she also questions our assumptions about our own identity, not only our sexual identity, but also our desires and freedom to accomplish our dreams within the set rules of an organized society which, in *In the Mothers' Land,* seems to be to be akin to what North America might have become, if Native Americans had evolved separately into a modern society.

Comparisons with Margaret Atwood's *The Handmaid's Tale* spring to mind, but, whereas Atwood's book leads us into a terrifying journey into the near future, Vonarburg's heroine portrait of her own environment is a far gentler one. The masterful rendering of a child's curious mind at the onset of the book, trying to make sense of the rules and explanations provided to her by adults, is especially powerful, and so is the portrait of a society that could serve as a pointer for the renewal of our contemporary society. However, once again the reader is left in a state of famine as the story appears to be in want of a sequel or are we to assume that the author either got bored with her main protagonist and grants us the freedom to imagine our own ending.

Her latest novel, *Les Voyageurs malgreux,* is her most ambitious to date and has been widely praised. It takes place in a North American dystopia where Québec Francophones live in an enclave in a part of Montreal, the only other remaining French-speaking regions being an independent Louisiana and a mythic Kingdom of Sags.

The oneiric sequences are very powerful even if rather longish and resolved too slowly; their lack of directions and clues, for the purpose of suspense, requires some patience from any reader fed on routine space opera, especially since they turn into a continuously unexplained mystery. *Les Voyageurs malgreux* is a dystopia that is not linked to our history even though the reader might expect everything to revert to a certain normality especially since the central character seems to be heavily inspired by the author's personal biography. It has, like Robert Charles Wilson's *Mysterium,* a fully Canadian-inspired context while retaining a universal appeal that demonstrates that SF can be independent of context and, as mainstream literature, related to a national identity. In this regard, *Les Voyageurs malgreux* succeeds in bringing us science fiction that is neither preaching nor esoteric while opening a window onto another school of science fiction.

—Henry Leperlier

VONNEGUT, Kurt, Jr.

Nationality: American. **Born:** Indianapolis, Indiana, 11 November 1922. **Education:** Cornell University, Ithaca, New York, 1940-42; Carnegie Institute, Pittsburgh, 1943; University of Chicago, 1945-47. **Military Service:** Served in the United States Army Infantry, 1942-45; Purple Heart. **Family:** Married 1) Jane Marie Cox in 1945 (divorced 1979), one son and two daughters; 2) Jill Krementz in 1979, one daughter. **Career:** Police reporter, Chicago City News Bureau, 1946; worked in public relations for the General Electric Company, Schenectady, New York, 1947-50. Since 1950, freelance writer. Since 1965, teacher, Hopefield School, Sandwich, Massachusetts. Visiting lecturer, Writers Workshop, University of Iowa, Iowa City, 1965-67, and Harvard University, Cambridge, Massachusetts, 1970-71; visiting professor, City University of New York, 1973-74. **Awards:** Guggenheim fellowship, 1967; American Academy grant, 1970. M.A.: University of Chicago, 1971; Litt. D.: Hobart and William Smith Colleges, Geneva, New York, 1974. **Member:** American Academy, 1973. **Agent:** Donald C. Farber, 99 Park Avenue, New York, New York 10016, U.S.A.

SCIENCE FICTION PUBLICATIONS

Novels

Player Piano. New York, Scribner, 1952; London, Macmillian, 1953; as *Utopia 14,* New York, Bantam, 1954.
The Sirens of Titan. New York, Dell, 1959; London, Gollancz, 1962.
Cat's Cradle. New York, Holt Rinehart, and London, Gollancz, 1963.
Slaughterhouse-Five; or, The Children's Crusade: A Duty-Dance with Death. New York, Delacorte Press, 1969; London, Cape, 1970.
Breakfast of Champions; or, Goodbye, Blue Monday. New York, Delacorte, and London, Cape, 1973.
Dead-Eye Dick. New York, Delacorte Press, 1982; London, Cape, 1983.
Galápagos. Franklin Center, Pennsylvania, Franklin Library, and London, Cape, 1985.
Hocus Pocus. Franklin Center, Pennsylvania, Franklin Library; as *Hocus Pocus; or, What's the Hurry, Son?,* New York, Putnam, and London, Cape, 1990.

Short Stories

Canary in a Cat House. Greenwich, Connecticut, Fawcett, 1961.
Welcome to the Monkey House: A Collection of Short Works. New York, Delacorte Press, 1968; London, Cape, 1969.

OTHER PUBLICATIONS

Novels

Mother Night. Greenwich, Connecticut, Fawcett, 1962; London, Cape, 1968.
God Bless You, Mr. Rosewater; or, Pearls before Swine. New York, Holt Rinehart, and London, Cape, 1965.
Slapstick; or, Lonesome No More! New York, Delacorte, and London, Cape, 1976.
Jailbird. New York, Delacorte, and London, Cape, 1979.
Bluebeard. Franklin Center, Pennsylvania, Franklin Library, and London, Cape, 1988.

Plays

Happy Birthday, Wanda June (as *Penelope,* produced Cape Cod, Massachusetts, 1960; revised version, as *Happy Birthday, Wanda June,* produced New York, 1970; London, 1977). New York, Delacorte, 1970; London, Cape, 1973.
The Very First Christmas Morning, in Better Homes and Gardens (Des Moines, Iowa), December 1962.
Between Time and Timbuktu; or, Prometheus-5: A Space Fantasy (televised, 1972; produced New York, 1976). New York, Delacorte, 1972; London, Panther, 1975.
Fortitude, in *Wampeters, Foma, and Granfalloons,* 1974.
Timesteps (produced Edinburgh, 1979).
God Bless You, Mr. Rosewater, adaptation of his own novel (produced New York, 1979).

Television Plays: *"Auf Wiedersehen,"* with Valentine Davies, 1958; *Between Time and Timbuktu,* 1972.

Other

Wampeters, Foma and Granfalloons: (Opinions). New York,
Delacorte, 1974; London, Cape, 1975.
Sun Moon Star. New York, Harper, and London, Hutchinson, 1980.
Palm Sunday: An Autobiographical Collage. New York, Delacorte,
and London, Cape, 1981.
Fates Worse Than Death. Nottingham, Spokesman, 1980.
*Fates Worse Than Death: An Autobiographical Collage of the
1980's.* New York, Putnam, and London, Cape, 1991.
Nothing Is Lost Save Honor: Two Essays. Jackson, Mississippi,
Nouveau Press, 1984.
Who Am I This Time? Minneapolis, Minnesota, Redpath Press,
1987.
Conversations with Kurt Vonnegut (interviews), edited by Will-
iam Rodney Allen. Jackson, University of Mississippi Press,
1988.

*

Bibliography: *Kurt Vonnegut, Jr.: A Descriptive Bibliography and
Annotated Secondary Checklist* by Asa B. Pieratt, Jr., and Jerome
Klinkowitz, Hamden, Connecticut, Shoe String Press, 1974; *Kurt
Vonnegut: A Comprehensive Bibliography* by Pieratt, Jr., Julie
Huffman-Klinkowitz, and Jerome Klinkowitz, Hamden, Connecti-
cut, Archon, 1987.

Critical Studies: *Kurt Vonnegut, Jr.* by Peter J. Reed, New York,
Warner, 1972; *Kurt Vonnegut: Fantasist of Fire and Ice* by David
H. Goldsmith, Bowling Green, Ohio, Popular Press, 1972; *The
Vonnegut Statement* edited by Jerome Klinkowitz and John Somer,
New York, Delacorte, 1973, London, Panther, 1975, *Vonnegut in
America: An introduction to the Life and Work of Kurt Vonnegut*
edited by Klinkowitz and Donald L. Lawler, New York, Delacorte
Press, 1977, and *Kurt Vonnegut* by Klinkowitz, London, Methuen,
1982; *Kurt Vonnegut, Jr.* by Stanley Schatt, Boston, Twayne, 1976;
Kurt Vonnegut by James Lundquist, New York, Ungar, 1977;
Vonnegut: A Preface to His Novels by Richard Giannone, Port
Washington, New York, Kennikat Press, 1977; *Kurt Vonnegut: The
Gospel from Outer Space* by Clark Mayo, San Bernardino, Cali-
fornia, Borgo Press, 1977; *Vonnegut's Duty-Dance with Death:
Theme and Structure in Slaughterhouse-Five* by Monica Loeb,
Umeå, Sweden, Umeå Studies in the Humanities, 1979.

*   *   *

What is Kurt Vonnegut's relationship to SF? It would be misleading to say that he began as a SF writer and later drifted away
from the "lodge." Vonnegut never identified with the "lodge,"
and he has continued to use SF as a mine of metaphors for his
sad, zany chronicles of the disintegration of middle-American
culture. The bizarre post-holocaust scene of *Cat's Cradle* shrinks
in *Deadeye Dick* to the depopulation of Midland City by a neutron bomb, but the weirdness of Vonnegut's fiction is characteristically SF.

One way to go wrong is to take straight Eliot Rosewater's much-
quoted drunken speech (in *God Bless You, Mr. Rosewater*) to a SF
writer's convention ("I love you sons of bitches. . . . You're all I
read any more. . . . You're the only ones with guts enough to really
care about the future. . . ."). Eliot is compassionate and humane, to
be sure, but he is also a drunken lunatic. And even Eliot admits that

SF writers can't "write for sour apples," while claiming that Kilgore
Trout, the dean of hacks, is "the greatest writer alive today."

Another way to go wrong is to misread Vonnegut's remark that,
since writing *Player Piano*, he has "been a sore-headed occupant
of a file drawer labeled 'science fiction,'" and that he wants out,
"particularly since so many serious critics regularly mistake the
drawer for a urinal." The urinal mistake is not Vonnegut's: he attributes it to critics who didn't take enough science courses in college, and he goes on to provide a clear-headed and sympathetic
account of the SF writer's "lodge" and the SF branch of the publishing industry.

Perhaps the best approach to mapping Vonnegut's SF connection is to consider Donald Lawler's analysis of *The Sirens of
Titan.* Lawler claims that the "narrative shell" of *Sirens* is "space
opera," and that it serves Vonnegut as "an enabling form of satire." Lawler is right to see the satirical punch of the novel as
arising from its SF form and content; however, the SF form
opposite to the "shaggy dog story" Lawler finds in the novel is
the apocalypse, the kind of SF story that portrays a catastrophic
transformation of the human scene in order to reveal the purpose of human history.

One of the most ambitious of SF's apocalyptic fictions is Arthur
C. Clarke's *Childhood's End*, published five years before *The Sirens of Titan.* In 1978, Vonnegut called Clarke's novel one of SF's
few masterpieces. ("All of the others were written by me," he said.)
Childhood's End portrays the end of human evolution on earth,
revealing that the latent destiny of humankind is to transform its
last generation into a collective immaterial entity that will soar away
from earth and join the Overmind, a godlike union of similar "racial" consciousnesses that is gradually taking over the universe.
Compared to Clarke's grandiose concept, the apocalyptic revelation of *Sirens* is a shaggy dog indeed, for its plot discloses that 50
thousand years of human history have had one trivial purpose: to
ensure the delivery of a repair part to the spacecraft of an alien
courier stranded on Titan. Not only that, the courier discovers that
the message he has spent his being to carry from one end of the
galaxy to the other is merely "Greetings."

The foregoing illustrates one way in which Vonnegut uses SF
conventions—by writing against them, often to the point of parody.
SF stories, whether they end well or badly for their protagonists,
generally embody a romantic concept of human purpose. Immanent or extrinsic, fated or born of the human struggle with nature,
the destiny of humankind is noble and meaningful: to dominate
and make sense of the universe. *The Sirens of Titan* uses SF motifs to counter this tradition. Its hero, Malachi Constant ("the eternal pilgrim"), learns, along with Winston Niles Rumfoord and the
rest of mankind, that the "outward push" is pointless, that there is
no meaning to the universe, and that there is no god but "God the
Utterly Indifferent."

Another indicator of Vonnegut's relationship to SF is, of course,
the feckless SF writer Kilgore Trout, who appears regularly in
Vonnegut's fiction. Promised his freedom in *Breakfast of Champions* (which was supposed to be Vonnegut's final novel), he was
pressed into service again for *Jailbird* and revived anonymously
for *Hocus Pocus.* In *Galápagos*, he appears briefly to his son, the
million-year-old narrator. Trout knows and cares little about science, writes terribly, and has earned neither critical nor popular acclaim: his books can be found, remaindered and misleadingly titled,
only in pornographic bookstores. His fate as a SF writer is far
worse than that of the late Theodore Sturgeon, but his name is almost certainly a wicked parody of Sturgeon's.

Trout, however, is clearly also an alter ego of Vonnegut. His novel *2BRO2B*, so admired by Eliot Rosewater, appears to involve the situation of *Player Piano*, Vonnegut's first novel, with the addition of Ethical Suicide Parlors for population control, themselves an appurtenance of the *Playboy* story "Welcome to the Monkey House" (written about the same time as *God Bless You, Mr. Rosewater*). Trout may be partly a foul-smelling old hack, but he is also a lovable eccentric whose fictions are based on big, imaginative concepts like that of Sturgeon's *The Cosmic Rape*, which saw its title parodied and its plot inverted in Vonnegut's notorious "The Big Space Fuck," published in *Again, Dangerous Visions* (edited by Harlan Ellison, New York, Doubleday, 1972; London, Millington, 1976).

Kilgore Trout is perhaps Vonnegut's chief SF metaphor—the writer whose vision outstrips his knowledge and his craft. In that his condition is Sturgeon's—but also Vonnegut's, and any writer's. Perhaps he also represents any writer's (and any reader's) fear of becoming an old, derelict failure—or of actually being one already. Perhaps he embodies some nagging fear of his creator that what he has created might just possibly be a bunch of worthless, second-rate SF.

Vonnegut's SF (many of the early stories, *Player Piano, The Sirens of Titan, Cat's Cradle, Slaughterhouse-Five,* and *Galápagos*) is not second-rate. *Player Piano*, perhaps, has suffered unfair competition from the major dystopian novels of its time: *1984, Fahrenheit 451,* and *The Space Merchants,* all of which have similar plots involving the rebellion of an insider against an oppressive social order. But, like the others, the story of Paul Proteus has a unique target—automated production—and, like the others, it presents a plausible vision of post-industrial society. *The Sirens of Titan* is not only the parody of apocalyptic SF discussed above: published at the beginning of the age of space, it is a satirical critique of a society obsessed with technological accomplishments that lead to little more than "empty heroics, low comedy, and pointless death."

Cat's Cradle, with its story that counterpoints the careless disposal of a doomsday weapon with the history of a harmless cult religion, is perhaps even stronger in its denunciation of the follies of technological society. The discoverer of Ice-Nine, the substance that destroys the planet by freezing all its water, irresponsibly leaves the fatal chunk to his three less-than-normal offspring. Dr. Felix Hoenikker was already the "father of the A-Bomb," a scientist who would play with any dangerous research idea suggested by the military sources of his funding. Contrasted with him is the playful Bokonon, inventor of a religion he acknowledges to be lies and illusions (or a fiction), but knows will relieve the miserable lives of the inhabitants of his poor Caribbean island. Bokonon is a holy fool who has created a warm extended family; Hoenikker is a man of reason who has neglected his children. The dreams of reason prove more dangerous than the illusions of religion.

Slaughterhouse-Five is the perfect marriage of Vonnegut's SF with his more "mundane" themes. "Billy Pilgrim has come unstuck in time." Unlike the purposeful time travelers of SF convention (but much like the Winston Niles Rumfoord of *Sirens,* jerked around by the chrono-synclastic infundibulum), this unlikely hero lives all the moments of his life simultaneously, including his P.O.W. captivity in Dresden during the firebombing, and his captivity in an exhibit on the planet Tralfamador. From this perspective, optometrist Billy sees that the universe is mechanically preordained, and that the solution is to live only the happy moments. Billy, of course, is regarded as a harmless lunatic (especially since he is a devoted

fan of SF writer Kilgore Trout). However, it is not the holy fools and lunatic dreamers who run the death camps and firebomb Dresden: a different kind of madman has polluted the stream of reason that trickles so weakly in a Billy, a Bokonon, and an Eliot Rosewater.

With *Slaughterhouse-Five,* Vonnegut's fiction becomes more personal, and the line begins to blur between fictional narrative and autobiographical essay. The auctorial voice becomes more direct, and hard to distinguish from those of first-person narrators who are clearly, unlike Trout, projections of Vonnegut. In the much-maligned *Breakfast of Champions,* the author-narrator actually appears in a cocktail lounge occupied by several of the novel's characters, and, at its conclusion, he confronts a pathetic Kilgore Trout. Though he tries to dismiss Trout, however, Vonnegut's SF roots will not disappear so easily. In *Slapstick,* he employs a Troutian conceit (telepathic intelligence-boosting between twins) and a vague post-holocaust setting to articulate the idea of artificial extended families as an antidote for the rootlessness of contemporary Americans. In *Deadeye Dick,* a freak neutron bomb accident is a metaphor for the demolition of the rich cultural matrix of a place much like the Indianapolis of Vonnegut's youth.

Vonnegut's most recent novels continue to address audiences familiar with SF conventions. *Galápagos,* Vonnegut's answer to Swift's *Voyage to the Land of the Houyhnhms,* Wells's *Time Machine,* and Stewart's *Earth Abides,* takes the post-holocaust fiction into new territories of rational absurdity. Its million-year-old narrator (the ghost of Kilgore Trout's son) unfolds for us the saga of how the human species was saved (sort of) when a plague rendered virtually all women permanently sterile. By chance, a small, motley group ends up stranded in the Galápagos Archipelago and is unafflicted by the plague. Their descendants, we are told, evolve into creatures who can digest seaweed and swim with flippers, whose brains are not of the big, dangerous sort possessed by their ancestors—and who do not know they are going to die. Most of the story's actual events take place in the 20th century, and those events would seem to justify the conclusion that humanity's curious devolution would not be such a bad outcome.

While *Bluebeard,* the story of the Armenian-American minimalist painter who appeared briefly in *Breakfast of Champions,* is not explicitly connected with Vonnegut's SF, the same cannot be said of *Hocus Pocus.* The involute saga of Eugene Debs Hartke, Vietnam hero, fired college teacher, prison warden, and TB victim, is narrated in the year 2001. Several other allusions to Arthur C. Clarke suggest that we are to take the story as another of Vonnegut's peeks at the contrast between our millennial pretensions and our cultural and economic decay. The novel plays promiscuously with elements of Vonnegut's fictional cosmos and the often depressing world of our daily newspapers and the detritus of our popular culture, and the effects often seem inexplicable. Why, for instance, is an ostentatious vulgarian clearly modeled on Malcolm Forbes given the name Arthur K. Clarke? The answer might be found in the text of the anonymous "Protocols of the Elders of Tralfamadore" stowed in Hartke's footlocker, a Troutian big-concept story that reveals the origin of life and religion in a conspiracy of superhuman aliens. Or it might not.

Vonnegut has been writing about two things since the beginning—the loss of old Indianapolis, a symbol of middle America, and its way of life (noble in spite of racism, pretentiousness, and abuse and neglect of the poor); and what seems to be replacing it (a racist, pretentious, exploitative vulgarity). Vonnegut, by his own admission not a member of the "lodge" and not a reader of SF pulps as a youngster, may not be a "licensed" SF writer. Yet he remains an ornament to SF, for without the SF devices that shape his fictions, he could not have made them what they are. If his chronicle of contemporary America's endless Great Depression has enduring value, it is largely due to Vonnegut's quirky dialect of the language of SF.

—John P. Brennan

WAINWRIGHT, Ken. *See* TUBB, E.C.

WALDROP, Howard

Nationality: American. **Born:** Houston, Mississippi, 15 September 1946. **Education:** Arlington High School, Texas, 1962-65; University of Texas, Arlington, 1965-70, 1972-74. **Military Service:** Served as an information specialist in the United States Army, 1970-72. **Career:** Linotype operator, *Arlington Daily News*, 1965-68; advertising copywriter, Lindell-Keyes, Dallas, 1972; auditory research subject, Dynastat Inc., Austin, 1975-80. **Awards:** Nebula award, 1980; World Fantasy award, 1981. **Agent:** Joseph Elder Agency, P.O. Box 298, Warwick, New York 10990. **Address:** P.O. Box 49335, Austin, Texas 78765, U.S.A.

SCIENCE FICTION PUBLICATIONS

Novels

The Texas-Israeli War: 1999, with Jake Saunders. New York, Ballantine, 1974.
Them Bones. New York, Ace, 1984; London, Legend, 1989.
A Dozen Tough Jobs. Willimantic, Connecticut, Zeising, 1989.

Short Stories

Howard Who?: Twelve Outstanding Stories of Speculative Fiction. Garden City, New York, Doubleday, 1986.
All about Strange Monsters of the Recent Past: Neat Stories. Kansas City, Missouri, Ursus, 1987; expanded as *Strange Monsters of the Recent Past,* New York, Ace, 1991.
Strange Things in Close-up: The Nearly Complete Howard Waldrop. London, Legend, 1989.
Night of the Cooters: More Neat Stories. Kansas City, Missouri, Ursus, 1990; expanded, London, Legend, 1991.
You Could Go Home Again. New Castle, Virginia, Cheap Street, 1993.

*   *   *

Howard Waldrop is one of science fiction's most distinctive stylists, one of the very few who might truly be called unique. Working predominantly in the shorter forms Waldrop has amassed an acclaimed body of work which consistently surprises, enlightens, and entertains.

It isn't possible to define a typical Waldrop story in terms more precise than "odd"—take "Fin-de-Cycle," in which the Dreyfus Affair that racked France in 1895 is viewed by characters including painter Henri Rousseau, Alfred Jarry, and film pioneer Georges Melies, as everyone cycles around Paris. Or "Flying Saucer Rock 'n' Roll," the partially true story of a Doo-wop singing contest between rival gangs that is interrupted by a UFO and causes a massive power failure along the whole East Coast of the U.S. Or the last of the Dodos, in Depression-era Mississippi, "The Ugly Chickens."

Waldrop's hallmarks are multiple, not least being his eclecticism: Dinosaurs, jazz, UFOs, rock 'n' roll, cowboys, comics, the movies; second must be the phenomenal research involved in these stories, which reveals itself in Waldrop's apparent belief that if it's been researched use it, don't waste it. The *Wild Cards* story "Thirty Minutes over Broadway" runs to 37 pages and is followed up with annotations covering a further 12 pages and detailing everything from the aircraft specs used in the story to the comic book and B-movie allusions of character names.

It is this depth that makes even a weaker Waldrop story such as the novella "A Dozen Tough Jobs" entertaining on one level. Some of the allusions are clumsy in this retelling of the labours of Hercules—here a paroled convict called Houlka Lee, narrated by the young black servant I.O. Lace—but others are more subtle. Waldrop avoids a direct retelling of the labours, preferring instead to focus on the social interactions of 1920s Mississippi so that in typical Waldrop fashion the story eventually says more about I.O. than about Houlka. What makes this charming but apparently lightweight story important is the revelation it casts upon Howard Waldrop as a Southern Writer. His blend of savagery and romance is tied strongly to a sense of place, so that after "A Dozen Tough Jobs" for all its weaknesses, it becomes hard to conceive of Hercules' labours taking place anywhere but Spunt County, Mississippi in 1927.

Waldrop's only solo novel, *Them Bones,* is also set in the South, albeit an alternative Louisiana where the Arabs and Aztecs rule and neither Christianity nor the Roman Empire ever happened. Ostensibly a time-travel novel, this is a detailed picture of Amerindian culture as it might have been. As in "The Ugly Chickens," the reader feels a sense of loss at this.

The games Waldrop plays with history make his stories amusing and entertaining in themselves, as in "Ike at the Mike," in which young Senator E. Aaron Presley watches the jazz performance of legendary musicians Ike Eisenhower and Louis Armstrong. The story moves along from this, however—via little asides about President Kennedy (and without ever saying so, directly hints that this might be Robert Kennedy) being the "first two-term president since Huey "Kingfish" Long—to an analysis of the importance of this music to people, of its power and its resonance. And when, at the end, you discover that the story doesn't actually have a plot of any sort, its absence has been made superfluous by the emotional intensity of Waldrop's exposition.

Music of one form or another, along with most other forms of popular culture, is a significant element in Waldrop's fiction. One of the many stories to deal directly with it is "Do Ya, Do Ya Wanna, Wanna Dance"—a romantic story about youthful idealism and dreams from the viewpoint of 20 years on. The first paragraph is in typical Waldrop voice: "The light was so bad in the bar that everyone there looked like they had been painted by Thomas Hart Benton, or carved from dirty bars of soap with rusty spoons." Later, the narrator joins his friends and notes pithily, "I seemed *not* to have interrupted a conversation."

This easy, conversational style and the historical games belie the dark heart of Waldrop. By denying the accepted significance of historical events, Waldrop might be seen to offer a new innocence which penetrates to objective truth. His stories frequently begin in light, but quickly threaten some ultimate catastrophe. Occasionally the general foreboding is built on real evidence, such as one particularly nasty scene in "Do Ya, Do Ya Wanna, Wanna Dance," but in most of Waldrop's stories it is the character's fears that the reader feels, and it may never be clear on what basis these are founded. Ultimately, for the Waldropian character one finds a transition from the aesthetic to the religious and, frequently, a sense of self-recognition, which is the essence of the Southern grotesque, and Howard Waldrop's unique contribution to science fiction. Other writers, outlaw fantasists such as Leigh Kennedy, Steven Utley, George R.R. Martin, etc., and non-genre authors such as T. Corraghessan Boyle may have done it intermittently, but only Waldrop has done it to such extent.

—Kev P. McVeigh

WALLACE, F(loyd) L.

Nationality: American. **Address:** Lives in California.

SCIENCE FICTION PUBLICATIONS

Novel

Address: Centauri. New York, Gnome Press, 1955.

Short Stories

Worlds in Balance. Melbourne, Atlas, 1955.

OTHER PUBLICATIONS

Novels

Three Times a Victim. New York, Ace, 1957.
Wired for Scandal. New York, Ace, 1959.

*   *   *

Still a hazy figure in the history of science fiction, F.L. Wallace was one of the field's most outstanding and least appreciated writers during the 1950s. His only SF novel, *Address: Centauri,* is a minor work that was an expansion of his very good story "Accidental Flight" (*Galaxy,* 1952). Wallace's other SF stories are of high quality, characterized by a depth and a thoroughness uncommon to the field in the 1950s. Among his most noteworthy stories are "Delay in Transit"; "Big Ancestor," a powerful commentary on the human race and its future direction; "Student Body," which features one of the very best descriptions and development of an alien lifeform in all of science fiction; "Bolden's Pets," wherein Wallace brilliantly employs the unique concept of positive parasitism; "Mezzerow Loves Company"; "Tangle Hold"; and "The Impossible Voyage Home."

—Martin H. Greenberg

WALLACE, Ian

Pseudonym for John W(allace) Pritchard. **Nationality:** American. **Born:** Chicago, Illinois, 4 December 1912. **Education:** University of Michigan, Ann Arbor, B.A. in English 1934, M.A. in edu-

cational psychology 1939, graduate study 1949-51; Wayne University, now Wayne State University, Detroit, education certificate 1936, Ed. D. 1957. **Military Service:** Served as a clinical psychologist in the United States Army during World War II: Captain. **Family:** Married Elizabeth Paul in 1938; two sons. **Career:** Psychology technician, clinical psychologist, department head, administrative assistant, director, and divisional director, Board of Education, Detroit, 1934-74; now retired. Part-time lecturer in education, Wayne State University, 1955-74. Lives in Asheville, North Carolina. **Address:** c/o DAW Books, 375 Hudson Street, New York, New York 10014, U.S.A.

SCIENCE FICTION PUBLICATIONS

Novels (series: Croyd; Pan Sagittarius; St. Cyr and U. Tuli)

Croyd: A Downtime Fantasy. New York, Putnam, 1967.
Dr. Orpheus: A Downtime Myth (St. Cyr). New York, Putnam, 1968.
Deathstar Voyage: A Downtime Mystery Cruise (Croyd/Pan). New York, Putnam, 1969; London, Dobson, 1972.
The Purloined Prince (St. Cyr). New York, McCall, 1971.
Pan Sagittarius. New York, Putnam, 1973.
A Voyage to Dari (Croyd/Pan). New York, DAW, 1974.
The World Asunder (Pan). New York, DAW, 1976; London, Dobson, 1978.
The Sign of the Mute Medusa (St. Cyr). New York, Popular Library, 1977.
Z-Sting (Croyd). New York, DAW, 1978.
Heller's Leap (Croyd/St. Cyr). New York, DAW, 1979.
The Lucifer Comet (Croyd). New York, DAW, 1980.
The Rape of the Sun. New York, DAW, 1982.
Megalomania (Croyd). New York, DAW, 1989.

OTHER PUBLICATIONS AS JOHN W(ALLACE) PRITCHARD

Novel

Every Crazy Wind. New York, Dodd Mead, 1952.

Other

Frank Cody, A Realist in Education, with others. New York, Macmillan, 1943.
Off to Work, with Paul H. Voelker. Pittsburgh, Stanwic House, 1962.
Public Education in Detroit, with Katherine Beamer. Detroit, Detroit Public Schools, 1963.
Detroit: A Manual for Citizens. Detroit, Board of Education, 1968.
On Their Way: A Teacher's Guide for off to Work, with Paul H. Voelker. Detroit, Board of Education, 1968.
Author-editor-publisher of numerous Detroit Board of Education textbooks and teaching guides, 1942-74.

*

Ian Wallace comments:
I aim my books at well-educated or self-educated minds. For them, I try to write pleasurable, frequently startling, coherently designed stories, taking advantage of fantasy to enlarge their scope,

but disciplining the tales with logic and with scientific and philosophic theory. I try to portray humans living at the highest levels of their humanity, entailing many-sided intelligence, emotion intelligently guided and expressed, and human fellow-feeling for all the different kinds of humans (including some weird-bodied instances on other planets); that, for me, is both a moral issue and a taste preference.

*   *   *

Ian Wallace is best known for his two science fiction series: the Croyd series of space operas and the St. Cyr futuristic detective series. The first book in the Croyd series is the most well known. Croyd is a humanoid with psychic powers that the rulers of the human Galaxy put to use as a secret agent. But, in *Croyd*, Croyd finds his body invaded by a gnurl—an alien agent—whose mission is to destroy the Galaxy. Croyd finds his identity transferred into the body of a female human. Croyd has two missions: to regain possession of his own superior body and to stop the destruction of the Galaxy before it's too late.

Dr. Orpheus features Croyd's powers of traveling "uptime" and "downtime" to defeat both a human agent who is attempting to weaken humanity with a drug called Anagonon—its effects make users unquestioning slaves—and the alien race behind the plot who see humanity as the ideal mammalian food-sources to implant their eggs. Only Croyd's time-travelling powers, which take him to ancient Greece to discover a vital clue, foil the plot within a plot.

A Voyage to Dari is the most ambitious of the Croyd novels; Wallace almost attempts too much. With the loss of his powers, Croyd still attempts to deal with a political confrontation modeled on India and colonial Britain. Added to the mix is a space-dwelling alien who adopts medieval imagery as its mental universe. Although the plot is sometimes muddled, the sheer alienness of the action makes reading *A Voyage to Dari* compulsive.

Z-Sting begins with Croyd in old age. He has eliminated war with his Comcord system. When a nation on the planet reaches a certain discord quotient, the Comcord system would trigger Z-sting: the offending nation would be surrounded and isolated from the rest of the world. But something has gone wrong with the system, and Croyd, with the help of his great-granddaughter, discovers a monstrous plot that threatens the whole human order.

In *Megalomania*, Croyd finds a threat to the galaxy from within its own government. Croyd is the leader of Sol Galaxy. His first minister, Dino Trigg, lusts for Croyd's position. When Croyd easily beats Trigg in the galactic elections, Trigg devises a plot to destroy Sol Galaxy with the Magellanic Clouds, which he will use to form a new galaxy. The scope of this space opera is cosmic and the action leaves the reader breathless.

The St. Cyr series lacks the galaxy-spanning scale of the Croyd books, but makes up for that with clever detection and careful plotting. *Deathstar Voyage* introduces Claudine St. Cyr, a 25th-century policewoman, whose mission is to bodyguard the king of Ligeria from the assassins plotting to kill him. The action takes place on a huge starship called *Eiland*, whose atomic pile is threatening to explode because of sabotage. St. Cyr's must identify the assassins, solve several bizarre murders, and solve the crisis of the *Eiland* before everything blows up. Wallace concocts a spellbinding mystery in *Deathstar Voyage*. *The Purloined Prince* is a delicious mystery in which St. Cyr is threatened with death for most of the book, but she has the grit to continue her investigation and solve the mystery.

The Sign of the Mute Medusa is a less flamboyant book. St. Cyr investigates a series of disappearances that might be murders in a domed city on Planet Turquoise. Much is made of the political struggle of the Haves—the ruling class—and the Have-nots—the rebels. The plotting is ingenious but the political subplots are heavy handed and diminish the book's enjoyment. The first two St. Cyr books are entertaining because of Wallace's light touch and sense of fun. But *The Sign of the Mute Medusa* is too slight to carry Wallace's ponderous political message.

The best St. Cyr is *Heller's Leap*, in which Claudine solves the murder of Klaus Heller, a survivor of a journey through a black hole. The bonus is that Wallace brings Croyd into the action to help St. Cyr solve the mystery and prevent the destruction of a planet. This union of Wallace's two most famous characters makes *Heller's Leap* one of his best novels.

Wallace's non-series books vary in quality. In *The World Asunder*, long philosophical speeches replace action. *The Rape of the Sun* starts promisingly with aliens who steal our Solar System as a present to their Princess, but then gets bogged down in pseudo-profound dialogue. The best of Wallace's non-series books is *The Lucifer Comet*, in which a battle between Good and Evil avoids the mind-deadening dialogues of many of Wallace's books and concentrates on the characters of Prometheus and Lucifer. Wallace's novels blend Van Vogtian plotting with E.E. Smith's comic scale to produce space operas with action as vast as the galaxies.

—George Kelley

WALTERS, Hugh

Pseudonym for Walter Llewellyn Hughes. **Nationality:** British. **Born:** Bilston, Staffordshire, 15 June 1910. **Education:** St. Martin's School; Bilston Central School; Dudley Grammar School, 1923-26; Wednesbury College, 1939-41; Wolverhampton Polytechnic, 1941-43. **Family:** Married 1) Doris Higgins in 1933, one son and one daughter; 2) Susan Hughes in 1977. **Career:** Since 1954, managing director, Bransteds Ltd., engineers, and chairman, Walter Hughes Ltd., furnishings. Justice of the Peace, 1947-74. **Agent:** John Farquharson Ltd., 162-168 Regent Street, London W1R 5TB, England.

<small>SCIENCE FICTION PUBLICATIONS</small>

Novels (for children; series: Chris Godfrey in all titles)

Blast off at Woomera. London, Faber, 1957; as *Blast-off at 0300*, New York, Criterion, 1958.
The Domes of Pico. London, Faber, 1958; as *Menace from the Moon*, New York, Criterion, 1959.
Operation Columbus. London, Faber, 1960; as *First on the Moon*, New York, Criterion, 1960.
Moon Base One. London, Faber, 1961; as *Outpost on the Moon*, New York, Criterion, 1962.
Expedition Venus. London, Faber, 1962; New York, Criterion, 1963.
Destination Mars. London, Faber, 1963; New York, Criterion, 1964.
Terror by Satellite. London, Faber, and New York, Criterion, 1964.
Journey to Jupiter. London, Faber, 1965; New York, Criterion, 1966.

977

Mission to Mercury. London, Faber, and New York, Criterion, 1965.

Spaceship to Saturn. London, Faber, and New York, Criterion, 1967.

The Mohole Mystery. London, Faber, 1968; as *The Mohole Menace,* New York, Criterion, 1969.

Nearly Neptune. London, Faber, 1969; as *Neptune One Is Missing,* New York, Washburn, 1970.

First Contact? London, Faber, 1971; Nashville, Nelson, 1973.

Passage to Pluto. London, Faber, and Nashville, Nelson, 1973.

Tony Hale, Space Detective. London, Faber, 1973.

Murder on Mars. London, Faber, 1975.

Boy Astronaut. London, Abelard-Schumann, 1977.

The Caves of Drach. London, Faber, 1977.

The Last Disaster. London, Faber, 1978.

The Blue Aura. London, Faber, 1979.

First Family on the Moon. London, Abelard, 1979.

The Dark Triangle. London, Faber, 1981.

School on the Moon. London, Abelard, 1981.

P-K. London, Severn House, 1986.

*

Hugh Walters comments:

(1981) All my books are for young people in the 9-11 and 11-16 age groups. I believe that books for this readership should 1) entertain, which is the primary object; 2) educate painlessly (astronomy, mathematics, geology, etc.); 3) inspire the young people of today to become the scientists and technicians of tomorrow.

* * *

Hugh Walters has devoted his entire writing career to children's SF, and the results have been mixed. At first, his novels were welcomed as filling a void in SF publishing, being praised as the way SF should be written for children. Gradually critical opinion shifted as Walter's fiction came to be seen as repetitive, formula-bound, and even carelessly written; and the attention it received from the review media in both SF and children's literature virtually ceased. In the face of critical neglect and sometimes even open scorn, the wonder is that Walter's novels continue to be published and have retained popularity for as long as they have. Obviously, his publishers are satisfied that the young audience Walters writes for does read and enjoy his novels and, ignoring adult disapproval, even puts pressure upon librarians to keep his books in circulation and order new titles as they appear. This phenomenon is readily understood once it is perceived that Walter's fiction is the result of his attempt to wed the formulas and expectations of boy's series books and SF. In other words, Walter's SF manifests both the strengths and weaknesses of children's series fiction writing.

On one hand, Walters's SF celebrates the exploits of youthful, dashing, and resourceful protagonists that boys chaffing under the dullness of their routine-filled lives enthusiastically identify with. In *Operation Columbus,* Chris Godfrey, hero of Walters's SF, is the first person on the moon and he also magnanimously saves the life of his young Russian rival, Serge Smyslov, who had previously disabled Chris's space craft. Chris then pilots the Russian space ship safely to earth in spite of not being familiar with the controls. In *Terror by Satellite,* Tony Hale, who appears in some of the Godfrey books, is the remaining link between earth and the Observatory, the space satellite taken over by its crazed commander,

Hendriks, who threatens to destroy earth; through his skill in electronics Tony proves indispensable as Chris successfully retakes control of the Observatory. Walters is clearly a knowledgeable author of children's books, and is careful to balance Chris, the public-school boy born to privilege and noblesse oblige, with Tony, the son of lower-class shop-keeping parents. In this way, many different kinds of young readers may be able to identify with Walters's protagonists. Further, although he does emphasize action and the various dangers of space exploration—emphases obviously intended to capture the attention of young readers—Walters does not neglect space technology and weaponry. Described in detail, these are usually up-to-date or plausibly extrapolated so that youngsters looking for "nuts and bolts SF" are readily satisfied.

On the other hand, Walters's SF exhibits the weaknesses characteristic of most series fiction: conventional, two-dimensional characterization, repetitive and predictable plotting, and dull, pedestrian writing. As a result of these weaknesses, Walters has been denied major status. At the same time, however, it would be unfair to dismiss Walters as just another author of series SF, another Victor Appleton II or John Blaine. For, in view of his strengths, it is clear that Walters's work is definitely a cut or two above typical series SF.

—Francis J. Molson

WATKINS, William Jon

Nationality: American. **Born:** Coaldale, Pennsylvania, 19 July 1942. **Education:** Neshaminy High School, Langehorne, Pennsylvania; Rutgers University, New Brunswick, New Jersey, B.S. 1964, M. Ed. 1965. **Family:** Married Sandra Lee Preno in 1961; three children. **Career:** Instructor, Delaware Valley College, Doyleston, Pennsylvania, 1965-68; high school teacher, Asbury Park, New Jersey, 1968-69. Instructor, 1969-70, assistant professor, 1970-71, and since 1971, associate professor of humanities, Brookdale Community College, Lincroft, New Jersey. **Awards:** Per Se award, for play, 1970. **Address:** 1406 Garven Avenue, Ocean, New Jersey 07712, U.S.A.

SCIENCE FICTION PUBLICATIONS

Novels (series: Legrange League)

Ecodeath, with Gene Snyder. Garden City, New York, Doubleday, 1972.

Clickwhistle. Garden City, New York, Doubleday, 1973.

The God Machine. Garden City, New York, Doubleday, and London, Angus and Robertson, 1973.

The Litany of Sh'reev, with Gene Snyder. Garden City, New York, Doubleday, 1976.

What Rough Beast. Chicago, Playboy Press, 1980.

The Centrifugal Rickshaw Dancer (Legrange). New York, Popular Library, 1985.

Going to See the End of the Sky (Legrange). New York, Popular Library, 1986.

The Last Deathship off Antares. New York, Popular Library, 1989.

Other Publications

Novel

A Fair Advantage (for children). Englewood Cliffs, New Jersey, Prentice-Hall, 1975.

Plays

The Judas Wheel (produced Warrensburg, Missouri, 1970), bound with *We Regret to Inform You,* by Grace Cavalier. New York, Smith, 1969.
A King of a Hole: A One-Act Play. Elgin, Illinois, Performance, 1974.

Poetry

Five Poems. Chula Vista, California, Word Press, 1968.

Other

Tracker: The Story of Tom Brown Jr., with Tom Brown Jr. Englewood Cliffs, New Jersey, Prentice-Hall, 1978.
The Psychic Experiment Book. Englewood Cliffs, New Jersey, Prentice-Hall, 1980.
The Psychic Diet Book. Asbury Park, New Jersey, Grappling Press, 1980.
Suburban Wilderness. New York, Putnam, 1981.
Who's Who in New Jersey Wrestling. Asbury Park, New Jersey, Grappling Press, 1981.

*   *   *

William Jon Watkins's novels, two of which were written with Gene Snyder, show man as a corrupt evildoer who creates his own doomsday crises in which he barely avoids the total extinction of human life on Earth.

In *Ecodeath,* Earth is about to die from water pollution. Two characters, Watkins and Snyder, start out as opponents but soon pool forces in order to rescue humankind. They use teleportation and finally link their mindpower to transport a small group of survivors to a pollution-free parallel earth of the future by telekinesis. Humankind survives because Watkins realizes that time implies parallel worlds existing simultaneously in infinity.

In *Clickwhistle,* extraterrestrial beings take possession of the minds of killer whales to send computerized commands to atomic missiles stored in submarines. Dr. Pearson, a dolphin authority, defeats the aliens with the help of dolphins, but other human beings are either evil-doers or slaves of dark political powers. Intrigue and betrayal run rampant while Orcas and dolphins battle. Earth is saved when dolphins triumph, but humans will forever live in fear of political bosses.

The God Machine shows perpetual and total warfare between a totalitarian worldwide state machine of Orwell's *Nineteen Eighty-Four* type and a highly technological underground opponent. Sophisticated weapons and tactics improve with the need to accelerate extermination. A reduction machine, the "micronizer," is central to several plot twists. Ecological negligence is the trademark of the status quo. An unbreathable atmosphere makes the use of masks and air filters universal. Neither side is a definite winner in the end.

In *The Litany of Sh'reev,* Sh'reev uses mental powers to heal and save lives while a chronic state of revolutionary wars wrecks civilization. Empire is run by the will of an absolute and totalitar-

ian ruler who destroys extant royal families to seize their wealth. The revolutionaries are ESPers who reject the increase of oppression. Sh'reev gets his spiritual power from Tao techniques. His mind fuses with those of the sick and dying in a state called Sh'aela. Eternal Return in its Eastern version provides further existences for Sh'reev.

The central action of *What Rough Beast* is the hunt for one huge, extraterrestrial, telekinetic, furry humanoid female who lands on Earth in order to help humans acquire her talents. Corporation mentality as the villainous hunter is aided by an almost sentient computer, Slic 1000, and his offspring Tad. There is an ironical twist when corporational man, dominated by a rigid mentality, becomes a dehumanized animal backbiting other corporate members in the struggle for power and rewards while the computers become humanized. The hero and savior is Lth, the alien furry female whose telepathic abilities merge with Tad in order to confer superhuman status upon humans. Humankind is saved when sentient microcomputers become an implanted standard stabilizing device in human brains.

Although Watkins's novels are simply constructed and appropriate for juvenile audiences, they deal with the vital issue of human's chances of survival. In each instance, they bring a catastrophic end upon themselves and an environment they can neither preserve nor duplicate, and avoid self-annihilation by the slightest margin. Watkins implies that humankind, part angel but mostly beast, is on a cyclical course and will probably repeat its past mistakes. In *What Rough Beast,* Watkins introduces two new solutions to the "scorpion syndrome," man against himself. One is Lth's Superwoman mentality; the other is brain microcomputer implantation. In both cases, Watkins suggests that man cannot be his own master.

—Eric A. Fontaine

WATSON, Ian

Nationality: British. **Born:** North Shields, Northumberland, 20 April 1943. **Education:** Tynemouth School, 1948-59; Balliol College, Oxford, 1960-65, B.A. (honours) in English 1963, B.Litt. 1965, M.A. 1966. **Family:** Married Judith Jackson in 1962; one daughter. Lecturer, University College, Dar es Salaam, Tanzania, 1965-67, and Tokyo University of Education, 1967-70; lecturer, 1970-75, and senior lecturer in Complementary Studies, 1975-76, Birmingham Polytechnic Art and Design Centre; features editor and regular contributor, *Foundation,* London, 1975-90; writer-in-residence, Nene College, Northampton, 1984. Since 1983, European editor, *Science Fiction Writers of America Bulletin.* **Awards:** Prix Apollo (France), 1975; Orbit award, 1976; British Science Fiction Association award, 1978; Southern Arts Association bursary, 1978. **Address:** Daisy Cottage, Moreton Pinkney, near Daventry, Northamptonshire, NN11 6SQ England.

Science Fiction Publications

Novels (series: Black Current; Mana; Warhammer 40,000; Yaleen)

The Embedding. London, Gollancz, 1973; New York, Scribner, 1975.

The Jonah Kit. London, Gollancz, 1975; New York, Scribner, 1976.
Orgasmachine. Paris, Editions Champ Libre, 1976.
The Martin Inca. London, Gollancz, and New York, Scribner, 1977.
Alien Embassy. London, Gollancz, 1977; New York, Ace, 1978.
Miracle Visitors. London, Gollancz, and New York, Ace, 1978.
God's World. London, Gollancz, 1979; New York, Carroll and Graf, 1990.
The Gardens of Delight. London, Gollancz, 1980; New York, Timescape, 1982.
Under Heaven's Bridge, with Michael Bishop. London, Gollancz, 1981; New York, Ace, 1982.
Deathhunter. London, Gollancz, 1981; New York, St. Martin's Press, 1986.
Chekhov's Journey. London, Gollancz, 1983; New York, Carroll and Graf, 1989.
The Books of the Black Current. Garden City, New York, Doubleday, 1986.
  The Book of the River. London, Gollancz, 1984; New York, DAW, 1986.
  The Book of the Stars. London, Gollancz, 1984; New York, DAW, 1986.
  The Book of Being. London, Gollancz, 1985; New York, DAW, 1986.
Converts. London, Panther, 1984; New York, St. Martin's Press, 1985.
Queenmagic, Kingmagic. London, Gollancz, and New York, St. Martin's Press, 1988.
The Power. London, Headline, 1987.
The Fire Worm. London, Gollancz, 1988.
Meat. London, Headline, 1988.
Whores of Babylon. London, Grafton, 1988.
The Flies of Memory. London, Gollancz, 1990; New York, Carroll and Graf, 1991.
Inquisitor (Warhammer). Brighton, West Sussex, Games Workshop, 1990.
Space Marine (Warhammer). London, Boxtree, 1993.
Lucky's Harvest (Mana). London, Gollancz, 1993.
The Fallen Moon: The Second Book of Mana. London, Gollancz, 1994.

Short Stories

Japan Tomorrow. Osaka, Bunken, 1975.
The Very Slow Time Machine: Science Fiction Stories. London, Gollancz, and New York, Ace, 1979.
Sunstroke and Other Stories. London, Gollancz, 1982.
The Book of Ian Watson (includes nonfiction). Willimantic, Connecticut, Ziesing, 1985.
Slow Birds and Other Stories. London, Gollancz, 1985.
Evil Water and Other Stories. London, Gollancz, 1987.
Salvage Rites and Other Stories. London, Gollancz, 1989.
Stalin's Teardrops and Other Stories. Brighton, West Sussex, Games Workshop, 1991.
Nanoware Time, with *The Persistence of Vision,* by John Varley. New York, Tor, 1991.
The Coming of Vertumnus and Other Stories. London, Gollancz, 1994.

OTHER PUBLICATIONS

Other

Japan: A Cat's Eye View (for children). Osaka, Bunken, 1969.

Editor, *Pictures at an Exhibition.* Cardiff, Greystoke Mobray, 1981.
Editor, with Pamela Sargent, *Afterlives: An Anthology of Stories about Life after Death.* New York, Vintage, 1986.
Editor, with Michael Bishop, *Changes: Stories of Metamorphosis: An Anthology of Speculative Fiction about Startling Metamorphoses, Both Psychological and Physical.* New York, Ace, 1983.

*

Manuscript Collection: Science Fiction Foundation, North-East London Polytechnic.

Ian Watson comments:

My books are all primarily about the relationship between reality and consciousness (testing out this theme variously by way of linguistics, speculation about cetacean intelligence, evolution, novel life forms, the UFO mythos, etc.) and whether any kind of ultimate understanding of the nature of reality and the reason for life and the universe may or may not be arrived at. Intersecting this is frequently—particularly in my earlier books—a strong socio-political underpinning to events. A dialectic of history and transcendence is at work. I regard my fiction as a research programme, in fictional form, into the nature of existence and the nature of knowledge.

*   *   *

The best of British science fiction in the 1950s was preoccupied with disasters, ravaging civilization with floods, earthquakes, droughts, and the like. Although many of these novels were excellent works of fiction, there was little concern with stylistic content until *New Worlds* magazine and the "new wave" introduced surrealism, non-linear plots, and other experiments into the genre. In the aftermath, a handful of writers found a successful balance between the two extremes and launched successful careers. One of these was Ian Watson, whose popularity and productivity have waned somewhat in the 1990s, but who is unquestionably one of the more original and inventive writers in the genre.

Ian Watson's fiction often explores the very nature of reality as it is perceived by humans, how our minds work, what we believe we know about the universe and how that belief stands up in practice, how we deal with our own mortality. His approach is often highly sophisticated, intelligent, and metaphysical, sometimes so original in concept and execution that casual readers become confused or alienated from his work. It is unfortunate that even as his critical success has grown, his commercial viability appears to have declined in the United States.

Watson's debut novel was *The Embedding,* which examined the role of language in shaping our existence, and the callous manner in which we make use of other human beings for our own purposes. On the one hand we have a group of children who have been deliberately exposed only to an artificial language; on the other, aliens willing to trade technology for human brains which may be the key to a transcendent experience. Virtually every party in this novel intends to sacrifice the welfare of others in return for some perceived advantage. Having presented his observations, Watson leaves it to the reader to draw conclusions.

The Jonah Kit is thematically similar. The universe is defined by our perception of it, and if we change what we believe to be true, the truth itself alters. A Soviet experiment involving the imprinting of human intelligence in whales takes an unexpected twist when they appear to have become a link with another form of intelligence. A mysterious virus inadvertently brought back from Mars is the catalyst for dramatic changes in *The Martian Inca,* raising the question of what it means to be a human being.

Alien Embassy presents an innovative way around the lightspeed limit. Humanity reaches the stars by means of psychic projection, gathering information, contacting other intelligent species, and transforming human society to what appears to be a near Utopia. The appearance is deceiving, however. Information is "managed" by a few for the assumed good of the many. There is a new caste system, censorship of ideas, conflict where there should have been cooperation. This atmosphere of repression becomes crucial when it appears that humanity itself may be on the brink of a transformation. Perhaps the most accessible of Watson's early novels, it was also a thoughtful work that raised and examined important questions.

Miracle Visitors used the UFO phenomenon as the springboard for another examination of multiple realities. The novel also contains some very humorous sequences although, as with its predecessors, the central focus is always serious. *The Gardens of Delight* is an intellectual puzzle set within a standard SF plot framework. A starship lands on a bizarre world that one crew member recognizes as that of the famous Bosch painting. *Under Heaven's Bridge,* written in collaboration with Michael Bishop, deals with efforts to establish communication with a species facing imminent destruction, and raises the question of just what do we mean by "intelligence."

Deathhunter is set in a society that views death as an experience to be met willingly. The protagonist has helped many people end their lives, but he questions his own life experience when involved in an attempt to capture death literally personified. *Chekhov's Journey* was less impressive but still an interesting story. A Russian stage crew uses hypnosis to help an actor identify with Chekhov, convincing him that he is the writer's reincarnation, but what "Chekhov" remembers is a radically different past than the one in the history books.

The Black Current trilogy: *The Book of the River, The Book of the Stars,* and *The Book of Being,* is Watson's most ambitious and in many ways most successful work to date. The opening volume is set on a world divided by a river into two rival societies, one repressive and male-dominated, the other less autocratic, dominated by women. Intercourse between the two societies is limited because the river is occupied by an enigmatic alien intelligence that drives men insane if they venture into its reach. The trilogy, which involves the battle between two omnipotent intelligences whose conflict threatens the entire universe, is much more straightforwardly adventurous than Watson's other novels, but retains a serious examination of the nature of the universe.

Queenmagic, Kingmagic also plays with realities, this time in the context of fantasy, a world whose natural laws are based on the game of chess. An amusing and cleverly constructed entertainment, it retains echoes of Watson's continuing interest in the nature of the universe. *The Flies of Memory* is a first contact story with some of the strangest aliens of all time. The Flies arrive on Earth but communication with humans is peripheral and unsatisfactory. The visitors spend most of their time wandering around the planet, "remembering" things. And those human artifacts that are remembered abruptly vanish. Are the aliens destroying or stealing them, or are they salvaging souvenirs from a doomed world?

Watson has also proven to be a skillful and prolific short-story writer. One of his earliest, "The Very Slow Time Machine," is a unique look at time paradoxes. "Thy Milk like Blood" raises a number of ethical questions in a new context, as does "The Roentgen Refugees." "Looking Down on You" plays with neurotic fear of heights. The protagonist of "Talk of the Town" can communicate with a community gestalt. Other outstanding stories include "Returning Home," "Slow Birds," "We Remember Babylon," "On the Dream Channel Panel," "In the Upper Cretaceous with the Summerfire Brigade," and the "Emir's Clock." Watson has also dabbled in the supernatural, most notably with "Salvage Rites."

—Don D'Ammassa

WATT-EVANS, Lawrence

Pseudonym for Lawrence Watt Evans (no hyphen). **Nationality:** American. **Born:** 26 July 1954. **Education:** Princeton University, Princeton, New Jersey, 1972-74, 1975-77 (no degree). **Family:** Married Julie F. McKenna in 1977; one daughter and one son. **Career:** Laborer, Griffith Ladder, Bedford Massachusetts, 1973; lab assistant, Mellon Institute of Science, Pittsburgh, Pennsylvania, 1976. **Awards:** Hugo award, for short story, 1988; *Asimov's* Reader's award, 1987, 1989. **Member:** SFWA, 1982; Horror Writers Association, 1988 (president, 1994-). **Agent:** Russell Galen, Scovil Chichak Galen, 381 Park Ave. South, Suite 1020, New York, New York 10016. **Address:** 5 Solitaire Court, Gaithersburg, Maryland, 20878, U.S.A.

SCIENCE FICTION PUBLICATIONS

Novels (series: War Surplus, Lords of Dûs, Legend of Ethshar, Three World Trilogy)

The Lure of the Basilisk (Dûs). New York, Ballantine, 1980; London, Grafton, 1987.
The Seven Altars of Dûsarra (Dûs). New York, Ballantine, 1981; London, Grafton, 1987.
The Cyborg and the Sorcerers (War Surplus). New York, Ballantine, 1982; London, Grafton, 1990.
The Sword of Bheleu (Dûs). New York, Ballantine, 1983; London, Grafton, 1987.
The Book of Silence (Dûs). New York, Ballantine, 1984; London, Grafton, 1987.
The Chromosomal Code. New York, Avon, 1984.
The Misenchanted Sword (Ethshar). New York, Ballantine, 1985; London, Grafton, 1988.
Shining Steel. New York, Avon, 1986.
With a Single Spell (Ethshar). New York, Ballantine, 1987; London, Grafton, 1988.
The Wizard and the War Machine (War Surplus). New York, Ballantine, 1987; London, Grafton, 1990.
Denner's Wreck. New York, Avon, 1988.
Nightside City. New York, Ballantine, 1989.
The Unwilling Warlord (Ethshar). New York, Ballantine, 1989; London, Grafton, 1991.
The Nightmare People. New York, Onyx, 1990.
The Blood of a Dragon (Ethshar). New York, Ballantine, 1991.
The Rebirth of Wonder. Newark, New Jersey, Wildside Press, Tor, 1992.
Taking Flight (Ethshar). New York, Ballantine, 1993.

The Spell of the Black Dagger (Ethshar). New York, Ballantine, 1993.

Split Heirs, with Esther Friesner. New York, Tor, 1993.

Out of This World (Three World). New York, Ballantine, 1994.

In the Empire of Shadow (Three World). New York, Ballantine, 1995.

Short Stories

Crosstime Traffic. New York, Ballantine, 1992.

OTHER PUBLICATIONS

Other

Editor, *Newer York: Stories of Science Fiction and Fantasy about the World's Greatest City.* New York, Roc, 1991.

*

Lawrence Watt-Evans comments:

I grew up reading science fiction; both my parents had read it in the old pulps, and stuck with it into the paperbacks and eventual hardcovers. I started with comic books, myself—the earliest thing I remember reading is a story called "Last of the Tree People," in *Adventures into The Unknown #105.* I think I was five.

By second grade, though, I was sneaking paperbacks into school and reading them during the more boring subjects. I worked through Heinlein's *Green Hills of Earth* and Bradbury's *October Country,* and in third grade through Asimov and Conklin's *Fifty Short Science Fiction Tales.*

Yes, those were adult books; I didn't know there *were* SF books aimed at kids. I didn't find any until I was in fifth grade.

Anyway, I thought those books were pretty neat, and after Miss Conroy, my second-grade teacher, praised my writing ability, I also thought I'd like to write stuff like that myself.

So I started trying.

My first SF story was sort of a swipe of Will Stanton's "Barney," except I changed the bad-guy lab rat to a good-guy lab mouse, which eliminated most of the plot. I got as far as putting this in an envelope addressed to the editor at *F&SF,* and even swiped a stamp to put on it, but never had the nerve to mail it. I was eight.

Sometime around then I told my parents that I wanted to be a writer, and they talked me out of it—pointed out that most writers didn't make a living at it, that it was very hard to break in, and so on. I gave up the idea of writing professionally.

But I kept writing; I couldn't help it. All through elementary school and junior high and high school, I wrote SF stories that swiped ideas freely from Niven and McCaffrey, I wrote alternate-history porno, sword-and-sorcery, all sorts of stuff—and I never let anyone see it, never submitted it anywhere, all those years. I eventually burned a lot of it.

But in 1972 I finally got up my nerve to send something out, and started collecting rejection slips.

At that point, I intended to be an architect. I'd gotten admitted to Princeton's architecture school; writing was to be just a hobby.

Except then I flunked out of Princeton, and that was that for a career in architecture, and I had absolutely no idea what else I might want to do—except write, of course. But I couldn't make a living at writing, everyone told me.

Still, it was something to do to fill in for a few months. At the time, Princeton had a fairly generous readmission policy, but the university did require that a prospective readmittee be off-campus for a full year before returning. I figured I'd spend the year writing, and the resulting rejection slips would demonstrate my serious intent to the readmissions officer.

So I collected seventy-two rejections slips . . . and an acceptance.

All of a sudden, people took my writing more seriously—which meant I could use it as a way to get out of working. If I wrote a novel during the summer of 1976, my parents wouldn't insist I get a summer job. So I wrote what became, three drafts later, *The Cyborg and the Sorcerers.*

And after I dropped out of Princeton again to get married in 1977 I wrote *The Lure of the Basilisk* to avoid getting a job. Worked for almost two years before my wife got fed up and I had to go to work.

And then *The Lure of the Basilisk* sold, and I never again had to worry about getting a job. Here we are, sixteen years later, and I'm *still* writing in order to avoid working.

Which I think is one reason I've been successful at it—I don't take it very seriously. I write for fun. I'm not trying to teach any lessons or create any great art; I'm just having fun, writing what I please. The only pressure is to bring in enough money that I don't need to get a day job.

An that's easy. My parents were dead wrong, back in 1962; writing is *easy.* It just took some practice to get the hand of it.

For me, anyway. When my parents died, we found evidence in their papers that my father had tried writing SF back in the 1940s and had failed miserably at it. That's probably why they tried to talk me out of it.

So why do I write? Because it beats working. And why do I write science fiction and fantasy? Because I grew up reading it, that's all, and because it's fun, I can reshape the world to fit my story, rather than being forced to fit the story to the world.

So I don't have any brilliant insights into the meaning of science fiction or the importance of literature or any of that stuff, which always strikes me as pointless pomposity; I write for fun, for people who read for fun. That doesn't mean my work's necessarily empty or frivolous; I do not use "fun" here to mean "mindless fun"—the adjective is not redundant.

What it does mean is that I write first to entertain, both my audience and myself, and everything else is directed to that end.

It seems to work.

*   *   *

Lawrence Watt-Evans has made his reputation primarily as a writer of fantasy fiction, first with a series of four adventures about a superhuman warriors exploits in a ruined world, the Lord of the Dus series, more effectively with the ongoing tapestry of Ethshar novels that started with *The Misenchanted Sword* and has continued with *The Unwilling Warlord, Taking Flight,* and others. The wide popularity of the latter series has obscured the fact that he has also produced a substantial body of science fiction, including the Hugo award-winning short story, "Why I Left Harry's All-Night Hamburgers."

The first of his SF novels was *Shining Steel,* set on a world colonized by people who chose to flee Earth in order to establish a theocratic state. There they split into numerous factions, each labeling all others as heretical, and the colony world becomes a ferment of constant internecine war, purges, and persecutions. Then Earth rediscovers them and sends those most insidious of corruptors, trading companies offering luxuries, indulgences, and modern weaponry, and the face of the world seems on the verge of changing forever. Unfortunately for the newcomers, they underestimate the determination of a man convinced God is at his side.

The Chromosomal Code is set on an almost unrecognizable future Earth. It appears that Earth, humanity specifically, was part of an experiment conducted by an alien race that has now progressed to a new stage. The protagonist is one of the few human survivors who escaped the end of the world, a man who has concealed in his genetic makeup a secret that could tip the balance in an interstellar war. *Denner's Wreck* is similar in some ways, although the villains in this case are humans made immortal through the use of clones. A group of them comes to a remote planet as a kind of vacation from galactic society, and they spend several centuries meddling in the local affairs, establishing themselves as near deities. Their holiday only comes to an end when a hero arises among the local population to challenge their authority.

Watt-Evans's best SF novel is unquestionably *Nightside City*. The setting is an enormous city built on the dark side of a planet which appeared to have stopped rotating relative to its sun. But the founders miscalculated, the city is moving steadily toward the light, and with its first touch the residents begin to flee. Carlisle Hsing is a private detective whose attention is attracted by the fact that someone is clandestinely buying up all of the abandoned property. She hears rumors that there is a plan to restore eternal darkness to the city, but suspects ulterior motives when it is clear someone is desperate to make certain no one finds out just what those plans are. One of the more interesting transplants of the private investigator story to SF.

The division between science fiction and fantasy blurs in some of Watt-Evans's fiction. *The Cyborg and the Sorcerers* and its sequel, *The Wizard and the War Machine,* are clearly fantasy in tone, but owe more to SF in plot and setting. A cyborg sent to combat the enemies of Earth and steal their technology returns to find the Earth has been destroyed, so he diverts to another planet where it appears that magic works and finds a new home and a new identity. In the sequel, another of his kind shows up, an equally singleminded cyborg who is convinced that his adopted world is an enemy of the now vanished Earth. The protagonist has to use both technological and magical powers to prevent the newcomer from destroying the planet. The two traditions jar a bit, but the smooth execution of both stories slides the reader past the rough spots.

More recently, *Out of This World* began a new trilogy that ties other disparate settings into a coherent whole. There are a multitude of universes, and an ancient war between good and evil is waging in them all, although the forms both sides take vary depending on the realm. The protagonist lives in our contemporary world, but his complacency is shattered when mythical creatures emerge through a gateway in his basement demanding his assistance in overcoming a demon in their own universe, and an Edward E. Smithian starship crashes nearby, having come from a third universe where the two sides contend using gigantic space fleets and storybook superweapons. A group of people cross over into one of the alternate universes and find their escape route closed, setting the stage for the next volume.

The most famous of Watt-Evans's short stories is "Why I Left Harry's All-Night Hamburgers," about a restaurant that has customers from different alternate histories. "The Drifter" concerns a man who has become unstuck in the time lines and who keeps slipping from one version of history to another, so quickly he can't keep track of things. Several of his best stories play with time and history, including "Storm Trooper," "Real Time," and "Truth, Justice, and the American Way." "Windwagon Smith and the Martians" is about an American entrepreneur who helps Martians find a way to travel about on their sand covered planet. Other stories of note include "The Final Folly of Captain Dancy," "Pickman's Modem," "Dread Vengeance," "The Frog Wizard," and "Hearts and Flowers." Lawrence Watt-Evans is first and foremost a storyteller who uses a clear, no-nonsense narrative style that is particular effective because of his tendency to understate melodramatic situations, particularly in his latter work, and the sense of good humor that pervades even the darkest of his visions. He is also the author of the superior supernatural novel *The Nightmare People,* which involves a new monster that emerges after the last vampire is killed, and has written scripts for graphic novels.

—Don D'Ammassa

WEBB, Ron. *See* WEBB, Sharon.

WEBB, Sharon

Pseudonym: Ron Webb. **Nationality:** American. **Born:** Tampa, Florida, 29 February 1936. **Education:** Attended Tampa public schools; Florida Southern College, Lakeland, 1953-56; Miami-Dade College School of Nursing, 1970-72. **Family:** Married Bryan Webb in 1956; three children. **Career:** Freelance writer, 1959-65; registered nurse, Baptist Hospital, Miami 1972-73, and in Blairsville, Georgia, 1973-81. Since 1979, freelance writer. **Agent:** Merrilee Heifetz, Writers House, Inc., 21 West 26th Street, New York, New York 10010. **Address:** Route 2, Box 2600, Blairsville, Georgia 30512, U.S.A.

SCIENCE FICTION PUBLICATIONS

Novels (series: Earth Song trilogy)

Earth Song trilogy:
  Earthchild. New York, Atheneum, 1982.
  Earth Song. New York, Atheneum, 1983.
  Ram Song. New York, Atheneum, 1984.
The Adventures of Terra Tarkington. New York, Bantam, 1985.
The Halflife. New York, Tor, 1990.

OTHER PUBLICATIONS

Novels

Pestis 18. New York, Tor, 1987.

Other

RN. New York, Zebra, 1981.

*

Manuscript Collection: University of Georgia, Athens.

Sharon Webb comments:

The sciences I studied in nursing school gave me the confidence to write something that I had loved since childhood: science fiction. Thirty stories and three SF books later, I can look back and see that this "tool" of science, while useful to the genre, is not essential to the writing of it. The real tool of SF is the use of metaphor to describe the human condition, and it is this, I believe, that explains the seductiveness of science fiction for the reader.

*   *   *

Sharon Webb's first publication in a science fiction magazine was a short poem called "Atomic Reaction" in the May 1963 issue of *The Magazine of Fantasy and Science Fiction,* during the short but potent editorial reign of Avram Davidson. Her first science fiction short story, "The Girl with the 100-Proof Eyes," appeared in the July 1964 issue of the same magazine. Both bore the pseudonym Ron Webb. She also sold some suspense stories under that name. But it was not until the publication in 1979 of "Hitch on the Bull Run," the first of her Terra Tarkington stories in *Isaac Asimov's Science Fiction Magazine,* that her SF career can really be said to have been launched.

These stories, collected and novelized in *The Adventures of Terra Tarkington,* concern the escapades of a member of the Interstellar Nurses Corps whose assignment, far from the human-populated portions of the galaxy, involves her with strange life-forms and stranger circumstances, including a political struggle between the intelligence agencies of competing galactic powers. The stories are deftly plotted and written, filled with delightfully outrageous ideas and characters, and stand among the most enjoyable of science fiction humor series. Like much of her fiction, they draw on Webb's long experience as a registered nurse for background.

Not all of Webb's fiction is humorous, however. Also in 1979, *Asimov's* published "Sharing Time in the Gallery," the story of a petty crook who attempts to sell fake paintings to extra-terrestrial art collectors. It is an effective example of the biter bit story, with a nice edge to its point of view. With the 1980 publication of "Variation on a Theme from Beethoven," she established herself as a writer of considerable serious ability.

It was this story that formed the basis for her first novel-length work, *Earthchild,* the beginning of the Earth Song trilogy, which continued with *Earth Song* and *Ram Song.* Although published ostensibly as juveniles, these novels, as with many so-called young adult science fiction works, concern themselves with distinctly adult ideas.

In the relatively near future, a process is discovered that can endow humans with apparent immortality, barring violent death. But, the recipient must be treated while still in his mid-teens, thus robbing adults of the process's benefits. Many of the potential immortals must face a personal sacrifice; the price of prolonging life is the complete loss of artistic creativity. The novel concerns 15-year-old Kurt Kraus, a budding musician who arrives at orchestra rehearsal one day only to learn that the Mouat-Gari process has already secretly been administered to the world's population. His immortality is assured. His career as a musician is ended.

Webb paints a frightening picture of a world in which adults are faced with the knowledge that they will die while children never will. Incidents of child abuse increase. Mobs mindlessly attack and inflict horrible deaths on children. At last, for their own protection, children have to be isolated from the general adult population. But the future has begun, and a very changed one it is for humankind.

Kurt becomes a leader of the society that emerges from these changes and begins to realize what the loss of art means to humanity. The only solution to that problem lies in yet another change. From now on, youngsters who show the promise of creativity will be given a choice: they may opt for immortality or they may choose a short, natural life-span, with the ability to express their creativity. Whichever their choice, there is no turning back. In *Ram Song,* set some 10,000 years in the future, the conflicts that arise are those of evolution and the nature of the universe itself.

Two main interests govern Webb's choices of story ideas and themes: her lifelong career in medicine (she is a registered nurse), and her love of music (she plays guitar). Her stories usually draw on physical settings familiar to her, either her native Tampa, Florida, or the environs of Chattanooga, Tennessee, Atlanta, or the Blue Ridge Mountains of Georgia where she and her husband now live. Even the rather *outre* settings of the Bull Run stories are often only satiric extrapolations of the sorts of hospital environments she worked in for so many years.

Her latest two books are not science fiction novels, but medical thrillers. *Pestis 18* deals with a terrorist threat to release a deadly experimental virus. It's a tautly plotted and written story. Her most recent novel, *The Halflife,* though also ostensibly a medical thriller, contains a sufficiency of science fictional touches to warrant discussion here. It concerns a government experiment to implant constructed personalities in the subconscious of certain subjects when they are teenagers. Years later it is hoped these personalities (unsuspected even by their hosts) can be activated and used as couriers by the CIA. The experiment goes wrong when it turns out that some of the subjects are victims of Multiple Personality Syndrome. These subjects integrate the constructed personality into their library of identities with dangerous results, at least one of them becoming a murderer. One of the subjects is a trance medium, and it is the relationship between her spirit contact and the constructed personality that gives rise to conflict. The novel explores its ideas deftly and interestingly but never once falters in maintaining its pace or suspense.

One of Webb's outstanding tools as a writer is her style. On the surface, it is simply a pleasing, unobtrusive style that does its job without drawing much attention to itself. But on closer examination, it is remarkable for the way in which it serves such a range of technical needs. Science fiction can boast far too many styles that are much flashier than hers, but few are more practical in serving the requirements of both writer and reader.

—Gerald W. Page

————

WEIGHT, Frank. *See* **TUBB, E.C.**

————

WEINBAUM, Stanley G(rauman)

Nationality: American. **Born:** Louisville, Kentucky, in 1902. **Education:** Public schools in Milwaukee; University of Wisconsin, Madison, B. Chem. Engr. 1923. **Family:** Married Margaret Weinbaum. **Career:** Worked as movie theater manager. **Died:** 14 December 1935.

<small>SCIENCE FICTION PUBLICATIONS</small>

Novels

The New Adam. Chicago, Ziff-Davis, 1939; London, Sphere, 1974.
The Black Flame. Reading, Pennsylvania, Fantasy Press, 1948.
The Dark Other. Los Angeles, Fantasy, 1950.

Short Stories

Dawn of Flame and Other Stories. Milwaukee, Wisconsin, Milwaukee Fictioneers, 1936.
A Martian Odyssey and Others. Reading, Pennsylvania, Fantasy Press, 1949; as *The Best of Stanley G. Weinbaum,* London, Sphere, 1977.
The Red Peri. Reading, Pennsylvania, Fantasy Press, 1952.
A Martian Odyssey. New York, Lancer, 1962.
A Martian Odyssey and Other Science-Fiction Tales, edited by Sam Moskowiz. Westport, Connecticut, Hyperion Press, 1974.
The Best of Stanley G. Weinbaum. New York, Ballantine, 1974; London, Sphere, 1977.

*

Critical Study: *After Ten Years: A Tribute to Stanley G. Weinbaum* edited by Gerry de la Ree and Sam Moskowitz, Westwood, New Jersey, de la Ree, 1945.

* * *

It is now formulaic to include the term "tragic death" with each mention of the name Stanley G. Weinbaum. His total career as a writer lasted from the publication of "A Martian Odyssey" in the July 1934 issue of *Wonder Stories* to his death in December 1935. Almost every critic who discusses the early years of pulp science fiction singles out Weinbaum as a unique voice who never had the chance to develop fully his powers as a writer. While one can never know just how far these powers would have in fact developed, a number of conclusions can be drawn, based on the short stories published during Weinbaum's career and a number of stories published after his death.

With his very first story, Weinbaum managed to break a number of standard formulae in pulp fiction. "A Martian Odyssey" not only attempted to portray aliens as creatures unlike man but went so far as to present one such creature in a highly sympathetic light. Weinbaum seems to have been one of the first, if not the first, to realize that aliens may differ from humans in not only their outer appearance but their inner thought processes as well. His invention of the big birdlike creature Tweel in "A Martian Odyssey" stands as a major step in the genre because it undertakes the difficult task of describing the actions of a creature that clearly thinks differ-

ently. Given its nonhuman nature, Weinbaum uses a human character's interaction with Tweel to bring out the alien's basic nature. While both the human character and the reader begin the story amused at the weird actions of Tweel, this amusement is changed to admiration and respect by the end of the story. Tweel first grasps the possibility of communication between alien and human, and is able to make use of the human language while the human character gives up any chance of comprehending Tweel's. Tweel shows the greater understanding of the other aliens on Mars, and looks more at home on Mars, even though he too is an explorer from another planet. In other words, with Tweel readers were given an alternative to the murderous aliens of H.G. Wells, and many writers were soon imitating Weinbaum.

But Weinbaum's stories were not successful simply because he had invented a new attitude toward aliens. In the stories that followed (all in *Wonder Stories*), Weinbaum continued to emphasize the fact that his aliens lived by systems of logic that were different from man's, and it is the fact that these different systems were both strange and internally consistent that won him a wide audience. The care with which Weinbaum created new aliens and described their alienness was unique to the pulp fiction of its time. Thus, even in a story such as "Paradise Planet," in which alien forms on Venus do menace humans, the threat originates in the nature of life on Venus and not in some anthropomorphic desire to rape and pillage humanity.

As *Wonder Stories* continued to publish stories by Weinbaum almost monthly, a second reason for his popularity became apparent: his stories contained a good deal of humor. This humor was often achieved at the expense of human character and human science. Thus in a series of stories based on a delightfully "mad" scientist named Professor Haskel van Manderpootz ("The Worlds of If," "The Ideal," and "The Point of View"), inventions constantly appear that seem to have no other reason for existence than the fact that they constantly complicate the life of Dixon Wells, a young and somewhat lovesick romantic.

Weinbaum's treatment of aliens and his use of humor, however, did not free him from all of the pulp formulas. In "Pygmalion's Spectacles," for example, Weinbaum refuses to bring the story to its logical, tragic conclusion. A young man, while wearing spectacles that allow the wearer to take full part in an illusion, falls in love with a dream woman. When the dream ends and he must take off the glasses, he remains in love with the woman. Weinbaum, however, begs the whole issue of illusion and reality when at the end of the story a living counterpart of the dream woman is produced. Given the strength with which Weinbaum evokes the dream world and the sadness that the hero undergoes with its loss, one feels that "Pygmalion's Spectacles" could have been a better story. Weinbaum's ties to pulp fiction can also be seen in *The Black Flame,* which contains two versions of the same story. The first version, "Dawn of Flame," is a competent but uninspired story of the innocent young man who meets the exotic and erotic immortal woman. Reminiscent of H. Rider Haggard's *She,* the story contains some powerfully sexual scenes but basically remains a formula story. In the second version, "The Black Flame," however, Weinbaum rewrites the story and adds the paraphernalia of a pulp story complete with happy ending. The mixture of these two separate traditions was less than successful, and "The Black Flame" seems to be constantly struggling to make up its mind as to exactly what it wants to be.

On those occasions when Weinbaum does completely overcome his pulp environment, however, the fiction he produces is both sensitive and moving. In "The Adoptive Ultimate," he refuses to opt for the happy ending, and in *The New Adam,* Weinbaum takes the stock superman character and turns him into a sympathetic character who is alone in a world of mere humans. Because of the first-person narration, the reader is able to see a side of such a character that rarely was portrayed before Weinbaum's treatment, and never so carefully or intimately. Lester del Rey calls the hero of *The New Adam* "a rather helpless failure," but such a characterization refuses to take into account what caused that failure, what it was in the nature of being a superman that led to it. And it is Weinbaum's investigation of exactly these questions in a sympathetic and painstaking manner that makes the novel so readable.

Works like *The New Adam* are rare in SF. Too often they are ignored when they do appear, and such was particularly true during the great age of the pulps. Weinbaum is remembered best for his aliens and the strange worlds he created for his stories in *Wonder Stories.* Thus, "A Martian Odyssey" remains Stanley Weinbaum's best-known work. While such stories have had a significant effect on the direction science fiction was to take in the 1940s, *The New Adam* deserves far more notice than it has received to date.

—Stephen H. Goldman

WEINER, Andrew

Nationality: Canadian/British. **Born:** London, England, 17 June 1949. **Education:** University of Sussex, 1967-70, B.A. in social psychology; London School of Economics, 1972-73, M.Sc. in social psychology. **Family:** Married Barbara Moses in 1973; one son. **Career:** Copywriter, Ogilvy and Mather, London, 1970-72. Lecturer in psychology, Dawson College, Montreal, Canada, 1975-77. Since 1977, freelance writer. **Agent:** Richard Curtis, 171 East 74th Street, New York, New York 10021, U.S.A. **Address:** 26 Summerhill Gardens, Toronto, Ontario M47 1B4, Canada.

SCIENCE FICTION PUBLICATIONS

Novel

Station Gehenna. New York, Congdon and Weed, 1987.

Short Stories

Distant Signals and Other Stories. Vancouver, British Columbia, Porcépic Press, 1989.

*

Andrew Weiner comments:

I suppose I am primarily a short-story writer, having published only one novel in almost two decades (I recently completed a second novel which is now with my agent). I grew up reading mainly short SF in preference to novels, and even now I think there are very few good SF novels being written and published.

I write in a number of modes: experimental, humorous, apocalyptic. Sometimes these overlap. In a sense all my stories, however apparently conventional in form, are experiments, since I'm never sure how they're going to turn out or even, in many cases, why I am writing them at all.

I think that what I write is less "science fiction" than a more or less skillful imitation of the "real" thing. Actually, I think this is probably true of almost every writer of my generation (e.g., post-1945), but some of us are more aware of it than others. I am personally unable to take aliens, distant planets, faster-than-light spaceships, mental powers, etc. *seriously,* although they can serve as convenient props. In this I place myself in a line of descent from Dick, Aldiss, Ballard, Sheckley, and Malzberg, as well as such "mainstream" writers of SF as Vonnegut and Walter Tevis. For want of a better word, I would call this self-conscious imitation of "real" SF "postmodern."

Actually I rarely write about outer space (the whole idea gives me vertigo) or the far future. I do, however, make heavy use of aliens, usually a metaphor for exploring the human mind.

*   *   *

While Andrew Weiner is not new to science fiction readers, his name has only recently come to prominence. After publishing stories in various magazines, Weiner published a science fiction thriller, *Station Gehenna,* which tells the story of a team on the planet Gehenna that tries to terraform the hostile planet into a hospitable one. Special agent Victor Lewin finds evidence that a murder has been committed, and the novel, part of the "Isaac Asimov presents" series, owes much to the whodunnit genre.

Weiner's first collection of short stories, *Distant Signals,* was published by the Canadian Porcépic Press and as such belongs to the new sophisticated school of Canadian science fiction with the likes of Candas Jane Dorsey and Élisabeth Vonarburg. The opening work, "The News from D Street," is one of Weiner's best stories, with many overtones of *film noir.* An agent is asked to find a missing person, and in typical *film noir* fashion we do not learn the agent's name until the fifth page. Only gradually do the science fiction elements come into the story, in the same way that missing clues come slowly together to a private investigator in a film. The more information we get about the surroundings, the less they seem to make sense, and we have to wait until the end of the story when, as in a thriller, we are given the solution we had been suspecting for several pages.

"Klein's Machine," from the same collection, could not be more different in style, setting, and technique. Philip Herbert Klein is a 23-year-old on a bus, his eyes blank and "the remains of a bright green crushed flower in his left hand." Unable either to answer any questions or to remember how he found himself on a bus with a one-way ticket from New York to San Francisco, Klein is stopped in Ohio and transferred to a state mental hospital. The "patient," according to a psychiatrist's report, while "suffering a classical dissociative reaction of amnesia coupled with fugue state," claims to have been "travelling in time." We are then shown Klein's own diary, in which he gives an account of his secret experiments with a time travel machine and his successful attempts at making a hamster travel through time and return. However, Klein cannot remember anything about his own trip into the future, so with the help of sodium pentathol, he is induced into reliving his travel experience into a future society where there are only machines and everything is in the hands of a computer because "the people have gone now, all gone away to other worlds." The reader is left to decide for himself whether Klein has really traveled in time. In "Empire of the Sun," Weiner turns to poetic prose that might deter readers in search of an easy-to-follow plot. A succession of tableaux that should be read as a film script, the story becomes clear only after several readings.

Weiner's penchant for ambiguity, for a blurring of the divide between reality and imagination, finds its highest expression in the title story, "Distant Signals." A faded movie star, Vance Macoby, is hired by mysterious investors to act again in a TV series that was cancelled after six episodes in 1961. The investors want Macoby to shoot new episodes of the series in which the character played by Macoby is an amnesiac gunslinger who wanders from town to town in search of his lost identity. Weiner has written a perfect blend of film noir and comedy while teaching us a lesson about our own place in the universe.

While adhering to the Canadian SF tendency of writing "soft" science fiction, Andrew Weiner definitely positions himself even more on the edge than his compatriots. His novella "Eternity, Baby," published in *Tesseracts 4,* is all the more remarkable since, although published in an anthology that purports to reflect Canadian science fiction or speculative fiction, it would clearly disappoint hard-core devotees of the genre; the story revolves around a teenager, Simon Nagel, falling in love with Elena Layton who is going out with one of his friends, Gil Daniels. Gil and Simon belong to one of those numerous bands, here interestingly enough called the Avengers (for a lost youth, no doubt), that most teenagers set up as a matter of course as part of their growing years. They do not produce anything original until the day when Simon falls in love at first sight with Elena and is instantly inspired into writing a superb hit that propels them, briefly, on the road to stardom. Only, Simon never has the courage to tell Elena that he is in love with her, even when Gil and her have a falling out.

But the memory persists, not of Elena, but of the image that he keeps of her in his mind. And unknown to everyone else, she reappears to him later, near every performing stage and meets him to make love, every night. This is magic realism at its best, with emotions that touch us directly, although it should be obvious that Andrew Weiner uses this story to resolve a latent dream and desire from his youth, a dream that most of us had as teenagers; for the Elena that he sees is not even connected to the real one, it is all in his mind, the real one still being there back home; "Eternity Baby" is an attempt to bridge the gap between two different types of fiction, magic realism and speculative SF, but whether science fiction readers and, as importantly, publishers are ready to embrace it remains to be seen. To quote one of Candas Jane Dorsey's definitions of Canadian SF, it is a "mood piece."

In fact, Andrew Weiner has lately declared himself not to be a science fiction writer and to prefer a "quiet and dignified obscurity to one involving publication with spaceships on the cover." Certainly, as is the case with many genre writers, one does not have to exclude the other.

—Henry Leperlier

WELLMAN, Manly Wade

Pseudonyms: Gabriel Barclay; John Cotten; Levi Crow; Manuel Fernez; Gans T. Field; Hampton Wells; Wade Wells. **Nationality:** American. **Born:** Kamundongo, Angola, 21 May 1903; brother of the writer Paul I. Wellman. **Education:** Wichita State University, Kansas, A.B. 1926; Columbia University, New York, B.Lit. 1927. **Family:** Married Frances Obrist in 1930; one son. **Career:** Reporter and feature writer, *Wichita Beacon,* 1927-30, and *Eagle,* 1930-34; assistant project supervisor, WPA Writers Project, New York, 1936-38; instructor of creative writing, Elon College, North Carolina, 1962-70, and University of North Carolina evening college, Chapel Hill, 1963-73. **Awards:** Ellery Queen award, 1946; Mystery Writers of America award, 1955; World Fantasy award, 1975, 1980; H.P. Lovecraft award, 1975; British Fantasy award, 1984. **Died:** 5 April 1986.

SCIENCE FICTION PUBLICATIONS

Novels (series: Captain Future; Silver John; John Thunstone)

The Invading Asteroid. New York, Stellar, 1932.
Romance in Black: A Thrilling Novel (as Gans T. Field). London, Utopian, 1946.
Sojarr of Titan: A Complete Scientifiction Novel. New York, Crestwood, 1949.
The Beasts from Beyond: A Complete Book-Length Novel of Amazing Adventure. Manchester, World, 1950.
Devil's Planet: A New and Original Novel of Martian Adventure. Manchester, World, 1951.
Twice in Time. New York, Avalon, 1957; with selected stories, introduction by Karl Edward Wagner, New York, Baen, 1988.
Giants from Eternity. New York, Avalon, 1959.
The Dark Destroyers. New York, Avalon, 1959.
Island in the Sky. New York, Avalon, 1961.
The Solar Invasion (Captain Future). New York, Popular Library, 1968.
Sherlock Holmes's War of the Worlds, with Wade Wellman. New York, Warner, 1975.
The Beyonders. New York, Warner, 1977.
The Old Gods Waken (Silver John). Garden City, New York, Doubleday, 1979.
After Dark (Silver John). Garden City, New York, Doubleday, 1980.
The Lost and the Lurking (Silver John). Garden City, New York, Doubleday, 1981.
The Hanging Stones (Silver John). Garden City, New York, Doubleday, 1982.
What Dreams May Come (Thunstone). Garden City, New York, Doubleday, 1983.
The Voice of the Mountain (Silver John). Garden City, New York, Doubleday, 1984.
The School of Darkness (Thunstone). Garden City, New York, Doubleday, 1985.
Cahena: A Dream of the Past. Garden City, New York, Doubleday, 1986.

Short Stories

Who Fears the Devil? (Silver John). Sauk City, Wisconsin, Arkham House, 1963; as *John the Balladeer,* edited by Karl Edward Wagner, New York, Baen, 1988.
A True Story of the Revolting and Bloody Crimes of Sergeant Stanlas, U.S.A. Wichita, Kansas, Four Ducks Press, 1964.
Worse Things Waiting. Chapel Hill, North Carolina, Carcosa, 1973.

Lonely Vigils (Thunstone). Chapel Hill, North Carolina, Carcosa, 1981.

Valley So Low: Southern Mountain Stories, edited by Karl Edward Wagner. Garden City, New York, Doubleday, 1987.

OTHER PUBLICATIONS

Novels

A Double Life (novelization of screenplay). Chicago, Century, 1947.

Find My Killer. New York, Farrar Straus, 1947; London, Sampson Low, 1948.

Fort Sun Dance. New York, Dell, and London, Corgi, 1955.

Candle of the Wicked. New York, Putnam, 1960.

Not at These Hands. New York, Putnam, 1962.

Novels (for children)

The Sleuth Patrol. New York, Nelson, 1947.

The Mystery of Lost Valley. New York, Nelson, 1948.

The Raiders of Beaver Lake. New York, Nelson, 1950.

The Haunts of Drowning Creek. New York, Holiday House, 1951.

Wild Dogs of Drowning Creek. New York, Holiday House, 1952.

The Last Mammoth. New York, Holiday House, 1953.

Gray Riders: Jeb Stuart and His Men. New York, Aladdin, 1954.

Rebel Mail Runner. New York, Holiday House, 1954.

Flag on the Levee. New York, Washburn, 1955.

To Unknown Lands. New York, Holiday House, 1956.

Young Squire Morgan. New York, Washburn, 1956.

Lights over Skeleton Ridge. New York, Washburn, 1957.

The Ghost Battalion: A Story of the Iron Scouts. New York, Washburn, 1958.

Ride, Rebels! Adventures of the Iron Scouts. New York, Washburn, 1959.

Appomattox Road: Final Adventures of the Iron Scouts. New York, Washburn, 1960.

Third String Center. New York, Washburn, 1960.

Rifles at Ramsour's Mill: A Tale of the Revolutionary War. New York, Washburn, 1961.

Battle for King's Mountain. New York, Washburn, 1962.

Clash on the Catawba. New York, Washburn, 1962.

The River Pirates. New York, Washburn, 1963.

Settlement on Shocco: Adventures in Colonial Carolina. Winston-Salem, North Carolina, Blair, 1963.

The South Fork Rangers. New York, Washburn, 1963.

The Master of Scare Hollow. New York, Washburn, 1964.

The Great Riverboat Race: A Tale of the Natchez and the Robert E. Lee. New York, Washburn, 1965.

Mystery at Bear Paw Gap. New York, Washburn, 1965.

Battle at Bear Paw Gap. New York, Washburn, 1966.

The Specter of Bear Paw Gap. New York, Washburn, 1966.

Jamestown Adventure. New York, Washburn, 1967.

Brave Horse: The Story of Janus. Williamsburg, Virginia, Colonial Williamsburg, 1968.

Carolina Pirate. New York, Washburn, 1968.

Frontier Reporter. New York, Washburn, 1969.

Mountain Feud. New York, Washburn, 1969.

Napoleon of the West: A Story of the Aaron Burr Conspiracy. New York, Washburn, 1970.

Fast Break Five. New York, Washburn, 1971.

Play

Many Are the Hearts: A Play in One Act. Raleigh, North Carolina Confederate Centennial Commission, 1961.

Other

Giant in Gray: A Biography of Wade Hampton of South Carolina. New York, Scribner, 1949.

Dead and Gone: Classic Crimes of North Carolina. Chapel Hill, University of North Carolina Press, 1954.

Rebel Boast: First at Bethel—Last at Appomattox. New York, Holt, 1956.

Fastest on the River. New York, Holt, 1957.

The Life and Times of Sir Archie, with Elizabeth Amis Blanchard. Chapel Hill, University of North Carolina Press, 1958.

The County of Warren, North Carolina, 1586-1917. Chapel Hill, University of North Carolina Press, 1959.

They Took Their Stand: The Founders of the Confederacy. New York, Putnam, 1959.

The Rebel Songster, with Frances Wellman. New York, Heritage House, 1959.

Harpers Ferry, Prize of War. Charlotte, North Carolina, McNally and Loftin, 1960.

The County of Gaston, with Robert F. Cope. Gastonia, North Carolina, Gaston County Historical Society, 1961.

The County of Moore 1847-1947. Southern Pines, North Carolina, Moore County Historical Association, 1962.

Winston-Salem in History: The Founders. Winston-Salem, North Carolina, Blair, 1966.

The Kingdom of Madison: A Southern Mountain Fastness and Its People. Chapel Hill, University of North Carolina Press, 1973.

The Story of Moore County. Southern Pines, North Carolina, Moore County Historical Association, 1974.

*

Manly Wade Wellman commented:

I came to America from an African wilderness, but with strong family heritage and association in the American West and South. I began by wanting to write of the fantastic, the imaginative. I wrote in other fields, too, but now I've returned to that first love. A writer must find himself out all alone, must understand himself, use himself in all he writes. More than by years or ability or reputation, your life is measured by the work you do. You pave your road by your writing, and travel it always into new wonders and perils and joys and sorrows. You find and use things out of sight and sound of all others. It's part of you, like the blood in your veins, the breath in your nostrils.

I look back on more than half a century of writing, and hope to keep on until they say the last words over me.

*   *   *

The bulk of Manly Wade Wellman's writing has been outside the science fiction field. A popular writer during the heyday of the SF pulps, he is best known today as a fantasy author and for his fiction and nonfiction work in the field of Southern regionalism.

Wellman began selling SF as early as 1927 with "Back to the Beast" in *Weird Tales.* In 1930, he turned to writing as a full-time profession, and in 1934, moved to New York in order to be closer to his markets. After "Outlaws on Callisto" made the cover of the April 1936 *Astounding Stories,* Wellman became a client of the noted agent Julius Schwartz, under whose direction he became part of the Better Publications stable. There Wellman became a regular contributor to *Thrilling Wonder Stories* and *Startling Stories.* These popular pulps, aimed at an adolescent readership, were well suited to Wellman's brisk, simple narrative style, and the bulk of his SF appeared in these and similar pulps. Most of his SF books are reprints of his earlier work, although recently he had begun to write fantasy.

Wellman's first book publication was *The Invading Asteroid.* It set the tone for the sort of space opera Wellman was to become known for. He created a consistent futuristic setting of the 30th century, and utilized this for some 16 of his stories. Wellman's 30th century was pretty much the same as the 20th, with the addition of interplanetary travel and extraterrestrials. Nonetheless, so well liked was Wellman's future world that fans cried "plagiarism" when Nelson Bond used certain of these elements for a story of his own, and Wellman had to explain that Bond had done so with his permission.

Sojarr of Titan is a "Tarzan of outer space" pastiche written at editor Leo Margulies's request. *The Beasts from Beyond* made use of the idea of invasion at the intersection point of bubble universes that Wellman returned to in *The Beyonders. Devil's Planet,* part of his 30th-century series, is a murder mystery set on Mars that teams a human and an android as detectives, and appears to be the archetype of Asimov's *Caves of Steel. Twice in Time* is a novel of a man who travels through time to become Leonardo da Vinci. It is Wellman's most important SF work and remains a superior time-travel novel. The 1988 Baen Books edition restores the original and superior text of the 1940 magazine version of *Twice in Time*— it also includes "The Timeless Tomorrow," an excellent novelette about Nostradamus. *The Dark Destroyers* has Earthmen throwing off the yoke of extraterrestrial conquest. In *Giants from Eternity,* Pasteur, Darwin, Newton, Edison, and Curie are brought back to life to combat an alien growth that threatens to engulf the Earth. In *Island in the Sky* a future gladiator rebels against a technological dictatorship that holds Earth in thrall. A final reprint from the pulp days, *The Solar Invasion* is Wellman's one fling at writing a Captain Future episode.

During the 1960s, Wellman collaborated with his son, Wade Wellman, for a series of droll pastiches that placed Doyle's Sherlock Holmes and Watson alongside Professor Challenger in the London of Wells's *War of the Worlds.* These were expanded and collected as *Sherlock Holmes's War of the Worlds,* a book that ranks among the best of the Holmes pastiches. *The Beyonders* is a routine novel of invasion by creatures from another dimension, with the saving charm of its Southern mountain setting.

While even the best of Wellman's SF seems naive and badly dated to modern readers, the same is not true for his fantasy writing, which remains some of the finest in the genre. The best of his short fantasy fiction has been collected in *Who Fears the Devil?, Worse Things Waiting, Lonely Vigils, Valley So Low,* and *John the Balladeer. Worse Things Waiting* collects the best of Wellman's fantasy/horror short fiction from the pulp era, while *Lonely Vigils* collects the cases of three occult investigators, Judge Pursuivant, Professor Enderby, and John Thunstone, whose separate series originally appeared in *Weird Tales* and *Strange Stories. Valley So Low* collects the best of his Southern mountain fantasy stories, all written during the last 15 years of his career. *Who Fears the Devil?* collects the adventures of a wandering balladeer, named simply "John," who confronts supernatural evil in the Southern Appalachians. The stories originally appeared in *The Magazine of Fantasy and Science*

Fiction during the 1950s. Wellman revised the stories, not for the better, for their book publication. The original versions are presented in *John the Balladeer,* in addition to the six new John stories Wellman wrote later in life.

When Warner rejected a proposed sequel to *The Beyonders,* Wellman revived John and rewrote his SF outline into the fantasy novel, *The Old Gods Waken.* This was the first in a series of fantasy novels written for Doubleday. John also stars in *After Dark, The Lost and the Lurking, The Hanging Stones,* and *The Voice of the Mountain.* Delving further into his back pages, Wellman reintroduced Judge Pursuivant in *The Hanging Stones,* then brought back John Thunstone as the hero of *What Dreams May Come* and *The School of Darkness.* Wellman, however, was far better with short fiction, and these later novels suffer from paucity of content and tiresome padding. *Cahena,* his final novel, is a historical fantasy/adventure set during the Islamic conquest of Northern Africa. Wellman had worked on it for years, but the novel he considered would be his magnum opus was a bust. His monument is his short fantasy/horror fiction, the best of which can stand proudly with the best in this genre, while his John stories remain true classics of American fantasy.

—Karl Edward Wagner

WELLS, H(erbert) G(eorge)

Nationality: British. **Born:** Bromley, Kent, 21 September 1866. **Education:** Mr. Morley's Bromley Academy until age 13: certificate in bookkeeping; apprentice draper, Rodgers and Denyer, Windsor, 1880; pupil-teacher at a school in Wookey, Somerset, 1880; apprentice chemist in Midhurst, Sussex, 1880-81; apprentice draper, Hyde's Southsea Drapery Emporium, Hampshire, 1881-83; student/assistant, Midhurst Grammar School, 1883-84; studied at Normal School (now Imperial College) of Science, London (editor, *Science School Journal*), 1884-87; teacher, Holt Academy, Wrexham, Wales, 1887-88, and at Henley House School, Kilburn, London, 1889; B.Sc. (honours) in zoology 1890, and D.Sc. 1943, University of London. **Family:** Married 1) his cousin Isabel Mary Wells in 1891 (separated 1894; divorced 1895); 2) Amy Catherine Robbins in 1895 (died 1927), two sons; had one daughter by Amber Reeves, and one son by Rebecca West, the writer Anthony West. **Career:** Tutor, University Tutorial College, London, 1890-93; full-time writer from 1893; theatre critic, *Pall Mall Gazette,* London, 1895; member of the Fabian Society, 1903-08; Labour candidate for Parliament, for the University of London, 1922, 1923; lived mainly in France, 1924-33. International president, PEN, 1934-46, D. Lit.: University of London, 1936. Honorary fellow, Imperial College of Science and Technology, London. **Died:** 13 August 1946.

SCIENCE FICTION PUBLICATIONS

Novels

The Time Machine: An Invention. London, Heinemann, and New York, Holt, 1895; as *The Definitive Machine: A Critical Edition of H.G. Wells's Scientific Romance,* edited by Harry M. Geduld, Bloomington, Indiana University Press, 1987.

The Wonderful Visit. London, Dent, and New York, Macmillan, 1895.

The Island of Doctor Moreau. London, Heinemann, and New York, Stone and Kimball, 1896.

The Invisible Man: A Grotesque Romance. London, Pearson, and New York, Arnold, 1897.

The War of the Worlds. London, Heinemann, and New York, Harper, 1898.

When the Sleeper Wakes. London and New York, Harper, 1899; revised edition, as *The Sleeper Awakes*, London, Nelson, 1910.

The First Men in the Moon. Indianapolis, Bowen-Merrill, and London, Newnes, 1901.

The Sea Lady: A Tissue of Moonshine. London, Methuen, and New York, Appleton, 1902.

The Food of the Gods, and How It Came to Earth. London, Macmillan, and New York, Scribner, 1904.

In the Days of the Comet. London, Macmillan, and New York, Century, 1906.

The War in the Air, and Particularly How Mr. Bert Smallways Fared While It Lasted. London, Bell, and New York, Macmillan, 1908.

The World Set Free: A Story of Mankind. London, Macmillan, and New York, Dutton, 1914.

The Undying Fire. London, Cassell, and New York, Macmillan, 1919; with nonfiction as *The Undying Fire, and Philosophical and Theological Speculations*, London, Unwin, 1925.

Men like Gods. London, Cassell, and New York, Macmillan, 1923.

The Dream. London, Cape, and New York, Macmillan, 1924.

Mr. Blettsworthy on Rampole Island. London, Benn, and New York, Doubleday, 1928.

The Autocracy of Mr. Parham: His Remarkable Adventures in This Changing World. London, Heinemann, and New York, Doubleday, 1930.

The Shape of Things to Come: The Ultimate Revolution. London, Hutchinson, and New York, Macmillan, 1933.

The Croquet Player: A Story. London, Chatto and Windus, 1936; New York, Viking Press, 1937.

Star Begotten: A Biological Fantasia. London, Chatto and Windus, and New York, Viking Press, 1937.

The Camford Visitation. London, Methuen, 1937.

The Brothers. London, Chatto and Windus, and New York, Viking Press, 1938.

The Holy Terror. London, Joseph, and New York, Simon and Schuster, 1939.

Short Stories

The Stolen Bacillus and Other Incidents. London, Methuen, 1895.

Select Conversations with an Uncle (Now Extinct) and Two Other Reminiscences. London, Lane, and New York, Merriman, 1895.

The Plattner Story and Others. London, Methuen, 1897.

Thirty Strange Stories. New York, Arnold, 1897.

Tales of Space and Time. London, Harper, and New York, Doubleday, 1899.

A Cure for Love: A Story of the Days to Come (Anno Domini 2090). New York, Scott, 1899.

The Vacant Country: A Story of the Days to Come. New York, Kent, 1899.

Twelve Stories and a Dream. London, Macmillan, 1903; New York, Scribner, 1905.

The Country of the Blind and Other Stories. London, Nelson, 1911; revised edition of *The Country of the Blind*, London, Golden Cockerel Press, 1939.

The Door in the Wall and Other Stories. New York, Kennerley, 1911; London, Richards, 1915.

The Star. London, Simplified Speling Sosieti, 1912(?).

Tales of the Unexpected [of Life and Adventure; of Wonder], edited by J.D. Beresford. London, Collins, 3 vols., 1922-23.

The Short Stories of H.G. Wells. London, Benn, 1927; Garden City, New York, Doubleday, 1929; as *Famous Short Stories of H.G. Wells*, Garden City, New York, Doubleday, 1938; as *The Complete Short Stories of H.G. Wells*. London, Benn, and New York, St. Martin's Press, 1987.

The Favorite Short Stories of H.G. Wells. Garden City, New York, Doubleday Doran, 1937.

28 Science Fiction Stories. New York, Dover, 1952.

Selected Short Stories. London, Penguin, 1958.

The Valley of Spiders. London, Fontana, 1964.

The Cone; Another Collection of Horror Stories. London, Fontana, 1965.

Best Science Fiction Stories of H.G. Wells. New York, Dover, 1966.

The Man with the Nose and the Other Uncollected Short Stories, edited by J.R. Hammond. London, Athlone Press, 1984.

The H.G. Wells Science Fiction Treasury. New York, Chatham River, 1984.

OTHER PUBLICATIONS

Novels

The Wheels of Chance. London, Dent, and New York, Macmillan, 1896.

Love and Mr. Lewisham: A Story of a Very Young Couple. New York, Stokes, and London, Harper, 1900.

A Modern Utopia. London, Chapman and Hall, and New York, Scribner, 1905.

Kipps: A Monograph. New York, Scribner, and London, Macmillan, 1905.

Tono-Bungay. New York, Duffield, 1908; London, Macmillan, 1909.

Ann Veronica. London, Unwin, and New York, Harper, 1909.

The History of Mr. Polly. London, Nelson, and New York, Duffield, 1910.

The New Machiavelli. New York, Duffield, 1910; London, Lane, 1911.

Marriage. London, Macmillan, and New York, Duffield, 1912.

The Passionate Friends. London, Macmillan, and New York, Harper, 1913.

The Wife of Sir Isaac Harman. London and New York, Macmillan, 1914.

Boon: The Mind of the Race, the Wild Asses of the Devil, and the Last Trump (as Reginald Bliss). London, Unwin, and New York, Doran, 1915.

Bealby: A Holiday. London, Methuen, and New York, Macmillan, 1915.

The Research Magnificent. London and New York, Macmillan, 1915.

Mr. Britling Sees It Through. London, Cassell, and New York, Macmillan, 1916.

The Soul of a Bishop. London, Cassell, and New York, Macmillan, 1917.

Joan and Peter. London, Cassell, and New York, Macmillan, 1918.

The Secret Places of the Heart. London, Cassell, and New York, Macmillan, 1922.

Christina Alberta's Father. London, Cape, and New York, Macmillan, 1925.

The World of William Clissold. London, Benn, 3 vols., and New York, Doran, 2 vols., 1926.

Meanwhile: The Picture of a Lady. London, Benn, and New York, Doran, 1927.

The King Who Was a King: The Book of a Film. London, Benn, and New York, Doubleday, 1929.

The Adventures of Tommy (for children). London, Harrap, and New York, Stokes, 1929.

The Bulpington of Blup. London, Hutchinson, 1932; New York, Macmillan, 1933.

Stories of Men and Women in Love (omnibus). London, Hutchinson, 1933.

Brynhild. London, Methuen, and New York, Scribner, 1937.

Apropos of Dolores. London, Cape, and New York, Scribner, 1938.

The Holy Terror. London, Joseph, and New York, Simon and Schuster, 1939.

Babes in the Darkling Wood. London, Secker and Warburg, and New York, Alliance, 1940.

All Aboard for Ararat. London, Secker and Warburg, 1940; New York, Alliance, 1941.

You Can't Be Too Careful: A Sample of Life 1901-1951. London, Secker and Warburg, 1941; New York, Putnam, 1942.

The Desert Daisy (for children), edited by Gordon N. Ray. Urbana, University of Illinois Press, 1957.

The Wealth of Mr. Waddy, edited by Harris Wilson. Carbondale, Southern Illinois University Press, 1969.

Plays

Kipps, with Rudolf Besier, adaptation of the novel by Wells (produced London, 1912).

The Wonderful Visit, with St. John Ervine, adaptation of the novel by Wells (produced London, 1921).

Hoopdriver's Holiday, adaptation of his novel *The Wheels of Chance,* edited by Michael Timko. Lafayette, Indiana, Purdue University English Department, 1964.

Screenplays: *H.G. Wells Comedies (Bluebottles, The Tonic, Daydreams),* with Frank Wells, 1928; *Things to Come,* 1936; *The Man Who Could Work Miracles,* 1936.

Other

Text-Book of Biology. London, Clive, 2 vols., 1893.

Honours Physiography, with R.A. Gregory. London, Hughes, 1893.

Certain Personal Matters: A Collection of Material, Mainly Autobiographical. London, Lawrence and Bullen, 1897.

Anticipations of the Reaction of Mechanical and Scientific Progress upon Human Life and Thought. London, Chapman and Hall, 1901; New York, Harper, 1902.

The Discovery of the Future (lecture). London, Unwin, 1902; New York, Huebsch, 1913; revised edition, London, Cape, 1925.

Mankind in the Making. London, Chapman and Hall, 1903; New York, Scribner, 1904.

The Future in America: A Search after Realities. London, Chapman and Hall, and New York, Harper, 1906.

Faults of the Fabian (lecture). Privately printed, 1906.

Socialism and the Family. London, Fifield, 1906; Boston, Ball, 1908.

Reconstruction of the Fabian Society. Privately printed, 1906.

This Misery of Boots. London, Fabian Society, 1907; Boston, Ball, 1908.

Will Socialism Destroy the Home? London, Independent Labour Party, 1907.

New Worlds for Old. London, Constable, and New York, Macmillan, 1908; revised edition, London, Constable, 1914.

First and Last Things: A Confession of Faith and Rule of Life. London, Constable, and New York, Putnam, 1908; revised edition, London, Cassell, 1917; London, Watts, 1929.

Floor Games (for children). London, Palmer, 1911; Boston, Small Maynard, 1912.

The Labour Unrest. London, Associated Newspapers, 1912.

War and Common Sense. London, Associated Newspapers, 1913.

Liberalism and Its Party. London, Good, 1913.

Little Wars (children's games). London, Palmer, and Boston, Small Maynard, 1913.

An Englishman Looks at the World, Being a Series of Unrestrained Remarks upon Contemporary Matters. London, Cassell, 1914; as *Social Forces in England and America,* New York, Harper, 1914.

The War That Will End War. London, Palmer, and New York, Duffield, 1914; reprinted in part as *The War and Socialism,* London, Clarion Press, 1915.

The Peace of the World. London, Daily Chronicle, 1915.

What Is Coming? A Forecast of Things after the War. London, Cassell, and New York, Macmillan, 1916.

The Elements of Reconstruction. London, Nisbet, 1916.

War and the Future. London, Cassell, 1917; as *Italy, France, and Britain at War,* New York, Macmillan, 1917.

God the Invisible King. London, Cassell, and New York, Macmillan, 1917.

A Reasonable Man's Peace. London, Daily News, 1917.

In the Fourth Year: Anticipations of a World Peace. London, Chatto and Windus, and New York, Macmillan, 1918; abridged edition, as *Anticipations of a World Peace,* Chatto and Windus, 1918.

British Nationalism and the League of Nations. London, League of Nations Union, 1918.

History Is One. Boston, Ginn, 1919.

The Outline of History, Being a Plain History of Life and Mankind. London, Newnes, 2 vols., and New York, Macmillan, 2 vols., 1920 (and later revisions).

Russia in the Shadows. London, Hodder and Stoughton, 1920; New York, Doran, 1921.

The Salvaging of Civilisation. London, Cassell, and New York, Macmillan, 1921.

The New Teaching of History, with a Reply to Some Recent Criticisms of "The Outline of History." London, Cassell, 1921.

Washington and Hope of Peace. London, Collins, 1922; as *Washington and the Riddle of Peace,* New York, Macmillan, 1922.

The World, Its Debts, and the Rich Men. London, Finer, 1922.

A Short History of the World. London, Cassell, and New York, Macmillan, 1922; revised edition, London, Penguin, 1946.

Socialism and the Scientific Motive (lecture). Privately printed, 1923.

The Story of a Great Schoolmaster, Being a Plain Account of the Life and Ideas of Sanderson of Oundle. London, Chatto and Windus, and New York, Macmillan, 1924.

The P.R. Parliament. London, Proportional Representation Society, 1924.

A Year of Prophesying. London, Unwin, 1924; New York, Macmillan, 1925.

Works (Atlantic Edition). London, Unwin, and New York, Scribner, 28 vols., 1924.

A Forecast of the World's Affairs. New York, Encyclopaedia Britannica, 1925.

Works (Essex Edition). London, Benn, 24 vols., 1926-27.

Mr. Belloc Objects to "The Outline of History." London, Watts, 1926.

Democracy under Revision (lecture). London, Hogarth Press, and New York, Doran, 1927.

Wells' Social Anticipations, edited by H.W. Laidler. New York, Vanguard Press, 1927.

In Memory of Amy Catherine Wells. Privately printed, 1927.

The Way the World Is Going: Guesses and Forecasts of the Years Ahead. London, Benn, 1928; New York, Doubleday, 1929.

The Open Conspiracy: Blue Prints for a World Revolution. London, Gollancz, and New York, Doubleday, 1928; revised edition, London, Hogarth Press, 1930; revised edition, as *What Are We to Do with Our Lives?,* London, Heinemann, and New York, Doubleday, 1931.

The Common Sense of World Peace (lecture). London, Hogarth Press, 1929.

Imperialism and the Open Conspiracy. London, Faber, 1929.

The Science of Life: A Summary of Contemporary Knowledge about Life and Its Possibilities, with Julian Huxley and G.P. Wells. London, Amalgamated Press, 3 vols., 1930; New York, Doubleday, 4 vols., 1931; revised edition, as *Science of Life Series,* London, Cassell, 9 vols., 1934-37.

The Problem of the Troublesome Collaborator. Privately printed, 1930.

Settlement of the Trouble Between Mr. Thring and Mr. Wells: A Footnote to The Problem of the Troublesome Collaborator. Privately printed, 1930.

The Way to World Peace. London, Benn, 1930.

The Work, Wealth, and Happiness of Mankind. New York, Doubleday, 2 vols., 1931; London, Heinemann, 1 vol., 1932; revised edition, Heinemann, 1934; as *The Outline of Man's Work and Wealth,* Doubleday, 1936.

After Democracy: Addresses and Papers on the Present World Situation. London, Watts, 1932.

What Should Be Done—Now. New York, Day, 1932.

Experiment in Autobiography: Discoveries and Conclusions of a Very Ordinary Brain (since 1866). London, Gollancz-Cresset Press, 2 vols., and New York, Macmillan, 1 vol., 1934.

Stalin-Wells Talk: The Verbatim Record, and A Discussion, with others. London, New Statesman and Nation, 1934.

The New America: The New World. London, Cresset Press, and New York, Macmillan, 1935.

The Anatomy of Frustration: A Modern Synthesis. London, Cresset Press, and New York, Macmillan, 1936.

The Idea of a World Encyclopaedia. London, Hogarth Press, 1936.

World Brain. London, Methuen, and New York, Doubleday, 1938.

Travels of a Republican Radical in Search of Hot Water. London, Penguin, 1939.

The Fate of Homo Sapiens: An Unemotional Statement of the Things That Are Happening to Him Now and of the Immediate Possibilities Confronting Him. London, Secker and Warburg, 1939; as *The Fate of Man,* New York, Alliance, 1939.

The New World Order, Whether It Is Obtainable, How It Can Be Obtained, and What Sort of World a World at Peace Will Have to Be. London, Secker and Warburg, and New York, Knopf, 1940.

The Rights of Man; or, What Are We Fighting For? London, Penguin, 1940.

The Common Sense of War and Peace: World Revolution or War Unending? London, Penguin, 1940.

The Pocket History of the World. New York, Pocket Books, 1941.

Guide to the New World: A Handbook of Constructive World Revolution. London, Gollancz, 1941.

The Outlook for Homo Sapiens (revised versions of *The Fate of Homo Sapiens* and *The New World Order*). London, Secker and Warburg, 1942.

Science and the World-Mind. London, New Europe, 1942.

Phoenix: A Summary of the Inescapable Conditions of World Reorganization. London, Secker and Warburg, 1942; Girard, Kansas, Haldeman Julius, n.d.

A Thesis on the Quality of Illusion in the Continuity of Individual Life of the Higher Metazoa, with Particular Reference to the Species Homo Sapiens. Privately printed, 1942.

The Conquest of Time. London, Watts, 1942.

The New Rights of Man. Girard, Kansas, Haldeman Julius, 1942.

Crux Ansata: An Indictment of the Roman Catholic Church. London, Penguin, 1943; New York, Agora, 1944.

The Mosley Outrage. London, Daily Worker, 1943.

'42 to '44: A Contemporary Memoir upon Human Behavior during the Crisis of the World Revolution. London, Secker and Warburg, 1944.

Marxism vs. Liberalism (interview with Stalin). New York, Century, 1945.

The Happy Turning: A Dream of Life. London, Heinemann, 1945.

Mind at the End of Its Tether. London, Heinemann, 1945.

Mind at the End of Its Tether, and The Happy Turning. New York, Didier, 1945.

Henry James and H.G. Wells: A Record of Their Friendship, Their Debate on the Art of Fiction, and Their Quarrel, edited by Leon Edel and Gordon N. Ray. Urbana, University of Illinois Press, and London, Hart Davis, 1958.

Arnold Bennett and H.G. Wells: A Record of a Personal and Literary Friendship, edited by Harris Wilson. London, Hart Davis, 1960.

George Gissing and H.G. Wells: Their Friendship and Correspondence, edited by Royal A. Gettman. London, Hart Davis, 1961.

Journalism and Prophecy 1893-1946, edited W. Warren Wagar. Boston, Houghton Mifflin, 1964; revised edition, London, Bodley Head, 1965.

Early Writings in Science and Science Fiction, edited by Robert M. Philmus and David Y. Hughes. Berkeley, University of California Press, 1975.

H.G. Wells's Literary Criticism, edited by Patrick Parrinder and Robert M. Philmus. Brighton, Sussex, Harvester Press, and Totowa, New Jersey, Barnes and Noble, 1980.

H.G. Wells in Love, edited by G.P. Wells. London, Faber, 1984.

The Discovery of the Future, with The Common-Sense of World Peace and The Human Adventure, edited by Patrick Parrinder. London, PNL, 1989.

Bernard Shaw and H.G. Wells, edited by J. Percy Smith (correspondence). Toronto, University of Toronto Press, 1995.

Editor, with G.R.S. Taylor and Frances Evelyn Warwick, *The Great State: Essays in Construction.* London, Harper, 1912; as *Socialism and the Great State,* New York, Harper, 1914.

*

Bibliography: *H.G. Wells: A Comprehensive Bibliography,* London, H.G. Wells Society, 1966, revised editions, 1968, 1986; *Herbert George Wells: An Annotated Bibliography of His Works* by J.R. Hammond, New York, Garland, 1977; *H.G. Wells: A Reference Guide* by William J. Scheick and J. Randolf Cox, Boston, 1988.

Manuscript Collection: University of Illinois, Urbana.

Critical Studies (selection): *The World of H.G. Wells* by Van Wyck Brooks, New York, Mitchell Kennerley, and London, T. Fisher Unwin, 1915; *H.G. Wells: A Biography,* London, Longman, 1951; *The Early H.G. Wells: A Study of the Scientific Romances* by Bernard Bergonzi, Manchester, Manchester University Press, 1961, and *H.G. Wells: A Collection of Critical Essays* edited by Bergonzi, Englewood Cliffs, New Jersey, Prentice Hall, 1976; *H.G. Wells: An Outline* by F.K. Chaplin, London, P.R. Macmillan, 1961; *H.G. Wells and the World State* by W. Warren Wagar, New Haven, Connecticut, Yale University Press, 1961; *The Life and Thought of H.G. Wells* by Julius Kagarlitsky (translated by Moura Budberg), London, Sidgwick and Jackson, 1966; *H.G. Wells* by Richard Hauer Costa, New York, Twayne, 1967, revised edition, 1985; *H.G. Wells: His Turbulent Life and Times* by Lovat Dickson, London, Macmillan, 1969; essay in *A Soviet Heretic* by Yevgeny Zamyatin (translated by Mirra Ginsburg), Chicago, University of Chicago Press, 1970; *H.G. Wells* by Patrick Parrinder, Edinburgh, Oliver and Boyd, 1970, New York, Capricorn, 1977, and *H.G. Wells: The Critical Heritage* edited by Parrinder, London, Routledge, 1972; *The Time Traveller: The Life of H.G. Wells* by Norman and Jeanne Mackenzie, London, Weidenfeld and Nicolson, 1973, as *H.G. Wells: A Biography,* New York, Simon and Schuster, 1973; *H.G. Wells: Critic of Progress* by Jack Williamson, Baltimore, Mirage Press, 1973; *H.G. Wells and Rebecca West* by Gordon N. Ray, New Haven, Connecticut, Yale University Press, and London, Macmillan, 1974; *The Scientific Romances of H.G. Wells* by Stephen Gill, Cornwall, Ontario, Vesta, 1975; *Anatomies of Egotism: A Reading of the Last Novels of H.G. Wells* by Robert Bloom, Lincoln, University of Nebraska Press, 1977; *H.G. Wells and Modern Science Fiction* edited by Darko Suvin and Robert M. Philmus, Lewisburg, Pennsylvania, Buckness University Press, 1977; *H.G. Wells: A Pictorial Biography* by Frank Wells, London, Jupiter, 1977; *The H.G. Wells Scrapbook* edited by Peter Haining, London, New English Library, 1978; *Who's Who in H.G. Wells* by Brian Ash, London, Elm Tree, 1979; *H.G. Wells, Discoverer of the Future: The Influence of Science on His Thought* by Roslynn D. Haynes, New York, New York University Press, and London, Macmillan, 1980; *H.G. Wells: Interviews and Recollections* edited by J.R. Hammond, London, Macmillan, 1980; *The Science Fiction of H.G. Wells: A Concise Guide* by P.H. Niles, Clifton Park, New York, Auriga, 1980; *The Science Fiction of H.G. Wells* by Frank McConnell, New York, Oxford University Press, 1981; *H.G. Wells and the Culminating Ape: Biological Themes and Imaginative Obsessions* by Peter Kemp, London, Macmillan, and New York, St. Martin's Press, 1982; *The Logic of Fantasy: H.G. Wells and Science Fiction* by John Huntington, New York, Columbia University Press, 1982; *H.G. Wells* by Robert Crossley, Mercer Island, Washington, Starmont House, 1984; *The Splintering Frame: The Later Fiction of H.G. Wells* by William J. Scheick, Victoria, University of Victoria English Literary Studies, 1984; *H.G. Wells: Aspects of a Life* by Anthony West, London, Hutchinson, and New York, Random House, 1984; *H.G. Wells* by John Batchelor, London, Cambridge University Press, 1985; *H.G. Wells: Desperately Mortal: A Biography* by David C. Smith, New Haven, Connecticut, Yale University Press, 1986; *H.G. Wells: Reality and Beyond* edited by Michael Mullin, Champaign, Illinois, Public Library, 1986; *The Prophetic Soul: A Reading of Things to Come* by Leon Stover, Jefferson, North Carolina, and London, McFarland, 1987; *H.G. Wells* by Michael Draper, London, Macmillan, and New York, St. Martin's Press, 1987; *H.G. Wells* by Christopher Martin, Hove, Wayland, 1988; *H.G. Wells under Revision* edited by Patrick Parrinder and Christopher Rolfe, Selinsgrove, Pennsylvania, and London, Susquehanna University Presses, 1990; *H.G. Wells* by Brian Murray, New York, Continuum, 1990; *Critical Essays on H.G. Wells* edited by John Huntington, Boston, G.K. Hall, 1991; *H.G. Wells and the Short Story* by J.R. Hammond, New York, St. Martin's Press, 1992; *The Invisible Man: The Life and Liberties of H.G. Wells* by Michael Coren, New York, Random House, 1993; *A Critical Edition of The War of the Worlds: H.G. Wells's Scientific Romance* edited by David Hughes and Harry M. Geduld, Bloomington, Indiana University Press, 1993; *The Critical Response to H.G. Wells* edited by William J. Scheick, Westport, Greenwood Press, 1995.

*   *   *

On the 20th anniversary of H.G. Wells's death, Godfrey Smith spoke of him as a substantial figure in our "literate subconscious." Numerous readers, in other words, have encountered Wells's writings either directly or indirectly (in works influenced by or responding to his books). This is especially true in the science fiction genre, which for at least 20 years after Wells's death derived much of its inspiration and shape from his fin de siècle scientific romances. If these once original and innovative romances seem less stimulating or adaptable within the genre as practiced today, the recollection of them is still hallowed, as is evident in recent science fiction stories which either allude to them specifically or include their author as a character.

When, in 1895, Wells appeared upon the literary scene with four books, including *The Time Machine* and *The Stolen Bacillus, and Other Incidents,* reviewers were generally skeptical. Distrustful of such productivity and confused by seeming inconsistencies in authorial point of view, reviewers tended to speak of Wells's potentiality rather than of his achievement in these works. During the following year *The Island of Dr. Moreau,* featuring vivisection, fostered both doubts concerning Wells's potentiality and concerns over his transgression of good taste in using a sensational subject for the purpose of commercial gain. Undaunted, Wells published four more books in 1897, including *The Invisible Man, Thirty Strange Stories,* and *The Plattner Story and Others*—all to a mixed critical reception. Edmond Gosse then typically lamented that Wells was wasting his considerable talents in "little horrible stories about monsters." Finding more to praise than to criticize in *The War of the Worlds,* reviewers in 1898 at last seemed to be more aligned with Wells's extensive readership, whose enthusiastic enjoyment of his romances had not been diminished in the least and perhaps had been nurtured by such equivocal commentary in newspapers and periodicals. During the 20th century, these same works would emerge as the most favored of Wells's oeuvre, not only among general readers but also among academic critics.

The deeper meanings of these works are now better appreciated. Today *The Time Machine* seems not only a Marxist satire on the English class system but also, among other possible interpretations, a dire representation of the non-utopian thrust of evolution. At present, *The Island of Dr. Moreau* seems less a Swiftian satire on the deity or on the Frankensteinian impulse to usurp the deity's power than, say, a Stevensonian portrait of divided human sensibilities or a Huxleyan portrait of the evolutionary process. If *The Invisible Man* allegorizes the dangerous intersection of scientific mastery and human limitation, it also demonstrates the alienation of the modern individual and the "invisible" subtleties of Wells's narrative method. And *The War of the Worlds* has now emerged as a critique of British imperialism that also dramatizes a psychological battle within its narrator.

Wells's short fiction likewise enjoyed a popular readership and a strong critical reception during his career, which accounts for the frequently reprinted 1927 edition of his collected short stories. With the single exception of the 1904 lost-race tale "The Country of the Blind," however, Wells's short fiction has received little critical scrutiny. Nevertheless, these works contain a wealth of overlooked opportunities for appreciating Wells's science fictional art. Wells, for instance, uses a bathysphere portal in "In the Abyss" (a tale of a suboceanic civilization), a window in "The Plattner Story" (a tale of another dimension), a doorway in "The Remarkable Case of Davidson's Eyes" (a tale of invisibility), and a viewing apparatus in "The Crystal Egg" (a tale of extraterrestrial contact), among many other instances, to represent the transitional state of human perception during the turn of the century.

If Wells's later science fiction has never been as ardently received as his earlier romances, many of these works, like the short fiction, represent substantial literary experiments in the genre. *When the Sleeper Wakes* (1899) insists on the need for a different future by parodying the inheritance convention of Victorian fiction; *The First Men in the Moon* (1901) jumbles reliable and unreliable narration to resist the reader's desire for certainty and to emphasize the thought process. *The Food of the Gods* (1904) disorients conventional expectations by transferring the reader's sympathy to creatures who threaten the ordinary world. *In the Days of the Comet* (1906) shatters the formula for the Victorian suspense novel in order to foster in the reader a new consciousness similar to the post-comet change in ideas undergone by the characters in the novel. *Men like Gods* (1923) recasts *Pilgrim's Progress* in Utopian terms, and *The Dream* (1924) in turn recasts *Men Like Gods* to hint at a core of undetected timeless truth within time-bound literary techniques. *Star Begotten* (1937), an extraterrestrial version of the New Testament nativity story, represents Wells's attempt at a new species of science fiction that demonstrates the open-ended, multi-dimensional capacity of the genre to express ongoing human possibilities.

The influences on Wells are many, including his early exposure to the thought of Charles Darwin, Thomas Huxley, and Karl Marx, and to the narrative techniques of Edgar Allan Poe, Nathaniel Hawthorne, Charles Dickens, and Robert Louis Stevenson. Wells's influence on other authors, whether they be sympathetic or unsympathetic to his work, are legion both within and without the genre of science fiction. To point to works by Aldous Huxley, George Orwell, Evgeny Zamyatin, and Jorge Luis Borges is not even to glimpse the proverbial tip of the iceberg of his influence. As W. Warren Wagar aptly indicated in his entry on Wells for the 3rd edition of this volume, "One may wonder if even one significant writer in the genre anywhere in the world in this century has missed reading H. G. Wells." And we may further wonder to what extent, in one way or another, many of these authors wittingly or unwittingly responded in their own work to the example of H.G. Wells.

—William Scheick

WELLS, John J. *See* **BRADLEY, Marion Zimmer; COULSON, Juanita.**

———

WERNHEIM, John. *See* **FEARN, John Russell.**

———

WEST, Douglas. *See* **TUBB, E.C.**

———

WHITE, James

Nationality: British. **Born:** Belfast, Northern Ireland, 7 April 1928. **Education:** St. John's Primary School, 1935-41, and St. Joseph's Secondary Technical School, 1942-43, both Belfast. **Family:** Married Margaret Sarah Martin in 1955; one daughter and two sons. **Career:** Salesman and manager in several tailoring stores, Belfast, 1943-65. Technical clerk, 1965-66, publicity assistant, 1966-68, and publicity officer, 1968-84, Shorts Aircraft, Belfast. Patron, Irish Science Fiction Association, 1974; council member, British Science Fiction Association, 1975. **Awards:** Europa award, 1972. **Agent:** Pamela Buckmaster, Carnell Literary Agency, Danescroft, Goose Lane, Little Hallingbury, Bishop's Stortford, Hertfordshire CM22 7RG, England. **Address:** 2 West Drive, Portstewart BT55 7ND, Northern Ireland.

SCIENCE FICTION PUBLICATIONS

Novels (series: Sector General)

The Secret Visitors. New York, Ace, 1957; London, Digit, 1961.
Second Ending. New York, Ace, 1962.
Hospital Station (Sector). New York, Ballantine, 1962; London, Corgi, 1967.
Star Surgeon (Sector). New York, Ballantine, 1963; London, Corgi, 1967.
The Escape Orbit. New York, Ace, 1965; as *Open Prison,* London, Four Square, 1965.
The Watch Below. New York, Ballantine, and London, Whiting and Wheaton, 1966.
All Judgment Fled. London, Rapp and Whiting, 1968; New York, Walker, 1969.
Tomorrow Is Too Far. New York, Ballantine, and London, Joseph, 1971.
Lifeboat. New York, Ballantine, 1972; as *Dark Inferno,* London, Joseph, 1972.
The Dream Millennium. London, Joseph, and New York, Ballantine, 1974.
Underkill: A Science Fiction Novel. London, Corgi, 1979.
Ambulance Ship (Sector). New York, Ballantine, 1979; expanded edition, London, Corgi, 1980.

Star Healer (Sector). New York, Ballantine, 1985; London, Orbit, 1987.

Code Blue—Emergency (Sector). New York, Ballantine, 1987; London, Orbit, 1989.

Federation World. New York, Ballantine, 1988; London, Orbit, 1990.

The Silent Stars Go By. New York, Ballantine, 1991.

The Genocidal Healer (Sector General). New York, Ballantine, 1992.

Short Stories (series: Sector General)

Deadly Litter. New York, Ballantine, 1964; London, Corgi, 1968.

The Aliens among Us. New York, Ballantine, 1969; London, Corgi, 1970.

Major Operation (Sector). New York, Ballantine, 1971; London, Orbit, 1987.

Monsters and Medics (includes *Second Ending*). London, Corgi, and New York, Ballantine, 1977.

Future Past. New York, Ballantine, 1982; revised edition, London, Orbit, 1988.

Sector General. New York, Ballantine, 1983; London, Orbit, 1987.

The Interpreter, bound with *A Novacon Garland,* by David Langford. Birmingham, England, Birmingham Science Fiction Group, 1985.

*

James White comments:

I have always felt that the best stories are those in which ordinary people are faced with extraordinary situations, and my early attraction to science fiction, both as a very young reader and later as a writer, was that it was the only genre which allowed ordinary people to be faced with truly extraordinary situations. My favourite of these is the one in which Earth-human characters make first contact with an extraterrestrial species. The attempts to understand the behaviour and thought processes of the aliens frequently illuminate the human condition as well, and the problem of learning to understand and adapt to a totally alien viewpoint places in proper perspective the very minor differences of skin pigmentation and politics which bedevil our own culture. ·

*   *   *

One of the most memorable of James White's many intriguing settings is to be found in *The Watch Below*: a colony survives for several generations trapped inside the hull of a tanker torpedoed during World War II. In their effort to keep themselves sane, one of the things the first generation does is to attempt to recall every story any of them has ever read. One survivor has read a few works in the relatively new genre of science fiction. He particularly remembers a Doc Smith novel with a character "who was a winged dragon with scales, claws, four extensible eyes, and a lot of other visually horrifying features and who was more human than some of the human characters." Now, since *The Watch Below* is a "first contact" story, there are reasons of plot for this introduction of this tribute to the idea of interspecific brotherhood. But beyond this, the tradition of the fraternity of all intelligent life which first took firm hold in magazine SF in the mid-1930s is one which has had a marked impact on White himself as an author.

Most of White's stories involve extraterrestrials, and these beings are a varied lot indeed, including creatures indistinguishable from terrestrials in *The Secret Visitors,* aquatic life-forms in *The Watch Below,* chlorine-breathers in *Open Prison,* and giant cater-

pillar-like tree-dwellers in *All Judgment Fled.* All these varieties together, and others besides, can be found at once in *Hospital Station* and the other books in White's series about Sector Twelve General Hospital, a multi-environmental hospital in deep space with staff and patients from a diverse galactic culture. Indeed, as an author White is quite fond of the field of medicine, perhaps seeing in it a paradigm of the cooperation and fellowship that should embrace all intelligent beings. Even outside the Sector General series, physicians are important characters in *The Secret Visitors, The Watch Below, All Judgment Fled,* and *Underkill.*

But soldiers figure almost as prominently as doctors in White's work. One section of *Hospital Station* is given over to the hero's realization that the Monitor Corps performs a necessary police function. White is not happy about this fact of life. Indeed, in at least three different books characters are relieved to have it turn out that the life-forms they were forced to kill are only animals, and not intelligent beings after all. And beyond such justified violence, White's work also depicts some conflicts based on honest misunderstanding, and others stemming from deliberate selfishness and greed. But with one exception, the accent in White's work is not on the existence of such abominations but on the possibility of doing something about them. White's stories almost always close with harmony restored, or at least with such a restoration anticipated. This stubborn optimism has been one of White's trademarks.

A second trademark, already alluded to, is his inventiveness regarding environments. If his most brilliant achievement in this area is the sunken tanker in *The Watch Below,* other instances are almost equally imaginative—the prison planet of *Open Prison,* the alien starship overrun with laboratory animals in *All Judgment Fled,* the energy-poor world of the "powerdown" in *Underkill,* and others.

White's work does have its defects. His human characters are too much alike, and sometimes their actions are inadequately motivated. Often White's extraterrestrials have incongruously human—indeed, Western—psychologies, whatever their external forms. White's fascinating environments are also sometimes a little too visibly contrived. Until fairly recently, the single most serious accusation that could be brought against White was his utopianism, his seeming belief that no group of intelligent beings could willfully persist in wrongdoing once they had had the right path pointed out to them. White, however, effectively countered any such accusation with *Underkill,* a novel presumably growing out of White's experience of the civil unrest in his home of Northern Ireland. In this novel, extra-terrestrials—playing as it were the part of an Old Testament Yahweh—find mankind so depraved (particularly by the ethnic and sectarian hatreds that lead to terrorism) that they see no solution but to destroy all the earth's population save for a chosen remnant of ten million, and to start over with those. Unlike other White books, *Underkill* is charged with a bitterness and forcefulness reminiscent of Jonathan Swift. However, after this aberration, White's next several books went back with no obvious difficulty to the seeming utopianism of the Sector General series. This return to a familiar path could have been based on commercial considerations, since *Underkill* failed to find an American publisher. (Presumably its bitterness was judged to be unviable in an American market that was beginning to emerge from the gloom of much Vietnam-era SF.) In any case, *Underkill* makes it clear that in his other books, White is presenting a view of human relations as they ought to be, not as he actually takes them to be. White is not naive—merely hopeful.

—Patrick L. McGuire

WHITE, Ted

Pseudonyms: Ron Archer; Norman Edwards. **Nationality:** American. **Born:** Theodore Edward White, Washington, D.C., 4 February 1938. **Education:** Public schools in Falls Church, Virginia. **Family:** Married 1) Sylvia Dees in 1958; 2) Robin Postal in 1966; one child; 3) Companion of Gwayne Naug. **Career:** Head of foreign department, Scott Meredith Literary Agency, 1963; assistant editor, 1963-67, and associate editor, 1967-68, *Fantasy and Science Fiction;* associate editor, Lancer Books, 1966; managing editor, 1969, and editor, 1970-78, *Amazing* and *Fantastic;* co-editor, *Void* fan magazine, 1959-68; editor, *Heavy Metal,* New York, 1979-81. **Awards:** Hugo award, for criticism, 1968. **Agent:** Henry Morrison Inc., 320 McLain Street, Bedford Hills, New York 10705, U.S.A.

SCIENCE FICTION PUBLICATIONS

Novels (series: Qanar)

Invasion from 2500 (with Terry Carr as Norman Edwards). Derby, Connecticut, Monarch, 1964.
Android Avenger. New York, Ace, 1965.
Phoenix Prime (Qanar). New York, Lancer, 1966.
The Sorceress of Qar (Qanar). New York, Lancer, 1966.
The Jewels of Elsewhen. New York, Belmont, 1967.
Lost in Space (novelization of TV play; as Ron Archer, with Dave Van Arnam). New York, Pyramid, 1967.
Secret of the Marauder Satellite (for children). Philadelphia, Westminster Press, 1967.
Sideslip, with Dave Van Arnam. New York, Pyramid, 1968.
Captain America: The Great Gold Steal. New York, Bantam, 1968.
The Spawn of the Death Machine. New York, Paperback Library, 1968.
No Time like Tomorrow (for children). New York, Crown, 1969.
By Furies Possessed: A Novel of Tomorrow. New York, Signet, 1970.
Star Wolf! (Qanar). New York, Lancer, 1971.
Trouble on Project Ceres (for children). Philadelphia, Westminster Press, 1971.
Forbidden World: A Science Fiction Novel, with David F. Bischoff. New York, Popular Library, 1978.
Phoenix: A Novel, with Marv Wolfman. New York, Pyramid, 1977.

OTHER PUBLICATIONS

Other

Editor, *The Best from Amazing Stories.* New York, Manor, 1973; London, Hale, 1976.
Editor, *The Best from Fantastic.* New York, Manor, 1973; London, Hale, 1976.

*   *   *

Ted White is the author of over a dozen novels and a greater number of short stories, and he acted as editor of both *Amazing* and *Fantastic* magazines for several years, where he was a contro-

versial but undeniably influential editor who changed the flavor of both magazines. Although he remains active in SF fandom, he has produced no new fiction in over a decade.

White's debut novel was *Android Avenger.* Bob Tanner is a perfectly ordinary guy, or so he thinks. One day his body starts acting independently of his mind and he discovers that he is an android, part human, part machine, equipped with deadly weapons and programmed to be an assassin. Tanner's career is continued in *The Spawn of the Death Machine.* Reactivated after a period of dormancy, controlled by a computer, Tanner sets out to explore a future where civilization has fallen and New York City is inhabited by cannibals and beasts of prey. In due course he realizes that the computer controlling him is responsible for the devastation and that he is the unwitting agent of its plot to win control of the world. Both novels are entertaining potboilers, though neither measures up to the quality of White's better work.

White's most popular series started with *Phoenix Prime.* Max Quest discovers that he has superhuman powers but, more importantly, earns the enmity of other supermen who don't want any more competition for primacy above the human race. Although he is too powerful for them to destroy, the Others use their own powers to transport him to another dimension, a world where his own abilities are muted and where magic works. The story continues in *The Sorceress of Qar.* Two heroic supermen battle the further plottings of the Others against the backdrop of a primitive world where magic really works. The sequel lacked the spirited plotting of its predecessor, and was followed by an even weaker third volume, *Star Wolf!* The son of Max Quest is shunned by his tribe, so he sets off on his own to find a way to cross the barrier between universes and find his father.

White's most accomplished novel was written in collaboration with Dave Van Arnam. *Sideslip* is an alternate history story of considerable skill and originality. The protagonist, Ron Archer, inadvertently crosses from one reality to another, finds himself in a version of New York City where Adolf Hitler rules America and aliens from outer space are an accepted part of everyday life. Archer is not there by chance, however, but at the bidding of a mysterious presence using him as the fulcrum to change the course of galactic history. Somewhat similar in theme is *The Jewels of Elsewhen,* which has one of the most effective openings in the field. This time the protagonist discovers that all of his fellow passengers on the subway have turned into manikins, and when he emerges, the laws of nature seem to have been altered. Although not quite as polished as *Sideslip,* this is White's most inventive novel. *By Furies Possessed* is a superior alien invasion story, this time in the form of amorphous parasites that seize control of their hosts. White avoided a contemporary setting and placed his story in a future where Earth is part of an interstellar civilization, which gives a decidedly different tone to the novel.

The remaining novels are of considerably less interest. With Terry Carr, White wrote the minor potboiler *Invasion from 2500* under the name Norman Edwards. *Lost in Space* is a novel based on the ludicrous television series, written with Dave Van Arnam as by Ron Archer. *The Great Gold Steal* is an adventure of the Marvel comics hero Captain America, pitting him against three villains who plan to steal the entire gold reserve of the U.S. *Forbidden World,* written with David Bischoff, is an episodic adventure story about a world whose inhabitants have been isolated into separate cultures. White also wrote two novels for younger readers. *Trouble on Project Ceres* is a standard spy thriller set within a government project to develop a method of farming the desert. *Secret of the Marauder*

Satellite is a much better work. A young space explorer assigned to police up the junk orbiting the Earth uncovers evidence of an alien creature living in orbit.

White's shorter fiction includes his inventive pastiche of Doc Savage and other pulp heroes, "Doc Phoenix," which was supposed to be the first of several adventures. "Junk Patrol" shows one of the perils of living off the Earth. America has adopted apartheid as a solution to social problems in "A Girl Like You" and racism appears as a theme again in "Things Are Tough All Over," where cannibalism is acceptable so long as it isn't whites being eaten. Ron Archer, hero of *Sideslip,* has further amusing adventures in "Wednesday, Noon," "It Could Be Anywhere," and "4:48 PM, October 6, 197-, Late Afternoon on Christopher Street." White indulges in nostalgia for the works of Leigh Brackett in "Under the Mad Sun" and takes pot shots at nationalism in "Saboteur."

Although most of White's fiction is oriented toward action and conflict, there is a frequent undercurrent of serious concerns. White indicts most of the obvious ills of the world, racism and other prejudices, obsession with wealth and power, exploitation of the less fortunate. Unlike some writers, he never allows those concerns to interfere with the story's pace or plot. He published no single work memorable enough to establish him as a lasting writer in the field, although some of his novels indicate he had the potential to become one should he return to writing.

—Don D'Ammassa

WHITEFORD, Wynne (Noel)

Nationality: Australian. **Born:** East Melbourne, Australia, 23 December 1915. **Education:** Royal Melbourne Institute of Technology, 1939-41; Melbourne University, 1948-50. **Family:** Married Laurel Miriam Fairey in 1949 (died 1978). **Career:** Proprietor, Wynray Studios, Prahran, Victoria, 1933-35; aircraft assembler, Commonwealth Aircraft Corporation, Fisherman's Bend, Victoria, 1939-43. Reporter, *Australian Motor Sports,* then technical editor, *Australian Motor Manual,* Melbourne, 1953-57. Lived in New York and London, 1957-60. Editor of newsletter and organizer of trade displays, Soil Conservation Authority of Victoria, 1961-65. President, Eastern Writers Group, 1962-85, 1991. Editor, *Zest* anthologies, Melbourne, 1989 and 1990. **Awards:** Epicurean and Cultural Society Short Story award, 1987; Ditmar award, 1990. **Agent:** Cherry Weiner, 28 Kipling Way, Manalapan, New Jersey 07726, U.S.A. **Address:** "Illalangi," 3 Stringybark Road, Eltham, Victoria 3095, Australia.

Science Fiction Publications

Novels

Breathing Space Only. St. Kilda, Victoria, Void Publications, 1980; New York, Ace, 1986.
Sapphire Road. St. Kilda, Victoria, Cory and Collins, 1982; New York, Ace, 1986.
Thor's Hammer. St. Kilda, Victoria, Cory and Collins, 1983; New York, Ace, 1985.

The Hyades Contact. New York, Ace, 1987.
Lake of the Sun. New York, Ace, 1989.
The Specialist. New York, Ace, 1990.

*

Wynne Whiteford comments:

My work has been mostly of the type described as "hard" science fiction. It is generally set in near-future environments extrapolated from present-day trends.

Until a few years ago, I had written fiction only in my spare time. I had my first three novels published in Australia in 1980, 1982, and 1983. I then took extended leave from Leader Newspapers, for whom I was working at the time, and took copies of these novels to New York publishers. Ace accepted the three and asked for more. Returning to Australia, I came to an arrangement with Leader Newspapers to work three days a week (later two) at their busiest times of the week, leaving myself more time for writing. After selling another novel in the U.S.A., I switched to full-time writing of fiction. Early experience in engineering plants has given me, I think, a solid basis for realistic mechanical descriptions. My wife Laurel, to whom I was married for 27 years, was a psychologist, and this gave me an interest in studying people, their motives, reactions, characteristics, etc., which has been very helpful. I now share a house with historical novelist Gwayne Naug in bushland. It has taken me a long time to work out a smooth technique in writing fiction. If I write fast, the story flows out naturally, but I forget to make some points along the way. If I write slowly and carefully, the narrative seems to creak with changes of mood and tempo. Now, I build a story slowly, by notes in files, then write one draft, *fast,* straight through from beginning to end, directly onto the machine. For the final draft, I use two IBM Selectrics, on desks reachable from a single swivel chair, one to try out doubtful sentences before committing them to the "clean" draft—saves a lot of retyping.

*   *   *

Wynne Whiteford's emergence in the 1980s as Australia's most reliable producer of SF thrillers, of old-fashioned "good reads," marks the third and most productive phase of a writing career that, in hindsight, goes back surprisingly far, to the brief flirtation during the 1930s and the frequent publication of short stories in the 1950s. The major phase was sparked off by the excitement of the WorldCon in Melbourne.

The first of Whiteford's novels, *Breathing Space Only,* was greeted with some enthusiasm. It employs an identifiable local scene, the Kosciusko region, and is set not unbelievably two or three hundred years hence as a last outpost of civilization above the smog of the plains below, in which are burning opencast coal fields. If one goes to this high country in summer one may easily get the feeling of being happily placed above the dull heat of the less fortunate Australians below; in Whiteford's future time, those unfortunates are known as Perms (Permissives), ridden by disease and divided into warring tribes. The upland scientific community is somewhat paranoid, and when an attempt is made to contact them by a returning starship's satellite they observe radio silence. A small group risks establishing contact and, after executing a dangerous mission into Perm territory, three of them have the opportunity of leaving Earth and attaining immortality. In this novel, the idea of humans modified into huge four-armed creatures (tetrabrachs) is first proposed; it is used again in Whiteford's later novels.

Sapphire Road is set further in the future than *Breathing Space Only,* although it could be part of the same history. Action is divided between Earth and Alcenar, one of the colonized planets of Alpha Centaurus. On Earth, following some dim catastrophe, power has devolved to the southern hemisphere. The watchword is "Stability" and progress is slow. The hero, industrialist Max Vanmore, has to cope with the murder of his family in central Australia before embarking in quest of sapphires on the distant planet. He races in his Indian friend Rajendra Naryan's ship in competition with his clandestine enemy, Captain Kranzen of the National Stability Council, who commands a military vessel. The plot is in outline not unlike one of Bob Shaw's thrillers, although the exposition is managed somewhat clumsily. To compensate, there is a memorable character, Bianca Baru, one of several notable humans in Whiteford's work whose physical modification causes mingled attraction and repulsion to the Earth-normal types. A giant from the high-gravity planet Chiron, Bianca accompanies Vanmore and Naryan to Alcenar.

Thor's Hammer gives the hero, Kingston Hannam, two unusual female companions in the tradition of Bianca. Hannam has been given a mission to find a fellow-employee, Slade Anton, who has disappeared after making a threat. Anton suggested that he might hurl an asteroid at the earth, since he believes that the future lies exclusively with the colony planets. Anton's former girl friend, Gail Busentil, has a "domehead" appearance: she is a superwoman with computer-enhanced brainpower and surgically increased height and breasts; the other woman helper, Yetta, is a dwarf. The denizens of Ceres are over-sized and another leading character, Yetta's partner in prospecting, Des Marston, has had his legs amputated in an accident. One begins to get the impression that the author thinks the future will be a paradise for freaks. Certainly, with such talents as his helpers command, Hannam has to exhibit little intelligence to perform his mission.

In *The Hyades Contact* we have a long-delayed completion to a story of first contact with a superior cat-like species which began in three chapters presented first as short stories in *Void* collections of 1978 and 1979. These chapters register effectively the shock of encountering fast-moving, highly-intelligent carnivores who have superior technology, the Kesrii. After failing to outmaneuver them in space, the humans are settled on a colony planet, which they call Terranova. The colonists divide between those who wish to go back to the home planets and those who wish to settle. The principal hero, Connor, is one of the latter; he marries a doctor, Zella, and their baby is rendered super-intelligent, thanks to the child-birth help of a female Kesrii. Much of the interest of the story lies in the growth of the colony as relatively primitive energy sources are developed to ensure its continued viability. When a second colony is discovered, of greyish eight-armed "droms," also dumped on the planet by the Kesrii, the encounter proves disastrous: they murder one of the humans but are in turn destroyed (*War of the Worlds* style) by his micro-organisms. The humans come to accept that they are a second-rate species, but unlike the droms they at least have a future. Whitefordian freaks in this novel include Nordstrom, over 200 years old, who has a cybernetic body; Sven, a squat giantess from a heavy planet; and Dr. Voll, who has been adapted to life on a space station and needs an exoskeleton to survive in Earth gravity: basically he is a brain with a very small body.

Whiteford's two most recent novels are both set mainly on Mars, but they do not share quite the same history. *Lake of the Sun* is a relatively simple but satisfying story of first contact: the main complication is that, when Earthmen meet Martians, they find there are two Martian races. The *ashti* are cyclopian, having one large eye; the *vora* have two eyes, larger than the Terran ones, although they share a remote Terran ancestry. (The Terrans themselves have already begun to adapt their bodies to their altered circumstances.) Ancient and modern humans meet after the subterranean denizens of Mars hear the explosions of colonists testing for minerals near the surface. Whiteford develops his thriller plot in a natural and convincing fashion: the conclusion is guardedly optimistic and sounds a warning heard also in Robert L. Forward's cheela books, that an encounter with a race that has developed superior technology might take away "our" future. *The Specialist,* set later in the colonists' future on Mars (it begins in 2095), ignores the idea of surviving Martian races and substitutes that of genetically engineered superhuman races. Whiteford's hero does not seem to look back to Robert Sheckley's famous "Specialist": the alienated humanoids in the book—giant Siamese twins and tetrabrachs and clones—leave Lance Garrith behind when they go space-voyaging. Lance, a generalist when considered as a top Earth newscaster, is allowed to survive as a specialist for his reporting skills after he has inconveniently penetrated the secret society of new people that has been able to develop on the margins of the apparently closed bubble-city life of Mars but would have found Earth inimical to them long before their plans could have matured. This novel is a splendid showcase for the author's own specialty: presenting close encounters with giants, grotesques, and aliens (especially women).

—Michael J. Tolley

WILDER, Cherry

Pseudonym for Cherry Barbara Grimm, née Lockett. **Nationality:** New Zealander. **Born:** Auckland, 3 September 1930. **Education:** Canterbury University College, Christchurch, B.A. 1952. **Family:** Married 1) A.J. Anderson in 1952; 2) H.K.F. Grimm in 1963 (died 1992), two daughters. **Career:** Lived in Australia, 1954-76: high school teacher, editorial assistant, theatre director; regular reviewer for *Sydney Morning Herald* and *The Australian,* 1964-74. **Awards:** Australia Council grant, 1973, 1975. **Agents:** James Frenkel & Associates, 414 S. Randall Ave., Madison, Wisconsin 53775, U.S.A.; Thomas Schlück, Hinter Der Worth 12, 30827 Garbsen, Germany. **Address:** Behring Str. 5, 65191 Wiesbaden, Germany.

SCIENCE FICTION PUBLICATIONS

Novels (series: Torin)

The Luck of Brin's Five (Torin). New York, Atheneum, 1977; London, Angus and Robertson, 1979.
The Nearest Fire (Torin). New York, Atheneum, 1980.
Second Nature. New York, Timescape, 1982; London, Allen and Unwin, 1986.
The Tapestry Warriors (Torin). New York, Atheneum, 1983.

Novels (series: Rulers of Hylor in all titles)

A Princess of the Chameln. New York, Atheneum, 1984; London, Allen and Unwin, 1986.

Yorath the Wolf. New York, Atheneum, 1984; London, Allen and Unwin, 1986.
The Summer's King. New York, Atheneum, 1986; London, Allen and Unwin, 1987.
Cruel Designs. London, Piatkus, 1988.

Short Stories

Dealers in Light and Darkness. Cambridge, Massachusetts, Edgewood Press, 1995.

OTHER PUBLICATIONS

Other

Translator, *Venice,* edited by Hans Hoeper and Heinz Vestner. Singapore, APA Productions, and New York, Prentice-Hall, 1992.

*

Manuscript Collection: de Grummond Collection, University of Southern Mississippi, Hattiesburg.

*   *   *

Cherry Wilder's first novel, *The Luck of Brin's Five,* describes the first encounter on the planet Torin with a visitor from Earth. The narrator was 12 years "shown" when this happened; he is a marsupial humanoid, who reckons his age not from birth but from the date of leaving the maternal pouch. Wilder's trilogy about the marsupial planet Torin thus recreates the kind of wonder with which the first Anglo-Celtic visitors observed the Earth's marsupial continent, Australia—land of the kangaroo and the platypus. Wilder herself migrated from New Zealand to Australia as a young adult, and reported long afterwards that "the strangeness of the Australian landscape suggested still other worlds." In each novel about the Moruians of Torin, a brief prologue describes scenery and interactions on Torin as a visiting human would perceive them. The adventures of *The Luck of Brin's Five* are then narrated by a Moruian bush weaver, Dorn Brinroyan. Without delaying the plot and the interweaving subplots, he illuminates (as if in passing) the traditional five-member family in Torin's marsupial humanoid civilization: three adults of mating age, one elderly person ("the ancient") and one person with an abnormality ("the luck"). Torin's local customs and extraordinary surroundings are richly present and totally convincing. But in the second Torin novel, *The Nearest Fire,* the narrator, Yolo Harn, is a miner whose upbringing was altogether different. She reveals that Moruian town-dwellers consider pair-marriages normal, and moreover have no fear of "fire-metal-magic" and no knowledge of other traditions that Dorn considered universal. Yolo is an "omor", the sturdiest and most muscular class of the Moruians—females with special training and diet, who are medically rendered sterile. *The Tapestry Warriors* then gives a third class's viewpoint: the narrator Rovan Wentroy and other young ruling-class "grandees" prove to be alienated from their elders in a way unknown among weavers and "townees."

This strategy of transforming the stranger of one volume into the narrator of another is also used in Wilder's "Rulers of Hylor" trilogy. In the first novel, *A Princess of the Chameln,* invaders from

Mel'Nir threaten the ruling houses of the Chameln lands. The princess Aidris flees into exile and works incognita in the stables of neighbouring Athron as a "kedran" or female soldier. Battles against the armies of Mel'Nir are seen from Aidris's viewpoint. But the sequel, *Yorath the Wolf,* is told by a Mel'Nir prince—also in exile, and thought to have been killed at birth. The third novel, *The Summer's King,* tells of King Sharn, who is Aidris's co-ruler.

Both the Torin and the Hylor trilogies were first published as "juveniles," and have conflicts and a villain in every volume. Throughout each trilogy, one powerful individual opposes the villain on behalf of society. The Moruians of Torin have "psychic" rather than magical powers; nevertheless, their champion is popularly known as "Magician" and "Great Diviner" as well as "Maker of Engines." But in Hylor the two opponents are truly magicians, since this is a fantasy world, where magical trees speak with princesses and where the fairy or "Light" people are genuinely terrifying. In contrast to conventional tales, like that of Merlin versus Morgan Le Fay, Wilder tells of male villains (in Torin, the Great Elder and the Juran; in Hylor, Rosmer); her good "magicians" (in Torin, Nantgeeb; in Hylor, Guenna) are female. Moreover, both Torin and Hylor follow an undemanding religion centred on a "Great Mother" or "Goddess," and one of Rosmer's villainies is to invent a religion with a male god, which vilifies women as "half-made." Wilder's unconventionality on this point is obviously feminist; but, like her strong awareness of differing viewpoints, it also seems appropriate to her origins "down under," since the Earth's southern hemisphere is regarded as upside-down in relation to the United States and Europe.

Anglo-Celts first settled "down under" little more than 200 years ago, and even today derive their culture chiefly from the northern hemisphere. Thus, they are paradoxically aware of their own surroundings as familiar and natural and yet at the same time exotic and "wrong" (with Christmas in summer and Easter in autumn). This sense both of wrongness and of being very distant in space from one's cultural origins is the imaginative core of *Second Nature,* Wilder's novel about the somewhat mutated descendants of some Earth people whose spaceship crashlanded on the planet Rhomary 265 years earlier. The pioneer and frontier legends of the United States are well known, and unconsciously influence many plots in science fiction. In *Second Nature,* instead, the characteristic myths of Australian history have inspired the plot, which is essentially about the lost becoming found. A second spaceship from Earth has gone astray and broken apart above Rhomary; the survivors, in their emergency capsules, are unaware of the marooned human settlers already on Rhomary, with their fruitless longing for Earth ships to arrive. A gigantic marine species, "the Vail", is one of three non-human intelligent life-forms so far encountered on Rhomary, and the Vail, too, has become lost—mourned as extinct, in consequence of a 10-year drought. Rhomary's deserts and droughts, the waiting for ships from "Home," the wanderers lost in the bush, and even the inland sea (which Australian explorers believed in but never found) correspond closely to Anglo-Celtic Australian legends. Like Australia, Rhomary also has unexpected fauna—including a domesticated species called "parmels," resembling camels, but six-legged and with extendible flaps on either side. This kind of detail, and Wilder's skilfully ample-seeming prose, cause her readers to feel welcome and cared for, nerving them, in all her novels, to assimilate a wealth of strangeness and a sometimes daunting number of characters and relationships.

Rhomary's most aggressive settlers are brawny sailor lasses, who recall to mind the strong female omors of Torin and the military "kedrans" and "sword lilies" of Hylor. But *Second Nature* describes only two physical skirmishes and its only villain is prejudice, resulting from religious bigotry. There is greater conflict in *Signs of Life* (the forthcoming sequel), where a large body of Rhomary's new castaways not only experience strife among themselves but also disastrously bungle their first contact with the Rhomarian settlers. Not only deaths from misadventure but also a murder and an accidental killing occur, providing temptations to minor warfare. But Wilder's fiction never celebrates the triumph of good by violence; rather, the emphasis is once again on the lost becoming found. Meanwhile, those who have read *Second Nature* will feel somewhat like old inhabitants of Rhomary, possessing enough detailed knowledge to make sense of discoveries which baffle the raw new community of castaways in *Signs of Life,* struggling to adjust its own elements and to assess dangers from the local fauna.

Three more tales about Rhomary appear in Wilder's first collection of short stories, *Dealers in Light and Darkness,* where the title-story tells more about the meddling offworld "spirit beings" who contrived a male Messiah for Rhomary, while "The Ballad of Hilo Hill" fleshes out the legend of a circumnavigating sea-cook, which surfaces in both the Rhomary novels. The nature of consciousness in androids (known as "oxper" or auxiliary personnel) is explored in *Signs of Life;* and *Dealers in Light and Darkness* handles a similar theme in three stories about the cybernetic "Todd-Gorman Research" centre (attenuated by catastrophe to the story-title "Odd Man Search"). Among the three remaining stories, "Something Coming Through" is set in the future, in a land where death is the penalty for carrying tobacco; a reprieve comes serendipitously through the influence of smoke from a different kind of leaf. And in the opening story, "Kaleidoscope," a cataclysm thrusts an elderly man and woman from our own culture into another reality where they succour an Aztec boy-prince and never fully comprehend his forbearance toward them.

When Wilder writes about other worlds and the future, her novels are notable for the absence of male brutality. It is otherwise in her horror novel *Cruel Designs,* which is set in our own world and era, in 20th-century Germany, when a house of evil influence and *Jugendstil* design brings out the worst in an abusive father whose family rents it. Other chillingly effective horror stories are Wilder's "Anzac Day," "The House on Cemetery Street," and "The Gingerbread House." The collection, *Dealers in Light and Darkness,* is very welcome, as are the recent reprintings in various anthologies of Wilder's stories from magazines. But other collections are still needed to represent Wilder's full range as a seductively skilful teller of stories.

—Yvonne Rousseau

WILHELM, Kate (Gertrude)

Nationality: American. **Born:** Kate Gertrude Meredith, Toledo, Ohio, 8 June 1928. **Family:** Married 1) Joseph B. Wilhelm in 1947 (divorced 1962), two sons; 2) Damon Knight, *q.v.,* in 1963, one son. **Career:** Co-director, Milford Science Fiction Writers Conference, 1963-72; lecturer, Clarion Science Fiction Writers Conference, since 1968, and Tulane University, New Orleans, 1971. **Awards:** Nebula award, 1968, 1986, 1987; Hugo award, 1977;

Jupiter award, 1977; *Locus* award, 1977. **Agent:** Brandt and Brandt, 1501 Broadway, New York, New York 10036. **Address:** 1645 Horn Lane, Eugene, Oregon 97404, U.S.A.

SCIENCE FICTION PUBLICATIONS

Novels (series: Meiklejohn and Leidl)

The Clone, with Ted Thomas. New York, Berkley, 1965; London, Hale, 1968.
The Nevermore Affair. Garden City, New York, Doubleday, 1966.
The Killer Thing. Garden City, New York, Doubleday, 1967; as *The Killing Thing,* London, Jenkins, 1967.
Let the Fire Fall. Garden City, New York, Doubleday, 1969; abridged edition, London, Panther, 1972.
The Year of the Cloud, with Ted Thomas. Garden City, New York, Doubleday, 1970.
Abyss: Two Novellas. Garden City, New York, Doubleday, 1971.
Margaret and I: A Novel. Boston, Little Brown, 1971.
The Clewiston Test. New York, Farrar Straus, 1976; London, Hutchinson, 1977.
Where Late the Sweet Birds Sang. New York, Harper, 1976; London, Arrow, 1977.
Fault Lines: A Novel. New York, Harper, 1977; London, Hutchinson, 1978.
Juniper Time: A Novel. New York, Harper, 1979; London, Hutchinson, 1980.
A Sense of Shadow. Boston, Houghton Mifflin, 1981.
Welcome, Chaos. Boston, Houghton Mifflin, 1983; London, Gollancz, 1986.
Huysman's Pets. New York, Bluejay, and London, Gollancz, 1986.
Crazy Time. New York, St. Martin's Press, 1988.
The Dark Door (Meiklejohn and Leidl). New York, St. Martin's Press, 1988; London, Gollancz, 1990.
Cambio Bay. New York, St. Martin's Press, 1990; London, Hale, 1991.
Sweet, Sweet Poison (Meiklejohn and Leidl). New York, St. Martin's Press, 1990; London, Hale, 1991.

Short Stories

The Mile-Long Spaceship. New York, Berkley, 1963; as *Andover and the Android,* London, Dobson, 1966.
The Downstairs Room and Other Speculative Fiction. Garden City, New York, Doubleday, 1968.
Infinity Box: A Collection of Speculative Fiction. New York, Harper, 1975; London, Arrow, 1979; title story bound with *He Who Shapes,* by Roger Zelazny, New York, Tor, 1989.
Somerset Dreams and Other Fictions. New York, Harper, 1978; London, Hutchinson, 1979.
Listen, Listen. Boston, Houghton Mifflin, 1981.
Children of the Wind: Five Novellas. New York, St. Martin's Press, 1989; London, Hale, 1990.
The Girl Who Fell into the Sky. Eugene, Oregon, Pulphouse, 1991.
State of Grace. Eugene, Oregon, Pulphouse, 1991.
Naming the Flowers. Eugene, Oregon, Axolotl Press, 1992.
And the Best Angels Sing: Stories. New York, St. Martin's Press, 1992.
A Flush of Shadows: Five Short Novels. New York, St. Martin's Press, 1995.

OTHER PUBLICATIONS

Novels

More Bitter Than Death. New York, Simon and Schuster, 1963;
   London, Hale, 1965.
City of Cain. Boston, Little Brown, 1974; London, Gollancz, 1975.
Oh, Susannah! Boston, Houghton Mifflin, 1982.
The Hamlet Trap (Meiklejohn and Leidl). New York, St. Martin's
   Press, 1987; London, Gollancz, 1988.
Smart House (Meiklejohn and Leidl). New York, St. Martin's Press,
   and London, Gollancz, 1989.
Death Qualified: A Mystery of Chaos. New York, St. Martin's
   Press, 1991.
Seven Kinds of Death (Meiklejohn and Leidl). New York, St.
   Martin's Press, 1992.
Justice for Some. New York, St. Martin's Press, 1993.
The Best Defense. New York, St. Martin's Press, 1994.

Other

Better Than One, with Damon Knight. Boston, Noreascon II, 1980.
The Hills Are Dancing, with Richard Wilhelm. Minneapolis,
   Corroboree Press, 1985.

Editor, *Nebula Award Stories 9.* London, Gollancz, 1974; New
   York, Harper, 1975.
Editor, *Clarion SF.* New York, Berkley, 1977.

*

Manuscript Collection: Syracuse University, New York.

*   *   *

Kate Wilhelm has said that about half of her published work is
science fiction, although much of the rest contains elements of fantasy. Her first novel was a mystery; later works such as *Margaret
and I* and *Fault Lines* are novels of contemporary life, although
Margaret and I makes use of a fantastic element by portraying the
protagonist's subconscious as a separate character. Wilhelm is a
writer who skillfully uses genre elements—suspenseful plots, scientific or technological notions, and slick prose—to produce fiction as satisfying and as well rounded as any being written today.

Wilhelm's technique, in most of her work, is to introduce a character or set of characters in a commonplace setting, then to reveal
the unusual or uncommon elements of the story through the
thoughts and actions of the people in it. Her characters are some of
the most fully realized people to be found in science fiction. Her
style is the smooth, almost slick manner of so much women's magazine fiction (several Wilhelm stories have in fact appeared in
Redbook), complete with the details of domestic and everyday life;
this manner of telling her stories makes the contrast and tension
between the usual and the unusual even more striking.

This technique can be seen in Wilhelm's first novel, *More Bitter
Than Death.* A young couple, Eve and Grant, return to Grant's
home, where the body of Grant's murdered mother has been found.
Eve must come to terms with her husband, who is one of those
suspected of the murder, and Grant must deal with long-suppressed
feelings about his home and family. The problems raised here are
resolved by the book's conclusion, although in her later work
Wilhelm's characters find answers more difficult to come by, life

more complex, and reconciliations more problematic. The problem
Eve and Grant face, that of having to understand the past and to
reconcile it with their future hopes in the midst of unusual events,
is present in Wilhelm's later work, and is especially prominent in
her science fiction. These same problems are depicted movingly in
the novella "Somerset Dreams," ostensibly a story about dream research in a dying town.

In two early science fiction novels, Wilhelm writes about standard science-fictional themes. In *The Killer Thing,* a computerized
robot that is trying to kill all life must be destroyed; in *Let the Fire
Fall,* an alien landing on Earth and the rise of a new religion are
shown. *The Killer Thing* displays Wilhelm's mastery of the technique of suspense. Although it is set in the familiar future of colonized planets so common in SF, the book shows the author's concern with the moral issues raised by space travel and human greed.
Let the Fire Fall begins in the familiar, almost cozy, environs of a
small American city. This novel is written in an uncharacteristically
breezy style; the author's strong opinions about organized religion
and cults are not concealed, and the new religion is much like some
rather disturbing present-day cults. These books, and early pieces
such as "The Mile-Long Spaceship" and "Stranger in the House,"
are better than average stories, but it is in later works that Wilhelm
shows her real strengths.

Wilhelm, unlike many writers, is a master of both the novel and
shorter forms of fiction. Her short story "Baby, You Were Great"
shows a world where it is possible, through brain-implanted electrodes, to live a celebrity's life vicariously and to feel all her emotions as well. Her Nebula Award-winning "The Planners" concerns
biological research, and "The Funeral" depicts a rigid future society. But these stories are not simply intellectual adventures comfortably removed from us in time. "The Planners" shows a scientist who does not fully comprehend the moral and ethical implications of his research, "The Funeral" reveals the crippling constraints
in which adults often place children, and "Baby, You Were Great"
takes place in a world uncomfortably like our own.

Wilhelm's work gains much of its strength by showing us life
as it is lived, as so many works of science fiction do not. Her stories are easily accessible, but they are not escapist entertainments
that one can read and then put aside; the issues she raises are present
in our lives. She is a concerned writer, but she does not moralize
and she does not lapse into despair. Many of her works, notably
City of Cain, a novel about a plot to build an underground city
where experiments are to be conducted on survivors of atomic and
environmental disasters, show the dangers of excessive power
thoughtlessly used. One especially strong novella, "The Infinity
Box," shows the way power can corrupt from the inside; the story
is made more disturbing by the fact that the protagonist begins as a
likeable, intelligent, and sympathetically portrayed man who is altered and changed simply by having the power to enter another
person's mind. *Where Late the Sweet Birds Sang* (Hugo Award,
1977) has been called, by many critics, the best treatment of cloning in science fiction. But this novel is also about the often destructive strategies human beings can employ in order to survive,
and it shows the author's concern with the damage we have done
to the earth, a theme present in much of her work.

Wilhelm's abilities as a writer of science fiction are at their height
in *The Clewiston Test* and *Juniper Time.* *The Clewiston Test* is both
a feminist novel and a psychological thriller that presents some of
the issues of women's lives in the context of a suspenseful story.
The isolation of the protagonist, Anne Clewiston, who is recovering from a serious accident, is symbolic of the isolation felt by so

many women; the scientific project in the novel is used as a plot device to illuminate the personal conflicts of the characters, as well as to present issues about human experimentation. *Juniper Time* tells the story of two people, Jean Brighton and Arthur Cluny, who are the children of astronauts. The two grow up in a drought-plagued world in which the dream of space exploration, the goal to which their fathers had devoted themselves, has died. The conflicts in the book reflect our own predicament; we must live with our technology, however uneasily, and cannot turn back, but we must also conserve what is valuable of the past, and keep future hopes from being perverted to unworthy and shortsighted ends.

Welcome, Chaos is another fine novel that unites many of Wilhelm's concerns and techniques; this book explores the dilemmas that immortality might raise. In an earlier novella, "April Fool's Day Forever," the author also dealt with immortality; there, the price of endless life turned out to be the loss of the bond with the collective unconscious and all creative forces. In *Welcome, Chaos,* Wilhelm, in the context of a thriller, asks some difficult questions: What if the serum that makes immortality possible kills half of those people who are exposed to it? Should such a serum be limited to only a few? How might its protection against the effects of radiation affect the willingness of nations to use nuclear weapons? It is to Wilhelm's credit that she attempts to give answers, however tentative, to these questions.

In recent years, Wilhelm has published several highly praised mystery and suspense novels, while continuing to write science fiction in the shorter lengths. Some of these mysteries use ideas that border on being science fictional notions; her novel *Death Qualified: A Mystery of Chaos* uses chaos theory, computers, and the possibility of superhuman powers to produce a work that is as much science fiction as it is a novel of suspense. Her series of mystery novels featuring the characters Constance Leidl and Charlie Meiklejohn are often centered around science fictional ideas; in *Smart House,* a fully automated house is the site of a murder, while *Sweet, Sweet Poison* is set near an experimental farm. Notable examples of Wilhelm's recent short science fiction include the Nebula Award-winning "Forever Yours, Anna," a haunting tale of time travel that (characteristically for this writer) is told from the point-of-view of a man who gradually realizes how he is connected to the central events of the story; "Naming the Flowers," a love story involving a short-lived human mutant; "And the Angels Sing," a character study of a man who discovers an alien; and "I Know What You're Thinking," in which a woman comes to realize that her telepathic abilities are not shared by other people.

The writer Karen Joy Fowler has said of Wilhelm: "I know of no other writer who conveys so successfully the twin truths of our lives—that the world is at once so much better and so much worse than we imagine it to be." In her science fiction—indeed, in all of her work—Kate Wilhelm holds a mirror to our world, and in her work we can see the dilemmas present in our uneasy, late-20th-century lives.

—Pamela Sargent

WILLIAMS, John A(lfred)

Pseudonym: J. Dennis Gregory. **Nationality:** American. **Born:** Jackson, Mississippi, 5 December 1925. **Education:** Central High School, Syracuse, New York; Syracuse University, A.B. 1950. **Mili-**

tary **Service:** Served in the United States Navy, 1943-46. **Family:** Married 1) Carolyn Clopton in 1947 (divorced), two sons; 2) Lorrain Isaac in 1965, one son. **Career:** Member of the public relations department, Doug Johnson Associates, Syracuse, 1952-54, and Arthur P. Jacobs Company; staff member, CBS, Hollywood and New York, 1954-55; publicity director, Comet Press Books, New York, 1955-56; publisher and editor, *Negro Market Newsletter,* New York, 1956-57; staff member, Abelard-Schuman, publishers, New York, 1957-58; director of information, American Committee on Africa, New York, 1958; European correspondent, *Ebony* and *Jet* magazines, 1958-59; announcer, WOV Radio, New York, 1959; Africa correspondent, *Newsweek,* New York, 1964-65. Regents Lecturer, University of California, Santa Barbara, 1972; distinguished professor of English, LaGuardia Community College, City University of New York, 1973-75; visiting professor, University of Hawaii, summer 1974, and Boston University, 1978-79. Since 1979, professor of English and journalism, Rutgers University, New Brunswick, New Jersey. Member of the editorial board, *Audience,* Boston, 1970-72; contributing editor, *American Journal,* New York, 1972. **Awards:** American Academy grant, 1962; Syracuse University Outstanding Achievement award, 1970; National Endowment for the Arts grant, 1977; Before Columbus Foundation award, 1983. Litt.D.: Southeastern Massachusetts University, North Dartmouth, 1978. **Address:** 693 Forest Avenue, Teaneck, New Jersey 07666, U.S.A.

SCIENCE FICTION PUBLICATIONS

Novels

sons of darkness, sons of light: A Novel of Some Probability. Boston, Little Brown, 1969; London, Eyre and Spottiswoode, 1970.
Captain Blackman: A Novel. Garden City, New York, Doubleday, 1972.

OTHER PUBLICATIONS

Novels

The Angry Ones. New York, Ace, 1960; as *One for New York,* Chatham, New Jersey, Chatham Bookseller, 1975.
Night Song. New York, Farrar Straus, 1961; London, Collins, 1962.
Sissie. New York, Farrar Straus, 1963; as *Journey out of Anger,* London, Eyre and Spottiswoode, 1968.
The Man Who Cried I Am. Boston, Little Brown, 1967; London, Eyre and Spottiswoode, 1968.
Mothersill and the Foxes. New York, Doubleday, 1975.
The Junior Bachelor Society. New York, Doubleday, 1976.
! Click Song. Boston, Houghton Mifflin, 1982.
The Berhama Account. New York, New Horizon Press, 1985.
Jacob's Ladder. New York, Thunder's Mouth Press, 1987.

Other

Africa: Her History, Lands, and People. New York, Cooper Square, 1962.
The Protectors (on narcotics agents; as J. Dennis Gregory), with Harry J. Anslinger. New York, Farrar Straus, 1964.
This Is My Country, Too. New York, New American Library, 1964; London, New English Library, 1966.

The Most Native of Sons: A Bibliography of Richard Wright. New York, Doubleday, 1970.

The King God Didn't Save: Reflections on the Life and Death of Martin Luther King, Jr. New York, Coward McCann, 1970; London, Eyre and Spottiswoode, 1971.

Flashbacks: A Twenty-Year Diary of Article Writing. New York, Doubleday, 1973.

Minorities in the City. New York, Harper, 1975.

If I Stop I'll Die: The Comedy and Tragedy of Richard Pryor, with Dennis A. Williams. New York, Thunder's Mouth Press, 1991.

Ways In: Approaches to Reading and Writing about Literature, with Gilbert H. Muller. New York, McGraw-Hill, 1994.

Editor, *The Angry Black.* New York, Lancer, 1962.

Editor, *Beyond the Angry Black.* New York, Cooper Square, 1967.

Editor, with Charles F. Harris, *Amistad I and II.* New York, Knopf, 2 vols., 1970-71.

Editor, with Gilbert H. Muller, *Introduction to Literature.* New York, McGraw-Hill, 1985; revised as *The McGraw-Hill Introduction to Literature,* 1995.

Editor, with Gilbert H. Muller, *Bridges: Literature across Cultures,* New York, McGraw-Hill, 1994.

*

Manuscript Collection: Syracuse University, New York; University of Rochester, New York.

Critical Study: *The Evolution of a Black Writer: John A. Williams* by Earl Cash, New York, Third Press, 1974.

*   *   *

Three of the nine novels by John A. Williams are revolutionary fiction, or "awful warning" stories. He writes at a high level of prestige in the mainstream of American fiction. His principal characters are African Americans. The three novels in question present a progress of plots and themes from warning story to virtually apocalyptic race revolution triumph. In every case, the science-fictionally extraordinary events of these works are actual and real, but Williams also always stops short of describing in much detail either their process or their completion. Perhaps he regards the events he predicts as obscene and believes they should not be described (for example, the "King Alfred" plan of *The Man Who Cried I Am*); or perhaps the stories are more effective as warnings when details are left to readers' imaginations. Because they are novels of character, they are especially effective in depicting the meaning of radical social and political changes on the lives of individuals.

The books present protagonists who are victims of a national racist conspiracy, ones who are agents provocateur in violent revolutionary acts, and protagonists who overthrow a racist Caucasian U.S. government. These novels are about a fictional revolutionary intervention in the history of racial discrimination against Africans in Europe and America. As such, they belong to a body of works that depict extraordinary events or racial revolutions in whole nations, especially the United States, that either preserve racist governments or change forever the political and economic structures of the Euro-American nations. Notable examples are Raymond Patterson's poem, "After the Thousand-Day Rebellion" (*Transatlantic Monthly,* winter/spring 1972), George Samuel Schuyler's *Black No More* (1931), William Melvin Kelley's *A Different Drum-*

mer (1959), Ronald Fair's *Many Thousand Gone* (1965), and Sam Greenlee's *The Spook Who Sat by the Door* (1969).

The Man Who Cried I Am is the most celebrated of all of Williams's novels. Its hero is the rising African American writer Max Reddick, World War II veteran, who, in the pre-civil rights era, laboriously works his way up through jobs as a journalist to recognition as a great contemporary novelist, much like James Baldwin or Ralph Ellison. Meanwhile, his several relationships with women are never completely happy ones—a microcosm of the situation of his race, his personal life is nearly hopelessly unsettled. Moreover, he has contracted a progressive rectal cancer, baldly symbolic of the metaphoric "ass-reaming" non-white peoples, especially Africans, have received historically from Europeans and Americans. The tragedy of Reddick's personal health is parallelled and ultimately overshadowed by the threat of genocide to the African American population when he learns of a scheme by the U.S. leaders that would put the Nazi extermination of six million Jews in the shade—to kill 22 million African Americans. The plan is called "King Alfred," and included as stage one is the legal process of detention of this massive population. Indeed, Williams's novel was a long way from being merely fictional. Title II, "Emergency Detention," of the McCarran "Internal Security Act of [September 23] 1950" (cosponsored by Richard Nixon, among others) provided the enabling legislation for such mass incarceration, at the U.S. president's order. The Title II sections of the act were repealed on September 25, 1971, four years after the publication of *The Man Who Cried I Am.*

The second of Williams's three speculative novels of revolution, *sons of darkness, sons of light* [lowercase letters deliberate]: *A Novel of Some Probability,* he called a "pot-boiler." It is nevertheless a well-made novel about the character Eugene Browning, possessor of a Ph.D. in political science, with a lovely wife and two children. He works in the New York-based Institute for Racial Justice. He is locally effective, but racial justice on a national scale is nowhere in prospect. Therefore, Browning hires a mafia hit of a white New York policeman who has escaped penalty for the flagrant murder, during an arrest process, of a sixteen-year-old black youth. Simultaneously, and not connected to Browning except as inspiration, a secret movement of African Americans, armed with weapons and explosives, seals off and takes over Manhattan. The novel ends as they present fair and equitable demands for minorities. The reader is sure they will not be met because they require immense social and economic change. The reader knows, therefore, that the takeover of New York will be re-enacted in all the major cities of the United States in a national race war.

Captain Blackman was dismissed by a few critics as minor Williams fiction because its nearly 200-year-old principal character, Abraham Blackman, "doesn't develop." Williams, however, had a revolutionary political agenda in writing it. Employing the device of the fabulously long-lived protagonist, used by Henry James in *The Sense of the Past* (1916) and Virginia Woolf in *Orlando* (1929), to dramatize the connection of historical events to the present, Williams has "Blackman" enlisted as a soldier in all the American wars from the Revolutionary War to the Vietnam conflict. The culturally psychotic treatment of black soldiers in war after war repeats itself. Pathetically eager to die for America and its promises of equality in all the earlier wars, black soldiers by the 1970s have left patriotism behind in favor of a plan for revolution that uses "fish," blacks that can pass for Caucasian, located in key positions in the U.S. nuclear defense system. These people capture and nullify America's nuclear retaliation capability. The United States will be helpless if its enemies attack. The novel is satirical and angry. It predicts the certain end of white America's political and economic dominance of its African American population.

—John Pfeiffer

WILLIAMS, Paul O(sborne)

Nationality: American. **Born:** Chatham, New Jersey, 17 January 1935. **Education:** Principia College, Elsah, Illinois, B.A. 1956; University of Pennsylvania, Philadelphia, M.A. 1958, Ph.D. 1962. **Family:** Married 1) Nancy Ellis in 1961 (divorced 1984), one daughter and one son; 2) Kerry Lynn Blau in 1985. **Career:** Instructor, 1961-62, and assistant professor of English, 1962-64, Duke University, Durham, North Carolina. Assistant professor, 1964-68, associate professor, 1968-77, professor of English, 1977-81, and since 1981, Cornelius and Muriel Wood Professor of Humanities, Principia College. **Member:** Board of Trustees, Village of Elsah, 1969-75; president, Greater St. Louis Historical Association, 1975, and Thoreau Society, 1977; director, Elsah Museum, 1981-84. **Awards:** John W. Campbell award, 1983. **Address:** c/o Historic Elsah Foundation, Box 117, Elsah, Illinois 62028, U.S.A.

SCIENCE FICTION PUBLICATIONS

Novels (series: Pelbar)

Pelbar series:
  The Breaking of Northwall. New York, Ballantine, 1981; London, Orbit, 1985.
  The Ends of the Circle. New York, Ballantine, 1981; London, Orbit, 1986.
  The Dome in the Forest. New York, Ballantine, 1981; London, Orbit, 1986.
  The Fall of the Shell. New York, Ballantine, 1982.
  An Ambush of Shadows. New York, Ballantine, 1983.
  The Song of the Axe. New York, Ballantine, 1984.
  The Sword of Forbearance. New York, Ballantine, 1985.
Gifts of the Gorboduc Vandal. New York, Ballantine, 1989.

OTHER PUBLICATIONS

Other

Elsah: A Historic Guidebook, with Charles B. Hosmer. Elsah, Illinois, Historic Elsah Foundation, 1967, second edition, 1967.
The McNair Family of Elsah, Illinois: Uncommon Common Men. Elsah, Illinois, Historic Elsah Foundation, 1982.
Frederick Oakes Sylvester: The Artist's Encounter with Elsah. Elsah, Illinois, Historic Elsah Foundation, 1986.
A Third-Generation Minister and a Pencilmaker's Son. Boston, Christian Science Publishing Society, 1991.

*　　*　　*

Like novels such as The City and The Stars, Earth Abides, and Canticle for Leibowitz, the Pelbar novels foreground a group of fairly well-developed characters, whose decisions become critical for the survival of human civilization, against a background of one or more societies who have made different decisions about their priorities and the nature of civilization. Williams's protagonists must debate such related questions as: what are the characteristics of a viable, enduring human society? once established, can expansion occur without war? Given the scope of the seven novels, Williams also has room to grapple with questions such as: what is the ethical foundation of a viable, enduring human society? can that foundation be openly debated and simultaneously provide a firm foundation? can a society oppose oppressors with violence without becoming oppressors themselves? how will the next generation become leaders and know when to fight and when to negotiate, when to uphold tradition and the established methods of maintaining order and safety and when to change?

Hypothesizing a nuclear war in the year 2006, Williams sets his Pelbar cycle 1000 years later as several of the surviving societies in the former U.S. have become large enough to begin expanding beyond their borders. During the 20 years covered by the novels, these societies must decide whether to compete or to cooperate for resources, products, and knowledge. Although societies from southwestern Canada to mid-Atlantic islands are depicted, the action of the novels radiates out from the Heartland and the three walled cities the Pelbar have built along the Mississippi River between the Missouri and Ohio rivers' confluences.

The first four volumes depict the literal and figurative opening of the walled Pelbar cities, necessitated by their own internal growing conservatism and dissension and by contact with their neighboring societies. The crisis of leaving the security of their cities is reflected in the titles of the first and fourth volumes—The Breaking of Northwall and The Fall of The Shell. The last three volumes relate the formation and expansion of the HeartRiver Federation throughout Urstadge (the United States and southwestern Canada). The diplomatic and spiritual leadership of the Pelbar is threatened by the discovery of two legacies from the 20th-century American civilization—weaponry, including nuclear warheads, and the Bible, the source text of their ethics.

In addition to these being political novels and epic stories of reunification, individual novels echo the cycle's movement from fragmentation to federation by depicting journeys of psychological and physical discovery. Five of the novels are bildungsroman (1-4, 6); with considerable overlap, four of the novels trace the difficult marriage of two Pelbar, Ahroe and Stel (2, 3, 5, 7). The bildungsroman are characterized by high adventure, miraculous escapes, and reunited lovers. The young adults, frequently traveling alone, become leaders as they learn self-reliance and forbearance and learn what drives people apart and what holds them together. They experience the wide variety of ways in which survivors shaped new societies—tribal societies of migrating, running hunters; agricultural societies dependent on slaves; a legalistic society that has replaced justice and religion with a dependence on laws; an oppressive, violent society based on fear and superstition surrounding the worship of a giant statue; an oligarchy dedicated to restoring order through scientific principles; and even a technocracy of the "ancients" who have survived for generations in a sealed dome.

The story of Ahroe and Stel begins as a bildungsroman but becomes a narrative of the movement toward unification as Ahroe becomes a Pelbar guard captain and then a leader in the treaty agreements and the federation conferences. The relationship between the couple epitomizes one of the central tensions in the design and maintenance of the Pelbar society which is based on mutual respect: how do you design a society for both the traditionalist and the individualist, the diplomat and the poet? As Ahroe becomes more dedicated to preserving the federation, she becomes more conservative and shortsighted; her husband Stel draws away from her in order to preserve his independent creativity as an inventor and religious thinker. Heated public debates, political intrigue, and personal losses characterize these novels.

Overall, the cycle reveals that unification requires the combined skills of different heroes—the visionary, the inventor/technician, the diplomat, the social leader, the rebel, the explorer, the military strategist, the warrior, the physician. *The Fall of the Shell* is the best way to sample the series in a single novel. Although it does not treat the marriage of Ahroe and Stel, it does deal with the themes of reunification, marriage, the uses of technology, and the concept that each society has a design. Williams uses the nautilus shell and the Mississippi River as symbols of the beauty, limitations, and potentiality of human society. The river gives access to a variety of human societies and greater knowledge of the single religion that underlies all of the Urstadge societies. The ambiguity of the shell suggests that it can either shelter or inhibit life.

Amateur archaeologist and historian, scholar, teacher, and poet, Paul O. Williams appeared suddenly in the public science fiction world with the seven-novel Pelbar cycle, published between 1981 and 1985 by Ballantine. In 1983 he won the John W. Campbell Award for Best New Writer at the World Science Fiction Convention in Baltimore. Since 1985, Williams has published only one additional science fiction novel, *The Gifts of the Gorboduc Vandal*, 1989. Although a galactic space story, it, too, explores how isolated cultures adapt to change and to knowledge of other ethical, political, and ecological systems.

Williams's concentrated period of creativity in science fiction can perhaps be best explained if the novels are seen as a coalescence of his interests and previous publications. Prominent are his knowledge of archaeology and history, especially of Native American material; his scholarship in 19th-century American romanticism, especially Thoreau; his study of American western expansion, particularly Bernard DeVoto's *Course of Empire;* the architecture of Bernard Maybeck; his nature poems and haiku and his study of nature first-hand and in books such as *The Tangled Wing: Biological Constraints on The Human Spirit;* and his clear love for the immensity of the land and the symbolism and power of the Mississippi River, a feature he watched from the limestone cliffs just north of St. Louis where he lived for many years. The cycle is rich in detail about political systems, social structures, games, architecture, dress, food, battles, technology, music, art, and education.

—Elizabeth Cummins

WILLIAMS, Robert Moore

Pseudonym: Russell Storm; E.K. Jarvis. **Nationality:** American. **Born:** Farmington, Missouri, 19 June 1907. **Education:** University of Missouri Columbia, B.A. in journalism. **Family:** Married Margaret Jelley in 1938 (divorced 1952); one daughter. **Career:** Full-time writer, 1937-72. **Died:** 1977.

SCIENCE FICTION PUBLICATIONS

Novels (series: Jongor; Zanthar)

The Chaos Fighters. New York, Ace, 1955.
Conquest of the Space Sea. New York, Ace, 1955.
Doomsday Eve. New York, Ace, 1957.
The Blue Atom. New York, Ace, 1958.
World of the Masterminds. New York, Ace, 1960.
The Day They H-Bombed Los Angeles. New York, Ace, 1961.
The Darkness before Tomorrow. New York, Ace, 1962.
King of the Fourth Planet. New York, Ace, 1962.
Walk up the Sky. New York, Avalon, 1962.
The Star Wasps. New York, Ace, 1963.
Flight From Yesterday. New York, Ace, 1963.
The Lunar Eye. New York, Ace, 1964.
The Second Atlantis. New York, Ace, 1965.
Vigilante, 21st Century. New York, Lancer, 1967.
Zanthar of the Many Worlds. New York, Lancer, 1967.
Zanthar at the Edge of Never. New York, Lancer, 1968.
The Bell from Infinity. New York, Lancer, 1968.
Zanthar at Moon's Madness. New York, Lancer, 1968.
Zanthar at Trip's End. New York, Lancer, 1969.
Beachhead Planet. New York, Dell, and London, Sidgwick and Jackson, 1970.
Love Is Forever—We Are for Tonight (autobiographic novel). New York, Curtis, 1970.
Jongor of Lost Land. New York, Popular Library, 1970.
Return of Jongor. New York, Popular Library, 1970.
Jongor Fights Back. New York, Popular Library, 1970.
Now Comes Tomorrow. New York, Curtis, and London, Sidgwick and Jackson, 1971.
Seven Tickets to Hell. New York, Popular Library, 1972.

Short Stories

The Void Beyond, and Other Stories. New York, Ace, 1958.
To the End of Time, and Other Stories. New York, Ace, 1960.
When Two Worlds Meet: Stories of Men on Mars. New York, Curtis, 1970.

* * *

During the editorship of Ray Palmer in the 1940s, *Amazing Stories* and *Fantastic Adventures* were juvenile action pulps principally written by a stable of writers under their own bylines and an assortment of house names. Robert Moore Williams was part of this stable, producing scores of stories, including a few under the name Russell Storm. (It is not clear which stories he wrote under house names, but it's probable that most of the stories published prior to 1951 under the name E.K. Jarvis are his.) Even today, Williams is largely associated with these magazines and their juvenile policy, but the truth is he was one of only a handful of writers of those years who were able to cut across policy boundaries and sell stories to almost all the existing science fiction magazines. He appeared often, for example, in both *Thrilling Wonder* and *Startling,* and also in John Campbell's *Astounding* (Campbell thought enough of his talents to mention him in his essay for Lloyd Eshbach's *Of Worlds Beyond*). In fact, of these writers, Williams is unique in sustaining a continuous career as an SF writer through to the 1970s.

Although Williams wrote almost 200 stories, it is possible from one of his collections to get a good feel for his approaches and talent. The stories in *When Two Worlds Meet* are linked through a common background of Earthman conflict although the background details of Mars and the Martians are inconsistent. The title story tells of an Earthman who tries to learn the secret behind a "god weapon" that allows one race to subjugate another. "Aurochs Came Walking" concerns a shaman's crystal ball that turns out to be a control device for a machine built by ancient Martians. In "The Sound of Bugles," Martians show an Earthman the secret of creating such resources as food and housing from pure thought. The weakest story in the book is probably "When the Spoilers Came," marred by an unconvincing and rather sentimental resolution, something not especially common in the fiction of Williams, whose romantic streak more often manifested itself as a mildly ironic cynicism. "The Final Frontier," in which a dying Martian wields strange powers to thwart exploitative Earthmen, is only technically better. The best story in the book is "On Pain of Death," a suspense story about a group of Earthmen trapped in a strange prison that may be either a particularly efficient machine or a test of their worthiness to live.

Again and again, Williams's fiction deals with machines that bestow godlike powers, or ordinary humans who possess a special rapport with machines or elemental energies. In "The Night the General Left Us," a mathematician's love of machines is returned by a model rocket that attacks a general who orders the man arrested. "The Smallness beyond Thought" deals with an eccentric hermit whose ability to grow food without water is related to his ability to sense the flow of electromagnetic and less familiar forms of energy.

It should not be assumed that Williams is playing with the traditional SF theme of the superman. Rather, his work expresses a basically mystical view of the world. This is borne out by "The Grove of God" (*Other Worlds*, 1956), whose editor described it as too taboo-breaking for other magazines. An expedition of space explorers from Earth lands on a planet where they discover godlike humans living in a primitive paradise. They discover that the planet is actually Earth, to which they have returned through some sort of application of Lorenz-Fitzgerald principle that none of the scientists seems to have been aware of. The narrative is as awkward and downright clumsy as the idea, something surprising in the work of a professional as experienced as Williams. Ironically, another story by him in that issue ("The Steogar" as by Russell Storm) deals more effectively with similar material: a research scientist at a government installation acquires godlike abilities through the agency of a miraculous invention.

Williams turned to novels for the growing paperback markets in 1955 with *The Chaos Fighters*. During the next 15 years Williams produced almost 30 books. By and large they were not too different from the mass of his magazine fiction and they abound with such concepts as aliens trying to control human destiny, Earthmen exploiting alien planets, and humans with miraculous powers. Williams did manage, in *The Day They H-Bombed Los Angeles* and *The Second Atlantis*, to find interesting ways to destroy Southern California. The Jongor series consist of Burroughs-like lost-land stories, and the Zanthar series are about a super-scientist who seems as interested in the occult as in physics. The last, appropriately called *Zanthar at Trip's End*, has him coping with a machine that blows the souls out of people's bodies.

The strangest of Williams's books, however, is a slim volume titled *Love Is Forever, We Are for Tonight*. Although it's called science fiction on one cover and a "strange and fantastic novel of a

man trapped in an inner world of fear and evil" on the other, the book is autobiography with no pretense of being fiction. It begins with some fairly evocative description of his childhood and youth but soon focuses on Williams's interest in and experiences with such things as dianetics, hallucinogenic gases, and communes (in the 1950s). The style reminds one of Ray Palmer's in his editorials for *Other Worlds*, but Palmer's delightful flamboyance and self-directed humor are missing and missed. The book is often vague and evasive, but some facts about the man crop up and the portions dealing with dianetics, while not particularly revealing, might hold interest for anyone curious about the impact of that cult on the SF field.

Williams doesn't seem to have very often probed deeply into any of his ideas or themes, and this makes some of his work, while perfectly readable on the surface, seem disturbingly incomplete. His best works tend to be stories of adventure and suspense, such as "On Pain of Death," and stories about determined human beings trying to survive, such as "Last Ship Out," where two disfigured survivors of atomic war try to battle their way on board a spaceship bound for Mars. The story is slight but compact and straightforward and very readable. It satisfies more than the ponderous "Grove of God," reminding us that Williams is more likely to be at his best writing about people and situations than about ideas.

—Gerald W. Page

WILLIAMS, Walter Jon

Also writes as Jon Williams. **Nationality:** American. **Born:** 1953.

SCIENCE FICTION PUBLICATIONS

Novels (series: Crown Jewels; Hardwired)

Ambassador of Progress. New York, Tor, 1984; London, Orbit, 1987.
Knight Moves. New York, Tor, 1985; London, Orbit, 1987.
Hardwired. New York, Tor, 1986; London, Macdonald, 1987.
Voice of the Whirlwind (Hardwired). New York, Tor, 1987; London, Orbit, 1989.
The Crown Jewels. New York, Tor, 1987.
The House of Shards (Crown Jewels). New York, Tor, 1988.
Angel Station. New York, Tor, 1989; London, Orbit, 1990.
Days of Atonement. New York, Tor, 1991; London, Grafton, 1992.
Aristoi. New York, Tor, 1992, London, Grafton, 1993.
Wall, Stone, Craft. Eugene, Oregon, Pulphouse, 1993.
Metropolitan. New York, HarperPrism, 1995.
Rock of Ages. New York, Tor, 1995.

Short Stories

Solip:System. Eugene, Oregon, Axolotl, 1989.
Facets. New York, Tor, 1990; London, Grafton, 1992.
Elegy for Angels and Dogs, bound with *The Graveyard Heart*, by Roger Zelazny. New York, Tor, 1990; London, Grafton, 1992.
Dinosaurs. Eugene, Oregon, Pulphouse, 1991.

Other

Hardwired: The Source Book. Berkeley, California, Talsorian Games, 1989.

*   *   *

Walter Jon Williams has proved himself a versatile and imaginative novelist since he turned to writing science fiction, having already published some C.S. Forester-type sea stories under the name Jon Williams. He has written cyberpunk, light-hearted Zelaznyesque adventure and alternate histories with equal panache. The worlds he envisions are frequently part of galaxy-spanning civilizations; he takes delight in exploring all facets of his created universes, from kitchen implements to the laws of physics, with such skill that the narrative rarely slows.

Ambassador of Progress (1984) was a strong debut, depicting the second rise of a human spacefaring civilization and the efforts of the ambassadors to a complex, intransigent culture to reintroduce concepts like the scientific method. It was followed by *Knight Moves* (1985), a philosophical science fantasy leavened with humor. Doran Falkner, after providing humanity with unlimited energy, rockets to new planets and freedom from disease and aging to those who desire them, has retired after purchasing most of Earth to encourage the rise of centaurs, satyrs, and other products of bioengineering. He is called into the field again to investigate reports of teleportation among the mindless creatures of a distant planet, and finds love and enemies on the way to a satisfying discovery of the causes behind the teleportation, which promise to reinvigorate a complacent, spoiled humanity. This pleasing, poignant story has been compared with the works of Clifford Simak and Roger Zelazny.

Hardwired (1986) is a cyberpunk thriller in which two cyborg rebels fight back against the profiteering and oppression of the corporate Orbitals who control a postwar America. The gritty style and high-tech details prompt comparisons with Gibson's *Neuromancer,* though Williams's elegant command of the language slips through the noir tone now and then.

Voice of the Whirlwind (1987) takes place in the same universe, 200 hundred years later. The corporations are more powerful than ever, and the addition of the Powers, an alien race over whom the "policorps" fight for the right to share exclusive commerce, creates an oppressively Byzantine society. The hero is the clone of a mercenary, Steward, who was once involved in espionage and counterespionage for various policorps; unfortunately, when the clone is "awakened," he learns that his memories do not include those of the first Steward's last 15 years. "Beta" Steward is drawn into the same entanglements without the knowledge of the various players' roles and goals.

The Crown Jewels (1987) is a manneristic farce starring gentleman burglar Drake Maijstral. The Human Constellation has successfully broken away from the Kosali Empire, though social and political commerce with the aliens still thrives. Describing Maijstral's attempt to steal a vial containing the Emperor's potent semen and the misadventures of a rival burglar in a chatty, conversational style, the omniscient narrator frequently steps back from the action to comment on such issues as training in politesse or the nature of philistinism. *House of Shards* (1988) and *Rock of Ages* (1995) provide further adventures with Maijstral and his loyal Kosali servant Roman.

Angel Station (1989) is a high-tech First Contact story in which Williams's intention, he says, was to have contact made by "a couple of confused teenagers on the run from the law, and to have the aliens they encountered be in almost as desperate a situation as they were." Ubu Roy, who possesses four arms and total recall, and Beautiful Maria, a navigational "witch" with the psychic power to control the flow of electrons, become unfortunate rivals of the ruthless de Suarez clan, who race them for control of commerce with the hive-mind aliens. The alien named Twelve is vividly drawn, and Williams draws humor and pathos from predictable scenes such as Twelve's exposure to human motion pictures.

Days of Atonement (1991), a police procedural and one of Williams's finest novels, features the powerfully conflicted anti-hero Loren Hawn, police chief of a New Mexico mining town. As in many of Williams's novels, several chapters are devoted to establishing character and setting before the real plot begins, when a man known to be 20 years dead stumbles into the police station and dies in Loren's arms, victim of a shooting. Loren finds that the scientists of a nearby particle-physics laboratory are involved, and when the dead corpse mysteriously disappears from the medical examiner's office, he suspects that a bizarre form of time travel may be related. The novel investigates problems of justice and moral values through the eyes of a provincial and deeply flawed character, and Loren's redemption at the height of a shockingly violent climax is both surprising and satisfying.

Aristoi (1992) depicts a distant future whose wealth and comforts rely on nanotechnology and the wisdom of the elite Aristoi, superhumans who use their split personalities for multitasking every project from planet governance to opera composition. Aristos Gabriel is torn away from his hedonistic life of creativity and free love when he learns that a renegade Aristos has established a planet on which humans live in primitive squalor, reintroducing guns and disease. Williams employs such narrative techniques as the use of parallel columns of dialogue to represent simultaneous spoken and mental conversations (a game going back to Alfred Bester's *The Demolished Man*) to dramatize typographically different states of mind and modes of communication. This is a thoughtful and vividly depicted novel.

Wall, Stone, Craft (1993) proposes that Lord Byron was a military man, not a poet, when he met Mary Wollstonecraft and Percy Shelley. This alternate history is admirably constructed, filled with drama, passion, and sacrifice.

Metropolitan (1995) creates a magical substance called plasm, the scientific explanation for which is charming if forced. A future, or possible alternative, Earth has become rather implausibly converted into a vast urban sprawl, in whose interstices plasm can be found and channelled by the force of human will. Less like electricity than a genie in a bottle, plasm is desired above all other resources because it can be converted into anything the mind directs: a force for building construction or the giver of health and long life. Poverty-stricken minority woman Aiah discovers a limitless plasm well, which she is supposed to report to Plasm Authority but instead turns over to the deposed radical reformer Constantine in return for a hefty fee. They become partners in a plan to transform the sick and corrupted world, starting with the destruction of the Shield that covers the megalopolis and blocks out vision of the heavens. Aiah's character is well thought out, and she remains likeable even as her ambition and discovery of the good life tempt her into corruption.

Williams's other works include independently published novellas *Solip:System* (1989), *Elegy for Angels and Dogs* (1990), and

Dinosaurs (1991). *Facets* (1990), with an introduction by Roger Zelazny, collects a representative variety of short stories, chiefly cyberpunk, though there are forays into human-alien contact and a fine alternate history, "No Spot of Ground," in which Edgar Allan Poe is a general in the Confederate army. His short stories have garnered several awards and found home in the *Year's Best Science Fiction* series.

Williams's fiction is characterized by complex plotting, claustrophobic sets placed against a galactic sprawl of a backdrop, and a powerful sense of justified paranoia. His future societies are crowded with surveillance systems, corrupt political corporations and a multiplicity of antagonists wrapped in Byzantine scheming. The social and technological synecologies of the worlds he depicts are often dark and Darwinian.

The human body becomes a political locus in his fiction; people are bioengineered for specialized subversive tasks or non-Terran environments, or addicted to weird chemicals, or given wetware implants in order to carry out corporate plots. Though characters may develop superhuman traits because of these specialties, Williams skillfully avoids making them cartoonish. A character in *Angel Station,* for example, who has been given eidetic memory in order to improve his navigational skills cannot help remembering all the moments of personal pain in his life, as well. The posthuman tropes of Williams's imagination provide not only a cynical view of what technology may offer, but a source of suffering and sacrifice for his character-driven dramas.

Williams often employs the image of hurricanes or whirlwinds, suggesting people buffeted by powers beyond their control. Yet these same characters often grow to identify with the whirlwind and discover the ambition to gain power, often through the use of Zen koans and other techniques of bodily and mental self-control. Williams's fiction explores the related themes of power and corruptibility and concludes again and again that moral responsibility and self-control are necessary for a creative and happy society, a conclusion that has led to comparisons with Frank Herbert's *Dune.*

At the heart of all these issues lies a concern for the boundaries between oneself and the Other. His characters seek distinctions between the human and the alien. *Angel Station,* for example, raises the question of whether learning to understand an alien makes one less than or better than human. *Knight Moves* discovers that cultural stagnation is dehumanizing, and *Aristoi* dramatizes the political justifications for benevolent despotism on the one hand and non-interference in nasty, brutish, character-building human evolution on the other.

Williams is disturbed by the variety of ways in which people use and betray each other, though he concludes that personal and political manipulation will remain with us no matter how we evolve. However, he tries to avoid simplistic oppositions of Good and Evil, and his narrative techniques support this strategy. For example, Williams for the most part eschews commentary by an Olympian narrator, preferring to present foreshadowing and conflicts of motivation through character behavior and dialogue. His protagonists, too, are never paragons of virtue, but can blame themselves for the difficulties they face. He also frequently intercuts scenes with parallel rising suspense in achronological order, forcing the reader to focus on affinities between apparently dissimilar themes. His plots are usually structured as mysteries in which a puzzle must be solved, which makes the inevitable showdown between opposing forces more intriguing and less Manichaean. His protagonists champion human rights and progressive ways of thinking supported by a live-and-let-live philosophy. In this belief in progress, Williams finds his most powerful and passionate theme, the sadness and desirability and necessity of seeing ways of life change forever.

—Fiona Kelleghan

WILLIAMSON, Jack

Pseudonym: Will Stewart. **Nationality:** American. **Born:** John Stewart Williamson, Bisbee, Arizona, 29 April 1908. **Education:** Richland High School, New Mexico; West Texas State University, Canyon, 1928-30; University of New Mexico, Albuquerque, 1931-32; Eastern New Mexico University, Portales, B.A. (summa cum laude), M.A. 1957; University of Colorado, Boulder, Ph.D. 1964. **Military Service:** Weather forecaster in the United States Army, 1942-45: Staff Sargeant. **Family:** Married Blanche Slaten Harp in 1947; two step-children. Writer from 1928; wire editor, *Portales News Tribune,* 1947; created comic strip *Beyond Mars, New York Sunday News,* 1952-55; instructor in English, New Mexico Military Institute, Roswell, 1958-60, and University of Colorado, 1960; professor of English, Eastern New Mexico University, 1960-77, now retired. **Member:** President, Science Fiction Writers of America, 1978-80. **Awards:** Pilgrim award, 1973; Grand Master Nebula award, 1975; Hugo award, for non-fiction, 1985. Guest of Honor, 35th World Science Fiction Convention, 1977. **Agent:** Eleanor Wood, 111 Eighth Avenue, Suite 1501, New York, New York 10011, U.S.A. **Address:** Box 761, Portales, New Mexico 88130, U.S.A.

SCIENCE FICTION PUBLICATIONS

Novels (series: Cuckoo's Saga; Jim Eden; Legion of Space; Seetee; Starchild)

The Legion of Space. Reading, Pennsylvania, Fantasy Press, 1947; London, Sphere, 1977.
Darker Than You Think. Reading, Pennsylvania, Fantasy Press, 1948; London, Sphere, 1976.
The Humanoids. New York, Simon and Schuster, 1949; London, Museum Press, 1953; expanded edition, Garden City, New York, Doubleday, 1980.
The Green Girl. New York, Avon, 1950.
Dragon's Island. New York, Simon and Schuster, 1951; London, Museum Press, 1954; as *The Not-Men: A Science-Fiction Novel,* New York, Tower, 1968.
The Legion of Time (includes *The Legion of Time* and *After World's End*). Reading, Pennsylvania, Fantasy Press, 1952; published in 2 volumes, London, Digit, 1961; as *Two Complete Novels: The Legion of Time, After World's End,* New York, Galaxy Magabook, 1963.
Dome around America. New York, Ace, 1955; London, Faber, 1964.
Star Bridge, with James E. Gunn. New York, Gnome Press, 1955; London, Sidgwick and Jackson, 1978.
The Trial of Terra. New York, Ace, 1962.
The Starchild Trilogy, with Frederik Pohl. Garden City, New York, Doubleday, 1977; London, Penguin, 1980.

The Reefs of Space. New York, Ballantine, 1964; London, Dobson, 1965.

Golden Blood. New York, Lancer, 1964.

The Reign of Wizardry. New York, Lancer, 1964.

Starchild. New York, Ballantine, 1965; London, Dobson, 1966.

Rogue Star. New York, Ballantine, 1969; London, Dobson, 1972.

Bright New Universe. New York, Ace, 1967; London, Sidgwick and Jackson, 1969.

Trapped in Space (for children). Garden City, New York, Doubleday, 1968.

The Moon Children. New York, Putnam, 1972; Morley, Yorkshire, Elmfield Press, 1975.

Farthest Star (Cuckoo's Saga), with Frederik Pohl. New York, Ballantine, 1975; London, Pan, 1976.

The Power of Blackness. New York, Berkley, 1976; London, Sphere, 1978.

Brother to Demons, Brother to God. Indianapolis, Bobbs Merrill, 1979; London, Sphere, 1981.

Three from the Legion. Garden City, New York, Doubleday, 1979.

Seetee. New York, Jove, 1979.

> *Seetee Shock* (as Will Stewart). New York, Simon and Schuster, 1950; Kingswood, Surrey, World's Work, 1954; bylined as Jack Williamson, New York, Lancer, 1968.

> *Seetee Ship* (as Will Stewart). New York, Gnome Press, 1951; bylined as Jack Williamson, New York, Lancer, 1968.

The Humanoid Touch. Huntington Woods, Michigan, Phantasia Press, 1980; London, Sphere, 1982.

Manseed. New York, Ballantine, 1982; London, Sphere, 1986.

The Queen of the Legion. New York, Timescape, 1983; London, Sphere, 1984.

The Saga of Cuckoo, with Frederik Pohl (includes *Wall around a Star* and *Farthest Star*). Garden City, New York, Doubleday, 1983.

Lifeburst. New York, Ballantine, 1984; London, Sphere, 1987.

Firechild. New York, Bluejay, 1986; London, Methuen, 1988.

Land's End, with Frederik Pohl. New York, Tor, 1988.

Mazeway. Norwalk, Connecticut, Easton Press, and London, Mandarin, 1990.

The Singers of Time, with Frederik Pohl. Garden City, New York, Doubleday, 1991.

The Undersea Trilogy, with Frederik Pohl. Riverdale, New York, Baen, 1992.

> *Undersea Quest* (Eden), with Frederik Pohl. New York, Gnome Press, 1954; London, Dobson, 1966.

> *Undersea Fleet* (Eden), with Frederik Pohl. New York, Gnome Press, 1956; London, Dobson, 1968.

> *Undersea City* (Eden), with Frederik Pohl. Hicksville, New York, Gnome Press, 1958; London, Dobson, 1968.

Beachhead. New York, Tor, 1992.

Demon Moon. New York, Tor, 1994.

Short Stories

The Girl from Mars, with Miles J. Breuer. New York, Stellar, 1929.

Lady in Danger. London, Utopian, 1945.

The Cometeers (Legion; includes *The Cometeers* and *One against the Legion*). Reading, Pennsylvania, Fantasy Press, 1950; *One against the Legion* published separately, New York, Pyramid, 1967; title story published separately, London, Sphere, 1977.

The Pandora Effect. New York, Ace, 1969.

People Machines. New York, Ace, 1971.

The Great Illusion, with others. Wallsend, Tyne and Wear, Fantasy Booklet, 1973.

The Early Williamson. Garden City, New York, Doubleday, 1975; London, Sphere, 1978.

Dreadful Sleep. Chicago, Weinberg, 1977.

The Best of Jack Williamson. New York, Ballantine, 1978.

The Alien Intelligence. New Orleans, P.D.A., 1980.

The Birth of a New Republic, with Miles J. Breuer. New Orleans, P.D.A., 1981.

Into the Eighth Decade. Eugene, Oregon, Pulphouse, 1990.

OTHER PUBLICATIONS

Other

Science Fiction Comes to College: A Preliminary Survey of Courses Offered. Portales, New Mexico, Williamson, 1971; expanded editions, 1971-72.

Teaching SF. Portales, New Mexico, privately published, 1972; expanded editions, as *Teaching Science Fiction: Education for Tomorrow,* 1972-75.

H.G. Wells, Critic of Progress. Baltimore, Mirage Press, 1973.

Wonder's Child: My Life in Science Fiction. New York, Bluejay, 1984.

Beyond Mars (comic strips; with Lee Elias). El Cajon, California, Blackthorne, 2 vols., 1987-88.

Editor, *Teaching Science Fiction for Tomorrow.* Philadelphia, Owlswick Press, 1980.

*

Bibliography: *Jack Williamson: A Primary and Secondary Bibliography* by Robert E. Myers, Boston, Hall, 1980.

Manuscript Collection: Golden Library, Eastern New Mexico University, Portales.

Critical Study: *Jack Williamson: An Interview* by Larry McCaffrey, Dallas, Texas, Northouse, 1988.

Jack Williamson comments:

(1991) I began writing at 20, hardly half-educated but dazzled with visions of science and intoxicated with science fiction as a device for exploring the possible. In all the years since, the known universe has vastly expanded and science fiction has grown as fast. Now at 83 I'm still held by the unfolding of science and still excited about science fiction. As a career, it has been rewarding. Though in the first few decades the pay in money was meager, there were always rich compensations in the satisfactions of creating, in the fine friendships, in the opportunities to observe the explosions of scientific knowledge and the human impacts of science and technology. The writers and readers of science fiction form a special community, still tiny when I first discovered it, inhabited by the most able and interesting people I have known. Belonging to it has been a privilege.

* * *

Williamson's early life was spent in a covered wagon on one of the last frontiers, that of rural New Mexico. His first story, "The

Metal Man" (1928), resulted from reading one of the first numbers of *Amazing Stories*. In a crude but enthusiastic way, it established one of Williamson's leitmotifs: the interface between man and machine, as the hero becomes a technological object, a "person-machine." After several early novels that have never been published in book form (e.g., "The Stone from the Green Star") Williamson first earned a reputation as a master of space opera with *The Legion of Space* (1934). This novel put Williamson in the same rank with such galaxy-conquerors as John W. Campbell and E.E. "Doc" Smith; but the novel resembles those of his contemporaries only in its exuberance. Unlike Campbell and Smith, Williamson was not espousing either technocracy, as Campbell did, or the joys of physics unchecked by any intellectual bound, as Smith did. Williamson is neither pro- nor anti-technology; while there is a great deal of gimcrack physics scattered throughout the text, the central device that allows the heros to conquer their foes, AKKA, can be activated only by a few scraps and an act of will; its operation is never explained. *The Legion of Space* is important because it is the first sign that SF was moving away from the epic of technocracy; although it is what Alexei Panshin would call a lost-race novel of space (much of the action is standard lost-race adventure transported to the jungle-covered moon of Jupiter, Titan), it is still an advance over other, duller works of the time and can still be read with pleasure. Its sequels are better written but less entertaining. Williamson was one of the few writers of the 1930s who could write with equal facility for the *Astounding* of F. Orlin Tremaine and the *Astounding* of John Campbell. It is generally forgotten that *One against the Legion* was published in Campbell's *Astounding*. Campbell prodded Williamson to excellence in much the same way as he prodded other writers; Williamson's best work dates from this period, and the only novel that Williamson produced after 1948 that achieves excellence is a result of a Campbell-inspired fragment of 1941.

Williamson's three great works deal with the same theme: the eternal tension of society. Man, Aristotle teaches, is a social animal; it is the degree to which an individual must participate in society without abandoning free will that Williamson seeks to find in *Darker Than You Think, The Humanoids,* and *Star Bridge.*

Darker Than You Think is a result of the two years Williamson spent in psychoanalysis in the late 1930s. Ostensibly, it concerns a war between lycanthropy and humanity for dominance; but the werewolves are seen as agents of freedom, creatures that put the lie to scientific and psychoanalytic explanations with mystical truth that transcends attempts at rationalization. But freedom, in this novel, requires a price, a sum of dependence, of eternal vigilance. It is as if the werewolves were organised anarchists, determined to preserve absolute liberty with a new order. Added to this, Williamson has produced what is the best explanation of lycanthropy extent (it depends on probablistic physics, a theme deepened in *The Humanoids*). *Darker Than You Think* is an excellent thriller as well, being the finest novel of the occult produced by a science fiction writer.

Williamson continued his search for controlling agents in his best work, *The Humanoids*. In two ancillary works designed to match each other as thesis and antithesis, "With Folded Hands" and "The Equalizer," Williamson ruminated on the use and abuse of technology. The former introduces a classic dystopian theme, that of robots following a categorical imperative to its logical limit; the latter shows that technology can preserve as well as destroy free will. But these two novellas are two halves of a larger whole; they cannot be read apart, and consequently they lose some of their artistic impact. Only in *The Humanoids* does Williamson attempt a synthesis; and he does this by relying on the old Campbellian warhorse, that of psionic power, as Williamson combines metaphysics with particle physics and the laws of probability to produce a new unified field theory. It is hard for the modern reader to accept psionics with the willingness of those in the late 1940s; but Williamson transcends mere reciting of psionic power to examine the epistemological foundations behind that power. Williamson also examines the fate of those who have accepted the humanoid categorical imperative, producing an examination of the middle ground between the two cultures of pure technocracy and pure mysticism that still retains its impact. *The Humanoids* is Williamson's best novel, a classic dystopia and the single best work on robot instrumentalities outside the work of Isaac Asimov.

Williamson began a rapid decline after *The Humanoids;* for the next dozen years, he produced works only in collaboration. These collaborations with Frederik Pohl are minor entertainments; the earlier novels such as *Undersea City* are competent juveniles, but quickly reach a nadir with *Starchild,* the worst novel of either author. Williamson's other "collaboration" is not one at all, but is instead the completion of a Williamson fragment by James Gunn. This novel, *Star Bridge,* is Williamson's last important work, an examination of the processes of political change no less searching than his examination of psychoanalysis in *Darker Than You Think* and of technology in *The Humanoids*. The dialectic between individual and society here is less distinct; the chief representative of individualism is an assassin who does not know what he stands for, the society a corporate state whose internal dynamic has been spent.

After *Star Bridge,* Williamson began a creative drought which lasted 27 years. During this period Williamson's only important work was nonfiction; he began an academic career in the late 1950s, his dissertation forming part of *H.G. Wells, Critic of Progress.* Williamson's novels during this period returned to stories that would have achieved minor billing in *Planet Stories;* such a work as *The Power of Blackness* suffers from a black hero so characterless that Williamson can find no other descriptive qualities for him than the color of his skin. By the 1980s, Williamson was reduced to writing unneeded sequels to his major works; *The Humanoid Touch* is a minor, darker pastiche of *The Humanoids,* while *The Queen of the Legion* is a frothy conceit lacking in the force of its predecessors.

Manseed marked a new phase in Williamson's career. This tale of a latent superman struggling to discover the limits of his powers, while seriously flawed, marked a new seriousness in Williamson's career. Williamson followed *Manseed* with a collaboration with Frederik Pohl, *Wall around a Star,* one of the few novels to use linguistics as the scientific base for its intricate plot.

Lifeburst is his most important novel since *The Humanoids*. In *Lifeburst,* Williamson returns to his eternal theme—in relations between man and the world. *Lifeburst* is a surprisingly dark exploration of galactic power politics, with the power struggles between clans used as a metaphor for sexual and social tension. Gritty and imaginative, *Lifeburst* is to Williamson what *Capriccio* was to Richard Strauss: an autumnal masterpiece that ensures that Williamson, unlike most writers of his generation, remains a major force in science fiction.

—Martin Morse Wooster

WILLIS, Connie

Nationality: American. **Born:** Constance E. Willis, Denver, Colorado, 31 December 1945. **Education:** University of Northern Colorado, Greeley, B.A. in English and elementary education 1967. **Family:** Married Courtney W. Willis in 1967; one daughter. **Career:** Teacher in elementary and junior high schools, Branford, Connecticut, 1967-69; substitute teacher, Woodland Park, Colorado, 1974-81. Since 1982, full-time writer. **Awards:** National Endowment for the Arts grant, 1982; Nebula award, 1982 (twice), 1988, 1989; Hugo award, 1982, 1988; John W. Campbell award, 1988. **Agent:** Ralph Vicinanza, 111 8th Avenue, Suite 1501, New York, New York 10011. **Address:** 1716 13th Avenue, Greeley, Colorado 80631, U.S.A.

SCIENCE FICTION PUBLICATIONS

Novels

Water Witch: A Novel, with Cynthia Felice. New York, Ace, 1982.
Lincoln's Dreams. New York, Bantam, 1987; London, Grafton, 1988.
Light Raid, with Cynthia Felice. New York, Ace, 1989.
Doomsday Book. New York, Bantam, and London, New English Library, 1992.
Uncharted Territory. New York, Bantam, and London, New English Library, 1994.
Remake. New York, Bantam, 1995.

Short Stories

Fire Watch. New York, Bluejay, 1985.
Distress Call. Arvada, Colorado, Roadkill Press, 1991.
Daisy, in the Sun. Eugene, Oregon, Pulphouse, 1991.
Impossible Things. New York, Bantam, 1994.

Other

Editor, *The New Hugo Winners, Volume III,* with Martin Harry Greenberg as anonymous co-editor. Riverdale, New York, Baen, 1994.

*

Connie Willis comments:

I love the short story. People are constantly telling me how the short story is dying and how it is economically impossible to make a career out of writing short stories, but I still love the short story, and I've been writing them for 20 years. I think I like the variety of moods, styles, and themes I can explore in the short story, which I have always felt was the most successful form of science fiction. It is necessary to work with only a few characters, to create worlds with only a few words and hints of background, and to make everything in the story do double duty. It's an exciting challenge. I have written everything from screwball comedies to mysteries to fairytales and have found to my delight that science fiction welcomes them all.

I have always been fascinated by the problem of time and our place in it, and science fiction has allowed me to explore that theme in a variety of ways. I have written stories that involve the impact of the past on the present and on the future and on the far-reaching and sometimes devastating effects time travel would have on us. My story "Fire Watch" and my new novel *Doomsday Book* concern a history department at Oxford that has time travel at its disposal. Time travel can be a wonderful aid to history, but the lessons to be learned are not always simple or painless ones. The theme of time is one of endless possibilities and I find the stories unfolding one after the other as if I hadn't even begun.

*   *   *

Connie Willis established early in her career a reputation as one of the most reliably skillful writers, particularly at shorter length, in the genre. In recent years, her abilities as a novelist have improved dramatically; and she is one of those rare authors who attracted a widely based following even though her books vary greatly from one to the next. Willis has consistently been one of the least predictable writers, ranging from science fiction to fantasy to horror. It is in science fiction, however, that her talents are best displayed, as her Hugo and Nebula awards attest.

Her first novel, *Water Witch,* written in collaboration with Cynthia Felice, was an interesting but not outstanding story of a shrewd and not particularly honest con artist on a planet where water is in short supply. Although the novel made little impression when it appeared, the publication of the collection *Fire Watch* three years later apparently caused readers to focus on the steady creation of an impressive body of work.

The title story concerns a man who travels back through time to the London Blitz as part of his training to study history. He becomes involved with the effort to save an historic cathedral from destruction, waiting on the roof during each air raid to extinguish incendiary bombs before they can do any great damage. He becomes involved emotionally with his fellow defenders and ultimately learns more about himself than he does about the Blitz. In "A Letter from the Clearys" Willis illustrates the strongest point of her fiction, her ability to create utterly convincing characters, in this case a young woman struggling for mental equilibrium in the aftermath of a nuclear war.

"The Sidon in the Mirror" is set in a small mining colony on the surface of a burnt-out star. The reader is exposed to the unravelling of the various relationships among the staff and patrons of a bordello catering to the miners. Rather than dwell on grotesqueries, however, Willis forces our attention to the human characters that exist beneath the facade. "The Curse of Kings" is somewhat more conventional. Archeologists on a primitive world uncover a fabulous treasure, but a mysterious and fatal illness begins to claim members of their party.

Her skill at the shorter form continues to improve with experience. "Daisy, in the Sun" involves the survival of consciousness following the extinction of our sun. "Blued Moon" is untypical of her work, a quite funny tale of what happens when the disposal of industrial waste affects the laws of probability. "Samaritan" is set in a future where most of the organized churches have combined into one ecumenical body. A minister and his assistant differ when their orangutan servant apparently requests baptism. Predictably, many members of the congregation are appalled at the idea of accepting an "animal" as a member, and the minister himself is torn between conflicting emotions. More recently, her "The Swartzchild Radius" has won her a host of new fans, and "The Last of the Winnebagos" is one of the most poignant stories of the near future ever to appear in the field.

Two solo novels also appeared during this period. *Lincoln Dreams* is not properly science fiction at all, but this haunting tale of a woman who shares the dreams of the Civil War period has definite fantastic overtones, and the powerful characterizations and sure-handed plotting foreshadowed even more significant works that were clearly within the field. *Light Raid* is more conventionally science fiction, although its setting is only superficially familiar. North America is split into warring factions, and phantasmagorical attacks are frequently launched through the skies of one city-state or another. The protagonist is a young woman who seeks to clear her parents' name, after some mysterious organization brands them as traitors.

Three novels published in the early 1990s propelled Willis to a position of major importance in the field. The award-winning *The Doomsday Book* is a time-travel story, alternating between a near future and the distant past. A research project using a time machine has stranded its subject and a devastating plague is spreading through the world. The story alternates between the two time periods, following the adventures of two sets of characters linked by the threats to their lives. *Uncharted Territory* is a much shorter, less ambitious work, ostensibly an adventure story about two explorers on an alien world, but more interested in the byplay of their personalities than their personal exploits. The application of technology to art, artistic freedom from censorship, and "political correctness" are all examined in *Remake*. The protagonist is a technician hired to expurgate any depiction of smoking from classic motion pictures, using highly sophisticated computers. Although intellectually opposed to the task, he needs the money. At the same time, he becomes involved with a young woman determined to become an actress, even though all motion pictures are now created entirely by electronic interpolation of historic actors.

Other science fiction of note includes "Death on the Nile" and "Close Encounter." Willis has also written some unusually effective traditional ghost stories, most notably "The Service for the Burial of the Dead," "Distress Call," and "Substitution Trick." Versatility, a strong grasp of the complexity of the human character, and a highly accessible style mark Willis as one of the premier stylists in the genre. Her notable mastery of the novel-length tale has already established her as one of the preeminent writers of the 1990s.

—Don D'Ammassa

WILSON, Colin (Henry)

Nationality: British. **Born:** Leicester, 26 June 1931. **Education:** Gateway Secondary Technical School, Leicester, 1942-47. **Military Service:** Served in the Royal Air Force, 1949-50. **Family:** Married 1) Dorothy Betty Troop in 1951 (marriage dissolved), one son; 2) Pamela Joy Stewart in 1973, two sons and one daughter. **Career:** Laboratory assistant, Gateway School, 1948-49; tax collector, Leicester and Rugby, 1949-50; labourer and hospital porter in London, 1951-53; salesman for the magazines *Paris Review* and *Merlin,* Paris, 1953. Since 1954, full-time writer. British Council Lecturer in Germany, 1957; writer-in-residence, Hollins College, Virginia, 1966-67; visiting professor, University of Washington, Seattle, 1968; professor, Institute of the Mediterranean (Dowling

College, New York), Mallorca, 1969; visiting professor, Rutgers University, New Brunswick, New Jersey, 1974. **Agent:** David Bolt Associates, 12 Heath Drive, Send, Surrey, GU23 7EP. **Address:** Tetherdown, Trewallock Lane, Gorran Haven, Cornwall PL26 6NT, England.

SCIENCE FICTION PUBLICATIONS

Novels (series: Spider World)

The Mind Parasites. London, Barker, and Sauk City, Wisconsin, Arkham House, 1967.
The Philosopher's Stone. London, Barker, 1969; New York, Crown, 1971.
The Space Vampires. London, Hart-Davis MacGibbon, and New York, Random House, 1976; as *The Space Vampires, Filmed as Life Force,* London, Granada, 1985; as *Life Force,* New York, Warner, 1985.
The Personality Surgeon. Sevenoaks, Kent, New English Library, 1985; San Francisco, Mercury House, 1986.
Spider World:
  The Tower. London, Grafton, 1987; as *Spider World: [The Desert; The Tower; The Fortress],* New York, Ace, 3 vols., 1988-89.
  The Delta. London, Grafton, 1987; New York, Ace, 1990.
  The Magician. London, HarperCollins, 1992.

Short Stories

The Return of the Lloigor. London, Village Press, 1974.

OTHER PUBLICATIONS

Novels

Ritual in the Dark. London, Gollancz, and Boston, Houghton Mifflin, 1960.
Adrift in Soho. London, Gollancz, and Boston, Houghton Mifflin, 1961.
The World of Violence. London, Gollancz, 1963; as *The Violent World of Hugh Greene,* Boston, Houghton Mifflin, 1963.
The Sex Diary of Gerard Sorme. New York, Dial Press, 1963; as *Man without a Shadow: The Diary of an Existentialist,* London, Barker, 1963; as *The Sex Diary of a Metaphysician,* Berkeley, California, Ronin Press, 1989.
Necessary Doubt. London, Barker, and New York, Trident Press, 1964.
The Glass Cage. London, Barker, 1966; New York, Random House, 1967.
The Killer. London, New English Library, 1970; as *Lingard,* New York, Crown, 1970.
The God of the Labyrinth. London, Hart-Davis, 1970; as *The Hedonists,* New York, Signet, 1971.
The Black Room. London, Weidenfeld and Nicolson, 1971; New York, Pyramid, 1975.
The Schoolgirl Murder Case. London, Hart-Davis MacGibbon, and New York, Crown, 1974.
The Janus Murder Case. London, Granada, 1984.
The Magician from Siberia. London, Hale, 1988.

Plays

Viennese Interlude (produced Scarborough, Yorkshire, and London, 1960).

Strindberg (as *Pictures in a Bath of Acid,* produced Leeds, Yorkshire, 1971; as *Strindberg: A Fool's Decision,* produced London, 1975). London, Calder and Boyars, 1970; New York, Random House, 1972.

Mysteries (produced Cardiff, 1979).

Mozart's Journey to Prague (produced London, 1991). Nottingham, Paupers' Press, 1992.

Other

The Outsider. London, Gollancz, and Boston, Houghton Mifflin, 1956.

Religion and the Rebel. London, Gollancz, and Boston, Houghton Mifflin, 1957.

The Age of Defeat. London, Gollancz, 1959; as *The Stature of Man,* Boston, Houghton Mifflin, 1959.

Encyclopaedia of Murder, with Patricia Pitman. London, Barker, 1961; New York, Putnam, 1962.

The Strength to Dream: Literature and the Imagination. London, Gollancz, and Boston, Houghton Mifflin, 1962.

Origins of the Sexual Impulse. London, Barker, and New York, Putnam, 1963.

Rasputin and the Fall of the Romanovs. London, Barker, and New York, Farrar Straus, 1964.

Brandy of the Damned: Discoveries of a Musical Eclectic. London, Baker, 1964; expanded as *Chords and Discords: Purely Personal Opinions on Music,* New York, Crown, 1966; augmented edition, as *Colin Wilson on Music,* London, Pan, 1967.

Beyond the Outsider: The Philosophy of the Future. London, Barker, and Boston, Houghton Mifflin, 1965.

Eagle and Earwig (essays). London, Baker, 1965.

Introduction to the New Existentialism. London, Hutchinson, 1966; Boston, Houghton Mifflin, 1967; as *The New Existentialism,* London, Wildwood House, 1980.

Sex and the Intelligent Teenager. London, Arrow, 1966; New York, Pyramid, 1968.

Voyage to a Beginning: A Preliminary Autobiography. New York, Crown, and London, Cecil and Amelia Woolf, 1969.

Bernard Shaw: A Reassessment. London, Hutchinson, and New York, Atheneum, 1969.

A Casebook of Murder. London, Frewin, 1969; New York, Cowles, 1970.

Poetry and Mysticism. San Francisco, City Lights, 1969; expanded edition, London, Hutchinson, 1970.

The Strange Genius of David Lindsay, with E.H. Visiak and J.B. Pick. London, Barker, 1970; Wilson's essay expanded as *The Haunted Man,* San Bernardino, California, Borgo Press, 1979.

The Occult. New York, Random House, and London, Hodder and Stoughton, 1971.

New Pathways in Psychology: Maslow and the Post-Freudian Revolution. London, Gollancz, and New York, Taplinger, 1972.

Order of Assassins: The Psychology of Murder. London, Hart-Davis, 1972.

L'Amour: The Ways of Love, photographs by Piero Rimaldi. New York, Crown, 1972.

Strange Powers. London, Latimer New Dimensions, 1973; New York, Random House, 1975.

Three by Tolkien. London, Covent Garden Press-Inca, 1973; Santa Barbara, California, Capra Press, 1974.

Hesse—Reich—Borges: Three Essays. Philadelphia, Leaves of Grass, 1974.

Hermann Hesse. London, Village Press, 1974.

Wilhelm Reich. London, Village Press, 1974.

Jorge Luis Borges. London, Village Press, 1974.

A Book of Booze. London, Gollancz, 1974.

The Unexplained. Lake Oswego, Oregon, Lost Pleiade Press, 1975.

Mysterious Powers. London, Aldus, and Danbury, Connecticut, Danbury Press, 1975; bound with *Spirits and Spirit Worlds,* by Roy Stemman as *They Had Strange Powers,* Garden City, New York, Doubleday, 1975.

The Craft of the Novel. London, Gollancz, 1975; Salem, New Hampshire, Salem House, 1986.

Enigmas and Mysteries. London, Aldus, and Danbury, Connecticut, Danbury Press, 1976.

The Geller Phenomenon. London, Aldus, and Danbury, Connecticut, Danbury Press, 1976.

Mysteries: An Investigation into the Occult, the Paranormal, and the Supernatural. London, Hodder and Stoughton, and New York, Putnam, 1978.

Science Fiction as Existentialism. Hayes, Middlesex, Bran's Head, 1978.

Starseekers. London, Hodder and Stoughton, 1980; Garden City, New York, Doubleday, 1981.

The War against Sleep: The Philosophy of Gurdjieff. Wellingborough, Northamptonshire, Aquarian Press, 1980; revised and expanded as *G.I. Gurdjieff: The War against Sleep,* 1986.

Frankenstein's Castle—Double Brain, Door to Wisdom. Sevenoaks, Kent, Ashgrove Press, 1980.

Anti-Sartre, with an Essay on Camus. San Bernardino, California, Borgo Press, 1981.

The Quest for Wilhelm Reich. London, Granada, and Garden City, New York, Doubleday, 1981.

Witches. Limpsfield, Surrey, Dragon's World, 1981; New York, A and W, 1982.

Poltergeist! A Study in Destructive Haunting. Sevenoaks, Kent, New English Library, 1981; New York, Putnam, 1982.

Access to Inner Worlds: The Story of Brad Absetz. London, Rider, 1983.

Encyclopaedia of Modern Murder 1962-1982, with Donald Seaman. London, Barker, 1983; New York, Putnam, 1984.

Psychic Detectives: The Story of Psychometry and Paranormal Crime Detection. London, Pan, 1984; San Francisco, Mercury House, 1985.

A Criminal History of Mankind. London, Granada, and New York, Putnam, 1984.

Lord of the Underworld: Jung and the Twentieth Century. Wellingborough, Northamptonshire, Aquarian Press, 1984.

The Essential Colin Wilson. London, Harrap, 1985; Berkeley, California, Celestial Arts, 1986.

Existential Essays, edited by Howard F. Dossor. Bath, Ashgrove Press, 1985.

Afterlife: An Investigation of the Evidence of Life after Death. London, Harrap, 1985; Garden City, New York, Doubleday, 1987.

The Bicameral Critic, edited by Howard F. Dossor. Bath, Avon, Ashgrove Press, and Salem, New Hampshire, Salem House, 1985.

Rudolf Steiner: The Man and His Vision. Wellingborough, Northamptonshire, Aquarian Press, 1985.

The Laurel and Hardy Theory of Consciousness. Mill Valley, California, Brigg, 1986.

Scandal! An Encyclopaedia, with Donald Seaman. London, Weidenfeld and Nicolson, and New York, Stein and Day, 1986; as *An Encyclopedia of Scandal,* London, Grafton, 1987.

An Essay on the "New" Existentialism. Nottingham, Paupers' Press, 1986.

Alister Crowley: The Nature of the Beast. Wellingborough, Northamptonshire, Aquarian Press, 1987.

The Musician as "Outsider." Nottingham, Paupers' Press, 1987.

The Encyclopedia of Unsolved Mysteries, with Damon Wilson. London, Harrap, 1987; Chicago, Contemporary Books, 1988; as *Unsolved Mysteries,* New York, Galahad, 1992; expanded as *Unsolved Mysteries Past and Present,* Chicago, Contemporary Books, 1992; London, Headline, 1993.

Jack the Ripper: Summing Up and Verdict, with Robin Odell, edited by Joe Gaute. London, and New York, Bantam, 1987.

Beyond the Occult. London, Bantam, 1988; New York, Carroll and Graf, 1989.

Existentially Speaking: Essays on the Philosophy of Literature. San Bernardino, California, Borgo Press, 1989.

Autobiographical Reflections. Nottingham, Paupers' Press, 1988.

The Mammoth Book of True Crime, edited by Howard Dossor. London, Robinson, and New York, Carroll and Graf, 1988.

The Misfits: A Study of Sexual Outsiders. London, Grafton, 1988; New York, Carroll and Graf, 1989.

The Decline and Fall of Leftism. Nottingham, Paupers' Press, 1989.

Lord Halifax's Ghost Book. London, Bellew, 1989.

Written in Blood: A History of Forensic Detection. London, Equation, 1989; as *Written in Blood: Detectives and Detection,* New York, Warner, 1991.

Music, Nature, and the Romantic Outsider. Nottingham, Paupers' Press, 1990.

The Mammoth Book of True Crime 2, edited by Damon Wilson. London, Robinson, and New York, Carroll and Graf, 1990.

The Serial Killers, with Donald Seaman. New York, Carroll and Graf, 1990; revised, London, True Crime, 1992.

Marriage and London, with Paris, Leicester, London Again. Nottingham, Paupers' Press, 1991.

The Strange Life of P.D. Ouspensky. London, Aquarian, 1993.

Editor, *Colin Wilson's Men of Mystery.* London, W.H. Allen, 1977; as *Dark Dimensions: A Celebration of the Occult,* New York, Everest House, 1977.

Editor, with John Grant, *The Book of Time.* Newton Abbot, Devon, Westbridge, 1980.

Editor, with John Grant, *The Directory of Possibilities.* Exeter, Webb and Bower, and New York, Rutledge Press, 1981; as *Mysteries: A Guide to the Unknown: Past, Present, Future,* London, Chancellor, 1994.

Editor, with Christopher Evans, *The Book of Great Mysteries.* London, Robinson, 1986; New York, Dorset, 1990.

Editor, with Ronald Duncan, *Marx Refuted: The Verdict of History.* Bath, Avon, Ashgrove, 1987.

Editor, with Damon Wilson, *Murder in the 1930s.* London, Robinson, and New York, Carroll and Graf, 1992.

Editor, with Damon Wilson and Rowland Wilson, *World Famous Murders.* London, Robinson, 1993; as *World Famous Crimes,* New York, Carroll and Graf, 1995.

Editor, with Damon Wilson, *Murder in the 1940s.* London, Robinson, and New York, Carroll and Graf, 1993.

*

Bibliography: *The Work of Colin Wilson: An Annotated Bibliography and Guide* by Colin Stanley, San Bernardino, California, Borgo Press, 1989.

Manuscript Collection: University of California, Riverside; University of Texas, Austin.

Critical Studies: *The Angry Decade* by Kenneth Allsop, London, Owen, 1958; *The World of Colin Wilson* by Sidney Campion, London, Muller, 1963; "The Novels of Colin Wilson" by R.H.W. Dillard, in *Hollins Critic* (Hollins College, Virginia), October 1967; *Colin Wilson* by John A. Weigel, New York, Twayne, 1975; *Colin Wilson: The Outsider and Beyond* by Clifford P. Bendau, San Bernardino, California, Borgo Press, 1979; *The Novels of Colin Wilson* by Nicolas Tredell, London, Vision Press, 1982; *An Odyssey of Freedom: Four Themes in Colin Wilson's Novels* by K. Gunnar Bergstrom, Uppsala, Sweden, University of Uppsala, 1983; *Colin Wilson: Two Essays: The English Existentialist* by John Moorhouse and *Spiders and Outsiders* by Paul Newman, edited by Colin Stanley, Nottingham, Paupers' Press, 1990; *Colin Wilson: The Man and His Mind* by Howard Dossor, Shaftsbury, Element, 1990; *"The Nature of Freedom" and Other Essays* by Colin Stanley, Nottingham, Paupers' Press, 1990; *Colin Wilson, the Positive Approach: A Response to a Critic* by Michael Trowell, Nottingham, Paupers' Press, 1990; *Human Nature Stained: Colin Wilson and the Existential Study of Modern Murder* by Jeffrey Smalldon, Nottingham, Paupers' Press, 1991; *The Guerilla Philosopher: Colin Wilson and Existentialism* by Tim Dalgleish, Nottingham, Paupers' Press, 1993; *Two Essays on Colin Wilson: World Rejection and Criminal Romantics and From Outsider to Post-Tragic Man* by Gary Lachman, Nottingham, Paupers' Press, 1994.

Colin Wilson comments:

I would prefer to describe my three SF novels *The Mind Parasites, The Philosopher's Stone,* and *The Space Vampires* as philosophical fiction, and feel that it is a pity that such a classification does not yet exist. When it finally does, we shall have a new type of fiction, designed to explore the same field as philosophy, and to appeal to the reader's intelligence. After all, we agree that philosophy is an "adventure of ideas" that can open breathtaking vistas to the human mind; why should these vistas not provide the excitement in works of fiction?

The Mind Parasites was written as a result of a challenge by H.P. Lovecraft's friend and publisher August Derleth. I had remarked in an interview that I thought Lovecraft an appalling stylist, and Derleth challenged me to see if I could do better. I took over much of the Lovecraft "Cthulhu" machinery, but used the novel to explore a theme that has always been central to my work since my first book *The Outsider:* that there is something basically wrong with human beings, something that Christian theologians had in mind when they talked of original sin. As machines, we are hopelessly inefficient. None of us ever lives up to our full potentialities. Yet it also seems to me that what is wrong is not seriously wrong. It is due to the strange woodenness of human consciousness, its almost hypnotic fixity. You could compare this mechanical defect to a clock whose hands are loose, so that it is useless as a clock—

yet all it requires is for someone to tighten the hands. So, in *The Mind Parasites,* I developed a myth of some invisible parasites that live in the human mind, draining our vitality, keeping us permanently below our proper level. On a plot level, the central question of the book is: how could we combat parasites who are in the mind, so that they knew what we are thinking even as we think it?

In *The Philosopher's Stone,* I was again concerned with the problem of the invisible blocks to human evolution, but this time I accepted Shaw's challenge to write a parable about longevity— his belief that, if we could simply be galvanised by a sense of necessity, we would find it perfectly natural to live to be at least 300. Stravinsky had once made the interesting remark that rats fed on a diet of ecstasy live far longer. It struck me that if we could find some way of widening man's narrow consciousness, so that he can see the distant horizons that allure every poet, we would experience such a sense of enthusiasm and purpose that our lives would automatically be extended far beyond the present range. In the novel, a scientist accidentally discovers a brain operation that will unblock the hidden powers of the mind (at that time, I was toying with the idea that the secret of inspiration lay in the pre-frontal lobes, whereas I was later inclined to place it in the right brain). But even when this new freedom has been achieved by one or two people, they realise that some force seems to be actively opposed to the evolution of human consciousness. And once again I drew upon Lovecraft for my invisible monsters—the "Ancient Old Ones" who prefer human beings to remain hypnotised, and who symbolise original sin.

The Space Vampires is probably my best SF novel as science fiction. Its basic idea is the perception that some people seem to drain your energy, leaving you exhausted, while others seem to impart vitality. I am convinced that this is so, and that we actually feed on one another's energies far more than we realise. In the novel, aliens who have been found in the asteroid belt in a state of suspended animation are brought back to Earth; when awakened, they prove to be energy-vampires who live by sucking human vitality. The interesting logistic problem is that they can also transfer themselves into the bodies of their victims, so that the hunters are faced with an interesting problem in detection: how would you track down a criminal who can move from body to body?

The novel has the dubious distinction of having inspired one of the worst movies ever made, *Life Force.* It should have been a masterpiece, written by Dan O'Bannon (of *Alien*) and directed by Tobe Hooper. But the film makers seem to have been inspired to overkill by the 30 million dollars they had to spend on it, and neglected the story-line (without which any film is bound to be a flop) for spectacular special effects, thus demonstrating once again that low-budget movies (like *Alien*) have a better start in life than movies that are born with a silver spoon in their mouths.

My greatest regret is that the flop led to the cancellation of a sequel, *Return of the Space Vampires,* which I planned to write with my old friend A.E. Van Vogt. . . .

Spider World is fantasy rather than science fiction, and was planned in three large volumes. Planned casually as a collaboration with a friend, and designed as an 80-thousand-word novel, it startled me by going its own way and quickly developing into a 200,000-word "first part" (beginning with *The Desert* and ending with *The Delta*). The second "volume" of *Spider World* is entitled *The Magician,* and its first half, consisting of *The Assassins* and *The Living Dead* was published in 1991, followed by the second half, *Shadowland;* these were succeeded by a third volume, *New Earth,* also planned in three parts. In its finished form, the total work should be about twice as long as Tolkien's *Lord of the Rings.*

The theme of the first part—an earth of the future, taken over by giant spiders who breed human beings for food—soon transformed itself into my basic obsession, a study of precisely what is wrong with human beings: what is it that means that we are at our best under crisis, and that happiness—lack of crisis, challenge—bores us and causes us to degenerate? I am still hoping to live long enough to pin down the answer, and express it with such clarity that the human race will suddenly wake up to its basic potentialities. Never addicted to what Shaw called "the modest cough of the minor poet," I become increasingly aware as I grow older that my fundamental ambition is to be the least pessimistic writer who has ever lived.

* * *

Colin Wilson is an enormously energetic and eclectic writer whose works include nonfiction and fiction of many classes. For his worldview he acknowledges a seminal and continuing influence of Bernard Shaw, whose long science fantasy play *Back to Methuselah* is a sort of mainspring for Wilson's science fiction novels.

In the preface to *The Mind Parasites* Wilson remarks that the work is his first attempt at fantasy and likely his last. It was not. Several more have followed it. In *The Mind Parasites,* Professor Gilbert Austin discovers a counter-life entity competing with humanity for life energy from the wellspring of creation. Throughout history the parasites have masked from men mankind's own true powers—which are enormous, even godlike. Austin and his cohorts turn the tide of battle in favor of man, after themselves becoming considerably advanced in this "natural" power. Similarly, in *The Philosopher's Stone,* Howard Lester seeks and finds the answer to the problem of death. The power of the will to live has been blocked by the "Old Ones," a superspecies millions of years old that caused and then intercepted the evolution of man. Long asleep, the Old Ones may soon awaken. Lester hopes to lead men to confront them as "Masters" where they once served the Old Ones as slaves. *The Space Vampires* streamlines in style and strategy a similar tale. Spaceship Commander Carlsen discovers a gigantic interstellar craft carrying perverted aliens from the star-system Rigel. These creatures cheat death by absorbing life energy from host species such as humanity. Fortunately for mankind, sane Rigelians catch up with the vampire Rigelians just in time. Carlsen acts as a medium for the saviours, and in the process learns wholesome means by which mankind can be "immortal."

There are an enthusiasm and bright-eyed bombast about these tales that make it not unrewarding to read them as parodies of science fiction. This may account for a number of the elements common in the three works, though one need not forego taking them seriously as well. Each is furnished with a preface acknowledging a debt to H.P. Lovecraft or August Derleth. Each manifests considerable erudition exhibiting Wilson's encyclopaedic knowledge of the occult as well as the arts and history, anthropology, and science: ancient mythologies are found to have considerable basis in fact. Each story presents an intellectual power fantasy. The hero, in whom a panoply of parapsychological abilities is emerging, seems torn between visions of mankind as mean, gullible, and cowardly, and man with a destiny of vaulting grandeur. These heroes, after lifting the yoke of mental slavery from both themselves and humanity, win a form of personal transcendence, a step in the direction of joining the advanced intelligent life that lives throughout the universe.

In the books of the Spider World series thus far in print, *The Desert, The Tower, The Fortress, The Delta,* and *The Magician,*

Wilson writes science fiction for young adults, and thanks his three children for helping to form the guidelines. Mostly worthy of the warm reviews it received, the series in its compromise for younger readers eschews detailed description and analyses of the sexual behavior of its characters. Otherwise it imagines, as in earlier works, a universe imbued with a Shavian life force engaged in creative evolution. In the not-too-distant future, a vegetable embodiment of the life force comes to earth, and causes a riot in the evolution of earth's flora and fauna. Much of the human species has fled to Alpha Centauri. Ten centuries in the future Naill is born, who as a young man special mental powers, is fated to encounter and neutralize the species of now fully sentient giant spiders that has enslaved most of the remaining humans. In the events of *The Magician* humans and spiders end their antagonism and become allies, with Naill as the lord of both humans and spiders. However, their peace is broken almost immediately by the mysterious and horrible predations of a sinister "person" known only as "the Magician," though the novel ends before full engagement with the Magician has occurred. The overarching theme of the series is that humanity has a chance to solve what Wilson contends is its abiding problem: Man must learn to know and control his own mind so that the control he so easily exerts over the material world can avoid yet another catastrophe like those that fill human history.

The Spider World series is a respectable reprise of the earlier works. *The Space Vampires* (alternate title: *Life Force*) is the shortest and slickest. *The Philosopher's Stone* bogs us down and seems precisely repetitive of *The Mind Parasites* whose patient narrative, nicely deployed scenic hyperboles, and wonderful message were Wilson's first, and best attempt after all.

—John R. Pfeiffer

WILSON, F(rancis) Paul

Nationality: American. **Born:** Jersey City, New Jersey, 17 May 1946. **Family:** Married Mary Murphy in 1969; two daughters. **Career:** Since 1974, physician, Cedar Bridge Medical Group, Bricktown, New Jersey. **Awards:** Prometheus award, 1979. **Agent:** Albert Zuckerman, Writers House, 21 West 26th Street, New York, New York 10010, U.S.A.

SCIENCE FICTION PUBLICATIONS

Novels (series: LaNague Federation in all titles)

Healer. Garden City, New York, Doubleday, 1976; London, Sidgwick and Jackson, 1977.
Wheels within Wheels: A Novel of the LaNague Federation. Garden City, New York, Doubleday, 1979; London, Sidgwick and Jackson, 1980.
An Enemy of the State. Garden City, New York, Doubleday, 1980.
The LaNague Chronicles (includes *Healer, Wheels within Wheels,* and *An Enemy of the State).* Riverdale, New York, Baen, 1992.

Short Stories as F. Wilson (series: LaNague)

Dydeetown World (LaNague). Norwich, Connecticut, Easton Press, 1989.

The Tery (LaNague). New York, Baen, 1990.
Soft and Others: 16 Stories of Wonder and Dread. New York, Tor, 1989.
Ad Statum Perspicuum. Eugene, Oregon, Pulphouse, 1990.

OTHER PUBLICATIONS

Novels (series: The Adversary)

The Keep (Adversary). New York, Morrow, 1981; London, New English Library, 1982.
The Tomb. Binghamton, New York, Whispers Press, 1984; London, New English Library, 1985.
The Touch. New York, Putnam, and London, New English Library, 1986.
Black Wind. New York, Tor, 1988; London, M. Joseph, 1989.
Reborn: A Novel (Adversary). Arlington Heights, Illinois, Dark Harvest, and London, New English Library, 1990.
Reprisal: A Novel (Adversary). Arlington Heights, Illinois, Dark Harvest, 1991.
Sibs. Arlington Heights, Illinois, Dark Harvest, 1991; as *Sister Night,* London, New English Library, 1993.
Nightworld: A Novel. London, New English Library, and Arlington Heights, Illinois, Dark Harvest, 1992.
The Select. New York, Morrow, 1994.

Short Stories

Midnight Mass. Eugene, Oregon, Axolotl Press, 1990.
Pelts. Round Top, New York, Footsteps Press, 1990.
Buckets. Eugene, Oregon, Pulphouse, 1991.
The Barrens. Newark, New Jersey, Wildside Press, 1992.

Editor, *Freak Show.* New York, Pocket Books, 1992.

*

F. Paul Wilson comments:

I spent the 1970s writing science fiction, spent the 1980s writing horror of a cosmic sort (with occasional side trips back into SF). I'm not sure what the 1990s will bring, but I feel I've said most of what I have to say in the field of supernatural horror. Maybe it's time to move closer to home, come down to street level, to the here-and-now. The new novel *Sibs* is, I believe, a sign post on the road I'm traveling. We'll see where it takes me. (1993)

*   *   *

F. Paul Wilson's first stories were relatively undistinguished formula pieces for *Analog* magazine, but he quickly distinguished himself with a few outstanding works, most notably "Pard" and "Lipidleggin'." "Pard" dealt with the symbiotic relationship between a human and an alien, both immortal and with unique mental powers that allow them to fulfill a unique role in human history. This story was later incorporated into Wilson's first novel, *Healer,* in which the paired intelligences must deal with an interstellar psionic plague which drives entire populations into madness. A natural catastrophe would be bad enough, but the plague is actually a weapon wielded by another consciousness, against which even the Healer may find his abilities inadequate. The larger than life nature of the character makes identification difficult, but Wilson keeps the plot moving so quickly, the flaw is largely invisible.

Wilson's second novel, *Wheels within Wheels,* was a combination of scientific puzzle with conventional mystery. An alien race incapable of violent acts or conscious lies admits to having murdered a human being, but will not explain the circumstances. Twenty years later, the victim's daughter arrives to investigate. The alien culture is fascinating and the resolution is both plausible and clever, but the story's pacing is slow at times. *An Enemy of the State,* set against the same interstellar civilization, was more in the mold of his early magazine stories, a fairly routine interplanetary political thriller with lots of overt action, occasionally interspersed with short but somewhat obtrusive observations by the author. Again, a single human being must take command of the destiny of the entire race. At about the same time, Wilson produced *The Tery,* pitting some physically unprepossessing aliens against a fanatical human religious cult with predictable but very engaging results. One of Wilson's better stories, it was originally published as a novella in Dell's short-lived "Binary Star" series, later reprinted as an independent novel.

In 1981, Wilson's *The Keep* catapulted him into the public eye. Marketed as a horror novel, it is all of that and arguably SF as well; certainly it is not easily classifiable. Nazi soldiers occupy an ancient castle during World War II, where they inadvertently free an ageless evil presence that has been imprisoned there. When it begins to slay members of their party, they resort to using a Jewish academic and his daughter in an attempt to determine the nature of the menace they face. The internal tensions among the Nazi officers is particularly well handled, and the story succeeds on a number of levels. On the surface, *The Keep* is a vampire novel, but Wilson turns the theme around. The monster is only one aspect of a duality that involves an ageless warrior who has lived secretly among the human race. Now the two must meet again in what may be the last battle between them. The popularity of the novel resulted in a mediocre though occasionally interesting film version, but it certainly established his reputation. Almost 10 years later, Wilson would write a sequel of sorts, *Reborn,* also marketed as horror but even more clearly science fiction. An aging scientist has died and mysteriously leaves his entire fortune to a young man whom he seemed never to have known. The recipient investigates to satisfy his own curiosity, and learns that he is the result of an illegal experiment in cloning. Although there are horrific elements, the fantastic elements are held at arm's length and the book could as easily have been marketed as science fiction. The story is continued in *Reprisal.*

Having established himself as a horror writer of some importance, most of Wilson's novels during the past several years have been in that field. A shipload of hideous creatures menaces modern America in *The Tomb.* The horror is less overt in *The Touch* and almost nonexistent in traditional terms in the thoughtful *Black Wind.* Another straight science fiction novel, *Dydeetown World,* also appeared during this period and is an interesting tour of a strange culture, written in the style of a traditional private investigator story, but with some unique twists and turns. It is also one of Wilson's rare forays into humor, although the whimsy is always subservient to the plot. The novel, though aimed at an adult audience, gained considerable acclaim as a book for younger readers.

Although most of his later novels are horror or suspense, he continues to use some of the devices of science fiction in their construction. Most notable of these is *Night World,* essentially a global catastrophe novel with supernatural causes that brings to an apparent conclusion the sequence begun with *The Keep.* The final battle, judgment day, dawns suddenly, or rather refuses to dawn at all. Night envelopes the entire world in defiance of natural law.

Volcanoes and earth tremors disturb the earth's crust, and from the fissures rise hoards of deadly insects with a taste for human flesh. The counterbalance to the evil Rasalom is the immortal Glaeken, but the latter's powers have weakened and it appears the evil force from another universe will conquer the human race.

Wilson continued to write short fiction in both the horror and SF genres during the late 1980s. One of his more interesting is a horror novella, "Midnight Mass," set in a world where vampires have taken control, a theme Richard Matheson examined earlier in *I Am Legend.* He provided a new twist to the Batman character with "Definitive Therapy." Other short stories worth noting include "Kids," "Soft," "Traps," "Cuts," "Bugs," and "The Last One Mo' Once Golden Revival." The best of his short fiction has been collected in *Soft and Others.*

Wilson has stated in print that he doesn't wish to be labeled as a writer in any particular genre, that he wishes to be free to use styles, themes, and subject matter that appeal to him, rather than those that fit a particular market. Certainly he has proven to be capable of wide-ranging styles; *Dydeetown World, Black Wind,* and *The Keep* read like the works of three entirely different writers. The one thing they all have in common is strong narrative technique and a sense that the author genuinely admires his protagonists. Unfortunately, Wilson's future in science fiction is questionable, as his interests have clearly moved in another direction.

—Don D'Ammassa

WILSON, Gabriel. *See* **CUMMINGS, Ray.**

WILSON, Richard

Nationality: American. **Born:** Huntington Station, New York, 23 September 1920. **Education:** Brooklyn College, 1935-36; University of Chicago, 1947-48. **Military Service:** Served in the United States Army Signal Corps and Air Force, 1942-46. **Family:** Married 1) Jessica Gould in 1941 (divorced 1944); 2) Doris Owens in 1950 (divorced 1967); 3) Frances Daniels in 1967 (divorced 1982); one son and one stepdaughter. **Career:** Reporter, copyreader, and assistant drama critic, Fairchild Publications, New York, 1941-42; Chief of Bureau, Transradio Press, Chicago, Washington, D.C. and New York, 1946-51; reporter, and deputy to the North American editor, Reuters, New York, 1951-64; director, Syracuse University News Bureau, New York, 1964-80, and university editor, 1980-82. **Awards:** Nebula award, 1968. **Died:** 1987(?).

SCIENCE FICTION PUBLICATIONS

Novels

The Girls from Planet 5. New York, Ballantine, 1955; London, Hale, 1968.

And Then the Town Took Off. New York, Ace, 1960.
30-Day Wonder. New York, Ballantine, 1960; London, Icon, 1963.

Short Stories

Those Idiots from Earth: Ten Science Fiction Stories. New York, Ballantine, 1957.
Time out for Tomorrow. New York, Ballantine, 1962; London, Mayflower, 1967.
The Kid from Ozone Park and Other Stories. Polk City, Iowa, Drumm, 1987.
Aunt Fritzi. Polk City, Iowa, Drumm, 1987.

OTHER PUBLICATIONS

Plays

Jack and Jill (produced Syracuse, New York, 1965).
Another Time, in *Modern Radio Production.* Belmont, California, Wadsworth, 1985.

Radio Play: *Inside Story (X Minus One* series), 1955.

Other

Syracuse University: The Critical Years (vol. 3 of university history). Syracuse, New York, Syracuse University, 1984.
Adventures in the Space Trade, bound with *Richard Wilson Checklist,* by Chris Drumm. Polk City, Iowa, Drumm, 1986.

*

Manuscript Collection: Bird Library, Syracuse University, New York.

*   *   *

Richard Wilson's career as a writer breaks quite nicely into two stages. In his early years, Wilson was a satirical humorist in the mode of Henry Kuttner and Robert Sheckley, whose stories were frequently infused with a grim humor and a sharp eye for humanity's foibles. The three novels written at this time are cases in point. *The Girls from Planet 5* takes a pair of old standby plots and fuses them, with delightful results. America has become a matriarchy, where only one state still upholds the macho ideal—Texas, naturally. Into this strife-ridden world come invaders from another world, but invaders who are actually beautiful women. Frustrated by their loss of preeminence, the Texan patriarchs are not willing to become a minor backwater in an increasingly female universe. Aliens appear again in *And Then the Town Took Off,* a shorter novel that details the effect upon the citizens of Superior, Ohio, when their city uproots itself from Earth and rises into space to become a separate planet. This rollicking escapade pokes amusing if unconscious fun at James Blish's famous "Cities in Flight" series. The third and best of the novels is *30-Day Wonder,* which takes what should be an ideal situation and turns it completely around. The Monolithians are alien visitors who express their determination to obey scrupulously all human laws and regulations, and ensure that all humans in their vicinity will do the same. The effect on rush-hour traffic of several automobiles sedately travelling well within

the speed limit is just the beginning of an increasingly taxing month for the human race.

Although most of Wilson's early short stories, such as "Those Idiots from Earth," were satirical or actively funny, his most well-known story of that period was very serious. The heroine of "Love" is a blind human girl living on Mars, who is in love with one of the despised Martian natives. When her father forbids her to have anything further to do with him, she runs off for one last meeting, and together they discover an ancient artifact that may well cure her sight. It is a touching tale told somewhat awkwardly, but effective.

The awkwardness left during the years that followed, and several of Wilson's more recent works are outstanding. "Mother to the World" won a Nebula award for its tender, effective portrayal of the last man on Earth and the last woman, a gentle but retarded individual whose tolerance and flexibility overcome the horrors of their situation. Wilson returned to the last man theme in "A Man Spekith," in which a disc jockey and a computer remain in orbit, looking down over the corpse of the Earth. "See Me Not" is one of the few recent treatments of invisibility that contains any novelty. "The Carson Effect" portrays a wave of philanthropy on the eve of the last day of the world, an ending that is miscalculated and never happens, much to the consternation of those who have given away their fortunes. "The Story Writer" is a complex, engrossing story that contains enough complexity for a brace of novels. An aging successful pulp writer sits in flea markets, writing stories for people as a whim, until he finds himself a character in one of his own stories, the tale of the meeting of our own race and another that has reached us through another plane of existence in their flight from a ravaged homeworld. The last few stories to appear by Wilson before his death employed a rich, witty style that demonstrated his continued growth as a writer. It is unfortunate that we will never know how much further he would have progressed.

—Don D'Ammassa

WILSON, Robert Anton

Nationality: American. **Born:** Brooklyn, New York, 18 January 1932. **Education:** Brooklyn Polytechnic Institute; New York University, Paideia University, B.S., M.A. 1978, Ph.D. 1981. **Family:** Married Arlen Riley in 1959; four children. Engineering aide, Ebasco Inc., New York, 1950-56; salesman, Doubleday Publishers, 1957; copywriter, Popular Club, Passaic, New Jersey, 1959-62; sales manager, Antioch Bookplate, Yellow Springs, Ohio, 1962-65; astrology columnist, *National Mirror,* and editor, *Jaguar,* 1965; associate editor, *Playboy,* Chicago, 1965-71. **Agent:** Al Zuckerman, Writers House, 21 West 26th Street, New York, New York 10010, U.S.A.

SCIENCE FICTION PUBLICATIONS

Novels (series: Illuminatus; Schrödinger's Cat)

Masks of the Illuminati. New York, Timescape, and London, Sphere, 1981.
The Earth Will Shake. Los Angeles, Tarcher, 1982.

The Illuminatus! Trilogy. New York, Dell, 1984.
>   *The Eye in the Pyramid.* New York, Dell, 1975; London, Sphere, 1976.
>   *The Golden Apple.* New York, Dell, 1975; London, Sphere, 1976.
>   *Leviathan.* New York, Dell, 1975; London, Sphere, 1976.

The Widow's Son. New York, Bluejay, 1985.
Schrödinger's Cat Trilogy. New York, Dell, 1988.
>   *The Universe Next Door.* New York, Pocket Books, 1979; London, Sphere, 1980.
>   *The Trick Top Hat.* New York, Pocket Books, and London, Sphere, 1981.
>   *The Homing Pigeons.* New York, Pocket Books, 1981; London, Sphere, 1982.

Nature's God. New York, Roc, 1991.
Reality Is What You Can Get Away With: A Screenplay. New York, Dell, 1992.

OTHER PUBLICATIONS

Novel

The Sex Magicians. Chatsworth, California, Sheffield House, 1973.

Plays

Illuminatus! (produced Liverpool, 1976; London, 1977; Seattle, 1978).
Wilhelm Reich in Hell (produced Dublin, 1985).

Other

Playboy's Book of Forbidden Words. Chicago, Playboy Press, 1972.
Sex and Drugs. Chicago, Playboy Press, 1973; London, Mayflower, 1975.
The Book of the Breast. Chicago, Playboy Press, 1974.
Cosmic Trigger: Final Secret of the Illuminati. Berkeley, California, And/Or Press, 1977; London, Abacus, 1979.
Neuropolitics, with Timothy Leary. Culver City, California, Peace Press, 1977; as *Neuropolitique,* with Leary and George A. Koopman, Las Vegas, Falcon Press, 1988.
The Illuminati Papers. Berkeley, California, And/Or Press, 1980; London, Sphere, 1982.
Right Where You Sitting Now: Further Tales of the Illuminati. Berkeley, California, And/Or Press, 1982; revised edition, Berkeley, Ronin, 1992.
Prometheus Rising. Santa Monica, California, Falcon Press, 1983.
Natural Law; or, Don't Put a Rubber on Your Willy. Port Townsend, Washington, Loompanics Unlimited, 1986.
Wilhelm Reich in Hell. Phoenix, Arizona, Falcon Press, 1987.
The New Inquisition: Irrational Rationalism and the Citadel of Science. Phoenix, Arizona, Falcon Press, 1988.
Coincidance: A Head Test. Phoenix, Arizona, Falcon Press, 1989.
Ishtar Rising; or, Why the Goddess Went to Hell and What to Expect Now That She's Returning. Las Vegas, Falcon Press, 1989.
Quantum Psychology: How Brain Software Programs You and Your World. Phoenix, Arizona, Falcon Press, 1990.

Editor, with Rudy Rucker and Peter Lamborn Wilson, *Semiotext[e] SF.* Brooklyn, New York, Autonomedia, 1989.

*

Robert Anton Wilson comments:

I define my writing as guerilla ontology—that is, a literary expression of the discoveries of physical relativity (Einstein), cultural relativity (anthropology), neurological relativity (Korzybski, Leary) and the new head-spaces opened to us by psychedelics, bio-feedback, scientific study of yoga, etc. Each of my books presents not one map of reality, but several; the humor, the suspense, and the philosophical meaning (if any) derive from the search for the one reality, never quite found, which will synthesize or include all the alternative reality-tunnels presented. As in quantum physics, the isolated observer or omniscient narrator does not exist in my world; it is a participatory universe in which each entity projects/creates its own surrounding experiential continuum.

*   *   *

"George, you're too serious. Don't you know how to play? Did you ever think that life is maybe a game? There is no difference between life and a game, you know."

Games of all kinds and at all levels abound throughout Robert Anton Wilson's books. The most famous of his books, *Illuminatus,* is on one level a detective story, the most formal of literary games, as is *Masks of the Illuminati* (with a denouement revealed by Albert Einstein and James Joyce yet!) Simultaenously he plays the game of parody (Tolkien, Ian Fleming, and Ayn Rand to name but three) and his own mind-game with the reader, Operation Mindfuck, which tries to break down "the mind-forged manacles" of unconscious dogma, to make the reader move into new points of view: "reality-tunnels" to use Wilson's terms.

Some readers will find that last level, Wilson's philosophical pretensions, ludicrous and absurd. But insofar as he is serious about anything, Wilson is serious about showing people the limits that their own assumptions place on them. To this end Wilson makes a mockery of all political viewpoints (including the capitalist anarchism he espouses) and all religions (including the Discordianism he helped popularise). In his nonfiction he does his best to justify the "Trancedental Agnosticism" that came to him as a result of drinking too deeply of too many Springs of Ultimate Wisdom, from hearing too many Ultimate Truths. *Prometheus Rising* and *Quantum Psychology* are practical handbooks of his peculiar philosophy although *The Illuminati Papers* and *Coincidance* may be more easily accesible to the casual reader.

The True Believers who infest these more dogmatic decades may find Wilson's relativism too, too "sixties," but they too are clearly depicted in Wilson's hilarious disection of "normal primate behaviour." He is especially funny concerning "scientific" dogmatism in *The New Inquisition, The Widow's Son,* and the article "The Persecution and Assasination of the Parapsychologists as Performed by the Inmates of the American Association for the Advancement of Science under the Direction of the Amazing Randi" (reprinted in *Right Where You are Sitting Now*).

And for those who find the quantum physics (which provides the structure, such as it is, for the *Schrödinger's Cat* sequence), the philosophy, the literary references and history a little heavy you can just lie back and enjoy the scenery, while Wilson, stealing from any source that pleases him (from Lovecraft and Tolkien to "Elephant Doody Comix") and throwing out the lunatic touches of characterisation that make the patchwork structures of the novels shine.

Wilson's viewpoint is determinedly optimistic (as his subjectivist philosophy would advise) as shown by his essays (in *The Illuminati Papers*) on the conquest of stupidity and on Buckminster

Fuller. Yet there is in his novels alongside the jugglers and buffoons a sense of pain and tragedy that is not diminished by his belief in the pointlessness of suffering. To quote Wilson again: "It isn't true unless it makes you laugh, but you don't understand it until it makes you cry."

The best "sampler" works for those who want to explore Wilson's fiction before tackling the huge mass ans in jokes on *Illuminatue* and *Schrödinger's Cat* are *Masks of the Illuminati* and the (so far incomplete) historical sequence *The Earth Will Shake, The Widow's Son,* and *Nature's God.*

—Michael Cule

WILSON, Robert Charles

Nationality: Canadian. **Born:** 1953. Lives in Vancouver, British Columbia. **Address:** c/o Doubleday, 666 Fifth Avenue, New York, New York 10103, U.S.A.

SCIENCE FICTION PUBLICATIONS

Novels

A Hidden Place. New York, Bantam, 1986; London, Orbit, 1990.
Memory Wire. New York, Bantam, 1988; London, Orbit, 1990.
Gypsies. Garden City, New York, Doubleday, 1989; London, Orbit, 1990.
The Divide. Garden City, New York, Doubleday, and London, Orbit, 1990.
A Bridge of Years. Garden City, New York, Doubleday, 1991.
The Harvest. New York, Bantam, and London, New English Library, 1993.
Mysterium. New York, Bantam, 1994.

*   *   *

Robert Charles Wilson is an extraordinarily gifted writer with a deep understanding of the importance of love, in all its forms, in human relationships. For these reasons he has often been compared to Theodore Sturgeon. Although he has published a number of short stories, his strength comes out mainly in his novels. *A Hidden Place,* his first novel, hallmarked him as a significantly talented writer. Travis Fisher, after his mother's death, moves into his aunt's house in a small prairie town, Haute Montagne, during the Great Depression. There, with his new found sweetheart, Nancy Wilcox, he falls under the spell of Anna Blaise, a strange and mysteriously radiant woman. Anna Blaise is from another universe and only half present, for she must be reunited with her "male part," Bone, in order to return home. In the meantime, Bone, an amnesiac hobo travelling on the railroads, is becoming distantly aware of his true nature. All the protagonists in *A Hidden Place* are estranged persons. Travis is estranged from his family, Nancy from her own town, Anna and Bone from each other and from their world while all the inhabitants of Haute Montagne strive to belong and conserve their position in the small community and not fall into the rejection that is Nancy and Travers' lot. However, *A Hidden Place* is not a nostalgic novel, for Wilson manages to keep it paced and have its plot

progressing briskly while combining romance and suspense without falling into the trap of an ordinary love story.

Wilson's second novel, *Memory Wire,* is an incursion into the world of cyberpunk. It is a slight departure from the usually realistic and contemporary setting that Wilson tends to lay out at the beginning of all his other novels. *Memory Wire* catapults us into the next century right from the beginning when volunteers are employed to function as human video-recorders by TV news networks after having been dotted with implants. Once again, Wilson deals with the theme of alienation, the inescapable condition of the main characters: Keller is the all seeing angel who is transformed into an unfeeling being for the main purpose of forgetting his past. Teresa, contrary to Keller, is trying to recapture her past through "oneiriltihs," extraterrestrial dreaming jewels discovered in the Amazone that enable one to remember one's past extremely accurately. All this makes up for a tense thriller in which love, described in a touching and delicate way, occupies a central place.

Gypsies, Wilson's third novel, is an excellent book slightly marred by the apparent determination of its author to explain all scientific events with words that have more to do with magic and fantasy than science fiction. It tells of siblings with the ability to travel between parallel universes who, up till now, have been living most of their lives in our reality/universe. Since they are the products of genetic research and government funding from another universe, it is puzzling, if not irritating, to find a constant reference to magic, spells, and words usually more associated with pure fantasy rather than science fiction. It is quite possible that Wilson, whose science fiction relies much more on "soft sciences" (such as psychology and sociology), feels uncomfortable with the use of scientific terminology in *Gypsies;* nevertheless, it is a science fiction novel that deals with human suffering: in an attempt to prevent them from using their powers and therefore to protect them from their former masters, two of the protagonists were often beat up by their parents, and this has left permanent scars that are explored movingly in the novel. As in many of his works, Wilson does not shy away from going deep into his characters' psyche and for this purpose often puts them into realistic situations, even if it is to escape the science fiction atmosphere for a while; in fact, this departure makes the return to the science-fiction aspect of the story all the more alluring and compelling. A good example is to be found in Karen's painful and truthful phone conversations with her estranged and "normal" husband. *The Divide,* set in Toronto, presents John Shaw, who has been transformed by U.S. research into a super-being gifted with hypersensory organs and intelligence. The project has been dropped, but now John Shaw's health is deteriorating, and Benjamin, his alternate persona, is taking control of John's mind. His split personality will kill him unless he finds a way of fusing his two minds. The novel is reminiscent of *A Hidden Place* with its theme of split personalities and inner reconciliation. In *The Divide,* Wilson engages in a bolder description of love while succeeding in writing a melancholic story about the search for oneself.

With his latest novel, *Mysterium,* Wilson shows that he belongs to a rare breed in the SF and mainstream literary world: the enduring one. He manages to produce a new novel on a regular basis (roughly one every eight months) and never disappoints, not because he does what his readers might expect from him but because he manages to renew himself while, at the same time, being able to bring science fiction into what is a seemingly ordinary world. *Mysterium* takes place in one of the most tranquil and uneventful environments, a small Michigan town where in one swoop his inhabitants, the village, and the surrounding countryside are catapulted into a frightening dystopia.

His favorite underlying theme is the cause of it all: government scientific experiments gone haywire. But here no one in this universe will have to suffer the consequences since the victims have all been zapped to an alternative North America, another country that makes our own society appear as the most homely and friendly one on earth.

For the inhabitants of Two Rivers, it is as if the rest of the world has physically vanished from the face of the earth; this is quite a feat from Wilson who manages to bring a totally new twist on one of SF's overused themes, a postholocaust society, but a holocaust where the protagonists do not suffer directly, not at first, a holocaust in a controlled environment; and instead of just having to survive on their own, they have to learn a new history, new ways and how to deal with the seemingly moral dilemma of loyalty to the old or the new world and its rulers.

But, not for one minute could we believe that they have been spared. On the contrary, little by little it appears that the rest of the world has been spared a descent into hell. The normal surroundings of all the protagonists turn into a terrifying world, not as gruesome as Stephen King's, but with a certainty that things will never be the same again. Robert Charles Wilson has written a well-crafted thriller while bringing us totally three-dimensional characters with whom we can readily identify or of whom we can disapprove. In this dystopia, ruled by zealots and secret police, and from which there is no escape, there is only room for survivors with higher moral virtues and the rebuilding of one's dreams.

Undoubtedly, Wilson will be one of the few writers of the last two decades that will easily survive his own era, very much like all his main protagonists. His treatment of contemporary themes, such as alienation and the loss of identity and his ability to explore skillfully the whole range of human emotions puts him in the same league with many SF and mainstream writers who have managed to resist the passage of time.

—Henry Leperlier

WINGRAVE, Anthony. *See* **WRIGHT, S. Fowler.**

WINGROVE, David (John)

Nationality: British. **Born:** London, England, 1 September 1954. **Education:** Battersea Grammar School, 1965-71; University of Kent, Canterbury, 1979-84, First Class Honours Degree, English and American literature. **Family:** Common law wife, Susan Oudôt; three daughters. **Career:** Worked in banking, 1971-79. Editor, *Vector* magazine, 1977-79. **Member:** Membership secretary, British Science Fiction Association, 1976-77. **Awards:** Science Fiction Achievement award (Hugo), 1987. **Agent:** Hilary Rubinstein, A.P. Watt, 20 John Street, London WC1N 2DR, England.

SCIENCE FICTION PUBLICATIONS

Novels (series: Chung Kuo in all titles)

The Middle Kingdom. London, New English Library, 1989; New York, Delacorte, 1990.
The Broken Wheel. London, New English Library, 1990; New York, Delacorte, 1991.
The White Mountain. London, New English Library, 1991; New York, Delacorte, 1992.
The Stone Within. London, New English Library, 1991; New York, Dell, 1993.
Beneath the Tree of Heaven. London, New English Library, 1993; New York, Dell, 1994.
White Moon, Red Dragon. London, Hodder and Stoughton, 1994.

OTHER PUBLICATIONS

Other

The Immortals of Science Fiction. London, Pierrot, 1980.
Apertures: A Study of the Writings of Brian W. Aldiss, with Brian Griffin. Westport, Connecticut, Greenwood Press, 1984.
The Science Fiction Source Book. Harlow, Essex, England, Longman, and New York, Van Nostrand Reinhold, 1984.
The Science Fiction Film Source Book. Harlow, Essex, England, Longman, 1985.
Trillion Year Spree: The History of Science Fiction, with Brian Aldiss. London, Gollancz, and New York, Atheneum, 1986.

*

David Wingrove comments:

If writing about the future is to have any prodromic significance, it must—in its themes and subject matter—address what is happening to our world right now. Over population, the destruction of the ecosystem, and man's tendency to seek rigid authoritarian solutions to the problems he creates are symptoms of a world seriously out of balance. In my eight-volume novel, *Chung Kuo,* I seek to illuminate some of these matters in an involving and, I hope, entertaining manner. If the sequence is about anything, it is about the search for balance—for a system of behaviour that can accommodate peacefully and healthily all the people we are.

*   *   *

David Wingrove's *Chung Kuo* is a large work which, on publication of the final volume, will portray 60 years of a future history of the human race. From a short story written in 1983, *Chung Kuo* expanded in intermediate stages (to one novel, then two novels) before attaining a form that satisfied the author—an eight-volume novel of which six volumes have thus far appeared.

The world of *Chung Kuo* is a world in stasis. The Han—or Chinese—utterly dominate the globe, and Earth's population inhabit vast, continent-spanning cities, 300 levels high and completely cut off from the outside. There are seven great regional Cities, each ruled by its T'ang, and together these absolute rulers constitute the Council of the Seven. *Chung Kuo's* society is rigidly stratified, its governing apparatus strictly authoritarian, and the Seven see their task as maintaining this state of affairs, thus resisting change.

But the very existence of *Chung Kuo* is based on a huge lie: that the ancient Chinese defeated the Roman Empire and went on to conquer the world. The founders of *Chung Kuo* devoted immense effort in fabricating a complex alternative history and erasing the truth, which was that in the mid-21st century the Western nations collapsed into chaos and war and were subjugated by a resurgent China led by a ruthless tyrant, Tsao Ch'un, at the cost of billions of lives and the obliteration of entire cultures. Tsao Ch'un was himself overthrown by his seven ministers who went on to establish their own power as the Council of the Seven and to complete the global hegemony of Chung Kuo. And Humanity was physically confined within the Cities, and mentally imprisoned by the strictures and codes of Han culture, by its imposed homogeneity.

Volume one, *The Middle Kingdom,* begins over a century later, with Earth's population more than 34 billion and rising, with demands that the 114-year-old Edict of Technological Control be moderated, and with undercurrents of political opposition to the rule of the Seven. Chung Kuo is ripe for change.

Change is one of David Wingrove's main themes and is continually shadowed by its corollary, the search for balance. This duality is openly stated in the prologue of *The Middle Kingdom:*

> Uncharacteristically, Li Shai Tung put his hands to his face. He had been having dreams. Dreams in which he saw the Cities burning. Dreams in which old friends were dead—brutally murdered in their beds, their children's bodies torn and bloodied on the nursery floor.
>
> In his dreams he saw the darkness bubble up into the bright-lit levels. Saw the whole edifice slide down into the mire of chaos. Saw it clearly as he saw his hands, now, before his face.
>
> Yet it was more than dreams. It was what would happen—unless they acted.
>
> Li Shai Tung, T'ang, Ruler of City Europe, one of the Seven, shuddered.

Li Shai Tung's resistance to change brings him (and by extension, the Seven) into conflict with its proponents. First are the Dispersionists, a political faction led by Berdichev, Wyatt, and Lehmann, wealthy businessmen in City Europe. After six years of confrontation, both overt and covert, Wyatt and Lehmann are dead, Berdichev has fled to Mars, and the Dispersionists are a spent force. But the rulers have not come through unharmed: by the end of *The Middle Kingdom,* four of the Seven are dead, replaced by young, inexperienced heirs, and Li Shai Tung's elder son has been assassinated.

Other opponents to the rule of the Seven come to the fore. In volume two, *The Broken Wheel,* revolutionaries called the Ping Tiao carry out acts of sabotage and terrorism against the state. But when, at the start of volume three, *The White Mountain,* they help to destroy a major fortress/barracks in City Europe, killing thousands of innocents, the backlash from the T'ang's security forces almost wipes them out. Soon after, another revolutionary group, the *Yu,* rises to prominence and by the end of *The White Mountain* has established a reputation for moral discrimination by assassinating only those responsible for corruption or murder.

David Wingrove's vast story of a world undergoing catastrophic change is also a story of movers, shakers, and victims, and of ambiguity and contradiction. Even though Li Shai Tung, and later his younger son, Li Yuan, are absolute rulers, they are not archetypal

monstrous tyrants. Both display dignity and compassion, qualities somewhat lacking in the Dispersionists and particularly in one of their main allies, Howard DeVore, a major in the T'ang's security forces. DeVore later emerges as the Seven's leading adversary, conducting a shadowy, almost secret war against the entire edifice of *Chung Kuo,* and becoming a personification of change—or at least its dark, masculine, Yang aspect.

This dark aspect of change resonates strongly with the very character of *Chung Kuo:* it is a society where yin and yang are severely out of balance, where the latter dominates the former and contributes to the atmosphere of wrongness and oppression, to the sense that a gentler aspect of human nature is missing.

Given the large cast of characters introduced in the first three volumes of *Chung Kuo,* and the devious (and often overlapping) intrigues in which they are involved, it is no surprise that the author chose to adopt a clear, straightforward prose style. Nothing is obscured, and with the open use of metaphor and leitmotif Wingrove has reached levels of meaning seldom encountered in science fiction. But before all matters of connotation comes the story itself, and through clarity of expression David Wingrove has thus far created a highly readable, genuinely enjoyable epic rich in symbolism.

—Michael Cobley

WINIKI, Ephraim. *See* **FEARN, John Russell.**

WINNARD, Frank. *See* **TUBB, E.C.**

WINTER, H.G. *See* **BATES, Harry.**

WITKIEWICZ, Stanislaw

Pseudonym: Witkacy. **Nationality:** Polish. **Born:** Krakow, 24 February 1885. **Career:** Painter and playwright. **Died:** Committed suicide, 18 September 1939.

SCIENCE FICTION PUBLICATIONS

Novels

Nienasycenie. Warsaw, Dom Ksiazky Polskiej, 1930; translated by Louis Iribarne as *Insatiability: A Novel in Two Parts,* Urbana, Illinois, University of Illinois Press, 1977.

Plays

Wariat i zakonnica. N.p., n.d.; translated by Daniel C. Gerould and C. S. Durer as *The Madman and the Nun and Other Plays,* Seattle, University of Washington Press, 1968.
"The Cuttlefish," in *Treasury of the Theatre 2,* edited by Bernard F. Dukore and John Gassner, n.p., 1969.
Tropical Madness: Four Plays. N.p., 1972.
The End of the World. N.p., n.d.

OTHER PUBLICATIONS

Short Stories

In a Little Country House, translated by Stefania E. Gross and Allen S. White. N.p., 1973.

Plays

The Mother and Other Unsavory Plays, edited and translated by Daniel C. Gerould and C. S. Durer. London, Quartet, 1985; New York, Applause, 1993.

Other

Beelzebub Sonata: Plays, Essays, and Document, edited by Daniel C. Gerould and Jadwiga Kosicka. New York, Performing Arts Journal Publications, 1980.
The Witkiewicz Reader, edited and translated by Daniel C. Gerould. Evanston, Illinois, Northwestern University Press, 1992; London, Quartet, 1993.

*   *   *

Labelled old-fashioned by his peers but avant-garde and prophetic by modern critics, a precursor of the Theater of the Absurd, and a forewarner of Hitler-like aberrations and Red Chinese power, Stanislaw Witkiewicz defies categorization. At times parodying Shakespeare, Ibsen, Chekhov, Stendhal, or Strindberg, Witkacy combines the wit and urbanity of an Oscar Wilde with the dramatic sensitivity and the sense of the absurd of a Samuel Beckett, the artistic perception of unity in fragmentation of a Picasso with the Renaissance conception of individual discord, disintegration, lunacy, and crisis as microcosmic reflections of the world at large. In both novels and plays he paints horrifying images of anti-utopias, characterized by exploding violence, the destruction of the individual, and the emergence of a totalitarian state of insect-like automatons. These mechanized men in mass are summed up most graphically in "the mobile yellow wall," a solid block of completely depersonalized Chinese soldiers who encircle Poland in *Insatiability.* The way "They" destroy art, language, creativity, and individuality, and harness man's sexual energies to produce a neutral social machine, bland, boring, and bogged down in mindless bureaucratic red tape and senseless cruelty, is Orwellian in conception. So too is his emphasis on fear tactics and collective madness. He envisions the destruction of contemporary civilization by mechanization and egalitarian levelling, with clone-like technocrats the wave of the future, a "dusk of mechanized grayness," not physical dissolution only but psychological too. The title of one of his plays destroyed during World War II sums up his final vision: *The End of the World.*

In a childhood play, "Cockroaches," a preview of his adult concerns, an army of identical gray insects from America invades a city, while in "The Cuttlefish," a Renaissance pope, a modern artist, and a potential dictator debate ethical, political, and artistic relativity. In "The Mother," the individuals are bloodsuckers, ultimately trapped in a room with no exits, dominated by a giant tube used by the mechanized workers of the State to suck out life. In "The Crazy Locomotive," set against a hurtling cinematic backdrop, the machine that will supposedly carry man to higher knowledge ends up in a headlong collision, death, and a pile of human and mechanical debris with "no help possible." They suggests a vast conspiracy, a dread and secret menace that bans art and crushes artists. In "The Madman and the Nun" the authorities, represented by a Freudian psychologist, imprison the artist, imposing physical and psychological restraints on his humanity, but at the end are forced to question their own sanity and the sanity of all systems which limit the individual. "The Water Hen" ends in revolution, with grenades exploding, heaps of corpses in the street, advocates of community property "banging away in fine style," and thinking man resigned to his fate, playing out a card hand amid chaos, the final call a "Pass." "The Shoemakers" envisions revolution after revolution—capitalism overturned by a fascist coup followed by a worker's rebellion in turn overthrown by nameless, identical technocrats who annihilate freedom and uniqueness and make boredom the ultimate reality.

Like his plays, Witkacy's novels are a kaleidoscopic mixture of the erotic, the philosophical, and the apocalyptic. They follow the adventures and musings of an artist who struggles against domination, but who ultimately fails, partly due to his own weakness, partly due to the disintegration of society around him, partly due to historical inevitability. "Farewell to Autumn," set in an unspecified future world, concentrates on a period of change, with metaphorical winter coming, an old regime failing, and "the amorphous anthill" dominating. As a bourgeois democratic revolution is followed by the reign of "Levellers," the artist hero seeks escape in cocaine and sex and faraway places, but finally succumbs to the horror of the new system: petty regimentation, a drab daily routine, and futile, fatal boredom. In a number of his works, Witkacy focuses on the debilitating power of drugs that paralyze those individuals who might have stood against the State. In "Sluts and Butterflies" he portrays whites, in the face of the vitality of primitives, resorting to pills as substitutes for real feelings; "Mother" includes a cocaine party, a sign of social decadence and a refusal to face facts; *Insatiability* predicts the Chinese use of a very special pill (and accompanying mystic pseudo-philosophy) to pacify and lull the European enemy populace, and thereby to effect the takeover of Russia and then Poland. Witkacy's most famous novel, *Insatiability* is a black comedy of chaos and loss, with the hero seeking personal identity in a world where identity is slowly but definitely being annihilated. The government has become a sport, news reporting false, women dominant, sexuality absurd, madness the norm. The Chinese, "flawless, fearless machines," threaten Poland and all of Western culture, first with painless palliatives, then with the possibility of crossbreeding to produce an Oriental-Occidental hybrid that is totally deindividualized. In this work, as is true throughout Witkacy's canon, sexual perversions, emasculated males and destructive, insatiable females are harbingers of totalitarian sterility, and images of the insect world sum up collective society. At their victory banquet the Chinese serve rats' tails in a bedbug sauce; Witkacy's childhood nightmare is realized; the world is in chains, and lunacy prevails. The fate of the individual and of society follow parallel courses; decapitation of victors and victims occurs after the human mind has already become extinct.

Witkacy's tone is mocking, irreverent, ironic. He depicts man baffled by an inexplicable universe, waging a hopeless battle for identity and control. Images of imprisonment, restraint, confinement are played off against those of stifled creativity. His characters are oversexed misfits, the lunatic fringe (the bastions of sanity in a world gone mad)—neurotic artists, criminals, demonic women, and mathematical geniuses, indulging in self-gratification, seeking thrills and oblivion, but sometimes making a last frenzied stand before being engulfed by historical inevitability. His works are full of fake deaths and resurrected corpses, as fantasy and psychological realism meet in a symbolic, metaphorical world of the grotesque. His style is an incredibly varied hodgepodge of forms: a new language of insults and obscenities, allusions, puns, jokes in mock Russian, parody, polemic, digression, political and philosophical argument, buffoonery, free-for-alls, cabaret routines, accelerated and decelerated tempos, anti-climaxes, sight gags, masks, and disclosures and exposures; although the triple puns, multiple connotations, and amazing manipulation of sound and meaning are lost in translation, his style remains impressively versatile. His future includes a Ministry of the Mechanization of Culture, a Department of Metaphysical Absurdity, a Commissariat of Sexual Nonsense, a Council for the production of Handmade Crap, and an organization of Vigilant Youth. Characters split in two, corpses prove dummies or return unscathed, the aging process is eliminated, and time and space are confused.

His works are not science fiction as we generally envision it; but they are science fiction in the sense of fantastic creations that project political worlds that could well (and in some cases did) evolve in the very near future.

—Gina Macdonald

WODHAMS, Jack

Pseudonym: Trudy Rose. **Nationality:** Australian. **Born:** Dagenham, Essex, England, 3 September 1931; immigrated to Australia in 1955. **Career:** Has worked as a weighing-machine mechanic, brush salesman, a porter in mental hospital, taxi and truck driver, bartender, welder, and magician's assistant. Currently mailvan driver, Brisbane. Guest of Honor, Melbourne Science Fiction Convention, 1968. **Address:** P.O. Box 48, Caboolture, Queensland 4510, Australia.

SCIENCE FICTION PUBLICATIONS

Novels

The Authentic Touch. New York, Curtis, 1971.
Looking for Blücher. St. Kilda, Victoria, Void, 1980.
Ryn. St. Kilda, Victoria, Cory and Collins, 1982.

Short Stories

Future War. St. Kilda, Victoria, Cory and Collins, 1982.

*

Jack Wodhams comments:

Why do I write SF? I write SF because it is a genre that isn't a genre. Someone selecting a romance can anticipate heartthrob; a western a shootout; a whodunnit clues to a killer. SF abides by no such predictable format. SF permits its writer to explore where that writer will, be it *20,000 Leagues under the Sea,* or what it would be like to be an Invisible Man, or how it might feel to voyage in space, to discover other worlds, to encounter other sentient beings.

Past, present, future. Techniques, methods, inventions, laws, societies, ways of life. To a high degree an SF writer may declare the rules of the tale she or he would unfold. When a reader picks up a collection of SF short stories, it is with the certain knowledge that no two will match in time, place, or circumstance. Each will carry its own distinct thought, idea, aspect, that cannot beforehand be preemptively presumed.

SF is simply the most interesting, beguiling, stimulating literature to exercise the mind. It certainly provides grand exercise for the mind of a writer.

*   *   *

It is well known that science fiction generally tends to emphasise content at the expense of style, but it is not always appreciated that this has had a positive influence on narrative techniques. Writers have been encouraged to develop different methods, better adapted to its needs than established storytelling procedures. Wodhams is one such writer. The way his stories are constructed would not be necessary and would not have evolved in traditional short story writing.

Smooth, effortless, controlled, a typical Wodhams story moves irresistibly ahead, carried mostly by dialog with a minimum of description and explanation. (True, sometimes the author intrudes to fill in background or state principles when it is called for: thus "Station 2152" begins with three pages of historic introduction.) There may be a single firm viewpoint or a focus of action, but more often there are frequent scene changes as the action unfolds through related events. Minor characters tend to be cyphers, no more than voices overheard by which we know what is going on, their feelings and motivations irrelevant—one of the common naive objections often raised to science fiction—but this is not to be seen as a fault. The effect at its best is of the story happening, not being reported. It has much in common with film scripting but it emerged naturally in science fiction as the field matured and a sophisticated readership developed.

Wodhams's stories usually grow out of and are motivated by an original scientific premise, or take a sceptical closer look at a familiar speculation, reevaluating the chances. They may bring out new objections or difficulties or turn a familiar argument around. Thus "Roadbreakers" sees a time when road transport is obsolete and conflicting interests compete to redevelop now useless highways. "The Token Pole" imagines the reduction of forests reversed, world climate changing with too high rainfall, deserts being seen as a threatened resource.

Some are in the venerable Dangerous Invention tradition. Thus "Stormy Bellwether" disturbingly sets out the bad news about person-to-person television. "The Fugelman of Recall" has criminal exploitation of a memory recording and transfer process. "The Empty Balloon" looks at a mindreading equivalent working on subvocalised verbal thinking, an uncomfortable possibility, with a spy plot. In "Androtomy and the Scion" a cloned duplicate brain, in rapport with the original, gives new powers for coercion to ever-present authority. "Split Personality" has an even more macabre atrocity, an expendable felon dissected into living right and left halves remaining in mental communication and used for interstellar communication.

Many other stories show some of the social implications of new technology, especially its use for oppression by the state or for private antisocial acts. Thus "Whosawatsa" explores the utter ruin of traditional assumptions, conventions, and legal structure implicit in human gender reversal. Its impact in areas like adultery, divorce, inheritance, custody is given a brisk once-over. "The Form Master" brings out the negative side of the coming world data bank, its use for fraud by selective use of false input. In "Sprog" the inventor of a system of predicting future events cannot get a hearing and resorts to exploiting the gullible as an ordinary fortune-teller. In "The Cure-All Merchant" behavior modification drugs have been refined into effective specifics for all common problems. But a practitioner treats patients just as well by suggestion.

One group of stories looks at hazards and misuses of matter-transmission devices. "There is a Crooked Man" shows future crime and detection in action. In "Wrong Rabbit" communication is accidentally opened with another world. "Top Billing" looks at what happens if people can be duplicated as well as transmitted. "Hey but no Presto" shows a future form of hijacking.

Among the stories of the interstellar future "Starhunger" stands out as an excellent look at the need to reach the stars, the drive for habitable new worlds, and the danger of failure. "Mostly Meantime" shows an age of interstellar relations of many worlds, but restricted as we ought to assume by the limiting velocity so that communication is a long term matter.

"Picaper" is a reprise of the hardboiled private eye story in the context of advanced technology: a culture where, for instance, automation of road traffic eliminates the human driver, where security systems should be impenetrable and privacy scarcely exists so that no antisocial act should be undetected . . . yet new opportunities will appear for crime, here impersonation by electronic simulation.

Some stories illuminate the picture of future war at the footslogger level common in the cruder kind of science fiction. Thus in "Pet" the dehumanised eunuch soldier, a mere robot killer to the command, keeps a civilian captive as his own property and is ultimately led to desert and join the human race.

Wodhams's booklength works, less successful, are written with much the same techniques. *Ryn,* really outside our sphere with its supernatural theme of a form of reincarnation, has the viewpoint character's consciousness inexplicably located in an infant and vainly attempting somehow to get some control of the situation.

In *Looking for Blücher* no real background rationale is given but the central character (an astronaut isolated in space? An experimental subject?), using a device to let him experience hallucinatory adventures, finds his fantasy worlds invaded by independent actors, a nuisance and then a danger. Observers are led to intervene leading to successive disasters in various fantasy environments. An amusing book, full of uncharacteristic wordplay, and the constant slippage between first and third person as the dreamer deals with his other persona is an unusual element. But none of the principals could be judged rational, and when anything can happen there is little to sustain interest.

The Authentic Touch is better. It does call for a lot of assumptions: there is a peaceful, affluent future world, to begin with, implying the solution of many obvious problems not mentioned; and cheap instant interstellar transit is available. But these basics are

conventionally allowed. In this context there is a thriving tourist industry, and an earthlike planet is used to establish not the usual kind of resorts but simulations of selected past eras, from imperial Rome to early 20th-century Europe.

Visitors participate, living and working like ordinary people in one of these societies in a radical change from their normal lives. Naturally nothing ever works quite as planned: the different cultures are not fully isolated so there can be contacts damaging to the illusion, and ultimately a puppet monarch can take his role seriously and start a war. But apart from that, on the personal level a number of tourists have unexpected changes of scene, and following their fortunes keeps up the pace.

Wodhams does not care to discuss his work. "I rather fancy that I scribble mainly because I have the talent," he commented; "I write because I can, just as a man who can play the piano will play the piano because he can play the piano."

—Graham Stone

WOLF, Gary K.

Nationality: American. **Born:** Berwyn, Illinois, 24 January 1941. **Education:** University of Illinois, Urbana, B.S. 1963. M.S. 1969. **Military Service:** Served in the United States Air Force, in Vietnam, 1963-69: Major. **Career:** Vice-president and creative director, Crosson Austin Wolf, advertising and public relations, Amherst, New Hampshire. President, Cry Wolf! Inc., writing consultants, Harvard, Massachusetts. **Agent:** William Reiss, John Hawkins and Associates, 71 West 23rd Street, Suite 1600, New York, New York 10010. **Address:** c/o Cry Wolf! Inc., Box 436, Harvard, Massachusetts 01451, U.S.A.

SCIENCE FICTION PUBLICATIONS

Novels (series: Roger Rabbit)

Killerbowl. Garden City, New York, Doubleday, 1975; London, Sphere, 1976.
A Generation Removed. Garden City, New York, Doubleday, 1977.
The Resurrectionist. Garden City, New York, Doubleday, 1979.

OTHER PUBLICATIONS

Novels

Who Censored Roger Rabbit? New York, St. Martin's Press, 1981.
Who P-P-P-Plugged Roger Rabbit? New York, Villard, 1991.

*   *   *

Gary K. Wolf is primarily known as the author of *Who Censored Roger Rabbit?,* the hilarious hardboiled detective pastiche that was the source for the enormously successful fantasy motion picture *Who Framed Roger Rabbit?* (1988). The Touchstone film, which was produced by Steven Spielberg and directed by Robert Zemeckis, differs significantly from the original, but many of the movies' funniest bits come directly from the novel. Although not science fiction and thus beyond the scope of this essay, *Who Censored Roger Rabbit?* is far and away Wolf's best full-length work. Appearing in 1981, it was also, for a decade at least, the author's first step away from science fiction as no other genre fiction has appeared under his name since. In 1991, Wolf finished a sequel, entitled *Who P-P-P-Plugged Roger Rabbit?*

Wolf began his genre-writing career in the early 1970s as the author of a number of serious and often experimental short stories, several of which appeared in Damon Knight's highly regarded *Orbit* original anthology series. His first published SF work, "Love Story," opens with a marriage ceremony, during which the couple involved are required to relive briefly their pasts. Their civilization at first seems typically dystopian—conception occurs artificially, each fetus is properly programmed, children are raised in state facilities—yet Wolf cleverly reverses the situation, making it clear that the children are both well cared for and happy. We briefly tour a culture where there is no excess population, where everyone is content and virtually immortal. Our protagonists grow to adulthood, fall in love, and live together. Eventually they decide to have children and, their twin babies born artificially, they prepare for marriage. "Love Story" ends with a jolt. The priest at the ceremony hands them each a wafer. Eucharist-like, symbolic of their love, poisoned. They give up immortality to provide space for their babies.

"Dissolve" argues that television, because of its documentary-like quality and its oversimplification of moral problems, is drastically distorting our view of reality. The story jumps montage-like between a TV talk-show discussion of the problem, a number of typical television programs, and a young couple living in a bombed-out TV studio after an atomic war. The girl is dying from radiation sickness, but the boy, immersed in the simplistic television mind set, seems to think that he can save her by making a video-tape in which she is cured. A grim story, it is very effective and even more believable today than it was in 1973. Equally powerful is "The Bridge Builder," a gripping story set in a world where the main transportation system is the Bridge, a matter transmitter. The protagonist builds bridges, repairs them, and is, in fact, fatally addicted to their use.

In "Therapy" Wolf began to show the talent for madcap humor that was to blossom in *Who Censored Roger Rabbit?* "Therapy" is a slight, funny piece about a computer marriage counselor, one of its less successful cases, and a robot elevator that thinks it's the computer's mother. "Slammer" and "Dr. Rivet and Supercon Sal" are both wildly comic tales reminiscent of Ron Goulart. The first concerns a prissy momma's boy who, mistakenly arrested for breaking into his own car and interred in a city reserved entirely for criminals, decides to stay there and become one. The second details the adventures of two shysters out to make a fast buck. He's a failure with people, but can do anything with machines. She's just the reverse. Their partner in crime is a rogue robot kitchenette. The story ends with one of the most hilarious chase scenes in recent fiction.

Wolf's science fiction novels, as a rule, are not of the same quality as his short fiction. *Killerbowl,* the best of them, is set in the world of street football, a cross between our current sport and guerilla warfare. The playing field covers several square city blocks, knives, clubs, and rifles are routinely issued, and the millions of fans keep statistics not only on touchdowns but also on kills. T.R. Mann, a veteran quarterback, has been marked for assassination because he isn't bloody enough. The novel is effective, but seems

derivative of William Harrison's well-known story "Roller Ball Murder" (1973). Less successful are *A Generation Removed,* which involves a near-future American where only those under 20 can hold political office and where those over 55 are "euthed," and *The Resurrectionist,* which details the adventures of a Bridge (see "The Bridge Builder") who must rescue a defector lost in the lines during transmission. Both novels suffer from weaknesses of plot, characterization, and style. All three books involve basically the same character motivation: a competent, middle-aged protagonist, while working for the System, discovers it to be corrupt and, finding himself in jeopardy, sets out vigilante-style to destroy it.

Wolf is a talented but uneven writer who has produced his best science fiction at the shorter lengths, most notably in such slightly experimental stories as "Dissolve" and "The Bridge Builder," and in the broad comedy of "Slammer" and "Dr. Rivet." Wolf's talent for broad, often slapstick humor has best shown itself in *Who Censored Roger Rabbit?*

—Michael M. Levy

WOLFE, Bernard

Nationality: American. **Born:** New Haven, Connecticut, 28 September 1915. **Education:** Yale University, New Haven, 1931-36, B.A. 1935 (Phi Beta Kappa). **Family:** Married Dolores Michaels in 1964. **Career:** Taught at Bryn Mawr College, Pennsylvania, 1936; Trotsky's secretary, Mexico, 1937; served in the United States Merchant Marine, 1937-39; editor, *Mechanix Illustrated,* New York, 1944-45; ghostwriter for Billy Rose's syndicated column, "Pitching Horseshoes," 1947-50; taught creative writing, University of California, Los Angeles, 1966-68. Screenwriter, Universal-International Productions, and Tony Curtis Productions, Hollywood. **Died:** 27 October 1985.

SCIENCE FICTION PUBLICATIONS

Novel

Limbo. New York, Random House, 1952; abridged edition, as *Limbo '90,* London, Secker and Warburg, 1953.

OTHER PUBLICATIONS

Novels

Really the Blues, with Mezz Mezzrow. New York, Random House, 1946; London, Musicians Press, 1947.
The Late Risers: Their Masquerade. New York, Random House, 1954; London, Consul, 1962; as *Everything Happens at Night,* New York, New American Library, 1963.
In Deep. New York, Knopf, 1957; London, Secker and Warburg, 1958.
The Great Prince Died. New York, Scribner, and London, Cape, 1959; as *Trotsky Dead,* Los Angeles, Wollstonecraft, 1975.
The Magic of Their Singing. New York, Scribner, 1961.
Come On out, Daddy. New York, Scribner, 1963.

Memoirs of a Not Altogether Shy Pornographer. New York, Doubleday, 1972.
Logan's Gone. Los Angeles, Nash, 1974.
Lies. Los Angeles, Wollstonecraft, 1975.

Short Stories

Move Up, Dress Up, Drink Up, Burn Up. New York, Doubleday, 1968.

Plays

Television Plays: *Assassin!,* 1955; *The Ghost Writer,* 1955; *The Five Who Shook the Mighty,* 1956.

Other

Full Disclosure, edited by Annette Welles. Los Angeles, Wollstonecraft, 1975.
Julie: The Life and Times of John Garfield. Los Angeles, Wollstonecraft, 1976.

Translator, with Alice Backer, *The Plot,* by Egon Hostovsky. London, Cassell, 1961.

*

Critical Study: *Bernard Wolfe* by Carolyn Geduld, New York, Twayne, 1972.

* * *

A lifelong enemy of science fiction, to judge from his comments in Harlan Ellison's *Again, Dangerous Visions,* Bernard Wolfe wrote a few science fiction stories and a celebrated dystopian novel. The stories are tightly written, but *Limbo* is a masterpiece.

Zany, action-packed, *Limbo* is formally and conceptually complex and unremittingly analytical, both politically and psychologically. Most effectively of Wolfe's novels, it argues Dr. Edmund Bergler's acceptance of ambivalence opposition to "pseudo-aggression." Alongside Korzybskian semantics, cybernetics, and various technological fantasies (van Vogt is cited by name in the Afterword), Bergler's neo-Freudian theories are entertained in an entertaining manner. Besides its Dantesque associations, the novel's title signifies voluntary amputation, the absurdist idea for literal "disarmament" Dr. Martine left behind in a journal when he deserted World War III's automated carnage. Self-exiled among the relatively primitive Mandunji for 18 years, he has perfected their traditional cure for evil spirits, lobotomy. When civilization invades his island in 1990, Martine feels compelled to return to the mainland, where he finds the postwar "Inland Strip" and its great power rival, the "East Union," have taken his gallows humor seriously.

As in Plato's *Republic,* the state is the individual writ large; only Martine, as its unwitting begetter, can end this travesty, after he comes to know himself. Others are little more than extensions of him, for or against the prosthetic limbs that are more dangerous than their originals. Tom, son of his loins, is the ultimate pacifist, a basket case, and a spokesman for the Anti-Pros. Children of Martine's thought are his former colleague, now President Helder (hero) and the charismatic Theo (god) whose wartime amputation by Martine started the whole chain of ideas. Performing a social

lobotomy, Martine removes both party "heads," returning with Theo to his tropical island. There, his healthy native son, Rambo (for Arthur Rimbaud), is leading a similar revolution against singleminded solutions.

Not a prediction of 1990, *Limbo* is a metaphorical extension of a literal malaise, most dangerous among the technologically sophisticated whose dependence on their tools blinds them to their own responsibility. Self-amputation is no answer to the human dilemma, rather a symptom of it. This central absurdity is the most important of many estranging devices integrated into a thoroughly modernist novel; its vision of wholeness and balance is both its form and its substance. Wolfe does not simply arouse anxiety about the uncontrollable, or appease it with an appeal to contemplate the artwork. *Limbo* locates the trouble's source in the individual, whose recognition of the problem is the necessary first step toward its solution.

This therapy may not have worked for Wolfe, whose subsequent novels belabored Berglerian analysis without winning much of an audience. Nor has post-1952 American society been self-evidently more able to laugh at and accept its ambivalence. The book's acceptance in SF circles is marginal; reviewed at arm's length, it has often been ignored in historical studies of the genre. Though its direct influence is questionable, *Limbo* is still a harbinger of more stylish, sexy, complex novels to come. On its literary merits, *Limbo* is the "great American dystopia."

—David N. Samuelson

WOLFE, Gene (Rodman)

Nationality: American. **Born:** Brooklyn, New York, 7 May 1931. **Education:** Texas A and M University, College Station, 1949, 1952; University of Houston, B.S. 1956; Miami University. **Military Service:** Served in the United States Army, 1952-54. **Family:** Married Rosemary Frances Dietsch in 1956; two sons and two daughters. **Career:** Project engineer, Procter and Gamble, 1956-72; senior editor, *Plant Engineering,* Barrington, Illinois, 1972-84. **Awards:** Nebula award, 1973, 1982; Rhysling award, for verse, 1978; *Locus* award, 1982, 1987; World Fantasy award, 1982; British Science Fiction Association award, 1982; British Fantasy award, 1983; John W. Campbell Memorial award, 1984. **Agent:** Virginia Kidd, Box 278, Milford, Pennsylvania 18337. **Address:** P.O. Box 69, Barrington, Illinois 60010, U.S.A.

SCIENCE FICTION PUBLICATIONS

Novels (series: Book of the Long Sun; Book of the New Sun; Latro)

Operation ARES. New York, Berkley, 1970; London, Dobson, 1977.
The Shadow of the Torturer (New Sun). New York, Simon and Schuster, 1980; London, Arrow, 1986.
The Claw of the Conciliator (New Sun). New York, Timescape, 1981; London, Legend, 1991.
The Sword of the Lictor (New Sun). New York, Timescape, and London, Sidgwick and Jackson, 1982.
The Citadel of the Autarch (New Sun). New York, Timescape, and London, Sidgwick and Jackson, 1983.

Free Live Free. Willimantic, Connecticut, Ziesing, 1984; London, Gollancz, 1985.

Soldier of the Mist (Latro). New York, Tor, and London, Gollancz, 1986.

The Urth of the New Sun. London, Gollancz, and New York, Tor, 1987.

There Are Doors. New York, Tor, 1988; London, Gollancz, 1989.

Soldier of Arete (Latro). New York, Tor, 1989; London, New English Library, 1990.

Castleview. New York, Tor, 1990; London, New English Library, 1991.

Nightside the Long Sun. New York, Tor, and London, New English Library, 1993.

Lake of the Long Sun. New York, Tor, and London, New English Library, 1994.

Litany of the Long Sun (omnibus). New York, Guild America, 1994.

Caldé of the Long Sun. New York, Tor, and London, New English Library, 1994.

Short Stories

The Fifth Head of Cerberus. New York, Scribner, 1972.

The Island of Doctor Death and Other Stories and Other Stories. New York, Pocket Books, 1980.

Gene Wolfe's Book of Days. Garden City, New York, Doubleday, 1981; London, Arrow, 1985.

The Castle of the Otter. Willimantic, Connecticut, Ziesing, 1982.

The Wolfe Archipelago. Willimantic, Connecticut, Ziesing, 1983.

Bibliomen: Ten Characters Waiting for a Book. New Castle, Virginia, Cheap Street, 1984.

Plan[e]t Engineering. Cambridge, Massachusetts, NESFA Press, 1984.

The Boy Who Hooked the Sun (New Sun). New Castle, Virginia, Cheap Street, 1985.

Empires of Foliage and Flower (New Sun). New Castle, Virginia, Cheap Street, 1987.

The Arimaspian Legacy. New Castle, Virginia, Cheap Street, 1987.

Storeys from the Old Hotel. Worcester Park, Surrey, Kerosina, 1988; New York, Tor, 1992.

Endangered Species. Norwalk, Connecticut, Easton Press, 1989; London, Orbit, 1990.

Seven American Nights, bound with *Sailing to Byzantium,* by Robert Silverberg. New Yor, Tor, 1989.

Slow Children at Play. New Castle, Virginia, Cheap Street, 1989.

The Death of Doctor Island, bound with *Fugue State,* by John M. Ford. New York, Tor, 1990.

The Old Woman Whose Rolling Pin Is the Sun. New Castle, Virginia, Cheap Street, 1991.

The Hero as Werwolf. Eugene, Oregon, Pulphouse, 1991.

Young Wolfe: A Collection of Early Stories. Weston, Ontario, United Mythologies Press, 1992.

Castle of Days (includes *Gene Wolfe's Book of Days* and *The Castle of the Otter*). New York, Tor, 1992.

OTHER PUBLICATIONS

Novels

Peace. New York, Harper, 1975; London, Chatto and Windus, 1985.

The Devil in a Forest (for children). Chicago, Follett, 1976; London, Panther, 1985.

Pandora by Holly Hollander. New York, Tor, 1990.

Poetry

For Rosemary. Worcester Park, Surrey, Kerosina, 1988.

Other

Letters Home. Weston, Ontario, United Mythologies Press, 1991.

Gene Wolfe's Orbital Thoughts (quotations), edited by Rosemary Wolfe. Weston, Ontario, United Mythologies Press, 1992.

*

Bibliography: in *The Castle of the Otter,* 1982.

Manuscript Collection: Merril Collection, Toronto Public Library, Canada.

Gene Wolfe comments:

I am frequently called an *Orbit* writer, by which the callers appear to mean an obscurantist. I do not feel the term is justified. I try to bring pleasure to my readers on more than one level; but that, I think, is a characteristic of virtually all good fiction. I avoid private symbolism, and usually provide more than enough clues for such small puzzles as I set. If I show a man lying when it is to his advantage to lie, I assume that my reader is intelligent enough to see that the man in question is a liar—and so on.

My heroes are often boys or young men trying to find a place in the world (Tacky Babcock in "The Island of Doctor Death and Other Stories," Mark in *The Devil in a Forest,* Number Five in *The Fifth Head of Cerberus* and so on); perhaps despite a conscious conviction to the contrary, I feel that the most adventurous years are between 10 and 30. But I have written about old women too, and young ones, aliens, and middle-aged men. Recently I wrote a story—"The War beneath the Tree"—in which the chief character was an automated teddy bear.

I think I am still at least as much a reader as a writer. I like Proust, Chesterton, Dickens (I've done a Dickens story: "Our Neighbor by David Copperfield"), Washington Irving, Lewis Carroll (not just *Alice*), Kipling, Maugham, Wells, John Fowles, R.A. Lafferty, Ursula K. Le Guin, Kate Wilhelm, Jorge Luis Borges, Tolkien, and C.S. Lewis. If you like half or more of those writers (for example, Maugham as far as the 'h') you should probably try me. Trembling, I throw myself on the mercy of the court.

*   *   *

Launched by space opera and comic books, as so many science fiction writers have been, Gene Wolfe adds myth, history, religion, and literary allusions from Dickens to Borges to the fuel which propels his fiction. The result is speculative fiction of the highest literary octane. Best known for his *Book of the New Sun,* a five-volume masterwork, he also excels at the novella, and has a long bibliography of fine novels and short stories. His most important novels are *Peace* (1975), the five-volume *The Book of the New Sun* (1980-87), the two-volume *Soldier of the Mist* series (1986 and 1989), and the still-unfolding *The Book of the Long Sun* (1993-). Equally important are his novellas. These include the three-novella cycle *The Fifth Head of Cerberus* (1972); another three-novella cycle beginning with "The Island of Doctor Death and Other Stories" (1970-78), "Tracking Song" (1975), and "Seven American Nights" (1978), all collected in *The Island of Doctor Death and Other Stories and Other Stories;* "The Detective of Dreams" (1980), collected in *Endangered Species,* and "The Haunted Boarding House" (1990) and "The Sailor Who Sailed after the Sun" (1992), uncollected. Among his major short stories are "The Hero as Werwolf" (1975), "Feather Tigers" (1973), and "The Toy Theatre" (1971), collected in *The Island of Doctor Death and Other Stories and Other Stories* (1980), "The Last Thrilling Wonder Story" (1982) and "Parkroads—A Review" (1987), collected in *Endangered Species.* These works represent the finest of a very fine ouevre.

Wolfe's fictions are characterized by complexity and ambiguity, and by their meticulously crafted and luminously metaphorical prose style. Lonely or disturbed children, settings of great antiquity or futurity, alien or inverted myths and legends, and nonhuman sentient beings appear repeatedly as motifs in Wolfe's fiction to illustrate his recurring themes of isolation, memory, faith, and the search for self and human identity.

His central technique is the limited viewpoint, used to illustrate and develop all his stylistic and thematic elements. Most typically, Wolfe employs a first-person narrator who cannot escape the limitations of his subjective vision. Perhaps this narrator has the perfect memory of Severian in *The Book of the New Sun* or the short-term-only memory of the narrator of *The Soldier of the Mist.* Perhaps he is insane ("Fifth Head of Cerberus") or limited by his culture ("Tracking Song"). Because the narrator is always unreliable, his story is always ambiguous, and the reality he perceives is peculiar only to his own consciousness.

But Wolfe typically multiplies the ambiguities by framing his narrators. For instance, Severian's huge saga of "a summer more than normally turbulent" (*Citadel* 308) has been translated, according to the appendix to *Shadow of the Torturer,* from "a tongue that has not yet achieved existence." What we read has been filtered not only by Severian's consciousness, but by a translator's. "Seven American Nights" comprises a diary written by an unreliable narrator, enclosed in a frame which suggests that the diary may be a partial or complete forgery. *Peace* uses stories within stories within stories: for example, the novel's narrator relates a childhood memory of a story his housekeeper heard from an Irish maid, and through each change in narrator the stories themselves must surely change. *Peace,* although not science fiction, and probably not fantasy, is typical of Wolfe's writing as a whole. Its plot structure is that of a meditation, either by a dead man as his life passes before his eyes (the more common interpretation), or of a middle-aged man in response to the Thematic Apperception Test (the interpretation I prefer). The novel is a collection of its narrator's most emotionally powerful memories and these evocative memories reveal the core of his emotional being. As Wolfe weaves this novel, he uses his unreliable narrator and framing devices to give memory the ambiguous and metaphorical texture which is its nature, as he shows an isolated man searching for self-definition, holding the reader's attention through his beautiful language and character development, as well as through the fascinating stories his narrator tells.

Gene Wolfe's greatest literary accomplishment thus far is his monumental five-volume *The Book of the New Sun,* consisting of: *The Shadow of the Torturer* (1980), *The Claw of the Conciliator* (1981), *The Sword of the Lictor* (1981), *The Citadel of the Autarch* (1982), and *The Urth of the New Sun* (1987). These volumes follow the fortunes of Severian, a young man who forgets nothing, exiled from the Torturers' Guild, but given a powerful sword and a book that contains the secrets of life. He finds a miraculous gem and goes on a quest to return it to its rightful owners. He has many adventures along the way, is made king, travels far beyond the Urth, and returns with a new sun to save humankind.

Using a number of repeated motifs—of mazes, giantism, gates, caves, roses, claws, cannibalism, and suns, to name the most common—Wolfe transforms his coming-of-age story, quest story, and save-the-world story into a densely imagined work of Christian symbolism in the tradition of C.S. Lewis. Severian himself is a Christ figure: he raises the dead, is raised from the dead himself, and brings salvation, in the form of a new sun to replace the dying one. A torturer seems an unlikely Christ figure, but only by understanding sin can he take on the sins of the world, only by understanding death and evil can he understand eternal life and goodness. The novel's science fictional speculations about time ultimately gloss Christian themes of neo-Platonism and Boethian precognition with free will.

What makes this series great is neither its exciting questing and testing story, nor its complex symbolism, but that it combines both so seamlessly, using intriguing science fictional speculations about genetic engineering and time travel, rich characterization, vivid settings, and fine prose style to do so.

As vast as *The Book of the New Sun* is, it may be seen as part of an even larger entity. Wolfe's next project was an historical fantasy series about an Ancient Roman soldier, brain damaged in fighting the Greeks. Latro or Lucius suffers two lasting effects from his injury: he loses his long-term memory, retaining only 24 hours at a time, and he sees gods and goddesses where others cannot. He copes with both effects by writing about them each day before he can forget it, but without any memory of the day before. The two novels in the series are *Soldier of the Mist* and *Soldier of Arete,* but they end with even less closure than is typical of Wolfe, suggesting that more volumes were planned. As John Clute points out in *The Encyclopedia of Science Fiction,* this series is a mirror image of *The Book of the New Sun.* It takes place in the distant past rather than the distant future, and its narrator has, instead of a prodigious memory, very little memory at all. Where total recall gives *The Book of the New Sun* a baroque style in which everything seems connected, amnesia lends the Latro novels disjointedness and an appropriate classical spareness. Such a disjointed, fragmentary narrative is as difficult for a reader as, for instance, the disjointed viewpoint of the idiot in Faulkner's *Sound and the Fury* (though just as valid), suggesting why the series didn't sell as well as *The Book of the New Sun.* The opposites of the Latro books develop parallel themes, however, of neo-Platonic Christianity and the piercing through from mundane reality into a higher spiritual plane.

We see this theme again in *The Book of the Long Sun,* which shares more than a similar title. This series, still unfolding, so far comprises *Nightside the Long Sun* (1993), *Lake of the Long Sun* (1994), and *Caldé of the Long Sun* (1994), with a fourth, and possibly final, volume, *Exodus from the Long Sun.* The *New Sun* volumes follow the quest of Patera Silk, a young priest impelled by a visionary moment of enlightenment to save his parish church or manteion from Blood, the man who has bought it. All action takes place on a generation ship, the Whorl. This series takes place in the same universe as *The Book of the New Sun* and there are a number of parallels between the series. Silk, savior as thief, shares much with Severian, savior as torturer. They also share an atmosphere both antique and futuristic. As in *The Book of the New Sun,* Silk and his people have a medieval approach to religion, in that they see the world as a vast metaphor for the greater reality of their faith. Again, as in the other series, the spiritual plane is the most important one. Indeed, the three series form a vast literary structure suitable to the vastness of their themes.

The Fifth Head of Cerberus shows Wolfe's command of story, symbol, speculation, character, setting and style on a smaller stage. This three-novella cycle grew from the title novella, and is published with two connected novellas, "'A Story,' by John V. Marsch" and "V.R.T.," in book form. The novellas share two common worlds, Sainte Croix and Sainte Anne; a common character, John V. Marsch; and common themes of humanity, identity, and memory. The first, "The Fifth Head of Cerberus," is the coming of age of a young man, a clone in a city of clones on the world of Sainte Croix, stagnating in a cultural and genetic backwater. "'A Story,' by John V. Marsch" is a myth about Sainte Croix's sister planet, Sainte Anne, about a twin in a world of shape-changers. "V.R.T." is a collection of documents tracing Marsch's anthropological tour and possible transformation on Sainte Anne and his subsequent imprisonment on Sainte Croix.

The novellas use their science-fictional speculations about cloning, aliens, and shape changing to raise many questions: to what extent do memory, genetic variation, and experience determine humanity and identity? What are the limits of humanity and what are humanity's responsibilities to other species? Can one person or culture ever really understand another? Can we ever truly determine the difference between perception and reality? While none of these questions can be answered, Wolfe uses three storytelling styles and three perspectives to show how complex and important these questions are. The first novella is a formal narrative and a reflective memoir of an historical past, the second a reconstruction of a cultural artifact, occurring in mythic dreamtime, and the third a collection of documents written in the present moment of recorded conversation and the journalistic immediate past.

The richness of style, content, and theme present in *The Book of the New Sun* and *The Fifth Head of Cerberus*, Wolfe's best known and most reprinted works, is present in all his writing, including works considered as minor, if only in comparison to the works named above. Gene Wolfe's fiction demands concentration, intelligence, and an ability to relish ambiguity to give up its rewards, but those rewards are always worth the effort. Further, there is every indication that his work is only getting better as his remarkable career continues.

—Joan Gordon

WOLLHEIM, Donald A(llen)

Pseudonym: David Grinnell. **Nationality:** American. **Born:** New York City, 1 October 1914. **Education:** New York University, B.A. **Family:** Married Elsie Balter in 1943; one daughter. **Career:** Editor, *Stirring Science Stories*, 1941-42, *Cosmic Stories*, 1941, *Out of This World Adventures*, 1950, *10 Story Fantasy*, 1951; editor, Avon Books, 1947-52, and Ace Books, 1952-67; editorial consultant, *Saturn*, 1957-58. Publisher and editor, DAW Books, from 1971. **Awards:** Hugo award, for editing, 1964, and Special award, 1975; 33rd World Science Fiction Convention award, 1975; World Fantasy award, 1981; British Fantasy award, 1984. **Died:** 2 November 1990.

SCIENCE FICTION PUBLICATIONS

Novels (for children: series: Mike Mars)

The Secret of Saturn's Rings. Philadelphia, Winston, 1954.
The Secret of the Martian Moons. Philadelphia, Winston, 1955.
One against the Moon. Cleveland, World, 1956.
The Secret of the Ninth Planet. Philadelphia, Winston, 1959.
Mike Mars:
    Mike Mars, Astronaut. Garden City, New York, Doubleday, 1961.
    Mike Mars Flies the X-15. Garden City, New York, Doubleday, 1961.
    Mike Mars at Cape Canaveral. Garden City, New York, Doubleday, 1961; as *Mike Mars at Cape Kennedy,* New York, Paperback Library, 1966.
    Mike Mars in Orbit. Garden City, New York, Doubleday, 1961.
    Mike Mars Flies the Dyna-Soar. Garden City, New York, Doubleday, 1962.
    Mike Mars, South Pole Spaceman. Garden City, New York, Doubleday, 1962.
    Mike Mars and the Mystery Satellite. Garden City, New York, Doubleday, 1963.
    Mike Mars around the Moon. Garden City, New York, Doubleday, 1964.

Novels as David Grinnell (series: Ajax Calkins)

Across Time. New York, Avalon, 1957.
Edge of Time. New York, Avalon, 1958.
The Martian Missile. New York, Avalon, 1959.
Destiny's Orbit (Calkins). New York, Avalon, 1961.
Destination: Saturn (Calkins), with Lin Carter. New York, Avalon, 1967.
To Venus! To Venus!. New York, Ace, 1970.

Short Stories

Two Dozen Dragon Eggs. Reseda, California, Powell, 1969; London, Dobson, 1977.
The Men from Ariel. Cambridge, Massachusetts, NESFA Press, 1982.

OTHER PUBLICATIONS

Other

Lee de Forest: Advancing the Electronic Age (for children). Chicago, Encyclopaedia Britannica Press, 1962.
The Universe Makers: Science Fiction Today. New York, Harper, 1971; London, Gollancz, 1972.
Up There and Other Strange Directions. Cambridge, Massachusetts, NESFA, 1988.

Editor, *The Pocket Book of Science-Fiction.* New York, Pocket Books, 1943.
Editor, *Portable Tales of Science.* New York, Viking Press, 1945.
Editor, *Avon Bedside Companion: A Treasury of Tales for the Sophisticated.* New York, Avon, 1947.
Editor, *Avon Detective Mysteries 3.* New York, Avon, 1947.
Editor, *Avon Fantasy Reader 1-18.* New York, Avon, 18 vols., 1947-52; selections edited with George Ernsberger published as *The Avon Fantasy Reader* [and *2nd Reader*], 2 vols., 1969.

Editor, *Avon Western Reader 3-4*. New York, Avon, 2 vols., 1947.

Editor, *Where the Girls Were Different and Other Stories,* by Erskine Caldwell. New York, Avon, 1948.

Editor, *Yesterday's Love and Eleven Other Stories,* by James T. Farrell. New York, Avon, 1948.

Editor, *Yvette and Other Stories,* by Guy de Maupassant. New York, Avon, 1949.

Editor, *Avon Book of New Stories of the Great Wild West.* New York, Avon, 1949.

Editor, *The Fox Woman and Other Stories,* by A. Merritt. New York, Avon, 1949.

Editor, *The Girl with the Hungry Eyes and Other Stories.* New York, Avon, 1949.

Editor, *A Hell of a Good Time and Other Stories,* by James T. Farrell. New York, Avon, 1950.

Editor, *The Avon All-American Fiction Reader.* New York, Avon, 1951.

Editor, *Avon Science Fiction Reader 1-3.* New York, Avon, 3 vols., 1951-52.

Editor, *Flight into Space.* New York, Fell, 1950; London, Cherry Tree, 1951.

Editor, *Every Boy's Book of Science-Fiction.* New York, Fell, 1951.

Editor, *Giant Mystery Reader.* New York, Avon, 1951.

Editor, *Hollywood Bedside Reader.* New York, Avon, 1951.

Editor, *Let's Go Naked.* New York, Pyramid, 1952.

Editor, *Prize Science Fiction.* New York, McBride, 1953; as *Prize Stories of Space and Time,* London, Weidenfeld and Nicolson, 1953.

Editor, *Adventures in the Far Future.* New York, Ace, 1954.

Editor, *Tales of Outer Space.* New York, Ace, 1954.

Editor, *The Ultimate Invader and Other Science-Fiction: Stories from the Four Corners of Time.* New York, Ace, 1954.

Editor, *Adventures on Other Planets.* New York, Ace, 1955.

Editor, *Terror in the Modern Vein.* New York, Hanover House, 1955; abridged edition, as *Terror [and More Terror] in the Modern Vein,* London, Digit, 2 vols., 1961.

Editor, *The End of the World.* New York, Ace, 1956.

Editor, *The Earth in Peril.* New York, Ace, 1957.

Editor, *Men on the Moon.* New York, Ace, 1958.

Editor, *The Hidden Planet: Science-Fiction Adventures on Venus.* New York, Ace, 1959.

Editor, *The Macabre Reader.* New York, Ace, 1959; London, Digit, 1960.

Editor, *More Macabre.* New York, Ace, 1961.

Editor, *More Adventures on Other Planets.* New York, Ace, 1963.

Editor, *Swordsmen in the Sky.* New York, Ace, 1964.

Editor, with Terry Carr, *World's Best Science Fiction 1965* [to *1971*]. New York, Ace, 1965-71; 1968 to 1971 vols. published London, Gollancz, 4 vols., 1969-71; first 4 vols. published as *World's Best Science Fiction: First* [to *Fourth*] Series, Ace, 1970.

Editor, *Operation Phantasy: The Best from the Phantagraph.* Rego Park, New York, Phantagraph Press, 1967.

Editor, *A Quintet of Sixes.* New York, Ace, 1969.

Editor, *Ace Science Fiction Reader.* New York, Ace, 1971; as *Trilogy of the Future,* London, Sidgwick and Jackson, 1972.

Editor, with Arthur W. Saha, *The 1972* [to *1990*] *Annual World's Best SF.* New York, DAW, 19 vols., 1972-90; first 8 vols. published as *Wollheim's World's Best SF 1-8,* 8 vols., 1977-85; 1974-75 vols. published as *The World's Best Short Stories 1-2,* Morley, Yorkshire, Elmfield Press, 1975-76; *World's Best SF 4-6,* London, Dobson, 3 vols., 1979-81.

Editor, *The Best from the Rest of the World: European Science Fiction.* Garden City, New York, Doubleday, 1976.

Editor, The DAW Science Fiction Reader. New York, DAW, 1976.

Editor, Fanciful Tales of Time and Space, Fall 1936. West Warwick, Rhode Island, Marc A. Michaud, 1977.

*

Manuscript Collections: Syracuse University, New York; University of Wyoming, Laramie (includes correspondence).

*   *   *

Although Donald A. Wollheim made his first sale while still in his teens ("The Man from Ariel," *Wonder Stories,* January 1934) and wrote about 20 volumes of science fiction, his greatest impact on SF has been in capacities other than that of author. Wollheim was one of the pioneering fan publishers in the 1930s, founded the influential Fantasy Amateur Press Association (which still exists), and was a founding member of the original Futurian Society. The Futurians, founded in New York in 1938, were an odd combination of science fiction club, radical political movement, communal residential society, and literary mutual aid association. At one point, Futurians controlled no fewer than seven SF pulp magazines—*Stirring Science Stories* and *Cosmic Stories* edited by Wollheim, *Super Science Stories* and *Astonishing* edited by Frederik Pohl, and *Future, Science Fiction,* and *Science Fiction Quarterly* edited by Robert A.W. Lowndes.

Since the Futurians numbered among their membership such young talents as James Blish, Damon Knight, Isaac Asimov, Judith Merril, and Richard Wilson, in addition to the three editors, there was a constant flow of material into the magazines. Wollheim's *Stirring* was the most interesting of the seven, divided into science fiction and fantasy sections. Wollheim later edited *The Pocket Book of Science Fiction* (1943), generally regarded as the first significant SF anthology, and helped A.A. Wyn in the creation of Ace Books in 1952. At Ace, Wollheim was known for his keen choices and successful mixture of commercially popular and artistically valid works. Besides publishing many important new SF writers, he was responsible for publication of the first mass-market editions of Tolkien's *The Lord of the Rings* and of many of the science fiction works of Edgar Rice Burroughs. In 1972, Wollheim left Ace to create DAW books, the first mass publisher devoted entirely to SF. At DAW, Wollheim continued his formula of mixing pulp-style adventure series with significant works.

Notwithstanding the greater importance of Wollheim's work as editor and publisher, his own production of fiction was substantial. In the 1950s, he wrote three juvenile novels in the "Secret of. . . ." series; all are set in the intermediate near future and deal with the exploration of the solar system. In the 1960s, Wollheim produced eight novels featuring the juvenile hero Mike Mars; these are set even closer in the future than the previous series. Among Wollheim's other novels, many readers have found amusement in *Destiny's Orbit* and its sequel *Destination: Saturn.* These amusing space opera-comedies feature Ajax Calkins, introduced in a series of short stories written by Wollheim under the pseudonym Martin Pearson. Also of interest is the novel *Edge of Time,* regarded by many as the definitive (although far from the first) treatment of the macro micro-universe theme.

A good collection of Wollheim's shorter fiction is *Two Dozen Dragon Eggs.* The short stories tend toward extreme simplicity of plot and minimal characterization, concentrating on a mix of atmosphere and "idea." "The Rag Thing" and "Mimic," probably Wollheim's two best stories, are both included in this collection. Wollheim's short critical volume, *The Universe Makers: Science Fiction Today,* is one of the most cohesive and convincing statements of philosophy to date in the context of science fiction.

His own works remain for the most part out of print, and apparently of only passing significance. His contribution as an editor and publisher, however, will continue to affect literature both within and beyond the SF field. He was responsible for the publication of early works—in many cases, first novels—by authors as diverse as Ursula K. Le Guin, Robert Silverberg, Roger Zelazny, Marion Zimmer Bradley, and Thomas M. Disch. He was a major force in the popularization of science fiction to a mass audience between the 1950s and 1980s.

—Richard A. Lupoff

WOLVERTON, Dave

Nationality: American. **Born:** Springfield, Illinois, 1957. **Career:** Has worked variously as a farmer, trapper, meatcutter, grocery store manager, prison guard, missionary, bookkeeper, ice-cream maker, technical writer, and documentation department manager for a computer company. **Awards:** Writers of the Future Grand prize, 1987.

SCIENCE FICTION PUBLICATIONS

Novels (series: Serpent Catch; Star Wars)

On My Way to Paradise. New York, Spectra, Bantam, 1989.
Serpent Catch. New York, Spectra, Bantam, 1991.
Path of the Hero (Serpent Catch). New York, Spectra, Bantam, 1993.
The Courtship of Princess Leia (Star Wars). New York and London, Bantam, 1994.
The Golden Queen. New York, Tor, 1994.
Beyond the Gate. New York, St. Martin's, 1995.

OTHER PUBLICATIONS

Other

Editor, *L. Ron Hubbard Presents Writers of the Future,* vols. 9-10. Los Angeles, Bridge Publications, 1993-94.

*   *   *

While still a student at Brigham Young University in 1987, Dave Wolverton received the top prize in the "Writers of the Future" awards, given annually to 14 yet-unpublished SF writers who showed promise. Less than a decade later, he has proved the judges on target; known for his dynamic settings and attention-grabbing plots, Wolverton has added several novels to the upper tier of contemporary science fiction. *On My Way to Paradise,* a first novel based on the novella which garnered him the 1987 award, hooked

readers with its positive portrayal of men and women fighting both to survive and maintain their humanity against the rising tide of technological progress. Since then, such novels as *Serpent Catch* and *The Golden Queen* have continued Wolverton's contribution of morally grounded works of science fiction and fantasy.

Wolverton's debut novel, *On My Way to Paradise* (1989), was highly praised for its insightful appraisal of the brutality of modern warfare. In the novel, Wolverton pits Angelo, a Panamanian pharmacologist against the Allied Earth Marines' Military Intelligence as he is forced to extreme action by his sense of justice and frees a captured intelligence officer from the military's clutches. Fleeing an Earth that has been torn apart by wars of political ideology, the couple moves to a corporate-owned planet engaged in a genocidal war. There, they struggle to preserve their positive human attributes in a violent world where dehumanizing technological advances reign supreme.

The moon of a gas giant is the setting for *Serpent Catch* (1991). In this action-filled science fiction novel, the observers become the observed as several top scientists—themselves the result of genetic engineering—studying Earth's various developmental eras in a secluded scientific setting are invaded by alien beings who force the scientists to take part into their own experiments. Genetically advanced homo sapiens must match wits with dinosaurs, sea creatures, as well as their dapper cousins, the Neanderthals, as separate experimental worlds collide.

In *The Golden Queen* (1994), Wolverton moves further into the realm of fantasy. Professional bodyguard Gallen O'Day and his coworker, Orick (a talking bear), are drawn into a courtly conspiracy on their small planet as a perfect human clone called Lady Everynne tries to stop the Queen of the insect-like Dronons from reengineering the human race. Amid an involved discussion of advances in genetic research, Wolverton weaves a quest, a cast of fantastic characters, and a classic battle between good and evil that is won in true fairy-tale fashion.

In addition to writing thought-provoking science fiction for adults, Wolverton has added to the *Star Wars* series with *The Courtship of Princess Leia,* which takes place after the *Star Wars* movies but before the three-novel series by author Timothy Zahn. While still warring with the Empire, the New Republic is given the chance to ally itself with a planetary consortium if Princess Leia will marry the consortium's Prince Isolder. Although favoring the alliance, Han Solo does not favor losing his beloved; the discovery of the Empire's dark forces maneuvering behind the scenes sends these two rivals for Leia's affections, along with Luke Skywalker and Leia herself, into danger at the outer reaches of the galaxy.

—Pamela Shelton

WOMACK, Jack

Nationality: American. **Born:** Lexington, Kentucky, 8 January 1956. **Education:** Transylvania University, Lexington, Kentucky, 1974-75, 1976-77. **Career:** Worked in various New York City bookstores, 1977-89; managing editor, *Labor Unity,* Amalgamated Clothing and Textile Workers Union, 1989-95. **Awards:** Philip K. Dick award, 1994. **Agent:** John Ware, 392 Central Park West, New York, New York 10025. **Address:** 515 W. 111th St. #5E, New York, New York 10025, U.S.A.

SCIENCE FICTION PUBLICATIONS

Novels (series: Dryco Chronicles in all titles)

Ambient. New York, Weidenfeld and Nicolson, 1987; London, Unwin Hyman, 1988.
Terraplane: A Novel. New York, Weidenfeld and Nicolson, 1988; London, Unwin Hyman, 1989.
Heathern. London, Unwin Hyman, and New York, Tor, 1990.
Elvissey. New York, Tor, and London, HaperCollins, 1993.
Random Acts of Senseless Violence. London, HarperCollins, 1993; New York, Atlantic Monthly Press, 1994.

*

Jack Womack comments:

I began writing because there was nothing else I could do.

When I wrote *Ambient* I set the action 30 years ahead of the present because the way I saw the contemporary world and the way that world actually was did not yet correspond.

Now they do, and that is why my new work is set in the present. The attitude and perspective remain the same, however.

I've always tried to write about what is just outside the door.

My art is a funhouse mirror, and whether you are scared, delighted, or left cold is up to you.

* * *

In the summer of 1995's Oklahoma City bombing, Jack Womack's astringent fictional visions of a future New York, future un-United States, future world, do not seem as far fetched as they might have only eight short years ago when *Ambient,* the first of his projected six-part Dryco Chronicles, appeared. The world has become a harsher, nastier place in those eight years, and the casually violent horrors Womack has his narrators notice, almost in passing and with a lack of affect that is terrifying in its implications, are among us, if not in quite such overwhelming mass as Womack's novels represent them. One of the questions his works raise is the perennial one of science fictional prescience, and how it works. The New York he projects (and projected from the first, in 1987) is rendered so as to provide the imagination with the sights, sounds, and feel of Sarajevo, say, as we visit it every night on our TV screens. As Womack puts it: "When I wrote *Ambient* I set the action thirty years ahead of the present because the way I saw the contemporary world and the way that world actually worked did not yet correspond. Now they do. . . ."

Womack sees himself as a specifically New York writer just as he sees New York as *the* city, of today and of the future. Certainly, except for some movement into the country and to Russia at the beginning of *Terraplane* and into heartland U.S.A. and London in *Elvissey,* all his books are set there. He identifies with the "fringe" point of view he assimilated from reading Charles Fort, and argues that "New York gives me the benefit of being an outsider and an insider at the same point." Certainly, his narrators tend to be outsiders even when they desperately wish to identify themselves as insiders. One of their problems, which is also a touchstone of the whole series, is that corporate America, identified in all the novels but *Random Acts of Senseless Violence* as Dryco, can only make use of or destroy them. Thus, if and when it does assimilate them it has already made them over in its own image, at which point they lose the power of speech and stop narrating, or it has done its

best to destroy them, at which point they lose the power of speech and stop narrating. Sometimes Dryco, as a symbol of complexly evocative evil, manages to do both.

Womack began writing his first novel, *Ambient,* in 1983; it was published in 1987. It now stands third chronologically in the series, which reads best in the following order: *Heathern* (1990), *Random Acts of Senseless Violence* (1994), *Ambient* (1987), *Terraplane* (1988), and *Elvissey* (1993). Womack promises that the final novel, to be set about 15 years after *Elvissey* will eventually appear, but he has now begun writing novels set in the present, and whether or not they could be called science fiction is moot. Womack puts it this way: "I don't know if I'll ever do anything else specifically science fiction after that last volume in the Dryco Chronicles, but I think everything I do will be in some degree science fiction." This is an interesting comment, as Womack came to write SF without really realizing it; yet I would hazard that any reader with an SF background who came upon *Ambient* or any others of the series immediately identified them as SF. It seems that even if he began writing without consciously knowing the protocols of SF tropes, he had a sure grasp of them (possibly from reading Fort). Since his work was received as SF, he began to learn more about the conventions of the genre, but it appears he didn't have to make many changes in his basic approach, and it's possible that he will have a greater influence on the field than it has had on him.

Although Womack's fiction fits many of the definitions of postmodernism, even, or perhaps especially, in terms of postmodernism's interest in the fragmentation of the subject, he has nevertheless found ways to develop real empathy in the reader for the fragmenting egos he reveals in operation. Many of the characters are monsters, but the ones who count are still human, and we find ourselves caring about what happens to them.

Heathern is set during, or just after, a monetary collapse toward the end of the century, neatly termed "the Readjustment" by those on top (as Womack reveals in his latest novel, *Random Acts of Senseless Violence,* those below the top aren't in any position to name what is happening, they merely suffer it; that only a very few truly gain from the widespread destruction is one of Womack's purest extrapolations from what is happening in America today). During this time of chaos, Thatcher and Susie Dryden, who began as drug runners, manage to gain control of most of corporate America as well as what's left of its political power. Like the writings of William Gibson, whose work Womack did not read until he was informed that he was writing leading-edge science fiction, the Dryco Chronicles imagine a future in which certain large multinationals have more power in the world than do any national governments (this is even true, in *Terraplane,* of Russia, where government has essentially become a business, and one willing to play the game with Dryco as U.S. representative). In one of his many black jokes, Womack has Dryco choose the happy face doodle as its corporate logo. Watching one of its early commercials, Joanna, the narrator, asks: "'Does it mean anything?'" Her superviser answers: "'Does the signifier need the sign? It's meaning-packed at the core level.'" One of the savage delights of Womack's fiction is the way many of its worst offenders utilize (and corrupt) theory for the corporate agenda.

Thatcher Dryden, a good old boy from Tennessee, whose belief in Elvis as God signals a certain strangeness, runs his corporation with all the finesse and paranoia of a mini-Hitler. For him, and those who follow him, "the Readjustment" is a gift from God. As Joanna points out when she sees some of the "normal" violence in the streets, she can't evince concern "toward those who'd lost that we might win." Throughout the series, characters are forced to recognize this aspect of life under the corporation; most either do not care or are unable to break away from the corporate agenda, if only because to do so would be to lose all chance of whatever safety is left in the brutal world Womack has imagined. At the end of *Heathern,* as she prepares to leave the safety of Dryco, Joanna points out to Thatcher that he'd "see to it if [the world] wasn't" "[g]etting worse all the time," thus setting the tone for the whole sequence.

Heathern and the other novels are fascinating for the way they confront the violence of late capitalism head-on, with a wit and understanding that matches if not surpasses anything to be found in the theoretical writings of, say, Frederic Jameson. Random Acts of Senseless Violence is set at about the same time as *Heathern,* only down among the people who suffer the ravages of "the Readjustment." The innocence and naiveté of its 12-year-old narrator show up the kind of rhetoric that attempts to explain and defend what economic and social Darwinism are doing to most of the populace.

Lola Hart, just turned 12, decides to keep a diary as the novel begins. For six months she does keep it, keeping track of a descent into hell that depends upon two related events: "the Readjustment" (although neither she nor her parents know that's what it will be called); and her fateful meeting with some street-wise kids in the new neighbourhood her family is forced to move to when their money gets low. Womack masterfully captures the voice of the naive, private school kid at the beginning, and he lets the changes in her language, partly due to her initiation into street life and lingo by the other girls, be the most specific marker of the changes she goes through. Fearful at first, she ends up a revengeful killer, yet she never loses our sympathy. In *Random Acts of Senseless Violence* perhaps more than in any of his novels, Womack demonstrates that the pity is in the horror.

Random Acts provides the necessary overview of how "the Readjustment" destroyed what might be called middleclass life in the U.S. of Womack's future, observing how a young girl of "good family" learns to survive, at least for awhile, by sluffing all she has learned about "proper behavior" in her private school and among her "class-mates." The language she achieves is not just a version of black street talk but an extrapolation thereof. As we watch her change, we also watch her world do so, and note, as she does, what happens to those who can't: they die.

Ambient is set sometime later, in the next century. Reading the series in proper order, we begin to recognize how certain characters reappear in some of the volumes, while others continue to influence what is happening after they have disappeared. As is true of most of Womack's novels, love plays a strange and arbitrary role in Ambient. It begins with Thatcher Dryden's son trying to kill off his father and take over the corporation; it ends with Seamus O'Malley achieving control almost by mistake; in between, there is violence galore, and some frightening glimpses of how jaded about such violence the people at the top have become. Then there are the ambients, who have their own language and their own philosophy of bodily change. They seem important, and even appear to follow the sayings of Joanna, but they also disappear from the series in the following novels, so perhaps their presence is something of a metaphysical decoy; although it is also presented as one of many responses to the discovery that Christianity was based on a lie and the concommitant loss of faith that followed (in this extrapolation Womack seems to have gone against the grain of American political developments during the past decade).

Seamus, "Shameless" as he is called by the woman he loves, actually has a moral code, unlike those he works for. It is the moral

code, in fact, of the "shamus," the private eye seeking a kind of justice in an unjust world—and Seamus is a "private eye" upon that world of the future, seeing it with a kind of innocent clarity, not unjudging but not blindly judgmental either. Perhaps the whole Private Eye tradition is one of Womack's many ironic intertexts here. What Seamus sees is just how powerful, and possibly necessary, Dryco has become.

With *Terraplane,* Womack extends his vision to an other, and separate, reality, a parallel history in which there was no civil war, slaves only received their freedom in the early 20th century, and racism is much more direct than in contemporary, or his future, America. The narrator this time is Luther Biggerstaff, a black retired General, who survived the Civil War in New York (maintained for at least three decades by Dryco because it's good for business), and now works for Dryco. A Russian invention flings him, Dryco's best bodyguard, Jake (first seen as a teenage recruit in Heathern), and the Russian Jake falls in love with, into this parallel world in its 1939. This new world is one of Womack's most startling and successful narrative moves in the sequence, for it allows him to balance the horrors of a future we can all too easily imagine against those of a past that may be even worse, and is at least as bad.

Part of the richness of the novel derives from the clash between the future-speak readers have become accustomed to and the commonplaces of an earlier "white" America; but there is also the clash of a bottom-line egalitarianism versus the violent racism of a country that never wanted to give up slavery. Both lead to violence, and Womack plays the ironies implicit in his imagined context for all they're worth. It seems that the only way to survive in either culture is by being tougher and meaner than anyone else.

At the end, Luther and a woman from the other world drive back to his world through a huge Tesla Coil at the 1939 World's Fair, opening a "gate" between the two worlds that Dryco seeks to exploit. In *Elvissey,* a way is found, for by then, some 15 years later, it's the mid-fifties there, and so that world's Elvis must be somewhere, to be plucked up and brought back to bring the followers of the Church of Elvis into the Dryco fold. *Elvissey* is narrated by Isobel, a black woman who has long worked for Dryco and is an old friend of Judy, now one of the bosses at Dryco (both appear at an earlier time in the later written Random Acts); she is having problems with her husband, John, a bodyguard trained under Jake. Womack's careful construction of the whole series becomes clearer with each additional novel, and he has made sure to set up resonant connections among them through such characterological developments.

"Whitened" by special treatments, and sent with John to find the other world's Elvis, Isobel experiences the postwar America there as a warped vision of what television's all-white TV eye saw. In fact, in that America, something akin to the final solution has been applied to the blacks. Most SF authors are satisfied to imagine one future per book, good or bad. In Womack's SF there's a bad future, but he then imagines another, worse, "past" and its "future," and brings people from the first to the second. Having carefully adumbrated a corporate warfare future where there is an essential racial equality among those who survive, he takes two successful blacks (in Dryco's terms, which are not gentle), and confronts them with the worst fears of U.S. apartheid. They survive; their pitiful few, and our somewhat more numerous, illusions do not. The worst that can be expected of human nature, especially the fear of the other, is displayed in all its nakedness in these books.

Elvissey takes us as far into the next century as Womack has ventured thus far. It is in many ways his most complex novel, giving all three of its central characters a near-tragic depth. But it is not a tragedy, rather a kind of tragicomedy, black yet desperately hopeful. Isobel is trained in the language of that other 1950s, which leads to moments of subtle comic menace as she speaks "their" language while thinking hers. John is more locked into his position as a guard, someone trained not to feel. Elvis is both more dangerous and more troubled than we might expect of such a character. Womack develops both his background and his response to the chance of becoming a god with complex sympathy. The novel continues to develop the dangers of corporate rule in the future, and offers a smidgen of hope that individuality might still find ways to thrive in a world of pure consumption and violent envy.

Womack is now writing a contemporary novel, yet all his work helps us to comprehend just how much we are living in the nightmare side of the future invented in our near past. That is a scarey SF thought, and it is the consistent ambience of all his novels. He is undoubtedly one of the most interesting writers to emerge in the field in the past decade.

—Douglas Barbour

———

WOODCOTT, Keith. *See* **BRUNNER, John.**

———

WOODS, Lawrence. *See* **LOWNDES, Robert A.W.**

———

WORTH, Peter. *See* **PHILLIPS, Rog.**

———

WRIGHT, Austin Tappan

Nationality: American. **Born:** Hanover, New Hampshire, 20 August 1883. **Education:** Harvard University, Cambridge, Massachusetts, A.B. 1905, LL.B. 1908. **Career:** Corporation and admiralty lawyer: practiced with firm of Brandeis Dunbar and Nutter, Boston, 1908-16; Professor of Law, University of California, Berkeley, 1916-24, and University of Pennsylvania, Philadelphia, 1924-31. **Died:** 18 September 1931.

SCIENCE FICTION PUBLICATIONS

Novel

Islandia. New York, Farrar and Rinehart, 1942.

*

Critical Studies: *An Introduction to Islandia* by Basil Davenport, New York Farrar and Rinehart, 1942; *The Islandian World of Austin Wright* by Lawrence Clark Powell, privately printed, 1957.

*   *   *

The reputation of Austin Tappan Wright rests on only one work, but it is safe to say there is nothing quite like *Islandia* in all of literature. If one can make a fine semantic distinction between science fiction and speculative fiction, Wright's novel is more the latter than the former. His "speculation" is in the area of geography and, spinning off that, sociology and cultural anthropology.

Islandia is a nation located on the southern half of the Karain subcontinent in the southern hemisphere. It is civilized but isolationist, and for it Wright has created the most detailed and in-depth of all fictional cultures. There are discernible elements of Japan, Madagascar, Indonesia, and India, but the sum total is curiously more Western than Eastern, more homey than exotic. Islandia is revealed to the reader in all its richness by the action of the novel, which takes place in the early part of this century. The country has decided to end its isolation from the rest of the world, and a few representatives of other governments are allowed in. One of these is a young American diplomat, John Lang; we learn about Islandia through his eyes as he travels the country and becomes acquainted and involved with her people.

The novel is peripherally a remarkable portrait of the nationalistic power plays that were occurring at the turn of the century, and a fine character sketch of an intelligent, moral young American confronted with values different from his own. But it is Islandia and the wonderful cast of characters with which it is peopled that is Wright's most notable achievement.

—Baird Searles

———

WRIGHT, Kenneth. *See* **del REY, Lester.**

———

WRIGHT, S(ydney) Fowler

Pseudonyms: Sydney Fowler; Alan Seymour; Anthony Wingrave. **Nationality:** British. **Born:** 6 January 1874. **Education:** King Edward's School, Birmingham. **Family:** Married 1) Nellie Ashbarry in 1895 (died 1918), three sons and three daughters; 2) Truda Hancock in 1920, one son and three daughters. **Career:** Accountant in Birmingham from 1895. Editor, *Poetry* (later *Poetry and the Play*) magazine, Birmingham, 1920-32. **Died:** 25 February 1965.

SCIENCE FICTION PUBLICATIONS

Novels (series: Marguerite Cranleigh; War of 1938; Martin Webster)

The Amphibians: A Romance of 500,000 Years Hence. London, Merton Press, 1925.

Deluge: A Romance (Webster). London, Fowler Wright, 1927; New York, Cosmopolitan, 1928.

The Island of Captain Sparrow. London, Gollancz, and New York, Cosmopolitan, 1928.

The World Below (includes *The Amphibians*). London, Collins, 1929; New York, Longman, 1930; published as *The Dwellers*, London, Panther, 1954.

Dawn (Webster). New York, Cosmopolitan, 1929; London, Harrap, 1930.

Dream; or, The Simian Maid (Cranleigh). London, Harrap, 1931.

The Bell Street Murders (as Syndey Fowler). London, Harrap, 1931; as Fowler Wright, New York, Macaulay, 1931.

Beyond the Rim. London, Jarrolds, 1932.

Power. London, Jarrolds, 1933.

Prelude in Prague: A Story of the War of 1938. London, Newnes, 1935; as *The War of 1938*, New York, Putnam, 1936.

The Vengeance of Gwa (as Anthony Wingrave). London, Butterworth, 1935; as Fowler Wright, London, Books of Today, 1945.

Four Days War (War of 1938). London, Hale, 1936.

Megiddo's Ridge (War of 1938). London, Hale, 1937.

The Screaming Lake. London, Hale, 1937.

The Hidden Tribe. London, Hale, 1938.

The Adventure of Wyndham Smith. London, Jenkins, 1938.

The Adventure of the Blue Room (as Sydney Fowler). London, Rich and Cowan, 1945.

Spiders' War: A Fantasy Novel (Cranleigh). New York, Abelard Press, 1954.

Short Stories

The New Gods Lead. London, Jarrolds, 1932; expanded as *The Throne of Saturn*, Sauk City, Wisconsin, Arkham House, 1949; London, Heinemann, 1951.

The Witchfinder. London, Books of Today, 1945.

Justice, and The Rat: Two Famous Stories. London, Books of Today, 1945.

OTHER PUBLICATIONS

Novels

Elfwin. London, Harrap, and New York, Longman, 1930.

Seven Thousand in Israel. London, Jarrolds, 1931.

Red Ike, with J.M. Denwood. London, Hutchinson, 1931; as *Under the Brutchstone*, New York, Coward McCann, 1931.

Lord's Right in Languedoc. London, Jarrolds, 1933.

David. London, Butterworth, 1934.

Ordeal of Barata. London, Jenkins, 1939.

The Siege of Malta: Founded on an Unfinished Romance by Sir Walter Scott. London, Muller, 1942.

Novels as Sydney Fowler

The King against Anne Bickerton. London, Harrap, 1930; as *The Case of Anne Bickerton*, by Fowler Wright, New York, Boni, 1930; as *Rex V. Anne Bickerton*, London, Penguin, 1947.

By Saturday. London, Lane, 1931.

The Hanging of Constance Hillier. London, Jarrolds, 1931; as Fowler Wright, New York, Macaulay, 1932.

Crime & Co (as Fowler Wright). New York, Macaulay, 1931; as *The Hand-Print Mystery*, London, Jarrolds, 1932.

Arresting Delia. London, Jarrolds, 1933; as Fowler Wright, New York, Macaulay, 1933.

The Secret of the Screen. London, Jarrolds, 1933.

Who Else But She? London, Jarrolds, 1934.

Three Witnesses. London, Butterworth, 1935.

The Attic Murder. London, Butterworth, 1936.

Was Murder Done? London, Butterworth, 1936.

Post-Mortem Evidence. London, Butterworth, 1936.

Four Callers in Razor Street. London, Jenkins, 1937.

The Jordans Murder. London, Jenkins, 1938; as Fowler Wright, New York, Curl, 1939.

The Murder in Bethnal Square. London, Jenkins, 1938.

The Wills of Jane Kanwhistle. London, Jenkins, 1939.

The Rissole Mystery. London, Rich and Cowan, 1941.

A Bout with the Mildew Gang. London, Eyre and Spottiswoode, 1941.

Second Bout with the Mildew Gang. London, Eyre and Spottiswoode, 1942.

Dinner in New York. London, Eyre and Spottiswoode, 1943.

The End of the Mildew Gang. London, Eyre and Spottiswoode, 1944.

Too Much for Mr. Jellipot. London, Eyre and Spottiswoode, 1945.

Who Murdered Reynard? London, Rich and Cowan, 1947.

With Cause Enough? London, Harvill Press, 1954.

Poetry

Scenes from the Morte d'Arthur (as Alan Seymour). London, Erskine MacDonald, 1919.

Some Songs of Bilitis. Birmingham, Poetry, 1921.

The Song of Songs and Other Poems. London, Merton Press, 1925; New York, Cosmopolitan, 1929.

The Ballad of Elaine. London, Merton Press, 1926.

The Riding of Lancelot: A Narrative Poem. London, Fowler Wright, 1929.

Other

Police and Public: A Political Pamphlet. London, Fowler Wright, 1929.

The Life of Walter Scott: A Biography. London, Poetry League, 1932; New York, Haskell House, 1971.

Should We Surrender Colonies? London, Readers' Library, 1939.

Editor, *Voices on the Wind: An Anthology of Contemporary Verse*. London, Merton Press, 3 vols., 1922-24.

Editor, *Poets of Merseyside: An Anthology of Present-Day Liverpool Poetry*. London, Merton Press, 1923.

Editor, with R. Crompton Rhodes, *Poems: Chosen by Boys and Girls*. Oxford, Blackwell, 4 vols., 1923-24.

Editor, *Birmingham Poetry 1923-24*. London, Merton Press, 1924.

Editor, *From Overseas: An Anthology of Contemporary Dominion and Colonial Verse*. London, Merton Press, 1924.

Editor, *Some Yorkshire Poets*. London, Merton Press, 1924.

Editor, *A Somerset Anthology of Modern Verse 1924*. London, Merton Press, 1924.

Editor, *The County Series* (verse anthologies). London, Fowler Wright, 13 vols., 1927-30.

Editor, *The Last Days of Pompeii: A Redaction,* by Edward Bulwer-Lytton. London, Vision Press, 1948.

Translator, *The Inferno,* by Dante. London, Fowler Wright, 1928.
Translator, *Marguerite de Valois,* by Andre Dumas *père.* London, Temple, 1947.
Translator, *The Purgatorio,* by Dante. Edinburgh, Oliver and Boyd, 1954.

* * *

S. Fowler Wright escaped his life as an accountant and poetry magazine editor with tales of fantasy, adventure, detection, and disaster. This prolific and versatile author began writing fantasy at 50.

His early novels reflect the influence of H.G. Wells. Wright, however, had such a pessimistic view of man's devolution that most human beings and their social customs vanish with dramatic flourishes. *The World Below* features a time-machine trip 500,000 years ahead to encounter Amphibians, delicate, web-footed, and cerebral, and Dwellers, gigantic seekers of knowledge through scientific investigation. The hero is most like the lizard-like Killers, who boil and eat victims. Much of the conversation between him and his amphibian companion reveals man's mistreatment of other living things, while many of the adventures show how close he is to bestiality when he throws reason aside in panic.

In *Beyond the Rim* descendants of British Puritans live in an Antarctic theocracy, raided occasionally by the Anabaptist horde from the volcanic hell nearby. The explorers include two strong women, one of whom remains while the other and her lover return home, but never to tell the real story. Similarly, in *The Island of Captain Sparrow* Charlton Fogle is shipwrecked where a pirate established a kingdom for his men and their women. Already present were a race of satyrs, providing meat, and a tribe of handsome natives decimated by disease brought by the outsiders. Charlton and Marcelle, intended for Sparrow's ugly, vicious heir, fall in love. At the book's spectacular climax the giant rokas, birds used for agricultural work, turn on the pirates, leaving the young lovers and the last native child to start over.

Deluge narrates a cataclysmic flood in which a hero and two heroines survive the barbarity to which most civilized people descend and found a new order. Martin Webster and Claire Arlington are among the few who adapt to living with nature. Because she is the kind of woman men put on a pedestal, Helen Webster also survives with her children. Some men—a murderer among them—become humane while others degenerate into ravaging, rapacious beasts which must be exterminated. At the end of this engrossing novel, Wright surprises his readers by allowing Martin to have both women. What's more—with noble psychological struggles—the women love each other. In Dawn, its sequel, Wright goes back in time to introduce new characters and repeat the flood's horrors. Defeat of the threatening gang and escape from another flood promise a future.

In *Dream* and its sequel, *Spiders' War,* Marguerite Leinster enjoys dangerous adventures with the help of a psychologist-magician. In the first she dreams of an ape-girl fighting off the river rats that challenge human supremacy. In *Spiders' War* she goes into a future where the threat to divided humanity stalks in the form of giant spiders. Her man, a scholar of 20th-century history, is also a warrior-leader. Together they organize three hostile groups against the intelligent monsters. *The Vengeance of Gwa* contrasts similar groups, ranging from starving barbarism to bored perfection, in a tale of an evil queen and her well-deserved end.

Prelude in Prague, Four Days War, and *Megiddo's Ridge* form a trilogy dealing with an ugly near-future in which Germany conquers Europe, by the use of a freezing gas, air raids, and political terrorism. In this apocalyptic disaster culminating in the destruction of the powerful forces of Von Teufel, Wright creates and kills a large cast of interesting characters, including a double agent and a woman pilot. He also vents anger at British underestimation of Germany, lack of preparation for war, and callousness about highway moralities. As in *Deluge* he warns readers that, while they vegetate, their neighbors hover a step from savagery.

In addition, Wright produced numerous short stories—light fantasy, medieval romance, mystery, and satire. Among the best are "Justice" and "Original Sin," a short version of *The Adventure of Wyndham Smith.* Society can be so perfect that only mass suicide can abolish boredom. So often does Wright annihilate mankind that it is not surprising that the heroine of his last story, "The Better Choice," prefers to remain a cat.

—Mary S. Weinkauf

WYLIE, Philip (Gordon)

Pseudonym: Leatrice Homesley. **Nationality:** American. **Born:** Beverly, Massachusetts, 12 May 1902. **Education:** Montclair High School, New Jersey; Princeton University, New Jersey, 1920-23. **Military Service:** Member of the board, Office of Facts and Figures, 1942; with Bureau of Personnel, United States Army Air Force, 1945. **Family:** Married 1) Sally Ondeck in 1928 (divorced 1937), one daughter; 2) Frederica Ballard in 1938. **Career:** Staff member, *The New Yorker,* 1925-27; advertising manager, Cosmopolitan Book Corporation, 1927-28; screenwriter, Paramount Pictures, 1931-33, and MGM, 1936-37; editor, Farrar and Rinehart, publishers, New York, 1944. **Member:** Authors Guild Council, 1945. Consultant to the Federal Civil Defense Administration, 1949-71. **Awards:** Freedom Foundation Gold Medal, 1953; Hyman Memorial Trophy, 1959. D.Litt.: University of Miami; Florida State University, Tallahassee. **Died:** 26 October 1971.

SCIENCE FICTION PUBLICATIONS

Novels (series: Bronson Beta)

Gladiator. New York, Knopf, 1930.
The Murderer Invisible. New York, Farrar and Rinehart, 1931.
When Worlds Collide (Bronson Beta), with Edwin Balmer. New York, Stokes, and London, Paul, 1933.
After Worlds Collide (Bronson Beta), with Edwin Balmer. New York, Stokes, and London, Paul, 1934.
Night unto Night. New York, Farrar and Rinehart, 1944.
The Disappearance. New York, Rinehart, and London, Gollancz, 1951.
Tomorrow! New York, Rinehart, 1954.
Triumph. Garden City, New York, Doubleday, 1963.
Los Angeles: A.D. 2017 (novelization of TV play). New York, Popular Library, 1971.
The End of the Dream. Garden City, New York, Doubleday, 1972; Morley, Yorkshire, Elmfield Press, 1975.

Short Stories

The Answer. New York, Rinehart, and London, Muller, 1956.

OTHER PUBLICATIONS

Novels

Heavy Laden. New York, Knopf, 1928.
Babes and Sucklings. New York, Knopf, 1929; as *The Party,* New York, Popular Library, 1966(?).
Blondy's Boy Friend (as Leatrice Homesley). New York, Chelsea House, 1930.
Footprint of Cinderella. New York, Farrar and Rinehart, 1931; as *9 Rittenhouse Square,* New York, Popular Library, 1964(?).
Five Fatal Words, with Edwin Balmer. New York, Long and Smith, 1932; London, Paul, 1933.
The Savage Gentleman. New York, Farrar and Rinehart, 1932.
Finnley Wrenn: A Novel in a New Manner. New York, Farrar and Rinehart, 1934.
The Golden Hoard, with Edwin Balmer. New York, Stokes, 1934.
As They Reveled. New York, Farrar and Rinehart, 1936.
Too Much of Everything. New York, Farrar and Rinehart, and London, Chapman and Hall, 1936.
The Shield of Silence, with Edwin Balmer. New York, Stokes, 1936; London, Collins, 1937.
An April Afternoon. New York, Farrar and Rinehart, 1938.
Danger Mansion. Los Angeles, Bantam, 1941.
The Other Horseman. New York, Farrar and Rinehart, 1942.
Corpses at Indian Stones. New York, Farrar and Rinehart, 1943.
Opus 21. New York, Rinehart, 1949; London, Consul, 1962.
They Were Both Naked. Garden City, New York, Doubleday, 1965.
A Resourceful Lady. New York, Popular Library, 1966.
The Spy Who Spoke Porpoise. Garden City, New York, Doubleday, 1969.

Short Stories

The Big Ones Get Away! New York, Farrar and Rinehart, 1940.
Salt Water Daffy. New York, Farrar and Rinehart, 1941.
Fish and Tin Fish: Crunch and Des Strike Back. New York, Farrar and Rinehart, 1944.
Fifth Mystery Book, with others. New York, Farrar and Rinehart, 1944.
Selected Short Stories. New York, Editions for the Armed Services, 1946.
Crunch and Des: Stories of Florida Fishing. New York, Rinehart, 1948.
Three to Be Read. New York, Rinehart, 1952; *Experiment in Crime* and *The Smuggled Atom Bomb* published separately, New York, Avon, 2 vols., 1956.
The Best of Crunch and Des. New York, Rinehart, 1954.
Treasure Cruise and Other Crunch and Des Stories. New York, Rinehart, 1956.
Autumn Romance. New York, Lancer, 1965.

Plays

Screenplays: *Island of Lost Souls,* with Waldemar Young, 1932; *The Invisible Man,* with R.C. Sherriff, 1933; *Murders in the Zoo,* 1933; *The King of the Jungle,* with Fred Niblo, Jr., 1933; *Death in Paradise Canyon,* with Saul Elkins and Norman Foster, 1936.

Other

The Army Way: A Thousand Pointers for New Soldiers, with William W. Muir. New York, Farrar and Rinehart, 1940.
Generation of Vipers. New York, Farrar and Rinehart, 1942; revised edition, Rinehart, and London, Muller, 1955.

An Essay on Morals. New York, Rinehart, 1947.
Denizens of the Deep: True Tales of Deep-Sea Fishing. New York, Rinehart, 1953.
The Innocent Ambassadors. New York, Rinehart, 1957; London, Muller, 1958.
The Lerner Marine Laboratory at Bimini, Bahamas. New York, American Museum of Natural History, 1960.
The Magic Animal. Garden City, New York, Doubleday, 1968.
Sons and Daughters of Mom. Garden City, New York, Doubleday, 1971.

*

Manuscript Collection: Princeton University, New Jersey.

Critical Study: *Philip Wylie* by Truman Frederick Keefer, Boston, Twayne, 1977.

*   *   *

Philip Wylie's SF represents only a small portion of his prolific output of magazine stories, novels, polemics, and screenplays. Wylie consciously and carefully placed himself in the "popular" market where his strongly moralistic and iconoclastic eye could not only observe and criticise but where his work would be read by large numbers. For, unlike the satirist, Wylie passionately believed that his pen could contribute to the sweeping away of cant and the creation of a modern and sane society.

Gladiator was accepted for publication in 1928 but Wylie's publishers held it for two years until he had produced two non-science fiction works. In it and in *The Murderer Invisible* he set the pattern for his ventures in the SF idiom. In both novels, the scientific projections (a genetically produced superman and an invisible man) are put in place quickly and without fuss as in H.G. Wells's novels, and the real stress lies on what the innovation can reveal about human nature and human society. Hugo Danner, the superman in *Gladiator,* observes the futility of human greed and of things like fraternity parties, football games, and the stock market. Through Hugo, Wylie poses the problem of what could be done to improve the lot of man even by a superman if the masses would not change themselves. In *The Murderer Invisible,* moral issues emerge because a scientist, William Carpenter, seriously wronged in a previous career on the commodities market, develops invisibility with intentions of a fair revenge and further use for the good of mankind. But he becomes a megalomaniac and attempts to take over the world for its own good. In these novels Wylie keeps calling his characters back to reckonings of conscience and analyses of the society that they are trying to change. These real and central concerns of his work are continued in *The Savage Gentleman,* a novel about a child educated away from mankind that offers a Tarzan-like variation on the single-man-against-society theme of the earlier novels.

Wylie's most optimistic venture into SF comes in two novels written in collaboration with Edwin Balmer, *When Worlds Collide* and *After Worlds Collide.* In these cosmic disaster stories two planets—a gas giant and an Earthlike planet in orbit about it—enter the solar system and destroy the Earth when the gas giant brushes against it. *When Worlds Collide* chronicles the discovery of the threat and the desperate efforts of a group of scientists to build rockets to get themselves onto Bronson Beta, the smaller of the invaders. Several parties succeed and the second novel deals with their survival on Bronson Beta, their discovery of a high civilisation there, and the conflicts between the American party and a Japanese-Chinese-

Soviet party which has also survived. These novels contain a good deal of Wylie's most careful scientific prognostication in astronomy, Earth physics, and in the prediction of human behaviour in times of extreme crisis, although the extrapolations about rocketry and interplanetary travel are considerably flawed.

Time spent in Hollywood, war work, and the pursuit of other kinds of writing leave a gap in Wylie's SF output until the 1951 publication of *The Disappearance.* The simple but very elegant premise of this novel is a world in which all of the women disappear in an instant from the world of men and all of the men disappear from the world of the women. Although no real explanation is offered for this split in the stream of reality, the device is a perfect instrument for some very carefully considered opinions on the roles of the sexes, particularly in modern America. Wylie cleverly sets a great deal of the novel in a family unit very much like his own, which lives in Miami and has all the domestic complications that society tends to produce. On one level the novel is fascinating because chapters taking place in exactly the same surroundings trace the varied collapse of the two worlds, the men having an all-out atomic war and a return to savagery while the women struggle with technological collapse. But in addition to the outward struggle there runs through the book some very serious contemplation of the double standard and the fragility of male-female relationships.

Wylie's next three SF works deal in various ways with his deep concern for the dangers of nuclear war, a phenomenon about which he was particularly well informed because of his activities in civil defence organisation. *Tomorrow!* is a detailed portrait of a nuclear attack on an American city and the civil defence response. He is heavily critical of the failure to face and prepare for this inevitability, and his realistically detailed picture of the carnage is both blunt and sobering. *The Answer* is a brief allegory in which both the Americans and the Russians bring down an angel in their bomb tests. The angel was carrying the message "Love one another" to mankind. *Triumph* paints the most horrible picture of holocaust, in which virtually the only survivors in the northern hemisphere are 14 people in a supershelter prepared by a farsighted millionaire.

Wylie's posthumous legacy to mankind, *The End of the Dream,* is his prediction of the pollution death of the world. Like John Brunner's novel of the same year, *The Sheep Look Up, The End of the Dream* ties together projections of man's mistreatment of the environment to foresee mass deaths from air pollution in the cities, a rice blight which leaves most of the world starving, and a particularly horrible mutation of an ocean leech which sucks the life from millions. *The End of the Dream* is a fitting culmination of Wylie's career, for it combines his anger against human foolishness with his obvious desire to warn and thus influence the future positively. From *Gladiator* to *The End of the Dream* Philip Wylie has used the science fiction mode and the style of the popular writer to reach and caution the widest possible audience in his lifelong crusade to save man from his own foolishness and blinkered views.

—Peter A. Brigg

WYNDHAM, John

Pseudonym for J.B. Harris. **Other Pseudonyms:** John Beynon; Johnson Harris. Also wrote as John Wyndham Parkes Lucas Beynon Harris. **Nationality:** British. **Born:** Knowle, Warwickshire, 10 July 1903. **Education:** Bedales School, Petersfield, Hampshire; also read for the Bar. **Military Service:** Served in the Royal Signals during World War II. **Family:** Married Grace Wilson in 1963. **Died:** 11 March 1969.

SCIENCE FICTION PUBLICATIONS

Novels

The Secret People (as John Beynon). London, Newnes, 1935; as John Beynon Harris, New York, Lancer, 1964; as John Wyndham, London, M. Joseph, 1972.
Planet Plane (as John Beynon). London, Newnes, 1936; revised edition, as *Stowaway to Mars: An Outstanding Adventure Novel of the First Interplanetary Flight to Mars,* London, Nova, 1953; as John Wyndham, London, M. Joseph, 1974.
The Day of the Triffids. Garden City, New York, Doubleday, and London, M. Joseph, 1951; as *Revolt of the Triffids,* New York, Popular Library, 1952; as *The Triffids,* adapted by Patrick Nobes (for children), London, Hutchinson, 1973.
The Kraken Wakes. London, M. Joseph, 1953; as *Out of the Deeps,* New York, Ballantine, 1953.
The Chrysalids. New York, Ballantine, and London, M. Joseph, 1955.
The Midwich Cuckoos. London, M. Joseph, 1957; New York, Ballantine, 1958; as *Village of the Damned,* Ballantine, 1960.
The Outward Urge (as John Wyndham and Lucas Parkes). London, M. Joseph, and New York, Ballantine, 1959.
Trouble with Lichen. London, M. Joseph, and New York, Ballantine, 1960.
Chocky. New York, Ballantine, and London, M. Joseph, 1968.
Web. London, M. Joseph, 1979; adapted by Joc Potter and Andy Hopkins (for children), London, Penguin, 1991.

Short Stories

Love in Time (as Johnson Harris). London, Utopian, 1946.
Jizzle. London, Dobson, 1954.
The Seeds of Time. London, M. Joseph, 1956.
Tales of Gooseflesh and Laughter. New York, Ballantine, 1956.
Consider Her Ways and Others. London, M. Joseph, 1961.
The Infinite Moment. New York, Ballantine, 1961.
The Best of John Wyndham. London, Sphere, 1973; as *The Man from Beyond and Other Stories.* London, M. Joseph, 1975.
Meteor: Short Stories, adapted by Patrick Nobes (for children). Oxford, Oxford University Press, 1991.

Short Stories as John Beynon

Sleepers of Mars. London, Coronet, 1973.
Wanderers of Time. London, Coronet, 1973.
Exiles on Asperus. London, Coronet, 1979; as John Wyndham, London, Severn House, 1979.

OTHER PUBLICATIONS

Novels

Foul Play Suspected (as John Beynon). London, Newnes, 1935.

Poetry

'Melia Ann: A Fantasy of the W.I. Taunton, Somerset, Wessex Press, 1953.

* * *

Beginning in 1930, J.B. Harris published—primarily in the United States and under several pseudonyms—a great many short stories and several novels. Eventually it was the novel *The Day of the Triffids* that, in 1951, brought Harris wide public recognition and permanently affixed to him the pseudonym under which he had published it: John Wyndham. Wyndham is justifiably considered to be the truest disciple of H.G. Wells in English literature. He himself said that of all science fiction he was most influenced by two of Wells's novels, *The Time Machine* and *War of the Worlds.* Indeed, Wyndham more than once dealt with themes raised in those novels, such as displacement in time and invasion from outerspace, though Wells's influence on Wyndham was not restricted to thematic borrowing.

Wyndham loved to write about perfectly familiar things—some everyday occurrence—and let the fantastic element help him uncover unprecedented and unforeseen possibilities in that daily routine. Only one of his novels, *The Outward Urge,* deals with other worlds. In his other novels and stories the action is set on Earth and in time frames not all that distant from ours. Nor does he burden us with technical minutiae. Being a firm opponent of the Jules Verne school of SF, resurrected and modernized in the U.S. by Hugo Gernsback, Wyndham uses technical—and other—detail only insofar as he or any other writer needs it: for the sake of credibility, realism, authenticity. In addition Wyndham has the ability—decidedly not within any other writer's reach—to compel us to suspend disbelief by being true to human character. Damon Knight correctly observed that Wyndham achieved his objective with down-to-earth means, that is, making us believe the most unbelievable things simply because they happened to people whom we all knew well. Wyndham's imagination is very tactile, sequential, logical. He follows the Wellsian method of the "single premise." In each of his books there is, then, one fantastic assumption; something in the world has changed and all subsequent changes follow as a consequence. Wyndham has the inventiveness to illustrate with many examples the impact of an event on all realms of life. All this causes Wyndham's fantasy novels to be part of the basic current of literature. He has no use for space opera; instead he practices a special kind of "realism in fantasy." One of his tasks has been the exploration of possibilities created by application of science fiction motifs to various types of short stories. That is the guiding principle behind the collection *The Seeds of Time.* Here again there can be no doubt about the influence of H.G. Wells.

The influence of Wells also determined the basic theme of Wyndham's writings. He is usually concerned with some catastrophe, cosmic or social, which results in the discovery of hitherto hidden dangers in daily life, in the revelation of character under novel circumstances, in the disclosure of defects in the society. In searching for his "single fantastic premise" Wyndham displays a degree of imagination which belies his ostensibly traditional manner. In *The Day of the Triffids,* which remains Wyndham's best-known novel, he showed his greatest originality. The novel deals with the disintegration of the social order under the impact of two events—a rain of meteors which has blinded most of the human race, and the appearance of mobile carnivorous plants. In two other novels Wyndham writes about the invasion of Earth by beings from other planets. In the first of these, *The Kraken Wakes,* invaders from space who can exist only under conditions of enormous pressure, establish a bridgehead deep under the ocean. In an attempt to wipe out the human race, they melt down the polar ice caps; the resultant flooding of the continents almost brings about the desired end. All this occurs under Cold War conditions, with mutual suspicion between the great powers preventing them from joining forces against the invaders. In the final analysis the catastrophe is caused by human divisiveness. In *The Midwich Cuckoos* the subject matter is not so much invasion as a kind of "penetration" from space. Here the non-Earthlings isolate the village of Midwich and a few other places on Earth from their surroundings and put their inhabitants to sleep. Nine months later there appear in those localities children of non-Earthly origin who are evidently destined to become the rulers of all mankind. Their intellectual and spiritual superiority is such that the Earthlings submit without protest, even to the point of taking actions clearly detrimental to themselves. What makes these children from outer space so superior is their capacity to communicate constantly with each other by telepathy. Thus, while remaining individual beings, they form at the same time a formidable collective force. Anything learned by one becomes immediately part of everyone's knowledge. And the group also has the ability to channel everyone's will in one direction. Eventually this colony of extraplanetary spawn becomes so dangerous to Earth that it must be destroyed.

Telepathy is a rather common theme in Wyndham's fiction. It serves as a means of demonstrating its relationship to various forms of collectivism. The collectivism of the non-Earthlings in *The Midwich Cuckoos,* for instance, reminds one of a fascist order. *The Chrysalids* provides an example of another sort of collectivist order. *The Chrysalids* takes place many centuries after a devastating nuclear war. Enclaves of life are cut off from one another by vast areas of radioactive contamination. Random mutations are occurring. As a result people, animals, and plants become so grotesquely disfigured that their hideousness exceeds even that which Wells anticipated in *The Island of Doctor Moreau.* These circumstances have given rise to puritanical communities seeking salvation by suppressing anything "different." Should anything new turn out to be superior to the old, these puritans are all the more eager to suppress it. They are convinced that they themselves represent the only kind of perfection possible, and at the very thought that elsewhere there might live people of a different color, they fly into a rage. Nevertheless, life, movement, progress win out even here. These horrible, monstrous families produce children similar to those who tried to control Midwich. They differ in one respect, though; they hate cruelty. According to Wyndham these children who feel themselves to be members of one single family will not merely rebuild the old world: they will build a new and better one. *Trouble with Lichen* is the least interesting of Wyndham's novels. Taking the theme of Shaw's *Back to Methuselah,* he discusses the possibilities a vastly extended life expectancy could open for mankind.

—Julius Kagarlitsky

Y

YARBRO, Chelsea Quinn

Pseudonyms: Terry Nelson Bonner; Vanessa Pryor. **Nationality:** American. **Born:** Berkeley, California, 15 September 1942. **Education:** Attended San Francisco State College, 1960-63. **Family:** Married Donald P. Simpson in 1969 (divorced 1982). **Career:** Theatre manager and playwright, Mirthmakers Children's Theatre, San Francisco, 1961-64; children's counsellor, 1963; cartographer, C.E. Erickson and Associates, Oakland, California, 1963-70; composer; card and palm reader, 1974-78. **Member:** Secretary, Science Fiction Writers of America, 1970-72; president, Horror Writers of America, 1988-89. **Agent:** Ellen Levine Literary Agency, 15 East 26th Street, Suite 1801, New York, New York 10010, U.S.A.

SCIENCE FICTION PUBLICATIONS

Novels

Time of the Fourth Horseman. Garden City, New York, Doubleday, 1976; London, Sidgwick and Jackson, 1980.
False Dawn. Garden City, New York, Doubleday, 1978; London, Sidgwick and Jackson, 1979.
Ariosto. New York, Pocket Books, 1980.
Hyacinths. Garden City, New York, Doubleday, 1983.
Nomads (novelization of screenplay). New York, Bantam, 1984.
Crown of Empire. New York, Baen, 1994.

Short Stories (series: Saint-Germain)

Cautionary Tales. Garden City, New York, Doubleday, 1978; expanded edition, New York, Warner, and London, Sidgwick and Jackson, 1980.
On Saint Hubert's Thing. New Castle, Virginia, Cheap Street, 1982.
Signs and Portents. Santa Cruz, California, Dream Press, 1984.
The Spider Glass (Saint-Germain). Eugene, Oregon, Pulphouse, 1991.

OTHER PUBLICATIONS

Novels (series: Atta Olivia Clemens; Charity; Charlie Moon; Saint-Germain)

Ogilvie, Tallant, and Moon (as C.Q. Yarbro; Moon). New York, Putnam, 1976; as *Bad Medicine,* New York, Jove, 1990.
Hôtel Transylvania: A Novel of Forbidden Love (Saint-Germain). New York, St. Martin's Press, 1978; London, New English Library, 1981.
The Palace: A Historical Horror Novel (Saint-Germain). New York, St. Martin's Press, 1978; London, New English Library, 1981.
Music When Sweet Voices Die (as C.Q. Yarbro; Moon). New York, Putnam, 1979; as *False Notes,* New York, Berkley, 1990.
Blood Games: A Novel of Historical Horror (Saint-Germain). New York, St. Martin's Press, 1979.

Dead and Buried (novelization of screenplay). New York, Warner, and London, Star, 1980.
Sins of Omission. New York, New American Library, 1980.
Path of the Eclipse: A Historical Horror Novel (Saint-Germain). New York, St. Martin's Press, 1981.
Tempting Fate (Saint-Germain). New York, St. Martin's Press, 1982.
A Taste of Wine (as Vanessa Pryor). New York, Pocket Books, 1982.
The Godforsaken. New York, Warner, 1983.
The Making of Australia 5: The Outback (as Terry Nelson Bonner). New York, Dell, 1983.
Locadio's Apprentice (for children). New York, Harper, 1984.
Four Horses for Tishtry (for children). New York, Harper, 1985.
A Mortal Glamour. New York, Bantam, 1985.
To the High Redoubt. New York, Popular Library, 1985.
Floating Illusions (for children). New York, Harper, 1986.
A Baroque Fable. New York, Berkley, 1986.
A Flame in Byzantium (Clemens). New York, Tor, 1987.
Firecode. New York, Popular Library, 1987.
Taji's Syndrome. New York, Popular Library, 1988.
Crusader's Torch (Clemens). New York, Tor, 1988.
Beastnights. New York, Warner, 1989.
A Candle for D'Artagnan (Clemens). New York, Tor, 1989.
The Law in Charity. Garden City, New York, Doubleday, 1989.
Out of the House of Life. (Saint-Germain). New York, Tor, 1990.
Poison Fruit (as C.Q. Yarbro; Moon). New York, Jove, 1991.
Cat's Claw (as C.Q. Yarbro; Moon). New York, Jove, 1992.
Charity, Colorado. New York, M. Evans, 1993.
Darker Jewels (Saint-Germain). New York, Tor, 1993.
Better in the Dark (Saint-Germain). New York, Tor, 1993.

Short Stories

The Saint-Germain Chronicles. New York, Pocket Books, 1983.

Other (series: Michael)

CQY. New Castle, Virginia, Cheap Street, 1982.
Messages from Michael on the Nature of the Evolution of the Human Soul. Chicago, Playboy Press, 1979.
More Messages from Michael. New York, Berkley, 1986.
Michael's People. New York, Berkley, 1988.

Editor, with Thomas N. Scortia, *Two Views of Wonder.* New York, Ballantine, 1973.

*

Chelsea Quinn Yarbro comments:

My work, for the most part, has to do with some aspect of love and survival, though that should be interpreted in its broadest sense. Music has very much influenced me, not only as subject matter, but structurally as well. Since I make my living as a writer, I do, in a pragmatic sense, write for money. However, I regard writing as an art, and feel that within certain realistic limitations a part of my responsibility is to maintain and protect the integrity of my work.

* * *

Chelsea Quinn Yarbro has written well-received works in a wide range of popular genres, including not only science fiction and fantasy but also mysteries and, most recently, a historical novel set in the American West. Her science fiction novels tend to combine elements of the medical thriller with those of the "disaster" novel. In these works she employs stark language to explore dire consequences of scientific or technological developments. Yarbro is best known, however, for elaborate fantasy narratives that blend aspects of the historical romance with the horror novel. Both types of fiction reflect her fascination with the darker aspects of human nature.

The danger of tampering with the natural order, even with noble intentions, provides the common theme of Yarbro's best science fiction. A collection of her early short stories, for example, is aptly titled *Cautionary Tales. Time of the Fourth Horseman,* her first published science fiction novel, could itself be described as a cautionary narrative. A secret project sponsored by the government is attempting to ease severe overpopulation by fostering the controlled re-emergence of such diseases as cholera, polio and diphtheria. But these efforts result in the unforeseen outbreak of a new form of polio that is particularly virulent and highly contagious. The novel recounts the discovery of this ill-conceived plan by a young physician, Dr. Natalie Lebbreau, whose husband is in charge of the research and whose son is among its first casualties. *Time of the Fourth Horseman* reflects two of Yarbro's strengths as a novelist: her ability to create sympathetic characters and her skill in fashioning a compelling plot.

Yarbro's next science fiction novel, *False Dawn,* contains several of the same elements: ecological disaster, a strong heroine, and a struggle for survival against overwhelming odds. *False Dawn* depicts an even bleaker future in which the earth has been devastated by a series of natural and human-caused disasters. The narrative centers on two individuals: Thea, a mutant woman, and Evan Montague, the deposed (and reformed) leader of a gang of marauding "pirates." Paired by chance, the two wander through the ravaged wilderness of the western United States in search of a rumored oasis. Yarbro balances the story of their struggles against both human enemies and nature with the slow growth of a warm and mutually respectful love between the two protagonists. On one level, the novel has a disturbing ending, as the lovers' hope of a refuge proves futile. But their concern for and commitment to each other soften the harshness of the conclusion. Yarbro's powerful but restrained depiction of the horrors of this future, joined with her treatment of a love that survives in a brutal world, makes this an excellent introduction to her science fiction.

Yarbro's other science fiction novels repeat the basic concerns and themes of the first two books. *Hyacinths,* for example, postulates a future in which artificially induced dreams serve as the major source of mass entertainment. In this work disaster results from the government's attempt to use these dreams for propaganda. *Taji's Syndrome* returns to the medical subject matter of her first novel. Genetic tampering leads to the emergence of a new disease that almost always proves fatal but leaves its rare survivors with psychokinetic powers. Moral issues are both less clearly defined and more important in *Taji's Syndrome* than in *Time of the Fourth Horseman.* The action centers on powerful interests with two opposed purposes, one wishing to eradicate the disease and the other (lured by the new powers of the survivors) wishing to foster its spread.

In the field of fantasy, Yarbro has proved particularly adept as a writer of horror novels. *The Godforsaken* combines the horror theme of lycanthropy with the human atrocities of the Spanish Inquisition. She has also written several strong horror novels set in the contemporary world, among them *Sins of Omission* and *Nomads.* But her reputation as a fantasist rests most solidly on her novels about vampirism, especially her series based on the exploits of the vampire Francois Rgoczy, Count of Saint Germain. While the writing in her science fiction is generally controlled and even austere, in her historical horror-fantasies, Yarbro employs far more elaborate language and provides lengthy, detailed descriptions of the time and places in which they are set.

Yarbro's Saint Germain series invites comparison with the vampire novels of Ann Rice and Fred Saberhagen. Saint Germain emerges as a noble, sympathetic character, an alien to be engaged and understood rather than a monster to be feared and destroyed. The villains of the various novels that comprise the series are the human characters. In *Hôtel Transylvania,* the novel that introduces Saint Germain, the villain is the leader of a satanic cult who would destroy the count's lover. Other villains include Savanarola (*The Palace*), a priestess of the goddess Kali (*Path of the Eclipse*), and even Joseph McCarthy (*The Saint-Germain Chronicles*).

More recently, Yarbro has begun a new vampire series featuring Atta Olivia Clemens, who was Saint Germain's lover in Imperial Rome in *Blood Games.* Strong and intelligent, Olivia calls to mind not only Saint Germain but also characters such as Thea and Dr. Lebbreau from Yarbro's science fiction novels. *A Flame in Byzantium,* the first novel in the projected series, involves Olivia in the court intrigues of Constantinople. *Crusader's Torch* requires her to travel from Tyre to Rome during the Crusades. These novels, however, seem more historical romances about a vampire than fantastic fictions that make use of historical settings. The early novels in the St. Germain series, particularly *Hôtel Transylvania* and *Path of the Eclipse,* offer more compelling examples of Yarbro's skill as a writer of horrific fantasy.

In an epilogue to *Hôtel Transylvania,* Yarbro has written that the vampire reflects "a generally ambivalent attitude about immortality" and speaks "to some hidden part of ourselves." That ambivalence permeates her vampire fantasies, much as an ambivalence about science and technology, particularly when they are controlled by political purposes, is central to her science fiction. Yarbro's ability to explore such dark themes in novels that successfully blend elements of other popular genres (such as the medical thriller and the historical romance) has earned her a reputation as a writer of consistently entertaining and occasionally superior science fiction and fantasy.

—Dennis M. Kratz

YEFREMOV, Ivan

Nationality: Russian. **Born:** 1907. **Died:** 1972.

SCIENCE FICTION PUBLICATIONS

Novels

Tumannost' Andromedy. Gvardina, Idz.-vo Tsiolkam Molodaia, 1958; translated by George Hanna as *Andromeda: A Space Age Tale,* Moscow, Foreign Languages Publishing House, 1959.
The Hour of the Bull. N.p., n.d.

Short Stories

Vstrecha nad Tuskarori. N.p., 1944; translated by M. Nicholas and
N. Nicholas as *A Meeting over Tuscarora and Other Adventure
Stories,* London, Hutchinson, 1946.
Stories, translated by Ovidii Gorchakov. Moscow, Foreign Lan-
guages Publishing House, 1954.
The Heart of the Serpent. N.p., n.d.

OTHER

Novels

Na Kraiu Oikumeny. Moscow, Molodaia Gvardiia, 1952; translated
by George Hanna as *The Land of Foam,* Moscow, Foreign
Lanugages Publishing House, 1957; Boston, Houghton Mifflin,
1959.

*   *   *

Ivan Yefremov, with degrees in geology and biology, was professor of paleontology at the Paleontological Institute in Moscow.
His first book of stories was *A Meeting over Tuscarora,* hovering
between folk legends, sea and historical romance, scientific popularization, and SF. His first "cosmic" novella was "Stellar Ships"
(*Stories*), but it is *Andromeda* which is his breakthrough, the bearer
of the post-Stalinist "thaw" in SF, and the supreme achievement of
its first phase (1957-63). *Andromeda* achieved this position after a
long and acrimonious public debate, unheard of in the former USSR
since the enthronement of dogmatic literary policy and the Stalinist
purges of the 1930s. Against violent ideological opposition, this debate resulted in 1957-58 in the victory of the new wave, which wanted
to build upon the pristine Soviet tradition, in abeyance since the Leninist
1920s. The opinion of "warm stream" critics, and of the thousands of
readers who wrote to the author, newspapers, and periodicals, that this
was a liberating turning-point in Soviet SF, finally prevailed.

Andromeda creatively revived the classical utopian and socialist
vision, which looks forward to a unified, affluent, humanist, classless, and stateless world. The novel is situated in year 408 of the
Era of the Great Ring, when mankind has established communica-
tional contact with inhabitants of distant constellations who pass
information to each other through a ring of inhabited systems. The
Earth itself is administered—by analogy with the associative centers of the human brain—by an Astronautic Council and an Economic Council which tallies all plans with existing possibilities;
their specialized research academies correspond to man's sensory
centers. Within this framework of the body politic, Yefremov concentrates on new ethical relationships of disalienated men. For all
the theatrical loftiness of his characters, whose emotions are rarely
less than sublime, they can learn through painful mistakes and failures, as distinct from the desperado and superman clichés of "socialist realism" or much American SF after Gernsback.

The novel's strong narrative sweep full of action, from fistfights
to encounters with electrical predators and a robot-spaceship from
the Andromeda nebula, is imbued with the joy and romance of cognition. Yefremov's strong anthropocentric bent places the highest
value on creativity, a simultaneous adventure of deed, thought, and
feeling, resulting in physical and ethical beauty. Even his title indicates not only a constellation but also the chained Greek beauty
rescued from a monster (here, class egotism and violence, personi-

fied in the novel as a bull, and often bearing hallmarks of Stalinism)
by a flying hero endowed with superior science. Astronautics thus
don't evolve into a new uncritical cult, but are claimed as a humanist discipline, in one of the most significant fusions of physical
sciences, social sciences, ethics, and art established as the norm
for Yefremov's new people. Such a connection is embodied even
in the compositional oscillation between cosmic and terrestrial chapters, where the "astronautic" Erg-Nisa subplot is finally integrated
with the "earthly" Darr-Veda subplot by means of the creative beauty
of science united to art (Mven-Chara and Renn-Evda). Furthermore,
this future is not the arrested, pseudo-perfect end of history—that
weak point of optimistic utopianism. Freed from economic and
power worries, people must still redeem time through a dialectics
of personal creativity and societal teamwork mediated by functional
beauty, shown in Dar's listening to the "Cosmic Symphony in F-mi-
nor, Color Tone 4.75 μ." Creativity is always countered by entropy,
and self-realization paid for in effort and suffering. In fact, several very
interesting approaches to a Marxist "optimistic tragedy" can be found
in *Andromeda,* e.g., in Mven's "happy Fall"; the failed and destructive
"null-space" experiment finally leads to great advances. Significantly,
the accent on beauty and responsible freedom places at the center of
the novel female heroines, interacting with the heroes and contributing
to the emotional motivation of new utopian ethics—in contrast to SF
in the United States during those times.

True, *Andromeda* has somewhat dated. In a number of places its
dialogue, motivation, and rhythm flag, and it falls back on melodrama and preaching. Yefremov's characters tend to be plaster-of-
Paris statuesque, and his incidents often exploit the quantitatively
grandiose: Mven blows up a satellite and half a mountain, Veda
loses the greatest anthropological find ever; Erg is manly, Nisa is
pure. One feels in *Andromeda* the presence of an unsophisticated
reader, who is, as Yefremov wrote, "still attracted to the externals,
decorations, and theatrical effects of the genre," and the presence
of the erotic, philosophic, and literary taboos of the cultural context. Yefremov's epistemology is a naive anthropocentrism: the 19th-
century view of man as subject and the universe as object of a
cognition that is ever expanding, if necessary through a basic social change yet without major existential consequences. Doubt and
the menace of entropy are only external enemies—e.g., the electric
predators of a far-off planet; if any epistemological opaqueness ever
becomes internalized in a man, then he is a melodramatic villain,
such as Pour Hyss.

Yefremov's ideology is thus receptive only to a certain romantically codified range of creativity. His limitations are more clearly
manifested in his later works. In *The Heart of the Serpent* Terrans
meeting a fluorine-based mankind put an end to its loneliness by
promising to transmute fluorine into oxygen. This story—an
avowed counterblast to Leinster's "First Contact" with its aggressive and acquisitive presuppositions—might be a legitimate paci-
fist-socialist allegory for changing US capitalist meritocrats into
Russian socialist ones, yet it is curiously ethnocentric. Yefremov's
last SF novel, *The Hour of the Bull,* demonstrates this even more
clearly. Though he took from Lem and the Strugatskys the device
of showing heroes (and heroines) facing anti-utopia, his old
preachiness reaches monumental proportions; and the fascist regime of Tormans seems nearer to US pulp SF of the 1930s and
1940s, or indeed to the weirdnesses of Lindsay (from whom the
planet's name is taken), than to either the reactionary capitalism or
Maoism which Yefremov declared he wanted to hit in one fell
swoop. Such parochial views preclude a full development of imaginative SF vistas.

Yet any discussion of such vistas in Soviet SF was made possible by Yefremov's pioneering effort. *Andromeda* has polyphonic scope and a large number of protagonists; it is Tolstoian rather than Flaubertain. Not limited to the consciousness of one central hero, it is one of the first utopias in world literature which successfully shows new characters creating, and being created by, a new society, i.e., the personal working out of a collective utopia (analogous to what Scott did for the historical novel). Yefremov's unfolding the narration as if the anticipated future was already a normative present unites the classic "looking backward" of utopian anticipations with the modern Einsteinian conception of different coordinate systems with autonomous norms: 20th-century science and the age-old Russian folk dreams of a just and happy society meet in his novel. This meeting made it a nodal point of the Russian and socialist SF tradition, and enabled it to usher in the second Golden Age of Soviet SF—an age which closed with the 1960s.

—Darko Suvin

YERMAKOV, Nicholas. *See* **HAWKE, Simon.**

YOLEN, Jane (Hyatt)

Nationality: American. **Born:** New York City, 11 February 1939. **Education:** Staples High School, Westport, Connecticut, graduated 1956; Smith College, Northampton, Massachusetts, B.A. 1960; New School for Social Research, New York; University of Massachusetts, Amherst, 1975-78, M.Ed. 1976. **Family:** Married David W. Stemple in 1962; one daughter and two sons. **Career:** Staff member, *This Week* magazine and *Saturday Review,* New York, 1960-61; assistant editor, Gold Medal Books, New York, 1961-62; associate editor, Rutledge Books, New York, 1962-63; assistant editor, Alfred A. Knopf Juvenile Books, New York, 1963-65; lecturer in Education, Smith College, 1979-84. Columnist ("Children's Bookfare"), *Daily Hampshire Gazette,* Northampton, Massachusetts, 1972-80. Massachusetts delegate, Democratic National Convention, Miami, 1972. Member of the Board of Directors, Society of Children's Book Writers since 1974, and Children's Literature Association, 1977-79; president, Science-Fiction Writers of America, 1986-88. **Awards:** Society of Children's Book Writers Golden Kite award, 1974; Christopher award, 1978; University of Minnesota Kerlan award, 1988. LL.D.: College of Our Lady of the Elms, Chicopee, Massachusetts, 1980. **Agent:** Marilyn Marlow, Curtis Brown, 10 Astor Place, New York, New York 10003. **Address:** 31 School Street, Box 27, Hatfield, Massachusetts 01038, U.S.A.

SCIENCE FICTION PUBLICATIONS

Novels (series: Great Alta)

Cards of Grief. New York, Ace, 1984; London, Orbit, 1986.

The Books of Great Alta. New York, Guild America, 1990.
  Sister Light, Sister Dark. New York, Tor, 1988; London, Orbit, 1989.
  White Jenna. New York, Tor, 1989.
Briar Rose. New York, Tor, 1992; London, Pan, 1994.

Novels for young adults (series: Pit Dragons)

The Wizard of Washington Square. New York, World, 1969.
The Magic Three of Solatia. New York, Crowell, 1974.
The Mermaid's Three Wisdoms. New York, Collins and World, 1978.
The Robot and Rebecca: The Mystery of the Code-carrying Kids. New York, Random House, 1980.
The Boy Who Spoke Chimp. New York, Knopf, 1981.
Dragon's Blood (Pit Dragons). New York, Delacorte Press, 1982; London, MacRae, 1983.
Heart's Blood (Pit Dragons). New York, Delacorte Press, and London, MacRae, 1984.
A Sending of Dragons (Pit Dragons). London, MacRae, and New York, Delacorte Press, 1987.
The Devil's Arithmetic. New York, Viking Kestrel, 1988.
The Faery Flag: Stories and Poems of Fantasy and the Supernatural. New York, Orchard, 1989.
The Dragon's Boy. New York, Harper and Row, 1990.
Wizard's Hall. San Diego, Harcourt Brace, 1991.
The Wild Hunt. San Diego, Harcourt Brace, 1995.

Short Stories

Dream Weaver (for young adults). Cleveland, Ohio, Collins, 1979.
Neptune Rising: Songs and Tales of the Undersea Folk (for young adults). New York, Philomel, 1982.
Tales of Wonder. New York, Schocken, 1983; London, Orbit, 1987.
Dragonfield and Other Stories. New York, Ace, 1985; London, Orbit, 1988.
Merlin's Booke. New York, Ace, 1986.
The Lady and the Merman: A Tale. Easthampton, Massachusetts, Pennyroyal Press, 1979.
The Whitethorne Wood and Other Magicks. Ottawa, Ontario, Triskell Press, 1984.
The Sword and the Stone. Eugene, Oregon, Pulphouse, 1991.
Storyteller. Cambridge, Massachusetts, NESFA Press, 1992.
Here There Be Dragons (for young adults). San Diego, Harcourt Brace, 1993.
Here There Be Unicorns (for young adults). San Diego, Harcourt Brace, 1994.

OTHER PUBLICATIONS

Fiction (for children)

The Witch Who Wasn't. New York, Macmillan, and London, Collier Macmillan, 1964.
Gwinellen, The Princess Who Could Not Sleep. New York, Macmillan, 1965.
Trust a City Kid, with Anne Huston. New York, Lothrop, 1966; London, Dent, 1967.
Isabel's Noel. New York, Funk and Wagnalls, 1967.
The Emperor and the Kite. Cleveland, World, 1967; London, Macdonald, 1969.

The Minstrel and the Mountain. Cleveland, World, and Edinburgh, Oliver and Boyd, 1968.

Greyling. Cleveland, World, 1968; London, Bodley Head, 1969.

The Longest Name on the Block. New York, Funk and Wagnalls, 1968.

The Inway Investigators; or, The Mystery at McCracken's Place. New York, Seabury Press, 1969.

The Seventh Mandarin. New York, Seabury Press, and London, Macmillan, 1970.

Hobo Toad and the Motorcycle Gang. New York, World, 1970.

The Bird of Time. New York, Crowell, 1971.

The Girl Who Loved the Wind. New York, Crowell, 1972; London, Collins, 1973.

The Girl Who Cried Flowers and Other Tales. New York, Crowell, 1974.

Rainbow Rider. New York, Crowell, 1974; London, Collins, 1975.

The Adventures of Eeka Mouse. Middletown, Connecticut, Xerox, 1974.

The Boy Who Had Wings. New York, Crowell, 1974.

The Little Spotted Fish. New York, Seabury Press, 1975.

The Transfigured Hart. New York, Crowell, 1975.

The Moon Ribbon and Other Tales. New York, Crowell, 1976; London, Dent, 1977.

Milkweed Days. New York, Crowell, 1976.

The Sultan's Perfect Tree. New York, Parents' Magazine Press, 1977.

The Seeing Stick. New York, Crowell, 1977.

The Lady and the Merman. Easthampton, Massachusetts, Pennyroyal Press, 1977.

The Hundredth Dove and Other Tales. New York, Crowell, 1977; London, Dent, 1979.

The Giants' Farm. New York, Seabury Press, 1977.

Hannah Dreaming. Springfield, Massachusetts, Springfield Museum of Fine Arts, 1977.

No Bath Tonight. New York, Crowell, 1978.

The Simple Prince. New York, Parents' Magazine Press, 1978.

Spider Jane. New York, Coward McCann, 1978.

The Giants Go Camping. New York, Seabury Press, 1979.

Spider Jane on the Move. New York, Coward McCann, 1980.

Mice on Ice. New York, Dutton, 1980.

Commander Toad in Space. New York, Coward McCann, 1980.

Shirlick Holmes and the Case of the Wandering Wardrobe. New York, Coward McCann, 1981.

Uncle Lemon's Spring. New York, Dutton, 1981.

Brothers of the Wind. New York, Philomel, 1981.

The Gift of Sarah Barker. New York, Viking Press, 1981.

The Acorn Quest. New York, Crowell, 1981.

The Robot and Rebecca and the Missing Owser. New York, Knopf, 1981.

Sleeping Ugly. New York, Coward McCann, 1981.

Commander Toad and the Planet of the Grapes. New York, Coward McCann, 1982.

Commander Toad and the Big Black Hole. New York, Coward McCann, 1983.

Children of the Wolf. New York, Viking Kestrel, 1984.

The Stone Silenus. New York, Philomel, 1984.

Commander Toad and the Dis-Asteroid. New York, Coward McCann, 1985.

Commander Toad and the Intergalactic Spy. New York, Coward McCann, 1986.

Piggins. San Diego, Harcourt Brace, 1987; London, Piccadilly Press, 1988.

Owl Moon. New York, Philomel, 1987.

Commander Toad and the Space Pirates. New York, Putnam, 1987.

Picnic with Piggins. San Diego, Harcourt Brace, 1988.

Piggins and the Royal Wedding. San Diego, Harcourt Brace, 1989.

Dove Isabeau. San Diego, Harcourt Brace, 1989.

Baby Bear's Bedtime Book. San Diego, Harcourt Brace, 1990.

Dinosaur Dances. New York, Putnam, 1990.

Elfabet: An ABC of Elves. Boston, Little Brown, 1990.

Sky Dogs. San Diego, Harcourt Brace, 1990.

All Those Secrets of the World. Boston, Little Brown, 1991.

Grandad Bill's Song. New York, Philomel, 1991.

Greyling. New York, Philomel, 1991.

Letting Swift River Go. Boston, Little Brown, 1991.

Wings. San Diego, Harcourt Brace, 1991.

Eeny, Meeny, Miney, Mole. San Diego, Harcourt Brace, 1992.

Encounter. San Diego, Harcourt Brace, 1992.

Honkers. Boston, Little Brown, 1993.

Mouse's Birthday. New York, Putnam, 1993.

Good Griselle: An Original Tale. San Diego, Harcourt Brace, 1994.

Old Dame Counterpane. New York, Philomel, 1994.

And Twelve Chinese Acrobats, with Jean Gralley. New York, Philomel, 1994.

Beneath the Ghost Moon. Boston, Little Brown, 1994.

The Girl in the Golden Bower. Boston, Little Brown, 1995.

The Ballad of the Pirate Queens. San Diego, Harcourt Brace, 1995.

Before the Storm. Honesdale, Pennsylvania, Wordsong, 1995.

Play

Robin Hood, music by Barbara Green (produced Boston, 1967).

Poetry

See This Little Line? New York, McKay, 1963.

It All Depends. New York, Funk and Wagnalls, 1969.

An Invitation to the Butterfly Ball: A Counting Rhyme. New York, Parents' Magazine Press, 1976; Kingswood, Surrey, World's Work, 1978.

All in the Woodland Early: An ABC Book, music by the author. Cleveland, Collins, 1979.

How Beastly! A Menagerie of Nonsense Poems. New York, Collins, 1980.

Dragon Night and Other Lullabies. New York, Methuen, 1980; London, Methuen, 1981.

Ring of Earth: A Child's Book of Seasons. San Diego, Harcourt Brace, 1986.

The Three Bear Rhyme Book. San Diego, Harcourt Brace, 1987.

Best Witches: Poems for Halloween. New York, Putnam, 1989.

Bird Watch. New York, Philomel, 1990.

What Rhymes with Moon? New York, Philomel, 1993.

Raining Cats and Dogs. San Diego, Harcourt Brace, 1993.

Animal Fair: Poems. San Diego, Harcourt Brace, 1994.

The Three Bears Holiday Rhyme Book. San Diego, Harcourt Brace, 1995.

Other

Pirates in Petticoats. New York, McKay, 1963.

World on a String: The Story of Kites. Cleveland, World, 1968.

Friend: The Story of George Fox and the Quakers. New York, Seabury Press, 1972.

The Wizard Islands. New York, Crowell, 1973.

Writing Books for Children. Boston, *The Writer,* 1973; revised edition, 1983.

Ring Out! A Book of Bells. New York, Seabury Press, 1974; London, Evans, 1978.

Simple Gifts: The Story of the Shakers. New York, Viking Press, 1976.

Touch Magic: Fantasy, Faerie, and Folklore in the Literature of Childhood. New York, Philomel, 1981.

The Sleeping Beauty (retelling). New York, Knopf, 1986.

Guide to Writing for Children. Boston, *The Writer,* 1989.

Tam Lin: An Old Ballad (retelling). San Diego, Harcourt Brace, 1990.

A Letter from Phoenix Farm. Katonah, New York, Owen, 1992.

Welcome to the Green House. New York, Putnam, 1993.

Editor, *The Fireside Song Book of Birds and Beasts,* music by Barbara Green. New York, Simon and Schuster, 1972.

Editor, *Zoo 2000: Twelve Stories of Science Fiction and Fantasy Beasts.* New York, Seabury Press, 1973; London, Gollancz, 1975.

Editor, *Rounds about Rounds,* music by Barbara Green, illustrated by Gail Gibbons. New York, Watts, 1977; London, Watts, 1978.

Editor, *Shape Shifters: Fantasy and Science Fiction Tales about Humans Who Can Change Their Shapes.* New York, Seabury Press, 1978.

Editor, *The Lullaby Songbook,* music arranged by Adam Stemple, illustrated by Charles Mikolaycak. San Diego, Harcourt Brace, 1986.

Editor, with Martin H. Greenberg and Charles G. Waugh, *Dragons and Dreams: A Collection of New Fantasy and Science Fiction Stories.* New York, Harper, 1986.

Editor, *Favorite Folktales from around the World.* New York, Pantheon, 1986.

Editor, with Martin H. Greenberg and Charles G. Waugh, *Spaceships and Spells.* New York, Harper, 1987.

Editor, with Martin H. Greenberg, *Werewolves: A Collection of Original Stories.* New York, Harper, 1988.

Editor, with Martin H. Greenberg, *Things That Go Bump in the Night.* New York, Harper, 1989.

Editor, *The Lap-Time Song and Play Book.* San Diego, Harcourt Brace, 1989.

Editor, with Martin H. Greenberg, *Vampires.* New York, HarperCollins, 1991.

Editor, *2041 A.D.: Twelve Stories about the Future by Top Science Fiction Writers.* New York, Delacorte Press, 1991.

Editor, *Hark! A Christmas Sampler.* New York, Putnam, 1991; as *A Christmas Treasury,* London, Hutchinson, 1991.

Editor, *Street Rhymes around the World.* Honesdale, Pennsylvania, Wordsong, 1992.

Editor, *Weather Report: Poems.* Honesdale, Pennsylvania, Wordsong, 1993.

Editor, *Jane Yolen's Songs of Summer.* Honesdale, Pennsylvania, Caroline House, 1993.

Editor, with Martin H. Greenberg, *Xanadu [1]-3.* New York, Tor, 3 vols., 1993-94.

Editor, *Sleep Rhymes around the World.* Honesdale, Pennsylvania, Wordsong, 1994.

Editor, with Martin H. Greenberg, *The Haunted House: A Collection of Original Stories.* New York, HarperCollins, 1995.

Editor, *Alphabestiary: Animal Poems from A to Z.* Honesdale, Pennsylvania, Wordsong, 1995.

*

Manuscript Collection: Kerlan Collection, University of Minnesota, Minneapolis.

*   *   *

Jane Yolen is first and foremost a storyteller. When one reads her works, the words transcend the eye and settle on the ear, as in her retelling of the ancient Scottish ballad of *Tam Lin.* Her choice and placement of words, her polished prose, maintains the rhythm of the ballad while rendering it in narrative text. Though *Tam Lin* is a picture book, Yolen accomplishes the same quality of a story being told, rather than read, in her adult works.

Yolen is not only an accomplished storyteller but an acknowledged authority on folklore. In her book of essays *Touch Magic: Fantasy, Faerie, and Folklore in the Literature of Childhood,* she posits that "These four functions of myth and folklore should establish the listening to and learning of the old tales as being among the most basic elements of our education: creating a landscape of allusion, enabling us to understand our own and other cultures from the inside out, providing an adaptable tool of therapy, and stating in symbolic or metaphoric terms the abstract truths of our common human existence." Combining her creativity with the solid grounding in folklore, Yolen is able to devise stories that resonate to our deepest understanding of myth while being set in worlds of her own creation.

Versatility is a hallmark of Yolen's work, and she has written more than 100 books ranging across genres and levels of appeal. Among her strongest works are those that are science fiction or fantasy. Her adult companion books *Sister Light, Sister Dark* and *White Jenna* share an interesting structure. The books are comprised of "The Myth," a terse, polished, and formal presentation that foreshadows the action; "The Legend," an account closer to the action but removed to the level of a tale told over time and passed from listener to listener; and "The Story," the actual unfolding of the tale. Sections called "The History" are from the writings of an imagined historian/folklorist and reveal the battles that rage in academia over interpretation of history and myth. Yolen's structure provides a tongue-in-cheek deflation of such behaviors.

A group of strong mountain women, outcasts from neighboring villages because they were deformed or because the village had too many females, has evolved into a society scattered across the landscape in mountain fortresses called Hames. They are united in their belief in The Book of Light by the Great Alta. Each light sister has a dark sister, visible only when there is light, called from the dark at maturity. *Sister Light, Sister Dark* tells of Jenna, a baby who came to Selden Hame under unusual circumstances and who as she reached maturity seemed to be the fulfillment of a prophecy foretelling the coming of a leader known by various names—the Anna, the White One, etc. Jenna's meeting with Carum, an exiled prince, her slaying of two evil brothers, and the destruction of Nill's Hame provide adventurous and thought-provoking reading.

White Jenna continues the saga, with Jenna setting out to warn the Hames of coming destruction. She meets Sorrel, one of the Grenna, and becomes "cocooned in time in the circle." In this underworld she meets Alta, named for the Goddess, and learns that "Time has come for the world to turn." Jenna's part in this is to fulfill the prophecy, overcoming evil. The setting and action are original while incorporating archetypes from our world.

Yolen's first book assembled directly for adults is *Tales of Wonder,* a collection of short stories that exemplifies the wide range of the author's talents. Some are witty, such as "Boris Chernevsky's Hands," some inexpressibly sad, as "Names." The collection contains the story "The Cards of Grief," which was later expanded into a novel, though other stories are complete in themselves and are reminiscent of traditional folk and fairy tale, as in "The Girl Who Loved the Wind." In the introductory essay, which recounts her process of creation, Yolen writes, "I would *like* to believe that there is that of faerie in each of us, a little trickle or stream that, if we could but tap it, would lead us back to the great wellspring of magic we share with every human being, every creature—and the world." Such a sentiment underlies the power of Jane Yolen's writing and explains her ability to reach the reader in many forms.

For her acclaimed young adult fantasy series, The Pit Dragon Trilogy, Yolen created an austere world, Austar IV. Once a penal colony, it is now a harsh world of masters and slaves. Its economy is based on gambling on the fighting pit dragons. *Dragon's Blood* begins the chronicle with Jakkin, a young bonder, stealing a dragon's egg and raising the young dragon to be a fighter in the pits. His success results in his attaining the status of master. In *Heart's Blood,* the story develops much more complexity. Jakkin and his love, Akki, become enmeshed in a rebel plot to overthrow the government. When it all turns sour, Jakkin and Akki are saved only by Heart's Blood's sacrifice of her life, resulting in their new ability to communicate on the level of a dragon. *A Sending of Dragons* completes the cycle, with Jakkin and Akki captured by a race of people who are also able to communicate by mind-sending. Yolen explores many moral complexities within the plot, such as the true meaning of freedom, the possibility of good going awry through venal desires, and one's responsibility for others.

Venturing onto the worn pathway of the tales of King Arthur, Yolen breaks her own trail in *The Dragon's Boy.* For the reader steeped in the lore King Arthur, *The Dragon's Boy* will be a splendid uncovering of clues to characters and ideas as the story unfolds in a new setting, and as Yolen plays with language and ideas in clever ways.

All of Yolen's work is saturated with her knowledge, her wit, and her belief in the importance of story. In her own words, "Knowing that . . . magic has consequences, whether it is the magic of wonder, the magic of language, or the magic of challenging a waiting mind, . . . It is up to the artist, the writer, the storyteller to reach out and touch that awesome magic. Touch magic—and pass it on."

—M. Jean Greenlaw

YOUNG, Robert F(ranklin)

Nationality: American. **Born:** Silver Creek, New York, 8 June 1915. **Military Service:** Served in the United States Army during World War II. **Family:** Married Regina M. Sadusky in 1941; one daughter. **Career:** Inspector in a nonferrous foundry. **Died:** 1986.

SCIENCE FICTION PUBLICATIONS

Novels

La Quête de la Sainte Grille. Paris, Opta, 1975.
Starfinder. New York, Pocket Books, 1980.
The Last Yggdrasill. New York, Ballantine, 1982.
Eridahn. New York, Ballantine, 1983.
The Vizier's Second Daughter. New York, DAW, 1985.

Short Stories

The Worlds of Robert F. Young. New York, Simon and Schuster, 1965; London, Gollancz, 1966.
A Glass of Stars. Jacksonville, Illinois, Harris Wolfe, 1968.
Le Pays d'esprit. Paris, Oswald, 1982.

*

Robert F. Young commented:

(1985) My books and stories deal with a variety of subjects. My motive in writing most of them stems in part from a fascination for science fiction dating from the long-ago years when I discovered Edgar Rice Burroughs and H.G. Wells, and in part from the genre's capability of providing a writer with the opportunity to make the impossible seem possible.

*   *   *

In an introductory essay to Robert F. Young's *A Glass of Stars,* Fritz Leiber remarks: "And I say that the field to which Robert F. Young has many times proven his claim is that of romantic love. The magic potion of which he is master creator is the love philter." It could be further noted that the potion is not meant merely for the characters in his stories, but to captivate the audience that reads them. Young's realm is the realm of boy meets girl, not in some bygone era but on other worlds or in a future mired in the sins of our own time, crass commercialism and the violation of the environment. Almost always Young surveys his domain with the force of his sense of humor, inserting it at the proper junctures so as not to allow "boy meets girl" to become soap opera. Young skillfully weaves his plots in such a manner that the reader can only smile at the fact that the man and woman are together, living happily ever after, in the end.

An especially fine example of Young's plot-twisting talent is the story "L'Arc de Jeanne," which takes place on the planet Ciel Bleu, near the key city of Fleur du Sud. This is a planet committed to the Psycho-Phenomenalist Church. We find it under attack by the forces of the evil tyrant O'Riordan. All that stands in the way of conquest is a young maiden who rides a "magnificent black stallion" and is armed with what appears to be a magic bow and arrow. O'Riordan wants the maiden captured, and sends a computer-selected young man guaranteed to be irresistible to the maiden, to win her affection. The story evolves in such a manner that Young's Joan of Arc must burn at the stake, yet Young manages the plot so that the story ends happily.

Young's conservation concerns show forth in "To Fell a Tree." A young treeman has the task of felling a glorious 1000-foot tree, a job his company has been hired to do by a rather greedy village. The tree is so enormous that he must live in the tree for a number of days in order to bring it down. While in the tree he meets a dryad, the spirit of the tree, who is seen slowly dying as the tree is cut down, the sap of which looks just like blood. Young's talent as a weaver of words is revealed in this story, along with his passionate concern for nature's living forms.

Young, a shrewd commentator on the crassness of commercialism, had a special fondness for the crudities of the automotive world. In "Romance in a Twenty-First-Century Used-Car-Lot," the auto industry has managed to miniaturize cars sufficiently so that they can be worn as clothing, and then convinced the public that not wearing them is obscene. Those who don't wear cars are called nudists and consigned to a nudist colony. "It wasn't hard to do," Howard Highways tells Arabella Grille, "because people had been wearing their cars unconsciously all along." Then there is Emily ("Emily and the Bards Sublime"), an assistant curator of a museum. She is extremely fond of the android poets, especially Lord Tennyson. One day she is told that the poets must go to make room for a display of 20th-century art—cars, that is. Mr. Brandon tells her she will be taking over the new exhibit; "Mr. Brandon handed her the big book he was carrying. *An Analysis of the Chrome Motif in Twentieth Century Art.* Read it religiously, Miss Meredith. It's the most important book of our century.'"

However, Young's first love was romance, and he was willing to go to, or to manipulate, the ends of time to bring his loved ones together. "The Dandelion Girl," "The Girl Who Made Time Stop," and "Mine Eyes Have Seen the Glory" are all examples of first-rate stories that entail clever use of the intricacies of time as the fourth dimension. Young's gift as a storyteller is brought out in these tales, for by the end of each story the reader has been moved to believe in the possibility of romantic love even when it entails bending the known laws of physics.

In *Starfinder,* Young also makes much use of the intricacies of time travel. The book deals with giant creatures—space whales—who can dive into the past, spaceships constructed from the carcasses of these creatures, and one man's relationship to both the spacecraft and one of the creatures. Young takes full advantage of the paradoxes of time travel as he spins yet another story of romance across the eons. The reader should be forewarned, however, that Young's romanticism takes something of a rather sexist turn in its portrayal of one of the most important female characters and the planet she helps rule. Several segments of *Starfinder* were first published in short story versions over a number of years.

—Mitchell Aboulafia

Z

ZAGAT, Arthur Leo

Nationality: American. **Born:** New York City, in 1895. **Education:** City College of New York, B.A.; Bordeaux University; Fordham University Law School, New York, LL.D. **Military Service:** Served in the United States Army during World War I, and with the Office of War Information during World War II. **Family:** Married Ruth Zagat; one daughter. **Career:** Founded Writers Workshop at New York University. **Member:** of the Council, Authors League of America. **Died:** 3 April 1949.

SCIENCE FICTION PUBLICATIONS

Novel

Seven out of Time. Reading, Pennsylvania, Fantasy Press, 1949.

*   *   *

Arthur Leo Zagat is essentially an early-1930s figure, to be seen in the context of science fiction broadening, diversifying, and acquiring a definite character as more magazines emerged.

His relatively small SF output reflected a personal interest in futuristic ideas; as with many others of the time whose overall output was trivial hack work, he showed originality and vision in science fiction. Every cliché began as an inspiration. Though his stories ranged over a variety of themes, his main contribution was to space flight. This was then something predicted for the indefinite future, but it was a vision that excited that generation as no other. The spectacular progress of aviation had made a profound impression, clearly made obvious the pace of technological change, and raised imagination from the ground.

Interplanetary travel had a long literary tradition, but, aside from its use as a springboard to introduce a utopia or a reflection on man's follies, its emphasis had always been on the initial problems to be solved. By the time SF was firmly established, readers had gone over that ground many times and were ready to go beyond it. Early 1930s science fiction tried to imagine regular traffic between worlds, and settled into a picture analogous to ocean shipping as it had been in earlier times when it was more hazardous and maritime countries more remote and diverse. Zagat helped build up the image of a dangerous yet established trade, of interplanetary shipping lines and business rivalries, of a rough spaceport district analogous to the traditional waterfront, of a rough frontier class of spacemen, with occasional piracy and clashes with natives, or a well-disciplined space service to keep order.

Inevitably this led to the repetitive action stories Tucker aptly tagged space opera. It tended to trivialise space flight by glossing over the problems, though it popularised the concept. Its rather optimistic view had a strong appeal in its time. Zagat's stories such as "The Great Dome on Mercury," "Spoor of the Bat," and "The Cavern of the Shining Pool" were good entertainment, and added to the movement's repertory of expectations. World-scale conflict of East and West, another standard theme, was exploited in "The Death-Cloud," "The Green Ray," and "Flight of the Silver Eagle," dated, but showing what then seemed good probabilities: a world shrunk by better communications, conflict mainly airborne, deathrays, and other devices.

And there are many other themes, all fairly new and treated originally—unEarthlike life, the amorphous "The Menace from Andromeda," logically evolved; a nonhuman intelligent race in "The Emperor of the Stars" sympathetically treated without humanising it; invisible subterranean beings in "Beyond the Spectrum"; machine intelligence in "The Revolt of the Machines"; the world depopulated and left to a few chance survivors in "When the Sleepers Woke"; big business replacing traditional state power in "Exiles of the Moon" and "Lost in Time"; glimpses of future custom and folklore, even sport, in "Sunward Flight"; dangerous inventions in "The Lanson Screen," the defensive shield that became a deadly prison.

Zagat's only book, *Seven out of Time,* drew on elements he had used before and clearly suffers from spinning out the suspense in a six-part serial. The early chapters with their missing-person plot and eerie touches contrast with the strange remote world of millions of years hence, where the group of dehumanised monsters evolved from us try to recover the insights and motivations they have lost by studying their kidnapped people of our own and earlier times. Dated and plausible only as symbolic fantasy even in 1939, it has merit for the message it presents even today.

The volume of SF still appearing in the general fiction magazines through the 1930s is generally overlooked, but it was considerable and, though mostly less original, it has interest. *Seven out of Time* first ran in *Argosy* which had a long history of including science fiction on its merits. Perhaps a better novel serialised there, never made a book, is "Drink We Deep," though hampered by its use of the primitive diary-letter form. This mystery with seemingly supernatural elements developed into a wild extravaganza of early SF fancies, with size-change to bring the leading characters from everyday America into a miniature people's realm under a lake, with scientific marvels and a possible menace to the human world, plot elements reminiscent of Burroughs or Merritt, and some memorable scenes. The 1939-41 series of six tales beginning with "Tomorrow" was discontinued without resolution, perhaps because its background of a future America enslaved by the Yellow Peril came to be less a stock theme than an uncomfortable possibility. But its treatment with a group of children growing into Noble Savages in a wilderness retreat to lead revolt was an unusual concept.

Zagat's first works were written with Nat Schachner, whose role cannot be distinguished. The writing is conventional, the human interest elementary, with characterisation going little beyond stock figures. But it is competent, good of its kind in its time, and it has conviction.

—Graham Stone

ZAHN, Timothy

Nationality: American. **Born:** Chicago, Illinois, 1 September 1951. **Education:** Michigan State University, East Lansing, 1969-73, B.A. in physics 1973; University of Illinois, Urbana, 1973-79, M.S. in physics 1975. **Family:** Married Anna L. Zahn in 1979; one son. **Career:** Since 1980, full-time writer. **Awards:** Hugo award, 1984. **Agent:** Russell Galen, Scott Meredith Literary Agency, 845 Third Avenue, New York, New York 10022. **Address:** 2014 Vawter Street, Apt. 2, Urbana, Illinois 61801, U.S.A.

SCIENCE FICTION PUBLICATIONS

Novels (series: Blackcollar; Cobra; Star Wars)

The Blackcollar. New York, DAW, 1983; London, Arrow, 1986.
A Coming of Age. New York, Bluejay, 1985.
Spinneret. New York, Bluejay, 1985; London, Arrow, 1987.
The Backlash Mission (Blackcollar). New York, DAW, 1986; London, Legend, 1988.
Triplet. New York, Baen, 1987; London, Legend, 1988.
Cobra Bargain. New York, Baen, 1988; London, Legend, 1989.
Deadman Switch. New York, Baen, 1988.
Warhorse. New York, Baen, 1990.
Heir to the Empire (Star Wars). New York and London, Bantam, 1991.
Cobras Two. Riverdale, New York, Baen, 1992.
　Cobra. New York, Baen, 1985.
　Cobra Strike. New York, Baen, 1986.
Dark Force Rising (Star Wars). New York and London, Bantam, 1992.
The Last Command (Star Wars). New York and London, Bantam, 1993.
Conqueror's Pride. New York, Bantam, 1994.

Short Stories

Cascade Point and Other Stories. New York, Bluejay, 1986; as *Cascade Point*, New York, Baen, 1987; title story bound with *Hardfought* by Greg Bear, New York, Tor, 1988.
Time Bomb and Zahndry Others. New York, Baen, 1988.
Distant Friends and Others. New York, Baen, 1992.

*

Timothy Zahn comments:

There are as many definitions of "science fiction" as there are writers, readers, and critics; but to me the important word here is "fiction," and fiction means telling a story. I enjoy speculating in my stories—playing the "if-then" game—and when I can make a point about humanity or society as well I feel I am helping, in a small way, to fulfill the promise of depth and richness that science fiction has always offered its readers. But the basic story must be worth reading; must hold the readers' attention and firmly draw them into the world the writer has created. Otherwise any message is likely to be lost, or never read at all.

The number-one goal in my writing, therefore, is to entertain my audience—to entertain with high adventure, as in *The Blackcollar;* to entertain with details of an unusual society, as in *A Coming of Age;* to entertain with scientific-puzzle stories, as in many of my shorter stories. But the entertainment must be there. Always. It's part of the job.

*　　*　　*

Timothy Zahn started his career primarily as a short story writer for *Analog* magazine during the early 1980s. Although most of his early stories are reasonably entertaining, they were largely formulaic. His blend of sound extrapolation of scientific principles and well-paced, convincing plots began to mark his work as unusual in such stories as "Between a Rock and a High Place," an exceptional story of a disastrous accident in space, "The Cassandra," and "When Johnny Comes Marching Home." The most noteworthy of these, and still his best single shorter work, was "Cascade Point," which won the Hugo award. It deals with a strange phenomenon associated with travel at faster-than-light speeds during which human beings are able to see alternate versions of themselves.

His first novel, *Blackcollar,* also demonstrated another of his recurring concerns—technological augmentation of the human body and the role of the professional soldier in society. Earth has been subjugated by alien conquerors despite the best efforts of the elite Blackcollar units to defend humanity. A generation later, one man learns that some of these supersoldiers have survived, and sets out to use them to overthrow the invaders. Their limited but genuine success is plausible, and the story as a whole is convincing and fast-moving entertainment. Zahn returned to this setting for a sequel, *Backlash Mission.* The secret to the success of the Blackcollars is their use of a secret drug. The secret of its manufacture has been lost, but there is a rumored storehouse deep in alien territory. Although the fast-paced action of the first novel was repeated here, the results are less satisfactory, essentially reprising the original story.

A Coming of Age was both more ambitious and more successful. A colony world has recovered from near chaos when newborn children begin demonstrating telekinetic abilities, which thankfully disappear as they grow older. A well-constructed mystery story is superimposed over this background, but the real focus of the novel is the exploration of the implications of the society that resulted from these unusual conditions.

The plight of the returned soldier during peacetime was examined in some of Zahn's earliest stories, and now two of these were incorporated into what became the first of the *Cobra* series. Jonny Moreau has had powerful weapons surgically implanted in his body, and his deadly abilities create an artificial barrier between himself and his neighbors, until a fresh alien menace, the Troft, alters the situation. Moreau returns in *Cobra Strike,* a generation later, although the novel is more concerned with one of his sons. Humans and the Troft have become reconciled to one another, but they are both menaced by the appearance of a new race. The third in the series, *Cobra Bargain,* returns to an examination of antimilitary sentiment, balanced by a renewed danger of warfare, and embellished by the battle for and against the inclusion of women in the all-male Cobra forces.

Spinneret concerns the discovery of remnants of the technology of a vanished alien race and is a much more sophisticated novel than most of those which preceded it. One strain of the plot is the obvious mystery surrounding the artifacts, while the primary conflict is among various human—and alien—interests attempting to gain power through control of knowledge. Zahn blurred the borders between science fiction and fantasy with *Triplet.* A newly discovered planet contains gates leading to two other worlds, in one of which there exists a technology so sophisticated that it is indistinguishable from magic, and in the other, magic itself holds sway. *Triplet* is an ambitious work that makes some interesting contrasts, but which suffers from the inconsistency of atmosphere required by the plot.

The questions of ethics raised in *Deadman Switch* give an already excellent hard-science-fiction novel an extra dimension. A resource-rich string of moons that has been unapproachable for generations proves attainable only at the cost of two human lives, one to penetrate the system, one to allow departure. As a consequence, condemned criminals are used as sacrifices to expediency by a civilization intent upon exploiting the situation. The ethical problem becomes the primary focus when one of the "criminals" is discovered to be innocent.

Warhorse, also an expansion of two early short stories, presents a similar conflict of interest. Humanity's expansion to the stars causes contact with the Tampies, a star-traveling species that has used bioengineering to breed living spaceships. Both species feel that they are destined to shape the future for all life in the universe, and the massive differences in cultural outlook inevitably lead to conflict. *Warhorse* and *Deadman Switch* are both serious and thoughtful novels as well as fast-paced adventure stories.

Although Zahn has shifted his emphasis to novels, he still writes occasional short stories, the most interesting of which in recent years have been "Evidence of Things Not Seen," "Black Thoughts at Midnight," and "The Hand That Rocks the Casket."

A recent project is a trilogy of novels set in the years following the events of the "Star Wars" movies, consisting of *Heir to the Empire, Dark Force Rising,* and *The Last Command.* Although necessarily restricted by the requirements of character and setting, Zahn has done an admirable job of capturing the pace and feel of the films, and introduces an interesting and suitably malevolent new villain. His gift for producing fast-paced, credible space adventures is perfectly suited for this particular setting and these are the most successful of several attempts to add on to the original sequence.

Subsequently, Zahn started a new series entirely of his own creation with *Conqueror's Pride.* The human race is the leading force in a powerful interstellar civilization that runs into trouble after a new space-traveling race refuses to communicate, instead destroying a small contingent of advanced military vessels, almost effortlessly. One of the crew is taken prisoner, and his family mounts a major effort to rescue him. Their efforts are proscribed by the government, which is reluctant to do anything that might lead the enemy to human-occupied worlds. This rousing action story also includes a well-contrived mystery involving the nature of the aliens, who seem to be able to communicate instantly over interstellar distances, in defiance of known science. There's a partial resolution in this opening volume, but the story remains decidedly incomplete.

Adventure-oriented science fiction has experienced an apparent decline in popularity during the past few years, perhaps because there are so few talented writers whose interests lie in that direction. Timothy Zahn has all the talents necessary to reverse that trend, because even his most melodramatic plots are intelligently constructed and unravelled.

—Don D'Ammassa

ZAMYATIN, Yevgeny

Nationality: Russian. **Born:** Lebedyan, 1 February 1884. **Education:** Voronezh Gymnasium, graduated 1902; St. Petersburg Polytechnical Institute (studies deferred when he was arrested and exiled for revolutionary activities in 1905 and again in 1911), graduated in naval engineering. **Career:** Writer, beginning in 1908; lecturer, Polytechnical Institute. Wrote *My,* which was circulated in manuscript but banned from publication in Russia, in 1920. When an unauthorized portion of the work appeared in a Russian emigré journal (1927), Zamyatin was silenced as a writer. Shortly thereafter, he went into voluntary exile in France, where he spent the remainder of his life. **Died:** 10 March 1937.

Science Fiction Publications

NOVELS

My. Praha, Lazarov, 1929; translated by Gregory Zilboorg as *We,* New York, Dutton, 1924.

OTHER PUBLICATIONS

Novels

Na kulichkakh. Petrograd, Izd.-vo Petrograd, 1923; translated by Walker Ford as *A Godforsaken Hole,* Ann Arbor, Michigan, Ardis, 1988.

Short Stories

The Dragon, edited and translated by Mirra Ginsburg. New York, Random House, 1966; London, Gollancz, 1972; as *The Dragon and Other Stories,* Harmondsworth, Middlesex, Penguin, 1975.
Islanders, and the Village of Men, translated by Sophie Fuller and Julian Sacchi. Edinburgh, Salamander Press, 1984.

Other

A Soviet Heretic: Essays, edited and translated by Mirra Ginsburg. Chicago, University of Chicago Press, 1970; London, Quartet, 1991.

* * *

Yevgeny Zamyatin wrote some 40 books of fiction, fables, plays, and essays. After the October Revolution he became a prominent figure in key literary groups, but from 1921 he incurred much critical disfavor, eventually culminating in a campaign of vilification, especially after *We* was published in an émigré journal. He died in Paris shunned both by Soviet officialdom and right-wing émigrés.

As all early Soviet SF, *We* (written in 1920) deals with the relation of the new Heavens and the old Earth. It incorporates significant features of Zamyatin's novella satirizing life-crushing bourgeois respectability and clerical philistinism written in England during World War I (sex coupons, Taylorite "table of compulsory salvation" through minutely regulated daily occupations). In *We* the Revolution, sunlike principle of life and movement, is opposed to Entropy, principle of dogmatic evil and death. Zamyatin thought of himself as a utopian, more revolutionary than the latter-day Bolsheviks. He is thus not primarily anti-Soviet—even though the increasingly dogmatic high priest of Soviet letters thought so. Extrapolating the repressive possibilities of every strong state and technocratic setup, including the socialist ones, Zamyatin describes a Unique State 12 centuries hence having for its leader "the Benefactor" (a prototype for Orwell), where art is a public utilitarian service, and science a guide for linear, undeviating happiness.

Zamyatin's sarcasm against abstract utopian prescriptions takes on Dostoevskian and Shchedrinian overtones against the totally rationalized city. The only irrational element left is people, like the narrator, the mathematician and rocketship builder D-503, and the temptress from the underground movement who for a moment makes of him a deviant. But man has a built-in instinct for slavery, the rebellion fails, and all the citizen "Numbers" are subjected to brain surgery removing the possibility of harmful imagination.

A practicing scientist committed to the scientific method, Zamyatin could not seriously blame it for the deformation of life. How was it then that a certain rationalism, claiming to be scientific, became harmful? Zamyatin could answer this only in mythical terms: the victory of any lofty ideal causes it to turn repressive. To the extent that *We* equates Leninist communism with institutionalized Christianity and models its fable on an inevitable Fall from Eden ending in ironical crucifixion, it has a strong anti-utopian streak. Instead of motivations, it advances through powerful recurring images, unable to reconcile rationalism and irrationalism, science and art (including the art of love). Zamyatin's political ideology conflicts here with his experimental approach: a meaningful exploration would have to be conducted in terms of the least alienating utopia imaginable—one in which there is no misuse of natural sciences by a dogmatic science of man.

Yet the basic values of *We* imply a stubborn vision of a classless new moral world free from all social alienations, a vision common to Anarchism and libertarian Marxism. Zamyatin confronts absolutistic control—extrapolated from both tsarist-bourgeois and early socialist state practices—with a utopian-socialist norm. As he wrote: "We do not turn to those who reject the present in the name of a return to the past, nor to those hopelessly stupefied by the present, but to those who can see the far-off tomorrow—and in the name of tomorrow, in the name of man, we judge the present." His novel brought to SF the realization that the new world cannot be a static changeless paradise of a new religion—albeit of steel, mathematics, and interplanetary flights. The materialist utopia must subject itself to a constant scrutiny; its values are for Zamyatin centered in an ever-developing human personality and expressed in irreducible and subversive erotic passion. For all its resolute one-sidedness, the uses of Zamyatin's bitter and paradoxical warning in a dialectical utopianism seem obvious.

The expressionistic language of *We,* manipulated for speed and economy ("a high voltage of every word"), helps to subsume the protagonist's defeat under the novel's concern for the integrity of man's knowledge (science) and practice (love and art). By sensitively subjecting the deformities it describes to the experimental examination and hyperbolic magnification of SF, Zamyatin's method makes it possible to identify and cope with them. In his own vocabulary, the protagonist's defeat is of the day but not necessarily of the epoch. The defeat in the novel *We* is not the defeat of the novel itself, but an exasperated shocking of the reader into thought and action. Zamyatin's encyclopedic knowledge embraced the SF tradition before and after Wells, from the utopias through the planetary and underground novels to the anticipations of Odoevsky, About, Bellamy, Morris, Lasswitz, Willbrandt, Jack London, and most notably Anatole France. *We* is thus a document of an acute clash between the "cold" and the "warm" utopia: it probably fails to attain full consistency because of the one-sided assumptions, but Zamyatin remains a heretic socialist.

Zamyatin also wrote the SF story "A Story about the Most Important Thing," interleaving developments on three levels—an episode of the Russian civil war, the death of a caterpillar, and four people on a dying "star" (planet, asteroid?) rushing toward destruction on Earth. Its lyrical investigation of the kinds of love and death that are "the most important thing" doesn't quite come off, but presents an interesting literary experiment.

—Darko Suvin

ZEBROWSKI, George

Nationality: American. **Born:** Villach, Austria, 28 December 1945. **Education:** Harpur College, State University of New York, Binghamton, B.A. in philosophy. **Career:** Copy editor, *Binghamton Evening Press,* 1967; filtration plant operator, New York, 1969-70; lecturer in science fiction, State University of New York, Binghamton, 1971; editor, *SFWA Bulletin,* 1970-75, and 1983-1991; general editor and consultant, Crown Publishers, Inc., New York, 1983-86. Freelance writer, editor, consultant, and lecturer. **Agent:** Richard Curtis Associates, Inc., 171 East 74th Street, New York, New York 10021, U.S.A. **Address:** c/o Richard Curtis Associates, Inc.

SCIENCE FICTION PUBLICATIONS

Novels (series: Omega Point; Bernal One)

The Omega Point. New York, Ace, 1972; London, New English Library, 1974.
The Star Web. Toronto, Laser, 1975.
Ashes and Stars. New York, Ace, 1977; London, New English Library, 1978.
Macrolife. New York, Harper, 1979; London, Orbit, 1980.
The Omega Point Trilogy (includes *The Omega Point* and *Ashes and Stars,* both revised, and *Mirror of Minds*). New York, Ace, 1983.
Sunspacer (for children; Bernal One). New York, Harper, 1984.
The Stars Will Speak (for children; Bernal One). New York, Harper, 1985.
Stranger Suns. New York, Bantam, 1991.
The Killing Star, with Charles Pellegrino. New York, Morrow, 1995.
The Sunspacers Trilogy (includes *Sunspacer, The Stars Will Speak,* and the previously unpublished in book form *Behind the Stars*). Clarkston, White Wolf, n.d.
A Fury Scorned, with Pamela Sargent. New York, Pocket Books, n.d.

Short Stories

The Monadic Universe. New York, Ace, 1977; augmented edition, 1985.
A Silent Shout (for children). Tulsa, Educational Development Corporation, 1979.
The Firebird (for children). Tulsa, Educational Development Corporation, 1979.
Adrift in Space (for children). Tulsa, Educational Development Corporation, 1979.

OTHER PUBLICATIONS

Other

Editor, *Tomorrow Today.* Santa Cruz, California, Unity Press, 1975.

Editor, with Thomas N. Scortia, *Human-Machines: An Anthology of Stories about Cyborgs.* New York, Vintage, 1975; London, Hale, 1977.

Editor, with Jack Dann, *Faster Than Light: An Original Anthology about Interstellar Travel.* New York, Harper, 1976.

Editor, *The Best of Thomas N. Scortia.* Garden City, New York, Doubleday, 1981.

Editor, with Isaac Asimov and Martin H. Greenberg, *Creations: The Quest for Origins in Story and Science.* New York, Crown, 1983; London, Harrap, 1984.

Editor, *Nebula Awards [20-22].* San Diego, California, Harcourt, 1985, 1987-88.

Editor, *Synergy [1-4]: New Science Fiction.* San Diego, California, Harcourt, 1987-89.

Editor, *Classics of Modern Science Fiction,* New York, Crown, 1984-85, 10 volumes.

*

Bibliography: *The Work of George Zebrowski: An Annotated Bibliography and Guide* by Jeffrey M. Elliot, San Bernardino, California, Borgo Press, 1986, 1990, revised, 1996.

Manuscript Collection: Paskow Science Fiction Collection, Temple University, Philadelphia.

George Zebrowski comments:

I have been described as a "hard SF writer with literary intent"—which makes me sound like a difficult person about to commit a crime of some sort. What "literary" means in this description, I believe, is that I pay attention to the writerly virtues of style, characterization, and lucid storytelling, as much as I do to what makes a work science fiction—its scientific facts, speculative ideas, and philosophical considerations. Nothing wrong with that; I wouldn't think much of any hard SF writer who deliberately leaves all that out.

James Blish, a favorite writer of mine, once said that SF should be hard (thoroughgoing) all the way through—in its ideas and literary virtues, which seems to me to be beyond argument as a prescription. It's the ideal I started with as a writer.

The knowledge of what one does as an SF writer can be clearly stated, but not easily practiced. One writes fiction that deals with the human impact of possible future changes in science and technology. Even if you remove science and technology, you still have "the human impact of possible future change." You might remove future, since many SF works are set in the present or past, but you can still substitute "imaginary but plausible" here and not violate the spirit of SF. The "human impact" makes it literature; the "plausible imaginary changes" makes it SF. How well the literary and science-fictional conceits come out depends on the ambition and skill of the writer.

*   *   *

Like Olaf Stapledon before him, George Zebrowski paints his fictive vistas with the brush of aeons, adding and subtracting galaxies and centuries with great slashing strokes. Not for him are the crabbed miniatures of most science fiction novelists, whose collective vision barely extends over the next hill. Zebrowski is concerned with the "big picture," the long-term fate of mankind, the end (and the beginning) of things, the how and where and particularly the *why* of life, the universe, and everything. Where so many of his compatriots are now producing western, mystery, and mainstream novels with SF trappings, sequel upon sequel upon inanity, *this*

author has written and continues to pen brilliant *science* fictions which could be presented in no other conceivable form.

Beginning life as the child of Polish parents displaced by World War II, Zebrowski grew up in England, Manhattan, Miami, and the Bronx, even then a wasteland of broken dreams and deadened hopes. He began reading science fiction at an early age, and was writing his first stories in the 1960s. In 1970 he published "The Water Sculptor," the first of a hundred stories which quickly earned him numerous award nominations. The author's first novel, *The Omega Point* (1972), later expanded into *The Omega Point Trilogy,* provided an initial showcase for Zebrowski's cosmic visions of man and the universe. These early fictions pale, however, before the sweep and impact of the writer's first major novel, *Macrolife,* which would ensure him a place in the SF Hall of Fame even if he never wrote another word.

Zebrowski had penned the first drafts of *Macrolife* as early as 1964, although the book was not completed until 15 years later. In a near-future Earth, the discovery of bulerite (named for the Bulero family) has revolutionized architecture and economics. Lightweight, versatile, stronger than steel, bulerite has enabled the construction of huge cityplexes, and facilitated the exploration of near-Earth space, with the subsequent colonization of Mars, the asteroids, and several of the larger moons in the Solar System. Unknown to the Buleros, however, bulerite is inherently unstable, and as structures made of the element begin to disintegrate or explode, they pull civilization down with it. Three of the Buleros—Richard, Sam, and Janet—escape to Asterome, a followed-out 10-mile-long asteroid in Earth orbit, along with other scattered refugees from the devastated planet below. Earth is enveloped in an impenetrable cloud, with no hope of any life surviving the incessant lightning storms raging over its surface.

Asterome represents the first stage of macrolife, a self-sufficient, self-contained structure that will eventually spread intelligent life to every part of the universe. Eventually, Asterome leaves the Solar System, traveling to nearby stars, and utilizing the raw materials from their planets to construct new macrolife globes as its own compartments become crowded, or as social divisions develop among the populace. The flexibility of this arrangement, and the gradual lengthening of lifespans, enable humanity to grow literally without limits, to avoid frictions that might lead to war, to develop intellectually and emotionally in ways never before contemplated. Eventually, an alien macrolife unit is located, one of many such structures traversing the galaxy, and contact is made, to the mutual benefit of both races. The mental links between these groups seem to promise another stage of development of mankind.

A hundred billion years later, all intelligence has merged into one group mind. But the universe is winding down toward ultimate nullity, when all matter will collapse into the final explosion. John Bulero, a clone of Samuel Bolero, suddenly finds his consciousness reconstituted for some ultimate decision. Is there something more? the intelligences ask. Can anything survive the final debacle? The answers to these questions lead Bulero to the third level of macrolife, a consciousness so powerful that it can create its own universes, can transcend time and space itself.

Zebrowski's next major novel, *Stranger Suns,* represents a further 15 years of effort, an early draft having been published in much abridged form in 1975. Juan Obrion and his three companions discover an abandoned alien spaceship buried deep in the Antarctic ice. The ship admits them, then abruptly takes off for an unknown destination. The explorers discover matter replicators within the ship that solve their immediate problems of food and water supply, but no sign of the race which had constructed the vessel. They determine that the aliens have built a network of way stations within the suns of both our galaxy and its neighbors; these sophisticated facilities have similarly been abandoned, as have the surface structures found on a barren planet at the end of the chain. Eventually Juan and his friends determine that a set of black panels in the ship's bowels connect directly through hyperspace to similar panels on two other vessels left within the Solar System, one buried in the Amazon jungle, the other on the Moon, and to other alien vessels and facilities, enabling instantaneous movement through tremendous distances.

However, nothing in Zebrowski's works is ever quite what it seems, because the very act of moving back and forth through the portals alters either the viewer or the viewed in ways which are sometimes subtly, sometimes grossly skewed from the original. Eye color may be changed, or the outcome of a football game—or the fundamental history of the world as Obrion has known it. Why did the alien race develop this alternate mode of transportation? Why have all their facilities been abandoned? Where have they gone? Can mankind use these structures to ensure its survival? The answers to these questions lead Obrion and company on a strange odyssey beyond the universe to an existence outside time and space as we know it.

The author's third major work, *The Killing Star* (with Charles Pellegrino), poses another curious question: if the universe is filled with intelligent life, as Carl Sagan and many other scientists have proposed, must they necessarily be as friendly as has been postulated? And if they're not friendly, or even if they're just a little bit afraid of what we might do to them in the future, won't they do it to us first? Within the first few pages of this gripping adventure set a hundred years hence, most of humanity is wiped out by an unseen alien race which has decided to dispose of a potential problem with humanity before it arises. By accelerating rocks and other debris to near-light speeds, the unseen enemies create devastating bombs that home in on all radio emissions in the solar system, eliminating 99% of the human species within a few minutes. All that survive are isolated outposts and ships, and these are quickly targeted for "mop-up" operations by the alien intruders. The bulk of this gripping saga deals with the efforts of the remnants of humanity to survive and fight back, countering the overwhelming alien presence with new and innovative scientific discoveries.

Zebrowski has penned more than just these three novels, of course. His young adult series, *The Sunspacers Trilogy,* has been well-received in the juvenile market. His numerous short stories include significant works of science fiction, horror, fantasy, and mainstream fiction. His editorial credits include numerous original and reprint anthologies, and long service as coeditor of the *Bulletin of the Science Fiction Writers of America.* Forthcoming are several collections of his essays, including groundbreaking pieces on Eastern European SF.

Most of his fiction focuses on man's attempts to rise from the mud of his mundane existence and lift his face to the stars. If our race is to survive the wars and chances of planet-bound existence, he seems to be saying, we must leave this place for the limitless reaches of outer space, and we must find new challenges for the species as a whole. Life on Earth is inherently flawed, for by creating a world on the edge of collapse we have imperiled our own future existence. In Zebrowski's cosmos, limited or unlimited, Earth (the soil) is Hell, the stars (the universe) are Heaven, and humanity can become either god or devil, savior or destroyer, as he or she so chooses.

—Robert Reginald

ZEIGFRIED, Karl. *See* FANTHORPE, R. Lionel.

———

ZELAZNY, Roger (Joseph)

Pseudonym: Harrison Denmark. **Nationality:** American. **Born:** Cleveland, Ohio, 13 May 1937. **Education:** Noble School, 1943-49, Shore Junior High School, 1949-52, and Euclid Senior High School, 1952-55, all Euclid, Ohio; Western Reserve University, Cleveland (Foster Poetry award, 1957, 1959), 1955-59, B.A. in English 1959; Columbia University, New York, 1959-60, M.A. 1962. **Military Service:** Served in the Ohio National Guard, 1960-63, and the United States Army Reserve, 1963-66. **Family:** Married 1) Sharon Steberl in 1964 (divorced 1966); 2) Judith Callahan in 1966, two sons and one daughter. **Career:** Claims representative, Cleveland, 1963-65, and claims specialist, Baltimore, 1965-69, Social Security Administration. Since 1969, freelance writer and lecturer. Secretary-Treasurer, Science Fiction Writers of America, 1967-68. **Awards:** Nebula award, 1965 (twice), 1975; Hugo award, for novel, 1966, 1968, for story, 1976, 1982; Prix Apollo, 1972; American Library Association award, 1976; *Locus* award, 1984, 1986. Guest of Honor, 32nd World Science Fiction Convention, 1974, and Australian National Science Fiction Convention, 1978. **Died:** 14 June 1995.

SCIENCE FICTION PUBLICATIONS

Novels (series: Amber; Divlish; Millennial Contest; Wizard World)

This Immortal. New York, Ace, 1966; London, Hart Davis, 1967.
The Dream Master. New York, Ace, 1966; London, Hart Davis, 1968.
Lord of Light. Garden City, New York, Doubleday, 1967; London, Faber, 1968.
Isle of the Dead. New York, Ace, 1969; London, Rapp and Whiting, 1970.
Creatures of Light and Darkness. Garden City, New York, Doubleday, 1969; London, Faber, 1970.
Damnation Alley. New York, Putnam, 1969; London, Faber, 1971.
Nine Princes in Amber. Garden City, New York, Doubleday, 1970; London, Faber, 1972.
Jack of Shadows. New York, Walker, 1971; London, Faber, 1973.
The Guns of Avalon (Amber). Garden City, New York, Doubleday, 1972; London, Faber, 1974.
Today We Choose Faces. New York, New American Library, 1973; London, Millington, 1974.
To Die in Italbar. Garden City, New York, Doubleday, 1973; London, Faber, 1975.
Sign of the Unicorn (Amber). Garden City, New York, Doubleday, 1975; London, Faber, 1977.
Doorways in the Sand. New York, Harper, 1976; London, W.H. Allen, 1977.
The Hand of Oberon (Amber). Garden City, New York, Doubleday, 1976; London, Faber, 1978.
Bridge of Ashes. New York, New American Library, 1976.

Deus Irae, with Philip K. Dick. Garden City, New York, Doubleday, 1976; London, Gollancz, 1977.

The Courts of Chaos (Amber). Garden City, New York, Doubleday, 1978; London, Faber, 1980.

The Chronicles of Amber (omnibus). Garden City, New York, Doubleday, 2 vols., 1979.

Roadmarks. New York, Ballantine, 1979; London, Futura, 1981.

Coils, with Fred Saberhagen. New York, Tor, 1980; London, Penguin, 1984.

The Changing Land; A Novel of Divlish the Damned. New York, Ballantine, 1981.

Eye of Cat. San Francisco, Underwood-Miller, 1982; London, Sphere, 1984.

Trumps of Doom (Amber). New York, Arbor House, 1985; London, Sphere, 1986.

Blood of Amber. New York, Arbor House, 1986; London, Sphere, 1987.

A Dark Traveling (for children). New York, Walker, 1987; as *A Dark Travelling,* London, Hutchinson, 1989.

Sign of Chaos (Amber). New York, Arbor House, 1987; London, Sphere, 1988.

Knight of Shadows (Amber). New York, Morrow, 1989; London, Orbit, 1991.

Wizard World. New York, Baen, 1989.

    Changeling. New York, Ace, 1980.

    Madwand. Huntington Woods, Michigan, Phantasia Press, 1981.

The Black Throne, with Fred Saberhagan. New York, Baen, 1990.

The Mask of Loki, with Thomas T. Thomas. New York, Baen, 1990.

Bring Me the Head of Prince Charming, with Robert Sheckley (Millennial Contest). New York, Bantam, 1991; London, Pan Books, 1994.

Prince of Chaos (Amber), New York, Morrow, 1991; London, Orbit, 1993.

Flare, with Thomas T. Thomas. New York, Baen, 1992.

A Night in the Lonesome October. New York, Morrow, 1993; London, Orbit, 1994.

If at Fauste You Don't Succeed, with Robert Sheckley (Millennial Contest). New York, Bantam, 1993.

A Farce to Be Reckoned With, with Robert Sheckley (Millennial Contest). New York, Bantam, 1995.

Short Stories (series: Amber; Divlish)

Four for Tomorrow. New York, Ace, 1967; as *A Rose for Ecclesiastes,* London, Hart Davis, 1969.

The Doors of His Face, the Lamps of His Mouth, and Other Stories. Garden City, New York, Doubleday, 1971; London, Faber, 1973; title story published separately as *The Doors of His Face, the Lamps of His Mouth,* Eugene, Oregon, Pulphouse, 1991.

My Name Is Legion. New York, Ballantine, 1976; London, Faber, 1979.

The Bells of Shoredan (Divlish). San Francisco, Underwood-Miller, 1979.

The Last Defender of Camelot. San Francisco, Underwood-Miller, 1980; with other stories, New York, Pocket Books, 1980; London, Sphere, 1986.

For a Breath I Tarry. San Francisco, Underwood-Miller, 1980.

A Rhapsody in Amber. New Castle, Virginia, Cheap Street, 1981.

Dilvish the Damned. New York, Ballantine, 1982.

Unicorn Variations. New York, Pocket Books, 1983.

Frost and Fire. New York, Morrow, 1989.

He Who Shapes, bound with *The Infinity Box,* by Kate Wilhelm. New York, Tor, 1989.

Home Is the Hangman, bound with *We, in Some Strange Power's Employ, Move on a Rigorous Line,* by Samuel R. Delany. New York, Tor, 1990.

The Graveyard Heart, bound with *Elegy for Angels and Dogs,* by Walter Jon Williams. New York, Tor, 1990.

Gone to Earth. Eugene, Oregon, Pulphouse, 1992.

Here There Be Dragons, illustrated by Vaughn Bodè. Hampton Falls, New Hampshire, Donald Grant, 1992.

Way up High, illustrated by Vaughn Bodè. Hampton Falls, New Hampshire, Donald Grant, 1992.

OTHER PUBLICATIONS

Poetry

Poems. N.p., Discon, 1974.

When Pussywillows Last in the Catyard Bloomed. Carlton, Australia, Nostrilia Press, 1980.

To Spin Is Miracle Cat. San Francisco, Underwood-Miller, 1982.

Other

The Authorized Illustrated Book of Roger Zelazny, edited and adapted by Byron Preiss, illustrated by Gray Morrow. New York, Baronet, 1978; as *The Illustrated Zelazny,* New York, Ace, 1979.

Roger Zelazny's Visual Guide to Castle Amber, with Neil Randall. New York, Avon, 1988.

Wilderness, with Gerald Hausman. New York, Forge, 1994.

Editor, *Nebula Award Stories Three.* Garden City, New York, Doubleday, and London, Gollancz, 1968.

Editor, *Warriors of Blood and Dreams.* New York, AvoNova, 1995.

*

Bibliography: *Roger Zelazny: A Primary and Secondary Bibliography* by Joseph L. Sanders, Boston, Hall, 1980; *Amber Dreams: A Roger Zelazny Bibliography* by Daniel J.H. Levack, Columbia, Pennsylvania, Underwood-Miller, 1983.

Manuscript Collections: George Arents Research Library, Syracuse University, New York; Special Collections, University of Maryland, Baltimore.

Critical Studies: *A Reader's Guide to Roger Zelazny* by Carl B. Yoke, West Linn, Oregon, Starmont House, 1979; *Roger Zelazny* by Theodore Krulik, New York, Unger, 1986.

Roger Zelazny commented:

(1991) My earlier writing involved considerable use of mythological materials. I have, however, attempted to diversify over the years. I write both fantasy and science fiction, as well as mixtures of the two. My objectives vary from book to book, but in general I begin with character in mind rather than plot. Among my personal favorites are the *Lord of Light* and *Doorways in the Sand.*

*   *   *

A writer who constantly challenged himself, Roger Zelazny is difficult to categorize. He successfully wrote both fantasy and "hardcore" science fiction; he created works of both light and serious tone; he was adept at all lengths; and he tackled most of the standard science fiction themes. Even his style changed since he published his first short story in 1962—from one that was highly mythic and richly poetic to one that was more controlled, economical, and precise. Yet despite the wide variation in tone, content, and style of his work, there are definite and consistent characteristics in his writing. Certain themes recur; certain kinds of characters reappear. Perhaps it is in his characterization that the threads which link his works are most easily seen.

Zelazny's ability to create believable characters is probably his single most important contribution to science fiction. Even though his protagonists usually possess some ability or talent which makes them "larger-than-life," they remain entirely credible. They prize their self-reliance, personal integrity, and individualism. They must develop their own unique abilities and talents. And, since growth is a result of experience, the psychological growth of the characters is directly linked to their adventures. Frequently, Zelazny's stories begin with his protagonist disillusioned, alienated, or geographically isolated, and, whatever the circumstances, the specific conditions of his situation set him off on some kind of quest. In addition to attaining some physical objective, however, Zelazny's heroes are also set off unconsciously on a psychological quest which is to achieve a metamorphosis of a personality, to raise their level of consciousness. If successful, this new maturity brings the disparate elements of their personalities into harmony, gives them a broader and deeper knowledge of themselves and the worlds in which they live, and creates the possibility for love. Of Zelazny's best works, the Amber novels, both series, "A Rose for Ecclesiastes," and "The Doors of His Face, the Lamps of His Mouth" use protagonists who achieve metamorphosis in the course of the story, while *Lord of Light* and *This Immortal* tell stories which could not happen until after their protagonists have achieved this growth.

Zelazny's recurrent themes are integrally related to the psychological quests of his heroes. Vanity, greed, power, guilt, and revenge block metamorphosis and must be overcome before it can occur. Immortality permits a character to achieve a fuller realization of his capabilities. Zelazny recognized that as long as a healthy person lives, psychological growth will continue. Love and fertility, in all their possible forms, are the positive benefits of metamorphosis. Self-reliance, personal integrity, and individualism are the keys to achieving it. Renewal, or restoration, which appears so frequently in Zelazny's stories, is an encompassing theme which signals both physical and psychological success.

Zelazny's most important works are the stories "A Rose for Ecclesiastes," "The Doors of His Face, the Lamps of His Mouth," "Home Is the Hangman," "Unicorn Variation," "Permafrost," and "24 Views of Mt. Fuji, by Hokusai," and the novels *This Immortal, The Dream Master, Lord of Light,* and the ten Amber books. "A Rose for Ecclesiastes" and "The Doors of His Face, the Lamps of His Mouth" are renewal stories, and both Gallinger, the conceited Earth poet, and Carlton Davits, the bankrupt baitman, must overcome their vanity in order to achieve personality metamorphosis. Each does, and in the process Gallinger saves the Martians from racial suicide and restores fertility to the planet, whilst Davits brings both his and his ex-wife's personalities into harmony and creates a healthy relationship. "Home Is the Hangman," one of Zelazny's "no-name detective" stories, presents a unique twist on the metamorphosis motif. In it, the Hangman, a combination telefactor and computer, returns to Earth after many years in space to show its teachers that it has overcome the neurosis they created for it. The anthropomorphic machine has successfully integrated the elements of its personality, while, ironically, one of its teachers, Jessie Brockden, is so overpowered by guilt that he believes that the machine has returned to kill him. "Unicorn Variation" is a whimsical story about a man who plays chess with a beer-guzzling unicorn. The fate of the human race rests on the outcome of the game, but George Martin gets help from a sasquatch. The story is wonderfully fanciful and one of Zelazny's most imaginative works.

This Immortal presents a protagonist, Conrad Nomikos, who has already achieved maturity by the time the story begins, so the focus of the story shifts from achieving metamorphosis to the role of the hero in restoring the irradiated Earth. A revolutionary group believes that the Vegans, a superior alien culture, are about to begin a wholesale exploitation of the planet, when in they truth are testing Conrad's worth to inherit and subsequently restore it.

The Dream Master presents the only instance in Zelazny's writing where a protagonist fails to achieve metamorphosis. Because his particular personality fault, once again pride, continues to dominate, Dr. Charles Render, a neuroparticipation therapist, is ultimately drawn into the madness of one of his patients. His vanity has prevented him from seeing the limits of his abilities. In one of Zelazny's more interesting attempts to expand a novel through the use of myth, he linked Render to the Scandinavian *ragnarok* and Eileen, his patient, to Arthurian legend. The *ragnarok* represents Render's view of the world and signifies the psychologically deterministic course of his life. The Arthurian material characterizes Eileen's chivalric and highly idealized view of the world. Though the concept is ingenious, the use of symbolic mythic sequences tends to confuse meaning for the perceptive reader rather than clarify it. In addition to illustrating the dangers inherent in allusion, it also illustrates the danger of assuming that Zelazny was attempting to translate whole bodies of myth into science fiction.

Lord of Light, undoubtedly Zelazny's best novel, also treats renewal—in this case the renewal of a society. By the time the story begins, Sam, the protagonist, has long since passed on to a higher state of consciousness. The world of Urath is ruled by colonists who have virtually become gods. They patterned the new after the Hindu culture that they left behind on Earth, and they have achieved virtual immortality because they have the technology for body transfer. Unfortunately, their power has corrupted them. They exploit the masses, their own descendants, and refuse to let them share their technological benefits. Society is repressive and stagnant, and Sam sets out to change it. Of course, he accomplishes his reform mission.

Both sets of Amber novels treat the physical and psychological sides of renewal—the restoration of the land and the metamorphosis of personality. In the first series, Corwin, the protagonist, journeys from youthful and romantic idealism to pragmatism in the course of his adventures to keep the universe from being absorbed back into chaos. In the process, he learns that the most important reason for living is psychologically healthy human relationships.

Both the first and second Amber series dramatize Zelazny's form and-chaos philosophy and stress how man should relate to these basic forces of the universe. The second series, Merlin's Story, probes the relationship between these forces in great detail. Corwin's son, Merlin, must reestablish a balance between Form and Chaos while he achieves his own destiny—to become the King of Chaos. Maintaining a balance between the principal generators of reality, the Pattern, for Form, and the Logrus, for Chaos, would not seem to be much of a challenge except that both have become sentient and are consciously playing against each other for advantage. Set against this is the bildungsroman of Merlin's education for kingship, complete with his transformation.

The Amber novels are not only a major fantasy work, they are also an excellent window on Zelazny's talents. Criticized by some who felt that he had not achieved the stature projected for him when he broke into the field more than 20 years ago, Zelazny had, perhaps more than any other writer, brought the techniques, style, and language of mainstream literature to science fiction and fantasy. There is no question about his stature. He was a major author who wrote several major works, but his greatest contribution may be that he brought characters who are psychologically credible, who are sympathetic, who have depth and scope, to a literature famous for its cardboard figures.

Zelazny's stories of the early 1980s showed two interesting lines of development. In *Changeling, Madwand,* and *Eye of Cat,* he consciously used Jungian imagery and concepts to shape his stories, much as he did earlier in "The Doors of His Face, the Lamps of His Mouth." Such usage reinforces the renewal theme, which pervades his work and which is evident in these stories, especially in the personality growth of his characters. This technique is very similar to what he did in his early writing with mythology.

His work during this period also leans strongly towards fantasy, but it is fantasy that has been hedged. That is, he takes great care to treat the worlds of these stories as if they were simply governed by physical laws different from our own. Magic, supernatural events, and other motifs and devices usually left unexplained in fantasy are treated as if they were a normal part of another reality in these worlds. In *Changeling* and *Madwand,* for instance, magic is a skill. There are different forms of it, there are rules to govern its use, and there are various degrees of adeptness in its practice. In short, Zelazny provided means for his characters to tap into and use the basic forces that govern their story worlds. Though these forces are different from our own, he implied that lying beneath all sets is something common. In these works, Zelazny probed the question of reality and offered differing scenarios as possibilities.

In addition to the second Amber series, Zelazny's other notable work in the 80s includes the award-winning, "Permafrost" and "24 Views of Mt. Fuji, by Hokusai." Both of these stories explore male-female relationships that have gone bad.

In "Permafrost," a man returns to an ice cave where his female friend perished, to clean up evidence of her demise and to claim a treasure in rare crystals. While he did not murder her, he chose to grab a bag of the crystals rather than save her. He discovers that she has not died. Rather, she has become part of the permafrost that girds the planet and acquired special abilities that permit her to arrange a most fitting revenge for him.

In "24 Views of Mt. Fuji, by Hokusai," a dying Japanese-American woman goes on a quest to discover herself and to rid the world of her husband who has transferred his being into an enormous data-net. She chooses her humanity over virtual electronic immortality when she realizes that the potential of such an existence has changed her husband into a megalomaniac. Behind these broken romances is yet another exploration of reality. Both the woman merged with the permafrost and the husband whose being has been transferred to a data-net pose questions about the reality and preservation of our identities.

Both of these stories show the hand of a master craftsman. Their writing is lean and precise, their worlds are original, and their themes demonstrate Zelazny's investigation of imagined alternatives to our own concept of reality. *Prince of Chaos,* the final novel of Merlin's Story, makes a particular point of examining the limits of reason and discusses, at various times, the validity of other means of knowing.

Zelazny's published works from 1990 to 1995 include several collaborations, an anthology, and an excellent novel, *A Night in the Lonesome October.* He wrote two novels with Thomas T. Thomas, *The Mask of Loki,* and *Flare.* Both are interesting and merge the talents of the two writers quite well, but neither reaches the level of Zelazny's best work. The same can be said of Zelazny's collaboration with Robert Sheckley on three comic novels, *Bring Me the Head of Prince Charming, If at Faust You Don't Succeed,* and *A Farce to Be Reckoned With.* The humor is broad and focuses on the eternal fantasy contest between good and evil, except that the battle is complicated by bureaucracy, personality, and contemporary issues. Zelazny also collaborated with Gerald Hausman on *Wilderness,* a poetic retelling of the legendary mountainmen John Colter and Hugh Glass. The book is fascinating and lyrical.

A Night in the Lonesome October is a brilliant, dark gem. Told by Snuff, a brave and loyal dog, the story chronicles the events surrounding that night in October, which turns out to be October 31, when Black Magic will try to summon the Elder Gods back to the world. The players gather, some to assure that the Elder Gods will return and some to be sure that they will not. Among the players are: Snuff's master, a knife-wielding man named Jack who walks the streets of London at night collecting grisly parts for a rite that will take place immediately after the death of the moon, a witch, a Count who sleeps by day, a Good Doctor and his Hulking Experimental Man made from body parts, a mad monk, a vengeful vicar, a shapeshifting man named Larry Talbot, a Great Detective strangely reminiscent of Sherlock Holmes, a rat named Bubo, a squirrel named Cheeter, an owl named Nightwind, a snake named Needle, and a cat named Graymalk. Snuff calculates the patterns of the game that will focus the conflict between good and evil and keeps track of the players involved. The players must collect the icons that will shift the balance when applied properly. When the gate finally begins to open a tentacle appears in the dark mass and there is a reptilian smell (very reminiscent of the evil creature in Henry Kuttner's *Dark World*), but the forces of good rally and close it, until the next time. *A Night in the Lonesome October* is told in a brilliantly simple style that reflects its point of view. It is bizarre and comic, and the text perfectly matches Gahan Wilson's illustrations for the novel

Roger Zelazny passed away on June 14, 1995, shortly after the appearance of an anthology of fantastic martial arts stories entitled *Warriors of Blood and Dream.* He left behind several unfinished projects and unpublished manuscripts. Among them were an untitled novel based on a fragment left by Alfred Bester when he died in 1987, a CD/ROM game with Jane Lindskold, a science fiction novel entitled *Donnerjack,* the outline for a fantasy novel, an anthology honoring Jack Williamson that he was editing, and four completed stories in what was to be a collection of short stories tying up the loose ends of the Amber novels.

—Carl B. Yoke

ZETFORD, Tully. *See* **BULMER, Kenneth.**

ZINDELL, David

Nationality: American. **Born:** 1956. **Address:** c/o Donald I. Fine Inc, 19 West 21st Street, New York, New York 10010, U.S.A.

SCIENCE FICTION PUBLICATIONS

Novel

Neverness. New York, Fine, 1988; London, Grafton, 1989.
The Broken God. London, HarperCollins, 1993; New York, Bantam, 1994.

*   *   *

In common with writers such as Karen Joy Fowler and Robert (Touzalin) Reed, David Zindell first properly came to public attention through the L. Ron Hubbard Writers of the Future contest, where he was one of the quarterly winners with his story "Shanidar." However, it was with *Neverness,* his first and so far only novel, that he achieved wider fame, including being shortlisted for the 1988 Arthur C. Clarke award in the United Kingdom.

As a debut novel, *Neverness* is in many respects a remarkable tour de force, a complex mixture of fantasy and science fiction, drawing on the author's knowledge of mathematics and anthropology to create a strange and exotic society. Focussing on Mallory Ringness, a wayward novitiate in the semi-mystical Order of Pilots (reminiscent of the Knights Templar), the first part of the novel follows his quest to discover the Solid State Entity, a vast galactic brain composed of planet-sized biocomputers. That he so quickly achieves what others, more capable, have failed to do is clearly the major flaw of the novel, as is the rapidity with which what might have been the climax of another fictional work is disposed of, in the first third of the book. Nevertheless, Zindell manages to create a very real sense of what the Entity is, and how Ringness had achieved the impossible in his manipulation, as a Pilot, of the laws of space and time, leaving the reader with the temporary sense of having grasped the most arcane intricacies of mathematical calculation.

Ironically, considering that this section of the novel is so soon dismissed, it is undoubtedly the confrontation with the Solid State Entity, rather than Ringness's subsequent exploration of his own world, which remains in the reader's mind. The remainder of the novel is devoted to a search for the key to immortality, Ringness's death and subsequent resurrection as a human biocomputer, akin to the entity he discovered, and to the retrieval of knowledge lost by his culture. Yet somehow the impetus of the early part of the novel is rarely recaptured, except perhaps in Zindell's descriptions of the ice city of *Neverness,* one of the more remarkable imaginary cities in recent SF and fantasy literature.

If *Neverness* was the story of a man metamorphosing into a god, which is Zindell's perception of his story, then *The Broken God,* and its two projected sequels, *The Wild* and *War in Heaven,* are intended to be about the religion which develops in the wake of events in *Neverness.* Narrated once again by Ringness, who this time acts as a kind of omnscient viewpoint, *The Broken God* fo-

cuses on Danlo, the son that Ringess abandoned during *Neverness.* We first see Danlo as the adopted son of the Alaloi, a culture genetically altered to withstand intense cold. After they die from a strange illness, Danlo treks across the ice to Neverness to attempt to fulfil his destiny as a Pilot, like his father. The story then takes on the aspect of a coming-of-age novel, as Danlo is rescued by kindly aliens, the Fravashi, who educate him, and then undergoes trials in order to enter the Academy. Here he meets Hanuman li Tosh, who will eventually become the leader of a powerful cult built around the story of Mallory Ringess's disappearence, while Danlo will become the cult's fiercest opponent.

With two books published, Zindell's preoccupations have become ever clearer. He has been quoted as saying that "most science fiction writers take easy potshots at religion" and his novels attempt to discover whether matter and spirit can be separated. He creates a cybernetic religion which represents as orthodox, a view which is currently radical, namely the downloading of personality to computer program, but then places this in conflict with a fresh religion in which man has transcended his own physicality. At the same time, while *Neverness* perhaps stumbled at times under the weight of the philosophical and mathematical concepts it was obliged to carry, *The Broken God* is, by comparison, a more dramatic and apparently more plot-driven novel. This is, by comparison with other more conventional novels, an illusion, but Zindell has the knack of creating complex and believable characters and generating immense drama while dealing with subjects that might seem not to lend themslves to fast-moving plots. The dense, allusive, and philosophical nature of his writing provides immensely satisfying reading, and it is to be regretted that more people aren't aware of an author who is really becoming one of SF's best kept secrets.

—Maureen Speller

ZOLINE, Pamela

Nationality: American. **Born:** Chicago, Illinois, in 1941. **Education:** Slade School of Fine Art, London. **Career:** Artist and illustrator; group show, Young Contemporaries, 1966. Lives in Colorado. **Address:** c/o Coffee House Press, 27 North Fourth Street, Suite 400, Minneapolis, Minnesota 55401, U.S.A.

SCIENCE FICTION PUBLICATIONS

Short Stories

Busy about the Tree of Life, and Other Stories. London, Women's Press, 1988; as *The Heat Death of the Universe and Other Stories,* Kingston, New York, McPherson, 1988.

OTHER PUBLICATIONS

Novel

Annika and the Wolves: A Fairy Tale. Minneapolis, Minnesota, Coffee House Press, 1985.

*

Critical Studies: "Generic Exhaustion and the 'Heat Death' of Science Fiction" by Elizabeth Hewitt, in *Science-Fiction Studies* 21, 1994.

*   *   *

Pamela Zoline, while highly regarded within the SF field, remains obscure. This situation is due not only to a low profile, but also a low output: the five stories collected in *Busy about the Tree of Life* were written over a period of 20 years. More remains unpublished, such as the extracts from a novel reportedly in Harlan Ellison's final *Dangerous Visions* anthology.

Zoline has never been a full-time writer; Brian Aldiss and Harry Harrison stated in their introduction to *Decade: The 1960s* that she was "primarily an artist." In this capacity she illustrated for the magazine *New Worlds* in the late 1960s, including the serial of Thomas M. Disch's *Camp Concentration.* Recently she has been working with her husband on designing a "radical mountain community" in Telluride, Colorado, where they live, and also has been composing "a real-time, interactive Computer Opera, *The Life and Death of Harry Houdini.* She describes herself as "neither a writer who paints nor a painter who writes."

Her first story, "The Heat Death of the Universe," published in 1967, was instantly acclaimed as one of the best of the New Wave fictions. Brian Aldiss described it as "superlative" in the first edition of *Billion Year Spree.*

"The Heat Death of the Universe" is, like Zoline's illustrations for *Camp Concentration,* a collage, incorporating dictionary definitions of concepts as diverse as ontology, love, and entropy. It also shows Zoline's fascination with lists, not only in the numbering of each paragraph (there are 54 in all) but in passages where the protagonist, a young housewife named Sarah Boyle, suddenly gets the urge to buy one of every cleaning product in the local supermarket, which she does "deliberately and with a careful ecstasy."

"The Heat Death of the Universe" describes American suburbia from an alien perspective. The theme of the trapped housewife has seldom been presented so bizarrely: Sarah responds to domestic tedium by imagining a household organized on Dada principles, or writing comments about the Nitrogen cycle on the lid of the diaper bin (in "Blushing Pink Nitetime lipstick"). She is, however, a metaphor, a microcosm of the universe itself, for as with the process of entropy the universe tends towards maximum disorder, so Sarah, exhausted after a children's party, breaks down into chaos. The heat death of the universe takes place in a Californian kitchen, as physics and sociology collide in one of the most elegantly written stories in the SF canon.

Zoline's second story, "The Holland of the Mind," published in 1969, again used collage techniques for a psychological investigation, this time into the failure of a marriage. A young American couple vacation in Holland; their increasing alienation is reflected by extracts from travel guides, art histories, particularly on Rembrandt and Vermeer, phrasebooks, even instructions for artificial respiration.

"Sheep," first published in 1981, is a longer, more experimental piece, with not only the familiar samples, from such sources as recipe books and husbandry manuals, but also a long, typographically distinct essay on "The Virtues of Wool," which initially appears to have had all the vowels coloured in by a child (as the author explains, clothes moths have eaten holes in the fabric of the text). The rest of "Sheep" is equally zany, as a spy narrative meets cowboys meets the pastoral, all occurring within the context of a sleepless night, in which a woman counts 259 sheep.

"Instructions for Exiting This Building in Case of Fire" is the most political of Zoline's published tales, concentrating upon her recurrent theme of children. The story is concerned with an entirely novel way of preventing war, in which the children of prominent politicians throughout the world are kidnapped and resettled in enemy territory: "Russian, American and Chinese children have been scattered over the planet like grains of rice; in Northern Ireland such is the nature of the horrid conflict that Catholic and Protestant babies have been exchanged and reworked so that they are often living down the street from their biological natural parents."

Five stories is a small oeuvre in terms of SF, where authors' bibliographies can include hundreds of items. Yet few writers can claim to have such a consistently high standard, precisely because Zoline has not wasted her words. She has not published in quantity, yet should her one book be measured in the SF quality scales, it would prove weightier than a pile of trilogies and decalogies.

—Lucy Sussex

READING LIST

Aldiss, Brian, *Billion Year Spree: A History of Science Fiction*. London, Weidenfeld and Nicolson, and New York, Doubleday, 1973.

Aldiss, Brian, *Science Fiction Art*. New York, Bounty, 1975; London, Hart Davis, 1976.

Aldiss, Brian, *Science Fiction as Science Fiction*. Frome, Somerset, Bran's Head, 1978.

Aldiss, Brian, *Trillion Year Spree: The History of Science Fiction*, with David Wingrove. London, Gollancz, and New York, Atheneum, 1986.

Aldiss, Brian, and Harry Harrison, editors, *Hell's Cartographers: Some Personal Histories of Science Fiction Writers*. London, Weidenfeld and Nicolson, and New York, Harper, 1975.

Aldiss, Brian, and Harry Harrison, editors, *SF Horizons*. New York, Arno Press, 1975.

Amis, Kingsley, *New Maps of Hell: A Survey of Science Fiction*. New York, Harcourt Brace, 1960; London, Gollancz, 1961.

Anderson, Craig W., *Science Fiction Films of the Seventies*. Jefferson, North Carolina, McFarland, 1985.

Armitt, Lucy, editor, *Where No Man Has Gone Before: Essays on Women and Science Fiction*. London and New York, Routledge, 1991.

Armytage, W.H.G., *Yesterday's Tomorrows: A Historical Survey of Future Societies*. London, Routledge, 1968.

Ash, Brian, *Faces of the Future: The Lessons of Science Fiction*. London, Elek, and New York, Taplinger, 1975.

Ash, Brian, editor, *The Visual Encyclopedia of Science Fiction*. New York, Harmony, and London, Pan, 1977.

Ash, Brian, *Who's Who in Science Fiction*. London, Elm Tree, and New York, Taplinger, 1976.

Ashley, Michael, editor, *The History of the Science Fiction Magazine*. London, New English Library, 4 vols., 1974-76; vols. 1 and 2, Chicago, Regnery, 1976.

Ashley, Michael, *The Illustrated Book of Science Fiction Lists*. New York, Simon and Shuster, 1983.

Bailey, J.O., *Pilgrims through Space and Time: Trends and Patterns in Scientific and Utopian Fiction*. New York, Argus, 1947.

Barnes, Myra, *Linguistics and Language in Science Fiction-Fantasy*. New York, Arno Press, 1975.

Barr, Marleen S., and Nicholas Smith, editors, *Women and Utopia: Critical Interpretations*. Lanham, Maryland, University Press of America, 1983.

Barron, Neil, editor, *Anatomy of Wonder 4: A Critical Guide to Science Fiction*. New Providence, New Jersey, Bowker, 1995.

Barron, Neil, editor, *Fantasy Literature: A Reader's Guide*. New York, Garland, 1990.

Baxter, John, *Science Fiction in the Cinema*. New York, A.S. Barnes, and London, Zwemmer, 1970.

Benson, Michael, *Vintage Science Fiction Films, 1896-1949*. Jefferson, North Carolina, McFarland, 1985.

Berger, Harold L., *Science Fiction and the New Dark Age*. Bowling Green, Ohio, Popular Press, 1976.

Bleiler, Everett F., *The Checklist of Fantastic Literature*. Chicago, Shasta, 1948; revised edition; as *The Checklist of Science-Fiction and Supernatural Fiction*, Glen Rock, New Jersey, Firebell, 1978.

Bleiler, Everett F., *The Guide to Supernatural Fiction: A Full Description of 1,775 Books from 1750-1960*. Kent, Ohio, Kent State University Press, 1983.

Bleiler, Everett F., editor, *Science Fiction Writers: Critical Studies of the Major Authors from the Early Nineteenth Century to the Present Day*. New York, Scribner, 1982.

Bleiler, Everett F., editor, *Supernatural Fiction Writers: Fantasy and Horror*. New York, Scribner, 1985.

Bleiler, Everett F., and Richard J. Bleiler, *Science Fiction: The Early Years*. Kent, Ohio, Kent State University Press, 1990.

Bleiler, Richard J., *The Index to Adventure Magazine*. Mercer Island, Washington, Starmont House, 1990.

Blish, James, *The Issue at Hand: Studies in Contemporary Magazine Science Fiction*. Chicago, Advent, 1964.

Blish, James, *More Issues at Hand: Critical Studies in Contemporary Science Fiction*. Chicago, Advent, 1970 (as William Atheling, Jr.).

Bova, Ben, editor, *Closeup, New Worlds*, with Trudy E. Bell. New York, St. Martin's Press, 1977.

Bova, Ben, *Notes to a Science Fiction Writer*. New York, Scribner, 1975; revised edition, Boston, Houghton Mifflin, 1981.

Bova, Ben, *Through Eyes of Wonder: Science Fiction and Science* (for children). Reading, Massachusetts, Addison-Wesley, 1975.

Bova, Ben, *Viewpoint*. Cambridge, Massachusetts, NESFA Press, 1977.

Boyajian, Jerry, and Kenneth R. Johnson, *Index to the Science Fiction Magazines, 1979-81*. Cambridge, Massachusetts, Twaci Press, 3 vols., 1981-82.

Bradley, Marion Zimmer, Norman Spinrad, and Alfred Bester, *Expedition Perilous: Three Essays on Science Fiction*. San Bernardino, California, Borgo Press, 1983.

Bretnor, Reginald, editor, *The Craft of Science Fiction*. New York, Harper, 1976.

Bretnor, Reginald, editor, *Modern Science Fiction: Its Meaning and Its Future*. New York, Coward-McCann, 1953; revised edition, Chicago, Advent, 1979.

Bretnor, Reginald, editor, *Science Fiction, Today and Tomorrow*. New York, Harper, 1974.

Brians, Paul, *Nuclear Holocausts: Atomic War in Fiction 1895-1984*. Kent, Ohio, Kent State University Press, 1987.

Briney, R.E., and Edward Wood, *SF Bibliographies: An Annotated Bibliography of Bibliographic Works on Science Fiction and Fantasy Fiction*. Chicago, Advent, 1972.

Brosnan, John, *Future Tense: The Cinema of Science Fiction*. London, Macdonald and Jane's, 1978; New York, St. Martin's Press, 1979; revised edition as *The Primal Screen: A History of Science Fiction Film*, London, Orbit, 1991; Boston, Little Brown, 1995.

Brown, Charles N., William G. Contento, and Hal W. Hall, *Science Fiction, Fantasy, and Horror: A Comprehensive Bibliography of Books and Short Fiction Published in the English Language 1984-[1990]*. Oakland, California, Locus Press, 1986-- (annual volume).

Brown, E.J., *Brave New World, 1984, and We: Essays on Anti-Utopia*. Ann Arbor, Michigan, Ardis, 1976.

Budrys, Algis, *Benchmarks: Galaxy Bookshelf*. Carbondale, Southern Illinois University Press, 1985.

Bukatman, Scott, *Terminal Identity: The Virtual Subject in Postmodern Science Fiction*. Durham, North Carolina, Duke University Press, 1993.

Burgess, Michael, *A Guide to Science Fiction and Fantasy in the Library of Congress Classification Scheme*. San Bernardino, California, Borgo Press, 1984; 2nd edition, 1988.

Burgess, Michael, *A Reference Guide to Science Fiction, Fantasy, and Horror*. Boulder, Colorado, Libraries Unlimited, 1992.

Cawthorn, James, and Michael Moorcock, *Fantasy: The 100 Best Books*. New York, Carroll and Graf, and London, Xanadu, 1988.

Chalker, Jack L., and Mark Owings, *The Science-Fantasy Publishers: A Critical and Bibliographic History*. Westminster, Maryland, Mirage Press, 1991; revised edition, 1992.

Clareson, Thomas D., editor, *Many Futures, Many Worlds: Theme and Form in Science Fiction*. Kent, Ohio, Kent State University Press, 1977.

Clareson, Thomas D., *Science Fiction Criticism: An Annotated Checklist*. Kent, Ohio, Kent State University Press, 1972.

Clareson, Thomas D., *Science Fiction in America, 1870's to 1930's: An Annotated Bibliography of Primary Sources*. Westport, Connecticut, Greenwood Press, 1984.

Clareson, Thomas D., *SF: A Dream of Other Worlds*. College Station, Texas A and M University, 1973.

Clareson, Thomas D., editor, *SF: The Other Side of Realism: Essays on Modern Fantasy and Science Fiction*. Bowling Green, Ohio, Popular Press, 1971.

Clareson, Thomas D., *Understanding Contemporary American Science Fiction: The Formative Period (1926-1970)*. Columbia, University of South Carolina Press, 1990.

Clareson, Thomas D., editor, *Voices for the Future: Essays on Major Science Fiction Writers*. Bowling Green, Ohio, Popular Press, 2 vols., 1976-79; vol. 3, edited with Thomas L. Wymer, 1983.

Clarke, I.F., *The Pattern of Expectation 1644-2001*. London, Cape, 1979.

Clarke, I.F., *The Tale of the Future*. London, Library Association, 1961.

Clarke, I.F., *Voices Prophesying War 1763-1984*. London, Oxford University Press, 1966; revised edition as *Voices Prophesying War: Future Wars, 1763-3749*, London, Oxford University Press, 1992.

Clute, John, and Peter Nicholls, editors, *The Encyclopedia of Science Fiction*, 2nd edition. New York, St. Martin's Press, 1993.

Contento, William, *Index to Science Fiction Anthologies and Collections*. Boston, Hall, and London, Prior, 1978.

Contento, William, *Index to Science Fiction Anthologies and Collections 1977-1983*. Boston, Hall, 1984.

Cottrill, Tim, Martin H. Greenberg, and Charles G. Waugh, *Science Fiction and Fantasy Series and Sequels: A Bibliography*. New York, Garland, 1986.

Cowart, David, and Thomas L. Wymer, editors, *Twentieth-Century American Science Fiction Writers*. Detroit, Gale, 2 vols., 1981.

Currey, L.W., *Science Fiction and Fantasy Authors: A Bibliography of First Printings of their Fiction and Selected Non-Fiction*. Boston, Hall, 1979.

Davies, Philip John, editor, *Science Fiction, Social Conflict, and War*. Manchester, Manchester University Press, 1990.

Day, Bradford M., *The Complete Checklist of Science Fiction Magazines*. New York, Science Fiction and Fantasy Publications, 1961.

Day, Bradford M., *An Index on the Weird and Fantastical in Magazines*. Privately printed, 1953.

Day, Bradford M., *The Supplemental Checklist of Fantastic Literature*. Denver, New York, Science Fiction and Fantasy Publications, 1963.

de Camp, L. Sprague, *Science-Fiction Handbook*. New York, Hermitage House, 1953; revised edition, with Catherine Crook de Camp, Philadelphia, Owlslick Press, 1975.

Delany, Samuel R., *The Jewel-Hinged Jaw: Notes on the Language of Science Fiction*. Elizabethtown, New York, Dragon Press, 1977.

Delany, Samuel R., *Starboard Wine: More Notes on the Language of Science Fiction*. Pleasantville, New York, Dragon Press, 1984.

del Rey, Lester, *The World of Science Fiction 1926-1976: The History of a Subculture*. New York, Ballantine, 1979.

Dunn, Thomas P., and Richard D. Erlich, editors, *Clockwork Worlds: Mechanical Environments in SF*. Westport, Connecticut, Greenwood Press, 1982.

Elliott, Robert C., *The Shape of Utopia: Studies in a Literary Genre*. Chicago, University of Chicago Press, 1970.

Eshbach, Lloyd Arthur, editor, *Of Worlds Beyond: The Science of Science-Fiction Writing*. Reading, Pennsylvania, Fantasy Press, 1947; London, Dobson, 1965.

Fischer, William B., *The Empire Strikes Out: Kurd Lasswitz, Hans Dominik, and the Development of German Science Fiction*. Bowling Green, Ohio, Popular Press, 1984.

Fletcher, Marilyn, editor, *Reader's Guide to Twentieth-Century Science Fiction*. Chicago, American Library Association, 1989.

Fletcher, Marilyn, *Science Fiction Short Story Index 1950-79*. Chicago, American Library Association, 2nd edition, 1981.

Frank, Alan, *The Science Fiction and Fantasy Film Handbook*. Totowa, New Jersey, Barnes and Noble, and London, Batsford, 1982.

Franklin, H. Bruce, editor, *Future Perfect: American Science Fiction of the Nineteenth Century*. New York, Oxford University Press, 1966; London, Oxford University Press, 1968.

Franson, Donald, and Howard DeVore, *A History of the Hugo, Nebula, and International Fantasy Awards*. Dearborn Heights, Michigan, DeVore, 1975.

Fredericks, Casey, *The Future of Eternity: Mythologies of Science Fiction and Fantasy*. Bloomington, Indiana University Press, 1982.

Frewin, Anthony, *One Hundred Years of Science Fiction Illustration 1840-1940*. London, Jupiter, 1974; New York, Pyramid, 1975.

Garber, Eric, and Lyn Paleo, *Uranian Worlds: A Reader's Guide to Alternate Sexuality in Science Fiction and Fantasy*. Boston, Hall, 1983; 2nd edition, 1990.

Gerber, Richard, *Utopian Fantasy: A Study of English Utopian Fiction Since the End of the Nineteenth Century*. London, Routledge, 1955; New York, McGraw Hill, 1973.

Gernsback, Hugo, *Evolution in Modern Science Fiction*. New York, Gernsback, 1952.

Gifford, Denis, *Science Fiction Film*. London, Studio Vista, and New York, Dutton, 1971.

Glad, John, *Extrapolations from Dystopia: A Critical Study of Soviet Science Fiction*. Kingston, New Jersey, Kingston Press, 1982.

Glut, Donald F., *The Frankenstein Legend*. Metuchen, New Jersey, Scarecrow Press, 1973.

Goswami, Amit and Maggie, *The Cosmic Dancers: Exploring the Physics of Science Fiction*. New York, Harper, 1983.

Goulart, Ron, *Cheap Thrills: An Informal History of the Pulp Magazines*. New Rochelle, New York, Arlington House, 1972.

Grebens, G.V., *Ivan Efremov's Theory of Soviet Science Fiction*. New York, Vantage Press, 1978.

Green, Roger Lancelyn, *Into Other Worlds: Spaceflight in Fiction from Lucian to Lewis*. London and New York, Abelard Schuman, 1957.

Green, Scott E., *Contemporary Science Fiction, Fantasy, and Horror Poetry: A Resource Guide and Biographical Dictionary*. New York, Greenwood Press, 1989.

Greenberg, Martin H., editor, *Fantastic Lives: Autobiographical Essays by Notable Science Fiction Writers*. Carbondale, Southern Illinois University Press, 1981.

Greenland, Colin, *The Entropy Exhibition: Michael Moorcock and the British "New Wave" in Science Fiction*. London and Boston, Routledge, 1983.

Griffiths, John, *Three Tomorrows: American, British, and Soviet Science Fiction*. New York, Barnes and Noble, and London, Macmillan, 1980.

Gunn, James E., *Alternate Worlds: The Illustrated History of Science Fiction*. Englewood Cliffs, New Jersey, Prentice Hall, 1975.

Gunn, James E., *The Discovery of the Future: The Ways Science Fiction Developed*. College Station, Texas A and M University, 1975.

Gunn, James E., *Inside Science Fiction: Essays on Fantastic Literature*. San Bernardino, California, Borgo Press, 1992.

Gunn, James E., editor, *The New Encyclopedia of Science Fiction*. New York and London, Viking Press, 1988.

Gunn, James E., editor, *The Road to Science Fiction*. New York, New American Library, 4 vols., 1977-82.

Hall, H.W., *Science Fiction and Fantasy Reference Index 1879-1985: An International Author and Subject Index to History and Criticism*. Detroit, Gale, 2 vols., 1987.

Hall, H.W., *Science Fiction and Fantasy Research Index* (annual). Privately printed, 1982--.

Hall, H.W., *Science Fiction Book Review Index 1923-73; 1974-79; 1980-84*. Detroit, Gale, 3 vols., 1975-85.

Hall, Hal W., *Science/Fiction Collections: Fantasy, Supernatural and Weird Tales*. New York, Haworth Press, 1983.

Hall, Hal W., *The Science Fiction Magazines: A Bibliographical Checklist of Titles and Issues through 1983*. Bryan, Texas, SFBRI, 1983.

Harbottle, Philip, and Stephen Holland, *Vultures of the Void: A History of British Science Fiction Publishing, 1946-1956,* San Bernardino, California, Borgo Press, 1993.

Hardy, Phil, editor, *The Overlook Film Encyclopedia: Science Fiction*. New York, Overlook, 1994.

Harrison, Harry, *Great Balls of Fire!* London, Pierrot, and New York, Grosset and Dunlap, 1977.

Hartwell, David G., *Age of Wonders: Exploring the World of Science Fiction*. New York, Walker, 1985.

Hassler, Donald M., *Comic Tones in Science Fiction: The Art of Compromise with Nature*. Westport, Connecticut, Greenwood Press, 1982.

Hillegas, Mark R., *The Future as Nightmare: H.G. Wells and the Anti-Utopians*. New York, Oxford University Press, 1967.

Hoffman, Stuart, *An Index to "Unknown" and "Unknown Worlds" by Author and by Title*. Black Earth, Wisconsin, Sirius Press, 1955.

Hollister, Bernard C., and Deane C. Thompson, *Grokking the Future: Science Fiction in the Classroom*. Dayton, Ohio, Pflaum, 1973.

Ikin, Van, editor, *Australian Science Fiction*. Brisbane, University of Queensland Press, 1982; Chicago, Academy, 1984.

Isaacs, Leonard, *Darwin to Double Helix: The Biological Theme in Science Fiction*. London, Butterworth, 1977.

Jakubowski, Maxim, and Edward James, editors, *The Profession of Science Fiction: Writers on Their Craft and Ideas*. London, Macmillan, 1991.

Jakubowski, Maxim, and Malcolm Edwards, *The SF Book of Lists*. New York, Berkley, 1983.

Jarvis, Sharon, editor, *Inside Outer Space: Science Fiction Professionals Look at Their Craft*. New York, Ungar, 1984.

Johnson, William, editor, *Focus on the Science Fiction Film*. Englewood Cliffs, New Jersey, Prentice Hall, 1972.

Justice, Keith L., *Science Fiction Master Index of Names*. Jefferson, North Carolina, McFarland, 1986.

Ketterer, David, *Canadian Science Fiction and Fantasy,* Bloomington, Indiana University Press, 1992.

Ketterer, David, *New Worlds for Old: The Apocalyptic Imagination, Science Fiction, and American Literature*. Bloomington, Indiana University Press, 1974.

King, Betty, *Women of the Future: The Female Main Character in Science Fiction*. Metuchen, New Jersey, Scarecrow Press, 1984.

Klai , Dragon, *The Plot of the Future: Utopia and Dystopia in Modern Drama*. Ann Arbor, University of Michigan Press, 1992.

Knight, Damon, *The Futurians*. New York, Day, 1977.

Knight, Damon, *In Search of Wonder*. Chicago, Advent, 1956, revised edition, 1967.

Knight, Damon, editor, *Turning Points: Essays on the Art of Science Fiction*. New York, Harper, 1977.

Kyle, David, *The Illustrated Book of Science Fiction Ideas and Dreams*. London, Hamlyn, 1977.

Kyle, David, *A Pictorial History of Science Fiction*. London, Hamlyn, 1976.

Lasky, Melvin J., *Utopia and Revolution*. Chicago, University of Chicago Press, 1976.

Lawler, Donald L., *Approaches to Science Fiction*. Boston, Houghton Mifflin, 1978.

Le Guin, Ursula K., *The Language of the Night: Essays on Fantasy and Science Fiction,* edited by Susan Wood. New York, Putnam, 1979; revised edition, New York, HarperCollins, 1992.

Locke, George, *Voyages in Space: A Bibliography of Interplanetary Fiction 1801-1914*. London, Ferret Fantasy, 1975.

Lowndes, Robert A.W., *Three Faces of Science Fiction*. Boston, NESFA Press, 1973.

Lundwall, Sam J., *Science Fiction: An Illustrated History*. New York, Grosset and Dunlap, 1978.

Lundwall, Sam J., *Science Fiction: What It's All About*. New York, Ace, 1971.

Lynn, Ruth Nadelman, *Fantasy for Children and Young Adults: An Annotated Bibliography*. New York, Bowker, 1979; 2nd edition, 1983; 3rd edition, 1989.

Magill, Frank N., editor, *Science Fiction, Alien Encounter*. Pasadena, California, Salem Press, 1981.

Magill, Frank N., editor, *Survey of Science Fiction Literature*. Englewood Cliffs, New Jersey, Salem Press, 5 vols., 1979; bibliographical supplement, 1982.

Magill, Frank N., and Keith Neilson, editors, *Survey of Modern Fantasy Literature*. Englewood Cliffs, New Jersey, Salem Press, 5 vols., 1983.

Malmgren, Carl D., *Worlds Apart: Narratology of Science Fiction*. Bloomington, Indiana University Press, 1991.

Malzberg, Barry N., *The Engines of the Night: Science Fiction in the Eighties*. New York, Doubleday, 1982.

Matthew, Robert, *Japanese Science Fiction*. London, Routledge, 1989.

McCaffery, Larry, editor, *Across the Wounded Galaxies: Interviews with Contemporary American Science Fiction Writers*. Urbana, University of Illinois Press, 1990.

McCaffery, Larry, editor, *Storming the Reality Studio: A Casebook of Cyberpunk and Postmodern Science Fiction*. Durham, North Carolina, Duke University Press, 1991.

McGuire, Patrick L., *Red Stars: Political Aspects of Soviet Science Fiction*. Ann Arbor, Michigan, UMI Research Press, 1985.

Menville, Douglas, *A Historical and Critical Survey of the Science-Fiction Film*. New York, Arno Press, 1975.

Menville, Douglas, R. Reginald, and Mary A. Burgess, *Futurevisions: The New Golden Age of the Science Fiction Film.* North Hollywood, California, Newcastle, 1985.

Meyers, Walter E., *Aliens and Linguists.* Athens, University of Georgia Press, 1980.

Miller, Fred D., Jr., and Nicholas D. Smith, editors, *Thought Probes: Philosophy Through Science Fiction.* Englewood Cliffs, New Jersey, Prentice Hall, 1981.

Moore, Patrick, *Science and Fiction.* London, Harrap, 1957.

Moskowitz, Sam, *Explorers of the Infinite: Shapers of Science Fiction.* Cleveland, World, 1963.

Moskowitz, Sam, *The Immortal Storm: A History of Science Fiction Fandom.* Atlanta, Atlanta Science Fiction Organization Press, 1954.

Moskowitz, Sam, editor, *Science Fiction by Gaslight: A History and Anthology of Science Fiction in Popular Magazines 1891-1911.* Cleveland, World, 1968.

Moskowitz, Sam, *Seekers of Tomorrow: Masters of Modern Science Fiction.* Cleveland, World, 1966.

Moskowitz, Sam, *Strange Horizons: The Spectrum of Science Fiction.* New York, Scribner, 1976.

Moskowitz, Sam, editor, *Under the Moons of Mars: A History and Anthology of "The Scientific Romance" in the Munsey Magazines.* New York, Holt Rinehart, 1970.

Myers, Robert E., editor, *The Intersection of Science Fiction and Philosophy: Critical Studies.* Westport, Connecticut, Greenwood Press, 1983.

Naha, Ed, *The Science Fictionary: An A-Z Guide to the World of SF Authors, Films, and TV Shows.* New York, Seaview Books, 1980.

New England Science Fiction Association, *The NESFA Index to the Science Fiction Magazines and Original Anthologies 1979-80.* Cambridge, Massachusetts, NESFA Press, 1982.

Newman, John, and Michael Unsworth, *Future War Novels: An Annotated Bibliography of Works in English Published Since 1946.* Phoenix, Oryx Press, 1984.

Nicholls, Peter, editor, *Science Fiction at Large.* London, Gollancz, 1976; New York, Harper, 1977; as *Explorations of the Marvellous,* London, Fontana, 1978.

Nicholls, Peter, David Langford, and Brian M. Stableford, *The Science in Science Fiction.* London, Joseph, 1982; New York, Knopf, 1983.

Nicolson, Marjorie Hope, *Voyages to the Moon.* New York, Macmillan, 1948.

The Octopus Encyclopaedia of Science Fiction. London, Octopus, and Baltimore, Hoen, 1978.

Page, Michael, and Robert Ingpen, *Encyclopedia of Things That Never Were.* New York, Viking Press, 1987.

Panshin, Alexei and Cory, *SF in Dimension: A Book of Explorations.* Chicago, Advent, 1976.

Panshin, Alexei and Cory, *The World Beyond the Hill: Science Fiction and the Quest for Transcendence,* Los Angeles, Jeremy P. Tarcher, 1989.

Parish, James Robert, and Michael R. Pitts, *The Great Science Fiction Pictures.* Metuchen, New Jersey, Scarecrow Press, 1977.

Parish, James Robert, and Michael R. Pitts, *The Great Science Fiction Pictures II.* Metuchen, New Jersey, Scarecrow Press, 1990.

Parrinder, Patrick, editor, *Science Fiction: A Critical Guide.* London, Longman, 1979.

Parrinder, Patrick, *Science Fiction: Its Criticism and Teaching.* London, Methuen, 1980.

Pfeiffer, John R., *Fantasy and Science Fiction: A Critical Guide.* Palmer Lake, Colorado, Filter Press, 1971.

Philmus, Robert, *Into the Unknown: The Evolution of Science Fiction from Francis Godwin to H.G. Wells.* Berkeley, University of California Press, 1970; 2nd edition, 1983.

Pierce, Hazel, *A Literary Symbiosis: Science Fiction/Fantasy/Mystery.* Westport, Connecticut, Greenwood Press, 1983.

Pierce, John J., *Great Themes of Science Fiction: A Study in Imagination and Evolution.* New York, Greenwood Press, 1987.

Platt, Charles, *Dream Makers: The Uncommon People Who Write Science Fiction.* New York, Berkley, 2 vols., 1980-83; revised edition, as *Dream Makers: Science Fiction and Fantasy Writers at Work,* New York, Ungar, and London, Xanadu, 1987.

Porter, Andrew, editor, *Experiment Perilous: Three Essays on Science Fiction.* New York, Algol Press, 1976.

Porush, David, *The Soft Machine: Cybernetic Fiction.* New York, Methuen, 1985.

Pringle, David, *Imaginary People: A Who's Who of Modern Fictional Characters.* London, Grafton, 1987; New York, World Almanac, 1988.

Pringle, David, *Modern Fantasy: The Hundred Best Novels: An English-Language Selection 1949-84.* New York, Carroll and Graf, and London, Xanadu, 1985.

Pringle, David, *Science Fiction: The Hundred Best Novels: An English-Language Selection 1949-84.* New York, Carroll and Graf, and London, Xanadu, 1985.

Pringle, David, *The Ultimate Guide to Science Fiction.* New York, Pharos Books, and London, Grafton, 1990.

Rabkin, Eric S., *The Fantastic in Literature.* Princeton, New Jersey, Princeton University Press, 1976.

Rabkin, Eric S., Martin H. Greenberg, and Joseph D. Olander, editors, *The End of the World.* Carbondale, Southern Illinois University Press, 1983.

Rabkins, Eric S., Martin H. Greenberg, and Joseph D. Olander, editors, *No Place Else: Explorations in Utopian and Dystopian Fiction.* Carbondale, Southern Illinois University Press, 1983.

Reginald, R., *Contemporary Science Fiction Authors.* New York, Arno Press, 1975.

Reginald, R., *Science Fiction and Fantasy Awards.* San Bernardino, California, Borgo Press, 1981; 2nd edition, as *Reginald's Science Fiction and Fantasy Awards: A Comprehensive Guide to the Awards and Their Winners,* with Daryl F. Mallett, 1991.

Reginald, R., *Science Fiction and Fantasy Literature: A Checklist 1700-1974.* Detroit, Gale, 2 vols., 1979.

Reilly, Robert, editor, *The Transcendent Adventure: Studies of Religion in Science Fiction/Fantasy.* Westport, Connecticut, Greenwood Press, 1984.

Robbins, Leonard A., *The Pulp Magazine Index.* Mercer Island, Washington, Starmont House, 1988-.

Robinson, Roger, *Who's Hugh? An SF Reader's Guide to Pseudonyms.* Harold Wood, Essex, Beccon, 1987.

Rock, James A., *Who Goes There? A Bibliographic Dictionary of Pseudonymous Literature in the Fields of Fantasy and Science Fiction.* Bloomington, Indiana, Rock, 1979.

Roemer, Kenneth M., *The Obsolete Necessity: America in Utopian Writings 1888-1900.* Kent, Ohio, Kent State University Press, 1976.

Rogers, Alva, *A Requiem for Astounding.* Chicago, Advent, 1964.

Rose, Mark, editor, *Science Fiction: A Collection of Critical Essays.* Englewood Cliffs, New Jersey, Prentice Hall, 1976.

Rose, Mark, *Alien Encounters: Anatomy of Science Fiction.* Cambridge, Massachusetts, Harvard University Press, 1981.

Rosenberg, Betty, and Diana Tixier Herald, *Genreflecting: A Guide to Reading Interests in Genre Fiction.* Boulder, Colorado, Libraries Unlimited, 3rd edition, 1991.

Rosinsky, Natalie M., *Feminist Futures: Contemporary Women's Speculative Fiction.* Ann Arbor, Michigan, UMI Research Press, 1984.

Rottensteiner, Franz, *The Science Fiction Book: An Illustrated History.* New York, Seabury Press, and London, Thames and Hudson, 1975.

Ruddick, Nicholas, *Ultimate Island: On the Nature of British Science Fiction.* Westport, Connecticut, Greenwood, 1993.

Sadoul, Jacques, *2000 A.D.: Illustrations from the Golden Age of Science Fiction Pulps.* Chicago, Regnery, and London, Souvenir Press, 1975.

Samuelson, David N., *Visions of Tomorrow: Six Journeys from Outer to Inner Space.* New York, Arno Press, 1975.

Sargent, Lyman T., *British and American Utopian Literature 1516-1975.* Boston, Hall, 1979.

Schlobin, Roger, *The Literature of Fantasy: A Comprehensive Annotated Bibliography of Modern Fantasy Fiction.* New York, Garland, 1979.

Schlobin, Roger C., *Urania's Daughters: A Checklist of Women Science Fiction Writers 1697-1982.* Mercer Island, Washington, Starmont House, 1983.

Scholes, Robert, *Structural Fabulation.* Notre Dame, Indiana, University of Notre Dame Press, 1975.

Scholes, Robert, and Eric S. Rabkin, *Science Fiction: History, Science, Vision.* New York, Oxford University Press, 1977.

Schweitzer, Darrell, and Jeffrey M. Elliot, editors, *Science Fiction Voices 1-4.* San Bernardino, California, Borgo Press, 4 vols., 1979-82.

Searles, Baird, and others, *A Reader's Guide to Science Fiction [Fantasy].* New York, Avon, 2 vols., 1979-82.

Senn, Bryan, and John Johnson, *Fantastic Cinema Subject Guide: A Topical Index to 2,500 Horror, Science Fiction, and Fantasy Films.* Jefferson, North Carolina, McFarland, 1992.

Shipman, David, *A Pictorial History of Science Fiction Films.* London, Hamlyn, 1985.

Slusser, George E., Eric S. Rabkin, and Robert Scholes, editors, *Coordinates: Placing Science Fiction and Fantasy.* Carbondale, Southern Illinois University Press, 1983.

Smith, Clark Ashton, *Planets and Dimensions: Collected Essays,* edited by Charles K. Wolfe. Baltimore, Mirage Press, 1973.

Smith, Nicholas D., editor, *Philosophers Look at Science Fiction.* Chicago, Nelson Hall, 1982.

Spinrad, Norman, *Science Fiction in the Real World.* Carbondale, Southern Illinois University Press, 1990.

Stableford, Brian M., *Masters of Science-Fiction: Essays on Six Science-Fiction Authors.* San Bernardino, California, Borgo Press, 1981.

Stableford, Brian M., *Scientific Romance in Britain 1890-1950.* New York, St. Martin's, 1985.

Stableford, Brian M., *The Sociology of Science Fiction.* San Bernardino, California, Borgo Press, 1987.

Staicar, Tom, editor, *Critical Encounters 2: Writers and Themes in Science Fiction.* New York, Ungar, 1982.

Staicar, Tom, editor, *The Feminine Eye: Science Fiction and the Women Who Write It.* New York, Ungar, 1982.

Stone, Graham, *Australian Science Fiction Index 1925-1967.* Canberra, Australian Science Fiction Association, 1968; *Supplement 1968-1975,* Sydney, Australian Science Fiction Association, 1976.

Suvin, Darko, *Metamorphoses of Science Fiction.* New Haven, Connecticut, Yale University Press, 1979.

Suvin, Darko, *Positions and Presuppositions in Science Fiction.* Kent, Ohio, Kent State University Press, 1988.

Suvin, Darko, *Russian Science Fiction 1956-1974: A Bibliography.* Elizabethtown, New York, Dragon Press, 1976.

Todorov, Tzvetan, *The Fantastic: A Structural Approach to a Literary Genre,* translated by Richard Howard. Cleveland, Press of Case Western Reserve University, 1973.

Tuck, Donald H., *The Encyclopedia of Science Fiction and Fantasy.* Chicago, Advent, 3 vols., 1974-83.

Tymn, Marshall B., *American Fantasy and Science Fiction: Toward a Bibliography of Works Published in the United States 1948-1973.* West Linn, Oregon, FAX, 1979.

Tymn, Marshall B., *Index to Stories in Thematic Anthologies of Science Fiction.* Boston, Hall, 1978.

Tymn, Marshall B., editor, *Science Fiction: A Teacher's Guide and Resource Book.* San Bernardino, California, Borgo Press, 1988.

Tymn, Marshall B., editor, *The Science Fiction Reference Book.* Mercer Island, Washington, Starmont, 1981.

Tymn, Marshall B., and Mike Ashley, editors, *Science Fiction, Fantasy, and Weird Fiction Magazines.* Westport, Connecticut, Greenwood Press, 1985.

Tymn, Marhsall B., Roger C. Schlobin, and L.W. Currey, *A Research Guide to Science Fiction Studies.* New York, Garland, 1977.

Tymn, Marshall, B., and Roger C. Schlobin, *The Year's Scholarship in Science Fiction and Fantasy 1972-1975.* Kent, Ohio, Kent State University Press, 1979.

Tymn, Marshall B., and Roger C. Schlobin, editors, *The Year's Scholarship in Science Fiction and Fantasy: 1976-1979.* Kent, Ohio, Kent State University Press, 1983.

University of California, Riverside, *Dictionary Catalog of the J. Lloyd Eaton Collection of Science Fiction and Fantasy Literature.* Boston, Hall, 3 vols., 1982.

Urang, Gunnar, *Shadows of Heaven: Religion and Fantasy in the Writings of C.S. Lewis, Charles Williams, and J.R.R. Tolkien.* Philadelphia, Pilgrim Press, and London, SCM Press, 1971.

Wagar, W. Warren, *Terminal Visions: The Literature of Last Things.* Bloomington, Indiana University Press, 1982.

Walker, Paul, *Speaking of Science Fiction* (interviews). Oradell, New Jersey, Luna, 1978.

Walsh, Chad, *From Utopia to Nightmare.* New York, Harper, and London, Bles, 1962.

Warner, Harry, Jr., *All Our Yesterdays: An Informal History of Science Fiction Fandom in the Forties.* Chicago, Advent, 1969.

Warrick, Patricia S., *The Cybernetic Imagination in Science Fiction.* Cambridge, Massachusetts, MIT Press, 1980.

Weinberg, Robert, *A Biographical Dictionary of Science Fiction and Fantasy Artists.* New York, Greenwood Press, 1988.

Weinberg, Robert, *The Weird Tales Story.* West Linn, Oregon, FAX, 1977.

Weinberg, Robert, and Edward P. Berglund, *Reader's Guide to the Cthulhu Mythos.* Albuquerque, Silver Scarab Press, 1973.

Weinberg, Robert, and Lohr McKinstry, *The Hero Pulp Index.* Evergreen, Colorado, Opar Press, 1971.

Wells, Stuart, III, *The Science Fiction and Heroic Fantasy Author Index.* Duluth, Purple Unicorn, 1978.

Wertham, Frederic, *The World of Fanzines: A Special Form of Communication.* Carbondale, Southern Illinois University Press, 1973.

Willingham, Ralph, *Science Fiction and the Theatre.* Westport, Connecticut, Greenwood Press, 1993.

Willis, Donald C., *Horror and Science Fiction Films: A Checklist.* Metuchen, New Jersey, Scarecrow Press, 1972.

Willis, Donald C., *Horror and Science Fiction Films II.* Metuchen, New Jersey, Scarecrow Press, 1982.

Willis, Donald C., *Horror and Science Fiction Films III.* Metuchen, New Jersey, Scarecrow Press, 1982.

Willis, Donald, C., editor, *Variety's Complete Science Fiction Reviews.* New York, Garland, 1985.

Wilson, Colin, *Science Fiction as Existentialism.* Hayes, Middlesex, Bran's Head, 1978.

Wilson, Colin, *The Strength to Dream: Literature and the Imagination.* London, Gollancz, and Boston, Houghton Mifflin, 1962.

Wingrove, David, editor, *The Science Fiction Film Source Book.* London and New York, Longman, 1985.

Wingrove, David, editor, *The Science Fiction Source Book.* New York, Van Nostrand Reinhold, 1984.

Wolfe, Gary K., *Critical Terms for Science Fiction and Fantasy: A Glossary and Guide to Scholarship.* New York, Greenwood Press, 1986.

Wolfe, Gary K., *The Known and the Unknown: The Iconography of Science Fiction.* Kent, Ohio, Kent State University Press, 1979.

Wolfe, Gary K., editor, *Science Fiction Dialogues.* Chicago, Academy, 1982.

Wollheim, Donald A., *The Universe Makers: Science Fiction Today.* New York, Harper, 1971; London, Gollancz, 1972.

Wolmark, Jenny, *Aliens and Others: Science Fiction, Feminism and Postmodernism.* Iowa City, University of Iowa Press, 1994.

Wright, Gene, *The Science Fiction Image: The Illustrated Encyclopedia of Science Fiction in Film, Television, Radio, and the Theater.* New York, Facts on File, and London, Columbus, 1983.

Wymer, Thomas L., and others, *Intersections: The Elements of Fiction in Science Fiction.* Bowling Green, Ohio, Popular Press, 1978.

Wysocki, R.J., *The Science Fiction, Fantasy, Weird, Hero Magazine Checklist.* Westlake, Ohio, Wysocki, 1985.

Ynetma, Sharon K., *More Than 100 Women Science Fiction Writers.* Freedom, California, Crossing Press, 1988.

Yoke, Carl B., and Donald M. Hassler, editors, *Death and the Serpent: Immortality in Science Fiction and Fantasy.* Westport, Connecticut, Greenwood Press, 1985.

NATIONALITY INDEX

Below is the list of entrants divided by nationality. The nationalities were chosen largely from information supplied by the entrants. A small number of entrants submitted two nationalities (e.g., American and British) and thus are listed under both. It should be noted that "British" was used for all English entrants and for any other British entrant who chose that designation over a more specific one, such as "Scottish."

AMERICAN

Max Adeler
Roger MacBride Allen
Kevin J. Anderson
Poul Anderson
Piers Anthony
Christopher Anvil
Eleanor Arnason
Isaac Asimov
Robert Lynn Asprin
A.A. Attanasio
Sharon Baker
John Barnes
Steven Barnes
Neal Barrett, Jr.
T.J. Bass
John Calvin Batchelor
Harry Bates
Greg Bear
Charles Beaumont
Edward Bellamy
Gregory Benford
Alfred Bester
Lloyd Biggle
Eando Binder
David F. Bischoff
Michael Bishop
Terry Bisson
James P. Blaylock
James Blish
Robert Bloch
Michael Blumlein
Nelson S. Bond
J.F. Bone
Anthony Boucher
Ben Bova
John Boyd
Leigh Brackett
Ray Bradbury
Marion Zimmer Bradley
Reginald Bretnor
David Brin
Fredric Brown
Rosel George Brown
Edward Bryant
Lois McMaster Bujold
Emma Bull
David R. Bunch
Edgar Rice Burroughs
William S. Burroughs
F.M. Busby
Octavia E. Butler
Pat Cadigan

Martin Caidin
Ernest Callenbach
John W. Campbell, Jr.
Orson Scott Card
Jayge Carr
Terry Carr
Lin Carter
Cleve Cartmill
Jeffrey A. Carver
Jack L. Chalker
Louis Charbonneau
Suzy McKee Charnas
C.J. Cherryh
Rob Chilson
Hal Clement
Mark Clifton
Stanton A. Coblentz
Theodore R. Cogswell
Glen Cook
Alfred Coppel
Juanita Coulson
Robert Coulson
Arthur Byron Cover
Michael Crichton
John Crowley
Ray Cummings
Brian C. Daley
Jack Dann
Avram Davidson
Chan Davis
L. Sprague de Camp
Miriam Allen deFord
Joseph H. Delaney
Samuel R. Delany
Lester del Rey
Lester Dent
Gene Deweese
Philip K. Dick
Gordon R. Dickson
Paul G. Di Filippo
Thomas M. Disch
Stephen R. Donaldson
Ignatius Donnelly
Sonya Dorman
Gardner Dozois
David A. Drake
Diane Duane
David Duncan
David Eddings
G.C. Edmondson
George Alec Effinger
Phyllis Eisenstein
Gordon Eklund

Suzette Haden Elgin
Mircea Eliade
Harlan Ellison
Ru Emerson
Carol Emshwiller
Sylvia Engdahl
M.J. Engh
George Allan England
Steve Erickson
Lloyd Arthur Eshbach
E. Everett Evans
Paul W. Fairman
Ralph Milne Farley
Philip José Farmer
Raymond E. Feist
Cynthia Felice
Jack Finney
Homer Eon Flint
William R. Forstchen
Robert L. Forward
Alan Dean Foster
M.A. Foster
Karen Joy Fowler
Gardner F. Fox
Pat Frank
Gertrude Friedberg
Raymond Z. Gallun
Daniel F. Galouye
Craig Shaw Gardner
Randall Garrett
Hugo Gernsback
David Gerrold
Mark S. Geston
William Gibson
Alexis A. Gilliland
Charlotte Perkins Gilman
Tom Godwin
H.L. Gold
Stephen Goldin
Lisa Goldstein
Felix C. Gotschalk
Ron Goulart
Charles L. Grant
Richard Grant
Joseph Green
William Greenleaf
Russell M. Griffin
Wyman Guin
James E. Gunn
Isidore Haiblum
Jack C. Haldeman
Joe Haldeman
Edward Everett Hale
Austin Hall
Edmond Hamilton
Elizabeth Hand
Charles L. Harness
Harry Harrison
Simon Hawke
Robert A. Heinlein
Zenna Henderson

Joe L. Hensley
Frank Herbert
Russell Hoban
Edward D. Hoch
Lee Hoffman
H.M. Hoover
Robert Hoskins
L. Ron Hubbard
Barry Hughart
Zach Hughes
Evan Hunter
Dean Ing
Alexander Jablokov
Harvey Jacobs
John Jakes
Laurence M. Janifer
K.W. Jeter
Neil R. Jones
Raymond F. Jones
Janet Kagan
James Kahn
Anna Kavan
David H. Keller
Leo P. Kelley
James Patrick Kelly
Leigh Kennedy
John Kessel
Alexander Key
Daniel Keyes
Lee Killough
Otis Adelbert Kline
Damon Knight
Norman L. Knight
Dean R. Koontz
C.M. Kornbluth
William Kotzwinkle
Nancy Kress
Michael P. Kube-McDowell
Michael Kurland
Katherine Kurtz
Henry Kuttner
R.A. Lafferty
Geoffrey A. Landis
Sterling E. Lanier
Joe R. Lansdale
Philip Latham
Keith Laumer
Ursula K. Le Guin
Fritz Leiber
Stephen Leigh
Murray Leinster
Madeleine L'Engle
Milton Lesser
Jonathan Lethem
Ira Levin
Jacqueline Lichtenberg
Alice Lightner
Brad Linaweaver
Jack London
Frank Belknap Long
Barry Longyear

H.P. Lovecraft
Robert A.W. Lowndes
Richard A. Lupoff
Elizabeth A. Lynn
C.C. MacApp
R.A. MacAvoy
John D. MacDonald
Katherine MacLean
Barry N. Malzberg
Laurence Manning
George R.R. Martin
Richard Matheson
Julian May
Ardath Mayhar
Bruce McAllister
Jack McDevitt
Maureen F. McHugh
Vonda N. McIntyre
Richard M. McKenna
Patricia A. McKillip
Dean McLaughlin
Mike McQuay
S.P. Meek
David Meltzer
R.M. Meluch
Richard C. Meredith
A. Merritt
Sam Merwin, Jr.
P. Schuyler Miller
Walter M. Miller, Jr.
Judith Moffett
Thomas F. Monteleone
C.L. Moore
Ward Moore
John Morressy
Janet E. Morris
James Morrow
Pat Murphy
Ed Naha
Ray Nelson
Kris Neville
Larry Niven
William F. Nolan
John Norman
Andre Norton
Warren Norwood
Alan E. Nourse
Philip Francis Nowlan
Charles G. Oberndorf
Kevin O'Donnell, Jr.
Andrew J. Offutt
Chad Oliver
Rebecca Ore
Raymond A. Palmer
Edgar Pangborn
Alexei Panshin
Paul Park
Steve Perry
Emil Petaja
Rog Phillips
Marge Piercy

Daniel Manus Pinkwater
H. Beam Piper
Doris Piserchia
Edgar Allan Poe
Frederik Pohl
Rachel Pollack
Arthur Porges
Jerry Pournelle
Tim Powers
Fletcher Pratt
Paul Preuss
Geo Proctor
Tom Purdom
Thomas Pynchon
Ayn Rand
Marta Randall
Tom Reamy
Michael Reaves
Kit Reed
Robert Reed
Mike Resnick
Mack Reynolds
Walt and Leigh Richmond
Frank M. Robinson
Kim Stanley Robinson
Spider Robinson
Ross Rocklynne
Michaela Roessner
William Rotsler
Victor Rousseau
Rudy Rucker
Kristine Kathryn Rusch
Joanna Russ
Fred Saberhagen
Margaret St. Clair
James Sallis
Jessica Amanda Salmonson
Pamela Sargent
Elizabeth Scarborough
Nat Schachner
Hilbert Schenck
Stanley Schmidt
James H. Schmitz
Thomas N. Scortia
Melissa Scott
Hank Searls
Luis P. Senarens
Rod Serling
Garrett P. Serviss
Jack Sharkey
Richard S. Shaver
Robert Sheckley
Lucius Shepard
T.L. Sherred
Wilmar H. Shiras
John Shirley
Susan Shwartz
Robert Silverberg
Clifford D. Simak
Curt Siodmak
John Sladek

William M. Sloane
Joan Slonczewski
Clark Ashton Smith
Cordwainer Smith
E.E. Smith
Evelyn E. Smith
George O. Smith
George H. Smith
Thorne Smith
Jerry Sohl
Martha Soukup
Norman Spinrad
Nancy Springer
Steven Spruill
Margaret St. Clair
Christopher Stasheff
Neal Stephenson
Bruce Sterling
Francis Stevens
George R. Stewart
G. Harry Stine
Frank R. Stockton
Craig Strete
Theodore Sturgeon
Michael Swanwick
John Taine
Stephen Tall
Judith Tarr
William Tenn
Sheri S. Tepper
Walter Tevis
Ted Thomas
Robert Thurston
James Tiptree, Jr.
Louis Trimble
Wilson Tucker
Harry Turtledove
Lisa Tuttle
Mark Twain
Kathy Tyers
Steven Utley
Jack Vance
Sydney J. Van Scyoc
A.E. van Vogt
John Varley
A. Hyatt Verrill
Joan D. Vinge
Vernor Vinge
Kurt Vonnegut, Jr.
Howard Waldrop
F.L. Wallace
Ian Wallace
William Jon Watkins
Lawrence Watt-Evans
Sharon Webb
Stanley G. Weinbaum
Manly Wade Wellman
Ted White
Kate Wilhelm
John A. Williams
Paul O. Williams

Robert Moore Williams
Walter Jon Williams
Jack Williamson
Connie Willis
F. Paul Wilson
Richard Wilson
Robert Anton Wilson
Gary K. Wolf
Bernard Wolfe
Gene Wolfe
Donald A. Wollheim
Dave Wolverton
Jack Womack
Austin Tappan Wright
Philip Wylie
Chelsea Quinn Yarbro
Jane Yolen
Robert F. Young
Arthur Leo Zagat
Timothy Zahn
George Zebrowski
Roger Zelazny
Pamela Zoline
Anna Kavan

ARGENTINE
Jorge Luis Borges

AUSTRALIAN
John Baxter
Damien Broderick
Frank Bryning
A. Bertram Chandler
Erle Cox
Terry Dowling
Greg Egan
M. Barnard Eldershaw
Lee Harding
David Lake
Sean McMullen
Gerald Murnane
Lucy Sussex
George Turner
Wynne Whiteford
Jack Wodhams

AUSTRIAN
Herbert W. Franke

BRITISH
Douglas Adams
Mark Adlard
Brian W. Aldiss
Kingsley Amis
Edwin L. Arnold
Frank Aubrey
Wilhelmina Baird
J.G. Ballard
Iain M. Banks
Stephen Baxter
Barrington John Bayley

J.D. Beresford
Christopher Blayre
Christine Brooke-Rose
John Brosnan
Eric Brown
John Brunner
Kenneth Bulmer
Edward Bulwer-Lytton
Katharine Burdekin
Anthony Burgess
Samuel Butler
Paul Capon
Angela Carter
Charles Chilton
John Christopher
Arthur C. Clarke
D.G. Compton
Michael G. Coney
Storm Constantine
Edmund Cooper
Richard Cowper
Robert Cromie
John Keir Cross
Peter Dickinson
Arthur Conan Doyle
Lawrence Durrell
E.R. Eddison
R. Lionel Fanthorpe
Mick Farren
John Russell Fearn
Nicholas Fisk
Michael Frayn
Neil Gaiman
David Garnett
David A. Gemmell
Mary Gentle
Peter George
John Gloag
William Golding
Rex Gordon
Stuart Gordon
Colin Greenland
John R. Gribbin
George Griffith
Nicola Griffith
Lindsay Gutteridge
H. Rider Haggard
M. John Harrison
H.F. Heard
James Herbert
Philip E. High
Christopher Hodder-Williams
William Hope Hodgson
James P. Hogan
Robert Holdstock
Fred and Geoffrey Hoyle
Trevor Hoyle
Aldous Huxley
C.J. Cutcliffe Hyne
Richard Jefferies
D.F. Jones

Diana Wynne Jones
Gwyneth A. Jones
Colin Kapp
Garry Kilworth
Vincent King
Rudyard Kipling
John Kippax
Nigel Kneale
David Langford
E.C. Large
Tanith Lee
Doris Lessing
C.S. Lewis
David Lindsay
John Lymington
George MacDonald
R.W. Mackelworth
Charles Eric Maine
Phillip Mann
Douglas R. Mason
David I. Masson
Paul J. McAuley
Ian McDonald
J.T. McIntosh
Michael Moorcock
Alan Moore
Patrick Moore
William Morris
Jeff Noon
George Orwell
Mervyn Peake
Charles Platt
Terry Pratchett
Christopher Priest
J.B. Priestley
John Rackham
Keith Roberts
Eric Frank Russell
Geoff Ryman
Sarban
Josephine Saxton
Arthur Sellings
Bob Shaw
Charles Sheffield
Mary Shelley
M.P. Shiel
Nevil Shute
Brian Stableford
Olaf Stapledon
Andrew M. Stephenson
Peter Tate
William F. Temple
Emma Tennant
D.M. Thomas
Patrick Tilley
J.R.R. Tolkien
E.C. Tubb
Ian Watson
Andrew Weiner
H.G. Wells
James White

Colin Wilson
David Wingrove
S. Fowler Wright
John Wyndham

CANADIAN
Charles de Lint
Candas Jane Dorsey
Wayland Drew
Dave Duncan
Leslie Gadallah
Phyllis Gotlieb
Terence M. Green
Monica Hughes
Crawford Kilian
Donald Kingsbury
Judith Merril
Robert J. Sawyer
Daniel Sernine
S.M. Stirling
Élisabeth Vonarburg
Andrew Weiner
Robert Charles Wilson

CZECH
Karel Capek
Franz Kafka
Josef Nesvadba

FRENCH
René Barjavel
Pierre Boulle
Michel Jeury
Gérard Klein
André Maurois
Maurice Renard
Vercors
Jules Verne

GERMAN
Otto Gail
Wolfgang Jeschke
Bernhard Kellermann
Kurd Lasswitz

IRISH
Lord Dunsany

Alun Llewellyn
Anne McCaffrey
Joseph O'Neill

ITALIAN
Dino Buzzati
Italo Calvino

JAPANESE
Kobo Abé
Shin'ichi Hoshi
Sakyo Komatsu
Haruki Murakami

LITHUANIAN
Algis Budrys

NEW ZEALANDER
M.K. Joseph
Cherry Wilder

POLISH
Stanislaw Lem
Stanislaw Witkiewicz

RUSSIAN
Aleksandr Belyaev
Valery Bryusov
Mikhail Bulgakov
Vladimir Mayakovsky
Boris and Arkady Strugatsky
Alexey Tolstoy
Konstantin Tsiolkovsky
Ilya Varshavsky
Ivan Yefremov
Yevgeny Zamyatin

SCOTTISH
Sheila MacLeod

SWEDISH
Karin Boye
Sam J. Lundwall

THAI
Somtow Sucharitkul

TITLE INDEX

The following list includes the titles of all novels and short stories (designated "s") cited as science fiction publications. The name in parenthesis is meant to direct the user to the appropriate entry, where full publication information is given. The term "series" indicates a recurring distinctive word or phrase (or name) in the titles of the entrant's books; series characters are also listed here, even if their names do not appear in specific titles of works.

10th Victim (Sheckley), 1966
100th Millennium (Brunner), 1959
1,000-Year Plan (Asimov), 1955
1,000-Year Voyage (Fearn, as Statten), 1954
13th Immortal (Silverberg), 1957
1945 (Forstchen), 1995
1964 (A. Moore), n.d.
1976: The Year of Terror (George H. Smith), 1961
1985 (Burgess), 1978
200 Years to Christmas (McIntosh), 1961
2000 Years On (Fearn, as Statten), 1950
2001: A Space Odyssey (Clarke), 1968
2010: Odyssey Two (Clarke), 1982
2018 (Lundwall), 1975
2061: Odyssey Three (Clarke), 1988
21st Century Sub (F. Herbert), 1956
3 for Space (s Nolan), 1992
30-Day Wonder (Richard Wilson), 1960
334 (Disch), 1972
40-Minute War (J. Morris), 1984
500 Millions of the Begum (Verne), 1879
57th Franz Kafka (s Rucker), 1983
6 x H (s Heinlein), 1961
9 Lives of Catseye Gomez (s Hawke), 1991
97th Step (Perry), 1989
98.4 (Hodder-Williams), 1969
99% (Gloag), 1944

A for Andromeda (F. and G. Hoyle), 1962
A Planet Called Krishna (de Camp), 1966
Aarn Munro series (Campbell), from 1947
Abandon Galaxy (Fox, as Somers), 1967
Abandonati (Kilworth), 1988
Abbs (Hyne), 1929
Abduction (Bischoff), 1990
Ability Quotient (Reynolds), 1975
Abode of Life (Stine, as Correy), 1982
Abominable Earthman (s Pohl), 1963
Abominations of Yondo (s Clark Ashton Smith), 1960
About Time (s Finney), 1986
Above All Else (Shiel), 1943
Abraxas Marvel Circus (Leigh), 1990
Absolute at Large (Capek), 1927
Abyss (Card), 1989
Abyss (Wilhelm), 1971
Academy of Terror (C. Grant, as Charles), 1986
Acceptable Time (L'Engle), 1989
Accidental Earth (Kelley), 1970
Account of a Meeting with Denizens of Another World, 1871 (Langford), 1979
Account Settled (Fearn, as Russell), 1949

Ace of Love (Lansdale), 1981
Achilles' Choice (S. Barnes, Niven), 1991
Achon! (S. Gordon), 1987
Across a Billion Years (Silverberg), 1969
Across Realtime (V. Vinge), 1986
Across the Ages (Fearn, as Statten), 1952
Across the Frames (Anthony), 1992
Across the Sea of Stars (s Clarke), 1959
Across the Sea of Suns (Benford), 1984
Across Time (Wollheim, as Grinnell), 1957
Actions and Reactions (s Kipling), 1909
Active Measures (Drake, J. Morris), 1985
Ad Statum Perspicuum (s F. Wilson), 1990
Adam in Moonshine (Priestley), 1927
Adam Link series (s Binder), from 1950
Addams Family (Sharkey), 1965
Address: Centauri (F.L. Wallace), 1955
Adept (Kurtz), 1991
Adrift in Space (s Zebrowski), 1979
Adulthood Rites (O. Butler), 1988
Adventure of Cobbler's Rune (s Le Guin), 1982
Adventure of the Blue Room (S. Wright, as Fowler), 1945
Adventure of the Peerless Peer by John H. Watson, M.D (Farmer), 1974
Adventure of Wyndham Smith (S. Wright), 1938
Adventures (Resnick), 1985
Adventures of a Solicitor (s Hyne, as Chesney), 1898
Adventures of a Two-Minute Werewolf (DeWeese), 1983
Adventures of Alyx (s Russ), 1983
Adventures of Captain Hatteras (Verne), 1876
Adventures of Doctor Esterhazy (s Davidson), 1991
Adventures of Smoke Bailey (s Morrow), 1983
Adventures of Terra Tarkington (Webb), 1985
Adventures of the Rat Family (s Verne), 1993
Adventures of Una Persson and Catherine Cornelius in the Twentieth Century (Moorcock), 1976
Adversary (May), 1984
Aelita (Tolstoy), 1957
Aestival Tide (Hand), 1992
Affair with Genius (s J. Green), 1969
Affirmation (Priest), 1981
After 12,000 Years (Coblentz), 1950
After Dark (Wellman), 1980
After Doomsday (P. Anderson), 1962
After London (Jefferies), 1885
After Long Silence (Tepper), 1987
After Many a Summer (Huxley), 1939
After Some Tomorrow (Reynolds), 1967
After Such Knowledge series (Blish), from 1991
After the Fact (Saberhagen), 1988
After Things Fell Apart (Goulart), 1970

Alternate Martians (Chandler), 1965
Alternate Orbits (s Chandler), 1971
Alternating Currents (s Pohl), 1956
Alternities (Kube-McDowell), 1988
Aluminum Man (Edmondson), 1975
Alvin Maker series (Card), from 1988
Always Coming Home (Le Guin), 1985
Always the Blackknight (Hoffman), 1970
Alyx (s Russ), 1976
Amalgamemnon (Brooke-Rose), 1984
Amazon Planet (Reynolds), 1975
Amazon Strikes Again (Fearn), 1954
Amazon's Diamond Quest (Fearn), 1953
Ambassador of Progress (W. Williams), 1984
Amber series (Zelazny), from 1970
Ambient (Womack), 1987
Ambulance Ship (J. White), 1979
Ambush at Corellia (Allen), 1995
Ambush of Shadows (P. Williams), 1983
American Ghosts and Old World Wonders (s A. Carter), 1993
American Gun Club (Verne), 1874
American Revolutionary (Cover), 1985
Ammonite (N. Griffith), 1993
Amnesia Moon (Lethem), 1995
Among the Dead and Other Events Leading Up to the Apocalypse
    (s Bryant), 1973
Amorica (Sucharitkul, as Somtow), 1994
Amphibian (Belyaev), 1959
Amphibians (S. Wright), 1925
Amsirs and the Iron Thorn (Budrys), 1967
Amtrak Wars series (Tilley), from 1984
Anackire (Lee), 1983
Analogue Men (Knight), 1962
Anarch Lords (Chandler), 1981
Anarchistic Colossus (van Vogt), 1977
Anasazi (s Ing), 1980
Ancient (Bischoff), 1994
Ancient Light (Gentle), 1987
Ancient, My Enemy (s Dickson), 1974
Ancient of Days (Bishop), 1985
. . . And All the Stars a Stage (Blish), 1971
And Chaos Died (Russ), 1970
And Don't Forget the One Red Rose (s Davidson), 1986
And Eternity (Anthony), 1990
And Not Make Dreams Your Master (Goldin), 1981
. . . and Others Shall Be Born (Long), 1968
. . . and Some Were Human (s del Rey), 1948
And Strange at Ecbatan the Trees (Bishop), 1976
And the Best Angels Sing (s Wilhelm), 1992
And the Devil Will Drag You Under (Chalker), 1979
And the Gods Laughed (s F. Brown), 1987
And Then the Town Took Off (Richard Wilson), 1960
And Then There'll Be Fireworks (Elgin), 1981
Andover and the Android (s Wilhelm), 1966
Android (Fanthorpe, as Zeigfreid), 1962
Android at Arms (Norton), 1971
Android Avenger (T. White), 1965
Android Planet (Mason, as Rankine), 1976
Androids (Long), 1969
Andromeda (Yefremov), 1959
Andromeda Breakthrough (F. and G. Hoyle), 1964

Andromeda Gun (Boyd), 1974
Andromeda series (F. and G. Hoyle), from 1962
Andromeda Strain (Crichton), 1969
Angado (Tubb), 1984
Angel of Pain (Stableford), 1991
Angel of the Revolution (G. Griffith), 1893
Angel series (Kilworth), from 1993
Angel Station (W. Williams), 1989
Angel with the Sword (Cherryh), 1985
Angels & Visitations (s Gaiman), 1993
Angels and Spaceships (s F. Brown), 1954
Angry Candy (s Ellison), 1988
Angry Espers (Biggle), 1961
Angry Ghost (Dent, as Robeson), 1977
Angry Planet (Cross), 1945
Animal Castle (Lee), 1972
Animal Farm (Orwell), 1945
Animal People (Coblentz), 1970
Anita (s Roberts), 1970
Anjani the Mighty (Fearn, as Titan), 1951
Annals of Klepsis (Lafferty), 1983
Annals of the Black Company (Cook), 1986
Annals of the Heechee (Pohl), 1987
Annals of the Time Patrol (P. Anderson), 1984
Annals of the Witch World (Norton), 1994
Anne and the Ripper of Siam (s Sucharitkul), n.d.
Annerton Pit (Dickinson), 1977
Annihilation (Fearn, as Statten), 1950
Annihilation Factor (Bayley), 1972
Annihilist (Dent, as Robeson), 1968
Annwn series (George H. Smith), from 1961
Anomalous Phenomenon, and Homeward Bound (Verne), 1965
Anomaly (Sohl), 1971
Anome (Vance), 1973
Another End (King), 1971
Another Heaven, Another Earth (Hoover), 1981
Another Kind (s Oliver), 1955
Another Tree in Eden (David Duncan), 1956
Answer (s Wylie), 1956
Antarctic Mystery (Verne), 1898
Anthem (Rand), 1938
Anthonology (s Anthony), 1985
Anthony Shriek; or, Lovers from a Darker Realm (Salmonson),
    1992
Anthropol series (Trimble), from 1968
Anti-Death League (Amis), 1966
Anti-Ice (Baxter), 1993
Anti-Man (Koontz), 1970
Antic Earth (Charbonneau), 1967
Antigeos series (Capon), from 1950
Antigrav (Fisk), 1978
Antinomy (s S. Robinson), 1980
Antiquities (s Crowley), 1993
Anton York—Immortal (s Binder), 1965
Ants Who Took away Time (Kotzwinkle), 1978
Anubis Gates (Powers), 1983
Anvil (Drake), 1993
Anvil (Stirling), 1993
Anvil of Stars (Bear), 1992
Anvil of Time (Silverberg), 1969
Any Old Iron (Burgess), 1989

Anything Box (s Henderson), 1965
Anything Tree (Rackham), 1970
Anything You Can Do . . . (Garrett, as Darrel T. Langart), 1963
Anywhen (s Blish), 1970
Apartheid, Superstrings, and Mordecai Thubana (Bishop), 1989
Ape and Essence (Huxley), 1948
Apocalypse (Springer), 1989
Apocalypses (s Lafferty), 1977
Apollo's War (Thurston), 1987
Apostle of the Cylinder (Rousseau), 1918
Apparitions of Things to Come (s Bellamy), 1990
Appointment at Bloodstar (Goldin, E.E. Smith), 1978
Apprentice Adept series (Anthony), from 1980
Approaching Oblivion (s Ellison), 1974
April Witch (s Bradbury), 1988
Aquarius Mission (Caidin), 1978
Aquila and the Iron Horse (Sucharitkul, as Somtow), 1988
Aquila and the Sphinx (Sucharitkul, as Somtow), 1988
Aquiliad series (Sucharitkul), from 1983
Arabian Nights series (Gardner), from 1991
Arafel's Saga (Cherryh), 1983
Araminta Station (Vance), 1987
Ararat (D.M. Thomas), 1983
Arc d'X (Erickson), 1993
Arc of the Dream (Attanasio), 1986
Arc One series (M. Hughes), from 1984
Arc Riders (Drake), 1995
Arc Riders (J. Morris), 1995
Archangel (Kilworth), 1994
Archer's Goon (Diana Wynne Jones), 1984
Archipelago (Lafferty), 1979
Architecture of Desire (Gentle), 1991
Arcot, Morey, and Wade series (Campbell), from 1973
Arctic Bride (s Meek), 1944
Arcturus Landing (Dickson), 1978
Ardneh's World (Saberhagen), 1988
Ardor on Aros (Offutt), 1973
Arena (Forstchen), 1994
Arena of Antares (Bulmer, as Akers), 1974
Argentis (Tubb, as Shaw), 1952
Argo (Lafferty), 1992
Argonaut Affair (Hawke), 1987
Argus Steps In (Sernine), 1990
Arimaspian Legacy (s G. Wolfe), 1987
Ariosto (Yarbro), 1980
Aristoi (W. Williams), 1992, London, Grafton, 1993
Ark Sakura (Abé), 1988
Arm of the Starfish (L'Engle), 1965
Armada of Antares (Bulmer, as Akers), 1976
Armageddon 2419 A.D (Nowlan), 1962
Armageddon Crazy (Farren), 1989
Armed Camps (K. Reed), 1969
Armies of Elfland (s P. Anderson), 1992
Armlet of the Gods (Eshbach), 1986
Armor of Light (Scott), 1988
Around the World in Eighty Days (Verne), 1873
Around the World under Water (Senarens), 1893
Arrive at Easterwine (Lafferty), 1971
Arrow from Earth (Busby), 1995
Arrows of Hercules (de Camp), 1965
Arrows of the Sun (Tarr), 1993

Ars Magica (Tarr), 1989
Arsenal of Miracles (Fox), 1964
Arslan (Engh), 1976
Art of the Sword (Emerson), 1994
Artery of Fire (Scortia), 1972
Arthur Gordon Pym (Poe), 1841
Artifact (Benford), 1985
Artificial Fire (s A. Carter), 1988
Artificial Kid (Sterling), 1980
Artificial Things (s Fowler), 1986
Arwen series (s Bradley), from 1974
As on a Darkling Plain (Bova), 1972
As the Curtain Falls (Chilson), 1974
As the Green Star Rises (L. Carter), 1975
As You Were (s Kuttner), 1955
Ascendancies (Compton), 1980
Ascension (C. Grant), 1977
Ascension Factor (F. Herbert), 1988
Ascian in Rose (de Lint), 1987
Asgard series (Stableford), from 1982
Ashes and Stars (Zebrowski), 1977
Ashes, Ashes (Barjavel), 1967
Asleep in the Afternoon (Large), 1938
Assassin Gambit (Forstchen), 1988
Assault on the Gods (Goldin), 1977
Assemblers of Infinity (K. Anderson), 1993
Assignment in Eternity (s Heinlein), 1953
Assignment in Nowhere (Laumer), 1968
Assignment: Hellhole (Offutt, as Cleve), 1983
Assignment: Nor'Dyren (Van Scyoc), 1973
Asteroid Man (Fanthorpe), 1960
Astra series (Norton), from 1954
Astral Fortress (Rotsler), 1981
Astral Mirror (s Bova), 1985
Astral Quest (Mason, as Rankine), 1975
Astronauts Must Not Land (Brunner), 1963
Asutra (Vance), 1974
Asylum Piece (s Kavan), 1940
Asylum World (Jakes), 1969
At Any Price (Drake), 1985
At Sea (s Hodgson), 1993
At the Back of the North Wind (G. MacDonald), 1870
At the Earth's Core (E. Burroughs), 1922
At the Edge of the World (s Dunsany), 1970
At the End of the Endless Stream (Komatsu), 1966
At the Eye of the Ocean (Schenck), 1980
At the Mountains of Madness (s Lovecraft), 1964
At the Narrow Passage (Meredith), 1973
At the North Pole (Verne), 1874
At the Seventh Level (Elgin), 1972
At Winter's End (Silverberg), 1988
Atlantean Chronicles series (Bradley), from 1983
Atlantean Nights Entertainment (Pangborn), 1980
Atlantic Abomination (Brunner), 1960
Atlantis (s Delany), 1995
Atlas Shrugged (Rand), 1957
Atom-War on Mars (Tubb), 1952
Atomic Fantasy (Capek), 1948
Atomic Nemesis (Fanthorpe, as Zeigfreid), 1962
Atoms and Evil (s Bloch), 1962
Atoms of Empire (s Hyne), 1904

Aton series (Anthony), from 1967
Atrocity Exhibition (s Ballard), 1970
Attack from Atlantis (del Rey), 1953
Attack of the Giant Baby (s K. Reed), 1981
Attar series (Joe Haldeman), from 1975
Attar's Revenge (Joe Haldeman, as Graham), 1975
Attic Child (Hoskins, as Corren), 1979
Attila the Pun (Pinkwater), 1981
Augmented Agent (s Vance), 1986
Aunt Fritzi (s Richard Wilson), 1987
Aunt Maria (Diana Wynne Jones), 1991
Aurelia (Lafferty), 1982
Austin, Steve series (Caidin), from 1972
Authentic Touch (Wodhams), 1971
Autocracy of Mr. Parham (Wells), 1930
Automated Goliath (Temple), 1962
Automatic Horse (s Hubbard), 1994
Autumn Angels series (Cover), from 1975
Autumn Land (s Simak), 1990
Avaryan Rising series (Tarr), from 1986
Avatar (P. Anderson), 1978
Avenger of Antares (Bulmer, as Akers), 1975
Avenger series (Goulart), from 1974
Avengers Battle the Earth-Wrecker (Binder), 1967
Avengers of Carrig (Brunner), 1969
Avenging Goddess (s Fanthorpe), 1964
Avenging Martian (Fearn, as Statten), 1951
Aventine (s Killough), 1982
Awakeners series (Tepper), from 1987
Awakening (Meredith), 1979
Away and Beyond (s van Vogt), 1952
Away Is a Strange Place to Be (Hoover), 1990
Awful Egg (Dent, as Robeson), 1978
Axiomatic (Egan), 1995
Ayesha (Haggard), 1905
Azazel (s Asimov), 1988

Babel-17 (Delany), 1966
Back to the Future Part III (Gardner), 1990
Back to the Future Part II (Gardner), 1989
Back to the Stone Age (E. Burroughs), 1937
Back to the Time Trap (Laumer), 1992
Back-yard War (Fisk), 1990
Backlash (Fisk), 1988
Backlash Mission (Zahn), 1986
Backward in Time (Kelley), 1979
Bad Day for Ali Baba (Gardner), 1991
Bad Place (Koontz), 1990
Bad Sister (Tennant), 1978
Badger in the Bag (s de Lint), 1985
Bag of Surprises (s Hoshi), 1989
Bagful of Dreams (s Vance), 1979
Balance of Power (Stableford), 1979
Ballad of Beta-2 (Delany), 1965
Balling Machine (Offutt, as Douglas), 1971
Ballroom of the Skies (J. MacDonald), 1952
Balook (Anthony), 1990
Baltimore Gun Club (Verne), 1874
Bander Snatch (O'Donnell), 1979
Bane of the Black Sword (Moorcock), 1977
Barbarana (Offutt, as Cleve), 1970

Barbarian of World's End (L. Carter), 1977
Barbarians of Mars (Moorcock, as Bradbury), 1965
Barbary (McIntyre), 1986
Barbie Murders (s Varley), 1980
Bard's Tale series (Emerson), from 1993
Barefoot in the Head (Aldiss), 1969
Barking Dogs (T. Green), 1988
Barnard's Planet (Boyd), 1975
Barnes/Moffat series (Bradley), from 1972
Barnstormer in Oz (Farmer), 1982
Barnum System series (Goulart), from 1970
Baron in the Trees (s Calvino), 1959
Barons of Behavior (Purdom), 1972
Barrayar (Bujold), 1991
Barrier 346 (Fanthorpe, as Zeigfreid), 1965
Barrier World (Charbonneau), 1970
Barron, Ron series (R. Jones), from 1952
Barsac Mission (Verne), 1960
Barsoom Project (S. Barnes, Niven), 1989
Barton series (Busby), from 1973
Basileus (J. Morris), 1985
Bastaard Revolution (Stine), 1988
Bastable, Oswald series (Moorcock), from 1978
Bastard Prince (Kurtz), 1994
Bat Hardin series (Reynolds), from 1974
Batman in the Black Egg of Atlantis (Barrett), 1992
Batman series (Gardner), from 1989
Batman series (Hawke), from 1991
Batman: Captured by the Engines (Lansdale), 1991
*batteries Not Included (Drew), 1987
Battle Circle series (Anthony), from 1978
Battle for the Stars (Hamilton), 1961
Battle of Forever (van Vogt), 1971
Battle on Mercury (del Rey, as Van Lhin), 1953
Battle on Venus (Temple), 1963
Battle Station (s Bova), 1987
Battle That Ended the Century (s Lovecraft), 1934
Battlecry (J. Barnes), 1992
Battlefield Earth (Hubbard), 1982
Battlestar Galactica 5 (Resnick), 1980
Battlestar Galactica 6 (Hawke, as Yermakov), 1982
Battlestar Galactica 7 (Hawke, as Yermakov), 1982
Battlestar Galactica series (Goulart), from 1983
Battlestar Galactica series (Thurston), from 1978
Battletech series (Mayhar), from 1987
Bazaar of the Bizarre (s Leiber), 1978
Beachhead (Williamson), 1992
Beachhead Planet (R. Williams), 1970
Beamriders! (Caidin), 1989
Beanstalk (Rackham), 1973
Bear's Fantasies (s Bear), 1992
Beard's Roman Women (Burgess), 1976
Bearing an Hourglass (Anthony), 1984
Bears Discover Fire (s Bisson), 1993
B.E.A.S.T. (Maine), 1966
Beast (van Vogt), 1963
Beast Master series (Norton), from 1959
Beast That Shouted Love at the Heart of the World (s Ellison), 1969
Beastchild (Koontz), 1970
Beastmarks (s Attanasio), 1984

Beasts (Crowley), 1976
Beasts from Beyond (Wellman), 1950
Beasts of Antares (Bulmer, as Akers), 1980
Beasts of Kohl (Rackham), 1966
Beasts of the Mist (Proctor), 1986
Beatrice (Haggard), 1890
Beautiful Biting Machine (s Lee), 1984
Beautiful Soup (Jacobs), 1993
Beauty (Tepper), 1991
Beauty and the Beast (Emerson), 1990
Because It Is Absurd (Belyaev), 1971
Beckoning Lights (M. Hughes), 1982
Becoming Alien (Ore), 1988
Bedlam Planet (Brunner), 1968
Beepers from Outer Space (DeWeese), 1985
Beetle in the Anthill (Strugatsky), 1980
Before Adam (London), 1906
Before the Dawn (Taine), 1934
Before the Universe (s Kornbluth, Pohl), 1980
Beggars series (Kress), from 1993
Beginning Place (Le Guin), 1980
Beginnings (s Dickson), 1988
Begum's Fortune (Verne), 1879
Behind the Walls of Terra (Farmer), 1970
Behold the Man (Moorcock), 1969
Behold the Stars (Bulmer), 1965
Being Alien (Ore), 1989
Belgariad series (Eddings), from 1982
Believers' World (Lowndes), 1961
Bell from Infinity (R. Williams), 1968
Bell Street Murders (S. Wright, as Fowler), 1931
Bell Tree (Hoover), 1982
Bells of Shoredan (s Zelazny), 1979
Belly of the Wolf (MacAvoy), 1994
Beloved Son (Turner), 1978
Belshazzar (Haggard), 1930
Beneath the Shattered Moons (Bishop), 1977
Beneath the Tree of Heaven (Wingrove), 1993
Beneath Your Very Boots (Hyne), 1889
Benita (Haggard), 1906
Berlin (de Lint), 1989
Bernal One series (Zebrowski), from 1984
Bernhard the Conqueror (Lundwall), 1973
Berserker series (Holdstock), from 1977
Berserker series (Saberhagen), from 1969
Best Ye Breed (Reynolds), 1978
Bestsellers Guaranteed (s Lansdale), 1993
Betrayal, The Rebirth and The Vindication (Cherryh), 1989
Betrothed (s Lee), 1968
Better Mantrap (s Shaw), 1982
Bettyann (Neville), 1970
Between Planets (Heinlein), 1951
Between the Strokes of Night (Sheffield), 1985
Between Two Worlds (s T. Carr), 1986
Bevis (Jefferies), 1882
Bewitchments of Love and Hate (Constantine), 1988
Beyond (s Sturgeon), 1960
Beyond (Strugatsky), n.d.
Beyond Another Sun (Godwin), 1971
Beyond Apollo (Malzberg), 1972
Beyond Bedlam (s Guin), 1973

Beyond Capella (Rackham), 1971
Beyond Earth's Gates (Kuttner and C.L. Moore, as Padgett), 1954
Beyond Eden (David Duncan), 1955
Beyond Heaven's River (Bear), 1980
Beyond Infinity (s Nourse), 1964
Beyond Sanctuary (J. Morris), 1985
Beyond the Barrier (Knight), 1964
Beyond the Barrier of Space (Fanthorpe, as Torro), 1969
Beyond the Beyond (s P. Anderson), 1969
Beyond the Black Enigma (Fox, as Bart Somers), 1965
Beyond the Blue Event Horizon (Pohl), 1980
Beyond the Burning Lands (Christopher), 1971
Beyond the Curve (s Abé), 1991
Beyond the Dar al-Harb (s Dickson), 1985
Beyond the Dark River (M. Hughes), 1979
Beyond the Eleventh Hour (R. Gordon, as Hough), 1961
Beyond the Fall of Night (Benford), 1990
Beyond the Farthest Star (E. Burroughs), 1964
Beyond the Fields We Know (s Dunsany), 1972
Beyond the Galactic Lens (Tubb, as Kern), 1975
Beyond the Galactic Rim (s Chandler), 1963
Beyond the Gate (Wolverton), 1995
Beyond the Gates of Dream (s L. Carter), 1969
Beyond the Imperium (Laumer), 1981
Beyond the Moon (Hamilton), 1950
Beyond the Planet Earth (Tsiolkovsky), 1960
Beyond the Resurrection (Eklund), 1973
Beyond the Rim (S. Wright), 1932
Beyond the Safe Zone (s Silverberg), 1986
Beyond the Silver Sky (Bulmer), 1961
Beyond the Stars (Cummings), 1963
Beyond the Tomorrow Mountains (Engdahl), 1973
Beyond the Vanishing Point (Cummings), 1958
Beyond the Veil (Fanthorpe, as Thanet), 1964
Beyond the Veil (J. Morris), 1985
Beyond the Veil of Stars (R. Reed), 1994
Beyond the Void (Fanthorpe, as Muller), 1965
Beyond the Wall of Sleep (s Lovecraft), 1943
Beyond Thirty (s E. Burroughs), 1955
Beyond This Horizon (Heinlein), 1948
Beyond Time (Fanthorpe, as Muller), 1962
Beyond Wizardwall (J. Morris), 1986
Beyonders (Wellman), 1977
Bible Stories for Adults (s Morrow), 1995
Bibliomen (s G. Wolfe), 1984
Bicentennial Man (s Asimov), 1976
Bid Time Return (Matheson), 1975
Big Bang (Goulart), 1982
Big Black Mark (Chandler), 1975
Big Death (Maine), 1978
Big Jump (Brackett), 1955
Big Lifters (Ing), 1988
Big Orange Splot (Pinkwater), 1977
Big Planet series (Vance), from 1957
Big Show (s Laumer), 1972
Big Time (Leiber), 1961
Big U (N. Stephenson), 1984
Big X (Searls), 1959
Bill, the Galactic Hero series (H. Harrison), from 1965
Bill, the Galactic Hero series (Bischoff), from 1991
Billenium (s Ballard), 1962

Billion Days of Earth (Piserchia), 1976
Billy Pink's Private Detective Agency (Kilworth), 1993
Binary Z (Mason, as Rankine), 1969
Bio of a Space Tyrant series (Anthony), from 1983
Bioblast! (Gallun), 1985
BiPohl (Pohl), 1982
Bird of Time (Effinger), 1986
Birds of Kinship series (Cowper), from 1978
Birds of Prey (Drake), 1984
Birth of a New Republic (s Williamson), 1981
Birth of Fire (Pournelle), 1976
Birth of Flux and Anchor (Chalker), 1985
Birth of the People's Republic of Antarctica (Batchelor), 1983
Birthgrave series (Lee), from 1978
Birthright (Resnick), 1982
Birthstone (D.M. Thomas), 1980
Bishop's Heir (Kurtz), 1984
Bitter Gold Hearts (Cook), 1988
Bitter Pill (Chandler), 1974
Bitter Reflection (s Fanthorpe), 1964
Black Air (s K. Robinson), 1991
Black Avengers (Fearn, as Statten), 1953
Black Bargain (Fearn, as Statten), 1953
Black Beast (Springer), 1982
Black Carousel (C. Grant), 1995
Black Chariots (Goulart, as Robeson), 1974
Black Cloud (F. and G. Hoyle), 1957
Black Company series (Cook), from 1984
Black Corridor (Moorcock), 1969
Black Current series (Watson), from 1984
Black Dragon series (MacAvoy), from 1983
Black Druid (s Long), 1975
Black Easter (Blish), 1968
Black Easter: The Day After Judgement (Blish), 1980
Black Egg of Atlantis (Barrett), 1992
Black Flame (Weinbaum), 1948
Black Fox (Heard), 1950
Black Galaxy (Leinster), 1954
Black Genesis (Hubbard), 1986
Black God's Shadow (s C.L. Moore), 1977
Black Grail (Broderick), 1986
Black Heart and White Heart; and, The Wizard (s Haggard), 1924
Black Hole (A. Foster), 1979
Black in Time (Jakes), 1970
Black Infinity (Fanthorpe, as Brett), 1961
Black Knight of the Iron Sphere (Eklund, E. E. Smith), 1979
Black Legion of Callisto (L. Carter), 1972
Black Lion (Fanthorpe), 1979
Black Magician (Edmondson), 1986
Black Maria (Diana Wynne Jones), 1991
Black Milk (R. Reed), 1989
Black Mountains (Saberhagen), 1971
Black Opal (Aubrey, as Ash), 1915
Black Roads (Hensley), 1976
Black Sorcerer of the Black Castle (s Offutt), 1976
Black Star (L. Carter), 1973
Black Star Passes (Campbell), 1953
Black Star Rising (Pohl), 1985
Black Steel (Perry), 1992
Black Suits from Outer Space (DeWeese), 1985
Black Throne (Saberhagen, Zelazny), 1990

Black Tower (Lupoff), 1988
Black Trillium (Bradley, May, Norton), 1990
Black Unicorn (Lee), 1991
Black Venus (s A. Carter), 1985
Black Venus's Tale (s A. Carter), 1980
Black Wheel (Merritt), 1947
Black Wine (s C. Grant), 1986
Black-Wing of Mars (Fearn, as Statten), 1953
Blackcollar series (Zahn), from 1983
Blackman's Burden (Reynolds), 1972
Blackthorne, Lincoln series (C. Grant), from 1984
Blade of the Guillotine (Cover), 1986
Blade, Richard series (Nelson), from 1979
Blade Runner (W. Burroughs), 1979
Bladerunner (Nourse), 1974
Bladerunner: Do Androids Dream of Electric Sheep? (Dick), 1982
Blades of Mars (Moorcock, as Bradbury), 1965
Bladesman of Antares (Bulmer, as Akers), 1975
Blake of the "Rattlesnake" (Jefferies), 1895
Blake's Progress (Nelson), 1975
Blake's Seven series (T. Hoyle), from 1977
Blal (s van Vogt), 1976
Blaze of Glory (Hawke), 1995
Blazon (Bulmer), 1970
Bleeding Man (s Strete), 1977
Blessing of Pan (Dunsany), 1926
Blind Circle (Renard), 1928
Blind Geometer (s K. Robinson), 1986
Blind Men and the Elephant (Griffin), 1982
Blind Needle (T. Hoyle), 1994
Blind Spot (Flint, Hall), 1951
Blind Voices (Reamy), 1978
Blind Worm (Stableford), 1970
Blindfold (K. Anderson), 1995
Blindfold from the Stars (High), 1979
Blindman's World (s Bellamy), 1898
Blob (Bischoff), 1988
Blob (s May, as Thorpe), 1982
Bloch and Bradbury (s Bloch, Bradbury), 1969
Blockade of Sinitron (s Mason), 1966
Blood (Moorcock), 1995
Blood and Burning (s Budrys), 1978
Blood and Fire (Naha, as McGann), 1991
Blood and Gingerbread (s Sladek), 1990
Blood Countess (Goulart, as Robeson), 1975
Blood County (Piserchia, as Selby), 1981
Blood Fever (K. Reed, as Hyde), 1982
Blood Fountain (Proctor), 1985
Blood Heritage series (Tepper), from 1986
Blood Kin (Naha, as McGann), 1989
Blood Music (Bear), 1985
Blood of a Dragon (Watt-Evans), 1991
Blood of Amber (Zelazny), 1986
Blood of Roses (Lee), 1990
Blood of the Lamb (Monteleone), 1992
Blood Opera series (Lee), from 1992
Blood Red Game (Moorcock), 1970
Blood River (Tilley), 1988
Blood River Down (C. Grant, as Fenn), 1986
Blood Runs Cold (s Bloch), 1961
Blood series (Killough), from 1987

Blood Siege (Stine), 1990
Blood Sky (s Nolan), 1991
Blood Trillium (May), 1992
Blood Vengance (Stirling), 1994
Blood Wedding (Goulart), 1976
Blooded on Arachne (s Bishop), 1982
Bloodfeuds (Stirling), 1993
Bloodhype (A. Foster), 1973
Bloodletter (Jeter), 1993
Bloodlinks (Killough), 1988
Bloodname (Thurston), 1991
Bloodstar Conspiracy (E.E. Smith), 1978
Bloodstar Conspiracy (Goldin), 1978
Bloodstone (Gemmell), 1994
Bloodwind (C. Grant), 1982
Bloodworld (Janifer), 1968
Bloody Chamber (s A. Carter), 1979
Bloody Sun (Bradley), 1964
Blow My Mind (Fox), 1970
Blown (Farmer), 1969
Blowout! (F. Robinson, Scortia), 1987
Blue Adept (Anthony), 1981
Blue Atom (R. Williams), 1958
Blue Barbarians (Coblentz), 1958
Blue Champagne (s Varley), 1986
Blue Face (Edmondson), 1972
Blue Hawk (Dickinson), 1976
Blue Juggernaut (Fanthorpe, as Fane), 1965
Blue Moose (Pinkwater), 1975
Blue Star (Pratt), 1969
Blue Thing (Pinkwater), 1977
Blue Tyson (s Dowling), 1992
Blue World (Vance), 1966
Bluesong (Van Scyoc), 1983
Boat of a Million Years (P. Anderson), 1989
Boats of the "Glen Carrig" (Hodgson), 1907
Bodelan Way (Trimble), 1974
Bodily Functions (s Aldiss), 1991
Body of Glass (Piercy), 1992
Body Snatchers (Finney), 1955
Bogey Men (s Bloch), 1963
Bolo series (Laumer), from 1976
Bolts: A Robot Dog (Key), 1966
Bone Dance (Bull), 1991
Bone Forest (s Holdstock), 1991
Bones (Tepper), 1987
Bones of God (Leigh), 1986
Bones of Zora (de Camp), 1983
Bonkers Clocks (Fisk), 1985
Book of Atrix Wolfe (McKillip), 1995
Book of Being (Watson), 1985
Book of Dreams (Vance), 1981
Book of Isle series (Springer), from 1977
Book of Kells (MacAvoy), 1985
Book of Morgaine (Cherryh), 1979
Book of Ptath (van Vogt), 1947
Book of Rack the Healer (Z. Hughes), 1973
Book of Silence (Watt-Evans), 1984
Book of Skaith (Brackett), 1976
Book of Skulls (Silverberg), 1972
Book of Suns (Springer), 1977

Book of the Beast (Lee), 1988
Book of the Damned (s Lee), 1988
Book of the Dead (Lee), 1991
Book of the Long Sun series (G. Wolfe), from 1993
Book of the Mad (Lee), 1993
Book of the New Sun series (G. Wolfe), from 1980
Book of the River (Watson), 1984
Book of the Stars (Watson), 1984
Book of Vale (Springer), 1984
Book of Wonder (s Dunsany), 1912
Book of Wraeththu series (Constantine), from 1987
Books of Great Alta (Yolen), 1990
Books of the Black Current (Watson), 1986
Boosted Man (Bulmer, as Zetford), 1974
Border, Breed Nor Birth (Reynolds), 1972
Border War (Shirley, as Drum), 1985
Borderline (Vercors), 1954
Borders of Infinity (s Bujold), 1989
Borgel (Pinkwater), 1990
Born Leader (McIntosh), 1954
Born of Luna (Fearn, as Statten), 1951
Born of Man and Woman (s Matheson), 1954
Born to Exile (s Eisenstein), 1978
Born under Mars (Brunner), 1967
Born with the Dead (s Silverberg), 1974
Borrowed Month (s Stockton), 1887
Boss of Terror (Dent, as Robeson), 1976
Bound in Time (D.F. Jones), 1981
Bow Down to Nul (Aldiss), 1960
Box of Nothing (Dickinson), 1985
Boy Adventurers in the Unknown Land (Verrill), 1924
Boy Adventures in the Land of the Monkey Men (Verrill), 1923
Boy in Darkness (s Peake), 1976
Boy Who Hooked the Sun (s G. Wolfe), 1985
Boy Who Spoke Chimp (Yolen), 1981
Boys from Brazil (Levin), 1976
Brain Child (Turner), 1991
Brain Machine (George O. Smith), 1968
Brain Plant series (Meltzer), from 1969
Brain Rose (Kress), 1990
Brain-Stealers (Leinster), 1954
Brain Twister (Garrett, Janifer, as Phillips), 1962
Brain Wave (P. Anderson), 1954
Brain World (Reynolds), 1978
Brainrose (Kress), 1991
Brains of Earth (Vance), 1966
Brains of Rats (s Blumlein), 1989
Brainz, Inc. (Goulart), 1985
Brak series (Jakes), from 1968
Bram Stoker's Dracula (Saberhagen), 1992
Branch (Resnick), 1984
Brand New World (Cummings), 1964
Brand of the Werewolf (Dent, as Robeson), 1965
Brass Dragon (Bradley), 1969
Brave Free Men (Vance), 1973
Brave Little Toaster (s Disch), 1986
Brave Little Toaster Goes to Mars (s Disch), 1988
Brave New World (Huxley), 1932
Breakaway (Tubb), 1999
Breakfast in the Ruins (Moorcock), 1972
Breakfast of Champions (Vonnegut), 1973

Breaking Earth (s Laumer), 1981
Breaking of Northwall (P. Williams), 1981
Breaking Point (s Gunn), 1972
Breaking Strain (Preuss), 1987
Breakout series (Lake), from 1976
Breakthrough (Cowper), 1967
Breath of Suspension (Jablokov), 1994
Breathing Space Only (Whiteford), 1980
Brede's Tale (s May), 1982
Breed to Come (Norton), 1972
Breeds of Man (Busby), 1988
Brethren (Haggard), 1904
Briar Rose (Yolen), 1992
Brick Moon (s Hale), 1899
Bride (McIntyre), 1985
Bride of the Slime Monster (Gardner), 1990
Bridge of Ashes (Zelazny), 1976
Bridge of Birds (Hughart), 1984
Bridge of Light (Verrill), 1950
Bridge of Lost Desire (s Delany), 1987
Bridge of Years (Robert Charles Wilson), 1991
Bridgehead (Drake), 1986
Bridging the Galaxies (s Niven), 1993
Brigade (Shirley), 1982
Brigadier Ffellowes series (s Lanier), from 1972
Brigands of the Moon (Cummings), 1931
Bright New Universe (Williamson), 1967
Brightness Falls from the Air (Tiptree), 1985
Brill/Maxwell series (Killough), from 1979
Bring Back Yesterday (Chandler), 1961
Bring Me the Head of Prince Charming (Sheckley, Zelazny), 1991
Bring the Jubilee (W. Moore), 1953
Brinkman (Goulart), 1981
Briton or Boer? (G. Griffith), 1897
Broke Down Engine and Other Troubles with Machines (s Goulart), 1971
Broken Cycle (Chandler), 1975
Broken God (Zindell), 1993
Broken Land (McDonald), 1992
Broken Lands (Saberhagen), 1968
Broken Sword (P. Anderson), 1954
Broken Symmetries (Preuss), 1983
Broken Wheel (Wingrove), 1990
Bromelaid (Pratchett), 1993
Bromius Phenomenon (Mason, as Rankine), 1973
Bronson Beta series (Wylie), from 1993
Brontomek! (Coney), 1976
Bronwyn's Bane (Scarborough), 1983
Bronze King (Charnas), 1985
Bronze of Eddarta (Garrett), 1983
Brooks, Clifford series (Fearn), from 1953
Broops! Down the Chimney (Fisk), 1991
Brothel in Rosenstrasse (Moorcock), 1982
Brother (s Simak), 1986
Brother Assassin (Saberhagen), 1969
Brother Death (Perry), 1992
Brother Esau (Gribbin), 1982
Brother John (Kelley), 1971
Brother Jonathan (Kilian), 1985
Brother Mouse (s F. Brown), 1987
Brother to Demons, Brother to God (Williamson), 1979

Brother to Dragons (Sheffield), 1992
Brother to Shadows (Norton), 1993
Brothers (Wells), 1938
Brothers in Arms (Bujold), 1989
Brothers of Earth (Cherryh), 1976
Brothers of the Head (Aldiss), 1977
Buck Rogers series (Lupoff), from 1978
Buck Rogers series (Niven), from 1980
Buck Rogers series (Pournelle), from 1980
Budry's Inferno (s Budrys), 1963
Buffalo Gals and Other Animal Presences (s Le Guin), 1987
Buffalo Gals, Won't You Come out Tonight (s Le Guin), 1994
Bug Jack Barron (Spinrad), 1969
Bug Wars (Asprin), 1979
Bugs (Sladek), 1989
Bull and the Spear (Moorcock), 1973
Bull Chief (Holdstock, as Carlsen), 1977
Bully! (s Resnick), 1990
Bumsider (MacApp), 1972
Bunch! (s Bunch), 1993
Burn, Witch, Burn! (Merritt), 1933
Burning (Gunn), 1972
Burning Bright (Scott), 1993
Burning Chrome (s Gibson), 1986
Burning Mountain (Coppel), 1983
Burning Realm (Reaves), 1988
Burning Ring (Burdekin), 1927
Burning Tears of Sassurum (Baker), 1988
Burning World (Ballard), 1964
Burying the Shadow (Constantine), 1992
Businessman (Disch), 1984
Busy about the Tree of Life (s Zoline), 1988
But What of Earth? (Anthony, R. Coulson), 1976
But Who Can Replace a Man? (s Aldiss), 1965
Butterfly Planet (High), 1971
Button Bright (Kurland), 1990
Buy Jupiter (s Asimov), 1975
Buying Time (Joe Haldeman), 1989
Bwana, and Bully! (s Resnick), 1991
By Airship to Ophir (Aubrey, as Ash), 1911
By Bizarre Hands (s Lansdale), 1989
By Furies Possessed (T. White), 1970
By Rocket to the Moon (Gail), 1931
By the Light of the Green Star (L. Carter), 1974
By the Time I Get to Nashville (C. Grant, as Fenn), 1994
Bypass to Otherness (s Kuttner), 1961
Byte Beautiful (s Tiptree), 1985
Byworlder (P. Anderson), 1971
Byzantium's Crown (Shwartz), 1987
Byzantium's Heirs series (Shwartz), from 1987

Cachalot (A. Foster), 1980
Cache (s Farmer), 1981
Cache from Outer Space (Farmer), 1962
Caduceus Wild (W. Moore), 1978
Cadwal Chronicles series (Vance), from 1987
Caesar's Column (Donnelly, as Boisgilbert), 1890
Cage (Stirling), 1989
Cage a Man (Busby), 1973
Cageworld series (Kapp), from 1982
Cahena (Wellman), 1986

Cal (s Asimov), 1991
Calculated Risk (Maine), 1960
Caldé of the Long Sun (G. Wolfe), 1994
Calendar of the Trees (s de Lint), 1984
Calenture (Constantine), 1994
Calibrated Alligator (s Silverberg), 1969
California Iceberg (H. Harrison), 1975
California Voodoo Game (S. Barnes, Nivae), 1992
Call of Earth (Card), 1993
Call of the Cosmos (s Tsiolkovsky), 1961
Call of the Savage (Kline), 1937
Call of the Werewolf (s Fanthorpe), 1958
Call of the Wild (s Fanthorpe), 1965
Call to Arms (A. Foster), 1991
Call to Battle (Hawke), 1993
Call to the Edge (s McMullen), 1992
Callahan's Place series (s S. Robinson), from 1977
Caller from Overspace (Lymington), 1979
Calling Captain Future (Hamilton), 1969
Calling Dr. Patchwork (Goulart), 1978
Calling of the Three (Emerson), 1990
Callipygia (L. Carter), 1988
Callisto series (L. Carter), from 1972
Caltraps of Time (s Masson), 1968
Calver, Derek series (Chandler), from 1961
Calvin Nullifier (DeWeese), 1987
Calvin Willeford series (DeWeese), from 1985
Camber of Culdi (Kurtz), 1976
Camber the Heretic (Kurtz), 1981
Camberwell Miracle (Beresford), 1933
Cambio Bay (Wilhelm), 1990
Camelot 30K (Forward), 1993
Camford Visitation (Wells), 1937
Camp Concentration (Disch), 1968
Can You Feel Anything When I Do This? (s Sheckley), 1971
Canary in a Cat House (s Vonnegut), 1961
Cancer Machine (s Binder), 1941
Candy Man (King), 1971
Canon Tellis series (L'Engle), from 1965
Canopus in Argos (Lessing), from 1979
Canopy of Time (s Aldiss), 1959
Canticle for Leibowitz (W. Miller), 1960
Cape (Caidin), 1971
Capitol (s Card), 1979
Capricious Robot (s Hoshi), 1986
Capricorn Games (s Silverberg), 1976
Capricorn One (Goulart), 1978
Captain (Norman), 1992
Captain America: The Great Gold Steal (T. White), 1968
Captain Blackman (J. Williams), 1972
Captain Future series (Hamilton), from 1969
Captain Future series (Wellman), from 1968
Captain Ishmael (G. Griffith), 1901
Captive Scorpio (Bulmer, as Akers), 1978
Captive Universe (H. Harrison), 1969
Captives of the Flame (Delany), 1963
Captives of the Moon (P. Moore), 1960
Car Warriors series (Drake), from 1992
Caravan (Goldin), 1975
Cards of Grief (Yolen), 1984

Carmen Dog (Emshwiller), 1988
Carnacki, the Ghost-Finder (s Hodgson), 1910
Carnadyne Horde (Offutt, as Cleve), 1984
Carnelian Cube (de Camp), 1948
Carnelian Cube (Pratchett), 1983
Carnelian Throne (J. Morris), 1979
Carnival of Destruction (Stableford), 1993
Carpathian Castle (Verne), 1963
Carpet People (Pratchett), 1971
Carson of Venus (E. Burroughs), 1939
Carstairs, Eric series (L. Carter), from 1979
Cart & Cwidder (Diana Wynne Jones), 1975
Cartoon Crimes (Goulart, as Robeson), 1974
Carve the Sky (Jablokov), 1991
Casablanca (Moorcock), 1989
Cascade Point (s Zahn), 1986
Case against Tomorrow (s Pohl), 1957
Case and the Dreamer (s Sturgeon), 1974
Case of Charles Dexter Ward (Lovecraft), 1951
Case of Conscience (Blish), 1958
Case of Painter's Ear (s Brunner), 1991
Case of the Toxic Spell Dump (Turtledove), 1993
Case of the Vanishing Boy (Key), 1979
Casey Agonistes (s McKenna), 1973
Castaways of Tanagar (Stableford), 1981
Castaways' World (Brunner), 1963
Casting Fortune (s Ford), 1989
Castle in the Air (Diana Wynne Jones), 1990
Castle Keeps (Offutt), 1972
Castle of Crossed Destinies (Calvino), 1977
Castle of Dark (Lee), 1978
Castle of Days (s G. Wolfe), 1992
Castle of Iron (de Camp), 1950
Castle of the Carpathians (Verne), 1893
Castle of the Otter (s G. Wolfe), 1982
Castle of Wizardry (Eddings), 1984
Castle Roogna (Anthony), 1979
Castle Tourmandyne (M. Hughes), 1995
Castleview (G. Wolfe), 1990
Cat Karina (Coney), 1982
Cat series (J. Vinge), from 1982
Cat Who Walks through Walls (Heinlein), 1985
Cat's Cradle (Vonnegut), 1963
Cat's Pawn series (Gadallah), from 1987
Cat-a-lyst (A. Foster), 1991
Cataclysm (Fearn, as Statten), 1951
Catacomb Years (Bishop), 1979
Catalyst (Fearn, as Statten), 1951
Catalyst (Harness), 1980
Catastrophe Planet (Laumer), 1966
Catch a Falling Star (Brunner), 1968
Catch the Star Winds (s Chandler), 1969
Caterpillar's Question (Anthony, Farmer), 1992
Catface (Simak), 1978
Catfang (Fisk), 1981
Cathouse (s Ing), 1990
Cats of Ulthar (s Lovecraft), 1935
Catseye (Norton), 1961
Catspaw (J. Vinge), 1988
Catwings (Le Guin), 1988
Catwings Return (Le Guin), 1989

Catwitch (Tuttle), 1983
Catwoman (Asprin), 1992
Caution! Inflammable! (s Scortia), 1975
Cautionary Tales (s Yarbro), 1978
Cave Girl (E. Burroughs), 1925
Cave of Cornelius (Capon), 1959
Caverns (O'Donnell), 1981
Caverns of the Moon (P. Moore), 1964
Caves of Karst (Hoffman), 1969
Caves of Mars (Petaja), 1965
Caves of Steel (Asimov), 1954
Caviar (s Sturgeon), 1955
Celestial Blueprint (s Farmer), 1962
Celestial Steam Locomotive (Coney), 1983
Cellars (Shirley), 1982
Cemetery World (Simak), 1973
Centaur Aisle (Anthony), 1982
Centauri Device (M. Harrison), 1974
Centigrade 233 (s Benford), 1990
Centre Cannot Hold (Stableford), 1990
Centrifugal Rickshaw Dancer (Watkins), 1985
Centurion's Vengeance (s Fanthorpe), 1961
Century of Progress (Saberhagen), 1983
Century of the Manikin (Tubb), 1972
Century's End (Griffin), 1981
Cerberus (s Budrys), 1989
Cerberus: A Wolf in the Fold (Chalker), 1982
Ceremony (Cook), 1986
Ceres Solution (Shaw), 1981
Cerin Songweaver series (s de Lint), from 1979
Chain of Attack (DeWeese), 1987
Chain of Chance (Lem), 1978
Chain Reaction (Hodder-Williams), 1959
Chaining the Lady (Anthony), 1978
Chains of Gold (Springer), 1986
Chalk Giants (Roberts), 1974
Challenge (Bulmer), 1954
Challenge from Beyond (s Leinster, Long), 1954
Challenge of Beyond (s Merritt), 1954
Challenge the Hellmaker (Richmond), 1976
Challengers of the Unknown (Goulart), 1977
Challenges (s Bova), 1993
Chamber of Horrors (s Bloch), 1966
Chameleon Corps and Other Shape Changers (s Goulart), 1972
Champion of Garathorm (Moorcock), 1973
Chance and Other Gestures of the Hand of Fate (s Springer), 1987
Change (Longyear), 1994
Change Song (Hoffman), 1972
Change the Sky (s St. Clair), 1974
Change War series (Leiber), from 1961
Changed Man, Flux (s Card), 1992-93
Changeling (Leigh), 1989
Changeling (s van Vogt), 1967
Changeling (Zelazny), 1980
Changeling Earth (Saberhagen), 1973
Changeling Sea (McKillip), 1988
Changeling Star series (Carver), from 1989
Changeling Worlds (Bulmer), 1959
Changelings of Chaan (Lake), 1985
Changes series (Dickinson), from 1969
Changewar (s Leiber), 1983

Changewinds series (Chalker), from 1987
Changing Land (Zelazny), 1981
Channel's Destiny (Lichtenberg), 1982
Chantry Guild (Dickson), 1988
Chanur series (Cherryh), from 1982
Chanur's Homecoming (Cherryh), 1986
Chanur's Legacy (Cherryh), 1992
Chanur's Venture (Cherryh), 1984
Chaos (Fanthorpe, as Bell), 1964
Chaos Chronicles series (Carver), from 1994
Chaos Fighters (R. Williams), 1955
Chaos in Lagrangia (Reynolds), 1984
Chaos Mode (Anthony), 1994
Chaos series (Kapp), from 1972
Chaos Weapon (Kapp), 1977
Chapayeca (Edmondson), 1971
Chapter House (F. Herbert), 1985
Chariot of Apollo (s Fanthorpe), 1962
Chariots of Ra (Bulmer), 1972
Charisma (Coney), 1975
Charles Fort Never Mentioned Wombats (DeWeese, R. Coulson), 1977
Charmed Life (Diana Wynne Jones), 1977
Charon: A Dragon at the Gate (Chalker), 1982
Charwoman's Shadow (Dunsany), 1926
Chase of the Golden Meteor (Verne), 1909
Chased across the Sahara (Senarens), 1893
Chateau d'If (s Vance), 1990
Chauvinisto (Merwin), 1976
Checkpoint Lambda (Leinster), 1966
Cheetah Girl (s Blayre), 1923
Chekhov's Journey (Watson), 1983
Chernevog (Cherryh), 1990
Chess with a Dragon (Gerrold), 1987
Chessboard Planet (Kuttner and C.L. Moore, as Padgett), 1956
Chessmen of Mars (E. Burroughs), 1922
Chicago Red (Meluch), 1990
Chieftain (Norman), 1991
Chieftain of Andor (Offutt), 1976
Child Christopher and Goldilind the Fair (W. Morris), 1895
Child Garden (Ryman), 1989
Child of Fortune (Spinrad), 1985
Child of Storm (Haggard), 1913
Child of Time (Asimov), 1991
Child of Time (Silverberg), 1992
Childe Cycle series (Dickson), from 1963
Childhood's End (Clarke), 1953
Children of Atlantis (Harding), 1975
Children of Flux and Anchor (Chalker), 1986
Children of Morrow (Hoover), 1973
Children of the Atom (s Shiras), 1953
Children of the Lens (E.E. Smith), 1954
Children of the Rainbow (T. Green), 1992
Children of the Stars series (J. Coulson), from 1981
Children of the Thunder (Brunner), 1989
Children of the Wind (s Wilhelm), 1989
Children of Tomorrow (van Vogt), 1970
Children's Country (Burdekin), 1929
Children's Crusade (Naha, as Drumm), 1987
Children's Hour (Pournelle, Stirling), 1991
Chiller (Benford, as Blake), 1993

Chimaera's Copper (Anthony), 1990
China Mountain Zhang (McHugh), 1992
Chocky (Wyndham), 1968
Choice of Destinies (Scott), 1986
Choice of Gods (Simak), 1971
Chorale (Malzberg), 1978
Chorus Skating (A. Foster), 1994
Chosen Few (s Stockton), 1895
Chrestomanci series (Diana Wynne Jones), from 1977
Chrestomathy (s Laumer), 1984
Christening Quest (Scarborough), 1985
Christina Enchanted (Platt, as St. James), 1980
Christmas Eve (Kornbluth), 1956
Christmas Stories of George MacDonald (G. MacDonald), 1981
Christmas Wreck (s Stockton), 1886
Chromosomal Code (Watt-Evans), 1984
Chromosome Game (Hodder-Williams), 1984
Chronicles of Amber (Zelazny), 1979
Chronicles of Castle Brass (Moorcock), 1985
Chronicles of Corum (Moorcock), 1978
Chronicles of Morgaine (Cherryh), 1985
Chronicles of Morgan, Prince of Hed (McKillip), 1981
Chronicles of Narnia series (Lewis), from 1973
Chronicles of Pern (s McCaffrey), 1993
Chronicles of Rodriguez (Dunsany), 1922
Chronicles of the Deryni series (Kurtz), from 1970
Chronicles of the Star Kings (Hamilton), 1986
Chronicles of Thomas Covenant the Unbeliever (Donaldson), 1993
Chronicles of Tornor series (Lynn), from 1979
Chronocules (Compton), 1970
Chronolysis (Jeury), 1980
Chronoplane Wars series (Kilian), from 1978
Chronopolis (s Ballard), 1971
Chronosequence (Schenck), 1988
Chrysalids (Wyndham), 1955
Chthon (Anthony), 1967
Chung Kuo series (Wingrove), from 1989
Cineverse series (Gardner), from 1989
Cinnabar (Bryant), 1976
Circuit-Breaker (MacLeod), 1978
Circumpolar! (Lupoff), 1984
Circus of Hells (P. Anderson), 1970
Circus series (Longyear), from 1980
Circus World (s Longyear), 1980
Cirque (T. Carr), 1977
Citadel of Fear (Stevens), 1970
Citadel of the Autarch (G. Wolfe), 1983
Cities in Flight series (Blish), from 1955
Cities of the Red Night (W. Burroughs), 1981
Citizen in Space (s Sheckley), 1955
Citizen of the Galaxy (Heinlein), 1957
Citizen Phaid (Farren), 1987
City (J. Herbert), 1994
City (s Simak), 1952
City and the Stars (Clarke), 1956
City at the Edge of Time (J. Morris), 1988
City at World's End (Hamilton), 1951
City Come a-Walkin' (Shirley), 1980
City Dwellers (Platt), 1970
City in the Autumn Stars (Moorcock), 1986
City in the North (Randall), 1976

City in the Sea (Tucker), 1951
City in the Sky (Siodmak), 1974
City in the Stars (Rotsler), 1981
City Machine (Trimble), 1972
City, Not Long After (Murphy), 1989
City of a Million Legends (Lichtenberg), 1985
City of a Thousand Suns (Delany), 1965
City of Baraboo (Longyear), 1980
City of Brass (s Hoch), 1971
City of Darkness (Bova), 1976
City of Gold and Lead (Christopher), 1967
City of Illusions (Le Guin), 1967
City of No Return (Tubb), 1954
City of Sorcery (Bradley), 1984
City of the Beast (Moorcock), 1970
City of the Chasch (Vance), 1968
City of the Singing Flame (s Clark Ashton Smith), 1981
City of the Sun (Stableford), 1978
City of Truth (Morrow), 1991
City on the Edge of Forever (Ellison), 1977
City on the Moon (Leinster), 1957
City Outside the World (L. Carter), 1977
City under the Sea (Bulmer), 1957
City under the Sea (Fairman), 1963
City Who Fought (McCaffrey, Stirling), 1993
Civil War Secret Agent (Perry), 1984
Claimed! (Stevens), 1966
Clan and Crown (Pournelle), 1982
Clane series (van Vogt), from 1957
Clans of the Alphane Moon (Dick), 1964
Clansman of Andor (Offutt), 1979
Clarion (Greenleaf), 1988
Clash by Night (s Kuttner, C.L. Moore), 1980
Clash of Cymbals (Blish), 1959
Clash of Star-Kings (Davidson), 1966
Clash of the Titans (A. Foster), 1981
Claw of the Conciliator (G. Wolfe), 1981
Clay's Ark (O. Butler), 1984
Cleopatra (Haggard), 1889
Cleopatra Crisis (Hawke), 1990
Clewiston Test (Wilhelm), 1976
Clickwhistle (Watkins), 1973
Cliffs (O'Donnell), 1986
Climate, Incorporated (Fearn), 1987
Climbing Olympus (K. Anderson), 1994
Clipjoint (Baird), 1994
Clipper of the Clouds (Verne), 1887
Clique (Hawke, as Yermakov), 1982
Cloak of Aesir (s Campbell), 1952
Clock of Time (s Finney), 1958
Clocks of Iraz (de Camp), 1971
Clockwork Orange (Burgess), 1962
Clockwork Traitor (Goldin, E.E. Smith), 1977
Clockwork's Pirates (Goulart), 1971
Clone (Cowper), 1972
Clone (T. Thomas, Wilhelm), 1965
Cloned Lives (Sargent), 1976
Close Encounters with the Deity (s Bishop), 1986
Close to Critical (Clement), 1964
Closed System (Z. Hughes), 1986
Closed Worlds (Hamilton), 1968

Convoy Strike (Naha, as McGann), 1990
Cool War (Pohl), 1981
Copulation Explosion (Fox), 1970
Copy Shop (Evelyn E. Smith), 1985
Copyright Violation (s S. Robinson), 1990
Coramonde series (Daley), from 1977
Core (Preuss), 1993
Corellian Trilogy series (Allen), from 1995
Cormac mac Art series (Offutt), from 1975
Cornelius Calendar (s Moorcock), 1993
Cornelius Chronicles (Moorcock), 1977
Cornelius, Jerry series (Moorcock), from 1968
Corona (Bear), 1984
Corpse (Farren), 1986
Corpus Earthling (Charbonneau), 1960
Corridors of Time (P. Anderson), 1965
Corum series (Moorcock), from 1973
Corundum's Woman (Offutt, as Cleve), 1982
Cory series (Siodmak), from 1943
Coscuin Chronicles series (Lafferty), from 1971
Cosmic Carnival of Stanislaw Lem (s Lem), 1981
Cosmic Carousel (s Garnett), 1976
Cosmic Checkmate (MacLean), 1962
Cosmic Computer (Piper), 1964
Cosmic Encounter (van Vogt), 1980
Cosmic Engineers (Simak), 1950
Cosmic Exodus (Fearn, as Holt), 1953
Cosmic Eye (Reynolds), 1969
Cosmic Flame (Fearn, as Statten), 1950
Cosmic Geoide, and One Other (Taine), 1949
Cosmic Kaleidoscope (s Shaw), 1976
Cosmic Manhunt (de Camp), 1954
Cosmic Perspective, Custer's Last Stand (s Stableford), 1985
Cosmic Puppets (Dick), 1957
Cosmic Rape (Sturgeon), 1958
Cosmic Spies (McIntosh), 1972
Cosmic Trilogy (Lewis), 1990
Cosmicomics (Calvino), 1968
Costigan's Needle (Sohl), 1953
Count Brass series (Moorcock), from 1973
Count-Down (Maine), 1959
Count Geiger's Blues (Bishop), 1992
Count Zero (Gibson), 1986
Counter-Clock World (Dick), 1967
Counterfeit Man (s Nourse), 1963
Counterfeit World (Galouye), 1964
Counterfeits (Kelley), 1967
Countersolar! (Lupoff), 1987
Counting the Cost (Drake), 1987
Country Love and Poison Rain (Tate), 1973
Country of Crimson Clouds (Strugatsky), n.d.
Country of the Blind (s Wells), 1911
Course of the Heart (M. Harrison), 1992
Courts of Chaos (Zelazny), 1978
Courtship of Princess Leia (Wolverton), 1994
Courtship Rite (Kingsbury), 1982
Covenant of Justice (Gerrold), 1994
Covenant, Thomas series (Donaldson), from 1977
Cowboy Heaven (Goulart), 1979
Coyote Stories (s de Lint), 1993
Crack (Tennant), 1978

Crack in Space (Dick), 1966
Crack in the Sky (Lupoff), 1976
Crack of Doom (Cromie), 1895
Cracken at Critical (Aldiss), 1987
Crackpot (Goulart), 1977
Cradle (Clarke), 1988
Cradle of the Sun (Stableford), 1969
Craft of Light (Emerson), 1993
Cranleigh, Marguerite series (S. Wright), from 1931
Crash (Ballard), 1973
Crash (Lundwall), 1982
Crashcourse (Baird), 1993
Crashing Suns (s Hamilton), 1965
Crashlander (s Niven), 1995
Crater of Fear (P. Moore), 1962
Crawford, Homer series (Reynolds), from 1972
Crawling Chaos (s Lovecraft), 1992
Crawling Fiend (s Fanthorpe, as Fane), 1960
Cray series (Eisenstein), from 1979
Crazy Time (Wilhelm), 1988
Creator (s Simak), 1946
Creator (s Simak), 1993
Creature from Beyond Infinity (Kuttner), 1968
Creature from the Black Lagoon (s May, as Thorpe), 1981
Creature from the Black Lagoon (Fearn, as Statten), 1954
Creatures of Light and Darkness (Zelazny), 1969
Creatures of the Abyss (Leinster), 1961
Creed (J. Herbert), 1990
Creep, Shadow! (Merritt), 1934
Crewel Lye (Anthony), 1985
Criminal Croesus (G. Griffith), 1904
Crimson Capsule (Coblentz), 1967
Crimson Planet (Fanthorpe, as Muller), 1961
Crimson Serpent (Dent, as Robeson), 1974
Crimson Witch (Koontz), 1971
Crisis 2000 (Maine), 1955
Crisis in 2140 (Piper), 1957
Crisis of Empire series (Allen), from 1989
Crisis of Empire series (Drake), from 1988
Crisis on Cheiron (J. Coulson), 1967
Crisis on Conshelf Ten (M. Hughes), 1975
Crisis on Doona (McCaffrey), 1992
Crisis! (s Gunn), 1986
Critical Mass (s Kornbluth), 1977
Critical Mass (s Pohl), 1977
Critical Threshold (Stableford), 1977
Crompton Divided (Sheckley), 1978
Crooked House (Monteleone), 1987
Croquet Player (Wells), 1936
Cross of Fire (Malzberg), 1982
Cross the Stars (Drake), 1984
Crossroads of Time (Norton), 1956
Crosstime Agent (Norton), 1975
Crosstime Traffic (s Watt-Evans), 1992
Crown Jewels series (W. Williams), from 1987
Crown of Dalemark (Diana Wynne Jones), 1993
Crown of Empire (Yarbro), 1994
Crown of Stars (s Tiptree), 1988
Crown of the Sword God (Bulmer, as Norvil), 1980
Croyd series (I. Wallace), from 1967
Crucible of Time (Brunner), 1983

Cruel Designs (Wilder), 1988
Cruiser Dreams (J. Morris), 1981
Crunch Bunch (Bischoff), 1985
Cry Horror! (s Lovecraft), 1958
Cryptozoic! (Aldiss), 1968
Crystal Drop (M. Hughes), 1992
Crystal Express (s Sterling), 1989
Crystal Gryphon (Norton), 1972
Crystal Horde (Taine), 1952
Crystal Line (McCaffrey), 1992
Crystal Memory (Leigh), 1987
Crystal Palace (Eisenstein), 1988
Crystal series (Forstchen), from 1988
Crystal Singer (McCaffrey), 1982
Crystal Star (McIntyre), 1994
Crystal Witness (Tyers), 1989
Crystal World (Ballard), 1966
Crystals of Air and Water (Goldin), 1989
Crystalworld (Haiblum), 1992
Cube Root of Uncertainty (s Silverberg), 1970
Cuckoo's Egg (Cherryh), 1985
Cuckoo's Saga series (Pohl), from 1975
Cuckoo's Saga series (Williamson), from 1975
Cugel's Saga (Vance), 1983
Cult of Loving Kindness (Park), 1991
Cultural Survey series (Biggle), from 1968
Culture series (Banks), from 1987
Cunningham Equations (Edmondson), 1986
Cunningham series (Edmondson), from 1986
Cure for Cancer (Moorcock), 1971
Cure for Love (s Anno Domini 2090), 1899
Curious Fragments (s London), 1975
Curious Quests of Brigadier Ffellowes (s Lanier), 1986
Currents of Space (Asimov), 1952
Curse (C. Grant), 1977
Curse of the Khan (s Fanthorpe), 1966
Curse of the Obelisk (Goulart), 1987
Curse of the Totem (s Fanthorpe), 1962
Curse of the Wise Woman (Dunsany), 1933
Cursed (Dave Duncan), 1995
Cursed (England), 1919
Custodians (s Cowper), 1976
Cutter (s Bryant), 1991
Cutting Edge (Dave Duncan), 1992
CV series (Knight), from 1985
Cyber Way (A. Foster), 1990
Cyberbooks (Bova), 1989
Cyberiad (s Lem), 1974
Cybernetic Brains (R. Jones), 1962
Cybernetic Controller (Bulmer), 1952
Cyborg (Caidin), 1972
Cyborg and the Sorcerers (Watt-Evans), 1982
Cyborg IV (Caidin), 1975
Cyborg King (Goulart), 1981
Cycle of Fire (Clement), 1957
Cycle of Nemesis (Bulmer), 1967
Cyclops in the Sky (Fanthorpe, as Roberts), 1960
Cygnet and the Firebird (McKillip), 1993
Cygnet; series (McKillip), from 1991
Cylon Death Machine (Thurston), 1979
Cyrion (Lee), 1982

Cyteen series (Cherryh), from 1988
Czar of Fear (Dent, as Robeson), 1968

Daedalus series (Stableford), from 1976
Dag Fletcher series (Mason), from 1966
Dagger (Drake), 1988
Dagger and the Cross (Tarr), 1991
Dagger in the Sky (Dent, as Robeson), 1969
Dagger Magic (Kurtz), 1995
Dagger of the Mind (Shaw), 1979
Dagon and Other Macabre Tales (s Lovecraft), 1965
Dahut (P. Anderson), 1988
Daily Voices (s Goldstein), 1989
Daisy, in the Sun (s Willis), 1991
Dalemark series (Diana Wynne Jones), from 1975
d'Alembert family series (Goldin, E.E. Smith), from 1976
Daleth Effect (H. Harrison), 1970
Damia (McCaffrey), 1992
Damia's Children (McCaffrey), 1993
Damiano (MacAvoy), 1984
Damiano's Lute (MacAvoy), 1984
Damnation Alley (Zelazny), 1969
Damnbanna (s Springer), 1992
Damned & Fancy (Brosnan), 1995
Damned series (A. Foster), from 1991
Dance Band on the Titanic (s Chalker), 1988
Dance Dance Dance (Murakami), 1994
Dance of the Apocalypse (Eklund), 1976
Dance of the Hag (Leigh), 1983
Dance the Eagle to Sleep (Piercy), 1970
Dancer from Atlantis (P. Anderson), 1971
Dancers at the End of Time series (Moorcock), from 1972
Dancers in the Afterglow (Chalker), 1978
Dancers of Arun (Lynn), 1979
Dancers of Noyo (St. Clair), 1973
Dancing Gods series (Chalker), from 1984
Dancing with Myself (s Sheffield), 1993
Dandelion Caper (DeWeese), 1986
Danger from Vega (Rackham), 1966
Danger—Human (s Dickson), 1970
Danger Moon (s Pohl, as MacCreigh), 1953
Danger Planet (Hamilton, as Sterling), 1968
Danger: Dinosaurs! (Hunter, as Marsten), 1953
Danger! (s Doyle), 1918
Dangerous Games (Randall), 1980
Dangerous Love (s Farley), 1946
Darcy, Jade series (Goldin), from 1988
Dare (Farmer), 1965
Dare to Go A-Hunting (Norton), 1990
Daredevils, Ltd (Goulart), 1987
Darfstellar (s W. Miller), 1982
Dark (J. Herbert), 1980
Dark Beasts (s Long), 1963-64
Dark Between the Stars (P. Anderson), 1981
Dark Between the Stars (Broderick), 1991
Dark Beyond the Stars (F. Robinson), 1991
Dark Boundaries (Fearn, as Lorraine), 1953
Dark Brotherhood (s Lovecraft), 1966
Dark Carnival (s Bradbury), 1947
Dark Castle series (Lee), from 1978
Dark Continuum (Fanthorpe, as Muller), 1964

Dark Cry of the Moon (s C. Grant), 1986
Dark Dance (Lee), 1992
Dark December (Coppel), 1960
Dark Design (Farmer), 1977
Dark Destroyers (Wellman), 1959
Dark Dimensions (Chandler), 1971
Dark Dominion (David Duncan), 1954
Dark Door (Wilhelm), 1988
Dark Force Rising (Zahn), 1992
Dark Future (Stableford, as Craig), 1991
Dark Hills, Hollow Clocks (s Kilworth), 1990
Dark Horizon (Jeter), 1993
Dark Inferno (J. White), 1972
Dark Intruder (s Bradley), 1964
Dark is the Sun (Farmer), 1979
Dark Lady (Resnick), 1987
Dark Light Years (Aldiss), 1964
Dark Messiah (Caidin), 1990
Dark Mind (Kapp), 1965
Dark Mirror (Duane), 1993
Dark Night in Toyland (s Shaw), 1989
Dark of the Woods (Koontz), 1970
Dark Other (Weinbaum), 1950
Dark Piper (Norton), 1968
Dark Planet (Rackham), 1971
Dark Prince (Gemmell), 1991
Dark Satanic (Bradley), 1972
Dark Seeker (Jeter), 1987
Dark Side (Z. Hughes), 1987
Dark Side of Earth (s Bester), 1964
Dark Side of the Moon (s Vance), 1986
Dark Side of the Sun (Pratchett), 1976
Dark Star (A. Foster), 1974
Dark Stars and Other Illuminations (s Monteleone), 1981
Dark Sun, Bright Sun (Fisk), 1986
Dark Sun series (Hawke), from 1993
Dark Symphony (Koontz), 1970
Dark Tides (s Russell), 1962
Dark Traveling (Zelazny), 1987
Dark Universe (Galouye), 1961
Dark Wing (MacLean), 1979
Dark World (C.L. Moore), 1965
Dark World (Kuttner), 1965
Darkchild (Van Scyoc), 1982
Darkening Island (Priest), 1972
Darker Drink (s Fanthorpe), 1962
Darker Passions (s Bryant), 1992
Darker Than You Think (Williamson), 1948
Darkest America series (Barrett), from 1986
Darkest of Nights (Maine), 1962
Darkfall (Koontz), 1984
Darkling Wind (Sucharitkul), 1985
Darkness and Dawn (England), 1914
Darkness and the Light (Stapledon), 1942
Darkness at Sethanon (Feist), 1986
Darkness before Tomorrow (R. Williams), 1962
Darkness Comes (Koontz), 1984
Darkness, I (Lee), 1994
Darkness in My Soul (Koontz), 1972
Darkness on Diamondia (van Vogt), 1972
Darkness upon the Ice (Forstchen), 1985

Darkover series (Bradley), from 1979
Darkwar series (Cook), from 1985
Darkworld Detective (Reaves), 1982
Darya of the Bronze Age (L. Carter), 1981
Darzek, Jan series (Biggle), from 1963
Daughter of Elysium (Slonczewski), 1993
Daughter of Regals (Donaldson), 1984
Daughter of the Bear King (Arnason), 1987
Daughter of the Empire (Feist), 1987
Daughters of Earth (s Merril), 1968
Daughters of the Sunstone (Van Scyoc), 1985
Davy (Pangborn), 1964
Dawn (O. Butler), 1987
Dawn (S. Wright), 1929
Dawn in Andromeda (Large), 1956
Dawn of Flame (s Weinbaum), 1936
Dawn of the Mutants (Fanthorpe, as Roberts), 1959
Dawn Palace (Hoover), 1988
Dawn's Uncertain Light (Barrett), 1989
Dawning Light (Garrett), 1959
Dawning Light (Silverberg and Garrett, as Randall), 1959
Dawnman Planet (Reynolds), 1966
Day after Judgment (Blish), 1971
Day after Tomorrow (Heinlein), 1951
Day after Tomorrow (Reynolds), 1976
Day before Forever, and Thunderhead (Laumer), 1968
Day before Tomorrow (Klein), 1972
Day Boy and the Night Girl (G. MacDonald), 1988
Day by Night (Lee), 1980
Day for Damnation (Gerrold), 1984
Day It Rained Forever (s Bradbury), 1959
Day Million (s Pohl), 1970
Day of Forever (s Ballard), 1967
Day of the Burning (Malzberg), 1974
Day of the Dissonance (A. Foster), 1984
Day of the Dragonstar (Bischoff, Monteleone), 1983
Day of the Drones (Lightner), 1969
Day of the Giants (del Rey), 1959
Day of the Klesh (M.A. Foster), 1979
Day of the Ness (Norton), 1975
Day of the Star Cities (Brunner), 1965
Day of the Triffids (Wyndham), 1951
Day of Their Return (P. Anderson), 1973
Day of Timestop (Farmer), 1968
Day of Wrath (O'Neill), 1936
Day of Wrath (Stableford), 1971
Day Star (Geston), 1972
Day the Machines Stopped (Anvil), 1964
Day the Martians Came (s Pohl), 1988
Day the World Died (Fanthorpe, as Muller), 1962
Day the World Stopped (Coblentz), 1968
Day They H-Bombed Los Angeles (R. Williams), 1961
Daybreak . . . 2250 A.D (Norton), 1954
Daybreak on a Different Mountain (Greenland), 1984
Daybreak series (Greenland), from 1987
Daymaker (G. Jones, as Halam), 1987
Daymares (s F. Brown), 1968
Days Between Stations (Erickson), 1985
Days of Atonement (W. Williams), 1991
Days of Glory (Stableford), 1971
Days of Grass (Lee), 1985

Dayworld series (Farmer), from 1986
De Bracy's Drug (Tubb, as Gridban), 1953
De Helden van de Highway (s Ellison), 1973
Dead in the West (Lansdale), 1986
Dead Moon (Kelley), 1979
Dead Morn (Anthony), 1990
Dead-Eye Dick (Vonnegut), 1982
Deadline to Pluto (Fearn, as Statten), 1951
Deadly Dwarf (Dent, as Robeson), 1968
Deadly Eyes (J. Herbert), 1983
Deadly Image (Cooper), 1958
Deadly Litter (s J. White), 1964
Deadly Mantis (s May, as Thorpe), 1982
Deadly Quicksilver Lies (Cook), 1994
Deadly Silents (Killough), 1981
Deadly Sky (Fairman, as Jorgensen), 1971
Deadly Sky (Piserchia), 1983
Deadman Switch (Zahn), 1988
Deadwalk (Goulart), 1976
Dealers in Light and Darkness (s Wilder), 1995
Dealing in Futures (s Joe Haldeman), 1985
Dealings with the Fairies (G. MacDonald), 1867
Dean Koontz Omnibus (Koontz), 1993
Dean R. Koontz (Koontz), 1992
Dear Hill (G. Jones), 1980
Death Box (Tolstoy), 1938
Death Bringer (Tilley), 1989
Death by Gaslight (Kurland), 1982
Death Cell (Goulart), 1971
Death Chants (s Strete), 1988
Death Dream (Bova), 1994
Death God's Citadel (J. Coulson), 1980
Death Has Two Faces (s Fanthorpe), 1964
Death in Florence (Effinger), 1978
Death in Silver (Dent, as Robeson), 1968
Death in the Spirit House (Strete), 1988
Death into Life (Stapledon), 1946
Death Is a Dream (Tubb), 1967
Death Machine (Goulart, as Robeson), 1975
Death Note (s Fanthorpe), 1958
Death of Doctor Island (s G. Wolfe), 1990
Death of Grass (Christopher), 1956
Death of Sleep (McCaffrey), 1990
Death of the Dragon (Komatsu), 1976
Death Quest (Hubbard), 1985
Death Sentence (Kelley), 1979
Death Sleep (Sohl), 1983
Death Watch (Compton), 1981
Death Wears a White Face (Tubb), 1979
Death's Acolyte (Proctor), 1985
Death's Arms (Jeter), 1987
Death's Deputy (Hubbard), 1948
Death's Master (Lee), 1979
Deathbeast (Gerrold), 1978
Deathbird Stories (s Ellison), 1975
Deathgame (Goulart), 1976
Deathhunter (Watson), 1981
Deathknight (Offutt), 1990
Deathless Amazon (Fearn), 1955
Deathstar Voyage (I. Wallace), 1969
Deathwish World (Ing, Reynolds), 1986

Deathworld series (H. Harrison), from 1960
Deathworms of Kratos (Cooper, as Avery), 1975
Deceivers (Bester), 1981
Deception (Bischoff), 1991
Decision at Doona (McCaffrey), 1969
Decreation (Fearn, as Statten), 1952
Deep (Crowley), 1975
Deep Fix (s Moorcock, as Colvin), 1966
Deep Freeze (Z. Hughes), 1992
Deep Range (Clarke), 1957
Deep Reaches of Space (Chandler), 1964
Deep Space (s Russell), 1954
Deep Waters (s Hodgson), 1967
Deep Wizardry (Duane), 1985
Deeper Sea (Jablokov), 1992
Deeper Than the Darkness (Benford), 1970
Deepwater Dreams (Van Scyoc), 1991
Defiance (Bulmer), 1963
Defiant Agents (Norton), 1962
Definitely Maybe (Strugatsky), 1978
Delaney, Mike series (Maine), from 1957
Delia of Vallia (Bulmer, as Akers), 1982
Delikon (Hoover), 1977
Delirium's Mistress (Lee), 1986
Delta (C. Wilson), 1987
Deluge (S. Wright), 1927
Deluge Drivers (A. Foster), 1987
Delusion World (Dickson), 1961
Delusion's Master (Lee), 1981
Demolished Man (Bester), 1953
Demon (Varley), 1984
Demon Breed (Schmitz), 1968
Demon in the Mirror (Offutt), 1977
Demon in the Skull (Pohl), 1984
Demon Island (Goulart, as Robeson), 1975
Demon Lord of Karanda (Eddings), 1988
Demon Moon (Williamson), 1994
Demon of Cawnpore (Verne), 1887
Demon of Scattery (P. Anderson), 1979
Demon Princes series (Vance), from 1964
Demon Seed (Koontz), 1973
Demon with a Glass Hand (s Ellison), 1986
Demon's World (Bulmer), 1964
Demons (Bulmer), 1965
Demons at Rainbow Bridge (Chalker), 1989
Demons Don't Dream (Anthony), 1993
Demons of the Dancing Gods (Chalker), 1984
Demons of the Sea (s Hodgson), 1992
Demu Trilogy (Busby), 1980
Denner's Wreck (Watt-Evans), 1988
Denver Is Missing (D.F. Jones), 1971
Denver's Double (G. Griffith), 1901
Departures (s Turtledove), 1993
Depression or Bust (Reynolds), 1974
Derai (Tubb), 1968
Derrick Devil (Dent, as Robeson), 1973
Dervish Daughter (Tepper), 1986
Deryni series (Kurtz), from 1970
Descent of Anansi (S. Barnes, Niven), 1982
Desert Moments (s de Lint), 1991
Desert of Ice (Verne), 1874

Desert of Stolen Dreams (s Silverberg), 1981
Design for Great Day (A. Foster, Russell), 1995
Desolation Road (McDonald), 1988
Desperate Games (Boulle), 1973
Destination Infinity (Kuttner, C.L. Moore), 1958
Destination Luna (P. Moore), 1955
Destination Moon (Fanthorpe, as Kenton), 1959
Destination Moon (s Heinlein), 1979
Destination: Saturn (L. Carter and Wollheim, as Grinnell), 1967
Destination: Universe! (s van Vogt), 1952
Destination: Void (F. Herbert), 1966
Destined Maid (G. Griffith), 1898
Destiny Dice (Bischoff), 1985
Destiny Doll (Simak), 1971
Destiny Makers (Turner), 1993
Destiny of the Sword (Dave Duncan), 1988
Destiny Past (Garnett, as Lee), 1974
Destiny Times Three (Leiber), 1956
Destiny's Orbit (Wollheim, as Grinnell), 1961
Destroy the U.S.A (Leinster), 1950
Destruction of the Temple (Malzberg), 1974
Deus Irae (Dick, Zelazny), 1976
Deus X (Spinrad), 1992
Deviates (R. Jones), 1959
Devil and the Doctor (Keller), 1940
Devil and the Floral Dance (D.M. Thomas), 1978
Devil from the Depths (s Fanthorpe), 1961
Devil Genghis (Dent, as Robeson), 1974
Devil in the Drain (Pinkwater), 1984
Devil Is Dead (Lafferty), 1971
Devil on My Back (M. Hughes), 1984
Devil on the Moon (Dent, as Robeson), 1970
Devil, Poor Devil! (Burdekin, as Constantine), 1934
Devil-Tree of El Dorado (Aubrey), 1896
Devil World (Eklund), 1979
Devil's Arithmetic (Yolen), 1988
Devil's Children (Dickinson), 1970
Devil's Day (Blish), 1990
Devil's Game (P. Anderson), 1980
Devil's Planet (Wellman), 1951
Devil's Tor (Lindsay), 1932
Devolutionist, and The Emancipatrix (Flint), 1965
Devouring Fire (Fearn, as Statten), 1951
Dhalgren (Delany), 1975
Dhalgren series (Gotlieb), from 1976
di Stefano, Angelo series (Janifer), from 1968
Diaboliad (s Bulgakov), 1972
Diabolist (Fairman, as Jorgensen), 1973
Diabols (Mackelworth), 1969
Dialing the Wind (C. Grant), 1988
Dialogue with Darkness (s P. Anderson), 1985
Diamond Age (N. Stephenson), 1995
Diamond Contessa (Bulmer), 1983
Diamond Mask (May), 1994
Diamond Moon (Preuss), 1990
Diamond Throne (Eddings), 1989
Dick for All Seasons (Z. Hughes, as Kane), 1970
Dickson! (s Dickson), 1984
"Die, Chameleon!" (Thurston), 1985
Dies Irae series (Stableford), from 1971
Difference Engine (Gibson, Sterling), 1990

Different Flesh (Turtledove), 1988
Different Light (Lynn), 1978
Difficulty with Dwarves (Gardner), 1987
Diggers (Pratchett), 1991
Digging Leviathan (Blaylock), 1984
Digital Wristwatch of Philip K. Dick (s Lupoff), 1985
Digits and Dastards (s Pohl), 1966
Dilation Effect (Mason), 1971
Dilbia series (Dickson), from 1961
Dilemmas: The Secret (s Clarke), 1989
Dilke, Matthew series (Gutteridge), from 1971
Dilvish series (Zelazny), from 1982
Dilvish the Damned (s Zelazny), 1982
Dimension of Horror (Nelson, as Lord), 1979
Dimension of Miracles (Sheckley), 1968
Dimension Thirteen (s Silverberg), 1969
Dimensioneers (Piserchia), 1982
Dimensions (Shaw), 1994
Dinner at Deviant's Palace (Powers), 1985
Dinosaur Beach (Laumer), 1971
Dinosaur Empire (Leigh), 1995
Dinosaur Junction (G. Jones, as Halam), 1992
Dinosaur Planet Survivors (McCaffrey), 1984
Dinosaur series (Leigh), from 1992
Dinosaur series (Sawyer), from 1992
Dinosaur Tales (s Bradbury), 1983
Dinosaurs (s W. Williams), 1991
Diploids, and Other Flights of Fancy (s MacLean), 1962
Dirdir (Vance), 1969
Direct Descent (F. Herbert), 1980
Dirge for Sabis (Cherryh), 1989
Dirk Gently series (Adams), from 1987
Dirty Tricks (s Effinger), 1978
Dirty Work (s Cadigan), 1993
Disagreement with Death (Gardner), 1989
Disappearance (Wylie), 1951
Disappearing Dwarf (Blaylock), 1983
Disaster (Hubbard), 1987
Disaster Area (s Ballard), 1967
Displaced Person (Harding), 1979
Dispossessed (Le Guin), 1974
Distant Friends (s Zahn), 1992
Distant Signals (s Weiner), 1989
Distant Stars (s Delany), 1981
Distant Suns (Moorcock), 1975
Distress Call (s Willis), 1991
Divergence (Sheffield), 1991
Diversity of Creatures (s Kipling), 1917
Divide (Robert Charles Wilson), 1990
Divide and Rule (s de Camp), 1948
Divine Endurance (G. Jones), 1984
Divine Invasion (Dick), 1981
DNA Cowboys series (Farren), from 1976
Do Androids Dream of Electric Sheep? (Dick), 1968
Doc Caliban series (Farmer), from 1969
Doc Savage series (Dent), from 1933
Doc Savage series (Farmer), from 1991
Dr. Adder series (Jeter), from 1984
Dr. Bloodmoney (Dick), 1965
Dr. Bones series (Leigh), from 1988
Dr. Cyclops (Kuttner), 1967

Dragon at War (Dickson), 1992

Dragon Circle series (Gardner), from 1994

Dragon Dance (Christopher), 1986

Dragon Hoard (Lee), 1971

Dragon in the Sea (F. Herbert), 1956

Dragon in the Sword (Moorcock), 1986

Dragon Knight (Dickson), 1990

Dragon Lord (Drake), 1979

Dragon Magic (Norton), 1972

Dragon Masters (Vance), 1963

Dragon Never Sleeps (Cook), 1988

Dragon on a Pedestal (Anthony), 1983

Dragon on the Border (Dickson), 1992

Dragon Rigger (Carver), 1993

Dragon series (Dickson), from 1992

Dragon Tears (Koontz), 1992

Dragon, the Earl, And The Troll (Dickson), 1994

Dragon Waiting (Ford), 1983

Dragon's Blood (Yolen), 1982

Dragon's Boy (Yolen), 1990

Dragon's Egg series (Forward), from 1980

Dragon's Island (Williamson), 1951

Dragon's Teeth (Killough), 1990

Dragonard series (Jakes), from 1967

Dragondance (Christopher), 1986

Dragondrums (McCaffrey), 1979

Dragonfield (s Yolen), 1985

Dragonflight (McCaffrey), 1968

Dragonflight series (Lee), from 1991

Dragonhiker's Guide to Battlefield Covenant at Dune's Edge (s Langford), 1988

Dragonquest (McCaffrey), 1971

Dragonrider series (McCaffrey), from 1968

Dragonriders of Pern (McCaffrey), 1978

Dragonrogue (L. Carter), 1984

Dragons and Nightmares (s Bloch), 1968

Dragons in the Stars (Carver), 1992

Dragons of Heorot (Pournelle), 1995

Dragonsdawn (McCaffrey), 1988

Dragonsinger (McCaffrey), 1977

Dragonslayer (Drew), 1981

Dragonsong (McCaffrey), 1976

Dragonstar series (Bischoff, Monteleone), from 1983

Dragonworld (Reaves), 1979

Draka series (Stirling), from 1988

Dramaturges of Yan (Brunner), 1972

Dramocles (Sheckley), 1983

Drastic Dragon of Draco, Texas (Scarborough), 1986

Draught of Eternity (Rousseau, as Egbert), 1924

Drawing of the Dark (Powers), 1979

Dread Brass Shadows (Cook), 1990

Dread Companion (Norton), 1970

Dread Empire series (Cook), from 1979

Dreadful Sanctuary (Russell), 1951

Dreadful Sleep (s Williamson), 1977

Dream (S. Wright), 1931

Dream (Wells), 1924

Dream Baby (McAllister), 1989

Dream, Benjamin's Dream, Benjamin's Bicentennial Blast (s Asimov), 1976

Dream Catcher (M. Hughes), 1986

Dream Chariots (Bulmer, as Norvil), 1977

Dream Cycle of H.P. Lovecraft (s Lovecraft), 1995

Dream Dancer (J. Morris), 1980

Dream Master (Zelazny), 1966

Dream Millennium (J. White), 1974

Dream of Debs (s London), 1912(s ?)

Dream of John Ball (W. Morris), 1888

Dream of Kinship (Cowper), 1981

Dream of Wessex (Priest), 1977

Dream of X (Hodgson), 1977

Dream Park series (S. Barnes, Niven), from 1981

Dream Weaver (s Yolen), 1979

Dream Years (Goldstein), 1985

Dream-Quest of Unknown Kadath (Lovecraft), 1955

Dreamer's Tales (s Dunsany), 1910

Dreamers (Gunn), 1980

Dreamfields (Jeter), 1976

Dreaming City (Moorcock), 1972

Dreaming Dragons (Broderick), 1980

Dreaming Earth (Brunner), 1963

Dreaming Jewels (Sturgeon), 1950

Dreaming Place (de Lint), 1990

Dreams and Fancies (s Lovecraft), 1962

Dreams of Dark and Light (s Lee), 1986

Dreams of Earth and Heaven (s Tsiolkovsky), n.d.

Dreams of Steel (Cook), 1990

Dreams That Burn in the Night (Strete), 1982

Dreams Underfoot (s de Lint), 1993

Dreams with Sharp Teeth (s Ellison), 1991

Dreamships (Scott), 1992

Dreamsnake (McIntyre), 1978

Dreamspy (Lichtenberg), 1989

Dreamstone (Cherryh), 1983

Drenai series (Gemmell), from 1984

Drew, Clayton series (Fearn), from 1950

Driftglass (s Delany), 1971

Drink Down the Moon (de Lint), 1990

Drinking Sapphire Wine (Lee), 1977

Drive-In (Lansdale), 1988

Drive-In 2 (Lansdale), 1989

Drone Man (s Merritt), 1948

Drought (Ballard), 1965

Drought on Ziax II (Morressy), 1978

Drowned Ammet (Diana Wynne Jones), 1977

Drowned Man's Reel (s de Lint), 1988

Drowned World (Ballard), 1962

Drowners (Kilworth), 1991

Drowning Towers (Turner), 1988

Drowntide (Van Scyoc), 1987

Drug of Choice (Crichton, as Lange), 1970

Druid (s Fanthorpe, as Brett), 1959

Druid Stones (Fox, as Majors), 1967

Druids' World (George H. Smith), 1967

Drums of Darkness (Bradley), 1976

Drums of Tapajos (Meek), 1961

Drunkard's Walk (Pohl), 1960

Dryco Chronicles (Womack), from 1987

Dueling Machine (Bova), 1969

Dumarest series (Tubb), from 1967

Duncan and Mallory series (Asprin), from 1988

Dune series (F. Herbert), from 1965

Dune Storybook (J. Vinge), 1984
Dungeon series (de Lint), from 1989
Dungeon series (Lupoff), from 1988
Dunjer series (Haiblum), from 1977
Dunwich Horror (s Lovecraft), 1945
Duplicated Man (Blish), 1959
Duplicated Man (Lowndes), 1959
Duplicators (Leinster), 1964
Durdane series (Vance), from 1973
Dushau series (Lichtenberg), from 1985
Dusk of Demons (Christopher), 1994
Dust Destroyer (Fearn, as Statten), 1953
Dust of Death (Dent, as Robeson), 1969
Dust of Far Suns (s Vance), 1981
Dweller in the Gulf (s Clark Ashton Smith), 1987
Dwellers (S. Wright), 1954
Dwellers in the Mirage (Merritt), 1932
Dwellers of the Deep (Malzberg, as O'Donnell), 1970
Dydeetown World (s F. Wilson), 1989
Dying Earth series (s Vance), from 1950
Dying for Tomorrow (s Moorcock), 1978
Dying Inside (Silverberg), 1972
Dying of the Light (Martin), 1977
Dynasty of Doom (Tubb, as Grey), 1953
Dyno-Depressant (Fearn, as Gridban), 1953

E Pluribus Unicorn (s Sturgeon), 1953
Eagles' Nest (Kavan), 1957
Ealdwood series (Cherryh), from 1981
Earl Aubec (s Moorcock), 1993
Early del Rey (s del Rey), 1975
Early Fears (s Bloch), 1994
Early Harvest (s Bear), 1988
Early Lafferty (s Lafferty), 1990
Early Long (s Long), 1975
Early Pohl (s Pohl), 1976
Early Romances of William Morris in Prose and Verse (s W. Morris), 1907
Early Science Fiction Stories of Thomas M. Disch (s Disch), 1977
Early Williamson (s Williamson), 1975
Earth (Brin), 1990
Earth 2 (Fearn, as Statten), 1955
Earth Abides (Stewart), 1949
Earth Book of Stormgate (s P. Anderson), 1978
Earth Cult (T. Hoyle), 1979
Earth Descended (s Saberhagen), 1981
Earth Dreams (J. Morris), 1982
Earth Enslaved (Tubb, as Kern), 1974
Earth Factor X (van Vogt), 1976
Earth Gods Are Coming (Bulmer), 1960
Earth Has Been Found (D.F. Jones), 1979
Earth Hive (Perry), 1992
Earth in Twilight (Piserchia), 1981
Earth Is Heaven (Tubb), 1982
Earth Is Room Enough (s Asimov), 1957
Earth Lords (Dickson), 1989
Earth Magic (Panshin), 1978
Earth-Shaker (L. Carter), 1982
Earth Song trilogy (Webb), from 1982
Earth-Thunder (Tilley), 1990
Earth Tripper (Kelley), 1973

Earth Two (Kelley), 1979
Earth Unaware (Reynolds), 1968
Earth War (Reynolds), 1963
Earth Will Shake (Robert Anton Wilson), 1982
Earth's Last Citadel (Kuttner, C.L. Moore), 1964
Earth's Last Fortress (s van Vogt), 1960
Earth's Long Shadow (Bulmer), 1962
Earth's Other Shadow (s Silverberg), 1973
Earthblood (R. Brown, Laumer), 1966
Earthborn (Card), 1995
Earthbound (Lesser), 1952
Earthbound (Matheson, as Swanson), 1989
Earthchild (Piserchia), 1977
Earthchild (Webb), 1982
Earthclan (Brin), 1987
Earthdark (M. Hughes), 1977
Earthdoom! (Langford), 1987
Earthfall (Card), 1995
Earthfall (Tubb), 1977
Earthgrip (s Turtledove), 1991
Earthlight (Clarke), 1955
Earthman, Come Home (Blish), 1955
Earthman, Go Home (s Ellison), 1964
Earthman, Go Home! (P. Anderson), 1960
Earthman on Venus (Farley), 1950
Earthman's Burden (s Anderson, Dickson), 1957
Earthminds series (Sargent), from 1980
Earthseed (Sargent), 1983
Earthsong (Elgin), 1994
Earthstrings (Rackham), 1972
Earthwind (Holdstock), 1977
Earthworks (Aldiss), 1965
Earthwreck! (Scortia), 1974
East of Laughter (Lafferty), 1988
East of Midnight (Lee), 1977
East Wind Coming (Cover), 1979
Eater of Worlds (Tubb, as Kern), 1974
Eaters of the Dead (Crichton), 1976
Ebezenum series (Gardner), from 1986
Ecce and Old Earth (Vance), 1991
Echo in the Skull (Brunner), 1959
Echo Round His Bones (Disch), 1967
Echo Vector (Kahn), 1987
Echoes of the Well of Souls (Chalker), 1993
Echoes of Thunder (Dann, Jack C. Haldeman), 1991
Eclipse (Shirley), 1985
Eclipse Corona (Shirley), 1990
Eclipse Express (Fearn, as Statten), 1952
Eclipse of Dawn (Eklund), 1971
Eclipse Penumbra (Shirley), 1988
Eclipses (Felice), 1983
Eclipsing Binaries (E.E. Smith), 1984
Eclipsing Binaries (Goldin), 1983
Ecodeath (Watkins), 1972
Ecolog (Nelson), 1977
Ecotopia (Callenbach), 1975
Ecotopia Emerging (Callenbach), 1981
Eden (Lem), 1989
Eden Cycle (Gallun), 1974
Eden, Jim series (Pohl, Williamson), from 1954
Edge (s Beaumont), 1966

Edge of Forever (s Oliver), 1971
Edge of Running Water (Sloane), 1939
Edge of Time (Wollheim, as Grinnell), 1958
Edison's Conquest of Mars (Serviss), 1947
Egg of the Glak (s Jacobs), 1969
Egg-Shaped Thing (Hodder-Williams), 1966
Egypt (Crowley), 1987
Eight Against Utopia (Mason), 1967
Eight Days of Luke (Diana Wynne Jones), 1975
Eight Fantasms and Magics (s Vance), 1969
Eight Keys to Eden (Clifton), 1960
Eight Skilled Gentlemen (Hughart), 1991
Eighty-Minute Hour (Aldiss), 1974
Einstein Intersection (Delany), 1967
Elak of Atlantis (s Kuttner), 1985
Elana series (Engdahl), from 1970
Electric Crocodile (Compton), 1970
Electric Forest (Lee), 1979
Electric Kid (Kilworth), 1994
Electric Sword Swallowers (Bulmer), 1971
Elegy for Angels and Dogs (s W. Williams), 1990
Element 79 (s F. and G. Hoyle), 1967
Elenium series (Eddings), from 1989
Elephant Song (Longyear), 1982
Elephant Vanishes (s Murakami), 1993
Elephantasm (Lee), 1993
Eleventh Commandment (del Rey), 1962
Elfin Lights (s Eshbach), n.d.
Elfin Ship series (Blaylock), from 1982
Elissa (Haggard), 1917
Elite (s Holdstock), 1984
Elixir of Hate (England), 1976
Elliptical Grave (s Lafferty), 1989
Ellison Wonderland (s Ellison), 1962
Eloise (Tubb), 1975
Elric of Melniboné series (Moorcock), from 1963
Elsewhere, Elsewhen, Elsehow (s deFord), 1971
Elvenbane (Norton), 1991
Elvenblood (Norton), 1995
Elvira's Zoo (s Sargent), 1979
Elvissey (Womack), 1993
Embedding (Watson), 1973
Embryo (Charbonneau), 1976
Emma Tupper's Diary (Dickinson), 1971
Emperor and Clown (Dave Duncan), 1992
Emperor for the Legion (Turtledove), 1987
Emperor of Mars (Fearn), 1950
Emperor of the Last Days (Goulart), 1977
Emperor of the World (Hyne), 1915
Emperor, Swords, Pentacles (Gotlieb), 1982
Empery (Kube-McDowell), 1987
Emphatically Not SF, Almost (s Bishop), 1990
Emphyrio (Vance), 1969
Empire (Campbell, Simak), 1951
Empire (Delany), 1978
Empire (s Piper), 1981
Empire Builders (Bova), 1993
Empire Dreams (s McDonald), 1988
Empire of Chaos (Bulmer), 1953
Empire of Fear (Stableford), 1988
Empire of the Atom (van Vogt), 1957

Empire of the Eagle (Shwartz), 1993
Empire of the East series (Saberhagen), from 1968
Empire of the Nine (Farmer), 1988
Empire of the World (Hyne), 1910
Empire of Time (Kilian), 1978
Empire of Two Worlds (Bayley), 1972
Empire series (Feist), from 1987
Empire Star (Delany), 1966
Empires of Flux and Anchor (Chalker), 1984
Empires of Foliage and Flower (s G. Wolfe), 1987
Empress Irene series (Chandler), from 1965
Empress of Earth (Scott), 1987
Empress of Outer Space (Chandler), 1965
Emprise (Kube-McDowell), 1985
Empty People (Malzberg, as O'Donnell), 1969
Empty World (Christopher), 1977
Enchanted Duplicator (s Shaw), 1954
Enchanted Pilgrimage (Simak), 1975
Enchanted Village (s van Vogt), 1979
Enchanter's Endgame (Eddings), 1984
Enchantments of Flesh and Spirit (Constantine), 1987
Enchantress from the Stars (Engdahl), 1970
Enchantress of World's End (L. Carter), 1975
Encounter at Farpoint (Gerrold), 1987
Encounter in Space (Bulmer), 1952
Encounter Three (Caidin), 1978
Encounters (Resnick), 1993-95
End as a Hero (Laumer), 1985
End Bringers (Mason), 1973
End of All Songs (Moorcock), 1976
End of an Era (Sawyer), 1994
End of Eternity (Asimov), 1955
End of Exile (Bova), 1975
End of the Dream (Wylie), 1972
End of the Dreams (s Gunn), 1975
End of the Empire (Gilliland), 1983
End of the Game (Tepper), 1987
End of the Matter (A. Foster), 1977
End of the Tunnel (Capon), 1959
End of the World News (Burgess), 1982
End of This Day's Business (Burdekin), 1989
End Run (Forstchen, Stasheff), 1994
Endangered Species (s G. Wolfe), 1989
Ender Wiggin series (Card), from 1985
Endgame Enigma (Hogan), 1987
Endless Shadow (Brunner), 1964
Endless Universe (Bradley), 1979
Endless Voyage (Bradley), 1975
Ends (s Dickson), 1988
Ends of the Circle (P. Williams), 1981
Ends of the Earth (s Shepard), 1991
Enemies from Beyond (s Laumer), 1967
Enemies of the System (Aldiss), 1978
Enemy Mine (Gerrold, Longyear), 1985
Enemy Mine (Longyear), 1985
Enemy of My Enemy (Davidson), 1966
Enemy of the State (F. Wilson), 1980
Enemy Stars (P. Anderson), 1959
Enemy within the Skull (Tubb, as Kern), 1974
Enemy Within (C. Grant, as Charles), 1987
Enemy Within (Hubbard), 1986

Energy Pirate (F. and G. Hoyle), 1982
Engine Summer (Crowley), 1979
Engineer Garin and His Death Ray (Tolstoy), 1987
Engineman (E. Brown), 1994
Engines of God (McDevitt), 1994
English Assassin (Moorcock), 1972
English at the North Pole (Verne), 1874
Enigma (Kube-McDowell), 1986
Enigma from Tantalus (Brunner), 1965
Enigma Score (Tepper), 1989
Enormous Hourglass (Goulart), 1976
Enquiries of Doctor Eszterhazy (s Davidson), 1975
Ensign Flandry (P. Anderson), 1966
Enslaved Brains (Binder), 1965
Enterprise 2115 (Tubb, as Grey), 1954
Enterprise: The First Adventure (McIntyre), 1986
Entropy Effect (McIntyre), 1981
Entropy Tango (Moorcock), 1981
Entry to Elsewhen (s Brunner), 1972
Envoy to New Worlds (s Laumer), 1963
Eon series (Bear), from 1985
Epic Tales of the Five series (Duane), from 1979
Epiphany (Hawke, as Yermakov), 1982
Episodes of the Argo (s Lafferty), 1990
Epitaph in Rust (Powers), 1976
Equal Rites (Pratchett), 1987
Equality (Bellamy), 1897
Equality: In the Year 2000 (Reynolds), 1977
Equator (Aldiss), 1961
Erasmus Magister (Sheffield), 1982
Erewhon (S. Butler), 1872
Erewhon Revisited Twenty Years Later, Both by the Original Dis-
   coverer of the Country and by His Son (S. Butler), 1901
Eric Brighteyes (Haggard), 1891
Eric of the Strong Heart (Rousseau), 1925
Eric of Zanthodon (L. Carter), 1982
Eridahn (Young), 1983
Eros at Nadir (Resnick), 1986
Eros at Zenith (Resnick), 1984
Eros Descending (Resnick), 1985
Erthring series (Drew), from 1984
Ervool (s Leiber), 1980
Escape (Rusch), 1995
Escape across the Cosmos (Fox), 1964
Escape Attempt (Strugatsky), 1962
Escape from Kathmandu (s K. Robinson), 1988
Escape from Loki (Farmer), 1991
Escape from Macho (Offutt, as Cleve), 1982
Escape from New York (McQuay), 1981
Escape from Splatterbang (Fisk), 1978
Escape from the Planet of the Apes (Pournelle), 1974
Escape into Space (Tubb), 1969
Escape on Venus (E. Burroughs), 1946
Escape Orbit (J. White), 1965
Escape Plans (G. Jones), 1986
Escape Plus (s Bova), 1984
Escape to Infinity (Fanthorpe, as Zeigfreid), 1963
Escape to the Wild Wood (Mann), 1993
Escape to Tomorrow (Effinger), 1975
Escape to Witch Mountain (Key), 1968
Escape Velocity (Stasheff), 1983

Escape! (Bova), 1970
Escapement (Maine), 1956
E.S.P. Worm (Anthony), 1970
Esper (Blish), 1958
Esper Transfer (Proctor), 1978
Essential Ellison (s Ellison), 1987
E.T. series (Kotzwinkle), from 1982
Eternal Champion series (Moorcock), from 1970
Eternal Conflict (Keller), 1949
Eternal Frontiers (Schmitz), 1973
Eternal Light (McAuley), 1991
Eternal Lover (E. Burroughs), 1925
Eternal Savage (E. Burroughs), 1963
Eternity (Bear), 1988
Eternity (Ing, Reynolds), 1984
Eternity Brigade (Goldin), 1980
Ethan of Athos (Bujold), 1986
Ethical Culture series (Turner), from 1978
Euphor Unfree (Mason), 1977
Eva (Dickinson), 1988
Eva Fairdeath (Lee), 1994
Eve of Saint Venus (Burgess), 1964
Eve's Diary (Twain), 1906
Evening and the Morning and the Night (s O. Butler), 1991
Evenor (s G. MacDonald), 1972
Event (s Roberts), 1989
Everybody Come to Cosmo's (Goulart), 1988
Evil Eye (Fisk), 1982
Evil Gnome (Dent, as Robeson), 1976
Evil in the Family (Hoskins, as Corren), 1972
Evil Is Live Spelled Backwards (Offutt), 1970
Evil That Men Do (Brunner), 1969
Evil Water (s Watson), 1987
Ex Oblivione (s Lovecraft), 1969
Excalibur! (Jakes), 1980
Excess of Enchantments (Gardner), 1988
Exchameleon series (Goulart), from 1987
Exchange of Gifts (s McCaffrey), 1995
Excommunication (s Aldiss), 1975
Exile (Kotzwinkle), 1987
Exile (Kube-McDowell), 1992
Exile Kiss (Effinger), 1991
Exile of Time (Cummings), 1964
Exile on Vlahil (Mayhar), 1984
Exile Waiting (McIntyre), 1975
Exile's Gate (Cherryh), 1988
Exiled in Space (Fanthorpe, as Torro), 1968
Exiles at the Well of Souls (Chalker), 1978
Exiles of Glory (Pournelle), 1978
Exiles of the Stars (Norton), 1971
Exiles of Time (Bond), 1949
Exiles on Asperus (s Wyndham, as Beynon), 1979
Exiles series (Bova), from 1971
Exit Earth (Caidin), 1987
Exit Funtopia (Farren), 1989
Exit Humanity (Fanthorpe, as Brett), 1960
Exit Life (Fearn, as Gridban), 1953
Exode series (Sernine), from
Exorcists (Fanthorpe, as Muller), 1965
Expanded Universe (s Heinlein), 1980
Expedition to Earth (s Clarke), 1953

Expendables series (Cooper), from 1975
Experiment in Terra (Goulart), 1984
Expletives Deleted (s A. Carter), 1992
Exploits (Resnick), 1993-95
Exploits of Ebenezum (Gardner), 1987
Explorations (s P. Anderson), 1981
Explorers (s Kornbluth), 1954
Explorers in Hell (Drake, J. Morris), 1989
Explorers into Infinity (Cummings), 1965
Exterminator (s W. Burroughs), 1960
Extinction Bomber (R. Gordon, as Hough), 1956
Extra (s Ordinary) People (s Russ), 1984
Extra Man (Tubb, as Grey), 1954
Extract from Captain Stormfield's Visit to Heaven (Twain), 1909
Extracts from Adam's Diary (Twain), 1904
Extraterrestrial Tales (Fisk), 1991
Extraterritorial (Morressy), 1977
Extro (Bester), 1975
Eyas (Kilian), 1982
Eye (s F. Herbert), 1985
Eye Among the Blind (Holdstock), 1976
Eye for Eye (s Card), 1990
Eye in the Pyramid (Robert Anton Wilson), 1975
Eye in the Sky (Dick), 1957
Eye of Cat (Zelazny), 1982
Eye of Karnak (Fanthorpe, as Muller), 1962
Eye of the Comet (Sargent), 1984
Eye of the Heron (Le Guin), 1982
Eye of the Monster (Norton), 1962
Eye of the Queen (Mann), 1982
Eye of the Vulture (Goulart), 1977
Eye of the Zodiac (Tubb), 1975
Eyes of Amber (s J. Vinge), 1979
Eyes of Darkness (Koontz, as Nichols), 1981
Eyes of Fire (Bishop), 1980
Eyes of Heisenberg (F. Herbert), 1966
Eyes of Sarsis (Offutt), 1980
Eyes of the Overworld (s Vance), 1966
Eyes series (S. Gordon), from 1973

Fabulous Riverboat (Farmer), 1971
Façade (Rusch), 1993
Face (Vance), 1979
Face in the Abyss (Merritt), 1931
Face in the Dark (s Fanthorpe), 1961
Face in the Night (Fanthorpe, as Brett), 1962
Face of Fear (Fanthorpe, as Torro), 1963
Face of Fear (Koontz, as Coffey), 1977
Face of Heaven (Stableford), 1976
Face of the Waters (Silverberg), 1991
Face of X (Fanthorpe, as Roberts), 1960
Faceless Man (Vance), 1978
Faceless Planet (Fanthorpe, as Brett), 1960
Faces (s Kennedy), 1986
Faces in the Flames (Tate), 1976
Facets (s W. Williams), 1990
Facing the Flag (Verne), 1897
Fade-out (Tilley), 1975
Faded Sun series (Cherryh), from 1978
Faerie Tale (Feist), 1988
Faery Flag (Yolen), 1989

Faery in Shadow (Cherryh), 1993
Faery Lands Forlorn (Dave Duncan), 1991
Fafhrd and the Gray Mouser series (Leiber), from 1968
Fahrenheit 451 (Bradbury), 1953
Fair in Emain Macha (s de Lint), 1990
Fairy Tales of George MacDonald (G. MacDonald), 1904
Faith of Tarot (Anthony), 1980
Falcon (Bull), 1989
Falcon Guard (Thurston), 1991
Falcons of Narabedla (Bradley), 1964
Falkenberg series (Pournelle), from 1976
Falkenberg's Legion series (Stirling), from 1991
Falklands Whale (Boulle), 1984
Fall into Darkness (Hawke, as Yermakov), 1982
Fall of Atlantis (Bradley), 1987
Fall of Chronopolis (Bayley), 1974
Fall of Colossus (D.F. Jones), 1974
Fall of Moondust (Clarke), 1961
Fall of Princes (Tarr), 1988
Fall of the Dream Machine (Koontz), 1969
Fall of the Families (Mann), 1987
Fall of the Republic (Kilian), 1987
Fall of the Shell (P. Williams), 1982
Fall of the Sky Lords (Brosnan), 1991
Fall of the Towers series (Delany), from 1970
Fall of the White Ship Avatar (Daley), 1987
Fall of Winter (Jack C. Haldeman), 1985
Fallen Angels (Niven, Pournelle), 1991
Fallen Country (Sucharitkul), 1986
Fallen Moon (Watson), 1994
Fallen Spaceman (Harding), 1973
Fallible Fiend (de Camp), 1973
Falling Astronauts (Malzberg), 1971
Falling Free (Bujold), 1988
Falling Torch (Budrys), 1959
Falling Toward Forever (Eklund), 1975
Falling Woman (Murphy), 1986
False Dawn (Yarbro), 1978
False Fatherland (Chandler), 1968
False Mirror (A. Foster), 1992
False Night (Budrys), 1954
Familiar Spirit (Tuttle), 1983
Fang, The Gnome (Coney), 1988
Fangs of the Hooded Demon (C. Grant, as Marsh), 1988
Fantasies of Harlan Ellison (s Ellison), 1979
Fantasma (Monteleone), 1987
Fantasms and Magics (s Vance), 1978
Fantastic Island (Dent, as Robeson), 1966
Fantastic Tales (Eliade), 1969
Fantastic Voyage (Asimov), 1966
Fantastic Voyage II (Asimov), 1987
Fantastico (Fisk), 1994
Fantasy (s P. Anderson), 1981
Fantasy Short Stories (s Hubbard), 1993
Fanthorpe Flame Mass (Fanthorpe), 1961
Far above Rubies (s G. MacDonald), 1899
Far and Away (s Boucher), 1955
Far Call (Dickson), 1978
Far Ends of Time (Asimov), 1979
Far from Home (s Tevis), 1981
Far Frontier (Rotsler), 1980

Far Future Calling (s Stapledon), 1980
Far Out (s Knight), 1961
Far-Out Worlds of A.E. van Vogt (s van Vogt), 1968
Far Rainbow (Strugatsky), 1967
Far Side of Evil (Engdahl), 1971
Far Stars (s Russell), 1961
Far Sunset (Cooper), 1967
Far Traveller (Chandler), 1977
Far-Seer (Sawyer), 1992
Farce to Be Reckoned With (Sheckley, Zelazny), 1995
Farewell, Earth's Bliss (Compton), 1966
Farewell Horizontal (Jeter), 1989
Farewell to Yesterday's Tomorrow (s Panshin), 1975
Farfetch (Lichtenberg), 1985
Farmer Flight to Opar (Farmer), 1976
Farmer in the Sky (Heinlein), 1950
Farnham's Freehold (Heinlein), 1964
Farside Cannon (Allen), 1988
Farthest Shore (Le Guin), 1972
Farthest Star (Pohl, Williamson), 1975
Fat Men from Space (Pinkwater), 1976
Fatal Fire (Bulmer), 1962
Fatapouis and Thinifers (s Maurois), 1940
Fateful Lightning (Forstchen), 1993
Father of Lies (Brunner), 1968
Father of Stones (Shepard), 1989
Father to the Man (Gribbin), 1989
Father to the Stars (s Farmer), 1981
Fattypuffs and Thinifers (s Maurois), 1941
Fault Lines (Wilhelm), 1977
Faust Eric (Pratchett), 1990
Faustine (Tennant), 1992
Faustus Hexagram series (Broderick), from 1986
Fear (Hubbard), 1957
Fear and Trembling (s Bloch), 1989
Fear, and Typewriter in the Sky (Hubbard), 1977
Fear, and Ultimate Adventure (Hubbard), 1970
Fear Cay (Dent, as Robeson), 1966
Fear That Man (Koontz), 1969
Fear Today, Gone Tomorrow (s Bloch), 1971
Feast of St. Dionysus (s Silverberg), 1975
Feast Unknown (Farmer), 1969
Feather Stroke (Van Scyoc), 1989
Feathered Octopus (Dent, as Robeson), 1970
Federation (s Piper), 1981
Federation World (J. White), 1988
Feelies (Farren), 1978
Feersum Endjinn (Banks), 1994
Feighan, McGill series (O'Donnell), from 1981
Fellowship of the HAND (Hoch), 1973
Fellowship of the Talisman (Simak), 1978
Female Man (Russ), 1975
Female War (Perry), 1993
Fenris Device (Stableford), 1974
Fetch (Holdstock), 1991
Fetish (s Bryant), 1991
Fever Dream and Other Fantasies (s Bloch), 1970
Fever Dreams (s Bradbury), 1970
Few Last Words (s Sallis), 1969
Fiasco (Lem), 1987
Fiddling for Waterbuffaloes (s Sucharitkul, as Somtow), 1992

Field of Ice (Verne), 1875
Fiends (Fanthorpe), 1959
Fiery Angel (Bryusov), 1930
Fifth Child (Lessing), 1988
Fifth Head of Cerberus (s G. Wolfe), 1972
Fifth Millennium series (Stirling), from 1985
Fifth Planet (F. and G. Hoyle), 1963
Fifty-One Tales (s Dunsany), 1915
Fight for Life (Leinster), 1947
Fighting Man of Mars (E. Burroughs), 1931
Figment of a Dream (s Keller), 1962
Final Battle (Lupoff), 1990
Final Blackout (Hubbard), 1948
Final Circle of Paradise (Strugatsky), 1976
Final Command (Norwood), 1986
Final Countdown (Caidin), 1980
Final Encyclopedia (Dickson), 1984
Final Magic (Anthony), 1992
Final Programme (Moorcock), 1968
Final Reflection (Ford), 1984
Final War (s Keller), 1949
Final War (s Malzberg, as O'Donnell), 1969
Find the Changeling (Benford, Eklund), 1980
Find the Feathered Serpent (Hunter), 1952
Finder (Bull), 1994
Fingalnan Conspiracy (Mason, as Rankine), 1973
Fingers of Darkness (s Fanthorpe), 1961
Finish Line (Goldin), 1976
Finished (Haggard), 1917
Fire and Hemlock (Diana Wynne Jones), 1985
Fire and Stone (Le Guin), 1989
Fire at the Center (Proctor), 1981
Fire-Eater (Goulart), 1970
Fire from the Wine-Dark Sea (s Sucharitkul), 1983
Fire in His Hands (Cook), 1984
Fire in the Abyss (S. Gordon), 1983
Fire in the Heavens (George O. Smith), 1958
Fire in the Sun (Effinger), 1989
Fire Mask (C. Grant), 1991
Fire on the Border (O'Donnell), 1990
Fire on the Mountain (Bisson), 1988
Fire Past the Future (Maine), 1959
Fire Pattern (Shaw), 1984
Fire Time (P. Anderson), 1974
Fire upon the Deep (V. Vinge), 1992
Fire Watch (s Willis), 1985
Fire Worm (Watson), 1988
Fireball series (Christopher), from 1981
Firebird (Harness), 1981
Firebird (s Zebrowski), 1979
Firebird series (Tyers), from 1987
Firebrand (Bradley), 1987
Firechild (Williamson), 1986
Fireclown (Moorcock), 1965
Firedance (S. Barnes), 1993
Firefight 2000 (s Ing), 1987
Fireflood (s McIntyre), 1979
Firefly (Anthony), 1990
Firefly (Stableford), 1994
Firehand (Norton), 1994
Firemantle (Mackelworth), 1968

Fires of Azeroth (Cherryh), 1979
Fires of Scorpio (Bulmer, as Akers), 1983
Fireship (s J. Vinge), 1978
Fireworks (s A. Carter), 1974
First Channel (Lichtenberg), 1980
First Chronicles of Druss the Legend (s Gemmell), 1993
First Chronicles of Thomas Covenant the Unbeliever (Donaldson), 1993
First Cycle (Kurland, Piper), 1982
First Family (Tilley), 1985
First He Died (Simak), 1953
First Lensman (E.E. Smith), 1950
First Men in the Moon (Wells), 1901
First on Mars (R. Gordon), 1957
First One and Twenty (s Gloag), 1946
First Person, Peculiar (s Sherred), 1972
First Through Time (R. Gordon), 1962
First to the Stars (R. Gordon), 1959
First, You Fight (Naha, as Drumm), 1984
Fish Dinner in Memison (Eddison), 1941
Fish Soup (Le Guin), 1992
Fisherman of the Inland Sea (s Le Guin), 1994
Fistful of Digits (Hodder-Williams), 1968
Fittest (McIntosh), 1955
Five against Arlane (Purdom), 1967
Five Against Venus (Latham), 1952
Five Faces of Fear (Fanthorpe, as Thorpe), 1960
Five Gold Bands (Vance), 1963
Five Steps to Tomorrow (Binder), 1970
Five to Twelve (Cooper), 1968
Five Way Secret Agent (Reynolds), 1975
Five-Twelfths of Heaven (Scott), 1985
Fize of the Gabriel Ratchets (Norwood), 1983
Flame Goddess (Fanthorpe, as Roberts), 1961
Flame Is Green (Lafferty), 1971
Flame of Iridar (L. Carter), 1967
Flame upon the Ice (Forstchen), 1984
Flamers (Fisk), 1979
Flames (Stapledon), 1947
Flames of Desire (George H. Smith, as Deer), 1963
Flaming Falcons (Dent, as Robeson), 1968
Flandry, Dominic series (P. Anderson), from 1959
Flare (Zelazny), 1992
Flash Gordon (Cover), 1980
Flash Gordon series (Goulart), from 1974
Flat Earth series (Lee), from 1978
Flat Earth series (Lupoff), from 1984
Flatland (s Sladek), 1982
Flatlander (s Niven), 1995
Fleet Action (Forstchen), 1994
Flesh (Farmer), 1960
Flesh in the Furnace (Koontz), 1972
Fleshpots of Sansato (Temple), 1968
Flexing the Warp (Norwood), 1983
Fliers of Antares (Bulmer, as Akers), 1975
Flies of Memory (Watson), 1990
Flight from Nevèryon (Delany), 1985
Flight from Rebirth (McIntosh), 1971
Flight From Yesterday (R. Williams), 1963
Flight in Yiktor (Norton), 1986
Flight into Yesterday (Harness), 1953

Flight of Exiles (Bova), 1972
Flight of the Dragonfly (Forward), 1984
Flight of the Horse (s Niven), 1973
Flight of the Valkyries (s Fanthorpe), 1958
Flight of Time (Capon), 1960
Flight of Vengeance (Norton), 1992
Flight to the Lonesome Place (Key), 1971
Flinx in Flux (A. Foster), 1988
Floating City, and The Blockade Runners (Verne), 1874
Floating Gods (M. Harrison), 1983
Floating Island (Verne), 1896
Floating Zombie (D.F. Jones), 1975
Florians (Stableford), 1976
Flow My Tears, The Policeman Said (Dick), 1974
Flower of Doradil (Rackham), 1970
Flowerdust (G. Jones), 1993
Flowers for Algernon (Keyes), 1966
Fluger (Piserchia), 1980
Fluke (J. Herbert), 1977
Flush of Shadows (s Wilhelm), 1995
Flux (Baxter), 1993
Flux (Goulart), 1974
Flying Fortunes in an Encounter with Rubberface! (Cross), 1952
Flying Legion (England), 1920
Flying Sorcerers (Gerrold, Niven), 1971
Fog (J. Herbert), 1975
Fog Horn (s Bradbury), 1977
Folk of the Fringe (s Card), 1989
Folsom Flint (s Keller), 1969
Food for Demons (s Evans), 1971
Food of Death (s Dunsany), 1974
Food of the Gods, and How It Came to Earth (Wells), 1904
Fool's Hill (Lupoff), 1978
Fool's Run (McKillip), 1987
Fools (Cadigan), 1992
Fools' Harvest (Cox), 1939
Footfall (Niven, Pournelle), 1985
Footprints on Sand (s de Camp), 1981
Footsteps (s Ellison), 1989
F.P.1. Does Not Reply (Siodmak), 1933
For a Breath I Tarry (s Zelazny), 1980
For Crown and Kingdom (Proctor), 1987
For England's Sake (Cromie), 1889
For Fear of the Night (C. Grant), 1988
For Love of Mother-Not (A. Foster), 1983
For Texas and Zed (Z. Hughes), 1976
For the Flag (Verne), 1897
Forbidden (Fanthorpe, as Brett), 1963
Forbidden Area (Frank), 1956
Forbidden Garden (Taine), 1947
Forbidden Planet (Fanthorpe, as Muller), 1961
Forbidden Tower (Bradley), 1977
Forbidden World (Bischoff, T. White), 1978
Force 97X (Fanthorpe, as Torro), 1965
Force of Arms (Stine), 1990
Foreign Bodies (s Aldiss), 1981
Foreign Constellations (s Brunner), 1980
Foreigner series (Cherryh), from 1994
Forerunner series (Norton), from 1973
Forest House (Bradley), 1993
Forest of Peldain (Bayley), 1985

Forest of the Night (Sucharitkul, as Somtow), 1992
Forests of the Night (s Lee), 1989
Forever City (Lupoff), 1988
Forever Drug (Perry), 1995
Forever Machine (Clifton), 1958
Forever Man (Dickson), 1986
Forever War (Joe Haldeman), 1975
Forge (Drake, Stirling), 1991
Forge of God series (Bear), from 1987
Forgetful Robot (Fairman), 1968
Forgotten Beasts of Eld (McKillip), 1974
Forgotten Dimension (Garnett), 1975
Forgotten Door (Key), 1965
Forgotten News (s Finney), 1983
Forgotten Planet (George H. Smith), 1965
Forgotten Planet (Leinster), 1954
Forgotten Sea of Mars (s Resnick), 1965
Forlorn Hope (Drake), 1984
Formula 29X (Fanthorpe, as Torro), 1963
Forsake the Sky (Powers), 1986
Forschungskreuzer Saumarez (Bulmer), 1960
Fort Privilege (K. Reed), 1985
Fortress (Drake), 1987
Fortress in the Eye of Time (Cherryh), 1995
Fortress of Death (Naha, as McGann), 1991
Fortress of Frost and Fire (Emerson), 1993
Fortress of Solitude (Dent, as Robeson), 1968
Fortress of the Pearl (Moorcock), 1989
Fortress Unvanquishable, Save for Sacnoth (s Dunsany), 1910
Fortune for Kregen (Bulmer, as Akers), 1979
Fortune of Fear (Hubbard), 1986
Fortunes of Brak (s Jakes), 1980
Forty Thousand in Gehenna (Cherryh), 1983
Forward in Time (s Bova), 1973
Forward! (s Dickson), 1985
Fossil (Clement), 1993
Fossil Hunter (Sawyer), 1993
Found Wanting (L. Carter), 1985
Foundation series (Asimov), from 1951
Fountains of Paradise (Clarke), 1979
Four Came Back (Caidin), 1968
Four-Day Planet (Piper), 1961
Four Day Weekend (George H. Smith), 1966
Four Days War (S. Wright), 1938). London, Hale, 1936
Four-Dimensional Nightmare (s Ballard), 1963
Four Encounters (s Stapledon), 1976
Four for Tomorrow (s Zelazny), 1967
Four from Planet 5 (Leinster), 1959
Four Hundred Billion Stars series (McAuley), from 1988
Four Lords of the Diamond (Chalker), 1983
Four Lords of the Diamond series (Chalker), from 1981
Four Prose Poems (s Lovecraft), 1987
Four-Sided Triangle (Temple), 1949
Four Stories (s Lafferty), 1983
Four Ways to Forgiveness (s Le Guin), 1995
Fourth "R." (George O. Smith), 1959
Fourth Book of Jorkens (s Dunsany), 1947
Fourth Hemisphere (Lake), 1980
Fourth Horseman (Nourse), 1983
Fourth Mansions (Lafferty), 1969
Fox, the Dog, and the Griffin (P. Anderson), 1966

Fox Thief of Llarn (Fox), 1966
Fox Woman (Merritt), 1946
Foxes of First Dark (Kilworth), 1990
Fracas Factor (Reynolds), 1978
Fractal Mode (Anthony), 1992
Frankenbagel Monster (Pinkwater), 1986
Frankenstein (s May, as Thorpe), 1977
Frankenstein Factory (Hoch), 1975
Frankenstein Meets Wolfman (s May, as Thorpe), 1981
Frankenstein Papers (Saberhagen), 1986
Frankenstein Unbound (Aldiss), 1973
Frankenstein Wheel (Fairman), 1972
Frankenstein; or, The Modern Prometheus (Shelley), 1818
Fratricide Is a Gas (Gutteridge), 1975
Freckled Shark (Dent, as Robeson), 1972
Free Live Free (G. Wolfe), 1984
Free Zone (*Unology, a Literary Work Consisting of One Volume), 1989
Freedom Beach (Kelly, Kessel), 1985
Freedom's Landing (McCaffrey), 1995
Friday (Heinlein), 1982
Friends Come in Boxes (Coney), 1973
Friendship Song (Springer), 1992
From a Changeling Star (Carver), 1989
From Afar (s Fearn), 1982
From Carthage Then I Came (Mason), 1966
From Death to the Stars (Hubbard), 1953
From Hell (A. Moore), n.d.
From Outer Space (Clement), 1957
From Realms Beyond (Fanthorpe, as Brett), 1963
From Sea to Shining Star (s Chandler), 1989
From the Clouds to the Mountains (s Verne), 1874
From the Earth to the Moon (Verne), 1869
From the Heart of Darkness (s Drake), 1983
From the Land of Fear (s Ellison), 1967
From the Oceans, from the Stars (s Clarke), 1962
From the Twilight Zone (s Serling), 1970(s ?)
From This Day Forward (s Brunner), 1972
From Time to Time (Finney), 1995
Frontier of the Dark (Chandler), 1984
Froomb! (Lymington), 1964
Frost and Fire (s Zelazny), 1989
Frost Dancers (Kilworth), 1992
Frostworld and Dreamfire (Morressy), 1977
Frozen Limit (Fearn, as Gridban), 1954
Frozen Planet (Fanthorpe, as Torro), 1960
Frozen Planet (P. Moore), 1954
Frozen Planet of Azuron (F. and G. Hoyle), 1982
Frozen Sky (Harding), 1975
Frozen Tomb (s Fanthorpe, as Brett), 1962
Fugitive from Time (High), 1978
Fugitive of the Stars (Hamilton), 1965
Fugitive of Time (Tubb, as Gridban), 1953
Fugitive Worlds (Shaw), 1989
Fugue for a Darkening Island (Priest), 1972
Fugue State (Ford), 1990
Fulfilments of Fate and Desire (Constantine), 1989
Fun with Your New Head (s Disch), 1971
Fundamental Disch (s Disch), 1980
Funeral for the Eyes of Fire (Bishop), 1975
Funhouse (Koontz, as West), 1980

Funnyfingers and Cabrito (s Lafferty), 1976
Fur Magic (Norton), 1968
Furies (Charnas), 1994
Furies (Roberts), 1966
Furious Future (s Budrys), 1964
Furious Gulf (Benford), 1994
Further Adventures of Halley's Comet (Batchelor), 1980
Furthest (Elgin), 1971
Fury (Kuttner, C.L. Moore), 1950
Fury Bombs (Hoskins, as Wilson), 1983
Fury from Earth (McLaughlin), 1963
Fury Out of Time (Biggle), 1965
Fury Scorned (Sargent), 1996
Fury Scorned (Zebrowski), n.d.
Fusion Fire (Tyers), 1988
Future Crime (s Bova), 1990
Future Glitter (van Vogt), 1973
Future History, Incorporating The Mercenary and West of Honor
    (Pournelle), 1990
Future History series (Heinlein), from 1950
Future Imperfect (Burgess), 1994
Future Imperfect (s Gunn), 1964
Future Past (s J. White), 1982
Future Quintet (s Bova), 1994
Future Sanctuary (Harding), 1976
Future Tense (s Vance), 1964
Future Times Three (Barjavel), 1970
Future War (s Wodhams), 1982
Futureworld (Rotsler, as Hall), 1976
Fuzzies series (Mayhar), from 1982
Fuzzies series (Piper), from 1962

G-Bomb (Fearn, as Statten), 1952
Gabriel (Tuttle), 1987
Gabriel and the Creatures (s Heard), 1952
Gabriel's Body (Siodmak), 1992
Gadget Man (Goulart), 1971
Gaea series (Varley), from 1979
Gaia's Toys (Ore), 1995
Gaian Expedient (Drew), 1985
Galactiad (Tubb, as Kern), 1983
Galactic Breed (Brackett), 1955
Galactic Center series (Benford), from 1977
Galactic Cluster (s Blish), 1959
Galactic Derelict (Norton), 1959
Galactic Diplomat (s Laumer), 1965
Galactic Dreams (s H. Harrison), 1994
Galactic Effectuator (s Vance), 1980
Galactic Intrigue (Bulmer), 1953
Galactic Medal of Honor (Reynolds), 1976
Galactic Midway series (Resnick), from 1982
Galactic Milieu series (May), from 1987
Galactic Odyssey (Laumer), 1967
Galactic Patrol (E.E. Smith), 1950
Galactic Pot-Healer (Dick), 1969
Galactic Rejects (Offutt), 1973
Galactic Sibyl Sue Blue (R. Brown), 1968
Galactic Storm (Brunner, as Hunt), 1951
Galactic Takeover Bid (McIntosh), 1973
Galactic Tours (Shaw), 1981
Galactic Troubadours (Lightner), 1965

Galactic Warriors (Bischoff), 1985
Galactic Whirlpool (Gerrold), 1980
Galápagos (Vonnegut), 1985
Galaxies (Malzberg), 1975
Galaxies Like Grains of Sand (s Aldiss), 1960
Galaxy 5 series (Kelley), from 1979
Galaxy 666 (Fanthorpe, as Torro), 1963
Galaxy Builder (Laumer), 1984
Galaxy Jane (Goulart), 1986
Galaxy Mission (Hamilton), 1969
Galaxy of Strangers (s Biggle), 1976
Galaxy of the Lost (Tubb, as Kern), 1973
Galaxy Primes (E.E. Smith), 1965
Galaxy's End (Lupoff), 1988
Gallagher's Glacier (Richmond), 1970
Gallery of His Dreams (s Rusch), 1991
Gallicenae (P. Anderson), 1987
Gambles with Destiny (s G. Griffith), 1899
Game Beyond (Scott), 1984
Game of Empire (P. Anderson), 1985
Game-Players of Titan (Dick), 1963
Game's End (K. Anderson), 1992
Gamearth (K. Anderson), 1989
Gamearth Trilogy (K. Anderson), from 1989
Gameplay (K. Anderson), 1989
Gameplayers of Zan (M.A. Foster), 1977
Games of Neith (St. Clair), 1960
Gamesman (Malzberg), 1975
Gamester Wars series (Forstchen), from 1987
Gaming Magi series (Bischoff), from 1985
Gandalara series (Garrett), from 1986
Ganymede series (Resnick), from 1967
Ganymede Takeover (Dick), 1967
Ganymede Takeover (Nelson), 1967
Gap series (Donaldson), from 1990
Garan the Eternal (s Norton), 1972
Garbage World (Platt), 1967
Garden of Rama (Clarke), 1991
Garden of Winter (Eklund), 1980
Garden on the Moon (Boulle), 1965
Gardens of Delight (Watson), 1980
Gardens One to Five (Tate), 1971
Garin Death Ray (Tolstoy), 1955
Garin series (Turtledove), from 1979
Garments of Caean (Bayley), 1976
Garrett Files series (Cook), from 1987
Gas (Platt), 1970
Gate of Ivrel (Cherryh), 1976
Gate of the Cat (Norton), 1987
Gate of Time (Farmer), 1966
Gate of Worlds (Silverberg), 1967
Gate to Women's Country (Tepper), 1988
Gates of Creation (Farmer), 1966
Gates of Eden (Stableford), 1983
Gates of Heaven (Preuss), 1980
Gates of Hell (Cherryh, J. Morris), 1986
Gates of Lucifer series (Eshbach), from 1986
Gates of the Universe (DeWeese, R. Coulson), 1975
Gates of Time (Barrett), 1970
Gateway (Pohl), 1977
Gateway to Elsewhere (Leinster), 1954

Gateway to Never (Chandler), 1978
Gateway Trip (s Pohl), 1990
Gath (Tubb), 1968
Gather, Darkness! (Leiber), 1950
Gather in the Hall of the Planets (Malzberg, as O'Donnell), 1971
Geis of the Gargoyle (Anthony), 1995
Gemini God (Kilworth), 1981
Gender Genocide (Cooper), 1972
Gene Wolfe's Book of Days (s G. Wolfe), 1981
General series (Drake), from 1991
General series (Stirling), from 1991
Generation Removed (Wolf), 1977
Generation Warriors (McCaffrey), 1991
Genesis Machine (Hogan), 1978
Genesis Shield (Spruill), 1985
Genetic Bomb (Offutt), 1975
Genetic Buccaneer (Tubb, as Kern), 1974
Genetic General (Dickson), 1960
Genetic Soldier (Turner), 1994
Genial Dinosaur (Fearn, as Gridban), 1954
Genius Loci (s Clark Ashton Smith), 1948
Genius Unlimited (Rackham, as Phillifent), 1972
Genocidal Healer (J. White), 1992
Genocides (Disch), 1965
Gentle Giants of Ganymede (Hogan), 1978
Genus Homo (de Camp, P. Miller), 1950
Geodesic Dreams (s Dozois), 1992
Geodyssey series (Anthony), from 1993
Georgia on My Mind (s Sheffield), 1995
Gertha's Lovers (W. Morris), 1905
Get off the Unicorn (s McCaffrey), 1977
Get Off My World (Binder), 1971
Get Off My World! (s Leinster), 1966
Get Out of My Sky; and, There Shall Be No Darkness (s Blish), 1980
Geta (Kingsbury), 1984
Getaway World (E.E. Smith, Goldin), 1977
Getaway World (Goldin), 1977
Getting Home (s Busby), 1987
Getting into Death (s Disch), 1973
Gholan Gate (Tubb, as Kern), 1974
Ghost Breaker (s Goulart), 1971
Ghost Dancers (Naha, as Drumm), 1987
Ghost King (Gemmell), 1988
Ghost Kings (Haggard), 1908
Ghost Light (s Leiber), 1984
Ghost Pirates (Hodgson), 1909
Ghost Rider (s Fanthorpe), 1959
Ghost Warriors (Naha, as McGann), 1990
Ghostlight (Bradley), 1995
Ghosts (s Dunsany), 1993
Ghosts of Epidoris (Tubb, as Kern), 1975
Ghosts of Sleath (J. Herbert), 1994
Ghosts of the Heaviside Layer (s Dunsany), 1980
Ghosts of Wind and Shadow (s de Lint), 1990
Ghostwood (de Lint), 1990
Ghoul (s Hubbard), 1991
Giant Cold (Dickinson), 1984
Giant of World's End (L. Carter), 1969
Giant Stumbles (Lymington), 1960
Giants from Eternity (Wellman), 1959

Giants in the Dust (Oliver), 1976
Giants of Universal Park (F. and G. Hoyle), 1982
Giants' Star (Hogan), 1981
Gift (Dickinson), 1973
Gift from Earth (Niven), 1968
Gift of the Manti (Bone), 1977
Gifts of the Child Christ (G. MacDonald), 1882
Gifts of the Gorboduc Vandal (P. Williams), 1989
Giggling Ghosts (Dent, as Robeson), 1971
Gilden-Fire (s Donaldson), 1981
Gilgamesh series (Silverberg), from 1984
Gilpin's Space (Bretnor), 1986
Ginger Star (Brackett), 1974
Girl from Mars (s Williamson), 1929
Girl from Tomorrow (Fanthorpe, as Zeigfreid), 1966
Girl in the Golden Atom (Cummings), 1922
Girl Who Fell into the Sky (s Wilhelm), 1991
Girl Who Heard Dragons (s McCaffrey), 1985
Girl Who Was Plugged In (s Tiptree), 1989
Girl with a Symphony in Her Fingers (Coney), 1975
Girl with the Jade Green Eyes (Boyd), 1978
Girls from Planet 5 (Richard Wilson), 1955
Give Daddy the Knife, Darling (Lymington), 1969
Give Warning to the World (Brunner), 1974
Gladiator (Wylie), 1930
Gladiator-at-Law (Kornbluth, Pohl), 1955
Glamour (Priest), 1984
Glass and Amber (s Cherryh), 1987
Glass Eyes and Cotton Strings (s de Lint), 1982
Glass Hammer (Jeter), 1985
Glass Man (Goulart, as Robeson), 1975
Glass of Dyskornis (Garrett), 1982
Glass of Stars (s Young), 1968
Globalhead (s Sterling), 1992
Glogauer, Karl series (Moorcock), from 1969
Gloriana (Moorcock), 1978
Glorious Pool (T. Smith), 1934
Glory (Coppel), 1993
Glory Game (Laumer), 1973
Glory Lane (A. Foster), 1987
Glory Planet (Chandler), 1964
Glory Road (Heinlein), 1963
Glory Season (Brin), 1993
Glory That Was (de Camp), 1960
Glory's War (Coppel), 1995
Glow of Candles (s C. Grant), 1981
Glue Factory (Meltzer), 1969
Gnome There Was (s Kuttner and C.L. Moore, as Padgett), 1950
Go Tell the Spartans (Pournelle, Stirling), 1991
Goblin Mirror (Cherryh), 1992
Goblin Reservation (Simak), 1968
Goblin Tower (de Camp), 1968
Goblins (C. Grant), 1994
God Box (Longyear), 1989
God Emperor of Dune (F. Herbert), 1981
G.O.D., Inc. series (Chalker), from 1987
God Killers (Baxter), 1968
God Machine (Caidin), 1968
God Machine (Watkins), 1973
God Makers (F. Herbert), 1972
God of Tarot (Anthony), 1979

God's Nose (s Knight), 1991
God's World (Watson), 1979
Godbody (Sturgeon), 1986
Godbond (Springer), 1988
Goddess of Ganymede (Resnick), 1967
Goddess of Mars (Fearn), 1950
Goddess of the Night (s Fanthorpe), 1963
Godfire (Felice), 1978
Godling, Go Home! (s Silverberg), 1964
Godmother series (Scarborough), from 1994
Godmother's Apprentice (Scarborough), 1995
Godolphin (Bulwer-Lytton), 1833
Gods and Golems (s del Rey), 1973
Gods Laughed (s P. Anderson), 1982
Gods, Men, and Ghosts (s Dunsany), 1972
Gods of Darkness (Fanthorpe, as Zeigfreid), 1962
Gods of Mars (E. Burroughs), 1918
Gods of Pegana (s Dunsany), 1905
Gods of Riverworld (Farmer), 1986
Gods of the Greataway (Coney), 1984
Gods of the Well of Souls (Chalker), 1994
Gods of Xuma (Lake), 1978
Gods or Demons? (Lightner), 1973
Gods Themselves (Asimov), 1972
Godspeed (Sheffield), 1993
Godwhale (Bass), 1974
Godzilla (s May, as Thorpe), 1977
G.O.G. 666 (Taine), 1954
Going to See the End of the Sky (Watkins), 1986
Gold (s Asimov), 1995
Gold and Iron (Slaves of the Klau), 1982
Gold at Starbow's End (s Pohl), 1972
Gold Coast (K. Robinson), 1988
Gold-Finder (G. Griffith), 1898
Gold of Akada (Fearn, as Titan), 1951
Gold Ogre (Dent, as Robeson), 1969
Gold Star (Z. Hughes), 1983
Gold the Man (J. Green), 1971
Gold Tooth (Taine), 1927
Gold Unicorn (Lee), 1994
Goldcamp Vampire; or, The Sanguinary Sourdough (Scarborough), 1987
Golden (Shepard), 1993
Golden Age (Lesser and Fairman, as Chase), 1959
Golden Amazon series (Fearn), from 1944
Golden Apple (Robert Anton Wilson), 1975
Golden Apples of the Sun (s Bradbury), 1953
Golden Aquarians (M. Hughes), 1994
Golden Barge (Moorcock), 1979
Golden Blight (England), 1916
Golden Blood (Williamson), 1964
Golden Bottle (Donnelly), 1892
Golden Chalice (Fanthorpe), 1961
Golden City (Verrill), 1916
Golden Dream (Mayhar), 1982
Golden Enemy (Key), 1969
Golden Fleece (Sawyer), 1990
Golden Gate (s Lafferty), 1982
Golden Grove (Kress), 1984
Golden Helix (s Sturgeon), 1979
Golden Horn (Tarr), 1985

Golden Key (G. MacDonald), n.d.
Golden Man (s Dick), 1980
Golden Naginata (Salmonson), 1982
Golden People (Saberhagen), 1964
Golden Peril (Dent, as Robeson), 1970
Golden Queen (Wolverton), 1994
Golden Scorpio (Bulmer, as Akers), 1978
Golden Space (Sargent), 1982
Golden Swan (Springer), 1983
Golden Sword (J. Morris), 1977
Golden Thread (Charnas), 1989
Golden Torc (May), 1982
Golden Trillium (Norton), 1993
Golden Vanity (Pollack), 1980
Golden Warrior (s Fanthorpe, as Roberts), 1958
Golden Wings (s W. Morris), 1904
Golden Witchbreed (Gentle), 1983
Goldenwing series (Coppel), from 1993
Golem^{100} (Bester), 1980
Goliah (s London), 1973
Gondwane Epic series (L. Carter), from 1974
Gone to Earth (s Zelazny), 1992
Good-bye to Earth (Kelley), 1979
Good Leviathan (Boulle), 1979
Good Neighbors (s Pangborn), 1972
Good News from Outer Space (Kessel), 1989
Good Omens (Gaiman, Pratchett), 1990
Good Omens (Pratchett), 1990
Good Taste (s Asimov), 1976
Goodbye Jupiter (Komatsu), 1982
Gor series (Norman), from 1966
Gordon, John series (Hamilton), from 1949
Gorgon (s Lee), 1985
Gorgon Child (S. Barnes), 1989
Gorgon Festival (Boyd), 1972
Gormenghast series (Peake), from 1946
Gormenghast series (s Peake), from 1976
Goslings (Beresford), 1913
Gosseyn, Gilbert series (van Vogt), from 1948
Grail of Hearts (Shwartz), 1992
Grain Kings (s Roberts), 1976
Gráinne (Roberts), 1987
Grand Adventure (s Farmer), 1984
Grand Illusion (Fearn, as Statten), 1953
Grand Jubilee (Elgin), 1981
Grand Wheel (Bayley), 1977
Grandon, Robert series (Kline), from 1929
Grandverger series (Sernine), from
Grass series (Tepper), from 1989
Grasshoppers and Wild Honey (s Lafferty), 1992
Grave (C. Grant), 1981
Graveyard Heart (s Zelazny), 1990
Graveyard of the Damned (s Fanthorpe), 1962
Gravity's Angels (s Swanwick), 1991
Gravity's Rainbow (Pynchon), 1973
Gray Lensman (E.E. Smith), 1951
Gray Magic (Norton), 1967
Gray, Maurice series (P. Moore), from 1955
Gray Prince (Vance), 1974
Graymantle (Morressy), 1981
Grayspace Beast (Eklund), 1976

Great 24-Hour Thing (Offutt), 1971
Great Alta series (Yolen), from 1988
Great Central Library series (Tiptree), from 1985
Great Divide (F. Robinson), 1982
Great Explosion (Russell), 1962
Great Fetish (de Camp), 1978
Great Fog (s Heard), 1944
Great Illusion (s Gallun), 1973
Great Illusion (s Hamilton, Williamson), 1973
Great Imperium series (L. Carter), from 1966
Great Pirate Syndicate (G. Griffith), 1899
Great Rock 'n' Roll Swindle (Moorcock), 1980
Great Sky River (Benford), 1987
Great Stone of Sardis (Stockton), 1898
Great Time Machine Hoax (Laumer), 1964
Great Wall of China (s Kafka), 1933
Great War Syndicate (Stockton), 1889
Great Weather Syndicate (G. Griffith), 1906
Great Works of Time (Crowley), 1991
Greatest Adventure (Taine), 1929
Greatheart Silver (Farmer), 1982
Greatwinter series (McMullen), from 1994
Green Brain (F. Herbert), 1966
Green Drift (Lymington), 1965
Green Eagle (Dent, as Robeson), 1968
Green Eyes (Shepard), 1984
Green Fire (Taine), 1928
Green Gene (Dickinson), 1973
Green Girl (Williamson), 1950
Green Hills of Earth (s Heinlein), 1951
Green Magic (s Vance), 1979
Green Man (Amis), 1969
Green Mars (K. Robinson), 1988
Green Millennium (Leiber), 1953
Green Odyssey (Farmer), 1957
Green Pearl (Vance), 1985
Green Planet series (Petaja), from 1967
Green Queen (St. Clair), 1956
Green Star series (L. Carter), from 1972
Greencomber (Tate), 1979
Greener Than You Think (W. Moore), 1947
Greenmagic (Kilian), 1992
Greenmantle (de Lint), 1988
Greenthieves (A. Foster), 1994
Greks Bring Gifts (Leinster), 1964
Gremlins 2 (Bischoff), 1990
Gremlins, Go Home! (Bova, Dickson), 1974
Grenfell and Wright series (P. Moore), from 1952
Grey Havens (Tolkien), 1990
Grey Horse (MacAvoy), 1987
Grey Ones (Lymington), 1960
Greybeard (Aldiss), 1964
Greylorn (s Laumer), 1968
Griffin's Egg (Swanwick), 1990
Grimes, John series (Chandler), from 1964
Grimm's World (V. Vinge), 1969
Grinny (Fisk), 1973
Grip of Fear (s Fanthorpe), 1961
Gripping Hand (Niven, Pournelle), 1993
Ground Zero Man (Shaw), 1971
Grounded (Bischoff), 1993

Group Feast (Saxton), 1971
Growing Up in Tier 3000 (Gotschalk), 1975
Growing Up Weightless (Ford), 1993
Grunts! A Fantasy with Attitude (Gentle), 1992
Gryb (s van Vogt), 1976
Gryphon (Kilian), 1989
Gryphon in Glory (Norton), 1981
Gryphon's Eyrie (Norton), 1984
Guardian (Monteleone), 1980
Guardian of Isis (M. Hughes), 1981
Guardians (Christopher), 1970
Guardians of the Gate (Trimble), 1972
Guardians of the Three series (Duane), from 1989
Guardians of the Tomb (s Fanthorpe, as Roberts), 1958
Guardians of the West (Eddings), 1987
Guardians of Time (s P. Anderson), 1960
Guards! Guards! (Pratchett), 1989
Guernica Night (Malzberg), 1974
Guided Tour (s Dickson), 1988
Gulliver of Mars (Arnold), 1964
Gummetch and Friends (s Leiber), 1992
Gun for Dinosaur (s de Camp), 1963
Gun, with Occasional Music (Lethem), 1994
Gunner Cade (Merril, Kornbluth, as Judd), 1952
Gunpowder God (Piper), 1978
Guns of Avalon (Zelazny), 1972
Guns of the South (Turtledove), 1992
Guts and Glory (Stine), 1991
Gutta-Percha Willie, The Working Genius (G. MacDonald), 1873
Guy from Hell (Strugatsky), 1976
Guys from Space (Pinkwater), 1989
Gwen, in Green (Z. Hughes, as Zachary), 1974
Gwilan's Harp (s Le Guin), 1981
Gypsies (Robert Charles Wilson), 1989
Gypsy series (Goulart), from 1977

Habit Is an Old Horse (s McCaffrey), 1986
Hacker and the Ants (Rucker), 1994
Hadon of Ancient Opar (Farmer), 1974
Hag's Tapestry (s Salmonson), 1984
Hail Hibbler (Goulart), 1980
Hain series (Le Guin), from 1966
Halcyon Drift (Stableford), 1972
Half a Sky (Lafferty), 1984
Half Past Human (Bass), 1971
Half the Day Is Night (McHugh), 1994
Halfblood Chronicles series (Norton), from 1991
Halflife (Webb), 1990
Halfling (s Brackett), 1973
Haljan series (Cummings), from 1931
Hall of the Mountain King (Tarr), 1986
Halloween Tree (Bradbury), 1972
Hamelin Plague (Chandler), 1963
Hammer (Drake, Stirling), 1992
Hammer and the Cross (H. Harrison), 1993
Hammer of God (Clarke), 1993
Hammer's Slammers series (Drake), from 1979
Hampdenshire Wonder (Beresford), 1911
Han Solo series (Daley), from 1979
Hand from Gehenna (s Fanthorpe, as Nobel), 1964
Hand of Doom (Fanthorpe), 1960

Hand of Ganz (Haiblum), 1985
Hand of Havoc (Tubb, as Grey), 1954
Hand of Oberon (Zelazny), 1976
Hand of Zei (de Camp), 1963
Handful of Darkness (s Dick), 1955
Handful of Men series (Dave Duncan), from 1992
Handful of Time (s R. Brown), 1963
Hands of Llyr (Norton), 1994
Hands of Orlac (Renard), 1929
Hanging Stones (Wellman), 1982
Hanlon, George series (Evans), from 1953
Haploids (Sohl), 1952
Happy Ending (s F. Brown), 1990
Hard Landing (Budrys), 1993
Hard Sell (s Anthony), 1990
Hard to Be a God (Strugatsky), 1973
Hard Way Up (s Chandler), 1972
Hard-Boiled Wonderland and the End of the World (Murakami),
   1991
Hardfought (Bear), 1988
Hardwired Angel (Dorsey), 1987
Hardwired series (W. Williams), from 1986
Harem of Aman Akbar (Scarborough), 1984
Harlan Ellison's Dream Corridor Special (s Ellison), 1995
Harm's Way (Greenland), 1993
Harmless Ghosts (s Salmonson), 1990
Harold Shea series (s Stasheff), from 1993
Harp of the Grey Rose (de Lint), 1985
Harper Hall of Pern (McCaffrey), 1984
Harpist in the Wind (McKillip), 1979
Harpy Thyme (Anthony), 1993
Harrowing of Gwynedd (Kurtz), 1989
Harry Challenge series (Goulart), from 1984
Hart's Hope (Card), 1983
Harvest (Robert Charles Wilson), 1993
Harvest of Stars (P. Anderson), 1993
Hasan (Anthony), 1979
Hashish-Eater (s Clark Ashton Smith), 1989
Hate Genius (Dent, as Robeson), 1979
Hatrack River (Card), 1988
Haunted (J. Herbert), 1988
Haunted and the Haunters (s Bulwer-Lytton), 1905
Haunted Earth (Koontz), 1973
Haunted House, and Calderon the Courtier (s Bulwer-Lytton), 1882
Haunted Pampero (s Hodgson), 1980
Haunted Pool (s Fanthorpe, as Thorpe), 1958
Haunted Stars (Hamilton), 1960
Haunted Woman (Lindsay), 1922
Haunter of the Dark (s Lovecraft), 1951
Haunting of Jessica Raven (G. Jones, as Halam), 1994
Hauser's Memory (Siodmak), 1968
Hautley Quicksilver series (L. Carter), from 1968
Have Space Suit—Will Travel (Heinlein), 1958
Have You Seen These? (s Asimov), 1974
Haven of Darkness (Tubb), 1977
Havengore series (Geston), from 1967
Hawk among the Sparrows (s McLaughlin), 1976
Hawk in Silver (Gentle), 1977
Hawk Queen series (Gemmell), from 1995
Hawkmistress! (Bradley), 1982
Hawkmoon (Moorcock), 1992

Hawksbill Station (Silverberg), 1968
Hawkshaw (Goulart), 1972
He Owned the World (Maine), 1960
He, She, and It (Piercy), 1991
He Who Shapes (s Zelazny), 1989
Heads (Bear), 1990
Heads of Cerberus (Stevens), 1952
Healer (Dickinson), 1983
Healer (F. Wilson), 1976
Healer (Meltzer), 1969
Healer's War (Scarborough), 1988
Heart of a Dog (Bulgakov), 1968
Heart of Red Iron (Gotlieb), 1989
Heart of Stone (s Lafferty), 1983
Heart of the Comet (Benford, Brin), 1986
Heart of the Serpent (s Yefremov), n.d.
Heart of the Tiger (Forstchen), 1995
Heart of the World (Haggard), 1895
Heart Readers (Rusch), 1993
Heart's Blood (Yolen), 1984
Heart-Beast (Lee), 1992
Heartbeeps (Koontz, as Hill), 1981
Heartfires (s de Lint), 1994
Hearts, Hands, and Voices (McDonald), 1992
Hearts of Three (London), 1918
Hearts of Wood (s Kotzwinkle), 1986
Heartsease (Dickinson), 1969
Heat Death of the Universe (s Zoline), 1988
Heathern (Womack), 1990
Heatseeker (s Shirley), 1989
Heaven Belt series (J. Vinge), from 1978
Heaven Chronicles (J. Vinge), 1991
Heaven Makers (F. Herbert), 1968
Heavenly Host (s Asimov), 1975
Heavy Time (Cherryh), 1991
Heavy Weather (Sterling), 1994
Hector Servadac (Verne), 1877
Hedgework and Guessery (s de Lint), 1991
Heechee series (Pohl), from 1977
Hefn series (Moffett), from 1991
Hegira (Bear), 1979
Heir of Sea and Fire (McKillip), 1978
Heir to the Empire (Zahn), 1991
Heirs of Babylon (Cook), 1972
Heirs of Hammerfell (Bradley), 1989
Heirs of Saint Camber series (Kurtz), from 1989
Heirs to the Warlock series (Stasheff), from 1993
Hell Fruit (Fearn, as Rose), 1953
Hell Has Wings (s Fanthorpe), 1962
Hell House (Matheson), 1971
Hell on Earth (Naha, as Drumm), 1986
Hell Planet (Tubb), 1954
Hell's Gate (Koontz), 1970
Hell's Pavement (Knight), 1955
Hellburner (Cherryh), 1992
Helle on Wheels (s Nolan), 1993
Heller's Leap (I. Wallace), 1979
Hellfire Rebellion (Hawke), 1990
Hellflower (George O. Smith), 1953
Hellhound Project (Goulart), 1975
Helliconia series (Aldiss), from 1982

Hello America (Ballard), 1981
Hello, Lemuria, Hello (Goulart), 1979
Hello Summer, Goodbye (Coney), 1975
Hellquad (Goulart), 1984
Hellspark (Kagan), 1988
Hellstar (Perry, Reaves), 1984
Hellstone (Spruill), 1980
Hellstrom's Hive (F. Herbert), 1973
Hemingway Hoax (Joe Haldeman), 1990
Her Majesty's Wizard (Stasheff), 1986
Her Smoke Rose up Forever (s Tiptree), 1990
Herbert West, the Reanimator (s Lovecraft), 1977
Hercules Text (McDevitt), 1986
Herds (Goldin), 1975
Here Abide Monsters (Norton), 1973
Here There Be Dragons (s Yolen), 1993
Here There Be Dragons (s Zelazny), 1992
Here There Be Unicorns (s Yolen), 1994
Hereafter Gang (Barrett), 1991
Heretics of Dune (F. Herbert), 1984
Heritage of Flight (Shwartz), 1989
Heritage of Hastur (Bradley), 1975
Heritage of Stars (Simak), 1977
Heritage of the Star (Engdahl), 1973
Heritage Universe series (Sheffield), from 1990
Herland (Gilman), 1979
Hermes 3000 (Kotzwinkle), 1972
Hermes Fall (Baxter), 1978
Hermetech (Constantine), 1991
Hero as Werwolf (s G. Wolfe), 1991
Hero Curse (Perry), 1991
Hero of Downways (Coney), 1973
Hero! (Dave Duncan), 1991
Heroes and Horrors (s Leiber), 1978
Heroes and Villains (A. Carter), 1969
Heroes in Hell series (Cherryh), from 1985
Heroes in Hell series (Drake), from 1989
Heroes in Hell series (J. Morris), from 1986
Heroics (Effinger), 1979
Heroine of the World (Lee), 1989
Heroines (s Kelly), 1990
Herold Childe series (Farmer), from 1968
Herovit's World (Malzberg), 1973
Herr Nightingale and the Satin Woman (Kotzwinkle), 1978
Hestia (Cherryh), 1979
Heu-Heu; or, The Monster (Haggard), 1924
Hex (Dent, as Robeson), 1969
Hex Witch of Seldom (Springer), 1989
Hexwood (Diana Wynne Jones), 1993
Hidden City (de Lint), 1990
Hidden City (Eddings), 1994
Hidden Ones (G. Jones), 1988
Hidden Place (Robert Charles Wilson), 1986
Hidden Side of the Moon (s Russ), 1987
Hidden Tribe (S. Wright), 1938
Hidden Universe (s Farley), 1950
Hidden Variables (s Sheffield), 1981
Hidden World (Coblentz), 1957
Hidden World (S. Gordon), 1988
Hidden Worlds of Zandra (Rotsler), 1983
Hide and Seek (Preuss), 1989

Hideaway (Koontz), 1992
Hierarchies (Rackham, as Phillifent), 1973
Hiero Desteen series (Lanier), from 1973
Hieros Gamos of Sam and An Smith (Saxton), 1969
High Crusade (P. Anderson), 1960
High Crystal (Caidin), 1974
High Deryni (Kurtz), 1973
High Hex (Janifer), 1969
High Justice (s Pournelle), 1977
High Moon (Duane), 1992
High-Rise (Ballard), 1975
High Sorcery (s Norton), 1970
High Spy (R. Coulson), 1987
High Steel (Dann, Jack C. Haldeman), 1993
High Tension (s Ing), 1982
High Vacuum (Maine), 1957
High Way Home (Fisk), 1973
High Wizardry (Duane), 1990
Highlander (Kilworth, as Douglas), 1986
Highway of Eternity (Simak), 1986
Highways in Hiding (George O. Smith), 1956
Highwood (Barrett), 1972
Hills Have Eyes, Part 2 (Garnett, as Ferring), 1984
His Level Best (s Hale), 1872
His Majesty's Elephant (Tarr), 1993
His Master's Voice (Lem), 1983
Histories of King Kelson series (Kurtz), from 1984
History of the Runestaff (Moorcock), 1979
Hitchhiker series (Adams), from 1979
Hive series (Bass), from 1971
Hobbit (Tolkien), 1937
Hocus Pocus (Vonnegut), 1990
Hogfoot Right and Bird-Hands (s Kilworth), 1993
Hoka series (P. Anderson), from 1975
Hoka! (s Anderson, Dickson), 1983
Holding Wonder (s Henderson), 1971
Hole in Space (s Niven), 1974
Hole in the Head (Fisk), 1991
Hole in the World (Lymington), 1974
Hole in the Zero (Joseph), 1967
Hollow Earth (Rucker), 1990
Hollow Land (s W. Morris), 1897
Hollow Lands (Moorcock), 1974
Hollowing (Holdstock), 1993
Holmes-Dracula File (Saberhagen), 1978
Holocaust for Hire (Goulart), 1979
Holocaust Horror (Bischoff), 1991
Holy Flower (Haggard), 1915
Holy Terror (Wells), 1939
Home by the Sea (s Cadigan), 1991
Home from the Shore (Dickson), 1978
Home Is the Hangman (s Zelazny), 1990
Home Is the Martian (Bulmer, as Kent), 1954
Home Sweet Home: 2010 A.D (Ing, Reynolds), 1984
Homebrew (s P. Anderson), 1976
Homecoming (Longyear), 1989
Homecoming series (Card), from 1992
Homefaring (s Silverberg), 1983
Homegoing (Pohl), 1989
Homesmind (Sargent), 1984
Homeward and Beyond (s P. Anderson), 1975

I Want the Stars (Purdom), 1964
I Was a Class 2 Werewolf (Pinkwater), 1992
I Was a Second Grade Werewolf (Pinkwater), 1983
I Will Fear No Evil (Heinlein), 1970
I, Zombie (Piserchia, as Selby), 1982
I.Q. Merchant (Boyd), 1972
I--Alien (Reaves), 1978
Icarus Descending (Hand), 1993
Ice (Kavan), 1967
Ice and Iron (Tucker), 1974
Ice Crown (Norton), 1970
Ice Desert (Verne), 1937
Ice Monkey (s M. Harrison), 1983
Ice People (Barjavel), 1970
Ice Prophet series (Forstchen), from 1983
Ice Schooner (Moorcock), 1969
Iceborn (s Benford), 1989
Icehenge (K. Robinson), 1984
Iceman (Felice), 1991
Icequake series (Kilian), from 1979
Icerigger (A. Foster), 1974
Iceworld (Clement), 1953
Iceworld Connection (Offutt, as Cleve), 1983
Identifying the Object (s G. Jones), 1993
Identity Matrix (Chalker), 1982
Identity Plunderers (Haiblum), 1984
Idle Pleasures (s Effinger), 1983
Iduna's Universe (Tubb), 1979
If All Else Fails . . . (s Strete), 1980
If at Faust You Don't Succeed (Sheckley, Zelazny), 1993
If I Pay Thee Not in Gold (Anthony), 1993
If I Were Dictator (Dunsany), 1934
If the Stars Are Gods (Benford, Eklund), 1977
If This Is Winnetka, You Must Be Judy (s Busby), 1992
Igniting the Reaches (Drake), 1994
Ill Fate Marshalling (Cook), 1988
Ill Met in Lankhmar (s Leiber), 1990
Ill Wind (K. Anderson), 1995
Illearth War (Donaldson), 1977
Illegal Rebirth of Billy the Kid (Ore), 1991
Illuminatus series (Robert Anton Wilson), from 1975
Illustrated Man (s Bradbury), 1951
Image of the Beast (Farmer), 1968
Image of Voices (Norwood), 1982
Imaginary Magnitude (s Lem), 1984
Imago (O. Butler), 1989
Immigrant (s Simak), 1991
Immortal (Gunn), 1970
Immortal of World's End (L. Carter), 1976
Immortality Delivered (Sheckley), 1958
Immortality Inc. (Sheckley), 1959
Immortality Option (Hogan), 1993
Immortals (Barjavel), 1974
Immortals (Fanthorpe, as Brett), 1962
Immortals (Farley), 1946
Immortals (Gunn), 1962
Immortals of Mercury (s Clark Ashton Smith), 1932
Impact-20 (s Nolan), 1963
Imperator Plot (Spruill), 1983
Imperial Earth (Clarke), 1975
Imperial Lady (Norton, Shwartz), 1989

Imperial Stars (Goldin, E.E. Smith), 1976
Imperium series (Laumer), from 1965
Implosion (D.F. Jones), 1967
Impossible Man (s Ballard), 1966
Impossible Things (s Willis), 1994
Impossible World (Binder), 1970
Impossible? (s Janifer), 1968
Impossibles (Garrett, Janifer, as Phillips), 1963
In a Dark Dream (C. Grant), 1989
In Alien Flesh (s Benford), 1986
In and Out of Quandary (s Hoffman), 1982
In Another Country (s Silverberg), 1990
In Caverns Below (Coblentz), 1975
In Darkness Waiting (Shirley), 1988
In Deep (s Knight), 1963
In Iron Years (s Dickson), 1980
In Mask and Motley (s de Lint), 1983
In Other Worlds (Attanasio), 1984
In Our Hands, The Stars (H. Harrison), 1970
In Quest of Qulara (Offutt, as Cleve), 1983
In Solitary (Kilworth), 1977
In the 4th Dimension (Cummings), 1981
In the Beginning (Christopher), 1972
In the Beginning (s Leiber), 1983
In the Bone (s Dickson), 1987
In the Caves of Exile (Emerson), 1988
In the Country of Tattooed Men (s Kilworth), 1993
In the Days of the Comet (Wells), 1906
In the Drift (Swanwick), 1985
In the Empire of Shadow (Watt-Evans), 1995
In the Enclosure (Malzberg), 1973
In the Face of My Enemy (Delaney), 1985
In the Footsteps of the Abominable Snowman (s Nesvadba), 1970
In the Garden (s Greenland), 1991
In the Green Star's Glow (L. Carter), 1976
In the Hall of the Martian Kings (s Varley), 1978
In the Hands of Glory (Eisenstein), 1981
In the Hollow of the Deep-Sea Wave (s Kilworth), 1989
In the Kingdom of the Beasts (Stableford), 1971
In the Land of the Dead (Jeter), 1989
In the Light of Sigma Draconis (Arnason), 1992
In the Mothers' Land (Vonarburg), 1992
In the Ocean of Night (Benford), 1977
In the Penal Settlement (s Kafka), 1949
In the Pocket (s Malzberg, as O'Donnell), 1971
In the Problem Pit (s Pohl), 1976
In the Red Lord's Reach (Eisenstein), 1989
In the Steps of the Master (Bradley), 1973
In the Valley of the Statues (s Holdstock), 1982
In the Wet (Shute), 1953
In Viriconium (M. Harrison), 1982
In-World (Fanthorpe, as Roberts), 1960
Inadequate Adept (Hawke), 1993
Incandescent Ones (F. and G. Hoyle), 1977
Incarnations of Immortality series (Anthony), from 1985
Incident on Ath (Tubb), 1978
Incomplete Enchanter (de Camp), 1941
Inconstant Moon (s Niven), 1973
Incorporated Knight series (de Camp), from 1987
Incredible Planet (Campbell), 1949
Incredible Shrinking Man (Matheson), 1988

Incredible Tide (Key), 1970
Incredulist (s Fanthorpe, as Roberts), 1954
Incubated Girl (Jefferies), 1896
Indiana Jones and the Temple of Doom (Kahn), 1984
Indiana Jones series (Caidin), from 1993
Indoctrinaire (Priest), 1970
Infernal Desire Machines of Dr. Hoffman (A. Carter), 1972
Infernal Devices (Jeter), 1987
Inferno (F. and G. Hoyle), 1973
Inferno (Fearn, as Statten), 1950
Inferno (Niven, Pournelle), 1976
Inferno (Resnick), 1993
Infinite Battle (Bischoff), 1985
Infinite Cage (Laumer), 1972
Infinite Dreams (s Joe Haldeman), 1978
Infinite Man (Galouye), 1973
Infinite Moment (s Wyndham), 1961
Infinite Summer (s Priest), 1979
Infinite Worlds of Maybe (del Rey and Fairman, as del Rey), 1966
Infinitive of Go (Brunner), 1980
Infinity Box (s Wilhelm), 1975
Infinity Concerto (Bear), 1984
Infinity Gambit (Hogan), 1991
Infinity Hold (Longyear), 1989
Infinity Link (Carver), 1984
Infinity Machine (Fanthorpe, as Muller), 1962
Informal Biography of Scrooge McDuck (s Chalker), 1974
Inherit the Stars (Hogan), 1977
Inheritor (Bradley), 1984
Inheritors (Chandler), 1978
Inheritors (Golding), 1955
Inheritors of Earth (Anderson, Eklund), 1974
Inland series (G. Jones), from 1987
Inn of the Hairy Toad (s Resnick), 1985
Inner Cosmos (Fearn, as Statten), 1952
Inner Wheel (Roberts), 1970
Innervisions (Gribbin), 1993
Innsmouth Heritage (s Stableford), 1992
Inquestor series (Sucharitkul), from 1982
Inquisitor (Watson), 1990
Insane City (Bulmer), 1971
Insatiability (Witkiewicz), 1977
Insect Invasion (Cummings), 1967
Inside Outside (Farmer), 1964
Instrumentality series (Cordwainer Smith), from 1963
Intangibles Inc. (s Aldiss), 1969
Integral Trees (Niven), 1984
Intelligence Gigantic (Fearn), 1943
Inter Ice Age Four (Abé), 1970
Interesting Times (Pratchett), 1994
Interface (Adlard), 1971
Interface (N. Stephenson, as Bury), 1994
Interloper (Fearn, as Statten), 1953
Intermind (Sellings, as Luther), 1967
Interpreter (Aldiss), 1961
Interpreter (s J. White), 1985
Interstellar Empire series (Brunner), from 1976
Interstellar Patrol series (Hamilton), from 1964
Interstellar Two-Five (Mason, as Rankine), 1966
Intervention (May), 1987
Interworld (Haiblum), 1977

Into Deepest Space (F. and G. Hoyle), 1974
Into Plutonian Depths (Coblentz), 1950
Into the Aether (Lupoff), 1974
Into the Alternate Universe (Chandler), 1964
Into the Eighth Decade (s Williamson), 1990
Into the Green (de Lint), 1993
Into the Nebula (DeWeese), 1995
Into the Out Of (A. Foster), 1986
Into the Sea of Stars (Forstchen), 1986
Into the Slave Nebula (Brunner), 1968
Into the Tenth Millennium (Capon), 1956
Into the Twilight Zone (s Serling), 1976
Intrepid Enchanter (de Camp), 1979
Intruder (Thurston), 1990
Intruders (Fanthorpe, as Fane), 1963
Intuit (s Clement), 1987
Invader (Cherryh), 1995
Invader from Space (P. Moore), 1963
Invader on My Back (High), 1968
Invaders (s Laumer), 1967
Invaders Are Coming! (Nourse), 1959
Invaders from Earth (Silverberg), 1958
Invaders from Rigel (Pratt), 1960
Invaders from the Centre (Stableford), 1990
Invaders from the Infinite (Campbell), 1961
Invaders of Space (Leinster), 1964
Invaders on the Moon (Neville), 1970
Invaders series (Laumer), from 1967
Invaders! (s Dickson), 1985
Invading Asteroid (Wellman), 1932
Invasion (Koontz, as Wolfe), 1975
Invasion from 2500 (T. Carr and T. White, as Edwards), 1964
Invasion of Mars (Serviss), 1969
Invasion of the Body Snatchers (Finney), 1973
Invasion: Earth (H. Harrison), 1982
Inverted World (Priest), 1974
Investigation (Lem), 1974
Invincible (Lem), 1973
Invincible Barriers (Silverberg, as Osborne), 1958
Invisibility Affair (DeWeese and R. Coulson, as Thomas Stratton), 1967
Invisible Cities (Calvino), 1974
Invisible Death (L. Carter), 1975
Invisible Man (Wells), 1897
Invitation to the Game (M. Hughes), 1990
Involuntary Immortals (Phillips), 1959
Involution Ocean (Sterling), 1977
Ion War (Kapp), 1978
Ipomoea (Rackham), 1969
Ireta series (McCaffrey), from 1978
Iron Angel series (Morressy), from 1980
Iron Cage (Norton), 1974
Iron Dragon's Daughter (Swanwick), 1993
Iron Dream (Spinrad), 1972
Iron Heel (London), 1907
Iron Lion (Dickinson), 1972
Iron Lords (Offutt), 1979
Iron Man (Rotsler), 1979
Iron Master (Tilley), 1987
Iron Skull (Goulart, as Robeson), 1975
Iron Star (Taine), 1930

Iron Tears (s Lafferty), 1992
Iron Thorn (Budrys), 1968
Ironbrand (Morressy), 1980
Ironhand's Daughter (Gemmell), 1995
Irrational Numbers (s Effinger), 1976
Is THAT What People Do? (s Sheckley), 1984
Isaac Asimov's Caliban (Allen), 1993
Isaac Asimov's Inferno (Allen), 1994
Isaac Asmiov's Robot City (Cover), 1988
Isis series (M. Hughes), from 1980
Island (Huxley), 1962
Island Called Moreau (Aldiss), 1981
Island Earth (R. Jones), 1952
Island in the Lake (Mayhar), 1993
Island in the Sky (Wellman), 1961
Island of Captain Sparrow (S. Wright), 1928
Island of Doctor Death (s G. Wolfe), 1980
Island of Doctor Moreau (Wells), 1896
Island of Dr. Moreau (Goulart, as Silva), 1977
Island of Fear (P. Moore), 1954
Island People (Coblentz), 1971
Island Snatchers (George H. Smith), 1978
Island under the Earth (Davidson), 1969
Islandia (A. Wright), 1942
Islands (Randall), 1976
Islands in the Net (Sterling), 1988
Islands in the Sky (Clarke), 1952
Islands of Space (Campbell), 1956
Islands of Tomorrow (Busby), 1994
Isle of Glass (Tarr), 1985
Isle of Lies (Shiel), 1909
Isle of the Dead (Zelazny), 1969
Isle of View (Anthony), 1990
Isle of Women (Anthony), 1993
Isotope Man (Maine), 1957
It (s Sturgeon), 1948
It Came from Outer Space (s May, as Thorpe), 1982
It Came from Schenectady (s Longyear), 1984
It Was the Day of the Robot (Long), 1963
It's a Mad, Mad, Mad Galaxy (s Laumer), 1968
It's All in Your Mind (Bloch), 1971
Ivanhoe Gambit (Hawke), 1984
Ivory (Resnick), 1988
Ivory and the Horn (s de Lint), 1995
Ivory Child (Haggard), 1916
Ivory Valley (Hyne), 1938

Jack-in-the-Box Planet (Hoskins), 1978
Jack of Eagles (Blish), 1952
Jack of Shadows (Zelazny), 1971
Jack of Swords (Tubb), 1976
Jack series (de Lint), from 1987
Jack the Bodiless (May), 1992
Jackals (C. Grant), 1994
Jacket (The Star Rover), 1915
Jade Man's Eyes (s Moorcock), 1973
Jagged Orbit (Brunner), 1969
Jagger, The Dog from Elsewhere (Key), 1976
Jaguar Hunter (s Shepard), 1987
Jake Murchison series (s Cartmill), from 1975
James P. Hogan's Entoverse (Hogan), 1991

James P. Hogan's The Giants Novels (Hogan), 1991
Jamie (s Bradley), 1993
Jamie the Red (Dickson), 1984
Jan in India (Kline), 1974
Jan series (Kline), from 1966
Jandar of Callisto (L. Carter), 1972
Janissaries series (Pournelle), from 1979
Janus Syndrome (Mason), 1969
Japan Sinks (Komatsu), 1976
Japan Tomorrow (s Watson), 1975
Jargoon Pard (Norton), 1974
Jaws That Bite, The Claws That Catch (Coney), 1975
Jedi Academy Trilogy (P. Anderson), from 1994
Jehad (Hawke, as Yermakov), 1984
Jekyll Legacy (Norton), 1990
JEM (Pohl), 1979
Jenny Villiers (Priestley), 1947
Jeremy Case (DeWeese), 1976
Jericho 52 (Caidin), 1979
Jerusalem Commands (Moorcock), 1992
Jerusalem Fire (Meluch), 1985
Jerusalem Man (Gemmell), 1988
Jester at Scar (Tubb), 1970
Jesus Incident (F. Herbert), 1979
Jesus on Mars (Farmer), 1979
Jet Morgan series (Chilton), from 1954
Jewel in the Skull (Moorcock), 1967
Jewel of Arwen (s Bradley), 1974
Jewel of Bas (Brackett), 1990
Jewel of Jarhen (Tubb, as Kern), 1974
Jewel of the Moon (s Kotzwinkle), 1985
Jewels of Aptor (Delany), 1962
Jewels of Elsewhen (T. White), 1967
Jinian series (Tepper), from 1985
Jinx on a Terran Inheritance (Daley), 1985
Jirel of Joiry (s C.L. Moore), 1969
Jitterbug (McQuay), 1984
Jizzle (s Wyndham), 1954
Job (Heinlein), 1984
Jodinareh (Offutt, as Cleve), 1970
Joe Mauser (Reynolds), 1986
John Carstairs, Space Detective (s Long), 1949
John Carter of Mars (s E. Burroughs), 1940
John Collier and Fredric Brown Went Quarrelling through My Head
     (s Salmonson), 1989
John E. Muller
John Gayther's Garden (s Stockton), 1902
John the Balladeer (s Wellman), 1988
Johnny and the Dead (Pratchett), 1993
Johnny Mnemonic (Bisson), 1995
Jolson, Ben series (Goulart), from 1968
Jonah (J. Herbert), 1981
Jonah Kit (Watson), 1975
Jondelle (Tubb), 1973
Jongor series (R. Williams), from 1970
Jonuta Rising! (Offutt, as Cleve), 1983
Jorian series (de Camp), from 1968
Jorkens series (s Dunsany), from 1931
Journal of Nicholas the American (Kennedy), 1986
Journey (Randall), 1978
Journey between Worlds (Engdahl), 1970

Journey beyond Tomorrow (Sheckley), 1962
Journey from Flesh (Hawke, as Yermakov), 1981
Journey into Darkness (Long), 1967
Journey into Space (Chilton), 1954
Journey into Terror (Effinger), 1975
Journey into the Interior of the Earth (Verne), 1975
Journey of Joenes (Sheckley), 1978
Journey through the Empty (Hoover), 1990
Journey to Mars (Tubb), 1954
Journey to Membliar (Baker), 1987
Journey to the Center (Stableford), 1982
Journey to the Centre of the Earth (Verne), 1872
Journey to the Goat Star (s Aldiss), 1991
Journey to the North Pole (Verne), 1875
Journey to the Underground World (L. Carter), 1979
Jovial Ghosts: The Misadventures of Topper (T. Smith), 1933
Joy in Our Cause (s Emshwiller), 1974
Joy Makers (Gunn), 1961
Joyleg (Davidson, W. Moore), 1962
Joyous Invasions (s Sturgeon), 1965
Judas Cross (Sheffield), 1994
Judas Mandala (Broderick), 1982
Judas Rose (Elgin), 1987
Judges of Hades (s Hoch), 1971
Judgment Day (Stine), 1992
Judgment Night (s C.L. Moore), 1952
Judgment of Dragons (Gotlieb), 1980
Judgment of Eve (Pangborn), 1966
Judgment on Janus (Norton), 1963
Judson's Eden (Laumer), 1991
Juggernaut (Fanthorpe, as Fane), 1960
Julia and the Bazooka (s Kavan), 1970
Junction (Dann), 1981
Jungle (s Drake), 1991
Jungle Girl (E. Burroughs), 1932
Jungle of Stars (Chalker), 1976
Juniper Time (Wilhelm), 1979
Junk Day (Sellings), 1970
Junkyard Planet (Piper), 1963
Jupiter Equilateral (Rackham), 1954
Jupiter Laughs (s Cooper), 1979
Jupiter Legacy (H. Harrison), 1970
Jupiter Project (Benford), 1975
Jurassic Park series (Crichton), from 1990
Justice (Drake), 1992
Justice, and The Rat (s S. Wright), 1945
Justice City (Compton), 1994
Justice of Revenge (G. Griffith), 1901
Juxtaposition (Anthony), 1982

Kaeti series (s Roberts), from 1986
Kaheesh (Sohl, as Butler), 1983
Kairos (G. Jones), 1988
Kaleidoscope (s Turtledove), 1990
Kaleidoscope Century (J. Barnes), 1995
Kalevala series (Petaja), from 1966
Kalimantan (s Shepard), 1990
Kalin (Tubb), 1969
Kallocain (Boye), 1966
Kampus (Gunn), 1977
Kamus series (Shirley), from 1988

Kandar (Bulmer), 1969
Kane and Pendrake series (Spruill), from 1978
Kane, Michael series (Moorcock), from 1981
Kar-Chee Reign (Davidson), 1966
Kar Kaballa (George H. Smith), 1969
Karma Corps (Barrett), 1984
Karns, Joe series (DeWeese, R. Coulson), from 1975
Kedrigern series (Morressy), from 1986
Keep Off the Grass (England), 1919
Keep the Giraffe Burning (s Sladek), 1977
Keeper of the City (Duane), 1989
Keeper of the Isis Light (M. Hughes), 1980
Keepers of the Gate (Spruill), 1977
Keepers of the Secrets (Farmer), 1983
Kellory the Warlock (L. Carter), 1984
Kelly Country (Chandler), 1983
Kelly series (Drake), from 1983
Kelwin (Barrett), 1970
Kenmore, Joe series (Leinster), from 1953
Kennedy, Cap series (Tubb), from 1973
Kent Montana series (C. Grant), from 1988
Kerrion Empire series (J. Morris), from 1980
Kesrick (L. Carter), 1982
Key of the Keplian (Norton), 1995
Key out of Time (Norton), 1963
Key to Irunium (Bulmer), 1967
Key to Midnight (Koontz, as Nichols), 1979
Key to Venudine (Bulmer), 1968
Keys to the Dimensions series (Bulmer), from 1967
Khadaji series (Perry), from 1985
Khadaji series (Reaves), from 1988
Khan's Persuasion (Felice), 1991
Khi to Freedom (Mayhar), 1983
Khyber Connection (Hawke), 1986
Kid from Ozone Park (s Richard Wilson), 1987
Kif Strike Back (Cherryh), 1985
Kill Ratio (Drake, J. Morris), 1987
Kill Station (Duane), 1992
Kill the Dead (Lee), 1980
Kill the Editor (S. Robinson), 1991
Killashandra series (McCaffrey), from 1982
Killbird (Z. Hughes), 1980
Killer (Drake), 1985
Killer Comet (P. Moore), 1978
Killer Mice (s K. Reed), 1976
Killer Pine (Gutteridge), 1973
Killer Planet (Shaw), 1989
Killer Station (Caidin), 1984
Killer Thing (Wilhelm), 1967
Killer to Come (Merwin), 1953
Killerbowl (Wolf), 1975
Killing Joke (A. Moore), n.d.
Killing Machine (Vance), 1964
Killing Star (Zebrowski), 1995
Killing Thing (Wilhelm), 1967
Killobyte (Anthony), 1993
Kindly Ones (Scott), 1987
Kindred (O. Butler), 1979
King (Norman), 1993
King and Joker (Dickinson), 1976
King beyond the Gate (Gemmell), 1985

King David's Spaceship (Pournelle), 1980
King Death's Garden (G. Jones, as Halam), 1986
King Dragon (Offutt), 1980
King Javan's Year (Kurtz), 1992
King Kobold (Stasheff), 1971
King Kobold Revived (Stasheff), 1984
King Kong (s May, as Thorpe), 1977
King Kull (s L. Carter), 1967
King Maker (Dent, as Robeson), 1975
King of Argent (Rackham, as Phillifent), 1973
King of Elfland's Daughter (Dunsany), 1924
King of Eolim (R. Jones), 1975
King of Morning, Queen of Day (s McDonald), 1991
King of Satan's Eyes (C. Grant, as Marsh), 1984
King of Terrors (s Bloch), 1977
King of the Dead (Aubrey), 1903
King of the Dead (MacAvoy), 1991
King of the Fourth Planet (R. Williams), 1962
King of the Hill (s McAuley), 1991
King of the Murgos (Eddings), 1988
King of the Scepter'd Isle (Coney), 1989
King of the Slavers (Offutt, as Cleve), 1985
King of the Stars (Kelley), 1979
King of the Swords (Moorcock), 1971
King of Ys series (P. Anderson), from 1988
King Solomon's Mines (Haggard), 1885
King Victor series (Dickinson), from 1976
King's Blood Four (Tepper), 1983
King's Buccaneer (Feist), 1992
King's Justice (Kurtz), 1985
King's Oak (s Cromie), 1897
Kingdom Come (Shirley, as Drum), 1984
Kingdom of Kevin Malone (Charnas), 1993
Kingdom of the Cats (Gotlieb), 1985
Kingdom of the Grail (Attanasio), 1992
Kingdoms of the Wall (Silverberg), 1992
Kings in Hell (Cherryh, J. Morris), 1987
Kingsbane (Morressy), 1982
Kingslayer (Hubbard), 1949
Kinship with the Stars (s P. Anderson), 1991
Kinsman series (Bova), from 1976
Kirinyaga (s Resnick), 1992
Kirlian Quest (Anthony), 1978
Kiteworld (Roberts), 1985
Kittatinny (Russ), 1978
Kleinzeit (Hoban), 1974
Klekton series (Jakes), from 1970
Knave, Gerald series (Janifer), from 1979
Knave of Dreams (Norton), 1975
Knight and Knave of Swords (s Leiber), 1988
Knight Flandry (P. Anderson), 1980
Knight Moves (W. Williams), 1985
Knight of Ghosts and Shadows (P. Anderson), 1974
Knight of Shadows (Zelazny), 1989
Knight of the Swords (Moorcock), 1971
Knights of Dark Renown (Gemmell), 1989
Knights of the Limits (s Bayley), 1978
Known Space series (Niven), from 1966
Konrad (Garnett, as Ferring), 1990
Kothar series (Fox), from 1969
Krakatit (Capek), 1924

Kraken Wakes (Wyndham), 1953
Kranton series (J. Coulson), from 1978
Kreativity for Kats (s Leiber), 1990
Kren series (Lichtenberg), from 1982
Krispos series (Turtledove), from 1991
Kronk (Cooper), 1971
Krono (Harness), 1988
Kroy series (s Le Guin), from 1982
Krozair of Kregen (Bulmer, as Akers), 1977
Krull (A. Foster), 1983
Kuldesak (Cowper), 1972
Kundalini Equation (S. Barnes), 1986
Kyerol series (McKillip), from 1984
Kylix series (L. Carter), from 1971
Kyrannon series (Mayhar), from 1980
Kyrik series (Fox), from 1975
Kyyra series (Schmidt), from 1976

La Quête de la Sainte Grille (Young), 1975
Labyrinth of Dreams (Chalker), 1987
Lacey and His Friends (s Drake), 1986
Ladder in the Sky (Brunner), 1962
Ladies from Hell (s Roberts), 1979
Ladies' Day; and, This Crowded Earth (Bloch), 1968
Lady and the Merman (s Yolen), 1979
Lady and the Tiger (s Stockton), 1992
Lady Decides (Keller), 1950
Lady from L.U.S.T. series (Fox), from 1969
Lady in Danger (s Williamson), 1945
Lady of Blossholme (Haggard), 1909
Lady of Han-Gilen (Tarr), 1987
Lady of the Heavens (Haggard), 1908
Lady of the Snowmist (Offutt), 1983
Lady of the Trillium (Bradley), 1995
Lady Sally's House series (S. Robinson), from 1991
Lady Slings the Booze (S. Robinson), 1992
Ladyhawke (J. Vinge), 1985
Lafferty in Orbit (s Lafferty), 1991
Lagrangia series (Reynolds), from 1979
Laid in the Future (Fox), 1970
Lair (J. Herbert), 1979
Lake of Gold (G. Griffith), 1903
Lake of the Long Sun (G. Wolfe), 1994
Lake of the Sun (Whiteford), 1989
Lallia (Tubb), 1971
Lamp for Medusa (Tenn), 1968
LaNague Federation series (F. Wilson), from 1976
LaNague series (s F. Wilson), from 1989
Land and Overland series (Shaw), from 1986
Land beyond the Gate (Eshbach), 1984
Land Beyond the Map (Bulmer), 1965
Land Fit for Heroes series (Mann), from 1993
Land Leviathan (Moorcock), 1974
Land of Always-Night (Dent, as Robeson), 1966
Land of Dreams (Blaylock), 1987
Land of Fear (Dent, as Robeson), 1973
Land of Hidden Men (E. Burroughs), 1963
Land of Mist (Doyle), 1925
Land of Terror (Dent, as Robeson), 1933
Land of Terror (E. Burroughs), 1944
Land of the Giants series (Leinster), from 1968

Land of Unreason (de Camp), 1942
Land That Time Forgot (s E. Burroughs), 1924
Land under England (O'Neill), 1935
Land's End (Pohl, Williamson), 1988
Landfall Is a State of Mind (Mason), 1968
Landscape with Landscape (s Murnane), 1985
Languages of Pao (Vance), 1958
Lani People (Bone), 1962
Lankar of Callisto (L. Carter), 1975
Larger than Life (Buzzati), 1962
Lark in the Morning (s de Lint), 1987
Larque on the Wing (Springer), 1994
Last Alien (C. Grant, as Charles), 1987
Last Amazon (Chandler), 1984
Last and First Men (Stapledon), 1930
Last Arabian Night (Gardner), 1993
Last Astronaut (Fanthorpe, as Torro), 1963
Last Battle (Lewis), 1956
Last Book of Wonder (s Dunsany), 1916
Last Call (Powers), 1992
Last Call of Mourning (C. Grant), 1979
Last Castle (Vance), 1967
Last Coin (Blaylock), 1988
Last Command (Zahn), 1993
Last Communion series (Hawke, as Yermakov), from 1981
Last Continent (Cooper), 1969
Last Day of Creation (Jeschke), 1982
Last Days of the Edge of the World (Stableford), 1978
Last Deathship off Antares (Watkins), 1989
Last Defender of Camelot (s Zelazny), 1980
Last Dream (s Dickson), 1986
Last Fathom (Caidin), 1967
Last Gasp (T. Hoyle), 1983
Last Guardian (Gemmell), 1989
Last Hurrah of the Golden Horde (s Spinrad), 1970
Last Leap (s Galouye), 1964
Last Legends of Earth (Attanasio), 1989
Last Magician (s Keller), 1978
Last Magicians (Jakes), 1969
Last Man (Shelley), 1826
Last Man on Earth (Fanthorpe, as Fane), 1960
Last Martian (Fearn, as Statten), 1952
Last Master (Dickson), 1984
Last Men in London (Stapledon), 1932
Last Miracle (Shiel), 1906
Last of the Country House Murders (Tennant), 1974
Last of the Great Race (Coblentz), 1964
Last Orders (s Aldiss), 1977
Last Planet (Norton), 1955
Last President (Kurland), 1980
Last Refuge (Scarborough), 1992
Last Revolution (Dunsany), 1951
Last Shuttle to Planet Earth (Mason, as Rankine), 1980
Last Space Ship (Leinster), 1949
Last Stand of the DNA Cowboys (Farren), 1989
Last Starfighter (A. Foster), 1984
Last Starship from Earth (Boyd), 1968
Last Sword of Power (Gemmell), 1988
Last Transaction (Malzberg), 1977
Last Valkyrie (Fanthorpe, as Roberts), 1961
Last Yggdrasill (Young), 1982

Late Knight Edition (s Knight), 1985
Lathe of Heaven (Le Guin), 1971
Latro series (G. Wolfe), from 1986
Laughter in Space (Fearn, as Statten), 1952
Laughter in the Leaves (s de Lint), 1984
Laughter of a Ghoul (s Bloch), 1977
Lava (O'Donnell), 1982
Lavalite World (Farmer), 1977
Lavender-Green Magic (Norton), 1974
Lavondyss (Holdstock), 1988
Law for the Stars (Morressy), 1976
Laxham Haunting (Lymington), 1976
Lazarus Effect (F. Herbert), 1983
Le Pays d'esprit (s Young), 1982
Leaves of Time (Barrett), 1971
Leese Webster (Le Guin), 1979
Leeshore (R. Reed), 1987
Left Hand of Darkness (Le Guin), 1969
Left to His Own Devices (s Gentle), 1994
Legacy (Bear), 1995
Legacy (Bone), 1976
Legacy (Schmitz), 1979
Legacy of Earth (J. Coulson), 1989
Legacy of Heorot (S. Barnes, Niven, Pournelle), 1987
Legacy of Lehr (Kurtz), 1986
Legacy of the Stars (Hoskins, as Gregory), 1979
Legend (Gemmell), 1984
Legend of Ethshar series (Watt-Evans), from 1985
Legend of Miaree (Z. Hughes), 1974
Legends from the End of Time (s Moorcock), 1976
Legends of Saint Camber series (Kurtz), from 1976
Legends of the Jade Phoenix series (Thurston), from 1995
Legion (C. Grant), 1979
Legion of Space series (Williamson), from 1947
Legion of the Lost (Fanthorpe, as Torro), 1962
Legion of the Super-Heroes (s Hamilton), 1992
Legion of Time (Williamson), 1952
Legion of Videssos (Turtledove), 1987
Legions of Antares (Bulmer, as Akers), 1981
Legions of Hell (Cherryh), 1987
Legrange League series (Watkins), from 1985
Leiber Chronicles (s Leiber), 1990
Lens of the World (MacAvoy), 1990
Lensman series (E.E. Smith), from 1948
Leopard's Daughter (Killough), 1987
Leopard's Tooth (Kotzwinkle), 1976
Lepidus the Centurion (Arnold), 1901
Ler series (M.A. Foster), from 1975
Less Than Human (Platt, as Clarke), 1986
Lest Darkness Fall (de Camp), 1941
Lest Earth Be Conquered (Long), 1966
Lest We Forget Thee, Earth (Silverberg, as Knox), 1958
Let the Fire Fall (Wilhelm), 1969
Let the Spacemen Beware! (P. Anderson), 1963
Letters from Atlantis (Silverberg), 1990
Letters from Home (s Cadigan, Fowler, Murphy), 1991
Leviathan (Robert Anton Wilson), 1975
Leviathan's Deep (J. Carr), 1979
Liar! (s Asimov), 1977
Liar's Dice (Naha, as McGann), 1990
Liberty's World (Killough), 1985

Lie Destroyer (Fearn, as Statten), 1953
Lies, Inc. (Dick), 1984
Lieut. Gullivar Jones (Arnold), 1905
Life during Wartime (Shepard), 1987
Life Everlasting (s Keller), 1947
Life for Kregen (Bulmer, as Akers), 1979
Life for the Stars (Blish), 1962
Life Force (C. Wilson), 1985
Life Force (Z. Hughes), 1988
Life in Interstellar Environment (s Tsiolkovsky), n.d.
Life in the Day of . . . (s F. Robinson), 1981
Life, The Universe, and Everything (Adams), 1982
Life with Lancelot (s Rackham, as Phillifent), 1973
Life-Form (A. Foster), 1995
Lifeboat (Dickson), 1978
Lifeboat (H. Harrison), 1977
Lifeboat (J. White), 1972
Lifeboat Earth (Schmidt), 1978
Lifeburst (Williamson), 1984
Lifekeeper (McQuay), 1980
Lifeline (K. Anderson), 1990
Lifeship (Dickson, H. Harrison), 1976
Lifter (Kilian), 1986
Light a Last Candle (King), 1969
Light at the End of the Universe (s T. Carr), 1976
Light Benders (Lymington, as Chance), 1968
Light Fantastic (Pratchett), 1986
Light Fantastic (s Bester), 1976
Light from a Lone Star (s Vance), 1985
Light on the Sound (Sucharitkul), 1982
Light Princess (G. MacDonald), 1961
Light Raid (Felice, Willis), 1989
Light That Never Was (Biggle), 1972
Lightning (Koontz), 1988
Lightning World (Fanthorpe, as Thorpe), 1960
Lights in the Sky Are Stars (F. Brown), 1953
Like Nothing on Earth (s Russell), 1975
Lilith (G. MacDonald), 1895
Lilith: A Snake in the Grass (Chalker), 1981
Lilliput Legion (Hawke), 1989
Limbo '90 (B. Wolfe), 1953
Limbo (B. Wolfe), 1952
Limits (s Niven), 1985
Lincoln Hunters (Tucker), 1958
Lincoln's Dreams (Willis), 1987
Line to Tomorrow (s Kuttner and C.L. Moore, as Padgett), 1954
Liners of Time (Fearn), 1947
Lion Game (Schmitz), 1973
Lion Men of Mongo (Goulart, as Steffanson), 1974
Lion of Boaz-Jachin and Jachin-Boaz (Hoban), 1973
Lion of Comarre, and Against the Fall of Night (Clarke), 1968
Lion of Macedon (Gemmell), 1990
Lion, The Witch, and the Wardrobe (Lewis), 1950
Lion Time in Timbuctoo (s Silverberg), 1991
Liquid Death (Fearn, as Griff), 1953
Lisa Kane (Lupoff), 1976
Listen, Listen (s Wilhelm), 1981
Listen! The Stars! (Brunner), 1963
Listeners (Gunn), 1972
Listeners (Leinster), 1969
Listening to Brahms (s Charnas), 1991

Litany of Sh'reev (Watkins), 1976
Litany of the Long Sun (G. Wolfe), 1994
Little, Big (Crowley), 1981
Little Black Box (Dick), 1990
Little Country (de Lint), 1991
Little Fuzzy (Piper), 1962
Little Green Spaceman (Fisk), 1974
Little Heroes (Spinrad), 1987
Little Knowledge (Bishop), 1977
Little Lost Robot (s Asimov), 1977
Little People (Christopher), 1966
Little Sister of the Apocalypse (K. Reed), 1994
Little Tours of Hell (s Saxton), 1986
Lives and Times of Jerry Cornelius (s Moorcock), 1976
Lives of Christopher Chant (Diana Wynne Jones), 1988
Lives You Wished to Lead But Never Dared (s Hubbard), 1978
Living Demons (s Bloch), 1967
Living Fire (s Fisk), 1987
Living God (Dave Duncan), 1994
Living Way Out (s Guin), 1967
Living World (Tubb, as Maddox), 1954
Lizard Lords (Coblentz), 1964
Lizard Music (Pinkwater), 1976
Llana of Gathol (E. Burroughs), 1948
Loafers of Refuge (J. Green), 1965
Lodge of the Lynx (Kurtz), 1992
Logan series (Nolan), from 1967
Lone Star (Perry), 1995
Lonely Astronomer (Fearn, as Gridban), 1954
Lonely Vigils (s Wellman), 1981
Long after Midnight (s Bradbury), 1976
Long Afternoon of Earth (Aldiss), 1962
Long ARM of Gil Hamilton (s Niven), 1976
Long Dark Tea-Time of the Soul (Adams), 1988
Long Eureka (s Sellings), 1968
Long Habit of Living (Joe Haldeman), 1989
Long Loud Silence (Tucker), 1952
Long Night (Caidin), 1956
Long Night (s P. Anderson), 1983
Long Night of the Grave (C. Grant), 1986
Long Orbit (Farren), 1988
Long Patrol (Goulart), 1984
Long Result (Brunner), 1965
Long Shot for Rosinante (Gilliland), 1981
Long Sleep (Koontz, as Hill), 1975
Long Tomorrow (Brackett), 1955
Long Trip to Teatime (Burgess), 1976
Long Twilight (Laumer), 1969
Long View (Busby), 1976
Long Voyage (Klein), 1964
Long Way Home (P. Anderson), 1975
Long Winter (Christopher), 1962
Longest Voyage (s P. Anderson), 1991
Look Away (s Effinger), 1990
Look into the Sun (Kelly), 1989
Look out for Space (Nolan), 1985
Looking Backward, 2000-1887 (Bellamy), 1888
Looking Backward, from the Year 2000 (Reynolds), 1973
Looking for Blücher (Wodhams), 1980
Lord Darcy series (Garrett), from 1967
Lord Darcy series (Kurland), from 1988

Lord Foul's Bane (Donaldson), 1977
Lord Grandith series (Farmer), from 1969
Lord Kalvan of Otherwhen (Piper), 1965
Lord Kelvin's Machine (Blaylock), 1992
Lord of Atlantis (Fearn), 1991
Lord of Death, and The Queen of Life (Flint), 1965
Lord of Labour (G. Griffith), 1911
Lord of Light (Zelazny), 1967
Lord of the Flies (Golding), 1954
Lord of the Green Planet (Petaja), 1967
Lord of the Rings series (Tolkien), from 1954
Lord of the Sea (Shiel), 1901
Lord of the Spiders (Moorcock), 1970
Lord of the Trees (Farmer), 1970
Lord of the Troll-Bats (Gilliland), 1992
Lord of the Two Lands (Tarr), 1993
Lord of Thunder (Norton), 1962
Lord of Tranerica (Coblentz), 1966
Lord Tedric series (E.E. Smith), from 1978
Lord Tedric series (Eklund), from 1979
Lord Tyger (Farmer), 1970
Lord Valentine's Castle (Silverberg), 1980
Lordly Ones (s Roberts), 1986
Lords and Ladies (Pratchett), 1992
Lords of Creation (Binder), 1949
Lords of Dûs series (Watt-Evans), from 1980
Lords of the Middle Dark (Chalker), 1986
Lords of the Psychon (Galouye), 1963
Lords of the Starship (Geston), 1967
Lords of the Triple Moons (Mayhar), 1983
Lords Temporal (Delaney), 1987
Lore of the Witch World (s Norton), 1980
Loremasters (Gadallah), 1988
Lori (Bloch), 1989
Los Angeles: A.D. 2017 (Wylie), 1971
Losers' Night (s P. Anderson), 1991
Lost—A Moon (Capon), 1956
Lost and the Lurking (Wellman), 1981
Lost Battalion (Stine), 1989
Lost Boys (Card), 1992
Lost Boys (Gardner),1987
Lost Cavern (s Heard), 1948
Lost Comet (Coblentz), 1964
Lost Continent (Hyne), 1900
Lost Continent (s E. Burroughs), 1963
Lost Crown (Gemmell), 1989
Lost Dorsai (s Dickson), 1980
Lost Dryad (s Stockton), 1912
Lost Face (s Nesvadba), 1971
Lost Futures (Tuttle), 1992
Lost in Space (George O. Smith), 1959
Lost in Space (T. White, as Archer), 1967
Lost in the Land of Fire (Senarens), 1893
Lost in Time and Space with Lefty Feep (s Bloch), 1987
Lost Legacy (s Heinlein), 1960
Lost Millennium (Richmond), 1967
Lost Moons (s Vance), 1982
Lost Oasis (Dent, as Robeson), 1965
Lost on Venus (E. Burroughs), 1935
Lost Perception (Galouye), 1966
Lost Princess (G. MacDonald), 1895

Lost Race of Mars (Silverberg), 1960
Lost Regiment series (Forstchen), from 1990
Lost Souls (Bear), 1982
Lost Star (Hoover), 1979
Lost World (Crichton), 1995
Lost World (Doyle), 1912
Lost World of Time (L. Carter), 1969
Lost Worlds (s Clark Ashton Smith), 1944
Lost Worlds (s L. Carter), 1980
Lost Worlds of Cronus (Kapp), 1982
Lost: Fifty Suns (s van Vogt), 1979
Lottery Night (s Sucharitkul), n.d.
Lotus Caves (Christopher), 1969
Love Ain't Nothing But Sex Misspelled (s Ellison), 1968
Love among the Xoids (s Sladek), 1984
Love and Napalm (s Ballard), 1972
Love and Sleep (Crowley), 1994
Love Conquers All (Saberhagen), 1979
Love Eternal (Haggard), 1918
Love in Time (s Wyndham, as Harris), 1946
Love Is Forever--We Are for Tonight (R. Williams), 1970
Love Not Human (s Dickson), 1981
Lovecraft's Book (Lupoff), 1985
Lovelock (Card), 1994
Lovely (Meltzer), 1969
Lovers (Farmer), 1961
Low-Flying Aircraft (s Ballard), 1976
Luana (A. Foster), 1974
Lucifer Comet (I. Wallace), 1980
Lucifer Jones series (Resnick), from 1985
Lucifer's Hammer (Niven, Pournelle), 1977
Luck Machine (Tubb), 1980
Luck of Brin's Five (Wilder), 1977
Lucky Starr series (Asimov), from 1952
Lucky's Harvest (Watson), 1993
Luna series (Heinlein), from 1966
Lunar Attack (Mason, as Rankine), 1975
Lunar Eye (R. Williams), 1964
Lunar Justice (Harness), 1991
Lunatics of Terra (s Sladek), 1984
Lunching with the AntiChrist (s Moorcock), 1995
Lure of the Basilisk (Watt-Evans), 1980
Luren series (Lichtenberg), from 1988
Lurid Dreams (Harness), 1990
Lurker at the Threshold (Lovecraft), 1945
Lurking Fear (s Lovecraft), 1947
Lute series (MacAvoy), from 1985
Lycanthia (Lee), 1981
Lydyard, David series (Stableford), from 1990
Lyon's Pride (McCaffrey), 1994
Lyonesse series (Vance), from 1983
Lyrica (Monteleone), 1987
Lysbeth (Haggard), 1901
Lythande (s Bradley), 1986

M33 in Andromeda (s van Vogt), 1971
Macabre Ones! (Fanthorpe, as Fane), 1964
Macedon series (Gemmell), from 1990
MacFarlane, Stephen series (Cross), from 1945
Machiavelli Interface (Perry), 1986
Machine in Shaft Ten (s M. Harrison), 1975

Machine Sex (s Dorsey), 1988
Machine that Thought (s Gallun, as Callahan), 1942(?)
Machineries of Joy (s Bradbury), 1964
Machines and Men (s Roberts), 1973
Macrocosmic Conflict (Bischoff), 1986
Macrolife (Zebrowski), 1979
Macroscope (Anthony), 1969
Mad Empress of Callisto (L. Carter), 1975
Mad Goblin (Farmer), 1970
Mad God's Amulet (Moorcock), 1969
Mad Mesa (Dent, as Robeson), 1972
Mad Metropolis (High), 1966
Madame Two Swords (Lee), 1988
Madbond (Springer), 1987
Madlands (Jeter), 1991
Madouc (Vance), 1989
Madwand (Zelazny), 1981
Maelstrom (Preuss), 1988
Magic Camera (Pinkwater), 1974
Magic Casement (Dave Duncan), 1990
Magic Cottage (J. Herbert), 1986
Magic Goes Away (Niven), 1978
Magic Island (Dent, as Robeson), 1977
Magic Labyrinth (Farmer), 1980
Magic Man (s Beaumont), 1965
Magic Meadow (Key), 1975
Magic Moscow Moose series (Pinkwater), from 1975
Magic of Xanth (Anthony), 1981
Magic Spectacles (Blaylock), 1991
Magic Spectacles (s Cowper), 1986
Magic Three of Solatia (Yolen), 1974
Magic Time (K. Reed), 1980
Magic Wagon (Lansdale), 1986
Magician (C. Wilson), 1992
Magician (Feist), 1982
Magician of Mars (Hamilton), 1969
Magician's Gambit (Eddings), 1983
Magician's Nephew (Lewis), 1955
Magicians (Gunn), 1976
Magicians (Priestley), 1954
Magicians of Caprona (Diana Wynne Jones), 1980
Magnetic Brain (Fearn, as Gridban), 1953
Magnificent Gallery (Monteleone), 1987
Magnificent Showboats of the Lower Vissel River (Vance), 1983
Magnificent Wilf (Dickson), 1995
Magnus d'Armand series (Stasheff), from 1979
Mahatma and the Hare (Haggard), 1911
Mahogany Trinrose (Lichtenberg), 1981
Main Experiment (Hodder-Williams), 1964
Maiwa's Revenge (Haggard), 1888
Majii (Dent, as Robeson), 1971
Majipoor series (Silverberg), from 1980
Major Corby and the Unidentified Flapping Object (DeWeese), 1979
Major Operation (s J. White), 1971
Make Room! Make Room! (H. Harrison), 1966
Maker of Universes (Farmer), 1965
Makeshift God (Griffin), 1979
Makeshift Rocket (P. Anderson), 1962
Making of the Lesbian Horse (s Priest), 1979
Making of the Representative for Planet 8 (Lessing), 1982
Makra Choria (Mayhar), 1987

Makropoulos Secret (Capek), 1925
Malacia Tapestry (Aldiss), 1976
Malady of Magicks (Gardner), 1986
Malafrena (Le Guin), 1979
Male Response (Aldiss), 1961
Mallorean series (Eddings), from 1987
Mallworld (Sucharitkul), 1981
Malone, Kenneth J. series (Garrett), from 1962
Malzberg at Large (s Malzberg), 1979
Man Divided (Stapledon), 1950
Man-Eater (s E. Burroughs), 1955
Man from Atlantis (Goulart, as Robeson), 1974
Man from Beyond (Fanthorpe, as Muller), 1965
Man from Beyond (s Wyndham), 1975
Man from Earth (s Dickson), 1983
Man from Maybe (Kelley), 1974
Man from Mundania (Anthony), 1989
Man from P.I.G (H. Harrison), 1968
Man from Tomorrow (Fearn, as Statten), 1952
Man from Tomorrow (Tucker), 1955
Man from U.N.C.L.E.: The Thousand Coffins Affair (T. Carr), 1965
Man in a Cage (Stableford), 1975
Man in Duplicate (Fearn, as Statten), 1953
Man in the High Castle (Dick), 1962
Man in the Maze (Silverberg), 1969
Man in the Tree (Knight), 1984
Man-Kzin Wars series (Ing), from 1988
Man-Kzin Wars series (Niven), from 1988
Man-Kzin Wars series (Pournelle), 1988
Man-Kzin Wars series (Stirling), 1989
Man Obsessed (Nourse), 1955
Man of Bronze (Dent, as Robeson), 1933
Man of Earth (Budrys), 1958
Man of His Word series (Dave Duncan), from 1990
Man of Many Minds (Evans), 1953
Man of Metal (Fanthorpe, as Torro), 1970
Man of the Future (s Bryant), 1990
Man of Two Worlds (F. Herbert), 1986
Man of Two Worlds (Fearn, as Statten), 1953
Man of Two Worlds (R. Jones), 1963
Man on the Meteor (Cummings), 1952
Man Plus series (Pohl), from 1976
Man Returned (Broderick), 1965
Man Rides Through (Donaldson), 1987
Man, the Hunted Animal (Rotsler, as Arrow), 1976
Man the Worlds Rejected (s Dickson), 1986
Man Who Ate the Phoenix (s Dunsany), 1949
Man Who Ate the World (s Pohl), 1960
Man Who Awoke (Manning), 1975
Man Who Came Back (Fanthorpe, as Thanet), 1964
Man Who Conquered Time (Fanthorpe, as Muller), 1962
Man Who Corrupted Earth (Edmondson), 1980
Man Who Couldn't Die (s Fanthorpe), 1960
Man Who Couldn't Sleep (Maine), 1958
Man Who Counts (P. Anderson), 1978
Man Who Fell to Earth (Tevis), 1963
Man Who Folded Himself (Gerrold), 1973
Man Who Had No Idea (s Disch), 1982
Man Who Japed (Dick), 1956
Man Who Limped (s Kline), 1946
Man Who Loved Mars (L. Carter), 1973

Man Who Loved Morlocks (Lake), 1981
Man Who Loved the Midnight Lady (s Malzberg), 1980
Man Who Made Models (s Lafferty), 1984
Man Who Mastered Time (Cummings), 1929
Man Who Melted (Dann), 1984
Man Who Never Missed (Perry), 1985
Man Who Owned the World (Maine), 1961
Man Who Pulled Down the Sky (J. Barnes), 1986
Man Who Shook the Earth (Dent, as Robeson), 1969
Man Who Sold the Moon (s Heinlein), 1950
Man Who Upset the Universe (Asimov), 1955
Man Who Used the Universe (A. Foster), 1983
Man Who Wanted Stars (McLaughlin), 1965
Man with a Thousand Names (van Vogt), 1974
Man with Nine Lives (Ellison), 1960
Man with the Nose (s Wells), 1984
Man with Three Eyes (G. Griffith), n.d.
Man without a Planet (Fairman, as del Rey), 1969
Man without a Planet (L. Carter), 1966
Man Without a Planet (del Rey), 1969
Man's Understanding (s Hyne), 1933
Mana series (Watson), from 1993
Manalone (Kapp), 1977
Mandala (Bischoff), 1983
Mandricardo (L. Carter), 1987
ManFac (Caidin), 1981
Manhattan Project (Bischoff), 1986
Manhounds of Antares (Bulmer, as Akers), 1974
Manhuntress (Offutt and Proctor, as Cleve), 1982
Manifest Destiny (s Longyear), 1980
Mankind on the Run (Dickson), 1956
Mankind under the Leash (Disch), 1966
Manlib (Offutt, as Cleve), 1974
Manna (Gloag), 1940
Manna (Stine, as Correy), 1984
Manseed (Williamson), 1982
Manshape (Brunner), 1982
Mansions of Space (Morressy), 1983
Mantis (Jeter), 1987
Many Waters (L'Engle), 1986
Many Worlds of Andre Norton (s Norton), 1974
Many Worlds of Barry Malzberg (s Malzberg), 1975
Many Worlds of Magnus Ridolph (s Vance), 1966
Many Worlds of Poul Anderson (s P. Anderson), 1974
Maori (A. Foster), 1988
Maps in a Mirror (s Card), 1990
Maracot Deep (s Doyle), 1929
Marathon Photograph (s Simak), 1986
Marauders series (Naha, as McGann), from 1989
March of the Robots (Fanthorpe, as Brett), 1961
Marching Morons (s Kornbluth), 1959
Marching through Georgia (Stirling), 1988
Marco Polo and the Sleeping Beauty (Davidson), 1988
Mareland Chronicles (Vonarburg), 1993
Margaret and I (Wilhelm), 1971
Marginalia (s Lovecraft), 1944
Marianne series (Tepper), from 1985
Marîd Audran series (Effinger), from 1987
Marie (Haggard), 1912
Marion Isle (Haggard), 1929
Marion's Wall (Finney), 1973

Mark of the Beast (Fanthorpe, as Muller), 1964
Mark of the Cat (Norton), 1992
Mark of the Moderately Vicious Vampire (C. Grant, as Fenn), 1992
Marooned (Caidin), 1964
Marooned in Realtime (V. Vinge), 1986
Marooned on Eden (Forward), 1993
Marooned on Mars (del Rey), 1952
Marriages between Zones Three, Four, and Five (Lessing), 1980
Marriner, Elspeth series (Merwin), from 1951
Mars (Bova), 1992
Mars Is My Destination (Long), 1962
Mars Monopoly (Sohl), 1956
Mars Plus (Pohl), 1994
Mars series (Brackett), from 1953
Mars series (E. Burroughs), from 1917
Mars series (K. Robinson), from 1988
Mars series (Kline), from 1960
Mars series (L. Carter), from 1971
Mars You Have in Me (s Dowling), 1992
Mars--The Red Planet (Farren), 1990
Martian Chronicles (s Bradbury), 1950
Martian Martyrs (s Binder, as Coleridge), 1942
Martian Missile (Wollheim, as Grinnell), 1959
Martian Odyssey (s Weinbaum), 1949
Martian Rainbow (Forward), 1991
Martian Sphinx (Brunner), 1965
Martian Time-Slip (Dick), 1964
Martian Visitors (Long), 1964
Martian Way (s Asimov), 1955
Martians, Go Home (F. Brown), 1955
Martin Inca (Watson), 1977
Martin Magnus series (Temple), from 1955
Marune: Alastor 933 (Vance), 1975
Marvelman (A. Moore), n.d.
Marvelous Palace (s Belyaev, Boulle), 1977
Mary of Marion Isle (Haggard), 1929
Mask (Koontz, as West), 1981
Mask (Perry), 1994
Mask (S. Gordon), 1990
Mask for the General (Goldstein), 1987
Mask of Chaos (Jakes), 1970
Mask of Circe (Kuttner, C.L. Moore), 1971
Mask of Loki (Zelazny), 1990
Mask of the Sun (Saberhagen), 1979
Maske: Thaery (Vance), 1976
Masks of Scorpio (Bulmer, as Akers), 1984
Masks of the Illuminati (Robert Anton Wilson), 1981
Masks of the Martyrs (Chalker), 1988
Masks of Time (Silverberg), 1968
Masque World (Panshin), 1969
Master and Margarita (Bulgakov), 1967
Master Mind of Mars (E. Burroughs), 1928
Master Must Die (Fearn, as Gridban), 1953
Master of Life and Death (Silverberg), 1957
Master of Misfit (Offutt and Proctor, as Cleve), 1982
Master of Norriya (Drew), 1985
Master of Paxwax (Mann), 1986
Master of Space (Clarke), 1961
Master of Space and Time (Rucker), 1984
Master of the Dark Gate (Jakes), 1970
Master of the Moon (P. Moore), 1952

Master of the Stars (Hoskins), 1976
Master of the World (Verne), 1914
Master Weed (Another Adventure of the Space Puppet), 1954
Masters of Everon (Dickson), 1980
Masters of Evolution (Knight), 1959
Masters of Flux and Anchor (Chalker), 1985
Masters of Space (E.E. Smith), 1979
Masters of Terror, Volume One (s Hodgson), 1977
Masters of the Maze (Davidson), 1965
Masters of the Pit (Moorcock), 1971
Masters of the Vortex (E.E. Smith), 1968
Masters of Time (s van Vogt), 1950
Mastodonia (Simak), 1978
Matadora (Perry), 1986
Matilda's Stepchildren (Chandler), 1979
Mating Center (Long), 1961
Mating Cry (van Vogt), 1960
Matrix (Mason), 1970
Matter of Metalaw (Stine, as Correy), 1986
Matter of Taste (Saberhagen), 1990
Matter of Time (Cook), 1985
Matter, Space, and Time series (Cummings), from 1922
Matter's End (s Benford), 1995
Maturity (s Sturgeon), 1979
Maurai and Kith (s P. Anderson), 1982
Maureen Birbaum, Barbarian Swordperson (Effinger), 1993
Mauser, Joe series (Reynolds), from 1963
Mavin Manyshaped series (Tepper), from 1985
Maximum Effort (Edmondson), 1987
Maxwell, Johnny series (Pratchett), from 1992
Maxwell's Demons (s Bova), 1978
Mayday Orbit (P. Anderson), 1961
Mayenne (Tubb), 1973
Mayfair Magician (G. Griffith), 1905
Mayflies (O'Donnell), 1979
Mayflower series (Card), from 1994
Maza of the Moon (Kline), 1930
Maze in the Mirror (Chalker), 1989
Maze of Death (Dick), 1970
Maze of Stars (Brunner), 1991
Mazes of Scorpio (Bulmer, as Akers), 1982
Mazeway (Williamson), 1990
McAndrew Chronicles (s Sheffield), 1983
McKie, Jorj X. series (F. Herbert), from 1970
M.D. (Disch), 1991
Meat (Watson), 1988
Mechanical Monarch (Tubb), 1958
Mechasm (Sladek), 1969
Med Service series (Leinster), from 1959
Meddlers (Bone), 1976
Medicine for Melancholy (s Bradbury), 1959
M*E*D*U*S*A (J. Morris), 1986
Medusa Encounter (Preuss), 1990
Medusa Frequency (Hoban), 1987
Medusa: A Tiger by the Tail (Chalker), 1983
Medusa's Children (Shaw), 1977
Meeting at Infinity (Brunner), 1961
Meeting over Tuscarora (s Yefremov), 1946
Meeting Place (s Beresford), 1929
Meeting with Medusa (s Clarke), 1988
Meetings in Infinity (s Kessel), 1992

Megalomania (I. Wallace), 1989
Megiddo's Ridge (S. Wright), 1938
Meiklejohn and Leidl series (Wilhelm), from 1988
Melancholy Elephants (s S. Robinson), 1984
Melome (Tubb), 1983
Melvinge of the Megaverse series (Lupoff), from 1992
Memoirs Found in a Bathtub (Lem), 1973
Memoirs of a Space Traveler (s Lem), 1982
Memoirs of a Survivor (Lessing), 1974
Memoirs of Alcheringia (Drew), 1984
Memories (McQuay), 1987
Memories of the Body (s Tuttle), 1992
Memories of the Space Age (s Ballard), 1988
Memory (s Lovecraft), 1969
Memory and Dream (de Lint), 1994
Memory Cathedral (Dann), 1995
Memory of Earth (Card), 1992
Memory of Whiteness (K. Robinson), 1985
Memory Wire (Robert Charles Wilson), 1988
Men and the Mirror (s Rocklynne), 1973
Men at Arms (Pratchett), 1993
Men from Ariel (s Wollheim), 1982
Men from P.I.G. and R.O.B.O.T (H. Harrison), 1974
Men in the Jungle (Spinrad), 1967
Men Inside (Malzberg), 1973
Men into Space (Leinster), 1960
Men like Gods (Wells), 1923
Men Like Rats (Chilson), 1989
Men, Martians, and Machines (s Russell), 1955
Men of Avalon (s Keller), 1935(?)
Men of the Deep Waters (s Hodgson), 1914
Menace from Earth (s Heinlein), 1959
Menace from Mercury (Fanthorpe, as La Salle), 1954
Menace from the Past (Tubb, as Maddox), 1954
Menace of the Saucers (Binder), 1969
Menace under Marswood (Lanier), 1983
Mendelov Conspiracy (Caidin), 1969
Mental Wizard (Dent, as Robeson), 1970
Mention My Name in Atlantis (Jakes), 1972
Mer-Cycle (Anthony), 1991
Mercenary (Anthony), 1984
Mercenary (Pournelle), 1977
Mercenary from Tomorrow (Reynolds), 1968
Merchanter series (Cherryh), from 1982
Merchants of Disaster (Dent, as Robeson), 1969
Merchants' War (Pohl), 1984
Mercy Men (Nourse), 1968
Mercycle (Anthony), 1992
Meridian Days (E. Brown), 1992
Merlin Dreams (Dickinson), 1988
Merlin Dreams in the Mondream Wood (s de Lint), 1992
Merlin's Booke (s Yolen), 1986
Merlin's Game (Saberhagen), 1995
Merlin's Mirror (Norton), 1975
Mermaid Reef (s Fanthorpe), 1959
Mermaid's Three Wisdoms (Yolen), 1978
Merman's Children (P. Anderson), 1979
Merovingen Nights series (Cherryh), from 1985
Merry Christmas, Ms. Minerva (Cooper), 1978
Mesklin series (Clement), from 1954
Message from the Eocene (St. Clair), 1964

Messages Found in an Oxygen Bottle (s Shaw), 1986
Messenger Chronicles (Kelly), from 1984
Messenger of Zhuvastou (Offutt), 1973
Messiah at the End of Time (Moorcock), 1978
Messiah Choice (Chalker), 1985
Messiah of the Cylinder (Rousseau), 1917
Messiah series (Caidin), from 1986
Metaconcert (May), 1988
Metal Angel (Springer), 1992
Metal Eater (Tubb, as Sheldon), 1954
Metal Giants (s Hamilton), 1935(s ?)
Metal Master (Dent, as Robeson), 1973
Metal Monster (Merritt), 1946
Metallic Muse (s Biggle), 1972
Metamorphosis (s Kafka), 1937
Metaphase (McIntyre), 1992
Meteor (Capek), 1935
Meteor (s Wyndham), 1991
Meteor Men (s Laumer, as LeBaron), 1968
Meteor Menace (Dent, as Robeson), 1964
Methuselah's Children (Heinlein), 1958
Metrognome (s A. Foster), 1990
Metropolitan (W. Williams), 1995
Mezentian Gate (Eddison), 1958
Michaelmas (Budrys), 1977
Micro Infinity (Fanthorpe, as Muller), 1962
Micro Men (Fearn, as Statten), 1950
Microscopic Ones (Fanthorpe, as Brett), 1960
Midas (Jeschke), 1987
Midas Deep (Brosnan), 1983
Midas Man (Dent, as Robeson), 1970
Midas World (s Pohl), 1983
Middle Kingdom (Wingrove), 1989
Middle of Nowhere (Gerrold), 1995
Midnight (Koontz), 1989
Midnight at the Well of Souls (Chalker), 1977
Midnight Pleasures (s Bloch), 1987
Midnight's Sun (Kilworth), 1990
Midsummer Century (Blish), 1972
Midsummer Tempest (P. Anderson), 1974
Midway Between (Norwood), 1984
Midwich Cuckoos (Wyndham), 1957
Midworld (A. Foster), 1975
Mightiest Machine (Campbell), 1947
Mighty Good Road (Scott), 1990
Mike Mars series (Wollheim), from 1961
Mile beyond the Moon (s Kornbluth), 1958
Mile-Long Spaceship (s Wilhelm), 1963
Miles Vorkosigan series (Bujold), from 1986
Military Dimension (s Drake), 1991
Millennial Contest series (Sheckley, Zelazny), from 1991
Millennium (Bova), 1976
Millennium (Varley), 1983
Million Cities (McIntosh), 1963
Million Open Doors (J. Barnes), 1992
Million Year Hunt (Bulmer), 1964
Mimics of Dephene (Tubb, as Kern), 1975
Mind behind the Eye (J. Green), 1972
Mind Cage (van Vogt), 1957
Mind Fields (s Ellison), 1994
Mind Force (Fanthorpe, as Brett), 1961

Mind from Outer Space (Binder), 1972
Mind Master (Gunn), 1982
Mind Net (Franke), 1974
Mind of Mr. Soames (Maine), 1961
Mind of My Mind (O. Butler), 1977
Mind Parasites (C. Wilson), 1967
Mind Pool (Sheffield), 1993
Mind-Riders (Stableford), 1976
Mind Spider (s Leiber), 1961
Mind Switch (Knight), 1965
Mind Thing (F. Brown), 1961
Mind-Twisters Affair (R. Coulson and DeWeese, as Stratton), 1967
Mind Warpers (Russell), 1965
Mind Wizards of Callisto (L. Carter), 1975
Mindbenders (Fisk), 1987
Mindblast (Duane), 1991
Mindbond (Springer), 1987
Mindbridge (Joe Haldeman), 1976
Mindflight (Goldin), 1978
Mindkiller (S. Robinson), 1982
Mindkiller series (S. Robinson), from 1982
Mindmix (Kelley), 1972
Mindplayers (Cadigan), 1987
Minds, Machines, and Evolution (s Hogan), 1988
Mindspan (s Dickson), 1986
Mindswap (Sheckley), 1966
Mindworm (s Kornbluth), 1955
Miners in the Sky (Leinster), 1967
Minervan Experiment series (Hogan), from 1981
Mining the Oort (Pohl), 1992
Minotaur Maze (s Sheckley), 1990
Mirabile (s Kagan), 1991
Miracle of Rare Design (Resnick), 1994
Miracle Visitors (Watson), 1978
Mirkheim (P. Anderson), 1977
Mirror Dance (Bujold), 1994
Mirror for Observers (Pangborn), 1954
Mirror Friend, Mirror Foe (Asprin), 1979
Mirror Image (Coney), 1972
Mirror in the Sky (Garnett), 1969
Mirror Maze (Hogan), 1989
Mirror of Destiny (Norton), 1995
Mirror of Her Dreams (Donaldson), 1987
Mirror Sun Rising (McMullen), 1995
Mirror to the Sky (Geston), 1992
Mischief Malicious (s and Murder Most Strange), 1991
Misenchanted Sword (Watt-Evans), 1985
Misplaced Legion (Turtledove), 1987
Misplaced Persons (Harding), 1979
Miss Ludington's Sister (Bellamy), 1884
Missing Angel (Cox), 1947
Missing Heart (s Cowper), 1982
Missing Man (MacLean), 1975
Missing Men of Saturn (Latham), 1953
Mission (Tilley), 1981
Mission Earth series (Hubbard), from 1985
Mission in Guemo (R. Gordon), 1953
Mission of Gravity (Clement), 1954
Mission to a Star (Long), 1964
Mission to Mars (P. Moore), 1955
Mission to Moulokin (A. Foster), 1979

Mission to Pactolus R (Mason), 1978
Mission to the Heart Stars (Blish), 1965
Mission to the Moon (del Rey), 1956
Mission to the Stars (Bulmer, as Kent), 1953
Mission to the Stars (van Vogt), 1955
Mission to Universe (Dickson), 1965
Mission: Interplanetary (van Vogt), 1952
Mission: Manstop (s Neville), 1971
Missionaries (Compton), 1972
Missionary and the Witch Doctor (s Haggard), 1920
Mrs. Aladdin (Rousseau), 1925
Mr. Adam (Frank), 1946
Mr. Blettsworthy on Rampole Island (Wells), 1928
Mister da V. (s K. Reed), 1967
Mister E (Jeter), 1991
Mr. Jorkens Remembers Africa (s Dunsany), 1934
Mister Justice (Piserchia), 1973
Mr. Mergenthwirker's Lobblies (s Bond), 1946
Mr. Merlin 1-2 (Rotsler), 1981
Mr. Murder (Koontz), 1993
Mr. Pye (Peake), 1953
Mistress of Mistresses (Eddison), 1935
Mistress of the Empire (Feist), 1992
Mists of Avalon (Bradley), 1982
Mists of Dawn (Oliver), 1952
Mists of Doom (Offutt), 1977
Mixed Feelings (s Effinger), 1974
Mixed Men (van Vogt), 1952
M'Lady Witch (Stasheff), 1994
Moat series (Niven, Pournelle), from 1993
Mockingbird (Tevis), 1980
Mode series (Anthony), from 1991
Model Village (Fisk), 1990
Moderan (Bunch), 1971
Modular Man (Allen), 1992
Molecular Cafe (s Strugatsky), 1968
Molecule Men and The Monster of Loch Ness (F. and G. Hoyle), 1972
Molly Zero (Roberts), 1980
Molt Brother (Lichtenberg), 1982
Moment of Eclipse (s Aldiss), 1970
Moment of the Magician (A. Foster), 1984
Mona Lisa Overdrive (Gibson), 1988
Monadic Universe (s Zebrowski), 1977
Monday Begins on Saturday (Strugatsky), 1977
Monella series (Aubrey), from 1896
Monitor Found in Orbit (s Coney), 1974
Monitor, the Miners, and the Shree (Killough), 1980
Monitors (Laumer), 1966
Monkey Planet (Boulle), 1964
Monkey Station (Mayhar), 1989
Monkeys Have No Tails in Zamboanga (s Meek), 1935
Monster (s Bond), 1953
Monster from Earth's End (Leinster), 1959
Monster from out of Time (Long), 1970
Monster Maker (Fisk), 1979
Monster Men (E. Burroughs), 1929
Monster of Metelaze (Tubb, as Kern), 1973
Monster of the Prophecy (s Clark Ashton Smith), 1983
Monsters (Dent, as Robeson), 1965
Monsters (s van Vogt), 1965

Monsters and Medics (s J. White), 1977
Monsters and Such (s Leinster), 1959
Monsters in Orbit (s Vance), 1965
Monsters of Juntonheim (Hamilton), 1950
Monstrous Regiment series (Constantine), from 1990
Monte Cristo (Jakes), 1970
Montezuma's Daughter (Haggard), 1893
Montezuma's Strip (s A. Foster), 1995
Monument (Biggle), 1974
Moon (J. Herbert), 1985
Moon and the Face (McKillip), 1985
Moon Base (Tubb), 1964
Moon Called (Norton), 1982
Moon Children (Williamson), 1972
Moon Dance (Sucharitkul, as Somtow), 1990
Moon-Flash (McKillip), 1984
Moon Goddess and the Son (Kingsbury), 1987
Moon Is a Harsh Mistress (Heinlein), 1966
Moon Is a Meadow (s de Lint), 1980
Moon Is Hell! (s Campbell), 1951
Moon Magic series (Norton), from 1966
Moon Maid (s E. Burroughs), 1926
Moon Maiden (Serviss), 1978
Moon Men (s E. Burroughs), 1962
Moon Metal (Serviss), 1900
Moon Mirror (s Norton), 1988
Moon Moth (s Vance), 1976
Moon Odyssey (Mason, as Rankine), 1975
Moon of Ice (Linaweaver), 1988
Moon of Israel (Haggard), 1918
Moon of Mutiny (del Rey), 1961
Moon of Three Rings (Norton), 1966
Moon on an Iron Meadow (Tate), 1974
Moon People (Coblentz), 1964
Moon Pool (Merritt), 1919
Moon Raiders (P. Moore), 1978
Moon Wolf (s Fanthorpe), 1964
Moon's Wife (Attanasio), 1993
Moon-Voyage (Verne), 1877
Moonbase One (R. Jones), 1972
Moonbeast (van Vogt), 1969
Moonferns and Starsongs (s Silverberg), 1971
Moonheart series (s de Lint), from 1984
Moonlight (de Lint), 1990
Moons for Sale (Fearn, as Gridban), 1953
Moons of Triopus (Mason, as Rankine), 1968
Moonstar Odyssey (Gerrold), 1977
Moonstone and Tiger Eye (s Charnas), 1992
Moorcock's Book of Martyrs (s Moorcock), 1976
Moosepire (Pinkwater), 1986
Mordant's Need series (Donaldson), from 1987
Mordred (Niven, Pournelle), 1980
More Nightmares (s Bloch), 1962
More than Fire (Farmer), 1993
More Than Human (Sturgeon), 1953
More Than One Universe (s Clarke), 1991
More Than Superhuman (s van Vogt), 1971
More Than the Sum of His Parts (s Joe Haldeman), 1991
More Things in Heaven (Brunner), 1973
Moreau's Other Island (Aldiss), 1980
Moreta, Dragonlady of Pern (McCaffrey), 1983

Morgaine series (Cherryh), from 1979
Morgan, Alan series (Fox), from 1964
Morgan series (Haiblum), from 1984
Morlock Night (Jeter), 1979
Morning Star (Haggard), 1910
Morningstar (Gemmell), 1992
Morphodite series (M.A. Foster), from 1981
Morreion (s Vance), 1992
Morrow series (Hoover), from 1973
Mort (Pratchett), 1987
Mortal Engines (s Lem), 1977
Mortals and Monsters (s del Rey), 1965
Mortenhoe, Katherine series (Compton), from 1974
Mortuary (s Clark Ashton Smith), 1971
Mostly Harmless (Adams), 1992
Mote in God's Eye (Niven, Pournelle), 1974
Mote in Time's Eye (Klein), 1973
Mother Earth (McQuay), 1985
Mother Lode (Z. Hughes), 1991
Mother of Storms (J. Barnes), 1994
Mother of Toads (s Clark Ashton Smith), 1987
Motherlines series (Charnas), from 1974
Motion Menace (Dent, as Robeson), 1971
Mountain Cage (s Sargent), 1983
Mountains of Majipoor (Silverberg), 1995
Mouvar's Magic (Anthony), 1992
Movement of Mountains (Blumlein), 1987
Moving Mars (Bear), 1993
Moving Pictures (Pratchett), 1990
Mudd's Angels (s Blish), 1978
Muddle Earth (Brunner), 1993
Muffin Fiend (Pinkwater), 1986
Mulengro (de Lint), 1985
Muliplex Man (Hogan), 1992
Müller-Fokker Effect (Sladek), 1970
Multi-Man (Fearn, as Statten), 1954
Multiface (Adlard), 1975
Multiple Man (Bova), 1976
Multitude of Monsters (Gardner), 1986
Mummy (s May, as Thorpe), 1981
Mummy and Miss Nitocris (G. Griffith), 1906
Mummy and the Girl (G. Griffith), n.d.
Murasaki (P. Anderson), 1992
Murder and Magic (s Garrett), 1979
Murder in the Clinic (s Hamilton), 1946
Murder Madness (Leinster), 1931
Murder of the Missing Link (Vercors), 1955
Murder of the U.S.A. (Leinster, as Jenkins), 1946
Murderer Invisible (Wylie), 1931
Murry, Meg series (L'Engle), from 1962
Mush, a Dog from Space (Pinkwater), 1995
Mutant (s Kuttner and C.L. Moore, as Padgett), 1953
Mutant Hell (Bischoff, as Grant), 1991
Mutant Season (Silverberg), 1989
Mutant Weapon (Leinster), 1959
Mutants (Neville), 1966
Mutants (s Dickson), 1970
Mutants Amok series (Bischoff, as Grant), from 1991
Mutants Are Coming (Haiblum), 1984
Mutants Rebel (Tubb), 1953
Mute (Anthony), 1981

Mutiny in Space (Davidson), 1964
Mutiny on the Bounty (Verne), 1879
My (Zamyatin), 1929
My Brother's Keeper (s Cadigan), 1992
My Brother's Keeper (Sheffield), 1982
My Country, 'Tis Not Only of Thee (s Aldiss), 1987
My Enemy, My Ally (Duane), 1984
My Experiences in the Third World War (s Moorcock), 1980
My Heart Leaps Up (Lafferty), 1986-1990
My Lady of the Nile (Rousseau), 1923
My Lady Tongue (s Sussex), 1990
My Little Helliad (J. Morris), 1988
My Lord Barbarian (Offutt), 1977
My Madness (s Kavan), 1990
My Name Is Legion (s Zelazny), 1976
My Science Project (McQuay), 1985
My Talks with Dean Spanley (Dunsany), 1936
Mysteries of the Worm (s Bloch), 1981
Mysterious Doom (s Salmonson), 1992
Mysterious Island (Verne), 1874-76
Mysterious Planet (del Rey, as Wright), 1953
Mysterious Stranger (Twain), 1916
Mysterium (Robert Charles Wilson), 1994
Mystery of Arthur Gordon Pym (Verne), 1961
Mystery of the Japanese Clock (s Leiber), 1982
Mystery of the Third Mine (Lowndes), 1953
Mystery on Happy Bones (Dent, as Robeson), 1979
Mystery on the Snow (Dent, as Robeson), 1972
Mystery under the Sea (Dent, as Robeson), 1968
Mystic Mullah (Dent, as Robeson), 1965
Myth series (Asprin), from 1978
Mythago series (Holdstock), from 1984
Mythmaster (Kelley), 1973
Myths, Legends, and True History (s Landis), 1991
Myths of the Near Future (s Ballard), 1982

N-Space (s Niven), 1990
Nada the Lily (Haggard), 1892
Nail Down the Stars (Morressy), 1973
Naked Came the Robot (Longyear), 1988
Naked Lunch (W. Burroughs), 1959
Naked Sun (Asimov), 1957
Naked to the Stars (Dickson), 1961
Naming the Flowers (s Wilhelm), 1992
Nanoware Time (s Watson), 1991
Nantucket Slayrides (s Shepard), 1989
Naphar series (Baker), from 1984
Napoleon Wager (Forstchen), 1993
Narabedla Ltd. (Pohl), 1988
Narrative of Arthur Gordon Pym of Nantucket (Poe), 1838
Narrow Land (s Vance), 1982
Nash, Gilbert series (Tucker), from 1953
Native Tongue (Elgin), 1984
Native Tongue series (Elgin), from 1987
Natives of Space (s Clement), 1965
Natural State (Knight), 1975
Nature's God (Robert Anton Wilson), 1991
Nautilus (McIntyre), 1994
Nautilus Sanction (Hawke), 1985
Navigator of Rhada (Coppel, as Gilman), 1969
Navigator's Sindrome series (J. Carr), from 1983

Nazhuret of Sordaling series (MacAvoy), from 1990
Neanderthal Planet (s Aldiss), 1970
Nearest Fire (Wilder), 1980
Nebogipfel at the End of Time (s Lupoff), 1979
Nebula Alert (Chandler), 1967
Nebula Maker (Stapledon), 1976
Nebula X (Fearn, as Statten), 1950
Necrom (Farren), 1991
Necromancer (Dickson), 1962
Necromancer Nine (Tepper), 1983
Necroville (McDonald), 1994
Nectar of Heaven (Tubb), 1981
Ned Feldman, Space Pirate (Pinkwater), 1994
Nedao series (Emerson), from 1987
Needle (Clement), 1950
Needle in a Timestack (s Silverberg), 1966
Needle series (Clement), from 1950
Negative Minus (Fanthorpe), 1963
Negative Ones (Fanthorpe, as Muller), 1965
Neighbor of the Beast (C. Grant, as Fenn), 1992
Nemesis (Asimov), 1989
Nemesis (Fanthorpe, as Fane), 1964
Nemesis from Terra (Brackett), 1961
Nemesis of Evil (L. Carter), 1975
Nemo (Goulart), 1977
Neon Twilight (Bryant), 1990
Neptune Crossing (Carver), 1994
Neptune Rising (s Yolen), 1982
Neptune's Cauldron (Coney), 1981
Neq, the Sword (Anthony), 1975
Nerilka's Story (McCaffrey), 1986
Nerves (del Rey), 1956
Nest of Nightmares (s Tuttle), 1986
Nestling (C. Grant), 1982
Nets of Space (Petaja), 1969
Neural Atrocity (Farren), 1977
Neuromancer (Gibson), 1984
Neuron World (Fanthorpe), 1965
Neutral Stars (Kippax), 1973
Neutron Star (s Niven), 1968
Never Let Up (Maine), 1964
Never the Same Door (Mason, as Rankine), 1967
Nevermore Affair (Wilhelm), 1966
Neverness (Zindell), 1988
Nevèryon series (Delany), from 1983
Nevèrÿona (Delany), 1983
New Adam (Weinbaum), 1939
New America (s P. Anderson), 1982
New Arrivals, Old Encounters (s Aldiss), 1979
New Atlantis (s Le Guin), 1989
New Bodies for Old (Renard), 1923
New Eden (Hyne), 1892
New Found Land (Christopher), 1983
New Gods Lead (s S. Wright), 1932
New King (s Shiel), 1980
New Legends (Bear), 1995
New Life (s Binder, as Coleridge), 1942
New Messiah (Cromie), 1902
New Pleasure (Gloag), 1933
New Satellite (Fearn, as Statten), 1951
New Springtime series (Silverberg), from 1988

New World series (Kahn), from 1980
Neweden series (Leigh), from 1981
Newhome series (Randall), from 1978
News from Elsewhere (s Cooper), 1968
News from Nowhere (W. Morris), 1890
Newton and the Quasi-Apple (Schmidt), 1975
Next Chapter (Maurois), 1927
Next Crusade (Cromie), 1896
Next Door to the Sun (Coblentz), 1960
Next of Kin (Russell), 1959
Next Stop the Stars (s Silverberg), 1962
Next Wave series (Allen), from 1992
Nexus (McQuay), 1989
Nice Day for Screaming (s Schmitz), 1965
Nick and the Glimmung (Dick), 1988
Nick of Time (Effinger), 1985
Nick of Time series (Effinger), from 1986
Nidor series (Garrett, Silverberg), from 1957
Night and the Enemy (s Ellison), 1987
Night Chills (Koontz), 1976
Night Face (P. Anderson), 1978
Night Fear (s Long), 1979
Night Gallery (s Serling), 1971
Night Gallery 2 (s Serling), 1972
Night Gift (McKillip), 1976
Night Hunter (Reaves), 1995
Night in the Lonesome October (Zelazny), 1993
Night in the Netherhells (Gardner), 1987
Night Land (Hodgson), 1912
Night Life of the Gods (T. Smith), 1931
Night Man (Jeter), 1990
Night Mare (Anthony), 1983
Night Monsters (s Leiber), 1969
Night Moves (s Powers), 1986
Night Ocean (s Lovecraft), 1982
Night of Delusions (Laumer), 1972
Night of Fire and Blood (Kelley), 1979
Night of Kadar (Kilworth), 1978
Night of Light (Farmer), 1966
Night of Masks (Norton), 1964
Night of Power (S. Robinson), 1985
Night of the Big Heat (Lymington), 1959
Night of the Cooters (s Waldrop), 1990
Night of the Dragonstar (Bischoff, Montelone), 1985
Night of the Living 'Gator! (Lupoff), 1992
Night of the Saucers (Binder), 1971
Night of the Wolf (Long), 1972
Night of the Wolf (s Leiber), 1966
Night Relics (Blaylock), 1994
Night Ride and Other Journeys (s Beaumont), 1960
Night Runner (Hoskins, as Kerr), 1979
Night Screams (Malzberg), 1979
Night Slaves (Sohl), 1965
Night Songs (C. Grant), 1984
Night Spiders (s Lymington), 1964
Night Things (Monteleone), 1980
Night-Threads series (Emerson), from 1990
Night unto Night (Wylie), 1944
Night Vision (Jeter), 1985
Night Walk (Shaw), 1967
Night's Black Agents (s Leiber), 1947

NYPD 2025 (George H. Smith, as Stryker), 1985

O Master Caliban! (Gotlieb), 1976
Oak and the Ram (Moorcock), 1973
Oak King's Daughter (s de Lint), 1979
Oath of Fealty (Niven, Pournelle), 1981
Oath of the Renuciates (Bradley), 1984
Oathbound Wizard (Stasheff), 1993
Oaths and Miracles (Kress), 1995
Observers (Knight), 1988
Occam's Razor (David Duncan), 1957
Ocean on Top (Clement), 1973
Ocean Under the Ice (Forward), 1994
Octagon (Saberhagen), 1981
Octagon Magic (Norton), 1967
October Country (s Bradbury), 1955
October the First Is Too Late (F. and G. Hoyle), 1966
October's Baby (Cook), 1980
Odd Jobs series (Goulart), from 1978
Odd John (Stapledon), 1935
Odd Warlock Out (Stasheff), 1989
Oddkins (Koontz), 1988
Odious Ones (Sohl), 1959
Odyssey of Nine (Fearn, as Statten), 1953
Odyssey series (Clarke), from 1968
Odyssey to Earthdeath (Kelley), 1968
Of Alien Bondage (Offutt, as Cleve), 1982
Of All Possible Worlds (s Tenn), 1955
Of Earth Foretold (Bulmer), 1961
Of Godlike Power (Reynolds), 1966
Of Man and Mantra (Anthony), 1986
Of Men and Monsters (Tenn), 1968
Of Other Worlds (s Lewis), 1966
Of Space/Time and the River (s Benford), 1985
Of the Fall (McAuley), 1989
Of Time and Stars (s Clarke), 1972
Off Center (s Knight), 1965
Off-Planet (s Simak), 1988
Off-Worlders (Baxter), 1966
Ogre Downstairs (Diana Wynne Jones), 1974
Ogre, Ogre (Anthony), 1982
Old Captivity (Shute), 1940
Old Die Rich (s Gold), 1955
Old Friend of the Family (Saberhagen), 1979
Old Funny Stuff (s Effinger), 1989
Old Gods Waken (Wellman), 1979
Old Man in New World (s Stapledon), 1944
Old Nathan (s Drake), 1991
Old Tin Sorrows (Cook), 1989
Old Woman Whose Rolling Pin Is the Sun (s G. Wolfe), 1991
Ole Doc Methuselah (s Hubbard), 1970
O'Leary series (Laumer), from 1966
Olga Romanoff (G. Griffith), 1894
Omega Cage (Perry, Reaves), 1988
Omega Man (Matheson), 1971
Omega Point series (Zebrowski), from 1972
Omega Worm (Mason), 1976
Omens of Kregen (Bulmer, as Akers), 1985
Omha Abides (MacApp), 1968
Omicron Invasion (Goldin), 1984
Omnibus of Time (s Farley), 1950

Omnicron Invasion (E.E. Smith), 1984
Omnificence Factor (Z. Hughes), 1994
Omnivore (Anthony), 1968
On a Pale Horse (Anthony), 1983
On a Planet Alien (Malzberg), 1974
On Alien Wings (Goulart), 1975
On My Way to Paradise (Wolverton), 1989
On Saint Hubert's Thing (s Yarbro), 1982
On Stranger Tides (Powers), 1987
On the Beach (Shute), 1957
On the Far Side of the Cadillac Desert with the Dead Folks (s Lansdale), 1991
On the Flip Side (Fisk), 1983
On the Moon (Tsiolkovsky), n.d.
On the Red World (Kelley), 1979
On the Run (Dickson), 1979
On the Seas of Destiny (Emerson), 1989
On the Symb-Socket Circuit (Bulmer), 1972
On Wheels (Jakes), 1973
On Wings of Magic (Norton), 1994
On Wings of Song (Disch), 1979
Once Departed (Reynolds), 1970
Once There Was a Giant (s Laumer), 1971
Once Upon a Time in the East (C. Grant, as Fenn), 1993
One against Herculum (Sohl), 1959
One against the Legion (s Williamson), 1967
One against the Moon (Wollheim), 1956
One Against Eternity (van Vogt), 1955
One-Eye (S. Gordon), 1973
One Human Minute (s Lem), 1986
One Hundred and Two H-Bombs (s Disch), 1966
One in Three Hundred (McIntosh), 1954
One is One (Mason, as Rankine), 1968
One King's Way (H. Harrison), 1995
One Land, One Duke (Emerson), 1992
One Man's Universe (s Sheffield), 1993
One Million Centuries (Lupoff), 1967
One Million Tomorrows (Shaw), 1970
One of Our Asteroids Is Missing (Silverberg, as M. Knox), 1964
One Side Laughing (s Knight), 1991
One Step from Earth (s H. Harrison), 1970
One Tree (Donaldson), 1982
One Winter in Eden (s Bishop), 1984
Ones Who Walk Away from Omelas (s Le Guin), 1993
Only Begotten Daughter (Morrow), 1990
Only Child (Hoover), 1992
Only You Can Save Mankind (Pratchett), 1992
Opal-Eyed Fan (Norton), 1977
Opar series (Farmer), from 1974
Open Prison (J. White), 1965
Opener of the Way (s Bloch), 1945
Operation ARES (G. Wolfe), 1970
Operation Chaos (P. Anderson), 1971
Operation High Dragon (Stine), 1989
Operation Interstellar (George O. Smith), 1950
Operation Iron Fist (Stine), 1989
Operation Nuke (Caidin), 1973
Operation Steel Band (Stine), 1988
Operation Terror (Leinster), 1962
Operation Time Search (Norton), 1967
Operation Umanaq (Mason, as Rankine), 1973

Operation Venus (Fearn), 1950
Operation: Outer Space (Leinster), 1954
Ophiuchi Hotline (Varley), 1977
Opium Generals (s Moorcock), 1984
Opoponax Invasion (Brosnan), 1993
Optiman (Stableford), 1980
Options (Sheckley), 1975
Or All the Seas with Oysters (s Davidson), 1962
ORA: CLE (O'Donnell), 1984
Oracle (Resnick), 1992
Oracle series (Resnick), from 1991
Orange County series (K. Robinson), from 1984
Orbit One (Fanthorpe, as Muller), 1962
Orbit Unlimited (s P. Anderson), 1961
Orbital Resonance (J. Barnes), 1991
Orbitsville series (Shaw), from 1975
Orc's Opal (Anthony), 1990
Orchard (C. Grant), 1986
Orchid Cage (Franke), 1973
Ordeal (Shute), 1939
Ordeal in Otherwhere (Norton), 1964
Organ Bank Farm (Boyd), 1970
Orgasmachine (Watson), 1976
Orion series (Bova), from 1984
Orion Shall Rise (P. Anderson), 1983
Orn (Anthony), 1971
Orphan of Creation (Allen), 1988
Orphan Star (A. Foster), 1977
Orphans of the Sky (s Heinlein), 1963
Orsinian Tales (s Le Guin), 1976
Orthe series (Gentle), from 1983
Orvis (Hoover), 1987
Ossian's Ride (F. and G. Hoyle), 1959
Other (Dickson), 1994
Other Americas (s Spinrad), 1988
Other Days, Other Eyes (Shaw), 1972
Other Dimensions (s Clark Ashton Smith), 1970
Other Eyes Watching (Fearn, as Cross), 1946
Other Foot (Knight), 1966
Other Half of the Planet (Capon), 1952
Other Human Race (Piper), 1964
Other Log of Phileas Fogg (Farmer), 1973
Other Passenger (s Cross), 1944
Other Place Sort (s Priestley), 1953
Other Side of Green Hills (Cross), 1947
Other Side of Here (Leinster), 1955
Other Side of Nowhere (Leinster), 1964
Other Side of the Sky (s Clarke), 1958
Other Side of the Sun (Capon), 1950
Other Side of Time (Laumer), 1965
Other Sinbad (Gardner), 1991
Other Sky (s Laumer), 1968
Other Time (Ing, Reynolds), 1984
Other Times, Other Worlds (s J. MacDonald), 1978
Other Voices (Greenland), 1988
Other World (Dent, as Robeson), 1968
Other Worlds of Clifford Simak (s Simak), 1962
Otherness (s Brin), 1994
Ou Lu Khen and the Beautiful Madwoman (Salmonson), 1985
Our Ancestors (s Calvino), 1980
Our Best (s Kornbluth), 1987

Our Children's Children (Simak), 1974
Our Friends from Frolix 8 (Dick), 1970
Our Lady of Darkness (Leiber), 1977
Our Lady of the Harbour (s de Lint), 1991
Out (Brooke-Rose), 1964
Out (Meltzer), 1969
Out from Ganymede (s Malzberg), 1974
Out of Bounds (s Merril), 1960
Out of Chaos (McIntosh), 1965
Out of My Head (s Bloch), 1986
Out of My Mind (s Brunner), 1967
Out of Space and Time (s Clark Ashton Smith), 1942
Out of Sync (Haiblum), 1990
Out of the Darkness (Fanthorpe), 1960
Out of the Dead City (Delany), 1968
Out of the Deeps (Wyndham), 1953
Out of the Everywhere and Other Extraordinary Visions (s Tiptree), 1981
Out of the Mouth of the Dragon (Geston), 1969
Out of the Mouths of Graves (s Bloch), 1979
Out of the Night (Fanthorpe, as Muller), 1965
Out of the Silence (Cox), 1925
Out of the Silent Planet (Lewis), 1938
Out of the Silent Sky (s Biggle), 1977
Out of the Storm (s Hodgson), 1975
Out of the Sun (Bova), 1968
Out of the Unknown (s van Vogt), 1948
Out of Their Minds (Simak), 1970
Out of This World (Leinster), 1958
Out of This World (Watt-Evans), 1994
Out of Time (Hogan), 1993
Out on Blue Six (McDonald), 1989
Out There Where the Big Ships Go (s Cowper), 1980
Outcasts of Heaven Belt (J. Vinge), 1978
Outerworld (Haiblum), n.d.
Outland (A. Foster), 1981
Outlanders series (Coblentz), from 1964
Outlaw World (Hamilton), 1969
Outlaws of Mars (Kline), 1960
Outlaws of the Air (G. Griffith), 1895
Outlaws of the Moon (Hamilton), 1969
Outnumbering the Dead (Pohl), 1991
Outpassage (J. Morris), 1988
Outpost Mars (Merril, Kornbluth, as Judd), 1952
Outpost of Jupiter (del Rey), 1963
Outposter (Dickson), 1972
Outreach (Lichtenberg), 1986
Outside (Norton), 1974
Outside the Universe (Hamilton), 1964
Outsider and Others (s Lovecraft), 1939
Outward Bound (J. Coulson), 1982
Outward Urge (Wyndham), 1959
Outworlder (L. Carter), 1971
Ova Hamlet Papers (s Lupoff), 1979
Over the Edge (s Ellison), 1970
Over the Hills and Far Away (s Dunsany), 1974
Overkill (Crichton), 1972
Overlay (Malzberg), 1972
Overloaded Man (s Ballard), 1967
Overlords of War (Klein), 1973
Overman Culture (Cooper), 1971

Perilous Galaxy (Fanthorpe, as Muller), 1962
Perilous Seas (Dave Duncan), 1991
Peripheral Vision (s Fowler), 1990
Permutation City (Egan), 1994
Perrin, Michael series (Bear), from 1984
Perry's Planet (Jack C. Haldeman), 1980
Persistence of Vision (s Varley), 1978
Persistence of Vision (s Varley), 1991
Personal Darkness (Lee), 1993
Personal Demon (Bischoff), 1985
Personality Surgeon (C. Wilson), 1985
Pet (C. Grant), 1986
Peter Nevsky and the True Story of the Russian Moon Landing
    (Batchelor), 1993
Petrified Planet (Fearn, as Statten), 1951
Phaeton Condition (Mason), 1973
Phaid the Gambler (Farren), 1986
Phantastes (G. MacDonald), 1858
Phantom Banjo (Scarborough), 1991
Phantom City (Dent, as Robeson), 1966
Phantom Crusader (s Fanthorpe, as Brett), 1963
Phantom of the Lunch Wagon (Pinkwater), 1992
Phantom Ones (Fanthorpe, as Torro), 1961
Phantom Piper (Kilworth), 1994
Phantom Universe (Garnett), 1975
Phantoms (Koontz), 1983
Phase IV (Malzberg), 1973
Phase Two (Richmond), 1979
Phaze Doubt (Anthony), 1990
Phenomena X (Fanthorpe, as Muller), 1966
Philip K. Dick Is Dead (Bishop), 1988
Philosopher's Stone (C. Wilson), 1969
Phobos, The Robot Planet (Capon), 1955
Phoenix (Cowper), 1968
Phoenix (T. White), 1977
Phoenix and the Mirror (Davidson), 1969
Phoenix in Obsidian (Moorcock), 1970
Phoenix in the Ashes (s J. Vinge), 1985
Phoenix of Megaron (Mason, as Rankine), 1976
Phoenix Prime (T. White), 1966
Phoenix Ship (Richmond), 1969
Phoenix without Ashes (Bryant, Ellison), 1975
Phra the Phonecian (Arnold), 1910
Phthor (Anthony), 1975
Phule series (Asprin), from 1990
Picking the Ballad's Bones (Scarborough), 1991
Pickle Creature (Pinkwater), 1979
Picnic on Nearside (s Varley), 1984
Picnic on Paradise (Russ), 1968
Piece of Martin Cann (Janifer), 1968
Piecework (s Brin), 1991
Piers Anthony's Hasan (Anthony), 1977
Pig Ignorant (Fisk), 1991
Pilgermann (Hoban), 1983
Pilgrim Project (Searls), 1964
Pilgrim series (Saberhagen), from 1987
Pilgrimage (s Henderson), 1961
Pilgrimage to Earth (s Sheckley), 1957
Pilgrims of the Rhine (s Bulwer-Lytton), 1834
Pillars of Eternity (Bayley), 1982
Pimpernel Plot (Hawke), 1984

Pink Elephants and Hairy Toads (s Resnick), 1991
Pink of Fading Neon (s Blaylock), 1986
Pioneer 1990 (Fearn, as Statten), 1953
Pioneers (Mann), 1988
Pirate of the Pacific (Dent, as Robeson), 1967
Pirate of World's End (L. Carter), 1978
Pirate's Ghost (Dent, as Robeson), 1971
Pirates of Rosinante (Gilliland), 1982
Pirates of the Thunder (Chalker), 1987
Pirates of Venus (E. Burroughs), 1934
Pirates of Zan (Leinster), 1959
Pirx the Pilot series (s Lem), from 1979
Pit Dragons series (Yolen), from 1982
Pitman's Progress (Mason), 1976
Pixilated Peeress (de Camp), 1991
Place Named Hell (George H. Smith, as Deer), 1963
Place of Dead Roads (W. Burroughs), 1983
Place of Silver Silence (Mayhar), 1988
Plague Daemon (Stableford, as Craig), 1990
Plague from Space (H. Harrison), 1965
Plague of Angels (Tepper), 1993
Plague of Demons (Laumer), 1965
Plague of Pythons (Pohl), 1965
Plague of Sound (Goulart, as Steffanson), 1974
Plague Ship (Norton, as North), 1956
Plains (Murnane), 1982
Planet Buyer (Cordwainer Smith), 1964
Planet Called Treason (Card), 1979
Planet Called Utopia (McIntosh), 1979
Planet Explorer (Leinster), 1957
Planet for Texans (Piper), 1958
Planet in Peril (Christopher), 1959
Planet Killers (Silverberg), 1959
Planet Mappers (Evans), 1955
Planet Murderer (Offutt, as Cleve), 1984
Planet of Death (F. and G. Hoyle), 1982
Planet of Death (Silverberg), 1967
Planet of Dread (Tubb, as Kern), 1974
Planet of Exile (Le Guin), 1966
Planet of Fear (P. Moore), 1977
Planet of Fire (P. Moore), 1969
Planet of Flowers (Norwood), 1984
Planet of Judgment (Joe Haldeman), 1977
Planet of Light (R. Jones), 1953
Planet of No Return (P. Anderson), 1957
Planet of No Return (H. Harrison), 1981
Planet of Peril (Kline), 1929
Planet of Robot Slaves (H. Harrison), 1989
Planet of the Apes (Boulle), 1963
Planet of the Apes series (Effinger), from 1974
Planet of the Apes series (Rotsler), from 1976
Planet of the Damned series (H. Harrison), from 1962
Planet of the Double Sun (s N. Jones), 1967
Planet of the Dreamers (J. MacDonald), 1953
Planet of the Voles (Platt), 1977
Planet of Treachery (E.E. Smith), 1982
Planet of Treachery (Goldin), 1982
Planet of Whispers (Kelly), 1984
Planet of Your Own (Brunner), 1966
Planet of Youth (Coblentz), 1952
Planet on the Table (s K. Robinson), 1986

Planet Patrol (Dorman), 1978
Planet Pirate series (McCaffrey), from 1990
Planet Plane (Wyndham, as Beynon), 1936
Planet Poachers (Lightner), 1965
Planet Run (Dickson, Laumer), 1967
Planet Savers (Bradley), 1962
Planet Seekers (Fanthorpe, as Barton), 1964
Planet Story (H. Harrison), 1979
Planet Strappers (Gallun), 1961
Planet Wizard (Jakes), 1969
Planetary Agent X (Reynolds), 1965
Planeteers (s Campbell), 1966
Planetfall (Tubb, as Hunt), 1951
Planetfall series (Cover), from 1988
Planetoid Disposals Ltd (Tubb, as Gridban), 1953
Planets for Sale (van Vogt), 1954
Planets in Peril (Hamilton), 1969
Planets Three (s Pohl), 1982
Plantos Affair (Mason, as Rankine), 1971
Plan[e]t Engineering (s G. Wolfe), 1984
Plasm (Platt), 1987
Plattner Story (s Wells), 1897
Platypus of Doom and Other Nihilists (s Cover), 1976
Player of Games (Banks), 1988
Player Piano (Vonnegut), 1952
Players at the Game of People (Brunner), 1980
Players of Null-A (van Vogt), 1970
Playgrounds of the Mind (s Niven), 1991
Pleasant Dreams—Nightmares (s Bloch), 1960
Pleasure Us! (Offutt, as Cleve), 1971
Pliocene Exile series (May), from 1981
Plot against Earth (Silverberg, as Knox), 1959
Plunder (Goulart), 1972
Plunge into Space (Cromie), 1890
Pluribus (Kurland), 1975
Pnume (Vance), 1970
Podkayne of Mars (Heinlein), 1963
Pohlstars (s Pohl), 1984
Point Ultimate (Sohl), 1955
Points of Departure (s Murphy), 1990
Poison Belt (Doyle), 1913
Poison Island (Dent, as Robeson), 1971
Poisoned Pussy (Fox), 1969
Polar Fleet (Norwood), 1985
Polar Treasure (Dent, as Robeson), 1965
Polesotechnic League series (P. Anderson), from 1963
Police Patrol: 2000 A.D (Reynolds), 1977
Police Your Planet (del Rey, as Van Lhin), 1956
Pollen (Noon), 1995
Pollinators of Eden (Boyd), 1969
Polly Charms the Sleeping Woman (s Davidson), 1977
Poltergeist series (Kahn), from 1982
Polymath (Brunner), 1974
Pool of Fire (Christopher), 1968
Port Eternity (Cherryh), 1982
Port of Peril (Kline), 1949
Port of Saints (W. Burroughs), 1973
Portent (G. MacDonald), 1864
Portent (J. Herbert), 1992
Porter, Harry series (Naha), from 1980
Portraits of His Children (s Martin), 1987

Poseidonis (s Clark Ashton Smith), 1973
Positive Charge (s Richmond), 1970
Positronic Man (Asimov, Silverberg), 1992
Possessors (Christopher), 1965
Post-Holocaust America series (Pangborn), from 1964
Postman (Brin), 1985
Postmarked the Stars (Norton), 1969
Power (F. Robinson), 1956
Power (Janifer), 1974
Power (S. Wright), 1933
Power (Watson), 1987
Power Ball (Lymington), 1981
Power Lines (McCaffrey, Scarborough), 1994
Power of Blackness (Williamson), 1976
Power of Three (Diana Wynne Jones), 1976
Power of Time (s Saxton), 1985
Power of X (Sellings), 1968
Power Sphere (Fanthorpe, as Brett), 1963
Power That Preserves (Donaldson), 1977
Powers series (McCaffrey, Scarborough), from 1993
Practice Effect (Brin), 1984
Prayer Machine (Hodder-Williams), 1976
Predator 2: A Novel (Hawke), 1990
Preferred Risk (del Rey and Pohl, as McCann), 1955
Prelude in Prague (S. Wright), 1935
Prelude to Mars (Clarke), 1965
Prelude to Space (Clarke), 1951
Prentice Alvin (Card), 1989
Preposterous Adventures of Swimmer (Key), 1973
Prescott, Dray series (Bulmer), from 1972
Preserver (M.A. Foster), 1985
Preserving Machine (s Dick), 1969
Press Enter (s Varley), 1990
Pressure Man (Z. Hughes), 1980
Pretender (Anthony), 1979
Prey (Naha, as Drumm), 1987
Prey (Perry), 1994
Price of Oranges (s Kress), 1992
Pride of Chanur (Cherryh), 1982
Pride of Monsters (s Schmitz), 1970
Priest (Disch), 1994
Priests of Psi (s F. Herbert), 1980
Primal Urge (Aldiss), 1961
Prime Number (s H. Harrison), 1970
Primitive (Tubb), 1977
Prince Alcouz and the Magician (s Clark Ashton Smith), 1977
Prince Caspian (Lewis), 1951
Prince in Waiting series (Christopher), from 1970
Prince of Chaos (Zelazny), 1991
Prince of Mercenaries (Pournelle), 1989
Prince of Morning Bells (Kress), 1981
Prince of Peril (Kline), 1930
Prince of Scorpio (Bulmer, as Akers), 1974
Prince of Sparta (Pournelle, Stirling), 1993
Prince of the Blood (Feist), 1989
Prince of the North (Turtledove), 1994
Prince on a White Horse (Lee), 1982
Prince Raynor (s Kuttner), 1987
Prince with the Silver Hand (Moorcock), 1993
Prince Zaleski (s Shiel), 1895
Princes of Earth (Kurland), 1978

Princes of the Air (Ford), 1982
Princess and Curdie (G. MacDonald), 1882
Princess and the Goblin (G. MacDonald), 1871
Princess and the Lord of Night (Bull), 1994
Princess Daphne (Blayre as Heron-Allen), 1885
Princess Hynchatti and Some Other Surprises (s Lee), 1972
Princess of Flames (Emerson), 1986
Princess of Mars (E. Burroughs), 1917
Princess of the Atom (Cummings), 1950
Princess of the Chameln (Wilder), 1984
Prism (Petaja), 1968
Prison of Night (Tubb), 1977
Prison Satellite (Kelley), 1979
Prison Ship (Caidin), 1989
Prisoner (Disch), 1969
Prisoner of Blackwood Castle (Goulart), 1984
Prisoner of Fire (Cooper), 1974
Prisoner of Zhamanak (de Camp), 1982
Prisoners of Power (Strugatsky), 1977
Prisoners of Space (del Rey and Fairman, as del Rey), 1968
Prisoners of the Sky (MacApp), 1969
Prisoners of the Stars (Asimov), 1979
Pritcher Mass (Dickson), 1972
Private Cosmos (Farmer), 1968
Private Life of Adam and Eve (s Twain), 1931
Private School series (C. Grant), from 1986
Private Universe (s Maurois), 1932
Privateers series (Bova), from 1985
Pro (Dickson), 1978
Probability Corner (Richmond), 1977
Prodigal Sun (High), 1964
Productions of Time (Brunner), 1967
Professor Challenger series (Doyle), from 1892
Professor Dowell's Head (Belyaev), 1980
Professor Jameson series (s N. Jones), from 1967
Profundis (Cowper), 1979
Project Barrier (s Galouye), 1968
Project Jupiter (F. Brown), 1954
Project Pendulum (Silverberg), 1987
Project Pope (Simak), 1981
Projection Barrier (Fanthorpe, as Zeigfreid), 1964
Prometheans (s Bova), 1986
Prometheus Crisis (F. Robinson, Scortia), 1975
Prometheus Man (Nelson), 1982
Promise (M. Hughes), 1989
Promised Land (Stableford), 1974
Promontory Goats (s Lafferty), 1988
Propeller Island (Verne), 1961
Prophet (Resnick), 1993
Prose Bowl (Malzberg), 1980
Prostho Plus (s Anthony), 1971
Protector (Niven), 1973
Protectorate (Farren), 1984
Proteus Operation (Hogan), 1985
Proteus series (Sheffield), from 1978
Proud Enemy (Busby), 1975
Proud Helios (Scott), 1995
Proud Man (Burdekin, as Constantine), 1934
Proud Robot (s Kuttner and C.L. Moore, as Padgett), 1983
Proxima Project (Rackham), 1968
Proxy Intelligence and Other Mind Benders (s van Vogt), 1971

Pruzy's Pot (s Sturgeon), 1986
Pry, Charles series (Large), from 1937
Psi High (s Nourse), 1967
Psi Hunt (Kurland), 1980
Psion (J. Vinge), 1982
Psionic Menace (Brunner), 1963
Pstalemate (del Rey), 1971
Psychedelic-40 (Charbonneau), 1965
Psychlone (Bear), 1979
Psycho Makers (George H. Smith, as Jason), 1965
Psychodrome series (Hawke), from 1987
Psychopath Plague (Spruill), 1978
Psychotechnic League series (P. Anderson), from 1981
Pugnacious Peacemaker (s Turtledove), 1990
Pulling Through (Ing), 1983
Puppet Masters (Heinlein), 1951
Puppies of Terra (Disch), 1978
Purchase of the North Pole (Verne), 1890
Pure Blood (McQuay), 1985
Purgatory (Resnick), 1993
Purity Plot (E.E. Smith), 1980
Purity Plot (Goldin), 1978
Purloined Planet (L. Carter), 1969
Purloined Prince (I. Wallace), 1971
Purple Book (s Farmer), 1982
Purple Cloud (Shiel), 1901
Purple Dragon (Dent, as Robeson), 1978
Purple Pterodactyls (s de Camp), 1979
Purple Sapphire (Taine), 1924
Purple Sapphire and Other Posthumous Papers (s Blayre), 1921
Purple Wizard (Fearn, as Gridban), 1953
Purple Zombie (Goulart, as Robeson), 1974
Purrfect Plunder (Offutt, as Cleve), 1982
Pursuit of Miracles (s Turner), 1990
Pursuit on Ganymede (Resnick), 1968
Puzzle of the Space Pyramids (Binder), 1971
Puzzle Planet (Lowndes), 1961
Pyramids (Pratchett), 1989
Pyramids (Saberhagen), 1987

Q Colony (Thurston), 1985
Q series (T. Hoyle), from 1977
Qanar series (T. White), from 1966
Qfwfq series (Calvino), from 1968
Quag Keep (Norton), 1978
Quality of Mercy (Compton), 1965
Quantrill, Ted series (Ing), from 1981
Quarantine (Egan), 1992
Quarantine World (s Leinster), 1992
Quarreling, They Met the Dragon (Baker), 1984
Quatermass (Kneale), 1979
Quayle's Invention (Taine), 1927
Queen of Air and Darkness (s P. Anderson), 1973
Queen of Angels (Bear), 1990
Queen of Atlantis (Aubrey), 1899
Queen of Sorcery (Eddings), 1982
Queen of Springtime (Silverberg), 1989
Queen of Stones (Tennant), 1982
Queen of the Dawn (Haggard), 1925
Queen of the Legion (Williamson), 1983
Queen of the States (Saxton), 1986

Queen of the Swords (Moorcock), 1971
Queen Sheba's Ring (Haggard), 1910
Queen's Squadron (Meluch), 1992
Queenmagic, Kingmagic (Watson), 1988
Queensblade (Shwartz), 1988
Quench the Burning Stars (Bulmer), 1970
Quest beyond the Stars (Hamilton), 1969
Quest Crosstime (Norton), 1965
Quest for Lost Heroes (Gemmell), 1990
Quest for Saint Camber (Kurtz), 1986
Quest for Tanelorn (Moorcock), 1975
Quest for the Future (van Vogt), 1970
Quest for the Well of Souls (Chalker), 1978
Quest for the White Duck series (C. Grant), from 1986
Quest for the White Witch (Lee), 1978
Quest, Gregory series (P. Moore), from 1956
Quest of Kadji (L. Carter), 1971
Quest of Qui (Dent, as Robeson), 1966
Quest of the DNA Cowboys (Farren), 1976
Quest of the Gypsy (Goulart), 1976
Quest of the Spaceways (P. Moore), 1955
Quest of the Spider (Dent, as Robeson), 1935
Quest of the Three Worlds (Cordwainer Smith), 1966
Questing of Kedrigern (Morressy), 1987
Question and Answer (P. Anderson), 1978
Question of Time (Saberhagen), 1992
Question Quest (Anthony), 1991
Quests of Simon Ark (s Hoch), 1984
Quickening (s Bishop), 1991
Quicks around the Zodiac (s Leiber), 1983
Quicksand (Brunner), 1967
Quicksilver's Knight (Stasheff), 1995
Quiet Night of Fear (C. Grant), 1981
Quiet of Stone (Leigh), 1984
Quiet Pools (Kube-McDowell), 1990
Quiet Woman (Priest), 1990
Quillian Sector (Tubb), 1978
Quincunx of Time (Blish), 1973
Quintara Marathon series (Chalker), from 1989
Quirke, Adam series (Fearn), from 1953
Quozl (A. Foster), 1989
Quy Effect (Sellings), 1966

R Is for Rocker (s Bradbury), 1962
R-Master (Dickson), 1973
Rabelaisian Reprise (J. Carr), 1988
Race across the Stars (Offutt, as Cleve), 1984
Race Against Time (Anthony), 1973
Rachel in Love (s Murphy), 1992
Rack the Healer series (Z. Hughes), from 1973
Radar Alert (Fanthorpe, as Zeigfreid), 1963
Radio Beasts (Farley), 1964
Radio Detectives under the Sea (Verrill), 1922
Radio Free Albemuth (Dick), 1985
Radio Man series (Farley), from 1946
Radio Planet (Farley), 1964
Radium Seekers (Aubrey, as Ash), 1905
Radix (Attanasio), 1981
Radix Tetrad series (Attanasio), from 1984
Raft (Baxter), 1991
Rafters Were Singing (s de Lint), 1986

Rag, A Bone, and a Hank of Hair (Fisk), 1980
Rage for Revenge (Gerrold), 1989
Ragged Astronauts (Shaw), 1986
Ragged Edge (Christopher), 1966
Ragged World (Moffett), 1991
Ragnarok (Compton, Gribbin), 1991
Ragnarok series (Godwin), from 1958
Raid of "Le Vengeur" (s G. Griffith), 1974
Raiders from the Rings (Nourse), 1962
Raiders on Mars (P. Moore), 1959
Rain Ghost (Kilworth), 1989
Rain in the Doorway (T. Smith), 1933
Rainbow and the Rose (Shute), 1958
Rainbow Man (Engh), 1993
Rains of Eridan (Hoover), 1977
Raising the Stones (Tepper), 1990
Rajah's Sapphire (Shiel), 1896
Rakehells of Heaven (Boyd), 1969
Rally Cry (Forstchen), 1990
Ralph 124C41+ (Gernsback), 1925
Ram Song (Webb), 1984
Rama series (Clarke), from 1973
Ramon and Morgan series (McQuay), from 1985
Ramsgate Paradox (Tall), 1976
Ranald Bannerman's Boyhood (G. MacDonald), 1871
Random Acts of Senseless Violence (Womack), 1993
Random Factor (Maine), 1971
Ranger Boys in Space (Clement), 1956
Ranks of Bronze (Drake), 1986
Rape of the Sun (I. Wallace), 1982
Raphael (MacAvoy), 1984
Rapture Effect (Carver), 1987
Rats and Gargoyles (Gentle), 1990
Rats series (J. Herbert), from 1974
Raven (C. Grant), 1993
Raven Walking (Gardner), 1994
Ravens of the Moon (C. Grant), 1978
Rax (Coney), 1975
Ray Bradbury (s Bradbury), 1975
Re-Entry (Preuss), 1981
Re: Colonized Planet 5, Shikasta (Lessing), 1979
Reach for Tomorrow (s Clarke), 1956
Reactor XK9 (Fanthorpe, as Muller), 1963
Reade, Frank, Jr., series (Senarens), from 1884
Real Life Mr Newman (s Moorcock), 1979
Real People (Beresford), 1929
Real-Time World (s Priest), 1974
Reality Forbidden (High), 1967
Reality Is What You Can Get Away With (Robert Anton Wilson), 1992
Reality Trip and Other Implausibilities (s Silverberg), 1972
Realms of Tartarus (Stableford), 1977
Realtime Interrupt (Hogan), 1995
Realtime series (V. Vinge), from 1984
Re-Animator (s Lovecraft), 1991
Reap the East Wind (Cook), 1987
Reap The Whirlwind (Cherryh), 1989
Reaper Man (Pratchett), 1991
Reasonable World (Knight), 1991
Reavers of Skaith (Brackett), 1976
Reaving Road (Dave Duncan), 1992

Rebel Attack (Bischoff, as Grant), 1991
Rebel Dynasty: Volume 1 (Busby), 1987
Rebel Dynasty: Volume 2 (Busby), 1988
Rebel in Time (H. Harrison), 1983
Rebel of Antares (Bulmer, as Akers), 1980
Rebel of Rhada (Coppel, as Gilman), 1968
Rebel Passion (Burdekin), 1929
Rebel Worlds (P. Anderson), 1969
Rebel's Quest (Busby), 1985
Rebellious Stars (Asimov), 1954
Rebels' Seed (Busby), 1986
Rebirth of Wonder (Watt-Evans), 1992
Recall Not Earth (MacApp), 1970
Recalled to Life (Silverberg), 1962
Recipe for Diamonds (Hyne), 1893
Recruit for Andromeda (Lesser), 1959
Red Alert (George), 1959
Red as Blood (s Lee), 1983
Red Clay, Tom series (Ore), from 1988
Red Dust (McAuley), 1993
Red Eve (Haggard), 1911
Red Hart Magic (Norton), 1976
Red Hawk (Lynn), 1983
Red Insects (Fearn, as Statten), 1951
Red Iron Nights (Cook), 1991
Red Journey Back (Cross), 1954
Red Line the Stars (Norton), 1993
Red Magician (Goldstein), 1982
Red Mars (K. Robinson), 1992
Red Men of Mars (Fearn), 1950
Red Moon (Goulart, as Robeson), 1974
Red Moon series (Bradley), from 1973
Red Noise (s Sladek), 1982
Red One (s London), 1918
Red Orc's Rage (Farmer), 1991
Red Peri (s Weinbaum), 1952
Red Planet (Chilton), 1956
Red Planet (Heinlein), 1949
Red Prophet (Card), 1988
Red Skull (Dent, as Robeson), 1967
Red Snow (Dent, as Robeson), 1969
Red Spider (Dent, as Robeson), 1979
Red Tape War (Chalker, Effinger, Resnick), 1991
Red Terrors (Dent, as Robeson), 1976
Red Twilight, World's End (Rousseau), 1991
Red Wizard (Springer), 1990
Redbeard (Resnick), 1969
Rediscovery (Bradley), 1993
Rediscovery of Man (s Cordwainer Smith), 1988
Redmagic (Kilian), 1995
Reduction in Arms (Purdom), 1971
Redward Edward Papers (s Davidson), 1978
Redworld (Harness), 1986
Reefs (O'Donnell), 1981
Reefs of Earth (Lafferty), 1968
Reefs of Space (Pohl), 1964
Reefs of Space (Williamson), 1964
Reel (Janifer), 1983
Refugee (Anthony), 1983
Regan's Planet (Silverberg), 1964
Rehearsal Night (Long), 1981

Reign of Wizardry (Williamson), 1964
Reigning Cats and Dogs (Lee), 1995
Relatives (Effinger), 1973
Reluctant King (de Camp), 1985
Reluctant Shaman (s de Camp), 1970
Reluctant Sorcerer series (Hawke), from 1992
Reluctant Swordsman (Dave Duncan), 1988
Reluctant Voyagers (Vonarburg), 1995
Remake (Willis), 1995
Remaking History (s K. Robinson), 1991
Remaking of Sigmund Freud (Malzberg), 1985
Remarkable Exploits of Lancelot Biggs, Spaceman (s Bond), 1950
Remarkables (R. Reed), 1992
Remember Tomorrow (s Kuttner), 1954
Remembrance for Kedrigern (Morressy), 1990
Renaissance (R. Jones), 1951
Renaissance (van Vogt), 1979
Rendezvous in Averoigne (s Clark Ashton Smith), 1988
Rendezvous on a Lost World (Chandler), 1961
Rendezvous with Rama (Clarke), 1973
Renegade of Callisto (L. Carter), 1978
Renegade of Kregen (Bulmer, as Akers), 1976
Renegade Star (Fearn, as Statten), 1951
Renegades of Pern (McCaffrey), 1989
Renegades of Time (R. Jones), 1975
Renfro and Dipple series (Norton), from 1961
RenSime (Lichtenberg), 1984
Repairmen of Cyclops (Brunner), 1965
Report from Paradise (Twain), 1952
Report on Probability A (Aldiss), 1968
Reproductive System (Sladek), 1968
Republic of the Southern Cross (s Bryusov), 1918
Requiem (s Heinlein), 1992
Requiem for a Ruler of Worlds (Daley), 1985
Rescue Mission (Rotsler), 1981
Rescue Run (McCaffrey), 1991
Rescued from Paradise (Forward), 1995
Rest in Agony (Fairman, as Jorgensen), 1963
Rest of the Robots (s Asimov), 1964
Restaurant at the End of the Universe (Adams), 1980
Restoree (McCaffrey), 1967
Resurgam (s Fanthorpe), 1957
Resurrected Man (Tubb), 1954
Resurrection Day (Dent, as Robeson), 1969
Resurrection Days (Tucker), 1981
Resurrection, Inc (K. Anderson), 1988
Resurrection of Roger Diment (Mason), 1972
Resurrectionist (Wolf), 1979
Retief series (Laumer), from 1963
Return (Fanthorpe, as Torro), 1964
Return (Haiblum), 1973
Return (s Fanthorpe, as Brett), 1959
Return from Rainbow Bridge (s K. Robinson), 1989
Return from the Stars (Lem), 1980
Return from Witch Mountain (Key), 1978
Return of Jongor (R. Williams), 1970
Return of Nathan Brazil (Chalker), 1980
Return of Skull-Face (Lupoff), 1977
Return of the King (Tolkien), 1955
Return of the Lloigor (s C. Wilson), 1974
Return of the Moose (Pinkwater), 1979

Return of Zeus (Fanthorpe, as Muller), 1962
Return to Earth (Hoover), 1980
Return to Eddarta (Garrett), 1985
Return to Eden (H. Harrison), 1988
Return to Nevèryon (s Delany), 1989
Return to Otherness (s Kuttner), 1962
Return to Rocheworld (Forward), 1993
Return to the Stars (Hamilton), 1970
Return to Tomorrow (Harding), 1976
Return to Tomorrow (Hubbard), 1954
Returning Creation (J. Morris), 1984
Reunion (Gribbin), 1991
Revelation (Bischoff), 1991
Revelations (Malzberg), 1972
Revenant (Z. Hughes, as Zachary), 1988
Revenants (Tepper), 1984
Revenge of the Fluffy Bunnies (Gardner), 1990
Revenge of the Rose (Moorcock), 1991
Revenge of the Senior Citizens, **Plus (s K. Reed), 1986
Reverse Universe (Tubb, as Gridban), 1952
Revolt in 2100 (s Heinlein), 1953
Revolt of Aphrodite (Durrell), 1974
Revolt of the Galaxy (Goldin, E.E. Smith), 1985
Revolt of the Triffids (Wyndham), 1952
Revolt of the Unemployables (Nelson), 1978
Revolt on Alpha C (Silverberg), 1955
Revolution (Beresford), 1921
Revolution from Rosinante (Gilliland), 1981
Revolving Boy (Friedberg), 1966
Rhada series (Coppel), from 1968
Rhapsody in Amber (s Zelazny), 1981
Rhapsody in Black (Stableford), 1973
Rhialto the Marvellous (s Cherryh, Vance), 1984
Rhythm of the Spheres (s Merritt), 1948
Richard Matheson (s Matheson), 1989
Riches and Power (s Leiber), 1982
Riddle of Stars (McKillip), 1979
Riddle of the Tower (Beresford), 1944
Riddle of the Wren (de Lint), 1984
Riddle-Master of Hed (McKillip), 1978
Riddley Walker (Hoban), 1980
Rider at the Gate (Cherryh), 1995
Riders of the Purple Wage (s Farmer), 1992
Riders of the Winds (Chalker), 1988
Riding the Torch (Spinrad), 1978
Riftwar series (Feist), from 1982
Right Hand of Dextra (Lake), 1977
Rim of Morning (Sloane), 1964
Rim of the Unknown (s Long), 1972
Rim Worlds series (Chandler), from 1961
Rime Isle (s Leiber), 1977
Rimrunners (Cherryh), 1989
Ring (Anthony), 1968
Ring (Baxter), 1994
Ring around the Sun (Simak), 1953
Ring of Charon (Allen), 1990
Ring of Garamas (Mason, as Rankine), 1971
Ring of Ritornel (Harness), 1968
Ring of Swords (Arnason), 1993
Ring of Truth (Lake), 1982
Ring of Violence (Mason), 1968

Ring-Rise, Ring-Set (M. Hughes), 1982
Ringing Changes (s Lafferty), 1984
Rings of Ice (Anthony), 1974
Rings of Saturn (Cover), 1985
Rings of Tantalus (Cooper, as Avery), 1975
Rings of the Master series (Chalker), from 1986
Ringstones (s Sarban), 1951
Ringtime (s Disch), 1983
Ringworld (Niven), 1970
Ringworld Engineers (Niven), 1979
Rissa series (Busby), from 1976
Rite of Passage (Panshin), 1968
Rites of Ohe (Brunner), 1963
Rithian Terror (Knight), 1965
Rituals of Infinity (Moorcock), 1971
Rival Rigellians (Reynolds), 1967
River and the Dream (R. Jones), 1977
River of Dancing Gods (Chalker), 1984
River of Eternity (Farmer), 1983
River of Time (s Brin), 1986
River Wall (Garrett), 1986
Riverrun series (Sucharitkul, as Somtow), from 1991
Rivers of Time (s de Camp), 1993
Riverworld series (Farmer), from 1971
Rivets and Sprockets (Key), 1964
Road Ghost (Naha, as Drumm), 1985
Road to Corlay (Cowper), 1978
Road to the Rim (Chandler), 1967
Road War (Shirley, as Drum), 1985
Roadmarks (Zelazny), 1979
Roads of Heaven (Scott), 1988
Roadside Picnic, Tale of the Troike (Strugatsky), 1977
Roar Devil (Dent, as Robeson), 1977
Robby Hoenig series (Dickson), from 1960
Robert Sheckley Omnibus (s Sheckley), 1973
Robert Silverberg's Time Tours (Cover), 1991
Robocop (Naha), 1987
Robocop II (Naha), 1990
Robot and Rebecca (Yolen), 1980
Robot City: Odyssey (Kube-McDowell), 1987
Robot City: Refuge (Chilson), 1988
Robot Dreams (s Asimov), 1986
Robot in the Closet (Goulart), 1981
Robot Jox (Thurston), 1989
Robot Novels (Asimov), 1972
Robot Revolt (Fisk), 1981
Robot Visions (s Asimov), 1990
Robot Who Looked Like Me (s Sheckley), 1978
Robots and Aliens series (Leigh), from 1989
Robots and Changelings (s del Rey), 1958
Robots and Empire (Asimov), 1985
Robots, Androids, and Mechanical Oddities (s Dick), 1984
Robots Have No Tails (s Kuttner and C.L. Moore, as Padgett), 1952
Robots of Dawn (Asimov), 1983
Robots series (Asimov), from 1954
Robur the Conqueror (Verne), 1887
Rocannon's World (Le Guin), 1966
Rocheworld series (Forward), from 1984
Rock of Ages (W. Williams), 1995
Rock of Three Planets (Lightner), 1963

Rock series (Lightner), from 1965
Rocket from Infinity (del Rey and Fairman, as del Rey), 1966
Rocket Jockey (del Rey, as St. John), 1952
Rocket Man (Stine, as Correy), 1955
Rocket Pilot (del Rey), 1955
Rocket Ship Galileo (Heinlein), 1947
Rocket to Limbo (Nourse), 1957
Rocket to Luna (Hunter, as Marsten), 1953
Rockets in Ursa Major (F. and G. Hoyle), 1969
Rockets to Nowhere (del Rey, as St. John), 1954
Rod of Light (Bayley), 1984
Rod Serling's Night Gallery Reader (s Serling), 1987
Rodent Mutation (Fanthorpe, as Fane), 1961
Roderick series (Sladek), from 1980
Roger's Rangers (Pournelle), 1983
Rogers' Rangers (Niven), 1983
Rogue Bolo (Laumer), 1986
Rogue Dragon (Davidson), 1965
Rogue Emperor (Kilian), 1988
Rogue in Space (F. Brown), 1957
Rogue Moon (Budrys), 1960
Rogue Planet (Tubb), 1976
Rogue Powers (Allen), 1986
Rogue Queen (de Camp), 1951
Rogue Reynard (Norton), 1947
Rogue Ship (van Vogt), 1965
Rogue Star (Pohl, Williamson), 1969
Roller Coaster World (Bulmer), 1972
Rolling Hot (Drake), 1989
Rolling Stones (Heinlein), 1952
Rolltown (Reynolds), 1976
Roma Mater (P. Anderson), 1986
Roman Twilight (s Fanthorpe, as Trent), 1963
Romance in Black (Wellman, as Field), 1946
Romance of Golden Star (G. Griffith), 1897
Romance of the Equator (s Aldiss), 1980
Romanoff, Olga series (G. Griffith), from 1893
Romulan Prize (Hawke), 1993
Romulan Way (Duane), 1987
Roots of the Mountains (W. Morris), 1889
Rork! (Davidson), 1965
Rose (s Harness), 1966
Rose for Armageddon (Schenck), 1982
Rose for Ecclesiastes (s Zelazny), 1969
Rose-Red City (Dave Duncan), 1987
Rose Sea (Stirling), 1994
Rosemary's Baby (Levin), 1967
Rosemary's Brain (s Soukup), 1992
Rosinante series (Gilliland), from 1981
Rosy Cheeks (Z. Hughes, as Kanto), 1969
Rough Shaking (G. MacDonald), 1890
Round the Moon (Verne), 1976
Rounded with Sleep (Chilson), 1990
Rowan series (McCaffrey), from 1990
Rubicon Beach (Erickson), 1986
Ruby Knight (Eddings), 1990
Ruins of Isis (Bradley), 1978
Rule Golden, Natural State, The Dying Man (Knight), 1967
Rule of the Door and Other Fanciful Regulations (s Biggle), 1967
Rule of the Pagbeasts (McIntosh), 1956
Ruler of the World (McIntosh), 1976

Rulers of Darkness (Spruill), 1995
Rulers of Hylor series (Wilder), from 1984
Rumors of Spring (R. Grant), 1987
Run, Come See Jerusalem! (Meredith), 1976
Run for the Stars (s Ellison), 1991
Run to Chaos Keep (Chalker), 1991
Runaway Robot (del Rey and Fairman, as del Rey), 1964
Runaway World (Coblentz), 1961
Runes of the Lyre (Mayhar), 1982
Runestaff series (Moorcock), from 1967
Rusalka series (Cherryh), from 1989
Russian Hide-and-Seek (Amis), 1980
Russian Quartet series (D.M. Thomas), from 1983
Russian Spring (Spinrad), 1991
Rx for Tomorrow (s Nourse), 1971
Ryder Hook series (Bulmer), from 1974
Ryn (Wodhams), 1982
Rynosseros series (s Dowling), from 1990

S Is for Space (s Bradbury), 1966
Sabella (Lee), 1980
Saber and Shadow (Stirling), 1992
Sable Moon (Springer), 1981
Sacred Locomotive Flies (Lupoff), 1971
Sacred Skull (G. Griffith), 1908
Saga of Cuckoo (Pohl, Williamson), 1983
Saga of Grittel Sundotha (Mayhar), 1985
Saga of Lost Earths (Petaja), 1966
Saga of Pliocene Exile (May), 1981
Sailing Bright Eternity (Benford), 1995
Sailing to Byzantium (s Silverberg), 1985
Sailing to Utopia (Moorcock), 1993
Sailor on the Seas of Fate (Moorcock), 1976
Saint Camber (Kurtz), 1978
St. Cyr and U. Tuli series (I. Wallace), from 1968
St. Francis Effect (Z. Hughes), 1976
Saint-Germain series (s Yarbro), from 1991
Saint, Jane series (Saxton), from 1986
Saints and Strangers (s A. Carter), 1986
Saliva Tree and Other Strange Growths (s Aldiss), 1966
Saltflower (Van Scyoc), 1971
Salvage Rites (s Watson), 1989
Sam Gunn, Unlimited (Bova), 1992
Sam Space series (Nolan), from 1971
Same to You Doubled (s Sheckley), 1974
Samuri Wizard (Hawke), 1991
San Diego Lightfoot Sue (s Reamy), 1980
Sanctuary in the Sky (Brunner), 1960
Sandkings (s Martin), 1981
Sands of Eternity (s Fanthorpe), 1963
Sands of Mars (Clarke), 1951
Sandworld (Lupoff), 1976
Sandwriter series (M. Hughes), from 1985
Santaroga Barrier (F. Herbert), 1968
Santiago (Resnick), 1986
Sapphire Road (Whiteford), 1982
Sapphire Rose (Eddings), 1991
Saraband of Lost Time (R. Grant), 1985
Sardonyx Net (Lynn), 1981
Sargasso of Space (Norton, as North), 1955
Sargasso Ogre (Dent, as Robeson), 1967

Sassinak (McCaffrey), 1990
Satan's Daughter (George H. Smith), 1961
Satan's World (P. Anderson), 1969
Satana Enslaved (Offutt, as Cleve), 1982
Satellite (Fanthorpe), 1960
Satellite 54-Zero (Mason), 1971
Satellite City (Reynolds), 1975
Saturn Game (s P. Anderson), 1989
Saturn over the Water (Priestley), 1961
Saturn Patrol (Tubb, as Lang), 1951
Saunders, Scott series (P. Moore), from 1977
Savage Pellucidar (s E. Burroughs), 1963
Savage Scorpio (Bulmer, as Akers), 1978
Savage Season (Lansdale), 1990
Scalehunter's Beautiful Daughter (Shepard), 1988
Scanner Darkly (Dick), 1977
Scarlet Dream (C.L. Moore), 1981
Scarlet Plague (London), 1915
Scatter of Stardust (s Tubb), 1972
Scavenger Hunt (Goldin), 1975
Scavengers in Space (Nourse), 1959
Scepter of Chance (Klein), 1986
Scheherazade's Night Out (Gardner), 1992
Scheme of Things (del Rey and Fairman, as del Rey), 1966
Schismatrix (Sterling), 1985
Scholars and Soldiers (s Gentle), 1989
School of Darkness (Wellman), 1985
Schooners of the Sun (Klein), 1961
Schrödinger's Cat series (Robert Anton Wilson), from 1979
Schrödinger's Kitten (s Effinger), 1992
Science Metropolis (Fearn, as Statten), 1952
Science of Power (Emerson), 1995
Scissors Cut Paper Wrap Stone (McDonald), 1994
Scop (Malzberg), 1976
Scorpion God (s Golding), 1971
Scorpion's Treasure (Sernine), 1990
Scourge of Screamers (Galouye), 1968
Scourge of the Atom (Fearn, as Gridban), 1953
Scourge of the Blood Cult (George H. Smith), 1961
Screaming Face (Lymington), 1963
Screaming Lake (S. Wright), 1937
Screwtop (s McIntyre), 1989
Scroll of Lucifer (Eshbach), 1990
Scudder's Game (Compton), 1988
Sea and Summer (Turner), 1987
Sea Angel (Dent, as Robeson), 1970
Sea Beasts (Chandler), 1971
Sea Demons (Rousseau, as Egbert), 1924
Sea Girl (Cummings), 1930
Sea Hag (Drake), 1989
Sea-Horse in the Sky (Cooper), 1969
Sea King series (Springer), from 1987
Sea Kissed (s Bloch), 1945
Sea Lady (Wells), 1902
Sea Magician (Dent, as Robeson), 1970
Sea of Glass (Longyear), 1987
Sea Siege (Norton), 1957
Sea Thing (s van Vogt), 1970
Sea's Furthest End (Broderick), 1993
Seagulls under Glass (s Tate), 1975
Sealed Sarcophagus (s Fanthorpe), 1965

Séance for a Vampire (Saberhagen), 1994
SeaQuest DSV (Duane), 1993
Search for Dinosaurs (Bischoff), 1984
Search for Kä (Garrett), 1984
Search for the Sun! (Kapp), 1982
Search for Zei (de Camp), 1962
Search the Sky (Kornbluth, Pohl), 1954
Seas of Ernathe (Carver), 1976
Season for Slaughter (Gerrold), 1992
Season of the Spellsong (A. Foster), 1985
Season to Be Wary (s Serling), 1967
Seasons in Flight (s Aldiss), 1984
Second Atlantis (R. Williams), 1965
Second Book of Fritz Leiber (s Leiber), 1975
Second Chronicles of Thomas Covenant the Unbeliever
    (Donaldson), 1994
Second Contact (Resnick), 1990
Second Deluge (Serviss), 1912
Second Empire series (Pournelle), from 1973
Second Ending (J. White), 1962
Second Game (MacLean), 1981
Second Great Dune Trilogy (F. Herbert), 1987
Second Nature (Wilder), 1982
Second Satellite (Latham, as Richardson), 1956
Second Stage Lensmen (E.E. Smith), 1953
Second Trip (Silverberg), 1972
Second War of the Worlds (George H. Smith), 1976
Secret Agent of Terra (Brunner), 1962
Secret Ascension (Bishop), 1987
Secret Books of Paradys series (Lee), from 1982
Secret Galactics (van Vogt), 1974
Secret Harmonies (McAuley), 1989
Secret in the Sky (Dent, as Robeson), 1967
Secret Martians (Sharkey), 1960
Secret of Life (Rucker), 1985
Secret of Saturn's Rings (Wollheim), 1954
Secret of Sinharat (Brackett), 1964
Secret of the Black Hole (P. Moore), 1980
Secret of the Black Planet (s Lesser), 1965
Secret of the Earth Star (s Kuttner), 1991
Secret of the Lona (Leigh), 1988
Secret of the Lost Race (Norton), 1959
Secret of the Marauder Satellite (T. White), 1967
Secret of the Martian Moons (Wollheim), 1955
Secret of the Ninth Planet (Wollheim), 1959
Secret of the Old Forest (Buzzati), n.d.
Secret of the Red Spot (Binder), 1971
Secret of the Runestaff (Moorcock), 1969
Secret of the Snows (s Fanthorpe), 1957
Secret of the Sunless World (MacApp, as Capps), 1969
Secret of This Book (s Aldiss), 1995
Secret of Wilhelm Storitz (Verne), 1963
Secret of ZI (Bulmer), 1958
Secret People (R. Jones), 1956
Secret People (Wyndham, as Beynon), 1935
Secret Scorpio (Bulmer, as Akers), 1977
Secret Sea (Monteleone), 1979
Secret Sharer (s Silverberg), 1988
Secret Songs (s Leiber), 1968
Secret under Antarctica (Dickson), 1963
Secret under the Caribbean (Dickson), 1964

Secret under the Sea (Dickson), 1960
Secret Visitors (J. White), 1957
Secrets of Stardeep (Jakes), 1969
Secrets of the Deep (Dickson), 1985
Secrets of the Vase (Fearn, as James), 1955
Section G: United Planets (Reynolds), 1976
Sector General series (J. White), from 1962
Secular Wizard (Stasheff), 1995
Seed of Earth (Silverberg), 1962
Seed of Evil (s Bayley), 1979
Seed of Light (Cooper), 1959
Seed of Stars (Kippax), 1972
Seed of the Dreamers (Petaja), 1970
Seed of the Gods (Z. Hughes), 1974
Seedling Stars (s Blish), 1957
Seeds of Change (Monteleone), 1975
Seeds of Life (Taine), 1951
Seeds of Time (s Wyndham), 1956
Seeker (Bischoff), 1976
Seekers of Shar Nuhn (Mayhar), 1980
Seeklight (Jeter), 1975
Seeress of Kell (Eddings), 1991
Seetee Alert! (Tubb, as Kern), 1974
Seetee series (Williamson, as Stewart), from 1950
Seg the Bowman (Bulmer, as Akers), 1984
Select Conversations with an Uncle (s Wells), 1895
Selections from Deep Space (s Russell), 1955
Selkie (Bischoff, Sheffield), 1982
Sending of Dragons (Yolen), 1987
Sense of Obligation (H. Harrison), 1967
Sense of Shadow (Wilhelm), 1981
Sensitive Dependence on Initial Contitions (s K. Robinson), 1991
Sensitives (Charbonneau), 1968
Sentenced to Prism (A. Foster), 1985
Sentinel (s Clarke), 1983
Sentinel Stars (Charbonneau), 1963
Sentinels from Space (Russell), 1953
Sepulchre (J. Herbert), 1987
Seren Cenacles (Norwood), 1983
Serpent Catch series (Wolverton), from 1991
Serpent Mage (Bear), 1986
Serpent's Blood (Stableford), 1995
Serpent's Egg (Lafferty), 1987
Serpent's Reach (Cherryh), 1980
Serpent's Tooth (s Norton), 1987
Servant of the Empire (Feist), 1990
Servants of the Wankh (Vance), 1969
Servants of Twilight (Koontz), 1988
Serving in Time (Eklund), 1975
Set of Wheels (Thurston), 1983
Seven Agate Devils (Dent, as Robeson), 1973
Seven Altars of Dûsarra (Watt-Evans), 1981
Seven American Nights (s G. Wolfe), 1989
Seven Conquests (s P. Anderson), 1969
Seven Days to Never (Frank), 1957
Seven Footprints to Satan (Merritt), 1928
Seven from the Stars (Bradley), 1962
Seven out of Time (Zagat), 1949
Seven Sexes (s Tenn), 1968
Seven Spears of the W'dch'ck (C. Grant, as Fenn), 1988
Seven Spells to Sunday (Norton), 1979

Seven Steps to the Arbiter (Hubbard), 1975
Seven Steps to the Sun (F. and G. Hoyle), 1970
Seven Tickets to Hell (R. Williams), 1972
Seven Views of Olduvai Gorge (s Resnick), 1994
Seventeen Virgins (s Vance), 1979
Seventh Sword series (Dave Duncan), from 1988
Sex and the High Command (Boyd), 1970
Sex Life on the Planet Mars (s F. Brown), 1986
Sex Pill (Offutt, as Williams), 1968
Sex Sphere (Rucker), 1984
Sex War (Merwin), 1960
Sexodus (George H. Smith, as Jason), 1963
Sexorcist (Offutt, as Cleve), 1974
Sexual Chemistry (s Stableford), 1991
Shades of Darkness (Cowper), 1986
Shadow (Dave Duncan), 1987
Shadow Dancers (Chalker), 1987
Shadow Games (Cook), 1989
Shadow Girl (Cummings), 1946
Shadow Hunter (Murphy), 1982
Shadow Man (Fanthorpe, as Barton), 1966
Shadow Man (Scott), 1995
Shadow of a Dark Queen (Feist), 1994
Shadow of All Night Falling (Cook), 1979
Shadow of Alpha (C. Grant), 1976
Shadow of Earth (Eisenstein), 1979
Shadow of Heaven (Shaw), 1969
Shadow of Sorcery (Offutt), 1993
Shadow of the Torturer (G. Wolfe), 1980
Shadow of the Well of Souls (Chalker), 1994
Shadow of the Wolf (Holdstock, as Carlsen), 1977
Shadow on the Doorstep (s Blaylock), 1987
Shadow on the Hearth (Merril), 1950
Shadow Out of Time (s Lovecraft), 1968
Shadow over Innsmouth (s Lovecraft), 1936
Shadow over Mars (Brackett), 1951
Shadow People (St. Clair), 1969
Shadow Play (s Beaumont), 1964
Shadow Shaia (Gilliland), 1990
Shadow's End (Tepper), 1994
Shadow's Son (Stirling), 1991
Shadowbreed (Garnett, as Ferring), 1991
Shadowfire (Lee), 1978
Shadowfires (Koontz, as Nichols), 1987
Shadowkeep (A. Foster), 1984
Shadowline (Cook), 1982
Shadowman (Proctor), 1980
Shadows in the Sun (Oliver), 1954
Shadows Linger (Cook), 1984
Shadows Out of Hell (Offutt), 1980
Shadows with Eyes (s Leiber), 1962
Shadowspawn (Offutt), 1987
Shadrach in the Furnace (Silverberg), 1976
Shaggy Planet (Goulart), 1972
Shakehole (Mackelworth), 1981
Shakespeare's Planet (Simak), 1976
Shambleau (s C.L. Moore), 1953
Shame of Man (Anthony), 1994
Shann Lantree series (Norton), from 1960
Shape Changer (Laumer), 1972
Shape of Space (s Niven), 1969

Shape of Things to Come (Wells), 1933
Shapechanger Scenario (Hawke), 1988
Shaper series (Sterling), from 1985
Shapes in the Fire (Shiel), 1896
Shards of Honor (Bujold), 1986
Shards of Space (s Sheckley), 1962
Sharp End (Drake), 1993
Sharpest Edge (Stirling), 1986
Sharra's Exile (Bradley), 1981
Shatterday (s Ellison), 1980
Shattered Chain (Bradley), 1976
Shattered Horse (Sucharitkul, as Somtow), 1986
Shattered People (Hoskins), 1975
Shattered Sphere (Allen), 1994
Shattered World series (Reaves), from 1984
She series (Haggard), from 1886
Shea, Harold series (de Camp, Pratt), from 1941
Sheep Look Up (Brunner), 1972
Shelter (O'Donnell), 1987
Sheltered Lives (Oberndorf), 1992
Shepherd Moon (Hoover), 1984
Sherlock Holmes's War of the Worlds (Wellman), 1975
Shield (P. Anderson), 1963
Shield of Time (s P. Anderson), 1990
Shift Key (Brunner), 1987
Shining Ones (Eddings), 1993
Shining Ones (Preuss), 1991
Shining Steel (Watt-Evans), 1986
Ship from Outside (Chandler), 1963
Ship of Ishtar (Merritt), 1926
Ship of Shadows (s Leiber), 1979
Ship of Strangers (Shaw), 1978
Ship series (McCaffrey), from 1969
Ship That Sailed the Time Stream (Edmondson), 1965
Ships of Durostorum (Bulmer), 1970
Ships of Earth (Card), 1994
Ships to the Stars (s Leiber), 1964
Shiva Descending (Benford, Rotsler), 1980
Shivering World (Tyers), 1991
Shock series (s Matheson), from 1961
Shock Wave (Richmond), 1967
Shockwave Rider (Brunner), 1975
Shon the Taken (Lee), 1979
Shoot at the Moon (Temple), 1966
Shore of Women (Sargent), 1986
Shores of Another Sea (Oliver), 1971
Shores of Death (Moorcock), 1970
Shores of Kansas (Chilson), 1976
Shores of Space (s Matheson), 1957
Shores of Tomorrow (s Silverberg), 1976
Short, Sharp Shock (K. Robinson), 1990
Short Stories (s London), 1960
Shot into Infinity (Gail), 1975
Showboat World (Vance), 1975
Shrine (J. Herbert), 1983
Shrinking Man (Matheson), 1956
Shrouded Abbot (s Fanthorpe), 1964
Shrouded Planet (Silverberg and Garrett, as Randall), 1957
Shudderchild (Norwood), 1987
Shunned House (s Lovecraft), 1928
Shuttered Room and Other Pieces (s Lovecraft), 1959

Shuttle Down (Stine, as Correy), 1981
Sibyl Sue Blue series (R. Brown), from 1966
Sideshow (Tepper), 1992
Sideslip (T. White), 1968
Sidewise in Time (s Leinster), 1950
Siege of the Unseen (van Vogt), 1959
Siege of Wonder (Geston), 1976
Siege Perilous (del Rey and Fairman, as del Rey), 1966
Sierra Madre (Stine), 1988
Sight of Proteus (Sheffield), 1978
Sign for the Sacred (Constantine), 1993
Sign of Chaos (Zelazny), 1987
Sign of the Burning Hart (Keller), 1938
Sign of the Labrys (St. Clair), 1963
Sign of the Moonbow (Offutt), 1977
Sign of the Mute Medusa (I. Wallace), 1977
Sign of the Unicorn (Zelazny), 1975
Signs and Portents (s Yarbro), 1984
Signs and Wonders (s Beresford), 1921
Silence and Solitude (Scott), 1986
Silence Is Deadly (Biggle), 1977
Silence Leigh series (Scott), from 1988
Silent City (Vonarburg), 1988
Silent Invaders (Silverberg), 1963
Silent Multitude (Compton), 1966
Silent Shout (s Zebrowski), 1979
Silent Sky (s Biggle), 1979
Silent Speakers (Sellings), 1963
Silent Stars Go By (J. White), 1991
Silent Thunder (s Ing), 1991
Silent Voice (Hodder-Williams), 1977
Silicon Man (Platt), 1991
Silistra series (J. Morris), from 1977
Silk Roads and Shadows (Shwartz), 1988
Silkie (van Vogt), 1969
Silmarillion (Tolkien), 1977
Silver Chair (Lewis), 1953
Silver Eggheads (Leiber), 1962
Silver Glove (Charnas), 1988
Silver Horse (Lynn), 1984
Silver John series (Wellman), from 1979
Silver Locusts (s Bradbury), 1951
Silver Metal Lover (Lee), 1981
Silver Pillow (s Disch), 1987
Silver Spike (Cook), 1989
Silver Sun (Springer), 1980
Silver Thread of Madness (s Salmonson), 1989
Silver Warriors (Moorcock), 1973
Silvered Cage (Fearn, as Blayn), 1955
Silverthorn (Feist), 1985
Sime/Gen series (Lichtenberg), from 1974
Simeon series (Tate), from 1969
Simon Ark series (s Hoch), from 1971
Simulacra (Dick), 1964
Simulacron-3 (Galouye), 1964
Sin in Space (Kornbluth, Merril), 1961
Sin of Origin (J. Barnes), 1988
Sinbad and the Eye of the Tiger (Rotsler, as Hall), 1977
Sinbad: The Thirteenth Voyage (Lafferty), 1989
Sinful Ones (Leiber), 1953
Singers of Time (Pohl, Williamson), 1991

Singing Citadel (s Moorcock), 1970
Singing Stones (J. Coulson), 1968
Single Combat (Ing), 1983
Singularity Project (Busby), 1993
Sinister Barrier (Russell), 1943
Sinister Ray (s Dent), 1987
Sins of the Blood (Rusch), 1994
Sins of the Fathers (Schmidt), 1976
Sioux Spaceman (Norton), 1960
Sipstrassi series (Gemmell), from 1987
Sir Bevis series (Jefferies), from 1881
Sir Gibbie (G. MacDonald), 1879
Sir Harold and the Gnome King (s de Camp), 1991
Sir Harold and the Monkey King (s Stasheff), 1993
Sirens of Titan (Vonnegut), 1959
Sirian Experiments (Lessing), 1981
Sirius (Stapledon), 1944
Siscoe, Nick and Ross Block series (Haiblum), from 1984
Sister Light, Sister Dark (Yolen), 1988
Sisters (s Bear), 1992
Sisters and Strangers (Tennant), 1990
Siva! (Richmond), 1979
Six Gates from Limbo (McIntosh), 1968
Six-Gun Solution (Hawke), 1991
Six Matches (s Strugatsky), n.d.
Six Weeks in the Great Whirlpool (Senarens), 1893
Six Worlds Yonder (s Russell), 1958
Sixth Column (Heinlein), 1949
Sixth Winter (Gribbin), 1979
Skeeve series (Asprin), from 1984
Skeleton-in-Waiting (Dickinson), 1989
Skeleton Key (C. Grant, as Charles), 1986
Skies Discrowned (Powers), 1976
Skin and Bones (T. Smith), 1933
Skirmish (s Simak), 1977
Skull of the Marquis de Sade (s Bloch), 1965
Sky Is Filled with Ships (Meredith), 1969
Sky Lords series (Brosnan), from 1988
Sky Pirates of Callisto (L. Carter), 1973
Skybreaker (G. Jones, as Halam), 1990
Skyclimber (Gallun), 1981
Skyfall (H. Harrison), 1976
Skylark series (E.E. Smith), from 1946
Skynappers (Brunner), 1960
Skyport (Siodmak), 1959
Skyripper (Drake), 1983
Skyrocket Steele series (Goulart), from 1980
Skyship (Brosnan), 1981
Slag Like Me (Longyear), 1994
Slan (van Vogt), 1946
Slaughterhouse-Five (Vonnegut), 1969
Slave Planet (Janifer), 1963
Slave Ship (Pohl), 1957
Slave Ship from Sergan (Tubb, as Kern), 1973
Slavers of Space (Brunner), 1960
Slaves of Heaven (Cooper), 1974
Slaves of Ijax (Fearn), 1948
Slaves of Sleep (Hubbard), 1948
Slaves of Spiegel (Pinkwater), 1982
Slaves of the Klau (Vance), 1958
Slaves of the Spectrum (Bulmer, as Kent), 1954

Slaves of the Volcano God (Gardner), 1989
Sleep Eaters (Lymington), 1963
Sleeper Awakes (Wells), 1910
Sleepers of Mars (s Wyndham, as Beynon), 1973
Sleeping Sorceress (Moorcock), 1971
Sleepside Story (s Bear), 1988
Sleepwalker's World (Dickson), 1971
Slight Detour (Stasheff), 1994
Slightly Off Center (s Barrett), 1992
Slippery (s Lafferty), 1985
Slipt (A. Foster), 1984
Slitherers (Fearn), 1984
Slow Birds (s Watson), 1985
Slow Children at Play (s G. Wolfe), 1989
Slow Dancing through Time (s Dozois, Jack C. Haldeman), 1990
Slow Fall to Dawn (Leigh), 1981
Slow Freight (Busby), 1991
Slow Funeral (Ore), 1994
Slow River (N. Griffith), 1995
Slow Sculpture (s Sturgeon), 1982
Slumming in Voodooland (s Stableford), 1991
Small Assassin (s Bradbury), 1962
Small Changes (s Clement), 1969
Small Gods (Pratchett), 1992
Smile (s Bradbury), 1991
Smile on the Void (S. Gordon), 1981
Smith and the Pharaohs (s Haggard), 1920
Smoke Ring (Niven), 1987
Snail on the Slope (Strugatsky), 1980
Snake in His Bosom (s Lafferty), 1983
Snakegod (Goulart), 1976
Snarkout Boys series (Pinkwater), from 1982
Sneak Preview (Bloch), 1971
Snoggle (Priestley), 1971
Snow Crash (N. Stephenson), 1992
Snow Queen series (J. Vinge), from 1980
Snow White and the Giants (McIntosh), 1968
Snow-White Soliloquies (MacLeod), 1970
Snowbrother (Stirling), 1985
Snows of Ganymede (P. Anderson), 1958
So Bright the Vision (s Simak), 1968
So Close to Home (s Blish), 1961
So Long, and Thanks for All the Fish (Adams), 1984
So You Want to Be a Wizard? (Duane), 1983
Sodom and Gomorrah Business (Malzberg), 1974
Soft and Others (s F. Wilson), 1989
Soft Come the Dragons (s Koontz), 1970
Soft Machine (W. Burroughs), 1961
Soft Targets (Ing), 1979
Soft Whisper of the Dead (C. Grant), 1982
Softly by Moonlight (Fanthorpe, as Fane), 1963
Software series (Rucker), from 1982
Sojan (s Moorcock), 1977
Sojarr of Titan (Wellman), 1949
Solar Invasion (Wellman), 1968
Solar Lottery (Dick), 1955
Solar Queen series (Norton), from 1955
Solarians (Spinrad), 1966
Solaris (Lem), 1970
Sold—For a Spaceship (High), 1973
Soldier, Ask Not (Dickson), 1967

Space Pirates (Eklund, E.E. Smith), 1979
Space Plague (George O. Smith), 1957
Space Plague (Lightner), 1966
Space Platform (Leinster), 1953
Space Police series (Kelley), from 1979
Space Prison (Godwin), 1960
Space Puppet series (Rackham), from 1954
Space Salvage (Bulmer), 1953
Space Scavengers (s Cartmill), 1975
Space Search (Reynolds), 1984
Space Skimmer (Gerrold), 1972
Space Sorcerers (McIntosh), 1972
Space Station No. 1 (Long), 1957
Space Swimmers (Dickson), 1967
Space, Time, and Nathaniel (s Aldiss), 1957
Space-Time Juggler (Brunner), 1963
Space Trap (Fanthorpe, as Bell), 1964
Space Trap (J. Coulson), 1976
Space Trap (M. Hughes), 1983
Space Treason (Bulmer), 1952
Space Tug (Leinster), 1953
Space Vampires (C. Wilson), 1976
Space Viking (Piper), 1963
Space Visitor (Reynolds), 1977
Space War (s N. Jones), 1967
Space War Blues (Lupoff), 1978
Space Warp (Fearn, as Statten), 1952
Space Willies (Russell), 1958
Space Winners (Dickson), 1965
Space: 1999 series (Mason), from 1975
Spaceburger (Pinkwater), 1993
Spacehawk, Inc (Goulart), 1974
Spacehounds of IPC (E.E. Smith), 1947
Spaceling (Piserchia), 1978
Spacemen, Go Home (Lesser), 1962
Spacepaw (Dickson), 1969
Spaceship Built of Stone (s Tuttle), 1987
Spaceship for the King (Pournelle), 1973
Spaceship Medic (H. Harrison), 1970
Spacetime Donuts (Rucker), 1981
Spaceways (Maine), 1953
Spaceways Satellite (Maine), 1958
Spaceways series (Edmondson), from 1985
Spaceways series (Jack C. Haldeman), from 1983
Spaceways series (Offutt and Proctor, as Cleve), from 1982
Spacial Delivery (Dickson), 1961
Spartan Planet (Chandler), 1969
Spawn of Laban (Tubb, as Kern), 1974
Spawn of the Death Machine (T. White), 1968
Speaker for the Dead (Card), 1986
Speaking in Tongues (s McDonald), 1992
Speaking of Dinosaurs (High), 1974
Spear (J. Herbert), 1978
Spear of Heaven (Tarr), 1994
Special Deliverance (Simak), 1982
Special Delivery (Neville), 1967
Special Mission (Fanthorpe, as Muller), 1963
Specialist (Whiteford), 1990
Specials (Charbonneau), 1967
Specimens (Saberhagen), 1976
Specter Is Haunting Texas (Leiber), 1969

Specterworld (Haiblum), 1991
Spectral Manifestations (s Hodgson), 1984
Spectre of Darkness (Fanthorpe, as Muller), 1965
Spectrum of a Forgotten Sun (Tubb), 1976
Spell Bound (Emerson), 1990
Spell for Chameleon (Anthony), 1977
Spell of the Black Dagger (Watt-Evans), 1993
Spell of the Witch World (s Norton), 1972
Spell Sword (Bradley), 1974
Spellcoats (Diana Wynne Jones), 1979
Spellsinger (A. Foster), 1983
Spellsinger at the Gate (A. Foster), 1983
Spellsinger Scherzo (A. Foster), 1987
Spellsinger series (A. Foster), from 1983
Sphere (Crichton), 1987
Sphinx (D.M. Thomas), 1986
Sphinx (Lindsay), 1923
Spider Glass (s Yarbro), 1991
Spider in the Bath (Lymington), 1975
Spider Play (Killough), 1986
Spider World series (C. Wilson), from 1987
Spider-Man (Duane), 1994
Spiders' War (S. Wright), 1954
Spindoc (Perry), 1994
Spinner (Piserchia), 1980
Spinneret (Zahn), 1985
Spirit of Bambatse (Haggard), 1906
Spirit of Dorsai (s Dickson), 1979
Spirit Ring (Bujold), 1992
Spirits of Flux and Anchor (Chalker), 1984
Spiritwalk (s de Lint), 1992
Spiteful Planet (s Hoshi), 1978
Splendid Chaos (Shirley), 1988
Splinter of the Mind's Eye (A. Foster), 1978
Split Heirs (Watt-Evans), 1993
Split Infinity (Anthony), 1980
Split Second (Kilworth), 1979
Spock, Messiah! (Cogswell), 1976
Spock Must Die! (s Blish), 1970
Spock's World (Duane), 1988
Spoils of War (A. Foster), 1993
Spook Hole (Dent, as Robeson), 1972
Spook Legion (Dent, as Robeson), 1967
Spot of Life (Hall), 1965
Spotted Men (Dent, as Robeson), 1977
Sprockets series (Key), from 1963
Spy in Space (P. Moore), 1977
Square Deal (Drake), 1992
Square Root of Man (s Tenn), 1968
Square Root of Tomorrow (s Cooper), 1970
Squares of the City (Brunner), 1965
Squeaking Goblin (Dent, as Robeson), 1969
Stadium Beyond the Stars (Lesser), 1960
Stained-Glass World (Bulmer), 1976
Stainless Steel Rat series (H. Harrison), from 1961
Stalin's Teardrops (s Watson), 1991
Stalk (J. Morris), 1994
Stalker from the Stars (Goulart), 1978
Stalkers (Shirley, as Drum), 1984
Stalking the Nightmare (s Ellison), 1982
Stalking the Unicorn (Resnick), 1987

Stalking the Wild Resnick (s Resnick), 1991
Stalking Time (Naha, as Drumm), 1986
Stand Alone Stan (Mann), 1994
Stand on Zanzibar (Brunner), 1968
Standing Joy (Guin), 1969
Star (s Wells), 1912(?)
Star-Anchored, Star-Angered (Elgin), 1979
Star Beast (Heinlein), 1954
Star Begotten (Wells), 1937
Star Born (Norton), 1957
Star Bridge (Gunn, Williamson), 1955
Star Bright (Caidin), 1980
Star Brothers (Bova), 1990
Star Circus (Lightner), 1977
Star City (Bulmer, as Zetford), 1974
Star Colony (Laumer), 1981
Star Conquerors (Bova), 1959
Star Courier (Chandler), 1977
Star-Crowned Kings (Chilson), 1975
Star Diaries (s Lem), 1976
Star Dog (Lightner), 1973
Star Driver (Stine, as Correy), 1980
Star Dwellers (Blish), 1961
Star Fall series (Bischoff), from 1980
S.T.A.R. Flight (Tubb), 1969
Star Fox (P. Anderson), 1965
Star Gate (Norton), 1958
Star Gold (Kelley), 1979
Star Griffin (Kurland), 1987
Star Guard (Norton), 1955
Star Hawks series (Goulart), from 1980
Star Healer (J. White), 1985
Star Hounds series (Bischoff), from 1985
Star Hunter (Norton), 1961
Star Ka'at series (Norton), from 1966
Star King (Vance), 1964
Star Kings (Hamilton), 1949
Star Light (Clement), 1971
Star Light, Star Bright (s Bester), 1976
Star Loot (Chandler), 1980
Star Magicians (L. Carter), 1966
Star Maker (Stapledon), 1937
Star Man's Son, 2250 A.D (Norton), 1952
Star Mill (Petaja), 1966
Star of Danger (Bradley), 1965
Star of Gypsies (Silverberg), 1986
Star of Hesiock (Mason, as Rankine), 1980
Star of Life (Hamilton), 1959
Star Pit (s Delany), 1989
Star Prince Charlie (Anderson, Dickson), 1975
Star Probe (J. Green), 1976
Star Quest (Koontz), 1968
Star Rangers (Norton), 1953
Star Rebel (Busby), 1984
Star Rider (Piserchia), 1974
Star Rigger series (Carver), from 1978
Star Road (s Dickson), 1973
Star Rogue (L. Carter), 1970
Star Rover (London), 1915
Star Seekers (Lesser), 1953
Star Shine (s F. Brown), 1956

Star Sister (J. Coulson), 1990
Star Slaver (Edmondson and Offutt, as Cleve), 1983
Star Smashers of the Galaxy Rangers (H. Harrison), 1973
Star Songs of an Old Primate (s Tiptree), 1978
Star-Spangled Future (s Spinrad), 1979
Star Spring (Bischoff), 1982
Star Surgeon (J. White), 1963
Star Surgeon (Nourse), 1960
Star Treasure (Laumer), 1971
Star Trek series (A. Foster), from 1974
Star Trek series (Bear), from 1984
Star Trek series (Bischoff), from 1993
Star Trek series (Cogswell), from 1976
Star Trek series (DeWeese), from 1987
Star Trek series (Duane), from 1984
Star Trek series (Eklund), from 1978
Star Trek series (Ford), from 1984
Star Trek series (Gerrold), from 1980
Star Trek series (Hawke), from 1993
Star Trek series (Jack C. Haldeman), from 1980
Star Trek series (Jeter), from 1993
Star Trek series (Joe Haldeman), from 1977
Star Trek series (McIntyre), from 1981
Star Trek series (Reynolds), from 1968
Star Trek series (Rotsler), from 1982
Star Trek series (Stine), from 1982
Star Trek: Deep Space Nine series (Scott), from 1995
Star Trek: Voyager series (Rusch), from 1995
Star Trove (Bulmer), 1970
Star Venturers (Bulmer), 1969
Star Virus (Bayley), 1970
Star Voyager Academy (Forstchen), 1994
Star Wars series (A. Foster), from 1976
Star Wars series (Allen), from 1995
Star Wars series (K. Anderson), from 1994
Star Wars series (J. Vinge), from 1983
Star Wars series (Kahn), from 1987
Star Wars series (McIntyre), from 1994
Star Wars series (Tyers), from 1994
Star Wars series (Wolverton), from 1994
Star Wars series (Zahn), from 1991
Star Wasps (R. Williams), 1963
Star Watchman (Bova), 1964
Star Ways (P. Anderson), 1956
Star Web (Zebrowski), 1975
Star Well (Panshin), 1968
Star Winds (Bayley), 1978
Star Witches (Lymington), 1965
Star Wolf! (T. White), 1971
Star-Search (Kapp), 1983
Starblood (Koontz), 1972
Starbrat (Morressy), 1972
Starbridge 7 (Emerson), 1995
Starbridge trilogy (Park), from 1987
Starburst (Pohl), 1982
Starburst (s Bester), 1958
Starcats series (Gotlieb), from 1980
Starchild series (Pohl, Williamson), from 1964
Starcrossed (Bova), 1975
Stardance series (S. Robinson), from 1979
Stardeath (Tubb), 1983

Stardreamer (s Cordwainer Smith), 1971
Stardrift (Morressy), 1975
Stardrift and Other Fantastic Flotsam (s Petaja), 1971
Stardroppers (Brunner), 1972
Stardust series (Tall), from 1976
Stardust Voyages (s Tall), 1975
Starfarers (McIntyre), 1989
Starfarers series (McIntyre), from 1989
Starfinder (Young), 1980
Starfire (Preuss), 1988
Starfishers series (Cook), from 1982
Starflight 3000 (Mackelworth), 1972
Starfollowers of Coramonde (Daley), 1979
Starhaven (Silverberg, as Jorgenson), 1958
Starhiker (Dann), 1977
Starhunt (Gerrold), 1985
Starjacked! (Greenleaf), 1987
Stark, Eric John series (Brackett), from 1976
Starkahn of Rhada (Coppel, as Gilman), 1970
Starless World (Eklund), 1978
Starlight (s Bester), 1976
Starliner (Drake), 1992
Starman (A. Foster), 1984
Starman Jones (Heinlein), 1953
Starman's Quest (Silverberg), 1959
Starmasters' Gambit (Klein), 1973
Starmen (Brackett), 1952
Starmen of Llyrdis (Brackett), 1976
Starmind (S. Robinson), 1995
StarMother (Van Scyoc), 1976
Starpirate's Brain (Goulart), 1987
Starquake (Forward), 1985
Starry Rift (s Tiptree), 1986
Stars Are Also Fire (P. Anderson), 1994
Stars Are Ours (Bulmer), 1953
Stars Are Ours! (Norton), 1954
Stars Are the Styx (s Sturgeon), 1979
Stars in My Pocket Like Grains of Sand (Delany), 1984
Stars in Shroud (Benford), 1978
Stars, Like Dust (Asimov), 1951
Stars Must Wait (Laumer), 1990
Stars, My Destination (Bester), 1957
Stars series (P. Anderson), from 1993
Stars Will Speak (Zebrowski), 1985
Stars' End (Cook), 1982
Starsea Invaders series (Stine), from 1993
Starseed (S. Robinson), 1991
Starseed on Gye Moor (Lymington), 1977
Starseekers (Garnett), 1971
Starshadows (s Sargent), 1977
Starshine (s Sturgeon), 1966
Starship (Aldiss), 1959
Starship (s P. Anderson), 1982
Starship and Haiku (Sucharitkul), 1981
Starship Death (Garrett), 1982
Starship Sapphire (Offutt, as Cleve), 1984
Starship through Space (Stine, as Correy), 1954
Starship Troopers (Heinlein), 1959
Starship Troupers series (Stasheff), from 1991
Starsilk (Van Scyoc), 1984
Starstormers (Fisk), 1980

Starstormers series (Fisk), from 1980
Starswarm (s Aldiss), 1964
Start of the End of It All (s Emshwiller), 1990
Startide Rising (Brin), 1983
Startling Worlds of Henry Kuttner (Kuttner), 1987
Starwings (Proctor), 1984
Starwolf series (Hamilton), from 1967
Starworld (H. Harrison), 1981
State of Grace (s Wilhelm), 1991
State of the Art (Banks), 1989
Statement of Randolph Carter (s Lovecraft), 1976
Station Gehenna (Weiner), 1987
Station in Space (s Gunn), 1958
Stationfall (Cover), 1989
Stations of the Nightmare (Farmer), 1982
Stations of the Tide (Swanwick), 1991
Status Civilization (Sheckley), 1960
Stealer of Souls (s Moorcock), 1963
Steam Bird (s Schenck), 1988
Steam-Driven Boy and Other Strangers (s Sladek), 1973
Steam House (Verne), 1880-81
Steampunk Trilogy (s Di Filippo), 1995
Steel (Drake, Stirling), 1993
Steel Beach (Varley), 1992
Steel Brother (s Dickson), 1985
Steel Crocodile (Compton), 1970
Steel Magic (Norton), 1965
Steel of Raithskar (Garrett), 1981
Steel, the Mist, and the Blazing Sun (Anvil), 1980
Steel Tsar (Moorcock), 1981
Steel Valentine (s Lansdale), 1991
Steele series (Hawke), from 1989
Stella Fregelius (Haggard), 1904
Stellar Assignment (Tubb), 1979
Stellar Fist (Proctor), 1989
Stellar Legion (Tubb), 1954
Stellar Ranger series (Perry), from 1994
Step to the Stars (del Rey), 1954
Stepford Wives (Levin), 1972
Stephen Archer (G. MacDonald), 1883
Steppe (Anthony), 1976
Steppin' Out, Summer '68 (s Lansdale), 1992
Steps of the Sun (Tevis), 1983
Stepsons of Terra (Silverberg), 1958
Still Forms on Foxfield (Slonczewski), 1980
Still I Persist in Wondering (s Pangborn), 1978
Still Life (Tepper, as Horlak), 1989
Still River (Clement), 1987
Still, Small Voice of Trumpets (Biggle), 1968
Stir of Echoes (Matheson), 1958
Stochastic Man (Silverberg), 1975
Stolen Bacillus and Other Incidents (s Wells), 1895
Stolen Faces (Bishop), 1977
Stolen Sphere (Cross), 1953
Stolen Submarine (G. Griffith), 1904
Stolen Sun (Petaja), 1967
Stolen Throne (Turtledove), 1995
Stone Dogs (Stirling), 1990
Stone Drum (s de Lint), 1989
Stone Giant (Blaylock), 1989
Stone God Awakens (Farmer), 1970

Stone in Heaven (P. Anderson), 1979
Stone Man (Dent, as Robeson), 1976
Stone That Never Came Down (Brunner), 1973
Stone Within (Wingrove), 1991
Stonehenge (H. Harrison), 1972
Stones of Nomuru (de Camp), 1988
Stones of Power (Gemmell), 1992
Stopping at Slowyear (s Pohl), 1991
Store of Infinity (s Sheckley), 1960
Storeys from the Old Hotel (s G. Wolfe), 1988
Stories by Mama Lansdale's Youngest Boy (s Lansdale), 1991
Stories from the Twilight Zone (s Serling), 1960
Stories from The Other Passenger (s Cross), 1961
Stories of Ray Bradbury (s Bradbury), 1980
Stork Factor (Z. Hughes), 1975
Storm God's Fury (s Fanthorpe, as Fane), 1962
Storm Lord (Lee), 1976
Storm of Wings (M. Harrison), 1980
Storm over Vallia (Bulmer, as Akers), 1985
Storm over Warlock (Norton), 1960
Storm Seed (J. Morris), 1990
Storm Warriors (Stableford, as Craig), 1991
Stormbringer (Moorcock), 1965
Stormqueen! (Bradley), 1978
Storms of Victory (Norton), 1991
Storms of Victory (Pournelle), 1987
Story of Pepita and Corindo (s Cowper), 1982
Story of the Gardener series (Mann), from 1986
Story of the Glittering Plain (W. Morris), 1891
Story of the Stone (Hughart), 1988
Story of the Unknown Church (s W. Morris), 1902
Story of Ulla (s Arnold), 1895
Storyteller (s Yolen), 1992
Storyteller and the Jann (Goldin), 1988
Stowaway to Mars (Wyndham), 1953
Stranded (Norwood), 1989
Strange Attractors (Carver), 1995
Strange Devices of the Sun and Moon (Goldstein), 1993
Strange Doings (s Lafferty), 1972
Strange Eons (Bloch), 1978
Strange Highways (s Koontz), 1995
Strange Invaders (Llewellyn), 1934
Strange Journeys of Colonel Polders (Dunsany), 1950
Strange Monsters of the Recent Past (s Waldrop), 1991
Strange Ones (Fanthorpe, as Torro), 1963
Strange Papers of Dr. Blayre (s Blayre), 1932
Strange Relations (s Farmer), 1960
Strange Seas and Shores (s Davidson), 1971
Strange Shadows (s Clark Ashton Smith), 1989
Strange Stories of Hospitals (s Aubrey, as Ashley), 1898
Strange Story (Bulwer-Lytton), 1862
Strange Things in Close-up (s Waldrop), 1989
Strange Wine (s Ellison), 1978
Strange Worlds (s Farley), 1952
Stranger (s Dickson), 1987
Stranger in a Strange Land (Heinlein), 1961
Stranger in the Shadow (s Fanthorpe), 1966
Stranger Suns (Zebrowski), 1991
Stranger Than You Think (s Edmondson), 1965
Strangers (Dozois), 1978
Strangers (Koontz), 1986

Strangers from Earth (s P. Anderson), 1961
Strangers in Paradise (Anvil), 1970
Strangers in the Universe (s Simak), 1956
Strangler's Moon (Goldin, E.E. Smith), 1976
Strata (Pratchett), 1981
Stray Lamb (T. Smith), 1929
Street (Kilworth, as Douglas), 1988
Street Magic (Reaves), 1991
Streetlethal (S. Barnes), 1983
Strength of Stones (Bear), 1981
Strength of the Strong (s London), 1911
Stress of Her Regard (Powers), 1989
Stress Pattern (Barrett), 1974
Stricken Field (Dave Duncan), 1993
Strings (Dave Duncan), 1990
Striped Holes (Broderick), 1988
Stroka Prospekt (s Lupoff), 1982
Struggle in Space (Belyaev), 1965
Strum Again? (Scarborough), 1992
Study in Sorcery (Kurland), 1989
Stunts (C. Grant), 1990
Sturgeon in Orbit (s Sturgeon), 1964
Suaine and the Crow-God (S. Gordon), 1975
Subb (MacApp), 1971
Submarine Mystery (Dent, as Robeson), 1971
Subspace Encounter (Eshbach, E.E. Smith), 1983
Subspace Explorers (E.E. Smith), 1965
Subterfuge (Maine), 1959
Such (Brooke-Rose), 1966
Such Stuff as Screams Are Made Of (s Bloch), 1979
Sudden Star (Sargent), 1979
Sudden Wild Magic (Diana Wynne Jones), 1992
Sugar Festival (Park), 1989
Sugar in the Air (Large), 1937
Sugar Rain (Park), 1989
Suicide, Inc (Goulart), 1985
Suicide Plague (Naha), 1982
Suiciders (McIntosh), 1973
Suldrun's Garden (Vance), 1983
Summer King, Winter Fool (Goldstein), 1994
Summer Queen (J. Vinge), 1991
Summer's King (Wilder), 1986
Summertide (Sheffield), 1990
Summit (D.M. Thomas), 1987
Sun and Shadow (s Bradbury), 1957
Sun Destroyers (Rocklynne), 1973
Sun Makers (Fearn, as Statten), 1950
Sun Saboteurs (Knight), 1961
Sun Smasher (Hamilton), 1959
Sun's End series (Lupoff), from 1984
Sunbound (Felice), 1981
Sunburst (Fisk), 1980
Sunburst (Gotlieb), 1964
Sundance (s Silverberg), 1974
Sundered Worlds (Moorcock), 1965
Sundering Flood (W. Morris), 1897
Sundiver (Brin), 1980
Sundrinker (Z. Hughes), 1987
Sunfall (s Cherryh), 1981
Sung in Blood (Cook), 1990
Sung in Shadow (Lee), 1983

Sunken World (Coblentz), 1948
Sunless World (s N. Jones), 1967
Sunrise on Mercury (s Silverberg), 1975
Suns of Scorpio (Bulmer, as Akers), 1973
Sunspacer series (Zebrowski), from 1984
Sunstone Scrolls series (Van Scyoc), from 1982
Sunstroke (s Watson), 1982
Sunwaifs (Van Scyoc), 1981
Sunworld (Kelley), 1979
Super Barbarians (Brunner), 1962
Superluminal (McIntyre), 1983
Superman III (Kotzwinkle), 1983
Supermind (Garrett and Janifer, as Phillips), 1963
Supermind (van Vogt), 1977
Supernova (Allen), 1991
Support Your Local Wizard (Duane), 1990
Surface Action (Drake), 1990
Surgeons of a Planet (Klein), 1960
Surrender the Galactica! (Thurston), 1988
Surveillance (May), 1988
Survey Ship (Bradley), 1980
Survival Game (Kapp), 1976
Survival Kit (s Pohl), 1979
Survival Margin (Maine), 1968
Survival Project (Fanthorpe, as Muller), 1966
Survival Ship (s Merril), 1974
Survival World (Long), 1971
Survival! (s Dickson), 1984
Survivor (J. Herbert), 1976
Survivor (Janifer), 1977
Survivor (O. Butler), 1978
Survivor and Others (s Lovecraft), 1957
Survivor of Mars (s Fearn), 1982
Survivor series (Janifer), from 1977
Survivors (Bradley), 1979
Survivors (Godwin), 1958
Suspension (Fanthorpe, as Fane), 1964
Svaha (de Lint), 1989
Svend and His Brethren (s W. Morris), 1901
Swain, Mathew series (McQuay), from 1981
Swallow (D.M. Thomas), 1984
Swallow (Haggard), 1899
Swan Song (Stableford), 1975
Swastika Night (Burdekin, as Constantine), 1937
Swatting at the Cosmos (s Morrow), 1990
Sweeney's Island (Christopher), 1964
Sweet Dreams (Frayn), 1973
Sweet Dreams, Sweet Princes (Reynolds), 1986
Sweet Evil (Platt), 1977
Sweet Silver Blues (Cook), 1987
Sweet, Sweet Poison (Wilhelm), 1990
Sweets from a Stranger (s Fisk), 1982
Swiftly Tilting Planet (L'Engle), 1978
Sword (Drake, Stirling), 1995
Sword Above the Night (Lymington), 1962
Sword and the Dagger (Mayhar), 1987
Sword and the Lion (Emerson, as Roberta Cray), 1993
Sword and the Stallion (Moorcock), 1974
Sword and the Stone (s Yolen), 1991
Sword for Kregen (Bulmer, as Akers), 1979
Sword of Aldones (Bradley), 1962

Sword of Aradel (Key), 1977
Sword of Arhapal (Sernine), 1990
Sword of Bheleu (Watt-Evans), 1983
Sword of Forbearance (P. Williams), 1985
Sword of Knowledge series (Cherryh), from 1989
Sword of Rhiannon (Brackett), 1953
Sword of the Dawn (Moorcock), 1968
Sword of the Demon (Lupoff), 1977
Sword of the Gael (Offutt), 1975
Sword of the Lictor (G. Wolfe), 1982
Sword of the Samurai (Perry, Reaves), 1984
Sword of the Spirits (Christopher), 1972
Sword of Tomorrow (s Kuttner), 1955
Sword of Welleran (s Dunsany), 1908
Sword of Winter (Randall), 1983
Sword Smith (Arnason), 1978
Sword Swallower (Goulart), 1968
Swordbearer (Cook), 1982
Swords against Death (s Leiber), 1970
Swords against Wizardry (s Leiber), 1968
Swords and Deviltry (Leiber), 1970
Swords and Ice Magic (s Leiber), 1977
Swords in the Mist (s Leiber), 1968
Swords of Corum Omnibus (Moorcock), 1986
Swords of Lankhmar (Leiber), 1968
Swords of Mars (E. Burroughs), 1936
Swords of Raemllyn series (Proctor), from 1985
Swords of the Barbarians (Bulmer), 1970
Swords of the Legion (Turtledove), 1987
Swords of Zinjaban (de Camp), 1991
Swords series (Bulmer), from 1970
Swords series (Saberhagen), from 1983
Swords Trilogy (Moorcock), 1977
Swords' Masters (s Leiber), 1990
Swordships of Scorpio (Bulmer, as Akers), 1973
Swordsman of Mars (Kline), 1960
Swordswoman (Salmonson), 1982
Sybaris and Other Homes (s Hale), 1869
Sylvia (Vercors), 1962
Symbol of Terra (Tubb), 1984
Syn (R. Jones), 1969
Synaptic Manhunt (Farren), 1976
Syndic (Kornbluth), 1953
Synners (Cadigan), 1991
Synthajoy (Compton), 1968
Synthetic Man (Sturgeon), 1957
Synthetic Men of Mars (E. Burroughs), 1940
Synthetic Ones (Fanthorpe, as Roberts), 1961
Systemic Shock (Ing), 1981
Syzygy (Coney), 1973
Syzygy (Pohl), 1982

t zero (Calvino), 1969
Tactics of Conquest (Malzberg), 1974
Tactics of Mistake (Dickson), 1971
Tail of the Arabian, Knight (C. Grant, as Marsh), 1986
Take Back Plenty (Greenland), 1990
Takeoff (Kornbluth), 1952
Takeoff Too! (s Garrett), 1987
Takeoff! (s Garrett), 1980
Takeover (Edmondson), 1984

Taking Flight (Watt-Evans), 1993
Tale of the House of the Wolfings (W. Morris), 1888
Tale of the Troika (Strugatsky), 1977
Tale of Three Lions, and On Going Back (Haggard), 1887
Tale of Time City (Diana Wynne Jones), 1987
Tale of Two Clocks (Schmitz), 1962
Talent for the Invisible (Goulart), 1973
Talent for War (McDevitt), 1989
Talents, Incorporated (Leinster), 1962
Tales from a Vanished Country (s Lynn), 1990
Tales from Gavagan's Bar (s de Camp), 1953
Tales from Night's Black Agents (s Leiber), 1961
Tales from Planet Earth (s Clarke), 1989
Tales from the Flat Earth (s Lee), 1987
Tales from the Nightside: Dark Fantasy (s C. Grant), 1981
Tales from the White Hart (s Clarke), 1957
Tales from Underwood (s Keller), 1952
Tales in a Jugular Vein (s Bloch), 1965
Tales of Chicago (Lafferty), 1992
Tales of Gooseflesh and Laughter (s Wyndham), 1956
Tales of Known Space (s Niven), 1975
Tales of Midnight (Lafferty), 1992
Tales of Narnia (Lewis), 1987
Tales of Nevèryon (s Delany), 1979
Tales of Science and Sorcery (s Clark Ashton Smith), 1964
Tales of Space and Time (s Wells), 1899
Tales of Ten Worlds (s Clarke), 1962
Tales of the Flying Mountains (s P. Anderson), 1970
Tales of the Galactic Midway (Resnick), 1982
Tales of the Grotesque and Arabesque (s Poe), 1840
Tales of the Occult (Eliade), 1970
Tales of the Quintana Roo (s Tiptree), 1986
Tales of the Scientific Crime Club (Cummings), 1979
Tales of the Unexpected (s Wells), 1922-23
Tales of the Velvet Comet (Resnick), 1984
Tales of Three Hemispheres (s Dunsany), 1919
Tales of Three Planets (s E. Burroughs), 1964
Tales of Wonder (s Dunsany), 1916
Tales of Wonder (s Fearn), 1983
Tales of Wonder (s Yolen), 1983
Talking Car (Fisk), 1988
Talking Man (Bisson), 1986
Talons of Scorpio (Bulmer, as Akers), 1983
Tam, Son of the Tiger (Kline), 1962
Tam Tinkern series (s de Lint), from 1980
Tama series (Cummings), from 1965
Tamastara (s Lee), 1984
Tambu (Asprin), 1979
Tamuli series (Eddings), from 1992
Tanar of Pellucidar (E. Burroughs), 1930
Tangents (s Bear), 1989
Tango Charlie and Foxtrot Romeo (s Varley), 1984
Tapestry of Magics (Daley), 1983
Tapestry of Time (Cowper), 1982
Tapestry Warriors (Wilder), 1983
Tar-Aiym Krang (A. Foster), 1972
Tara of the Twilight (L. Carter), 1979
Target (Drake, J. Morris), 1989
Target: Terra (Janifer), 1968
Tarot series (Anthony), from 1979
Tarrano, the Conqueror (Cummings), 1930

Tartarus series (Greenleaf), from 1983
Tarzan and the Valley of Gold (Leiber), 1966
Tarzan series (E. Burroughs), from 1914
Tarzan series (Farmer), from 1974
Tatham Mound (Anthony), 1991
Tatja Grimm's World (V. Vinge), 1987
Tau Zero (P. Anderson), 1970
Tcity series (Adlard), from 1971
Tea Party (C. Grant), 1985
Tea with the Black Dragon (MacAvoy), 1983
Technicolor Time Machine (H. Harrison), 1967
Technos (Tubb), 1972
Tehanu (Le Guin), 1990
Telempath (S. Robinson), 1976
Telepath (Sellings), 1962
Telepathist (Brunner), 1965
Telepower (Hoffman), 1967
Television Detective (s Keller), 1938
Telly Is Watching You (Fisk), 1989
Telnarian Histories series (Norman), from 1991
Telzey Amberdon series (Schmitz), from 1964
Templar Treasure (Kurtz), 1993
Temple of Fire (Aubrey, as Ashley), 1905
Temple of Truth (Tubb), 1985
Temporary Agency (Pollack), 1994
Tempus (s J. Morris), 1987
Tempus Unbound (J. Morris), 1989
Ten Deadly Men (Fairman, as Jorgensen), 1976
Ten from Infinity (Fairman, as Jorgensen), 1963
Ten from Tomorrow (s Tubb), 1966
Ten Little Wizards (Kurland), 1988
Ten Million Years to Friday (Lymington), 1967
Ten Thousand Light-Years from Home (s Tiptree), 1973
Ten Times One Is Ten (s Hale, as Ingham), 1971
Ten Years to Doomsday (Kurland), 1964
Tenth Planet (Cooper), 1973
Terminal Beach (s Ballard), 1964
Terminal Café (McDonald), 1994
Terminal Experiment (Sawyer), 1995
Terminal Man (Crichton), 1972
Terminal Road (Shirley, as Drum), 1986
Terminal Velocity (Shaw), 1991
Terra Data (Tubb), 1980
Terra Magica series (L. Carter), from 1982
Terran Federation series (Piper), from 1961
Terraplane (Womack), 1988
Terrible Swift Sword (Forstchen), 1992
Terridae (Tubb), 1981
Terror (Pohl), 1986
Terror in the Navy (Dent, as Robeson), 1969
Terror on the Moons of Jupiter (Rotsler), 1981
Terror Star (P. Moore), 1979
Terror Version (Lymington), 1982
Tery (s F. Wilson), 1990
Test of Fire (Bova), 1982
Test of Honor (Bujold), 1987
Testament of Andros (s Blish), 1977
Testing (Oberndorf), 1993
Texas-Israeli War: 1999 (Waldrop), 1974
Textermination (Brooke-Rose), 1991
Texts of Festival (Farren), 1973

Tharkol, Lord of the Unknown (Hamilton), 1950
That Hideous Strength (Lewis), 1945
That Man on Beta (Lupoff, as Steele), 1979
The Enchanter Compleated (de Camp), 1980
The Floating Continent (de Camp), 1966
The Next Wave series (Leigh), from 1991
The Queen of Zamba (de Camp), 1977
Theatre of Timesmiths (Kilworth), 1984
Thebes of the Hundred Gate (s Silverberg), 1991
Their Master's War (Farren), 1987
T. H. E. M (Edmondson), 1974
Them Bones (Waldrop), 1984
Then Beggars Could Ride (Nelson), 1976
Thendara House (Bradley), 1983
There Are Doors (G. Wolfe), 1988
There Is No Darkness (Jack C. Haldeman, Joe Haldeman), 1983
There Shall Be Darkness (s C.L. Moore), 1954
There Was a Knock (s Hoshi), 1984
There Will Be Time (P. Anderson), 1972
Thermals of August (s Bryant), 1992
These Savage Futurians (High), 1967
They (Kipling), 1904
They Fly at Çiron (Delany), 1993
They Never Came Back (Fanthorpe, as Brett), 1962
They Shall Have Stars (Blish), 1956
They Walked like Men (Simak), 1962
They'd Rather Be Right (Clifton), 1957
Thief of Thoth (L. Carter), 1968
Thieves of Light (Kube-McDowell, as Hudson), 1987
Thieves' World series (Asprin), from 1986
Thieves' World series (Dickson), from 1984
Thieves' World series (Drake), from 1988
Thieves' World--Shadowspawn series (Offutt), from 1987
Thieves' World--Tempus series (J. Morris), from 1989
Thing (A. Foster), 1982
Thing (s Campbell), 1952
Thing from Another World (s Campbell), 1953
Thing from Sheol (s Fanthorpe, as Fane), 1963
Thing in the Cellar (s Keller), 1940
Thing of the Past (Fearn, as Gridban), 1953
Things beyond Midnight (s Nolan), 1984
Thinking Seat (Tate), 1969
Thinktank That Leaked (Hodder-Williams), 1979
Third Eagle (MacAvoy), 1989
Third Ear (Siodmak), 1971
Third Eye (s Cogswell), 1968
Third from the Sun (s Matheson), 1955
Third Level (s Finney), 1957
Thirst! (Maine), 1977
Thirteen O'Clock and Other Zero Hours (s Kornbluth), 1970
Thirty-first of February (s Bond), 1949
Thirty-First of June (Priestley), 1961
Thirty Strange Stories (s Wells), 1897
This above All (Shiel), 1933
This Darkening Universe (Biggle), 1976
This Fortress World (Gunn), 1955
This Immortal (Zelazny), 1966
This Is the Way the World Begins (McIntosh), 1977
This Is the Way the World Ends (Morrow), 1986
This Perfect Day (Levin), 1970
This Sentient Earth (T. Hoyle), 1979

This Star Shall Abide (Engdahl), 1972
This Strange Tomorrow (Long), 1966
This Time of Darkness (Hoover), 1980
This World Is Taboo (Leinster), 1961
Thongor series (L. Carter), from 1966
Thor's Hammer (Whiteford), 1983
Thorburn Enterprise (Mason, as Rankine), 1977
Thorn (Saberhagen), 1980
Thorns (Silverberg), 1967
Those Gentle Voices (Effinger), 1976
Those Idiots from Earth (s Richard Wilson), 1957
Those of My Blood (Lichtenberg), 1988
Those Who Favor Fire (Randall), 1984
Those Who Watch (Silverberg), 1967
Those Who Watch over Earth (Sernine), 1990
Thought Projector (s Keller), 1929
Thought-Reading Machine (Maurois), 1938
Thousand-Headed Man (Dent, as Robeson), 1964
Thousand Shrine Warrior (Salmonson), 1984
Thousandstar (Anthony), 1980
Threats . . . and Other Promises (s V. Vinge), 1988
Three against the Witch World (Norton), 1965
Three Corners to Nowhere (Caidin), 1975
Three Eternals (s Binder), 1949
Three-Eyes (S. Gordon), 1975
Three Eyes of Evil (van Vogt), 1973
Three Faces of Time (Long), 1969
Three Faces of Time (Merwin), 1955
Three from the Legion (Williamson), 1979
Three Hearts and Three Lions (P. Anderson), 1961
Three-Legged Hootch Dancer (Resnick), 1983
Three Lines of Old French (s Merritt), 1937
Three of Swords (s Leiber), 1989
Three Plusketeers and the Garden Slugs (s de Lint), 1985
Three-Ring Psychus (Shirley), 1980
Three Steps Spaceward (Long), 1963
Three Stigmata of Palmer Eldritch (Dick), 1965
Three Suns of Amara (Temple), 1962
Three Survived (Silverberg), 1969
Three to Conquer (Russell), 1956
Three to Dorsai! (Dickson), 1975
Three World series (Watt-Evans), from 1994
Three Worlds of Futurity (s St. Clair), 1964
Three Worlds to Conquer (P. Anderson), 1964
Threshold (Le Guin), 1980
Threshold of Eternity (Brunner), 1959
Threshold series (J. Morris), from 1990
Thrice upon a Time (Hogan), 1980
Throme of the Erril of Sheril (McKillip), 1973
Throne of Madness (Sucharitkul), 1983
Throne of Saturn (s S. Wright), 1949
Through a Glass, Clearly (s Asimov), 1967
Through Channels (Matheson), 1989
Through Darkest America (Barrett), 1986
Through Darkest Resnick with Gun and Camera (s Resnick), 1990
Through Elegant Eyes (s Lafferty), 1983
Through Space and Time with Ferdinand (s Bretnor, as Briarton), 1962
Through the Barrier (Fanthorpe, as Torro), 1963
Through the Breach (Drake), 1995
Through the Eye of a Needle (Clement), 1978

Time's Last Gift (Farmer), 1972
Time's Rub (s Benford), 1984
Timebinder series (Nelson), from 1976
Timefall (Kahn), 1987
Timejumper (Greenleaf), 1980
Timekeeper Conspiracy (Hawke), 1984
Timeless Ones (Fanthorpe, as Torro), 1963
Timelike Infinity (Baxter), 1992
Timeliner (Maine), 1955
Timeliner series (Meredith), from 1973
Timeliner Trilogy (Meredith), 1987
Timemaster (Forward), 1992
Timequest (Nelson), 1985
Times without Number (Brunner), 1962
Timescape (Benford), 1980
Timescoop (Brunner), 1969
Timeservers (Griffin), 1985
Timeslip! (Leinster), 1967
Timestop! (Farmer), 1970
Timestorm (Dickson), 1992
Timetipping (s Dann), 1980
Timetracks (s Laumer), 1972
Timewars series (Hawke), from1984
Timewinders (Kapp), 1980
Tin Angel (Goulart), 1973
Tin Men (Frayn), 1965
Tin Soldier (s J. Vinge), 1990
Tin Woodman (Bischoff), 1979
Titan (s P. Miller), 1952
Titan (Varley), 1979
Titan's Daughter (Blish), 1961
Tithonian Factor (s Cowper), 1984
Titus Alone (Peake), 1959
Titus Books (Peake), 1983
Titus Groan (Peake), 1946
Titus Unbound (s Peake), 1977
Tlon, Uqbar, Orbis Tertius (s Borges), 1983
To Challenge Chaos (Stableford), 1972
To Conquer Chaos (Brunner), 1964
To Control the Stars (Hoskins), 1977
To Demons Bound (Proctor), 1985
To Die in Italbar (Zelazny), 1973
To Escape the Stars (Hoskins), 1978
To Fear the Lion (Bova), 1994
To Here and the Easel (s Sturgeon), 1973
To Keep the Ship (Chandler), 1978
To Kill a Shadow (Shirley, as Drum), 1984
To Live Again (Silverberg), 1969
To Live Forever (Vance), 1956
To Make Death Love Us (Strete, as Falconer), 1987
To Marry Medusa (s Sturgeon), 1987
To-morrow's Yesterday (Gloag), 1932
To Open the Sky (Silverberg), 1967
To Outrun Doomsday (Bulmer), 1967
To Prime the Pump (Chandler), 1971
To Renew the Ages (R. Coulson), 1976
To Ride Pegasus (s McCaffrey), 1973
To Sail beyond the Sunset (Heinlein), 1987
To Sail the Century Sea (Edmondson), 1981
To Save the Sun series (Bova), from 1992
To Sing Strange Songs (s Bradbury), 1979

To the End of Time (Stapledon), 1953
To the End of Time (s R. Williams), 1960
To the Haunted Mountains (Emerson), 1987
To the Land of the Living (Silverberg), 1989
To the Land of the Electric Angel (Rotsler), 1976
To the Resurrection Station (Arnason), 1986
To the Stars (s Hubbard), 1995
To the Stars series (H. Harrison), from 1981
To the Sun? A Journey through Planetary Space (Verne), 1878
To the Tombaugh Station (Tucker), 1960
To the Ultimate (Fearn, as Statten), 1952
To the Vanishing Point (A. Foster), 1988
To The Magic Born (Stasheff), 1986
To Venus in Five Seconds (Jefferies), 1897
To Venus! To Venus! (Wollheim, as Grinnell), 1970
To Walk the Night (Sloane), 1937
To Worlds Beyond (s Silverberg), 1965
To Your Scattered Bodies Go (Farmer), 1971
Today We Choose Faces (Zelazny), 1973
Tom O'Bedlam (Silverberg), 1985
Tom Swift series (Rotsler), from 1981
Tomato Cain (s Kneale), 1949
Tomb (s Lovecraft), 1969
Tombs of Atuan (Le Guin), 1971
Tombs of Kobol (Thurston), 1979
Tomoe Gozen series (Salmonson), from 1981
Tomorrow and Tomorrow (Eldershaw), 1947
Tomorrow and Tomorrow (Hunter), 1956
Tomorrow and Tomorrow, and The Fairy Chessmen (Kuttner and C.L. Moore, as Padgett), 1951
Tomorrow and Tomorrow and Tomorrow (Eldershaw), 1983
Tomorrow Came (s Cooper), 1963
Tomorrow City (M. Hughes), 1978
Tomorrow Is Too Far (J. White), 1971
Tomorrow Knight (Kurland), 1976
Tomorrow Lies in Ambush (s Shaw), 1973
Tomorrow Might Be Different (Reynolds), 1975
Tomorrow People (Merril), 1960
Tomorrow Plus X (Tucker), 1957
Tomorrow Testament (Longyear), 1983
Tomorrow Times Seven (s Pohl), 1959
Tomorrow! (Wylie), 1954
Tomorrow's Gift (s Cooper, as Avery), 1958
Tomorrow's Heritage (J. Coulson), 1981
Tomorrow's Son (Hoskins), 1977
Tomorrow's World (Hunter, as Collins), 1956
Tongues of the Moon (Farmer), 1964
Tonight We Steal the Stars (Jakes), 1969
Too Many Magicians (Garrett), 1967
Tool of the Trade (Joe Haldeman), 1987
Tooth-Gnasher Superflash (Pinkwater), 1981
Topper series (T. Smith), from 1926
Topsy-Turvy (Verne), 1890
Torch of Honor series (Allen), from 1985
Torched! (Baxter), 1986
Torin series (Wilder), from 1977
Tormented City (Tubb, as Grey), 1953
Torrent of Faces (Blish, Knight), 1967
Torture Garden (s Bloch), 1967
Tortured Planet (Lewis), 1958
Torturing Mr. Amberwell (s Disch), 1985

Voyage to Amaltheia (Strugatsky), 1962
Voyage to Arcturus (Lindsay), 1920
Voyage to Dari (I. Wallace), 1974
Voyage to the Bottom of the Sea (R. Jones), 1965
Voyage to the Bottom of the Sea (Sturgeon), 1961
Voyage to the City of the Dead (A. Foster), 1984
Voyage to the Island of the Articoles (Maurois), 1928
Voyage to the Moon (Verne), 1923
Voyage to the Red Planet (Bisson), 1990
Voyage to Venus (Perelandra), 1953
Voyager in Night (Cherryh), 1984
Voyagers series (Bova), from 1981
Vril: The Power of the Coming Race (Bulwer-Lytton), 1972
Vulcan Treasure (Rotsler), 1986
Vulcan's Hammer (Dick), 1960
Vurt (Noon), 1993

Wagered World (Janifer), 1969
Wailing Asteroid (Leinster), 1960
Waiting for the End of the World (Harding), 1983
Waiting World (Fanthorpe), 1958
Waking of the Stone (Lymington), 1978
Waking the Moon (Hand), 1994
Waldo, and Magic Inc. (Heinlein), 1950
Waldo, Genius in Orbit (Heinlein), 1958
Walk through To-morrow (Fanthorpe, as Zeigfreid), 1962
Walk to the End of the World (Charnas), 1974
Walk up the Sky (R. Williams), 1962
Walkabout Woman (Roessner), 1988
Walkers on the Sky (Lake), 1976
Walking Shadow (s Fanthorpe, as Fane), 1964
Walking Shadow (Stableford), 1979
Wall (Mayhar), 1987
Wall (Tubb, as Grey), 1953
Wall around a Star (Pohl), 1983
Wall around Eden (Slonczewski), 1989
Wall Around the World (s Cogswell), 1962
Wall of Serpents (de Camp), 1960
Wall of Years (A. Stephenson), 1979
Wall, Stone, Craft (W. Williams), 1993
Walpurgis III (Resnick), 1982
Wanderer (Leiber), 1964
Wanderer in Space (P. Moore), 1961
Wanderer of Space (Fearn, as Statten), 1950
Wanderer's Necklace (Haggard), 1914
Wanderers of Time (s Wyndham, as Beynon), 1973
Wandering Variables (Trimble), 1972
Wanderings of Wuntvor (Gardner), 1989
Wandl, the Invader (Cummings), 1961
Wankh (Vance), 1986
Wanting Factor (DeWeese), 1980
Wanting Seed (Burgess), 1962
War against the Chtorr series (Gerrold), from 1983
War against the Rull (van Vogt), 1959
War Birds (Meluch), 1989
War Fever (s Ballard), 1990
War for the Lot (Lanier), 1969
War for the Oaks (Bull), 1987
War Games (Stableford), 1981
War Games of Zelos (Cooper, as Avery), 1975
War Hound and the World's Pain (Moorcock), 1981

War in Outer Space (Rotsler), 1981
War in the Air (Wells), 1908
War Machine (Allen), 1989
War Machine (Drake), 1989
War of 1938 series (S. Wright), from 1935
War of Dreams (A. Carter), 1974
War of Nerves (Joe Haldeman, as Graham), 1975
War of Omission (O'Donnell), 1982
War of Shadows (Chalker), 1979
War of the Gods on Earth series (Offutt), from 1979
War of the Maelstrom (Chalker), 1988
War of the Roses (s Fowler), 1991
War of the Sky Lords (Brosnan), 1989
War of the Wing-Men (P. Anderson), 1958
War of the Wizards series (Offutt), from 1977
War of the Worlds (Wells), 1898
War of Two Worlds (P. Anderson), 1959
War Surplus series (Watt-Evans), from 1982
War with the Gizmos (Leinster), 1958
War with the Newts (Capek), 1937
War with the Robots (s H. Harrison), 1962
Warblade (Garnett, as Ferring), 1993
Warbots series (Stine), from 1988
'Ware Hawk (Norton), 1983
Wargames (Bischoff), 1983
Warhammer 40,000 series (Watson), from 1990
Warhammer series (Stableford), from 1989
Warhammer-Konrad series (Garnett), from 1991
Warhorse (Zahn), 1990
Warlock (Cook), 1985
Warlock (Koontz), 1972
Warlock at the Wheel (s Diana Wynne Jones), 1984
Warlock of Rhada (Coppel, as Gilman), 1985
Warlock of the Witch World (Norton), 1967
Warlock series (Stasheff), from 1969
Warlock's Gift (Mayhar), 1982
Warlord of Antares (Bulmer, as Akers), 1988
Warlord of Kor (T. Carr), 1963
Warlord of Mars (E. Burroughs), 1919
Warlord of the Air (Moorcock), 1971
Warlord! (J. Morris), 1987
Warlord's World (Anvil), 1975
Warlords of Xuma (Lake), 1983
Warm Worlds and Otherwise (s Tiptree), 1975
Warped (Jeter), 1995
Warren Peace series (Shaw), from 1977
Warrior (Drake), 1991
Warrior of Llarn (Fox), 1964
Warrior of Mars (Fearn), 1950
Warrior of Mars (Moorcock, as Bradbury), 1981
Warrior of Scorpio (Bulmer, as Akers), 1973
Warrior of World's End (L. Carter), 1974
Warrior Shield (Stine), 1992
Warrior Who Carried Life (Ryman), 1985
Warrior Woman (Bradley), 1985
Warrior's Apprentice (Bujold), 1986
Warrior's Blood (Niven), 1981
Warrior's Blood (Pournelle), 1981
Warrior's World (Niven, Pournelle), 1981
Warriors of Dawn (M.A. Foster), 1975
Warriors of Day (Blish), 1953

Warriors of Mars (Moorcock, as Bradbury), 1965
Warriors of the Storm (Chalker), 1987
Warriors of the Way series (H. Harrison), from 1993
Wars of Vis series (Lee), from 1976
Wartide (J. Barnes), 1992
Wasp (Russell), 1957
Watch Below (J. White), 1966
Watch on Peter (Rackham), 1964
Watchbird (s Sheckley), 1990
Watchers (Koontz), 1987
Watchers at the Well (Chalker), 1994
Watchers of the Dark (Biggle), 1966
Watchers of the Forest (s Fanthorpe), 1958
Watchers Out of Time (s Lovecraft), 1974
Watchers series (S. Gordon), from 1987
Watching World (Fanthorpe), 1966
Watchman series (Bova), from 1964
Watchmen (A. Moore), 1987
Watchmen (Bova), 1994
Watchstar (Sargent), 1980
Watchstar Trilogy (Sargent), 1996
Watchtower (Lynn), 1979
Water in the Air (G. Jones), 1977
Water Is Wide (s Le Guin), 1976
Water of the Wondrous Isles (W. Morris), 1897
Water of Thought (Saberhagen), 1965
Water Witch (Felice, Willis), 1982
Water-Walker (s F. Brown), 1990
Waters of Centaurus (R. Brown), 1970
Waters of Death Presents Thunder Jim Wade (s Kuttner), 1992
Waters of Lethe (s Keller), 1937
Wave Rider (s Schenck), 1980
Wave without a Shore (Cherryh), 1981
Waves (M.A. Foster), 1980
Way Back (Chandler), 1976
Way Down the Hill (s Powers), 1986
Way Home (s Sturgeon), 1955
Way of the Clans (Thurston), 1991
Way of the Gods (s Kuttner), 1954
Way of the Pilgrim (Dickson), 1987
Way Station (Simak), 1963
Way up High (s Zelazny), 1992
Waylander (Gemmell), 1986
Waylander II (Gemmell), 1992
We (Zamyatin), 1924
We All Died at Breakaway Station (Meredith), 1969
We Can Build You (Dick), 1972
We Can Remember It for You Wholesale (s Dick), 1990
We Claim These Stars (P. Anderson), 1959
We Could Do Worse (s Benford), 1988
We, in Some Strange Power's Employ, Move on a Rigorous Line (s Delany), 1990
We Open on Venus (Stasheff), 1994
We, The Venusians (Rackham), 1965
We Who Are about to . . . (Russ), 1977
Wealth of the Void (Fearn, as Statten), 1954
Weapon from Beyond (Hamilton), 1967
Weapon Shop series (van Vogt), from 1947
Weathermakers (Bova), 1967
Weathermonger (Dickinson), 1968
Web (Wyndham), 1979

Web between the Worlds (Sheffield), 1979
Web of Angels (Ford), 1980
Web of Darkness (Bradley), 1984
Web of Defeat (C. Grant, as Fenn), 1987
Web of Everywhere (Brunner), 1974
Web of Light (Bradley), 1983
Web of Sand (Tubb), 1979
Web of the Chozen (Chalker), 1978
Web of the Magi (s Cowper), 1980
Web of the Spider (Offutt), 1981
Web of the Witch World (Norton), 1964
Web of Time (Harding), 1980
Web of Wizardry (J. Coulson), 1978
Webster, Martin series (S. Wright), from 1927
Weeping May Tarry (del Rey, R. Jones), 1978
Weeping Sky (Harding), 1977
Weigher of Souls (Maurois), 1931
Weird of the White Wolf (Moorcock), 1977
Weird Shadow over Innsmouth (s Lovecraft), 1944
Weisman Experiment (Mason, as Rankine), 1969
Welcome, Chaos (Wilhelm), 1983
Welcome to Mars (Blish), 1967
Welcome to the Monkey House (s Vonnegut), 1968
Well at the World's End (W. Morris), 1896
Well of Darkness (Garrett), 1983
Well of Shiuan (Cherryh), 1978
Well of the Unicorn (Pratt, as Fletcher), 1948
Well of the Worlds (Kuttner and C.L. Moore, as Padgett), 1953
Well World series (Chalker), from 1977
Wempires (Pinkwater), 1991
Were-Wrath (s Norton), 1984
Wereblood (Turtledove, as Iverson), 1979
Werenight (Turtledove, as Iverson), 1979
Werewolf Among Us (Koontz), 1973
Werewolf at Large (s Fanthorpe), 1960
Werewolf Principle (Simak), 1967
Werewolves of Kregen (Bulmer, as Akers), 1985
Werewolves of London (Stableford), 1990
West, Julian series (Bellamy), from 1889
West, Julian series (Reynolds), from 1973
West of Eden series (H. Harrison), from 1984
West of Honor (Pournelle), 1976
West of January (Dave Duncan), 1989
West of the Moon (Lake), 1988
West of the Sun (Pangborn), 1953
Westlin Wind (s de Lint), 1989
Westminster Disaster (F. and G. Hoyle), 1978
Wetbones (Shirley), 1991
Wetware (Rucker), 1988
Whale of the Victoria Cross (Boulle), 1983
"What Dreams May Come . . ." (Beresford), 1941
What Dreams May Come (Matheson), 1978
What Dreams May Come (Wellman), 1983
What Entropy Means to Me (Effinger), 1972
What Happened to the Corbetts (Shute), 1939
What Mad Universe (F. Brown), 1949
What Made Stevie Crye? (Bishop), 1984
What Rough Beast (Watkins), 1980
What Strange Stars and Skies (s Davidson), 1965
What the Moon Brings (s Lovecraft), 1970
What's Become of Screwloose? (s Goulart), 1971

Wind from the North (O'Neill), 1934
Wind from the Sun (s Clarke), 1972
Wind in Cairo (Tarr), 1989
Wind in the Door (L'Engle), 1973
Wind of Liberty (Bulmer), 1962
Wind series (Meluch), from 1981
Wind Whales of Ishmael (Farmer), 1971
Wind's Twelve Quarters (s Le Guin), 1975
Windhaven (Martin), 1981
Windhaven (Tuttle), 1981
Windhover Tapes series (Norwood), from 1982
Windows (Compton), 1979
Windows of Forever (Morressy), 1975
Winds of Altair (Bova), 1973
Winds of Change (s Asimov), 1983
Winds of Darkover (Bradley), 1970
Winds of Gath (Tubb), 1967
Winds of Limbo (Moorcock), 1969
Winds of Mars (Hoover), 1995
Winds of Time (Oliver), 1957
Windwalker series (Mayhar), from 1987
Wine of the Dreamers (J. MacDonald), 1951
Wine of Violence (Morrow), 1981
Wing Commander series (Forstchen), from 1994
Winged Man (van Vogt), 1966
Wingman (Pinkwater), 1975
Wings (Pratchett), 1990
Wings of Flame (Springer), 1985
Wings of Pegasus (McCaffrey), 1991
Winners (s P. Anderson), 1981
Winter in Eden (H. Harrison), 1986
Winter Moon (Koontz), 1994
Winter of the Wolf (MacAvoy), 1993
Winter of the World (P. Anderson), 1975
Winter Players (Lee), 1976
Winter's Children (Coney), 1974
Winter's Youth (Gloag), 1934
Winterlong series (Hand), from 1990
Winterwood and Other Hauntings (s Roberts), 1989
Wisdom's Daughter (Haggard), 1923
Wise Woman (G. MacDonald), 1875
Wish Goes to Slumber Land (Cooper), 1960
Wishbringer (Gardner), 1988
Wishing Smith (Hyne), 1939
Wishing Well (s de Lint), 1993
Wishing Well (s Heard), 1953
Witch Doctor (Stasheff), 1994
Witch Hill (Bradley), 1990
Witch Mountain series (Key), from 1968
Witch of the Dark Gate (Jakes), 1972
Witch Queen of Lochlann (George H. Smith), 1969
Witch Week (Diana Wynne Jones), 1982
Witch World series (Norton), from 1963
Witch's Business (Diana Wynne Jones), 1974
Witch's Eye (C. Grant, as Charles), 1986
Witches Abroad (Pratchett), 1991
Witches of Karres (Schmitz), 1966
Witches of Kregen (Bulmer, as Akers), 1985
Witches Trilogy (Pratchett), 1995
Witchfinder (s S. Wright), 1945
Witching Hour (s Gunn), 1970

With a Finger in My I (s Gerrold), 1972
With a Single Spell (Watt-Evans), 1987
With a Strange Device (Russell), 1964
With Friends Like These. . . (s A. Foster), 1977
With Mercy Toward None (Cook), 1985
With the Night Mail (Kipling), 1909
Without Sorcery (s Sturgeon), 1948
Witling (V. Vinge), 1976
Wizard (Haggard), 1896
Wizard (Varley), 1980
Wizard and the War Machine (Watt-Evans), 1987
Wizard Crystal (Pinkwater), 1973
Wizard in Absentia (Stasheff), 1993
Wizard in Bedlam (Stasheff), 1979
Wizard in Mind (Stasheff), 1995
Wizard in Rhyme series (Stasheff), from 1993
Wizard of 4th Street (Hawke), 1987
Wizard of Anharitte (Kapp), 1973
Wizard of Camelot (Hawke), 1993
Wizard of Earthsea (Le Guin), 1968
Wizard of Lemuria (L. Carter), 1965
Wizard of Linn (van Vogt), 1962
Wizard of Lovecraft's Cafe (Hawke), 1993
Wizard of Rue Morgue (Hawke), 1990
Wizard of Santa Fe (Hawke), 1991
Wizard of Starship Poseidon (Bulmer), 1963
Wizard of Sunset Strip (Hawke), 1989
Wizard of Venus (s E. Burroughs), 1970
Wizard of Washington Square (Yolen), 1969
Wizard of Whitechapel (Hawke), 1988
Wizard of Woodworld (Kilworth), 1987
Wizard of Zao (L. Carter), 1978
Wizard series (Hawke), from 1987
Wizard Spawn (Cherryh), 1989
Wizard World series (Zelazny), from 1980
Wizard; and, Black Heart and White Heart (s Haggard), 1907
Wizard's Apprentice (Sucharitkul, as Somtow), 1993
Wizard's Eleven (Tepper), 1984
Wizard's Hall (Yolen), 1991
Wizardry series (Duane), from 1983
Wizards of Senchuria (Bulmer), 1969
Wizards' Worlds (s Norton), 1989
Wizenbeak series (Gilliland), from 1986
Wolf and Iron (Dickson), 1990
Wolf Flow (Jeter), 1992
Wolf Hollow Bubbles (s Keller), 1934
Wolf in Shadow (Gemmell), 1987
Wolf Man (s May, as Thorpe), 1977
Wolf Moon (de Lint), 1988
Wolf's-Head and the Queen (W. Morris), 1931
Wolfbane (Kornbluth, Pohl), 1959
Wolfe Archipelago (s G. Wolfe), 1983
Wolfhead (Harness), 1978
Wolfling (Dickson), 1969
Wolfshead (Norton), 1977
Wolves of Memory (Effinger), 1981
Woman a Day (Farmer), 1960
Woman against the World (G. Griffith), 1903
Woman from Another Planet (Long), 1960
Woman of Flowers (Shwartz), 1987
Woman of the Iron People (Arnason), 1991

Woman of the Wood (s Merritt), 1948
Woman on the Edge of Time (Piercy), 1976
Woman Who Is the Midnight Wind (s T. Green), 1987
Woman Who Loved the Moon (s Lynn), 1981
Women as Demons (s Lee), 1989
Wonder (Beresford), 1917
Wonder Effect (s Kornbluth), 1962
Wonder Effect (s Pohl), 1962
Wonder Stick (Coblentz), 1929
Wonder War (Janifer), 1964
Wonderbolt (Capon), 1955
Wonderful Adventures of Arthur Gordon Pym (Poe), 1861
Wonderful Adventures of Phra the Phoenician (Arnold), 1890
Wonderful Alexander and the Catwings (Le Guin), 1994
Wonderful Visit (Wells), 1895
Wonderful World of Robert Sheckley (s Sheckley), 1979
Wonderworlds (s Nolan), 1977
Wood beyond the World (W. Morris), 1894
Wood Magic (Jefferies), 1881
Wooden Spaceships (Shaw), 1988
Wooden Star (s Tenn), 1968
Woodrow Wilson Dime (Finney), 1968
Woodworld series (Kilworth), from 1988
Word for World Is Forest (Le Guin), 1976
Work of Art (s Blish), 1993
World Aflame (Bulmer), 1954
World Aflame (Tubb, as Kern), 1974
World and Thorinn (Knight), 1980
World Asunder (I. Wallace), 1976
World at Bay (Capon), 1953
World at Bay (Tubb), 1954
World at the End of Time (Pohl), 1990
World Below (S. Wright), 1929
World Between (s Vance), 1965
World Between (Spinrad), 1979
World Called Solitude (Goldin), 1981
World Ends in Hickory Hollow (Mayhar), 1985
World Enough and Time (Kahn), 1980
World Grabbers (Fairman), 1964
World in Peril (Chilton), 1960
World in Winter (Christopher), 1962
World Inside (Silverberg), 1971
World Jones Made (Dick), 1956
World Masters (G. Griffith), 1903
World Menders (Biggle), 1971
World of a Thousand Colors (s Silverberg), 1982
World of A (van Vogt), 1948
World of Chance (Dick), 1956
World of Chthon series (Platt), from 1987
World of Difference (Cooper), 1980
World of Difference (Turtledove), 1990
World of George MacDonald (s G. MacDonald), 1978
World of If (Phillips), 1951
World of Mists (P. Moore), 1956
World of Null-A (van Vogt), 1969
World of Promise (Tubb), 1980
World of Ptavvs (Niven), 1966
World of Shadows (Harding), 1975
World of the Future (Fanthorpe, as Zeigfreid), 1964
World of the Gods (Fanthorpe, as Torro), 1960
World of the Masterminds (R. Williams), 1960

World of the Starwolves (Hamilton), 1968
World of Tiers series (Farmer), from 1965
World of Tomorrow (Fanthorpe, as Zeigfreid), 1963
World of Women (Beresford), 1913
World out of Time (Niven), 1976
World Out of Mind (McIntosh), 1953
World Peril of 1910 (G. Griffith), 1907
World Set Free (Wells), 1914
World Shuffler (Laumer), 1970
World Swappers (Brunner), 1959
World That Never Was (Fanthorpe, as Zeigfreid), 1963
World Where Sex Was Born (Z. Hughes, as Kanto), 1968
World without Children (Knight), 1970
World without End (Joe Haldeman), 1979
World without Men (Maine), 1958
World without Stars (P. Anderson), 1966
World Wreckers (Bradley), 1971
World's Desire (Haggard), 1890
World's End (J. Vinge), 1984
World's End series (L. Carter), from 1969
World's Fair 1992 (Silverberg), 1970
World's Fair Goblin (Dent, as Robeson), 1969
Worlds Apart (Cowper), 1974
Worlds Apart (Joe Haldeman), 1983
Worlds Apart (Kelley), 1979
Worlds Apart (McIntosh), 1958
Worlds Enough and Time (Joe Haldeman), 1992
Worlds for the Taking (Bulmer), 1966
Worlds in Balance (s F.L. Wallace), 1955
Worlds of A.E. van Vogt (s van Vogt), 1974
Worlds of Anne McCaffrey (s McCaffrey), 1981
Worlds of Clifford Simak (s Simak), 1960
Worlds of Eclos (R. Gordon), 1961
Worlds of Frank Herbert (s F. Herbert), 1970
Worlds of Fritz Leiber (s Leiber), 1976
Worlds of George O. Smith (s George O. Smith), 1982
Worlds of H. Beam Piper (s Piper), 1983
Worlds of Jack Vance (s Vance), 1973
Worlds of Poul Anderson (s P. Anderson), 1974
Worlds of Robert F. Young (s Young), 1965
Worlds of the Imperium (Laumer), 1962
Worlds of the Wall (MacApp), 1969
Worlds of Theodore Sturgeon (s Sturgeon), 1972
Worlds of Wonder (Stapledon), 1949
Worlds series (Joe Haldeman), from 1981
Worlds to Conquer (Fearn, as Statten), 1952
Worlds Within (Phillips), 1950
Worlds Within (s Fearn), 1982
Worlds without End (s Simak), 1964
Worlds: A Novel of the Near Future (Joe Haldeman), 1981
Worldwar series (Turtledove), from 1994
Worm Charmers (Fisk), 1989
Worm Ouroboros (Eddison), 1922
Worms of Kukumlima (Pinkwater), 1981
Wormwood (s Dowling), 1991
Worse Things Waiting (s Wellman), 1973
Worthing Chronicle series (Card), from 1979
Worthing Saga (Card), 1990
Wounded Land (Donaldson), 1980
Wounded Sky (Duane), 1983
Wraeththu (Constantine), 1993

Wraith Board (Bischoff), 1985
Wraiths of Time (Norton), 1976
Wreath of Stars (Shaw), 1976
Wrecks of Time (Moorcock), 1967
Wright, Jack series (Senarens), from 1891
Wrinkle in the Skin (Christopher), 1965
Wrinkle in Time (L'Engle), 1962
Writers of the Purple Sage (s Lansdale), 1994
Wrong End of Time (Brunner), 1971
Wulfsyarn (Mann), 1990
Wuntvor series (Gardner), from 1987
Wyoming Sun (s Bryant), 1980
Wyrd Sisters (Pratchett), 1988
Wyrldmaker (Bisson), 1981
Wyrms (Card), 1987
Wyst: Alastor 1716 (Vance), 1978
Wyvern (Attanasio), 1988

X Factor (Norton), 1965
X Files series (C. Grant), from 1994
X-Machine (Fanthorpe, as Muller), 1962
Xan (Tilley), 1985
Xanth series (Anthony), from 1977
Xanthe and the Robots (MacLeod), 1977
Xeelee series (Baxter), from 1992
Xélucha (s Shiel), 1975
Xeno (D.F. Jones), 1979
Xenocide (Card), 1991
Xenogenesis (s deFord), 1969
Xenogenesis series (O. Butler), from 1987
Xiccarph (s Clark Ashton Smith), 1972
Xolotl (s Sheckley), 1991
Xorandor series (Brooke-Rose), from 1986
X, Y (Blumlein), 1993

Yank at Valhalla (Hamilton), 1950
Yankee at the Court of King Arthur (Twain), 1889
Yarrow (de Lint), 1986
Yates series (Drake), from 1987
Year 2018! (Blish), 1957
Year Before Yesterday (Aldiss), 1987
Year Dot (Lymington), 1972
Year for Love (George H. Smith), 1965
Year of the Cloud (T. Thomas), 1970
Year of the Cloud (Wilhelm), 1970
Year of the Comet (Christopher), 1955
Year of the Painted World (Mackelworth), 1975
Year of the Quiet Sun (Tucker), 1970
Year of the Ransom (P. Anderson), 1988
Year of the Unicorn (Norton), 1965
Year When Stardust Fell (R. Jones), 1958
Years of the City (Pohl), 1984
Yellow Cloud (Dent, as Robeson), 1971
Yellow Danger (Shiel), 1898
Yellow Fraction (R. Gordon), 1969
Yellow God (Haggard), 1908
Yellow Peril (Shiel), 1929
Yesterday and Tomorrow (s Verne), 1965

Yesterday's Children (Gerrold), 1972
Yesterday's Men (Turner), 1983
Ylana of Callisto (L. Carter), 1977
Yobgorble, Mystery Monster of Lake Ontario (Pinkwater), 1979
Yoke of Magic (Proctor), 1985
Yoke of Shen (Proctor and Offutt, as Cleve), 1983
Yonder (s Beaumont), 1958
Yonder Comes the Other End of Time (Elgin), 1986
Yorath the Wolf (Wilder), 1984
You Could Go Home Again (s Waldrop), 1993
You Remember Me! (Fisk), 1984
You Sane Men (Janifer), 1965
You Shall Know Them (Vercors), 1953
You Will Never Be the Same (s Cordwainer Smith), 1963
You're All Alone (Leiber), 1972
Young Bleys (Dickson), 1991
Young Blood (Stableford), 1992
Young Men Are Coming! (Shiel), 1937
Young Rissa (Busby), 1984
Young Student (s Cowper), 1982
Young Unicorns (L'Engle), 1968
Young Warriors (Thurston), 1980
Young Wolfe (s G. Wolfe), 1992
Yours Truly, Jack the Ripper (s Bloch), 1962
Youth Madness (Coblentz), 1944
Youth without Youth (Eliade), 1989
Yurth Burden (Norton), 1978
Yvgenie (Cherryh), 1991

Z Formations (Fearn, as Shaw), 1953
Z-Sting (I. Wallace), 1978
Zandra series (Rotsler), from 1978
Zanoni (Bulwer-Lytton), 1 volume, 1842
Zanoni, Zicci (Bulwer-Lytton), 1912
Zanthar series (R. Williams), from 1967
Zanthodon (L. Carter), 1980
Zanzibar Cat (s Russ), 1983
Zap Gun (Dick), 1967
Zaragoz (Stableford, as Craig), 1989
Zarkon series (L. Carter), from 1975
Zarsthor's Bane (Norton), 1978
Zelde M'Tana (Busby), 1980
Zelerod's Doom (Lichtenberg), 1986
Zen Gun (Bayley), 1983
Zenda Vendetta (Hawke), 1985
Zenya (Tubb), 1974
Zero Hour (Fearn, as Statten), 1953
Zero Minus X (Fanthorpe, as Zeigfreid), 1962
Zero Stone series (Norton), from 1968
Zhorani (Bulmer, as Maras), 1953
Ziax II series (Morressy), from 1974
Zimiamvia (Eddison), 1992
Zoboa (Caidin), 1986
Zodiac (N. Stephenson), 1988
Zone Null (Franke), 1974
Zone Yellow (Laumer), 1990
Zork Chronicles (Effinger), 1990
Zothique (s Clark Ashton Smith), 1970

NOTES ON
ADVISER AND CONTRIBUTORS

ABOULAFIA, Mitchell. Professor of philosophy and humanities, University of Houston, Clear Lake City. Author of *The Self-Winding Circle: A Study of Hegel's System*, 1982; and *The Mediating Self: Mead, Sartre, and Self-Determination*, 1986. **Essay:** Robert F. Young.

ALDISS, Brian. See his own entry. **Essays:** Franz Kafka; Mary Shelley.

ARBUR, Rosemarie. Associate professor of English, Lehigh University, Bethlehem, Pennsylvania. Author of *Leigh Brackett, Marion Zimmer Bradley, Anne McCaffrey: A Primary and Secondary Bibliography*, 1982; *Computer-Assisted Preparation of Texts*, 1982; *Marion Zimmer Bradley: A Reader's Guide*, 1985; and articles in journals and collections. **Essay:** Leigh Brackett.

BAILEY, K. V. Freelance writer. Author of *The Listening Schools*, 1957; *The Earth Is Your Spaceship*, 1959; *Education and Heritage*, 1976; *Other Worlds and Alderney*, 1982; and articles in journals and anthologies. **Essays:** James P. Blaylock; Olaf Stapledon.

BARBOUR, Douglas. Professor of English, University of Alberta, Edmonton; poetry editor, *Canadian Forum*. Author of several books of poetry, including *Visible Visions: The Selected Poems*, 1984; and *Worlds Out of Words: The SF Novels of Samuel R. Delany*, 1979; and articles on Delany, J.R.R. Tolkien, and Roger Zelazny. **Essays:** Terence Green; Lucy Sussex; Jack Womack.

BARNES, Myra. Teacher. Author of *Linguistics and Language in Science Fiction-Fantasy*, 1975. **Essay:** Hank Searls.

BARR, Marleen S. Assistant professor of English, Virginia Polytechnic Institute and State University, Blacksburg. Author of *Alien to Femininity: Women and Contemporary Science Fiction*. Editor of *Future Females: A Critical Anthology*, 1981; *Women and Utopia Critical Interpretations* (with Nicholas Smith), 1983; and the feminist SF issue of *Women's Studies International Forum*, June 1984. **Essay:** Suzy McKee Charnas.

BARRETT, David V. Freelance writer since 1991. Researcher and writer on religious and esoteric subjects. Former teacher of religious studies and English, computer programmer, intelligence analyst for the U.K. government Communications Headquarters and the U.S. National Security Agency, and computer journalist. Editor of *Vector*, 1985-89. Chairman of the 1990 Milford Writers' Conference. Administrator and chairman, 1992-95, of the judges of the Arthur C. Clarke Award for science fiction. Author of *Digital Dreams*, 1990; *The Encyclopedia of Prediction*, 1992; *Destiny and Your Dreams*, 1992; *Astrology and Fortune-Telling*, 1994; a series of six books on divination, 1995; and forthcoming major studies of alternative religions, 1996; and secret societies, 1997; and of short fiction. Author of reviews and articles for *Independent, Times Literary Supplement, Literary Review, New Scientist, New Statesman and Society, City Limits, Gnosis, British Book News*, and contributor to several encyclopedia on SF and fantasy. Fretless bass player for a rock-folk band. **Essays:** Stephen Baxter; John Gribbin; Christopher Hodder-Williams; Rachel Pollack.

BARTH, Melissa E. Professor of English, Appalachian State University, Boone, North Carolina. Author of *A Reader's Guide to Stephen R. Donaldson; A Reader's Guide to Orson Scott Card;* of essays on numerous contemporary American and British authors; and of book reviews, biographical essays, and several textbooks. **Essays:** Italo Calvino; John Varley.

BARTTER, Martha A. Associate professor of English, Northeast Missouri State University, Kirksville. **Essays:** Lois McMaster Bujold; M.J. Engh.

BEATIE, Bruce A. Professor of German and comparative literature, Cleveland State University, Ohio. **Essay:** E.E. (Doc) Smith.

BENET, Sydonie. Chicago-based freelance writer. **Essays:** Nicola Griffith; Kristine Kathryn Rusch.

BISHOP, E.R. Associate professor of mathematics, Acadia University, Wolfville, Nova Scotia. **Essay:** Paul Park.

BISHOP, Michael. See his own entry. **Essay:** Steven Utley.

BLACKFORD, Russell. Federal labor relations representative for Australian universities. Author of *The Tempting of the Witch King* (a fantasy novel), 1983; and of SF and fantasy stories. Regular contributor of articles to *Science Fiction: A Review of Speculative Literature*. Co-editor of *Urban Fantasies*. **Essays:** John Calvin Batchelor; William S. Burroughs.

BLANSFIELD, Karen Charmaine. Freelance writer. Has taught at East Carolina University, Greenville, North Carolina, and University of Delaware, Newark. Author of reviews in *Mid-American Review* and *San Francisco Chronicle*. Former assistant editor of journal *Teaching English in the Two-Year College*. **Essay:** E.C. Large.

BOGSTAD, Janice M. Librarian, McIntyre Library, University of Wisconsin-Eau Claire. Author of *An Introduction to Fantasy and Science Fiction* (with F.J. Lemoine), 1985; and of articles and book reviews in journals. Former editor of magazine *Janus*. **Essays:** Gene DeWeese; Ru Emerson; Carol Emshwiller; M.A. Foster; Ardath Mayhar; Maureen F. McHugh; R.M. Meluch; Joan Slonczewski.

BOSKY, Bernadette Lynn. Holds M.A. and almost-Ph.D. in English, Duke University; lives in Yonkers, New York. Teacher of literature and composition. Freelance writer and proofreader. Regular reviewer of fantasy, science fiction, and horror in *Publishers Weekly* and small-press magazines in the field. Contributor of articles on topics from 17th-century alchemy to self-esteem, including studies of Stephen King, Peter Straub, and Charles Williams. Also author of fiction, including an erotic science fiction novella. **Essays:** Philip K. Dick (with Arthur D. Hlavaty); David A. Drake; Suzette Haden Elgin; Joe R. Lansdale; Rebecca Ore; Tim Powers; Richard S. Shaver.

BRAZIER, Paul. British SF critic. **Essays:** Harry Harrison; Geoff Ryman.

BRENNAN, John P. Associate professor of English and director of graduate studies, Indiana University-Purdue University, Fort Wayne. Author of articles on Ursula K. Le Guin, C.M. Kornbluth, George Orwell, and Frederik Pohl. **Essays:** John Brunner; James P. Hogan; L. Ron Hubbard; Spider Robinson; Norman Spinrad; Kurt Vonnegut, Jr.

BRIGG, Peter. Associate professor of English, University of Guelph, Guelph, Ontario. Author of *J.G. Ballard* and *A Shanghai Year.* Contributor of chapters to books on Ursula K. Le Guin, Arthur C. Clarke, and Robertson Davies. Author of articles in *Science-Fiction Studies, Extrapolation, Mosaic, Foundation, English Studies in Canada, Canadian Literature, World Literature Written in English, Canadian Drama, Educational Theatre Journal;* and of encyclopedia entries in *Survey of Science Fiction Literature, Twentieth-Century Science Fiction Writers, Survey of Modern Fantasy Literature,* and *The International Dictionary of the Theatre.* **Essays:** J.G. Ballard; Lester del Rey; Phyllis Gotlieb; Philip Wylie.

BRIN, David. See his own entry. **Essay:** Greg Bear.

BRINEY, R.E. Professor of computer science and chairman of Computer Science Department, Salem State College, Massachusetts; editor, *Rohmer Review;* a founder, Advent publishers. Author of *SF Bibliographies* (with Edward Wood), 1972; of essays in *The Mystery Writer's Art,* 1971; *The Conan Grimoire,* 1971; and *The Mystery Story,* 1976; and of articles and bibliographies in journals. Editor of *Master of Villainy: A Biography of Sax Rohmer,* 1972; co-editor of *Multiplying Villainies: Selected Mystery Criticism* by Anthony Boucher, 1973. Contributing editor, *Encyclopedia of Mystery and Detection,* 1976, and *Encyclopedia of Frontier and Western Fiction,* 1983; also contributing editor of the journal *Views and Reviews,* 1972-75; member of the editorial board, Mystery Library, 1975-80, and Collection of Mystery Classics, 1985. **Essays:** Juanita Coulson; Robert Coulson; Henry Kuttner; Rog Phillips; Frank M. Robinson; Francis Stevens.

BRIZZI, Mary Turzillo. Professor emeritus of English literature, Kent State University, Kent, Ohio. Author of *A Reader's Guide to Philip José Farmer* and *A Reader's Guide to Anne Inez McCaffrey.* Author of short fiction and poetry for *SF Age, Asimov's, Fantasy and Science Fiction, Interzone,* and numerous anthologies. **Essays:** Philip José Farmer; H.F. Heard; Anne McCaffrey.

BRUNNER, John. See his own entry. **Essay:** Rudyard Kipling.

BURGESS, Scott. Doctoral candidate in computer science, Oregon State University. Author of *The Work of Reginald Bretnor: An Annotated Bibliography and Guide* and *The Work of Dean Ing: An Annotated Bibliography and Guide,* both from Borgo Press. **Essays:** Reginald Bretnor; Stephen Leigh.

BUTRYM, Alexander J. Associate professor of English, Seton Hall University, South Orange, New Jersey; director of program to train teachers in technical writing, Fund for the Improvement of Post-Secondary Education. Author of "For Suffering Humanity: Ethics of Scientists in SF," in *The Transcendent Adventure,* edited by Robert Reilly, 1984. **Essay:** Sam J. Lundwall.

CARTER, Gay E. Reference/documents librarian, University of Houston, Clear Lake City. **Essays:** Phyllis Eisenstein; Vonda N. McIntyre.

CARTER, Steven R. Teacher in San Juan, Puerto Rico. Author of articles on mystery fiction, black literature, and science fiction in *Dimensions of Detective Fiction, Popular Culture Association Newsletter,* and *Armchair Detective.* **Essay:** Ayn Rand.

CHAPMAN, Edgar L. Associate professor of English and for-

eign languages, Bradley University, Peoria, Illinois. Author of *The Magic Labyrinth of Philip José Farmer,* 1984; and of articles on numerous science fiction writers; and of a book on Robert Silverberg. **Essays:** John Crowley; Mike McQuay.

CHAUVETTE, Cathy. Program coordinator, Fairfax County Public Library, Virginia. Author of book reviews in *School Library Journal;* and of other articles. **Essay:** Tanith Lee.

COBLEY, Michael. Freelance writer. Author of short stories and articles in various SF magazines. **Essay:** David Wingrove.

COLBERT, Robert E. Associate professor of English, Louisiana State University, Shreveport. Author of articles on the criticism of Brian Aldiss and James Blish; of articles on authors Stanley Elkin, Saul Bellow, F.R. Leavis, and Ford Madox Ford; and of conference papers on Doris Lessing's SF and C.M. Kornbluth's satire. **Essay:** Russell M. Griffin.

COLEMAN, Rosemary. Associate professor of literature, Illinois Benedictine College, Lisle. **Essays:** Peter Tate; Ilya Varshavsky.

COLLINGS, Michael R. Professor of English, Pepperdine University, Malibu. Poet, short story writer, novelist, playwright, and critic. Author of *Piers Anthony,* 1984; *Brian W. Aldiss,* 1986; and *In the Image of God: Theme, Characterization, and Landscape in the Fiction of Orson Scott Card.* Editor of *Reflections on the Fantastic: Selected Essays from the Fourth International Conference on the Fantastic in the Arts,* 1987. **Essay:** Orson Scott Card.

COUGHLAN, Gary. Teacher. **Essay:** Patrick Moore.

COWPER, Richard. See his own entry. **Essay:** George Orwell.

COX, F. Brett. Assistant professor of English, Gordon College, Barnesville, Georgia. Author of articles in *New England Quarterly, The New York Review of Science Fiction,* and other journals. **Essays:** John Kessel; Jack McDevitt; James Morrow.

COX, J. Randolph. Reference and documents librarian, and associate professor, St. Olaf College, Northfield, Minnesota; reviewer of popular culture for *Choice.* Author of *Man of Magic and Mystery: A Guide to the Works of Walter B. Gibson,* 1989; *Masters of Mystery and Detective Fiction,* 1989; and of bibliographies and studies of John Buchan, M.R. James, the Nick Carter authors, George Harmon Coxe, and others for *Dime Novel Roundup, Baker Street Journal, English Literature in Transition, Armchair Detective,* and other journals. Contributor of the dime novel sections to *Mystery, Detective and Espionage Magazines,* 1983, and *Detective and Mystery Fiction: An International Bibliography of Secondary Sources,* 1985. Editor of *H.G. Wells: A Reference Guide,* with William J. Scheick, 1989. **Essays:** Ron Goulart; Luis P. Senarens.

CULE, Michael. Actor. Appeared in the stage and TV versions of *The Hitch-Hiker's Guide to the Galaxy.* **Essays:** Jack L. Chalker; David Eddings; Randall Garrett; David Langford; Robert Anton Wilson.

CUMMINS, Elizabeth. Assistant professor of English, University of Missouri, Rolla; member of the editorial board, *Extrapolation.* Author of *Ursula K. Le Guin: A Primary and Secondary Bib-*

liography, 1983; and an article on Darko Suvin in *Essays in Arts and Sciences,* August 1980. **Essay:** Paul O. Williams.

CURRIER, Catherine M. Account services manager, Ebsco Subscription Services. Author of papers on SF issues. **Essays:** Douglas Adams; John M. Ford; Janet Kagan; Nancy Springer; Kathy Tyers.

CUSHING, Charles. Adult services librarian, Hamilton Public Library, Ontario. **Essay:** Charles L. Harness.

D'AMMASSA, Don. Assistant vice-president, Data Processing, Taunton Silversmiths; book reviewer for *Science Fiction Chronicle* since 1986; book reviewer for *Mystery Science* since 1989. Past editor of *Mythologies.* Author of *Blood Beast,* 1988; and of numerous short stories and articles. **Essays:** Roger Macbride Allen; Kevin J. Anderson; Piers Anthony; Wilhelmina Baird; Steven Barnes; Neal Barrett, Jr.; Barrington John Bayley; Alfred Bester; David F. Bischoff; Robert Bloch; J.F. Bone; Ben Bova; Edward Bryant; David R. Bunch; Anthony Burgess; Paul Capon; Terry Carr; Jeffrey A. Carver; A. Bertram Chandler; Rob Chilson; Mark Clifton; D.G. Compton; Glen Cook; Alfred Coppel; Brian C. Daley; L. Sprague de Camp; Joseph H. Delaney; Peter Dickinson; Paul Di Filippo; Wayland Drew; Dave Duncan; G.C. Edmondson; Gordon Eklund; E. Everett Evans; Mick Farren; William R. Forstchen; Leslie Gadallah; Craig Shaw Gardner; Stephen Goldin; Lisa Goldstein; Rex Gordon; Stuart Gordon; Charles L. Grant; William Greenleaf; Isidore Haiblum; Jack C. Haldeman; Simon Hawke; James Herbert; Philip E. High; Christopher Hodder-Williams; Robert Holdstock; Fred and Geoffrey Hoyle; Barry Hughart; Harvey Jacobs; James Patrick Kelly; Lee Killough; Damon Knight; Nancy Kress; Brad Linaweaver; Barry Longyear; Richard Lupoff; Laurence Manning; George R.R. Martin; Ian McDonald; Richard M. McKenna; Dean McLaughlin; Thomas F. Monteleone; Michael Moorcock; C.L. Moore; John Morressy; Janet Morris; Ed Naha; Ray Nelson; Alan E. Nourse; Charles Oberndorf; Doris Piserchia; Jerry Pournelle; Terry Pratchett; Paul Preuss; Christopher Priest; John Rackham; Robert Reed; Mike Resnick; Sarban; Robert J. Sawyer; Elizabeth Scarborough; Hilbert Schenck; William M. Sloane; George H. Smith; George O. Smith; Martha Soukup; G. Harry Stine; Michael Swanwick; Stephen Tall; Sheri S. Tepper; Ted Thomas; Robert Thurston; Patrick Tilley; Vercors; Ian Watson; Lawrence Watt-Evans; Ted White; Connie Willis; F. Paul Wilson; Richard Wilson; Timothy Zahn.

DRAKE, David A. See his own entry. **Essay:** Arthur Porges.

DUNN, Thomas P. Professor of English, Miami University, Oxford, Ohio; member of the editorial board, *Extrapolation.* Author of various articles on science fiction. Editor, with Richard D. Erlich, *The Mechanical God: Machines in Science Fiction,* 1982; and *Clockwork Worlds: Mechanized Environments in SF,* 1983. **Essays:** C.J. Cherryh; H.M. Hoover; Kevin O'Donnell, Jr.; James Tiptree, Jr.

EDWARDS, Karren C. Teacher. **Essay:** Frank Aubrey.

EISENSTEIN, Alex. Author of several SF short stories with Phyllis Eisenstein. **Essay:** C.M. Kornbluth.

FEELEY, Gregory. Freelance writer and critic. Author of a forth-

coming biography of James Blish, *Alchemy under Pressure;* and of the novel *The Oxygen Barons,* 1990. **Essays:** James Blish; Avram Davidson; Felix C. Gotschalk; Richard Grant; Donald Kingsbury.

FONTAINE, Eric A. Freelance writer and critic. Author of articles on French and Latin American literature. **Essay:** William Jon Watkins.

FRANE, Jeff. Freelance writer. Author of *Fritz Leiber,* 1980. Co-editor of *A Fantasy Reader,* 1981. **Essay:** Elizabeth A. Lynn.

FRANKLIN, H. Bruce. John Cotton Dana Professor of English and American Studies, Rutgers University, Newark. Consulting editor, *Science-Fiction Studies.* Editor of *Future Perfect: American Science Fiction of the Nineteenth Century,* 1966 (revised 1968, 1978); author of *Robert A. Heinlein: America as Science Fiction,* 1980; and *War Stars: The Superweapon and the American Imagination,* 1988. Pilgrim Award recipient, 1983.

FRATZ, D. Douglas. Former publisher and editor of critical literary journal *QUANTUM-Science Fiction & Fantasy Review* (formerly *THRUST-Science Fiction & Fantasy Review*), which was nominated for the Hugo Award in 1980 for best fanzine, and 1988-91 for best semiprozine in the science fiction field. Author of numerous articles and book reviews in *QUANTUM/THRUST, Science Fiction Eye, Washington Post Book World, Science Fiction Age, Fantasy Review,* and other journals in the field; and of contributed entries to *The Dictionary of Biography on British Science Fiction and Fantasy* and *The Encyclopedia Galactica.* Environmental scientist with numerous publications in scientific and public policy journals. Lives in Gaithersburg, Maryland. **Essays:** D.G. Compton; Elizabeth Hand; Alexander Jablokov; Michael P. Kube-McDowell; Geoffrey A. Landis; Charles Platt; Kim Stanley Robinson; Jessica A. Salmonson.

GAAR, Alice Carol. Associate university librarian, Florida State University Library, Tallahassee. Co-author of *Deutsche Stunden,* 1964; and of articles in *Robert A. Heinlein,* 1978, *Quarber Merkur, Science Fiction Studies,* and *SForum.* Contributor of reviews and poems. **Essay:** Herbert W. Franke.

GARNER, John V. High school language director. **Essay:** Mark S. Geston.

GILLINGS, Walter. Editor and publisher of British science fiction from the 1930s; editor of *Tales of Wonder, Scientification, Fantasy Review, Science Fantasy,* and *Cosmos Science-Fantasy Review;* associate editor of Utopian Publications; and founding director of Nova Publications. Died in 1979. **Essays:** S.P. Meek; Eric Frank Russell; Garrett P. Serviss; A. Hyatt Verrill.

GOLDMAN, Stephen H. Associate professor of English, University of Kansas, Lawrence. Author of articles in *Survey of Science Fiction,* and *Science-Fiction Studies.* Died in 1991. **Essays:** Tom Godwin; James E. Gunn; Daniel Keyes; Stanley G. Weinbaum.

GORDON, Joan. Associate professor of English, Nassau Community College, Garden City, New York. Teacher of science fiction; scholar of feminist SF and vampires. Author of *Joe Haldeman,* 1980; and *Gene Wolfe,* 1986. **Essay:** Gene Wolfe.

GOUGH, John. Lecturer in mathematics education, Victoria College, Malven. Author of writing manuals and numerous articles on children's literature, teaching, and mathematics education. **Essay:** George MacDonald.

GREENBERG, Martin H. Professor of Regional Analysis, University of Wisconsin, Green Bay; series co-editor of Alternatives (Southern Illinois University Press) and Writers of the Twenty-First Century (Taplinger). Coauthor of *Index to Stories in Thematic Anthologies of Science Fiction,* 1978. Editor of more than 100 anthologies and single-author collections. **Essays:** Christopher Anvil; Chan Davis; F.L. Wallace.

GREENLAND, Colin. See his own entry. **Essays:** Mervyn Peake; Walter Tevis.

GREENLAW, M. Jean. Regents Professor of Education, University of North Texas, Denton. **Essay:** Jane Yolen.

GUNN, James. Retired professor of English, University of Kansas, Lawrence. Author of some 30 books of and about science fiction. Former president of the Science Fiction Writers of America and the Science Fiction Research Association. His best known novels are *The Immortals, The Joy Makers, The Listeners, Kampus,* and *The Dreamers;* and best known critical works are *Alternate Worlds: An Illustrated History of Science Fiction, The Road to Science Fiction,* and *Isaac Asimov: The Foundations of Science Fiction* (Hugo Award), which has recently been revised for Scarecrow Press. Pilgrim Award recipient, 1976. **Essay:** Isaac Asimov.

HALL, Hal W. Head, Special Formats Division, Texas A and M University, College Station. Compiler of *Science Fiction Book Review Index 1923-73, 1974-79,* and annual volumes since 1980; and of the annual *Science Fiction and Fantasy Research Index.* Guest editor, *Science Fiction Collections,* 1983.

HAMMERTON, Max. Professor emeritus of psychology, University of Newcastle. Author of *Statistics for the Human Sciences,* 1975; and of over 50 technical papers in various psychological journals; and of papers on other subjects, including science fiction writers. **Essays:** Robert L. Forward; Harry Turtledove.

HARBOTTLE, Philip J. Local government officer. Author of publication on John Russell Fearn *The Multi-Man,* 1968; *Vultures of the Void* (with Stephen Holland), 1991; *British Science Fiction Paperbacks* (with Holland), 1991; and *The Work of John Russell Fearn.* Research consultant and contributor, *The Visual Encyclopaedia of Science Fiction,* 1977. Editor, *The Best of E.E. "Doc" Smith,* 1975. **Essay:** John Russell Fearn.

HARTWELL, David G. Consulting editor, Tor Books and William Morrow, New York. Author of *Age of Wonders: Exploring the World of Science Fiction,* 1985. Editor (with Kathryn Kramer) of *Spirits of Christmas,* 1989. Former SF editor for Signet-New American Library, Berkley-Putnam, and Timescape-Pocket Books. **Essays:** Peter George; Frank R. Stockton.

HASSLER, Donald M. Professor of English, Kent State University, Kent, Ohio; editor, *Extrapolation* since 1990. President, Science Fiction Research Association, 1985-86. Author of *The Comedian as the Letter D: Erasmus Darwin's Comic Materialism,*

1973; *Erasmus Darwin,* 1974; *Comic Tones in Science Fiction: The Art of Compromise with Nature,* 1982; and *Hal Clement,* 1982. Editor of *Patterns of the Fantastic,* 2 vols., 1983-84; and co-editor of *Death and the Serpent: Immortality in Science Fiction and Fantasy,* 1985. Author of *Isaac Asimov,* 1991, winner of the Eaton Award; and of edition of Arthur Machen's letters. **Essays:** Harry Bates; Hal Clement; Raymond Z. Gallun; David H. Keller; Norman L. Knight; Murray Leinster; Nat Schachner; Stanley Schmidt.

HATFIELD, Len. Instructor in English, Indiana University at Bloomington; book review editor, *Victorian Studies.* Author of articles on William Butler Yeats and May Sinclair and of reviews to *Fantasy Review.* Assistant editor, *College English,* 1982-84. **Essay:** D.M. Thomas.

HECHT, Sharon-Ilona. Technical editor for a NASA contractor. **Essay:** M.K. Joseph.

HERBERT, Rosemary. Former reference librarian, Harvard University, Cambridge, Massachusetts; instructor, The Experimental College, Tufts University, Massachusetts. Author of book of photographs; and of collection of interviews of mystery writers. **Essays:** Arthur Conan Doyle; Ursula K. Le Guin; Margaret St. Clair; Evelyn E. Smith.

HILLS, Norman L. Director of data processing, Servi Share, Inc. Author of articles on Charles L. Harness and Fritz Leiber. **Essays:** Lawrence Durrell; Fritz Leiber.

HLAVATY, Arthur D. Holds A.B. in philosophy, Swarthmore College, and M.S. in information science, University of North Carolina; lives in Yonkers, New York. Freelance writer and editor/publisher of *Derogatory Reference.* Nominated 12 times for the Best Fan Writer Hugo Award. **Essays:** Philip K. Dick (with Bernadette Lynn Bosky); Theodore Sturgeon.

HOLM, Janis Butler. Associate professor of English, Ohio University. Author of exploratory essays on early modern gender relations. Editor of 16th-century domestic conduct book, *The Mirror of Modestie;* associate editor of film journal, *Wide Angle.* **Essay:** Sheila MacLeod.

HUGHES, Terry. Freelance writer. **Essay:** Lee Hoffman.

HULL, Elizabeth Anne. Associate professor of English, William Rainey Harper College, Palatine, Illinois. North American secretary, World SF; and editor of *World SF Newsletter.* Author of essays in *Clockwork Worlds, Extrapolation, Essays in Arts and Sciences, Destinies,* and *Starlog Science Fiction Yearbook;* contributor to *Locus, Science Fiction Chronicle,* and *Fantasy Review.* **Essays:** Lloyd Biggle, Jr.; Judith Merril.

HUNT, Marvin W. Graduate student in English, University of North Carolina at Chapel Hill. Author of travel narrative "The Road to Key West," in the Winston-Salem *Journal,* December 1984. **Essays:** Paul W. Fairman; Tom Purdom; Louis Trimble.

IKIN, Van. Lecturer in English, University of Western Australia, Nedlands; editor of *Science Fiction: A Review of Speculative Literature;* SF columnist for *Sydney Morning Herald.* Editor of *Australian Science Fiction,* 1982; and *Glass Reptile Breakout and Other*

Australian Speculative Stories, 1990. **Essays:** John Baxter; Frank Bryning; Terry Dowling; Lee Harding; George Turner.

JAKUBOWSKI, Maxim. Publisher, writer, and owner of Murder One crime bookshop, London. Series editor of Blue Murder crime imprint; editor of *New Crimes; The Detective Directory;* and of many other books on crime fiction, science fiction, fantasy, film, and music. Contributor of reviews and articles to numerous journals and newspapers, including *The Times, Time Out,* and *The Observer.*

JAMES, Edward. Senior lecturer of history and co-director, Centre for Medieval Studies, University of York. Editor, *Foundation.* Author of *The Merovingian Archaeology of South-West Gaul,* 2 vols., 1977; *The Origins of France,* 1982; *Gregory of Tours: The Life of the Fathers,* 1985; *The Franks,* 1988; and of numerous articles on various subjects, including the history of science fiction; and of reviews of science fiction. Editor, *Visigothic Spain,* 1980; and *The Profession of Science Fiction,* with Maxim Jakubowski, 1991. **Essays:** Christine Brooke-Rose; John Gribbin; Gwyneth Jones; Ian McDonald.

JONES, Anne Hudson. Associate professor of literature and medicine, Institute for the Medical Humanities, University of Texas Medical Branch, Galveston; editor-in-chief, *Literature and Medicine;* member of the editorial board, *Medical Heritage.* Author of several articles on feminist science fiction, and on literature and medical ethics. Editor of *Literature and Medicine: Images of Healers,* 1983. **Essay:** Katherine MacLean.

JURKIEWICZ, Kenneth. Assistant professor of English, Central Michigan University, Mount Pleasant. Author of articles on space movies, Ramsey Campbell, and Saki. **Essays:** Pierre Boulle; Curt Siodmak.

KAGARLITSKY, Julius. Freelance critic; member of the editorial board, Library of Modern SF. Author of *The Life and Thought of H.G. Wells,* 1966; *What Does It Mean, SF?,* 1974; *Western Theatre of the 18th Century in the Eyes of Russian Critics,* 1976; *Shakespeare and Voltaire,* 1980; and *Theatre for All Ages,* 1986. Editor, 15-volume edition of works by H.G. Wells, 1964. Former professor, State Theatrical Institute, Moscow. Pilgrim Award recipient, 1972. **Essay:** John Wyndham.

KELLEGHAN, Fiona. Librarian and associate professor, University of Miami. Lecturer at SF conferences on SF humor and camouflage in fantastic fiction and film. Author of articles on Alfred Bester, John Kessel, and cat food in *Science-Fiction Studies, Extrapolation,* and *Journal for the Fantastic in the Arts;* and of articles on SF, fantasy, and horror in *Genre Collections* (forthcoming), edited by Milton T. Wolf; and of essays on Harry Harrison and John Kessel for *Magill's Guide to Science Fiction and Fantasy Literature* (forthcoming). **Essays:** Jonathan Lethem; Walter Jon Williams.

KELLEY, George. Professor of business administration, Erie Community College. Contributor to *The Oxford Companion to Mystery Fiction, Twentieth Century Mystery Writers, Twentieth Century Western Writers,* and the previous three editions of *Twentieth Century Science Fiction Writers.* Lives in North Tonawanda, New York. **Essays:** Michael Bishop; Miriam Allen deFord; Gardner

Dozois; Cynthia Felice; M. John Harrison; Joe L. Hensley; Trevor Hoyle; Zach Hughes; Dean Ing; K.W. Jeter; Leo P. Kelley; Crawford Kilian; William Kotzwinkle; Milton Lesser; Jack Sharkey; T.L. Sherred; Robert Silverberg; Christopher Stasheff; Emma Tennant; Ian Wallace.

KETTERER, David. Professor of English, Concordia University, Montreal. Author of *New Worlds for Old: The Apocalyptic Imagination, Science Fiction, and American Literature,* 1974; *The Rationale of Deception in Poe,* 1979; *Frankenstein's Creation: The Book, the Monster, and Human Reality,* 1979; *Imprisoned in a Tesseract: The Life and Work of James Blish,* 1987; *Edgar Allan Poe: Life, Work, and Criticism,* 1989; and *Canadian Science Fiction and Fantasy,* 1992. Editor of *The Science Fiction of Mark Twain,* 1984; and Charles Heber Clark's *A Family Memoir,* 1995. **Essay:** Max Adeler.

KINCAID, Paul. Reviews editor, *Vector,* 1985-90. Coordinator, British Science Fiction Association, 1986-89. Author of *Keith Roberts,* 1983; and of short stories and reviews in various journals, including *Times Literary Supplement, Vector,* and *Foundation.* **Essays:** Iain M. Banks; Terry Bisson; John Brosnan; Steve Erickson; Karen J. Fowler; Gwyneth Jones; Christopher Priest; Keith Roberts; Josephine Saxton; Bob Shaw; Thorne Smith; Neal Stephenson.

KLEIN, Gérard. See his own entry. Editor, Editions Robert Laffont, Paris, and consultant economist. **Essay:** Michel Jeury.

KOHLER, Vince. Staff writer and SF reviewer, *The Oregonian,* Portland. **Essay:** John Kippax.

KRATZ, Dennis M. Professor of arts and humanities, University of Texas, Dallas. Author of *Mocking Epic: Waltharius, Alexandreis and the Problem of Christian Heroism,* 1980; *Waltharius and Ruodlieb,* 1984; *The Romances of Alexander,* 1991; and of numerous articles on fantasy, science fiction, and medieval literature. **Essays:** Lin Carter; John Sladek; Chelsea Quinn Yarbro.

LAKE, David. See his own entry. **Essays:** Russell Hoban; C.S. Lewis.

LARBALESTIER, Justine. Member of Department of English, University of Sydney. Author of articles on science fiction and related topics. **Essay:** Michael Blumlein.

LASKOWSKI, William. Associate professor of English, Jamestown College. Author of book on Rupert Brooke; and of essays on Jack Vance and George Orwell. **Essays:** Larry Niven; Jack Vance.

LAWLER, Donald L. Professor of English, East Carolina University, Greenville, North Carolina; editor of *Victorians Institute Journal.* Co-author of *Vonnegut in America,* 1977; and author of *Approaches to Science Fiction,* 1978; and of articles on 19th- and 20th-century British and American writers. Contributing editor, *Survey of Science Fiction Literature,* 1979; consulting editor, *Survey of Modern Fantasy Literature,* 5 vols., 1983; and editor of an edition of Oscar Wilde's *The Picture of Dorian Gray.* **Essays:** Anthony Boucher; Otis Adelbert Kline; Kris Neville; J.R.R. Tolkien.

LAWSON, John I. Electronic specialist, Fairfax County Public

Library, Virginia. Book reviewer for *School Library Journal.* Author of various articles and reviews. **Essay:** Alan Dean Foster.

LEAHY, Mark Warwick. Graduate student, University of Adelaide, South Australia. **Essay:** Sylvia Engdahl.

LEPERLIER, Henry D. Journalist, *LA,* Ireland; translator teacher, and broadcaster. Computer consultant. Ph.D. candidate in comparative literature, University of Sherbrooke, Quebec. Author of numerous articles and reviews on politics, the arts, and linguistics. **Essays:** Candace Jane Dorsey; Daniel Sernine; S.M. Stirling; Elisabeth Vonarburg; Andrew Weiner; Robert Charles Wilson.

LEVY, Michael M. Professor of English, University of Wisconsin-Stout. Author of *Natalie Babbitt* (1991); and of the first book-length study of Babbitt. Also author of modern science fiction chapter for fourth edition of the award-winning reference book *Anatomy of Wonder,* 1995; and of science fiction year-in-review essays for the annual reference books *What Do I Read Next?* and *Science Fiction and Fantasy Book Review Annual*; also co-editor of *Science Fiction and Fantasy Book Review Annual.* Contributor of numerous articles and reviews on science fiction and children's literature. **Essays:** Eleanor Arnason; Warren Norwood; Philip Francis Nowlan; Lucius Shepard; Gary K. Wolf.

LEWIS, Arthur O. Professor emeritus of English, Pennsylvania State University, University Park; member of the advisory board, *Alternative Futures.* Author of numerous books, including *Of Men and Machines,* 1963; *American Utopias: Selected Short Fiction,* 1971; and *Utopian Literature in the Pennsylvania State University Libraries: A Selected Bibliography,* 1984. Editor of *Utopian Literature,* 41 vols., 1971 and the SF issue, 1976, and Utopian Studies issue, 1981; and of *Journal of General Education.* **Essays:** Edward Bulwer-Lytton; Ernest Callenbach; Ignatius Donnelly; Edward Everett Hale; Richard Jefferies; Joseph O'Neill; Marge Piercy; Steven Spruill.

LOWENKOPF, Shelly. Adjunct professor, Professional Writing Program, University of Southern California, Los Angeles. Author of more than 40 books (fiction and nonfiction); and of numerous essays and reviews. Former director, Dell Publishing, California Office, and former editor-in-chief, American Bibliographical Center-Clio Press and Ross-Erickson Inc. **Essay:** Madeleine L'Engle.

LUNAN, Duncan. Freelance writer, lecturer, and critic. Author of *Man and the Stars* (in U.S. as *Interstellar Contact*), 1974, *New Worlds for Old,* 1979, and *Man and the Planets,* 1983 (all nonfiction); and of many articles and papers. Also author of 24 short stories. **Essays:** Charles Chilton; Joe Haldeman.

LUPOFF, Richard A. See his own entry. **Essays:** Edwin L. Arnold; Robert Asprin; Eando Binder; Edgar Rice Burroughs; Stanton A. Coblentz; George Allan England; Hugo Gernsback; H.L. Gold; Michael Kurland; Frank Belknap Long; Sam Merwin, Jr.; Raymond A. Palmer; Wilmar H. Shiras; Donald A. Wollheim.

LYNCH, Peter. Houston-based freelance writer. **Essay:** Victor Rousseau.

MACDONALD, Andrew. Academic director of Intensive English and English as a Second Language, Loyola University, New Or-

leans. Author of articles on Ben Jonson, Shakespeare, English as a second language, SF, and popular culture. **Essays:** Martin Caidin (with Gina Macdonald); Doris Lessing; Nevil Shute.

MACDONALD, Gina. Assistant professor of English, Loyola University, New Orleans. Author of articles on Shakespeare, Robert Greene, English as a second language, popular culture, and SF. **Essays:** Kingsley Amis; Martin Caidin (with Andrew Macdonald); William Golding; Frank Herbert; Robert Hoskins; Aldous Huxley; Stanislaw Lem; Douglas R. Mason; Thomas Pynchon; Arthur Sellings; Somtow Sucharitkul; Boris and Arkady Strugatsky (with Darko Suvin); Stanislaw Witkiewicz.

MACRAE, Cathi. Young adult librarian, Boulder Public Library, Colorado. Author of *Presenting Young Adult Fantasy;* and of young adult book review column in *Wilson Library Bulletin;* and of other articles. **Essays:** R.A. MacAvoy; Patricia McKillip.

MAKI, Shinji. Freelance writer and critic. Author of articles and reviews in Japanese prozines. Editor of *SF Bibliophile,* a fanzine for booklovers. **Essay:** Shin'ichi Hoshi.

MALLETT, Daryl F. Freelance writer/editor. Contributing editor and series editor, Borgo Press, San Bernardino, California; series editor, SFRA Press; associate editor, *Other Worlds,* and Gryphon Publications; contributing writer, *Overstreet's Fan Magazine;* editor/publisher, Angel Enterprises. **Essays:** David Brin; Susan Shwartz.

McGUIRE, Patrick L. Civil servant, U.S. federal government. Author of *Red Stars: Political Aspects of Soviet Science Fiction,* 1985; and of articles on Joe Haldeman, the Strugatskys, C.J. Cherryh, and Poul Anderson. Consulting editor, *Survey of Science Fiction Literature,* 1979; translator of works on Soviet SF. **Essays:** Keith Laumer; Vernor Vinge; James White.

McKITTERICK, Christopher. Graduate student, University of Kansas, Lawrence. **Essay:** James Gunn.

McVEIGH, Kev P. Coordinator, British Science Fiction Association; editor, *Vector,* since 1989. **Essays:** Storm Constantine; Leigh Kennedy; Judith Moffett; Pat Murphy; Jeff Noon; Michaela Roessner; Howard Waldrop.

MEYERING, Sheryl L. Assistant professor of English, Southern Illinois University, Edwardsville. Author of *Charlotte Perkins Gilman: The Woman and Her Work,* 1989; *Sylvia Plath: A Reference Guide,* 1990; *Studies in the Short Fiction of Willa Cather*; and of various articles and reviews. **Essay:** Charlotte Perkins Gilman.

MEYERS, Walter E. Professor of English, North Carolina State University, Raleigh; member of the editorial board, *Science-Fiction Studies.* Author of *Aliens and Linguists,* 1980. Consulting editor, *Survey of Science Fiction Literature,* 1979. **Essays:** T.J. Bass; Rosel George Brown; H. Rider Haggard; Ward Moore; James H. Schmitz.

MIESEL, Sandra. Freelance writer; holds master's degrees in biochemistry and medieval history. Author of *Against Time's Arrow: The High Crusade of Poul Anderson,* 1978; *Dreamrider,* 1982; *Shaman,* 1989; and of numerous articles about the SF field. Editor of six SF collections; co-editor of two SF anthologies. Since 1983 has focused on journalism, producing hundreds of articles for Catholic publications. Lives in Indianapolis. **Essays:** Poul Anderson; Gordon R. Dickson; Alexis A. Gilliland; Zenna Henderson; R.A. Lafferty; Fred Saberhagen; Wilson Tucker.

MILLER, Richard W. Associate professor of philosophy, University of Missouri, Rolla. **Essay:** H. Beam Piper.

MIYAWAKI, Toshifumi. Professor of American literature, Seikei University, Tokyo, Japan. Author of various essays on F. Scott Fitzgerald, Nathaniel Hawthorne, Sinclair Lewis, and Haruki Murakami; translator of *Paris Was Yesterday* by Janet Flanner (forthcoming). **Essay:** Haruki Murakami.

MOLSON, Francis J. Professor of English, Central Michigan University, Mount Pleasant. Author of chapters on SF for children in *Anatomy of Wonder, The Art and Aesthetics of Fantasy,* and *The Science Fiction Reference Book;* and of articles on Ursula K. Le Guin, Emily Dickinson, Frances Hodgson Burnett, and other writers. **Essays:** Monica Hughes; Alexander Key; Alice Lightner; Hugh Walters.

MORAN, Daniel Keys. Science fiction writer and critic. Author of *The Armageddon Blues,* 1988; *Emerald Eyes,* 1988; and *The Long Run,* 1989. **Essay:** David Gerrold.

MORRISSEY, Thomas J. Professor of English and director of college writing, State University of New York College, Plattsburgh. Author of articles and reviews for *Science-Fiction Studies, Eire-Ireland, Centennial Review,* and *Children's Literature;* and of poetry for *Green Fuse* and *Blue Line.* **Essay:** Pamela Sargent.

MURRAY, Will. Editorial director of Odyssey Publications; and freelance writer. Author or co-author of *The Man Behind Doc Savage,* 1974; *The Duende History of The Shadow Magazine,* 1979; and *The Assasin's Handbook.* Author of articles in *Starlog, Lovecraft Studies, Crypt of Cthulhu, Xenophile, Etchings and Odysseys;* and of fiction in *Ellery Queen's Mystery Magazine, Eldritch Tales,* and other periodicals. Past editor of magazines *Duende* and *Skullduggery.* **Essays:** Lester Dent; Clark Ashton Smith; John Taine.

NELLIS, Marilyn K. Assistant professor, Liberal Studies Center, Clarkson University, Potsdam, New York. **Essay:** James Kahn.

NICHOLS, Ian. English teacher, Churchlands Senior High, Australia. *Analyzing the Trooper in Heinlein,* 1986, *Moorcock and the New Wave,* 1987, *Conan the Messiah,* 1985, and *Mythology and Samuel R. Delany,* 1988. **Essays:** A.A. Attanasio; Raymond E. Feist.

OLIVER, Chad. See his own entry. **Essays:** Edmond Hamilton; Ross Rocklynne.

OLSEN, Lance. Director of creative writing, University of Idaho, Moscow. Author of eight books of criticism and fiction, including the novel *Tonguing the Zeitgeist.* **Essay:** William Gibson.

ORODENKER, Richard. Associate professor of English, Peirce Junior College, Philadelphia. Author of criticism and fiction in *North American Review, Benzene, Studies in Short Fiction,* and other

publications. **Essay:** F.M. Busby.

PAGE, Gerald W. Writer and editor. Author of many SF and fantasy stories since 1963. Editor of anthologies *Year's Best Horror Stories 4-7; Nameless Places;* and *Heroic Fantasy* (with Hank Reinhardt); former editor of *Witchcraft and Sorcery Magazine;* and consultant editor of *Amazing.* **Essays:** Nelson S. Bond; Gardner F. Fox; Neil R. Jones; Raymond F. Jones; Lisa Tuttle; Sharon Webb; Robert Moore Williams.

PARKIN-SPEER, Diane. Professor of English, Southwest Texas State University, San Marcos. Author of articles on 16th- and 17th-century English literature, history of ideas, and the relation of law and literature. **Essays:** Alexei Panshin; Sydney J. Van Scyoc.

PATTEN, Frederick. Catalogue librarian in an aerospace technical library. Author of the guide to comic books, *Magazines for Libraries;* and of reviews of SF in *Library Journal, Science Fiction, Locus,* and other publications. Publisher and co-editor of *Delap's F&SF Reviews,* 1975-77. **Essay:** C.C. MacApp.

PAUL, Terri. Senior scientific programmer, McDonnell Douglas Technical Services Company, Houston. Author of articles on Frederik Pohl, women in SF, time travel, and technical writing. **Essay:** Rudy Rucker.

PEIPPO, Kathleen. Holds B.A. in journalism, University of Minnesota, and M.A. in organizational leadership, College of St. Catherine. Freelance writer. **Essay:** Melissa Scott.

PERKINS, Michael. Author of novels *Evil Companions* and *Dark Matter;* also author of critical studies *The Secret Record* and *The Good Parts.* Editor of Tompkins Square Press, Croton Press, Ulster Arts,* and *Masquerade Newsletter.* **Essays:** Thomas M. Disch; David Meltzer.

PFEIFFER, John R. Professor of English, Central Michigan University, Mount Pleasant; bibliographer, *Shaw Annual.* Author of *Fantasy and Science Fiction: A Critical Guide,* 1971; and of essays on John Brunner, Ursula K. Le Guin, Aldous Huxley, and others; co-author of chapter on the modern period in *Anatomy of Wonder,* 1976 (revised 1981, 1987). Special editor of "GBS and Science Fiction" issue of *Shaw Review.* **Essays:** Octavia Butler; John Christopher; John A. Williams; Colin Wilson.

PHILLIPS, Gene. Librarian. Author of fantasy stories. **Essays:** Kenneth Bulmer; Colin Kapp; Emil Petaja.

PHILMUS, Robert M. Professor of English, Concordia University, Montreal; editor, *Science-Fiction Studies.* Author of *Into the Unknown: The Evolution of Science Fiction from Francis Godwin to H.G. Wells,* 1970 (2nd edition 1983); and chapter on early SF in *Anatomy of Wonder,* 1976 (revised 1981). Co-editor of *H.G. Wells: Early Writings in Science and Science Fiction,* 1975; *H.G. Wells and Modern Science Fiction,* 1977; and *H.G. Wells's Literary Criticism,* 1980.

PIERCE, Hazel. Professor emeritus of English, Kearney State College, Nebraska; member of the editorial board, *Platte Valley Review.* Author of *Philip K. Dick,* 1982; *A Literary Symbiosis: Science Fiction/Fantasy/Mystery,* 1983; and of essays on Isaac Asimov,

Ray Bradbury, and Dick in *Writers of the 21st Century* volumes; and of essays on William Blake and Lord Byron. **Essays:** George Alec Effinger; Kurd Lasswitz; Phillip Mann; A.E. Van Vogt.

PIERCE, John J. Associate editor, *Private Label.* Author of essays on Cordwainer Smith. Editor of *The Best of Cordwainer Smith,* 1975; *Norstrilia,* 1975; *The Best of Murray Leinster,* 1978; and *The Best of Raymond Z. Gallun,* 1978. Former editor of *Galaxy;* and of fanzines *Renaissance and Tension, Apprehension,* and *Dissension.* **Essays:** Otto Gail; Bernhard Kellermann.

PRATT, Nick. Freelance photographer; book reviewer. **Essay:** R.W. Mackelworth.

PRONZINI, Bill. Author of over 50 novels, several nonfiction books, and collections; and author of numerous stories, articles, essays, and thematic anthologies. **Essays:** Charles Beaumont; Cleve Cartmill; Edward D. Hoch; Evan Hunter.

QUINN, Joseph A. Associate professor of English, University of Windsor, Ontario. Author of articles and reviews in *Chesterton Review, University of Windsor Review, Christianity and Literature,* and *Alternative Futures.* **Essay:** Alun Llewellyn.

REGINALD, Robert. Professor, California State University, San Bernardino; publisher, Borgo Press. Author of 80 books and over 150 articles; editor of 650 books. Pilgrim Award recipient, 1993; Collector's Award recipient, 1993. **Essays:** Arthur B. Cover; R. Lionel Fanthorpe; Katherine Kurtz; Bruce McAllister; William F. Nolan; Michael Reaves; Brian Stableford; George Zebrowski.

REILLY, Robert. Professor of English, Rider College, Lawrenceville, New Jersey. Author of *The Transcendent Adventure: Studies of Religion in Science Fiction/Fantasy,* 1984; and of articles on Ray Bradbury, Robert Silverberg, and Roger Zelazny. **Essays:** D.F. Jones; Vincent King.

RIES, Lawrence R. Assistant director, University Without Walls, Skidmore College, Saratoga Springs, New York. Author of *Wolf Masks: Violence in Contemporary Poetry,* 1977. **Essay:** Sterling E. Lanier.

ROBU, Cornel. Lecturer in literature, University of Cluj-Napoca, Romania. Editor of the first reprint and critical edition, with an afterword in English, of the first Romanian SF novel, *In anul 4000 sau O c l torie la Venus,* 1986 ("In the year 4000 or A Voyage to Venus") by Victor Anestin (1875-1918), the earliest SF writer proper in Romania. Editor of summarizing anthology of postwar Romanian science fiction, *Timpul este umbra noastr* ("Time is Our Shadow"), also with an afterword in English. Also author of entry on Romania and contributor of ideas to the entry on "the sense of wonder" for *The Encyclopedia of Science Fiction,* edited by John Clute and Peter Nicholls, 1993. Articles on "sense of wonder" and the sublime in SF appeared in English, including "A Key to Science Fiction: The Sublime," in *Foundation,* No. 42, 1988; and of "'The Sense of Wonder' Is 'A Sense Sublime'," in *SFRA Review,* No. 211, 1994. Currently working on *Revisiting the Sense of Wonder,* a study of the connection between science fiction and the sublime. **Essay:** Mircea Eliade.

ROSENBERG, Aaron. Doctoral student in English, University

of Kansas. Recently presented a paper on "Fantasy as Genre" at The Sixteenth International Conference for the Fantastic in the Arts. **Essay:** Stephen R. Donaldson.

ROTTENSTEINER, Franz. Freelance editor, translator, and literary agent. Editor of Suhrkamp's Fantastic Library series (12-24 annual vols.). Author of *The Science Fiction Book,* 1975; and *The Fantasy Book,* 1978. Editor of *View from Another Shore: European SF,* 1973; *The Slaying of the Dragon: Modern Tales of the Playful Imagination,* 1984; and *Microworlds* by Stanislaw Lem, 1984; and of numerous anthologies in German. **Essays:** Karin Boye; Dino Buzzati; Wyman Guin; Wolfgang Jeschke; Maurice Renard.

ROUSSEAU, Yvonne. Freelance writer and editor. Joint editor of *Australian Science Fiction Review, 1986-91.* Author of *The Murders at Hanging Rock,* 1980; of commentary to *The Secret of Hanging Rock,* 1987; and of numerous critical articles and several short stories. **Essay:** Cherry Wilder.

RUDDICK, Nicholas. Associate professor of English, University of Regina, Canada. Science fiction division head, International Association for the Fantastic in the Arts, since 1988. Author of *Christopher Priest,* 1989; *British Science Fiction: A Chronology 1478-1990;* and of numerous articles on British and American poetry and fiction. Editor of *State of the Fantastic.*

RUSS, Joanna. See her own entry. **Essay:** H.P. Lovecraft.

SAMMONS, Todd H. Associate professor of English, University of Hawaii, Manoa. Author of numerous articles on and reviews of science fiction. **Essays:** Julian May; Charles Sheffield.

SAMUELSON, David N. Professor of English, California State University, Long Beach; member of the editorial board, *Science Fiction Studies* and *Survey of Science Fiction Literature.* Author of *Visions of Tomorrow: Six Voyages from Outer to Inner Space,* 1974; *Arthur C. Clarke: A Primary and Secondary Bibliography,* 1984; and of essays and reviews in newspapers and journals. **Essays:** John Boyd; Walter M. Miller, Jr.; Bernard Wolfe.

SANDERS, Joe. Professor of English, Lakeland Community College, Mentor, Ohio; associate editor of *The Year's Scholarship in Science Fiction, Fantasy, and Horror Literature* since 1980. Author of *Roger Zelazny: A Primary and Secondary Bibliography;* nine essays in *Survey of Fantasy Literature,* 1983; and of article on Richard Condon in *Extrapolation,* 1984. **Essays:** Neil Gaiman; Alan Moore; John Shirley; Bruce Sterling.

SARGENT, Pamela. See her own entry. **Essays:** Jack Dann; Kate Wilhelm.

SATTY, Harvey J. President of the Olaf Stapledon Society. Author of *Olaf Stapledon: A Bibliography* (with Curtis C. Smith), 1984. **Essay:** John Gloag.

SCARBOROUGH, John. Professor of classics and ancient history, University of Wisconsin, Madison. Author of *Roman Medicine,* 1969; *Facets of Hellenic Life,* 1976; "Medicine in Science Fiction," in *The Science Fiction Encyclopedia,* 1979; *Pharmacy's Ancient Heritage,* 1985; *Greek and Latin Origins of Medical Termi-*

nologies, 1992; and of articles on H. Rider Haggard, John Wyndham, Stanislaw Lem, Piers Anthony, and Erich von Däniken. Editor of *Symposium on Byzantine Medicine,* 1984; and *Folklore and Folk Medicines,* 1987. **Essay:** Josef Nesvadba.

SCHEICK, William J. Professor of English, University of Texas at Austin. Editor (with J. Randolph Cox) of *H.G. Wells: A Reference Guide,* 1988. **Essay:** H.G. Wells.

SCHLOBIN, Roger C. Professor of English, North Central Campus, Purdue University; internationally recognized scholar of the fantastic in the arts. Holds Ph.D. in medieval literature, Ohio State University; author of six books; and editor of over 50 books. Also author of over 100 essays, various poems, fiction, reviews, and bibliographies on such varied topics as fantasy literature, pedagogy, science fiction, medieval literature, linguistics, and microcomputer hardware and software. Co-founder of International Association and its Conference for the Fantastic in the Arts and of the "Year's Scholarship in Science Fiction and Fantasy"; editor of *The Journal of the Fantastic in the Arts.* Author of the first original fantasy novel to be published on the Internet: *Fire and Fur: The Last Sorcerer Dragon.* **Essays:** Lord Dunsany; Andre Norton.

SCHUYLER, William M., Jr. Professor of philosophy, University of Louisville, Kentucky. Author of articles and chapters on philosophy and SF. **Essay:** Diane Duane.

SEARLES, Baird. Owner and manager, The Science Fiction Shop, New York; film columnist, *Amazing;* and book columnist, *Isaac Asimov's Science Fiction Magazine.* Author or co-author of study of Heinlein, *The Science Fiction Quiz Book,* 1974; *A Reader's Guide to Science Fiction [Fantasy],* 2 vols., 1979-82; and numerous reviews. Died in 1993. **Essays:** A. Merritt; Austin Tappan Wright.

SEIDEL, Kathryn Lee. Dean of Arts and Sciences and professor of English, University of Central Florida. Author of articles and books on Zora Neale Hurston, Marge Piercy, Gail Godwin, and others. **Essay:** Dean R. Koontz.

SHELTON, Pamela. Michigan-based freelance writer. **Essays:** John Barnes; Emma Bull; Pat Cadigan; Steve Perry; Dave Wolverton.

SHWARTZ, Susan. See her own entry. **Essays:** Marion Zimmer Bradley; Jayge Carr; Jacqueline Lichtenberg; Judith Tarr.

SLUSSER, George. Professor, Center for Bibliographical Studies and Research, Eaton Program for Science Fiction and Fantasy Studies, University of California, Riverside. Pilgrim Award recipient, 1986. **Essays:** Samuel R. Delany; Robert A. Heinlein; Gérard Klein.

SMITH, Curtis C. Professor of literature, University of Houston, Clear Lake City. Author of *Olaf Stapledon: A Bibliography* (with Harvey J. Satty), 1984. Editor of *Twentieth-Century Science Fiction Writers,* 1981 (2nd edition 1986). **Essays:** Laurence M. Janifer; Philip Latham; Jack London; Robert A.W. Lowndes; Mack Reynolds.

SNYDER, Carol L. Associate professor of humanities, Univer-

sity of Houston, Clear Lake City. **Essay:** Joanna Russ.

SNYDER, Judith. Teacher and freelance writer. **Essay:** Gertrude Friedberg.

SPELLER, Maureen Kincaid. Freelance editor. Administrator, British Science Fiction Association, 1989-91, since 1993. Author of reviews in *Vector* and other journals. **Essays:** Eric Brown; Charles de Lint; David Gemmell; Diana Wynne Jones; David Zindell.

STABLEFORD, Brian M. See his own entry.

STAPLES, Katherine. Translator of works by Henri Rousseau; and of *Les Illuminations* by Arthur Rimbaud. **Essay:** J.T. McIntosh.

STAVANS, Ilan. Assistant professor of Latin American letters, Baruch College, City University of New York. Author of *Talia y el cielo,* 1989; *Prontuario,* 1991; *Imagining Columbus: The Literary Voyage,* 1992; and of fiction and criticism in *New York Times, Diario 16, Science-Fiction Studies,* and other journals and newspapers. **Essay:** Jorge Luis Borges.

STEPHENSEN-PAYNE, Philippa. Freelance writer. **Essay:** Nicholas Fisk.

STONE, Graham. Bookseller. Author of *Australian Science Fiction Index 1925-1967,* 1968 (supplement 1976); *Index to British Science Fiction Magazines 1934-1953,* 1980; and *Notes on Australian Science Fiction,* 1991. **Essays:** Christopher Blayre; Erle Cox; Ray Cummings; Lloyd Arthur Eshbach; P. Schuyler Miller; Jack Wodhams; Arthur Leo Zagat.

STOVER, Leon. Ph.D., Litt. D., professor emeritus of anthropology, Illinois Institute of Technology, Chicago. Presently completing a six-volume series, *The Annotated H.G. Wells,* critical editions of the scientific romances. **Essays:** John W. Campbell, Jr.; George R. Stewart; Jules Verne.

SULLIVAN, C.W., III. Professor of English and director of Graduate Studies in English, East Carolina University. Immediate past president, International Association for the Fantastic in the Arts; and editor of *The Children's Folklore Review.* Author of *Welsh Celtic Myth in Modern Fantasy,* 1989; editor of *Science Fiction for Young Readers,* 1993; and co-editor of *Herbal and Magical Medicine: Traditional Healing Today,* 1992; also author of articles on mythology, folklore, fantasy, and science fiction for a variety of anthologies and journals. **Essays:** E.R. Eddison; Harlan Ellison; Pat Frank; John Norman; Andrew Offutt; Kit Reed.

SUSSEX, Lucy. See her own entry. **Essays:** Katherine Burdekin; Pamela Zoline.

SUVIN, Darko. Professor of English and comparative literature, McGill University, Montreal. Author of *Russian Science Fiction 1956-74: A Bibliography,* 1976; *Metamorphoses of Science Fiction,* 1979; *Victorian Science Fiction in the UK: The Discourses of Knowledge and of Power,* 1983; *To Brecht and Beyond,* 1984; *The Long March,* 1987; *Positions and Presuppositions in Science Fiction,* 1988; and *Azmizana Arkadija,* 1990. Editor of *Other Worlds,*

Other Seas, 1970; *Science-Fiction Studies* (with R.D. Mullen) 2 vols., 1976-78; and *H.G. Wells and Modern Science Fiction* (with Robert M. Philmus), 1977. Pilgrim Award recipient, 1979. **Essays:** Edward Bellamy; Aleksandr Belyaev; Valery Bryusov; Samuel Butler; Karel Capek; Robert Cromie; George Griffith; C.J. Cutcliffe Hyne; Vladimir Mayakovsky; Boris and Arkady Strugatsky (with Gina Macdonald); Alexey Tolstoy; Konstantin Tsiolkovsky; Ivan Yefremov; Yevgeny Zamyatin.

SWANK, Paul. Assistant professor of educational psychology, University of Houston, University Park. **Essay:** Fletcher Pratt.

TALBOT, Norman. Professor of English, University of Newcastle, New South Wales; managing editor, Nimrod Publications. Author of several books of poetry, including *The Kelly Haiku;* and of works of literary criticism. Editor of anthologies of poetry, criticism, and prose. **Essay:** William Morris.

TATSUMI, Takayuki. Associate professor of English, Keio University, Tokyo, Japan. Contributing editor, *Science-Fiction Eye, Science-Fiction Studies,* and *Paradoxa.* Author of *Cyberpunk America,* 1988; *The Contemporary Rhetoric of Science Fiction,* 1992; *Metafiction as Ideology,* 1993; *A Manifesto for Japanoids: On Japanese Postmodern Science Fiction,* 1993; and *Disfiguration of Genres: A Reading in the Rhetoric of Edgar Allan Poe,* 1995. Co-author of *Storming the Reality Studio,* 1991. Editor of *Cyborg Feminism: Haraway, Delany, Salmonson,* 1991; and *The Best Essays of Isaac Asimov,* 1993. Co-recipient of the fifth Pioneer Award (SFRA), 1994. **Essay:** Edgar Allan Poe.

THURSTON, Robert. See his own entry. **Essays:** Richard C. Meredith; James Sallis.

TOLLEY, Michael J. Reader in English, University of Adelaide, South Australia; editorial adviser, *Blake Studies.* Author of 20 essays on Blake; and of reviews for *SF&F Book Review* and *Fantasy Review,* mainly on Australian writing. Co-editor of *William Blake's Designs for Edward Young's Night Thoughts,* 2 vols., 1980; and *The Stellar Gauge: Essays on Science Fiction Writers,* 1980. **Essays:** Mark Adlard; Damien Broderick; Angela Carter; Michael G. Coney; Michael Frayn; Joseph Green; Lindsay Gutteridge; David Lake; John D. MacDonald; Sean McMullen; Gerald Murnane; Wynne Whiteford.

TUCKER, Frank H. Professor emeritus of history, Colorado College, Colorado Springs. Author of *The White Conscience,* 1969; a chapter in *Robert A. Heinlein,* 1978; *The Frontier Spirit and Progress,* 1980; and of articles in *Russian Affairs, Japanese Affairs, Intellect;* and *Extrapolation.* **Essays:** Kobo Abé; Sakyo Komatsu; André Maurois.

TURNER, George. See his own entry. **Essays:** J.D. Beresford; M. Barnard Eldershaw.

TUTTLE, Lisa. See her own entry. **Essay:** Tom Reamy.

TUZAR, Jana I. Doctoral student, University of Chicago. **Essay:** Mikhail Bulgakov.

UTLEY, Steven. See his own entry. **Essay:** Ralph Milne Farley.

VARDEMAN, Robert E. Freelance writer; president of the Cenotaph Corporation. Editor, *SFWA Forum,* 1978-79; vice-president, SFWA, 1979-80. Author of more than 90 books, including *Sandcats of Rhyl,* 1978; *Colors of Chaos,* 1988; and *Space Vectors,* 1990; and of short stories in various science fiction and horror anthologies. **Essay:** George W. Proctor.

WAGNER, Karl Edward. Freelance writer. Editor of *Carcosa.* Author of *Darkness Weaves,* 1970; *Death Angel's Shadow,* 1973; *Bloodstone,* 1975; *Dark Crusade,* 1976; *Legion from the Shadows,* 1976; *Night Winds,* 1978; *The Road of Kings,* 1978; *In a Lonely Place,* 1983; *Killer* (with David A. Drake), 1985; *The Book of Kane,* 1985; and *Why Not You and I?,* 1987. Editor of *The Year's Best Horror Stories 8-20; Echoes of Valor 1-3; Intensive Scare;* and of authorized Conan series. **Essay:** Manly Wade Wellman.

WALLMANN, Jeffrey. Instructor in English, University of Nevada, Reno. Author of more than 220 novels, in such genres as mystery, science fiction, western, and historical romance, under 22 pseudonyms. Also author of more than 100 short stories, novelettes, and articles. **Essay:** Barry Malzberg.

WATSON, Ian. See his own entry. **Essay:** David I. Masson.

WAY, Douglas E. Retired businessman. **Essay:** Austin Hall and Homer Eon Flint.

WAY, Karen G. Teaching assistant, Department of English, Rutgers University, New Brunswick, New Jersey. Past editor of *Lovejoy's Guidance Digest.* **Essays:** J.B. Priestley; Walt and Leigh Richmond; E.C. Tubb.

WEBB, Janeen. Senior lecturer (professor) of literature, Australian Catholic University, Melbourne. Specialist in comparative literature, children's literature, and speculative fiction. Co-editor of *Australian Science Fiction Review,* 1987-91. Consultant and contributor to *Encyclopedia of Science Fiction,* edited by John Clute and Peter Nicholls. Author of over 75 articles, essays and reviews in journals, including *Omni, Foundation, New York Review of Science Fiction, Meanjin, The Age, Metascience, International Review Journal for the History, Philosophy and Social Studies of Science, Australian Science Fiction Review,* and *Journal of Myth, Fantasy, and Romanticism.* Author of *Trends in the Modern Novel; Modern Australian Drama* (with G. McKay); and *Storylines.* Also author of critical biographies of William Gibson, Angela Carter, and Thomas Keneally for the *Borgo Press Modern Authors* series. **Essays:** Greg Egan.

WEEDMAN, Jane B. Assistant professor of English, Texas Tech University, Lubbock. Author of *Samuel R. Delany,* 1982; and of articles on Delany, James White, and E.E. Smith. Editor of *Women Worldwalkers: New Dimensions of Science Fiction and Fantasy.* **Essays:** Anna Kavan; Mark Twain.

WEINKAUF, Mary S. Professor of English and head of the department, Dakota Wesleyan University, Mitchell, South Dakota. Author of *Early Poems by a Late Beginner,* 1976; *Lew Archer, Humanist Priest,* 1985; studies of S. Fowler Wright and Ngaio Marsh; and of articles and reviews in *Fantasy and Science Fiction Book Review, SFRA Newsletter, Extrapolation, Studies in English Literature, Texas Quarterly,* and other periodicals. **Essays:** René

Barjavel; Craig Strete; S. Fowler Wright.

WELCH, Dennis M. Associate professor of English and humanities, Virginia Polytechnic and State University, Blacksburg. Author of articles on Alfred Tennyson, Theodore Sturgeon, William Blake, and Percy Bysshe Shelley. **Essay:** Theodore Cogswell.

WHITE, Fred D. Assistant professor of English, University of Santa Clara, California. Author of *Composition: Art and Craft,* and of articles in *San Jose Studies, Arizona Quarterly, Journal of English Teaching Techniques, The Writing Instructor,* and other publications. **Essay:** Robert Sheckley.

WILCOX, Robert H. Professor emeritus, Glendale College, Arizona. Former consulting editor, *Amazing;* and editor-in-chief, Industrial Publications, New York. **Essays:** Fredric Brown; Louis Charbonneau; Frederick Pohl; Clifford D. Simak; William F. Temple.

WILDER, Cherry. See her own entry. **Essays:** Colin Greenland; Ira Levin.

WINGROVE, David. See his own entry. **Essays:** Richard Cowper; David Garnett; Mary Gentle; Gary Kilworth; Paul McAuley; Andrew M. Stephenson.

WOLFE, Gary K. Professor of humanities, Roosevelt University, Chicago. Author of *The Known and the Unknown: The Iconography of Science Fiction,* 1979; *Elements of Research,* 1979; *David Lindsay,* 1982; *Critical Terms for Science Fiction and Fantasy,* 1986; and of articles and reviews for books and periodicals. Pilgrim Award recipient, 1987. **Essays:** Brian Aldiss; Sharon Baker; Gregory Benford; Ray Bradbury; Edmund Cooper; John Keir Cross; Jack Finney; William Hope Hodgson; Nigel Kneale; David Lindsay; John Lymington; Richard Matheson; Chad Oliver; Daniel

Manus Pinkwater; Rod Serling; M.P. Shiel; Cordwainer Smith; Jerry Sohl.

WOLFE, Gene. See his own entry. **Essay:** Algis Budrys.

WOOSTER, Martin Morse. Washington editor, *Reason.* Author of articles in *Esquire, Wall Street Journal, Chicago Tribune, Fantasy Review, Toronto Star, Boston Globe,* and other publications. **Essays:** William Rotsler; Jack Williamson.

WYGANT, Alice Chambers. Reference librarian, Moody Medical Library, Galveston, Texas. Died. **Essay:** Sonya Dorman.

YOKE, Carl B. Assistant to the associate vice-president for the Extended University, and associate professor of English, Kent State University, Ohio; associate editor of *Extrapolation.* Author of *A Reader's Guide to Roger Zelazny and Andre Norton: Proponents of Individualism;* and of articles on John Jakes, Daniel Galouye, Michael Crichton, Joan Vinge, Charles Eric Maine, Henry Kuttner, C.L. Moore, A. Merritt, Michael Moorcock, and other SF and fantasy writers. Co-editor of *Death and the Serpent: Immortality in Science Fiction and Fantasy,* 1985. **Essays:** Michael Crichton; Daniel F. Galouye; John Jakes; Charles Eric Maine; Joan D. Vinge; Roger Zelazny.

ZAKI, Hoda M. Assistant professor of political science, Hampton University, Virginia. Reviewer for *Hypatia: A Journal of Feminist Philosophy;* Hampton and Newport News *Daily Press,* and the National Women's Studies Association's *Newsletter.* **Essay:** Marta Randall.

ZEBROWSKI, George. See his own entry. **Essays:** Arthur C. Clarke; David Duncan; Edgar Pangborn; Thomas N. Scortia; William Tenn.